CLASSICS OF PHILOSOPHY

CLASSICS OF PHILOSOPHY

THIRD EDITION

LOUIS P. POJMAN
LEWIS VAUGHN

New York • Oxford
OXFORD UNIVERSITY PRESS
2011

Oxford University Press, Inc., publishes works that further Oxford University's
objective of excellence in research, scholarship, and education.

Oxford   New York
Auckland   Cape Town   Dar es Salaam   Hong Kong   Karachi
Kuala Lumpur   Madrid   Melbourne   Mexico City   Nairobi
New Delhi   Shanghai   Taipei   Toronto

With offices in
Argentina   Austria   Brazil   Chile   Czech Republic   France   Greece
Guatemala   Hungary   Italy   Japan   Poland   Portugal   Singapore
South Korea   Switzerland   Thailand   Turkey   Ukraine   Vietnam

Published by Oxford University Press, Inc.
198 Madison Avenue, New York, New York, 10016
http://www.oup.com

Oxford is a registered trademark of Oxford University Press.

Credits—Fig. 12.1 © National Gallery, London / Art Resource, New York;
Fig. 15.1 Image Select / Art Resource, New York;
Fig. 18.1 Foto Marburg / Art Resource, New York;
Fig. 34.1 © Estate of Fred Stein / Art Resource, New York.

Library of Congress Cataloging-in-Publication Data

Classics of philosophy / [edited by] Louis P. Pojman, Lewis Vaughn.—3rd ed.
    p. cm.
  Includes bibliographical references.
  ISBN 978-0-19-973729-1 (acid-free paper)
1. Philosophy.   I. Pojman, Louis P.   II. Vaughn Lewis.
  B72.C54 2011
  100—dc22

                                                    2010015821

Printing number: 9 8 7

Printed in the United States of America
on acid-free paper

Dedicated to
William Lawhead and Wallace Matson
whose love of the classics
has inspired me

CONTENTS

---

* Selection reprinted in its entirety.

PREFACE

The last edition of this text set a high standard. It was the largest collection of writings in Western philosophy, providing students with unabridged or substantial texts of classic works while keeping as close to the heart of the canon as possible in the space provided. It spanned over 2,500 years of philosophical thought, from Thales to Rawls. It retained elements that helped set the book apart from its competitors—namely, the selections from the pre-Socratics and contemporary philosophy. All this is true of the new edition. But in many ways the new improves significantly on the old while keeping the price reasonable.

IMPROVEMENTS TO THE THIRD EDITION

This revision contains 20 complete works and more than 70 selections by 49 authors, each of which is introduced by a brief essay. It enlarges many of the existing readings, adds some important philosophers, and includes just enough pedagogy to help students without diminishing their own direct experience with the text. Specifically, improvements include:

- Expanding Aristotle's *Posterior Analytics*, *On the Soul*, *Metaphysics*, and *Nicomachean Ethics*; Berkeley's *Of the Principles of Human Knowledge*; and Hume's *Treatise on Human Nature*
- Adding selections from Maimonides and Schopenhauer as well as Kant's *Critique of Pure Reason*
- Including review questions for each chapter
- Providing online resources:
  - **Instructor's Resources** that include (1) brief summaries for each reading, (2) essay questions for the selections, (3) objective test questions covering the work of each philosopher, and (4) a time line highlighting the lives of the authors.
  - **Student Resources** that feature (1) autograded quizzes covering each author, (2) review questions for each chapter, (3) a time line featuring the authors in the text, and (4) helpful web links.

This new *Classics of Philosophy*, then, should give students easier access to more of philosophy's greatest works in a more economical package. It should also offer an alternative to teachers who want a high-quality anthology of Western classics that includes the best of the pre-Socratics as well as a sampling of influential contemporary philosophy.

ACKNOWLEDGMENTS

The evolution of this text began in the last edition with the help of many able philosophers—most notably, Wallace Matson, Bill Lawhead, Jim Landesman, and Stanley Obitts.

This new edition has been developed with the help of other philosophical notables, including Marshell Bradley, Sam Houston State University; Matthew Daude Laurents, Austin Community College; Gary Elkins, Toccoa Falls College; Matthew W. Hallgarth, Tarleton State University; Bruce Hauptli, Florida International University; Severin Kitanov, Salem State College; Kevin Kukla, University of Alabama; Edward McGushin, Saint Anselm College; John Meadors, Mississippi College; Joseph Novak, University of Waterloo; Jonathan Parsons, College of DuPage; Konstantin Pollok, University of South Carolina; Jeremy Sabol, Stanford University; James Van Slyke, Azusa Pacific University; and Brenda Wirkus, John Carroll University. From the beginning, the work has been inspired and supported by Robert Miller, Oxford University Press's distinguished philosophy editor, and along the way he has been aided by editorial assistants, including (for this edition) Christina Mancuso, Kristin Maffei, and Lauren Roth.

Lewis Vaughn

TIME LINE

THE ANCIENT PERIOD

Philosophers	Dates	Major Figures and Events
Thales*	c. 624–545 B.C.	Thales predicts solar eclipse, 585 B.C.
Anaximander	c. 612–545 B.C.	Lao-tzu, c. 575 B.C.
Anaximenes	c. 585–528 B.C.	Buddha, c. 563–483 B.C.
Pythagoras	c. 580–496 B.C.	Confucius, 551–479 B.C.
Xenophanes	c. 570–478 B.C.	
Heraclitus	c. 540–480 B.C.	Republic of Rome established, c. 508 B.C.
Parmenides	c. 515–450 B.C.	Sophocles, c. 496–406 B.C.
Anaxagoras	500–428 B.C.	Battle of Marathon, 490 B.C.
Empedocles	c. 495–435 B.C.	
Zeno the Eleatic	c. 490–430 B.C.	Parthenon built in Athens, 438 B.C.
Portagoras	c. 490–420 B.C.	
Gorgias	c. 483–375 B.C.	Peloponnesian War, 431–404 B.C.
Socrates	c. 470–399 B.C.	Trial and death of Socrates, 399 B.C.
Democritus	c. 460–370 B.C.	
Plato	c. 427–347 B.C.	Plato founds the Academy, c. 388 B.C.
Aristotle	384–322 B.C.	Aristotle founds the Lyceum, 334 B.C.
Pyrrho	c. 360–270 B.C.	Death of Alexander the Great, 323 B.C.

*Philosophers whose names appear in **boldface** appear in this volume.

THE ANCIENT PERIOD

Philosophers	Dates	Major Figures and Events
Epicurus	341–270 B.C.	Epicurus opens school in Athens, 306 B.C.
Zeno the Stoic	c. 336–264 B.C.	Zeno opens school at the Stoa, 301 B.C. Rome conquers the Greek world, 200–128 B.C. Caesar is dictator of Rome, 49–44 B.C. Jesus Christ, c. 4 B.C.–A.D. 30
Epictetus	c. 50–130	Romans destroy Temple in Jerusalem, 70
Marcus Aurelius	121–180	
Sextus Empiricus	c. 200	
Plotinus	205–270	

THE MEDIEVAL PERIOD

Philosophers	Dates	Major Figures and Events
		Constantine grants tolerance to Christianity, 313
Augustine	354–430	Theodosius I makes Christianity the state religion of Rome, 392
Boethius	c. 480–524	Fall of the Roman Empire in the West, 476
John Scotus Erigena	c. 810–877	Muhammad, c. 570–632
Avicenna	980–1037	
Anselm	1034–1109	
Al-Ghazali	1058–1111	
Peter Abelard	1079–1142	William of Normandy conquers England, 1066 Start of the Crusades, 1096
Averroës	1126–1198	University of Paris founded, 1160

THE MEDIEVAL PERIOD

Philosophers	Dates	Major Figures and Events
Moses Maimonides	1135–1204	Oxford University founded, 1167 Cambridge University founded, 1209
Thomas Aquinas	1225–1274	
Meister Eckhart	c. 1260–1327	Dante Alighieri, 1265–1321
John Duns Scotus	c. 1266–1308	The Black Death ravages Europe, 1347–1351
William of Ockham	c. 1285–1349	

THE MODERN PERIOD

Philosophers	Dates	Major Figures and Events
		Johann Gutenberg invents the printing press, 1445 Leonardo da Vinci, 1452–1519
Thomas Hobbes	1588–1679	
René Descartes	1596–1650	The reign of Louis XIV in France, 1643–1715
Blaise Pascal	1623–1662	
Benedict (Baruch) Spinoza	1632–1677	Johann Sebastian Bach, 1685–1750
John Locke	1632–1704	*Two Treatises on Government*, 1689
Isaac Newton	1642–1727	Publication of *Principia Mathematica*, 1687
Gottfried Wilhelm Leibniz	1646–1716	
George Berkeley	1685–1753	Wolfgang Amadeus Mozart, 1756–1791
Voltaire	1694–1778	*Candide*, 1759
David Hume	1711–1776	Ludwig van Beethoven, 1770–1827

THE MODERN PERIOD

Philosophers	Dates	Major Figures and Events
Jean-Jacques Rousseau	1712–1778	American Revolution, 1775–1783
Adam Smith	1723–1790	*The Wealth of Nations*, 1776
Immanuel Kant	1724–1804	*Critique of Pure Reason*, 1781
Edmund Burke	1729–1797	French Revolution, 1789–92
William Paley	1743–1805	
Jeremy Bentham	1748–1832	Industrial Revolution in England, c. 1790 Napoleon crowns himself emperor of France, 1804
Mary Wollstonecraft	1759–1797	Charles Darwin, 1809–1882 Richard Wagner, 1813–1883
Georg W. F. Hegel	1770–1831	Fyodor Dostoevsky, 1821–1881 Leo Tolstoy, 1828–1910
Arthur Schopenhauer	1788–1860	Second French Revolution, 1830 Opium War in China, 1839
Auguste Comte	1798–1857	Italian Revolution, 1848
John Stuart Mill	1806–1873	*On Liberty*, 1859 Darwin's *Origin of Species*, 1859
Søren Kierkegaard	1813–1855	*Fear and Trembling*, 1841
Karl Marx	1818–1883	*The Communist Manifesto*, 1848 Sigmund Freud, 1856–1939
Friedrich Engels	1820–1895	American Civil War, 1861–1865 Bismark unites Germany, 1870 C. G. Jung, 1875–1961
Friedrich Nietzsche	1844–1900	Pablo Picasso, 1881–1973 James Joyce, 1882–1941 Virginia Woolf, 1882–1941 The Dreyfus Affair (France), 1899

THE CONTEMPORARY PERIOD

Philosophers	Dates	Major Figures and Events
Charles S. Peirce	1839–1914	Albert Einstein presents theory of relativity, 1905
William James	1842–1910	
W. K. Clifford	1845–1879	
Gottlob Frege	1848–1925	First World War, 1914–1918
Edmund Husserl	1859–1938	
Henri Bergson	1859–1941	Russian Communist Revolution, 1917
John Dewey	1859–1952	Gandhi begins his crusade for Indian independence, 1919
Alfred North Whitehead	1861–1947	Joseph Stalin becomes general secretary of the Communist party, 1922
Bertrand Russell	1872–1970	The Great Depression, 1929–1939 Spanish Civil War, 1936–1939
G. E. Moore	1873–1958	
Ludwig Wittgenstein	1889–1951	Second World War, 1939–1945
Martin Heidegger	1889–1976	Dropping of the atomic bomb on Hiroshima August 6, 1945
Rudolph Carnap	1891–1970	India gains independence, 1947
Gilbert Ryle	1900–1976	Israel becomes a nation, 1949
Karl Popper	1902–1994	People's Republic of China under Mao Tse-tung established, 1949 Crick and Watson identify the structure of DNA, 1953
John Wisdom	1904–1993	Korean War, 1950–1953
Jean-Paul Sartre	1905–1980	Cuban Missile Crisis, 1962

THE CONTEMPORARY PERIOD

Philosophers	Dates	Major Figures and Events
Nelson Goodman	1906–1998	Assassination of John F. Kennedy, 1963
Simone de Beauvoir	1908–1986	
Willard V. O. Quine	1908–2000	War in Vietnam, 1954–1975
A. J. Ayer	1910–1989	Assassination of Martin Luther King, Jr., 1968
Philippa Foot	b. 1920	
John Rawls	b. 1921	*A Theory of Justice*, 1971
Thomas Kuhn	1922–1996	The fall of the Soviet Union, 1991
Michel Foucault	1926–1984	Apartheid ends in South Africa, 1994
Thomas Nagel	b. 1937	Islamic terrorist attacks on U.S. World Trade Center and Pentagon September 11, 2001

CLASSICS OF PHILOSOPHY

Part One

THE

ANCIENT

PERIOD

1

THE PRE-SOCRATICS

INTRODUCTION

Philosophy begins with wonder, and even now it is wonder that causes philosophers to philosophize. At first they wondered about the obvious difficulties and then they gradually progressed to puzzle about the greater ones, for example, the behavior of the moon and sun and stars and the coming to be of the universe. Whoever is puzzled and in a state of wonder believes he is ignorant (this is why the lover of myths is also in a way a philosopher, since myths are made up of wonders). And so, if indeed they pursued philosophy to escape ignorance, they were obviously pursuing scientific knowledge in order to know and not for the sake of any practical need.[1]

(ARISTOTLE)

They looked into the heavens and wondered how the universe had come about. They pondered the structure of the world. Is there one fundamental substance that underlies all of reality or are there many substances? What is the really *real*, and not just a matter of appearance?

The first philosophers were Greeks of the sixth century B.C. living on the Ionian coast of the Aegean Sea, in Miletus, Colophon, Samos, and Ephesus. Other people in other

---

[1] Aristotle, *Metaphysics* 1.2 982b.

3

cultures had wondered about these questions, but usually religious authority or myth had imposed an answer. Typically, as in the Hebrews' Genesis 1 or the Greek Hesiod's *Theogony*, the world order was said to have arisen from God or the gods. Now a break occurred. Here for the first time a pure philosophical and scientific inquiry was allowed to flourish. The Great Civilizations of Egypt, China, Assyria, Babylon, Israel, and Persia, not to mention those of the Incas, Mayans, and Africans, had produced art and artifacts and government of advanced sorts, but nowhere, with the possible exception of India, was anything like philosophy or science developed. Ancient India was the closest civilization to produce philosophy, but it was always connected with religion, with the question of salvation or the escape from suffering. Ancient Chinese thought, led by Confucius (551–475 B.C.), had a deep ethical dimension. But no epistemology or formulated logic. Now Greek philosophy, especially from Socrates on, also had a practical bent and was concerned with ethics, but it went deeper and further than ethics, asking for the nature of all things, aiming at knowledge and understanding for its own sake, seeking systematic understanding of metaphysics, and using experiment and logical argument, rather than religion or intuition alone, to reach its conclusions. Indeed, Socrates was the first to develop dialectical argument (the "Socratic Method") and Aristotle invented formal logic, the system of syllogisms.

The first Greek philosophers were materialists and naturalists, sometimes called *Hylicists* (from the Greek *hulé*, which means matter), for they rejected spiritual and religious causes and sought naturalistic explanations of reality. The standard date for the beginning of philosophy is May 23, 585 B.C., when, according to Herodotus, Thales of Miletus (625–545 B.C.) on the coast of Asia Minor (then called Ionia, now Turkey) predicted a solar eclipse.[2] What has the prediction of an eclipse to do with philosophy? Thales used mathematical and astronomical investigation to make his prediction. In this sense he may have been the first scientist, and since at this early stage of development science cannot be separated from philosophy, the prediction of the solar eclipse serves as a clothespin holding one end of the long sheet of the history of philosophy to the clothesline of world history.

Thales, who was an engineer by training, asked, "What is the nature of reality? What is the ultimate explanation of all that is?" and speculated and experimented in order to come up with the answer. What was his answer? "Water." Water is necessary for the production and sustenance of life. Water is everywhere; look past the coastline and you'll find a sea of water, dig under the ground and you're bound to find water. It rises as mist from the sea and falls down to earth as rain. Heat water and it becomes a gas like air, freeze it and it becomes solid. So Thales concluded that earth was just especially solid water, a hard flat cork which floated in a sea of liquid of the same substance. It is the first recorded attempt to give a naturalistic answer to the question "What is reality?"

A simple beginning? No doubt, but it is worth quoting Friedrich Nietzsche here.

> Greek philosophy seems to begin with a preposterous fancy, with the proposition that water is the origin and mother-womb of all things. Is it really necessary to stop there and become serious? Yes, and for three reasons: Firstly, because the proposition does enunciate something about the origin of things; secondly, because it does so without figure and fable; thirdly, because in it is contained, although only in the chrysalis state, the idea—Everything is one. The first-mentioned

---

[2]Discussed and quoted in G. S. Kirk and J. E. Raven, *The Presocratic Philosophers* (Cambridge: Cambridge University Press, 1957), pp. 74–81.

reason leaves Thales still in the company of religious and superstitious people; the second, however, takes him out of this company and shows him to us as a natural philosopher; but by virtue of the third, Thales becomes the first Greek philosopher.[3]

After Thales his fellow Ionian Anaximander (c. 612–545 B.C.) rejected the idea that water was the root substance and hypothesized that ultimate reality could not be equated with any one material substance, but was neutral between them, yet underlying all matter. It was an unknown boundless material substance (*Apeiron*), the *Infinite* or *Boundless*.

Anaximander asserted that the source and elements of existing things is the *infinite*. He was the first to introduce this name for the source. He says that it is neither water nor any of the other so-called "elements," but of another nature which is infinite, from which all the heavens and the world-order in them arise.

No mention is made of the gods, nor of a beginning nor end of reality.

Everything either is a beginning or has a beginning. But there is no beginning of the infinite; for if there were, it would limit it. Moreover, since it is a beginning, it is unbegotten and indestructible. For there must be a point at which what has come into being reaches completion, and a point at which all perishing ceases. Hence, as we say, there is no source of *the Infinite*, but it appears to be the source of all the rest and "encompasses all things" and "steers all things," as those assert who do not recognize other causes besides the infinite. And this, they say, is divine; for it is "deathless" and "imperishable" as Anaximander puts it, and most of the physicists agree with him.

The Infinite is externally in motion and the source of time, space, matter and mind. An opposition of forces keeps the world in its revolving place. These opposites "make reparation to one another for their injustice," creating an exterior homeostasis or equilibrium of forces.

Into those things from which existing things have their coming into being, their passing away, too, takes place, according to what must be; for they make reparation to one another for their injustice according to the ordinance of time.[4]

Analogously, health is an inner homeostasis, an equilibrium of opposing forces within us. Our world is only one of many worlds produced by the Infinite in its eternal motion, a motion which is perpetually whirling. This Whirl separates as in a vortex or whirlpool in which heavy objects move to the bottom and light to the top. Hence the colder elements, earth and water, move downward and the lighter ones, fire and air, upward. This seems to be the beginning of the idea of Natural Law in which natural causes, blind and impersonal, replace the gods. Wind, not Zeus, causes lightning. He rejected Thales notion of a stationary flat earth and suggested that the earth was a revolving, cylindrical body, whose flat top was our home.[5]

---

[3]Friedrich Nietzsche quoted in ed. L. Miller, *Questions That Matter* (New York: McGraw-Hill, 1987), p. 61.

[4]Quoted by Simplicius in his *Physics*. Quoted in John Mansley Robinson, *An Introduction to Early Greek Philosophy* (New York: Houghton Mifflin Company, 1968), p. 34.

[5]Alcameon developed this thought, applying it to health: The essence of health lies in the "equality" of the powers—moist, dry, cold, hot, bitter, sweet, and the rest—whereas the cause of sickness is the "supremacy of one" among these. For the rule of any one of them is a cause of destruction . . . while health is the proportionate mixture of the qualities. Quoted in Robinson, *Introduction*, p. 35.

Rejecting the anthropocentric notions of the religious and mythological explanations and anticipating Darwin by 2500 years, Anaximander put forth a theory of evolution based on the need for species to adapt to their environment. Human beings evolved from fish or fish-like creatures who had to adapt to land and so developed the characteristics we now have.

Anaximander's disciple Anaximenes (585–528 B.C.) accepted his teacher's notion that reality is infinite, but observing evaporation and condensation and how breath animated both humans and animals, he posited air as the ultimate substance. "Just as our soul, being air, keeps us together in order, so also breath and air encompass the whole cosmos."

One other philosopher from the Ionian coast deserves mention. Xenophanes (c. 570– c. 478 B.C.) noted the anthropomorphic nature of the gods, their immorality, their stealings, adulteries, and deceivings, their ethnic qualities, suggesting that each culture creates its gods in its own image.

> The Ethiopians make their gods black and snub-nosed. The Thracians make theirs have grey-eyes and red-hair. And if oxen and horses and lions had hands and could paint with their hands, and produce works of art as men do, horses would paint the forms of the gods like horses, and oxen like oxen, and make their bodies in the image of their own.[6]

He argued that there was one God beyond all these mythological and anthropomorphic counterfeits, who seeks, hears and thinks all over. "He remains forever in the same place, without moving; nor is it fitting for him to go about from one place to another. But without labor he sets all things in motion by his intelligent willpower."

PYTHAGORAS

The first philosopher of which we have substantial information is Pythagoras of Samos (580–496 B.C.), who settled in Croton in southern Italy, where he founded the first community of philosophers. Pythagoras either visited Egypt himself or learned from those who did, since the Greek historian Herodotus points to similarities between his ideas and the Egyptians' (religious customs forbidding people to wear wool in temples and belief in an afterlife).[7] It could be argued that not Thales but Pythagoras was the father of philosophy, for with him a comprehensive study of the fundamental questions of philosophy first takes place: What is reality? How does one come to know the truth? How shall I live my life? Here is an early document on what he taught:

> First he said that the soul is immortal; second, that it migrates into other kinds of animals; third, that the same events are repeated in cycles, nothing being new in the strict sense; and finally, that all things with souls should be regarded as related to each other. Pythagoras seems to have been the first to introduce these ideas into Greece.[8]

Pythagoras rejected the Hylicist's materialism and opted for a refined spiritualism, a mathematical mysticism, aiming at the purification of the whole person, body and soul.

---

[6]Quoted in Robinson, *Introduction*, p. 52.
[7]See Richard McKirahan, Jr., *Philosophy Before Socrates* (82–87) for a lucid discussion of this point.
[8]Diogenes Laertius viii.5 quoted in Robinson, *Introduction*, p. 57.

Knowledge (or Science) and Music would purify the soul and Gymnastics and Medicine, the body. All living things (including plant life) had souls and were related to one another and involved in the transmigration of souls. Pythagoreans generally despised the body as inferior to the soul, which they sought to purify by ascetic practices. They were vegetarians, eating neither meat nor eggs nor beans, nor drinking wine. A story circulated in the ancient world that when Pythagoras noticed a man beating a dog, he cried to him to desist, claiming that he recognized in the dog the "voice of a dear friend."

Pythagoras related morality to the harmony of the soul. A good soul has a proper order of standards and impulses within itself like beautiful music and the sublime system of the heavens. Pythagoreans were renowned for their mutual friendship, altruism, integrity, devotion to duty. At the end of each day they asked themselves what wrongs they had committed, what duties they had neglected, what good they had done.

Pythagoras is the first person on record to hold the doctrine of universal brotherhood, which led him to provide equal opportunity for men and women. Two centuries before Plato's famous declaration of this doctrine in the *Republic* Pythagoras accepted women on an equal basis with men, admitting them into his school. He also called for, and himself practiced, humane treatment of slaves. He was reputed to have never chastised a slave.

Under the government of the Pythagoreans, Croton succeeded in establishing an intellectual aristocracy over a territory about four times the size of Attica, which was destroyed by the democratic party in the second half of the fifth century B.C. The democrats massacred the Pythagoreans, surrounding their assembly house, in which the leadership was lodged, and burning it to the ground.

Pythagoras's fundamental doctrine was that the world is really not material but made up of numbers. Numbers are things and constitute the essence of reality. The original "one," being fire, sets the surrounding cold air in motion, drawing it upon itself and limiting it. From numbers the world is created:

> From numbers points, from points lines, from lines plane figures, from plane figures solid figures, from these sensible bodies, of which the elements are four: fire, water, earth, and air. These change and are wholly transformed; and from them arises a cosmos animate, intelligent, and spherical, embracing earth (itself spherical and inhabited all around) as its center.

Pythagoras was led to this doctrine by his musical studies. He recognized that the pitch of tones depends on the length of the strings on musical instruments and that musical harmony is determined by definite mathematical propositions. The recognition of this fact led the Pythagoreans to the soul, which was not contained in matter itself but was suprasensual. Thus the anthropological dualism of body and soul was extended to the cosmic dualism of matter and form, or, as they expressed it, of the unlimited and the limited. Hence number was for them something essentially different from water for Thales, or the Apeiron for Anaximander or air for Anaximenes; it was something opposed to matter and distinguished from it although closely connected with it, something which limits it and gives it shape. Matter, as such, was presupposed by the Pythagoreans, and they seem to have imagined it in a way that combined Anaximander's Unbounded and Anaximene's air. Matter is unlimited breath, that is, the endless expanse of air beyond the cosmos from which the world draws its breath.

Now that number was established as a world-principle, they proceeded to make remarkable speculations on its nature. They drew distinctions between straight and not-straight, unity and duality, and thus derived two further pairs of opposites, whose number was later rather arbitrarily extended up to ten. Individual numbers were considered particularly sacred. One (1) is the paradoxical point, both the limited and the unlimited, 2 is the line, 3 the plane, 4 the solid, 5 physical qualities, 6 animation, 7 intelligence, 8 health, 9 love and wisdom, 10 the sacred Decad, by which they were accustomed to take oaths. From their experiments with numbers they were led to the discovery of the "Pythagorean Theorem" (the sum of the squares of the sides of a right angle triangle are equal to the square of the hypotenuse). Theophrastus tells us that the Pythagoreans were the first to speak of the spherical shape of the earth, the harmony of the spheres and planetary motion. Pythagoras supposed there to be a Central Fire around which the round earth revolved.

Mystic and mathematician, Pythagoras held that we are strangers and pilgrims in the world, that the body is the tomb of the soul, that the visible world of matter is appearance, which must be overcome if we are to know reality. In this life there are three types of people who come to the Olympic Games. The lowest class is made up of those who come to buy and sell, the next above them are those who compete. Best of all, however, are those who come simply to look on. These three types of people correspond to three parts of the soul: the love of gain, of honor, and of wisdom. We must aim at Purification from the world, which comes about through the disinterested pursuit of philosophy. We will meet all these ideas again in Plato, who seems have been influenced by Pythagoras.

Pythagoras apparently wrote nothing, so we cannot study his writings.

THE ELEATICS

With Parmenides (540–470 B.C.) a further advance in philosophical discourse took place. Parmenides observed that nature is constantly changing and noted that such flux was inimical to the idea of knowledge: to have knowledge there must be permanence, something which is unchanging. He theorized that the real world was unchanging on the order of Pythagoras's number, whereas the apparent, illusory world was the world of change. The senses grasped the changing world of unreality or *Non-being*, whereas reason alone could grasp the real world of *Being*. Being never comes into existence, nor does it cease to be, for it always is. It cannot be divided or added onto, for it is whole and complete in itself, one. It is unmoved and undisturbed, for motion and disturbance are forms of becoming. Being is. It doesn't become. It is self-identical and uncaused. This view is sometimes called Absolute Idealism: there is an Absolute Idea which makes up all there is, and all change is illusory. All is One and Permanently at Rest.

Three theses can be identified in Parmenides' work.

1. That which is, is and cannot not-be; that which is not, is not and cannot be. The real is and cannot be nonexistent.
2. That which is can be thought or known and truly named. That which is not, cannot. Thinking and the thought that it is are the same thing.
3. That which is, is one and cannot be many. The real is unique. There is no second thing besides it. It is also indivisible. It does not contain a plurality of distinct parts.

Being or Reality is one, immaterial, continuous, indivisible, motionless, beginningless, imperishable, and everywhere. It is wholly indeterminate and can only be described in negative terms. It cannot be created nor pass away. It cannot be created, for if it were, it would have to be created from Nothing, which is impossible. It cannot be destroyed, for if it could, then something could become nothing, which is impossible. When thought has negated all that can be negated, it is Being which remains, the unique, godlike One.

Parmenides' most famous disciple was Zeno of Elea (c. 490–c. 430 B.C.), who defended the Eleatic Idealism against those who claimed that there were both multiplicity and motion. Zeno is the first philosopher we know of who self-consciously makes use of the law of noncontradiction to argue against his opponents. Using universally acceptable premises, he develops a series of paradoxes which leads to the conclusion that there is no motion or multiplicity. One of his paradoxes, *The Line*, attempts to show that motion does not exist.

The Eleatics held that a line was one, whereas their opponents held that it was divisible into parts, discrete units. Zeno argues that if a line was divisible into units, it must be divisible into an infinite number of discrete units, so that each unit must be infinitely small. But if there were an infinite number of these units, then if we multiplied them, we would get a line which was infinitely large, for the smallest magnitude multiplied by infinity becomes an infinite magnitude. So what started out as a finite line turns out to be infinitely long, which is a contradiction.

> A second paradox is his Arrow Paradox: the Argument Against Movement. If everything is at rest when it is in a place equal to itself, and if the moving object is always in the present and therefore in a place equal to itself, then the moving arrow is motionless.[9]

Consider an arrow flying from one place to another. Does it really move? No, movement is only an illusion. Consider.

1. The arrow could not move in the place in which it is not.
2. But neither could it move in the place where it is.
3. For this is "a place equal to itself."
4. Everything is always at Rest when it is "at a place equal to itself."
5. But the flying arrow is always at the place where it is.
6. Therefore the flying arrow is always at Rest and cannot move.

A body must either be moving in a place where it is or where it is not. It can't be moving in a place where it is not, for it is not there. But if it is in place, it cannot be moving. For the arrow is at rest at any point in the trajectory and what is at rest at any point cannot move. Therefore the flying arrow cannot be moving.

All of the paradoxes have the same form. Any quantity of space must either be indivisible or divisible ad infinitum. If it is composed of indivisible units, these must have magnitude which can't be divided. If it is composed of divisible units, it must be divisible ad infinitum and we are faced with the contradiction of supposing that an infinite number of parts can be added up to make a finite sum total.

Zeno's paradoxes were in part aimed at destroying Pythagorean doctrines that motion and plurality could be explained by mathematics and logic. He showed that logic led to

---

[9] Aristotle, *Physics* 6.9, 239.

paradoxes that undermined the notions of motion and plurality. In this he vindicated the Eleatic doctrine that Reality was One, immovable, eternal, and uncreated.

HERACLITUS

Heraclitus (535–475 B.C.) of Ephesus, a cynical, aloof, solitary aristocrat, sometimes called "the weeping philosopher," was contemptuous of democracy ("most men are bad") and scornful of the Pythagorean and Eleatic Idealism and set forth an opposing philosophy ("Pythagoras claimed for his own wisdom what was but a knowledge of many things and an art of mischief"). Rejecting the notion that only Being is, he posited that only Becoming is ("nothing ever is, everything is becoming"). All things are in perpetual flux (Greek *panta rhei*), and permanence is an illusion. There is a single principle at work in the universe. It is fire. "Mind is fire." Fire, an infinite mass of substance, uncreated and eternal, is identical with the universe.

> The world order was not made by a god or a man, but always was and is and will be an ever-living fire.[10]

Fire consumes fuel, thus changing all, but is in constant flux. Transforming all that it comes in contact with, fire replaces Anaximander's Unlimited. Reality is like a stream of fire in constant motion. Nothing is stable. All comes from fire and to fire it shall return. At the same time Heraclitus posited *logos* (reason) as the lawlike process which governed the world.

The world follows an orderly process, though one of conflict and survival of the fittest. Hence war is reason's way of justice in the world. It is the "father of all and the king of all."

The logos, as the rational principle of the universe, has independent existence and according to it all things come into existence. It perpetually confronts people, calling on them to awake from their sleep of illusion. "To those who are awake the world-order is one, common to all, but the sleeping turn aside each into a world of his own."

The logos is hidden in humanity. We become intelligent "by drawing in the divine logos when we breathe." In sleep we are separated from the source of our being and forget. Further, Heraclitus said that the laws of the city were but a reflection of the logos which runs through all things.

> It is necessary for men who speak with common sense to place reliance on what is common to all, as a city relies upon law, and even more firmly. For all human laws are nourished by the one divine law. For it governs as far as it will, and it is sufficient for all things and outlasts them.

THE PLURALISTS: EMPEDOCLES AND THE ATOMISTS

Three philosophers rejected both the absolute monism of the Eleatics and the spiritual dynamics of Heraclitus. The first was Empedocles (ca. 450 B.C.) who argued that the world was made up of different combinations of four basic elements, water, earth, air, and fire.

---

[10]This and the following quotations are from Diogenes Laertius ix.

At the center of the universe there are two forces: attraction and repulsion, called "Love" and "Hate," which are in constant strife. When Love prevails, all things tend toward unity. When Hate prevails, all things separate, individuate. An eternal cosmological battle is waged, so that as one seems to be winning, the other experiences a resurgence.

According to Empedocles it is literally the case that "Love makes the world go round." But, so does Hate.

The second reaction to the Eleatics was that of the materialists, who hearkened back to the Milesians. Leucippus (c. 450 B.C.) and his more famous disciple, Democritus (c. 460–370 B.C.) taught that the ultimate constituents of the world were atoms (from the Greek *a* for "not" and *tome* for "cut" or "separable"). They were simple, indestructible, internally solid, homogeneous particles which are perpetually in motion in the void of empty space. Their combination and interaction account for all that is. Materialists were hedonists who believed that the only thing that is good is pleasure and the only thing bad is pain. They did not believe in the gods or in immortality.

ANAXAGORAS OF CLAZOMENAE

Anaxagoras (500–428 B.C.) was the first philosopher to make his home in Athens. He reintroduced pluralism, going against the Eleatic stream of monism, but he also rejected Empedocles's notion of the four elements (earth, fire, air, and water) of which all things were composed. They failed to account for the infinite variety and differentiation of the world of experience. Instead Anaxagoras taught that all things contain a portion of everything else.

> In everything there is a portion of everything. For how else could hair come from what is not hair? or flesh from what is not flesh? unless hair and flesh as well as teeth, eyes, and bone, et cetera are contained in food?[11]

Nous is a material (airy) substance but it is the purest and most rarefied of things, having power over all else. As an efficient cause, Nous sets up a rotary motion in the undifferentiated mass of being and causes separation and differentiation.

Anaxagoras was accused of uttering blasphemy in saying that the sun was a red hot stone and the moon was made of earth, for the Athenians regarded the heavenly bodies as gods. He was condemned, tried, found guilty of blasphemy, but escaped Athens to another country.

Socrates heard someone reading from a book of Anaxagoras. He was struck by the phrase, "Mind orders all things," and got hold of the book. Although the book proved a disappointment, concerning itself mainly with mechanical causation, it was a catalyst in turning Socrates away from speculations about the physical world and toward the study of human existence.

FOR FURTHER READING

Copleston, Frederick. *A History of Philosophy*, vol. 1 (Doubleday, 1962).

Freeman, Kathleen, ed. and trans. *Ancilla to the Pre-Socratic Philosophers* (Harvard University Press, 1948).

---

[11] Diels and Kranz, *Fragments of the Presocratic Philosophers* (henceforth "DK") 59 B 11.

Furley, David, and R. E. Allen, eds. *Studies in Presocratic Philosophy*, 2 vols. (Routledge & Kegan Paul, 1970).

Guthrie, W. K. C. *A History of Greek Philosophy*, 6 vols. (Cambridge University Press, 1962–1981).

Hussey, Edward. *The Presocratics* (Scribners, 1972).

Irwin, Terrence. *A History of Western Philosophy: Classical Thought* (Oxford University Press, 1989).

Jones, W. T. *Selections from Early Greek Philosophy* (Harcourt Brace Jovanovich, 1970).

Matson, Wallace. *A New History of Philosophy* (Harcourt Brace Jovanovich, 1987).

McKirahan, Richard D. *Philosophy Before Socrates: An Introduction with Texts and Commentary* (Hackett Publishing Co., 1994).

Robinson, John Mansley. *An Introduction to Early Greek Philosophy* (Houghton Mifflin, 1968).

Stace, W. T. *A Critical History of Greek Philosophy* (Macmillan, 1920), reprint St. Martin's Press, 1967).

READINGS

Here are some important texts concerning the Pre-Socratic philosophers. These texts are usually divided into "testimonies," or reports about the Pre-Socratics from ancient authorities, and "fragments," or quotations from the Pre-Socratics themselves. The texts below are numbered sequentially; in brackets is the number of the testimony (A-number) or fragment (B-number) in the standard sourcebook, Hermann Diels, *Fragmente der Vorsokratiker*, edited by Walther Kranz (6th ed., Dublin, 1951). Words believed to be direct quotations are put in boldface; sources of testimonies are given in parentheses.

THALES

1. [A12] Of the first philosophers, the majority thought the sources of all things were found only in the class of matter. For that of which all existing things consist, and that from which they come to be first and into which they perish last—the substance continuing but changing in its properties—*this*, they say, is the element and source of existing things. Accordingly they do not think anything either comes to be or perishes, inasmuch as this nature is always preserved. . . . For there is a certain nature, either one or more than one, from which everything else comes to be while this is preserved. All, however, do not agree on the number and character of this source, but Thales, the originator of this kind of theory, says it is water (and that is why he asserts that the earth floats on water), perhaps getting this conception from observing that everything derives its nourishment from what is moist and that the hot itself arises from and lives off it (and the thing from which the hot comes to be is the source of everything else). He gets his conception both from this fact and from the fact that the seeds of all things have a moist nature, and also the fact that water is the principle of growth for moist things. (Aristotle)

2. (1) Thales of Miletus, one of the Seven Wise Men, is said to have been the first to pursue natural philosophy. He said the beginning and end of the world was water. (2) For from this the world is composed when it is condensed and in turn dissolved, and the world is borne on it. From it come earthquakes, windstorms, and the motions of the heavenly bodies. (3) And things of the world travel and flow as they are carried around by the nature of the

first agent of their coming to be. And this is God, which has neither beginning nor end. (4) By occupying himself with the study and explanation of the heavenly bodies, Thales became the founder of astronomy among the Greeks. (Hippolytus)

3. [A22] It appears from what is recounted of him that Thales too understood the soul to be a source of motion, since he said the loadstone has a soul because it moves iron. . . . Some say that [soul] is mixed in the universe; this is perhaps the reason Thales said **all things are full of gods**. (Aristotle)

ANAXIMANDER

1. [A9] Of those who say the principle is one and in motion and boundless, Anaximander, the son of Praxiades, of Miletus, the successor and student of Thales, said the source and element of existing things was **the boundless**, being the first one to apply this term to the source. And he says it is neither water nor any of the so-called elements, but some other boundless [or: indefinite] nature, from which come to be all the heavens and the world-orders in them: [BI] From what things existing objects come to be, to them too does their destruction take place, according to what must be: for they give recompense and pay restitution to each other for their injustice according to the ordinance of Time, using these rather poetic terms. (Simplicius)

2. [A10] After [Thales] Anaximander, who was his companion, said **the boundless** contained the whole cause of coming to be and perishing of the world, from which he says the heavens are separated and generally all the world orders, which are countless. And he declared perishing to take place and much earlier coming to be, all these recurring from an infinite time past. He says the earth is cylindrical in shape, and its depth is one third of its width. He says that that part of **the everlasting** which is generative of hot and cold separated off at the coming to be of the world-order and from

this a sort of sphere of flame grew around the air about the earth like bark around a tree. This subsequently broke off and was closed into individual circles to form the sun, the moon, and the stars. He also says that in the beginning man was generated from animals of a different species [namely fish], inferring this from the fact that other animals quickly come to eat on their own, while man alone needs to be nursed for a long time. For this reason man would never have survived if he had originally had his present form. (Pseudo-Plutarch)

3. [A11] (3) The earth is suspended, supported by nothing, staying there because it maintains equal distance from everything. Its shape is concave, round, like a column drum. We walk on one of its surfaces, and there is another surface opposite. (4) The heavenly bodies are circles of fire, separated from the cosmic fire, surrounded by air. There are certain flute-like passages for breathing holes, through which the heavenly bodies appear. Accordingly, when the holes are blocked there are eclipses. (5) The moon appears to be waxing or waning by turns according to whether the passages are being blocked or opened. The circle of the sun is twenty-seven times <that of the earth;> that of the moon <eighteen times>. The sun is the highest body, and lowest are the circles of the fixed stars. (6) Living creatures arose from the moist being evaporated by the sun. In the beginning man was similar to a different kind of animal, namely a fish. (7) Winds come to be from the lightest vapors of air which are separated off and moved after being gathered, and rains from the vapor drawn up from the things under the sun [text corrupt]. Lightning occurs when wind as it breaks out of clouds rends them. He was born in the third year of the forty-second Olympiad [610]. (Hippolytus)

ANAXIMENES

1. [A7] (1) Anaximenes, he too being from Miletus, the son of Eurystratus, said boundless air is the source, from which the things that are,

were, and will be, and gods and divinities all come to be, and the rest come from the off-spring of these. (2) This is the character of air: when it is very uniform it is imperceptible to sight, but it is discerned by being cold, hot, damp, or in motion. It is always in motion; for it would not undergo all the changes it does without moving. (3) For being condensed or thinned it changes its appearance: when it is dispersed to become thinner, it becomes fire; when, on the other hand, air is condensed it becomes winds, and from air cloud is produced by **felting**, when it is condensed still more water, still more earth, and when it is condensed as much as possible stones. So the main contraries of generation are hot and cold. (4) The earth is flat **riding on air**, likewise the sun and moon and the other heavenly bodies, which are fiery **float on air** because of their flatness. (5) The heavenly bodies came to be from earth because of the moisture arising from it, which being thinned comes to be fire, and from fire floating aloft the heavenly bodies are composed. There are also some earthy natures in the place of the stars which are carried around with them. (6) He denies that the heavenly bodies move under the earth, as others suppose, but he says they turn around the earth **like a felt cap** around our head. The sun is hidden not by going under the earth, but by being covered by the higher parts of the earth and by being a greater distance away from us. The stars do not heat us because of their great distance. (7) The winds are generated when the condensed air is lifted up and carried along. Being collected and compacted still more clouds are generated and thus turn to water. And hail is produced when water from clouds is frozen as it travels downward; and snow, when more moisture-laden particles are solidified. (8) Lightning is produced when clouds are rent by the force of winds, for when they are rent the flash is bright and fiery. A rainbow is produced when the rays of the sun fall on thickened air. . . . (9) These are the views of Anaximenes, who flourished around the first year of the fifty-eighth Olympiad [548/7]. (Hippolytus)

2. [B1] Or just as Anaximenes of old thought, let us not leave the cold or the hot in substance, but let us view them as common properties of matter which supervene on changes. For he says what is contracted and condensed is cold, what is thin and **loose** (using this very term) is hot. Hence it is not inappropriate to say that man emits hot and cold from his mouth. For the breath is cooled when it is compressed and condensed by the lips, but when the mouth is relaxed it becomes hot as it leaves the mouth because of being rarefied. (Plutarch)

HERACLITUS

THE WORD (LOGOS)

1. [B1] **Of this Word being forever[1] uncomprehending do men prove to be, both before they hear and once they have heard. For although all things happen according to this Word they are like the unexperienced experiencing words and deeds such as I explain dividing each thing according to its nature and showing how it is. Other men are unaware of what they do when they are awake just as they are forgetful of what they do when they are asleep.**

2. [B40] **Collecting information does not teach understanding. Else it would have taught Hesiod and Pythagoras, as well as Xenophanes and Hecataeus.**

3. [B50] **Listening not to me but to the Word it is wise to agree that all things are one.**

---

[1]This sentence was famous in antiquity for being ambiguous: does "forever" go with the preceding or the following words? Syntactic ambiguity is one of many kinds of word-play Heraclitus uses. Compare the ambiguity in **8** [B12]: who or what is staying the same?

THE WORLD IS EVERLIVING FIRE

4. [B30] This world order, the same of all, no god nor man did create, but it ever was and is and will be: everliving fire, kindling in measures and being quenched in measures.

5. [B31a] The turnings of fire: first sea, and of sea half is earth, half firewind.

6. [B90] All things are an exchange for fire and fire for all things, as goods for gold and gold for goods.

7. [B60] The road up and down [= the course out and back] is one and the same.

8. [B12] On those stepping into rivers staying the same other and other waters flow.

9. [A6] Heraclitus says, I believe, that all things march on and nothing stands still and comparing things to the flow of a river he says you could not step twice into the same river. (Plato)[2]

10. All things move and are in flux. (Plato)

11. [B10] Collections: wholes, not wholes; brought together, pulled apart; in tune, out of tune; from all things one and from one all things.

12. [B51] They do not understand how differing from itself it agrees: backturning connection as of a bow or a lyre.

13. [B88] As the same thing in us is living and dead, waking and sleeping, young and old. For these things having changed around are those, and those in turn having changed around are these.

SOUL IS FIRE

14. [B36] To souls it is death to become water, to water death to become earth, but from earth water is born, and from water soul.

15. [B119] The character of man is his destiny.

16. [B114] Speaking with sense we must trust in the common sense of all, as a city trusts in its wall, and with even more trust. For all human laws are nourished by the one divine law. For it prevails as far as it will and provides enough for all and to spare.

17. [B67] God is day night, winter summer, war peace, satiety hunger; it alters just as <fire> when it is mixed with incense is named according to the aroma of each.

18. [B93] The Lord whose oracle is at Delphi neither reveals nor conceals, but gives a sign.

PARMENIDES

THE WAY OF TRUTH

1. [B2] Come now and I shall tell, and do you attend hearing,
which are the only two ways of inquiry for thinking:
the one: that it is and that it is not possible not to be,
is the path of Persuasion (for she attends on Truth);
the other: that it is not and that it is right it should not be,
this I declare to you is an utterly inscrutable track,
for neither would you know what is not (for it cannot be accomplished),
nor could you declare it [i.e., express it; or: point it out].

2. [B6] It is right to say and to think that what-is is [or: it is right that what is for saying and thinking should *be*], for it is able to be [or: it is for being]
and nothing is not. These things I bid you consider.
From this first way of inquiry I withheld you,
but now from this one, which mortals knowing nothing
wander, two-beaded. For helplessness in their

---

[2]This testimony and the following one are perhaps the most famous sayings attributed to Heraclitus. They are, however, likely to be only interpretations of **8** [B12].

breasts directs a wandering mind; and
they are borne
both deaf and blind, dazed, undiscerning
tribes,
by whom to be and not to be are thought
to be the same
and not the same, and the path of all
[men/ things] is backward-turning.

3. [B7] Never shall this prevail, that things that
are not are.
But you, withhold your thought from this
way of inquiry,
nor let habit born of long experience force
you along this way,
to ply an unseeing eye and echoing ear
and tongue. But judge by reasoning the
contentious refutation
spoken by me.

4. [B8]. . . only one tale is left of the way:
that it is; and on this are posted
very many signs that [i] what-is is
ungenerated and imperishable,
[ii] a whole of one kind, [iii] unperturbed
and [iv] complete.

[i] Never was it, nor shall it be, since it
now *is*, all together,
one, continuous. For what birth would you
seek of it?
Where [or: how], whence did it grow? Not
from what-is-not will I allow
you to say or to think; for it is not sayable
or thinkable
that it is not. And what need would have
stirred it
later or earlier, starting from nothing, to
grow?
Thus it must be completely or not
at all.
Nor ever from what-is-not will the
strength of faith allow
anything to come to be beside it.
Wherefore neither to come to be
nor to perish did Justice permit it by
loosening its shackles,

but she holds it fast. And the decision
concerning these things comes to this:
it is or it is not. Thus the decision is made,
as is necessary,
to leave the one way unthought,
unnamed—for it is not a true
way—the other to be and to be true.
And how would what-is be hereafter? How
would it have come to be?
For if it has come to be, it *is* not, and
similarly if it is ever about to be.
Thus coming to be is quenched and
perishing unheard of.

[ii] Nor is it divisible, since all is alike,
nor is there any more here, which would
keep it from holding together,
nor any less, but all is full of what-is.
Thus it is all continuous, for what-is
cleaves to what-is.

[iii] Further, motionless in the limits of
great bonds
it is without starting and stopping, since
coming to be and perishing
wandered very far away, and true faith
banished them.
Remaining the same in the same by itself
it stays,
and thus it remains steadfast there; for
mighty Necessity
holds it in the bonds of a limit, which
confines it round about.

[iv] Wherefore it is not right for what-is to
be incomplete;
for it is not needy; if it were it would lack
everything.
The same thing is for thinking and is
wherefore there is thought.
For not without what-is, to which it is
directed,
will you find thought. For nothing else
either is or shall be
beside what-is, since Fate shackled it

to be whole and unmoved. In relation to
this have all things been named,

which mortals established, trusting them
to be true:

coming to be and perishing, being and not
being,

changing place and exchanging bright color.

Yet since there is a final limit, it is complete,

in every direction like to the mass of a
well-rounded ball,

equally balanced from the center in all
directions. For it is not right

for there to be any more or any less here
or there.

For neither is there what-is-not, which
might stop it from reaching

its like, nor is there what-is in such a way
that there would be of what-is

here more and there less, since all is inviolate.

For being equal to itself in every direction, it
meets with equal limits.

THE WAY OF OPINION

[B8, continued] Here I cease from faithful
account and thought

about truth; from this point on learn
mortal opinions,

hearing the deceptive ordering of my words.

For they made up their minds to name
two forms,

of which it is not right to name one—this
is where they have gone astray—

and they distinguished contraries in body
and set signs

apart from each other, to this form the
ethereal fire of flame,

being gentle, very light, everywhere the
same as itself,

not the same as the other; but also that
one by itself

contrarily, unintelligent night, a dense
body and heavy.

I declare to you this ordering to be
completely likely,

so that no judgment of mortals will ever
surpass you.

ANAXAGORAS

THE PRIMEVAL CHAOS

1. [B1] Together were all things, boundless
both in quantity and in smallness; for the
small was boundless too. And as all things
were together nothing was manifest by reason of its smallness. For air and aether dominated all things, both being boundless. For
these things are the greatest in the totality
both in quantity and in size.

2. [B4b] Before these things were separated,
when they were all together, not so much as
a color was manifest. For the mixture of all
things prevented it, of the wet and the dry,
of the hot and the cold, and of the bright
and dark, since much earth was in it and
seeds countless in number which were not
at all like one another. For no one thing of
them appeared like to any other. Since these
things were so, one must believe that all
things were present in the totality.

MIXTURE AND SEPARATION

3. [B8] Things in the one world-order are not isolated from each other, nor are they cut off by
an axe—neither the hot from the cold nor the
cold from the hot.

4. [B10] Because Anaxagoras discovered the ancient doctrine that nothing comes from what
in no way is, he rejected coming to be, introducing separation in its place. For he said all
things are mixed with each other, and as they
increase they are separated. For example, in
the same seed there are hair, nails, veins, ar-
teries, sinews, and bones, and although they
happen to be invisible because of their micro-
scopic size, as they grow they gradually become distinct. **For how, he says, would
hair grow from not-hair and flesh from**

not-flesh? He attributes this not only to bodies but to colors. For example, black is present in white and white in black. He ascribes the same thing to weights: with the heavy he holds that light is mixed and likewise the heavy with the light. (Scholium on Gregory of Nazianzus)

5. [B17] **Coming to be and perishing the Greeks do not understand correctly. For no object comes to be or perishes, but it is mixed together from existing objects and separated back into them. And thus they should really call coming to be "mixture" and perishing "separation."**

COSMIC MIND RULES ALL THINGS

6. [B12] **Everything else has a portion of everything, but mind is boundless and autonomous and mixed with no object, but it is alone all by itself. If it were not by itself, but were mixed with something else, it would have a portion of all objects, if it were mixed with any; for there is a portion of everything in everything, as I said earlier. And the things mixed with it would hinder it from ruling any object in the way it does when it is alone by itself. For it is the finest of all objects and the purest, and it exercises complete oversight over everything and prevails above all. And all things that have soul, both the larger and the smaller, these does mind rule. And mind took control of the whole revolution, so that it revolved in the beginning. And first it began to revolve from a small revolution, and now it has a greater revolution, and it will have a still greater one. And things mixed together and separated and things distinguished, all these did mind comprehend. And what things were to be—what things were but now are not, and what things now are, and what things will be—all these did mind set in order, as well as this revolution, with which the stars, the sun, the moon, the air, and the aether which were being separated now revolve. For this revolution made things separate. And from the rare is separated the dense, from the cold the hot,** from the dark the bright, and from the wet the dry. But there are many portions of many things. And nothing is completely separated nor distinguished the one from the other except mind. Mind is all alike, both the larger and the smaller. But no other thing is like anything else, but in whatever thing some portion predominates, each one was and is most manifestly that.

EMPEDOCLES

THE FOUR ELEMENTS

1. [B6] **The four roots [elements] of all things hear first:**
Shining Zeus [fire], life-giving Hera [earth? air?],
Hades [air? earth?],
and Nestis [water], who by her tears moistens the mortal spring.

2. [B8] **I shall tell you another thing: there is no birth of any of all**
mortal things, neither any end of destructive death,
but only mixture and separation of mixed things exist,
and birth is a term applied to them by men.

THE COSMIC CYCLE

3. [B17] **I shall speak a double tale: at one time they [the roots] grew to be one alone**
from many, and at another time it grew apart to be many from one
And double is the birth of mortal things, and double the demise;
for the confluence of all things begets and destroys the one [generation],
while the other having been nurtured while things were growing apart fled away.
And these things never cease continually alternating,
at one time all coming together into one by Love,
at another time each being borne apart by the enmity of Strife.

<Thus, inasmuch as they are wont to
  become one from many,>
and in turn with the one growing apart
  they produce many,
they are born and they do not enjoy a
  steadfast life;
but inasmuch as they never cease
  continually alternating,
they are ever immobile in the cycle.

4. [B35]. . . when Strife reached the innermost
  depth
of the vortex, and Love comes to be in the
  middle of the circle,
there all these things combine to be one
  thing alone,
not suddenly, but joining together willingly
  each from its own place.
When these things are mingled the myriad
  races of mortal things flow out,
and many things stay unmixed in contrast
  to the things that are being blended,
which Strife holds still suspended; for not
  perfectly
yet had he withdrawn to the uttermost
  bounds of the circle,
but some of his limbs remained within
  while some had withdrawn.
As far as he would run ahead, so far
  would advance
the gentle immortal press of blameless
  Love.
And suddenly those things grew mortal
  which before were wont to be
  immortal,
and what was before unblended became
  mixed, exchanging paths.
When these things are mingled the myriad
  races of mortal things flow out,
fitted with all sorts of shapes, a marvel to
  behold.

REINCARNATION

5. [B115] There is an oracle of necessity, an ancient decree of the gods,
everlasting, sealed by broad oaths:
when one in his crimes stains his own
limbs with innocent blood
and wrongfully forswears himself,
one of those spirits who have inherited
  long life,
thrice ten thousand seasons he is exiled
  from the blessed gods,
through time growing to be all kinds of
  creatures,
going from one difficult path of life to
  another.
For mighty aether drives him into sea,
sea spews him onto the surface of the
  earth, and earth to the rays
of shining sun, who casts him into the
  whirls of aether.
One passes him to another; all abhor him.
Of these I too am now one, a fugitive and
  wanderer from the gods,
a devotee of raving Strife.·

LEUCIPPUS AND DEMOCRITUS

ATOMS AND THE VOID

1. [Leucippus A6] Leucippus and his companion Democritus say the elements are **the full** and **the empty**, calling them **what-is** and **what-is-not**, respectively, and of these the full and solid what-is, the empty and rare are what-is-not. For this reason they say that what-is is no more than what-is-not: because void *is* no less than body. . . . And just as those who made the underlying substance one in number generated other things from the affections of this (positing the rare and the dense as sources of these affections), in the same way [the atomists] say the differences [of their atoms] are the causes of all other things. Now they say these are three: shape, order, and position. For they say what-is differs by contour, **contact**, and **rotation**. Of these contour is shape, contact is order, and rotation is position. For instance, A differs from N in shape, AN from NA in order, and Z from N in position. (Aristotle)

2. [Democritus A37] [Democritus] calls place by these names: **the empty** [or: the void], **not-thing** [*ouden*] and **the boundless**, and each of the substances by these: **thing** [*den*], **the compact**, and **what-is**. He thinks

the substances are so small as to escape our senses. But they have all kinds of forms and shapes and differences of size. Thus from these as from elements he can create the visible and perceptible masses by compounding. (Aristotle from Simplicius)

3. [B156] **Thing** [*den*] **is no more than nothing** [*mêden*].

HUMAN PERCEPTION

4. [B11] **Of understanding there are two kinds, one legitimate, one bastard. Of the bastard kind are all these: sight, hearing, smell, taste, touch. And there is the legitimate kind, which is distinct from this. [. . .] Whenever the bastard kind is no longer able to see any smaller or to hear, smell, taste, or perceive by touch** . . . [sc. the legitimate kind takes over to make] **finer** [discriminations].

5. [B9] Sometimes Democritus rejects things that appear to the senses and says none of them appears in truth, but only in opinion, but the truth about things is that there are atoms and the void: **By convention,** he says, **there is sweet, by convention bitter; by convention hot, by convention cold; by convention color; but in reality atoms and the void.** (Sextus Empiricus)

FORMATION OF COMPOUNDS

6. [A37, continued] They struggle and travel in the void because of dissimilarity and the other aforementioned differences, and as they travel they strike each other and become entangled in such a way as to produce mutual contact and proximity, but this does not in any way create a genuinely single nature from them. For it is completely absurd to think two or more things could ever come to be one. The reason he gives for these substances cohering for a certain time

is that the bodies connect together and grasp hold of each other. For some of them are angular, some hooked, some concave, some convex, and some have countless other differences. Thus he thinks they hold out and cohere so long as some more powerful force from the surrounding area does not appear to shake and scatter them apart.

THE ORIGIN OF THE COSMOS

7. [Leucippus A1] [Leucippus says] the worlds come to be in this way: **by being cut off from the boundless,** many bodies having all sorts of shapes travel into a **great void,** which being gathered together produce a single vortex, in which, striking each other and spinning every which way the like are separated apart to the like. When they are no longer able to travel around in equilibrium because of the multitude, the light ones retreat to the void outside as if they were sifted, while the rest **cohere** and becoming entangled move in unison with each other so as to make a primary spherical structure. And this like a **membrane** stands apart, containing in itself all sorts of bodies. As the bodies spin around in response to the resistance of the middle, the surrounding membrane becomes attenuated as a result of the adjacent bodies being continually eroded as they come in contact with the vortex. And so the earth comes to be, when the bodies borne to the center **cohere.** And the membrane-like container in turn grows by an influx of bodies from outside, and being borne by the vortex, it captures whatever bodies it comes in contact with. Some of these becoming entangled form structures, at first moist and muddy, which then, being dried out as they are carried about with the revolution of the world, are ignited to produce the substance of the stars. (Diogenes Laertius)

REVIEW QUESTIONS

1. How did the inquiries of the Pre-Socratics differ from the way other cultures had posed and answered questions about the world? What role did religion play in the intellectual progress of most of the Great Civilizations? What role did it play in the philosophical investigations of the Pre-Socratics?

2. What are Parmenides' doctrines concerning change and the world of Being? Why are Parmenides' views considered a form of absolute idealism?

3. According to Heraclitus, what is the nature of the universe? Was it created, or has it always been? What is the role of logos in the world?

4. According to Empedocles, of what is the universe composed? What is his doctrine of love and hate?

5. What is the central doctrine of Leucippus and Democritus? How is their insight related to modern physics?

2

PLATO

The safest general characterization of the European philosophical tradition is that it consists of a series of footnotes to Plato.

(ALFRED NORTH WHITEHEAD)

Plato is Philosophy, and Philosophy is Plato. . . . Out of Plato comes all things that are still written and debated among men of thought.

(RALPH WALDO EMERSON)

Plato (427–347 B.C.) is generally recognized as the Father of Philosophy, the first systematic metaphysician and epistemologist, the first philosopher to set forth a comprehensive treatment of the entire domain of philosophy from ontology to ethics and aesthetics. He was born into an Athenian aristocratic family at the end of the Periclean Golden Age of Greek democracy.[1] During much of his life, Athens was at war with Sparta, the Greek city state to the south. He was Socrates' disciple, the developer of his teacher's ideas, the founder of the first university and school of philosophy (the Academy in Athens), Aristotle's teacher, and an adviser to kings, Dionysius and Dion. His goal may have been to found the ideal state, described in Book V of the *Republic*, where philosophers ruled with justice. Among his important works are the *Euthyphro*, *Apology*, *Crito*, *Phaedo*, *Meno*, and *Republic*, which are included in this part of our book. Most of his books are dialogues in which Socrates is the key spokesman and interlocutor, who seeks an understanding of difficult concepts.

---

[1] Pericles (495–429 B.C.) was the great Athenian general and statesman under whose leadership Athens developed into a humane democracy and prospered materially and culturally.

Socrates (c. 470–399 B.C.), the son of Sophroniscus, an Athenian stone cutter, and Phanenarete, a midwife, one of the most important yet enigmatic figures in philosophy, was the inspiration for Plato's thought. At one time a follower of the "Pre-Socratic" cosmologists (perhaps of Anaxagoras), he later turned from cosmological speculation about the heavens to consider ethics, how we ought to live. He wrote nothing, but his ideas are conveyed to us by Plato. In the early dialogues, such as the *Euthyphro*, *Apology*, and *Crito*, Plato may be reporting Socrates' own thoughts, if not his own words, but as Plato developed his own philosophy, he continued to use Socrates as his mouthpiece. After the infamous trial and execution of Socrates in 399 B.C., Plato, then twenty-eight, abandoned thoughts for a political career, traveled, and then began his career as a philosopher.

What were Plato's distinctive ideas? The most famous idea is the *Theory of Forms*, an instance of the idea of the *One and the Many*. What do the *many* similar things have in common? The *one* Form. All beautiful things have in common participation in the form of the Beautiful; all good things have in common participation in the Form of the Good.

What do all triangles or green objects have in common? Triangles come in different shapes and sizes. It is true that all triangles are closed plain figures with three sides and three angles adding up to 180 degrees, but the sides may be different sizes and the shape of the triangle may be isosceles or scalene. Even before we can articulate the definition of a triangle we seem to know one when we see it. Regarding green objects, we cannot even define their common property—*green*. We cannot help a blind person understand what it is or even describe it to one who knows what green is. It is an unanalyzable simple property. All green things have this undefinable property in common. Now let us go from perceptual objects (triangles, colors, chairs, and tables) to abstract ideas: friendship, equality, justice, beauty, goodness. What do all exemplars of each of these properties have in common? Plato's *Theory of Forms* (sometimes referred to as his "Theory of Ideas") seeks to give us a satisfactory answer to this question.

Aristotle tells us how Plato first came upon this theory:

> The Theory of forms occurred to Plato because he was persuaded of the truth of Heraclitus' doctrine that all things accessible to the senses are always in a state of flux, so that if knowledge or thought is to have an object there must besides things accessible to the senses be certain other entities which persist; for there is no knowledge of things which are in a state of flux. Socrates occupied himself with the moral virtues, and was the first to look for general definitions in this area. There are two things which may fairly be ascribed to Socrates, arguments by analogy and general definitions, both of which are concerned with the starting point of knowledge. But whereas Socrates made neither the universal nor the definition exist separately, others gave them a separate existence and this was the sort of thing to which they gave the name of Forms. So for them it followed by almost the same argument that there are forms for everything to which general words apply.[2]

Whereas Socrates sought clear definitions of concepts in order to have a common basis for discussion (how can we even settle on an understanding of what a "just society" will be if we have different definitions of *justice*?), Plato went beyond *verbal* definitions and posited a comprehensive theory of reality.

According to Plato, every significant word (noun, adjective, and verb) and thing partakes of and derives its identity from a Form or Forms. The Forms are single, common to all objects and abstract terms, perfect as the particulars or exemplars are not, independent

[2]Aristotle, *Metaphysics*, 1078.

of any particulars and yet their cause, having objective existence (they are the truly real, while particulars are only apparently so). While independent of the human mind, they are intelligible and can be known by the mind alone and not by sense experience. The Forms are divine, eternal, simple, indissoluble, unchanging, self-subsisting reality, existing outside space and time. They are the cause of all that is.

We will encounter Plato's ideas of the Forms in his dialogues *Phaedo* and *Republic*.

Related to Plato's theory of the Forms is his doctrine of *Innate Ideas and the Theory of Recollection*. In the dialogue *Meno*, Plato, through his spokesman Socrates, seeks to prove that we are born with innate ideas of the Forms. The dialogue begins with Meno raising a puzzle about learning: how do you know when you have found the answer to a question you are asking? Either (1) you don't know the answer and so won't know when you've found it; or (2) you already know the answer, in which case why make an inquiry in the first place? Socrates sets about to solve this riddle about the impossibility of learning through the theory of recollection of knowledge. The specific question Meno raises is whether virtue can be taught. He calls one of Meno's slaves, an uneducated boy, who will be the test case as to whether learning takes place through recollecting knowledge learned in a previous existence. He will argue that in provoking the correct answers from the slave he demonstrates that we have innate ideas which must have been learned in a previous existence. This method of evoking implicit knowledge from the student is now referred to as the "Socratic method" of teaching, though it need not include a theory of innate ideas.

Our first reading, the *Euthyphro*, deals with the question "What is piety?" and raises the issue of whether the god or gods love the good because it is good or whether the good is good because the god loves it.

FOR FURTHER READING

By Plato

The Dialogues of Plato, 4th ed., revised by D. J. Allan and H. E. Dale (Oxford University Press, 1953). Jowett's translation is still among the best, literary and accurate.

Plato: The Collected Dialogues, ed. Edith Hamilton and Huntington Cairns (Princeton University Press, 1982). This complete set of Plato's dialogues is the best single-volume collection of his works. The translations are typically excellent.

Plato's Republic, trans. G. M. A. Grube (Hackett, 1980). This is an accessible, accurate translation.

About Socrates

Benson, Hugh, ed. *Essays on the Philosophy of Socrates* (Oxford University Press, 1992).

Guthrie, W. K. C. *The History of Greek Philosophy*, vol. III (Cambridge University Press, 1969).

Kraut, Richard. *Socrates and the State* (Princeton University Press, 1984).

Taylor, A. E. *Socrates* (Methuen, 1933).

Vlastos, Gregory. *Socrates, Ironist and Moral Philosopher* (Cornell University Press, 1991).

Vlastos, Gregory, ed. *The Philosophy of Socrates* (Doubleday, 1971).

About Plato

Annas, Julia. *An Introduction to Plato's Republic* (Oxford University Press, 1981).

Crombie, I. M. *An Examination of Plato's Doctrines*, 2 vols. (Humanities Press, 1963, 1969).

Grube, G. M. A. *Plato's Thought* (Methuen, 1935). An insightful discussion of Plato's thought, especially of the Forms.

Guthrie, W. K. C. *The History of Greek Philosophy*, vols. IV & V (Cambridge University Press, 1975, 1978).

Irwin, Terrance. *Plato's Moral Theory: Early and Middle Dialogues* (Clarendon Press, 1977). A complex, advanced but rich scholarly work.

Kraut, Richard, ed. *The Cambridge Companion to Plato* (Cambridge University Press, 1992).

Ross, W. D. *Plato's Theory of Ideas* (Oxford University Press, 1951). This book traces the theory of the Forms from the early dialogues to the Laws. A brilliant analysis.

Taylor, A. E. *Plato: The Man and His Work* (Methuen, 1950). A splendid exposition of the entire Platonic corpus.

Vlastos, Gregory, ed. *Plato: A Collection of Critical Essays*, 2 vols. (Doubleday, 1970, 1971).

About the Period

Jones, W. T. *The Classical Mind* (Harcourt, Brace, 1952). A helpful overview of the ancient Greeks and their culture.

Renault, Mary. *The Last of the Wine* (Pantheon, 1956). A novel depicting Athens in the days of Socrates.

25–35

EUTHYPHRO

Socrates and Euthyphro meet at the entrance to the law courts, and to Euthyphro's surprised question—"What has taken you from your haunts in the Lyceum?"—Socrates answers that a charge has been brought against him which is rather a grand one, that of corrupting the youth of Athens, and that the prosecutor knows just how it is done and how. Socrates is doing it. But why, he asks in turn, is Euthyphro here? The reason, the latter answers, is that he is prosecuting his own father on a charge of murder. Socrates' astonishment at this does not disturb him. He is by profession an interpreter of religion, a theologian, and he tells Socrates that with his special insight into what is right and wrong he knows that he is acting in the spirit of true piety. When Socrates asks what then is piety, he gives the answer characteristic of the orthodox everywhere—in effect, "Piety is thinking as I do." His sincerity is as patent as his conceit. He really believes that he ought to prosecute his father who though certainly not a murderer is not free from blame.

The conversation that follows is chiefly an attempt to define piety, and comes to nothing, but in the course of it Socrates makes a distinction fundamental in reasoning and often disregarded, that the good is not good because the gods approve it, but the gods approve it because it is good.

The real interest of the dialogue, however, is the picture of Socrates just before his trial. There is no question that he realized the danger he was in, but Plato, who knew him best of all, shows him engaging humorously and ironically and keenly in a discussion completely removed from his own situation. Just at the end he says that if only Euthyphro will instruct him in what true piety is he will tell his accuser that he has become the pupil of a great theologian and is going to lead a better life. But Euthyphro, by this time in no mood to define anything, gives up. "Another time, then, Socrates," he says and hurries away.

2 *Euthyphro.* This, Socrates, is something new? What has taken you from your haunts in the Lyceum, and makes you spend your time at the royal porch? You surely cannot have a case at law, as I have, before the Archon-King.

Socrates. My business, Euthyphro, is not what is known at Athens as a case at law; it is a criminal prosecution.

b *Euthyphro.* How is that? You mean that somebody is prosecuting you? I never would believe that you were prosecuting anybody else.

Socrates. No indeed.

Euthyphro. Then somebody is prosecuting you?

Socrates. Most certainly.

Euthyphro. Who is it?

Socrates. I am not too clear about the man myself, Euthyphro. He appears to me to be a young man, and unknown. I think, however, that they call him Meletus, and his deme is Pitthos, if you happen to know anyone named Meletus of that deme—a hook-nosed man with long straight hair, and not much beard.

Euthyphro. I don't recall him, Socrates. But c tell me, of what does he accuse you?

Socrates. His accusation? It is no mean charge. For a man of his age it is no small thing to have settled a question of so much importance. He says, in fact, that he knows the method by which young people are corrupted, and knows who the persons are that do it. He is, quite possibly, a wise man, and, observing that my ignorance has led me to corrupt his generation, comes like a child to his mother to accuse me to the d city. And to me he appears to be the only one who begins his political activity aright, for the right way to begin is to pay attention to the young, and make them just as good as possible—precisely as the able farmer will give his atten-3 tion to the young plants first, and afterward care for the rest. And so Meletus no doubt begins by clearing us away, the ones who ruin, as he says, the tender shoots of the young. That done, he obviously will care for the older generation, and will thus become the cause, in the highest and widest measure, of benefit to the state. With such a notable beginning, his chances of success look good.

Euthyphro. I hope so, Socrates, but I'm very much afraid it will go the other way. When he starts to injure you, it simply looks to me like the beginning at the hearth to hurt the state. But tell me what he says you do to corrupt the young.

Socrates. It sounds very queer, my friend, b when first you hear it. He says I am a maker of gods; he charges me with making new gods, and not believing in the old ones. These are his grounds for prosecuting me, he says.

Euthyphro. I see it, Socrates. It is because you say that ever and anon you have the spiritual sign! So he charges you in this indictment with introducing novelties in religion, and that is the reason why he comes to court with this slanderous complaint, well knowing how easily such matters can be misrepresented to the crowd. For my own part, when I speak in the Assembly about c matters of religion, and tell them in advance what will occur, they laugh at me as if I were a madman, and yet I never have made a prediction that did not come true. But the truth is, they are jealous of all such people as ourselves. No, we must not worry over them, but go to meet them.

Socrates. Dear Euthyphro, if we were only laughed at, it would be no serious matter. The Athenians, as it seems to me, are not very much disturbed if they think that so-and-so is clever, so long as he does not impart his knowledge to anybody else. But the moment they suspect that he is giving his ability to others, they get angry, whether out of jealousy, as you say, or, it may be, for some other reason. d

Euthyphro. With regard to that, I am not very eager to test their attitude to me.

Socrates. Quite possibly you strike them as a man who is chary of himself, and is unwilling to impart his wisdom; as for me, I fear I am so kindly they will think that I pour out all I have to everyone, and not merely without pay—nay, rather, glad to offer something if it would induce someone to hear me. Well then, as I said just now, if they were going to laugh at me, as you say they do at you, it wouldn't be at all unpleasant to spend the time laughing and joking in court. But if they take the matter seriously, then there is no knowing how it will turn out. Only you prophets can e tell!

Euthyphro. Well, Socrates, perhaps no harm will come of it at all, but you will carry your case as you desire, and I think that I shall carry mine.

Socrates. Your case, Euthyphro? What is it? Are you prosecuting, or defending?

Euthyphro. Prosecuting.

Socrates. Whom?

Euthyphro. One whom I am thought a maniac to be attacking.

Socrates. How so? Is it someone who has wings to fly away with?

Euthyphro. He is far from being able to do that; he happens to be old, a very old man.

Socrates. Who is it, then?

Euthyphro. It is my father.

Socrates. Your father, my good friend?

Euthyphro. Just so.

Socrates. What is the complaint? Of what do you accuse him?

Euthyphro. Of murder, Socrates.

Socrates. Good heavens, Euthyphro! Surely the crowd is ignorant of the way things ought to go. I fancy it is not correct for any ordinary person to do that [to prosecute his father on this charge], but only for a man already far advanced in point of wisdom.

Euthyphro. Yes, Socrates, by heaven! Far advanced!

Socrates. And the man your father killed, was he a relative of yours? Of course he was? You never would prosecute your father, would you, for the death of anybody who was not related to you?

Euthyphro. You amuse me, Socrates. You think it makes a difference whether the victim was a member of the family, or not related, when the only thing to watch is whether it was right or not for the man who did the deed to kill him. If he was justified, then let him go; if not, you have to prosecute him, no matter if the man who killed him shares your hearth, and sits at table with you. The pollution is the same if, knowingly, you associate with such a man, and do not cleanse yourself, and him as well, by bringing him to justice. The victim in this case was a laborer of mine, and when we were cultivating land in Naxos, we employed him on our farm. One day he had been drinking, and became enraged at one of our domestics, and cut his throat; whereupon my father

bound him hand and foot, and threw him into a ditch. Then he sent a man to Athens to find out from the seer what ought to be done—meanwhile paying no attention to the man who had been bound, neglecting him because he was a murderer and it would be no great matter even if he died. And that was just what happened. Hunger, cold, and the shackles finished him before the messenger got back from visiting the seer. That is why my father and my other kin are bitter at me when I prosecute my father as a murderer. They say he did not kill the man, and had he actually done it, the victim was himself a murderer, and for such a man one need have no consideration. They say that for a son to prosecute his father as a murderer is unholy. How ill they know divinity in its relation, Socrates, to what is holy or unholy!

Socrates. But you, by heaven! Euthyphro, you think that you have such an accurate knowledge of things divine, and what is holy and unholy, that, in circumstances such as you describe, you can accuse your father? You are not afraid that you yourself are doing an unholy deed?

Euthyphro. Why, Socrates, if I did not have an accurate knowledge of all, I should be good for nothing, and Euthyphro would be no different from the general run of men.

Socrates. Well then, admirable Euthyphro, the best thing I can do is to become your pupil, and challenge Meletus before the trial comes on. Let me tell him that in the past I have considered it of great importance to know about things divine, and that now, when he asserts that I erroneously put forward my own notions and inventions on this head, I have become your pupil. I could say, Come Meletus, if you agree that Euthyphro has wisdom in such matters, you must admit as well that I hold the true belief, and must not prosecute. If you do not, you must lodge your complaint, not against me, but against my aforesaid master; accuse him of corrupting the elder generation, me and his own father—me by his instruction, his father by correcting and chastising him.

And if he would not yield, would neither quit the suit nor yet indict you rather than myself, then I would say the same in court as when I challenged him!

Euthyphro. Yes, Socrates, by heaven! If he undertook to bring me into court, I guess I would find out his rotten spot, and our talk there would concern him sooner by a long shot than ever it would me!

Socrates. Yes, my dear friend, that I know, and so I wish to be your pupil. This Meletus, I perceive, along presumably with everybody else, appears to overlook you, but sees into me so easily and keenly that he has attacked me for impiety. So, in the name of heaven, tell me now about the matter you just felt sure you knew quite thoroughly. State what you take piety and impiety to be with reference to murder and all other cases. Is not the holy always one and the same thing in every action, and, again, is not the unholy always opposite to the holy, and like itself? And as unholiness does it not always have its one essential form, which will be found in everything that is unholy?

Euthyphro. Yes, surely, Socrates.

Socrates. Then tell me. How do you define the holy and the unholy?

Euthyphro. Well then, I say that the holy is what I am now doing, prosecuting the wrongdoer who commits a murder or a sacrilegious robbery, or sins in any point like that, whether it be your father, or your mother, or whoever it may be. And not to prosecute would be that such is the law. It is one I have already given to others; I tell them that the right procedure must be not to tolerate the impious man, no matter who. Does not mankind believe that Zeus is the most excellent and just among the gods? And these same men admit that Zeus shackled his own father [Cronus] for swallowing his [other] sons unjustly, and that Cronus in turn had gelded his father [Uranus] for like reasons. But now they are enraged at me when I proceed against my father for wrongdoing, and so they contradict themselves in what they say about the gods and what they say of me.

Socrates. There, Euthyphro, you have the reason why the charge is brought against me. It is because, whenever people tell such stories about the gods, I am prone to take it ill, and, so it seems, that is why they will maintain that I am sinful. Well, now, if you who are so well versed in matters of the sort entertain the same beliefs, then necessarily, it would seem, I must give in, for what could we urge who admit that, for our own part, we are quite ignorant about these matters? But, in the name of friendship, tell me! Do you actually believe that these things happened so?

Euthyphro. Yes, Socrates, and things even more amazing, of which the multitude does not know.

Socrates. And you actually believe that war occurred among the gods, and there were dreadful hatreds, battles, and all sorts of fearful things like that? Such things as the poets tell of, and good artists represent in sacred places; yes, and at the great Panathenaic festival the robe that is carried up to the Acropolis is all inwrought with such embellishments? What is our position, Euthyphro? Do we say that these things are true?

Euthyphro. Not these things only, Socrates, but, as I just now said, I will, if you wish, relate to you many other stories about the gods, which I am certain will astonish you when you hear them.

Socrates. I shouldn't wonder. You shall tell me all about them when we have the leisure at some other time. At present try to tell me more clearly what I asked you a little while ago, for, my friend, you were not explicit enough before when I put the question. What is holiness? You merely said that what you are now doing is a holy deed—namely, prosecuting your father on a charge of murder.

Euthyphro. And, Socrates, I told the truth.

Socrates. Possibly. But, Euthyphro, there are many other things that you will say are holy.

Euthyphro. Because they are.

Socrates. Well, bear in mind that what I asked of you was not to tell me one or two out of all the numerous actions that are holy; I wanted you to tell me what is the essential form of holiness which makes all holy actions holy. I believe you held that there is one ideal form by which unholy things are all unholy, and by which all holy things are holy. Do you remember that?

Euthyphro. I do.

Socrates. Well then, show me what, precisely, this ideal is, so that, with my eye on it, and using it as a standard, I can say that any action done by you or anybody else is holy if it resembles this ideal, or, if it does not, can deny that it is holy.

Euthyphro. Well, Socrates, if that is what you want, I certainly can tell you.

Socrates. It is precisely what I want.

Euthyphro. Well then, what is pleasing to the gods is holy, and what is not pleasing to them is unholy.

Socrates. Perfect, Euthyphro! Now you give me just the answer that I asked for. Meanwhile, whether it is right I do not know, but obviously you will go on to prove your statement true.

Euthyphro. Indeed I will.

Socrates. Come now, let us scrutinize what we are saying. What is pleasing to the gods, and the man that pleases them, are holy; what is hateful to the gods, and the man they hate, unholy. But the holy and unholy are not the same; the holy is directly opposite to the unholy. Isn't it so?

Euthyphro. It is.

Socrates. And the matter clearly was well stated.

Euthyphro. I accept it, Socrates; that was stated.

Socrates. Was it not also stated, Euthyphro, that the gods revolt and differ with each other, and that hatreds come between them?

Euthyphro. That was stated.

Socrates. Hatred and wrath, my friend—what kind of disagreement will produce them? Look at the matter thus. If you and I were to differ about numbers, on the question which of two was the greater, would a disagreement about that make us angry at each other, and make enemies of us? Should we not settle things by calculation, and so come to an agreement quickly on any point like that?

Euthyphro. Yes, certainly.

Socrates. And similarly if we differed on a question of greater length or less, we would take a measurement, and quickly put an end to the dispute?

Euthyphro. Just that.

Socrates. And so, I fancy, we should have recourse to scales, and settle any question about a heavier or lighter weight?

Euthyphro. Of course.

Socrates. What sort of thing, then, is it about which we differ, till, unable to arrive at a decision, we might get angry and be enemies to one another? Perhaps you have no answer ready, but listen to me. See if it is not the following—right and wrong, the noble and the base, and good and bad. Are not these the things about which we differ, till, unable to arrive at a decision, we grow hostile, when we do grow hostile, to each other, you and I and everybody else?

Euthyphro. Yes, Socrates, that is where we differ, on these subjects.

Socrates. What about the gods, then, Euthyphro? If, indeed, they have dissensions, must it not be on these subjects?

Euthyphro. Quite necessarily.

Socrates. Accordingly, my noble Euthyphro, by your account some gods take one thing to be right, and others take another, and similarly with the honorable and the base, and good and bad. They would hardly be at variance with each other, if they did not differ on these questions. Would they?

Euthyphro. You are right.

Socrates. And what each one of them thinks noble, good, and just, is what he loves, and the opposite is what he hates?

Euthyphro. Yes, certainly.

Socrates. But it is the same things, so you say, that some of them think right, and others wrong, and through disputing about these they are at variance, and make war on one another. Isn't it so?

Euthyphro. It is.

Socrates. Accordingly, so it would seem, the same things will be hated by the gods and loved by them; the same things would alike displease and please them.

Euthyphro. It would seem so.

Socrates. And so, according to this argument, the same things, Euthyphro, will be holy and unholy.

Euthyphro. That may be.

Socrates. In that case, admirable friend, you have not answered what I asked you. I did not ask you to tell me what at once is holy and unholy, but it seems that what is pleasing to the gods is also hateful to them. Thus, Euthyphro, it would not be strange at all if what you now are doing in punishing your father were pleasing to Zeus, but hateful to Cronus and Uranus, and welcome to Hephaestus, but odious to Hera, and if any other of the gods disagree about the matter, satisfactory to some of them, and odious to others.

Euthyphro. But, Socrates, my notion is that, on this point, there is no difference of opinion among the gods—not one of them but thinks that if a person kills another wrongfully, he ought to pay for it.

Socrates. And what of men? Have you never c heard a man contending that someone who has killed a person wrongfully, or done some other unjust deed, ought not to pay the penalty?

Euthyphro. Why! There is never any end to their disputes about these matters; it goes on everywhere, above all in the courts. People do all kinds of wrong, and then there is nothing they will not do or say in order to escape the penalty.

Socrates. Do they admit wrongdoing, Euthyphro, and, while admitting it, deny that they ought to pay the penalty?

Euthyphro. No, not that, by any means.

Socrates. Then they will not do and say quite everything. Unless I am mistaken, they dare not say or argue that if they do wrong they should not d pay the penalty. No, I think that they deny wrongdoing. How about it?

Euthyphro. It is true.

Socrates. Therefore they do not dispute that anybody who does wrong should pay the penalty. No, the thing that they dispute about is likely to be who is the wrongdoer, what he did, and when.

Euthyphro. That is true.

Socrates. Well then, isn't that precisely what goes on among the gods, if they really do have quarrels about right and wrong, as you say they do? One set will hold that some others do wrong, and the other set deny it? For that other thing, my friend, I take it no one, whether god or man, will dare to say—that the wrongdoer should not pay e the penalty!

Euthyphro. Yes, Socrates, what you say is true—in the main.

Socrates. It is the individual act, I fancy, Euthyphro, that the disputants dispute about, both

men and gods, if gods ever do dispute. They differ on a certain act; some hold that it was rightly done, the others that it was wrong. Isn't it so?

Euthyphro. Yes, certainly.

Socrates. Then come, dear Euthyphro, teach 9 me as well, and let me grow more wise. What proof have you that all the gods think that your servant died unjustly, your hireling, who, when he had killed a man, was shackled by the master of the victim, and perished, dying because of his shackles before the man who shackled him could learn from the seers what ought to be done with him? What proof have you that for a man like him it is right for a son to prosecute his father, and indict him on a charge of murder? Come on. Try to make it clear to me beyond all doubt that under these conditions the gods must all consider this action to be right. If you can adequately prove it to me, I will never cease from praising you for b your wisdom.

Euthyphro. But, Socrates, that, very likely, would be no small task, although I could indeed make it very clear to you.

Socrates. I understand. You think that I am duller than the judges; obviously you will demonstrate to them that what your father did was wrong, and that the gods all hate such deeds.

Euthyphro. I shall prove it absolutely, Socrates, if they will listen to me.

Socrates. They are sure to listen if they think c that you speak well. But while you were talking, a notion came into my head, and I asked myself, Suppose that Euthyphro proved to me quite clearly that all the gods consider such a death unjust; would I have come one whit the nearer for him to knowing what the holy is, and what is the unholy? The act in question, seemingly, might be displeasing to the gods, but then we have just seen that you cannot define the holy and unholy in that way, for we have seen that a given thing may be displeasing, and also pleasing, to gods. So on this point, Euthyphro, I will let you off; if you like, the gods shall all consider the act unjust, and they all shall hate it. But suppose that we now correct our definition, and say what the gods all hate is d unholy, and what they love is holy, whereas what some of them love, and others hate, is either both or neither. Are you willing that we now define the holy and unholy in this way?

Euthyphro. What is there to prevent us, Socrates?

Socrates. Nothing to prevent me, Euthyphro. As for you, see whether when you take this definition you can quite readily instruct me, as you promised.

Euthyphro. Yes, I would indeed affirm that holiness is what the gods all love, and its opposite is what the gods all hate, unholiness.

Socrates. Are we to examine this position also, Euthyphro, to see if it is sound? Or shall we let it through, and thus accept our own and others' statement, and agree to an assertion simply when somebody says that a thing is so? Must we not look into what the speaker says?

Euthyphro. We must. And yet, for my part, I regard the present statement as correct.

Socrates. We shall soon know better about that, my friend. Now think of this. Is what is holy holy because the gods approve it, or do they approve it because it is holy?

Euthyphro. I do not get your meaning.

Socrates. Well, I will try to make it clearer. We speak of what is carried and the carrier, do we not, of led and leader, of the seen and that which sees? And you understand that in all such cases the things are different, and how they differ?

Euthyphro. Yes, I think I understand.

Socrates. In the same way what is loved is one thing, and what loves is another?

Euthyphro. Of course.

Socrates. Tell me now, is what is carried 'carried' because something carries it, or is it for some other reason?

Euthyphro. No, but for that reason.

Socrates. And what is led, because something leads it? And what is seen, because something sees it?

Euthyphro. Yes, certainly.

Socrates. Then it is not because a thing is seen that something sees it, but just the opposite—because something sees it, therefore it is seen. Nor because it is led, that something leads it, but because something leads it, therefore it is led. Nor

because it is carried, that something carries it, but because something carries it, therefore it is carried. Do you see what I wish to say, Euthyphro? It is this. Whenever an effect occurs, or something is effected, it is not the thing effected that gives rise to the effect; no, there is a cause, and then comes this effect. Nor is it because a thing is acted on that there is this effect; no, there is a cause for what it undergoes, and then comes this effect. Don't you agree?

Euthyphro. I do.

Socrates. Well then, when a thing is loved, is it not in process of becoming something, or of undergoing something, by some other thing?

Euthyphro. Yes, certainly.

Socrates. Then the same is true here as in the previous cases. It is not because a thing is loved that they who love it love it, but it is loved because they love it.

Euthyphro. Necessarily.

Socrates. Then what are we to say about the holy, Euthyphro? According to your argument, is it not loved by all the gods?

Euthyphro. Yes.

Socrates. Because it is holy, or for some other reason?

Euthyphro. No, it is for that reason.

Socrates. And so it is because it is holy that it is loved; it is not holy because it is loved.

Euthyphro. So it seems.

Socrates. On the other hand, it is beloved and pleasing to the gods just because they love it?

Euthyphro. No doubt of that.

Socrates. So what is pleasing to the gods is not the same as what is holy, Euthyphro, nor, according to your statement, is the holy the same as what is pleasing to the gods. They are two different things.

Euthyphro. How may that be, Socrates?

Socrates. Because we are agreed that the holy is loved because it is holy, and is not holy because it is loved. Isn't it so?

Euthyphro. Yes.

Socrates. Whereas what is pleasing to the gods is pleasing to them just because they love it, such being its nature and its cause. Its being loved of the gods is not the reason of its being loved.

Euthyphro. You are right.

Socrates. But suppose, dear Euthyphro, that what is pleasing to the gods and what is holy were not two separate things. In that case if holiness were loved because it was holy, then also what was pleasing to the gods would be loved because it pleased them. And on the other hand, if what was pleasing to them pleased because they loved it, then also the holy would be holy because they loved it. But now you see that it is just the opposite, because the two are absolutely different from each other, for the one [what is pleasing to the gods] is of a sort to be loved because it is loved, whereas the other [what is holy] is loved because it is of a sort to be loved. Consequently, Euthyphro, it looks as if you had not given me my answer—as if when you were asked to tell the nature of the holy, you did not wish to explain the essence of it. You merely tell an attribute of it, namely, that it appertains to holiness to be loved by all the gods. What it *is*, as yet you have not said. So, if you please, do not conceal this from me. No, begin again. Say what the holy is, and never mind if gods do love it, nor if it has some other attribute; on that we shall not split. Come, speak out. Explain the nature of the holy and unholy.

Euthyphro. Now, Socrates, I simply don't know how to tell you what I think. Somehow everything that we put forward keeps moving about us in a circle, and nothing will stay where we put it.

Socrates. Your statements, Euthyphro, look like the work of Daedalus, founder of my line. If I had made them, and they were my positions, no doubt you would poke fun at me, and say that, being in his line, the figures I construct in words run off, as did his statues, and will not stay where they are put. Meanwhile, since they are your definitions, we need some other jest, for in fact, as you see yourself, they will not stand still.

Euthyphro. But, Socrates, it seems to me that the jest is quite to the point. This tendency in our statements to go in a circle, and not to stay in one place, it is not I who put it there. To my mind, it is you who are the Daedalus; so far as I am concerned, they would have held their place.

Socrates. If so, my friend, I must be more expert in his art than he, in that he merely made his own works capable of moving, whereas I give this power not merely to my own, but, seemingly, to the works of other men as well. And the rarest thing about my talent is that I am an unwilling artist, since I would rather see our arguments stand fast and hold their ground than have the art of Daedalus plus all the wealth of Tantalus to boot. But enough of this. And since, to my mind, you are languid, I will myself make bold with you to show how you might teach me about holiness. Do not weaken. See if you do not think that of necessity all that is holy is just.

Euthyphro. Yes, I do.

Socrates. Well then, is all justice holy too? Or, granted that all holiness is just, is justice not all holy, but some part of it is holy, and some part of it is not?

Euthyphro. I do not follow, Socrates.

Socrates. And yet you surpass me in your wisdom not less than by your youth. I repeat, you are languid through your affluence in wisdom. Come, lucky friend, exert yourself? What I have to say is not so hard to grasp. I mean the very opposite of what the poet wrote.

Zeus, who brought that all to pass, and made it all to grow,
You will not name, for where fear is, there too is reverence.[1]

On that I differ from the poet. Shall I tell you why?

Euthyphro. By all means.

Socrates. I do not think that 'where fear is, there too is reverence.' For it seems to me that there are many who fear sickness, poverty, and all the like, and so are afraid, but have no reverence whatever for the things they are afraid of. Does it not seem so to you?

Euthyphro. Yes, certainly.

Socrates. Where, however, you have reverence, there you have fear as well. Is there anybody who has reverence and a sense of shame about an act, and does not at the same time dread and fear an evil reputation?

---

[1] Stasinus, fr. 20.

Euthyphro. Yes, he will be afraid of it.

Socrates. So it is not right to say that 'where fear is, there too is reverence.' No, you may say that where reverence is, there too is fear—not, however, that where fear is, there always you have reverence. Fear, I think, is wider in extent than reverence. Reverence is a part of fear, as the uneven is a part of number; thus you do not have the odd wherever you have number, but where you have the odd you must have number. I take it you are following me now?

Euthyphro. Yes, indeed.

Socrates. Well then, what I asked you was like that. I asked you if wherever justice is, there is holiness as well; or, granted that wherever there is holiness, there is justice too, if where justice is, the holy is not always to be found. Thus holiness would be a part of justice. Shall we say so, or have you a different view?

Euthyphro. No, that is my opinion. I think that you are clearly right.

Socrates. Then see what follows. If holiness is a part of justice, it seems to me that we must find out what part of justice it is. Suppose, for instance, in our case just now, you had asked me what part of number is the even, and which the even number is. I would have said it is the one that corresponds to the isosceles, and not to the scalene. Does it not seem so to you?

Euthyphro. It does.

Socrates. Then try to show me in this way what part of the just is holiness, so that we may tell Meletus to cease from wronging me, and to give up prosecuting me for irreligion, because we have adequately learned from you of piety and holiness, and the reverse.

Euthyphro. Well then, Socrates, I think that the part of justice which is religious and is holy is the part that has to do with the service of the gods; the remainder is the part of justice that has to do with the service of mankind.

Socrates. And what you say there, Euthyphro, to me seems excellent. There is one little point, however, on which I need more light. I am not yet quite clear about the thing which you call 'service.' I suppose you do not mean the sort of care we give to other things. The 'service' of the gods is not like that—the sort of thing we have in mind when we assert that it is not everybody who knows how to care for horses. It is the horseman that knows, is it not?

Euthyphro. Yes, certainly.

Socrates. I suppose it is the special care that appertains to horses?

Euthyphro. Yes.

Socrates. In the same way, it is not everyone who knows about the care of dogs; it is the huntsman.

Euthyphro. True.

Socrates. The art of the huntsman is the care of dogs.

Euthyphro. Yes.

Socrates. And that of the herdsman is the care of cattle.

Euthyphro. Yes, certainly.

Socrates. And in the same way, Euthyphro, holiness and piety mean caring for the gods? Do you say so?

Euthyphro. I do.

Socrates. And so the aim of all this care and service is the same? I mean it thus. The care is given for the good and welfare of the object that is served. You see, for instance, how the horses that are cared for by the horseman's art are benefited and made better. Don't you think so?

Euthyphro. Yes, I do.

Socrates. And so no doubt the dogs by the art of the huntsman, the cattle by that of the herdsman, and in like manner all the rest. Unless, perhaps, you think that the care may tend to injure the object that is cared for?

Euthyphro. By heaven, not I!

Socrates. The care aims at its benefit?

Euthyphro. Most certainly.

Socrates. Then holiness, which is the service of the gods, must likewise aim to benefit the gods and make them better? Are you prepared to say that when you do a holy thing you make some deity better?

Euthyphro. By heaven, not I!

Socrates. Nor do I fancy, Euthyphro, that you mean it so—far from it. No, it was on this account that I asked just what you meant by service of the gods, supposing that, in fact, you did not mean that sort of care.

Euthyphro. And, Socrates, you were right. I do not mean it so.

Socrates. Good. And now what kind of service of the gods will holiness be?

Euthyphro. Socrates, it is the kind that slaves give to their masters.

Socrates. I understand. It seems to be a kind of waiting on the gods.

Euthyphro. Just that.

Socrates. See if you can tell me this. The art which serves physicians, what results does it serve to produce? Don't you think that it is health?

Euthyphro. I do.

Socrates. Further, what about the art that serves the shipwrights? What result does it serve to produce?

Euthyphro. Obviously, Socrates, the making of a ship.

Socrates. And that which serves the builders serves the building of a house?

Euthyphro. Yes.

Socrates. Now tell me, best of friends, about the service of the gods. What result will this art serve to produce? You obviously know, since you profess to be the best informed among mankind on things divine!

Euthyphro. Yes, Socrates, I say so, and I tell the truth.

Socrates. Then tell me, I adjure you, what is that supreme result which the gods produce when they employ our services?

Euthyphro. They do many things and noble, Socrates.

Socrates. Just as the generals do, my friend. All the same you would have no trouble in summing up what they produce, by saying it is victory in war. Isn't it so?

Euthyphro. Of course.

Socrates. And the farmers too, I take it, produce many fine results, but the net result of their production is the food they get from the earth.

Euthyphro. Yes, surely.

Socrates. Well now, of the many fine and noble things which the gods produce, what is the sum of their production?

Euthyphro. Just a little while ago I told you, Socrates, that the task is not a light one to learn precisely how all these matters stand. I will, however, simply tell you this. If anyone knows how to say and do things pleasing to the gods in prayer and sacrifice, that is holiness, and such behavior serves the family in private life together with the common interests of the state. To do the opposite of things pleasing to the gods is impious, and this it is that upsets all and ruins everything.

Socrates. Surely, Euthyphro, if you had wished, you could have summed up what I asked for much more briefly. But the fact is that you are not eager to instruct me. That is clear. But a moment since, you were on the very point of telling me—and you slipped away. Had you given the answer, I would now have learned from you what holiness is, and would be content. As it is—for perforce the lover must follow the loved one wherever he leads the way—once more, how do you define the holy, and what is holiness? Don't you say that it is a science of sacrifice and prayer?

Euthyphro. I do.

Socrates. Well, and is not sacrifice a giving to the gods, and prayer an asking them to give?

Euthyphro. Precisely, Socrates.

Socrates. By this reasoning, holiness would be the science of asking from the gods and giving to them.

Euthyphro. Quite right, Socrates; you have caught my meaning perfectly.

Socrates. Yes, my friend, for I have my heart set on your wisdom, and give my mind to it, so that nothing you say shall be lost. Now, tell me, what is this service to the gods? You say it is to ask of them and give to them?

Euthyphro. I do.

Socrates. And hence to ask aright will be to ask them for those things of which we stand in need from them?

Euthyphro. What else?

Socrates. And, on the other hand, to give aright will be to give them in return those things which they may need to receive from us? I take it there would be no art in offering anyone a gift of something that he did not need.

Euthyphro. True, Socrates.

Socrates. And therefore, Euthyphro, holiness will be a mutual art of commerce between gods and men.

Euthyphro. An art of commerce, if you like to call it so.

Socrates. Well, I do not like it if it is not so. But tell me what advantage could come to the gods from the gifts which they receive from us? Everybody sees what they give us. No good that we possess but is given by them. What advantage can they gain by what they get from us? Have we so much the better of them in this commerce that we get all good things from them, and they get nothing from us?

Euthyphro. What! Socrates. Do you suppose that the gods gain anything by what they get from us?

Socrates. If not, then what would be the meaning, Euthyphro, of these gifts to the gods from us?

Euthyphro. What do you think they ought to mean but worship, honor, and, as I just now said, good will?

Socrates. So, Euthyphro, the holy is what pleases them, not what is useful to them, nor yet what the gods love?

Euthyphro. I believe that what gives them pleasure is precisely what they love.

Socrates. And so once more, apparently the holy is that which the gods love.

Euthyphro. Most certainly.

Socrates. After that, will you be amazed to find your statements walking off, and not staying where you put them? And will you accuse me as the Daedalus who makes them move, when you are yourself far more expert than Daedalus, and make them go round in a circle? Don't you see that our argument has come full circle to the point where it began? Surely you have not forgotten how in what was said before we found that holiness and what is pleasing to the gods were not the same, but different from each other. Do you not remember?

Euthyphro. I do.

Socrates. And are you not aware now that you say that what the gods love is holy? But is not what the gods love just the same as what is pleasing to the gods?

Euthyphro. Yes, certainly.

Socrates. Well then, either we were wrong in our recent conclusion, or if that was right, our position now is wrong.

Euthyphro. So it seems.

Socrates. And so we must go back again, and start from the beginning to find out what the holy is. As for me, I never will give up until I know. Ah! Do not spurn me, but give your mind with all your might now at length to tell me the absolute truth, for if anybody knows, of all mankind, it is you, and one must not let go of you, you Proteus, until you tell. If you did not know precisely what is holy and unholy, it is unthinkable that for a simple hireling you ever would have moved to prosecute your aged sire on a charge of murder. No, you would have feared to risk the wrath of the gods on the chance that you were not doing right, and would have been afraid of the talk of men. But now I am sure that you think you know exactly what is holy and what is not. So tell me, peerless Euthyphro, and do not hide from me what you judge it to be.

Euthyphro. Another time, then, Socrates, for I am in a hurry, and must be off this minute.

Socrates. What are you doing, my friend? Will you leave, and dash me down from the mighty expectation I had of learning from you what is holy and what is not, and so escaping from Meletus' indictment? I counted upon showing him that now I had gained wisdom about things divine from Euthyphro, and no longer out of ignorance made rash assertions and forged innovations with regard to them, but would lead a better life in future.

THE APOLOGY

17a I don't know* how you, fellow Athenians,* have been affected by my accusers, but for my part I felt myself almost transported by them, so persuasively did they speak. And yet hardly a word they have said is true. Among their many falsehoods, one especially
5 astonished me: their warning that you must† be careful not to be taken in by me, because I am a clever
b speaker. It seemed to me the height of impudence on their part not to be embarrassed at being refuted straight away by the facts, once it became apparent that I was not a clever speaker at all—unless indeed
5 they call a 'clever' speaker one who speaks the truth. If that is what they mean, then I would admit to being an orator, although not on a par with them.

As I said, then, my accusers have said little or nothing true; whereas from me you shall hear the whole truth, though not, I assure you, fellow Athenians, in language adorned with fine words and
c phrases or dressed up, as theirs was: you shall hear my points made spontaneously in whatever words occur to me—persuaded as I am that my case is just. None of you should expect anything to be put differently, because it would not, of course, be at all
5 fitting at my age, gentlemen, to come before you with artificial speeches, such as might be composed by a young lad.

One thing, moreover, I would earnestly beg of you, fellow Athenians. If you hear me defending myself with the same arguments I normally use at the bankers' tables in the market-place (where many of
10 you have heard me) and elsewhere, please do not be
d surprised or protest on that account. You see, here is the reason: this is the first time I have ever appeared before a court of law, although I am over 70; so I am literally a stranger to the diction of this place. And if I really were a foreigner, you would naturally
5 excuse me, were I to speak in the dialect and style
18a in which I had been brought up; so in the present case as well I ask you, in all fairness as I think, to disregard my manner of speaking—it may not be as

good, or it may be better—but to consider and attend simply to the question whether or not my case is just; because that is the duty of a judge, as it is an 5 orator's duty to speak the truth.

To begin with, fellow Athenians, it is fair that I should defend myself against the first set of charges falsely brought against me by my first accusers, and then turn to the later charges and the more recent b ones. You see, I have been accused before you by many people for a long time now, for many years in fact, by people who spoke not a word of truth. It is those people I fear more than Anytus and his crowd, though they too are dangerous. But those others are more so, gentlemen: they have taken hold of most 5 of you since childhood, and made persuasive accusations against me, yet without an ounce more truth in them. They say that there is one Socrates, a 'wise man',* who ponders what is above the earth and investigates everything beneath it, and turns the weaker c argument into the stronger.*

Those accusers who have spread such rumour about me, fellow Athenians, are the dangerous ones, because their audience believes that people who inquire into those matters also fail to acknowledge the gods.* Moreover, those accusers are numerous, and 5 have been denouncing me for a long time now, and they also spoke to you at an age at which you would be most likely to believe them, when some of you were children or young lads; and their accusations simply went by default for lack of any defence. But the most absurd thing of all is that one cannot even get to know their names or say who they were— d except perhaps one who happens to be a comic playwright.* The ones who have persuaded you by malicious slander, and also some who persuade others because they have been persuaded themselves, are all very hard to deal with; one cannot put any of them 5 on the stand here in court, or cross-examine anybody, bur one must literally engage in a sort of shadowboxing to defend oneself, and cross-examine without

From *Plato: Defence of Socrates, Euthyphro, Crito,* trans. David Gallop (Oxford: Oxford University Press, 1997).

anyone to answer. You too, then, should allow, as I just said, that I have two sets of accusers: one set who have accused me recently, and the other of long standing to whom I was just referring. And please grant that I need to defend myself against the latter first, since you too heard them accusing me earlier, and you heard far more from them than from these recent critics here.

Very well, then. I must defend myself, fellow Athenians, and in so short a time* must try to dispel the slander which you have had so long to absorb. That is the outcome I would wish for, should it be of any benefit to you and to me, and I should like to succeed in my defence*—though I believe the task to be a difficult one, and am well aware of its nature. But let that turn out as God wills: I have to obey the law* and present my defence.

Let us examine, from the beginning, the charge that has given rise to the slander against me—which was just what Meletus relied upon when he drew up this indictment. Very well then, what were my slanderers actually saying when they slandered me? Let me read out their deposition, as if they were my legal accusers:

'Socrates is guilty of being a busybody, in that he inquires into what is beneath the earth and in the sky, turns the weaker argument into the stronger, and teaches others to do the same.'

The charges would run something like that. Indeed, you can see them for yourselves, enacted in Aristophanes' comedy: in that play, a character called 'Socrates' swings around, claims to be walking on air,* and talks a lot of other nonsense on subjects of which I have no understanding, great or small.

Not that I mean to belittle knowledge of that sort, if anyone really is learned in such matters—no matter how many of Meletus' lawsuits I might have to defend myself against—but the fact is, fellow Athenians, those subjects are not my concern at all.* I call most of you to witness yourselves, and I ask you to make that quite clear to one another, if you have ever heard me in discussion (as many of you have). Tell one another, then, whether any of you has ever heard me discussing such subjects, either briefly or at length; and as a result you will realize that the other things said about me by the public are equally baseless.

In any event, there is no truth in those charges. Moreover, if you have heard from anyone that I undertake to educate people and charge fees, there is no truth in that either—though for that matter I do think it also a fine thing if anyone *is* able to educate people, as Gorgias of Leontini, Prodicus of Ceos, and Hippias of Elis profess to. Each of them can visit any city, gentlemen, and persuade its young people, who may associate free of charge with any of their own citizens they wish, to leave those associations, and to join with them instead, paying fees and being graceful into the bargain.

On that topic, there is at present another expert here, a gentleman from Paros; I heard of his visit, because I happened to run into a man who has spent more money on sophists* than everyone else put together—Callias, the son of Hipponicus. So I questioned him, since he has two sons himself.

'Callias,' I said, 'if your two sons had been born as colts or calves, we could find and engage a tutor who could make them both excel superbly in the required qualities—and he'd be some sort of expert in horse-rearing or agriculture. But seeing that they are actually human, whom do you intend to engage as their tutor? Who has knowledge of the required human and civic qualities? I ask, because I assume you've given thought to the matter, having sons yourself. Is there such a person,' I asked, 'or not?'

'Certainly,' he replied.

'Who is he?' I said; 'Where does he come from, and what does he charge for tuition?'

'His name is Evenus, Socrates,' he replied; 'He comes from Paros, and he charges 5 minas.'*

I thought Evenus was to be congratulated, if he really did possess that skill and imparted it for such a modest charge. I, at any rate, would certainly be giving myself fine airs and graces if I possessed that knowledge. But the fact is, fellow Athenians, I do not.

Now perhaps one of you will interject: 'Well then, Socrates, what is the difficulty in your case? What is the source of these slanders against you? If you are not engaged in something out of the ordinary, why ever has so much rumour and talk arisen about you? It would surely never have arisen, unless you were up to something different from most people. Tell us what it is, then, so that we don't jump to conclusions about you.'

That speaker makes a fair point, I think; and so I will try to show you just what it is that has earned me my reputation and notoriety. Please hear me out. Some of you will perhaps think I am joking, but I assure you that I shall be telling you the whole truth.

You see, fellow Athenians, I have gained this reputation on account of nothing but a certain sort of wisdom. And what sort of wisdom is that? It is a human kind of wisdom, perhaps, since it might just be true that I have wisdom of that sort. Maybe the people I just mentioned* possess wisdom of a superhuman kind; otherwise I cannot explain it. For my part, I certainly do not possess that knowledge; and whoever says I do is lying and speaking with a view to slandering me—

Now please do not protest, fellow Athenians, even if I should sound to you rather boastful. I am not myself the source of the story I am about to tell you, but I shall refer you to a trustworthy authority. As evidence of my wisdom, if such it actually be, and of its nature, I shall call to witness before you the god at Delphi.*

You remember Chaerephon, of course. He was a friend of mine from youth, and also a comrade in your patty, who shared your recent exile and restoration.* You recall too what sort of man Chaerephon was, how impetuous he was in any undertaking. Well, on one occasion he actually went to the Delphic oracle, and had the audacity to put the following question to it—as I said, please do not make a disturbance, gentlemen—he went and asked if there was anyone wiser than myself; to which the Pythia responded* that there was no one. His brother here will testify to the court about that story, since Chaerephon himself is deceased.

Now keep in mind why I have been telling you this: it is because I am going to explain to you the origin of the slander against me. When I heard the story, I thought to myself: 'What ever is the god saying? What can his riddle mean?* Since I am all too conscious of not being wise in any matter, great or small, what ever can he mean by pronouncing me to be the wisest? Surely he cannot be lying: for him that would be out of the question.'*

So for a long time I was perplexed about what he could possibly mean. But then, with great reluctance, I proceeded to investigate the matter somewhat as follows. I went to one of the people who had a reputation for wisdom, thinking there, if anywhere, to disprove the oracle's utterance and declare to it: 'Here is someone wiser than I am, and yet you said that I was the wisest.'

So I interviewed this person—I need not mention his name, but he was someone in public life; and when I examined him, my experience went something like this, fellow Athenians: in conversing with him, I formed the opinion that, although the man was thought to be wise by many other people, and especially by himself, yet in reality he was not. So I then tried to show him that he thought himself wise without being so. I thereby earned his dislike, and that of many people present; but still, as I went away, I thought to myself: 'I am wiser than that fellow, anyhow. Because neither of us, I dare say, knows anything of great value; but he thinks he knows a thing when he doesn't; whereas I neither know it in fact, nor think that I do. At any rate, it appears that I am wiser than he in just this one small respect: if I do not know something, I do not think that I do.'

Next, I went to someone else, among people thought to be even wiser than the previous man, and I came to the same conclusion again; and so I was disliked by that man too, as well as by many others.

Well, after that I went on to visit one person after another. I realized, with dismay and alarm, that I was making enemies; but even so, I thought it my duty to attach the highest importance to the god's business; and therefore, in seeking the oracle's meaning, I had to go on to examine all those with any reputation for knowledge. And upon my word,* fellow Athenians—because I am obliged to speak the truth before the court—I truly did experience something like this: as I pursued the god's inquiry, I found those held in the highest esteem were practically the most defective, whereas men who were supposed to be their inferiors were much better off in respect of understanding.

Let me, then, outline my wanderings for you, the various 'labours' I kept undertaking,* only to find that the oracle proved completely irrefutable. After I had done with the politicians, I turned to the poets—including tragedians, dithyrambic poets,* and the rest—thinking that in their company I would be shown up as more ignorant than they were. So I picked up the poems over which I thought they had taken the most trouble, and questioned them about their meaning, so that I might also learn something from them in the process.

Now I'm embarrassed to tell you the truth, gentlemen, but it has to be said. Practically everyone else present could speak better than the poets themselves about their very own compositions. And so, once more, I soon realized this truth about them too:* it was not from wisdom that they composed their works, but from a certain natural aptitude and inspiration, like that of seers and soothsayers*—because those people too utter many fine words, yet know nothing of the matters on which they pronounce. It was obvious to me that the poets were in much the same situation; yet at the same time I realized that because of their compositions they thought themselves the wisest people in other matters as well, when they were not. So I left, believing that I was ahead of them in the same way as I was ahead of the politicians.

Then, finally, I went to the craftsmen, because I was conscious of knowing almost nothing myself, but felt sure that amongst them, at least, I would find much valuable knowledge. And in that expectation I was not disappointed: they did have knowledge in fields where I had none, and in that respect they were wiser than I. And yet, fellow Athenians, those able craftsmen seemed to me to suffer from the same failing as the poets: because of their excellence at their own trade, each claimed to be a great expert also on matters of the utmost importance; and this arrogance of theirs seemed to eclipse their wisdom. So I began to ask myself, on the oracle's behalf, whether I should prefer to be as I am, neither wise as they are wise, nor ignorant as they are ignorant, or to possess both their attributes; and in reply, I told myself and the oracle that I was better off as I was.

The effect of this questioning, fellow Athenians, was to earn me much hostility of a very vexing and trying sort, which has given rise to numerous slanders, including this reputation I have for being 'wise'—because those present on each occasion imagine me to be wise regarding the matters on which I examine others. But in fact, gentlemen, it would appear that it is only the god who is truly wise; and that he is saying to us, through this oracle, that

human wisdom is worth little or nothing.* It seems that when he says 'Socrates', he makes use of my name, merely taking me as an example—as if to say, 'The wisest amongst you, human beings, is anyone like Socrates who has recognized that with respect to wisdom he is truly worthless.'

That is why, even to this day, I still go about seeking out and searching into anyone I believe to be wise, citizen or foreigner, in obedience to the god. Then, as soon as I find that someone is not wise, I assist the god* by proving that he is not. Because of this occupation, I have had no time at all for any activity to speak of, either in public affairs or in my family life; indeed, because of my service to the god, I live in extreme poverty.

In addition, the young people who follow me around of their own accord,† the ones who have plenty of leisure because their parents are wealthiest, enjoy listening to people being cross-examined. Often, too, they copy my example themselves, and so attempt to cross-examine others. And I imagine that they find a great abundance of people who suppose themselves to possess some knowledge, but really know little or nothing. Consequently, the people they question are angry with me, though not with themselves, and say that there is a nasty pestilence abroad called 'Socrates', who is corrupting the young.

Then, when asked just what he is doing or teaching, they have nothing to say, because they have no idea what he does; yet, rather than seem at a loss, they resort to the stock charges against all who pursue intellectual inquiry, trotting out 'things in the sky and beneath the earth', 'failing to acknowledge the gods', and 'turning the weaker argument into the stronger'. They would, I imagine, be loath to admit the truth, which is that their pretensions to knowledge have been exposed, and they are totally ignorant. So because these people have reputations to protect, I suppose, and are also both passionate and numerous, and have been speaking about me in a vigorous and persuasive style, they have long been filling your ears with vicious slander. It is on the strength of all this that Meletus, along with Anytus and Lycon, has proceeded against me: Meletus is aggrieved for the poets, Anytus for the craftsmen and politicians, and Lycon for the orators.* And so, as I began by saying, I should be surprised if I could rid your minds of this slander in so short a time, when so much of it has accumulated.

There is the truth for you, fellow Athenians. I have spoken it without concealing anything from you, major or minor, and without glossing over anything. And yet I am virtually certain that it is my very candour that makes enemies for me—which goes to show that I am right: the slander against me is to that effect, and such is its explanation. And whether you look for one now or later, that is what you will find.

So much for my defence before you against the charges brought by my first group of accusers. Next, I shall try to defend myself against Meletus, good patriot that he claims to be, and against my more recent critics. So once again, as if they were a fresh set of accusers, let me in turn review their deposition. It runs something like this:

'Socrates is guilty of corrupting the young, and of failing to acknowledge the gods acknowledged by the city, but introducing new spiritual beings* instead.'

Such is the charge: let us examine each item within it.

Meletus says, then, that I am guilty of corrupting the young. Well I reply, fellow Athenians, that Meletus is guilty of trifling in a serious matter, in that he brings people to trial on frivolous grounds, and professes grave concern about matters for which he has never cared at all.* I shall now try to prove to you too that that is so.

Step forward, Meletus, and answer me. It is your chief concern, is it not, that our younger people shall be as good as possible?

—It is.

Very well, will you please tell the judges who influences them for the better—because you must obviously know, seeing that you care? Having discovered me, as you allege, to be the one who is corrupting them, you bring me before the judges here and accuse me. So speak up, and tell the court who has an improving influence.

You see, Meletus, you remain silent, and have no answer. Yet doesn't that strike you as shameful, and as proof in itself of exactly what I say—that you have never cared about these matters at all? Come then, good fellow, tell us who influences them for the better.

—The laws.

Yes, but that is not what I'm asking, excellent fellow. I mean, which *person*, who already knows the laws to begin with?

—These gentlemen, the judges, Socrates.

What are you saying, Meletus? Can these people educate the young, and do they have an improving influence?

—Most certainly.

All of them, or some but not others?

—All of them.

My goodness, what welcome news, and what a generous supply of benefactors you speak of! And how about the audience here in court? Do they too have an improving influence, or not?

—Yes, they do too.

And how about members of the Council?*

—Yes, the Councillors too.

But in that case, how about people in the Assembly, its individual members, Meletus? They won't be corrupting their youngers, will they? Won't they all be good influences as well?

—Yes, they will too.

So every person in Athens, it would appear, has an excellent influence on them except for me, whereas I alone am corrupting them. Is that what you're saying?

—That is emphatically what I'm saying.

Then I find myself, if we are to believe you, in a most awkward predicament. Now answer me this. Do you think the same is true of horses? Is it everybody who improves them, while a single person spoils them? Or isn't the opposite true: a single person, or at least very few people, namely the horse-trainers, can improve them; while lay people spoil them,* don't they, if they have to do with horses and make use of them? Isn't that true of horses as of all other animals, Meletus? Of course it is, whether you and Anytus deny it or not. In fact, I dare say our young people are extremely lucky if only one person is corrupting them, while everyone else is doing them good.

All right, Meletus. Enough has been said to prove that you never were concerned about the young. You betray your irresponsibility plainly, because you have not cared at all about the charges on which you bring me before this court.

Furthermore, Meletus, tell us, in God's name, whether it is better to live among good fellow citizens or bad ones. Come sir, answer: I am not asking a hard question. Bad people have a harmful impact upon their closest companions at any given time, don't they, whereas good people have a good one?

—Yes.

Well, is there anyone who wants to be harmed by his companions rather than benefited?—Be a good fellow and keep on answering, as the law requires you to. Is there anyone who wants to be harmed?

—Of course not.

Now tell me this. In bringing me here, do you claim that I am corrupting and depraving the young intentionally or unintentionally?

—Intentionally, so I maintain.

Really, Meletus? Are you so much smarter at your age than I at mine as to realize that the bad have a harmful impact upon their closest companions at any given time, whereas the good have a beneficial effect? Am I, by contrast, so far gone in my stupidity as not to realize that if I make one of my companions vicious, I risk incurring harm at his hands? And am I, therefore, as you allege, doing so much damage intentionally?

That I cannot accept from you, Meletus, and neither could anyone else, I imagine. Either I am not corrupting them—or if I am, I am doing so unintentionally;* so either way your charge is false. But if I am corrupting them unintentionally, the law does not require me to be brought to court for such mistakes, but rather to be taken aside for private instruction and admonition—since I shall obviously stop doing unintentional damage, if I learn better. But you avoided association with me and were unwilling to instruct me. Instead you bring me to court, where the law requires you to bring people who need punishment rather than enlightenment.

Very well, fellow Athenians. That part of my case is now proven: Meletus never cared about these matters, either a lot or a little. Nevertheless, Meletus, please tell us in what way you claim that I am corrupting our younger people. That is quite obvious, isn't it, from the indictment you drew up? It is by teaching them not to acknowledge the gods acknowledged by the city, but to accept new spiritual beings instead? You mean, don't you, that I am corrupting them by teaching them that?*

—I most emphatically do.

Then, Meletus, in the name of those very gods we are now discussing, please clarify the matter further for me, and for the jury here. You see, I cannot make out what you mean. Is it that I am teaching people to acknowledge that some gods exist—in which case it follows that I do acknowledge their existence myself as well, and am not a complete atheist, hence am not guilty on that count—and yet that those gods are not the ones acknowledged by the city, but different ones? Is that your charge against me—namely, that they are different? Or are you saying that I acknowledge no god at all myself, and teach the same to others?

—I am saying the latter: you acknowledge no gods at all.

What ever makes you say that, Meletus, you strange fellow? Do I not even acknowledge, then, with the rest of mankind, that the sun and the moon are gods?*

—By God, he does not, members of the jury, since he claims that the sun is made of rock, and the moon of earth!

My dear Meletus, do you imagine that it is Anaxagoras you are accusing?* Do you have such contempt for the jury, and imagine them so illiterate as not to know that books by Anaxagoras of Clazomenae are crammed with such assertions? What's more, are the young learning those things from me when they can acquire them at the bookstalls,* now and then, for a drachma at most, and so ridicule Socrates if he claims those ideas for his own, especially when they are so bizarre? In God's name, do you really think me as crazy as that? Do I acknowledge the existence of no god at all?

—By God no, none whatever.

I can't believe you, Meletus—nor, I think, can you believe yourself. To my mind, fellow Athenians, this fellow is an impudent scoundrel who has framed this indictment out of sheer wanton impudence and insolence. He seems to have devised a sort of riddle in order to try me out: 'Will Socrates the Wise tumble to my nice self-contradiction?* Or shall I fool him along with my other listeners?' You see, he seems to me to be contradicting himself in the indictment. It's as if he were saying: 'Socrates is guilty of not acknowledging gods, but of acknowledging gods'; and yet that is sheer tomfoolery.

I ask you to examine with me, gentlemen, just how that appears to be his meaning. Answer for us, Meletus; and the rest of you, please remember my initial request not to protest if I conduct the argument in my usual manner.*

Is there anyone in the world, Meletus, who acknowledges that human phenomena exist, yet does not acknowledge human beings?—Require him to answer, gentlemen, and not to raise all kinds of confused objections. Is there anyone who does not acknowledge horses, yet does acknowledge equestrian phenomena? Or who does not acknowledge that musicians exist, yet does acknowledge musical phenomena?*

There is no one, excellent fellow: if you don't wish to answer, I must answer for you, and for the jurors here. But at least answer my next question yourself. Is there anyone who acknowledges that spiritual phenomena exist, yet does not acknowledge spirits?

—No.

How good of you to answer—albeit reluctantly and under compulsion from the jury. Well now, you say that I acknowledge spiritual beings* and teach others to do so. Whether they actually be new or old is no matter: I do at any rate, by your account, acknowledge spiritual beings, which you have also mentioned in your sworn deposition. But if I acknowledge spiritual beings, then surely it follows quite inevitably that I must acknowledge spirits. Is that not so?—Yes, it is so: I assume your agreement, since you don't answer. But we regard spirits, don't we, as either gods or children of gods? Yes or no?

—Yes.

Then given that I do believe in spirits, as you say, if spirits are gods of some sort, this is precisely what I claim when I say that you are presenting us with a riddle and making fun of us: you are saying that I do not believe in gods, and yet again that I do believe in gods, seeing that I believe in spirits.

On the other hand, if spirits are children of gods,* some sort of bastard offspring from nymphs—or from whomever they are traditionally said, in each case, to be born—then who in the world could ever believe that there were children of gods, yet no gods? That would be just as absurd as accepting the existence of children of horses and asses†—namely, mules—yet rejecting the existence of horses or asses!

In short, Meletus, you can only have drafted this† either by way of trying us out, or because you were at a loss how to charge me with a genuine offence. How could you possibly persuade anyone with even the slightest intelligence that someone who accepts spiritual beings does not also accept divine ones,† and again that the same person also accepts neither spirits nor gods nor heroes? There is no conceivable way.

But enough, fellow Athenians. It needs no long defence, I think, to show that I am not guilty of the charges in Meletus' indictment; the foregoing will suffice. You may be sure, though, that what I was saying earlier is true: I have earned great hostility among many people. And that is what will convict me, if I am convicted: not Meletus or Anytus, but the slander and malice of the crowd. They have certainly convicted many other good men as well, and I imagine they will do so again; there is no risk of their stopping with me.

Now someone may perhaps say: 'Well then, are you not ashamed, Socrates, to have pursued a way of life which has now put you at risk of death?'

But it may be fair for me to answer him as follows: 'You are sadly mistaken, fellow, if you suppose that a man with even a grain of self-respect should reckon up the risks of living or dying, rather than simply consider, whenever he does something, whether his actions are just or unjust, the deeds of a good man or a bad one. By your principles, presumably, all those demigods who died in the plain of Troy* were inferior creatures—yes, even the son of Thetis,* who showed so much scorn for danger, when the alternative was to endure dishonour. Thus, when he was eager to slay Hector, his mother, goddess that she was, spoke to him—something like this, I fancy:

My child, if thou dost avenge the murder of thy friend, Patroclus, And dost slay Hector, then straightway [so runs the poem]

Shalr thou die thyself, since doom is prepared for thee

Next after Hector's.

But though he heard that, he made light of death and danger, since he feared far more to live as a base man, and to fail to avenge his dear ones. The poem goes on:

> Then straightway let me die, once I have given the wrongdoer
> His deserts, lest I remain here by the beak-prowed ships,
> An object of derision, and a burden upon the earth.

Can you suppose that he gave any thought to death or danger?

You see, here is the truth of the matter, fellow Athenians. Wherever a man has taken up a position because he considers it best, or has been posted there by his commander, that is where I believe he should remain, steadfast in danger, taking no account at all of death or of anything else rather than dishonour. I would therefore have been acting absurdly, fellow Athenians, if when assigned to a post at Potidaea, Amphipolis, or Delium* by the superiors you had elected to command me, I remained where I was posted on those occasions at the risk of death, if ever any man did; whereas now that the god assigns me, as I became completely convinced, to the duty of leading the philosophical life by examining myself and others, I desert that post from fear of death or anything else. Yes, that would be unthinkable; and then I truly should deserve to be brought to court for failing to acknowledge the gods' existence, in that I was disobedient to the oracle, was afraid of death, and thought I was wise when I was not.

After all, gentlemen, the fear of death amounts simply to thinking one is wise when one is not: it is thinking one knows something one does not know. No one knows, you see, whether death may not in fact prove the greatest of all blessings for mankind; but people fear it as if they knew it for certain to be the greatest of evils. And yet† to think that one knows what one does not know must surely be the kind of folly which is reprehensible.

On this matter especially, gentlemen, that may be the nature of my own advantage over most people. If I really were to claim to be wiser than anyone in any respect, it would consist simply in this: just as I do not possess adequate knowledge of life in Hades,* so I also realize that I do not possess it; whereas acting unjustly in disobedience to one's betters, whether god or human being, is something I *know* to be evil

and shameful. Hence I shall never fear or flee from something which may indeed be a good for all I know, rather than from things I know to be evils.

Suppose, therefore, that you pay no heed to Anytus, but are prepared to let me go. He said I need never have been brought to court in the first place; but that once I had been, your only option was to put me to death.* He declared before you that, if I got away from you this time, your sons would all be utterly corrupted by practising Socrates' teachings. Suppose, in the face of that, you were to say to me:

'Socrates, we will nor listen to Anytus this time. We are prepared to let you go—but only on this condition: you are to pursue that quest of yours and practise philosophy no longer; and if you are caught doing it any more, you shall be put to death.'

Well, as I just said, if you were prepared to let me go on those terms, I should reply to you as follows:

'I have the greatest fondness and affection for you, fellow Athenians, but I will obey my god rather than you; and so long as I draw breath and am able, I shall never give up practising philosophy, or exhorting and showing the way to any of you whom I ever encounter, by giving my usual sort of message. "Excellent friend," I shall say; "You are an Athenian. Your city is the most important and renowned for its wisdom and power; so are you not ashamed that, while you take care to acquire as much wealth as possible, with honour and glory as well, yet you take no care or thought for understanding or truth, or for the best possible state of your soul?"

'And should any of you dispute that, and claim that he does take such care, I will not let him go straight away nor leave him, but I will question and examine and put him to the test; and if I do not think he has acquired goodness, though he says he has, I shall say, "Shame on you, for setting the lowest value upon the most precious things, and for rating inferior ones more highly!" That I shall do for anyone I encounter, young or old, alien or fellow citizen; but all the more for the latter, since your kinship with me is closer.'

Those are my orders from my god, I do assure you. Indeed, I believe that no greater good has ever befallen you in our city than my service to my god; because all I do is to go about persuading you, young and old alike, not to care for your bodies or for your wealth so intensely as for the greatest possible well-being of your souls. 'It is not wealth', I tell you, 'that produces goodness; rather, it is from goodness that wealth, and all other benefits for human beings, accrue to them in their private and public life.'*

If, in fact, I am corrupting the young by those assertions, you may call them harmful. But if anyone claims that I say anything different, he is talking nonsense. In the face of that I should like to say: 'Fellow Athenians, you may listen to Anytus or not, as you please; and you may let me go or not, as you please, because there is no chance of my acting otherwise, even if I have to die many times over—'

Stop protesting, fellow Athenians! Please abide by my request* that you not protest against what I say, but hear me out; in fact, it will be in your interest, so I believe, to do so. You see, I am going to say some further things to you which may make you shout out—although I beg you not to.

You may be assured that if you put to death the sort of man I just said I was, you will not harm me more than you harm yourselves. Meletus or Anytus would not harm me at all; nor, in fact, could they do so, since I believe it is out of the question for a better man to be harmed by his inferior. The latter may, of course, inflict death or banishment or disenfranchisement; and my accuser here, along with others no doubt, believes those to the great evils. But I do not. Rather, I believe it a far greater evil to try to kill a man unjustly, as he does now.

At this point, therefore, fellow Athenians, so far from pleading on my own behalf, as might be supposed, I am pleading on yours, in case by condemning me you should mistreat the gift which God has bestowed upon you—because if you put me to death, you will not easily find another like me. The fact is, if I may put the point in a somewhat comical way, that I have been literally attached by God to our city, as if to a horse—a large thoroughbred, which is a bit sluggish because of its size, and needs to be aroused by some sort of gadfly. Yes, in me, I believe, God has attached to our city just such a creature—the kind which is constantly alighting everywhere on you, all day long, arousing, cajoling, or reproaching each and every one of you. You will not easily acquire another such gadfly, gentlemen; rather, if you take my advice, you will spare my life. I dare say, though, that you will get angry, like people who are awakened from their doze. Perhaps you will heed Anytus, and give

me a swat: you could happily finish me off, and then spend the rest of your life asleep—unless God, in his compassion for you, were to send you someone else.

That I am, in fact, just the sort of gift that God would send to our city, you may recognize from this: it would not seem to be in human nature* for me to have neglected all my own affairs, and put up with the neglect of my family for all these years, but constantly minded your interests, by visiting each of you in private like a father or an elder brother, urging you to be concerned about goodness. Of course, if I were gaining anything from that, or were being paid to urge that course upon you, my actions could be explained. But in fact you can see for yourselves that my accusers, who so shamelessly level all those other charges against me, could not muster the impudence to call evidence that I ever once obtained payment, or asked for any. It is I who can call evidence sufficient, I think, to show that I am speaking the truth—namely, my poverty.

Now it may perhaps seem peculiar that, as some say, I give this counsel by going around and dealing with others' concerns in private, yet do not venture to appear before the Assembly, and counsel the city about your business in public. But the reason for that is one you have frequently heard me give in many places: it is a certain divine or spiritual sign* which comes to me, the very thing to which Meletus made mocking allusion in his indictment. It has been happening to me ever since childhood: a voice of some sort which comes, and which always—whenever it does come—restrains me from what I am about to do, yet never gives positive direction. That is what opposes my engaging in politics—and its opposition is an excellent thing, to my mind; because you may be quite sure, fellow Athenians, that if I had tried to engage in politics,[†] I should have perished long since, and should have been of no use either to you or to myself.

And please do not get angry if I tell you the truth. The fact is that there is no person on earth whose life will be spared by you or by any other majority, if he is genuinely opposed to many injustices and unlawful acts, and tries to prevent their occurrence in our city. Rather, anyone who truly fights for what is just, if he is going to survive for even a short time, must act in a private capacity rather than a public one.

I will offer you conclusive evidence of that—not just words, but the sort of evidence that you respect, namely, actions. Just hear me tell my experiences, so that you may know that I would not submit to a single person for fear of death, contrary to what is just; nor would I do so, even if I were to lose my life on the spot. I shall mention things to you which are vulgar commonplaces of the courts; yet they are true.

Although I have never held any other public office in our city, fellow Athenians, I have served on its Council. My own tribe, Antiochis, happened to be the presiding commission* on the occasion when you wanted† a collective trial for the ten generals who had failed to rescue the survivors from the naval battle.* That was illegal, as you all later recognized. At the time I was the only commissioner opposed to your acting illegally, and I voted against the motion. And though its advocates were prepared to lay information against me and have me arrested, while you were urging them on by shouting, I believed that I should face danger in siding with law and justice, rather than take your side for fear of imprisonment or death, when your proposals were contrary to justice.

Those events took place while our city was still under democratic rule. But on a subsequent occasion, after the oligarchy had come to power, the Thirty* summoned me and four others to the round chamber,* with orders to arrest Leon the Salaminian, and fetch him from Salamis* for execution; they were constantly issuing such orders, of course, to many others, in their wish to implicate as many as possible in their crimes. On that occasion, however, I showed, once again not just by words, but by my actions, that I couldn't care less about death—if that would not be putting it rather crudely—but that my one and only care was to avoid doing anything sinful or unjust. Thus, powerful as it was, that regime did not frighten me into unjust action: when we emerged from the round chamber, the other four went off to Salamis and arrested Leon, whereas I left them and went off home. For that I might easily have been put to death, had the regime not collapsed shortly afterwards. There are many witnesses who will testify before you about those events.

Do you imagine, then, that I would have survived all these years if I had been regularly active in pub-

lic life, and had championed what was right in a manner worthy of a brave man, and valued that above all else, as was my duty? Far from it, fellow Athenians: I would not, and nor would any other man. But in any public undertaking, that is the sort of person that I, for my part, shall prove to have been throughout my life; and likewise in my private life, because I have never been guilty of unjust association with anyone, including those whom my slanderers allege to have been my students.*

I never, in fact, was anyone's instructor* at any time. But if a person wanted to hear me talking, while I was engaging in my own business, I never grudged that to anyone, young or old; nor do I hold conversation only when I receive payment, and not otherwise. Rather, I offer myself for questioning to wealthy and poor alike, and to anyone who may wish to answer in response to questions from me. Whether any of those people acquires a good character or not, I cannot fairly be held responsible, when I never at any time promised any of them that they would learn anything from me, nor gave them instruction. And if anyone claims that he ever learnt anything from me, or has heard privately something that everyone else did not hear as well, you may be sure that what he says is untrue.

Why then, you may ask, do some people enjoy spending so much time in my company? You have already heard, fellow Athenians: I have told you the whole truth—which is that my listeners enjoy the examination of those who think themselves wise but are not, since the process is not unamusing. But for me, I must tell you, it is a mission which I have been bidden to undertake by the god, through oracles and dreams,* and through every means whereby a divine injunction to perform any task has ever been laid upon a human being.*

That is not only true, fellow Athenians, but is easily verified—because if I do corrupt any of our young people, or have corrupted others in the past, then presumably, when they grew older, should any of them have realized that I had at any time given them bad advice in their youth, they ought now to have appeared here themselves to accuse me and obtain redress. Or else, if they were unwilling to come in person, members of their families—fathers, brothers, or other relations—had their relatives suffered any harm at my hands, ought now to put it on record and obtain redress.

10 In any case, many of those people are present, e whom I can see: first there is Crito, my contemporary and fellow demesman, father of Critobulus here; then Lysanias of Sphettus, father of Aeschines here; next, Epigenes' father, Antiphon from Cephisia, is present; then again, there are others here whose brothers have spent time with me in these studies: Nicostratus, son of Theozotides, brother of 5 Theodotus—Theodotus himself, incidentally, is deceased, so Nicostratus could not have come at his brother's urging; and Paralius here, son of Demodocus, whose brother was Theages; also present is 34a Ariston's son, Adimantus, whose brother is Plato here;* and Aeantodorus, whose brother is Apollodorus here.

There are many others I could mention to you, from whom Meletus should surely have called some 5 testimony during his own speech. However, if he forgot to do so then, let him call it now—I yield the floor to him—and if he has any such evidence, let him produce it. But quite the opposite is true, gentlemen: you will find that they are all prepared to support me, their corruptor, the one who is, according to Meletus and Anytus, doing their relatives misb chief. Support for me from the actual victims of corruption might perhaps be explained; but what of the uncorrupted—older men by now, and relatives of my victims? What reason would they have to support me, apart from the right and proper one, which is that they know very well that Meletus is lying, 5 whereas I am telling the truth?

There it is, then, gentlemen. That, and perhaps more of the same, is about all I have to say in my defence. But perhaps, among your number, there may be c someone who will harbour resentment when he recalls a case of his own: he may have faced a less serious trial than this one, yet begged and implored the jury, weeping copiously, and producing his children here, along with many other relatives and loved ones, 5 to gain as much sympathy as possible. By contrast, I shall do none of those things, even though I am running what might be considered the ultimate risk. Perhaps someone with those thoughts will harden his heart against me; and enraged by those same

thoughts, he may cast his vote against me in anger. d Well, if any of you are so inclined—not that I expect it of you, but if anyone *should* be—I think it fair to answer him as follows:

'I naturally do have relatives, my excellent friend, because—in Homer's own words*—I too was "not born of oak nor of rock", but of human parents; and 5 so I do have relatives—including my sons,* fellow Athenians. There are three of them: one is now a youth, while two are still children. Nevertheless, I shall not produce any of them here, and then entreat you to vote for my acquittal.'

And why, you may ask, will I do no such thing? 10 Not out of contempt or disrespect for you, fellow e Athenians—whether or not I am facing death boldly is a different issue. The point is that with our reputations in mind—yours and our whole city's, as well as my own—I believe that any such behaviour would be ignominious, at my age and with the reputation I possess; that reputation may or may not, in fact, be deserved, but at least it is believed that Socrates 5 stands out in some way from the run of human be-35a ings. Well, if those of you who are believed to be pre-eminent in wisdom, courage, or any other form of goodness, are going to behave like that, it would be demeaning.

I have frequently seen such men when they face judgment: they have significant reputations, yet they put on astonishing performances, apparently in the 5 belief that by dying they will suffer something unheard of—as if they would be immune from death, so long as you did not kill them! They seem to me to put our city to shame: they could give any for-b eigner the impression that men preeminent among Athenians in goodness, whom they select from their own number to govern and hold other positions, are no better than women.* I say this, fellow Athenians, because none of us† who has even the slightest reputation should behave like that; nor should you put 5 up with us if we try to do so. Rather, you should make one thing clear: you will be far more inclined to convict one who stages those pathetic charades and makes our city an object of derision, than one who keeps his composure.

But leaving reputation aside, gentlemen, I do not 10 think it right to entreat the jury, nor to win acquittal c in that way, instead of by informing and persuading them. A juror does not sit to dispense justice as a favour, but to determine where it lies. And he has sworn, not that he will favour whomever he pleases, but that he will try the case according to law. We should not, then, accustom you to transgress your oath, nor should you become accustomed to doing so: neither of us would be showing respect towards the gods. And therefore, fellow Athenians, do not require behaviour from me towards you which I consider neither proper nor right nor pious—more especially now, for God's sake, when I stand charged by Meletus here with impiety: because if I tried to persuade and coerce you with entreaties in spite of your oath, I clearly *would* be teaching you not to believe in gods; and I would stand literally self-convicted, by my defence, of failing to acknowledge them. But that is far from the truth: I do acknowledge them, fellow Athenians, as none of my accusers do;* and I trust to you, and to God, to judge my case as shall be best for me and for yourselves.

*

For many reasons, fellow Athenians, I am not dismayed by this outcome[1]—your convicting me, I mean—and especially because the outcome has come as no surprise to me. I wonder far more at the number of votes cast on each side, because I did not think the margin would be so narrow. Yet it seems, in fact, that if a mere thirty votes had gone the other way, I should have been acquitted.* Or rather, even as things stand, I consider that I have been cleared of Meletus' charges. Nor only that, but one thing is obvious to everyone: if Anytus had not come forward with Lycon to accuse me, Meletus would have forfeited 1,000 drachmas, since he would not have gained one-fifth of the votes cast.*

But anyhow, this gentleman demands the death penalty for me. Very well, then: what alternative penalty* shall I suggest to you, fellow Athenians? Clearly, it must be one I deserve. So what do I deserve to incur or to pay, for having taken it into my head not to lead an inactive life? Instead, I have neglected the things that concern most people—making money, managing an estate, gaining military or civic honours, or other positions of power, or joining political clubs and parties which have formed in our city. I thought myself, in truth, too honest to survive if I engaged in those things. I did not pursue a course, therefore, in which I would be of no use to you or to myself. Instead, by going to each individual privately, I tried to render a service for you which is—so I maintain—the highest service of all. Therefore that was the course I followed: I tried to persuade each of you not to care for any of his possessions rather than care for himself, striving for the utmost excellence and understanding; and not to care for our city's possessions rather than for the city itself; and to care about other things in the same way.

So what treatment do I deserve for being such a benefactor? If I am to make a proposal truly in keeping with my deserts, fellow Athenians, it should be some benefit; and moreover, the sort of benefit that would be fitting for me. Well then, what *is* fitting for a poor man who is a benefactor, and who needs time free for exhorting you? Nothing could be more fitting,† fellow Athenians, than to give such a man regular free meals in the Prytaneum;* indeed, that is far more fitting for him than for any of you who may have won an Olympic race with a pair or a team of horses: that victor brings you only the appearance of success, whereas I bring you the reality; besides, he is not in want of sustenance, whereas I am. So if, as justice demands, I am to make a proposal in keeping with my deserts, that is what I suggest: free meals in the Prytaneum.

Now, in proposing this, I may seem to you, as when I talked about appeals for sympathy, to be speaking from sheer effrontery. But actually I have no such motive, fellow Athenians. My point is rather this: I am convinced that I do not treat any human being unjustly, at least intentionally*—but I cannot make you share that conviction, because we have conversed together so briefly. I say this, because if it were the law here, as in other jurisdictions, that a capital case must not be tried in a single day, but over several,* I think you could have been convinced; but as things stand, it is not easy to clear oneself of such grave allegations in a short time.

Since, therefore, I am persuaded, for my part, that I have treated no one unjustly, I have no intention

---

[1]The verdict was 'Guilty'. Socrates here begins his second speech, proposing an alternative to the death penalty demanded by the prosecution.

whatever of so treating myself, nor of denouncing myself as deserving ill, or proposing any such treatment for myself. Why should I do that? For fear of the penalty Meletus demands for me, when I say that I don't know if that is a good thing or a bad one?* In preference to that, am I then to choose one of the things I know very well to be bad, and demand that instead? Imprisonment, for instance? Why should I live in prison, in servitude to the annually appointed prison commissioners?* Well then, a fine, with imprisonment until I pay? That would amount to what I just mentioned, since I haven't the means to pay it.

Well then, should I propose banishment? Perhaps that is what you would propose for me. Yet I must surely be obsessed with survival, fellow Athenians, if I am so illogical as that. You, my fellow citizens, were unable to put up with my discourses and arguments, but they were so irksome and odious to you that you now seek to be rid of them. Could I not draw the inference, in that case, that others will hardly take kindly to them? Far from it, fellow Athenians. A fine life it would be for a person of my age to go into exile, and spend his days continually exchanging one city for another, and being repeatedly expelled—because I know very well that wherever I go, the young will come to hear me speaking, as they do here. And if I repel them, they will expel me themselves, by persuading their elders; while if I do not repel them, their fathers and relatives will expel me on their account.*

Now, perhaps someone may say: 'Socrates, could you not be so kind as to keep quiet and remain inactive, while living in exile?' This is the hardest point of all of which to convince some of you. Why? Because, if I tell you that that would mean disobeying my god, and that is why I cannot remain inactive, you will disbelieve me and think that I am practising a sly evasion.* Again, if I said that if really is the greatest benefit for a person to converse every day about goodness, and about the other subjects you have heard me discussing when examining myself and others—and that an unexamined life is no life for a human being to live*—then you would believe me still less when I made those assertions. But the facts, gentlemen, are just as I claim them to be, though it is not easy to convince you of them. At the same time, I am not accustomed to think of myself as deserving anything bad. If I had money, I would have proposed a fine of as much as I could afford: that would have done me no harm at all. But the fact is that I have none—unless you wish to fix the penalty at a sum I could pay. I could afford to pay you 1 mina, I suppose, so I suggest a fine of that amount—

One moment, fellow Athenians. Plato here, along with Crito, Critobulus, and Apollodorus, is urging me to propose 30 minas,* and they are saying they will stand surety for that sum. So I propose a fine of that amount, and these people shall be your sufficient guarantors of its payment.

*

For the sake of a slight gain in time, fellow Athenians, you will incur infamy and blame from those who would denigrate our city, for putting Socrates to death[2]—a 'wise man'—because those who wish to malign yon will say I am wise, even if I am not; in any case, had you waited only a short time, you would have obtained that outcome automatically. You can see, of course, that I am now well advanced in life, and death is not far off. I address that not to all of you, but to those who condemned me to death;* and to those same people I would add something further.

Perhaps you imagine, gentlemen, that I have been convicted for lack of arguments of the sort I could have used to convince you, had I believed that I should do or say anything* to gain acquittal. But that is far from true. I have been convicted, not for lack of arguments, but for lack of brazen impudence and willingness to address you in such terms as you would most like to be addressed in—that is to say, by weeping and wailing, and doing and saying much else that I claim to be unworthy of me—the sorts of thing that you are so used to hearing from others. But just as I did not think during my defence that I should do anything unworthy of a free man because I was in danger, so now I have no regrets about defending myself as I did; I should far rather present such a defence and die, than live by defending myself in that other fashion.

---

[2]The jury has now voted for the death penalty, and Socrates begins his final speech.

In court, as in warfare, neither I nor anyone else should contrive to escape death at any cost. On the battlefield too, it often becomes obvious that one could avoid death by throwing down one's arms and flinging oneself upon the mercy of one's pursuers. And in every sort of danger there are many other means of escaping death, if one is shameless enough to do or to say anything. I suggest that it is not death that is hard to avoid, gentlemen, but wickedness is far harder, since it is fleeter of foot than death.* Thus, slow and elderly as I am, I have now been overtaken by the slower runner; while my accusers, adroit and quick-witted as they are, have been overtaken by the faster, which is wickedness. And so I take my leave, condemned to death by your judgment, whereas they stand for ever condemned to depravity and injustice as judged by Truth.* And just as I accept my penalty, so must they. Things were bound to turn out this way, I suppose, and I imagine it is for the best.

In the next place, to those of you who voted against me, I wish to utter a prophecy. Indeed, I have now reached a point at which people are most given to prophesying—that is, when they are on the point of death.* I warn you, my executioners, that as soon as I am dead retribution will come upon you*—far more severe, I swear, than the sentence you have passed upon me. You have tried to kill me for now, in the belief that you will be relieved from giving an account of your lives. But in fact, I can tell you, you will face just the opposite outcome. There will be more critics to call you to account, people whom I have restrained for the time being though you were unaware of my doing so. They will be all the harder on you since they are younger, and you will rue it all the more—because if you imagine that by putting people to death you will prevent anyone from reviling you for not living rightly, you are badly mistaken. That way of escape is neither feasible nor honourable. Rather, the most honourable and easiest way is not the silencing of others, but striving to make oneself as good a person as possible. So with that prophecy to those of you who voted against me, I take my leave.

As for those who voted for my acquittal, I should like to discuss the outcome of this case while the officials are occupied, and I am not yet on the way to the place where I must die. Please bear with me, gentlemen, just for this short time: there is no reason why we should not have a word with one another while that is still permitted.

Since I regard you as my friends, I am willing to show you the significance of what has just befallen me. You see, gentlemen of the jury—and in applying that term to you, I probably use it correctly*—something wonderful has just happened to me. Hitherto, the usual prophetic voice from my spiritual sign was continually active, and frequently opposed me even on trivial matters, if I was about to do anything amiss. But now something has befallen me, as you can see for yourselves, which one certainly might consider—and is generally held—to be the very worst of evils. Yet the sign from God did not oppose me, either when I left home this morning, or when I appeared here in court, or at any point when I was about to say anything during my speech; and yet in other discussions it has very often stopped me in mid-sentence. This time, though, it has not opposed me at any moment in anything I said or did in this whole business.

Now, what do I take to be the explanation for that? I will tell you: I suspect that what has befallen me is a blessing, and that those of us who suppose death to be an evil cannot be making a correct assumption. I have gained every ground for that suspicion, because my usual sign could not have failed to oppose me, unless I were going to incur some good result.

And let us also reflect upon how good a reason there is to hope that death is a good thing. It is, you see, one or other of two things: either to be dead is to be nonexistent, as it were, and a dead person has no awareness whatever of anything at all; or else, as we are told, the soul undergoes some sort of transformation, or exchanging of this present world for another. Now if there is, in fact, no awareness in death, but it is like sleep—the kind in which the sleeper does not even dream at all*—then death would be a marvellous gain. Why, imagine that someone had to pick the night in which he slept so soundly that he did not even dream, and to compare all the other nights and days of his life with that one; suppose he had to say, upon consideration, how many days or nights in his life he had spent better and more agreeably than that night; in that case, I think he would find them easy to count compared with his other days and nights—even if he were the

Great King of Persia,* let alone an ordinary person. Well, if death is like that, then for my part I call it a gain; because on that assumption the whole of time would seem no longer than a single night.

On the other hand, if death is like taking a trip from here to another place, and if it is true, as we are told, that all of the dead do indeed exist in that other place, why then, gentlemen of the jury, what could he a greater blessing than that? If upon arriving in Hades, and being rid of these people who profess to be 'jurors', one is going to find those who are truly judges, and who are also said to sit in judgment there*—Minos, Rhadamanthys, Aeacus, Triptolemus, and all other demigods who were righteous in their own lives—would that be a disappointing journey?

Or again, what would any of you not give to share the company of Orpheus and Musaeus, of Hesiod and Homer? I say 'you,' since I personally would be willing to die many times over, if those tales are true. Why? Because my own sojourn there would be wonderful, if I could meet Palamedes, or Ajax, son of Telamon, or anyone else of old who met their death through an unjust verdict. Whenever I met them, I could compare my own experiences with theirs— which would be not unamusing, I fancy—and best of all, I could spend time questioning and probing people there, just as I do here, to find out who among them is truly wise, and who thinks he is without being so.

What would one not give, gentlemen of the jury, to be able to question the leader of the great expedition against Troy,* or Odysseus, or Sisyphus, or countless other men and women* one could mention? Would it not be unspeakable good fortune to converse with them there, to mingle with them and question them? At least that isn't a reason, presumably, for people in that world to put you to death— because amongst other ways in which people there are more fortunate than those in our world, they have become immune from death for the rest of time, if what we are told is actually true.

Moreover, you too, gentlemen of the jury, should be of good hope in the face of death, and fix your minds upon this single truth: nothing can harm a good man, either in life or in death; nor are his fortunes neglected by the gods. In fact, what has befallen me

has come about by no mere accident; rather, it is clear to me that it was better I should die now and be rid of my troubles.* That is also the reason why the divine sign at no point turned me back; and for my part, I bear those who condemned me, and my accusers, no ill will at all—though, to be sure, it was not with that intent that they were condemning and accusing me, but with intent to harm me—and they are culpable for that. Still, this much I ask of them.* When my sons come of age, gentlemen, punish them: give them the same sort of trouble that I used to give you, if you think they care for money or anything else more than for goodness, and if they think highly of themselves when they are of no value. Reprove them, as I reproved you, for failing to care for the things they should, and for thinking highly of themselves when they are worthless. If you will do that, then I shall have received my own just deserts from you, as will my sons.

But enough. It is now time to leave—for me to die, and for you to live—though which of us has the better destiny is unclear to everyone, save only to God.*

NOTES

I don't know: it is striking that the *Defence of Socrates* begins, as it ends, with a disavowal of knowledge. See note on 42a.

fellow Athenians: Socrates addresses his judges in this way, instead of the more usual 'gentlemen of the jury', partly because he will later refuse to recognize those who voted against him as 'jurors' at all. See note on 40a. The mode of address may also appeal, as do portions of his speech (29d–e, 34e–35b), to the jurors' pride as Athenian citizens.

a 'wise man': sophos has generally been rendered 'wise', and *sophia* 'wisdom'. A different word (*phronēsis*), often given as 'wisdom', has been translated 'understanding'. Although Plato draws no clear-cut distinction between these terms, they tend to have different resonances in his usage. In particular, (i) *sophia*, unlike *phronēsis*, can cover expertise in specific fields of knowledge, as well as 'wisdom' in general; and (ii) irony can often be heard in its use. In some contexts, therefore, 'expert', 'learned', 'clever', or 'smart' will capture the flavour of *sophos* better than 'wise'.

18c *turns the weaker argument into the stronger:* Socrates' reputation for skill in argument enabled Aristophanes to caricature him as an instructor in logical trickery. Cf. *Clouds* 112–15. The play also features a debate between Right and Wrong, in which the latter prevails (889–1104). Chicanery in argument is brilliantly satirized, and contrasted with the methods of Socrates, in Plato's *Euthydemus*, 'Turning the weaker argument into the stronger' was evidently regarded as a trade mark of the late fifth-century sophistic movement. Training in it is reported by Aristotle to have been offered by the famous sophist Protagoras, and to have been unpopular (*Rhetoric* 1402a23–6). For the sophists, see also note on 20a, and Introduction, pp. xviii–xix.

fail to acknowledge the gods: 'failing to acknowledge the gods' was one of the formal charges against Socrates, quoted at 24b–c. It is ambiguous, since the verb translated 'acknowledge' could mean either 'worship' or 'believe', or some combination of the two. Belief seems more likely to be in point here, since an interest in scientific explanation was associated, in Socrates' time as in ours, with atheism. Cf. especially *Clouds* 358–427. When Socrates responds to the charge, it is taken to mean not that he fails to worship the gods, but that he denies their existence (26c).

18d *one who happens to be a comic playwright:* the reference is to Aristophanes, for whom see 19c, note on 18c, Index of Names, and Introduction, pp. viii, xviii–xix.

19a *in so short a time:* speeches in Athenian lawcourts were timed. Socrates reflects on the constraint this places on lawyers, and contrasts their life with the leisure of philosophers, at *Theaetetus* 172d–e. Because a jury has limited time in which to learn, and no first-hand experience of the events about which they must judge, their verdicts can at best express 'true belief' as distinct from 'knowledge' (cf. *Theaetetus* 201a–c).

I should like to succeed in my defence: this is in direct conflict with the testimony of Xenophon, that Socrates had no serious interest in acquittal. See note on 41d, and Introduction, pp. xvi–xvii.

I have to obey the law: this is one of several places in the *Defence* in which Socrates registers his respect for the law. For others, see Introduction, p. xxxii.

swings around, claims to be walking on air: this de- 19c scribes Socrates' first appearance in the *Clouds* (223–5), where he is swung around in a basket in the air, and says he is walking on air and thinking about the sun.

those subjects are not my concern at all: in the 19d *Phaedo* (96a–b) Socrates recounts his early intellectual development, and professes to have been interested, as a young man, in questions about the physical world. That story need not be taken to contradict his present statement, which does not mean that he had no interest in scientific matters, but only that they were not the subject of his own distinctive inquiries.

sophists: professional educators who offered instruc- 20a tion in many subjects. Socrates' present reference to eminent sophists is tinged with irony. Plato's *Protagoras* is devoted to contrasting their approach to education with that of Socrates. See also Index of Names, s.vv. Evenus, Gorgias, Hippias, Prodicus, Introduction, p. xix, and notes on 18c, 33a.

be charges 5 minas: a mina equalled 100 silver 20b drachmas. At the end of the fifth century a drachma was roughly equivalent to one day's pay for a man employed in public works. Evenus' fees were therefore not as 'modest' as Socrates pretends. They were ten times the amount charged by Prodicus for his 50-drachma course on names. Socrates compares that with a course for only 1 drachma, which was all he could afford himself (*Cratylus* 384b). We cannot seriously assess Evenus' fees without knowing more of the nature and duration of his course. In any case, Socrates is slyly insinuating that tuition which genuinely provided what Evenus claimed to impart would have been a bargain at any price.

the people I just mentioned: the sophists mentioned 20e at 19e.

the god at Delphi: for Delphi, see Introduction, p. xix. The god Apollo, though nowhere named in the *Defence*, is the deity whose servant Socrates claims to be (*Phaedo* 85b). In what follows, however, when he speaks of 'the god', it is not always clear whether he means Apollo, or a personal God distinct from any deity of traditional Greek religion. Direct reference to Apollo is clearly intended at 21b, 21e, 22a, 23a–c. Later, however (28e, 30a, 30e, 31a, 35d, 41d–42a), the reference is less definite, and 'God' or 'my god' has been used in the translation. See also notes on 42a and *Crito* 54e.

21a *your recent exile and restoration:* politicians of the democratic party had fled from Athens during the regime of the Thirty Tyrants. They returned under an amnesty in 403 when the Thirty were overthrown. See also Index of Names, s.v. Chaerephon.

the Pythia responded: see Introduction, p. xix. The verb used here for 'response' of the priestess seems to have been used originally for the picking up of a bean, i.e. drawing a lot, but nothing is known of the procedure in Chaerephon's case.

21b *What can his riddle mean?:* Heraclitus (early fifth-century philosopher) recognized the riddling character of the Delphic oracle, when he declared: 'the lord whose oracle is in Delphi neither indicates clearly nor conceals, but gives a sign' (fragment 93, trans. T. M. Robinson, *Heraclitus* (Toronto, 1987), 57, 143–4). Socrates' determination to probe the god's 'riddle' is in keeping with this tradition. For riddles see also note on 27a.

out of the question: a solemn expression, suggesting a religious prohibition, a violation of the divine order of things, and therefore unthinkable. Cf. 30d and *Phaedo* 61c–d. The belief that lying or deceit is 'out of the question' for a deity remained a basic conviction of Plato, strongly at variance with poetic tradition. Cf. *Republic* 382c–e.

22a *upon my word:* literally, 'by the dog!', a favourite Socratic oath, which may have originated as a euphemism. It occurs also at *Phaedo* 99a, and at *Gorgias* 482b, where it is linked with 'the god of the Egyptians'. See E. R. Dodds, ed., *Gorgias* (Oxford, 1959), 262–3.

the various 'labours' I kept undertaking: Socrates alludes to the labours of Heracles, twelve tasks of prodigious difficulty imposed upon a hero of legendary strength and courage.

dithyrambic poets: the dithyramb was an emotionally 22b powerful lyric poem, performed by a chorus of singers and dancers. It was believed by Aristotle to have been the genre from which tragic drama had evolved.

I soon realized this truth about them too: Socrates speaks as if the conclusion he is about to draw regarding the poets was one he had already drawn regarding the politicians. He had not, however, ascribed divine inspiration to the latter in our text. Only in the *Meno* (99b–e) is that conclusion explicitly drawn for politicians. For a possible explanation, and its implications for the dating of the *Defence*, see De Strycker and Slings (Bibliography, item 16), 66, 282–3.

seers and soothsayers: the comparison reflects the 22c important Platonic theme that poetry is the product of divine inspiration, not of genuine knowledge. It is typical of those who are inspired to be unable to give a rational explanation of their achievements. The theme is echoed in the *Meno* at the expense of politicians (see previous note), and is elaborated for poets in the *Ion* (533d–535a). For a related line of thought, cf. *Timaeus* 71e–72b.

human wisdom is worth little or nothing: philoso- 23a phy, embodied in Socrates, is here depicted as an intermediate state between human ignorance and divine knowledge. The philosopher lies between most human beings and God, in that he is conscious of his ignorance, aspires to knowledge, but has not yet attained it. The same idea, which underlies the traditional definition of philosophy as 'love of wisdom', appears at *Symposium* 204a–c.

I assist the god: for 'service' to the gods, see *Euthy-* 23b *phro* 13d–14b, where the notion is differently interpreted, and Socrates' own conception of 'service to God' is not allowed to surface. See also note on 20e, and Introduction, pp. xiii–xiv.

Meletus . . . for the poets . . . Anytus for the crafts- 24a *men . . . Lycon for the orators:* it is not clear why Socrates aligns his accusers in this way. Meletus may have been the son of a poet of the same name. Anytus speaks for craftsmen as well as politicians, perhaps because he was a master-tanner, and can thus represent 'business men in government' (Burnet (Bibliography, item 9), 99). Lycon was a politician with no special reputation as an orator, though Diogenes Laertius (ii. 38) calls him a 'demagogue'. See also Index of Names, s.vv. Anytus, Lycon, Meletus.

24c *Socrates is guilty . . . new spiritual beings:* Plato's version of the indictment differs from those of Xenophon (*Memorabilia* i. 1. 1) and Diogenes Laertius (ii. 40), which are probably historically more accurate. Plato reverses the order of the charges, placing 'corrupting the young' first. This perhaps reflects the greater importance attached by him to that charge, and the greater seriousness of Socrates' defence against it. See note on 26b and Introduction, p. xviii.

never cared at all: Socrates' repeated references to 'caring' in his interrogation of Meletus (cf. 24d, 25c) contain a play upon his accuser's name, whose first syllable is also the root of verbs and nouns for 'care'.

25a *the Council:* the Athenian Council was a body of 500, with fifty members from each of the ten tribes, elected annually by lot from citizens over the age of 30. In conjunction with the magistrates it carried on state business, and prepared an agenda for the Assembly (for which see note on *Euthyphro* 3c). See also note on 32b below.

25b *a single person . . . lay people spoil them:* this line of thought is of great importance for the argument of the *Crito*. See, especially, 47b–48a.

26a *I am doing so unintentionally:* Socrates' denial that he corrupts the young intentionally (cf. 37a) relies upon the principle that human beings never intentionally follow a course of action which they know or believe to be harmful to themselves. Since, in Socrates' view, all wrongdoing is harmful to the agent, it follows that all wrongdoing is unintentional, and curable by the removal of ignorance. This doctrine, one of the so-called Socratic Paradoxes, is often summarized in the slogan 'Virtue is Knowledge'. It is elaborated in the *Meno* (77b–78a) and *Protagoras* (352a–358b).

26b *I am corrupting them by teaching them that:* here the two counts of Meletus' indictment are linked, in that 'corrupting the youth' consisted in teaching them atheistic doctrines. This enables Socrates to dispose of the whole indictment by arguing that the charge of atheism was self-contradictory. That charge had stemmed partly from his enemies' total ignorance of philosophical inquiry (23d). But it still remains for him to meet the charge of 'corruption' independently of its connection with atheistic teaching. This he will do below, especially at 29d–31b and 33a–34b). For the relation between the two counts of the indictment, see also note on 24c and Introduction, p. xviii.

the sun and the moon are gods: the sun and moon, 26d even though not the objects of an official cult at Athens, were widely believed to be divine. In the *Cratylus* (397c–d) the belief is attributed by Socrates to 'the earliest people in Greece'. Cf. *Laws* 886d–e, 887d–e. In the *Symposium* (220d) Socrates is reported to have addressed a prayer to the sun at sunrise, and he expressly calls the sun, and other heavenly bodies, 'gods' at *Republic* 508a.

do you imagine that it is Anaxagoras you are accusing?: according to one tradition, Anaxagoras (for whom see Index of Names) had been prosecuted for heresies regarding the composition of the sun and moon. The historicity and the date of Anaxagoras' trial are controversial, and the present text does not prove that it ever occurred. But if it did, Meletus betrays his ignorance by raking up an old charge that had no relevance to Socrates' beliefs or behaviour.

at the bookstalls: literally 'from the *orchēstra*' The 26c *orchēstra* was an area in the Agora. The young men may have heard Anaxagoras' works being read aloud there, just as Socrates says he once heard a book of Anaxagoras being read *(Phaedo* 97b). If so, the charge of a drachma will have been for hearing Anaxagoras' doctrines rather than for buying his books.

a . . . riddle . . . my nice self-contradiction: the 'rid- 27a dle' which Socrates attributes to Meletus consists in the self-contradictory statement 'Socrates acknowledges gods and does not acknowledge gods'. Greek riddles often take the form of paradoxes generated by apparent self-contradiction. The challenge is to find a subject which is both X and not-X at the same rime. Compare our 'when is a door not a door?' An elaborate riddle of this type, comprising no fewer than six self-contradictory descriptions, is mentioned at *Republic* 479b–c. For Greek riddles in general, see D. Gallop in *Ionian Philosophy,* ed. K. J. Boudouris (Athens, 1989), 123–35.

27b   *in my usual manner:* i.e. by question-and-answer, cf. 17c–d. In the following interrogation, as at 20a–b, Socrates also shows his fondness for homespun examples and analogies.

musicians . . . musical phenomena: Socrates refers specifically to players of the *aulos,* which is commonly translated 'flute', but has no English equivalent. The instrument more closely resembled an oboe or clarinet.

27c   *spiritual phenomena . . . spiritual beings:* Socrates' logic is suspect. Here he picks up the exact language of Meletus' indictment (24b–c), which had referred to 'spiritual beings' (*daimonia*) but had not used the noun translated 'phenomena' (*pragmata*) essential to the analogies in 27b. Yet, on the strength of those analogies, Meletus is now compelled to admit that Socrates accepts the existence of 'spirits' (*daimones*). For the status of 'spirits', as intermediate between the human and the divine, see *Symposium* 202d–203a, and note on 23a.

27d   *children of gods:* spirits were sometimes begotten by gods through union with nymphs or mortals. In Socrates' comical analogy, horses correspond to gods, asses to their sexual partners, and mules to spirits. The Greek for 'mule' (*hēmionos,* meaning 'half-ass') is of the same form as the word for 'demigod' (*hēmitheos*), used of Achilles and other heroes at 28c below. The verbal parallel may have suggested the analogy to Plato. The present argument is loosely paraphrased by Aristotle at *Rhetoric* I41a5–12.

28c   *the plain of Troy:* site of the legendary war between the Greeks and Trojans, which is the context of Homer's *Iliad.*

the son of Thetis: Achilles, heroic Greek warrior in the Trojan War. As the offspring of a goddess mother by a mortal father, he is referred to as a 'demigod'. The words quoted are a version of lines from *Iliad* xviii. 95–104. See also Index of Names, s.vv. Hector, Patroclus, Thetis.

28e   *Potidaea, Amphipolis, or Delium:* Potidaea, in Thrace, was the scene of a campaign in 432 BC recounted in

Thucydides i. 56–65. Socrates' endurance of extreme hardship there is described in Plato's *Symposium* 219e–220e. For the battle of Delium (424 BC), cf. Thucydides iv. 90; and for Socrates' selfless bravery in it, see Plato's *Symposium* 221a–b, *Laches* 181b. The fighting at Amphipolis is probably a battle in 422 BC described in Thucydides v. 2.

29b   *life in Hades:* for Hades, see Index of Names. For ignorance of the afterlife, cf. *Phaedo* 66e–67a, 68a–b. See also note on 42a.

29c   *I need never have been brought to court . . . death:* Anytus would have preferred Socrates to leave Athens voluntarily, rather than face formal charges. But since Socrates was unwilling to abandon his activities, an indictment was needed. It became necessary for the prosecution to seek the death penalty, in the expectation that the defence would propose exile as an alternative. Socrates here shows that he well understood the plan. Later (37d–38b) he refuses to oblige its proponents. Cf. *Crito* 45c.

30b   *It is not wealth . . . public life:* this translation, which is the usual one, makes Socrates utter what some scholars have thought an inappropriate sentiment. Burnet (Bibliography, item 9, 124) remarked that, having stressed the extreme poverty resulting from his service to God (23c, 31b–c), Socrates could 'hardly recommend virtue as a good investment'. Instead, Burnet takes the sentence to mean that only through goodness does wealth or anything else become beneficial to human beings. This idea is developed at *Meno* 87e–89a, *Euthydemus* 279a–281e, *Laws* 661a–d, and in the pseudo-Plātonic *Eryxias.* However, Burnet's view, although favoured by several recent writers, places an almost impossible strain upon the Greek. Translated in the usual way, the sentence must mean that goodness is generally (though not always or necessarily) attended by prosperity and other external goods. That position is defended at *Republic* 612b–613e, and by Aristotle (*Politics* 1323a38–b7). Socrates need not be taken to mean that one should seek goodness *in order to* acquire wealth etc. (so he is far from advocating virtue as an 'investment'), but only that those who acquire goodness will normally acquire other benefits as well. Reading the text thus, De Strycker and Slings (Bibliography, item 16, 138–40) aptly compare it with

Christ's words in Matthew 6: 33: 'Seek ye first the Kingdom of God and His righteousness, and all these things shall be added unto you.'

30c *abide by my request:* cf. 17c–d.

31b *it would not seem to be in human nature:* Socrates argues that the purely benevolent nature of his mission points to its divine origin. It is not natural for human beings, but only for God, to act solely for the benefit of another. Cf. *Euthyphro* 3d, 15a, and Introduction, p. xiv.

31d *a certain divine or spiritual sign:* Socrates here confirms that his well-known mysterious 'sign' had been used to substantiate the charge of 'introducing new spiritual realities'. Cf. *Euthyphro* 3b with note. At 40b and 41d the *absence* of the sign will be taken as significant. For the implications of this, see Introduction, p. xxiii. Other allusions to the sign in Plato occur at *Euthydemus* 272e, *Republic* 496c, *Theaetetus* 151a, *Phaedrus* 242b–c. A very different account is given by Xenophon in *Memorabilia* i. 1. 1–9, iv. 8. 1–2, and *Defence of Socrates* 12–13. There it is not limited to warnings against Socrates' own intended actions, but enables him to counsel others. See also the pseudo-Platonic *Theages* (128d–131a). Xenophon assimilates the sign to traditional divination, and attributes to Socrates heaven-sent premonitions of events that are unpredictable on the basis of scientific knowledge.

32b *the presiding commission:* fifty representatives from each of the ten tribes who made up the Council (see note on 25a) took turns during the year to provide an executive for the entire body. In this capacity they were called *prutaneis,* and the tribe in office at any given time was said to 'preside' (*prutaneuein*). They met and dined in the 'round chamber' (see 32c with note).

a collective trial . . . the naval battle: in 406 BC, after a sea-battle off the Ionian coast at Arginusae, several Athenian commanders were charged for their failure to rescue the shipwrecked survivors and recover the dead. A motion to try them collectively was endorsed by the Council and referred to the Assembly. Although a collective trial was unconstitutional, the motion was passed by the Assembly after a stormy debate, and six surviving commanders were convicted and executed. The debate, to which

Socrates alludes here, is recounted in vivid detail by Xenophon (*Hellenica* i. 7). See Introduction, p. xxxii.

the Thirty: see Introduction, pp. vii–viii. 32c

the round chamber: a building (*tholos*) also called the 'sunshade' (*skia*) from its shape. It was commandeered as a seat of government by the Thirty.

Salamis: an island separated by a narrow channel from the coast of Attica.

those whom my slanderers allege to have been my 33a *students:* Socrates is probably alluding, especially, to two of his former associates who had become notorious enemies of the Athenian democracy, Alcibiades and Critias. The former was a brilliant but wayward politician, who had turned against Athens and helped her enemies. He plays a major role in Plato's *Symposium* (212d–223a). The latter was an unscrupulous oligarch, who had become a leading member of the Thirty Tyrants. In the light of their subsequent villainous careers, Socrates was widely suspected of having 'corrupted' them. Xenophon (*Memorabilia* i. 2. 24–47) refutes this belief at length. According to him, 'politics had brought them to Socrates, and for politics they left him' (i. 2. 47).

I never . . . was anyone's instructor: Socrates here, in effect, contrasts himself with the sophists, in that he did not set himself up as a professional teacher. See note on 20a and Introduction, p. xix.

through oracles and dreams: for example, the Del- 33c phic oracle, whose answer had led Socrates to undertake his mission. Dreams had long been believed to be a source of divine communication with human beings, and are often so treated by Plato, cf. *Crito* 44a–b, *Phaedo* 60e–61b. See note on 40d, and D. Gallop, *Aristotle on Sleep and Dreams* (Peterborough, 1991), 7–11.

and through every means . . . human being: additional means of divine communication may include divine appearances of gods to human beings, and perhaps also human intelligence, conceived as a god-given faculty. See Introduction, p. xxiii.

Plato here: Plato's name occurs in his dialogues only 34a here, at 38b below, and at *Phaedo* 59b, where it is noted that he was absent at Socrates' death owing to illness.

34d *in Homer's own words:* the quotation is from *Odyssey,* xix. 163.

my sons: at the time of his trial Socrates had two little boys, Sophroniscus and Menexenus, and an older son, Lamprocles (*Phaedo* 116b).

35b *no better than women:* this is one of many disparaging remarks in Plato about women. Open displays of emotion, especially grief, are regarded as distinctively female, an indulgence of the 'female side' of our nature. Cf. *Phaedo* 60a, 117d–e, *Republic* 387e, 395d, 469d, 605d–e. For Socrates and women, see note on 41c below.

35d *I do acknowledge them . . . as none of my accusers do:* Socrates displays religious faith of an order shared by none of his accusers. For a similar argument in relation to the charges against him, cf. 29a, and see Introduction, p. xxi.

36a *if a mere thirty votes . . . I should have been acquitted:* with a jury of 500, this implies that the vote was 280–220, since at the time of Socrates' trial an evenly split vote (250–250) would have secured his acquittal. Diogenes Laertius (ii. 41) says that Socrates was condemned 'by 281 votes more than those for acquittal'. This cannot be reconciled with the present text. Probably Diogenes, or his source, assumed a jury of 501, and meant that there were 281 votes for condemnation, i.e. 61 more than those for acquittal. Odd-numbered juries are not, however, attested in the first half of the fourth century.

36b *he would not have gained one-fifth of the votes cast:* a minimum proportion of votes was required, on pain of a fine, in order to discourage frivolous prosecutions. Socrates playfully postulates an equal division of the negative votes amongst his three accusers. Each would then be credited with only 93⅓ votes, i.e. less than one-fifth of the total jury of 500.

what alternative penalty: the court had to decide between the penalty demanded by the prosecution and a counter-penalty proposed by the defence, with no option of substituting a different one. Socrates' accusers would probably have expected him to propose exile. Socrates recognizes that that was what the court would probably have preferred (37c), but refuses to oblige them.

36d *free meals in the Prytaneum:* the Prytaneum was the building on the north-east slope of the Acropolis, in which hospitality was given to honoured guests of the state, and to Olympic victors and other sports-heroes. Hence, in proposing that he be given free meals there, Socrates is asking for treatment normally reserved for persons of outstanding distinction. Moreover, he is brazen enough to propose it in order that he may continue the very activity for which he has just been convicted. The jury had no power to grant such a request, as he well knew. Indeed, he obviously half-expected to he held in contempt of court (37a). His comparison of a philosopher's claim to public recognition with the claims of sports-heroes recalls a poem by Xenophanes. See J. H. Lesher, *Xnophanes of Colophon* (Toronto, 1992), 55–61, 74.

37a *I do not treat any human being unjustly, at least intentionally:* cf. 26a with note.

as in other jurisdictions . . . over several: this was the law at Sparta, because of the irrevocability of capital punishment. In the *Laws* (855c–856a) Plato proposes a legal procedure requiring capital cases to be tried over three consecutive days.

37b *I don't know if that is a good thing or a bad one:* cf. 29a–b.

37c *the annually appointed prison commissioners:* literally, 'the Eleven', a commission responsible for prisons and state executions.

37e *If I repel them . . . will expel me on their account:* it is not cleat (*a*) why young people in other cities should get rid of Socrates by putting pressure on their parents, if his ideas repel them, or (*b*) why he should expect such a different reception from the one he had enjoyed from the youth of Athens. On the other hand, if he does not repel them, it is not obvious why their elders should regard him less favourably than the relatives whom he had named as supporters at 33d–34a. Perhaps he had reason to believe that other communities would be less tolerant than Athens of free intellectual inquiry.

38a *you will . . . think that I am practising a sly evasion:* Socrates refers to his 'irony' (*eirōneia*), a charge made by his enemies, and often interpreted as an insincere disavowal of knowledge. For its supposed relevance to the *Euthyphro,* see Introduction, p. xv. Although its role is different in the present passage, the notion of insincerity is still present. The jury will imagine that Socrates is invoking God's will only as a pretext for refusing to give up philosophy.

an unexamined life is no life for a human being to live: the most celebrated line in the *Defence.* Note that Socrates' examination of others is inseparable from examination of himself (cf. 28e). 'Examining' therefore includes 'being examined'. Its importance for a worthwhile *human* life reminds us of the removal of the false conceit of knowledge, which Socrates had earlier (20d) called 'a *human* kind of wisdom'. See notes on 23a, 23b, and Introduction, p. xx.

38b *30 minas:* this seems to have been a normal amount for a fine, and was a considerable sum. See note on 20b. According to Xenophon, however, Socrates refused to propose any fine, or allow his friends to do so, on the ground that that would have been an admission of guilt *(Defence of Socrates* 23).

38d *those who condemned me to death:* Diogenes Laertius (ii. 42) says that the death sentence was passed with an accession of eighty fresh votes. If so, the vote would have been 360–140. See note on 36a.

do or say anything: this phrase, repeated at 39a, also occurs in the argument of *Euthyphro* 8c–d, that no one will be so shameless as to admit wrongdoing, yet try to escape punishment. Here Socrates uses it to make the point that he was not willing to pay any price to secure acquittal.

39b *fleeter of foot than death:* literally, 'runs faster than death'. The Greek words form an alliterative jingle, which may have been proverbial.

as judged by Truth: for the personification of 'truth', cf. *Crito* 48a, *Symposium* 201c, *Phaedo* 91c, *Republic* 597e.

39c *when they are on the point of death:* for prophecy when death is imminent, cf. Socrates' comparison of himself with the prophetic swans of Apollo in the *Phaedo* (85a–b).

as soon as I am dead retribution will come upon you: this section has an aggressive, almost vengeful tone, in curious contrast with the forgiving spirit of 41d.

Socrates' 'avengers' may be the youthful disciples who had used his methods of cross-examination upon others (23c). But there is no evidence that such activities intensified after his death. According to Diogenes Laertius (ii. 106, iii. 6), Plato and other disciples swiftly betook themselves to Megara.

in applying that term to you, I probably use it cor- 40a *rectly:* only at this point does Socrates begin to address (some of) his jurors as 'gentlemen of the jury'. See note on 17a. Those who voted against him are not 'judges', properly speaking, because they have failed to judge him according to the principles they were sworn to observe (35c–d, cf. 18a).

the kind in which the sleeper does not even dream 40d *at all:* literally 'does not even see a dream'. In Greek idiom, dreams are always 'seen', a usage which reflects the archaic view of the dream as a figure experienced in a distinctive mode of vision. See note on 33c, and E. R. Dodds, *The Greeks and the Irrational* (Berkeley, 1951), 104–6.

the Great King of Persia: this monarch embodied the 40e popular ideal of happiness (cf. *Gorgias* 470e, *Euthydemus* 274a). Socrates does not claim that a night of dreamless sleep is 'happy', but only that very few days or nights in anyone's life, even the Great King's, are spent 'better and more agreeably' (40d). He expects happiness or 'good fortune' *(eudaimonia)* only on his alternative hypothesis, an afterlife in which he can meet and cross-examine heroes of the past (41c).

who are also said to sit in judgment there: for the judges 41a see Index of Names, s.vv. Aeacus, Minos, Rhadamanthys, Triptolemus. It is not clear whether Socrates envisages them merely as judging disputes among the dead, or as passing judgment upon the earthly life of those who enter Hades. If the latter, he may be thinking of an 'appeal' in the next world against his unjust treatment in this one. Just such an idea is elaborated by Plato in the closing myth of the *Gorgias* (523a–527a).

the leader of the great expedition against Troy: 41c Agamemnon, chief of the Greek forces in the Trojan War. Cf. 28c with note.

countless other men and women: at *Symposium* 215d Socrates' audience is said to include women, and the same dialogue features his own encounter with Diotima, a wise woman from Mantinea. In the present passage he probably imagines himself examining wise women of bygone ages, or mythical figures such as Diotima. The whole passage seems to be inspired by the visit of Odysseus to the underworld in Homer's *Odyssey,* Book xi, and his encounters with the souls of the dead.

41d *better I should die now and be rid of my troubles:* by his 'troubles', Socrates probably means the infirmities of old age. A wish to escape these was, according to Xenophon, what motivated his conduct at his trial. Contrast, however, what Plato makes him say at 19a, and see Introduction, pp. xvi–xvii.

this much I ask of them: it would he odd if Socrates 41e meant to restrict his final request to the jurors who had voted against him. Also surprising, given what he had said of them at 39b–d, is the suggestion that, if his sons are properly admonished, he will have received his 'just deserts' from them. It seems better to take his final request as intended for the whole jury.

unclear to everyone, save only to God: Socrates' 42a closing words show him to be free from the false conceit of knowledge (cf. 21d, 23b), specifically knowledge about death (cf. 29a–b). They express a serene faith in God, which also marks the end of the *Crito.* See notes on 20e and *Crito* 54e.

CRITO

43a   *Socrates.* Why have you come at this hour, Crito? It's still very early, isn't it?

   Crito. Yes, very.

   Socrates. About what time?

   Crito. Just before daybreak.

5   *Socrates.* I'm surprised the prison-warder was willing to answer the door.

   Crito. He knows me by now, Socrates, because I come and go here so often; and besides, I've done him a small favour.

   Socrates. Have you just arrived, or have you been here for a while?

10   *Crito.* For quite a while.

b   *Socrates.* Then why didn't you wake me up right away instead of sitting by me in silence?

   Crito. Well *of course* I didn't wake you, Socrates! I only wish I weren't so sleepless and 5 wretched myself. I've been marvelling all this time as I saw how peacefully you were sleeping, and I deliberately kept from waking you, so that you could pass the time as peacefully as possible. I've often admired your disposition in the past, in fact all your life; but more than ever in your present plight, you bear it so easily and patiently.

10   *Socrates.* Well, Crito, it really would be tiresome for a man of my age to get upset if the time has come when he must end his life.

   Crito. And yet others of your age, Socrates, are c overtaken by similar troubles, but their age brings them no relief from being upset at the fate which faces them.

   Socrates. That's true. But tell me, why *have* you come so early?

   Crito. I bring painful news, Socrates—not 5 painful for you, I suppose, but painful and hard for me and all your friends—and hardest of all for me to bear, I think.

   Socrates. What news is that? Is it that the ship has come back from Delos,* the one on whose return I must die?

d   *Crito.* Well no, it hasn't arrived yet, but I think it will get here today, judging from reports of people who've come from Sunium,* where they disembarked. That† makes it obvious that it will get 5 here today; and so tomorrow, Socrates, you will have to end your life.

   Socrates. Well, may that be for the best, Crito. If it so please the gods, so be it. All the same, I don't think it will get here today.

   Crito. What makes you think that? 44a

   Socrates. I'll tell you. You see, I am to die on the day after the ship arrives, am I not?

   Crito. At least that's what the authorities say.

   Socrates. Then I don't think it will get here on 5

From *Plato: Defence of Socrates, Euthyphro, Crito,* trans. David Gallop (Oxford: Oxford University Press, 1997).

the day that is just dawning, but on the next one. I infer that from a certain dream I had in the night*—a short time ago, so it may be just as well that you didn't wake me.

Crito. And what was your dream?

Socrates. I dreamt that a lovely, handsome woman approached me, robed in white. She called me and said:

'Socrates,

Thou shalt reach fertile Phthia upon the third day.'*

Crito. What a curious dream, Socrates.

Socrates. Yet its meaning is clear, I think, Crito.

Crito. All too clear, it would seem. But please, Socrates, my dear friend, there is still time to take my advice, and make your escape—because if you die, I shall suffer more than one misfortune: not only shall I lose such a friend as I'll never find again, but it will look to many people, who hardly know you or me, as if I'd abandoned you—since I could have rescued you if I'd been willing to put up the money. And yet what could be more shameful than a reputation for valuing money more highly than friends? Most people won't believe that it was you who refused to leave this place yourself, despite our urging you to do so.

Socrates. But why should we care so much, my good Crito, about what most people believe? All the most capable people, whom we should take more seriously, will think the matter has been handled exactly as it has been.

Crito. Yet surely, Socrates, you can see that one must heed popular opinion too. Your present plight shows by itself that the populace can inflict not the least of evils, but just about the worst, if someone has been slandered in their presence.

Socrates. Ah Crito, if only the populace *could* inflict the worst of evils! Then they would also be capable of providing the greatest of goods, and a fine thing that would be. But the fact is that they can do neither: they are unable to give anyone understanding or lack of it,* no matter what they do.

Crito. Well, if you say so. But tell me this, Socrates: can it be that you are worried for me and your other friends, in case the blackmailers* give us trouble, if you escape, for having smuggled you out of here? Are you worried that we

might be forced to forfeit all our property as well, or pay heavy fines, or even incur some further penalty? If you're afraid of anything like that, put it out of your mind. In rescuing you we are surely justified in taking that risk, or even worse if need be. Come on, listen to me and do as I say.

Socrates. Yes, those risks do worry me, Crito—amongst many others.

Crito. Then put those fears aside—because no great sum is needed to pay people who are willing to rescue you and get you out of here. Besides, you can surely see that those blackmailers are cheap, and it wouldn't take much to buy them off. My own means are available to you and would be ample, I'm sure. Then again, even if—out of concern on my behalf—you think you shouldn't be spending my money, there are visitors here who are ready to spend theirs. One of them, Simmias from Thebes, has actually brought enough money for this very purpose, while Cebes and quite a number of others are also prepared to contribute. So, as I say, you shouldn't hesitate to save yourself on account of those fears.

And don't let it trouble you, as you were saying in court,* that you wouldn't know what to do with yourself if you went into exile. There will be people to welcome you anywhere else you may go: if you want to go to Thessaly,* I have friends there who will make much of you and give you safe refuge, so that no one from anywhere in Thessaly will trouble you.

Next, Socrates, I don't think that what you propose—giving yourself up, when you could be rescued—is even just. You are actually hastening to bring upon yourself just the sorts of thing which your enemies would hasten to bring upon you—indeed, they have done so—in their wish to destroy you.

What's more, I think you're betraying those sons of yours.* You will be deserting them, if you go off when you could be raising and educating them: as far as you're concerned, they will fare as best they may. In all likelihood, they'll meet the sort of fate which usually befalls orphans once they've lost their parents. Surely, one should either not have children at all, or else see the toil and trouble of their upbringing and education through to the end; yet you seem to me to prefer the easiest path. One should rather choose the path that a good and resolute man would choose, particularly if one professes to cultivate goodness* all one's life. Frankly, I'm ashamed for you and for us, your friends: it may appear that this whole predicament of yours has been handled with a certain feebleness on our part. What with the bringing of your case to court when that could have been avoided,* the actual conduct of the trial, and now, to crown it all, this absurd outcome of the business, it may seem that the problem has eluded us through some fault or feebleness on our part—in that we failed to save you, and you failed to save yourself, when that was quite possible and feasible, if we had been any use at all.

Make sure, Socrates, that all this doesn't turn out badly, and a disgrace to you as well as us. Come now, form a plan—or rather, don't even plan, because the time for that is past, and only a single plan remains. Everything needs to be carried out during the coming night; and if we go on waiting around, it won't be possible or feasible any longer. Come on, Socrates, do all you can to take my advice, and do exactly what I say.

Socrates. My dear Crito, your zeal will be invaluable if it should have right on its side; but otherwise, the greater it is, the harder it makes matters. We must therefore consider whether or not the course you urge should be followed—because it is in my nature, not just now for the first time but always, to follow nothing within me but the principle* which appears to me, upon reflection, to be best.

I cannot now reject the very principles that I previously adopted, just because this fate has overtaken me; rather, they appear to me much the same as ever, and I respect and honour the same ones that I did before. If we cannot find better ones to maintain in the present situation, you can be sure that I won't agree with you—not even if the power of the populace threatens us, like children, with more bogeymen* than it does now, by visiting us with imprisonment, execution, or confiscation of property.

What, then, is the most reasonable way to consider the matter? Suppose we first take up the point you make about what people will think. Was it always an acceptable principle that one should pay heed to some opinions but not to others, or was it not? Or was it acceptable before I had to die, while now it is exposed as an idle assertion made for the sake of talk, when it is really childish nonsense? For my part, Crito, I'm eager to look into this together with you, to see whether the principle is to be viewed any differently, or in the same way, now that I'm in this position, and whether we should disregard or follow it.

As I recall, the following principle always used to be affirmed by people who thought they were talking sense: the principle, as I was just saying, that one should have a high regard for some opinions held by human beings, but not for others. Come now, Crito: don't you think that was a good principle? I ask because you are not, in all foreseeable likelihood, going to die tomorrow, and my present trouble shouldn't impair your judgement. Consider, then: don't you think it a good principle, that one shouldn't respect all human opinions, but only some and not others; or, again, that one shouldn't respect everyone's opinions, but those of some people, and not those of others? What do you say? Isn't that a good principle?

Crito. It is.

Socrates. And one should respect the good ones, but not the bad ones?

Crito. Yes.

Socrates. And good ones are those of people with understanding, whereas bad ones are those of people without it?

Crito. Of course.

Socrates. Now then, once again, how were such points established?* When a man is in training, and concentrating upon that, does he pay heed to the praise or censure or opinion of each and every man, or only to those of the individual who happens to be his doctor or trainer?

Crito. Only to that individual's.

Socrates. Then he should fear the censures, and welcome the praises of that individual, but not those of most people.*

Crito. Obviously.

Socrates. So he must base his actions and exercises, his eating and drinking, upon the opinion of the individual, the expert supervisor, rather than upon everyone else's.

Crito. True.

Socrates. Very well. If he disobeys that individual and disregards his opinion and his praises, bur respects those of most people, who are ignorant, he'll suffer harm, won't he?

Crito. Of course.

5 *Socrates.* And what is that harm? What does it affect? What element within the disobedient man?

Crito. Obviously, it affects his body, because that's what it spoils.

Socrates. A good answer. And in other fields too, Crito—we needn't go through them all, but they surely include matters of just and unjust, ho-10 nourable and dishonourable, good and bad, the subjects of our present deliberation—is it the d opinion of most people that we should follow and fear, or is it that of the individual authority— assuming that some expert exists* who should be respected and feared above all others? If we don't follow that person, won't we corrupt and impair 5 the element which (as we agreed) is made better by what is just, but is spoilt by what is unjust?* Or is there nothing in all that?

Crito. I accept it myself, Socrates.

Socrates. Well now, if we spoil the part of us that is improved by what is healthy but corrupted 10 by what is unhealthy, because it is not expert e opinion that we are following, are our lives worth living once it has been corrupted? The part in question is, of course, the body, isn't it?

Crito. Yes.

Socrates. And are our lives worth living with 5 a poor or corrupted body?

Crito. Definitely not.

Socrates. Well then, are they worth living if the element which is impaired by what is unjust and benefited by what is just has been corrupted? Or do we consider the element to which justice 48a or injustice belongs, whichever part of us it is, to be of less value than the body?

Crito. By no means.

Socrates. On the contrary, it is more precious?

Crito. Far more.

5 *Socrates.* Then, my good friend, we shouldn't care all that much about what the populace will say of us, but about what the expert on matters of justice and injustice will say, the individual authority, or Truth.* In the first place, then, your proposal that we should care about popular opinion regarding just, honourable, or good ac- 10 tions, and their opposites, is mistaken.

'Even so,' someone might say, 'the populace has the power to put us to death.'

Crito. That's certainly clear enough; one might b say that, Socrates.

Socrates. You're right. But the principle we've rehearsed, my dear friend, still remains as true as it was before—for me at any rate. And now consider this further one, to see whether or not it still holds good for us. We should attach the highest value, shouldn't we, not to living, but to living 5 well?

Crito. Why yes, that still holds.

Socrates. And living well is the same as living honourably or justly?* Does that still hold or not?

Crito. Yes, it does.

Socrates. Then in the light of those admissions, 10 we must ask the following question: is it just, or is it not, for me to try to get out of here, when c Athenian authorities are unwilling to release me? Then, if it does seem just, let us attempt it; but if it doesn't, let us abandon the idea.

As for the questions you raise about expenses and reputation and bringing up children, I suspect they are the concerns of those who cheerfully put 5 people to death, and would bring them back to life if they could, without any intelligence, namely, the populace. For us, however, because our principle so demands, there is no other question to ask except the one we just raised: shall we be acting justly—we who are rescued as well as d the rescuers themselves—if we pay money and do favours to those who would get me out of here? Or shall we in truth be acting unjustly if we do all those things? And if it is clear that we shall be acting unjustly in taking that course, then the question whether we shall have to die through standing firm and holding our peace, or suffer in 5 any other way, ought not to weigh with us in comparison with acting unjustly.

Crito. I think that's finely *said*, Socrates; but do please consider what we should *do*.

Socrates. Let's examine that question together, dear friend; and if you have objections to any- e thing I say, please raise them, and I'll listen to you—otherwise, good fellow, it's time to stop telling me, again and again, that I should leave

here against the will of Athens. You see, I set
great store upon persuading you as to my course
of action, and not acting against your will. Come
now, just consider whether you find the starting-
point of our inquiry acceptable, and try to answer
my questions according to your real beliefs.

Crito. All right, I'll try.

Socrates. Do we maintain that people should on
no account whatever do injustice willingly? Or may
it be done in some circumstances but not in others?
Is acting unjustly in no way good or honourable, as
we frequently agreed in the past? Or have all those
former agreements been jettisoned during these last
few days? Can it be, Crito, that men of our age have
long failed to notice, as we earnestly conversed with
each other, that we ourselves were no better than
children? Or is what we then used to say true above
all else? Whether most people say so or not, and
whether we must be treated more harshly or more
leniently than at present, isn't it a fact, all the same,
that acting unjustly is utterly bad and shameful for
the agent? Yes or no?

Crito. Yes.

Socrates. So one must not act unjustly at all.

Crito. Absolutely not.

Socrates. Then, even if one is unjustly treated,
one should not return injustice,* as most people believe—given that one should act not unjustly at all.

Crito. Apparently not.

Socrates. Well now, Crito, should one ever ill-
treat anybody or not?

Crito. Surely not, Socrates.

Socrates. And again, when one suffers ill-treatment, is it just to return it, as most people maintain, or isn't it?

Crito. It is not just at all.

Socrates. Because there's no difference, I take
it, between ill-treating people and treating them
unjustly.

Crito. Correct.

Socrates. Then one shouldn't return injustice
or ill-treatment to any human being, no matter
how one may be treated by that person. And in
making those admissions, Crito, watch our that
you're not agreeing to anything contrary to your
real beliefs.* I say that, because I realize that the
belief is held by few people, and always will be.
Those who hold it share no common counsel with

those who don't; but each group is bound to regard the other with contempt when they observe
one another's decisions. You too, therefore,
should consider very carefully whether you share
that belief with me, and whether we may begin
our deliberations from the following premiss: neither doing nor returning in justice is ever right,
nor should one who is ill-treated defend himself
by retaliation. Do you agree? Or do you dissent
and not share my belief in that premiss? I've long
been of that opinion myself, and I still am now;
but if you've formed any different view, say so,
and explain it. If you stand by our former view,
however, then listen to my next point.

Crito. Well, I do stand by it and share that
view, so go ahead.

Socrates. All right, I'll make my next point—
or rather, ask a question. Should the things one
agrees with someone else be done, provided they
are just,* or should one cheat?

Crito. They should be done.

Socrates. Then consider what follows. If we
leave this place without having persuaded our
city, are we or are we not ill-treating certain people, indeed people whom we ought least of all to
be ill-treating? And would we be abiding by the
things we agreed,* those things being just, or not?

Crito. I can't answer your question, Socrates,
because I don't understand it.

Socrates. Well, look at it this way. Suppose we
were on the point of running away from here, or
whatever else one should call it.* Then the Laws,
or the State of Athens, might come and confront
us, and they might speak as follows:

'Please tell us, Socrates, what do you have in
mind? With this action you are attempting, do you
intend anything short of destroying us,* the Laws
and the city as a whole, to the best of your ability? Do you think that a city can still exist without being overturned, if the legal judgments rendered within it possess no force, but are nullified
or invalidated by individuals?'

What shall we say, Crito, in answer to that and
other such questions? Because somebody, particularly a legal advocate,* might say a great deal
on behalf of the law that is being invalidated here,
the one requiring that judgments, once rendered,
shall have authority.* Shall we tell them: 'Yes,

that is our intention, because the city was treating us unjustly, by not judging our case correctly'? Is that to be our answer, or what?

Crito. Indeed it is, Socrates.

5 *Socrates.* And what if the Laws say: 'And was that also part of the agreement between you and us, Socrates? Or did you agree to abide by whatever judgments the city rendered?'

Then, if we were surprised by their words, perhaps they might say: 'Don't be surprised at what we are saying, Socrates, but answer us, seeing that
10 you like to use question-and-answer.* What com-
d plaint, pray, do you have against the city and ourselves, that you should now attempt to destroy us? In the first place, was it not we who gave you birth? Did your father not marry your mother and beget you under our auspices? So will you inform those of us here who regulate marriages whether you have any criticism of them as poorly framed?'

5 'No, I have none,' I should say.

'Well then, what of the laws dealing with children's upbringing and education, under which you were educated yourself? Did those of us Laws who are in charge of that area not give proper direction, when they required your father to educate
e you in the arts and physical training?'*

'They did,' I should say.

'Very good. In view of your birth, upbringing, and education, can you deny, first, that you belong to us as our offspring and slave, as your fore-
5 bears also did? And if so, do you imagine that you are on equal terms with us in regard to what is just, and that whatever treatment we may accord to you, it is just for you to do the same thing back to us? You weren't on equal terms with your father, or your master (assuming you had one), making it just for you to return the treatment you re-
51a ceived—answering back when you were scolded, or striking back when you were struck, or doing many other things of the same sort. Will you then have licence against your fatherland and its Laws, if we try to destroy you, in the belief that that is
5 just? Will you try to destroy us in return, to the best of your ability? And will you claim that in doing so you are acting justly, you who are genuinely exercised about goodness? Or are you, in your wisdom, unaware that, in comparison with your mother and father and all your other

forebears, your fatherland is more precious and
b venerable, more sacred and held in higher esteem among gods, as well as among human beings who have any sense; and that you should revere your fatherland, deferring to it and appeasing it when it is angry,* more than your own father? You must either persuade it, or else do whatever it commands;* and if it ordains that you must submit to certain treatment, then you must hold your peace
5 and submit to it: whether that means being beaten or put in bonds, or whether it leads you into war to be wounded or killed,* you must act accordingly, and that is what is just; you must neither give way nor retreat, nor leave your position;* rather, in warfare, in court, and everywhere else, you must do whatever your city or fatherland commands, or else persuade it as to what is truly
10 just;* and if it is sinful to use violence against
c your mother or father, it is far more so to use it against your fatherland.'*

What shall we say to that, Crito? That the Laws are right or not?

Crito. I think they are.
5

Socrates. 'Consider then, Socrates,' the Laws might go on, 'whether the following is also true: in your present undertaking you are not proposing to treat us justly. We gave you birth, upbringing, and education, and a share in all the benefits
d we could provide for you along with all your fellow citizens. Nevertheless, we proclaim, by the formal granting of permission, that any Athenian who wishes, once he has been admitted to adult status,* and has observed the conduct of city business and ourselves, the Laws, may—if he is dissatisfied with us—go wherever he pleases* and take his property. Not one of us Laws hinders or
5 forbids that: whether any of you wishes to emigrate to a colony, or to go and live as an alien elsewhere, he may go wherever he pleases and
e keep his property, if we and the city fail to satisfy him.

'We do say, however, that if any of you remains here after he has observed the system by which we dispense justice and otherwise manage our city, then he has agreed with us by his conduct to obey whatever orders we give him. And
5 thus we claim that anyone who fails to obey is guilty on three counts: he disobeys us as his

parents; he disobeys those who nurtured him; and after agreeing to obey us he neither obeys nor persuades us if we are doing anything amiss, even though we offer him a choice, and do not harshly 52a insist that he must do whatever we command. Instead, we give him two options: he must either persuade us or else do as we say; yet he does neither. Those are the charges, Socrates, to which we say you too will be liable if you carry out your 5 intention; and among Athenians, you will be not the least liable, but one of the most.'

And if I were to say, 'How so?' perhaps they could fairly reproach me, observing that I am actually among those Athenians who have made that agreement with them most emphatically.

b 'Socrates,' they would say, 'we have every indication that you were content with us, as well as with our city, because you would never have stayed home here, more than is normal for all other Athenians,* unless you were abnormally content. 5 You never left our city for a festival—except once to go to the Isthmus*—nor did you go elsewhere for other purposes, apart from military service. You never travelled abroad, as other people do; nor were you eager for acquaintance with a differ- c ent city or different laws: we and our city sufficed for you. Thus, you emphatically opted for us, and agreed to be a citizen on our terms. In particular, you fathered children in our city, which would suggest that you were content with it.

'Moreover, during your actual trial it was open to you, had you wished, to propose exile as your 5 penalty; thus, what you are now attempting to do without the city's consent, you could then have done with it. On that occasion, you kept priding yourself that it would not trouble you if you had to die: you would choose death ahead of exile, so you said.* Yet now you dishonour those words, and show no regard for us, the Laws, in your ef- d fort to destroy us. You are acting as the meanest slave would act, by trying to run away* in spite of those compacts and agreements you made with us, whereby you agreed to be a citizen on our terms.

'First, then, answer us this question: are we 5 right in claiming that you agreed, by your conduct if not verbally, that you would be a citizen on our terms? Or is that untrue?'

What shall we say in reply to that, Crito? Mustn't we agree?

Crito. We must, Socrates.

Socrates. 'Then what does your action amount to,' they would say, 'except breaking the com- e pacts and agreements you made with us? By your own admission, you were not coerced or tricked into making them, or forced to reach a decision in a short time: you had seventy years* in which it was open to you to leave if you were not happy with us, or if you thought those agreements un- 5 fair. Yet you preferred neither Lacedaemon nor Crete*—places you often say are well governed— 53a nor any other Greek or foreign city: in fact, you went abroad less often than the lame and the blind or other cripples. Obviously, then, amongst Athenians you were exceptionally content with our city and with us, its Laws—because who would care for a city apart from its laws? Won't you, 5 then, abide by your agreements now? Yes you will, if you listen to us, Socrates; and then at least you won't make yourself an object of derision by leaving the city.

'Just consider: if you break those agreements, and commit any of those offences, what good will you do yourself or those friends of yours? Your 10 friends, pretty obviously, will risk being exiled b themselves, as well as being disenfranchised or losing their property. As for you, first of all, if you go to one of the nearest cities, Thebes or Megara*—they are both well governed—you will 5 arrive as an enemy of their political systems, Socrates: all who are concerned for their own cities will look askance at you, regarding you as a subverter of laws.* You will also confirm your jurors in their judgment, making them think they c decided your case correctly: any subverter of laws, presumably, might well be thought to be a corrupter of young, unthinking people.

'Will you, then, avoid the best-governed cities and the most respectable of men? And if so, will your life be worth living? Or will you associate 5 with those people, and be shameless enough to converse with them? And what will you say to them, Socrates? The things you used to say here, that goodness and justice are most precious to mankind, along with institutions and laws? Don't you think that the predicament of Socrates will cut an ugly figure? Surely you must.

'Or will you take leave of those spots, and go to stay with those friends of Crito's up in Thessaly?* That, of course, is a region of the utmost disorder and licence; so perhaps they would enjoy hearing from you about your comical escape from gaol, when you dressed up in some outfit, wore a leather jerkin or some other runaway's garb, and altered your appearance. Will no one observe that you, an old man with probably only a short time left to live, had the nerve to cling so greedily to life by violating the most important laws? Perhaps not, so long as you don't trouble anyone. Otherwise, Socrates, you will hear a great deal to your own discredit. You will live as every person's toady and lackey; and what will you be doing—apart from living it up in Thessaly, as if you had travelled all the way to Thessaly to have dinner? As for those principles of yours about justice and goodness in general—tell us, where will they be then?

'Well then, is it for your children's sake that you wish to live, in order to bring them up and give them an education? How so? Will you bring them up and educate them by taking them off to Thessaly and making foreigners of them, so that they may gain that advantage too? Or if, instead of that, they are brought up here, will they be better brought up and educated just because you are alive, if you are not with them? Yes, you may say, because those friends of yours will take care of them. Then will they take care of them if you travel to Thessaly, but not take care of them if you travel to Hades?* Surely if those professing to be your friends are of any use at all, you must believe that they will.

'No, Socrates, listen to us, your own nurturers: do not place a higher value upon children, upon life, or upon anything else, than upon what is just, so that when you leave for Hades, this may be your whole defence before the authorities there; to take that course seems neither better nor more just or holy, for you or for any of your friends here in this world. Nor will it be better for you when you reach the next. As things stand, you will leave this world (if you do) as one who has been treated unjustly not by us Laws, but by human beings;* whereas if you go into exile, thereby shamefully returning injustice for injustice and ill-treatment for ill-treatment, breaking the agreements and compacts you made with us, and inflicting harm upon the people you should least harm—yourself, your friends, your fatherland, and ourselves—then we shall be angry with you in your lifetime; and our brother Laws in Hades will not receive you kindly there, knowing that you tried, to the best of your ability, to destroy us too. Come then, do not let Crito persuade you to take his advice rather than ours.'

That, Crito, my dear comrade, is what I seem to hear them saying, I do assure you. I am like the Corybantic revellers* who think they are still hearing the music of pipes: the sound of those arguments is ringing loudly in my head, and makes me unable to hear the others. As far as these present thoughts of mine go, then, you may be sure chat if you object to them, you will plead in vain. None the less, if you think you will do any good, speak up.

Crito. No, Socrates, I've nothing to say.

Socrates. Then let it be, Crito, and let us act accordingly, because that is the direction in which God* is guiding us.

NOTES

the ship has come back from Delos: the small island of Delos was sacred to the god Apollo. A mission sailed there annually from Athens to commemorate her deliverance by Theseus from servitude to King Minos of Crete. No executions could be carried out in Athens until the sacred ship returned (*Phaedo* 58b–c).

Sunium: the headland at the south-eastern extremity of Artica, about 50 kilometres from Athens. The winds were unfavourable at the time (*Phaedo* 58c), so the ship may have been taking shelter at Sunium when the travellers left it there.

a certain dream I had in the night: see notes on *Defence* 33c, 40d.

Thou shalt . . . third day: in Homer's *Iliad* (ix. 363) Achilles says, 'on the third day I may return to fertile Phthia', meaning that he can get home in three days. In Socrates' dream 'Phthia' becomes a symbol for the 'home' to which he will return after his death.

44d *they are unable to give anyone understanding or lack of it:* the implication, that understanding and ignorance are the greatest good and the worst of evils, is Socrates' constant theme in the *Defence*. See Introduction, p. xx. For the translation 'understanding', see note on *Defence* 18b.

44c *the blackmailers:* Athens had no public prosecutors. Prosecutions were undertaken by private citizens, who sometimes threatened legal action for personal, political, or financial gain. The word *sukophantēs* means, literally, 'one who shows figs'. It is uncertain how it acquired its legal sense. One theory connects it with revealing the fruit on a fig-tree by shaking the tree, hence extorting money by accusation or blackmail. The sense of 'toady', borne by its modern derivative 'sycophant", was not present in the Greek word.

45b *as you were saying in court:* cf. *Defence* 37c–d.

45c *Thessaly.* the region of northern Greece, lying 200–300 kilometres north-west of Africa. According to Diogenes Laertius (ii. 25) Socrates refused invitations from residents of Crannon and Larissa, two cities in Thessaly.

those sons of yours: see note on *Defence* 34d.

45d *if one professes to cultivate goodness:* a palpable hit at Socrates, who has professed to care for nothing else. The blow will be effectively parried, however, at 51a and 53c. See Introduction, pp. xxxi–xxxii.

45e *when that could have been avoided:* see *Defence* 29c with note.

46b *to follow nothing within me but the principle:* the word translated 'principle' (*logos*) can also mean 'argument', and is sometimes so rendered here. But in what follows Socrates seems to be thinking of principles that must guide his conduct, rather than the arguments by which those principles had been established. By calling a principle something 'within him', Socrates virtually personifies it as a force motivating his actions.

46c *more bogeymen:* Socrates compares death and other terrors with bogeys used to frighten children. Cf.

Phaedo 77d–e. He will also distinguish serious, adult argument from childish nonsense (46d, 49b). The 'bogeys' mentioned are all standard instruments of law enforcement. For the implication of this, see Introduction, p. xxxiii.

47a *how were such points established?:* this evidently refers to discussions held between Socrates and Crito on previous occasions (cf. 46c–d, 48b, 49a–b). The method of establishing the point is argument by analogy, a favourite Socraric technique. See also next note.

47b *not those of most people:* this passage recalls the arguments of *Defence* 20a–c, 25a–c, that only one person, or very few, can possess expertise in any given field, whereas the majority are ignorant. It also anticipates the important argument of the *Theaetetus* (152a–179d), which attacks the thesis that all truth is subjective, and that one man's opinion is as true as another's.

47d *assuming that some expert exists:* the idea that there is an expert in moral matters, comparable with the doctor in health matters, is fundamental to all of Plato's ethical and political thought. Such expertise is the province of the philosopher, and is the aim of all Socratic inquiry. The role of the moral expert affects the way in which the arguments of the *Crito* are structured. See note on 49b, and Introduction, p. xxvi.

the element which . . . is made better by what is just, but is spoilt by what is unjust: this element is what is referred to in the *Defence* (29e), and often elsewhere, as the 'soul' (*psuchē),* that precious part of human beings whose good condition constitutes their true well-being, and must therefore be of paramount concern. Here, as often in Plato, the effect of wrongdoing upon the soul is compared with the effect of unhealthy practices upon the body. Cf. *Republic* 444c–445b.

48a *Truth:* see note on *Defence* 39b.

48b *living well is the same as living honourably or justly:* this equation puts Plato's ethical theory in a nutshell. A full defence of it is not undertaken in the *Crito*. See Introduction, p. xxi.

49b *one should not return injustice:* this clearly follows from the general principle that one should not act unjustly in any circumstances whatever. It is because the principle, and particularly the inference drawn from it here, would be widely denied, that Socrates has argued for trusting the moral expert rather than majority opinion. See Introduction, p. xxvi.

49d *contrary to your real beliefs:* Socrates often insists that his respondents answer according to their real beliefs. Where they fail or refuse to do so, discussion proves futile, because—as he says here—they share 'no common counsel', i.e. no basis for joint deliberation.

49e *provided they are just:* for the interpretation of this important proviso, and its role in the argument, see Introduction, p. xxviii.

50a *would we be abiding by the things we agreed:* the notion of an agreement between the citizen and the state is often said to prefigure the 'Social Contract' theory of political obligation, according to which the individual surrenders some degree of personal liberty in return for benefits from the state. Note, however, that the agreement is here made between the individual and the state, not between individuals and one another. In this respect the present theory differs from the version of the 'Social Contract' put forward at *Republic* 358e–359b.

or whatever else one should call it: it is implied that any other word would be a mere euphemism for 'running away', a term of contempt for deserting soldiers or runaway slaves. Cf. 52d, 53d. Fleeing in battle is treated by Socrates as a paradigm of cowardice (*Defence* 28e, 39a). In the *Phaedo* (62b) deserting one's post provides an analogy for committing suicide, as it does here for breaking gaol. All of these acts involve disobedience to higher authority: military commanders, courts of law, or God.

50b *With this action you are attempting, do you intend anything short of destroying us. . .?:* in raising this question, the Laws are often thought to be using a generalizing argument of the form 'what would happen if everyone were to break the law?' since only on that hypothesis would the laws and the state be 'destroyed'. No such argument, however, need be read into the text. See Introduction, p. xxx.

particularly a legal advocate: it was customary in Athens to appoint a public advocate to defend laws which it was proposed to abrogate. By alluding to

this procedure, the Laws perhaps insinuate the absurdity of 'abrogating' the fundamental principle that they go on to mention. See next note.

the one requiring that judgments, once rendered, shall have authority: these words have been read as referring to a specific law passed when the Athenian democracy was restored after the fall of the Thirty Tyrants in 403 (Burnet (Bibliography, item 9), 201). It had reinstated judgments made by the democratic courts before the regime of the Thirty. But it would be pointless to invoke a law framed specifically to uphold judgments made five years before Socrates' own trial. The Laws are better understood as invoking a basic general principle upon which any legal system must depend. See Introduction, pp. xxix–xxx.

question-and-answer: the Laws allude to Socrates' 50c much-vaunted preference for this method, to which he had referred in the *Defence* (e.g. 17c, 27b, 33b, 41c).

in the arts and physical training: the standard com- 50e ponents of traditional Athenian education, in terms of which Plato discusses education in the *Republic*, Books ii–iii.

you should revere your fatherland, deferring to it 51b *and appeasing it when it is angry:* in a cascade of patriotic rhetoric, the Laws here demand a degree of subservience that has often been found offensive. Indeed, their talk of 'appeasement' suggests precisely the kind of grovelling behaviour with which Socrates had refused to demean himself in court (*Defence* 34d–35b). Although he is made to raise no objection to their present speech, we need not suppose that Plato would have endorsed every word of it, or meant his readers to do so. The Laws speak only from their own point of view. See Introduction, p. xxxiii.

You must either persuade it, or else do whatever it commands: the Laws claim that the city remains open to persuasion, an important point repeated twice below (51b–c, 51e–52a). They do not, however, say explicitly how Socrates might have 'persuaded' the city, or identify the 'command' relevant to his case. The 'command' is, presumably, the death sentence passed upon him. Since he had failed to 'persuade' the jury to acquit him or to substitute an alternative penalty, it is that command which, according to the Laws, he is now obliged to obey.

being beaten or put in bonds . . . to be wounded or killed: it is notable that all the examples in this passage are of things that the obedient citizen must *suffer,* not of things that he must *do.* For the significance of this point, see Introduction, p. xxviii.

you must neither give way nor retreat, nor leave your position: once again, the Laws use military metaphors for dereliction of duty. See note on 50a.

51c *or else persuade it as to what is truly just:* the language hints at a conception of 'natural' justice which transcends the dictates of the law. Socrates must obey the city's commands, unless he can persuade it that he has *moral* right on his side.

against your fatherland: the analogy between doing violence to one's country and doing it to one's parents has been subtly reinforced, throughout this speech, by the fact that the word often translated 'country' (*patris*) is cognate with 'father' (*patēr*).

51d *once he has been admitted to adult status:* admission to Athenian citizenship was not automatic, but required formal registration by males at the age of 17 or 18, with proof of age and parental citizenship. The procedure is described, and its implications for the argument of the Laws well discussed, by Kraut (Bibliography, item 20), 154–7.

may . . . go wherever he pleases: this line of argument would not be available to any state which controls its borders by means of passports.

52b *more than is normal for all other Athenians:* Phaedrus, in the Platonic dialogue named after him (230c–d), remarks that Socrates never so much as sets foot outside the city walls. Socrates replies that he is a lover of learning, and cannot learn anything from the trees and open country, as he can from people in town.

except once to go to the Isthmus: the Isthmus was the strip of land linking the Peloponnese with the rest of Greece. Socrates may have attended the Isthmian Games, which were held every two years at Corinth.

52c *you would choose death ahead of exile, so yon said:* cf. *Defence* 37c–d.

52d *trying to run away:* see note on 50a.

seventy years: an exaggeration. Socrates was only 70 52e at the time of his trial (*Defence* 17d), He could hardly have had the option of leaving Athens for another city before he came of age.

neither Lacedaemoi nor Crete: Lacedaemon was the official name for the territory of Sparta. Sparta and Crete were both authoritarian and 'closed' societies, which forbade their citizens to live abroad. Plato's attitude towards them is not uncritical. Accounts of the Spartan way of life occur at *Hippias Major* 283a–286a and *Protagoras* 342a–343c, both heavily spiced with irony. In the latter passage Crete is conjoined with Sparta, and speakers from both states appear in Plato's *Laws,* which is set in Crete. For comparison of their political systems with that of Athens, see Kraut (Bibliography, item 20), 177–80, 215–28.

Thebes or Megara: Thebes was the chief city in 53b Boeotia, the region lying to the north-west of Artica; Megara was on the Isthmus (see note on 52b). Both lay within easy reach of Athens.

a subverter of laws: in support of this claim, see Introduction, p. xxx.

Thessaly: see note on 45c. 53d

Hades: see Index of Names. 54a

treated unjustly not by us Laws, but by human be- 54c *ings:* for an explanation of this highly questionable distinction, see Introduction, p. xxxi. The Laws never concede that they have wronged Socrates. They had thought it just to destroy him (51a), and remain unpersuaded that they have done anything amiss (51e).

the Corybantic revellers: the Corybantes performed 54d orgiastic rites and dances to the sound of pipe and drum music. Their music sometimes induced a state of frenzy in emotionally disordered people, which was followed by a deep sleep from which the patients awoke cured. Socrates compares the arguments of the Laws with Corybantic music, which continues to ring in the ears even when the instruments have ceased to play.

God: or 'the god'. Socrates may be referring to his 54e own guiding deity; but a deeper, monotheistic note seems audible in his final words, as also at the close of the *Defence.* See note on *Defence* 42a.

PHAEDO

Phaedo, a disciple of Socrates, relates to his friend Echecrates Socrates' last conversation before he drank the hemlock. Cebes and Simmias, two of Socrates' disciples, inquire on the nature of the soul and whether it is immortal. Socrates attempts to prove that the soul is indeed immortal. We enter the dialogue as Cebes asks about the moral permissibility of suicide.

'Well then, Socrates, on just what ground do they say it's forbidden to kill oneself? Because—to answer the question you were just asking—I certainly did hear from Philolaus, when he was living with us, and earlier from several others, that one ought not to do that; but I've never heard anything definite about it from anyone.'

'Well you must take heed,' he said; 'as maybe you will hear. Perhaps, though, it will seem a matter for wonder to you if this alone of all things is unqualified, and it never happens as other things do sometimes and for some people, that it is better for a man to be dead than alive; and for those for whom it is better to be dead, perhaps it seems a matter for wonder to you if for these men it is not holy to do good to themselves, but they must await another benefactor.'

Cebes chuckled at this. 'Hark at that, now!' he said, speaking in his own dialect.

'Well yes,' said Socrates, 'it would seem unreasonable, put that way; but perhaps there is, in fact, some reason for it. The reason given in mysteries on the subject, that we men are in some sort of prison, and that one ought not to release oneself from it or run away, seems to me a lofty idea and not easy to penetrate; but still, Cebes, this much seems to me well said: it is gods who care for us, and for the gods we men are among their belongings. Don't you think so?'

'I do,' said Cebes.

'Well, if one of your belongings were to kill itself, without your signifying that you wanted it to die, wouldn't you be vexed with it, and punish it, if you had any punishment at hand?'

'Certainly.'

'So perhaps, in that case, it isn't unreasonable that one should not kill oneself until God sends some necessity, such as the one now before us.'

'Yes, that does seem fair,' said Cebes. 'But then what you were saying just now—that philosophers should be willing to die lightly—that seems odd, if what we were just saying, that it is God who cares for us, and that we are his belongings, is well founded. Because it's unreasonable that the wisest of men should not be resentful at quitting this service, where they're directed by the best directors there are—the gods; since a man of that sort, surely, doesn't believe he'll care for himself any better on becoming free. A stupid man would perhaps believe that: he would think he should escape from his master, and wouldn't reflect that a good master is not one to escape from, but to stay with as long as possible, and so his escape would be irrational; but a man of intelligence would surely always want to be with one better than himself. Yet in that case, Socrates, the very opposite of what was said just now seems likely: it's the wise who should be resentful at dying, whereas the foolish should welcome it.'

When Socrates heard this he seemed to me pleased at Cebes' persistence, and looking at us he said: 'There goes Cebes, always hunting down arguments, and not at all willing to accept at once what anyone may say.'

'Well yes,' said Simmias; 'but this time, Socrates, I think myself there's something in what

Reprinted from Plato's *Phaedo,* translated by David Gallop (1975) by permission of Oxford University Press.

Cebes says: why, indeed, should truly wise men want to escape from masters who are better than themselves, and be separated from them lightly? So I think it's at you that Cebes is aiming his argument, because you take so lightly your leaving both ourselves and the gods, who are good rulers by your own admission.'

b 'What you both say is fair,' he said; 'as I take you to mean that I should defend myself against these charges as if in a court of law.'

'Yes, exactly,' said Simmias.

'Very well then,' he said; 'let me try to defend myself more convincingly before you than I did before the jury. Because if I didn't believe, Simmias and Cebes, that I shall enter the presence, first, of other gods both wise and good, and next of dead men better than those in this world, then I should be wrong not to be resentful at death; but as it is, be assured that I expect to join the company of good c men—although that point I shouldn't affirm with absolute conviction; but that I shall enter the presence of gods who are very good masters, be assured that if there's anything I should affirm on such matters, it is that. So that's why I am not so resentful, but rather am hopeful that there is something in store for those who've died—in fact, as we've long been told, something far better for the good than for the wicked.'

'Well then, Socrates,' said Simmias, 'do you mean to go off keeping this thought to yourself, or d would you share it with us too? We have a common claim on this benefit as well, I think; and at the same time your defence will be made, if you persuade us of what you say.'

'All right, I'll try,' he said, 'But first let's find out what it is that Crito here has been wanting to say, for some time past, I think.'

'Why Socrates,' said Crito, 'it's simply that the man who's going to give you the poison has been telling me for some time that you must be warned to talk as little as possible: he says people get heated through talking too much, and one must bring nothing of that sort in contact with the poison; people doing that sort of thing are sometimes e obliged, otherwise, to drink twice or even three times.'

'Never mind him,' said Socrates. 'Just let him prepare his stuff so as to give two doses, or even three if need be.'

'Yes, I pretty well knew it,' said Crito; 'but he's been giving me trouble for some while.'

'Let him be,' he said. 'Now then, with you for my jury I want to give my defence, and show with what good reason, as it seems to me, a man who has truly spent his life in philosophy feels confident when about to die, and is hopeful that, when he has 64 died, he will win very great benefits in the other world. So I'll try, Simmias and Cebes, to explain how this could be.

'Other people may well be unaware that all who actually engage in philosophy aright are practising nothing other than dying and being dead. Now if this is true, it would be odd indeed for them to be eager in their whole life for nothing but this, and yet to be resentful when it comes, the very thing they'd long been eager for and practised.'

Simmias laughed at this and said: 'Goodness, Socrates, you've made me laugh, even though I wasn't much inclined to laugh just now. I imagine b that most people, on hearing that, would think it very well said of philosophers—and our own countrymen would quite agree—that they are, indeed, verging on death, and that they, at any rate, are well aware that this is what philosophers deserve to undergo.'

'Yes, and what they say would be true, Simmias, except for their claim to be aware of it themselves; because they aren't aware in what sense genuine philosophers are verging on death and deserving of it, and what kind of death they deserve. Anyway, c let's discuss it among ourselves, disregarding them: do we suppose that death is something?'

'Certainly,' rejoined Simmias.

'And that it is nothing but the separation of the soul from the body? And that being dead is this: the body's having come to be apart, separated from the soul, alone by itself, and the soul's being apart, alone by itself, separated from the body? Death can't be anything else but that, can it?'

'No, it's just that.'

'Now look, my friend, and see if maybe you agree with me on these points; because through them I d think we'll improve our knowledge of what we're examining. Do you think it befits a philosophical man to be keen about the so-called pleasures of, for example, food and drink?'

'Not in the least, Socrates,' said Simmias.

'And what about those of sex?'

'Not at all.'

'And what about the other services to the body? Do you think such a man regards them as of any value? For instance, the possession of smart clothes and shoes, and the other bodily adornments—do you think he values them highly, or does he disdain them,
e except in so far as he's absolutely compelled to share in them?'

'I think the genuine philosopher disdains them.'

'Do you think in general, then, that such a man's concern is not for the body, but so far as he can stand aside from it, is directed towards the soul?'

'I do.'

'Then is it clear that, first, in such matters as these the philosopher differs from other men in releasing
65 his soul, as far as possible, from its communion with the body?'

'It appears so.'

'And presumably, Simmias, it does seem to most men that someone who finds nothing of that sort pleasant, and takes no part in those things, doesn't deserve to live; rather, one who cares nothing for the pleasures that come by way of the body runs pretty close to being dead.'

'Yes, what you say is quite true.'

'And now, what about the actual gaining of wisdom? Is the body a hindrance or not, if one enlists
b it as a partner in the quest? This is the sort of thing I mean: do sight and hearing afford men any truth, or aren't even the poets always harping on such themes, telling us that we neither hear nor see anything accurately? And yet if these of all the bodily senses are neither accurate nor clear, the others will hardly be so; because they are, surely, all inferior to these. Don't you think so?'

'Certainly.'

'So when does the soul attain the truth? Because plainly, whenever it sets about examining anything in company with the body, it is completely taken in by it.'

'That's true.'   c

'So isn't it in reasoning, if anywhere at all, that any of the things that *are* become manifest to it?

'Yes.'

'And it reasons best, presumably, whenever none of these things bothers it, neither hearing nor sight nor pain, nor any pleasure either, but whenever it comes to be alone by itself as far as possible, disregarding the body, and whenever, having the least possible communion and contact with it, it strives for that which is.'

'That is so.'

'So there again the soul of the philosopher utterly disdains the body and flees from it, seeking rather to   d come to be alone by itself?'

'It seems so.'

'Well now, what about things of this sort, Simmias? Do we say that there is something *just*, or nothing?'

'Yes, we most certainly do!'

'And again, something *beautiful*, and *good*?'

'Of course.'

'Now did you ever yet see any such things with your eyes?'

'Certainly not.'

'Well did you grasp them with any other bodily sense-perception? And I'm talking about them all— about largeness, health, and strength, for example— and, in short, about the Being of all other such things, what each one actually is; is it through the body that   e their truest element is viewed, or isn't it rather thus: whoever of us is prepared to think most fully and minutely of each object of his inquiry, in itself, will come closest to the knowledge of each?'

'Yes, certainly.'

'Then would that be achieved most purely by the man who approached each object with his intellect alone as far as possible, neither adducing sight in his thinking, nor dragging in any other sense to accompany his reasoning; rather, using his intellect alone   66 by itself and unsullied, he would undertake the hunt for each of the things that are, each alone by itself and unsullied; he would be separated as far as possible from his eyes and ears, and virtually from his whole body, on the ground that it confuses the soul, and doesn't allow it to gain truth and wisdom when in partnership with it: isn't it this man, Simmias, who will attain that which is, if anyone will?'

'What you say is abundantly true, Socrates,' said Simmias.

'For all these reasons, then, some such view as this must present itself to genuine philosophers, so that they say such things to one another as these: "There now, it looks as if some sort of track is leading us, together with our reason, astray in our inquiry: as long as we possess the body, and our soul is contaminated by such an evil, we'll surely never adequately gain what we desire—and that, we say, is truth. Because the body affords us countless distractions, owing to the nurture it must have; and again, if any illnesses befall it, they hamper our pursuit of that which is. Besides, it fills us up with lusts and desires, with fears and fantasies of every kind, and with any amount of trash, so that really and truly we are, as the saying goes, never able to think of anything at all because of it. Thus, it's nothing but the body and its desires that brings wars and factions and fighting; because it's over the gaining of wealth that all wars take place, and we're compelled to gain wealth because of the body, enslaved as we are to its service; so for all these reasons it leaves us no leisure for philosophy. And the worst of it all is that if we do get any leisure from it, and turn to some inquiry, once again it intrudes everywhere in our researches, setting up a clamour and disturbance, and striking terror, so that the truth can't be discerned because of it. Well now, it really has been shown us that if we're ever going to know anything purely, we must be rid of it, and must view the objects themselves with the soul by itself; it's then, apparently, that the thing we desire and whose lovers we claim to be, wisdom, will be ours—when we have died, as the argument indicates, though not while we live. Because, if we can know nothing purely in the body's company, then one of two things must be true: either knowledge is nowhere to be gained, or else it is for the dead; since then, but no sooner, will the soul be alone by itself apart from the body. And therefore while we live, it would seem that we shall be closest to knowledge in this way— if we consort with the body as little as possible, and do not commune with it, except in so far as we must, and do not infect ourselves with its nature, but remain pure from it, until God himself shall release us; and being thus pure, through separation from the body's folly, we shall probably be in like company, and shall know through our own selves all that is unsullied—and that, I dare say, is what the truth is; because never will it be permissible for impure to touch pure." Such are the things, I think, Simmias, that all who are rightly called lovers of knowledge must say to one another, and must believe. Don't you agree?'

'Emphatically, Socrates?'

'Well then, if that's true, my friend,' said Socrates, 'there's plenty of hope for one who arrives where I'm going, that there, if anywhere, he will adequately possess the object that's been our great concern in life gone by; and thus the journey now appointed for me may also be made with good hope by any other man who regards his intellect as prepared, by having been, in a manner, purified.'

'Yes indeed,' said Simmias.

'Then doesn't purification turn out to be just what's been mentioned for some while in our discussion—the parting of the soul from the body as far as possible, and the habituating of it to assemble and gather itself together, away from every part of the body, alone by itself, and to live, so far as it can, both in the present and in the hereafter, released from the body, as from fetters?'

'Yes indeed.'

'And is it just this that is named "death"—a release and parting of soul from body?'

'Indeed it is.'

'And it's especially those who practise philosophy aright, or rather they alone, who are always eager to release it, as we say, and the occupation of philosophers is just this, isn't it—a release and parting of soul from body?'

'It seems do.'

'Then wouldn't it be absurd, as I said at the start, for a man to prepare himself in his life to live as close as he can to being dead, and then to be resentful when this comes to him?'

'It would be absurd, of course.'

'Truly then, Simmias, those who practise philosophy aright are cultivating dying, and for them least of all men does being dead hold any terror. Look at it like this: if they've set themselves at odds with the body at every point, and desire to possess their soul alone by itself, wouldn't it be quite illogical if they were afraid and resentful when this came about—if, that is, they didn't go gladly to the place where, on arrival, they may hope to attain what they longed for throughout life, namely wisdom—and to be rid of the company of that with which they'd set themselves at odds? Or again, many have been willing to enter Hades of their own accord, in quest of human loves, of wives and sons who have died, led by this hope, that there they would see and be united with those they desired; will anyone, then, who truly longs for wisdom, and who firmly holds the same hope, that nowhere but in Hades will he attain it in any way worth mentioning, be resentful at dying; and will he not go there gladly? One must suppose so, my friend, if he's truly a lover of wisdom; since this will be his firm belief, that nowhere else but there will he attain wisdom purely. Yet if that is so, wouldn't it, as I said just now, be quite illogical if such a man were afraid of death?'

'Yes, quite illogical!'

'Then if you see a man resentful that he is going to die, isn't this proof enough for you that he's no lover of wisdom after all, but what we may call a lover of the body? And this same man turns out, in some sense, to be a lover of riches and of prestige, either one of these or both.'

'It's just as you say.'

'Well now, Simmias, isn't it also true that what is named "bravery" belongs especially to people of the disposition we have described?'

'Most certainly.'

'And then temperance too, even what most people name "temperance"—not being excited over one's desires, but being scornful of them and well-ordered—belongs, doesn't it, only to those who utterly scorn the body and live in love of wisdom?'

'It must.'

'Yes, because if you care to consider the bravery and temperance of other men, you'll find it strange.'

'How so, Socrates?'

'You know, don't you, that all other men count death among great evils?'

'Very much so.'

'Is it, then, through being afraid of greater evils that the brave among them abide death, whenever they do so?'

'It is.'

'Then, it's through fearing and fear that all men except philosophers are brave; and yet it's surely illogical that anyone should be brave through fear and cowardice.'

'It certainly is.'

'And what about those of them who are well-ordered? Aren't they in this same state, temperate through a kind of intemperance? True, we say that's impossible; but still that state of simple-minded temperance does turn out in their case to be like this: it's because they're afraid of being deprived of further pleasures, and desire them, that they abstain from some because they're overcome by others. True, they call it "intemperance" to be ruled by pleasures, but still that's what happens to them: they overcome some pleasures because they're overcome by others. And this is the sort of thing that was just mentioned: after a fashion, they achieve temperance because of intemperance.'

'Yes, so it seems.'

'Yes, Simmias, my good friend; since this may not be the right exchange with a view to goodness, the exchanging of pleasures for pleasures, pains for pains, and fear for fear, greater for lesser ones, like coins; it may be, rather, that this alone is the right coin, for which one should exchange all these things—wisdom; and the buying and selling of all things for that, or rather with that, may be real bravery, temperance, justice, and, in short, true goodness in company with wisdom, whether pleasures and fears and all else of that sort be added or taken away; but as for their being parted from wisdom and exchanged for one another, goodness of that sort may be a kind of illusory facade, and fit for slaves indeed, and may have nothing healthy or true about it; whereas, truth to tell, temperance, justice, and bravery may in fact be a kind of purification of all such things, and wisdom itself a kind of purifying rite. So it really looks as if those who established our initiations are no mean people, but have in fact long been saying in riddles that whoever arrives in Hades unadmitted to the rites, and uninitiated, shall lie in the slough, while he who arrives there purified and initiated shall dwell with gods. For truly there are, so say those concerned with the initiations, "many who bear the wand, but few who are devotees". Now these latter, in my view, are none other than those who have practised philosophy aright. And it's to be among them that I myself have striven, in every way I could, neglecting nothing during my life within my power. Whether I have striven aright and we have achieved anything, we shall, I think, know for certain, God willing, in a little while, on arrival yonder.

'There's my defence, then, Simmias and Cebes, to show how reasonable it is for me not to take it hard or be resentful at leaving you and my masters here, since I believe that there also, no less than here, I shall find good masters and companions; so if I'm any more convincing in my defence to you than to the Athenian jury, it would be well.'

When Socrates had said this, Cebes rejoined: 'The other things you say, Socrates, I find excellent; but what you say about the soul is the subject of much disbelief: men fear that when it's been separated from the body, it may no longer exist anywhere, but that on the very day a man dies, it may be destroyed and perish, as soon as it's separated from the body; and that as it goes out, it may be dispersed like breath or smoke, go flying off, and exist no longer anywhere at all. True, if it did exist somewhere, gathered together alone by itself, and separated from those evils you were recounting just now, there'd be plenty of hope, Socrates, and a fine hope it would be, that what you say is true; but on just this point, perhaps, one needs no little reassuring and convincing, that when the man has died, his soul exists, and that it possesses some power and wisdom.'

'That's true, Cebes,' said Socrates, 'but then what are we to do? Would you like us to speculate on these very questions, and see whether this is likely to be the case or not?'

'For my part anyway,' said Cebes, 'I'd gladly hear whatever opinion you have about them.'

'Well,' said Socrates, 'I really don't think anyone listening now, even if he were a comic poet, would say that I'm talking idly, and arguing about things that don't concern me. If you agree, then, we should look into the matter.

'Let's consider it, perhaps, in this way: do the souls of men exist in Hades when they have died, or do they not? Now there's an ancient doctrine, which we've recalled, that they do exist in that world, entering it from this one, and that they re-enter this world and are born again from the dead; yet if this is so, if living people are born again from those who have died, surely our souls would have to exist in that world? Because they could hardly be born again, if they didn't exist; so it would be sufficient evidence for the truth of these claims, if it really became plain that living people are born from the dead and from nowhere else; but if that isn't so, some other argument would be needed.'

'Certainly,' said Cebes.

'Well now, consider the matter, if you want to understand more readily, in connection not only with mankind, but with all animals and plants; and, in general, for all things subject to coming-to-be, let's see whether everything comes to be in this way: opposites come to be only from their opposites—in the case of all things that actually have an opposite—as, for example, the beautiful is opposite, of course, to the ugly, just to unjust, and so on in countless other cases. So let's consider this: is it necessary that whatever has an opposite comes to be only from its opposite? For example, when a thing comes to be larger, it must, surely, come to be larger from being smaller before?'

'Yes.'

'And again, if it comes to be smaller, it will come to be smaller later from being larger before?'

'That's so.'

'And that which is weaker comes to be, presumably, from a stronger, and that which is faster from a slower?'

'Certainly.'

'And again, if a thing comes to be worse, it's from a better, and if more just, from a more unjust?'

'Of course.'

'Are we satisfied, then, that all things come to be in this way, opposite things from opposites?'

'Certainly.'

'Now again, do these things have a further feature of this sort: between the members of every pair of opposites, since they are two, aren't there two processes of coming-to-be, from one to the other, and back again from the latter to the former? Thus, between a larger thing and a smaller, isn't there increase and decrease, so that in the one case we speak of "increasing" and in the other of "decreasing"?'

'Yes.'

'And similarly with separating and combining, cooling and heating, and all such; even if in some cases we don't use the names, still in actual fact mustn't the same principle everywhere hold good: they come to be from each other, and there's a process of coming-to-be of each into the other?'

'Certainly.'

c   'Well then, is there an opposite to living, as sleeping is opposite to being awake?'

'Certainly.'

'What is it?'

'Being dead.'

'Then these come to be from each other, if they are opposites; and between the pair of them, since they are two, the processes of coming-to-be are two?'

'Of course.'

'Now then,' said Socrates, 'I'll tell you one of the couples I was just mentioning, the couple itself and

d   its processes; and you tell me the other. My couple is sleeping and being awake: being awake comes to be from sleeping, and sleeping from being awake, and their processes are going to sleep and waking up. Is that sufficient for you or not?'

'Certainly.'

'Now it's for you to tell me in the same way about life and death. You say, don't you, that being dead is opposite to living?'

'I do.'

'And that they come to be from each other?'

'Yes.'

'Then what is it that comes to be from that which is living?'

'That which is dead.'

'And what comes to be from that which is dead?'

'I must admit that it's that which is living.'

'Then it's from those that are dead, Cebes, that living things and living people are born?'

e   'Apparently.'

'Then our souls do exist in Hades.'

'So it seems.'

'Now *one* of the relevant processes here is obvious, isn't it? For dying is obvious enough, surely?'

'It certainly is.'

'What shall we do then? Shan't we assign the opposite process to balance it? Will nature be lame in this respect? Or must we supply some process opposite to dying?'

'We surely must.'

'What will this be?'

'Coming to life again.'

'Then if there *is* such a thing as coming to life

72   again, wouldn't this, coming to life again, be a process from dead to living people.'

'Certainly.'

'In that way too, then, we're agreed that living people are born from the dead no less than dead people from the living; and we thought that, if this were the case, it would be sufficient evidence that the souls of the dead must exist somewhere, whence they are born again.'

'I think, Socrates, that that must follow from our admissions.'

'Then look at it this way, Cebes, and you'll see, I think, that our admissions were not mistaken. If there were not perpetual reciprocity in coming to be,   b between one set of things and another, revolving in a circle, as it were—if, instead, coming-to-be were a linear process from one thing into its opposite only, without any bending back in the other direction or reversal, do you realize that all things would ultimately have the same form: the same fate would overtake them, and they would cease from coming to be?'

'What do you mean?'

'It's not at all hard to understand what I mean. If, for example, there were such a thing as going to sleep, but from sleeping there were no reverse process of waking up, you realize that everything would ultimately make Endymion seem a mere trifle: he'd be nowhere, because the same fate as his, sleeping,   c would have overtaken everything else. Again, if everything were combined, but not separated, then Anaxagoras' notion of "all things together" would soon be realized. And similarly, my dear Cebes, if all things that partake in life were to die, but when they'd died, the dead remained in that form, and didn't come back to life, wouldn't it be quite inevitable that everything would ultimately be dead, and nothing would live? Because if the living things   d came to be from the other things, but the living things were to die, what could possibly prevent everything from being completely spent in being dead?'

'Nothing whatever, in my view, Socrates,' said Cebes; 'what you say seems to be perfectly true.'

'Yes, it certainly is true, Cebes, as I see it; and we're not deceived in making just those admissions: there really is such a thing as coming to life again, living people *are* born from the dead, and the souls of the dead exist.'   e

'Yes, and besides, Socrates,' Cebes replied, 'there's also that theory you're always putting forward, that our learning is actually nothing but recollection; according to that too, if it's true, what we are now reminded of we must have learned at some former time. But that would be impossible, unless our souls existed somewhere before being born in this human form; so in this way too, it appears that the soul is something immortal.'

'Yes, what are the proofs of those points, Cebes?' put in Simmias. 'Remind me, as I don't recall them very well at the moment.'

'One excellent argument,' said Cebes, 'is that when people are questioned, and if the questions are well put, they state the truth about everything for themselves—and yet unless knowledge and a correct account were present within them, they'd be unable to do this; thus, if one takes them to diagrams or anything else of that sort, one has there the plainest evidence that this is so.'

'But if that doesn't convince you, Simmias,' said Socrates, 'then see whether maybe you agree if you look at it this way. Apparently you doubt whether what is called "learning" is recollection?'

'I don't *doubt* it,' said Simmias; 'but I do need to undergo just what the argument is about, to be "reminded". Actually, from the way Cebes set about stating it, I do almost recall it and am nearly convinced; but I'd like, none the less, to hear now how you set about stating it yourself.'

'I'll put it this way. We agree, I take it, that if anyone is to be reminded of a thing, he must have known that thing at some time previously.'

'Certainly.'

'Then do we also agree on this point: that whenever knowledge comes to be present in this sort of way, it is recollection? I mean in some such way as this: if someone, on seeing a thing, or hearing it, or getting any other sense-perception of it, not only recognizes that thing, but also thinks of something else, which is the object not of the same knowledge but of another, don't we then rightly say that he's been "reminded" of the object of which he has got the thought?'

'What do you mean?'

'Take the following examples: knowledge of a man, surely, is other than that of a lyre?'

'Of course.'

'Well now, you know what happens to lovers, whenever they see a lyre or cloak or anything else their loves are accustomed to use: they recognize the lyre, and they get in their mind, don't they, the form of the boy whose lyre it is? And that is recollection. Likewise, someone seeing Simmias is often reminded of Cebes, and there'd surely be countless other such cases.'

'Countless indeed!' said Simmias.

'Then is something of that sort a kind of recollection? More especially, though, whenever it happens to someone in connection with things he's since forgotten, through lapse of time or inattention?'

'Certainly.'

'Again now, is it possible, on seeing a horse depicted or a lyre depicted, to be reminded of a man; and on seeing Simmias depicted, to be reminded of Cebes?'

'Certainly.'

'And also, on seeing Simmias depicted, to be reminded of Simmias himself?'

'Yes, that's possible.'

'In all these cases, then, doesn't it turn out that there is recollection from similar things, but also from dissimilar things?'

'It does.'

'But whenever one is reminded of something from similar things, mustn't one experience something further: mustn't one think whether or not the thing is lacking at all, in its similarity, in relation to what one is reminded of?'

'One must.'

'Then consider whether this is the case. We say, don't we, that there is something *equal*—I don't mean a log to a log, or a stone to a stone, or anything else of that sort, but some further thing beyond all those, the equal itself: are we to say that there *is* something or nothing?'

'We most certainly are to say that there *is*,' said Simmias; 'unquestionably!'

'And do we know *what it is*?'

'Certainly.'

'Where did we get the knowledge of it? Wasn't it from the things we were just mentioning: on seeing logs or stones or other equal things, wasn't it from these that we thought of that object, it being different from them? Or doesn't it seem different to you? Look at it this way: don't equal stones and logs, the very same ones, sometimes seem equal to one, but not to another?'

'Yes, certainly.'

c 'But now, did the equals themselves ever seem to you unequal, or equality inequality?'

'Never yet, Socrates.'

'Then those equals and the equal itself, are not the same.'

'By no means, Socrates, in my view.'

'But still, it is from *those* equals, different as they are from *that* equal, that you have thought of and got the knowledge of it?'

'That's perfectly true.'

'It being either similar to them or dissimilar?'

'Certainly.'

'Anyway, it makes no difference; so long as on seeing one thing, one does, from this sight, think of
d another, whether it be similar or dissimilar, this must be recollection.'

'Certainly.'

'Well now, with regard to the instances in the logs, and, in general, the equals we mentioned just now, are we affected in some way as this: do they seem to us to be equal in the same way as *what it is* itself? Do they fall short of it at all in being like the equal, or not?'

'Very far short of it.'

'Then whenever anyone, on seeing a thing, thinks to himself, "this thing that I now see seeks to be like
e another of the things that are, but falls short, and cannot be like that object: it is inferior", do we agree that the man who thinks this must previously have known the object he says it resembles but falls short of?'

'He must.'

'Now then, have we ourselves been affected in just this way, or not, with regard to the equals and the equal itself?'

'Indeed we have.'

'Then we must previously have known the equal, before that time when we first, on seeing the equals,
75 thought that all of them were striving to be like the equal but fell short of it.'

'That is so.'

'Yet we also agree on this: we haven't derived the thought of it, nor could we do so, from anywhere

but seeing or touching or some other of the senses—I'm counting all these as the same.'

'Yes, they are the same, Socrates, for what the argument seeks to show.'

'But of course it is *from* one's sense-perceptions that one must think that all the things in the sense-
b perceptions are striving for *what equal is*, yet are inferior to it; or how shall we put it?'

'Like that.'

'Then it must, surely, have been before we began to see and hear and use the other senses that we got knowledge of the equal itself, of *what it is*, if we were going to refer the equals from our sense-perceptions to it, supposing that all things are doing their best to be like it, but are inferior to it.'

'That must follow from what's been said before, Socrates.'

'Now we were seeing and hearing, and were possessed of our other senses, weren't we, just as soon as we were born?'

'Certainly.'

'But we must, we're saying, have got our knowl-
c edge of the equal *before* these?'

'Yes.'

'Then it seems that we must have got it before we were born.'

'It seems so.'

'Now if, having got it before birth, we were born in possession of it, did we know, both before birth and as soon as we were born, not only the equal, the larger and the smaller, but everything of that sort? Because our present argument concerns the beautiful itself, and the good itself, and just and holy, no less than the equal; in fact, as I say, it concerns every-
d thing on which we set this seal, "*what it is*", in the questions we ask and in the answers we give. And so we must have got pieces of knowledge of all those things before birth.'

'That is so.'

'Moreover, if having got them, we did not on each occasion forget them, we must always be born knowing, and must continue to know throughout life: because this is knowing—to possess knowledge one has got of something, and not to have lost it; or isn't loss of knowledge what we mean by "forgetting", Simmias?'

'Certainly it is, Socrates.' e

'But on the other hand, I suppose that if, having got them before birth, we lost them on being born, and later on, using the senses about the things in question, we regain those pieces of knowledge that we possessed at some former time, in that case wouldn't what we call "learning" be the regaining of knowledge belonging to us? And in saying that this was being reminded, shouldn't we be speaking correctly?'

'Certainly.'

76 'Yes, because it did seem possible, on sensing an object, whether by seeing or hearing or getting some other sense-perception of it, to think from this of some other thing one had forgotten—either a thing to which the object, though dissimilar to it, was related, or else something to which it was similar; so, as I say, one of two things is true: *either* all of us were born knowing those objects, and we know them throughout life; *or* those we speak of as "learning" are simply being reminded later on, and learning would be recollection.'

'That's quite true, Socrates.'

'Then which do you choose, Simmias? That we
b are born knowing, or that we are later reminded of the things we'd gained knowledge of before?'

'At the moment, Socrates, I can't make a choice.'

'Well, can you make one on the following point, and what do you think about it? If a man knows things, can he give an account of what he knows or not?'

'Of course he can, Socrates.'

'And do you think everyone can give an account of those objects we were discussing just now?'

'I only wish they could,' said Simmias; 'but I'm afraid that, on the contrary, this time tomorrow there may no longer be any man who can do so properly.'

c 'You don't then, Simmias, think that everyone knows those objects?'

'By no means.'

'Are they, then, reminded of what they once learned?'

'They must be.'

'When did our souls get the knowledge of those objects? Not, at any rate, since we were born as human beings.'

'Indeed not.'

'Earlier, then.'

'Yes.'

'Then our souls did exist earlier, Simmias, before entering human form, apart from bodies; and they possessed wisdom.'

'Unless maybe, Socrates, we get those pieces of knowledge at the very moment of birth; that time still remains.'

'Very well, my friend; but then at what other time, d may I ask, do we lose them? We aren't born with them, as we agreed just now. Do we then lose them at the very time at which we get them? Or have you any other time to suggest?'

'None at all, Socrates. I didn't realize I was talking nonsense.'

'Then is our position as follows, Simmias? If the objects we're always harping on exist, a beautiful, and a good and all such Being, and if we refer all the things from our sense-perceptions to that Being, finding again what was formerly ours, and if we com- e pare these things with that, then just as surely as those objects exist, so also must our soul exist before we are born. On the other hand, if they don't exist, this argument will have gone for nothing. Is this the position? Is it equally necessary that those objects exist, and that our souls existed before birth, and if the former don't exist, then neither did the latter?'

'It's abundantly clear to me, Socrates,' said Simmias, 'that there's the same necessity in either case, and the argument takes opportune refuge in the view that our soul exists before birth, just as surely as the Being of which you're now speaking. Because I my- 77 self find nothing so plain to me as that all such objects, beautiful and good and all the others you were speaking of just now, *are* in the fullest possible way; so in my view it's been adequately proved.'

'And what about Cebes?' said Socrates. 'We must convince Cebes too.'

'It's adequate for him, I think,' said Simmias; 'though he's the most obstinate of people when it comes to doubting arguments. But I think he's been sufficiently convinced that our soul existed before we were born. Whether it will still exist, however, after we've died, doesn't seem, even to me, to have b been shown, Socrates; but the point Cebes made just now still stands—the popular fear that when a man dies, his soul may be dispersed at that time, and that

that may be the end of its existence. Because what's to prevent it from coming to be and being put together from some other source, and from existing before it enters a human body, yet when it has entered one, and again been separated from it, from then meeting its end, and being itself destroyed?'

'You're right, Simmias,' said Cebes. 'It seems that half, as it were, of what is needed has been shown—that our soul existed before we were born; it must also be shown that it will exist after we've died, no less than before we were born, if the proof is going to be complete.'

'That's been proved already, Simmias and Cebes,' said Socrates, 'if you will combine this argument with the one we agreed on earlier, to the effect that all that is living comes from that which is dead. Because if the soul does have previous existence, and if when it enters upon living and being born, it must come from no other source than death and being dead, surely it must also exist after it has died, given that it has to be born again? So your point has been proved already. But even so, I think you and Simmias would like to thrash out this argument still further; you seem afraid, like children, that as the soul goes out from the body, the wind may literally blow it apart and disperse it, especially when someone happens not to die in calm weather but in a high wind.'

Cebes laughed at this, and said: 'Try to reassure us, Socrates, as if we were afraid; or rather, not as if we were afraid ourselves—but maybe there's a child inside us, who has fears of that sort. Try to persuade him, then, to stop being afraid of death, as if it were a bogey-man.'

'Well, you must sing spells to him every day,' said Socrates, 'till you've charmed it out of him.'

'And where', he said, 'shall we find a charmer for such fears, Socrates, now that you're leaving us?'

'Greece is a large country, Cebes, which has good men in it, I suppose; and there are many foreign races too. You must ransack all of them in search of such a charmer, sparing neither money nor trouble, because there's no object on which you could more opportunely spend your money. And you yourselves must search too, along with one another; you may not easily find anyone more capable of doing this than yourselves.'

'That shall certainly be done,' said Cebes; 'but let's go back to the point where we left off, if you've no objection.'

'Of course not; why should I?'

'Good.'

'Well then,' said Socrates, 'mustn't we ask ourselves something like this: What kind of thing is liable to undergo this fate—namely, dispersal—and for what kind of thing should we fear lest it undergo it? And what kind of thing is not liable to it? And next, mustn't we further ask to which of these two kinds soul belongs, and then feel either confidence or fear for our own soul accordingly?'

'That's true.'

'Then is it true that what has been put together and is naturally composite is liable to undergo this, to break up at the point at which it was put together; whereas if there be anything incomposite, it alone is liable, if anything is, to escape this?'

'That's what I think,' said Cebes.

'Well now, aren't the things that are constant and unvarying most likely to be the incomposite, whereas things that vary and are never constant are likely to be composite?'

'I think so.'

'Then let's go back to those entities to which we turned in our earlier argument. Is the Being itself, whose being we give an account of in asking and answering questions, unvarying and constant, or does it vary? Does the equal itself, the beautiful itself, *what each thing is* itself, that which *is*, ever admit of any change whatever? Or does *what each of them is*, being uniform alone by itself, remain unvarying and constant, and never admit of any kind of alteration in any way or respect whatever?'

'It must be unvarying and constant, Socrates,' said Cebes.

'But what about the many beautiful things, such as men or horses or cloaks or anything else at all of that kind? Or equals, or all things that bear the same name as those objects? Are they constant, or are they just the opposite of those others, and practically never constant at all, either in relation to themselves or to one another?'

'That is their condition,' said Cebes; 'they are never unvarying.'

79 'Now these things you could actually touch and see and sense with the other senses, couldn't you, whereas those that are constant you could lay hold of only by reasoning of the intellect; aren't such things, rather, invisible and not seen?'

'What you say is perfectly true.'

'Then would you like us to posit two kinds of beings, the one kind seen, the other invisible?'

'Let's posit them.'

'And the invisible is always constant, whereas the seen is never constant?'

'Let's posit that too.'

b 'Well, but we ourselves are part body and part soul, aren't we?'

'We are.'

'Then to which kind do we say that the body will be more similar and more akin?'

'That's clear to anyone: obviously to the seen.'

'And what about the soul? Is it seen or invisible?'

'It's not seen by men, at any rate, Socrates.'

'But we meant, surely, things seen and not seen with reference to human nature; or do you think we meant any other?'

'We meant human nature.'

'What do we say about soul, then? Is it seen or unseen?'

'It's not seen.'

'Then it's invisible?'

'Yes.'

'Then soul is more similar than body to the invisible, whereas body is more similar to that which is seen.'

c 'That must be so, Socrates.'

'Now weren't we saying a while ago that whenever the soul uses the body as a means to study anything, either by seeing or hearing or any other sense—because to use the body as a means is to study a thing through sense-perception—then it is dragged by the body towards objects that are never constant; and it wanders about itself, and is confused and dizzy, as if drunk, in virtue of contact with things of a similar kind?'

'Certainly.'

d 'Whereas whenever it studies alone by itself, it departs yonder towards that which is pure and always existent and immortal and unvarying, and in virtue of its kinship with it, enters always into its company, whenever it has come to be alone by itself, and whenever it may do so; then it has ceased from its wandering and, when it is about those objects, it is always constant and unvarying, because of its contact with things of a similar kind; and this condition of it is called "wisdom", is it not?'

'That's very well said and perfectly true, Socrates.'

'Once again, then, in the light of our earlier and present arguments, to which kind do you think that soul is more similar and more akin?'

e

'Everyone, I think, Socrates, even the slowest learner, following this line of inquiry, would agree that soul is totally and altogether more similar to what is unvarying than to what is not.'

'And what about the body?'

'That is more like the latter.'

'Now look at it this way too: when soul and body are present in the same thing, nature ordains that the one shall serve and be ruled, whereas the other shall rule and be master; here again, which do you think is similar to the divine and which to the mortal? Don't you think the divine is naturally adapted for ruling and domination, whereas the mortal is adapted for being ruled and for service?'

80

'I do.'

'Which kind, then, does the soul resemble?'

'Obviously, Socrates, the soul resembles the divine, and the body the mortal.'

'Consider, then, Cebes, if these are our conclusions from all that's been said: soul is most similar to what is divine, immortal, intelligible, uniform, indissoluble, unvarying, and constant in relation to itself; whereas body, in its turn, is most similar to what is human, mortal, multiform, non-intelligible, dissoluble, and never constant in relation to itself. Have we anything to say against those statements, my dear Cebes, to show that they're false?'

b

'We haven't.'

'Well then, that being so, isn't body liable to be quickly dissolved, whereas soul must be completely indissoluble, or something close to it?'

'Of course.'

c

'Now you're aware that when a man has died, the part of him that's seen, his body, which is situated in the seen world, the corpse as we call it, although liable to be dissolved and fall apart and to disinte-

soul purified

grate, undergoes none of these things at once, but remains as it is for a fairly long time—in fact for a very considerable time, even if someone dies with his body in beautiful condition, and in the flower of youth; why, the body that is shrunken and embalmed, like those who've been embalmed in Egypt, remains

d almost entire for an immensely long time; and even should the body decay, some parts of it, bones and sinews and all such things, are still practically immortal; isn't that so?'

'Yes.'

'Can it be, then, that the soul, the invisible part, which goes to another place of that kind, noble, pure and invisible, to "Hades" in the true sense of the word, into the presence of the good and wise god— where, God willing, my own soul too must shortly enter—can it be that this, which we've found to be a thing of such a kind and nature, should on separation from the body at once be blown apart and per-

e ish, as most men say? Far from it, my dear Cebes and Simmias; rather, the truth is far more like this: suppose it is separated in purity, while trailing nothing of the body with it, since it had no avoidable commerce with it during life, but shunned it; suppose too that it has been gathered together alone into itself, since it always cultivated this—nothing else but the right practice of philosophy, in fact, the cul-

81 tivation of dying without complaint—wouldn't this be the cultivation of death?'

'It certainly would.'

'If it is in that state, then, does it not depart to the invisible, which is similar to it, the divine and immortal and wise; and on arrival there, isn't its lot to be happy, released from its wandering and folly, its fears and wild lusts, and other ills of the human condition, and as is said of the initiated, does it not pass the rest of time in very truth with gods? Are we to say this, Cebes, or something else?'

'This, most certainly!', said Cebes.

'Whereas, I imagine, if it is separated from the body when it has been polluted and made impure, because it has always been with the body, has served

b and loved it, and been so bewitched by it, by its passions and pleasures, that it thinks nothing else real save what is corporeal—what can be touched and seen, drunk and eaten, or used for sexual enjoyment—yet it has been accustomed to hate and shun

and tremble before what is obscure to the eyes and invisible, but intelligible and grasped by philosophy;

c do you think a soul in that condition will separate unsullied, and alone by itself?'

'By no means.'

'Rather, I imagine, it will have been interspersed with a corporeal element, ingrained in it by the body's company and intercourse, through constant association and much training?'

'Certainly.'

'And one must suppose, my friend, that this element is ponderous, that it is heavy and earthy and is seen; and thus encumbered, such a soul is weighed down, and dragged back into the region of the seen, through fear of the invisible and of Hades; and it

d roams among tombs and graves, so it is said, around which some shadowy phantoms of souls have actually been seen, such wraiths as souls of that kind afford, souls that have been released in no pure condition, but while partaking in the seen; and that is just why they are seen.'

'That's likely, Socrates.'

'It is indeed, Cebes; and they're likely to be the souls not of the good but of the wicked, that are compelled to wander about such places, paying the penalty for their former nurture, evil as it was. And they wander about until, owing to the desire of the corporeal element attendant upon them, they are once more imprisoned in a body; and they're likely to be imprisoned in whatever types of character they may

e have cultivated in their lifetime.'

'What types can you mean, Socrates?'

'Those who have cultivated gluttony, for example, and lechery, and drunkenness, and have taken no pains to avoid them, are likely to enter the forms

82 of donkeys and animals of that sort. Don't you think so?'

'What you say is very likely.'

'Yes, and those who've preferred injustice, tyranny, and robbery will enter the forms of wolves and hawks and kites. Where else can we say that such souls will go?'

'Into such creatures, certainly,' said Cebes.

'And isn't the direction taken by the others as well obvious in each case, according to the affinities of their training?'

'Quite obvious, of course.'

'And aren't the happiest among these and the ones who enter the best place, those who have practised popular and social goodness, "temperance" and "justice" so-called, developed from habit and training, but devoid of philosophy and intelligence?'

'In what way are these happiest?'

'Because they're likely to go back into a race of tame and social creatures similar to their kind, bees perhaps, or wasps or ants; and to return to the human race again, and be born from those kinds as decent men.'

'That's likely.'

'But the company of gods may not rightly be joined by one who has not practised philosophy and departed in absolute purity, by any but the lover of knowledge. It's for these reasons, Simmias and Cebes, my friends, that true philosophers abstain from all bodily desires, and stand firm without surrendering to them; it's not for any fear of poverty or loss of estate, as with most men who are lovers of riches; nor again do they abstain through dread of dishonour or ill-repute attaching to wickedness, like lovers of power and prestige.'

'No, that would ill become them, Socrates,' said Cebes.

'Most certainly it would! And that, Cebes, is just why those who have any care for their own souls, and don't live fashioning the body, disregard all those people; they do not walk in the same paths as those who, in their view, don't know where they are going; but they themselves believe that their actions must not oppose philosophy, or the release and purifying rite it affords, and they are turned to follow it, in the direction in which it guides them.'

'How so, Socrates?'

'I'll tell you. Lovers of knowledge recognize that when philosophy takes their soul in hand, it has been literally bound and glued to the body, and is forced to view the things that are as if through a prison, rather than alone by itself; and that it is wallowing in utter ignorance. Now philosophy discerns the cunning of the prison, sees how it is effected through desire, so that the captive himself may co-operate most of all in his imprisonment. As I say, then, lovers of knowledge recognize that their soul is in that state when philosophy takes it in hand, gently reassures it and tries to release it, by showing that

inquiry through the eyes is full of deceit, and deceitful too is inquiry through the ears and other senses; and by persuading it to withdraw from these, so far as it need not use them, and by urging it to collect and gather itself together, and to trust none other but itself, whenever, alone by itself, it thinks of any of the things that are, alone by *itself*; and not to regard as real what it observes by other means, and what varies in various things; that kind of thing is sensible and seen, whereas the object of its own vision is intelligible and invisible. It is, then, just because it believes it should not oppose this release that the soul of the true philosopher abstains from pleasures and desires and pains, so far as it can, reckoning that when one feels intense pleasure or fear, pain or desire, one incurs harm from them not merely to the extent that might be supposed—by being ill, for example, or spending money to satisfy one's desires—but one incurs the greatest and most extreme of all evils, and does not take it into account.'

'And what is that, Socrates?' said Cebes.

'It's that the soul of every man, when intensely pleased or pained at something, is forced at the same time to suppose that whatever most affects it in this way is most clear and most real, when it is not so; and such objects especially are things seen, aren't they?'

'Certainly.'

'Well, isn't it in this experience that soul is most thoroughly bound fast by body?'

'How so?'

'Because each pleasure and pain fastens it to the body with a sort of rivet, pins it there, and makes it corporeal, so that it takes for real whatever the body declares to be so. Since by sharing opinions and pleasures with the body, it is, I believe, forced to become of like character and nurture to it, and to be incapable of entering Hades in purity; but it must always exit contaminated by the body, and so quickly fall back into another body, and grow in it as if sown there, and so have no part in communing with the divine and pure and uniform.'

'What you say is perfectly true, Socrates,' said Cebes.

'It's for these reasons, then, Cebes, that those who deserve to be called "lovers of knowledge" are orderly and brave; it's not for the reasons that count with most people, or do you think it is?'

84   'No, indeed I don't.'

'Indeed not; but the soul of a philosophic man would reason as we've said: it would not think that while philosophy should release it, yet on being released, it should of itself surrender to pleasures and pains, to bind it to the body once again, and should perform the endless task of a Penelope working in reverse at a kind of web. Rather, securing rest from these feelings, by following reasoning and being ever within it, and by beholding what is true and divine b and not the object of opinion, and being nurtured by it, it believes that it must live thus for as long as it lives, and that when it has died, it will enter that which is akin and of like nature to itself, and be rid of human ills. With that kind of nurture, surely, Simmias and Cebes, there's no danger of its fearing that on separation from the body it may be rent apart, blown away by winds, go flying off, and exist no longer anywhere at all.'

When Socrates had said this, there was silence for c a long time. To judge from his appearance, Socrates himself was absorbed in the foregoing argument, and so were most of us; but Cebes and Simmias went on talking to each other in a low voice. When he noticed them, Socrates asked: 'What is it? Can it be that you find something lacking in what's been said? It certainly still leaves room for many misgivings and objections, if, that is, one's going to examine it adequately. If it's something else you're considering, never mind; but if you have some difficulty about these matters, don't hesitate to speak for your-d selves and explain it, if you think what was said could be improved in any way; or again, enlist me too, if you think you'll get out of your difficulty any better with my help.'

Simmias replied: 'All right, Socrates, I'll tell you the truth. For some time each of us has had difficulties, and has been prompting and telling the other to question you, from eagerness to hear, but hesitating to make trouble, in case you should find it unwelcome in your present misfortune.'

When Socrates heard this, he chuckled and said: 'Dear me, Simmias! I'd certainly find it hard to con-e vince other people that I don't regard my present lot as a misfortune, when I can't convince even you two, but you're afraid that I'm more ill-humoured now than in my earlier life; you must, it seems, think I have a poorer power of prophecy than the swans, who when they realize they must die, then sing more 5 fully and sweetly than they've ever sung before, for 85 joy that they are departing into the presence of the god whose servants they are. Though indeed mankind, because of their own fear of death, malign the swans, and say that they sing their farewell song in distress, lamenting their death; they don't reflect 5 that no bird sings when it is hungry or cold or suffering any other distress, not even the nightingale herself, nor the swallow, nor the hoopoe, birds that are reputed to sing lamentations from distress. But, as I see it, neither they nor the swans sing in distress, b but rather, I believe, because, belonging as they do to Apollo, they are prophetic birds with foreknowledge of the blessings of Hades, and therefore sing and rejoice more greatly on that day than ever before. Now I hold that I myself am a fellow-servant 5 of the swans, consecrated to the same god, that I possess prophetic power from my master no less than theirs, and that I'm departing this life with as good a cheer as they do. No; so far as that goes, you should say and ask whatever you wish, for as long as eleven Athenian gentlemen allow.'

'Thank you,' said Simmias; 'then I'll tell you my 10 difficulty, and Cebes here in his turn will say where c he doesn't accept what's been said. I think, Socrates, as perhaps you do too, that in these matters certain knowledge is either impossible or very hard to come by in this life; but that even so, not to test what is said about them in every possible way, without leaving off till one has examined them exhaustively from 5 every aspect, shows a very feeble spirit; on these questions one must achieve one of two things: either learn or find out how things are; or, if that's impossible, then adopt the best and least refutable of human doctrines, embarking on it as a kind of raft, and d risking the dangers of the voyage through life, unless one could travel more safely and with less risk, on a securer conveyance afforded by some divine doctrine. So now I shan't scruple to put my question, since you tell me to, and then I shan't reproach 5 myself at a later time for failing to speak my mind now. In my view, Socrates, when I examine what's

been said, either alone or with Cebes here, it doesn't
10 seem altogether adequate.'

e   'Maybe your view is correct, my friend,' said
Socrates; 'but tell me, in what way inadequate?'

'I think in this way,' he said; 'one could surely
use the same argument about the attunement of a lyre
and its strings, and say that the attunement is some-
5 thing unseen and incorporeal and very lovely and di-
86 vine in the tuned lyre, while the lyre itself and
its strings are corporeal bodies and composite and
earthy and akin to the mortal, Now, if someone
5 smashed the lyre, or severed and snapped its strings,
suppose it were maintained, by the same argument
as yours, that the attunement must still exist and not
have perished—because it would be inconceivable
that when the strings had been snapped, the lyre and
the strings themselves, which are of mortal nature,
should still exist, and yet that the attunement, which
b has affinity and kinship to the divine and the immortal, should have perished—and perished before the
mortal; rather, it might be said, the attunement itself
must still exist somewhere, and the wood and the
5 strings would have to rot away before anything happened to it. And in point of fact, Socrates, my own
belief is that you're aware yourself that something
of this sort is what we actually take the soul to be:
our body is kept in tension, as it were, and held together by hot and cold, dry and wet, and the like,
c and our soul is a blending and attunement of these
same things, when they're blended with each other
in due proportion. If, then, the soul proves to be some
kind of attunement, it's clear that when our body is
5 unduly relaxed or tautened by illnesses and other
troubles, then the soul must perish at once, no matter how divine it may be, just like other attunements,
those in musical notes and in all the products of
craftsmen; whereas the remains of each body will
d last for a long time, until they're burnt up or rot away.
Well, consider what we shall say in answer to that
argument, if anyone should claim that the soul, being a blending of the bodily elements, is the first
thing to perish in what is called death.'

5   At this Socrates looked at us wide-eyed, as he often used to, and said with a smile: 'Simmias' remarks
are certainly fair. So if any of you is more resourceful than I am, why doesn't he answer him? Because
he really seems to be coming to grips with the argu-

ment in no mean fashion, However, before answering I think we should first hear from Cebes here what   e
further charge he has to bring against the argument,
so that in the intervening period we may be thinking what to say; then, when we've heard them both,
either we can agree with them, if it seems they're at
all in tune; or if not, we can enter a plea for the argument at that point. Come on then, Cebes, tell us   5
what's been troubling you.'

'I certainly will,' said Cebes. 'You see, the argument seems to me to remain where it was, and to be
open to the same charge as we made before. As to
the existence of our soul even before it entered its   87
present form, I don't take back my admission that
this has been very neatly, and, if it's not presumptuous to say so, very adequately proved; but I don't
think the same about its still existing somewhere
when we've died. Not that I agree with Simmias' ob-   5
jection that soul isn't stronger and longer-lived than
body: because I think it far superior in all those ways.
"Why then", the argument would say, "are you still
in doubt, when you can see that the weaker part still
exists after the man has died? Don't you think the   b
longer-lived part must still be preserved during that
time?"

'Well, consider if there's anything in my reply to
that; because it seems that, like Simmias, I too need
an image. What's being said, I think, is very much
as if someone should offer this argument about a
man—a weaver who has died in old age—to show   5
that the man hasn't perished but exists somewhere
intact, and should produce as evidence the fact that
the cloak he had woven for himself, and worn, was
intact and had not perished; and if anyone doubted   c
him, he should ask which class of thing is longer-
lived, a man, or a cloak in constant use and wear;
and on being answered that a man is much longer-
lived, should think it had been proved that the man
must therefore surely be intact, seeing that something   5
shorter-lived hadn't perished. Yet in fact, Simmias,
this isn't so: because you too must consider what I'm
saying. Everyone would object that this is a simple-
minded argument. Because this weaver, though he'd
woven and worn out many such cloaks, perished af-   d
ter all of them, despite their number, but still, presumably, before the last one; and yet for all that a
man is neither lesser nor weaker than a cloak.

'The relation of soul to body would, I think, admit of the same comparison: anyone making the same points about them, that the soul is long-lived, while the body is weaker and shorter-lived, would in my view argue reasonably; true indeed, he might say, every soul wears out many bodies, especially in a life of many years—because, though the body may decay and perish while the man is still alive, still the soul will always weave afresh what's being worn out; nevertheless, when the soul does perish, it will have to be wearing its last garment, and must perish before that one alone; and when the soul has perished, then at last the body will reveal its natural weakness, moulder away quickly, and be gone. So we've no right as yet to trust this argument, and feel confident that our soul still exists somewhere after we've died. Indeed, were one to grant the speaker even more than what you say, allowing him not only that our souls existed in the time before we were born, but that nothing prevents the souls of some, even after we've died, from still existing and continuing to exist, and from being born and dying over and over again— because soul is so strong by nature that it can endure repeated births—even allowing all that, were one not to grant the further point that it does not suffer in its many births, and does not end by perishing completely in one of its deaths, and were one to say that no one can know this death or detachment from the body which brings perishing to the soul—since none of us can possibly perceive it—well, if that's the case, then anyone who's confident in face of death must be possessed of a foolish confidence, unless he can prove that soul is completely immortal and imperishable; otherwise, anyone about to die must always fear for his own soul, lest in its present disjunction from the body it perish completely.' ...

'Well now, to proceed. First remind me of what you were saying, in case I prove not to have remembered. Simmias, I believe, is doubtful and afraid that the soul, though more divine and lovelier than the body, may still perish before it, being a kind of attunement. Whereas Cebes, I thought, agreed with me in this much, that soul is longer-lived than body; but he held that no one could be sure whether the soul, after wearing out many bodies time and again, might not then perish itself, leaving its last body behind, and whether death might not be just this, the perishing of

soul—since body, of course, is perishing incessantly and never stops. Aren't those the points, Simmias and Cebes, that we have to consider?'

They both agreed that they were.

'Then do you reject all of the previous arguments, or only some of them?'

'Some of them,' they said, 'but not others.'

'Well what do you say, then, about the argument in which we said that learning was recollection, and that this being so, our souls must exist somewhere else before being imprisoned in the body?'

'For my part,' said Cebes, 'I was wonderfully convinced by it at the time, and remain so now, as by no other argument.'

'And I'm of the same mind,' said Simmias; 'and I'd be very surprised if I ever came to think otherwise about that.'

To this Socrates answered: 'But you'll have to think otherwise, my Theban friend, if you stick to this idea that attunement is a composite thing, and that soul is a kind of attunement composed of the bodily elements held in tension; because you surely won't allow yourself to say that an attunement existed as a composite, before the elements of which it was to be composed; or will you?'

'Certainly not, Socrates.'

'Then do you see that this is implied by your assertion, when you say that the soul exists before entering human form and body, yet that it is a composite of things that don't yet exist? Surely your attunement isn't, in fact, the same kind of thing as that to which you liken it: rather, the lyre, and its strings and notes, come into being first, as yet untuned, whereas the attunement is put together last of all, and is the first to perish. So how's this theory of yours going to harmonize with that one?'

'In no way,' said Simmias.

'Yet surely, if there's one theory that ought to be in harmony, it's a theory about attunement.'

'So it ought,' said Simmias.

'Well, this one of yours isn't in harmony; but see which of the theories you prefer: that learning is recollection, or that soul is attunement.'

'The former, by a long way, Socrates. Because I acquired the latter without any proof, but from a certain likelihood and plausibility about it, whence its appeal for most people, but I'm aware that arguments basing their proofs upon likelihoods are impostors, and if one doesn't guard against them, they completely deceive one, in geometry as well as in all other subjects. But the argument about recollection and learning has come from a hypothesis worthy of acceptance. Because it was, of course, asserted that our soul existed even before it entered the body, just as surely as its object exists—the Being, bearing the name of "*what it is*"; and this, I'm convinced, I have accepted rightly and for adequate reason. So it would seem, consequently, that I must allow neither myself nor anyone else to say that soul is attunement.'

'Again now, look at it this way, Simmias. Do you think it befits an attunement, or any other compound, to be in any state other than that of the elements of which it's composed?'

'Certainly not.'

'Nor yet, I presume, to act, or be acted upon, in any way differently from the way they may act or be acted upon?'

He assented.

'An attunement therefore should not properly direct the things of which it's composed, but should follow them.'

He agreed.

'Then an attunement can't possibly undergo contrary movement or utter sound or be opposed in any other way to its own parts.'

'It can't possibly.'

'Again now, isn't it natural for every attunement to be an attunement just as it's been tuned?'

'I don't understand.'

'Isn't it the case that if it's been tuned more and to a greater extent, assuming that to be possible, it will be more an attunement and a greater one; whereas if less and to a smaller extent, it will be a lesser and smaller one?'

'Certainly.'

'Well, is this the case with soul—that even in the least degree, one soul is either to a greater extent and more than another, or to a smaller extent and less, just itself—namely, a soul?'

'In no way whatever.'

'Well, but is one soul said to have intelligence and goodness and to be good, while another is said to have folly and wickedness and to be bad? And are we right in saying those things?'

'Quite right.'

'Then what will any of those who maintain that soul is attunement say these things are, existing in our souls—goodness and badness? Are they, in turn, a further attunement and non-attunement? And is one soul, the good one, tuned, and does it have within itself, being an attunement, a further attunement, whereas the untuned one is just itself, and lacking a further attunement within it?'

'I couldn't say myself,' said Simmias; 'but obviously anyone maintaining the hypothesis would say something of that sort.'

'But it's already been agreed that no one soul is more or less a soul than another; and this is the admission that no one attunement is either more or to a greater extent, or less or to a smaller extent, an attunement than another. Isn't that so?'

'Certainly.'

'But that which is neither more nor less an attunement has been neither more nor less tuned; is that so?'

'It is.'

'But does that which has been neither more nor less tuned participate in attunement to a greater or to a smaller degree, or to an equal degree?'

'To an equal degree.'

'But then, given that no one soul is either more or less itself, namely a soul, than another, it hasn't been more or less tuned either?'

'That is so.'

'And this being its condition, surely it couldn't participate more either in non-attunement or in attunement?'

'Indeed not.'

'And this again being its condition, could any one soul participate to a greater extent than another in badness or goodness, assuming that badness is non-attunement, while goodness is attunement?'

'It couldn't.'

'Or rather, surely, following sound reasoning, Simmias, no soul will participate in badness, assuming it is attunement; because naturally an attunement, being completely itself, namely an attunement, could never participate in non-attunement.'

'No indeed.'

'Nor then, of course, could a soul, being completely a soul, participate in badness.'

'How could it, in view of what's already been said?'

'By this argument, then, we find that all souls of all living things will be equally good, assuming that 10 it's the nature of souls to be equally themselves, namely souls.'

'So it seems to me, Socrates.'

'Yes, and do you approve of this assertion, or b think this would happen to the argument, if the hypothesis that soul is attunement were correct?'

'Not in the least.'

'Again now, would you say that of all the things 5 in a man it is anything but soul, especially if it's a wise one, that rules him?'

'I wouldn't.'

'Does it comply with the bodily feelings or does it oppose them? I mean, for example, when heat and thirst are in the body, by pulling the opposite way, away from drinking, and away from eating when it 10 feels hunger; and surely in countless other ways we c see the soul opposing bodily feelings, don't we?'

'We certainly do.'

'And again, didn't we agree earlier that if it is at- 5 tunement, it would never utter notes opposed to the tensions, relaxations, strikings, and any other affections of its components, but would follow and never dominate them?'

'We did of course agree.'

'Well now, don't we find it, in fact, operating in 10 just the opposite way, dominating all those alleged d sources of its existence, and opposing them in almost everything throughout all of life, mastering them in all kinds of ways, sometimes disciplining more harshly and painfully with gymnastics and medicine, sometimes more mildly, now threatening and now admonishing, conversing with our appetites and pas- 5 sions and fears, as if with a separate thing? That, surely, is the sort of thing Homer has represented in the *Odyssey*, where he says that Odysseus:

Striking his breast, reproved his heart with the
words:
e *"Endure, my heart; e'en worse thou didst once*
endure."

Do you think he'd have composed that, with the idea that the soul was attunement, the sort of thing that could be led by the feelings of the body rather than

something that could lead and master them, being it- self far too divine a thing to rank as attunement?' 5

'Goodness no, Socrates, I don't!'

'In no way at all then, my friend, do we approve of the thesis that soul is a kind of attunement; be- 95 cause it seems that we should agree neither with the divine poet Homer nor with ourselves.'

'That is so.'

'Well then,' said Socrates, 'we seem to have pla- cated the Theban lady Harmonia moderately well; 5 but now, how about the question of Cadmus? How and with what argument, Cebes, shall we placate him?'

'You'll find a way, I think,' said Cebes; 'at any rate this argument of yours against attunement has surprised me beyond expectation. Because when Simmias was speaking in his perplexity, I was very much wondering if anyone would be able to handle b his argument; so it seemed to me quite remarkable that it immediately failed to withstand the first as- sault of your own argument. Accordingly, I shouldn't wonder if the argument of Cadmus suffered the same fate.'

'No big talking, my friend,' said Socrates, 'in case 5 some evil eye should turn the coming argument to rout. But that shall be God's concern; for ourselves, let's come to close quarters, in Homeric fashion, and try to see if, in fact, there's anything in what you say. The sum and substance of what you're after is surely this: you want it proved that our soul is im- c perishable and immortal, if a philosophic man about to die, confidently believing that after death he'll fare much better yonder than if he were ending a life lived differently, isn't to be possessed of a senseless and foolish confidence. As for showing that the soul is 5 something strong and god-like, and existed even be- fore we were born as men, nothing prevents all that, you say, from indicating not immortality, but only that soul is long-lived and existed somewhere for an immense length of time in the past, and knew and did all kinds of things; even so, it was none the more immortal for all that, but its very entry into a human d body was the beginning of its perishing, like an ill- ness: it lives this life in distress, and finally perishes in what is called death. And, you say, it makes no difference, so far as our individual fears are con-

cerned, whether it enters a body once or many times:
anyone who neither knows nor can give proof that
it's immortal should be afraid, unless he has no
sense.

'Something like this, Cebes, is what I think you're
saying; and I'm purposely reviewing it more than
once, so that nothing may escape us, and so that you
may add or take away anything you wish.'

To this Cebes replied: 'No, there's nothing at
present that I want to take away or add; those are my
very points.'

Here Socrates paused for a long time examining
something in his own mind. He then said: 'It's no
trivial matter, this quest of yours, Cebes: it calls for
a thorough inquiry into the whole question of the reason for coming-to-be and destruction. So I will, if
you like, relate my own experiences on these matters: and then, if any of the things I say seem helpful to you, you can use them for conviction on the
points you raise.'

'Well, I certainly should like that,' said
Cebes.

'Then listen to my story. When I was young,
Cebes, I was remarkably keen on the kind of wisdom known as natural science; it seemed to me
splendid to know the reasons for each thing, why
each thing comes to be, why it perishes, and why it
exists. And I was always shifting back and forth, examining, for a start, questions like these: is it, as
some said, whenever the hot and the cold give rise
to putrefaction, that living creatures develop? And is
it blood that we think with, or air, or fire? Or is it
none of these, but the brain that provides the senses
of hearing and seeing and smelling, from which
memory and judgement come to be; and is it from
memory and judgement, when they've acquired stability, that knowledge comes to be accordingly?
Next, when I went on to examine the destruction of
these things, and what happens in the heavens and
the earth, I finally judged myself to have absolutely
no gift for this kind of inquiry. I'll tell you a good
enough sign of this: there had been things that I previously did know for sure, at least as I myself and
others thought; yet I was then so utterly blinded by
this inquiry, that I unlearned even those things I formerly supposed I knew, including, amongst many
other things, why it is that a human being grows.

That, I used earlier to suppose, was obvious to everyone: it was because of eating and drinking; whenever, from food, flesh came to accrue to flesh, and
bone to bone, and similarly on the same principle the
appropriate matter came to accrue to each of the
other parts, it was then that the little bulk later came
to be big; and in this way the small human being
comes to be large. That was what I supposed then:
reasonably enough, don't you think?'

'I do,' said Cebes.

'Well, consider these further cases: I used to suppose it was an adequate view, whenever a large man
standing beside a small one appeared to be larger just
by a head; similarly with two horses. And, to take
cases even clearer than these, it seemed to me that
ten was greater than eight because of the accruing of
two to the latter, and that two cubits were larger than
one cubit, because of their exceeding the latter by
half.'

'Well, what do you think about them now?' said
Cebes.

'I can assure you that I'm far from supposing I
know the reason for any of these things, when I
don't even accept from myself that when you add
one to one, it's either the one to which the addition
is made that's come to be two, or the one that's
been added *and* the one to which it's been added,
that have come to be two, because of the addition
of one to the other. Because I wonder if, when they
were apart from each other, each was one and they
weren't two then; whereas when they came close
to each other, this then became a reason for their
coming to be two—the union in which they were
juxtaposed. Nor again can I any longer be persuaded, if you divide one, that this has now become
a reason for its coming to be two, namely division;
because if so, we have a reason opposite to the previous one for its coming to be two; then it was their
being brought close to each other and added, one
to the other; whereas now it's their being drawn
apart, and separated each from the other. Why, I
can't even persuade myself any longer that I know
why it is that one comes to be; nor, in short, why
anything else comes to be, or perishes, or exists,
following that method of inquiry. Instead I rashly
adopt a different method, a jumble of my own, and
in no way incline towards the other.

'One day, however, I heard someone reading from a book he said was by Anaxagoras, according to which it is, in fact, Intelligence that orders and is the reason for everything. Now this was a reason that pleased me; it seemed to me, somehow, to be a good thing that Intelligence should be the reason for everything. And I thought that, if that's the case, then Intelligence in ordering all things must order them and place each individual thing in the best way possible; so if anyone wanted to find out the reason why each thing comes to be or perishes or exists, this is what he must find out about it: how is it best for that thing to exist, or to act or be acted upon in any way? On this theory, then, a man should consider nothing else, whether in regard to himself or anything else, but the best, the highest good; though the same man must also know the worse, as they are objects of the same knowledge. Reckoning thus, I was pleased to think I'd found, in Anaxagoras, an instructor to suit my own intelligence in the reason for the things that are. And I thought he'd inform me, first, whether the earth is flat or round, and when he'd informed me, he'd go on to expound the reason why it must be so, telling me what was better—better, that is, that it should be like this; and if he said it was in the centre, he'd go on to expound the view that a central position for it was better. If he could make these things clear to me, I was prepared to hanker no more after any other kind of reason. What's more, I was prepared to find out in just the same way about the sun, the moon, and the stars, about their relative velocity and turnings and the other things that happen to them, and how it's better for each of them to act and be acted upon just as they are. Because I never supposed that, having said they were ordered by Intelligence, he'd bring in any reason for them other than its being best for them to be just the way they are; and I supposed that in assigning the reason for each individual thing, and for things in general, he'd go on to expound what was best for the individual, and what was the common good for all; nor would I have sold these hopes for a large sum, but I made all haste to get hold of the books and read them as quickly as I could, so that I might know as quickly as possible what was best and what was worse.

'Well, my friend, these marvellous hopes of mine were dashed; because, as I went on with my reading, I beheld a man making no use of his Intelligence at all, nor finding in it any reasons for the ordering of things, but imputing them to such things as air and aether and water and many other absurdities. In fact, he seemed to me to be in exactly the position of someone who said that all Socrates' actions were performed with his intelligence, and who then tried to give the reasons for each of my actions by saying, first, that the reason why I'm now sitting here is that my body consists of bones and sinews, and the bones are hard and separated from each other by joints, whereas the sinews, which can be tightened and relaxed, surround the bones, together with the flesh and the skin that holds them together; so that when the bones are turned in their sockets, the sinews by stretching and tensing enable me somehow to bend my limbs at this moment, and that's the reason why I'm sitting here bent in this way; or again, by mentioning other reasons of the same kind for my talking with you, imputing it to vocal sounds, air currents, auditory sensations, and countless other such things, yet neglecting to mention the true reasons: that Athenians judged it better to condemn me, and therefore I in my turn have judged it better to sit here, and thought it more just to stay behind and submit to such penalty as they may ordain. Because, I dare swear, these sinews and bones would long since have been off in Megara or Boeotia, impelled by their judgement of what was best, had I not thought it more just and honourable not to escape and run away, but to submit to whatever penalty the city might impose. But to call such things "reasons" is quite absurd. It would be quite true to say that without possessing such things as bones and sinews, and whatever else I possess, I shouldn't be able to do what I judged best; but to call these things the reasons for my actions, rather than my choice of what is best, and that too though I act with intelligence, would be a thoroughly loose way of talking. Fancy being unable to distinguish two different things: the reason proper, and that without which the reason could never be a reason! Yet it's this latter that most people call a reason, appearing to me to be feeling it over blindfold, as it were, and applying a wrong name to it. That's why one man makes the earth stay in position by means of the heaven, putting a whirl around it; while another presses down the air as a base, as if with a flat kneading-trough. Yet the power by which they're now situated in the best way that they could be placed, this they neither look for nor credit with any supernatural strength; but they think they'll one day discover an Atlas stronger and more immortal than this, who does more to hold everything together. That it's the good or binding, that genuinely does bind and hold things together, they don't believe at all. Now I should most gladly have become anyone's pupil, to learn the truth about a reason of that sort; but since I was deprived of this, proving unable either to find it for myself or to learn it from anyone else, would you like me, Cebes, to give you a display of how I've conducted my second voyage in quest of the reason?'

'Yes, I'd like that immensely,' he said.

'Well then, it seemed to me next, since I'd wearied of studying the things that are, that I must take care not to incur what happens to people who observe and examine the sun during an eclipse; some of them, you know, ruin their eyes, unless they examine its image in water or something of that sort. I had a similar thought: I was afraid I might be completely blinded in my soul, by looking at objects with my eyes and trying to lay hold of them with each of my senses. So I thought I should take refuge in theories, and study in them the truth of the things that are. Perhaps my comparison is, in a certain way, inept; as I don't at all admit that one who examines in theories the things that are is any more studying them in images than one who examines them in concrete. But anyhow, this was how I proceeded: hypothesizing on each occasion the theory I judge strongest, I put down as true whatever things seem to me to accord with it, both about a reason and about everything else; and whatever do not, I put down as not true. But I'd like to explain my meaning more clearly; because I don't imagine you understand it as yet.'

'Not entirely, I must say!' said Cebes.

'Well, this is what I mean: it's nothing new, but what I've spoken of incessantly in our earlier discussion as well as at other times. I'm going to set about displaying to you the kind of reason I've been dealing with; and I'll go back to those much harped-on entities, and start from them, hypothesizing that a beautiful, itself by itself, is something, and so are a good and a large and all the rest. If you grant me that and agree that those things exist, I hope that from them I shall display to you the reason, and find out that soul is immortal.'

'Well, you may certainly take that for granted,' said Cebes, 'so you couldn't be too quick to conclude.'

'Then look at what comes next to those things, and see if you think as I do. It seems to me that if anything else is beautiful besides the beautiful itself, it is beautiful for no reason at all other than that it participates in that beautiful; and the same goes for all of them. Do you assent to a reason of that kind?'

'I do.'

'Then I no longer understand nor can I recognize those other wise reasons; but if anyone gives me as the reason why a given thing is beautiful either its having a blooming colour, or its shape, or something else like that, I dismiss those other things—because all those others confuse me—but in a plain, artless, and possibly simple-minded way, I hold this close to myself: nothing else makes it beautiful except that beautiful itself, whether by its presence or communion or whatever the manner and nature of the relation may be; as I don't go so far as to affirm that, but only that it is by the beautiful that all beautiful things are beautiful. Because that seems to be the safest answer to give both to myself and to another, and if I hang on to this, I believe I'll never fall: it's safe to answer both to myself and to anyone else that it is by the beautiful that beautiful things are beautiful; or don't you agree?'

'I do.'

'Similarly it's by largeness that large things are large, and larger things larger, and by smallness that smaller things are smaller?'

'Yes.'

'Then you too wouldn't accept anyone's saying that one man was larger than another by a head, and that the smaller was smaller by that same thing; but you'd protest that you for your part will say only that everything larger than something else is larger by nothing but largeness, and largeness is the reason for its being larger; and that the smaller is smaller by nothing but smallness, and smallness is the reason for its being smaller. You'd be afraid, I imagine, of meeting the following contradiction: if you say that someone is larger and smaller by a head, then, first, the larger will be larger and the smaller smaller by the same thing; and secondly, the head, by which the larger man is larger, is itself a small thing; and it's surely monstrous that anyone should be large by something small; or wouldn't you be afraid of that?'

'Yes, I should,' said Cebes laughing.

'Then wouldn't you be afraid to say that ten is greater than eight by two, and that this is the reason for its exceeding, rather than that it's by numerousness, and because of numerousness? Or that two cubits are larger than one cubit by half, rather than by largeness? Because, of course, there'd be the same fear.'

'Certainly,' he said.

'And again, wouldn't you beware of saying that when one is added to one, the addition is the reason for their coming to be two, or when one is divided, that division is the reason? You'd shout loudly that you know no other way in which each thing comes to be, except by participating in the peculiar Being of any given thing in which it does participate; and in these cases you own no other reason for their coming to be two, save participation in twoness: things that are going to be two must participate in that, and whatever is going to be one must participate in oneness. You'd dismiss those divisions and additions and other such subtleties, leaving them as answers to be given by people wiser than yourself; but you, scared of your own shadow, as the saying is, and of your inexperience, would hang on to that safety of the hypothesis, and answer accordingly. But if anyone hung on to the hypothesis itself, you would dismiss him, and you wouldn't answer till you should have examined its consequences, to see if, in your view, they are in accord or discord with each other; and when you had to give an account of the hypothesis itself, you would give it in the same way, once again hypothesizing another hypothesis, whichever should seem best of those above, till you came to something adequate; but you wouldn't jumble things as the contradiction-mongers do, by discussing the starting-point and its consequences at the same time, if, that is, you wanted to discover any of the things that are. For them, perhaps, this isn't a matter of the least thought or concern; their wisdom enables them to mix everything up together, yet still be pleased with themselves; but you, if you really are a philosopher, would, I imagine, do as I say.'

'What you say is perfectly true,' said Simmias and Cebes together.

Echecrates. Goodness, Phaedo, there was reason to say that! It seems marvellous to me how clearly he put things, even for someone of small intelligence.

Phaedo. Exactly, Echecrates. That was how it seemed to everyone there.

Echecrates. And to us who weren't there but are now hearing it. Tell us, though, what were the things that were said next?

Phaedo. As I recall, when these points had been granted him, and it was agreed that each of the forms *was* something, and that the other things, partaking in them, took the name of the forms themselves, he next asked: 'If you say that that is so, then whenever you say that Simmias is larger than Socrates but smaller than Phaedo, you mean then, don't you, that both things are in Simmias, largeness and smallness?'

'I do.'

'Well anyhow, do you agree that Simmias' overtopping of Socrates isn't expressed in those words according to the truth of the matter? Because it isn't, surely, by nature that Simmias overtops him, by virtue, that is of his being Simmias, but by virtue of the largeness that he happens to have. Nor again does he overtop Socrates became Socrates is Socrates, but because of smallness that Socrates has in relation to his largeness?'

'True.'

'Nor again is he overtopped by Phaedo in virtue of Phaedo's being Phaedo, but because of largeness that Phaedo has in relation to Simmias' smallness?'

'That is so.'

'So that's how Simmias takes the name of being both small and large; it's because he's between the two of them, submitting his smallness to the largeness of the one for it to overtop, and presenting to the other his largeness which overtops the latter's smallness.'

At this he smiled, and added: 'That sounds as if I'm going to talk like a book. But anyway, things are surely as I say.'

He agreed.

5 'My reason for saying this is that I want you to think as I do. Now it seems to me that not only is largeness itself never willing to be large and small at the same time, but also that the largeness in us never admits the small, nor is it willing to be over-topped. Rather, one of two things must happen: ei-
e ther it must retreat and get out of the way, when its opposite, the small, advances towards it; or else, upon that opposite's advance, it must perish. But what it is not willing to do is to abide and admit smallness, and thus be other than what it was. Thus I, having admitted and abided smallness, am still
5 what I am, this same individual, only small; whereas the large in us, while being large, can't endure to be small. And similarly, the small that's in us is not willing ever to come to be, or to be, large. Nor will any other of the opposites, while still being what it
103 was, at the same time come to be, and be, its own opposite, If that befalls it, *either* it goes away *or* it perishes.'

'I entirely agree,' said Cebes.

On hearing this, one of those present—I don't re-
5 member for sure who it was—said: 'But look here, wasn't the very opposite of what's now being said agreed in our earlier discussion: that the larger comes to be from the smaller, and the smaller from the larger, and that coming-to-be is, for opposites, just this—they come to be from their opposites. Whereas now I think it's being said that this could never
10 happen.'

Socrates turned his head and listened. 'It's splen-
b did of you to have recalled that,' he said; 'but you don't realize the difference between what's being said now and what was said then. It was said then that one opposite *thing* comes to be from another op-posite *thing*; what we're saying now is that the op-
5 posite *itself* could never come to be opposite to it-self, whether it be the opposite in us or the opposite in nature. Then, my friend, we were talking about things that *have* opposites, calling them by the names they take from them; whereas now we're talking about the opposites themselves, from whose pres-ence in them the things so called derive their names.

It's these latter that we're saying would never be c willing to admit coming-to-be from each other.'

With this he looked towards Cebes and said: 'Cebes, you weren't troubled, I suppose, by any of the things our friend here said, were you?'

'No, not this time,' said Cebes; 'though I don't 5 deny that many things do trouble me.'

'We've agreed, then, unreservedly on this point: an opposite will never be opposite to itself.'

'Completely.'

'Now please consider this further point, and see 10 if you agree with it. Is there something you call hot, and again cold?'

'There is.'

'Do you mean the same as snow and fire?'

'No, most certainly not.' d

'Rather, the hot is something different from fire, and the cold is something different from snow?'

'Yes.'

'But this I think you will agree: what is snow will 5 never, on the lines of what we were saying earlier, admit the hot and still be what it was, namely snow, and also hot; but at the advance of the hot, it will ei-ther get out of the way or perish.'

'Certainly.'

'And again fire, when cold advances, will either 10 get out of the way or perish; but it will never endure to admit the coldness, and still be what it was, namely fire and also cold.'

'That's true.' e

'The situation, then, in some cases of this kind, is as follows: not only is the form itself entitled to its own name for all time; but there's something else too, which is not the same as the form, but which, whenever it exists, always has the character of that 5 form. Perhaps what I mean will be clearer in this fur-ther example: the odd must, surely, always be given this name that we're now using, mustn't it?'

'Certainly.'

'But is it the only thing there is—this is my ques-tion—or is there something else, which is not the 104 same as the odd, yet which one must also always call odd, as well as by its own name, because it is by na-ture such that it can never be separated from the odd? I mean the sort of thing that happens to threeness, and to many other instances. Consider the case of 5 threeness. Don't you think it must always be called both by its own name and by that of the odd, although the odd is not the same as threeness? They aren't the same, yet threeness and fiveness and half the entire number series are by nature, each of them, always odd, although they are not the same as the odd. And again, two and four and the whole of the other row of numbers, though not the same as the even, are still, each of them, always even. Do you agree or not?'

'Of course.'

'Look closely then at what I want to show. It is this: apparently it's not only the opposites we spoke of that don't admit each other. This is also true of all things which, although not opposites to each other, always have the opposites. These things too, it seems, don't admit whatever form may be opposite to the one that's in them, but when it attacks, *either* they perish *or* they get out of the way. Thus we shall say, shan't we, that three will sooner perish, will undergo anything else whatever, sooner than abide coming to be even, while remaining three?'

'Indeed we shall,' said Cebes.

'Moreover, twoness isn't opposite to threeness.'

'Indeed not.'

'Then not only do the forms that are opposites not abide each other's attack; but there are, in addition, certain other things that don't abide the opposites' attack.'

'Quite true.'

'Then would you like us, if we can, to define what kinds these are?'

'Certainly.'

'Would they, Cebes, be these: things that are compelled by whatever occupies them to have not only its own form, but always the form of some opposite as well?'

'What do you mean?'

'As we were saying just now. You recognize, no doubt, that whatever the form of three occupies must be not only three but also odd.'

'Certainly.'

'Then, we're saying, the form opposite to the character that has that effect could never go to a thing of that kind.'

'It couldn't.'

'But it was that of odd that had that effect?'

'Yes.'

'And opposite to this is that of the even?'

'Yes.'

'So that of the even will never come to three.'

'No, it won't.'

'Three, then, has no part in the even.'

'No part.'

'So threeness is uneven.'

'Yes.'

'So what I was saying we were to define, the kind of things which, while not opposite to a given thing, nevertheless don't admit it, the opposite in question—as we've just seen that threeness, while not opposite to the even, nevertheless doesn't admit it, since it always brings up its opposite, just as twoness brings up the opposite of the odd, and the fire brings up the opposite of the cold, and so on in a great many other cases—well, see whether you would define them thus: it is not only the opposite that doesn't admit its opposite; there is also that which brings up an opposite into whatever it enters itself; and that thing, the very thing that brings it up, never admits the quality opposed to the one that's brought up. Recall it once more: there's no harm in hearing it several times. Five won't admit the form of the even, nor will ten, its double, admit that of the odd. This, of course, is itself also the opposite of something else; nevertheless, it won't admit the form of the odd. Nor again will one-and-a-half, and the rest of that series, the halves, admit the form of the whole; and the same applies to a third, and all that series. Do you follow and agree that that is so?'

'I agree most emphatically, and I do follow.'

'Then please repeat it from the start; and don't answer in the exact terms of my question, but in imitation of my example. I say this, because from what's now being said I see a different kind of safeness beyond the answer I gave initially, the old safe one. Thus, if you were to ask me what it is, by whose presence in a body, that body will be hot, I shan't give you the old safe, ignorant answer, that it's *hotness*, but a subtler answer now available, that it's *fire*. And again, if you ask what it is, by whose presence in a body, that body will ail, I shan't say that it's *illness*, but *fever*. And again, if asked what it is, by whose presence in a number, that number will be odd, I shan't say *oddness*, but *oneness*; and so on. See whether by now you have an adequate understanding of what I want.'

'Yes, quite adequate.'

'Answer then, and tell me what it is, by whose presence in a body, that body will be living.'

'Soul.'

'And is this always so?'

'Of course.'

'Then soul, whatever it occupies, always comes to that thing bringing life?'

'It comes indeed.'

'And is there an opposite to life, or is there none?'

'There is.'

'What is it?'

'Death.'

'Now soul will absolutely never admit the opposite of what it brings up, as has been agreed earlier?'

'Most emphatically,' said Cebes.

'Well now, what name did we give just now to what doesn't admit the form of the even?'

'Un-even.'

'And to that which doesn't admit the just, and to whatever doesn't admit the musical?'

'Un-musical, and un-just.'

'Well then, what do we call whatever doesn't admit death?'

'Im-mortal.'

'But soul doesn't admit death?'

'No.'

'Then soul is immortal.'

'It's immortal.'

'Very well. May we say that this much has been proved? Or how does it seem to you?'

'Yes, and very adequately proved, Socrates.'

'Now what about this, Cebes? If it were necessary for the uneven to be imperishable, three would be imperishable, wouldn't it?'

'Of course.'

'Or again, if the un-hot were necessarily imperishable likewise, then whenever anyone brought hot against snow, the snow would get out of the way, remaining intact and unmelted? Because it couldn't perish, nor again could it abide and admit the hotness.'

'True.'

'And in the same way, I imagine, if the un-coolable were imperishable, then whenever something cold attacked the fire, it could never be put out nor could it perish, but it would depart and go away intact.'

'It would have to.'

'Then aren't we compelled to say the same thing about the immortal? If the immortal is also imperishable, it's impossible for soul, whenever death attacks it, to perish. Because it follows from what's been said before that it won't admit death, nor will it be dead, just as we said that three will not be even, any more than the odd will be; and again that fire will not be cold, any more than the hotness in the fire will be. "But", someone might say, "what's to prevent the odd, instead of coming to be even, as we granted it didn't, when the even attacks, from perishing, and there coming to be even in its place?" Against one who said that, we could not contend that it doesn't perish; because the uneven is not imperishable. If that had been granted us, we could easily have contended that when the even attacks, the odd and three depart and go away. And we could have contended similarly about fire and hot and the rest, couldn't we?'

'Certainly we could.'

'So now, about the immortal likewise: if it's granted us that it must also be imperishable, then soul, besides being immortal, would also be imperishable; but if not, another argument would be needed.'

'But there's no need of one, on that score at least. Because it could hardly be that anything else wouldn't admit destruction if the immortal, being everlasting, is going to admit destruction.'

'Well God anyway,' said Socrates, 'and the form of life itself, and anything else immortal there may be, never perish, as would, I think, be agreed by everyone.'

'Why yes, to be sure; by all men and still more, I imagine, by gods.'

'Then, given that the immortal is also indestructible, wouldn't soul, if it proves to be immortal, be imperishable as well?'

'It absolutely must be imperishable.'

'Then when death attacks a man, his mortal part, it seems, dies; whereas the immortal part gets out of the way of death, departs, and goes away intact and undestroyed.'

'It appears so.'

'Beyond all doubt then, Cebes, soul is immortal and imperishable, and our souls really will exist in Hades.'

'Well, Socrates, for my part I've no further objection, nor can I doubt the arguments at any point. But if Simmias here or anyone else has anything to say, he'd better not keep silent; as I know of no future occasion to which anyone wanting to speak or hear about such things could put it off.'

'Well no,' said Simmias; 'nor have I any further ground for doubt myself, as far as the arguments go; though in view of the size of the subject under discussion, and having a low regard for human weakness, I'm bound to retain some doubt in my mind about what's been said.'

'Not only that, Simmias,' said Socrates; 'what you say is right, so the initial hypotheses, even if they're acceptable to you people, should still be examined more clearly: if you analyse them adequately, you will, I believe, follow the argument to the furthest point to which man can follow it up; and if you get that clear, you'll seek nothing further.'

'What you say is true.'

'But this much it's fair to keep in mind, friends: if a soul *is* immortal, then it needs care, not only for the sake of this time in which what we call "life" lasts, but for the whole of time; and if anyone is going to neglect it, now the risk *would* seem fearful. Because if death were a separation from everything, it would be a godsend for the wicked, when they died, to be separated at once from the body and from their own wickedness along with the soul; but since, in fact, it is evidently immortal, there would be no other refuge from ills or salvation for it, except to become as good and wise as possible. For the soul enters Hades taking nothing else but its education and nurture, which are, indeed, said to do the greatest benefit or harm to the one who has died, at the very outset of his journey yonder.

'Now it is said that when each man has died, the spirit allotted to each while he was living proceeds to bring him to a certain place, where those gathered must submit to judgement, and then journey to Hades with the guide appointed to conduct those in this world to the next; and when they have experienced there the things they must, and stayed there for the time required, another guide conveys them back here during many long cycles of time. So the journey is not as Aeschylus' Telephus describes it: he says it

is a simple path that leads to Hades, but to me it seems to be neither simple nor single. For then there would be no need of guides; since no one, surely, could lose the way anywhere, if there were only a single road. But in fact it probably has many forkings and branchings; I speak from the evidence of the rites and observances followed here. Now the wise and well-ordered soul follows along, and is not unfamiliar with what befalls it; but the soul in a state of desire for the body, as I said earlier, flutters around it for a long time, and around the region of the seen, and after much resistance and many sufferings it goes along, brought by force and against its will by the appointed spirit. And on arriving where the others have gone, if the soul is unpurified and has committed any such act as engaging in wrongful killings, or performing such other deeds as may be akin to those and the work of kindred souls, everyone shuns and turns aside from it, and is unwilling to become its travelling companion or guide; but it wanders by itself in a state of utter confusion, till certain periods of time have elapsed, and when these have passed, it is taken perforce into the dwelling meet for it; but the soul that has passed through life with purity and moderation finds gods for travelling companions and guides, and each inhabits the region that befits it.

'Now there are many wondrous regions in the earth, and the earth itself is of neither the nature nor the size supposed by those who usually describe it, as someone has convinced me.'

Here Simmias said: 'What do you mean by that, Socrates? I've heard many things about the earth too, but not these that convince you; so I'd be glad to hear them).'

'Well, Simmias, I don't think the skill of Glaucus is needed to relate what they are; although to prove them true does seem to me too hard for the skill of Glaucus—I probably couldn't do it myself, and besides, even if I knew how to, I think the life left me, Simmias, doesn't suffice for the length of the argument. Still, nothing prevents me from telling of what I've been convinced the earth is like in shape, and of its regions.'

'Well, even that is enough,' said Simmias.

'First then, I've been convinced that if it is round and in the centre of the heaven, it needs neither air nor any other such force to prevent its falling, but the uniformity of the heaven in every direction with itself is enough to support it, together with the equilibrium of the earth itself; because a thing in equilibrium placed in the middle of something uniform will be unable to incline either more or less in any direction, but being in a uniform state it will remain without incline. So that's the fast thing of which I've been convinced.'

'And rightly so,' said Simmias.

'And next, that it is of vast size, and that we who dwell between the Phasis River and the Pillars of Heracles inhabit only a small part of it, living around the sea like ants or frogs around a marsh, and that there are many others living elsewhere in many such places. For there are many hollows all over the earth, varying in their shapes and sizes, into which water and mist and air have flowed together; and the earth itself is set in the heaven, a pure thing in pure surroundings, in which the stars are situated, and which most of those who usually describe such things name "aether"; it's from this that these elements are the dregs, and continually flow together into the hollows of the earth. Now we ourselves are unaware that we live in its hollows, and think we live above the earth—just as if someone living at the bottom of the ocean were to think he lived above the sea, and seeing the sun and the stars through the water, were to imagine that the sea was heaven, and yet through slowness and weakness had never reached the surface of the sea, nor emerged, stuck his head up out of the sea into this region here, and seen how much purer and fairer it really is than their world, nor had heard this from anyone else who had seen it. Now this is just what has happened to us: living in some hollow of the earth, we think we live above it, and we call the air "heaven", as if this were heaven and the stars moved through it; whereas the truth is just the same—because of our weakness and slowness, we are unable to pass through to the summit of the air; for were anyone to go to its surface, or gain wings and fly aloft, he would stick his head up and see— just as here the fishes of the sea stick their heads up and see the things here, so he would see the things up there; and if his nature were able to bear the vision, he would realize that this is the true heaven, the genuine light, and the true earth. For this earth of ours, and its stones and all the region here, are corrupted and eaten away, as are things in the sea by the brine; nor does anything worth mentioning grow in the sea, and practically nothing is perfect, but there are eroded rocks and sand and unimaginable mud and mire, wherever there is earth as well, and things are in no way worthy to be compared with the beauties in our world. But those objects in their turn would be seen to surpass the things in our world by a far greater measure still; indeed, if it is proper to tell a tale, it's worth hearing, Simmias, what the things upon the earth and beneath the heaven are actually like.'

'Why yes, Socrates,' said Simmias, 'we'd be glad to hear this tale.'

'Well then, my friend, first of all the true earth, if one views it from above, is said to look like those twelve-piece leather balls, variegated, a patchwork of colours, of which our colours here are, as it were, samples that painters use. There the whole earth is of such colours, indeed of colours far brighter still and purer than these: one portion is purple, marvellous for its beauty, another is golden, and all that is white is whiter than chalk or snow; and the earth is composed of the other colours likewise, indeed of colours more numerous and beautiful than any we have seen. Even its very hollows, full as they are of water and air, give an appearance of colour, gleaming among the variety of the other colours, so that its general appearance is of one continuous multicoloured surface. This being its nature, things that grow on it, trees and flowers and fruit, grow in proportion; and again, the mountains contain stones likewise, whose smoothness, transparency, and beauty of colour are in the same proportion; it is from these that the little stones we value, sardian stones, jaspers, emeralds, and all such, are pieces; but there, every single one is like that, or even more beautiful still. This is because the stones there are pure, and not corroded or corrupted, like those here, by mildew and brine due to the elements that have flowed together, bringing ugliness and disease to stones and earth, and to plants and animals as well. But the true earth is adorned with all these things, and with gold and silver also, and with the other things of that kind as well. For they are plainly visible, being many in number, large, and everywhere upon the earth; happy, therefore, are they who behold the sight of it.

Among many other living things upon it there are men, some dwelling inland, some living by the air, as we live by the sea, and some on islands surrounded by the air and lying close to the mainland; and in a word, what the water and the sea are to us for our needs, the air is to them; and what air is for us, aether is for them. Their climate is such that they are free from sickness and live a far longer time than people here, and they surpass us in sight, hearing, wisdom, and all such faculties, by the extent to which air surpasses water for its purity, and aether surpasses air. Moreover, they have groves and temples of gods, in which gods are truly dwellers, and utterances and prophecies, and direct awareness of the gods; and communion of that kind they experience face to face. The sun and moon and stars are seen by them as they really are, and their happiness in all else accords with this.

'Such is the nature of the earth as a whole and its surroundings; but in it there are many regions within the hollows it has all around it, some deeper and some more extended than the one in which we dwell, some deeper but with a narrower opening than our own region, and others that are shallower in depth but broader than this one. All these are interconnected underground in every direction, by passages both narrower and wider, and they have channels through which abundant water flows from one into another, as into mixing bowls, and continuous underground rivers of unimaginable size, with waters hot and cold, and abundant fire and great rivers of fire, and many of liquid mud, some purer and some more miry, like the rivers of mud in Sicily that flow ahead of the lava-stream, and the lava-stream itself; with these each of the regions is filled, as the circling stream happens to reach each one on each occasion. All of this is kept moving back and forth by a kind of pulsation going on within the earth; and the nature of this pulsation is something like this: one of the openings in the earth happens to be especially large, and perforated right through the earth; it is this that Homer spoke of as:

> *A great way off, where lies the deepest pit beneath earth;*

and it is this that he, and many other poets have elsewhere called Tartarus. Now into this opening all the rivers flow together, and from it they flow out again; and each acquires its character from the nature of the earth through which it flows. The reason why all the streams flow out there, and flow in, is that this liquid has neither bottom nor resting place. So it pulsates and surges back and forth, and the air and the breath enveloping it do the same; because they follow it, when it rushes towards those areas of the earth and again when it returns to these; and just as in breathing the current of breath is continuously exhaled and inhaled, so there the breath pulsating together with the liquid causes terrible and unimaginable winds, as it passes in and out. Now when the water recedes into the so-called "downward" region, it flows along the courses of those streams through the earth and fills them, as in the process of irrigation; and when it leaves there again and rushes back here, then it fills these ones here once more; these, when filled, flow through the channels and through the earth, and reaching the regions into which a way has been made for each, they make seas and lakes and rivers and springs; and then dipping again beneath the earth, some circling longer and more numerous regions, and others fewer and shorter ones, they discharge once more into Tartarus, some a long way and others a little below where the irrigation began; but all flow in below the point of outflow, some across from where they poured out, and some in the same part; and there are some that go right round in a circle, coiling once or even many times around the earth like serpents, and then, after descending as far as possible, discharge once more. It is possible to descend in either direction as far as the middle but no further; because the part on either side slopes uphill for both sets of streams.

'Now there are many large streams of every kind; *journey of soul* but among their number there happen to be four in particular, the largest of which, flowing outermost and round in a circle, is the one called Oceanus; across from this and flowing in the opposite direction is Acheron, which flows through other desert regions, and in particular, flowing underground, reaches the Acherusian Lake, where the souls of most of those who have died arrive, and where, after they have stayed for certain appointed periods, some longer, some shorter, they are sent forth again into the generation of living things. The third river issues between these two, and near the point of is-sue it pours into a huge region all ablaze with fire, and forms a lake larger than our own sea, boiling with water and mud; from there it proceeds in a cir-cle, turbid and muddy, and coiling about within the earth it reaches the borders of the Acherusian Lake, amongst other places, but does not mingle with its water; then, after repeated coiling underground, it discharges lower down in Tartarus; this is the river they name Pyriphlegethon, and it is from this that the lava-streams blast fragments up at various points upon the earth. Across from this again issues the fourth river, first into a region terrible and wild, it is said, coloured bluish-grey all over, which they name the Stygian region, and the river as it discharges forms a lake, the Styx; when it has poured in there, and gained terrible powers in the water, it dips be-neath the earth, coils round and proceeds in the op-posite direction to Pyriphlegethon, which it encoun-ters in the Acherusian Lake from the opposite side; nor does the water of this river mingle with any other, but it too goes round in a circle and discharges into Tartarus opposite to Pyriphlegethon; and its name, according to the poets, is Cocytus.

'Such, then, is their nature. Now when those who have died arrive at the region to which the spirit con-veys each one, they first submit to judgement, both those who have lived honourable and holy lives and those who have not. Those who are found to have lived indifferently journey to Acheron, embark upon certain vessels provided for them, and on these they reach the lake; there they dwell, undergoing purga-tion by paying the penalty for their wrong-doings, and are absolved, if any has committed any wrong, and they secure reward for their good deeds, each according to his desert; but all who are found to be incurable because of the magnitude of their offences, through having committed many grave acts of sac-rilege, or many wrongful and illegal acts of killing, or any other deeds that may be of that sort, are hurled by the appropriate destiny into Tartarus, whence they nevermore emerge. Those, again, who are found guilty of curable yet grave offences, such as an act of violence in anger against a father or a mother, and have lived the rest of their lives in penitence, or who have committed homicide in some other such fash-ion, must fall into Tartarus; and when they have

fallen and stayed there for a year, the surge casts them forth, the homicides by way of Cocytus, and those who have assaulted father or mother by way of Pyriphlegethon; then, as they are carried along and draw level with the Acherusian Lake, they cry out and call, some to those they killed, others to those they injured; calling upon them, they beg and be-seech them to allow them to come forth into the lake and to receive them; and if they persuade them, they come forth and cease from their woes; but if not, they are carried back into Tartarus, and from there again into the rivers, and they do not cease from these sufferings till they persuade those they have wronged; for this is the penalty imposed upon them by their judges. But as for those who are found to have lived exceptionally holy lives, it is they who are freed and delivered from these regions within the earth, as from prisons, and who attain to the pure dwelling above, and make their dwelling above ground. And among their number, those who have been adequately purified by philosophy live bodiless for the whole of time to come, and attain to dwelling places fairer even than these, which it is not easy to reveal, nor is the time sufficient at present. But it is for the sake of just the things we have related, Sim-mias, that one must do everything possible to have part in goodness and wisdom during life; for fair is the prize and great the hope.

'Now to insist that these things are just as I've re-lated them would not be fitting for a man of intelli-gence; but that either this or something like it is true about our souls and their dwellings, given that the soul evidently is immortal, this, I think, *is* fitting and worth risking, for one who believes that it is so—for a noble risk it is—so one should repeat such things to oneself like a spell; which is just why I've so pro-longed the tale. For these reasons, then, any man should have confidence for his own soul, who dur-ing his life has rejected the pleasures of the body and its adornments as alien, thinking they do more harm than good, but has devoted himself to the pleasures of learning, and has decked his soul with no alien adornment, but with its own, with temperance and justice, bravery, liberality, and truth, thus awaiting the journey he will make to Hades, whenever des-tiny shall summon him. Now as for you, Simmias and Cebes and the rest, you will make your several journeys at some future time, but for myself, "e'en now", as a tragic hero might say, "destiny doth summon me"; and it's just about time I made for the bath: it really seems better to take a bath before drinking the poison, and not to give the women the trouble of washing a dead body.'

b   When he'd spoken, Crito said: 'Very well, Socrates: what instructions have you for these others or for me, about your children or about anything else? What could we do, that would be of most service to you?'

'What I'm always telling you, Crito,' said he, 'and nothing very new: if you take care of yourselves, your actions will be of service to me and mine, and to yourselves too, whatever they may be, even if you make no promises now; but if you take no care for yourselves, and are unwilling to pursue your lives along the tracks, as it were, marked by our present and earlier discussions, then even if you make many firm promises at this time, you'll do no good at all.'

c   'Then we'll strive to do as you say,' he said; 'but in what fashion are we to bury you?'

'However you wish,' said he; 'provided you catch me, that is, and I don't get away from you.' And with this he laughed quietly, looked towards us and said: 'Friends, I can't persuade Crito that I am Socrates here, the one who is now conversing and arranging each of the things being discussed; but he imagines I'm that dead body he'll d see in a little while, so he goes and asks how he's to bury me! But as for the great case I've been arguing all this time, that when I drink the poison, I shall no longer remain with you, but shall go off and depart for some happy state of the blessed, this, I think, I'm putting to him in vain, while comforting you and myself alike. So please stand surety for me with Crito, the opposite surety to that which he stood for me with the judges: his guarantee was that I *would* stay behind, whereas you must guarantee that, when I die, I shall *not* stay behind, but shall go off and depart; then Crito e will bear it more easily, and when he sees the burning or interment of my body, he won't be distressed for me, as if I were suffering dreadful things, and won't say at the funeral that it is Socrates they are laying out or bearing to the grave

or interring. Because you can be sure, my dear Crito, that misuse of words is not only troublesome in itself, but actually has a bad effect on the soul. Rather, you should have confidence, and say you are burying my body; and bury it however you please, and think most proper.'

116

After saying this, he rose and went into a room to take a bath, and Crito followed him but told us to wait. So we waited, talking among ourselves about what had been said and reviewing it, and then again dwelling on how great a misfortune had befallen us, literally thinking of it as if we were deprived of a father and would lead the rest of our life as orphans. After he'd bathed and his children had been brought to him—he had two little sons and one b big one—and those women of his household had come, he talked with them in Crito's presence, and gave certain directions as to his wishes; he then told the women and children to leave, and himself returned to us.

By now it was close to sunset, as he'd spent a long time inside. So he came and sat down, fresh from his bath, and there wasn't much talk after that. Then the prison official came in, stepped up to him and said: 'Socrates, I shan't reproach you as I re- c proach others for being angry with me and cursing, whenever by order of the rulers I direct them to drink the poison. In your time here I've known you for the most generous and gentlest and best of men who have ever come to this place; and now especially, I feel sure it isn't with me that you're angry, but with others, because you know who are responsible. Well now, you know the message I've come to bring: good-bye, then, and try to bear the inevitable as eas- d ily as you can.' And with this he turned away in tears, and went off.

Socrates looked up at him and said: 'Good-bye to you too, and we'll do as you say.' And to us he added: 'What a civil man he is! Throughout my time here he's been to see me, and sometimes talked with me, and been the best of fellows; and now how generous of him to weep for me! But come on, Crito, let's obey him: let someone bring in the poison, if it has been prepared; if not, let the man prepare it.'

Crito said: 'But Socrates, I think the sun is still e on the mountains and hasn't yet gone down. And besides, I know of others who've taken the draught long after the order had been given them, and after dining well and drinking plenty, and even in some cases enjoying themselves with those they fancied. Be in no hurry, then: there's still time left.'

Socrates said: 'It's reasonable for those you speak of to do those things—because they think they gain by doing them; for myself, it's reasonable not to do them; because I think I'll gain nothing by taking the draught a little later: I'll only earn my own ridicule by clinging to life, and being sparing when there's nothing more left. Go on now; do as I ask, and nothing else.'

Hearing this, Crito nodded to the boy who was standing nearby. The boy went out, and after spending a long time away he returned, bringing the man who was going to administer the poison, and was carrying it ready-pounded in a cup. When he saw the man, Socrates said: 'Well, my friend, you're an expert in these things: what must one do?'

'Simply drink it' he said, 'and walk about till a heaviness comes over your legs; then lie down, and it will act of itself.' And with this he held out the cup to Socrates.

He took it perfectly calmly, Echecrates, without a tremor, or any change of colour or countenance; but looking up at the man, and fixing him with his customary stare, he said: 'What do you say to pouring someone a libation from this drink? Is it allowed or not?'

'We only prepare as much as we judge the proper dose, Socrates,' he said.

'I understand,' he said; 'but at least one may pray to the gods, and so one should, that the removal from this world to the next will be a happy one; that is my own prayer: so may it be.' With these words he pressed the cup to his lips, and drank it off with good humour and without the least distaste.

Till then most of us had been fairly well able to restrain our tears; but when we saw he was drinking, that he'd actually drunk it, we could do so no longer. In my own case, the tears came pouring out in spite of myself, so that I covered my face and wept

for myself—not for him, no, but for my own misfortune in being deprived of such a man for a companion. Even before me, Crito had moved away, when he was unable to restrain his tears. And Apollodorus, who even earlier had been continuously in tears, now burst forth into such a storm of weeping and grieving, that he made everyone present break down except Socrates himself.

But Socrates said: 'What a way to behave, my strange friends! Why, it was mainly for this reason that I sent the women away, so that they shouldn't make this sort of trouble; in fact, I've heard one should die in silence. Come now, calm yourselves and have strength.'

When we heard this, we were ashamed and checked our tears. He walked about, and when he said that his legs felt heavy he lay down on his back—as the man told him—and then the man, this one who'd given him the poison, felt him, and after an interval examined his feet and legs; he then pinched his foot hard and asked if he could feel it, and Socrates said not. After that he felt his shins once more; and moving upwards in this way, he showed us that he was becoming cold and numb. He went on feeling him, and said that when the coldness reached his heart, he would be gone.

By this time the coldness was somewhere in the region of his abdomen, when he uncovered his face—it had been covered over—and spoke; and this was in fact his last utterance: 'Crito,' he said, 'we owe a cock to Asclepius: please pay the debt, and don't neglect it.'

'It shall be done,' said Crito; 'have you anything else to say?'

To this question he made no answer, but after a short interval he stirred, and when the man uncovered him his eyes were fixed; when he saw this, Crito closed his mouth and his eyes.

And that, Echecrates, was the end of our companion, a man who, among those of his time we knew, was—so we should say—the best, the wisest too, and the most just.

MENO

70   *Meno.* Can you tell me, Socrates, whether virtue is acquired by teaching or by practice; or if neither by teaching nor by practice, then whether it comes to man by nature, or in what other way?

Socrates. There was a time, Meno, when the Thessalians were famous among the other Hellenes for their riches and their riding; but now, if b I am not mistaken, they are famous also for their wisdom, especially at Larisa, which is the native city of your friend Aristippus. And this is Gorgias' doing; for when he came there, he imbued with the love of wisdom the flower of the c Aleuadae, among them your admirer Aristippus, and the other chiefs of the Thessalians. And he has taught you the habit of answering questions in the grand and bold style, which is natural to those who know, and may be expected from one who is himself ready and willing to be questioned on any subject by any Hellene, and answers all comers. How different is our lot! my dear Meno. 71 Here at Athens there is a dearth of the commodity, and all wisdom seems to have emigrated from us to you. I am certain that if you were to ask any Athenian whether virtue was natural or acquired, he would laugh in your face, and say: 'Stranger, you have far too good an opinion of me, if you think that I can answer your question. For I literally do not know what virtue is, and much less whether it is acquired by teaching or not.'

b   And I myself, Meno, living as I do in this region of poverty am as poor as the rest of the world; and I confess with shame that I know literally nothing about virtue; and when I do not know the 'quid' of anything how can I know the 'quale'? How, if I knew nothing at all of Meno, could I tell if he was handsome, or the opposite; rich and noble, or the reverse of rich and noble? Do you think that I could?

Men. No, indeed. But are you in earnest, Socrates, in saying that you do not know what virtue is? And am I to carry back this report of c you to Thessaly?

Soc. Not only that, my dear boy, but you may say further that I have never come across anyone else who did, in my judgement.

Men. Then you have never met Gorgias when d he was at Athens?

Soc. Yes, I have.

Men. And did you not think that he knew?

Soc. I have not a good memory, Meno, and therefore I cannot now tell what I thought of him at the time. I dare say that he does know, and that you know what he said: please, therefore, to remind me of what he said; or, if you would rather, tell me your own view; for I suspect that you and he think much alike.

Men. Very true.

Soc. Then as he is not here, never mind him, and do you tell me. I adjure you, Meno, be generous, and tell me what you say that virtue is; for I shall esteem myself truly fortunate if I find that I have been mistaken, and that you and Gorgias do really have this knowledge, when I have been just saying that I have never met anybody who had.

Men. There will be no difficulty, Socrates, in e answering your question. Let us take first the virtue of a man—he should know how to administer the state, and in the administration of it should benefit his friends and harm his enemies; and he must also be careful not to suffer harm himself. A woman's virtue, if you wish to know about that, may also be easily described: her duty is to order her household and keep properly what is indoors, and obey her husband. Every age, every condition of life, young or old, male or fe- 72 male, bond or free, has a different virtue: there are virtues numberless, and consequently there is no difficulty about definitions; for there is a virtue relative to the actions and ages of each of us in all that we do. And I take it the same may be said of vice, Socrates.

Soc. How fortunate I am, Meno! When I ask you for one virtue, you present me with a swarm of them, which are in your keeping. Suppose that I carried on the figure of the swarm, and asked of you, What is the nature of the bee? and you answered that there are many different kinds of bees, and I replied: But are there many different kinds of bees because they differ quâ bees; or, not differing quâ bees, are they distinguished from one another by something else, some quality such as beauty, or size, or some other such attribute? How would you answer me?

Men. I should answer that bees do not differ from one another, quâ bees.

Soc. And if I went on to say: That is what I desire to know, Meno; tell me what is the quality in which they do differ, but are all alike;—you would presumably be able to answer?

Men. I should.

Soc. And so of the virtues, however many and different they may be, they have all a common form which makes them virtues; and on this he who would answer the question, 'What is virtue?' would do well to have his eye fixed: Do you understand?

Men. I am beginning to understand; but I do not as yet take hold of the question as I could wish.

Soc. When you say, Meno, that there is one virtue of a man, another of a woman, and so on, does this apply only to virtue, or would you say the same of health, and size, and strength? Or is the nature of health always the same, whether in man or woman?

Men. I should say that health is the same, both in man and woman.

Soc. And is not this true of size and strength? If a woman is strong, she will be strong by reason of the same form and of the same strength subsisting in her which there is in the man. I mean to say that strength, as strength, whether of man or woman, is the same. Is there any difference?

Men. I think not.

Soc. And will not virtue, as virtue, be the same, whether in a child or in an old man, in a woman or in a man?

Men. I cannot help feeling, Socrates, that this case is different from the others.

Soc. But why? Were you not saying that the virtue of a man was to order a state, and the virtue of a woman was to order a household?

Men. I did say so.

Soc. And can either household or state or anything be well ordered without temperance and without justice?

Men. Certainly not.

Soc. Then they who order a state or a house temperately and justly order them with temperance and justice?

Men. Certainly.

Soc. Then both men and women, if they are to be good men and women, must have the same virtues of temperance and justice?

Men. Clearly.

Soc. And could either a young man or an elder one ever become good, while they were intemperate and unjust?

Men. Certainly not.

Soc. They must be temperate and just?

Men. Yes.

Soc. Then all human beings are good in the same way, and become good by possession of the same virtues?

Men. Such is the inference.

Soc. And they surely would not have been good in the same way, unless their virtue had been the same?

Men. They would not.

Soc. Then now that the sameness of all virtue has been proven, try and remember what Gorgias, and you with him, say that virtue is.

Men. I know not what to say, but that virtue is the power of governing mankind—if you really want to have one definition of them all.

Soc. That is indeed what I want. Now consider this point; can virtue as you define it be the virtue of a child or a slave, Meno? Can the child govern his father, or the slave his master; and would he who governed be any longer a slave?

Men. I think not, Socrates.

Soc. No, indeed; there would be small reason in that. Yet once more, fair friend; according to you, virtue is 'the power of governing'; but shall we not add 'justly and not unjustly'?

Men. Yes, Socrates; I agree there; for justice is virtue.

Soc. Would you say 'virtue', Meno or 'a virtue'?

Men. What do you mean?

Soc. I mean as I might say about anything; that roundness, for example, is 'a figure' and not simply 'figure', and I should adopt this mode of speaking, because there are other figures.

Men. Quite right; and that is just what I say about virtue—that there are other virtues as well as justice.

Soc. What are they? tell me the names of them, as I would tell you the names of the other figures if you asked me.

Men. Courage and temperance and wisdom and a noble way of life are virtues, it seems to me; and there are many others.

Soc. Yes, Meno; and again we are in the same case: in searching after one virtue we have found many, though not in the same way as before; but we have been unable to find the common virtue which runs through them all.

Men. Why, Socrates, even now I am not able to help you in your inquiry and get at one common notion of virtue as in the other cases.

Soc. No wonder; but I will try to get us nearer if I can. You perhaps understand that this reasoning applies universally: suppose that someone asked you the question which I asked before: Meno, what is figure? if you answered 'roundness', he would reply to you, in my way of speaking, by asking whether roundness is 'figure' or 'a figure'; and you would, of course, answer 'a figure'.

Men. Certainly.

Soc. And for this reason—that there are other figures?

Men. Yes.

Soc. And if he proceeded to ask, What other figures are there? you would have told him.

Men. I should.

Soc. And if he similarly asked what colour is, and you answered whiteness, and the questioner rejoined, Would you say that whiteness is colour or a colour? you would reply, A colour, because there are other colours as well.

Men. I should.

Soc. And if he had said, Tell me what they are?—you would have told him of other colours which are colours just as much as whiteness.

Men. Yes.

Soc. And suppose that he were to pursue the matter in my way, he would say: Ever and anon we are landed in particulars, but that is not what I want; tell me then, since you call them by a common name, and say that they are all figures even when opposed to one another, what is that common nature which you designate as figure—which contains round no less than straight, and, you say, belongs to one no more than to the other—that would be your mode of speaking?

Men. Yes.

Soc. And in speaking thus, do you mean to say that the round is no more round than straight, or the straight no more straight than round?

Men. Of course not.

Soc. You only assert that the round figure is figure no more than the straight, nor the straight than the round?

Men. Very true.

Soc. To what then do we give the name of figure? Try and answer. Suppose that when a person asked you this question either about figure or colour, you were to reply, My good sir, I do not understand what you want, or know what you mean; he would look rather astonished and say: Do you not understand that I am looking for that which is identical in all the particulars? And then he might put the question in another form: Meno, he might say, what is there identical in the round, the straight, and everything else that you call a figure? Could you not answer that question, Meno? I wish that you would try; the attempt will be good practice for the answer about virtue.

Men. I would rather that you should answer, Socrates.

Soc. Shall I indulge you?

Men. By all means.

Soc. And then you will tell me about virtue?

Men. I will.

Soc. Then I must do my best, for there is a prize to be won.

Men. Certainly.

Soc. Well, I will try and explain to you what figure is. What do you say to this answer?—

Figure is the only thing which accompanies colour. Will you be satisfied with it, as I am sure that I should be if you would let me have a similar definition of virtue?

Men. But, Socrates, it is such an artless answer.

Soc. Why artless?

Men. Because, according to you, figure is that which always accompanies colour. Very well; but if a person were to say that he does not know what colour is, any more than what figure is—what sort of answer would you have given him?

Soc. In my opinion, the truth. And if he were a philosopher of the eristic and contentious sort, I should say to him: You have my answer, and if I am wrong, your business is to take up the argument and refute me. But if we were friends, and were talking as you and I are now, I ought of course to reply in a milder strain and more in the dialectician's vein; that is to say, I should not only speak the truth, but I should make use of premises which the person interrogated would be willing to admit. And this is the way in which I shall endeavour to approach you. You will acknowledge, will you not, that there is such a thing as an end, or termination, or extremity?—all which words I use in the same sense, although I am aware that Prodicus might disagree on this point: but still you, I imagine, would speak of a thing as ended or terminated—that is all which I am saying—nothing subtle.

Men. Yes, I should; and I believe that I understand your meaning.

Soc. And you would speak of a surface and also of a solid, as for example in geometry.

Men. Yes.

Soc. Well then, you are now in a condition to understand my definition of figure. I define figure to be always that in which the solid finds its limit; or, more concisely, the limit of solid.

Men. And now, Socrates, what is colour?

Soc. You are outrageous, Meno, in thus plaguing a poor old man to give you an answer, when you will not take the trouble of remembering what is Gorgias' definition of virtue.

Men. When you have told me what I ask, I will tell you, Socrates.

Soc. A man who was blindfolded has only to hear you talking, and he would know that you are a beautiful creature and still have lovers.

Men. Why do you think so?

Soc. Why, because you always speak in imperatives, like proud beauties who reign with absolute power so long as they are in their prime; and also, I suspect, you have found out that I have a weakness for beauty, and therefore to humour you I must answer.

Men. Please do.

Soc. Would you like me to answer you after the manner of Gorgias, in which you may find it easiest to follow me?

Men. I should like nothing better.

Soc. Do not he and you and Empedocles say that there are certain effluences from existing things?

Men. Certainly.

Soc. And passages into which and through which the effluences pass.

Men. Exactly.

Soc. And some of the effluences fit into the passages, and some of them are too small or too large?

Men. True.

Soc. And there is such a thing as sight?

Men. Yes.

Soc. And now, as Pindar says, 'read my meaning':—colour is an effluence of figures, commensurate with sight, and palpable to sense.

Men. That, Socrates, appears to me to be an admirable answer.

Soc. Why, yes, because it happens to be one which you have been in the habit of hearing: and your wit will have discovered, I suspect, that you may explain in the same way the nature of sound and smell, and of many other similar phenomena.

Men. Quite true.

Soc. The answer, Meno, was in the solemn language of tragedy, and therefore was more acceptable to you than the other answer about figure.

Men. Yes.

Soc. And yet, O son of Alexidemus, I cannot help thinking that the other was the better; and I believe that you would be of the same opinion, if you would only stay and be initiated, and were not compelled, as you said yesterday, to go away before the mysteries.

Men. But I will stay, Socrates, if you will give me many such answers.

Soc. Well then, for my own sake as well as for yours, I will do my very best; but I am afraid that I shall not be able to give you very many as good. And now, in your turn, you are to fulfil your promise, and tell me what virtue is in the universal; and do not make a singular into a plural, as the facetious always say of those who break a thing, but leave virtue whole and sound when you tell me its nature. I have given you the pattern.

Men. Well then, Socrates, virtue, as I take it, is when he, who desires things which are lovely, is able to provide them for himself; so the poet says, and I say too that 'virtue is the desire of things that are lovely, with power to attain them'.

Soc. And does he who desires the things that are lovely also desire the good?

Men. Certainly.

Soc. Then are there some who desire the evil and others who desire the good? Do not all men, my dear sir, desire good?

Men. I think not.

Soc. There are some who desire evil?

Men. Yes.

Soc. Do you mean that they think the evils which they desire, to be good; or do they know that they are evil and yet desire them?

Men. Both, I think.

Soc. And do you really imagine, Meno, that a man knows evils and desires them notwithstanding?

Men. Certainly I do.

Soc. Desire is of possession?

Men. Yes, of possession.

Soc. And does he think that evils do good to him who possesses them, or does he know that their presence does harm?

Men. There are some who think that the evils do them good, and others who know that they do harm.

Soc. And, in your opinion, do those who think that they do them good know that they are evils?

Men. I would not go so far as that.

Soc. Is it not obvious that those who are ignorant of their nature do not desire them, but desire what they suppose to be goods although they are really evils; and therefore if in their ignorance they suppose the evils to be goods they really desire goods?

Men. In that case, no doubt.

Soc. Again, those who, as you say, desire evils, and think that evils are hurtful to the possessor of them, presumably know that they will be hurt by them?

Men. They must know it.

Soc. And must they not suppose that those who are hurt are miserable in proportion to the hurt which is inflicted upon them?

Men. How can it be otherwise?

Soc. But are not the miserable ill fated?

Men. Yes, indeed.

Soc. And does anyone desire to be miserable and ill fated?

Men. I should say not, Socrates.

Soc. But if there is no one who desires to be miserable, there is no one, Meno, who desires evil; for what is misery but the desire and possession of evil?

Men. That appears to be the truth, Socrates, and I admit that nobody desires evil.

Soc. And yet, were you not saying just now that virtue is the desire and power of attaining good?—[Yes, I did say so.]—But of this definition one part, the desire, is common to all, and one man is no better than another in that respect?—[Clearly.]—It is obvious then that if one man is indeed better than another, he must be better in the power of attaining good?

Men. Exactly.

Soc. Then, according to your definition, virtue would appear to be the power of attaining good?

Men. I entirely approve, Socrates, of the manner in which you now view this matter.

Soc. Then let us see whether what you now say is true from another point of view; for very likely you may be right:—You affirm virtue to be the power of attaining goods?

Men. Yes.

Soc. And the goods which you mean are such as health and wealth?

Men. And the possession of gold and silver, and having office and honour in the state.

Soc. Those are what you would call goods?

Men. Yes, I should include all those.

Soc. Then, according to Meno, who is the
d hereditary friend of the great king, virtue is the
power of getting silver and gold; and would you
add that they must be gained piously, justly, or
do you deem this to be of no consequence? And
is any mode of acquisition, even if unjust, equally
to be deemed virtue?

Men. Not virtue, Socrates.

Soc. But vice?

Men. Yes.

Soc. Then justice or temperance or piety, or
e some other part of virtue, as would appear, must
accompany the acquisition, and without them the
mere acquisition of goods will not be virtue.

Men. Why, how can there be virtue without
these?

Soc. On the other hand, the failure to acquire
gold and silver in an unjust way for oneself or another, or in other words the want of them, may be
equally virtue?

Men. True.

Soc. Then the acquisition of such goods is no
79 more virtue than the non-acquisition and want of
them, but it seems that whatever is accompanied
by justice or honesty is virtue, and whatever is
devoid of any such quality is vice.

Men. It cannot be otherwise, in my judgement.

Soc. And were we not saying just now that
justice, temperance, and the like, were each of
them a part of virtue?

Men. Yes.

Soc. And so, Meno, this is the way in which
you mock me.

Men. Why do you say that, Socrates?

Soc. Why, because a short while ago I asked
you not to break up virtue and offer it to me in
little pieces, and I gave you patterns according to
which you were to frame your answer; and you
have forgotten already, and tell me that virtue is
b the power of attaining goods with justice; and justice you acknowledge to be a part of virtue.

Men. Yes.

Soc. Then it follows from your own admissions, that virtue consists in doing with one part
of virtue whatever a man does do; for justice and

the like are said by you to be parts of virtue, each
and all of them. Let me explain further. Did not
I ask you to tell me the nature of virtue as a
whole? And you are very far from telling me this,
but declare every action to be virtue which is done c
with a part of virtue; as though you had told me
the nature of virtue as a whole, so that I should
recognize it even when you fritter it away into little pieces. And, therefore, my dear Meno, I fear
that I must begin again and repeat the same question: What is virtue? for otherwise I can only say
that every action done with a part of virtue is
virtue; what else is the meaning of saying that
every action done with justice is virtue? Ought I
not to ask the question over again; for can anyone who does not know the nature of virtue know
the nature of a part of virtue?

Men. No; I do not say that he can.

Soc. Do you remember how, in the example
of figure, we rejected any answer given in terms d
which were as yet unexplained or unadmitted?

Men. Yes, Socrates; and we were quite right
in doing so.

Soc. But then, my friend, do not suppose that
while the nature of virtue as a whole is still undetermined, you can explain it to anyone by reference to some part of virtue; or indeed explain
anything at all in that fashion. We should only
have to ask over again the old question, What is e
this virtue of yours? Am I not right?

Men. I believe that you are.

Soc. Then begin again, and answer me, What,
according to you and your friend Gorgias, is the
definition of virtue?

Men. O Socrates, I used to be told, before I
knew you, that you were always doubting your- 80
self and making others doubt; and now you are
casting your spells over me, and I am simply getting betwitched and enchanted, and am at my
wits' end. And if I may venture to make a jest
upon you, you seem to me both in your appearance and in your power over others to be very like
the flat torpedo fish, who torpifies those who
come near him and touch him, as you have now
torpified me, I think. For my soul and my tongue
are really torpid, and I do not know how to answer you; and though I have been delivered of an b
infinite variety of speeches about virtue before now,

and to many persons—and very good speeches they were, as I thought—at this moment I cannot even say what virtue is. And I think that you are very wise in not voyaging and going away from home, for if you did in other places as you do in Athens, you would be cast into prison as a magician.

Soc. You are a rogue, Meno, and had all but caught me.

Men. What do you mean, Socrates?

c   *Soc.* I can tell why you made a simile about me.

Men. Why?

Soc. In order that I might make another simile about you. For I know that all beautiful youths like to have similes made about them—as well they may, since beautiful images, I take it, are naturally evoked by beauty—but I shall not return the compliment. As to my being a torpedo, if the torpedo is itself torpid as well as the cause of torpidity in others, then indeed I am a torpedo, but

d   not otherwise; for I perplex others, not because I am clear, but because I am utterly perplexed myself. And now I know not what virtue is, and you seem to be in the same case, although you did once perhaps know before you touched me. However, I have no objection to join with you in the inquiry.

Men. And how will you investigate, Socrates, that of which you know nothing at all? Where can you find a starting-point in the region of the unknown? And even if you happen to come full upon what you want, how will you ever know that this is the thing which you did not know?

Soc. I know, Meno, what you mean; but just

e   see what a tiresome dispute you are introducing. You argue that a man cannot inquire either about that which he knows, or about that which he does not know; for if he knows, he has no need to inquire; and if not, he cannot; for he does not know the very subject about which he is to inquire.

81   *Men.* Well, Socrates, and is not the argument sound?

Soc. I think not.

Men. Why not?

Soc. I will tell you why: I have heard from certain men and women skilled in things divine that—[Here Socrates pauses to change the tone of the dialogue.]

Men. What did they say?

Soc. They spoke of a glorious truth, as I conceive.

Men. What is it? and who are they?

Soc. Some of them are priests and priestesses, who have striven to learn how to give a reasonable account of the things with which they b concern themselves: there are poets also, like Pindar, and the many others who are inspired. And they say—mark, now, and see whether their words are true—they say that the soul of man is immortal, and at one time has an end, which is termed dying, and at another time is born again, but is never destroyed. And the moral is, that a man ought to live always in perfect holiness. 'For in the ninth year Persephone sends the souls of c those from whom she has received the penalty of ancient crime back again from beneath into the light of the sun above, and these are they who become noble kings and mighty men and great in wisdom and are for ever called saintly heroes.'

The soul, then, as being immortal and having been born again many times, and having seen all things that exist, whether in this world or in the world below, has knowledge of them all; and it is no wonder that she should be able to call to remembrance all that she ever knew about virtue, and about everything; for as all nature is akin, and the soul has learned all things, there is no difficulty in a man eliciting out of a single rec- d ollection all the rest—the process generally called 'learning'—if he is strenuous and does not faint; for all inquiry and all learning is but recollection.

And therefore we ought not to listen to this eristic argument about the impossibility of inquiry: for it will make us idle, and it is sweet to the sluggard; but the other doctrine will make us e active and inquisitive. In that confiding, I will gladly inquire with you into the nature of virtue.

Men. Yes, Socrates; but what do you mean by saying that we do not learn, and that what we call learning is only a process of recollection? Can you teach me how this is?

Soc. I told you, Meno, just now that you were a rogue, and now you ask whether I can teach you, when I am saying that there is no teaching, but 82 only recollection; and thus you imagine that you will expose me in a contradiction.

Men. Indeed, Socrates, I protest that I had no such intention. I only asked the question from habit; but if you can prove to me that what you say is true, I wish that you would.

Soc. It will be no easy matter, but I am willing to do my best for you. Suppose that you call one of your numerous attendants, whichever you like, that I may demonstrate on him.

Men. Certainly. Come hither, boy.

Soc. He is Greek, and speaks Greek, does he not?

Men. Yes, indeed; he was born in the house.

Soc. Attend now, and observe whether he learns of me or only remembers.

Men. I will.

Soc. Tell me, boy, do you know that a figure like this is a square?

Boy. I do.

Soc. And you know that a square figure has these four lines equal?

Boy. Certainly.

Soc. And these lines which I have drawn through the middle of the square are also equal?

Boy. Yes.

Soc. A square may be of any size?

Boy. Certainly.

Soc. And if one side of the figure be of two feet, and the other side be of two feet, how much will the whole be? Let me explain: if in one direction the space was of two feet, and in the other direction of one foot, the whole would be of two feet taken once?

Boy. Yes.

Soc. But since this side is also of two feet, there are twice two feet?

Boy. There are.

Soc. Then the square is of twice two feet?

Boy. Yes.

Soc. And how many are twice two feet? count and tell me.

Boy. Four, Socrates.

Soc. And might there not be another square twice as large as this, and having like this the lines equal?

Boy. Yes.

Soc. And of how many feet will that be?

Boy. Of eight feet.

Soc. And now try and tell me the length of the line which forms the side of that double square: this is two feet—what will that be?

Boy. Clearly, Socrates, it will be double.

Soc. Do you observe, Meno, that I am not teaching the boy anything, but only asking him questions; and now he fancies that he knows how long a line is necessary in order to produce a figure of eight square feet; does he not?

Men. Yes.

Soc. And does he really know?

Men. Certainly not.

Soc. He only guesses that because the square is double, the line is double.

Men. True.

Soc. Observe him while he recalls the steps in regular order. (*To the Boy.*) Tell me, boy, do you assert that a double space comes from a double line? Remember that I am not speaking of an oblong, but of a figure equal every way, and twice the size of this—that is to say of eight feet; and I want to know whether you still say that a double square comes from a double line?

Boy. Yes.

Soc. But does not this line become doubled if we add another such line here?

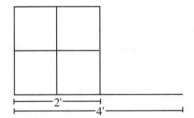

Boy. Certainly.

Soc. And four such lines will make a space containing eight feet?

Boy. Yes.

Soc. Let us describe such a figure: Would you not say that this is the figure of eight feet?

Boy. Yes.

Soc. And are there not these four divisions in the figure, each of which is equal to the figure of four feet?

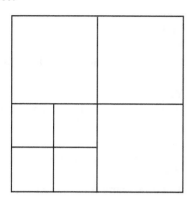

Boy. True.

Soc. And is not that four times four?

Boy. Certainly.

Soc. And four times is not double?

Boy. No, indeed.

Soc. But how much?

Boy. Four times as much.

Soc. Therefore the double line, boy, has given a space, not twice, but four times as much.

Boy. True.

c *Soc.* Four times four are sixteen—are they not?

Boy. Yes.

Soc. What line would give you a space of eight feet, as this gives one of sixteen feet;—do you see?

Boy. Yes.

Soc. And the space of four feet is made from this half line?

Boy. Yes.

Soc. Good; and is not a space of eight feet twice the size of this, and half the size of the other?

Boy. Certainly.

Soc. Such a space, then, will be made out of a line greater than this one, and less than that one?

Boy. Yes; I think so.

d *Soc.* Very good; I like to hear you say what you think. And now tell me, is not this a line of two feet and that of four?

Boy. Yes.

Soc. Then the line which forms the side of eight feet ought to be more than this line of two feet, and less than the other of four feet?

Boy. It ought.

Soc. Try and see if you can tell me how much it will be.

Boy. Three feet.

Soc. Then if we add a half to this line of two, that will be the line of three. Here are two and there is one; and on the other side, here are two also and there is one: and that makes the figure of which you speak?

e

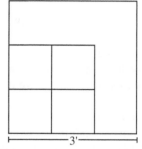

Boy. Yes.

Soc. But if there are three feet this way and three feet that way, the whole space will be three times three feet?

Boy. That is evident.

Soc. And how much are three times three feet?

Boy. Nine.

Soc. And how much is the double of four?

Boy. Eight.

Soc. Then the figure of eight is not made out of a line of three?

Boy. No.

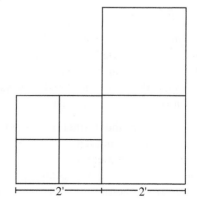

84 *Soc.* But from what line?—tell me exactly; and if you would rather not reckon, try and show me the line.

Boy. Indeed, Socrates, I do not know.

Soc. Do you see, Meno, what advances he has made in his power of recollection? He did not know at first, and he does not know now, what is the side of a figure of eight feet: but then he thought that he knew, and answered confidently as if he knew, and had no difficulty; now he has a difficulty, and neither knows nor fancies that he knows.

b *Men.* True.

Soc. Is he not better off in knowing his ignorance?

Men. I think that he is.

Soc. If we have made him doubt, and given him the 'torpedo's shock,' have we done him any harm?

Men. I think not.

Soc. We have certainly, as would seem, assisted him in some degree to the discovery of the truth; and now he will wish to remedy his ignorance, but then he would have been ready to tell

c all the world again and again that the double space should have a double side.

Men. True.

Soc. But do you suppose that he would ever have enquired into or learned what he fancied that he knew, though he was really ignorant of it, until he had fallen into perplexity under the idea that he did not know, and had desired to know?

Men. I think not, Socrates.

Soc. Then he was the better for the torpedo's touch?

Men. I think so.

[Although the slave boy has never been educated, he possesses innate knowledge of geometry. Socrates claims that all he is doing is helping the slave bring to consciousness that which he already knows. That is, education is recollection of innate ideas.]

Soc. Mark now the farther development. I shall only ask him, and not teach him, and he shall share the enquiry with me: and do you watch and see if you find me telling or explaining anything to him, instead of eliciting his opinion. Tell me,

boy, is not this a square of four feet which I have d drawn?

Boy. Yes.

Soc. And now I add another square equal to the former one?

Boy. Yes.

Soc. And a third, which is equal to either of them?

Boy. Yes.

Soc. Suppose that we fill up the vacant corner?

Boy. Very good.

Soc. Here, then, there are four equal spaces?

Boy. Yes.

Soc. And how many times larger is this space e than this other?

Boy. Four times.

Soc. But it ought to have been twice only, as you will remember.

Boy. True.

Soc. And does not this line, reaching from corner to corner, bisect each of these spaces? 85 [BDEF]

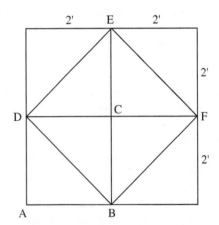

Boy. Yes.

Soc. And are there not here four equal lines which contain this space? [BD, DE, EF, and FB]

Boy. There are.

Soc. Look and see how much this space is.

Boy. I do not understand.

Soc. Has not each interior line cut off half of the four spaces? [BD, DE, EF, and FB]

Boy. Yes.

Soc. And how many spaces are there in this section? [BDEF]

Boy. Four.

Soc. And how many in this? [ABCD]

Boy. Two.

Soc. And four is how many times two?

Boy. Twice.

Soc. And this space is of how many feet? [BDEF]

Boy. Of eight feet.

Soc. And from what line do you get this figure?

Boy. From this. [BDEF]

Soc. That is, from the line which extends from corner to corner of the figure of four feet?

Boy. Yes.

Soc. And that is the line which the learned call the diagonal. And if this is the proper name, then you, Meno's slave, are prepared to affirm that the double space is the square of the diagonal?

Boy. Certainly, Socrates.

Soc. What do you say of him, Meno? Were not all these answers given out of his own head?

Men. Yes, they were all his own.

Soc. And yet, as we were just now saying, he did not know?

Men. True.

Soc. But still he had in him those notions of his—had he not?

Men. Yes.

Soc. Then he who does not know may still have true notions of that which he does not know?

Men. He has.

Soc. And at present these notions have just been stirred up in him, as in a dream; but if he were frequently asked the same questions, in different forms, he would know as well as any one at last?

Men. I dare say.

Soc. Without any one teaching him he will recover his knowledge for himself, if he is only asked questions?

Men. Yes.

Soc. And this spontaneous recovery of knowledge in him is recollection?

Men. True.

Soc. And this knowledge which he now has must he not either have acquired or always possessed?

Men. Yes.

Soc. But if he always possessed this knowledge he would always have known; or if he has acquired the knowledge he could not have acquired it in this life, unless he has been taught geometry; for he may be made to do the same with all geometry and every other branch of knowledge. Now, has any one ever taught him all this? You must know about him, if, as you say, he was born and bred in your house.

Men. And I am certain that no one ever did teach him.

Soc. And yet he has the knowledge?

Men. The fact, Socrates, is undeniable.

Soc. But if he did not acquire the knowledge in this life, then he must have had and learned it at some other time?

Men. Clearly.

Soc. Which must have been the time when he was not a man?

Men. Yes.

Soc. And if there are always to be true thoughts in him, both while he is and while he is not a man, which only need to be awakened into knowledge by putting questions to him, his soul must remain always possessed of this knowledge; for he must always either be or not be a man.

Men. Obviously.

Soc. And if the truth of all things always exists in the soul, then the soul is immortal. Wherefore be of good cheer, and try to discover by recollection what you do not now know, or rather what you do not remember.

Men. I feel, somehow, that I like what you are saying.

Soc. And I too like what I am saying. Some things I have said of which I am not altogether confident. But that we shall be better and braver and less helpless if we think that we ought to inquire, than we should have been if we thought that there was no knowing and no duty to seek to know what we do not know;—that is a belief for which I am ready to fight, in word and deed, to the utmost of my power.

REPUBLIC

The first chapter consists of a typical early Platonic dialogue: it was possibly originally written separately from the rest of the book. No firm conclusions are reached about the ostensible purpose of the inquiry—to discover the nature of morality—but the arguments are lively and interesting and raise issues that will recur later in the book. Once the scene has been set, Socrates whittles away at the unthinking acceptance of conventional views on morality (represented by Cephalus and Polemarchus) before dealing more vigorously with the robust assault on convention (and on Socrates himself) delivered by the sophist Thrasymachus. Socrates accepts neither conventional nor unconventional views unless they survive his logical scrutiny; the ground is prepared for Plato's stress throughout Republic on the importance of reason for morality.

CHAPTER 1
CONVENTION UNDER ATTACK

SOCRATES

327a Yesterday I went down to the Piraeus with Glaucon the son of Ariston to worship the goddess and also because I wanted to see how they would conduct the festival on this, its first performance. I was certainly impressed with the splendour of the procession made by the local people, but I have to say that the Thracians rose to the occasion just as well in their pro- b cession. Once our worshipping and watching were over, we were starting to make our way back to town, when Polemarchus the son of Cephalus spotted us from a distance setting off home, and he told his slave to run over to us and tell us to wait for him. The boy came up behind me, caught hold of my coat, and said, 'Polemarchus wants you to wait.'

I turned around and asked where his master was. 'There,' he said, 'coming up behind you. Please wait.'

'All right, we will,' said Glaucon.

c Polemarchus soon caught up with us, and so did Glaucon's brother Adeimantus, Niceratus the son of Nicias, and some others; they had all apparently been at the procession.

'Socrates,' Polemarchus said, 'it looks to me as though the two of you are setting off back to town.'

'That's right,' I replied.

'Well,' he said, 'do you see how many of us there are?'

'Of course.'

'You'd better choose, then,' he said, 'between overpowering us and staying here.'

'Well, there *is* one further possibility,' I pointed out. 'We might convince you to let us leave.'

'Can you convince people who don't listen?' he asked.

'Impossible,' Glaucon replied.

'Then I think you should know that we won't be listening to you.'

'Anyway,' Adeimantus added, 'don't you realize 328a that there's going to be a horseback torch-race this evening for the goddess?'

'Horseback?' I said. 'That's unusual. Do you mean there'll be a horse-race in which they'll carry torches and pass them on to one another?'

'Precisely,' Polemarchus said. 'And they're also putting on an all-night celebration, which should be worth seeing. We're going to go out to watch it after dinner, and lots of young men will be there too, whom we shall be talking to. So you must do as we suggest and stay.' b

'It looks as though we'd better stay,' said Glaucon.

'Well, if you think so,' I said, 'then that's what we should do.'

So we went to Polemarchus' house, and there we found his brothers Lysias and Euthydemus, and also Thrasymachus of Chalcedon, Charmantides of Paeania, and Cleitophon the son of Aristonymus. Polemarchus' father Cephalus was in the house too; I

Reprinted from Plato's *Republic*, translated by Robin Waterfield (1993) by permission of Oxford University Press.

c thought he looked very old, but then I hadn't seen him for quite a while. He was sitting on a chair with a cushion, and wearing a chaplet, since he had just been making a ritual offering in the courtyard. Some other chairs had been placed in a circle there, so we sat down beside him.

As soon as Cephalus saw me, he said hello and then went on, 'Socrates, unfortunately for us, you're not in the habit of coming down to the Piraeus. You should, you know. I mean, if I still had the strength to make the journey up to town easily, you wouldn't have to come here, because I'd be visiting you. But as things are, you should come here more often. In my case, you see, declining interest in physical plea-sures is exactly matched by increasing desire for and enjoyment of conversation. So please do as I ask: by all means spend time with these young men who are your companions, but treat us too as your friends—as your very close friends—and come here to visit us.'

'I certainly will, Cephalus,' I replied. 'I do in fact enjoy talking with very old people, because I think we ought to learn from them. They've gone on ahead of us, as it were, on a road which we too will prob-ably have to travel, and we ought to find out from them what the road is like—whether it is rough and hard, or easy and smooth. And I'd be especially glad to ask you your opinion about it, since you've reached the time of life the poets describe as being "on the threshold of old age". Is it a difficult period of one's life, would you say, or what?'

329a 'Of course I'll tell you my opinion, Socrates,' he said. 'You see, it's not uncommon for some of us old men of approximately the same age to get to-gether (and so vindicate the ancient proverb!). These gatherings are invariably used for grumbling, by those who miss the pleasures of youth. They remind themselves of their love lives, drinking, feasting, and the like, and consequently complain of having been robbed of things that are important and claim that in those days they used to live well, whereas nowadays they aren't even alive. Others bleat about how their families treat old age like dirt; in fact, this is the main reason they go on and on about all the evils for which old age is responsible. But to my mind, Socrates, they are holding an innocent responsible. If old age were to blame, then I too would have had the same experiences as them—at least as far as old age is concerned—and so would everyone else who has

reached this age. But in the past I, at any rate, have met others like myself who do not feel this way. In particular, I was once with Sophocles the poet when someone asked him, "How do you feel about sex, Sophocles? Are you still capable of having sex with a woman?" He replied, "Be quiet, man! To my great delight, I have broken free of that, like a slave who has got away from a rabid and savage master." I thought at the time that this was a good response, and I haven't changed my mind. I mean, there's no doubt that in old age you get a great deal of peace and freedom from things like sex. When the desires lose their intensity and ease up, then what happens is absolutely as Sophocles described—freedom from a great many demented masters. However, the one thing responsible for this, and for one's relationship with relatives as well, is not a person's old age, Socrates, but his character. If someone is self-disciplined and good-tempered, old age isn't too much of a burden; otherwise, it's not just a question of old age, Socrates—such a person will find life dif-ficult when he's young as well.'

I was filled with admiration for him and his words, and because I wanted him to continue, I tried to provoke him by saying, 'Cephalus, I think that most people would react to what you're saying with scepticism; they'd think that you're finding old age easy to bear not because of your character, but be-cause of your great wealth. The rich have many con-solations, they say.'

'You're right,' he said, 'they are sceptical. And they do have a point, though not as important a point as they imagine. The story about Themistocles is rel-evant here—how when the man from Seriphus was rudely saying that his fame was due not to his own merits but to his city, he replied, "It's true that I wouldn't have become famous if I were a Seriphian, but it's also true that you wouldn't if you were an Athenian." The same principle applies to people who aren't rich and are finding old age hard to bear. It's true that a good man wouldn't find old age particu-larly easy to bear if he were poor, but it's also true that a bad man would never be content with himself even if he were wealthy.'

'Did you inherit most of your wealth, Cephalus,' I asked, 'or did you make it yourself?'

'What's that you say, Socrates?' he asked. 'Make it myself? As a businessman, I come between my grandfather and my father. My grandfather (after whom I'm named) inherited assets approximately equal to what I have now, and increased them considerably; my father Lysanias, however, decreased them to less than they are now. It'll make me happy if I leave these sons of mine not less, but a little more than I inherited.'

'I'll tell you why I asked,' I said. 'It was because I got the impression that you don't particularly care for money, and this is usually the mark of someone who hasn't made it himself, whereas people who have made it themselves are twice as attached to it as anyone else. Poets are attached to their own compositions, fathers to their sons; in the same way, businessmen are concerned about money not only because it's useful (which is why everyone else is interested in it), but also because it is the product of their own labours. This makes them irritating to be with, since money is the only thing they're prepared to think highly of.'

'You're right,' he said.

'Yes,' I said. 'But there's another question I wanted to ask you. What do you think is the greatest benefit you've gained from being rich?'

'Something which many people might find implausible,' he answered. 'You see, Socrates, when thoughts of death start to impinge on a person's mind, he entertains fears and worries about things which never occurred to him before. In the past he used to laugh at the stories that are told about what goes on in Hades—about how someone who has done wrong here is bound to be punished there—but now they trouble his mind, in case they might be true. This might be due to the weakness of old age or it might be because, now that he's closer to the next world, he sees it more clearly; the result is that he becomes filled with anxiety and fear, and starts to make calculations and to see if he has wronged anyone in any way. Anyone who discovers that during his life he has committed a lot of crimes wakes up constantly in terror from his dreams, as children do, and also lives in dread; on the other hand, anyone who is aware of no wrong in himself faces the future with confidence and optimism which, as Pindar says as well, "comforts him in old age". To my mind, Socrates, he expresses it beautifully when he says that anyone who has spent his life behaving morally and justly has "Sweet hope as a companion,

joyfully fostering his heart, comforting him in old age—hope which steers, more than anything else does, men's fickle intention." This is incredibly well put. And this is the context in which I value the possession of money so highly—at least for a decent, orderly person. I mean, the possession of money has a major role to play if one is to avoid cheating or lying against one's better judgment, and also avoid the fear of leaving this life still owing some ritual offerings to a god or some money to someone. It serves a lot of other purposes too, but all things considered I'd say that for an intelligent person, Socrates, wealth is particularly useful in this far from insignificant context.'

'A thoroughly commendable sentiment, Cephalus,' I said. 'But what about this thing you mentioned, doing right? Shall we say that it is, without any qualification, truthfulness and giving back anything one has borrowed from someone? Or might the performance of precisely these actions sometimes be right, but sometimes wrong? This is the kind of thing I mean. I'm sure everyone would agree that if you'd borrowed weapons from a friend who was perfectly sane, but he went insane and then asked for the weapons back, you shouldn't give them back, and if you were to given them back you wouldn't be doing right, and neither would someone who was ready to tell the whole truth to a person like that.'

'You're right,' he agreed.

'It follows that this isn't the definition of morality, to tell the truth and to give back whatever one has borrowed.'

'Yes, it is, Socrates,' Polemarchus interjected. 'At least, it is if we're to believe Simonides.'

'Well now,' said Cephalus, 'I shall pass the discussion on to you two, since it's time for me to attend to the ceremony.'

'And shall I be your heir?' asked Polemarchus.

'Of course,' he said with a chuckle, and promptly left for the ceremony.

In a manner strongly reminiscent of Plato's earlier dialogues, Socrates draws inferences about morality by assuming that it is an area of expertise, and that what holds good for other areas of expertise will hold good for morality as well. Polemarchus could have denied that morality has a single field of operation, as crafts do:

morality might have some broader function in human relationships, or its purpose might be something general, like promoting happiness. Lacking this insight, Polemarchus is tied into paradoxical knots. In a startling anticipation of Christian ethics (prefigured in the dialogues Crito and Gorgias), Socrates finally concludes that it is never right to harm anyone under any circumstances.

e 'Well then,' I told him, 'now that you've inherited the discussion, tell us what it is that Simonides says which you think is an accurate statement about morality.'

'That it is right to give anyone back what you owe them,' he said. 'In my opinion, this is a fine remark.'

'Well,' I said, 'it isn't easy to disagree with Simonides: he's a clever man—superhumanly so. But while *you* may understand what he means by this, Polemarchus, I don't. I mean, he obviously doesn't mean what we were talking about a moment ago, the returning of something one has been 332a lent to someone insane who's asking for it back. And yet something lent is owed, wouldn't you say?'

'Yes,'

'And if the person asking for it back is insane, it's inconceivable that it should be given back, isn't it?'

'True,' he replied.

'Then apparently it wasn't this, but something else, that Simonides meant by the assertion that it is right to give back what is owed.'

'Yes, of course it was something else,' he said. 'His view is that friends owe friends good deeds, not bad ones.'

'I see,' I said. 'So if someone gives money back to someone who lent it to him, and this repayment and returning turns out to be harmful, and both the b giver and the receiver are friends, then this is not a case of giving back what is owed: is this Simonides' meaning, according to you?'

'Yes, exactly.'

'Now, should we give back what is owed to our enemies?'

'Oh, yes,' he said. 'What is owed to them—yes, absolutely. And what an enemy owes an enemy, I think, is also what is appropriate—something bad.'

'There was apparently a certain obscurity, then, in Simonides' definition of morality,' I remarked. 'How typical of a poet! Although, as it turns out, he c meant that it is right to give back to people what is appropriate for them, he called it what is owed to them.'

'I'm surprised you thought any different,' he said.

'But listen,' I said, 'suppose he were asked, "So, Simonides, take the art that we know as medicine. What is it? What does it give that is owed and appropriate, and to what does it give it?" What do you suppose his reply to us would be?'

'Obviously,' he answered, 'he'd reply that it is the art of giving drugs, food, and drink to bodies.'

'What about cookery? What art do we say it is? What does it give that is owed and appropriate, and to what does it give it?'

'It gives taste to cooked food.' d

'All right. So which art—the art of giving what to what—might we call morality?'

'In order to be consistent with what was said earlier, Socrates,' he replied, 'it has to be the art of giving benefit and harm to friends and enemies respectively.'

'So Simonides claims that morality is doing good to one's friends and harm to one's enemies, does he?'

'I think so.'

'Now, where sickness and health are concerned, who is best able to do good to his friends and harm to his enemies when they aren't well?'

'A doctor.'

'And where the risks of a sea voyage are con- e cerned, when friends are on board a ship?'

'A ship's captain.'

'And what about a moral person? In which walk of life or for what activity is he best able to benefit his friends and harm his enemies?'

'In fighting against enemies and in support of friends, I'd say.'

'All right. Now, my dear Polemarchus, a doctor is no use unless people are ill.'

'True.'

'And a captain is no use unless people are on a sea voyage.'

'Quite so.'

'Is a moral person, then, no use to anyone who is not at war?'

'No, I don't agree with that.'

'So morality is useful during times of peace too?'

333a 'Yes.'

'And so is farming. Yes?'

'Yes.'

'To provide us with crops?'

'Yes.'

'And shoemaking too?'

'Yes.'

'To provide us with shoes, I imagine you'd say?'

'Exactly.'

'All right, then. What can we use morality for? What does it provide us with? What would you say morality is good for in times of peace?'

'For business contracts, Socrates.'

'By business contracts do you mean when people enter into association with one another, or what?'

'Yes, when people enter into association with one another.'

'So when there's a move to make in backgam-

b mon, is it a moral person, or an expert backgammon player, who is a good and useful associate?'

'An expert backgammon player.'

'And when it's a question of the positioning of bricks and stones, is a moral person a better and more useful associate than a builder?'

'Not at all.'

'Well, what kind of association is it that people enter into for which a moral person is a better associate than a builder or a musician? I mean, analogously to how a musician is better than a moral person when it comes to an association over melodies.'

'An association involving money, in my opinion.'

'Yes, Polemarchus, but what about when money is put to use? When you jointly need to buy or sell a horse, for instance, then I suppose an expert in

c horses is a better associate, don't you think?'

'I suppose so.'

'And if you need to buy or sell a ship, then it's a shipwright or a sailor?'

'You could be right.'

'For what joint usage of money, then, is a moral person more useful than anyone else?'

'When we want to put it on deposit and have it in safe keeping, Socrates.'

'You mean when you don't want to put it to use, but just to have it in store?'

'Yes.'

'So morality is useful in relation to money at pre- d
cisely the time when money is not in use?'

'So it seems.'

'Furthermore, when a pruning-knife needs to be kept safe, then morality is useful (whether you're on your own or have an associate); but when it needs using, then it's viticulture that is useful. Yes?'

'I suppose so.'

'And would you also say that when a shield or a lyre needs to be protected and kept unused, then morality is useful, whereas when they need using, then military or musical expertise is useful?'

'Of course.'

'In every instance, then, morality is useless when anything is being used, and useful when anything is not being used.'

'So it seems.'

'Morality can't be a very important thing, then, e
can it, my friend, if it is useful for useless objects. And there's another point for us to consider. In a fight—a boxing-match or any other kind of fight—isn't it the person who is expert at hitting who is also expert at protecting himself?'

'Yes.'

'And isn't it the person who knows how to give protection from a disease who is also the expert at secretly inducing the disease?'

'I would say so.'

'Moreover, it's one and the same person who's 334a
good at protecting an army and at stealing the enemy's plans and outwitting the rest of his projects, isn't it?'

'Yes,'

'So anything one is good at protecting, one is also good at stealing.'

'So it seems.'

'If a moral person is good at protecting money, therefore, he's also good at stealing it.'

'That's what the argument suggests, anyway,' he said.

'Morality has been exposed, then,' I said. 'A moral person is a kind of thief, apparently. You probably got this notion from Homer. He speaks warmly b
of Autolycus, Odysseus' grandfather on his mother's side, and also says that he surpassed everyone "at theft and perjury". So the view that morality is a kind

of stealing is yours, Homer's, and Simonides'—with the qualification that it must be done to benefit friends and harm enemies. Was this what you meant?'

'It most certainly was not,' he said, 'but I'm no longer sure what I meant. I do still think this, however—that morality lies in helping one's friends and harming one's enemies.'

'When you say "friends", do you mean those who appear to a person to be good, or those who genuinely are good (even if they don't appear to be)? And likewise for enemies.'

'It seems plausible to suggest', he said, 'that one treats as friends those one regards as good, and as enemies those one regards as bad.'

'Isn't it common to make mistakes about this, and think that people are good when they aren't, and vice versa?'

'Yes.'

'When this happens, then, doesn't one regard good people as enemies and bad people as friends?'

'Yes.'

'But all the same, in these circumstances it's right for one to help bad people and harm good people, is it?'

'Apparently.'

'But good people are moral and not the kind to do wrong.'

'True.'

'On your line of reasoning, then, it's right to harm people who do no wrong.'

'Not at all, Socrates,' he said. 'My reasoning must be flawed, I suppose.'

'It's right to harm wrongdoers, then,' I said, 'and to help those who do right?'

'That sounds better.'

'But since there are lots of people who are completely mistaken, Polemarchus, then it will commonly turn out to be right for people to harm friends (whom they regard as bad) and to help enemies (whom they regard as good). And in affirming this, we'll be contradicting what we said Simonides meant.'

'Yes,' he said, 'that is a consequence of what we're saying. Let's change tack, however: we're probably making a wrong assumption about friends and enemies.'

'What assumption, Polemarchus?'

'That someone who appears good is a friend.'

'What shall we change that to instead?' I asked.

'That someone who doesn't just appear good, but actually *is* good, is a friend; and that someone who seems good, but actually isn't, is an apparent friend, not a genuine one. And the same goes for enemies.'

'So on this line of reasoning, it's a good man who is a friend, and a bad man who is an enemy.'

'Yes.'

'You're telling us, then, that our original description of morality, when we said that it was right to do good to a friend and harm to an enemy, was incomplete. Now you want us to add that it is right to do good to a friend, provided he is good, and to harm an enemy, provided he is bad. Is that right?'

'Yes,' he said, 'I think that's a good way to put it.'

'Can a moral person harm *anyone*?' I asked.

'Yes, he can,' he replied. 'He has to harm bad men, people who are his enemies.'

'When horses are harmed, do they improve or deteriorate?'

'Deteriorate.'

'In respect of a state of goodness for dogs or of a state of goodness for horses?'

'In respect of a state of goodness for horses.'

'So the same goes for dogs too: when they are harmed, they deteriorate in respect of what it is to be a good dog, not in respect of what it is to be a good horse. Is that right?'

'No doubt about it.'

'And where people are concerned, my friend, shouldn't we say that when they're harmed they deteriorate in respect of what it is to be a good human?'

'Yes.'

'And isn't a moral person a good human?'

'There's no doubt about that either.'

'It necessarily follows, Polemarchus, that people who are harmed become less moral.'

'So it seems.'

'Now, can musicians use music to make people unmusical?'

'Impossible.'

'Can skilled horsemen use their skill to make people bad horsemen?'

'No.'

'So can moral people use morality to make people immoral? Or in general can good people use their goodness to make people bad?'

'No, that's impossible.'

'I imagine this is because cooling things down, for instance, is not the function of warmth but of its opposite.'

'Yes.'

'And moistening things is not the function of dryness but of its opposite.'

'Yes.'

'So harming people is not the function of a good person, but of his opposite.'

'I suppose so.'

'And is a moral person a good person?'

'Of course.'

'It is not the job of a moral person, then, Polemarchus, to harm a friend or anyone else; it is the job of his opposite, an immoral person.'

'I think you're absolutely correct, Socrates,' he said.

'So the claim that it's right and moral to give back to people what they are owed—if this is taken to mean that a moral person owes harm to his enemies and help to his friends—turns out to be a claim no clever person would make. I mean, it's false: we've found that it is never right to harm anyone.'

'I agree,' he said.

'You and I will join forces, then,' I said, 'to combat anyone who asserts that it is the view of Simonides or Bias or Pittacus or anyone else who is so sublimely clever.'

'Yes,' he said, 'I'm ready to play my part in the battle.'

'Do you know whose view I think it is,' I said, 'that it's right to help one's friends and harm one's enemies?'

'Whose?' he asked.

'I think it was Periander or Perdiccas or Xerxes or Ismenias of Thebes or someone else like that— a rich man who fancied himself to be vastly powerful.'

'You're quite right,' he said.

'All right,' I said. 'Now that we've found that being moral and doing right don't consist in this, can we come up with an alternative definition?'

Thrasymachus now bursts into the picture. Plato's portrait of Thrasymachus is patently unfavourable, but his position is at least forcefully argued and defended. Socrates first shows that his position— that morality is a convention to enable the stronger party to get the weaker party to act to the stronger party's advantage—cannot be universally true. Thrasymachus intends his view to be a cynical comment on the dog-eat-dog nature of the real world, but is now forced to admit that his views only really apply to ideal, infallible rulers. With a weak inference based on the art of medicine, Socrates concludes that no arts, including morality, are self-serving, but that they all look out for their subjects' interests.

Now, Thrasymachus had often made as if to interrupt us in mid-sentence and pounce on the argument, but he'd always been restrained by his neighbours, who had wanted to hear the discussion out. But when we did come to a break, and I'd asked this question, he could no longer remain silent: like a wild animal, he crouched and hurled himself at us as if to tear us apart.

Polemarchus and I were terrified and panic-stricken, but Thrasymachus bellowed out for all to hear, 'What a lot of drivel, Socrates! Why are you deferentially bowing and scraping to each other like simpletons? If you really want to know what morality is, then don't just ask questions and look for applause by refuting any and every answer you get, because you've realized that it's easier to ask questions than it is to answer them. No, state an opinion yourself: say what you think morality is. And make sure you state your view clearly and precisely, without saying that it is duty or benefit or profit or gain or advantage; I won't let you get away with any rubbish like that.'

I was scared stiff at his words, and I looked at him in fear. I think that if I hadn't seen him before he saw me, I'd have been unable to speak. But in fact I had got in the first look, when he originally began to get furious at the discussion, and so I was able to respond to him. 'Thrasymachus,' I said, trembling with fear, 'please don't be cross with us. If Polemarchus and I are going wrong anywhere in the course of investigating the ideas, I assure you that we don't mean to. You can imagine that, if we were looking for money, we wouldn't under any circumstances choose to defer to each other in the course of the search and ruin our chances of finding it. It is morality we are looking for, however, and this is more valuable than pots of money; so you shouldn't think that we'd be so stupid as to give in to each other and not do our level best to discover it. Believe me, Thrasymachus, we're doing all we can. If we lack competence—which I suppose is the case—then pity is a far more reasonable feeling for you experts to have for us than impatience.'

337a

He erupted into highly sarcastic laughter at my words and said, 'God, there goes Socrates again, pretending to be an ignoramus! I knew this would happen; I even told the others here some time ago that you wouldn't be prepared to express opinions, and would feign ignorance and do anything rather than answer a question put to you.'

'That's because you're clever, Thrasymachus,' I said. 'You were well aware of the fact that if you were to ask someone what twelve is, and were to add as a rider to the question, "And just make sure you

b avoid saying that twelve is two times six, or three times four, or six times two, or four times three. I won't let you get away with any nonsense like that"— well, I'm sure it was obvious to you that no one would answer a question phrased like that. But suppose this person said, "What do you mean, Thrasymachus? You don't want me to give any of the answers you've mentioned? But what if twelve really is one of those things, Thrasymachus? Shall I still avoid that answer—that is, not tell the truth? Or what would you

c have me do?" How would you respond to this?'

'Well,' he said, 'it's not as if the two cases were similar.'

'Why not?' I replied. 'Anyway, even if they aren't, and it's only that the person you've asked thinks they are, do you think that makes any difference? Won't he still state his opinion, whether or not we rule it out?'

'That's what you're going to do as well, is it?' he asked. 'Respond with one of the answers I ruled out?'

'I wouldn't be surprised if I decided to do that, once I'd looked into the matter,' I said.

d 'What if I were to demonstrate that there's another answer you can give about morality,' he asked,

'which isn't any of those answers and is better than any of them? What penalty would you expect?'

'The penalty which is appropriate for ignorance, of course,' I said, 'which is learning from an expert. That's the penalty I expect.'

'Don't be naïve,' he said. 'You can't just learn: you must pay for it too.'

'If I ever have the money, I will,' I said.

'He has it,' said Glaucon. 'We'll all help Socrates out financially, so as far as the money is concerned, Thrasymachus, go ahead and speak.'

'Oh yes, sure!' he said. 'So that Socrates can get e his way and not make any claims himself, while he attacks and criticizes someone else's claims.'

'That's because I have no choice, Thrasymachus,' I explained. 'How can anyone express a view when he's not only ignorant, but also admits his ignorance? Moreover, when he's been forbidden to mention any opinion he might happen to hold by a man of considerable calibre? No, it's you who ought to speak, really, since you do claim to have knowledge and to be able 338a to express it. So please do what I'm asking: if you state your view, you'll be doing me a favour, and also generously teaching Glaucon here and all the others too.'

My words prompted Glaucon and the others to urge him to do what I was asking, and although it was clear that Thrasymachus wanted to be heard (since he thought he had an impressive position to state, which would win him acclaim), yet he continued to dissemble and to argue that it should be me who stated my position. Eventually, however, he gave in, and then added, 'Now you can see what b Socrates is good at—he refuses to do any teaching himself, but he goes around learning from other people and doesn't even give them thanks in return.'

'You're quite right to say that I learn from other people, Thrasymachus,' I said, 'but quite wrong to say that I don't repay them with gratitude. I pay what I can—and compliments are all I can give, since I don't have money. If I think someone has a good idea, I'm quick to applaud it—as you'll find out very soon when you tell us your opinion, since I'm sure it will be a good one.'

'All right, then, listen to this,' he said. 'My claim is that morality is nothing other than the advantage c of the stronger party . . . Well, why aren't you applauding? No, you won't let yourself do that.'

'First I need to understand your meaning,' I told him. 'I don't yet. You say that right is the advantage of the stronger party, but what on earth do you mean by this, Thrasymachus? Surely you're not claiming, in effect, that if Poulydamas the pancratiast is stronger than us and it's to his advantage, for the sake of his physique, to eat beef, then this food is advantageous, and therefore right, for us too, who are weaker than him?'

'Foul tactics, Socrates,' he said, 'to interpret what I say in the way which allows you unscrupulously to distort it most.'

'No, you've got me wrong, Thrasymachus,' I said, 'I just want you to explain yourself better.'

'Don't you know, then,' he said, 'that some countries are dictatorships, some are democracies, and some are aristocracies?'

'Of course I do.'

'And that what has power in any given country is the government?'

'Yes.'

'Now, each government passes laws with a view to its own advantage: a democracy makes democratic laws, a dictatorship makes dictatorial laws, and so on and so forth. In so doing, each government makes it clear that what is right and moral for its subjects is what is to its own advantage; and each government punishes anyone who deviates from what is advantageous to itself as if he were a criminal and a wrongdoer. So, Socrates, that is what I claim morality is: it is the same in every country, and it is what is to the advantage of the current government. Now, of course, it's the current government which has power, and the consequence of this, as anyone who thinks about the matter correctly can work out, is that morality is everywhere the same—the advantage of the stronger party.'

'Now I see what you mean,' I said. 'And I'll try to see whether or not your claim is true. Your position too, Thrasymachus, is that morality is advantage—despite the fact that you ruled this answer out for me—except that you immediately add "of the stronger party".'

'Hardly a trivial addition,' he said.

'Whether or not it is important isn't yet clear. What *is* clear is that we must try to find out whether your claim is true. The point is that I agree that morality is some kind of advantage, but you are qualifying this and claiming that it is the advantage of the stronger party; since I haven't made up my mind about this qualified version, we must look into the matter.'

'Go ahead,' he said.

'All right,' I said. 'Here's a question for you: you're also claiming, I assume, that obedience to the government is right?'

'Yes, I am.'

'And is the government in every country infallible, or are they also capable of error?'

'They are certainly capable of error,' he said.

'So when they turn to legislation, they sometimes get it right, and sometimes wrong?'

'Yes, I suppose so.'

'When they get it right, the laws they make will be to their advantage, but when they get it wrong, the laws will be to their disadvantage. Is that what you're saying?'

'Yes.'

'And you're also saying that their subjects must act in accordance with any law that is passed, and that this constitutes doing right?'

'Of course.'

'Then it follows from your line of argument that it is no more right to act to the advantage of the stronger party than it is to do the opposite, to act to their disadvantage.'

'What are you saying?' he asked.

'Exactly the same as you, I think; but let's have a closer look. We're agreed that sometimes, when a government orders its subjects to do things, it is utterly mistaken about its own best interest, but that it's right for the subjects to act in accordance with any order issued by the government. Isn't that what we agreed?'

'Yes, I suppose so.'

'Then you must also suppose', I continued, 'that you have agreed that it is right to do things which are not to the advantage of the government and the stronger party. When the rulers mistakenly issue orders which are bad for themselves, and since you claim that it is right for people to act in conformity with all the government's orders, then, my dear Thrasymachus, doesn't it necessarily follow that it is right to do the opposite of what your position affirmed? I mean, the weaker party is being ordered to do what is disadvantageous to the stronger party, obviously.'

340a 'Yes, Socrates,' said Polemarchus, 'that's perfectly clear.'

'Of course,' Cleitophon interrupted, 'if you're going to act as a witness for Socrates.'

'There's no need for a witness,' Polemarchus replied. 'Thrasymachus himself admits that rulers sometimes issue orders which are bad for themselves, and that it's right for people to carry out these orders.'

'That's because Thrasymachus maintained that it was right to carry out the rulers' instructions, Polemarchus.'

b 'Yes, Cleitophon, and he also maintained that right is the advantage of the stronger party. And once he'd affirmed both of these propositions, he also agreed that sometimes the stronger party tells the weaker party, which is subject to it, to do things which are disadvantageous to it. And from these premisses it follows that morality is no more what is advantageous to the stronger party than it is what is disadvantageous to the stronger party.'

'But,' Cleitophon said, 'what he meant by the advantage of the stronger party was what the stronger party *thinks* is to its advantage. This is what he was maintaining the weaker party ought to do, and this is what he was maintaining morality is.'

'But that's not what he said,' Polemarchus remarked.

c 'Never mind, Polemarchus,' I said. 'If this is what Thrasymachus is saying now, then let's accept it as his view. But do please tell me, Thrasymachus: *did* you mean to define morality as what appears to the stronger party to be to its advantage, whether or not it really is to its advantage? Is that how we are to understand your meaning?'

'Absolutely not!' he protested. 'Do you suppose I would describe someone who makes mistakes as the stronger party when he is making a mistake?'

'Yes,' I replied, 'I did think you were saying this, when you agreed that rulers are not infallible, but also make mistakes.'

d 'That's because you're a bully in discussions, Socrates,' he said. 'I mean, to take the first example that comes to mind, do you describe someone who makes mistakes about his patients as a doctor in virtue of the fact that he makes mistakes? Or do you describe someone who makes mistakes in his calculations as a mathematician, at precisely the time when he is making a mistake, and in virtue of the mistake that he is making? It's true that the expression is in our language: we say that a doctor or a mathematician or a teacher makes mistakes; but in fact, in my opinion, to the extent that each of them e is what we call him, he never makes mistakes. And the consequence of this is that, strictly speaking— and you're the stickler for verbal precision—no professional makes mistakes: a mistake is due to a failure of knowledge, and for as long as that lasts he is not a professional. Professional, expert, ruler—no ruler makes a mistake at precisely the time when he is ruling, despite the universal usage of expressions like "The doctor made a mistake" or "The ruler made a mistake". So, when I stated my position to you recently, you should appreciate that I too was speaking like that; but the most precise formulation is in fact that a ruler, to the extent that he is a ruler, does 341a not make mistakes; and in not making mistakes he passes laws which are in his best interest; and any subject of his should act in conformity with these laws. Consequently, as I said in the first place, my position is that morality is acting to the advantage of the stronger party.'

'Well, Thrasymachus,' I said, 'so you think I'm a bully, do you?'

'Yes, I do,' he said.

'And that's because you think my questions were premeditated attempts to wrong you?'

'I'm certain of it,' he said. 'And you won't gain any advantage from it, firstly because I'm aware of b your unscrupulous tactics, and secondly because as long as I am aware of them, you won't be able to use the argument to batter me down.'

'My dear Thrasymachus,' I protested, 'the idea would never even occur to me! But we must make sure that this situation doesn't arise again, so please would you make something perfectly clear? Is it, according to you, the ruler and the stronger person in the loose sense, or in what you were just calling the precise sense, whose interest, since he is the stronger party, it is right for the weaker party to act in?'

'I'm talking about the ruler in the most precise sense possible,' he replied. 'You can do anything you like, as far as I'm concerned, so try your unscrupulous and bullying tactics on that, if you can! But you don't stand a chance.'

'Do you think I'm crazy enough to try to shave a lion and bully Thrasymachus?' I asked.

'Well, you tried just now,' he said, 'even though you're a nonentity at that too.'

'That's enough of that sort of remark,' I said. 'But let's take this doctor you were talking about a short while ago—the one who's a doctor in the strict sense of the term. Is he a businessman, or someone who attends to sick people? Think about the genuine doctor, please.'

'He attends to sick people,' he replied.

'What about a ship's captain? Is the true captain in charge of sailors or a sailor?'

'In charge of sailors.'

'In other words, we shouldn't take any account of the fact that he is on board a ship and describe him as a sailor. I mean, it isn't because he's on a ship that he's called a captain, but because of his expertise and because he has authority over the sailors.'

'True,' he said.

'Now, does each of the various parties in these situations have a particular advantage to gain?'

'Yes.'

'And isn't it the case,' I went on, 'that the *raison d'être* of a branch of expertise is to consider the welfare and interest of each party and then procure it?'

'Yes, that is what expertise is for,' he answered.

'Is there anything which is in the interest of any branch of expertise except being as perfect as possible?'

'I don't understand the question.'

'For instance,' I said, 'suppose you were to ask me whether it's enough for the body just to be the body, or whether it needs anything else. I'd reply, "There's no doubt at all that it needs something else. That's why the art of medicine has been invented, because the body is flawed and it isn't enough for it to be like that. The branch of expertise has been developed precisely for the purpose of procuring the body's welfare." Would this reply of mine be correct, do you think, or not?' I asked.

'Yes, it would,' he said.

'Well now, is medicine itself flawed? Are all branches of expertise imperfect? For instance, eyes need sight and ears need hearing, and that's why they need a branch of expertise to consider their welfare in precisely these respects and to procure it. Is expertise itself somehow inherently flawed as well, so that each branch of expertise needs a further branch to consider its welfare, and this supervisory branch needs yet another one, and so on *ad infinitum*? Or does every art consider its own interest and welfare? Or is the whole question of it, or another art, being needed to consider its welfare in view of its flaws irrelevant, in the sense that no branch of expertise is flawed or faulty in the slightest, and it's inappropriate for any branch of expertise to investigate the welfare of anything other than its own area of expertise? In other words, any branch of expertise is flawless and perfect, provided it's a genuine branch of expertise—that is, as long as it wholly is what it is, nothing more and nothing less. Please consider this issue with the same strict use of language we were using before, and tell me: am I right or not?'

'I think you're right,' he said.

'It follows, then,' I said, 'that medicine does not consider the welfare of medicine, but the welfare of the body.'

'Yes,' he said.

'And horsemanship considers the welfare of horses, not of horsemanship. In short, no branch of expertise considers its own advantage, since it isn't deficient in any respect: it considers the welfare of its area of expertise.'

'So it seems,' he said.

'But surely, Thrasymachus, the branches of expertise have authority and power over their particular areas of expertise.'

He gave his assent to this with extreme reluctance.

'So no branch of knowledge considers or enjoins the advantage of the stronger party, but the advantage of the weaker party, which is subject to it.'

Eventually, he agreed to this too, although he tried to argue against it. Once he'd agreed, however, I said, 'Surely, then, no doctor, in his capacity as doctor, considers or enjoins what is advantageous to the doctor, but what is advantageous to the patient? I mean, we've agreed that a doctor, in the strict sense of the term, is in charge of bodies, not a businessman. Isn't that what we agreed?'

He concurred.

'And a ship's captain too is, strictly speaking, in charge of sailors, not a sailor?'

He agreed.

'So since captains are like this and wield authority in this way, they won't consider and enjoin the interest of the captain, but what is advantageous to the sailor, the subject.'

He reluctantly agreed.

'Therefore, Thrasymachus,' I said, 'no one in any other kind of authority either, in his capacity as ruler, considers or enjoins his own advantage, but the advantage of his subject, the person for whom he practises his expertise. Everything he says and everything he does is said and done with this aim in mind and with regard to what is advantageous to and appropriate for this person.'

Socrates has tried to reduce Thrasymachus' position to the relatively trivial claims that rulers rule in their own interest, and that morality is obeying rulers. Thrasymachus therefore changes his formulation, but not his tack. The important thing about morality being to someone else's advantage, he says, is that it shows that morality is a bad thing, and weak, and unprofitable to its possessor. Socrates' inability (or possibly artificial refusal) to distinguish higher-order arts from lower-order ones results in the strange position that profit-making is a separate art, so that (again) no art—or at least no art other than profit-making—seeks the profit or advantage of the artisan.

Once we'd reached this point in the discussion, it was perfectly clear to everyone that the definition of morality had been turned upside down. Thrasymachus didn't respond to my last remarks, but instead said, 'Tell me, Socrates, do you have a nurse?'

'What?' I asked. 'Shouldn't you come up with some response rather than this question?'

'The point is,' he said, 'that she takes no notice of your runny nose and lets it dribble on when it needs wiping, when you can't even tell her the difference between sheep and shepherd.'

'I haven't the faintest idea what you're getting at,' I said.

'What I'm getting at is your notion that shepherds or cowherds consider what is good for their sheep or their cows, and fatten them up and look after them, with any aim in mind other than what is good for their masters and for themselves; and also at your supposition that the attitude which people with political authority—who are the real rulers—have towards their subjects differs in the slightest from how one might feel about sheep, and that what they consider day and night is anything other than their own advantage and how to gain it. You're so far off understanding right and wrong, and morality and immorality, that you don't even realize that morality and right are actually good for someone else—they are the advantage of the stronger party, the ruler—and bad for the underling at the receiving end of the orders. Nor do you realize that the opposite is true for immorality: the wrongdoer lords it over those moral simpletons—that's what they are, really—while his subjects do what is to his advantage, since he is stronger, and make him happy by doing his bidding, but don't further their own happiness in the slightest.

'You fool, Socrates, don't you see? In any and every situation, a moral person is worse off than an immoral one. Suppose, for instance, that they're doing some business together, which involves one of them entering into association with the other: by the time the association is dissolved, you'll never find the moral person up on the immoral one—he'll be worse off. Or again, in civic matters, if there's a tax on property, then a moral person pays more tax than an immoral one even when they're both equally well off; and if there's a hand-out, then the one gets nothing, while the other makes a lot. And when each of them holds political office, even if a moral person loses out financially in no other way, his personal affairs deteriorate through neglect, while his morality stops him making any profit from public funds, and moreover his family and friends fall out with him over his refusal to help them out in unfair ways; in all these respects, however, an immoral person's experience is the opposite.

'I'm talking about the person I described a short while ago, the one with the power to secure huge advantages for himself. This is the person you should consider, if you want to assess the extent to which immorality rather than morality is personally advantageous—and this is something you'll appreciate most easily if you look at immorality in its most perfect form and see how it enhances a wrongdoer's life beyond measure, but ruins the lives of his victims, who haven't the stomach for crime, to the same degree. It's dictatorship I mean, because whether it takes stealth or overt violence, a dictator steals what doesn't belong to him—consecrated and unconsecrated objects, private possessions, and public property—and does so not on a small scale, but comprehensively. Anyone who is caught committing the merest fraction of these crimes is not only punished, but thoroughly stigmatized as well: small-scale criminals who commit these kinds of crimes are called temple-robbers, kidnappers, burglars, thieves, and robbers. On the other hand, when someone appropriates the assets of the citizen body and then goes on to rob them of their very freedom and enslave them, then denigration gives way to congratulation, and it isn't only his fellow citizens who call him happy, but anyone else who hears about his consummate wrongdoing does so as well. The point is that immorality has a bad name because people are afraid of being at the receiving end of it, not of doing it.

'So you see, Socrates, immorality—if practised on a large enough scale—has more power, licence, and authority than morality. And as I said at the beginning, morality is really the advantage of the stronger party, while immorality is profitable and advantageous to oneself.'

After flooding our ears, like an attendant in the baths, with this torrential gush of words, Thrasymachus was thinking of leaving. No one there would let him go, however: they forced him to stay and justify what he'd been saying. I myself was particularly insistent. 'My dear Thrasymachus,' I said, 'you surely aren't thinking of leaving? You can't just pelt us with words, so to speak, and then leave before adequately demonstrating—or before finding out yourself—whether or not they're true. Or do you think that what you're attempting to define is a trivial matter, and not how anyone can live his life in the most rewarding manner?'

'Am I disagreeing with you?' Thrasymachus protested.

'You do give that impression,' I replied, 'unless it's just us you don't care about in the slightest, and you don't spare a thought for whether our ignorance of what you're claiming to know will make us live better or worse lives. No, Thrasymachus, please do your best to enlighten us too: it won't turn out badly for you to do so many of us a favour. I'll tell you my position: I'm not convinced. I do not think that immorality is more profitable than morality, not even if it is given free rein and never prevented from getting its own way; and even if I grant you your immoral person, Thrasymachus, with the power to do wrong either by wealth or by brute force, for my part I'm still not convinced that it is more profitable than morality. It's possible that someone else here feels the same, and that I'm not alone; so, Thrasymachus, you must come up with a good enough argument to convince us that rating morality higher than immorality is a mistake.'

'How do you expect me to do that?' he asked. 'If what I've just been saying doesn't convince you, what else can I do? Do you want me to spoonfeed the argument into your mind?'

'No, I certainly don't want you to do that,' I said. 'Above all, I'd like you to be consistent; or if you do change your mind, I'd like you to do so openly, without trying to deceive us. What's happening, you see, Thrasymachus—I mean, we haven't completed our investigation of what you were saying before— is that although you started by trying to define the true doctor, you didn't maintain the same level of precision when you subsequently turned to the true shepherd. You don't think that the reason a shepherd, in his capacity as shepherd, herds sheep is what is best for the sheep; you think he's like a dinner-guest when a meal is due, and is interested only in indulging himself—or alternatively that he behaves like a businessman rather than a shepherd, and is interested only in making money. But of course the sole concern of shepherding is to procure the best for what is in its charge, since its own best state has been sufficiently procured, as we know, as long as it wholly and entirely is shepherding. The same reasoning, *I* thought, was what compelled us not long ago to conclude that all authority (whether political or non-political), *qua* authority, considers what is best for nothing except its subjects, its wards. But do you think that people with political authority— the "real" rulers—exercise authority willingly?'

'I most definitely do not *think* so,' he replied. 'I'm absolutely certain of it!'

'But, Thrasymachus,' I said, 'don't you realize that no other form of authority is willingly exercised by its holder? People demand wages, on the grounds that the power isn't going to benefit *them*, but those who are in their charge. I mean, tell me this: when we want to distinguish one branch of expertise from another, don't we do so by distinguishing what it is capable of doing? And please, Thrasymachus, make sure that your reply expresses what you really believe; otherwise, we won't make any progress.'

346a

'Yes, that's how we distinguish it,' he said.

'And doesn't every branch of expertise have its own particular benefit to bestow as well, rather than one which it shares with other branches of expertise? For instance, medicine confers health, naval captaincy confers safety at sea, and so on.'

'Yes.'

b

'And isn't an income conferred by expertise at earning money? I mean, this is what it is capable of doing. You surely don't identify medicine and captaincy, do you? We must do as you suggested and make precise distinctions, so if a ship's captain recovers from illness because seafaring is good for him, does this lead you to call what he does medicine?'

'Of course not,' he said.

'Nor, I imagine, if someone recovers from illness while earning money, do you describe moneymaking skill as medical skill.'

'Of course not.'

'Well, suppose someone earns money while restoring health? Does this make you describe medicine as moneymaking?'

c

'No.'

'We've agreed that every branch of expertise has its own particular benefit to bestow, haven't we?'

'Yes, I grant you that,' he said.

'So if there's any benefit which the practitioners of every branch of expertise share, then obviously this benefit must come from something which is the same for all of them, and which they all equally make use of, over and above making use of their own particular expertise.'

'I suppose so,' he said.

'And it's our view that practitioners of branches of expertise benefit by earning money because they make use of the skill of moneymaking in addition to their own particular skill.'

He reluctantly agreed.

'It follows that no one benefits, in the sense of earning money, as a result of practising his own branch of expertise. Instead, given that our enquiry has to be conducted with precision, we should say that medicine creates health, while moneymaking creates an income, and that building creates a house, while moneymaking may accompany building and create an income, and so on for the other branches of expertise: each of them has its own job to do and benefits what is in its charge. But leaving wages aside, is there any benefit which a practitioner gains from his expertise?'

d

'Apparently not,' he said.

'And what about when he works for free? Does he in fact fail to confer any benefit at that time?'

e

'No, I think he does.'

'So, Thrasymachus, it's now clear that no branch of expertise or form of authority procures benefit for itself; as we were saying some time ago, it procures and enjoins benefit for its subject. It considers the advantage of its subject, the weaker party, not that of the stronger party. That, my dear Thrasymachus, is why I was proposing just now that no one willingly chooses authority and the task of righting other people's wrongs; they ask to be paid for it, because anyone who works properly with his expertise consistently fails to work for his own welfare, and also fails to legislate for his own welfare when he gives instructions as a professional. It isn't *his* welfare, but that of his subject, which is his concern. This presumably explains why it is necessary to pay people with money or prestige before they are prepared to hold authority, or to punish them if they refuse.'

347a

'What do you mean, Socrates?' asked Glaucon. 'I recognize your two modes of payment, but I don't know what punishment you are referring to and how it replaces payment.'

'Then you don't know what kind of payment is needed to induce truly excellent people to be prepared to rule,' I said. 'Don't you realize that to say that someone is interested in prestige or money is thought—and rightly thought—to be insulting?'

b

'Yes, I know that,' he said.

'Well,' I explained, 'that's why neither money nor prestige tempts good people to accept power. You see, if they overtly require money for being in charge, they'll be called hired hands, and if they covertly make money for themselves out of the possession of power, they'll be called thieves; and they don't want either of these alternatives. On the other hand, they won't do it for prestige either, since they aren't ambitious. So one has to pressurize them and threaten them with punishment, otherwise they'll never assume power; and this is probably the origin of the conventional view that it's shameful to *want* to take power on, rather than waiting until one has no choice. The ultimate punishment for being unwilling to assume authority oneself is to be governed by a worse person, and it is fear of this happening, I think, which prompts good men to assume power occasionally. On these occasions, they don't embark upon government with the expectation of gaining some advantage or benefit from it: their attitude is that they have no choice in the matter, in the sense that they haven't been able to find people better than themselves, or even their equals, to whom they might entrust the task. The chances are that were a community of good men to exist, the competition to avoid power would be just as fierce as the competition for power is under current circumstances. In such a community, it would be glaringly obvious that any genuine ruler really is incapable of considering his own welfare, rather than that of his subject, and the consequence would be that anyone with any sense would prefer receiving benefit to all the problems that go with conferring it. So anyway, I utterly disagree with Thrasymachus' assertion that morality is the advantage of the stronger party; but we've examined that topic enough for the time being.'

Thrasymachus has also claimed that immorality is more rewarding than morality. Socrates now attacks this claim, which is also the target of much of the rest of Republic. In an argument which is rather too clever for its own good, Socrates first argues that an immoral person's behaviour resembles that of bad, stupid people in other areas of expertise, rather than that of good, intelligent people. The argument exploits an ambiguity in superiority, which can mean 'doing better than' or 'having more than'; and, by means of the analogy between morality and skill, it assumes that an immoral person is a failure

where a moral person succeeds. In fact, however, moral and immoral people have different goals.

'Thrasymachus' current claim, however, is that a life of crime is better than a life of integrity, and this seems to me to be a far more important assertion. Do you have a preference, Glaucon?' I asked. 'Which view do you think is closer to the truth?'

'I think a moral life is more rewarding.'

'Did you hear Thrasymachus' recent long list of the advantages of an immoral life?' I asked.

'I did,' he answered, 'but I'm not convinced.'

'Shall we try to convince him, then, if we possibly can, of the falsehood of his claim?'

'Yes, of course, let's,' he said.

'Well,' I said, 'if we counter his claim by drawing up an alternative list of all the advantages of morality, and then he responds to that, and we respond to his response, we'll find ourselves in the position of having to add up advantages and measure the lengths of our respective lists, and before we know it we'll need jurors to adjudicate for us. On the other hand, if we conduct the investigation as we did just now, by trying to win each other's consent, then we'll be our own jurors *and* claimants.'

'Quite so,' he said.

'Which plan do you like, then?' I asked.

'The latter,' he said.

'All right, then, Thrasymachus,' I said, 'let's go back to the beginning. Could you please confirm for us that your claim is that perfect immorality is more profitable than perfect morality?'

'Yes, that's my claim,' he said, 'and I've explained why too.'

'And here's another question about them: do you think that one of them is a good state and the other is a bad one?'

'Of course.'

'That is, morality is a good state, and immorality a bad one?'

'Don't be so naïve, Socrates,' he said. 'Would I say that when I'm claiming that it's immorality which is profitable, not morality?'

'What *is* your position, then?'

'The opposite of what you said,' he replied.

'That morality is bad?'

'No, it's sheer simplicity.'

'So you're saying that immorality is duplicity, are you?'

'No, it's sound judgement,' he said.

'Do you really think that criminals are clever, good people, Thrasymachus?'

'Yes, if their criminality is able to manifest in a perfect form and they are capable of dominating countries and nations. I suppose you think I was talking about pickpockets. Actually,' he added, 'activities like that are rewarding too, if you can get away with them, but they're insignificant—unlike the ones I've just mentioned.'

'Yes, I see what you mean,' I said. 'But I'm surprised you count immorality as a form of goodness and cleverness, and morality as the opposite.'

'Nevertheless, that's exactly what I do.'

'You've come up with a rather intractable idea this time,' I commented. 'It's not easy to know how to respond to it. If you were proposing that immorality is profitable, but also conceding (as others do) that it's contemptible and bad, then our conversation could proceed against a background of convention. However, since you've made the enterprising suggestion that it's to be classified along with goodness and cleverness, you're obviously going to say that it is a fine, effective quality, and will attribute to it all the other properties which we tend to ascribe to morality.'

'Your prophecy couldn't be more accurate,' he said.

'All the same,' I said, 'I musn't be put off. I must continue with the discussion and carry on with the investigation, as long as I feel that you're speaking your mind. I mean, I get the impression, Thrasymachus, that now you aren't toying with us in the slightest, but are expressing your beliefs about the way things truly are.'

'What does it matter to you whether or not it's what I believe?' he said. 'Why don't you just tackle what I'm saying?'

'It doesn't matter to me at all,' I said. 'But here's another question I'd like you to try to answer, over and above what you've already said. Do you think a moral person would wish to set himself up as superior to another moral person?'

'Of course he wouldn't,' he replied. 'Otherwise he wouldn't be the civilized simpleton he is.'

'Well, would he want to set himself up as superior to moral behaviour?'

'Again, no,' he replied.

'Would he, or would he not, want and intend to set himself up as superior to an immoral person?'

'He would intend to,' he replied, 'but he wouldn't be able to.'

'I'm not asking whether he'd be able to do it,' I said. 'My question is: isn't it the case that a moral person does not intend or wish to set himself up as superior to another moral person, but only to an immoral person?'

'That's correct,' he said.

'What about an immoral person? Does he want to set himself up as superior to a moral person and to moral behaviour?'

'Of course,' he replied. 'He wants to gain the upper hand in everything.'

'So will an immoral person also try to set himself up as superior to another immoral person and to immoral behaviour? In short, will he struggle to gain the upper hand over everyone else in everything?'

'Yes.'

'Let's put it this way,' I said. 'A moral person doesn't set himself up as superior to people who are like him, but only to people who are unlike him; an immoral person, on the other hand, sets himself up as superior to people who are like him as well as to people who are unlike him.'

'You couldn't have put it better,' he said.

'Now, an immoral person is clever and good, and a moral person is neither clever nor good. Isn't that right?'

'Yes, you've put that well too,' he said.

'So is it the case that an immoral person also *resembles* a clever, good person, while a moral person does not?' I asked.

'Naturally,' he replied. 'Since that's the type of person he is, then of course he resembles others of the same type; and of course a moral person does not resemble them.'

'Fine. So each of them is of the same type as people he resembles?'

'That goes without saying,' he said.

'All right, Thrasymachus. Do you acknowledge that some people are musical and some aren't?'

'I do.'

'Which ones are clever and which aren't?'

'The musical ones are clever, of course, and the unmusical ones aren't.'

'And if someone is clever at something, isn't he also good at it, and bad at it if he isn't clever at it?'

'Yes.'

'And doesn't the same apply to medicine?'

'Yes.'

'Do you think, then, Thrasymachus, that when a musical person is tuning a lyre—tightening and slackening the strings—he would want to set himself up as superior to, and gain the upper hand over, another musical person?'

'No, I don't think so.'

'As superior to an unmusical person, then?'

'Inevitably,' he said.

350a 'And what about a doctor? Do you think that in dietary matters he would have the slightest desire to set himself up as superior to another doctor or to medical practice?'

'Of course not.'

'But as superior to non-medical people and practice?'

'Yes.'

'Consider any instance of knowledge or ignorance. Do you think that the actions or words of anyone who is knowledgeable in anything are motivated by a desire to surpass the actions or words of another person with the same knowledge? Don't you think that his actions and words would be identical to those of someone like him in the same circumstances?'

'Yes, I suppose that's bound to be the case,' he said.

'What about an ignoramus? Wouldn't he try to b set himself up as superior to knowledgeable people and to ignorant people equally?'

'I suppose so.'

'A knowledgeable person is clever, isn't he?'

'Yes.'

'And a clever person is good?'

'Yes.'

'So it's if someone is good and clever that he won't want to set himself up as superior to people who are like him, but only to people who are unlike him and have nothing in common with him.'

'So it seems.'

'If someone is bad and ignorant, however, he'll want to set himself up as superior to people who are like him as well as to people who are unlike him.'

'I suppose so.'

'Well, Thrasymachus,' I said, 'we found that it was an immoral person who sets himself up as superior to people who are like him as well as to people who are unlike him, didn't we? Isn't that what you said?'

'I did,' he replied.

'And a moral person won't set himself up as su- c perior to people who are like him, but only to people who are unlike him?'

'Yes.'

'It follows,' I said, 'that it is a moral person who resembles a clever, good person, and an immoral person who resembles a bad, ignorant person.'

'It looks that way.'

'And we agreed that each of them is of the same type as people he is like.'

'Yes, we did.'

'We've proved, then, that it is a moral person who is good and clever, whereas an immoral person is ignorant and bad.'

Socrates launches an attack on the effectiveness of immoral behaviour. Criminals fall out with one another, and therefore cannot act in concert; an immoral individual, such as Thrasymachus' dictator, falls out with himself. Thrasymachus meekly accepts this idea (which prefigures the psychology and the definition of morality which will occur later in Republic) because he accepts that immorality is essentially destructive of concord.

Now, although Thrasymachus did concede all these points, it wasn't as easy as I'm making it sound by describing it: he was hauled along with great re- d luctance, sweating profusely (since it was the hot season). And I also saw then something I'd never seen before—a red-faced Thrasymachus.

So anyway, we agreed that morality was a good state and was knowledge, and that immorality was a bad state and was ignorance. Next I said, 'All right. We may have settled that issue, but we also have before us the claim that immorality is effective. Do you remember, Thrasymachus?'

'Yes, I remember,' he replied. 'But I'm not satisfied with the statements you've just been making. I could address them, but I'm sure that if I did, you'd claim that I was holding forth like an orator. So either let me say what I want and for as long as I want, or go on with your questions, if you insist on doing that, and I'll go on saying "All right" and nodding and shaking my head as if I were listening to old women telling stories.'

'But you must never go against what you actually believe,' I said.

'Why shouldn't I?' he said. 'It makes you happy. You won't let me speak—do you want more from me than that?'

'No, not at all,' I replied. 'If you'll do what you said, that's fine, and I'll ask the questions.'

'Go ahead, then.'

'Well, here's the question I was getting at just now; I think it's the logical next one for our investigation. When morality is compared with immorality, what do we learn about morality? I mean, the suggestion was made that immorality is more powerful and more effective than morality; but the fact that we've now established that morality is a good state and is knowledge will make it easy to prove, I think, that it's also more effective than immorality, given that immorality is ignorance, as everyone knows by now. However, I don't want our investigation to be couched in such abstract terms, Thrasymachus, but rather as follows: would you agree that it is wrong for a community to undertake the domination of other communities, to deprive other communities of their freedom, and to keep a number of other communities subservient to itself?'

'Of course it is,' he said. 'And the better the community—the more perfectly immoral—the more it will act in exactly that way.'

'I appreciate that this is your position,' I said, 'but what I'm doing is exploring an aspect of it and asking whether a community which is stronger than another community will retain its power if it doesn't have morality, or whether it can do so only if it has morality.'

'If your recent assertion was correct,' he replied, 'that morality is knowledge, then it will take morality; but if I'm right, it takes immorality.'

'Thrasymachus,' I said, 'I'm really pleased that you're not just nodding and shaking your head, but are giving these excellent answers.'

'I'm doing it to make you happy,' he said.

'Thank you. You'll carry on making me happy if you answer this question of mine. Do you think that a community or an army or pirates or thieves or any other band which forms for the purpose of wrongdoing would be capable of doing anything if the members of the band wrong one another?'

'Of course not,' he said.

'But if they don't wrong one another, then they stand a better chance of success?'

'Yes.'

'Because immorality makes for mutual conflict, hatred, and antagonism, while moral behaviour makes for concord and friendship. Is that right?'

'I'll grant you that: I don't want to quarrel with you,' he said.

'Thank you, Thrasymachus. Now here's another question for you. If it's a function of immorality to generate hatred in its train, then whenever it arises among people—people from any walk of life—won't it make them hate one another and clash with one another and be incapable of doing things together?'

'Yes.'

'What about when it arises between two people? Won't it make them quarrel with and feel hatred and hostility towards not only each other but also moral people?'

'It will.'

'And, Thrasymachus, if immorality arises within a single person, it won't lose its power, surely, will it? Won't it retain it in an undiminished form?'

'I dare say it does,' he said.

'Evidently, then, its power is twofold. First, its occurrence makes things incapable of co-ordinated action, because of their internal conflict and dissension; second, as well as generating internal hostility, it generates hostility between them and anything which is completely different from them—that is, anything which is moral. And this is the case whether it arises in a community, a family, an army, or anything else. Isn't this right?'

'Yes.'

'And when it arises within a single individual, it will, I suppose, produce exactly the same results—

the results it is inherently bound to have. First, it will make him incapable of action, because of internal dissension and discord; second, as well as generating internal hostility, it will generate hostility between him and moral people. Right?'

'Yes.'

'Now, my friend, aren't the gods moral beings?'

'I dare say.'

b   'Therefore, an immoral person will be an enemy of the gods, Thrasymachus, and a moral person will be in their favour.'

'That's right, indulge yourself,' he said. 'And don't worry: I won't contradict what you're saying. I mean, I don't want to fall out with our friends here.'

'All right, then,' I went on. 'You'll treat me to all the food I still need to be satisfied, if you continue to answer my questions as you have been just now. I mean, we've found that moral people are more expert at getting things done, are better at it, and are more capable of it, and that immoral people are not capable of acting together at all. Moreover, if we ever claim that immoral people have been effective c   and have performed some concerted action together, then we are not telling the whole truth, because if they were absolutely immoral, they'd have been at one another's throats; there was obviously a degree of morality in them, which enabled them to refrain from wrongdoing one another as well as their victims and which allowed them to do what they did. Immorality had only half perverted them when they embarked upon their misdeeds, since people who are rotten through and through and are perfectly immoral are perfectly incapable of doing anything either. I d   now see that all this is correct, and that your original position was quite wrong.'

At last Socrates turns to a direct refutation of Thrasymachus' claim that immorality is rewarding. Everything has a particular job to do, and the good state of anything is what enables it to do its job well. Therefore, if morality is a good state, it enables one to do a good job at life—to live well, and be happy and fulfilled. The argument is, as with most of the arguments in this chapter, as weak or as strong as the pervasive analogy between morality and skill or being good at something.

'However, we must also look into the postponed issue of whether moral people have a better and a more fulfilled life than immoral people. I must say that at the moment it does look to me as though they do, on the basis of what we've been saying. All the same, we must look more closely at the matter, since what is at stake is far from insignificant: it is how one should live one's life.'

'Go ahead with your investigation, then,' he said.

'All right,' I said. 'Tell me, please: do you think that a horse has a function?'

'Yes.'   e

'And would you say that a horse's function, or anything else's function, is what can be done only with that thing, or can be done best only with that thing?'

'I don't understand,' he said.

'Look at it this way: can you see with anything except eyes?'

'Of course not.'

'And can you hear with anything except ears?'

'No.'

'Would it be right, then, for us to say that these are their functions?'

'Yes.'

'Now, you could cut a vine-twig with a short-   353a sword or a cobbler's knife or plenty of other things, couldn't you?'

'Of course.'

'But I should think that the best tool for the job would be a pruning-knife, the kind made especially for this purpose.'

'True.'

'Shall we say that this is its function, then?'

'Yes.'

'No doubt you can now see the point of the question I asked a moment ago, whether the function of anything is what it alone can do, or what it can do better than anything else.'

'Yes, I can,' he said. 'And I agree that this is anything's function.'   b

'All right,' I said. 'Now, don't you think that anything which has been endowed with a function also has a state of being good? Let's go back to the same examples. We're saying that eyes have a function?'

'Yes.'

'And do eyes also have a state of being good?'

'Yes, that too.'

'And do ears have a function?'

'Yes.'

'And a state of being good as well?'

'Yes, that too.'

'And does the same go for everything else?'

'Yes.'

c 'Now then, could eyes do a good job if they weren't in their own special good state, but were instead in a bad state?'

'Of course not,' he replied. 'I suppose you mean if they were blind instead of capable of seeing.'

'I mean whatever their good state is,' I said. 'You've answered a question I haven't yet asked. At the moment I'm asking only whether it is thanks to its own special state of goodness that anything with a job to do performs its function well, and thanks to badness that it does its job badly.'

'Well, that's true,' he said.

'And in the absence of their goodness, will ears do their job badly?'

'Yes.'

d 'And so on, on the same principle, for everything else?'

'I think so.'

'All right, now here's the next point to think about. Does the mind have a function—something you couldn't do with anything else? Consider, for instance, management, the exercise of authority, planning, and so on: would it be right for us to ascribe them to anything except the mind or to say that they were the particular province of anything except the mind?'

'No.'

'And what about one's way of life? Won't we say that this is a function of the mind?'

'Absolutely,' he said.

'And do we also think that the mind has a good state?'

'Yes.'

e 'Will the mind, then, Thrasymachus, ever perform its functions well in the absence of its own special goodness? Or is that impossible?'

'Yes, it's impossible.'

'Therefore, management and authority will inevitably be handled badly by a bad mind, whereas a good mind will do all these things well.'

'Inevitably.'

'Now, we agreed that morality is a good mental state, and that immorality is a bad state.'

'We did.'

'So a moral mind and a moral person will live a good life, and an immoral person will live a bad life.'

'Apparently,' he said, 'on your line of reasoning.'

'Now, anyone who lives a good life is happy and fulfilled, and anyone who doesn't is the opposite.'

'Of course.'

'Therefore, a moral person is happy, whereas an immoral person is unhappy.'

354a

'I dare say,' he said.

'Now, no one is well off because they're unhappy, but because they're happy.'

'Of course.'

'Therefore, my dear Thrasymachus, immorality is never more rewarding than morality.'

'There's your treat, Socrates,' he said, 'for this festival of Bendis.'

'And the meal was provided by you, Thrasymachus,' I said, 'since you were kind to me and stopped being cross. I've not had a proper meal, however—but that's my fault, not yours. I think b I've behaved like those gluttons who can't wait to taste every dish that's served up, before they've given themselves a proper chance to enjoy the previous one. I gave up before we discovered what we set out to discover—the nature of morality—and I embarked instead on an investigation into whether it was a bad state and ignorance, or whether it was knowledge and a good state; then later, when the idea cropped up that immorality was more profitable than morality, I couldn't resist turning to that next. Consequently, the effect of our discussion on me has been ignorance. I mean, if I don't know what morality actually is, it's going to be difficult for me to know whether or not it is good, and whether its possession makes someone unhappy or happy.'

CHAPTER 2
THE CHALLENGE TO SOCRATES

Glaucon and Adeimantus (Plato's brothers) now become Socrates' interlocutors for the rest of the book. Socrates has claimed (352d–354a) that morality enables us to prosper; they demand a full justification of this claim. Instead of the more usual views that morality is (a) not good, but a lesser evil (Glaucon), and (b) valued only for its external rewards (Adeimantus), they challenge

Socrates to prove that morality is intrinsically good and rewarding, and that it contributes towards a moral person's happiness.

357a At this point, I thought I'd be exempt from further talking, but apparently that was only the preamble. You see, it's not in Glaucon's nature to cut and run from anything, and on this occasion he refused to accept Thrasymachus' capitulation, but said, 'Socrates, do you want us *really* to be convinced that in all cir-
b cumstances morality is better than immorality or merely to pretend to be?'

'If it were up to me,' I replied, 'I'd prefer your conviction to be genuine.'

'Well,' he remarked, 'your behaviour is at odds with your wishes, then. I mean, here's a question for you. Don't you describe as good something which is welcomed for its own sake, rather than because its consequences are desired? Enjoyment, for instance, and all those pleasures which are harmless and whose future consequences are only enjoyable?'

'Yes,' I agreed, ' "good" seems to me the right description for that situation.'

c 'And what about things which are welcome not just for their own sakes, but also for their consequences? Intelligence, sight, and health, for instance, are evidently welcomed for both reasons.'

'Yes,' I said.

'And isn't there, in your experience,' he asked, 'a third category of good things—the category in which we find exercise, medical treatment, and any moneymaking job like being a doctor? All these things are regarded as nuisances, but beneficial, and are not welcomed for their own sakes, but for their financial
d rewards and other consequences.'

'Yes,' I agreed, 'there is this third category as well. What of it.'

'To which category do you think morality belongs?' he asked.

358a 'In my opinion,' I replied, 'it belongs in the best category—the category which anyone who expects to be happy should welcome both for its own sake and for its consequences.'

'That's not the usual view,' he said, 'which consigns morality to the nuisance category of things which have to be done for the sake of financial reward and for the prospect of making a good impres-

sion, but which, taken in isolation, are so trying that one should avoid them.'

'I'm aware of this view,' I said, 'and it's the reason why Thrasymachus has been running morality down all this time, and praising immorality. But I'm slow on the uptake, apparently.'

'All right, then,' he said, 'listen to what I have to b say too, and see if you agree with me. The point is that Thrasymachus gave up too soon, in my opinion: you charmed him into docility as if he were a snake. The arguments that have been offered about both morality and immorality leave *me* unsatisfied, however, in the sense that I still want to hear a definition of them both, and to be told what the effect is of the occurrence of each of them in the mind—each of them in isolation, without taking into consideration financial reward or any other consequence they might have.

'So if it's all right with you, what I'll do is revive Thrasymachus' position. First, I'll explain the usual c view of the nature and origin of morality; second, I'll claim that it is only ever practised reluctantly, as something necessary, but not good; third, I'll claim that this behaviour is reasonable, because people are right to think that an immoral person's life is much better than a moral person's life.

'Now, I don't agree with any of this, Socrates, but I don't know what to think. My ears are ringing from listening to Thrasymachus and countless others, but I've never yet heard the kind of support for morality, as being preferable to immorality, that I'd like d to hear, which is a hymn to the virtues it possesses in and of itself. If I can get this from anyone, it'll be you, I think. That is why I'll speak at some length in praise of the immoral life; by doing so, I'll be showing you the kind of rejoinder I want you to develop when you criticize immorality and commend morality. What do you think of this plan?'

'I thoroughly approve,' I replied. 'I mean, I can't think of another topic which any thinking person would more gladly see cropping up again and again in his conversations.'

'That's wonderful,' he said. 'Well, I promised I'd e talk first about the nature and origin of morality, so here goes. The idea is that although it's a fact of nature that doing wrong is good and having wrong done to one is bad, nevertheless the disadvantages of having it done to one outweigh the benefits of doing it. Consequently, once people have experienced both committing wrong and being at the receiving end of it, they see that the disadvantages are unavoidable and the benefits are unattainable; so they decide that the most profitable course is for them to enter into a contract with one another, guaranteeing that no wrong will be committed or received. They then set about making laws and decrees, and from then on they use the terms "legal" and "right" to describe anything which is enjoined by their code. So that's the origin and nature of morality, on this view: it is a compromise between the ideal of doing wrong without having to pay for it, and the worst situation, which is having wrong done to one while lacking the means of exacting compensation. Since morality is a compromise, it is endorsed because, while it may not be good, it does gain value by preventing people from doing wrong. The point is that any real man with the ability to do wrong would never enter into a contract to avoid both wronging and being wronged: he wouldn't be so crazy. Anyway, Socrates, that is what this view has to say about the nature and origin of morality and so on.

'As for the fact that morality is only ever practised reluctantly, by people who lack the ability to do wrong—this would become particularly obvious if we performed the following thought-experiment. Suppose we grant both types of people—moral and immoral—the scope to do whatever they want, and we then keep an eye on them to see where their wishes lead them. We'll catch our moral person redhanded: his desire for superiority will point him in the same direction as the immoral person, towards a destination which every creature naturally regards as good and aims for, except that people are compelled by convention to deviate from this path and respect equality.

'They'd have the scope I'm talking about especially if they acquired the kind of power which, we hear, an ancestor of Gyges of Lydia once acquired. He was a shepherd in the service of the Lydian ruler of the time, when a heavy rainstorm occurred and an earthquake cracked open the land to a certain extent, and a chasm appeared in the region where he was pasturing his flocks. He was fascinated by the sight, and went down into the chasm and saw there, as the

story goes, among other artefacts, a bronze horse, which was hollow and had windows set in it; he stooped and looked in through the windows and saw a corpse inside, which seemed to be that of a giant. The corpse was naked, but had a golden ring on one finger; he took the ring off the finger and left. Now, the shepherds used to meet once a month to keep the king informed about his flocks, and our protagonist came to the meeting wearing the ring. He was sitting down among the others, and happened to twist the ring's bezel in the direction of his body, towards the inner part of his hand. When he did this, he became invisible to his neighbours, and to his astonishment they talked about him as if he'd left. While he was fiddling about with the ring again, he turned the bezel outwards, and became visible. He thought about this and experimented to see if it was the ring which had this power; in this way he eventually found that turning the bezel inwards made him invisible and turning it outwards made him visible. As soon as he realized this, he arranged to be one of the delegates to the king; once he was inside the palace, he seduced the king's wife and with her help assaulted and killed the king, and so took possession of the throne.

'Suppose there were two such rings, then—one worn by our moral person, the other by the immoral person. There is no one, on this view, who is ironwilled enough to maintain his morality and find the strength of purpose to keep his hands off what doesn't belong to him, when he is able to take whatever he wants from the market-stalls without fear of being discovered, to enter houses and sleep with whomever he chooses, to kill and to release from prison anyone he wants, and generally to act like a god among men. His behaviour would be identical to that of the other person: both of them would be heading in the same direction.

'Now this is substantial evidence, it would be claimed, that morality is never freely chosen. People do wrong whenever they think they can, so they act morally only if they're forced to, because they regard morality as something which isn't good for one personally. The point is that everyone thinks the rewards of immorality far outweigh those of morality—and they're right, according to the proponent of this view. The sight of someone with that kind of scope refusing all those opportunities for wrongdoing and never laying a finger on things that didn't belong to him would lead people to think that he was in an extremely bad way, and was a first-class fool as well—even though their fear of being wronged might make them attempt to mislead others by singing his praises to them in public.

'That's all I have to say on this. As for actually assessing the lives of the people we're talking about, we'll be able to do that correctly if we make the gap between a moral person and an immoral person as wide as possible. That's the only way to make a proper assessment. And we should set them apart from each other by leaving their respective immorality and morality absolutely intact, so that we make each of them a consummate professional. In other words, our immoral person must be a true expert. A top-notch ship's captain, for instance, or doctor, recognizes the limits of his branch of expertise and undertakes what is possible while ignoring what is impossible; moreover, if he makes a mistake, he has the competence to correct it. Equally, our immoral person must get away with any crimes he undertakes in the proper fashion, if he is to be outstandingly immoral; getting caught must be taken to be a sign of incompetence, since the acme of immorality is to give an impression of morality while actually being immoral. So we must attribute consummate immorality to our consummate criminal, and if we are to leave it intact, we should have him equipped with a colossal reputation for morality even though he is a colossal criminal. He should be capable of correcting any mistakes he makes. He must have the ability to argue plausibly, in case any of his crimes are ever found out, and to use force wherever necessary, by making use of his courage and strength and by drawing on his fund of friends and his financial resources.

'Now that we've come up with this sketch of an immoral person, we must conceive of a moral person to stand beside him—someone who is straightforward and principled, and who, as Aeschylus says, wants genuine goodness rather than merely an aura of goodness. So we must deprive him of any such aura, since if others think him moral, this reputation will gain him privileges and rewards, and it will become unclear whether it is morality or the rewards

and privileges which might be motivating him to be what he is. We should strip him of everything except morality, then, and our portrait should be of someone in the opposite situation to the one we imagined before. I mean, even though he does no wrong at all, he must have a colossal reputation for immorality, so that his morality can be tested by seeing whether or not he is impervious to a bad reputation and its consequences; he must unswervingly follow his path until he dies—a saint with a lifelong reputation as a sinner. When they can both go no further in morality and immorality respectively, we can decide which of them is the happier.'

'My dear Glaucon,' I said, 'I'm very impressed at how industriously you're ridding each of them of defects and getting them ready for assessment. It's as if you were working on statues.'

'I'm doing the best I can,' he replied. 'And now that we've established what the two of them are like, I'm sure we won't find it difficult to specify what sort of life is in store for either of them. That's what I must do, then—and if my words are rather coarse, Socrates, please remember that the argument is not mine, but stems from those who prefer immorality to morality.

'Here's what they'll say: for a moral person in the situation I've described, the future holds flogging, torture on the rack, imprisonment in chains, having his eyes burnt out, and every ordeal in the book, up to and including being impaled on a stake. Then at last he'll realize that one's goal should be not actual morality, but the appearance of morality. In fact, that phrase of Aeschylus' has far more relevance for an immoral person, in the sense that, as they will claim, it is really an immoral person who wants genuine immorality rather than merely an aura of immorality, because his occupation takes account of the way things are and his life is not concerned with appearances. He is the one who "reaps the harvest of wise plans which grow in his mind's deep furrow"—and what he plans is first to use his reputation for morality to gain control over his country, and then to marry a woman from any family he wants, to have his children marry whomever he wants, to deal and do business with whomever he wants, and, over and above all this, to secure his own benefit by ensuring that his lack of distaste for crime makes him a financial

profit. If he's challenged privately or publicly, he wins the day and comes off better than his enemies;
c because he gains the upper hand, he gets rich; he therefore does good to his friends and harm to his enemies, and the religious rites he performs and the offerings he makes to the gods are not just adequate but magnificent; his service to the gods and to the men he favours is far better than a moral person's; and consequently it is more appropriate for the gods to smile on him rather than on a moral person, and more likely that they will. And this, Socrates, is why both gods and men provide a better life for an immoral person than for a moral person, according to this view.'

d After Glaucon's speech, I was intending to make some reply to what he'd been saying, but his brother Adeimantus asked, 'Surely you don't consider that an adequate treatment of the issue, do you, Socrates?'

'Why shouldn't I?' I said.

'It's precisely the most important point which has been omitted,' he said.

'Well,' I said, 'as the saying goes, a man and his brother should stick together. So if Glaucon here has left anything out, you should back him up. As far as I'm concerned, however, even what he's already said is enough to floor me and make me a totally ineffective ally of morality.'

e 'Rubbish,' he said. 'But don't let that stop you listening to what I have to say as well. In order to clarify Glaucon's meaning, we also have to go into the arguments for the opposite of his point—the arguments in favour of morality and against immorality. As you know, fathers point out to their sons the importance of morality and impress it upon them (as every guardian impresses it upon his ward) by
363a singing the praises not of morality itself but of the good reputation it brings. The inducement they offer is that power, good marriage, and all the things Glaucon mentioned a moment ago come to someone who is thought to be moral as a result of this reputation: if a moral persons gets them, it is because he is well thought of.

'They have more to say about the consequences of reputation. They adduce being well thought of by the gods, and then they have benefits galore to talk of, all the ones the gods are said to award to just people. There are, for instance, the statements of noble

Hesiod and of Homer. Hesiod says that the gods make "oaks bear acorns on their outsides and bees
b in their centres" for moral people; and he says that "their wooly sheep are weighed down by their fleeces", and that they gain many other advantages. Homer makes very similar claims: "As of some righteous king," he says, "who pleases the gods by upholding justice, and the dark earth bears wheat and barley, the trees hang heavy with fruit, the sheep
c steadily give birth, and the sea-waters yield fish."

'Musaeus and his son claim that the gods give moral people even more exciting advantages. Once they've transported them, in their account, to Hades and got them reclining on couches for the party they've laid on for just people, they next have them spending eternity wearing chaplets on their heads and drinking, on the assumption that the best possi-
d ble reward for goodness is perpetual intoxication. Others have the gods' rewards for morality lasting even longer: they say that the legacy left behind by a person who is just and keeps his promises is that his children's children are better people.

'These, and others like them, are the glowing terms in which they speak of morality. As for unjust and immoral people, they bury them in Hades in a kind of mud and force them to carry water in sieves, and they make sure that while they remain alive they are thought badly of; and they claim that all the pun-
e ishments which Glaucon specified for people who, despite being moral, are thought to be immoral are destined for immoral people. They have no novel punishments to add to this list, however.

'Anyway, that's how morality is commended and immorality condemned. But there's also another point for you to take into consideration, Socrates. It's the sort of thing ordinary people say to one another about morality and immorality, but it occurs in the 364a poets as well. They all unanimously go on and on about how self-discipline and morality may be commendable, but are also difficult and troublesome, whereas self-indulgence and immorality are enjoyable and easily gained, and it's only in people's minds and in convention that they are contemptible. They also say that, on the whole, immorality is more rewarding than morality; and whereas they're perfectly ready to admire bad men, if they're affluent and powerful in other respects as well, and to award them political office and personal prestige, they have disrespect and look down on people who are in any way powerless or are poor, even while admitting their moral superiority to the others.

'The most astonishing thing of all, however, is what gets said about the gods and goodness—that the gods often assign misfortune and a terrible life to good people, and the opposite to the other type of person. Beggar-priests and soothsayers knock on the doors of wealthy households and try to persuade the owners that (as long as there's some enjoyable feasting involved) the gods have granted them the power to use rituals and spells to expiate any sin committed by a person or by any of his ancestors, and that if anyone has an enemy he'd like to hurt, then it'll cost hardly anything to injure him—and it makes no difference whether the target is a moral or an immoral person—by means of certain incantations and formulae, since they can persuade the gods, they say, to do their bidding.

'The poets are called on to support all these claims. Some people concede that vice involves nothing arduous, on the grounds that "There's no difficulty in choosing vice in abundance: the road is smooth and it's hardly any distance to where it lives. But the gods have put sweat in the way of goodness", and a long, rough, steep road. Others cite Homer in support of the idea that humans can influence the gods, pointing out that he too said, "Even the gods themselves can be moved by entreaty: men appeal to them by means of rites and softly spoken prayers, libations and sacrifices, and influence them, when a crime has been committed and a wrong has been done." They come up with a noisy mob of books written by Musaeus and Orpheus (who are descended from the Moon and the Muses, they say), which are source-books for their rituals; and they convince whole countries as well as individuals that there are in fact ways to be free and cleansed of sin. While we remain on earth, this involves rituals and enjoyable diversions, which also work for us after we have died and which they call initiations. These initiations, they say, free us from all the terrors of the other world, but ghastly things await anyone who didn't take part in the rituals.

'This, my dear Socrates,' he went on, 'is the kind of thing that gets said—and at this kind of length—

about how highly gods and men regard virtue and vice. Can we tell what the effect of being exposed to all this is on a young mind which is naturally gifted and is capable of working out, as a result of flitting (so to speak) from one idea to another and dipping into them all, what type of person he has to be and what road he has to take to have as good a life as possible? He would probably follow Pindar and ask himself, " 'Is it honesty or crooked deceit that enables me to scale the higher wall' and so live my life surrounded by secure defences? What I hear is people telling me that, unless I also gain a reputation for morality, my actually being moral will do me no good, but will be a source of private troubles and public punishments. On the other hand, an immoral person who has managed to get a reputation for morality is said to have a wonderful life. Therefore, since the experts tell me that 'Appearance overpowers reality' and is responsible for happiness, I must wholeheartedly devote myself to appearance. I must surround myself with an illusion of goodness. This must be my front, what people see of me, but behind me I must have on a leash that cunning, subtle fox of which Archilochus, the greatest of all experts, speaks. Someone might object, 'But it's not easy to cloak one's badness for ever.' That's because no important project is easy, we shall reply; nevertheless, everything we hear marks this as the road to take if we are to be happy. To help us with our disguise, we shall form clubs and pressure-groups, and we can acquire skill at political and forensic speaking from teachers of the art of persuasion. Consequently, by a combination of persuasion and brute force, we shall dominate others without being punished for it."

' "But you can't hide from the gods, or overpower them." "Well, suppose there are no gods, or suppose they aren't bothered in the slightest about human affairs: then why should we in our turn bother about hiding from them? On the other hand, if the gods do exist, and do care for us, then our only sources of knowledge and information about them are tradition and the poets who have described their lineage. And these are precisely the people who are telling us that the gods can be persuaded and influenced by 'rites and softly spoken prayers' and offerings. Their credibility in one respect stands or falls with their credibility in the other respect. So if we listen to them, our course is to do wrong and then make offerings to the gods from the proceeds of our crimes. The point is that if we behave morally, then the most that we'll avoid is being punished by the gods, but we'll also pass up the opportunity for making a profit from our immorality; if we are immoral, however, we'll not only get rich, we'll win the gods over with our entreaties and get off scot-free, for all the crimes we commit and wrong we do."

' "But we'll pay in Hades for the crimes we've committed here on earth—or if we don't ourselves, then our children's children will." He'll think about it and then reply, "No, my friend, we won't. Initiations are very effective and the gods whose domain is exoneration have a great deal of power: that is the message we are given by very important countries and by the offspring of the gods, who have become poets and the gods' interpreters, and who reveal that this is so."

'Is there any argument left, then, which might persuade us not to choose out-and-out immorality, but to prefer morality? I mean, if we combine immorality with a fraudulent, but specious, façade, then we can do as we please in this world and in the next, in the presence of both gods and men. This is what both ordinary people and outstanding people are telling us. So after all these arguments, Socrates, is there any strategy to enable someone with potential—whether it is due to mental attributes or wealth or physique or lineage—to be prepared to rate morality highly, rather than laugh when he hears it being praised?

'I tell you, if there's anyone who can not only refute the arguments I've been stating, but is also secure in his knowledge that morality is best, then what he feels for immoral people is not anger but a large measure of forgiveness. He knows that people abstain from wrong either because, by divine dispensation, they instinctively find it distasteful, or because of some realization they've come to, and that otherwise no one chooses to be moral, although people find fault with immorality when cowardice or old age or some other form of weakness prevents them from doing wrong. This is obviously the case: the first of these people to gain power is the first to behave immorally—and as immorally as he possibly can.

'One thing is responsible for all this, and it is the same thing which constituted the starting-point of this whole discussion. Both Glaucon and I, Socrates, are saying to you, "My friend, we can start with those original heroes whose writings are extant and end with our contemporaries, but we find that not a single one of you self-styled supporters of morality has ever found fault with immorality or commended morality except in terms of the reputation, status, and rewards which follow from them. What each of them does on its own, however, and what the effect is of its occurrence in someone's mind, where it is hidden from the eyes of both gods and men, has never been adequately explained either in poetry or in everyday conversation; nor has it ever been proven that the worst possible thing that can occur in the mind is immorality, and that morality is the best. If this is how all of you had approached the matter from the outset, and if you had started trying to convince us when we were young, then we wouldn't now be defending ourselves against one another's wrongdoing, but everyone would be his own best defender, since he'd be afraid that if he did wrong he'd be opening his doors to the worst of all possible residents."

'That, Socrates, is what Thrasymachus—though he's not the only one, of course—might say on the subject of morality and immorality, and he'd probably have even more to add. Now, *I* think he's crudely misrepresenting their functions, but the reason I've taken his argument as far as I can is, to be perfectly candid, because I want to hear you making the opposite claims. It's not enough just to demonstrate that morality is better than immorality. Why does one of them, in and of itself, make anyone who possesses it bad, while the other one, in and of itself, makes him good? And, as Glaucon suggested, don't bring reputation into it. You see, if you leave them with reputations which genuinely reflect their natures, and don't attribute to each of them reputations which fail to do justice to them, then we'll accuse you of praising a reputation for morality rather than morality itself, and of criticizing a reputation for immorality rather than immorality itself; and we'll claim that what you're recommending is being immoral and getting away with it, and that you actually agree with Thrasymachus that morality is good for someone else—that it is the advantage of the stronger party—while it is immorality that is to one's own advantage and profit, but is disadvantageous to the weaker party.

'So, since it is your expressed opinion that morality is one of those paramount good things which are worth having not just for their consequences, but also and especially for themselves (like sight, hearing, intelligence—health, of course—and any other good things which are not just thought to be worth while, but are inherently so), then this is the aspect of morality which you should pay tribute to. You should show how morality is worth while in and of itself for anyone who possesses it and how immorality harms him, and leave others to praise rewards and reputations. I mean, I can accept the fact that others praise morality and criticize immorality in these terms, by eulogizing or abusing their reputations and rewards, but I won't put up with that from you (unless you insist), because this and this alone is what you've spent your whole life investigating. So it's not enough just to demonstrate that morality is better than immorality: show us why one of them, in and of itself, makes anyone who possesses it good, whether or not it is hidden from the eyes of gods and men, while the other one, in and of itself, and whether or not it is hidden from the eyes of gods and men, makes him bad.'

CHAPTER 3
FUNDAMENTALS OF INNER POLITICS

In order to meet the challenge issued in the last chapter, Plato begins to imagine the constitution of a community which will correspond to human psychology and make it easier to understand morality. The first community consists of workers alone living a life of rude and primitive health, each with a single talent and therefore a single job, responding cooperatively to one another's selfish needs. In political terms, economics underpins society; in psychological terms, our desires or needs are fundamental.

Now, I've always admired Glaucon's and Adeimantus' temperaments, but I was particularly delighted with them on this occasion, once I'd heard what they had to say. 'Like father, like sons,' I remarked. 'The first line of the elegiac poem which Glaucon's lover composed when you distinguished yourselves at the battle of Megara wasn't wrong in addressing you as "sons of Ariston, godlike offspring of an eminent sire". I think this is quite right: "godlike" is certainly the word for your state, if you can speak like that in support of immorality, and yet remain unconvinced that it is better than morality. I *do* think that you really are unconvinced; my evidence is what I know of your characters from other occasions. If I'd had to judge from your words alone, I would have doubted it. But it's precisely because I don't doubt it that I'm in a quandary. On the one hand, I can't come to the assistance of morality, since I am incompetent—as is proven by the fact that although I thought the points I'd made to Thrasymachus had shown that morality was better than immorality, you weren't satisfied. On the other hand, I can't not come to morality's assistance, since I'm afraid that it might actually be sacrilegious to stand idly by while morality is being denigrated and not try to assist as long as one has breath in one's body and a voice to protest with. Anyway, the best thing is for me to offer it whatever help I can.'

Glaucon and the others begged me to do everything I could to help; they implored me not to abandon the discussion, but to make a thorough enquiry into the nature of both morality and immorality, and to search out the truth about their expediency. I told them what occurred to me: 'We're undertaking an investigation which, in my opinion, requires care and sharp eyesight. Now, we're not experts,' I pointed out, 'so I suggest we conduct the investigation as follows. Suppose we were rather short-sighted and had been told to read small writing from a long way off, and then one of us noticed the same letters written elsewhere in a larger size and on a larger surface: I'm sure we'd regard this as a godsend and would read them there before examining the smaller ones, to see if they were really identical.'

'Of course we would,' said Adeimantus. 'But how is this analogous to our investigation into morality, Socrates, in your view?'

'I'll tell you,' I replied. 'Wouldn't we say that morality can be a property of whole communities as well as of individuals?'

'Yes,' he said.

'And a community is larger than a single person?'

'Yes,' he said.

'It's not impossible, then, that morality might exist on a larger scale in the larger entity and be easier to discern. So, if you have no objection, why don't we start by trying to see what morality is like in communities? And then we can examine individuals too, to see if the larger entity is reflected in the features of the smaller entity.'

'I think that's an excellent idea,' he said.

'Well,' I said, 'the theoretical observation of a community in the process of formation would enable us to see its morality and immorality forming too, wouldn't it?'

'I should think so,' he said.

'And once the process is complete, we could expect to see more easily what we're looking for?'

'Yes, much more easily.'

'Are we agreed, then, on the necessity of trying to see this plan through? I'm asking because I think it'll take a lot of work. So are you sure?'

'Yes, we are,' said Adeimantus. 'Please do what you're proposing.'

'Well,' I said, 'a community starts to be formed, I suppose, when individual human beings find that they aren't self-sufficient, but that each of them has plenty of requirements which he can't fulfil on his own. Do you have an alternative suggestion as to why communities are founded?'

'No,' he said.

'So people become involved with various other people to fulfil various needs, and we have lots of needs, so we gather lots of people together and get them to live in a single district as our associates and assistants. And then we call this living together a community. Is that right?'

'Yes.'

'And people trade goods with one another, because they think they'll be better off if each gives or receives something in exchange, don't they?'

'Yes.'

'All right, then,' I said. 'Let's construct our theoretical community from scratch. Apparently, its cause is our neediness.'

'Of course.'

'And the most basic and most important of our needs is that we are provided with enough food for existence and for life.'

'Absolutely.'

'The second most important is our need for somewhere to live, and the third is our need for clothing and so on.'

'True.'

'All right,' I said. 'How will our community cope with all this provisioning? Mustn't one member of it be a farmer, another a builder, and another a weaver? Is that all the people we need to look after our bodily needs? Shall we add a shoemaker to it as well?'

'Yes.'

'And there we'd have our community. Reduced to its bare essentials, it would consist of four or five people.'

'So it seems.'

'Well now, should each of them make what he produces publicly available for everyone? For instance, although the farmer is only one person, should he supply all four people with food? Should he spend four times as long and work four times as hard on supplying food and share it out, or should he ignore everyone else and spend a quarter of his time producing only a quarter of this amount of food for himself, and divide the other three-quarters between getting a house and clothes and shoes for himself, and not have all the bother of associating with other people, but look after his own affairs on his own?'

Adeimantus said, 'It looks as though the first alternative is simpler, Socrates.'

'That's not surprising, of course,' I said. 'I mean, it occurred to me while you were speaking that, in the first place, different people are inherently suitable for different activities, since people are not particularly similar to one another, but have a wide variety of natures. Don't you agree?'

'I do.'

'And is success a more likely consequence of an individual working at several jobs or specializing in only one?'

'Of his specializing in only one,' he said.

'Now, here's another obvious point, I'm sure—that missing the critical opportunity has a deleterious effect.'

'Yes, obviously.'

'The reason being that the work isn't prepared to wait for the worker to make time for it. No, it's cruc cial for the worker to fall in with the work and not try to fit it into his spare time.'

'Yes, that's crucial.'

'So it follows that productivity is increased, the quality of the products is improved, and the process is simplified when an individual sets aside his other pursuits, does the one thing for which he is naturally suited, and does it at the opportune moment.'

'Absolutely.'

'We need more than four citizens, then, Adeimantus, to supply the needs we mentioned. I mean, if the farmer's going to have a good plough, he will appar-

d ently not be making it himself, and the same goes for his hoe and all the rest of his farming implements. Moreover, the builder won't be making his own tools either, and he too needs plenty of them; nor, by the same token, will the weaver and the shoemaker. True?'

'True.'

'So plenty of other craftsmen—joiners, metal-workers, and so on—will join our little settlement and swell its population.'

'Yes.'

'It still won't be very big, though, even when we've added shepherds and other herdsmen—who are also needed, otherwise the farmers won't have oxen to plough with, and there'll be no draught-

e animals for them and the builders to use for pulling things, and no leather or wool for the weavers and shoemakers.'

'No,' he said, 'but it won't be small either with all that lot.'

'Now, it's practically impossible to build the actual community in a place where it will have no need of imports,' I pointed out.

'Yes, that's too much to expect.'

'Then they'll need more people, to bring in what it needs from elsewhere.'

'Yes.'

'But if their man goes empty-handed, in the sense of taking nothing with him which satisfies the re-

371a quirements of the people from whom they're trying to get what they need, then he'll depart empty-handed, won't he?'

'I should say so.'

'Then their home production must not only be enough to satisfy their own requirements, but must also be of a type and a quantity which satisfies the requirements of the people they need.'

'Yes, it must.'

'So our community had better increase the number of its farmers and other craftsmen.'

'Yes.'

'And also the number of its workers, I suppose, who import and export all the different kinds of goods—which is to say, merchants. Don't you agree?'

'Yes.'

'We'll need merchants too, then.'

'Certainly.'

'And if they deal with overseas countries, then a great many other people will be needed—experts in all sea-related work.'   b

'Yes, we'll certainly need a lot of them.'

'Now, within the actual community, how will people trade their produce with one another? I mean, that was why we established an association and founded a community in the first place.'

'They'll trade by buying and selling, obviously,' he said.

'Then a consequence of this is that we'll have a market-place and coinage as a system of trading.'

'Yes.'

'So if a farmer or one of the other producers c brings some of his produce to the market-place, but doesn't arrive at the same time as the people who want to trade with him, won't he be sitting in the market-place neglecting his own work?'

'No,' he replied, 'because there are people who notice the situation and take it on themselves to supply this service; in properly organized communities, they tend to be those who are physically the weakest and who are therefore unsuited for any other kind of work. Their job is to stay there in the market-place and to give people who want to sell something money in exchange for their goods, and then to give d goods in exchange for money to people who want to buy something.'

'So this need', I said, 'gives rise to stallholders in our community. I mean, aren't people who stay put in a market-place and do the job of buying and selling called "stallholders", as distinct from those who travel from community to community, who are called "merchants"?'

'Yes, that's right.'

'I think there's another category of worker too, e consisting of people who don't really deserve to join

our community for their mental abilities, but who are physically strong enough to undertake hard labour. They sell the use of their strength, "pay" is the name of the reward they get for this, and that is why they're called "paid hands", I suppose, don't you?'

'Yes.'

'With paid hands as well, then, our community has reached its limit, I should think.'

'I agree.'

'Well, Adeimantus, our community has certainly grown. Is it now just right?'

'I suppose so.'

'Does it contain morality and immorality, then? If so, where and thanks to which of the people we've considered?'

372a 'I've no idea, Socrates,' he said, 'unless it has something to do with how these people treat one another.'

'You might be right,' I said. 'We must look into your idea: it deserves to be taken seriously. Let's start by considering how people who've been provided for like this will live. Surely they'll spend their time producing food, wine, clothes, and shoes, won't they? Once they've built their houses, they'll turn to production, which they'll invariably work at in the summer naked and with bare feet, and in the winter with adequate protective clothing and footwear.
b Their food will be barley-meal and wheat-meal, which will sometimes be cooked and sometimes pulped, and the resulting honest fare of barley-cakes and wheat-cakes will be served up on reeds or on clean leaves, as they and their children, wearing chaplets and singing hymns to the gods, recline on carpets of bryony and myrtle and eat their fill, while drinking wine. They'll enjoy having sex, except that
c concern about poverty or war will stop them procreating beyond their means.'

At this point Glaucon interrupted and said, 'This diet you're giving them dispenses with savouries, apparently.'

'You're right,' I said. 'I was forgetting that they'll also have savouries—salt, obviously, and olives and cheese—and they'll boil up the kinds of roots and vegetables which country stews are made of. We'll serve them with desserts too, I suppose, of figs, chick-peas, and beans; and they'll roast myrtle-berries and acorns in the fire as they sip their drinks. And so, it seems, their life will pass

in peace and good health, and at their death in old d age they will pass on a similar way of life to their offspring.'

'Socrates,' he remarked, 'isn't this exactly the fodder you'd lay on if you were devising a community for pigs?'

'What would you suggest, then, Glaucon?' I asked.

'Nothing abnormal,' he replied. 'I think they should recline on couches, if they're to be comfortable, and eat from tables, and have the kinds of e savouries and desserts which are in current usage.'

Realistically, there is more to human life than the first community can provide—more to the human psyche than mere needs. The community is expanded to include non-necessary needs, until it threatens the integrity of others with which it comes into contact, and is itself threatened in the same way. It therefore needs guardians, to protect its integrity. The job of protection requires passion and love of knowledge.

'All right,' I said. 'I see. We're not just investigating the origins of a community, apparently, but of an indulgent community. Well, that may not be wrong: if we extend our enquiry like that, we might perhaps see how morality and immorality take root in communities. Now, I think that the true community—the one in a healthy condition, as it were—is the one we've described; but if you want us to inspect an inflamed community as well, so be it. There's no reason not to. I mean, some people apparently won't be satisfied with the pro- 373a visions and the lifestyle we've described, but will have all sorts of furniture like couches and tables, and a wide selection of savouries, perfumes, incense, prostitutes, and pastries. Moreover, the essential requirements can no longer be restricted to the houses and clothing and shoes we originally mentioned; no, we have to invent painting and ornamentation, and get hold of gold and ivory and so on. Don't you agree?' b

'Yes,' he said.

'So we have to increase the size of our community once again. That healthy community will no longer do; it must become bloated and distended with occupations which leave the essential requirements of a community behind—for instance, with all kinds of hunters and imitators. Among the latter will be hordes of people concerned with shapes and colours, and further hordes concerned with music (poets and their dependants—rhapsodes, actors, dancers, producers), and manufacturers of all kinds of contraptions and all sorts of things, especially women's cosmetics. Furthermore, we'll need c a larger number of workers—don't you think?—such as children's attendants, nurses, nannies, hairdressers, barbers, and savoury-cooks and meat-cooks too. And that's not the end of it: we'll need pig-farmers as well— a job which didn't exist in our previous community, since there was no need of it, but which will be needed in the present one—and huge numbers of cows and sheep, if they are to be eaten, won't we?'

'Of course.'

d 'And with this lifestyle won't we be in far greater need of doctors than we were before?'

'Yes.'

'And, of course, although the inhabitants of our former community could live off the produce of the land, the land will be too small now, don't you think?'

'I agree.'

'So we'll have to take a chunk of our neighbours' land, if we're going to have enough for our herds and our crops, won't we? And suppose they too have stopped limiting themselves to necessities and have gone in for the uncontrolled acquisition of innumerable possessions: then they'll have to take a chunk of our land too, won't they?'

e 'That's more or less inevitable, Socrates,' he replied.

'And the next step will be war, Glaucon, don't you think?'

'I agree,' he said.

'Now, let's not commit ourselves yet to a view on whether the effects of war are good or bad,' I said. 'All we're saying at the moment is that we've now discovered the origin of war. It is caused by those factors whose occurrence is the major cause of a community's troubles, whether it's the community as a whole which is afflicted or any individual member of it.'

'Yes.'

'We need another sizeable increase in our com- 374a munity, then, Glaucon—an army-sized increase. We need an army to go out and defend all the community's property and all the people we were talking about a moment ago against invaders.'

'But can't the inhabitants do this themselves?' he asked.

'No,' I replied. 'At any rate, they can't if the proposition we all—including you—agreed to when we were forming our community was correct. The proposition was, if you remember, that it is impossible for one person to work properly at more than one area of expertise.'

'You're right.'

'Well,' I said, 'don't you think that warfare re- b quires expertise?'

'I certainly do,' he answered.

'So should we take more trouble over our shoe-makers than we do over our soldiers?'

'Not at all.'

'Well now, we prohibited a shoemaker from simultaneously undertaking farming or weaving or building, but had him concentrating exclusively on shoemaking, to ensure quality achievements in shoemaking; and we similarly allotted every single person just one job—the one for which he was naturally suited, and which he was to work at all his life, setting aside his other pursuits, so as not to miss the opportunities which are critical for quality achieve- c ment. Isn't it crucial, however, that the achievements of warfare are of a high standard? Or is soldiering so easy that someone can be expert at it while carrying on with his farming or shoemaking or whatever his profession might be, despite the fact that no one could even become a competent backgammon-player or dice-player if he took it up only in his spare time and didn't concentrate on it for years, starting when he was a young man? Does someone just have to pick up a shield (or whatever military implement d or instrument it may be) and he instantaneously becomes a competent fighter in a heavy infantry engagement (or in whatever form of armed conflict it may be)? This would be unique, since no other implement makes a person a craftsman or an athlete if he just holds it, and no other implement is the slightest good to anyone unless he's acquired the knowledge of how to use it and has devoted sufficient attention to it.'

'Yes,' he said, 'if tools could do that, they'd be highly prized.'

'Now,' I said, 'the amount of time allotted just to it, and also the degree of professionalism and training, should reflect the supreme importance of the guardians' work.'

'I certainly think so,' he said.

'And a natural talent for the job would help too, wouldn't it?'

'Of course.'

'Our job, then, if we're up to it, would seem to be to select which people and what types of person have a natural gift for protecting our community.'

'Yes, it is.'

'We've certainly taken on an awesome task, then,' I said. 'Still, we mustn't be intimidated; we must do the best we can.'

'I agree.'

'Well,' I went on, 'do you think there's any difference, as far as suitability for guarding is concerned, between the nature of the best type of dog and that of a well-born young man?'

'What are you getting at?'

'That both of them have to be acutely perceptive, quick on their feet (so as to chase after anything they do perceive) and strong as well, in the case they have to fight someone they've cornered.'

'Yes,' he said, 'they need all these qualities.'

'And a good fighter must be brave, of course.'

'That goes without saying.'

'Now, you'll never find courage without passion, in a horse or a dog or any other creature, will you? I mean, you must have noticed how indomitable and invincible passion is. It always takes passion in a mind to make it capable of facing any situation without fear and without yielding, doesn't it?'

'Yes.'

'It's obvious what physical attributes a guardian must have, then.'

'Yes.'

'And the importance of a passionate temperament is also clear.'

'Again, yes.'

'Well, aren't people of this type bound to behave like brutes to one another and to the rest of their fellow citizens, Glaucon?' I asked.

'Yes, it certainly won't be easy to stop them,' he replied.

'However, they should really behave with civilized gentleness towards their friends and neighbours and with ferocity towards their enemies. Otherwise,

it won't be a question of waiting for others to come and destroy them: they'll do the job first themselves!'

'True,' he said.

'What shall we do, then?' I asked. 'Where are we going to find a character that is simultaneously gentle and high-spirited, when gentleness and passion are opposites?'

'Yes, they do seem to be mutually exclusive.'

'And yet if a guardian is deprived of either of them he can't be a good guardian. We seem to be faced with an impasse; it turns out that a good guardian is an impossibility.'

'I suppose so.'

I was stuck. I surveyed the course of the discussion and then said, 'We deserve to be stuck, Glaucon. We haven't kept to the analogy we proposed.'

'What do you mean?'

'We've overlooked the fact that the supposedly impossible type of character, which contains these opposite qualities, does exist.'

'Where?'

'In animals. You could find the combination primarily—though not exclusively—in the animal we used as an analogy for our guardian. I mean, as I'm sure you know, there's no creature more gentle towards people it knows and recognizes, and no creature more savage towards strangers, then the best type of dog; and this is due to its innate character.'

'Yes, I'm aware of that.'

'So it *is* a possibility, then,' I said. 'We're not looking for something unnatural in looking for a guardian of this type.'

'No, I suppose not.'

'Now, don't you think there's another quality which a would-be guardian needs as well? Don't you think that in addition to being naturally passionate he should also have a philosopher's love of knowledge?'

'Why?' he asked. 'I don't see why.'

'Take dogs again,' I said. 'It's noticeable that they have a remarkable feature.'

'What?'

'They get fierce with strangers even before the slightest harm has been done them, and they welcome familiar people even if they've never been benefited by them. Has this never struck you as surprising?'

'I hadn't really thought about it until now,' he said. 'But yes, they do clearly do that.'

'But don't you think that this feature shows how naturally smart they are and how genuinely they love knowledge?'

'How?'

'Because', I explained, 'their sole criterion for the friendliness or hostility of what they see is whether or not they have learnt to recognize it. Now, anything that relies on familiarity and unfamiliarity to define what is congenial and what is alien must prize learning, mustn't it?'

'Yes,' he said, 'inevitably.'

'Well,' I went on, 'isn't loving learning the same thing as loving knowledge?'

'Yes, it is,' he said.

'So why don't we stick our necks out and suggest that the same goes for a human being too—that if he's going to be gentle with his friends and acquaintances, he must be an innate lover of knowledge and learning?'

'All right,' he said.

'Anyone who is going to be a truly good guardian of our community, then, will have a philosopher's love of knowledge, and will be passionate, quick on his feet, and strong.'

'Absolutely,' he said.

CHAPTER 4
PRIMARY EDUCATION
FOR THE GUARDIANS

The would-be guardians have natural aptitude, but how should their characters be moulded? (Academic-education is reserved for the few, and for when they are older.) Plato begins with the stories they hear from childhood onwards. These inculcate values, so they must hear only morally sound stories, which will help them gain the appropriate social attitudes, such as respect for their parents, the desire for political unity, and, above all, correct beliefs about God, who is good, straight-forward, and unchanging. Any stories which could inculcate the wrong attitudes in any of these respects are to be censored.

'So those are his attributes. But how are we going to bring these people up? What education shall we give them? If we look into these issues, does it further the overall purpose of our enquiry, which is to see how morality and immorality arise in society? We have to be careful not to leave out any relevant argument or to swamp the discussion with too many topics.'

It was Glaucon's brother who said, 'I expect the consideration of these issues will substantially further it.'

'In that case, my dear Adeimantus' I said, 'we must certainly not give up, even if the investigation turns out to be rather lengthy.'

'No, we mustn't.'

'All right, then, let's devise a theoretical education for these people, as if we were making up a story and weren't worried about time.'

'Yes, that's a good idea.'

'How shall we educate them, then? Or is it hard to improve on the educational system which has evolved over a long period of time? This, as you known, consists of exercise for the body and cultural studies for the mind.'

'Yes.'

'And shall we begin the cultural programme before the physical one?'

'Of course.'

'Cultural studies include literature, don't you think?' I asked.

'I do.'

'Aren't there two kinds of literature, true and false?'

'Yes.'

'Should we include both kinds in our educational system, and start with the untrue kind?'

'I don't understand what you're getting at,' he said.

'Don't you realize,' I asked, 'that we start by telling children stories which are, by and large, untrue, though they contain elements of truth? And stories precede physical exercise in our education of children.'

'True.'

'Which is why I suggested that cultural studies should be taken up before physical exercise.'

'It was a good suggestion,' he said.

'Now, do you appreciate that the most important stage of any enterprise is the beginning, especially when something young and sensitive is involved?

b You see, that's when most of its formation takes place, and it absorbs every impression that anyone wants to stamp upon it.'

'You're absolutely right.'

'Shall we, then, casually allow our children to listen to any old stories, made up by just anyone, and to take into their minds views which, on the whole, contradict those we'll want them to have as adults?'

'No, we won't allow that at all.'

'So our first job, apparently, is to oversee the work of the story-writers, and to accept any good story they write, but reject the others. We'll let nurses and c mothers tell their children the acceptable ones, and we'll have them devote themselves far more to using these stories to form their children's minds than they do to using their hands to form their bodies. However, we'll have to disallow most of the stories they currently tell.'

'Which stories?' he asked.

'If we examine the grander kind of story,' I said, 'that will give us insights into the more lightweight d kind as well, because the same principle must be involved and both kinds are bound to have the same effect, don't you think?'

'That sounds fine to me,' he replied, 'but I don't even understand which stories you're describing as grander.'

'The ones which Hesiod, Homer, and their fellow poets tell us. In the past, it's always been the poets who've composed untrue stories to tell people, and it's no different nowadays.'

'Which stories?' he asked. 'And what's their defect, in your view?'

'There is no defect which one ought to condemn more quickly and more thoroughly,' I replied, 'especially if the lies have no redeeming feature.'

'Yes, but what *is* the defect?'

e 'Using the written word to give a distorted image of the nature of the gods and heroes, just as a painter might produce a portrait which completely fails to capture the likeness of the original.'

'Yes,' he said, 'it's quite right to find fault with that sort of thing. But how do they do that? What kinds of things do they say?'

'First and most important, since the subject is so important,' I said, 'there is no redeeming feature to 378a the lies which Hesiod repeats, about Uranus' deeds and Cronus' revenge on Uranus. Then there are

Cronus' deeds and what his son did to him. Now, I think that even if these stories are true, they oughtn't to be told so casually to young people and people who lack discrimination; it's better to keep silent, and if one absolutely has to speak, to make them esoteric secrets told to as few people as possible, who are to have sacrificed no mere piglet, but something so large and rare that the smallest conceivable number of people get to hear them.'

'Yes,' he said, 'these stories are definitely dangerous.'

'And we must censor them in our community, b Adeimantus,' I said. 'No young person is to hear stories which suggest that were he to commit the vilest of crimes, and were he to do his utmost to punish his father's crimes, he wouldn't be doing anything out of the ordinary, but would simply be behaving like the first and the greatest gods.'

'No, I absolutely agree,' he said. 'I share your view that these stories are unsuitable and shouldn't be repeated.'

'And that's not all,' I said. 'The stories which have gods fighting and scheming and battling against one another are utterly unsuitable too, because c they're just as untrue. If the prospective guardians of our community are to loathe casual quarrels with one another, we must take good care that battles between gods and giants and all the other various tales of gods and heroes coming to blows with their relatives and friends don't occur in the stories they hear and the pictures they see. No, if we're somehow to convince them that fellow citizens never fall out with one another, that this is wrong, then that is the kind d of story they must hear, from childhood onwards, from the community's elders of both sexes; and the poets they'll hear when they're older must be forced to tell equivalent stories in their poetry. But we'd better not admit into our community the story of Hera being tied up by her son, or the episode when Hephaestus is hurled away by his father for trying to save his mother from a beating, or any of the battles between the gods which Homer has in his poetry, whether or not their intention is allegorical. The point is that a young person can't tell when something is allegorical and when it isn't, and any idea admitted by a person of that age tends to become almost ineradicable and permanent. All things considered, e then, that is why a very great deal of importance should be placed upon ensuring that the first stories they hear are best adapted for their moral improvement.'

'Yes, that makes sense,' he said. 'But suppose we were once again to be asked, in this context as well, what stories we meant, how would we respond?'

'Adeimantus,' I said, 'you and I are not making up stories at the moment; we're founding a community. Founders ought to know the broad outlines within which their poets are to compose stories, so that they can exclude any compositions which do not conform to those outlines; but they shouldn't themselves make stories up.'

'You're right,' he said. 'But that's precisely the point: what are these guidelines for talking about the gods?'

'They'd be something like this,' I said. 'Whatever the type of poetry—epic, lyric, or tragic—God must of course always be portrayed as he really is.'

'Yes, he must.'

'Well, isn't God good, in fact, and shouldn't he be described as such?'

'Of course.'

'And nothing good is harmful, is it?'

'I don't think so.'

'Now, can anything harmless cause damage?'

'No, of course not.'

'Can anything incapable of causing damage do anything bad?'

'Again, no.'

'And something which never does bad couldn't be responsible for bad, could it?'

'Of course not.'

'Well now, is goodness beneficial?'

'Yes.'

'And it's responsible for doing good, then?'

'Yes.'

'So goodness is not responsible for everything: it's responsible for things that are in a good state, but bad things cannot be attributed to it.'

'Exactly,' he said. . . .

CHAPTER 5
THE GUARDIANS' LIFE AND DUTIES

This chapter covers various topics, which are loosely strung together, in a sketchy form, because Plato is in pursuit of morality, and other features of the community are of less interest to him in this context. Still, important points are made. First, the guardians are divided into guardians proper, who are to rule, and auxiliaries, who are the militia. Selection of full guardians will take years (see also Chapter 10) of checking that they always have the community's best interests at heart. We now have three classes—guardians, auxiliaries, and workers—whom we may call the castes of gold, silver, and copper or iron. The members of the castes have to believe that this is the way God wants them to be, but there is a little room for change.

'So much for our educational principles. I mean, we don't have to describe in detail the guardians' dances, hunts, sporting competitions, and horse-races: it's fairly obvious that these activities must conform to the same principles, and their elucidation shouldn't cause any problems now.'

'No, I suppose they shouldn't,' he said.

'All right,' I said. 'What do we have to decide about next? Shouldn't we decide which members of this particular class will be the rulers and which will be the subjects?'

'Of course.'

'It's obvious that the older ones should be the rulers and the younger ones the subjects, isn't it?'

'Yes.'

'And only the best of the older ones?'

'Yes, that's obvious too.'

'Now, the best farmers are the most accomplished farmers, aren't they?'

'Yes.'

'And in the present case, since we're after the best guardians, they must be those who are particularly good at safeguarding the community, mustn't they?'

'Yes.'

'They not only have to have the intelligence and the competence for the job, but they also have to care for the community, wouldn't you say?'

'Yes.'

'Now, you care most for things that happen to be dear to you.'

'Inevitably.'

'And something is particularly dear to you if you regard your interests and its interests as identical, and if you think that your success and failure follow from its success and failure.'

'Yes,' he said.

'It follows that we should select from among the guardians men who particularly strike us, on investigation, as being the type to devote their whole lives to wholeheartedly doing what they regard as advantageous to the community, and to completely refusing to do anything they regard as disadvantageous to it.'

'Yes, they would make suitable rulers,' he said.

'I think we'll have to watch them at every stage of their lives, then, to make sure that they're good at safeguarding this idea and aren't magically or forcibly induced to shed and forget the notion that it's essential to do what's best for the community.'

'What do you mean by this shedding?' he asked.

'I'll explain,' I said. 'It seems to me that the departure of an idea from a person's mind can be either intentional or unintentional. It's intentional if the idea is false and the person learns better, and unintentional whenever the idea is true.'

'I understand intentional loss,' he said, 'but I still don't understand unintentional loss.'

'But don't you think that the loss of good things is unintentional, while the loss of bad things is intentional?' I asked. 'And don't you think that being deceived about the truth is a bad thing, while having a grasp of the truth is good? And don't you think that having a grasp of the truth is having a belief that matches the way things are?'

'Yes, you're right,' he said. 'I agree that the loss of a true belief is unintentional.'

'So when this happens, it's the result of robbery, magic, or brute force, wouldn't you say?'

'I don't understand again,' he said.

'I suppose I am talking pompously,' I said. 'When I talk of a person being robbed of a belief, I mean that he's persuaded by an argument to change his mind, or time causes him to forget it: in either case, he doesn't notice the departure of the belief. I should think you understand now, don't you?'

'Yes,'

'And when I talk of a person being forced out of a belief, I mean that pain or suffering makes him change his mind.'

'Yes, I understand that too,' he said, 'and you're right.'

'And I'm sure you'd agree that anyone who changes his mind because he's been beguiled by

pleasure or terrified by threats has had magic used on him.'

'Yes,' he said, 'any deception is a form of magic, I suppose.'

'As I was starting to say a moment ago, then, we must try to discover which of our guardians are particularly good at safeguarding within themselves the belief that they should only ever pursue courses of action which they think are in the community's best interests. We must watch them from childhood onwards, and set them tasks which maximize the possibility of their forgetting a belief like this and being misled; those who bear the belief in mind and prove hard to mislead are the ones we should select, while excluding the others. Do you agree?'

'Yes.'

'And we should also set them tough and painful assignments and ordeals, and watch for exactly the same things.'

'Right,' he said.

'Now, we'll have to invent a selection procedure for our third category, magic, as well,' I said, 'and observe how they perform. People test a foal's nervousness by introducing it to noise and commotion, and in the same way we must bring our guardians, while they're young, face to face with fear and then shift them into facing pleasure. People use fire to test gold, but our test must be far more thorough, and must show us how well they resist magic and whether they remain graceful whatever the situation, keep themselves and their cultural education intact, and display rhythm and harmony throughout; if they're capable of doing this, their value to themselves and to the community will be very high. Anyone who emerges without impurities from every single test—as a child, as a young man, and as an adult—should be made a ruler and guardian of our community, and should be honoured in life and in death, in the sense of being awarded the most privileged of funerals and tombs. Anyone who gets corrupted, however, should be excluded. So, Glaucon,' I concluded, 'I think that this is how we should select and appoint our rulers and guardians. These are just guidelines, though: I haven't gone into details.'

'I agree,' he said. 'It must be something like this.'

'And we really and truly could hardly go wrong if we reserved the term "guardian" in its fullest sense for these people, who ensure that neither the desire nor the capacity for harming the community arises, whether from external enemies or from internal friends. As for the young men we've been calling guardians up to now, we should strictly call them auxiliaries and assistants of the guardians and their decision-making, don't you think?'

'Yes, I do,' he said.

'Now,' I said, 'can we devise one of those lies—the kind which crop up as the occasion demands, which we were talking about not long ago—so that with a single noble lie we can indoctrinate the rulers themselves, preferably, but at least the rest of the community?'

'What sort of lie?' he asked.

'Nothing too outlandish,' I replied, 'just a tall story about something which happened all over the place in times past (at least, that's what the poets claim and have persuaded us to believe), but which hasn't happened in our lifetimes and I'm not sure it could, and people would need a great deal of convincing about it.'

'You seem reluctant to tell us the story,' he remarked.

'And you'll see that my reluctance was well founded', I said, 'when I do tell you about it.'

'Don't worry,' he said. 'Just talk.'

'What I'm saying is . . . I'm not sure where to find the gall or the words to tell the story . . . I'll be trying above all to convince the rulers themselves and the military, and secondarily the rest of the community, that all the nurture and education we provided happened to them in a kind of dream-world; in actual fact, they were at that time being formed and nurtured deep inside the earth, and their weaponry and their equipment in general were also being made there. When they were finished products, the earth, their mother, sent them up above ground; and now in their policy-making they must regard the country they find themselves in as their mother and their nurse, they must defend her against invasion, and they should think of the rest of the inhabitants of the community as their earth-born brothers.'

'I'm not surprised you were ashamed to tell us the lie before,' he remarked.

'I had good reason,' I said. 'All the same, do please listen to the rest of the story as well. "Al-

though all of you citizens are brothers," we'll continue the tale by telling them, "nevertheless, during the kneading phase, God included gold in the mixture when he was forming those of you who have what it takes to be rulers (which is why the rulers have the greatest privileges), silver when he was forming the auxiliaries, and iron and copper when he was forming the farmers and other workers. Now, despite the fact that in general your offspring will be similar in kind to yourselves, nevertheless, because you're all related, sometimes a silver child might be born to a gold parent, a gold one to a silver parent, and so on: any of them might be produced by any of the others. Therefore, of all his instructions to the rulers, there is none that God stresses more than this: there is no aspect of their work as guardians which they shall be so good at or dedicated to as watching over the admixture of elements in the minds of the children of the community. If one of their own children is born with a nature tinged with copper or iron, they shall at all costs avoid feeling sorry for it: they shall assign it the status appropriate to its nature and banish it to the workers or the farmers. On the other hand, if a child born to a worker or a farmer has a nature tinged with gold or silver, they shall honour it and elevate it to the rank of either guardian or auxiliary, because of an oracle which states that the community will be destroyed when it has a copper or iron guardian." Can you think of any tactics to make them believe this story?'

'No, not for this particular lot, anyway,' he said, 'but I can for the immediately succeeding generations and all the generations to follow.'

'I've got a pretty good idea of what you're getting at,' I said.

'It would help them care even more for the community and for one another. But the future of all this will be decided by popular consensus, not by us.'

Within the community, the guardians and auxiliaries are to live an alert, military life (which resembles that of the Spartans), without owning property, which would corrupt them (by turning them into members of the lower class) and cause the downfall of the community. It is true that they will not be happy in the common, materialistic sense of the term, but arguably they will have the greatest happiness (see Chapter 12). In any case, the happiness of the whole is more important than that of any of its parts.

'What we can do, however, is arm these earth-born men and mobilize them under the leadership of their rulers. They must go and look for the best location within the community for their barracks, a location from where they can control any disobedience to the laws on the part of the internal inhabitants, and repel the assault of an external enemy who falls on the community like a wolf on a flock of sheep. When they've occupied the site, they must sacrifice to the appropriate gods and construct shelters, don't you think?'

'Yes,' he said.

'And these shelters should provide adequate protection whatever the weather?'

'Of course,' he said. 'I mean, these are their living-quarters you're talking about, I think.'

'Yes,' I said, 'but military quarters, not places of business.'

'*Now* what distinction are you getting at?' he asked.

'I'll try to explain,' I answered. 'Consider, for example, the dogs which shepherds train to act as their auxiliaries, to help them look after their flocks: there could be nothing more dreadful or despicable than for these dogs, thanks to their nature or thanks to the shepherds' training, to be capable of being influenced by indiscipline or hunger or some other bad habit to try to harm the sheep and behave like wolves rather than sheepdogs.'

'It goes without saying that this would be dreadful,' he said.

'So we must do everything possible to guard against the possibility of our auxiliaries treating the inhabitants of our community like that and using their greater power to behave like brutal despots rather than well-intentioned allies.'

'Yes, we must,' he said.

'Wouldn't a really excellent education have equipped them to take the maximum amount of care?'

'But they did receive an excellent education,' he said.

'That's not something we should stake our lives on, my dear Glaucon,' I said. 'But we should stand firmly by our present position, that whatever constitutes a proper education, it is the chief factor in the guardians' treating themselves and their wards in a civilized fashion.'

'That's right,' he said.

'Now, doesn't it make sense to say that this education isn't all they need? That in addition their living-quarters and their property in general should be designed not to interfere with their carrying out their work as guardians as well as possible or to encourage them to commit crimes against their fellow citizens?'

'Yes, it does.'

'I wonder if they'd turn out as we want if their lifestyle and living-quarters were somewhat as follows,' I said. 'See what you think. In the first place, none of them is to have any private property, except what is absolutely indispensable. In the second place, none of them is to have living-quarters and store-rooms which are not able to be entered by anyone who wants to. Their provisions (which should be suitable in quantity for self-controlled and courageous warriors) are to be their stipend, paid by their fellow citizens for their guarding, the amount being fixed so that, at the end of a year, there is no excess or shortfall. There will be shared mess-halls for them to go to, and their lives will be communal, as if they were on campaign. We'll tell them that the permanent presence in their minds of divine gold and silver, which they were granted by the gods, means that they have no need of earthly gold and silver as well; and we'll add that it is sacrilegious for them to adulterate and contaminate that heavenly possession by owning the earthly variety, because in the past this earthly variety, which is accepted as currency by the masses, has provoked many acts of desecration, whereas theirs is untainted. So, unlike any of their fellow citizens, they are not permitted to have any contact or involvement with gold and silver: they are not to come under the same roof as gold and silver, or wear them on their bodies, or drink from gold and silver cups. These precepts will guarantee not only their own integrity, but also the integrity of the community which is in their safe keeping. If they do come to own land and homes and money, they will be estate-managers and farmers instead of guardians; they will become despots, and enemies rather than allies of the inhabitants of the community; they will spend their lives hating and being hated, plotting and being plotted against; they will have internal enemies to fear more, and more intensely, than their external enemies. With private property, they will be racing ever closer to the ruin of themselves and the whole community. All this confirms the importance of our stated arrangements for the guardians' living-quarters and so on,' I concluded, 'so shall we enshrine them in law, or not?'

'We certainly must,' said Glaucon.

419a   Adeimantus came in with an objection: 'Tell me, Socrates,' he said. 'How are you going to reply to the accusation that you're not making these men at all happy, and moreover you're making it their own fault? In a real sense, the community belongs to them, but they don't derive any benefit from the community. Others own estates, build beautiful mansions and stock them with suitable furniture, perform their own special religious rites, entertain, and of course own the items you were just talking about, gold and silver, and everything else without which happiness is, on the usual view, impossible. Instead of all this, a critic might say, their role in our community really is just like that of auxiliary troops—mercenaries—

420a with nothing to do except maintain a garrison.'

'Yes,' I agreed. 'And they don't even get paid like other auxiliary troops: they get no more than their provisions. Consequently, they can't even take a trip for personal reasons out of town if they want to, or give presents to mistresses, or spend money on anything else they might want to, as so-called happy people can. You're leaving all this out of your accusation, and plenty of other things too.'

'All right,' he said. 'Please assume that the accusation includes them.'

b   'So you're asking how we'll defend ourselves, are you?'

'Yes.'

'I don't think we need to change direction at all to come across a suitable defence,' I said. 'We'll reply that although it wouldn't surprise us in the slightest if in fact there were no people happier than these men, all the same we're not constructing our community with the intention of making one group within it especially happy, but to maximize the happiness of the community as a whole. We thought we'd be most likely to find morality in a community

like ours and also immorality in a community with the worst possible management, and that once we'd examined them we'd reach the decision which is the c original purpose of our investigation. What we're doing at the moment, we think, is forming a community which is happy as a whole, without hiving off a few of its members and making them the happy ones; and before long we'll be looking at a community in the opposite condition.

'Suppose we were painting a statue and someone came up and criticized us for not using the most beautiful paint for the creature's most beautiful features, because the eyes are the most beautiful part and they hadn't been painted purple but black. It would be perfectly reasonable, in our opinion, for us to reply to this critic by saying, "My dear chap, you can't ex- d pect us to paint beautiful eyes in a way which stops them looking like eyes, or to do that to the other parts of the body either. Don't you think that if we treat every single part in an appropriate fashion, we're making the creature as a whole beautiful? Likewise, in the present case, please don't force us to graft the sort of happiness on to the guardians which will make them anything but guardians. You see, we know we e could dress our farmers in soft clothes and golden jewellery and tell them to work the land only when they have a mind to, and we know we could have our potters lie basking in their kiln-fire's warmth on a formal arrangement of couches, drinking and feasting with their wheel beside them as a table, and doing pottery only as much as they feel like, and we know we could make everyone else happy in this sort of way, and so have a community which was happy overall; but please don't advise us to do so, because if we follow your recommendation, then our farmers won't be farmers and our potters won't be potters and 421a no one else will retain that aspect of himself which is a constituent of a community. Now, this isn't so important where the rest of the community is concerned. I mean, if cobblers go to the bad and degenerate and pretend to be other than what they are, it's not catastrophic for a community; but if the people who guard a community and its laws ignore their essence and start to pose, then obviously they're utterly destroying the community, despite the fact that its good management and happiness are crucially in their hands and their hands alone."

'Now, if we're creating genuine guardians, who can hardly harm their community, and the originator of that other idea is talking about a certain kind of farmer and people who are, as it were, happy to fill their stomachs on holiday, but aren't members of a community, then he's not talking about a community, but something else. What we have to consider is whether our intention in putting the guardians in place is to maximize their happiness, or whether we ought to make the happiness of the community as a whole our goal and should, by fair means and foul, convince these auxiliaries and guardians that their task is to ensure that they, and everyone else as well, are the best at their own jobs. Then, when the community as a whole is flourishing and rests on a fine foundation, we can take it for granted that every group within it will find happiness according to its nature.'

'I'm sure you're right,' he said.

The continued integrity, unity, and stability of the community require the guardians to prevent the workers neglecting their work by becoming too rich or too poor, and to keep the population from becoming too great. Since they lack the material resources for prolonged warfare, diplomacy and the threat of their military prowess will be the preferred means of resolving conflicts with other states. To save discussing every possible topic, Plato stresses the overall importance of education: good men, with an understanding of principle, will not need endless rules to guide their lives. Once you have a good system of education and a good political system, beware of change and innovation.

'Well, I wonder if a closely related idea of mine will also strike you as sensible,' I said.

'What is it?'

'That there are other factors which corrupt the rest of the workers and make them bad at their jobs.'

'What factors?'

'Affluence and poverty,' I replied.

'What do you mean?'

'This is what I mean. If a potter gets rich, do you think he'll still be willing to devote himself to his profession?'

'Not at all,' he answered.

'He'll become less hard-working and less conscientious than before, won't he?'

'Considerably less.'

'Then he'll be a worse potter?'

'Again, considerably worse,' he said.

'But if he's so poor that he lacks the means to provide himself with tools and other essentials for his job, then he's going to be turning out inferior products and he'll not be able to provide his sons (or whoever else is apprenticed to him) with adequate training.'

'Of course.'

'Both affluence and poverty, then, are causes of degeneration in the products and the practitioners of a craft.'

'So it seems.'

'So we've come up with more things which the guardians must at all costs prevent from sneaking into the community without their noticing it.'

'What things?'

'Affluence and poverty,' I said. 'The first brings indulgence, indolence, and innovation; the second entails miserliness and bad workmanship, as well as also bringing innovation.'

'Quite so,' he said. 'But, Socrates, here's a question for you. How will our community be capable of waging war if its coffers are empty, especially if it has to face an enemy who is large and wealthy?'

'Obviously it would be easier to have two such opponents ranged against us than one, relatively speaking,' I said.

'What are you getting at?' he asked.

'Chiefly this,' I said. 'If they do have to fight, won't it be a case of warriors versus plutocrats?'

'Yes,' he said.

'Well, Adeimantus,' I went on, 'don't you think that a single boxer who has received the best possible training can easily take on two non-boxers who are rich and fat?'

'Maybe not at the same time,' he answered.

'Not even if it were possible for him to draw back and then turn around and strike whichever opponent is bearing down on him first?' I asked. 'And what about if he could do this over and over again in the sunshine and stifling heat? Under these circumstances, couldn't he overcome even more opponents of the kind we're postulating?'

'Without a doubt,' he said. 'It wouldn't be at all surprising.'

'Well, don't you think that rich people are better and more experienced boxers than they are soldiers?'

'I do,' he replied.

'Our warriors will, then, in all likelihood, have no difficulty in taking on two or three times the number of rich opponents.'

'I'll concede the point,' he said. 'I think you're right.'

d   'All right, then. Suppose they send a herald to one of the two communities with the following true message: "We have no use for gold and silver; it is taboo for us, though not for you. Side with us in the war, and you can have the other side's assets." Do you think that anyone who received this message would choose the option of fighting tough, lean dogs rather than siding with the dogs against fat, tender sheep?'

'No, I don't. But if all the assets of all the other communities are gathered up by a single community, then don't you think this situation might entail some danger for our asset-free community?'

'It's naïve of you to think that any community other than the one we're constructing deserves the name,' I said.

'What should I call them?' he asked.

'They should have a more capacious title,' I replied, 'since each of them is not so much a community as a great many communities, as in the game. Minimally, they contain two warring communities—one consisting of the rich and one of the poor. Then each of these two contains quite a number of further communities. It would be quite wrong to treat this plurality as a unity. However, if you treat them as a plurality and offer one section's assets and power and personnel to another section, then you'll always have a lot of allies and few enemies. And as long as your community's administration retains its discipline and is arranged in accordance with our recent regulations, it will have no equal. I don't mean that it will merely have the reputation of having no equal, but that it really won't, even if its militia numbers no more than a thousand. You'll be hard put to find a community of this size in Greece or abroad which is actually single, though there are plenty of communities which are far larger in size and which might be thought to be single. Do you agree, or not?'

'I most certainly do,' he said.

'Now, this could also provide our rulers with the best criterion for deciding on the appropriate size for the community,' I said, 'and how much territory they should reserve for a community of this size, without expanding any further.'

'What criterion?' he asked.

'To allow growth as long as growth doesn't jeopardize its unity,' I said, 'but no further. This is the criterion I'm thinking of.'

'It's a good one,' he commented.

'So here's another instruction we'll be giving the guardians,' I said. 'They are to do everything possible to guard against the community either being small or merely appearing large, and to ensure that it is just the right size and is a unity.'

'I suppose you think that's a simple instruction for them to carry out,' he said.

'And here's an even simpler one,' I said, 'which we mentioned earlier as well. We were talking of the necessity of banishing to the other ranks any inferior child who is born to the guardians, and of having any outstanding child who is born to the other ranks join the guardians. And the point of this idea was that every single member of the community, from the other ranks as well as any of the guardians, has to dedicate himself to the single job for which he is naturally suited, because this specialization of function will ensure that every person is not a plurality but a unity, and thus that the community as a whole develops as a unity, not a plurality.'

'Oh yes, that's simpler—hardly worth mentioning!' he said.

'As a matter of fact, my dear Adeimantus,' I said, 'the instructions we're giving them are not as numerous or as difficult as they might seem: they're all simple, provided they follow the saying and "stick to the one thing that's important"—or rather, not important so much as decisive.'

'What is this thing?' he asked.

'Their education and upbringing,' I replied. 'If they receive a good education which makes them moderate, then they'll easily discover everything we're talking about for themselves—and everything we've missed out so far as well, such as what they are to do with their wives, and what to do about marriage and childbirth, and how all these matters have to be dealt with in accordance with the proverbial saying that friends share everything they can.'

'Yes, that would be best,' he said.

'Now, provided our community's constitution is given a good initial start,' I said, 'then it'll get into a spiral of growth. I mean, a good educational system, if maintained, engenders people of good character; and then people of good character, if they in their turn receive the benefits of an education of this kind, become even better than their predecessors in every respect, but especially—as is the case with other creatures too—in that they produce better children.'

'Yes, that seems reasonable,' he said.

'To put it succinctly, then, the government of the community must adhere to this educational system, and make sure that its integrity is not subtly compromised; they should constantly be on their guard against innovations which transgress our regulations about either physical exercise or cultural studies. They should look out for these to the best of their ability, and should worry if they hear the claim that "the most popular song is the one which happens to be on singers' lips at the moment", in case the poet might commonly be taken to be talking not about new songs, but a new type of singing, and might be commended for doing so. This kind of thing should be frowned on, however, and it surely is not what the poet meant. The point is that caution must be taken in adopting an unfamiliar type of music: it is an extremely risky venture, since any change in the musical modes affects the most important laws of a community. This is what Damon claims, and I believe him.'

'You can count me as another convert to this view,' said Adeimantus.

'So now we know where the guardians should build their lookout post,' I said. 'It's in the field of music and culture.'

'Yes,' he said. 'At any rate, indiscipline can easily creep in here without being noticed.'

'Yes,' I agreed. 'because it's not taken seriously and is assumed to have no harmful effects.'

'That's because it doesn't,' he said, 'except that it gradually establishes itself and then silently seeps into people's mannerisms and habits, which become the basis from which it erupts, now enlarged, into their business dealings with one another, which in turn become the basis from which it assaults the laws and the constitution with gross indecency, Socrates, until it eventually throws everything into chaos in both the private and the public spheres.'

'Really?' I asked.

'I think so,' he said.

'Our original position was correct, then: the children of our community must engage in more lawful amusements right from the start, because when pastimes become lawless and children follow suit, it is impossible for them to grow into law-abiding, exemplary adults. Yes?'

'Of course,' he said.

'Therefore, when children play in a proper manner right from the start, and their cultural education introduces them to the orderliness of law, there is the opposite result: lawfulness accompanies them in everything they do, guides their growth, and corrects any aspect of the community which was formerly aberrant.'

'You're right,' he said.

'And they therefore rediscover those apparently trivial rules which their predecessors had completely lost.'

'What rules?'

'For example, that one should be silent in the presence of people older than oneself. Younger people should also give up their seats for their elders, stand up when they enter the room, and look after their parents. Then there are the rules about hairstyle, clothing, footwear, and in general the way one presents oneself, and so on and so forth. Do you agree?'

'Yes.'

'But in my opinion only an idiot would legislate on these matters. I don't think these rules come into being, and I don't think they would remain in force either, through being formulated and written down.'

'How could they?'

'Anyway, Adeimantus,' I said, 'education is the factor which determines a person's subsequent direction in life. I mean, doesn't like always attract like?'

'Of course.'

'And I suppose we'd say that the final result is a single, dynamic whole, whether or not it's good.'

'Naturally,' he said.

'And that's why I for one wouldn't try to legislate further than we already have done in this area,' I said.

'It makes sense not to,' he remarked.

'Now then,' I said, 'what on earth shall we do about the world of the agora? I mean the commercial deals people make with one another and, of course, contracts with labourers, lawsuits for slander and assault, indictments, empanelling juries, the collecting or paying of any money due for renting space in the agora or the port, and any business which concerns the general regulation of the agora or the city or the ports or whatever. Shall we take it on ourselves to make any rules and regulations about these matters?'

'It isn't right to tell truly good men what to do,' he said. 'They won't have any difficulty, in the majority of cases, in finding out which matters need legal measures.'

'No, my friend, they won't,' I said, 'as long as, by God's will, the laws we've already discussed are preserved intact.'

'Otherwise,' he said, 'they'll spend their whole lives making rule after rule, and then trying to improve them, in the hope that they'll hit on a successful formula.'

'You mean they'll live like people who are ill, but lack the discipline to give up a way of life that is bad for them,' I said.

'That's it.'

'And what a nice time *they* have! All their treatments get them nowhere (except that they increase the variety and seriousness of their ailments) and they're constantly expecting every medicine they are recommended to make them better.'

'Yes, that's typical of this kind of invalid,' he said.

'And here's another nice feature of theirs,' I said. 'The thing they can abide least of all is someone telling the truth—that until they stop getting drunk, stuffing themselves, whoring, and doing no work, no medicine or cautery or surgery, and no spell or amulet or anything like that either, is going to do them the slightest good.'

'That's not at all nice,' he said. 'There's nothing nice about getting angry at good advice.'

'You don't think highly of this type of person, it seems,' I commented.

'No, I certainly don't.'

'And you also won't think highly of a whole community, then, if it carries on in the equivalent way we mentioned a moment ago. I mean, wouldn't you describe as identical the actions of all those badly governed states which forewarn their citizens not to interfere with the general political system and threaten with death anyone who does so, while anyone who treats them, despite the condition of their government, in a way which pleases them a great deal, and who gets into their good books by flattering them and anticipating their wishes and by being good at satisfying these wishes, is accounted and acclaimed by them a man of virtue and high skill?'

'Yes, I think they're doing exactly the same,' he said, 'and I've got nothing good to say about them at all.'

'And what about people who are prepared, and even determined, to look after such communities? Don't you admire their courage—and their casual attitude?'

'Yes, I do,' he replied, 'except when they're deluded into imagining that they're true statesmen simply because the masses think highly of them.'

'What do you mean?' I asked. 'Don't you feel compassion for them? I mean, do you suppose there's any way in which a man who is incapable of measuring can avoid thinking he's four cubits tall when others (who are just as ignorant) are frequently telling him he is?'

'No, he can't,' he said.

'Don't be so hard on them, then: they're the nicest of people. They make the kinds of laws we mentioned a short while ago and then try to improve them, and constantly expect the next breach of contract to be the last one, and likewise for the other crimes we mentioned just now, because they are unaware that in fact they're slashing away at a kind of Hydra.'

'Yes, that's exactly what they're doing,' he said.

'So I wouldn't have thought that in either a badly governed or a well-governed community a genuine legislator need occupy himself with laws and administration of this kind. In the one community they can't help and don't accomplish anything; in the other some of them will be obvious and others will follow automatically from habits the citizens will already have acquired.'

'Is there any legislation for us still to see to, then?' he asked.

'Not for us,' I replied, 'but Delphic Apollo still has to make the most important, valuable, and fundamental laws.'

'Which ones?' he asked.

'How to site temples, how to conduct sacrifices, and how in general to worship the gods, deities, and heroes. Then there's the burial of the dead and all the services we have to perform to propitiate those who have gone to the other world. You see, we aren't experts in this area, and in founding our city we won't—if we have any sense—trust anyone else's advice or consult any arbiter except our ancestral one. Apollo is, of course, the traditional arbiter in this area for the whole human race, and he performs his function as arbiter from his seat at the earth's navel.'

'That's a good idea,' he said. 'We must do as you suggest.'

CHAPTER 6
INNER AND OUTER MORALITY

Plato now locates the four presumed elements of goodness in the community he has imagined. The thought and resourcefulness of the guardians, as they take care of the community as a whole, are its wisdom; the lawful bravery of the auxiliaries is its courage; the lower orders tolerating the control of the rulers is its self-discipline; the members of the three classes doing what they are best equipped to do, without usurping the functions of others, is its morality, because (as Plato supposes morality must) it allows the other elements of goodness to exist.

'So there you are, Adeimantus,' I said. 'Your community seems to have been founded. The next thing for you to do is to get hold of a bright enough light and explore the community—you should invite your brother and Polemarchus and the rest of us to join you—to see if we can locate morality and immorality within it, discover how they differ from each other, and find out which of them is a prerequisite for happiness, whether or not its possession is hidden from the eyes of gods and men.'

'Rubbish,' said Glaucon. 'You promised you'd do the investigating, on the grounds that it was sacrilegious for you not to do everything you could to assist morality.'

'You're right,' I said. 'Thanks for the reminder. But you should still help me while I do so.'

'We will,' he said.

'I think I know how we'd better conduct the search,' I said. 'I assume that if the community has been founded properly, it has everything it takes to be good.'

'Necessarily,' he replied.

'Obviously, then, it has wisdom, courage, self-discipline, and morality.'

'Obviously.'

'And clearly, as we go about our search, we'll discover some of these elements and there'll be some we have yet to discover.'

'Of course.'

'Now, imagine any set of four things, and imagine we're exploring something for one of the four. Either we'd recognize it straight away and that would do the job, or we would recognize the one we're looking for by first recognizing the other three, in the sense that whatever is left is bound to be the one we're looking for.'

'Right,' he said.

'Well, we're faced with a set of four things here, so the principles of exploration are the same. Yes?'

'Obviously.'

'Now, the first thing which I think is visible here is wisdom. And there's a peculiarity in its case.'

'What?' he asked.

'Well, I do think that the community we've described really is wise. I mean, it's resourceful, isn't it?'

'Yes.'

'And this thing, resourcefulness, is obviously a kind of knowledge. I mean, it's not ignorance which makes people resourceful; it's knowledge.'

'Obviously.'

'Now, there are many branches of knowledge in our community, of all different kinds.'

'Naturally.'

'So is it the knowledge its carpenters have which makes the community deserve to be described as wise and resourceful?'

c   'No, that only entitles us to call it good at carpentry,' he replied.

'It shouldn't be called wise, then, because of its knowledge of carpentry and because it is resourceful at ensuring the excellence of its furniture.'

'Certainly not.'

'Because it knows how to make mental implements, then, or anything like that?'

'Definitely not that either,' he said.

'And the fact that it knows how to grow crops only entitles us to describe it as good at agriculture.'

'That's what I think.'

'All right,' I said. 'Is there a branch of knowledge which some of the inhabitants of the community we've just founded have, which enables it to think

d   resourcefully about the whole community, not just some element of it, and about enhancing the whole community's domestic and foreign policies?'

'There certainly is.'

'What is it?' I asked. 'And which of the citizens have it?'

'It is guardianship,' he replied, 'and the people who have it are those rulers—the ones we not long ago called guardians in the strict sense of the word.'

'And what description does this branch of knowledge earn the community, in your opinion?'

'Resourceful and genuinely wise,' he answered.

'Now, do you think that in our community metal-

e   workers will outnumber these true guardians, or the other way round?' I asked.

'There'll be far more metalworkers,' he said.

'And wouldn't these guardians be outnumbered by any of the other acknowledged categories of experts?' I asked.

'Yes, by a long way.'

'So when a community is founded on natural principles, the wisdom it has as a whole is due to the smallest grouping and section within it and to the knowledge possessed by this group, which is the authoritative and ruling section of the community. And we also find that this category, which is naturally the

429a   least numerous, is the one which inherently possesses the only branch of knowledge which deserves to be called wisdom.'

'You're absolutely right,' he said.

'So we've somehow stumbled across one of the four qualities we were looking for and found whereabouts in the community it is located.'

'*I* think it's clear enough, anyway,' he said.

'Now, it's not too hard to spot courage and to see which section of the community possesses it and enables the community to be described as courageous.'

'Why?'

'The only feature of a community which might justify describing it as either cowardly or courageous', I   b answered, 'is its defensive and military arm.'

'Yes, that's the only one,' he agreed.

'The point is', I went on, 'that whether the rest of its inhabitants are cowardly or brave wouldn't affect the nature of the community either way, I imagine.'

'No, it wouldn't.'

'Again, then, it is a section of a community that earns it the right to be called courageous. This section possesses the ability to retain under all circumstances the notion that the things and kinds of things   c to be feared are precisely those things and kinds of things which during their education the legislator pronounced fearful. Isn't this what you call courage?'

'I haven't understood your point,' he said. 'Please could you repeat it.'

'I'm saying that courage is a sort of retention,' I explained.

'What do you mean, retention?'

'I mean the retention of the notion, which has been inculcated by law through the agency of education, about what things and what kinds of things are to be feared. And by its retention "under all circumstances" I meant keeping it intact and not losing   d it whether one is under the influence of pain or pleasure, desire or aversion. I can tell you what strikes me as analogous, if you like.'

'Yes, please.'

'Well,' I said, 'you know how when dyers want to dye wool purple, they first select something which is naturally white, rather than any other colour; then they subject it to a lengthy preparatory treatment designed to ensure that the colour will take as well as possible; and when it's in the required condition,   e they dye it. Anything dyed in this way holds its colour, and the colour can't be washed out, whether or not one uses solvent. But you know what happens to anything which isn't dyed in this way, when something of another colour is dyed, or when something white is dyed without having been treated first.'

'Yes,' he said. 'The dye washes out and they look ridiculous.'

'So I want you to imagine', I said, 'that we too were doing our best to achieve something similar, when we selected our militia and put them through their cultural and physical education. You should assume that the educational programme was designed for one purpose only: to indoctrinate them so thoroughly that the laws take in them like a dye, so that their notions about what is to be feared and about everything else hold fast (which requires a suitable character as well as a suitable upbringing), with the dye being incapable of being washed out by those solvents which are so frighteningly good at scouring—pleasure, which is a more efficient cleanser than any soda and lye, and pain and aversion and desire, which outclass any solvent. So this ability to retain under all circumstances a true and lawful notion about what is and is not to be feared is what I'm calling courage. That's how I'll use the term, unless you have an alternative suggestion.'

'No, I don't,' he said. 'I mean, I think your idea is that any true notion about these matters which is formed in an animal or a slave without the benefit of education is not really lawful, and I suppose you'd find some other name for it, not courage.'

'You're quite right,' I said.

'I accept your definition of courage, then.'

'Accept it by all means,' I said, 'but as a definition of the kind of courage a community has; then your acceptance will be all right. We'll go into the subject more thoroughly later, if you want; you see, at the moment our quarry is morality, not courage, which I think we've explored enough.'

'That's fine by me,' he said.

'Well, we've still got two qualities to detect in the community,' I said, 'self-discipline and the purpose of the whole enquiry, morality.'

'Quite so.'

'Can we somehow locate morality and not bother any more about self-discipline?'

'I don't know if we can,' he said, 'and anyway I wouldn't like morality to be discovered first if that entails dropping the search for self-discipline. I'd be grateful if you'd look for self-discipline before morality.'

'Then it's my duty to do so, of course,' I said.

'Go on, then,' he said.

'All right,' I said. 'From my point of view, we're faced here with a closer similarity to some kind of harmony and attunement than we were before.'

'Why?'

'To be self-disciplined', I replied, 'is somehow to order and control the pleasures and desires. Hence the opaque expression "self-mastery"; and there are other expressions which hint at its nature. Yes?'

'Absolutely,' he said.

'Isn't the phrase "self-mastery" absurd? I mean, anyone who is his own master is also his own slave, of course, and vice versa, since it's the same person who is the subject in all these expressions.'

'Of course.'

'What this expression means, I think,' I continued, 'is that there are better and worse elements in a person's mind, and when the part which is naturally better is in control of the worse part, then we use this phrase "self-mastery" (which is, after all, complimentary). But when, as a result of bad upbringing or bad company, the smaller better part is defeated by the superior numbers of the worse part, then we use critical and deprecatory language and describe someone in this state as lacking self-mastery and discipline.'

'That sounds plausible,' he said.

'Have a look at our new community, then,' I said, 'and you'll find that the first of these alternatives is attributable to it. I mean, you must admit the justice of describing it as having self-mastery, since anything whose better part rules its worse part should be described as having self-discipline and self-mastery.'

'Yes, I can see the truth of what you're saying,' he said.

'Now, children, women, slaves, and (among so-called free men) the rabble who constitute the majority of the population are the ones who evidently experience the greatest quantity and variety of forms of desire, pleasure, and pain.'

'Yes.'

'Whereas simple and moderate forms, which are guided by the rational mind with its intelligence and true beliefs, are encountered only in those few people who have been endowed with excellence by their nature and their education.'

'True,' he said.

'And is it clear to you that this is a property of your community, where the desires of the common majority are controlled by the desires and the intelligence of the minority of better men?'

'It is,' he said.

'So if any community deserves to be described as having mastered pleasure and desire, and as having self-mastery, it is this one.'

'Without the slighest doubt,' he said.

'So it also deserves to be called self-disciplined, doesn't it?'

'Yes, indeed,' he said.

'Moreover, it is in this community, more than in any other conceivable community, that the rulers and their subjects agree on who the rulers should be, don't you think?'

'Definitely,' he said.

'In a situation like this, then, is it the rulers or the subjects of the community who, in your opinion, possess self-discipline?'

'Both,' he replied.

'Is it clear to you, then,' I asked, 'that our recent conjecture that self-discipline resembles a kind of attunement wasn't bad?'

'Why?'

'Because unlike courage and wisdom, both of which imbued the community with their respective qualities while being properties of only a part of the community, self-discipline literally spans the whole octaval spread of the community, and makes the weakest, the strongest, and the ones in between all sing in unison, whatever criterion you choose in order to assess their relative strengths—intelligence, physical strength, numerical quantity, wealth, and so on. And the upshot is that we couldn't go wrong if we claimed that self-discipline was this unanimity, a harmony between the naturally worse and naturally better elements of society as to which of them should rule both in a community and in every individual.'

'I certainly agree,' he said.

'All right,' I said. 'We've detected three of the qualities in our community, as far as we can tell. But there's one final way in which a community achieves goodness. What precisely is morality? I mean, morality is this missing type of goodness, clearly.'

'Clearly.'

'We must now imitate hunters surrounding a thicket, Glaucon, and make sure that morality doesn't somehow elude us and disappear into obscurity. I mean, we know it's somewhere round here. Keep your eyes peeled and try to spot it. If you see it before I do, let me know where it is.'

'I wish I could,' he said. 'But in fact it would be more realistic of you to regard me as someone who follows in your footsteps and can see things only when they're pointed out to him.'

'Follow me, then,' I said, 'and pray for success.'

'I will,' he said. 'You have only to lead on.'

'Now, we're in a rather rugged and overcast spot, it seems,' I said. 'At any rate, it's gloomy and hunting won't be easy. Still, we must carry on.'

'Yes, we must,' he said.

I caught a glimpse of something and shouted, "Hurray! Glaucon, I believe we're on its trail! I don't think it will get clean away from us.'

'That's good news,' he said.

'What a stupid state to find ourselves in!' I exclaimed.

'What do you mean?'

'It looks as though it's been curled up at our feet all the time, right from the beginning, my friend, and we didn't see it, but just made absolute fools of ourselves. You know how people sometimes go in search of something they're holding in their hands all the time? That's what we've been like. We've been looking off into the distance somewhere, instead of at our quarry, and that was why we didn't notice it, I suppose.'

'What do you mean?'

'I'll tell you,' I said. 'I think it's been the subject of our discussion all along and we just didn't appreciate that we were in a sense talking about it.'

'What a long preamble,' he said, 'when I'm so keen to hear what you're getting at!'

'All right,' I said. 'See if you think there's anything in what I say. From the outset, when we first started to found the community, there's a principle we established as a universal requirement—and this, or some version of it, is in my opinion morality. The principle we established, and then repeated time and again, as you'll remember, is that every individual has to do just one of the jobs relevant to the community, the one for which his nature has best equipped him.'

'Yes, that's what we said.'

'Furthermore, the idea that morality is doing one's own job and not intruding elsewhere is commonly
b voiced, and we ourselves have often said it.'

'Yes, we have.'

'So, Glaucon,' I said, 'it seems likely that this is in a sense what morality is—doing one's own job. Do you know what makes me think so?'

'No,' he answered. 'Please tell me.'

'We've examined self-discipline, courage, and wisdom,' I said, 'and it occurs to me that this principle is what is left in the community, because it is the principle which makes it possible for all those other qualities to arise in the community, and its continued presence allows them to flourish in safety
c once they have arisen. And we did in fact say that if we found the other three, then whatever was left would be morality.'

'Yes, that's necessarily so,' he said.

'But if we had to decide which of these qualities it was whose presence is chiefly responsible for the goodness of the community,' I said, 'it would be hard to decide whether it's the unanimity between rulers
d and subjects, or the militia's retention of the lawful notion about what is and is not to be feared, or the wise guardianship which is an attribute of the rulers, or the fact that it is an attribute of every child, woman, slave, free person, artisan, ruler, and subject that each individual does his own job without intruding elsewhere, that is chiefly responsible for making it good.'

'Yes, of course that would be a difficult decision,' he said.

'When it comes to contributing to a community's goodness, then, there's apparently a close contest between the ability of everyone in a community to do their own jobs and its wisdom, self-discipline, and courage.'

'There certainly is,' he said.

'And wouldn't you say that anything which rivals these qualities in contributing towards a commu-
e nity's goodness must be morality?'

'Absolutely.'

'See if you also agree when you look at it from this point of view. Won't you be requiring the rulers

to adjudicate when lawsuits occur in the community?'

'Of course.'

'And won't their most important aim in doing so be to ensure that people don't get hold of other people's property and aren't deprived of their own?'

'Yes.'

'Because this is right?'

'Yes.'

'So from this point of view too we are agreed that morality is keeping one's own property and keeping to one's own occupation.'
434a

'True.'

'See if you agree with me on this as well: if a joiner tried to do a shoemaker's job, or a shoemaker a carpenter's, or if they swapped tools or status, or even if the same person tried to do both jobs, with all the tools and so on of both jobs switched around, do you think that much harm would come to the community?'

'Not really,' he said.

'On the other hand, when someone whom nature has equipped to be an artisan or to work for money in some capacity or other gets so puffed up by his b wealth or popularity or strength or some such factor that he tries to enter the military class, or when a member of the militia tries to enter the class of policy-makers and guardians when he's not qualified to do so, and they swap tools and status, or when a single person tries to do all these jobs simultaneously, then I'm sure you'll agree that these interchanges and c intrusions are disastrous for the community.'

'Absolutely.'

'There's nothing more disastrous for the community, then, than the intrusion of any of the three classes into either of the other two, and the interchange of roles among them, and there could be no more correct context for using the term "criminal".'

'Indubitably.'

'And when someone commits the worst crimes against his own community, wouldn't you describe this as immorality?'

'Of course.'

'Then this is what immorality is. Here's an alternative way of putting it. Isn't it the case (to put it the other way round) that when each of the three classes—the one that works for a living, the auxiliaries, and the guardians—performs its proper function and does its own job in the community, then this is morality and makes the community a moral one?'

d   'Yes, I think that's exactly right,' he said.

The existence of conflict within a person's mind proves that there are different 'parts' to the mind. On examination, we can claim that there are three parts. Plato's description of them is rather hard to pin down, and the discussion in this section should be supplemented by reference to 580d–588a, 602c–605c, and Chapter II as a whole. He distinguishes a part which includes our desires or wants or instinctive appetites; our intellect, which uses both pure and applied thinking; and our passionate, assertive, proud, brave side, which (in non-Platonic terms) enhances or defends our 'sense of I'. This is Plato's famous theory of the tripartite mind, which recurs in *Phaedrus* and *Timaeus*. Since all three parts have aims and objectives and distinctive pleasures, the most profitable way to think of them is to describe them as forms of desire: instinctive desire; the desire for one's overall good; and the desire for good results based on one's self-image.

'Let's not be too inflexible about it yet,' I warned. 'If we also conclude that this type of thing constitutes morality in the case of individual human beings as well, then we'll have no reservations. I mean, how could we under those circumstances? However, if we find that it doesn't apply to humans as well, then we'll have to take the enquiry into new areas. So let's now wind up that aspect of the enquiry which is based on the idea we had that it would be easier to detect the nature of morality in an individual human being if we first tried to observe it in something larger and to watch its operation there. We decided that the larger thing was a community, and so we founded as good a community as we could, because we were well

e   aware that it would have to be a good community for morality to exist in it. What we have to do now is apply the results we found in the case of the community to an individual. If there's a match, that will be fine; but if we find something different in the case of an individual, then we'll return to the community to test the new result. With luck, the friction of compar-

435a   ing the two cases will enable morality to flare up from

these fire-sticks, so to speak, and once it's become visible we'll make it more of a force in our own lives.'

'That's a viable notion,' he said. 'We should do as you suggest.'

'Well,' I said, 'if a single property is predicated of two things of different sizes, then in so far as it's the same predicate, is it in fact dissimilar or similar in the two instances?'

'Similar,' he said.

'So in respect of the actual type of thing moral-   b ity is, a moral person will be no different from a moral community, but will resemble it.'

'Yes,' he said.

'Now, we decided that a community was moral when each of the three natural classes that exist within it did its own job, and also that certain other states and conditions of the same three classes made it self-disciplined and courageous and wise.'

'True.'

'It follows, my friend, that we should expect an individual to have the same three classes in himself,   c and that the same conditions make him liable to the same predicates as the community receives.'

'That's absolutely inevitable,' he said.

'Glaucon,' I said, 'now we're faced with another simple enquiry, to see whether or not the mind contains these three features.'

'It hardly seems to me to be a simple one,' he remarked. 'But then it's probably a true saying, Socrates, that anything fine is difficult.'

'I think that's right,' I said. 'In fact, I have to tell you, Glaucon, that in my opinion we'll never com-   d pletely understand this issue by relying on the kinds of methods we've employed so far in our discussion: a longer and fuller approach is needed. Still, we can hope to come up with something which is in keeping with what we've already said in the earlier stages of our enquiry.'

'Shouldn't we be content with that?' he asked. 'I for one would be satisfied with that for the time being.'

'And it'll do perfectly well for me too,' I said.

'No flagging, then,' he said. 'On with the enquiry.'

'Well, here's something we're bound to agree on,   e aren't we?' I asked. 'That we do contain the same kinds of features and characteristics as the community. I mean, where else could it have got them from?

When the general population of a community consists of people who are reputedly passionate—Thracians and Scythians, for example, and almost any northerner—it would be absurd to think that passion arises in this community from any other source. And the same goes for love of knowledge, for which our country has a strong reputation; and being mercenary might be claimed to be a particular characteristic of Phoenicians and Egyptians.'

'Certainly.'

'This is a matter of fact, then,' I said, 'and it wasn't hard to discover.'

'No.'

'But here's a hard one: is there just a single thing which we use for doing everything, or are there three and we use different things for different tasks? Do we learn with one of our aspects, get worked up with another, and with a third desire the pleasures of eating, sex, and so on, or do we use the whole of our mind for every task we actually get going on? These questions won't be easy to answer satisfactorily.'

'I agree,' he said.

'Well, let's approach an answer by trying to see whether these aspects are the same as one another or are different.'

'How?'

'It's clear that the same one thing cannot simultaneously either act or be acted on in opposite ways in the same respect and in the same context. And consequently, if we find this happening in the case of these aspects of ourselves, we'll know that there are more than one of them.'

'All right.'

'What about this, then?'

'What?'

'Is it possible for the same thing to be simultaneously at rest and in motion in the same respect?' I asked.

'Of course not.'

'Let's take a closer look before agreeing, otherwise we'll start arguing later. My assumption is that if someone claims that a person who is standing still, but moving his hands and head, is the same person simultaneously being still and moving, we won't approve of this way of putting it, as opposed to saying that one part of him is still, and another part of him is moving. Yes?'

'Yes.'

'So even if the advocate of the claim were to get even more subtle and ingeniously maintain that when a top is spinning round with its peg fixed in place, then this is definitely a case of something simultaneously being still and moving as a whole, or that the same goes for anything else which spins round on one spot, we wouldn't accept this assertion. We'll say that in this situation these objects are not still and moving in the same respects. We'll point out that they include an axis and a circumference, and that they may be still in respect of their axes (in the sense that they're not tipping over at all), but they have circular motion in respect of their circumferences; and we'll add that when one of these objects tips its upright to the right or left or front or back while simultaneously spinning round, then it has no stillness in any respect.'

'Yes, that's right,' he said.

'No assertion of this kind will put us off, then, or make us in the slightest inclined to believe that the same thing could ever simultaneously be acted on or exist or act in opposite ways in the same respect and in the same context.'

'I won't be put off, anyway,' he said.

'That's as may be,' I said. 'But let's not feel compelled to have all the bother of going through every single one of these arguments and proving them false. Let's assume that we're right and carry on, with the understanding that if we ever turn out to have been mistaken, all the conclusions we draw on the basis of this assumption will be invalidated.'

'Yes, that's what we'd better do,' he said.

'Wouldn't you count assent and dissent,' I asked, 'seeking and avoidance, and liking and disliking, as all pairs of opposites? It'll make no difference whether you think of them as ways of acting or of being acted on.'

'Yes, they're opposites,' he answered.

'What about thirst and hunger and the desires generally,' I went on, 'and what about wishing and wanting? Wouldn't you say that all these things belong somewhere among the sets we've just mentioned? For example, won't you describe the mind of anyone who is in a state of desire as seeking to fulfil his desires, or as liking whatever the desired object is? Or again, to the extent that it wants to get hold of something, don't you think it is internally assenting to this thing, as if in response to a question, and is longing for it to happen?'

'Yes, I do.'

'And what about the states of antipathy, reluctance, or unwillingness? Won't we put these states in the opposite category, which includes dislike and aversion?'

'Of course.'

d 'Under these circumstances, then, won't we say that there is a category which consists of the desires, and that the most conspicuous desires are the ones called thirst and hunger?'

'Yes,' he said.

'And the one is desire for drink, the other desire for food?'

'Yes.'

'Now, is thirst, in itself, the mental desire for anything more than the object we mentioned? For example, is thirst thirst for a hot drink or a cold one, a lot of drink or a little, or in short for any particular kind of drink at all? Doesn't it take heat in addition to thirst e to give it the extra feature of being desire for something cold, and cold to make it desire for something hot? Doesn't it take a thirst which has been aggravated into becoming strong to produce the desire for a lot of drink, and doesn't it take a weak thirst to produce the desire for a little drink? The actual state of being thirsty, however, cannot possibly be desire for anything other than its natural object, which is just drink; and the same goes for hunger and food.'

'Yes,' he said. 'Each desire is for its natural object only, and the desire for an object of this or that type is a result of some addition.'

438a 'It should be quite impossible, then,' I said, 'for anyone to catch us unawares and rattle us with the claim that no one desires drink, but a good drink, and no one desires food, but good food. Everyone desires good, they say, so if thirst is a desire, it must be desire for a good drink or whatever; and so on for the other desires.'

'There might seem to be some plausibility to the claim,' he remarked.

'But there are only two categories of things whose nature is to be relative,' I said. 'The first category consists, in my opinion, of things which have particular qualities and whose correlates have particular qualities; the second category consists of things b which are just what they are and whose correlates are just what they are.'

'I don't understand,' he said.

'Don't you realize', I said, 'that anything which is greater is greater than something?'

'Yes.'

'Than something smaller?'

'Yes.'

'Whereas anything which is a lot greater is relative to something which is a lot smaller. Agreed?'

'Yes.'

'And anything which was once greater (or will be) is relative to something which was once smaller (or will be), isn't it?'

'Of course,' he said.

'And the same goes for more in relation to less, c and double in relation to half (and all similar numerical relations); also for heavier in relation to lighter, quicker in relation to slower, and moreover hot in relation to cold, and so on and so forth, don't you think?'

'Yes.'

'And what about the branches of knowledge? Isn't it the same story? Knowledge in itself is knowledge of information in itself (or whatever you choose to call the object of knowledge), but a particular branch of knowledge, knowledge qualified, is knowledge of a particular qualified kind of thing. d Here's an example: when the knowledge of making houses was developed, didn't it differ from the rest of the branches of knowledge and consequently gain its own name, building?'

'Of course.'

'And didn't it do so by virtue of the fact that it is a particular kind of knowledge, a kind which none of the other branches of knowledge is?'

'Yes.'

'And wasn't it when its object came into being as a particular kind of thing that it too came into being as a particular kind of knowledge? And doesn't the same go for all the other branches of expertise and knowledge?'

'Yes, it does.'

'I wonder if you've grasped my meaning now,' I said. 'You should think of this as the point I was trying to make before, when I said that there are two categories of things whose nature it is to be relative: some are only themselves and are related to objects which are only themselves; others have particular qualities and are related to objects with particular qualities. I don't mean to imply that their quality is the same as the quality of their objects—that knowledge of health and illness is itself healthy and ill, and knowledge of evil and good is itself evil and good. I mean that when knowledge occurs whose object is not the unqualified object of knowledge, but an object with a particular quality (say, health and illness), then the consequence is that the knowledge itself also acquires a particular quality, and this is why it is no longer called just plain knowledge: the qualification is added, and it is called medical knowledge.'

'I do understand,' he said, 'and I agree as well.'

'As for thirst, then,' I said, 'don't you think it finds its essential place among relative things? And what it essentially is, of course, is thirst . . .'

'. . . for drink,' he said. 'Yes, I agree.'

'So for drink of a particular kind there is also thirst of a particular kind; but thirst in itself is not thirst for a lot of drink or a little drink, or a beneficial drink or a harmful drink, or in short for drink of any particular kind. Thirst in itself is essentially just thirst for drink in itself.'

'Absolutely.'

'When someone is thirsty, then, the only thing— in so far as he is thirsty—that his mind wants is to drink. This is what it longs for and strives for.'

'Clearly.'

'So imagine an occasion when something is making it resist the pull of its thirst: isn't this bound to be a different part of it from the thirsty part, which is impelling it towards drink as if it were an animal? I mean, we've already agreed that the same one thing cannot thanks to the same part of itself simultaneously have opposite effects in the same context.'

'No, it can't.'

'As an analogy, it isn't in my opinion right to say that an archer's hands are simultaneously pushing the bow away and pulling it closer. Strictly, one hand is pushing it away and the other is pulling it close.'

'I quite agree,' he said.

'Now, do we know of cases where thirsty people are unwilling to drink?'

'Certainly,' he said. 'It's a common occurrence.'

'What could be the explanation for these cases?' I asked. 'Don't we have to say that their mind contains a part which is telling them to drink, and a part which is telling them not to drink, and that this is a different part and overcomes the part which is telling them to drink?'

'I think so,' he said.

'And those occasions when thirst and so on are countermanded occur thanks to rationality, whereas the pulls and impulses occur thanks to afflictions and diseased states, don't they?'

'I suppose so.'

'So it wouldn't be irrational of us to expect that these are two separate parts,' I said, 'one of which we can describe as rational, and the other as irrational and desirous. The first is responsible for the mind's capacity to think rationally, and the second— which is an ally of certain satisfactions and pleasures—for its capacity to feel lust, hunger, and thirst, and in general to be stirred by desire.'

'No, it wouldn't be irrational,' he said. 'This would be a perfectly reasonable view for us to hold.'

'Let's have these, then,' I said, 'as two distinct aspects of our minds. What about the passionate part, however, which is responsible for the mind's capacity for passion? Is it a third part, or might it be interchangeable with one of the other two?'

'I suppose it might be the same as the desirous part,' he said.

'But there's a story I once heard which seems to me to be reliable,' I said, 'about how Leontius the son of Aglaeon was coming up from the Piraeus, outside the North Wall but close to it, when he saw some corpses with the public executioner standing near by. On the one hand, he experienced the desire to see them, but at the same time he felt disgust and averted his gaze. For a while, he struggled and kept his hands over his eyes, but finally he was overcome by the desire; he opened his eyes wide, ran up to the corpses, and said, "There you are, you wretches! What a lovely sight! I hope you feel satisfied!"'

'Yes, I've heard the story too,' he said.

'Now, what it suggests', I said, 'is that it's possible for anger to be at odds with the desires, as if they were different things.'

'Yes, it does,' he agreed.

'And that's far from being an isolated case, isn't it?' I asked. 'It's not at all uncommon to find a per-

son's desires compelling him to go against his reason, and to see him cursing himself and venting his
passion on the source of the compulsion within him.
It's as if there were two warring factions, with passion fighting on the side of reason. But I'm sure you
wouldn't claim that you had ever, in yourself or in
anyone else, met a case of passion siding with the
desires against the rational mind, when the rational
mind prohibits resistance.'

'No, I certainly haven't,' he said.

'And what about when you feel you're in the wrong?'
I asked. 'If someone who in your opinion has a right to
do so retaliates by inflicting on you hunger and cold and
so on, then isn't it the case that, in proportion to your
goodness of character, you are incapable of getting angry at this treatment and your passion, as I say, has no
inclination to get worked up against him?'

'True,' he said.

'But suppose you feel you're being wronged. Under these circumstances, your passion boils and
rages, and fights for what you regard as right. Then
hunger, cold, and other sufferings make you stand
firm and conquer them, and only success or death
can stop it fighting the good fight, unless it is recalled by your rational mind and calmed down, as a
dog is by a shepherd.'

'That's a very good simile,' he said. 'And in fact
the part we've got the auxiliaries to play in our community is just like that of dogs, with their masters
being the rulers, who are, as it were, the shepherds
of the community.'

'Yes, you've got it,' I said. 'That's exactly what
I mean. But there's something else here too, and I
wonder if you've noticed it as well.'

'What is it?'

'That we're getting the opposite impression of the
passionate part from what we did before. Previously,
we were thinking that it was an aspect of the desirous
part, but now that seems to be way off the mark, and
we're saying that when there's mental conflict, it is
far more likely to fight alongside reason.'

'Absolutely,' he said.

'Is it different from the rational part, then, or is it
a version of it, in which case there are two, not three,
mental categories—the rational and the desirous? Or
will the analogy with the community hold good?
Three classes constituted the community—the one

which works for a living, the auxiliaries, and the policy-makers—so is there in the mind as well a third
part, the passionate part, which is an auxiliary of
the rational part, unless it is corrupted by bad
upbringing?'

'It must be a third party,' he said.

'Yes,' I said, '*if* we find that it's as distinct from
the rational part as it is from the desirous part.'

'But that's easy,' he said. 'Just look at children.
It's evident that from the moment of their birth they
have a copious supply of passion, but I'm not convinced that some of them ever acquire reason, and it
takes quite a time for most of them to do so.'

'Yes, you've certainly put that well,' I said. 'And
animals provide further evidence of the truth of what
you're saying. Moreover, we can adduce the passage
from Homer we quoted earlier: "He struck his breast
and spoke sternly to his heart." Clearly, Homer here
has one distinct part rebuking another distinct part—
the part which has thought rationally about what is
better and worse rebuking the part whose passion is
irrationally becoming aroused.'

'You're absolutely right,' he said.

'It's not been easy,' I said, 'but we've made it to
the other shore: we've reached the reasonable conclusion that the constituent categories of a community and of any individual's mind are identical in nature and number.'

'Yes, they are.'

Since the three mental parts are precisely analogous
to the three social classes of Plato's community,
Plato now analyses individual wisdom, courage,
self-discipline, and morality in ways which precisely parallel his analysis of their civic manifestations. Morality, then, is an inner state and has little
to do with external appearances. It is harmony between the parts of a person's mind under the leadership of his or her intellect; immorality is anarchy
and civil war between the parts. The remaining
question, whether morality or immorality is rewarding, is raised, but then deferred to Chapter 11.

'Isn't it bound to follow that the manner and cause
of a community's and an individual's wisdom are
identical?'

'Naturally.'

'And that the manner and cause of a community's and an individual's courage are identical, and that the same goes for every other factor which contributes in both cases towards goodness?'

'Inevitably.'

'So no doubt, Glaucon, we'll also be claiming that human morality is the same in kind as a community's morality.'

'Yes, that's absolutely inevitable too.'

'We can't have forgotten, however, that a community's morality consists in each of its three constituent classes doing its own job.'

'No, I'm sure we haven't,' he said.

'So we should impress upon our minds the idea that the same goes for human beings as well. Where each of the constituent parts of an individual does its own job, the individual will be moral and will do *his* own job.'

'Yes, we certainly should do that,' he said.

'Since the rational part is wise and looks out for the whole of the mind, isn't it right for it to rule, and for the passionate part to be its subordinate and its ally?'

'Yes.'

'Now—to repeat—isn't it the combination of culture and exercise which will make them attuned to each other? The two combined provide fine discussions and studies to stretch and educate the rational part, and music and rhythm to relax, calm, and soothe the passionate part.'

'Absolutely.'

'And once these two parts have received this education and have been trained and conditioned in their true work, then they are to be put in charge of the desirous part, which is the major constituent of an individual's mind and is naturally insatiably greedy for things. So they have to watch over it and make sure that it doesn't get so saturated with physical pleasures (as they are called) that in its bloated and strengthened state it stops doing its own job, and tries to dominate and rule over things which it is not equipped by its hereditary status to rule over, and so plunges the whole of everyone's life into chaos.'

'Yes, indeed,' he said.

'Moreover, these two are perfect for guarding the entire mind and the body against external enemies, aren't they?' I asked. 'The rational part will do the planning, and the passionate part the fighting. The passionate part will obey the ruling part and employ its courage to carry out the plans.'

'True.'

'I imagine, then, that it is the passionate part of a person which we are taking into consideration when we describe him as courageous: we're saying that neither pain nor pleasure stops his passionate part retaining the pronouncements of reason about what is and is not to be feared.'

'That's right,' he agreed.

'And the part we take into consideration when we call him wise is that little part—his internal ruler, which made these pronouncements—which knows what is advantageous for each of the three parts and for their joint unity.'

'Yes.'

'And don't we call him self-disciplined when there's concord and attunement between these same parts—that is, when the ruler and its two subjects unanimously agree on the necessity of the rational part being the ruler and when they don't rebel against it?'

'Yes, that's exactly what self-discipline is, in both a community and an individual,' he said.

'And we're not changing our minds about the manner and cause of morality.'

'Absolutely not.'

'Well,' I said, 'have we blunted the edge of our notion of morality in any way? Do we have any grounds for thinking that our conclusions about its nature in a community don't apply in this context?'

'I don't think so,' he replied.

'If there's still any doubt in our minds,' I said, 'we can eradicate it completely by checking our conclusion against everyday cases.'

'What cases?'

'Take this community of ours and a person who resembles it by virtue of both his nature and his upbringing, and suppose, for instance, we had to state whether, in our opinion, a person of this type would steal money which had been deposited with him. Is it conceivable to you that anyone would think our man capable of this, rather than any other type of person?'

'No one could think that,' he said.

'And he could have nothing to do with temple-robbery, theft, and betrayal either of his personal friends or, on a public scale, of his country, could he?'

'No, he couldn't.'

'Moreover, nothing could induce him to break an oath or any other kind of agreement.'

'No, nothing.'

'And he's the last person you'd expect to find committing adultery, neglecting his parents, and failing to worship the gods.'

'Yes, of course,' he said.

'And isn't the reason for all of this the fact that each of his constituent parts does its own job as ruler or subject?'

'Yes, that's the only reason.'

'Do you need to look any further for morality, then? Don't you think it can only be the capacity we've come up with, which enables both people and communities to be like this?'

'I for one certainly don't need to look any further,' he said.

'Our dream has finally come true, then. We said we had a vague impression that we had probably—with the help of some god—stumbled across the origin and some kind of outline of morality right at the start of our foundation of the community.'

'Absolutely.'

'It turns out, then, Glaucon—and this is why it was so useful—that the idea that a person who has been equipped by nature to be a shoemaker or a joiner or whatever should make shoes or do joinery or whatever was a dreamt image of morality.'

'So it seems.'

'And we've found that in real life morality is the same kind of property, apparently, though not in the field of external activities. Its sphere is a person's inner activity: it is really a matter of oneself and the parts of oneself. Once he has stopped his mental constituents doing any job which is not their own or intruding on one another's work; once he has set his own house in order, which is what he really should be concerned with; once he is his own ruler, and is well regulated, and has internal concord; once he has treated the three factors as if they were literally the three defining notes of an octave—low, high, and middle—and has created a harmony out of them and however many notes there may be in between; once he has bound all the factors together and made himself a perfect unity instead of a plurality, self-disciplined and internally attuned: then and only then does he act—if he acts—to acquire property or look after his body or play a role in government or do some private business. In the course of this activity, it is conduct which preserves and promotes this inner condition of his that he regards as moral and describes as fine, and it is the knowledge which oversees this conduct that he regards as wisdom; however, it is any conduct which disperses this condition that he regards as immoral, and the thinking which oversees this conduct that he regards as stupidity.'

'You're absolutely right, Socrates,' he said.

'All right,' I said. 'I imagine that we'd regard as no more than the truth the claim that we had found out what it is to be a moral person and a moral community, and had discovered what morality actually is when it occurs in them.'

'Yes, we certainly would,' he said.

'Shall we make the claim, then?'

'Yes.'

'So be it,' I said. 'Next, I suppose, we should consider immorality.'

'Obviously.'

'Isn't it bound to involve these three factors being in conflict, intruding into one another's work, and exchanging roles, and one part rebelling against the mind as a whole in an improper attempt to usurp rulership—improper because its natural function is to be dominated unless it belongs to the ruling class? Our position, I'm sure, will be that it is disruption and disorder of the three parts along these lines that constitutes not only immorality, but also indiscipline, cowardice, and stupidity—in a word, badness of any kind.'

'Precisely,' he said.

'Now that morality and immorality are in plain view, doesn't that mean that wrongdoing and immoral conduct, and right conduct too, are as well?' I asked.

'Why?'

'Because their role in the mind happens to be identical to that of healthy or unhealthy factors in the body,' I said.

'In what sense?'

'Healthy factors engender health, and unhealthy ones illness.'

'Yes.'

d 'Well, doesn't moral behaviour engender morality, while immoral behaviour engenders immorality?'

'Inevitably.'

'But you create health by making the components of a body control and be controlled as nature intended, and you create disease by subverting this natural order.'

'Yes.'

'Doesn't it follow,' I said, 'that you create morality by making the components of a mind control and be controlled as nature intended, and immorality by subverting this natural order?'

'Absolutely,' he said.

'Goodness, then, is apparently a state of mental health, bloom, and vitality; badness is a state of men-
e tal sickness, deformity, and infirmity.'

'That's right.'

'Isn't it the case, therefore, that goodness is a consequence of good conduct, badness of bad conduct?'

'Necessarily.'

'Now we come to what is, I suppose, the final topic. We have to consider whether moral conduct,
445a fine behaviour, and being moral (whether or not the person is known to be moral) are rewarding, or whether it is wrongdoing and being immoral (provided that the immoral person doesn't have to pay for his crimes and doesn't become a better person as a result of being punished).'

'It seems to me that it would be absurd to consider that topic now, Socrates,' he said. 'Life isn't thought to be worth living when the natural constitution of the body is ruined, even if one has all the food and drink and wealth and power in the world. So how could it be worth living when the natural constitution of the very life-force within us is dis-
b rupted and ruined? How could life be worth living if a person's chosen course of action is to avoid the path which will lead him away from badness and immorality and towards the possession of morality and goodness, given the evident accuracy of our descriptions of both of these states?'

'Yes, it is absurd,' I agreed. 'All the same, since we've reached a point which affords the clearest pos-

sible view of the truth of these matters, we shouldn't give up now.'

'I couldn't agree more,' he said. 'Giving up should be the last thing on our minds.'

'Come and join me here, then,' I said, 'and you'll c see, I think, all the types of badness there are—at least, the ones that are worth seeing.'

'I'm coming,' he said. 'You have only to tell me.'

'Well,' I said, 'the impression I get from the vantage-point we've reached at this point of our discussion is that while there's only one kind of goodness, there are countless types of badness, of which four are worth mentioning.'

'What do you mean?' he asked.

'There are probably as many types of character,' I said, 'as there are identifiable forms of political system.'

'And how many is that?'

'There are five types of political system,' I d replied, 'and five types of character.'

'Please tell me what they are,' he said.

'All right,' I said. 'One of the forms of political system would be the one we've described. There are two possible ways of referring to it, however: if a single outstanding individual arises within the ruling class, it's called a kingship; but if there is a plurality of rulers, it's called an aristocracy.'

'True,' he said.

'This is the first of the types of political system I had in mind,' I said. 'The point is that whether there is a single ruler in the community, or whether there are more than one, they won't disturb any of the com- e munity's important laws, since they'll have been brought up and educated in the manner we've explained.'

'No, it's implausible to think that they will,' he said. . . .

CHAPTER 9
THE SUPREMACY OF GOOD

. . . 'I'm sure you remember when, as a result of distinguishing three aspects within the mind, we defined morality, self-discipline, courage, and wisdom,' I said.

'If I didn't,' he said, 'then we might as well stop right now.'

'Do you also remember how we prefaced our discussion of those qualities?'

'How?'

'We said that it would take a different route, a longer one, to reach the best possible vantage-point and that they would be plainly visible to anyone who went that way, but that it was possible to come up with arguments which were in keeping with the kinds of discussions we'd already been having. You said that would do, and we proceeded at the time on that basis. I think the argument was defective, in terms of precision, but it's up to you to say whether you were happy with it.'

'Yes, I was happy enough with it,' he said, 'and so was everyone else.'

'But in these sorts of matters, my friend,' I said, 'anything which misses the truth by even a tiny amount is nowhere near "enough". Anything less than perfect is not up to the mark at all, though people occasionally think it's adequate and that they don't need to look any further.'

'Yes, a great many people feel this,' he said, 'because they're lazy.'

'But it's a completely inappropriate feeling for a guardian of a community and its laws to have,' I said.

'I suppose so,' he said.

'Then a guardian had better take the longer route, Adeimantus,' I said, 'and put just as much effort into his intellectual work as his physical exercise. Otherwise, as we said a moment ago, he'll never see that fundamental field of study through to the end—and it's not just fundamental, but particularly appropriate for him.'

'Are you implying that morality and the other qualities we discussed are not the most important things there are—that there's something even more fundamental than them?' he asked.

'It's not only more fundamental,' I said, 'but it's exactly the kind of thing which requires viewing as a completely finished product, without skimping and looking merely at an outline, as we did just now. I mean, wouldn't it be absurd to devote extremes of energy and effort to getting as precise and clear a picture as possible of insignificant matters, and then not to think that the most important matters deserve the utmost precision too?'

'An excellent sentiment,' he said. 'But surely you don't expect to get away without being asked what this fundamental field of study of yours is, and what it is concerned with?'

'No, I don't,' I answered. 'Go ahead and ask your questions. In actual fact, you've not infrequently been told what it is, but it's either slipped your mind for the moment, or you're intending to make trouble for me by attacking my position. I incline towards the latter alternative, since you've often been told that the most important thing to try to understand is the character of goodness, because this is where anything which is moral (or whatever) gets its value and advantages from. It can hardly have escaped your notice that this is my position, and you must know what I'm going to add: that our knowledge of goodness is inadequate. And you appreciate, I'm sure, that there's absolutely no point in having expert knowledge of everything else, but lacking knowledge of goodness, just as there isn't in having anything else either, unless goodness comes with it. I mean, do you think there's any advantage in owning everything in the world except good things, or in understanding everything else except goodness, and therefore failing to understand anything worth while and good?'

'I certainly don't,' he said.

'Now, it can't have escaped your notice either that the usual view of goodness is that it's pleasure, while there's also a more ingenious view around, that it's knowledge.'

'Of course it hasn't.'

'As you also know, however, my friend, the people who hold the latter view are incapable of explaining exactly *what* knowledge constitutes goodness, but are forced ultimately to say that it is knowledge of goodness.'

'And so to make complete fools of themselves,' he remarked.

'Of course they do,' I said. 'First they tell us off for not knowing what goodness is, then they talk to us as if we did know what it is. I mean, to say it's knowledge of goodness is to assume that we understand what they're saying when they use the term "goodness".'

'You're absolutely right,' he said.

'What about the definition of goodness as pleasure? Aren't its proponents just as thoroughly misguided as the others? I mean, they too are forced to make a concession, in this case that there are bad pleasures, aren't they?'

'Certainly.'

'So their position ends up being that it is possible for a single thing to be both good and bad, doesn't it?'

'Naturally.'

'It's clear, therefore, that there's plenty of scope for serious disagreement where goodness is concerned. Yes?'

'Of course.'

'Well, isn't it also clear that whereas (whether it's a matter of doing something, or owning something, or having a certain reputation) people usually prefer the appearance of morality and right, even if there's no reality involved, yet no one is content with any possession that is only apparently good? It's the reality of goodness they want; no one thinks at all highly of mere appearance in this sphere.'

'Yes, that's perfectly clear,' he said.

'So here we have something which everyone, whatever their temperament, is after, and which is the goal of all their activities. They have an inkling of its existence, but they're confused about it and can't adequately grasp its nature or be as certain and as confident about it as they can about other things, and consequently they fail to derive any benefit even from those other activities. When something of this kind and this importance is involved, can we allow the best members of our community, the ones to whom we're going to entrust everything, to be equally in the dark?'

'Certainly not,' he protested.

'Anyway,' I said, 'I imagine that anyone who is ignorant about the goodness of moral and right conduct would make a second-rate guardian of morality and right, and I suspect that no one will fully understand them until he knows about their relation to goodness.'

'Your suspicion is right,' he said.

'So the constitution and organization of our community will be perfect only if they are overseen by the kind of guardian who has this knowledge, won't they?'

'Necessarily,' he said. 'But Socrates, do *you* identify goodness with knowledge or pleasure, or with something else?'

'Just listen to him!' I exclaimed. 'It's been perfectly obvious all along that other people's views on the matter weren't going to be enough for you.'

'That's because I don't think it's right, Socrates,' he said, 'for someone who's devoted so much time to the matter to be in a position to state others' beliefs, but not his own.'

'But do you think it's right', I responded, 'for someone to talk as if he knew what he doesn't know?'

'Of course not,' he said. 'Not as if he knew, but as if he'd formed opinions—he should be prepared to say what he thinks.'

'But aren't ideas which aren't based on knowledge always defective, in your experience?' I asked. 'The best of them are blind. I mean, don't people who have a correct belief, but no knowledge, strike you as exactly like blind people who happen to be taking the right road?'

'Yes,' he said.

'Well, do you want to see things which are defective, blind, and deformed,' I asked, 'when you could be getting lucid, correct views from elsewhere?'

Socrates professes himself incapable of defining goodness and proposes a simile instead. This is the Simile of the Sun, the first of the three great, and justly famous, interconnected images which Plato uses to convey some of his core views. The Sun consists of an extended analogy between the visible and intelligible realms: just as the sun is the source of light and growth, and is responsible for sight and seeing, and is the acme of the visible realm, so goodness is the source of truth and reality, and is responsible for knowledge and knowing, and is the acme of the intelligible realm. Belief, on the other hand, is like partial sight.

'Socrates,' said Glaucon, 'please don't back away from the finishing-line, so to speak. We'd be happy with the kind of description of goodness that you gave of morality, self-discipline, and so on.'

'So would I, Glaucon,' I said, 'very happy. But I'm afraid it'll be more than I can manage, and that my malformed efforts will make me ridiculous. What I suggest, my friends, is that we forget about trying to define goodness itself for the time being. You see, I don't at the moment think that our current impulse is enough to take us to where I'd like to see us go. However, I am prepared to talk about something which seems to me to be the child of goodness and to bear a very strong resemblance to it. Would you like me to do that? If not, we can just forget it.'

'Please do,' he said. 'You can settle your account by discussing the father another time.'

'I hope I can make the repayment,' I said, 'and you can recover the debt, rather than just the interest, as you are now. Anyway, as interest on your account, here's an account of the child of goodness. But please be careful that I don't cheat you—not that I intend to—by giving you a counterfeit description of the child.'

'We'll watch out for that as best we can,' he replied. 'Just go ahead, please.'

'First I want to make sure that we're not at cross purposes,' I said, 'and to remind you of something that came up earlier, though you've often heard it on other occasions as well.'

'What?' he asked.

'As we talk,' I said, 'we mention and differentiate between a lot of beautiful things and a lot of good things and so on.'

'Yes, we do.'

'And we also talk about beauty itself, goodness itself and so on. All the things we refer to as a plurality on those occasions we also conversely count as belonging to a single class by virtue of the fact that they have a single particular character, and we say that the *x* itself is "what really is".'

'True.'

'And we say that the first lot is visible rather than intelligible, whereas characters are intelligible rather than visible.'

'Absolutely.'

'With what aspect of ourselves do we see the things we see?'

'With our sight,' he replied.

'And we use hearing for the things we hear, and so on for all the other senses and the things we perceive. Yes?'

'Of course.'

'Well, have you ever stopped to consider', I asked, 'how generous the creator of the senses was when he created the domain of seeing and being seen?'

'No, not really,' he said.

'Look at it this way. Are hearing and sound deficient? Do they need an extra something to make

the one hear and the other be heard—some third thing without which hearing won't hear and sound won't be heard?'

'No,' he answered.

'And in my opinion', I went on, 'the same goes for many other domains, if not all: they don't need anything like this. Or can you point to one that does?'

'*I* can't,' he said.

'But do you realize that sight and the visible realm *are* deficient?'

'How?'

'Even if a person's eyes are capable of sight, and he's trying to use it, and what he's trying to look at is coloured, the sight will see nothing and the colours will remain unseen, surely, unless there is also present an extra third thing which is made specifically for this purpose.'

'What is this thing you're getting at?' he asked.

'It's what we call light,' I said.

'You're right,' he said.

'So if light has value, then because it links the sense of sight and the ability to be seen, it is far and away the most valuable link there is.'

'Well, it certainly does have value,' he said.

'Which of the heavenly gods would you say is responsible for this? Whose light makes it possible for our sight to see and for the things we see to be seen?'

'My reply will be no different from what yours or anyone else's would be,' he said. 'I mean, you're obviously expecting the answer, "the sun".'

'Now, there are certain conclusions to be drawn from comparing sight to this god.'

'What?'

'Sight and the sun aren't to be identified: neither the sense itself nor its location—which we call the eye—is the same as the sun.'

'True.'

'Nevertheless, there's no sense-organ which more closely resembles the sun, in my opinion, than the eye.'

'The resemblance is striking.'

'Moreover, the eye's ability to see has been bestowed upon it and channelled into it, as it were, by the sun.'

'Yes.'

'So the sun is not to be identified with sight, but is responsible for sight and is itself within the visible realm. Right?'

'Yes,' he said.

'The sun is the child of goodness I was talking about, then,' I said. 'It is a counterpart to its father, goodness. As goodness stands in the intelligible realm to intelligence and the things we know, so in the visible realm the sun stands to sight and the things we see.'

'I don't understand,' he said. 'I need more detail, please.'

'As you know,' I explained, 'when our eyes are directed towards things whose colours are no longer bathed in daylight, but in artificial light instead, then they're less effective and seem to be virtually blind, as if they didn't even have the potential for seeing clearly.'

'Certainly,' he said.

'But when they're directed towards things which are lit up by the sun, then they see clearly and obviously do have that potential.'

'Of course.'

'Well, here's how you can think about the mind as well. When its object is something which is lit up by truth and reality, then it has—and obviously has—intelligent awareness and knowledge. However, when its object is permeated with darkness (that is, when its object is something which is subject to generation and decay), then it has beliefs and is less effective, because its beliefs chop and change, and under these circumstances it comes across as devoid of intelligence.'

'Yes, it does.'

'Well, what I'm saying is that it's goodness which gives the things we know their truth and makes it possible for people to have knowledge. It is responsible for knowledge and truth, and you should think of it as being within the intelligible realm, but you shouldn't identify it with knowledge and truth, otherwise you'll be wrong: for all their value, it is even more valuable. In the other realm, it is right to regard light and sight as resembling the sun, but not to identify either of them with the sun; so in this realm it is right to regard knowledge and truth as resembling goodness, but not to identify either of them with goodness, which should be rated even more highly.'

'You're talking about something of inestimable value,' he said, 'if it's not only the source of knowledge and truth, but is also more valuable than them.

I mean, you certainly don't seem to be identifying it with pleasure!'

'How could you even think it?' I exclaimed. 'But we can take our analogy even further.'

'How?'

'I think you'll agree that the ability to be seen is not the only gift the sun gives to the things we see. It is also the source of their generation, growth, and nourishment, although it isn't actually the process of generation.'

'Of course it isn't.'

'And it isn't only the known-ness of the things we know which is conferred upon them by goodness, but also their reality and their being, although goodness isn't actually the state of being, but surpasses being in majesty and might.'

'It's way beyond human comprehension, all right,' was Glaucon's quite amusing comment.

'It's your fault for forcing me to express my views on the subject,' I replied.

'Yes, and please don't stop,' he said. 'If you've left anything out of your explanation of the simile of the sun, then the least you could do is continue with it.'

'There are plenty of omissions, in fact,' I said.

'Don't leave any gaps,' he said, 'however small.'

'I think I'll have to leave a lot out,' I said, 'but I'll try to make it as complete as I can at the moment.'

'All right,' he said.

The image of the Line, in which now follows, is expressly (509c) supposed to supplement the Sun.

$$| \underline{\quad} | \underline{\quad\quad} | \underline{\quad\quad} | \underline{\quad\quad} |$$

A   B   C   D

As *A* stands to *B* in terms of clarity and opacity, so *C* stands to *D* as well. *A* consists of likenesses, which are identified by conjecture; *B* consists of the solid things of the material world, which are identified confidently; *C* and *D* consist of the types, which are knowable, but the two sections are distinguished because of a difference in methodology. As *B* stands to *A* in terms of truth, so *C* and *D* together stand to *A* and *B* together. *A* and *B* together constitute the visible realm, which is the realm of belief; *C* and *D* together constitute the intelligible realm, which is the realm of knowledge.

'So bear in mind the two things we've been talking about,' I said, 'one of which rules over the intelligible realm and its inhabitants, while the other rules over the visible realm—I won't say over the heavens in case you think I'm playing clever word-games. Anyway, do you understand this distinction between visible things and intelligible things?'

'Yes.'

'Well, picture them as a line cut into two unequal sections and, following the same proportion, subdivide both the section of the visible realm and that of the intelligible realm. Now you can compare the sections in terms of clarity and unclarity. The first section in the visible realm consists of likenesses, by which I mean a number of things: shadows, reflections (on the surface of water or on anything else which is inherently compact, smooth, and bright), and so on. Do you see what I'm getting at?'

'I do.'

'And you should count the other section of the visible realm as consisting of the things whose likenesses are found in the first section: all the flora and fauna there are in the world, and every kind of artefact too.'

'All right.'

'I wonder whether you'd agree,' I said, 'that truth and lack of truth have been the criteria for distinguishing these sections, and that the image stands to the original as the realm of beliefs stands to the realm of knowledge?'

'Yes,' he said, 'I certainly agree.'

'Now have a look at how to subdivide the section which belongs to the intelligible realm.'

'How?'

'Like this. If the mind wants to explore the first subdivision, it can do so only by using those former originals as likenesses and by taking things for granted on its journey, which leads it to an end-point, rather than to a starting-point. If it wants to explore the second subdivision, however, it takes things for granted in order to travel to a starting-point where nothing needs to be taken for granted, and it has no involvement with likenesses, as before, but makes its approach by means of types alone, in and of themselves.'

'I don't quite understand what you're saying,' he said.

'You will if I repeat it,' I said, 'because this preamble will make it easier to understand. I'm sure you're aware that practitioners of geometry, arithmetic, and so on take for granted things like numerical oddness and evenness, the geometrical figures, the three kinds of angle, and any other things of that sort which are relevant to a given subject. They act as if they know about these things, treat them as basic, and don't feel any further need to explain them either to themselves or to anyone else, on the grounds that there is nothing unclear about them. They make them the starting-points for their subsequent investigations, which end after a coherent chain of reasoning at the point they'd set out to reach in their research.'

'Yes, I'm certainly well aware of this,' he said.

'So you must also be aware that in the course of their discussions they make use of visible forms, despite the fact that they're not interested in visible forms as such, but in the things of which the visible forms are likenesses: that is, their discussions are concerned with what it is to be a square, and with what it is to be a diagonal (and so on), rather than with the diagonal (and so on) which occurs in their diagrams. They treat their models and diagrams as likenesses, when these things have likenesses themselves, in fact (that is, shadows and reflections on water); but they're actually trying to see squares and so on in themselves, which only thought can see.'

'You're right,' he said.

'So it was objects of this type that I was describing as belonging to the intelligible realm, with the rider that the mind can explore them only by taking things for granted, and that its goal is not a starting-point, because it is incapable of changing direction and rising above the things it is taking for granted. And I went on to say that it used as likenesses those very things which are themselves the originals of a lower order of likenesses, and that relative to the likenesses, the originals command respect and admiration for their distinctness.'

'I see,' he said. 'You're talking about the objects of geometry and related occupations.'

'Now, can you see what I mean by the second subdivision of the intelligible realm? It is what reason grasps by itself, thanks to its ability to practise dialectic. When it takes things for granted, it doesn't treat them as starting-points, but as basic in the strict sense—as platforms and rungs, for example. These serve it until it reaches a point where nothing needs to be taken for granted, and which is the starting-point for everything. Once it has grasped this starting-point, it turns around and by a process of depending on the things which depend from the starting-point, it descends to an end-point. It makes absolutely no use of anything perceptible by the senses: it aims for types by means of types alone, in and of themselves, and it ends its journey with types.'

'I don't quite understand,' he said. 'I mean, you're talking about crucial matters here, I think. I do understand, however, that you want to mark off that part of the real and intelligible realm which is before the eyes of anyone who knows how to practise dialectic as more clear than the other part, which is before the eyes of practitioners of the various branches of expertise, as we call them. The latter make the things they take for granted their starting-points, and although they inevitably use thought, not the senses, to observe what they observe, yet because of their failure to ascend to a starting-point—because their enquiries rely on taking things for granted—you're saying that they don't understand these things, even though they are intelligible, when related to a starting-point. I take you to be describing what geometers and so on do as thinking rather than knowing, on the grounds that thinking is the intermediate state between believing and knowing.'

'There's nothing wrong with your understanding,' I said. 'And you should appreciate that there are four states of mind, one for each of the four sections. There's knowledge for the highest section and thought for the second one; and you'd better assign confidence to the third one and conjecture to the final one. You can make an orderly progression out of them, and you should regard them as possessing as much clarity as their objects possess truth.'

'I see,' he said. 'That's fine with me: I'll order them in the way you suggest.'

The final image, the Allegory of the Cave, is the longest and most famous of the three. It is introduced rather abruptly, but is meant to fit in with the preceding two images (517b–c, 532a–d). Further details of the fit are a matter of dispute, although the broad outlines are clear enough. Like all the great images of the world's greatest literature, Plato's Cave manages simultaneously to appear transparent and yet unexpectedly rich and surprising. Those readers who believe that philosophy is a dry academic pursuit will be surprised at its presentation here as a pursuit which frees us from a terrible slavery; but for Plato and his peers philosophy is a way of life, not just a course of study.

'Next,' I said, 'here's a situation which you can use as an analogy for the human condition—for our education or lack of it. Imagine people living in a cavernous cell down under the ground; at the far end of the cave, a long way off, there's an entrance open to the outside world. They've been there since childhood, with their legs and necks tied up in a way which keeps them in one place and allows them to look only straight ahead, but not to turn their heads. There's firelight burning a long way further up the cave behind them, and up the slope between the fire and the prisoners there's a road, beside which you should imagine a low wall has been built—like the partition which conjurors place between themselves and their audience and above which they show their tricks.'

'All right,' he said.

'Imagine also that there are people on the other side of this wall who are carrying all sorts of artefacts. These artefacts, human statuettes, and animal models carved in stone and wood and all kinds of materials stick out over the wall; and as you'd expect, some of the people talk as they carry these objects along, while others are silent.'

'This is a strange picture you're painting,' he said, 'with strange prisoners.'

'They're no different from us,' I said. 'I mean, in the first place, do you think they'd see anything of themselves and one another except the shadows cast by the fire on to the cave wall directly opposite them?'

'Of course not,' he said. 'They're forced to spend their lives without moving their heads.'

'And what about the objects which were being carried along? Won't they only see their shadows as well?'

'Naturally.'

'Now, suppose they were able to talk to one another: don't you think they'd assume that their words applied to what they saw passing by in front of them?'

'They couldn't think otherwise.'

"And what if sound echoed off the prison wall opposite them? When any of the passers-by spoke, don't you think they'd be bound to assume that the sound came from a passing shadow?'

'I'm absolutely certain of it,' he said.

c   'All in all, then,' I said, 'the shadows of artefacts would constitute the only reality people in this situation would recognize.'

'That's absolutely inevitable,' he agreed.

'What do you think would happen, then,' I asked, 'if they were set free from their bonds and cured of their inanity? What would it be like if they found that happening to them? Imagine that one of them has been set free and is suddenly made to stand up, to turn his head and walk, and to look towards the firelight. It hurts him to do all this and he's too dazzled to be capable of making out the objects whose shadows he'd formerly been looking at. And suppose someone tells him that what he's been seeing all this time has no substance, and that he's now closer to reality and is seeing more accurately, because of the greater reality of the things in front of his eyes—what do you imagine his reaction would be? And what do you think he'd say if he were shown any of the passing objects and had to respond to being asked what it was? Don't you think he'd be bewildered and would think that there was more reality in what he'd been seeing before than in what he was being shown now?'

'Far more,' he said.

e   'And if he were forced to look at the actual firelight, don't you think it would hurt his eyes? Don't you think he'd turn away and run back to the things he could make out, and would take the truth of the matter to be that these things are clearer than what he was being shown?'

'Yes,' he agreed.

'And imagine him being dragged forcibly away from there up the rough, steep slope,' I went on, 'without being released until he's pulled out into the sunlight. Wouldn't this treatment cause him pain and distress? And once he's reached the sunlight, he wouldn't be able to see a single one of the things

516a

which are currently taken to be real, would he, because his eyes would be overwhelmed by the sun's beams?'

'No, he wouldn't,' he answered, 'not straight away.'

'He wouldn't be able to see things up on the surface of the earth, I suppose, until he'd got used to his situation. At first, it would be shadows that he could most easily make out, then he'd move on to the reflections of people and so on in water, and later he'd be able to see the actual things themselves. Next, he'd feast his eyes on the heavenly bodies and the heavens themselves, which would be easier at night: he'd look at the light of the stars and the moon, rather b than at the sun and sunlight during the daytime.'

'Of course.'

'And at last, I imagine, he'd be able to discern and feast his eyes on the sun—not the displaced image of the sun in water or elsewhere, but the sun on its own, in its proper place.'

'Yes, he'd inevitably come to that,' he said.'

'After that, he'd start to think about the sun and he'd deduce that it is the source of the seasons and the yearly cycle, that the whole of the visible realm is its domain, and that in a sense everything which c he and his peers used to see is its responsibility.'

'Yes, that would obviously be the next point he'd come to,' he agreed.

'Now, if he recalled the cell where he'd originally lived and what passed for knowledge there and his former fellow prisoners, don't you think he'd feel happy about his own altered circumstances, and sorry for them?'

'Definitely.'

'Suppose that the prisoners used to assign prestige and credit to one another, in the sense that they rewarded speed at recognizing the shadows as they passed, and the ability to remember which ones normally come earlier and later and at the same time as which other ones, and expertise at using this as a basis for guessing which ones would arrive next. Do d you think our former prisoner would covet these honours and would envy the people who had status and power there, or would he much prefer, as Homer describes it, "being a slave labouring for someone else—someone without property", and would put up with anything at all, in fact, rather than share their beliefs and their life?'

'Yes, I think he'd go through anything rather than live that way,' he said.

'Here's something else I'd like your opinion about,' I said. 'If he went back underground and sat down again in the same spot, wouldn't the sudden transition from the sunlight mean that his eyes would be overwhelmed by darkness?'

'Certainly,' he replied.

'Now, the process of adjustment would be quite long this time, and suppose that before his eyes had settled down and while he wasn't seeing well, he had once again to compete against those same old prisoners at identifying those shadows. Wouldn't he make a fool of himself? Wouldn't they say that he'd come back from his upward journey with his eyes ruined, and that it wasn't even worth trying to go up there? And wouldn't they—if they could—grab hold of anyone who tried to set them free and take them up there and kill him?'

'They certainly would,' he said.

'Well, my dear Glaucon,' I said, 'you should apply this allegory, as a whole, to what we were talking about before. The region which is accessible to sight should be equated with the prison cell, and the firelight there with the light of the sun. And if you think of the upward journey and the sight of things up on the surface of the earth as the mind's ascent to the intelligible realm, you won't be wrong—at least *I* don't think you'd be wrong, and it's my impression that you want to hear. Only God knows if it's actually true, however. Anyway, it's my opinion that the last thing to be seen—and it isn't easy to see either—in the realm of knowledge is goodness; and the sight of the character of goodness leads one to deduce that it is responsible for everything that is right and fine, whatever the circumstances, and that in the visible realm it is the progenitor of light and of the source of light, and in the intelligible realm it is the source and provider of truth and knowledge. And I also think that the sight of it is a prerequisite for intelligent conduct either of one's own private affairs or of public business.'

'I couldn't agree more,' he said.

'All right, then,' I said. 'I wonder if you also agree with me in not finding it strange that people who've travelled there don't want to engage in human business: there's nowhere else their minds would ever rather be than in the upper region—which is hardly surprising, if our allegory has got this aspect right as well.'

'No, it's not surprising,' he agreed.

'Well, what about this?' I asked. 'Imagine someone returning to the human world and all its misery after contemplating the divine realm. Do you think it's surprising if he seems awkward and ridiculous while he's still not seeing well, before he's had time to adjust to the darkness of his situation, and he's forced into a contest (in a lawcourt or wherever) about the shadows of morality or the statuettes which cast the shadows, and into a competition whose terms are the conceptions of morality held by people who have never seen morality itself?'

'No, that's not surprising in the slightest,' he said.

'In fact anyone with any sense,' I said, 'would remember that the eyes can become confused in two different ways, as a result of two different sets of circumstances: it can happen in the transition from light to darkness, and also in the transition from darkness to light. If he took the same facts into consideration when he also noticed someone's mind in such a state of confusion that it was incapable of making anything out, his reaction wouldn't be unthinking ridicule. Instead, he'd try to find out whether this person's mind was returning from a mode of existence which involves greater lucidity and had been blinded by the unfamiliar darkness, or whether it was moving from relative ignorance to relative lucidity and had been overwhelmed and dazzled by the increased brightness. Once he'd distinguished between the two conditions and modes of existence, he'd congratulate anyone he found in the second state, and feel sorry for anyone in the first state. If he did choose to laugh at someone in the second state, his amusement would be less absurd than when laughter is directed at someone returning from the light above.'

'Yes,' he said, 'you're making a lot of sense.'

Since the Cave was expressly introduced as being relevant to education, its immediate educational implications are now drawn out. We all have the capacity for knowledge (in the Platonic sense, not just information), and education should develop that potential. But since it requires knowledge of goodness to manage a community well, then those who gain such knowledge have to 'return to the cave': paradoxically, those who least want power are the ones who should have it.

'Now, if this is true,' I said, 'we must bear in mind that education is not capable of doing what some people promise. They claim to introduce knowledge into a mind which doesn't have it, as if they were introducing sight into eyes which are blind.'

'Yes, they do,' he said.

'An implication of what we're saying at the moment, however,' I pointed out, 'is that the capacity for knowledge is present in everyone's mind. If you can imagine an eye that can turn from darkness to brightness only if the body as a whole turns, then our organ of understanding is like that. Its orientation has to be accompanied by turning the mind as a whole away from the world of becoming, until it becomes capable of bearing the sight of real being and reality at its most bright, which we're saying is goodness. Yes?'

'Yes.'

'That's what education should be,' I said, 'the art of orientation. Educators should devise the simplest and most effective methods of turning minds around. It shouldn't be the art of implanting sight in the organ, but should proceed on the understanding that the organ already has the capacity, but is improperly aligned and isn't facing the right way.'

'I suppose you're right,' he said.

'So although the mental states which are described as good generally seem to resemble good physical states, in the sense that habituation and training do in fact implant them where they didn't use to be, yet understanding (as it turns out) is undoubtedly a property of something which is more divine: it never loses its power, and it is useful and beneficial, or useless and harmful, depending on its orientation. For example, surely you've noticed how the petty minds of those who are acknowledged to be bad, but clever, are sharp-eyed and perceptive enough to gain insights into matters they direct their attention towards. It's not as if they weren't sharp-sighted, but their minds are forced to serve evil, and consequently the keener their vision is, the greater the evil they accomplish.'

'Yes, I've noticed this,' he said.

'However,' I went on, 'if this aspect of that kind of person is hammered at from an early age, until

the inevitable consequences of incarnation have been knocked off it—the leaden weights, so to speak, which are grafted on to it as a result of eating and similar pleasures and indulgences and which turn the sight of the mind downwards—if it sheds these weights and is reoriented towards the truth, then (and we're talking about the same organ and the same people) it would see the truth just as clearly as it sees the objects it faces at the moment.'

'Yes, that makes sense,' he said.

'Well, doesn't this make sense as well?' I asked. 'Or rather, isn't it an inevitable consequence of what we've been saying that uneducated people, who have no experience of truth, would make incompetent administrators of a community, and that the same goes for people who are allowed to spend their whole lives educating themselves? The first group would be no good because their lives lack direction: they've got no single point of reference to guide them in all their affairs, whether private or public. The second group would be no good because their hearts wouldn't be in the business: they think they've been transported to the Isles of the Blessed even while they're still alive.'

'True,' he said.

'Our job as founders, then,' I said, 'is to make sure that the best people come to that fundamental field of study (as we called it earlier): we must have them make the ascent we've been talking about and see goodness. And afterwards, once they've been up there and had a good look, we mustn't let them get away with what they do at the moment.'

'Which is what?'

'Staying there,' I replied, 'and refusing to come back down again to those prisoners, to share their work and their rewards, no matter whether those rewards are trivial or significant.'

'But in that case,' he protested, 'we'll be wronging them: we'll be making the quality of their lives worse and denying them the better life they could be living, won't we?'

'You're again forgetting, my friend,' I said, 'that the point of legislation is not to make one section of a community better off than the rest, but to engineer this for the community as a whole. Legislators should persuade or compel the members of a community to mesh together, should make every individual share with his fellows the benefit which he is capable of

520a contributing to the common welfare, and should ensure that the community does contain people with this capacity; and the purpose of all this is not for legislators to leave people to choose their own directions, but for them to use people to bind the community together.'

'Yes, you're right,' he said. 'I was forgetting.'

'I think you'll also find, Glaucon,' I said, 'that we won't be wronging any philosophers who arise in our b community. Our remarks, as we force them to take care of their fellow citizens and be their guardians, will be perfectly fair. We'll tell them that it's reasonable for philosophers who happen to occur in other communities not to share the work of those communities, since their occurrence was spontaneous, rather than planned by the political system of any of the communities in question, and it's fair for anything which arises spontaneously and doesn't owe its nurture to anyone or anything to have no interest in repaying anyone for having provided its nourishment. "We've bred *you*, however," we'll say, "to act, as it were, as the hive's leaders and kings, for your own good as well as that of the rest of the community. You've received a better and more thorough education than c those other philosophers, and you're more capable of playing a part in both spheres. So each of you must, when your time comes, descend to where the rest of the community lives, and get used to looking at things in the dark. The point is that once you become acclimatized, you'll see infinitely better than the others there; your experience of genuine right, morality, and goodness will enable you to identify every one of the images and recognize what it is an image of. And then the administration of our community—ours as well as yours—will be in the hands of people who are awake, as distinct from the norm nowadays of communities being governed by people who shadow-box and fall out with one another in their dreams over who should rule, as if that were a highly desirable thing to do. No, d the truth of the matter is this: the less keen the would-be rulers of a community are to rule, the better and less divided the administration of that community is bound to be, but where the rulers feel the opposite, the administration is bound to be the opposite."'

'Yes,' he said.

'And do you think our wards will greet these views of ours with scepticism and will refuse to join in the work of government when their time comes,

when they can still spend most of their time living with one another in the untainted realm?'

'No, they couldn't,' he answered. 'They're fair- e minded people, and the instructions we're giving them are fair. However, they'll undoubtedly approach rulership as an inescapable duty—an attitude which is the opposite of the one held by the people who have power in communities at the moment.'

'You're right, Glaucon,' I said. 'You'll only have a well-governed community if you can come up with 521a a way of life for your prospective rulers that is preferable to ruling! The point is that this is the only kind of community where the rulers will be genuinely well off (not in material terms, but they'll possess the wealth which is a prerequisite of happiness—a life of virtue *bad* and intelligence), whereas if government falls into the *outcome* hands of people who are impoverished and starved of any good things of their own, and who expect to wrest some good for themselves from political office, a well-governed community is an impossibility. I mean, when rulership becomes something to fight for, a domestic and internal war like this destroys not only the perpetrators, but also the rest of the community.'

'You're absolutely right,' he said.

'Apart from the philosophical life,' I said, 'is there b any way of life, in your opinion, which looks down on political office?'

'No, definitely not,' he answered.

'In fact, political power should be in the hands of people who aren't enamoured of it. Otherwise their rivals in love will fight them for it.'

'Of course.'

'There's no one you'd rather force to undertake the guarding of your community, then, than those who are experts in the factors which contribute towards the good government of a community, who don't look to politics for their rewards, and whose life is better than the political life. Agreed?'

'Yes,' he said. . . .

CHAPTER 11
WARPED MINDS, WARPED SOCIETIES

. . . 'All there is left for us to do', I said, 'is study 517a an actual dictatorial person, to try to see how he evolves out of the democratic type, what he's like once he does exist, and whether his life is happy or unhappy.'

'Yes, that's right,' he said.

'Well, there's still a deficiency to remedy, I think,' I said.

'What?'

'I don't think we've finished distinguishing the various kinds of desires or finding out how many different kinds there are. And as long as this job remains unfinished, our enquiry will be veiled in obscurity.'

'But it's not too late, is it?' he asked.

'No. The thing about them I want to have out in the open is that some of the unnecessary pleasures and desires strike me as lawless. We probably all contain these pleasures and desires, but they can be kept under control by convention and by the co-operation of reason and the better desires. Some people, in fact, control them so well that they get rid of them altogether or leave only a few of them in a weakened state, but they remain stronger and more numerous in others.'

'What pleasures and desires are you thinking of?' he asked.

'The ones that wake up while we're asleep,' I replied. 'When all the rest of the mind—the rational, regulated, controlling part—is asleep, then if the wild, unruly part is glutted with food or drink, it springs up and longs to banish sleep and go and satisfy its own instincts. I'm sure you're aware of how in these circumstances nothing is too outrageous: a person acts as if he were totally lacking in moral principle and unhampered by intelligence. In his dreams, he doesn't stop at trying to have sex with his mother and with anyone or anything else—man, beast, or god; he's ready to slaughter anything; there's nothing he wouldn't eat. In short, he doesn't hold back from anything, however bizarre or disgusting.'

'You're quite right,' he said.

'On the other hand, I imagine, when someone who's self-disciplined and who keeps himself healthy goes to sleep, he's made sure that his rational mind is awake and has eaten its fill of fine ideas and arguments, which he's brought to an agreed conclusion within himself. Since he hasn't either starved or over-indulged his desirous part, it can settle down to sleep and not bother the best part of him with its feelings of pleasure or pain, and consequently the best part is free to get on with the enquiries it carries out all by itself, when it is secluded and untarnished by anything else, and to try to fulfil its impulse for perceiving something in the past or present or future that it doesn't know. He's also calmed down his passionate part and doesn't go to bed in an emotionally disturbed state because he's been angry with someone. In other words, he's quietened down two aspects of himself, but woken up the third—the one in which intelligence resides—and that's how he takes his rest; and, as you know, in this state he can maximize his contact with the truth and minimize the lawlessness of the visions he sees in his dreams.'

'I'm sure you're absolutely right,' he said.

'Now, we've wandered rather far from the main course of the argument, but the point I'm trying to get across is this: every one of us—even someone who seems very restrained—contains desires which are terrible, wild, and lawless, and this category of desire becomes manifest during sleep. Do you agree? Do you think I have a point?'

'Yes, I do agree.'

'Well, remember the nature of the democratic man, as we described him: his formative childhood upbringing was by a skinflint of a father who valued only desires which helped him make money, and despised all the unnecessary ones with their frivolity and frippery, wasn't it?'

'Yes.'

'But then he fell in with a more elegant crowd, consisting of people who indulge in the desires we've just been describing, and his dislike of his father's meanness drove him to all kinds of outrageous behaviour, and to modelling himself on them. However, he was essentially better than these corrupters of his, and since he was being pulled in both directions, he found between the two ways of life a compromise in which he drew on each of them to a reasonable extent, in his opinion, and lived a life which wasn't miserly, but at the same time wasn't lawless either. And that's how he made the transition from being oligarchic to being democratic.'

'Yes, that's what we thought earlier, and it still seems valid,' he said.

'Now imagine', I said, 'that our democratic type has grown older and has a son who's been brought up, in his turn, in his father's ways.'

'All right.'

'And imagine that the same thing happens to him as happened to his father: he's attracted by complete lawlessness (although the people who are advertising it to him call it complete freedom), his father and his family in general reinforce the desires he settled on as a compromise, and others reinforce his lawless side. When these black magicians, these creators of dictators, realize that there's only one way they're going to gain control of the young man, they arrange matters until they implant in him a particular lust, to champion the rest of his desires which are too idle to do more than share out anything that readily comes their way. And don't you think this kind of lust is exactly like a great, winged drone?'

'Yes, that seems to me to be a perfect description of it,' he said.

'Then the rest of the desires buzz in a swarm around their champion, reeking of incense and perfumes, laden with garlands, overflowing with wine, and offering all the indulgent pleasures that go with that kind of social life. Under their caring nurture, he grows to his fullest extent and gains a sting whose poison is unfulfilled longing. This inner champion now takes frenzy for his bodyguard and runs amok. If he finds that the person contains any apparently good beliefs or desires which still cause him to feel shame, he kills them and banishes them, until he's purged the person of self-discipline and imported frenzy in its place.'

'That's a perfect description of a dictatorial type's evolution,' he said.

'And isn't this also the kind of reason why lust is traditionally called a dictator?' I asked.

'I suppose so,' he said.

'Now, there's something dictatorial about a drunken person's arrogance too, isn't there, Adeimantus?' I asked.

'Yes, there is.'

'And people who are insane and mentally disturbed try to dominate the gods, let alone other human beings, and expect to be able to do so.'

'Yes,' he agreed.

'So strictly speaking, Adeimantus,' I said, 'the dictatorial type is the result of someone's nature or conditioning—or both—making him a drunken, lustful maniac.'

'Absolutely.'

'So that's how the dictatorial type evolves, apparently. Now, what's his life like?'

'At the risk of sounding like a tease,' he said, 'it's you who'll have to tell me.'

'All right,' I said. 'I think he proceeds to give himself over to feasting and revelry, parties and prostitutes, and all the activities which typically indicate that the dictator lust has taken up residence within a person and is in complete control of his mind.'

'Yes, that's bound to happen,' he agreed.

'Every day and every night, terrible desires with prodigious appetites branch out in large numbers from the main stem, don't they?'

'Yes, they do.'

'So his income is soon exhausted.'

'Of course.'

'And then he starts borrowing and working his way through his estate.'

'Naturally.'

'And when there's nothing left, his young brood of desires is bound to clamour long and loud. He's driven by the stinging swarm of his desires (and especially by lust, the captain of the bodyguard the others form) to run amok—to see if there's anyone he can steal anything from by deceit or by force. Yes?'

'Definitely,' he said.

'He has no choice: he can either filch from every available source, or be racked with agonizing pains.'

'Agreed.'

'Now, every passing pleasant sensation he feels takes precedence over the ones which are in the past and steals from them, so by the same token he expects to take precedence over his parents, despite being younger than them, and to steal from them, in the sense of appropriating his father's property once he's exhausted his own. Yes?'

'Of course,' he agreed.

'And if his parents refused to hand it over to him, he'd initially resort to obtaining money from them on false pretences, wouldn't he?'

'Absolutely.'

'And if that didn't work, he'd turn to robbery with violence?'

'I think so,' he said.

'If his elderly parents resisted and fought back, Adeimantus, do you think he'd be circumspect and hesitant about doing anything dictatorial?'

'No, I don't hold out much hope for the parents of someone like this,' he said.

'Would he really beat up his mother, who's cared for him for years, Adeimantus, and whom he could never have lived without, for the sake of his latest

dispensable girlfriend, whom he's just fallen in love
c with? Would he really beat up his aged, indispensable father, who may not be much to look at any
more, but whose affection has lasted for so many
years, for the sake of his latest alluring, but dispensable, boyfriend? Would he honestly let his parents
be dominated by them, if he had them all living together in the same house?'

'Yes, he certainly would,' he said.

'What a happy thing it is, then,' I exclaimed, 'to
be the parent of a dictator!'

'That's right,' he agreed.

d 'What happens when there's none of his parents'
property left, but a large number of pleasures have
gathered together in a swarm within him? Won't he
first turn his hand to a bit of burglary or to mugging
travellers late at night, and then try emptying out a
temple? At the same time a gang of beliefs which
had until recently been suppressed, but now form
lust's bodyguard, come to his assistance to enable
him to overpower all the views about good and bad
behaviour he'd been brought up to hold and which
he'd assumed to comprise morality. This gang consists of attitudes which had formerly—during the period when there was still a democratic government
within him, and he was still subject to the laws and
e to his father—broken free only at night, while he was
asleep. Once he's under the dictatorship of lust, however, his constant waking state is one that was formerly rare and restricted to dreams: there's no form
of murder, however vile, that he isn't willing to commit; there's nothing he won't eat, no deed he isn't
ready to perform. Lust lives within him like a dicta-
575a tor, with no regard for law and convention. It uses
its absolute power to influence the person in whom
it lives, as an autocrat influences his community, to
stop at nothing as long as the result is the perpetua-
tion of itself and the pandemonium it generates.
Some of this pandemonium is the result of bad company, and has therefore been introduced from outside; the rest is the result of the person's own practice of the same bad habits, and so has been released
and set free internally. Don't you think this is how
he lives?'

'Yes,' he said.

'Now, if people of this kind form a small propor-
b tion of a community's population, while the rest are
self-disciplined,' I said, 'then they leave and serve

in the bodyguard of a dictator somewhere else, or as
mercenaries in some war or other. But if they occur
in a time of peace and stability, they stay in their
community and commit lots of trivial crimes.'

'What sort of crimes do you mean?'

'They're thieves, burglars, pickpockets, muggers,
temple-robbers, kidnappers; if they have any ability
at public speaking, they might be sycophants, and
they're the kind of people who commit perjury in
court and take bribes.'

'Yes, these are trivial crimes, as long as there c
aren't many people committing them,' he said.

'Anything trivial is only trivial in comparison
with something important,' I went on, 'and all these
crimes are (as the saying goes) well wide of the mark
of dictatorship in the effect they have on how rotten
and unhappy a community is. In fact, it's when these
people and their followers start to form a significant
proportion of a community's population, and realize
how many there are of them, that they—assisted by
the folly of the people—become the ones to whom
the dictator we discussed owes his origin: he is simply whichever one of them has the greatest and most
thriving dictator in his own mind.'   d

'Yes, that's likely,' he agreed. 'Dictatorship
would come most naturally to him.'

'There's no problem if they're happy to defer to
him, but if the community refuses to submit, then,
if he can, it'll be his fatherland's turn for the same
punishment he inflicted on his mother and father
before. He'll bring new friends in from abroad and,
for all her long-standing care, he'll make sure that
his motherland (as the Cretans call their country)
and fatherland are kept and maintained—in a state
of enslavement to these new friends of his. After
all, that's how the desire of this sort of person is
fulfilled.'

'Yes, it is, absolutely,' he said.   e

'Now, don't people of this sort behave like dictators in their private lives even before they gain political power?' I asked. 'Take their relationships with
others, for instance. They either go about with people who flatter them and are ready to carry out their
every whim, or they're deferential themselves, if
they want something from someone. As long as   576a
that's the case, there's nothing they wouldn't do to
make him believe they're his friends, but once
they've got what they want, they're distant again.'

'Definitely.'

'They never have any friends, then, throughout their lives: they can only be masters or slaves. Dictatorial people can never experience freedom and true friendship.'

'No.'

'We couldn't exactly call them reliable, could we?'

'Of course not.'

'And, assuming that our earlier conclusions about the nature of morality were correct, we'd have to say that there's no one more immoral than them.'

'Well, our earlier conclusions *are* right,' he said.

'In short, then,' I said, 'the worst type of person is one whose waking life resembles the dreams we discussed.'

'Yes.'

'He's the product of absolute power falling into the hands of an inherently dictatorial person, and the longer he spends as a dictator, the worse he becomes.'

'Glaucon took over the job of talking with me, and said, 'Yes, that's bound to happen.'

CHAPTER 12
HAPPINESS AND UNHAPPINESS

Plato now declares himself to be in a position to adjudicate the relative happiness or unhappiness of the five types of individuals. As usual, he starts by looking at the equivalent communities. Happiness is circumscribed by a number of properties—freedom, lack of need, lack of fear—and it is concluded that a community ruled by a dictator, and a dictatorial person (especially if he becomes an actual dictator), are in the most miserable condition. On the weak basis of the fact that in the previous chapter the five types were presented as a series of degenerations, with the dictator at the bottom, the happiness and unhappiness of the five types are now ranked according to the order of degeneration.

576c 'Now,' I continued, 'won't we find that the worst person is also the unhappiest person? And won't we find—whatever most people think—that it's the most enduring and thorough dictator who has the most enduring and thorough unhappiness?'

'Yes,' he said, 'that's inevitable.'

'Now, isn't it the case', I asked, 'that a dictatorial person is the counterpart of a community which is ruled by a dictator, and a democratic person corresponds to a community with a democratic government, and so on for the rest?'

'Of course.'

d 'So we can compare the state of goodness and the happiness of one type of community with another and apply the results to their corresponding human types, can we?'

'Of course.'

'How does the state of goodness of a community which is ruled by a dictator compare, then, with that of the one we described first, with its kings?'

'They're at opposite ends of the scale,' he answered. 'One is the best type of community, the other is the worst.'

'I don't need to ask which is which,' I said, 'because it's obvious. But now what about their happiness and unhappiness? Would you come up with the same estimate, or a different one? We shouldn't be rushed into a decision by our impressions of just one person, the dictator himself, or by the few people who constitute his immediate circle. We should visit the community and see all the sights, immerse ourselves thoroughly in it and look everywhere, and then express an opinion.'

'That's a good suggestion,' he said. 'And everyone would see that a community under a dictator is as unhappy as any community can be, while a community under kingship is the happiest one possible.'

'And suppose I were to make the same suggestion as regards their human equivalents too,' I said. 'Would that be a good suggestion? I'd be expecting 577a someone to come up with his assessment of their happiness and unhappiness only if he has the ability to gain insights into a person by using his mind to take on that person's characteristics. Rather than childishly looking from the outside and being won over by the ostentatious façade a dictator presents to the outside world, he should be capable of insight. Suppose we found someone who's not only this good at assessment, but who has also lived in close proximity with a dictator, and has been an eyewitness to what goes on inside a dictator's house and how he treats the various members of his household, because these are the best circumstances for seeing a dictab tor stripped of his pompous clothing; and suppose he'd also seen how a dictator reacts to the risks involved in political life. Would I be right to claim that we should all listen to what this person has to say? Should we ask him to draw on all this firsthand experience to tell us how a dictator fares, as regards happiness and unhappiness, compared with our other types?'

'Yes, that would be a very good idea as well,' he said.

'Shall we pretend, then', I said, 'that *we* are expert assessors, and have in the past met dictators? Otherwise, there'll be no one to answer our questions for us.'

'Yes, let's.'

c 'All right, then,' I said, 'here's how you'd better proceed with the enquiry. You should bear in mind the equivalence between community and individual and submit them one after another to a detailed examination; then you'll be in a position to describe the attributes either or both of them have.'

'What attributes?' he asked.

'Starting with a community,' I said, 'do you think a community which is ruled by a dictator is free or oppressed?'

'It's impossible to imagine a more complete state of oppression,' he replied.

'But some of its members are evidently free and are doing the oppressing.'

'Yes,' he said, 'but they're the minority. Wretched servitude, with no civil rights, is pretty much the universal condition of the citizen body—certainly of the truly good elements.'

d 'Given the correspondence between individual and community,' I said, 'then isn't his structure necessarily identical? Oppression and servitude must pervade his mind, with the truly good parts of it being oppressed, and an evil, crazed minority doing the oppressing.'

'Necessarily,' he agreed.

'Well, do you think a mind in this condition is free or enslaved?'

'Enslaved, I'd say—definitely.'

'Then again, a community which is enslaved and ruled by a dictator is hardly ever free to do what it wants, is it?'

'I quite agree.'

e 'What about a mind which is ruled by an inner dictator, then? Treating the mind as a single whole, it'll hardly ever be free to do what it wants, will it? It'll constantly be subject to the overpowering whims of its lust, and this will make it highly inconsistent and fickle.'

'Of course.'

'And would a community under a dictator be poor or well off?'

'Poor.'

'So a person with a dictatorial mind is bound to 578a be in a constant state of poverty and need.'

'Yes,' he agreed.

'Now, isn't fear ever-present in communities and individuals of this sort?'

'It certainly is.'

'Is there any other community, do you think, where you'd come across more moaning, complaining, grievances, and hardships?'

'No, definitely not.'

'Would you come across more of them in any other type of individual, do you think? Or has the limit been reached with this dictatorial type and the frenzy caused by his desires and lusts?'

'Of course it has,' he said.

'I imagine all this was the kind of evidence which led you to conclude that the community is as un- b happy as any community can be.'

'Do you disagree?' he asked.

'Not at all,' I replied. 'But what does the same evidence lead you to think about a dictatorial person?'

'That he is far unhappier than any of the other types,' he answered.

'Now you've made a claim I *do* disagree with,' I said.

'Why?' he asked.

'I don't think he's that outstandingly unhappy,' I said.

'Who is, then?'

'I should think you'd agree that here's an even more miserable person than the one we've been discussing.'

'Who?'

'A dictatorial person who can't remain a private c citizen all his life,' I said, 'but has the misfortune to end up, by force of circumstance, as an actual dictator.'

'If I'm to be consistent with our earlier argument,' he said, 'I have to admit that you're right.'

'Yes,' I said, 'but it's important for us not to rely on assumptions in these sorts of cases. We're looking into the most important issue there is—which kind of life is good, and which is bad—so we must conduct a really thorough investigation, and I think I see how to proceed.'

'You're quite right,' he said.

'Well, I wonder what you'll make of my idea that we should start the investigation by bearing in mind d the following points.'

'Which ones?'

'Every single wealthy citizen in a community owns a lot of slaves. In this respect—that they have a number of people under their control—they resemble dictators; the only difference is that dictators control larger numbers of people.'

'That's right.'

'Well, do you appreciate that these slave-owners aren't in a state of fear? They aren't afraid of their slaves, are they?'

'What reason would they have to be?'

'None,' I answered. 'But do you realize shy?'

'Yes. It's because behind every single citizen is the community as a whole.'

e 'Exactly,' I said. 'Now, imagine that a man who owns fifty or more slaves is plucked by some god from his community—wife, children, and all—and deposited in some isolated spot along with all his property, especially his slaves. There are no other free men around to help him. Would he be afraid of his slaves killing him and his family? And if so, how frightened do you think he'd be?'

'He'd be absolutely terrified, I expect,' he replied.

579a 'What he'd have to do, then, despite their being his slaves, is immediately get on the right side of some of them, make them extravagant promises, and give them their freedom, whatever misgivings he may have. In fact, he'd end up being dependent on the goodwill of his servants, wouldn't he?'

'It's either that or be killed,' he said, 'so he doesn't really have a choice.'

'And what do you think would happen if this god also surrounded him with a lot of neighbours in nearby settlements, and these neighbours of his couldn't abide anyone presuming to be anyone else's master, and punished with extreme severity any case they came across of this kind of oppression?'

'He'd be in an even worse trap,' he said, 'with all b those enemies hemming him in on every side.'

'Well, is there any difference between this and the prison a dictator finds himself in, because of all the fears and lusts his nature, as we've described it, makes him liable to? He may be greedy for new experiences, but he's the only person in the community who can't travel abroad or see all the sights every other free man longs to see. Instead, he lives like a woman, buried indoors most of the time, resenting any of his fellow citizens who go abroad and c see something worth while.'

'Absolutely,' he said.

'So these are the kinds of troubles which swell the harvest of evils reaped by the individual who, in your recent assessment, is as unhappy as anyone can be—the dictatorial type, whose bad government is restricted to himself—when he can't remain a private citizen all his life, but is forced by some misfortune to take on the government of others, despite his inability to control even himself. This is like someone ill with spastic paralysis being forced to enter the public arena and spend his life competing as an athlete against others or fighting in wars.'   d

'That's a perfect analogy, Socrates,' he said. 'You're quite right.'

'There's nothing but misery in a dictator's life, then, is there, Glaucon?' I asked. 'You thought you'd identified the worst life possible, but there's even more hardship in his, isn't there?'

'Definitely,' he said.

'The truth of the matter, then, even if people deny it, is that a real dictator is actually a real slave—judging by the extent of his obsequiousness and servitude—and a flatterer of the worst kinds of people. His desires are completely insatiable as well: any expert observer of the totality of the mind can see that   e a dictator is actually never fulfilled and is therefore poor. Moreover, fear pervades his whole life, and he's convulsed with constant pains. This is what he's like, if his condition resembles that of the community he rules over—and it does, doesn't it?'

'Yes, it does,' he agreed.

'And we haven't finished with his attributes yet: 580a there are also all the ones we mentioned earlier, which he's not only bound to have, but bound to have even more thoroughly than before because of being in office. He's resentful, unreliable, immoral, friendless, and unjust; and he gives room and board to every vice. And the result of all this is not just the extreme wretchedness of his own condition; these attributes of his also rub off on people who come near him.'

'That's beyond all reasonable doubt,' he said.

'All right, then,' I continued. 'Now is the time for you to play the part of the judge with overall author-ity and reveal your verdict. Of the five types—regal, timocratic, oligarchic, democratic, and dictatorial—which comes first, in your opinion, in the contest of happiness? Which comes second? You'd better grade all five of them.'

'It's an easy decision to make,' he said, 'because the order in which they made their entrance, like troupes of dancers on a stage, corresponds to how I rate them. That's my estimate of where they come on the scale of goodness and badness, and of happi-ness and unhappiness.'

'Shall we hire a town crier, then,' I asked, 'or shall I be the one to proclaim that the son of Aris-ton has judged the happiest person to be the best and most moral person—that is, the person who pos-sesses the highest degree of regal qualities and who rules as king over himself? And that he has also judged the unhappiest person to be the worst and most immoral person—that is, the person who pos-sesses the highest degree of dictatorial qualities and rules as completely as possible as a dictator over himself and his community?'

'*You* make the announcement,' he said.

'And can I add a rider that this is so whether or not their condition is hidden from the eyes of god and men?' I asked.

'You can,' he said.

A second proof of the philosopher's happiness proceeds on the basis of the threefold division of the human mind (Chapter 6) and the correspond-ing types of individual—philosophical, competi-tive, avaricious. Each enjoys different things, and each claims that what he or she enjoys is best. However, the philosopher's claim is the most au-thoritative since he has the experience and intel-ligence to decide the issue.

'All right, then,' I said. 'That's the first proof, but I wonder how the second one strikes you.'

'What is it?'

'I think the correspondence between the three classes into which the community was divided and the threefold division of everyone's mind provides the basis for a further argument,' I said.

'What argument?'

'It seems to me that each of the three mental cat-egories has its own particular pleasure, so that there are three kinds of pleasure as well. The same would also go for desires and motivations.'

'What do you mean?' he said.

'We found that one part is the intellectual part of a person, another is the passionate part, and the third has so many manifestations that we couldn't give it a single label which applied to it and it alone, so we named it after its most prevalent and powerful as-pect: we called it the desirous part, because of the intensity of our desires for food, drink, sex, and so on, and we also referred to it as the mercenary part, because desires of this kind invariably need money for their fulfilment.'

'And we were right,' he said.

'What if we said that what it enjoys, what it cares for, is profit? This would be the best way for us to clarify the issue for ourselves: we could keep our ref-erences to this part of the mind concise, and call it mercenary and avaricious. Would that description hit the mark?'

'I think so,' he said.

'And isn't our position that the passionate part al-ways has its sights set wholly on power, success, and fame?'

'Yes.'

'So it would be fair for us to call it competitive and ambitious, wouldn't it?'

'Perfectly fair.'

'And it's patently obvious that our intellectual part is entirely directed at every moment towards knowing the truth of things, and isn't interested in the slightest in money and reputation.'

'Certainly.'

'So we'd be right to call it intellectual and philo-sophical, wouldn't we?'

'Of course.'

'Now, sometimes this intellectual part is the mo-tivating aspect of one's mind; sometimes—as cir-cumstances dictate—it's one of the other two. Yes?'

'Yes,' he said.

'Which is why we're also claiming that there are three basic human types—the philosophical, the competitive, and the avaricious.'

'Exactly.'

'And it also explains why there are three kinds of pleasure as well, one for each of the human types, doesn't it?'

'Yes.'

'Now, I'm sure you're aware', I said, 'that if you were to approach representatives of these three types one by one and ask them which of these ways of life was the most enjoyable, they'd each swear by their own way of life, wouldn't they? A money-minded person wouldn't think that respect or learning, and their pleasures, were anywhere near as important as making money, unless there was also a profit to be made out of them, would he?'

'True,' he said.

'Then again, an ambitious person would regard enjoyment of money as vulgar,' I continued, 'and would think that only some concomitant respect could redeem enjoyment of intellectual activities from being an impractical waste of time, wouldn't he?'

'Yes,' he agreed.

'What about a philosopher?' I asked. 'How do you think he rates other pleasures compared with knowing the truth of things and with constantly employing his intellect and feeling that kind of pleasure? Doesn't he think they miss the mark by a long way? Doesn't he describe them as necessary, in the strict sense that, apart from intellectual pleasures, he needs only those which are unavoidable?'

'We can be perfectly certain about that,' he replied.

'Now, when people are arguing about the various pleasures which accompany aspects of themselves,' I said, 'and even about the kind of life one should lead, and when the only criterion they're using is where a way of life comes on the scale of pleasure and distress, rather than on the scales of right and wrong or good and bad, then how can we know who has truth on his side?'

'I really couldn't tell you,' he said.

'Well, look at it this way. What does it take to make a good decision? Doesn't it take experience, intelligence, and rationality? Aren't these the best means of reaching a decision?'

'Of course,' he said.

'All right, then. Which of the three men has had the greatest exposure to all the pleasures we've mentioned? Do you think the avaricious type understands the truth of things and has therefore had more experience of intellectual pleasure than a philosopher has of the pleasure of moneymaking?'

'There's a world of difference,' he replied. 'From his earliest years onward a philosopher has inevitably experienced both the other kinds of pleasure; there's never been any reason, however, for an avaricious person to experience the sweetness of intellectual pleasure and it remains unfamiliar to him—in fact, even if he wanted to get a taste of it, he'd find it difficult.'

'In other words,' I commented, 'a philosopher's experience of both intellectual and moneymaking pleasures puts him in a better position than an avaricious person, anyway.'

'A far better position.'

'And how does he compare with an ambitious person? Is he more familiar with the enjoyment of respect than an ambitious person is with the enjoyment of intelligence?'

'But anyone can get respect: it's a result of attaining one's objective,' he said. 'Respect is showered on people for their wealth, their courage, and their intelligence: all three types are familiar with what it's like to enjoy being respected, at any rate. But only a philosopher can have found out by experience what it's like to enjoy contemplating reality.'

'As far as experience is concerned, then,' I said, 'it's a philosopher who's in the best position to make a decision.'

'By far the best position,' he agreed.

'And he's the only one who'll be in a position to combine experience and intelligence.'

'Naturally.'

'Moreover, the resources for making a decision are available only to a philosopher, not to an avaricious or an ambitious person.'

'What resources?'

'We did say that decisions require rational argumentation, didn't we?'

'Yes.'

'And rational argumentation is a particularly important resource in this context.'

'Of course.'

'Now, if money and wealth were the best means of making decisions, then the likes and dislikes of the avaricious type would necessarily be closest to the truth.'

'Yes.'

'And if prestige, success, and courage were best, it would be the likes and dislikes of the ambitious, competitive type. Yes?'

'Obviously.'

'But since it takes experience, intelligence and rationality. . . ?'

'Then it's the philosophical type, with his appreciation of rationality, whose tastes are closest to the truth,' he said.

'Of the three kinds of pleasure, the most enjoyable, then, is that which belongs to the intellectual part of the mind; one's life becomes most enjoyable when this part of the mind is one's motivating force.'

'Of course,' he said. 'I mean, when a thoughtful person recommends his own way of life, he ought to be taken seriously.'

'Which way of life—which pleasure—comes second, in his assessment?'

'Obviously the pleasure which accompanies the military, ambitious life, since it differs less from his own way of life than the moneymaking one does.'

'Apparently, then, the way of life pursued by the avaricious type comes last, in his estimate. Yes?'

'Of course,' he said.

The third proof of the philosopher's happiness is again concerned with pleasure. In a suggestive fashion, Plato distinguishes between true (genuine) pleasures and false (illusory) pleasures. The vast majority of so-called pleasures are actually only relief from pain—a state intermediate between pleasure and pain. Genuine pleasures are pure, unsullied by pain in this way. They are, above all, the pleasures of the mind, since the things of the rational mind, being more real, offer more real or genuine satisfaction. Since only the philosopher is familiar with these mental pleasures, then only he has true pleasure. Since morality is the rule of the rational mind, then a moral life is far happier and more desirable—involves far more true pleasure—than the immoral life of a dictator. In fact, one could say that a philosopher was 729 times happier than a dictator!

'That makes it two, then, one after another: immorality has twice been defeated by morality. In Olympic fashion, here's the third round—for Zeus the Saviour and Zeus of Olympus. I wonder whether you agree that only the philosopher's pleasure is true and pure, while the others are illusory; I seem to remember having heard some clever fellow or other expressing this idea. And in fact that would be the most important and serious fall of the whole competition.'

'It certainly would. But what are you getting at?'

'I'll find out, if you'll help my investigation by answering my questions,' I said.

'Go ahead,' he said.

'All right,' I said. 'Pain is the opposite of pleasure, wouldn't you say?'

'Yes.'

'And is there a state which involves no pleasure or pain?'

'Yes, there certainly is.'

'It's an intermediate state in which the mind isn't active in either of these ways, isn't it? What do you think?'

'I agree,' he said.

'Now, can you remember what people say when they're ill?' I asked.

'What?'

'They claim that health really is the most pleasant thing in the world, but that they didn't appreciate the fact until they got ill.'

'Yes, that's familiar,' he said.

'And you're aware that when people are in great pain they say that the most pleasant thing in the world would be for the pain to end.'

'Yes.'

'And you've come across all sorts of other situations, I should think, in which people are feeling pain and claim that there is nothing more pleasant than the remission and absence of pain. It's not pleasure whose praises they sing in these situations.'

'That's because under these circumstances remission does become pleasant and desirable, I suppose,' he remarked.

'And it follows that when someone stops feeling pleasure, the remission of pleasure will be painful.'

'I suppose so,' he said.

'So the intermediate state, as we called it a moment ago—the state of inactivity—will at different times be both pleasure and pain.'

'So it seems.'

'Is it possible for anything to be both of two things if it is neither of those two things?'

'I don't think so.'

'Now, the mental feelings of pleasure and pain are both activities, aren't they?'

'Yes.'

584a 'And didn't we just find that the state which involves no pain or pleasure is actually a state of *in*activity which falls between the two?'

'Yes, we did.'

'How can it be right, then, to regard absence of pain as pleasant, or absence of pleasure as painful?'

'It can't be.'

'There's no reality here, then, just some superficial effect,' I said. 'Inactivity merely appears pleasant and painful on those occasions, because it's being contrasted respectively with pain and with pleasure. These appearances aren't reliable in the slightest: they're a kind of deception.'

'Yes, that *is* what the argument suggests,' he said.

b 'Well, I'd like to show you pleasures which aren't products of pain,' I said. 'I'm worried about the possibility of your currently regarding all pleasure as the cessation of pain, and all pain as the cessation of pleasure, and thinking that this is how things are.'

'Where shall I look?' he asked. 'What pleasures are you talking about?'

'If you'd care to consider the enjoyment of smells,' I replied, 'you'd see particularly clear examples, though there are plenty of other cases too. The point is that there's no preceding feeling of pain, and yet you can suddenly get an incredibly intense pleasure at a scent, which also leaves no distress behind when it's over.'

'That's true,' he said.

c 'So we'd better resist the notion that pure pleasant pleasure is escape from pain, and pure pain is escape from pleasure.'

'Yes.'

'All the same,' I went on, 'I dare say that most so-called pleasures—the most intense ones, anyway—which reach the mind through the body are of this kind: in some way or other they involve escape from pain.'

'True.'

'And doesn't the same go for anticipatory pleasure and distress, which happen before the event as a result of expectations?'

'Yes.'

'Do you know what they're like—what the best d analogy for them is?' I asked.

'What?' he answered.

'You know how things can be high, low, or in between?' I asked.

'Yes.'

'Well, someone moving from the bottom of anything to the middle is bound to get an impression of upward motion, isn't he? And once he's standing at the halfway point and looking down to where he travelled from, then if he hasn't seen the true heights, he's bound to think he's reached the top, isn't he?'

'Yes, I'd certainly have to agree with that,' he said.

'And if he retraced his steps, he'd think—rightly—that he was travelling downwards, wouldn't e he?' I asked.

'Of course.'

'And all these experiences of his would be due to his ignorance of the true nature of high, middle, and low, wouldn't they?'

'Obviously.'

'So would you think it odd for people who have never experienced truth, and who therefore have unreliable views about a great many subjects, to be in the same position where pleasure, pain, and the intermediate state are concerned? They not only hold the correct opinion that they are feeling pain, and do 585a in fact feel pain, when they move into a state of pain, but they're also certain about the satisfaction and pleasure they feel when they move away from pain and into the intermediate state. But they're being misled: there's no difference between people who've never experienced pleasure comparing pain with absence of pain, and people who've never experienced white comparing black with grey.'

'No, I don't find this at all odd,' he replied. 'In fact, I'd be far more surprised if it didn't happen.'

'Here's something for you to think about,' I said. 'Aren't hunger, thirst, and so on states in which the b body is lacking something?'

'Naturally.'

'While stupidity and unintelligence are states in which the mind is lacking something?'

'Yes.'

'So food and intelligence are the sources of satisfaction in these cases?'

'Of course.'

'Is it the case that the more real something is, the more it can be a source of true satisfaction? Or is it the less real it is?'

'Obviously it's the more real it is.'

'Well, is reality present in a purer form in things like bread, drink, savouries, and food in general, do you think, or in things like true belief, knowledge, intelligence, and in short in all the things that constitute goodness? Here's another issue to help you decide. There are objects which never alter, never perish, and are never deceptive, and which are not only like that in themselves, but are found in an environment which is also like that; on the other hand, there are objects which are constantly altering and are perishable, and which are not only like that in themselves, but are found in an environment which is also like that. Which class of objects, do you think, contains a higher degree of reality.'

'The class of objects which never alter is far superior in this respect,' he replied.

'And isn't the reality of that which never alters just as knowable as it is real?'

'Yes.'

'And just as true?'

'Again, yes.'

'If it were less true, it would be less real as well, wouldn't it?'

'Necessarily.'

'To sum up, then, the kinds of things which tend to the body are less true and less real than the kinds of things which tend to the mind. Yes?'

'Yes, certainly.'

'And don't you think the same goes for the body, compared to the mind?'

'I do.'

'Is it the case, then, that an object which is satisfied by more real things, and which is itself more real, is more really satisfied than an object which is satisfied by less real things, and which is itself less real?'

'Of course.'

'Therefore, assuming that being satisfied by things which accord with one's nature is pleasant, an object which is really satisfied more (that is, by more real things) would be enabled more really and truly to feel true pleasure, while an object which comes by less real things would be less truly and steadily satisfied and would come by a less dependable and less true version of pleasure.'

'That's absolutely inevitable,' he agreed.

'It turns out, then, that people to whom intelligence and goodness are unfamiliar, whose only interest is self-indulgence and so on, spend their lives moving aimlessly to and fro between the bottom and the halfway point, which is as far as they reach. But they never travel any further towards the true heights: they've never even looked up there, let alone gone there; they aren't really satisfied by anything real; they don't experience steady, pure pleasure. They're no different from cattle: they spend their lives grazing, with their eyes turned down and heads bowed towards the ground and their tables. Food and sex are their only concerns, and their insatiable greed for more and more drives them to kick and butt one another to death with their horns and hoofs of iron, killing one another because they're seeking satisfaction in unreal things for a part of themselves which is also unreal—a leaky vessel they're trying to fill.'

'Socrates,' Glaucon declared, 'you've given an inspired and perfect description of the life most people lead.'

'Isn't it also inevitable that the pleasures they're involved with are, in fact, combinations of pleasure and pain, mere effigies of true pleasure? Like those illusory paintings, the pleasure and pain are vivid only because of the contrast between them, and their intensity is therefore no more than apparent. They impregnate people with an insane lust for the pleasure they offer, and these fools fight over them, as the Trojans in Stesichorus' story, out of ignorance of the truth, fought over the mere apparition of Helen.'

'Yes, something like that's bound to be the case,' he said.

'What about the passionate part of the mind? Won't the situation be more or less the same for anyone who brings its desires to a successful conclusion? He's either ambitious, in which case he's motivated by resentment and seeks satisfaction in status; or he's competitive, in which case he relies on force and seeks satisfaction in success; or he's bad-tempered, in which case he resorts to anger and seeks satisfaction in an angry outburst. But none of these involve reason and intelligence.'

'Again, yes, something like that's bound to be the case,' he said.

'All right, then,' I said. 'Shall we confidently state that, where avarice and competitiveness are concerned, any desire which succeeds in attaining its objective will get the truest pleasure available to it when it is guided by truth, which is to say when it follows the leadership of knowledge and reason in its quest for those pleasures to which intelligence directs it? And shall we add that the pleasures it gets will also be the ones which are particularly suitable for it—that is, if suitability and benefit coincide?'

'Well, they do coincide,' he said.

'It follows that when the whole mind accepts the leadership of the philosophical part, and there's no internal conflict, then each part can do its own job and be moral in everything it does, and in particular can enjoy its own pleasures, and thus reap as much benefit and truth from pleasure as is possible for it.'

'Exactly.'

'When one of the other two parts is in control, however, it not only fails to attain its own pleasure, but it also forces the other parts to go after unsuitable, false pleasures.'

'Right,' he agreed.

'Now, the further removed something is from philosophy and reason, the more it'll have an effect of this kind.'

'Certainly.'

'And aren't things separated from law and order to the same extent that they're separated from reason?'

'Obviously.'

'And didn't we find that it's the lustful, dictatorial desires which are the furthest removed from law and order?'

'We certainly did.'

'While the regal, restrained desires are closest to them?'

'Yes.'

'The more of a dictator a person is, then, the greater the distance between him and pleasure which is both true and suitable; the more of a king a person is, the shorter the distance.'

'Necessarily.'

'It follows that there is no life less enjoyable than a dictator's, and no life more enjoyable than a king's.'

'No doubt about it.'

'Do you know, in fact, how much less enjoyable a dictator's life is than a king's?' I asked.

'No. Please tell me,' he replied.

'There are three kinds of pleasure, apparently, and one of them is genuine, while two are spurious. A dictator, in his flight from law and reason, crosses over into the land beyond the spurious pleasures and settles down with his bodyguard of slavish pleasures. Perhaps the best way to describe the extent of his degeneration, which isn't all that easy to describe, is as follows.'

'How?' he asked.

'The dictator occupies the third place in the series which starts with the oligarchic type, since the democratic type comes in between them.'

'Yes.'

'So the pleasure he beds down with is also, assuming the truth of our earlier conclusions, a reflection three places away from oligarchic pleasure. Yes?'

'Yes.'

'Moreover, counting from the regal type (and assuming that aristocracy and kingship belong to the same category), it's the oligarchic type's turn to come third.'

'Yes.'

'It follows', I said, 'that a dictator's distance from true pleasure is, in numerical terms, triple a triple.'

'I suppose so.

'So it appears', I said, 'that the reflection which constitutes a dictator's pleasure is a plane number based on the quantity of the linear number.'

'Yes, definitely.'

'And the extent of the distance can be expressed as a square and a cube.'

'It can be a mathematician, anyway,' he said.

'So suppose you wanted to put it the other way round and state how far a king is from a dictator in terms of the truth of pleasure, the completed multiplication would show that his life is 729 times more pleasant than a dictator's. And a dictator is that much more wretched than a king.'

'You've had to spout some complex mathematics,' he remarked, 'to describe the difference, in terms of pleasure and distress, between the two men—the moral one and the immoral one.'

'Yes, but I'm right,' I said, 'and it's a number which suits lives, assuming that days, nights, months, and years are related to lives.'

'Well, they certainly are,' he said.

'Now, if this is how decisive a victory a good, moral person wins over a bad, immoral one on the field of pleasure, just think how infinitely more resounding his victory will be on the field of elegance and propriety of life, and of goodness.'

'Yes, that's absolutely right,' he said.

Plato concludes that he has responded to the challenge of Chapter 2: he has demonstrated that morality is intrinsically rewarding and desirable. He rounds this off with a graphic image of the tripartite mind as consisting of three creatures: a human being (reason), a lion (passion), and a mutable monster (desire). Morality feeds the human being, tames the lion, and subdues the monster; immorality—especially if it goes undiscovered—makes one a monster. Self-discipline (as a result of the educational programme of Chapters 4 and 10) is best, but the externally imposed discipline of law and convention is a good second best. One must use the imaginary community as a paradigm on which to model one's own inner constitution.

'All right,' I said. 'At this point in the argument,
b let's remind ourselves of the original assertion which started us off on our journey here. Wasn't it someone saying that immorality was rewarding if you were a consummate criminal who gave an impression of morality? Wasn't that the asssertion?'

'Yes, it was.'

'Well, now that we've decided what effect moral and immoral conduct have,' I said, 'we can engage him in conversation.'

c 'What shall we say?' he asked.

'Let's construct a theoretical model of the mind, to help him see what kind of idea he's come up with.'

'What sort of model?' he asked.

'Something along the lines of those creatures who throng the ancient myths,' I said, 'like the Chimera, Scylla, Cerberus, and so on, whose form is a composite of the features of more than one creature.'

'Yes, that's how they're described,' he said.

'Make a model, then, of a creature with a single— if varied and many-headed—form, arrayed all around with the heads of both wild and tame animals, and possessing the ability to change over to a different set of heads and to generate all these new bits from its own body.'

'That would take some skilful modelling,' he re-
d marked, 'but since words are a more plastic material than wax and so on, you may consider the model constructed.'

'A lion and a man are the next two models to make, then. The first of the models, however, is to be by far the largest, and the second the second largest.'

'That's an easier job,' he said. 'It's done.'

'Now join the three of them together until they become one, as it were.'

'All right,' he said.

'And for the final coat, give them the external appearance of a single entity. Make them look like a person, so that anyone incapable of seeing what's in-
e side, who can see only the external husk, will see a single creature, a human being.'

'It's done,' he said.

'Now, we'd better respond to the idea that this person gains from doing wrong, and loses from doing right, by pointing out to its proponent that this is tantamount to saying that we're rewarded if we indulge and strengthen the many-sided beast and the
589a lion with all its aspects, but starve and weaken the man, until he's subject to the whims of the others, and can't promote familiarity and compatibility between the other two, but lets them bite each other, fight, and try to eat each other.'

'Yes, that's undoubtedly what a supporter of immorality would have to say,' he agreed.

'So the alternative position, that morality is profitable, is equivalent to saying that our words and be-
b haviour should be designed to maximize the control the inner man has within us, and should enable him to secure the help of the leonine quality and then tend to the many-headed beast as a farmer tends to his crops—by nurturing and cultivating its tame aspects, and by stopping the wild ones growing. Then he can ensure that they're all compatible with one another, and with himself, and can look after them all equally, without favouritism.'

'Yes, that's exactly what a supporter of morality has to say,' he agreed.

'Whichever way you look at it, then, a supporter of morality is telling the truth, and a supporter of im-
c morality is wrong. Whether your criterion is pleasure, reputation, or benefit, a supporter of morality is right, and a critic of morality is unreliable and doesn't know what he's talking about.'

'I quite agree: he doesn't in the slightest,' he said.

'But he doesn't mean to make a mistake, so let's be gentle with him. Here's a question we can ask him, to try to win him over: "My friend, don't you think that this is also what accounts for conventional standards of what is and is not acceptable? Things are acceptable when they subject the bestial aspects of our nature to the human—or it might be more accurate to say the divine—part of ourselves, but they're objectionable when they cause the oppression of our tame side under the savage side." Will he agree, do you think?'

'Well, I'll be recommending him to,' he answered.

'So what follows from this argument? Can there be any profit in the immoral acquisition of money, if this entails the enslavement of the best part of oneself to the worst part? The point is, if there's no profit in someone selling his son or daughter into slavery—slavery under savage and evil men—for even a great deal of money, then what happens if he cruelly enslaves the most divine part of himself to the vilest, most godless part? Isn't unhappiness the result? Isn't the deadly business he's being paid for far more terrible than what Eriphyle did when she accepted the necklace as the price for her husband's death?'

'Yes, by a long way,' Glaucon said. 'I mean, I'll answer on behalf of our supporter of immorality.'

'Now, do you think the reason for the traditional condemnation of licentiousness is the same—because it allows that fiend, that huge and many-faceted creature, greater freedom than it should have?'

'Obviously,' he said.

'And aren't obstinacy and bad temper considered bad because they distend and invigorate our leonine, serpentine side to a disproportionate extent?'

'Yes.'

'Whereas a spoilt, soft way of life is considered bad because it makes this part of us so slack and loose that it's incapable of facing hardship?'

'Of course.'

'And why are lack of independence and autonomy despised? Isn't it still to do with the passionate part, because we have to subordinate it to the unruly beast and, from our earliest years, get the lion used to being insulted and to becoming a monkey instead of a lion—and all for the sake of money and to satisfy our greed?'

'Yes.'

'What about mundane, manual labour? Why do you think it has a bad name? Isn't it precisely because there's an inherent weakness in the truly good part of the person which makes him incapable of controlling his internal beasts, so that all he does is pander to them, and all he can learn is their whims?'

'I suppose that's right,' he said.

'The question is, how can a person in this condition become subject to the kind of rulership which is available to a truly good person? By being the slave, we suggest, of a truly good person, whose divine element rules within him. But we're not suggesting, as Thrasymachus did about subjects, that his status as a subject should do him harm; we're saying that subjection to the principle of divine intelligence is to everyone's advantage. It's best if this principle is part of a person's own nature, but if it isn't, it can be imposed from outside, to foster as much unanimity and compatibility between us as might be possible when we're all governed by the same principle.'

'You're right,' he said.

'It's also clear', I continued, 'that this is the function of law: this is why every member of a community has the law to fall back on. And it explains why we keep children under control and don't allow them their freedom until we've formed a government within them, as we would in a community. What we do is use what is best in ourselves to cultivate the equivalent aspect of a child, and then we let him go free once the equivalent part within him has been established as his guardian and ruler.'

'Yes, that's clear,' he said.

'Is there any conceivable argument, then, Glaucon, which will enable us to claim that immorality or licentiousness is rewarding, when the result of any kind of shameful behaviour may be a richer or otherwise more powerful person, but is certainly a worse person?'

'No, there isn't,' he replied.

'And how can it be profitable for a person's immorality to go unnoticed and unpunished? The consequence of a criminal getting away with his crimes is that he becomes a worse person. If he's found out and punished, however, then his bestial side is tamed and pacified, his tame side is liberated, and in short his mental state becomes as good as it can be. And, in so far as the mind is a more valuable asset than the body, it's more important for the mind to acquire self-discipline, morality, and intelligence than it is for the body to become fit, attractive, and healthy.'

'You're absolutely right,' he said.

c 'Then anyone with any sense will put all his energies, throughout his life, into achieving this goal. In the first place, he'll value only those intellectual pursuits which have the effect we've described on the mind, and regard any others as trivial, won't he?'

'Obviously,' he said.

'In the second place,' I went on, 'there's more to his attitude towards the care and condition of his body than simply the fact that he won't give himself over to bestial and irrational pleasure and make that the whole point of his life. He won't, in fact, be interested in physical health and he won't take the pursuit of physical fitness, health, and beauty seriously

d unless they also lead to self-discipline. We'll find him, throughout his life, attuning his body in order to make music with his mind.'

'Yes, that's exactly what it takes to be a true virtuoso,' he said.

'And won't the same attunement and harmony guide his acquisition of money? He's hardly going to be swayed by the usual standards of happiness and amass an inexhaustible pile of money, along with its inexhaustible troubles, is he?'

'I don't think so,' he said.

'What he'll do, however,' I said, 'is keep an eye

e on his own inner society and watch out for trouble brewing among its members, caused by his having either too much or too little property. He'll stick to this guiding principle as much as possible, and increase and decrease his assets accordingly.'

'Exactly,' he agreed.

592a 'And the same consideration will also guide his attitude towards honours. He won't hesitate to accept and experience those which will, in his view, make him a better person, but in his private life as well as in public life he'll avoid those which he thinks would cause the downfall of his established constitution.'

'If that's what's important to him,' he said, 'he's unlikely to have anything to do with government.'

'Actually,' I said, 'he certainly will, in his own community. But I agree that he probably won't in the country of his birth, short of divine intervention.'

'I see,' he said. 'You mean that he will in the community we've just been founding and describing, which can't be accommodated anywhere in the world, and therefore rests at the level of ideas.'

'It may be, however,' I replied, 'that it is retained b in heaven as a paradigm for those who desire to see it and, through seeing it, to return from exile. In fact, it doesn't make the slightest bit of difference whether it exists or will exist anywhere: it's still the only community in whose government he could play a part.'

'Yes, I suppose so,' he said.

CHAPTER 13
POETRY AND UNREALITY

Plato now launches his notorious attack on poetry (with painting introduced in a supporting role); the critique is supplementary to that of Chapter 4. The attack begins with the claim that artistic products are two stages removed from reality and truth, and that they represent things as they appear to be, not as they are. It is easy to be a master of representing appearances, since it involves no understanding of any of the things represented, no penetration beyond the surface of things to their function or to whether or not they serve some moral purpose.

'You know,' I said, 'the issue of poetry is the main 595a consideration—among many others—which convinces me that the way we were trying to found our community was along absolutely the right lines.'

'What are you thinking of?' he asked.

'That we flatly refused to admit any representational poetry. I mean, its total unacceptability is even clearer, in my opinion, now that we've distinguished b the different aspects of the mind.'

'How is it clearer?'

'Well, this is just between ourselves: please don't denounce me to the tragic playwrights and all the other representational poets. But it looks as though this whole genre of poetry deforms its audience's minds, unless they have the antidote, which is recognition of what this kind of poetry is actually like.'

'What do you mean? What do you have in mind?' he asked.

'It's fairly clear,' I said, 'that all these fine tragedians trace their lineage back to Homer: they're Homer's students and disciples, ultimately. And this makes it difficult for me to say what I have to say, because I've had a kind of fascinated admiration for Homer ever since I was young. Still, we should value truth more than we value any person, so, as I say, I'd better speak out.'

'Yes,' he said.

'And you'll listen to what I have to say, or rather respond to any questions I ask?'

'Yes. Go ahead and ask them.'

'Can you tell me what representation basically is? You see, I don't quite understand its point myself.'

'And I suppose I do!' he said.

'It wouldn't surprise me if you did,' I said. 'Just because a person can't see very well, it doesn't mean that he won't often see things before people with better eyesight than him.'

'That's true,' he said. 'All the same, I'd be too shy to explain any views I did have in front of you, so please try to come up with an answer yourself.'

'All right. Shall we get the enquiry going by drawing on familiar ideas? Our usual position is, as you know, that any given plurality of things which have a single name constitutes a single specific type. Is that clear to you?'

'Yes.'

'So now let's take any plurality you want. Would it be all right with you if we said that there were, for instance, lots of beds and tables?'

'Of course.'

'But these items of furniture comprise only two types—the type of bed and the type of table.'

'Yes.'

'Now, we also invariably claim that the manufacture of either of these items of furniture involves the craftsman looking to the type and then making the beds or tables (or whatever) which we use. The point is that the type itself is not manufactured by any craftsman. How could it be?'

'It couldn't.'

'There's another kind of craftsman, too. I wonder what you think of him.'

'What kind?'

'He makes everything—all the items which every single manufacturer makes.'

'He must be extraordinarily gifted.'

'Wait: you haven't heard the half of it yet. It's not just a case of his being able to manufacture all the artefacts there are: every plant too, every creature (himself included), the earth, the heavens, gods, and every-

thing in the heavens and in Hades under the earth—all these are made and created by this one man!'

'He really must be extraordinarily clever,' he said.

'Don't you believe me?' I asked. 'Tell me, do you doubt that this kind of craftsman could exist under any circumstances, or do you admit the possibility that a person could—in one sense, at least—create all these things? I mean, don't you realize that you yourself could, under certain circumstances, create all these things?'

'What circumstances?' he asked.

'I'm not talking about anything complicated or rare,' I said. 'It doesn't take long to create the circumstances. The quickest method, I suppose, is to get hold of a mirror and carry it around with you everywhere. You'll soon be creating everything I mentioned a moment ago—the sun and the heavenly bodies, the earth, yourself, and all other creatures, plants, and so on.'

'Yes, but I'd be creating appearances, not actual real things,' he said.

'That's a good point,' I said. 'You've arrived just in time to save the argument. I mean, that's presumably the kind of craftsman a painter is. Yes?'

'Of course.'

'His creations aren't real, according to you; but do you agree that all the same there's a sense in which even a painter creates a bed?'

'Yes,' he said, 'he's another one who creates an apparent bed.'

'What about a joiner who specializes in making beds? Weren't we saying a short while ago that what he makes is a particular bed, not the type, which is (on our view) the real bed?'

'Yes, we were.'

'So if there's no reality to his creation, then it isn't real; it's similar to something real, but it isn't actually real. It looks as though it's wrong to attribute full reality to a joiner's or any artisan's product, doesn't it?'

'Yes,' he said, 'any serious student of this kind of argument would agree with you.'

'It shouldn't surprise us, then, if we find that even these products are obscure when compared with the truth.'

'No, it shouldn't.'

'Now, what about this representer we're trying to understand? Shall we see if these examples help us?' I asked.

'That's fine by me,' he said.

'Well, we've got these three beds. First, there's the real one, and we'd say, I imagine, that it is the product of divine craftsmanship. I mean, who else could have made it?'

'No one, surely.'

'Then there's the one the joiner makes.'

'Yes,' he said.

'And then there's the one the painter makes. Yes?'

'Yes, agreed.'

'These three, then—painter, joiner, God—are responsible for three different kinds of bed.'

'Yes, that's right.'

'Now, God has produced only that one real bed.

c The restriction to only one might have been his own choice, or it might just be impossible for him to make more than one. But God never has, and never could, create two or more such beds.'

'Why not?' he asked.

'Even if he were to make only two such beds,' I said, 'an extra one would emerge, and both the other two would be of that one's type. It, and not the two beds, would be the real bed.'

'Right,' he said.

'God realized this, I'm sure. He didn't want to be

d a kind of joiner, making a particular bed: he wanted to be a genuine creator and make a genuine bed. That's why he created a single real one.'

'I suppose that's right.'

'Shall we call him its progenitor, then, or something like that?'

'Yes, he deserves the name,' he said, 'since he's the maker of this and every other reality.'

'What about a joiner? Shall we call him a manufacturer of beds?'

'Yes.'

'And shall we also call a painter a manufacturer and maker of beds and so on?'

'No, definitely not.'

'What do you think he does with beds, then?'

e 'I think the most suitable thing to call him would be a representer of the others' creations,' he said.

'Well, in that case,' I said, 'you're using the term "represanter" for someone who deals with things which are, in fact, two generations away from reality, aren't you?'

'Yes,' he said.

'The same goes for tragic playwrights, then, since they're representers: they're two generations away from the throne of truth, and so are all other representers.'

'I suppose so.'

'Well, in the context of what we're now saying about representation, I've got a further question about painters. Is it, in any given instance, the actual reality that they try to represent, or is it the craftsmen's products?'

'The craftsmen's products,' he said.

'Here's another distinction you'd better make: do they try to represent them as they are, or as they appear to be?'

'What do you mean?' he asked.

'I'll tell you. Whether you look at a bed from the side or straight on or whatever, it's still just as much a bed as it ever was, isn't it? I mean, it doesn't actually alter it at all: it just *appears* to be different, doesn't it? And the same goes for anything else you can mention. Yes.'

'Yes,' he agreed. 'It seems different, but isn't actually.'

'So I want you to consider carefully which of

b these two alternatives painting is designed for in any and every instance. Is it designed to represent the facts of the real world or appearances? Does it represent appearance or truth?'

'Appearance,' he said.

'It follows that representation and truth are a considerable distance apart, and a representer is capable of making every product there is only because his contact with things is slight and is restricted to how they look. Consider what a painter does, for instance: we're saying that he doesn't have a clue about shoe-making or joinery, but he'll still paint pictures of ar-

c tisans working at these and all other areas of expertise, and if he's good at painting he might paint a joiner, have people look at it from far away, and deceive them—if they're children or stupid adults—by making it look as though the joiner were real.'

'Naturally.'

'I think the important thing to bear in mind about cases like this, Glaucon, is that when people tell us they've met someone who's mastered every craft, and is the world's leading expert in absolutely every branch of human knowledge, we should reply that

598a

they're being rather silly. They seem to have met the kind of illusionist who's expert at representation and, thanks to their own inability to evaluate knowledge, ignorance, and representation, to have been so thoroughly taken in as to believe in his omniscience.'

'You're absolutely right,' he said.

'Now, we'd better investigate tragedy next,' I said, 'and its guru, Homer, because one does come across the claim that there's no area of expertise, and nothing relevant to human goodness and badness either—and nothing to do with the gods even—that these poets don't understand. It is said that a good poet must understand the issues he writes about, if his writing is to be successful, and that if he didn't understand them, he wouldn't be able to write about them. So we'd better try to decide between the alternatives. Either the people who come across these representational poets are being taken in and are failing to appreciate, when they see their products, that these products are two steps away from reality and that it certainly doesn't take knowledge of the truth to create them (since what they're creating are appearances, not reality); or this view is valid, and in fact good poets are authorities on the subjects most people are convinced they're good at writing about.'

'Yes, this definitely needs looking into,' he said.

'Well, do you think that anyone who was capable of producing both originals and images would devote his energy to making images, and would make out that this is the best things he's done with his life?'

'No, I don't.'

'I'm sure that if he really knew about the things he was copying in his representations, he'd put far more effort into producing real objects than he would into representations, and would try to leave behind a lot of fine products for people to remember him by, and would dedicate himself to being the recipient rather than the bestower of praise.'

'I agree,' he said. 'He'd gain a lot more prestige and do himself a great deal more good.'

'Well, let's concentrate our interrogation of Homer (or any other poet you like) on a single area. Let's not ask him whether he can tell us of any patients cured by any poet in ancient or modern times, as Asclepius cured his patients, or of any students

any of them left to continue his work, as Asclepius left his sons. And even these questions grant the possibility that a poet might have had some medical knowledge, instead of merely representing medical terminology. No, let's not bother to ask him about any other areas of expertise either. But we do have a right to ask Homer about the most important and glorious areas he undertakes to expound—warfare, tactics, politics, and human education. Let's ask him, politely, "Homer, maybe you aren't two steps away from knowing the truth about goodness; maybe you aren't involved in the manufacture of images (which is what we called representation). Perhaps you're actually only one step away, and you do have the ability to recognize which practices—in their private or their public lives—improve people and which ones impair them. But in that case, just as Sparta has its Lycurgus and communities of all different sizes have their various reformers, please tell us which community has you to thank for improvements to its government. Which community attributes the benefits of its good legal code to you? Italy and Sicily name Charondas in this respect, we Athenians name Solon. Which country names you?" Will he have any reply to make?'

'I don't think so,' said Glaucon. 'Even the Homeridae themselves don't make that claim.'

'Well, does history record that there was any war fought in Homer's time whose success depended on his leadership or advice?'

'No.'

'Well, then, are a lot of ingenious inventions attributed to him, as they are to Thales of Miletus and Anacharsis of Scythia? I mean the kinds of inventions which have practical applications in the arts and crafts and elsewhere. He is, after all, supposed to be good at creating things.'

'No, there's not the slightest hint of that sort of thing.'

'All right, so there's no evidence of his having been a public benefactor, but what about in private? In there any evidence that, during his lifetime, he was a mentor to people, and that they used to value him for his teaching and then handed down to their successors a particular Homeric way of life? This is what happened to Pythagoras: he wasn't only held in extremely high regard for his teaching during his lifetime, but his successors even now call their way of life Pythagorean and somehow seem to stand out from all other people.'

'No, there's no hint of that sort of thing either,' he said. 'I mean, Homer's associate Creophylus' cultural attainments would turn out to be even more derisory than his name suggests they are, Socrates, if the stories about Homer are true. You see, Creophylus is said to have more or less disregarded Homer during his lifetime.'

'Yes, that *is* what we're told,' I agreed. 'But, Glaucon, if Homer really had been an educational expert whose products were better people—which is to say, if he had knowledge in this sphere and his abilities were not limited to representation—don't you think he'd have been surrounded by hordes of associates, who would have admired him and valued his company highly? Look at Protagoras of Abdera, Prodicus of Ceos, and all the rest of them: they can use their exclusive tuition to make their contemporaries believe that without them in charge of their education they won't be capable of managing their own estates, let alone their communities, and they're so appreciated for this expertise of theirs that their associates almost carry them around on their heads. So if Homer or Hesiod had been able to help people's moral development, would their contemporaries have allowed them to go from town to town reciting their poems? Wouldn't they have kept a tighter grip on them than on their money, and tried to force them to stay with them in their homes? And if they couldn't persuade them to do that, wouldn't they have danced attendance on them wherever they went, until they'd gained as much from their teaching as they could?'

'I don't think anyone could disagree with you, Socrates,' he said.

'So shall we classify all poets, from Homer onwards, as representers of images of goodness (and of everything else which occurs in their poetry), and claim that they don't have any contact with the truth? The facts are as we said a short while ago: a painter creates an illusory shoemaker, when not only does he not understand anything about shoemaking, but his audience doesn't either. They just base their conclusions on the colours and shapes they can see.'

'Yes.'

'And I should think we'll say that the same goes for a poet as well: he uses words and phrases to block in some of the colours of each area of expertise, although all he understands is how to represent things in a way which makes other superficial people, who base their conclusions on the words they can hear, think that he's written a really good poem about shoemaking or military command or whatever else it is that he's set to metre, rhythm, and music. It only takes these features to cast this powerful a spell: that's what they're for. But when the poets' work is stripped of its musical hues and expressed in plain words, I think you've seen what kind of impression it gives, so you know what I'm talking about.'

'I do,' he said.

'Isn't it', I asked, 'like what noticeably happens when a young man has alluring features, without actually being goodlooking, and then this charm of his deserts him?'

'Exactly,' he said.

'Now, here's another point to consider. An image-maker, a representer, understands only appearance, while reality is beyond him. Isn't that our position?'

'Yes.'

'Let's not leave the job half done: let's give this idea the consideration it deserves.'

'Go on,' he said.

'What a painter does, we're saying, is paint a picture of a horse's reins and a bit. Yes?'

'Yes.'

'While they're made by a saddler and a smith, aren't they?'

'Yes.'

'Does a painter know what the reins and the bit have to be like? Surely even their makers, the smith and the saddler, don't know this, do they? Only the horseman does, because he's the one who knows how to make use of them.'

'You're quite right.'

'In fact, won't we claim that it's a general principle?'

'What?'

'That whatever the object, there are three areas of expertise: usage, manufacture, and representation.'

'Yes.'

'Now, is there any other standard by which one assesses the goodness, fineness, and rightness of anything (whether it's a piece of equipment or a creature or an activity) than the use for which it was made, by man or by nature?'

'No.'

'It's absolutely inevitable, then, that no one knows the ins and outs of any object more than the person who makes use of it. He has to be the one to tell the manufacturer how well or badly the object he's using fares in actual usage. A pipe-player, for example, tells a pipe-maker which of his pipes do what they're supposed to do when actually played, and goes on to instruct him in what kinds of pipes to make, and the pipe-maker does what he's told.'

'Of course.'

'So as far as good and bad pipes are concerned, it's a knowledgeable person who gives the orders, while the other obeys the orders and does the manufacturing. Right?'

'Yes.'

'Justified confidence, then, is what a pipe-maker has about goodness and badness (as a result of spending time with a knowledgeable person and having to listen to him), while knowledge is the province of the person who makes use of the pipes.'

'Yes.'

'Which of these two categories does our representer belong to? Does he acquire knowledge about whether or not what he's painting is good or right from making use of the object, or does he acquire true belief because of having to spend time with a knowledgeable person and being told what to paint?'

'He doesn't fit either case.'

'As far as goodness and badness are concerned, then, a representer doesn't have either knowledge or true beliefs about whatever it is he's representing.'

'Apparently not.'

'How nicely placed a poetic representer is, then, to know what he's writing about!'

'Not really.'

'No, because all the same, despite his ignorance of the good and bad aspects of things, he'll go on representing them. But what he'll be representing, apparently, is whatever appeals to a large, if ignorant, audience.'

'Naturally.'

'Here are the points we seem to have reached a reasonable measure of agreement on, then: a representer knows nothing of value about the things he represents; representation is a kind of game, and shouldn't be taken seriously; and those who compose tragedies in iambic and epic verse are, without exception, outstanding examples of representers.'

'Yes.'

Since poetry deals with appearances, it appeals to—and fattens up—the lower part of the mind, not the rational part. It makes us indulge in emotional feelings which hamper reason, even when we would not normally sanction those feelings. Reason uses measurement to combat some illusory appearances, and calculation of benefit to combat unnecessary feelings. In short, poetry does nothing to establish an ordered, moral inner constitution, and if one is already established, it threatens to subvert it. Until or unless it can be proven that feelings foster philosophy, rather than hinder it, we must be extremely wary of them.

'So the province of representation is indeed two steps removed from truth, isn't it?' I said.

'Yes.'

'But on which of the many aspects of a person does it exert its influence?'

'What are you getting at?'

'Something like this. One and the same object appears to vary in size depending on whether we're looking at it from close up or far away.'

'Yes.'

'And the same objects look both bent and straight depending on whether we look at them when they're in water or out of it, and both concave and convex because sight gets misled by colouring. Our mind obviously contains the potential for every single kind of confusion like this. It's because illusory painting aims at this afflicting in our natures that it can only be described as sorcery; and the same goes for conjuring and all trickery of that sort.'

'True.'

'Now, methods have evolved of combating this—measuring, counting, and weighing are the most elegant of them—and consequently of ending the reign within us of apparent size, number, and weight, and replacing them with something which calculates and measures, or even weighs. Right?'

'Of course.'

'And this, of course, is the job of the rational part of the mind, which is capable of performing calculations.'

'Yes.'

'Now, it's not uncommon for the mind to have made its measurements, and to be reporting that *x* is larger than *y* (or smaller than it, or the same size as it), but still to be receiving an impression which contradicts its measurements of these very objects.'

'Yes.'

'Well, didn't we say that it's impossible for a single thing to hold contradictory beliefs at the same time about the same objects?'

'Yes, we did, and we were right.'

603a 'So the part of the mind whose views run counter to the measurements must be different from the part whose views fall in with the measurements.'

'Yes.'

'But it's the best part of the mind which accepts measurements and calculations.'

'Of course.'

'The part which opposes them, therefore, must be a low-grade part of the mind.'

'Necessarily.'

'Well, all that I've been saying has been intended to bring us to the point where we can agree that not only does painting—or rather representation in general—produce a product which is far from truth, but it also forms a close, warm, affectionate relationship with a part of us which is, in its turn, far from intel-
b ligence. And nothing healthy or authentic can emerge from this relationship.'

'Absolutely,' he said.

'A low-grade mother like representation, then, and an equally low-grade father produce low-grade children.'

'I suppose that's right.'

'Does this apply only to visual representation,' I asked, 'or to aural representation as well—in other words, to poetry?'

'I suppose it applies to poetry as well,' he said.

'Well, we'd better not rely on mere suppositions based on painting,' I said. 'Let's also get close
c enough to that part of the mind which poetic representation consorts with to see whether it's of low or high quality.'

'Yes, we should.'

'We'd better start by having certain ideas out in the open. We'd say that representational poetry represents people doing things, willingly or unwillingly, and afterwards thinking that they've been successful or unsuccessful, and throughout feeling distressed or happy. Have I missed anything out?'

'No, nothing.'

'Well, does a person remain internally unanimous throughout all this? We found that, in the case of d sight, there's conflict and people have contradictory views within themselves at the same time about the same objects. Is it like that when one is doing things too? Is there internal conflict and dissent? But it occurs to me that there's really no need for us to decide where we stand on this issue now, because we've already done so, perfectly adequately, in an earlier phase of the discussion, when we concluded that, at any given moment, our minds are teeming with countless thousands of these kinds of contradictions.'

'That's right,' he said.

'Yes,' I said. 'But that earlier discussion of ours was incomplete, and I think it's crucial that we fin- e ish it off now.'

'What have we left out?' he asked.

'If a good man meets with a misfortune such as losing a son or something else he values very highly, we've already said, as you know, that he'll endure this better than anyone else.'

'Yes.'

'But here's something for us to think about. Will he feel no grief, or is that impossible? If it's impossible, is it just that he somehow keeps his pain within moderate bounds?'

'The second alternative is closer to the truth,' he said.

'But now I've got another question for you about him. Do you think he'll be more likely to fight and 604a resist his distress when his peers can see him, or when he's all alone by himself in some secluded spot?'

'He'll endure pain far better when there are people who can see him, of course,' he said.

'When he's all alone, however, I imagine he won't stop himself expressing a lot of things he'd be ashamed of anyone hearing, and doing a lot of things he'd hate anyone to see him do.'

'That's right,' he agreed.

'Isn't it the case that reason and convention recommend resistance, while the actual event pushes b him towards distress?'

'True.'

'When a person is simultaneously pulled in opposite directions in response to a single object, we're bound to conclude that he has two sides.'

'Of course.'

'One of which is prepared to let convention dictate the proper course of action, isn't it?'

'Can you explain how?'

'Convention tells us, as you know, that it's best to remain as unruffled as possible when disaster strikes and not to get upset, on the grounds that it's never clear whether an incident of this nature is good or bad, that nothing positive is gained by taking it badly, that no aspect of human life is worth bothering about a great deal, and that grief blocks our access to the very thing we need to have available as quickly as possible in these circumstances.'

'What do you have in mind?' he asked.

'The ability to think about the incident', I replied, 'and, under the guidance of reason, to make the best possible use of one's situation, as one would in a game of dice when faced with how the dice had fallen. When children bump into things, they clutch the hurt spot and spend time crying; instead of behaving like that, we should constantly be training our minds to waste no time before trying to heal anything which is unwell, and help anything which has fallen get up from the floor—to banish mourning by means of medicine.'

'Yes, that's the best way to deal with misfortune,' he said.

'Now, our position is that the best part of our minds is perfectly happy to be guided by reason like this.'

'That goes without saying.'

'Whereas there's another part of our minds which urges us to remember the bad times and to express our grief, and which is insatiably greedy for tears. What can we say about it? That it's incapable of listening to reason, that it can't face hard work, that it goes hand in hand with being frightened of hardship?'

'Yes, that's right.'

'Now, although the petulant part of us is rich in a variety of representable possibilities, the intelligent and calm side of our characters is pretty well constant and unchanging. This makes it not only difficult to represent, but also difficult to understand when it is represented, particularly when the audience is the kind of motley crowd you find crammed into a theatre, because they're simply not acquainted with the experience that's being represented to them.'

'Absolutely.'

'Evidently, then, a representational poet has nothing to do with this part of the mind: his skill isn't made for its pleasure, because otherwise he'd lose his popular appeal. He's concerned with the petulant and varied side of our characters, because it's easy to represent.'

'Obviously.'

'So we're now in a position to see that we'd be perfectly justified in taking hold of him and placing him in the same category as a painter. He resembles a painter because his creations fall short of truth, and a further point of resemblance is that the part of the mind he communicates with is not the best part, but something else. Now we can see how right we'd be to refuse him admission into any community which is going to respect convention, because now we know which part of the mind he wakes up. He destroys the rational part by feeding and fattening up this other part, and this is equivalent to someone destroying the more civilized members of a community by presenting ruffians with political power. There's no difference, we'll claim, between this and what a representational poet does: at a personal level, he establishes a bad system of government in people's minds by gratifying their irrational side, which can't even recognize what size things are—an object which at one moment it calls big, it might call small the next moment—by creating images, and by being far removed from truth.'

'Yes.'

'However, we haven't yet made the most serious allegation against representational poetry. It has a terrifying capacity for deforming even good people. Only a very few escape.'

'Yes, that *is* terrifying. Does it really do that?'

'Here's my evidence: you can make up your own mind. When Homer or another tragedian represents the grief of one of the heroes, they have him deliver a lengthy speech of lamentation or even have him sing a dirge and beat his breast; and when we listen to all this, even the best of us, as I'm sure you're aware, feels pleasure. We surrender ourselves, let ourselves be carried along, and share the hero's pain; and then we enthuse about the skill of any poet who makes us feel particularly strong feelings.'

'Yes, I'm aware of this, of course.'

'However, you also appreciate that when we're afflicted by trouble in our own lives, then we take pride in the opposite—in our ability to endure pain without being upset. We think that this is manly behaviour, and that only women behave in the way we were sanctioning earlier.'

'I realize that,' he said.

'So,' I said, 'instead of being repulsed by the sight of the kind of person we'd regret and deplore being ourselves, we enjoy the spectacle and sanction it. Is this a proper way to behave?'

'No, it certainly isn't,' he said. 'It's pretty unreasonable, I'd say.'

'I agree,' I said, 'and here's even more evidence.'

'What?'

'Consider this. What a poet satisfies and gratifies on these occasions is an aspect of ourselves which we forcibly restrain when tragedy strikes our own lives—an aspect which hungers after tears and the satisfaction of having cried until one can cry no more, since that is what it is in its nature to want to do. When the part of us which is inherently good has been inadequately trained in habits enjoined by reason, it relaxes its guard over this other part, the part which feels sad. Other people, not ourselves, are feeling these feelings, we tell ourselves, and it's no disgrace for us to sanction such behaviour and feel sorry for someone who, even while claiming to be good, is over-indulging in grief; and, we think, we are at least profiting from the pleasure, and there's no point in throwing away the pleasure by spurning the whole poem or play. You see, few people have the ability to work out that we ourselves are bound to store the harvest we repeat from others: these occasions feed the feeling of sadness until it is too strong for us easily to restrain it when hardship occurs in our own lives.'

'You're absolutely right,' he said.

'And doesn't the same go for humour as well? If there are amusing things which you'd be ashamed to do yourself, but which give you a great deal of pleasure when you see them in a comic representation or hear about them in private company—when you don't find them loathsome and repulsive—then isn't this exactly the same kind of behaviour as we uncovered when talking about feeling sad? There's a part of you which wants to make people laugh, but your reason restrains it, because you're afraid of being thought a vulgar clown. Nevertheless, you let it have its way on those other occasions, and you don't realize that the almost inevitable result of giving it energy in this other context is that you become a comedian in your own life.'

'Yes, that's very true,' he said.

'And the same goes for sex, anger, and all the desires and feelings of pleasure and distress which, we're saying, accompany everything we do: poetic representation has the same effect in all these cases too. It irrigates and tends to these things when they should be left to wither, and it makes them our rulers when they should be our subjects, because otherwise we won't live better and happier lives, but quite the opposite.'

'I can't deny the truth of what you're saying,' he said.

'Therefore, Glaucon,' I went on, 'when you come across people praising Homer and saying that he is the poet who has educated Greece, that he's a good source for people to learn how to manage their affairs and gain culture in their lives, and that one should structure the whole of one's life in accordance with his precepts, you ought to be kind and considerate: after all, they're doing the best they can. You should concede that Homer is a supreme poet and the original tragedian, but you should also recognize that the only poems we can admit into our community are hymns to the gods and eulogies of virtuous men. If you admit the entertaining Muse of lyric and epic poetry, then instead of law and the shared acceptance of reason as the best guide, the kings of your community will be pleasure and pain.'

'You're quite right,' he agreed.

'So,' I said, 'since we've been giving poetry another hearing, there's our defence: given its nature, we had good grounds for banishing it earlier from our community. No rational person could have done any different. However, poetry might accuse us of insensitivity and lack of culture, so we'd better also tell her that there's an ancient quarrel between poetry and philosophy. There are countless pieces of evidence for this enmity between them, but here are just a few: there's that "bitch yelping and baying at her master"; there's "featuring prominently in the idle chatter of fools";

there's "control by a crowd of know-alls"; there are those whose "subtle notions" lead them to realize that they do indeed have "notional incomes". All the same, we ought to point out that if the kinds of poetry and representation which are designed merely to give pleasure can come up with a rational argument for their inclusion in a well-governed community, we'd be delighted—short of compromising the truth as we see it, which wouldn't be right—to bring them back from exile: after all, we know from our own experience all about their spell. I mean, haven't *you* ever fallen under the spell of poetry, Glaucon, especially when the spectacle is provided by Homer?'

'I certainly have.'

'Under these circumstances, then, if our allegations met a poetic rebuttal in lyric verse or whatever, would we be justified in letting poetry return?'

'Yes.'

'And I suppose we'd also allow people who champion poetry because they like it, even though they can't compose it, to speak on its behalf in prose, and to try to prove that there's more to poetry than mere pleasure—that it also has a beneficial effect on society and on human life in general. And we won't listen in a hostile frame of mind, because we'll be the winners if poetry turns out to be beneficial as well as enjoyable.'

'Of course we will,' he agreed.

'And if it doesn't, Glaucon, then we'll do what a lover does when he thinks that a love affair he's involved in is no good for him: he reluctantly detaches himself. Similarly, since we've been conditioned by our wonderful societies until we have a deep-seated love for this kind of poetry, we'll be delighted if there proves to be nothing better and closer to the truth than it. As long as it is incapable of rebutting our allegations, however, then while we listen to poetry we'll be chanting these allegations of ours to ourselves as a precautionary incantation against being caught once more by that childish and pervasive love. Our message will be that the commitment appropriate for an important matter with access to the truth shouldn't be given to this kind of poetry. People should, instead, be worried about the possible effects, on one's own inner political system, of listening to it and should tread cautiously; and they should let our arguments guide their attitude towards poetry.'

'I couldn't agree more,' he said.

'You see, my dear Glaucon,' I said, 'what's in the balance here is absolutely crucial—far more so than people think. It's whether one becomes a good or a bad person, and consequently has the calibre not to be distracted by prestige, wealth, political power, or even poetry from applying oneself to morality and whatever else goodness involves.'

'Looking back over our discussion,' he said, 'I can only agree with you. And I think anyone else would do the same as well.'

REVIEW QUESTIONS

1. In the *Republic,* what is Plato's argument that morality is advantageous to those who practice it? If his concern is with individual character, why does he spend so much time discussing an imaginary community?

2. What is Plato's theory of ideas, or forms? What is his chain of reasoning leading to this theory?

3. In *Meno,* what is Socrates' explanation of how we can know when we have found the answer to a question we are asking? What does Socrates try to demonstrate with his conversation with the slave boy?

4. In the *Euthyphro,* Socrates asks, in effect, whether the good is good because the gods approve of it or whether the gods approve of it because it is good. What is his answer? What are the implications of his answer for morality?

5. According to Plato, what is the relationship between virtue and knowledge? between wrongdoing and ignorance?

6. In the *Apology,* What is Socrates' explanation of why men fear death? How does knowledge dispel fear of death?

3

ARISTOTLE

Aristotle (384–322 B.C.), son of a physician, student in Plato's Academy for twenty years, teacher of Alexander the Great, rivals Plato as the most important philosopher in the Western tradition. He started the second great university, the Lyceum, nicknamed "Peripatetic" because he and the students frequently walked in the courtyard while conversing. Reputed to have written 400 books, he was an encyclopedic scholar and writer. The Father of Logic, a great biologist and physicist, writer of the second great work on ethics (accepting the *Republic* as the first) and great works on political philosophy, he made significant contributions to every area of philosophy. He stammered. He wrote his treatise *Ethics* (included below) to his son Nicomachus. After Alexander's death, finding himself unpopular in Athens, charged with the crime of impiety, he fled the city, "lest the Athenians sin twice against philosophy" (the first time was in executing Socrates).

COMPARISON OF ARISTOTLE'S THOUGHT WITH PLATO'S

Both Plato and Aristotle sought knowledge as a good in its own right. Both were *teleologists* in that they believed in a universal goal for all things, the Good or the *final cause*. In this they differ from modern science (nature knows no purposes), especially Darwinian evolution where chance or random selection and survival of the fittest replace rational order. Aristotle believed in teleology because of the regularity in generation, astronomy, and physical behavior. Nature has unconscious purposes.

Whereas Plato was mystical, an idealist, loved abstract ideas, and scorned the physical, empirical, and sensual, Aristotle was more commonsensical, loved facts, physics, biology,

202

[handwritten margin note: epistemologist — how do we know things?]

and scientific observation. Plato offers us grand allegories and myths to convey a comprehensive world view, whereas Aristotle sought to remove myth and symbol from philosophy, substituting rational explanation and logical precision.

Aristotle's main disagreement with Plato is over the theory of the Forms. He criticizes it from various points of view—as a logician he offers a different analysis of predication; as an ontologist and epistemologist he argues that it is the concrete particular, not the universal or form, that is substance in the primary sense, and that provides the starting point in our investigation of form. Third, as a physicist he points out that the separate and transcendent forms are useless in accounting for change and coming into existence. Plato's Forms belong to the world of unchanging being, but the study of change involves the investigator of forms in the changing objects of the world of becoming. Aristotle shifted the focus from the study of pure, immutable being to physics, the study of Nature (and natural change).

[handwritten margin notes: ontology — nature of being & existence; predication — relationship between things]

Aristotle sets forth three basic ingredients for the explanation of change:

a. The Substrata (Substance)—that which persists through change.
b. The Privation or absence of form.
c. The Form which appears in the process of change, always a part of the concrete thing.

Change consists in a substratum (matter) acquiring a form which it didn't previously possess. Non-being is associated with privation, and the substratum, since it is always in existence, is in itself free of non-being. But since form follows privation, there is a sense in which we do have a creation out of non-being. Before matter and form merge in an individual, they are only potential; in becoming a particular they are acutalized. The result is *Substance* ("primary substance"), a particular individual. Hence Aristotle brings Plato's Forms down from heaven to concrete reality. Universals do not have any existence of their own as individuals but only subsist in things (we can refer to them only apart from things as abstractions, i.e., an ideal triangle or horse).

Aristotle complains that Plato's Forms neither cause movement nor change. Change and motion are especially related to physics. It is in this regard that Aristotle offers an alternative account to what has gone before (*Physics* I, II).

Aristotle's Metaphysics

Aristotle inherited from earlier philosophers of Nature the view that change takes place between opposites of one kind or another. This provides the basis of his own general theory of form or privation. Change takes place between a pair of opposites, such as hot and cold, one of which represents the form and the other the privation. But a third factor is necessary, i.e., that which is subject to or undergoes the change (*hypokeimenon*, substratum or matter). For example, boiling a kettle of water—there is an underlying matter that begins in the form of water and is changed to air (matter is *qualityless* and never present—a sort of nonbeing). Here we have two causes: (1) Form—change either from the form to the privation or vice versa and (2) Matter (substratum). Aristotle adds two more types: (3) Efficient or Moving Cause, and (4) Final or End Cause (*telos*), ending with four types of causes:

1. Matter or Material Cause—the substratum out of which the change occurs, the underlying subject which persists through change (e.g., the bronze or wood out of which a statue is made—the Greek word for matter is *hule* = wood).

2. Formal Cause—the essence of the thing, that from or to which a thing changes [shape] (e.g., the statue is a figure of Athene or Apollo).
3. Efficient Cause—the moving or proximate cause (the sculptor who makes the statue).
4. The Final or End Cause (*telos*)—the goal or purpose (the sculptor has in mind) toward which the change is moving (e.g., the statue is to represent Athene or Apollo as a symbol for worship and admiration).

The formal cause is Socrates' essence (his reason, being a bipedal animala, etc.); the material cause is his mother; the efficient cause is his father, whose semen does not contribute the matter of the embryo (which is the mother's) but serves to activate the matter; the final cause is his end, a fully functioning reality as a mature philosopher.

Some of the implications of the theory are:

1. No conscious purpose exists in Nature (*Physics* 119b). Nature does not deliberate but there are nevertheless *unconscious* purposes or ends in nature.
2. Nature fulfills its ends only as a general rule, not as an absolute rule without exceptions (there are mistakes). As Aristotle says, Natural processes take place "always or for the most part."
3. Nevertheless, final causes exist in nature in spite of the fact that nature does not deliberate because of the regularity of natural change. First the movements of the heavenly bodies provide a model of regularity and uniformity; then there is uniformity in the reproduction of natural species, in that each kind produces its own kind, man generating man, mice generating mice, oak trees generating oak trees; and regularity is also to be found in the natural movements of the four elements, earth always falling and fire rising when nothing impedes their motion. Therefore it would seem reasonable to conclude via induction that Nature is not random or haphazard but exhibits order and regularity and if these, then Ends, though not conscious ones.
4. Aristotle's craftsman is reminiscent of Plato's demiurge (*Timaeus*) with the difference that Aristotle goes a lot further in trying to demythologize and naturalize explicitly this process—more a metaphor for Aristotle. It's not clear how literal Plato believes his explanation to be, but Aristotle clearly views his metaphors as such Nature has its ends not from without but from within (inner *telos*).

Another way to look at change is in terms of *potentiality* and *actuality*. For example, take a tree: the seed of the tree is *potentially* the mature tree (acorn, the oak). Similarly the fetus is potentially the adult human; a piece of wood, potentially the table; a piece of marble, potentially the statue of Apollo.

In each instance it is the relatively formless matter, the shapeless wood or marble that may be said to possess potentiality. Qualityless matter, the abstraction, is pure potentiality. But relatively formless matter possesses potentialities in different senses and to different degrees. (e.g., a fetus is potentially a man to a higher degree than earth, fire, air, and water are potentially a man).

Aristotle's point in tying potentiality and actuality together is to show that even the relatively formless matter is potentially what the end product is actually. Form is not something transcendent and separate, as Plato claimed, but something that is gradually acquired and brought to actuality during the process of change. That is, Aristotle did not hold that something came out of nothing [*ex nihilo nihil fit*, nothing comes from nothing], but all coming into existence is relative: something comes from something else which is potentially what it later is actually. In each case the substratum acquires a new form. Hence in a sense a seed is and is not a tree—potentially it is but actually it is not.

Finally, we say a word about Aristotle's *Ethics* and *Politics*, which are included as our two final readings in this chapter. After a general discussion of the nature of ethics, Aristotle turns to the nature of virtue. Virtues are simply those characteristics that enable individuals to live well in communities. In order to achieve a state of well-being (*eudaimonia*, usually translated happiness), proper social institutions are necessary. Thus the moral person cannot really exist apart from a flourishing political setting that enables the individual to develop the requisite virtues for the good life. Ethics is thus a species of politics.

Next, Aristotle distinguishes moral virtues from intellectual ones. Whereas the intellectual virtues may be taught directly, the moral ones must be lived in order to be learned. By living well we acquire the right habits. These habits are in fact the virtues, which are to be sought as the best guarantee to the happy life. But, again, happiness requires that one be lucky enough to live in a flourishing state. The morally virtuous life consists in living in moderation, according to the "golden mean."

Politics rivals the *Republic* as the greatest political treatise of ancient philosophy. It consists of a series of essays which discuss the definitions and structure of the state, as well as criticize Plato's Utopianism and forms of democracy. Aristotle argues for aristocracy (rule by the excellent) as the best form of government.

In our first reading, *Categories*, Aristotle offers a theory of predication, that is an explanation of how the terms of language apply to things in the world (the Greek word *kategoriai* from which we derive the word 'categories' comes from the verb meaning 'to predicate'). Aristotle argues that underlying all reality is substance, fundamental and independent reality. Everything else depends for its existence on substance.

FOR FURTHER READING

Ackrill, J. L. *Aristotle the Philosopher* (Oxford University Press, 1981).
Allan, D. J. *The Philosophy of Aristotle* (Oxford University Press, 1970).
Barnes, Jonathan. *Aristotle* (Oxford University Press, 1982).
Barnes, Jonathan. *The Complete Works of Aristotle*, 2 vols. (Princeton University Press, 1984).
Guthrie, W. K. C. *A History of Greek Philosophy*, vol. VI (Cambridge University Press, 1981).
Irwin, Terrance. *Aristotle's First Principles* (Oxford University Press, 1988).
Rorty, A. O., ed. *Essays on Aristotle's Ethics* (University of California Press, 1980).
Ross, W. D. *Aristotle* (1923; reprint, Meridian Books, 1959).
Taylor, A. E. *Aristotle* (Dover, 1955).

CATEGORIES

1ª   1. When things have only a name in common and the definition of being which corresponds to the name is different, they are called *homonymous*. Thus, for example, both a man and a picture are animals. These have only a name in common and the definition of being which corresponds to the name is different; for if one is to say what being an animal is for each of them, one will give two distinct definitions.   5

Reprinted from Aristotle's *Categories*, translated by J. L. Ackrill (1963) by permission of Oxford University Press.

When things have the name in common and the definition of being which corresponds to the name is the same, they are called *synonymous*. Thus, for example, both a man and an ox are animals. Each of these is called, by a common name, an animal, and the definition of being is also the same; for if one is to give the definition of each—what being an animal is for each of them—one will give the same definition.

When things get their name from something, with a difference of ending, they are called *paronymous*. Thus, for example, the grammarian gets his name from grammar, the brave get theirs from bravery.

2. Of things that are said, some involve combination while others are said without combination. Examples of those involving combination are: man runs, man wins; and of those without combination: man, ox, runs, wins.

Of things there are: (*a*) some are *said of* a subject but are not *in* any subject. For example, man is said of a subject, the individual man, but is not in any subject. (*b*) Some are in a subject but are not said of any subject. (By 'in a subject' I mean what is in something, not as a part, and cannot exist separately from what it is in.) For example, the individual knowledge-of-grammer is in a subject, the soul, but is not said of any subject; and the individual white is in a subject, the body (for all colour is in a body), but is not said of any subject. (*c*) Some are both said of a subject and in a subject. For example, knowledge is in a subject, the soul, and is also said of a subject, knowledge-of-grammar. (*d*) Some are neither in a subject nor said of a subject, for example, the individual man or the individual horse—for nothing of this sort is either in a subject or said of a subject. Things that are individual and numerically one are, without exception, not said of any subject, but there is nothing to prevent some of them from being in a subject—the individual knowledge-of-grammar is one of the things in a subject.

3. Whenever one thing is predicated of another as of a subject, all things said of what is predicated will be said of the subject also. For example, man is predicated of the individual man, and animal of man; so animal will be predicated of the individual man also—for the individual man is both a man and an animal.

The differentiae of genera which are different and not subordinate one to the other are themselves different in kind. For example, animal and knowledge: footed, winged, aquatic, two-footed, are differentiae of animal, but none of these is a differentia of knowledge; one sort of knowledge does not differ from another by being two-footed. However, there is nothing to prevent genera subordinate one to the other from having the same differentiae. For the higher are predicated of the genera below them, so that all differentiae of the predicated genus will be differentiae of the subject also.

4. Of things said without any combination, each signifies either substance or quantity or qualification or a relative or where or when or being-in-a-position or having or doing or being-affected. To give a rough idea, examples of substance are man, horse; of quantity: four-foot, five-foot; of qualification: white, grammatical; of a relative: double, half, larger; of where: in the Lyceum, in the market-place; of when: yesterday, last-year; of being-in-a-position: is-lying, is-sitting; of having: has-shoes-on, has-armour-on; of doing: cutting, burning; of being-affected: being-cut, being-burned.

None of the above is said just by itself in any affirmation, but by the combination of these with one another an affirmation is produced. For every affirmation, it seems, is either true or false; but of things said without any combination none is either true or false (e.g. man, white, runs, wins).

5. A *substance*—that which is called a substance most strictly, primarily, and most of all—is that which is neither said of a subject nor in a subject, e.g. the individual man or the individual horse. The species in which the things primarily called substances are, are called *secondary substances*, as also are the genera of these species. For example, the individual man belongs in a species, man, and animal is a genus of the species; so these—both man and animal—are called secondary substances.

It is clear from what has been said that if something is said of a subject both its name and its definition are necessarily predicated of the subject. For example, man is said of a subject, the individual man, and the name is of course predicated (since you will be predicating man of the individual man), and also the definition of man will be predicated of the individual man (since the individual man is also a man). Thus both the name and the definition will be predicated of the subject. But as for things which are in a subject, in most cases neither the name nor the definition is predicated of the subject. In some cases there is nothing to prevent the name from being predicated of the subject, but it is impossible for the definition to be predicated. For example, white, which is in a subject (the body), is predicated of the subject; for a body is called white. But the definition of white will never be predicated of the body.

All the other things are either said of the primary substances as subjects or in them as subjects. This is clear from an examination of cases. For example, animal is predicated of man and therefore also of the individual man; for were it predicated of none of the individual men it would not be predicated of man at all. Again, colour is in body and therefore also in an individual body; for were it not in some individual body it would not be in body at all. Thus all the other things are either said of the primary substances as subjects or in them as subjects. So if the primary substances did not exist it would be impossible for any of the other things to exist.

Of the secondary substances the species is more a substance than the genus, since it is nearer to the primary substance. For if one is to say of the primary substance what it is, it will be more informative and apt to give the species than the genus. For example, it would be more informative to say of the individual man that he is a man than that he is an animal (since the one is more distinctive of the individual man while the other is more general); and more informative to say of the individual tree that it is a tree than that it is a plant. Further, it is because the primary substances are subjects for all the other things and all the other things are predicated of them or are in them, that they are called substances most of all. But as the primary substances stand to the other things, so the species stands to the genus: the species is a subject for the genus (for the genera are predicated of the species but the species are not predicated reciprocally of the genera). Hence for this reason too the species is more a substance than the genus.

But of the species themselves—those which are not genera—one is no more a substance than another: it is no more apt to say of the individual man that he is a man than to say of the individual horse that it is a horse. And similarly of the primary substances one is no more a substance than another: the individual man is no more a substance than the individual ox.

It is reasonable that, after the primary substances, their species and genera should be the only other things called secondary substances. For only they, of things predicated, reveal the primary substance. For if one is to say of the individual man what he is, it will be in place to give the species or the genus (though more informative to give man than animal); but to give any of the other things would be out of place—for example, to say white or runs or anything like that. So it is reasonable that these should be the only other things called substances. Further, it is because the primary substances are subjects for everything else that they are called substances most strictly. But as the primary substances stand to everything else, so the species and genera of the primary substances stand to all the rest: all the rest are predicated of these. For if you will call the individual man grammatical, then you will call both a man and an animal grammatical; and similarly in other cases.

It is a characteristic common to every substance not to be in a subject. For a primary substance is neither said of a subject nor in a subject. And as for secondary substances, it is obvious at once that they are not in a subject. For man is said of the individual man as subject but is not in a subject: man is not *in* the individual man. Similarly, animal also is said of the individual man as subject, but animal is not *in* the individual man. Further, while there is nothing to prevent the name of what is in a subject from being sometimes predicated of the subject, it is impossible for the definition to be predicated. But the definition of the secondary substances, as well as the name, is predicated of the subject: you will predicate the definition of man of the individual man, and also that of animal. No substance, therefore, is in a subject.

This is not, however, peculiar to substance, since the differentia also is not in a subject. For footed and two-footed are said of man as subject but are not in a subject; neither two-footed nor footed is *in* man. Moreover, the definition of the differentia is predicated of that of which the differentia is said. For example, if footed is said of man the definition of footed will also be predicated of man; for man is footed.

30 We need not be disturbed by any fear that we may be forced to say that the parts of a substance, being in a subject (the whole substance), are not substances. For when we spoke of things *in a subject* we did not mean things belonging in something as *parts*.

It is a characteristic of substances and differentiae that all things called from them are so called syn-
35 onymously. For all the predicates from them are predicated either of the individuals or of the species. (For from a primary substance there is no predicate, since it is said of no subject; and as for secondary substances, the species is predicated of the individual, the genus both of the species and of the indi-
3ᵇ1 vidual. Similarly, differentiae too are predicated both of the species and of the individuals.) And the primary substances admit the definition of the species and of the genera, and the species admits that of the genus; for everything said of what is predicated will
5 be said of the subject also. Similarly, both the species and the individuals admit the definition of the differentiae. But synonymous things were precisely those with both the name in common and the same definition. Hence all the things called from substances and differentiae are so called synonymously.

10 Every substance seems to signify a certain 'this'. As regards the primary substances, it is indisputably true that each of them signifies a certain 'this'; for the thing revealed is individual and numerically one. But as regards the secondary substances, though it appears from the form of the name—when one speaks
15 of man or animal—that a secondary substance likewise signifies a certain 'this', this is not really true; rather, it signifies a certain qualification—for the subject is not, as the primary substance is, one, but man and animal are said of many things. However, it does not signify simply a certain qualification, as white does. White signifies nothing but a qualification,
20 whereas the species and the genus mark off the qualification of substance—they signify substance of a certain qualification. (One draws a wider boundary with the genus than with the species, for in speaking of animal one takes in more than in speaking of man.)

Another characteristic of substances is that there is nothing contrary to them. For what would be contrary
25 to a primary substance? For example, there is nothing

contrary to an individual man, nor yet is there anything contrary to man or to animal. This, however, is not peculiar to substance but holds of many other things also, for example, of quantity. For there is nothing contrary to four-foot or to ten or to anything of this kind—unless someone were to say that many is contrary to few or large to small; but still there is noth-
30 ing contrary to any *definite* quantity.

Substance, it seems, does not admit of a more and a less. I do not mean that one substance is not more a substance than another (we have said that it is), but that any given substance is not called more, or less,
35 that which it is. For example, if this substance is a man, it will not be more a man or less a man either than itself or than another man. For one man is not more a man than another, as one pale thing is more
4ᵇ1 pale than another and one beautiful thing more beautiful than another. Again, a thing is called more, or less, such-and-such than itself; for example, the body that is pale is called more pale now than before, and the one that is hot is called more, or less, hot. Substance, however, is not spoken of thus. For a man is not called more a man now than before, nor is anything else that is a substance. Thus substance does
5 not admit of a more and a less.

It seems most distinctive of substance that what is numerically one and the same is able to receive
10 contraries. In no other case could one bring forward anything, numerically one, which is able to receive contraries. For example, a colour which is numerically one and the same will not be black and white, nor will numerically one and the same action be bad and good; and similarly with everything else that is
15 not substance. A substance, however, numerically one and the same, is able to receive contraries. For example, an individual man—one and the same—becomes pale at one time and dark at another, and hot and cold, and bad and good.
20

Nothing like this is to be seen in any other case, unless perhaps someone might object and say that statements and beliefs are like this. For the same statement seems to be both true and false. Suppose, for
25 example, that the statement that somebody is sitting is true; after he has got up this same statement will be false. Similarly with beliefs. Suppose you believe truly that somebody is sitting; after he has got up you
30 will believe falsely if you hold the same belief about

him. However, even if we were to grant this, there is still a difference in the *way* contraries are received. For in the case of substances it is by themselves changing that they are able to receive contraries. For what has become cold instead of hot, or dark instead of pale, or good instead of bad, has changed (has altered); similarly in other cases too it is by itself undergoing change that each thing is able to receive contraries. Statements and beliefs, on the other hand, themselves remain completely unchangeable in every way; it is because the *actual thing* changes that the contrary comes to belong to them. For the statement that somebody is sitting remains the same; it is because of a change in the actual thing that it comes to be true at one time and false at another. Similarly with beliefs. Hence at least the *way* in which it is able to receive contraries—through a change in itself—would be distinctive of substance, even if we were to grant that beliefs and statements are able to receive

contraries. However, this is not true. For it is not because they themselves receive anything that statements and beliefs are said to be able to receive contraries, but because of what has happened to something else. For it is because the actual thing exists or does not exist that the statement is said to be true or false, not because it is able itself to receive contraries. No statement, in fact, or belief is changed at all by anything. So, since nothing happens in them, they are not able to receive contraries. A substance, on the other hand, is said to be able to receive contraries because it itself receives contraries. For it receives sickness and health, and paleness and darkness; and because it itself receives the various things of this kind it is said to be able to receive contraries. It is, therefore, distinctive of substance that what is numerically one and the same is able to receive contraries. This brings to an end our discussion of substance.

POSTERIOR ANALYTICS (ANALYTICA POSTERIORA)

BOOK I

1. All instruction given or received by way of argument proceeds from pre-existent knowledge. This becomes evident upon a survey of all the species of such instruction. The mathematical sciences and all other speculative disciplines are acquired in this way, and so are the two forms of dialectical reasoning, syllogistic and inductive; for each of these latter make use of old knowledge to impart new, the syllogism assuming an audience that accepts its premisses, induction exhibiting the universal as implicit in the clearly known particular. Again, the persuasion exerted by rhetorical arguments is in principle the same, since they use either example, a kind of induction, or enthymeme, a form of syllogism.

The pre-existent knowledge required is of two kinds. In some cases admission of the fact must be assumed, in others comprehension of the meaning of the term used, and sometimes both assumptions are essential. Thus, we assume that every predicate can

be either truly affirmed or truly denied of any subject, and that 'triangle' means so and so; as regards 'unit' we have to make the double assumption of the meaning of the word and the existence of the thing. The reason is that these several objects are not equally obvious to us. Recognition of a truth may in some cases contain as factors both previous knowledge and also knowledge acquired simultaneously with that recognition—knowledge, this latter, of the particulars actually falling under the universal and therein already virtually known. For example, the student knew beforehand that the angles of every triangle are equal to two right angles; but it was only at the actual moment at which he was being led on to recognize this as true in the instance before him that he came to know 'this figure inscribed in the semicircle' to be a triangle. For some things (viz. the singulars finally reached which are not predicable of anything else as subject) are only learnt in this way, i.e. there is here no recognition through a middle of a minor term as subject to a major. Before he was

Reprinted from Aristotle's *Posterior Analytics*, translated by G. R. G. Mure by permission of Oxford University Press.

led on to recognition or before he actually drew a conclusion, we should perhaps say that in a manner he knew, in a manner not.

If he did not in an unqualified sense of the term know the existence of this triangle, how could he know without qualification that its angles were equal to two right angles? No: clearly he knows not without qualification but only in the sense that he knows universally. If this distinction is not drawn, we are faced with the dilemma in the Meno: either a man will learn nothing or what he already knows; for we cannot accept the solution which some people offer. A man is asked, 'Do you, or do you not, know that every pair is even?' He says he does know it. The questioner then produces a particular pair, of the existence, and so a fortiori of the evenness, of which he was unaware. The solution which some people offer is to assert that they do not know that every pair is even, but only that everything which they know to be a pair is even: yet what they know to be even is that of which they have demonstrated evenness, i.e. what they made the subject of their premiss, viz. not merely every triangle or number which they know to be such, but any and every number or triangle without reservation. For no premiss is ever couched in the form 'every number which you know to be such', or 'every rectilinear figure which you know to be such': the predicate is always construed as applicable to any and every instance of the thing. On the other hand, I imagine there is nothing to prevent a man in one sense knowing what he is learning, in another not knowing it. The strange thing would be, not if in some sense he knew what he was learning, but if he were to know it in that precise sense and manner in which he was learning it.

2. We suppose ourselves to possess unqualified scientific knowledge of a thing, as opposed to knowing it in the accidental way in which the sophist knows, when we think that we know the cause on which the fact depends, as the cause of that fact and of no other, and, further, that the fact could not be other than it is. Now that scientific knowing is something of this sort is evident—witness both those who falsely claim it and those who actually possess it, since the former merely imagine themselves to be, while the latter are also actually, in the condition described. Consequently the proper object of

unqualified scientific knowledge is something which cannot be other than it is.

There may be another manner of knowing as well—that will be discussed later. What I now assert is that at all events we do know by demonstration. By demonstration I mean a syllogism productive of scientific knowledge, a syllogism, that is, the grasp of which is eo ipso such knowledge. Assuming then that my thesis as to the nature of scientific knowing is correct, the premisses of demonstrated knowledge must be true, primary, immediate, better known than and prior to the conclusion, which is further related to them as effect to cause. Unless these conditions are satisfied, the basic truths will not be 'appropriate' to the conclusion. Syllogism there may indeed be without these conditions, but such syllogism, not being productive of scientific knowledge, will not be demonstration. The premisses must be true: for that which is non-existent cannot be known—we cannot know, e.g. that the diagonal of a square is commensurate with its side. The premisses must be primary and indemonstrable; otherwise they will require demonstration in order to be known, since to have knowledge, if it be not accidental knowledge, of things which are demonstrable, means precisely to have a demonstration of them. The premisses must be the causes of the conclusion, better known than it, and prior to it; its causes, since we possess scientific knowledge of a thing only when we know its cause; prior, in order to be causes; antecedently known, this antecedent knowledge being not our mere understanding of the meaning, but knowledge of the fact as well. Now 'prior' and 'better known' are ambiguous terms, for there is a difference between what is prior and better known in the order of being and what is prior and better known to man. I mean that objects nearer to sense are prior and better known to man; objects without qualification prior and better known are those further from sense. Now the most universal causes are furthest from sense and particular causes are nearest to sense, and they are thus exactly opposed to one another. In saying that the premisses of demonstrated knowledge must be primary, I mean that they must be the 'appropriate' basic truths, for I identify primary premiss and basic truth. A 'basic truth' in a demonstration is an immediate proposition. An immediate proposition is one which has no other proposition prior to it. A proposition is either part of an enunciation, i.e. it predicates a single attribute of a single subject. If a proposition is dialectical, it assumes either part indifferently; if it is demonstrative, it lays down one part to the definite exclusion of the other because that part is true. The term 'enunciation' denotes either part of a contradiction indifferently. A contradiction is an opposition which of its own nature excludes a middle. The part of a contradiction which conjoins a predicate with a subject is an affirmation; the part disjoining them is a negation. I call an immediate basic truth of syllogism a 'thesis' when, though it is not susceptible of proof by the teacher, yet ignorance of it does not constitute a total bar to progress on the part of the pupil: one which the pupil must know if he is to learn anything whatever is an axiom. I call it an axiom because there are such truths and we give them the name of axioms par excellence. If a thesis assumes one part or the other of an enunciation, i.e. asserts either the existence or the non-existence of a subject, it is a hypothesis; if it does not so assert, it is a definition. Definition is a 'thesis' or a 'laying something down', since the arithmetician lays it down that to be a unit is to be quantitatively indivisible; but it is not a hypothesis, for to define what a unit is is not the same as to affirm its existence.

Now since the required ground of our knowledge—i.e. of our conviction—of a fact is the possession of such a syllogism as we call demonstration, and the ground of the syllogism is the facts constituting its premises, we must not only know the primary premises—some if not all of them—beforehand, but know them better than the conclusion: for the cause of an attribute's inherence in a subject always itself inheres in the subject more firmly than that attribute; e.g. the cause of our loving anything is dearer to us than the object of our love. So since the primary premises are the cause of our knowledge—i.e. of our conviction—it follows that we know them better—that is, are more convinced of them—than their consequences, precisely because of our knowledge of the latter is the effect of our knowledge of the premises. Now a man cannot believe in anything more than in the things he knows, unless he has either actual knowledge of it or something better than actual knowledge. But we are faced with this paradox if a student whose belief rests on demonstration has not prior knowledge; a man must believe in some, if not in all, of the basic truths more than in the conclusion. Moreover, if a man sets out to acquire the scientific knowledge that comes through demonstration, he must not only have a better knowledge of the basic truths and a firmer conviction of them than of the connexion which is being demonstrated: more than this, nothing must be more certain or better known to him than these basic truths in their character as contradicting the fundamental premises which lead to the opposed and erroneous conclusion. For indeed the conviction of pure science must be unshakable.

3. Some hold that, owing to the necessity of knowing the primary premises, there is no scientific knowledge. Others think there is, but that all truths are demonstrable. Neither doctrine is either true or a necessary deduction from the premises. The first school, assuming that there is no way of knowing other than by demonstration, maintain that an infinite regress is involved, on the ground that if behind the prior stands no primary, we could not know the posterior through the prior (wherein they are right, for one cannot traverse an infinite series): if on the other hand—they say—the series terminates and there are primary premises, yet these are unknowable because incapable of demonstration, which according to them is the only form of knowledge. And since thus one cannot know the primary premises, knowledge of the conclusions which follow from them is not pure scientific knowledge nor properly knowing at all, but rests on the mere supposition that the premises are true. The other party agree with them as regards knowing, holding that it is only possible by demonstration, but they see no difficulty in holding that all truths are demonstrated, on the ground that demonstration may be circular and reciprocal.

Our own doctrine is that not all knowledge is demonstrative: on the contrary, knowledge of the immediate premises is independent of demonstration. (The necessity of this is obvious; for since we must know the prior premises from which the demonstration is drawn, and since the regress must end in immediate truths, those truths must be indemonstrable.) Such, then, is our doctrine, and in addition we maintain that besides scientific knowledge there is its originative source which enables us to recognize the definitions.

Now demonstration must be based on premises prior to and better known than the conclusion; and the same things cannot simultaneously be both prior and posterior to one another: so circular demonstration is clearly not possible in the unqualified sense of 'demonstration', but only possible if 'demonstration' be extended to include that other method of argument which rests on a distinction between truths prior to us and truths without qualification prior, i.e. the method by which induction produces knowledge. But if we accept this extension of its meaning, our definition of unqualified knowledge will prove faulty; for there seem to be two kinds of it. Perhaps, however, the second form of demonstration, that which proceeds from truths better known to us, is not demonstration in the unqualified sense of the term.

The advocates of circular demonstration are not only faced with the difficulty we have just stated: in addition their theory reduces to the mere statement that if a thing exists, then it does exist—an easy way of proving anything. That this is so can be clearly shown by taking three terms, for to constitute the circle it makes no difference whether many terms or few or even only two are taken. Thus by direct proof, if A is, B must be; if B is, C must be; therefore if A is, C must be. Since then—by the circular proof—if A is, B must be, and if B is, A must be, A may be substituted for C above. Then 'if B is, A must be'='if B is, C must be', which above gave the conclusion 'if A is, C must be': but C and A have been identified. Consequently the upholders of circular demonstration are in the position of saying that if A is, A must be—a simple way of proving anything. Moreover, even such circular demonstration is impossible except in the case of attributes that imply one another, viz. 'peculiar' properties.

Now, it has been shown that the positing of one thing—be it one term or one premiss—never involves a necessary consequent: two premises constitute the first and smallest foundation for drawing a conclusion at all and therefore a fortiori for the demonstrative syllogism of science. If, then, A is implied in B and C, and B and C are reciprocally implied in one another and in A, it is possible, as has been shown in my writings on the syllogism, to prove all the assumptions on which the original conclusion rested, by circular demonstration in the first figure. But it has also been shown that in the other figures either no conclusion is possible, or at least none which proves both the original premises. Propositions the terms of which are not convertible cannot be circularly demonstrated at all, and since convertible terms occur rarely in actual demonstrations, it is clearly frivolous and impossible to say that demonstration is reciprocal and that therefore everything can be demonstrated.

4. Since the object of pure scientific knowledge cannot be other than it is, the truth obtained by demonstrative knowledge will be necessary. And since demonstrative knowledge is only present when we have a demonstration, it follows that demonstration is an inference from necessary premises. So we must consider what are the premises of demonstration—i.e. what is their character: and as a preliminary, let us define what we mean by an attribute 'true in every instance of its subject', an 'essential' attribute, and a 'commensurate and universal' attribute. I call 'true in every instance' what is truly predicable of all instances—not of one to the exclusion of others—and at all times, not at this or that time only; e.g. if animal is truly predicable of every instance of man, then if it be true to say 'this is a man', 'this is an animal' is also true, and if the one be true now the other is true now. A corresponding account holds if point is in every instance predicable as contained in line. There is evidence for this in the fact that the objection we raise against a proposition put to us as true in every instance is either an instance in which, or an occasion on which, it is not true. Essential attributes are (1) such as belong to their subject as elements in its essential nature (e.g. line thus belongs to triangle, point to line; for the very being or 'substance' of triangle and line is composed of these elements, which are contained in the formulae defining triangle and line): (2) such that, while they belong to certain subjects, the subjects to which they belong are contained in the attribute's own defining formula. Thus straight and curved belong to line, odd and even, prime and compound, square and oblong, to number; and also the formula defining any one of these attributes contains its subject—e.g. line or number as the case may be.

Extending this classification to all other attributes, I distinguish those that answer the above description as belonging essentially to their respective subjects; whereas attributes related in neither of these two ways to their subjects I call accidents or 'coincidents'; e.g. musical or white is a 'coincident' of animal.

Further (a) that is essential which is not predicated of a subject other than itself: e.g. 'the walking [thing]' walks and is white in virtue of being something else besides; whereas substance, in the sense of whatever signifies a 'this somewhat', is not what it is in virtue of being something else besides. Things, then, not predicated of a subject I call essential; things predicated of a subject I call accidental or 'coincidental'.

In another sense again (b) a thing consequentially connected with anything is essential; one not so connected is 'coincidental'. An example of the latter is 'While he was walking it lightened': the lightning was not due to his walking; it was, we should say, a coincidence. If, on the other hand, there is a consequential connexion, the predication is essential; e.g. if a beast dies when its throat is being cut, then its death is also essentially connected with the cutting, because the cutting was the cause of death, not death a 'coincident' of the cutting.

So far then as concerns the sphere of connexions scientifically known in the unqualified sense of that term, all attributes which (within that sphere) are essential either in the sense that their subjects are contained in them, or in the sense that they are contained in their subjects, are necessary as well as consequentially connected with their subjects. For it is impossible for them not to inhere in their subjects either simply or in the qualified sense that one or other of a pair of opposites must inhere in the subject; e.g. in line must be either straightness or curvature, in number either oddness or evenness. For within a single identical genus the contrary of a given attribute is either its privative or its contradictory; e.g. within number what is not odd is even, inasmuch as within this sphere even is a necessary consequent of not-odd. So, since any given predicate must be either affirmed or denied of any subject, essential attributes must inhere in their subjects of necessity.

Thus, then, we have established the distinction between the attribute which is 'true in every instance' and the 'essential' attribute.

I term 'commensurately universal' an attribute which belongs to every instance of its subject, and to every instance essentially and as such; from which it clearly follows that all commensurate universals inhere necessarily in their subjects. The essential attribute, and the attribute that belongs to its subject as such, are identical. E.g. point and straight belong to line essentially, for they belong to line as such; and triangle as such has two right angles, for it is essentially equal to two right angles.

An attribute belongs commensurately and universally to a subject when it can be shown to belong to any random instance of that subject and when the subject is the first thing to which it can be shown to belong. Thus, e.g. (1) the equality of its angles to two right angles is not a commensurately universal attribute of figure. For though it is possible to show that a figure has its angles equal to two right angles, this attribute cannot be demonstrated of any figure selected at haphazard, nor in demonstrating does one take a figure at random—a square is a figure but its angles are not equal to two right angles. On the other hand, any isosceles triangle has its angles equal to two right angles, yet isosceles triangle is not the primary subject of this attribute but triangle is prior. So whatever can be shown to have its angles equal to two right angles, or to possess any other attribute, in any random instance of itself and primarily—that is the first subject to which the predicate in question belongs commensurately and universally, and the demonstration, in the essential sense, of any predicate is the proof of it as belonging to this first subject commensurately and universally: while the proof of it as belonging to the other subjects to which it attaches is demonstration only in a secondary and unessential sense. Nor again (2) is equality to two right angles a commensurately universal attribute of isosceles; it is of wider application.

BOOK II

8. We must now start afresh and consider which of these conclusions are sound and which are not, and what is the nature of definition, and whether essential nature is in any sense demonstrable and definable or in none.

Now to know its essential nature is, as we said, the same as to know the cause of a thing's existence, and the proof of this depends on the fact that a thing must have a cause. Moreover, this cause is either identical with the essential nature of the thing or distinct from it; and if its cause is distinct from it, the essential nature of the thing is either demonstrable or indemonstrable. Consequently, if the cause is distinct from the thing's essential nature and demonstration is possible, the cause must be the middle term, and, the conclusion proved being universal and affirmative, the proof is in the first figure. So the method just examined of proving it through another essential nature would be one way of proving essential nature, because a conclusion containing essential nature must be inferred through a middle which is an essential nature just as a 'peculiar' property must be inferred through a middle which is a 'peculiar' property; so that of the two definable natures of a single thing this method will prove one and not the other.

Now it was said before that this method could not amount to demonstration of essential nature—it is actually a dialectical proof of it—so let us begin again and explain by what method it can be demonstrated. When we are aware of a fact we seek its reason, and though sometimes the fact and the reason dawn on us simultaneously, yet we cannot apprehend the reason a moment sooner than the fact; and clearly in just the same way we cannot apprehend a thing's definable form without apprehending that it exists, since while we are ignorant whether it exists we cannot know its essential nature. Moreover we are aware whether a thing exists or not sometimes through apprehending an element in its character, and sometimes accidentally, as, for example, when we are aware of thunder as a noise in the clouds, of eclipse as a privation of light, or of man as some species of animal, or of the soul as a self-moving thing. As often as we have accidental knowledge that the thing exists, we must be in a wholly negative state as regards awareness of its essential nature; for we have not got genuine knowledge even of its existence, and to search for a thing's essential nature when we are unaware that it exists is to search for nothing. On the other hand, whenever we apprehend an element in the thing's character there is less difficulty. Thus it follows that the degree of our knowledge of a thing's essential nature is determined by the sense in which we are aware that it exists. Let us then take the following as our first instance of being aware of an element in the essential nature. Let A be eclipse, C the moon, B the earth's acting as a screen. Now to ask whether the moon is eclipsed or not is to ask whether or not B has occurred. But that is precisely the same as asking whether A has a defining condition; and if this condition actually exists, we assert that A also actually exists. Or again we may ask which side of a contradiction the defining condition necessitates: does it make the angles of a triangle equal or not equal to two right angles? When we have found the answer, if the premises are immediate, we know fact and reason together; if they are not immediate, we know the fact without the reason, as in the following example: let C be the moon, A eclipse, B the fact that the moon fails to produce shadows though she is full and though no visible body intervenes between us and her. Then if B, failure to produce shadows in spite of the absence of an intervening body, is attributable A to C, and eclipse, is attributable to B, it is clear that the moon is eclipsed, but the reason why is not yet clear, and we know that eclipse exists, but we do not know what its essential nature is. But when it is clear that A is attributable to C and we proceed to ask the reason of this fact, we are inquiring what is the nature of B: is it the earth's acting as a screen, or the moon's rotation or her extinction? But B is the definition of the other term, viz. in these examples, of the major term A; for eclipse is constituted by the earth acting as a screen. Thus, (1) 'What is thunder?' 'The quenching of fire in cloud', and (2) 'Why does it thunder?' 'Because fire is quenched in the cloud', are equivalent. Let C be cloud, A thunder, B the quenching of fire. Then B is attributable to C, cloud, since fire is quenched in it; and A, noise, is attributable to B; and B is assuredly the definition of the major term A. If there be a further mediating cause of B, it will be one of the remaining partial definitions of A.

We have stated then how essential nature is discovered and becomes known, and we see that, while there is no syllogism—i.e. no demonstrative syllogism—of essential nature, yet it is through syllogism, viz. demonstrative syllogism, that essential nature is exhibited. So we conclude that neither can the essential nature of anything which has a cause distinct from itself be known without demonstration, nor can it be demonstrated; and this is what we contended in our preliminary discussions.

9. Now while some things have a cause distinct from themselves, others have not. Hence it is evident that there are essential natures which are immediate, that is are basic premisses; and of these not only that they are but also what they are must be assumed or revealed in some other way. This too is the actual procedure of the arithmetician, who assumes both the nature and the existence of unit. On the other hand, it is possible (in the manner explained) to exhibit through demonstration the essential nature of things which have a 'middle', i.e. a cause of their substantial being other than that being itself; but we do not thereby demonstrate it.

10. Since definition is said to be the statement of a thing's nature, obviously one kind of definition will be a statement of the meaning of the name, or of an equivalent nominal formula. A definition in this sense tells you, e.g. the meaning of the phrase 'triangular character'. When we are aware that triangle exists, we inquire the reason why it exists. But it is difficult thus to learn the definition of things the existence of which we do not genuinely know-the cause of this difficulty being, as we said before, that we only know accidentally whether or not the thing exists. Moreover, a statement may be a unity in either of two ways, by conjunction, like the Iliad, or because it exhibits a single predicate as inhering not accidentally in a single subject.

That then is one way of defining definition. Another kind of definition is a formula exhibiting the cause of a thing's existence. Thus the former signifies without proving, but the latter will clearly be a quasi-demonstration of essential nature, differing from demonstration in the arrangement of its terms. For there is a difference between stating why it thunders, and stating what is the essential nature of thunder; since the first statement will be 'Because fire is quenched in the clouds', while the statement of what the nature of thunder is will be 'The noise of fire being quenched in the clouds'. Thus the same statement takes a different form: in one form it is continuous demonstra-

tion, in the other definition. Again, thunder can be defined as noise in the clouds, which is the conclusion of the demonstration embodying essential nature. On the other hand the definition of immediates is an indemonstrable positing of essential nature.

We conclude then that definition is (a) an indemonstrable statement of essential nature, or (b) a syllogism of essential nature differing from demonstration in grammatical form, or (c) the conclusion of a demonstration giving essential nature.

Our discussion has therefore made plain (1) in what sense and of what things the essential nature is demonstrable, and in what sense and of what things it is not; (2) what are the various meanings of the term definition, and in what sense and of what things it proves the essential nature, and in what sense and of what things it does not; (3) what is the relation of definition to demonstration, and how far the same thing is both definable and demonstrable and how far it is not.

19. As regards syllogism and demonstration, the definition of, and the conditions required to produce each of them, are now clear, and with that also the definition of, and the conditions required to produce, demonstrative knowledge, since it is the same as demonstration. As to the basic premisses, how they become known and what is the developed state of knowledge of them is made clear by raising some preliminary problems.

We have already said that scientific knowledge through demonstration is impossible unless a man knows the primary immediate premisses. But there are questions which might be raised in respect of the apprehension of these immediate premisses: one might not only ask whether it is of the same kind as the apprehension of the conclusions, but also whether there is or is not scientific knowledge of both; or scientific knowledge of the latter, and of the former a different kind of knowledge; and, further, whether the developed states of knowledge are not innate but come to be in us, or are innate but at first unnoticed. Now it is strange if we possess them from birth; for it means that we possess apprehensions more accurate than demonstration and fail to notice them. If on the other hand we acquire them and do not previously possess them, how could we apprehend and learn without a basis of pre-existent knowledge? For that is impossible, as we used to find in the case of demonstration. So it emerges that neither can we possess them from birth, nor can they come to be in us if we are without knowledge of them to the extent of having no such developed state at all. Therefore we must possess a capacity of some sort, but not such as to rank higher in accuracy than these developed states. And this at least is an obvious characteristic of all animals, for they possess a congenital discriminative capacity which is called sense-perception. But though sense-perception is innate in all animals, in some the sense-impression comes to persist, in others it does not. So animals in which this persistence does not come to be have either no knowledge at all outside the act of perceiving, or no knowledge of objects of which no impression persists; animals in which it does come into being have perception and can continue to retain the sense-impression in the soul: and when such persistence is frequently repeated a further distinction at once arises between those which out of the persistence of such sense-impressions develop a power of systematizing them and those which do not. So out of sense-perception comes to be what we call memory, and out of frequently repeated memories of the same thing develops experience; for a number of memories constitute a single experience. From experience again—i.e. from the universal now stabilized in its entirety within the soul, the one beside the many which is a single identity within them all—originate the skill of the craftsman and the knowledge of the man of science, skill in the sphere of coming to be and science in the sphere of being.

We conclude that these states of knowledge are neither innate in a determinate form, nor developed from other higher states of knowledge, but from sense-perception. It is like a rout in battle stopped by first one man making a stand and then another, until the original formation has been restored. The soul is so constituted as to be capable of this process.

Let us now restate the account given already, though with insufficient clearness. When one of a number of logically indiscriminable particulars has made a stand, the earliest universal is present in the soul: for though the act of sense-perception is of the particular, its content is universal—is man, for example, not the man Callias. A fresh stand is made among these rudimentary universals, and the process does not cease until the indivisible concepts, the true universals, are established: e.g. such and such a species of animal is a step towards the genus animal, which by the same process is a step towards a further generalization.

Thus it is clear that we must get to know the primary premisses by induction; for the method by which even sense-perception implants the universal is inductive. Now of the thinking states by which we grasp truth, some are unfailingly true, others admit of error—opinion, for instance, and calculation, whereas scientific knowing and intuition are always true: further, no other kind of thought except intuition is more accurate than scientific knowledge, whereas primary premisses are more knowable than demonstrations, and all scientific knowledge is discursive. From these considerations it follows that there will be no scientific knowledge of the primary premisses, and since except intuition nothing can be truer than scientific knowledge, it will be intuition that apprehends the primary premisses-a result which also follows from the fact that demonstration cannot be the originative source of demonstration, nor, consequently, scientific knowledge of scientific knowledge. If, therefore, it is the only other kind of true thinking except scientific knowing, intuition will be the originative source of scientific knowledge. And the originative source of science grasps the original basic premiss, while science as a whole is similarly related as originative source to the whole body of fact.

PHYSICS

BOOK II

1. Of things that exist, some exist by nature, some from other causes. By nature the animals and their parts exist, and the plants and the simple bodies (earth, fire, air, water)—for we say that these and the like exist by nature.

All the things mentioned plainly differ from things which are *not* constituted by nature. For each of them has within itself a principle of motion and of stationariness (in respect of place, or of growth and decrease, or by way of alteration). On the other hand, a bed and a coat and anything else of that sort, *qua* receiving these designations—i.e. in so far as they are products of art—have no innate impulse to change. But in so far as they happen to be composed of stone or of earth or of a mixture of the two, they *do* have such an impulse, and just to that extent—which seems to indicate that nature is a principle or cause of being moved and of being at rest in that to which it belongs primarily, in virtue of itself and not accidentally.

I say 'not accidentally', because (for instance) a man who is a doctor might himself be a cause of health to himself. Nevertheless it is not in so far as he is a patient that he possesses the art of medicine: it merely has happened that the same man is doctor and patient—and that is why these attributes are not always found together. So it is with all other artificial products. None of them has in itself the principle of its own production. But while in some cases (for instance houses and the other products of manual labour) that principle is in something else external to the thing, in others—those which may cause a change in themselves accidentally—it lies in the things themselves (but not in virtue of what they are).

Nature then is what has been stated. Things have a nature which have a principle of this kind. Each of them is a substance; for it is a subject, and nature is always in a subject.

The term 'according to nature' is applied to all these things and also to the attributes which belong to them in virtue of what they are, for instance the property of fire to be carried upwards—which is not a nature nor has a nature but is by nature or according to nature.

What nature is, then, and the meaning of the terms 'by nature' and 'according to nature', has been stated. *That* nature exists, it would be absurd to try to prove; for it is obvious that there are many things of this kind, and to prove what is obvious by what is not is the mark of a man who is unable to distinguish what is self-evident from what is not. (This state of mind is clearly possible. A man blind from birth might reason about colours.) Presumably therefore such persons must be talking about words without any thought to correspond.

Some identify the nature or substance of a natural object with that immediate constituent of it which taken by itself is without arrangement, e.g. the wood is the nature of the bed, and the bronze the nature of the statue.

As an indication of this Antiphon points out that if you planted a bed and the rotting wood acquired the power of sending up a shoot, it would not be a bed that would come up, but *wood* which shows that the arrangement in accordance with the rules of the art is merely an accidental attribute, whereas the substance is the other, which, further, persists continuously through the process.

But if the material of each of these objects has itself the same relation to something else, say bronze (or gold) to water, bones (or wood) to earth and so on, *that* (they say) would be their nature and substance. Consequently some assert earth, others fire or air or water or some or all of these, to be the nature of the things that are. For whatever any one of them supposed to have this character—whether one thing or more than one thing—this or these he declared to be the whole of substance, all else being its affections, states, or dispositions. Every such thing they held to be eternal (for it could not pass into anything

Reprinted from Aristotle's *Physics*, translated by R. P. Hardie & P. K. Gaye by permission of Oxford University Press.

else), but other things to come into being and cease to be times without number.

This then is one account of nature, namely that it is the primary underlying matter of things which have in themselves a principle of motion or change.

Another account is that nature is the shape or form which is specified in the definition of the thing.

For the word 'nature' is applied to what is according to nature and the natural in the same way as 'art' is applied to what is artistic or a work of art. We should not say in the latter case that there is anything artistic about a thing, if it is a bed only potentially, not yet having the form of a bed; nor should we call it a work of art. The same is true of natural compounds. What is potentially flesh or bone has not yet its own nature, and does not exist by nature, until it receives the form specified in the definition, which we name in defining what flesh or bone is. Thus on the second account of nature, it would be the shape or form (not separable except in statement) of things which have in themselves a principle of motion. (The combination of the two, e.g. man, is not nature but by nature.)

The form indeed is nature rather than the matter; for a thing is more properly said to be what it is when it exists in actuality than when it exists potentially. Again man is born from man but not bed from bed. That is why people say that the shape is not the nature of a bed, but the wood is—if the bed sprouted, not a bed but wood would come up. But even if the shape *is* art, then on the same principle the shape of man is nature. For man is born from man.

Again, nature in the sense of a coming-to-be proceeds towards nature. For it is not like doctoring, which leads not to the art of doctoring but to health. Doctoring must start from the art, not lead to it. But it is not in this way that nature is related to nature. What grows *qua* growing grows from something into something. Into what then does it grow? Not into that from which it arose but into that to which it tends. The shape then is nature.

Shape and nature are used in two ways. For the privation too is in a way form. But whether in unqualified coming to be there is privation, i.e. a contrary, we must consider later.

2. We have distinguished, then, the different ways in which the term 'nature' is used.

The next point to consider is how the mathematician differs from the student of nature; for natural bodies contain surfaces and volumes, lines and points, and these are the subject-matter of mathematics.

Further, is astronomy different from natural science or a department of it? It seems absurd that the student of nature should be supposed to know the nature of sun or moon, but not to know any of their essential attributes, particularly as the writers on nature obviously do discuss their shape and whether the earth and the world are spherical or not.

Now the mathematician, though he too treats of these things, nevertheless does not treat of them as the limits of a natural body; nor does he consider the attributes indicated as the attributes of such bodies. That is why he separates them; for in thought they are separable from motion, and it makes no difference, nor does any falsity result, if they are separated. The holders of the theory of Forms do the same, though they are not aware of it; for they separate the objects of natural science, which are less separable than those of mathematics. This becomes plain if one tries to state in each of the two cases the definitions of the things and of their attributes. Odd and even, straight and curved, and likewise number, line, and figure, do not involve motion; not so flesh and bone and man—*these* are defined like snub nose, not like curved.

Similar evidence is supplied by the more natural of the branches of mathematics, such as optics, harmonics, and astronomy. These are in a way the converse of geometry. While geometry investigates natural lines but not *qua* natural, optics investigates mathematical lines, but *qua* natural, not *qua* mathematical.

Since two sorts of thing are called nature, the form and the matter, we must investigate its objects as we would the essence of snubness, that is neither independently of matter nor in terms of matter only. Here too indeed one might raise a difficulty. Since there are two natures, with which is the student of nature concerned? Or should he investigate the combination of the two? But if the combination of the two, then also each severally. Does it belong then to the same or to different sciences to know each severally?

If we look at the ancients, natural science would seem to be concerned with the *matter*. (It was only

very slightly that Empedocles and Democritus
20 touched on form and essence.)

But if on the other hand art imitates nature, and
it is the part of the same discipline to know the form
and the matter up to a point (e.g. the doctor has a
knowledge of health and also of bile and phlegm, in
which health is realized and the builder both of the
25 form of the house and of the matter, namely that it
is bricks and beams, and so forth): if this is so, it
would be the part of natural science also to know nature in both its senses.

Again, that for the sake of which, or the end, belongs to the same department of knowledge as the
means. But the nature is the end or that for the sake
of which. For if a thing undergoes a continuous
30 change toward some end, that last stage is actually
that for the sake of which. (That is why the poet was
carried away into making an absurd statement when
he said 'he has the end for the sake of which he was
born'. For not every stage that is last claims to be an
end, but only that which is best.)

For the arts make their material (some simply
35 make it, others make it serviceable), and we use
everything as if it was there for our sake. (We also
are in a sense an end. 'That for the sake of which'
may be taken in two ways, as we said in our work
194ᵇ1 *On Philosophy*.) The arts, therefore, which govern
the matter and have knowledge are two, namely the
art which uses the product and the art which directs
the production of it. That is why the using art also
is in a sense directive; but it differs in that it knows
the form, whereas the art which is directive as being
5 concerned with production knows the matter. For the
helmsman knows and prescribes what sort of form a
helm should have, the other from what wood it
should be made and by means of what operations.
In the products of art, however, we make the material with a view to the function, whereas in the products of nature the matter is there all along.

Again, matter is a relative thing—for different
forms there is different matter.

10 How far then must the student of nature know the
form or essence? Up to a point, perhaps, as the doctor must know sinew or the smith bronze (i.e. until
he understands the purpose of each); and the student
of nature is concerned only with things whose forms
are separable indeed, but do not exist apart from mat-

ter. Man is begotten by man and by the sun as well.
The mode of existence and essence of the separable
it is the business of first philosophy to define.   15

3. Now that we have established these distinctions, we must proceed to consider causes, their character and number. Knowledge is the object of our inquiry, and men do not think they know a thing till
they have grasped the 'why' of it (which is to grasp
its primary cause). So clearly we too must do this as   20
regards both coming to be and passing away and
every kind of natural change, in order that, knowing
their principles, we may try to refer to these principles each of our problems.

In one way, then, that out of which a thing comes
to be and which persists, is called a cause, e.g. the   25
bronze of the statue, the silver of the bowl, and the
genera of which the bronze and the silver are species.

In another way, the form or the archetype, i.e. the
definition of the essence, and its genera, are called
causes (e.g. of the octave the relation of 2:1, and generally number), and the parts in the definition.

Again, the primary source of the change or rest;   30
e.g. the man who deliberated is a cause, the father is
cause of the child, and generally what makes of what
is made and what changes of what is changed.

Again, in the sense of end or that for the sake of
which a thing is done, e.g. health is the cause of walking about. ('Why is he walking about?' We say: 'To
be healthy', and, having said that, we think we have
assigned the cause.) The same is true also of all the   35
intermediate steps which are brought about through
the action of something else as means towards the
end, e.g. reduction of flesh, purging, drugs, or sur-   195ᵇ1
gical instruments are means towards health. All these
things are for the sake of the end, though they differ from one another in that some are activities, others instruments.

This then perhaps exhausts the number of ways
in which the term 'cause' is used.

As things are called causes in many ways, it follows that there are several causes of the same thing   5
(not merely accidentally), e.g. both the art of the
sculptor and the bronze are causes of the statue.
These are causes of the statue *qua* statue, not in virtue
of anything else that it may be—only not in the same
way, the one being the material cause, the other the
cause whence the motion comes. Some things cause

each other reciprocally, e.g. hard work causes fitness and *vice versa*, but again not in the same way, but the one as end, the other as the principle of motion. Further the same thing is the cause of contrary results. For that which by its presence brings about one result is sometimes blamed for bringing about the contrary by its absence. Thus we ascribe the wreck of a ship to the absence of the pilot whose presence was the cause of its safety.

All the causes now mentioned fall into four familiar divisions. The letters are the causes of syllables, the material of artificial products, fire and the like of bodies, the parts of the whole, and the premisses of the conclusion, in the sense of 'that from which'. Of these pairs the one set are causes in the sense of what underlies, e.g. the parts, the other set in the sense of essence—the whole and the combination and the form. But the seed and the doctor and the deliberator, and generally the maker, are all sources whence the change or stationariness originates, which the others are causes in the sense of the end or the good of the rest; for that for the sake of which tends to be what is best and the end of the things that lead up to it. (Whether we call it good or apparently good makes no difference.)

Such then is the number and nature of the kinds of cause.

Now the modes of causation are many, though when brought under heads they too can be reduced in number. For things are called causes in many ways and even within the same kind one may be prior to another; e.g. the doctor and the expert are causes of health, the relation 2:1 and number of the octave, and always what is inclusive to what is particular. Another mode of causation is the accidental and its genera, e.g. in one way Polyclitus, in another a sculptor is the cause of a statue, because being Polyclitus and a sculptor are accidentally conjoined. Also the classes in which the accidental attribute is included; thus a man could be said to be the cause of a statue or, generally, a living creature. An accidental attribute too may be more or less remote, e.g. suppose that a pale man or a muscial man were said to be the cause of the statue.

All causes, both proper and accidental, may be spoken of either as potential or as actual; e.g. the cause of a house being built is either a house-builder or a house-builder building.

Similar distinctions can be made in the things of which the causes are causes, e.g. of this statue or of a statue or of an image generally, of this bronze or of bronze or of material generally. So too with the accidental attributes. Again we may use a complex expression for either and say, e.g., neither 'Polyclitus' nor a 'sculptor' but 'Polyclitus, the sculptor'.

All these various uses, however, come to six in number, under each of which again the usage is twofold. It is either what is particular or a genus, or an accidental attribute or a genus of that, and these either as a complex or each by itself; and all either as actual or as potential. The difference is this much, that causes which are actually at work and particular exist and cease to exist simultaneously with their effect, e.g. this healing person with this being-healed person and that housebuilding man with that being-built house; but this is not always true of potential causes—the house and the housebuilder do not pass away simultaneously.

In investigating the cause of each thing it is always necessary to seek what is most precise (as also in other things): thus a man builds because he is a builder, and a builder builds in virtue of his art of building. This last cause then is prior; and so generally.

Further, generic effects should be assigned to generic causes, particular effects to particular causes, e.g. statue to sculptor, this statue to this sculptor; and powers are relative to possible effects, actually operating causes to things which are actually being effected.

This must suffice for our account of the number of causes and the modes of causation.

4. But chance and spontaneity are also reckoned among causes: many things are said both to be and to come to be as a result of chance and spontaneity. We must inquire therefore in what manner chance and spontaneity are present among the causes enumerated, and whether they are the same or different, and generally what chance and spontaneity are.

Some people even question whether there are such things or not. They say that nothing happens by chance, but that everything which we ascribe to chance or spontaneity has some definite cause, e.g. coming by chance into the market and finding there a man whom one wanted but did not expect to meet is due to one's wish to go and buy in the market. Similarly, in other so-called cases of chance it is always possible, they maintain, to find something which is the cause; but not chance, for if chance were real, it would seem strange indeed, and the question might be raised, why on earth none of the wise men of old in speaking of the causes of generation and decay took account of chance; whence it would seem that they too did not believe that anything is by chance. But there is a further circumstance that is surprising. Many things both come to be and are by chance and spontaneity, and although all know that each of them can be ascribed to some cause (as the old argument said which denied chance), nevertheless they all speak of some of these things as happening by chance and others not. For this reason they ought to have at least referred to the matter in some way or other.

Certainly the early physicists found no place for chance among the causes which they recognized—love, strife, mind, fire, or the like. This is strange, whether they supposed that there is no such thing as chance or whether they thought there is but omitted to mention it—and that too when they sometimes used it, as Empedocles does when he says that the air is not always separated into the highest region, but as it may chance. At any rate he says in his cosmogony that 'it happened to run that way at that time, but it often ran otherwise'. He tells us also that most of the parts of animals came to be by chance.

There are some who actually ascribe this heavenly sphere and all the worlds to spontaneity. They say that the vortex arose spontaneously, i.e. the motion that separated and arranged the universe in its present order. This statement might well cause surprise. For they are asserting that chance is not responsible for the existence or generation of animals and plants, nature or mind or something of the kind being the cause of them (for it is not any chance thing that comes from a given seed but an olive from one kind and a man from another); and yet at the same time they assert that the heavenly sphere and the divinest of visible things arose spontaneously, having no such cause as is assigned to animals and plants. Yet if this is so, it is a fact which deserves to be dwelt upon, and something might well have been said about it. For besides the other absurdities of the statement, it is the more absurd that people should make it when they see nothing coming to be spontaneously in the heavens, but much happening by chance among the things which as they say are not due to chance; whereas we should have expected exactly the opposite.

Others there are who believe that chance is a cause, but that it is inscrutable to human intelligence, as being a divine thing and full of mystery.

Thus we must inquire what chance and spontaneity are, whether they are the same or different, and how they fit into our division of causes.

5. First then we observe that some things always come to pass in the same way, and others for the most part. It is clearly of neither of these that chance, or the result of chance, is said to be the cause—neither of that which is by necessity and always, nor of that which is for the most part. But as there is a third class of events besides these two—events which all say are by chance—it is plain that there is such a thing as chance and spontaneity; for we know that things of this kind are due to chance and that things due to chance are of this kind.

Of things that come to be, some come to be for the sake of something, others not. Again, some of the former class are in accordance with intention, others not, but both are in the class of things which are for the sake of something. Hence it is clear that even among the things which are outside what is necessary and what is for the most part, there are some in connexion with which the phrase 'for the sake of something' is applicable. (Things that are for the sake of something include whatever may be done as a result of thought or of nature.) Things of this kind, then, when they come to pass accidentally are said to be by chance. For just as a thing is something either in virtue of itself or accidentally, so may it be a cause. For instance, the housebuilding faculty is in virtue of itself a cause of a house, whereas the pale or the musical is an accidental cause. That which is *per se* cause is determinate, but the accidental cause is indeterminable; for the possible attributes of an individual are innumerable. As we said, then, when a thing of this kind comes to pass among events which are for the sake of something, it is said to be spontaneous or by chance. (The distinction between the two must be made later—for the present it is sufficient if it is plain that both are in the sphere of things done for the sake of something.)

Example: A man is engaged in collecting subscriptions for a feast. He would have gone to such and such a place for the purpose of getting the money, if he had known. He actually went there for another purpose, and it was only accidentally that he got his money by going there; and this was not due to the fact that he went there as a rule or necessarily, nor is the end effected (getting the money) a cause present in himself—it belongs to the class of things that are objects of choice and the result of thought. It is when these conditions are satisfied that the man is said to have gone by chance. If he had chosen and gone for the sake of this—if he always or normally went there when he was collecting payments—he would not be said to have gone by chance.

It is clear then that chance is an accidental cause in the sphere of those actions for the sake of something which involve choice. Thought, then, and chance are in the same sphere, for choice implies thought.

It is necessary, no doubt, that the causes of what comes to pass by chance be indefinite; and that is why chance is supposed to belong to the class of the indefinite and to be inscrutable to man, and why it might be thought that, in a way, nothing occurs by chance. For all these statements are correct, as might be expected. Things *do*, in a way, occur by chance, for they occur accidentally and chance is an accidental cause. But it is not the cause without qualification of anything; for instance, a housebuilder is the cause of a house; accidentally, a fluteplayer may be so.

And the causes of the man's coming and getting the money (when he did not come for the sake of that) are innumerable. He may have wished to see somebody or been following somebody or avoiding somebody, or may have gone to see a spectacle. Thus to say that chance is unaccountable is correct. For an account is of what holds always or for the most part, whereas chance belongs to a third type of event. Hence, since causes of this kind are indefinite, chance too is indefinite. (Yet in some cases one might raise the question whether *any* chance fact might be the cause of the chance occurrence, e.g. of health the fresh air or the sun's heat may be the cause,

but having had one's hair cut *cannot*; for some accidental causes are more relevant to the effect than others.)

Chance is called good when the result is good, evil when it is evil. The terms 'good fortune' and 'ill fortune' are used when either result is of considerable magnitude. Thus one who comes within an ace of some great evil or great good is said to be fortunate or unfortunate. The mind affirms the presence of the attribute, ignoring the hair's breadth of difference. Further, it is with reason that good fortune is regarded as unstable; for chance is unstable, as none of the things which result from it can hold always or for the most part.

Both are then, as I have said, accidental causes—both chance and spontaneity—in the sphere of things which are capable of coming to pass not simply, nor for the most part and with reference to such of these as might come to pass for the sake of something.

6. They differ in that spontaneity is the wider. Every result of chance is from what is spontaneous, but not everything that is from what is spontaneous is from chance.

Chance and what results from chance are appropriate to agents that are capable of good fortune and of action generally. Therefore necessarily chance is in the sphere of actions. This is indicated by the fact that good fortune is thought to be the same, or nearly the same, as happiness, and happiness to be a kind of action, since it is well-doing. Hence what is not capable of action cannot do anything by chance. Thus an inanimate thing or a beast or a child cannot do anything by chance, because it is incapable of choice; nor can good fortune or ill fortune be ascribed to them, except metaphorically, as Protarchus, for example, said that the stones of which altars are made are fortunate because they are held in honour, while their fellows are trodden under foot. Even these things, however, can in a way be affected by chance, when one who is dealing with them does something to them by chance, but not otherwise.

The spontaneous on the other hand is found both in the beasts and in many inanimate objects. We say, for example, that the horse came spontaneously, because, though his coming saved him, he did not come for the sake of safety. Again, the tripod fell spontaneously, because, though it stood on its feet so as to serve for a seat, it did not fall so as to serve for a seat.

Hence it is clear that events which belong to the general class of things that may come to pass for the sake of something, when they come to pass not for the sake of what actually results, and have an external cause, may be described by the phrase 'from spontaneity'. These spontaneous events are said to be from chance if they have the further characteristics of being the objects of choice and happening to agents capable of choice. This is indicated by the phrase 'in vain', which is used when one thing which is for the sake of another, does not result in it. For instance, taking a walk is for the sake of evacuation of the bowels; if this does not follow after walking, we say that we have walked in vain and that the walking was vain. This implies that what is naturally for the sake of an end is in vain, when it does not effect the end for the sake of which it was the natural means—for it would be absurd for a man to say that he had bathed in vain because the sun was not eclipsed, since the one was not done for the sake of the other. Thus the spontaneous is even according to its derivation the case in which the thing itself happens in vain. The stone that struck the man did not fall for the sake of striking him; therefore it fell spontaneously, because it might have fallen by the action of an agent and for the sake of striking. The difference between spontaneity and what results by chance is greatest in things that come to be by nature; for when anything comes to be contrary to nature, we do not say that it came to be by chance, but by spontaneity. Yet strictly this too is different from the spontaneous proper; for the cause of the latter is external, that of the former internal.

198ᵃ1 We have now explained what chance is and what spontaneity is, and in what they differ from each other. Both belong to the mode of causation 'source of change', for either some natural or some intelligent agent is always the cause; but in this sort of causation the number of possible causes is infinite.

Spontaneity and chance are causes of effects which, though they might result from intelligence or nature, have in fact been caused by something accidentally. Now since nothing which is accidental is prior to what is *per se*, it is clear that no accidental cause can be prior to a cause *per se*. Spontaneity and chance, therefore, are posterior to intelligence and nature. Hence, however true it may be that the heavens are due to spontaneity, it will still be true that intelligence and nature will be prior causes of this universe and of many things in it besides.

7. It is clear then that there are causes, and that the number of them is what we have stated. The number is the same as that of the things comprehended under the question 'why'. The 'why' is referred ultimately either, in things which do not involve motion, e.g. in mathematics, to the 'what' (to the definition of straight line or commensurable or the like); or to what initiated a motion, e.g. 'why did they go to war?—because there had been a raid'; or we are inquiring 'for the sake of what?'—'that they may rule'; or in the case of things that come into being, we are looking for the matter. The causes, therefore, are these and so many in number.

Now, the causes being four, it is the business of the student of nature to know about them all, and if he refers his problems back to all of them, he will assign the 'why' in the way proper to his science—the matter, the form, the mover, that for the sake of which. The last three often coincide; for the what and that for the sake of which are one, while the primary source of motion is the same in species as these. For man generates man—and so too, in general, with all things which cause movement by being themselves moved; and such as are not of this kind are no longer inside the province of natural science, for they cause motion not by possessing motion or a source of motion in themselves, but being themselves incapable of motion. Hence there are three branches of study, one of things which are incapable of motion, the second of things in motion, but indestructible, the third of destructible things.

The question 'why', then, is answered by reference to the matter, to the form, and to the primary moving cause. For in respect of coming to be it is mostly in this last way that causes are investigated—'what comes to be after what? what was the primary agent or patient?' and so at each step of the series.

Now the principles which cause motion in a natural way are two, of which one is not natural, as it has no principle of motion in itself. Of this kind is whatever causes movement, not being itself moved, such as that which is completely unchangeable, the primary reality, and the essence of a thing, i.e. the form; for this is the end or that for the sake of which. Hence since nature is for the sake of something, we must know this cause also. We must explain the 'why' in all the senses of the term, namely, that from this that will necessarily result ('from this' either without qualification or for the most part); that this must be so if that is to be so (as the conclusion presupposes the premisses); that this was the essence of the thing; and because it is better thus (not without qualification, but with reference to the substance in each case).

8. We must explain then first why nature belongs to the class of causes which act for the sake of something; and then about the necessary and its place in nature, for all writers ascribe things to this cause, arguing that since the hot and the cold and the like are of such and such a kind, therefore certain things *necessarily* are and come to be—and if they mention any other cause (one friendship and strife, another mind), it is only to touch on it, and then good-bye to it.

A difficulty presents itself: why should not nature work, not for the sake of something, nor because it is better so, but just as the sky rains, not in order to make the corn grow, but of necessity? (What is drawn up must cool, and what has been cooled must become water and descend, the result of this being that the corn grows.) Similarly if a man's crop is spoiled on the threshing-floor, the rain did not fall for the sake of this—in order that the crop might be spoiled—but that result just followed. Why then should it not be the same with the parts in nature, e.g. that our teeth should come up of necessity—the front teeth sharp, fitted for tearing, the molars broad and useful for grinding down the food—since they did not arise for this end, but it was merely a coincident result; and so with all other parts in which we suppose that there is purpose? Wherever then all the parts came about just what they would have been if they had come to be for an end, such things survived, being organized spontaneously in a fitting way; whereas those which grew otherwise perished and continue to perish, as Empedocles says his 'man-faced ox-progeny' did.

Such are the arguments (and others of the kind) which may cause difficulty on this point. Yet it is impossible that this should be the true view. For teeth and all other natural things either invariably or for the most part come about in a given way; but of not one of the results of chance or spontaneity is this true. We do not ascribe to chance or mere coincidence the frequency of rain in winter, but frequent rain in summer we do; nor heat in summer but only if we have it in winter. If then, it is agreed that things are either the result of coincidence or for the sake of something, and these cannot be the result of coincidence or spontaneity, it follows that they must be for the sake of something; and that such things are all due to nature even the champions of the theory which is before us would agree. Therefore action for an end is present in things which come to be and are by nature.

Further, where there is an end, all the preceding steps are for the sake of that. Now surely as in action, so in nature; and as in nature, so it is in each action, if nothing interferes. Now action is for the sake of an end; therefore the nature of things also is so. Thus if a house, e.g., had been a thing made by nature, it would have been made in the same way as it is now by art; and if things made by nature were made not only by nature but also by art, they would come to be in the same way as by nature. The one, then, is for the sake of the other; and generally art in some cases completes what nature cannot bring to a finish, and in others imitates nature. If, therefore, artificial products are for the sake of an end, so clearly also are natural products. The relation of the later to the earlier items is the same in both.

This is most obvious in the animals other than man: they make things neither by art nor after inquiry or deliberation. That is why people wonder whether it is by intelligence or by some other faculty that these creatures work,—spiders, ants, and the like. By gradual advance in this direction we come to see clearly that in plants too that is produced which is conducive to the end—leaves, e.g. grow to provide shade for the fruit. If then it is both by nature and for an end that the swallow makes its nest and the spider its web, and plants grow leaves for the sake of the fruit and send their roots down (not up) for the sake of nourishment, it is plain that this kind of cause is operative in things which come to be and are by nature. And since nature is twofold, the matter and the form, of which the latter is the end, and since all the rest is for the sake of the end, the form must be the cause in the sense of that for the sake of which.

Now mistakes occur even in the operations of art: the literate man makes a mistake in writing and the doctor pours out the wrong dose. Hence clearly mistakes are possible in the operations of nature also. If then in art there are cases in which what is rightly produced serves a purpose, and if where mistakes occur there was a purpose in what was attempted, only it was not attained, so must it be also in natural products, and monstrosities will be failures in the purposive effort. Thus in the original combinations the 'ox-progeny', if they failed to reach a determinate end must have arisen through the corruption of some principle, as happens now when the seed is defective.

Further, seed must have come into being first, and not straightway the animals: what was 'undifferentiated first' was seed.

Again, in plants too we find that for the sake of which, though the degree of organization is less. Were there then in plants also olive-headed vine-progeny, like the 'man-headed ox-progeny', or not? An absurd suggestion; yet there must have been, if there were such things among animals.

Moreover, among the seeds anything must come to be at random. But the person who asserts this entirely does away with nature and what exists by nature. For those things are natural which, by a continuous movement originated from an internal principle, arrive at some end: the same end is not reached from every principle; nor any chance end, but always the tendency in each is towards the same end, if there is no impediment.

The end and the means towards it may come about by chance. We say, for instance, that a stranger has come by chance, paid the ransom, and gone away, when he does so as if he had come for that purpose, though it was not for that that he came. This is accidental, for chance is an accidental cause, as I remarked before. But when an event takes place always or for the most part, it is not accidental or by chance. In natural products the sequence is invariable, if there is no impediment.

It is absurd to suppose that purpose is not present because we do not observe the agent deliberating. Art does not deliberate. If the ship-building art were in the wood, it would produce the same results by nature. If, therefore, purpose is present in art, it is present also in nature. The best illustration is a doctor doctoring himself: nature is like that.

It is plain then that nature is a cause, a cause that operates for a purpose.

9. As regards what is of necessity, we must ask whether the necessity is hypothetical, or simple as well. The current view places what is of necessity in the process of production, just as if one were to suppose that the wall of a house necessarily comes to be because what is heavy is naturally carried downwards and what is light to the top, so that the stones and foundations take the lowest place, with earth above because it is lighter, and wood at the top of all as being the lightest. Whereas, though the wall does not come to be *without* these, it is not *due* to these, except as its material cause: it comes to be for the sake of sheltering and guarding certain things. Similarly in all other things which involve that for the sake of which: the product cannot come to be without things which have a necessary nature, but it is not due to these (except as its material); it comes to be for an end. For instance, why is a saw such as it is? To effect so-and-so and for the sake of so-and-so. This end, however, cannot be realized unless the saw is made of iron. It is, therefore, necessary for it to be of iron, if we are to have a saw and perform the operation of sawing. What is necessary then, is necessary on a hypothesis, not as an end. Necessity is in the matter, while that for the sake of which is in the definition.

Necessity in mathematics is in a way similar to necessity in things which come to be through the operation of nature. Since a straight line is what it is, it is necessary that the angles of a triangle should equal two right angles. But not conversely; though if the angles are *not* equal to two right angles, then the straight line is not what it is either. But in things which come to be for an end, the reverse is true. If the end is to exist or does exist, that also which precedes it will exist or does exist; otherwise just as there, if the conclusion is not true, the principle will not be true, so here the end or that for the sake of which will not exist. For this too is itself a principle, but of the reasoning, not of the action. (In mathematics the principle is the principle of the reasoning only, as there is no action.) If then there is to be a house, such-and-such things must be made or be there already or exist, or generally the matter relative to the end, bricks and stones if it is a house. But the end is not due to these except as the matter, nor will it come to exist because of them. Yet if they do not exist at all, neither will the house, or the saw—the former in the absence of stones, the latter in the absence of iron—just as in the other case the principles will not be true, if the angles of the triangle are not equal to two right angles.

The necessary in nature, then, is plainly what we call by the name of matter, and the changes in it. Both causes must be stated by the student of nature, but especially the end; for that is the cause of the matter, not *vice versa*; and the end is that for the sake of which, and the principle starts from the definition or essence: as in artificial products, since a house is of such-and-such a kind, certain things must *necessarily* come to be or be there already, or since health is this, these things must necessarily come to be or be there already, so too if man is this, then these; if these, then those. Perhaps the necessary is present also in the definition. For if one defines the operation of sawing as being a certain kind of dividing, then this cannot come about unless the saw has teeth of a certain kind; and these cannot be unless it is of iron. For in the definition too there are some parts that stand as matter.

BOOK III

1. Nature is a principle of motion and change, and it is the subject of our inquiry. We must therefore see that we understand what motion is; for if it were unknown, nature too would be unknown.

When we have determined the nature of motion, our task will be to attack in the same way the terms which come next in order. Now motion is supposed to belong to the class of things which are continuous; and the infinite presents itself first in the continuous—that is how it comes about that the account of the infinite is often used in definitions of the continuous; for what is infinitely divisible is continuous. Besides these, place, void, and time are thought to be necessary conditions of motion.

Clearly, then, for these reasons and also because the attributes mentioned are common to everything and universal, we must first take each of them in hand and discuss it. For the investigation of special attributes comes after that of the common attributes.

To begin then, as we said, with motion.

Some things are in fulfilment only, others in potentiality and in fulfilment—one being a 'this', another so much, another such and such, and similarly for the other categories of being. The term 'relative' is applied sometimes with reference to excess and defect, sometimes to agent and patient, and generally to what can move and what can be moved. For what can cause movement is relative to what can be moved, and *vice versa*.

There is no such thing as motion over and above the things. It is always with respect to substance or to quantity or to quality or to place that what changes changes. But it is impossible, as we assert, to find anything common to these which is neither 'this' nor quantity nor quality nor any of the other predicates. Hence neither will motion and change have reference to something over and above the things mentioned; for there *is* nothing over and above them.

Now each of these belongs to all its subjects in either of two ways: namely, substance—the one is its form, the other privation; in quality, white and black; in quantity, complete and incomplete. Similarly, in respect of locomotion, upwards and downwards or light and heavy. Hence there are as many types of motion or change as there are of being.

We have distinguished in respect of each class between what is in fulfilment and what is potentially; thus the fulfilment of what is potentially, as such, is motion—e.g. the fulfilment of what is alterable, as alterable, is alteration; of what is increasable and its opposite, decreasable (there is no common name for both), increase and decrease; of what can come to be and pass away, coming to be and passing away; of what can be carried along, locomotion.

That this is what motion is, is clear from what follows: when what is buildable, in so far as we call it such, is in fulfilment, it is being built, and that is building. Similarly with learning, doctoring, rolling, jumping, ripening, aging.

The same thing can be both potential and fulfilled, not indeed at the same time or not in the same respect, but e.g. potentially hot and actually cold. Hence such things will act and be acted on by one another in many ways: each of them will be capable at the same time of acting and of being acted upon. Hence, too, what effects motion as a natural agent can be moved: when a thing of this kind causes motion, it is itself also moved. This, indeed, has led some people to suppose that every mover is moved. But this question depends on another set of arguments, and the truth will be made clear later. It *is* possible for a thing to cause motion, though it is itself incapable of being moved.

It is the fulfilment of what is potential when it is already fulfilled and operates not as itself but as movable, that is motion. What I mean by 'as' is this: bronze is potentially a statue. But it is not the fulfilment of bronze as *bronze* which is motion. For to be bronze and to be a certain potentiality are not the same. If they were identical without qualification, i.e. in definition, the fulfilment of bronze as bronze *would* be motion. But they are not the same, as has been said. (This is obvious in contraries. To be capable of health and to be capable of illness are not the same; for if they were there would be no difference between being ill and being well. Yet the subject both of health and of sickness—whether it is humour or blood—is one and the same.)

We can distinguish, then, between the two—just as colour and visible are different—and clearly it is the fulfilment of what is potential as potential that is motion.

It is evident that this is motion, and that motion occurs just when the fulfilment itself occurs, and neither before nor after. For each thing is capable of being at one time actual, at another not. Take for instance the buildable: the actuality of the buildable as buildable is the process of building. For the actuality must be either this or the house. But when there is a house, the buildable is no longer there. On the other hand, it *is* the buildable which is *being* built. Necessarily, then, the actuality is the process of building. But building is a kind of motion, and the same account will apply to the other kinds also.

2. The soundness of this definition is evident both when we consider the accounts of motion that the others have given, and also from the difficulty of defining it otherwise.

One could not easily put motion and change in another genus—this is plain if we consider where some people put it: they identify motion with difference or inequality or not being; but such things are not necessarily moved, whether they are different or unequal or non-existent. Nor is change either to or from *these* rather than to or from their opposites.

The reason why they put motion into these genera is that it is thought to be something indefinite, and the principles in the second column are indefinite because they are privative: none of them is either a 'this' or such or comes under any of the other categories. The reason why motion is thought to be indefinite is that it cannot be classed as a potentiality or as an actuality—a thing that is merely *capable* of having a certain size is not necessarily undergoing change, nor yet a thing that is *actually* of a certain size, and motion is thought to be a sort of *actuality*, but incomplete, the reason for this view being that the potential whose actuality it is is incomplete. This is why it is hard to grasp what motion is. It is necessary to class it with privation or with potentiality or with simple actuality, yet none of these seems possible. There remains then the suggested mode of definition, namely that it is a sort of actuality, or actuality of the kind described, hard to grasp, but not incapable of existing.

Every mover too is moved, as has been said— every mover, that is, which is capable of motion, and whose immobility is rest (for when a thing is subject to motion its immobility is rest). For to act on the movable as such is just to move it. But this it does by contact, so that at the same time it is also acted on. Hence motion is the fulfilment of the movable as movable, the cause being contact with what can move, so that the mover is also acted on. The mover will always transmit a form, either a 'this' or such or so much, which, when it moves, will be the principle and cause of the motion, e.g. the actual man begets man from what is potentially man.

3. The solution of the difficulty is plain: motion is in the movable. It is the fulfilment of this potentiality by the action of that which has the power of causing motion; and the actuality of that which has the power of causing motion is not other than the actuality of the movable; for it must be the fulfilment of *both*. A thing is capable of causing motion because

it *can* do this, it is a mover because it actually *does* it. But it is on the movable that it is capable of acting. Hence there is a single actuality of both alike, just as one to two and two to one are the same interval, and the steep ascent and the steep descent are one—for these are one and the same, although their definitions are not one. So it is with the mover and the moved.

This view has a dialectical difficulty. Perhaps it is necessary that there should be an actuality of the agent and of the patient. The one is agency and the other patiency; and the outcome and end of the one is an action, that of the other a passion. Since then they are both motions, we may ask: *in* what are they, if they are different? Either both are in what is acted on and moved, or the agency is in the agent and the patiency in the patient. (If we ought to call the latter also 'agency', the word would be used in two senses.)

Now, in the latter case, the motion will be in the mover, for the same account will hold of mover and moved. Hence either *every* mover will be moved, or, though having motion, it will not be moved.

If on the other hand both are in what is moved and acted on—both the agency and the patiency (e.g. both teaching and learning, though they are two, in the learner), then, first, the actuality of each will not be present *in* each, and, a second absurdity, a thing will have two motions at the same time. How will there be two alterations of quality in *one* subject towards *one* form? The thing is impossible: the actualization will be one.

But (someone will say) it is contrary to reason to suppose that there should be one identical actualization of two things which are different in kind. Yet there will be, if teaching and learning are the same, and agency and patiency. To teach will be the same as to learn, and to act the same as to be acted on— the teacher will necessarily be learning everything

that he teaches, and the agent will be acted on. It is not absurd that the actualization of one thing should be in another. Teaching is the activity of a person who can teach, yet the operation is performed in something—it is not cut adrift from a subject, but is of one thing in another.

There is nothing to prevent two things having one and the same actualization (not the same in being, but related as the potential is to the actual).

Nor is it necessary that the teacher should learn, even if to act and to be acted on are one and the same, provided they are not the same in respect of the account which states their essence (as raiment and dress), but are the same in the sense in which the road from Thebes to Athens and the road from Athens to Thebes are the same, as has been explained above. For it is not things which are in any way the same that have all their attributes the same, but only those to be which is the same. But indeed it by no means follows from the fact that teaching is the same as learning, that to learn is the same as to teach, any more than it follows from the fact that there is one distance between two things which are at a distance from each other, that being here at a distance from there and being there at a distance from here are one and the same. To generalize, teaching is not the same as learning, or agency as patiency, in the full sense, though they belong to the same subject, the motion; for the actualization of this in that and the actualization of that through the action of this differ in definition.

What then motion is, has been stated both generally and particularly. It is not difficult to see how each of its types will be defined—alteration is the fulfilment of the alterable as alterable (or, more scientifically, the fulfilment of what can act and what can be acted on, as such)—generally and again in each particular case, building, healing. A similar definition will apply to each of the other kinds of motion.

ON THE SOUL

BOOK II

412a 1. Let the foregoing suffice as our account of the views concerning the soul which have been handed on by our predecessors; let us now dismiss them and make as it were a completely fresh start, endeavouring to give, a precise answer to the question, What
5 is soul? i.e. to formulate the most general possible definition of it.

We are in the habit of recognizing, as one determinate kind of what is, substance, and that in several senses, (a) in the sense of matter or that which in itself is not 'a this', and (b) in the sense of form or essence, which is that precisely in virtue of which a thing is called 'a this', and thirdly (c) in the sense of that which is compounded of both (a) and (b).
10 Now matter is potentiality, form actuality; of the latter there are two grades related to one another as e.g. knowledge to the exercise of knowledge.

Among substances are by general consent reckoned bodies and especially natural bodies; for they are the principles of all other bodies. Of natural bodies some have life in them, others not; by life we mean self-nutrition and growth (with its correlative decay). It follows that every natural body which has
15 life in it is a substance in the sense of a composite.

But since it is also a body of such and such a kind, viz. having life, the body cannot be soul; the body is the subject or matter, not what is attributed to it. Hence the soul must be a substance in the sense of
20 the form of a natural body having life potentially within it. But substance is actuality, and thus soul is the actuality of a body as above characterized. Now the word actuality has two senses corresponding respectively to the possession of knowledge and the actual exercise of knowledge. It is obvious that the
25 soul is actuality in the first sense, viz. that of knowledge as possessed, for both sleeping and waking presuppose the existence of soul, and of these waking corresponds to actual knowing, sleeping to knowledge possessed but not employed, and, in the history of the individual, knowledge comes before its employment or exercise.

That is why the soul is the first grade of actuality 412b of a natural body having life potentially in it. The body so described is a body which is organized. The parts of plants in spite of their extreme simplicity are 'organs'; e.g. the leaf serves to shelter the pericarp, the pericarp to shelter the fruit, while the roots of plants are analogous to the mouth of animals, both serving for the absorption of food. If, then, we have to give a general formula applicable to all kinds of soul, we must 5 describe it as the first grade of actuality of a natural organized body. That is why we can wholly dismiss as unnecessary the question whether the soul and the body are one: it is as meaningless as to ask whether the wax and the shape given to it by the stamp are one, or generally the matter of a thing and that of which it is the matter. Unity, has many senses (as many as 'is' has), but the most proper and fundamental sense of both is the relation of an actuality to that of which it is the actuality. We have now given an answer to the question, What is soul?—an answer which applies to 10 it in its full extent. It is substance in the sense which corresponds to the definitive formula of a thing's essence. That means that it is 'the essential whatness' of a body of the character just assigned. Suppose that what is literally an 'organ', like an axe, were a natural body, its 'essential whatness', would have been its essence, and so its soul; if this disappeared from it, it would have ceased to be an axe, except in name. As 15 it is, it is just an axe; it wants the character which is required to make its whatness or formulable essence a soul; for that, it would have had to be a natural body of a particular kind, viz. one having in itself the power of setting itself in movement and arresting itself. Next, apply this doctrine in the case of the 'parts' of the living body. Suppose that the eye were an animal—sight would have been its soul, for sight is the substance or 20 essence of the eye which corresponds to the formula, the eye being merely the matter of seeing; when seeing is removed the eye is no longer an eye, except in

Reprinted from Aristotle's *On the Soul*, translated by J. A. Smith (1956) by permission of Oxford University Press.

name—it is no more a real eye than the eye of a statue or of a painted figure. We must now extend our consideration from the 'parts' to the whole living body; for what the departmental sense is to the bodily part which is its organ, that the whole faculty of sense is to the whole sensitive body as such.

25 We must not understand by that which is 'potentially capable of living' what has lost the soul it had, but only what still retains it; but seeds and fruits are bodies which possess the qualification. Consequently, while waking is actuality in a sense corresponding to the cutting and the seeing, the soul is actuality in the sense corresponding to the power of sight and the power in the tool; the body corresponds to what exists in potentiality; as the pupil plus the 413a power of sight constitutes the eye, so the soul plus the body constitutes the animal.

From this it indubitably follows that the soul is 5 inseparable from its body, or at any rate that certain parts of it are (if it has parts)—for the actuality of some of them is nothing but the actualities of their bodily parts. Yet some may be separable because they are not the actualities of any body at all. Further, we have no light on the problem whether the soul may not be the actuality of its body in the sense in which the sailor is the actuality of the ship.

10 This must suffice as our sketch or outline determination of the nature of soul.

2. Since what is clear or logically more evident emerges from what in itself is confused but more observable by us, we must reconsider our results from this point of view. For it is not enough for a definitive formula to express as most now do the mere fact; it must include and exhibit the ground also. At pres-15 ent definitions are given in a form analogous to the conclusion of a syllogism; e.g. What is squaring? The construction of an equilateral rectangle equal to a given oblong rectangle. Such a definition is in form equivalent to a conclusion. One that tells us that squaring is the discovery of a line which is a mean proportional between the two unequal sides of the given 20 rectangle discloses the ground of what is defined.

We resume our inquiry from a fresh starting-point by calling attention to the fact that what has soul in it differs from what has not, in that the former displays life. Now this word has more than one sense, and provided any one alone of these is found in a thing we say that thing is living. Living, that is, may 25 mean thinking or perception or local movement and rest, or movement in the sense of nutrition, decay and growth. Hence we think of plants also as living, for they are observed to possess in themselves an originative power through which they increase or decrease in all spatial directions; they grow up and down, and everything that grows increases its bulk alike in both directions or indeed in all, and contin-30 ues to live so long as it can absorb nutriment.

This power of self-nutrition can be isolated from the other powers mentioned, but not they from it—in mortal beings at least. The fact is obvious in plants; for it is the only psychic power they possess.

This is the originative power the possession of 413b which leads us to speak of things as living at all, but it is the possession of sensation that leads us for the first time to speak of living things as animals; for even those beings which possess no power of local movement but do possess the power of sensation we call animals and not merely living things.

The primary form of sense is touch, which be-5 longs to all animals. just as the power of self-nutrition can be isolated from touch and sensation generally, so touch can be isolated from all other forms of sense. (By the power of self-nutrition we mean that departmental power of the soul which is common to plants and animals: all animals whatsoever are observed to have the sense of touch.) What the explanation of these two facts is, we must discuss 10 later. At present we must confine ourselves to saying that soul is the source of these phenomena and is characterized by them, viz. by the powers of self-nutrition, sensation, thinking, and motivity.

Is each of these a soul or a part of a soul? And if a part, a part in what sense? A part merely distin-15 guishable by definition or a part distinct in local situation as well? In the case of certain of these powers, the answers to these questions are easy, in the case of others we are puzzled what to say. just as in the case of plants which when divided are observed to continue to live though removed to a distance from one another (thus showing that in their case the soul of each individual plant before division was actually one, potentially many), so we notice a similar result in other varieties of soul, i.e. in insects which have 20 been cut in two; each of the segments possesses both sensation and local movement; and if sensation, necessarily also imagination and appetition; for, where there is sensation, there is also pleasure and pain, and, where these, necessarily also desire.

25 We have no evidence as yet about mind or the power to think; it seems to be a widely different kind of soul, differing as what is eternal from what is perishable; it alone is capable of existence in isolation from all other psychic powers. All the other parts of soul, it is evident from what we have said, are, in spite of certain statements to the contrary, incapable of separate existence though, of course, distinguishable by definition. If opining is distinct from per-
30 ceiving, to be capable of opining and to be capable of perceiving must be distinct, and so with all the other forms of living above enumerated. Further,
414a some animals possess all these parts of soul, some certain of them only, others one only (this is what enables us to classify animals); the cause must be considered later.' A similar arrangement is found also within the field of the senses; some classes of animals have all the senses, some only certain of them, others only one, the most indispensable, touch.
5 Since the expression 'that whereby we live and perceive' has two meanings, just like the expression 'that whereby we know'—that may mean either (a) knowledge or (b) the soul, for we can speak of knowing by or with either, and similarly that whereby we are in health may be either (a) health or (b) the body or some part of the body; and since of the two terms thus contrasted knowledge or health is the name of
10 a form, essence, or ratio, or if we so express it an actuality of a recipient matter—knowledge of what is capable of knowing, health of what is capable of being made healthy (for the operation of that which is capable of originating change terminates and has its seat in what is changed or altered); further, since it is the soul by or with which primarily we live, perceive, and think:—it follows that the soul must be a ratio or formulable essence, not a matter or subject. For, as we said, the word substance has three mean-
15 ings—form, matter, and the complex of both—and of these three what is called matter is potentiality, what is called form actuality. Since then the complex here is the living thing, the body cannot be the actuality of the soul; it is the soul which is the actuality of a certain kind of body. Hence the rightness of the view that the soul cannot be without a body,
20 while it cannot he a body; it is not a body but something relative to a body. That is why it is in a body, and a body of a definite kind. It was a mistake, therefore, to do as former thinkers did, merely to fit it into a body without adding a definite specification of the kind or character of that body. Reflection confirms the observed fact; the actuality of any given thing
25 can only be realized in what is already potentially that thing, i.e. in a matter of its own appropriate to it. From all this it follows that soul is an actuality or formulable essence of something that possesses a potentiality of being besouled.

4. It is necessary for the student of these forms of soul first to find a definition of each, expressive
415a of what it is, and then to investigate its derivative
15 properties, &c. But if we are to express what each is, viz. what the thinking power is, or the perceptive, or the nutritive, we must go farther back and first give an account of thinking or perceiving, for in the order of investigation the question of what an agent does precedes the question, what enables it to do
20 what it does. If this is correct, we must on the same ground go yet another step farther back and have some clear view of the objects of each; thus we must start with these objects, e.g. with food, with what is
25 perceptible, or with what is intelligible.

It follows that first of all we must treat of nutrition and reproduction, for the nutritive soul is found along with all the others and is the most primitive and widely distributed power of soul, being indeed that one in virtue of which all are said to have life. The acts in which it manifests itself are reproduction and the use of food-reproduction, I say, because for any living thing that has reached its normal development and which is unmutilated, and whose mode of generation is not spontaneous, the most natural act is the production of another like itself, an animal producing an animal, a plant a plant, in order that, as far as its nature allows, it may partake in the eter-
415b nal and divine. That is the goal towards which all things strive, that for the sake of which they do whatsoever their nature renders possible. The phrase 'for the sake of which' is ambiguous; it may mean either (a) the end to achieve which, or (b) the being in whose interest, the act is done. Since then no living thing is able to partake in what is eternal and divine
5

by uninterrupted continuance (for nothing perishable can for ever remain one and the same), it tries to achieve that end in the only way possible to it, and success is possible in varying degrees; so it remains not indeed as the self-same individual but continues its existence in something like itself—not numerically but specifically one.

The soul is the cause or source of the living body. The terms cause and source have many senses. But the soul is the cause of its body alike in all three senses which we explicitly recognize. It is (a) the source or origin of movement, it is (b) the end, it is (c) the essence of the whole living body. ·

That it is the last, is clear; for in everything the essence is identical with the ground of its being, and here, in the case of living things, their being is to live, and of their being and their living the soul in them is the cause or source. Further, the actuality of whatever is potential is identical with its formulable essence.

It is manifest that the soul is also the final cause of its body. For Nature, like mind, always does whatever it does for the sake of something, which something is its end. To that something corresponds in the case of animals the soul and in this it follows the order of nature; all natural bodies are organs of the soul. This is true of those that enter into the constitution of plants as well as of those which enter into that of animals. This shows that that the sake of which they are is soul. We must here recall the two senses of 'that for the sake of which', viz. (a) the end to achieve which, and (b) the being in whose interest, anything is or is done.

We must maintain, further, that the soul is also the cause of the living body as the original source of local movement. The power of locomotion is not found, however, in all living things. But change of quality and change of quantity are also due to the soul. Sensation is held to be a qualitative alteration, and nothing except what has soul in it is capable of sensation. The same holds of the quantitative changes which constitute growth and decay; nothing grows or decays naturally except what feeds itself, and nothing feeds itself except what has a share of soul in it.

Empedocles is wrong in adding that growth in plants is to be explained, the downward rooting by the natural tendency of earth to travel downwards, and the upward branching by the similar natural tendency of fire to travel upwards. For he misinterprets up and down; up and down are not for all things what they are for the whole Cosmos: if we are to distinguish and identify organs according to their functions, the roots of plants are analogous to the head in animals. Further, we must ask what is the force that holds together the earth and the fire which tend to travel in contrary directions; if there is no counteracting force, they will be torn asunder; if there is, this must be the soul and the cause of nutrition and growth. By some the element of fire is held to be the cause of nutrition and growth, for it alone of the primary bodies or elements is observed to feed and increase itself. Hence the suggestion that in both plants and animals it is it which is the operative force. A concurrent cause in a sense it certainly is, but not the principal cause, that is rather the soul; for while the growth of fire goes on without limit so long as there is a supply of fuel, in the case of all complex wholes formed in the course of nature there is a limit or ratio which determines their size and increase, and limit and ratio are marks of soul but not of fire, and belong to the side of formulable essence rather than that of matter.

Nutrition and reproduction are due to one and the same psychic power. It is necessary first to give precision to our account of food, for it is by this function of absorbing food that this psychic power is distinguished from all the others. The current view is that what serves as food to a living thing is what is contrary to it—not that in every pair of contraries each is food to the other: to be food a contrary must not only be transformable into the other and vice versa, it must also in so doing increase the bulk of the other. Many a contrary is transformed into its other and vice versa, where neither is even a quantum and so cannot increase in bulk, e.g. an invalid into a healthy subject. It is clear that not even those contraries which satisfy both the conditions mentioned above are food to one another in precisely the same sense; water may be said to feed fire, but not fire water. Where the members of the pair are elementary bodies only one of the contraries, it would appear, can be said to feed the other. But there is a difficulty here. One set of thinkers assert that like fed, as well as increased in amount, by like. Another set, as we have said, maintain the very reverse, viz. that what feeds and what is fed are contrary to one another; like, they argue, is incapable of being affected by like; but food is changed in the process of digestion, and change is always to what is opposite or to what is intermediate. Further, food is acted upon by what is nourished by it, not the other way round, as timber is worked by a carpenter and not conversely; there is a change in the carpenter but it is merely a change from not-working to working. In answering this problem it makes all the difference whether we mean by 'the food' the 'finished' or the 'raw' product. If we use the word food of both, viz. of the completely undigested and the completely digested matter, we can justify both the rival accounts of it; taking food in the sense of undigested matter, it is the contrary of what is fed by it, taking it as digested it is like what is fed by it. Consequently it is clear that in a certain sense we may say that both parties are right, both wrong.

Since nothing except what is alive can be fed, what is fed is the besouled body and just because it has soul in it. Hence food is essentially related to what has soul in it. Food has a power which is other than the power to increase the bulk of what is fed by it; so far forth as what has soul in it is a quantum, food may increase its quantity, but it is only so far as what has soul in it is a 'this-somewhat' or substance that food acts as food; in that case it maintains the being of what is fed, and that continues to be what it is so long as the process of nutrition continues. Further, it is the agent in generation, i.e. not the generation of the individual fed but the reproduction of another like it; the substance of the individual fed is already in existence; the existence of no substance is a self-generation but only a self-maintenance.

Hence the psychic power which we are now studying may be described as that which tends to maintain whatever has this power in it of continuing such as it was, and food helps it to do its work. That is why, if deprived of food, it must cease to be.

The process of nutrition involves three factors, (a) what is fed, (b) that wherewith it is fed, (c) what does the feeding; of these (c) is the first soul, (a) the body which has that soul in it, (b) the food. But since it is

right to call things after the ends they realize, and the end of this soul is to generate another being like that in which it is, the first soul ought to be named the reproductive soul. The expression (b) 'wherewith it is fed' is ambiguous just as is the expression 'wherewith the ship is steered'; that may mean either (i) the hand or (ii) the rudder, i.e. either (i) what is moved and sets in movement, or (ii) what is merely moved. We can apply this analogy here if we recall that all food must be capable of being digested, and that what produces digestion is warmth; that is why everything that has soul in it possesses warmth.

We have now given an outline account of the nature of food; further details must be given in the appropriate place.

5. Having made these distinctions let us now speak of sensation in the widest sense. Sensation depends, as we have said, on a process of movement or affection from without, for it is held to be some sort of change of quality. Now some thinkers assert that like is affected only by like; in what sense this is possible and in what sense impossible, we have explained in our general discussion of acting and being acted upon.

Here arises a problem: why do we not perceive the senses themselves as well as the external objects of sense, or why without the stimulation of external objects do they not produce sensation, seeing that they contain in themselves fire, earth, and all the other elements, which are the direct or indirect objects is so of sense? It is clear that what is sensitive is only potentially, not actually. The power of sense is parallel to what is combustible, for that never ignites itself spontaneously, but requires an agent which has the power of starting ignition; otherwise it could have set itself on fire, and would not have needed actual fire to set it ablaze.

In reply we must recall that we use the word 'perceive' in two ways, for we say (a) that what has the power to hear or see, 'sees' or 'hears', even though it is at the moment asleep, and also (b) that what is actually seeing or hearing, 'sees' or 'hears'. Hence 'sense' too must have two meanings, sense potential, and sense actual. Similarly 'to be a sentient' means either (a) to have a certain power or (b) to manifest a certain activity. To begin with, for a time, let us speak as if there were no difference between

(i) being moved or affected, and (ii) being active, for movement is a kind of activity-an imperfect kind, as has elsewhere been explained. Everything that is acted upon or moved is acted upon by an agent which is actually at work. Hence it is that in one sense, as has already been stated, what acts and what is acted upon are like, in another unlike, i.e. prior to and during the change the two factors are unlike, after it like.

But we must now distinguish not only between what is potential and what is actual but also different senses in which things can be said to be potential or actual; up to now we have been speaking as if each of these phrases had only one sense. We can speak of something as 'a knower' either (a) as when we say that man is a knower, meaning that man falls within the class of beings that know or have knowledge, or (b) as when we are speaking of a man who possesses a knowledge of grammar; each of these is so called as having in him a certain potentiality, but there is a difference between their respective potentialities, the one (a) being a potential knower, because his kind or matter is such and such, the other (b), because he can in the absence of any external counteracting cause realize his knowledge in actual knowing at will. This implies a third meaning of 'a knower' (c), one who is already realizing his knowledge—he is a knower in actuality and in the most proper sense is knowing, e.g. this A. Both the former are potential knowers, who realize their respective potentialities, the one (a) by change of quality, i.e. repeated transitions from one state to its opposite under instruction, the other (b) by the transition from the inactive possession of sense or grammar to their active exercise. The two kinds of transition are distinct.

Also the expression 'to be acted upon' has more than one meaning; it may mean either (a) the extinction of one of two contraries by the other, or (b) the maintenance of what is potential by the agency of what is actual and already like what is acted upon, with such likeness as is compatible with one's being actual and the other potential. For what possesses knowledge becomes an actual knower by a transition which is either not an alteration of it at all (being in reality a development into its true self or actuality) or at least an alteration in a quite different sense from the usual meaning.

Hence it is wrong to speak of a wise man as being 'altered' when he uses his 'wisdom, just as it would be absurd to speak of a builder as being altered when he is using his skill in building a house.

What in the case of knowing or understanding leads from potentiality to actuality ought not to be called teaching but something else. That which starting with the power to know learns or acquires knowledge through the agency of one who actually knows and has the power of teaching either (a) ought not to be said 'to be acted upon' at all or (b) we must recognize two senses of alteration, viz. (i) the substitution of one quality for another, the first being the contrary of the second, or (ii) the development of an existent quality from potentiality in the direction of fixity or nature.

In the case of what is to possess sense, the first transition is due to the action of the male parent and takes place before birth so that at birth the living thing is, in respect of sensation, at the stage which corresponds to the possession of knowledge. Actual sensation corresponds to the stage of the exercise of knowledge. But between the two cases compared there is a difference; the objects that excite the sensory powers to activity, the seen, the heard, &c., are outside. The ground of this difference is that what actual sensation apprehends is individuals, while what knowledge apprehends is universals, and these are in a sense within the soul. That is why a man can exercise his knowledge when he wishes, but his sensation does not depend upon himself a sensible object must be there. A similar statement must be made about our knowledge of what is sensible-on the same ground, viz. that the sensible objects are individual and external.

A later more appropriate occasion may be found thoroughly to clear up all this. At present it must be enough to recognize the distinctions already drawn; a thing may be said to be potential in either of two senses, (a) in the sense in which we might say of a boy that he may become a general or (b) in the sense in which we might say the same of an adult, and there are two corresponding senses of the term 'a potential sentient'. There are no separate names for the two stages of potentiality; we have pointed out that they are different and how they are different. We cannot help using the incorrect terms 'being acted upon or altered' of the two transitions involved. As we have said, has the power of sensation is potentially like what the perceived object is actually; that is, while at the beginning of the process of its being acted upon the two interacting factors are dissimilar, at the end the one acted upon is assimilated to the other and is identical in quality with it.

12. The following results applying to any and every sense may now be formulated.

(A) By a 'sense' is meant what has the power of receiving into itself the sensible forms of things without the matter. This must be conceived of as taking place in the way in which a piece of wax takes on the impress of a signet-ring without the iron or gold; we say that what produces the impression is a signet of bronze or gold, but its particular metallic constitution makes no difference: in a similar way the sense is affected by what is coloured or flavoured or sounding, but it is indifferent what in each case the substance is; what alone matters is what quality it has, i.e. in what ratio its constituents are combined.

(B) By 'an organ of sense' is meant that in which ultimately such a power is seated.

The sense and its organ are the same in fact, but their essence is not the same. What perceives is, of course, a spatial magnitude, but we must not admit that either the having the power to perceive or the sense itself is a magnitude; what they are is a certain ratio or power in a magnitude. This enables us to explain why objects of sense which possess one of two opposite sensible qualities in a degree largely in excess of the other opposite destroy the organs of sense; if the movement set up by an object is too strong for the organ, the equipoise of contrary qualities in the organ, which just is its sensory power, is disturbed; it is precisely as concord and tone are destroyed by too violently twanging the strings of a lyre. This explains also why plants cannot perceive. In spite of their having a portion of soul in them and obviously being affected by tangible objects themselves; for undoubtedly their temperature can be lowered or raised. The explanation is that they have no mean of contrary qualities, and so no principle in them capable of taking on the forms of sensible objects without their matter; in the case of plants the affection is an affection by form-and-matter together. The problem might be raised: Can what cannot smell be said to be affected by smells or what cannot see by colours, and so on? It might be said that a smell is just what can be smelt, and if it produces any effect it can only be so as to make something smell it,

and it might be argued that what cannot smell cannot be affected by smells and further that what can smell can be affected by it only in so far as it has in it the power to smell (similarly with the proper objects of all the other senses). Indeed that this is so is made quite evident as follows. Light or darkness, sounds and smells leave bodies quite unaffected; what does affect bodies is not these but the bodies which are their vehicles, e.g. what splits the trunk of a tree is not the sound of the thunder but the air which accompanies thunder. Yes, but, it may be objected, bodies are affected by what is tangible and by flavours. If not, by what are things that are without soul affected, i.e. altered in quality? Must we not, then, admit that the objects of the other senses also may affect them? Is not the true account this, that all bodies are capable of being affected by smells and sounds, but that some on being acted upon, having no boundaries of their own, disintegrate, as in the instance of air, which does become odorous, showing that some effect is produced on it by what is odorous? But smelling is more than such an affection by what is odorous—what more? Is not the answer that, while the air owing to the momentary duration of the action upon it of what is odorous does itself become perceptible to the sense of smell, smelling is an observing of the result produced?

BOOK III

4. Turning now to the part of the soul with which the soul knows and thinks (whether this is separable from the others in definition only, or spatially as well) we have to inquire (1) what differentiates this part, and (2) how thinking can take place.

If thinking is like perceiving, it must be either a process in which the soul is acted upon by what is capable of being thought, or a process different from but analogous to that. The thinking part of the soul must therefore be, while impassible, capable of receiving the form of an object; that is, must be potentially identical in character with its object without being the object. Mind must be related to what is thinkable, as sense is to what is sensible.

Therefore, since everything is a possible object of thought, mind in order, as Anaxagoras says, to dominate, that is, to know, must be pure from all admixture;

for the co-presence of what is alien to its nature is a hindrance and a block: it follows that it too, like the sensitive part, can have no nature of its own, other than that of having a certain capacity. Thus that in the soul which is called mind (by mind I mean that whereby the soul thinks and judges) is, before it thinks, not actually

25 any real thing. For this reason it cannot reasonably be regarded as blended with the body: if so, it would acquire some quality, e.g. warmth or cold, or even have an organ like the sensitive faculty: as it is, it has none. It was a good idea to call the soul 'the place of forms', though (1) this description holds only of the intellective soul, and (2) even this is the forms only potentially, not actually.

Observation of the sense-organs and their em-

30 ployment reveals a distinction between the impassi-
429b bility of the sensitive and that of the intellective faculty. After strong stimulation of a sense we are less able to exercise it than before, as e.g. in the case of a loud sound we cannot hear easily immediately after, or in the case of a bright colour or a powerful odour we cannot see or smell, but in the case of mind thought about an object that is highly intelligible renders it more and not less able afterwards to think objects that are less intelligible: the reason is that while the faculty of sensation is dependent upon the body,

5 mind is separable from it.

Once the mind has become each set of its possible objects, as a man of science has, when this phrase is used of one who is actually a man of science (this happens when he is now able to exercise the power on his own initiative), its condition is still one of potentiality, but in a different sense from the potentiality which preceded the acquisition of knowledge by learning or discovery: the mind too is then able to think itself.

10 Since we can distinguish between a spatial magnitude and what it is to be such, and between water and what it is to be water, and so in many other cases (though not in all; for in certain cases the thing and its form are identical), flesh and what it is to be flesh are discriminated either by different faculties, or by the same faculty in two different states: for flesh necessarily involves matter and is like what is snub-nosed, a this in a this. Now it is by means of the sensitive

15 faculty that we discriminate the hot and the cold, i.e. the factors which combined in a certain ratio consti-

tute flesh: the essential character of flesh is apprehended by something different either wholly separate from the sensitive faculty or related to it as a bent line to the same line when it has been straightened out.

Again in the case of abstract objects what is 20 straight is analogous to what is snub-nosed; for it necessarily implies a continuum as its matter: its constitutive essence is different, if we may distinguish between straightness and what is straight: let us take it to be two-ness. It must be apprehended, therefore, by a different power or by the same power in a different state. To sum up, in so far as the realities it knows are capable of being separated from their matter, so it is also with the powers of mind.

The problem might be suggested: if thinking is a 25 passive affection, then if mind is simple and impassible and has nothing in common with anything else, as Anaxagoras says, how can it come to think at all? For interaction between two factors is held to require a precedent community of nature between the factors. Again it might be asked, is mind a possible object of thought to itself? For if mind is thinkable per se and what is thinkable is in kind one and the same, then either (a) mind will belong to everything, or (b) 30 mind will contain some element common to it with all other realities which makes them all thinkable.

(1) Have not we already disposed of the difficulty about interaction involving a common element, when we said that mind is in a sense potentially whatever is thinkable, though actually it is nothing until it has thought? What it thinks must be in it just as characters may be said to be on a writingtablet on which as yet nothing actually stands written: this is exactly what happens with mind. 430a

(Mind is itself thinkable in exactly the same way as its objects are. For (a) in the case of objects which involve no matter, what thinks and what is thought 5 are identical; for speculative knowledge and its object are identical. (Why mind is not always thinking we must consider later.) (b) In the case of those which contain matter each of the objects of thought is only potentially present. It follows that while they will not have mind in them (for mind is a potentiality of them only in so far as they are capable of being disengaged from matter) mind may yet be thinkable

5. Since in every class of things, as in nature as 10 a whole, we find two factors involved, (1) a matter

which is potentially all the particulars included in the class, (2) a cause which is productive in the sense that it makes them all (the latter standing to the former, as e.g. an art to its material), these distinct elements must likewise be found within the soul.

And in fact mind as we have described it is what it is what it is by virtue of becoming all things, while there is another which is what it is by virtue of making all things: this is a sort of positive state like light; for in a sense light makes potential colours into actual colours.

Mind in this sense of it is separable, impassible, unmixed, since it is in its essential nature activity (for always the active is superior to the passive factor, the originating force to the matter which it forms).

Actual knowledge is identical with its object: in the individual, potential knowledge is in time prior to actual knowledge, but in the universe as a whole it is not prior even in time. Mind is not at one time knowing and at another not. When mind is set free from its present conditions it appears as just what it is and nothing more: this alone is immortal and eternal (we do not, however, remember its former activity because, while mind in this sense is impassible, mind as passive is destructible), and without it nothing thinks.

METAPHYSICS (METAPHYSICA)

BOOK I

1. All men by nature desire to know. An indication of this is the delight we take in our senses; for even apart from their usefulness they are loved for themselves; and above all others the sense of sight. For not only with a view to action, but even when we are not going to do anything, we prefer seeing (one might say) to everything else. The reason is that this, most of all the senses, makes us know and brings to light many differences between things.

By nature animals are born with the faculty of sensation, and from sensation memory is produced in some of them, though not in others. And therefore the former are more intelligent and apt at learning than those which cannot remember; those which are incapable of hearing sounds are intelligent though they cannot be taught, e.g. the bee, and any other race of animals that may be like it; and those which besides memory have this sense of hearing can be taught.

The animals other than man live by appearances and memories, and have but little of connected experience; but the human race lives also by art and reasonings. Now from memory experience is produced in men; for the several memories of the same thing produce finally the capacity for a single experience. And experience seems pretty much like science and art, but really science and art come to men *through* experience; for 'experience made art', as Polus says, 'but inexperience luck'. Now art arises when from many notions gained by experience one universal judgement about a class of objects is produced. For to have a judgement that when Callias was ill of this disease this did him good, and similarly in the case of Socrates and in many individual cases, is a matter of experience; but to judge that it has done good to all persons of a certain constitution, marked off in one class, when they were ill of this disease, e.g. to phlegmatic or bilious people when burning with fever—this is a matter of art.

With a view to action experience seems in no respect inferior to art, and men of experience succeed even better than those who have theory without experience. (The reason is that experience is knowledge of individuals, art of universals, and actions and productions are all concerned with the individual; for the physician does not cure *man*, except in an incidental way, but Callias or Socrates or some other called by some such individual name, who happens to be a man. If, then, a man has the theory without the experience, and recognizes the universal but does not know the individual included in this, he will often fail to cure; for it is the individual that is to be cured.) But yet we think that *knowledge* and *understanding* belong to art rather than to experience, and we suppose artists to be wiser than men of experience (which implies that Wisdom depends in all cases rather on knowledge); and this because the former know the cause, but the latter do not. For men of experience know that the thing is so, but do not know why, while the others know the 'why' and the cause. Hence we think also that the master-workers in each craft are more honourable and know in a truer sense and are wiser than the manual workers, because they know the causes of the things that are done (we think the manual workers are like certain lifeless things which act indeed, but act without knowing what they do, as fire burns—but while the lifeless things perform each of their functions by a natural tendency, the labourers perform them through habit); thus we view them as being wiser not in virtue of being able to act, but of having the theory for themselves and knowing the causes. And in general it is a sign of the man who knows and of the man who does not know, that the former can teach, and therefore we think art more truly knowledge than experience is; for artists can teach, and men of mere experience cannot.

Again, we do not regard any of the senses as Wisdom; yet surely these give the most authoritative knowledge of particulars. But they do not tell us the 'why' of anything—e.g. why fire is hot; they only say *that* it is hot.

At first he who invented any art whatever that went beyond the common perceptions of man was naturally admired by men, not only because there was something useful in the inventions, but because he was thought wise and superior to the rest. But as more arts were invented, and some were directed to the necessities of life, others to recreation, the inventors of the latter were naturally always regarded as wiser than the inventors of the former, because their branches of knowledge did not aim at utility. Hence when all such inventions were already established, the sciences which do not aim at giving pleasure or at the necessities of life were discovered, and first in the places where men first began to have leisure. This is why the mathematical arts were

founded in Egypt; for there the priestly caste was allowed to be at leisure.

We have said in the *Ethics*[1] what the difference is between art and science and the other kindred faculties; but the point of our present discussion is this, that all men suppose what is called Wisdom to deal with the first causes and the principles of things; so that, as has been said before, the man of experience is thought to be wiser than the possessors of any sense-perception whatever, the artist wiser than the men of experience, the master-worker than the mechanic, and the theoretical kinds of knowledge to be more of the nature of Wisdom than the productive. Clearly then Wisdom is knowledge about certain principles and causes.

2. Since we are seeking this knowledge, we must inquire of what kind are the causes and the principles, the knowledge of which is Wisdom. If one were to take the notions we have about the wise man, this might perhaps make the answer more evident. We suppose first, then, that the wise man knows all things, as far as possible, although he has not knowledge of each of them in detail; secondly, that he who can learn things that are difficult, and not easy for man to know, is wise (sense-perception is common to all, and therefore easy and no mark of Wisdom); again, that he who is more exact and more capable of teaching the causes is wiser, in every branch of knowledge; and that of the sciences, also, that which is desirable on its own account and for the sake of knowing it is more of the nature of Wisdom than that which is desirable on account of its results, and the superior science is more of the nature of Wisdom than the ancillary; for the wise man must not be ordered but must order, and he must not obey another, but the less wise must obey *him*.

Such and so many are the notions, then, which we have about Wisdom and the wise. Now of these characteristics that of knowing all things must belong to him who has in the highest degree universal knowledge; for he knows in a sense all the instances that fall under the universal. And these things, the most universal, are on the whole the hardest for men to know; for they are farthest from the senses. And

---

[1] 1139[b] 14-1141[b] 8.

the most exact of the sciences are those which deal most with first principles; for those which involve fewer principles are more exact than those which involve additional principles, e.g. arithmetic than geometry. But the science which investigates causes is also *instructive*, in a higher degree, for the people who instruct us are those who tell the causes of each thing. And understanding and knowledge pursued for their own sake are found most in the knowledge of that which is most knowable (for he who chooses to know for the sake of knowing will choose most readily that which is most truly knowledge, and such is the knowledge of that which is most knowable); and the first principles and the causes are most knowable; for by reason of these, and from these, all other things come to be known, and not these by means of the things subordinate to them. And the science which knows to what end each thing must be done is the most authoritative of the sciences, and more authoritative than any ancillary science; and this end is the good of that thing, and in general the supreme good in the whole of nature. Judged by all the tests we have mentioned, then, the name in question falls to the same science; this must be a science that investigates the first principles and causes; for the good, i.e. the end, is one of the causes.

That it is not a science of production is clear even from the history of the earliest philosophers. For it is owing to their wonder that men both now begin and at first began to philosophize; they wondered originally at the obvious difficulties, then advanced little by little and stated difficulties about the greater matters, e.g. about the phenomena of the moon and those of the sun and of the stars, and about the genesis of the universe. And a man who is puzzled and wonders thinks himself ignorant (whence even the lover of myth is in a sense a lover of Wisdom, for the myth is composed of wonders); therefore since they philosophized in order to escape from ignorance, evidently they were pursuing science in order to know, and not for any utilitarian end. And this is confirmed by the facts; for it was when almost all the necessities of life and the things that make for comfort and recreation had been secured, that such knowledge began to be sought. Evidently then we do not seek it for the sake of any other advantage; but as the man is free, we say, who exists for his own

sake and not for another's, so we pursue this as the only free science, for it alone exists for its own sake.

Hence also the possession of it might be justly regarded as beyond human power; for in many ways human nature is in bondage, so that according to Simonides 'God alone can have this privilege', and it is unfitting that man should not be content to seek the knowledge that is suited to him. If, then, there is something in what the poets say, and jealousy is natural to the divine power, it would probably occur in this case above all, and all who excelled in this knowledge would be unfortunate. But the divine power cannot be jealous (nay, according to the proverb, 'bards tell many a lie'), nor should any other science be thought more honourable than one of this sort. For the most divine science is also most honourable; and this science alone must be, in two ways, most divine. For the science which it would be most meet for God to have is a divine science, and so is any science that deals with divine objects; and this science alone has both these qualities; for (1) God is thought to be among the causes of all things and to be a first principle, and (2) such a science either God alone can have, or God above all others. All the sciences, indeed, are more necessary than this, but none is better.

Yet the acquisition of it must in a sense end in something which is the opposite of our original inquiries. For all men begin, as we said, by wondering that things are as they are, as they do about self-moving marionettes, or about the solstices or the incommensurability of the diagonal of a square with the side; for it seems wonderful to all who have not yet seen the reason, that there is a thing which cannot be measured even by the smallest unit. But we must end in the contrary and, according to the proverb, the better state, as is the case in these instances too when men learn the cause; for there is nothing which would surprise a geometer so much as if the diagonal turned out to be commensurable.

We have stated, then, what is the nature of the science we are searching for, and what is the mark which our search and our whole investigation must reach.

3. Evidently we have to acquire knowledge of the original causes (for we say we know each thing only when we think we recognize its first cause), and

causes are spoken of in four senses. In one of these we mean the substance, i.e. the essence (for the 'why' is reducible finally to the definition, and the ultimate 'why' is a cause and principle); in another the matter or substratum, in a third the source of the change, and in a fourth the cause opposed to this, the purpose and the good (for this is the end of all generation and change). We have studied these causes sufficiently in our work on nature,[2] but yet let us call to our aid those who have attacked the investigation of being and philosophized about reality before us. For obviously they too speak of certain principles and causes; to go over their views, then, will be of profit to the present inquiry, for we shall either find another kind of cause, or be more convinced of the correctness of those which we now maintain.

Of the first philosophers, then, most thought the principles which were of the nature of matter were the only principles of all things. That of which all things that are consist, the first from which they come to be, the last into which they are resolved (the substance remaining, but changing in its modifications), this they say is the element and this the principle of things, and therefore they think nothing is either generated or destroyed, since this sort of entity is always conserved, as we say Socrates neither comes to be absolutely when he comes to be beautiful or musical, nor ceases to be when he loses these characteristics, because the substratum, Socrates himself, remains. Just so they say nothing else comes to be or ceases to be; for there must be some entity—either one or more than one—from which all other things come to be, it being conserved.

Yet they do not all agree as to the number and the nature of these principles. Thales, the founder of this type of philosophy, says the principle is water (for which reason he declared that the earth rests on water), getting the notion perhaps from seeing that the nutriment of all things is moist, and that heat itself is generated from the moist and kept alive by it (and that from which they come to be is a principle of all things). He got his notion from this fact, and from the fact that the seeds of all things have a moist nature, and that water is the origin of the nature of moist things.

[2]*Phys.* ii. 3, 7.

Some think that even the ancients who lived long before the present generation, and first framed accounts of the gods, had a similar view of nature; for they made Ocean and Tethys the parents of creation, and described the oath of the gods as being by water, to which they give the name of Styx; for what is oldest is most honourable, and the most honourable thing is that by which one swears. It may perhaps be uncertain whether this opinion about nature is primitive and ancient, but Thales at any rate is said to have declared himself thus about the first cause. Hippo no one would think fit to include among these thinkers, because of the paltriness of his thought.

Anaximenes and Diogenes make air prior to water, and the most primary of the simple bodies, while Hippasus of Metapontium and Heraclitus of Ephesus say this of fire, and Empedocles says it of the four elements (adding a fourth—earth—to those which have been named); for these, he says, always remain and do not come to be, except that they come to be more or fewer, being aggregated into one and segregated out of one.

Anaxagoras of Clazomenae, who, though older than Empedocles, was later in his philosophical activity, says the principles are infinite in number; for he says almost all the things that are made of parts like themselves, in the manner of water or fire, are generated and destroyed in this way, only by aggregation and segregation, and are not in any other sense generated or destroyed, but remain eternally.

From these facts one might think that the only cause is the so-called material cause; but as men thus advanced, the very facts opened the way for them and joined in forcing them to investigate the subject. However true it may be that all generation and destruction proceed from some one or (for that matter) from more elements, why does this happen and what is the cause? For at least the substratum itself does not make itself change; e.g. neither the wood nor the bronze causes the change of either of them, nor does the wood manufacture a bed and the bronze a statue, but something else is the cause of the change. And to seek this is to seek the second cause, as *we* should say—that from which comes the beginning of the movement. Now those who at the very beginning set themselves to this kind of inquiry, and said the substratum was one,[3] were not at all dissatisfied with themselves; but some at least of those who maintain it to be one[4]—as though defeated by this search for the second cause—say the one and nature as a whole is unchangeable not only in respect of generation and destruction (for this is a primitive belief, and all agreed in it), but also of all other change; and this view is peculiar to them. Of those who said the universe was one, then, none succeeded in discovering a cause of this sort, except perhaps Parmenides, and he only inasmuch as he supposes that there is not only one but also in some sense two causes. But for those who make more elements[5] it is more possible to state the second cause, e.g. for those who make hot and cold, or fire and earth, the elements; for they treat fire as having a nature which fits it to move things, and water and earth and such things they treat in the contrary way.

When these men and the principles of this kind had had their day, as the latter were found inadequate to generate the nature of things men were again forced by the truth itself, as we said,[6] to inquire into the next kind of cause. For it is not likely either that fire or earth or any such element should be the reason why things manifest goodness and beauty both in their being and in their coming to be, or that those thinkers should have supposed it was; nor again could it be right to entrust so great a matter to spontaneity and chance. When one man[7] said, then, that reason was present—as in animals, so throughout nature—as the cause of order and of all arrangement, he seemed like a sober man in contrast with the random talk of his predecessors. We know that Anaxagoras certainly adopted these views, but Hermotimus of Clazomenae is credited with expressing them earlier. Those who thought thus stated that there is a principle of things which is at the same time the cause of beauty, and that sort of cause from which things acquire movement.

4. One might suspect that Hesiod was the first to look for such a thing—or some one else who put love or desire among existing things as a principle, as Parmenides, too, does; for he, in constructing the genesis of the universe, says:—

Love first of all the Gods she planned.

And Hesiod says:—

First of all things was chaos made, and then
Broad-breasted earth, . . .
And love, 'mid all the gods pre-eminent,

which implies that among existing things there must be from the first a cause which will move things and bring them together. How these thinkers should be arranged with regard to priority of discovery let us be allowed to decide later;[8] but since the contraries of the various forms of good were also perceived to be present in nature—not only order and the beautiful, but also disorder and the ugly, and bad things in greater number than good, and ignoble things than beautiful—therefore another thinker introduced friendship and strife, each of the two the cause of one of these two sets of qualities. For if we were to follow out the view of Empedocles, and interpret it according to its meaning and not to its lisping expression, we should find that friendship is the cause of good things, and strife of bad. Therefore, if we said that Empedocles in a sense both mentions, and is the first to mention, the bad and the good as principles, we should perhaps be right, since the cause of all goods is the good itself.

These thinkers, as we say, evidently grasped, and to this extent, two of the causes which we distinguished in our work on nature[9]—the matter and the source of the movement—vaguely, however, and with no clearness, but as untrained men behave in fights; for they go round their opponents and often strike fine blows, but they do not fight on scientific principles, and so too these thinkers do not seem to know what they say; for it is evident that, as a rule, they make no use of their causes except to a small extent. For Anaxagoras uses reason as a *deus ex*

---

[3]Thales, Anaximenes, and Heraclitus.
[4]The Eleatics.
[5]The reference is probably to Empedocles.
[6]18.
[7]Anaxagoras.

---

[8]The promise is not fulfilled.
[9]*Phys.* ii. 3, 7.

machina for the making of the world, and when he is at a loss to tell from what cause something necessarily is, then he drags reason in, but in all other cases ascribes events to anything rather than to reason.[10] And Empedocles, though he uses the causes to a greater extent than this, neither does so sufficiently nor attains consistency in their use. At least, in many cases he makes love segregate things, and strife aggregate them. For whenever the universe is dissolved into its elements by strife, fire is aggregated into one, and so is each of the other elements; but whenever again under the influence of love they come together into one, the parts must again be segregated out of each element.

Empedocles, then, in contrast with his predecessors, was the first to introduce the dividing of this cause, not positing one source of movement, but different and contrary sources. Again, he was the first to speak of four material elements; yet he does not *use* four, but treats them as two only; he treats fire by itself, and its opposites—earth, air, and water—as one kind of thing. We may learn this by study of his verses.

This philosopher then, as we say, has spoken of the principles in this way, and made them of this number. Leucippus and his associate Democritus say that the full and the empty are the elements, calling the one being and the other non-being—the full and solid being being, the empty non-being (whence they say being no more is than non-being, because the solid no more is than the empty); and they make these the material causes of things. And as those who make the underlying substance one generate all other things by its modifications, supposing the rare and the dense to be the sources of the modifications, in the same way these philosophers say the differences in the elements are the causes of all other qualities. These differences, they say, are three—shape and order and position. For they say the real is differentiated only by 'rhythm' and 'inter-contact' and 'turning'; and of these rhythm is shape, inter-contact is order, and turning is position; for A differs from N in shape, AN from NA in order, H from H in position. The question of movement—whence or how it is to belong to things—these thinkers, like the others, lazily neglected.

Regarding the two causes, then, as we say, the inquiry seems to have been pushed thus far by the early philosophers.

5. Contemporaneously with these philosophers and before them, the so-called Pythagoreans, who were the first to take up mathematics, not only advanced this study, but also having been brought up in it they thought its principles were the principles of all things. Since of these principles numbers are by nature the first, and in numbers they seemed to see many resemblances to the things that exist and come into being—more than in fire and earth and water (such and such a modification of numbers being justice, another being soul and reason, another being opportunity—and similarly almost all other things being numerically expressible); since, again, they saw that the modifications and the ratios of the musical scales were expressible in numbers;—since, then, all other things seemed in their whole nature to be modelled on numbers, and numbers seemed to be the first things in the whole of nature, they supposed the elements of numbers to be the elements of all things, and the whole heaven to be a musical scale and a number. And all the properties of numbers and scales which they could show to agree with the attributes and parts and the whole arrangement of the heavens, they collected and fitted into their scheme; and if there was a gap anywhere, they readily made additions so as to make their whole theory coherent. E.g. as the number 10 is thought to be perfect and to comprise the whole nature of numbers, they say that the bodies which move through the heavens are ten, but as the visible bodies are only nine, to meet this they invent a tenth—the 'counter-earth'. We have discussed these matters more exactly elsewhere.[11]

But the object of our review is that we may learn from these philosophers also what they suppose to be the principles and how these fall under the causes we have named. Evidently, then, these thinkers also consider that number is the principle both as matter for things and as forming both their modifications and their permanent states, and hold that the elements

---

[10]Cf. Pl. *Phaedo*, 98 BC, *Laws*, 967 B–D.

[11]*De Caelo*, ii. 13.

of number are the even and the odd, and that of these the latter is limited, and the former unlimited; and that the One proceeds from both of these (for it is both even and odd), and number from the One; and that the whole heaven, as has been said, is numbers.

20 Other members of this same school say there are ten principles, which they arrange in two columns of cognates—limit and unlimited, odd and even, one and plurality, right and left, male and female, rest-25 ing and moving, straight and curved, light and darkness, good and bad, square and oblong. In this way Alcmaeon of Croton seems also to have conceived the matter, and either he got this view from them or they got it from him; for he expressed himself sim-30 ilarly to them. For he says most human affairs go in pairs, meaning not definite contrarieties such as the Pythagoreans speak of, but any chance contrarieties, e.g. white and black, sweet and bitter, good and bad, great and small. He threw out indefinite suggestions about the other contrarieties, but the Pythagoreans declared both how many and which their contrari-986ᵇ eties are.

From both these schools, then, we can learn this much, that the contraries are the principles of things; and how many these principles are and which they are, we can learn from one of the two schools. But how these principles can be brought together under the causes we have named has not been clearly and 5 articulately stated by them; they seem, however, to range the elements under the head of matter; for out of these as immanent parts they say substance is composed and moulded.

From these facts we may sufficiently perceive the meaning of the ancients who said the elements of nature were more than one; but there are some who spoke of the universe as if it were one entity, though 10 they were not all alike either in the excellence of their statement or in its conformity to the facts of nature. The discussion of them is in no way appropriate to our present investigation of causes, for they do not, like some of the natural philosophers, assume being to be one and yet generate it out of the one as out of matter, but they speak in another way; those others 15 add change, since they generate the universe, but these thinkers say the universe is unchangeable. Yet *this* much is germane to the present inquiry: Parmenides seems to fasten on that which is one in definition,

Melissus on that which is one in matter, for which reason the former says that it is limited, the latter that it is unlimited; while Xenophanes, the first of these par-20 tisans of the One (for Paramenides is said to have been his pupil), gave no clear statement, nor does he seem to have grasped the nature of either of these causes, but with reference to the whole material universe he says the One is God. Now these thinkers, as we said, must be neglected for the purposes of the present in-25 quiry—two of them entirely, as being a little too naïve, viz. Xenophanes and Melissus; but Parmenides seems in places to speak with more insight. For, claiming that, besides the existent, nothing non-existent exists, he thinks that of necessity one thing exists, viz. the existent and nothing else (on this we have spoken 30 more clearly in our work on nature),[12] but being forced to follow the observed facts, and supposing the existence of that which is one in definition, but more than one according to our sensations, he now posits two causes and two principles, calling them hot and cold, i.e. fire and earth; and of these he ranges the hot with 987ᵃ the existent, and the other with the nonexistent.

From what has been said, then, and from the wise men who have now sat in council with us, we have got thus much—on the one hand from the earliest philosophers, who regard the first principle as cor-5 poreal (for water and fire and such things are bodies), and of whom some suppose that there is one corporeal principle, others that there are more than one, but both put these under the head of matter; and on the other hand from some who posit both this cause and besides this the source of movement, which we have got from some as single and from others as twofold.

Down to the Italian school, then, and apart from it, philosophers have treated these subjects rather ob-10 scurely, except that, as we said, they have in fact used two kinds of cause, and one of these—the source of movement—some treat as one and others as two. But the Pythagoreans have said in the same way that there are two principles, but added this 15 much, which is peculiar to them, that they thought that finitude and infinity were not attributes of certain other things, e.g. of fire or earth or anything else

---

[12] *Phys.* i. 3.

of this kind, but that infinity itself and unity itself were the substance of the things of which they are predicated. This is why number was the substance of all things. On this subject, then, they expressed themselves thus; and regarding the question of essence they began to make statements and definitions, but treated the matter too simply. For they both defined superficially and thought that the first subject of which a given definition was predicable was the substance of the thing defined, as if one supposed that 'double' and '2' were the same, because 2 is the first thing of which 'double' is predicable. But surely to be double and to be 2 are not the same; if they are, one thing will be many—a consequence which they actually drew. From the earlier philosophers, then, and from their successors we can learn thus much.

6. After the systems we have named came the philosophy of Plato, which in most respects followed these thinkers, but had peculiarities that distinguished it from the philosophy of the Italians. For, having in his youth first become familiar with Cratylus and with the Heraclitean doctrines (that all sensible things are ever in a state of flux and there is no knowledge about them), these views he held even in later years. Socrates, however, was busying himself about ethical matters and neglecting the world of nature as a whole but seeking the universal in these ethical matters, and fixed thought for the first time on definitions; Plato accepted his teaching, but held that the problem applied not to sensible things but to entities of another kind—for this reason, that the common definition could not be a definition of any sensible thing, as they were always changing. Things of this other sort, then, he called Ideas, and sensible things, he said, were all named after these, and in virtue of a relation to these; for the many existed by participation in the Ideas that have the same name as they. Only the name 'participation' was new; for the Pythagoreans say that things exist by 'imitation' of numbers, and Plato says they exist by participation, changing the name. But what the participation or the imitation of the Forms could be they left an open question.

Further, besides sensible things and Forms he says there are the objects of mathematics, which occupy an intermediate position, differing from sensible things in being eternal and unchangeable, from Forms in that there are many alike, while the Form itself is in each case unique.

Since the Forms were the causes of all other things, he thought their elements were the elements of all things. As matter, the great and the small were principles; as essential reality, the One; for from the great and the small, by participation in the One, come the Numbers.

But he agreed with the Pythagoreans in saying that the One is substance and not a predicate of something else; and in saying that the Numbers are the causes of the reality of other things he agreed with them; but positing a dyad and constructing the infinite out of great and small, instead of treating the infinite as one, is peculiar to him; and so is his view that the Numbers exist apart from sensible things, while *they* say that the things themselves are Numbers, and do not place the objects of mathematics between Forms and sensible things. His divergence from the Pythagoreans in making the One and the Numbers separate from things, and his introduction of the Forms, were due to his inquiries in the region of definitions (for the earlier thinkers had no tincture of dialectic), and his making the other entity besides the One a dyad was due to the belief that the numbers, except those which were prime, could be neatly produced out of the dyad as out of some plastic material.

Yet what *happens* is the contrary; the theory is not a reasonable one. For they make many things out of the matter, and the form generates only once, but what we observe is that one table is made from one matter, while the man who applies the form, though he is one, makes many tables. And the relation of the male to the female is similar; for the latter is impregnated by one copulation, but the male impregnates many females; yet these are analogues of those first principles.

Plato, then, declared himself thus on the points in question; it is evident from what has been said that he has used only two causes, that of the essence and the material cause (for the Forms are the causes of the essence of all other things, and the One is the cause of the essence of the Forms); and it is evident what the underlying matter is, of which the Forms are predicated in the case of sensible things, and the

One in the case of Forms, viz. that this is a dyad, the great and the small. Further, he has assigned the cause of good and that of evil to the elements, one to each of the two, as we say some of his predecessors sought to do, e.g. Empedocles and Anaxagoras.

7. Our review of those who have spoken about first principles and reality and of the way in which they have spoken, has been concise and summary; but yet we have learnt *this* much from them, that of those who speak about 'principle' and 'cause' no one has mentioned any principle except those which have been distinguished in our work on nature, but all evidently have some inkling of *them*, though only vaguely. For some speak of the first principle as matter, whether they suppose one or more first principles, and whether they suppose this to be a body or to be incorporeal; e.g. Plato spoke of the great and the small, the Italians of the infinite, Empedocles of fire, earth, water, and air, Anaxagoras of the infinity of things composed of similar parts. These, then, have all had a notion of this kind of cause, and so have all who speak of air or fire or water, or something denser than fire and rarer than air; for some have said the prime element is of this kind.

These thinkers grasped this cause only; but certain others have mentioned the source of movement, e.g. those who make friendship and strife, or reason, or love, a principle.

The essence, i.e. the substantial reality, no one has expressed distinctly. It is hinted at chiefly by those who believe in the Forms; for they do not suppose either that the Forms are the matter of sensible things, and the One the matter of the Forms, or that they are the source of movement (for they say these are causes rather of immobility and of being at rest), but they furnish the Forms as the essence of every other thing, and the One as the essence of the Forms.

That for whose sake actions and changes and movements take place, they assert to be a cause in a way, but not in this way, i.e. not in the way in which it is its *nature* to be a cause. For those who speak of reason or friendship class these causes as goods; they do not speak, however, as if anything that exists either existed or came into being for the same of these, but as if movements started from these. In the same way those who say the One or the existent is the good, say that it is the cause of substance, but not

that substance either is or comes to be for the sake of this. Therefore it turns out that in a sense they both say and do not say the good is a cause; for they do not call it a cause *qua* good but only incidentally.

All these thinkers, then, as they cannot pitch on another cause, seem to testify that we have determined rightly both how many and of what sort the causes are. Besides this it is plain that when the causes are being looked for, either all four must be sought thus or they must be sought in one of these four ways. Let us next discuss the possible difficulties with regard to the way in which each of these thinkers has spoken, and with regard to his situation relatively to the first principles.

8. Those, then, who say the universe is one and posit one kind of thing as matter, and as corporeal matter which has spatial magnitude, evidently go astray in many ways. For they posit the elements of bodies only, not of incorporeal things, though there are also incorporeal things. And in trying to state the causes of generation and destruction, and in giving a physical account of all things, they do away with the cause of movement. Further, they err in not positing the substance, i.e. the essence, as the cause of anything, and besides this in lightly calling any of the simple bodies except earth the first principle, without inquiring how they are produced out of one another,—I mean fire, water, earth, and air. For some things are produced out of each other by combination, others by separation, and this makes the greatest difference to their priority and posteriority. For (1) in a way the property of being most elementary of all would seem to belong to the first thing from which they are produced by combination, and *this* property would belong to the most fine-grained and subtle of bodies. For this reason those who make fire the principle would be most in agreement with this argument. But each of the other thinkers agrees that the element of corporeal things is of this sort. At least none of those who named one element claimed that earth was the element, evidently because of the coarseness of its grain. (Of the other three elements each has found some judge on its side; for some maintain that fire, others that water, others that air is the element. Yet why, after all, do they not name earth also, as most men do? For people say all things are earth. And Hesiod says earth was produced first

of corporeal things; so primitive and popular has the opinion been.) According to this argument, then, no one would be right who either says the first principle is any of the elements other than fire, or supposes it to be denser than air but rarer than water. But (2) if that which is later in generation is prior in nature, and that which is concocted and compounded is later in generation, the contrary of what we have been saying must be true—water must be prior to air, and earth to water.

So much, then, for those who posit one cause such as we mentioned; but the same is true if one supposes more of these, as Empedocles says the matter of things is four bodies. For he too is confronted by consequences some of which are the same as have been mentioned, while others are peculiar to him. For we see these bodies produced from one another, which implies that the same body does not always remain fire or earth (we have spoken about this in our works on nature[13]); and regarding the cause of movement and the question whether we must posit one or two, he must be thought to have spoken neither correctly nor altogether plausibly. And in general, change of quality is necessarily done away with for those who speak thus, for on their view cold will not come from hot nor hot from cold. For if it did there would be something that accepted the contraries themselves, and there would be some one entity that became fire and water, which Empedocles denies.

As regards Anaxagoras, if one were to suppose that he said there were two elements, the supposition would accord thoroughly with an argument which Anaxagoras himself did not state articulately, but which he must have accepted if any one had led him on to it. True, to say that in the beginning all things were mixed is absurd both on other grounds and because it follows that they must have existed before in an unmixed form, and because nature does not allow any chance thing to be mixed with any chance thing, and also because on this view modifications and accidents could be separated from substances (for the same things which are mixed can be separated); yet if one were to follow him up, piecing together what he means, he would perhaps be seen to be somewhat modern in his views. For when nothing was separated out, evidently nothing could be truly asserted of the substance that then existed. I mean, e.g., that it was neither white nor black, nor grey nor any other colour, but of necessity colourless; for if it had been coloured, it would have had one of these colours. And similarly, by this same argument, it was flavourless, nor had it any similar attribute; for it could not be either of any quality or of any size, nor could it be any definite kind of thing. For if it were, one of the particular forms would have belonged to it, and this is impossible, since all were mixed together; for the particular form would necessarily have been already separated out, but he says all were mixed except reason, and this alone was unmixed and pure. From this it follows, then, that he must say the principles are the One (for this is simple and unmixed) and the Other, which is of such a nature as we suppose the indefinite to be before it is defined and partakes of some form. Therefore, while expressing himself neither rightly nor clearly, he means something like what the later thinkers say and what is now more clearly seen to be the case.

But these thinkers are, after all, at home only in arguments about generation and destruction and movement; for it is practically only of this sort of substance that they seek the principles and the causes. But those who extend their vision to all things that exist, and of existing things suppose some to be perceptible and others not perceptible evidently study both classes, which is all the more reason why one should devote some time to seeing what is good in their views and what bad from the standpoint of the inquiry we have now before us.

The 'Pythagoreans' treat of principles and elements stranger than those of the physical philosophers (the reason is that they got the principles from non-sensible things, for the objects of mathematics, except those of astronomy, are of the class of things without movement); yet their discussions and investigations are all about nature; for they generate the heavens, and with regard to their parts and attributes and functions they observe the phenomena, and use up the principles and the causes in explaining these, which implies that they agree with the others, the physical philosophers, that the *real* is just all that which is perceptible and contained by the so-called

---

[13]*De Caelo*, iii. 7.

'heavens'. But the causes and the principles which they mention are, as we said, sufficient to act as steps even up to the higher realms of reality, and are more suited to these than to theories about nature. They do not tell us at all, however, how there can be movement if limit and unlimited and odd and even are the only things assumed, or how without movement and change there can be generation and destruction, or the bodies that move through the heavens can do what they do.

Further, if one either granted them that spatial magnitude consists of these elements, or this were proved, still how would some bodies be light and others have weight? To judge from what they assume and maintain they are speaking no more of mathematical bodies than of perceptible; hence they have said nothing whatever about fire or earth or the other bodies of this sort, I suppose because they have nothing to say which applies *peculiarly* to perceptible things.

Further, how are we to combine the beliefs that the attributes of number, and number itself, are causes of what exists and happens in the heavens both from the beginning and now, and that there is no other number than this number out of which the world is composed? When in one particular region they place opinion and opportunity, and, a little above or below, injustice and decision or mixture, and allege, as proof, that each of these is a number, and that there happens to be already in this place a plurality of the extended bodies composed of numbers, because these attributes of number attach to the various places—this being so, is this number, which we must suppose each of these abstractions to be, the same number which is exhibited in the material universe, or is it another than this? Plato says it is different; yet even he thinks that both these bodies and their causes are numbers, but that the *intelligible* numbers are causes, while the others are *sensible*.

9. Let us leave the Pythagoreans for the present; for it is enough to have touched on them as much as we have done. But as for those who posit the Ideas as causes, firstly, in seeking to grasp the causes of the things around us, they introduced others equal in number to these, as if a man who wanted to count things thought he would not be able to do it while they were few, but tried to count them when he had added to their number. For the Forms are practically equal to—or not fewer than—the things, in trying to explain which these thinkers proceeded from them to the Forms. For to each thing there answers an entity which has the same name and exists apart from the substances, and so also in the case of all other groups there is a one over many, whether the many are in this world or are eternal.

Further, of the ways in which we prove that the Forms exist, none is convincing; for from some no inference necessarily follows, and from some arise Forms even of things of which we think there are no Forms. For according to the arguments from the existence of the sciences there will be Forms of all things of which there are sciences, and according to the 'one over many' argument there will be Forms even of negations, and according to the argument that there is an object for thought even when the thing has perished, there will be Forms of perishable things; for we have an image of these. Further, of the more accurate arguments, some lead to Ideas of relations, of which we say there is no independent class, and others introduce the 'third man'.

And in general the arguments for the Forms destroy the things for whose existence we are more zealous than for the existence of the Ideas; for it follows that not the dyad but number is first, i.e. that the relative is prior to the absolute—besides all the other points on which certain people by following out the opinions held about the Ideas have come into conflict with the principles of the theory.

Further, according to the assumption on which our belief in the Ideas rests, there will be Forms not only of substances but also of many other things (for the concept is single not only in the case of substances but also in the other cases, and there are sciences not only of substance but also of other things, and a thousand other such difficulties confront them). But according to the necessities of the case and the opinions held about the Forms, if Forms can be shared in there must be Ideas of substances only. For they are not shared in incidentally, but a thing must share in its Form as in something not predicated of a subject (by 'being shared in incidentally' I mean that e.g. if a thing shares in 'double itself', it shares also in 'eternal', but incidentally; for 'eternal' happens to be predicable of the 'double'). Therefore the Forms will be substance; but the same terms indicate substance in this and in the ideal world (or what will be the meaning of saying that there is something apart from the particulars—the one over many?). And if the Ideas and the particulars that share in them have the same form, there will be something common to these; for why should '2' be one and the same in the perishable 2's or in those which are many but eternal, and not the same in the '2 itself' as in the particular 2? But if they have not the same form, they must have only the name in common, and it is as if one were to call both Callias and a wooden image a 'man', without observing any community between them.[14]

Above all one might discuss the question what on earth the Forms contribute to sensible things, either to those that are eternal or to those that come into being and cease to be. For they cause neither movement nor any change in them. But again they help in no wise either towards the knowledge of the other things (for they are not even the substance of these, else they would have been in them), or towards their being, if they are not *in* the particulars which share in them; though if they were, they might be thought to be causes, as white causes whiteness in a white object by entering into its composition. But this argument, which first Anaxagoras and later Eudoxus and certain others used, is very easily upset; for it is not difficult to collect many insuperable objections to such a view.

But, further, all other things cannot come from the Forms in any of the usual senses of 'from'. And to say that they are patterns and the other things share in them is to use empty words and poetical metaphors. For what is it that works, looking to the Ideas? And anything can either be, or become, like another without being copied from it, so that whether Socrates exists or not a man like Socrates might come to be; and evidently this might be so even if Socrates were eternal. And there will be several patterns of the same thing, and therefore several Forms; e.g. 'animal' and 'two-footed' and also 'man himself' will be Forms of man. Again, the Forms are patterns not only of sensible things, but of Forms themselves also; i.e. the genus, as genus of various

species, will be so; therefore the same thing will be pattern and copy.

Again, it would seem impossible that the substance and that of which it is the substance should exist apart; how, therefore, could the Ideas, being the substances of things, exist apart? In the *Phaedo*[15] the case is stated in this way—that the Forms are causes both of being and of becoming; yet when the Forms exist, still the things that share in them do not come into being, unless there is something to originate movement; and many other things come into being (e.g. a house or a ring) of which we say there are no Forms. Clearly, therefore, even the other things can both be and come into being owing to such causes as produce the things just mentioned.[16]

Again, if the Forms are numbers, how can they be causes? Is it because existing things are other numbers, e.g. one number is man, another is Socrates, another Callias? Why then are the one set of numbers causes of the other set? It will not make any difference even if the former are eternal and the latter are not. But if it is because things in this sensible world (e.g. harmony) are ratios of numbers, evidently the things between which they are ratios are some one class of things. If, then, this—the matter—is some definite thing, evidently the numbers themselves too will be ratios of something to something else. E.g. if Callias is a numerical ratio between fire and earth and water and air, his Idea also will be a number of certain other underlying things; and man-himself, whether it is a number in a sense or not, will still be a numerical ratio of certain things and not a number proper, nor will it be a kind of number merely because it is a numerical ratio.

Again, from many numbers one number is produced, but how can one Form come from many Forms? And if the number comes not from the many numbers themselves but from the units in them, e.g. in 10,000, how is it with the units? If they are specifically alike, numerous absurdities will follow, and also if they are not alike (neither the units in one number being themselves like one another nor those in other numbers being all like to all); for in what will they differ, as they are without quality? This is

[14]With 990[b] 2–991[a] 8 Cf. xiii. 1078[b] 34–1079[b] 3.

[15]IQQ C–E.
[16]With 991[a] 8–[b] 9 Cf. xiii. 1079[b] 12–1080[a] 8.

not a plausible view, nor is it consistent with our thought on the matter.

Further, they must set up a second kind of number (with which arithmetic deals), and all the objects which are called 'intermediate' by some thinkers; and how do these exist or from what principles do they proceed? Or why must they be intermediate between the things in this sensible world and the things-themselves?

Further, the units in 2 must each come from a prior 2; but this is impossible.

Further, why is a number, when taken all together, one?

Again, besides what has been said, if the units are *diverse* the Platonists should have spoken like those who say there are four, or two, elements; for each of these thinkers gives the name of element not to that which is common, e.g. to body, but to fire and earth, whether there is something common to them, viz. body, or not. But in fact the Platonists speak as if the One were *homogeneous* like fire or water; and if this is so, the numbers will not be substances. Evidently, if there is a One-itself and this is a first principle, 'one' is being used in more than one sense; for otherwise the theory is impossible.

When we wish to reduce substances to their principles, we state that lines come from the short and long (i.e. from a kind of small and great), and the plane from the broad and narrow, and body from the deep and shallow. Yet how then can either the plane contain a line, or the solid a line or a plane? For the broad and narrow is a different class from the deep and shallow. Therefore, just as number is not present in these, because the many and few are different from these, evidently no other of the higher classes will be present in the lower. But again the broad is not a genus which includes the deep, for then the solid would have been a species of plane.[17] Further, from what principle will the presence of the *points* in the line be derived? Plato even used to object to this class of things as being a geometrical fiction. He gave the name of principle of the line—and this he often posited—to the indivisible lines. Yet these must have a limit; therefore the argument from which the existence of the line follows proves also the existence of the point.

In general, though philosophy seeks the cause of perceptible things, we have given this up (for we say nothing of the cause from which change takes its start), but while we fancy we are stating the substance of perceptible things, we assert the existence of a second class of substances, while our account of the way in which they are the substances of perceptible things is empty talk; for 'sharing', as we said before,[18] means nothing.

Nor have the Forms any connexion with what we see to be the cause in the case of the arts, that for whose sake both all mind and the whole of nature are operative[19]—with this cause which we assert to be one of the first principles; but mathematics has come to be identical with philosophy for modern thinkers, though they say that it should be studied for the sake of other things.[20]

Further, one might suppose that the substance which according to them underlies as matter is too mathematical, and is a predicate and differentia of the substance, i.e. of the matter, rather than the matter itself; i.e. the great and the small are like the rare and the dense which the physical philosophers speak of, calling these the primary differentiae of the substratum; for these are a kind of excess and defect. And regarding movement, if the great and the small are to *be* movement, evidently the Forms will be moved; but if they are not to be movement, whence did movement come? The whole study of nature has been annihilated.

And what is thought to be easy—to show that all things are one—is not done; for what is proved by the method of setting out instances[21] is not that all things are one but that there is a One-itself,—if we grant all the assumptions. And not even this follows, if we do not grant that the universal is a genus; and this in some cases it cannot be.

Nor can it be explained either how the lines and planes and solids that come after the numbers exist

[17]With 992ᵃ 10–19 Cf. xiii. 1085ᵃ 9–19.

[18]991ᵃ 20–22.
[19]*sc.* the final cause.
[20]Cf. Plato, *Rep.* vii. 531 D, 533 B–E.
[21]For this Platonic method Cf. vii. 1031ᵇ 21, xiii. 1086ᵇ 9, xiv. 1090ᵃ 17.

or can exist, or what significance they have; for these can neither be Forms (for they are not numbers), nor the intermediates (for those are the objects of mathematics), nor the perishable things. This is evidently a distinct fourth class.

In general, if we search for the elements of existing things without distinguishing the many senses in which things are said to exist, we cannot find them, especially if the search for the elements of which things are made is conducted in this manner. For it is surely impossible to discover what 'acting' or 'being acted on', or 'the straight', is made of, but if elements can be discovered at all, it is only the elements of substances; therefore either to seek the elements of all existing things or to think one has them is incorrect.

And how could we *learn* the elements of all things? Evidently we cannot start by knowing anything before. For as he who is learning geometry, though he may know other things before, knows none of the things with which the science deals and about which he is to learn, so is it in all other cases. Therefore if there is a science of all things, such as some assert to exist, he who is learning this will know nothing before. Yet all learning is by means of premises which are (either all or some of them) known before—whether the learning be by demonstration or by definitions; for the elements of the definition must be known before and be familiar; and learning by induction proceeds similarly. But again, if the science were actually innate, it were strange that we are unaware of our possession of the greatest of sciences.

Again, how is one to *come to know* what all things are made of, and how is this to be made *evident*? This also affords a difficulty; for there might be a conflict of opinion, as there is about certain syllables; some say *za* is made out of *s* and *d* and *a*, while others say it is a distinct sound and none of those that are familiar.

Further, how could we know the objects of sense without having the sense in question? Yet we ought to, if the elements of which all things consist, as complex sounds consist of the elements proper to sound, are the same.

10. It is evident, then, even from what we have said before, that all men seem to seek the causes named in the *Physics*,[22] and that we cannot name any beyond these; but they seek these vaguely; and though in a sense they have all been described before, in a sense they have not been described at all. For the earliest philosophy is, on all subjects, like one who lisps, since it is young and in its beginnings. For even Empedocles says bone exists by virtue of the ratio in it. Now this is the essence and the substance of the thing. But it is similarly necessary that flesh and each of the other tissues should be the ratio of its elements, or that not one of them should; for it is on account of this that both flesh and bone and everything else will exist, and not on account of the matter, which *he* names—fire and earth and water and air. But while he would necessarily have agreed if another had said this, he has not said it clearly.

On these questions our views have been expressed before; but let us return to enumerate the difficulties that might be raised on these same points; for perhaps we may get from them some help towards our later difficulties. . . .

BOOK VII

1. There are several senses in which a thing may be said to 'be', as we pointed out previously in our book on the various senses of words;' for in one sense the 'being' meant is 'what a thing is' or a 'this', and in another sense it means a quality or quantity or one of the other things that are predicated as these are. While 'being' has all these senses, obviously that which 'is' primarily is the 'what', which indicates the substance of the thing. For when we say of what quality a thing is, we say that it is good or bad, not that it is three cubits long or that it is a man; but when we say what it is, we do not say 'white' or 'hot' or 'three cubits long', but 'a man' or 'a 'god'. And all other things are said to be because they are, some of them, quantities of that which is in this primary sense, others qualities of it, others affections of it, and others some other determination of it. And so one might even raise the question whether the words 'to walk', 'to be healthy', 'to sit' imply that each of these things

---

[22]ii. 3, 7.

is existent, and similarly in any other case of this sort; for none of them is either self-subsistent or capable of being separated from substance, but rather, if anything, it is that which walks or sits or is healthy that is an existent thing. Now these are seen to be more real because there is something definite which underlies them (i.e. the substance or individual), which is implied in such a predicate; for we never use the word 'good' or 'sitting' without implying this. Clearly then it is in virtue of this category that each of the others also is. Therefore that which is primarily, i.e. not in a qualified sense but without qualification, must be substance.

Now there are several senses in which a thing is said to be first; yet substance is first in every sense—(1) in definition, (2) in order of knowledge, (3) in time. For (3) of the other categories none can exist independently, but only substance. And (1) in definition also this is first; for in the definition of each term the definition of its substance must be present. And (2) we think we know each thing most fully, when we know what it is, e.g. what man is or what fire is, rather than when we know its quality, its quantity, or its place; since we know each of these predicates also, only when we know what the quantity or the quality is.

And indeed the question which was raised of old and is raised now and always, and is always the subject of doubt, viz. what being is, is just the question, what is substance? For it is this that some assert to be one, others more than one, and that some assert to be limited in number, others unlimited. And so we also must consider chiefly and primarily and almost exclusively what that is which is in this sense.

2. Substance is thought to belong most obviously to bodies; and so we say that not only animals and plants and their parts are substances, but also natural bodies such as fire and water and earth and everything of the sort, and all things that are either parts of these or composed of these (either of parts or of the whole bodies), e.g. the physical universe and its parts, stars and moon and sun. But whether these alone are substances, or there are also others, or only some of these, or others as well, or none of these but only some other things, are substances, must be considered. Some think the limits of body, i.e. surface, line, point, and unit, are substances, and more so than body or the solid.

Further, some do not think there is anything substantial besides sensible things, but others think there are eternal substances which are more in number and more real; e.g. Plato posited two kinds of substance-the Forms and objects of mathematics-as well as a third kind, viz. the substance of sensible bodies. And Speusippus made still more kinds of substance, beginning with the One, and assuming principles for each kind of substance, one for numbers, another for spatial magnitudes, and then another for the soul; and by going on in this way he multiplies the kinds of substance. And some say Forms and numbers have the same nature, and the other things come after them— lines and planes—until we come to the substance of the material universe and to sensible bodies.

Regarding these matters, then, we must inquire which of the common statements are right and which are not right, and what substances there are, and whether there are or are not any besides sensible substances, and how sensible substances exist, and whether there is a substance capable of separate existence (and if so why and how) or no such substance, apart from sensible substances; and we must first sketch the nature of substance.

3. The word 'substance' is applied, if not in more senses, still at least to four main objects; for both the essence and the universal and the genus, are thought to be the substance of each thing, and fourthly the substratum. Now the substratum is that of which everything else is predicated, while it is itself not predicated of anything else. And so we must first determine the nature of this; for that which underlies a thing primarily is thought to be in the truest sense its substance. And in one sense matter is said to be of the nature of substratum, in another, shape, and in a third, the compound of these. (By the matter I mean, for instance, the bronze, by the shape the pattern of its form, and by the compound of these the statue, the concrete whole.) Therefore if the form is prior to the matter and more real, it will be prior also to the compound of both, for the same reason.

We have now outlined the nature of substance, showing that it is that which is not predicated of a stratum, but of which all else is predicated. But we must not merely state the matter thus; for this is not enough. The statement itself is obscure, and further, on this view, matter becomes substance. For if this is not substance, it baffles us to say what else is. When all else is stripped off evidently nothing but matter remains. For while the rest are affections, products, and potencies of bodies, length, breadth, and depth are quantities and not substances (for a quantity is not a substance), but the substance is rather that to which these belong primarily. But when length and breadth and depth are taken away we see nothing left unless there is something that is bounded by these; so that to those who consider the question thus matter alone must seem to be substance. By matter I mean that which in itself is neither a particular thing nor of a certain quantity nor assigned to any other of the categories by which being is determined. For there is something of which each of these is predicated, whose being is different from that of each of the predicates (for the predicates other than substance are predicated of substance, while substance is predicated of matter). Therefore the ultimate substratum is of itself neither a particular thing nor of a particular quantity nor otherwise positively characterized; nor yet is it the negations of these, for negations also will belong to it only by accident.

If we adopt this point of view, then, it follows that matter is substance. But this is impossible; for both separability and 'thisness' are thought to belong chiefly to substance. And so form and the compound of form and matter would be thought to be substance, rather than matter. The substance compounded of both, i.e. of matter and shape, may be dismissed; for it is posterior and its nature is obvious. And matter also is in a sense manifest. But we must inquire into the third kind of substance; for this is the most perplexing.

1029ᵇ · Some of the sensible substances are generally admitted to be substances, so that we must look first among these. For it is an advantage to advance to that which is more knowable. For learning proceeds for all in this way-through that which is less knowable by nature to that which is more knowable; and just as in conduct our task is to start from what is good for each and make what is without qualification good good for each, so it is our task to start from what is more knowable to oneself and make what is knowable by nature knowable to oneself. Now what is knowable and primary for particular sets of peo-

ple is often knowable to a very small extent, and has little or nothing of reality. But yet one must start from that which is barely knowable but knowable to oneself, and try to know what is knowable without qualification, passing, as has been said, by way of those very things which one does know.

4. Since at the start we distinguished the various marks by which we determine substance, and one of these was thought to be the essence, we must investigate this. And first let us make some linguistic remarks about it. The essence of each thing is what it is said to be propter se. For being you is not being musical, since you are not by your very nature musical. What, then, you are by your very nature is your essence.

Nor yet is the whole of this the essence of a thing; not that which is propter se as white is to a surface, because being a surface is not identical with being white. But again the combination of both—'being a white surface'—is not the essence of surface, because 'surface' itself is added. The formula, therefore, in which the term itself is not present but its meaning is expressed, this is the formula of the essence of each thing. Therefore if to be a white surface is to be a smooth surface, to be white and to be smooth are one and the same.

But since there are also compounds answering to the other categories (for there is a substratum for each category, e.g. for quality, quantity, time, place, and motion), we must inquire whether there is a formula of the essence of each of them, i.e. whether to these compounds also there belongs an essence, e.g. 'white man'. Let the compound be denoted by 'cloak'. What is the essence of cloak? But, it may be said, this also is not a propter se expression. We reply that there are just two ways in which a predicate may fail to be true of a subject propter se, and one of these results from the addition, and the other from the omission, of a determinant. One kind of predicate is not propter se because the term that is being defined is combined with another determinant, e.g. if in defining the essence of white one were to state the formula of white man; the other because in the subject another determinant is combined with that which is expressed in the formula, e.g. if 'cloak' meant 'white man', and one were to define cloak as white; white man is white indeed, but its essence is not to be white.

But is being-a-cloak an essence at all? Probably not. For the essence is precisely what something is; but when an attribute is asserted of a subject other than itself, the complex is not precisely what some 'this' is, e.g. white man is not precisely what some 'this' is, since thisness belongs only to substances. Therefore there is an essence only of those things whose formula is a definition. But we have a definition not where we have a word and a formula identical in meaning (for in that case all formulae or sets of words would be definitions; for there will be some name for any set of words whatever, so that even the Iliad will be a definition), but where there is a formula of something primary; and primary things are those which do not imply the predication of one element in them of another element. Nothing, then, which is not a species of a genus will have an essence—only species will have it, for these are thought to imply not merely that the subject participates in the attribute and has it as an affection, or has it by accident; but for ever thing else as well, if it has a name, there be a formula of its meaning— viz. that this attribute belongs to this subject; or instead of a simple formula we shall be able to give a more accurate one; but there will be no definition nor essence.

Or has 'definition', like 'what a thing is', several meanings? 'What a thing is' in one sense means substance and the 'this', in another one or other of the predicates, quantity, quality, and the like. For as 'is' belongs to all things, not however in the same sense, but to one sort of thing primarily and to others in a secondary way, so too 'what a thing is' belongs in the simple sense to substance, but in a limited sense to the other categories. For even of a quality we might ask what it is, so that quality also is a 'what a thing is',-not in the simple sense, however, but just as, in the case of that which is not, some say, emphasizing the linguistic form, that that is which is not is-not is simply, but is non-existent; so too with quality.

We must no doubt inquire how we should express ourselves on each point, but certainly not more than how the facts actually stand. And so now also, since it is evident what language we use, essence will belong, just as 'what a thing is' does, primarily and in the simple sense to substance, and in a secondary way to the other categories also,—not essence in the simple sense, but the essence of a quality or of a quantity. For it must be either by an equivocation that we say these are, or by adding to and taking from the meaning of 'are' (in the way in which that which is not known may be said to be known),—the truth being that we use the word neither ambiguously nor in the same sense, but just as we apply the word 'medical' by virtue of a reference to one and the same thing, not meaning one and the same thing, nor yet speaking ambiguously; for a patient and an operation and an instrument are called medical neither by an ambiguity nor with a single meaning, but with reference to a common end. But it does not matter at all in which of the two ways one likes to describe the facts; this is evident, that definition and essence in the primary and simple sense belong to substances. Still they belong to other things as well, only not in the primary sense. For if we suppose this it does not follow that there is a definition of every word which means the same as any formula; it must mean the same as a particular kind of formula; and this condition is satisfied if it is a formula of something which is one, not by continuity like the Iliad or the things that are one by being bound together, but in one of the main senses of 'one', which answer to the senses of 'is'; now 'that which is' in one sense denotes a 'this', in another a quantity, in another a quality. And so there can be a formula or definition even of white man, but not in the sense in which there is a definition either of white or of a substance.

6. We must inquire whether each thing and its essence are the same or different. This is of some use for the inquiry concerning substance; for each thing is thought to be not different from its substance, and the essence is said to be the substance of each thing.

Now in the case of accidental unities the two would be generally thought to be different, e.g. white man would be thought to be different from the essence of white man. For if they are the same, the essence of man and that of white man are also the same; for a man and a white man are the same thing, as people say, so that the essence of white man and that of man would be also the same. But perhaps it does not follow that the essence of accidental unities should be the same as that of the simple terms. For the extreme terms are not in the same way identical with the middle term. But perhaps this might be thought to follow, that the extreme terms, the accidents, should turn out to be the same, e.g. the essence of white and that of musical; but this is not actually thought to be the case.

But in the case of so-called self-subsistent things, is a thing necessarily the same as its essence? E.g. if there are some substances which have no other substances nor entities prior to them—substances such as some assert the Ideas to be?—If the essence of good is to be different from good-itself, and the essence of animal from animal-itself, and the essence of being from being-itself, there will, firstly, be other substances and entities and Ideas besides those which are asserted, and, secondly, these others will be prior substances, if essence is substance. And if the posterior substances and the prior are severed from each other, (a) there will be no knowledge of the former, and (b) the latter will have no being. (By 'severed' I mean, if the good-itself has not the essence of good, and the latter has not the property of being good.) For (a) there is knowledge of each thing only when we know its essence. And (b) the case is the same for other things as for the good; so that if the essence of good is not good, neither is the essence of reality real, nor the essence of unity one. And all essences alike exist or none of them does; so that if the essence of reality is not real, neither is any of the others. Again, that to which the essence of good does not belong is not good.—The good, then, must be one with the essence of good, and the beautiful with the essence of beauty, and so with all things which do not depend on something else but are self-subsistent and primary. For it is enough if they are this, even if they are not Forms; or rather, perhaps, even if they are Forms. (At the same time it is clear that if there are Ideas such as some people say there are, it will not be substratum that is substance; for these must be substances, but not predicable of a substratum; for if they were they would exist only by being participated in.)

Each thing itself, then, and its essence are one and the same in no merely accidental way, as is evident both from the preceding arguments and because to know each thing, at least, is just to know its essence, so that even by the exhibition of instances it becomes clear that both must be one.

(But of an accidental term, e.g. 'the musical' or 'the white', since it has two meanings, it is not true to say that it itself is identical with its essence; for both that to which the accidental quality belongs, and the accidental quality, are white, so that in a sense the accident and its essence are the same, and in a sense they are not; for the essence of white is not the same as the man or the white man, but it is the same as the attribute white.)

The absurdity of the separation would appear also if one were to assign a name to each of the essences; for there would be yet another essence besides the original one, e.g. to the essence of horse there will belong a second essence. Yet why should not some things be their essences from the start, since essence is substance? But indeed not only are a thing and its essence one, but the formula of them is also the same, as is clear even from what has been said; for it is not by accident that the essence of one, and the one, are one. Further, if they are to be different, the process will go on to infinity; for we shall have (1) the essence of one, and (2) the one, so that to terms of the former kind the same argument will be applicable.

Clearly, then, each primary and self-subsistent thing is one and the same as its essence. The sophistical objections to this position, and the question whether Socrates and to be Socrates are the same thing, are obviously answered by the same solution; for there is no difference either in the standpoint from which the question would be asked, or in that from which one could answer it successfully. We have explained, then, in what sense each thing is the same as its essence and in what sense it is not.

13. Let us return to the subject of our inquiry, which is substance. As the substratum and the essence and the compound of these are called substance, so also is the universal. About two of these we have spoken; both about the essence and about the substratum, of which we have said that it underlies in two senses, either being a 'this'—which is the way in which an animal underlies its attributes—or as the matter underlies the complete reality. The universal also is thought by some to be in the fullest sense a cause, and a principle; therefore let us attack the discussion of this point also. For it seems impossible that any universal term should be the name of a substance. For firstly the substance of each thing

is that which is peculiar to it, which does not belong to anything else; but the universal is common, since that is called universal which is such as to belong to more than one thing. Of which individual then will this be the substance? Either of all or of none; but it cannot be the substance of all. And if it is to be the substance of one, this one will be the others also; for things whose substance is one and whose essence is one are themselves also one.

Further, substance means that which is not predicable of a subject, but the universal is predicable of some subject always.

But perhaps the universal, while it cannot be substance in the way in which the essence is so, can be present in this; e.g. 'animal' can be present in 'man' and 'horse'. Then clearly it is a formula of the essence. And it makes no difference even if it is not a formula of everything that is in the substance; for none the less the universal will be the substance of something, as 'man' is the substance of the individual man in whom it is present, so that the same result will follow once more; for the universal, e.g. 'animal', will be the substance of that in which it is present as something peculiar to it. And further it is impossible and absurd that the 'this', i.e. the substance, if it consists of parts, should not consist of substances nor of what is a 'this', but of quality; for that which is not substance, i.e. the quality, will then be prior to substance and to the 'this'. Which is impossible; for neither in formula nor in time nor in coming to be can the modifications be prior to the substance; for then they will also be separable from it. Further, Socrates will contain a substance present in a substance, so that this will be the substance of two things. And in general it follows, if man and such things are substance, that none of the elements in their formulae is the substance of anything, nor does it exist apart from the species or in anything else; I mean, for instance, that no 'animal' exists apart from the particular kinds of animal, nor does any other of the elements present in formulae exist apart.

If, then, we view the matter from these standpoints, it is plain that no universal attribute is a substance, and this is plain also from the fact that no common predicate indicates a 'this', but rather a 'such'. If not, many difficulties follow and especially the 'third man'.

The conclusion is evident also from the following consideration. A substance cannot consist of substances present in it in complete reality; for things that are thus in complete reality two are never in complete reality one, though if they are potentially two, they can be one (e.g. the double line consists of two halves-potentially; for the complete realization of the halves divides them from one another); therefore if the substance is one, it will not consist of substances present in it and present in this way, which Democritus describes rightly; he says one thing cannot be made out of two nor two out of one; for he identifies substances with his indivisible magnitudes. It is clear therefore that the same will hold good of number, if number is a synthesis of units, as is said by some; for two is either not one, or there is no unit present in it in complete reality. But our result involves a difficulty. If no substance can consist of universals because a universal indicates a 'such', not a 'this', and if no substance can be composed of substances existing in complete reality, every substance would be incomposite, so that there would not even be a formula of any substance. But it is thought by all and was stated long ago that it is either only, or primarily, substance that can defined; yet now it seems that not even substance can. There cannot, then, be a definition of anything; or in a sense there can be, and in a sense there cannot. And what we are saying will be plainer from what follows.

14. It is clear also from these very facts what consequence confronts those who say the Ideas are substances capable of separate existence, and at the same 'time make the Form consist of the genus and the differentiae. For if the Forms exist and 'animal' is present in 'man' and 'horse', it is either one and the same in number, or different. (In formula it is clearly one; for he who states the formula will go through the formula in either case.) If then there is a 'man-in-himself' who is a 'this' and exists apart, the parts also of which he consists, e.g. 'animal' and 'two-footed', must indicate 'thises', and be capable of separate existence, and substances; therefore 'animal', as well as 'man', must be of this sort.

Now (1) if the 'animal' in 'the horse' and in 'man' is one and the same, as you are with yourself, (a) how will the one in things that exist apart be one, and how will this 'animal' escape being divided even from itself?

Further, (b) if it is to share in 'two-footed' and 'many-footed', an impossible conclusion follows; for contrary attributes will belong at the same time to it although it is one and a 'this'. If it is not to share in them, what is the relation implied when one says the animal is two-footed or possessed of feet? But perhaps the two things are 'put together' and are 'in contact', or are 'mixed'. Yet all these expressions are absurd.

But (2) suppose the Form to be different in each species. Then there will be practically an infinite number of things whose substance is animal'; for it is not by accident that 'man' has 'animal' for one of its elements. Further, many things will be 'animal-itself'. For (i) the 'animal' in each species will be the substance of the species; for it is after nothing else that the species is called; if it were, that other would be an element in 'man', i.e. would be the genus of man. And further, (ii) all the elements of which 'man' is composed will be Ideas. None of them, then, will be the Idea of one thing and the substance of another; this is impossible. The 'animal', then, present in each species of animals will be animal-itself. Further, from what is this 'animal' in each species derived, and how will it be derived from animal-itself? Or how can this 'animal', whose essence is simply animality, exist apart from animal-itself?

Further, (3) in the case of sensible things both these consequences and others still more absurd follow. If, then, these consequences are impossible, clearly there are not Forms of sensible things in the sense in which some maintain their existence.

BOOK XII

1. The subject of our inquiry is substance; for the principles and the causes we are seeking are those of substances. For if the universe is of the nature of a whole, substance is its first part; and if it coheres merely by virtue of serial succession, on this view also substance is first, and is succeeded by quality, and then by quantity. At the same time these latter are not even being in the full sense, but are qualities and movements of it—or else even the not-white and the not-straight would be being; at least we say even

these *are*, e.g. 'there is a not-white'.[23] Further, none of the categories other than substance can exist apart. And the early philosophers also in practice testify to the primacy of substance; for it was of substance that they sought the principles and elements and causes. The thinkers of the present[24] day tend to rank universals as substances (for genera are universals, and these they tend to describe as principles and substances, owing to the abstract nature of their inquiry); but the thinkers of old ranked particular things as substances, e.g. fire and earth, not what is common to both, body.

There are three kinds of substance—one that is sensible (of which one subdivision is eternal and another is perishable; the latter is recognized by all men, and includes e.g. plants and animals), of which we must grasp the elements, whether one or many; and another that is immovable, and this certain thinkers assert to be capable of existing apart, some dividing it into two, others identifying the Forms and the objects of mathematics, and others positing, of these two, only the objects of mathematics.[25] The former two kinds of substance are the subject of physics (for they imply movement); but the third kind belongs to another science, if there is no principle common to it and to the other kinds.

2. Sensible substance is changeable. Now if change proceeds from opposites or from intermediates, and not from all opposites (for the voice is not-white [but it does not therefore change to white]), but from the contrary, there must be something underlying which changes into the contrary state; for the *contraries* do not change. Further, something persists, but the contrary does not persist; there is, then, some third thing besides the contraries, viz. the matter. Now since changes are of four kinds—either in respect of the 'what' or of the quality or of the quantity or of the place, and change in respect of 'this-ness' is simple generation and destruction, and change in quantity is increase and diminution, and change in respect of an affection is alteration, and

---

[23]This is an implication of the ordinary type of judgement, '*x* is not white'.

[24]The Platonists.

[25]The three views appear to have been held respectively by Plato, Xenocrates, and Speusippus.

change of place is motion, changes will be from given states into those contrary to them in these several respects. The matter, then, which changes must be capable of both states. And since that which 'is' has two senses, we must say that everything changes from that which is potentially to that which is actually, e.g. from potentially white to actually white, and similarly in the case of increase and diminution. Therefore not only can a thing come to be, incidentally, out of that which is not, but also all things come to be out of that which is, but is potentially, and is not actually. And this is the 'One' of Anaxagoras; for instead of 'all things were together'—and the 'Mixture' of Empedocles and Anaximander and the account given by Democritus—it is better to say 'all things were together potentially but not actually'. Therefore these thinkers seem to have had some notion of matter. Now all things that change have matter, but different matter; and of eternal things those which are not generable but are movable in space have matter—not matter for generation, however, but for motion from one place to another.

One might raise the question from what sort of non-being generation proceeds; for 'non-being' has three senses. If, then, one form of nonbeing exists potentially, still it is not by virtue of a potentiality for any and every thing, but different things come from different things; nor is it satisfactory to say that 'all things were together'; for they differ in their matter, since otherwise why did an infinity of things come to be, and not one thing? For 'reason' is one, so that if matter also were one, that must have come to be in actuality which the matter was in potency.[26] The causes and the principles, then, are three, two being the pair of contraries of which one is definition and form and the other is privation, and the third being the matter.

3. Note, next, that neither the matter nor the form comes to be—and I mean the last matter and form. For everything that changes is something and is changed by something and into something. That by which it is changed is the immediate mover; that which is changed, the matter; that into which it is changed, the form. The process, then, will go on to

infinity, if not only the bronze comes to be round but also the round or the bronze comes to be; therefore there must be a stop.

Note, next, that each substance comes into being out of something that shares its name. (Natural objects and other things both rank as substances.) For things come into being either by art or by nature or by luck or by spontaneity. Now art is a principle of movement in something other than the thing moved, nature is a principle in the thing itself (for man begets man), and the other causes are privations of these two.

There are three kinds of substance—the matter, which is a 'this' in appearance (for all things that are characterized by contact and not by organic unity are matter and substratum, e.g. fire, flesh, head; for these are all matter, and the last matter is the matter of that which is in the full sense substance); the nature, which is a 'this' or positive state towards which movement takes place; and again, thirdly, the particular substance which is composed of these two, e.g. Socrates or Callias. Now in some cases the 'this' does not exist apart from the composite substance, e.g. the form of house does not so exist, unless the art of building exists apart (nor is there generation and destruction of these forms, but it is in another way that the house apart from its matter, and health, and all ideals of art, exist and do not exist); but if the 'this' exists apart from the concrete thing, it is only in the case of natural objects. And so Plato was not far wrong when he said that there are as many Forms as there are kinds of natural object (if there *are* Forms distinct from the things of this earth). The moving causes exist as things preceding the effects, but causes in the sense of definitions are simultaneous with their effects. For when a man is healthy, then health also exists; and the shape of a bronze sphere exists at the same time as the bronze sphere. (But we must examine whether any form also survives afterwards. For in some cases there is nothing to prevent this; e.g. the soul may be of this sort—not all soul but the reason; for presumably it is impossible that *all* soul should survive.) Evidently then there is no necessity, on this ground at least, for the existence of the Ideas. For man is begotten by man, a given man by an individual father; and similarly in the arts; for the medical art is the formal cause of health.

---

[26]*sc.* an undifferentiated unity.

4. The causes and the principles of different things are in a sense different, but in a sense, if one speaks universally and analogically, they are the same for all. For one might raise the question whether the principles and elements are different or the same for substances and for relative terms, and similarly in the case of each of the categories. But it would be paradoxical if they were the same for all. For then from the same elements will proceed relative terms and substances. What then will this common element be? For (1) (a) there is nothing common to and distinct from substance and the other categories, viz. those which are predicated; but an element is prior to the things of which it is an element. But again (b) substance is not an element in relative terms, nor is any of these an element in substance. Further, (2) how can all things have the same elements? For none of the elements can be the same as that which is composed of elements, e.g. b or a cannot be the same as ba. (None, therefore, of the intelligibles, e.g. being or unity, is an element; for these are predicable of each of the compounds as well.) None of the elements, then, will be either a substance or a relative term; but it must be one or other. All things, then, have not the same elements.

Or, as we are wont to put it, in a sense they have and in a sense they have not; e.g. perhaps the elements of perceptible bodies are, as *form*, the hot, and in another sense the cold, which is the *privation*; and, as *matter*, that which directly and of itself potentially has these attributes; and substances comprise both these and the things composed of these, of which these are the principles, or any unity which is produced out of the hot and the cold, e.g. flesh or bone; for the product must be different from the elements. These things then have the same elements and principles (though specifically different things have specifically different elements); but *all* things have not the same elements in this sense, but only analogically; i.e. one might say that there are three principles—the firm, the privation, and the matter. But each of these is different for each class; e.g. in colour they are white, black, and surface, and in day and night they are light, darkness, and air.

Since not only the elements present in a thing are causes, but also something external, i.e. the moving cause, clearly while 'principle' and 'element' are different both are causes, and 'principle' is divided into these two kinds[27] and that which acts as producing movement or rest is a principle and a substance. Therefore analogically there are three elements, and four causes and principles; but the elements are different in different things, and the proximate moving cause is different for different things. Health, disease, body; the moving cause is the medical art. Form, disorder of a particular kind, bricks; the moving cause is the building art. And since the moving cause in the case of natural things is—for man, for instance, man, and in the products of thought the form or its contrary, there will be in a sense three causes, while in a sense there are four. For the medical art is in some sense health, and the building art is the form of the house, and man begets man;[28] further, besides these there is that which as first of all things moves all things.

5. Some things can exist apart and some cannot, and it is the former that are substances. And therefore all things have the same causes,[29] because, without substances, modifications and movements do not exist. Further, these causes will probably be soul and body, or reason and desire and body.

And in yet another way, analogically identical things are principles, i.e. actuality and potency; but these also are not only different for different things but also apply in different ways to them. For in some cases the same thing exists at one time actually and at another potentially, e.g. wine or flesh or man does so. (And these two fall under the above-named causes.[30] For the form exists actually, if it can exist apart, and so does the complex of form and matter, and the privation, e.g. darkness or disease; but the matter exists potentially; for this is that which can become qualified either by the form or by the privation.) But the distinction of actuality and potentiality applies in another way to cases where the matter of cause and of effect is not the same, in some

---

[27] i.e. the principles which are elements and those which are not.

[28] i.e. the efficient cause is identical with the formal.

[29] i.e. the causes of substance are the causes of all things.

[30] i.e. the division into potency and actuality stands in a definite relation to the previous division into matter, form, and privation.

of which cases the form is not the same but different; e.g. the cause of man is (1) the elements in man (viz. fire and earth as matter, and the peculiar form), and further (2) something else outside, i.e. the father, and (3) besides these the sun and its oblique course, which are neither matter nor form nor privation of man nor of the same species with him, but moving causes.

Further, one must observe that some causes can be expressed in universal terms, and some cannot. The proximate principles of all things are the 'this' which is proximate in actuality, and another which is proximate in potentiality.[31] The universal causes, then, of which we spoke[32] do not *exist*. For it is the individual that is the originative principle of the individuals. For while man is the originative principle of man universally, there *is* no universal man, but Peleus is the originative principle of Achilles, and your father of you, and this particular *b* of this particular *ba*, though *b* in general is the originative principle of *ba* taken without qualification.

Further, if the causes of substances are the causes of all things, yet different things have different causes and elements, as was said[33]; the causes of things that are not in the same class, e.g. of colours and sounds, of substances and quantities, are different except in an analogical sense; and those of things in the same species are different, not in species, but in the sense that the causes of different individuals are different, your matter and form and moving cause being different from mine, while in their universal definition they are the same. And if we inquire what are the principles or elements of substances and relations and qualities—whether they are the same or different—clearly when the names of the causes are used in several senses the causes of each are the same, but when the senses are distinguished the causes are not the same but different, except that in the following senses the causes of all are the same. They are (1) the same or analogous in this sense, that matter, form, privation, and the moving cause are common to all things; and (2) the causes of substances may be treated as causes of all things in this sense, that when substances are removed all things are removed; further, (3) that which is first in respect of complete reality is the cause of all things. But in another sense there are different first causes, viz. all the contraries which are neither generic nor ambiguous terms; and, further, the matters of different things are different. We have stated, then, what are the principles of sensible things and how many they are, and in what sense they are the same and in what sense different.

6. Since there were[34] three kinds of substance, two of them physical and one unmovable, regarding the latter we must assert that it is necessary that there should be an eternal unmovable substance. For substances are the first of existing things, and if they are all destructible, all things are destructible. But it is impossible that movement should either have come into being or cease to be (for it must always have existed), or that time should. For there could not be a before and an after if time did not exist. Movement also is continuous, then, in the sense in which time is; for time is either the same thing as movement or an attribute of movement. And there is no continuous movement except movement in place, and of this only that which is circular is continuous.

But if there is something which is capable of moving things or acting on them, but is not actually doing so, there will not necessarily be movement; for that which has a potency need not exercise it. Nothing, then, is gained even if we suppose eternal substances, as the believers in the Forms do, unless there is to be in them some principle which can cause change; nay, even this is not enough, nor is another substance besides the Forms enough; for if it is not to *act*, there will be no movement. Further, even if it acts, this will not be enough, if its essence is potency; for there will not be *eternal* movement, since that which is potentially may possibly not be. There must, then, be such a principle, whose very essence is actuality. Further, then, these substances must be without matter; for they must be eternal, if *anything* is eternal. Therefore they must be actuality.

---

[31]e.g. the proximate causes of a child are the individual father (who on Aristotle's view is the efficient and contains the formal cause) and the germ contained in the individual mother (which is the material cause).
[32]In 1. 17.
[33]In 1070[b] 17.

---

[34]Cf. 1069[a] 30.

Yet there is a difficulty; for it is thought that everything that acts is able to act, but that not everything that is able to act acts, so that the potency is prior. But if this is so, nothing that is need be; for it is possible for all things to be capable of existing but not yet to exist.

Yet if we follow the theologians who generate the world from night, or the natural philosophers who say that 'all things were together',[35] the same impossible result ensues. For how will there be movement, if there is no actually existing cause? Wood will surely not move itself—the carpenter's art must act on it; nor will the menstrual blood nor the earth set themselves in motion, but the seeds must act on the earth and the *semen* on the menstrual blood.

This is why some suppose eternal actuality—e.g. Leucippus[36] and Plato[37]; for they say there is always movement. But why and what this movement is they do not say, nor, if the world moves in this way or that, do they tell us the cause of its doing so. Now nothing is moved at random, but there must always be something present to move it; e.g. as a matter of fact a thing moves in one way by nature, and in another by force or through the influence of reason or something else. (Further, what sort of movement is primary? This makes a vast difference.) But again for Plato, at least, it is not permissible to name here that which he sometimes supposes to be the source of movement—that which moves itself;[38] for the soul is later, and coeval with the heavens, according to his account.[39] To suppose potency prior to actuality, then, is in a sense right, and in a sense not; and we have specified these senses.[40] That actuality is prior is testified by Anaxagoras (for his 'reason' is actuality) and by Empedocles in his doctrine of love and strife, and by those who say that there is always movement, e.g. Leucippus. Therefore chaos or night did not exist for an infinite time, but the same things have always existed (either passing through a cycle of changes or obeying some other law), since actuality is prior to potency. If, then, there is a constant cycle, something must always remain,[41] acting in the same way. And if there is to be generation and destruction, there must be something else[42] which is always acting in different ways. This must, then, act in one way in virtue of itself, and in another in virtue of something else—either of a third agent, therefore, or of the first. Now it must be in virtue of the first. For otherwise this again causes the motion both of the second agent and of the third. Therefore it is better to say 'the first'. For it was the cause of eternal uniformity; and something else is the cause of variety, and evidently both together are the cause of eternal variety. This, accordingly, is the character which the motions actually exhibit. What need then is there to seek for other principles?

7. Since (1) this is a possible account of the matter, and (2) if it were not true, the world would have proceeded out of night and 'all things together' and out of non-being, these difficulties may be taken as solved. There is, then, something which is always moved with an unceasing motion, which is motion in a circle; and this is plain not in theory only but in fact. Therefore the first heaven[43] must be eternal. There is therefore also something which moves it. And since that which is moved and moves is intermediate, there is something which moves without being moved, being eternal, substance, and actuality. And the object of desire and the object of thought move in this way; they move without being moved. The primary objects of desire and of thought are the same. For the apparent good is the object of appetite, and the real good is the primary object of rational wish. But desire is consequent on opinion rather than opinion on desire; for the thinking is the starting-point. And thought is moved by the object of thought, and one of the two columns of opposites is in itself the object of thought; and in this, substance is first, and in substance, that which is simple and exists actually. (The one and the simple are not the same; for 'one' means a measure, but 'simple' means that the thing itself has a certain nature.) But the beautiful, also, and that which is in itself desirable are in the

---

[35] Anaxagoras.
[36] Cf. *De Caelo*, iii. 300^b 8.
[37] Cf. *Timaeus*, 30 A.
[38] Cf. *Phaedrus*, 245 c; *Laws*, 894 E.
[39] Cf. *Timaeus*, 34 B.
[40] Cf. 1071^b 22–26.

[41] i.e. the sphere of the fixed stars.
[42] i.e. the sun. Cf. *De Gen. et Corr*. ii. 336^a 23 ff.
[43] i.e. the outer sphere of the universe, that in which the fixed stars are set.

same column; and the first in any class is always best, or analogous to the best.

That a final cause may exist among unchangeable entities is shown by the distinction of its meanings. For the final cause is (*a*) some being for whose good an action is done, and (*b*) something at which the action aims; and of these the latter exists among unchangeable entities though the former does not. The final cause, then, produces motion as being loved, but all other things move by being moved.

Now if something is moved it is capable of being otherwise than as it is. Therefore if its actuality is the primary form of spatial motion, then in so far as it is subject to change, in *this* respect it is capable of being otherwise—in place, even if not in substance. But since there is something which moves while itself unmoved, existing actually, this can in no way be otherwise than as it is. For motion in space is the first of the kinds of change, and motion in a circle the first kind of spatial motion; and this the first mover *produces*.[44] The first mover, then, exists of necessity; and in so far as it exists by necessity, its mode of being is good, and it is in this sense a first principle. For the necessary has all these senses—that which is necessary perforce because it is contrary to the natural impulse, that without which the good is impossible, and that which cannot be otherwise but can exist only in a single way.

On such a principle, then, depend the heavens and the world of nature. And it is a life such as the best which we enjoy, and enjoy for but a short time (for it is ever in this state, which we cannot be), since its actuality is also pleasure. (And for this reason[45] are waking, perception, and thinking most pleasant, and hopes and memories are so on account of these.) And thinking in itself deals with that which is best in itself, and that which is thinking in the fullest sense with that which is best in the fullest sense. And thought thinks on itself because it shares the nature of the object of thought; for it becomes an object of thought in coming into contact with and thinking its

objects, so that thought and object of thought are the same. For that which is *capable* of receiving the object of thought, i.e. the essence, is thought. But it is *active* when it *possesses* this object. Therefore the possession rather than the receptivity is the divine element which thought seems to contain, and the act of contemplation is what is most pleasant and best. If, then, God is always in that good state in which we sometimes are, this compels our wonder; and if in a better this compels it yet more. And God *is* in a better state. And life also belongs to God; for the actuality of thought is life, and God is that actuality; and God's self-dependent actuality is life most good and eternal. We say therefore that God is a living being, eternal, most good, so that life and duration continuous and eternal belong to God; for this *is* God.

Those who suppose, as the Pythagoreans and Speusippus do, that supreme beauty and goodness are not present in the beginning, because the beginnings both of plants and of animals are *causes*, but beauty and completeness are in the *effects* of these, are wrong in their opinion. For the seed comes from other individuals which are prior and complete, and the first thing is not seed but the complete being; e.g. we must say that before the seed there is a man—not the man produced from the seed, but another from whom the seed comes.

It is clear then from what has been said that there is a substance which is eternal and unmovable and separate from sensible things. It has been shown also that this substance cannot have any magnitude, but is without parts and indivisible (for it produces movement through infinite time, but nothing finite has infinite power; and, while every magnitude is either infinite or finite, it cannot, for the above reason, have finite magnitude, and it cannot have infinite magnitude because there is no infinite magnitude at all). But it has also been shown that it is impassive and unalterable; for all the other changes are posterior to change of place.

8. It is clear, then, why these things are as they are. But we must not ignore the question whether we have to suppose one such substance or more than one, and if the latter, how many; we must also mention, regarding the opinions expressed by others, that they have said nothing about the number of the substances that can even be clearly stated. For the theory of Ideas

---

[44]If it had any movement, it would have the first. But it produces this and therefore cannot share in it; for if it did, we should have to look for something that is prior to the first mover and imparts this motion to it.

[45]*sc.* because they are activities or actualities.

has no special discussion of the subject; for those who speak of Ideas say the Ideas are numbers, and they speak of numbers now as unlimited, now as limited by the number 10; but as for the reason why there should be just so many numbers, nothing is said with any demonstrative exactness. We however must discuss the subject, starting from the presuppositions and distinctions we have mentioned. The first principle or primary being is not movable either in itself or accidentally, but produces the primary eternal and single movement. But since that which is moved must be moved by something, and the first mover must be in itself unmovable, and eternal movement must be produced by something eternal and a single movement by a single thing, and since we see that besides the simple spatial movement of the universe, which we say the first and unmovable substance produces, there are other spatial movements—those of the planets—which are eternal (for a body which moves in a circle is eternal and unresting; we have proved these points in the physical treatises), each of *these* movements also must be caused by a substance both unmovable in itself and eternal. For the nature of the stars[46] is eternal just because it is a certain kind of substance, and the mover is eternal and prior to the moved, and that which is prior to a substance must be a substance. Evidently, then, there must be substances which are of the same number as the movements of the stars, and in their nature eternal, and in themselves unmovable, and without magnitude, for the reason before mentioned.[47]

That the movers are substances, then, and that one of these is first and another second according to the same order as the movements of the stars, is evident. But in the number of the movements we reach a problem which must be treated from the standpoint of that one of the mathematical sciences which is most akin to philosophy—viz. of astronomy; for this science speculates about substance which is perceptible but eternal, but the other mathematical sciences, i.e. arithmetic and geometry, treat of no substance. That the movements are more numerous than the bodies that are moved is evident to those who have given even moderate atten-

tion to the matter; for each of the planets has more than one movement. But as to the actual number of these movements, we now—to give some notion of the subject—quote what some of the mathematicians say, that our thought may have some definite number to grasp; but, for the rest, we must partly investigate for ourselves, partly learn from other investigators, and if those who study this subject form an opinion contrary to what we have now stated, we must esteem both parties indeed, but follow the more accurate.

Eudoxus supposed that the motion of the sun or of the moon involves, in either case, three spheres, of which the first is the sphere of the fixed stars, and the second moves in the circle which runs along the middle of the zodiac, and the third in the circle which is inclined across the breadth of the zodiac; but the circle in which the moon moves is inclined at a greater angle than that in which the sun moves. And the motion of the planets involves, in each case, four spheres, and of these also the first and second are the same as the first two mentioned above (for the sphere of the fixed stars is that which moves all the other spheres, and that which is placed beneath this and has its movement in the circle which bisects the zodiac is common to all), but the *poles* of the third sphere of each planet are in the circle which bisects the zodiac, and the motion of the fourth sphere is in the circle which is inclined at an angle to the equator of the third sphere; and the poles of the third sphere are different for each of the other planets, but those of Venus and Mercury are the same.

Callippus made the position of the spheres the same as Eudoxus did, but while he assigned the same number as Eudoxus did to Jupiter and to Saturn, he thought two more spheres should be added to the sun and two to the moon, if one is to explain the observed facts; and one more to each of the other planets.

But it is necessary, if all the spheres combined are to explain the observed facts, that for each of the planets there should be other spheres (one fewer than those hitherto assigned) which counteract those already mentioned and bring back to the same position the outermost sphere of the star which in each case is situated below[48] the star in question; for only

---

[46]This is to be understood as a general term including both fixed stars and planets.
[47]Cf. ll. 5–11.

[48]i.e. inwards from, the universe being thought of as a system of concentric spheres encircling the earth.

thus can all the forces at work produce the observed motion of the planets. Since, then, the spheres involved in the movement of the planets themselves are—eight for Saturn and Jupiter and twenty-five for the others, and of these only those involved in the movement of the lowest-situated planet need not be counteracted, the spheres which counteract those of the outermost two planets will be six in number, and the spheres which counteract those of the next four planets will be sixteen; therefore the number of all the spheres—both those which move the planets and those which counteract these—will be fifty-five. And if one were not to add to the moon and to the sun the movements we mentioned, the whole set of spheres will be forty-seven in number.

Let this, then, be taken as the number of the spheres, so that the unmovable substances and principles also may probably be taken as just so many; the assertion of *necessity* must be left to more powerful thinkers. But if there can be no spatial movement which does not conduce to the moving of a star, and if further every being and every substance which is immune from change and in virtue of itself has attained to the best must be considered an end, there can be no other being apart from these we have named, but this must be the number of the substances. For if there are others, they will cause change as being a final cause of movement; but there cannot *be* other movements besides those mentioned. And it is reasonable to infer this from a consideration of the bodies that are moved; for if everything that moves is for the sake of that which is moved, and every movement belongs to something that is moved, no movement can be for the sake of itself or of another movement, but all the movements must be for the sake of the stars. For if there is to be a movement for the sake of a movement, this latter also will have to for the sake of something else; so that since there cannot be an infinite regress, the end of every movement will be one of the divine bodies which move through the heaven.

(Evidently there is but one heaven. For if there are many heavens as there are many men, the moving principles, of which each heaven will have one, will be one in form but in *number* many. But all things that are many in number have matter; for one and the same definition, e.g. that of man, applies to

many things, while Socrates is one. But the primary essence has not matter; for it is complete reality. So the unmovable first mover is one both in definition and in number; so too, therefore, is that which is moved always and continuously; therefore there is one heaven alone.)

Our forefathers in the most remote ages have handed down to their posterity a tradition, in the form of a myth, that these bodies are gods and that the divine encloses the whole of nature. The rest of the tradition has been added later in mythical form with a view to the persuasion of the multitude and to its legal and utilitarian expediency; they say these gods are in the form of men or like some of the other animals, and they say other things consequent on and similar to these which we have mentioned. But if one were to separate the first point from these additions and take it alone—that they thought the first substances to be gods, one must regard this as an inspired utterance, and reflect that, while probably each art and each science has often been developed as far as possible and has again perished, these opinions, with others, have been preserved until the present like relics of the ancient treasure. Only thus far, then, is the opinion of our ancestors and of our earliest predecessors clear to us.

9. The nature of the divine thought involves certain problems; for while thought is held to be the most divine of things observed by us, the question how it must be situated in order to have that character involves difficulties. For if it thinks of nothing, what is there here of dignity? It is just like one who sleeps. And if it thinks, but this depends on something else, then (since that which is its substance is not the act of thinking, but a potency) it cannot be the best substance; for it is through thinking that its value belongs to it. Further, whether its substance is the faculty of thought or the act of thinking, what does it think of? Either of itself or of something else; and if of something else, either of the same thing always or of something different. Does it matter, then, or not, whether it thinks of the good or of any chance thing? Are there not some things about which it is incredible that it should think? Evidently, then, it thinks of that which is most divine and precious, and it does not change; for change would be change for the worse, and this would be already a movement.

1074ᵇ

First, then, if 'thought' is not the act of thinking but a potency, it would be reasonable to suppose that the continuity of its thinking is wearisome to it. Secondly, there would evidently be something else more precious than thought, viz. that which is thought of. For both thinking and the act of thought will belong even to one who thinks of the worst thing in the world, so that if this ought to be avoided (and it ought, for there are even some things which it is better not to see than to see), the act of thinking cannot be the best of things. Therefore it must be of itself that the divine thought thinks (since it is the most excellent of things), and its thinking is a thinking on thinking.

But evidently knowledge and perception and opinion and understanding have always something else as their object, and themselves only by the way. Further, if thinking and being thought of are different, in respect of which does goodness belong to thought? For to *be* an act of thinking and to *be* an object of thought are not the same thing. We answer that in some cases the knowledge is the object. In the productive sciences it is the substance or essence of the object, matter omitted, and in the theoretical sciences the definition or the act of thinking is the object. Since, then, thought and the object of thought are not different in the case of things that have not matter, the divine thought and its object will be the same, i.e. the thinking will be one with the object of its thought.

A further question is left—whether the object of the divine thought is composite; for if it were, thought would change in passing from part to part of the whole. We answer that everything which has not matter is indivisible—as human thought, or rather the thought of composite beings, is in a certain period of time (for it does not possess the good at this moment or at that, but its best, being something *different* from it, is attained only in a whole period of time), so throughout eternity is the thought which has *itself* for its object.

10. We must consider also in which of two ways the nature of the universe contains the good and the highest good, whether as something separate and by itself, or as the order of the parts. Probably in both ways, as an army does; for its good is found both in its order and in its leader, and more in the latter; for he does not depend on the order but it depends on him. And all things are ordered together somehow, but not all alike—both fishes and fowls and plants; and the world is not such that one thing has nothing to do with another, but they are connected. For all are ordered together to one end, but it is as in a house, where the freemen are least at liberty to act at random, but all things or most things are already ordained for them, while the slaves and the animals do little for the common good, and for the most part live at random; for this is the sort of principle that constitutes the nature of each. I mean, for instance, that all must at least come to be dissolved into their elements,[49] and there are other functions similarly in which all share for the good of the whole.

We must not fail to observe how many impossible or paradoxical results confront those who hold different views from our own, and what are the views of the subtler thinkers, and which views are attended by fewest difficulties. All make all things out of contraries. But neither 'all things' nor 'out of contraries' is right; nor do these thinkers tell us how all the things in which the contraries are present can be made out of the contraries; for contraries are not affected by one another. Now for us this difficulty is solved naturally by the fact that there is a third element.[50] These thinkers however make one of the two contraries matter; this is done for instance by those who make the unequal matter for the equal, or the many matter for the one. But this also is refuted in the same way; for the one matter which underlies any pair of contraries is contrary to nothing. Further, all things, except the one, will, on the view we are criticizing, partake of evil; for the bad itself is one of the two elements. But the other school does not treat the good and the bad even as principles; yet in all things the good is in the highest degree a principle. The school we first mentioned is right in saying that is a principle, but *how* the good is a principle they do not say—whether as end or as mover or as form.

---

[49] *sc.* in order that higher forms of being may be produced by new combinations of the elements.

[50] i.e. the substratum.

1075ᵇ   Empedocles also has a paradoxical view; for he identifies the good with love, but this is a principle both as mover (for it brings things together) and as matter (for it is part of the mixture). Now even if it happens that the same thing is a principle both as matter and as mover, still the being, at least, of the two is not the same. In which respect then is love a principle? It is paradoxical also that strife should be imperishable; the nature of his 'evil' is just strife.

Anaxagoras makes the good a motive principle; for his 'reason' moves things. But it moves them for an end, which must be something other than it, except according to *our* way of stating the case; for, on our view, the medical art is in a sense health. It is paradoxical also not to suppose a contrary to the good, i.e. to reason. But all who speak of the contraries make no use of the contraries, unless we bring their views into shape. And why some things are perishable and others imperishable, no one tells us; for they make all existing things out of the same principles. Further, some make existing things out of the non-existent; and others to avoid the necessity of this make all things one.

Further, why should there always be becoming, and what is the cause of becoming?—this no one tells us. And those who suppose two principles must suppose another, a superior principle, and so must those who believe in the Forms; for why did things come to participate, or why do they participate, in the Forms? And all other thinkers[51] are confronted by the necessary consequence that there is something contrary to Wisdom, i.e. to the highest knowledge; but *we* are not. For there is nothing contrary to that which is primary; for all contraries have matter, and

things that have matter exist only potentially; and the ignorance which is contrary to any knowledge leads to an object contrary to the object of the knowledge; but what is primary has no contrary.

Again, if besides sensible things no others exist, there will be no first principle, no order, no becoming, no heavenly bodies, but each principle will have a principle before it, as in the accounts of the theologians and all the natural philosophers. But if the Forms or the numbers are to exist, they will be causes of nothing; or if not that, at least not of movement. Further, how is extension, i.e. a *continuum*, to be produced out of unextended parts? For number will not, either as mover or as form, produce a *continuum*. But again there cannot be any *contrary* that is also essentially a productive or moving principle; or it would be possible not to be.[52] Or at least its action would be posterior to its potency. The world, then, would not be eternal. But it is; one of these premisses, then, must be denied. And we have said how this must be done. Further, in virtue of what the numbers, or the soul and the body, or in general the form and the thing, are one—of this no one tells us anything; nor can any one tell, unless he says, as we do, that the mover makes them one. And those who say mathematical number is first and go on to generate one kind of substance after another and give different principles for each, make the substance of the universe a mere series of episodes (for one substance has no influence on another by its existence or non-existence), and they give us many governing principles; but the world refuses to be governed badly.

'The rule of many is not good; one ruler let there be.'

---

[51]The special reference is to Plato; Cf. *Rep.* 477.

[52]Since contraries must contain matter, and matter implies potentiality and contingency.

NICOMACHEAN ETHICS

BOOK I

1094ª1   1. Every art and every inquiry, and similarly every action and choice, is thought to aim at some good; and for this reason the good has rightly been declared to be that at which all things aim. But a certain difference is found among ends; some are activities, others are products apart from the activities that produce them. Where there are ends apart from the actions, it is the nature of the products to be better than the activities. Now, as there are many actions, arts, and sciences, their ends also are many; the end of the medical art is health, that of shipbuilding a vessel, that of strategy victory, that of economics wealth. But where such arts fall under a single capacity—as bridle-making and the other arts concerned with the equipment of horses fall under the art of riding, and this and every military action under strategy, in the same way other arts fall under yet others—in all of these the ends of the master arts are to be preferred to all the subordinate ends; for it is for the sake of the former that the latter are pursued. It makes no difference whether the activities themselves are the ends of the actions, or something else apart from the activities, as in the case of the sciences just mentioned.

2. If, then, there is some end of the things we do, which we desire for its own sake (everything else being desired for the sake of this), and if we do not choose everything for the sake of something else (for at that rate the process would go on to infinity, so that our desire would be empty and vain), clearly this must be the good and the chief good. Will not the knowledge of it, then, have a great influence on life? Shall we not, like archers who have a mark to aim at, be more likely to hit upon what we should? If so, we must try, in outline at least, to determine what it is, and of which of the sciences or capacities it is the object. It would seem to belong to the most authoritative art and that which is most truly the master art. And politics appears to be of this nature; for it is this that ordains which of the sciences should be studied

1094ᵇ

in a state, and which each class of citizens should learn and up to what point they should learn them; and we see even the most highly esteemed of capacities to fall under this, e.g. strategy, economics, rhetoric; now, since politics uses the rest of the sciences, and since, again, it legislates as to what we are to do and what we are to abstain from, the end of this science must include those of the others, so that this end must be the good for man. For even if the end is the same for a single man and for a state, that of the state seems at all events something greater and more complete both to attain and to preserve; for though it is worth while to attain the end merely for one man, it is finer and more godlike to attain it for a nation or for city-states. These, then, are the ends at which our inquiry, being concerned with politics, aims.

3. Our discussion will be adequate if it has as much clearness as the subject-matter admits of; for precision is not to be sought for alike in all discussions, any more than in all the products of the crafts. Now fine and just actions, which political science investigates, exhibit much variety and fluctuation, so that they may be thought to exist only by convention, and not by nature. And goods also exhibit a similar fluctuation because they bring harm to many people; for before now men have been undone by reason of their wealth, and others by reason of their courage. We must be content, then, in speaking of such subjects and with such premises to indicate the truth roughly and in outline, and in speaking about things which are only for the most part true and with premises of the same kind to reach conclusions that are no better. In the same spirit, therefore, should each of our statements be *received*; for it is the mark of an educated man to look for precision in each class of things just so far as the nature of the subject admits: it is evidently equally foolish to accept probable reasoning from a mathematician and to demand from a rhetorician demonstrative proofs.

Now each man judges well the things he knows, and of these he is a good judge. And so the man who

Reprinted from Aristotle's *Nicomachean Ethics*, translated by W. D. Ross by permission of Oxford University Press.

has been educated in a subject is a good judge of that subject, and the man who has received an all-round education is a good judge in general. Hence a young man is not a proper hearer of lectures on political science; for he is inexperienced in the actions that occur in life, but its discussions start from these and are about these; and, further, since he tends to follow his passions, his study will be vain and unprofitable, because the end aimed at is not knowledge but action. And it makes no difference whether he is young in years or youthful in character; the defect does not depend on time, but on his living and pursuing each successive object as passion directs. For to such persons, as to the incontinent, knowledge brings no profit; but to those who desire and act in accordance with a rational principle knowledge about such matters will be of great benefit.

These remarks about the student, the way in which our statements should be received, and the purpose of the inquiry, may be taken as our preface.

4. Let us resume our inquiry and state, in view of the fact that all knowledge and choice aims at some good, what it is that we say political science aims at and what is the highest of all goods achievable by action. Verbally there is very general agreement; for both the general run of men and people of superior refinement say that it is happiness, and identify living well and faring well with being happy; but with regard to what happiness is they differ, and the many do not give the same account as the wise. For the former think it is some plain and obvious thing, like pleasure, wealth, or honour; they differ, however, from one another—and often even the same man identifies it with different things, with health when he is ill, with wealth when he is poor; but, conscious of their ignorance, they admire those who proclaim some great thing that is above their comprehension. Now some thought that apart from these many goods there is another which is good in itself and causes the goodness of all these as well. To examine all the opinions that have been held would no doubt be somewhat fruitless: it is enough to examine those that are most prevalent or that seem to have some reason in their favour.

Let us not fail to notice, however, that there is a difference between arguments from and those to the first principles. For Plato, too, was right in raising this question and asking, as he used to do, 'are we on the way from or to the first principles?' There is a difference, as there is in a race-course between the course from the judges to the turning-point and the way back. For, while we must begin with what is familiar, things are so in two ways—some to us, some without qualification. Presumably, then, we must begin with things familiar to us. Hence any one who is to listen intelligently to lectures about what is noble and just and, generally, about the subjects of political science must have been brought up in good habits. For the facts are the starting-point, and if they are sufficiently plain to him, he will not need the reason as well; and the man who has been well brought up has or can easily get starting-points. And as for him who neither has nor can get them, let him hear the words of Hesiod:[1]

Far best is he who knows all things himself;
Good, he that hearkens when men counsel right;
But he who neither knows, nor lays to heart
Another's wisdom, is a useless wight.

5. Let us, however, resume our discussion from the point at which we digressed. To judge from the lives that men lead, most men, and men of the most vulgar type, seem (not without some reason) to identify the good, or happiness, with pleasure; which is the reason why they love the life of enjoyment. For there are, we may say, three prominent types of life—that just mentioned, the political, and thirdly the contemplative life. Now the mass of mankind are evidently quite slavish in their tastes, preferring a life suitable to beasts, but they get some reason for their view from the fact that many of those in high places share the tastes of Sardanapallus. But people of superior refinement and of active disposition identify happiness with honour; for this is, roughly speaking, the end of the political life. But it seems too superficial to be what we are looking for, since it is thought to depend on those who bestow honour rather than on him who receives it, but the good we divine to be something of one's own and not easily taken from one. Further, men seem to pursue honour in order that they may be assured of their merit; at least it is by men of practical wisdom that they seek to be

---

[1] *Works and Days* 293–7.

honoured, and among those who know them, and on the ground of their excellence; clearly, then, according to them, at any rate, excellence is better. And perhaps one might even suppose this to be, rather than honour, the end of the political life. But even this appears somewhat incomplete; for possession of excellence seems actually compatible with being asleep, or with lifelong inactivity, and, further, with the greatest sufferings and misfortunes; but a man who was living so no one would call happy, unless he were maintaining a thesis at all costs. But enough of this; for the subject has been sufficiently treated even in ordinary discussions. Third comes the contemplative life, which we shall consider later.

The life of money-making is one undertaken under compulsion, and wealth is evidently not the good we are seeking; for it is merely useful and for the sake of something else. And so one might rather take the aforenamed objects to be ends; for they are loved for themselves. But it is evident that not even these are ends—although many arguments have been thrown away in support of them. Let us then dismiss them.

6. We had perhaps better consider the universal good and discuss thoroughly what is meant by it, although such an inquiry is made an uphill one by the fact that the Forms have been introduced by friends of our own. Yet it would perhaps be thought to be better, indeed to be our duty, for the sake of maintaining the truth even to destroy what touches us closely, especially as we are philosophers; for, while both are dear, piety requires us to honour truth above our friends.

The men who introduced this doctrine did not posit Ideas of classes within which they recognized priority and posteriority (which is the reason why they did not maintain the existence of an Idea embracing all numbers); but things are called good both in the category of substance and in that of quality and in that of relation, and that which is *per se*, i.e. substance, is prior in nature to the relative (for the latter is like an offshoot and accident of what is); so that there could not be a common Idea set over all these goods. Further, since things are said to be good in as many ways as they are said to be (for things are called good both in the category of substance, as God and reason, and in quality, e.g. the virtues, and

in quantity, e.g. that which is moderate, and in relation, e.g. the useful, and in time, e.g. the right opportunity, and in place, e.g. the right locality and the like), clearly the good cannot be something universally present in all cases and single; for then it would not have been predicated in all the categories but in one only. Further, since of the things answering to one Idea there is one science, there would have been one science of all the goods; but as it is there are many sciences even of the things that fall under one category, e.g. of opportunity (for opportunity in war is studied by strategy and in disease by medicine), and the moderate in food is studied by medicine and in exercise by the science of gymnastics. And one might ask the question, what in the world they *mean* by 'a thing itself', if in man himself and in a particular man the account of man is one and the same. For in so far as they are men, they will in no respect differ; and if this is so, neither will there be a difference in so far as they are good. But again it will not be good any the more for being eternal, since that which lasts long is no whiter than that which perishes in a day. The Pythagoreans seem to give a more plausible account of the good, when they place the one in the column of goods; and it is they that Speusippus seems to have followed.

But let us discuss these matters elsewhere; an objection to what we have said, however, may be discerned in the fact that the Platonists have not been speaking about *all* goods, and that the goods that are pursued and loved for themselves are called good by reference to a single Form, while those which tend to produce or to preserve these somehow or to prevent their contraries are called so by reference to these, and in a different sense. Clearly, then, goods must be spoken of in two ways, and some must be good in themselves, the others by reason of these. Let us separate, then, things good in themselves from things useful, and consider whether the former are called good by reference to a single Idea. What sort of goods would one call good in themselves? Is it those that are pursued even when isolated from others, such as intelligence, sight, and certain pleasures and honours? Certainly, if we pursue these also for the sake of something else, yet one would place them among things good in themselves. Or is nothing other than the Idea good in itself? In that case the Form will be empty. But if the things we have named are also things good in themselves, the account of the good will have to appear as something identical in them all, as that of whiteness is identical in snow and in white lead. But of honour, wisdom, and pleasure, just in respect of their goodness, the accounts are distinct and diverse. The good, therefore, is not something common answering to one Idea.

But then in what way are things called good? They do not seem to be like the things that only chance to have the same name. Are goods one, then, by being derived from one good or by all contributing to one good, or are they rather one by analogy? Certainly as sight is in the body, so is reason in the soul, and so on in other cases. But perhaps these subjects had better be dismissed for the present; for perfect precision about them would be more appropriate to another branch of philosophy. And similarly with regard to the Idea; even if there is some one good which is universally predictable of goods or is capable of separate and independent existence, clearly it could not be achieved or attained by man; but we are now seeking something attainable. Perhaps, however, some one might think it worth while to have knowledge of it with a view to the goods that *are* attainable and achievable; for having this as a sort of pattern we shall know better the goods that are good for us, and if we know them shall attain them. This argument has some plausibility, but seems to clash with the procedure of the sciences; for all of these, though they aim at some good and seek to supply the deficiency of it, leave on one side the knowledge of *the* good. Yet that all the exponents of the arts should be ignorant of, and should not even seek, so great an aid is not probable. It is hard, too, to see how a weaver or a carpenter will be benefited in regard to his own craft by knowing this 'good itself', or how the man who has viewed the Idea itself will be a better doctor or general thereby. For a doctor seems not even to study health in this way, but the health of man, or perhaps rather the health of a particular man; for it is individuals that he is healing. But enough of these topics.

7. Let us again return to the good we are seeking, and ask what it can be. It seems different in different actions and arts; it is different in medicine, in strategy, and in the other arts likewise. What then is the good of each? Surely that for whose sake everything else is done. In medicine this is health, in strategy victory, in architecture a house, in any other sphere something else, and in every action and choice the end; for it is for the sake of this that all men do whatever else they do. Therefore, if there is an end for all that we do, this will be the good achievable by action, and if there are more than one, these will be the goods achievable by action.

So the argument has by a different course reached the same point; but we must try to state this even more clearly. Since there are evidently more than one end, and we choose some of these (e.g. wealth, flutes, and in general instruments) for the sake of something else, clearly not all ends are complete ends; but the chief good is evidently something complete. Therefore, if there is only one complete end, this will be what we are seeking, and if there are more than one, the most complete of these will be what we are seeking. Now we call that which is in itself worthy of pursuit more complete than that which is worthy of pursuit for the sake of something else, and that which is never desirable for the sake of something else more complete than the things that are desirable both in themselves and for the sake of that other thing, and therefore we call complete without qualification that which is always desirable in itself and never for the sake of something else.

Now such a thing happiness, above all else, is held to be; for this we choose always for itself and never for the sake of something else, but honour, pleasure, reason, and every excellence we choose indeed for themselves (for if nothing resulted from them we should still choose each of them), but we choose them also for the sake of happiness, judging that through them we shall be happy. Happiness, on the other hand, no one chooses for the sake of these, nor, in general, for anything other than itself.

From the point of view of self-sufficiency the same result seems to follow; for the complete good is thought to be self-sufficient. Now by self-sufficient we do not mean that which is sufficient for a man by himself, for one who lives a solitary life, but also for parents, children, wife, and in general for his friends and fellow citizens, since man is sociable by nature. But some limit must be set to this; for if we extend our requirement to ancestors and descendants and friends' friends we are in for an infinite series. Let us examine this question, however, on another occasion; the self-sufficient we now define as that which when isolated makes life desirable and lacking in nothing; and such we think happiness to be; and further we think it most desirable of all things, without being counted as one good thing among others—if it were so counted it would clearly be made more desirable by the addition of even the least of goods; for that which is added becomes an excess of goods, and of goods the greater is always more desirable. Happiness, then, is something complete and self-sufficient, and is the end of action.

Presumably, however, to say that happiness is the chief good seems a platitude, and a clearer account of what it is is still desired. This might perhaps be given, if we could first ascertain the function of man. For just as for a flute-player, a sculptor, or any artist, and, in general, for all things that have a function or activity, the good and the 'well' is thought to reside in the function, so would it seem to be for man, if he has a function. Have the carpenter, then, and the tanner certain functions or activities, and has man none? Is he naturally functionless? Or as eye, hand, foot, and in general each of the parts evidently has a function, may one lay it down that man similarly has a function apart from all these? What then can this be? Life seems to be common even to plants, but we are seeking what is preculiar to man. Let us exclude, therefore, the life of nutrition and growth. Next there would be a life of perception, but *it* also seems to be common even to the horse, the ox, and every animal. There remains, then, an active life of the element that has a rational principle (of this, one part has such a principle in the sense of being obedient to one, the other in the sense of possessing one and exercising thought); and as this too can be taken in two ways, we must state that life in the sense of activity is what we mean; for this seems to be the more proper sense of the term. Now if the function of man is an activity of soul in accordance with, or not without, rational principle, and if we say a so-and-so and a good so-and-so have a function which is the same in kind, e.g. a lyre-player and a good lyre-player, and so without qualification in all cases, eminence in respect of excellence being added to the function (for the function of a lyre-player is to play the lyre, and that of a good lyre-player is to do so well): if this is the case, [and we state the function of man to be a certain kind of life, and this to be an activity or actions of the soul implying a rational principle, and the function of a good man to be the good and noble performance of these, and if any action is well performed when it is performed in accordance with the appropriate excellence: if this is the case,][2] human good turns out to be activity of soul in conformity with excellence, and if there are more than one excellence, in conformity with the best and most complete.

But we must add 'in a complete life'. For one swallow does not make a summer, nor does one day; and so too one day, or a short time, does not make a man blessed and happy.

Let this serve as an outline of the good; for we must presumably first sketch it roughly, and then later fill in the details. But it would seem that any one is capable of carrying on and articulating what has once been well outlined, and that time is a good discoverer or partner in such a work; to which facts the advances of the arts are due; for any one can add what is lacking. And we must also remember what has been said before, and not look for precision in all things alike, but in each class of things such precision as accords with the subject-matter, and so much as is appropriate to the inquiry. For a carpenter and a geometer look for right angles in different ways; the former does so in so far as the right angle is useful for his work, while the latter inquires what it is or what sort of thing it is; for he is a spectator of the truth. We must act in the same way, then, in all other matters as well, that our main task may not be subordinated to minor qustions. Nor must we demand the cause in all matters alike; it is enough in some cases that the *fact* be well established, as in the case of the first principles; the fact is a primary thing or first principle. Now of first principles we see some by induction, some by perception, some by a certain habituation, and others too in other ways. But each set of principles we must try to investigate in the natural way, and we must take pains to determine them correctly, since they have a great influence on what follows. For the beginning is

1098ª1

1098ᵇ1

---

[2]Excised by Bywater.

thought to be more than half of the whole, and many of the questions we ask are cleared up by it.

8. We must consider it, however, in the light not only of our conclusion and our premises, but also of what is commonly said about it; for with a true view all the facts harmonize, but with a false one they[3] soon clash. Now goods have been divided into three classes, and some are described as external, others as relating to soul or to body; and we call those that relate to soul most properly and truly goods. But we are positing actions and activities relating to soul.[4] Therefore our account must be sound, at least according to this view, which is an old one and agreed on by philosophers. It is correct also in that we identify the end with certain actions and activities; for thus it falls among goods of the soul and not among external goods. Another belief which harmonizes with our account is that the happy man lives well and fares well; for we have practically defined happiness as a sort of living and faring well. The characteristics that are looked for in happiness seem also, all of excellence, some with practical wisdom, others with a kind of philosophic wisdom, others with these, or one of these, accompanied by pleasure or not without pleasure; while others include also external prosperity. Now some of these views have been held by many men and men of old, others by a few persons; and it is not probable that either of these should be entirely mistaken, but rather that they should be right in at least some one respect or even in most respects.

With those who identify happiness with excellence or some one excellence our account is in harmony; for to excellence belongs activity in accordance with excellence. But it makes, perhaps, no small difference whether we place the chief good in possession or in use, in state or in activity. For the state may exist without producing any good result, as in a man who is asleep or in some other way quite inactive, but the activity cannot; for one who has the activity will of necessity be acting, and acting well. And as in the Olympic Games it is not the most beautiful and the strongest that are crowned but those who compete (for it is some of these that are victorious),

so those who act rightly win the noble and good things in life.

Their life is also in itself pleasant. For pleasure is a state of soul, and to each man that which he is said to be a lover of is pleasant; e.g. not only is a horse pleasant to the lover of horses, and a spectacle to the lover of sights, but also in the same way just acts are pleasant to the lover of justice and in general excellent acts to the lover of excellence. Now for most men their pleasures are in conflict with one another because these are not by nature pleasant, but the lovers of what is noble find pleasant the things that are by nature pleasant; and excellent actions are such, so that these are pleasant for such men as well as in their own nature. Their life, therefore, has no further need of pleasure as a sort of adventitious charm, but has its pleasure in itself. For, besides what we have said, the man who does not rejoice in noble actions is not even good; since no one would call a man just who did not enjoy acting justly, nor any man liberal who did not enjoy liberal actions; and similarly in all other cases. If this is so, excellent actions must be in themselves pleasant. But they are also *good* and *noble*, and have each of these attributes in the highest degree, since the good man judges well about these attributes and he judges in the way we have described. Happiness then is the best, noblest, and most pleasant thing, and these attributes are not severed as in the inscription at Delos—

> Most noble is that which is justest, and best is
>   health;
> But pleasantest is it to win what we love.

For all these properties belong to the best activities; and these, or one—the best—of these, we identify with happiness.

Yet evidently, as we said, it needs the external goods as well; for it is impossible, or not easy, to do noble acts without the proper equipment. In many actions we use friends and riches and political power as instruments; and there are some things the lack of which takes the lustre from blessedness, as good birth, satisfactory children, beauty; for the man who is very ugly in appearance or ill-born or solitary and childless is hardly happy, and perhaps a man would be still less so if he had thoroughly bad children or

---

[3]Omitting τὰλ ηθες.
[4]Omitting ψυχικάς.

friends or had lost good children or friends by death. As we said, then, happiness seems to need this sort of prosperity in addition; for which reason some identify happiness with good fortune, though others identify it with excellence.

9. For this reason also the question is asked, whether happiness is to be acquired by learning or by habituation or some other sort of training, or comes in virtue of some divine providence or again by chance. Now if there is *any* gift of the gods to men, it is reasonable that happiness should be god-given, and most surely god-given of all human things inasmuch as it is the best. But this question would perhaps be more appropriate to another inquiry; happiness seems, however, even if it is not god-sent but comes as a result of excellence and some process of learning or training, to be among the most godlike things; for that which is the prize and end of excellence seems to be the best thing and something god-like and blessed.

It will also on this view be very generally shared; for all who are not maimed as regards excellence may win it by a certain kind of study and care. But if it is better to be happy thus than by chance, it is reasonable that the facts should be so, since everything that depends on the action of nature is by nature as good as it can be, and similarly everything that depends on art or any cause, and especially if it depends on the best of all causes. To entrust to chance what is greatest and most noble would be a very defective arrangement.

The answer to the question we are asking is plain also from the definition[5]; for it has been said to be a certain kind of activity of soul. Of the remaining goods, some are necessary and others are naturally co-operative and useful as instruments. And this will be found to agree with what we said at the outset; for we stated the end of political science to be the best end, and political science spends most of its pains on making the citizens to be of a certain character, viz. good and capable of noble acts.

It is natural, then, that we call neither ox nor horse nor any other of the animals happy; for none of them is capable of sharing in such activity. For this reason

also a boy is not happy; for he is not yet capable of such acts, owing to his age; and boys who are called happy are being congratulated by reason of the hopes we have for them. For there is required, as we said, not only complete excellence but also a complete life, since many changes occur in life, and all manner of chances, and the most prosperous may fall into great misfortunes in old age, as is told of Priam in the Trojan Cycle; and one who has experienced such chances and has ended wretchedly no one calls happy.

10. Must no one at all, then, be called happy while he lives; must we, as Solon says, see the end? Even if we are to lay down this doctrine, is it also the case that a man is happy when he is *dead*? Or is not this quite absurd, especially for us who say that happiness is an activity? But if we do not call the dead man happy, and if Solon does not mean this, but that one can then safely *call* a man blessed as being at last beyond evils and misfortunes, this also affords matter for discussion; for both evil and good are thought to exist for a dead man, as much as for one who is alive but not aware of them; e.g. honours and dishonours and the good or bad fortunes of children and in general of descendants. And this also presents a problem; for though a man has lived blessedly up to old age and has had a death worthy of his life, many reverses may befall his descendants— some of them may be good and attain the life they deserve, while with others the opposite may be the case; and clearly too the degrees of relationship between them and their ancestors may vary indefinitely. It would be odd, then, if the dead man were to share in these changes and become at one time happy, at another wretched; while it would also be odd if the fortunes of the descendants did not for *some* time have *some* effect on the happiness of their ancestors.

But we must return to our first difficulty; for perhaps by a consideration of it our present problem might be solved. Now if we must see the end and only then call a man blessed, not as being blessed but as having been so before, surely it is odd that when he is happy the attribute that belongs to him is not to be truly predicated of him because we do not wish to call living men happy, on account of the changes that may befall them, and because we have assumed happiness to be something permanent and

---

[5]Omitting κατ᾽ ἀρετήν.

100ᵇ1 by no means easily changed, while a single man may suffer many turns of fortune's wheel. For clearly if we were to follow his fortunes, we should often call the same man happy and again wretched, making the happy man out to be a 'chameleon and insecurely based'. Or is this following his fortunes quite wrong? Success or failure in life does not depend on these, but human life, as we said, needs these as well, while excellent activities or their opposites are what determine happiness or the reverse.

The question we have now discussed confirms our definition. For no function of man has so much permanence as excellent activities (these are thought to be more durable even than knowledge), and of these themselves the most valuable are more durable because those who are blessed spend their life most readily and most continuously in these; for this seems to be the reason why we do not forget them. The attribute in question, then, will belong to the happy man, and he will be happy throughout his life; for always, or by preference to everything else, he will do and contemplate what is excellent, and he will bear the chances of life most nobly and altogether decorously, if he is 'truly good' and 'foursquare beyond reproach'.

Now many events happen by chance, and events differing in importance; small pieces of good fortune or of its opposite clearly do not weigh down the scales of life one way or the other, but a multitude of great events if they turn out well will make life more blessed (for not only are they themselves such as to add beauty to life, but the way a man deals with them may be noble and good), while if they turn out ill they crush and maim blessedness; for they both bring pain with them and hinder many activities. Yet even in these nobility shines through, when a man bears with resignation many great misfortunes, not through insensibility to pain but through nobility and greatness of soul.

If activities are, as we said, what determines the character of life, no blessed man can become miserable; for he will never do the acts that are hateful and mean. For the man who is truly good and wise, we think, bears all the chances of life becomingly and always makes the best of circumstances, as a good general makes the best military use of the army at his command and a shoemaker makes the best

shoes out of the hides that are given him; and so with all other craftsmen. And if this is the case, the happy man can never become miserable—though he will not reach *blessedness*, if he meet with fortunes like those of Priam.

Nor, again, is he many-coloured and changeable; for neither will he be moved from his happy state easily or by any ordinary misadventures, but only by many great ones, nor, if he has had many great misadventures, will he recover his happiness in a short time, but if at all, only in a long and complete one in which he has attained many splendid successes.

Why then should we not say that he is happy who is active in conformity with complete excellence and is sufficiently equipped with external goods, not for some chance period but throughout a complete life? Or must we add 'and who is destined to live thus and die as befits his life'? Certainly the future is obscure to us, while happiness, we claim, is an end and something in every way final. If so, we shall call blessed those among living men in whom these conditions are, and are to be, fulfilled—but blessed *men*. So much for these questions.

11. That the fortunes of descendants and of all a man's friends should not affect his happiness at all seems a very unfriendly doctrine, and one opposed to the opinions men hold; but since the events that happen are numerous and admit of all sorts of difference, and some come more near to us and others less so, it seems a long—indeed an endless—task to discuss each in detail; a general outline will perhaps suffice. If, then, as some of a man's own misadventures have a certain weight and influence on life while others are, as it were, lighter, so too there are differences among the misadventures of all our friends, and it makes a difference whether the various sufferings befall the living or the dead (much more even than whether lawless and terrible deeds are presupposed in a tragedy or done on the stage), this difference also must be taken into account; or rather, perhaps, the fact that doubt is felt whether the dead share in any good or evil. For it seems, from these considerations, that even if anything whether good or evil penetrates to them, it must be something weak and negligible, either in itself or for them, or if not, at least it must be such in degree and kind as not to make happy those who are not happy nor to

take away their blessedness from those who are. The good or bad fortunes of friends, then, seem to have some effects on the dead, but effects of such a kind and degree as neither to make the happy unhappy nor to produce any other change of the kind.

12. These questions having been answered, let us consider whether happiness is among the things that are praised or rather among the things that are prized; for clearly it is not to be placed among *potentialities*. Everything that is praised seems to be praised because it is of a certain kind and is related somehow to something else; for we praise the just or brave man and in general both the good man and excellence itself because of the actions and functions involved, and we praise the strong man, the good runner, and so on, because he is of a certain kind and is related in a certain way to something good and important. This is clear also from the praises of the gods; for it seems absurd that the gods should be referred to our standard, but this is done because praise involves a reference, as we said, to something else. But if praise is for things such as we have described, clearly what applies to the best things is not praise, but something greater and better, as is indeed obvious; for what we do to the gods and the most godlike of men is to call them blessed and happy. And so too with good things; no one praises happiness as he does justice, but rather calls it blessed, as being something more divine and better.

Eudoxus also seems to have been right in his method of advocating the supremacy of pleasure; he thought that the fact that, though a good, it is not praised indicated it to be better than the things that are praised, and that this is what God and the good are; for by reference to these all other things are judged. Praise is appropriate to excellence; for as a result of excellence men tend to do noble deeds (*encomia* are bestowed on acts, whether of the body or of the soul—but perhaps nicety in these matters is more proper to those who have made a study of encomia); but to us it is clear from what has been said that happiness is among the things that are prized and complete. It seems to be so also from the fact that it is a first principle; for it is for the sake of this that we all do everything else, and the first principle and cause of goods is, we claim, something prized and divine.

13. Since happiness is an activity of soul in accordance with complete excellence, we must consider the nature of excellence; for perhaps we shall thus see better the nature of happiness. The true student of politics, too, is thought to have studied this above all things; for he wishes to make his fellow citizens good and obedient to the laws. As an example of this we have the lawgivers of the Cretans and the Spartans, and any others of the kind that there may have been. And if this inquiry belongs to political science, clearly the pursuit of it will be in accordance with our original plan. But clearly the excellence we must study is human excellence; for the good we were seeking was human good and the happiness human happiness. By human excellence we mean not that of the body but that of the soul; and happiness also we call an activity of soul. But if this is so, clearly the student of politics must know somehow the facts about soul, as the man who is to heal the eyes must know about the whole body also; and all the more since politics is more prized and better than medicine; but even among doctors the best educated spend much labour on acquiring knowledge of the body. The student of politics, then, must study the soul, and must study it with these objects in view, and do so just to the extent which is sufficient for the questions we are discussing; for further precision is perhaps something more laborious than our purposes require.

Some things are said about it, adequately enough, even in the discussions outside our school, and we must use these; e.g. that one element in the soul is irrational and one has a rational principle. Whether these are separated as the parts of the body or of anything divisible are, or are distinct by definition but by nature inseparable, like convex and concave in the circumference of a circle, does not affect the present question.

Of the irrational element one division seems to be widely distributed, and vegetative in its nature, I mean that which causes nutrition and growth; for it is this kind of power of the soul that one must assign to all nurslings and to embryos, and this same power to full-grown creatures; this is more reasonable than to assign some different power to them. Now the excellence of this seems to be common to all and not specifically human; for this part or faculty seems to function most in sleep, while goodness and badness are least manifest in sleep (whence comes the saying that the happy are not better off than the wretched for half their lives; and this happens naturally enough, since sleep is an inactivity of the soul in that respect in which it is called good or bad), unless perhaps to a small extent some of the movements actually penetrate, and in this respect the dreams of good men are better than those of ordinary people. Enough of this subject, however; let us leave the nutritive faculty alone, since it has by its nature no share in human excellence.

There seems to be also another irrational element in the soul—one which in a sense, however, shares in a rational principle. For we praise the reason of the continent man and of the incontinent, and the part of their soul that has reason, since it urges them aright and towards the best objects; but there is found in them also another natural element beside reason, which fights against and resists it. For exactly as paralysed limbs when we choose to move them to the right turn on the contrary to the left, so is it with the soul; the impulses of incontinent people move in contrary directions. But while in the body we see that which moves astray, in the soul we do not. No doubt, however, we must none the less suppose that in the soul too there is something beside reason, resisting and opposing it. In what sense it is distinct from the other elements does not concern us. Now even this seems to have a share in reason, as we said; at any rate in the continent man it obeys reason—and presumably in the temperate and brave man it is still more obedient; for in them it speaks, on all matters, with the same voice as reason.

Therefore the irrational element also appears to be two-fold. For the vegetative element in no way shares in reason, but the appetitive and in general the desiring element in a sense shares in it, in so far as it listens to and obeys it; this is the sense in which we speak of paying heed to one's father or one's friends, not that in which we speak of 'the rational' in mathematics.[6] That the irrational element is in some sense persuaded by reason is indicated also by the giving of advice and by all reproof and exhortation. And if this element also must be said to have reason, that which has reason also will be twofold, one subdivision having it in the strict sense and in itself, and the other having a tendency to obey as one does one's father.

Excellence too is distinguished into kinds in accordance with this difference; for we say that some excellences are intellectual and others moral,[7] philosophic wisdom and understanding and practical wisdom being intellectual, liberality and temperance moral. For in speaking about a man's character we do not say that he is wise or has understanding but that he is good-tempered or temperate; yet we praise the wise man also with respect to his state; and of states we call those which merit praise excellences.

BOOK II

1. Excellence, then, being of two kinds, intellectual and moral, intellectual excellence in the main owes both its birth and its growth to teaching (for which reason it requires experience and time), while moral excellence comes about as a result of habit, whence also its name is one that is formed by a slight variation from the word for 'habit'.[8] From this it is also plain that none of the moral excellences arises in us by nature; for nothing that exists by nature can form a habit contrary to its nature. For instance the stone which by nature moves downwards cannot be habituated to move upwards, not even if one tries to train it by throwing it up ten thousand times; nor can fire be habituated to move downwards, nor can anything else that by nature behaves in one way be trained to behave in another. Neither by nature, then, nor contrary to nature do excellences arise in us; rather we are adapted by nature to receive them, and are made perfect by habit.

Again, of all the things that come to us by nature we first acquire the potentiality and later exhibit the activity (this is plain in the case of the senses; for it was not by often seeing or often hearing that we got

---

[6]Λόγον ἔχειν means (i) 'possess reason', (ii) 'pay heed to', 'obey', (iii) 'be rational' (in the mathematical sense).

[7]'Moral', here and hereafter, is used in the archaic sense of 'pertaining to character or *mores*'.

[8]ηθική from ἔθις.

these senses, but on the contrary we had them before we used them, and did not come to have them by using them); but excellences we get by first exercising them, as also happens in the case of the arts as well. For the things we have to learn before we can do, we learn by doing, e.g. men become builders by building and lyre-players by playing the lyre; so too we become just by doing just acts, temperate by doing temperate acts, brave by doing brave acts.

This is confirmed by what happens in states; for legislators make the citizens good by forming habits in them, and this is the wish of every legislator; and those who do not effect it miss their mark, and it is in this that a good constitution differs from a bad one.

Again, it is from the same causes and by the same means that every excellence is both produced and destroyed, and similarly every art; for it is from playing the lyre that both good and bad lyre-players are produced. And the corresponding statement is true of builders and of all the rest; men will be good or bad builders as a result of building well or badly. For if this were not so, there would have been no need of a teacher, but all men would have been born good or bad at their craft. This, then, is the case with the excellences also; by doing the acts that we do in our transactions with other men we become just or unjust, and by doing the acts that we do in the presence of danger, and being habituated to feel fear or confidence, we become brave or cowardly. The same is true of appetites and feelings of anger; some men become temperate and good-tempered, others self-indulgent and irascible, by behaving in one way or the other in the appropriate circumstances. Thus, in one word, states arise out of like activities. This is why the activities we exhibit must be of a certain kind; it is because the states correspond to the differences between these. It makes no small difference, then, whether we form habits of one kind or of another from our very youth; it makes a very great difference, or rather *all* the difference.

2. Since, then, the present inquiry does not aim at theoretical knowledge like the others (for we are inquiring not in order to know what excellence is, but in order to become good, since otherwise our inquiry would have been of no use), we must examine the nature of actions, namely how we ought to do

them; for these determine also the nature of the states that are produced, as we have said. Now, that we must[9] act according to right reason is a common principle and must be assumed—it will be discussed later, i.e. both what it is, and how it is related to the other excellences. But this must be agreed upon beforehand, that the whole account of matters of conduct must be given in outline and not precisely, as we said at the very beginning that the accounts we demand must be in accordance with the subject-matter; matters concerned with conduct and questions of what is good for us have no fixity, any more than matters of health. The general account being of this nature, the account of particular cases is yet more lacking in exactness; for they do not fall under any art or set of precepts, but the agents themselves must in each case consider what is appropriate to the occasion, as happens also in the art of medicine or of navigation.

But though our present account is of this nature we must give what help we can. First, then, let us consider this, that it is the nature of such things to be destroyed by defect and excess, as we see in the case of strength and of health (for to gain light on things imperceptible we must use the evidence of sensible things); both excessive and defective exercise destroys the strength, and similarly drink or food which is above or below a certain amount destroys the health, while that which is proportionate both produces and increases and preserves it. So too is it, then, in the case of temperance and courage and the other excellences. For the man who flies from and fears everything and does not stand his ground against anything becomes a coward, and the man who fears nothing at all but goes to meet every danger becomes rash; and similarly the man who indulges in every pleasure and abstains from none becomes self-indulgent, while the man who shuns every pleasure, as boors do, becomes in a way insensible; temperance and courage, then, are destroyed by excess and defect, and preserved by the mean.

But not only are the sources and causes of their origination and growth the same as those of their destruction, but also the sphere of their activity will be the same; for this is also true of the things which are

---

[9]Reading πράττειν δεῖν.

more evident to sense, e.g. of strength; it is produced by taking much food and undergoing much exertion, and it is the strong man that will be most able to do these things. So too is it with the excellences; by abstaining from pleasures we become temperate, and it is when we have become so that we are most able to abstain from them; and similarly too in the case of courage; for by being habituated to despise things that are terrible and to stand our ground against them we become brave, and it is when we have become so that we shall be most able to stand our ground against them.

3. We must take as a sign of states the pleasure or pain that supervenes on acts; for the man who abstains from bodily pleasures and delights in this very fact is temperate, while the man who is annoyed at it is self-indulgent, and he who stands his ground against things that are terrible and delights in this or at least is not pained is brave, while the man who is pained is a coward. For moral excellence is concerned with pleasures and pains; it is on account of pleasure that we do bad things, and on account of pain that we abstain from noble ones. Hence we ought to have been brought up in a particular way from our very youth, as Plato says, so as both to delight in and to be pained by the things that we ought; for this is the right education.

Again, if the excellences are concerned with actions and passions, and every passion and every action is accompanied by pleasure and pain, for this reason also excellence will be concerned with pleasures and pains. This is indicated also by the fact that punishment is inflicted by these means; for it is a kind of cure, and it is the nature of cures to be effected by contraries.

Again, as we said but lately, every state of soul has a nature relative to and concerned with the kind of things by which it tends to be made worse or better; but it is by reason of pleasures and pains that men become bad, by pursuing and avoiding these—either the pleasures and pains they ought not or when they ought not or as they ought not, or by going wrong in one of the other similar ways that reason can distinguish. Hence men even define the excellences as certain states of impassivity and rest; not well, however, because they speak absolutely, and do not say 'as one ought' and 'as one ought

not' and 'when one ought or ought not', and the other things that may be added. We assume, then, that this kind of excellence tends to do what is best with regard to pleasures and pains, and badness does the contrary.

The following facts also may show us that they are concerned with these same things. There being three objects of choice and three of avoidance, the noble, the advantageous, the pleasant, and their contraries, the base, the injurious, the painful, about all of these the good man tends to go right and the bad man to go wrong, and especially about pleasure; for this is common to the animals, and also it accompanies all objects of choice; for even the noble and the advantageous appear pleasant.

Again, it has grown up with us all from our infancy; this is why it is difficult to rub off this passion, engrained as it is in our life. And we measure even our actions, some of us more and others less, by pleasure and pain. For this reason, then, our whole inquiry must be about these; for to feel delight and pain rightly or wrongly has no small effect on our actions.

Again, it is harder to fight with pleasure than with anger, to use Heraclitus' phrase, but both art and excellence are always concerned with what is harder; for even the good is better when it is harder. Therefore for this reason also the whole concern both of excellence and of political science is with pleasures and pains; for the man who uses these well will be good, he who uses them badly bad.

That excellence, then, is concerned with pleasures and pains, and that by the acts from which it arises it is both increased and, if they are done differently, destroyed, and that the acts from which it arose are those in which it actualizes itself—let this be taken as said.

4. The question might be asked, what we mean by saying that we must become just by doing just acts, and temperate by doing temperate acts; for if men do just and temperate acts, they are already just and temperate, exactly as, if they do what is grammatical or musical they are proficient in grammar and music.

Or is this not true even of the arts? It is possible to do something grammatical either by chance or under the guidance of another. A man will be proficient in grammar, then, only when he has both done something grammatical and done it grammatically; and this means doing it in accordance with the grammatical knowledge in himself.

Again, the case of the arts and that of the excellences are not similar; for the products of the arts have their goodness in themselves, so that it is enough that they should have a certain character, but if the acts that are in accordance with the excellences have themselves a certain character it does not follow that they are done justly or temperately. The agent also must be in a certain condition when he does them; in the first place he must have knowledge, secondly he must choose the acts, and choose them for their own sakes, and thirdly his action must proceed from a firm and unchangeable character. These are not reckoned in as conditions of the possession of the arts, except the bare knowledge; but as a condition of the possession of the excellences, knowledge has little or no weight, while the other conditions count not for a little but for everything, i.e. the very conditions which result from often doing just and temperate acts.

Actions, then, are called just and temperate when they are such as the just or the temperate man would do; but it is not the man who does these that is just and temperate, but the man who also does them *as* just and temperate men do them. It is well said, then, that it is by doing just acts that the just man is produced, and by doing temperate acts the temperate man; without doing these no one would have even a prospect of becoming good.

But most people do not do these, but take refuge in theory and think they are being philosophers and will become good in this way, behaving somewhat like patients who listen attentively to their doctors, but do none of the things they are ordered to do. As the latter will not be made well in body by such a course of treatment, the former will not be made well in soul by such a course of philosophy.

5. Next we must consider what excellence is. Since things that are found in the soul are of three kinds—passions, faculties, states—excellence must be one of these. By passions I mean appetite, anger, fear, confidence, envy, joy, love, hatred, longing, emulation, pity, and in general the feelings that are accompanied by pleasure or pain; by faculties the things in virtue of which we are said to be capable of feeling these, e.g. of becoming angry or being pained or feeling pity; by states the things in virtue of which we stand well or badly with reference to the passions, e.g. with reference to anger we stand badly if we feel it violently or too weakly, and well if we feel it moderately; and similarly with reference to the other passions.

Now neither the excellences nor the vices are *passions*, because we are not called good or bad on the ground of our passions, but are so called on the ground of our excellences and our vices, and because we are neither praised nor blamed for our passions (for the man who feels fear or anger is not praised, nor is the man who simply feels anger blamed, but the man who feels it in a certain way), but for our excellences and our vices we *are* praised or blamed.

Again, we feel anger and fear without choice, but the excellences are choices or involve choice. Further, in respect of the passions we are said to be moved, but in respect of the excellences and the vices we are said not to be moved but to be disposed in a particular way.

For these reasons also they are not *faculties* 1; for we are neither called good nor bad, nor praised nor blamed, for the simple capacity of feeling the passions; again, we have the faculties by nature, but we are not made good or bad by nature; we have spoken of this before.

If, then, the excellences are neither passions nor faculties, all that remains is that they should be *states*.

Thus we have stated what excellence is in respect of its genus.

6. We must, however, not only describe it as a state, but also say what sort of state it is. We may remark, then, that every excellence both brings into good condition the thing of which it is the excellence and makes the work of that thing be done well; e.g. the excellence of the eye makes both the eye and its work good; for it is by the excellence of the eye that we see well. Similarly the excellence of the horse makes a horse both good in itself and good at running and at carrying its rider and at awaiting the attack of the enemy. Therefore, if this is true in every case, the excellence of man also will be the state which makes a man good and which makes him do his own work well.

How this is to happen we have stated already, but it will be made plain also by the following consideration of the nature of excellence. In everything that is continuous and divisible it is possible to take more, less, or an equal amount, and that either in terms of the thing itself or relatively to us; and the equal is an intermediate between excess and defect. By the intermediate in the object I mean that which is equidistant from each of the extremes, which is one and the same for all men; by the intermediate relatively to us that which is neither too much nor too little—and this is not one, nor the same for all. For instance, if ten is many and two is few, six is intermediate, taken in terms of the object; for it exceeds and is exceeded by an equal amount; this is intermediate according to arithmetical proportion. But the intermediate relatively to us is not to be taken so; if ten pounds are too much for a particular person to eat and two too little, it does not follow that the trainer will order six pounds; for this also is perhaps too much for the person who is to take it, or too little—too little for Milo, too much for the beginner in athletic exercises. The same is true of running and wrestling. Thus a master of any art avoids excess and defect, but seeks the intermediate and chooses this— the intermediate not in the object but relatively to us.

If it is thus, then, that every art does its work well—by looking to the intermediate and judging its works by this standard (so that we often say of good works of the art that it is not possible either to take away or to add anything, implying that excess and defect destroy the goodness of works of art, while the mean preserves it; and good artists, as we say, look to this in their work), and if, further, excellence is more exact and better than any art, as nature also is, then it must have the quality of aiming at the intermediate. I mean moral excellence; for it is this that is concerned with passions and actions, and in these there is excess, defect, and the intermediate. For instance, both fear and confidence and appetite and anger and pity and in general pleasure and pain may be felt both too much and too little, and in both cases not well; but to feel them at the right times, with reference to the right objects, towards the right people, with the right aim, and in the right way, is what is both intermediate and best, and this is characteristic of excellence. Similarly with regard to actions also

there is excess, defect, and the intermediate. Now excellence is concerned with passions and actions, in which excess is a form of failure, and so is defect, while the intermediate is praised and is a form of success; and both these things are characteristics of excellence. Therefore excellence is a kind of mean, since it aims at what is intermediate.

Again, it is possible to fail in many ways (for evil belongs to the class of the unlimited, as the Pythagoreans conjectured, and good to that of the limited), while to succeed is possible only in one way (for which reason one is easy and the other difficult—to miss the mark easy, to hit it difficult); for these reasons also, then, excess and defect are characteristic of vice, and the mean of excellence;

For men are good in but one way, but bad in many.

Excellence, then, is a state concerned with choice, lying in a mean relative to us, this being determined by reason and in the way in[10] which the man of practical wisdom would determine it. Now it is a mean between two vices, that which depends on excess and that which depends on defect; and again it is a mean because the vices respectively fall short of or exceed what is right in both passions and actions, while excellence both finds and chooses that which is intermediate. Hence in respect of its substance and the account which states its essence is a mean, with regard to what is best and right it is an extreme.

But not every action nor every passion admits of a mean; for some have names that already imply badness, e.g. spite, shamelessness, envy, and in the case of actions adultery, theft, murder; for all of these and suchlike things imply by their names that they are themselves bad, and not the excesses or deficiencies of them. It is not possible, then, ever to be right with regard to them; one must always be wrong. Nor does goodness or badness with regard to such things depend on committing adultery with the right woman, at the right time, and in the right way, but simply to do any of them is to go wrong. It would be equally absurd, then, to expect that in unjust, cowardly, and self-indulgent action there should be a mean, an excess, and a deficiency; for at that rate there would be a mean of excess and of deficiency, an excess of excess, and a deficiency of deficiency. But as there

---

[10]Reading ὡς ἄν.

is no excess and deficiency of temperance and courage because what is intermediate is in a sense an extreme, so too of the actions we have mentioned there is no mean nor any excess and deficiency, but however they are done they are wrong; for in general there is neither a mean of excess and deficiency, nor excess and deficiency of a mean.

7. We must, however, not only make this general statement, but also apply it to the individual facts. For among statements about conduct those which are general apply more widely, but those which are particular are more true, since conduct has to do with individual cases, and our statements must harmonize with the facts in these cases. We may take these cases from the diagram. With regard to feelings of fear and confidence courage is the mean; of the people who exceed, he who exceeds in fearlessness has no name (many of the states have no name), while the man who exceeds in confidence is rash, and he who exceeds in fear and falls short in confidence is a coward. With regard to pleasures and pains—not all of them, and not so much with regard to the pains—the mean is temperance, the excess self-indulgence. Persons deficient with regard to the pleasures are not often found; hence such persons also have received no name. But let us call them 'insensible'.

With regard to giving and taking of money the mean is liberality, the excess and the defect prodigality and meanness. They exceed and fall short in contrary ways to one another:[11] The prodigal exceeds in spending and falls short in taking, while the mean man exceeds in taking and falls short in spending. (At present we are giving a mere outline or summary, and are satisfied with this; later these states will be more exactly determined.) With regard to money there are also other dispositions—a mean, magnificence (for the magnificent man differs from the liberal man; the former deals with large sums, the latter with small ones), an excess, tastelessness and vulgarity, and a deficiency, niggardliness; these differ from the states opposed to liberality, and the mode of their difference will be stated later.

With regard to honour and dishonour the mean is proper pride, the excess is known as a sort of empty vanity, and the deficiency is undue humility; and as we said liberality was related to magnificence, differing from it by dealing with small sums, so there is a state similarly related to proper pride, being concerned with small honours while that is concerned with great. For it is possible to desire small honours[12] as one ought, and more than one ought, and less, and the man who exceeds in his desires is called ambitious, the man who falls short unambitious, while the intermediate person has no name. The dispositions also are nameless, except that that of the ambitious man is called ambition. Hence the people who are at the extremes lay claim to the middle place; and we ourselves sometimes call the intermediate person ambitious and sometimes unambitious, and sometimes praise the ambitious man and sometimes the unambitious. The reason of our doing this will be stated in what follows; but now let us speak of the remaining states according to the method which has been indicated.

With regard to anger also there is an excess, a deficiency, and a mean. Although they can scarcely be said to have names, yet since we call the intermediate person good-tempered let us call the mean good temper; of the persons at the extremes let the one who exceeds be called irascible, and his vice irascibility, and the man who falls short an inirascible sort of person, and the deficiency inirascibility.

There are also three other means, which have a certain likeness to one another, but differ from one another: for they are all concerned with intercourse in words and actions, but differ in that one is concerned with truth in this sphere, the other two with pleasantness; and of this one kind is exhibited in giving amusement, the other in all the circumstances of life. We must therefore speak of these too, that we may the better see that in all things the mean is praiseworthy, and the extremes neither praiseworthy nor right, but worthy of blame. Now most of these states also have no names, but we must try, as in the other cases, to invent names ourselves so that we may be clear and easy to follow. With regard to truth, then, the intermediate is a truthful sort of person and the mean may be called truthfulness, while the pre-

---

[11]Reading ἐναντίως δὲ αὐτοῖς.

[12]Reading μικρᾶς τιμῆς.

tence which exaggerates is boastfulness and the person characterized by it a boaster, and that which understates is mock modesty and the person characterized by it mock-modest. With regard to pleasantness in the giving of amusement the intermediate person is ready-witted and the disposition ready wit, the excess is buffoonery and the person characterized by it a buffoon, while the man who falls short is a sort of boor and his state is boorishness. With regard to the remaining kind of pleasantness, that which is exhibited in life in general, the man who is pleasant in the right way is friendly and the mean is friendliness, while the man who exceeds is an obsequious person if he has no end in view, a flatterer if he is aiming at his own advantage, and the man who falls short and is unpleasant in all circumstances is a quarrelsome and surly sort of person.

There are also means in the passions and concerned with the passions; since shame is not an excellence, and yet praise is extended to the modest man. For even in these matters one man is said to be intermediate, and another to exceed, as for instance the bashful man who is ashamed of everything; while he who falls short or is not ashamed of anything at all is shameless, and the intermediate person is modest. Righteous indignation is a mean between envy and spite, and these states are concerned with the pain and pleasure that are felt at the fortunes of our neighbours; the man who is characterized by righteous indignation is pained at undeserved good fortune, the envious man, going beyond him, is pained at all good fortune, and the spiteful man falls so far short of being pained that he even rejoices. But these states there will be an opportunity of describing elsewhere; with regard to justice, since it has not one simple meaning, we shall, after describing the other states, distinguish its two kinds and say how each of them is a mean; and similarly we shall treat also of the rational excellences.

8. There are three kinds of disposition, then, two of them vices, involving excess and deficiency and one an excellence, viz. the mean, and all are in a sense opposed to all; for the extreme states are contrary both to the intermediate state and to each other, and the intermediate to the extremes; as the equal is greater relatively to the less, less relatively to the greater, so the middle states are excessive relatively to the deficiencies, deficient relatively to the excesses, both in passions and in actions. For the brave man appears rash relatively to the coward, and cowardly relatively to the rash man; and similarly the temperate man appears self-indulgent relatively to the insensible man, insensible relatively to the self-indulgent, and the liberal man prodigal relatively to the mean man, mean relatively to the prodigal. Hence also the people at the extremes push the intermediate man each over to the other, and the brave man is called rash by the coward, cowardly by the rash man, and correspondingly in the other cases.

These states being thus opposed to one another, the greatest contrariety is that of the extremes to each other, rather than to the intermediate; for these are further from each other than from the intermediate, as the great is further from the small and the small from the great than both are from the equal. Again, to the intermediate some extremes show a certain likeness, as that of rashness to courage and that of prodigality to liberality; but the extremes show the greatest unlikeness to each other; now contraries are defined as the things that are furthest from each other, so that things that are further apart are more contrary.

To the mean in some cases the deficiency, in some the excess is more opposed; e.g. it is not rashness, which is an excess, but cowardice, which is a deficiency, that is more opposed to courage, and not insensibility, which is a deficiency, but self-indulgence, which is an excess, that is more opposed to temperance. This happens from two reasons, one being drawn from the thing itself; for because one extreme is nearer and liker to the intermediate, we oppose not this but rather its contrary to the intermediate. E.g., since rashness is thought liker and nearer to courage, and cowardice more unlike, we oppose rather the latter to courage; for things that are further from the intermediate are thought more contrary to it. This, then, is one cause, drawn from the thing itself; another is drawn from ourselves; for the things to which we ourselves more naturally tend seem more contrary to the intermediate. For instance, we ourselves tend more naturally to pleasures, and hence are more easily carried away towards self-indulgence than towards propriety. We describe as contrary to the mean, then, the states into which we are more inclined to lapse; and therefore self-indulgence, which is an excess, is the more contrary to temperance.

9. That moral excellence is a mean, then, and in what sense it is so, and that it is a mean between two vices, the one involving excess, the other deficiency, and that it is such because its character is to aim at what is intermediate in passions and in actions, has been sufficiently stated. Hence also it is no easy task to be good. For in everything it is no easy task to find the middle, e.g. to find the middle of a circle is not for every one but for him who knows; so, too, any one can get angry—that is easy—or give or spend money; but to do this to the right person, to the right extent, at the right time, with the right aim, and in the right way, *that* is not for every one, nor is it easy; that is why goodness is both rare and laudable and noble.

Hence he who aims at the intermediate must first depart from what is the more contrary to it, as Calypso advises—

Hold the ship out beyond that surf and spray.[13]

For of the extremes one is more erroneous, one less so; therefore, since to hit the mean is hard in the extreme, we must as a second best, as people say, take the least of the evils; and this be done best in the way we describe.

But we must consider the things towards which we ourselves also are easily carried away; for some of us tend to one thing, some to another; and this will be recognizable from the pleasure and the pain we feel. We must drag ourselves away to the contrary extreme; for we shall get into the intermediate state by drawing well away from error, as people do in straightening sticks that are bent.

Now in everything the pleasant or pleasure is most to be guarded against; for we do not judge it impartially. We ought, then, to feel towards pleasure as the elders of the people felt towards Helen, and in all circumstances repeat their saying; for if we dismiss pleasure thus we are less likely to go astray. It is by doing this, then, (to sum the matter up) that we shall best be able to hit the mean.

---

[13]*Odyssey* XII 219.

But this is no doubt difficult, and especially in individual cases; for it is not easy to determine both how and with whom and on what provocation and how long one should be angry; for we too sometimes praise those who fall short and call them good-tempered, but sometimes we praise those who get angry and call them manly. The man, however who deviates little from goodness is not blamed, whether he do so in the direction of the more or of the less, but only the man who deviates more widely; for *he* does not fail to be noticed. But up to what point and to what extent a man must deviate before he becomes blameworthy it is not easy to determine by reasoning, any more than anything else that is perceived by the senses; such things depend on particular facts, and the decision rests with perception. So much, then, makes it plain that the intermediate state is in all things to be praised, but that we must incline sometimes towards the excess, sometimes towards the deficiency; for so shall we most easily hit the mean and what is right.

BOOK III

1. Since excellence is concerned with passions and actions, and on voluntary passions and actions praise and blame are bestowed, on those that are involuntary forgiveness, and sometimes also pity, to distinguish the voluntary and the involuntary is presumably necessary for those who are studying excellence and useful also for legislators with a view to the assigning both of honours and of punishments.

Those things, then, are thought involuntary, which take place under compulsion or owing to ignorance; and that is compulsory of which the moving principle is outside, being a principle in which nothing is contributed by the person who acts or is acted upon, e.g. if he were to be carried somewhere by a wind, or by men who had him in their power.

But with regard to the things that are done from fear of greater evils or for some noble object (e.g. if a tyrant were to order one to do something base, having one's parents and children in his power, and if one did the action they were to be saved, but otherwise would be put to death), it may be debated whether such actions are involuntary or voluntary.

Something of the sort happens also with regard to the throwing of goods overboard in a storm; for in the abstract no one throws goods away voluntarily, but on condition of its securing the safety of himself and his crew any sensible man does so. Such actions, then, are mixed, but are more like voluntary actions; for they are worthy of choice at the time when they are done, and the end of an action is relative to the occasion. Both the terms, then, 'voluntary' and 'involuntary', must be used with reference to the moment of action. Now the man acts voluntarily; for the principle that moves the instrumental parts of the body in such actions is in him, and the things of which the moving principle is in a man himself are in his power to do or not to do. Such actions, therefore, are voluntary, but in the abstract perhaps involuntary; for no one would choose any such act in itself.

For such actions men are sometimes even praised, when they endure something base or painful in return for great and noble objects gained; in the opposite case they are blamed, since to endure the greatest indignities for no noble end or for a trifling end is the mark of an inferior person. On some actions praise indeed is not bestowed, but forgiveness is, when one does what he ought not under pressure which overstrains human nature and which no one could withstand. But some acts, perhaps, we cannot be forced to do, but ought rather to face death after the most fearful sufferings; for the things that forced Euripides' Alcmaeon to slay his mother seem absurd. It is difficult sometimes to determine what should be chosen at what cost, and what should be endured in return for what gain, and yet more difficult to abide by our decisions; for as a rule what is expected is painful, and what we are forced to do is base, whence praise and blame are bestowed on those who have been compelled or have not.

What sort of acts, then, should be called compulsory? We answer that without qualification actions are so when the cause is in the external circumstances and the agent contributes nothing. But the things that in themselves are involuntary, but now and in return for these gains are worthy of choice, and whose moving principle is in the agent, are in themselves involuntary, but now and in return for these gains voluntary. They are more like voluntary acts; for actions are in the class of particulars, and the particular acts here are voluntary. What sort of things are to be chosen in return for what it is not easy to state; for there are many differences in the particular cases.

But if some one were to say that pleasant and noble objects have a compelling power, forcing us from without, all acts would be for him compulsory; for it is for these objects that all men do everything they do. And those who act under compulsion and unwillingly act with pain, but those who do acts for their pleasantness and nobility do them with pleasure; it is absurd to make external circumstances responsible, and not oneself, as being easily caught by such attractions, and to make oneself responsible for noble acts but the pleasant objects responsible for base acts. The compulsory, then, seems to be that whose moving principle is outside, the person compelled contributing nothing.

Everything that is done by reason of ignorance is non-voluntary; it is only what produces pain and regret that is involuntary. For the man who has done something owing to ignorance, and feels not the least vexation at his action, has not acted voluntarily, since he did not know what he was doing, nor yet involuntarily, since he is not pained. Of people, then, who act by reason of ignorance he who regrets is thought an involuntary agent, and the man who does not regret may, since he is different, be called a non-voluntary agent; for, since he differs from the other, it is better that he should have a name of his own.

Acting by reason of ignorance seems also to be different from acting in ignorance; for the man who is drunk or in a rage is thought to act as a result not of ignorance but of one of the causes mentioned, yet not knowingly but in ignorance.

Now every wicked man is ignorant of what he ought to do and what he ought to abstain from, and error of this kind makes men unjust and in general bad; but the term 'involuntary' tends to be used not if a man is ignorant of what is to his advantage—for it is not ignorance in choice that makes action involuntary (it makes men wicked), nor ignorance of the universal (for that men are blamed), but ignorance of particular circumstances of the action and the objects with which it is concerned. For it is on these that both pity and forgiveness depend, since the person who is ignorant of any of these acts involuntarily.

Perhaps it is just as well, therefore, to determine their nature and number. A man may be ignorant, then, of who he is, what he is doing, what or whom he is acting on, and sometimes also what (e.g. what instrument) he is doing it with, and to what end (e.g. for safety), and how he is doing it (e.g. whether gently or violently). Now of all of these no one could be ignorant unless he were mad, and evidently also he could not be ignorant of the agent; for how could he not know himself? But of what he is doing a man might be ignorant, as for instance people say 'it slipped out of their mouths as they were speaking',[14] or 'they did not know it was a secret', as Aeschylus said of the mysteries, or a man might say he 'let it go off when he merely wanted to show its working', as the man did with the catapult. Again, one might think one's son was an enemy, as Merope did, or that a pointed spear had a button on it, or that a stone was pumice-stone; or one might give a man a draught to save him, and really kill him; or one might want to touch a man, as people do in sparring, and really strike him. The ignorance may relate, then, to any of these things, i.e. of the circumstances of the action, and the man who was ignorant of any of these is thought to have acted involuntarily, and especially if he was ignorant on the most important points; and these are thought to be what[15] he is doing and with what aim. Further,[16] the doing of an act that is called involuntary in virtue of ignorance of this sort must be painful and involve regret.

Since that which is done under compulsion or by reason of ignorance is involuntary, the voluntary would seem to be that of which the moving principle is in the agent himself, he being aware of the particular circumstances of the action. Presumably acts done by reason of anger or appetite are not rightly called involuntary. For in the first place, on that showing none of the other animals will act voluntarily, nor will children; and secondly, is it meant that we do not do voluntarily *any* of the acts that are due to appetite or anger, or that we do the noble acts voluntarily and the base acts involuntarily? Is not this absurd, when one and the same thing is the cause? But it would surely be odd to describe as involuntary the things one ought to desire; and we ought both to be angry at certain things and to have an appetite for certain things, e.g. for health and for learning. Also what is involuntary is thought to be painful, but what is in accordance with appetite is thought to be pleasant. Again, what is the difference in respect of involuntariness between errors committed upon calculation and those committed in anger? Both are to be avoided, but the irrational passions are thought not less human than reason is, and therefore also the actions which proceed from anger or appetite are the man's actions. It would be odd, then, to treat them as involuntary.

2. Both the voluntary and the involuntary having been delimited, we must next discuss choice; for it is thought to be most closely bound up with excellence and to discriminate characters better than actions do.

Choice, then, seems to be voluntary, but not the same thing as the voluntary; the latter extends more widely. For both children and the other animals share in voluntary action, but not in choice, and acts done on the spur of the moment we describe as voluntary, but not as chosen.

Those who say it is appetite or anger or wish or a kind of opinion do not seem to be right. For choice is not common to irrational creatures as well, but appetite and anger are. Again, the incontinent man acts with appetite, but not with choice; while the continent man on the contrary acts with choice, but not with appetite. Again, appetite is contrary to choice, but not appetite to appetite. Again, appetite relates to the pleasant and the painful, choice neither to the painful nor to the pleasant.

Still less is it anger; for acts due to anger are thought to be less than any other objects of choice.

But neither is it wish, though it seems near to it; for choice cannot relate to impossibles, and if any one said he chose them he would be thought silly; but there may be a wish even for impossibles, e.g. for immortality. And wish may relate to things that could in no way be brought about by one's own efforts, e.g. that a particular actor or athlete should win in a competition; but no one chooses such things, but only the things that he thinks could be brought about

---

[14]Reading λέγοντας . . . αὑτούς.

[15]Reading δοκεῖ ὃ καὶ οὗ ἕνεκα.

[16]Reading δέ.

by his own efforts. Again, wish relates rather to the end, choice to what contributes to the end; for instance, we wish to be healthy, but we choose the acts which will make us healthy, and we wish to be happy and say we do, but we cannot well say we choose to be so; for, in general, choice seems to relate to the things that are in our own power.

For this reason, too, it cannot be opinion; for opinion is thought to relate to all kinds of things, no less to eternal things and impossible things than to things in our own power; and it is distinguished by its falsity or truth, not by its badness or goodness, while choice is distinguished rather by these.

Now with opinion in general perhaps no one really says it is identical. But it is not identical even with any kind of opinion; for by choosing what is good or bad we are men of a certain character, which we are not by holding certain opinions. And we choose to get or avoid something good or bad, but we have opinions about what a thing is or whom it is good for or how it is good for him; we can hardly be said to opine to get or avoid anything. And choice is praised for being related to the right object rather than for being rightly related to it, opinion for being truly related to its object. And we choose what we best know to be good, but we opine what we do not know at all; and it is not the same people that are thought to make the best choices and to have the best opinions, but some are thought to have fairly good opinions, but by reason of vice to choose what they should not. If opinion precedes choice or accompanies it, that makes no difference; for it is not this that we are considering, but whether it is *identical* with some kind of opinion.

What, then, or what kind of thing is it, since it is none of the things we have mentioned? It seems to be voluntary, but not all that is voluntary to be an object of choice. Is it, then, what has been decided on by previous deliberation? For choice involves reason and thought. Even the name seems to suggest that it is what is chosen before other things.[17]

3. Do we deliberate about everything, and is everything a possible subject of deliberation, or is deliberation impossible about some things? We ought presumably to call not what a fool or a madman would deliberate about, but what a sensible man would deliberate about, a subject of deliberation. Now about eternal things no one deliberates, e.g. about the universe or the incommensurability of the diagonal and the side of a square. But no more do we deliberate about the things that involve movement but always happen in the same way, whether of necessity or by nature or from any other cause, e.g. the solstices and the risings of the stars; nor about things that happen now in one way, now in another, e.g. droughts and rains; nor about chance events, like the finding of treasure. But we do not deliberate even about all human affairs; for instance, no Spartan deliberates about the best constitution for the Scythians. For none of these things can be brought about by our own efforts.

We deliberate about things that are in our power and can be done; and these are in fact what is left. For nature, necessity, and chance are thought to be causes, and also thought and everything that depends on man. Now every class of men deliberates about the things that can be done by their own efforts. And in the case of exact and self-contained sciences there is no deliberation, e.g. about the letters of the alphabet (for we have no doubt how they should be written); but the things that are brought about by our own efforts, but not always in the same way, are the things about which we deliberate, e.g. questions of medical treatment or of money-making. And we do so more in the case of the art of navigation than in that of gymnastics, inasmuch as it has been less exactly worked out, and again about other things in the same ratio, and more also in the case of the arts than in that of the sciences; for we have more doubt about the former. Deliberation is concerned with things that happen in a certain way for the most part, but in which the event is obscure, and with things in which it is indeterminate. We call in others to aid us in deliberation on important questions, distrusting ourselves as not being equal to deciding.

We deliberate not about ends but about what contributes to ends. For a doctor does not deliberate whether he shall heal, nor an orator whether he shall convince, nor a statesman whether he shall produce law and order, nor does any one else deliberate about his end. Having set the end they consider how and

---

[17] 'προαίρεσις' connected with 'πρὸ ἑτέρων αἱρετόν'.

by what means it is to be attained; and if it seems to be produced by several means they consider by which it is most easily and best produced, while if it is achieved by one only they consider how it will be achieved by this and by what means *this* will be achieved, till they come to the first cause, which in the order of discovery is last. For the person who deliberates seems to inquire and analyse in the way described as though he were analysing a geometrical construction (not all inquiry appears to be deliberation—for instance mathematical inquiries—but all deliberation is inquiry), and what is last in the order of analysis seems to be first in the order of becoming. And if we come on an impossibility, we give up the search, e.g. if we need money and this cannot be got; but if a thing appears possible we try to do it. By 'possible' things I mean things that might be brought about by our own efforts; and these in a sense include things that can be brought about by the efforts of our friends, since the moving principle is in ourselves. The subject of investigation is sometimes the instruments, sometimes the use of them; and similarly in the other cases—sometimes the means, sometimes the mode of using it or the means of bringing it about. It seems, then, as has been said, that man is a moving principle of actions; now deliberation is about the things to be done by the agent himself, and actions are for the sake of things other than themselves. For the end cannot be a subject of deliberation, but only what contributes to the ends; nor indeed can the particular facts be a subject of it, as whether this is bread or has been baked as it should; for these are matters of perception. If we are to be always deliberating, we shall have to go on to infinity.

The same thing is deliberated upon and is chosen, except that the object of choice is already determinate, since it is that which has been decided upon as a result of deliberation that is the object of choice. For every one ceases to inquire how he is to act when he has brought the moving principle back to himself and to the ruling part of himself; for this is what chooses. This is plain also from the ancient constitutions, which Homer represented; for the kings announced their choices to the people. The object of choice being one of the things in our own power which is desired after deliberation, choice will be deliberate desire of things in our own power; for when we have decided as a result of deliberation, we desire in accordance with our deliberation.

We may take it, then, that we have described choice in outline, and stated the nature of its objects and the fact that it is concerned with what contributes to the ends.

4. That *wish* is for the end has already been stated; some think it is for the good, others for the apparent good. Now those who say that the good is the object of wish must admit in consequence that that which the man who does not choose aright wishes for is not an object of wish (for if it is to be so, it must also be good; but it was, if it so happened, bad); while those who say the apparent good is the object of wish must admit that there is no natural object of wish, but only what seems so to each man. Now different things appear so to different people, and, if it so happens, even contrary things.

If these consequences are unpleasing, are we to say that absolutely and in truth the good is the object of wish, but for each person the apparent good; that that which is in truth an object of wish is an object of wish to the good man, while any chance thing may be so to the bad man, as in the case of bodies also the things that are in truth wholesome are wholesome for bodies which are in good condition, while for those that are diseased other things are wholesome—or bitter or sweet or hot or heavy, and so on; since the good man judges each class of things rightly, and in each the truth appears to him? For each state of character has its own ideas of the noble and the pleasant, and perhaps the good man differs from others most by seeing the truth in each class of things, being as it were the norm and measure of them. In most things the error seems to be due to pleasure; for it appears a good when it is not. We therefore choose the pleasant as a good, and avoid pain as an evil.

5. The end, then, being what we wish for, the things contributing to the end what we deliberate about and choose, actions concerning the latter must be according to choice and voluntary. Now the exercise of the excellences is concerned with these. Therefore excellence also is in our own power, and so too vice. For where it is in our power to act it is also in our power not to act, and *vice versa*; so that,

if to act, where this is noble, is in our power, not to
10 act, which will be base, will also be in our power,
and if not to act, where this is noble, is in our power,
to act, which will be base, will also be in our power.
Now if it is in our power to do noble or base acts,
and likewise in our power not to do them, and this
was what being good or bad meant, then it is in our
power to be virtuous or vicious.

15 The saying that 'no one is voluntarily wicked nor
involuntarily blessed' seems to be partly false and
partly true; for no one is involuntarily blessed, but
wickedness *is* voluntary. Or else we shall have to
dispute what has just been said, at any rate, and deny
that man is a moving principle or begetter of his ac-
20 tions as of children. But if these facts are evident and
we cannot refer actions to moving principles other
than those in ourselves, the acts whose moving principles are in us must themselves also be in our power
and voluntary.

Witness seems to be borne to this both by individuals in their private capacity and by legislators
themselves; for these punish and take vengeance on
those who do wicked acts (unless they have acted
under compulsion or as a result of ignorance for
25 which they are not themselves responsible), while
they honour those who do noble acts, as though they
meant to encourage the latter and deter the former.
But no one is encouraged to do the things that are
neither in our power nor voluntary; it is assumed that
there is no gain in being persuaded not to be hot or
in pain or hungry or the like, since we shall experience these feelings none the less. Indeed, we punish
a man for his very ignorance, if he is thought responsible for the ignorance, as when penalties are
doubled in the case of drunkenness; for the moving
30 principle is in the man himself, since he had the
power of not getting drunk and his getting drunk was
the cause of his ignorance. And we punish those who
are ignorant of anything in the laws that they ought
to know and that is not difficult, and so too in the
14ª1 case of anything else that they are thought to be ignorant of through carelessness; we assume that it is
in their power not to be ignorant, since they have the
power of taking care.

But perhaps a man is the kind of man not to take
care. Still they are themselves by their slack lives re-
5 sponsible for becoming men of that kind, and men

are themselves responsible for being unjust or self-
indulgent, in that they cheat or spend their time in
drinking bouts and the like; for it is activities exercised on particular objects that make the corresponding character. This is plain from the case of
people training for any contest or action; they practise the activity the whole time. Now not to know
that it is from the exercise of activities on particular
objects that states of character are produced is the
mark of a thoroughly senseless person. Again, it is 10
irrational to suppose that a man who acts unjustly
does not wish to be unjust or a man who acts self-
indulgently to be self-indulgent. But if without being ignorant a man does the things which will make
him unjust, he will be unjust voluntarily. Yet it does
not follow that if he wishes he will cease to be unjust and will be just. For neither does the man who 15
is ill become well on those terms—although[18] he
may, perhaps, be ill voluntarily, through living incontinently and disobeying his doctors. In that case
it was *then* open to him not to be ill, but not now,
when he has thrown away his chance, just as when
you have let a stone go it is too late to recover it;
but yet it was in your power to throw it, since the
moving principle was in you. So, too, to the unjust
and to the self-indulgent man it was open at the be- 20
ginning not to become men of this kind, and so they
are such voluntarily; but now that they have become
so it is not possible for them not to be so.

But not only are the vices of the soul voluntary, but
those of the body also for some men, whom we accordingly blame; while no one blames those who are
ugly by nature, we blame those who are so owing to
want of exercise and care. So it is, too, with respect to 25
weakness and infirmity; no one would reproach a man
blind from birth or by disease or from a blow, but rather
pity him, while every one would blame a man who
was blind from alcoholism or some other form of self-
indulgence. Of vices of the body, then, those in our
own power are blamed, those not in our power are not.
And if this be so, in the other cases also the vices that 30
are blamed must be in our own power.

Now some one may say that all men aim at the
apparent good, but have no control over how things
appear to him; but the end appears to each man in a

---

[18]Reading καίτοι εἰ

^{1114^b1} form answering to his character. We reply that if each man is somehow responsible for the state he is in, he will also be himself somehow responsible for how things appear; but if not, no one is responsible for his own evildoing, but everyone does evil acts through ignorance of the end, thinking that by these he will get what is best, and the aiming at the end is not self-chosen but one must be born with an eye, as it were, by which to judge rightly and choose what is truly good, and he is well endowed by nature who is well endowed with this. For it is what is greatest and most noble, and what we cannot get or learn from another, but must have just such as it was when given us at birth, and to be well and nobly endowed with this will be complete and true natural endowment. If this is true, then, how will excellence be more voluntary than vice? To both men alike, the good and the bad, the end appears and is fixed by nature or however it may be, and it is by referring everything else to this that men do whatever they do.

Whether, then, it is not by nature that the end appears to each man such as it does appear, but something also depends on him, or the end is natural but because the good man does the rest voluntarily excellence is voluntary, vice also will be none the less voluntary; for in the case of the bad man there is equally present that which depends on himself in his actions even if not in his end. If, then, as is asserted, the excellences are voluntary (for we are ourselves somehow part-causes of our states of character, and it is by being persons of a certain kind that we assume the end to be so and so), the vices also will be voluntary; for the same is true of them.

With regard to the excellences in *general* we have stated their genus in outline, viz. that they are means and that they are states, and that they tend by their own nature to the doing of the acts by which they are produced, and that they are in our power and voluntary, and act as right reason prescribes. But actions and states are not voluntary in the same way; for we are masters of our actions from the beginning right to the end, if we know the particular facts, but though we control the beginning of our states the ^{1115^a1} gradual progress is not obvious, any more than it is in illnesses; because it was in our power, however, to act in this way or not in this way, therefore the states are voluntary.

Let us take up the several excellences, however, and say which they are and what sort of things they are concerned with and how they are concerned with them; at the same time it will become plain how many they are. And first let us speak of courage.

6. That it is a mean with regard to fear and confidence has already been made evident; and plainly the things we fear are terrible things, and these are, to speak without qualification, evils; for which reason people even define fear as expectation of evil. Now we fear all evils, e.g. disgrace, poverty, disease, friendlessness, death, but the brave man is not thought to be concerned with all; for to fear some things is even right and noble, and it is base not to fear them—e.g. disgrace; he who fears this is good and modest, and he who does not is shameless. He is, however, by some people called brave, by an extension of the word; for he has in him something which is like the brave man, since the brave man also is a fearless person. Poverty and disease we perhaps ought not to fear, nor in general the things that do not proceed from vice and are not due to a man himself. But not even the man who is fearless of these is brave. Yet we apply the word to him also in virtue of a similarity; for some who in the dangers of war are cowards are liberal and are confident in face of the loss of money. Nor is a man a coward if he fears insult to his wife and children or envy or anything of the kind; nor brave if he is confident when he is about to be flogged. With what sort of terrible things, then, is the brave man concerned? Surely with the greatest; for no one is more likely than he to stand his ground against what is dreadful. Now death is the most terrible of all things; for it is the end, and nothing is thought to be any longer either good or bad for the dead. But the brave man would not seem to be concerned even with death in *all* circumstances, e.g. at sea or in disease. In what circumstances, then? Surely in the noblest. Now such deaths are those in battle; for these take place in the greatest and noblest danger. And this agrees with the ways in which honours are bestowed in city-states and at the courts of monarchs. Properly, then, he will be called brave who is fearless in face of a noble death, and of all emergencies that involve death; and the emergencies of war are in the highest degree of this kind. Yet at sea also, and in disease, the brave man is fearless,

15ᵇ1 but not in the same way as the seamen; for he has given up hope for safety, and is disliking the thought of death in this shape, while they are hopeful because of their experience. At the same time, we show courage in situations where there is the opportunity of showing prowess or where death is noble; but in these forms of death neither of these conditions is fulfilled.

7. What is terrible is not the same for all men; but we say there are things terrible even beyond human strength. These, then, are terrible to every one—at least to every sensible man; but the terrible things that are *not* beyond human strength differ in magnitude and degree, and so too do the things that inspire confidence. Now the brave man is as dauntless as man may be. Therefore, while he will fear even the things that are not beyond human strength, he will fear them as he ought and as reason directs, and[19] he will face them for the sake of what is noble; for this is the end of excellence. But it is possible to fear these more, or less, and again to fear things that are not terrible as if they were. Of the faults that are committed one consists in fearing what one should not, another in fearing as we should not, another in fearing when we should not, and so on; and so too with respect to the things that inspire confidence. The man, then, who faces and who fears the right things and with the right aim, in the right way and at the right time, and who feels confidence under the corresponding conditions, is brave; for the brave man feels and acts according to the merits of the case and in whatever way reason directs. Now the end of every activity is conformity to the corresponding state. This is true, therefore, of the brave man as well as of others. But courage is noble.[20] Therefore the end also is noble; for each thing is defined by its end. Therefore it is for a noble end that the brave man endures and acts as courage directs.

Of those who go to excess he who exceeds in fearlessness has no name (we have said previously that many states have no names), but he would be a sort of madman or insensible person if he feared nothing, neither earthquakes nor the waves, as they say the Celts do not; while the man who exceeds in confidence about what really is terrible is rash. The rash man, however, is also thought to be boastful and only a pretender to courage; at all events, as the brave man *is* with regard to what is terrible, so the rash man wishes to *appear*; and so he imitates him in situations where he can. Hence also most of them are a mixture of rashness and cowardice; for, while in these situations they display confidence, they do not hold their ground against what is really terrible. The man who exceeds in fear is a coward; for he fears both what he ought not and as he ought not, and all the similar characterizations attach to him. He is lacking also in confidence; but he is more conspicuous for his excess of fear in painful situations. The coward, then, is a despairing sort of person; for he fears everything. The brave man, on the other hand, has the opposite disposition; for confidence is the mark of a hopeful disposition. The coward, the rash man, and the brave man, then, are concerned with the same objects but are differently disposed towards them; for the first two exceed and fall short, while the third holds the middle, which is the right, position; and rash men are precipitate, and wish for dangers beforehand but draw back when they are in them, while brave men are keen in the moment of action, but quiet beforehand.

As we have said, then, courage is a mean with respect to things that inspire confidence or fear, in the circumstances that have been stated; and it chooses or endures things because it is noble to do so, or because it is base not to do so. But to die to escape from poverty or love or anything painful is not the mark of a brave man, but rather of a coward; for it is softness to fly from what is troublesome, and such a man endures death not because it is noble but to fly from evil.

8. Courage, then, is something of this sort, but the name is also applied to five other kinds. (1) First comes political courage; for this is most like true courage. Citizens seem to face dangers because of the penalties imposed by the laws and the reproaches they would otherwise incur, and because of the honours they win by such action; and therefore those peoples seem to be bravest among whom cowards are held in dishonour and brave men in honour. This is the kind of courage that Homer depicts, e.g. in Diomede and in Hector:

---

[19]Reading ὡς ὁ λόγος, ὑπομενεῖ τε.
[20]Reading ἀνδρείῳ δή · ἠδ' ἀνδρεία.

*First will Polydamas be to heap reproach on
   me then.*[21]

and

*For Hector one day 'mid the Trojans shall utter
   his vaulting harangue:
"Afraid was Tydeides, and fled from my face,"*[22]

This kind of courage is most like that which we described earlier, because it is due to excellence; for it is due to shame and to desire of a noble object (i.e. honour) and avoidance of disgrace, which is ignoble. One might rank in the same class even those who are compelled by their rulers; but they are inferior, inasmuch as they act not from shame but from fear, and to avoid not what is disgraceful but what is painful; for their masters compel them, as Hector does:

*But if I shall spy any dastard that cowers far
   from the fight,
Vainly will such an one hope to escape from
   the dogs.*[23]

And those who give them their posts, and beat them if they retreat, do the same, and so do those who draw them up with trenches or something of the sort behind them; all of these apply compulsion. But one ought to be brave not under compulsion but because it is noble to be so.

(2) Experience with regard to particular facts is also thought to be courage; this is indeed the reason why Socrates thought courage was knowledge. Other people exhibit this quality in other dangers, and soldiers exhibit it in the dangers of war; for there seem to be many empty alarms in war, of which these have had the most comprehensive experience; therefore they seem brave, because the others do not know the nature of the facts. Again, their experience makes them most capable of doing without being done to, since they can use their arms and have the kind that are likely to be best both for doing and for not being done to; therefore they fight like armed men against unarmed or like trained athletes against amateurs; for in such contests too it is not the bravest men that fight best, but those who are strongest and have their bodies in the best condition. Soldiers turn cowards, however, when the danger puts too great a strain on them and they are inferior in numbers and equipment; for they are the first to fly, while citizen-forces die at their posts, as in fact happened at the temple of Hermes. For to the latter flight is disgraceful and death is preferable to safety on those terms; while the former from the very beginning faced the danger on the assumption that they were stronger, and when they know the facts they fly, fearing death more than disgrace; but the brave man is not that sort of person.

(3) Passion also is sometimes reckoned as courage; those who act from passion, like wild beasts rushing at those who have wounded them, are thought to be brave, because brave men also are passionate; for passion above all things is eager to rush on danger, and hence Homer's 'put strength into his passion' and 'aroused their spirit and passion' and 'bitter spirit in his nostrils' and 'his blood boiled'.[24] For all such expressions seem to indicate the stirring and onset of passion. Now brave men act for the sake of the noble, but passion aids them; while wild beasts act under the influence of pain; for they attack because they have been wounded or because they are afraid, since if they are in a forest they do not come near one. Thus they are not brave because, driven by pain and passion, they rush on danger without foreseeing any of the perils, since at that rate even asses would be brave when they are hungry; for blows will not drive them from their food; and lust also makes adulterers do many daring things. [Those creatures are not brave, then, which are driven on to danger by pain or passion.][25] The courage that is due to passion seems to be the most natural, and to be courage if choice and aim be added.

Men, then, as well as beasts, suffer pain when they are angry, and are pleased when they exact their revenge; those who fight for these reasons, however, are pugnacious but not brave; for they do not act for the sake of the noble nor as reason directs, but from feeling; they have, however, something akin to courage.

---

[21] *Iliad* XXII 100.
[22] *Iliad* VIII 148.
[23] See *Iliad* II 391; XV 348.
[24] See *Iliad* V 470; XI 11; XVI 529; *Odyssey* XXIV 318.
[25] Excised in Bywater.

(4) Nor are sanguine people brave; for they are confident in danger only because they have conquered often and against many foes. Yet they closely resemble brave men, because both are confident; but brave men are confident for the reasons stated earlier, while these are so because they think they are the strongest and can suffer nothing. (Drunken men also behave in this way; they become sanguine). When their adventures do not succeed, however, they run away; but it was the mark of a brave man to face things that are, and seem, terrible for a man, because it is noble to do so and disgraceful not to do so. Hence also it is thought the mark of a braver man to be fearless and undisturbed in sudden alarms than to be so in those that are foreseen; for it must have proceeded more from a state of character, because less from preparation; for acts that are foreseen may be chosen by calculation and reason, but sudden actions in accordance with one's state of character.

(5) People who are ignorant also appear brave, and they are not far removed from those of a sanguine temper, but are inferior inasmuch as they have no self-reliance while these have. Hence also the sanguine hold their ground for a time; but those who have been deceived fly if they know or suspect that things are different as happened to the Argives when they fell in with the Spartans and took them for Sicyonians.

9. We have, then, described the character both of brave men and of those who are thought to be brave.

Though courage is concerned with confidence and fear, it is not concerned with both alike, but more with the things that inspire fear; for he who is undisturbed in face of these and bears himself as he should towards these is more truly brave than the man who does so towards the things that inspire confidence. It is for facing what is painful, then, as has been said, that men are called brave. Hence also courage involves pain, and is justly praised; for it is harder to face what is painful than to abstain from what is pleasant. Yet the end which courage sets before it would seem to be pleasant, but to be concealed by the attending circumstances, as happens also in athletic contests; for the end at which boxers aim is pleasant—the crown and the honours—but the blows they take are distressing to flesh and blood, and painful, and so is their whole exertion; and because the blows and the exertions are many the end, which is but small, appears to have nothing pleasant in it. And so, if the case of courage is similar, death and wounds will be painful to the brave man and against his will, but he will face them because it is noble to do so or because it is base not to do so. And the more he is possessed of excellence in its entirety and the happier he is, the more he will be pained at the thought of death; for life is best worth living for such a man, and he is knowingly losing the greatest goods, and this is painful. But he is none the less brave, and perhaps all the more so, because he chooses noble deeds of war at that cost. It is not the case, then, with all the excellences that the exercise of them is pleasant, except in so far as it reaches its end. But it is quite possible that the best soldiers may be not men of this sort but those who are less brave but have no other good; for these are ready to face danger, and they sell their life for trifling gains.

So much, then, for courage; it is not difficult to grasp its nature in outline, at any rate, from what has been said.

10. After courage let us speak of temperance; for these seem to be the excellences of the irrational parts. We have said that temperance is a mean with regard to pleasures (for it is less, and not in the same way, concerned with pains); self-indulgence also is manifested in the same sphere. Now, therefore, let us determine with what sort of pleasures they are concerned. We may assume the distinction between bodily pleasures and those of the soul, such as love of honour and love of learning; for the lover of each of these delights in that of which he is a lover, the body being in no way affected, but rather the mind; but men who are concerned with such pleasures are called neither temperate nor self-indulgent. Nor, again, are those who are concerned with the other pleasures that are not bodily; for those who are fond of hearing and telling stories and who spend their days on anything that turns up are called gossips, but not self-indulgent, nor are those who are pained at the loss of money or of friends.

Temperance must be concerned with bodily pleasures, but not all even of these; for those who delight in objects of vision, such as colours and shapes and painting, are called neither temperate nor self-indulgent; yet it would seem possible to delight even in these either as one should or to excess or to a deficient degree.

And so too is it with objects of hearing; no one calls those who delight extravagantly in music or acting self-indulgent, nor those who do so as they ought temperate.

Nor do we apply these names to those who delight in odour, unless it be incidentally; we do not call those self-indulgent who delight in the odour of apples or roses or incense, but rather those who delight in the odour of unguents or of dainty dishes; for self-indulgent people delight in these because these remind them of the objects of their appetite. And one may see even other people, when they are hungry, delighting in the smell of food; but to delight in this kind of thing is the mark of the self-indulgent man; for these are objects of appetite to him.

Nor is there in animals other than man any pleasure connected with these senses except incidentally. For dogs do not delight in the scent of hares, but in the eating of them, but the scent told them the hares were there; nor does the lion delight in the lowing of the ox, but in eating it; but he perceived by the lowing that it was near, and therefore appears to delight in the lowing; and similarly he does not delight because he sees 'a stag or a wild goat',[26] but because he is going to make a meal of it. Temperance and self-indulgence, however, are concerned with the kind of pleasures that the other animals share in, which therefore appear slavish and brutish; these are touch and taste. But even of taste they appear to make little or no use; for the business of taste is the discriminating of flavours, which is done by wine-tasters and people who season dishes; but they hardly take pleasure in making these discriminations, or at least self-indulgent people do not, but in the actual enjoyment, which in all cases comes through touch, both in the case of food and in that of drink and in that of sexual intercourse. This is why a certain gourmand prayed that his throat might become longer than a crane's, implying that it was the contact that he took pleasure in. Thus the sense with which self-indulgence is connected is the most widely shared of the senses; and self-indulgence would seem to be

justly a matter of reproach, because it attaches to us not as men but as animals. To delight in such things, then, and to love them above all others, is brutish. For even of the pleasures of touch the most liberal have been eliminated, e.g. those produced in the gymnasium by rubbing and by the consequent heat; for the contact characteristic of the self-indulgent man does not affect the whole body but only certain parts.

11. Of the appetites some seem to be common, others to be peculiar to individuals and acquired; e.g. the appetite for food is natural, since every one who is without it craves for food or drink, and sometimes for both, and for love also (as Homer says) if he is young and lusty; but not every one craves for this or that kind of nourishment or love, nor for the same things. Hence such craving appears to be our very own. Yet it has of course something natural about it; for different things are pleasant to different kinds of people, and some things are more pleasant to every one than chance objects. Now in the natural appetites few go wrong, and only in one direction, that of excess; for to eat or drink whatever offers itself till one is surfeited is to exceed the natural amount, since natural appetite is the replenishment of one's deficiency. Hence these people are called belly-gods, this implying that they fill their belly beyond what is right. It is people of entirely slavish character that become like this. But with regard to the pleasures peculiar to individuals many people go wrong and in many ways. For while the people who are fond of so and so are so called because they delight either in the wrong things, or more than most people do, or in the wrong way, the self-indulgent exceed in all three ways; they both delight in some things that they ought not to delight in (since they are hateful), and if one ought to delight in some of the things they delight in, they do so more than one ought and than most men do.

Plainly, then, excess with regard to pleasures is self-indulgence and is culpable; with regard to pains one is not, as in the case of courage, called temperate for facing them or self-indulgent for not doing so, but the self-indulgent man is so called because he is pained more than he ought at not getting pleasant things (even his pain being caused by pleasure), and the temperate man is so called because he is not

---

[26] *Iliad* III 24.

pained at the absence of what is pleasant and at his abstinence from it.

The self-indulgent man, then, craves for all pleasant things or those that are most pleasant, and is led by his appetite to choose these at the cost of everything else; hence he is pained both when he fails to get them and when he is craving for them (for appetite involves pain); but it seems absurd to be pained for the sake of pleasure. People who fall short with regard to pleasures and delight in them less than they should are hardly found; for such insensibility is not human. Even the other animals distinguish different kinds of food and enjoy some and not others; and if there is any one who finds nothing pleasant and nothing more attractive than anything else, he must be something quite different from a man; this sort of person has not received a name because he hardly occurs. The temperate man occupies a middle position with regard to these objects. For he neither enjoys the things that the self-indulgent man enjoys most—but rather dislikes them—nor in general the things that he should not, nor anything of this sort to excess, nor does he feel pain or craving when they are absent, or does so only to a moderate degree, and not more than he should, nor when he should not, and so on; but the things that, being pleasant, make for health or for good condition, he will desire moderately and as he should, and also other pleasant things if they are not hindrances to these ends, or contrary to what is noble, or beyond his means. For he who neglects these conditions loves such pleasures more than they are worth, but the temperate man is not that sort of person, but the sort of person that right reason prescribes.

12. Self-indulgence is more like a voluntary state than cowardice. For the former is actuated by pleasure, the latter by pain, of which the one is to be chosen and the other to be avoided; and pain upsets and destroys the nature of the person who feels it, while pleasure does nothing of the sort. Therefore self-indulgence is more voluntary. Hence also it is more a matter of reproach; for it is easier to become accustomed to its objects, since there are many things of this sort in life, and the process of habituation to them is free from danger, while with terrible objects the reverse is the case. But cowardice would seem to be voluntary in a different degree from its particular

manifestations; for it is itself painless, but in these we are upset by pain, so that we even throw down our arms and disgrace ourselves in other ways; hence our acts are even thought to be done under compulsion. For the self-indulgent man, on the other hand, the particular acts are voluntary (for he does them with craving and desire), but the whole state is less so; for no one craves to be self-indulgent.

The name self-indulgence is applied also to childish faults; for they bear a certain resemblance to what we have been considering. Which is called after which, makes no difference to our present purpose; plainly, however, the later is called after the earlier. The transference of the name seems not a bad one; for that which desires what is base and which develops quickly ought to be kept in a chastened condition,[27] and these characteristics belong above all to appetite and to the child, since children in fact live at the beck and call of appetite, and it is in them that the desire for what is pleasant is strongest. If, then, it is not going to be obedient and subject to the ruling principle, it will go to great lengths; for in an irrational being the desire for pleasure is insatiable and tries every source of gratification, and the exercise of appetite increases its innate force, and if appetites are strong and violent they even expel the power of calculation. Hence they should be moderate and few, and should in no way oppose reason—and this is what we call an obedient and chastened state—and as the child should live according to the direction of his tutor, so the appetitive element should live according to reason. Hence the appetitive element in a temperate man should harmonize with reason; for the noble is the mark at which both aim, and the temperate man craves for the things he ought, as he ought, and when he ought; and this is what reason directs.

Here we conclude our account of temperance.

BOOK VI

1. Since we have previously said that one ought to choose that which is intermediate, not the excess nor

---

[27] ἀκόλαστος ('self-indulgent') is connected with κολάζειν ('chasten,' 'punish').

the defect, and that the intermediate is determined by the dictates of the right rule, let us discuss the nature of these dictates. In all the states of character we have mentioned, as in all other matters, there is a mark to which the man who has the rule looks, and heightens or relaxes his activity accordingly, and there is a standard which determines the mean states which we say are intermediate between excess and defect, being in accordance with the right rule. But such a statement, though true, is by no means clear; for not only here but in all other pursuits which are objects of knowledge it is indeed true to say that we must not exert ourselves nor relax our efforts too much nor too little, but to an intermediate extent and as the right rule dictates; but if a man had only this knowledge he would be none the wiser e.g. we should not know what sort of medicines to apply to our body if some one were to say 'all those which the medical art prescribes, and which agree with the practice of one who possesses the art'. Hence it is necessary with regard to the states of the soul also not only that this true statement should be made, but also that it should be determined what is the right rule and what is the standard that fixes it.

We divided the virtues of the soul and a said that some are virtues of character and others of intellect. Now we have discussed in detail the moral virtues; with regard to the others let us express our view as follows, beginning with some remarks about the soul. We said before that there are two parts of the soul—that which grasps a rule or rational principle, and the irrational; let us now draw a similar distinction within the part which grasps a rational principle. And let it be assumed that there are two parts which grasp a rational principle—one by which we contemplate the kind of things whose originative causes are invariable, and one by which we contemplate variable things; for where objects differ in kind the part of the soul answering to each of the two is different in kind, since it is in virtue of a certain likeness and kinship with their objects that they have the knowledge they have. Let one of these parts be called the scientific and the other the calculative; for to deliberate and to calculate are the same thing, but no one deliberates about the invariable. Therefore the calculative is one part of the faculty which grasps a rational principle. We must, then, learn what is the best state of each of these two parts; for this is the virtue of each.

2. The virtue of a thing is relative to its proper work. Now there are three things in the soul which control action and truth—sensation, reason, desire.

Of these sensation originates no action; this is plain from the fact that the lower animals have sensation but no share in action.

What affirmation and negation are in thinking, pursuit and avoidance are in desire; so that since moral virtue is a state of character concerned with choice, and choice is deliberate desire, therefore both the reasoning must be true and the desire right, if the choice is to be good, and the latter must pursue just what the former asserts. Now this kind of intellect and of truth is practical; of the intellect which is contemplative, not practical nor productive, the good and the bad state are truth and falsity respectively (for this is the work of everything intellectual); while of the part which is practical and intellectual the good state is truth in agreement with right desire.

The origin of action—its efficient, not its final cause—is choice, and that of choice is desire and reasoning with a view to an end. This is why choice cannot exist either without reason and intellect or without a moral state; for good action and its opposite cannot exist without a combination of intellect and character. Intellect itself, however, moves nothing, but only the intellect which aims at an end and is practical; for this rules the productive intellect, as well, since every one who makes makes for an end, and that which is made is not an end in the unqualified sense (but only an end in a particular relation, and the end of a particular operation)—only that which is done is that; for good action is an end, and desire aims at this. Hence choice is either desiderative reason or ratiocinative desire, and such an origin of action is a man. (It is to be noted that nothing that is past is an object of choice, e.g. no one chooses to have sacked Troy; for no one deliberates about the past, but about what is future and capable of being otherwise, while what is past is not capable of not having taken place; hence Agathon is right in saying

For this alone is lacking even to God,
To make undone things that have once been done.)

The work of both the intellectual parts, then, is truth. Therefore the states that are most strictly those in respect of which each of these parts will reach truth are the virtues of the two parts.

3. Let us begin, then, from the beginning, and discuss these states once more. Let it be assumed that the states by virtue of which the soul possesses truth by way of affirmation or denial are five in number, i.e. art, scientific knowledge, practical wisdom, philosophic wisdom, intuitive reason; we do not include judgement and opinion because in these we may be mistaken.

Now what scientific knowledge is, if we are to speak exactly and not follow mere similarities, is plain from what follows. We all suppose that what we know is not even capable of being otherwise; of things capable of being otherwise we do not know, when they have passed outside our observation, whether they exist or not. Therefore the object of scientific knowledge is of necessity. Therefore it is eternal; for things that are of necessity in the unqualified sense are all eternal; and things that are eternal are ungenerated and imperishable. Again, every science is thought to be capable of being taught, and its object of being learned. And all teaching starts from what is already known, as we maintain in the Analytics also; for it proceeds sometimes through induction and sometimes by syllogism. Now induction is the starting-point which knowledge even of the universal presupposes, while syllogism proceeds from universals. There are therefore starting-points from which syllogism proceeds, which are not reached by syllogism; it is therefore by induction that they are acquired. Scientific knowledge is, then, a state of capacity to demonstrate, and has the other limiting characteristics which we specify in the Analytics, for it is when a man believes in a certain way and the starting-points are known to him that he has scientific knowledge, since if they are not better known to him than the conclusion, he will have his knowledge only incidentally.

Let this, then, be taken as our account of scientific knowledge.

5. Regarding practical wisdom we shall get at the truth by considering who are the persons we credit with it. Now it is thought to be the mark of a man of practical wisdom to be able to deliberate well about what is good and expedient for himself, not in some particular respect, e.g. about what sorts of thing conduce to health or to strength, but about what sorts of thing conduce to the good life in general. This is shown by the fact that we credit men with practical wisdom in some particular respect when they have calculated well with a view to some good end which is one of those that are not the object of any art. It follows that in the general sense also the man who is capable of deliberating has practical wisdom. Now no one deliberates about things that are invariable, nor about things that it is impossible for him to do. Therefore, since scientific knowledge involves demonstration, but there is no demonstration of things whose first principles are variable (for all such things might actually be otherwise), and since it is impossible to deliberate about things that are of necessity, practical wisdom cannot be scientific knowledge nor art; not science because that which can be done is capable of being otherwise, not art because action and making are different kinds of thing. The remaining alternative, then, is that it is a true and reasoned state of capacity to act with regard to the things that are good or bad for man. For while making has an end other than itself, action cannot; for good action itself is its end. It is for this reason that we think Pericles and men like him have practical wisdom, viz. because they can see what is good for themselves and what is good for men in general; we consider that those can do this who are good at managing households or states. (This is why we call temperance (sophrosune) by this name; we imply that it preserves one's practical wisdom (sozousa tan phronsin). Now what it preserves is a judgement of the kind we have described. For it is not any and every judgement that pleasant and painful objects destroy and pervert, e.g. the judgement that the triangle has or has not its angles equal to two right angles, but only judgements about what is to be done. For the originating causes of the things that are done consist in the end at which they are aimed; but the man who has been ruined by pleasure or pain forthwith fails to see any such originating cause—to see that for the sake of this or because of this he ought to choose and do whatever he chooses and does; for vice is destructive of the originating cause of action.) Practical wisdom, then, must be a reasoned and true state of capacity to act with regard to human goods. But further, while there is such a thing as excellence

in art, there is no such thing as excellence in practical wisdom; and in art he who errs willingly is preferable, but in practical wisdom, as in the virtues, he is the reverse. Plainly, then, practical wisdom is a virtue and not an art. There being two parts of the soul that can follow a course of reasoning, it must be the virtue of one of the two, i.e. of that part which forms opinions; for opinion is about the variable and so is practical wisdom. But yet it is not only a reasoned state; this is shown by the fact that a state of that sort may forgotten but practical wisdom cannot.

6. Scientific knowledge is judgement about things that are universal and necessary, and the conclusions of demonstration, and all scientific knowledge, follow from first principles (for scientific knowledge involves apprehension of a rational ground). This being so, the first principle from which what is scientifically known follows cannot be an object of scientific knowledge, of art, or of practical wisdom; for that which can be scientifically known can be demonstrated, and art and practical wisdom deal with things that are variable. Nor are these first principles the objects of philosophic wisdom, for it is a mark of the philosopher to have demonstration about some things. If, then, the states of mind by which we have truth and are never deceived about things invariable or even variable are scientific knowlededge, practical wisdom, philosophic wisdom, and intuitive reason, and it cannot be any of the three (i.e. practical wisdom, scientific knowledge, or philosophic wisdom), the remaining alternative is that it is intuitive reason that grasps the first principles.

7. Wisdom (1) in the arts we ascribe to their most finished exponents, e.g. to Phidias as a sculptor and to Polyclitus as a maker of portrait-statues, and here we mean nothing by wisdom except excellence in art; but (2) we think that some people are wise in general, not in some particular field or in any other limited respect, as Homer says in the Margites,

Him did the gods make neither a digger nor yet a ploughman
Nor wise in anything else.

Therefore wisdom must plainly be the most finished of the forms of knowledge. It follows that the wise man must not only know what follows from the first principles, but must also possess truth about the first principles. Therefore wisdom must be intuitive reason combined with scientific knowledge—scientific knowledge of the highest objects which has received as it were its proper completion.

Of the highest objects, we say; for it would be strange to think that the art of politics, or practical wisdom, is the best knowledge, since man is not the best thing in the world. Now if what is healthy or good is different for men and for fishes, but what is white or straight is always the same, any one would say that what is wise is the same but what is practically wise is different; for it is to that which observes well the various matters concerning itself that one ascribes practical wisdom, and it is to this that one will entrust such matters. This is why we say that some even of the lower animals have practical wisdom, viz. those which are found to have a power of foresight with regard to their own life. It is evident also that philosophic wisdom and the art of politics cannot be the same; for if the state of mind concerned with a man's own interests is to be called philosophic wisdom, there will be many philosophic wisdoms; there will not be one concerned with the good of all animals (any more than there is one art of medicine for all existing things), but a different philosophic wisdom about the good of each species.

But if the argument be that man is the best of the animals, this makes no difference; for there are other things much more divine in their nature even than man, e.g., most conspicuously, the bodies of which the heavens are framed. From what has been said it is plain, then, that philosophic wisdom is scientific knowledge, combined with intuitive reason, of the things that are highest by nature. This is why we say Anaxagoras, Thales, and men like them have philosophic but not practical wisdom, when we see them ignorant of what is to their own advantage, and why we say that they know things that are remarkable, admirable, difficult, and divine, but useless; viz. because it is not human goods that they seek.

Practical wisdom on the other hand is concerned with things human and things about which it is possible to deliberate; for we say this is above all the work of the man of practical wisdom, to deliberate well, but no one deliberates about things invariable, nor about things which have not an end, and that a good that can be brought about by action. The man who is without qualification good at deliberating is the man who is capable of aiming in accordance with calculation at the best for man of things attainable by action. Nor is practical wisdom concerned with universals only—it must also recognize the particulars; for it is practical, and practice is concerned with particulars. This is why some who do not know, and especially those who have experience, are more practical than others who know; for if a man knew that light meats are digestible and wholesome, but did not know which sorts of meat are light, he would not produce health, but the man who knows that chicken is wholesome is more likely to produce health.

Now practical wisdom is concerned with action; therefore one should have both forms of it, or the latter in preference to the former. But of practical as of philosophic wisdom there must be a controlling kind.

8. Political wisdom and practical wisdom are the same state of mind, but their essence is not the same. Of the wisdom concerned with the city, the practical wisdom which plays a controlling part is legislative wisdom, while that which is related to this as particulars to their universal is known by the general name 'political wisdom'; this has to do with action and deliberation, for a decree is a thing to be carried out in the form of an individual act. This is why the exponents of this art are alone said to 'take part in politics'; for these alone 'do things' as manual labourers 'do things'.

Practical wisdom also is identified especially with that form of it which is concerned with a man himself—with the individual; and this is known by the general name 'practical wisdom'; of the other kinds one is called household management, another legislation, the third politics, and of the latter one part is called deliberative and the other judicial. Now knowing what is good for oneself will be one kind of knowledge, but it is very different from the other kinds; and the man who knows and concerns himself with his own interests is thought to have practical wisdom, while politicians are thought to be busybodies; hence the word of Euripides,

But how could I be wise, who might at ease,
Numbered among the army's multitude,
Have had an equal share?
For those who aim too high and do too much.

Those who think thus seek their own good, and consider that one ought to do so. From this opinion, then, has come the view that such men have practical wisdom; yet perhaps one's own good cannot exist without household management, nor without a form of government. Further, how one should order one's own affairs is not clear and needs inquiry.

What has been said is confirmed by the fact that while young men become geometricians and mathematicians and wise in matters like these, it is thought that a young man of practical wisdom cannot be found. The cause is that such wisdom is concerned not only with universals but with particulars, which become familiar from experience, but a young man has no experience, for it is length of time that gives experience; indeed one might ask this question too, why a boy may become a mathematician, but not a philosopher or a physicist. It is because the objects of mathematics exist by abstraction, while the first principles of these other subjects come from experience, and because young men have no conviction about the latter but merely use the proper language, while the essence of mathematical objects is plain enough to them?

Further, error in deliberation may be either about the universal or about the particular; we may fall to know either that all water that weighs heavy is bad, or that this particular water weighs heavy.

That practical wisdom is not scientific knowledge is evident; for it is, as has been said, concerned with the ultimate particular fact, since the thing to be done is of this nature. It is opposed, then, to intuitive reason; for intuitive reason is of the limiting premises, for which no reason can be given, while practical wisdom is concerned with the ultimate particular, which is the object not of scientific knowledge but of perception-not the perception of qualities peculiar to one sense but a perception akin to that by which we perceive that the particular figure before us is a triangle; for in that direction as well as in that of the major premiss there will be a limit. But this is rather perception than practical wisdom, though it is another kind of perception than that of the qualities peculiar to each sense.

12. Difficulties might be raised as to the utility of these qualities of mind. For (1) philosophic wisdom will contemplate none of the things that will

make a man happy (for it is not concerned with any coming into being), and though practical wisdom has this merit, for what purpose do we need it? Practical wisdom is the quality of mind concerned with things just and noble and good for man, but these are the things which it is the mark of a good man to do, and we are none the more able to act for knowing them if the virtues are states of character, just as we are none the better able to act for knowing the things that are healthy and sound, in the sense not of producing but of issuing from the state of health; for we are none the more able to act for having the art of medicine or of gymnastics. But (2) if we are to say that a man should have practical wisdom not for the sake of knowing moral truths but for the sake of becoming good, practical wisdom will be of no use to those who are good; again it is of no use to those who have not virtue; for it will make no difference whether they have practical wisdom themselves or obey others who have it, and it would be enough for us to do what we do in the case of health; though we wish to become healthy, yet we do not learn the art of medicine. (3) Besides this, it would be thought strange if practical wisdom, being inferior to philosophic wisdom, is to be put in authority over it, as seems to be implied by the fact that the art which produces anything rules and issues commands about that thing.

These, then, are the questions we must discuss; so far we have only stated the difficulties.

(1) Now first let us say that in themselves these states must be worthy of choice because they are the virtues of the two parts of the soul respectively, even if neither of them produce anything.

(2) Secondly, they do produce something, not as the art of medicine produces health, however, but as health produces health; so does philosophic wisdom produce happiness; for, being a part of virtue entire, by being possessed and by actualizing itself it makes a man happy.

(3) Again, the work of man is achieved only in accordance with practical wisdom as well as with moral virtue; for virtue makes us aim at the right mark, and practical wisdom makes us take the right means. (Of the fourth part of the soul—the nutritive—there is no such virtue; for there is nothing which it is in its power to do or not to do.)

(4) With regard to our being none the more able to do because of our practical wisdom what is noble and just, let us begin a little further back, starting with the following principle. As we say that some people who do just acts are not necessarily just, i.e. those who do the acts ordained by the laws either unwillingly or owing to ignorance or for some other reason and not for the sake of the acts themselves (though, to be sure, they do what they should and all the things that the good man ought), so is it, it seems, that in order to be good one must be in a certain state when one does the several acts, i.e. one must do them as a result of choice and for the sake of the acts themselves. Now virtue makes the choice right, but the question of the things which should naturally be done to carry out our choice belongs not to virtue but to another faculty. We must devote our attention to these matters and give a clearer statement about them. There is a faculty which is called cleverness; and this is such as to be able to do the things that tend towards the mark we have set before ourselves, and to hit it. Now if the mark be noble, the cleverness is laudable, but if the mark be bad, the cleverness is mere smartness; hence we call even men of practical wisdom clever or smart. Practical wisdom is not the faculty, but it does not exist without this faculty. And this eye of the soul acquires its formed state not without the aid of virtue, as has been said and is plain; for the syllogisms which deal with acts to be done are things which involve a starting-point, viz. 'since the end, i.e. what is best, is of such and such a nature', whatever it may be (let it for the sake of argument be what we please); and this is not evident except to the good man; for wickedness perverts us and causes us to be deceived about the starting-points of action. Therefore it is evident that it is impossible to be practically wise without being good.

13. We must therefore consider virtue also once more; for virtue too is similarly related; as practical wisdom is to cleverness—not the same, but like it—so is natural virtue to virtue in the strict sense. For all men think that each type of character belongs to its possessors in some sense by nature; for from the very moment of birth we are just or fitted for self-control or brave or have the other moral qualities; but yet we seek something else as that which is good in the strict sense—we seek for the presence of such

qualities in another way. For both children and brutes have the natural dispositions to these qualities, but without reason these are evidently hurtful. Only we seem to see this much, that, while one may be led astray by them, as a strong body which moves with-out sight may stumble badly because of its lack of sight, still, if a man once acquires reason, that makes a difference in action; and his state, while still like what it was, will then be virtue in the strict sense. Therefore, as in the part of us which forms opinions there are two types, cleverness and practical wisdom, so too in the moral part there are two types, natural virtue and virtue in the strict sense, and of these the latter involves practical wisdom. This is why some say that all the virtues are forms of practical wisdom, and why Socrates in one respect was on the right track while in another he went astray; in thinking that all the virtues were forms of practical wisdom he was wrong, but in saying they implied practical wisdom he was right. This is confirmed by the fact that even now all men, when they define virtue, after naming the state of character and its objects add 'that (state) which is in accordance with the right rule'; now the right rule is that which is in accordance with practi-cal wisdom. All men, then, seem somehow to divine that this kind of state is virtue, viz. that which is in accordance with practical wisdom. But we must go a little further. For it is not merely the state in accor-dance with the right rule, but the state that implies the presence of the right rule, that is virtue; and prac-tical wisdom is a right rule about such matters. Socrates, then, thought the virtues were rules or ra-tional principles (for he thought they were, all of them, forms of scientific knowledge), while we think they involve a rational principle.

It is clear, then, from what has been said, that it is not possible to be good in the strict sense without practical wisdom, nor practically wise without moral virtue. But in this way we may also refute the di-alectical argument whereby it might be contended that the virtues exist in separation from each other; the same man, it might be said, is not best equipped by nature for all the virtues, so that he will have al-ready acquired one when he has not yet acquired an-other. This is possible in respect of the natural virtues, but not in respect of those in respect of which a man is called without qualification good; for with

the presence of the one quality, practical wisdom, will be given all the virtues. And it is plain that, even if it were of no practical value, we should have needed it because it is the virtue of the part of us in question; plain too that the choice will not be right without practical wisdom any more than without virtue; for the one deter, mines the end and the other makes us do the things that lead to the end.

But again it is not supreme over philosophic wis-dom, i.e. over the superior part of us, any more than the art of medicine is over health; for it does not use it but provides for its coming into being; it issues or-ders, then, for its sake, but not to it. Further, to main-tain its supremacy would be like saying that the art of politics rules the gods because it issues orders about all the affairs of the state.

BOOK VII

1. Let us now make a fresh beginning and point out that of moral states to be avoided there are three kinds—vice, incontinence, brutishness. The con-traries of two of these are evident,—one we call virtue, the other continence; to brutishness it would be most fitting to oppose superhuman virtue, a heroic and divine kind of virtue, as Homer has represented Priam saying of Hector that he was very good,

For he seemed not, he,
The child of a mortal man, but as one that of God's
*   seed came.*

Therefore if, as they say, men become gods by excess of virtue, of this kind must evidently be the state opposed to the brutish state; for as a brute has no vice or virtue, so neither has a god; his state is higher than virtue, and that of a brute is a different kind of state from vice.

Now, since it is rarely that a godlike man is found—to use the epithet of the Spartans, who when they admire any one highly call him a 'godlike man'—so too the brutish type is rarely found among men; it is found chiefly among barbarians, but some brutish qualities are also produced by disease or de-formity; and we also call by this evil name those men who go beyond all ordinary standards by reason of vice. Of this kind of disposition, however, we must later make some mention, while we have discussed vice before we must now discuss incontinence and softness (or effeminacy), and continence and endurance; for we must treat each of the two neither as identical with virtue or wickedness, nor as a different genus. We must, as in all other cases, set the observed facts before us and, after first discussing the difficulties, go on to prove, if possible, the truth of all the common opinions about these affections of the mind, or, failing this, of the greater number and the most authoritative; for if we both refute the objections and leave the common opinions undisturbed, we shall have proved the case sufficiently.

Now (1) both continence and endurance are thought to be included among things good and praiseworthy, and both incontinence and soft, ness among things bad and blameworthy; and the same man is thought to be continent and ready to abide by the result of his calculations, or incontinent and ready to abandon them. And (2) the incontinent man, knowing that what he does is bad, does it as a result of passion, while the continent man, knowing that his appetites are bad, refuses on account of his rational principle to follow them (3) The temperate man all men call continent and disposed to endurance, while the continent man some maintain to be always temperate but others do not; and some call the self indulgent man incontinent and the incontinent man self-indulgent indiscriminately, while others distinguish them. (4) The man of practical wisdom, they sometimes say, cannot be incontinent, while sometimes they say that some who are practically wise and clever are incontinent. Again (5) men are said to be incontinent even with respect to anger, honour, and gain.—These, then, are the things that are said.

2. Now we may ask (1) how a man who judges rightly can behave incontinently. That he should behave so when he has knowledge, some say is impossible; for it would be strange—so Socrates thought—if when knowledge was in a man something else could master it and drag it about like a slave. For Socrates was entirely opposed to the view in question, holding that there is no such thing as incontinence; no one, he said, when he judges acts against what he judges best—people act so only by reason of ignorance. Now this view plainly contradicts the observed facts, and we must inquire about what happens to such a man; if he acts by reason of ignorance, what is the manner of his ignorance? For that the man who behaves incontinently does not, before he gets into this state, think he ought to act so, is evident. But there are some who concede certain of Socrates' contentions but not others; that nothing is stronger than knowledge they admit, but not that on one acts contrary to what has seemed to him the better course, and therefore they say that the incontinent man has not knowledge when he is mastered by his pleasures, but opinion. But if it is opinion and not knowledge, if it is not a strong conviction that resists but a weak one, as in men who hesitate, we sympathize with their failure to stand by such convictions against strong appetites; but we do not sympathize with wickedness, nor with any of the other blameworthy states. Is it then practical wisdom whose resistance is mastered? That is the strongest of all states. But this is absurd; the same man will be at once practically wise and incontinent, but no one would say that it is the part of a practically wise man to do willingly the basest acts. Besides, it has been shown before that the man of practical wisdom is one who will act (for he is a man concerned with the individual facts) and who has the other virtues.

(2) Further, if continence involves having strong and bad appetites, the temperate man will not be continent nor the continent man temperate; for a temperate man will have neither excessive nor bad appetites. But the continent man must; for if the appetites are good, the state of character that restrains us from following them is bad, so that not all continence will be good; while if they are weak and not bad, there is nothing admirable in resisting them, and if they are weak and bad, there is nothing great in resisting these either.

(3) Further, if continence makes a man ready to stand by any and every opinion, it is bad, i.e. if it makes him stand even by a false opinion; and if incontinence makes a man apt to abandon any and every opinion, there will be a good incontinence, of which Sophocles' Neoptolemus in the Philoctetes will be an instance; for he is to be praised for not standing by what Odysseus persuaded him to do, because he is pained at telling a lie.

(4) Further, the sophistic argument presents a difficulty; the syllogism arising from men's wish to

expose paradoxical results arising from an opponent's view, in order that they may be admired when they succeed, is one that puts us in a difficulty (for thought is bound fast when it will not rest because the conclusion does not satisfy it, and cannot advance because it cannot refute the argument). There is an argument from which it follows that folly coupled with incontinence is virtue; for a man does the opposite of what he judges, owing to incontinence, but judges what is good to be evil and something that he should not do, and consequence he will do what is good and not what is evil.

(5) Further, he who on conviction does and pursues and chooses what is pleasant would be thought to be better than one who does so as a result not of calculation but of incontinence; for he is easier to cure since he may be persuaded to change his mind. But to the incontinent man may be applied the proverb 'when water chokes, what is one to wash it down with?' If he had been persuaded of the lightness of what he does, he would have desisted when he was persuaded to change his mind; but now he acts in spite of his being persuaded of something quite different.

(6) Further, if incontinence and continence are concerned with any and every kind of object, who is it that is incontinent in the unqualified sense? No one has all the forms of incontinence, but we say some people are incontinent without qualification.

3. Of some such kind are the difficulties that arise; some of these points must be refuted and the others left in possession of the field; for the solution of the difficulty is the discovery of the truth. (1) We must consider first, then, whether incontinent people act knowingly or not, and in what sense knowingly; then (2) with what sorts of object the incontinent and the continent man may be said to be concerned (i.e. whether with any and every pleasure and pain or with certain determinate kinds), and whether the continent man and the man of endurance are the same or different; and similarly with regard to the other matters germane to this inquiry. The starting-point of our investigation is (a) the question whether the continent man and the incontinent are differentiated by their objects or by their attitude, i.e. whether the incontinent man is incontinent simply by being concerned with such and such objects, or, instead, by his attitude, or,

instead of that, by both these things; (b) the second question is whether incontinence and continence are concerned with any and every object or not. The man who is incontinent in the unqualified sense is neither concerned with any and every object, but with precisely those with which the self-indulgent man is concerned, nor is he characterized by being simply related to these (for then his state would be the same as self-indulgence), but by being related to them in a certain way. For the one is led on in accordance with his own choice, thinking that he ought always to pursue the present pleasure; while the other does not think so, but yet pursues it.

(1) As for the suggestion that it is true opinion and not knowledge against which we act incontinently, that makes no difference to the argument; for some people when in a state of opinion do not hesitate, but think they know exactly. If, then, the notion is that owing to their weak conviction those who have opinion are more likely to act against their judgement than those who know, we answer that there need be no difference between knowledge and opinion in this respect; for some men are no less convinced of what they think than others of what they know; as is shown by the of Heraclitus. But (a), since we use the word 'know' in two senses (for both the man who has knowledge but is not using it and he who is using it are said to know), it will make a difference whether, when a man does what he should not, he has the knowledge but is not exercising it, or is exercising it; for the latter seems strange, but not the former.

(b) Further, since there are two kinds of premisses, there is nothing to prevent a man's having both premisses and acting against his knowledge, provided that he is using only the universal premiss and not the particular; for it is particular acts that have to be done. And there are also two kinds of universal term; one is predicable of the agent, the other of the object; e.g. 'dry food is good for every man', and 'I am a man', or 'such and such food is dry'; but whether 'this food is such and such', of this the incontinent man either has not or is not exercising the knowledge. There will, then, be, firstly, an enormous difference between these manners of knowing, so that to know in one way when we act incontinently would not seem anything strange, while to know in the other way would be extraordinary.

And further (c) the possession of knowledge in another sense than those just named is something that happens to men; for within the case of having knowledge but not using it we see a difference of state, admitting of the possibility of having knowledge in a sense and yet not having it, as in the instance of a man asleep, mad, or drunk. But now this is just the condition of men under the influence of passions; for outbursts of anger and sexual appetites and some other such passions, it is evident, actually alter our bodily condition, and in some men even produce fits of madness. It is plain, then, that incontinent people must be said to be in a similar condition to men asleep, mad, or drunk. The fact that men use the language that flows from knowledge proves nothing; for even men under the influence of these passions utter scientific proofs and verses of Empedocles, and those who have just begun to learn a science can string together its phrases, but do not yet know it; for it has to become part of themselves, and that takes time; so that we must suppose that the use of language by men in an incontinent state means no more than its utterance by actors on the stage. (d) Again, we may also view the cause as follows with reference to the facts of human nature. The one opinion is universal, the other is concerned with the particular facts, and here we come to something within the sphere of perception; when a single opinion results from the two, the soul must in one type of case affirm the conclusion, while in the case of opinions concerned with production it must immediately act (e.g. if 'everything sweet ought to be tasted', and 'this is sweet', in the sense of being one of the particular sweet things, the man who can act and is not prevented must at the same time actually act accordingly). When, then, the universal opinion is present in us forbidding us to taste, and there is also the opinion that 'everything sweet is pleasant', and that 'this is sweet' (now this is the opinion that is active), and when appetite happens to be present in us, the one opinion bids us avoid the object, but appetite leads us towards it (for it can move each of our bodily parts); so that it turns out that a man behaves incontinently under the influence (in a sense) of a rule and an opinion, and of one not contrary in itself, but only incidentally—for the appetite is contrary, not the opinion—to the right rule. It also foltows that

this is the reason why the lower animals are not incontinent, viz. because they have no universal judgement but only imagination and memory of particulars.

The explanation of how the ignorance is dissolved and the incontinent man regains his knowledge, is the same as in the case of the man drunk or asleep and is not peculiar to this condition; we must go to the students of natural science for it. Now, the last premiss both being an opinion about a perceptible object, and being what determines our actions this a man either has not when he is in the state of passion, or has it in the sense in which having knowledge did not mean knowing but only talking, as a drunken man may utter the verses of Empedocles. And because the last term is not universal nor equally an object of scientific knowledge with the universal term, the position that Socrates sought to establish actually seems to result; for it is not in the presence of what is thought to be knowledge proper that the affection of incontinence arises (nor is it this that is 'dragged about' as a result of the state of passion), but in that of perceptual knowledge.

This must suffice as our answer to the question of action with and without knowledge, and how it is possible to behave incontinently with knowledge.

BOOK X

6. Now that we have spoken of the excellences, the forms of friendship, and the varieties of pleasure, what remains is to discuss in outline the nature of happiness, since this is what we state the end of human nature to be. Our discussion will be the more concise if we first sum up what we have said already. We said, then, that it is not a state; for if it were it might belong to some one who was asleep throughout his life, living the life of a plant, or, again, to some one who was suffering the greatest misfortunes. If these implications are unacceptable, and we must rather class happiness as an activity, as we have said before, and if some activities are necessary and desirable for the sake of something else, while others are so in themselves, evidently happiness must be placed among those desirable in themselves, not among those desirable for the sake of something else; for happiness does not lack

anything, but is self-sufficient. Now those activities are desirable in themselves from which nothing is sought beyond the activity. And of this nature excellent actions are thought to be; for to do noble and good deeds is a thing desirable for its own sake.

Pleasant amusements also are thought to be of this nature; we choose them not for the sake of other things; for we are injured rather than benefited by them, since we are led to neglect our bodies and our property. But most of the people who are deemed happy take refuge in such pastimes, which is the reason why those who are ready-witted at them are highly esteemed at the courts of tyrants; they make themselves pleasant companions in the tyrant's favourite pursuits, and that is the sort of man they want. Now these things are thought to be of the nature of happiness because people in despotic positions spend their leisure in them, but perhaps such people prove nothing; for excellence and thought, from which good activities flow, do not depend on despotic position; nor, if these people, who have never tasted pure and generous pleasure, take refuge in the bodily pleasures, should these for that reason be thought more desirable; for boys, too, think the things that are valued among themselves are the best. It is to be expected, then, that, as different things seem valuable to boys and to men, so they should to bad men and to good. Now, as we have often maintained, those things are both valuable and pleasant which are such to the good man; and to each man the activity in accordance with his own state is most desirable, and, therefore, to the good man that which is in accordance with excellence. Happiness, therefore, does not lie in amusement; it would, indeed, be strange if the end were amusement, and one were to take trouble and suffer hardship all one's life in order to amuse oneself. For, in a word, everything that we choose we choose for the sake of something else—except happiness, which is an end. Now to exert oneself and work for the sake of amusement seems silly and utterly childish. But to amuse oneself in order that one may exert oneself, as Anacharsis puts it, seems right; for amusement is a sort of relaxation, and we need relaxation because we cannot work continuously. Relaxation, then, is not an end; for it is taken for the sake of activity.

1177ª1

The happy life is thought to be one of excellence; now an excellent life requires exertion, and does not consist in amusement. And we say that serious things are better than laughable things and those connected with amusement, and that the activity of the better of any two things—whether it be two parts or two men—is the better; but the activity of the better is *ipso facto* superior and more of the nature of happiness. And any chance person—even a slave—can enjoy the bodily pleasures no less than the best man; but no one assigns to a slave a share in happiness—unless he assigns to him also a share in human life. For happiness does not lie in such occupations, but, as we have said before, in excellent activities.

7. If happiness is activity in accordance with excellence, it is reasonable that it should be in accordance with the highest excellence; and this will be that of the best thing in us. Whether it be intellect or something else that is this element which is thought to be our natural ruler and guide and to take thought of things noble and divine, whether it be itself also divine or only the most divine element in us, the activity of this in accordance with its proper excellence will be complete happiness. That this activity is contemplative we have already said.

Now this would seem to be in agreement both with what we said before and with the truth. For this activity is the best (since not only is intellect the best thing in us, but the objects of intellect are the best of knowable objects); and, secondly, it is the most continuous, since we can contemplate truth more continuously than we can *do* anything. And we think happiness has pleasure mingled with it, but the activity of wisdom is admittedly the pleasantest of excellent activities; at all events philosophy is thought to offer pleasures marvellous for their purity and their enduringness, and it is to be expected that those who know will pass their time more pleasantly than those who inquire. And the self-sufficiency that is spoken of must belong most to the contemplative activity. For while a wise man, as well as a just man and the rest, needs the necessaries of life, when they are sufficiently equipped with things of that sort the just man needs people towards whom and with whom he shall act justly, and the temperate man, the brave man, and each of the others is in the same case, but the wise man, even when by himself, can contemplate truth, and the better the wiser he is; he can perhaps do so better if he has fellow-workers, but still he is the most self-sufficient. And this activity alone would seem to be loved for its own sake; for nothing arises from it apart from the contemplating, while from practical activities we gain more or less apart from the action. And happiness is thought to depend on leisure; for we are busy that we may have leisure, and make war that we may live in peace. Now the activity of the practical excellences is exhibited in political or military affairs, but the actions concerned with these seem to be unleisurely. Warlike actions are completely so (for no one chooses to be at war, or provokes war, for the sake of being at war; any one would seem absolutely murderous if he were to make enemies of his friends in order to bring about battle and slaughter); but the action of the statesman is also unleisurely, and—apart from the political action itself—aims at despotic power and honours, or at all events happiness, for him and his fellow citizens—a happiness different from political action, and evidently sought as being different. So if among excellent actions political and military actions are distinguished by nobility and greatness, and these are unleisurely and aim at an end and are not desirable for their own sake, but the activity of intellect, which is contemplative, seems both to be superior in worth and to aim at no end beyond itself, and to have its pleasure proper to itself (and this augments the activity), and the self-sufficiency, leisureliness, unweariedness (so far as this is possible for man), and all the other attributes ascribed to the blessed man are evidently those connected with this activity, it follows that this will be the complete happiness of man, if it be allowed a complete term of life (for none of the attributes of happiness is *in*complete).

But such a life would be too high for man; for it is not in so far as he is man that he will live so, but in so far as something divine is present in him; and by so much as this is superior to our composite nature is its activity superior to that which is the exercise of the other kind of excellence. If intellect is divine, then, in comparison with man, the life according to it is divine in comparison with human life. But we must not follow those who advise us, being men, to think of human things and, being mortal, of mortal things, but must, so far as we can, make ourselves immortal, and strain every nerve to live in accordance with the best thing in us; for even if it be small in bulk, much more does it in power and worth surpass everything. This would seem, too, to be each man himself, since it is the authoritative and better part of him. It would be strange, then, if he were to choose not the life of himself but that of something else. And what we said before will apply now; that which is proper to each thing is by nature best and most pleasant for each thing; for man, therefore, the life according to intellect is best and pleasantest, since intellect more than anything else *is* man. This life therefore is also the happiest.

8. But in a secondary degree the life in accordance with the other kind of excellence is happy; for the activities in accordance with this befit our human estate. Just and brave acts, and other excellent acts, we do in relation to each other, observing what is proper to each with regard to contracts and services and all manner of actions and with regard to passions; and all of these seem to be human. Some of them seem even to arise from the body, and excellence of character to be in many ways bound up with the passions. Practical wisdom, too, is linked to excellence of character, and this to practical wisdom, since the principles of practical wisdom are in accordance with the moral excellences and rightness in the moral excellences is in accordance with practical wisdom. Being connected with the passions also, the moral excellences must belong to our composite nature; and the excellences of our composite nature are human; so, therefore, are the life and the happiness which correspond to these. The excellence of the intellect is a thing apart; we must be content to say this much about it, for to describe it precisely is a task greater than our purpose requires. It would seem, however, also to need external equipment but little, or less than moral excellence does. Grant that both need the necessaries, and do so equally, even if the statesman's work is the more concerned with the body and things of that sort; for there will be little difference there; but in what they need for the exercise of their activities there will be much difference. The liberal man will need money for the doing of his liberal deeds, and the just man too will need it for the returning of services (for wishes are hard to discern, and even people who are not just pretend to

wish to act justly); and the brave man will need power if he is to accomplish any of the acts that correspond to his excellence, and the temperate man will need opportunity; for how else is either he or any of the others to be recognized? It is debated, too, whether the choice or the deed is more essential to excellence, which is assumed to involve both; it is surely clear that its completion involves both; but for 178ᵇ1 deeds many things are needed, and more, the greater and nobler the deeds are. But the man who is contemplating the truth needs no such thing, at least with a view to the exercise of his activity; indeed they are, one may say, even hindrances, at all events to his contemplation; but in so far as he is a man and lives 5 with a number of people, he chooses to do excellent acts; he will therefore need such aids to living a human life.

But that complete happiness is a contemplative activity will appear from the following consideration as well. We assume the gods to be above all other beings blessed and happy; but what sort of actions 10 must we assign to them? Acts of justice? Will not the gods seem absurd if they make contracts and return deposits, and so on? Acts of a brave man, then, confronting dangers and running risks because it is noble to do so? Or liberal acts? To whom will they 15 give? It will be strange if they are really to have money or anything of the kind. And what would their temperate acts be? Is not such praise tasteless, since they have no bad appetites? If we were to run through them all, the circumstances of action would be found trivial and unworthy of gods. Still, every one supposes that they *live* and therefore that they are active; we cannot suppose them to sleep like Endymion. Now if you take away from a living be- 20 ing action, and still more production, what is left but contemplation? Therefore the activity of God, which surpasses all others in blessedness, must be contemplative; and of human activities, therefore, that which is most akin to this must be most of the nature of happiness.

This is indicated, too, by the fact that the other animals have no share in happiness, being com- 25 pletely deprived of such activity. For while the whole life of the gods is blessed, and that of men too in so far as some likeness of such activity belongs to them, none of the other animals is happy, since they in no way share in contemplation. Happiness extends, then, just so far as contemplation does, and those to whom contemplation more fully belongs are more truly happy, not accidentally, but in virtue of the contemplation; for this is in itself precious. Happiness, 30 therefore, must be some form of contemplation.

But, being a man, one will also need external prosperity; for our nature is not self-sufficient for the purpose of contemplation, but our body also must be healthy and must have food and other attention. Still, we must not think that the man who is to be happy 1179ᵃ1 will need many things or great things, merely because he cannot be blessed without external goods; for self-sufficiency and action do not depend on excess, and we can do noble acts without ruling earth and sea; for even with moderate advantages one can act excellently (this is manifest enough; for private persons are thought to do worthy acts no less than despots— indeed even more); and it is enough that we should have so much as that; for the life of the man who is 5 active in accordance with excellence will be happy. Solon, too, was perhaps sketching well the happy man when he described him as moderately furnished with externals but as having done (as Solon thought) the noblest acts, and lived temperately; for one can with but moderate possessions do what one ought. 10 Anaxagoras also seems to have supposed the happy man not to be rich nor a despot, when he said that he would not be surprised if the happy man were to seem to most people a strange person; for they judge by 15 externals, since these are all they perceive. The opinions of the wise seem, then, to harmonize with our arguments. But while even such things carry some conviction, the truth in practical matters is discerned from the facts of life; for these are the decisive factor. We must therefore survey what we have already 20 said, bringing it to the test of the facts of life, and if it harmonizes with the facts we must accept it, but if it clashes with them we must suppose it to be mere theory. Now he who exercises his intellect and cultivates it seems to be both in the best state and most dear to the gods. For if the gods have any care for human affairs, as they are thought to have, it would 25 be reasonable both that they should delight in that which was best and most akin to them (i.e. intellect) and that they should reward those who love and honour this most, as caring for the things that are dear

30 to them and acting both rightly and nobly. And that all these attributes belong most of all to the wise man is manifest. He, therefore, is the dearest to the gods. And he who is that will presumably be also the happiest; so that in this way too the wise man will more than any other be happy.

9. If these matters and the excellences, and also friendship and pleasure, have been dealt with sufficiently in outline, are we to suppose that our pro-

1179ᵇ1 gramme has reached its end? Surely, as is said, where there are things to be done the end is not to survey and recognize the various things, but rather to do them; with regard to excellence, then, it is not enough to know, but we must try to have and use it, or try any other way there may be of becoming good. Now if arguments were in themselves enough to make

5 men good, they would justly, as Theognis says, have won very great rewards, and such rewards should have been provided; but as things are, while they seem to have power to encourage and stimulate the generous-minded among the young, and to make a character which is gently born, and a true lover of what is noble, ready to be possessed by excellence,

10 they are not able to encourage the many to nobility and goodness. For these do not by nature obey the sense of shame, but only fear, and do not abstain from bad acts because of their baseness but through fear of punishment; living by passion they pursue their own pleasures and the means to them, and avoid the opposite pains, and have not even a conception of what is noble and truly pleasant, since they have

15 never tasted it. What argument would remould such people? It is hard, if not impossible, to remove by argument the traits that have long since been incorporated in the character; and perhaps we must be content if, when all the influences by which we are thought to become good are present, we get some tincture of excellence.

20 Now some think that we are made good by nature, others by habituation, others by teaching. Nature's part evidently does not depend on us, but as a result of some divine causes is present in those who are truly fortunate; while argument and teaching, we may suspect, are not powerful with all men, but the soul of the student must first have been cultivated by means of habits for noble joy and noble hatred,

25 like earth which is to nourish the seed. For he who

lives as passion directs will not hear argument that dissuades him, nor understand it if he does; and how can we persuade one in such a state to change his ways? And in general passion seems to yield not to argument but to force. The character, then, must somehow be there already with a kinship to excellence, loving what is noble and hating what is base. 30

But it is difficult to get from youth up a right training for excellence if one has not been brought up under right laws; for to live temperately and hardily is not pleasant to most people, especially when they are young. For this reason their nurture and occupations should be fixed by law; for they will not be painful when they have become customary. But it is surely 1180ᵃ1 not enough that when they are young they should get the right nurture and attention; since they must, even when they are grown up, practise and be habituated to them, we shall need laws for this as well, and generally speaking to cover the whole of life; for most people obey necessity rather than argument, and punishments rather than what is noble. 5

This is why some think that legislators ought to stimulate men to excellence and urge them forward by the motive of the noble, on the assumption that those who have been well advanced by the formation of habits will attend to such influences; and that punishments and penalties should be imposed on those who disobey and are of inferior nature, while the incurably bad should be completely banished. A good man (they think), since he lives with his mind 10 fixed on what is noble, will submit to argument, while a bad man, whose desire is for pleasure, is corrected by pain like a beast of burden. This is, too, why they say the pains inflicted should be those that are most opposed to the pleasures such men love.

However that may be, if (as we have said) the 15 man who is to be good must be well trained and habituated, and go on to spend his time in worthy occupations and neither willingly nor unwillingly do bad actions, and if this can be brought about if men live in accordance with a sort of intellect and right order, provided this has force,—if this be so, the paternal command indeed has not the required force or compulsive power (nor in general has the command 20 of one man, unless he be a king or something similar), but the law *has* compulsive power, while it is at the same time an account proceeding from a sort of practical wisdom and intellect. And while people hate *men* who oppose their impulses, even if they oppose them rightly, the law in its ordaining of what is good is not burdensome.

In the Spartan state alone, or almost alone, the legislator seems to have paid attention to questions of nurture and occupations; in most states such matters have been neglected, and each man lives as he pleases, Cyclops-fashion, 'to his own wife and children dealing law'.[28] Now it is best that there should be a public and proper care for such matters; but if they are neglected by the community it would seem right for each man to help his children and friends towards excellence, and that they should be able or at least choose, to do this.[29]

It would seem from what has been said that he can do this better if he makes himself capable of legislating. For public care is plainly effected by laws, and good care by good laws; whether written or unwritten would seem to make no difference, nor whether they are laws providing for the education of individuals or of groups—any more than it does in the case of music or gymnastics and other such pursuits. For as in cities laws and character have force, so in households do the injunctions and the habits of the father, and these have even more because of the tie of blood and the benefits he confers; for the children start with a natural affection and disposition to obey. Further, individual education has an advantage over education in common, as individual medical treatment has; for while in general rest and abstinence from food are good for a man in a fever, for a particular man they may not be; and a boxer presumably does not prescribe the same style of fighting to all his pupils. It would seem, then, that the detail is worked out with more precision if the care is particular to individuals; for each person is more likely to get what suits his case.

But individuals[30] can be best cared for by a doctor or gymnastic instructor or any one else who has the universal knowledge of what is good for every one or for people of a certain kind (for the sciences both are said to be, and are, concerned with what is common); not but what some particular detail may perhaps be well looked after by an unscientific person, if he has studied accurately in the light of experience what happens in each case, just as some people seem to be their own best doctors, though they could give no help to any one else. None the less, it will perhaps be agreed that if a man does wish to become master of an art or science he must go to the universal, and come to know it as well as possible; for, as we have said, it is with this that the sciences are concerned.

And surely he who wants to make men, whether many or few, better by his care must try to become capable of legislating, if it is through laws that we can become good. For to get anyone whatever—anyone who is put before us—into the right condition is not for the first chance comer; if anyone can do it, it is the man who knows, just as in medicine and all other matters which give scope for care and practical wisdom.

Must we not, then, next examine whence or how one can learn how to legislate? Is it, as in all other cases, from statesmen? Certainly it was thought to be a part of statesmanship. Or is a difference apparent between statesmanship and the other sciences and faculties? In the others the same people are found offering to teach the faculties and practising them, e.g. doctors or painters; but while the sophists profess to teach politics, it is practised not by any of them but by the politicians, who would seem to do so by dint of a certain faculty and experience rather than of thought; for they are not found either writing or speaking about such matters (though it were a nobler occupation perhaps than composing speeches for the law-courts and the assembly), nor again are they found to have made statesmen of their own sons or any other of their friends. But it was to be expected that they should if they could; for there is nothing better than such a skill that they could have left to their cities, or could choose to have for themselves, or, therefore, for those dearest to them. Still, experience seems to contribute not a little; else they could not have become politicians by familiarity with politics; and so it seems that those who aim at knowing about the art of politics need experience as well.

---

[28] *Odyssey* IX 114.
[29] Placing καὶ δρᾶν αὐτὸ δύνασθαι after συμβάλλε''' σθαι.
[30] Reading καθ' ἕνα.

But those of the sophists who profess the art seem to be very far from teaching it. For, to put the matter generally, they do not even know what kind of thing it is nor what kinds of things it is about; otherwise they would not have classed it as identical with rhetoric or even inferior to it, nor have thought it easy to legislate by collecting the laws that are thought well of; they say it is possible to select the best laws, as though even the selection did not demand intelligence and as though right judgement were not the greatest thing, as in matters of music. For while people experienced in any department judge rightly the works produced in it, and understand by what means or how they are achieved, and what harmonizes with what, the inexperienced must be content if they do not fail to see whether the work has been well or ill made—as in the case of painting. Now laws are as it were the works of the political art; how then can one learn from them to be a legislator, or judge which are best? Even medical men do not seem to be made by a study of text-books. Yet people try, at any rate, to state not only the treatments, but also how particular classes of people can be cured and should be treated—distinguishing the various states; but while this seems useful to experienced people, to the ignorant it is valueless. Surely, then, while collections of laws, and of constitutions also, may be serviceable to those who can study them and judge what is good or bad and what enactments suit what circumstances, those who go through such collections without a practised faculty will not have right judgement (unless it be spontaneous), though they may perhaps become more intelligent in such matters.

Now our predecessors have left the subject of legislation to us unexamined; it is perhaps best, therefore, that we should ourselves study it, and in general study the question of the constitution, in order to complete to the best of our ability the philosophy of human nature. First, then, if anything has been said well in detail by earlier thinkers, let us try to review it; then in the light of the constitutions we have collected let us study what sorts of influence preserve and destroy states, and what sorts preserve or destroy the particular kinds of constitution, and to what causes it is due that some are well and others ill administered. When these have been studied we shall perhaps be more likely to see which constitution is best, and how each must be ordered, and what laws and customs it must use. Let us make a beginning of our discussion.

POLICS

BOOK I

1. Every state is a community of some kind, and every community is established with a view to some good; for everyone always acts in order to obtain that which they think good. But, if all communities aim at some good, the state or political community, which is the highest of all, and which embraces all the rest, aims at good in a greater degree than any other, and at the highest good.

Some people think that qualifications of a statesman, king, householder, and master are the same, and that they differ, not in kind, but only in the number of their subjects. For example, the ruler over a few is called a master; over more, the manager of a household; over a still larger number, a statesman or king, as if there were no difference between a great household and a small state. The distinction which is made between the king and the statesman is as follows: When the government is personal, the ruler is a king; when, according to the rules of the political science, the citizens rule and are ruled in turn, then he is called a statesman.

But all this is a mistake, as will be evident to any one who considers the matter according to the method which has hitherto guided us. As in other departments of science, so in politics, the compound should always be resolved into the simple elements or least parts of the whole. We must therefore look at the elements of which the state is composed, in order that we may see in what the different kinds of rule differ from one another, and whether any scientific result can be attained about each one of them.

2. He who thus considers things in their first growth and origin, whether a state or anything else, will obtain the clearest view of them. In the first place there must be a union of those who cannot exist without each other; namely, of male and female, that the race may continue (and this is a union which is formed, not of choice, but because, in common with other animals and with plants, mankind have a natural desire to leave behind them an image of themselves), and of natural ruler and subject, that both may be preserved. For that which can foresee by the exercise of mind is by nature lord and master, and that which can with its body give effect to such foresight is a subject, and by nature a slave; hence master and slave have the same interest. Now nature has distinguished between the female and the slave. For she is not niggardly, like the smith who fashions the Delphian knife for many uses; she makes each thing for a single use, and every instrument is best made when intended for one and not for many uses. But among barbarians no distinction is made between women and slaves, because there is no natural ruler among them: they are a community of slaves, male and female. That is why the poets say,—

It is meet that Hellenes should rule over
barbarians;

as if they thought that the barbarian and the slave were by nature one.

Out of these two relationships the first thing to arise is the family, and Hesiod is right when he says,—

First house and wife and an ox for the plough,

for the ox is the poor man's slave. The family is the association established by nature for the supply of men's everyday wants, and the members of it are called by Charondas, 'companions of the cupboard', and by Epimenides the Cretan, 'companions of the manger'. But when several families are united, and the association aims at something more than the supply of daily needs, the first society to be formed is the village. And the most natural form of the village appears to be that of a colony from the family, composed of the children and grandchildren, who are said to be 'suckled with the same milk'. And this is the

reason why Hellenic states were originally governed by kings; because the Hellenes were under royal rule before they came together, as the barbarians still are. Every family is ruled by the eldest, and therefore in the colonies of the family the kingly form of government prevailed because they were of the same blood. As Homer says:

Each one gives law to his children and to
his wives.

For they lived dispersedly, as was the manner in ancient times. That is why men say that the Gods have a king, because they themselves either are or were in ancient times under the rule of a king. For they imagine not only the forms of the Gods but their ways of life to be like their own.

When several villages are united in a single complete community, large enough to be nearly or quite self-sufficing, the state comes into existence, originating in the bare needs of life, and continuing in existence for the sake of a good life. And therefore, if the earlier forms of society are natural, so is the state, for it is the end of them, and the nature of a thing is its end. For what each thing is when fully developed, we call its nature, whether we are speaking of a man, a horse, or a family. Besides, the final cause and end of a thing is the best, and to be self-sufficing is the end and the best.

Hence it is evident that the state is a creation of nature, and that man is by nature a political animal. And he who by nature and not by mere accident is without a state, is either a bad man or above humanity; he is like the

Tribeless, lawless, hearthless one,

whom Homer denounces—the natural outcast is forthwith a lover of war; he may be compared to an isolated piece at draughts.

Now, that man is more of a political animal than bees or any other gregarious animals is evident. Nature, as we often say, makes nothing in vain, and man is the only animal who has the gift of speech. And whereas mere voice is but an indication of pleasure or pain, and is therefore found in other animals (for their nature attains to the perception of pleasure and pain and the intimation of them to one another, and no further), the power of speech is intended to set forth the expedient and inexpedient, and therefore likewise the just and the unjust. And it is a characteristic of man that he alone has any sense of good and evil, of just and unjust, and the like, and the association of living beings who have this sense makes a family and a state.

Further, the state is by nature clearly prior to the family and to the individual, since the whole is of necessity prior to the part; for example, if the whole body be destroyed, there will be no foot or hand, except homonymously, as we might speak of a stone hand; for when destroyed the hand will be no better than that. But things are defined by their function and power; and we ought not to say that they are the same when they no longer have their proper quality, but only that they are homonymous. The proof that the state is a creation of nature and prior to the individual is that the individual, when isolated, is not self-sufficing; and therefore he is like a part in relation to the whole. But he who is unable to live in society, or who has no need because he is sufficient for himself, must be either a beast or a god: he is no part of a state. A social instinct is implanted in all men by nature, and yet he who first founded the state was the greatest of benefactors. For man, when perfected, is the best of animals, but, when separated from law and justice, he is the worst of all; since armed injustice is the more dangerous, and he is equipped at birth with arms, meant to be used by intelligence and excellence, which he may use for the worst ends. That is why, if he has not excellence, he is the most unholy and the most savage of animals, and the most full of lust and gluttony. But justice is the bond of men in states; for the administration of justice, which is the determination of what is just, is the principle of order in political society.

1253ᵇ 3. Seeing then that the state is made up of households, before speaking of the state we must speak of the management of the household. The parts of household management correspond to the persons who compose the household, and a complete household consists of slaves and freemen. Now we should begin by examining everything in its fewest possible elements; and the first and fewest possible parts of a family are master and slave, husband and wife, father and children. We have therefore to consider what each of these three relations is and ought to be:—I mean the relation of master and servant, the marriage relation (the conjunction of man and wife has no name of its own), and, thirdly, the paternal relation (this also has no proper name). And there is another element of a household, the so-called art of getting wealth, which, according to some, is identical with household management, according to others, a principal part of it; the nature of this art will also have to be considered by us.

Let us first speak of master and slave, looking to the needs of practical life and also seeking to attain some better theory of their relation than exists at present. For some are of the opinion that the rule of a master is a science, and that the management of a household, and the mastership of slaves, and the political and royal rule, as I was saying at the outset, are all the same. Others affirm that the rule of a master over slaves is contrary to nature, and that the distinction between slave and freeman exists by convention only, and not by nature; and being an interference with nature is therefore unjust.

4. Property is a part of the household, and the art of acquiring property is a part of the art of managing the household; for no man can live well, or indeed live at all, unless he is provided with necessaries. And as in the arts which have a definite sphere the workers must have their own proper instruments for the accomplishment of their work, so it is in the management of a household. Now instruments are of various sorts; some are living, others lifeless; in the rudder, the pilot of a ship has a lifeless, in the lookout man, a living instrument; for in the arts the servant is a kind of instrument. Thus, too, a possession is an instrument for maintaining life. And so, in the arrangement of the family, a slave is a living possession, and property a number of such instruments; and the servant is himself an instrument for instruments. For if every instrument could accomplish its own work, obeying or anticipating the will of others, like the statues of Daedalus, or the tripods of Hephaestus, which, says the poet,

of their own accord entered the assembly of
the Gods;

if, in like manner, the shuttle would weave and the 1254ᵃ plectrum touch the lyre, chief workmen would not want servants, nor masters slaves. Now the instruments commonly so called are instruments of production, whilst a possession is an instrument of action. From a shuttle we get something else besides the use of it, whereas of a garment or of a bed there is only the use. Further, as production and action are different in kind, and both require instruments, the instruments which they employ must likewise differ in kind. But life is action and not production, and therefore the slave is the minister of action. Again, a possession is spoken of as a part is spoken of; for the part is not only a part of something else, but wholly belongs to it; and this is also true of a possession. The master is only the master of the slave; he does not belong to him, whereas the slave is not only the slave of his master, but wholly belongs to him. Hence we see what is the nature and office of a slave; he who is by nature not his own but another's man, is by nature a slave; and he may be said to be another's man who, being a slave, is also a possession. And a possession may be defined as an instrument of action, separable from the possessor.

5. But is there any one thus intended by nature to be a slave, and for whom such a condition is expedient and right, or rather is not all slavery a violation of nature?

There is no difficulty in answering this question, on grounds both of reason and of fact. For that some should rule and others be ruled is a thing not only necessary, but expedient; from the hour of their birth, some are marked out for subjection, others for rule.

And there are many kinds both of rulers and subjects (and that rule is the better which is exercised over better subjects—for example, to rule over men is better than to rule over wild beasts; for the work is better which is executed by better workmen, and where one man rules and another is ruled, they may be said to have a work); for in all things which form a composite whole and which are made up of parts, whether continuous or discrete, a distinction between the ruling and the subject element comes to light. Such a duality exists in living creatures, originating from nature as a whole; even in things which have no life there is a ruling principle, as in a musical mode. But perhaps this is matter for a more popular investigation. A living creature consists in the first place of soul and body, and of these two, the one is

by nature the ruler and the other the subject. But then we must look for the intentions of nature in things which retain their nature, and not in things which are corrupted. And therefore we must study the man who is in the most perfect state both of body and soul, for in him we shall see the true relation of the two; although in bad or corrupted natures the body will often appear to rule over the soul, because they are in an evil and unnatural condition. At all events we may firstly observe in living creatures both a despotical and a constitutional rule; for the soul rules the body with a despotical rule, whereas the intellect rules the appetites with a constitutional and royal rule. And it is clear that the rule of the soul over the body, and of the mind and the rational element over the passionate, is natural and expedient; whereas the equality of the two or the rule of the inferior is always hurtful. The same holds good of animals in relation to men; for tame animals have a better nature than wild and all tame animals are better off when they are ruled by man; for then they are preserved. Again, the male is by nature superior, and the female inferior; and the one rules, and the other is ruled; this principle, of necessity, extends to all mankind. Where then there is such a difference as that between soul and body, or between men and animals (as in the case of those whose business is to use their body, and who can do nothing better), the lower sort are by nature slaves, and it is better for them as for all inferiors that they should be under the rule of a master. For he who can be, and therefore is, another's, and he who participates in reason enough to apprehend, but not to have, is a slave by nature. Whereas the lower animals cannot even apprehend reason; they obey their passions. And indeed the use made of slaves and of tame animals is not very different; for both with their bodies minister to the needs of life. Nature would like to distinguish between the bodies of freemen and slaves, making the one strong for servile labour, the other upright, and although useless for such services, useful for political life in the arts both of war and peace. But the opposite often happens—that some have the souls and others have the bodies of freemen. And doubtless if men differed from one another in the mere forms of their bodies as much as the statues of the Gods do from men, all would acknowledge that the inferior class should be slaves of the superior. And if this is true of the body, how much more just that a similar distinction should exist in the soul? But the beauty of the body is seen, whereas the beauty of the soul is not seen. It is clear, then, that some men are by nature free, and others slaves, and that for these latter slavery is both expedient and right.

6. But that those who take the opposite view have in a certain way right on their side, may be easily seen. For the words slavery and slave are used in two senses. There is a slave or slavery by convention as well as by nature. The convention is a sort of agreement—the convention by which whatever is taken in war is supposed to belong to the victors. But this right many jurists impeach, as they would an orator who brought forward an unconstitutional measure; they detest the notion that, because one man has the power of doing violence and is superior in brute strength, another shall be his slave and subject. Even among philosophers there is a difference of opinion. The origin of the dispute, and what makes the views invade each other's territory, is as follows: in some sense excellence, when furnished with means, has actually the greatest power of exercising force: and as superior power is only found where there is superior excellence of some kind, power seems to imply excellence, and the dispute to be simply one about justice (for it is due to one party identifying justice with goodwill, while the other identifies it with the mere rule of the stronger). If these views are thus set out separately, the other views have no force or plausibility against the view that the superior in excellence ought to rule, or be master. Others, clinging, as they think, simply to a principle of justice (for convention is a sort of justice), assume that slavery in accordance with the custom of war is just, but at the same moment they deny this. For what if the cause of the war be unjust? And again, no one would ever say that he is a slave who is unworthy to be a slave. Were this the case, men of the highest rank would be slaves and the children of slaves if they or their parents chanced to have been taken captive and sold. That is why people do not like to call themselves slaves, but confine the term to foreigners. Yet, in using this language, they really mean the natural slave of whom we spoke at first; for it must be admitted that some are slaves everywhere, others

nowhere. The same principle applies to nobility. People regard themselves as noble everywhere, and not only in their own country, but they deem foreigners noble only when at home, thereby implying that there are two sorts of nobility and freedom, the one absolute, the other relative. The Helen of Theodectes says:

> Who would presume to call me servant who
> am on both sides sprung from the stem of
> the Gods?

What does this mean but that they distinguish freedom and slavery, noble and humble birth, by the two principles of good and evil? They think that as men and animals beget men and animals, so from good men a good man springs. Nature intends to do this often but cannot.

We see then that there is some foundation for this difference of opinion, and that all are not either slaves by nature or freemen by nature, and also that there is in some cases a marked distinction between the two classes, rendering it expedient and right for the one to be slaves and the others to be masters: the one practising obedience, the others exercising the authority and lordship which nature intended them to have. The abuse of this authority is injurious to both; for the interests of part and whole, of body and soul, are the same, and the slave is a part of the master, a living but separated part of his bodily frame. Hence, where the relation of master and slave between them is natural they are friends and have a common interest, but where it rests merely on convention and force the reverse is true.

7. The previous remarks are quite enough to show that the rule of a master is not a constitutional rule, and that all the different kinds of rule are not, as some affirm, the same as each other. For there is one rule exercised over subjects who are by nature free, another over subjects who are by nature slaves. The rule of a household is a monarchy, for every house is under one head: whereas constitutional rule is a government of freemen and equals. The master is not called a master because he has science, but because he is of a certain character, and the same remark applies to the slave and the freeman. Still there may be a science for the master and a science for the slave. The science of the slave would be such as the

man of Syracuse taught, who made money by instructing slaves in their ordinary duties. And such a knowledge may be carried further, so as to include cookery and similar menial arts. For some duties are of the more necessary, others of the more honourable sort; as the proverb says, 'slave before slave, master before master'. But all such branches of knowledge are servile. There is likewise a science of the master, which teaches the use of slaves; for the master as such is concerned, not with the acquisition, but with the use of them. Yet this science is not anything great or wonderful; for the master need only know how to order that which the slave must know how to execute. Hence those who are in a position which places them above toil have stewards who attend to their households while they occupy themselves with philosophy or with politics. But the art of acquiring slaves, I mean of justly acquiring them, differs both from the art of the master and the art of the slave, being a species of hunting or war. Enough of the distinction between master and slave.

1256ᵃ   8. Let us now inquire into property generally, and into the art of getting wealth, in accordance with our usual method, for a slave has been shown to be a part of property. The first question is whether the art of getting wealth is the same as the art of managing a household or a part of it, or instrumental to it; and if the last, whether in the way that the art of making shuttles is instrumental to the art of weaving, or in the way that the casting of bronze is instrumental to the art of the statuary, for they are not instrumental in the same way, but the one provides tools and the other material; and by material I mean the substratum out of which any work is made; thus wool is the material of the weaver, bronze of the statuary. Now it is easy to see that the art of household management is not identical with the art of getting wealth, for the one uses the material which the other provides. For the art which uses household stores can be no other than the art of household management. There is, however, a doubt whether the art of getting wealth is a part of household management or a distinct art. If the getter of wealth has to consider whence wealth and property can be procured, but there are many sorts of property and riches, then are husbandry, and the care and provision of food in general, parts of the art of household management or

distinct arts? Again, there are many sorts of food, and therefore there are many kinds of lives both of animals and men; they must all have food, and the differences in their food have made differences in their ways of life. For of beasts, some are gregarious, others are solitary; they live in the way which is best adapted to sustain them, accordingly as they are carnivorous or herbivorous or omnivorous: and their habits are determined for them by nature with regard to their ease and choice of food. But the same things are not naturally pleasant to all of them; and therefore the lives of carnivorous or herbivorous animals further differ among themselves. In the lives of men too there is a great difference. The laziest are shepherds, who lead an idle life, and get their subsistence without trouble from tame animals; their flocks having to wander from place to place in search of pasture, they are compelled to follow them, cultivating a sort of living farm. Others support themselves by hunting, which is of different kinds. Some, for example, are brigands, others, who dwell near lakes or marshes or rivers or a sea in which there are fish, are fishermen, and others live by the pursuit of birds or wild beasts. The greater number obtain a living from the cultivated fruits of the soil. Such are the modes of subsistence which prevail among those whose industry springs up of itself, and whose food is not acquired by exchange and retail trade—there is the shepherd, the husbandman, the brigand, the   1256ᵇ
fisherman, the hunter. Some gain a comfortable maintenance out of two employments, eking out the deficiencies of one of them by another: thus the life of a shepherd may be combined with that of a brigand, the life of a farmer with that of a hunter. Other modes of life are similarly combined in any way which the needs of men may require. Property, in the sense of a bare livelihood, seems to be given by nature herself to all, both when they are first born, and when they are grown up. For some animals bring forth, together with their offspring, so much food as will last until they are able to supply themselves; of this the vermiparous or oviparous animals are an instance; and the viviparous animals have up to a certain time a supply of food for their young in themselves, which is called milk. In like manner we may infer that, after the birth of animals, plants exist for their sake, and that the other animals exist for the

sake of man, the tame for use and food, the wild, if not all, at least the greater part of them, for food, and for the provision of clothing and various instruments. Now if nature makes nothing incomplete, and nothing in vain, the inference must be that she has made all animals for the sake of man. And so, from one point of view, the art of war is a natural art of acquisition, for the art of acquisition includes hunting, an art which we ought to practise against wild beasts, and against men who, though intended by nature to be governed, will not submit; for war of such a kind is naturally just.

Of the art of acquisition then there is one kind which by nature is a part of the management of a household, in so far as the art of household management must either find ready to hand, or itself provide, such things necessary to life, and useful for the community of the family or state, as can be stored. They are the elements of true riches; for the amount of property which is needed for a good life is not unlimited, although Solon in one of his poems says that

No bound to riches has been fixed for man.

But there is a boundary fixed, just as there is in the other arts; for the instruments of any art are never unlimited, either in number or size, and riches may be defined as a number of instruments to be used in a household or in a state. And so we see that there is a natural art of acquisition which is practised by managers of households and by statesmen, and the reason for this.

1257ᵃ 9. There is another variety of the art of acquisition which is commonly and rightly called an art of wealth-getting, and has in fact suggested the notion that riches and property have no limit. Being nearly connected with the preceding, it is often identified with it. But though they are not very different, neither are they the same. The kind already described is given by nature, the other is gained by experience and art.

Let us begin our discussion of the question with the following considerations. Of everything which we possess there are two uses: both belong to the thing as such, but not in the same manner, for one is the proper, and the other the improper use of it. For example, a shoe is used for wear, and is used for exchange; both are uses of the shoe. He who gives a shoe in exchange for money or food to him who wants one, does indeed use the shoe as a shoe, but this is not its proper use, for a shoe is not made to be an object of barter. The same may be said of all possessions, for the art of exchange extends to all of them, and it arises at first from what is natural, from the circumstance that some have too little, others too much. Hence we may infer that retail trade is not a natural part of the art of getting wealth; had it been so, men would have ceased to exchange when they had enough. In the first community, indeed, which is the family, this art is obviously of no use, but it begins to be useful when the society increases. For the members of the family originally had all things in common; later, when the family divided into parts, the parts shared in many things, and different parts in different things, which they had to give in exchange for what they wanted, a kind of barter which is still practised among barbarous nations who exchange with one another the necessaries of life and nothing more; giving and receiving wine, for example, in exchange for corn, and the like. This sort of barter is not part of the wealth-getting art and is not contrary to nature, but is needed for the satisfaction of men's natural wants. The other form of exchange grew, as might have been inferred, out of this one. When the inhabitants of one country became more dependent on those of another, and they imported what they needed, and exported what they had too much of, money necessarily came into use. For the various necessaries of life are not easily carried about, and hence men agreed to employ in their dealings with each other something which was intrinsically useful and easily applicable to the purposes of life, for example, iron, silver, and the like. Of this the value was at first measured simply by size and weight, but in process of time they put a stamp upon it, to save the trouble of weighing and to mark the value.

When the use of coin had once been discovered, 1257ᵇ out of the barter of necessary articles arose the other art of wealth-getting, namely, retail trade; which was at first probably a simple matter, but became more complicated as soon as men learned by experience whence and by what exchanges the greatest profit might be made. Originating in the use of coin, the art of getting wealth is generally thought to be chiefly concerned with it, and to be the art which produces riches and wealth, having to consider how they may be accumulated. Indeed, riches is assumed by many to be only a quantity of coin, because the arts of getting wealth and retail trade are concerned with coin. Others maintain that coined money is a mere sham, a thing not natural, but conventional only, because, if the users substitute another commodity for it, it is worthless, and because it is not useful as a means to any of the necessities of life, and, indeed, he who is rich in coin may often be in want of necessary food. But how can that be wealth of which a man may have a great abundance and yet perish with hunger, like Midas in the fable, whose insatiable prayer turned everything that was set before him into gold?

Hence men seek after a better notion of riches and of the art of getting wealth, and they are right. For natural riches and the natural art of wealth-getting are a different thing; in their true form they are part of the management of a household; whereas retail trade is the art of producing wealth, not in every way, but by exchange. And it is thought to be concerned with coin; for coin is the unit of exchange and the limit of it. And there is no bound to the riches which spring from this art of wealth-getting. As in the art of medicine there is no limit to the pursuit of health, and as in the other arts there is no limit to the pursuit of their several ends, for they aim at accomplishing their ends to the uttermost (but of the means there is a limit, for the end is always the limit), so, too, in this art of wealth-getting there is no limit of the end, which is riches of the spurious kind, and the acquisition of wealth. But the art of wealth-getting which consists in household management, on the other hand, has a limit; the unlimited acquisition of wealth is not its business. And, therefore, from one point of view, all riches must have a limit; nevertheless, as a matter of fact, we find the opposite to be the case; for all getters of wealth increase their hoard of coin without limit. The source of the confusion is the near connexion between the two kinds of wealth-getting; in both, the instrument is the same, although the use is different, and so they pass into one another; for each is a use of the same property, but with a difference: accumulation is the end in the one case, but there is a further end in the other. Hence some persons are led to believe that getting wealth

is the object of household management, and the whole idea of their lives is that they ought either to increase their money without limit, or at any rate not to lose it. The origin of this disposition in men is that they are intent upon living only, and not upon living well; and, as their desires are unlimited, they also desire that the means of gratifying them should be without limit. Those who do aim at a good life seek the means of obtaining bodily pleasures; and, since the enjoyment of these appears to depend on property, they are absorbed in getting wealth: and so there arises the second species of wealth-getting. For, as their enjoyment is in excess, they seek an art which produces the excess of enjoyment; and, if they are not able to supply their pleasures by the art of getting wealth, they try other causes, using in turn every faculty in a manner contrary to nature. The quality of courage, for example, is not intended to make wealth, but to inspire confidence; neither is this the aim of the general's or of the physician's art; but the one aims at victory and the other at health. Nevertheless, some men turn every quality or art into a means of getting wealth; this they conceive to be the end, and to the promotion of the end they think all things must contribute.

Thus, then, we have considered the art of wealth-getting which is unnecessary, and why men want it; and also the necessary art of wealth-getting, which we have seen to be different from the other, and to be a natural part of the art of managing a household, concerned with the provision of food, not, however, like the former kind, unlimited, but having a limit.

10. And we have found the answer to our original question, Whether the art of getting wealth is the business of the manager of a household and of the statesman or not their business?—viz. that wealth is presupposed by them. For as political science does not make men, but takes them from nature and uses them, so too nature provides them with earth or sea or the like as a source of food. At this stage begins the duty of the manager of a household, who has to order the things which nature supplies—he may be compared to the weaver who has not to make but to use wool, and to know, too, what sort of wool is good and serviceable or bad and unserviceable. Were this otherwise, it would be difficult to see why the art of getting wealth is a part of the management of a

household and the art of medicine not; for surely the members of a household must have health just as they must have life or any other necessity. The answer is that as from one point of view the master of the house and the ruler of the state have to consider about health, from another point of view not they but the physician has to; so in one way the art of household management, in another way the subordinate art, has to consider about wealth. But, strictly speaking, as I have already said, the means of life must be provided beforehand by nature; for the business of nature is to furnish food to that which is born, and the food of the offspring is always what remains over of that from which it is produced. That is why the art of getting wealth out of fruits and animals is always natural.

There are two sorts of wealth-getting, as I have said; one is a part of household management, the other is retail trade: the former is necessary and honourable, while that which consists in exchange is justly censured; for it is unnatural, and a mode by 1258ᵇ which men gain from one another. The most hated sort, and with the greatest reason, is usury, which makes a gain out of money itself, and not from the natural object of it. For money was intended to be used in exchange, but not to increase at interest. And this term interest, which means the birth of money from money, is applied to the breeding of money because the offspring resembles the parent. That is why of all modes of getting wealth this is the most unnatural.

11. Enough has been said about the theory of wealth-getting; we will now proceed to the practical part. Such things may be studied by a free man, but will only be practised from necessity. The useful parts of wealth-getting are, first, the knowledge of live-stock—which are most profitable, and where, and how—as for example, what sort of horses or sheep or oxen or any other animals are most likely to give a return. A man ought to know which of these pay better than others, and which pay best in particular places, for some do better in one place and some in another. Secondly, husbandry, which may be either tillage or planting, and the keeping of bees and of fish, or fowl, or of any animals which may be useful to man. These are the divisions of the true or proper art of wealth-getting and come first. Of the

other, which consists in exchange, the first and most important division is commerce (of which there are three kinds—ship-owning, the conveyance of goods, exposure for sale—these again differing as they are safer or more profitable), the second is usury, the third, service for hire—of this, one kind is employed in the mechanical arts, the other in unskilled and bodily labour. There is still a third sort of wealth-getting intermediate between this and the first or natural mode which is partly natural, but is also concerned with exchange, viz. the industries that make their profit from the earth, and from things growing from the earth which, although they bear no fruit, are nevertheless profitable; for example, the cutting of timber and all mining. The art of mining itself has many branches, for there are various kinds of things dug out of the earth. Of the several divisions of wealth-getting I now speak generally; a minute consideration of them might be useful in practice, but it would be tiresome to dwell upon them at greater length now.

Those occupations are most truly arts in which there is the least element of chance; they are the meanest in which the body is most maltreated, the most servile in which there is the greatest use of the body, and the most illiberal in which there is the least need of excellence.

Works have been written upon these subjects by various persons; for example, by Chares the Parian, 1259ᵃ and Apollodorus the Lemnian, who have treated of Tillage and Planting, while others have treated of other branches; anyone who cares for such matters may refer to their writings. It would be well also to collect the scattered stories of the ways in which individuals have succeeded in amassing a fortune; for all this is useful to persons who value the art of getting wealth. There is the anecdote of Thales the Milesian and his financial scheme, which involves a principle of universal application, but is attributed to him on account of his reputation for wisdom. He was reproached for his poverty, which was supposed to show that philosophy was of no use. According to the story, he knew by his skill in the stars while it was yet winter that there would be a great harvest of olives in the coming year; so, having a little money, he gave deposits for the use of all the olive-presses in Chios and Miletus, which he hired at a low price because no one bid against him. When the harvest-time came, and many were wanted all at once and of a sudden, he let them out at any rate which he pleased, and made a quantity of money. Thus he showed the world that philosophers can easily be rich if they like, but that their ambition is of another sort. He is supposed to have given a striking proof of his wisdom, but, as I was saying, his scheme for getting wealth is of universal application, and is nothing but the creation of a monopoly. It is an art often practised by cities when they are in want of money; they make a monopoly of provisions.

There was a man of Sicily, who, having money deposited with him, bought up all the iron from the iron mines; afterwards, when the merchants from their various markets came to buy, he was the only seller, and without much increasing the price he gained 200 per cent. Which when Dionysius heard, he told him that he might take away his money, but that he must not remain at Syracuse, for he thought that the man had discovered a way of making money which was injurious to his own interests. He made the same discovery as Thales; they both contrived to create a monopoly for themselves. And statesmen as well ought to know these things; for a state is often as much in want of money and of such schemes for obtaining it as a household, or even more so; hence some public men devote themselves entirely to finance.

12. Of household management we have seen that there are three parts—one is the rule of a master over slaves, which has been discussed already, another of a father, and the third of a husband. A husband and father, we saw, rules over wife and children, both free, but the rule differs, the rule over his children being a royal, over his wife a constitutional rule. For although there may be exceptions to the order of nature, the male is by nature fitter for command than the female, just as the elder and full-grown is superior to the younger and more immature. But in most constitutional states the citizens rule and are ruled by turns, for the idea of a constitutional state implies that the natures of the citizens are equal, and do not differ at all. Nevertheless, when one rules and the other is ruled we endeavour to create a difference of outward forms and names and titles of respect, which may be illustrated by the saying of Amasis about his foot-pan. The relation of the male to the female is always of this kind. The rule of a father over his children is royal, for he rules by virtue both of love and of the respect due to age, exercising a kind of royal power. And therefore Homer has appropriately called Zeus 'father of Gods and men', because he is the king of them all. For a king is the natural superior of his subjects, but he should be of the same kin or kind with them, and such is the relation of elder and younger, of father and son.

13. Thus it is clear that household management attends more to men than to the acquisition of inanimate things, and to human excellence more than to the excellence of property which we call wealth, and to the excellence of freemen more than to the excellence of slaves. A question may indeed be raised, whether there is any excellence at all in a slave beyond those of an instrument and of a servant—whether he can have the excellences of temperance, courage, justice, and the like; or whether slaves possess only bodily services. And, whichever way we answer the question, a difficulty arises; for, if they have excellence, in what will they differ from freemen? On the other hand, since they are men and share in rational principle, it seems absurd to say that they have no excellence. A similar question may be raised about women and children, whether they too have excellences; ought a woman to be temperate and brave and just, and is a child to be called temperate, and intemperate, or not? So in general we may ask about the natural ruler, and the natural subject, whether they have the same or different excellences. For if a noble nature is equally required in both, why should one of them always rule, and the other always be ruled? Nor can we say that this is a question of degree, for the difference between ruler and subject is a difference of kind, which the difference of more and less never is. Yet how strange is the supposition that the one ought, and that the other ought not, to have excellence! For if the ruler is intemperate and unjust, how can he rule well? if the subject, how can he obey well? If he is licentious and cowardly, he will certainly not do what is fitting. It is evident, therefore, that both of them must have a share of excellence, but varying as natural subjects also vary among themselves. Here the very constitution of the soul has shown us the way; in it one part naturally rules, and the other is subject, and

the excellence of the ruler we maintain to be different from that of the subject—the one being the excellence of the rational, and the other of the irrational part. Now, it is obvious that the same principle applies generally, and therefore almost all things rule and are ruled according to nature. But the kind of rule differs—the freeman rules over the slave after another manner from that in which the male rules over the female, or the man over the child; although the parts of the soul are present in all of them, they are present in different degrees. For the slave has no deliberative faculty at all; the woman has, but it is without authority, and the child has, but it is immature. So it must necessarily be supposed to be with the excellences of character also; all should partake of them, but only in such manner and degree as is required by each for the fulfilment of his function. Hence the ruler ought to have excellence of character in perfection, for his function, taken absolutely, demands a master artificer, and reason is such an artificer; the subjects, on the other hand, require only that measure of excellence which is proper to each of them. Clearly, then, excellence of character belongs to all of them; but the temperance of a man and of a woman, or the courage and justice of a man and of a woman, are not, as Socrates maintained, the same; the courage of a man is shown in commanding, of a woman in obeying. And this holds of all other excellences, as will be more clearly seen if we look at them in detail, for those who say generally that excellence consists in a good disposition of the soul, or in doing rightly, or the like, only deceive themselves. Far better than such definitions is the mode of speaking of those who, like Gorgias, enumerate the excellences. All classes must be deemed to have their special attributes; as the poet says of women,

Silence is a woman's glory,

but this is not equally the glory of man. The child is imperfect, and therefore obviously his excellence is not relative to himself alone, but to the perfect man and to his teacher, and in like manner the excellence of the slave is relative to a master. Now we determined that a slave is useful for the wants of life, and therefore he will obviously require only so much excellence as will prevent him from failing in his func-

1260ᵇ

tion through cowardice or lack of self-control. Someone will ask whether, if what we are saying is true, excellence will not be required also in the artisans, for they often fail in their work through the lack of self-control. But is there not a great difference in the two cases? For the slave shares in his master's life; the artisan is less closely connected with him, and only attains excellence in proportion as he becomes a slave. The meaner sort of mechanic has a special and separate slavery; and whereas the slave exists by nature, not so the shoemaker or other artisan. It is manifest, then, that the master ought to be the source of such excellence in the slave, and not a mere possessor of the art of mastership which trains the slave in his functions. That is why they are mistaken who forbid us to converse with slaves and say that we should employ command only, for slaves stand even more in need of admonition than children.

So much for this subject; the relations of husband and wife, father and child, their several excellences, what in their intercourse with one another is good, and what is evil, and how we may pursue the good and escape the evil, will have to be discussed when we speak of the different forms of government. For, inasmuch as every family is a part of a state, and these relationships are the parts of a family, and the excellence of the part must have regard to the excellence of the whole, women and children must be trained by education with an eye to the constitution, if the excellences of either of them are supposed to make any difference in the excellences of the state. And they must make a difference: for the children grow up to be citizens, and half the free persons in a state are women.

Of these matters, enough has been said; of what remains, let us speak at another time. Regarding, then, our present inquiry as complete, we will make a new beginning. And, first, let us examine the various theories of a perfect state.

BOOK II

1. Our purpose is to consider what form of political community is best of all for those who are most able to realize their ideal of life. We must therefore examine not only this but other constitutions,

both such as actually exist in well-governed states, and any theoretical forms which are held in esteem, so that what is good and useful may be brought to light. And let no one suppose that in seeking for something beyond them we are anxious to make a sophistical display at any cost; we only undertake this inquiry because all the constitutions which now exist are faulty.

We will begin with the natural beginning of the subject. The members of a state must either have all things or nothing in common, or some things in common and some not. That they should have nothing in common is clearly impossible, for the constitution is a community, and must at any rate have a common place—one city will be in one place, and the citizens are those who share in that one city. But should a well-ordered state have all things, as far as may be, in common, or some only and not others? For the citizens might conceivably have wives and children and property in common, as Socrates proposes in the Republic of Plato. Which is better, our present condition, or one conforming to the law laid down in the Republic?

2. There are many difficulties in the community of women. And the principle on which Socrates rests the necessity of such an institution evidently is not established by his arguments. Further, as a means to the end which he ascribes to the state, the scheme, taken literally, is impracticable, and how we are to interpret it is nowhere precisely stated. I am speaking of the supposition from which the argument of Socrates proceeds, that it is best for the whole state to be as unified as possible. Is it not obvious that a state may at length attain such a degree of unity as to be no longer a state?—since the nature of a state is to be a plurality, and in tending to greater unity, from being a state, it becomes a family, and from being a family, an individual; for the family may be said to be more one than the state, and the individual than the family. So that we ought not to attain this greatest unity even if we could, for it would be the destruction of the state. Again, a state is not made up only of so many men, but of different kinds of men; for similars do not constitute a state. It is not like a military alliance. The usefulness of the latter depends upon its quantity even where there is no difference in quality (for mutual protection is the end

aimed at), just as a greater weight depresses the scale more (in like manner, a state differs from a nation, when the nation has not its population organized in villages, but lives an Arcadian sort of life); but the elements out of which a unity is to be formed differ in kind. That is why the principle of reciprocity, as I have already remarked in the Ethics, is the salvation of states. Even among freemen and equals this is a principle which must be maintained, for they cannot all rule together, but must change at the end of a year or some other period of time or in some order of succession. The result is that upon this plan they all govern; just as if shoemakers and carpenters were to exchange their occupations, and the same persons did not always continue shoemakers and carpenters. And since it is better that this should be so in politics as well, it is clear that while there should be continuance of the same persons in power where this is possible, yet where this is not possible by reason of the natural equality of the citizens, and at the same time it is just that all should share in the government (whether to govern be a good thing or a bad),—in these cases this is imitated. Thus the one party rules and the others are ruled in turn, as if they were no longer the same persons. In like manner when they hold office there is a variety in the offices held. Hence it is evident that a city is not by nature one in that sense which some persons affirm; and that what is said to be the greatest good of cities is in reality their destruction; but surely the good of things must be that which preserves them. Again, from another point of view, this extreme unification of the state is clearly not good; for a family is more self-sufficing than an individual, and a city than a family, and a city only comes into being when the community is large enough to be self-sufficing. If then self-sufficiency is to be desired, the lesser degree of unity is more desirable than the greater.

3. But, even supposing that it were best for the community to have the greatest degree of unity, this unity is by no means proved to follow from the fact of all men saying 'mine' and 'not mine' at the same instant of time, which, according to Socrates, is the sign of perfect unity in a state. For the word 'all' is ambiguous. If the meaning be that every individual says 'mine' and 'not mine' at the same time, then perhaps the result at which Socrates aims may be in

some degree accomplished; each man will call the same person his own son and the same person his own wife, and so of his property and of all that falls to his lot. This, however, is not the way in which people would speak who had their wives and children in common; they would say 'all' but not 'each'. In like manner their property would be described as belonging to them, not severally but collectively. There is an obvious fallacy in the term 'all': like some other words, 'both', 'odd', 'even', it is ambiguous, and even in abstract argument becomes a source of logical puzzles. That all persons call the same thing mine in the sense in which each does so may be a fine thing, but it is impracticable; or if the words are taken in the other sense, such a unity in no way conduces to harmony. And there is another objection to the proposal. For that which is common to the greatest number has the least care bestowed upon it. Everyone thinks chiefly of his own, hardly at all of the common interest; and only when he is himself concerned as an individual. For besides other considerations, everybody is more inclined to neglect something which he expects another to fulfil; as in families many attendants are often less useful than a few. Each citizen will have a thousand sons who will not be his sons individually, but anybody will be equally the son of anybody, and will therefore be neglected by all alike. Further, upon this principle, every one will use the word 'mine' of one who is prospering or the reverse, however small a fraction he may himself be of the whole number; the same boy will be my son, so and so's son, the son of each of the thousand, or whatever be the number of the citizens; and even about this he will not be positive; for it is impossible to know who chanced to have a child, or whether, if one came into existence, it has survived. But which is better—for each to say 'mine' in this way, making a man the same relation to two thousand or ten thousand citizens, or to use the word 'mine' as it is now used in states? For usually the same person is called by one man his own son whom another calls his own brother or cousin or kinsman—blood relation or connexion by marriage—either of himself or of some relation of his, and yet another his clansman or tribesman; and how much better it is to be the real cousin of somebody than to be a son after Plato's fashion! Nor is there any way of pre-

venting brothers and children and fathers and mothers from sometimes recognizing one another; for children are born like their parents, and they will necessarily be finding indications of their relationship to one another. Geographers declare such to be the fact; they say that in part of Upper Libya, where the women are common, nevertheless the children who are born are assigned to their respective fathers on the ground of their likeness. And some women, like the females of other animals—for example, mares and cows—have a strong tendency to produce offspring resembling their parents, as was the case with the Pharsalian mare called Honest Wife.

4. Other difficulties, against which it is not easy for the authors of such a community to guard, will be assaults and homicides, voluntary as well as involuntary, quarrels and slanders, all of which are most unholy acts when committed against fathers and mothers and near relations, but not equally unholy when there is no relationship. Moreover, they are much more likely to occur if the relationship is unknown than if it is known and, when they have occurred, the customary expiations of them can be made if the relationship is known, but not otherwise. Again, how strange it is that Socrates, after having made the children common, should hinder lovers from carnal intercourse only, but should permit love and familiarities between father and son or between brother and brother, than which nothing can be more unseemly, since even without them love of this sort is improper. How strange, too, to forbid intercourse for no other reason than the violence of the pleasure, as though the relationship of father and son or of brothers with one another made no difference.

This community of wives and children seems better suited to the husbandmen than to the guardians, for if they have wives and children in common, they will be bound to one another by weaker ties, as a subject class should be, and they will remain obedient and not rebel. In a word, the result of such a law would be just the opposite of that which good laws ought to have, and the intention of Socrates in making these regulations about women and children would defeat itself. For friendship we believe to be the greatest good of states and what best preserves them against revolutions; and Socrates particularly praises the unity of the state which seems and is said by him to be created by friendship. But the unity which he commends would be like that of the lovers in the Symposium, who, as Aristophanes says, desire to grow together in the excess of their affection, and from being two to become one, in which case one or both would certainly perish. Whereas in a state having women and children common, love will be diluted; and the father will certainly not say 'my son', or the son 'my father'. As a little sweet wine mingled with a great deal of water is imperceptible in the mixture, so, in this sort of community, the idea of relationship which is based upon these names will be lost; there is no reason why the so-called father should care about the son, or the son about the father, or brothers about one another. Of the two qualities which chiefly inspire regard and affection—that a thing is your own and that it is precious—neither can exist in such a state as this.

Again, the transfer of children as soon as they are born from the rank of husbandmen or of artisans to that of guardians, and from the rank of guardians into a lower rank, will be very difficult to arrange; the givers or transferrers cannot but know whom they are giving and transferring, and to whom. And the previously mentioned assaults, unlawful loves, homicides, will happen more often among them; for they will no longer call the members of the class they have left brothers, and children, and fathers, and mothers, and will not, therefore, be afraid of committing any crimes by reason of consanguinity. Touching the community of wives and children, let this be our conclusion.

5. Next let us consider what should be our arrangements about property: should the citizens of the perfect state have their possessions in common or not? This question may be discussed separately from the enactments about women and children. Even supposing that the women and children belong to individuals, according to the custom which is at present universal, may there not be an advantage in 1263ᵃ having and using possessions in common? E.g. (1) the soil may be appropriated, but the produce may be thrown for consumption into the common stock; and this is the practice of some nations. Or (2), the soil may be common, and may be cultivated in common, but the produce divided among individuals for their private use; this is a form of common property

which is said to exist among certain foreigners. Or (3), the soil and the produce may be alike common.

When the husbandmen are not the owners, the case will be different and easier to deal with; but when they till the ground for themselves the question of ownership will give a world of trouble. If they do not share equally in enjoyments and toils, those who labour much and get little will necessarily complain of those who labour little and receive or consume much. But indeed there is always a difficulty in men living together and having all human relations in common, but especially in their having common property. The partnerships of fellow-travellers are an example to the point; for they generally fall out over everyday matters and quarrel about any trifle which turns up. So with servants: we are most liable to take offence at those with whom we most frequently come into contact in daily life.

These are only some of the disadvantages which attend the community of property; the present arrangement, if improved as it might be by good customs and laws, would be far better, and would have the advantages of both systems. Property should be in a certain sense common, but, as a general rule, private; for, when everyone has a distinct interest, men will not complain of one another, and they will make more progress, because everyone will be attending to his own business. And yet by reason of goodness, and in respect of use, 'Friends', as the proverb says, 'will have all things common'. Even now there are traces of such a principle, showing that it is not impracticable, but, in well-ordered states, exists already to a certain extent and may be carried further. For, although every man has his own property, some things he will place at the disposal of his friends, while of others he shares the use with them. The Lacedaemonians, for example, use one another's slaves, and horses, and dogs, as if they were their own; and when they lack provisions on a journey, they appropriate what they find in the fields throughout the country. It is clearly better that property should be private, but the use of it common; and the special business of the legislator is to create in men this benevolent disposition. Again, how immeasur- 1263ᵇ ably greater is the pleasure, when a man feels a thing to be his own; for surely the love of self is a feeling implanted by nature and not given in vain, although selfishness is rightly censured; this, however, is not the mere love of self, but the love of self in excess, like the miser's love of money; for all, or almost all, men love money and other such objects in a measure. And further, there is the greatest pleasure in doing a kindness or service to friends or guests or companions, which can only be rendered when a man has private property. These advantages are lost by excessive unification of the state. The exhibition of two excellences, besides, is visibly annihilated in such a state: first, temperance towards women (for it is an honourable action to abstain from another's wife for temperance sake); secondly, liberality in the matter of property. No one, when men have all things in common, will any longer set an example of liberality or do any liberal action; for liberality consists in the use which is made of property.

Such legislation may have a specious appearance of benevolence; men readily listen to it, and are easily induced to believe that in some wonderful manner everybody will become everybody's friend—especially when someone is heard denouncing the evils now existing in states, suits about contracts, convictions for perjury, flatteries of rich men and the like, which are said to arise out of the possession of private property. These evils, however, are due not to the absence of communism but to wickedness. Indeed, we see that there is much more quarrelling among those who have all things in common, though there are not many of them when compared with the vast numbers who have private property.

Again, we ought to reckon not only the evils from which the citizens will be saved, but also the advantages which they will lose. The life which they are to lead appears to be quite impracticable. The error of Socrates must be attributed to the false supposition from which he starts. Unity there should be, both of the family and of the state, but in some respects only. For there is a point at which a state may attain such a degree of unity as to be no longer a state, or at which, without actually ceasing to exist, it will become an inferior state, like harmony passing into unison, or rhythm which has been reduced to a single foot. The state, as I was saying, is a plurality, which should be united and made into a community by education; and it is strange that the author of a system of education which he thinks will make the state virtuous, should expect to improve his citizens by regulations of this sort, and not by philosophy or by customs and laws, like those which prevail at Sparta and Crete respecting common meals, whereby the legislator has made property common. Let us remember that we should not disregard the experience of ages; in the multitude of years these things, if they were good, would certainly not have been unknown; for almost everything has been found out, although sometimes they are not put together; in other cases men do not use the knowledge which they have. Great light would be thrown on this subject if we could see such a form of government in the actual process of construction; for the legislator could not form a state at all without distributing and dividing its constituents into associations for common meals, and into phratries and tribes. But all this legislation ends only in forbidding agriculture to the guardians, a prohibition which the Lacedaemonians try to enforce already.

But, indeed, Socrates has not said, nor is it easy to decide, what in such a community will be the general form of the state. The citizens who are not guardians are the majority, and about them nothing has been determined: are the husbandmen, too, to have their property in common? Or is each individual to have his own? and are their wives and children to be individual or common? If, like the guardians, they are to have all things in common, in what do they differ from them, or what will they gain by submitting to their government? Or upon what principle would they submit, unless indeed the governing class adopt the ingenious policy of the Cretans, who give their slaves the same institutions as their own, but forbid them gymnastic exercises and the possession of arms. If, on the other hand, the inferior classes are to be like other cities in respect of marriage and property, what will be the form of the community? Must it not contain two states in one, each hostile to the other? He makes the guardians into a mere occupying garrison, while the husbandmen and artisans and the rest are real citizens. But if so the suits and quarrels, and all the evils which Socrates affirms to exist in other states, will exist equally among them. He says indeed that, having so good an education, the citizens will not need many laws, for example laws about the city or about the

1264ᵃ

markets; but then he confines his education to the guardians. Again, he makes the husbandmen owners of the property upon condition of their paying a tribute. But in that case they are likely to be much more unmanageable and conceited than the Helots, or Penestae, or slaves in general. And whether community of wives and property be necessary for the lower equally with the higher class or not, and the questions akin to this, what will be the education, form of government, laws of the lower class, Socrates has nowhere determined: neither is it easy to discover this, nor is their character of small importance if the common life of the guardians is to be maintained.

Again, if Socrates makes the women common, and retains private property, the men will see to the fields, but who will see to the house? And who will do so if the agricultural class have both their property and their wives in common? Once more: it is absurd to argue, from the analogy of animals, that men and women should follow the same pursuits, for animals have not to manage a household. The government, too, as constituted by Socrates, contains elements of danger; for he makes the same persons always rule. And if this is often a cause of disturbance among the meaner sort, how much more among high-spirited warriors? But that the persons whom he makes rulers must be the same is evident; for the gold which the God mingles in the souls of men is not at one time given to one, at another time to another, but always to the same: as he says, God mingles gold in some, and silver in others, from their very birth; but brass and iron in those who are meant to be artisans and husbandmen. Again, he deprives the guardians even of happiness, and says that the legislator ought to make the whole state happy. But the whole cannot be happy unless most, or all, or some of its parts enjoy happiness. In this respect happiness is not like the even principle in numbers, which may exist only in the whole, but in neither of the parts; not so happiness. And if the guardians are not happy, who are? Surely not the artisans, or the common people. The Republic of which Socrates discourses has all these difficulties, and others quite as great.

6. The same, or nearly the same, objections apply to Plato's later work, the Laws, and therefore we had better examine briefly the constitution which is therein described. In the Republic, Socrates has definitely settled in all a few questions only; such as the community of women and children, the community of property, and the constitution of the state. The population is divided into two classes—one of husbandmen, and the other of warriors; from this latter is taken a third class of counsellors and rulers of the state. But Socrates has not determined whether the husbandmen and artisans are to have a share in the government, and whether they, too, are to carry arms and share in the military service, or not. He certainly thinks that the women ought to share in the education of the guardians, and to fight by their side. The remainder of the work is filled up with digressions foreign to the main subject, and with discussions about the education of the guardians. In the Laws there is hardly anything but laws; not much is said about the constitution. This, which he had intended to make more of the ordinary type, he gradually brings round to the other form. For with the exception of the community of women and property, he supposes everything to be the same in both states; there is to be the same education; the citizens of both are to live free from servile occupations, and there are to be common meals in both. The only difference is that in the Laws, the common meals are extended to women, and the warriors number 5000, but in the Republic only 1000.

The discourses of Socrates are never commonplace; they always exhibit grace and originality and thought; but perfection in everything can hardly be expected. We must not overlook the fact that the number of 5000 citizens, just now mentioned, will require a territory as large as Babylon, or some other huge site, if so many persons are to be supported in idleness, together with their women and attendants, who will be a multitude many times as great. In framing an ideal we may assume what we wish, but should avoid impossibilities.

It is said that the legislator ought to have his eye directed to two points—the people and the country. But neighbouring countries also must not be forgotten by him, firstly because the state for which he legislates is to have a political and not an isolated life. For a state must have such a military force as will be serviceable against her neighbours, and not merely useful at home. Even if such a life is not accepted, ei-

1265ª

ther for individuals or states, still a city should be formidable to enemies, whether invading or retreating.

There is another point: Should not the amount of property be defined in some way which differs from this by being clearer? For Socrates says that a man should have so much property as will enable him to live temperately, which is only a way of saying to live well; this is too general a conception. Further, a man may live temperately and yet miserably. A better definition would be that a man must have so much property as will enable him to live not only temperately but liberally; if the two are parted, liberality will combine with luxury; temperance will be associated with toil. For liberality and temperance are the only eligible qualities which have to do with the use of property. A man cannot use property with mildness or courage, but temperately and liberally he may; and therefore the practice of these excellences is inseparable from property. There is an absurdity, too, in equalizing the property and not regulating the number of citizens; the population is to remain unlimited, and he thinks that it will be sufficiently equalized by a certain number of marriages being unfruitful, however many are born to others, because he finds this to be the case in existing states. But greater care will be 1265ᵇ required than now; for among ourselves, whatever may be the number of citizens, the property is always distributed among them, and therefore no one is in want; but, if the property were incapable of division as in the Laws, the supernumeraries, whether few or many, would get nothing. One would have thought that it was even more necessary to limit population than property; and that the limit should be fixed by calculating the chances of mortality in the children, and of sterility in married persons. The neglect of this subject, which in existing states is so common, is a never-failing cause of poverty among the citizens; and poverty is the parent of revolution and crime. Pheidon the Corinthian, who was one of the most ancient legislators, thought that the families and the number of citizens ought to remain the same, although originally all the lots may have been of different sizes; but in the Laws the opposite principle is maintained. What in our opinion is the right arrangement will have to be explained hereafter.

There is another omission in the Laws: Socrates does not tell us how the rulers differ from their subjects; he only says that they should be related as the warp and the woof, which are made out of different wools. He allows that a man's whole property may be increased fivefold, but why should not his land also increase to a certain extent? Again, will the good management of a household be promoted by his arrangement of homesteads? for he assigns to each individual two homesteads in separate places, and it is difficult to live in two houses.

The whole system of government tends to be neither democracy nor oligarchy, but something in a mean between them, which is usually called a polity, and is composed of the heavy-armed soldiers. Now, if he intended to frame a constitution which would suit the greatest number of states, he was very likely right, but not if he meant to say that this constitutional form came nearest to his first state; for many would prefer the Lacedaemonian, or, possibly, some other more aristocratic government. Some, indeed, say that the best constitution is a combination of all existing forms, and they praise the Lacedaemonian because it is made up of oligarchy, monarchy, and democracy, the king forming the monarchy, and the council of elders the oligarchy, while the democratic element is represented by the Ephors; for the Ephors are selected from the people. Others, however, declare the Ephorate to be a tyranny, and find the element of democracy in the common meals and in the habits of daily life. In the Laws it is maintained that the best constitution is made up of democracy and 1266ᵃ tyranny, which are either not constitutions at all, or are the worst of all. But they are nearer the truth who combined many forms; for the constitution is better which is made up of more numerous elements. The constitution proposed in the Laws has no element of monarchy at all; it is nothing but oligarchy and democracy, leaning rather to oligarchy. This is seen in the mode of appointing magistrates; for although the appointment of them by lot from among those who have been already selected combines both elements, the way in which the rich are compelled by law to attend the assembly and vote for magistrates or discharge other political duties, while the rest may do as they like, and the endeavour to have the greater number of the magistrates appointed out of the richer classes and the highest officers selected from those who have the greatest incomes, both these are oligarchical features. The oligarchical principle prevails also in the choice of the council, for all are compelled to choose, but the compulsion extends only to the choice out of the first class, and of an equal number out of the second class and out of the third class, but not in this latter case to all the voters but to those from the third or fourth class; and the selection of candidates out of the fourth class is only compulsory on the first and second. Then, from the persons so chosen, he says that there ought to be an equal number of each class selected. Thus a preponderance will be given to the better sort of people, who have the larger incomes, because some of the lower classes, not being compelled, will not vote. These considerations, and others which will be adduced when the time comes for examining similar constitutions, tend to show that states like Plato's should not be composed of democracy and monarchy. There is also a danger in electing the magistrates out of a body who are themselves elected; for, if but a small number choose to combine, the elections will always go as they desire. Such is the constitution which is described in the Laws. . . .

BOOK III

1. He who would inquire into the essence and attributes of various kinds of government must first of all determine what a state is. At present this is a disputed question. Some say that the state has done a certain act; others, not the state, but the oligarchy or the tyrant. And the legislator or statesman is concerned entirely with the state, a government being an arrangement of the inhabitants of a state. But a state is composite, like any other whole made up of many parts—these are the citizens, who compose it. 1275ᵃ It is evident, therefore, that we must begin by asking, Who is the citizen, and what is the meaning of the term? For here again there may be a difference of opinion. He who is a citizen in a democracy will often not be a citizen in an oligarchy. Leaving out of consideration those who have been made citizens, or who have obtained the name of citizen in any other accidental manner, we may say, first, that a citizen is not a citizen because he lives in a certain place,

for resident aliens and slaves share in the place; nor is he a citizen who has legal rights to the extent of suing and being sued; for this right may be enjoyed under the provisions of a treaty. Resident aliens in many places do not possess even such rights completely, for they are obliged to have a patron, so that they do but imperfectly participate in the community, and we call them citizens only in a qualified sense, as we might apply the term to children who are too young to be on the register, or to old men who have been relieved from state duties. Of these we do not say quite simply that they are citizens, but add in the one case that they are not of age, and in the other, that they are past the age, or something of that sort; the precise expression is immaterial, for our meaning is clear. Similar difficulties to those which I have mentioned may be raised and answered about disfranchised citizens and about exiles. But the citizen whom we are seeking to define is a citizen in the strictest sense, against whom no such exception can be taken, and his special characteristic is that he shares in the administration of justice, and in offices. Now of offices some are discontinuous, and the same persons are not allowed to hold them twice, or can only hold them after a fixed interval; others have no limit of time—for example, the office of juryman or member of the assembly. It may, indeed, be argued that these are not magistrates at all, and that their functions give them no share in the government. But surely it is ridiculous to say that those who have the supreme power do not govern. Let us not dwell further upon this, which is a purely verbal question; what we want is a common term including both juryman and member of the assembly. Let us, for the sake of distinction, call it 'indefinite office', and we will assume that those who share in such office are citizens. This is the most comprehensive definition of a citizen, and best suits all those who are generally so called.

But we must not forget that things of which the underlying principles differ in kind, one of them being first, another second, another third, have, when regarded in this relation, nothing, or hardly anything, worth mentioning in common. Now we see that governments differ in kind, and that some of them are prior and that others are posterior; those which are faulty or perverted are necessarily posterior to those 1275ᵇ which are perfect. (What we mean by perversion will be hereafter explained.) The citizen then of necessity differs under each form of government; and our definition is best adapted to the citizen of a democracy; but not necessarily to other states. For in some states the people are not acknowledged, nor have they any regular assembly, but only extraordinary ones; and law-suits are distributed by sections among the magistrates. At Lacedaemon, for instance, the Ephors determine suits about contracts, which they distribute among themselves, while the elders are judges of homicide, and other causes are decided by other magistrates. A similar principle prevails at Carthage; there certain magistrates decide all causes. We may, indeed, modify our definition of the citizen so as to include these states. In them it is the holder of a definite, not an indefinite office, who is juryman and member of the assembly, and to some or all such holders of definite offices is reserved the right of deliberating or judging about some things or about all things. The conception of the citizen now begins to clear up.

He who has the power to take part in the deliberative or judicial administration of any state is said by us to be a citizen of that state; and, speaking generally, a state is a body of citizens sufficing for the purposes of life.

2. But in practice a citizen is defined to be one of whom both the parents are citizens (and not just one, i.e. father or mother); others insist on going further back; say to two or three or more ancestors. This is a short and practical definition; but there are some who raise the further question of how this third or fourth ancestor came to be a citizen. Gorgias of Leontini, partly because he was in a difficulty, partly in irony, said that mortars are what is made by the mortar-makers, and the citizens of Larissa are those who are made by the magistrates; for it is their trade to 'make Larissaeans'. Yet the question is really simple, for, if according to the definition just given they shared in the government, they were citizens. This is a better definition than the other. For the words, 'born of a father or mother who is a citizen', cannot possibly apply to the first inhabitants or founders of a state.

There is a greater difficulty in the case of those who have been made citizens after a revolution, as by Cleisthenes at Athens after the expulsion of the tyrants, for he enrolled in tribes many metics, both strangers and slaves. The doubt in these cases is, not who is, but whether he who is ought to be a citizen; and there will still be a further doubt, whether he who ought not to be a citizen, is one in fact, for what ought not to be is what is false. Now, there are some who hold office, and yet ought not to hold office, whom we describe as ruling, but ruling unjustly. And the citizen was defined by the fact of his holding some kind of rule or office—he who holds a certain sort of office fulfils our definition of a citizen. It is evident, therefore, that the citizens about whom the doubt has arisen must be called citizens.

3. Whether they ought to be so or not is a question which is bound up with the previous inquiry. For a parallel question is raised respecting the state, whether a certain act is or is not an act of the state; for example, in the transition from an oligarchy or a tyranny to a democracy. In such cases persons refuse to fulfil their contracts or any other obligations, on the ground that the tyrant and not the state, contracted them; they argue that some constitutions are established by force, and not for the sake of the common good. But this would apply equally to democracies, and then the acts of the democracy will be neither more nor less acts of the state in question than those of an oligarchy or of a tyranny. This question runs up into another:—on what principle shall we ever say that the state is the same, or different? It would be a very superficial view which considered only the place and the inhabitants (for the soil and the population may be separated, and some of the inhabitants may live in one place and some in another). This, however, is not a very serious difficulty; we need only remark that the word 'state' is ambiguous.

It is further asked: When are men, living in the same place, to be regarded as a single city—what is the limit? Certainly not the wall of the city, for you might surround all Peloponnesus with a wall. Babylon, we may say, is like this, and every city that has the compass of a nation rather than a city; Babylon, they say, had been taken for three days before some part of the inhabitants become aware of the fact. This difficulty may, however, with advantage be deferred to another occasion; the statesman has to consider the size of the state, and whether it should consist of more than one race or not.

Again, shall we say that while the race of inhabitants remains the same, the city is also the same, although the citizens are always dying and being born, as we call rivers and fountains the same, although the water is always flowing away and more coming? Or shall we say that the generations of men, like the rivers, are the same, but that the state changes? For, since the state is a partnership, and is a partnership of citizens in a constitution, when the form of the government changes, and becomes different, then it may be supposed that the state is no longer the same, just as a tragic differs from a comic chorus, although the members of both may be identical. And in this manner we speak of every union or composition of elements as different when the form of their composition alters; for example, a scale containing the same sounds is said to be different, accordingly as the Dorian or the Phrygian mode is employed. And if this is true it is evident that the sameness of the state consists chiefly in the sameness of the constitution, and it may be called or not called by the same name, whether the inhabitants are the same or entirely different. It is quite another question, whether a state ought or ought not to filfil engagements when the form of government changes.

4. There is a point nearly allied to the preceding: Whether the excellence of a good man and a good citizen is the same or not. But before entering on this discussion, we must certainly first obtain some general notion of the excellence of the citizen. Like the sailor, the citizen is a member of a community. Now, sailors have different functions, for one of them is a rower, another a pilot, and a third a look-out man, a fourth is described by some similar term; and while the precise definition of each individual's excellence applies exclusively to him, there is, at the same time, a common definition applicable to them all. For they have all of them a common object, which is safety in navigation. Similarly, one citizen differs from another, but the salvation of the community is the common business of them all. This community is the constitution; the excellence of the citizen must therefore be relative to the constitution of which he is a member. If, then, there are many forms of government, it is evident that there is not one single excellence of the good citizen which is perfect excellence. But we say that the good man is he who has one single excellence which is perfect excellence. Hence it is evident that the good citizen need not of necessity possess the excellence which makes a good man.

The same question may also be approached by another road, from a consideration of the best constitution. If the state cannot be entirely composed of good men, and yet each citizen is expected to do his own business well, and must therefore have excellence, still, inasmuch as all the citizens cannot be alike, the excellence of the citizen and of the good man cannot coincide. All must have the excellence of the good citizen—thus, and thus only, can the state be perfect; but they will not have the excellence of a good man, unless we assume that in the good state all the citizens must be good.

Again, the state, as composed of unlikes, may be compared to the living being: as the first elements into which a living being is resolved are soul and body, as soul is made up of rational principle and appetite, the family of husband and wife, property of master and slave, so of all these, as well as other dissimilar elements, the state is composed; and therefore the excellence of all the citizens cannot possibly be the same, any more than the excellence of the leader of a chorus is the same as that of the performer who stands by his side. I have said enough to show why the two kinds of excellence cannot be absolutely the same.

But will there then be no case in which the excellence of the good citizen and the excellence of the good man coincide? To this we answer that the good ruler is a good and wise man, but the citizen need not be wise. And some persons say that even the education of the ruler should be of a special kind; for are not the children of kings instructed in riding and military exercises? As Euripides says:

No subtle arts for me, but what the state requires.

As though there were a special education needed for a ruler. If the excellence of a good ruler is the same as that of a good man, and we assume further that the subject is a citizen as well as the ruler, the excellence of the good citizen and the excellence of the good man cannot be absolutely the same, although in some cases they may; for the excellence of a ruler differs from that of a citizen. It was the sense of this difference which made Jason say that 'he felt hungry when he was not a tyrant', meaning that he could not endure to live in a private station. But, on the other hand, it may be argued that men are praised for knowing both how to rule and how to obey, and he is said to be a citizen of excellence who is able to do both well. Now if we suppose the excellence of a good man to be that which rules, and the excellence of the citizen to include ruling and obeying, it cannot be said that they are equally worthy of praise. Since, then, it is sometimes thought that the ruler and the ruled must learn different things and not the same, but that the citizen must know and share in them both, the inference is obvious. There is, indeed, the rule of a master, which is concerned with menial offices—the master need not know how to perform these, but may employ others in the execution of them: the other would be degrading; and by the other I mean the power actually to do menial duties, which vary much in character and are executed by various classes of slaves, such, for example, as handicraftsmen, who, as their name signifies, live by the labour of their 1277ᵇ hands—under these the mechanic is included. Hence in ancient times, and among some nations, the working classes had no share in the government—a privilege which they only acquired under extreme democracy. Certainly the good man and the statesman and the good citizen ought not to learn the crafts of inferiors except for their own occasional use; if they habitually practise them, there will cease to be a distinction between master and slave.

But there is a rule of another kind, which is exercised over freemen and equals by birth—a constitutional rule, which the ruler must learn by obeying, as he would learn the duties of a general of cavalry by being under the orders of a general of cavalry, or the duties of a general of infantry by being under the orders of a general of infantry, and by having had the command of a regiment and of a company. It has been well said that he who has never learned to obey cannot be a good commander. The excellence of the two is not the same, but the good citizen ought to be capable of both; he should know how to govern like a freeman, and how to obey like a freeman—these are the excellences of a citizen. And, although the temperance and justice of a ruler are distinct from those of a subject, the excellence of a good man will include both; for the excellence of the good man who

is free and also a subject, e.g. his justice, will not be one but will comprise distinct kinds, the one qualifying him to rule, the other to obey, and differing as the temperance and courage of men and women differ. For a man would be thought a coward if he had no more courage than a courageous woman, and a woman would be thought loquacious if she imposed no more restraint on her conversation than the good man; and indeed their part in the management of the household is different, for the duty of the one is to acquire, and of the other to preserve. Practical wisdom is the only excellence peculiar to the ruler: it would seem that all other excellences must equally belong to ruler and subject. The excellence of the subject is certainly not wisdom, but only true opinion; he may be compared to the maker of the flute, while his master is like the flute-player or user of the flute.

From these considerations may be gathered the answer to the question, whether the excellence of the good man is the same as that of the good citizen, or different, and how far the same, and how far different.

5. There still remains one more question about the citizen: Is he only a true citizen who has a share of office, or is the mechanic to be included? If they who hold no office are to be deemed citizens, not every citizen can have this excellence; for this man is a citizen. And if none of the lower class are citizens, in which part of the state are they to be placed? For they are not resident aliens, and they are not foreigners. May we not reply, that as far as this objec- 1278ᵃ tion goes there is no more absurdity in excluding them than in excluding slaves and freedmen from any of the above-mentioned classes? It must be admitted that we cannot consider all those to be citizens who are necessary to the existence of the state; for example, children are not citizens equally with grown-up men, who are citizens absolutely, but children, not being grown up, are only citizens on a certain assumption. In ancient times, and among some nations, the artisan class were slaves or foreigners, and therefore the majority of them are so now. The best form of state will not admit them to citizenship; but if they are admitted, then our definition of the excellence of a citizen will not apply to every citizen, nor to every free man as such, but only to those

who are freed from necessary services. The necessary people are either slaves who minister to the wants of individuals, or mechanics and labourers who are the servants of the community. These reflections carried a little further will explain their position; and indeed what has been said already is of itself, when understood, explanation enough.

Since there are many forms of government there must be many varieties of citizens, and especially of citizens who are subjects; so that under some governments the mechanic and the labourer will be citizens, but not in others, as, for example, in so-called aristocracies, if there are any, in which honours are given according to excellence and merit; for no man can practise excellence who is living the life of a mechanic or labourer. In oligarchies the qualification for office is high, and therefore no labourer can ever be a citizen; but a mechanic may, for an actual majority of them are rich. At Thebes there was a law that no man could hold office who had not retired from business for ten years. But in many states the law goes to the length of admitting aliens; for in some democracies a man is a citizen though his mother only be a citizen; and a similar principle is applied to illegitimate children among many. Nevertheless they make such people citizens because of the dearth of legitimate citizens (for they introduce this sort of legislation owing to lack of population); so when the number of citizens increases, first the children of a male or a female slave are excluded; then those whose mothers only are citizens; and at last the right of citizenship is confined to those whose fathers and mothers are both citizens.

Hence, as is evident, there are different kinds of citizens; and he is a citizen in the fullest sense who shares in the honours of the state. Compare Homer's words 'like some dishonoured stranger'; he who is excluded from the honours of the state is no better than an alien. But when this exclusion is concealed, then its object is to deceive their fellow inhabitants.

1278^b As to the question whether the excellence of the good man is the same as that of the good citizen, the considerations already adduced prove that in some states the good man and the good citizen are the same, and in others different. When they are the same it is not every citizen who is a good man, but only the statesman and those who have or may have, alone

or in conjunction with others, the conduct of public affairs.

6. Having determined these questions, we have next to consider whether there is only one form of government or many, and if many, what they are, and how many, and what are the differences between them.

A constitution is the arrangement of magistracies in a state, epecially of the highest of all. The government is everywhere sovereign in the state, and the constitution is in fact the government. For example, in democracies the people are supreme, but in oligarchies, the few; and, therefore, we say that these two constitutions also are different: and so in other cases.

First, let us consider what is the purpose of a state, and how many forms of rule there are by which human society is regulated. We have already said, in the first part of this treatise, when discussing household management and the rule of a master, that man is by nature a political animal. And therefore, men, even when they do not require one another's help, desire to live together; not but that they are also brought together by their common interests in so far as they each attain to any measure of well-being. This is certainly the chief end, both of individuals and of states. And mankind meet together and maintain the political community also for the sake of mere life (in which there is possibly some noble element so long as the evils of existence do not greatly overbalance the good). And we all see that men cling to life even at the cost of enduring great misfortune, seeming to find in life a natural sweetness and happiness.

There is no difficulty in distinguishing the various kinds of rule; they have been often defined already in our popular discussions. The rule of a master, although the slave by nature and the master by nature have in reality the same interests, is nevertheless exercised primarily with a view to the interest of the master, but accidentally considers the slave, since, if the slave perish, the rule of the master perishes with him. On the other hand, the government of a wife and children and of a household, which we have called household management, is exercised in the first instance for the good of the governed or for the common good of both parties, but essentially for 1279^a

the good of the governed, as we see to be the case in medicine, gymnastic, and the arts in general, which are only accidentally concerned with the good of the artists themselves. For there is no reason why the trainer may not sometimes practise gymnastics, and the helmsman is always one of the crew. The trainer or the helmsman considers the good of those committed to his care. But, when he is one of the persons taken care of, he accidentally participates in the advantage, for the helmsman is also a sailor, and the trainer becomes one of those in training. And so in politics: when the state is framed upon the principle of equality and likeness, the citizens think that they ought to hold office by turns. Formerly, as is natural, everyone would take his turn of service; and then again, somebody else would look after this interest, just as he, while in office, had looked after theirs. But nowadays, for the sake of the advantage which is to be gained from the public revenues and from office, men want to be always in office. One might imagine that the rulers, being sickly, were only kept in health while they continued in office; in that case we may be sure that they would be hunting after places. The conclusion is evident: that governments which have a regard to the common interest are constituted in accordance with strict principles of justice, and are therefore true forms; but those which regard only the interest of the rulers are all defective and perverted forms, for they are despotic, whereas a state is a community of freemen.

7. Having determined these points, we have next to consider how many forms of government there are, and what they are; and in the first place what are the true forms, for when they are determined the perversions of them will at once be apparent. The words constitution and government have the same meaning, and the government, which is the supreme authority in states, must be in the hands of one, or of a few, or of the many. The true forms of government, therefore, are those in which the one, or the few, or the many, govern with a view to the common interest; but governments which rule with a view to the private interest, whether of the one, or of the few, or of the many, are perversions. For the members of a state, if they are truly citizens, ought to participate in its advantages. Of forms of government in which one rules, we call that which regards the common interest, kingship; that in which more than one, but not many, rule, aristocracy; and it is so called, either because the rulers are the best men, or because they have at heart the best interests of the state and of the citizens. But when the many administer the state for the common interest, the government is called by the generic name—a constitution. And there is a reason for this use of language. One man or a few may excel in excellence; but as the number increases it becomes more difficult for them to attain perfection in every kind of excellence, though they may in military excellence, for this is found in the masses. Hence in a constitutional government the fighting-men have the supreme power, and those who possess arms are the citizens. 1279[b]

Of the above-mentioned forms, the perversions are as follows:—of kingship, tyranny; of aristocracy, oligarchy; of constitutional government, democracy. For tyranny is a kind of monarchy which has in view the interest of the monarch only; oligarchy has in view the interest of the wealthy; democracy, of the needy: none of them the common good of all.

8. But there are difficulties about these forms of government, and it will therefore be necessary to state a little more at length the nature of each of them. For he who would make a philosophical study of the various sciences, and is not only concerned with practice, ought not to overlook or omit anything, but to set forth the truth in every particular. Tyranny, as I was saying, is monarchy exercising the rule of a master over the political society; oligarchy is when men of property have the government in their hands; democracy, the opposite, when the indigent, and not the men of property, are the rulers. And here arises the first of our difficulties, and it relates to the distinction just drawn. For democracy is said to be the government of the many. But what if the many are men of property and have the power in their hands? In like manner oligarchy is said to be the government of the few; but what if the poor are fewer than the rich, and have the power in their hands because they are stronger? In these cases the distinction which we have drawn between these different forms of government would no longer hold good.

Suppose, once more, that we add wealth to the few and poverty to the many, and name the governments accordingly—an oligarchy is said to be that in which the few and the wealthy, and a democracy that in which the many and the poor are the rulers—there will still be a difficulty. For, if the only forms of government are the ones already mentioned, how shall we describe those other governments also just mentioned by us, in which the rich are the more numerous and the poor are the fewer, and both govern in their respective states?

The argument seems to show that, whether in oligarchies or in democracies, the number of the governing body, whether the greater number, as in a democracy, or the smaller number, as in an oligarchy, is an accident due to the fact that the rich everywhere are few, and the poor numerous. But if so, there is a misapprehension of the causes of the difference between them. For the real difference between democracy and oligarchy is poverty and wealth. Wherever men rule by reason of their wealth, whether they be few or many, that is an oligarchy, and where the poor rule, that is a democracy. But in fact the rich are few and the poor many; for few are well-to-do, whereas freedom is enjoyed by all, and wealth and freedom are the grounds on which the two parties claim power in the state.

9. Let us begin by considering the common definitions of oligarchy and democracy, and what is oligarchical and democratic justice. For all men cling to justice of some kind, but their conceptions are imperfect and they do not express the whole idea. For example, justice is thought by them to be, and is, equality—not, however, for all, but only for equals. And inequality is thought to be, and is, justice; neither is this for all, but only for unequals. When the persons are omitted, then men judge erroneously. The reason is that they are passing judgement on themselves, and most people are bad judges in their own case. And whereas justice implies a relation to persons as well as to things, and a just distribution, as I have already said in the Ethics, implies the same ratio between the persons and between the things, they agree about the equality of the things, but dispute about the equality of the persons, chiefly for the reason which I have just given—because they are bad judges in their own affairs; and secondly, because both the parties to the argument are speaking of a limited and partial justice, but imagine themselves to be speaking of absolute justice. For the one

party, if they are unequal in one respect, for example wealth, consider themselves to be unequal in all; and the other party, if they are equal in one respect, for example free birth, consider themselves to be equal in all. But they leave out the capital point. For if men met and associated out of regard to wealth only, their share in the state would be proportioned to their property, and the oligarchical doctrine would then seem to carry the day. It would not be just that he who paid one mina should have the same share of a hundred minae, whether of the principal or of the profits, as he who paid the remaining ninety-nine. But a state exists for the sake of a good life, and not for the sake of life only: if life only were the object, slaves and brute animals might form a state, but they cannot, for they have no share in happiness or in a life based on choice. Nor does a state exist for the sake of alliance and security from injustice, nor yet for the sake of exchange and mutual intercourse; for then the Tyrrhenians and the Carthaginians, and all who have commercial treaties with one another, would be the citizens of one state. True, they have agreements about imports, and engagements that they will do no wrong to one another, and written articles of alliance. But there are no magistracies common to the contracting parties; different states have each their own magistracies. Nor does one state take care that the citizens of the other are such as they ought to be, nor see that those who come under the terms of the treaty do no wrong or wickedness at all, but only that they do no injustice to one another. Whereas, those who care for good government take into consideration political excellence and defect. Whence it may be further inferred that excellence must be the care of a state which is truly so called, and not merely enjoys the name: for without this end the community becomes a mere alliance which differs only in place from alliances of which the members live apart; and law is only a convention, 'a surety to one another of justice', as the sophist Lycophron says, and has no real power to make the citizens good and just.

This is obvious; for suppose distinct places, such as Corinth and Megara, to be brought together so that their walls touched, still they would not be one city, not even if the citizens had the right to intermarry, which is one of the rights peculiarly characteristic of states. Again, if men dwelt at a distance from one another, but not so far off as to have no intercourse, and there were laws among them that they should not wrong each other in their exchanges, neither would this be a state. Let us suppose that one man is a carpenter, another a farmer, another a shoemaker, and so on, and that their number is ten thousand: nevertheless, if they have nothing in common but exchange, alliance, and the like, that would not constitute a state. Why is this? Surely not because they are at a distance from one another; for even supposing that such a community were to meet in one place, but that each man had a house of his own, which was in a manner his state, and that they made alliance with one another, but only against evil-doers; still an accurate thinker would not deem this to be a state, if their intercourse with one another was of the same character after as before their union. It is clear then that a state is not a mere society, having a common place, established for the prevention of mutual crime and for the sake of exchange. These are conditions without which a state cannot exist; but all of them together do not constitute a state, which is a community of families and aggregations of families in well-being, for the sake of a perfect and self-sufficing life. Such a community can only be established among those who live in the same place and intermarry. Hence there arise in cities family connexions, brotherhoods, common sacrifices, amusements which draw men together. But these are created by friendship, for to choose to live together is friendship. The end of the state is the good life, and these are the means towards it. And the state is the union of families and villages 1281ᵃ in a perfect and self-sufficing life, by which we mean a happy and honourable life.

Our conclusion, then, is that political society exists for the sake of noble actions, and not of living together. Hence they who contribute most to such a society have a greater share in it than those who have the same or a greater freedom or nobility of birth but are inferior to them in political excellence; or than those who exceed them in wealth but are surpassed by them in excellence.

From what has been said it will be clearly seen that all the partisans of different forms of government speak of a part of justice only.

10. There is also a doubt as to what is to be the supreme power in the state:—Is it the multitude? Or the wealthy? Or the good? Or the one best man? Or a tyrant? Any of these alternatives seems to involve disagreeable consequences. If the poor, for example, because they are more in number, divide among themselves the property of the rich—is not this unjust? No, by heaven (will be the reply), for the supreme authority justly willed it. But if this is not extreme injustice, what is? Again, when in the first division all has been taken, and the majority divide anew the property of the minority, is it not evident, if this goes on, that they will ruin the state? Yet surely, excellence is not the ruin of those who possess it, nor is justice destructive of a state; and therefore this law of confiscation clearly cannot be just. If it were, all the acts of a tyrant must of necessity be just; for he only coerces other men by superior power, just as the multitude coerce the rich. But is it just then that the few and the wealthy should be the rulers? And what if they, in like manner, rob and plunder the people—is this just? If so, the other case will likewise be just. But there can be no doubt that all these things are wrong and unjust.

Then ought the good to rule and have supreme power? But in that case everybody else, being excluded from power, will be dishonoured. For the offices of a state are posts of honour; and if one set of men always hold them, the rest must be deprived of them. Then will it be well that the one best man should rule? That is still more oligarchical, for the number of those who are dishonoured is thereby increased. Someone may say that it is bad in any case for a man, subject as he is to all the accidents of human passion, to have the supreme power, rather than the law. But what if the law itself be democratic or oligarchical, how will that help us out of our difficulties? Not at all; the same consequences will follow.

11. Most of these questions may be reserved for another occasion. The principle that the multitude ought to be in power rather than the few best might seem to be solved and to contain some difficulty and perhaps even truth. For the many, of whom each in- 1281ᵇ dividual is not a good man, when they meet together may be better than the few good, if regarded not individually but collectively, just as a feast to which many contribute is better than a dinner provided out

of a single purse. For each individual among the many has a share of excellence and practical wisdom, and when they meet together, just as they become in a manner one man, who has many feet, and hands, and senses, so too with regard to their character and thought. Hence the many are better judges than a single of music and poetry; for some understand one part, and some another, and among them they understand the whole. There is a similar combination of qualities in good men, who differ from any individual of the many, as the beautiful are said to differ from those who are not beautiful, and works of art from realities, because in them the scattered elements are combined, although, if taken separately, the eye of one person or some other feature in another person would be fairer than in the picture. Whether this principle can apply to every democracy, and to all bodies of men, is not clear. Or rather, by heaven, in some cases it is impossible to apply; for the argument would equally hold about brutes; and wherein, it will be asked, do some men differ from brutes? But there may be bodies of men about whom our statement is nevertheless true. And if so, the difficulty which has been already raised, and also another which is akin to it—viz. what power should be assigned to the mass of freemen and citizens, who are not rich and have no personal merit—are both solved. There is still a danger in allowing them to share the great offices of state, for their folly will lead them into error, and their dishonesty into crime. But there is a danger also in not letting them share, for a state in which many poor men are excluded from office will necessarily be full of enemies. The only way of escape is to assign to them some deliberative and judicial functions. For this reason Solon and certain other legislators give them the power of electing to offices, and of calling the magistrates to account, but they do not allow them to hold office singly. When they meet together their perceptions are quite good enough, and combined with the better class they are useful to the state (just as impure food when mixed with what is pure sometimes makes the entire mass more wholesome than a small quantity of the pure would be), but each individual, left to himself, forms an imperfect judgement. On the other hand, the popular form of government involves certain difficulties. In the first place, it might be objected that he who can judge of the healing of a sick man would be one who could himself heal his disease, and make him whole—that is, in other words, the physician; and so in all professions and arts. As, then, the physician ought to be called to account by physicians, so ought men in general to be called to account by their peers. But physicians are of three kinds:—there is the ordinary practitioner, and there is the master physician, and thirdly the man educated in the art: in all arts there is such a class; and we attribute the power of judging to them quite as much as to professors of the art. Secondly, does not the same principle apply to elections? For a right election can only be made by those who have knowledge; those who know geometry, for example, will choose a geometrician rightly, and those who know how to steer, a pilot; and, even if there be some occupations and arts in which private persons share in the ability to choose, they certainly cannot choose better than those who know. So that, according to this argument, neither the election of magistrates, nor the calling of them to account, should be entrusted to the many. Yet possibly these objections are to a great extent met by our old answer, that if the people are not utterly degraded, although individually they may be worse judges than those who have special knowledge, as a body they are as good or better. Moreover, there are some arts whose products are not judged of solely, or best, by the artists themselves, namely those arts whose products are recognized even by those who do not possess the art; for example, the knowledge of the house is not limited to the builder only; the user, or, in other words, the master, of the house will actually be a better judge than the builder, just as the pilot will judge better of a rudder than the carpenter, and the guest will judge better of a feast than the cook.

This difficulty seems now to be sufficiently answered, but there is another akin to it. That inferior persons should have authority in greater matters than the good would appear to be a strange thing, yet the election and calling to account of the magistrates is the greatest of all. And these, as I was saying, are functions which in some states are assigned to the people, for the assembly is supreme in all such

1282^a

matters. Yet persons of any age, and having but a small property qualification, sit in the assembly and deliberate and judge, although for the great officers of state, such as treasurers and generals, a high qualification is required. This difficulty may be solved in the same manner as the preceding, and the present practice of democracies may be really defensible. For the power does not reside in the juryman, or counsellor, or member of the assembly, but in the court, and the council, and the assembly, of which the aforesaid individuals—counsellor, assemblyman, juryman—are only parts or members. And for this reason the many may claim to have a higher authority than the few; for the people, and the council, and the courts consist of many persons, and their property collectively is greater than the property of one or of a few individuals holding great offices. But enough of this.

The discussion of the first question shows nothing so clearly as that laws, when good, should be 1282ᵇ supreme; and that the magistrate or magistrates should regulate those matters only on which the laws are unable to speak with precision owing to the difficulty of any general principle embracing all particulars. But what are good laws has not yet been clearly explained; the old difficulty remains. The goodness or badness, justice or injustice, of laws varies of necessity with the constitutions of states. This, however, is clear, that the laws must be adapted to the constitutions. But, if so, true forms of government will of necessity have just laws, and perverted forms of government will have unjust laws.

12. In all sciences and arts the end is a good, and the greatest good and in the highest degree a good in the most authoritative of all—this is the political science of which the good is justice, in other words, the common interest. All men think justice to be a sort of equality; and to a certain extent they agree with what we have said in our philosophical works about ethics. For they say that what is just is just for someone and that it should be equal for equals. But there still remains a question: equality or inequality of what? Here is a difficulty which calls for political speculation. For very likely some persons will say that offices of state ought to be unequally distributed according to superior excellence, in whatever respect, of the citizen, although there is no other

difference between him and the rest of the community; for those who differ in any one respect have different rights and claims. But, surely, if this is true, the complexion or height of a man, or any other advantage, will be a reason for his obtaining a greater share of political rights. The error here lies upon the surface, and may be illustrated from the other arts and sciences. When a number of flute-players are equal in their art, there is no reason why those of them who are better born should have better flutes given to them; for they will not play any better on the flute, and the superior instrument should be reserved for him who is the superior artist. If what I am saying is still obscure, it will be made clearer as 1283ᵃ we proceed. For if there were a superior flute-player who was far inferior in birth and beauty, although either of these may be a greater good than the art of flute-playing and may excel flute-playing in a greater ratio than he excels the others in his art, still he ought to have the best flutes given to him, unless the advantages of wealth and birth contribute to excellence in flute-playing, which they do not. Moreover, upon this principle any good may be compared with any other. For if a given height may be measured against wealth and against freedom, height in general may be so measured. Thus if A excels in height more than B in excellence, even if excellence in general excels height still more, all goods will be comparable; for if a certain amount is better than some other, it is clear that some other will be equal. But since no such comparison can be made, it is evident that there is good reason why in politics men do not ground their claim to office on every sort of inequality. For if some be slow, and others swift, that is no reason why the one should have little and the others much; it is in gymnastic contests that such excellence is rewarded. Whereas the rival claims of candidates for office can only be based on the possession of elements which enter into the composition of a state. And therefore the well-born, or free-born, or rich, may with good reason claim office; for holders of offices must be freemen and tax-payers: a state can be no more composed entirely of poor men than entirely of slaves. But if wealth and freedom are necessary elements, justice and valour are equally so; for without the former qualities a state cannot exist at all, without the latter not well.

BOOK VII

1. He who would duly inquire about the best form of a state ought first to determine which is the most eligible life; while this remains uncertain the best form of the state must also be uncertain; for, in the natural order of things, those men may be expected to lead the best life who are governed in the best manner of which their circumstances admit. We ought therefore to ascertain, first of all, which is the most generally eligible life, and then whether the same life is or is not best for the state and for individuals.

Assuming that enough has been already said in discussions outside the school concerning the best life, we will now only repeat what is contained in them. Certainly no one will dispute the propriety of that partition of goods which separates them into three classes, viz. external goods, goods of the body, and goods of the soul, or deny that the happy man must have all three. For no one would maintain that he is happy who has not in him a particle of courage or temperance or justice or practical wisdom, who is afraid of every insect which flutters past him, and will commit any crime, however great, in order to gratify his lust for meat or drink, who will sacrifice his dearest friend for the sake of half a farthing, and is as feeble and false in mind as a child or a madman. These propositions are almost universally acknowledged as soon as they are uttered, but men differ about the degree or relative superiority of this or that good. Some think that a very moderate amount of excellence is enough, but set no limit to their desires for wealth, property, power, reputation, and the like. To them we shall reply by an appeal to facts, which easily prove that mankind does not acquire or preserve the excellences by the help of external goods, but external goods by the help of the excellences, and that happiness, whether consisting in pleasure or excellence, or both, is more often found with those who are most highly cultivated in their mind and in their character, and have only a moderate share of external goods, than among those who possess external goods to a useless extent but are deficient in higher qualities; and this is not only a matter of experience, but, if reflected upon, will easily appear to be in accordance with reason. For, whereas external goods have a limit, like any other instrument, and all things useful are useful for a purpose, and where there is too much of them they must either do harm, or at any rate be of no use, to their possessors, every good of the soul, the greater it is, is also of greater use, if the epithet useful as well as noble is appropriate to such subjects. No proof is required to show that the best state of one thing in relation to another corresponds in degree of excellence to the interval between the natures of which we say that these very states are states: so that, if the soul is more noble than our possessions or our bodies, both absolutely and in relation to us, it must be admitted that the best state of either has a similar ratio to the other. Again, it is for the sake of the soul that goods external and goods of the body are desirable at all, and all wise men ought to choose them for the sake of the soul, and not the soul for the sake of them.

Let us acknowledge then that each one has just so much of happiness as he has of excellence and wisdom, and of excellent and wise action. The gods are a witness to us of this truth, for they are happy and blessed, not by reason of any external good, but in themselves and by reason of their own nature. And herein of necessity lies the difference between good fortune and happiness; for external goods come of themselves, and chance is the author of them, but no one is just or temperate by or through chance. In like manner, and by a similar train of argument, the happy state may be shown to be that which is best and which acts rightly; and it cannot act rightly without doing right actions, and neither individual nor state can do right actions without excellence and wisdom. Thus the courage, justice, and wisdom of a state have the same form and nature as the qualities which give the individual who possesses them the name of just, wise or temperate.

This much may suffice by way of preface: for I could not avoid touching upon these questions, neither could I go through all the arguments affecting them; these are the business of another science.

Let us assume then that the best life, both for individuals and states, is the life of excellence, when excellence has external goods enough for the performance of good actions. If there are any who dispute our assertion, we will in this treatise pass them over, and consider their objections hereafter.

2. There remains to be discussed the question, whether the happiness of the individual is the same as that of the state, or different. Here again there can be no doubt—no one denies that they are the same. For those who hold that the well-being of the individual consists in his wealth, also think that riches make the happiness of the whole state, and those who value most highly the life of a tyrant deem that city the happiest which rules over the greatest number; while they who approve an individual for his excellence say that the more excellent a city is, the happier it is. Two points here present themselves for consideration: first, which is the more desirable life, that of a citizen who is a member of a state, or that of an alien who has no political ties; and again, which is the best form of constitution or the best condition of a state, either on the supposition that political privileges are desirable for all, or for a majority only? Since the good of the state and not of the individual is the proper subject of political thought and speculation, and we are engaged in a political discussion, while the first of these two points has a secondary interest for us, the latter will be the main subject of our inquiry.

Now it is evident that that form of government is best in which every man, whoever he is, can act best and live happily. But even those who agree in thinking that the life of excellence is the most desirable raise a question, whether the life of business and politics is or is not more desirable than one which is wholly independent of external goods, I mean than a contemplative life, which by some is maintained to be the only one worthy of a philosopher. For these two lives—the life of the philosopher and the life of the statesman—appear to have been preferred by those who have been most keen in the pursuit of excellence, both in our own and in other ages. Which is the better is a question of no small moment; for the wise man, like the wise state, will necessarily regulate his life according to the best end. There are some who think that while a despotic rule over others is the greatest injustice, to exercise a constitutional rule over them, even though not unjust, is a great impediment to a man's individual well-being. Others take an opposite view; they maintain that the true life of man is the practical and political, and that every excellence admits of being practised, quite as

1324ᵇ

much by statesmen and rulers as by private individuals. Others, again, are of the opinion that arbitrary and tyrannical rule alone makes for happiness; indeed, in some states the entire aim both of the laws and of the constitution is to give men despotic power over their neighbours. And, therefore, although in most cities the laws may be said generally to be in a chaotic state, still, if they aim at anything, they aim at the maintenance of power: thus in Lacedaemon and Crete the system of education and the greater part of the laws are framed with a view to war. And in all nations which are able to gratify their ambition military power is held in esteem, for example among the Scythians and Persians and Thracians and Celts. In some nations there are even laws tending to stimulate the warlike virtues, as at Carthage, where we are told that men obtain the honour of wearing as many armlets as they have served campaigns. There was once a law in Macedonia that he who had not killed an enemy should wear a halter, and among the Scythians no one who had not slain his man was allowed to drink out of the cup which was handed round at a certain feast. Among the Iberians, a warlike nation, the number of enemies whom a man has slain is indicated by the number of obelisks which are fixed in the earth round his tomb; and there are numerous practices among other nations of a like kind, some of them established by law and others by custom. Yet to a reflecting mind it must appear very strange that the statesman should be always considering how he can dominate and tyrannize over others, whether they are willing or not. How can that which is not even lawful be the business of the statesman or the legislator? Unlawful it certainly is to rule without regard to justice, for there may be might where there is no right. The other arts and sciences offer no parallel; a physician is not expected to persuade or coerce his patients, nor a pilot the passengers in his ship. Yet most men appear to think that the art of despotic government is statesmanship, and what men affirm to be unjust and inexpedient in their own case they are not ashamed of practising towards others; they demand just rule for themselves, but where other men are concerned they care nothing about it. Such behaviour is irrational; unless the one party is, and the other is not, born to serve, in which case men have a right to command, not indeed all their fellows, but only those who are intended to be subjects; just as we ought not to hunt men, whether for food or sacrifice, but only those animals which may be hunted for food or sacrifice, that is to say, such wild animals as are eatable. And surely there may be a city happy in isolation, which we will assume to be well-governed (for it is quite possible that a city thus isolated might be well-administered and have good laws); but such a city would not be constituted with any view to war or the conquest of enemies—all that sort of thing must be excluded. Hence we see very plainly that warlike pursuits, although generally to be deemed honourable, are not the supreme end of all things, but only means. And the good lawgiver should inquire how states and races of men and communities may participate in a good life, and in the happiness which is attainable by them. His enactments will not be always the same; and where there are neighbours he will have to see what sort of studies should be practised in relation to their several characters, or how the measures appropriate in relation to each are to be adopted. The end at which the best form of government should aim may be properly made a matter of future consideration.

3. Let us now address those who, while they agree that the life of excellence is the most desirable, differ about the manner of practising it. For some renounce political power, and think that the life of the freeman is different from the life of the statesman and the best of all; but others think the life of the statesman best. The argument of the latter is that he who does nothing cannot do well, and that acting well is identical with happiness. To both we say: 'you are partly right and partly wrong.' The first class are right in affirming that the life of the freeman is better than the life of the despot; for there is nothing noble in having the use of a slave, in so far as he is a slave; or in issuing commands about necessary things. But it is an error to suppose that every sort of rule is despotic like that of a master over slaves, for there is as great a difference between rule over freemen and rule over slaves as there is between slavery by nature and freedom by nature, about which I have said enough at the commencement of this treatise. And it is equally a mistake to place inactivity above action, for happiness is activity, and the actions of the just and wise are the realization of much that is noble.

But perhaps someone, accepting these premises, may still maintain that supreme power is the best of all things, because the possessors of it are able to perform the greatest number of noble actions. If so, the man who is able to rule, instead of giving up anything to his neighbour, ought rather to take away his power; and the father should care nothing for his son, nor the son for his father, nor friend for friend; they should not bestow a thought on one another in comparison with this higher object, for the best is the most desirable and 'acting well' is the best. There might be some truth in such a view if we assume that robbers and plunderers attain the chief good. But this can never be; their hypothesis is false. For the actions of a ruler cannot really be honourable, unless he is as much superior to other men as a man is to a woman, or a father to his children, or a master to his slaves. And therefore he who violates the law can never recover by any success, however great, what he has already lost in departing from excellence. For equals the honourable and the just consist in sharing alike, as is just and equal. But that the unequal should be given to equals, and the unlike to those who are like, is contrary to nature, and nothing which is contrary to nature is good. If, therefore, there is anyone superior in excellence and in the power of performing the best actions, he is the man we ought to follow and obey, but he must have the capacity for action as well as excellence.

If we are right in our view, and happiness is assumed to be acting well, the active life will be the best, both for every city collectively, and for individuals. Not that a life of action must necessarily have relation to others, as some persons think, nor are those ideas only to be regarded as practical which are pursued for the sake of practical results, but much more the thoughts and contemplations which are independent and complete in themselves; since acting well, and therefore a certain kind of action, is an end, and even in the case of external actions the directing mind is most truly said to act. Neither, again, is it necessary that states which are cut off from others and choose to live alone should be inactive; for activity, as well as other things, may take place by sections; there are many ways in which the sections of a state act upon one another. The same thing is equally true of every individual. If this were otherwise, the gods and the universe, who have no external actions over and above their own energies, would be far enough from perfection. Hence it is evident that the same life is best for each individual, and for states and for mankind collectively.

1331ᵇ   13. Returning to the constitution itself, let us seek to determine out of what and what sort of elements the state which is to be happy and well-governed should be composed. There are two things in which all well-being consists: one of them is the choice of a right end and aim of action, and the other the discovery of the actions which contribute towards it; for the means and the end may agree or disagree. Sometimes the right end is set before men, but in practice they fail to attain it; in other cases they are successful in all the contributory factors, but they propose to themselves a bad end; and sometimes they fail in both. Take, for example, the art of medicine; physicians do not always understand the nature of health, and also the means which they use may not effect the desired end. In all arts and sciences both the end and the means should be equally within our control.

The happiness and well-being which all men manifestly desire, some have the power of attaining, but 1332ᵃ to others, from some accident or defect of nature, the attainment of them is not granted; for a good life requires a supply of external goods, in a less degree when men are in a good state, in a greater degree when they are in a lower state. Others again, who possess the conditions of happiness, go utterly wrong from the first in the pursuit of it. But since our object is to discover the best form of government, that, namely, under which a city will be best governed, and since the city is best governed which has the greatest opportunity of obtaining happiness, it is evident that we must clearly ascertain the nature of happiness.

We maintain, and have said in the Ethics, if the arguments there adduced are of any value, that happiness is the realization and perfect exercise of excellence, and this not conditional, but absolute. And I use the term 'conditional' to express that which is indispensable, and 'absolute' to express that which is good in itself. Take the case of just actions; just punishments and chastisements do indeed spring from a good principle, but they are good only because we cannot do without them—it would be better that neither individuals nor states should need anything of the sort—but actions which aim at honour and advantage are absolutely the best. The conditional action is only the choice of a lesser evil; whereas these are the foundation and creation of good. A good man may make the best even of poverty and disease, and the other ills of life; but he can only attain happiness under the opposite conditions (for this also has been determined in the Ethics, that the good man is he for whom, because he is excellent, the things that are absolutely good are good; it is also plain that his use of these goods must be excellent and in the absolute sense good). This makes men fancy that external goods are the cause of happiness, yet we might as well say that a brilliant performance on the lyre was to be attributed to the instrument and not to the skill of the performer.

It follows then from what has been said that some things the legislator must find ready to his hand in a state, others he must provide. And therefore we can only say: may our state be constituted in such a manner as to be blessed with the goods of which fortune disposes (for we acknowledge her power): whereas excellence and goodness in the state are not a matter of chance but the result of knowledge and choice. A city can be excellent only when the citizens who have a share in the government are excellent, and in our state all the citizens share in the government; let us then inquire how a man becomes excellent. For even if we could suppose the citizen body to be excellent, without each of them being so, yet the latter would be better, for in the excellence of each the excellence of all is involved.

There are three things which make men good and excellent; these are nature, habit, reason. In the first place, every one must be born a man and not some 1332ᵇ other animal; so, too, he must have a certain character, both of body and soul. But some qualities there is no use in having at birth, for they are altered by habit, and there are some gifts which by nature are made to be turned by habit to good or bad. Animals lead for the most part a life of nature, although in lesser particulars some are influenced by habit as well. Man has reason, in addition, and man only. For this reason nature, habit, reason must be in harmony with one another; for they do not always agree; men do many things against habit and nature, if reason persuades them that they ought. We have already determined what natures are likely to be most easily moulded by the hands of the legislator. All else is the work of education; we learn some things by habit and some by instruction.

14. Since every political society is composed of rulers and subjects, let us consider whether the relations of one to the other should interchange or be permanent. For the education of the citizens will necessarily vary with the answer given to this question. Now, if some men excelled others in the same degree in which gods and heroes are supposed to excel mankind in general (having in the first place a great advantage even in their bodies, and secondly in their minds), so that the superiority of the governors was undisputed and patent to their subjects, it would clearly be better that once for all the one class should rule and the others serve. But since this is unattainable, and kings have no marked superiority over their subjects, such as Scylax affirms to be found among the Indians, it is obviously necessary on many grounds that all the citizens alike should take their turn of governing and being governed. Equality consists in the same treatment of similar persons, and no government can stand which is not founded upon justice. For if the government is unjust everyone in the country unites with the governed in the desire to have a revolution, and it is an impossibility that the members of the government can be so numerous as to be stronger than all their enemies put together. Yet that governors should be better than their subjects is undeniable. How all this is to be effected, and in what way they will respectively share in the government, the legislator has to consider. The subject has been already mentioned. Nature herself has provided the distinction when she made a difference between old and young within the same species, of whom she fitted the one to govern and the other to be governed. No one takes offence at being governed when he is young, nor does he think himself better than his governors, especially if he will enjoy the same privilege when he reaches the required age.

1333ª   We conclude that from one point of view governors and governed are identical, and from another

different. And therefore their education must be the same and also different. For he who would learn to command well must, as men say, first of all learn to obey. As I observed in the first part of this treatise, there is one rule which is for the sake of the rulers and another rule which is for the sake of the ruled; the former is a despotic, the latter a free government. Some commands differ not in the thing commanded, but in the intention with which they are imposed. That is why many apparently menial offices are an honour to the free youth by whom they are performed; for actions do not differ as honourable or dishonourable in themselves so much as in the end and intention of them. But since we say that the excellence of the citizen and ruler is the same as that of the good man, and that the same person must first be a subject and then a ruler, the legislator has to see that they become good men, and by what means this may be accomplished, and what is the end of the perfect life.

Now the soul of man is divided into two parts, one of which has a rational principle in itself, and the other, not having a rational principle in itself, is able to obey such a principle. And we call a man in any way good because he has the excellences of these two parts. In which of them the end is more likely to be found is no matter of doubt to those who adopt our division; for in the world both of nature and of art the inferior always exists for the sake of the superior, and the superior is that which has a rational principle. This principle, too, in our ordinary way of making the division, is divided into two kinds, for there is a practical and a speculative principle. This part, then, must evidently be similarly divided. And there must be a corresponding division of actions; the actions of the naturally better part are to be preferred by those who have it in their power to attain to two out of the three or to all, for that is always to everyone the most desirable which is the highest attainable by him. The whole of life is further divided into two parts, business and leisure, war and peace, and of actions some aim at what is necessary and useful, and some at what is honourable. And the preference given to one or the other class of actions must necessarily be like the preference given to one or other part of the soul and its actions over the other; there must be war for the sake of peace, business for the sake of leisure, things useful and necessary for the sake of things honourable. All these points the statesman should keep in view when he frames his laws; he should consider the parts of the soul and their functions, and above all the better and the end; he should also remember the diversities of human lives and actions. For men must be able to engage in business and go to war, but leisure and peace are better; they must do what is necessary and indeed what is useful, but what is honourable is better. On such principles children and persons of every age which requires education should be trained. Whereas even the Greeks of the present day who are reputed to be best governed, and the legislators who gave them their constitutions, do not appear to have framed their governments with a regard to the best end, or to have given them laws and education with a view to all the excellences, but in a vulgar spirit have fallen back on those which promised to be more useful and profitable. Many modern writers have taken a similar view: they commend the Lacedaemonian constitution, and praise the legislator for making conquest and war his sole aim, a doctrine which may be refuted by argument and has long ago been refuted by facts. For most men desire empire in the hope of accumulating the goods of fortune; and on this ground Thibron and all those who have written about the Lacedaemonian constitution have praised their legislator, because the Lacedaemonians, by being trained to meet dangers, gained great power. But surely they are not a happy people now that their empire has passed away, nor was their legislator right. How ridiculous is the result, if, while they are continuing in the observance of his laws and no one interferes with them, they have lost the better part of life! These writers further err about the sort of government which the legislator should approve, for the government of freemen is nobler and implies more excellence than despotic government. Neither is a city to be deemed happy or a legislator to be praised because he trains his citizens to conquer and obtain dominion over their neighbours, for there is great harm in this. On a similar principle any citizen who could, should obviously try to obtain the power in his own state—the crime which the Lacedaemonians accuse king Pausanias of attempting, although he had such great honour already. No such principle and no

law having this object is either statesmanlike or useful or right. For the same things are best both for individuals and for states, and these are the things which the legislator ought to implant in the minds of his citizens. Neither should men study war with a view to the enslavement of those who do not deserve to be enslaved; but first of all they should provide against their own enslavement, and in the second place obtain empire for the good of the governed, and not for the sake of exercising a general despotism, and in the third place they should seek to be masters only over those who deserve to be slaves. Facts, as well as arguments, prove that the legislator should direct all his military and other measures to the provision of leisure and the establishment of peace. For most of these military states are safe only while they are at war, but fall when they have acquired their empire; like unused iron they lose their edge in time of peace. And for this the legislator is to blame, he never having taught them how to lead the life of peace.

15. Since the end of individuals and of states is the same, the end of the best man and of the best constitution must also be the same; it is therefore evident that there ought to exist in both of them the excellences of leisure; for peace, as has been often repeated, is the end of war, and leisure of toil. But leisure and cultivation may be promoted not only by those excellences which are practised in leisure, but also by some of those which are useful to business. For many necessaries of life have to be supplied before we can have leisure. Therefore a city must be temperate and brave, and able to endure: for truly, as the proverb says, 'There is no leisure for slaves,' and those who cannot face danger like men are the slaves of any invader. Courage and endurance are required for business and philosophy for leisure, temperance and justice for both, and more especially in times of peace and leisure, for war compels men to be just and temperate, whereas the enjoyment of good fortune and the leisure which comes with peace tend to make them insolent. Those then who seem to be the best-off and to be in the possession of every good, have special need of justice and temperance— for example, those (if such there be, as the poets say) who dwell in the Islands of the Blest; they above all will need philosophy and temperance and justice, and

all the more the more leisure they have, living in the midst of abundance. There is no difficulty in seeing why the state that would be happy and good ought to have these excellences. If it is disgraceful in men not to be able to use the goods of life, it is peculiarly disgraceful not to be able to use them in time of leisure—to show excellent qualities in action and war, and when they have peace and leisure to be no better than slaves. That is why we should not practise excellence after the manner of the Lacedaemonians. For they, while agreeing with other men in their conception of the highest goods, differ from the rest of mankind in thinking that they are to be obtained by the practice of a single excellence. And
1334ᵇ since these goods and the enjoyment of them are greater than the enjoyment derived from the excellences . . . and that for its own sake, is evident from what has been said; we must now consider how and by what means it is to be attained.

We have already determined that nature and habit and reason are required, and, of these, the proper nature of the citizens has also been defined by us. But we have still to consider whether the training of early life is to be that of reason or habit, for these two must accord, and when in accord they will then form the best of harmonies. Reason may be mistaken and fail in attaining the highest ideal of life, and there may be a like influence of habit. Thus much is clear in the first place, that, as in all other things, birth implies an antecedent beginning, and that there are beginnings whose end is relative to a further end. Now, in men reason and mind are the end towards which nature strives, so that the birth and training in custom of the citizens ought to be ordered with a view to them. In the second place, as the soul and body are two, we see also that there are two parts of the soul, the rational and the irrational, and two corresponding states—reason and appetite. And as the body is prior in order of generation to the soul, so the irrational is prior to the rational. The proof is that anger and wishing and desire are implanted in children from their very birth, but reason and understanding are developed as they grow older. For this reason, the care of the body ought to precede that of the soul, and the training of the appetitive part should follow: none the less our care of it must be for the sake of the reason, and our care of the body for the sake of the soul.

REVIEW QUESTIONS

1. What is Aristotle's theory of change? What are his four types of causes? In what way is his notion of cause teleological?

2. For Aristotle, what is a substance? What reasons does Aristotle give for believing in an eternal unmovable substance?

3. On what grounds does Aristotle maintain that essence, not matter, is what gives identity and individuality to substances?

4. What reasons does Aristotle give for rejecting Plato's theory of the Forms? How does his view of Universals differ from Plato's?

5. What is Aristotle's view of the soul? How does his notion of soul differ from that in Christianity or in Descartes? Why does he say that the question of whether the soul and body are one is unnecessary?

6. What does Aristotle mean by his assertion that *eudaimonia* (flourishing) is "an activity of the soul in accordance with excellence"? Is *eudaimonia* synonymous with happiness? How can a person achieve *eudaimonia*? Of what does flourishing consist?

7. According to Aristotle, what are virtues? How does he distinguish between moral virtues and intellectual virtues? How does one learn moral virtues?

4

EPICURUS

Epicurus (341–270 B.C.), a Greek philosopher who was born on the isle of Samos, lived much of his life in Athens, where he founded his very successful school of philosophy, called the "Garden." He was influenced by the materialist Democritus (c. 460–370 B.C.), who is the first philosopher known to believe that the world is made up of atoms. Epicurus added the concept of the "swerve" to atomic theory. Atoms cannot move in parallel lines, otherwise there would be no combinations or changes in bodies. So there must be infinitesimal swerves in their motion, causing collisions and combinations. Only a few fragments of Epicurus's writings are extant.

Epicurus identified good with pleasure and evil with pain. This doctrine (repeated later by Jeremy Bentham [1748–1832]) is called *hedonism* (from the Greek word for pleasure). But contrary to popular opinion, Epicurus was not what "Epicureanism" stands for today, a sensuous, profligate life style or gourmet tastes. Quite the opposite. Epicurus believed that the true life of pleasure consisted in an attitude of imperturbable emotional calm which needed only simple pleasures, a healthy diet, a prudent moral life (based on contractual agreement), and good friends. Prudence must constrain pleasure. Since only good or bad sensations (pleasures or pains) should concern us, and death is not a sensation, we should not fear death.

FOR FURTHER READING

Long, A. A. *Hellenistic Philosophy: Stoics, Epicureans, Sceptics*, 2nd ed. (University of California Press, 1985).

Long, A. A., and D. N. Sedley, eds. *The Hellenistic Philosophers* (Cambridge University Press, 1987).

Lucretius. *On the Nature of the Universe*, trans. R. E. Latham (Penguin Books, 1951).

Rist, John M. *Epicurus: An Introduction* (Cambridge University Press, 1972).

Saunders, Jason, ed. *Greek and Roman Philosophy After Aristotle* (Macmillan, 1966).

LETTER TO MENOECEUS

EPICURUS TO MENOECEUS

Let no one when young delay to study philosophy, nor when he is old grow weary of his study. For no one can come too early or too late to secure the health of his soul. And the man who says that the age for philosophy has either not yet come or has gone by is like the man who says that the age for happiness is not yet come to him, or has passed away. Wherefore both when young and old a man must study philosophy, that as he grows old he may be young in blessings through the grateful recollection of what has been, and that in youth he may be old as well, since he will know no fear of what is to come. We must then meditate on the things that make our happiness, seeing that when that is with us we have all, but when it is absent we do all to win it.

The things which I used unceasingly to commend to you, these do and practise, considering them to be the first principles of the good life. First of all believe that god is a being immortal and blessed, even as the common idea of a god is engraved on men's minds, and do not assign to him anything alien to his immortality or ill-suited to his blessedness: but believe about him everything that can uphold his blessedness and immortality. For gods there are, since the knowledge of them is by clear vision. But they are not such as the many believe them to be: for indeed they do not consistently represent them as they believe them to be. And the impious man is not he who denies the gods of the many, but he who attaches to the gods the beliefs of the many. For the statements of the many about the gods are not conceptions derived from sensation, but false suppositions, according to which the greatest misfortunes befall the wicked and the greatest blessings the good by the gift of the gods. For men being accustomed always to their own virtues welcome those like themselves, but regard all that is not of their nature as alien.

Become accustomed to the belief that death is nothing to us. For all good and evil consists in sensation, but death is deprivation of sensation. And therefore a right understanding that death is nothing to us makes the mortality of life enjoyable, not because it adds to it an infinite span of time, but because it takes away the craving for immortality. For there is nothing terrible in life for the man who has truly comprehended that there is nothing terrible in not living. So that the man speaks but idly who says that he fears death not because it will be painful when it comes, but because it is painful in anticipation. For that which gives no trouble when it comes, is but an empty pain in anticipation. So death, the most terrifying of ills, is nothing to us, since so long as we exist, death is not with us; but when death comes, then we do not exist. It does not then concern either the living or the dead, since for the former it is not, and the latter are no more.

But the many at one moment shun death as the greatest of evils, at another yearn for it as a respite from the evils in life. But the wise man neither seeks to escape life nor fears the cessation of life, for neither does life offend him nor does the absence of life seem to be any evil. And just as with food he does not seek simply the larger share and nothing else, but rather the most pleasant, so he seeks to enjoy not the longest period of time, but the most pleasant.

And he who counsels the young man to live well, but the old man to make a good end, is foolish, not merely because of the desirability of life, but also because it is the same training which teaches to live well and to die well. Yet much worse still is the man who says it is good not to be born, but

> "once born make haste to pass the gates of
> Death." [Theognis, 427]

For if he says this from conviction why does he not pass away out of life? For it is open to him to do so, if he had firmly made up his mind to this. But if he speaks in jest, his words are idle among men who cannot receive them.

We must then bear in mind that the future is neither ours, nor yet wholly not ours, so that we may

Reprinted from *The Extant Remains*, translated by Cyril Bailey (1926) by permission of Oxford University Press.

not altogether expect it as sure to come, nor abandon hope of it, as if it will certainly not come.

We must consider that of desires some are natural, others vain, and of the natural some are necessary and others merely natural; and of the necessary some are necessary for happiness, others for the repose of the body, and others for very life. The right understanding of these facts enables us to refer all choice and avoidance to the health of the body and the soul's freedom from disturbance, since this is the aim of the life of blessedness. For it is to obtain this end that we always act, namely, to avoid pain and fear. And when this is once secured for us, all the tempest of the soul is dispersed, since the living creature has not to wander as though in search of something that is missing, and to look for some other thing by which he can fulfil the good of the soul and the good of the body. For it is then that we have need of pleasure, when we feel pain owing to the absence of pleasure; but when we do not feel pain, we no longer need pleasure. And for this cause we call pleasure the beginning and end of the blessed life. For we recognize pleasure as the first good innate in us, and from pleasure we begin every act of choice and avoidance, and to pleasure we return again, using the feeling as the standard by which we judge every good.

And since pleasure is the first good and natural to us, for this very reason we do not choose every pleasure, but sometimes we pass over many pleasures, when greater discomfort accrues to us as the result of them: and similarly we think many pains better than pleasures, since a greater pleasure comes to us when we have endured pains for a long time. Every pleasure then because of its natural kinship to us is good, yet not every pleasure is to be chosen: even as every pain also is an evil, yet not all are always of a nature to be avoided. Yet by a scale of comparison and by the consideration of advantages and disadvantages we must form our judgement on all these matters. For the good on certain occasions we treat as bad, and conversely the bad as good.

And again independence of desire we think a great good—not that we may at all times enjoy but a few things, but that, if we do not possess many, we may enjoy the few in the genuine persuasion that those

have the sweetest pleasure in luxury who least need it, and that all that is natural is easy to be obtained, but that which is superfluous is hard. And so plain savours bring us a pleasure equal to a luxurious diet, when all the pain due to want is removed; and bread and water produce the highest pleasure, when one who needs them puts them to his lips. To grow accustomed therefore to simple and not luxurious diet gives us health to the full, and makes a man alert for the needful employments of life, and when after long intervals we approach luxuries, disposes us better towards them, and fits us to be fearless of fortune.

When, therefore, we maintain that pleasure is the end, we do not mean the pleasures of profligates and those that consist in sensuality, as is supposed by some who are either ignorant or disagree with us or do not understand, but freedom from pain in the body and from trouble in the mind. For it is not continuous drinkings and revellings, nor the satisfaction of lusts, nor the enjoyment of fish and other luxuries of the wealthy table, which produce a pleasant life, but sober reasoning, searching out the motives for all choice and avoidance, and banishing mere opinions, to which are due the greatest disturbance of the spirit.

Of all this the beginning and the greatest good is prudence. Wherefore prudence is a more precious thing even than philosophy: for from prudence are sprung all the other virtues, and it teaches us that it is not possible to live pleasantly without living prudently and honourably and justly, nor, again, to live a life of prudence, honour, and justice without living pleasantly. For the virtues are by nature bound up with the pleasant life, and the pleasant life is inseparable from them. For indeed who, think you, is a better man than he who holds reverent opinions concerning the gods, and is at all times free from fear of death, and has reasoned out the end ordained by nature? He understands that the limit of good things is easy to fulfil and easy to attain, whereas the course of ills is either short in time or slight in pain: he laughs at destiny, whom some have introduced as the mistress of all things. He thinks that with us lies the chief power in determining events, some of which happen by necessity and some by chance, and some are within our control; for while necessity cannot be called to account, he sees that chance is inconstant, but that which is in our control is subject to no master, and to it are naturally attached praise and blame. For, indeed, it were better to follow the myths about the gods than to become a slave to the destiny of the natural philosophers: for the former suggests a hope of placating the gods by worship, whereas the latter involves a necessity which knows no placation. As to chance, he does not regard it as a god as most men do (for in a god's acts there is no disorder), nor as an uncertain cause of all things: for he does not believe that good and evil are given by chance to man for the framing of a blessed life, but that opportunities for great good and great evil are afforded by it. He therefore thinks it better to be unfortunate in reasonable action than to prosper in unreason. For it is better in a man's actions that what is well chosen should fail, rather than that what is ill chosen should be successful owing to chance.

Meditate therefore on these things and things akin to them night and day by yourself, and with a companion like to yourself, and never shall you be disturbed waking or asleep, but you shall live like a god among men. For a man who lives among immortal blessings is not like to a mortal being.

PRINCIPAL DOCTRINES

I. The blessed and immortal nature knows no trouble itself nor causes trouble to any other, so that it is never constrained by anger or favour. For all such things exist only in the weak.

II. Death is nothing to us: for that which is dissolved is without sensation; and that which lacks sensation is nothing to us.

III. The limit of quantity in pleasures is the removal of all that is painful. Wherever pleasure is present, as long as it is there, there is neither pain of body nor of mind, nor of both at once.

IV. Pain does not last continuously in the flesh, but the acutest pain is there for a very short time, and even that which just exceeds the pleasure in the flesh does not continue for many days at once. But chronic illnesses permit a predominance of pleasure over pain in the flesh.

V. It is not possible to live pleasantly without living prudently and honourably and justly, nor again to live a life of prudence, honour, and justice without living pleasantly. And the man who does not possess the pleasant life, is not living prudently and honourably and justly, and the man who does not possess the virtuous life, cannot possibly live pleasantly.

VI. To secure protection from men anything is a natural good, by which you may be able to attain this end.

VII. Some men wished to become famous and conspicuous, thinking that they would thus win for themselves safety from other men. Wherefore if the life of such men is safe, they have obtained the good which nature craves; but if it is not safe, they do not possess that for which they strove at first by the instinct of nature.

VIII. No pleasure is a bad thing in itself: but the means which produce some pleasures bring with them disturbances many times greater than the pleasures.

IX. If every pleasure could be intensified so that it lasted and influenced the whole organism or the most essential parts of our nature, pleasures would never differ from one another.

X. If the things that produce the pleasures of profligates could dispel the fears of the mind about the phenomena of the sky and death and its pains, and also teach the limits of desires and of pains, we should never have cause to blame them: for they would be filling themselves full with pleasures from every source and never have pain of body or mind, which is the evil of life.

Reprinted from *The Extant Remains*, translated by Cyril Bailey (1926) by permission of Oxford University Press.

XI. If we were not troubled by our suspicions of the phenomena of the sky and about death, fearing that it concerns us, and also by our failure to grasp the limits of pains and desires, we should have no need of natural science.

XII. A man cannot dispel his fear about the most important matters if he does not know what is the nature of the universe but suspects the truth of some mythical story. So that without natural science it is not possible to attain our pleasures unalloyed.

XIII. There is no profit in securing protection in relation to men, if things above and things beneath the earth and indeed all in the boundless universe remain matters of suspicion.

XIV. The most unalloyed source of protection from men, which is secured to some extent by a certain force of expulsion, is in fact the immunity which results from a quiet life and the retirement from the world.

XV. The wealth demanded by nature is both limited and easily procured; that demanded by idle imaginings stretches on to infinity.

XVI. In but few things chance hinders a wise man, but the greatest and most important matters reason has ordained and throughout the whole period of life does and will ordain.

XVII. The just man is most free from trouble, the unjust most full of trouble.

XVIII. The pleasure in the flesh is not increased, when once the pain due to want is removed, but is only varied: and the limit as regards pleasure in the mind is begotten by the reasoned understanding of these very pleasures and of the emotions akin to them, which used to cause the greatest fear to the mind.

XIX. Infinite time contains no greater pleasure than limited time, if one measures by reason the limits of pleasure.

XX. The flesh perceives the limits of pleasure as unlimited and unlimited time is required to supply it. But the mind, having attained a reasoned understanding of the ultimate good of the flesh and its limits and having dissipated the fears concerning the time to come, supplies us with the complete life, and we have no further need of infinite time: but neither does the mind shun pleasure, nor, when circumstances begin to bring about the departure from life, does it approach its end as though it fell short in any way of the best life.

XXI. He who has learned the limits of life knows that that which removes the pain due to want and makes the whole of life complete is easy to obtain; so that there is no need of actions which involve competition.

XXII. We must consider both the real purpose and all the evidence of direct perception, to which we always refer the conclusions of opinion; otherwise, all will be full of doubt and confusion.

XXIII. If you fight against all sensations, you will have no standard by which to judge even those of them which you say are false.

XXIV. If you reject any single sensation and fail to distinguish between the conclusion of opinion as to the appearance awaiting confirmation and that which is actually given by the sensation or feeling, or each intuitive apprehension of the mind, you will confound all other sensations as well with the same groundless opinion, so that you will reject every standard of judgement. And if among the mental images created by your opinion you affirm both that which awaits confirmation and that which does not, you will not escape error, since you will have preserved the whole cause of doubt in every judgement between what is right and what is wrong.

XXV. If on each occasion instead of referring your actions to the end of nature, you turn to some other nearer standard when you are making a choice or an avoidance, your actions will not be consistent with your principles.

XXVI. Of desires, all that do not lead to a sense of pain, if they are not satisfied, are not necessary, but involve a craving which is easily dispelled, when the object is hard to procure or they seem likely to produce harm.

XXVII. Of all the things which wisdom acquires to produce the blessedness of the complete life, far the greatest is the possession of friendship.

XXVIII. The same conviction which has given us confidence that there is nothing terrible that lasts forever or even for long, has also seen the protection of friendship most fully completed in the limited evils of this life.

XXIX. Among desires some are natural and necessary, some natural but not necessary, and others neither natural nor necessary, but due to idle imagination.

XXX. Wherever in the case of desires which are physical, but do not lead to a sense of pain, if they are not fulfilled, the effort is intense, such pleasures are due to idle imagination, and it is not owing to their own nature that they fail to be dispelled, but owing to the empty imaginings of the man.

XXXI. The justice which arises from nature is a pledge of mutual advantage to restrain men from harming one another and save them from being harmed.

XXXII. For all living things which have not been able to make compacts not to harm one another or be harmed, nothing ever is either just or unjust; and likewise too for all tribes of men which have been unable or unwilling to make compacts not to harm or be harmed.

XXXIII. Justice never is anything in itself, but in the dealings of men with one another in any place whatever and at any time it is a kind of compact not to harm or be harmed.

XXXIV. Injustice is not an evil in itself, but only in consequence of the fear which attaches to the apprehension of being unable to escape those appointed to punish such actions.

XXXV. It is not possible for one who acts in secret contravention of the terms of the compact not to harm or be harmed, to be confident that he will escape detection, even if at present he escapes a thousand times. For up to the time of death it cannot be certain that he will indeed escape.

XXXVI. In its general aspect justice is the same for all, for it is a kind of mutual advantage in the dealings of men with one another: but with reference to the individual peculiarities of a country or any other circumstances the same thing does not turn out to be just for all.

XXXVII. Among actions which are sanctioned as just by law, that which is proved on examination to be of advantage in the requirements of men's dealings with one another, has the guarantee of justice, whether it is the same for all or not. But if a man makes a law and it does not turn out to lead to advantage in men's dealings with each other, then it no longer has the essential nature of justice. And even if the advantage in the matter of justice shifts from one side to the other, but for a while accords with the general concept, it is none the less just for that period in the eyes of those who do not confound themselves with empty sounds but look to the actual facts.

XXXVIII. Where, provided the circumstances have not been altered, actions which were considered just, have been shown not to accord with the general concept in actual practice, then they are not just. But where, when circumstances have changed, the same actions which were sanctioned as just no longer lead to advantage, there they were just at the time when they were of advantage for the dealings of fellow-citizens with one another; but subsequently they are no longer just, when no longer of advantage.

XXXIX. The man who has best ordered the element of disquiet arising from external circumstances has made those things that he could akin to himself and the rest at least not alien: but with all to which he could not do even this, he has refrained from mixing, and has expelled from his life all which it was of advantage to treat thus.

XL. As many as possess the power to procure complete immunity from their neighbours, these also live most pleasantly with one another, since they have the most certain pledge of security, and after they have enjoyed the fullest intimacy, they do not lament the previous departure of a dead friend, as though he were to be pitied.

REVIEW QUESTIONS

1. Does Epicurus deserve his reputation as a reckless, self-indulgent profligate? Why or why not? Does he encourage culinary or sexual excesses?
2. What is the relationship between pleasure and pain? What is Epicurus' philosophy of life?
3. What is his argument for why we should not fear death?
4. What is the aim of a blessed life? What is the good?
5. Why does Epicurus believe that it is not possible to live pleasantly without living virtuously? What is his view of morality (justice)?

5

❦

EPICTETUS

Epictetus (c. 50–c. 130), born a Greek slave in Asia Minor, was freed sometime after the death of Nero, in 68. He, along with all the philosophers, was expelled from Rome by the Emperor Domitian in 90 and died in northern Greece about 130. He was known as a kindly man, humble and charitable, especially to children. He was crippled in slavery, which may have influenced his motto: "Bear and forbear." He embraced Stoicism and taught that we should submit to our fate as God's sacred gift and design. Epictetus did not publish anything, but his pupil Flavius Arrianus recorded his teachings, the most famous of which is the *Encheiridion* (a handbook).

Stoicism was a Greek school of philosophy founded in circa 300 B.C. in Athens by Zeno of Citium and developed into the dominant philosophy of the Roman Empire. The word *stoa* from which "Stoic" derives is the Greek word for porch. Apparently Zeno lectured from the "painted porch," a public building in the Agora. The Stoics believed that we should resign ourselves to our fate, do our duty faithfully, and thereby acquire tranquillity of mind. The world is transient and unstable. We cannot change very much, but we can master our souls so that we attain tranquillity amidst the chaos all around us. Stoics were the first world citizens, "cosmopolitans," holding that a divine spark dwelt in every human being. Chrysippus (c. 280–206 B.C.), referred to in the text, was the third leader of the Stoics and credited with over 700 treatises.

PRINCIPAL IDEAS

I. Religious Materialists: Everything was made up of matter (monists—one versus many), including God. But there are degrees of condensation and rarefaction of matter

(Aristotle's four elements). The soul in every man was a rarefied divine spark, which was manifest in reason (*logos*).

II. The Universe is a Vast Animal whose soul is God, a divine fire, the Universal *Logos*. We are mini-animals whose soul is a mini-god, possessing as it does sparks of the divine fire. Universe is a spherical plenum held together by tension, the more tension the more value. Accordingly, the world consists of four kinds of beings:

1. Least tension—mere material objects, rocks and sand
2. A little more tension—plants
3. Moderate tension (souls)—animals
4. High tension (mini-cosmos)—man (rational animals)

III. Universalism: The Stoics were the first cosmopolitans, believing that all men were brothers under one Father, God.

In the things are true which are said by the philosophers about the kinship between God and man, what else remains for men to do than what Socrates did Never in reply to the question, to what country you belong, say that you are an Athenian or a Corinthian, but that you are a citizen of the world. . . . He then who has observed with intelligence the administration of the world, and has learned that the greatest and supreme and the most comprehensive community is that which is composed of men and God, and that from God have descended the seeds not only to my father and grandfather, but to all beings which are generated on the earth and are produced, and particularly to rational beings—for these only are by their nature formed to have communion with God, being by means of reason conjoined with him—why should not such a man call himself a citizen of the world, why not a son of God, and why should he be afraid of anything which happens among men? Is kinship with Caesar or with any other of the powerful in Rome sufficient to enable us to live in safety, and above contempt and without any fear at all? and to have God for your maker and father and guardian, shall not this release us from sorrows and fears? (Epictetus, *Discourses* Bk I, 9)

IV. Virtuous Character. Like Aristotle the Stoics placed primary emphasis on moral character. They found Socrates, Zeno, and Diogenes prime examples of moral virtue. One of the most famous Stoics was the Roman Emperor Marcus Aurelius (121–180) who said, "Be like the headland, on which the billows dash themselves continually; but it stands fast, till about its base the boiling breakers are lulled to rest." The following is his *Dedication to Duty:*

Hour by hour resolve to do the task of the hour carefully, with unaffected dignity, affectionately, freely and justly. You can avoid distractions that might interfere with such performance if every act is done as though it were the last act of your life. Free yourself from random aims and curb any tendency to let the passions of emotion, hypocrisy, self-love and dissatisfaction with your allotted share cause you to ignore the commands of reason.

V. Attitude to Death and Suicide. Death is not to be feared but the idea is to be used to concentrate the mind, transforming our lives. Live every day as though it were your last. (Seneca A.D.[RC] 3–65):

Life has carried some men with the greatest rapidity to the harbor, the harbor they were bound to reach if they tarried on the way, while others it has fretted and harassed. To such a life, as you are aware, one should not always cling. *For mere living is not a good, but living well.* Accordingly, the wise man will live as long as he ought, not as long as he can. He will mark in what place, with whom, and how he is to conduct his existence, and what he is about to do. He always reflects concerning the quality, and not the quantity of his life. As soon as there are many events in his life that give him trouble and disturb his peace of mind, he sets himself free. And this privilege is his, not only when the crisis is upon him, but as soon as Fortune seems to be playing him false; then he looks about carefully and sees whether he ought, or ought not, to end his life on that account. . . . He does not regard death with fear, as if it were a great loss; for no man can lose very much when but a driblet remains. It is not a question of dying earlier or later, but of dying well or ill. And dying well means escape from the danger of living ill.

The wise person will accept the inevitability of all good things coming to an end, including life, and treating life as a glorious banquet: having enjoyed to the full but now coming to a close, he or she retires gracefully, grateful for all the good things experienced. Death becomes a way of saying thank you to life. As Epictetus said, "If the room is smoky, if only moderately, I will stay; if there is too much smoke, I will go. Remember this, keep firm hold on it, the door is always open."

FOR FURTHER READING

Inwood, Brad. *Ethics and Human Action in Early Stoicism* (Clarendon Press, 1985).

Long, A. A. *The Hellenistic Philosophy: Stoics, Epicureans, Sceptics*, 2nd ed. (University of California Press, 1985).

Long, A. A., and D. N. Sedley, eds. *The Hellenistic Philosophers* (Cambridge University Press, 1987).

Marcus Aurelius. *The Meditations*, trans. G. M. A. Grube (Hackett Publishing Co., 1985).

Rist, John M., ed. *The Stoics* (University of California Press, 1978).

Sandbach, F. H. *The Stoics* (W. W. Norton, 1975).

ENCHEIRIDION

1. Some things are up to us, some are not up to us. Up to us are perception, intention, desire, aversion, and in sum, whatever are our own doings; not up to us are body, property, reputation, political office and in sum, whatever are not our own doings. And the things that are up to us are naturally free, unforbidding, unimpeding, while those not up to us are weak, slavish, forbidding, alien. Remember, then, that if you think naturally slavish things are free and that alien things are your own, you will be impeded, grieved, troubled, you will blame gods and men; but if you think that what is yours is yours and what is alien is alien, as it really is, nobody will ever compel you, nobody will forbid you, you will not blame anyone, you will not complain about anything,

you will not do a single thing unwillingly, you will have no enemy, no one will hurt you; for you will not suffer anything harmful.

If you are aiming for such great things, remember that you must not be moderate in exerting yourself to attain them: you must avoid some things altogether and postpone others for the time being. For if you want both to accomplish these aims, and also to achieve eminence and riches, it may come about that you will not get the latter because you were trying for the former, and certainly you will not get the former, which are the only things that produce freedom and well-being.

So take rigorous care to say to every menacing impression, "You are just an impression, not the real

Epictetus, *Encheiridion*, translation by Wallace I. Matson. Copyright © Wallace Matson 1996. This translation appears here in print for the first time.

thing at all." Then test it and consider it according to your rules—first and foremost this: whether it belongs among the things that are up to us or to those not up to us. And if it is something not up to us, be ready to say "It is nothing to me."

2. Remember that the aim of desire is to get what arouses the desire, the aim of aversion is to avoid that to which you are averse; and he who fails to get what he desires is miserable, and so is he who gets what he is averse to. So then, if you are averse only to things contrary to nature that are up to you, you will not get anything to which you are averse; but if you are averse to sickness or death or poverty, you will be miserable. So take your aversion away from everything that is not up to you and transfer it to things contrary to nature that are up to you. But for the time being, destroy desire altogether; for if you desire something not up to you, necessarily you will be unfortunate; as for things that are up to us, and would be good to desire, none of them is yet within your grasp. But only make use of selection and rejection, and these lightly, discreetly, and tentatively.

3. As for every thing that delights your mind or is useful or beloved, remember to describe it as it really is, starting with the smallest thing. If you are fond of a pot, say "It is a pot that I am fond of." For then, if it breaks, you will not be upset. If you kiss your child or your wife, say that you are kissing a human being. Then if they die you will not be upset.

4. Whenever you are about to undertake some activity, remind yourself what kind of activity it is. If you are going out to bathe, picture to yourself what goes on in baths—the splashers, the elbow-jabbers, the foul-mouths, the thieves. You will undertake the activity with more security, if you declare right away "I want to bathe *and* to keep my own will in accord with nature." And so with every activity. Thus, if anything gets in the way of your bathing, you will be ready to say: "But I did not want this only, but also to keep my will in accord with nature; I will not keep it, if I am upset by what happens."

5. It is not things that upset people but rather ideas about things. For example, death is nothing terrible, else it would have seemed so even to Socrates; rather it is the idea that death is terrible that is terrible. So whenever we are frustrated or upset or grieved, let us not blame others, but ourselves—that

is, our ideas. It is the act of a philosophically ignorant person to blame others for his own troubles. One who is beginning to learn blames himself. An educated person blames neither anyone else nor himself.

6. Do not pride yourself on superiority that is not your own. If a horse in its pride should say, "I am a fine horse," that could be tolerated. You however, when you boast "I have a fine horse," should realize that you are boasting about the excellence of a horse. What then is your own? The use of impressions. So, make use of your impressions in accord with nature, and then take pride; for your pride will be in a good thing that is your own.

7. When on a voyage the ship is anchored, you may go ashore to get fresh water, and on the way you may pick up a few shells and salad greens, but you have to keep your mind on the ship and continually turn around to look back and see whether the captain is summoning you; and if he summons, you must drop everything, or they will tie you up and dump you on board like a sheep. In life it is the same: if, instead of a shell or a radish, you are given a wife or a child, fine; but if the captain summons, get back on board, leave them behind, don't turn around. If you are old, never go very far from the ship, or you may miss the summons.

8. Don't seek for things to happen as you wish, but wish for things to happen as they do, and you will get on well.

9. Illness is an impediment of the body, but not of the will, as long as the will itself does not so wish. Lameness is an impediment of the leg, not of the will. And say this to yourself of every accident that befalls you; for you will find it an impediment to something else, not to yourself.

10. Whatever occasion befalls you, remember to turn around and look into yourself to see what power you have to make use of it. If you see a handsome boy or a beautiful girl, you will find the relevant power to be self-control. If labor is heaped on you, endurance is what you need; if abuse, forbearance. And thus habituating yourself, you will not be carried away by impressions.

11. Never say about anything that you have "lost it," but that you have "given it back." Your child has died? It has been given back. Your wife has died? She has been given back. "I have been deprived of

my estate." This too has been given back. "But the usurper is wicked." What concern is it of yours, through whom the gift was returned to the giver? For the time it is given to you, treat it as someone else's, as travellers do an inn.

12. If you want to make progress, shun these sorts of reasonings: "If I neglect my affairs, I shall have nothing to live on;" "if I don't punish my slave, he will be good for nothing." For it is better to attain freedom from sorrow and fear and then die of hunger than to live lavishly in vexation. It is better for your slave to be bad than for you to be unhappy. Begin with little things. A little oil has been spilled, a little wine has been swiped: say to yourself, "This is the price of peace, that of serenity." Nothing is gratis. When you call for your slave, consider that maybe he won't hear you, and even if he does he still won't do what you want him to do. But he is not so well off that your tranquillity should depend on him.

13. If you want to make progress, be content to appear stupid and foolish about externals, and don't wish to seem to know anything. And whenever you seem to be somebody to someone, distrust yourself. For be aware that it is not easy both to have your will in accordance with nature and to be on your guard about externals also; if you are to take care of the one it is absolutely necessary to neglect the other.

14. If you want your children and your wife and friends to live forever, you are a fool; for you want what is not up to you to be up to you, and what is not yours to be yours. Thus also if you want your slave not to do anything wrong, you are stupid; for you want badness not to be badness but something else. But if what you want is not to fail in getting what you desire, that you can bring about. So practise what you are capable of. Every person's master is the one who controls whether that person shall get what he wants and avoid what he doesn't want. Thus whoever wishes to be free should neither seek nor avoid anything that is up to others; otherwise he will necessarily be a slave.

15. Remember that you ought to conduct yourself as you do at a banquet. When something passed around reaches you, extend your hand and take it politely. If it is passing you by, don't grab. If it has not yet reached you, don't crave for it, but wait un-

til it gets to you. Thus toward children, thus toward women, thus toward jobs, thus toward riches; and in due time you will be worthy to dine with the gods. But if you do not take even the things set out for you, but despise them, then not only will you be a banquet companion of the gods, you will even be a co-ruler. By thus acting, Diogenes and Heraclitus and like men came to be called divine, and deservedly.

16. Whenever you see someone weeping in grief because his child is going away or he has lost his property, be careful not to be misled by the impression that he is in a bad way because of external things, but be ready to say at once "It is not the circumstances that distress him (for someone else would not be distressed), but the idea he has about them." Don't, of course, hesitate to condole with him in words, and, if there is occasion, even to groan with him; but take care not to groan inwardly.

17. Remember that you are an actor in a drama such as the playwright wishes it to be. If he wants it short, it will be short; if long, long. If he wants you to play a beggar, play even that capably; or a lame man, or a ruler, or a private person. For this is yours, to play the assigned role well. Casting is the business of another.

18. If a raven croaks unauspiciously, do not let the impression carry you away, but straightway draw a distinction and say: "This prophesies nothing for me, but either for my miserable body or my wretched property or my dubious reputation or my children or wife. But for *me* everything prophesies auspiciously, if I want it to; for, no matter what comes of this, it will be up to me to benefit from it."

19. You can be unbeatable if you never enter a contest in which it is not up to you who wins. Beware lest ever, seeing someone else preferred in honor or having great power or otherwise esteemed, you get carried away by impressions and deem him blessed. For since the essence of the good lies in the things up to us, neither jealousy nor envy has a place; and you yourself will not wish to be a praetor[1] or a senator or a consul, but a free man. There is but one way to this: contempt for things not up to us.

---

[1] Roman magistrate

20. Remember that it is not the man who curses you or the man who hits you that insults you, but the idea you have of them as insulting. So, whenever someone irritates you, realize that it is your own opinion that has irritated you. First of all, try not to be carried away by impressions; if you succeed just once in gaining time and avoiding hastiness, you will easily control yourself.

21. Let death and exile and all dreadful appearances be before your eyes every day, and most of all, death; and you will never deem anything trivial, nor desire anything excessively.

22. If you are eager for philosophy, be prepared from the beginning to be ridiculed and sneered at by the mob, who will say things like "All of a sudden he has come back to us a philosopher!" and "Where did he get that high brow?" But don't be a highbrow; hold fast to what seems best for you, as one who has been assigned to this territory by the god. And remember this: if you stay with it, the ones who ridicule you at first will admire you afterwards; but if they get the better of you, it will be your lot to be laughed at twice.

23. If ever it happens that you turn to externals because you want to please someone, realize that you have lost your bearings. It suffices to *be* a philosopher in all things; but if you also want to *appear* to be one, appear so to yourself and that will be enough.

24. Don't let reflections like this upset you: "I shall live without honor, a complete nobody." For suppose not being honored is an evil: you cannot be subjected to evil by another, any more than to shamefulness. Is it your business to acquire power or an invitation to a banquet? By no means. How then is this being without honor? How then will you be a complete nobody, when you ought to be somebody only with respect to those things that are up to you— the domain wherein it is given to you to be of the greatest worth? But your friends will get no help from you? What do you mean by help? They won't have a penny from you; nor will you make them Roman citizens. So who told you that these things are up to you, and not the business of others? Who can give to another things that he does not have himself? "Then get them," one says, "so that we can have them." If I can get them while preserving my self-respect and trustworthiness and high-mindedness, show me the way and I'll get them. But if you require me to be one who will lose my proper goods in order to produce worthless things for you,—just look, how partial and unfair you are. Which do you want more? Money, or a faithful and upright friend? Then you had better help me to acquire the characteristics of one and not require me to do the things that would ruin them.

"But my country, as far as its fate is up to me," one says, "will be helpless." Again, what kind of help do you mean? She will not get arcades or baths from you. So what? Neither does she get shoes from smiths nor weapons from shoemakers. It is enough if everyone fulfills his own task. If you make someone else into a faithful and upright citizen, have you done something for the state? "Yes." Then you yourself are not unhelpful if you are that one. "Then what status," one asks, "will I have in the city?" Whatever you are capable of, while conserving your faithfulness and uprightness. If in wishing to aid her you throw them away, what advantage will accrue to her when you have ended up shameless and faithless?

25. Has someone been honored above you at a feast or in form of address or in being invited to a conference? If these things are goods, you ought to rejoice that he succeeded in getting them; if they are evils, don't lament because you didn't get them. Remember that because you did not do the same things to succeed in getting things not up to you, you can not be considered worthy of getting an equal share. For how can one who does not hang around doorsteps be equal to one who does? One who does not march in the entourage, to one who does? One who does not praise, to one who does? So you would be unjust and immoderate if without paying the price for which these things are sold, you demanded them anyway. Well, how much does a head of lettuce sell for? An obol, maybe. Whoever lays down an obol gets his head of lettuce. You don't pay and you don't get one: don't suppose you are worse off than the buyer. For he has the lettuce, you have the obol you didn't spend.

The same thing applies here. You weren't invited to someone's banquet? You didn't pay the host the price he put on the dinner. It is sold for praise and service. So pay the charge, if it is to your advantage. But if you don't want to put it out and yet to get these things, you are greedy and stupid. So then you have nothing instead of the dinner? Oh yes, you have something: you didn't praise the fellow, which you didn't want to do; you didn't have to put up with his flunkies.

26. We can learn the will of nature by considering the matters about which we don't disagree with one another. For instance, when somebody else's miserable slave breaks a cup, you are ready right away to say "So it goes." But realize that when it is yours that gets broken, you ought to behave the same way you did when it was someone else's. Apply this to more important matters as well. Somebody else's child or wife has died; there is no one who would not say "That's life." But when his own child or wife dies, it is "Alas, woe is me!" We ought to remember what we feel when we hear the same thing about other people.

27. As a target is not set up for the purpose of being missed, so nothing in the world is intrinsically evil.

28. If someone were to hand over your body to just whomever happened along, you would be outraged. Why aren't you outraged at the fact that *you* turn over your own mind to whomever happens along—if he insults you and you let it upset and trouble you?

29. In every work examine the things that have to be done first and what is to follow, and only then get started on it. If you don't, you will go along eagerly at first, because you have given no consideration to what is coming next; later when difficulties appear the work will come to an ignoble halt. You want to win at Olympia? I do too, by the gods; for it is a fine thing. But look at what comes first, and what comes next, and then take on the work. You must keep discipline, diet, give up pastries, do the compulsory exercises at the set time in heat or in cold, never drink anything cold, take wine only with meals, completely submit yourself to your trainer as to your doctor, and then when the contest starts you have to wallow around in the mud, maybe dislocate your wrist or turn your ankle, swallow quantities of sand, perhaps sometimes be flogged,—and after all this you still lose. Taking it all into consideration,

go ahead and be an athlete, if you still want to. Otherwise you will be turning from one thing to another like children, who now play wrestlers, now gladiators, now trumpeters, then tragic actors; you too would be now athlete, now gladiator, then orator, then philosopher, nothing with your whole soul; but like a monkey you mimic every sight that you see as one thing after another intrigues you. For you have never proceeded with something in accord with investigation, after looking at it from all sides; but just at random and out of frivolous enthusiasm.

Thus some people, when they have seen a philosopher and have heard someone speaking the way Euphrates speaks (but who can speak like him?), wish to philosophize themselves. Man, consider first what kind of business this is. And then learn what your own nature is; can you bear it? Do you want to be a pentathlete or a wrestler? Look at your arms, your thighs, learn about your hips. One man is naturally fitted for one thing, another for another. Do you suppose you can do these things and keep on eating and drinking and enthusing and sulking just as you do now? You will have to go without sleep, labor, leave home, be despised by a slave, have everyone laugh at you, get the worse in everything, in honors, in jobs, in lawsuits, in every trifle. Look these things over and decide whether you want to exchange them for tranquillity, freedom, and peace; if not, don't go ahead, don't be, like a child, now philosopher, afterwards tax collector, then orator, finally Caesar's procurator. These things do not go together. You ought to be one man, good or evil; you must cultivate either your own guiding principle or externals; that is, apply yourself either to the inner man or to outward things: assume either the role of philosopher or of layman.

30. What is proper for us to do is for the most part defined by our social relationships. He is your father: this means that it is for you to look after him, to defer to him in all things, to put up with his abuse and his beatings. "But he is a bad father." Did nature then assign you to a *good* father? No, just to a father. "My brother is wronging me." Then keep up your relationship toward him; don't look at what he may be doing, but at what *you* should do to keep your will in accord with nature. No other person will hurt you unless *you* will it; you will be hurt to the

extent that you think you are hurt. Thus if you will make a habit of contemplating social relationships, you will discover what it is fitting to do as a neighbor, as a citizen, as a consul.

31. Concerning piety toward the gods, know that this is the main thing: have right beliefs about them—that they exist, that they run the world well and justly; and you have been appointed to obey them and to resign yourself to whatever happens and to follow willingly because you are led by the best judgment. Thus you will never blame the gods nor accuse them of unconcern. However, this can never come about unless you withdraw yourself from things not up to us and place good and evil exclusively in the class of things up to us. Thus, if you consider anything else to be good or evil, inevitably, when you fail to get what you want and stumble in to what you don't want, you will assign blame and hate those responsible. For it is natural for every creature to flee and avert itself from hurtful appearances and their causes, and on the other hand to go after and to admire the beneficial and their causes. So it is impossible for anyone who thinks he is being hurt to enjoy what he thinks is hurting him, just as enjoying harm itself is impossible. Consequently even a father is abused by his son, insofar as he does not give the child things that seem to be good; and Polyneices and Eteocles were made enemies of each other by the idea that having the tyranny would be a good thing. On this account also the farmer curses the gods, as do the sailor, the merchant, and those who have lost their wives and children. For wherever one's interest is, there also is one's piety. So, whoever concerns himself with desire and aversion as he ought, concerns himself in the same way with piety too. But libations and sacrifices and rites according to the traditions of the country are always appropriate, and they should be done with purity and not in a slovenly manner nor carelessly; neither stingily nor extravagantly.

32. When you go to a soothsayer, remember that you do not know *what* is going to happen—that is what you came to ask the seer about; but as to *how* it will be, you knew already before you arrived, since you are a philosopher. For if it is something not up to us, necessarily it will be neither good nor evil. So do not bring desire or aversion to the seer, nor approach him trembling, but recognizing that everything that will happen will be indifferent and nothing to you; whatever it may be, it will be possible to make good use of it; no one can prevent this. So approach the gods confidently, as your advisers; afterwards, when counsel has been given you, remember what counsellors you have adopted and whose advice you will be ignoring if, having heard them, you give no heed. Approach divination as Socrates thought proper: only about things where the inquiry exclusively concerns the facts of what is going to happen, and where neither reason nor any other art has resources for making the discovery. So, for example, if it is your duty to share the danger of your friend or your country, it is not right to ask a soothsayer whether you ought to share the danger. For if the diviner should tell you that the sacred omens are bad, it is clear that death or maiming of a limb of the body or exile is meant; reason chooses even so that you stand by your friend and your country, sharing the danger. Therefore give heed to the greater soothsayer, the Pythian Apollo, who expelled from his temple the man who did not come to the aid of his friend when he was being murdered.

33. Prescribe a certain character and type for yourself, and guard it both when you are by yourself and when you meet people. And be silent about most things, or chat only when necessary and about few matters. On rare occasions, when the time is ripe and you are called on to talk, talk—but not about banal topics; not about gladiators, or athletes, or horse races, or food and drink, such as you hear everywhere; and above all, not about blaming or praising or comparing people. If you can, lead the conversation around to something proper. But if you happen to be alone with strange people, be silent.

Laugh seldom and about few things and with restraint.

Totally abstain from taking oaths, if you can; if not, then refuse whenever circumstances allow.

Avoid celebrations, both public and private; but if the occasion calls you, be alert not to lapse into vulgarity. For know that if a companion is defiled, necessarily also one who keeps company with him will be defiled, even if he himself happens to be pure.

Partake of things having to do with the body only as far as bare need goes: such things as food, drink, clothing, housing, slaves. Dispense altogether with whatever has to do with reputation or luxury.

As to sex, be as pure as you can before marriage; but if you are aroused, indulge only to the extent that is customary. However, don't by any means be troublesome to those who do indulge, or censorious; and don't keep mentioning that you yourself can get along without it.

If someone tells you that somebody else is saying awful things about you, don't defend yourself against the accusations, but reply, "He must not know about the other faults that I have, if these are the only ones he mentioned."

It isn't necessary to attend shows for the most part. But if there is a proper occasion, do not appear to be more enthusiastic for anyone else than for yourself, that is, wish only that those things should happen that do happen and that only the winner should win; that way you will not be frustrated. Abstain altogether from shouting and ridiculing anyone or getting emotionally involved. And after the performance don't talk much about what happened, if it does not tend toward your improvement. For it would be evident from this that you were dazzled by the spectacle.

Don't attend authors' readings indiscriminately or eagerly; but if you are present, guard your decorum and dignity and at the same time be indulgent.

Whenever you are going to meet someone, especially one reputed to be important, consider what Socrates or Zeno would have done in the circumstances, and you will not be puzzled about how to use the occasion properly. When you are going to visit a powerful personage, propose to yourself that you will not find him at home, that you will be shut out, that the gates will be slammed in your face, that he will not notice you. And if nevertheless it is your duty to go, when you arrive bear with what happens and by no means say to yourself "It wasn't worth it." For it is unphilosophical to be troubled by externals.

In conversation avoid overmuch talk about your own deeds and dangers. For although it is pleasant for you to recall your own adventures, it may not be so for others to hear about what happened to you.

Also avoid raising laughter; for this is a slippery slope to vulgarity and at the same time sufficient to cancel the respect that others have for you. It is also dangerous to get into dirty talk. Whenever anything of this sort begins, if you get the opportunity, you might rebuke the person who starts it; or if not, make it clear by being silent or blushing and scowling that you are displeased by the talk.

34. When you receive an impression of a certain pleasure, be on your guard, just as you are with other impressions, lest you get carried away by it. Take your time with the thing, wait a while. Next call to mind both times—the time when you will enjoy the pleasure, and the time when, after enjoying it, you will change your mind and scold yourself; and set against these the thought of how, if you abstain, you will rejoice and praise yourself. But if it still seems to you to be the proper occasion to indulge, consider, lest you be overcome by the gentleness and sweetness of it and its seductiveness; set against it, how much better it will be to be conscious of yourself as having won this victory.

35. When you do something because you have recognized that it ought to be done, never go out of your way not to be seen doing it, not even if public opinion takes a different view of it. For if it isn't right for you to do, shun the deed itself; if it is right, why are you afraid of people who would be censuring you wrongly?

36. As the propositions "It is day" and "It is night" separately have truth values, but the conjunction of them has none, so also taking the bigger portion may be valid with respect to the body but invalid when the question is about what you must take care to do rightly when sharing a feast. So when you are dining with someone else, remember not only to look to which of the dishes set before you is good for your body, but also take care about what is seemly with regard to your host.

37. If you take on a role that is too much for you, you both disgrace yourself in it and neglect the one that you might have filled.

38. Just as in walking you pay attention not to step on a nail or to turn your ankle, pay attention not to hurt your ruling principle. And if we look out for this in all of our activities, we will take them on more securely.

39. For everyone the need of his body is the standard for possessions, as fitting the foot is for the shoe. So if you stop there, you will keep the measure; but

if you go beyond, necessarily it will be like going over the edge of a cliff—just as in the case of shoes, if you depart from the foot standard, you will get into gilded shoes and then purple ones and on to studding with jewels; there is no limit, once you have gone beyond the measure.

40. Women, soon after they have reached the age of fourteen, are called "ladies" by men. Accordingly when they see how there is going to be nothing else for them but sleeping with men, they start in to adorn themselves and they put all their hopes in that. So it is worth thinking about: how they can be brought to sense that they are honored for no other reason than that they appear chaste and modest?

41. It is the sign of a weak mind to spend too much time on things having to do with the body, such as exercising a lot, eating a lot, drinking a lot, excreting, sex. Such things should be done incidentally; let all your attention be concentrated on your mind.

42. Whenever someone treats you badly or says bad things about you, remember that he does it or says it thinking that he is doing the right thing. Now it is not possible for him to adhere to *your* conception of the right, but only his own. Whence it follows that if he has a wrong view of things, he, being deceived, is the one who is hurt. For if someone believes that a true proposition is false, it is not the proposition that suffers but the deceived believer. If you consider these things you will deal gently with the slanderer. On each occasion just say, "So it seemed to him."

43. Every thing has two handles, one by which it may be borne, one by which it cannot be borne. If your brother has done wrong, don't grasp this by the "wrongdoing" handle—it can't be borne by that one— but by the "brother", the "brought-up-together" handle, and thereby you will be able to bear it.

44. These sorts of arguments are invalid: "I am richer than you are, therefore I am better than you"; "I am more eloquent than you are, therefore I am better than you". But these are valid: "I am richer than you are, therefore my possessions are better than yours"; "I am more eloquent than you are, therefore my speech is better than yours" *You*, however, are neither your possessions nor your speech.

45. Someone bathes hurriedly: do not say "badly," but "hurriedly." Someone drinks a lot of wine: do not say "badly," but "a lot." For before you know what idea motivated him, how do you know whether he did badly? Thus it will happen that in some cases you receive intuitively certain impressions, whereas in other cases you merely consent.[2]

46. Never refer to yourself as a philosopher or chatter much with laymen about philosophical principles, but do what the principles prescribe. For example, at a banquet do not talk about how one ought to eat, but eat as you ought. Remember that Socrates altogether eschewed ostentation. When people came to him who wanted him to introduce them to philosophers, he did so, being quite content to be overlooked. And if an argument about some philosophical principle gets started among laymen, you should in most instances be silent; for there is great danger of straightway vomiting up what you have not digested. And if someone says to you that you know nothing, and you aren't hurt by the remark, you may then be sure that you are making a beginning at your task. Sheep brought to pasture don't show off to the shepherd how much they have eaten, but rather they digest their fodder internally and produce wool and milk on the outside. Likewise you should not show off your principles to laymen, but digest them and display the results.

47. When you have got adjusted to being frugal in supplying your body, do not brag about the fact. If you drink water, do not say every time you turn down wine that you drink only water. And if from time to time you want to train yourself to endure hardship, do it by yourself, not in front of people. Don't embrace statues;[3] but some time when you are terribly thirsty, take some cold water into your mouth and spit it out and don't tell anyone.

48. Position and character of a vulgar person: he never expects help or harm from himself, but only from outside. Position and character of a philosopher: he expects all help and harm to come from himself.

---

[2]Text and translation of the last sentence are uncertain.

[3]An allusion to Diogenes the Cynic, who in freezing weather stripped naked and threw his arms around a metal statue—in the marketplace of Athens, where people could see him.

Marks of one making progress: he blames nobody, he praises nobody, he complains about nobody, he accuses nobody, he never speaks of himself as if he were anybody or knew anything. If he is impeded or frustrated he blames himself. And if someone praises him, he smiles to himself at the person giving the praise; but if he is blamed, he offers no defense. He comports himself as invalids do, taking care not to move a damaged limb before it has healed. He has purged himself of all desire; he has concentrated aversion solely on things that are against nature but up to us. He takes things as they come. If he appears stupid or ignorant, he doesn't care. In sum, he guards against himself as against an enemy lying in wait.

49. If someone brags because he understands the books of Chrysippus and can explain them, say to yourself: "If Chrysippus had not written unclearly, this fellow would have nothing to brag about."

But what is it that I want? To learn nature and to follow her. So I ask, Who is the interpreter? And hearing that it is Chrysippus, I go to him. But I do not comprehend the writings; so I ask for *their* interpreter. And so far there has been nothing to be proud of. But if I should find the interpreter, it will remain to make use of the precepts; this alone is what one might be proud of. But if I am dazzled by the interpretation itself, what else have I ended up as, than a grammarian instead of a philosopher?—except that it is Chrysippus rather than Homer who is being interpreted. Better, then, that whenever anyone says "Read Chrysippus to me," I should blush, because I can't exhibit deeds that match and accord with his words.

50. Whatever principles are set before you, follow them as laws, the dishonoring of which would be impious. But don't worry about what anyone says about you; for this is not at all up to you.

51. How much time will you take yet before you judge yourself worthy of the best, and never step over the bounds discriminated by reason? You have been apprised of the philosophical principles to which you ought to subscribe, and you have subscribed. So what sort of teacher are you still waiting for, that you put off your own reformation until he gets here? You are no longer a child, but a grown man. If now you take no care and loaf and always keep putting things off and set one day after another on which to start attending to your own affairs, you will lose yourself,

making no progress but going on being a layman in life and in death. Right now, then, deem yourself worthy of living as an adult making progress. And let all that appears best to you be your inviolable law. And if some task is set for you, whether pleasant or glorious or inglorious, remember, that right now you are the contestant and here are the Olympic games, and there can't be any more delay, and that one day and one deed will determine whether progress is lost or saved. That is how Socrates became what he was: by attending in all things that he encountered to nothing other than reason. But you—even if you are not yet a Socrates, at least you ought to live as someone wishing to be like Socrates.

52. The primary and most essential topic in philosophy is that of the use of philosophical principles, for instance, not to lie. The secondary is that of proofs, for instance why one ought not to lie. Tertiary is of what gives certainty and consequence to the first two, for instance, why is this a proof? what indeed is a proof? implication? inconsistency? truth? falsity? The tertiary topic is required because of the secondary, the secondary because of the primary; but the one that is most necessary and that ought never to be neglected is the primary. But we turn them around: for we wrangle about the tertiary topics and bestow all our interest on them, while we altogether neglect the primary. And so we tell lies, and at the same time we are prepared to prove why lying is wrong.

53. On every occasion you ought to have the following ready for use:

Lead thou me on, O Zeus, and Destiny,
Wherever has been fixed by thy decree.
I shall come willingly; though if I fall
Into corruption,—no less, come I shall.
—CLEANTHES

Whoever yields with grace to what must be,
We deem him wise: he knows divinity.
—EURIPIDES

Well, Crito, if so it pleases the gods,
let it be so.
—SOCRATES

Anytus and Meletus can kill me, but they
cannot harm me.
—SOCRATES

REVIEW QUESTIONS

1. What does Epictetus mean by "it is not things that upset people but rather ideas about things"?
2. What is the point of Epictetus' distinction between what is up to us and what is not up to us? According to him, which things are and are not up to us?
3. What does he mean when he says that we ought to conduct ourselves as we would at a banquet?
4. Why shouldn't you be upset by the thought that you shall live without honor, a complete nobody?
5. What are Epictetus' views on laughter, oaths, luxury, and sex?

6

SEXTUS EMPIRICUS

We do not know where Sextus Empiricus lived, but he did write in Greek and lived around the year 200. We know next to nothing about his life except that he was the compiler and historian of ancient Skepticism, especially the teachings of Pyrrho (c. 360–270 B.C.) and the philosophy named after him, Pyrrhonism. Whereas the Academic Skeptics (the school originally founded by Plato) followed Socrates (who asserted that he knew only one thing—that he knew nothing) in claiming certainty about their lack of knowledge, the Pyrrhonists claimed that we could not even know that we knew nothing. For Sextus, "Skepticism is an ability to place in antithesis, in any manner whatever, appearances and judgments, and thus—because equality of force in the objects and arguments opposed—to come first of all to suspension of judgment and then to mental tranquillity."

Skeptics accept appearances, but not positive beliefs. Appearances of the way the world is are passive aspects of perceptions. One is forced, involuntarily, to see the world the way one does, but the skeptic *actively* refuses to draw conclusions from this regarding real existence. "While living undogmatically, we pay due respect to appearances."

Using a device called *tropes* (modes of balancing arguments), Skeptics called attention to the relativity and undecidability of beliefs and explanations. For every physical or nonphysical state of affairs, there were innumerable possibilities for its explanation, and there is no reason to suppose that we can know which is the correct explanation. While Skeptics conceded similarities in some appearances, they doubted whether these similarities led to essential knowledge. "It appears to us that honey is sweet. This we concede, for we experience sweetness through sensation. We doubt, however, whether it is sweet by reason of its essence, which is not a question of the appearance, but of that which is asserted of the appearance." They pointed out that animals and humans perceived things differently and that among humans enormous differences existed in judgment, evaluation, taste, ability, and habits. "Different men take delight in different deeds" and "If fair and wise meant both the same to all, Dispute and strife would be no more."

Different philosophies and religions offer equally dogmatic accounts of the origin of life and the nature of reality. There is relativity of knowledge and custom, so that it is impossible to decide the truth on these matters—or any matter. This inherent undecidability leads to a state of confusion. Here the Skeptics advised withholding assent or dissent regarding any opinion. The term they coined for this suspension of judgment was *Epochē*, a state of purposefully refusing to have an opinion on metaphysical matters. It was not that they denied the gods or the soul, but they refused to assent either to their existence or nonexistence. They espoused a deliberate agnosticism. Doubt all! Maintain an inner *aphasia* (silence) on metaphysical matters! Doubt, thus characterized as the purgation or laxative of the soul, cleanses the soul of the excrescences that befoul it. Ultimately, the Skeptics thought and claimed to have reached *Ataraxia* (tranquillity or imperturbability of soul), their version of peace of mind.

FOR FURTHER READING

Annas, Julia, and Jonathan Barnes, eds. *Modes of Scepticism: Ancient Texts and Modern Interpretations* (Cambridge University Press, 1985).

Barnes, Jonathan. *The Tolls of Scepticism* (Cambridge University Press, 1990).

Buryeat, Myles, ed. *The Skeptical Tradition* (University of California Press, 1983).

Frede, Michael. *Essays in Ancient Philosophy* (University of Minnesota Press, 1987).

Long, A. A. *Hellenistic Philosophy: Stoics, Epicureans, Sceptics* (University of California Press, 1985).

Stough, Charlotte. *Greek Skepticism: A Study in Epistemology* (University of California Press, 1969).

OUTLINES OF PYRRHONISM

BOOK 1 OF THREE

1. THE MAIN DIFFERENCE BETWEEN THE PHILOSOPHIES

When people search for something, the likely outcome is that either they find it or, not finding it, they accept that it cannot be found, or they continue to search. So also in the case of what is sought in philosophy, I think, some people have claimed to have found the truth, others have asserted that it cannot be apprehended, and others are still searching. Those who think that they have found it are the Dogmatists, properly so called—for example, the followers of Aristotle and Epicurus, the Stoics, and certain others. The followers of Cleitomachus and Carneades, as well as other Academics, have asserted that it cannot be apprehended. The Skeptics continue to search. Hence it is with reason that the main types of philosophy are thought to be three in number: the Dogmatic, the Academic, and the Skeptic. Concerning the first two it will best become others to speak; but concerning the Skeptic Way we shall now give an outline account, stating in advance that as regards none of the things that we are about to say do we firmly maintain that matters are absolutely as stated, but in each instance we are simply reporting, like a chronicler, what now appears to us to be the case.

Reprinted from *Sextus Empiricus, Outlines of Pyrrhonism,* translated by Benson Mates (Oxford University Press, 1996) by permission.

2. THE ACCOUNTS OF SKEPTICISM

One account of the Skeptic philosophy is called "general"; the other, "specific". In the general account we set forth the characteristic traits of Skepticism, stating its basic idea, its origins, arguments, criterion and goal, as well as the modes of *epochē* [suspension of judgment], and how we take the Skeptic statements, and the distinction between Skepticism and the competing philosophies. In the specific account we state objections to each part of so-called "philosophy." Let us, then, first take up the general account, beginning the exposition with the various terms for the Skeptic Way.

3. THE NOMENCLATURE OF THE SKEPTIC WAY

The Skeptic Way is called Zetetic ["questioning"] from its activity in questioning and inquiring, Ephectic ["suspensive"] from the *pathos* that arises concerning the subject of inquiry, Aporetic ["inclined to *aporiai*"] either, as some say, from its being puzzled and questioning about everything or from its being at a loss as to whether to assent or dissent, and Pyrrhonean because it appears to us that Pyrrho applied himself to Skepticism more vigorously and conspicuously than his predecessors did.

4. WHAT SKEPTICISM IS

The Skeptic Way is a disposition to oppose phenomena and noumena to one another in any way whatever, with the result that, owing to the equipollence among the things and statements thus opposed, we are brought first to *epochē* and then to *ataraxia*. We do not apply the term "disposition" in any subtle sense, but simply as cognate with "to be disposed." At this point we are taking as phenomena the objects of sense perception, thus contrasting them with the noumena. The phrase "in any way whatever" can modify both the word "disposition" (so as to make us take that word in a plain sense, as we said) and the phrase "to oppose phenomena and noumena"; for since we oppose these in various ways—phenomena to phenomena, noumena to noumena, or *alternando* phenomena to noumena, we say "in any way whatever" in order to include all such

oppositions. Or we can apply "in any way whatever" to "phenomena and noumena," in order that we may not have to inquire how the phenomena appear or the noumena are thought, but may take these terms in their plain senses. By "opposed" statements we simply mean inconsistent ones, not necessarily affirmative and negative. By "equipollence" we mean equality as regards credibility and the lack of it, that is, that no one of the inconsistent statements takes precedence over any other as being more credible. *Epochē* is a state of the intellect on account of which we neither deny nor affirm anything. *Ataraxia* is an untroubled and tranquil condition of the soul. In our remarks on the goal of Skepticism we shall come back to the question of how *ataraxia* enters the soul along with *epochē*.

5. THE SKEPTIC

The definition of the Pyrrhonean philosopher is implicitly contained in that of the Skeptic Way: he is the person who has the aforementioned disposition.

6. THE ORIGINS OF SKEPTICISM

We say that the causal origin of the Skeptic Way is the hope of attaining *ataraxia*. Certain talented people, upset by anomaly in "the facts" and at a loss as to which of these "facts" deserve assent, endeavored to discover what is true in them and what is false, expecting that by settling this they would achieve *ataraxia*. But the main origin of Skepticism is the practice of opposing to each statement an equal statement; it seems to us that doing this brings an end to dogmatizing.

7. DOES THE SKEPTIC DOGMATIZE?

When we say that the Skeptic does not dogmatize we are not using the term "dogma" as some do, in its more common meaning, "something that one merely agrees to", for the Skeptic does give assent to the *pathē* that are forced upon him by a *phantasia*; for example, when feeling hot (or cold) he would not say "I seem not to be hot (or cold)." But when we assert that he does not dogmatize, we use "dogma" in the sense, which others give it, of assent to one of the non-evident matters investigated by the sciences. For the Pyrrhonist assents to nothing that is non-evident. Not even in putting forward the Skeptic slogans about nonevident things does he dogmatize—slogans like "Nothing more" or "I determine nothing" or any of the others of which we shall speak later. For the dogmatizer propounds as certainty the things about which he is said to be dogmatizing, but the Skeptic does not put forward these slogans as holding absolutely. He considers that, just as the "All things are false" slogan says that together with the other things it is itself false, as does the slogan "Nothing is true," so also the "Nothing more" slogan says that it itself is no more the case than its opposite, and thus it applies to itself along with the rest. We say the same of the other Skeptic slogans. So that since the dogmatizer is one who posits the content of his dogmas as being true, while the Skeptic presents his skeptical slogans as implicitly self-applicable, the Skeptic should not be said to dogmatize thereby. But the most important point is that in putting forward these slogans he is saying what seems to him to be the case and is reporting his *pathos* without belief, not firmly maintaining anything concerning what exists externally.

8. DOES THE SKEPTIC HAVE A SYSTEM?

We proceed in the same way when asked whether the Skeptic has a system. If one defines a system as an attachment to a number of dogmas that agree with one another and with appearances, and defines a dogma as an assent to something non-evident, we shall say that the Skeptic does not have a system. But if one says that a system is a way of life that, in accordance with appearances, follows a certain rationale, where that rationale shows how it is possible to seem to live rightly ("rightly" being taken, not as referring only to virtue, but in a more ordinary sense) and tends to produce the disposition to suspend judgment, then we say that he does have a system. For we do follow a certain rationale that, in accord with appearances, points us toward a life in conformity with the customs of our country and its laws and institutions, and with our own particular *pathē*.

9. DOES THE SKEPTIC THEORIZE ABOUT NATURE?

We reply in the same vein if asked whether the Skeptic needs to theorize about nature. On the one hand, if there is a question of making an assertion with firm confidence about any of the matters dogmatically treated in physical theory, we do not theorize; but, on the other hand, in the course of opposing to every statement an equal statement, and in connection with *ataraxia*, we do touch upon physical theory. This, too, is the way we approach the logical and ethical parts of so-called "philosophy."

10. DO THE SKEPTICS DENY APPEARANCES?

Those who claim that the Skeptics deny appearances seem to me not to have heard what we say. For, as we stated above, we do not reject the things that lead us involuntarily to assent in accord with a passively received *phantasia,* and these are appearances. And when we question whether the external object is such as it appears, we grant that it does appear, and we are not raising a question about the appearance but rather about what is said about the appearance; this is different from raising a question about the appearance itself. For example, the honey appears to us to be sweet. This we grant, for we sense the sweetness. But whether it *is* sweet we question insofar as this has to do with the [philosophical] theory, for that theory is not the appearance, but something said about the appearance. And even when we do present arguments in opposition to the appearances, we do not put these forward with the intention of denying the appearances but by way of pointing out the precipitancy of the Dogmatists; for if the theory is so deceptive as to all but snatch away the appearances from under our very eyes, should we not distrust it in regard to the non-evident, and thus avoid being led by it into precipitate judgments?

11. THE CRITERION OF THE SKEPTIC WAY

That we hold to the appearances is obvious from what we say about the criterion of the Skeptic Way. The word "criterion" is used in two ways: first, for the criterion that is assumed in connection with belief about existence or nonexistence, and that we shall discuss in our objections; and second, for the criterion of action, by attention to which in the conduct of daily life we do some things and not others; it is of the latter that we are now speaking. Accordingly, we say that the criterion of the Skeptic Way is the appearance—in effect using that term here for the *phantasia*—for since this appearance lies in feeling and involuntary *pathos* it is not open to question. Thus nobody, I think, disputes about whether the external object appears this way or that, but rather about whether it is such as it appears to be.

Holding to the appearances, then, we live without beliefs but in accord with the ordinary regimen of life, since we cannot be wholly inactive. And this ordinary regimen of life seems to be fourfold: one part has to do with the guidance of nature, another with the compulsion of the *pathē*, another with the handing down of laws and customs, and a fourth with instruction in arts and crafts. Nature's guidance is that by which we are naturally capable of sensation and thought; compulsion of the *pathē* is that by which hunger drives us to food and thirst makes us drink; the handing down of customs and laws is that by which we accept that piety in the conduct of life is good and impiety bad; and instruction in arts and crafts is that by which we are not inactive in whichever of these we acquire. And we say all these things without belief.

12. WHAT IS THE GOAL OF SKEPTICISM?

After these remarks, our next task is to explain the goal of the Skeptic Way. Now the goal or end is that for the sake of which everything is done or considered, while it, in turn, is not done or considered for the sake of anything else; or, it is the ultimate object of the desires. We always say that as regards belief the Skeptic's goal is *ataraxia*, and that as regards things that are unavoidable it is having moderate *pathē*. For when the Skeptic set out to philosophize with the aim of assessing his *phantasiai*—that is, of determining which are true and which are false so as to achieve *ataraxia*—he landed in a controversy between positions of equal strength, and, being unable to resolve it, he suspended judgment. But while he was thus suspending judgment there followed by chance the sought-after *ataraxia* as regards belief.

For the person who believes that something is by nature good or bad is constantly upset; when he does not possess the things that seem to be good, he thinks he is being tormented by things that are by nature bad, and he chases after the things he supposes to be good; then, when he gets these, he falls into still more torments because of irrational and immoderate exultation, and, fearing any change, he does absolutely everything in order not to lose the things that seem to him good. But the person who takes no position as to what is by nature good or bad neither avoids nor pursues intensely. As a result, he achieves *ataraxia*.

Indeed, what happened to the Skeptic is just like what is told of Apelles the painter. For it is said that once upon a time, when he was painting a horse and wished to depict the horse's froth, he failed so completely that he gave up and threw his sponge at the picture—the sponge on which he used to wipe the paints from his brush—and that in striking the picture the sponge produced the desired effect. So, too, the Skeptics were hoping to achieve *ataraxia* by resolving the anomaly of phenomena and noumena, and, being unable to do this, they suspended judgment. But then, by chance as it were, when they were suspending judgment the *ataraxia* followed, as a shadow follows the body. We do not suppose, of course, that the Skeptic is wholly untroubled, but we do say that he is troubled only by things unavoidable. For we agree that sometimes he is cold and thirsty and has various feelings like those. But even in such cases, whereas ordinary people are affected by two circumstances—namely by the *pathē* themselves and not less by its seeming that these conditions are by nature bad—the Skeptic, by eliminating the additional belief that all these things are naturally bad, gets off more moderately here as well. Because of this we say that as regards belief the Skeptic's goal is *ataraxia*, but in regard to things unavoidable it is having moderate *pathē*. But some notable Skeptics have added "suspension of judgment during investigations" to these.

13. THE GENERAL MODES OF *EPOCHĒ*

Since we have been saying that *ataraxia* follows on suspending judgment about everything, the next thing would be to explain how we reach this suspension. Roughly speaking, one may say that it comes about through the opposition of things. We oppose phenomena to phenomena or noumena to noumena, or *alternando*. For instance, we oppose phenomena to phenomena when we say that the same tower appears round from a distance but square from close up; and noumena to noumena when, in reply to one who infers the existence of divine providence from the order of the heavenly bodies, we oppose the fact that often the good fare ill and the bad fare well, and deduce from this that divine providence does not exist; and noumena to phenomena, as when Anaxagoras argued, in opposition to snow's being white, that snow is frozen water and water is dark in color, and therefore snow is dark in color. Or, with a different concept of opposition, we sometimes oppose present things to present things, as in the foregoing examples, and sometimes present things to things past or to things future; for example, when somebody brings up an argument that we are not able to refute, we say to him: "Just as before the birth of the person who introduced the system which you follow, the argument supporting that system did not yet appear sound although it really was, so also it is possible that the opposite of the argument you now advance is really sound despite its not yet appearing so to us, and hence we should not yet assent to this argument that now seems so strong."

But in order that we may more accurately understand these oppositions, I shall set down the modes or arguments by means of which suspension of judgment is brought about, without, however, maintaining anything about their number or their force. For they may well be unsound, and there may be more than the ones I shall mention.

14. THE TEN MODES

The older Skeptics, according to the usual account, have handed down some modes, ten in number, through which it seems that suspension of judgment is brought about, and which they also synonymously call "arguments" or "points." And these modes are as follows: first, there is the one based on the variety of animals; second, the one based on the differences among human beings; third, that based on the differences in constitution of the sense organs; fourth, on the circumstances; fifth, on positions, distances and locations; sixth, on admixtures; seventh, on the quantity and constitution of the external objects; eighth, on relativity; ninth, on the frequency or infrequency of occurrence; and tenth, on ways of life, customs and laws, mythic beliefs and dogmatic opinions. We adopt this order without prejudice.

Superordinate to these are three modes, one based on what does the judging, another based on what is judged, and a third based on both. The first four of the ten modes are subordinate to the mode based on what does the judging, for that is either an animal or a human being or a sense and is in some circumstance; the seventh and tenth modes are referred to the mode based on what is judged; and the fifth, sixth, eighth, and ninth are referred to the one that is based on both. These three in turn are referred to the relativity mode, making it the most generic, with the three as specific and the ten as subordinate. We offer the foregoing comments, as plausible, concerning their number; concerning their content, we say the following.

The first argument, as we were saying, is that according to which the same *phantasiai* do not arise from the same things because of the difference of animals. This we conclude from the difference in the ways animals are produced and from the variety in the structures of their bodies. As concerns the ways they are produced, some animals are produced without sexual union, and others from intercourse. And, of those produced without sexual union, some come from fire, like the tiny creatures that appear in ovens, some from stagnant water, like mosquitoes, some from wine that is turning, like gnats, some from earth, like [. . .], some from slime, like frogs, some from mud, like worms, some from donkeys, like dung-beetles, some from greens, like caterpillars, some from fruit, like the gall insects in the wild fig tree, some from rotting animals, like bees from bulls and wasps from horses. Of animals produced by intercourse, some, the majority, come from homogeneous parents, and others, like mules, from heterogeneous parents. Again, of animals in general, some are born viviparously, like human beings; others oviparously, like birds: and still others just as lumps of flesh, like bears. So one would expect these dissimilarities and differences of origin to result in great contrariety of *pathē*, contributing incompatibility, disharmony, and conflict.

However, it is the differences among the most important parts of the body, especially those naturally fitted for judging and sensing, that can produce the greatest conflict of the *phantasiai*. Thus, things that appear white to us are said to be yellow by people with jaundice, and reddish by those with bloodshot eyes. Since, then, some animals have yellow eyes, others bloodshot eyes, others white, and still others some other color, it is likely, I think, that their perception of colors will be different. Further, if we look long and fixedly at the sun and then stoop down to a book, the letters seem to us golden and moving around. Since, then, some animals have by nature a luster of the eyes and emit a fine and quick stream of light, so as even to be able to see at night, we should expect that external objects would not affect them and us in the same way. And illusionists, by treating lamp wicks with copper rust and cuttle fish ink, make the bystanders appear now copper-colored and now black, just by a slight sprinkling of the mixture. It is surely all the more reasonable that, since differing humors are mixed in the eyes of animals, these animals will have differing *phantasiai* of the external objects. Also, when we press the eyeball on one side, the forms, shapes and sizes of the things seen appear elongated and narrowed. So it is likely that those animals that have elongated and slanting pupils (e.g., goats, cats, and such) will in their *phantasiai* experience the external objects as different from and unlike what animals with round pupils take them to be. Mirrors, too, because of their differing construction, sometimes show the external objects as very short, when the mirror is concave, and sometimes as long and narrow, when it is convex. And some show the head of the reflected person at the bottom, and the feet at the top. Since, then, some of the organs of sight are bulging with convexity and others are quite concave, while still others are in a flat plane, it is likely that because of this the *phantasiai*, too, are various, and that dogs, fish, lions, human beings, and locusts do not see the same things as equal in size or similar in shape, but in each case what is seen depends on the imprint created by the eye that receives the appearance.

The same argument holds for the other senses as well. For how could one say, with regard to touch, that animals are similarly affected whether their surfaces consist of shell, flesh, needles, feathers, or scales? And, as regards hearing, how could one say that perceptions are alike in animals with a very narrow auditory canal and in those with a very wide one, or in those with hairy ears and those with ears that are hairless? Indeed, even we find our hearing affected one way when our ears are plugged and another way when we use them ordinarily. Smell, too, will differ according to the variety of animals. For if we ourselves are affected in one way when we have a cold with a lot of phlegm, and in another way when the parts about the head are filled with an excess of blood (in the latter case being repelled and feeling virtually assaulted by things that seem to others to smell sweet), then, since some animals are flabby and phlegmatic by nature, others very rich in blood, and still others have a predominant excess of yellow or black bile, it is reasonable to suppose that this makes odiferous things appear differently in each case. So, too, with the objects of taste, since some animals have rough and dry tongues and others very moist. And when in a fever we ourselves have relatively dry tongues, we consider the food offered to us to be earthy, bad tasting, and bitter, and we feel thus because of the differing strength of the humors said to be in us. Since, then, the animals too have differing organs of taste, with different humors predominating, they would get differing taste *phantasiai* of the external objects. For, just as the same food, when digested, becomes in one place a vein, in another an artery, in another a bone, and in still another a tendon, and so on, showing a differing disposition depending on the difference of the parts receiving it; and just as water, one and the same in form, when applied to trees becomes bark in one place, branch in another, and blossom in another and thus finally fig, pomegranate, and each of the other fruits; and just as one and the same breath of the musician, when blown into a flute becomes here a high note and there a low note, and the same stroke of the hand on the lyre produces here a bass sound and there a treble one; so, too, it is likely that the external objects are perceived differently depending on the differing makeups of the animals having the *phantasiai*.

But one can see this more clearly from the preferences and aversions of animals. Thus, perfume seems very pleasant to human beings but intolerable to dung beetles and bees, and the application of olive oil is beneficial to human beings but kills wasps and bees. And to human beings sea water is unpleasant and even poisonous to drink, while to fish it is most pleasant and potable. And pigs bathe more happily in the worst stinking mud than in clear and pure water. And, of animals, some eat grass and others eat bushes, some eat wood and others seeds or meat or milk, some like their food aged and others fresh, and some like it raw and others like it prepared by cooking. And in general the things that are pleasant to some animals are unpleasant, repugnant and even poisonous to others. Thus, hemlock fattens quails and hyoscyamus fattens pigs, and pigs enjoy eating salamanders, as the deer enjoy eating poisonous creatures and swallows enjoy blister-beetles. Ants and mosquitoes, when swallowed by human beings, produce discomfort and stomach ache, whereas the she-bear, if she feels somehow weak, is strengthened by licking them up. The adder is stupefied by the mere touch of a branch of oak, and the bat by a leaf of the plane tree. The elephant fears the ram, the lion the rooster, sea-monsters the crackling of bursting beans, the tiger the sound of a drum. And it is possible to give further examples, but—that we may not seem more prolix than necessary—if the same things are unpleasant to some but pleasant to others, and if the pleasure and unpleasantness lie in the *phantasiai*, then differing animals receive different *phantasiai* from the external objects.

But if the same things do appear differently because of the difference of animals, then we shall be in a position to say how the external object looks to *us*, but we shall suspend judgment on how it is in nature. For we shall not be able to decide between our *phantasiai* and those of the other animals, since we are part of the dispute and thus are in need of someone to make the decision, rather than competent to pass judgment ourselves. Besides, we shall not be able to give preference, whether with or without proof, to our *phantasiai* over those of the non-rational animals. For in addition to the possibility of there being no such thing as a proof, as we shall point out, any purported proof will either be apparent or not apparent to us. And if, on the one hand, it is not apparent, then we shall not accept it with confidence. But if, on the other, it *is* apparent to us, then since

what is apparent to animals is the very matter in question, and the proof is apparent to us animals, the proof itself will be in question as to whether, as apparent, it is true. But it is absurd to try to settle the matter in question by means of the matter in question, since the same thing will be both credible and not credible, which is impossible—credible insofar as tending to prove, not credible insofar as needing proof. Therefore, we shall not have a proof justifying us in preferring our own *phantasiai* to those of the so-called "non-rational" animals. If, therefore, the *phantasiai* differ because of the difference of animals, and it is impossible to decide between them, then it is necessary to suspend judgment concerning the external objects.

But for good measure we go on to match up the so-called "non-rational" animals with human beings as regards *phantasiai*. For, after our serious arguments, we do not consider it unseemly to poke a little fun at the Dogmatists, wrapped, as they are, in the fog of their discussions with themselves. We usually take the non-rational animals as a group when comparing them with human beings, but since in groping for an argument the Dogmatists say that the comparison is unfair, we shall for even more good measure carry our joking still further and base the argument on just one animal—the dog, if you will—which seems to be the humblest of all. For we shall find that even in this case the animals that are the subject of the argument are not inferior to ourselves as regards the credibility of the appearances.

So, then, the Dogmatists acknowledge that this animal differs from us in sensation; for it perceives more by the sense of smell than we do, being able by this sense to track wild animals that it cannot see, and with its eyes it sees them more quickly than we do, and its sense of hearing is more acute. Next let us consider reasoning. One kind of reasoning is internal, the other is expressed. Let us first look at the internal kind. This, according to those Dogmatists who at the moment are our chief opponents—namely, the Stoics—seems to involve the following: acceptance of the familiar and avoidance of the alien, knowledge of the arts related to this, possession of the virtues pertaining to one's proper nature and of those having to do with the *pathē*. Now then, the dog, the animal upon which as an example we decided to base the argument, chooses what is congenial to him and avoids the harmful, hunting for food and withdrawing before the raised whip. Furthermore, he has the art, namely hunting, to provide the congenial. Nor is he without virtue. For certainly if justice is giving to each according to his deserts, the dog, who fawns on and guards his family and benefactors but wards off strangers and malefactors, would not be lacking in justice. And if he has this virtue, then in view of the unity of the virtues he has them all, which the wise tell us is not the case with the majority of mankind. And we see him valiant and smart in his defending, to which Homer bears witness when he depicts Odysseus as unknown to all the people of the household but recognized by the dog Argus alone. The dog was not deceived by the physical changes in the man, nor had he lost his "apprehensive *phantasia*," which he clearly retained better than the human beings did. And according to Chrysippus, who was certainly no friend of non-rational animals, the dog even shares in the celebrated Dialectic. In fact, this author says that the dog uses repeated applications of the fifth undemonstrated argument-schema when, arriving at a juncture of three paths, after sniffing at the two down which the quarry did not go, he rushes off on the third without stopping to sniff. For, says this ancient authority, the dog in effect reasons as follows: the animal either went this way or that way or the other; he did not go this way and he did not go that; therefore, he went the other. Furthermore, the dog is aware of and can deal with his own *pathē*. For when a thorn has got stuck in him, he hastens to remove it by rubbing his foot on the ground and by using his teeth. And when he has a wound anywhere he gently licks off the accumulated pus, since dirty wounds are hard to cure, while clean ones are easily healed. Indeed, he follows very well Hippocrates' prescription; since "immobility cures the foot," whenever his foot is injured he holds it up and keeps it undisturbed so far as possible. When he is troubled by humors that do not agree with him, he eats grass, and then regurgitates the uncongenial material along with it and gets well. Since, then, it is apparent that the animal upon which as an example we have rested the argument chooses what is congenial and avoids what is troublesome, and possesses the art of obtaining the congenial, and is aware of

and able to deal with his own *pathē*, and furthermore is not without virtue—in which elements consists the perfection of internal reasoning—the dog would thus far be without deficiency. Which, I suppose, is why certain philosophers [the Cynics] have honored themselves with the name of this animal.

Concerning reasoning as expressed externally it is not necessary at present to inquire, for even some of the Dogmatists have deprecated it as counterproductive to the acquisition of virtue, and for this reason they used to practice silence during their schooling. And anyhow, supposing that a person is unable to speak, no one will infer that he is non-rational. But leaving these points aside, we certainly observe animals, the subject of our discussion, uttering quite human sounds—jays, for instance, and others. And letting this too pass, even if we do not understand the utterances of the so-called "non-rational" animals it is not at all improbable that they are conversing although we do not understand. For when we hear the talk of barbarians we do not understand that either, and it seems to us undifferentiated sound. Moreover, we hear dogs making one sound when they are keeping people away and another when they are howling, and one sound when they are beaten and a different one when they are fawning. In general, if somebody were to study the matter he would find a great difference of sounds uttered by this and the other animals according to different circumstances, and so for that reason it may fairly be said that the so-called "non-rational" animals have their share of externally expressed reasoning. And if they are neither inferior to human beings in the acuteness of their senses nor in internal reasoning, nor, on top of that, in externally expressed reasoning, then as concerns *phantasiai* they are not less worthy of belief than we are. It is also possible to show this, I think, by basing the argument on each kind of non-rational animal. For instance, who would not say that birds excel in shrewdness and employ externally expressed reasoning? For they have knowledge not only of things present but also of the future, and by prophetic sounds or some other signs they reveal these things in advance to people who can understand them.

As I previously indicated, I have made this comparison for good measure, having sufficiently shown, I think, that we cannot prefer our own *phantasiai* to those of the non-rational animals. But if the non-rational animals are not less worthy of belief than we are when it comes to deciding about *phantasiai,* and the *phantasiai* differ depending on the variety of animals, then although I shall be able to say how each of the external objects appears to me, I shall be forced, for the reasons stated above, to suspend judgment as to how it is in nature.

Such, then, is the first mode of *epochē*. We said that the second was the one based on the differences among human beings. For even if it were granted, by way of supposition, that human beings are more to be believed than the non-rational animals, we shall find that even consideration of our own differences leads to suspension of judgment. For human beings are said to be composed of two elements, the soul and the body, and we differ from one another in respect to both of them. As regards the body, we differ in form and constitution. The body of a Scythian differs in form from that of an Indian, and the variation is produced, they say, by the differing relative strengths of the humors. Depending on this difference in relative strength of the humors there arise differing *phantasiai,* as we pointed out in the first mode. So, too, these humors produce a great difference in the choice and avoidance of things external. Indians like some things and we like others, and liking different things is an indication of receiving differing *phantasiai* from the external objects. In consequence of our peculiarities of makeup, we differ in such a way that some of us digest beef better than rock fish or get diarrhea from the weak wine of Lesbos. There was, it is said, an old woman of Attica who safely drank thirty drams of hemlock, and Lysis took four drams of opium without trouble. And Demophon, who waited table for Alexander, used to shiver in the sun or the bath, but felt warm in the shade; the Argive Athenagoras felt no pain when stung by scorpions and venomous spiders; the Psyllaeans, as they are called, are not harmed when bitten by asps or other snakes; nor are the Egyptian Tentyritae harmed by crocodiles. Further, the Egyptians who live along the Astapous river opposite Lake Meroe safely eat scorpions, snakes, and the like. And Rufinus of Chalcis, when he drank hellebore, neither threw up nor suffered any laxative effect, but he took it and digested it as though it were

something to which he was accustomed. Chrysermus the Herophilean, if he ever used pepper, risked a heart attack. And Soterichus the surgeon, whenever he smelled fried fish, got diarrhea. Andron the Argive was so immune to thirst that he even traveled through the Libyan desert without needing anything to drink. Tiberius Caesar could see in the dark, and Aristotle tells of a certain Thasian to whom it seemed that a human phantom was all the time leading him around.

Since there is so much variation among human beings as regards the body—and it suffices to mention only a few of the cases that the Dogmatists provide—it is likely that human beings will also differ among themselves as regards the soul. For the body is a kind of image of the soul, as indeed the art of Physiognomy shows. But the greatest indication of the vast and limitless difference in the intellect of human beings is the inconsistency of the various statements of the Dogmatists concerning what may be appropriately chosen, what avoided, and so on. The poets, too, have expressed themselves appropriately about these things. For Pindar says:

> The crowns and trophies of his storm-foot steeds
> Give joy to one; yet others find it joy
> To dwell in gorgeous chambers gold-bedecked;
> Some even take delight in voyaging
> O'er ocean's billows in a speeding barque.
>
> FRAG. 221 SNELL, AS TRANSLATED BY SIR J. E. SANDYS

And the poet says:

> One person delights in one activity, another
> in another.
>
> ODYSSEY 14.228

Tragedy, too, is full of such things:

> If the same things were beautiful and wise for
> everybody,
> There would be no disputatious strife among
> mankind.
>
> EURIPIDES, PHOENISSAE 499-500

And again,

> It is strange that the same thing should
> be pleasing to some mortals and
> hateful to others.
>
> ANON., FRAY. 462 NAUCK

Since, then, choice and avoidance are in pleasure and displeasure, and pleasure and displeasure lie in sense and *phantasia,* when the same things are chosen by some people and avoided by others it is logical for us to infer that these people are not affected alike by the same things, since if they would alike have chosen and avoided the same things. But if the same things produce different affects depending on the difference of human beings, this too would reasonably lead to suspension of judgment and we would, perhaps, be able to say what each of the external objects appears to be, relative to each difference, but we would not be able to state what it is in nature. For we shall either have to give credence to all human beings or to some. But if to all, we shall be attempting impossibilities and accepting contradictory statements. And if to some, let the Dogmatists tell us to whom we should give assent. The Platonist will say "to Plato" and the Epicurean "to Epicurus," and the others analogously, and thus with their unsettled disputes they bring us again to suspension of judgment. Anyone who says that we ought to give assent to the majority view is making a childish proposal, for no one is able to approach the whole human race and by talking with them find out what pleases the majority. Indeed, there may be peoples of whom we know nothing but among whom attributes that are most rare among us are common, while the attributes most common among us are rare among them; so that, for example, most of them feel no pain when bitten by spiders, while a few, on rare occasions, do; and analogously with the other "idiosyncrasies" previously mentioned. Of necessity, therefore, suspension of judgment comes in again, via the differences of human beings.

While the Dogmatists egoistically claim that in deciding the facts preference ought to be given to themselves above all other human beings, we realize that this claim of theirs is inappropriate since they themselves are part of the dispute. And if, giving preference to themselves, they make a decision about the appearances, by entrusting the decision to themselves they beg the question before the deciding is begun. In any case, in order to arrive at suspension of judgment by an argument dealing with only one person— their Ideal Sage, for example, who is expert at interpreting dreams—we take up the third mode in the list.

This mode is the one that we say is based on the difference of the senses. That the senses differ from one another is obvious from the start. For instance, to the eye it seems that paintings have hollows and prominences, but not to the touch. And for some people honey seems pleasant to the tongue but unpleasant to the eye; consequently, it is impossible to say without qualification whether it is pleasant or unpleasant. And likewise in the case of perfume, for it pleases the sense of smell but displeases the taste. So too with spurge juice: since it is painful to the eyes but painless to all the rest of the body, we will not be able to say without qualification whether, insofar as its nature is concerned, it is painful or painless to bodies. And rain water is beneficial to the eyes, but it is rough on the wind pipe and lungs, as is olive oil despite its being soothing to the skin. The sting-ray, when it touches the extremities, produces numbness, but it can touch the rest of the body harmlessly. Hence we shall not be able to say how each of these things is in its nature, but only how it appears to be in each instance.

More examples can be given, but in order not to delay carrying out the purpose of our essay, the following point needs to be made. Each thing that appears to us in sensation seems to affect us as complex; for example, the apple seems smooth, fragrant, sweet, yellow. But it is not evident whether it really has these and only these qualities, or whether, having only one quality, it appears differently depending on the different constitutions of the sense organs, or again whether it has more qualities than are apparent but some of them do not affect us. That it has one quality could be argued on the basis of what we previously said about the food taken up by the body and the water taken up by the tree and the air breathed into flutes and pipes and similar instruments; for the apple, too, may be of one form but appear differently because of the difference of the sense organs through which it is perceived. And that the apple has more qualities than those that appear to us, we can reason as follows. Suppose that someone is born having the senses of touch, smell, and taste, but can neither hear nor see. Then he will assume that the origin of his perceptions is not something visible or audible, but that it has only those three types of quality which he is capable of perceiving. And it is possible that we, with only our five senses, perceive only those qualities of the apple that we are fitted to perceive, and that perhaps there are other qualities, affecting other sense organs which we lack and for which we consequently cannot perceive any corresponding objects.

But nature, someone may say, has made the senses exactly proportionate to the objects of sense. But what is this "nature", seeing that there is so much unresolved controversy among the Dogmatists concerning its very existence? For anyone who decides this question, that is, whether nature exists, will have no credibility with them if he is an ordinary person, while if he is a philosopher he will be part of the controversy and instead of being a judge will be subject to judgment himself. So that if it is possible that only those qualities exist in the apple which we seem to perceive, or that there are more than these, or again that there are not even the ones that affect us, what the apple is like will be nonevident to us. The same argument holds also in the case of the other objects of sense. And since the senses do not apprehend the external objects, the intellect is not capable of doing so either, so that this argument, too, seems conducive to suspension of judgment concerning the external objects.

In order that we shall be able to reach suspension of judgment when basing the argument on each single sense or even disregarding the senses, we take up further the fourth mode of *epochē*. This is the one described as "based on circumstances," where by "circumstances" we mean conditions. We say that it is concerned with being in a natural or unnatural condition, with being awake or asleep, with dependence on age, on being in motion or at rest, on hating or loving, on being in need or satisfied, on being drunk or sober, on predispositions, on being courageous or fearful, on being distressed or cheerful. Thus, things affect us in dissimilar ways depending on whether we are in a natural or unnatural condition, as when people who are delirious or possessed by a god seem to hear spirits but we do not. Similarly, those people often say that they perceive odors of storax or frankincense or some such thing, and much else, too, although we do not sense them. And the same water that seems to us to be lukewarm seems boiling hot when poured on an inflamed place. And the same coat appears tawny-orange to people with bloodshot

eyes but not to me. Also, the same honey appears sweet to me but bitter to the jaundiced. Further, if someone says that an intermingling of certain humors produces, in persons who are in an unnatural condition, odd *phantasiai* of the external objects, it must be replied that since healthy people, too, have intermingled humors, it is possible that the external objects are in nature such as they appear to those persons who are said to be in an unnatural state, but that these humors are making the external objects appear to the healthy people to be other than they are. For to give the power of altering the external objects to some humors but not to others is arbitrary; since just as the healthy in a natural state have the nature of the healthy and in an unnatural state that of the sick, so too the sick in an unnatural state have the nature of the healthy and in a natural state that of the sick; so that credence should be given to these last, too, as being in a relatively natural state.

Different *phantasiai* come about, too, depending on whether we are asleep or awake. For when we are awake we do not imagine [*ou phantazometha*] what we imagine when we are asleep, nor when we are asleep do we imagine what we imagine when awake, so that whether the *phantasiai* are the case or are not the case is not absolute but relative, that is, relative to being asleep or awake. It is fair to say, then, that when asleep we see things that are not the case in the waking state, though not absolutely not the case. For they are the case in our sleep, just as what we see in our waking state is the case, though not in our sleep.

Depending on age, too, different *phantasiai* arise, since the same air seems cold to the aged but temperate to those who are in their prime, and the same color appears faint to older people but vivid to those in their prime, and likewise the same sound appears faint to the former but clearly audible to the latter. And people of differing ages are moved in different ways depending on their choices and aversions. For instance, children are interested in balls and hoops, but people in their prime prefer other things, and the elderly still others. From this we conclude that, also depending on differences of age, differing *phantasiai* arise from the same external objects.

Objects appear differently, too, depending on whether one is in motion or at rest. For things that we see as stationary when we are at rest seem to be moving when we are sailing by. Depending on liking and disliking, also: for some people are completely repelled by pork, while others eat it with the greatest of pleasure. Whence Menander, too, said:

> Look how his face appears now that he
>   has come to this—like an animal!
> It is acting justly that makes us fair.
>   *FRAG. 518 KOCK*

And many people who have ugly mistresses think them beautiful. Depending on hunger and satiety, too: since the same food seems very pleasant to the hungry but unpleasant to the sated. And depending on being drunk or sober: since things we consider shameful when we are sober appear to us not to be shameful when we are drunk. And depending on predispositions: since the same wine that appears sour to people who have previously eaten dates or figs seems sweet to those who have eaten nuts or chickpeas; and the vestibule of the bathhouse is warm to those entering from outside and cold to those leaving, if they have spent some time in it. And depending on being afraid or feeling courageous: since the same thing seems frightful and terrible to the timid but not at all so to the bold. And, finally, depending on being distressed or cheerful: since the same things that are annoying to people who are distressed are pleasant to those who are cheerful.

Since, therefore, there is so much anomaly depending on conditions, and human beings are in one condition at one time and another at another, how each external object appears to each person is easy to say, I suppose, but not how it is, since the anomaly is unresolved. For anyone resolving it is either in one of the aforementioned conditions or is in no condition at all. But to say that he is in no condition at all—for example, neither healthy nor sick, neither in motion nor at rest, nor of any particular age, and devoid of the other conditions as well—is completely absurd. But if he, being in some condition, makes a decision about the *phantasiai,* he will be part of the dispute and in other ways not a pure or fair judge of the external objects, because he has been contaminated by the conditions he is in. The waking person cannot compare the *phantasiai* of sleepers with those of people who are awake, nor can the healthy person compare those of the sick with those of the healthy. For we assent to things that are in the present and move us in the present, more than to things that are not in the present.

In another way, too, the anomaly of such *phantasiai* is unresolved. For anyone preferring one *phantasia* to another or one circumstance to another either does this without making a decision and without giving proof, or by making a decision and giving proof. But he will not do it without these means, for then he will not be credible, nor will he do it with them, either. For if he makes a decision about the *phantasiai,* he will certainly decide by means of a criterion. And certainly he will either say that this criterion is true or that it is false. But if he says that it is false, he will not be credible. And if he says that the criterion is true, either he will say this without proof or he will say it with proof. Again, if he says it without proof, he will not be credible; but if with proof, the proof will certainly need to be true if he is to be credible. When he affirms the truth of the proof which he is taking to establish the credibility of the criterion, will he have made a decision about this or not? If he has not made the decision, he will not be credible; and if he has made the decision, then it is obvious that he will say that he has decided by means of a criterion, in order that it may be maintained, and the criterion has need of a proof, in order that it may be shown to be true. And neither is it possible for a proof to be sound without the prior existence of a true criterion, nor for a criterion to be true without the previously confirmed proof. And thus the criterion and the proof fall into the circularity type of *aporia,* in which both are found not to be credible; for each, while it awaits the credibility of the other, is equally incredible with the other. Therefore, if nobody, with or without a proof and criterion, is able to give one *phantasia* preference over another, then the differing *phantasiai* that arise depending on the different conditions will be undecidable; so that this mode, too, leads to suspension of judgment concerning the nature of the external objects.

The fifth argument is that depending on positions, distances, and locations. For, depending on each of these, the same things appear different—for example, the same stoa viewed from either end appears tapering but from the middle completely symmetrical, and from afar the same boat appears small and stationary but from close up large and in motion, and the same tower appears round from afar but square from close up.

These depend on distances. But depending on locations: the same lamp-light appears dim in the sunshine but bright in the dark, and the same oar appears broken when it is in the water and straight when it is out, and the egg soft when it is in the bird but hard when it is in the air, and the ligure liquid in the lynx but hard in the air, and coral soft in the sea but hard in the air, and sound appears one way in a pipe, another in a flute, and still another when it is simply in the air.

And depending on positions: the same portrait appears smooth when tilted back, but when tilted forward a certain amount it seems to have depths and prominences. And the necks of pigeons appear different in color depending on the different angles of inclination.

Therefore, since everything apparent is viewed in some location and from some distance and in some position, each of which produces a great deal of variation in the *phantasiai*, as we have remarked above, we shall be forced also by this mode to have recourse to suspension of judgment. And anyone wishing to give preference to some of these *phantasiai* will be attempting the impossible. For if he makes his assertion simply and without proof, he will not be credible; whereas, supposing that he wishes to use a proof, if he says that the proof is false he will confute himself, while if he says that it is true he will need a proof of its being true, and again a proof of that, since it too must be true, and so on ad infinitum. But it is impossible to produce infinitely many proofs; and so he will not be able by means of a proof to give one *phantasia* preference over another. And if one cannot decide about the aforementioned *phantasiai* either with or without a proof, suspension of judgment results; for, I suppose, of any given thing we are able to say of what sort, relative to its particular position, distance, and place, it appears to be, but for the above reasons we cannot state of what sort it is in its nature.

The sixth mode is the one that depends on admixtures and according to which we conclude that, since none of the external objects affects us by itself but always in combination with something, it is perhaps possible to say what the mixture of the external object and that together with which it is observed is like, but we cannot do the same for the external object considered by itself. It is obvious from the start, I think, that none of the external objects affects us by itself, but always does so in combination with something, and that depending on this it is observed as different. Thus, our own complexion is seen as of one hue in warm air and as of another in cold air, and so we cannot say how our complexion is in nature, but only how it looks together with each of the two kinds of air. Further, the same sound appears one way in thin air and another in dense air, and spices are more pungent in the bathhouse and in the sun than in very cold air, and the body is light when immersed in water, but heavy in air.

In order to get away from just external admixtures: our eyes contain within themselves both membranes and liquids. Since things seen are not observed without these, they will not be accurately apprehended, for it is the mixture that we perceive, and because of this the jaundiced see everything yellow, while those with blood in the eyes see things as bloodred. And since the same sound appears of one quality in open places and of another in places that are narrow and winding, and of one quality in clear air and another in murky air, it is likely that we do not perceive the sound in and of itself; for the ears have narrow and winding passages and are contaminated by vaporous effluvia said to be conducted from places around the head. Moreover, since there are substances in the nostrils and in the areas of taste, we perceive the objects of taste and of smell together with these and not in and of themselves. Therefore, because of the admixtures the senses do not perceive precisely how the external objects are.

Nor does the intellect do so either, especially since its guides, the senses, go wrong; perhaps it too contributes some special admixture of its own to the reports of the senses; for we observe that there are humors situated around each of the places in which the Dogmatists suppose that the ruling part of the soul is located, whether the brain or the heart or whatever part of the animal anyone wants to put it in. And so by this mode also we see that, being unable to say anything about the nature of the external objects, we are forced to suspension of judgment.

The seventh mode, we said, is that depending on the quantity and constitution of the external objects, giving "constitution" its common meaning, namely, combination. It is obvious that by this mode, too, we are forced to suspend judgment about the nature of the objects. For example, shavings off a goat's horn appear white when observed by themselves and not in combination, but when they are combined in the substance of the horn they look black. And individual filings of a piece of silver appear black, but when united with the whole they affect us as white. And pieces of Taenarean marble look white when they are polished, but combined in the whole stone they appear yellow. And grains of sand when scattered appear rough, but when gathered together in a dune they affect our senses as soft. And hellebore, taken when fine and light, tends to choke one, but not when coarse. And wine, when drunk in moderation, strengthens us, but when taken in excess, disables the body. And food, similarly, exhibits different powers depending on the amount; often, indeed, by being taken in too great quantity it brings the body down with indigestion and diarrhea. So here, too, we shall be able to say of what quality the shaving of horn is, and of what quality the combination of many shavings is, and the same for the particle of silver and the combination of many particles, and for the bit of Taenarean marble and the combination of many bits, and we can make relative statements in the case of the grains of sand and the hellebore and the wine and the food, too, but we still cannot state the absolute nature of the things because of the anomaly of *phantasiai* depending on combination.

It seems that in general even beneficial things become harmful when they are used in immoderate quantities, and the things that seem hurtful when taken in excess are harmless in small quantities. The best indication of this point is what is observed in regard to the powers of medicines, in which the exact mixing of the simple drugs produces a compound that is beneficial, but the occasional slightest error in weighing, when overlooked, makes it not only not beneficial but even quite hurtful and often poisonous.

So the argument relating to quantities and constitutions muddles the existence of the external objects. Consequently this mode too may be expected to lead us around to suspension of judgment, for we are unable to say anything without qualification about the nature of the external objects.

The eighth mode is the one based on relativity, where we conclude that, since everything is in relation to something, we shall suspend judgment as to what things are in themselves and in their nature. But it must be noticed that here, as elsewhere, we use "are" for "appear to be," saying in effect "everything appears in relation to something." But this statement has two senses: first, as implying relation to what does the judging, for the object that exists externally and is judged appears in relation to what does the judging, and second, as implying relation to the things observed together with it, as, for example, what is on the right is in relation to what is on the left. And, indeed, we have taken into account earlier that everything is in relation to something: for example, as regards what does the judging, that each thing appears in relation to this or that animal or person or sense and in relation to such and such a circumstance; and as regards the things observed together with it, that each thing appears in relation to this or that admixture or manner or combination or quantity or position.

But it is also possible to prove by a special argument that everything is in relation to something, as follows. Do the things that are what they are by virtue of a difference differ from the things that are in relation to something, or not? If they do not differ, then they too are in relation to something; if they do differ, then, since whatever differs is in relation to something (for it is called what it is in relation to that from which it differs), the things that are what they are by virtue of a difference are in relation to something. And, according to the Dogmatists, of things that are, some are *summa genera*, others are *infimae species*, and others are genera and species. But all these are relative. Again, of things that are, some are pre-evident and others are non-evident, as they say; the appearances signify, and the non-evident things are signified by the appearances. For, according to them, "the appearances are a view of the non-evident." But what signifies and what is signified are relative. Therefore, everything is relative. Moreover, of things that are, some are similar and others are dissimilar, and some are equal and others are unequal; but these things are relative; therefore, everything is relative. And even the person who says that not all things are relative confirms the relativity of all things, for by the arguments he opposes to us he shows that the very relativity of all things is relative to us and not universal.

Now, when we have shown that all things are relative, the obvious result is that as concerns each external object we shall not be able to state how it is in its own nature and absolutely, but only how, in relation to something, it appears to be. It follows that we must suspend judgment about the nature of the objects.

In connection with the mode based on the constancy or infrequency of occurrence, which we say is the ninth in order, we consider such items as the following. The sun is certainly a much more marvelous thing than a comet. But since we see the sun all the time but the comet only infrequently, we marvel at the comet so much as even to suppose it a divine portent, but we do nothing like that for the sun. If, however, we thought of the sun as appearing infrequently and setting infrequently, and as illuminating everything all at once and then suddenly being eclipsed, we would find much to marvel at in the matter. And earthquakes are not equally troublesome to the person who is experiencing one for the first time and to the person who has become accustomed to them. And how marvelous is the sea to the person who sees it for the first time! And a beautiful human body that is seen suddenly and for the first time excites us more than if it were to become a customary sight. Things that are rare seem precious, but things that are familiar and easy to get do not. Indeed, if we thought of water as rare, how much more precious it would appear than all the things that do seem precious! And if we imagine gold simply scattered on the ground like stones, to whom do we think it would then be precious and worth hoarding away?

Since, then, the same things, depending on whether they occur frequently or infrequently, seem at one time marvelous or precious and at another time not, we infer that we shall perhaps be able to say how each of these appears when it occurs frequently or when it occurs infrequently, but that we shall not be able to state without qualification how each of the external objects is. And, accordingly, via this mode too we withhold assent as regards them.

The tenth mode, which is principally concerned with ethics, is the one depending on ways of life and on customs, laws, mythic beliefs, and dogmatic suppositions. A way of life is a chosen basis for living or for some particular action, adopted by one person or many—for example, by Diogenes or the Laconians. A law is a written agreement among the citizens, the violator of which is punished; a custom or common practice (for there is no difference) is the joint acceptance by a number of people of a certain way of acting, where the violator is not in all cases punished; thus, there is a law against adultery, and for us it is a custom not to have intercourse with a woman in public. A mythic belief is the acceptance of things that are not the case and are fictional—such as, among others, the myths about Cronus—and in which many people place credence. And a dogmatic supposition is the acceptance of something that seems to be established by analogy or some kind of proof, such as that there are atomic elements of things, or homoeomeries [ultimate particles of matter], or *minima,* or other things.

And we oppose each of these items sometimes to itself and sometimes to each of the others. For example, we oppose custom to custom thus: some of the Ethiopians tattoo their babies, but we do not. And the Persians think it becoming to wear brightly colored garments that reach to the feet, but we consider it unbecoming; and whereas the Indians have intercourse with women in public, most others consider this shameful. We oppose law to law thus: among the Romans, he who gives up his patrimony does not pay his father's debts; but among the Rhodians he always pays them; and among the Tauri of Scythia there was a law that foreigners were to be sacrificed to Artemis, but with us it is forbidden to kill a human being at the temple. And we oppose a way of life to a way of life when we set Diogenes's way of life in opposition to that of Aristippus, or that of the Laconians to that of the Italians. We oppose a mythical belief to a mythical belief when in one place we say that according to myth Zeus is the father of men and gods, while in another we say that it is Oceanus, referring to the line:

Oceanus, the source of the gods, and Tethys, the mother.

ILIAD 14.201

And we oppose dogmatic opinions to one another when we say that some people assert that there is just one element and others that there are infinitely many, and that some assert that the soul is mortal and others that it is immortal, and that some assert that our affairs are arranged by divine providence while others assert that they are not.

We also oppose custom to the other items—to law, for example, when we say that among the Persians sodomy is customary but among the Romans it is prohibited by law; and with us adultery is prohibited, but among the Massagetae it is by custom treated as a matter of indifference, as Eudoxus of Cnidos reports in the first book of his *Travels*; and with us it is forbidden to have intercourse with one's mother, whereas with the Persians this sort of marriage is very much the custom. And among the Egyptians men marry their sisters, which for us is prohibited by law. Custom is opposed to way of life when, whereas the majority of men have intercourse with their wives in some place apart, Crates did it with Hipparchia in public; and Diogenes went around with shoulders bare, while we dress in the usual way. And custom is opposed to mythical belief, as when the myths say that Cronus ate his own children, it being customary among us to take care of children; and whereas with us it is customary to worship the gods as being good and immune from evil, they are presented by the poets as being wounded by and envious of one another. Custom is also opposed to dogmatic opinion when with us it is the custom to pray to the gods for good things, whereas Epicurus says that the divinity does not care about us; and when Aristippus thinks it a matter of indifference whether one wears women's clothing, while we think this shameful.

We oppose way of life to law when, though there is a law against striking a free and well-born man, the pancratiasts hit one another because of their way of life, and when, though homicide is forbidden, the gladiators kill one another for the same reason.

Further, we oppose mythical belief to way of life when we point out that the myths say that Heracles in the house of Omphale "carded wool and endured slavery" and did these things which nobody would choose to do, even to a moderate degree, whereas Heracles's way of life was noble. We oppose way of life to dogmatic supposition when athletes undertake an onerous way of life for the sake of glory, on the supposition that glory is good, while many philosophers dogmatize that it is an evil thing. And we oppose law to mythical belief when the poets present the gods as practicing adultery and sodomy, while with us the law prohibits doing these things; and we oppose law to dogmatic opinion when the Chrysippeans say that intercourse with mothers or sisters is a matter of indifference, while the law prohibits these things. Further, we oppose mythical belief to dogmatic supposition when the poets say that Zeus came down and had intercourse with mortal women, whereas this is deemed by the Dogmatists to be impossible; and the poet says that Zeus, because of grief over Sarpedon,

Let fall a shower of blood upon the earth,
ILIAD 16.459

while it is a dogma of the philosophers that the divinity is impassive; and when the philosophers reject the myth of the hippocentaurs, while offering us the hippocentaur as a paradigm of nonexistence.

For each of the foregoing oppositions it was possible to take many other examples, but in an outline these will suffice. At any rate, since by this mode, too, so many anomalies in "the facts" have been shown, we shall not be able to say how any external object or state of affairs is in its nature, but only how it appears in relation to a given way of life or law or custom, and so forth. And so because of this mode, too, we must suspend judgment about the nature of the external "facts." Thus, via all ten modes we end up with suspension of judgment.

REVIEW QUESTIONS

1. What is *epochē?* How is it different from a simple denial of belief? What is *aphasia?*
2. What are appearances? Does the skeptic deny them?
3. What does Sextus Empiricus mean by "we live without beliefs but in accord with the ordinary regimen of life"?
4. What are the ten modes, and what does Sextus Empiricus hope to show with them?
5. What is the ultimate goal of skepticism?

7

PLOTINUS

Plotinus (205–270), the last great neo-Platonist, was born in Lykopolis, Egypt. He studied in Alexandria before traveling to Persia and India to learn Eastern wisdom, and then to Rome, where he established a school of philosophy. His most famous work is the *Enneads*, six groups of nine writings, from which our selections are taken. Plotinus died of leprosy.

As a Platonist he sought through mystical contemplation a supreme principle, the Good or One. The Good is infinite and overflows, producing the realm of the Intellect (*Nous*), the realm of Plato's Forms, which in turn overflows to produce the Divine Soul, the lowest of the emanations of the Good. The ascent of the soul to the highest goal demanded, not religious belief or ritual, but liberation from bodily needs (bodies are phantoms) and moral purity. One ascends upward through stages, first the realm of pure Soul, then the realm of the Intellect, and, finally, the Good or One. Plotinus thought his soul had ascended to the Good momentarily at various points in his later life.

Our first selection (*Ennead* I.6) describes the ascent of the soul to the Good. Our second (*Ennead* V.1) describes the first three hypostases.

ENNEAD I.6

BEAUTY

1. Beauty addresses itself chiefly to sight; but there is a beauty for the hearing too, as in certain combinations of words and in all kinds of music, for melodies and cadences are beautiful; and minds that lift themselves above the realm of sense to a higher order are aware of beauty in the conduct of life, in actions, in character, in the pursuit of the intellect; and there is the beauty of the virtues. What loftier beauty there may be, yet, our argument will bring to light.

What, then, is it that gives comeliness to material forms and draws the ear to the sweetness perceived in sounds, and what is the secret of the beauty there is in all that derives from Soul?

Is there some One Principle from which all take their grace, or is there a beauty peculiar to the embodied and another for the bodiless? Finally, is beauty one or many, what would such a Principle be?

Consider that some things, material shapes for instance, are gracious not by anything inherent but by something communicated, while others are lovely of themselves, as, for example, Virtue.

The same bodies appear sometimes beautiful, sometimes not; so that there is a good deal between being body and being beautiful.

What, then, is this something that shows itself in certain material forms? This is the natural beginning of our inquiry.

What is it that attracts the eyes of those to whom a beautiful object is presented, and calls them, lures them, toward it, and fills them with joy at the sight? If we possess ourselves of this, we have at once a standpoint for the wider survey.

Almost everyone declares that the symmetry of parts towards each other and towards a whole, with, besides, a certain charm of color, constitutes the beauty recognized by the eye, that in visible things, as indeed in all else, universally, the beautiful thing is essentially symmetrical, patterned.

But think what this means.

Only a compound can be beautiful, never anything devoid of parts; and only a whole; the several parts will have beauty, not in themselves, but only as working together to give a comely total. Yet beauty in an aggregate demands beauty in details; it cannot be constructed out of ugliness; its law must run throughout.

All the loveliness of colour and even the light of the sun being devoid of parts and so not beautiful by symmetry, must be ruled out of the realm of beauty. And how comes gold to be a beautiful thing? And lightning by night, and the stars, why are these so fair?

In sounds also the simple must be proscribed, though often in a whole noble composition each several tone is delicious in itself.

Again since the one face, constant in symmetry, appears sometimes fair and sometimes not, can we doubt that beauty is something more than symmetry, that symmetry itself owes its beauty to a remoter principle?

Turn to what is attractive in methods of life or in the expression of thought; are we to call in symmetry here? What symmetry is to be found in noble conduct, or excellent laws, in any form of mental pursuit?

What symmetry can there be in points of abstract thought?

The symmetry of being accordant with each other? but there may be accordance or entire identity where there is nothing but ugliness: the proposition that honesty is merely a generous artlessness chimes in the most perfect harmony with the proposition that morality means weakness of will; the accordance is complete.

Then again, all the virtues are a beauty of the soul, a beauty authentic beyond any of these others; but how does symmetry enter here? The soul, it is true, is not a simple unity, but still its virtue cannot have the symmetry of size or of number: what standard of measurement could preside over the compromise or the coalescence of the soul's faculties or purpose?

Plotinus, *The Six Enneads*, translated by Stephen MacKenna. Ennead I.6 was first published in London in 1908 and then published with the entire *Enneads* by the Medici Society of London in 1917. I have made slight changes to the text.

Finally, how by this theory would there be beauty in the Intellectual-Principle, essentially the solitary?

2. Let us, then, go back to the source, and indicate at once the Principle that bestows beauty on material things.

Undoubtedly this Principle exists; it is something that is perceived at the first glance, something which the soul names as from an ancient knowledge and, recognizing, welcomes it, enters into unison with it.

But let the soul fall in with the Ugly and at once it shrinks within itself, denies the thing, turns away from it, not accordant, resenting it.

Our interpretation is that the soul—by the very truth of its nature, by its affiliation to the noblest Existents in the hierarchy of Being—when it sees anything of that kin, or any trace of that kinship, thrills with an immediate delight, takes its own to itself, and thus stirs anew to the sense of its nature and of all its affinity.

But, is there any such likeness between the loveliness of this world and the splendors in the Supreme? Such likeness in the particulars would make the two orders alike: but what is there in common between beauty here and beauty There?

We hold that all the loveliness of this world comes by participating in the Ideal Form.

Every shapeless thing whose kind admits of pattern and form, as long as it remains outside of Reason and Idea, is ugly by that very isolation from the Divine-Thought. And this is the Absolute Ugly: an ugly thing is something that has not been entirely mastered by pattern, that is by Reason, the Matter not yielding at all points and in all respects to the Ideal Form.

But where the Idea-Form has entered, it has grouped and coordinated what from a diversity of parts was to become a unity: it has rallied confusion into co-operation: it has made the sum one harmonious coherence: for the Idea is a unity and what it molds must come to unity as far as multiplicity may.

So beauty enthrones itself on what has been brought into unity, giving itself to the parts as to the sum: when it lights on some natural unity, a thing of like parts, then it gives itself to that whole. Thus, for an illustration, there is the beauty, conferred by craftsmanship, of all a house with all its parts, and the beauty which some natural quality may give to a single stone.

This, then, is how the material thing becomes beautiful—by participating in the thought that flows from the Divine.

3. And the soul includes a faculty peculiarly addressed to Beauty—a power incomparably certain in the appreciating of its own, never in doubt whenever any lovely thing presents itself for judgment.

Or perhaps the soul itself acts immediately, affirming the Beautiful where it finds something accordant with the Ideal Form within itself, using this Idea as a canon of accuracy in its decision.

But what accordance is there between the material and that which antedates all Matter?

On what principle does the architect, when he finds the house standing before him correspondent with his inner ideal of a house, pronounce it beautiful? Is it not that the house before him, the stones apart, is the inner idea stamped upon the mass of exterior matter, the indivisible exhibited in diversity?

So with the perceptive faculty: discerning in certain objects the Ideal Form which has bound and controlled shapeless matter, opposed in nature to Idea, seeing further stamped upon the common shapes some shape excellent above the common, it gathers into unity what still remains fragmentary, catches it up and carries it within, no longer a thing of parts, and presents it to the Ideal-Principle as something concordant and congenial, a natural friend: the joy here is like that of a good man who discerns in a youth the early signs of a virtue consonant with the achieved perfection within his own soul.

The beauty of colour is also the outcome of a unification; it derives from shape, from the conquest of the darkness inherent in Matter by the pouring in of light, the unembodied, which is a Rational-Principle and an Ideal Form.

Hence it is that Fire itself is splendid beyond all material bodies, holding the rank of Ideal-Principle to the other elements, proceeding ever upwards, the subtlest and sprightliest of all bodies, as very near to the unembodied; itself alone admitting no other, all the others penetrated by it: for they take warmth but this is never cold; it has colour primarily; they receive the Form of colour from it: hence the splendor of its light, the splendor that belongs to the Idea. And all that has resisted and is but uncertainly held by its light remains outside of beauty, as not having absorbed the plentitude of the Form of colour.

And harmonies unheard in sound create the harmonies we hear, and wake the soul to the consciousness of beauty, showing it the one essence in another kind: for the measures of our sensible music are not arbitrary but are determined by the Principle whose labor is to dominate Matter and bring pattern into being.

Thus far of the beauties of the realm of sense, images and shadow-pictures, fugitives that have entered into Matter—to adorn, and to ravish, where they are seen.

4. But there are earlier and loftier beauties than these. In the sense-bound life we are no longer granted to know them, but the soul, taking no help from the organs, sees and proclaims them. To the vision of these we must mount, leaving sense to its own low place.

As it is not for those to speak of the graceful forms of the material world who have never seen them or known their grace—men born blind, let us suppose—in the same way those must be silent upon the beauty of noble conduct and of learning and all that order who have never cared for such things, nor may those tell of the splendor of virtue who have never known the face of Justice and of Moral-Wisdom beautiful beyond the beauty of Evening and of Dawn.

Such vision is for those only who see with the Soul's sight—and at the vision, they will rejoice, and awe will fall upon them and a trouble deeper than all the rest could ever stir, for now they are moving in the realm of Truth.

This is the spirit that Beauty must ever induce, wonderment and a delicious trouble, longing and love and a trembling that is all delight. For the unseen all this may be felt as for the seen; and this the Souls feel for it, every soul in some degree, but those the more deeply that are the more truly apt to this higher love—just as all take delight in the beauty of the body but all are not stung as sharply, and those only that feel the keener wound are known as Lovers.

5. These Lovers, then, lovers of the beauty outside of sense, must be made to declare themselves.

What do you feel in the presence of the grace you discern in actions, in manners, in sound morality, in all the works and fruits of virtue, in the beauty of souls? When you see that you yourselves are beautiful within, what do you feel? What is this Dionysian exultation that thrills through your being, this straining upwards of all your Soul, this longing to break away from the body and live sunken within the veritable self?

These are no other than the emotions of Souls under the spell of love.

But what is it that awakens all this passion? No shape, no colour, no grandeur of mass: all is for a Soul, something whose beauty rests upon no colour, for the moral wisdom the Soul enshrines and all the other colorless splendor of the virtues. It is that you find in yourself, or admire in another, loftiness of spirit; righteousness of life; disciplined purity; courage of the majestic face; gravity; modesty that goes fearless and tranquil and passionless; and, shining down upon all, the light of god-like Intellection.

All these noble qualities are to be reverenced and loved, no doubt, but what entitles them to be called beautiful?

They exist: they manifest themselves to us: anyone that sees them must admit that they have reality of Being; and is not Real-Being, really beautiful?

But we have not yet shown by what property in them they have wrought the Soul to loveliness: what is this grace, this splendor as of Light, resting upon all the virtues?

Let us take the contrary, the ugliness of the Soul, and set that against its beauty: to understand, at once, what this ugliness is and how it comes to appear in the Soul will certainly open our way before us.

Let us then suppose an ugly Soul, dissolute, unrighteous: teeming with all the lusts; torn by internal discord; beset by the fears of its cowardice and the envies of its pettiness; thinking, in the little thought it has, only of the perishable and the base; perverse in all its unclean pleasures; living the life of abandonment to bodily sensation and delighting in its deformity.

What must we think but that all this shame is something that has gathered about the Soul, some foreign bane outraging it, soiling it, so that, encumbered with all manner of turpitude, it has no longer a clean activity or a clean sensation, but commands only a life smoldering dully under the crust of evil; that, sunk in manifold death, it no longer sees what a Soul should see, may no longer rest in its own being, dragged ever as it is towards the outer, the lower, the darkness?

An unclean thing, I dare say; flickering hither and thither at the call of objects of sense, deeply infected with the taint of body, occupied always in Matter, and absorbing Matter into itself, in its commerce with the Ignoble it has trafficked away for an alien nature its own essential Idea.

If a man has been immersed in filth or daubed with mud his native comeliness disappears and all that is seen is the foul stuff besmearing him: his ugly condition is due to alien matter that has encrusted him, and if he is to win back his grace it must be his business to scour and purify himself and make himself what he was.

So, we may justly say, a Soul becomes ugly by something foisted upon it, by sinking itself into the alien, by a fall, a descent into body, into Matter. The dishonor of the Soul is in its ceasing to be clean and separate. Gold is degraded when it is mixed with earthly particles; if these be worked out, the gold with gold alone. And so the Soul; let it be but cleared of the desires that come by its too intimate converse with the body, emancipated from all the passions, purged of all that embodiment has thrust upon it, withdrawn, a solitary, to itself again—in that moment the ugliness that came only from the alien is stripped away.

6. For, as the ancient teaching was, moral discipline and courage and every virtue, not even excepting Wisdom itself, all is purification.

Hence the Mysteries with good reason adumbrate the immersion of the unpurified in filth, even in the Nether-World, since the unclean loves filth for its very filthiness, and swine foul of body find their joy in foulness.

What else is Sophrosune [Self-control], rightly so-called, but to take no part in the pleasures of the body, to break away from them as unclean and unworthy of the clean? So too, Courage is but being fearless of the death which is but the parting of the Soul from the body, an event which no one can dread whose delight is to be his unmingled self. And Magnanimity is but disregard for the lure of things here. And Wisdom is but the Act of the Intellectual-Principle withdrawn from the lower places and leading the Soul to the Above.

The Soul thus cleansed is all Idea and Reason, wholly free of body, intellectual, entirely of that divine order from which the wellspring of Beauty rises and all the race of Beauty.

Hence the Soul heightened to the Intellectual-Principle is beautiful to all its power. For Intellection and all that proceeds from Intellection are the Soul's beauty, a graciousness native to it and not foreign, for only with these is it truly Soul. And it is just to say that in the Soul's becoming a good and beautiful thing is its becoming like to God, for from the Divine comes all the Beauty and all the Good in beings.

We may even say that Beauty is the Authentic-Existence and Ugliness is the Principle contrary to Existence: and the Ugly is also the primal evil; therefore its contrary is at once good and beautiful, or is Good and Beauty: and hence the one method will discover to us the Beauty-Good and the Ugliness-Evil.

And Beauty, this Beauty which is also The Good, must be posed as The First: directly deriving from this First is the Intellectual-Principle which is preeminently the manifestation of Beauty; through the Intellectual-Principle Soul is beautiful. The beauty in things of a lower order—actions and pursuits for instance—comes by operation of the shaping Soul which is also the author of the beauty found in the world of sense. For the Soul, a divine thing, a fragment as it were of the Primal Beauty, makes beautiful to the fullness of their capacity all things whatsoever that it grasps and molds.

7. Therefore we must ascend again towards the Good, the desired of every Soul. Anyone that has seen This, knows what I intend when I say that it is beautiful. Even the desire of it is to be desired as a Good. To attain it is for those that will take the upward part, who will set all their forces towards it, who will divest themselves of all that we have put on in our descent: so, to those that approach the Holy Celebrations of the Mysteries, there are appointed purifications and the laying aside of the garments worn before, and the entry in nakedness—until, passing, on the upward way, all that is other than the God, each in the solitude of himself shall behold that solitary-dwelling Existence, the Apart, the Unmingled, the Pure, that from Which all things depend, for Which all look and live and act and know, the Source of Life and of Intellection and of Being.

And one that shall know this vision—with what passion of love shall he not be seized, with what pangs of desire, what longing to be molten into one with This, what wondering delight! If he that has never seen this Being must hunger for It as for all his welfare, he that has known must love and reverence It as the very Beauty; he will be flooded with awe and gladness, stricken by a salutary terror; he loves with a veritable love, with sharp desire; all other loves than this he must despise, and disdain all that once seemed fair.

This, indeed, is the mood even of those who, having witnessed the manifestation of Gods or Supernals, can never again feel the old delight in the comeliness of material forms: what then are we to think of one that contemplates Absolute Beauty in Its essential integrity, no accumulation of flesh and matter, no dweller on earth or in the heavens—so perfect Its purity—far above all such things in that they are non-essential, composite, not primal but descending from This?

Beholding this Being—the Choragos [Leader of the Chorus, ed.] of all Existence, the Self-Intent that ever gives forth and never takes—resting rapt, in the vision and possession of so lofty a loveliness, growing to Its likeness, what Beauty can the soul yet lack? For This, the Beauty supreme, the absolute, and the primal, fashions Its lovers to Beauty and makes them also worthy of love.

And for This, the sternest and the uttermost combat is set before the Souls; all our labor is for This, lest we be left without part in this noblest vision, which to attain is to be blessed in the blissful sight, which to fail is to fail utterly.

For not he that has failed of the joy that is in colour or in visible forms, not he that has failed of power or of honoring or of kingdom has failed, but only he that has failed of only This, for Whose winning he should renounce kingdoms and command over earth and ocean and sky, if only, spurning the world of sense from beneath his feet, and straining to This, he may see.

8. But what must we do? How lies the path? How come to vision of the inaccessible Beauty, dwelling as if in consecrated precincts, apart from the common ways where all may see, even the profane?

He that has the strength, let him arise and withdraw into himself, foregoing all that is known by the eyes, turning away for ever from the material beauty that once made his joy. When he perceives those shapes of grace that show in body, let him not pursue: he must know them for copies, vestiges, shadows, and hasten away towards That they tell of. For if anyone follow what is like a beautiful shape playing over water—is there not a myth telling in symbol of such a dupe, how he sank into the depths of the current and was swept away to nothingness? So too, one that is held by material beauty and will not break free shall be precipitated, not in body but in Soul, down to the dark depths loathed of the Intellective-Being, where, blind even in the Lower-World, he shall have commerce only with shadows, there as here.

"Let us flee then to the beloved Fatherland:" this is the soundest counsel. But what is this flight? How are we to gain the open sea? For Odysseus is surely a parable to us when he commands the flight from the sorceries of Circe or Calypso—not content to linger for all the pleasure offered to his eyes and all the delight of sense filling his days.

The Fatherland to us is There whence we have come, and There is The Father.

What then is our course, what the manner of our flight? This is not a journey for the feet; the feet bring us only from land to land; nor need you think of coach or ship to carry you away; all this order of things you must set aside and refuse to see: you must close the eyes and call instead upon another vision which is to be waked within you, a vision, the birthright of all, which few turn to use.

9. And this inner vision, what is its operation?

Newly awakened it is all too feeble to bear the ultimate splendor. Therefore the Soul must be trained—to the habit of remarking, first, all noble pursuits, then the works of beauty produced not by the labor of the arts but by the virtue of men known for their goodness: lastly, you must search the souls of those that have shaped these beautiful forms.

But how are you to see into a virtuous soul and know its loveliness?

Withdraw into yourself and look. And if you do not find yourself beautiful yet, act as does the creator of a statue that is to be made beautiful: he cuts away here, he smoothes there, he makes this line lighter, this other purer, until a lovely face has grown upon his work. So do you also: cut away all that is excessive, straighten all that is crooked, bring light to all that is overcast, labor to make all one glow of beauty and never cease chiselling your statue, until there shall shine out on you from it the godlike splendor of virtue, until you shall see the perfect goodness surely established in the stainless shrine.

When you know that you have become this perfect work, when you are self-gathered in the purity of your being, nothing from without clinging to the authentic man, when you find yourself wholly true to your essential nature, wholly that only veritable Light which is not measured by space, not narrowed to any circumscribed form nor again diffused as a thing void of term, but ever unmeasurable as something greater than all measure and more than all quantity—when you perceive that you have grown to this, you are now become very vision: now call up all your confidence, strike forward yet a step—you need a guide no longer—strain and see.

This is the only eye that sees the might Beauty. If the eye that adventures the vision be dimmed by vice, or weak, and unable in its cowardly blenching to see the uttermost brightness, then it sees nothing even though another point to what lies plain to sight before it. To any vision must be brought an eye adapted to what is to be seen, and having some likeness to it. Never did eye see the sun unless it had first become sunlike, and never can the soul have vision of the First Beauty unless itself be beautiful.

Therefore, first let each become godlike and each beautiful who cares to see God and Beauty. So, mounting, the Soul will come first to the Intellectual-Principle and survey all the beautiful Ideas in the Supreme and will avow that this is Beauty, that the Ideas are Beauty. For by their efficacy comes all Beauty else, but the offspring and essence of the Intellectual-Being. What is beyond the Intellectual-Principle we affirm to be the nature of Good radiating Beauty before it. So that, treating the Intellectual-Kosmos as one, the first is Beautiful: if we make distinction there, the Realm of Ideas constitutes the Beauty of the Intellectual Sphere; and The Good, which lies beyond, is the Fountain at once and Principle of Beauty: the Primal Good and the Primal Beauty have the one dwelling-place and, thus, always, Beauty's seat is There.

ENNEAD V.1

FIRST TRACTATE

THE THREE INITIAL HYPOSTASES

1. What can it be that has brought the souls to forget the father, God, and, though members of the Divine and entirely of that world, to ignore at once themselves and It?

The evil that has overtaken them has its source in self-will, in the entry into the sphere of process, and in the primal differentiation with the desire for self ownership. They conceived a pleasure in this freedom and largely indulged their own motion; thus they were hurried down the wrong path, and in the end, drifting further and further, they came to lose even the thought of their origin in the Divine. A child wrenched young from home and brought up during many years at a distance will fail in knowledge of its father and of itself: the souls, in the same way, no longer discern either the divinity or their own nature; ignorance of their rank brings self-depreciation; they misplace their respect, honouring everything more than themselves; all their awe and admiration is for the alien, and, clinging to this, they have broken apart, as far as a soul may, and they make light of what they have deserted; their regard for the mundane and their disregard of themselves bring about their utter ignoring of the divine.

Admiring pursuit of the external is a confession of inferiority; and nothing thus holding itself inferior to things that rise and perish, nothing counting itself less honourable and less enduring than all else it admires could ever form any notion of either the nature or the power of God.

A double discipline must be applied if human beings in this pass are to be reclaimed, and brought back to their origins, lifted once more towards the Supreme and One and First.

There is the method, which we amply exhibit elsewhere, declaring the dishonour of the objects which the Soul holds here in honour; the second teaches or recalls to the soul its race and worth; this latter is the leading truth, and, clearly brought out, is the evidence of the other.

It must occupy us now for it bears closely upon our enquiry to which it is the natural preliminary: the seeker is soul and it must start from a true notion of the nature and quality by which soul may undertake the search; it must study itself in order to learn whether it has the faculty for the enquiry, the eye for the object proposed, whether in fact we ought to seek; for if the object is alien the search must be futile, while if there is relationship the solution of our problem is at once desirable and possible.

2. Let every soul recall, then, at the outset the truth that soul is the author of all living things, that it has breathed the life into them all, whatever is nourished by earth and sea, all the creatures of the air, the divine stars in the sky; it is the maker of the sun; itself formed and ordered this vast heaven and conducts all that rhythmic motion; and it is a principle distinct from all these to which it gives law and movement and life, and it must of necessity be more honourable than they, for they gather or dissolve as soul brings them life or abandons them, but soul, since it never can abandon itself, is of eternal being.

How life was purveyed to the universe of things and to the separate beings in it may be thus conceived:

That great soul must stand pictured before another soul, one not mean, a soul that has become worthy to look, emancipate from the lure, from all that binds its fellows in bewitchment, holding itself in quietude. Let not merely the enveloping body be at peace, body's turmoil stilled, but all that lies around, earth at peace, and sea at peace, and air and the very heavens. Into that heaven, all at rest, let the great soul be conceived to roll inward at every point, penetrating, permeating, from all sides pouring in its light. As the rays of the sun throwing their brilliance upon a lowering cloud make it gleam all gold, so the soul entering the material expanse of the heavens has given life, has given immortality: what was abject it has lifted up; and the heavenly system, moved now in endless motion by the soul that leads it in wisdom, has become a living and a blessed thing; the soul domiciled within, it takes worth where, before the

soul, it was stark body—clay and water—or, rather, the blankness of Matter, the absence of Being, and, as an author says, "the execration of the Gods."

The Soul's nature and power will be brought out more clearly, more brilliantly, if we consider next how it envelops the heavenly system and guides all to its purposes: for it has bestowed itself upon all that huge expanse so that every interval, small and great alike, all has been ensouled.

The material body is made up of parts, each holding its own place, some in mutual opposition and others variously interdependent; the soul is in no such condition; it is not whittled down so that life tells of a part of the soul and springs where some such separate portion impinges; each separate life lives by the soul entire, omnipresent in the likeness of the engendering father, entire in unity and entire in diffused variety. By the power of the soul the manifold and diverse heavenly system is a unit: through soul this universe is a God: and the sun is a God because it is ensouled; so too the stars: and whatsoever we ourselves may be, it is all in virtue of soul; for "dead is viler than dung."

This, by which the gods are divine, must be the oldest God of them all: and our own soul is of that same Ideal nature, so that to consider it, purified, freed from all accruement, is to recognise in ourselves that same value which we have found soul to be, honourable above all that is bodily. For what is body but earth, and, taking fire itself, what [but soul] is its burning power? So it is with all the compounds of earth and fire, even with water and air added to them.

If, then, it is the presence of soul that brings worth, how can a man slight himself and run after other things? You honour the Soul elsewhere; honour then yourself.

3. The Soul once seen to be thus precious, thus divine, you may hold the faith that by its possession you are already nearing God: in the strength of this power make upwards towards Him: at no great distance you must attain: there is not much between.

But over this divine, there is still a diviner: grasp the upward neighbour of the soul, its prior and source.

Soul, for all the worth we have shown to belong to it, is yet a secondary, an image of the Intellectual-Principle: reason uttered is an image of the reason stored within the soul, and in the same way soul is an utterance of the Intellectual-Principle: it is even the total of its activity, the entire stream of life sent forth by that Principle to the production of further being; it is the forthgoing heat of a fire which has also heat essentially inherent. But within the Supreme we must see energy not as an overflow but in the double aspect of integral inherence with the establishment of a new being. Sprung, in other words, from the Intellectual-Principle, Soul is intellective, but with an intellection operation by the method of reasonings: for its perfecting it must look to that Divine Mind, which may be thought of as a father watching over the development of his child born imperfect in comparison with himself.

Thus its substantial existence comes from the Intellectual-Principle; and the Reason within it becomes Act in virtue of its contemplation of that prior; for its thought and act are its own intimate possession when it looks to the Supreme Intelligence; those only are soul-acts which are of this intellective nature and are determined by its own character; all that is less noble is foreign [traceable to Matter] and is accidental to the soul in the course of its peculiar task.

In two ways, then, the Intellectual-Principle enhances the divine quality of the soul, as father and as immanent presence; nothing separates them but the fact that they are not one and the same, that there is succession, that over against a recipient there stands the ideal-form received; but this recipient, Matter to the Supreme Intelligence, is also noble as being at once informed by divine intellect and uncompounded.

What the Intellectual-Principle must be is carried in the single word that Soul, itself so great, is still inferior.

4. But there is yet another way to this knowledge:

Admiring the world of sense as we look out upon its vastness and beauty and the order of its eternal march, thinking of the gods within it, seen and hidden, and the celestial spirits and all the life of animal and plant, let us mount to its archetype, to the yet more authentic sphere: there we are to contemplate all things as members of the Intellectual—eternal in their own right, vested with a self-springing consciousness and life—and, presiding over all these, the unsoiled Intelligence and the unapproachable wisdom.

That archetypal world is the true Golden Age, age of Kronos, who is the Intellectual-Principle as being the offspring or exuberance of God. For here is contained all that is immortal: nothing here but is Divine Mind; all is God; this is the place of every soul. Here is rest unbroken: for how can that seek change, in which all is well; what need that reach to, which holds all within itself; what increase can that desire, which stands utterly achieved? All its content, thus, is perfect, that itself may be perfect throughout, as holding nothing that is less than the divine, nothing that is less than intellective. Its knowing is not by search but by possession, its blessedness inherent, not acquired; for all belongs to it eternally and it holds the authentic Eternity imitated by Time which, circling round the Soul, makes towards the new thing and passes by the old. Soul deals with thing after thing—now Socrates; now a horse: always some one entity from among beings—but the Intellectual-Principle is all and therefore its entire content is simultaneously present in that identity: this is pure being in eternal actuality; nowhere is there any future, for every then is a now; nor is there any past, for nothing there has ever ceased to be; everything has taken its stand for ever, an identity well pleased, we might say, to be as it is; and everything, in that entire content, is Intellectual-Principle and Authentic Existence; and the total of all is Intellectual-Principle entire and Being entire. Intellectual-Principle by its intellective act establishes Being, which in turn, as the object of intellection, becomes the cause of intellection and of existence to the Intellectual-Principle—though, of course, there is another cause of intellection which is also a cause to Being, both rising in a source distinct from either.

Now while these two are coalescents, having their existence in common, and are never apart, still the unity they form is two-sided; there is Intellectual-Principle as against Being, the intellectual agent as against the object of intellection; we consider the intellective act and we have the Intellectual-Principle; we think of the object of that act and we have Being.

Such difference there must be if there is to be any intellection; but similarly there must also be identity [since, in perfect knowing, subject and object are identical.]

Thus the Primals [the first "Categories"] are seen to be: Intellectual-Principle; Existence; Difference; Identity: we must include also Motion and Rest: Motion provides for the intellectual act, Rest preserves identity as Difference gives at once a Knower and a Known, for, failing this, all is one, and silent.

So too the objects of intellection [the ideal content of the Divine Mind]—identical in virtue of the self-concentration of the principle which is their common ground—must still be distinct each from another; this distinction constitutes Difference.

The Intellectual Kosmos thus a manifold, Number and Quantity arise: Quality is the specific character of each of these ideas which stand as the principles from which all else derives.

5. As a manifold, then, this God, the Intellectual-Principle, exists within the Soul here, the Soul which once for all stands linked a member of the divine, unless by a deliberate apostasy.

Bringing itself close to the divine Intellect, becoming, as it were, one with this, it seeks still further: What Being, now, has engendered this God, what is the Simplex preceding this multiple; what the cause at once of its existence and of its existing as a manifold; what the source of this Number, this Quantity?

Number, Quantity, is not primal: obviously before even duality, there must stand the unity.

The Dyad is a secondary; deriving from unity, it finds in unity the determinant needed by its native indetermination: once there is any determination, there is Number, in the sense, of course, of the real [the archetypal] Number. And the soul is such a number or quantity. For the Primals are not masses or magnitudes; all of that gross order is later, real only to the sense-thought; even in seed the effective reality is not the moist substance but the unseen—that is to say Number [as the determinant of individual being] and the Reason-Principle [of the product to be].

Thus by what we call the Number and the Dyad of that higher realm, we mean Reason Principles and the Intellectual-Principle: but while the Dyad is, as regards that sphere, undetermined—representing, as it were, the underly [or Matter] of The One—the later Number [or Quantity]—that which rises from the Dyad [Intellectual-Principle] and The One—is not

Matter to the later existents but is their forming-Idea, for all of them take shape, so to speak, from the ideas rising within this. The determination of the Dyad is brought about partly from its object—The One—and partly from itself, as is the case with all vision in the act of sight: intellection [the Act of the Dyad] is vision occupied upon The One.

6. But how and what does the Intellectual-Principle see and, especially, how has it sprung from that which is to become the object of its vision?

The mind demands the existence of these Beings, but it is still in trouble over the problem endlessly debated by the most ancient philosophers: from such a unity as we have declared The One to be, how does anything at all come into substantial existence, any multiplicity, dyad, or number? Why has the Primal not remained self-gathered so that there be none of this profusion of the manifold which we observe in existence and yet are compelled to trace to that absolute unity?

In venturing an answer, we first invoke God Himself, not in loud word but in that way of prayer which is always within our power, leaning in soul towards Him by aspiration, alone towards the alone. But if we seek the vision of that great Being within the Inner Sanctuary—self-gathered, tranquilly remote above all else—we begin by considering the images stationed at the outer precincts, or, more exactly to the moment, the first image that appears. How the Divine Mind comes into being must be explained:

Everything moving has necessarily an object towards which it advances; but since the Supreme can have no such object, we may not ascribe motion to it: anything that comes into being after it can be produced only as a consequence of its unfailing self-intention; and, of course, we dare not talk of generation in time, dealing as we are with eternal Beings: where we speak of origin in such reference, it is in the sense, merely, of cause and subordination: origin from the Supreme must not be taken to imply any movement in it: that would make the Being resulting from the movement not a second principle but a third: the Movement would be the second hypostasis.

Given this immobility in the Supreme, it can neither have yielded assent nor uttered decree nor stirred in any way towards the existence of a secondary.

What happened then? What are we to conceive as rising in the neighbourhood of that immobility?

It must be a circumradiation—produced from the Supreme but from the Supreme unaltering—and may be compared to the brilliant light encircling the sun and ceaselessly generated from that unchanging substance.

All existences, as long as they retain their character, produce—about themselves, from their essence, in virtue of the power which must be in them—some necessary, outward-facing hypostasis continuously attached to them and representing in image the engendering archetypes: thus fire gives out its heat; snow is cold not merely to itself; fragrant substances are a notable instance; for, as long as they last, something is diffused from them and perceived wherever they are present.

Again, all that is fully achieved engenders: therefore the eternally achieved engenders eternally an eternal being. At the same time, the offspring is always minor: what then are we to think of the All-Perfect but that it can produce nothing less than the very greatest that is later than itself. The greatest, later than the divine unity, must be the Divine Mind, and it must be the second of all existence, for it is that which sees The One on which alone it leans while the First has no need whatever of it. The offspring of the prior to Divine Mind can be no other than that Mind itself and thus is the loftiest being in the universe, all else following upon it—the soul, for example, being an utterance and act of the Intellectual-Principle as that is an utterance and act of The One. But in soul the utterance is obscured, for soul is an image and must look to its own original: that Principle, on the contrary, looks to the First without mediation—thus becoming what it is—and has that vision not as from a distance but as the immediate next with nothing intervening, close to the One as Soul to it.

The offspring must seek and love the begetter; and especially so when begetter and begotten are alone in their sphere; when, in addition, the begetter is the highest good, the offspring [inevitably seeking its Good] is attached by a bond of sheer necessity, separated only in being distinct.

7. We must be more explicit:

The Intellectual-Principle stands as the image of The One, firstly because there is a certain necessity that the first should have its offspring, carrying onward much of its quality, in other words that there be something in its likeness as the sun's rays tell of the sun. Yet The One is not an Intellectual-Principle; how then does it engender an Intellectual-Principle?

Simply by the fact that in its self-quest it has vision: this very seeing is the Intellectual-Principle. Any perception of the external indicates either sensation or intellection, sensation symbolized by a line, intellection by a circle . . . [corrupt passage].

Of course the divisibility belonging to the circle does not apply to the Intellectual-Principle; all, there too, is a unity, though a unity which is the potentiality of all existence.

The items of this potentiality the divine intellection brings out, so to speak, from the unity and knows them in detail, as it must if it is to be an intellectual principle.

It has besides a consciousness, as it were, within itself of this same potentiality; it knows that it can of itself beget an hypostasis and can determine its own Being by the virtue emanating from its prior; it knows that its nature is in some sense a definite part of the content of that First; that it thence derives its essence, that its strength lies there and that its Being takes perfection as a derivative and a recipient from the First. It sees that, as a member of the realm of division and part, it receives life and intellection and all else it has and is, from the undivided and part-less, since that First is no member of existence, but can be the source of all on condition only of being held down by no one distinctive shape but remaining the undeflected unity.

And so the First is not a thing among the things contained by the Intellectual-Principle though the source of all. In virtue of this source, things of the later order are essential beings; for from that fact there is determination; each has its form: what has being cannot be envisaged as outside of limit; the nature must be held fast by boundary and fixity; though to the Intellectual Beings this fixity is no more than determination and form, the foundations of their substantial existence.

A being of this quality, like the Intellectual-Principle, must be felt to be worthy of the all-pure: it could not derive from any other than from the first principle of all; as it comes into existence, all other beings must be simultaneously engendered—all the beauty of the Ideas, all the Gods of the Intellectual realm. And it still remains pregnant with this offspring; for it has, so to speak, drawn all within itself again, holding them lest they fall away towards Matter to be "brought up in the House of Rhea" [in the realm of flux]. This is the meaning hidden in the Mysteries, and in the Myths of the gods: Kronos, as the wisest, exists before Zeus; he must absorb his offspring that, full within himself, he may be also an Intellectual-Principle manifest in some product of his plenty; afterwards, the myth proceeds, Kronos engenders Zeus, who already exists as the [necessary and eternal] outcome of the plenty there; in other words the offspring of the Divine Intellect, perfect within itself, is Soul [the life-principle carrying forward the Ideas in the Divine Mind].

Now, even in the Divine the engendered could not be the very highest; it must be a lesser, an image; it will be undetermined, as the Divine is, but will receive determination, and, so to speak, its shaping idea, from the progenitor.

Yet any offspring of the Intellectual-Principle must be a Reason-Principle; the thought of the Divine Mind must be a substantial existence: such then is that [Soul] which circles about the Divine Mind, its light, its image inseparably attached to it: on the upper level united with it, filled from it, enjoying it, participant in its nature, intellective with it, but on the lower level in contact with the realm beneath itself, or, rather, generating in turn an offspring which must lie beneath; of this lower we will treat later; so far we deal still with the Divine.

8. This is the explanation of Plato's Triplicity, in the passage where he names as the Primals the Beings gathered about the King of All, and establishes a Secondary containing the Secondaries, and a Third containing the Tertiaries.

He teaches, also, that there is an author of the Cause, that is of the Intellectual-Principle, which to him is the Creator who made the Soul, as he tells us, in the famous mixing bowl. This author of the causing principle, of the divine mind, is to him the Good, that which transcends the Intellectual-Principle and transcends Being: often too he uses the term "The Idea" to indicate Being and the Divine Mind. Thus

Plato knows the order of generation—from the Good, the Intellectual-Principle; from the Intellectual-Principle, the Soul. These teachings are, therefore, no novelties, no inventions of today, but long since stated, if not stressed; our doctrine here is the explanation of an earlier and can show the antiquity of these opinions on the testimony of Plato himself.

Earlier, Parmenides made some approach to the doctrine in identifying Being with Intellectual-Principle while separating Real Being from the realm of sense.

"Knowing and Being are one thing" he says, and this unity is to him motionless in spite of the intellection he attributes to it: to preserve its unchanging identity he excludes all bodily movement from it; and he compares it to a huge sphere in that it holds and envelops all existence and that its intellection is not an outgoing act but internal. Still, with all his affirmation of unity, his own writings lay him open to the reproach that his unity turns out to be a multiplicity.

The Platonic Parmenides is more exact; the distinction is made between the Primal One, a strictly pure Unity, and a secondary One which is a One-Many and a third which is a One-and-many; thus he too is in accordance with our thesis of the Three Kinds.

9. Anaxagoras, again, in his assertion of a Mind pure and unmixed, affirms a simplex First and a sundered One, though writing long ago he failed in precision.

Heraclitus, with his sense of bodily forms as things of ceaseless process and passage, knows the One as eternal and intellectual.

In Empedocles, similarly, we have a dividing principle, "Strife," set against "Friendship"—which is The One and is to him bodiless, while the elements represent Matter.

Later there is Aristotle; he begins by making the First transcendent and intellective but cancels that primacy by supposing it to have self-intellection. Further he affirms a multitude of other intellective beings—as many indeed as there are orbs in the heavens; one such principle as in—over to every orb—and thus his account of the Intellectual Realm differs from Plato's and, failing reason, he brings in necessity; though whatever reasons he had alleged there would always have been the objection that it would be more reasonable that all the spheres, as contributory to one system, should look to a unity, to the First.

We are obliged also to ask whether to Aristotle's mind all Intellectual Beings spring from one, and that one their First; or whether the Principles in the Intellectual are many.

If from one, then clearly the Intellectual system will be analogous to that of the universe of sense—sphere encircling sphere, with one, the outermost, dominating all—the First [in the Intellectual] will envelop the entire scheme and will be an Intellectual [or Archetypal] Kosmos; and as in our universe the spheres are not empty but the first sphere is thick with stars and none without them, so, in the Intellectual Kosmos, those principles of Movement will envelop a multitude of Beings, and that world will be the realm of the greater reality.

If on the contrary each is a principle, then the effective powers become a matter of chance; under what compulsion are they to hold together and act with one mind towards that work of unity, the harmony of the entire heavenly system? Again what can make it necessary that the material bodies of the heavenly system be equal in number to the Intellectual moving principles, and how can these incorporeal Beings be numerically many when there is no Matter to serve as the basis of difference?

For these reasons the ancient philosophers that ranged themselves most closely to the school of Pythagoras and of his later followers and to that of Pherekudes, have insisted upon this Nature, some developing the subject in their writings while others treated of it merely in unwritten discourses, some no doubt ignoring it entirely.

10. We have shown the inevitability of certain convictions as to the scheme of things:

There exists a Principle which transcends Being; this is The One, whose nature we have sought to establish in so far as such matters lend themselves to proof. Upon The One follows immediately the Principle which is at once Being and the Intellectual-Principle. Third comes the Principle, Soul.

Now just as these three exist for the system of Nature, so, we must hold, they exist for ourselves. I am not speaking of the material order—all that is separable—but of what lies beyond the sense realm in the same way as the Primals are beyond all the heavens; I mean the corresponding aspect of man, what Plato calls the Interior Man.

Thus our soul, too, is a divine thing, belonging to another order than sense; such is all that holds the rank of soul, but [above the life-principle] there is the soul perfected as containing Intellectual-Principle with its double phase, reasoning and giving the power to reason. The reasoning phase of the soul, needing no bodily organ for its thinking but maintaining, in purity, its distinctive Act that its thought may be uncontaminated—this we cannot err in placing, separate and not mingled into body, within the first Intellectual. We may not seek any point of space in which to seat it; it must be set outside of all space: its distinct quality, its separateness, its immateriality, demand that it be a thing alone, untouched by all of the bodily order. This is why we read of the universe that the Demiurge cast the soul around it from without—understand that phase of soul which is permanently seated in the Intellectual—and of ourselves that the charioteer's head reaches upwards towards the heights.

The admonition to sever soul from body is not, of course, to be understood spatially—that separation stands made in Nature—the reference is to holding our rank, to use of our thinking, to an attitude of alienation from the body in the effort to lead up and attach to the over-world, equally with the other, that phase of soul seated here and, alone, having to do with body, creating, moulding, spending its care upon it.

11. Since there is a Soul which reasons upon the right and good—for reasoning is an enquiry into the rightness and goodness of this rather than that—there must exist some permanent Right, the source and foundation of this reasoning in our soul; how, else, could any such discussion be held? Further, since the soul's attention to these matters is intermittent, there must be within us an Intellectual-Principle acquainted with that Right not by momentary act but in permanent possession. Similarly there must be also the principle of this principle, its cause, God. This Highest cannot be divided and allotted, must remain intangible but not bound to space, it may be present at many points, wheresoever there is anything capable of

accepting one of its manifestations; thus a centre is an independent unity; everything within the circle has its term at the centre; and to the centre the radii bring each their own. Within our nature is such a centre by which we grasp and are linked and held; and those of us are firmly in the Supreme whose collective tendency is There.

12. Possessed of such powers, how does it happen that we do not lay hold of them, but for the most part, let these high activities go idle—some, even, of us never bringing them in any degree to effect?

The answer is that all the Divine Beings are unceasingly about their own act, the Intellectual-Principle and its Prior always self-intent; and so, too, the soul maintains its unfailing movement; for not all that passes in the soul is, by that fact, perceptible; we know just as much as impinges upon the faculty of sense. Any activity not transmitted to the sensitive faculty has not traversed the entire soul: we remain unaware because the human being includes sense-perception; man is not merely a part [the higher part] of the soul but the total.

None the less every being of the order of soul is in continuous activity as long as life holds, continuously executing to itself its characteristic act: knowledge of the act depends upon transmission and perception. If there is to be perception of what is thus present, we must turn the perceptive faculty inward and hold it to attention there. Hoping to hear a desired voice, we let all others pass and are alert for the coming at last of that most welcome of sounds: so here, we must let the hearings of sense go by, save for sheer necessity, and keep the soul's perception bright and quick to the sounds from above.

REVIEW QUESTIONS

1. In what way is Plotinus a neo-Platonist? How did he further develop Plato's views?
2. For Plotinus, what is the nature of the soul?
3. What is the highest goal of the soul, and how is it reached?
4. According to Plotinus, what is self-control, courage, magnanimity, and wisdom?
5. What is the role of the intellect in the spiritual life?

Part Two

THE
MEDIEVAL
PERIOD

8

AUGUSTINE

Aurelius Augustinus (354–430), bishop of Hippo (now Annaba, Algeria), is perhaps the most influential philosopher between Aristotle and Aquinas. As a pagan rhetoretician, his career took him from his native Carthage in North Africa to Italy, first to Rome and then to Milan. After having been under the spell of the Manichaean religion, he became increasingly dissatisfied with its inability to answer philosophical problems. In 385 he was converted to Christianity and soon identified with a neo-Platonic version of the faith. In 395 he became bishop of Hippo. His numerous works include *On Free Will*, from which our first selection is taken, *Confessions*, from which our second selection is taken, and *The City of God*, from which our third selection is taken.

In *On Free Will*, the chief ethical problem for Augustine is the problem of Evil. What is its definition, source, and effect on human nature, and how is it to be remedied? Implicit in his thinking is Epicurus's puzzle: If God is willing to prevent evil and suffering but is unable so, then He is not omnipotent, and hence not worthy of worship. If God is able to prevent evil and suffering but unwilling, then He is not all good and still unworthy of worship. Augustine defines evil as "the absence of good." Since existence is good (since it is created by God), evil is the negative element of existence, a privation of existence. It is compared to a disease and wound (i.e., absence of health) that cease to exist when the cure comes, "for the wound or disease is not a substance, but a defect in the fleshly substance."

The source or cause of evil is the will, the falling away from the unchangeable good of a being made good but unchangeable. First, the angel Satan and all his followers fell from the high ideal, and then humanity, led by the first man, Adam, followed after. The angels and Adam were created with a will that permitted a free option between good and evil. They chose the latter and thereby limited the choice of all succeeding human beings. When the will ceases to adhere to what is above itself, its Source (God) and turns to what is lower (itself or created objects), it becomes evil, not because itself is evil, but because of the improper valuing of things.

Evil's power over man leads to ignorance of duty and lusting (*libido*) after what is hurtful, which in turn lead to error and suffering, which lead to fear. Error also leads to a false evaluation of values and virtues, which alone explains human pride or foolish joy in earthly success and goods. From these basic evils flow all other forms of misery. A just God must punish evil.

The answer to Epicurus's puzzle is that free will is a good, necessary for doing good, but, as such, it can be directed to evil (through false valuations—created things over the Creator). So it is not God's fault that man sinned and that, consequently, moral evil exists. But God does intervene and save an elect, so that the fall turns out to be a good thing for the elect (a *felix culpa*—a happy fault).

In our second reading "On Time and Eternity," Augustine reverentially ponders the paradoxes of time: "Provided that no one asks me, I know [what time is]. If I want to explain it, I do not know"; since the past no longer exists and the future is not yet, how can the time be measured? Normally we can only measure what exists, but only the fleeting present exists. But we cannot measure the present, since it is past as soon as we attempt to measure it. Juxtaposed with temporal extension is God's eternity, which never changes.

In our third selection from *The City of God*, Augustine responds to the charge that Christianity is responsible for the fall of the Roman Empire under Alaric in 412 and develops a Christian political philosophy.

FOR FURTHER READING

Armstrong, A. H., ed. *The Cambridge History of Later Greek and Early Medieval Philosophy* (Cambridge University Press, 1967), ch. 21–7.

Brown, Peter. *Augustine of Hippo* (University of California Press, 1967).

Chadwick, Henry. *Augustine* (Oxford University Press, 1986).

D'Arcy, M. C., ed. *Augustine: A Collection of Critical Essays* (Meridian, 1957).

Gilson, Etienne. *The Christian Philosophy of Saint Augustine*, trans. L. Lynch (Random House, 1960).

Kirwin, Christopher. *Augustine* (Routledge, 1989).

Meagher, E. *An Introduction to Augustine* (New York University Press, 1978).

Nash, Ronald. *The Light of the Mind: St. Augustine's Theory of Knowledge* (University of Kentucky Press, 1969).

ON FREE WILL

BOOK I

i, 1. *Evodius.*—Tell me, pray, whether God be not the author of evil. *Augustine.*—I shall tell you, if you will make it clear what you mean by evil in your question. For we are wont to use the word evil in two senses: the evil a man has done, and the evil he has suffered. *Evodius.*—I want to know about both kinds of evil. *Augustine.*—If you know or believe that God is good (and we may not think otherwise) he cannot do evil. Again, if we confess that God is just (and to deny that is sacrilegious) he gives rewards to the good just as he gives punishments to the wicked, but of course these punishments are evil to those who suffer them. Hence if no one is penalized unjustly—and this we must believe, seeing we believe that the universe is governed by divine providence—God is not the author of the evil a man does though he is the author of the evil a man suffers. *Ev.*—Is there then some other author of the kind of evil which we do not attribute to the action of God? *Aug.*—There certainly is, for we cannot say that it happens without an author. But if you ask who that is I cannot tell you. For there is no one single author. Every evil man is the author of his evil deeds. If you wonder how that is, consider what we have just said: evil deeds are punished by the justice of God. They would not be justly punished unless they were done voluntarily.

2. *Ev.*—I do not know whether anyone sins without being taught to do evil. If that is true I ask from whom have we learned to do wrong. *Aug.*—Is learning a good thing? *Ev.*—Who would venture to say it was a bad thing? *Aug.*—Perhaps it is neither good nor bad? *Ev.*—I think it is a good thing. *Aug.*— Quite right, at any rate if learning gives and stirs up knowledge, and if it is the only path to knowledge. Don't you agree that this is so? *Ev.*—I think that nothing but good is learned by education. *Aug.*—Yet possibly evil is also learned in this way, for learning [*disciplina*] is derived from the verb "to learn" *discere.* *Ev.*—How, then, are evils committed by a man if they are not learned? *Aug.*—Possibly because he turns away from learning and stands apart from it. However that may be, it is at least manifest that, since learning is good, evil cannot be learned. If it is learned, it must be a part of education, and education will not be good. But, as you yourself admit, it is good. Evil, therefore, is not learned, and it is vain to ask from whom we have learned to do evil. Or, if indeed evil is learned, that can only be in the sense that we learn to avoid deeds which ought not to be done. Hence to do evil is nothing but to stray away from education.

3. *Ev.*—I think there must be two kinds of education, one by which we learn to do well and one by which we learn to do evil. When you asked whether education was a good thing I replied that it was, because my enthusiasm for the good made me think of the education that teaches to do good. Now I have a suspicion that there is another kind, which I have no doubt is a bad thing. *Aug.*—At any rate you regard intelligence as entirely a good thing? *Ev.*—So good indeed that a man can have nothing better. I should never say that intelligence can possibly be evil. *Aug.*—If a man has been taught something but does not understand it, could you regard him as learned? *Ev.*—Certainly not. *Aug.*—If intelligence is entirely good and is the necessary result of learning, every one who learns does well and also arrives at intelligence, and so again does well. Whoever asks for the cause of our learning anything simply asks for the cause of our doing well. So do not look for any teacher of evil. If he is evil he is not a teacher. If he is a teacher he is not evil.

ii, 4. *Ev.*—Since you force me to agree that we are not taught to do evil, tell me the cause why we do evil. *Aug.*—That is a question that gave me great trouble when I was a young man. It wearied me and drove me into the arms of heretics. By that accident I was so afflicted and overwhelmed with such masses of vain fables that, had not my love of finding the truth obtained divine aid, I could never have found

Reprinted from *Augustine: Earlier Writings*, edited and translated by John H. S. Burleigh, 1953, used by permission of SCM Press and Westminster John Knox Press.

subjective — by time & circumstance

my way out or breathed the pure air of free inquiry. But I took the greatest pains to find deliverance from that quandary, so in discoursing with you I shall follow the order which led to my own deliverance. May God grant his aid, and give us to understand what we have first believed. The steps are laid down by the prophet who says: "Unless ye believe ye shall not understand" (Isa. 7:9 LXX). We know well that we must hold fast to that. We believe that all things which exist are from one God; and yet God is not the author of sins. The difficulty for the mind is this. If sins originate with souls which God has created, and which therefore have their origin from God, how are sins not to be charged against God at least mediately?

5. *Ev.*—Now you have plainly stated the problem that was troubling my mind, and which impelled me to ask my question. *Aug.*—Have courage, and hold to your faith. You cannot do better than believe even when you do not know the reason for your faith. To think the best of God is the truest foundation of piety. And to think the best of God means to believe that he is omnipotent and absolutely unchangeable, that he is the Creator of all good things, being himself more excellent than them all; that he is the most just ruler of all that he has created; that he had no assistance in creating as if he were not sufficient in himself. Hence he created all things of nothing. One, however, he did not create, but begat, One equal to himself, whom we call the only Son of God, whom we endeavour to describe more fully when we call him the Power and Wisdom of God. By him he made all things which are made of nothing. Having stated these articles of our faith let us strive with God's help to reach understanding of the problem which you have raised, and in this fashion.

iii, 6. You ask for the cause of our doing evil. First we must discuss what doing evil is. Tell me what you think about this. If you cannot put the whole thing briefly in a few words, at least indicate your opinion by naming some evil deeds one by one. *Ev.*—Adultery, homicide, sacrilege. I need mention no more. To enumerate all the others neither time nor my memory would be sufficient. But no one doubts that those I have mentioned are examples of evil deeds. *Aug.*—Tell me now why you think adultery is evil. Is it because it is forbidden by law? *Ev.*—It is not evil because it is forbidden by law. It is forbidden by law because it is evil. *Aug.*—Suppose someone were to press us, stressing the delights of adultery and asking why it is evil and why we think it worthy of condemnation. Do you think that people who wanted not only to believe that adultery is evil but also to know the reason why it is so, would be driven to appeal to the authority of the law? You and I believe without the slightest hesitation that adultery is evil, and I declare that all peoples and nations must believe that too. But our present endeavour is to obtain intelligent knowledge and assurance of what we have accepted in faith. Give this matter your best consideration and tell me the reason why you know that adultery is evil. *Ev.*—I know it is evil because I should not wish it to be committed with my own wife. Whoever does to another what he would not have done to himself does evil. *Aug.*—Suppose someone offered his wife to another, being willing that she should be corrupted by him in return for a similar licence allowed him with the other's wife. Would he have done no evil? *Ev.*—Far from that. He would have done great evil. *Aug.*—And yet his sin does not come under your general rule, for he does not do what he would not have done to him. You must find another reason to prove that adultery is evil.

7. *Ev.*—I think it evil because I have often seen men condemned on this charge. *Aug.*—But are not men frequently condemned for righteous deeds? Without going to other books, think of scripture history which excels all other books because it has divine authority. If we decide that condemnation is a certain indication of evil-doing, what an evil opinion we must adopt of the apostles and martyrs, for they were all thought worthy of condemnation for their faith. If whatever is condemned is evil, it was evil in those days to believe in Christ and to confess the Christian faith. But if everything is not evil which is condemned you must find another reason for teaching that adultery is evil. *Ev.*—I have no reply to make.

8. *Aug.*—Possibly the evil thing in adultery is lust. So long as you look for the evil in the outward act you discover difficulties. But when you understand that the evil lies in lust it becomes clear that even if a man finds no opportunity to lie with the wife of another but shows that he desires to do so and would do it if he got the chance, he is no less

guilty than if he were caught in the act. *Ev.*—Nothing is more manifest; and I now see that there is no need of lengthy argument to persuade me that the same is true of homicide, sacrilege and all other sins. For it is clear that lust alone dominates the whole realm of evil-doing. →"*libido*"

BOOK II

i, 1. *Evodius.*—Now explain to me, if it can be done, why God has given man free choice in willing, for if he had not received that freedom he would not have been able to sin. *Augustine.*—You hold it to be certainly known that it is God who has given man this power which you think ought not to have been given. *Ev.*—My impression is that we learned in the earlier book both that we have free will, and that our sinning is due to it. *Aug.*—I too remember that that became manifest to us. But now my question was whether you know that God gave us this power which we clearly have and which is the cause of our sinning. *Ev.*—No one else could have done so, I think. For we derive our origin from him, and from him we merit punishment or reward according as we sin or act rightly. *Aug.*—Here is another thing I desire to know. Do you know this quite distinctly, or do you merely believe it, without knowing it, because you allow yourself to be influenced by authority? *Ev.*—Undoubtedly I was first brought to believe this on the ground of authority. But what can be more true than to say that every good thing is from God, that justice is entirely good, and that it is just that sinners should be punished and well-doers rewarded. Hence it follows that it is by God that sinners are made unhappy and well-doers happy.

2. *Aug.*—I am not objecting: but I ask the question: how do you know that we derive our origin from God? You have not explained this though you have explained how we merit punishment or reward at his hand. *Ev.*—If it is accepted that God punishes sins, as it must be if it is true that all justice has its source in him, this alone would prove that we derive our origin from him. No doubt it is the characteristic of goodness to confer benefits on strangers, but it is not similarly the mark of justice to punish sins in those who are not under its immediate jurisdiction. Hence it is clear that we belong to him because

he is not only most kind in conferring benefits upon us, but also most just in his punishments. Moreover, from the statement I made and you accepted, that every good thing comes from God, it can be known that man also comes from God. For man, in so far as he is man, is good because he can live aright if he chooses to do so.

3. *Aug.*—Clearly if this is so, the problem you have posed is solved. If man is good, and if he would not be able to act rightly except by willing to do so, he ought to have free will because without it he would not be able to act rightly. Because he also sins through having free will, we are not to believe that God gave it to him for that purpose. It is, therefore, a sufficient reason why he ought to have been given it, that without it man could not live aright. That it was given for this purpose can be understood from this fact. If anyone uses his free will in order to sin, God punishes him. That would be unjust unless the will was free not only to live aright but also to sin. How could he be justly punished who uses his will for the purpose for which it was given? Now when God punishes a sinner what else do you suppose he will say to him than "Why did you not use your free will for the purpose for which I gave it to you, that is, in order to do right?" Justice is praised as a good thing because it condemns sins and honours righteous actions. How could that be done if man had not free will? An action would be neither sinful nor righteous unless it were done voluntarily. For the same reason both punishment and reward would be unjust, if man did not have free will. But in punishing and in rewarding there must have been justice since justice is one of the good things which come from God. God, therefore, must have given and ought to have given man free will.

ii, 4. *Ev.*—I admit now that God has given us free will. But don't you think, pray, that, if it was given for the purpose of well-doing, it ought not to have been possible to convert it to sinful uses? Justice itself was given to man so that he might live rightly, and it is not possible for anyone to live an evil life by means of justice. So no one ought to be able to sin voluntarily if free will was given that we might live aright. *Aug.*—God will, I hope, give me ability to answer you, or rather will give you the ability to answer your own question. Truth, which is the best master of all, will inwardly teach us both alike. But

I wish you would tell me this: I asked you whether you know with perfect certainty that God has given us free will and you replied that you did. Now if we allow that God gave it, ought we to say that he ought not to have given it? If it is uncertain whether he gave it, we rightly ask whether it was good that it was given. If then we find that it was good, we find also that it was given by him who bestows all good things on men. If, however, we find that it was not a good thing we know that it was not given by him whom it is impious to accuse. If it is certain that he has given it, we ought to confess that, however it was given, it was rightly given. We may not say that it ought not to have been given or that it ought to have been given in some other way. If he has given it his action cannot in any way be rightly blamed.

5. *Ev.*—I believe all that unshakably. Nevertheless, because I do not know it, let us inquire as if it were all uncertain. I see that because it is uncertain whether free will was given that men might do right since by it we can also sin, another uncertainty arises, namely whether free will ought to have been given to us. If it is uncertain that it was given that we should act righteously, it is also uncertain that it ought to have been given at all. Hence it will also be uncertain whether it was God who gave it. If it is uncertain that it ought to have been given, it is uncertain that it was given by him whom it is impious to believe has given anything which ought not to have been given. *Aug.*—At any rate you are quite certain that God exists. *Ev.*—I firmly believe it, but I do not know it. *Aug.*—We read in Scripture: "The fool hath said in his heart: there is no God" (Ps. 52:18). If such a fool were to say to you there is no God, and would not believe as you do, but wanted to know whether what you believe is true, would you simply go away and leave him, or would you think it your duty somehow to try to persuade him that what you believe is true, especially if he were really eager to know and not merely to argue obstinately? *Ev.*—Your last proviso tells me what I ought to reply to him. However absurd he might be he would assuredly agree that one ought not to dispute with an insidious and obstinate opponent about anything at all, least of all about a matter so important. He would admit that, and try to get me to believe that his inquiry was made in all good faith, and that in this matter there was

neither guile nor obstinacy in him. Then I would use an argument that ought to carry great weight with any fair-minded person. I should show him that, just as he wants his neighbour to believe him when he tells of the thoughts of his mind, which he of course knows, but which are quite concealed from his neighbour, so he ought to believe that God exists because that is taught in the books of great men who have left their testimony in writing that they lived with the Son of God, and because they have written that they saw things which could not have happened if there were no God. I should urge that he would be very foolish to blame me for believing them, when he wanted me to believe himself. And when he saw that he had no good ground for finding fault with me, he would find no reason for refusing to imitate my faith. *Aug.*—If you think the existence of God is sufficiently proved by the fact that we judge it not to be rash to believe the Scripture-writers, why don't you think we should similarly trust their authority in the matters we have begun to investigate as if they were uncertain or quite beyond our knowledge? So we should be spared much labour in investigation. *Ev.*—Yes. But we want to know and to understand what we believe.

6. *Aug.*—You remember the position we adopted at the beginning of our former discussion. We cannot deny that believing and knowing are different things, and that in matters of great importance, pertaining to divinity, we must first believe before we seek to know. Otherwise the words of the prophet would be vain, where he says: "Except ye believe ye shall not understand" (Isa. 7:9). Our Lord himself, both in his words and by his deeds, exhorted those whom he called to salvation first of all to believe. When he afterwards spoke of the gift that was to be given to believers he said, not: "This is life eternal that they may believe"; but: "This is life eternal that they may know thee, the only true God, and Jesus Christ whom thou hast sent" (John 17:3). To those who already believed he said: "Seek and ye shall find" (Matt. 7:7). He cannot be said to have found, who merely believes what he does not know. And no one is fit to find God, who does not first believe what he will afterwards learn to know. Wherefore, in obedience to the precepts of the Lord, let us press on in our inquiry. What we seek at his bidding we

shall find, as far as that can be done in this life, and by people such as we are. And he himself will demonstrate it to us. We must believe that these things are perceived and possessed by people of superior character even while they dwell on earth, and certainly, more clearly and perfectly, by all the good and pious after this life. So we must hope it will be with us, and, despising earthly and human things, we must in every way desire and love heavenly things.

BOOK III

45. God owes nothing to any man, for he gives everything gratuitously. If anyone says God owes him something for his merits, God did not even owe him existence. Nothing could be owing to one who did not yet exist. And what merit is there in turning to him from whom you derive existence, that you may be made better by him from whom you derive existence? Why do you ask him for anything as if you were demanding repayment of a debt? If you were unwilling to turn to him, the loss would not be his but yours. For without him you would be nothing, and from him you derive such existence as you have; but on condition that, unless you turn to him, you must pay him back the existence you have from him, and become, not indeed nothing, but miserable. All things owe him, first, their existence so far as they are natural things, and secondly, that they can become better if they wish, receiving additional gifts if they wish them and being what they ought to be. No man is guilty because he has not received this or that power. But because he does not do as he ought he is justly held guilty. Obligation arises if he has received free will and sufficient power.

46. No blame attaches to the Creator if any of his creatures does not do what he ought. Indeed, that the wrong-doer suffers as he ought redounds to the praise of the Creator. In the very act of blaming anyone for not doing as he ought, he is praised to whom the debt is owed. If you are praised for seeing what you ought to do, and you only see it in him who is unchangeable truth, how much more is he to be praised who has taught you what you ought to wish, has given you the power to do it, and has not allowed you to refuse to do it with impunity? If "oughtness" depends

upon what has been given, and man has been so made that he sins by necessity, then he ought to sin. So when he sins he does what he ought. But it is wicked to speak like that. No man's nature compels him to sin, nor does any other nature. No man sins when he suffers what he does not wish. If he has to suffer justly he does not sin in suffering unwillingly. He sinned in that he did something voluntarily which involved him in suffering justly what he did not wish. If he suffers unjustly, where is the sin? There is no sin in suffering something unjustly but in doing something unjustly. So, if no one is compelled to sin either by his own nature or by another, it remains that he sins by his own will. If you want to attribute his sin to the Creator you will make the sinner guiltless because he has simply obeyed the laws of the Creator. If the sinner can be rightly defended he is not a sinner, and there is no sin to attribute to the Creator. Let us then praise the Creator whether or not the sinner can be defended. If he is justly defended he is no sinner and we can therefore praise the Creator. If he cannot be defended, he is a sinner so far as he turns away from the Creator. Therefore praise the Creator. I find, therefore, no way at all, and I assert that there is none to be found, by which our sins can be ascribed to the Creator, our God. I find that he is to be praised even for sins, not only because he punishes them, but also because sin arises only when a man departs from his truth.

Evodius.—I most gladly approve all you have said, and assent with all my heart to the truth that there is no way at all of rightly ascribing our sins to our Creator. xvii, 47. But I should like to know, if possible, why those beings do not sin whom God knew beforehand would not sin, and why those others do sin whom he foresaw would sin. I do not now think that God's foreknowledge compels the one to sin and the other not to sin. But if there were no cause rational creatures would not be divided into classes as they are: those who never sin, those who continually sin, and the intermediary class of those who sometimes sin and sometimes are turned towards well-doing. What is the reason for this division? I do not want you to reply that it is the will that does it. What I want to know is what cause lies behind willing. There must be some reason why one class never wills to sin, another never lacks the will to sin, and another sometimes wills to sin and at other times does not so will. For they are all alike in nature. I seem to see that there must be some cause for this three-fold classification of rational beings according to their wills, but what it is I do not know.

48. *Augustine.*—Since will is the cause of sin, you now ask what is the cause of will. If I could find one, are you not going to ask for the cause of the cause I have found? What limit will there be to your quest, what end to inquiry and explanation? You ought not to push your inquiry deeper, for you must beware of imagining that anything can be more truly said than that which is written: "Avarice is the root of all evils" (I Tim. 6:10), that is, wanting more than is sufficient. That is sufficient which is demanded by the need of preserving any particular creature. Avarice, in Greek *philarguria*, derives its name from *argentum* [silver], because among the ancients coins were made of silver or more frequently with an admixture of silver. But avarice must be understood as connected not only with silver and money but with everything which is immoderately desired, in every case where a man wants more than is sufficient. Such avarice is cupidity, and cupidity is an evil will. An evil will therefore, is the cause of all evils. If it were according to nature it would preserve nature and not be hostile to it, and so it would not be evil. The inference is that the root of all evils is not according to nature. That is sufficient answer to all who want to accuse nature. But you ask what is the cause of this root. How then will it be the root of all evils? If it has a cause, that cause will be the root of evil. And if you find a cause, as I said, you will ask for a cause of that cause, and there will be no limit to your inquiry.

49. But what cause of willing can there be which is prior to willing? Either it is a will, in which case we have not got beyond the root of evil will. Or it is not a will, and in that case there is no sin in it. Either, then, will is itself the first cause of sin, or the first cause is without sin. Now sin is rightly imputed only to that which sins, nor is it rightly imputed unless it sins voluntarily. I do not know why you should want to inquire further, but here is a further point. If there is a cause of willing it is either just or unjust. If it is just, he who obeys it will not sin, if unjust he who does not obey it will not sin either.

xviii, 50. But it may perhaps be violent, and compel him against his will? Are we to repeat our reply over and over again? Remember how much we have spoken earlier about sin and free will. Perhaps it is difficult to commit everything to memory, but hold fast to this brief statement. Whatever be the cause of willing, if it cannot be resisted no sin results from yielding to it. If it can be resisted, and it is not yielded to, no sin results. Possibly it may deceive a man when he is off his guard? Let him then take care not to be deceived. Is the deception so great that he cannot possibly avoid it? In that case no sin results? No one commits sin in doing what there was no means of avoiding? Yes, indeed, sin does result, and that means he is able to be on his guard.

51. Nevertheless, some things are done in ignorance which are held to be wrong and worthy of correction, as we read in the divinely authoritative books. The apostle says: "I obtained mercy because I did it in ignorance" (I Tim. 1:13). And the prophet says: "Remember not the sins of my youth and of my ignorance" (Ps. 25:7). Wrong things are done by necessity when a man wills to do right and has not the power. For thus it is written: "The good that I would I do not, but the evil which I would not, that I do." Again: "To will is present with me; but how to perform that which is good I find not" (Rom. 7:18–19). And again: "The flesh lusteth against the spirit, and the spirit against the flesh; for these are contrary the one to the other, so that ye cannot do the things that ye would" (Gal. 5:17). These are the words of men emerging from deadly damnation. If this were a description of man's nature and not of the penalty of sin, his situation would not be sinful. If man has not departed from the natural state in which he was created, and which could not be made better, he is doing what he ought even when he does evil. But now man might be good if he were different. Because he is what he now is, he is not good, nor is it in his power to become good, either because he does not see what he ought to be, or, seeing it, has not the power to be what he sees he ought to be. Who can doubt that his is a penal state? Every just penalty is the penalty of sin and is called punishment. If the penalty is unjust, there is no doubt that it is, in fact, penalty, but it has been imposed on man by some unjust power that lords it over him. But it

is mad to have any doubt about the omnipotence or the justice of God. Therefore man's penalty is just and is recompense for sin. No unjust lord could have usurped dominion over man, as it were, without the knowledge of God. No one could have forced him in his weakness against his will either by terrorism or by actual affliction, so that man's punishment might be held to be unjust. It remains, therefore, that his punishment is just and comes to him because he is to be condemned.

52. It is not to be wondered at that man, through ignorance, has not the freedom of will to choose to do what he ought; or that he cannot see what he ought to do or fulfil it when he will, in face of carnal custom which, in a sense, has grown as strong, almost, as nature, because of the power of mortal succession. It is the most just penalty of sin that man should lose what he was unwilling to make a good use of, when he could have done so without difficulty if he had wished. It is just that he who, knowing what is right, does not do it should lose the capacity to know what is right, and that he who had the power to do what is right and would not should lose the power to do it when he is willing. In fact there are for every sinful soul these two penal conditions, ignorance and difficulty. From ignorance springs disgraceful error, and from difficulty comes painful effort. To approve falsehood instead of truth so as to err in spite of himself, and not to be able to refrain from the works of lust because of the pain involved in breaking away from fleshly bonds: these do not belong to the nature of man as he was created. They are the penalty of man as condemned. When we speak of the freedom of the will to do right, we are speaking of the freedom wherein man was created.

xix, 53. Here comes in the question which men, who are ready to accuse anything for their sins except themselves, are wont to cast up, murmuring amongst themselves. They say: If Adam and Eve sinned, what have we miserable creatures done to deserve to be born in the darkness of ignorance and in the toils of difficulty, that, in the first place, we should err not knowing what we ought to do, and, in the second place, that when the precepts of justice begin to be opened out to us, we should wish to obey them but by some necessity of carnal lust should not have the power? To them I reply: Keep quiet and stop murmuring against God. They might perhaps rightly complain if no man had ever been victorious over error and lust. And yet there is One present everywhere who, in many ways, by means of the creation that serves him as its Lord, calls back him who has gone astray, teaches him who believes, comforts him who has hope, exhorts the diligent, helps him who is trying and answers prayer. You are not held guilty because you are ignorant in spite of yourself, but because you neglect to seek the knowledge you do not possess. You are not held guilty because you do not use your wounded members but because you despise him who is willing to heal them. These are your own personal sins. To no man is it given to know how to seek to his advantage what to his disadvantage he does not know. He must humbly confess his weakness, so that as he seeks and makes his confession *he* may come to his aid who, in aiding, knows neither error nor difficulty.

54. All that a man does wrongfully in ignorance, and all that he cannot do rightly though he wishes, are called sins because they have their origin in the first sin of the will when it was free. These are its deserved consequences. We apply the name "tongue" not only to the member which we move in our mouth when we speak, but also to what follows from that motion, namely, words and language. Thus we speak of the Greek or the Latin tongue. So we apply the word "sin" not only to that which is properly called sin, that is, what is committed knowingly and with free will, but also to all that follows as the necessary punishment of that first sin. So we use the word "nature" in a double sense. Properly speaking, human nature means the blameless nature with which man was originally created. But we also use it in speaking of the nature with which we are born mortal, ignorant and subject to the flesh, which is really the penalty of sin. In this sense the apostle says: "We also were by nature children of wrath even as others" (Eph. 2:3).

xx, 55. As we are born from the first pair to a mortal life of ignorance and toil because they sinned and fell into a state of error, misery and death, so it most justly pleased the most high God, Governor of all things, to manifest from the beginning, from man's origin, his justice in exacting punishment, and in human history his mercy in remitting punishment. When the first man was condemned, happiness was

[handwritten marginalia: transcend — sin with Hope & God's love. 3 possible avenues for soul ① original to ② pre-exist ③ souls come in their own]

not so completely taken from him that he lost also his fecundity. Though his offspring was carnal and mortal, yet in its own way it could contribute some glory and ornament to the earth. That he should beget children better than himself would not have been equitable. But if any of Adam's race should be willing to turn to God, and so overcome the punishment which had been merited by the original turning away from God, it was fitting not only that he should not be hindered but that he should also receive divine aid. In this way also the Creator showed how easily man might have retained, if he had so willed, the nature with which he was created, because his offspring had power to transcend that in which he was born.

56. Again, if only one soul was originally created, and the souls of all men since born derive their origin from it, who can say that he did not sin when the first man sinned? If however souls are created separately in individual men as they are born, it appears not to be unreasonable but rather most appropriate and in accordance with right order that the ill desert of an earlier soul should determine the nature of those which are created afterwards, and that by its goodness a soul later created should deserve to regain the state which the earlier one had lost. There would be nothing unworthy about it if the Creator had determined to show in this way that the soul so far excelled in dignity every corporeal creature that one soul could start from the position to which another had fallen. The sinful soul reached an estate of ignorance and toil, which is rightly called penalty, because before the penalty it had been better. Even if a soul, before it sinned and even before it was born, was given a nature like that which another acquired after a guilty life, it has no small good for which to give thanks to its Creator, for even in its inchoate beginning it is better than any body however perfect. These are no mean advantages, not only to be a soul and so naturally to excel all bodies, but also to have the power with the aid of the Creator to cultivate itself, and with pious care to acquire all the virtues by which it may be liberated both from tormenting toil and from blinding ignorance. If that is so in the case of souls that are born, ignorance and toil will not be punishment for sin but a warning to improve themselves, and the beginning of their perfecting. It is no small thing to have been given, before there has been

any merit gained by any good work, the natural power to discern that wisdom is to be preferred to error and tranquillity to toil, and to know that these good things are to be reached not simply by being born but by earnestly seeking them. But if the soul will not act in this way it will rightly be held guilty of sin for not making a good use of the power it has received. Though it is born in ignorance and toilsomeness there is no necessity for it to remain in that state. Indeed it could not exist were not Almighty God the Creator of such souls. For before he was loved he made them. In love he restores them. And being loved he perfects them. To souls which do not yet exist he gives existence; and to those who love him who gives them existence he gives happiness too.

57. If, on the other hand, souls pre-exist in some secret place and are sent out to quicken and rule the bodies of individuals when they are born, their mission is to govern well the body which is born under the penalty of the sin of the first man, that is, mortality. They are to discipline it with the virtues, and subject it to an orderly and legitimate servitude, so that in due order and in the due time men may attain the place of heavenly perfection. When they enter this life and submit to wearing mortal members these souls must also undergo forgetfulness of their former existence and the labours of their present existence, with consequent ignorance and toil which in the first man were a punishment involving mortality and completing the misery of the soul. But for these souls ignorance and toil are opportunities for ministering to the restoration of the integrity of the body. The flesh coming from a sinful stock causes this ignorance and toil to infect the souls sent to it. Only in this sense are they to be called sins, and the blame for them is to be ascribed neither to the souls nor to their Creator. For he has given them power to do good in difficult duties, and has provided for them the way of faith where oblivion had brought blindness. Also and above all, he has given them the insight which every soul possesses; that it must seek to know what to its disadvantage it does not know, and that it must persevere in burdensome duties and strive to overcome the difficulty of well-doing, and implore the Creator's aid in its efforts. By the law without and by direct address to the heart within, he has commanded that effort be made, and he has pre-

pared the glory of the Blessed City for those who triumph over the devil, who with wicked persuasion overcame the first man and reduced him to his state of misery. That misery these souls undergo in lively faith in order to overcome the devil. No little glory is to be gained from the campaign to overcome the devil, waged by undergoing the punishment which he glories in having brought upon his victim, man. Whoever yields to love of the present life and takes no part in that campaign can by no means justly attribute the shame of his desertion to the command of his king. Rather the Lord of all will appoint his place with the devil, because he loved the base hire wherewith he bought his desertion.

58. But if souls existing in some place are not sent by the Lord God, but come of their own accord to inhabit bodies, it is easy to see that any ignorance or toil which is the consequence of their own choice cannot in any way be ascribed as blame to the Creator. He would be entirely without blame. If we accept the view that he himself sent souls, he did not take from them even in the state of ignorance and toil their freedom to ask and seek and endeavour, and was ever ready to give to those who ask, to demonstrate to those who seek and to open to those who knock. Similarly, on this other view, he would allow conquest over ignorance and difficulty on the part of earnest and rightminded souls to count as a crown of glory. He would not lay the ignorance or the difficulty to the charge of the negligent or of those who wished to defend their sins on the ground of their infirmity. But he would justly punish them because they would rather abide in ignorance and difficulty than reach truth and a life free from struggle by zeal in seeking and learning, and by humility in prayer and confession.

xxi, 59. Now there are these four opinions about the origin of the soul, viz., that it comes by propagation, that it is newly created with each individual who is born, that it exists somewhere beforehand and comes into the body of the newly-born either being divinely sent or gliding in of its own accord. None of these views may be rashly affirmed. Either that question, because of its obscurity and perplexity, has not been handled and illumined by catholic commentators on Holy Writ. Or, if it has been done, their writings have not come into our hands. God give us a true faith that will hold no false or unworthy opinion concerning the substance of the Creator. For by the path of piety we are wending our way towards him. If we hold any other opinion concerning him than the true one, our zeal will drive us not to beatitude but to vanity. There is no danger if we hold a wrong opinion about the creature, provided we do not hold it as if it were assured knowledge. We are not bidden to turn to the creature in order to be happy, but to the Creator himself. If we are persuaded to think otherwise of him than we ought to think or otherwise than what is true we are deceived by most deadly error. No man can reach the happy life by making for that which is not, or, if it does exist, does not make men happy.

60. That we may be able to enjoy and cleave to eternal truth in contemplation, a way out of temporalities has been prepared for our weakness, so that we may trust the past and the future so far as is sufficient for our journey towards eternal things. The discipline of faith is governed by the divine mercy, so that it may have supreme authority. Things present are perceived as transient so far as the creature is concerned. They consist in the mobility and mutability of body and soul. Of these things we cannot have any kind of knowledge unless they enter into our experience. If we are told on divine authority about the past or the future of any created thing we are to believe it without hesitation. No doubt some of this was past before we could have perceived it. Some of it has not yet reached our senses. Nevertheless we are to believe it, for it helps to strengthen our hope and call forth our love, inasmuch as it reminds us, through the ordered temporal series, that God does not neglect our liberation. If any error assumes the rôle of divine authority it is most reasonably refuted, if it is shown to hold or to affirm that there is any mutable form that is not the creation of God, or that there is any mutability in the substance of God; or if it contends that the substance of God is more or less than a Trinity. To understand that Trinity soberly and piously occupies all the watchful care of Christians, and that is the goal of every advance. Concerning the unity of the Trinity and the equality of persons and the properties of each, this is not the place to discourse. To relate some things which pertain to saving faith and which concern the

focus on future.

Lord our God, Author and Maker and Governor of all things, may give useful support to a childlike incipient purpose to rise from earthly to heavenly things. That is easy to do and it has already been done by many. But to handle the whole question so as to bring all human intelligence into the light of clear reason, as far as possible in this life, does not seem an easy task for any man's eloquence or even for any man's thought, much less ours. It is therefore not to be lightly attempted. Let us go on with what we have begun, so far as we have the permission and the help of God. All that we are told of past events concerning the creation, and all that is foretold concerning the future is to be believed without hesitation, because it helps to commend pure religion by stimulating in us sincere love to God and our neighbour. It is to be defended against unbelievers, either by wearing down their unbelief with the weight of authority, or by showing them, as far as possible, first, that it is not foolish to believe it, and, secondly, that it is foolish not to believe it. But false doctrine, not about past or future events so much as about the present and above all about unchangeable things, must be convincingly refuted by clear reasoning, so far as it is granted to us.

61. Of course when we are thinking of the series of temporal things, expectation of things to come is more important than research into things past. In the divine books also past events are narrated, but they carry with them the forecast or promise or attestation of things to come. In fact no one pays much attention to temporal prosperity or adversity when they are past. All anxiety and care are bestowed on what is hoped for in the future. By some intimate and natural mechanism of the mind things which have happened to us, after they are past, are accounted, in any reckoning of felicity and misery, as if they had never happened. What disadvantage is it to me not to know when I began to be, when I know that I exist now and do not cease to hope that I shall continue to exist? I am not so interested in the past as to dread as deadly error any false opinion I may entertain as to what actually transpired. But as to my future I direct my course, guided by the mercy of my Maker. But if I have any false belief or opinion about my future, or about him with whom I am to be for ever, I must with all my might beware of that error. Otherwise I shall not make

the necessary preparation, or I shall not be able to reach him who is the objective of my enterprise, because my outlook has been confused. If I were buying a garment it would be no disadvantage to me to have forgotten last winter, but it would be a disadvantage if I did not believe that cold weather was coming on. So it would be no disadvantage to my soul to forget anything that it may perhaps have endured, so long as it diligently observes and remembers all that may warn it to make preparation for the future. For example, it will do no harm to a man who is sailing to Rome to forget from what shore he set sail, so long as he knows all the time whither he is directing his course. It will do him no good to remember the shore from which he began his voyage, if he has made some false calculation about the port of Rome and runs upon rocks. So it is no disadvantage to me not to remember the beginning of my life, so long as I know the end where I am to find rest. Nor would any memory or guess concerning life's commencement be of any advantage to me if, holding unworthy opinions of God who is the sole end of the soul's labours, I should run upon the reefs of error.

62. What I have said is not to be taken to mean that I forbid those who have the ability to inquire whether, according to the divinely inspired Scriptures, soul is propagated from soul, or whether souls are created separately for all animate beings; whether they are sent at the divine behest from some place where they abide to animate and rule the body, or whether they insinuate themselves of their own accord. Such inquiries and discussions are justifiable if reason demands them in order to answer some necessary question, or if leisure from more necessary matters is available. I spoke as I did rather that no one in so great a problem should rashly become angry with another because he will not yield to his opinion, having grounds for hesitation based perhaps on a broader culture; or even that no one who has clear and certain understanding of these matters from Scripture should suppose that another has lost all hope for the future because he does not remember the soul's origin in the past.

xxii, 63. However that may be, whether that question is to be passed over entirely or to be deferred for later consideration, there is no obstacle preventing us from answering the question with which we are dealing at present in such a way as to make clear that by the upright, just, unshaken and changeless majesty and substance of the Creator souls pay the penalty for their own sins. These sins, as we have explained at great length, are to be ascribed to nothing but to their own wills, and no further cause for sins is to be looked for.

64. If ignorance and moral difficulty are natural to man, it is from that condition that the soul begins to progress and to advance towards knowledge and tranquillity until it reaches the perfection of the happy life. If by its own will it neglects to advance by means of good studies and piety—for the capacity to do so is not denied to it—it justly falls into a still graver state of ignorance and struggle, which is now penal, and is ranked among inferior creatures according to the appropriate and fitting government of the universe. Natural ignorance and natural impotence are not reckoned to the soul as guilt. The guilt arises because it does not eagerly pursue knowledge, and does not give adequate attention to acquiring facility in doing right. It is natural for an infant not to know how to speak and not to be able to speak. But that ignorance and inability are not only blameless according to the rules of the teachers, but are also attractive and pleasing to human feeling. In this case there is no faulty failure to acquire the power of speaking, nor, if possessed, was it lost through any fault. If we supposed that happiness was to be found in eloquence and it was thought criminal to commit a fault in speaking, as it is thought criminal to commit a fault in action, no one would put the blame on our infancy, though as infants we began to acquire eloquence. But clearly one would be deservedly blamed if by perversity of will one either remained in the infantile condition or fell back into it. In the same way, if ignorance of the truth and difficulty in doing right are natural to man, and he has to begin to rise from that condition to the happiness of wisdom and tranquillity, no one rightly blames him for the natural condition from which he started. But if he refuses to progress, or voluntarily falls back from the path of progress, he will justly and deservedly pay the penalty.

65. But his Creator is to be praised on all counts. He gave him the power to rise from such beginnings to ability to attain the chief good. He renders aid as he advances. He completes and perfects his advance. And if he sins, that is, if he refuses to rise from these beginnings to perfection or if he falls back from any progress he may have made, he imposes on him a most just condemnation according to his deserts. The soul was not created evil because it was not given all that it had power to become. All corporeal things however perfect are far inferior to the soul's beginning, though anyone who takes a sane view of things judges that they, too, are to be praised in their own kind. That the soul does not know what it should do is due to its not yet having received that gift. It will receive it if it makes a good use of what it has received. It has received the power to seek diligently and piously if it will. That it cannot instantly fulfil the duty it recognizes as duty, means that that is another gift it has not yet received. Its higher part first perceives the good it ought to do, but the slower and carnal part is not immediately brought over to that opinion. So by that very difficulty it is admonished to implore for its perfecting the aid of him whom it believes to be the author of its beginning. Hence he becomes dearer to it, because it has its existence not from its own resources but from his goodness, and by his mercy it is raised to happiness. The more it loves him from whom it derives its existence, the more surely it rests in him, and enjoys his eternity more fully. We do not rightly say of a young shoot of a tree that it is sterile, because several summers must pass before at the appointed time it reveals its fruitfulness. Why should not the Author of the soul be praised with due piety if he has given it so good a start that it may by zeal and progress reach the fruit of wisdom and justice, and has given it so much dignity as to put within its power the capacity to grow towards happiness if it will?

xxiii, 66. Against this reasoning, ignorant men are wont to repeat a calumny based upon the deaths of infants and certain bodily torments with which we often see them afflicted. They say: What need had the infant to be born if it was to die before it had acquired any merit in life? How is it to be reckoned in the future judgment, seeing that it cannot be put among the just since it performed no good works, nor among the evil because it never sinned? I reply: If you think of the all-embracing complexity of the universe, and the orderly connection of the whole creation throughout space and time, you will not believe that a man, whatsoever he may be, can be created superfluously. Why, not even the leaf of a tree is created superfluously. But it is idly superfluous to inquire about the merits of one who has done nothing to merit anything. There is no need to fear lest there be a life lived which is neither righteous nor sinful, nor that the judge will be able to pronounce sentence involving neither reward nor punishment.

67. At this point men are wont to ask what good the sacrament of Christ's Baptism can do to infants, seeing that many of them die after having been baptized but before they can know anything about it. In this case it is pious and right to believe that the infant is benefited by the faith of those who bring him to be consecrated. This is commended by the salutary authority of the Church, so that everyone may realize how beneficial to him is his faith, seeing that one man's faith can be made beneficial for another who has no faith of his own. The son of the widow of Nain could have had no advantage from any faith of his own, for, being dead, he had no faith. But his mother's faith procured him the benefit of being raised from the dead (Luke 7:11 ff.). How much more may the faith of another benefit an infant seeing that no faithlessness of its own can be imputed to it?

68. A greater complaint, and one with a show of pity about it, is often occasioned by the bodily torments which infants suffer, for by reason of their tender age they have committed no sins, at least if the souls which animate them have had no existence prior to their birth as human beings. People say: What evil have they done that they should suffer such things? As if innocence could have any merit before it has the power to do any hurt! Perhaps God is doing some good in correcting parents when their beloved children suffer pain and even death. Why should not such things happen? When they are past they will be for those who suffered them as if they never happened. And those on whose account they happened will be made better if they accept correction from temporal troubles and choose to live more righteously. Or, if they will not allow the sufferings of this life to turn their desire towards eternal life, they will be without excuse when they are punished at the last judgment. By the torments of their children parents have their hard hearts softened, their

faith exercised and their tenderness proved. Who knows what good compensation God has reserved in the secrecy of his judgments for the children themselves who, though they have not had the chance of living righteously, at least have committed no sin and yet have suffered? Not for nothing does the Church commend for honour as martyrs the children who were slain by the orders of Herod when he sought to slay the Lord Jesus Christ.

69. These casuists, who ask questions of that kind not because they want to examine them seriously but because they are loquacious and want to ventilate them, are wont also to trouble the faith of the less learned by pointing to the pains and labours of animals. What evil, they say, have the animals deserved that they suffer such woes, or what good can they hope for in having such troubles imposed on them? They say that or feel like that because they have a perverted sense of values. They are not able to see what the chief good is, and they want to have everything just as they conceive the chief good to be. They can think of no chief good except fine bodies like the celestial bodies which are not subject to corruption. And so without any sense of order they demand that the bodies of animals shall not suffer death or any corruption, as if forsooth they were not mortal, being lowly bodies, or were evil because celestial bodies are better. The pain which the animals suffer commends the vigour of the animal soul as admirable and praiseworthy after its own fashion. By animating and ruling the body of the animal it shows its desire for unity. For what is pain but a certain feeling that cannot bear division and corruption? Hence it is clearer than day that the animal soul is eager for unity in the whole body and is tenacious of unity. Neither gladly nor with indifference, but reluctantly and with obstinate resistance it meets bodily suffering which it is grieved to know destroys the unity and integrity of the body. We should never know what eagerness there is for unity in the inferior animal creation, were it not for the pain suffered by animals. And if we did not know that, we should not be made sufficiently aware that all things are framed by the supreme, sublime and ineffable unity of the Creator.

70. Indeed, if you give pious and diligent attention, every kind of creature which can come under the consideration of the human mind contributes to

our instruction, speaking by its diverse movements and feelings as in so many diverse tongues, everywhere proclaiming and insisting that the Creator is to be recognized. There is no creature that feels pain or pleasure which does not by some sort of unity attain a beauty appropriate to its own kind, or some sort of stability of nature. There is no creature sensitive to pain or pleasure which does not, simply by avoiding pain and seeking pleasure, show that it avoids its own destruction and seeks unity. In rational souls all desire for knowledge, which is the delight of the rational nature, refers its acquisitions to unity, and, in avoiding error, avoids nothing so much as the confusion of incomprehensible ambiguity. Why is ambiguity so detestable save that it has no certain unity? Hence it is clear that all things, whether they offend or are offended, whether they delight or are delighted, proclaim or suggest the unity of the Creator. But if ignorance and moral difficulty from which we must set out on the rational life are not natural to souls, they must be undertaken as a duty or imposed as a punishment. I think we have said enough about these matters now.

xxiv, 71. What sort of creature the first man was when created is a more important question than how his posterity was propagated. People seem to pose a very acute question when they say: If the first man was created wise, why has he been seduced? If he was created foolish how is God to escape being held to be the author of vice, since folly is the greatest vice of all? As if human nature might not receive some intermediate quality which can be called neither folly nor wisdom! Man begins to be either foolish or wise, and one or other of these terms must necessarily be applied to him, as soon as it becomes possible for him to have wisdom or to neglect it. Then his will is guilty, for his folly is his own fault. No one is so foolish as to call an infant foolish, though it would be even more absurd to call it wise. An infant can be called neither foolish nor wise though it is already a human being. So it appears that human nature receives an intermediate condition which cannot be rightly called either folly or wisdom. Similarly, if anyone was animated by a soul disposed as men are who lack wisdom through negligence, nobody could rightly call him foolish, because he would owe his condition not to his own

fault but to the nature with which he was endowed. Folly is not any kind of ignorance of things to be sought and avoided, but ignorance which is due to a man's own fault. We do not call an irrational animal foolish, because it has not received the power to be wise. Yet we often apply terms improperly where there is some similarity. Blindness is the greatest fault that eyes can have, yet it is not a fault in puppies, and is not properly called blindness.

72. If man was created such that, although he was not yet wise, he could at least receive a commandment which he ought to obey, it is not surprising that he could be seduced. Nor is it unjust that he pays the penalty for not obeying the commandment. Nor is his Creator the author of sins, for it was not yet a sin in man not to have wisdom, if that gift were not yet given him. But he had something that would enable him to attain what he did not have, provided he was willing to make a good use of it. It is one thing to be a rational being, another to be a wise man. Reason makes a man able to receive the precept to which he ought to be loyal, so that he may perform what is commanded. The rational nature grasps the precept, obedience to which brings wisdom. What nature contributes to the grasping of the precept, will contributes to obedience to it. As the merit of receiving the precept, so to speak, is to have a rational nature, so the merit of receiving wisdom is obedience to the precept. As soon as a man begins to have the power to receive the precept, he begins also to have the possibility of sinning. Before he becomes wise he sins in one or other of two ways. Either he does not fit himself to receive the precept, or, receiving it, he does not obey it. The wise man sins if he turns away from wisdom. The precept does not come from him on whom it is laid, but from him who gives it; so wisdom, too, comes not from him who is illumined, but from him who gives the light. Why then should not the Creator of man be praised? Man is good, and better than the cattle because he is capable of receiving the precept; better still when he has received the precept; and still better when he has obeyed it; best of all when he is made happy by the eternal light of wisdom. Sin, or evil, consists in neglect to receive the precept or to obey it, or to hold fast the contemplation of wisdom. So we learn that, even although the first man had been created wise, it was nevertheless

possible for him to be seduced. Because his sin was committed with his free will, a just penalty followed by divine law. As the apostle Paul says: "Saying they are wise they have become fools" (Rom. 1:22). It is pride that turns man away from wisdom, and folly is the consequence of turning away from wisdom. Folly is a kind of blindness, as he says: "Their foolish heart was darkened." Whence came this darkness, if not from turning away from the light of wisdom? And whence came the turning away, if not from the fact that man, whose good God is, willed to be his own good and so to substitute himself for God. Accordingly the Scriptures say: "Looking to myself, my soul is cast down" (Ps. 42:6. LXX). And again: "Taste and ye shall be as gods" (Gen. 3:5).

73. Some people are troubled by this question. Did folly cause the first man to depart from God, or did he become foolish by departing from God? If you answer that folly made him depart from wisdom, it will appear that he was foolish before he did so, so that folly is the cause of his doing so. If you reply that he became foolish by departing from wisdom, they ask whether he acted foolishly or wisely in departing. If wisely he did right and committed no sin. If foolishly there was folly already in him, they say, which made him depart from wisdom. For without folly he could do nothing foolishly. Clearly there is some middle state of transition from wisdom, to folly, which cannot be called either wisdom or folly; but it is not given to men to understand this except by way of contrast with both. No mortal becomes wise unless he passes from folly to wisdom. If there is folly in the actual transition it is not a good thing, but to say that would be mad. If there is wisdom in it, there must already be wisdom in a man before he makes the transition to wisdom. But that is equally absurd. Hence we learn that there is an intermediate state which may be said to be neither folly nor wisdom. In the same way when the first man passed from the citadel of wisdom to folly, the transition in itself was neither foolish nor wise. In the matter of sleeping and waking, to be asleep is not the same thing as to fall asleep, nor is to be awake the same thing as to awake. There is a transitional state between sleeping and waking as between folly and wisdom. But there is this difference. In the former case there is no intervention of will; in the latter the transition never takes

place except by the action of the will. That is why the consequence is just retribution.

xxv, 74. But the will is not enticed to do anything except by something that has been perceived. It is in a man's power to take or reject this or that, but it is not in his power to control the things which will affect him when they are perceived. We must admit, therefore, that the mind is affected by perceptions both of superior things and of inferior things. Thus the rational creature may take from either what it will, and, according to its deserts in making the choice, it obtains as a consequence either misery or happiness. In the Garden of Eden the commandment of God came to man's attention from above. From beneath came the suggestion of the serpent. Neither the commandment of God nor the suggestion of the serpent was in man's power. But if he has reached the healthy state of wisdom he is freed from all the shackles of moral difficulty, and has freedom not to yield to the enticing suggestions of inferior things. How free he is we can infer from the fact that even fools overcome them as they pass on to wisdom, though of course they have the difficulty of trying to do without the deadly sweetness of the pernicious things to which they have been accustomed.

75. Here it may be asked, if man had impressions from both sides, from the commandment of God and from the suggestion of the serpent, whence did the devil receive the suggestion to follow impiety which brought him down from his abode on high. If there was nothing in his experience to affect him he would not have chosen to do what he did. If nothing had come into his mind he would not have directed his purpose to wickedness. Whence then did the thought come into his mind to attempt things which made of a good angel a devil? Whoever wills wills something. He cannot exercise will unless some hint comes to him from outside through bodily sense, or some thought comes into his mind in some secret way. We must distinguish two kinds of experience. One proceeds from the will of another who uses persuasion, as, for example, when man sinned by consenting to the persuasion of the devil. The other kind springs from environment, mental and spiritual, or corporeal and sensational. The environment of the mind may be said to include the unchangeable Trinity, though the Trinity rather stands high above the mind. More

properly the environment of the mind is, first of all, the mind itself which enables us to know that we live, and, secondly, the body which the mind governs, moving the appropriate limb to accomplish any action that may be required. The environment of the senses is corporeal objects of all kinds.

76. The mind is not sovereign wisdom, for that is unchangeable. Yet in contemplating sovereign wisdom the mutable mind may behold itself and in a fashion come to know itself. But that cannot be unless a distinction is made. The mind is not as God is, and yet, next to God, it can give us satisfaction. It is better when it forgets itself in love for the unchangeable God, or indeed utterly contemns itself in comparison with him. But if the mind, being immediately conscious of itself, takes pleasure in itself to the extent of perversely imitating God, wanting to enjoy its own power, the greater it wants to be the less it becomes. Pride is the beginning of all sin, and the beginning of man's pride is revolt from God (Eccl. 10:12–13). To the devil's pride was added malevolent envy, so that he persuaded man to show the same pride as had proved the devil's damnation. So man had imposed on him a penalty which was corrective rather than destructive. As the devil had offered himself to man as a pattern of pride to be imitated, so the Lord, who promises us eternal life, offered himself as a pattern of humility for our imitation. Now that the blood of Christ is shed for us, after unspeakable toils and miseries, let us cleave to our Liberator with such love, let us be so enraptured with his brightness, that nothing coming into our experience from the lower realms may rob us of our vision of the higher things. And if any suggestion springing from a desire for the inferior should deflect our purpose, the eternal damnation and torments of the devil will recall us to the true path.

77. Such is the beauty of justice, such the pleasure of the eternal light, that is, of unchangeable truth and wisdom, that, even if we could not abide in it more than the space of a single day, for that day alone innumerable years of this life full of delights and abundance of temporal goods would be rightly and deservedly despised. Deep and unfeigned is the emotion expressed in these words: "One day in thy courts is better than thousands" (Ps. 84:10). These words can be understood in another sense. Thousands of days might be understood of mutable time, and by the expression "one day" changeless eternity might be denoted. I do not know whether I have omitted any point in replying, as God has deigned to give me the power, to your questions. Even if anything else occurs to you, moderation compels us now to bring this book to an end, and to take some rest after this disputation.

ON TIME AND ETERNITY

BOOK ELEVEN

The eternal Creator and the Creation in time. Augustine ties together his memory of his past life, his present experience, and his ardent desire to comprehend the mystery of creation. This leads him to the questions of the mode and time of creation. He ponders the mode of creation and shows that it was de nihilo and involved no alteration in the being of God. He then considers the question of the beginning of the world and time and shows that time and creation are cotemporal. But what is time? To this Augustine devotes a brilliant analysis of the subjectivity of time and the relation of all temporal process to the abiding eternity of God. From this, he prepares to turn to a detailed interpretation of Gen. 1:1, 2. [Translator's introduction]

CHAPTER I

1. Is it possible, O Lord, that, since thou art in eternity, thou art ignorant of what I am saying to thee? Or, dost thou see in time an event at the time it occurs? If not, then why am I recounting such a tale of things to thee? Certainly not in order to

Reprinted from St. Augustine's *Confessions*, translated by A. Outler.

acquaint thee with them through me; but, instead, that through them I may stir up my own love and the love of my readers toward thee, so that all may say, "Great is the Lord and greatly to be praised." I have said this before and will say it again: "For love of thy love I do it." So also we pray—and yet Truth tells us, "Your Father knoweth what things you need before you ask him." Consequently, we lay bare our feelings before thee, that, through our confessing to thee our plight and thy mercies toward us, thou mayest go on to free us altogether, as thou hast already begun; and that we may cease to be wretched in ourselves and blessed in thee—since thou hast called us to be poor in spirit, meek, mourners, hungering and athirst for righteousness, merciful and pure in heart. Thus I have told thee many things, as I could find ability and will to do so, since it was thy will in the first place that I should confess to thee, O Lord my God—for "Thou art good and thy mercy endureth forever."

CHAPTER II

2. But how long would it take for the voice of my pen to tell enough of thy exhortations and of all thy terrors and comforts and leadings by which thou didst bring me to preach thy Word and to administer thy sacraments to thy people? And even if I could do this sufficiently, the drops of time are very precious to me and I have for a long time been burning with the desire to meditate on thy law, and to confess in thy presence my knowledge and ignorance of it—from the first streaks of thy light in my mind and the remaining darkness, until my weakness shall be swallowed up in thy strength. And I do not wish to see those hours drained into anything else which I can find free from the necessary care of the body, the exercise of the mind, and the service we owe to our fellow men—and what we give even if we do not owe it.

3. O Lord my God, hear my prayer and let thy mercy attend my longing. It does not burn for itself alone but longs as well to serve the cause of fraternal love. Thou seest in my heart that this is so. Let me offer the service of my mind and my tongue—and give me what I may in turn offer back to thee. For "I am needy and poor"; thou art rich to all who

call upon thee—thou who, in thy freedom from care, carest for us. Trim away from my lips, inwardly and outwardly, all rashness and lying. Let thy Scriptures be my chaste delight. Let me not be deceived in them, nor deceive others from them. O Lord, hear and pity! O Lord my God, light of the blind, strength of the weak—and also the light of those who see and the strength of the strong—hearken to my soul and hear it crying from the depths. Unless thy ears attend us even in the depths, where should we go? To whom should we cry?

"Thine is the day and the night is thine as well." At thy bidding the moments fly by. Grant me in them, then, an interval for my meditations on the hidden things of thy law, nor close the door of thy law against us who knock. Thou hast not willed that the deep secrets of all those pages should have been written in vain. Those forests are not without their stags which keep retired within them, ranging and walking and feeding, lying down and ruminating. Perfect me, O Lord, and reveal their secrets to me. Behold, thy voice is my joy; thy voice surpasses in abundance of delights. Give me what I love, for I do love it. And this too is thy gift. Abandon not thy gifts and despise not thy "grass" which thirsts for thee. Let me confess to thee everything that I shall have found in thy books and "let me hear the voice of thy praise." Let me drink from thee and "consider the wondrous things out of thy law"—from the very beginning, when thou madest heaven and earth, and thenceforward to the everlasting reign of thy Holy City with thee.

4. O Lord, have mercy on me and hear my petition. For my prayer is not for earthly things, neither gold nor silver and precious stones, nor gorgeous apparel, nor honors and power, nor fleshly pleasures, nor of bodily necessities in this life of our pilgrimage: all of these things are "added" to those who seek thy Kingdom and thy righteousness.

Observe, O God, from whence comes my desire. The unrighteous have told me of delights but not such as those in thy law, O Lord. Behold, this is the spring of my desire. See, O Father, look and see—and approve! Let it be pleasing in thy mercy's sight that I should find favor with thee—that the secret things of thy Word may be opened to me when I knock. I beg this of thee by our Lord Jesus Christ, thy Son, the Man of thy right hand, the Son of Man;

whom thou madest strong for thy purpose as Mediator between thee and us; through whom thou didst seek us when we were not seeking thee, but didst seek us so that we might seek thee; thy Word, through whom thou madest all things, and me among them; thy only Son, through whom thou hast called thy faithful people to adoption, and me among them. I beseech it of thee through him who sitteth at thy right hand and maketh intercession for us, "in whom are hid all treasures of wisdom and knowledge." It is he I seek in thy books. Moses wrote of him. He tells us so himself; the Truth tells us so.

CHAPTER III

5. Let me hear and understand how in the beginning thou madest heaven and earth. Moses wrote of this; he wrote and passed on—moving from thee to thee—and he is now no longer before me. If he were, I would lay hold on him and ask him and entreat him solemnly that in thy name he would open out these things to me, and I would lend my bodily ears to the sounds that came forth out of his mouth. If, however, he spoke in the Hebrew language, the sounds would beat on my senses in vain, and nothing would touch my mind; but if he spoke in Latin, I would understand what he said. But how should I then know whether what he said was true? If I knew even this much, would it be that I knew it from him? Indeed, within me, deep inside the chambers of my thought, Truth itself—neither Hebrew, nor Greek, nor Latin, nor barbarian, without any organs of voice and tongue, without the sound of syllables—would say, "He speaks the truth," and I should be assured by this. Then I would confidently say to that man of thine, "You speak the truth." However, since I cannot inquire of Moses, I beseech thee, O Truth, from whose fullness he spoke truth; I beseech thee, my God, forgive my sins, and as thou gavest thy servant the gift to speak these things, grant me also the gift to understand them.

CHAPTER IV

6. Look around; there are the heaven and the earth. They cry aloud that they were made, for they change and vary. Whatever there is that has not been made, and yet has being, has nothing in it that was not there before. This having something not already existent is what it means to be changed and varied. Heaven and earth thus speak plainly that they did not make themselves: "We are, because we have been made; we did not exist before we came to be so that we could have made ourselves!" And the voice with which they speak is simply their visible presence. It was thou, O Lord, who madest these things. Thou art beautiful; thus they are beautiful. Thou art good, thus they are good. Thou art; thus they are. But they are not as beautiful, nor as good, nor as truly real as thou their Creator art. Compared with thee, they are neither beautiful nor good, nor do they even exist. These things we know, thanks be to thee. Yet our knowledge is ignorance when it is compared with thy knowledge.

CHAPTER V

7. But how didst thou make the heaven and the earth, and what was the tool of such a mighty work as thine? For it was not like a human worker fashioning body from body, according to the fancy of his mind, able somehow or other to impose on it a form which the mind perceived in itself by its inner eye (yet how should even he be able to do this, if thou hadst not made that mind?). He imposes the form on something already existing and having some sort of being, such as clay, or stone or wood or gold or such like (and where would these things come from if thou hadst not furnished them?). For thou madest his body for the artisan, and thou madest the mind which directs the limbs; thou madest the matter from which he makes anything; thou didst create the capacity by which he understands his art and sees within his mind what he may do with the things before him; thou gavest him his bodily sense by which, as if he had an interpreter, he may communicate from mind to matter what he proposes to do and report back to his mind what has been done, that the mind may consult with the Truth which presideth over it as to whether what is done is well done.

All these things praise thee, the Creator of them all. But how didst thou make them? How, O God, didst thou make the heaven and earth? For truly, neither in heaven nor on earth didst thou make heaven and earth—nor in the air nor in the waters, since all of these also belong to the heaven and the earth. Nowhere in the whole world didst thou make the whole world, because there was no place where it could be made before it was made. And thou didst not hold anything in thy hand from which to fashion the heaven and the earth, for where couldst thou have gotten what thou hadst not made in order to make something with it? Is there, indeed, anything at all except because thou art? Thus thou didst speak and they were made, and by thy Word thou didst make them all.

CHAPTER VI

8. But how didst thou speak? Was it in the same manner in which the voice came from the cloud saying, "This is my beloved Son"? For that voice sounded forth and died away; it began and ended. The syllables sounded and passed away, the second after the first, the third after the second, and thence in order, till the very last after all the rest; and silence after the last. From this it is clear and plain that it was the action of a creature, itself in time, which sounded that voice, obeying thy eternal will. And what these words were which were formed at that time the outer ear conveyed to the conscious mind, whose inner ear lay attentively open to thy eternal Word. But it compared those words which sounded in time with thy eternal Word sounding in silence and said: "This is different; quite different! These words are far below me; they are not even real, for they fly away and pass, but the Word of my God remains above me forever." If, then, in words that sound and fade away thou didst say that heaven and earth should be made, and thus madest heaven and earth, then there was already some kind of corporeal creature before heaven and earth by whose motions in time that voice might have had its occurrence in time. But there was nothing corporeal before the heaven and the earth; or if there was, then it is certain that already, without a time-bound voice, thou hadst created whatever it was out of which thou didst make the time-bound voice by which thou didst say, "Let the heaven and the earth be made!" For whatever it was out of which such a voice was made

simply did not exist at all until it was made by thee. Was it decreed by thy Word that a body might be made from which such words might come?

CHAPTER VII

9. Thou dost call us, then, to understand the Word—the God who is God with thee—which is spoken eternally and by which all things are spoken eternally. For what was first spoken was not finished, and then something else spoken until the whole series was spoken; but all things, at the same time and forever. For, otherwise, we should have time and change and not a true eternity, nor a true immortality.

This I know, O my God, and I give thanks. I know, I confess to thee, O Lord, and whoever is not ungrateful for certain truths knows and blesses thee along with me. We know, O Lord, this much we know: that in the same proportion as anything is not what it was, and is what it was not, in that very same proportion it passes away or comes to be. But there is nothing in thy Word that passes away or returns to its place; for it is truly immortal and eternal. And, therefore, unto the Word coeternal with thee, at the same time and always thou sayest all that thou sayest. And whatever thou sayest shall be made is made, and thou makest nothing otherwise than by speaking. Still, not all the things that thou dost make by speaking are made at the same time and always.

CHAPTER VIII

10. Why is this, I ask of thee, O Lord my God? I see it after a fashion, but I do not know how to express it, unless I say that everything that begins to be and then ceases to be begins and ceases when it is known in thy eternal Reason that it ought to begin or cease—in thy eternal Reason where nothing begins or ceases. And this is thy Word, which is also "the Beginning," because it also speaks to us. Thus, in the gospel, he spoke through the flesh; and this sounded in the outward ears of men so that it might be believed and sought for within, and so that it might be found in the eternal Truth, in which the good and only Master teacheth all his disciples.

There, O Lord, I hear thy voice, the voice of one speaking to me, since he who teacheth us speaketh to us. But he that doth not teach us doth not really speak to us even when he speaketh. Yet who is it that teacheth us unless it be the Truth immutable? For even when we are instructed by means of the mutable creation, we are thereby led to the Truth immutable. There we learn truly as we stand and hear him, and we rejoice greatly "because of the bridegroom's voice," restoring us to the source whence our being comes. And therefore, unless the Beginning remained immutable, there would then not be a place to which we might return when we had wandered away. But when we return from error, it is through our gaining knowledge that we return. In order for us to gain knowledge he teacheth us, since he is the Beginning, and speaketh to us.

CHAPTER IX

11. In this Beginning, O God, thou hast made heaven and earth—through thy Word, thy Son, thy Power, thy Wisdom, thy Truth: all wondrously speaking and wondrously creating. Who shall comprehend such things and who shall tell of it? What is it that shineth through me and striketh my heart without injury, so that I both shudder and burn? I shudder because I am unlike it; I burn because I am like it. It is Wisdom itself that shineth through me, clearing away my fog, which so readily overwhelms me so that I faint in it, in the darkness and burden of my punishment. For my strength is brought down in neediness, so that I cannot endure even my blessings until thou, O Lord, who hast been gracious to all my iniquities, also healest all my infirmities—for it is thou who "shalt redeem my life from corruption, and crown me with loving-kindness and tender mercy, and shalt satisfy my desire with good things so that my youth shall be renewed like the eagle's." For by this hope we are saved, and through patience we await thy promises. Let him that is able hear thee speaking to his inner mind. I will cry out with confidence because of thy own oracle, "How wonderful are thy works, O Lord; in wisdom thou hast made them all." And this Wisdom is the Beginning, and in that Beginning thou hast made heaven and earth.

CHAPTER X

12. Now, are not those still full of their old carnal nature who ask us: "What was God doing before he made heaven and earth? For if he was idle," they say, "and doing nothing, then why did he not continue in that state forever—doing nothing, as he had always done? If any new motion has arisen in God, and a new will to form a creature, which he had never before formed, how can that be a true eternity in which an act of will occurs that was not there before? For the will of God is not a created thing, but comes before the creation—and this is true because nothing could be created unless the will of the Creator came before it. The will of God, therefore, pertains to his very Essence. Yet if anything has arisen in the Essence of God that was not there before, then that Essence cannot truly be called eternal. But if it was the eternal will of God that the creation should come to be, why, then, is not the creation itself also from eternity?"

CHAPTER XI

13. Those who say these things do not yet understand thee, O Wisdom of God, O Light of souls. They do not yet understand how the things are made that are made by and in thee. They endeavor to comprehend eternal things, but their heart still flies about in the past and future motions of created things, and is still unstable. Who shall hold it and fix it so that it may come to rest for a little; and then, by degrees, glimpse the glory of that eternity which abides forever; and then, comparing eternity with the temporal process in which nothing abides, they may see that they are incommensurable? They would see that a long time does not become long, except from the many separate events that occur in its passage, which cannot be simultaneous. In the Eternal, on the other hand, nothing passes away, but the whole is simultaneously present. But no temporal process is wholly simultaneous. Therefore, let it see that all time past is forced to move on by the incoming future; that all the future follows from the past; and that all, past and future, is created and issues out of that which is forever present. Who will hold the heart of man that it may stand still and see how the eternity which al-

ways stands still is itself neither future nor past but expresses itself in the times that are future and past? Can my hand do this, or can the hand of my mouth bring about so difficult a thing even by persuasion?

CHAPTER XII

14. How, then, shall I respond to him who asks, "What was God doing before he made heaven and earth?" I do not answer, as a certain one is reported to have done facetiously (shrugging off the force of the question). "He was preparing hell," he said, "for those who pry too deep." It is one thing to see the answer; it is another to laugh at the questioner—and for myself I do not answer these things thus. More willingly would I have answered, "I do not know what I do not know," than cause one who asked a deep question to be ridiculed—and by such tactics gain praise for a worthless answer.

Rather, I say that thou, our God, art the Creator of every creature. And if in the term "heaven and earth" every creature is included, I make bold to say further: "Before God made heaven and earth, he did not make anything at all. For if he did, what did he make unless it were a creature?" I do indeed wish that I knew all that I desire to know to my profit as surely as I know that no creature was made before any creature was made.

CHAPTER XIII

15. But if the roving thought of someone should wander over the images of past time, and wonder that thou, the Almighty God, the All-creating and All-sustaining, the Architect of heaven and earth, didst for ages unnumbered abstain from so great a work before thou didst actually do it, let him awake and consider that he wonders at illusions. For in what temporal medium could the unnumbered ages that thou didst not make pass by, since thou art the Author and Creator of all the ages? Or what periods of time would those be that were not made by thee? Or how could they have already passed away if they had not already been? Since, therefore, thou art the Creator of all times, if there was any time before thou madest heaven and earth, why is it said that thou wast abstaining from working? For thou madest that

very time itself, and periods could not pass by before thou madest the whole temporal procession. But if there was no time before heaven and earth, how, then, can it be asked, "What wast thou doing then?" For there was no "then" when there was no time.

16. Nor dost thou precede any given period of time by another period of time. Else thou wouldst not precede all periods of time. In the eminence of thy ever-present eternity, thou precedest all times past, and extendest beyond all future times, for they are still to come—and when they have come, they will be past. But "Thou art always the Selfsame and thy years shall have no end." Thy years neither go nor come; but ours both go and come in order that all separate moments may come to pass. All thy years stand together as one, since they are abiding. Nor do thy years past exclude the years to come because thy years do not pass away. All these years of ours shall be with thee, when all of them shall have ceased to be. Thy years are but a day, and thy day is not recurrent, but always today. Thy "today" yields not to tomorrow and does not follow yesterday. Thy "today" is eternity. Therefore, thou didst generate the Coeternal, to whom thou didst say, "This day I have begotten thee." Thou madest all time and before all times thou art, and there was never a time when there was no time.

CHAPTER XIV

17. There was no time, therefore, when thou hadst not made anything, because thou hadst made time itself. And there are no times that are coeternal with thee, because thou dost abide forever; but if times should abide, they would not be times.

For what is time? Who can easily and briefly explain it? Who can even comprehend it in thought or put the answer into words? Yet is it not true that in conversation we refer to nothing more familiarly or knowingly than time? And surely we understand it when we speak of it; we understand it also when we hear another speak of it.

What, then, is time? If no one asks me, I know what it is. If I wish to explain it to him who asks me, I do not know. Yet I say with confidence that I know that if nothing passed away, there would be no past time; and if nothing were still coming, there would be no future time; and if there were nothing at all, there would be no present time.

But; then, how is it that there are the two times, past and future, when even the past is now no longer and the future is now not yet? But if the present were always present, and did not pass into past time, it obviously would not be time but eternity. If, then, time present—if it be time—comes into existence only because it passes into time past, how can we say that even this is, since the cause of its being is that it will cease to be? Thus, can we not truly say that time is only as it tends toward nonbeing?

CHAPTER XV

18. And yet we speak of a long time and a short time; but never speak this way except of time past and future. We call a hundred years ago, for example, a long time past. In like manner, we should call a hundred years hence a long time to come. But we call ten days ago a short time past; and ten days hence a short time to come. But in what sense is something long or short that is nonexistent? For the past is not now, and the future is not yet. Therefore, let us not say, "It is long"; instead, let us say of the past, "It was long," and of the future, "It will be long," And yet, O Lord, my Light, shall not thy truth make mockery of man even here? For that long time past: was it long when it was already past, or when it was still present? For it might have been long when there was a period that could be long, but when it was past, it no longer was. In that case, that which was not at all could not be long. Let us not, therefore, say, "Time past was long," for we shall not discover what it was that was long because, since it is past, it no longer exists. Rather, let us say that "time present was long, because when it was present it was long." For then it had not yet passed on so as not to be, and therefore it still was in a state that could be called long. But after it passed, it ceased to be long simply because it ceased to be.

19. Let us, therefore, O human soul, see whether present time can be long, for it has been given you to feel and measure the periods of time. How, then, will you answer me?

Is a hundred years when present a long time? But, first, see whether a hundred years can be present at once. For if the first year in the century is current, then it is present time, and the other ninety and nine are still future. Therefore, they are not yet. But, then, if the second year is current, one year is already past, the second present, and all the rest are future. And thus, if we fix on any middle year of this century as present, those before it are past, those after it are future. Therefore, a hundred years cannot be present all at once.

Let us see, then, whether the year that is now current can be present. For if its first month is current, then the rest are future; if the second, the first is already past, and the remainder are not yet. Therefore, the current year is not present all at once. And if it is not present as a whole, then the year is not present. For it takes twelve months to make the year, from which each individual month which is current is itself present one at a time, but the rest are either past or future.

20. Thus it comes out that time present, which we found was the only time that could be called "long," has been cut down to the space of scarcely a single day. But let us examine even that, for one day is never present as a whole. For it is made up of twenty-four hours, divided between night and day. The first of these hours has the rest of them as future, and the last of them has the rest as past; but any of those between has those that preceded it as past and those that succeed it as future. And that one hour itself passes away in fleeting fractions. The part of it that has fled is past; what remains is still future. If any fraction of time be conceived that cannot now be divided even into the most minute momentary point, this alone is what we may call time present. But this flies so rapidly from future to past that it cannot be extended by any delay. For if it is extended, it is then divided into past and future. But the present has no extension whatever.

Where, therefore, is that time which we may call "long"? Is it future? Actually we do not say of the future, "It is long," for it has not yet come to be, so as to be long. Instead, we say, "It will be long." When will it be? For since it is future, it will not be long, for what may be long is not yet. It will be long only when it passes from the future which is not as yet, and will have begun to be present, so that there can be something that may be long. But in that case, time present cries aloud, in the words we have already heard, that it cannot be "long."

CHAPTER XVI

21. And yet, O Lord, we do perceive intervals of time, and we compare them with each other, and we say that some are longer and others are shorter. We even measure how much longer or shorter this time may be than that time. And we say that this time is twice as long, or three times as long, while this other time is only just as long as that other. But we measure the passage of time when we measure the intervals of perception. But who can measure times past which now are no longer, or times future which are not yet—unless perhaps someone will dare to say that what does not exist can be measured? Therefore, while time is passing, it can be perceived and measured; but when it is past, it cannot, since it is not.

CHAPTER XVII

22. I am seeking the truth, O Father; I am not affirming it. O my God, direct and rule me.

Who is there who will tell me that there are not three times—as we learned when boys and as we have also taught boys—time past, time present, and time future? Who can say that there is only time present because the other two do not exist? Or do they also exist; but when, from the future, time becomes present, it proceeds from some secret place; and when, from times present, it becomes past, it recedes into some secret place? For where have those men who have foretold the future seen the things foretold, if then they were not yet existing? For what does not exist cannot be seen. And those who tell of things past could not speak of them as if they were true, if they did not see them in their minds. These things could in no way be discerned if they did not exist. There are therefore times present and times past.

CHAPTER XVIII

23. Give me leave, O Lord, to seek still further. O my Hope, let not my purpose be confounded. For if there are times past and future, I wish to know where they are. But if I have not yet succeeded in this, I still know that wherever they are, they are not

there as future or past, but as present. For if they are there as future, they are there as "not yet"; if they are there as past, they are there as "no longer." Wherever they are and whatever they are they exist therefore only as present. Although we tell of past things as true, they are drawn out of the memory—not the things themselves, which have already passed, but words constructed from the images of the perceptions which were formed in the mind, like footprints in their passage through the senses. My childhood, for instance, which is no longer, still exists in time past, which does not now exist. But when I call to mind its image and speak of it, I see it in the present because it is still in my memory. Whether there is a similar explanation for the foretelling of future events—that is, of the images of things which are not yet seen as if they were already existing—I confess, O my God, I do not know. But this I certainly do know: that we generally think ahead about our future actions, and this premeditation is in time present; but that the action which we premeditate is not yet, because it is still future. When we shall have started the action and have begun to do what we were premeditating, then that action will be in time present, because then it is no longer in time future.

24. Whatever may be the manner of this secret foreseeing of future things, nothing can be seen except what exists. But what exists now is not future, but present. When, therefore, they say that future events are seen, it is not the events themselves, for they do not exist as yet (that is, they are still in time future), but perhaps, instead, their causes and their signs are seen, which already do exist. Therefore, to those already beholding these causes and signs, they are not future, but present, and from them future things are predicted because they are conceived in the mind. These conceptions, however, exist now, and those who predict those things see these conceptions before them in time present.

Let me take an example from the vast multitude and variety of such things. I see the dawn; I predict that the sun is about to rise. What I see is in time present, what I predict is in time future—not that the sun is future, for it already exists; but its rising is future, because it is not yet. Yet I could not predict even its rising, unless I had an image of it in my mind; as, indeed, I do even now as I speak. But that dawn which I see in the sky is not the rising of the sun (though it does precede it), nor is it a conception in my mind. These two are seen in time present, in order that the event which is in time future may be predicted.

Future events, therefore, are not yet. And if they are not yet, they do not exist. And if they do not exist, they cannot be seen at all, but they can be predicted from things present, which now are and are seen.

CHAPTER XIX

25. Now, therefore, O Ruler of thy creatures, what is the mode by which thou teachest souls those things which are still future? For thou hast taught thy prophets. How dost thou, to whom nothing is future, teach future things—or rather teach things present from the signs of things future? For what does not exist certainly cannot be taught. This way of thine is too far from my sight; it is too great for me, I cannot attain to it. But I shall be enabled by thee, when thou wilt grant it, O sweet Light of my secret eyes.

CHAPTER XX

26. But even now it is manifest and clear that there are neither times future nor times past. Thus it is not properly said that there are three times, past, present, and future. Perhaps it might be said rightly that there are three times: a time present of things past; a time present of things present; and a time present of things future. For these three do coexist somehow in the soul, for otherwise I could not see them. The time present of things past is memory; the time present of things present is direct experience; the time present of things future is expectation. If we are allowed to speak of these things so, I see three times, and I grant that there are three. Let it still be said, then, as our misapplied custom has it: "There are three times, past, present, and future." I shall not be troubled by it, nor argue, nor object—always provided that what is said is understood, so that neither the future nor the past is said to exist now. There are

but few things about which we speak properly—and many more about which we speak improperly—though we understand one another's meaning.

CHAPTER XXI

27. I have said, then, that we measure periods of time as they pass so that we can say that this time is twice as long as that one or that this is just as long as that, and so on for the other fractions of time which we can count by measuring.

So, then, as I was saying, we measure periods of time as they pass. And if anyone asks me, "How do you know this?", I can answer: "I know because we measure. We could not measure things that do not exist, and things past and future do not exist." But how do we measure present time since it has no extension? It is measured while it passes, but when it has passed it is not measured; for then there is nothing that could be measured. But whence, and how, and whither does it pass while it is being measured? Whence, but from the future? Which way, save through the present? Whither, but into the past? Therefore, from what is not yet, through what has no length, it passes into what is now no longer. But what do we measure, unless it is a time of some length? For we cannot speak of single, and double, and triple, and equal, and all the other ways in which we speak of time, except in terms of the length of the periods of time. But in what "length," then, do we measure passing time? Is it in the future, from which it passes over? But what does not yet exist cannot be measured. Or, is it in the present, through which it passes? But what has no length we cannot measure. Or is it in the past into which it passes? But what is no longer we cannot measure.

CHAPTER XXII

28. My soul burns ardently to understand this most intricate enigma. O Lord my God, O good Father, I beseech thee through Christ, do not close off these things, both the familiar and the obscure, from my desire. Do not bar it from entering into them; but let their light dawn by thy enlightening mercy, O Lord. Of whom shall I inquire about these things?

And to whom shall I confess my ignorance of them with greater profit than to thee, to whom these studies of mine (ardently longing to understand thy Scriptures) are not a bore? Give me what I love, for I do love it; and this thou hast given me. O Father, who truly knowest how to give good gifts to thy children, give this to me. Grant it, since I have undertaken to understand it, and hard labor is my lot until thou openest it. I beseech thee, through Christ and in his name, the Holy of Holies, let no man interrupt me. "For I have believed, and therefore do I speak." This is my hope; for this I live: that I may contemplate the joys of my Lord. Behold, thou hast made my days grow old, and they pass away—and how I do not know.

We speak of this time and that time, and these times and those times: "How long ago since he said this?" "How long ago since he did this?" "How long ago since I saw that?" "This syllable is twice as long as that single short syllable." These words we say and hear, and we are understood and we understand. They are quite commonplace and ordinary, and still the meaning of these very same things lies deeply hid and its discovery is still to come.

CHAPTER XXIII

29. I once heard a learned man say that the motions of the sun, moon, and stars constituted time; and I did not agree. For why should not the motions of all bodies constitute time? What if the lights of heaven should cease, and a potter's wheel still turn round: would there be no time by which we might measure those rotations and say either that it turned at equal intervals, or, if it moved now more slowly and now more quickly, that some rotations were longer and others shorter? And while we were saying this, would we not also be speaking in time? Or would there not be in our words some syllables that were long and others short, because the first took a longer time to sound, and the others a shorter time? O God, grant men to see in a small thing the notions that are common to all things, both great and small. Both the stars and the lights of heaven are "for signs and seasons, and for days and years." This is doubtless the case, but just as I should not say that the circuit of that wooden wheel was a day, neither would that learned man say that there was, therefore, no time.

30. I thirst to know the power and the nature of time, by which we measure the motions of bodies, and say, for example, that this motion is twice as long as that. For I ask, since the word "day" refers not only to the length of time that the sun is above the earth (which separates day from night), but also refers to the sun's entire circuit from east all the way around to east—on account of which we can say, "So many days have passed" (the nights being included when we say, "So many days," and their lengths not counted separately)—since, then, the day is ended by the motion of the sun and by his passage from east to east, I ask whether the motion itself is the day, or whether the day is the period in which that motion is completed; or both? For if the sun's passage is the day, then there would be a day even if the sun should finish his course in as short a period as an hour. If the motion itself is the day, then it would not be a day if from one sunrise to another there were a period no longer than an hour. But the sun would have to go round twenty-four times to make just one day. If it is both, then that could not be called a day if the sun ran his entire course in the period of an hour; nor would it be a day if, while the sun stood still, as much time passed as the sun usually covered during his whole course, from morning to morning. I shall, therefore, not ask any more what it is that is called a day, but rather what time is, for it is by time that we measure the circuit of the sun, and would be able to say that it was finished in half the period of time that it customarily takes if it were completed in a period of only twelve hours. If, then, we compare these periods, we could call one of them a single and the other a double period, as if the sun might run his course from east to east sometimes in a single period and sometimes in a double period.

Let no man tell me, therefore, that the motions of the heavenly bodies constitute time. For when the sun stood still at the prayer of a certain man in order that he might gain his victory in battle, the sun stood still but time went on. For in as long a span of time as was sufficient the battle was fought and ended.

I see, then, that time is a certain kind of extension. But do I see it, or do I only seem to? Thou, O Light and Truth, wilt show me.

CHAPTER XXIV

31. Dost thou command that I should agree if anyone says that time is "the motion of a body"? Thou dost not so command. For I hear that no body is moved but in time; this thou tellest me. But that the motion of a body itself is time I do not hear; thou dost not say so. For when a body is moved, I measure by time how long it was moving from the time when it began to be moved until it stopped. And if I did not see when it began to be moved, and if it continued to move so that I could not see when it stopped, I could not measure the movement, except from the time when I began to see it until I stopped. But if I look at it for a long time, I can affirm only that the time is long but not how long it may be. This is because when we say, "How long?", we are speaking comparatively as: "This is as long as that," or, "This is twice as long as that"; or other such similar ratios. But if we were able to observe the point in space where and from which the body, which is moved, comes and the point to which it is moved; or if we can observe its parts moving as in a wheel, we can say how long the movement of the body took or the movement of its parts from this place to that. Since, therefore, the motion of a body is one thing, and the norm by which we measure how long it takes is another thing, we cannot see which of these two is to be called time. For, although a body is sometimes moved and sometimes stands still, we measure not only its motion but also its rest as well; and both by time! Thus we say, "It stood still as long as it moved," or, "It stood still twice or three times as long as it moved"—or any other ratio which our measuring has either determined or imagined, either roughly or precisely, according to our custom. Therefore, time is not the motion of a body.

CHAPTER XXV

32. And I confess to thee, O Lord, that I am still ignorant as to what time is. And again I confess to thee, O Lord, that I know that I am speaking all these things in time, and that I have already spoken of time a long time, and that "very long" is not long except when measured by the duration of time. How, then, do I know this, when I do not know what time is?

Or, is it possible that I do not know how I can express what I do know? Alas for me! I do not even know the extent of my own ignorance. Behold, O my God, in thy presence I do not lie. As my heart is, so I speak. Thou shalt light my candle; thou, O Lord my God, wilt enlighten my darkness.

CHAPTER XXVI

33. Does not my soul most truly confess to thee that I do measure intervals of time? But what is it that I thus measure, O my God, and how is it that I do not know what I measure? I measure the motion of a body by time, but the time itself I do not measure. But, truly, could I measure the motion of a body—how long it takes, how long it is in motion from this place to that—unless I could measure the time in which it is moving?

How, then, do I measure this time itself? Do we measure a longer time by a shorter time, as we measure the length of a crossbeam in terms of cubits? Thus, we can say that the length of a long syllable is measured by the length of a short syllable and thus say that the long syllable is double. So also we measure the length of poems by the length of the lines, and the length of the line by the length of the feet, and the length of the feet by the length of the syllable, and the length of the long syllables by the length of the short ones. We do not measure by pages—for in that way we would measure space rather than time—but when we speak the words as they pass by we say: "It is a long stanza, because it is made up of so many verses; they are long verses because they consist of so many feet; they are long feet because they extend over so many syllables; this is a long syllable because it is twice the length of a short one."

But no certain measure of time is obtained this way; since it is possible that if a shorter verse is pronounced slowly, it may take up more time than a longer one if it is pronounced hurriedly. The same would hold for a stanza, or a foot, or a syllable. From this it appears to me that time is nothing other than extendedness; but extendedness of what I do not know. This is a marvel to me. The extendedness may be of the mind itself. For what is it I measure, I ask thee, O my God, when I say either, roughly, "This time is longer than that," or, more precisely, "This is twice as long as that." I know that I am measuring time. But I am not measuring the future, for it is not yet; and I am not measuring the present because it is extended by no length; and I am not measuring the past because it no longer is. What is it, therefore, that I am measuring? Is it time in its passage, but not time past [*praetereuntia tempora, non praeterita*]? This is what I have been saying.

CHAPTER XXVII

34. Press on, O my mind, and attend with all your power. God is our Helper: "it is he that hath made us and not we ourselves." Give heed where the truth begins to dawn. Suppose now that a bodily voice begins to sound, and continues to flow. We can measure it only while it is sounding, for when it has ceased to sound it will be already past and there will not be anything there that can be measured. Let us measure it exactly; and let us say how much it is. But while it is sounding, it cannot be measured except from the instant when it began to sound, down to the final moment when it left off. For we measure the time interval itself from some beginning point to some end. This is why a voice that has not yet ended cannot be measured, so that one could say how long or how briefly it will continue. Nor can it be said to be equal to another voice or single or double in comparison to it or anything like this. But when it is ended, it is no longer. How, therefore, may it be measured? And yet we measure times; not those which are not yet, nor those which no longer are, nor those which are stretched out by some delay, nor those which have no limit. Therefore, we measure neither times future nor times past, nor times present, nor times passing by; and yet we do measure times.

35. Deus Creator omnium [God, Creator of all things]: this verse of eight syllables alternates between short and long syllables. The four short ones—that is, the first, third, fifth, and seventh—are single in relation to the four long ones—that is, the second, fourth, sixth, and eighth. Each of the long ones is double the length of each of the short ones. I affirm this and report it, and common sense perceives that this indeed is the case. By common sense, then, I measure a long syllable by a short one, and I

find that it is twice as long. But when one sounds after another, if the first be short and the latter long, how can I hold the short one and how can I apply it to the long one as a measure, so that I can discover that the long one is twice as long, when, in fact, the long one does not begin to sound until the short one leaves off sounding? That same long syllable I do not measure as present, since I cannot measure it until it is ended; but its ending is its passing away.

What is it, then, that I can measure? Where is the short syllable by which I measure? Where is the long one that I am measuring? Both have sounded, have flown away, have passed on, and are no longer. And still I measure, and I confidently answer—as far as a trained ear can be trusted—that this syllable is single and that syllable double. And I could not do this unless they both had passed and were ended. Therefore I do not measure them, for they do not exist any more. But I measure something in my memory which remains fixed.

36. It is in you, O mind of mine, that I measure the periods of time. Do not shout me down that it exists [objectively]; do not overwhelm yourself with the turbulent flood of your impressions. In you, as I have said, I measure the periods of time. I measure as time present the impression that things make on you as they pass by and what remains after they have passed by—I do not measure the things themselves which have passed by and left their impression on you. This is what I measure when I measure periods of time. Either, then, these are the periods of time or else I do not measure time at all.

What are we doing when we measure silence, and say that this silence has lasted as long as that voice lasts? Do we not project our thought to the measure of a sound, as if it were then sounding, so that we can say something concerning the intervals of silence in a given span of time? For, even when both the voice and the tongue are still, we review—in thought—poems and verses, and discourse of various kinds or various measures of motions, and we specify their time spans—how long this is in relation to that—just as if we were speaking them aloud. If anyone wishes to utter a prolonged sound, and if, in forethought, he has decided how long it should be, that man has already in silence gone through a span of time, and committed his sound to memory. Thus he begins to speak and his voice sounds until it reaches the predetermined end. It has truly sounded and will go on sounding. But what is already finished has already sounded and what remains will still sound. Thus it passes on, until the present intention carries the future over into the past. The past increases by the diminution of the future until by the consumption of all the future all is past.

CHAPTER XXVIII

37. But how is the future diminished or consumed when it does not yet exist? Or how does the past, which exists no longer, increase, unless it is that in the mind in which all this happens there are three functions? For the mind expects, it attends, and it remembers; so that what it expects passes into what it remembers by way of what it attends to. Who denies that future things do not exist as yet? But still there is already in the mind the expectation of things still future. And who denies that past things now exist no longer? Still there is in the mind the memory of things past. Who denies that time present has no length, since it passes away in a moment? Yet, our attention has a continuity and it is through this that what is present may proceed to become absent. Therefore, future time, which is nonexistent, is not long; but "a long future" is "a long expectation of the future." Nor is time past, which is now no longer, long; a "long past" is "a long memory of the past."

38. I am about to repeat a psalm that I know. Before I begin, my attention encompasses the whole, but once I have begun, as much of it as becomes past while I speak is still stretched out in my memory. The span of my action is divided between my memory, which contains what I have repeated, and my expectation, which contains what I am about to repeat. Yet my attention is continually present with me, and through it what was future is carried over so that it becomes past. The more this is done and repeated, the more the memory is enlarged—and expectation is shortened—until the whole expectation is exhausted. Then the whole action is ended and passed into memory. And what takes place in the entire psalm takes place also in each individual part of it

and in each individual syllable. This also holds in the even longer action of which that psalm is only a portion. The same holds in the whole life of man, of which all the actions of men are parts. The same holds in the whole age of the sons of men, of which all the lives of men are parts.

CHAPTER XXIX

39. But "since thy loving-kindness is better than life itself," observe how my life is but a stretching out, and how thy right hand has upheld me in my Lord, the Son of Man, the Mediator between thee, the One, and us, the many—in so many ways and by so many means. Thus through him I may lay hold upon him in whom I am also laid hold upon; and I may be gathered up from my old way of life to follow that One and to forget that which is behind, no longer stretched out but now pulled together again—stretching forth not to what shall be and shall pass away but to those things that are before me. Not distractedly now, but intently, I follow on for the prize of my heavenly calling, where I may hear the sound of thy praise and contemplate thy delights, which neither come to be nor pass away.

But now my years are spent in mourning. And thou, O Lord, art my comfort, my eternal Father. But I have been torn between the times, the order of which I do not know, and my thoughts, even the inmost and deepest places of my soul, are mangled by various commotions until I shall flow together into thee purged and molten in the fire of thy love.

CHAPTER XXX

40. And I will be immovable and fixed in thee, and thy truth will be my mold. And I shall not have to endure the questions of those men who, as if in a morbid disease, thirst for more than they can hold and say, "What did God make before he made heaven and earth?" or, "How did it come into his mind to make something when he had never before made anything?" Grant them, O Lord, to consider well what they are saying; and grant them to see that where there is no time they cannot say "never." When, therefore, he is said "never to have made"

something—what is this but to say that it was made in no time at all? Let them therefore see that there could be no time without a created world, and let them cease to speak vanity of this kind. Let them also be stretched out to those things which are before them, and understand that thou, the eternal Creator of all times, art before all times and that no times are coeternal with thee; nor is any creature, even if there is a creature "above time."

CHAPTER XXXI

41. O Lord my God, what a chasm there is in thy deep secret! How far short of it have the consequences of my sins cast me? Heal my eyes, that I may enjoy thy light. Surely, if there is a mind that so greatly abounds in knowledge and foreknowledge, to which all things past and future are as well known as one psalm is well known to me, that mind would be an exceeding marvel and altogether astonishing. For whatever is past and whatever is yet to come would be no more concealed from him than the past and future of that psalm were hidden from me when I was chanting it: how much of it had been sung from the beginning and what and how much still remained till the end. But far be it from thee, O Creator of the universe, and Creator of our souls and bodies—far be it from thee that thou shouldst merely know all things past and future. Far, far more wonderfully, and far more mysteriously thou knowest them. For it is not as the feelings of one singing familiar songs, or hearing a familiar song in which, because of his expectation of words still to come and his remembrance of those that are past, his feelings are varied and his senses are divided. This is not the way that anything happens to thee, who art unchangeably eternal, that is, the truly eternal Creator of minds. As in the beginning thou knewest both the heaven and the earth without any change in thy knowledge, so thou didst make heaven and earth in their beginnings without any division in thy action. Let him who understands this confess to thee; and let him who does not understand also confess to thee! Oh, exalted as thou art, still the humble in heart are thy dwelling place! For thou liftest them who are cast down and they fall not for whom thou art the Most High.

THE CITY OF GOD

DISORDER IN THE ORDER OF CREATION

All natures inasmuch as they are, and have therefore a rank and species of their own, and a kind of internal harmony, are certainly good. And when they are in the places assigned to them by the order of their nature, they preserve such being as they have received. And those things which have not received everlasting being, are altered for better or for worse, so as to suit the wants and motions of those things to which the Creator's law has made them subservient; and thus they tend in the divine providence to that end which is embraced in the general scheme of the government of the universe. So that, though the corruption of transitory and perishable things brings them to utter destruction, it does not prevent their producing that which was designed to be their result. And this being so, God, who supremely is, and who therefore created every being which has not supreme existence (for that which was made of nothing could not be equal to Him, and indeed could not be at all had He not made it), is not to be found fault with on account of the creature's faults, but is to be praised in view of the natures He has made.[1]

Thus the true cause of the blessedness of the good angels is found to be this, that they cleave to Him who supremely is. And if we ask the cause of the misery of the bad, it occurs to us, and not unreasonably, that they are miserable because they have forsaken Him who supremely is, and have turned to themselves who have no such essence. And this vice, what else is it called than pride? For "pride is the beginning of sin." They were unwilling, then, to preserve their strength for God; and as adherence to God was the condition of their enjoying an ampler being,

---

[1] *The City of God*, trans. Marcus Dods (Edinburgh: T. & T. Clark, 1871), Bk. XII, chap. v.

they diminished it by preferring themselves to Him. This was the first defect, and the first impoverishment, and the first flaw of their nature, which was created, not indeed supremely existent, but finding its blessedness in the enjoyment of the Supreme Being; whilst by abandoning Him it should become, not indeed no nature at all, but a nature with a less ample existence, and therefore wretched.

If the further question be asked, What was the efficient cause of their evil will? there is none. For what is it which makes the will bad, when it is the will itself which makes the action bad? And consequently the bad will is the cause of the bad action, but nothing is the efficient cause of the bad will. For if anything is the cause, this thing either has or has not a will. If it has, the will is either good or bad. If good, who is so left to himself as to say that a good will makes a will bad? For in this case a good will would be the cause of sin; a most absurd supposition. On the other hand, if this hypothetical thing has a bad will, I wish to know what made it so; and that we may not go on for ever, I ask at once, what made the *first* evil will bad? For that is not the first which was itself corrupted by an evil will, but that is the first which was made evil by no other will. For if it were preceded by that which made it evil, that will was first which made the other evil. But if it is replied, "Nothing made it evil; it always was evil," I ask if it has been existing in some nature. For if not, then it did not exist at all; and if it did exist in some nature, then it vitiated and corrupted it, and injured it, and consequently deprived it of good. And therefore the evil will could not exist in an evil nature, but in a nature at once good and mutable, which this vice could injure. For if it did no injury, it was no vice; and consequently the will in which it was, could not be called evil. But if it did injury, it did it by taking away or diminishing good. And therefore there could not be from eternity, as was suggested, an evil will in that thing in which there had been previously a natural good, which the evil will was able to diminish by corrupting it. If, then, it was not from eternity, who, I ask, made it? The only thing that can be suggested in reply is, that something which itself had no will, made the will evil. I ask, then, whether this thing was superior, inferior, or equal to it? If superior, then it is better. How, then, has it no will, and not rather a good will? The same reasoning applies if it was equal; for so long as two things have equally a good will, the one cannot produce in the other an evil will. Then remains the supposition that that which corrupted the will of the angelic nature which first sinned, was itself an inferior thing without a will. But that thing, be it of the lowest and most earthly kind, is certainly itself good, since it is a nature and being, with a form and rank of its own in its own kind and order. How, then, can a good thing be the efficient cause of an evil will? How, I say, can good be the cause of evil? For when the will abandons what is above itself, and turns to what is lower, it becomes evil—not because that is evil to which it turns, but because the turning itself is wicked. Therefore it is not an inferior thing which has made the will evil, but it is itself which has become so by wickedly and inordinately desiring an inferior thing. For if two men, alike in physical and moral constitution, see the same corporal beauty, and one of them is excited by the sight to desire an illicit enjoyment, while the other stedfastly maintains a modest restraint of his will, what do we suppose brings it about, that there is an evil will in the one and not in the other? What produces it in the man in whom it exists? Not the bodily beauty, for that was presented equally to the gaze of both, and yet did not produce in both an evil will. Did the flesh of the one cause the desire as he looked? But why did not the flesh of the other? Or was it the disposition? But why not the disposition of both? For we are supposing that both were of a like temperament of body and soul. Must we, then, say that the one was tempted by a secret suggestion of the evil spirit? As if it was not by his own will that he consented to this suggestion and to any inducement whatever! This consent, then, this evil will which he presented to the evil suasive influence—what was the cause of it, we ask? For, not to delay on such a difficulty as this, if both are tempted equally, and one yields and consents to the temptation, while the other remains unmoved by it, what other account can we give of the matter than this, that the one is willing, the other unwilling, to fall away from chastity? And what causes this but their own wills, in cases at least such as we are supposing, where the temperament is identical?[2]

---

[2]Ibid., Bk. XII, chap. vi.

This I do know, that the nature of God can never, nowhere, nowise be defective, and that natures made of nothing can. These latter, however, the more being they have, and the more good they do (for then they do something positive), the more they have efficient causes; but in so far as they are defective in being, and consequently do evil (for then what is their work but vanity?), they have deficient causes. And I know likewise, that the will could not become evil, were it unwilling to become so; and therefore its failings are justly punished, being not necessary, but voluntary. For its defections are not to evil things, but are themselves evil; that is to say, are not towards things that are naturally and in themselves evil, but the defection of the will is evil, because it is contrary to the order of nature, and an abandonment of that which has supreme being for that which has less. For avarice is not a fault inherent in gold, but in the man who inordinately loves gold, to the detriment of justice, which ought to be held in incomparably higher regard than gold. Neither is luxury the fault of lovely and charming objects, but of the heart that inordinately loves sensual pleasures, to the neglect of temperance, which attaches us to objects more lovely in their spirituality, and more delectable by their incorruptibility. Nor yet is boasting the fault of human praise, but of the soul that is inordinately fond of the applause of men, and that makes light of the voice of conscience. Pride, too, is not the fault of him who delegates power, nor of power itself, but of the soul that is inordinately enamoured of its own power, and despises the more just dominion of a higher authority. Consequently he who inordinately loves the good which any nature possesses, even though he obtain it, himself becomes evil in the good, and wretched because deprived of a greater good.[3]

THE NATURE OF SIN

But the character of the human will is of moment; because, if it is wrong, these motions of the soul will be wrong, but if it is right, they will be not merely blameless, but even praiseworthy. For the will is in

them all; yea, none of them is anything else than will. For what are desire and joy but a volition of consent to the things we wish? And what are fear and sadness but a volition of aversion from the things which we do not wish? But when consent takes the form of seeking to possess the things we wish, this is called desire; and when consent takes the form of enjoying the things we wish, this is called joy. In like manner, when we turn with aversion from that which we do not wish to happen, this volition is termed fear; and when we turn away from that which has happened against our will, this act of will is called sorrow. And generally in respect of all that we seek or shun, as a man's will is attracted or repelled, so it is changed and turned into these different affections. Wherefore the man who lives according to God, and not according to man, ought to be a lover of good, and therefore a hater of evil. And since no one is evil by nature, but whoever is evil is evil by vice, he who lives according to God ought to cherish towards evil men a perfect hatred, so that he shall neither hate the man because of his vice, nor love the vice because of the man, but hate the vice and love the man. For the vice being cursed, all that ought to be loved, and nothing that ought to be hated, will remain.[4]

But because God foresaw all things, and was therefore not ignorant that man also would fall, we ought to consider this holy city in connection with what God foresaw and ordained, and not according to our own ideas, which do not embrace God's ordination. For man, by his sin, could not disturb the divine counsel, nor compel God to change what He had decreed; for God's foreknowledge had anticipated both—that is to say, both how evil the man whom He had created good should become, and what good He Himself should even thus derive from him. For though God is said to change His determinations (so that in a topical sense the Holy Scripture says even that God repented), this is said with reference to man's expectation, or the order of natural causes, and not with reference to that which the Almighty had foreknown that He would do. Accordingly God, as it is written, made man upright, and consequently with a good will. For if he had not had a good will,

---

[3]Ibid., Bk. XII, chap. viii.

[4]Ibid., Bk. XIV, chap. vi.

he could not have been upright. The good will, then, is the work of God; for God created him with it. But the first evil will, which preceded all man's evil acts, was rather a kind of falling away from the work of God to its own works than any positive work. And therefore the acts resulting were evil, not having God, but the will itself for their end; so that the will or the man himself, so far as his will is bad, was as it were the evil tree bringing forth evil fruit. Moreover, the bad will, though it be not in harmony with, but opposed to nature, inasmuch as it is a vice or blemish, yet it is true of it as of all vice, that it cannot exist except in a nature, and only in a nature created out of nothing, and not in that which the Creator has begotten of Himself, as He begot the Word, by whom all things were made. For though God formed man of the dust of the earth, yet the earth itself, and every earthly material, is absolutely created out of nothing; and man's soul, too, God created out of nothing, and joined to the body, when He made a man. But evils are so thoroughly overcome by good, that though they are permitted to exist, for the sake of demonstrating how the most righteous foresight of God can make a good use even of them, yet good can exist without evil, as in the true and supreme God Himself, and as in every invisible and visible celestial creature that exists above this murky atmosphere; but evil cannot exist without good, because the natures in which evil exists, in so far as they are natures, are good. And evil is removed, not by removing any nature, or part of a nature, which had been introduced by the evil, but by healing and correcting that which had been vitiated and depraved. The will, therefore, is then truly free, when it is not the slave of vices and sins. Such was it given us by God; and this being lost by its own fault, can only be restored by Him who was able at first to give it.[5]

Our first parents fell into open disobedience because already they were secretly corrupted; for the evil act had never been done had not an evil will preceded it. And what is the origin of our evil will but pride? For "pride is the beginning of sin." And what is pride but the craving for undue exaltation? And this is undue exaltation, when the soul abandons Him to whom it ought to cleave as its end, and becomes a kind of end to itself. This happens when it becomes its own satisfaction. And it does so when it falls away from that unchangeable good which ought to satisfy it more than itself. This falling away is spontaneous; for if the will had remained stedfast in the love of that higher and changeless good by which it was illumined to intelligence and kindled into love, it would not have turned away to find satisfaction in itself, and so become frigid and benighted; the woman would not have believed the serpent spoke the truth, nor would the man have preferred the request of his wife to the command of God, nor have supposed that it was a venial transgression to cleave to the partner of his life even in a partnership of sin. The wicked deed, then—that is to say, the transgression of eating the forbidden fruit—was committed by persons who were already wicked. That "evil fruit" could be brought forth only by "a corrupt tree." But that the tree was evil was not the result of nature; for certainly it could become so only by the vice of the will, and vice is contrary to nature. Now, nature could not have been depraved by vice had it not been made out of nothing. Consequently, that it is a nature, this is because it is made by God; but that it falls away from Him, this is because it is made out of nothing. But man did not so fall away as to become absolutely nothing; but being turned towards himself, his being became more contracted than it was when he clave to Him who supremely is. Accordingly, to exist in himself, that is, to be his own satisfaction after abandoning God, is not quite to become a nonentity, but to approximate to that. And therefore the holy Scriptures designate the proud by another name, "self-pleasers." For it is good to have the heart lifted up, yet not to one's self, for this is proud, but to the Lord, for this is obedient, and can be the act only of the humble. There is, therefore, something in humility which, strangely enough, exalts the heart, and something in pride which debases it. This seems, indeed, to be contradictory, that loftiness should debase and lowliness exalt. But pious humility enables us to submit to what is above us; and nothing is more exalted above us than God; and therefore humility, by making us subject to God, exalts us. But pride, being a defect of nature, by the very act of refusing subjection and revolting from Him who is supreme, falls to a low condition; and

[5]Ibid., Bk. XIV, chap. xi.

then comes to pass what is written: "Thou castedst them down when they lifted up themselves." For he does not say, "when they had been lifted up, as if first they were exalted, and then afterwards cast down; but "when they lifted up themselves" even then they were cast down—that is to say, the very lifting up was already a fall. And therefore it is that humility is specially recommended to the city of God as it sojourns in this world, and is specially exhibited in the city of God, and the person of Christ its King; while the contrary vice of pride, according to the testimony of the sacred writings, specially rules his adversary the devil. And certainly this is the great difference which distinguishes the two cities of which we speak, the one being the society of the godly men, the other of the ungodly, each associated with the angels that adhere to their party, and the one guided and fashioned by love of self, the other by love of God.[6]

THE TWO CITIES

Accordingly, two cities have been formed by two loves: the earthly by the love of self, even to the contempt of God; the heavenly by the love of God, even to contempt of self. The former, in a word, glories in itself, the latter in the Lord. For the one seeks glory from men; but the greatest glory of the other is God, the witness of conscience. The one lifts up its head in its own glory; the other says to its God, "Thou art my glory, and the lifter up of mine head." In the one, the princes and the nations it subdues are ruled by the love of ruling; in the other, the princes and the subjects serve one another in love, the latter obeying, while the former take thought for all. The one delights in its own strength, represented in the persons of its rulers; the other says to its God, "I will love Thee, O Lord, my strength." And therefore the wise men of the one city, living according to man, have sought for profit to their own bodies or souls, or both, and those who have known God "glorified Him not as God, neither were thankful, but became vain in their imaginations, and their foolish heart was darkened; professing themselves to be wise"—that is, glorying in their own wisdom, and being possessed by pride—"they became fools, and changed the glory of the incorruptible God into an image made like to corruptible man, and to birds, and four-footed beasts, and creeping things." For they were either leaders or followers of the people in adoring images, "and worshipped and served the creature more than the Creator, who is blessed for ever." But in the other city there is no human wisdom, but only godliness, which offers due worship to the true God, and looks for its reward in the society of the saints, of holy angels as well as holy men, "that God may be all in all."[7]

We have already stated in the preceding books that God, desiring not only that the human race might be able by their similarity of nature to associate with one another, but also that they might be bound together in harmony and peace by the ties of relationship, was pleased to derive all men from one individual, and created man with such a nature that the members of the race should not have died, had not the two first (of whom the one was created out of nothing, and the other out of him) merited this by their disobedience; for by them so great a sin was committed, that by it the human nature was altered for the worse, and was transmitted also to their posterity, liable to sin and subject to death. And the kingdom of death so reigned over men, that the deserved penalty of sin would have hurled all headlong even into the second death, of which there is no end, had not the undeserved grace of God saved some therefrom. And thus it has come to pass, that though there are very many and great nations all over the earth, whose rites and customs, speech, arms, and dress, are distinguished by marked differences, yet there are no more than two kinds of human society, which we may justly call two cities, according to the language of our Scriptures. The one consists of those who wish to live after the flesh, the other of those who wish to live after the spirit; and when they severally achieve what they wish, they live in peace, each after their kind.[8]

First, we must see what it is to live after the flesh, and what to live after the spirit. For any one who either

---

[6]Ibid., Bk. XIV, chap. xiii.

[7]Ibid., Bk. XIV, chap. xxvii.
[8]Ibid., Bk. XIV, chap. i.

does not recollect, or does not sufficiently weigh, the language of sacred Scripture, may, on first hearing what we have said, suppose that the Epicurean philosophers live after the flesh, because they place man's highest good in bodily pleasure; and that those others do so who have been of opinion that in some form or other bodily good is man's supreme good; and that the mass of men do so who, without dogmatizing or philosophizing on the subject, are so prone to lust that they cannot delight in any pleasure save such as they receive from bodily sensations: and he may suppose that the Stoics, who place the supreme good of men in the soul, live after the spirit; for what is man's soul, if not spirit? But in the sense of the divine Scripture both are proved to live after the flesh.

Since, then, Scripture uses the word flesh in many ways, which there is not time to collect and investigate, if we are to ascertain what it is to live after the flesh (which is certainly evil, though the nature of flesh is not itself evil), we must carefully examine that passage of the epistle which the Apostle Paul wrote to the Galatians, in which he says, "Now the works of the flesh are manifest, which are these: adultery, fornication, uncleanness, lasciviousness, idolatry, witchcraft, hatred, variance, emulations, wrath, strife, seditions, heresies, envyings, murders, drunkenness, revellings, and such like: of the which I tell you before, as I have also told you in time past, that they which do such things shall not inherit the kingdom of God." This whole passage of the apostolic epistle being considered, so far as it bears on the matter in hand, will be sufficient to answer the question, what it is to live after the flesh. For among the works of the flesh which he said were manifest, and which he cited for condemnation, we find not only those which concern the pleasure of the flesh, as fornications, uncleanness, lasciviousness, drunkenness, revellings, but also those which, though they be remote from fleshly pleasure, reveal the vices of the soul. For who does not see that idolatries, witchcrafts, hatreds, variance, emulations, wrath, strife, heresies, envyings, are vices rather of the soul than of the flesh? For it is quite possible for a man to abstain from fleshly pleasures for the sake of idolatry or some heretical error; and yet, even when he does so, he is proved by this apostolic authority to be living after the flesh; and in abstaining from fleshly

pleasure, he is proved to be practising damnable works of the flesh. Who that has enmity has it not in his soul? or who would say to his enemy, or to the man he thinks his enemy, You have a bad flesh towards me, and not rather, You have a bad spirit towards me? In fine, if any one heard of what I may call "carnalities," he would not fail to attribute them to the carnal part of man; so no one doubts that "animosities" belong to the soul of man. Why then does the doctor of the Gentiles in faith and verity call all these and similar things works of the flesh, unless because, by that mode of speech whereby the part is used for the whole he means us to understand by the word flesh the man himself?[9]

When, therefore, man lives according to man, not according to God, he is like the devil. Because not even an angel might live according to an angel, but only according to God, if he was to abide in the truth, and speak God's truth and not his own lie. And of man, too, the same apostle says in another place, "If the truth of God hath more abounded through my lie";—"my lie," he said, and "God's truth." When, then, a man lives according to the truth, he lives not according to himself, but according to God; for He was God who said, "I am the truth." When, therefore, man lives according to himself—that is, according to man, not according to God—assuredly he lives according to a lie; not that man himself is a lie, for God is his author and creator, who is certainly not the author and creator of a lie, but because man was made upright, that he might not live according to himself, but according to Him that made him—in other words, that he might do His will and not his own; and not to live as he was made to live, that is a lie. For he certainly desires to be blessed even by not living so that he may be blessed. And what is a lie if this desire be not? Wherefore it is not without meaning said that all sin is a lie. For no sin is committed save by that desire or will by which we desire that it be well with us, and shrink from it being ill with us. That, therefore, is a lie which we do in order that it may be well with us, but which makes us more miserable than we were. And why is this, but because the source of man's happiness lies only

---

[9]Ibid., Bk. XIV, chap. ii.

in God, whom he abandons when he sins, and not in himself, by living according to whom he sins?

In enunciating this proposition of ours, then, that because some live according to the flesh and others according to the spirit there have arisen two diverse and conflicting cities, we might equally well have said, "because some live according to man, others according to God."[10]

THE HARMONY OF GOD'S ORDER

Whoever gives even moderate attention to human affairs and to our common nature, will recognise that if there is no man who does not wish to be joyful, neither is there any one who does not wish to have peace. For even they who make war desire nothing but victory—desire, that is to say, to attain to peace with glory. For what else is victory than the conquest of those who resist us? and when this is done there is peace. It is therefore with the desire for peace that wars are waged, even by those who take pleasure in exercising their warlike nature in command and battle. And hence it is obvious that peace is the end sought for by war. For every man seeks peace by waging war, but no man seeks war by making peace. For even they who intentionally interrupt the peace in which they are living have no hatred of peace, but only wish it changed into a peace that suits them better. They do not, therefore, wish to have no peace, but only one more to their mind. And in the case of sedition, when men have separated themselves from the community, they yet do not effect what they wish, unless they maintain some kind of peace with their fellow-conspirators. And therefore even robbers take care to maintain peace with their comrades, that they may with greater effect and greater safety invade the peace of other men. And if an individual happen to be of such unrivalled strength, and to be so jealous of partnership, that he trusts himself with no comrades, but makes his own plots, and commits depredations and murders on his own account, yet he maintains some shadow of peace with such persons as he is unable to kill, and from whom he wishes to conceal his deeds. In his own home, too, he makes it his aim to be at peace with his wife and children, and any other members of his household; for unquestionably their prompt obedience to his every look is a source of pleasure to him. And if this be not rendered, he is angry, he chides and punishes; and even by this storm he secures the calm peace of his own home, as occasion demands. For he sees that peace cannot be maintained unless all the members of the same domestic circle be subject to one head, such as he himself is in his own house. And therefore if a city or nation offered to submit itself to him, to serve him in the same style as he had made his house-hold serve him, he would no longer lurk in a brigand's hiding-places, but lift his head in open day as a king, though the same covetousness and wickedness should remain in him. And thus all men desire to have peace with their own circle whom they wish to govern as suits themselves. For even those whom they make war against they wish to make their own, and impose on them the laws of their own peace.

For the most savage animals encompass their own species with a ring of protecting peace. They cohabit, beget, produce, suckle, and bring up their young, though very many of them are not gregarious, but solitary—not like sheep, deer, pigeons, starlings, bees, but such as lions, foxes, eagles, bats. For what tigress does not gently purr over her cubs, and lay aside her ferocity to fondle them? What kite, solitary as he is when circling over his prey, does not seek a mate, build a nest, hatch the eggs, bring up the young birds, and maintain with the mother of his family as peaceful a domestic alliance as he can? How much more powerfully do the laws of man's nature move him to hold fellowship and maintain peace with all men so far as in him lies, since even wicked men wage war to maintain the peace of their own circle, and wish that, if possible, all men belonged to them, that all men and things might serve but one head, and might, either through love or fear, yield themselves to peace with him! It is thus that pride in its perversity apes God. It abhors equality with other men under Him; but, instead of His rule, it seeks to impose a rule of its own upon its equals. It abhors, that is to say, the just peace of God, and loves its own unjust peace; but it cannot help loving peace of one kind or other. For there is no vice so clean contrary to nature that it obliterates even the faintest traces of nature.

---

[10]Ibid., Bk. XIV, chap. iv.

He, then, who prefers what is right to what is wrong, and what is well-ordered to what is perverted, sees that the peace of unjust men is not worthy to be called peace in comparison with the peace of the just. And yet even what is perverted must of necessity be in harmony with, and in dependence on, and in some part of the order of things, for otherwise it would have no existence at all.[11]

The peace of the body then consists in the duly proportioned arrangements of its parts. The peace of the irrational soul is the harmonious repose of the appetites, and that of the rational soul the harmony of knowledge and action. The peace of body and soul is the well-ordered and harmonious life and health of the living creature. Peace between man and God is the well-ordered obedience of faith to eternal law. Peace between man and man is well-ordered concord. Domestic peace is the well-ordered concord between those of the family who rule and those who obey. Civil peace is a similar concord among the citizens. The peace of the celestial city is the perfectly ordered and harmonious enjoyment of God, and of one another in God. The peace of all things is the tranquillity of order. Order is the distribution which allots things equal and unequal, each to its own place. And hence, though the miserable, in so far as they are such, do certainly not enjoy peace, but are severed from that tranquillity of order in which there is no disturbance, nevertheless, inasmuch as they are deservedly and justly miserable, they are by their very misery connected with order. They are not, indeed, conjoined with the blessed, but they are disjoined from them by the law of order. And though they are disquieted, their circumstances are notwithstanding adjusted to them, and consequently they have some tranquillity of order, and therefore some peace. But they are wretched because, although not wholly miserable, they are not in that place where any mixture of misery is impossible. They would, however, be more wretched if they had not that peace which arises from being in harmony with the natural order of things. When they suffer, their peace is in so far disturbed; but their peace continues in so far as they do not suffer, and in so far as their nature continues to exist. As, then, there may be life without pain, while there cannot be pain without some kind of life, so there may be peace without war, but there cannot be war without some kind of peace, because war supposes the existence of some natures to wage it, and these natures cannot exist without peace of one kind or other.

And therefore there is a nature in which evil does not or even cannot exist; but there cannot be a nature in which there is no good. Hence not even the nature of the devil himself is evil, in so far as it is nature, but it was made evil by being perverted. Thus he did not abide in the truth, but could not escape the judgment of the Truth; he did not abide in the tranquillity of order, but did not therefore escape the power of the Ordainer. The good imparted by God to his nature did not screen him from the justice of God by which order was preserved in his punishment; neither did God punish the good which He had created, but the evil which the devil had committed. God did not take back all He had imparted to his nature, but something He took and something He left, that there might remain enough to be sensible of the loss of what was taken. And this very sensibility to pain is evidence of the good which has been taken away and the good which has been left. For, were nothing good left, there could be no pain on account of the good which had been lost. For he who sins is still worse if he rejoices in his loss of righteousness. But he who is in pain, if he derives no benefit from it, mourns at least the loss of health. And as righteousness and health are both good things, and as the loss of any good thing is a matter of grief, not of joy—if, at least, there is no compensation, as spiritual righteousness may compensate for the loss of bodily health—certainly it is more suitable for a wicked man to grieve in punishment than to rejoice in his fault. As, then, the joy of a sinner who has abandoned what is good is evidence of a bad will, so his grief for the good he has lost when he is punished is evidence of a good nature. For he who laments the peace his nature has lost is stirred to do so by some relics of peace which make his nature friendly to itself. And it is very just that in the final punishment the wicked and godless should in anguish bewail the loss of the natural advantages they enjoyed, and should perceive that they were most justly taken from them by that God whose benign liberality they had despised. God, then, the most wise Creator and most just Ordainer of all natures, who

---

[11] Ibid., Bk. XIX, chap. xii.

placed the human race upon earth as its greatest ornament, imparted to men some good things adapted
to this life, to wit, temporal peace, such as we can
enjoy in this life from health and safety and human
fellowship, and all things needful for the preservation
and recovery of this peace, such as the objects which
are accommodated to our outward senses, light, night,
the air, and waters suitable for us, and everything the
body requires to sustain, shelter, heal, or beautify it:
and all under this most equitable condition, that every
man who made a good use of these advantages suited
to the peace of his mortal condition, should receive
ampler and better blessings, namely, the peace of immortality, accompanied by glory and honour in an
endless life made fit for the enjoyment of God and
of one another in God; but that he who used the present blessings badly should both lose them and should
not receive the others.[12]

The whole use, then, of things temporal has a reference to this result of earthly peace in the earthly
community, while in the city of God it is connected
with eternal peace. And therefore, if we were irrational animals, we should desire nothing beyond the
proper arrangement of the parts of the body and the
satisfaction of the appetites—nothing, therefore, but
bodily comfort and abundance of pleasures, that the
peace of the body might contribute to the peace of
the soul. For if bodily peace be awanting, a bar is put
to the peace even of the irrational soul, since it cannot obtain the gratification of its appetites. And these
two together help out the mutual peace of soul and
body, the peace of harmonious life and health. For
as animals, by shunning pain, show that they love
bodily peace, and, by pursuing pleasure to gratify
their appetites, show that they love peace of soul, so
their shrinking from death is a sufficient indication
of their intense love of that peace which binds soul
and body in close alliance. But, as man has a rational soul, he subordinates all this which he has in common with the beasts to the peace of his rational soul,
that his intellect may have free play and may regulate his actions, and that he may thus enjoy the well-
ordered harmony of knowledge and action which
constitutes, as we have said, the peace of the ratio-

nal soul. And for this purpose he must desire to be
neither molested by pain, nor disturbed by desire, nor
extinguished by death, that he may arrive at some
useful knowledge by which he may regulate his life
and manners. But, owing to the liability of the human mind to fall into mistakes, this very pursuit of
knowledge may be a snare to him unless he has a divine Master, whom he may obey without misgiving,
and who may at the same time give him such help
as to preserve his own freedom. And because, so long
as he is in this mortal body, he is a stranger to God,
he walks by faith, not by sight; and he therefore refers
all peace, bodily or spiritual or both, to that peace
which mortal man has with the immortal God, so that
he exhibits the well-ordered obedience of faith to
eternal law. But as this divine Master inculcates two
precepts—the love of God and the love of our neighbour—and as in these precepts a man finds three
things he has to love—God, himself, and his neighbour—and that he who loves God loves himself
thereby, it follows that he must endeavour to get his
neighbour to love God, since he is ordered to love
his neighbour as himself. He ought to make this endeavour in behalf of his wife, his children, his household, all within his reach, even as he would wish his
neighbour to do the same for him if he needed it; and
consequently he will be at peace, or in well-ordered
concord, with all men, as far as in him lies. And this
is the order of this concord, that a man, in the first
place, injure no one, and, in the second, do good to
every one he can reach. Primarily, therefore, his own
household are his care, for the law of nature and of
society gives him readier access to them and greater
opportunity of serving them. And hence the apostle
says, "Now, if any provide not for his own, and specially for those of his own house, he hath denied the
faith, and is worse than an infidel." This is the origin of domestic peace, or the well-ordered concord
of those in the family who rule and those who obey.
For they who care for the rest rule—the husband the
wife, the parents the children, the masters the servants; and they who are cared for obey—the women
their husbands, the children their parents, the servants
their masters. But in the family of the just man who
lives by faith and is as yet a pilgrim journeying on
to the celestial city, even those who rule serve those
whom they seem to command; for they rule not from

---

[12]Ibid., Bk. XIX, chap. xiii.

a love of power, but from a sense of the duty they owe to others—not because they are proud of authority, but because they love mercy.[13]

THE EARTHLY SOJOURN OF THE CITIZEN OF HEAVEN

But the families which do not live by faith seek their peace in the earthly advantages of this life; while the families which live by faith look for those eternal blessings which are promised, and use as pilgrims such advantages of time and of earth as do not fascinate and divert them from God, but rather aid them to endure with greater ease, and to keep down the number of those burdens of the corruptible body which weigh upon the soul. Thus the things necessary for this mortal life are used by both kinds of men and families alike, but each has its own peculiar and widely different aim in using them. The earthly city, which does not live by faith, seeks an earthly peace, and the end it proposes, in the well-ordered concord of civic obedience and rule, is the combination of men's wills to attain the things which are helpful to this life. The heavenly city, or rather the part of it which sojourns on earth and lives by faith, makes use of this peace only because it must, until this mortal condition which necessitates it shall pass away. Consequently, so long as it lives like a captive and a stranger in the earthly city, though it has already received the promise of redemption, and the gift of the Spirit as the earnest of it, it makes no scruple to obey the laws of the earthly city, whereby the things necessary for the maintenance of this mortal life are administered; and thus, as this life is common to both cities, so there is a harmony between them in regard to what belongs to it. This heavenly city, then, while it sojourns on earth, calls citizens out of all nations, and gathers together a society of pilgrims of all languages, not scrupling about diversities in the manners, laws, and institutions whereby earthly peace is secured and maintained, but recognizing that, however various these are, they all tend to one and the same end of earthly peace. It therefore is so far from rescinding and abolishing these

diversities, that it even preserves and adapts them, so long only as no hindrance to the worship of the one supreme and true God is thus introduced. Even the heavenly city, therefore, while in its state of pilgrimage, avails itself of the peace of earth and, so far as it can without injuring faith and godliness, desires and maintains a common agreement among men regarding the acquisition of the necessaries of life, and makes this earthly peace bear upon the peace of heaven; for this alone can be truly called and esteemed the peace of the reasonable creatures, consisting as it does in the perfectly ordered and harmonious enjoyment of God and of one another in God. When we shall have reached that peace, this mortal life shall give place to one that is eternal, and our body shall be no more this animal body which by its corruption weighs down the soul, but a spiritual body feeling no want, and in all its members subjected to the will. In its pilgrim state the heavenly city possesses this peace by faith; and by this faith it lives righteously when it refers to the attainment of that peace every good action towards God and man; for the life of the city is a social life.[14]

But the peace which is peculiar to ourselves we enjoy now with God by faith, and shall hereafter enjoy eternally with Him by sight. But the peace which we enjoy in this life, whether common to all or peculiar to ourselves, is rather the solace of our misery than the positive enjoyment of felicity. Our very righteousness, too, though true in so far as it has respect to the true good, is yet in this life of such a kind that it consists rather in the remission of sins than in the perfecting of virtues. Witness the prayer of the whole city of God in its pilgrim state, for it cries to God by the mouth of all its members, "Forgive us our trespasses as we forgive those who trespass against us." And this prayer is efficacious not for those whose faith is "without works and dead," but for those whose faith "worketh by love." For as reason, though subjected to God, is yet "pressed down by the corruptible body," so long as it is in this mortal condition, it has not perfect authority over vice, and therefore this prayer is needed by the righteous. For though it exercises authority, the vices do not submit without a struggle. For however well

---

[13]Ibid., Bk. XIX, chap. xiv.

[14]Ibid., Bk. XIX, chap. xvii.

one maintains the conflict, and however thoroughly he has subdued these enemies, there steals in some evil thing, which, if it do not find ready expression in act, slips out by the lips, or insinuates itself into the thought; and therefore his peace is not full so long as he is at war with his vices. For it is a doubtful conflict he wages with those that resist, and his victory over those that are defeated is not secure, but full of anxiety and effort. Amidst these temptations, therefore, of all which it has been summarily said in the divine oracles, "Is not human life upon earth a temptation?" who but a proud man can presume that he so lives that he has no need to say to God, "Forgive us our trespasses"? And such a man is not great, but swollen and puffed up with vanity, and is justly resisted by Him who abundantly gives grace to the humble. Whence it is said, "God resisteth the proud, but giveth grace to the humble." In this, then, consists the righteousness of a man, that he submit himself to God, his body to his soul, and his vices, even when they rebel, to his reason, which either defeats or at least resists them; and also that he beg from God grace to do his duty, and the pardon of his sins, and that he render to God thanks for all the blessings he receives. But, in that final peace to which all our righteousness has reference, and for the sake of which it is maintained, as our nature shall enjoy a sound immortality and incorruption, and shall have no more vices, and as we shall experience no resistance either from ourselves or from others, it will not be necessary that reason should rule vices which no longer exist, but God shall rule the man, and the soul shall rule the body, with a sweetness and facility suitable to the felicity of a life which is done with bondage. And this condition shall there be eternal, and we shall be assured of its eternity; and thus the peace of this blessedness and the blessedness of this peace shall be the supreme good.[15]

---

[15]Ibid., Bk. XIX, chap. xxvii.

FOR FURTHER READING

Primary Sources

The main writings of St. Augustine are to be found in many editions and translations. The most commonly available are the following:

A Select Library of the Nicene and Post-Nicene Fathers, First Series, Edited by Philip Schaff. Vols. I–VIII. New York: The Christian Literature Publishing Co., 1886–90.

Fathers of the Church Series, New York: The Fathers of the Church, Inc., 1947–

Library of Christian Classics, Philadelphia: The Westminster Press, 1953–55, Vols. VI, VII, VIII.

Basic Writings of St. Augustine. 2 vols. Edited by Whitney J. Oates. New York: Random House, Inc., 1948.

The *Confessions* and *The City of God* are separately available in many inexpensive editions.

Secondary Sources

Bourke, Vernon J. *Augustine's Quest of Wisdom.* Milwaukee: The Bruce Publishing Co., 1947.

D'Arcy, M. C. (ed.). *A Monument to St. Augustine.* London: Sheed & Ward, 1934.

Cochrane, C. N. *Christianity and Classical Culture.* Oxford: The Clarendon Press, 1940.

REVIEW QUESTIONS

1. For Augustine, what is the problem of evil? What is his solution to it?
2. What is the ultimate cause of evil?
3. Does Augustine think that God's foreknowledge undermines free will? What does he say to those who seek a cause of the will itself?
4. What is Augustine's answer to those who ask "What was God doing before he made heaven and earth?"
5. What is Augustine's answer to those who blamed Christianity for the fall of the Roman Empire?

9

BOETHIUS

Boethius (c. 480–524), Roman patrician, consul of Rome, and minister to Ostrogoth King Theodoric, was known as "the last of the Roman philosophers and the first of the scholastic theologians." Next to Augustine he was the most influential thinker in the middle ages prior to Thomas of Aquinas. Until the thirteenth century Aristotle was known only through his translations. He set forth the famous definition of eternity as "perfect possession all at the same time of endless life" as well as the difference between conditional and simple necessity which Boethius discusses in our selection. Apparently a victim of political intrigue, Boethius was falsely accused of treason, tortured, imprisoned, and bludgeoned to death. While in prison he composed *The Consolation of Philosophy*, which Gibbon called "a golden volume not unworthy of the leisure of Plato or of Tully [Cicero]," from which the following selection is taken.

In *Consolation* Philosophy appears to Boethius as a woman of awe-inspiring beauty, "her eyes burning and keen beyond the usual power of ordinary mortals, whose color was full of life, and whose strength was still intact though she was so full of years that by no means would it be believed that she was of our generation." She then begins the process of applying spiritual medicine to Boethius's soul, leading him from his lonely despair to an understanding of and resignation to Providence. The healing process takes the form of a dialogue comparable to one of Plato's. In the last book of *Consolation*, Philosophy explains the meaning of chance and how free will can be reconciled with divine foreknowledge.

THE CONSOLATION OF PHILOSOPHY

CHANCE, FREE WILL AND FOREKNOWLEDGE

1. PHILOSOPHY DISCUSSES THE NATURE OF CHANCE

Here Philosophy made an end and was steering the conversation to certain other matters when I interrupted her, "I am learning in fact what you stated in words a while ago: the question of Providence is bound up in many others. I would ask you whether you think that chance exists at all, and what you think it is."

She replied, "I am eager to fulfill my promise and to open for you the way which you may return home. But these things, though very useful to know, are nevertheless rather removed from our proposed path, and we must be careful lest you, wearied of side trips, be not strong enough to complete the main journey."

"Have no fear about that," I said, "it will be satisfying to know these things in which I delight so much. At the same time, since every side of your argument has stood firm with unshaken credit, let there be nothing ambiguous about its sequel."

Then she said, "I will gratify you," and began to speak as follows: "If anyone define chance as the outcome of random motion produced by no sequence of causes, I am sure there is no such thing and consider it an empty, meaningless word, even if we refer by it to some actual event. For what place can be left for any random happening, seeing that God keeps everything in order? It is a true statement that nothing comes out of nothing. None of the ancients ever denied it, although they used it as a maxim of their natural philosophy with reference to material objects, not efficient causes. But if something were to arise from no cause, it would appear to have arisen out of nothing. Since this is impossible, then chance also, of the sort such as we just defined, cannot exist."

"Then," I asked, "Is there nothing which can justly be called chance or accident? Or is there something which, although unknown to common people, these words are fitting?"

"My philosopher, Aristotle," she replied, "defined it in his *Physics* briefly and close to the truth."

"In what way?" I asked.

"Whenever," she replied, "something is done with one intention but something else, other than what was intended, results from certain causes, that is called *chance*; as, for example, if a man, digging for the purpose of cultivating a field, finds a mass of buried gold. Such a thing is believed to have happened by chance, but not from nothing, for it has its own causes whose unforeseen and unexpected coincidence seems to have brought about a chance. For, had not the cultivator dug the ground and had not the depositor buried the money in that particular spot, the gold would not have been found. These then are the reasons for that profitable accident, which came about from the meeting and confluence of causes, not from the intention of the agents. For neither he who buried the gold nor he who worked the field intended that the gold should be found, but, as I said, it was a coincidence that the one happened to dig where the other had buried. Chance therefore may be defined as an unexpected result from the coincidence of certain causes in matter done for some other purpose. The order of the universe, advancing with inevitable sequence, brings about this coincidence and confluence of causes. This order emanates from its source, which is Providence, and disposes all things in their proper time and place. . . .

2. PHILOSOPHY ASSERTS THE EXISTENCE OF FREE WILL

"I agree with what you say," said I, "but is there any place for free will in this series of cohering causes, or does the chain of Fate bind the very movements of our minds as well?"

"There is free will," she replied, "nor could there be any reasoning nature without it. For any being that, by its nature, can use reason has a power of discernment with which it can judge any thing. By itself, therefore, it distinguishes between objects to

From *The Consolation of Philosophy*. Based on the translation of W. V. Cooper (London 1902).

be shunned and objects to be desired. Now, everyone seeks what he judges to be desirable, and flees what he deems should be shunned. Wherefore all who have reason have also within themselves freedom of desiring and refusing. But I do not lay it down that this freedom is equal in all beings. Heavenly and divine substances have at hand an acute judgment, an uncorrupted will, and the power to effect their desires. Human souls must be the more free the more they maintain themselves in the contemplation of the divine mind, less free when their attention is distracted towards material things, and less free still when they are tied to their earthly members. Indeed, the last stage is mere slavery, wherein the spirit is delivered over to vices and has fallen away from the possession of its reason. For when the mind's eye turns from the light of the highest truth to what is lower and less lucid, it is soon dimmed by the clouds of ignorance and becomes turbid through ruinous passions; by yielding and consenting to these passions, men increase the slavery which they have brought upon themselves and become in a certain way captive through their own freedom. But all these things are known in the sight of that Providence which foresees all things from eternity and disposes each according to its own deserts as predestined."

3. BOETHIUS CANNOT RECONCILE GOD'S FOREKNOWLEDGE WITH HUMAN FREE WILL

"Behold," I said, "I am now more confused than ever."

"What is it," she asked, "although I already have an idea of what is troubling you?"

"There seems," I replied, "to be such incompatibility between the existence of God's universal foreknowledge and that of man's free will. For, if God foresees all things and can in no wise be mistaken, then that which His Providence foresees as going to happen must result necessarily. Wherefore, if from eternity He foreknows not only men's deeds but also their designs and wishes, there will be no free will; for there can neither be any deed done nor wish formed except such as the infallible Providence of God has foreseen. For, if matters could ever be so turned as to result otherwise than was foreseen,

His foreknowledge of the future would never be certain but would rather be uncertain opinion, a thing which I deem impious to attribute to God. And, further, I cannot approve of that argument by which some men think they can solve this knotty problem: they say that a future event does not come to pass for the reason that Providence has foreseen it, but rather, on the contrary, since it is about to come to pass it cannot be hidden from divine Providence. In that way necessity is taken away from the events foreseen and attributed to the act of foreseeing, so that it is not necessary that what is forseen should actually happen but necessary that those things which are going to happen be also foreseen; as though, indeed, our problem was: What is the cause of what? Is God's foreknowledge the cause of the necessity of the future, or is the necessity of the future the cause of God's foreknowledge? Whereas we actually strive to prove this, that, howsoever this causal relation be ordered, the event of the things foreknown is necessary, even if foreknowledge itself does not seem to induce this necessity of the event into things to come.

"For, if a man is sitting, then the belief that he is sitting must be true and conversely, if the opinion that the man is sitting is true, then he must necessarily be sitting. There is therefore necessity in both cases: in the former the opinion must be true and in the latter the man must be sitting. However, he is not sitting because the opinion is true, but rather the opinion is true because his being seated preceded it.

"It is manifest that we should reason in like manner concerning Providence and future events. For, even if these are foreseen because they are about to happen, and do not happen because they are foreseen, it is nevertheless necessary both that what is about to happen should be foreseen by God and that what has been foreseen should happen as it was foreseen, and this last alone is enough to destroy free will. Yet how preposterous it is for us to say that the temporal event is the cause of eternal foreknowledge! Moreover, to hold that God foresees future things because they are about to happen is nothing else than to think that what has happened in the past is the cause of that highest Providence. Besides, just as when I really know that something exists it must needs exist, so also when I really know that something is about to come to pass it must needs come to pass. Thus it follows that the event of a thing foreknown is inevitable.

"Finally, if any one believes something which is actually not so, he has no knowledge but a fallacious opinion, a thing far removed from scientific truth. Wherefore, if any future thing is future in such a way that its event is not sure or necessary, how can it possibly be known beforehand that it will occur? For, just as knowledge itself is unmixed with falsity, so also that which is conceived by it cannot be otherwise than it is conceived. That is the reason why knowledge does not lie, because each matter must be just as knowledge understands it to be. What then? How does God foreknow uncertain future things? For, if He thinks they will inevitably happen while the possibility of their not happening exists, He is mistaken; and this is wicked to think or say. But if He judges these uncertain future events to be uncertain as they actually are, i.e., if He knows only that they may or may not occur, then one can hardly speak of fore*knowledge*, for He would know nothing certain and definite. Or wherein does it differ from that ridiculous prophecy of Tiresias in Horace's *Satires:*

Whatever I say shall either be or not be.

How, too, would God's Providence be better than man's opinion, if like mankind He judges uncertain those things whose events are uncertain? But if there can be nothing uncertain in that most certain Fount of all things, then those things which He has firmly foreknown as things which are going to happen will certainly happen. Wherefore there exists no liberty for human designs and actions. For the divine mind, foreseeing all things without the error of deception, restricts and binds each one of them to one single outcome.

"Once this has been admitted, it is plain what a destructive effect such an admission must have for all human affairs. In vain are rewards and punishments proposed for the good and the bad, for there are no free and voluntary actions of the mind to warrant them. And what we now judge most fair will prove to be most unfair in all respects, namely, to punish the wicked or reward the upright, since not their own will but the fixed necessity of the future forces them to do either good or evil. There will no longer be such things as virtues or vices but merely an indiscriminate mixture of merit and/or guilt. And nothing more criminal than this could be imagined: since the whole order of things proceeds from Providence and nothing is left to human designs, it follows that our vices as well as our virtues must be referred to the Author of all good things. Hence there is no reason to hope for or to pray against anything, for what could any man hope for or pray against when all that can be desired is merely a link in an inflexible chain of events? Thus there will be taken away that sole communication between God and man, namely, the right of prayer. . . .

4. PHILOSOPHY TRIES TO SHOW HOW FOREKNOWLEDGE AND FREE WILL MAY BE RECONCILED

Then Philosophy spoke, "This is an ancient complaint against Providence. Cicero argued against it when dealing with divination, and it is a matter about which you yourself have made long and frequent inquiries. But hitherto neither of you have developed it with sufficient diligence and precision. The reason why the solution of this problem has always remained hidden is the fact that the step-by-step process of human reasoning cannot attain to the act of simple insight which divine foreknowledge is. If our minds could somehow operate this latter way, there would be no doubt left at all. I will try to make this clear after I have explained your difficulties. Tell me why you reject the arguments of those who think that free will is not in any way hindered by foreknowledge, because they hold that foreknowledge is not the cause of the necessity in future things. Whence do *you* draw your evidence for the necessity of future things if not from the fact that things foreknown cannot but come to pass? If, then, as you yourself admitted a while back, foreknowledge imposes no necessity upon future things, what could possibly change voluntary acts into necessary ones? Let us assume for the sake of argument, so that you may see what follows, that there is no foreknowledge at all. Then, under the circumstances thus assumed, are the events resulting from free will bound by necessity?"

"Of course not."

"Now, let us assume that foreknowledge exists, but imposes no necessity upon things; then, I think, the same freedom of will shall be left, intact and absolute.

" 'But,' you will say, 'although foreknowledge does not establish any necessity for the event of future things, yet foreknowledge is a sign that they will necessarily come to pass.' It would plainly follow that the event of future things would be necessary even if there were no foreknowledge. For a sign merely points at what is; it does not bring into being that which it points out. Wherefore it must first be proved that nothing happens but of necessity before it can be demonstrated that foreknowledge is a sign of this necessity. Otherwise, if there is no necessity, foreknowledge cannot be a sign of that which does not exist. . . . Now how can it possibly be that things which are foreseen as about to happen should not take place? For apparently we refuse to believe that those events whose occurrence Providence has foreseen might actually not occur; nevertheless we choose to believe that such events, even when they actually occur, did not have to happen by a necessity inherent in their nature—which fact you may easily gather from the following example:

"We see many things occur before our eyes, for instance, those things which charioteers are seen to do when they drive and turn their chariots, and in like manner other things. Does any necessity compel any one of these things to happen as it does?"

"By no means, for all skills would be of no effect if all things took place by compulsion."

"Therefore, since these things have no necessity for occurring at the moment they happen, they cannot, before they actually occur, happen with necessity in the future. Wherefore there are certain things about-to-come-to-pass whose occurrence is absolutely free from any necessity. For I believe no one would say that the things which are done in the present were not about-to-be-done in the past before they were done. Thus these foreknown events occur freely. Just as knowledge of present things imposes no necessity upon them while they are being done, so foreknowledge does not impose any necessity upon future things. 'But', you say, 'this itself is dubious, whether there can be any foreknowledge of those things which do not occur nec-

essarily.' To you a 'foreknowledge of things which do not occur necessarily' implies a contradiction; you believe that if they are foreseen the necessity (of occurrence) follows, that without this necessity there can be no foreknowledge, that all knowledge is always knowledge of something certain, and that, if things which will not occur necessarily are foreknown as necessary, we are not dealing with the truth of knowledge but with the obscurity of opinion. For you believe that to judge anything as other than it is in fact is far removed from the integrity of true knowledge."

PHILOSOPHY DISCUSSES THE VARIOUS GRADES OF COGNITION

"The cause of your error is that everyone believes that all the things he knows come to his knowledge solely through their own nature and through a force inherent in them. But the opposite is true. For everything which is known is comprehended not according to its own force but rather according to the faculty of those who comprehend it. Let me make this plain by a brief example: the roundness of a body is recognized by sight in one way, and by touch in another way. Sight, remaining at a distance, takes in the whole body at once with all its diverging radii, while touch, clinging and conjoined, as it were, to the sphere, comprehends the roundness of the body as it passes inch by inch over the actual circumference. Likewise sense, imagination, reason, and insight all behold a man differently. For sense considers his figure as it is impressed on his body, while imagination considers the figure by itself without the body. Reason goes further than this: by contemplating only the universal aspects it investigates the species itself, which is represented in particular specimens. Higher still is the view of insight: reaching beyond the sphere of the material universe it beholds with the pure vision of the mind the Idea of Man in its simplicity.

"Herein the chief point for consideration is this: the higher power of comprehension includes the lower, but the lower can never raise itself to the higher. For the senses are capable of comprehending nothing but matter; imagination cannot look upon universal species; reason cannot grasp the simple

Idea; but insight seems to look down from above and, after having perceived the Idea, judges everything patterned after this Idea in the same way in which it comprehends the Idea itself, which can be known by no other faculty. For insight knows the universal grasped by reason, and the immaterial figure visualized by imagination, and the material object perceived by the senses, making use neither of reason nor of imagination nor of the senses but seeing with one grasp of the mind all things in their Idea, so to speak. Reason, too, when it views a universal, makes no use of the imagination of the senses, and yet it comprehends the objects both of imagination and of sensation. For it is reason which defines a universal resulting from its own mode of conception like this: man is a two-footed, rational animal. Though this is a universal notion, everybody knows that what reason thus considers not by an act of the imagination or of the senses but by an act of rational conception is a thing accessible to imagination and sense. Likewise, although imagination takes its beginning of seeing and forming figures from the senses, still without their aid it surveys each sensible thing not with a sensory but with an imaginary faculty of distinguishing. Do you see, then, that in the act of knowing all subjects employ their own faculty rather than that of the objects known? And this is only reasonable for, since every judgement formed is an act of the person who judges, every man must of necessity perform his own operation with his own and not another's faculty. . . .

5. PHILOSOPHY DISCUSSES THE DIFFERENCE BETWEEN HUMAN REASON AND DIVINE INSIGHT

"If, with regard to perceiving physical objects, although the qualities projected from without affect the sensory organs and although the body's passive reception, preceding the mind's energetic action, calls forth to itself the mind's activity and arouses the hitherto quiescent ideas within; if, I repeat, with regard to perceiving physical objects, the mind does not passively receive impressions from said objects but of its own power judges the reception dependent on the body, how much less do those beings which are free from all affections of the body follow in their judgment external objects, but rather they release the independent actions of their minds. For this reason many different manners of cognition have fallen to widely different substances. The senses alone, destitute of any knowledge but their own, have fallen to those living beings which are incapable of motion, like the shellfish of the sea and other low forms of life which live by clinging to rocks; while imagination has fallen to animals with the power of motion, who seem to be affected by a desire to seek certain things and to avoid others. But reason belongs to the human race alone, just as insight is God's alone. . . .

"Suppose then that sensation and imagination oppose reasoning, saying that those universals which reason pretends to contemplate do not exist, arguing that what is comprehensible to the senses and imagination cannot be universal; that therefore either the judgment of reason is true and nothing comprehensible exists or (since reason knows full well that there are many objects comprehensible to the senses and imagination) the conceptions of reason are empty because it holds the individual thing comprehensible to the sense to be something universal. If reason were to respond that it does, indeed, perceive the objects of sense and imagination from a universal point of view; that sense and imagination, on the other hand, cannot aspire to knowledge of universals since their manner of cognition goes no further than bodies and figures; and that in matters of knowledge it is best to trust to the stronger and more nearly perfect judgment—if such a trial by debate occurred should not we, who have the power not only to reason but also to imagine and perceive with the sense, approve reason's cause rather than the others'? We are dealing with a similar situation when human reason supposes that the divine insight cannot contemplate future things except as it (the human reason) conceives them. For you argue thus: 'If there are some things which do not occur necessarily and certainly, then it cannot be known in advance with certainty that these things will actually occur; therefore there can be no foreknowledge of these things for, if we believe that they can be foreknown, then everything happens by necessity.' If we, however, who partake of reason, could also share that power of judgment which is proper to the divine mind, we would think it most fitting that, just as we have decided that the senses and imagination should yield to human reason, so the latter should submit itself to the divine mind. Let us therefore raise ourselves, if we can, to that height of the loftiest intelligence. For there reason will see what she cannot intuit on her own, i.e., how foreknowledge sees distinctly and certainly even those things which occur without necessity and how such foreknowledge is not mere opinion but rather the simplicity of the highest knowledge, unencumbered by any finite bounds. . . .

6. PHILOSOPHY EXPLAINS THAT GOD'S INSIGHT VIEWS ALL THINGS IN THEIR ETERNAL DESIGN, WHILE HUMAN REASON CAN SEE THEM ONLY FROM A TEMPORAL VIEWPOINT

"Since then, as we have just now shown, everything that is known is apprehended not according to its own nature but according to that of the knower, let us examine now, so far as we lawfully may, what is the state of the divine substance, so that we may be able to learn also what its knowledge is. The common opinion, according to all men living, is that God is eternal. Let us therefore consider what eternity is, for this will make clear to us at the same time the divine nature and the divine knowledge. Now, eternity is the complete possession of an endless life enjoyed as one simultaneous whole; this will appear clearer from a comparison with temporal things. For whatever is living in time proceeds in the present from times past to times future; and nothing existing in time is so constituted as to embrace the whole span of its life at once, but it has not yet grasped tomorrow, while it has already lost yesterday. In this life of today you are living in no more than a fleeting, transitory moment. And so it is with everything that is subject to the condition of time: even if it should never have begun and would never cease to be—which Aristotle believed of the universe—even if its life were to be co-extensive with the infinity of time, yet it could not rightly be held to be eternal. For, even granted that it has an infinite lifetime, it does not embrace this life as a simultaneous whole; it does not now have a grasp of the future, which is yet to be lived through. What is rightly called eternal is that which grasps and possesses simultane-

ously the entire fullness of an unending life, a life which lacks nothing of the future and has lost nothing of the fleeting past. Such a being must necessarily always be its whole self, unchangingly present to itself, and the infinity of changing time must be as one present before him. Wherefore they are mistaken who, hearing that Plato thought this world had no beginning in time and would have no end, think that in this way the created universe is coeternal with the Creator. For to pass step by step through an unending life, a process ascribed by Plato to the universe, is one thing; to embrace simultaneously the whole of an unending life in one present, an act manifestly peculiar to the divine mind, is quite another thing. And, further, God should not be regarded as older than His creations by any quantity of time but rather by the peculiar quality of simplicity in His nature. For the infinite motion of temporal things tries to imitate the ever present immobility of His life, does not succeed in copying or equalling it, sinks from immobility into motion, and falls from the simplicity of the present to the infinite stretch of future and past; and since it cannot possess its life completely and simultaneously it seems to emulate, by the very fact that it somehow exists forever without ceasing, what it cannot fully attain and express, clinging as it does to the so-called present of this short and fleeting moment, which, inasmuch as it bears a certain resemblance to that abiding present, makes those to whom it comes appear to exist. But, since this present could not be abiding, it took to the infinite journey through time, and so it has come to pass that, by journeying on, it continues that life the fullness of which it could not grasp by staying. Thus if we would apply proper epithets to these subjects we would say, following Plato, that God is eternal, while the universe is perpetual.

"Since, then, every judgment comprehends the objects of its thought according to its own nature, and since God has an ever present and eternal state, His knowledge also, surpassing every temporal movement, remains in the simplicity of its own present and, embracing infinite lengths of past and future, views with its own simple comprehension all things as if they were taking place in the present. If you will weigh the foresight with which God discerns all things, you will rightly esteem it to be the knowledge of a never fading instant rather than a foreknowledge of the 'future.' It should therefore rather be called *pro*vision than *pre*vision because, placed high above lowly things, it looks out over all as from the loftiest mountain top. Why then do you demand that those things which are translucent to the divine mind's light be necessary if not even men make necessary the things they see? Because you can see present things, does your sight impose upon them any necessity?"

"Surely not."

"Yet, if one may not unworthily compare the human present with the divine, just as you see certain things in this, your temporal present, so God sees all things in His eternal present. Wherefore this divine foreknowledge does not change the nature or properties of things: it sees things present to its contemplation just as they will turn out some time in the future. Neither is there any confusion in its judgments of things: with one glimpse of the mind it distinguishes what will happen necessarily and what will happen non-necessarily. For example, when you observe at the same time a man walking on the earth and the sun rising in the sky, although you see both sights simultaneously, nevertheless you distinguish between them and judge that the one is moving voluntarily, the other necessarily; in like manner the intuition of God looks down upon all things without at all disturbing their nature, yet they are present to Him and future in relation to time. Wherefore it is not opinion but knowledge grounded in truth when He knows that something will occur in the future and knows as well that it will not occur of necessity. If you say at this point that what God sees as about to happen cannot but happen and that what cannot but happen happens, and you pin me down to this definition of necessity, I will confess a matter of the firmest truth but one which scarcely any one save a contemplator of the divine can reach: i.e., I shall answer that one and the same future event is necessary with respect to God's knowledge of it but absolutely free and unrestrained when it is examined in its own nature.

"For there are two kinds of necessity. One is simple: for instance, it is necessary that all men are mortal. The other is conditional: for instance, if you re-ally know that a man is walking, he must be walking. For what a man really knows cannot be otherwise than it is known to be. But the conditional kind of necessity by no means implies the simple kind, for the former is not based on the very nature of the thing called necessary but on the addition of an 'if.' For example, no necessity compels a man who is walking of his own accord to proceed, though it is necessary that, *if* he is walking, he should be proceeding. In the same way, if Providence sees any thing as present, that thing must be, though it has no necessity of its own nature; and, of course, God sees as present those future things which come to pass through free will. Therefore free acts, when referred to the divine intuition, become necessary in the conditional sense because God's knowledge provides that condition; on the other hand, viewed by themselves, they do not lose the perfect freedom of their nature. Without doubt, then, all things which God foreknows do come to pass, but certain of them proceed from free will. And these free acts, though they come to pass, do not by actually occurring lose their proper nature, because of which, before they come to pass, they could also not have come to pass. . . .

" 'But,' you will say, 'if it is within my power to change my mind I can make Providence void, for I may change what she foreknows.' To this I will answer that you can indeed change your mind but, since Providence truly sees in her present that you can change it, whether you will change it, and whither you may change it, you cannot avoid the divine foreknowledge any more than you can avoid the glance of an eye which is present, though you may by your free will turn yourself to various different actions. You will then say, 'Will the divine foreknowledge be altered by my own disposition, so that when I choose now one thing, now another, it too will seem to undergo alternations in its own cognition?' By no means; for the divine insight precedes the future and recalls it to the one present of its own proper cognition. It does not alternate, as you suppose, between this and that in its foreknowledge, but it is constantly preceding and grasping with one glance all mutations. This presence of comprehending and witnessing all things is not based on the actual occurrence of future events but on God's own peculiar simplicity—which fact also resolves that problem which you posed a little while ago when you said that it is shameful to maintain that our future acts are the cause of God's knowledge. For this power of knowledge to take cognizance, with one ever present glance, of all things has itself determined for each thing its mode of existence and owes nothing more to future things. Since this is so, mortal man's freedom of judgment remains inviolate and, because his will is free from any necessity, the laws which propose rewards and punishments are not unjust. God is the ever prescient spectator of all things, and the eternity of His vision, which is ever present, runs in unison with the future nature of our acts, dispensing rewards to the good, punishments to the evil. Hopes are not vainly put in God nor prayers vainly offered which, if they be right, must be effective. Therefore turn from vice, cultivate virtue, raise your heart to legitimate hope, direct humble prayers to the heavens. If you will only take notice and not dissemble, a great necessity for righteousness is laid upon you, since you live under the eyes of a Judge who discerns all."

REVIEW QUESTIONS

1. What is Boethius' argument for the existence of free will?
2. What is the purported conflict between free will and God's foreknowledge? How does Boethius try to reconcile them?
3. What is the difference between conditional and simple necessity?
4. How does God's view of events differ from human understanding of them?
5. What does Boethius mean by "the intuition of God looks down upon all things without at all disturbing their nature, yet they are present to Him and future in relation to time"?

10

ANSELM AND GAUNILO

St. Anselm (1033/34–1109) was abbot of Bec and later archbishop of Canterbury. He wrote several important treatises on theological subjects, including *Cur Deus Homo* (Why God Became Man). In this selection from his *Proslogium* he begins with the definition of God as "that than which nothing greater can be conceived." Today we might translate this as "the greatest possible being." From that definition Anselm proceeds to argue for the necessary existence of God, known as the *Ontological Argument* for the existence of God. Although a version of this argument can be found in Augustine, Anselm's rendition is more complete and better developed. Anselm believes that God's existence is so certain that only a fool would doubt or deny it. Yet he desires understanding to fulfill his faith. The Ontological Argument is the product of this desire.

Anselm's contemporary, Gaunilo, a Benedictine monk, sets forth the first objection to Anselm's argument, centering on a delectable lost island, one that is more excellent than all lands. Since it is better that such a perfect island exists in reality than simply in the mind alone, this Isle of the Blest must necessarily exist.

Anselm's reply to Gaunilo is included in our readings.

FOR FURTHER READING

Evans, G. R. *Anselm and Talking About God* (Oxford University Press, 1978).
Harshorne, C. *Anselm's Discovery* (Open Court, 1965).
Hick, John and Arthur McGill, eds. *The Many-Faced Arguments* (Macmillan, 1967).
Hopkins, Jasper. *A Companion to the Study of St. Anselm* (University of Minnesota Press, 1972).
Plantinga, Alvin, ed. *The Ontological Argument* (Doubleday, 1965).
Southern, R. W. *Saint Anselm: A Portrait in a Landscape* (Cambridge University Press, 1990).

PROSLOGIUM

ST. ANSELM'S PRESENTATION

*Truly there is a God, although
the fool hath said in his heart,
There is no God.*

And so, Lord, do thou, who dost give understanding and faith, give me, so far as thou knowest it to be profitable, to understand that thou art as we believe; and that thou art that which we believe. And, indeed, we believe that thou art a being than which nothing greater can be conceived. Or is there no such nature, since the fool hath said in his heart, there is no God? (Psalms xiii, I). But, at any rate, this very fool, when he hears of this being of which I speak—a being than which nothing greater can be conceived—understands what he hears, and what he understands is in his understanding; although he does not understand it to exist.

For, it is one thing for an object to be in the understanding, and another to understand that the object exists. When a painter first conceives of what he will afterwards perform, he has it in his understanding, but he does not yet understand it to be, because he has not yet performed it. But after he has made the painting, he both has it in his understanding, and he understands that it exists, because he has made it.

Hence, even the fool is convinced that something exists in the understanding, at least, than which nothing greater can be conceived. For, when he hears of this, he understands it. And whatever is understood, exists in the understanding. And assuredly that, than which nothing greater can be conceived, cannot exist in the understanding alone. For, suppose it exists in the understanding alone: then it can be conceived to exist in reality; which is greater.

Therefore, if that, than which nothing greater can be conceived, exists in the understanding alone, the very being, than which nothing greater can be conceived, is one, than which a greater can be conceived. But obviously this is impossible. Hence, there is no doubt that there exists a being, than which nothing greater can be conceived, and it exists both in the understanding and in reality.

God cannot be conceived not to exist.—God is that, than which nothing greater can be conceived.—That which can be conceived not to exist is not God.

And it assuredly exists so truly, that it cannot be conceived not to exist. For, it is possible to conceive of a being which cannot be conceived not to exist; and this is greater than one which can be conceived not to exist. Hence, if that, than which nothing greater can be conceived, can be conceived not to exist, it is not that, than which nothing greater can be conceived. But this is an irreconcilable contradiction. There is, then, so truly a being than which nothing greater can be conceived to exist, that it cannot even be conceived not to exist; and this being thou art, O Lord, our God.

So truly, therefore, dost thou exist, O Lord, my God, that thou canst not be conceived not to exist; and rightly. For, if a mind could conceive of a being better than thee, the creature would rise above the Creator; and this is most absurd. And, indeed, whatever else there is, except thee alone, can be conceived not to exist. To thee alone, therefore, it belongs to exist more truly than all other beings, and hence in a higher degree than all others. For, whatever else exists does not exist so truly, and hence in a less degree it belongs to it to exist. Why, then, has the fool said in his heart, there is no God (Psalms xiii, I), since it is so evident, to a rational mind, that thou dost exist in the highest degree of all? Why, except that he is dull and a fool?

How the fool has said in his heart what cannot be conceived.—A thing may be conceived in two ways: (1) when the word signifying it is con-

Reprinted by permission from Open Court Trade & Academic Books, a division of Carus Publishing Company, Peru, IL, from *St. Anselm: Basic Writings*, translated by S. N. Deane.

ceived; (2) when the thing itself is understood. As far as the word goes, God can be conceived not to exist; in reality he cannot.

But how has the fool said in his heart what he could not conceive; or how is it that he could not conceive what he said in his heart? since it is the same to say in the heart, and to conceive.

But, if really, nay, since really, he both conceived, because he said in his heart; and did not say in his heart, because he could not conceive; there is more than one way in which a thing is said in the heart or conceived. For, in one sense, an object is conceived, when the word signifying it is conceived; and in another, when the very entity, which the object is, is understood.

In the former sense, then, God can be conceived not to exist; but in the latter, not at all. For no one who understands what fire and water are can conceive fire to be water, in accordance with the nature of the facts themselves, although this is possible according to the words. So, then, no one who understands what God is can conceive that God does not exist; although he says these words in his heart, either without any or with some foreign, signification. For, God is that than which a greater cannot be conceived. And he who thoroughly understands this, assuredly understands that this being so truly exists, that not even in concept can it be non-existent. Therefore, he who understands that God so exists, cannot conceive that he does not exist.

I thank thee, gracious Lord, I thank thee; because what I formerly believed by thy bounty, I now so understand by thine illumination, that if I were unwilling to believe that thou dost exist, I should not be able not to understand this to be true.

GAUNILO'S CRITICISM

IN BEHALF OF THE FOOL

For example: it is said that somewhere in the ocean is an island, which, because of the difficulty, or rather the impossibility, of discovering what does not exist, is called the lost island. And they say that this island has an inestimable wealth of all manner of riches and delicacies in greater abundance than is told of the Islands of the Blest; and that having no owner or inhabitant, it is more excellent than all other countries, which are inhabited by mankind, in the abundance with which it is stored.

Now if some one should tell me that there is such an island, I should easily understand his words, in which there is no difficulty. But suppose that he went on to say, as if by a logical inference: "You can no longer doubt that this island which is more excellent than all lands exists somewhere, since you have no doubt that it is in your understanding. And since it is more excellent not to be in the understanding alone, but to exist both in the understanding and in reality, for this reason it must exist. For if it does not exist, any land which really exists will be more excellent than it; and so the island already understood by you to be more excellent will not be more excellent."

If a man should try to prove to me by such reasoning that this island truly exists, and that its existence should no longer be doubted, either I should believe that he was jesting, or I know not which I ought to regard as the greater fool: myself, supposing that I should allow this proof; or him, if he should suppose that he had established with any certainty the existence of this island. For he ought to show first that the hypothetical excellence of this island exists as a real and indubitable fact, and in no wise as any unreal object, or one whose existence is uncertain, in my understanding.

ST. ANSELM'S REJOINDER

APOLOGETIC

A criticism of Gaunilo's example, in which he tries to show that in this way the real existence of a lost island might be inferred from the fact of its being conceived.

But, you say, it is as if one should suppose an island in the ocean, which surpasses all lands in its fertility, and which, because of the difficulty, or rather the impossibility, of discovering what does not exist, is called a lost island; and should say that there can be no doubt that this island truly exists in reality, for this reason, that one who hears it described easily understands what he hears.

Now I promise confidently that if any man shall devise anything existing either in reality or in concept alone (except that than which a greater cannot be conceived) to which he can adapt the sequence of my reasoning, I will discover that thing, and will give him his lost island, not to be lost again.

But it now appears that this being than which a greater is inconceivable cannot be conceived not to be, because it exists on so assured a ground of truth; for otherwise it would not exist at all.

Hence, if any one says that he conceives this being not to exist, I say that at the time when he conceives of this either he conceives of a being than which a greater is inconceivable, or he does not conceive at all. If he does not conceive, he does not conceive of the non-existence of that of which he does not conceive. But if he does conceive, he certainly conceives of a being which cannot be even conceived not to exist. For if it could be conceived not to exist, it could be conceived to have a beginning and an end. But this is impossible.

He, then, who conceives of this being conceives of a being which cannot be even conceived not to exist; but he who conceives of this being does not conceive that it does not exist; else he conceives what is inconceivable. The nonexistence, then, of that than which a greater cannot be conceived is inconceivable.

REVIEW QUESTIONS

1. What is Anselm's ontological argument for the existence of God? What assumptions does Anselm bring to the argument?
2. What is the significance of the analogy with the painter?
3. Why does it matter to Anselm's argument whether existence is a perfection?
4. What is Gaunilo's criticism of the argument?
5. What is Anselm's response to Gaunilo?

11

MOSES MAIMONIDES

Moses Maimonides (Moses ben Maimon, 1138–1204) was an unsurpassed scholar of Jewish law and the most important Jewish philosopher in history. His comprehensive attempt to reconcile religious tradition with philosophy, especially Aristotelian thought, engages thinkers to this day. Maimonides was born in Cordova, Spain, a Muslim-ruled city whose intellectual life was among the liveliest and most permissive of the medieval world. That atmosphere changed in 1148, when the Muslim Almohads conquered Cordova and demanded that non-Muslims immediately convert or submit to exile or death. Having little choice, Maimonides and his family fled the city, traveling about for years, seeking refuge in Morocco, Palestine, and finally Egypt. In Cairo, he served as court physician and Egypt's foremost rabbinic leader, all the while writing the works that would influence generations to come. His preeminent authority as a rabbinic jurist was forever established by his *Book of the Commandments*; *the Commentary on the Mishneh*; and the fourteen-volume Code of Jewish Law, the *Mishneh Torah*. His credentials as a philosopher were secured by his masterpiece, *Guide for the Perplexed*.

Like ancient Greek thinkers and some philosophers of his day (including a few Arabic scholars), Maimonides sought truth through reason and tried to apply rational methods of inquiry not just to philosophy and science, but to religious and biblical beliefs. This approach led him to argue in the *Guide* that biblical and rabbinic writings embody, in figurative language, truths that can be discovered and demonstrated by philosophy. There can be no contradiction between religious texts and the deliverances of reason, although the former must be interpreted figuratively to agree with the latter. To interpret scripture literally is to fall into error. For example, scriptural language seems to suggest that God is corporeal and that He possesses essential attributes. But, Maimonides says, philosophy shows that these literal understandings are false, so the passages must be given a figurative meaning. God has no body and cannot be conceived of or described at all. We can only characterize God negatively (for instance, "God does not lack power" instead of "God is powerful"), which is simply a way of acknowledging that God is beyond our comprehension.

FOR FURTHER READING

Buijs, Joseph, ed. *Maimonides: A Collection of Critical Essays* (University of Notre Dame Press, 1988).
Davidson, Herbert. *Maimonides: The Man and His Works* (Oxford University Press, 2005).
Kraemer, J., ed. *Perspectives on Maimonides* (Oxford University Press, 1991).
Friedlander, M., trans. *The Guide for the Perplexed* (Dover Publications, 1956).
Pines, S., trans. *The Guide of the Perplexed* (University of Chicago Press, 1929).
Seeskin, Kenneth. *Searching for a Distant God* (Oxford University Press, 2000).
Seeskin, Kenneth. "Maimonides" *Stanford Encyclopedia of Philosophy* (Fall 2008). <http://plato.stanford.edu/entries/maimonides>.

GUIDE FOR THE PERPLEXED

PART 1

CHAPTER LVIII

This chapter is even more recondite than the preceding. Know that the negative attributes of God are the true attributes: they do not include any incorrect notions or any deficiency whatever in reference to God, while positive attributes imply polytheism, and are inadequate, as we have already shown. It is now necessary to explain how negative expressions can in a certain sense be employed as attributes, and how they are distinguished from positive attributes. Then I shall show that we cannot describe the Creator by any means except by negative attributes. An attribute does not exclusively belong to the one object to which it is related; while qualifying one thing, it can also be employed to qualify other things, and is in that case not peculiar to that one thing. E.g., if you see an object from a distance, and on enquiring what it is, are told that it is a living being, you have certainly learnt an attribute of the object seen, and although that attribute does not exclusively belong to the object perceived,

it expresses that the object is not a plant or a mineral. Again, if a man is in a certain house, and you know that something is in the house, but not exactly what, you ask what is in that house, and you are told, not a plant nor a mineral. You have thereby obtained some special knowledge of the thing; you have learnt that it is a living being, although you do not yet know what kind of a living being it is. The negative attributes have this in common with the positive, that they necessarily circumscribe the object to some extent, although such circumscription consists only in the exclusion of what otherwise would not be excluded. In the following point, however, the negative attributes are distinguished from the positive. The positive attributes, although not peculiar to one thing, describe a portion of what we desire to know, either some part of its essence or some of its accidents; the negative attributes, on the other hand, do not, as regards the essence of the thing which we desire to know, in any way tell us what it is, except it be indirectly, as has been shown in the instance given by us.

After this introduction, I would observe that,—as has already been shown—God's existence is ab-

Reprinted from *Guide for the Perplexed*, trans. M. Friedlander, Hebrew Publishing Co., 1881.

solute, that it includes no composition, as will be proved, and that we comprehend only the fact that He exists, not His essence. Consequently it is a false assumption to hold that He has any positive attribute; for He does not possess existence in addition to His essence; it therefore cannot be said that the one may be described as an attribute [of the other]; much less has He [in addition to His existence] a compound essence, consisting of two constituent elements to which the attribute could refer; still less has He accidents, which could be described by an attribute. Hence it is clear that He has no positive attribute whatever. The negative attributes, however, are those which are necessary to direct the mind to the truths which we must believe concerning God; for, on the one hand, they do not imply any plurality, and, on the other, they convey to man the highest possible knowledge of God; e.g., it has been established by proof that some being must exist besides those things which can be perceived by the senses, or apprehended by the mind; when we say of this being, that it exists, we mean that its non-existence is impossible. We then perceive that such a being is not, for instance, like the four elements, which are inanimate, and we therefore say that it is living, expressing thereby that it is not dead. We call such a being incorporeal, because we notice that it is unlike the heavens, which are living, but material. Seeing that it is also different from the intellect, which, though incorporeal and living, owes its existence to some cause, we say it is the first, expressing thereby that its existence is not due to any cause. We further notice, that the existence, that is the essence, of this being is not limited to its own existence; many existences emanate from it, and its influence is not like that of the fire in producing heat, or that of the sun in sending forth light, but consists in constantly giving them stability and order by well-established rule, as we shall show: we say, on that account, it has power, wisdom, and will, i.e., it is not feeble or ignorant, or hasty, and does not abandon its creatures; when we say that it is not feeble, we mean that its existence is capable of producing the existence of many other things; by saying that it is not ignorant, we mean "it perceives" or "it lives,"—for everything that perceives is living—by saying "it is not hasty, and does not abandon its creatures," we mean that

all these creatures preserve a certain order and arrangement; they are not left to themselves; they are not produced aimlessly, but whatever condition they receive from that being is given with design and intention. We thus learn that there is no other being like unto God, and we say that He is One, i.e., there arc not more Gods than one.

It has thus been shown that every attribute predicated of God either denotes the quality of an action, or—when the attribute is intended to convey some idea of the Divine Being itself, and not of His actions—the negation of the opposite. Even these negative attributes must not be formed and applied to God, except in the way in which, as you know, sometimes an attribute is negatived in reference to a thing, although that attribute can naturally never be applied to it in the same sense, as, e.g., we say, "This wall does not see." Those who read the present work are aware that, notwithstanding all the efforts of the mind, we can obtain no knowledge of the essence of the heavens—a revolving substance which has been measured by us in spans and cubits, and examined even as regards the proportions of the several spheres to each other and respecting most of their motions—although we know that they must consist of matter and form; but the matter not being the same as sublunary matter, we can only describe the heavens in terms expressing negative properties, but not in terms denoting positive qualities. Thus we say that the heavens are not light, not heavy, not passive and therefore not subject to impressions, and that they do not possess the sensations of taste and smell; or we use similar negative attributes. All this we do, because we do not know their substance. What, then, can be the result of our efforts, when we try to obtain a knowledge of a Being that is free from substance, that is most simple, whose existence is absolute, and not due to any cause, to whose perfect essence nothing can be superadded, and whose perfection consists, as we have shown, in the absence of all defects. All we understand is the fact that He exists, that He is a Being to whom none of His creatures is similar, who has nothing in common with them, who does not include plurality, who is never too feeble to produce other beings, and whose relation to the universe is that of a steersman to a boat; and even this is not a real relation, a real simile, but serves only to convey to us the idea that God rules the universe; that is, that He gives it duration, and preserves its necessary arrangement. This subject will be treated more fully. Praised be He! In the contemplation of His essence, our comprehension and knowledge prove insufficient; in the examination of His works, how they necessarily result from His will, our knowledge proves to be ignorance, and in the endeavour to extol Him in words, all our efforts in speech are mere weakness and failure! . . .

PART III

CHAPTER XX

It is generally agreed upon that God cannot at a certain time acquire knowledge which He did not possess previously; it is further impossible that His knowledge should include any plurality, even according to those who admit the Divine attributes. As these things have been fully proved, we, who assert the teaching of the Law, believe that God's knowledge of many things does not imply any plurality; His knowledge does not change like ours when the objects of His knowledge change. Similarly we say that the various events are known to Him before they take place; He constantly knows them, and therefore no fresh knowledge is acquired by Him. E.g., He knows that a certain person is non-existent at present, will come to existence at a certain time, will continue to exist for some time, and will then cease to exist. When this person, in accordance with God's foreknowledge concerning him, comes into existence, God's knowledge is not increased; it contains nothing that it did not contain before, but something has taken place that was known previously exactly as it has taken place. This theory implies that God's knowledge extends to things not in existence, and includes also the infinite. We nevertheless accept it, and contend that we may attribute to God the knowledge of a thing which does not yet exist, but the existence of which God foresees and is able to effect. But that which never exists cannot be an object of His knowledge; just as our knowledge does not comprise things which we consider as non-existing. A doubt has been raised, however, whether His knowl-

edge includes the infinite. Some thinkers assume that knowledge has the species for its object, and therefore extends at the same time to all individual members of the species. This view is taken by every man who adheres to a revealed religion and follows the dictates of reason. Philosophers, however, have decided that the object of knowledge cannot be a nonexisting thing, and that it cannot comprise that which is infinite. Since, therefore, God's knowledge does not admit of any increase, it is impossible that He should know any transient thing. He only knows that which is constant and unchangeable. Other philosophers raised the following objection: God does not know even things that remain constant; for His knowledge would then include a plurality according to the number of objects known; the knowledge of every thing being distinguished by a certain peculiarity of the thing. God therefore only knows His own essence.

My opinion is this: the cause of the error of all these schools is their belief that God's knowledge is like ours; each school points to something withheld from our knowledge, and either assumes that the same must be the case in God's knowledge, or at least finds some difficulty how to explain it. We must blame the philosophers in this respect more than any other persons, because they demonstrated that there is no plurality in God, and that He has no attribute that is not identical with His essence; His knowledge and His essence are one and the same thing; they likewise demonstrated, as we have shown, that our intellect and our knowledge are insufficient to comprehend the true idea of His essence. How then can they imagine that they comprehend His knowledge, which is identical with His essence; seeing that our incapacity to comprehend His essence prevents us from understanding the way how He knows objects? for His knowledge is not of the same kind as ours, but totally different from it and admitting of no analogy. And as there is an Essence of independent existence, which is, as the philosophers call it, the Cause of the existence of all things, or, as we say, the Creator of everything that exists beside Him, so we also assume that this Essence knows everything, that nothing whatever of all that exists is hidden from it, and that the knowledge attributed to this essence has nothing in common with our knowledge, just as that essence is in no way like our essence. The homonymity of the term "knowledge" misled people; [they forgot that] only the words are the same, but the things designated by them are different; and therefore they came to the absurd conclusion that that which is required for our knowledge is also required for God's knowledge.

Besides, I find it expressed in various passages of Scripture that the fact that God knows things while in a state of possibility, when their existence belongs to the future, does not change the nature of the possible in any way; that nature remains unchanged; and the knowledge of the realization of one of several possibilities does not yet effect that realization. This is likewise one of the fundamental principles of the Law of Moses, concerning which there is no doubt nor any dispute. Otherwise it would not have been said, "And thou shalt make a battlement for thy roof," etc. (Deut. xxii. 8), or "Lest he die in the battle, and another man take her" (*ibid.* xx. 7). The fact that laws were given to man, both affirmative and negative, supports the principle, that God's knowledge of future [and possible] events does not change their character. The great doubt that presents itself to our mind is the result of the insufficiency of our intellect. Consider in how many ways His knowledge is distinguished from ours according to all the teaching of every revealed religion. First, His knowledge is one, and yet embraces many different kinds of objects. Secondly, it is applied to things not in existence. Thirdly, it comprehends the infinite. Fourthly, it remains unchanged, though it comprises the knowledge of changeable things; whilst it seems [in reference to ourselves] that the knowledge of a thing that is to come into existence is different from the knowledge of the thing when it has come into existence; because there is the additional knowledge of its transition from a state of potentiality into that of reality. Fifthly, according to the teaching of our Law, God's knowledge of one of two eventualities does not determine it, however certain that knowledge may be concerning the future occurrence of the one eventuality.—Now I wonder what our knowledge has in common with God's knowledge, according to those who treat God's knowledge as an attribute. Is there anything else common to both besides the mere name? According to our theory that God's knowledge is not different from His essence,

there is an essential distinction between His knowledge and ours, like the distinction between the substance of the heavens and that of the earth. The Prophets have clearly expressed this. Comp. "For my thoughts are not your thoughts, neither are your ways my ways, said the Lord. For as the heavens are higher than the earth, so are my ways higher than your ways" (Isa. lv. 8–9). In short, as we cannot accurately comprehend His essence, and yet we know that His existence is most perfect, free from all admixture of deficiency, change, or passiveness, so we have no correct notion of His knowledge, because it is nothing but His essence, and yet we are convinced that He does not at one time obtain knowledge which He had not before; i.e., He obtains no new knowledge, He does not increase it, and it is not finite; nothing of all existing things escapes His knowledge, but their nature is not changed thereby; that which is possible remains possible. Every argument that seems to contradict any of these statements is founded on the nature of our knowledge, that has only the name in common with God's knowledge. The same applies to the term intention; it is homonymously employed to designate our intention towards a certain thing, and the intention of God. The term "management" (Providence) is likewise homonymously used of our management of a certain thing, and of God's management. In fact management, knowledge, and intention are not the same when ascribed to us and when ascribed to God. When these three terms are taken in both cases in the same sense, great difficulties must arise; but when it is noticed that there is a great difference whether a thing is predicated of God or of us, the truth will become clear. The difference between that which is ascribed to God and that which is ascribed to man is expressed in the words above mentioned, "And your ways are not my ways."

CHAPTER XXI

There is a great difference between the knowledge which the producer of a thing possesses concerning it, and the knowledge which other persons possess concerning the same thing. Suppose a thing is produced in accordance with the knowledge of the producer, the producer was then guided by his knowledge in the act of producing the thing. Other people, however, who examine this work and acquire a knowledge of the whole of it, depend for that knowledge on the work itself. E.g., An artisan makes a box in which weights move with the running of the water, and thus indicate how many hours have passed of the day and of the night. The whole quantity of the water that is to run out, the different ways in which it runs, every thread that is drawn, and every little ball that descends—all this is fully perceived by him who makes the clock; and his knowledge is not the result of observing the movements as they are actually going on; but, on the contrary, the movements are produced in accordance with his knowledge. But another person who looks at that instrument will receive fresh knowledge at every movement he perceives; the longer he looks on, the more knowledge does he acquire; he will gradually increase his knowledge till he fully understands the machinery. If an infinite number of movements were assumed for this instrument, he would never be able to complete his knowledge. Besides, he cannot know any of the movements before they take place, since he only knows them from their actual occurrence. The same is the case with every object, and its relation to our knowledge and God's knowledge of it. Whatever we know of the things is derived from observation; on that account it is impossible for us to know that which will take place in future, or that which is infinite.

Our knowledge is acquired and increased in proportion to the things known by us. This is not the case with God. His knowledge of things is not derived from the things themselves; if this were the case, there would be change and plurality in His knowledge; on the contrary, the things are in accordance with His eternal knowledge, which has established their actual properties, and made part of them purely spiritual, another part material and constant as regards its individual members, a third part material and changeable as regards the individual beings according to eternal and constant laws. Plurality, acquisition, and change in His knowledge is therefore impossible. He fully knows His unchangeable essence, and has thus a knowledge of all that results from any of His acts. If we were to try to understand in what manner this is done, it would be the same as if we tried to be the same as God, and to make our knowledge identical with His knowledge. Those who seek the truth, and admit what is true, must believe that nothing is hidden from God; that everything is revealed to His knowledge, which is identical with His essence; that this kind of knowledge cannot be comprehended by us; for if we knew its method, we would possess that intellect by which such knowledge could be acquired. Such intellect does not exist except in God, and is at the same time His essence. Note this well, for I think that this is an excellent idea, and leads to correct views; no error will be found in it; no dialectical argument; it does not lead to any absurd conclusion, nor to ascribing any defect to God. These sublime and profound themes admit of no proof whatever, neither according to our opinion who believe in the teaching of Scripture, nor according to the philosophers who disagree and are much divided on this question. In all questions that cannot be demonstrated, we must adopt the method which we have adopted in this question about God's Omniscience. Note it.

REVIEW QUESTIONS

1. What does Maimonides mean by the "negative attributes of God"? Why does he think that God can be discussed only negatively?
2. What is his argument that God cannot be described in positive terms?
3. For Maimonides, what is the difference between saying "God is powerful" and "God does not lack power"?
4. According to Maimonides, why doesn't God's knowledge ever change?
5. How is God's knowledge different from that of humans?

12

THOMAS AQUINAS

The Roman Catholic Dominican monk Thomas Aquinas (1225–1274) is considered by many to be the greatest theologian in Western religion. He was born in Roccasecca near the Italian town of Aquino, the son of the Count Aquino. While at the University of Naples, much to the horror of his noble parents, he decided to join the Dominicans, a mendicant (begging) order, considered by many to be a hotbed of religious fanatics. His parents had him kidnapped and carried off to a family castle at Monte San Giovanni. His family both appealed to his family loyalty and threatened him with punishment in hope of persuading him to quit the habit of a monk. One night his brothers sent a prostitute to his cell to offer herself for his pleasure. Thomas leaped up, grabbed a brand from the fire and chased her from his room. From that time onward he avoided the sight and company of women, except where it was necessary. Neither his mother's tears, his brothers' threats, nor the lure of a prostitute were sufficient to strip him of his determination to live a celibate, mendicant life, dedicated to the Church. He was kept under house arrest for more than a year before he was allowed to rejoin his fellow monks. He went to the Dominican school at Cologne where from 1248 to 1252 he studied under the renowned scholar and theologian Albert the Great. It was there he studied Aristotle's work, which had recently become available in Latin translation. A large man, slow in movement, stubborn, deliberate, methodical, imperturbable, his fellow students thought him stupid and unkindly gave him the nickname, "Dumb Ox." His teacher, Albert the Great, however, saw great promise in the youth, and declared, "You call him a Dumb Ox; I tell you the Dumb Ox will bellow so loud his bellowing will fill the world."

In 1252 Albert declared that Thomas was ready for advanced studies in philosophy and theology and sent him to the University of Paris where he received his Mastership in 1256.

During this time Thomas began teaching at the University of Paris and began developing an Aristotelian version of Catholic theology. His own writings are voluminous (over 8 million words of closely reasoned prose) and encyclopedic, dealing with questions of the problem of evil, truth, the nature of the soul, the existence and attributes of God, morality, and politics. He wrote two summations of theology: *On the Truth of the Catholic Faith Against the Gentiles (Summa Contra Gentiles)*, which was a handbook for missionaries seeking to convert Muslims and others to the Christian faith, and *Summa Theologica (Summation of Theology)*. On December 6, 1273, he had a deeply religious experience, after which he ceased to write. He reported, "All that I have written seems to me like straw compared to what has now been revealed to me." He died four months later.

The five arguments given in our first selection from the *Summa Theologica* are a posteriori arguments, that is, based on premises that can be known only by means of experience of the world (for example, that there is a world, events have causes, and so forth). Put simply, their strategies are as follows: The first argument begins with the fact that there is change and argues that there must be an Unmoved Mover which originates all change (or motion) but itself is not changed or moved. The second argument is from causation and argues that there must be a first cause to explain the existence of cause. The third argument is from contingency. It argues that since there are dependent beings (e.g., humans), there must be an independent or necessary being on whom the dependent beings rely for their subsistence. The fourth argument is from excellence, and it argues that since there are degrees of excellence, there must be a perfect being from whence come all excellences. The final argument is from the harmony of things. There is a harmony of nature which calls for an explanation. The only sufficient explanation is that there is a divine designer who planned such harmony.

Our second selection (Question 46) deals with the beginning and duration of creatures, and our fourth selection (Question 85) with how the soul knows.

In our final selection from the Second Part of the *Summa Theologica* is Aquina's classic treatise on Natural Law.

FOR FURTHER READING

Aquinas, Thomas. *Basic Writings of St. Thomas Aquinas*, trans. Anton Pegis (Random House, 1945).

Aquinas, Thomas. *Summa Theologiciae*, ed. Thomas Gilby (London, 1963–75), 60 vols.

Copleston, F. C. *Aquinas* (Penguin Books, 1955).

Davies, Brian. *The Thought of Thomas Aquinas* (Oxford University Press, 1992).

Gilson, Etienne. *The Christian Philosophy of St. Thomas Aquinas* (Random House, 1956).

Kenny, Anthony. *Aquinas* (Hill and Wang, 1980).

Kenny, Anthony. *The Five Ways: St. Thomas Aquinas' Proofs of God's Existence* (Routledge & Kegan Paul, 1969).

Kenny, Anthony, ed. *Aquinas: A Collection of Critical Essays* (Anchor Doubleday, 1969).

Kretzman, Norman, and Eleonore Stump, eds. *The Cambridge Companion to Aquinas* (Cambridge University Press, 1993).

SUMMA THEOLOGICA

QUESTION II. THE EXISTENCE OF GOD

FIRST ARTICLE. WHETHER THE EXISTENCE OF GOD IS SELF-EVIDENT?

We proceed thus to the First Article:—

Objection 1. It seems that the existence of God is self-evident. For those things are said to be self-evident to us the knowledge of which exists naturally in us, as we can see in regard to first principles. But a Damascene says, *the knowledge of God is naturally implanted in all.* Therefore the existence of God is self-evident.

Obj. 2. Further, those things are said to be self-evident which are known as soon as the terms are known, which the Philosopher says is true of the first principles of demonstration. Thus, when the nature of a whole and of a part is known, it is at once recognized that every whole is greater than its part, But as soon as the signification of the name *God* is understood, it is at once seen that God exists. For by this name is signified that thing than which nothing greater can be conceived. But that which exists actually and mentally is greater than that which exists only mentally. Therefore, since as soon as the name *God* is understood it exists mentally, it also follows that it exists actually. Therefore the proposition *God exists* is self-evident.

Obj. 3. Further, the existence of truth is self-evident. For whoever denies the existence of truth grants that truth does not exist: and, if truth does not exist, then the proposition *Truth does not exist* is true: and if there is anything true, there must be truth. But God is truth itself: *I am the way, the truth, and the life* (*Jo.* xiv. 6). Therefore *God exists* is self-evident.

On the contrary, No one can mentally admit the opposite of what is self-evident, as the Philosopher states concerning the first principles of demonstration. But the opposite of the proposition *God is* can be mentally admitted: *The fool said in his heart,* *There is no God* (*Ps.* lii. I). Therefore, that God exists is not self-evident.

I answer that, A thing can be self-evident in either of two ways: on the one hand, self-evident in itself, though not to us; on the other, self-evident in itself, and to us. A proposition is self-evident because the predicate is included in the essence of the subject: e.g., Man is an animal, for animal is contained in the essence of man. If, therefore, the essence of the predicate and subject be known to all, the proposition will be self-evident to all; as is clear with regard to the first principles of demonstration, the terms of which are certain common notions that no one is ignorant of, such as being and non-being, whole and part, and the like. If, however, there are some to whom the essence of the predicate and subject is unknown, the proposition will be self-evident in itself, but not to those who do not know the meaning of the predicate and subject of the proposition. Therefore, it happens, as Boethius says, that there are some notions of the mind which are common and self-evident only to the learned, as that incorporeal substances are not in space. Therefore I say that this proposition, *God exists*, of itself is self-evident, for the predicate is the same as the subject, because God is His own existence as will be hereafter shown. Now because we do not know the essence of God, the proposition is not self-evident to us, but needs to be demonstrated by things that are more known to us, though less known in their nature—namely, by His effects.

Reply Obj. I. To know that God exists in a general and confused way is implanted in us by nature, inasmuch as God is man's beatitude. For man naturally desires happiness, and what is naturally desired by man is naturally known by him. This, however, is not to know absolutely that God exists; just as to know that someone is approaching is not the same as to know that Peter is approaching, even though it is Peter who is approaching; for there are many who

Reprinted by permission from Thomas Aquinas, *Basic Writings of Thomas Aquinas*, translated by A. Pegis (New York: Random House, 1945).

God essence can't be understood but God signifies TW NGCB thought.

faith presupposes natural Knowledge compare w..

imagine that man's perfect good, which is happiness, consists in riches, and others in pleasures, and others in something else.

Reply Obj. 2. Perhaps not everyone who hears this name *God* understands it to signify something than which nothing greater can be thought, seeing that some have believed God to be a body. Yet, granted that everyone understands that by this name *God* is signified something than which nothing greater can be thought, nevertheless, it does not therefore follow that he understands that what the name signifies exists actually, but only that it exists mentally. Nor can it be argued that it actually exists, unless it be admitted that there actually exists something than which nothing greater can be thought; and this precisely is not admitted by those who hold that God does not exist.

Reply Obj. 3. The existence of truth in general is self-evident, but the existence of a Primal Truth is not self-evident to us.

SECOND ARTICLE. WHETHER IT CAN BE DEMONSTRATED THAT GOD EXISTS?

We proceed thus to the Second Article:—

Objection 1. It seems that the existence of God cannot be demonstrated. For it is an article of faith that God exists. But what is of faith cannot be demonstrated, because a demonstration produces scientific knowledge, whereas faith is of the unseen, as is clear from the Apostle (*Heb.* xi. I). Therefore it cannot be demonstrated that God exists.

Obj. 2. Further, essence is the middle term of demonstration. But we cannot know in what God's essence consists, but solely in what it does not consist, as Damascene says. Therefore we cannot demonstrate that God exists.

Obj. 3. Further, if the existence of God were demonstrated, this could only be from His effects. But His effects are not proportioned to Him, since He is infinite and His effects are finite, and between finite and infinite there is no proportion. Therefore, since a cause cannot be demonstrated by an effect not proportioned to it, it seems that the existence of God cannot be demonstrated.

On the contrary, The Apostle says: *The invisible things of Him are clearly seen, being understood by the things that are made* (*Rom.* i. 20). But this would not be unless the existence of God could be demonstrated through the things that are made; for the first thing we must know of anything is, whether it exists.

faith seeking understanding

I answer that, Demonstration can be made in two ways: One is through the cause, and is called *propter quid*, and this is to argue from what is prior absolutely. The other is through the effect, and is called a demonstration *quia*; this is to argue from what is prior relatively only to us. When an effect is better known to us than its cause, from the effect we proceed to the knowledge of the cause. And from every effect the existence of its proper cause can be demonstrated, so long as its effects are better known to us; because, since every effect depends upon its cause, if the effect exists, the cause must pre-exist. Hence the existence of God, in so far as it is not self-evident to us, can be demonstrated from those of His effects which are known to us.

Reply Obj. 1. The existence of God and other like truths about God, which can be known by natural reason, are not articles of faith, but are preambles to the articles; for faith presupposes natural knowledge, even as grace presupposes nature and perfection the perfectible. Nevertheless, there is nothing to prevent a man, who cannot grasp a proof, from accepting, as a matter of faith, something which in itself is capable of being scientifically known and demonstrated.

write about this

Reply Obj. 2. When the existence of a cause is demonstrated from an effect, this effect takes the place of the definition of the cause in proving the cause's existence. This is especially the case in regard to God, because, in order to prove the existence of anything, it is necessary to accept as a middle term the meaning of the name, and not its essence, for the question of its essence follows on the question of its existence. Now the names given to God are derived from His effects, as will be later shown. Consequently, in demonstrating the existence of God from His effects, we may take for the middle term the meaning of the name *God*. *meaning*

Reply Obj. 3. From effects not proportioned to the cause no perfect knowledge of that cause can be obtained. Yet from every effect the existence of the cause can be clearly demonstrated, and so we can

Infinity? Aquinas supposes universe is finite material things are spiritually finite.

demonstrate the existence of God from His effects; though from them we cannot know God perfectly as He is in His essence.

THIRD ARTICLE. WHETHER GOD EXISTS?

We proceed thus to the Third Article:—

Objection 1. It seems that God does not exist; because if one of two contraries be infinite, the other would be altogether destroyed. But the name God means that He is infinite goodness. If, therefore, God existed, there would be no evil discoverable; but there is evil in the world. Therefore God does not exist.

Obj. 2. Further, it is superfluous to suppose that what can be accounted for by a few principles has been produced by many. But it seems that everything we see in the world can be accounted for by other principles, supposing God did not exist. For all natural things can be reduced to one principle, which is nature; and all voluntary things can be reduced to one principle, which is human reason, or will. Therefore there is no need to suppose God's existence.

On the contrary, It is said in the person of God: *I am Who am* (Exod. iii. 14).

I answer that, The existence of God can be proved in five ways.

The first and more manifest way is the argument from motion. It is certain, and evident to our senses, that in the world some things are in motion. Now whatever is moved is moved by another, for nothing can be moved except it is in potentiality to that towards which it is moved; whereas a thing moves inasmuch as it is in act. For motion is nothing else than the reduction of something from potentiality to actuality. But nothing can be reduced from potentiality to actuality, except by something in a state of actuality. Thus that which is actually hot, as fire, makes wood, which is potentially hot, to be actually hot, and thereby moves and changes it. Now it is not possible that the same thing should be at once in actuality and potentiality in the same respect, but only in different respects. For what is actually hot cannot simultaneously be potentially hot; but it is simultaneously potentially cold. It is therefore impossible that in the same respect and in the same way a thing should be both mover and moved, i.e., that it should move itself. Therefore, whatever is moved must be moved by another. If that by which it is moved be itself moved, then this also must needs be moved by another, and that by another again. But this cannot go on to infinity, because then there would be no first mover, and, consequently, no other mover, seeing that subsequent movers move only inasmuch as they are moved by the first mover; as the staff moves only because it is moved by the hand. Therefore it is necessary to arrive at a first mover, moved by no other; and this everyone understands to be God.

The second way is from the nature of efficient cause. In the world of sensible things we find there is an order of efficient causes. There is no case known (neither is it, indeed, possible) in which a thing is found to be the efficient cause of itself; for so it would be prior to itself, which is impossible. Now in efficient causes it is not possible to go on to infinity, because in all efficient causes following in order, the first is the cause of the intermediate cause, and the intermediate is the cause of the ultimate cause, whether the intermediate cause be several, or one only. Now to take away the cause is to take away the effect. Therefore, if there be no first cause among efficient causes, there will be no ultimate, nor any intermediate, cause. But if in efficient causes it is possible to go on to infinity, there will be no first efficient cause, neither will there be an ultimate effect, nor any intermediate efficient causes; all of which is plainly false. Therefore it is necessary to admit a first efficient cause, to which everyone gives the name of God.

The third way is taken from possibility and necessity, and runs thus. We find in nature things that are possible to be and not to be, since they are found to be generated, and to be corrupted, and consequently, it is possible for them to be and not to be. But it is impossible for these always to exist, for that which can not-be at some time is not. Therefore, if everything can not-be, then at one time there was nothing in existence. Now if this were true, even now there would be nothing in existence, because that which does not exist begins to exist only through something already existing. Therefore, if at one time nothing was in existence, it would have been impossible for anything to have begun to exist; and thus even now nothing would be in existence—which is absurd. Therefore, not all beings are merely possible, but there must exist something the existence of which is necessary. But every necessary thing either has its necessity caused by another, or not. Now it is impossible to go on to infinity in necessary things which have their necessity caused by another, as has been already proved in regard to efficient causes. Therefore we cannot but admit the existence of some being having of itself its own necessity, and not receiving it from another, but rather causing in others their necessity. This all men speak of as God.

The fourth way is taken from the gradation to be found in things. Among beings there are some more and some less good, true, noble, and the like. But more and less are predicated of different things according as they resemble in their different ways something which is the maximum, as a thing is said to be hotter according as it more nearly resembles that which is hottest; so that there is something which is truest, something best, something noblest, and, consequently, something which is most being, for those things that are greatest in truth are greatest in being, as it is written in *Metaph.* ii. Now the maximum in any genus is the cause of all in that genus, as fire, which is the maximum of heat, is the cause of all hot things, as is said in the same book. Therefore there must also be something which is to all beings the cause of their being, goodness, and every other perfection; and this we call God.

The fifth way is taken from the governance of the world. We see that things which lack knowledge, such as natural bodies, act for an end, and this is evident from their acting always, or nearly always, in the same way, so as to obtain the best result. Hence it is plain that they achieve their end, not fortuitously, but designedly. Now whatever lacks knowledge cannot move towards an end, unless it be directed by some being endowed with knowledge and intelligence; as the arrow is directed by the archer. Therefore some intelligent being exists by whom all natural things are directed to their end; and this being we call God.

Reply Obj. 1. As Augustine says: *Since God is the highest good, He would not allow any evil to exist in His works, unless His omnipotence and goodness were such as to bring good even out of evil.* This is part of the infinite goodness of God, that He should allow evil to exist, and out of it produce good.

Reply Obj. 2. Since nature works for a determinate end under the direction of a higher agent, whatever is done by nature must be traced back to God as to its first cause. So likewise whatever is done voluntarily must be traced back to some higher cause other than human reason and will, since these can change and fail; for all things that are changeable and capable of defect must be traced back to an immovable and self-necessary first principle, as has been shown.

QUESTION XLVI. ON THE BEGINNING OF THE DURATION OF CREATURES

Next must be considered the beginning of the duration of creatures, about which there are three points for treatment: (1) Whether creatures always existed? (2) Whether that they began to exist is an article of Faith? (3) How God is said to have created heaven and earth in the beginning?

FIRST ARTICLE. WHETHER THE UNIVERSE OF CREATURES ALWAYS EXISTED?

We proceed thus to the First Article:—

Objection 1. It would seem that the universe of creatures, which is now called the world, had no beginning, but existed from eternity. For everything which begins to be had, before being, the possibility of being: otherwise its coming to be would have been impossible. If therefore the world began to be, before it began to be it was possible for it to be. But *that which can be* is matter, which is in potentiality to being, which results from a form, and to nonbeing, which results from privation of form. If therefore the world began to be, matter must have existed before the world. But matter cannot be without form: and if the matter of the world is joined to form, that *is* the world. Therefore the world existed before it began to be: which is impossible.

Obj. 2. Further, nothing which has power to be always, sometimes is and sometimes is not; because as far as the power of a thing lasts, so long does it exist. But every incorruptible thing has the power to be always, for its power does not extend to any determinate time. Therefore no incorruptible thing sometimes is, and sometimes is not. But everything, which has a beginning, at some time is, and at some time is not. Therefore no incorruptible thing begins to be. But there are many incorruptible things in the world, as the celestial bodies and all intellectual substances. Therefore the world did not begin to be.

Obj. 3. Further, what is ungenerated has no beginning. But the Philosopher proves that matter is ungenerated, and also that the heavens are ungenerated. Therefore the universe did not begin to be.

Obj. 4. Further, there is a vacuum where there is not a body, but there could be. But if the world began to be, there was first no body where the body of the world now is; and yet it could be there, otherwise it would not be there now. Therefore before the world there was a vacuum; which is impossible.

Obj. 5. Further, nothing begins anew to be moved except for the fact that either the mover or the thing moved is now otherwise than it was before. But what is now otherwise than it was before is moved. Therefore before every new motion there was a previous motion. Therefore motion always was; and therefore so also was the thing moved, because motion is only in a movable thing.

Obj. 6. Further, every mover is either natural or voluntary. But neither begins to move except by some pre-existing motion. For nature always operates in the same manner: hence unless some change precede either in the nature of the mover, or in the movable thing, there cannot arise from the natural mover a motion which was not there before. As for the will, without itself being changed, it puts off doing what it proposes to do; but this can be only by some imagined change, even if it involves only the passage of time. Thus he who wills to make a house to-morrow, and not to-day, awaits something which will be to-morrow, but is not to-day. At the very least he awaits for to-day to pass, and for to-morrow to come; and this cannot be without change, because time is the number of motion. Therefore it remains that before every new motion, there was a previous motion; and so the same conclusion follows as before.

Obj. 7. Further, whatever is always in its beginning, and always in its end, cannot cease and cannot begin; because what begins is not in its end, and what ceases is not in its beginning. But time is always in its beginning and end, because no part of time exists except *now*, which is the end of the past and the beginning of the future. Therefore time cannot begin or end, and consequently neither can motion, of which time is the number.

Obj. 8. Further, God is before the world either in the order of nature only, or also in duration. If in the order of nature only, therefore, since God is eternal, the world also is eternal. But if God is prior in duration, since what is prior and posterior in duration constitutes time, it follows that time existed before the world; which is impossible.

Obj. 9. Further, if there is a sufficient cause, there is an effect; for a cause from which there is no effect is an imperfect cause, requiring something else to make the effect follow. But God is the sufficient cause of the world: He is the final cause, by reason of His goodness, the exemplary cause by reason of His wisdom, and the efficient cause by reason of His power, as appears from the above. Since therefore God is eternal, the world also is eternal.

Obj. 10. Further, He who has an eternal action also has an eternal effect. But the action of God is His substance, which is eternal. Therefore the world is eternal.

On the contrary, It is said (*Jo.* xvii. 5), *Glorify Me, O Father, with Thyself with the glory which I had before the world was;* and (*Prov.* viii. 22), *The Lord possessed Me in the beginning of His ways, before He made anything from the beginning.*

I answer that, Nothing except God can be eternal. This statement is far from impossible. For it has been shown above that the will of God is the cause of things. Therefore, things are necessary according as it is necessary for God to will them, since the necessity of the effect depends on the necessity of the cause. Now it was shown above that, absolutely speaking, it is not necessary that God should will anything except Himself. It is not therefore necessary for God to will that the world should always exist; but supposing an eternal world to exist, it exists to the extent that God wills it to exist, since the being of the world depends on the will of God as on its cause. It is not therefore necessary for the world to be always; hence neither can it be proved demonstratively.

Nor are Aristotle's arguments absolutely demonstrative, but only relatively—viz., as against the

(1) first mover

arguments of some of the ancients who asserted that the world began to be in some actually impossible ways. This appears in three ways. First, because both in *Physics* viii. and in *De Caelo* i. he premises some opinions, such as those of Anaxagoras, Empedocles and Plato, and brings forward arguments to refute them. Secondly, because wherever he speaks of this subject, he quotes the testimony of the ancients, which is not the way of a demonstrator, but of one persuading of what is probable. Thirdly, because he expressly says that there are dialectical problems which we cannot solve demonstratively, as, *whether the world is eternal.*

Reply Obj. 1. Before the world existed, it was possible for the world to be, not, indeed, according to the passive power which is matter, but according to the active power of God. The world also, according as a thing is called absolutely possible, not in relation to any power, but from the sole relation of the terms which are not repugnant to each other; in which sense possible is opposed to impossible, as appears from the Philosopher.

Reply Obj. 2. Whatever has the power always to be, from the fact of having that power cannot sometimes be and sometimes not-be. However, before it received that power, it did not exist. Hence this argument, which is given by Aristotle, does not prove absolutely that incorruptible beings never began to be; it proves that they did not begin according to the natural process by which generable and corruptible beings begin to be.

Reply Obj. 3. Aristotle proves that *matter is ungenerated* from the fact that *it has not a subject* from which to derive its existence; and he proves that the heavens are ungenerated, because they have no contrary form from which to be generated. Hence it appears that no conclusion follows in either case, except that matter and the heavens did not begin by generation; as some said especially about the heavens. But what we say is that matter and the heavens were produced into being by creation, as appears above.

Reply Obj. 4. The notion of a vacuum is not only that *in which is nothing,* but also implies a space capable of holding a body and in which there is not a body, as appears from Aristotle. But we hold that there was no place or space before the world was.

Reply Obj. 5. The first mover was always in the same state, but the first movable thing was not always so, because it began to be whereas hitherto it was not. This, however, was not through change, but by creation, which is not change, as was said above. Hence it is evident that this argument, which Aristotle gives, is valid against those who admitted the existence of eternal movable things, but not eternal motion, as appears from the opinions of Anaxagoras and Empedocles. But we hold that motion always existed from the moment that movable things began to exist.

Reply Obj. 6. The first agent is a voluntary agent. And although He had the eternal will to produce some effect, yet He did not produce an eternal effect. Nor is it necessary for some change to be presupposed, not even because of imaginary time. For we must take into consideration the difference between a particular agent, that presupposes something and produces something else, and the universal agent, who produces the whole. The particular agent produces the form, and presupposes the matter; and hence it is necessary that it introduce the form in due proportion into a suitable matter. Hence it is logical to say that the particular agent introduces the form into such matter, and not into another, because of the different kinds of matter. But it is not logical to say so of God Who produces form and matter together; whereas it is logical to say of Him that He produces matter fitting to the form and to the end. Now a particular agent presupposes time just as it presupposes matter. Hence it is logically described as acting in a time *after* and not in a time *before,* according to an imaginary succession of time after time. But the universal agent, who produces both the thing and time, is not correctly described as acting now, and not before, according to an imaginary succession of time succeeding time, as if time were presupposed to His action; but He must be considered as giving time to His effect as much as and when He willed, and according to what was fitting to demonstrate His power. For the world leads more evidently to the knowledge of the divine creating power if it was not always, than if it had always been; since everything which was not always manifestly has a cause; whereas this is not so manifest of what always was.

Reply Obj. 7. As is stated in *Physics* iv., *before and after belong to time,* according as *they are found in motion*. Hence beginning and end in time must be taken in the same way as in motion. Now, granted the eternity of motion, it is necessary that any given moment in motion be a beginning and an end of motion; which need not be if motion has a beginning. The same applies to the *now* of time. Thus it appears that the view of the instant *now*, as being always the beginning and end of time, presupposes the eternity of time and motion. Hence Aristotle brings forward this argument against those who asserted the eternity of time, but denied the eternity of motion.

Reply Obj. 8. God is prior to the world by priority of duration. But the word *prior* signifies priority, not of time, but of eternity.—Or we may say that it signifies the eternity of imaginary time, and not of time really existing; much as, when we say that above the heavens there is nothing, the word *above* signifies only an imaginary place, according as it is possible to imagine other dimensions beyond those of the body of the heavens.

Reply Obj. 9. Just as the effect of a cause that acts by nature follows from it according to the mode of its form, so likewise it follows from the voluntary agent according to the form preconceived and determined by the agent, as appears from what was said above. Therefore, although God was from eternity the sufficient cause of the world, we may not hold that the world was produced by Him, except as preordained by His will—that is, that it should have being after non-being, in order more manifestly to declare its author.

Reply Obj. 10. Given the action, the effect follows according to the requirement of the form which is the principle of action. But in agents acting by will, what is conceived and preordained is considered as the form which is the principle of action. Therefore, from the eternal action of God an eternal effect does not follow; there follows only such an effect as God has willed, an effect, namely, which has being after non-being.

SECOND ARTICLE. WHETHER IT IS AN ARTICLE OF FAITH THAT THE WORLD BEGAN?

We proceed thus to the Second Article:—

Objection 1. It would seem that it is not an article of faith but a demonstrable conclusion that the world began. For everything that is made has a beginning of its duration. But it can be proved demonstratively that God is the producing cause of the world; indeed this is asserted by the more approved philosophers. Therefore it can be demonstratively proved that the world began.

Obj. 2. Further, if it is necessary to say that the world was made by God, it must have been made from nothing, or from something. But it was not made from something, or otherwise the matter of the world would have preceded the world; and against this are the arguments of Aristotle who held that the heavens are ungenerated. Therefore it must be said that the world was made from nothing; and thus it has being after non-being. Therefore it must have begun to be.

Obj. 3. Further, *everything which works by intellect works from some principle*, as is revealed in all works of human art. But God acts by intellect, and therefore His work has a principle, from which to begin. The world, therefore, which is His effect, did not always exist.

Obj. 4. Further, it appears manifestly that certain arts have developed, and certain parts of the world have begun to be inhabited at some fixed time. But this would not be the case if the world had always been in existence. Therefore it is manifest that the world did not always exist.

Obj. 5. Further, it is certain that nothing can be equal to God. But if the world had always been, it would be equal to God in duration. Therefore it is certain that the world did not always exist.

Obj. 6. Further, if the world always was, the consequence is that an infinite number of days preceded this present day. But it is impossible to traverse what is infinite. Therefore we should never have arrived at this present day; which is manifestly false.

Obj. 7. Further, if the world was eternal, generation also was eternal. Therefore one man was begotten of another in an infinite series. But the father is the efficient cause of the son. Therefore in efficient causes there could be an infinite series; which however is disproved in *Metaph.* ii.

Obj. 8. Further, if the world and generation always were, there have been an infinite number of men. But man's soul is immortal. Therefore an infinite number of human souls would now actually ex-

faith is of things that appear not. revelation illuminators augustine's argument here

ist, which is impossible. Therefore it can be known with certainty that the world began: it is not held by faith alone.

On the contrary, The articles of faith cannot be proved demonstratively, because *faith is of things that appear not*. But that God is the Creator of the world in such a way that the world began to be is an article of faith; for we say, *I believe in one God*, etc. And again, Gregory says that Moses prophesied of the past, saying, *In the beginning God created heaven and earth:* in which words the newness of the world is stated. Therefore the newness of the world is known only by revelation, and hence it cannot be proved demonstratively.

I answer that, That the world did not always exist we hold by faith alone: it cannot be proved demonstratively; which is what was said above of the mystery of the Trinity. The reason for this is that the newness of the world cannot be demonstrated from the world itself. For the principle of demonstration is the essence of a thing. Now everything, considered in its species, abstracts from *here* and *now;* which is why it is said that *universals are everywhere and always*. Hence it cannot be demonstrated that man, or the heavens, or a stone did not always exist.

Likewise, neither can the newness of the world be demonstrated from the efficient cause, which acts by will. For the will of God cannot be investigated by reason, except as regards those things which God must will of necessity; and what He wills about creatures is not among these, as was said above. But the divine will can be manifested by revelation, on which faith rests. Hence that the world began to exist is an object of faith, but not of demonstration or science. And it is useful to consider this, lest anyone, presuming to demonstrate what is of faith, should bring forward arguments that are not cogent; for this would give unbelievers the occasion to ridicule, thinking that on such grounds we believe the things that are of faith.

Reply Obj. 1. As Augustine says, the opinion of philosophers who asserted the eternity of the world was twofold. For some said that the substance of the world was not from God, which is an intolerable error; and therefore it is refuted by proofs that are cogent. Some, however, said that the world was eternal, although made by God. *For they hold that the world has a beginning, not of time, but of creation;* which means that, in a scarcely intelligible way, it was always made. And they try to explain their meaning thus: for just as, if a foot were always in the dust from eternity, there would always be a footprint which without doubt was caused by him who trod on it, so also the world always was, because its Maker always existed.* To understand this we must consider that an efficient cause which acts by motion of necessity precedes its effect in time; for the effect exists only in the end of the action, and every agent must be the beginning of action. But if the action is instantaneous and not successive, it is not necessary for the maker to be prior in duration to the thing made, as appears in the case of illumination. Hence it is held that it does not follow necessarily that if God is the active cause of the world, He must be prior to the world in duration; because creation, by which He produced the world, is not a successive change, as was said above.

Reply Obj. 2. Those who would hold that the world was eternal, would say that the world was made by God from nothing; not that it was made after nothing, according to what we understand by the term *creation*, but that it was not made from anything. And so some of them even do not reject the term creation, as appears from Avicenna.

Reply Obj. 3. This is the argument of Anaxagoras as reported in *Physics* iii. But it does not lead to a necessary conclusion, except as to that intellect which deliberates in order to find out what should be done; which procedure is like movement. Such is the human intellect, but not the divine intellect.

Reply Obj. 4. Those who hold the eternity of the world hold that some region was changed an infinite number of times from being uninhabitable to being inhabitable and *vice versa*. They also hold that the arts, by reason of various corruptions and accidents, were subject to an infinite succession of discovery and decay. Hence Aristotle says that it is absurd to base our opinion of the newness of the whole world on such particular changes.

Reply Obj. 5. Even supposing that the world always was, it would not be equal to God in eternity, as Boethius says; for the divine Being is all being simultaneously without succession, but with the world it is otherwise.

Reply Obj. 6. Passage is always understood as being from term to term. Whatever by-gone day we choose, from it to the present day there is a finite number of days which can be traversed. The objection is founded on the idea that, given two extremes, there is an infinite number of mean terms.

Reply Obj. 7. In efficient causes it is impossible to proceed to infinity *per se.* Thus, there cannot be an infinite number of causes that are *per se* required for a certain effect; for instance, that a stone be moved by a stick, the stick by the hand, and so on to infinity. But it is not impossible to proceed to infinity *accidentally* as regards efficient causes; for instance, if all the causes thus infinitely multiplied should have the order of only one cause, while their multiplication is accidental: *e.g.*, as an artificer acts by means of many hammers accidentally, because one after the other is broken. It is accidental, therefore, that one particular hammer should act after the action of another, and it is likewise accidental to this particular man as generator to be generated by another man; for he generates as a man, and not as the son of another man. For all men generating hold one grade in the order of efficient causes—viz., the grade of a particular generator. Hence it is not impossible for a man to be generated by man to infinity; but such a thing would be impossible if the generation of this man depended upon this man, and on an elementary body, and on the sun, and so on to infinity.

Reply Obj. 8. Those who hold the eternity of the world evade this argument in many ways. For some do not think it impossible for there to be an actual infinity of souls, as appears from the *Metaphysics* of Algazel, who says that such a thing is an accidental infinity. But this was disproved above. Some say that the soul is corrupted with the body. And some say that of all souls only one remains. But others, as Augustine says, asserted on this account a circulation of souls—viz., that souls separated from their bodies again return thither after a course of time. A fuller consideration of this matter will be given later. But be it noted that this argument considers only a particular case. Hence one might say that the world was eternal, or at least some creature, as an angel, but not man. But we are considering the question in general, namely, whether any creature can exist from eternity. . . .

QUESTION LXXXV. THE MODE AND ORDER OF UNDERSTANDING

We come now to consider the mode and order of understanding. Under this head there are eight points of inquiry: (1) Whether our intellect understands by abstracting species from the phantasms? (2) Whether the intelligible species abstracted from the phantasms are what our intellect understands, or that whereby it understands? (3) Whether our intellect naturally first understands the more universal? (4) Whether our intellect can know many things at the same time? (5) Whether our intellect understands by composition and division? (6) Whether the intellect can err? (7) Whether one intellect can understand the same thing better than another? (8) Whether our intellect understands the indivisible before the divisible?

FIRST ARTICLE. WHETHER OUR INTELLECT UNDERSTANDS CORPOREAL AND MATERIAL THINGS BY ABSTRACTION FROM PHANTASMS?

We proceed thus to the First Article:—

Objection 1. It would seem that our intellect does not understand corporeal and material things by abstraction from the phantasms. For the intellect is false if it understands a thing otherwise than as it is. Now the forms of material things do not exist in abstraction from the particular things represented by the phantasms. Therefore, if we understand material things by the abstraction of species from phantasms, there will be error in the intellect.

Obj. 2. Further, material things are those natural things which include matter in their definition. But nothing can be understood apart from that which enters into its definition. Therefore material things cannot be understood apart from matter. Now matter is the principle of individuation. Therefore material things cannot be understood by the abstraction of the universal from the particular; and this is to abstract intelligible species from the phantasm.

Obj. 3. Further, the Philosopher says that the phantasm is to the intellectual soul what color is to the sight. But seeing is not caused by abstraction of species from color, but by color impressing itself on the sight. Therefore neither does the act of understanding take place by the abstraction of something from the phantasms, but by the phantasms impressing themselves on the intellect.

Obj. 4. Further, the Philosopher says that there are two things in the intellectual soul—the possible intellect and the agent intellect. But it does not belong to the possible intellect to abstract the intelligible species from the phantasm, but to receive them already abstracted. Neither does it seem to be the function of the agent intellect, which is related to phantasms as light is to colors; since light does not abstract anything from colors, but rather acts on them. Therefore in no way do we understand by abstraction from phantasms.

Obj. 5. Further, the Philosopher says that *the intellect understands the species in the phantasms;* and not, therefore, by abstraction.

On the contrary, The Philosopher says that *things are intelligible in proportion as they are separable from matter.* Therefore material things must needs be understood according as they are abstracted from matter and from material images, namely phantasms.

I answer that, As stated above, the object of knowledge is proportionate to the power of knowledge. Now there are three grades of the cognitive powers. For one cognitive power, namely, the sense, is the act of a corporeal organ. And therefore the object of every sensitive power is a form as existing in corporeal matter; and since such matter is the principle of individuation, therefore every power of the sensitive part can have knowledge only of particulars. There is another grade of cognitive power which is neither the act of a corporeal organ, nor in any way connected with corporeal matter. Such is the angelic intellect, the object of whose cognitive power is therefore a form existing apart from matter; for though angels know material things, yet they do not know them save in something immaterial, namely, either in themselves or in God. But the human intellect holds a middle place; for it is not the act of an organ, and yet it is a power of the soul, which is the form of the body, as is clear from what we have said above. And therefore it is proper to it to know a form existing individually in corporeal matter, but not as existing in this individual matter. But to know what is in individual matter, yet not as existing in such matter, is to abstract the form from individual matter which is represented by the phantasms. Therefore we must needs say that our intellect understands material things by abstracting from phantasms; and that through material things thus considered we acquire some knowledge of immaterial things, just as, on the contrary, angels know material things through the immaterial.

But Plato, considering only the immateriality of the human intellect, and not that it is somehow united to the body, held that the objects of the intellect are separate Ideas, and that we understand, not by abstraction, but rather by participating in abstractions, as was stated above.

Reply Obj. 1. Abstraction may occur in two ways. First, by way of composition and division, and thus we may understand that one thing does not exist in some other, or that it is separate from it. Secondly, by way of a simple and absolute consideration; and thus we understand one thing without considering another. Thus, for the intellect to abstract one from another things which are not really abstract from one another, does, in the first mode of abstraction, imply falsehood. But, in the second mode of abstraction, for the intellect to abstract things which are not really abstract from one another, does not involve falsehood, as clearly appears in the case of the senses. For if we said that color is not in a colored body, or that it is separate from it, there would be error in what we thought or said. But if we consider color and its properties, without reference to the apple which is colored, or if we express in word what we thus understand, there is no error in such an opinion or assertion; for an apple is not essential to color, and therefore color can be understood independently of the apple. In the same way, the things which belong to the species of a material thing, such as a stone, or a man, or a horse, can be thought without the individual principles which do not belong to the notion of the species. This is what we mean by abstracting the universal from the particular, or the intelligible species from the phantasm; in other words, this is to consider the nature of the species apart from its individual principles represented by the phantasms. If, therefore, the intellect is said to be false when it understands a thing otherwise than as it is, that is so, if the word *otherwise* refers to the thing understood; for the intellect is false when it under-

[handwritten margin notes: "Plato reference" / "Species did not exist in matter" / "Two-fold matter"]

stands a thing to be otherwise than as it is. Hence, the intellect would be false if it abstracted the species of a stone from its matter in such a way as to think that the species did not exist in matter, as Plato held. But it is not so, if the word *otherwise* be taken as referring to the one who understands. For it is quite true that the mode of understanding, in one who understands, is not the same as the mode of a thing in being; since the thing understood is immaterially in the one who understands, according to the mode of the intellect, and not materially, according to the mode of a material thing.

Reply Obj. 2. Some have thought that the species of a natural thing is a form only, and that matter is not part of the species. If that were so, matter would not enter into the definition of natural things. Therefore we must disagree and say that matter is twofold, common and *signate,* or individual: common, such as flesh and bone; individual, such as this flesh and these bones. The intellect therefore abstracts the species of a natural thing from the individual sensible matter, but not from the common sensible matter. For example, it abstracts the species of *man* from *this flesh and these bones*, which do not belong to the species as such, but to the individual, and need not be considered in the species. But the species of man cannot be abstracted by the intellect from *flesh and bones*.

Mathematical species, however, can be abstracted by the intellect not only from individual sensible matter, but also from common sensible matter. But they cannot be abstracted from common intelligible matter, but only from individual intelligible matter. For sensible matter is corporeal matter as subject to sensible qualities, such as being cold or hot, hard or soft, and the like; while intelligible matter is substance as subject to quantity. Now it is manifest that quantity is in substance before sensible qualities are. Hence quantities, such as number, dimension, and figures, which are the terminations of quantity, can be considered apart from sensible qualities, and this is to abstract them from sensible matter. But they cannot be considered without understanding the substance which is subject to the quantity, for that would be to abstract them from common intelligible matter. Yet they can be considered apart from this or

that substance, and this is to abstract them from individual intelligible matter.

But some things can be abstracted even from common intelligible matter, such as *being, unity, potency, act,* and the like, all of which can exist without matter, as can be verified in the case of immaterial substances. And because Plato failed to consider the twofold kind of abstraction, as above explained, he held that all those things which we have stated to be abstracted by the intellect, are abstract in reality.

Reply Obj. 3. Colors, as being in individual corporeal matter, have the same mode of being as the power of sight; and therefore they can impress their own image on the eye. But phantasms, since they are images of individuals, and exist in corporeal organs, have not the same mode of being as the human intellect, as is clear from what we have said, and therefore they have not the power of themselves to make an impression on the possible intellect. But through the power of the agent intellect, there results in the possible intellect a certain likeness produced by the turning of the agent intellect toward the phantasms. This likeness represents what is in the phantasms, but includes only the nature of the species. It is thus that the intelligible species is said to be abstracted from the phantasm; not that the identical form which previously was in the phantasm is subsequently in the possible intellect, as a body transferred from one place to another.

Reply Obj. 4. Not only does the agent intellect illumine phantasms, it does more; by its power intelligible species are abstracted from phantasms. It illumines phantasms because, just as the sensitive part acquires a greater power by its conjunction with the intellectual part, so through the power of the agent intellect phantasms are made more fit for the abstraction of intelligible intentions from them. Now the agent intellect abstracts intelligible species from phantasms inasmuch as by its power we are able to take into our consideration the natures of species without individual conditions. It is in accord with their likenesses that the possible intellect is informed.

Reply Obj. 5. Our intellect both abstracts the intelligible species *from* phantasms, inasmuch as it considers the natures of things universally, and yet

[handwritten marginalia: Outside soul is material what is understood is in intellect] *[handwritten marginalia: words signify what is understood]*

understands these natures *in* the phantasms, since it cannot understand the things, of which it abstracts the species, without turning to phantasms, as we have said above.

SECOND ARTICLE. WHETHER THE INTELLIGIBLE SPECIES ABSTRACTED FROM PHANTASMS ARE RELATED TO OUR INTELLECT AS THAT WHICH IS UNDERSTOOD?

We proceed thus to the Second Article:—

Objection 1. It would seem that the intelligible species abstracted from phantasms are related to our intellect as that which is understood. For the understood in act is in the one who understands: since the understood in act is the intellect itself in act. But nothing of what is understood is in the actually understanding intellect save the abstracted intelligible species. Therefore this species is what is actually understood.

Obj. 2. Further, what is actually understood must be in something; or else it would be nothing. But it is not in something outside the soul; for, since what is outside the soul is material, nothing therein can be actually understood. Therefore what is actually understood is in the intellect. Consequently it can be nothing else than the aforesaid intelligible species.

Obj. 3. Further, the Philosopher says that *words are signs of the passions in the soul.* But words signify the things understood, for we express by word what we understand. Therefore these passions of the soul, viz., the intelligible species, are what is actually understood.

On the contrary, The intelligible species is to the intellect what the sensible species is to the sense. But the sensible species is not *what* is perceived, but rather that *by which* the sense perceives. Therefore the intelligible species is not what is actually understood, but that by which the intellect understands.

I answer that, Some have asserted that our intellectual powers know only the impressions made on them; as, for example, that sense is cognizant only of the impression made on its own organ. According to this theory, the intellect understands only its own impressions, namely, the intelligible species which it has received.

This is, however, manifestly false for two reasons. First, because the things we understand are also the objects of science. Therefore, if what we understand is merely the intelligible species in the soul, it would follow that every science would be concerned, not with things outside the soul, but only with the intelligible species within the soul; just as, according to the teaching of the Platonists, all the sciences are about Ideas, which they held to be that which is actually understood. Secondly, it is untrue, because it would lead to the opinion of the ancients who maintained that *whatever seems, is true,* and that consequently contradictories are true simultaneously. For if a power knows only its own impressions, it can judge only of them. Now a thing *seems* according to the impression made on the cognitive power. Consequently the cognitive power will always judge of its own impression as such; and so every judgment will be true. For instance, if taste perceived only its own impression, when anyone with a healthy taste perceives that honey is sweet, he would judge truly, and if anyone with a corrupt taste perceives that honey is bitter, this would be equally true; for each would judge according to the impression on his taste. Thus every opinion, in fact, every sort of apprehension, would be equally true.

Therefore it must be said that the intelligible species is related to the intellect as that by which it understands. Which is proved thus. Now action is twofold, as it is said in *Metaph.* ix: one which remains in the agent (for instance, to see and to understand), and another which passes into an external object (for instance, to heat and to cut). Each of these actions proceeds in virtue of some form. And just as the form from which proceeds an act tending to something external is the likeness of the object of the action, as heat in the heater is a likeness of the thing heated, so the form from which proceeds an action remaining in the agent is a likeness of the object. Hence that by which the sight sees is the likeness of the visible thing; and the likeness of the thing understood, that is, the intelligible species, is the form by which the intellect understands. But since the intellect reflects upon itself, by such reflection it understands both its own act of understanding, and the species by which it understands. Thus the intelligible species is secondarily that which is understood; but that which is primarily understood is the thing, of which the species is the likeness.

This also appears from the opinion of the ancient philosophers, who said that *like is known by like*. For they said that the soul knows the earth outside itself by the earth within itself; and so of the rest. If, therefore, we take the species of the earth instead of the earth, in accord with Aristotle who says *that a stone is not in the soul, but only the likeness of the stone,* it follows that by means of its intelligible species the soul knows the things which are outside it.

Reply Obj. 1. The thing understood is in the knower by its own likeness. It is in this sense that we say that the thing actually understood is the intellect in act, because the likeness of the thing understood is the form of the intellect, just as the likeness of a sensible thing is the form of the sense in act. Hence it does not follow that the abstracted intelligible species is what is actually understood; but rather that it is the likeness thereof.

Reply Obj. 2. In these words *the thing actually understood* there is a double meaning:—the thing which is understood, and the fact that it is understood. In like manner, the words *abstract universal* mean two things, the nature of a thing and its abstraction or universality. Therefore the nature itself which suffers the act of being understood, or the act of being abstracted, or the intention of universality, exists only in individuals; but that it is understood, abstracted or considered as universal is in the intellect. We see something similar to this in the senses. For the sight sees the color of the apple apart from its smell. If therefore it be asked where is the color which is seen apart from the smell, it is quite clear that the color which is seen is only in the apple; but that it be perceived apart from the smell, this is owing to the sight, inasmuch as sight receives the likeness of color and not of smell. In like manner, the humanity which is understood exists only in this or that man; but that humanity be apprehended without the conditions of individuality, that is, that it be abstracted and consequently considered as universal, befalls humanity inasmuch as it is perceived by the intellect, in which there is a likeness of the specific nature, but not of the individual principles.

Reply Obj. 3. There are two operations in the sensitive part. One is limited to immutation, and thus the operation of the senses takes place when the senses are impressed by the sensible. The other is formation, inasmuch as the imagination forms for itself an image of an absent thing, or even of something never seen. Both of these operations are found in the intellect. For in the first place there is the passion of the possible intellect as informed by the intelligible species; and then the possible intellect, as thus informed, then forms a definition, or a division, or a composition, which is expressed by language. And so, the notion signified by a *term* is a definition; and a *proposition* signifies the intellect's division or composition. Words do not therefore signify the intelligible species themselves; but that which the intellect forms for itself for the purpose of judging of external things.

THIRD ARTICLE. WHETHER THE MORE UNIVERSAL IS FIRST IN OUR INTELLECTUAL COGNITION?

We proceed thus to the Third Article:—

Objection 1. It would seem that the more universal is not first in our intellectual cognition. For what is first and more known in its own nature is secondarily and less known in relation to ourselves. But universals come first as regards their nature, because *that is first which does not involve the existence of its correlative.* Therefore universals are secondarily known by our intellect.

Obj. 2. Further, the composite precedes the simple in relation to us. But universals are the more simple. Therefore they are known secondarily by us.

Obj. 3. Further, the Philosopher says that the object defined comes in our knowledge before the parts of its definition. But the more universal is part of the definition of the less universal, as *animal* is part of the definition of *man.* Therefore universals are secondarily known by us.

Obj. 4. Further, we know causes and principles by their effects. But universals are principles. Therefore universals are secondarily known by us.

On the contrary, We must proceed from the universal to the singular.

I answer that, In our knowledge there are two things to be considered. First, that intellectual knowledge in some degree arises from sensible knowledge. Now because sense has singular and individual things for its object, and intellect has the universal

compare:
Universal vs.
distinct. Knowledge of senses first
SUMMA THEOLOGICA 469
sensible knowledge is prior to intellectual knowledge

for its object, it follows that our knowledge of the former comes before our knowledge of the latter. Secondly, we must consider that our intellect proceeds from a state of potentiality to a state of actuality; and that every power thus proceeding from potentiality to actuality comes first to an incomplete act, which is intermediate between potentiality and actuality, before accomplishing the perfect act. The perfect act of the intellect is complete knowledge, when the object is distinctly and determinately known; whereas the incomplete act is imperfect knowledge, when the object is known indistinctly, and as it were confusedly. A thing thus imperfectly known is known partly in act and partly in potentiality. Hence the Philosopher says that *what is manifest and certain is known to us at first confusedly; afterwards we know it by distinguishing its principles and elements*. Now it is evident that to know something that comprises many things, without a proper knowledge of each thing contained in it, is to know that thing confusedly. In this way we can have knowledge not only of the universal whole, which contains parts potentially, but also of the integral whole, for each whole can be known confusedly, without its parts being known distinctly. But to know distinctly what is contained in the universal whole is to know the less common; and thus to know *animal* indistinctly is to know it as *animal*, whereas to know *animal* distinctly is to know it as *rational* or *irrational animal*, that is, to know a man or a lion. And so our intellect knows *animal* before it knows man; and the same reason holds in comparing any more universal concept with the less universal.

Moreover, as sense, like the intellect, proceeds from potentiality to act, the same order of knowledge appears in the senses. For by sense we judge of the more common before the less common, in reference both to place and time. In reference to place, when a thing is seen afar off it is seen to be a body before it is seen to be an animal, and to be an animal before it is seen to be a man, and to be a man before it is seen to be Socrates or Plato. The same is true as regards time, for a child can distinguish man from not-man before he distinguishes this man from that, and therefore *children at first call all men fathers, and later on distinguish each one from the others*. The reason of this is clear: he who knows a thing indistinctly is in a state of potentiality as regards its

principle of distinction; just as he who knows *genus* is in a state of potentiality as regards *difference*. Thus it is evident that indistinct knowledge is midway between potentiality and act.

We must therefore conclude that knowledge of the singular and individual is prior, as regards us, to the knowledge of the universal, just as sensible knowledge is prior to intellectual knowledge. But in both sense and intellect the knowledge of the more common precedes the knowledge of the less common.

Reply Obj. 1. The universal can be considered in two ways. First, the universal nature may be considered together with the intention of universality. And since the intention of universality—viz., the relation of one and the same to many—is due to intellectual abstraction, the universal thus considered is subsequent in our knowledge. Hence it is said that the *universal animal is either nothing or something subsequent*. But according to Plato, who held that universals are subsistent, the universal considered thus would be prior to the particular, for the latter, according to him, are mere participations in the subsistent universals which he called Ideas.

Secondly, the universal can be considered according to the nature itself (for instance, *animality* or *humanity*) as existing in the individual. And thus we must distinguish two orders of nature: one, by way of generation and time; and thus the imperfect and the potential come first. In this way the more common comes first in the order of nature. This appears clearly in the generation of man and animal; for *the animal is generated before man*, as the Philosopher says. The other order is the order of perfection or of the intention of nature. For instance, act considered absolutely is naturally prior to potentiality, and the perfect to the imperfect; and thus the less common comes naturally before the more common, as man comes before animal. For the intention of nature does not stop at the generation of animal, but aims at the generation of man.

Reply Obj. 2. The more common universal may be compared to the less common as a whole, and as a part. As a whole, inasmuch as in the more universal there is potentially contained not only the less universal, but also other things; as in *animal* is contained not only *man* but also *horse*. As a part, inasmuch as the less common universal contains in its notion not only the more common, but also more;

as *man* contains not only *animal* but also *rational*. Therefore *animal* considered in itself is in our knowledge before *man*; but *man* comes before *animal* considered as a part of the notion of man.

Reply Obj. 3. A part can be known in two ways. First, absolutely considered in itself; and thus nothing prevents the parts from being known before the whole, as stones are known before a house is known. Secondly, as belonging to a certain whole; and thus we must needs know the whole before its parts. For we know a house confusedly before we know its different parts. So, likewise, that which defines is known before the thing defined is known; otherwise the thing defined would not be made known by the definition. But as parts of the definition they are known after. For we know man confusedly as man before we know how to distinguish all that belongs to human nature.

Reply Obj. 4. The universal, as understood with the intention of universality, is, in a certain manner, a principle of knowledge, in so far as the intention of universality results from the mode of understanding, which is by way of abstraction. But that which is a principle of knowledge is not of necessity a principle of being, as Plato thought, since at times we know a cause through its effect, and substance through accidents. Therefore the universal thus considered, according to the opinion of Aristotle, is neither a principle of being, nor a substance, as he makes clear. But if we consider the generic or specific nature itself as existing in the singular, thus in a way it has the character of a formal principle in regard to singulars; for the singular is the result of matter, while the nature of the species is from the form. But the generic nature is compared to the specific nature rather after the fashion of a material principle, because the generic nature is taken from that which is material in a thing, while the nature of the species is taken from that which is formal. Thus the notion of animal is taken from the sensitive part, whereas the notion of man is taken from the intellectual part. Thus it is that the ultimate intention of nature is towards the species and not the individual, or the genus; because the form is the end of generation, while matter is for the sake of the form. Neither is it necessary that the knowledge of any cause or principle should be subsequent in relation to us, since through sensible causes we sometimes become acquainted with unknown effects, and sometimes conversely.

QUESTION XCII. OF THE EFFECTS OF LAW

FIRST ARTICLE. WHETHER AN EFFECT OF LAW IS TO MAKE MEN GOOD?

We proceed thus to the First Article:—

Objection 1. It seems that it is not an effect of law to make men good. For men are good through virtue, since virtue, as stated in *Ethic.* ii. 6 is *that which makes its subject good.* But virtue is in man from God alone, because He it is Who *works it in us without us*, as we stated above in giving the definition of virtue. Therefore the law does not make men good.

Obj. 2. Further, Law does not profit a man unless he obeys it. But the very fact that a man obeys a law is due to his being good. Therefore in man goodness is presupposed to the law. Therefore the law does not make men good.

Obj. 3. Further, Law is ordained to the common good, as stated above. But some behave well in things regarding the community, who behave ill in things regarding themselves. Therefore it is not the business of the law to make men good.

Obj. 4. Further, some laws are tyrannical, as the Philosopher says. But a tyrant does not intend the good of his subjects, but considers only his own profit. Therefore law does not make men good.

On the contrary, The Philosopher says that the *intention of every lawgiver is to make good citizens.*

I answer that, As stated above, a law is nothing else than a dictate of reason in the ruler by whom his subjects are governed. Now the virtue of any subordinate thing consists in is being well subordinated to that by which it is regulated: thus we see that the virtue of the irascible and concupiscible faculties consists in their being obedient to reason; and accordingly *the virtue of every subject consists in his being well subjected to his ruler*, as the Philosopher says. But every law aims at being obeyed by those who are subject to it. Consequently it is evident that the proper effect of law is to lead its subjects to their proper virtue: and since virtue is that which makes its subject good, it follows that the proper effect of law is to make those to whom it is given, good, either simply or in some particular respect. For if the

natural law appointed by reason

intention of the lawgiver is fixed on true good, which is the common good regulated according to Divine justice, it follows that the effect of the law is to make men good simply. If, however, the intention of the lawgiver is fixed on that which is not simply good, but useful or pleasurable to himself, or in opposition to Divine justice; then the law does not make men good simply, but in respect to that particular government. In this way good is found even in things that are bad of themselves: thus a man is called a good robber, because he works in a way that is adapted to his end.

Reply Obj. 1. Virtue is twofold, as explained above, viz., acquired and infused. Now the fact of being accustomed to an action contributes to both, but in different ways; for it causes the acquired virtue; while it disposes to infused virtue, and preserves and fosters it when it already exists. And since law is given for the purpose of directing human acts; as far as human acts conduce to virtue, so far does law make men good. Wherefore the Philosopher says in the second book of the *Politics* that *lawgivers make men good by habituating them to good works.*

Reply Obj. 2. It is not always through perfect goodness of virtue that one obeys the law, but sometimes it is through fear of punishment, and sometimes from the mere dictate of reason, which is a beginning of virtue, as stated above.

Reply Obj. 3. The goodness of any part is considered in comparison with the whole; hence Augustine says that *unseemly is the part that harmonizes not with the whole.* Since then every man is a part of the state, it is impossible that a man be good, unless he be well proportionate to the common good: nor can the whole be well consistent unless its parts be proportionate to it. Consequently the common good of the state cannot flourish, unless the citizens be virtuous, at least those whose business it is to govern. But it is enough for the good of the community, that the other citizens be so far virtuous that they obey the commands of their rulers. Hence the Philosopher says that *the virtue of a sovereign is the same as that of a good man, but the virtue of any common citizen is not the same as that of a good man.*

Reply Obj. 4. A tyrannical law, through not being according to reason, is not a law, absolutely speaking, but rather a perversion of law; and yet in so far as it is something in the nature of a law, it aims at the citizens being good. For all it has in the nature of a law consists in its being an ordinance made by a superior to his subjects, and aims at being obeyed by them, which is to make them good, not simply, but with respect to that particular government.

QUESTION XCIV. THE NATURAL LAW

FIRST ARTICLE. WHETHER THE NATURAL LAW IS A HABIT?

We proceed thus to the First Article:—

Objection 1. It would seem that the natural law is a habit. For, as the Philosopher says, *there are three things in the soul, power, habit and passion.* But the natural law is not one of the soul's powers, nor is it one of the passions, as we may see by going through them one by one. Therefore the natural law is a habit.

Obj. 2. Further, Basil says that the *conscience or synderesis is the law of our mind,* which can apply only to the natural law. But *synderesis* is a habit, as was shown in the First Part. Therefore the natural law is a habit.

Obj. 3. Further, the natural law abides in man always, as will be shown further on. But man's reason, which the law regards, does not always think about the natural law. Therefore the natural law is not an act, but a habit.

On the contrary, Augustine says that *a habit is that whereby something is done when necessary.* But such is not the natural law, since it is in infants and in the damned who cannot act by it. Therefore the natural law is not a habit.

I answer that, A thing may be called a habit in two ways. First, properly and essentially, and thus the natural law is not a habit. For it has been stated above that the natural law is something appointed by reason, just as a proposition is a work of reason. Now that which a 7man does is not the same as that whereby he does it, for he makes a becoming speech by the habit of grammar. Since, then, a habit is that by which we act, a law cannot be a habit properly and essentially.

Secondly, the term habit may be applied to that which we hold by a habit. Thus *faith* may mean *that which we hold by faith.* Accordingly, since the precepts of the natural law are sometimes considered by reason actually, while sometimes they are in the reason only habitually, in this way the natural law may be called a habit. So, too, in speculative matters, the indemonstrable principles are not the habit itself whereby we hold these principles; they are rather the principles of which we possess the habit.

Reply Obj. 1. The Philosopher proposes there to discover the genus of virtue; and since it is evident that virtue is a principle of action, he mentions only those things which are principles of human acts, viz., powers, habits and passions. But there are other things in the soul besides these three: e.g., acts, as *to will* is in the one that wills; again, there are things known in the knower; moreover its own natural properties are in the soul, such as immortality and the like.

Reply Obj. 2. Synderesis is said to be the law of our intellect because it is a habit containing the precepts of the natural law, which are the first principles of human actions.

Reply Obj. 3. This argument proves that the natural law is held habitually; and this is granted.

To the argument advanced in the contrary sense we reply that sometimes a man is unable to make use of that which is in him habitually, because of some impediment. Thus, because of sleep, a man is unable to use the habit of science. In like manner, through the deficiency of his age, a child cannot use the habit of the understanding of principles, or the natural law, which is in him habitually.

SECOND ARTICLE. WHETHER THE NATURAL LAW CONTAINS SEVERAL PRECEPTS, OR ONLY ONE?

We proceed thus to the Second Article:—

Objection 1. It would seem that the natural law contains, not several precepts, but only one. For law is a kind of precept, as was stated above. If therefore there were many precepts of the natural law, it would follow that there are also many natural laws.

Obj. 2. Further, the natural law is consequent upon human nature. But human nature, as a whole, is one, though, as to its parts, it is manifold. Therefore, either there is but one precept of the law of nature because of the unity of nature as a whole, or there are many by reason of the number of parts of human nature. The result would be that even things relating to the inclination of the concupiscible power would belong to the natural law.

Obj. 3. Further, law is something pertaining to reason, as was stated above. Now reason is but one in man. Therefore there is only one precept of the natural law.

On the contrary, The precepts of the natural law in man stand in relation to operable matters as first principles do to matters of demonstration. But there are several first indemonstrable principles. Therefore there are also several precepts of the natural law.

I answer that, As was stated above, the precepts of the natural law are to the practical reason what the first principles of demonstrations are to the speculative reason, because both are self-evident principles. Now a thing is said to be self-evident in two ways: first, in itself; secondly, in relation to us. Any proposition is said to be self-evident in itself, if its predicate is contained in the notion of the subject; even though it may happen that to one who does not know the definition of the subject, such a proposition is not self-evident. For instance, this proposition, *Man is a rational being*, is, in its very nature, self-evident, since he who says *man says a rational being*; and yet to one who does not know what a man is, this proposition is not self-evident. Hence it is that, as Boethius says, certain axioms or propositions are universally self-evident to all; and such are the propositions whose terms are known to all, as, *Every whole is greater than its part*, and, *Things equal to one and the same are equal to one another*. But some propositions are self-evident only to the wise, who understand the meaning of the terms of such propositions. Thus to one who understands that an angel is not a body, it is self-evident that an angel is not circumscriptively in a place. But this is not evident to the unlearned, for they cannot grasp it.

Now a certain order is to be found in those things that are apprehended by men. For that which first falls under apprehension is *being*, the understanding of which is included in all things whatsoever a man apprehends. Therefore the first indemonstrable principle is that *the same thing cannot be affirmed and denied at the same time*, which is based on the notion of *being* and *not-being*: and on this principle all others are based, as is stated in *Metaph.* iv. Now as *being* is the first thing that falls under the apprehension absolutely, so good is the first thing that falls under the apprehension of the practical reason,

(1) natural law: good is to be done + promoted
(2) natural law preserve life
(3) natural to know truth

which is directed to action (since every agent acts for an end, which has the nature of good). Consequently, the first principle in the practical reason is one founded on the nature of good, viz., that *good is that which all things seek after*. Hence this is the first precept of law, that *good is to be done and promoted, and evil is to be avoided*. All other precepts of the natural law are based upon this; so that all the things which the practical reason naturally apprehends as man's good belong to the precepts of the natural law under the form of things to be done or avoided.

Since, however, good has the nature of an end, and evil, the nature of the contrary, hence it is that all those things to which man has a natural inclination are naturally apprehended by reason as being good, and consequently as objects of pursuit, and their contraries as evil, and objects of avoidance. Therefore, the order of the precepts of the natural law is according to the order of natural inclinations. For there is in man, first of all, an inclination to good in accordance with the nature which he has in common with all substances, inasmuch, namely, as every substance seeks the preservation of its own being, according to its nature; and by reason of this inclination, whatever is a means of preserving human life, and of warding off its obstacles, belongs to the natural law. Secondly, there is in man an inclination to things that pertain to him more specially, according to that nature which he has in common with other animals; and in virtue of this inclination, those things are said to belong to the natural law *which nature has taught to all animals*, such as sexual intercourse, the education of offspring and so forth. Thirdly, there is in man an inclination to good according to the nature of his reason, which nature is proper to him. Thus man has a natural inclination to know the truth about God, as to live in society; and in this respect, whatever pertains to this inclination belongs to the natural law: e.g., to shun ignorance, to avoid offending those among whom one has to live, and other such things regarding the above inclination.

Reply Obj. 1. All these precepts of the law of nature have the character of one natural law, inasmuch as they flow from one first precept.

Reply Obj. 2. All the inclinations of any parts whatsoever of human nature, e.g., of the concupiscible and irascible parts, in so far as they are ruled by

reason, belong to the natural law, and are reduced to one first precept, as was stated above. And thus the precepts of the natural law are many in themselves, but they are based on one common foundation.

Reply Obj. 3. Although reason is one in itself, yet it directs all things regarding man; so that whatever can be ruled by reason is contained under the law of reason.

FOURTH ARTICLE. WHETHER THE NATURAL LAW IS THE SAME IN ALL MEN?

not same for all

We proceed thus to the Fourth Article:—

Objection 1. It would seem that the natural law is not the same in all. For it is stated in the *Decretals* that *the natural law is that which is contained in the Law and the Gospel*. But this is not common to all men, because, as it is written (*Rom.* x. 16), *all do not obey the gospel*. Therefore the natural law is not the same in all men.

Obj. 2. Further, *Things which are according to the law are said to be just*, as is stated in *Ethics* v. But it is stated in the same book that nothing is so just for all as not to be subject to change in regard to some men. Therefore even the natural law is not the same in all men.

Obj. 3. Further, as was stated above, to the natural law belongs everything to which a man is inclined according to his nature. Now different men are naturally inclined to different things,—some to the desire of pleasures, others to the desire of honors, and other men to other things. Therefore, there is not one natural law for all.

On the contrary, Isidore says: *The natural law is common to all nations*.

I answer that, As we have stated above, to the natural law belong those things to which a man is inclined naturally; and among these it is proper to man to be inclined to act according to reason. Now it belongs to the reason to proceed from what is common to what is proper, as is stated in *Physics* i. The speculative reason, however, is differently situated, in this matter, from the practical reason. For, since the speculative reason is concerned chiefly with necessary things, which cannot be otherwise than they are, its proper conclusions, like the universal principles, contain the truth without fail. The practical reason, on the other hand, is concerned with contingent matters, which is the domain of human actions; and, consequently, although there is necessity in the common principles, the more we descend towards the particular, the more frequently we encounter defects. Accordingly, then, in speculative matters truth is the same in all men, both as to principles and as to conclusions; although the truth is not known to all as regards the conclusions, but only as regards the principles which are called *common notions*. But in matters of action, truth or practical rectitude is not the same for all as to what is particular, but only as to the common principles; and where there is the same rectitude in relation to particulars, it is not equally known to all.

It is therefore evident that, as regards the common principles whether of speculative or of practical reason, truth or rectitude is the same for all, and is equally known by all. But as to the proper conclusions of the speculative reason, the truth is the same for all, but it is not equally known to all. Thus, it is true for all that the three angles of a triangle are together equal to two right angles, although it is not known to all. But as to the proper conclusions of the practical reason, neither is the truth or rectitude the same for all, nor, where it is the same, is it equally known by all. Thus, it is right and true for all to act according to reason, and from this principle it follows, as a proper conclusion, that goods entrusted to another should be restored to their owner. Now this is true for the majority of cases. But it may happen in a particular case that it would be injurious, and therefore unreasonable, to restore goods held in trust; for instance, if they are claimed for the purpose of fighting against one's country. And this principle will be found to fail the more, according as we descend further towards the particular, e.g., if one were to say that goods held in trust should be restored with such and such a guarantee, or in such and such a way; because the greater the number of conditions added, the greater the number of ways in which the principle may fail, so that it be not right to restore or not to restore.

Consequently, we must say that the natural law, as to the first common principles, is the same for all, both as to rectitude and as to knowledge. But as to certain more particular aspects, which are conclusions, as it were, of those common principles, it is the same for all in the majority of cases, both as to rectitude and as to knowledge; and yet in some few

cases it may fail, both as to rectitude, by reason of certain obstacles (just as natures subject to generation and corruption fail in some few cases because of some obstacle), and as to knowledge, since in some the reason is perverted by passion, or evil habit, or an evil disposition of nature. Thus at one time theft, although it is expressly contrary to the natural law, was not considered wrong among the Germans, as Julius Caesar relates.

Reply Obj. 1. The meaning of the sentence quoted is not that whatever is contained in the Law and the Gospel belongs to the natural law, since they contain many things that are above nature; but that whatever belongs to the natural law is fully contained in them. Therefore Gratian, after saying that *the natural law is what is contained in the Law and the Gospel*, adds at once, by way of example, *by which everyone is commanded to do to others as he would be done by.*

Reply Obj. 2. The saying of the Philosopher is to be understood of things that are naturally just, not as common principles, but as conclusions drawn from them, having rectitude in the majority of cases, but failing in a few.

Reply Obj. 3. Just as in man reason rules and commands the other powers, so all the natural inclinations belonging to the other powers must needs be directed according to reason. Therefore it is universally right for all men that all their inclinations should be directed according to reason.

FIFTH ARTICLE. WHETHER THE NATURAL LAW CAN BE CHANGED?

We proceed thus to the Fifth Article:—

Objection 1. It would seem that the natural law can be changed. For on *Ecclus.* xvii. 9 (*He gave them instructions, and the law of life*) the *Gloss* says: *He wished the law of the letter to be written, in order to correct the law of nature.* But that which is corrected is changed. Therefore the natural law can be changed.

Obj 2. Further, the slaying of the innocent, adultery and theft are against the natural law. But we find these things changed by God: as when God commanded Abraham to slay his innocent son (*Gen.* xii. 2); and when He ordered the Jews to borrow and purloin the vessels of the Egyptians (*Exod.* xii. 35); and when He commanded Osee to take to himself *a wife of fornications* (*Osee* i. 2). Therefore the natural law can be changed.

Obj. 3. Further, Isidore says that *the possession of all things in common, and universal freedom, are matters of natural law*. But these things are seen to be changed by human laws. Therefore it seems that the natural law is subject to change.

On the contrary, It is said in the *Decretals: The natural law dates from the creation of the rational creature. It does not vary according to time, but remains unchangeable.*

I answer that, A change in the natural law may be understood in two ways. First, by way of addition. In this sense, nothing hinders the natural law from being changed, since many things for the benefit of human life have been added over and above the natural law, both by the divine law and by human laws.

Secondly, a change in the natural law may be understood by way of subtraction, so that what previously was according to the natural law, ceases to be so. In this sense, the natural law is altogether unchangeable in its first principles. But in its secondary principles, which, as we have said, are certain detailed proximate conclusions drawn from the first principles, the natural law is not changed so that what it prescribes be not right in most cases. But it may be changed in some particular cases of rare occurrence, through some special causes hindering the observance of such precepts, as was stated above.

Reply Obj. 1. The written law is said to be given for the correction of the natural law, either because it supplies what was wanting to the natural law, or because the natural law was so perverted in the hearts of some men, as to certain matters, that they esteemed those things good which are naturally evil; which perversion stood in need of correction.

Reply Obj. 2. All men alike, both guilty and innocent, die the death of nature; which death of nature is inflicted by the power of God because of original sin, according to *1 Kings* ii. 6: *The Lord killeth and maketh alive*. Consequently, by the command of God, death can be inflicted on any man, guilty or innocent, without any injustice whatever.—In like manner, adultery is intercourse with another's wife; who is allotted to him by the law emanating from God. Consequently intercourse with any woman, by the command of God, is neither adultery nor fornication.—The same applies to theft, which is the taking of another's property. For

whatever is taken by the command of God, to Whom all things belong, is not taken against the will of its owner, whereas it is in this that theft consists.—Nor is it only in human things that whatever is commanded by God is right; but also in natural things, whatever is done by God is, in some way, natural, as was stated in the First Part.

Reply Obj. 3. A thing is said to belong to the natural law in two ways. First, because nature inclines thereto: e.g., that one should not do harm to another. Secondly, because nature did not bring with it the contrary. Thus, we might say that for man to be naked is of the natural law, because nature did not give him clothes, but art invented them. In this sense, *the possession of all things in common and universal freedom* are said to be of the natural law, because, namely, the distinction of possessions and slavery were not brought in by nature, but devised by human reason for the benefit of human life. Accordingly, the law of nature was not changed in this respect, except by addition.

QUESTION XCV. HUMAN LAW

FIRST ARTICLE. WHETHER IT WAS USEFUL FOR LAWS TO BE FRAMED BY MEN?

We proceed thus to the First Article:—

Objection 1. It would seem that it was not useful for laws to be framed by men. For the purpose of every law is that man be made good thereby, as was stated above. But men are more to be induced to be good willingly by means of admonitions, than against their will, by means of laws. Therefore there was no need to frame laws.

Obj. 2. Further, As the Philosopher says, *men have recourse to a judge as to animate justice*. But animate justice is better than inanimate justice, which is contained in laws. Therefore it would have been better for the execution of justice to be entrusted to the decision of judges than to frame laws in addition.

Obj. 3. Further, every law is framed for the direction of human actions, as is evident from what has been stated above. But since human actions are about singulars, which are infinite in number, matters pertaining to the direction of human actions cannot be taken into sufficient consideration except by a wise man, who looks into each one of them. Therefore it would have been better for human acts to be directed by the judgment of wise men, than by the framing of laws. Therefore there was no need of human laws.

On the contrary, Isidore says: *Laws were made that in fear thereof human audacity might be held in check, that innocence might be safeguarded in the midst of wickedness, and that the dread of punishment might prevent the wicked from doing harm.* But these things are most necessary to mankind. Therefore it was necessary that human laws should be made.

I answer that, As we have stated above, man has a natural aptitude for virtue; but the perfection of virtue must be acquired by man by means of some kind of training. Thus we observe that a man is helped by diligence in his necessities, for instance, in food and clothing. Certain beginnings of these he has from nature, viz., his reason and his hands; but he has not the full complement, as other animals have, to whom nature has given sufficiently of clothing and food. Now it is difficult to see how man could suffice for himself in the matter of this training, since the perfection of virtue consists chiefly in withdrawing man from undue pleasures, to which above all man is inclined, and especially the young, who are more capable of being trained. Consequently a man needs to receive this training from another, whereby to arrive at the perfection of virtue. And as to those young people who are inclined to acts of virtue by their good natural disposition, or by custom, or rather by the gift of God, paternal training suffices, which is by admonitions. But since some are found to be dissolute and prone to vice, and not easily amenable to words, it was necessary for such to be restrained from evil by force and fear, in order that, at least, they might desist from evil-doing, and leave others in peace, and that they themselves, by being habituated in this way, might be brought to do willingly what hitherto they did from fear, and thus become virtuous. Now this kind of training, which compels through fear of punishment, is the discipline of laws. Therefore, in order that man might have peace and virtue, it was necessary for laws to be framed; for, as the Philosopher says, *as man is the most noble of animals if he be perfect in virtue, so he is the lowest of all, if he be severed from law and justice.* For man can use his reason to devise means of satisfying his lusts and evil passions, which other animals are unable to do.

Reply Obj. 1. Men who are well disposed are led willingly to virtue by being admonished better than by coercion; but men whose disposition is evil are not led to virtue unless they are compelled.

Reply Obj. 2. As the Philosopher says, *it is better that all things be regulated by law, than left to be decided by judges.* And this for three reasons. First, because it is easier to find a few wise men competent to frame right laws, than to find the many who would be necessary to judge rightly of each single case.—Secondly, because those who make laws consider long beforehand what laws to make, whereas judgment on each single case has to be pronounced as soon as it arises; and it is easier for man to see what is right, by taking many instances into consideration, than by considering one solitary instance.—Thirdly, because law-givers judge universally and about future events, whereas those who sit in judgment judge of things present, towards which they are affected by love, hatred, or some kind of cupidity; and thus their judgment becomes perverted.

Since, then, the animated justice of the judge is not found in every man, and since it can be bent, therefore it was necessary, whenever possible, for the law to determine how to judge, and for very few matters to be left to the decision of men.

Reply Obj. 3. Certain individual facts which cannot be covered by the law *have necessarily to be committed to judges,* as the Philosopher says in the same passage: *e.g., concerning something that has happened or not happened,* and the like.

SECOND ARTICLE. WHETHER EVERY HUMAN LAW IS DERIVED FROM THE NATURAL LAW?

We proceed thus to the Second Article:—

Objection 1. It would seem that not every human law is derived from the natural law. For the Philosopher says that *the legal just is that which originally was a matter of indifference.* But those things which arise from the natural law are not matters of indifference. Therefore the enactments of human laws are not all derived from the natural law.

Obj. 2. Further, positive law is divided against natural law, as is stated by Isidore and the Philosopher. But those things which flow as conclusions from the common principles of the natural law belong to the natural law, as was stated above. Therefore that which is established by human law is not derived from the natural law.

Obj. 3. Further, the law of nature is the same for all, since the Philosopher says that *the natural just is that which is equally valid everywhere.* If therefore human laws were derived from the natural law, it would follow that they too are the same for all; which is clearly false.

Obj. 4. Further, it is possible to give a reason for things which are derived from the natural law. But *it is not possible to give the reason for all the legal enactments of the lawgivers,* as the Jurist says. Therefore not all human laws are derived from the natural law.

On the contrary, Tully says: *Things which emanated from nature, and were approved by custom, were sanctioned by fear and reverence for the laws.*

I answer that, As Augustine says, *that which is not just seems to be no law at all.* Hence the force of a law depends on the extent of its justice. Now in human affairs a thing is said to be just from being right, according to the rule of reason. But the first rule of reason is the law of nature, as is clear from what has been stated above. Consequently, every human law has just so much of the nature of law as it is derived from the law of nature. But if in any point it departs from the law of nature, it is no longer a law but a perversion of law.

But it must be noted that something may be derived from the natural law in two ways: first, as a conclusion from principles; secondly, by way of a determination of certain common notions. The first way is like to that by which, in the sciences, demonstrated conclusions are drawn from the principles; while the second is likened to that whereby, in the arts, common forms are determined to some particular. Thus, the craftsman needs to determine the common form of a house to the shape of this or that particular house. Some things are therefore derived from the common principles of the natural law by way of conclusions: e.g., that *one must not kill* may be derived as a conclusion from the principle that *one should do harm to no man;* while some are derived therefrom by way of determination: e.g., the law of nature has it that the evil-doer should be punished, but that he be punished in this or that way is a determination of the law of nature.

Accordingly, both modes of derivation are found in the human law. But those things which are derived in the first way are contained in human law, not as emanating therefrom exclusively, but as having some force from the natural law also. But those things which are derived in the second way have no other force than that of human law.

Reply Obj. 1. The Philosopher is speaking of those enactments which are by way of determination or specification of the precepts of the natural law.

Reply Obj. 2. This argument holds for those things that are derived from the natural law by way of conclusion.

Reply Obj. 3. The common principles of the natural law cannot be applied to all men in the same way because of the great variety of human affairs; and hence arises the diversity of positive laws among various people.

Reply Obj. 4. These words of the Jurist are to be understood as referring to the decisions of rulers in determining particular points of the natural law; and to these determinations the judgment of expert and prudent men is related as to its principles, in so far, namely, as they see at once what is the best thing to decide. Hence the Philosopher says that, in such matters, *we ought to pay as much attention to the undemonstrated sayings and opinions of persons who surpass us in experience, age and prudence, as to their demonstrations.*

REVIEW QUESTIONS

1. What are the two objections that people give to deny the existence of God?
2. What are Aquinas' solutions to these two objections?
3. What is the central idea in each of the five arguments?
4. According to Aquinas, what is the first efficient cause? Why does he think that an infinite series of causes is impossible?
5. Why does Aquinas think that it is necessary that there be an Unmoved Mover?

13

WILLIAM OF OCKHAM

William of Ockham was born in Ockham, England, around 1285. He joined the Franciscan order and studied at Oxford University. In 1324 he was accused of heresy and was denied a license to teach. He was involved in theological controversies and took refuge in Munich under the protection of Emperor Ludwig of Bavaria. He died in 1349.

Ockham is best known for the "Law of Parsimony" or "Ockham's Razor": "Entities are not to be multiplied beyond necessity." In other words, other things being equal, we should always adopt the simpler explanation.

Ockham applied this principle to the problem of universals and particulars. All there is are particular things or substances. The notion of universals is an unnecessary invention. There is no real universal apart from the particular thing. This position is called nominalism as distinguished from realism, the view that universals exist apart from individual substances. Ockham has been viewed as the founder of nominalism. An early letter from the nominalist masters of the University of Paris to King Louis XI in 1473 sets forth the nominalist position.

> Those doctors are called Nominalists who do not multiply the things principally signified by terms in accordance with the multiplication of the terms. Realists, however, are those who contend on the contrary that things are multiplied according to the multiplicity of terms. For example, Nominalists say that divinity and wisdom are one and the same thing altogether, because everything which is in God, is God. But realists say that the divine wisdom is divided from divinity.
>
> Again, those are called Nominalists who show diligence and zeal in understanding all the properties of terms on which the truth and falsity of a sentence depends, and without which the perfect judgment of the truth and falsity of propositions cannot be made. These properties are: supposition, appellation, ampliation, restriction, exponible distribution. They especially understand

obligations and the nature of the insoluble, the true foundation of dialectical arguments and their failure. Being instructed in these things, they easily understand concerning any given argumentation whether it is good or bad. But the Realists neglect all these things, and they condemn them, saying, "We proceed to things, we have no concern for terms." Against them Master John Gerson said, "While you proceed to things, neglecting terms, you fall into complete ignorance of things themselves." This is in his treatise on the Magnificat; and he added that the said Realists involve themselves in inexplicable difficulties, since they seek difficulty where there is none, unless it is logical difficulty.[1]

FOR FURTHER READING

Boehner, P. *Collected Articles on Ockham* (St. Bonaventure University Press, 1956).
Hyman, Arthur, and James Walsh. *Philosophy in the Middle Ages* (Hackett Publishing Co., 1973).
Moody, E. A. *The Logic of William of Ockham* (New York, 1935).
Ockham. *Philosophical Writings*, ed. P. Boehner (Nelson Philosophical Texts, 1957).

SUMMA LOGICAE

PART I

CHAPTER 14: ON THE UNIVERSAL

It is not enough for the logician to have a merely general knowledge of terms; he needs a deep understanding of the concept of a term. Therefore, after discussing some general divisions among terms we should examine in detail the various headings under these divisions.

First, we should deal with terms of second intention and afterwards with terms of first intention. I have said that "universal," "genus," and "species" are examples of terms of second intention. We must discuss those terms of second intention which are called the five universals, but first we should consider the common term "universal." It is predicated of every universal and is opposed to the notion of a particular.

First, it should be noted that the term "particular" has two senses. In the first sense a particular is that which is one and not many. Those who hold that a universal is a certain quality residing in the mind which is predicable of many (not suppositing for itself, of course, but for the many of which it is predicated) must grant that, in this sense of the word, every universal is a particular. Just as a word, even if convention makes it common, is a particular, the intention of the soul signifying many is numerically one thing a particular; for although it signifies many things it is nonetheless one thing and not many.

In another sense of the word we use "particular" to mean that which is one and not many and which cannot function as a sign of many. Taking "particular" in this sense no universal is a particular, since every universal is capable of signifying many and of being predicated of many. Thus, if we take the term "universal" to mean that which is not one in number, as many do, then, I want to say that nothing is a universal. One could, of course, abuse the expression and say that a population constitutes a single universal because it is not one but many. But that would be puerile.

Reprinted from William of Ockham, *Ockham's Theory of Terms: Part I of the Summa Logicae*, translated by Michel Loux. © 1974 by the University of Notre Dame Press. Reprinted by permission.

---

[1] Translated by James J. Walsh from the text of Ehrle, *Der Sentenzenkommentater Peters von Candida* in *Philosophy in the Middle Ages*, ed. Arthur Hyman and James J. Walsh (Indianapolis: Hackett Publishing Co., 1973), p. 649f.

Therefore, it ought to be said that every universal is one particular thing and that it is not a universal except in its signification, in its signifying many things. This is what Avicenna means to say in his commentary on the fifth book of the *Metaphysics*. He says, "One form in the intellect is related to many things, and in this respect it is a universal; for it is an intention of the intellect which has an invariant relationship to anything you choose." He then continues, "Although this form is a universal in its relationship to individuals, it is a particular in its relationship to the particular soul in which it resides; for it is just one form among many in the intellect." He means to say that a universal is an intention of a particular soul. Insofar as it can be predicated of many things not for itself but for these many, it is said to be a universal; but insofar as it is a particular form actually existing in the intellect, it is said to be a particular. Thus "particular" is predicated of a universal in the first sense but not in the second. In the same way we say that the sun is a universal cause and, nevertheless, that it is really and truly a particular or individual cause. For the sun is said to be a universal cause because it is the cause of many things (i.e., every object that is generable and corruptible), but it is said to be a particular cause because it is one cause and not many. In the same way the intention of the soul is said to be a universal because it is a sign predicable of many things, but it is said to be a particular because it is one thing and not many.

But it should be noted that there are two kinds of universals. Some things are universal by nature; that is, by nature they are signs predicable of many in the same way that the smoke is by nature a sign of fire; weeping, a sign of grief; and laughter, a sign of internal joy. The intention of the soul, of course, is a universal by nature. Thus, no substance outside the soul, nor any accident outside the soul is a universal of this sort. It is of this kind of universal that I shall speak in the following chapters.

Other things are universals by convention. Thus, a spoken word, which is numerically one quality, is a universal; it is a sign conventionally appointed for the signification of many things. Thus, since the word is said to be common, it can be called a universal. But notice it is not by nature, but only by convention, that this label applies.

CHAPTER 15: THAT THE UNIVERSAL IS NOT A THING OUTSIDE THE MIND

But it is not enough just to state one's position; one must defend it by philosophical arguments. Therefore, I shall set forth some arguments for my view, and then corroborate it by an appeal to the authorities.

That no universal is a substance existing outside the mind can be proved in a number of ways:

No universal is a particular substance, numerically one; for if this were the case, then it would follow that Socrates is a universal; for there is no good reason why one substance should be a universal rather than another. Therefore no particular substance is a universal; every substance is numerically one and a particular. For every substance is either one thing and not many or it is many things. Now, if a substance is one thing and not many, then it is numerically one; for that is what we mean by "numerically one." But if, on the other hand, some substance is several things, it is either several particular things or several universal things. If the first alternative is chosen, then it follows that some substance would be several particular substances; and consequently that some substance would be several men. But although the universal would be distinguished from a single particular, it would not be distinguished from several particulars. If, however, some substance were to be several universal entities, I take one of those universal entities and ask, "Is it many things or is it one and not many?" If the second is the case then it follows that the thing is particular. If the first is the case then I ask, "Is it several particular things or several universal things?" Thus, either an infinite regress will follow or it will be granted that no substance is a universal in a way that would be incompatible with its also being a particular. From this it follows that no substance is a universal.

Again, if some universal were to be one substance existing in particular substances, yet distinct from them, it would follow that it could exist without them; for everything that is naturally prior to something else can, by God's power, exist without that thing; but the consequence is absurd.

Again, if the view in question were true, no individual would be able to be created. Something of the individual would pre-exist it, for the whole individual would not take its existence from nothing if the universal which is in it were already in something else. For the same reason it would follow that God could not annihilate an individual substance without destroying the other individuals of the same kind. If He were to annihilate some individual, he would destroy the whole which is essentially that individual and, consequently, He would destroy the universal which is in that thing and in others of the same essence. Consequently, other things of the same essence would not remain, for they could not continue to exist without the universal which constitutes a part of them.

Again, such a universal could not be construed as something completely extrinsic to the essence of an individual; therefore, it would belong to the essence of the individual; and consequently, an individual would be composed of universals, so that the individual would not be any more a particular than a universal.

Again, it follows that something of the essence of Christ would be miserable and damned, since that common nature really existing in Christ would be damned in the damned individual; for surely that essence is also in Judas. But this is absurd.

Many other arguments could be brought forth, but in the interests of brevity, I shall dispense with them. Instead, I shall corroborate my account by an appeal to authorities. First, in the seventh book of the *Metaphysics*, Aristotle is treating the question of whether a universal is a substance. He shows that no universal is a substance. Thus, he says, "it is impossible that substance be something that can be predicated universally."

Again, in the tenth book of the *Metaphysics*, he says, "Thus, if, as we argued in the discussions on substance and being, no universal can be a substance, it is not possible that a universal be a substance in the sense of a one over and against the many."

From these remarks it is clear that, in Aristotle's view, although universals can supposit for substances, no universal is a substance.

Again, the Commentator in his forty-fourth comment on the seventh book of the *Metaphysics* says, "In the individual, the only substance is the particular form and matter out of which the individual is composed."

Again, in the forty-fifth comment, he says, "Let us say, therefore, that it is impossible that one of those things we call universals be the substance of anything, although they do express the substances of things."

And, again, in the forty-seventh comment, "It is impossible that they (universals) be parts of substances existing of and by themselves."

Again, in the second comment on the eighth book of the *Metaphysics*, he says, "No universal is either a substance or a genus."

Again, in the sixth comment on the tenth book, he says, "Since universals are not substances, it is clear that the common notion of being is not a substance existing outside the mind."

Using these and many other authorities, the general point emerges: no universal is a substance regardless of the viewpoint from which we consider the matter. Thus, the viewpoint from which we consider the matter is irrelevant to the question of whether something is a substance. Nevertheless, the meaning of a term is relevant to the question of whether the expression "substance" can be predicated of the term. Thus, if the term "dog" in the proposition "The dog is an animal" is used to stand for the barking animal, the proposition is true; but if it is used for the celestial body which goes by that name, the proposition is false. But it is impossible that one and the same thing should be a substance from one viewpoint and not a substance from another.

Therefore, it ought to be granted that no universal is a substance regardless of how it is considered. On the contrary, every universal is an intention of the mind which, on the most probable account, is identical with the act of understanding. Thus, it is said that the act of understanding by which I grasp men is a natural sign of men in the same way that weeping is a natural sign of grief. It is a natural sign such that it can stand for men in mental propositions in the same way that a spoken word can stand for things in spoken propositions.

That the universal is an intention of the soul is clearly expressed by Avicenna in the fifth book of the *Metaphysics*, in which he comments, "I say, therefore, that there are three senses of 'universal.' For we say that something is a universal if (like 'man') it is actually predicated of many things; and we also call an intention a universal if it could be predicated of many." Then follows the remark, "An intention is also called a universal if there is nothing inconceivable in its being predicated of many."

From these remarks it is clear that the universal is an intention of the soul capable of being predicated of many. The claim can be corroborated by argument. For every one agrees that a universal is something predicable of many, but only an intention of the soul or a conventional sign is predicated. No substance is ever predicated of anything. Therefore, only an intention of the soul or a conventional sign is a universal; but I am not here using the term "universal" for conventional signs, but only for signs that are universals by nature. That substance is not capable of functioning as predicate is clear; for if it were, it would follow that a proposition would be composed of particular substances; and, consequently, the subject would be in Rome and the predicate in England which is absurd.

Furthermore, propositions occur only in the mind, in speech, or in writing; therefore, their parts can exist only in the mind, in speech, and in writing. Particular substances, however, cannot themselves exist in the mind, in speech, or in writing. Thus, no proposition can be composed of particular substances. Propositions are, however, composed of universals; therefore, universals cannot conceivably be substances.

CHAPTER 16: AGAINST SCOTUS' ACCOUNT OF THE UNIVERSAL

It may be clear to many that a universal is not a substance outside the mind which exists in, but is distinct from, particulars. Nevertheless, some want to claim that the universal is, in some way, outside the soul and in particulars; and while they do not want to say that a universal is really distinct from particulars, they say that it is formally distinct from particulars. Thus, they say that in Socrates there is human nature which is contracted to Socrates by an individual difference which is not really, but only formally, distinct from that nature. Thus, while there are not two things, one is not formally the other.

I do not find this view tenable:

First, in creatures there can never be any distinction outside the mind unless there are distinct things; if, therefore, there is any distinction between the nature and the difference, it is necessary that they really be distinct things. I prove my premise by the following syllogism: the nature is not formally distinct from itself; this individual difference is formally distinct from this nature; therefore, this individual difference is not this nature.

Again, the same entity is not both common and proper, but in their view the individual difference is proper and the universal is common; therefore, no universal is identical with an individual difference.

Again, opposites cannot be attributed to one and the same created thing, but *common* and *proper* are opposites; therefore, the same thing is not both common and proper. Nevertheless, that conclusion would follow if an individual difference and a common nature were the same thing.

Again, if a common nature were the same thing as an individual difference, there would be as many common natures as there are individual differences; and, consequently, none of those natures would be common, but each would be peculiar to the difference with which it is identical.

Again, whenever one thing is distinct from another it is distinguished from that thing either of and by itself or by something intrinsic to itself. Now, the humanity of Socrates is something different from the humanity of Plato; therefore, they are distinguished of and by themselves and not by differences that are added to them.

Again, according to Aristotle things differing in species also differ in number, but the nature of a man and the nature of a donkey differ in species of and by themselves; therefore, they are numerically distinguished of and by themselves; therefore, each of them is numerically one of and by itself.

Again, that which cannot belong to many cannot be predicated of many; but such a nature, if it really is the same thing as the individual difference, cannot belong to many since it cannot belong to any other particular. Thus, it cannot be predicable of many; but, then, it cannot be a universal.

Again, take an individual difference and the nature which it contracts. Either the difference between these two things is greater or less than the difference between two particulars. It is not greater because they do not differ really; particulars, however, do differ really. But neither is it less because then they would admit of one and the same definition, since two particulars, can admit of the same definition. Consequently, if one of them is, by itself, one in number, the other will also be.

Again, either the nature is the individual difference or it is not. If it is the difference I argue as follows: this individual difference is proper and not common; this individual difference is this nature; therefore this nature is proper and not common, but that is what I set out to prove. Likewise, I argue as follows: the individual difference is not formally distinct from the individual difference; the individual difference is the nature; therefore, the nature is not formally distinct from the individual difference. But if it be said that the individual difference is not the nature, my point has been proved; for it follows that if the individual difference is not the nature, the individual difference is not really the nature; for from the opposite of the consequent follows the opposite of the antecedent. Thus, if it is true that the individual difference really is the nature, then the individual difference is the nature. The inference is valid, for from a determinable taken with its determination (where the determination does not detract from or diminish the determinable) one can infer the determinable taken by itself; but "really" does not express a determination that detracts or diminishes. Therefore, it follows that if the individual difference is really the nature, the individual difference is the nature.

Therefore, one should grant that in created things there is no such thing as a formal distinction. All things which are distinct in creatures are really distinct and, therefore, different things. In regard to creatures modes of argument like the following ought never be denied; this is A; this is B; therefore, B is A; and this is not A; this is B; therefore, B is not A. Likewise, one ought never deny that, as regards creatures, there are distinct things where contradictory notions hold. The only exception would be the case where contradictory notions hold true because of some syncategorematic element or similar determination, but in the same present case this is not so.

Therefore, we ought to say with the philosophers that in a particular substance there is nothing substantial except the particular form, the particular matter, or the composite of the two. And, therefore, no one ought to think that in Socrates there is a humanity or a human nature which is distinct from Socrates and to which there is added an individual difference which contracts that nature. The only thing in Socrates which can be construed as substantial is that particular matter, this particular form, or the composite of the two. And, therefore, every essence and quiddity and whatever belongs to substance, if it is really outside the soul, is just matter, form, or the composite of these or, following the doctrine of the Peripatetics, a separated and immaterial substance.

REVIEW QUESTIONS

1. What is a universal? What is nominalism? What is realism?
2. What are two arguments that Ockham uses to try to show that "no universal is a substance existing outside the mind"?
3. What point does Ockham try to make by quoting Aristotle's *Metaphysics*?
4. What does Ockham mean by "the universal is an intention of the soul"? Why does he argue for this point?
5. How does Ockham argue against Dun s Scotus' account of universals?

Part Three

THE
MODERN
PERIOD

14

RENÉ DESCARTES

There was once a young man who was troubled because he discovered that many of the things he believed, many of which he had been taught by his elders and in school, were false or, at least, were unsupported by the evidence. Despite having the best education available, he found it filled with error. For some years he resolved that were he to obtain leisure time, he would use it not for entertainment or professional purposes but in order to rework his entire system of knowledge. He writes:

> I had been nourished on the humanities since childhood, and since I was given to believe that by their means a clear and certain knowledge could be obtained of all that is useful in life, I was extremely eager to learn them. But as soon as I had finished my course of study at the end of which one is normally admitted among the ranks of the learned, I completely altered my view on the matter. For I found myself embarrassed by so many doubts and errors, that it seemed to me that the only profit I had had from my efforts to acquire knowledge was the progressive discovery of my own ignorance. And yet I was in one of the most prestigious schools in Europe, and if knowledge existed anywhere, it must be in the scholars there. I had learned everything that the others were learning there, and, not content with the studies in which we were instructed, I had even perused all the books that came into my hands, treating of subjects considered advanced and esoteric. At the same time I knew that others regarded me with respect, even though some of these were as brilliant as any age has produced.
>
> Having studied with the best, and learned from them, I was confident that I should seek knowledge in myself, or at least in the great book of the world. I employed the rest of my youth in travel, in seeing courts and armies, in conversation with men of diverse temperaments and conditions, in collecting varied experiences, in testing myself in the various predicaments in which I was placed by fortune. In all circumstances I sought to bring my mind to bear on the things that came before it so that I might derive some profit from my experience. I had a passion to learn to

distinguish truth from falsehood in order to have clear insight into my actions and how to live my life.

So for nine years I did nothing but roam hither and thither, trying to be a spectator rather than an actor in all the comedies which the world displays. I considered the manners and customs of other men, and found nothing to give me settled convictions. I noticed in people's beliefs and customs as much diversity as I had earlier noticed in the views of philosophers. So much was this so, that I learned not to believe too firmly anything that I had been convinced of only by example and custom. I thus gradually freed myself from many errors that may obscure the light of nature in us and make us less capable of hearing reason. But after spending these years in the study of the book of the world and in trying to gain experience, the day came when I resolved to make my studies within myself, and use all of the powers of my mind to choose the path that I must follow.[1]

These are the words of the man considered to be the father of modern philosophy, René Descartes. Descartes was born in France in 1596 and educated by the Jesuits, an intellectually elite order in the Roman Catholic Church, in La Fleche. At seventeen he left school for Paris where he plunged into a fast-moving social life. After a few years of high society, he withdrew to a more contemplative life. In 1618 he became a soldier, serving in three different European armies. After four years he retired from the army and resumed his travels to Switzerland, Italy, and, finally Holland, where he settled and became a writer of philosophy. He reputedly did most of his research and writing, especially in winter, sitting up in bed. He became famous, and even the rulers of Europe wrote to him for advice. One of the rulers who admired him was Queen Christina of Sweden. She invited Descartes to visit her in Stockholm and teach her philosophy. Against the advice of friends, he moved to Stockholm. The queen insisted that the lessons be given three times a week at 5 A.M. in spite of his being a late night owl. He was not happy in Sweden and hated the cold weather, and a few months after he arrived, he caught pneumonia from which he died on February 11, 1650.

Descartes' classic work in the theory of knowledge is his *Meditations on First Philosophy*, written in Holland in November 1640. It is a short but tightly written set of six philosophical meditations, one for each day of the week (even philosophers should rest on the Sabbath). Each meditation is to occupy the mind in reflection for an entire day. Descartes begins by admitting that he has painfully discovered that many of his former beliefs were false. How can he be sure that his present beliefs won't suffer the same fate? He is revolted by the thought that he may be deceived in his beliefs and desires to know the truth. How shall he separate the true beliefs from the false? He decides that there is only one way. He must destroy his tottering, unstable house of "knowledge" and lay a new foundation upon which to construct an indestructible edifice. The method consists of doubting everything that can be doubted and then, upon the pure remainder of certain truth, beginning the process of constructing an indubitable system of knowledge. The result is a type of rationalism in which the only certainties are discovered by the mind through self-evident insight or reason.

---

[1] René Descartes, *Discourse on Method* in *The Philosophical Works of Descartes* vol. I, trans. Elizabeth Haldane and G. R. T. Ross (Dover Publications, 1911).

FOR FURTHER READING

Curley, E. M. *Descartes Against the Skeptics* (Harvard University Press, 1978).
Dicker, George. *Descartes* (Oxford University Press, 1992). A comprehensive treatment.
Doney, Willis, ed. *Descartes: A Collection of Critical Essays* (Doubleday, 1967).
Hooker, Michael, ed. *Descartes, Critical and Interpretative Essays* (Johns Hopkins Press, 1978).
Kenny, Anthony. *Descartes: A Study of His Philosophy* (Doubleday, 1967).
Markie, Peter. *Descartes' Gambit* (Cornell University Press, 1986).

MEDITATIONS ON FIRST PHILOSOPHY

In which are demonstrated the existence of God and the distinction between the human soul and the body.

FIRST MEDITATION

WHAT CAN BE CALLED INTO DOUBT

Some years ago I was struck by the large number of falsehoods that I had accepted as true in my childhood, and by the highly doubtful nature of the whole edifice that I had subsequently based on them. I realized that it was necessary, once in the course of my life, to demolish everything completely and start again right from the foundations if I wanted to establish anything at all in the sciences that was stable and likely to last. But the task looked an enormous one, and I began to wait until I should reach a mature enough age to ensure that no subsequent time of life would be more suitable for tackling such inquiries. This led me to put the project off for so long that I would now be to blame if by pondering over it any further I wasted the time still left for carrying it out. So today I have expressly rid my mind of all worries and arranged for myself a clear stretch of free time. I am here quite alone, and at last I will devote myself sincerely and without reservation to the general demolition of my opinions.

But to accomplish this, it will not be necessary for me to show that all my opinions are false, which is something I could perhaps never manage. Reason now leads me to think that I should hold back my assent from opinions which are not completely certain and indubitable just as carefully as I do from those which are patently false. So, for the purpose of rejecting all my opinions, it will be enough if I find in each of them at least some reason for doubt. And to do this I will not need to run through them all individually, which would be an endless task. Once the foundations of a building are undermined, anything built on them collapses of its own accord; so I will go straight for the basic principles on which all my former beliefs rested.

Whatever I have up till now accepted as most true I have acquired either from the senses or through the senses. But from time to time I have found that the senses deceive, and it is prudent never to trust completely those who have deceived us even once.

Yet although the senses occasionally deceive us with respect to objects which are very small or in the distance, there are many other beliefs about which doubt is quite impossible, even though they are derived from the senses—for example, that I am here, sitting by the fire, wearing a winter dressing-gown, holding this piece of paper in my hands, and so on. Again, how could it be denied that these hands or this whole body are mine? Unless perhaps I were to liken myself to madmen, whose brains are so damaged by the persistent vapours of melancholia that they firmly maintain they are kings when they are paupers, or say they are dressed in purple when they are naked, or that their heads are made of earthenware, or that they are pumpkins, or made of glass. But such people are insane, and I would be thought equally mad if I took anything from them as a model for myself.

A brilliant piece of reasoning! As if I were not a man who sleeps at night, and regularly has all the same experiences while asleep as madmen do when awake—indeed sometimes even more improbable

Composite things are doubtful
general and certain

ones. How often, asleep at night, am I convinced of just such familiar events—that I am here in my dressing-gown, sitting by the fire—when in fact I am lying undressed in bed! Yet at the moment my eyes are certainly wide awake when I look at this piece of paper; I shake my head and it is not asleep; as I stretch out and feel my hand I do so deliberately, and I know what I am doing. All this would not happen with such distinctness to someone asleep. Indeed! As if I did not remember other occasions when I have been tricked by exactly similar thoughts while asleep! As I think about this more carefully, I see plainly that there are never any sure signs by means of which being awake can be distinguished from being asleep. The result is that I begin to feel dazed, and this very feeling only reinforces the notion that I may be asleep.

dreams

Suppose then that I am dreaming, and that these particulars—that my eyes are open, that I am moving my head and stretching out my hands—are not true. Perhaps, indeed, I do not even have such hands or such a body at all. Nonetheless, it must surely be admitted that the visions which come in sleep are like paintings, which must have been fashioned in the likeness of things that are real, and hence that at least these general kinds of things—eyes, head, hands and the body as a whole—are things which are not imaginary but are real and exist. For even when painters try to create sirens and satyrs with the most extraordinary bodies, they cannot give them natures which are new in all respects; they simply jumble up the limbs of different animals. Or if perhaps they manage to think up something so new that nothing remotely similar has ever been seen before—something which is therefore completely fictitious and unreal—at least the colours used in the composition must be real. By similar reasoning, although these general kinds of things—eyes, head, hands and so on—could be imaginary, it must at least be admitted that certain other even simpler and more universal things are real. These are as it were the real colours from which we form all the images of things, whether true or false, that occur in our thought.

imagined vs real

This class appears to include corporeal nature in general, and its extension; the shape of extended things; the quantity, or size and number of these things; the place in which they may exist, the time through which they may endure, and so on.

extended things

So a reasonable conclusion from this might be that physics, astronomy, medicine, and all other disciplines which depend on the study of composite things, are doubtful; while arithmetic, geometry and other subjects of this kind, which deal only with the simplest and most general things, regardless of whether they really exist in nature or not, contain something certain and indubitable. For whether I am awake or asleep, two and three added together are five, and a square has no more than four sides. It seems impossible that such transparent truths should incur any suspicion of being false.

And yet firmly rooted in my mind is the long-standing opinion that there is an omnipotent God who made me the kind of creature that I am. How do I know that he has not brought it about that there is no earth, no sky, no extended thing, no shape, no size, no place, while at the same time ensuring that all these things appear to me to exist just as they do now? What is more, since I sometimes believe that others go astray in cases where they think they have the most perfect knowledge, may I not similarly go wrong every time I add two and three or count the sides of a square, or in some even simpler matter, if that is imaginable? But perhaps God would not have allowed me to be deceived in this way, since he is said to be supremely good. But if it were inconsistent with his goodness to have created me such that I am deceived all the time, it would seem equally foreign to his goodness to allow me to be deceived even occasionally; yet this last assertion cannot be made.

Perhaps there may be some who would prefer to deny the existence of so powerful a God rather than believe that everything else is uncertain. Let us not argue with them, but grant them that everything said about God is a fiction. According to their supposition, then, I have arrived at my present state by fate or chance or a continuous chain of events, or by some other means; yet since deception and error seem to be imperfections, the less powerful they make my original cause, the more likely it is that I am so imperfect as to be deceived all the time. I have no answer to these arguments, but am finally compelled to admit that there is not one of my former beliefs about which a doubt may not properly be raised; and this is not flippant or ill-considered conclusion, but is based on powerful and well thought-out reasons.

So in future I must withhold my assent from these former beliefs just as carefully as I would from obvious falsehoods, if I want to discover any certainty.

But it is not enough merely to have noticed this; I must make an effort to remember it. My habitual opinions keep coming back, and, despite my wishes, they capture my belief, which is as it were bound over to them as a result of long occupation and the law of custom. I shall never get out of the habit of confidently assenting to these opinions, so long as I suppose them to be what in fact they are, namely highly probable opinions—opinions which, despite the fact that they are in a sense doubtful, as has just been shown, it is still much more reasonable to believe than to deny. In view of this, I think it will be a good plan to turn my will in completely the opposite direction and deceive myself, by pretending for a time that these former opinions are utterly false and imaginary. I shall do this until the weight of preconceived opinion is counter-balanced and the distorting influence of habit no longer prevents my judgement from perceiving things correctly. In the meantime, I know that no danger or error will result from my plan, and that I cannot possibly go too far in my distrustful attitude. This is because the task now in hand does not involve action but merely the acquisition of knowledge.

I will suppose therefore that not God, who is supremely good and the source of truth, but rather some malicious demon of the utmost power and cunning has employed all his energies in order to deceive me. I shall think that the sky, the air, the earth, colours, shapes, sounds and all external things are merely the delusions of dreams which he has devised to ensnare my judgement. I shall consider myself as not having hands or eyes, or flesh, or blood or senses, but as falsely believing that I have all these things. I shall stubbornly and firmly persist in this meditation; and, even if it is not in my power to know any truth, I shall at least do what is in my power, that is, resolutely guard against assenting to any falsehoods, so that the deceiver, however powerful and cunning he may be, will be unable to impose on me in the slightest degree. But this is an arduous undertaking, and a kind of laziness brings me back to normal life. I am like a prisoner who is enjoying an imaginary freedom while asleep; as he begins to suspect that he is asleep, he dreads being woken up, and goes along with the pleasant illusion as long as he can. In the same way, I happily slide back into my old opinions and dread being shaken out of them, for fear that my peaceful sleep may be followed by hard labour when I wake, and that I shall have to toil not in the light, but amid the inextricable darkness of the problems I have now raised.

SECOND MEDITATION

THE NATURE OF THE HUMAN MIND, AND HOW IT IS BETTER KNOWN THAN THE BODY

So serious are the doubts into which I have been thrown as a result of yesterday's meditation that I can neither put them out of my mind nor see any way of resolving them. It feels as if I have fallen unexpectedly into a deep whirlpool which tumbles me around so that I can neither stand on the bottom nor swim up to the top. Nevertheless I will make an effort and once more attempt the same path which I started on yesterday. Anything which admits of the slightest doubt I will set aside just as if I had found it to be wholly false; and I will proceed in this way until I recognize something certain, or, if nothing else, until I at least recognize for certain that there is no certainty. Archimedes used to demand just one firm and immovable point in order to shift the entire earth; so I too can hope for great things if I manage to find just one thing, however slight, that is certain and unshakeable. *body is illusion*

I will suppose then, that everything I see is spurious. I will believe that my memory tells me lies, and that none of the things that it reports ever happened. I have no senses. Body, shape, extension, movement and place are chimeras. So what remains true? Perhaps just the one fact that nothing is certain. *True: nothing is certain* ←

Yet apart from everything I have just listed, how do I know that there is not something else which does not allow even the slightest occasion for doubt? Is there not a God, or whatever I may call him, who puts into me the thoughts I am now having? But why do I think this, since I myself may perhaps be the author of these thoughts? In that case am not I, at least, something? But I have just said that I have no senses and no body. This is the sticking point: what follows from this? Am I not so bound up with a body and with senses that I cannot exist without them? But I have convinced myself that there is absolutely nothing in the world, no sky, no earth, no minds, no bodies. Does it now follow that I too do not exist? No: if I convinced myself of something then I certainly existed. But there is a deceiver of supreme power and cunning who is deliberately and constantly deceiving me. In that case I too undoubtedly exist, if he is deceiving me; and let him deceive me as much as he can, he will never bring it about that I am nothing so long as I think that I am something. So after considering everything very thoroughly, I must finally conclude that this proposition, I am, I exist, is necessarily true whenever it is put forward by me or conceived in my mind.

But I do not yet have a sufficient understanding of what this 'I' is, that now necessarily exists. So I must be on my guard against carelessly taking something else to be this 'I,' and so making a mistake in the very item of knowledge that I maintain is the most certain and evident of all. I will therefore go back and meditate on what I originally believed myself to be, before I embarked on this present train of thought. I will then subtract anything capable of being weakened, even minimally, by the arguments now introduced, so that what is left at the end may be exactly and only what is certain and unshakeable.

What then did I formerly think I was? A man. But what is a man? Shall I say 'a rational animal'? No; for then I should have to inquire what an animal is, what rationality is, and in this way one question would lead me down the slope to other harder ones, and I do not now have the time to waste on subtleties of this kind. Instead I propose to concentrate on what came into my thoughts spontaneously and quite naturally whenever I used to consider what I was. Well, the first thought to come to mind was that I had a face, hands, arms and the whole mechanical structure of limbs which can be seen in a corpse, and which I called the body. The next thought was that I was nourished, that I moved about, that I engaged in sense-perception and thinking; and these actions I attributed to the soul. But as to the nature of this soul, either I did not think about this or else I imagined it to be something tenuous, like a wind or fire or ether, which permeated my more solid parts. As to the body, however, I had no doubts about it, but thought I knew its nature distinctly. If I had tried to

describe the mental conception I had of it, I would have expressed it as follows: by a body I understand whatever has a determinable shape and a definable location and can occupy a space in such a way as to exclude any other body; it can be perceived by touch, sight, hearing, taste or smell, and can be moved in various ways, not by itself but by whatever else comes into contact with it. For, according to my judgement, the power of self-movement, like the power of sensation or of thought, was quite foreign to the nature of a body; indeed, it was a source of wonder to me that certain bodies were found to contain faculties of this kind.

But what shall I now say that I am, when I am supposing that there is some supremely powerful and, if it is permissible to say so, malicious deceiver, who is deliberately trying to trick me in every way he can? Can I now assert that I possess even the most insignificant of all the attributes which I have just said belong to the nature of a body? I scrutinize them, think about them, go over them again, but nothing suggests itself; it is tiresome and pointless to go through the list once more. But what about the attributes I assigned to the soul? Nutrition or movement? Since now I do not have a body, these are mere fabrications. Sense-perception? This surely does not occur without a body, and besides, when asleep I have appeared to perceive through the senses many things which I afterwards realized I did not perceive through the senses at all. Thinking? At last I have discovered it—thought; this alone is inseparable from me. I am, I exist—that is certain. But for how long? For as long as I am thinking. For it could be that were I totally to cease from thinking, I should totally cease to exist. At present I am not admitting anything except what is necessarily true. I am, then, in the strict sense only a thing that thinks; that is, I am a mind, or intelligence, or intellect, or reason—words whose meaning I have been ignorant of until now. But for all that I am a thing which is real and which truly exists. But what kind of a thing? As I have just said—a thinking thing.

What else am I? I will use my imagination. I am not that structure of limbs which is called a human body, I am not even some thin vapour which permeates the limbs—a wind, fire, air, breath, or whatever I depict in my imagination; for these are things which I have supposed to be nothing. Let this

I exist and all images couldbe dreams. Thinking elurg doubts + w. sensory perceptions.

MEDITATIONS ON FIRST PHILOSOPHY | 493

supposition stand; for all that I am still something. And yet may it not perhaps be the case that these very things which I am supposing to be nothing, because they are unknown to me, are in reality identical with the 'I' of which I am aware? I do not know, and for the moment I shall not argue the point, since I can make judgements only about things which are known to me. I know that I exist; the question is, what is this 'I' that I know? If the 'I' is understood strictly as we have been taking it, then it is quite certain that knowledge of it does not depend on things of whose existence I am as yet unaware; so it cannot depend on any of the things which I invent in my imagination. And this very word 'invent' shows me my mistake. It would indeed be a case of fictitious invention if I used my imagination to establish that I was something or other; for imagining is simply contemplating the shape or image of a corporeal thing. Yet now I know for certain both that I exist and at the same time that all such images and, in general, everything relating to the nature of body, could be mere dreams and chimeras. Once this point has been grasped, to say 'I will use my imagination to get to know more distinctly what I am' would seem to be as silly as saying 'I am now awake, and see some truth; but since my vision is not yet clear enough, I will deliberately fall asleep so that my dreams may provide a truer and clearer representation.' I thus realize that none of the things that the imagination enables me to grasp is at all relevant to this knowledge of myself which I possess, and that the mind must therefore be most carefully diverted from such things if it is to perceive its own nature as distinctly as possible.

But what then am I? A thing that thinks. What is that? A thing that doubts, understands, affirms, denies, is willing, is unwilling, and also imagines and has sensory perceptions.

This is a considerable list, if everything on it belongs to me. But does it? Is it not one and the same 'I' who is now doubting almost everything, who nonetheless understands some things, who affirms that this one thing is true, denies everything else, desires to know more, is unwilling to be deceived, imagines many things even involuntarily, and is aware of many things which apparently come from the senses? Are not all these things just as true as the fact that I exist, even if I am asleep all the time, and even if he who created me is doing all he can to deceive me? Which of all these activities is distinct from my thinking? Which of them can be said to be separate from myself? The fact that it is I who am doubting and understanding and willing is so evident that I see no way of making it any clearer. But it is also the case that the 'I' who imagines is the same 'I'. For even if, as I have supposed, none of the objects of imagination are real, the power of imagination is something which really exists and is part of my thinking. Lastly, it is also the same 'I' who has sensory perceptions, or is aware of bodily things as it were through the senses. For example, I am now seeing light, hearing a noise, feeling heat. But I am asleep, so all this is false. Yet I certainly seem to see, to hear, and to be warmed. This cannot be false; what is called 'having a sensory perception' is strictly just this, and in this restricted sense of the term it is simply thinking.

From all this I am beginning to have a rather better understanding of what I am. But it still appears—and I cannot stop thinking this—that the corporeal things of which images are formed in my thought, and which the senses investigate, are known with much more distinctness than this puzzling 'I' which cannot be pictured in the imagination. And yet it is surely surprising that I should have a more distinct grasp of things which I realize are doubtful, unknown and foreign to me, than I have of that which is true and known—my own self. But I see what it is: my mind enjoys wandering off and will not yet submit to being restrained within the bounds of truth. Very well then; just this once let us give it a completely free rein, so that after a while, when it is time to tighten the reins, it may more readily submit to being curbed.

Let us consider the things which people commonly think they understand most distinctly of all; that is, the bodies which we touch and see. I do not mean bodies in general—for general perceptions are apt to be somewhat more confused—but one particular body. Let us take, for example, this piece of wax. It has just been taken from the honeycomb; it has not yet quite lost the taste of the honey; it retains some of the scent of the flowers from which it was gathered; its colour, shape and size are plain to see; it is hard, cold and can be handled without difficulty; if you rap it with your knuckle it makes a sound. In

wax changes shape & sensed / attorated / & intended / perceived by mind alone

short, it has everything which appears necessary to enable a body to be known as distinctly as possible. But even as I speak, I put the wax by the fire, and look: the residual taste is eliminated, the smell goes away, the colour changes, the shape is lost, the size increases; it becomes a liquid and hot; you can hardly touch it, and if you strike it, it no longer makes a sound. But does the same wax remain? It must be admitted that it does; no one denies it, no one thinks otherwise. So what was it in the wax that I understood with such distinctness? Evidently one of the features which I arrived at by means of the senses; for whatever came under taste, smell, sight, touch or hearing has now altered—yet the wax remains.

Perhaps the answer lies in the thought which now comes to mind; namely, the wax was not after all the sweetness of the honey, or the fragrance of the flowers, or the whiteness, or the shape, or the sound, but was rather a body which presented itself to me in these various forms a little while ago, but which now exhibits different ones. But what exactly is it that I am now imagining? Let us concentrate, take away everything which does not belong to the wax, and see what is left: merely something extended, flexible and changeable. But what is meant here by 'flexible' and 'changeable'? Is it what I picture in my imagination: that this piece of wax is capable of changing from a round shape to a square shape, or from a square shape to a triangular shape? Not at all; for I can grasp that the wax is capable of countless changes of this kind, yet I am unable to run through this immeasurable number of changes in my imagination, from which it follows that it is not the faculty of imagination that gives me my grasp of the wax as flexible and changeable. And what is meant by 'extended'? Is the extension of the wax also unknown? For it increases if the wax melts, increases again if it boils, and is greater still if the heat is increased. I would not be making a correct judgement about the nature of wax unless I believed it capable of being extended in many more different ways than I will ever encompass in my imagination. I must therefore admit that the nature of this piece of wax is in no way revealed by my imagination, but is perceived by the mind alone. (I am speaking of this particular piece of wax; the point is even clearer with regard to wax in general.) But what is this wax which is perceived by the mind alone? It is of course the same wax which I see, which I touch, which I picture in my imagination, in short the same wax which I thought it to be from the start. And yet, and here is the point, the perception I have of it is a case not of vision or touch or imagination—nor has it ever been, despite previous appearances—but of purely mental scrutiny; and this can be imperfect and confused, as it was before, or clear and distinct as it is now, depending on how carefully I concentrate on what the wax consists in.

But as I reach this conclusion I am amazed at how weak and prone to error my mind is. For although I am thinking about these matters within myself, silently and without speaking, nonetheless, the actual words bring me up short, and I am almost tricked by ordinary ways of talking. We say that we see the wax itself, if it is there before us, not that we judge it to be there from its colour or shape; and this might lead me to conclude without more ado that knowledge of the wax comes from what the eye sees, and not from the scrutiny of the mind alone. But then if I look out of the window and see men crossing the square, as I just happen to have done, I normally say that I see the men themselves, just as I say that I see the wax. Yet do I see any more than hats and coats which could conceal automatons? I judge that they are men. And so something which I thought I was seeing with my eyes is in fact grasped solely by the faculty of judgement which is in my mind.

However, one who wants to achieve knowledge above the ordinary level should feel ashamed at having taken ordinary ways of talking as a basis for doubt. So let us proceed, and consider on which occasion my perception of the nature of the wax was more perfect and evident. Was it when I first looked at it, and believed I knew it by my external senses, or at least by what they call the 'common' sense—that is, the power of imagination? Or is my knowledge more perfect now, after a more careful investigation of the nature of the wax and of the means by which it is known? Any doubt on this issue would clearly be foolish; for what distinctness was there in my earlier perception? Was there anything in it which an animal could not possess? But when I distinguish the wax from its outward forms—take the clothes off, as it were, and consider it naked—then although my judgement may still contain errors, at least my perception now requires a human mind.

But what am I to say about this mind, or about myself? (So far, remember, I am not admitting that there is anything else in me except a mind.) What, I ask, is this 'I' which seems to perceive the wax so distinctly? Surely my awareness of my own self is not merely much truer and more certain than my awareness of the wax, but also much more distinct and evident. For if I judge that the wax exists from the fact that I see it, clearly this same fact entails much more evidently that I myself also exist. It is possible that what I see is not really the wax; it is possible that I do not even have eyes with which to see anything. But when I see, or think I see (I am not here distinguishing the two), it is simply not possible that I who am now thinking am not something. By the same token, if I judge that the wax exists from the fact that I touch it, the same result follows, namely that I exist. If I judge that it exists from the fact that I imagine it, or for any other reason, exactly the same thing follows. And the result that I have grasped in the case of the wax may be applied to everything else located outside me. Moreover, if my perception of the wax seemed more distinct after it was established not just by sight or touch but by many other considerations, it must be admitted that I now know myself even more distinctly. This is because every consideration whatsoever which contributes to my perception of the wax, or of any other body cannot but establish even more effectively the nature of my own mind. But besides this, there is so much else in the mind itself which can serve to make my knowledge of it more distinct, that it scarcely seems worth going through the contributions made by considering bodily things.

I see that without any effort I have now finally got back to where I wanted. I now know that even bodies are not strictly perceived by the senses or the faculty of imagination but by the intellect alone, and that this perception derives not from their being touched or seen but from their being understood; and in view of this I know plainly that I can achieve an easier and more evident perception of my own mind than of anything else. But since the habit of holding on to old opinions cannot be set aside so quickly, I should like to stop here and meditate for some time on this new knowledge I have gained, so as to fix it more deeply in my memory.

THIRD MEDITATION

THE EXISTENCE OF GOD

I will now shut my eyes, stop my ears, and withdraw all my senses. I will eliminate from my thoughts all images of bodily things, or rather, since this is hardly possible, I will regard all such images as vacuous, false and worthless. I will converse with myself and scrutinize myself more deeply; and in this way I will attempt to achieve, little by little, a more intimate knowledge of myself. I am a thing that thinks: that is, a thing that doubts, affirms, denies, understands a few things, is ignorant of many things, is willing, is unwilling, and also which imagines and has sensory perceptions; for as I have noted before, even though the objects of my sensory experience and imagination may have no existence outside me, nonetheless the modes of thinking which I refer to as cases of sensory perception and imagination, in so far as they are simply modes of thinking, do exist within me—of that I am certain.

In this brief list I have gone through everything I truly know, or at least everything I have so far discovered that I know. Now I will cast around more carefully to see whether there may be other things within me which I have not yet noticed. I am certain that I am a thinking thing. Do I not therefore also know what is required for my being certain about anything? In this first item of knowledge there is simply a clear and distinct perception of what I am asserting; this would not be enough to make me certain of the truth of the matter if it could ever turn out that something which I perceived with such clarity and distinctness was false. So I now seem to be able to lay it down as a general rule that whatever I perceive very clearly and distinctly is true.

Yet I previously accepted as wholly certain and evident many things which I afterwards realized were doubtful. What were these? The earth, sky, stars, and everything else that I apprehended with the senses. But what was it about them that I perceived clearly? Just that the ideas, or thoughts, of such things appeared before my mind. Yet even now I am

God given nature is questioned.

defining volitions / judgments

not denying that these ideas occur within me. But there was something else which I used to assert, and which through habitual belief I thought I perceived clearly, although I did not in fact do so. This was that there were things outside me which were the sources of my ideas and which resembled them in all respects. Here was my mistake; or at any rate, if my judgement was true, it was not thanks to the strength of my perception.

But what about when I was considering something very simple and straightforward in arithmetic or geometry, for example that two and three added together make five, and so on? Did I not see at least these things clearly enough to affirm their truth? Indeed, the only reason for my later judgement that they were open to doubt was that it occurred to me that perhaps some God could have given me a nature such that I was deceived even in matters which seemed most evident. And whenever my preconceived belief in the supreme power of God comes to mind, I cannot but admit that it would be easy for him, if he so desired, to bring it about that I go wrong even in those matters which I think I see utterly clearly with my mind's eye. Yet when I turn to the things themselves which I think I perceive very clearly, I am so convinced by them that I spontaneously declare: let whoever can do so deceive me, he will never bring it about that I am nothing, so long as I continue to think I am something; or make it true at some future time that I have never existed, since it is now true that I exist; or bring it about that two and three added together are more or less than five, or anything of this kind in which I see a manifest contradiction. And since I have no cause to think that there is a deceiving God, and I do not yet even know for sure whether there is a God at all, any reason for doubt which depends simply on this supposition is a very slight and, so to speak, metaphysical one. But in order to remove even this slight reason for doubt, as soon as the opportunity arises I must examine whether there is a God, and, if there is, whether he can be a deceiver. For if I do not know this, it seems that I can never be quite certain about anything else.

First, however, considerations of order appear to dictate that I now classify my thoughts into definite kinds, and ask which of them can properly be said to be the bearers of truth and falsity. Some of my thoughts are as it were the images of things, and it is only in these cases that the term 'idea' is strictly appropriate—for example, when I think of a man, or a chimera, or the sky, or an angel, or God. Other thoughts have various additional forms: thus when I will, or am afraid, or affirm, or deny, there is always a particular thing which I take as the object of my thought, but my thought includes something more than the likeness of that thing. Some thoughts in this category are called volitions or emotions, while others are called judgements.

Now as far as ideas are concerned, provided they are considered solely in themselves and I do not refer them to anything else, they cannot strictly speaking be false; for whether it is a goat or a chimera that I am imagining, it is just as true that I imagine the former as the latter. As for the will and the emotions, here too one need not worry about falsity; for even if the things which I may desire are wicked or even nonexistent, that does not make it any less true that I desire them. Thus the only remaining thoughts where I must be on my guard against making a mistake are judgements. And the chief and most common mistake which is to be found here consists in my judging that the ideas which are in me resemble, or conform to, things located outside me. Of course, if I considered just the ideas themselves simply as modes of my thought, without referring them to anything else, they could scarcely give me any material for error.

Among my ideas, some appear to be innate, some to be adventitious, and others to have been invented by me. My understanding of what a thing is, what truth is, and what thought is, seems to derive simply from my own nature. But my hearing a noise, as I do now, or seeing the sun, or feeling the fire, comes from things which are located outside me, or so I have hitherto judged. Lastly, sirens, hippogriffs and the like are my own invention. But perhaps all my ideas may be thought of as adventitious, or they may all be innate, or all made up; for as yet I have not clearly perceived their true origin.

But the chief question at this point concerns the ideas which I take to be derived from things existing outside me: what is my reason for thinking that they resemble these things? Nature has apparently taught me to think this. But in addition I know by experience that these ideas do not depend on my will, and hence that they do not depend simply on me. Frequently I notice them even when I do not want to: now, for example, I feel the heat whether I want to or not, and this is why I think that this sensation or idea of heat comes to me from something other than myself, namely the heat of the fire by which I am sitting. And the most obvious judgement for me to make is that the thing in question transmits to me its own likeness rather than something else.

I will now see if these arguments are strong enough. When I say 'Nature taught me to think this', all I mean is that a spontaneous impulse leads me to believe it, not that its truth has been revealed to me by some natural light. There is a big difference here. Whatever is revealed to me by the natural light—for example that from the fact that I am doubting it follows that I exist, and so on—cannot in any way be open to doubt. This is because there cannot be another faculty both as trustworthy as the natural light and also capable of showing me that such things are not true. But as for my natural impulses, I have often judged in the past that they were pushing me in the wrong direction when it was a question of choosing the good, and I do not see why I should place any greater confidence in them in other matters.

Then again, although these ideas do not depend on my will, it does not follow that they must come from things located outside me. Just as the impulses which I was speaking of a moment ago seem opposed to my will even though they are within me, so there may be some other faculty not yet fully known to me, which produces these ideas without any assistance from external things; this is, after all, just how I have always thought ideas are produced in me when I was dreaming.

And finally, even if these ideas did come from things other than myself, it would not follow that they must resemble those things. Indeed, I think I have often discovered a great disparity between an object and its idea in many cases. For example, there are two different ideas of the sun which I find within me. One of them, which is acquired as it were from the senses and which is a prime example of an idea which I reckon to come from an external source, makes the sun appear very small. The other idea is based on astronomical reasoning, that is, it is derived from certain notions which are innate in me (or else it is constructed by me in some other way), and this idea shows the sun to be several times larger than the earth. Obviously both these ideas cannot resemble the sun which exists outside me; and reason persuades me that the idea which seems to have emanated most directly from the sun itself has in fact no resemblance to it at all.

All these considerations are enough to establish that it is not reliable judgement but merely some blind impulse that has made me believe up till now that there exist things distinct from myself which transmit to me ideas or images of themselves through the sense organs or in some other way.

But it now occurs to me that there is another way of investigating whether some of the things of which I possess ideas exist outside me. In so far as the ideas are considered simply as modes of thought, there is no recognizable inequality among them: they all appear to come from within me in the same fashion. But in so far as different ideas are considered as images which represent different things, it is clear that they differ widely. Undoubtedly, the ideas which represent substances to me amount to something more and, so to speak, contain within themselves more objective reality than the ideas which merely represent modes or accidents. Again, the idea that gives me my understanding of a supreme God, eternal, infinite, immutable, omniscient, omnipotent and the creator of all things that exist apart from him, certainly has in it more objective reality than the ideas that represent finite substances.

Now it is manifest by the natural light that there must be at least as much reality in the efficient and total cause as in the effect of that cause. For where, I ask, could the effect get its reality from, if not from the cause? And how could the cause give it to the effect unless it possessed it? It follows from this both that something cannot arise from nothing, and also that what is more perfect—that is, contains in itself more reality—cannot arise from what is less perfect. And this is transparently true not only in the case of effects which possess what the philosophers call actual or formal reality, but also in the case of ideas, where one is considering only what they call objective reality. A stone, for example, which previously did not exist, cannot begin to exist unless it is

cause & effect.

ex nihilo

idea comes from some cause. *what is primary idea?* *idea an archetype?* *what is the cause of ideas reality.*

produced by something which contains, either formally or eminently, everything to be found in the stone; similarly, heat cannot be produced in an object which was not previously hot, except by something of at least the same order, degree, or kind, of perfection as heat, and so on. But it is also true that the idea of heat, or of a stone, cannot exist in me unless it is put there by some cause which contains at least as much reality as I conceive to be in the heat or in the stone. For although this cause does not transfer any of its actual or formal reality to my idea, it should not on that account be supposed that it must be less real. The nature of an idea is such that of itself it requires no formal reality except what it derives from my thought, of which it is a mode. But in order for a given idea to contain such and such objective reality, it must surely derive it from some cause which contains at least as much formal reality as there is objective reality in the idea. For if we suppose that an idea contains something which was not in its cause, it must have got this from nothing; yet the mode of being by which a thing exists objective or representatively in the intellect by way of an idea, imperfect though it may be, is certainly not nothing, and so it cannot come from nothing.

And although the reality which I am considering in my ideas is merely objective reality, I must not on that account suppose that the same reality need not exist formally in the causes of my ideas, but that it is enough for it to be present in them objectively. For just as the objective mode of beings belongs to ideas by their very nature, so the formal mode of being belongs to the causes of ideas—or at least the first and most important ones—by their very nature. And although one idea may perhaps originate from another, there cannot be an infinite regress here; eventually one must reach a primary idea, the cause of which will be like an archetype which contains formally and in fact all the reality or perfection which is present only objectively or representatively in the idea. So it is clear to me, by the natural light, that the ideas in me are like pictures, or images which can easily fall short of the perfection of the things from which they are taken, but which cannot contain anything greater or more perfect.

The longer and more carefully I examine all these points, the more clearly and distinctly I recognize

objective + formal modes

their truth. But what is my conclusion to be? If the objective reality of any of my ideas turns out to be so great that I am sure the same reality does not reside in me, either formally or eminently, and hence that I myself cannot be its cause, it will necessarily follow that I am not alone in the world, but that some other thing which is the cause of this idea also exists. But if no such idea is to be found in me, I shall have no argument to convince me of the existence of anything apart from myself. For despite a most careful and comprehensive survey, this is the only argument I have so far been able to find.

Among my ideas, apart from the idea which gives me a representation of myself, which cannot present any difficulty in this context, there are ideas which variously represent God, corporeal and inanimate things, angels, animals and finally other men like myself.

As far as concerns the ideas which represent other men, or animals, or angels, I have no difficulty in understanding that they could be put together from the ideas I have of myself, of corporeal things and of God, even if the world contained no men besides me, no animals and no angels.

As to my ideas of corporeal things, I can see nothing in them which is so great or excellent as to make it seem impossible that it originated in myself. For if I scrutinize them thoroughly and examine them one by one, in the way in which I examined the idea of the wax yesterday, I notice that the things which I perceive clearly and distinctly in them are very few in number. The list comprises size, or extension in length, breadth and depth; shape, which is a function of the boundaries of this extension; position, which is a relation between various items possessing shape; and motion, or change in position; to these may be added substance, duration and number. But as for all the rest, including light and colours, sounds, smells, tastes, heat and cold and the other tactile qualities, I think of these only in a very confused and obscure way, to the extent that I do not even know whether they are true or false, that is, whether the ideas I have of them are ideas of real things or of non-things. For although, as I have noted before, falsity in the strict sense, or formal falsity, can occur only in judgements, there is another kind of falsity, material falsity, which occurs in ideas, when they represent non-things as

[handwritten margin note top left: it is something in me?]

[handwritten margin note top right: where does idea of infinite come from when I am finite?]

things. For example, the ideas which I have of heat and cold contain so little clarity and distinctness that they do not enable me to tell whether cold is merely the absence of heat or vice versa, or whether both of them are real qualities, or neither is. And since there can be no ideas which are not as it were of things, if it is true that cold is nothing but the absence of heat, the idea which represents it to me as something real and positive deserves to be called false; and the same goes for other ideas of this kind.

Such ideas obviously do not require me to posit a source distinct from myself. For on the one hand, if they are false, that is, represent non-things, I know by the natural light that they arise from nothing— that is, they are in me only because of a deficiency and lack of perfection in my nature. If on the other hand they are true, then since the reality which they represent is so extremely slight that I cannot even distinguish it from a non-thing, I do not see why they cannot originate from myself.

With regard to the clear and distinct elements in my ideas of corporeal things, it appears that I could have borrowed some of these from my idea of myself, namely substance, duration, number and anything else of this kind. For example, I think that a stone is a substance, or is a thing capable of existing independently, and I also think that I am a substance. Admittedly I conceive of myself as a thing that thinks and is not extended, whereas I conceive of the stone as a thing that is extended and does not think, so that the two conceptions differ enormously; but they seem to agree with respect to the classification 'substance'. Again, I perceive that I now exist, and remember that I have existed for some time; moreover, I have various thoughts which I can count; it is in these ways that I acquire the ideas of duration and number which I can then transfer to other things. As for all the other elements which make up the ideas of corporeal things, namely extension, shape position and movement, these are not formally contained in me, since I am nothing but a thinking thing; but since they are merely modes of a substance, and I am a substance, it seems possible that they are contained in me eminently.

So there remains only the idea of God; and I must consider whether there is anything in the idea which could not have originated in myself. By the word 'God' I understand a substance that is infinite, eternal, immutable, independent, supremely intelligent, supremely powerful, and which created both myself and everything else (if anything else there be) that exists. All these attributes are such that, the more carefully I concentrate on them, the less possible it seems that they could have originated from me alone. So from what has been said it must be concluded that God necessarily exists.

It is true that I have the idea of substance in me in virtue of the fact that I am a substance; but this would not account for my having the idea of an infinite substance, when I am finite, unless this idea proceeded from some substance which really was infinite.

And I must not think that, just as my conceptions of rest and darkness are arrived at by negating movement and light, so my perception of the infinite is arrived at not by means of a true idea but merely by negating the finite. On the contrary, I clearly understand that there is more reality in an infinite substance than in a finite one, and hence that my perception of the infinite, that is God, is in some way prior to my perception of the finite, that is myself. For how could I understand that I doubted or desired—that is, lacked something—and that I was not wholly perfect, unless there were in me some idea of a more perfect being which enabled me to recognize my own defects by comparison?

Nor can it be said that this idea of God is perhaps materially false and so could have come from nothing, which is what I observed just a moment ago in the case of the ideas of heat and cold, and so on. On the contrary, it is utterly clear and distinct, and contains in itself more objective reality than any other idea; hence there is no idea which is in itself truer or less liable to be suspected of falsehood. This idea of a supremely perfect and infinite being is, I say, true in the highest degree; for although perhaps one may imagine that such a being does not exist, it cannot be supposed that the idea of such a being represents something unreal, as I said with regard to the idea of cold. The idea is, moreover, utterly clear and distinct; for whatever I clearly and distinctly perceive as being real and true, and implying any perfection, is wholly contained in it. It does not matter that I do not grasp the infinite, or that there are countless

[handwritten margin notes right column: whatever I perceive as true is true even if I can't get infinite]

[Handwritten margin notes: "On the nature of God infinite not to be grasped. I understand infinite" (top left); "If I derived existence from myself" (top right); "prove that is God in me?" (left margin); "gradual increase of knowledge sign of imperfection" (left margin); "never infinity" (left margin); "God is already infinite" (left margin); "clear idea of the come from God" (bottom left)]

additional attributes of God which I cannot in any way grasp, and perhaps cannot even reach in my thought; for it is in the nature of the infinite not to be grasped by a finite being like myself. It is enough that I understand the infinite, and that I judge that all the attributes which I clearly perceive and know to imply some perfection—and perhaps countless others of which I am ignorant—are present in God either formally or eminently. This is enough to make the idea that I have of God the truest and most clear and distinct of all my ideas.

But perhaps I am something greater than I myself understand, and all the perfections which I attribute to God are somehow in me potentially, though not yet emerging or actualized. For I am now experiencing a gradual increase in my knowledge, and I see nothing to prevent its increasing more and more to infinity. Further, I see no reason why I should not be able to use this increased knowledge to acquire all the other perfections of God. And finally, if the potentiality for these perfections is already within me, why should not this be enough to generate the idea of such perfections?

But all this is impossible. First, though it is true that there is a gradual increase in my knowledge, and that I have many potentialities which are not yet actual, this is all quite irrelevant to the idea of God, which contains absolutely nothing that is potential; indeed, this gradual increase in knowledge is itself the surest sign of imperfection. What is more, even if my knowledge always increases more and more, I recognize that it will never actually be infinite, since it will never reach the point where it is not capable of a further increase; God, on the other hand, I take to be actually infinite, so that nothing can be added to his perfection. And finally, I perceive that the objective being of an idea cannot be produced merely by potential being, which strictly speaking is nothing, but only by actual or formal being.

If one concentrates carefully, all this is quite evident by the natural light. But when I relax my concentration, and my mental vision is blinded by the images of things perceived by the senses, it is not so easy for me to remember why the idea of a being more perfect than myself must necessarily proceed from some being which is in reality more perfect. I should therefore like to go further and inquire

whether I myself, who have this idea, could exist if no such being existed.

From whom, in that case, would I derive my existence? From myself presumably, or from my parents, or from some other beings less perfect than God; for nothing more perfect than God, or even as perfect, can be thought of or imagined.

Yet if I derived my existence from myself, then I should neither doubt nor want, nor lack anything at all; for I should have given myself all the perfections of which I have any idea, and thus I should myself be God. I must not suppose that the items I lack would be more difficult to acquire than those I now have. On the contrary, it is clear that, since I am a thinking thing or substance, it would have been far more difficult for me to emerge out of nothing than merely to acquire knowledge of the many things of which I am ignorant—such knowledge being merely an accident of that substance. And if I had derived my existence from myself, which is a greater achievement, I should certainly not have denied myself the knowledge in question, which is something much easier to acquire, or indeed any of the attributes which I perceive to be contained in the idea of God; for none of them seem any harder to achieve. And if any of them were harder to achieve, they would certainly appear so to me, if I had indeed got all my other attributes from myself, since I should experience a limitation of my power in this respect.

I do not escape the force of these arguments by supposing that I have always existed as I do now, as if it followed from this that there was no need to look for any author of my existence. For a lifespan can be divided into countless parts, each completely independent of the others, so that it does not follow from the fact that I existed a little while ago that I must exist now, unless there is some cause which as it were creates me afresh at this moment—that is, which preserves me. For it is quite clear to anyone who attentively considers the nature of time that the same power and action are needed to preserve anything at each individual moment of its duration as would be required to create that thing anew if it were not yet in existence. Hence the distinction between preservation and creation is only a conceptual one, and this is one of the things that are evident by the natural light.

I must therefore now ask myself whether I possess some power enabling me to bring it about that I who now exist will still exist a little while from now. For since I am nothing but a thinking thing—or at least since I am now concerned only and precisely with that part of me which is a thinking thing—if there were such a power in me, I should undoubtedly be aware of it. But I experience no such power, and this very fact makes me recognize most clearly that I depend on some being distinct from myself.

But perhaps this being is not God, and perhaps I was produced either by my parents or by other causes less perfect than God. No; for as I have said before, it is quite clear that there must be at least as much in the cause as in the effect. And therefore whatever kind of cause is eventually proposed, since I am a thinking thing and have within me some idea of God, it must be admitted that what caused me is itself a thinking thing and possesses the idea of all the perfections which I attribute to God. In respect of this cause one may again inquire whether it derives its existence from itself or from another cause. If from itself, then it is clear from what has been said that it is itself God, since if it has the power of existing through its own might, then undoubtedly it also has the power of actually possessing all the perfections of which it has an idea—that is, all the perfections which I conceive to be in God. If, on the other hand, it derives its existence from another cause, then the same question may be repeated concerning this further cause, namely whether it derives its existence from itself or from another cause, until eventually the ultimate cause is reached, and this will be God.

It is clear enough that an infinite regress is impossible here, especially since I am dealing not just with the cause that produced me in the past, but also and most importantly with the cause that preserves me at the present moment.

Nor can it be supposed that several partial causes contributed to my creation, or that I received the idea of one of the perfections which I attribute to God from one cause and the idea of another from another—the supposition here being that all the perfections are to be found somewhere in the universe but not joined together in a single being, God. On the contrary, the unity, the simplicity, or the insep-

arability of all the attributes of God is one of the most important of the perfections which I understand him to have. And surely the idea of the unity of all his perfections could not have been placed in me by any cause which did not also provide me with the ideas of the other perfections; for no cause could have made me understand the interconnection and inseparability of the perfections without at the same time making me recognize what they were.

Lastly, as regards my parents, even if everything I have ever believed about them is true, it is certainly not they who preserve me; and in so far as I am a thinking thing, they did not even make me; they merely placed certain dispositions in the matter which I have always regarded as containing me, or rather in my mind, for that is all I now take myself to be. So there can be no difficulty regarding my parents in this context. Altogether then, it must be concluded that the mere fact that I exist and have within me an idea of a most perfect being, that is, God, provides a very clear proof that God indeed exists.

the idea of a perfect being is proof.

It only remains for me to examine how I received this idea from God. For I did not acquire it from the senses; it has never come to me unexpectedly, as usually happens with the ideas of things that are perceivable by the senses, when these things present themselves to the external sense organs—or seem to do so. And it was not invented by me either; for I am plainly unable either to take away anything from it or to add anything to it. The only remaining alternative is that it is innate in me, just as the idea of myself is innate in me.

not from senses. not invented. is innate

And indeed it is no surprise that God, in creating me, should have placed this idea in men to be, as it were, the mark of the craftsman stamped on his work—not that the mark need be anything distinct from the work itself. But the mere fact that God created me is a very strong basis for believing that I am somehow made in his image and likeness, and that I perceive that likeness, which includes the idea of God, by the same faculty which enables me to perceive myself. That is, when I turn my mind's eye upon myself, I understand that I am a thing which is incomplete and dependent on another and which aspires without limit to ever greater and better things; but I also understand at the same time that he on whom I depend has within him all those greater

defining God: not deceiving

things, not just indefinitely and potentially but actually and infinitely, and hence that he is God. The whole force of the argument lies in this: I recognize that it would be impossible for me to exist with the kind of nature I have—that is, having within me the idea of God—were it not the case that God really existed. By 'God' I mean the very being the idea of whom is within me, that is, the possessor of all the perfections which I cannot grasp, but can somehow reach in my thought, who is subject to no defects whatsoever. It is clear enough from this that he cannot be a deceiver, since it is manifest by the natural light that all fraud and deception depend on some defect.

divine wonder

But before examining this point more carefully and investigating other truths which may be derived from it, I should like to pause here and spend some time in the contemplation of God; to reflect on his attributes, and to gaze with wonder and adoration on the beauty of this immense light, so far as the eye of my darkened intellect can bear it. For just as we believe through faith that the supreme happiness of the next life consists solely in the contemplation of the divine majesty, so experience tells us that this same contemplation, albeit much less perfect, enables us to know the greatest joy of which we are capable in this life.

FOURTH MEDITATION

TRUTH AND FALSITY *about God & my own shortcomings*

During these past few days I have accustomed myself to leading my mind away from the senses; and I have taken careful note of the fact that there is very little about corporeal things that is truly perceived, whereas much more is known about the human mind, and still more about God. The result is that I now have no difficulty in turning my mind away from imaginable things and towards things which are objects of the intellect alone and are totally separate from matter. And indeed the idea I have of the human mind, in so far as it is a thinking thing, which is not extended in length, breadth or height and has no other bodily characteristics, is much more distinct than the idea of any corporeal thing. And when I consider the fact that I have doubts, or that I am a thing that is incomplete and dependent, then there arises

in me a clear and distinct idea of a being who is independent and complete, that is, an idea of God. And from the mere fact that there is such an idea within me, or that I who possess this idea exist, I clearly infer that God also exists, and that every single moment of my entire existence depends on him. So clear is this conclusion that I am confident that the human intellect cannot know anything that is more evident or more certain. And now, from this contemplation of the true God, in whom all the treasures of wisdom and the sciences lie hidden, I think I can see a way forward to the knowledge of other things.

To begin with, I recognize that it is impossible that God should ever deceive me. For in every case of trickery or deception some imperfection is to be found; and although the ability to deceive appears to be an indication of cleverness or power, the will to deceive is undoubtedly evidence of malice or weakness, and so cannot apply to God.

Next, I know by experience that there is in me a faculty of judgement which, like everything else which is in me, I certainly received from God. And since God does not wish to deceive me, he surely did not give me the kind of faculty which would ever enable me to go wrong while using it correctly.

There would be no further doubt on this issue were it not that what I have just said appears to imply that I am incapable of ever going wrong. For if everything that is in me comes from God, and he did not endow me with a faculty for making mistakes, it appears that I can never go wrong. And certainly, so long as I think only of God, and turn my whole attention to him, I can find no cause of error or falsity. But when I turn back to myself, I know by experience that I am prone to countless errors. On looking for the cause of these errors, I find that I possess not only a real and positive idea of God, or a being who is supremely perfect, but also what may be described as a negative idea of nothingness, or of that which is farthest removed from all perfection. I realize that I am, as it were, something intermediate between God and nothingness, or between supreme being and non-being: my nature is such that in so far as I was created by the supreme being, there is nothing in me to enable me to go wrong or lead me astray; but in so far as I participate in nothingness or non-being, that is, in so far as I am not myself the supreme being and am lacking in countless respects, it is no

Judgement from God is not infinite in man.

Know only myself God

wonder that I make mistakes. I understand, then, that error as such is not something real which depends on God, but merely a defect. Hence my going wrong does not require me to have a faculty specially bestowed on me by God; it simply happens as a result of the fact that the faculty of true judgement which I have from God is in my case not infinite.

But this is still not entirely satisfactory. For error is not a pure negation, but rather a privation or lack of some knowledge which somehow should be in me. And when I concentrate on the nature of God, it seems impossible that he should have placed in me a faculty which is not perfect of its kind, or which lacks some perfection which it ought to have. The more skilled the craftsman the more perfect the work produced by him; if this is so, how can anything produced by the supreme creator of all things not be complete and perfect in all respects? There is, moreover, no doubt that God could have given me a nature such that I was never mistaken; again, there is no doubt that he always wills what is best. Is it then better that I should make mistakes than that I should not do so?

As I reflect on these matters more attentively, it occurs to me first of all that it is no cause for surprise if I do not understand the reasons for some of God's actions; and there is no call to doubt his existence if I happen to find that there are other instances where I do not grasp why or how certain things were made by him. For since I now know that my own nature is very weak and limited, whereas the nature of God is immense, incomprehensible and infinite, I also know without more ado that he is capable of countless things whose causes are beyond my knowledge. And for this reason alone I consider the customary search for final causes to be totally useless in physics; there is considerable rashness in thinking myself capable of investigating the impenetrable purposes of God.

It also occurs to me that whenever we are inquiring whether the works of God are perfect, we ought to look at the whole universe, not just at one created thing on its own. For what would perhaps rightly appear very imperfect if it existed on its own is quite perfect when its function as a part of the universe is considered. It is true that, since my decision to doubt everything, it is so far only myself and God whose existence I have been able to know with certainty; but after considering the immense power of God, I cannot deny that many other things have been made by him, or at least could have been made, and hence that I may have a place in the universal scheme of things.

Next, when I look more closely at myself and inquire into the nature of my errors (for these are the only evidence of some imperfection in me), I notice that they depend on two concurrent causes, namely on the faculty of knowledge which is in me, and on the faculty of choice or freedom of the will; that is, they depend on both the intellect and the will simultaneously. Now all that the intellect does is to enable me to perceive the ideas which are subjects for possible judgement; and when regarded strictly in this light, it turns out to contain no error in the proper sense of that term. For although countless things may exist without there being any corresponding ideas in me, it should not, strictly speaking, be said that I am deprived of these ideas, but merely that I lack them, in a negative sense. This is because I cannot produce any reason to prove that God ought to have given me a greater faculty of knowledge than he did; and no matter how skilled I understand a craftsman to be, this does not make me think he ought to have put into every one of his works all the perfections which he is able to put into some of them. Besides, I cannot complain that the will or freedom of choice which I received from God is not sufficiently extensive or perfect, since I know by experience that it is not restricted in any way. Indeed, I think it is very noteworthy that there is nothing else in me which is so perfect and so great that the possibility of a further increase in its perfection or greatness is beyond my understanding. If, for example, I consider the faculty of understanding, I immediately recognize that in my case it is extremely slight and very finite, and I at once form the idea of an understanding which is much greater—indeed supremely great and infinite; and from the very fact that I can form an idea of it, I perceive that it belongs to the nature of God. Similarly, if I examine the faculties or imagination, or any others, I discover that in my case each one of these faculties is weak and limited, while in the case of God it is immeasurable. It is only the will, or freedom of choice, which I experience within me to be so great that the idea of any greater faculty is beyond my grasp; so much so that it is above all in virtue of the will that I understand myself to bear in some way the image and likeness of God. For although God's will is incomparably greater than mine, both in virtue of the knowledge and power that accompany it and make it more firm and efficacious, and also in virtue of its object, in that it ranges over a greater number of items, nevertheless it does not seem any greater than mine when considered as will in the essential and strict sense. This is because the will simply consists in our ability to do or not do something (that is, to affirm or deny, to pursue or avoid); or rather, it consists simply in the fact that when the intellect puts something forward for affirmation or denial or for pursuit or avoidance, our inclinations are such that we do not feel we are determined by any external force. In order to be free, there is no need for me to be inclined both ways; on the contrary, the more I incline in one direction—either because I clearly understand that reasons of truth and goodness point that way, or because of a divinely produced disposition of my inmost thoughts—the freer is my choice. Neither divine grace nor natural knowledge ever diminishes freedom; on the contrary, they increase and strengthen it. But the indifference I feel when there is no reason pushing me in one direction rather than another is the lowest grade of freedom; it is evidence not of any perfection of freedom, but rather of a defect in knowledge or a kind of negation. For if I always saw clearly what was true and good, I should never have to deliberate about the right judgement or choice; in that case, although I should be wholly free, it would be impossible for me ever to be in a state of indifference.

From these considerations I perceive that the power of willing which I received from God is not, when considered in itself, the cause of my mistakes; for it is both extremely ample and also perfect of its kind. Nor is my power of understanding to blame; for since my understanding comes from God, everything that I understand I undoubtedly understand correctly, and any error here is impossible. So what then is the source of my mistakes? It must be simply this: the scope of the will is wider than that of the intellect; but instead of restricting it within the same limits, I extend its use to matters which I do not understand. Since the will is indifferent in such cases, it easily turns aside from what is true and good, and this is the source of my error and sin.

For example, during the past few days I have been asking whether anything in the world exists, and I have realized that from the very fact of my raising this question it follows quite evidently that I exist. I could not but judge that something which I understood so clearly was true; but this was not because I was compelled so to judge by any external force, but because a great light in the intellect was followed by a great inclination in the will, and thus the spontaneity and freedom of my belief was all the greater in proportion to my lack of indifference. But now, besides the knowledge that I exist, in so far as I am a thinking thing, an idea of corporeal nature comes into my mind; and I happen to be in doubt as to whether the thinking nature which is in me, or rather which I am, is distinct from this corporeal nature or identical with it. I am making the further supposition that my intellect has not yet come upon any persuasive reason in favour of one alternative rather than the other. This obviously implies that I am indifferent as to whether I should assert or deny either alternative, or indeed refrain from making any judgement on the matter.

What is more, this indifference does not merely apply to cases where the intellect is wholly ignorant, but extends in general to every case where the intellect does not have sufficiently clear knowledge at the time when the will deliberates. For although probable conjectures may pull me in one direction, the mere knowledge that they are simply conjectures, and not certain and indubitable reasons, is itself quite enough to push my assent the other way. My experience in the last few days confirms this: the mere fact that I found that all my previous beliefs were in some sense open to doubt was enough to turn my absolutely confident belief in their truth into the supposition that they were wholly false.

If, however, I simply refrain from making a judgement in cases where I do not perceive the truth with sufficient clarity and distinctness, then it is clear that I am behaving correctly and avoiding error. But if in such cases I either affirm or deny, then I am not using my free will correctly. If I go for the alternative which is false, then obviously I shall be in error; if I take the other side, then it is by pure chance that I arrive at the truth, and I shall still be at fault since it is clear by the natural light that the perception of the intellect should always precede the determination of the will. In this incorrect use of free will may be found the privation which constitutes the essence of error. The privation, I say, lies in the operation of the will in so far as it proceeds from me, but not in the faculty of will which I received from God, nor even in its operation, in so far as it depends on him.

And I have no cause for complaint on the grounds that the power of understanding or the natural light which God gave me is no greater than it is; for it is in the nature of a finite intellect to lack understanding of many things, and it is in the nature of a created intellect to be finite. Indeed, I have reason to give thanks to him who has never owed me anything for the great bounty that he has shown me, rather than thinking myself deprived or robbed of any gifts he did not bestow.

Nor do I have any cause for complaint on the grounds that God gave me a will which extends more widely than my intellect. For since the will consists simply of one thing which is, as it were, indivisible, it seems that its nature rules out the possibility of anything being taken away from it. And surely, the more widely my will extends, then the greater thanks I owe to him who gave it to me.

Finally, I must not complain that the forming of those acts of will or judgements in which I go wrong happens with God's concurrence. For in so far as these acts depend on God, they are wholly true and good; and my ability to perform them means that there is in a sense more perfection in men than would be the case if I lacked this ability. As for the privation involved—which is all that the essential definition of falsity and wrong consists in—this does not in any way require the concurrence of God, since it is not a thing; indeed, when it is referred to God as its cause, it should be called not a privation but simply a negation. For it is surely no imperfection in God that he has given me the freedom to assent or not to assent in those cases where he did not endow my intellect with a clear and distinct perception; but it is undoubtedly an imperfection in me to misuse that freedom and make judgements about matters which I do not fully understand. I can see, however, that God could easily have brought it about that with-

out losing my freedom, and despite the limitations in my knowledge, I should nonetheless never make a mistake. He could, for example, have endowed my intellect with a clear and distinct perception of everything about which I was ever likely to deliberate; or he could simply have impressed it unforgettably on my memory that I should never make a judgement about anything which I did not clearly and distinctly understand. Had God made me this way, then I can easily understand that, considered as a totality, I would have been more perfect than I am now. But I cannot therefore deny that there may in some way be more perfection in the universe as a whole because some of its parts are not immune from error, while others are immune, than there would be if all the parts were exactly alike. And I have no right to complain that the role God wished me to undertake in the world is not the principal one or the most perfect of all.

What is more, even if I have no power to avoid error in the first way just mentioned, which requires a clear perception of everything I have to deliberate on, I can avoid error in the second way, which depends merely on my remembering to withhold judgement on any occasion when the truth of the matter is not clear. Admittedly, I am aware of a certain weakness in me, in that I am unable to keep my attention fixed on one and the same item of knowledge at all times; but by attentive and repeated meditation I am nevertheless able to make myself remember it as often as the need arises, and thus get into the habit of avoiding error.

It is here that man's greatest and most important perfection is to be found, and I therefore think that today's meditation, involving an investigation into the cause of error and falsity, has been very profitable. The cause of error must surely be the one I have explained; for if, whenever I have to make a judgement, I restrain my will so that it extends to what the intellect clearly and distinctly reveals, and no further, then it is quite impossible for me to go wrong. This is because every clear and distinct perception is undoubtedly something, and hence cannot come from nothing, but must necessarily have God for its author. Its author, I say, is God, who is supremely perfect, and who cannot be a deceiver on pain of contradiction; hence the perception is undoubtedly true. So today I have learned not only what

triangle as eternal not my convention

precautions to take to avoid ever going wrong, but also what to do to arrive at the truth. For I shall unquestionably reach the truth, if only I give sufficient attention to all the things which I perfectly understand, and separate these from all the other cases where my apprehension is more confused and obscure. And this is just what I shall take good care to do from now on.

FIFTH MEDITATION

THE ESSENCE OF MATERIAL THINGS, AND THE EXISTENCE OF GOD CONSIDERED A SECOND TIME

There are many matters which remain to be investigated concerning the attributes of God and the nature of myself, or my mind; and perhaps I shall take these up at another time. But now that I have seen what to do and what to avoid in order to reach the truth, the most pressing task seems to be to try to escape from the doubts into which I fell a few days ago, and see whether any certainty can be achieved regarding material objects.

But before I inquire whether any such things exist outside me, I must consider the ideas of these things, in so far as they exist in my thought, and see which of them are distinct, and which confused.

Quantity, for example, or 'continuous' quantity as the philosophers commonly call it, is something I distinctly imagine. That is, I distinctly imagine the extension of the quantity (or rather of the thing which is quantified) in length, breadth and depth. I also enumerate various parts of the thin, and to these parts I assign various sizes, shapes, positions and local motions; and to the motions I assign various durations.

Not only are all these things very well known and transparent to me when regarded in this general way, but in addition there are countless particular features regarding shape, number, motion and so on, which I perceive when I give them my attention. And the truth of these matters is so open and so much in harmony with my nature, that on first discovering them it seems that I am not so much learning something new as remembering what I knew before; or it seems like noticing for the first time things which were long present within me although I had never turned my mental gaze on them before.

But I think the most important consideration at this point is that I find within me countless ideas of things which even though they may not exist anywhere outside me still cannot be called nothing; for although in a sense they can be thought of at will, they are not my invention but have their own true and immutable natures. When, for example, I imagine a triangle, even if perhaps no such figure exists, or has ever existed, anywhere outside my thought, there is still a determinate nature, or essence, or form of the triangle which is immutable and eternal, and not invented by me or dependent on my mind. This is clear from the fact that various properties can be demonstrated of the triangle, for example that its three angles equal two right angles, that its greatest side subtends its greatest angle, and the like; and since these properties are ones which I now clearly recognize whether I want to or not, even if I never thought of them at all when I previously imagined the triangle, it follows that they cannot have been invented by me.

It would be beside the point for me to say that since I have from time to time seen bodies of triangular shape, the idea of the triangle may have come to me from external things by means of the sense organs. For I can think up countless other shapes which there can be no suspicion of my ever having encountered through the senses, and yet I can demonstrate various properties of these shapes, just as I can with the triangle. All these properties are certainly true, since I am clearly aware of them, and therefore they are something, and not merely nothing; for it is obvious that whatever is true is something; and I have already amply demonstrated that everything of which I am clearly aware is true. And even if I had not demonstrated this, the nature of my mind is such that I cannot but assent to these things, at least so long as I clearly perceive them. I also remember that even before, when I was completely preoccupied with the objects of the senses, I always held that the most certain truths of all were the kind which I recognized clearly in connection with shapes, or numbers or other items relating to arithmetic or geometry, or in general to pure and abstract mathematics.

But if the mere fact that I can produce from my thought the idea of something entails that everything which I clearly and distinctly perceive to belong to that thing really does belong to it, is not this a possible basis for another argument to prove the existence of God? Certainly, the idea of God, or a supremely perfect being, is one which I find within me just as surely as the idea of any shape or number. And my understanding that it belongs to his nature that he always exists is no less clear and distinct than is the case when I prove of any shape or number that some property belongs to its nature. Hence, even if it turned out that not everything on which I have meditated in these past days is true, I ought still to regard the existence of God as having at least the same level of certainty as I have hitherto attributed to the truths of mathematics.

At first sight, however, this is not transparently clear, but has some appearance of being a sophism. Since I have been accustomed to distinguish between existence and essence in everything else, I find it easy to persuade myself that existence can also be separated from the essence of God, and hence that God can be thought of as not existing. But when I concentrate more carefully, it is quite evident that existence can no more be separated from the essence of God than the fact that its three angles equal two right angles can be separated from the essence of a triangle, or than the idea of a mountain can be separated from the idea of a valley. Hence it is just as much of a contradiction to think of God (that is, a supremely perfect being) lacking existence (that is, lacking a perfection), as it is to think of a mountain without a valley.

However, even granted that I cannot think of God except as existing, just as I cannot think of a mountain without a valley, it certainly does not follow from the fact that I think of a mountain with a valley that there is any mountain in the world; and similarly, it does not seem to follow from the fact that I think of God as existing that he does exist. For my thought does not impose any necessity on things; and just as I may imagine a winged horse even though no horse has wings, so I may be able to attach existence to God even though no God exists.

But there is a sophism concealed here. From the fact that I cannot think of a mountain without a valley, it does not follow that a mountain and valley exist anywhere, but simply that a mountain and a valley, whether they exist or not, are mutually in-

separable. But from the fact that I cannot think of God except as existing, it follows that existence is inseparable from God, and hence that he really exists. It is not that my thought makes it so, or imposes any necessity on any thing; on the contrary, it is the necessity of the thing itself, namely the existence of God, which determines my thinking in this respect. For I am not free to think of God without existence (that is, a supremely perfect without a supreme perfection) as I am free to imagine a horse with or without wings.

And it must not be objected at this point that while it is indeed necessary for me to suppose God exists, once I have made the supposition that he has all perfections (since existence is one of the perfections), nevertheless the original supposition was not necessary. Similarly, the objection would run, it is not necessary for me to think that all quadrilaterals can be inscribed in a circle; but given this supposition, it will be necessary for me to admit that a rhombus can be inscribed in a circle—which is patently false. Now admittedly, it is not necessary that I ever light upon any thought of God; but whenever I do choose to think of the first and supreme being, and bring forth the idea of god from the treasure house of my mind as it were, it is necessary that I attribute all perfections to him, even if I do not at that time enumerate them or attend to them individually. And this necessity plainly guarantees that, when I later realize that existence is a perfection, I am correct in inferring that the first and supreme being exists. In the same way, it is not necessary for me ever to imagine a triangle; but whenever I do wish to consider a rectilinear figure having just three angles, it is necessary that I attribute to it the properties which license the inference that its three angles equal no more than two right angles, even if I do not notice this at the time. By contrast, when I examine what figures can be inscribed in a circle, it is in no way necessary for me to think that this class includes all quadrilaterals. Indeed, I cannot even imagine this, so long as I am willing to admit only what I clearly and distinctly understand. So there is a great difference between this kind of false supposition and the true ideas which are innate in me, of which the first and most important is the idea of God. There are many ways in which I understand that this idea is not something fictitious which is dependent on my thought, but is an image of a true and immutable nature. First of all, there is the fact that, apart from God, there is nothing else of which I am capable of thinking such that existence belongs to its essence. Second, I cannot understand how there could be two or more Gods of this kind; and after supposing that one God exists, I plainly see that it is necessary that he has existed from eternity and will abide for eternity. And finally, I perceive many other attributes of God, none of which I can remove or alter.

But whatever method of proof I use, I am always brought back to the fact that it is only what I clearly and distinctly perceive that completely convinces me. Some of the things I clearly and distinctly perceive are obvious to everyone, while others are discovered only by those who look more closely and investigate more carefully; but once they have been discovered, the latter are judged to be just as certain as the former. In the case of a right-angled triangle, for example, the fact that the square on the hypotenuse is equal to the square on the other two sides is not so readily apparent as the fact that the hypotenuse subtends the largest angle; but once one has seen it, one believes it just as strongly. But as regards God, if I were not overwhelmed by preconceived opinions, and if the images of things perceived by the senses did not besiege my thought on every side, I would certainly acknowledge him sooner and more easily than anything else. For what is more self-evident than the fact that the supreme being exists, or that God, to whose essence alone existence belongs exists?

Although it needed close attention for me to perceive this, I am now just as certain of it as I am of everything else which appears most certain. And what is more, I see that the certainty of all other things depends on this, so that without it nothing can ever be perfectly known.

Admittedly my nature is such that so long as I perceive something very clearly and distinctly I cannot but believe it to be true. But my nature is also such that I cannot fix my mental vision continually on the same thing, so as to keep perceiving it clearly; and often the memory of a previously made judgement may come back, when I am no longer attending to the arguments which led me to make it. And so other arguments can now occur to me which might easily undermine my opinion, if I were unaware of God; and I should thus never have true and certain knowledge about anything, but only shifting and changeable opinions. For example, when I consider the nature of a triangle, it appears most evident to me, steeped as I am in the principles of geometry, that its three angles are equal to two right angles; and so long as I attend to the proof, I cannot but believe this to be true. But as soon as I turn my mind's eye away from the proof, then in spite of still remembering that I perceived it very clearly, I can easily fall into doubt about its truth, if I am unaware of God. For I can convince myself that I have a natural disposition to go wrong from time to time in matters which I think I perceive as evidently as can be. This will seem even more likely when I remember that there have been frequent cases where I have regarded things as true and certain, but have later been led by other arguments to judge them to be false.

Now, however, I have perceived that God exists, and at the same time I have understood that everything else depends on him, and that he is no deceiver; and I have drawn the conclusion that everything which I clearly and distinctly perceive is of necessity true. Accordingly, even if I am no longer attending to the arguments which led me to judge that this is true, as long as I remember that I clearly and distinctly perceived it, there are no counter-arguments which can be adduced to make me doubt it, but on the contrary I have true and certain knowledge about it. And I have knowledge not just of this matter, but of all matters which I remember ever having demonstrated, in geometry and so on. For what objections can now be raised? That the way I am made makes me prone to frequent error? But I now know that I am incapable of error in those cases where my understanding is transparently clear. Or can it be objected that I have in the past regarded as true certain many things which I afterwards recognized to be false? But none of these were things which I clearly and distinctly perceived: I was ignorant of this rule for establishing the truth, and believed these things for other reasons which I later discovered to be less reliable.

So what is left to say? Can one raise the objection I put to myself a while ago, that I may be dreaming, or that everything which I am now thinking has a little truth as what comes to the mind of one who is asleep? Yet even this does not change anything. For even though I might be dreaming, if there is anything which is evident to my intellect, then it is wholly true.

Thus I see plainly that the certainty and truth of all knowledge depends uniquely on my awareness of the true God, to such an extent that I was incapable of perfect knowledge about anything else until I became aware of him. And now it is possible for me to achieve full and certain knowledge of countless matters, both concerning God himself and other things whose nature is intellectual, and also concerning the whole of that corporeal nature which is the subject-matter of pure mathematics.

SIXTH MEDITATION

THE EXISTENCE OF MATERIAL THINGS, AND THE REAL DISTINCTION BETWEEN MIND AND BODY

It remains for me to examine whether material things exist. And at least I now know they are capable of existing, in so far as they are the subject-matter of pure mathematics, since I perceive them clearly and distinctly. For there is no doubt that God is capable of creating everything that I am capable of perceiving in this manner; and I have never judged that something could not be made by him except on the grounds that there would be a contradiction in my perceiving it distinctly. The conclusion that material things exist is also suggested by the faculty of imagination, which I am aware of using when I turn my mind to material things. For when I give more attentive consideration to what imagination is, it seems to be nothing else but an application of the cognitive faculty to a body which is intimately present to it, and which therefore exists.

To make this clear, I will first examine the difference between imagination and pure understanding. When I imagine a triangle, for example, I do not merely understand that it is a figure bounded by three lines, but at the same time I also see the three lines with my mind's eye as if they were present before me; and this is what I call imagining. But if I want to think of a chiliagon, although I understand that it is a figure consisting of a thousand sides just as well as I understand the triangle to be a three-sided figure, I do not in the same way imagine the thousand sides or see them as if they were present before me. It is true that since I am in the habit of imagining something whenever I think of a corporeal thing, I may construct in my mind a confused representation of some figure; but it is clear that this is not a chiliagon. For it differs in no way from the representation I should form if I were thinking of a myriagon, or any figure with very many sides. Moreover, such a representation is useless for recognizing the properties which distinguish a chiliagon from other polygons. But suppose I am dealing with a pentagon: I can of course understand the figure of a pentagon, just as I can the figure of a chiliagon, without the help of the imagination; but I can also imagine a pentagon, by applying my mind's eye to its five sides and the area contained within them. And in doing this I notice quite clearly that imagination requires a peculiar effort of mind which is not required for understanding; this additional effort of mind clearly shows the difference between imagination and pure understanding.

Besides this, I consider that this power of imagining which is in me, differing as it does from the power of understanding, is not a necessary constituent of my own essence, that is, of the essence of my mind. For if I lacked it, I should undoubtedly remain the same individual as I now am; from which it seems to follow that it depends on something distinct from myself. And I can easily understand that, if there does exist some body to which the mind is so joined that it can apply itself to contemplate it, as it were, whenever it pleases, then it may possibly be this very body that enables me to imagine corporeal things. So the difference between this mode of thinking and pure understanding may simply be this: when the mind understands, it in some way turns towards itself and inspects one of the ideas which are within it; but when it imagines, it turns towards the body and looks at something in the body which conforms

Senses first, reason later

to an idea understood by the mind or perceived by the senses. I can, as I say, easily understand that this is how imagination comes about, if the body exists; and since there is no other equally suitable way of explaining imagination that comes to mind, I can make a probable conjecture that the body exists. But this is only a probability; and despite a careful and comprehensive investigation, I do not yet see how the distinct idea of corporeal nature which I find in my imagination can provide any basis for a necessary inference that some body exists.

But besides that corporeal nature which is the subject-matter of pure mathematics, there is much else that I habitually imagine, such as colours, sounds, tastes, pain and so on—though not so distinctly. Now I perceive these things much better by means of the senses, which is how, with the assistance of memory, they appear to have reached the imagination. So in order to deal with them more fully, I must pay equal attention to the senses, and see whether the things which are perceived by means of that mode of thinking which I call 'sensory perception' provide me with any sure argument for the existence of corporeal things.

To begin with, I will go back over all the things which I previously took to be perceived by the senses, and reckoned to be true; and I will go over my reasons for thinking this. Next, I will set out my reasons for subsequently calling these things into doubt. And finally I will consider what I should now believe about them.

First of all then, I perceived by my senses that I had a head, hands, feet and other limbs making up the body which I regarded as part of myself, or perhaps even as my whole self. I also perceived by my senses that this body was situated among many other bodies which could affect it in various favourable or unfavourable ways; and I gauged the favourable effects by a sensation of pleasure, and the unfavourable ones by a sensation of pain. In addition to pain and pleasure, I also had sensations within me of hunger, thirst, and other such appetites, and also of physical propensities towards cheerfulness, sadness, anger and similar emotions. And outside me, besides the extension, shapes and movements of bodies, I also had sensations of their hardness and heat, and of the other tactile qualities. In addition, I had sensations of light, colours, smells, tastes and sounds, the variety of which enabled me to distinguish the sky, the earth, the seas, and all other bodies, one from another. Considering the ideas of all these qualities which presented themselves to my thought, although the ideas were, strictly speaking, the only immediate objects of my sensory awareness, it was not unreasonable for me to think that the items which I was perceiving through the senses were things quite distinct from my thought, namely bodies which produced the ideas. For my experience was that these ideas came to me quite without my consent, so that I could not have sensory awareness of any object, even if I wanted to, unless it was present to my sense organs; and I could not avoid having sensory awareness of it when it was present. And since the ideas perceived by the senses were much more lively and vivid and even, in their own way, more distinct than any of those which I deliberately formed through meditating or which I found impressed on my memory, it seemed impossible that they should have come from within me; so the only alternative was that they came from other things. Since the sole source of my knowledge of these things was the ideas themselves, the supposition that the things resembled the ideas was bound to occur to me. In addition, I remembered that the use of my senses had come first, while the use of my reason came only later; and I saw that the ideas which I formed myself were less vivid than those which I perceived with the senses and were, for the most part, made up of elements of sensory ideas. In this way I easily convinced myself that I had nothing at all in the intellect which I had not previously had in sensation. As for the body which by some special right I called 'mine', my belief that this body, more than any other, belonged to me had some justification. For I could never be separated from it, as I could from other bodies; and I felt all my appetites and emotions in, and on account of, this body; and finally, I was aware of pain and pleasurable ticklings in parts of this body, but not in other bodies external to it. But why should that curious sensation of pain give rise to a particular distress of mind; or why should a certain kind of delight follow on a tickling sensation? Again, why should that curious tugging in the stomach which I call hunger tell me that I should eat, or a dryness of the throat tell me to drink, and so on? I was not able to give any explanation of all this, except that nature taught me so. For there is absolutely no connection (at least that I can understand) between the tugging sensation and the decision to take food, or between the sensation of something causing pain and the mental apprehension of distress that arises from that sensation. These and other judgements that I made concerning sensory objects, I was apparently taught to make by nature; for I had already made up my mind that this was how things were, before working out any arguments to prove it.

Later on, however, I had many experiences which gradually undermined all the faith I had had in the senses. Sometimes towers which had looked round from a distance appeared square from close up; and enormous statues standing on their pediments did not seem large when observed from the ground. In these and countless other such cases, I found that the judgements of the external senses were mistaken. And this applied not just to the external senses but to the internal senses as well. For what can be more internal than pain? And yet I had heard that those who had had a leg or an arm amputated sometimes still seemed to feel pain intermittently in the missing part of the body. So even in my own case it was apparently not quite certain that a particular limb was hurting, even if I felt pain in it. To these reasons for doubting, I recently added two very general ones. The first was that every sensory experience I have ever thought I was having while awake I can also think of myself as sometimes having while asleep; and since I do not believe that what I seem to perceive in sleep comes from things located outside me, I did not see why I should be any more inclined to believe this of what I think I perceive while awake. The second reason for doubt was that since I did not know the author of my being (or at least was pretending not to), I saw nothing to rule out the possibility that my natural constitution made me prone to error even in matters which seemed to me most true. As for the reasons for my previous confident belief in the truth of the things perceived by the senses, I had no trouble in refuting them. For since I apparently had natural impulses towards many things which reason told me to avoid, I reckoned that a great deal of confidence should not be placed in what I was taught by nature. And despite the fact that the perceptions of the senses were not dependent on my

will, I did not think that I should on that account infer that they proceeded from things distinct from myself, since I might perhaps have a faculty not yet known to me which produced them.

But now, when I am beginning to achieve a better knowledge of myself and the author of my being, although I do not think I should heedlessly accept everything I seem to have acquired from the senses, neither do I think that everything should be called into doubt.

First, I know that everything which I clearly and distinctly understand is capable of being created by God so as to correspond exactly with my understanding of it. Hence the fact that I can clearly and distinctly understand one thing apart from another is enough to make me certain that the two things are distinct, since they are capable of being separated, at least by God. The question of what kind of power is required to being about such a separation does not affect the judgement that the two things are distinct. Thus, simply by knowing that I exist and seeing at the same time that absolutely nothing else belongs to my nature or essence except that I am a thinking thing, I can infer correctly that my essence consists solely in the fact that I am a thinking thing. It is true that I may have (or, to anticipate, that I certainly have) a body that is very closely joined to me. But nevertheless, on the one hand I have a clear and distinct idea of myself, in so far as I am simply a thinking, non-extended thing; and on the other hand I have a distinct idea of body, in so far as this is simply an extended, non-thinking thing. And accordingly, it is certain that I am really distinct from my body, and can exist without it.

Besides this, I find in myself faculties for certain special modes of thinking, namely imagination and sensory perception. Now I can clearly and distinctly understand myself as a whole without these faculties; but I cannot, conversely, understand these faculties without me, that is, without an intellectual substance to inhere in. This is because there is an intellectual act included in their essential definition; and hence I perceive that the distinction between them and myself corresponds to the distinction between the modes of a thing and the thing itself. Of course I also recognize that there are other faculties (like those of changing position, of taking on various shapes, and so on) which, like sensory perception and imagination, cannot be understood apart from some substance for them to inhere in, and hence cannot exist without it. But it is clear that these other faculties, if they exist, must be in a corporeal or extended substance and not an intellectual one; for the clear and distinct conception of them includes extension, but does not include any intellectual act whatsoever. Now there is in me a passive faculty of sensory perception, that is, a faculty for receiving and recognizing the ideas of sensible objects; but I could not make use of it unless there was also an active faculty, either in me or in something else, which produced or brought about these ideas. But this faculty cannot be in me, since clearly it presupposes no intellectual act on my part, and the ideas in question are produced without my cooperation and often even against my will. So the only alternative is that it is in another substance distinct from me—a substance which contains either formally or eminently all the reality which exists objectively in the ideas produced by this faculty (as I have just noted). This substance is either a body, that is, a corporeal nature, in which case it will contain formally and in fact everything which is to be found objective or representatively in the ideas; or else it is God, or some creature more noble than a body, in which case it will contain eminently whatever is to be found in the ideas. But since God is not a deceiver, it is quite clear that he does not transmit the ideas to me either directly from himself, or indirectly, via some creature which contains the objective reality of the ideas not formally but only eminently. For God has given me no faculty at all for recognizing any such source for these ideas; on the contrary, he has given me a great propensity to believe that they are produced by corporeal things. So I do not see how God could be understood to be anything but a deceiver if the ideas were transmitted from a source other than corporeal things. It follows that corporeal things exist. They may not all exist in a way that exactly corresponds with my sensory grasp of them, for in many cases the grasp of the senses is very obscure and confused. But at least they possess all the properties which I clearly and distinctly understand, that is, all those which, viewed in general terms, are comprised within the subject-matter of pure mathematics.

What of the other aspects of corporeal things which are either particular (for example that the sun is of such and such a size or shape), or less clearly understood, such as light or sound or pain, and so on? Despite the high degree of doubt and uncertainty involved here, the very fact that God is not a deceiver, and the consequent impossibility of there being any falsity in my opinions which cannot be corrected by some other faculty supplied by God, offers me a sure hope that I can attain the truth even in these matters. Indeed, there is no doubt that everything that I am taught by nature contains some truth. For if nature is considered in its general aspect, then I understand by the term nothing other than God himself, or the ordered system of created things established by God. And by my own nature in particular I understand nothing other than the totality of things bestowed on me by God.

There is nothing that my own nature teaches me more vividly than that I have a body, and that when I feel pain there is something wrong with the body, and that when I am hungry or thirsty the body needs food and drink, and so on. So I should not doubt that there is some truth in this.

Nature also teaches me, by these sensations of pain, hunger, thirst and so on, that I am not merely present in my body as a sailor is present in a ship, but that I am very closely joined and, as it were, intermingled with it, so that I and the body form a unit. If this were not so, I, who am nothing but a thinking thing, would not feel pain when the body was hurt, but would perceive the damage purely by the intellect, just as a sailor perceives by sight if anything in his ship is broken. Similarly, when the body needed food or drink, I should have an explicit understanding of the fact, instead of having confused sensations of hunger and thirst. For these sensations of hunger, thirst, pain and so on are nothing but confused modes of thinking which arise from the union and, as it were, intermingling of the mind with the body.

I am also taught by nature that various other bodies exist in the vicinity of my body, and that some of these are to be sought out and others avoided. And from the fact that I perceive by my senses a great variety of colours, sounds, smells and tastes, as well as differences in heat, hardness and the like, I am

[handwritten margin notes: "define nature more limited than God's gifts", "senses inform mind of phys safety", "Nature is not omniscient"]

correct in inferring that the bodies which are the source of these various sensory perceptions possess differences corresponding to them, though perhaps not resembling them. Also, the fact that some of the perceptions are agreeable to me while others are disagreeable makes it quite certain that my body, or rather my whole self, in so far as I am a combination of body and mind, can be affected by the various beneficial or harmful bodies which surround it.

There are, however, many other things which I may appear to have been taught by nature, but which in reality I acquired not from nature but from a habit of making ill-considered judgements; and it is therefore quite possible that these are false. Cases in point are the belief that any space in which nothing is occurring to stimulate my senses must be empty; or that the heat in a body is something exactly resembling the idea of heat which is in me; or that when a body is white or green, the selfsame whiteness or greenness which I perceive through my senses is present in the body; or that in a body which is bitter or sweet there is the selfsame taste which I experience, and so on; or, finally, that stars and towers and other distinct bodies have the same size and shape which they present to my senses, and other examples of this kind. But to make sure that my perceptions in this matter are sufficiently distinct, I must more accurately define exactly what I mean when I say that I am taught something by nature. In this context I am taking nature to be something more limited than the totality of things bestowed on me by God. For this includes many things that belong to the mind alone—for example my perception that what is done cannot be undone, and all other things that are known by the natural light; but at this stage I am not speaking of these matters. It also includes much that relates to the body alone, like the tendency to move in a downward direction, and so on; but I am not speaking of these matters either. My sole concern here is with what God has bestowed on me as a combination of mind and body. My nature, then, in this limited sense, does indeed teach me to avoid what induces a feeling of pain and to seek out what induces feelings of pleasure, and so on. But it does not appear to teach us to draw any conclusions from these sensory perceptions about things located outside us without waiting until the intellect has examined the matter. For knowledge of the truth about such things seems to belong to the mind alone, not to the combination of mind and body. Hence, although a star has no greater effect on my eye than the flame of a small light, that does not mean that there is any real or positive inclination in me to believe that the star is no bigger than the light; I have simply made this judgement from childhood onwards without any rational basis. Similarly, although I feel heat when I go near a fire and feel pain when I go too near, there is no convincing argument for supposing that there is something in the fire which resembles the heat, any more than for supposing that there is something which resembles the pain. There is simply reason to suppose that there is something in the fire, whatever it may eventually turn out to be, which produces in us the feelings of heat or pain. And likewise, even though there is nothing in any given space that stimulates the senses, it does not follow that there is no body there. In these cases and many others I see that I have been in the habit of misusing the order of nature. For the proper purpose of the sensory perceptions given me by nature is simply to inform the mind of what is beneficial or harmful for the composite of which the mind is a part; and to this extent they are sufficiently clear and distinct. But I misuse them by treating them as reliable touchstones for immediate judgements about the essential nature of the bodies located outside us; yet this is an area where they provide only very obscure information.

I have already looked in sufficient detail at how, notwithstanding the goodness of God, it may happen that my judgements are false. But a further problem now comes to mind regarding those very things which nature presents to me as objects which I should seek out or avoid, and also regarding the internal sensations, where I seem to have detected errors—e.g., when someone is tricked by the pleasant taste of some food into eating the poison concealed inside it. Yet in this case, what the man's nature urges him to go for is simply what is responsible for the pleasant taste, and not the poison, which his nature knows nothing about. The only inference that can be drawn from this is that his nature is not omniscient. And this is not surprising, since man is a limited thing, and so it is only fitting that his perfection should be limited.

Clock + body analogy

nature several meanings

And yet it is not unusual for us to go wrong even in cases where nature does urge us towards something. Those who are ill, for example, may desire food or drink that will shortly afterwards turn out to be bad for them. Perhaps it may be said that they go wrong because their nature is disordered, but this does not remove the difficulty. A sick man is no less one of God's creatures than a healthy one, and it seems no less a contradiction to suppose that he has received from God a nature which deceives him. Yet a clock constructed with wheels and weights observes all the laws of its nature just as closely when it is badly made and tells the wrong time as when it completely fulfils the wishes of the clockmaker. In the same way, I might consider the body of a man as a kind of machine equipped with and made up of bones, nerves, muscles, veins, blood and skin in such a way that, even if there were no mind in it, it would still perform all the same movements as it now does in those cases where movement is not under the control of the will or, consequently, of the mind. I can easily see that if such a body suffers from dropsy, for example, and is affected by the dryness of the throat which normally produces in the mind the sensation of thirst, the resulting condition of the nerves and other parts will dispose the body to take a drink, with the result that the disease will be aggravated. Yet this is just as natural as the body's being stimulated by a similar dryness of the throat to take a drink when there is no such illness and the drink is beneficial. Admittedly, when I consider the purpose of the clock, I may say that it is departing from its nature when it does not tell the right time; and similarly when I consider the mechanism of the human body, I may think that, in relation to the movements which normally occur in it, it too is deviating from its nature if the throat is dry at a time when drinking is not beneficial to its continued health. But I am well aware that 'nature' as I have just used it has a very different significance from 'nature' in the other sense. As I have just used it, 'nature' is simply a label which depends on my thought; it is quite extraneous to the things to which it is applied, and depends simply on my comparison between the idea of a sick man and a badly-made clock, and the idea of a healthy man and a well-made clock. But by 'nature' in the other sense I understand something which is really to be found in the things themselves; in this sense, therefore, the term contains something of the truth.

When we say, then, with respect to the body suffering from dropsy, that it has a disordered nature because it has a dry throat and yet does not need drink, the term 'nature' is here used merely as an extraneous label. However, with respect to the composite, that is, the mind united with this body, what is involved is not a mere label, but a true error of nature, namely that it is thirsty at a time when drink is going to cause it harm. It thus remains to inquire how it is that the goodness of God does not prevent nature, in this sense, from deceiving us.

The first observation I make at this point is that there is a great difference between the mind and the body, inasmuch as the body is by its very nature always divisible, while the mind is utterly indivisible. For when I consider the mind, or myself in so far as I am merely a thinking thing, I am unable to distinguish any parts within myself; I understand myself to be something quite single and complete. Although the whole mind seems to be united to the whole body, I recognize that if a foot or arm or any other part of the body is cut off, nothing has thereby been taken away from the mind. As for the faculties of willing, of understanding, of sensory perception and so on, these cannot be termed parts of the mind, since it is one and the same mind that wills, and understands and has sensory perceptions. By contrast, there is no corporeal or extended thing that I can think of which in my thought I cannot easily divide into parts; and this very fact makes me understand that it is divisible. This one argument would be enough to show me that the mind is completely different from the body, even if I did not already know as much from other considerations.

My next observation is that the mind is not immediately affected by all parts of the body, but only by the brain, or perhaps just by one small part of the brain, namely the part which is said to contain the 'common' sense. Every time this part of the brain is in a given state, it presents the same signals to the mind, even though the other parts of the body may be in a different condition at the time. This is established by countless observations, which there is no need to review here.

I observe, in addition, that the nature of the body is such that whenever any part of it is moved by another part which is some distance away, it can always be moved in the same fashion by any of the parts which lie in between, even if the more distant part does nothing. For example, in a cord ABCD, if one end D is pulled so that the other end A moves, the exact same movement could have been brought about if one of the intermediate points B or C had been pulled, and D had not moved at all. In similar fashion, when I feel a pain in my foot, physiology tells me that this happens by means of nerves distributed throughout the foot, and that these nerves are like cords which go from the foot right up to the brain. When the nerves are pulled in the foot, they in turn pull on inner parts of the brain to which they are attached, and produce a certain motion in them; and nature has laid it down that this motion should produce in the mind a sensation of pain, as occurring in the foot. But since these nerves, in passing from the foot to the brain, must pass through the calf, the thigh, the lumbar region, the back and the neck, it can happen that, even if it is not the part in the foot but one of the intermediate parts which is being pulled, the same motion will occur in the brain as occurs when the foot is hurt, and so it will necessarily come about that the mind feels the same sensation of pain. And we must suppose the same thing happens with regard to any other sensation.

My final observation is that any given movement occurring in the part of the brain that immediately affects the mind produces just one corresponding sensation; and hence the best system that could be devised is that it should produce the one sensation which, of all possible sensations, is most especially and most frequently conducive to the preservation of the healthy man. And experience shows that the sensations which nature has given us are all of this kind; and so there is absolutely nothing to be found in them that does not bear witness to the power and goodness of God. For example, when the nerves in the foot are set in motion in a violent and unusual manner, this motion, by way of the spinal cord, reaches the inner parts of the brain, and there gives the mind

its signal for having a certain sensation, namely the sensation of a pain as occurring in the foot. This stimulates the mind to do its best to get rid of the cause of the pain, which it takes to be harmful to the foot. It is true that God could have made the nature of man such that this particular motion in the brain indicated something else to the mind; it might, for example, have made the mind aware of the actual motion occurring in the brain, or in the foot, or in any of the intermediate regions; or it might have indicated something else entirely. But there is nothing else which would have been so conducive to the continued well-being of the body. In the same way, when we need drink, there arises a certain dryness in the throat; this sets in motion the nerves of the throat, which in turn move the inner parts of the brain. This motion produces in the mind a sensation of thirst, because the most useful thing for us to know about the whole business is that we need drink in order to stay healthy. And so it is in the other cases.

It is quite clear from all this that, notwithstanding the immense goodness of God, the nature of man as a combination of mind and body is such that it is bound to mislead him from time to time. For there may be some occurrence, not in the foot but in one of the other areas through which the nerves travel in their route from the foot to the brain, or even in the brain itself; and if this cause produces the same motion which is generally produced by injury to the foot, then pain will be felt as if it were in the foot. This deception of the senses is natural, because a given motion in the brain must always produce the same sensation in the mind; and the origin of the motion in question is much more often going to be something which is hurting the foot, rather than something existing elsewhere. So it is reasonable that this motion should always indicate to the mind a pain in the foot rather than in any other part of the body. Again, dryness of the throat may sometimes arise not, as it normally does, from the fact that a drink is necessary to the health of the body, but from some quite opposite cause, as happens in the case of the man with dropsy. Yet it is much better that it should mislead on this occasion than that it should always mislead when the body is in good health. And the same goes for the other cases.

This consideration is the greatest help to me, not only for noticing all the errors to which my nature is liable, but also for enabling me to correct or avoid them without difficulty. For I know that in matters regarding the well-being of the body, all my senses report the truth much more frequently than not. Also, I can almost always make use of more than one sense to investigate the same thing; and in addition, I can use both my memory, which connects present experiences with preceding ones, and my intellect, which has by now examined all the causes of error. Accordingly, I should not have any further fears about the falsity of what my senses tell me every day; on the contrary, the exaggerated doubts of the last few days should be dismissed as laughable. This applies especially to the principle reason for doubt, namely my inability to distinguish between being asleep and being awake. For I now notice that there is a vast difference between the two, in that dreams are never linked by memory with all the other actions of life as waking experiences are. If, while I am awake, anyone were suddenly to appear to me and then

disappear immediately, as happens in sleep, so that I could not see where he had come from or where he had gone to, it would not be unreasonable for me to judge that he was a ghost, or a vision created in my brain, rather than a real man. But when I distinctly see where things come from and where and when they come to me, and when I can connect my perceptions of them with the whole of the rest of my life without a break, then I am quite certain that when I encounter these things I am not asleep but awake. And I ought not to have even the slightest doubt of their reality if, after calling upon all the senses as well as my memory and my intellect in order to check them, I receive no conflicting reports from any of these sources. For from the fact that God is not a deceiver it follows that in cases like these I am completely free from error. But since the pressure of things to be done does not always allow us to stop and make such a meticulous check, it must be admitted that in this human life we are often liable to make mistakes about particular things, and we must acknowledge the weakness of our nature.

REVIEW QUESTIONS

1. What caused Descartes to begin the process of doubting everything?
2. Why does Descartes doubt his senses?
3. Why does he posit the idea of an evil genius who always deceives him?
4. What is the first thing that Descartes comes to know with certainty?
5. What are Descartes' arguments for the existence of God? What part does God play in Descartes' theory of knowledge?

15

THOMAS HOBBES

Thomas Hobbes (1588–1679) is the greatest English political philosopher, who gave classic expression to the idea that morality and politics arise out of a social contract. He was born on Good Friday, April 5, 1588, in Westbury, England, the son of an eccentric vicar. On the day of his birth, the Spanish Armada, the greatest naval fleet the world had seen up to that time, was spotted off the coast of southern England. The chronicler John Aubrey reports that Hobbes's mother, only seven months pregnant, startled by the news, fell into labor with Hobbes and delivered him. Hobbes wrote of this experience, "Unbeknownst to my mother at that time she gave birth to twins, myself and fear. And fear has been my constant companion throughout life." Hobbes's lifetime was filled with the dangers of war, the invading Spanish Armada, the religious wars of Europe, the Civil War in England. His political philosophy may be read as a cure against the fear and insecurity of people desperately in need of peace and tranquility.

Hobbes was educated at Oxford University and lived through an era of political revolutions as a scholar and tutor (he was tutor to Charles II of England). He was widely traveled and was in communication with most of the intellectual luminaries of his day, both on the Continent (Galileo, Gassendi, and Descartes) and in England (Francis Bacon, Ben Johnson, and William Harvey), and was regarded as a brilliant, if somewhat unorthodox and controversial, intellectual.

Hobbes is known today primarily for his masterpiece in political theory, *Leviathan* (1651), a book written during the English civil wars (1642–1646), sometimes referred to as "The Great Rebellion," which pitted the forces of monarchy (the Royalists) under Charles I against those of Parliament under Oliver Cromwell. Hobbes's work was intended to support the Royalists, because he believed that the monarchy was the best guarantee for an orderly and stable government. Yet the Royalists misconstrued his interpretation as supporting the rebels, no doubt because Hobbes rejected the usual grounds for the monarchy, the divine right of kings. For this reason, and because the book conveyed a materialist view of human nature, thought to be dangerous to religion, it was suppressed or violently attacked throughout Hobbes's lifetime.

What are the doctrines that his contemporaries found so controversial? First of all, Hobbes breaks from the medieval notion that the state is a natural organism, based on natural devotion and interdependence. He develops a moral and political theory based not on natural affection, but on psychological egoism. Hobbes argues that people are all egoists who always act in their own self-interest, to obtain gratification and avoid harm. However, we cannot obtain any of the basic goods because of the inherent fear of harm and death, the insecurity in an unregulated "state of nature," in which life is "solitary, poor, nasty, brutish and short." We cannot relax our guard, for everyone is constantly in fear of everyone else. In this state of anarchy the prudent person concludes that it really is in all our self-interest to make a contract to keep to a minimal morality of respecting human life, keeping covenants made, and obeying the laws of the society. This minimal morality, which Hobbes refers to as "The Laws of Nature," is nothing more than a set of maxims of prudence. In order to ensure that we all obey this covenant Hobbes proposes a strong sovereign or "Leviathan" to impose severe penalties on those who disobey the laws, for "covenants without sword are but words." The term "Leviathan" refers to the sea monster (or whale) referred to in the Book of Job:

> Let those curse the day who are skilled to rouse up Leviathan (3:8).
> Can you draw out Leviathan with a fishhook or press down his tongue with a cord?
> Can you put a rope in his nose or pierce his jaw with a hook?
> Will he make a covenant with you to take him for your servant for ever?
> His sneezings flash forth light, and his eyes are like the eyelids of the dawn.
> Out of his mouth go flaming torches; sparks of fire leap forth.
> Out of his nostrils comes forth smoke, as from a boiling pot and burning rushes.
> His breath kindles coals, and flame comes forth from his mouth.
> When he raises himself up the mighty are afraid; at the crashing they are beside themselves.
> Upon earth there is not his like, a creature without fear.
> He beholds everything that is high; he is king over all the sons of pride (Job 41).

The state is the great Leviathan, awesome and powerful, inspiring fear, but offering protection from violence and harm. We begin with Hobbes's discussion of human nature in Part I of *Leviathan* and move on through Part II on the Commonwealth.

FOR FURTHER READING

Gauthier, David. *The Logic of Leviathan: The Moral and Political Thought of Thomas Hobbes* (Clarendon Press, 1969)

Hampton, Jean. *Hobbes and the Social Contract* (Cambridge University Press, 1986).

Hobbes, Thomas. *Leviathan* (Penguin, 1986). Introduction by C. B. MacPherson. A useful introduction together with an inexpensive edition.

Kavka, Gregory. *Hobbesian Moral and Political Theory* (Princeton University Press, 1986). An advanced, thorough work.

Oakshott, Michael. *Hobbes on Civil Association* (University of California Press, 1975).

Peters, Richard. *Hobbes* (Penguin, 1956). A clear exposition of Hobbes's ideas.

Rogers, G. A. J., and Alan Ryan, eds. *Perspectives on Thomas Hobbes* (Oxford University Press, 1989).

Turnbull, Colin. *The Mountain People* (Simon & Schuster, 1972). A poignant account of a displaced people in northern Uganda whose social conditions reflect a Hobbesian state of nature.

Wolin, Sheldon S. *Politics and Vision* (Little, Brown, 1960). A perceptive history of Western political thought with a good chapter on Hobbes.

LEVIATHAN OR THE MATTER, FORM, & POWER OF A COMMONWEALTH ECCLESIASTICAL AND CIVIL

PART 1. OF MAN

CHAPTER 1. OF SENSE

Concerning the thoughts of man, I will consider them first singly, and afterwards in train, or dependence upon one another. Singly, they are every one a representation or appearance, of some quality, or other accident of a body without us; which is commonly called an object. Which object works on the eyes, ears, and other parts of a man's body; and by diversity of working, produces diversity of appearances.

The original of them all, is that which we call SENSE; (For there is no conception in a man's mind, which hath not at first, totally, or by parts, been begotten upon the organs of sense.) The rest are derived from that original.

To know the natural cause of sense, is not very necessary to the business now in hand; and I have elsewhere written of the same at large. Nevertheless, to fill each part of my present method, I will briefly deliver the same in this place.

The cause of sense, is the external body, or object, which presses the organ proper to each sense, either immediately, as in the taste and touch; or mediately, as in seeing, hearing, and smelling: which pressure, by the mediation of nerves, and other strings and membranes of the body, continued inwards to the brain and heart, causes there a resistance, or counter-pressure, or endeavour of the heart, to deliver it self: which endeavour, because outward, seems to be some matter without. And this seeming, or, fancy, is that which men call sense; and consists, as to the eye, in a light, or colour figured; to the ear, in a sound; to the nostril, in an odour; to the tongue and palate, in a savour; and to the rest of the body, in heat, cold, hardness, softness, and such other qualities as we discern by feeling. All which qualities called sensible, are in the object, that causes them, but so many several motions of the matter, by which it presses our organs diversely. Neither in us that are pressed, are they any thing else, but divers motions (for motion produces nothing but motion). But their appearance to us is fancy, the same waking, that dreaming. And as pressing, rubbing, or striking the eye, makes us fancy a light; and pressing the ear, produces a din; so do the bodies also we see, or hear, produce the same by their strong, though unobserved action. For if those colours and sounds were in the bodies, or objects that cause them, they could not be severed from them, as by glasses, and in echoes by reflection, we see they are; where we know the thing we see, is in one place; the appearance in another. And though at some certain distance, the real and very object seem invested with the fancy it begets in us; yet still the object is one thing, the image or fancy is another. So that sense in all cases, is nothing else but original fancy, caused (as I have said) by the pressure, that is, by the motion, of external things upon our eyes, ears, and other organs thereunto ordained.

But the philosophy-schools, through all the universities of Christendom, grounded upon certain texts of Aristotle, teach another doctrine; and say, for the cause of vision, that the thing seen, sends forth on every side a visible species (in English) a visible show, apparition, or aspect, or a being seen; the receiving whereof into the eye, is seeing. And for the cause of hearing, that the thing heard, sends forth an audible species, that is, an audible aspect, or audible being seen; which entering at the ear, maketh hearing. Nay for the cause of understanding also, they say the thing understood, sends forth intelligible species, that is, an intelligible being seen; which coming into the understanding, makes us understand. I say not this, as disapproving the use of universities: but because I am to speak hereafter of their office in a commonwealth, I must let you see on all occasions by the way, what things would be amended in them; amongst which the frequency of insignificant speech is one.

CHAPTER 2. OF IMAGINATION

That when a thing lies still, unless somewhat else stir it, it will lie still for ever, is a truth that no man doubts of. But that when a thing is in motion, it will eternally be in motion, unless somewhat else stay it, though the reason be the same (namely, that nothing can change it self) is not so easily assented to. For men measure, not only other men, but all other things, by themselves: and because they find themselves subject after motion to pain, and lassitude, think every thing else grows weary of motion, and seeks repose of its own accord; little considering, whether it be not some other motion, wherein that desire of rest they find in themselves, consists. From hence it is, that the schools say, heavy bodies fall downwards, out of an appetite to rest, and to conserve their nature in that place which is most proper for them; ascribing appetite and knowledge of what is good for their conservation (which is more than man has) to things inanimate, absurdly.

When a body is once in motion, it moves (unless something else hinder it) eternally; and whatsoever hinders it, cannot in an instant, but in time, and by degrees quite extinguish it: And as we see in the water, though the wind cease, the waves give not over rolling for a long time after; so also it happens in that motion, which is made in the internal parts of a man, then, when he sees, dreams &c. For after the object is removed, or the eye shut, we still retain an image of the thing seen, though more obscure then when we see it. And this is it, the Latins call imagination, from the image made in seeing; and apply the same, though improperly, to all the other senses. But the Greeks call it fancy; which signifies appearance, and is as proper to one sense, as to another. IMAGINATION therefore is nothing but decaying sense; and is found in men, and many other living creatures, as well sleeping, as waking.

The decay of sense in men waking, is not the decay of the motion made in sense; but an obscuring of it, in such manner as the light of the sun obscures the light of the stars; which stars do no less exercise their virtue, by which they are visible, in the day, than in the night. But because amongst many strokes, which our eyes, ears, and other organs receive from external bodies, the predominant only is sensible; therefore the light of the sun being predominant, we are not affected with the action of the stars. And any object being removed from our eyes, though the impression it made in us remain; yet other objects more present succeeding, and working on us, the imagination of the past is obscured, and made weak, as the voice of a man is in the noise of the day. From whence it followeth, that the longer the time is, after the sight or sense of any object, the weaker is the imagination. For the continual change of man's body destroys in time the parts which in sense were moved: so that distance of time, and of place, hath one and the same effect in us. For as at a great distance of place, that which we look at appears dim, and without distinction of the smaller parts; and as voices grow weak, and inarticulate; so also, after great distance of time, our imagination of the past is weak; and we lose (for example) of cities we have seen, many particular streets, and of actions, many particular circumstances. This decaying sense, when we would express the thing it self (I mean fancy it self), we call imagination, as I said before; but when we would express the decay, and signify that the sense is fading, old, and past, it is called memory. So that imagination and memory are but one thing, which for divers considerations hath divers names.

Much memory, or memory of many things, is called experience. Again, imagination being only of those things which have been formerly perceived by sense, either all at once, or by parts at several times; the former (which is the imagining the whole object, as it was presented to the sense) is simple imagination; as when one imagines a man, or horse, which he hath seen before. The other is compounded; as when from the sight of a man at one time, and of a horse at another, we conceive in our mind a Centaur. So when a man compounds the image of his own person, with the image of the actions of another man; as when a man imagines himself a Hercules or an Alexander (which happens often to them that are much taken with reading of romances) it is a compound imagination, and properly but a fiction of the mind. There be also other imaginations that rise in men (though waking) from the great impression made in sense: as from gazing upon the sun, the impression leaves an image of the sun before our eyes a long time after; and from being long and vehemently attent upon geometrical figures, a man shall in the dark (though awake) have the images of lines and angles before his eyes: which kind of fancy hath no particular name; as being a thing that doth not commonly fall into men's discourse.

The imaginations of them that sleep are those we call dreams. And these also (as all other imaginations) have been before, either totally or by parcels in the sense. And because in sense, the brain and nerves, which are the necessary organs of sense, are so benumbed in sleep, as not easily to be moved by the action of external objects, there can happen in sleep no imagination; and therefore no dream, but what proceeds from the agitation of the inward parts of man's body; which inward parts, for the connexion they have with the brain, and other organs, when they be distempered, do keep the same in motion; whereby the imaginations there formerly made, appear as if a man were waking; saving that the organs of sense being now benumbed, so as there is no new object, which can master and obscure them with a more vigorous impression, a dream must needs be more clear, in this silence of sense, than are our a waking thoughts. And hence it comes to pass, that it is a hard matter, and by many thought impossible to distinguish exactly between sense and dreaming. For my part, when I consider that in dreams, I do not often, nor constantly think of the same persons, places, objects, and actions that I do waking; nor remember so long a train of coherent thoughts, dreaming, as at other times; and because waking I often observe the absurdity of dreams, but never dream of the absurdities of my waking thoughts; I am well satisfied, that being awake, I know I dream not; though when I dream I think myself awake.

And seeing dreams are caused by the distemper of some of the inward parts of the body; divers distempers must needs cause different dreams. And

hence it is, that lying cold breeds dreams of fear, and raises the thought and image of some fearful object (the motion from the brain to the inner parts, and from the inner parts to the brain being reciprocal;) and that as anger causes heat in some parts of the body, when we are awake; so when we sleep the over heating of the same parts causes anger, and raiseth up in the brain the imagination of an enemy. In the same manner, as natural kindness, when we are awake, causes desire; and desire makes heat in certain other parts of the body; so also, too much heat in those parts, while we sleep, raiseth in the brain an imagination of some kindness shown. In sum, our dreams are the reverse of our waking imaginations; the motion when we are awake, beginning at one end; and when we dream, at another.

The most difficult discerning of a man's dream, from his waking thoughts, is then, when by some accident we observe not that we have slept: which is easy to happen to a man full of fearful thoughts; and whose conscience is much troubled; and that sleeps, without the circumstances, of going to bed, or putting off his clothes, as one that noddeth in a chair. For he that taketh pains, and industriously lays himself to sleep, in case any uncouth and exorbitant fancy come unto him, cannot easily think it other than a dream. We read of Marcus Brutus (one that had his life given him by Julius Caesar, and was also his favourite, and notwithstanding murdered him), how at Philippi, the night before he gave battle to Augustus Caesar, he saw a fearful apparition, which is commonly related by historians as a vision; but considering the circumstances, one may easily judge to have been but a short dream. For sitting in his tent, pensive and troubled with the horror of his rash act, it was not hard for him, slumbering in the cold, to dream of that which most affrighted him; which fear, as by degrees it made him wake; so also it must needs make the apparition by degrees to vanish; and having no assurance that he slept, he could have no cause to think it a dream, or any thing but a vision. And this is no very rare accident; for even they that be perfectly awake, if they be timorous, and superstitious, possessed with fearful tales, and alone in the dark, are subject to the like fancies; and believe they see spirits and dead men's ghosts walking in churchyards; whereas it is either their fancy only, or else the knavery of such persons, as make use of such superstitious fear, to pass disguised in the night, to places they would not be known to haunt.

From this ignorance of how to distinguish dreams, and other strong fancies, from vision and sense, did arise the greatest part of the religion of the Gentiles in time past, that worshipped satyrs, fawns, nymphs, and the like; and now-a-days the opinion that rude people have of fairies, ghosts, and goblins, and of the power of witches. For as for witches, I think not that their witchcraft is any real power; but yet that they are justly punished, for the false belief they have, that they can do such mischief, joined with their purpose to do it if they can: their trade being nearer to a new religion than to a craft or science. And for fairies, and walking ghosts, the opinion of them has I think been on purpose, either taught, or not confuted, to keep in credit the use of exorcism, of crosses, of holy water, and other such inventions of ghostly men. Nevertheless, there is no doubt, but God can make unnatural apparitions: But that he does it so often, as men need to fear such things, more than they fear the stay, or change, of the course of nature, which he also can stay, and change, is no point of Christian faith. But evil men under pretext that God can do any thing, are so bold as to say any thing when it serves their turn, though they think it untrue; it is the part of a wise man, to believe them no further, than right reason makes that which they say, appear credible. If this superstitious fear of spirits were taken away, and with it, prognostics from dreams, false prophecies, and many other things depending thereon, by which, crafty ambitious persons abuse the simple people, men would be much more fitted than they are for civil obedience.

And this ought to be the work of the schools: but they rather nourish such doctrine. For (not knowing what imagination, or the senses are), what they receive, they teach: some saying, that imaginations rise of themselves, and have no cause; others, that they rise most commonly from the will; and that good thoughts are blown (inspired) into a man by God, and evil thoughts by the Devil; or that good thoughts are poured (infused) into a man by God, and evil ones by the Devil. Some say the senses receive the species of things, and deliver them to the common sense; and the common sense delivers them over to the fancy, and the fancy to the memory, and the memory to the judgment, like handing of things from one to another, with many words making nothing understood.

The imagination that is raised in man (or any other creature endowed with the faculty of imagining) by words, or other voluntary signs, is that we generally call understanding; and is common to man and beast. For a dog by custom will understand the call, or the rating of his master; and so will many other beasts. That understanding which is peculiar to man, is the understanding not only his will, but his conceptions and thoughts, by the sequel and contexture of the names of things into affirmations, negations, and other forms of speech; and of this kind of understanding I shall speak hereafter.

CHAPTER 3. OF THE CONSEQUENCE OR TRAIN OF IMAGINATIONS

By Consequence, or train of thoughts, I understand that succession of one thought to another, which is called (to distinguish it from discourse in words) mental discourse.

When a man thinks on any thing whatsoever, his next thought after, is not altogether so casual as it seems to be. Not every thought to every thought succeeds indifferently. But as we have no imagination, whereof we have not formerly had sense, in whole, or in parts; so we have no transition from one imagination to another, whereof we never had the like before in our senses. The reason whereof is this. All fancies are motions within us, relics of those made in the sense: and those motions that immediately succeeded one another in the sense, continue also together after sense: insomuch as the former coming again to take place, and be predominant, the latter followeth, by coherence of the matter moved, in such manner, as water upon a plain table is drawn which way any one part of it is guided by the finger. But because in sense, to one and the same thing perceived, sometimes one thing, sometimes another succeeds, it comes to pass in time, that in the imagining of any thing, there is no certainty what we shall imagine next; only this is certain, it shall be something that succeeded the same before, at one time or another.

This train of thoughts, or mental discourse, is of two sorts. The first is unguided, without design, and inconstant; wherein there is no passionate thought, to govern and direct those that follow, to it self, as the end and scope of some desire, or other passion: in which case the thoughts are said to wander, and seem impertinent one to another, as in a dream. Such are commonly the thoughts of men, that are not only without company, but also without care of any thing; though even then their thoughts are as busy as at other times, but without harmony; as the sound which a lute out of tune would yield to any man; or in tune, to one that could not play. And yet in this wild ranging of the mind, a man may oft-times perceive the way of it, and the dependance of one thought upon another. For in a discourse of our present civil war, what could seem more impertinent, than to ask (as one did) what was the value of a Roman penny? Yet the coherence to me was manifest enough. For the thought of the war, introduced the thought of the delivering up the king to his enemies; the thought of that, brought in the thought of the delivering up of Christ; and that again the thought of the 30 pence, which was the price of that treason; and thence easily followed that malicious question, and all this in a moment of time; for thought is quick.

The second is more constant; as being regulated by some desire, and design. For the impression made by such things as we desire, or fear, is strong, and permanent, or (if it cease for a time), of quick return: so strong it is sometimes, as to hinder and break our sleep. From desire, arises the thought of some means we have seen produce the like of that which we aim at; and from the thought of that, the thought of means to that mean; and so continually, till we come to some beginning within our own power. And because the end, by the greatness of the impression, comes often to mind, in case our thoughts begin to wander, they are quickly again reduced into the way: which observed by one of the seven wise men, made him give men this precept, which is now worn out, *Respice finem*; that is to say, in all your actions, look often upon what you would have, as the thing that directs all your thoughts in the way to attain it.

The train of regulated thoughts is of two kinds; one, when of an effect imagined, we seek the causes, or means that produce it: and this is common to man and beast. The other is, when imagining any thing whatsoever, we seek all the possible effects, that can by it be produced; that is to say, we imagine what we can do with it, when we have it. Of which I have not at any time seen any sign, but in man only; for this is a curiosity hardly incident to the nature of any living creature that has no other passion but sensual, such as are hunger, thirst, lust, and anger. In sum, the discourse of the mind, when it is governed by design, is nothing but seeking, or the faculty of invention, which the Latins called *sagacitas*, and *solertia*; a hunting out of the causes, of some effect, present or past; or of the effects, of some present or past cause. Sometimes a man seeks what he hath lost; and from that place, and time, wherein he misses it, his mind runs back, from place to place, and time to time, to find where, and when he had it; that is to say, to find some certain, and limited time and place, in which to begin a method of seeking. Again, from thence, his thoughts run over the same places and times, to find what action, or other occasion might make him lose it. This we call remembrance, or calling to mind: the Latins call it *reminiscentia*, as it were a re-conning of our former actions.

Sometimes a man knows a place determinate, within the compass whereof he is to seek; and then his thoughts run over all the parts thereof, in the same manner as one would sweep a room, to find a jewel; or as a spaniel ranges the field, till he find a scent; or as a man should run over the alphabet, to start a rhyme.

Sometimes a man desires to know the event of an action; and then he thinks of some like action past, and the events thereof one after another; supposing like events will follow like actions. As he that foresees what will become of a criminal, reckons what he has seen follow on the like crime before; having this order of thoughts, the crime, the officer, the prison, the judge, and the gallows. Which kind of thoughts, is called foresight, and prudence, or providence; and sometimes wisdom; though such conjecture, through the difficulty of observing all circumstances, be very fallacious. But this is certain; by how much one man has more experience of things past, than another; by so much also he is more prudent, and his expectations the seldomer fail him. The present only has a being in nature; things past have a being in the memory only, but things to come have no being at all; the future being but a fiction of the mind, applying the sequels of actions past, to the actions that are present; which with most certainty is done by him that has most experience; but not with certainty enough. And though it be called prudence, when the event answers our expectation; yet in its own nature, it is but presumption. For the foresight of things to come, which is providence, belongs only to him by whose will they are to come. From him only, and supernaturally, proceeds prophecy. The best prophet naturally is the best guesser; and the best guesser, he that is most versed and studied in the matters he guesses at: for he hath most signs to guess by. . . .

CHAPTER 6. OF THE INTERIOR BEGINNINGS OF VOLUNTARY MOTIONS; COMMONLY CALLED THE PASSIONS; AND THE SPEECHES BY WHICH THEY ARE EXPRESSED

There be in animals, two sorts of motions peculiar to them: one called vital; begun in generation, and continued without interruption through their whole life; such as are the course of the blood, the pulse, the breathing, the concoction, nutrition, excretion, &c; to which motions there needs no help of imagination: the other is animal motion, otherwise called voluntary motion; as to go, to speak, to move any of our limbs, in such manner as is first fancied in our minds. That sense is motion in the organs and interior parts of man's body, caused by the action of the things we see, hear, &c.; and that fancy is but the relics of the same motion, remaining after sense, has been already said in the first and second chapters. And because going, speaking, and the like voluntary motions, depend always upon a precedent thought of whither, which way, and what; it is evident, that the imagination is the first internal beginning of all voluntary motion. And although unstudied men do not conceive any motion at all to be there, where the thing moved is invisible; or the space it is moved in, is (for the shortness of it) insensible; yet that doth not hinder, but that such motions are. For let a space be never so little, that which is moved over a greater space, whereof that little one is part, must first be moved over that. These small beginnings of motion,

within the body of man, before they appear in walking, speaking, striking, and other visible actions, are commonly called ENDEAVOR.

This endeavor, when it is toward something which causes it, is called APPETITE, or DESIRE; the latter, being the general name; and the other, oftentimes restrained to signify the desire of food, namely hunger and thirst. And when the endeavor is fromward something, it is generally called AVERSION. These words, appetite and aversion, we have from the Latins; and they both of them signify the motions, one of approaching, the other of retiring. So also do the Greek words for the same, which are [orme] and [aphorme]. For nature itself does often press upon men those truths, which afterwards, when they look for somewhat beyond nature, they stumble at. For the Schools find in mere appetite to go, or move, no actual motion at all: but because some motion they must acknowledge, they call it metaphorical motion; which is but an absurd speech: for though words may be called metaphorical; bodies and motions cannot.

That which men desire, they are also said to LOVE: and to HATE those things for which they have aversion. So that desire and love are the same thing; save that by desire, we always signify the absence of the object; by love, most commonly the presence of the same. So also by aversion, we signify the absence; and by hate, the presence of the object.

Of appetites and aversions, some are born with men; as appetite of food, appetite of excretion, and exoneration (which may also and more properly be called aversions, from somewhat they feel in their bodies); and some other appetites, not many. The rest, which are appetites of particular things, proceed from experience, and trial of their effects upon themselves or other men. For of things we know not at all, or believe not to be, we can have no further desire, than to taste and try. But aversion we have for things, not only which we know have hurt us, but also that we do not know whether they will hurt us, or not.

Those things which we neither desire, nor hate, we are said to contemn; CONTEMPT being nothing else but an immobility, or contumacy of the heart, in resisting the action of certain things; and proceeding from that the heart is already moved otherwise, by other more potent objects; or from want of experience of them.

And because the constitution of a man's body is in continual mutation, it is impossible that all the same things should always cause in him the same appetites, and aversions: much less can all men consent, in the desire of almost any one and the same object.

But whatsoever is the object of any man's appetite or desire, that is it which he for his part calls good: and the object of his hate and aversion, evil; and of his contempt, vile and inconsiderable. For these words of good, evil, and contemptible, are ever used with relation to the person that uses them: there being nothing simply and absolutely so; nor any common rule of good and evil, to be taken from the nature of the objects themselves; but from the person of the man (where there is no commonwealth); or (in a commonwealth) from the person that represents it; or from an arbitrator or judge, whom men disagreeing shall by consent set up, and make his sentence the rule thereof.

The Latin tongue has two words, whose significations approach to those of good and evil; but are not precisely the same; and those are pulchrum and turpe. Whereof the former signifies that, which by some apparent signs promises good; and the latter, that which promises evil. But in our tongue we have not so general names to express them by. But for pulchrum we say in some things, fair; in others, beautiful, or handsome, or gallant, or honorable, or comely, or amiable; and for turpe, foul, deformed, ugly, base, nauseous, and the like, as the subject shall require; all which words, in their proper places, signify nothing else but the mien, or countenance, that promises good and evil. So that of good there be three kinds; good in the promise, that is pulchrum; good in effect, as the end desired, which is called jucundum, delightful; and good as the means, which is called utile, profitable; and as many of evil: for evil in promise, is that they call turpe; evil in effect, and end, is molestum, unpleasant, troublesome; and evil in the means, inutile, unprofitable, hurtful.

As, in sense, that which is really within us, is, (as I have said before,) only motion, caused by the action of external objects, but in appearance; to the

sight, light and colour; to the ear, sound; to the nostril, odor, &c.: so, when the action of the same object is continued from the eyes, ears, and other organs to the heart, the real effect there is nothing but motion, or endeavor; which consists in appetite, or aversion, to or from the object moving. But the appearance, or sense of that motion, is that we either call delight, or trouble of mind.

This motion, which is called appetite, and for the appearance of it delight, and pleasure, seems to be a corroboration of vital motion, and a help thereunto; and therefore such things as caused delight, were not improperly called jucunda, from helping or fortifying; and the contrary, molesta, offensive, from hindering, and troubling the motion vital.

Pleasure therefore (or delight), is the appearance, or sense of good; and molestation or displeasure, the appearance, or sense of evil. And consequently all appetite, desire, and love, is accompanied with some delight more or less; and all hatred and aversion, with more or less displeasure and offence.

Of pleasures or delights, some arise from the sense of an object present; and those may be called pleasures of sense (the word sensual, as it is used by those only that condemn them, having no place till there be laws). Of this kind are all onerations and exonerations of the body; as also all that is pleasant, in the sight, hearing, smell, taste, or touch. Others arise from the expectation, that proceeds from foresight of the end, or consequence of things; whether those things in the sense please or displease. And these are pleasures of the mind of him that draws those consequences, and are generally called JOY. In the like manner, displeasures are some in the sense, and called PAIN; others in the expectation of consequences, and are called GRIEF.

These simple passions called appetite, desire, love, aversion, hate, joy, and grief, have their names for divers considerations diversified. As first, when they one succeed another, they are diversely called from the opinion men have of the likelihood of attaining what they desire. Secondly, from the object loved or hated. Thirdly, from the consideration of many of them together. Fourthly, from the alteration or succession it self.

For appetite, with an opinion of attaining, is called HOPE.

The same, without such opinion, DESPAIR.

Aversion, with opinion of hurt from the object, FEAR.

The same, with hope of avoiding that hurt by resistance, COURAGE.

Sudden courage, ANGER.

Constant hope, CONFIDENCE of ourselves.

Constant despair, DIFFIDENCE of ourselves.

Anger for great hurt done to another, when we conceive the same to be done by injury, INDIGNATION.

Desire of good to another, BENEVOLENCE, GOOD WILL, CHARITY. If to man generally, GOOD NATURE.

Desire of riches, COVETOUSNESS: a name used always in signification of blame; because men contending for them, are displeased with one another's attaining them; though the desire in itself, be to be blamed, or allowed, according to the means by which those riches are sought.

Desire of office, or precedence, AMBITION: a name used also in the worse sense, for the reason before mentioned.

Desire of things that conduce but a little to our ends, and fear of things that are but of little hindrance, PUSILLANIMITY.

Contempt of little helps and hindrances, MAGNANIMITY.

Magnanimity, in danger of death or wounds, VALOR, FORTITUDE.

Magnanimity, in the use of riches, LIBERALITY.

Pusillanimity, in the same, WRETCHEDNESS, MISERABLENESS, or PARSIMONY; as it is liked or disliked.

Love of persons for society, KINDNESS.

Love of persons for pleasing the sense only, NATURAL LUST.

Love of the same, acquired from rumination, that is, imagination of pleasure past, LUXURY.

Love of one singularly, with desire to be singularly beloved, THE PASSION OF LOVE. The same, with fear that the love is not mutual, JEALOUSY.

Desire, by doing hurt to another, to make him condemn some fact of his own, REVENGEFULNESS.

Desire to know why, and how, CURIOSITY; such as is in no living creature but man: so that man is distinguished, not only by his reason, but also by this singular passion from other animals; in whom the appetite of food, and other pleasures of sense, by predominance, take away the care of knowing causes; which is a lust of the mind, that by a perseverance of delight in the continual and indefatigable generation of knowledge, exceedeth the short vehemence of any carnal pleasure.

Fear of power invisible, feigned by the mind, or imagined from tales publicly allowed, RELIGION; not allowed, SUPERSTITION. And when the power imagined, is truly such as we imagine, TRUE RELIGION.

Fear, without the apprehension of why, or what, PANIC TERROR, called so from the fables, that make Pan the author of them; whereas in truth, there is always in him that so feareth, first, some apprehension of the cause, though the rest run away by example, every one supposing his fellow to know why. And there this passion happens to none but in a throng, or multitude of people.

Joy, from apprehension of novelty, ADMIRATION; proper to man, because it excites the appetite of knowing the cause.

Joy, arising from imagination of a man's own power and ability, is that exultation of the mind which is called GLORYING: which if grounded upon the experience of his own former actions, is the same with confidence: but if grounded on the flattery of others; or only supposed by himself, for delight in the consequences of it, is called VAINGLORY: which name is properly given; because a well grounded confidence begetteth attempt; whereas the supposing of power does not, and is therefore rightly called vain.

Grief, from opinion of want of power, is called DEJECTION of mind.

The vain-glory which consists in the feigning or supposing of abilities in ourselves, which we know are not, is most incident to young men, and nourished by the histories, or fictions of gallant persons; and is corrected oftentimes by age, and employment.

Sudden glory, is the passion which maketh those grimaces called LAUGHTER; and is caused either by some sudden act of their own, that pleases them; or by the apprehension of some deformed thing in another, by comparison whereof they suddenly applaud themselves. And it is incident most to them, that are conscious of the fewest abilities in themselves; who are forced to keep themselves in their own favour, by observing the imperfections of other men. And therefore much laughter at the defects of others, is a sign of pusillanimity. For of great minds, one of the proper works is, to help and free others from scorn; and compare themselves only with the most able.

On the contrary, sudden dejection, is the passion that causes WEEPING; and is caused by such accidents, as suddenly take away some vehement hope, or some prop of their power: and they are most subject to it, that rely principally on helps external, such as are women, and children. Therefore some weep for the loss of friends; others for their unkindness; others for the sudden stop made to their thoughts of revenge, by reconciliation. But in all cases, both laughter, and weeping, are sudden motions; custom taking them both away. For no man laughs at old jests; or weeps for an old calamity.

Grief, for the discovery of some defect of ability, is SHAME, or the passion that discovers itself in BLUSHING; and consists in the apprehension of some thing dishonorable; and in young men, is a sign of the love of good reputation, and commendable: in old men it is a sign of the same; but because it comes too late, not commendable.

The contempt of good reputation is called IMPUDENCE.

Grief, for the calamity of another, is PITY; and arises from the imagination that the like calamity may befall himself; and therefore is called also COMPASSION, and in the phrase of this present time a FELLOW-FEELING: and therefore for calamity arriving from great wickedness, the best men have the least pity; and for the same calamity, those have least pity, that think themselves least obnoxious to the same.

Contempt, or little sense of the calamity of others, is that which men call CRUELTY; proceeding from security of their own fortune. For, that any man should take pleasure in other men's great harms, without other end of his own, I do not conceive it possible.

Grief, for the success of a competitor in wealth, honour, or other good, if it be joined with endeavor to enforce our own abilities to equal or exceed him, is called EMULATION: but joined with endeavor to supplant, or hinder a competitor, ENVY.

When in the mind of man, appetites, and aversions, hopes, and fears, concerning one and the same thing, arise alternatively; and divers good and evil consequences of the doing, or omitting the thing propounded, come successively into our thoughts; so that sometimes we have an appetite to it; sometimes an aversion from it; sometimes hope to be able to do it; sometimes despair, or fear to attempt it; the whole sum of desires, aversions, hopes and fears continued till the thing be either done, or thought impossible, is that we call DELIBERATION.

Therefore of things past, there is no deliberation; because manifestly impossible to be changed: nor of things known to be impossible, or thought so; because men know, or think such deliberation vain. But of things impossible, which we think possible, we may deliberate; not knowing it is in vain. And it is called deliberation; because it is a putting an end to the liberty we had of doing, or omitting, according to our own appetite, or aversion.

This alternate succession of appetites, aversions, hopes and fears, is no less in other living creatures than in man: and therefore beasts also deliberate.

Early deliberation is then said to end, when that whereof they deliberate, is either done, or thought impossible; because till then we retain the liberty of doing, or omitting, according to our appetite, or aversion.

In deliberation, the last appetite, or aversion, immediately adhering to the action, or to the omission thereof, is that we call the WILL; the act (not the faculty) of willing. And beasts that have deliberation, must necessarily also have will. The definition of the will, given commonly by the Schools, that it is a rational appetite, is not good. For if it were, then could there be no voluntary act against reason. For a voluntary act is that, which proceeds from the will, and no other. But if instead of a rational appetite, we shall say an appetite resulting from a precedent deliberation, then the definition is the same that I have given here. Will therefore is the last appetite in deliberating. And though we say in common discourse, a man had a will once to do a thing, that nevertheless he forbore to do; yet that is properly but an inclination, which makes no action voluntary; because the action depends not of it, but of the last inclination, or appetite. For if the intervenient appetites, make any action voluntary; then by the same reason all intervenient aversions, should make the same action involuntary; and so one and the same action, should be both voluntary and involuntary.

By this it is manifest, that not only actions that have their beginning from covetousness, ambition, lust, or other appetites to the thing propounded; but also those that have their beginning from aversion, or fear of those consequences that follow the omission, are voluntary actions.

The forms of speech by which the passions are expressed, are partly the same, and partly different from those, by which we express our thoughts. And first, generally all passions may be expressed indicatively; as I love, I fear, I joy, I deliberate, I will, I command: but some of them have particular expressions by themselves, which nevertheless are not affirmations, unless it be when they serve to make other inferences, besides that of the passion they proceed from. Deliberation is expressed subjunctively; which is a speech proper to signify suppositions, with their consequences; as, if this be done, then this will follow; and differs not from the language of reasoning, save that reasoning is in general words; but deliberation for the most part is of particulars. The language of desire, and aversion, is imperative; as do this, forbear that; which when the party is obliged to do, or forbear, is command; otherwise prayer; or else counsel. The language of vain-glory, of indignation, pity and revengefulness, optative: but of the desire to know, there is a peculiar expression, called interrogative; as, what is it, when shall it, how is it done, and why so? other language of the passions I find none: for cursing, swearing, reviling, and the like, do not signify as speech; but as the actions of a tongue accustomed.

These forms of speech, I say, are expressions, or voluntary significations of our passions: but certain signs they be not; because they may be used arbitrarily, whether they that use them, have such passions or not. The best signs of passions present, are either in the countenance, motions of the body, actions, and ends, or aims, which we otherwise know the man to have.

And because in deliberation, the appetites, and aversions, are raised by foresight of the good and evil consequences, and sequels of the action whereof we deliberate; the good or evil effect thereof depends on the foresight of a long chain of consequences, of which very seldom any man is able to see to the end. But for so far as a man seeth, if the good in those consequences be greater than the evil, the whole chain is that which writers call apparent, or seeming good. And contrarily, when the evil exceeds the good, the whole is apparent, or seeming evil: so that he who hath by experience, or reason, the greatest and surest prospect of consequences, deliberates best himself; and is able when he will, to give the best counsel unto others.

Continual success in obtaining those things which a man from time to time desires, that is to say, continual prospering, is that men call FELICITY; I mean the felicity of this life. For there is no such thing as perpetual tranquillity of mind, while we live here; because life itself is but motion, and can never be without desire, nor without fear, no more than without sense. What kind of felicity God hath ordained to them that devoutly honour Him, a man shall no sooner know, than enjoy; being joys, that now are as incomprehensible, as the word of school-men beatifical vision is unintelligible.

The form of speech whereby men signify their opinion of the goodness of any thing, is PRAISE. That whereby they signify the power and greatness of any thing, is MAGNIFYING. And that whereby they signify the opinion they have of a man's felicity, is by the Greeks called for which we have no name in our tongue. And thus much is sufficient for the present purpose, to have been said of the PASSIONS.

CHAPTER 10. OF POWER, WORTH, DIGNITY, HONOUR, AND WORTHINESS

The power of a man (to take it universally) is his present means, to obtain some future apparent good; and is either original or instrumental.

Natural power, is the eminence of the faculties of body, or mind: as extraordinary strength, form, prudence, arts, eloquence, liberality, nobility. Instrumental are those powers, which acquired by these, or by fortune, are means and instruments to acquire more: as riches, reputation, friends, and the secret working of God, which men call good luck. For the nature of power, is in this point, like to fame, increasing as it proceeds; or like the motion of heavy bodies, which the further they go, make still the more haste.

The greatest of human powers, is that which is compounded of the powers of most men, united by consent, in one person, natural, or civil, that has the use of all their powers depending on his will; such as is the power of a common-wealth: or depending on the will of each particular; such as is the power of a faction or of divers factions leagued. Therefore to have servants, is power; to have friends, is power: for they are strengths united.

Also riches joined with liberality, is power; because it procureth friends, and servants: without liberality, not so; because in this case they defend not; but expose men to envy, as a prey.

Reputation of power, is power; because it draweth with it the adherence of those that need protection.

So is reputation of love of man's country (called popularity) for the same reason.

Also, what quality soever maketh a man beloved, or feared of many; or the reputation of such quality, is power; because it is a means to have the assistance, and service of many.

Good success is power; because it maketh reputation of wisdom, or good fortune; which makes men either fear him, or rely on him.

Affability of men already in power, is increase of power; because it gaineth love.

Reputation of prudence in the conduct of peace or war, is power; because to prudent men, we commit the government of ourselves, more willingly than to others.

Nobility is power, not in all places, but only in those commonwealths, where it has privileges: for in such privileges consists their power.

Eloquence is power, because it is seeming prudence.

Form is power; because being a promise of good, it recommendeth men to the favour of women and strangers.

The sciences, are small power; because not eminent; and therefore, not acknowledged in any man; nor are at all, but in a few, and in them, but of a few

things. For science is of that nature, as none can understand it to be, but such as in a good measure have attained it.

Arts of public use, as fortification, making of engines, and other instruments of war; because they confer to defence, and victory, are power: and though the true mother of them, be science, namely the mathematics; yet, because they are brought into the light, by the hand of the artificer, they be esteemed (the midwife passing with the vulgar for the mother) as his issue.

The value, or WORTH of a man, is as of all other things, his price; that is to say, so much as would be given for the use of his power: and therefore is not absolute; but a thing dependant on the need and judgment of another. An able conductor of soldiers, is of great price in time of war present, or imminent; but in peace not so. A learned and uncorrupt judge, is much worth in time of peace; but not so much in war. And as in other things, so in men, not the seller, but the buyer determines the price. For let a man (as most men do) rate themselves at the highest value they can; yet their true value is no more than it is esteemed by others.

The manifestation of the value we set on one another, is that which is commonly called honoring, and dishonoring. To value a man at a high rate, is to honour him; at a low rate, is to dishonor him. But high, and low, in this case, is to be understood by comparison to the rate that each man setteth on himself.

The public worth of a man, which is the value set on him by the commonwealth, is that which men commonly call DIGNITY. And this value of him by the commonwealth, is understood, by offices of command, judicature, public employment; or by names and titles, introduced for distinction of such value.

To pray to another, for aid of any kind, is to HONOUR; because a sign we have an opinion he has power to help; and the more difficult the aid is, the more is the honour.

To obey, is to honour, because no man obeys them, whom they think have no power to help, or hurt them. And consequently to disobey, is to dishonor.

To give great gifts to a man, is to honour him; because it is buying of protection, and acknowledging of power. To give little gifts, is to dishonor; because it is but alms, and signifies an opinion of the need of small helps.

CHAPTER 11. OF THE DIFFERENCE OF MANNERS

By manners I mean not decency of behavior; as how one man should salute another, or how a man should wash his mouth, or pick his teeth before company, and such other points of the small morals; but those qualities of mankind, that concern their living together in peace, and unity. To which end we are to consider, that the felicity of this life, consists not in the repose of a mind satisfied. For there is no such (utmost aim) nor summum bonum (greatest good) as is spoken of in the books of the old moral philosophers. Nor can a man any more live, whose desires are at an end, than he, whose senses and imaginations are at a stand. Felicity is a continual progress of the desire, from one object to another; the attaining of the former, being still but the way to the latter. The cause whereof is, that the object of man's desire, is not to enjoy once only, and for one instant of time; but to assure forever, the way of his future desire. And therefore the voluntary actions, and inclinations of all men, tend, not only to the procuring, but also to the assuring of a contented life; and differ only in the way: which arises partly from the diversity of passions, in divers men; and partly from the difference of the knowledge, or opinion each one has of the causes, which produce the effect desired.

So that in the first place, I put for a general inclination of all mankind, a perpetual and restless desire of power after power, that ceases only in death. And the cause of this, is not always that a man hopes for a more intensive delight, than he has already attained to; or that he cannot be content with a moderate power: but because he cannot assure the power and means to live well, which he hath present, without the acquisition of more. And from hence it is, that kings, whose power is greatest, turn their endeavors to the assuring it at home by laws, or abroad by wars: and when that is done, there succeeds a new desire; in some, of fame from new conquest; in others, ease and sensual pleasure; in others, of admiration, or being flattered for excellence in some art, or other ability of the mind.

Competition of riches, honour, command, or other power, inclines to contention, enmity, and war: because the way of one competitor, to the attaining of his desire, is to kill, subdue, supplant, or repel the other. Particularly, competition of praise, inclines to a reverence of antiquity. For men contend with the living, not with the dead; to these ascribing more than due, that they may obscure the glory of the other.

Desire of ease, and sensual delight, disposes men to obey a common power: because by such desires, a man doth abandon the protection might be hoped for from his own industry, and labour. Fear of death, and wounds, disposes to the same; and for the same reason. On the contrary, needy men, and hardy, not contented with their present condition; as also, all men that are ambitious of military command, are inclined to continue the causes of war; and to stir up trouble and sedition: for there is no honour military but by war; nor any such hope to mend an ill game, as by causing a new shuffle.

Desire of knowledge, and arts of peace, inclines men to obey a common power: For such desire, contains a desire of leisure; and consequently protection from some other power than their own.

Desire of praise, disposes to laudable actions, such as please them whose judgment they value; for of those men whom we contemn [despise], we contemn also the praises. Desire of fame after death does the same. And though after death, there be no sense of the praise given us on earth, as being joys, that are either swallowed up in the unspeakable joys of Heaven, or extinguished in the extreme torments of hell: yet is not such fame vain; because men have a present delight therein, from the foresight of it, and of the benefit that may redound thereby to their posterity: which though they now see not, yet they imagine; and any thing that is pleasure to the sense, the same also is pleasure in the imagination.

To have received from one, to whom we think ourselves equal, greater benefits than there is hope to requite, disposes to counterfeit love; but really secret hatred; and puts a man into the estate of a desperate debtor, that in declining the sight of his creditor, tacitly wishes him there, where he might never see him more. For benefits oblige, and obligation is thraldom; and unrequitable obligation, perpetual thraldom; which is to one's equal, hateful.

But to have received benefits from one, whom we acknowledge for superior, inclines to love; because the obligation is no new depression: and cheerful acceptation (which men call gratitude) is such an honour done to the obliger, as is taken generally for retribution. Also to receive benefits, though from an equal, or inferior, as long as there is hope of requital, disposes to love: for in the intention of the receiver, the obligation is of aid, and service mutual; from whence proceeds an emulation of who shall exceed in benefiting; the most noble and profitable contention possible; wherein the victor is placed with his victory, and the other revenged by confessing it.

To have done more hurt to a man, than he can, or is willing to expiate, inclines the doer to hate the sufferer. For he must expect revenge, or forgiveness; both which are hateful.

Fear of oppression, disposes a man to anticipate, or to seek aid by society: for there is no other way by which a man can secure his life and liberty.

Men that distrust their own subtlety, are in tumult and sedition, better disposed for victory, than they that suppose themselves wise, or crafty. For these love to consult, the other (fearing to be circumvented) to strike first. And in sedition, men being always in the precincts of battle, to hold together, and use all advantages of force, is a better stratagem, than any that can proceed from subtlety of wit.

Vain-glorious men, such as without being conscious to themselves of great sufficiency, delight in supposing themselves gallant men, are inclined only to ostentation; but not to attempt: because when danger or difficulty appears, they look for nothing but to have their insufficiency discovered.

Vain-glorious men, such as estimate their sufficiency by the flattery of other men, or the fortune of some precedent action, without assured ground of hope from the true knowledge of themselves, are inclined to rash engaging; and in the approach of danger, or difficulty, to retire if they can: because not seeing the way of safety, they will rather hazard their honour, which may be salved with an excuse; than their lives, for which no salve is sufficient.

Men that have a strong opinion of their own wisdom in matter of government, are disposed to ambition. Because without public employment in council or magistracy, the honour of their wisdom is lost. And therefore eloquent speakers are inclined to ambition; for eloquence seems wisdom, both to themselves and others.

Pusillanimity disposes men to irresolution, and consequently to lose the occasions, and fittest opportunities of action. For after men have been in deliberation till the time of action approach, if it be not then manifest what is best to be done, it is a sign, the difference of motives, the one way and the other, are not great: therefore not to resolve then, is to lose the occasion by weighing of trifles; which is pusillanimity.

Frugality (though in poor men a virtue) maketh a man unapt to achieve such actions, as require the strength of many men at once: for it weakeneth their endeavor, which is to be nourished and kept in vigor by reward.

Eloquence, with flattery, disposes men to confide in them that have it; because the former is seeming wisdom, the latter seeming kindness. Add to them military reputation, and it disposes men to adhere, and subject themselves to those men that have them. The two former, having given them caution against danger from him; the latter gives them caution against danger from others.

Want of science, that is, ignorance of causes, disposes, or rather constrains a man to rely on the advice, and authority of others. For all men whom the truth concerns, if they rely not on their own, must rely on the opinion of some other, whom they think wiser than themselves, and see not why he should deceive them.

CHAPTER 12. OF RELIGION

Seeing there are no signs, nor fruit of religion, but in many only; there is no cause to doubt, but that the seed of religion, is also only in man; and consists in some peculiar quality, or at least in some eminent degree thereof, not to be found in other living creatures.

And first, it is peculiar to the nature of man, to be inquisitive into the causes of the events they see, some more, some less; but all men so much, as to be curious in the search of the causes of their own good and evil fortune.

Secondly, upon the sight of any thing that hath a beginning, to think also it had a cause, which determined the same to begin, then when it did, rather than sooner or later.

Thirdly, whereas there is no other felicity of beasts, but the enjoying of their quotidian food, ease, and lusts; as having little or no foresight of the time to come, for want of observation, and memory of the order, consequence, and dependence of the things they see; man observes how one event hath been produced by another; and remembers in them antecedence and consequence; and when he cannot assure himself of the true causes of things (for the causes of good and evil fortune for the most part are invisible), he supposes causes of them, either such as his own fancy suggests; or trusts to the authority of other men, such as he thinks to be his friends, and wiser than himself.

The two first, make anxiety. For being assured that there be causes of all things that have arrived hitherto, or shall arrive hereafter; it is impossible for a man, who continually endeavors to secure himself against the evil he fears, and procure the good he desires, not to be in a perpetual solicitude of the time to come; so that every man, especially those that are over provident, are in an estate like to that of Prometheus. For as Prometheus (which interpreted, is, the prudent man) was bound to the hill Caucasus, a place of large prospect, where, an eagle feeding on his liver, devoured in the day, as much as was repaired in the night: so that man, which looks too far before him, in the care of future time, has his heart all the day long, gnawed on by fear of death, poverty, or other calamity; and has no repose, nor pause of his anxiety, but in sleep.

This perpetual fear, always accompanying mankind in the ignorance of causes, as it were in the dark, must needs have for object something. And therefore when there is nothing to be seen, there is nothing to accuse, either of their good, or evil fortune, but some power, or agent invisible: in which sense perhaps it was, that some of the old poets said, that the gods were at first created by human fear: which spoken of the gods (that is to say, of the many gods of the Gentiles) is very true. But the acknowledging of one God, eternal, infinite, and omnipotent, may more easily be derived, from the desire men

have to know the causes of natural bodies, and their several virtues, and operations; than from the fear of what was to befall them in time to come. For he that from any effect he seeth come to pass, should reason to the next and immediate cause thereof, and from thence to the cause of that cause, and plunge himself profoundly in the pursuit of causes; shall at last come to this, that there must be (as even the heathen philosophers confessed) one first mover; that is, a first, and an eternal cause of all things; which is that which men mean by the name of God: and all this without thought of their fortune; the solicitude whereof, both inclines to fear, and hinders them from the search of the causes of other things; and thereby gives occasion of feigning of as many gods, as there be men that feign them.

And for the matter, or substance of the invisible agents, so fancied; they could not by natural cogitation, fall upon any other conceit, but that it was the same with that of the soul of man; and that the soul of man, was of the same substance, with that which appears in a dream, to one that sleeps; or in a looking-glass, to one that is awake; which, men not knowing that such apparitions are nothing else but creatures of fancy, think to be real, and external substances; and therefore call them ghosts; as the Latins called them *imagines*, and *umbrae*, and thought them spirits, that is, thin aerial bodies; and this invisible agents, which they feared, to be like them; save that they appear, and vanish when they please. But the opinion that such spirits were incorporeal, or immaterial, could never enter into the mind of any man by nature; because, though men may put together words of contradictory signification, as spirit, and incorporeal; yet they can never have the imagination of any thing answering to them: and therefore, men that by their own meditation, arrive to the acknowledgment of one infinite, omnipotent, and eternal God, choose rather to confess he is incomprehensible, and above their understanding, than to define his nature by spirit incorporeal, and then confess their definition to be unintelligible: or if they give him such a title, it is not dogmatically, with intention to make the divine nature understood; but piously, to honour him with attributes, of significations, as remote as they can from the grossness of bodies visible.

Then, for the way by which they think these invisible agents wrought their effects; that is to say, what immediate causes they used, in bringing to pass, men that know not what it is that we call causing (that is, almost all men) have no other rule to guess by, but by observing, and remembering what they have seen to precede the like effect at some other time, or times before, without seeing between the antecedent and subsequent event, any dependence or connexion at all: and therefore from the like things past, they expect the like things to come; and hope for good or evil luck, superstitiously, from things that have no part at all in the causing of it: as the Athenians did for their war at Lepanto, demand another Phormio; the Pompeian faction for their war in Africa, another Scipio; and others have done in divers other occasions since. In like manner they attribute their fortune to a bystander, to a lucky or unlucky place, to words spoken, especially if the name of God be amongst them; as charming and conjuring (the liturgy of witches); insomuch as to believe, they have power to turn a stone into bread, bread into a man, or any thing into any thing.

Thirdly, for the worship which naturally men exhibit to powers invisible, it can be no other, but such expressions of their reverence, as they would use towards men; gifts, petitions, thanks, submission of body, considerate addresses, sober behavior, premeditated words, swearing (that is, assuring one another of their promises), by invoking them. Beyond that reason suggesteth nothing; but leaves them either to rest there; or for further ceremonies, to rely on those they believe to be wiser than themselves.

Lastly, concerning how these invisible powers declare to men the things which shall hereafter come to pass, especially concerning their good or evil fortune in general, or good or ill success in any particular undertaking, men are naturally at a stand; save that using to conjecture of the time to come, by the time past, they are very apt, not only to take casual things, after one or two encounters, for prognostics of the like encounter ever after, but also to believe the like prognostics from other men, of whom they have once conceived a good opinion.

And in these four things, opinion of ghosts, ignorance of second causes, devotion towards what men fear, and taking of things casual for prognostics, consists the natural seed of religion, which by reason of the different fancies, judgments, and passions of several men, hath grown up into ceremonies so different, that those which are used by one man, are for the most part ridiculous to another.

For these seeds have received culture from two sorts of men. One sort have been they, that have nourished, and ordered them, according to their own invention. The other have done it, by God's commandment, and direction: but both sorts have done it, with a purpose to make those men that relied on them, the more apt to obedience, laws, peace, charity, and civil society. So that the religion of the former sort, is a part of human politics; and teaches part of the duty which earthly kings require of their subjects. And the religion of the latter sort is divine politics; and contains precepts to those that have yielded themselves subjects in the kingdom of God. Of the former sort, were all the founders of commonwealths, and the lawgivers of the Gentiles: of the latter sort, were Abraham, Moses, and our blessed Savior; by whom have been derived unto us the laws of the kingdom of God.

And for that part of religion, which consists in opinions concerning the nature of powers invisible, there is almost nothing that has a name, that has not been esteemed amongst the Gentiles, in one place or another, a god, or devil; or by their poets feigned to be inanimated, inhabited, or possessed by some spirit or other.

The unformed matter of the world, was a god, by the name of Chaos.

The heaven, the ocean, the planets, the fire, the earth, the winds, were so many gods.

Men, women, a bird, a crocodile, a calf, a dog, a snake, an onion, a leek, deified. Besides that, they filled almost all places, with spirits called demons: the plains, with Pan, and Panises, or Satyrs; the woods, with Fawns, and Nymphs: the sea, with Tritons, and other Nymphs; every river, and fountain, with a ghost of his name, and with Nymphs; every house with its Lares or familiars; every man with his Genius; hell with ghosts, and spiritual officers, as Charon, Cerberus, and the Furies; and in the night time, all places with larvae, lemures, ghosts of men deceased, and a whole kingdom of fairies and bugbears. They have also ascribed divinity, and built temples to mere accidents, and qualities; such as are time, night, day, peace, concord, love, contention, virtue, honour, health, rust, fever, and the like; which when they prayed for, or against, they prayed to, as if there were ghosts of those names hanging over their heads, and letting fall, or withholding that good, or evil, for, or against which they prayed. They invoked also their own wit, by the name of Muses; their own ignorance, by the name of Fortune; their own lust, by the name of Cupid; their own rage, by the name Furies; their own privy members, by the name of Priapus, and attributed their pollutions, to Incubi, and Succubae: insomuch as there was nothing, which a poet could introduce as a person in his poem, which they did not make either a god, or a devil. . . .

CHAPTER 13. OF THE NATURAL CONDITION OF MANKIND AS CONCERNING THEIR FELICITY, AND MISERY

Nature hath made men so equal, in the faculties of body, and mind; as that though there be found one man sometimes manifestly stronger in body, or of quicker mind than another; yet when all is reckoned together, the difference between man, and man, is not so considerable, as that one man can thereupon claim to himself any benefit, to which another may not pretend, as well as he. For as to the strength of body, the weakest has strength enough to kill the strongest, either by secret machination, or by confederacy with others, that are in the same danger with himself.

And as to the faculties of the mind (setting aside the arts grounded upon words, and especially that skill of proceeding upon general, and infallible rules, called science; which very few have, and but in few things; as being not a native faculty, born with us; nor attained, [as prudence], while we look after somewhat else), I find yet a greater equality amongst men, than that of strength. For prudence, is but experience; which equal time, equally bestows on all men, in those things they equally apply themselves unto. That which may perhaps make such equality incredible, is but a vain conceit of one's own wisdom, which almost all men think they have in a greater degree, than the vulgar; that is, than all men but themselves, and a few others, whom by fame, or for concurring with themselves, they approve. For such is the nature of men, that howsoever they may acknowledge many others to be more witty, or more eloquent, or more learned; yet they will hardly believe there be many so wise as themselves: For they see their own wit at hand, and other men's at a distance. But this proves rather that men are in that point equal, than unequal. For there is not ordinarily a greater sign of the equal distribution of any thing, than that every man is contented with his share.

From this equality of ability, arises equality of hope in the attaining of our ends. And therefore if any two men desire the same thing, which nevertheless they cannot both enjoy, they become enemies; and in the way to their end (which is principally their own conservation, and sometimes their delectation only), endeavor to destroy, or subdue one another. And from hence it comes to pass, that where an invader hath no more to fear, than another man's single power; if one plant, sow, build, or possess a convenient seat, others may probably be expected to come prepared with forces united, to dispossess, and deprive him, not only of the fruit of his labour, but also of his life, or liberty. And the invader again is in the like danger of another.

And from this diffidence of one another, there is no way for any man to secure himself, so reasonable, as anticipation; that is, by force, or wiles, to master the persons of all men he can, so long, till he see no other power great enough to endanger him: and this is no more than his own conservation requires, and is generally allowed. Also because there be some, that taking pleasure in contemplating their own power in the acts of conquest, which they pursue farther than their security requires; if others, that otherwise would be glad to be at ease within modest bounds, should not by invasion increase their power, they would not be able, long time, by standing only on their defence, to subsist. And by consequence, such augmentation of dominion over men, being necessary to a man's conservation, it ought to be allowed him.

Again, men have no pleasure (but on the contrary a great deal of grief) in keeping company, where there is no power able to over-awe them all. For every man looks that his companion should value him, at the same rate he sets upon himself: and upon all signs of contempt, or undervaluing, naturally endeavors, as far as he dares (which amongst them that have no common power to keep them in quiet, is far enough to make them destroy each other), to extort a greater value from his condemners, by damage; and from others, by the example.

So that in the nature of man, we find three principal causes of quarrel. First, competition; secondly, diffidence; thirdly, glory.

The first, maketh men invade for gain; the second, for safety; and the third, for reputation. The first use violence, to make themselves masters of other men's persons, wives, children, and cattle; the second to defend them; the third, for trifles, as a word, a smile, a different opinion, and any other sign of undervalue, either direct in their persons, or by reflection in their kindred, their friends, their nation, their profession, or their name.

Hereby it is manifest, that during the time men live without a common power to keep them all in awe, they are in that condition which is called war; and such a war, as is of every man, against every man. For WAR, consists not in battle only, or the act of fighting; but in a tract of time, wherein the will to contend by battle is sufficiently known: and therefore the notion of time, is to be considered in the nature of war; as it is in the nature of weather. For as the nature of foul weather, lies not in a shower or two of rain; but in an inclination thereto of many days together: so the nature of war, consists not in actual fighting; but in the known disposition thereto, during all the time there is no assurance to the contrary. All other time is PEACE.

Whatsoever therefore is consequent to a time of war, where every man is enemy to every man; the same is consequent to the time; wherein men live without other security, than what their own strength, and their own invention shall furnish them withal. In such condition, there is no place for industry; because the fruit thereof is uncertain: and consequently no culture of the earth; no navigation, nor use of the commodities that may be imported by sea; no commodious building; no instruments of moving, and removing such things as require much force; no knowledge of the face of the earth; no account of time; no arts; no letters; no society; and which is worst of all, continual fear, and danger of violent death; and the life of man, solitary, poor, nasty, brutish, and short.

It may seem strange to some man, that has not well weighed these things; that nature should thus dissociate, and render men apt to invade, and destroy one another: and he may therefore, not trusting to this inference, made from the passions, desire perhaps to have the same confirmed by experience. Let him therefore consider with himself, when taking a journey, he arms himself, and seeks to go well accompanied; when going to sleep, he locks his doors; when even in his house he locks his chests; and this when he knows there be laws, and public officers, armed, to revenge all injuries shall be done him; what opinion he has of his fellow subjects, when he rides armed; of his fellow citizens, when he locks his doors; and of his children, and servants, when he locks his chests. Does he not there as much accuse mankind by his actions, as I do by my words? But neither of us accuse man's nature in it. The desires, and other passions of man, are in themselves no sin. No more are the actions, that proceed from those passions, till they know a law that forbids them: which till laws be made they cannot know: nor can any law be made, till they have agreed upon the person that shall make it.

It may peradventure be thought, there was never such a time, nor condition of war as this; and I believe it was never generally so, over all the world: but there are many places, where they live so now. For the savage people in many places of America, except the government of small families, the concord whereof depends on natural lust, have no government at all; and live at this day in that brutish manner, as I said before. Howsoever, it may be perceived what manner of life there would be, where there were no common power to fear; by the manner of life, which men that have formerly lived under a peaceful government, use to degenerate into, in a civil war.

But though there had never been any time, wherein particular men were in a condition of war one against another; yet in all times, kings, and persons of sovereign authority, because of their independency, are in continual jealousies, and in the state and posture of gladiators; having their weapons pointing, and their eyes fixed on one another; that is, their forts, garrisons, and guns upon the frontiers of their kingdoms; and continual spies upon their neighbours; which is a posture war. But because they uphold thereby, the industry of their subjects; there does not follow from it, that misery, which accompanies the liberty of particular men.

To this war of every man against every man, this also is consequent; that nothing can be unjust. The notions of right and wrong, justice and injustice have there no place. Where there is no common power, there is no law: where no law no injustice. Force, and fraud, are in war the two cardinal virtues. Justice, and injustice are none of the faculties neither of the body, nor mind. If they were, they might be in a man that were alone in the world, as well as his senses, and passions. They are qualities, that relate to men in society, not in solitude. It is consequent also to the same condition, that there be no propriety, no dominion, no mine and thine distinct; but only that to be every man's, that he can get; and for so long, as he can keep it. And thus much for the ill condition, which man by mere nature is actually placed in; though with a possibility to come out of it, consisting partly in the passions, partly in his reason.

The passions that incline men to peace, are fear of death; desire of such things as are necessary to commodious living; and a hope by their industry to obtain them. And reason suggests convenient articles of peace, upon which men may be drawn to agreement. These articles, are they, which otherwise are called the Laws of Nature: whereof I shall speak more particularly, in the two following chapters.

CHAPTER 14. OF THE FIRST AND SECOND NATURAL LAWS, AND OF CONTRACTS

The RIGHT OF NATURE, which writers commonly call *jus naturale*, is the liberty each man hath, to use his own power, as he will himself, for the preservation of his own nature; that is to say, of his own life; and consequently, of doing any thing, which in his own judgment, and reason, he shall conceive to be the aptest means thereunto.

By LIBERTY, is understood, according to the proper signification of the word, the absence of external impediments: which impediments, may oft take away part of a man's power to do what he would; but cannot hinder him from using the power

left him, according as his judgment, and reason shall dictate to him.

A LAW OF NATURE (*lex naturalis*), is a precept, or general rule, found out by reason, by which a man is forbidden to do that, which is destructive of his life, or taketh away the means of preserving the same; and to omit that, by which he thinks it may be best preserved. For though they that speak of this subject, use to confound jus, and lex, right and law; yet they ought to be distinguished; because RIGHT, consists in liberty to do, or to forbear; whereas LAW, determines, and binds to one of them: so that law, and right, differ as much, as obligation, and liberty; which in one and the same matter are inconsistent.

And because the condition of man (as hath been declared in the precedent chapter) is a condition of war of every one against every one; in which case every one is governed by his own reason; and there is nothing he can make use of that may not be a help unto him, in preserving his life against his enemies; it followeth, that in such a condition, every man has a right to every thing; even to one another's body. And therefore, as long as this natural right of every man to every thing endures, there can be no security to any man (how strong or wise soever he be) of living out the time, which nature ordinarily allows men to live. And consequently it is a precept, or general rule of reason, that every man, ought to endeavor peace, as far as he has hope of obtaining it; and when he cannot obtain it, that he may seek, and use, all helps, and advantages of war. The first branch of which rule, containeth the first, and fundamental law of nature; which is, to seek peace, and follow it. The second, the sum of the right of nature; which is, by all means we can, to defend ourselves.

From this fundamental law of nature, by which men are commanded to endeavor peace, is derived this second law; that a man be willing, when others are so too, as far-forth, as for peace, and defence of himself he shall think it necessary, to lay down this right to all things; and be contented with so much liberty against other men, as he would allow other men against himself. For as long as every man holds this right, of doing any thing he likes; so long are all men in the condition of war. But if other men will not lay down their right, as well as he; then there is no reason for any one, to divest himself of his: for that were to expose himself to prey (which no man is bound to) rather than to dispose himself to peace. This is that law of the Gospel; whatsoever you require that others should do to you, that do ye to them. And that law of all men, [what you would not have done to you, do not do to others].

To lay down a man's right to any thing, is to divest himself of the liberty, of hindering another of the benefit of his own right to the same. For he that renounces or passeth away his right, giveth not to any other man a right which he had not before; because there is nothing to which every man had not right by nature: but only stands out of his way, that he may enjoy his own original right, without hindrance from him; not without hindrance from another. So that the effect which redounds to one man, by another man's defect of right, is but so much diminution of impediments to the use of his own right original.

Right is laid aside, either by simply renouncing it; or by transferring it to another. By simply RENOUNCING; when he cares not to whom the benefit thereof redounds. By TRANSFERRING; when he intends the benefit thereof to some certain person, or persons. And when a man hath in either manner abandoned, or granted away his right; then is he said to be OBLIGED, or BOUND, not to hinder those, to whom such right is granted, or abandoned, from the benefit of it: and that he ought, and it is his DUTY, not to make void that voluntary act of his own: and that such hindrance is INJUSTICE, and INJURY, as being sine jure; the right being before renounced, or transferred. So that injury, or injustice, in the controversies of the world, is somewhat like to that, which in the disputations of scholars is called absurdity. For as it is there called an absurdity, to contradict what one maintained in the beginning: so in the world, it is called injustice, and injury, voluntarily to undo that, which from the beginning he had voluntarily done. The way by which a man either simply renounces, or transfers his right, is a declaration, or signification, by some voluntary and sufficient sign, or signs, that he doth so renounce, or transfer; or hath so renounced, or transferred the same, to him that accepts it. And these signs are either words only, or actions only; (as it happens most often) both words, and actions. And the same are the BONDS, by which men are bound, and obliged: bonds, that have their strength, not from

their own nature (for nothing is more easily broken than a man's word), but from fear of some evil consequence upon the rupture.

Whensoever a man transfers his right, or renounces it; it is either in consideration of some right reciprocally transferred to himself; or for some other good he hopes for thereby. For it is a voluntary act: and of the voluntary acts of every man, the object is some good to himself. And therefore there be some rights, which no man can be understood by any words, or other signs, to have abandoned, or transferred. As first a man cannot lay down the right of resisting them, that assault him by force, to take away his life; because he cannot be understood to aim thereby, at any good to himself. The same may be said of wounds, and chains, and imprisonment; both because there is no benefit consequent to such patience; as there is to the patience of suffering another to be wounded, or imprisoned: as also because a man cannot tell, when he sees men proceed against him by violence, whether they intend his death or not. And lastly the motive, and end for which this renouncing, and transferring of right is introduced, is nothing else but the security of a man's person, in his life, and in the means of so preserving life, as not to be weary of it. And therefore if a man by words, or other signs, seem to despoil himself of the end, for which those signs were intended; he is not to be understood as if he meant it, or that it was his will; but that he was ignorant of how such words and actions were to be interpreted.

The mutual transferring of right, is that which men call CONTRACT.

There is difference between transferring of right to the thing; and transferring, or tradition, that is, delivery of the thing it self. For the thing may be delivered together with the translation of the right; as in buying and selling with ready money; or exchange of goods, or lands: and it may be delivered some time after.

Again, one of the contractors, may deliver the thing contracted for on his part, and leave the other to perform his part at some determinate time after, and in the mean time be trusted; and then the contract on his part, is called PACT, or COVENANT: or both parts may contract now, to perform hereafter: in which cases, he that is to perform in time to come, being trusted, his performance is called keeping of promise, or faith; and the failing of performance (if it be voluntary) violation of faith.

When the transferring of right, is not mutual; but one of the parties transfers, in hope to gain thereby friendship, or service from another, or from his friends; or in hope to gain the reputation of charity, or magnanimity; or to deliver his mind from the pain of compassion; or in hope or reward in heaven; this is not contract, but GIFT, FREE-GIFT, GRACE: which words signify one and the same thing.

Signs of contract, are either express, or by inference. Express, are words spoken with understanding of what they signify: and such words are either of the time present, or past; as, I give, I grant, I have given, I have granted, I will that this be yours: or of the future; as, I will give, I will grant: which words of the future are called PROMISE.

Signs by inference, are sometimes the consequence of words; sometimes the consequence of silence; sometimes the consequences of actions; sometimes the consequence of forbearing an action: and generally a sign by inference, of any contract, is whatsoever sufficiently argues the will of the contractor.

Words alone, if they be of the time to come, and contain a bare promise, are an insufficient sign of a free-gift and therefore not obligatory. For if they be of the time to come, as, tomorrow I will give, they are a sign I have not given yet, and consequently that my right is not transferred, but remains till I transfer it by some other act. But if the words be of the time present, or past, as, I have given, or do give to be delivered tomorrow, then is my tomorrow's right given away to day; and that by the virtue of the words, though there were no other argument of my will. And there is a great difference in the signification of these words, *volo hoc tuum esse cras*, and *cras dabo*; that is, between I will that this be thine tomorrow, and, I will give it thee tomorrow: for the word I will, in the former manner of speech, signifies an act of the will present; but in the latter, it signifies a promise of an act of the will to come: and therefore the former words, being of the present, transfer a future right; the latter, that be of the future, transfer nothing. But if there be other signs of the will to transfer a right, besides words; then, though the gift be free, yet may the right be understood to pass by words of the future: as if a man pro-

pound a prize to him that comes first to the end of a race, the gift is free: and though the words be of the future, yet the right passeth: for if he would not have his words so be understood, he should not have let them run.

In contracts, the right passeth, not only where the words are of the time present, or past, but also where they are of the future: because all contract is mutual translation, or change of right; and therefore he that promises only, because he hath already received the benefit for which he promises, is to be understood as if he intended the right should pass: for unless he had been content to have his words so understood, the other would not have performed his part first. And for that cause, in buying, and selling, and other acts of contract, a promise is equivalent to a covenant; and therefore obligatory.

He that performs first in the case of a contract, is said to MERIT that which he is to receive by the performance of the other; and he hath it as due. Also when a prize is propounded to many, which is to be given to him only that wins; or money is thrown amongst many, to be enjoyed by them that catch it; though this be a free gift; yet so to win, or so to catch, is to merit, and to have it as DUE. For the right is transferred in the propounding of the prize, and in throwing down the money; though it be not determined to whom, but by the event of the contention. But there is between these two sorts of merit, this difference, that in contract, I merit by virtue of my own power, and the contractor's need; but in this case of free gift, I am enabled to merit only by the benignity of the giver: in contract, I merit at the contractor's hand that he should depart with his right; in this case of gift, I merit not that the giver should part with his right; but that when he has parted with it, it should be mine, rather than another's. . . .

If a covenant be made, wherein neither of the parties perform presently, but trust one another; in the condition of mere nature (which is a condition of war of every man against every man), upon an reasonable suspicion, it is void: but if there be a common power set over them both, with right and force sufficient to compel performance, it is not void. For he that performs first, has no assurance the other will perform after; because the bonds of words are too weak to bridle men's ambition, avarice, anger, and other passions, without the fear of some coercive power; which in the condition of mere nature, where all men are equal, and judges of the justness of their own fears, cannot possibly be supposed. And therefore he which performs first, does but betray himself to his enemy; contrary to the right (he can never abandon) of defending his life, and means of living.

But in a civil estate, where there is a power set up to constrain those that would otherwise violate their faith, that fear is no more reasonable; and for that cause, he which by the covenant is to perform first, is obliged so to do.

The cause of fear, which maketh such a covenant invalid, must be always something arising after the covenant made; as some new fact, or other sign of the will not to perform: else it cannot make the covenant void. For that which could not hinder a man from promising, ought not to be admitted as a hindrance of performing.

He that transfers any right, transfers the means of enjoying it, as far as lies in his power. As he that sells land, is understood to transfer the herbage, and whatsoever grows upon it; nor can he that sells a mill turn away the stream that drives it. And they that give to a man the right of government in sovereignty, are understood to give him the right of levying money to maintain soldiers; and of appointing magistrates for the administration of justice.

To make covenants with brute beasts, is impossible; because not understanding our speech, they understand not, nor accept of any translation of right; nor can translate any right to another: and without mutual acceptation, there is no covenant.

To make covenant with God, is impossible, but by mediation of such as God speaks to, either by revelation supernatural, or by his lieutenants that govern under him, and in his name: for otherwise we know not whether our covenants be accepted, or not. And therefore they that vow any thing contrary to any law of nature, vow in vain; as being a thing unjust to pay such vow. And if it be a thing commanded by the law of nature, it is not the vow, but the law that binds them.

The matter, or subject of a covenant, is always something that falls under deliberation (for to covenant, is an act of the will; that is to say an act, and the last act, of deliberation) and is therefore always understood to be something to come; and which is judged possible for him that covenants, to perform.

And therefore, to promise that which is known to be impossible, is no covenant. But if that prove impossible afterwards, which before was thought possible, the covenant is valid, and bind (though not to the thing it self), yet to the value; or, if that also be impossible, to the unfeigned endeavor of performing as much as is possible: for to more no man can be obliged.

Men are freed of their covenants two ways; by performing; or by being forgiven. For performance, is the natural end of obligation; and forgiveness, the restitution of liberty; as being a retransferring of that right, in which the obligation consisted.

Covenants entered into by fear, in the condition of mere nature, are obligatory. For example, if I covenant to pay a ransom, or service for my life, to an enemy; I am bound by it. For it is a contract, wherein one receives the benefit of life; the other is to receive money, or service for it; and consequently, where no other law (as in the condition, of mere nature) forbids the performance, the covenant is valid. Therefore prisoners of war, if trusted with the payment of their ransom, are obliged to pay it: and if a weaker prince, make a disadvantageous peace with a stronger, for fear; he is bound to keep it; unless (as hath been said before) there arises some new, and just cause of fear, to renew the war. And even in commonwealths, if I be forced to redeem myself from a thief by promising him money, I am bound to pay it, till the civil law discharge me. For whatsoever I may lawfully do without obligation, the same I may lawfully covenant to do through fear: and what I lawfully covenant, I cannot lawfully break.

A former covenant, makes void a later. For a man that hath passed away his right to one man today, hath it not to pass tomorrow to another: and therefore the later promise passeth no right, but is null.

A covenant not to defend myself from force, by force, is always void. For (as I have showed before) no man can transfer, or lay down his right to save himself from death, wounds, and imprisonment, (the avoiding whereof is the only end of laying down any right, and therefore the promise of not resisting force, in no covenant transfers any right; nor is obliging. For though a man may covenant thus, unless I do so, or so, kill me; he cannot covenant thus, unless I do so, or so, I will not resist you, when you come to kill me. For man by nature chooses the lesser evil, which is danger of death in resisting; rather than the greater, which is certain and present death in not resisting. And this is granted to be true by all men, in that they lead criminals to execution, and prison, with armed men, notwithstanding that such criminals have consented to the law, by which they are condemned.

A covenant to accuse one self, without assurance of pardon, is likewise invalid. For in the condition of nature, where every man is judge, there is no place for accusation: and in the civil state, the accusation is followed with punishment; which being force, a man is not obliged not to resist. The same is also true, of the accusation of those, by whose condemnation a man falls into misery; as of a father, wife, or benefactor. For the testimony of such an accuser, if it be not willingly given, is presumed to be corrupted by nature; and therefore not to be received: and where a man's testimony is not to be credited, he is not bound to give it. Also accusations upon torture, are not to be reputed as testimonies. For torture is to be used but as means of conjecture, and light, in the further examination, and search of truth: and what is in that case confessed, tends to the ease of him that is tortured, not to the informing of the torturers: and therefore ought not to have the credit of a sufficient testimony: for whether he deliver himself by true, or false accusation, he does it by the right of preserving his own life.

The force of words, being (as I have formerly noted) too weak to hold men to the performance of their covenants; there are in man's nature, but two imaginable helps to strengthen it. And those are either a fear of the consequence of breaking their word; or a glory, or pride in appearing not to need to break it. This latter is a generosity too rarely found to be presumed on, especially in the pursuers of wealth, command, or sensual pleasure; which are the greatest part of mankind. The passion to be reckoned upon, is fear; whereof there be two very general objects: one, the power of spirits invisible; the other, the power of those men they shall therein offend. Of these two, though the former be the greater power, yet the fear of the latter is commonly the greater fear. The fear of the former is in every man, his own religion: which hath place in the nature of man before civil society. The latter hath not so; at least not place enough, to keep men to their promises; because in

the condition of mere nature, the inequality of power is not discerned, but by the event of battle. So that before the time of civil society, or in the interruption thereof by war, there is nothing can strengthen a covenant of peace agreed on, against the temptations of avarice, ambition, lust, or other strong desire, but the fear of that invisible power, which they every one worship as God; and fear as a revenger of their perfidy. All therefore that can be done between two men not subject to civil power, is to put one another to swear by the God he fears: which swearing, or OATH, is a form of speech, added to a promise; by which he that promises, signifies, that unless he perform, he renounces the mercy of his God, or calleth to him for vengeance on himself. Such was the heathen form, Let Jupiter kill me else, as I kill this beast. So is our form, I shall do thus, and thus, so help me God. And this, with the rites and ceremonies, which every one uses in his own religion, that the fear of breaking faith might be the greater.

By this it appears, that an oath taken according to any other form, or rite, than his, that swears, is in vain; and no oath: and that there is no swearing by any thing which the swearer thinks not God. For though men have sometimes used to swear by their kings, for fear, or flattery; yet they would have it thereby understood, they attributed to them divine honour. And that swearing unnecessarily by God, is but profaning of his name: and swearing by other things, as men do in common discourse, is not swearing, but an impious custom, gotten by too much vehemence of talking.

It appears also, that the oath adds nothing to the obligation. For a covenant, if lawful, binds in the sight of God, without the oath, as much as with it: if unlawful, binds not at all; though it be confirmed with an oath.

CHAPTER 15. OF OTHER LAWS OF NATURE

From that law of nature, by which we are obliged to transfer to another, such rights, as being retained, hinder the peace of mankind, there followeth a third; which is this, that men perform their covenants made: without which, covenants are in vain, and but empty words; and the right of all men to all things remaining, we are still in the condition of war.

And in this law of nature, consists the fountain and original of JUSTICE. For where no covenant hath proceeded, there hath no right been transferred, and every man has right to every thing; and consequently, no action can be unjust. But when a covenant is made, then to break it is unjust: and the definition of INJUSTICE, is no other than the not performance of covenant. And whatsoever is not unjust, is just.

But because covenants of mutual trust, where there is a fear of not performance on either part (as hath been said in the former chapter), are invalid; though the original of justice be the making of covenants; yet injustice actually there can be none, till the cause of such fear be taken away; which while men are in the natural condition of war, cannot be done. Therefore before the names of just, and unjust can have place, there must be some coercive power, to compel men equally to the performance of their covenants, by the terror of some punishment, greater than the benefit they expect by the breach of their covenant; and to make good that propriety, which by mutual contract men acquire, in recompense of the universal right they abandon: and such power there is none before the erection of a commonwealth. And this is also to be gathered out of the ordinary definition of justice in the Schools: for they say, that justice is the constant will of giving to every man his own. And therefore where there is no own, that is, no propriety, there is no injustice; and where there is no coercive power erected, that is, where there is no commonwealth, there is no propriety; all men having right to all things: therefore where there is no commonwealth, there nothing is unjust. So that the nature of justice, consists in keeping of valid covenants: but the validity of covenants begins not but with the constitution of a civil power, sufficient to compel men to keep them: and then it is also that propriety begins.

The fool hath said in his heart, there is no such thing as justice; and sometimes also with his tongue; seriously alleging, that every man's conservation, and contentment, being committed to his own care, there could be no reason, why every man might not do what he thought conduced thereunto: and therefore also to make, or not make; keep, or not keep covenants, was not against reason, when it conduced to one's benefit. He does not therein deny, that there be covenants; and that they are sometimes broken, sometimes kept; and that such breach of them may be called injustice, and the observance of them justice: but he questions, whether injustice, taking away the fear of God (for the same fool hath said in his heart there is no God), may not sometimes stand with that reason, which dictates to every man his own good; and particularly then, when it conduces to such a benefit, as shall put a man in a condition, to neglect not only the dispraise, and revilings, but also the power of other men. The kingdom of God is gotten by violence: but what if it could be gotten by unjust violence? were it against reason so to get it, when it is impossible to receive hurt by it? and if it be not against reason, it is not against justice; or else justice is not to be approved for good. From such reasoning as this, successful wickedness hath obtained the name of virtue: and some that in all other things have disallowed the violation of faith; yet have allowed it, when it is for the getting of a kingdom. And the heathen that believed, that Saturn was deposed by his son Jupiter, believed nevertheless the same Jupiter to be the avenger of injustice: somewhat like a piece of law in Coke's *Commentaries on Littleton*;[1] where he says, if the right heir of the crown be attainted of treason; yet the crown shall descend to him, and eo instante the attender be void: from which instances a man will be very prone to infer; that when the heir apparent of a kingdom, shall kill him that is in possession, though his father; you may call it injustice, or by what other name you will; yet it can never be against reason, seeing all the voluntary actions of men tend to the benefit of themselves; and those actions are most reasonable, that conduce most to their ends. This specious reasoning is nevertheless false.

For the question is not of promises mutual, where there is no security of performance on either side; as when there is no civil power erected over the parties promising; for such promises are no covenants: but either where one of the parties has performed

---

[1] Sir Edward Coke (1552–1634) was the first Lord Chief Justice of England. His *Commentaries on Littleton*, refers to Sir Thomas de Littleton's (1407–1481) *Treatise on Tenures.*

already; or where there is a power to make him perform; there is the question whether it be against reason, that is, against the benefit of the other to perform, or not. And I say it is not against reason. For the manifestation whereof, we are to consider; first, that when a man doth a thing, which notwithstanding any thing can be foreseen, and reckoned on, tends to his own destruction, howsoever some accident which he could not expect, arriving may turn it to his benefit; yet such events do not make it reasonably or wisely done. Secondly, that in a condition of war, wherein every man to every man, for want of a common power to keep them all in awe, is an enemy, there is no man can hope by his own strength, or wit, to defend himself from destruction, without the help of confederates; where every one expects the same defence by the confederation, that any one else does: and therefore he which declares he thinks it reason to deceive those that help him, can in reason expect no other means of safety, than what can be had from his own single power. He therefore that breaks his covenant, and consequently declares that he thinks he may with reason do so, cannot be received into any society, that unite themselves for peace and defence, but by the error of them that receive him; nor when he is received, be retained in it, without seeing the danger of their error; which errors a man cannot reasonably reckon upon as the means of his security: and therefore if he be left, or cast out of society, he perishes; and if he live in society, it is by the errors of other men, which he could not foresee, nor reckon upon; and consequently against the reason of his preservation; and so, as all men that contribute not to his destruction, forbear him only out of ignorance of what is good for themselves.

As for the instance of gaining the secure and perpetual felicity of heaven, by any way; it is frivolous: there being but one way imaginable; and that is not breaking, but keeping of covenant.

And for the other instance of attaining sovereignty by rebellion; it is manifest, that though the event follow, yet because it cannot reasonably be expected, but rather the contrary; and because by gaining it so, others are taught to gain the same in like manner, the attempt thereof is against reason. Justice therefore, that is to say, keeping of covenant, is a rule of reason, by which we are forbidden to do any thing destructive to our life; and consequently a law of nature.

There be some that proceed further; and will not have the law of nature, to be those rules which conduce to the preservation of man's life on earth; but to the attaining of an eternal felicity after death; to which they think the breach of covenant may conduce; and consequently be just and reasonable (such are they that think it a work of merit to kill, or depose, or rebel against, the sovereign power constituted over them by their own consent). But because there is no natural knowledge of man's estate after death; much less of the reward that is then to be given to breach of faith; but only a belief grounded upon other men's saying, that they know it supernaturally, or that they know those, that knew them, that knew others, that knew it supernaturally; breach of faith cannot be called a precept of reason, or nature.

Others, that allow for a law of nature, the keeping of faith, do nevertheless make exception of certain persons; as heretics, and such as use not to perform their covenant to others: and this also is against reason. For if any fault of a man, be sufficient to discharge our covenant made; the same ought in reason to have been sufficient to have hindered the making of it.

The names of just, and unjust, when they are attributed to men, signify one thing; and when they are attributed to actions, another. When they are attributed to men, they signify conformity, or inconformity of manners, to reason. But when they are attributed to actions, they signify the conformity, or inconformity to reason, not of manners, or manner of life, but of particular actions. A just man therefore, is he that taketh all the care he can, that his actions may be all just: and an unjust man, is he that neglects it. And such men are more often in our language styled by the names of righteous, and unrighteous; than just, and unjust; though the meaning be the same. Therefore a righteous man, does not lose that title, by one, or a few unjust actions, that proceed from sudden passion, or mistake of things, or persons: nor does an unrighteous man, lose his character, for such actions, as he does, or forbears to do for fear: because his will is not framed by the justice, but by the apparent benefit of what he is to do. That which gives to human actions the relish of justice, is a certain nobleness or gallantness of courage (rarely found), by which a man scorns to be beholding for the contentment of his life, to fraud, or breach of promise. This justice of the manners, is that which is meant, where justice is called a virtue; and injustice a vice.

But the justice of actions denominates men, not just, but guiltless: and the injustice of the same (which is also called injury), gives them but the name of guilty.

Again, the injustice of manners, is the disposition, or aptitude to do injury; and is injustice before it proceed to act; and without supposing any individual person injured. But the injustice of an action (that is to say injury), supposes an individual person injured; namely him, to whom the covenant was made: and therefore many times the injury is received by one man, when the damage redounds to another. As when the master commands his servant to give money to a stranger; if it be not done, the injury is done to the master, whom he had before covenanted to obey; but the damage redounds to the stranger, to whom he had no obligation; and therefore could not injure him. And so also in commonwealths, private men may remit to one another their debts; but not robberies or other violences, whereby they are damaged; because the detaining of debt, is an injury to themselves; but robbery and violence, are injuries to the person of the commonwealth.

Whatsoever is done to a man, conformable to his own will signified to the doer, is no injury to him. For if he that doeth it, hath not passed away his original right to do what he please, by some antecedent covenant, there is no breach of covenant; and therefore no injury done him. And if he have; then his will to have it done being signified, is a release of that covenant: and so again there is no injury done him.

Justice of actions, is by writers divided into commutative, and distributive: and the former they say consists in proportion arithmetical; the latter in proportion geometrical. Commutative therefore, they place in the equality of value of the things contracted for; and distributive, in the distribution of equal benefit, to men of equal merit. As if it were injustice to sell dearer than we buy; or to give more to a man than he merits. The value of all things contracted for, is measured by the appetite of the contractors: and therefore the just value, is that which they be contented to give. And merit (besides that which is by covenant, where the performance on one part, mer-

its the performance of the other part, and falls under justice commutative, not distributive) is not due by justice; but is rewarded of grace only. And therefore this distinction, in the sense wherein it uses to be expounded, is not right. To speak properly commutative justice, is the justice of a contractor; that is, a performance of covenant, in buying, and selling; hiring, and letting to hire; lending, and borrowing; exchanging, bartering, and other acts of contract.

And distributive justice, the justice of an arbitrator; that is to say, the act of defining what is just. Wherein (being trusted by them that make him arbitrator) if he perform his trust, he is said to distribute to every man his own: and his is indeed just distribution, and may be called (though improperly) distributive justice; but more properly equity; which also is a law of nature, as shall be shown in due place.

As justice depends on antecedent covenant; so does GRATITUDE depend on antecedent grace; that is to say, antecedent free-gift: and is the fourth law of nature; which may be conceived in this form, that a man which receives benefit from another of mere grace, endeavor that he which giveth it, have no reasonable cause to repent him of his good will. For no man giveth, but with intention of good to himself; because gift is voluntary; and of all voluntary acts, the object is to every man his own good; of which if men see they shall be frustrated, there will be no beginning of benevolence, or trust; nor consequently of mutual help nor of reconciliation of one man to another; and therefore they are to remain still in the condition of war; which is contrary to the first and fundamental law of nature, which commands men to seek peace. The breach of this law, is called ingratitude; and hath the same relation to grace, that injustice hath to obligation by covenant.

A fifth law of nature, is COMPLAISANCE; that is to say, that every man strive to accommodate himself to the rest. For the understanding whereof, we may consider, that there is in men's aptness to society, a diversity of nature, rising from their diversity of affections; not unlike to that we see in stones brought together for building of an edifice. For as that stone which by the asperity, and irregularity of figure, takes more room from others, than itself fills; and for the hardness, cannot be easily made plain, and thereby hinders the building, is by the builders cast away as unprofitable, and troublesome: so also, a man that by asperity of nature, will strive to retain those things which to himself are superfluous, and to others necessary; and for the stubbornness of his passions, cannot be corrected, is to be left, or cast out of society, as cumbersome thereunto. For seeing every man, not only by right, but also by necessity of nature, is supposed to endeavor all he can, to obtain that which is necessary for his conservation; he that shall oppose himself against it, for things superfluous, is guilty of the war that thereupon is to follow; and therefore doth that, which is contrary to the fundamental law of nature, which commands to seek peace. The observers of this law, may be called SOCIABLE (the Latins call them *commodi*); the contrary, stubborn, unsociable, froward, intractable.

A sixth law of nature, is this, that upon caution of the future time, a man ought to pardon the offences past of them that repenting, desire it. For PARDON, is nothing but granting of peace; which though granted to them that persevere in their hostility, be not peace, but fear; yet not granted to them that give caution of the future time, is sign of an aversion to peace; and therefore contrary to the law of nature.

A seventh is, that in revenges (that is, retribution of evil for evil), men look not at the greatness of the evil past, but the greatness of the good to follow. Whereby we are forbidden to inflict punishment with any other design, than for correction of the offender, or direction of others. For this law is consequent to the next before it, that commands pardon, upon security of the future time. Besides, revenge without respect to the example, and profit to come, is a triumph, or glorying in the hurt of another, tending to no end (for the end is always somewhat to come); and glorying to no end, is vain-glory, and contrary to reason; and to hurt without reason, tends to the introduction of war; which is against the law of nature; and is commonly styled by the name of cruelty.

And because all signs of hatred, or contempt, provoke to fight; insomuch as most men choose rather to hazard their life, than not to be revenged; we may in the eighth place, for a law of nature, set down this precept, that no man by deed, word, countenance, or gesture, declare hatred, or contempt of another. The breach of which law, is commonly called contumely.

The question who is the better man, has no place in the condition of mere nature; where (as has been shewn before) all men are equal. The inequality that now is, has been introduced by the laws civil. I know that Aristotle in the first book of his *Politics*, for a foundation of his doctrine, maketh men by nature, some more worthy to command, meaning the wiser sort (such as he thought himself to be for his philosophy); others to serve (meaning those that had strong bodies, but were not philosophers as he); as if master and servant were not introduced by consent of men, but by difference of wit: which is not only against reason; but also against experience. For there are very few so foolish, that had not rather govern themselves, than be governed by others: nor when the wise in their own conceit, contend by force, with them who distrust their own wisdom, do they always, or often, or almost at any time, get the victory. If nature therefore have made men equal, that equality is to be acknowledged: or if nature have made men unequal; yet because men that think themselves equal, will not enter into conditions of peace, but upon equal terms, such as equality must be admitted. And therefore the ninth law of nature, I put this, that every man acknowledge other for his equal by nature. The breach of this precept is pride.

On this law, depends another, that at the entrance into conditions of peace, no man require to reserve to himself any right, which he is not content should be reserved to every one of the rest. As it is necessary for all men that seek peace, to lay down certain rights of nature; that is to say, not to have liberty to do all they list: so it is necessary for man's life, to retain some; as right to govern their own bodies; enjoy air, water, motion, ways to go from place to place; and all things else without which a man cannot live, or not live well. If in this case, at the making of peace, men require for themselves that which they would not have to be granted to others, they do contrary to the precedent law, that commands the acknowledgment of natural equality, and therefore also against the law of nature. The observers of this law are those we call modest, and the breakers arrogant men. The Greeks call the violation of this law [*pleonexia*]; that is, a desire of more than their share.

Also if a man be trusted to judge between man and man, it is a precept of the law of nature, that he deal equally between them. For without that, the controversies of men cannot be determined but by war. He therefore that is partial in judgment, doth what in him lies, to deter men from the use of judges, and arbitrators; and consequently (against the fundamental law of nature) is the cause of war.

The observance of this law, from the equal distribution to each man, of that which in reason belongs to him, is called EQUITY, and (as I have said before) distributive justice: the violation, acception of persons.

And from this followeth another law, that such things as cannot be divided, be enjoyed in common, if it can be; and if the quantity of the thing permit, without stint; otherwise proportionably to the number of them that have right. For otherwise the distribution is unequal, and contrary to equity.

But some things there be, that can neither be divided, nor enjoyed in common. Then, the law of nature, which prescribes equity, requires, that the entire right; or else (making the use alternate) the first possession, be determined by lot. For equal distribution, is of the law of nature; and other means of equal distribution cannot be imagined.

Of lots there be two sorts, arbitrary, and natural. Arbitrary, is that which is agreed on by the competitors: natural, is either primogeniture (which the Greek calls [kleronomia], which signifies, given by lot); or first seizure.

And therefore those things which cannot be enjoyed in common, nor divided, ought to be adjudged to the first possessor; and in some cases to the firstborn, as acquired by lot.

It is also a law of nature, that all men that mediate peace, be allowed safe conduct. For the law that commands peace, as the end, commands intercession, as the means; and to intercession the means is safe conduct.

And because, though men be never so willing to observe these laws, there may nevertheless arise questions concerning a man's action; first, whether it were done, or not done; secondly (if done), whether against the law, or not against the law; the former whereof, is called a question of fact; the latter a question of right; therefore unless the parties to the question, covenant mutually to stand to the sentence of another, they are as far from peace as ever. This other, to whose sentence they submit, is called an ARBITRATOR. And therefore it is of the law of nature, that they that are at controversy, submit their right to the judgment of an arbitrator.

And seeing every man is presumed to do all things in order to his own benefit, no man is a fit arbitrator in his own cause: and if he were never so fit; yet equity allowing to each party equal benefit, if one be admitted to be judge, the other is to be admitted also; and so the controversy, that is, the cause of war, remains, against the law of nature.

For the same reason no man in any cause ought to be received for arbitrator, to whom greater profit, or honour, or pleasure apparently arises out of the victory of one party, than of the other: for he hath taken (though an unavoidable bribe, yet) a bribe; and no man can be obliged to trust him. And thus also the controversy, and the condition of war remains, contrary to the law of nature.

And in a controversy of fact, the judge being to give no more credit to one, than to the other (if there be no other arguments), must give credit to a third; or to a third and fourth; or more: for else the question is undecided, and left to force, contrary to the law of nature.

These are the laws of nature, dictating peace, for a means of the conservation of men in multitudes; and which only concern the doctrine of civil society. There be other things tending to the destruction of particular men; as drunkenness, and all other parts of intemperance; which may therefore also be reckoned amongst those things which the law of nature hath forbidden; but are not necessary to be mentioned, nor are pertinent enough to this place.

And though this may seem too subtle a deduction of the laws of nature, to be taken notice of by all men; whereof the most part are too busy in getting food, and the rest too negligent to understand; yet to leave all men inexcusable, they have been contracted into one easy sum, intelligible, even to the meanest capacity; and that is, Do not that to another, which thou wouldest not have done to thyself; which shows him, that he has no more to do in learning the laws of nature, but, when weighing the actions of other men with his own, they seem too heavy, to put them into the other part of the balance, and his own into their place, that his own passions, and self-love, may add nothing to the weight; and then there is none of these laws of nature that will not appear unto him very reasonable.

The laws of nature oblige *in foro interno* [in conscience]; that is to say, they bind to a desire they should take place: but *in foro externo* [in civil law]; that is, to the putting them in act, not always. For he that should be modest, and tractable, and perform all he promises, in such time, and place, where no man else should do so, should but make himself a prey to others, and procure his own certain ruin, contrary to the ground of all laws of nature, which tend to nature's preservation. And again, he that having sufficient security, that others shall observe the same laws towards him, observes them not himself, seeks not peace, but war; and consequently the destruction of his nature by violence.

And whatsoever laws bind *in foro interno*, may be broken, not only by a fact contrary to the law, but also by a fact according to it, in case a man think it contrary. For though his action in this case, be according to the law; yet his purpose was against the law; which, where the obligations is *in foro interno*, is a breach.

The laws of nature are immutable and eternal; for injustice, ingratitude, arrogance, pride, iniquity, acception of persons, and the rest, can never be made lawful. For it can never be that war shall preserve life, and peace destroy it.

The same laws, because they oblige only to a desire, and endeavor, I mean an unfeigned and constant endeavor, are easy to be observed. For in that they require nothing but endeavor; he that endeavors their performance, fulfills them; and he that fulfills the law, is just.

And the science of them, is the true and only moral philosophy. For moral philosophy is nothing else but the science of what is good, and evil, in the conversation, and society of mankind. Good, and evil, are names that signify our appetites, and aversions; which in different tempers, customs, and doctrines of men, are different: and divers men, differ not only in their judgment, on the senses of what is pleasant, and unpleasant to the taste, smell, hearing, touch, and sight; but also of what is conformable, or disagreeable to reason, in the actions of common life. Nay, the same man, in divers times, differs from himself; and one time praises, that is, calleth good, what another time he dispraises, and calleth evil: from whence arise disputes, controversies, and at last war. And therefore so long a man is in the condition of mere nature (which is a condition of war), as private appetite is the measure of good, and evil: and consequently all men agree on this, that peace is good, and therefore also the way, or means of peace, which (as I have shewed before) are justice, gratitude, modesty, equity, mercy, and the rest of the laws of nature, are good; that is to say, moral virtues; and their contrary vices, evil. Now the science of virtue and vice, is moral philosophy; and therefore the true doctrine of the laws of nature, is the true moral philosophy. But the writers of moral philosophy, though they acknowledge the same virtues and vices; yet not seeing wherein consisted their goodness; nor that they come to be praised, as the means of peaceable, sociable, and comfortable living; place them in a mediocrity of passions: as if not the cause, but the degree of daring, made fortitude; or not the cause, but the quantity of a gift, made liberality.

These dictates of reason, men use to call by the name of laws; but improperly: for they are but conclusions, or theorems concerning what conduces to the conversion and defence of themselves; whereas law, properly, is the word of him, that by right hath command over others. But yet if we consider the same theorems, as delivered in the word of God, that by right commands all things; then are they properly called laws.

PART 2. OF COMMONWEALTH

CHAPTER 17. OF THE CAUSES, GENERATION, AND DEFINITION OF A COMMONWEALTH

The final cause, end, or design of men (who naturally love liberty, and dominion over others), in the introduction of that restraint upon themselves (in which we see them live in commonwealths), is the foresight of their own preservation, and of a more contented life thereby; that is to say, of getting themselves out from that miserable condition of war, which is necessarily consequent (as hath been shown), to the natural passions of men, when there is no visible power to keep them in awe, and tie them by fear of punishment to the performance of their covenants, and observation of those laws of nature set down in the fourteenth and fifteenth chapters.

For the laws of nature (as justice, equity, modesty, mercy, and [in sum] doing to others, as we would be done to), of themselves, without the terror of some power to cause them to be observed, are contrary to our natural passions, that carry us to partiality, pride, revenge, and the like. And covenants without the sword are but words, and of no strength to secure a man at all. Therefore notwithstanding the laws of nature (which every one hath then kept, when he has the will to keep them, when he can do it safely), if there be no power erected, or not great enough for our security; every man will, and may lawfully, rely on his own strength and art for caution against all other men. And in all places, where men have lived by small families, to rob and spoil one another, has been a trade, and so far from being reputed against the law of nature, that the greater spoils they gained, the greater was their honour; and men observed no other laws therein, but the laws of honour; that is, to abstain from cruelty, leaving to men their lives, and instruments of husbandry. And as small families did then; so now do cities and kingdoms which are but greater families (for their own security) enlarge their dominions, upon all pretenses of danger, and fear of invasion, or assistance that may be given to invaders, endeavor as much as they can, to subdue, or weaken their neighbors, by open force, and secret arts, for want of other caution, justly; and are remembered for it in after ages with honour.

Nor is it the joining together of a small number of men, that gives them this security; because in small numbers, small additions on the one side or the other, make the advantage of strength so great, as is sufficient to carry the victory; and therefore gives encouragement to an invasion. The multitude sufficient to confide in for our security, is not determined by any certain number, but by comparison with the enemy we fear; and is then sufficient, when the odds of the enemy is not of so visible and conspicuous moment, to determine the event of war, as to move him to attempt.

And be there never so great a multitude; yet if their actions be directed according to their particular judgments, and particular appetites, they can ex-pect thereby no defence, nor protection, neither against a common enemy, nor against the injuries of one another. For being distracted in opinions concerning the best use and application of their strength, they do not help, but hinder one another; and reduce their strength by mutual opposition to nothing: whereby they are easily, not only subdued by a very few that agree together; but also when there is no common enemy, they make war upon each other, for their particular interests. For if we could suppose a great multitude of men to consent in the observation of justice, and other laws of nature, without a common power to keep them all in awe; we might as well suppose all mankind to do the same; and then there neither would be, nor need to be any civil government, or commonwealth at all; because there would be peace without subjection.

Nor is it enough for the security, which men desire should last all the time of their life, that they be governed, and directed by one judgment, for a limited time; as in one battle, or one war. For though they obtain a victory by their unanimous endeavor against a foreign enemy; yet afterwards, when either they have no common enemy, or he that by one part is held for an enemy, is by another part held for a friend, they must needs by the difference of their interests dissolve, and fall again into a war amongst themselves.

It is true, that certain living creatures, as bees and ants, live sociably one with another (which are therefore by Aristotle numbered amongst political creatures); and yet have no other direction, than their particular judgments and appetites; nor speech, whereby one of them can signify to another, what he thinks expedient for the common benefit: and therefore some man may perhaps desire to know, why mankind cannot do the same. To which I answer,

First, that men are continually in competition for honour and dignity, which these creatures are not; and consequently amongst men there arises on that ground, envy and hatred, and finally war; but amongst these not so.

Secondly, that amongst these creatures, the common good differs not from the private; and being by nature inclined to their private, they procure thereby the common benefit. But man, whose joy consists in comparing himself with other men, can relish nothing but what is eminent.

Thirdly, that these creatures, having not (as man) the use of reason, do not see, nor think they see any fault, in the administration of their common business; whereas amongst men, there are very many, that think themselves wiser, and abler to govern the public, better than the rest; and these strive to reform and innovate, one this way, another that way; and thereby bring it into distraction and civil war.

Fourthly, that these creatures, though they have some use of voice, in making known to one another their desires, and other affections; yet they want that art of words, by which some men can represent to others, that which is good, in the likeness of evil; and evil, in the likeness of good; and augment, or diminish the apparent greatness of good and evil; discontenting men, and troubling their peace at their pleasure.

Fifthly, irrational creatures cannot distinguish between injury, and damage; and therefore as long as they be at ease, they are not offended with their fellows: whereas man is then most troublesome, when he is most at ease: for then it is that he loves to shew his wisdom, and control the actions of them that govern the commonwealth.

Lastly, the agreement of these creatures is natural; that of men, is by covenant only, which is artificial: and therefore it is no wonder if there be somewhat else required (besides covenant) to make their agreement constant and lasting; which is a common power, to keep them in awe, and to direct their actions to the common benefit.

The only way to erect such a common power, as may be able to defend them from the invasion of foreigners, and the injuries of one another, and thereby to secure them in such sort, as that by their own industry, and by the fruits of the earth, they may nourish themselves and live contentedly; is, to confer all their power and strength upon one man, or upon one assembly of men, that may reduce all their wills, by plurality of voices, unto one will: which is as much as to say, to appoint one man, or assembly of men, to bear their person; and every one to own, and acknowledge himself to be author of whatsoever he that so beareth their person, shall act, or cause to be acted, in those things which concern the common peace and safety; and therein to submit their wills, every one to his will, and their judgments, to his

judgment. This is more than consent, or concord; it is a real unity of them all, in one and the same person, made by covenant of every man with every man, in such manner, as if every man should say to every man, I authorize and give up my right of governing myself, to this man, or to this assembly of men, on this condition, that thou give up thy right to him, and authorize all his actions in like manner. This done, the multitude so united in one person, is called a COMMONWEALTH, in Latin CIVITAS. This is the generation of that great LEVIATHAN, or rather (to speak more reverently) of that mortal god, to which we owe under the immortal God, our peace and defence. For by this authority, given him by every particular man in the commonwealth, he hath the use of so much power and strength conferred on him, that by terror thereof, he is enabled to form the wills of them all, to peace at home, and mutual aid against their enemies abroad. And in him consists the essence of the commonwealth; which (to define it) is one person, of whose acts a great multitude, by mutual covenants one with another, have made themselves every one the author, to the end he may use the strength and means of them all, as he shall think expedient, for their peace and common defence.

And he that carries this person, is called SOVEREIGN, and said to have sovereign power; and every one besides, his SUBJECT.

The attaining to this sovereign power, is by two ways. One, by natural force; as when a man maketh his children, to submit themselves, and their children to his government, as being able to destroy them if they refuse; or by war subdues his enemies to his will, giving them their lives on that condition. The other, is when men agree amongst themselves, to submit to some man, or assembly of men, voluntarily, on confidence to be protected by him against all others. This latter, may be called a political commonwealth, or commonwealth by institution; and the former, a commonwealth by acquisition. And first, I shall speak of a commonwealth by institution.

CHAPTER 18. OF THE RIGHTS OF SOVEREIGNS BY INSTITUTION

A commonwealth is said to be instituted, when a multitude of men do agree, and covenant, every one, with every one, that to whatsoever man, or assembly of men, shall be given by the major part, the right to present the person of them all (that is to say, to be their representative); every one, as well he that voted for it, as he that voted against it, shall authorize all the actions and judgments, of that man, or assembly of men, in the same manner, as if they were his own, to the end, to live peaceably amongst themselves, and be protected against other men.

From this institution of a commonwealth are derived all the rights, and faculties of him, or them, on whom the sovereign power is conferred by the consent of the people assembled.

First, because they covenant, it is to be understood, they are not obliged by former covenant to any thing repugnant hereunto. And consequently they that have already instituted a commonwealth, being thereby bound by covenant, to own the actions, and judgments of one, cannot lawfully make a new covenant, amongst themselves, to be obedient to any other, in any thing whatsoever, without his permission. And therefore, they that are subjects to a monarch, cannot without his leave cast off monarchy, and return to the confusion of a disunited multitude; nor transfer their person from him that beareth it, to another man, or other assembly of men: for they are bound, every man to every man, to own, and be reputed author of all, that he that already is their sovereign, shall do, and judge fit to be done: so that any one man dissenting, all the rest should break their covenant made to that man, which is injustice: and they have also every man given the sovereignty to him that beareth their person; and therefore if they depose him, they take from him that which is his own, and so again it is injustice. Besides, if he that attempts to depose his sovereign, be killed, or punished by him for such attempt, he is author of his own punishment, as being by the institution, author of all his sovereign shall do: and because it is injustice for a man to do any thing, for which he may be punished by his own authority, he is also upon that title, unjust. And whereas some men have pretended for their disobedience to their sovereign, a new covenant, made, not with men, but with God; this also is unjust: for there is no covenant with God, but by mediation of somebody that represents God's person; which none doth but God's lieutenant, who hath the sovereignty under God. But this pretence of covenant with God, is so evident a lie, even in the pretenders' own consciences, that it is not only an act of an unjust, but also a vile, and unmanly disposition.

Secondly, because the right of bearing the person of them all, is given to him they make sovereign, by covenant only of one to another, and not of him to any of them; there can happen no breach of covenant on the part of the sovereign; and consequently none of his subjects, by any pretence of forfeiture, can be freed from his subjection. That he which is made sovereign maketh no covenant with his subjects beforehand, is manifest; because either he must make it with the whole multitude, as one party to the covenant; or he must make a several covenant with every man. With the whole, as one party, it is impossible; because as yet they are not one person: and if he make so many several covenants as there be men, those covenants after he hath the sovereignty are void, because what act soever can be pretended by any one of them for breach thereof, is the act both of himself, and of all the rest, because done in the person, and by the right of every one of them in particular. Besides, if any one, or more of them, pretend a breach of the covenant made by the sovereign at his institution; and others, or one other of his subjects, or himself alone, pretend there was no such breach, there is in this case, no judge to decide the controversy; it returns therefore to the sword again; and every man recovers the right of protecting himself by his own strength, contrary to the design they had in the institution. It is therefore in vain to grant sovereignty by way of precedent covenant. The opinion that any monarch receives his power by covenant, that is to say, on condition, proceeds from want of understanding this easy truth, that covenants being but words and breath, have no force to oblige, contain, constrain, or protect any man, but what it has from the public sword; that is, from the untied hands of that man, or assembly of men that hath the sovereignty, and whose actions are avouched by them all, and performed by the strength of them all, in him united. But when an assembly of men is made sovereign; then no man imagines any such covenant to have passed in the institution; for no man is so dull as to say, for example, the people of Rome made a covenant with the Romans, to hold the sovereignty on such or such conditions; which not performed, the Romans might lawfully depose the Roman people. That men see not the reason to be alike in a monarchy, and in a popular government, proceeds from the ambition of some, that are kinder to the government of an assembly, whereof they may hope to participate, than of monarchy, which they despair to enjoy.

Thirdly, because the major part hath by consenting voices declared a sovereign; he that dissented must now consent with the rest; that is, be contented to avow all the actions he shall do, or else justly be destroyed by the rest. For if he voluntarily entered into the congregation of them that were assembled, he sufficiently declared thereby his will, (and therefore tacitly covenanted) to stand to what the major part should ordain: and therefore if he refuse to stand thereto, or make protestation against any of their decrees, he does contrary to his covenant, and therefore unjustly. And whether he be of the congregation, or not; and whether his consent be asked, or not, he must either submit to their decrees, or be left in the condition of war he was in before; wherein he might without injustice be destroyed by any man whatsoever.

Fourthly, because every subject is by this institution author of all the actions, and judgments of the sovereign instituted; it follows, that whatsoever he doth, it can be no injury to any of his subjects; nor ought he to be by any of them accused of injustice. For he that doth any thing by authority from another, doth therein no injury to him by whose authority he acts: but by this institution of a commonwealth, every particular man is author of all the sovereign doth; and consequently he that complains of injury from his sovereign, complains of that whereof he himself is author; and therefore ought not to accuse any man but himself; no nor himself of injury; because to do injury to one's self, is impossible. It is true that they that have sovereign power, may commit iniquity; but not injustice, or injury in the proper signification.

Fifthly, and consequently to that which was said last, no man that hath sovereign power can justly be put to death, or otherwise in any manner by his subjects punished. For seeing every subject is author of the actions of his sovereign; he punishes another, for the actions committed by himself.

And because the end of this institution, is the peace and defence of them all; and whosoever has right to the end, has right to the means; it belongs of right, to whatsoever man, or assembly that hath the sovereignty, to be judge of both of the means of peace and defence; and also of the hindrances, and disturbances of the same; and to do whatsoever he shall think necessary to be done, both beforehand, for the preserving of peace and security, by prevention of discord at home, and hostility from abroad; and, when peace and security are lost, for the recovery of the same. And therefore,

Sixthly, it is annexed to the sovereignty, to be judge of what opinions and doctrines are averse, and what conducing to peace; and consequently on what occasions, how far, and what, men are to be trusted withal, in speaking to multitudes of people; and who shall examine the doctrines of all books before they be published. For the actions of men proceed from their opinions; and in the well-governing of opinions, consists the well-governing of men's actions, in order to their peace, and concord. And though in matter of doctrine, nothing ought to be regarded but the truth; yet this is not repugnant to regulating of the same by peace. For doctrine repugnant to peace, can no more be true, than peace and concord can be against the law of nature. It is true, that in a commonwealth, where by the negligence, or unskillfulness of governors, and teachers, false doctrines are by time generally received; the contrary truths may be generally offensive: Yet the most sudden, and rough bustling in of a new truth, that can be, does never break the peace, but only sometimes awake the war. For those men that are so remissly governed, that they dare take up arms, to defend, or introduce an opinion, are still in war; and their condition not peace, but only a cessation of arms for fear of one another; and they live as it were, in the precincts of battle continually. It belongs therefore to him that hath the sovereign power, to be judge, or constitute all judges of opinions and doctrines, as a thing necessary to peace; thereby to prevent discord and civil war.

Seventhly, is annexed to the sovereignty, the whole power of prescribing the rules, whereby every man may know, what goods he may enjoy, and what actions he may do, without being molested by any of his fellow-subjects; and this is it men call propriety. For before constitution of sovereign power (as hath already been shown) all men had right to all things; which necessarily causes war: and therefore this propriety, being necessary to peace, and depending on sovereign power, is the act of that power, in order to the public peace. These rules of propriety (or *meum* and *tuum* [mine and thine]) and of good, evil, lawful, and unlawful in the actions of subjects, are the civil laws; that is to say, the laws of each commonwealth in particular; though the name of civil law be now restrained to the ancient civil laws of the city of Rome; which being the head of a great part of the world, her laws at that time were in these parts the civil law.

Eighthly, is annexed to the sovereignty, the right of judicature; that is to say, of hearing and deciding all controversies, which may arise concerning law, either civil, or natural; or concerning fact. For without the decision of controversies, there is no protection of one subject, against the injuries of another; the laws concerning meum and tuum are in vain; and to every man remains, from the natural and necessary appetite of his own conservation, the right of protecting himself by his private strength, which is the condition of war; and contrary to the end for which every commonwealth is instituted.

Ninthly, is annexed to the sovereignty, the right of making war and peace with other nations, and commonwealths; that is to say, of judging when it is for the public good, and how great forces are to be assembled, armed, and paid for that end; and to levy money upon the subjects, to defray the expenses thereof. For the power by which the people are to be defended, consists in their armies; and the strength of an army, in the union of their strength under one command; which command the sovereign instituted, therefore hath; because the command of the militia, without other institution, maketh him that hath it sovereign. And therefore whosoever is made general of an army, he that hath the sovereign power is always generalissimo.

Tenthly, is annexed to the sovereignty, the choosing of all counsellors, ministers, magistrates, and officers, both in peace, and war. For seeing the sovereign is charged with the end, which is the common peace and defence, he is understood to have power to use such means, as he shall think most fit for his discharge.

Eleventhly, to the sovereign is committed the power of rewarding with riches, or honour; and of punishing with corporal, or pecuniary punishment, or with ignominy every subject according to the law he hath formerly made; or if there be no law made, according as he shall judge most to conduce to the encouraging of men to serve the commonwealth, or deterring of them from doing disservice to the same.

Lastly, considering what values men are naturally apt to set upon themselves; what respect they look for from others; and how little they value other men; from whence continually arise amongst them, emulation, quarrels, factions, and at last war, to the destroying of one another, and diminution of their strength against a common enemy; it is necessary that there be laws of honour, and a public rate of the worth of such men as have deserved, or are able to deserve well of the commonwealth; and that there be force in the hands of some or other, to put those laws in execution. But it hath already been shown, that not only the whole militia, or forces of the commonwealth; but also the judicature of all controversies, is annexed to the sovereignty. To the sovereign therefore it belongs also to give titles of honour; and to appoint what order of place, and dignity, each man shall hold; and what signs of respect, in public or private meetings, they shall give to one another.

These are the rights, which make the essence of sovereignty; and which are the marks, whereby a man may discern in what man, or assembly of men, the sovereign power is placed, and resides. For these are incommunicable, and inseparable. The power to coin money; to dispose of the estate and persons of infant heirs; to have preemption in markets; and all other statute prerogatives, may be transferred to the sovereign; and yet the power to protect his subjects be retained. But if he transfer the militia, he retains the judicature in vain, for want of execution of the laws: or if he grant away the power of raising money; the militia is in vain: or if he give away the government of doctrines, men will be frightened into rebellion with the fear of spirits. And so if we consider any one of the said rights, we shall presently see, that the holding of all the rest will produce no effect, in the conservation of peace and justice, the end for which all commonwealths are instituted. And this division is it, whereof it is said, a kingdom divided in itself cannot stand: for unless this division precede, division into opposite armies can never happen. If there had not first been an opinion received of the greatest part of England, that these powers were divided between the King, and the Lords, and the House of Commons, the people had never been divided and fallen into this civil war; first between those that disagreed in politics; and after between the dissenters about the liberty of religion; which have so instructed men in this point of sovereign right, that there be few now (in England) that do not see, that these rights are inseparable, and will be so generally acknowledged at the next return of peace;[2] and so continue, till their miseries are forgotten; and no longer, except the vulgar be better taught than they have hitherto been.

And because they are essential and inseparable rights, it follows necessarily, that in whatsoever words any of them seem to be granted away, yet if the sovereign power itself be not in direct terms renounced, and the name of sovereign no more given by the grantees to him that grants them, the grant is void: for when he has granted all he can, if we grant back the sovereignty, all is restored, as inseparably annexed thereunto.

This great authority being indivisible, and inseparably annexed to the sovereignty, there is little ground for the opinion of them, that say of sovereign kings, though they be singulis majores, of greater power than every one of their subjects, yet they be universis minores, of less power than them all together. For if by all together, they mean not the collective body as one person, then all together, and every one, signify the same; and the speech is absurd. But if by all together, they understand them as one person (which person the sovereign bears), then the power of all together, is the same with the sovereign's power; and so again the speech is absurd: which absurdity they see well enough, when the sovereignty is in an assembly of the people; but in a monarch they see it not; and yet the power of sovereignty is the same in whomsoever it be placed.

And as the power, so also the honour of the sovereign, ought to be greater, than that of any, or all the subjects. For in the sovereignty is the fountain of honour. The dignities of lord, earl, duke, and prince are his creatures. As in the presence of the master, the servants are equal, and without any honour at all; so are the subjects, in the presence of the sovereign. And though they shine some more, some less, when they are out of his sight; yet in his presence, they shine no more than the stars in the presence of the sun.

But a man may here object, that the condition of subjects is very miserable; as being obnoxious to the lusts, and other irregular passions of him, or them that have so unlimited a power in their hands. And commonly they that live under a monarch, think it the fault of monarchy; and they that live under the government of democracy, or other sovereign assembly, attribute all the inconvenience to that form of commonwealth; whereas the power in all forms, if they be perfect enough to protect them, is the same; not considering that the estate of man can never be without some incommodity or other; and that the greatest, that in any form of government can possibly happen to the people in general, is scarce sensible, in respect of the miseries, and horrible calamities, that accompany a civil war, or that dissolute condition of masterless men, without subjection to laws, and a coercive power to tie their hands from rapine and revenge: nor considering that the greatest pressure of sovereign governors, proceeds not from any delight, or profit they can expect in the damage or weakening of their subjects, in whose vigor, consists their own strength and glory; but in the restiveness of themselves, that unwillingly contributing to their own defence, make it necessary for their governors to draw from them what they can in time of peace, that they may have means on any emergent occasion, or sudden need, to resist, or take advantage on their enemies. For all men are by nature provided of notable multiplying glasses (that is their passions and self-love), through which, every little payment appears a great grievance; but are destitute of those prospective glasses (namely moral and civil science), to see afar off the miseries that hang over them, and cannot without such payments be avoided. . . .

---

[2]Hobbes wrote this work in the midst of the English civil war (1641–1646; 1648–1652) in which Parliament fought King Charles I (the Royalists), which Parliament won.

CHAPTER 21. OF THE LIBERTY OF SUBJECTS

LIBERTY, or FREEDOM, signifies (properly) the absence of opposition (by opposition, I mean external impediments of motion); and may be applied no less to irrational, and inanimate creatures, than to rational. For whatsoever is so tied, or environed, as it cannot move, but within a certain space, which space is determined by the opposition of some external body, we say it hath not liberty to go further. And so of all living creatures, whilst they are imprisoned, or restrained, with walls, or chains; and of the water whilst it is kept in by banks, or vessels, that otherwise would spread itself into a larger space, we use to say, they are not at liberty, to move in such manner, as without those external impediments they would. But when the impediment of motion, is in the constitution of the thing itself, we use not to say, it wants the liberty; but the power to move; as when a stone lies still, or a man is fastened to his bed by sickness.

And according to this proper, and generally received meaning of the word, a FREEMAN, is he, that in those things, which by his strength and wit he is able to do, is not hindered to do what he has a will to. But when the words free, and liberty, are applied to any thing but bodies, they are abused; for that which is not subject to motion, is not subject to impediment: and therefore, when it is said (for example) the way is free, no liberty of the way is signified, but of those that walk in it without stop. And when we say a gift is free, there is not meant any liberty of the gift, but of the giver, that was not bound by any law, or covenant to give it. So when we speak freely, it is not the liberty of voice, or pronunciation, but of the man, whom no law hath obliged to speak otherwise than he did. Lastly, from the use of the word free-will, no liberty can be inferred of the will, desire, or inclination, but the liberty of the man; which consists in this, that he finds no stop, in doing what he has the will, desire, or inclination to do.

Fear, and liberty are consistent; as when a man throws his goods into the sea for fear the ship should sink, he doth it nevertheless very willingly, and may refuse to do it if he will: it is therefore the action of one that was free: so a man sometimes pays his debt, only for fear of imprisonment, which because nobody hindered him from detaining, was the action of a man at liberty. And generally all actions which men do in commonwealths, for fear of the law, are actions, which the doers had liberty to omit.

Liberty, and necessity are consistent: as in the water, that hath not only liberty, but a necessity of descending by the channel; so likewise in the actions which men voluntarily do: which, because they proceed from their will, proceed from liberty; and yet, because every act of man's will, and every desire, and inclination proceeds from some cause, and that from another cause, in a continual chain (whose first link is in the hand of God the first of all causes), they proceed from necessity. So that to him that could see the connexion of those causes, the necessity of all men's voluntary actions, would appear manifest. And therefore God, that sees, and disposes all things, sees also that the liberty of man in doing what he will, is accompanied with the necessity of doing that which God will, and no more, nor less. For though men may do many things, which God does not command, nor is therefore author of them; yet they can have no passion, nor appetite to any thing, of which appetite God's will is not the cause. And did not his will assure the necessity of man's will, and consequently of all that on man's will depends, the liberty of men would be a contradiction, and impediment to the omnipotence and liberty of God. And this shall suffice (as to the matter in hand) of that natural liberty, which only is properly called liberty.

But as men, for the attaining of peace, and conservation of themselves thereby, have made an artificial man, which we call a commonwealth; so also have they made artificial chains, called civil laws, which they themselves, by mutual covenants, have fastened at one end, to the lips of that man, or assembly, to whom they have given the sovereign power; and at the other end to their own ears. These bonds in their own nature but weak, may nevertheless be made to hold, by the danger, though not by the difficulty of breaking them.

In relation to these bonds only it is, that I am to speak now, of the liberty of subjects. For seeing there is no commonwealth in the world, wherein there be rules enough set down, for the regulating of all the actions, and words of men (as being a thing impossible): it followeth necessarily, that in all kinds of actions, but the laws pretermitted, men have the liberty, of doing what their own reasons shall suggest, for the most profitable to themselves. For if we take liberty in the proper sense, for corporal liberty; that is to say, freedom from chains, and prison, it were very absurd for men to clamor as they do, for the liberty they so manifestly enjoy. Again, if we take liberty, for an exemption from laws, it is no less absurd, for men to demand as they do, that liberty, by which all other men may be masters of their lives. And yet as absurd as it is, this is it they demand; not knowing that the laws are of no power to protect them, without a sword in the hands of a man, or men, to cause those laws to be put in execution. The liberty of a subject, lies therefore only in those things, which in regulating their actions, the sovereign hath pretermitted: such as is the liberty to buy, and sell, and otherwise contract with one another; to choose their own abode, their own diet, their own trade of life, and institute their children as they themselves think fit; and the like.

Nevertheless we are not to understand, that by such liberty, the sovereign power of life and death, is either abolished, or limited. For it has been already shown, that nothing the sovereign representative can do to a subject, on what pretence soever, can properly be called injustice, or injury; because every subject is author of every act the sovereign doth; so that he never wants right to any thing, otherwise, than as he himself is the subject of God, and bound thereby to observe the laws of nature. And therefore it may, and doth often happen in commonwealths, that a subject may be put to death, by the command of the sovereign power; and yet neither do the other wrong: as when Jephtha caused his daughter to be sacrificed: in which, and the like cases, he that so dies, had liberty to do the action, for which he is nevertheless, without injury put to death. And the same holds also in a sovereign prince, that puts to death an innocent subject. For though the action be against the law of nature, as being contrary to equity (as was the killing of Uriah, by David); yet it was not an injury to Uriah; but to God. Not to Uriah, because the right to do what he pleased, was given him by Uriah himself: and yet to God, because David was God's subject; and prohibited all iniquity by the law of nature. Which distinction, David himself, when he repented the fact, evidently confirmed, saying, To thee only have I sinned. In the same manner, the people of

Athens, when they banished the most potent of their commonwealth for ten years, thought they committed no injustice; and yet they never questioned what crime he had done; but what hurt he would do; nay they commanded the banishment of they knew not whom; and every citizen bringing his oystershell into market place, written with the name of him he desired should be banished, without actual accusing him, sometimes banished an Aristides, for his reputation of justice; and sometimes a scurrilous jester, as Hyperbolus, to make a jest of it. And yet a man cannot say, the sovereign people of Athens wanted right to banish them; or an Athenian the liberty to jest, or to be just.[3]

The liberty, whereof there is so frequent and honorable mention, in the histories, and philosophy of the ancient Greeks, and Romans, and in the writings, and discourse of those that from them have received all their learning in the politics, is not the liberty of particular men; but the liberty of the commonwealth: which is the same with that, which every man then should have, if there were no civil laws, nor commonwealth at all. And the effects of it also be the same. For as amongst masterless men, there is perpetual war, of every man against his neighbor; no inheritance, to transmit to the son, nor to expect from the father; no propriety of goods, or lands; no security; but a full and absolute liberty in every particular man: so in states, and commonwealths not dependent on one another, every commonwealth (not every man) has an absolute liberty, to do what it shall judge (that is to say, what that man, or assembly that represents it, shall judge) most conducing to their benefit. But withall, they live in the condition of a perpetual war, and upon the confines of battle, with their frontiers armed, and cannons planted against their neighbors round about. The Athenians, and Romans were free; that is, free commonwealths: not that any particular men had the liberty to resist their own representative; but that their representative had the

---

[3]The Athenians in the fifth century B.C. expelled innocent men thought to be dangerous to the state. The names of the men deemed dangerous were written on pieces of broken pottery. The famous general Aristides was expelled in 483 B.C. but recalled a few years later. The demagogue Hyperbolus was expelled in 417 B.C.

liberty to resist, or invade other people. There is written on the turrets of the city of Lucca in great characters at this day, the word LIBERTAS; yet no man can thence infer, that a particular man has more liberty, or immunity from the service of the commonwealth there, than in Constantinople. Whether a commonwealth be monarchical, or popular, the freedom is still the same.

But it is an easy thing, for men to be deceived, by the specious name of liberty, and for want of judgment to distinguish, mistake that for their private inheritance, and birth right, which is the right of the public only. And when the same error is confirmed by the authority of men in reputation for their writings in this subject, it is no wonder if it produce sedition, and change of government. In these western parts of the world, we are made to receive our opinions concerning the institution, and rights of commonwealths, from Aristotle, Cicero, and other men, Greeks and Romans, that living under popular states, derived those rights, not from the principles of nature, but transcribed them into their books, out of the practice of their own commonwealths, which were popular; as the grammarians describe the rules of language, out of the practice of the time; or the rules of poetry, out of the poems of Homer and Virgil. And because the Athenians were taught (to keep them from desire of changing their government), that they were freemen, and all that lived under monarchy were slaves; therefore Aristotle puts it down in his *Politics*. In democracy, Liberty is to be supposed: for it is commonly held, that no man is Free in any other government. And as Aristotle; so Cicero, and other writers have ground their civil doctrine, on the opinions of the Romans, who were taught to hate monarchy, at first, by them that having deposed their sovereign, shared amongst them the sovereignty of Rome; and afterwards by their successors. And by reading of these Greek, and Latin authors, men from their childhood have gotten a habit (under a false show of liberty), of favoring tumults, and of licentious controlling the actions of their sovereigns; and again of controlling those controllers, with the effusion of so much blood; as I think I may truly say, there was never any thing so dearly bought, as these western parts have bought the learning of the Greek and Latin tongues.

To come now to the particulars of the true liberty of a subject; that is to say, what are the things, which though commanded by the sovereign, he may nevertheless, without injustice, refuse to do; we are to consider, what rights we pass away, when we make a commonwealth; or (which is all one), what liberty we deny ourselves, by owning all the actions (without exception) of the man, or assembly we make our sovereign. For in the act of our submission, consists both our obligation, and our liberty; which must therefore be inferred by arguments taken from thence; there being no obligation on any man, which arises not from some act of his own; for all men equally, are by nature free. And because such arguments, must either be drawn from the express words, I authorize all his actions, or from the intention of him that submits himself to his power (which intention is to be understood by the end for which he so submits); the obligation, and liberty of the subject, is to be derived, either from those words (or others equivalent); or else from the end of the institution of sovereignty, namely, the peace of the subjects within themselves, and their defence against a common enemy.

First therefore, seeing sovereignty by institution, is by covenant of every one to every one; and sovereignty by acquisition, by covenants of the vanquished to the victor, or child to the parent; it is manifest, that every subject has liberty in all those things, the right whereof cannot by covenant be transferred. I have shewn before the 14th chapter, that covenants, not to defend a man's own body, are void. Therefore, If the sovereign command a man (though justly condemned) to kill, wound, or maim himself; or not to resist those that assault him; or to abstain from the use of food, air, medicine, or any other thing, without which he cannot live; yet hath that man the liberty to disobey.

If a man be interrogated by the sovereign, or his authority, concerning a crime done by himself, he is not bound (without assurance of pardon) to confess it; because no man (as I have shown in the same chapter) can be obliged by covenant to accuse himself.

Again, the consent of a subject to sovereign power, is contained in these words, I authorize, or take upon me, all his actions; in which there is no restriction at all, of his own former natural liberty: for by allowing him to kill me, I am not bound to kill myself when he commands me. It is one thing to say, kill me, or my fellow, if you please; another thing to say, I will kill myself, or my fellow. It followeth therefore, that No man is bound by the words themselves, either to kill himself, or any other man; and consequently, that the obligation a man may sometimes have, upon the command of the sovereign to execute any dangerous, or dishonorable office, depends not on the words of our submission; but on the intention, which is to be understood by the end thereof. When therefore our refusal to obey, frustrates the end for which the sovereignty was ordained; then there is no liberty to refuse: otherwise there is.

Upon this ground, a man that is commanded as a soldier to fight against the enemy, though his sovereign have right enough to punish his refusal with death, may nevertheless in many cases refuse, without injustice; as when he substitutes a sufficient soldier in his place: for in this case he deserts not the service of the commonwealth. And there is allowance to be made for natural timorousness; not only to women (of whom no such dangerous duty is expected), but also to men of feminine courage. When armies fight, there is on one side, or both, a running away; yet when they do it not out of treachery, but fear, they are not esteemed to do it unjustly, but dishonorably. For the same reason, to avoid battle, is not injustice, but cowardice. But he that enrolls himself a soldier, or taketh imprest money, taketh away the excuse of a timorous nature; and is obliged, not only to go to the battle, but also not to run from it, without his captain's leave. And when the defence of the commonwealth, requires at once the help of all that are able to bear arms, every one is obliged; because otherwise the institution of the commonwealth, which they have not the purpose, or courage to preserve, was in vain.

To resist the sword of the commonwealth, in defence of another man, guilty, or innocent, no man hath liberty; because such liberty, takes away from the sovereign, the means of protecting us; and is therefore destructive of the very essence of government. But in case a great many men together, have already resisted the sovereign power unjustly, or committed some capital crime, for which every one of them expects death, whether have they not the liberty then to join together, and assist, and defend one another? Certainly they have: for they but defend their lives, which the guilty man may as well do, as the innocent. There was indeed injustice in the first breach of their duty; their bearing of arms subsequent to it, though it be to maintain what they have done, is no new unjust act. And if it be only to defend their persons, it is not unjust at all. But the offer of pardon taketh from them, to whom it is offered, the plea of self-defence, and maketh their perseverance in assisting, or defending the rest, unlawful.

As for other liberties, they depend on the silence of the law. In cases where the sovereign has prescribed no rule, there the subject hath the liberty to do, or forbear, according to his own discretion. And therefore such liberty is in some places more, and in some less; and in some times more, in other times less, according as they that have the sovereignty shall think most convenient. As for example, there was a time, when in England a man might enter into his own land (and dispossess such as wrongfully possessed it), by force. But in aftertimes, that liberty of forcible entry, was taken away by a statute made (by the king) in parliament. And in some places of the world, men have the liberty of many wives: in other places, such liberty is not allowed.

If a subject have a controversy with his sovereign, of debt, or of right of possession of lands or goods, or concerning any service required at his hands, or concerning any penalty, corporal, or pecuniary, grounded on a precedent law; he hath the same liberty to sue for his right, as if it were against a subject; and before such judges, as are appointed by the sovereign. For seeing the sovereign demands by force of a former law, and not by virtue of his power; he declares thereby, that he requires no more, than shall appear to be due by that law. The suit therefore is not contrary to the will of the sovereign; and consequently the subject hath the liberty to demand the hearing of his cause; and sentence, according to that law. But if he demand, or take any thing by pretence of his power; there lies, in that case, no action of law: for all that is done by him in virtue of his power, is done by the authority of every subject, and consequently, he that brings an action against the sovereign, brings it against himself.

If a monarch, or sovereign assembly, grant a liberty to all, or any of his subjects, which grant standing, he is disabled to provide for their safety, the grant is void; unless he directly renounce, or transfer the sovereignty to another. For in that he might openly (if it had been his will), and in plain terms, have renounced, or transferred it, and did not; it is to be understood it was not his will; but that the grant proceeded from ignorance of the repugnancy between such a liberty and the sovereign power: and therefore the sovereignty is still retained; and consequently all those powers, which are necessary to the exercising thereof; such as are the power of war, and peace, of judicature, of appointing officers, and councilors, of levying money, and the rest named in the 18th chapter.

The obligation of subjects to the sovereign, is understood to last as long, and no longer, than the power lasts, by which he is able to protect them. For the right men have by nature to protect themselves, when none else can protect them, can by no covenant be relinquished. The sovereignty is the soul of the commonwealth; which once departed from the body, the members do no more receive their motion from it. The end of obedience is protection; which, wheresoever a man sees it, either in his own, or in another's sword, nature applies his obedience to it, and his endeavor to maintain it. And though sovereignty, in the intention of them that make it, be immortal; yet is it in its own nature, not only subject to violent death, by foreign war; but also through the ignorance, and passions of men, it hath in it, from the very institution, many seeds of a natural mortality, by intestine discord.

If a subject be taken prisoner in war; or his person, or his means of life be within the guards of the enemy, and hath his life and corporal liberty given him, on condition to be subject to the victor, he hath liberty to accept the condition; and having accepted it, is the subject of him that took him; because he had no other way to preserve himself. The case is the same, if he be detained on the same terms, in a foreign country. But if a man be held in prison, or bonds, or is not trusted with the liberty of his body; he cannot be understood to be bound by covenant to subjection; and therefore may, if he can, make his escape by any means whatsoever.

If a monarch shall relinquish the sovereignty, both for himself, and his heirs; his subjects return to the absolute liberty of nature; because, though nature may declare who are his sons, and who are the nearest of his kin; yet it depends on his own will (as hath been said in the precedent chapter), who shall be his heir. If therefore he will have no heir, there is no sovereignty, nor subjection. The case is the same, if he die without known kindred, and without declaration of his heir. For then there can no heir be known, and consequently no subjection be due.

If the sovereign banish his subject; during the banishment, he is not subject. But he that is sent on a message, or hath leave to travel, is still subject; but it is, by contract between sovereigns, not by virtue of the covenant of subjection. For whosoever enters into another's dominion, is subject to all the laws thereof; unless he have a privilege by the amity of the sovereigns, or by special license.

If a monarch subdued by war, render himself subject to the victor; his subjects are delivered from their former obligation, and become obliged to the victor. But if he be held prisoner, or have not the liberty of his own body; he is not understood to have given away the right of sovereignty; and therefore his subjects are obliged to yield obedience to the magistrates formerly placed, governing not in their own name, but in his. For, his right remaining, the question is only of the administration; that is to say, of the magistrates and officers; which, if he have not means to name, he is supposed to approve those, which he himself had formerly appointed.

REVIEW QUESTIONS

1. According to Hobbes, in what sense are all persons equal?
2. What is the natural relationship between people in the state of nature? What are the characteristics of the state of nature?
3. What is the solution to the horrible state of nature? What is necessary to establish morality and law?
4. How does Hobbes define good and evil?
5. What is the Leviathan? Why does Hobbes use this image?

16

BLAISE PASCAL

Blaise Pascal (1623–1662), scientist, philosopher, and mathematician, was born in Clermont in Auvergne, France, the son of a nobleman who was a government official. A child prodigy, he learned Latin, Greek, mathematics, and science under his father's supervision. As a child he discovered Pythagoras's theorem. At sixteen he published a treatise on conic sections (projective geometry) and at eighteen invented a calculating machine. In 1646 he began work on the problem of the vacuum, which later led to his inventing the barometer. He made discoveries on the nature of probability, which, since his work was used to enhance gambling, troubled his soul.

Suddenly, on the night of November 23, 1654, he had a deeply religious experience. He calls it "The night of fire" and speaks of "joy, joy, joy, tears of joy!" and exhalts the "God of Abraham, God of Isaac, God of Jacob, not the God of the philosophers and scholars." From that time forward, he devoted his entire energies to his faith. Eight years earlier, he had already joined the Jansenists, a radical Catholic movement, seeking to purify the Church (for example, they proposed three yearly Lents, each consisting of forty days of fasting). Now he devoted his life to carrying out their ideals.

Pascal was struck with the insignificance of human life. Man is a creature of contradictions, a creature occupying a middle position in the universe between the infinitesimal and the infinite. He is an All in relation to Nothing, a Nothing in relation to the All. Man's condition is "inconstancy, boredom, anxiety . . . Man is only a reed, the weakest in nature, but he is a thinking reed."

Reprinted from Blaise Pascal, *Thoughts*, translated by W. F. Trotter (New York: Collier & Son, 1910).

What kind of chimera then is man? What novelty, what monster, what chaos, what subject of contradictions, what prodigy? Judge of all things, imbecile worm of the earth, depository of truth, sink of uncertainty and error, glory and scum of the universe.

When I consider the short duration of my life, swallowed up in the eternity before and after, the little space which I fill, and even can see, engulfed in the infinite immensity of space of which I am ignorant, and which knows me not, I am frightened, and am astonished being here rather than there, why now rather than then.

Pascal held that faith was the appropriate mode for apprehending God, announcing that "the heart has reasons of its own which the mind knows nothing of."

Know, then, proud man, what a paradox you are to yourself. Humble yourself, weak reason. Silence yourself, foolish nature, learn that man infinitely surpasses man, and hear from your master your real state which you do not know . . . Hear God.

In the famous section from his *Pensées* (Thoughts), Pascal argues that if we do a cost-benefit analysis of the matter, it turns out that it is eminently reasonable to get ourselves to believe that God exists, regardless of whether we have good evidence for that belief. The argument goes something like this: Regarding the proposition "God exists," reason is neutral. It can neither prove or disprove it. But we must make a choice on the matter, for not to choose for God is in effect to choose against him and lose the possible benefits that belief would bring. Since these benefits of faith promise to be infinite and the loss equally infinite, we must take a gamble on faith.

William James in his *Will to Believe* (see Chapter 31) asserts that he is following Pascal in his advocacy of the Will over Reason with regard to faith.

FOR FURTHER READING

Adams, A. *Grandeur and Illusion* (Weidenfeld, 1972).
Broome, J. H. *Pascal* (Arnold, 1965).
Krailsheimer, Alban. *Pascal* (Hill & Wang, 1980).
Mensard, J. *Pascal, His Life and Works* (Boivin, 1952).
Pascal, Blaise. *Pensees*, trans. A. J. Krailsheimer (Penguin, 1966).
Pascal, Blaise. *The Provincial Letters*, trans. A. J. Krailsheimer (Penguin, 1967).
Pascal, Blaise. *Thoughts*, trans. W. F. Trotter (Collier & Son, 1910).

PENSÉES

THE WAGER

Infinite—Nothing.—Our soul is cast into a body, where it finds number, time, dimension. Thereupon it reasons, calls this nature, necessity, and can believe nothing else.

Unity joined to infinity adds nothing to it, no more than one foot to an infinite measure. The finite is annihilated in the presence of the infinite, and becomes a pure nothing. So our spirit before God, so our justice before divine justice. There is not so great disproportion between our justice and that of God, as between unity and infinity.

The justice of God must be vast like His compassion. Now, justice to the outcast is less vast, and ought to offend our feelings less than mercy towards the elect.

We know that there is an infinite, and are ignorant of its nature. As we know it to be false that numbers are finite, it is therefore true that there is an infinity in number. But we do not know what it is. It is false that it is even, it is false that it is odd; for the addition of a unit can make no change in its nature. Yet it is a number, and every number is odd or even (this is certainly true of every finite number). So we may well know that there is a God without knowing what He is. Is there not one substantial truth, seeing there are so many things which are not the truth itself?

We know then the existence and nature of the finite, because we also are finite and have extension. We know the existence of the infinite, and are ignorant of its nature, because it has extension like us, but not limits like us. But we know neither the existence nor the nature of God, because He has neither extension nor limits.

But by faith we know His existence; in glory we shall know His nature. Now, I have already shown that we may well know the existence of a thing, without knowing its nature.

Let us now speak according to natural lights.

If there is a God, He is infinitely incomprehensible, since, having neither parts nor limits, He has no affinity to us. We are then incapable of knowing either what He is or if He is. This being so, who will dare to undertake the decision of the question? Not we, who have no affinity to Him.

Who then will blame Christians for not being able to give a reason for their belief, since they profess a religion for which they cannot give a reason? They declare, in expounding it to the world, that it is a foolishness, *stultitiam*; and then you complain that they do not prove it! If they proved it, they would not keep their words; it is in lacking proofs, that they are not lacking in sense. "Yes, but although this excuses those who offer it as such, and takes away from them the blame of putting it forward without reason, it does not excuse those who receive it." Let us then examine this point, and say, "God is, or He is not." But to which side shall we incline? Reason can decide nothing here. There is an infinite chaos which separates us. A game is being played at the extremity of this infinite distance where heads or tails will turn up. What will you wager? According to reason, you can do neither the one thing nor the other; according to reason, you can defend neither of the propositions.

Do not then reprove for error those who have made a choice; for you know nothing about it. "No, but I blame them for having made, not this choice, but a choice; for again both he who chooses heads and he who chooses tails are equally at fault, they are both in the wrong. The true course is not to wager at all."

—Yes; but you must wager. It is not optional. You are embarked. Which will you choose then; Let us see. Since you must choose, let us see which interests you least. You have two things to lose, the true and the good; and two things to stake, your reason and your will, your knowledge and your happiness; and your nature has two things to shun, error and misery. Your reason is no more shocked in choosing one rather than the other, since you must of necessity choose. This is one point settled. But your happiness? Let us weigh the gain and the loss in wagering that God is. Let us estimate these two chances. If you gain, you gain all; if you lose, you lose nothing. Wager then without hesitation that He is.—"That is very fine. Yes, I must wager; but I may perhaps wager too much."—Let us see. Since there is an equal risk of gain and of loss, if you had only to gain two lives, instead of one, you might still wager. But if there were three lives to gain, you would have to play (since you are under the necessity of playing), and you would be imprudent, when you are forced to play, not to chance your life to gain three at a game where there is an equal risk of loss and gain. But there is an eternity of life and happiness. And this being so, if there were an infinity of chances, of which one only would be for you, you would still be right in wagering one to win two, and you would act stupidly, being obliged to play, by refusing to stake one life against three at a game in which you had an infinity of an infinitely happy life to gain. But there is here an infinity of an infinitely happy life to gain, a chance of gain against a finite number of chances of loss, and what you stake is finite. It is all divided; wherever the infinite is and there is not an infinity of chances of loss against that of gain, there is no time to hesitate, you must give all. And thus, when one is forced to play, he must renounce reason to preserve his life, rather than risk it for infinite gain, as likely to happen as the loss of nothingness.

For it is no use to say it is uncertain if we will gain, and it is certain that we risk, and that the infinite distance between the *certainty* of what is staked and the *uncertainty* of what will be gained, equals the finite good which is certainly staked against the uncertain infinite. It is not so, as every player stakes a certainty to gain an uncertainty, and yet he stakes a finite certainty to gain a finite uncertainty, without transgressing against reason. There is not an infinite distance between the certainty staked and the uncertainty of the gain; that is untrue. In truth, there is an infinity between the certainty of gain and the certainty of loss. But the uncertainty of the gain is proportioned to the certainty of the stake according to the proportion of the chances of gain and loss. Hence it comes that, if there are as many risks on one side as on the other, the course is to play even; and then the certainty of the stake is equal of the uncertainty of the gain, so far is it from the fact that there is an infinite distance between them. And so our proposition is of infinite force, when there is the finite to stake in a game where there are equal risks of gain and of loss, and the infinite to gain. This is demonstrable; and if men are capable of any truths, this is one.

"I confess it, I admit it. But still is there no means of seeing the faces of the cards?"—Yes, Scripture and the rest, &c.—"Yes, but I have my hands tied and my mouth closed; I am forced to wager, and am not free. I am not released, and am so made that I cannot believe. What then would you have me do?"

"True. But at least learn your inability to believe, since reason brings you to this, and yet you cannot believe. Endeavour then to convince yourself, not by increase of proofs of God, but by the abatement of your passions. You would like to attain faith, and do not know the way; you would like to cure yourself of unbelief, and ask the remedy for it. Learn of those who have been bound like you, and who now stake all their possessions. These are people who know the way which you would follow, and who are cured of an ill of which you would be cured. Follow the way by which they began; by acting as if they believe, taking the holy water, having masses said, &c. Even this will naturally make you believe, and deaden your acuteness.—"But this is what I am afraid of."—And why? What have you to lose?

But to show you that this leads you there, it is this which will lessen the passions, which are your stumbling-blocks.

The end of this discourse.—Now what harm will befall you in taking this side? You will be faithful, honest, humble, grateful, generous, a sincere friend, truthful. Certainly you will not have those poisonous pleasures, glory and luxury; but will you not have others? I will tell you that you will thereby gain in this life, and that, at each step you take on this road, you will see so great certainty of gain, so much nothingness in what you risk, that you will at last recognize that you have wagered for something certain and infinite, for which you have given nothing.

"Ah! This discourse transports me, charms me," &c.

If this discourse pleases you and seems impressive, know that it is made by a man who has knelt, both before and after it, in prayer to that Being, infinite and without parts, before whom he lays all he has, for you also to lay before Him all you have for your own good and for His glory, so that strength may be given to lowliness.

REVIEW QUESTIONS

1. According to Pascal, why can we not know the existence or nature of God?
2. What does Pascal say regarding those who blame Christians for not producing evidence or proofs for the existence of God? Can God's existence be proved? Why or why not?
3. What is the wager Pascal advocates, and how does he calculate the cost-benefit ratio?
4. What advice does Pascal give to those who are unable to believe in God?
5. What is the relationship between our finitude and infinity? What is the infinite?

17

Baruch Spinoza

Baruch Spinoza (1632–1677) was born in Amsterdam, Holland, of a prosperous merchant family, Jews who had fled Portugal because of religious persecution. After an education in the Jewish tradition (the Hebrew Bible, the Talmud and Jewish codes, the works of Maimonides), as well as in Latin, Spinoza showed an inclination toward independent and heretical thinking. He fell into disfavor with the synagogue authorities for arguing that there is nothing in the Hebrew Bible to support the views that God has no body, that there are angels, or that the soul is immortal. He also maintained that Moses, alleged author of the first five books, was no guide to science or a final guide to theology. The authorities, after trying in vain to silence him with bribes and threats, excommunicated him in July 1656. Befriended by Christians, Spinoza left Amsterdam and eventually settled in the town of Voorburg and later in The Hague, where he worked as a lens grinder. During this period of his life, he encountered and was deeply influenced by the philosophies of Descartes and Hobbes.

In his major work, Spinoza sought to bring to philosophy the certainty of mathematical reasoning by beginning with absolutely certain truths and reasoning carefully and explicitly from them. Like Euclid's *Elements*, each of its five parts opens with definitions, axioms, and postulates and is followed by theorems proved from them. Informal remarks elaborating on the implications of the theorems follow in Scholia (Notes) and Appendices.

Spinoza published only two works during his lifetime, the *Principles of Descartes's Philosophy* and the *Theologico-Political Treatise*, but his genius was known to scholars in all parts of Europe. He was also respected as a man of unimpeachable character. On February 20, 1677, he died of pulmonary disease aggravated by inhaling glass dust from his lens grinding. He was buried in the New Church on the Spuy. *The Ethics* was published—at some risk—by Spinoza's friends a year after his death. A sizable selection from it is set forth here.

Spinoza concurred with Hobbes and Descartes in holding that all matter is governed by deterministic laws, while rejecting (as did Hobbes) dualism, the notion of a soul that is somehow a different kind of reality from matter. Most significantly, he rejected the common Judeo-Christian notion of God as creating and ruling the material world from outside—"transitive cause." Rather, he maintained, God is the *immanent* cause of all things—the world's inherent energy, which he also designated as Substance. In Part 1 (here reprinted complete) Spinoza demonstrates that rather than the two ultimate realities of Descartes, thought and extension, only one substance exists. This is God or Nature, which exists *necessarily*, not caused by anything prior to itself. Thought and extension are real, but not really distinct: they are two of the infinite *attributes* of God. All finite things are *modes* of God, not separate substances but depending on the one substance, somewhat as a wave depends on the ocean. Spinoza is thus a pantheist ("all-God-ist"). God, however, is not a person. Nor is He (or "It") providential; He *is* the deterministic way things go; free will—if it implies the possibility of altering the natural order—is an illusion. While we should love God, as the perfect (complete) being, God cannot love us or providentially take an interest in our lives.

In Part 2, "Of the Nature and Origin of the Mind," Spinoza demonstrates that the *mental* and the *physical* (thought and extension) are "one and the same, expressed in two ways": mind and body differ only conceptually. Parts 3 and 4 (not included in this work) deal with the nature of human affects (emotions, passions) and "human bondage" to them. Finally, Part 5 (part of which is reprinted below) deals with the power of the intellect to free us from this bondage. Here Spinoza argues that just as God is free from passions, we should be too (to the limited extent that this is possible for us); when we are, we may experience the "intellectual love of God," which, "manifested through the human mind, considered under the form of eternity," is "part of the infinite love with which God loves Himself," and is not "destroyed with the body."

FOR FURTHER READING

Allison, Henry. *Benedict de Spinoza* (Yale University Press, 1987).

Bennett, Jonathan. *A Study of Spinoza's Ethics* (Hackett, 1984).

Curley, E. M. *Behind the Geometrical Method: A Reading of Spinoza's Ethics* (Princeton University Press, 1988).

Curley, E. M. *Spinoza's Metaphysics: An Essay in Interpretation* (Harvard University Press, 1969).

Donagan, Alan. *Spinoza* (University of Chicago, 1989).

Kashhap, Paul, ed. *Studies in Spinoza* (University of California Press, 1972).

Hampshire, Stuart. *Spinoza* (Penguin Books, 1952).

Mandelbaum, Maurice, and Eugene Freeman, eds. *Spinoza: Essays in Interpretation* (Open Court Press, 1975).

Matson, Wallace. "Spinoza's Theory of Mind," *The Monist*, vol. 55 (1971). Reprinted in Mandelbaum & Freeman.

Wolfson, Harry. *The Philosophy of Spinoza: Unfolding the Latent Processes of His Reasoning* (Schocken, 1969).

THE ETHICS

II/45 ## FIRST PART OF THE ETHICS OF GOD

DEFINITIONS

D1: By cause of itself I understand that whose essence involves existence, *or* that whose nature cannot be conceived except as existing.

D2: That thing is said to be finite in its own kind that can be limited by another of the same nature.

For example, a body is called finite because we always conceive another that is greater. Thus a thought is limited by another thought. But a body is not limited by a thought nor a thought by a body

D3: By *substance* I understand what is in itself and is conceived through itself, that is, that whose concept does not require the concept of another thing, from which it must be formed.

D4: By attribute I understand what the intellect perceives of a substance, as constituting its essence.

D5: By mode I understand the affections of a substance, *or* that which is in another through which it is also conceived.

D6: By God I understand a being absolutely infinite, that is, a substance consisting of an infinity of attributes, of which each one expresses an eternal and infinite essence.

II/46 Exp.: I say absolutely infinite, not infinite in its own kind; for if something is only infinite in its own kind, we can deny infinite attributes of it [NS: (i.e., we can conceive infinite attributes which do not pertain to its nature)]; but if something is absolutely infinite, whatever expresses essence and involves no negation pertains to its essence.

D7: That thing is called free which exists from the necessity of its nature alone, and is determined to act by itself alone. But a thing is called necessary, or rather compelled, which is determined by another to exist and to produce an effect in a certain and determinate manner.

D8: By eternity I understand existence itself, insofar as it is conceived to follow necessarily from the definition alone of the eternal thing.

Exp.: For such existence, like the essence of a thing, is conceived as an eternal truth, and on that account cannot be explained by duration or time, even if the duration is conceived to be without beginning or end.

AXIOMS

A1: Whatever is, is either in itself or in another.

A2: What cannot be conceived through another, must be conceived through itself.

A3: From a given determinate cause the effect follows necessarily; and conversely, if there is no determinate cause, it is impossible for an effect to follow.

A4: The knowledge of an effect depends on, and involves, the knowledge of its cause.

A5: Things that have nothing in common with one another also cannot be understood through one another, *or* the concept of the one does not involve die concept of the other.

A6: A true idea must agree with its object. II/47

A7: If a thing can be conceived as not existing, its essence does not involve existence.

P1: *A substance is prior in nature to its affections.*
Dem.: This is evident from D3 and D5.

P2: *Two substances having different attributes have nothing in common with one another.*
Dem.: This is also evident from D3. For each must be in itself and be conceived through itself, *or* the concept of the one does not involve the concept of the other.

P3: *If things have nothing in common with one another, one of them cannot be the cause of the other.*

Dem.: If they have nothing in common with one another, then (by A5) they cannot be understood through one another, and so (by A4) one cannot be the cause of the other, q.e.d.

P4: *Two or more distinct things are distinguished from one another, either by a difference in the attributes of the substances or by a difference in their affections.*

Dem.: Whatever is, is either in itself or in another (by A1), that is (by D3 and D5), outside the intellect there is nothing except substances and their affections. Therefore, there is nothing outside the intellect through which a number of things can be distinguished from one another except substances, *or* what is the same (by D4), their attributes, and their affections, q.e.d.

P5: *In Nature there cannot be two or more substances of the same nature or attribute.*

Dem.: If there were two or more distinct substances, they would have to be distinguished from one another either by a difference in their attributes, or by a difference in their affections (by P4). If only by a difference in their attributes, then it will be conceded that there is only one of the same attribute. But if by a difference in their affections, then since a substance is prior in nature to its affections (by P1), if the affections are put to one side and [the substance] is considered in itself, that is (by D3 and A6), considered truly, one cannot be conceived to be distinguished from another, that is (by P4), there cannot be many, hut only one [of the same nature *or* attribute], q.e.d.

P6: *One substance cannot be produced by another substance.*

Dem.: In Nature there cannot be two substances of the same attribute (by P5), that is (by P2), which have something in common with each other. Therefore (by P3) one cannot be the cause of the other, *or* cannot be produced by the other, q.e.d.

Cor.: From this it follows that a substance cannot be produced by anything else. For in Nature there is nothing except substances and their affections, as is evident from A1, D3, and D5. But it cannot be produced by a substance (by P6). Therefore, substance absolutely cannot be produced by anything else, q.e.d.

Alternatively: This is demonstrated even more easily from the absurdity of its contradictory. For if a substance could be produced by something else, the knowledge of it would have to depend on the knowledge of its cause (by A4). And so (by D3) it would not be a substance.

P7: *It pertains to the nature of a substance to exist.*

Dem.: A substance cannot be produced by anything else (by P6C); therefore it will be the cause of itself, that is (by D1), its essence necessarily involves existence, or it pertains to its nature to exist, q.e.d.

P8: *Every substance is necessarily infinite.*

Dem.: A substance of one attribute does not exist unless it is unique (P5), and it pertains to its nature to exist (P7). Of its nature, therefore, it will exist either as finite or as infinite. But not as finite. For then (by D2) it would have to be limited by something else of the same nature, which would also have to exist necessarily (by P7), and so there would be two substances of the same attribute, which is absurd (by P5). Therefore, it exists as infinite, q.e.d.

Schol. 1: Since being finite is really, in part, a negation, and being infinite is an absolute affirmation of the existence of some nature, it follows from P7 alone that every substance must be infinite. [NS: For if we assumed a finite substance, we would, in part, deny existence to its nature, which (by P7) is absurd.]

Schol. 2: I do not doubt that the demonstration of P7 will be difficult to conceive for all who judge things confusedly, and have not been accustomed to know things through their first causes—because they do not distinguish between the modifications of substances and the substances themselves, nor do they know how things are produced. So it happens that they fictitiously ascribe to substances the beginning which they see that natural things have; for those who do not know the true causes of things confuse everything and without any conflict of mind feign that both trees and men speak, imagine that men are formed both from stones and from seed, and that any form whatever is changed into any other. So also, those who confuse the divine nature with the human easily ascribe human affects to God, particularly so long as they are also ignorant of how those affects are produced in the mind.

But if men would attend to the nature of substance, they would have no doubt at all of the truth of P7. Indeed, this proposition would be an axiom for everyone, and would be numbered among the common notions. For by substance they would understand what is in itself and is conceived through itself, that is, that the knowledge of which does not require the knowledge of any other thing. But by modifications they would understand what is in another, those things whose concept is formed from the concept of the thing in which they are.

This is how we can have true ideas of modifications which do not exist; for though they do not actually exist outside the intellect, nevertheless their essences are comprehended in another in such a way that they can be conceived through it. But the truth of substances is not outside the intellect unless it is in them themselves, because they are conceived through themselves.

Hence, if someone were to say that he had a clear and distinct, that is, true, idea of a substance, and nevertheless doubted whether such a substance existed, that would indeed be the same as if he were to say that he had a true idea, and nevertheless doubted whether it was false (as is evident to anyone who is sufficiently attentive). Or if someone maintains that a substance is created, he maintains at the same time that a false idea has become true. Of course nothing more absurd can be conceived. So it must be confessed that the existence of a substance, like its essence, is an eternal truth.

And from this we can infer in another way that there is only one [substance] of the same nature, which I have considered it worth the trouble of showing here. But to do this in order, it must be noted,

I. that the true definition of each thing neither involves nor expresses anything except the nature of the thing defined.

From which it follows,

II. that no definition involves or expresses any certain number of individuals,

since it expresses nothing other than the nature of the thing defined. For example, the definition of the triangle expresses nothing but the simple nature of the triangle, but not any certain number of triangles. It is to be noted,

III. that there must be, for each existing thing, a certain cause on account of which it exists.

Finally, it is to be noted,

IV. that this cause, on account of which a thing exists, either must be contained in the very nature and definition of the existing thing (*viz that it pertains to its nature to exist*) or must be outside it.

From these propositions it follows that if, in Nature, a certain number of individuals exists, there must be a cause why those individuals, and why neither more nor fewer, exist.

For example, if twenty men exist in Nature (*to make the matter clearer; I assume that they exist at the same time, and that no others previously existed in Nature*), it will not be enough (i.e., *to give a reason why twenty men exist*) to show the cause of human nature in general; but it will be necessary in addition to show the cause why not more and not fewer than twenty exist. For (by III) there must necessarily be a cause why each [NS: particular man] exists. But this cause (by II and III) cannot be contained in human nature itself, since the true definition of man does not involve the number 20. So (by IV) the cause why these twenty men exist, and consequently, why each of them exists, must necessarily be outside each of them. II/51

For that reason it is to be inferred absolutely that whatever is of such a nature that there can be many individuals [of that nature] must, to exist, have an external cause to exist. Now since it pertains to the nature of a substance to exist (by what we have already shown in this scholium), its definition must involve necessary existence, and consequently its existence must be inferred from its definition alone. But from its definition (as we have shown from II and III) the existence of a number of substances cannot follow. Therefore it follows necessarily from this, that there exists only one of the same nature, as was proposed.

P9: *The more reality or being each thing has, the more attributes belong to it.*

Dem.: This is evident from D4.

P10: *Each attribute of a substance must be conceived through itself.*

Dem.: For an attribute is what the intellect perceives concerning a substance, as constituting its essence (by D4); so (by D3) it must be conceived through itself, q.e.d.

II/52 Schol.: From these propositions it is evident that although two attributes may be conceived to be really distinct (i.e., one may be conceived without the aid of the other), we still cannot infer from that that they constitute two beings, *or* two different substances. For it is of the nature of a substance that each of its attributes is conceived through itself, since all the attributes it has have always been in it together, and one could not be produced by another, but each expresses the reality, *or* being of substance.

So it is far from absurd to attribute many attributes to one substance. Indeed, nothing in Nature is clearer than that each being must be conceived under some attribute, and the more reality, *or* being it has, the more it has attributes which express necessity, *or* eternity, and infinity. And consequently there is also nothing clearer than that a being absolutely infinite must be defined (as we taught in D6) as a being that consists of infinite attributes, each of which expresses a certain eternal and infinite essence.

But if someone now asks by what sign we shall be able to distinguish the diversity of substances, let him read the following propositions, which show that in Nature there exists only one substance, and that it is absolutely infinite. So that sign would be sought in vain.

P11: *God, or a substance consisting of infinite attributes, each of which expresses eternal and infinite essence, necessarily exists.*

Dem.: If you deny this, conceive, if you can, that God does not exist. Therefore (by A7) his essence does not involve existence. But this (by P7) is absurd. Therefore God necessarily exists, q.e.d.

Alternatively: For each thing there must be assigned a cause, *or* reason, both for its existence and for its nonexistence. For example, if a triangle exists, there must be a reason *or* cause why it exists; but if it does not exist, there must also be a reason
II/53 *or* cause which prevents it from existing, *or* which takes its existence away.

But this reason, *or* cause, must either be contained in the nature of the thing, or be outside it. For

example, the very nature of a square circle indicates the reason why it does not exist, namely, because it involves a contradiction. On the other hand, the reason why a substance exists also follows from its nature alone, because it involves existence (see P7). But the reason why a circle or triangle exists, or why it does not exist, does not follow from the nature of these things, but from the order of the whole of corporeal Nature. For from this [order] it must follow either that the triangle necessarily exists now or that it is impossible for it to exist now. These things are evident through themselves; from them it follows that a thing necessarily exists if there is no reason or cause which prevents it from existing. Therefore, if there can be no reason or cause which prevents God from existing, or which takes his existence away, it must certainly be inferred that he necessarily exists.

But if there were such a reason, *or* cause, it would have to be either in God's very nature or outside it, that is, in another substance of another nature. For if it were of the same nature, that very supposition would concede that God exists. But a substance which was of another nature [NS: than the divine] would have nothing in common with God (by P2), and therefore could neither give him existence nor take it away. Since, then, there can be, outside the divine nature, no reason, *or*, cause which takes away the divine existence, the reason will necessarily have to be in his nature itself, if indeed he does not exist. That is, his nature would involve a contradiction [NS: as in our second example]. But it is absurd to affirm this of a Being absolutely infinite and supremely perfect. Therefore, there is no cause, *or* reason, either in God or outside God, which takes his existence away. And therefore, God necessarily exists, q.e.d.

Alternatively: To be able not to exist is to lack power, and conversely, to be able to exist is to have power (as is known through itself). So, if what now necessarily exists are only finite beings, then finite beings are more powerful than an absolutely infinite Being. But this, as is known through itself, is absurd. So, either nothing exists or an absolutely infinite Being also exists. But we exist, either in ourselves, or in something else, which necessarily exists (see A1 and P7). Therefore an absolutely infinite Being—that is (by D6), God—necessarily exists, q.e.d.

II/54 Schol.: In this last demonstration I wanted to show God's existence a posteriori, so that the demonstration would be perceived more easily—but not because God's existence does not follow a priori from the same foundation. For since being able to exist is power, it follows that the more reality belongs to the nature of a thing, the more powers it has, of itself, to exist. Therefore, an absolutely infinite Being, *or* God, has, of himself, an absolutely infinite power of existing. For that reason, he exists absolutely.

Still, there may be many who will not easily be able to see how evident this demonstration is, because they have been accustomed to contemplate only those things that flow from external causes. And of these, they see that those which quickly come to be, that is, which easily exist, also easily perish. And conversely, they judge that those things to which they conceive more things to pertain are more difficult to do, that is, that they do not exist so easily. But to free them from these prejudices, I have no need to show here in what manner this proposition—*what quickly comes to be, quickly perishes*—is true, nor whether or not all things are equally easy in respect to the whole of Nature. It is sufficient to note only this, that I am not here speaking of things that come to be from external causes, but only of substances that (by P6) can be produced by no external cause.

For things that come to be from external causes—whether they consist of many parts or of few—owe all the perfection or reality they have to the power of the external cause; and therefore their existence arises only from the perfection of their external cause, and not from their own perfection. On the other hand, whatever perfection substance has is not owed to any external cause. So its existence must follow from its nature alone; hence its existence is nothing but its essence.

Perfection, therefore, does not take away the existence of a thing, but on the contrary asserts it. But imperfection takes it away. So there is nothing of whose existence we can be more certain than we are of the existence of an absolutely infinite, *or* perfect, Being—that is, God. For since his essence excludes all imperfection, and involves absolute perfection, by that very fact it takes away every cause of doubting his existence, and gives the greatest certainty concerning it. I believe this will be clear even to those who are only moderately attentive.

P12: *No attribute of a substance can be truly conceived from which it follows that the substance can be divided.* II/55

Dem.: For the parts into which a substance so conceived would be divided either will retain the nature of the substance or will not. If the first [NS: viz. they retain the nature of the substance], then (by P8) each part will have to be infinite, and (by P7) its own cause, and (by P5) each part will have to consist of a different attribute. And so many substances will be able to be formed from one, which is absurd (by P6). Furthermore, the parts (by P2) would have nothing in common with their whole, and the whole (by D4 and P10) could both be and be conceived without its parts, which is absurd, as no one will be able to doubt.

But if the second is asserted, namely, that the parts will not retain the nature of substance, then since the whole substance would be divided into equal parts, it would lose the nature of substance, and would cease to be, which (by P7) is absurd.

P13: *A substance which is absolutely infinite is indivisible.*

Dem.: For if it were divisible, the parts into which it would be divided will either retain the nature of an absolutely infinite substance or they will not. If the first, then there will be a number of substances of the same nature, which (by P5) is absurd. But if the second is asserted, then (as above [NS: P12]), an absolutely infinite substance will be able to cease to be, which (by P11) is also absurd.

Cor.: From these [propositions] it follows that no substance, and consequently no corporeal substance, insofar as it is a substance, is divisible.

Schol.: That substance is indivisible, is understood more simply merely from this, that the nature of substance cannot be conceived unless as infinite, and that by a part of substance nothing can be understood except a finite substance, which (by P8) implies a plain contradiction. II/56

P14: *Except God, no substance can be or be conceived.*

Dem.: Since God is an absolutely infinite being, of whom no attribute which expresses an essence of substance can be denied (by D6), and he necessarily exists (by P11), if there were any substance except God, it would have to be explained through some attribute of God, and so two substances of the same attribute would exist, which (by P5) is absurd. And so except God, no substance can be or, consequently, be conceived. For if it could be conceived, it would have to he conceived us existing. But this (by the first part of this demonstration) is absurd. Therefore, except for God no substance can be or be conceived, q.e.d.

Cor. 1: From this it follows most clearly, first, that God is unique, that is (by D6), that in Nature there is only one substance, and that it is absolutely infinite (as we indicated in P10S).

Cor. 2: It follows, second, that an extended thing and a thinking thing are either attributes of God, or (by A1) affections of God's attributes.

P15: *Whatever is, is in God, and nothing can be or be conceived without God.*

Dem.: Except for God, there neither is, nor can be conceived, any substance (by P14), that is (by D3), thing that is in itself and is conceived through itself. But modes (by D5) can neither be nor be conceived without substance. So they can be in the divine nature alone, and can be conceived through it alone. But except for substances and modes there is nothing (by A1). Therefore, [NS: everything is in God and] nothing can be or be conceived without God, q.e.d.

Schol.: [I.] There are those who feign a God, like man, consisting of a body and a mind, and subject to passions. But how far they wander from the true knowledge of God, is sufficiently established by what has already been demonstrated. Them I dismiss. For everyone who has to any extent contemplated the divine nature denies that God is corporeal. They prove this best from the fact that by body we understand any quantity, with length, breadth, and depth, limited by some certain figure. Nothing more absurd than this can be said of God, namely, of a being absolutely infinite. But meanwhile, by the other arguments by which they strive to demonstrate this same conclusion they clearly show that they entirely remove corporeal, *or* extended, substance itself from the divine nature. And they maintain that it has been created by God. But by what divine power could it

be created? They are completely ignorant of that. And this shows clearly that they do not understand what they themselves say. At any rate, I have demonstrated clearly enough—in my judgment, at least—that no substance can be produced or created by another thing (see P6C and P8S2). Next, we have shown (P14) that except for God, no substance can either be or be conceived, and hence [in P14C2] we have concluded that extended substance is one of God's infinite attributes. But to provide a fuller explanation, I shall refute my opponents' arguments, which all reduce to these.

[II.] *First*, they think that corporeal substance, insofar as it is substance, consists of parts. And therefore they deny that it can be infinite, and consequently, that it can pertain to God. They explain this by many examples, of which I shall mention one or two.

[i] If corporeal substance is infinite, they say, let us conceive it to be divided in two parts. Each part will be either finite or infinite. It the former, then an infinite is composed of two finite parts, which is absurd. If the latter [NS: i.e., if each part is infinite], then there is one infinite twice as large as another, which is also absurd, [ii] Again, if an infinite quantity is measured by parts [each] equal to a foot, it will consist of infinitely many such parts, as it will also, if it is measured by parts [each] equal to an inch. And therefore, one infinite number will be twelve times greater than another [NS: which is no less absurd], [iii] Finally, if we conceive that from one point of a certain infinite quantity two lines, say AB and AC, are extended to infinity, it is certain that, although in the beginning they are a certain, determinate distance apart, the distance between B and C is continuously increased, and at last, from being determinate, it will become indeterminable. Since these absurdities follow—so they think—from the fact that an infinite quantity is supposed, they infer that corporeal substance must be finite, and consequently cannot pertain to God's essence.

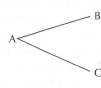

[III.] Their *second* argument is also drawn from God's supreme perfection. For God, they say, since he is a supremely perfect being, cannot be acted on. But corporeal substance, since it is divisible, can be acted on. It follows, therefore, that it does not pertain to God's essence.

[IV.] These are the arguments which I find Authors using, to try to show that corporeal substance is unworthy of the divine nature, and cannot pertain to it. But anyone who is properly attentive will find that I have already replied to them, since these arguments are founded only on their supposition that corporeal substance is composed of parts, which I have already (P12 and P13C) shown to be absurd. And then anyone who wishes to consider the matter rightly will see that all those absurdities (*if indeed they are all absurd, which I am not now disputing*), from which they wish to infer that extended substance is finite, do not follow at all from the fact that an infinite quantity is supposed, but from the fact that they suppose an infinite quantity to be measurable and composed of finite parts. So from the absurdities which follow from that they can infer only that infinite quantity is not measurable, and that it is not composed of finite parts. This is the same thing we have already demonstrated above (P12, etc.). So the weapon they aim at us, they really turn against themselves. If, therefore, they still wish to infer from this absurdity of theirs that extended substance must be finite, they are indeed doing nothing more than if someone feigned that a circle has the properties of a square, and inferred from that the circle has no center, from which all lines drawn to the circumference are equal. For corporeal substance, which cannot be conceived except as infinite, unique, and indivisible (sec P8, 5, and 12), they conceive to be composed of finite parts, to be many, and to be divisible, in order to infer that it is finite.

II/59

So also others, after they feign that a line is composed of points, know how to invent many arguments, by which they show that a line cannot be divided to infinity. And indeed it is no less absurd to assert that corporeal substance is composed of bodies, *or* parts, than that a body is composed of surfaces, the surfaces of lines, and the lines, finally, of points. All those who know that clear reason is infallible must confess this—particularly those who deny that there is a vacuum. For if corporeal substance could be so divided that its parts were really distinct, why, then, could one part not be annihilated, the rest remaining connected with one another as before? And why must they all be so fitted together that there is no vacuum? Truly, of things which are really distinct from one another, one can be, and

remain in its condition, without the other. Since, therefore, there is no vacuum in Nature (a subject I discuss elsewhere), but all its parts must so concur that there is no vacuum, it follows also that they cannot be really distinguished, that is, that corporeal substance, insofar as it is a substance, cannot be divided.

[V.] If someone should now ask why we are, by nature, so inclined to divide quantity, I shall answer that we conceive quantity in two ways: abstractly, *or* superficially, as we [NS: commonly] imagine it, or as substance, which is done by the intellect alone [NS: without the help of the imagination]. So if we attend to quantity as it is in the imagination, which we do often and more easily, it will be found to be finite, divisible, and composed of parts; but if we attend to it as it is in the intellect, and conceive it insofar as it is a substance, which happens [NS: seldom and] with great difficulty, then (as we have already sufficiently demonstrated) it will be found to be infinite, unique, and indivisible.

This will be sufficiently plain to everyone who knows how to distinguish between the intellect and the imagination—particularly if it is also noted that matter is everywhere the same, and that parts are distinguished in it only insofar as we conceive matter to be affected in different ways, so that its parts are distinguished only modally, but not really.

For example, we conceive that water is divided and its parts separated from one another—insofar as it is water, but not insofar as it is corporeal substance. For insofar as it is substance, it is neither separated nor divided. Again, water, insofar as it is water, is generated and corrupted, but insofar as it is substance, it is neither generated nor corrupted.

II/60

[VI.] And with this I think I have replied to the second argument also, since it is based on the supposition that matter, insofar as it is substance, is divisible, and composed of parts. Even if this [reply] were not [sufficient], I do not know why [matter] would be unworthy of the divine nature. For (by P14) apart from God there can be no substance by which [the divine nature] would be acted on. All things, I say, are in God, and all things that happen, happen only through the laws of God's infinite nature and follow (as I shall show) from the necessity of his essence. So it cannot be said in any way that God is acted on by another, or that extended substance is unworthy of the divine nature, even if it is supposed to be divisible, so long as it is granted to be eternal and infinite. But enough of this for the present.

P16: *Prom the necessity of the divine nature there must follow infinitely many things in infinitely many modes, (i.e., everything which can fall under an infinite intellect).*

Dem.: This proposition must be plain to anyone, provided he attends to the fact that the intellect infers from the given definition of any thing a number of properties that really do follow necessarily from it (that is, from the very essence of the thing); and that it infers more properties the more the definition of the thing expresses reality, that is, the more reality the essence of the defined thing involves. But since the divine nature has absolutely infinite attributes (by D6), each of which also expresses an essence infinite in its own kind, from its necessity there must follow infinitely many things in infinite modes (i.e., everything which can fall under an infinite intellect), q.e.d.

Cor. 1: From this it follows that God is the efficient cause of all things which can fall under an infinite intellect.

II/61   Cor. 2: It follows, second, that God is a cause through himself and not an accidental cause.

Cor. 3: It follows, third, that God is absolutely the first cause.

P17: *God acts from the laws of his nature alone, and is compelled by no one.*

Dem.: We have just shown (P16) that from the necessity of the divine nature alone, or (what is the same thing) from the laws of his nature alone, absolutely infite things follow, and in P15 we have demonstrated that nothing can be or be conceived without God, but that all things are in God. So there can be nothing outside him by which he is determined or compelled to act. Therefore, God acts from the laws of his nature alone, and is compelled by no one, q.e.d.

Cor. 1: From this it follows, first, that there is no cause, either extrinsically or intrinsically, which prompts God to action, except the perfection of his nature.

Cor. 2: It follows, second, that God alone is a free cause. For God alone exists only from the necessity of his nature (by P11 and P14C1), and acts from the necessity of his nature (by P17). Therefore (by D7) God alone is a free cause, q.e.d.

Schol.: [I.] Others think that God is a free cause because he can (so they think) bring it about that the things which we have said follow from his nature (i.e., which are in his power) do not happen or are not produced by him. But this is the same as if they were to say that God can bring it about that it would not follow from the nature of a triangle that its three angles are equal to two right angles; *or* that from a given cause the effect would not follow—which is absurd.   II/62

Further, I shall show later, without the aid of this proposition, that neither intellect nor will pertain to God's nature. Of course I know there are many who think they can demonstrate that a supreme intellect and a free will pertain to God's nature. For they say they know nothing they can ascribe to God more perfect than what is the highest perfection in us.

Moreover, though they conceive God to actually understand in the highest degree, they still do not believe that he can bring it about that all the things he actually understands exist. For they think that in that way they would destroy God's power. If he had created all the things in his intellect (they say), then he would have been able to create nothing more, which they believe to be incompatible with God's omnipotence. So they prefer to maintain that God is indifferent to all things, not creating anything except what he has decreed to create by some absolute will.

But I think I have shown clearly enough (see P16) that from God's supreme power, *or* infinite nature, infinitely many things in infinitely many modes, that is, all things, have necessarily flowed, or always follow, by the same necessity and in the same way as from the nature of a triangle it follows, from eternity and to eternity, that its three angles are equal to two right angles. So God's omnipotence has been actual from eternity and will remain in the same actuality to eternity. And in this way, at least in my opinion, God's omnipotence is maintained far more perfectly.

Indeed—to speak openly—my opponents seem to deny God's omnipotence. For they are forced to confess that God understands infinitely many creatable things, which nevertheless he will never be able to create. For otherwise, if he created everything he understood [NS: to be creatable] he would (according to them) exhaust his omnipotence and render himself imperfect. Therefore to maintain that God is perfect, they are driven to maintain at the same time that he cannot bring about everything to which his power extends. I do not see what could be feigned which would be more absurd than this or more contrary to God's omnipotence.

[II.] Further—to say something here also about the intellect and will which we commonly attribute to God—if will and intellect do pertain to the eternal essence of God, we must of course understand by each of these attributes something different from what men commonly understand. For the intellect and will which would constitute God's essence would have to differ entirely from our intellect and will, and could not agree with them in anything except the name. They would not agree with one another any more than do the dog that is a heavenly constellation and the dog that is a barking animal. I shall demonstrate this.

If intellect pertains to the divine nature, it will not be able to be (like our intellect) by nature either posterior to (as most would have it), or simultaneous with, the things understood, since God is prior in causality to all things (by P16C1). On the contrary, the truth and formal essence of things is what it is because it exists objectively in that way in God's intellect. So God's intellect, insofar as it is conceived to constitute God's essence, is really the cause both of the essence and of the existence of things. This seems also to have been noticed by those who asserted that God's intellect, will, and power are one and the same.

Therefore, since God's intellect is the only cause of things (viz. as we have shown, both of their essence and of their existence), he must necessarily differ from them both as to his essence and as to his existence. For what is caused differs from its cause precisely in what it has from the cause [NS: for that reason it is called the effect of such a cause]. For example, a man is the cause of the existence of another man, but not of his essence, for the latter is an eternal truth. Hence, they can agree entirely according to their essence. But in existing they must differ. And for that reason, if the existence of one perishes, the other's existence will not thereby perish. But if the essence of one could be destroyed, and become false, the other's essence would also be destroyed [NS: and become false].

So the thing that is the cause both of the essence and of the existence of some effect, must differ from

such an effect, both as to its essence and as to its existence. But God's intellect is the cause both of the essence and of the existence of our intellect. Therefore, God's intellect, insofar as it is conceived to constitute the divine essence, differs from our intellect both as to its essence and as to its existence, and cannot agree with it in anything except in name, as we supposed. The proof proceeds in the same way concerning the will, as anyone can easily see.

P18: *God is the immanent, not the transitive, cause of all things.*

Dem.: Everything that is, is in God, and must be conceived through God (by P15), and so (by P16C1) God is the cause of [NS: all] things, which are in him. That is the first [thing to be proven]. And then outside God there can be no substance (by P14), that is (by D3), thing which is in itself outside God. That was the second. God, therefore, is the immanent, not the transitive cause of all things, q.e.d.

P19: *God is eternal, or all God's attributes are eternal.*

Dem.: For God (by D6) is substance, which (by P11) necessarily exists, that is (by P7), to whose nature it pertains to exist, or (what is the same) from whose definition it follows that he exists; and therefore (by D8), he is eternal.

Next, by God's attributes are to be understood what (by D4) expresses an essence of the divine substance, that is, what pertains to substance. The attributes themselves, I say, must involve it itself. But eternity pertains to the nature of substance (as I have already demonstrated from P7). Therefore each of the attributes must involve eternity, and so, they are all eternal, q.e.d.

Schol.: This proposition is also as clear as possible from the way I have demonstrated God's existence (P11). For from that demonstration, I say, it is established that God's existence, like his essence, is an eternal truth. And then I have also demonstrated God's eternity in another way (*Descartes' Principles* IP19), and there is no need to repeat it here.

P20: *God's existence and his essence are one and the same.*

Dem.: God (by P19) and all of his attributes are eternal, that is (by D8), each of his attributes

II/63

II/64

expresses existence. Therefore, the same attributes of God which (by D4) explain God's eternal essence at the same time explain his eternal existence, that is, that itself which constitutes God's essence at the same time constitutes his existence. So his existence and his essence are one and the same, q.e.d.

Cor. 1: From this it follows, first, that God's existence, like his essence, is an eternal truth.

Cor. 2: It follows, second, that God, *or* all of God's attributes, are immutable. For if they changed as to their existence, they would also (by P20) change as to their essence, that is (as is known through itself), from being true become false, which is absurd.

P21: *All the things which follows form the absolute nature of any of God's attributes have always had to exist and be infinte, or are, through the same attribute, eternal and infinite.*

Dem.: If you deny this, then conceive (if you can) that in some attribute of God there follows from its absolute nature something that is finite and has a determinate existence, *or* duration, for example, God's idea in thought. Now since thought is supposed to be an attribute of God, it is necessarily (by P11) infinite by its nature. But insofar as it has God's idea, [thought] is supposed to be finite. But (by D2) [thought] cannot be conceived to be finite unless it is determined through thought itself. But [thought can] not [be determined] through thought itself, insofar as it constitutes God's idea, for to that extent [thought] is supposed to be finite. Therefore, [thought must be determined] through thought insofar as it does not constitute God's idea, which [thought] nevertheless (by P11) must necessarily exist. Therefore, there is thought which does not constitute God's idea, and on that account God's idea does not follow necessarily from the nature [of this thought] insofar as it is absolute thought (for [thought] is conceived both as constituting God's idea and as not constituting it). [That God's idea does not follow from thought, insofar as it is absolute thought] is contrary to the hypothesis. So if God's idea in thought, or anything else in any attribute of God (for it does not matter what example is taken, since the demonstration is universal), follows from the necessity of the absolute nature of the attribute itself, it must necessarily be infinite. This was the first thing to be proven.

Next, what follows in this way from the necessity of the nature of any attribute cannot have a determinate [NS: existence, or] duration. For if you deny this, then suppose there is, in some attribute of God, a thing which follows from the necessity of the nature of that attribute—for example, God's idea in thought—and suppose that at some time [this idea] did not exist or will not exist. But since thought is supposed to be an attribute of God, it must exist necessarily and be immutable (by P11 and P20C2). So beyond the limits of the duration of God's idea (for it is supposed that at some time [this idea] did not exist or will not exist) thought will have to exist without God's idea. But this is contrary to the hypothesis, for it is supposed that God's idea follows necessarily from the given thought. Therefore, God's idea in thought, or anything else which follows necessarily from the absolute nature of some attribute of God, cannot have a determinate duration, but through the same attribute is eternal. This was the second thing [NS: to be proven]. Note that the same is to be affirmed of any thing which, in some attribute of God, follows necessarily from God's absolute nature.

P22: *Whatever follows from some attribute of God insofar as it is modified by a modification which, through the same attribute, exists necessarily and is infinite, must also exist necessarily and be infinite.*

Dem.: The demonstration of this proposition proceeds in the same way as the demonstration of the preceding one.

P23: *Every mode which exists necessarily and is infinite has necessarily had to follow either from the absolute nature of some attribute of God, or from some attribute, modified by a modification which exists necessarily and is infinite.*

Dem.: For a mode is in another, through which it must be conceived (by D5), that is (by P15), it is in God alone, and can be conceived through God alone. So if a mode is conceived to exist necessarily and be infinite, [its necessary existence and infinity] must necessarily be inferred, *or* perceived through some attribute of God, insofar as that attribute is conceived to express infinity and necessity of existence, *or* (what is the same, by D8) eternity, that is (by D6 and P19), insofar as it is considered absolutely. Therefore, the mode, which exists necessarily and is infinite, has had to follow from the absolute nature of some attribute of God—either immediately (see P21) or by some mediating modification, which follows from its absolute nature, that is (by P22), which exists necessarily and is infinite, q.e.d.

P24: *The essence of things produced by God does not involve existence.*

Dem.: This is evident from D1. For that whose nature involves existence (considered in itself), is its own cause, and exists only from the necessity of its nature.

Cor.: From this it follows that God is not only the cause of things' beginning to exist, but also of their persevering in existing, *or* (to use a Scholastic term) God is the cause of the being of things. For—whether the things [NS: produced] exist or not—so long as we attend to their essence, we shall find that it involves neither existence nor duration. So their essence can be the cause neither of their existence nor of their duration, but only God, to whose nature alone it pertains to exist [, can be the cause] (by P14C1).

P25: *God is the efficient cause, not only of the existence of things, but also of their essence.*

II/68 Dem.: If you deny this, then God is not the cause of the essence of things; and so (by A4) the essence of things can be conceived without God. But (by P15) this is absurd. Therefore God is also the cause of the essence of things, q.e.d.

Schol.: This proposition follows more clearly from P16. For from that it follows that from the given divine nature both the essence of things and their existence must necessarily be inferred; and in a word, God must be called the cause of all things in the same sense in which he is called the cause of himself. This will be established still more clearly from the following corollary.

Cor.: Particular things are nothing but affections of God's attributes, *or* modes by which God's attributes are expressed in a certain and determinate way. The demonstration is evident from P15 and D5.

P26: *A thing which has been determined to produce an effect has necessarily been determined in this way by God; and one which has not been determined by God cannot determine itself to produce an effect.*

Dem.: That through which things are said to be determined to produce an effect must be something positive (as is known through itself). And so, God,

from the necessity of his nature, is the efficient cause both of its essence and of its existence (by P25 and 16); this was the first thing. And from it the second thing asserted also follows very clearly. For if a thing which has not been determined by God could determine itself, the first part of this [NS: proposition] would be false, which is absurd, as we have shown.

P27: *A thing which has been determined by God to produce an effect, cannot render itself undetermined.*

Dem.: This proposition is evident from A3.

P28: *Every singular thing, or any thing which is finite and has a determinate existence, can neither exist nor be determined to produce an effect unless it is determined to exist and produce an effect by another cause, which is also finite and has a determinate existence; and again, this cause also can neither exist nor be determined to produce an effect unless it is determined to exist and produce an effect by another, which is also finite and has a determinate existence, and so on, to infinity.*   II/69

Dem.: Whatever has been determined to exist and produce an effect has been so determined by God (by P26 and P24C). But what is finite and has a determinate existence could not have been produced by the absolute nature of an attribute of God; for whatever follows from the absolute nature of an attribute of God is eternal and infinite (by P21). It had, therefore, to follow either from God or from an attribute of God insofar as it is considered to be affected by some mode. For there is nothing except substance and its modes (by A1, D3, and D5) and modes (by P25C) are nothing but affections of God's attributes. But it also could not follow from God, or from an attribute of God, insofar as it is affected by a modification which is eternal and infinite (by P22). It had, therefore, to follow from, or be determined to exist and produce an effect by God or an attribute of God insofar as it is modified by a modification which is finite and has a determinate existence. This was the first thing to be proven.

And in turn, this cause, *or* this mode (by the same reasoning by which we have already demonstrated the first part of this proposition) had also to be determined by another, which is also finite and has a determinate existence; and again, this last (by the same reasoning) by another, and so always (by the same reasoning) to infinity, q.e.d.

II/70   Schol.: Since certain things had to be produced by God immediately, namely, those which follow necessarily from his absolute nature, and others (which nevertheless can neither be nor be conceived without God) had to be produced by the mediation of these first things, it follows:

I. That God is absolutely the proximate cause of the things produced immediately by him, and not [a proximate cause] in his own kind, as they say. For God's effects can neither be nor be conceived without their cause (by P15 and P24C).

II. That God cannot properly be called the remote cause of singular things, except perhaps so that we may distinguish them from those things that he has produced immediately, or rather, that follow from his absolute nature. For by a remote cause we understand one which is not conjoined in any way with its effect. But all things that are, are in God, and so depend on God that they can neither be nor be conceived without him.

P29: *In nature there is nothing contingent, but all things have been determined from the necessity of the divine nature to exist and produce an effect in a certain way.*

Dem.: Whatever is, is in God (by PI5); but God cannot be called a contingent thing. For (by P11) he exists necessarily, not contingently. Next, the modes of the divine nature have also followed from it necessarily and not contingently (by P16)—either insofar as the divine nature is considered absolutely (by P21) or insofar as it is considered to be determined to act in a certain way (by P28). Further, God is the cause of these modes not only insofar as they simply exist (by P24C), but also (by P26) insofar as they are considered to be determined to produce an effect. For if they have not been determined by God, then (by P26) it is impossible, not contingent, that they should determine themselves. Conversely (by P27) if they have II/71   been determined by God, it is not contingent, but impossible, that they should render themselves undetermined. So all things have been determined from the necessity of the divine nature, not only to exist, but to exist in a certain way, and to produce effects in a certain way. There is nothing contingent, q.e.d.

Schol.: Before I proceed further, I wish to explain here—or rather to advise [the reader]—what we must understand by *Natura naturans* and *Natura natatu-*

rata. For from the preceding I think it is already established that by *Natura naturans* we must understand what is in itself and is conceived through itself, *or* such attributes of substance as express an eternal and infinite essence, that is (by P14C1 and P17C2), God, insofar as he is considered free cause.

But by *Natura naturata* I understand whatever follows from the necessity of God's nature, *or* from any of God's attributes, that is, all the modes of God's attributes insofar as they are considered as things which are in God, and can neither be nor he conceived without God.

P30: *An actual intellect, whether finite or infinite, must comprehend (God's attributes and God's affections, and nothing else.*

Dem.: A true idea must agree with its object (by A6), that is (as is known through itself), what is contained objectively in the intellect must necessarily be in Nature. But in Nature (by P14C1) there is only one substance, namely, God, and there are no affections other than those which are in God (by P15) and which can neither be nor be conceived without God (by P15). Therefore, an actual intellect, whether finite or infinite, must comprehend God's attributes and God's affections, and nothing else, q.e.d.

P31: *The actual intellect, whether finite or infinite, like will, desire, love, and the like, must be referred to* Natura naturata, *not to* Natura naturans.

Dem.: By intellect (as is known through itself) we   II/72 understand not absolute thought, but only a certain mode of thinking, which mode differs from the others, such as desire, love, and the like, and so (by D5) must be conceived through absolute thought, that is (by P15 and D6), it must be so conceived through an attribute of God, which expresses the eternal and infinite essence of thought, that it can neither be nor be conceived without [that attribute]; and so (by P29S), like the other modes of thinking, it must be referred to *Natura naturata*, not to *Natura naturans*, q.e.d.

Schol.: The reason why I speak here of actual intellect is not because I concede that there is any potential intellect, but because, wishing to avoid all confusion, I wanted to speak only of what we perceive as clearly as possible, that is, of the intellection itself. We perceive nothing more clearly than that. For we can understand nothing that does not lead to more perfect knowledge of the intellection.

P32: *The will cannot be called a free cause, but only a necessary one.*

Dem.: The will, like the intellect, is only a certain mode of thinking. And so (by P28) each volition can neither exist nor be determined to produce an effect unless it is determined by another cause, and this cause again by another, and so on, to infinity. Even if the will be supposed to be infinite, it must still be determined to exist and produce an effect by God, not insofar as he is an absolutely infinite substance, but insofar as he has an attribute that expresses the infinite and eternal essence of thought (by P23). So in whatever way it is conceived, whether as finite or as infinite, it requires a cause by which it is determined to exist and produce an effect. And so (by D7) it cannot be called a free cause, but only a necessary or compelled one, q.e.d.

II/73   Cor. 1: From this it follows, first, that God does not produce any effect by freedom of the will.

Cor. 2: It follows, second, that will and intellect are related to God's nature as motion and rest are, and as are absolutely all natural things, which (by P29) must be determined by God to exist and produce an effect in a certain way. For the will, like all other things, requires a cause by which it is determined to exist and produce an effect in a certain way. And although from a given will, *or* intellect infinitely many things may follow, God still cannot be said, on that account, to act from freedom of the will, any more than he can be said to act from freedom of motion and rest on account of those things that follow from motion and rest (for infinitely many things also follow from motion and rest). So will does not pertain to God's nature any more than do the other natural things, but is related to him in the same way as motion and rest, and all the other things which, as we have shown, follow from the necessity of the divine nature and are determined by it to exist and produce an effect in a certain way.

P33: *Things could have been produced by God in no other way, and in no other order than they have been produced.*

Dem.: For all things have necessarily followed from God's given nature (by P16), and have been determined from the necessity of God's nature to exist and produce an effect in a certain way (by P29).

Therefore, if things could have been of another nature, or could have been determined to produce an effect in another way, so that the order of Nature was different, then God's nature could also have been other than it is now, and therefore (by P11) that [other nature] would also have had to exist, and consequently, there could have been two or more Gods, which is absurd (by P14C1). So things could have been produced in no other way and no other order, and so on, q.e.d.

Schol. 1: Since by these propositions I have   II/74
shown more clearly than the noon light that there is absolutely nothing in things on account of which they can be called contingent, I wish now to explain briefly what we must understand by contingent—but first, what [we must understand] by necessary and impossible.

A thing is called necessary either by reason of its essence or by reason of its cause. For a thing's existence follows necessarily either from its essence and definition or from a given efficient cause. And a thing is also called impossible from these same causes—namely, either because its essence, *or* definition, involves a contradiction, or because there is no external cause which has been determined to produce such a thing.

But a thing is called contingent only because of a defect of our knowledge. For if we do not know that the thing's essence involves a contradiction, or if we do know very well that its essence docs not involve a contradiction, and nevertheless can affirm nothing certainly about its existence, because the order of causes is hidden from us, it can never seem to us either necessary or impossible. So we call it contingent or possible.

Schol. 2: From the preceding it clearly follows that things have been produced by God with the highest perfection, since they have followed necessarily from a given most perfect nature. Nor does this convict God of any imperfection, for his perfection compels us to affirm this. Indeed, from the opposite, it would clearly follow (as I have just shown), that God is not supremely perfect; because if things had been produced by God in another way, we would have to attribute to God another nature, different from that which we have been compelled to attribute to him from the consideration of the most perfect being.

However, I have no doubt that many will reject this opinion as absurd, without even being willing to examine it—for no other reason than because they have been accustomed to attribute another freedom to God, far different from that we have taught (D7), namely, an absolute will. But I also have no doubt that, if they are willing to reflect on the matter, and consider properly the chain of our demonstrations, in the end they will utterly reject the freedom they now attribute to God, not only as futile, but as a great obstacle to science. Nor is it necessary for me to repeat here what I said in P17S.

Nevertheless, to please them, I shall show that even if it is conceded that will pertains to God's essence, it still follows from his perfection that things could have been created by God in no other way or order. It will be easy to show this if we consider, first, what they themselves concede, namely, that it depends on God's decree and will alone that each thing is what it is. For otherwise God would not be the cause of all things. Next, that all God's decrees have been established by God himself from eternity. For otherwise he would be convicted of imperfection and inconstancy. But since, in eternity, there is neither *when,* nor *before,* nor *after,* it follows, from God's perfection alone, that he can never decree anything different, and never could have, *or* that God was not before his decrees, and cannot be without them.

But they will say that even if it were supposed that God had made another nature of things, or that from eternity he had decreed something else concerning Nature and its order, no imperfection in God would follow from that.

Still, if they say this, they will concede at the same time that God can change his decrees. For if God had decreed, concerning Nature and its order, something other than what he did decree, that is, had willed and conceived something else concerning Nature, he would necessarily have had an intellect other than he now has, and a will other than he now has. And if it is permitted to attribute to God another intellect and another will, without any change of his essence and of his perfection, why can he not now change his decrees concerning created things, and nevertheless remain equally perfect? For his intellect and will concerning created things and their order are the same

in respect to his essence and his perfection, however his will and intellect may be conceived.

Further, all the philosophers I have seen concede that in God there is no potential intellect, but only an actual one. But since his intellect and his will are not distinguished from his essence, as they all also concede, it follows that if God had another actual intellect, and another will, his essence would also necessarily be other. And therefore (as I inferred at the beginning) if things had been produced by God otherwise than they now are, God's intellect and his will, that is (as is conceded), his essence, would have to be different [NS: from what it now is]. And this is absurd.

Therefore, since things could have been produced by God in no other way, and no other order, and since it follows from God's supreme perfection that this is true, no truly sound reason can persuade us to believe that God did not will to create all the things which are in his intellect, with that same perfection with which he understands them.

But they will say that there is no perfection or imperfection in things; what is in them, on account of which they are perfect or imperfect, and are called good or bad, depends only on God's will. And so, if God had willed, he could have brought it about that what is now perfection would have been the greatest imperfection, and conversely [NS: that what is now an imperfection in things would have been the most perfect]. How would this be different from saying openly that God, who necessarily understands what he wills, can bring it about by his will that he understands things in another way than he does understand them? As I have just shown, this is a great absurdity.

So I can turn the argument against them in the following way. All things depend on God's power. So in order for things to be able to be different, God's will would necessarily also have to be different. But God's will cannot be different (as we have just shown most evidently from God's perfection). So things also cannot be different.

I confess that this opinion, which subjects all things to a certain indifferent will of God, and makes all things depend on his good pleasure, is nearer the truth than that of those who maintain that God does all things for the sake of the good. For they seem to place something outside God, which does not depend on God, to which God attends, as a model, in what

II/75

II/76

he does, and at which he aims, as at a certain goal. This is simply to subject God to fate. Nothing more absurd can be maintained about God, whom we have shown to be the first and only free cause, both of the essence of all things, and of their existence. So I shall waste no time in refuting this absurdity.

P34: *God's power is his essence itself.*

II/77   Dem.: For from the necessity alone of God's essence it follows that God is the cause of himself (by P11) and (by P16 and P16C) of all things. Therefore, God's power, by which he and all things are and act, is his essence itself, q.e.d.

P35: *Whatever we conceive to be in God's power, necessarily exists.*

Dem.: For whatever is in God's power must (by P34) be so comprehended by his essence that it necessarily follows from it, and therefore necessarily exists, q.e.d.

P36: *Nothing exists front whose nature some effect does not follow.*

Dem.: Whatever exists expresses the nature, *or* essence of God in a certain and determinate way (by P25C), that is (by P34), whatever exists expresses in a certain and determinate way the power of God, which is the cause of all things. So (by P16), from [NS: everything which exists] some effect must follow, q.e.d.

APPENDIX

With these [demonstrations] I have explained God's nature and properties: that he exists necessarily; that he is unique; that he is and acts from the necessity alone of his nature, that (and how) he is the free cause of all things; that all things are in God and so depend on him that without him they can neither be nor be conceived; and finally, that all things have been predetermined by God, not from freedom of the will *or* absolute good pleasure, but from God's absolute nature, *or* infinite power. Further I have taken care, whenever the occasion arose, to remove prejudices that could prevent my demonstrations from being perceived. But because many prejudices remain that could, and can, be a great obstacle to men's

understanding the connection of things in the way I have explained it, I considered it worthwhile to submit them here to the scrutiny of reason. All the prejudices   II/78 I here undertake to expose depend on this one: that men commonly suppose that all natural things act, as men do, on account of an end; indeed, they maintain as certain that God himself directs all things to some certain end, for they say that God has made all things for man, and man that he might worship God.

So I shall begin by considering this one prejudice, asking *first* [I] why most people are satisfied that it is true, and why all are so inclined by nature to embrace it. *Then* [II] I shall show its falsity, *and finally* [III] how, from this, prejudices have arisen concerning *good* and *evil, merit* and *sin, praise* and *blame, order* and *confusion, beauty* and *ugliness,* and other things of this kind.

[I.] Of course this is not the place to deduce these things from the nature of the human mind. It will be sufficient here if I take as a foundation what everyone must acknowledge: that all men are born ignorant of the causes of things, and that they all want to seek their own advantage, and are conscious of this appetite. From these [assumptions] it follows, *first,* that men think themselves free, because they are conscious of their volitions and their appetite, and do not think, even in their dreams, of the causes by which they are disposed to wanting and willing, because they are ignorant of [those causes]. It follows, *second,* that men act always on account of an end, namely, on account of their advantage, which they want. Hence they seek to know only the final causes of what has been done, and when they have heard them, they are satisfied, because they have no reason to doubt further. But if they cannot hear them from another, nothing remains for them but to turn toward themselves, and reflect on the ends by which they are usually determined to do such things; so they necessarily judge the temperament of the other from their own temperament.

Furthermore, they find—both in themselves and outside themselves—many means that are very helpful in seeking their own advantage, for example, eyes for seeing, teeth for chewing, plants and animals for food, the sun for light, the sea for supporting fish [NS: and so with almost all other things whose natural causes they have no reason to doubt]. Hence, they consider all natural things as means to their own advantage. And knowing that they had found these means, not provided them for themselves, they had reason to believe that there was someone else who had prepared those means for their use. For after they considered things as means, they could not believe that the things had made themselves; but from the means they were accustomed to prepare for themselves, they had to infer that there was a ruler, or a number of rulers, of Nature, endowed with human freedom, who had taken care of all things for them, and made all things for their use.

And since they had never heard anything about the temperament of these rulers, they had to judge it from their own. Hence, they maintained that the gods direct all things for the use of men in order to bind men to them and be held by men in the highest honor. So it has happened that each of them has thought up from his own temperament different ways of worshiping God, so that God might love him above all the rest, and direct the whole of Nature according to the needs of their blind desire and insatiable greed. Thus this prejudice was changed into superstition, and struck deep roots in their minds. This was why each of them strove with great diligence to understand and explain the final causes of all things.

But while they sought to show that Nature does nothing in vain (i.e., nothing not of use to men), they seem to have shown only that Nature and the gods are as mad as men. See, I ask you, how the matter has turned out! Among so many conveniences in Nature they had to find many inconveniences: storms, earthquakes, diseases, and the like. These, they maintain, happen because the gods [NS: (whom they judge to be of the same nature as themselves)] are angry on account of wrongs done to them by men, *or* on account of sins committed in their worship. And though their daily experience contradicted this, and though infinitely many examples showed that conveniences and inconveniences happen indiscriminately to the pious and the impious alike, they did not on that account give up their long-standing prejudice. It was easier for them to put this among the other unknown things, whose use they were ignorant of, and so remain in the state of ignorance in which they had been born, than to destroy that whole construction, and think up a new one.

So they maintained it as certain that the judgments of the gods far surpass man's grasp. This alone, of course, would have caused the truth to be hidden from the human race to eternity, if mathematics, which is concerned not with ends, but only with the essences and properties of figures, had not shown men another standard of truth. And besides mathematics, we can assign other causes also (which it is unnecessary to enumerate here), which were able to bring it about that men [NS: —but very few, in relation to the whole human race—] would notice these common prejudices and be led to the true knowledge of things.

[II.] With this I have sufficiently explained what I promised in the first place [viz. why men are so inclined to believe that all things act for an end]. Not many words will be required now to show that Nature has no end set before it, and that all final causes are nothing but human fictions. For I believe I have already sufficiently established it, both by the foundations and causes from which I have shown this prejudice to have had its origin, and also by P16, P32C1, and C2, and all those [propositions] by which I have shown that all things proceed by a certain eternal necessity of Nature, and with the greatest perfection.

I shall, however, add this: this doctrine concerning the end turns Nature completely upside down. For what is really a cause, it considers as an effect, and conversely [NS: what is an effect it considers as a cause]. What is by nature prior, it makes posterior. And finally, what is supreme and most perfect, it makes imperfect. For—to pass over the first two, since they are manifest through themselves—as has been established in PP21–23, that effect is most perfect which is produced immediately by God, and the more something requires several intermediate causes to produce it, the more imperfect it is. But if the things which have been produced immediately by God had been made so that God would achieve his end, then the last things, for the sake of which the first would have been made, would be the most excellent of all.

Again, this doctrine takes away God's perfection. For if God acts for the sake of an end, he necessarily wants something which he lacks. And though the theologians and metaphysicians distinguish between an end of need and an end of assimilation, they nevertheless confess that God did all things for his own sake, not for the sake of the things to be created. For before creation they can assign nothing except God for whose sake God would act. And so they are necessarily compelled to confess that God lacked those things for the sake of which he willed to prepare means, and that he desired them. This is clear through itself.

Nor ought we here to pass over the fact that the Followers of this doctrine, who have wanted to show off their cleverness in assigning the ends of things, have introduced—to prove this doctrine of theirs—a new way of arguing: by reducing things, not to the impossible, but to ignorance. This shows that no other way of defending their doctrine was open to them. For example, if a stone has fallen from a roof onto someone's head and killed him, they will show, in the following way, that the stone fell in order to kill the man. For if it did not fall to that end, God willing it, how could so many circumstances have concurred by chance (for often many circumstances do concur at once)? Perhaps you will answer that it happened because the wind was blowing hard and the man was walking that way. But they will persist: why was the wind blowing hard at that time? why was the man walking that way at that same time? If you answer again that the wind arose then because on the preceding day, while the weather was still calm, the sea began to toss, and that the man had been invited by a friend, they will press on—for there is no end to the questions which can be asked: but why was the sea tossing? why was the man invited at just that time? And so they will not stop asking for the causes of causes until you take refuge in the will of God, that is, the sanctuary of ignorance.

II/81

Similarly, when they see the structure of the human body, they are struck by a foolish wonder, and because they do not know the causes of so great an art, they infer that it is constructed, not by mechanical, but by divine, or supernatural art, and constituted in such a way that one part does not injure another.

Hence it happens that one who seeks the true causes of miracles, and is eager, like an educated man, to understand natural things, not to wonder at them, like a fool, is generally considered an impious heretic and denounced as such by those whom the people honor as interpreters of Nature and the gods. For they know that if ignorance is taken away, then foolish wonder, the only means they have of arguing and defending their authority, is also taken away. But I leave these things, and pass on to what I have decided to treat here in the *third* place.

[III.] After men persuaded themselves that everything which happens, happens on their account, they had to judge that what is most important in each thing is what is most useful to them, and to rate as most excellent all those things by which they were most pleased. Hence, they had to form these notions, by which they explained natural things: *good, evil, order, confusion, warm, cold, beauty, ugliness*. And because they think themselves free, those notions have arisen: *praise* and *blame, sin* and *merit*. The latter I shall explain after I have treated human nature; but the former I shall briefly explain here.

Whatever conduces to health and the worship of God, they have called *good*; but what is contrary to these, *evil*.

And because those who do not understand the nature of things, but only imagine them, affirm nothing concerning things, and take the imagination for the intellect, they firmly believe, in their ignorance of things and of their own nature, that there is an order in things. For when things are so disposed that, when they are presented to us through the senses, we can easily imagine them, and so can easily remember them, we say that they are well-ordered; but if the opposite is true, we say that they are badly ordered, or confused.

II/82

And since those things we can easily imagine are especially pleasing to us, men prefer order to confusion, as if order were anything in Nature more than a relation to our imagination. They also say that God has created all things in order, and so, unknowingly attribute imagination to God—unless, perhaps, they mean that God, to provide for human imagination, has disposed all things so that men can very easily imagine them. Nor will it, perhaps, give them pause that infinitely many things are found which far surpass our imagination, and a great many which confuse it on account of its weakness. But enough of this.

The other notions are also nothing but modes of imagining, by which the imagination is variously affected; and yet the ignorant consider them the chief attributes of things, because, as we have already said, they believe all things have been made for their sake, and call the nature of a thing good or evil, sound or rotten and corrupt, as they are affected by it. For example, if the motion the nerves receive from objects presented through the eyes is conducive to health, the objects by which it is caused are called beautiful; those which cause a contrary motion are called ugly. Those which move the sense through the nose, they call pleasant-smelling or stinking; through the tongue, sweet or bitter, tasty or tasteless; through touch, hard or soft, rough or smooth, and the like; and finally, those which move the ears are said to produce noise, sound, or harmony. Men have been so mad as to believe that God is pleased by harmony. Indeed there are philosophers who have persuaded themselves that the motions of the heavens produce a harmony.

All of these things show sufficiently that each one has judged things according to the disposition of his brain; or rather, has accepted affections of the imagination as things. So it is no wonder (to note this, too, in passing) that we find so many controversies to have arisen among men, and that they have finally given rise to skepticism. For although human bodies II/83 agree in many things, they still differ in very many. And for that reason what seems good to one, seems bad to another; what seems ordered to one, seems confused to another; what seems pleasing to one, seems displeasing to another, and so on.

I pass over the [other notions] here, both because this is not the place to treat them at length, and because everyone has experienced this [variability] sufficiently for himself. That is why we have such sayings as "So many heads, so many attitudes," "everyone finds his own judgment more than enough," and "there are as many differences of brains as of palates." These proverbs show sufficiently that men judge things according to the disposition of their brain, and imagine, rather than understand them. For if men had understood them, the things would at least convince them all, even if they did not attract them all, as the example of mathematics shows.

We see, therefore, that all the notions by which ordinary people are accustomed to explain Nature are only modes of imagining, and do not indicate the nature of anything, only the constitution of the imagination. And because they have names, as if they were [notions] of beings existing outside the imagination, I call them beings, not of reason, but of imagination. So, all the arguments in which people try to use such notions against us can easily be warded off.

For many are accustomed to arguing in this way: if all things have followed from the necessity of God's most perfect nature, why are there so many imperfections in Nature? why are things corrupt to the point where they stink? so ugly that they produce nausea? why is there confusion, evil, and sin?

As I have just said, those who argue in this way are easily answered. For the perfection of things is to be judged solely from their nature and power; things are not more or less perfect because they please or offend men's senses, or because they are of use to, or are incompatible with, human nature.

But to those who ask "why God did not create all men so that they would be governed by the command of reason?" I answer only "because he did not lack material to create all things, from the highest degree of perfection to the lowest"; or, to speak more properly, "because the laws of his nature have been so ample that they sufficed for producing all things which can be conceived by an infinite intellect" (as I have demonstrated in P16).

These are the prejudices I undertook to note here. If any of this kind still remain, they can be corrected by anyone with only a little meditation. [NS: And so I find no reason to devote more time to these matters, and so on.]

SECOND PART OF THE ETHICS OF THE NATURE AND ORIGIN OF THE MIND

II/84

I pass now to explaining those things which must necessarily follow from the essence of God, or the infinite and eternal being—not, indeed, all of them, for we have demonstrated (IP16) that infinitely many things must follow from it in infinitely many modes, but only those that can lead us, by the hand, as it were, to the knowledge of the human mind and its highest blessedness.

DEFINITIONS

D1: By body I understand a mode that in a certain and determinate way expresses God's essence insofar as he is considered as an extended thing (see IP25C).

D2: I say that to the essence of any thing belongs that which, being given, the thing is [NS: also] necessarily posited and which, being taken away, the thing is necessarily [NS: also] taken away; or that without which the thing can neither be nor be conceived, and which can neither be nor be conceived without the thing.

D3: By idea I understand a concept of the mind which the mind forms because it is a thinking thing.

Exp.: *I say concept rather than perception, because the word perception seems to indicate that the mind is acted on by the object. But concept seems to express an action of the mind.*

D4: By adequate idea I understand an idea which, insofar as it is considered in itself, without relation to an object, has all the properties, *or* intrinsic denominations of a true idea.

Exp.: *I say intrinsic to exclude what is extrinsic, namely, the agreement of the idea with its object.*

D5: Duration is an indefinite continuation of existing.

Exp.: *I say indefinite because it cannot be determined at all through the very nature of the existing thing, nor even by the efficient cause, which necessarily posits the existence of the thing, and does not take it away.*

D6: By reality and perfection I understand the same thing.

D7: By singular things I understand things that are finite and have a determinate existence. And if a number of individuals so concur in one action that together they are all the cause of one effect, I consider them all, to that extent, as one singular thing.

AXIOMS

A1: The essence of man does not involve necessary existence, that is, from the order of Nature it can happen equally that this or that man does exist, or that he does not exist.

A2: Man thinks [NS: or, to put it differently, we know that we think].

A3: There are no modes of thinking, such as love, desire, or whatever is designated by the word affects of the mind, unless there is in the same individual the idea of the thing loved, desired, and the like. But there can be an idea, even though there is no other mode of thinking.

A4: We feel that a certain body [NS: our body] is affected in many ways.

A5: We neither feel nor perceive any singular things [NS: or anything of *Natura naturata*], except bodies and modes of thinking.

See the postulates after P13.

P1: *Thought is an attribute of God,* or *God is a thinking thing.*

Dem.: Singular thoughts, *or* this or that thought, are modes which express God's nature in a certain and determinate way (by IP25C). Therefore (by ID5) there belongs to God an attribute whose concept all singular thoughts involve, and through which they are also conceived. Therefore, thought is one of God's infinite attributes, which expresses an eternal and infinite essence of God (see ID6), *or* God is a thinking thing, q.e.d.

Schol.: This proposition is also evident from the fact that we can conceive an infinite thinking being. For the more things a thinking being can think, the more reality, *or* perfection, we conceive it to contain. Therefore, a being which can think infinitely many things in infinitely many ways is necessarily infinite in its power of thinking. So since we can conceive an infinite being by attending to thought alone, thought (by ID4 and D6) is necessarily one of God's infinite attributes, as we maintained.

P2: *Extension is an attribute of God,* or *God is an extended thing.*

Dem: The demonstration of this proceeds in the same way as that of the preceding proposition.

P3: *In God there is necessarily an idea, both of his essence and of everything which necessarily follows from his essence.*

Dem.: For God (by P1) can think infinitely many things in infinitely many modes, *or* (what is the same, by IP16) can form the idea of his essence and of all the things which necessarily follow from it. But whatever is in God's power necessarily exists (by IP35); therefore, there is necessarily such an idea, and (by IP15) it is only in God, q.e.d.

Schol.: By God's power ordinary people understand God's free will and his right over all things which are, things which on that account are commonly considered to be contingent. For they say that God has the power of destroying all things and reducing them to nothing. Further, they very often compare God's power with the power of kings.

But we have refuted this in IP32C1 and C2, and we have shown in IP16 that God acts with the same necessity by which he understands himself, that is, just as it follows from the necessity of the divine nature (as everyone maintains unanimously) that God understands himself, with the same necessity it also follows that God does infinitely many things in infinitely many modes. And then we have shown in IP34 that God's power is nothing except God's active essence. And so it is as impossible for us to conceive that God does not act as it is to conceive that he does not exist.

Again, if it were agreeable to pursue these matters further, I could also show here that power which ordinary people fictitiously ascribe to God is not only human (which shows that ordinary people conceive God as a man, or as like a man), but also involves lack of power. But I do not wish to speak so often about the same topic. I only ask the reader to reflect II/88 repeatedly on what is said concerning this matter in Part I, from P16 to the end. For no one will be able to perceive rightly the things I maintain unless he takes great care not to confuse God's power with the human power or right of kings. . . .

P4: *God's idea', from which infinitely many things follow in infinitely many modes, must be unique.*

Dem.: An infinite intellect comprehends nothing except God's attributes and his affections (by IP30). But God is unique (by IP14C1). Therefore God's idea, from which infinitely many things follow in infinitely many modes, must be unique, q.e.d.

P5: *The formal being of ideas admits God as a cause only insofar as he is considered as a thinking thing, and not insofar as he is explained by any other attribute. That is, ideas, both of God's attributes and of singular things, admit not the objects themselves, or the things perceived, as their efficient cause, but God himself insofar as he is a thinking thing.*

Dem.: This is evident from P3. For there we inferred that God can form the idea of his essence,

and of all the things that follow necessarily from it, solely from the fact that God is a thinking thing, and not from the fact that he is the object of his own idea. So the formal being of ideas admits God as its cause insofar as he is a thinking thing.

But another way of demonstrating this is the following. The formal being of ideas is a mode of thinking (as is known through itself), that is (by IP25C), a mode which expresses, in a certain way, God's nature insofar as he is a thinking thing. And so (by IP10) it involves the concept of no other attribute of God, and consequently (by IA4) is the effect of no other attribute than thought. And so the formal being II/89 of ideas admits God as its cause insofar as he is considered only as a thinking thing, and so on, q.e.d.

P6: *The modes of each attribute have God for their cause only insofar as he is considered under the attribute of which they are modes, and not insofar as he is considered under any other attribute.*

Dem.: For each attribute is conceived through itself without any other (by IP10). So the modes of each attribute involve the concept of their own attribute, but not of another one; and so (by IA4) they have God for their cause only insofar as he is considered under the attribute of which they are modes, and not insofar as he is considered under any other, q.e.d.

Cor.: From this it follows that the formal being of things which are not modes of thinking does not follow from the divine nature because [God] has first known the things; rather the objects of ideas follow and are inferred from their attributes in the same way and by the same necessity as that with which we have shown ideas to follow from the attribute of thought.

P7: *The order and connection of ideas is the same as the order and connection of things.*

Dem.: This is clear from IA4. For the idea of each thing caused depends on the knowledge of the cause of which it is the effect.

Cor.: From this it follows that God's [NS: actual] power of thinking is equal to his actual power of acting. That is, whatever follows formally from God's infinite nature follows objectively in God from his idea in the same order and with the same connection.

Schol.: Before we proceed further, we must recall II/90 here what we showed [NS: in the First Part], namely, that whatever can be perceived by an infinite intellect as constituting an essence of substance pertains to one substance only, and consequently that the thinking substance and the extended substance are one and the same substance, which is now comprehended under this attribute, now under that. So also a mode of extension and the idea of that mode are one and the same thing, but expressed in two ways. Some of the Hebrews seem to have seen this, as if through a cloud, when they maintained that God, God's intellect, and the things understood by him are one and the same.

For example, a circle existing in Nature and the idea of the existing circle, which is also in God, are one and the same thing, which is explained through different attributes. Therefore, whether we conceive Nature under the attribute of extension, or under the attribute of thought, or under any other attribute, we shall find one and the same order, or one and the same connection of causes, that is, that the same things follow one another.

When I said [NS: before] that God is the cause of the idea, say of a circle, only insofar as he is a thinking thing, and [the cause] of the circle, only insofar as he is an extended thing, this was for no other reason than because the formal being of the idea of the circle can be perceived only through another mode of thinking, as its proximate cause, and that mode again through another, and so on, to infinity. Hence, so long as things are considered as modes of thinking, we must explain the order of the whole of Nature, or the connection of causes, through the attribute of thought alone. And insofar as they are considered as modes of extension, the order of the whole of Nature must be explained through the attribute of extension alone. I understand the same concerning the other attributes.

So of things as they are in themselves, God is really the cause insofar as he consists of infinite attributes. For the present, I cannot explain these matters more clearly.

P8: *The ideas of singular things, or of modes, that do not exist must be comprehended in God's infinite idea in the same way as the formal essences of the singular things, or modes, are contained in God's attributes.*

II/91   Dem.: This proposition is evident from the preceding one, but is understood more clearly from the preceding scholium.

Cor.: From this it follows that so long as singular things do not exist, except insofar as they are comprehended in God's attributes, their objective being, or ideas, do not exist except insofar as God's infinite idea exists. And when singular things are said to exist, not only insofar as they are comprehended in God's attributes, but insofar also as they are said to have duration, their ideas also involve the existence through which they are said to have duration.

Schol.: If anyone wishes me to explain this further by an example, I will, of course, not be able to give one which adequately explains what I speak of here, since it is unique. Still I shall try as far as possible to illustrate the matter: the circle is of such a nature that the rectangles formed from the segments of all the straight lines intersecting in it are equal to one another. So in a circle there are contained infinitely many rectangles which are equal to one another. Nevertheless, none of them can be said to exist except insofar as the circle exists, nor also can the idea of any of these rectangles be said to exist except insofar as it is comprehended in the idea of the circle. Now of these infinitely many [rectangles] let two only, namely, 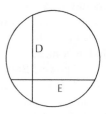 [those formed from the segments of lines] D and E, exist. Of course their ideas also exist now, not only insofar as they are only comprehended in the idea of the circle, but also insofar as they involve the existence of those rectangles. By this they are distinguished from the other ideas of the other rectangles.

P9: *The idea of a singular thing which actually exists has God for a cause not insofar as he is infinite, but insofar as he is considered to be affected by another idea of a singular thing which actually exists; and of this [idea] God is also the cause, insofar as he is affected by another third [NS: idea], and so on, to infinity.*   II/92

Dem.: The idea of a singular thing which actually exists is a singular mode of thinking, and distinct from the others (by P8C and S), and so (by P6) has God for a cause only insofar as he is a thinking thing. But not (by IP28) insofar as he is a thing thinking absolutely; rather insofar as he is considered to be affected by another [NS: determinate] mode of thinking. And God is also the cause of this mode, insofar as he is affected by another [NS: determinate mode of thinking], and so on, to infinity. But the order and connection of ideas (by P7) is the same as the order and connection of causes. Therefore, the cause of one singular idea is another idea, *or* God, insofar as he is considered to be affected by another idea; and of this also [God is the cause], insofar as he is affected by another, and so on, to infinity, q.e.d.

Cor.: Whatever happens in the singular object of any idea, there is knowledge of it in God, only insofar as he has the idea of the same object.

Dem.: Whatever happens in the object of any idea, there is an idea of it in God (by P3), not insofar as he is infinite, but insofar as he is considered to be affected by another idea of [NS: an existing] singular thing (by P9); but the order and connection of ideas (by P7) is the same as the order and connection of things; therefore, knowledge of what happens in a singular object will be in God only insofar as he has the idea of the same object, q.e.d.

P10: *The being of substance does not pertain to the essence of man, or substance does not constitute the form of man.*

Dem.: For the being of substance involves necessary existence (by IP7). Therefore, if the being of substance pertained to the essence of man, then substance being given, man would necessarily be given (by D2), and consequently man would exist necessarily, which (by A1) is absurd, q.e.d.

II/93

Schol.: This proposition is also demonstrated from IP5, namely, that there are not two substances of the same nature. Since a number of men can exist, what constitutes the form of man is not the being of substance. Further, this proposition is evident from the other properties of substance, namely, that substance is, by its nature, infinite, immutable, indivisible, and so forth, as anyone can easily see.

Cor.: From this it follows that the essence of man is constituted by certain modifications of God's attributes.

Dem.: For the being of substance does not pertain to the essence of man (by P10). Therefore, it is something (by IP15) which is in God, and which can neither be nor be conceived without God, *or* (by IP25C) an affection, *or* mode, which expresses God's nature in a certain and determinate way.

Schol.: Everyone, of course, must concede that nothing can either be or be conceived without God. For all confess that God is the only cause of all things, both of their essence and of their existence. That is, God is not only the cause of the coming to be of things, as they say, but also of their being.

But in the meantime many say that anything without which a thing can neither be nor be conceived pertains to the nature of the thing. And so they believe either that the nature of God pertains to the essence of created things, or that created things can be or be conceived without God—or what is more certain, they are not sufficiently consistent.

The cause of this, I believe, was that they did not observe the [proper] order of philosophizing. For they believed that the divine nature, which they should have contemplated before all else (because it is prior both in knowledge and in nature) is last in the order of knowledge, and that the things which are called objects of the senses are prior to all. That is why, when they contemplated natural things, they thought of nothing less than they did of the divine nature; and when afterwards they directed their minds to contemplating the divine nature, they could think of nothing less than of their first fictions, on which they had built the knowledge of natural things, because these could not assist knowledge of the divine nature. So it is no wonder that they have generally contradicted themselves.

II/94

But I pass over this. For my intent here was only to give a reason why I did not say that anything without which a thing can neither be nor be conceived pertains to its essence—namely, because singular things can neither be nor be conceived without God, and nevertheless, God does not pertain to their essence. But I have said that what necessarily constitutes the essence of a thing is that which, if it is given, the thing is posited, and if it is taken away, the thing is taken away, that is, the essence is what the thing can neither be nor be conceived without, and vice versa, what can neither be nor be conceived without the thing.

P11: *The first thing which constitutes the actual being of a human Mind is nothing but the idea of a singular thing which actually exists.*

Dem.: The essence of man (by P10C) is constituted by certain modes of God's attributes, namely (by A2), by modes of thinking, of all of which (by

A3) the idea is prior in nature, and when it is given, the other modes (to which the idea is prior in nature) must be in the same individual (by A3). And therefore an idea is the first thing which constitutes the being of a human mind. But not the idea of a thing which does not exist. For then (by P8C) the idea itself could not be said to exist. Therefore, it will be the idea of a thing which actually exists. But not of an infinite thing. For an infinite thing (by IP21 and 22) must always exist necessarily. But (by A1) it is absurd [that this idea should be of a necessarily existing object]. Therefore, the first thing which constitutes the actual being of a human mind is the idea of a singular thing which actually exists, q.e.d.

Cor.: From this it follows that the human mind is a part of the infinite intellect of God. Therefore, when we say that the human mind perceives this or that, we are saying nothing but that God, not insofar as he is infinite, but insofar as he is explained through the nature of the human mind, *or* insofar as he constitutes the essence of the human mind, has this or that idea; and when we say that God has this or that idea, not only insofar as he constitutes the nature of the human mind, but insofar as he also has the idea of another thing together with the human mind, then we say that the human mind perceives the thing only partially, *or* inadequately.

II/95

Schol.: Here, no doubt, my readers will come to a halt, and think of many things which will give them pause. For this reason I ask them to continue on with me slowly, step by step, and to make no judgment on these matters until they have read through them all.

P12: *Whatever happens in the object of the idea constituting the human mind must be perceived by the human mind, or there will necessarily be an idea of that thing in the mind; that is, if the object of the idea constituting a human mind is a body, nothing can happen in that body which is not perceived by the mind.*

Dem.: For whatever happens in the object of any idea, the knowledge of that thing is necessarily in God (by P9C), insofar as he is considered to be affected by the idea of the same object, that is (by PI 1), insofar as he constitutes the mind of some thing. Therefore, whatever happens in the object of the idea constituting the human mind, the knowledge of it is necessarily in God insofar as he constitutes

the nature of the human mind, that is (by P11C), knowledge of this thing will necessarily be in the mind, *or* the mind will perceive it, q.e.d.

Schol.: This proposition is also evident, and more clearly understood from P7S, which you should consult.

P13: *'The object of the idea constituting the human mind is the body,* or *a certain mode of extension which actually exists, and nothing else.*

II/96

Dem.: For if the object of the human mind were not the body, the ideas of the affections of the body would not be in God (by P9C) insofar as he constituted our mind, but insofar as he constituted the mind of another thing, that is (by P11C), the ideas of the affections of the body would not be in our mind; but (by A4) we have ideas of the affections of the body. Therefore, the object of the idea which constitutes the human mind is the body, and it (by P11) actually exists.

Next, if the object of the mind were something else also, in addition to the body, then since (by IP36) nothing exists from which there does not follow some effect, there would necessarily (by P12) be an idea in our mind of some effect of it. But (by A5) there is no idea of it. Therefore, the object of our mind is the existing body and nothing else, q.e.d.

Con: From this it follows that man consists of a mind and a body, and that the human body exists, as we are aware of it.

Schol.: From these [propositions] we understand not only that the human mind is united to the body, but also what should be understood by the union of mind and body. But no one will be able to understand it adequately, *or* distinctly, unless he first knows adequately the nature of our body. For the things we have shown so far are completely general and do not pertain more to man than to other individuals, all of which, though in different degrees, are nevertheless animate. For of each thing there is necessarily an idea in God, of which God is the cause in the same way as he is of the idea of the human body. And so, whatever we have said of the idea of the human body must also be said of the idea of any thing.

However, we also cannot deny that ideas differ among themselves, as the objects themselves do, and that one is more excellent than the other, and contains more reality, just as the object of the one is more excellent than the object of the other and contains more

II/97

reality. And so to determine what is the difference between the human mind and the others, and how it surpasses them, it is necessary for us, as we have said, to know the nature of its object, that is, of the human body. I cannot explain this here, nor is that necessary for the things I wish to demonstrate. Nevertheless, I say this in general, that in proportion as a body is more capable than others of doing many things at once, or being acted on in many ways at once, so its mind is more capable than others of perceiving many things at once. And in proportion as the actions of a body depend more on itself alone, and as other bodies concur with it less in acting, so its mind is more capable of understanding distinctly. And from these [truths] we can know the excellence of one mind over the others, and also see the cause why we have only a completely confused knowledge of our body, and many other things which I shall deduce from them in the following [propositions]. For this reason I have thought it worthwhile to explain and demonstrate these things more accurately. To do this it is necessary to premise a few things concerning the nature of bodies.

A1': All bodies either move or are at rest.

A2': Each body moves now more slowly, now more quickly.

L1: *Bodies are distinguished from one another by reason of Motion and rest, speed and slowness, and not by reason of substance.*

Dem.: I suppose that the first part of this is known through itself. But that bodies are not distinguished by reason of substance is evident both from IP5 and from IP8. But it is more clearly evident from those things which are said in IP15S.

II/98 L2: *All bodies agree in certain things.*

Dem.: For all bodies agree in that they involve the concept of one and the same attribute (by Dl), and in that they can move now more slowly, now more quickly, and absolutely, that now they move, now they are at rest.

L3: *A body which moves or is at rest must be determined to motion or rest by another body, which has also been determined to motion or rest by another, and that again by another, and so on, to infinity.*

Dem.: Bodies (by D1) are singular things which (by L1) are distinguished from one another by reason

of motion and rest; and so (by IP28), each must be determined necessarily to motion or rest by another singular thing, namely (by P6), by another body, which (by A1') either moves or is at rest. But this body also (by the same reasoning) could not move or be at rest if it had not been determined by another to motion or rest, and this again (by the same reasoning) by another, and so on, to infinity, q.e.d.

Cor.: From this it follows that a body in motion moves until it is determined by another body to rest; and that a body at rest also remains at rest until it is determined to motion by another.

This is also known through itself. For when I suppose that body A, say, is at rest, and do not attend to any other body in motion, I can say nothing about body A except that it is at rest. If afterwards it happens that body A moves, that of course could not have come about from the fact that it was at rest. For from that nothing else could follow but that body A would be at rest.

If, on the other hand, A is supposed to move, then II/99 as often as we attend only to A, we shall be able to affirm nothing concerning it except that it moves. If afterwards it happens that A is at rest, that of course also could not have come about from the motion it had. For from the motion nothing else could follow but that A would move. Therefore, it happens by a thing which was not in A, namely, by an external cause, by which [NS: the body in motion, A] has been determined to rest.

A1": All modes by which a body is affected by another body follow both from the nature of the body affected and at the same time from the nature of the affecting body, so that one and the same body may be moved differently according to differences in the nature of the bodies moving it. And conversely, different bodies may be moved differently by one and the same body.

A2": When a body in motion strikes against another which is at rest and cannot give way, then it is reflected, so that it continues to move, and the angle of the line of the reflected motion with the surface of the body at rest which it struck against will be equal to the angle which the line of the incident motion makes with the same surface.

This will be sufficient concerning the simplest bodies, which are distinguished from one another only by motion and rest, speed and slowness. Now let us move up to composite bodies.

II/100

DEFINITION: *When a number of bodies, whether of the same or of different size, are so constrained by other bodies that they lie upon one another, or if they so move, whether with the same degree or different degrees of speed, that they communicate their motions to each other in a certain fixed manner, we shall say that those bodies are united with one another and that they all together compose one body or individual, which is distinguished from the others by this union of bodies.*

A3″: As the parts of an individual, or composite body, lie upon one another over a larger or smaller surface, so they can be forced to change their position with more or less difficulty; and consequently the more or less will be the difficulty of bringing it about that the individual changes its shape. And therefore the bodies whose parts lie upon one another over a large surface, I shall call *hard*; those whose parts lie upon one another over a small surface, I shall call *soft*; and finally those whose parts are in motion, I shall *fluid*.

L4: *If, of a body, or of an individual, which is composed of a number of bodies, some are removed, and at the same time as many others of the same nature take their place, the [NS: body, or the] individual will retain its nature, as before, without any change of its form.*

Dem.: For (by L1) bodies are not distinguished in respect to substance; what constitutes the form of the individual consists [NS: only] in the union of the bodies (by the preceding definition). But this [NS: union] (by hypothesis) is retained even if a continual change of bodies occurs. Therefore, the individual will retain its nature, as before, both in respect to substance, and in respect to mode, q.e.d.

L5: *If the parts composing an individual become greater or less, but in such a proportion that they all keep the same ratio of motion and rest to each other as before, then the individual will likewise retain its nature, as before without any change of form.*

Dem.: The demonstration of this is the same as that of the preceding lemma.

L6: *If certain bodies composing an individual are compelled to alter the motion they have from one direction to another, but so that they can continue their motions and communicate them to each other in the same ratio as before, the individual will likewise retain its nature, without any change of form.*

II/101

Dem.: This is evident through itself. For it is supposed that it retains everything which, in its definition, we said constitutes its form. [NS: See the definition before L4.]

L7: *Furthermore, the individual so composed retains its nature, whether it, as a whole, moves or is at rest, or whether it moves in this or that direction, so long as each part retains its motion, and communicates it, as before, to the others.*

Dem.: This [NS: also] is evident from the definition preceding L4.

Schol.: By this, then, we see how a composite individual can be affected in many ways, and still preserve its nature. So far we have conceived an individual which is composed only of bodies which are distinguished from one another only by motion and rest, speed and slowness, that is, which is composed of the simplest bodies. But if we should now conceive of another, composed of a number of individuals of a different nature, we shall find that it can be affected in a great many other ways, and still preserve its nature. For since each part of it is composed of a number of bodies, each part will therefore (by L7) be able, without any change of its nature, to move now more slowly, now more quickly, and consequently communicate its motion more quickly or more slowly to the others.

II/102

But if we should further conceive a third kind of individual, composed [NS: of many individuals] of this second kind, we shall find that it can be affected in many other ways, without any change of its form. And if we proceed in this way to infinity, we shall easily conceive that the whole of nature is one individual, whose parts, that is, all bodies, vary in infinite ways, without any change of the whole individual.

If it had been my intention to deal expressly with body, I ought to have explained and demonstrated these things more fully. But I have already said that

I intended something else, and brought these things forward only because I can easily deduce from them the things I have decided to demonstrate.

POSTULATES

I. The human body is composed of a great many individuals of different natures, each of which is highly composite.

II. Some of the individuals of which the human body is composed are fluid, some soft, and others, finally, are hard.

III. The individuals composing the human body, and consequently, the human body itself, are affected by external bodies in very many ways.

IV. The human body, to be preserved, requires a great many other bodies, by which it is, as it were, continually regenerated.

V. When a fluid part of the human body is determined by an external body so that it frequently thrusts against a soft part [of the body], it changes its surface and, as it were, impresses on [the soft part] certain traces of the external body striking against [the fluid part].

VI. The human body can move and dispose external bodies in a great many ways.

P14: *The human mind is capable of perceiving a great many things, and is the more capable, the more its body can be disposed in a great many ways.*

Dem.: For the human body (by Post. 3 and 6) is affected in a great many ways by external bodies, and is disposed to affect external bodies in a great many ways. But the human mind must perceive everything which happens in the human body (by P12). Therefore, the human mind is capable of perceiving a great many things, and is the more capable [, NS: as the human body is more capable], q.e.d.

P15: *The idea that constitutes the formal being* [esse] *of the human mind is not simple, but composed of a great many ideas.*

Dem.: The idea that constitutes the formal being of the human mind is the idea of a body (by P13), which (by Post. 1) is composed of a great many highly composite individuals. But of each individual composing the body, there is necessarily (by P8C) an idea in God. Therefore (by P7), the idea of the human body is composed of these many ideas of the parts composing the body, q.e.d.

P16: *The idea of any mode in which the human body is affected by external bodies must involve the nature of the human body and at the same time the nature of the external body.*

Dem.: For all the modes in which a body is affected follow from the nature of the affected body, and at the same time from the nature of the affecting body (by A1″[II/99]). So the idea of them (by IA4) will necessarily involve the nature of each body. And so the idea of each mode in which the human body is affected by an external body involves the nature of the human body and of the external body, q.e.d.

Cor. 1: From this it follows, first, that the human mind perceives the nature of a great many bodies together with the nature of its own body.

Cor. 2: It follows, second, that the ideas which we have of external bodies indicate the condition of our own body more than the nature of the external bodies. I have explained this by many examples in the Appendix of Part I.

P17: *If the human body is affected with a mode that involves the nature of an external body, the human mind will regard the same external body as actually existing, or as present to it, until the body is affected by an affect that excludes the existence or presence of that body.*

Dem.: This is evident. For so long as the human body is so affected, the human mind (by P12) will regard this affection of the body, that is (by P16), it will have the idea of a mode that actually exists, an idea which involves the nature of the external body, that is, an idea which does not exclude, but posits, the existence or presence of the nature of the external body. And so the mind (by P16C1) will regard the external body as actually existing, or as present, until it is affected, and so on, q.e.d.

Cor.: Although the external bodies by which the human body has once been affected neither exist nor are present, the mind will still be able to regard them as if they were present.

Dem.: While external bodies so determine the fluid parts of the human body that they often thrust against the softer parts, they change (by Post. 5) their surfaces with the result (see A2″ after L3) that they are reflected from it in another way than they used to be before, and still later, when the fluid parts, by their spontaneous motion, encounter those new surfaces, they are reflected in the same way as when they were driven against those surfaces by the external bodies. Consequently, while, thus reflected, they continue to move, they will affect the human body with the same mode, concerning which the mind (by P12) will think again, that is (by P17), the mind will again regard the external body as present; this will happen as often as the fluid parts of the human body encounter the same surfaces by their spontaneous motion. So although the external bodies by which the human body has once been affected do not exist, the mind will still regard them as present, as often as this action of the body is repeated, q.e.d.

Schol.: We see, therefore, how it can happen (as it often does) that we regard as present things which do not exist. This can happen from other causes also, but it is sufficient for me here to have shown one through which I can explain it as if I had shown it through its true cause; still, I do not believe that I wander far from the true [cause] since all those postulates which I have assumed contain hardly anything which is not established by experience which we cannot doubt, after we have shown that the human body exists as we are aware of it (see P13C).

Furthermore (from P17C and P16C2), we clearly understand what is the difference between the idea of, say, Peter, which constitutes the essence of Peter's mind, and the idea of Peter which is in another man, say in Paul. For the former directly explains the essence of Peter's body, II/106 and does not involve existence, except so long as Peter exists; but the latter indicates the condition of Paul's body more than Peter's nature [NS: see P16C2], and therefore, while that condition of Paul's body lasts, Paul's mind will still regard Peter as present to itself, even though Peter does not exist.

Next, to retain the customary words, the affections of the human body whose ideas present external bodies as present to us, we shall call images of things, though they do not reproduce the [NS: external] fig-

ures of things. And when the mind regards bodies in this way, we shall say that it imagines.

And here, in order to begin to indicate what error is, I should like you to note that the imaginations of the mind, considered in themselves contain no error, or that the mind does not err from the fact that it imagines, but only insofar as it is considered to lack an idea which excludes the existence of those things which it imagines to be present to it. For if the mind, while it imagined nonexistent things as present to it, at the same time knew that those things did not exist, it would, of course, attribute this power of imagining to a virtue of its nature, not to a vice—especially if this faculty of imagining depended only on its own nature, that is (by ID7), if the mind's faculty of imagining were free.

P18: *If the human body has once been affected by two or more bodies at the same time, then when the mind subsequently imagines one of them, it will immediately recollect the others also.*

Dem.: The mind (by P17C) imagines a body because the human body is affected and disposed as it was affected when certain of its parts were struck by the external body itself. But (by hypothesis) the body was then so disposed that the mind imagined two [or more] bodies at once; therefore it will now also imagine two [or more] at once, and when the mind imagines one, it will immediately recollect the other also, q.e.d.

Schol.: From this we clearly understand what memory is. For it is nothing other than a certain II/10' connection of ideas involving the nature of things which are outside the human body—a connection which is in the mind according to the order and connection of the affections of the human body,

I say, *first* that the connection is only of those ideas which involve the nature of things outside the human body, but not of the ideas which explain the nature of the same things. For they are really (by P16) ideas of affections of the human body which involve both its nature and that of external bodies.

I say, *second*, that this connection happens according to the order and connection of the affections of the human body in order to distinguish it from the connection of ideas which happens according to the order of the intellect, by which the mind perceives things through their first causes, and which is the same in all men.

And from this we clearly understand why the mind, from the thought of one thing, immediately passes to the thought of another, which has no likeness to the first: as, for example, from the thought of the word *pomum* a Roman will immediately pass to the thought of the fruit [viz. an apple], which has no similarity to that articulate sound and nothing in common with it except that the body of the same man has often been affected by these two [NS: at the same time], that is, that the man often heard the word *pomum* while he saw the fruit.

And in this way each of us will pass from one thought to another, as each one's association has ordered the images of things in the body. For example, a soldier, having seen traces of a horse in the sand, will immediately pass from the thought of a horse to the thought of a horseman, and from that to the thought of war, and so on. But a farmer will pass from the thought of a horse to the thought of a plow, and then to that of a field, and so on. And so each one, according as he has been accustomed to join and connect the images of things this or that way, will pass from one thought to another. . . .

P19: *The human mind does not know the human body itself, nor does it know that it exists, except through ideas of affections by which the body is affected.*

II/108

Dem.: For the human mind is the idea itself, *or* knowledge of the human body (by P13), which (by P9) is indeed in God insofar as he is considered to be affected by another idea of a singular thing, or because (by Post. 4) the human body requires a great many bodies by which it is, as it were, continually regenerated; and [NS: because] the order and connection of ideas is (by P7) the same as the order and connection of causes, this idea will be in God insofar as he is considered to be affected by the ideas of a great many singular things. Therefore, God has the idea of the human

body, *or* knows the human body, insofar as he is affected by a great many other ideas, and not insofar as he constitutes the nature of the human mind, that is (by P11C), the human mind does not know the human body.

But the ideas of affections of the body are in God insofar as he constitutes the nature of the human mind, *or* the human mind perceives the same affections (by P12), and consequently (by P16) the human body itself, as actually existing (by P17).

Therefore to that extent only, the human mind perceives the human body itself, q.e.d.

P20: *There is also in God an idea,* or *knowledge, of the human mind, which follows in God in the same way and is related to God in the same way as the idea,* or *knowledge, of the human body.*

Dem.: Thought is an attribute of God (by P1), and so (by P3) there must necessarily be in God an idea both of [NS: thought] and of all of its affections, and consequently (by P11), of the human mind also. Next, this idea, *or* knowledge, of the mind does not follow in God insofar as he is infinite, but insofar as he is affected by another idea of a singular thing (by P9). But the order and connection of ideas is the same as the order and connection of causes (by P7). Therefore, this idea, *or* knowledge, of the mind follows in God and is related to God in the same way) as the idea, *or* knowledge, of the body, q.e.d.

P21: *This idea of the mind is united to the mind in the same way as the mind is united to the body.*

II/109

Dem.: We have shown that the mind is united to the body from the fact that the body is the object of the mind (see P12 and 13); and so by the same reasoning the idea of the mind must be united with its own object, that is, with the mind itself, in the same way as the mind is united with the body, q.e.d.

Schol.: This proposition is understood far more clearly from what is said in P7S; for there we have shown that the idea of the body and the body, that is (by P13), the mind and the body, are one and the same individual, which is conceived now under the attribute of thought, now under the attribute of extension. So the idea of the mind and the mind itself are one and the same thing, which is conceived under one and the same attribute, namely, thought. The idea of the mind, I say, and the mind itself follow in God from the same power of thinking and by the same necessity. For the idea of the mind, that is, the idea of the idea, is nothing but the form of the idea insofar as this is considered as a mode of thinking without relation to the object. For as soon as someone knows something, he thereby knows that he knows it, and at the same time knows that he knows that he knows, and so on, to infinity. But more on these matters later.

P22: *The human mind perceives not only the affections of the body, but also the ideas of these affections.*

Dem.: The ideas of the ideas of the affections follow in God in the same way and are related to God in the same way as the ideas themselves of the affections (this is demonstrated in the same way as P20). But the ideas of the affections of the body are in the human mind (by P12), that is (by P11C), in God, insofar as he constitutes the essence of the human mind. Therefore, the ideas of these ideas will be in God insofar as he has the knowledge, *or* idea, of the human mind, that is (by P21), they will be in the human mind itself, which for that reason perceives not only the affections of the body, but also their ideas, q.e.d.

P23. *The mind does not know itself, except insofar as it perceives the ideas of the affections of the body.*

Dem.: The idea, *or* knowledge, of the mind (by P20) follows in God in the same way, and is related to God in the same way as the idea, *or* knowledge, of the body. But since (by P19) the human mind does not know the human body itself, that is (by P11C), since the knowledge of the human body is not related to God insofar as he constitutes the nature of the human mind, the knowledge of the mind is also not related to God insofar as he constitutes the essence of the human mind. And so (again by P11C) to that extent the human mind does not know itself.

Next, the ideas of the affections by which the body is affected involve the nature of the human body itself (by P16), that is (by P13), agree with the nature of the mind. So knowledge of these

II/110

ideas will necessarily involve knowledge of the mind. But (by P22) knowledge of these ideas is in the human mind itself. Therefore, the human mind, to that extent only, knows itself, q.e.d.

P24: *The human mind does not involve adequate knowledge of the parts composing the human body.*

Dem.: The parts composing the human body pertain to the essence of the body itself only insofar as they communicate their motions to one another in a certain fixed manner (see the definition after L3C), and not insofar as they can be considered as individuals, without relation to the human body. For (by Post. 1) the parts of the human body are highly composite individuals, whose parts (by L4) can be separated from the human body and communicate their motions (see A1″ after L3) to other bodies in another manner, while the human body completely preserves its nature and form. And so the idea, *or* knowledge, of each part will be in God (by P3), insofar as he is considered to be affected by another idea of a singular thing (by P9), a singular thing which is prior, in the order of Nature, to the part itself (by P7). The same must also be said of each part of the individual composing the human body. And so, the knowledge of each part composing the human body is in God insofar as he is affected with a great many ideas of things, and not insofar as he has only the idea of the human body, that is (by P13), the idea which constitutes the nature of the human mind. And so, by (P11C) the human mind does not involve adequate knowledge of the parts composing the human body, q.e.d.

P25: *The idea of any affection of the human body does not involve adequate knowledge of an external body.*

Dem.: We have shown (P16) that the idea of an affection of the human body involves the nature of an external body insofar as the external body determines the human body in a certain fixed way. But insofar as the external body is an Individual which is not related to the human body, the idea, *or* knowledge, of it is in God (by P9) insofar as God is considered to be affected with the idea of another thing which (by P7) is prior in nature to the external body itself. So adequate

II/111

knowledge of the external body is not in God insofar as he has the idea of an affection of the human body, *or* the idea of an affection of the human body does not involve adequate knowledge of the external body, q.e.d.

P26: *The human mind does not perceive any external body as actually existing, except through the ideas of the affections of its own body.*

Dem.: If the human body is not affected by an external body in any way, then (by P7) the idea of the human body, that is (by P13) the human mind, is also not affected in any way by the idea of the existence of that body, *or* it does not perceive the existence of that external body in any way. But insofar as the human body is affected by an external body in some way, to that extent [the human mind] (by P16 and P16C1) perceives the external body, q.e.d.

Cor.: Insofar as the human mind imagines an external body, it does not have adequate knowledge of it.

Dem.: When the human mind regards external bodies through ideas of the affections of its own body, then we say that it imagines (see P17S); and the mind cannot in any other way (by P26) imagine external bodies as actually existing. And so (by P25), insofar as the mind imagines external bodies, it does not have adequate knowledge of them, q.e.d.

P27: *The idea of any affection of the human body does not involve adequate knowledge of the human body itself.*

Dem.: Any idea of any affection of the human body involves the nature of the human body insofar as the human body itself is considered to be affected with a certain definite mode (see P16). But insofar as the human body is an individual, which can be affected with many other modes, the idea of this [affection] and so on. (See P25D.). . .

P29: *The idea of the idea of any affection of the human body does not involve adequate knowledge of the human wind.*

Dem.: For the idea of an affection of the human body (by P27) does not involve adequate knowledge of the body itself, *or* does not express its nature adequately, that is (by P13), does not agree

adequately with the nature of the mind; and so (by IA6) the idea of this idea does not express the nature of the human mind adequately, *or* does not involve adequate knowledge of it, q.e.d.

Cor.: From this it follows that so long as the human mind perceives things from the common order of Nature, it does not have an adequate, but only a confused and mutilated knowledge of itself, of its own body, and of external bodies. For the mind does not know itself except insofar as it perceives ideas of the affections of the body (by P23). But it does not perceive its own body (by P19) except through the very ideas themselves of the affections [of the body], and it is also through them alone that it perceives external bodies (by P26). And so, insofar as it has these [ideas], then neither of itself (by P29), nor of its own body (by P27), nor of external bodies (by P25) does it have an adequate knowledge, but only (by P28 and P28S) a mutilated and confused knowledge, q.e.d.

Schol.: I say expressly that the mind has, not an adequate but only a confused [NS: and mutilated] knowledge, of itself, of its own body, and of external bodies, so long as it perceives things from the common order of Nature, that is, so long as it is determined externally, from fortuitous encounters with things, to regard this or that, and not so long as it is determined internally, from the fact that it regards a number of things at once, to understand their agreements, differences, and oppositions. For so often as it is disposed internally, in this or another way, then it regards things clearly and distinctly, as I shall show below.

P30: *We can have only an entirely inadequate knowledge of the duration of our body.*

Dem.: Our body's duration depends neither on its essence (by A1), nor even on God's absolute nature (by IP21). But (by IP28) it is determined to exist and produce an effect from such [NS: other] causes as are also determined by others to exist and produce an effect in a certain and determinate manner, and these again by others, and so to infinity. Therefore, the duration of our body depends on the common order of Nature and the constitution of things. But adequate knowledge of how things are constituted is in God, insofar as he has the ideas of all of them, and not insofar as he has only the idea of the human body (by P9C). So the knowledge of the duration of our body is quite inadequate in God, insofar as he is considered to constitute only the nature of the human mind, that is (by P11C), this knowledge is quite inadequate in our mind, q.e.d.

P31: *We can have only an entirely inadequate knowledge of the duration of the singular things which are outside us.*

Dem.: For each singular thing, like the human body, must be determined by another singular thing to exist and produce effects in a certain and determinate way, and this again by another, and so to infinity (by IP28). But since (in P30) we have demonstrated from this common property of singular things that we have only a very inadequate knowledge of the duration of our body, we shall have to draw the same conclusion concerning the duration of singular things [outside us], namely, that we can have only a very inadequate knowledge of their duration, q.e.d.

Cor.: From this it follows that all particular things are contingent and corruptible. For we can have no adequate knowledge of their duration (by P31), and that is what we must understand by the contingency of things and the possibility of their corruption (see IP33S1). For (by IP29) beyond that there is no contingency.

II/116

P32: *All ideas, insofar as they are related to God, are true.*

Dent.: For all ideas which are in God agree entirely with their objects (by P7C), and so (by 1A6) they are all true, q.e.d.

P33: *There is nothing positive in ideas on account of which they are called false.*

Dem.: If you deny this, conceive (if possible) a positive mode of thinking which constitutes the form of error, *or* falsity. This mode of thinking cannot be in God (by P32). But it also can neither be nor he conceived outside God (by IP15). And so there can be nothing positive in ideas on account of which they are called false, q.e.d.

P34: *Every idea which in us is absolute, or adequate and perfect, is true.*

Dem.: When we say that there is in us an adequate and perfect idea, we are saying nothing but that (by P11C) there is an adequate and perfect idea in God insofar as he constitutes the essence of our mind, and consequently (by P32) we are saying nothing but that such an idea is true, q.e.d.

P35: *Falsity consists in the privation of knowledge which inadequate,* or *mutilated and confused, ideas involve.*

Dem.: There is nothing positive in ideas which constitutes the form of falsity (by P33); but falsity cannot consist in an absolute privation (for it is minds, not bodies, which are said to err, or be deceived), nor also in absolute ignorance. For to be ignorant and to err are different. So it consists in the privation of knowledge which inadequate knowledge of things, *or* inadequate and confused ideas, involve, q.e.d.

II/117

Schol.: In P17S I explained how error consists in the privation of knowledge. But to explain the matter more fully, I shall give [NS: one or two examples]: men are deceived in that they think themselves free [NS: i.e., they think that, of their own free will, they can either do a thing or forbear doing it], an opinion which consists only in this, that they are conscious of their actions and ignorant of the causes by which they are determined. This, then, is their idea of freedom—that they do not know any cause of their actions. They say, of course, that human actions depend on the will, but these are only words for which they have no idea. For all are ignorant of what the will is, and how it moves the body; those who boast of something else, who feign seats and dwelling places of the soul, usually provoke either ridicule or disgust.

Similarly, when we look at the sun, we imagine it as about two hundred feet away from us, an error which does not consist simply in this imagining, but in the fact that while we imagine it in this way, we are ignorant of its true distance and of the cause of this imagining. For even if we later come to know that it is more six-hundred diameters of the earth away from us, we nevertheless imagine it as near. For we imagine the sun so near not because we do not know its true distance, but because an affection of our body involves the essence of the sun insofar as our body is affected by the sun. . . .

P36: *Inadequate and confused ideas follow with the same necessity as adequate, or clear and distinct ideas.*

Dem.: All ideas are in God (by IP15); and, insofar as they are related to God, are true (by P32), and (by P7C) adequate. And so there are no inadequate or confused ideas except insofar as they are related to the singular mind of sometime (see P24 and P28). And so all ideas—both the adequate and the inadequate—follow with the same necessity (by P6C), q.e.d.

P37: *What is common to all things* (on this see L2, above) *and is equally in the part and in the whole, does not constitute the essence of any singular thing.*

Dem.: If you deny this, conceive (if possible) that it does constitute the essence of some singular thing, say the essence of B. Then (by D2) it can neither be nor be conceived without B. But this is contrary to the hypothesis. Therefore, it does not pertain to the essence of B, nor does it constitute the essence of any other singular thing, q.e.d.

P38: *Those things which are common to all, and which are equally in the part and in the whole, can only be conceived adequately.*

Dem.: Let A be something which is common to all bodies, and which is equally in the part of each body and in the whole. I say that A can only be conceived adequately. For its idea (by P7C) will necessarily be adequate in God, both insofar as he has the idea of the human body and insofar as he has ideas of its affections, which (by P16, P25, and P27) involve in part both the nature of the human body and that of external bodies. That is (by P12 and P13), this idea will necessarily be adequate in God insofar as he constitutes the human mind, *or* insofar as he has ideas that are in the human mind. The mind, therefore (by P11C), necessarily perceives A adequately, and does so both insofar as it perceives itself and insofar as it perceives its own or any external body. Nor can A be conceived in another way, q.e.d.

Cor.: From this it follows that there are certain ideas, *or* notions, common to all men. For (by L2)

all bodies agree in certain things, which (by P38) must be perceived adequately, *or* clearly and distinctly, by all.

P39: *If something is common to, and peculiar to, the human body and certain external bodies by which the human body is usually affected, and is equally in the part and in the whole of each of them, its idea will also be adequate in the mind.*

Dem.: Let A be that which is common to, and peculiar to, the human body and certain external bodies, which is equally in the human body and in the same external bodies, and finally, which is equally in the part of each external body and in the whole. There will be an adequate idea of A in God (by P7C), both insofar as he has the idea of the human body, and insofar as he has ideas of the posited external bodies. Let it be posited now that the human body is affected by an external body through what it has in common with it, that is, by A; the idea of this affection will involve property A (by P16), and so (by P7C) the idea of this affection, insofar as it involves property A, will be adequate in God insofar as he is affected with the idea of the human body, that is (by P13), insofar as he constitutes the nature of the human mind. And so (by P11C), this idea is also adequate in the human mind, q.ed.

Cor.: From this it follows that the mind is the more capable of perceiving many things adequately as its body has many things in common with other bodies.

P40: *Whatever ideas follow in the mind from ideas which are adequate in the mind are also adequate.*

Dem.: This is evident. For when we say that an idea in the human mind follows from ideas which are adequate in it, we are saying nothing but that (by P11C) in the divine intellect there is an idea of which God is the cause, not insofar as he is infinite, nor insofar as he is affected with the ideas of a great many singular things, but insofar as he constitutes only the essence of the human mind [NS: and therefore, it must be adequate].

Schol. 1: With this I have explained the cause of those notions which are called *common*, and which are the foundations of our reasoning.

But some axioms, *or* notions, result from other causes which it would be helpful to explain by this method of ours. For from these [explanations] it would be established which notions are more useful than the others, and which are of hardly any use; and then, which are common, which are clear and distinct only to those who have no prejudices, and finally, which are ill-founded. Moreover, we would establish what is the origin of those notions they call *Second*, and consequently of the axioms founded on them, and other things I have thought about, from time to time, concerning these matters. But since I have set these aside for another treatise, and do not wish to give rise to disgust by too long a discussion, I have decided to pass over them here.

But not to omit anything it is necessary to know, I shall briefly add something about the causes from which the terms called *Transcendental* have had their origin—I mean terms like Being, Thing, and Something. These terms arise from the tact that the human body, being limited, is capable of forming distinctly only a certain number of images at the same time (I have explained what an image is in P17S). If that number is exceeded, the images will begin to be confused, and if the number of images the body is capable of forming distinctly in itself at once is greatly exceeded, they will all be completely confused with one another.

II/121

Since this is so, it is evident from P17C and P18, that the human mind will be able to imagine distinctly, at the same time, as many bodies as there can be images formed at the same time in its body. But when the images in the body are completely confused, the mind also will imagine all the bodies confusedly, without any distinction, and comprehend them as if under one attribute, namely, under the attribute of Being, Thing, and so forth. This can also be deduced from the fact that images are not always equally vigorous and from other causes like these, which it is not necessary to explain here. For our purpose it is sufficient to consider only one. For they all reduce to this: these terms signify ideas that are confused in the highest degree.

Those notions they call *Universal*, like Man, Horse, Dog, and the like, have arisen from similar causes, namely, because so many images (e.g., of men) are formed at one time in the human body that they surpass the power of imagining—not entirely, of course, but still to the point where the mind can imagine neither slight differences of the singular [men] (such as the color and size of each one, etc.) nor their determinate number, and imagines distinctly only what they all agree in, insofar as they affect the body. For the body has been affected most [NS: forcefully] by [what is common], since each singular has affected it [by this property]. And [NS: the mind] expresses this by the word *man*, and predicates it of infinitely many singulars. For as we have said, it cannot imagine a determinate number of singulars.

But it should be noted that these notions are not formed by all [NS: men] in the same way, but vary from one to another, in accordance with what the body has more often been affected by, and what the mind imagines or recollects more easily. For example, those who have more often regarded men's stature with wonder will understand by the word *man* an animal of erect stature. But those who have been accustomed to consider something else, will form another common image of men—for example, that man is an animal capable of laughter, or a featherless biped, or a rational animal.

And similarly concerning the others—each will form universal images of things according to the disposition of his body. Hence it is not surprising that so many controversies have arisen among the philosophers, who have wished to explain natural things by mere images of things.

Schol. 2: From what has been said above, it is clear that we perceive many things and form universal notions:

II/122

   I. from singular things which have been represented to us through the senses in a way which is mutilated, confused, and without order for the intellect (see P29C); for that reason I have been accustomed to call such perceptions knowledge from random experience;

  II. from signs, for example, from the fact that, having heard or read certain words, we recollect things, and form certain ideas of them, like those through which we imagine the things (P18S); these two ways of regarding things I shall henceforth call knowledge of the first kind, opinion or imagination;

 III. finally, from the fact that we have common notions and adequate ideas of the properties of things (see P38C, P39, P39C, and P40).

This I shall call reason and the second kind of knowledge.

[IV.] In addition to these two kinds of knowledge, there is (as I shall show in what follows) another, third kind, which we shall call intuitive knowledge. And this kind of knowing proceeds from an adequate idea of the formal essence of certain attributes of God to the adequate knowledge of the [NS: formal] essence of things.

I shall explain all these with one example. Suppose there are three numbers, and the problem is to find a fourth which is to the third as the second is to the first. Merchants do not hesitate to multiply the second by the third, and divide the product by the first, because they have not yet forgotten what they heard from their teacher without any demonstration, or because they have often found this in the simplest numbers, or from the force of the demonstration of P19 in Book VII of Euclid, namely, from the common property of proportionals. But in the simplest numbers none of this is necessary. Given the numbers 1, 2, and 3, no one fails to see that the fourth proportional number is 6—and we see this much more clearly because we infer the fourth number from the ratio which, in one glance, we see the first number to have to the second.

P41: *Knowledge of the first kind is the only cause of falsity, whereas knowledge of the second and of the third kind is necessarily true.*

II/123

Dem.: We have said in the preceding scholium that to knowledge of the first kind pertain all those ideas which are inadequate and confused; and so (by P35) this knowledge is the only cause of falsity. Next, we have said that to knowledge of the second and third kinds pertain those which are adequate; and so (by P34) this knowledge is necessarily true.

P42: *Knowledge of the second and third kinds, and not of the first kind, teaches us to distinguish the true from the false.*

Dem.: This proposition is evident through itself. For he who knows how to distinguish between the true and the false must have an adequate idea of the true and of the false, that is (P40S2), must know the true and the false by the second or third kind of knowledge.

P43: *He who has a true idea at the same time knows that he has a true idea, and cannot doubt the truth of the thing.*

Dem.: An idea true in us is that which is adequate in God insofar as he is explained through the nature of the human mind (by P11C). Let us posit, therefore, that there is in God, insofar as he is explained through the nature of the human mind, an adequate idea, A. Of this idea there must necessarily also be in God an idea which is related to God in the same way as idea A (by P20, whose demonstration is universal [NS: and can be applied to all ideas]). But idea A is supposed to be related to God insofar as he is explained through the nature of the human mind; therefore the idea of idea A must also be related to God in the same way, that is (by the same P11C), this adequate idea of idea A will be in the mind itself which has the adequate idea A. And so he who has an adequate idea, *or* (by P34) who knows a thing truly, must at the same time have an adequate idea, *or* true knowledge, of his own knowledge. That is (as is manifest through itself), he must at the same time be certain, q.e.d.

II/124

Schol.: In P21S I have explained what an idea of an idea is. But it should be noted that the preceding proposition is sufficiently manifest through itself. For no one who has a true idea is unaware that a true idea involves the highest certainty. For to have a true idea means nothing other than knowing a thing perfectly, *or* in the best way. And of course no one can doubt this unless he thinks that an idea is something mute, like a picture on a tablet, and not a mode of thinking, namely, the very [act of] understanding. And I ask, who can know that he understands some thing unless he first understands it? That is, who can know that he is certain about some thing unless he is first certain about it? What can there be which is clearer and more certain than a true idea, to serve as a standard of truth? As the light makes both itself and the darkness plain, so truth is the standard both of itself and of the false.

By this I think we have replied to these questions: if a true idea is distinguished from a false one, [NS: not insofar as it is said to be a mode of thinking, but] only insofar as it is said to agree with its object, then a true idea has no more reality or perfection than a false one (since they are distinguished only through the extrinsic denomination [NS: and not through the intrinsic denomination])—and so, does the man who has true ideas [NS: have any more reality or perfection] than he who has only false ideas? Again, why do men have false ideas? And finally, how can someone know certainly that he has ideas which agree with their objects?

To these questions, I say, 1 think I have already replied. For as far as the difference between a true and a false idea is concerned, it is established from P35 that the true is related to the false as being is to nonbeing. And the causes of falsity I have shown most clearly from P19 to P35S. From this it is also clear what is the difference between the man who has true ideas and the man who has only false ideas. Finally, as to the last, namely, how a man can know that he has an idea which agrees with its object? I have just shown, more than sufficiently, that this arises solely from his having an idea which does agree with its object—*or* that truth is its own standard. Add to this that our mind, insofar as it perceives things truly, is part of the infinite intellect of God (by P11C); hence, it is as necessary that the mind's clear and distinct ideas are true as that God's ideas are.

II/125

P44: *It is of the nature of reason to regard things as necessary, not as contingent.*

Dem.: It is of the nature of reason to perceive things truly (by P41), namely (by IA6), as they are in themselves, that is (by IP29), not as contingent but as necessary, q.e.d.

Cor. 1: From this it follows that it depends only on the imagination that we regard things as contingent, both in respect to the past and in respect to the future.

Schol.: I shall explain briefly how this happens. We have shown above (by P17 and P17C) that even though things do not exist, the mind still imagines them always as present to itself, unless causes occur which exclude their present existence. Next, we have shown (P18) that if the human body has once been affected by two external bodies at the same time, then afterwards, when the mind imagines one of them, it will immediately recollect the other also, that is, it will regard both as present to itself unless causes occur which exclude their present existence. Moreover, no one doubts but what we also imagine

time, namely, from the fact that we imagine some bodies to move more slowly than others, or more quickly, or with the same speed.

Let us suppose, then, a child, who saw Peter for the first time yesterday, in the morning, but saw Paul at noon, and Simon in the evening, and today again saw Peter in the morning. It is clear from P18 that as soon as he sees the morning light, he will immediately imagine the sun taking the same course through the sky as he saw on the preceding day, *or* he will imagine the whole day, and Peter together with the morning, Paul with noon, and Simon with the evening. That is, he will imagine the existence of Paul and of Simon with a relation to future time. On the other hand, if he sees Simon in the evening, he will relate Paul and Peter to the time past, by imagining them together with past time. And he will do this more uniformly, the more often he has seen them in this same order.

II/126

But if it should happen at some time that on some other evening he sees James instead of Simon, then on the following morning he will imagine now Simon, now James, together with the evening time, but not both at once. For it is supposed that he has seen one or the other of them in the evening, but not both at once. His imagination, therefore, will vacillate and he will imagine now this one, now that one, with the future evening time, that is, he will regard neither of them as certainly future, but both of them as contingently future.

And this vacillation of the imagination will be the same if the imagination is of things we regard in the same way with relation to past time or to present time. Consequently we shall imagine things as contingent in relation to present time as well as to past and future time.

Cor 2: It is of the nature of reason to perceive things under a certain species of eternity.

Dem.: It is of the nature of reason to regard things as necessary and not as contingent (by P44). And it perceives this necessity of things truly (by P41), that is (by IA6), as it is in itself. But (by IP16) this necessity of things is the very necessity of God's eternal nature. Therefore, it is of the nature of reason to regard things under this species of eternity.

Add to this that the foundations of reason are notions (by P38) which explain those things which are common to all, and which (by P37) do not explain the essence of any singular thing. On that account, they must be conceived without any relation to time, but under a certain species of eternity, q.e.d.

II/127 P45: *Each idea of each body, or of each singular thing which actually exists, necessarily involves an eternal and infinite essence of God.*

Dem.: The idea of a singular thing which actually exists necessarily involves both the essence of the thing and its existence (by P8C). But singular things (by IP15) cannot be conceived without God—on the contrary, because (by P6) they have God for a cause insofar as he is considered under the attribute of which the things are modes, their ideas must involve the concept of their attribute (by IA4), that is (by ID6), must involve an eternal and infinite essence of God, q.e.d.

Schol,: By existence here I do not understand duration, that is, existence insofar as it is conceived abstractly, and as a certain species of quantity. For I am speaking of the very nature of existence, which is attributed to singular things because infinitely many things follow from the eternal necessity of God's nature in infinitely many modes (see IP16). I am speaking, I say, of the very existence of singular things insofar as they are in God. For even if each one is determined by another singular thing to exist in a certain way, still the force by which each one perseveres in existing follows from the eternal necessity of God's nature. Concerning this, see IP24C.

P46: *The knowledge of God's eternal and infinite essence which each idea involves is adequate and perfect.*

Dem.: The demonstration of the preceding proposition is universal, and whether the thing is considered as a part or as a whole, its idea, whether of the whole or of a part (by P45), will involve God's eternal and infinite essence. So what gives knowledge of an eternal and infinite essence of God is common to all, and is equally in the part and in the whole. And so (by P38) this knowledge will be adequate, q.e.d.

II/128

P47: *The human mind has an adequate knowledge of God's eternal and infinite essence.*

Dem.: The human mind has ideas (by P22) from which it perceives (by P23) itself, (by P19) its own

body, and (by P16C1 and P17) external bodies as actually existing. And so (by P45 and P46) it has an adequate knowledge of God's eternal and infinite essence, q.e.d.

Schol.: From this we see that God's infinite essence and his eternity are known to all. And since all things are in God and are conceived through God, it follows that we can deduce from this knowledge a great many things which we know adequately, and so can form that third kind of knowledge of which we spoke in P40S2 and of whose excellence and utility we shall speak in Part V.

But that men do not have so clear a knowledge of God as they do of the common notions comes from the face that they cannot imagine God, as they can bodies, and that they have joined the name *God* to the images of things which they are used to seeing. Men can hardly avoid this, because they are continually affected by external bodies.

And indeed, most errors consist only in our not rightly applying names to things. For when someone says that the lines which are drawn from the center of a circle to its circumference are unequal, he surely understands (then at least) by a circle something different from what mathematicians understand. Similarly, when men err in calculating, they have certain numbers in their mind and different ones on the paper. So if you consider what they have in mind, they really do not err, though they seem to err because we think they have in their mind the numbers which are on the paper. If this were not so, we would not believe that they were erring, just as I did not believe that he was erring whom I recently heard cry out that his courtyard had flown into his neighbor's hen [NS: although his words were absurd], because what he had in mind seemed sufficiently clear to me [viz. that his hen had flown into his neighbor's courtyard].

II/129

And most controversies have arisen from this, that men do not rightly explain their own mind, or interpret the mind of the other man badly. For really, when they contradict one another most vehemently, they either have the same thoughts, or they are thinking of different things, so that what they think are errors and absurdities in the other are not.

P48: *In the mind there is no absolute, or free, will, but the mind is determined to will this or that by a cause which is also determined by another, and this again by another, and so to infinity.*

Dem.: The mind is a certain and determinate mode of thinking (by P11), and so (by IP17C2) cannot be a free cause of its own actions, *or* cannot have an absolute faculty of willing and not willing. Rather, it must be determined to willing this or that (by IP28) by a cause which is also determined by another, and this cause again by another, and so on, q.e.d.

Schol.: In this same way it is also demonstrated that there is in the mind no absolute faculty of understanding, desiring, loving, and the like. From this it follows that these and similar faculties are either complete fictions or nothing but metaphysical beings, *or* universals, which we are used to forming from particulars. So intellect and will are to this or that idea, or to this or that volition as 'stone-ness' is to this or that stone, or man to Peter or Paul.

We have explained the cause of men's thinking themselves free in the Appendix of Part I. But before I proceed further, it should be noted here that by will I understand a faculty of affirming and denying, and not desire. I say that I understand the fac-
II/130 ulty by which the mind affirms or denies something true or something false, and not the desire by which the mind wants a thing or avoids it.

But after we have demonstrated that these faculties are universal notions which are not distinguished from the singulars from which we form them, we must now investigate whether the volitions themselves are anything beyond the very ideas of things. We must investigate, I say, whether there is any other affirmation or negation in the mind except that which the idea involves, insofar as it is an idea—on this see the following proposition and also D3—so that our thought does not fall into pictures, For by ideas I understand, not the images which are formed at the back of the eye (and, if you like, in the middle of the brain), but concepts of thought [NS: or the objective being of a thing insofar as it consists only in thought].

P49: *In the mind there is no volition,* or *affirmation and negation, except that which the idea involves insofar as it is an idea.*

Dem.: In the mind (by P48) there is no absolute faculty of willing and not willing, but only singular volitions, namely, this and that affirmation, and this

and that negation. Let us conceive, therefore, some singular volition, say a mode of thinking by which the mind affirms that the three angles of a triangle are equal to two right angles.

This affirmation involves the concept, *or* idea, of the triangle, that is, it cannot be conceived without the idea of the triangle. For to say that A must involve the concept of B is the same as to say that A cannot be conceived without B. Further, this affirmation (by A3) also cannot be without the idea of the triangle. Therefore, this affirmation can neither be nor be conceived without the idea of the triangle.

Next, this idea of the triangle must involve this same affirmation, namely, that its three angles equal two right angles. So conversely, this idea of the triangle also can neither be nor be conceived without this affirmation.

So (by D2) this affirmation pertains to the essence of the idea of the triangle and is nothing beyond it. And what we have said concerning this volition (since we have selected it at random), must also be said concerning any volition, namely, that it is nothing apart from the idea, q.e.d.

Cor.: The will and the intellect are one and the same. II/131

Dem.: The will and the intellect are nothing apart from the singular volitions and ideas themselves (by P48 and P48S). But the singular volitions and ideas are one and the same (by P49). Therefore the will and the intellect are one and the same, q.e.d.

Schol.: [I.] By this we have removed what is commonly maintained to be the cause of error. Moreover, we have shown above that falsity consists only in the privation which mutilated and confused ideas involve. So a false idea, insofar as it is false, does not involve certainty. When we say that a man rests in false ideas, and does not doubt them, we do not, on that account, say that he is certain, but only that he does not doubt, or that he rests in false ideas because there are no causes to bring it about that his imagination wavers [NS: or to cause him to doubt them]. On this, sec P44S.

Therefore, however stubbornly a man may cling to something false [NS: so that we cannot in any way make him doubt it], we shall still never say that he is certain of it]. For by certainty we understand something positive (see P43 and P43S), not the privation of doubt. But by the privation of certainty, we understand falsity.

However, to explain the preceding proposition more fully, there remain certain things I must warn you of. And then I must reply to the objections which can be made against this doctrine of ours. And finally, to remove every uneasiness, I thought it worthwhile to indicate some of the advantages of this doctrine. Some, I say—for the most important ones will be better understood from what we shall say in Part V.

[II.] I begin, therefore, by warning my readers, first, to distinguish accurately between an idea, *or* concept, of the mind, and the images of things which we imagine. And then it is necessary to distinguish between ideas and the words by which we signify things. For because many people either completely confuse these three—ideas, images, and words—or do not distinguish them accurately enough, or carefully enough, they have been completely ignorant of this doctrine concerning the will. But it is quite necessary to know it, both for the sake of speculation and in order to arrange one's life wisely.

Indeed, those who think that ideas consist in images which are formed in us from encounters with [NS: external] bodies, are convinced that those ideas of things [NS: which can make no trace in our brains, or] of which we can form no similar image [NS: in our brain] are not ideas, but only fictions which we feign from a free choice of the will. They look on ideas, therefore, as mute pictures on a panel, and pre-occupied with this prejudice, do not see that an idea, insofar as it is an idea, involves an affirmation or negation.

And then, those who confuse words with the idea, or with the very affirmation which the idea involves, think that they can will something contrary to what they are aware of, when they only affirm or deny with words something contrary to what they are aware of. But these prejudices can easily be put aside by anyone who attends to the nature of thought, which does not at all involve the concept of extension. He will then understand clearly that an idea (since it is a mode of thinking) consists neither in the image of anything, nor in words. For the essence of words and of images is constituted only by corporeal motions, which do not at all involve the concept of thought.

It should suffice to have issued these few words of warning on this matter, so I pass to the objections mentioned above.

[III.A.(i)] The first of these is that they think it clear that the will extends more widely than the intellect, and so is different from the intellect. The reason why they think the will extends more widely than the intellect is that they say they know by experience that they do not require a greater faculty of assenting, *or* affirming, and denying, than we already have, in order to assent to infinitely many other things which we do not perceive—but they do require a greater faculty of understanding. The will, therefore, is distinguished from the intellect because the intellect is finite and the will is infinite.

[IIIA.(ii)] Second, it can be objected to us that experience seems to teach nothing more clearly than that we can suspend our judgment so as not to assent to things we perceive. This also seems to be confirmed from the fact that no one is said to be deceived insofar as he perceives something, but only insofar as he assents or dissents. For example, someone who feigns a winged horse does not on that account grant that there is a winged horse, that is, he is not on that account deceived unless at the same time he grants that there is a winged horse. Therefore, experience seems to teach nothing more clearly than that the will, *or* faculty of assenting, is free, and different from the faculty of understanding.

[III.A.(iii)] Third, it can be objected that one affirmation does not seem to contain more reality than another, that is, we do not seem to require a greater power to affirm that what is true, is true, than to affirm that something false is true. But [NS: with ideas it is different, for] we perceive that one idea has more reality, *or* perfection, than another. As some objects are more excellent than others, so also some ideas of objects are more perfect than others. This also seems to establish a difference between the will and the intellect.

[III.A.(iv)] Fourth, it can be objected that if man does not act from freedom of the will, what will happen if he is in a state of equilibrium, like Buridan's ass? Will he perish of hunger and of thirst? If I concede that he will, I would seem to conceive an ass, or a statue of a man, not a man. But if I deny that he will, then he will determine himself, and

II/132

II/133

consequently have the faculty of going where he wills and doing what he wills.

Perhaps other things in addition to these can be objected. But because I am not bound to force on you what anyone can dream, I shall only take the trouble to reply to these objections—and that as briefly as I can.

[III.B.(i)] To the first I say that I grant that the will extends more widely than the intellect, if by intellect they understand only clear and distinct ideas. But I deny that the will extends more widely than perceptions, *or* the faculty of conceiving. And indeed, I do not see why the faculty of willing should be called infinite, when the faculty of sensing is not. For just as we can affirm infinitely many things by the same faculty of willing (but one after another, for we cannot affirm infinitely many things at once), so also we can sense, *or* perceive, infinitely many bodies by the same faculty of sensing (viz. one after another [NS: and not at once]).

If they say that there are infinitely many things which we cannot perceive, I reply that we cannot reach them by any thought, and consequently, not by any faculty of willing. But, they say, if God willed to bring it about that we should perceive them also, he would have to give us a greater faculty of perceiving, but not a greater faculty of willing than he has given us. This is the same as if they said that, if God should will to bring it about that we understood infinitely many other beings, it would indeed be necessary for him to give us a greater intellect, but not a more universal idea of being, in order for us to embrace the same infinity of beings. For we have shown that the will is a universal being, *or* idea, by which we explain all the singular volitions, that is, it is what is common to them all.

Therefore, since they believe that this common *or* universal idea of all volitions is a faculty, it is not at all surprising if they say that this faculty extends beyond the limits of the intellect to infinity. For the universal is said equally of one, a great many, or infinitely many individuals.

[III.B(ii)] To the second objection I reply by - denying that we have a free power of suspending judgment. For when we say that someone suspends judgment, we are saying nothing but that he sees that he does not perceive the thing adequately. Suspen-

sion of judgment, therefore, is really a perception, not [an act of] free will.

To understand this clearly, let us conceive a child imagining a winged horse, and not perceiving anything else. Since this imagination involves the existence of the horse (by P17C), and the child does not perceive anything else which excludes the existence of the horse, he will necessarily regard the horse as present. Nor will he be able to doubt its existence, though he will not be certain of it.

We find this daily in our dreams, and I do not believe there is anyone who thinks that while he is dreaming he has a free power of suspending judgment concerning the things he dreams, and of bringing it about that he does not dream the things he dreams he sees. Nevertheless, it happens that even in dreams we suspend judgment, namely, when we dream that we dream.

Next, I grant that no one is deceived insofar as he perceives, that is, I grant that the imaginations of the mind, considered in themselves, involve no error. But I deny that a man affirms nothing insofar as he perceives. For what is perceiving a winged horse other than affirming wings of the horse? For if the mind perceived nothing else except the winged horse, it would regard it as present to itself, and would not have any cause of doubting its existence, or any faculty of dissenting, unless either the imagination of the winged horse were joined to an idea which excluded the existence of the same horse, or the mind perceived that its idea of a winged horse was inadequate. And then either it will necessarily deny the horse's existence, or it will necessarily doubt it.

[III.B.(iii)] As for the third objection, I think what has been said will be an answer to it too: namely, that the will is something universal, which is predicated of all ideas, and which signifies only what is common to all ideas, namely, the affirmation, whose adequate essence, therefore, insofar as it is thus conceived abstractly, must be in each idea and in this way only must be the same in all, but not insofar as it is considered to constitute the idea's essence; for in that regard the singular affirmations differ from one another as much as the ideas themselves do. For example, the affirmation which the idea of a circle involves differs from that which the idea of a triangle involves as much as the idea of the circle differs from the idea of the triangle.

Next, I deny absolutely that we require an equal power of thinking, to affirm that what is true is true, as to affirm that what is false is true. For if you consider the mind, they are related to one another as being to not-being. For there is nothing positive in ideas which constitutes the form of falsity (see P35, P35S, and P47S). So the thing to note here, above all, is how easily we are deceived when we confuse universals with singulars, and beings of reason and abstractions with real beings.

[III.B.(iv)] Finally, as far as the fourth objection is concerned, I say that I grant entirely that a man placed in such an equilibrium (viz. who perceives nothing but thirst and hunger, and such food and drink as are equally distant from him) will perish of hunger and thirst. If they ask me whether such a man should not be thought an ass, rather than a man, I say that I do not know—just as I also do not know how highly we should esteem one who hangs himself, or children, fools, and madmen, and so on.

[IV.] It remains now to indicate how much knowledge of this doctrine is to our advantage in life. We shall see this easily from the following considerations:

[A.] Insofar as it teaches that we act only from God's command, that we share in the divine nature, and that we do this the more, the more perfect our actions are, and the more and more we understand God. This doctrine, then, in addition to giving us complete peace of mind, also teaches us wherein our greatest happiness, *or* blessedness, consists: namely, in the knowledge of God alone, by which we are led to do only those things which love and morality advise. From this we clearly understand how far they stray from the true valuation of virtue, who expect

to be honored by God with the greatest rewards for their virtue and best actions, as for the greatest bondage—as if virtue itself, and the service of God, were not happiness itself, and the greatest freedom.

[B.] Insofar as it teaches us how we must bear ourselves concerning matters of fortune, *or* things which are not in our power, that is, concerning things which do not follow from our nature—that we must expect and bear calmly both good fortune and bad. For all things follow from God's eternal decree with the same necessity as from the essence of a triangle it follows that its three angles are equal to two right angles.

[C.] This doctrine contributes to social life, insofar as it teaches us to hate no one, to disesteem no one, to mock no one, to be angry at no one, to envy no one; and also insofar as it teaches that each of us should be content with his own things, and should be helpful to his neighbor, not from unmanly compassion, partiality, or superstition, but from the guidance of reason, as the time and occasion demand. I shall show this in the Fourth Part.

[D.] Finally, this doctrine also contributes, to no small extent, to the common society insofar as it teaches how citizens are to be governed and led, not so that they may be slaves, but that they may do freely the things which are best.

And with this I have finished what I had decided to treat in this scholium, and put an end to this our Second Part. In it I think that I have explained the nature and properties of the human mind in sufficient detail, and as clearly as the difficulty of the subject allows, and that I have set out doctrines from which we can infer many excellent things, which are highly useful and necessary to know, as will be established partly in what follows.

II/136

REVIEW QUESTIONS

1. Why does Spinoza reject dualism, the notion that the world contains two different kinds of stuff (matter and something else)?
2. How can the intellect free us from bondage?
3. Is Spinoza's God a person? Does his God intervene in human affairs? What is the relationship between God and humans?
4. In what way is Spinoza a pantheist?
5. How does Spinoza solve the mind-body problem (the nature of the relationship between the mental and the physical)?

18

GOTTFRIED WILHELM LEIBNIZ

G. W. Leibniz was born on July 1, 1646, in Leipzig. His father, a scholar and a professor of moral philosophy at the University of Leipzig, who apparently began to teach Leibniz as a small child, died when Leibniz was only six years old. Leibniz seems to have been largely self-taught, teaching himself Latin at the age of seven. Gaining admittance to his late father's library, he concentrated especially in the Church Fathers and in the Latin classics. Leibniz attended university from age fourteen to age twenty-one, first at the University of Leipzig and then the University of Altdorf, graduating with degrees in law and in philosophy. He was soon recognized as a talented young man of great promise and was offered a position on the faculty at the University of Altdorf. He declined the offer, choosing instead public service. Under the patronage of Baron Johann Christian von Boineburg, Leibniz entered the service of the Elector of Mainz and occupied a number of positions in Mainz and nearby Nuremburg. There he stayed until he was sent to Paris in spring 1672 on diplomatic business, a trip that deeply affected his intellectual development.

In Paris from 1672 to 1676 Leibniz made the acquaintance of such intellectual luminaries as Christian Huygens, who became his teacher and introduced him to other philosophers and scientists, such as Arnauld and Malebranche. It was in Paris that he laid the foundations for his work in calculus. Before Leibniz returned to Germany, in December 1676, he stopped in England and in Holland, where he met Spinoza. Both Boineburg and the Elector of Mainz had died while he was in Paris. Leibniz returned to the court of Hanover as a counselor, where he settled for the rest of his life.

Although recognized today as one of the leading philosophers of all time and one of two founders of calculus (with Newton), Leibniz was not popular in his own time. Newton accused him of stealing his invention of calculus (we know now that the two geniuses invented it independently, Leibniz publishing his work first in 1684, Newton in 1687), and many of his contemporaries (including the prestigious Royal Society) belittled his work. Bertrand Russell has written the following in this regard:

> Leibniz was one of the supreme intellects of all time, but as a human being he was not admirable. He had, it is true, the virtues that one would wish to find mentioned in a testimonial to a prospective employee: he was industrious, frugal, temperate, and financially honest. But he was wholly destitute of those higher philosophic virtues that are so notable in Spinoza. His best thought was not such as would win him popularity, and he left his records of it unpublished in his desk. . . . It was the popular Leibniz who invented the doctrine that this is the best of all possible worlds (to which F. H. Bradley added the sardonic comment, "and everything in it is a necessary evil"); it was this Leibniz that Voltaire caricatured as Doctor Pangloss.[1]

Leibniz published very little in his lifetime. A major work on Locke's *Essay* was withheld from publication when Locke died in 1704. His only systematic work is *Theodicy* (1710), whose thesis: "this is the best of all possible worlds" was satirized by Voltaire's *Candide*. In metaphysics, the "Discourse on Metaphysics," which I have included in this section, was written in 1686 but left unpublished. Themes from the "Discourse," however, appeared, somewhat transformed, in the "New System of Nature," which Leibniz published in 1695—the first public exposition of his metaphysical system. These themes appear further developed in later summaries of his doctrines, the unpublished "Principles of Nature and Grace" and "Monadology" (included here). Leibniz did extensive work in physics, writing "A Specimen of Dynamics" (1695), and inventing a calculating machine that could add, subtract, multiply, divide, and extract square roots. He was passionately interested in theology and sought to reconcile Catholicism with his own Protestant faith. He went even further, seeking to reconcile Cartesian dualism with Hobbesian materialism—and these with the major ideas of the medieval schoolmen.

Leibniz died in Hanover on November 14, 1716.

What were Leibniz's main ideas? They center on the idea of *substance*, on ultimate reality. Whereas Descartes thought there were three substances, God, mind (thought), and matter (extension), and Spinoza thought that there was only one, God or Nature (both thought and extension are attributes of God), Leibniz held that extension cannot be an attribute of a substance. For extension implies plurality and, so, can apply only to the aggregate of substances. Each single substance must be unextended. He held that there must be an infinite number of substances, which he called *monads*: simple, indivisible, substances that make up all of reality. The monad is without parts, windowless, and eternal. In a letter to Burcher de Volder, Leibniz describes them thus:

> Considering matters accurately, it must be said that there is nothing in things except simple substances, and, in them, nothing but perception and appetite. Moreover, matter and motion are not so much substances or things as they are the phenomena of permanent beings, the reality of which is located in the harmony of each percipient with itself (with respect to different times) and with different percipients.

In this passage Leibniz says the monad is immaterial, lacking spatial extension, containing only perception and desire (appetite). In fact, the monad is a soul. There are an infinite number of these entities, which are windowless in the sense that each one mirrors the entire

---

[1]Bertrand Russell, *A History of Western Philosophy* (New York: Simon & Schuster, 1945), p. 581.

universe from a particular point of view, some more clearly and distinctly than others, in hierarchical order. The monads never interact but function like an infinite set of clocks which keep perfect time, arranged by God in a preestablished harmony, so that each of us can communicate with the thoughts of other monads. A human body is composed entirely of monads, each of which is a soul, and as such, immortal, but there is a dominant monad (*soul*) which rules over the soulish monads.

Matter and space, as they appear to the senses, are unreal, but they are reflections of the arrangements of monads in an order that mirrors real but abstract relations.

Although this seems to lend itself to a deterministic world view, Leibniz was a theist, who recognized the need to explain how a good God could permit evil. He set forth the idea of a *theodicy*, or idea of the best of all worlds, in which God is thought to have contemplated an infinite set of worlds and chosen one with the best ratio of good over evil. It was not possible for God to create a better world than this one, so long as humans have free will—something of very high value.

> Let us suppose that the current of one and the same river carries along with it various boats, which differ among themselves only in cargo, some being laden with wood, others with stone, and some more, the others less. That being so, it will come about that the boats most heavily laden will go more slowly than the others, provided it be assumed that the wind or the oar, or some other similar means, assist them not at all . . . Let us now compare the force which the current exercises on boats, and communicates to them, with the action of God, who produces and conserves whatever is positive in creatures, . . . let us compare the inertia of matter with the natural imperfection of creatures, and the slowness of the laden boat with the defects to be found in the qualities and the action of the creature; and we shall find that there is nothing so just as this comparison. The current is the cause of the boat's movement, but not of its retardation; God is the cause of perfection in the nature and the actions of the creature, but the limitation of the receptivity of the creature is the cause of the defects there are in its action . . . God is no more the cause of sin than the river's current is the cause of the retardation of the boat.[2]

So although our nature may incline us one way or the other, an ineliminable input of choice, not God or circumstances, causes us to act in one way or another, for good or evil.

FOR FURTHER READING

Broad, C. D. *Leibniz: An Introduction* (Cambridge University Press, 1975).

Brown, Stuart. *Leibniz* (University of Minnesota Press, 1984).

Costabel, Pierre. *Leibniz and Dynamics* (Cornell University Press, 1973).

Frankfurt, Harry, ed. *Leibniz* (Doubleday, 1972).

Hick, John. *Evil and the God of Love* (Harper & Row, 1966).

Hooker, Michael, ed. *Leibniz: Critical and Interpretative Essays* (University of Minnesota Press, 1982).

Ishiguro, Hidé. *Leibniz's Philosophy of Logic and Language* (Cornell University Press, 1972).

Jolley, Nicholas. *Leibniz and Locke* (Oxford University Press, 1984).

Mates, Benson. *The Philosophy of Leibniz: Metaphysics and Language* (Oxford University Press, 1986).

Parkinson, G. H. R. *Logic and Reality in Leibniz's Metaphysics* (Oxford University Press, 1965).

Rescher, Nicholas. *The Philosophy of Leibniz* (Prentice-Hall, 1967).

Russell, Bertrand. *A Critical Exposition of the Philosophy of Leibniz* (George Allen & Unwin, 1900).

Woolhouse, R. S., ed. *Leibniz: Metaphysics and Philosophy of Science* (Oxford University Press, 1981).

---

[2]Leibniz, *Theodicy* Part I, Para 30.

DISCOURSE ON METAPHYSICS

I. CONCERNING THE DIVINE PERFECTION AND THAT GOD DOES EVERYTHING IN THE MOST DESIRABLE WAY

The conception of God which is the most common and the most full of meaning is expressed well enough in the words: God is an absolutely perfect being. The implications, however, of these words fail to receive sufficient consideration. For instance, there are many different kinds of perfection, all of which God possesses, and each one of them pertains to him in the highest degree.

We must also know what perfection is. One thing which can surely be affirmed about it is that those forms or natures which are not susceptible of it to the highest degree, say the nature of numbers or of figures, do not permit of perfection. This is because the number which is the greatest of all (that is, the sum of all the numbers), and likewise the greatest of all figures, imply contradictions. The greatest knowledge, however, and omnipotence contain no impossibility. Consequently power and knowledge do admit of perfection, and in so far as they pertain to God they have no limits.

Whence it follows that God who possesses supreme and infinite wisdom acts in the most perfect manner not only metaphysically, but also from the moral standpoint. And with respect to ourselves it can be said that the more we are enlightened and informed in regard to the work of God the more will we be disposed to find them excellent and conforming entirely to that which we might desire.

II. AGAINST THOSE WHO HOLD THAT THERE IS IN THE WORKS OF GOD NO GOODNESS, OR THAT THE PRINCIPLES OF GOODNESS AND BEAUTY ARE ARBITRARY

Therefore I am far removed from the opinion of those who maintain that there are no principles of goodness or perfection in the nature of things, or in the ideas which God has about them, and who say that the works of God are good only through the formal reason that God has made them. If this position were true, God, knowing that he is the author of things, would not have to regard them afterwards and find them good, as the Holy Scripture witnesses. Such anthropological expressions are used only to let us know that excellence is recognized in regarding the works themselves, even if we do not consider their evident dependence on their author. This is confirmed by the fact that it is in reflecting upon the works that we are able to discover the one who wrought. They must therefore bear in themselves his character. I confess that the contrary opinion seems to me extremely dangerous and closely approaches that of recent innovators who hold that the beauty of the universe and the goodness which we attribute to the works of God are chimeras of human beings who think of God in human terms. In saying, therefore, that things are not good according to any standard of goodness, but simply by the will of God, it seems to me that one destroys, without realizing it, all the love of God and all his glory; for why praise him for what he has done, if he would be equally praiseworthy in doing the contrary? Where will be his justice and his wisdom if he has only a certain despotic power, if arbitrary will takes the place of reasonableness, and if in accord with the definition of tyrants, justice consists in that which is pleasing to the most powerful? Besides it seems that every act of willing supposes some reason for the willing and this reason, of course, must precede the act. This is why, accordingly, I find so strange those expressions of certain philosophers who say that the eternal truths of metaphysics and Geometry, and consequently the principles of goodness, of justice, and of perfection, are effects only of the will of God. To me it seems that all these follow from his understanding, which does not depend upon his will any more than does his essence.

III. AGAINST THOSE WHO THINK THAT GOD MIGHT HAVE MADE THINGS BETTER THAN HE HAS

No more am I able to approve of the opinion of certain modern writers who boldly maintain that that which God has made is not perfect in the highest degree, and that he might have done better. It seems to me that the consequences of such an opinion are wholly inconsistent with the glory of God. *Uti minus malum habet rationem boni, ita minus bonum habet rationem mali.* I think that one acts imperfectly if he acts with less perfection than he is capable of. To show that an architect could have done better is to find fault with his work. Furthermore this opinion is contrary to the Holy Scriptures when they assure us of the goodness of God's work. For if comparative perfection were sufficient, then in whatever way God had accomplished this work, since there is an infinitude of possible imperfections, it would always have been good in comparison with the less perfect; but a thing is little praiseworthy when it can be praised only in this way.

I believe that a great many passages from the divine writings and from the holy fathers will be found favoring my position, while hardly any will be found in favor of that of these modern thinkers. Their opinion is, in my judgment, unknown to the writers of antiquity and is a deduction based upon the too slight acquaintaince which we have with the general harmony of the universe and with the hidden reasons for God's conduct. In our ignorance, therefore, we are tempted to decide audaciously that many things might have been done better.

These modern thinkers insist upon certain hardly tenable subtleties, for they imagine that nothing is so perfect that there might not have been something more perfect. This is an error. They think, indeed, that they are thus safeguarding the liberty of God. As if it were not the highest liberty to act in perfection according to the sovereign reason. For to think that God acts in anything without having any reason for his willing, even if we overlook the fact that such action seems impossible, is an opinion which conforms little to God's glory. For example, let us suppose that God chooses between A and B, and that he takes A without any reason for preferring it to B. I say that this action on the part of God is at least not praiseworthy, for all praise ought to be founded upon reason which *ex hypothesi* is not present here. My opinion is that God does nothing for which he does not deserve to be glorified.

IV. THAT LOVE FOR GOD DEMANDS ON OUR PART COMPLETE SATISFACTION WITH AND ACQUIESCENCE IN THAT WHICH HE HAS DONE

The general knowledge of this great truth that God acts always in the most perfect and most desirable manner possible, is in my opinion the basis of the love which we owe to God in all things; for he who loves seeks his satisfaction in the felicity or perfection of the object loved and in the perfection of his actions. *Idem velle et idem nolle vera amicitia est.* I believe that it is difficult to love God truly when one, having the power to change his disposition, is not disposed to wish for that which God desires. In fact those who are not satisfied with what God does seem to me like dissatisfied subjects whose attitude is not very different from that of rebels. I hold therefore, that on these principles, to act conformably to the love of God it is not sufficient to force oneself to be patient, we must be really satisfied with all that comes to us according to his will. I mean this acquiescence in regard to the past; for as regards the future one should not be a quietist with the arms folded, open to ridicule, awaiting that which God will do; according to the sophism which the ancients called λ∂γου ἄεργον, the lazy reason. It is necessary to act conformably to the presumptive will of God as far as we are able to judge of it, trying with all our might to contribute to the general welfare and particularly to the ornamentation and the perfection of that which touches us, or of that which is nigh and so to speak at our hand. For if the future shall perhaps show that God has not wished our good intention to have its way, it does not follow that he has not wished us to act as we have; on the contrary, since he is the best of all masters, he ever demands only the right intentions, and it is for him to know the hour and the proper place to let good designs succeed.

V. IN WHAT THE PRINCIPLES OF THE DIVINE PERFECTION CONSIST, AND THAT THE SIMPLICITY OF THE MEANS COUNTER-BALANCES THE RICHNESS OF THE EFFECTS

It is sufficient therefore to have this confidence in God, that he has done everything for the best and that nothing will be able to injure those who love him. To know in particular, however, the reasons which have moved him to choose this order of the universe, to permit sin, to dispense his salutary grace in a certain manner,—this passes the capacity of a finite mind, above all when such a mind has not come into the joy of the vision of God. Yet it is possible to make some general remarks touching the course of providence in the government of things. One is able to say, therefore, that he who acts perfectly is like an excellent Geometer who knows how to find the best construction for a problem; like a good architect who utilizes his location and the funds destined for the building in the most advantageous manner, leaving nothing which shocks or which does not display that beauty of which it is capable; like a good householder who employs his property in such a way that there shall be nothing uncultivated or sterile; like a clever machinist who makes his production in the least difficult way possible; and like an intelligent author who encloses the most of reality in the least possible compass.

Of all beings those which are the most perfect and occupy the least possible space, that is to say those which interfere with one another the least, are the spirits whose perfections are the virtues. That is why we may not doubt that the felicity of the spirits is the principal aim of God and that he puts this purpose into execution, as far as the general harmony will permit. We will recur to this subject again.

When the simplicity of God's way is spoken of, reference is specially made to the means which he employs, and on the other hand when the variety, richness and abundance are referred to, the ends or effects are had in mind. Thus one ought to be proportioned to the other, just as the cost of a building should balance the beauty and grandeur which is expected. It is true that nothing costs God anything, just as there is not cost for a philosopher who makes hypotheses in constructing his imaginary world, because God has only to make decrees in order that a real world come into being; but in matters of wisdom the decrees or hypotheses meet the expenditure in proportion as they are more independent of one another. The reason wishes to avoid multiplicity in hypotheses or principles very much as the simplest system is preferred in Astronomy.

VI. THAT GOD DOES NOTHING WHICH IS NOT ORDERLY, AND THAT IT IS NOT EVEN POSSIBLE TO CONCEIVE OF EVENTS WHICH ARE NOT REGULAR

The activities or the acts of will of God are commonly divided into ordinary and extraordinary. But it is well to bear in mind that God does nothing out of order. Therefore, that which passes for extraordinary is so only with regard to a particular order established among the created things, for as regards the universal order, everything conforms to it. This is so true that not only does nothing occur in this world which is absolutely irregular, but it is even impossible to conceive of such an occurrence. Because, let us suppose for example that some one jots down a quantity of points upon a sheet of paper helter skelter, as do those who exercise the ridiculous art of Geomancy; now I say that it is possible to find a geometrical line whose concept shall be uniform and constant, that is, in accordance with a certain formula, and which line at the same time shall pass through all of those points, and in the same order in which the hand jotted them down; also if a continuous line be traced, which is now straight, now circular, and now of any other description, it is possible to find a mental equivalent, a formula or an equation common to all the points of this line by virtue of which formula the changes in the direction of the line must occur. There is no instance of a face whose contour does not form part of a geometric line and which can not be traced entire by a certain mathematical motion. But when the formula is very complex, that which conforms to it passes for irregular. Thus we may say that in whatever manner God might have created the world, it would always have been regular and in a certain order. God, however, has chosen the most perfect, that is to say the one which is at the same time the simplest in hypotheses and the richest in phenomena, as might be the case with a geometric line, whose construction was easy, but whose properties and effects were extremely remarkable and of great significance. I use these comparisons to picture a certain imperfect resemblance to the divine wisdom, and to point out that which may at least raise our minds to conceive in some sort what cannot otherwise be expressed. I do not pretend at all to explain thus the great mystery upon which depends the whole universe.

VII. THAT MIRACLES CONFORM TO THE REGULAR ORDER ALTHOUGH THEY GO AGAINST THE SUBORDINATE REGULATIONS; CONCERNING THAT WHICH GOD DESIRES OR PERMITS AND CONCERNING GENERAL AND PARTICULAR INTENTIONS

Now since nothing is done which is not orderly, we may say that miracles are quite within the order of natural operations. We use the term natural of these operations because they conform to certain subordinate regulations which we call the nature of things. For it can be said that this nature is only a custom of God's which he can change on the occasion of a stronger reason than that which moved him to use these regulations. As regards general and particular intentions, according to the way in which we understand the matter, it may be said on the one hand that everything is in accordance with his most general intention, or that which best conforms to the most perfect order he has chosen; on the other hand, however, it is also possible to say that he has particular intentions which are exceptions to the subordinate regulations above mentioned. Of God's laws, however, the most universal, i.e., that which rules the whole course of the universe, is without exceptions.

It is possible to say that God desires everything which is an object of his particular intention. When we consider the objects of his general intentions, however, such as are the modes of activities of created things and especially of the reasoning creatures with whom God wishes to co-operate, we must make a distinction; for if the action is good in itself, we may say that God wishes it and at times commands it, even though it does not take place; but if it is bad in itself and becomes good only by accident through the course of events and especially after chastisement and satisfaction have corrected its malignity and rewarded the ill with interest in such a way that more perfection results in the whole train of circumstances than would have come if that ill had not occurred,—if all this takes place we must say that God permits the evil, and not that he desired it, al-

though he has co-operated by means of the laws of nature which he has established. He knows how to produce the greatest good from them.

VIII. IN ORDER TO DISTINGUISH BETWEEN THE ACTIVITIES OF GOD AND THE ACTIVITIES OF CREATED THINGS WE MUST EXPLAIN THE CONCEPTION OF AN INDIVIDUAL SUBSTANCE

It is quite difficult to distinguish God's actions from those of his creatures. Some think that God does everything; others image that he only conserves the force that he has given to created things. How far can we say either of these opinions is right?

In the first place since activity and passivity pertain properly to individual substances (*actiones sunt suppositorum*) it will be necessary to explain what such a substance is. It is indeed true that when several predicates are attributes of a single subject and this subject is not an attribute of another, we speak of it as an individual substance, but this is not enough, and such an explanation is merely nominal. We must therefore inquire what it is to be an attribute in reality of a certain subject. Now it is evident that every true predication has some basis in the nature of things, and even when a proposition is not identical, that is, when the predicate is not expressly contained in the subject, it is still necessary that it be virtually contained in it, and this is what the philosophers call *in-esse*, saying thereby that the predicate is in the subject. Thus the content of the subject must always include that of the predicate in such a way that if one understands perfectly the concept of the subject, he will know that the predicate appertains to it also. This being so, we are able to say that this is the nature of an individual substance or of a complete being, namely, to afford a conception so complete that the concept shall be sufficient for the understanding of it and for the deduction of all the predicates of which the substance is or may become the subject. Thus the quality of king, which belonged to Alexander the Great, an abstraction from the subject, is not sufficiently determined to constitute an individual, and does not contain the other qualities of the same subject, nor everything which the idea of this prince includes. God, however, seeing the individual concept, or haecceity, of Alexander, sees there at the same time the basis and the reason of all the predicates which can be truly uttered regarding him; for instance that he will conquer Darius and Porus, even to the point of knowing *a priori* (and not by experience) whether he died a natural death or by poison,—facts which we can learn only through history. When we carefully consider the connection of things we see also the possibility of saying that there was always in the soul of Alexander marks of all that had happened to him and evidences of all that would happen to him and trace even of everything which occurs in the universe, although God alone could recognize them all.

IX. THAT EVERY INDIVIDUAL SUBSTANCE EXPRESSES THE WHOLE UNIVERSE IN ITS OWN MANNER AND THAT IN ITS FULL CONCEPT IS INCLUDED ALL ITS EXPERIENCES TOGETHER WITH ALL THE ATTENDANT CIRCUMSTANCES AND THE WHOLE SEQUENCE OF EXTERIOR EVENTS

There follow from these considerations several noticeable paradoxes; among others that it is not true that two substances may be exactly alike and differ only numerically, *solo numero*, and that what St. Thomas says on this point regarding angels and intelligences (*quod ibi omne individuum sit species infima*) is true of all substances, provided that the specific difference is understood as Geometers understand it in the case of figures; again that a substance will be able to commence only through creation and perish only through annihilation; that a substance cannot be divided into two nor can one be made out of two, and that thus the number of substances neither augments nor diminishes through natural means, although they are frequently transformed. Furthermore every substance is like an entire world and like a mirror of God, or indeed of the whole world which it portrays, each one in its own fashion; almost as the same city is variously represented according to the various situations of him who is regarding it. Thus the universe is multiplied in some sort as many times as there are substances, and the glory of God is multiplied in the same way by

as many wholly different representations of his works. It can indeed be said that every substance bears in some sort the character of God's infinite wisdom and omnipotence, and imitates him as much as it is able to; for it expresses, although confusedly, all that happens in the universe, past, present and future, deriving thus a certain resemblance to an infinite perception or power of knowing. And since all other substances express this particular substance and accommodate themselves to it, we can say that it exerts its power upon all the others in imitation of the omnipotence of the creator.

X. THAT THE BELIEF IN SUBSTANTIAL FORMS HAS A CERTAIN BASIS IN FACT, BUT THAT THESE FORMS EFFECT NO CHANGES IN THE PHENOMENA AND MUST NOT BE EMPLOYED FOR THE EXPLANATION OF PARTICULAR EVENTS

It seems that the ancients, able men, who were accustomed to profound meditations and taught theology and philosophy for several centuries and some of whom recommend themselves to us on account of their piety, had some knowledge of that which we have just said and this is why they introduced and maintained the substantial forms so much decried today. But they were not so far from the truth nor so open to ridicule as the common run of our new philosophers imagine. I grant that the consideration of these forms is of no service in the details of physics and ought not to be employed in the explanation of particular phenomena. In regard to this last point, the schoolmen were at fault, as were also the physicians of times past who followed their example, thinking they had given the reason for the properties of a body in mentioning the forms and qualities without going to the trouble of examining the manner of operation; as if one should be content to say that a clock had a certain amount of clockness derived from its form, and should not inquire in what that clockness consisted. This is indeed enough for the man who buys it, provided he surrenders the care of it to someone else. The fact, however, that there was this misunderstanding and misuse of the substantial forms should not bring us to throw away something whose recognition is so necessary in metaphysics. Since without these we will not be able, I hold, to know the ultimate principles nor to lift our minds to the knowledge of the incorporeal natures and of the marvels of God. Yet as the geometer does not need to encumber his mind with the famous puzzle of the composition of the continuum, and as no moralist, and still less a jurist or a statesman has need to trouble himself with the great difficulties which arise in conciliating free will with the providential activity of God, (since the geometer is able to make all his demonstrations and the statesman can complete all his deliberations without entering into these discussions which are so necessary and important in Philosophy and Theology), so in the same way the physicist can explain his experiments, now using simpler experiments already made, now employing geometrical and mechanical demonstrations without any need of the general considerations which belong to another sphere, and if he employs the co-operation of God, or perhaps of some soul or animating force, or something else of a similar nature, he goes out of his path quite as much as that man who, when facing an important practical question would wish to enter into profound argumentations regarding the nature of destiny and of our liberty; a fault which men quite frequently commit without realizing it when they cumber their minds with considerations regarding fate, and thus they are even sometimes turned from a good resolution or from some necessary provision.

XI. THAT THE OPINIONS OF THE THEOLOGIANS AND OF THE SO-CALLED SCHOLASTIC PHILOSOPHERS ARE NOT TO BE WHOLLY DESPISED

I know that I am advancing a great paradox in pretending to resuscitate in some sort the ancient philosophy, and to recall *postliminio* the substantial forms almost banished from our modern thought. But perhaps I will not be condemned lightly when it is known that I have long meditated over the modern philosophy and that I have denoted much time to experiments in physics and to the demonstrations of geometry and that I, too, for a long time was persuaded of the baselessness of those "beings" which, however, I was finally obliged to take up again in

spite of myself and as though by force. The many investigations which I carried on compelled me to recognize that our moderns do not do sufficient justice to Saint Thomas and to the other great men of that period and that there is in the theories of the scholastic philosophers and theologians far more solidity than is imagined, provided that these theories are employed *à propos* and in their place. I am persuaded that if some careful and meditative mind were to take the trouble to clarify and direct their thoughts in the manner of analytic geometers, he would find a great treasure of very important truths, wholly demonstrable.

XII. THAT THE CONCEPTION OF THE EXTENSION OF A BODY IS IN A WAY IMAGINARY AND DOES NOT CONSTITUTE THE SUBSTANCE OF THE BODY

But to resume the thread of our discussion, I believe that he who will meditate upon the nature of substance, as I have explained it above, will find that the whole nature of bodies is not exhausted in their extension, that is to say, in their size, figure and motion, but that we must recognize something which corresponds to soul, something which is commonly called substantial form, although these forms effect no change in the phenomena, any more than do the souls of beasts, that is if they have souls. It is even possible to demonstrate that the ideas of size, figure and motion are not so distinctive as is imagined, and that they stand for something imaginary relative to our preceptions as do, although to a greater extent, the ideas of color, heat, and the other similar qualities in regard to which we may doubt whether they are actually to be found in the nature of the things outside of us. This is why these latter qualities are unable to constitute "substance" and if there is no other principle of identity in bodies than that which has just been referred to a body would not subsist more than for a moment.

The souls and the substance-forms of other bodies are entirely different from intelligent souls which alone know their actions, and not only do not perish through natural means but indeed always retain the knowledge of what they are; a fact which makes them alone open to chastisement or recompense, and makes them citizens of the republic of the universe whose monarch is God. Hence it follows that all the other creatures should serve them, a point which we shall discuss more amply later.

XIII. AS THE INDIVIDUAL CONCEPT OF EACH PERSON INCLUDES ONCE FOR ALL EVERYTHING WHICH CAN EVER HAPPEN TO HIM, IN IT CAN BE SEEN, *A PRIORI* THE EVIDENCES OR THE REASONS FOR THE REALITY OF EACH EVENT, AND WHY ONE HAPPENED SOONER THAN THE OTHER. BUT THESE EVENTS, HOWEVER CERTAIN, ARE NEVERTHELESS CONTINGENT, BEING BASED ON THE FREE CHOICE OF GOD AND OF HIS CREATURES. IT IS TRUE THAT THEIR CHOICES ALWAYS HAVE THEIR REASONS, BUT THEY INCLINE TO THE CHOICES UNDER NO COMPULSION OF NECESSITY

But before going further it is necessary to meet a difficulty which may arise regarding the principles which we have set forth in the preceding. We have said that the concept of an individual substance includes once for all everything which can ever happen to it and that in considering this concept one will be able to see everything which can truly be said concerning the individual, just as we are able to see in the nature of a circle all the properties which can be derived from it. But does it not seem that in this way the difference between contingent and necessary truths will be destroyed, that there will be no place for human liberty, and that an absolute fatality will rule as well over all our actions as over all the rest of the events of the world? To this I reply that a distinction must be made between that which is certain and that which is necessary. Every one grants that future contingencies are assured since God foresees them, but we do not say just because of that that they are necessary. But it will be objected, that if any conclusion can be deduced infallibly from some definition or concept, it is necessary; and now since we have maintained that everything which is to happen to anyone is already virtually included in his nature or concept, as all the properties are contained in the definition of a circle,

therefore, the difficulty still remains. In order to meet the objection completely, I say that the connection or sequence is of two kinds; the one, absolutely necessary, whose contrary implies contradiction, occurs in the eternal verities like the truths of geometry; the other is necessary only *ex hypothesi*, and so to speak by accident, and in itself it is contingent since the contrary is not implied. This latter sequence is not founded upon ideas wholly pure and upon the pure understanding of God, but upon his free decrees and upon the processes of the universe. Let us give an example. Since Julius Caesar will become perpetual Dictator and master of the Republic and will overthrow the liberty of Rome, this action is contained in his concept, for we have supposed that it is the nature of such a perfect concept of a subject to involve everything, in fact so that the predicate may be included in the subject *ut possit inesse subjecto*. We may say that it is not in virtue of this concept or idea that he is obliged to perform this action, since it pertains to him only because God knows everything. But it will be insisted in reply that his nature or form responds to this concept, and since God imposes upon him this personality, he is compelled henceforth to live up to it. I could reply by instancing the similar case of the future contingencies which as yet have no reality save in the understanding and will of God, and which, because God has given them in advance this form, must needs correspond to it. But I prefer to overcome a difficulty rather than to excuse it by instancing other difficulties, and what I am about to say will serve to clear up the one as well as the other. It is here that must be applied the distinction in the kind of relation, and I say that that which happens conformably to these decrees is assured, but that it is not therefore necessary, and if anyone did the contrary, he would do nothing impossible in itself, although it is impossible *ex hypothesi* that that other happen. For if anyone were capable of carrying out a complete demonstration by virtue of which he could prove this connection of the subject, which is Caesar, with the predicate, which is his successful enterprise, he would bring us to see in fact that the future dictatorship of Caesar had its basis in his concept or nature, so that one would see there a reason why he resolved to cross the Rubicon rather than to stop, and why he gained instead of losing the day at Pharsalus, and that it was reasonable and by consequence assured that this would occur, but one would not prove that it was necessary in itself, nor that the contrary implied a contradiction, almost in the same way in which it is reasonable and assured that God will always do what is best although that which is less perfect is not thereby implied. For it would be found that this demonstration of this predicate as belonging to Caesar is not as absolute as are those of numbers or of geometry, but that this predicate supposes a sequence of things which God has shown by his free will. This sequence is based on the first free decree of God which was to do always that which is the most perfect and upon the decree which God made following the first one, regarding human nature, which is that men should always do, although freely, that which appears to be the best. Now every truth which is founded upon this kind of decree is contingent, although certain, for the decrees of God do not change the possibilities of things and, as I have already said, although God assuredly chooses the best, this does not prevent that which is less perfect from being possible in itself. Although it will never happen, it is not its impossibility but its imperfection which causes him to reject it. Now nothing is necessitated whose opposite is possible. One will then be in a position to satisfy these kinds of difficulties, however great they may appear (and in fact they have not been less vexing to all other thinkers who have ever treated this matter), provided that he considers well that all contingent propositions have reasons why they are thus, rather than otherwise, or indeed (what is the same thing) that they have proof *a priori* of their truth, which render them certain and show that the connection of the subject and predicate in these propositions has its basis in the nature of the one and of the other, but he must further remember that such contingent propositions have not the demonstrations of necessity, since their reasons are founded only on the principle of contingency or of the existence of things, that is to say, upon that which is, or which appears to be the best among several things equally possible. Necessary truths, on the other hand, are founded upon the principle of contradiction, and upon the

possibility or impossibility of the essences themselves, without regard here to the free will of God or of creatures.

XIV. GOD PRODUCES DIFFERENT SUBSTANCES ACCORDING TO THE DIFFERENT VIEWS WHICH HE HAS OF THE WORLD, AND BY THE INTERVENTION OF GOD, THE APPROPRIATE NATURE OF EACH SUBSTANCE BRINGS IT ABOUT THAT WHAT HAPPENS TO ONE CORRESPONDS TO WHAT HAPPENS TO ALL THE OTHERS, WITHOUT, HOWEVER, THEIR ACTING UPON ONE ANOTHER DIRECTLY

After having seen, to a certain extent, in what the nature of substances consists, we must try to explain the dependence they have upon one another and their actions and passions. Now it is first of all very evident that created substances depend upon God who preserves them and can produce them continually by a kind of emanation just as we produce our thoughts, for when God turns, so to say, on all sides and in all fashions, the general system of phenomena which he finds it good to produce for the sake of manifesting his glory, and when he regards all the aspects of the world in all possible manners, since there is no relation which escapes his omniscience, the result of each view of the universe as seen from a different position is a substance which expresses the universe conformably to this view, provided God sees fit to render his thought effective and to produce the substance, and since God's vision is always true, our perceptions are always true and that which deceives us are our judgments, which are of us. Now we have said before, and it follows from what we have just said that each substance is a world by itself, independent of everything else excepting God; therefore, all our phenomena that is all things which are ever able to happen to us, are only consequences of our being. Now as the phenomena maintain a certain order conformably to our nature, or so to speak to the world which is in us (from whence it follows that we can, for the regulation of our conduct, make useful observations which are justified by the outcome of the future phenomena) and as we are thus able often to judge the future by the past without deceiving ourselves, we have sufficient grounds for saying that these phenomena are true and we will not be put to the task of inquiring whether they are outside of us, and whether others perceive them also.

Nevertheless it is most true that the perceptions and expressions of all substances intercorrespond, so that each one following independently certain reasons or laws which he has noticed meets others which are doing the same, as when several have agreed to meet together in a certain place on a set day, they are able to carry out the plan if they wish. Now although all express the same phenomena, this does not bring it about that their expressions are exactly alike. It is sufficient if they are proportional. As when several spectators think they see the same thing and are agreed about it, although each one sees or speaks according to the measure of his vision. It is God alone, (from whom all individuals emanate continually, and who sees the universe not only as they see it, but besides in a very different way from them) who is the cause of this correspondence in their phenomena and who brings it about that that which is particular to one, is also common to all, otherwise there would be no relation. In a way, then, we might properly say, although it seems strange, that a particular substance never acts upon another particular substance nor is it acted upon by it. That which happens to each one is only the consequence of its complete idea or concept, since this idea already includes all the predicates and expresses the whole universe. In fact nothing can happen to us except thoughts and perceptions, and all our thoughts and perceptions are but the consequence, contingent it is true, of our precedent thoughts and perceptions, in such a way that were I able to consider directly all that happens or appears to me at the present time, I should be able to see all that will happen to me or that will ever appear to me. This future will not fail me, and will surely appear to me even if all that which is outside of me were destroyed, save only that God and myself were left.

Since, however, we ordinarily attribute to other things an action upon us which brings us to perceive things in a certain manner, it is necessary to consider the basis of this judgment and to inquire what there is of truth in it.

XV. THE ACTION OF ONE FINITE SUBSTANCE UPON ANOTHER CONSISTS ONLY IN THE INCREASE IN THE DEGREES OF EXPRESSION OF THE FIRST COMBINED WITH A DECREASE IN THAT OF THE SECOND, IN SO FAR AS GOD HAS IN ADVANCE FASHIONED THEM SO THAT THEY SHALL ACT IN ACCORD

Without entering into a long discussion it is sufficient for reconciling the language of metaphysics with that of practical life to remark that we preferably attribute to ourselves, and with reason, the phenomena which we express the most perfectly, and that we attribute to other substances those phenomena which each one expresses the best. Thus a substance, which is of an infinite extension in so far as it expresses all, becomes limited in proportion to its more or less perfect manner of expression. It is thus then that we may conceive of substances as interfering with and limiting one another, and hence we are able to say that in this sense they act upon one another, and that they, so to speak, accommodate themselves to one another. For it can happen that a single change which augments the expression of the one may diminish that of the other. Now the virtue of a particular substance is to express well the glory of God, and the better it expresses it, the less is it limited. Everything when it expresses its virtue or power, that is to say, when it acts, changes to better, and expands just in so far as it acts. When therefore a change occurs by which several substances are affected (in fact every change affects them all) I think we may say that those substances, which by this change pass immediately to a greater degree of perfection, or to a more perfect expression, exert power and act, while those which pass to a lesser degree disclose their weakness and suffer. I also hold that every activity of a substance which has perception implies some pleasure, and every passion some pain, except that it may very well happen that a present advantage will be eventually destroyed by a greater evil, whence it comes that one may sin in acting or exerting his power and in finding pleasure.

XVI. THE EXTRAORDINARY INTERVENTION OF GOD IS NOT EXCLUDED IN THAT WHICH OUR PARTICULAR ESSENCES EXPRESS, BECAUSE THEIR EXPRESSION INCLUDES EVERYTHING. SUCH INTERVENTION, HOWEVER, GOES BEYOND THE POWER OF OUR NATURAL BEING OR OF OUR DISTINCT EXPRESSION, BECAUSE THESE ARE FINITE, AND FOLLOW CERTAIN SUBORDINATE REGULATIONS

There remains for us at present only to explain how it is possible that God has influence at times upon men or upon other substances by an extraordinary or miraculous intervention, since it seems that nothing is able to happen which is extraordinary or supernatural in as much as all the events which occur to the other substances are only the consequences of their natures. We must recall what was said above in regard to the miracles in the universe. These always conform to the universal law of the general order, although they may contravene the subordinate regulations, and since every person or substance is like a little world which expresses the great world, we can say that this extraordinary action of God upon this substance is nevertheless miraculous, although it is comprised in the general order of the universe in so far as it is expressed by the individual essence or concept of this substance. This is why, if we understand in our natures all that they express, nothing is supernatural in them, because they reach out to everything, an effect always expressing its cause, and God being the veritable cause of the substances. But as that which our natures express the most perfectly pertains to them in a particular manner, that being their special power, and since they are limited, as I have just explained, many things there are which surpass the powers of our natures and even of all limited natures. As a consequence, to speak more clearly, I say that the miracles and the extraordinary interventions of God have this peculiarity that they cannot be foreseen by any created mind however enlightened. This is because the distinct comprehension of the fundamental order surpasses them all, while on the other hand, that which is called natural depends upon less fundamental regulations which the creatures are able to understand. In order then

that my words may be as irreprehensible as the meaning I am trying to convey, it will be well to associate certain words with certain significations. We may call that which includes everything that we express and which expresses our union with God himself, nothing going beyond it, our essence. But that which is limited in us may be designated as our nature or our power and in accordance with this terminology that which goes beyond the natures of all created substances is supernatural.

XVII. AN EXAMPLE OF A SUBORDINATE REGULATION IN THE LAW OF NATURE WHICH DEMONSTRATES THAT GOD ALWAYS PRESERVES THE SAME AMOUNT OF FORCE BUT NOT THE SAME QUANTITY OF MOTION:—AGAINST THE CARTESIANS AND MANY OTHERS

I have frequently spoken of subordinate regulations, or of the laws of nature, and it seems that it will be well to give an example. Our new philosophers are unanimous in employing that famous law that God always preserves the same amount of motion in the universe. In fact it is a very plausible law, and in times past I held it for indubitable. But since then I have learned in what its fault consists. Monsieur Descartes and many other clever mathematicians have thought that the quantity of motion, that is to say the velocity multiplied by the mass[1] of the moving body, is exactly equivalent to the moving force, or to speak in mathematical terms that the force varies as the velocity multiplied by the mass. Now it is reasonable that the same force is always preserved in the universe. So also, looking to phenomena, it will be readily seen that a mechanical perpetual motion is impossible, because the force in

---

[1]This term is employed here for the sake of clearness. Leibniz did not possess the concept "mass," which was enunciated by Newton in the same year in which the present treatise was written, 1686. Leibniz uses the terms "body," "magnitude of body," etc. The technical expression "mass" occurs once only in the writings of Leibniz (in a treatise published in 1695), and was there doubtless borrowed from Newton. For the history of the controversy concerning the Cartesian and Leibnizian measure of force, see Mach's *Science of Mechanics*, Chicago, 1893, pp. 272 et seq.—*Trans.*

such a machine, being always diminished a little by friction and so ultimately destined to be entirely spent, would necessarily have to recoup its losses, and consequently would keep on increasing of itself without any new impulsion from without; and we see furthermore that the force of a body is diminished only in proportion as it gives up force, either to a contiguous body or to its own parts, in so far as they have a separate movement. The mathematicians to whom I have referred think that what can be said of force can be said of the quantity of motion. In order, however, to show the difference I make two suppositions: in the first place, that a body falling from a certain height acquires a force enabling it to remount to the same height, provided that its direction is turned that way, or provided that there are no hindrances. For instance, a pendulum will rise exactly to the height from which it has fallen, provided the resistance of the air and of certain other small particles do not diminish a little its acquired force.

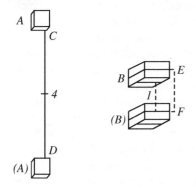

I suppose in the second place that it will take as much force to lift a body A weighing one pound to the height CD, four feet, as to raise a body B weighing four pounds to the height EF, one foot. These two suppositions are granted by our new philosophers. It is therefore manifest that the body A falling from the height CD acquires exactly as much force as the body B falling from the height EF, for the body B at F, having by the first supposition sufficient force to return to E, has therefore the force to carry a body of four pounds to the distance of one foot, EF. And likewise the body A at D, having the force to return to C, has also the force required to carry a body weighing one pound, its own weight, back to C, a distance of four feet. Now by the sec-

ond supposition the force of these two bodies is equal. Let us now see if the quantity of motion is the same in each case. It is here that we will be surprised to find a very great difference, for it has been proved by Galileo that the velocity acquired by the fall CD is double the velocity acquired by the fall EF, although the height is four times as great. Multiplying, therefore, the body A, whose mass is 1, by its velocity, which is 2 the product or the quantity of movement will be 2, and on the other hand, if we multiply the body B, whose mass is 4, by its velocity, which is 1, the product or quantity of motion will be 4. Hence the quantity of the motion of the body A at the point D is half the quantity of motion of the body B at the point F, yet their forces are equal, and there is therefore a great difference between the quantity of motion and the force. This is what we set out to show. We can see therefore how the force ought to be estimated by the quantity of the effect which it is able to produce, for example by the height to which a body of certain weight can be raised. This is a very different thing from the velocity which can be imparted to it, and in order to impart to it double the velocity we must have double the force. Nothing is simpler than this proof and Monsieur Descartes has fallen into error here, only because he trusted too much to his thoughts even when they had not been ripened by reflection. But it astonishes me that his disciples have not noticed this error, and I am afraid that they are beginning to imitate little by little certain Peripatetics whom they ridicule, and that they are accustoming themselves to consult rather the books of their master, than reason or nature.

XVIII. THE DISTINCTION BETWEEN FORCE AND THE QUANTITY OF MOTION IS, AMONG OTHER REASONS, IMPORTANT AS SHOWING THAT WE MUST HAVE RECOURSE TO METAPHYSICAL CONSIDERATIONS IN ADDITION TO DISCUSSIONS OF EXTENSION IF WE WISH TO EXPLAIN THE PHENOMENA OF MATTER

This consideration of the force, distinguished from the quantity of motion is of importance, not only in physics and mechanics for finding the real laws of nature and the principles of motion, and even for correcting many practical errors which have crept into the writings of certain able mathematicians, but also in metaphysics it is of importance for the better understanding of principles. Because motion, if we regard only its exact and formal meaning, that is, change of place, is not something entirely real, and when several bodies change their places reciprocally, it is not possible to determine by considering the bodies alone to which among them movement or repose is to be attributed, as I could demonstrate geometrically, if I wished to stop for it now. But the force, or the proximate cause of these changes is something more real, and there are sufficient grounds for attributing it to one body rather than to another, and it is only through this latter investigation that we can determine to which one the movement must appertain. Now this force is something different from size, from form or from motion, and it can be seen from this consideration that the whole meaning of a body is not exhausted in its extension together with its modifications as our moderns persuade themselves. We are therefore obliged to restore certain beings or forms which they have banished. It appears more and more clear that although all the particular phenomena of nature can be explained mathematically or mechanically by those who understand them, yet nevertheless, the general principles of corporeal nature and even of mechanics are metaphysical rather than geometric, and belong rather to certain indivisible forms or natures as the causes of the appearances, than to the corporeal mass or to extension. This reflection is able to reconcile the mechanical philosophy of the moderns with the circumspection of those intelligent and well-meaning persons who, with a certain justice, fear that we are becoming too far removed from immaterial beings and that we are thus prejudicing piety.

XIX. THE UTILITY OF FINAL CAUSES IN PHYSICS

As I do not wish to judge people in ill part I bring no accusation against our new philosophers who pretend to banish final causes from physics, but I am nevertheless obliged to avow that the consequences of such a banishment appear to me dangerous, especially when joined to that position which I refuted at the beginning of this treatise. That position seemed to go the length of discarding final causes entirely as though God proposed no end and no good in his activity, or as if good were not to be the object of his will. I hold on the contrary that it is just in this that the principle of all existences and of the laws of nature must be sought, hence God always proposes the best and most perfect. I am quite willing to grant that we are liable to err when we wish to determine the purposes or councils of God, but this is the case only when we try to limit them to some particular design, thinking that he has had in view only a single thing, while in fact he regards everything at once. As for instance, if we think that God has made the world only for us, it is a great blunder, although it may be quite true that he has made it entirely for us, and that there is nothing in the universe which does not touch us and which does not accommodate itself to the regard which he has for us according to the principle laid down above. Therefore when we see some good effect or some perfection which happens or which follows from the works of God we are able to say assuredly that God has purposed it, for he does nothing by chance, and is not like us who sometimes fail to do well. Therefore, far from being able to fall into error in this respect as do the extreme statesmen who postulate too much foresight in the designs of Princes, or as do commentators who seek for too much erudition in their authors, it will be impossible to attribute too much reflection to God's infinite wisdom, and there is no matter in which error is less to be feared provided we confine ourselves to affirmations and provided we avoid negative statements which limit the designs of God. All those who see the admirable structure of animals find themselves led to recognize the wisdom of the author of things and I advise those who have any sentiment of piety and indeed of true philosophy to hold aloof from the expressions of certain pretentious minds who instead of saying that eyes were made for seeing, say that we see because we find ourselves having eyes. When one seriously holds such opinions which hand everything over to material necessity or to a kind of chance (although either alternative ought to appear ridiculous to those who understand what we have explained above) it is difficult to recognize an intelligent author of nature. The effect should correspond to its cause and indeed it is best known through the recognition of its cause, so that it is reasonable to introduce a sovereign intelligence ordering things, and in place of making use of the wisdom of this sovereign being, to employ only the properties of matter to explain phenomena. As if in order to account for the capture of an important place by a prince, the historian should say it was because the particles of powder in the cannon having been touched by a spark of fire expanded with a rapidity capable of pushing a hard solid body against the walls of the place, while the little particles which composed the brass of the cannon were so well interlaced that they did not separate under this impact,—as if he should account for it in this way instead of making us see how the foresight of the conqueror brought him to choose the time and the proper means and how his ability surmounted all obstacles.

XX. A NOTEWORTHY DISQUISITION IN PLATO'S PHAEDO AGAINST THE PHILOSOPHERS WHO WERE TOO MATERIALISTIC

This reminds me of a fine disquisition by Socrates in Plato's Phaedo, which agrees perfectly with my opinion on this subject and seems to have been uttered expressly for our too materialistic philosophers. This agreement has led me to a desire to translate it although it is a little long. Perhaps this example will give some of us an incentive to share in many of the other beautiful and well balanced thoughts which are found in the writings of this famous author.[2]

XXI. IF THE MECHANICAL LAWS DEPENDED UPON GEOMETRY ALONE WITHOUT METAPHYSICAL INFLUENCES, THE PHENOMENA WOULD BE VERY DIFFERENT FROM WHAT THEY ARE

Now since the wisdom of God has always been recognized in the detail of the mechanical structures of certain particular bodies, it should also be shown in the general economy of the world and in the constitution of the laws of nature. This is so true that even

[2]There is a gap here in the MS., intended for the passage from Plato, the translation of which Leibniz did not supply.—*Trans.*

in the laws of motion in general, the plans of this wisdom have been noticed. For if bodies were only extended masses, and motion were only a change of place, and if everything ought to be and could be deduced by geometric necessity from these two definitions alone, it would follow, as I have shown elsewhere, that the smallest body on contact with a very large one at rest would impart to it its own velocity, yet without losing any of the velocity that it had. A quantity of other rules wholly contrary to the formation of a system would also have to be admitted. But the decree of the divine wisdom in preserving always the same force and the same total direction has provided for a system. I find indeed that many of the effects of nature can be accounted for in a twofold way, that is to say by a consideration of efficient causes, and again independently by a consideration of final causes. An example of the latter is God's decree to always carry out his plan by the easiest and most determined way. I have shown this elsewhere in accounting for the catoptric and dioptric laws, and I will speak more at length about it in what follows.

XXII. RECONCILIATION OF THE TWO METHODS OF EXPLANATION, THE ONE USING FINAL CAUSES, AND THE OTHER EFFICIENT CAUSES, THUS SATISFYING BOTH THOSE WHO EXPLAIN NATURE MECHANICALLY AND THOSE WHO HAVE RECOURSE TO INCORPOREAL NATURES

It is worth while to make the preceding remark in order to reconcile those who hope to explain mechanically the formation of the first tissue of an animal and all the interrelation of the parts, with those who account for the same structure by referring to final causes. Both explanations are good; both are useful not only for the admiring of the work of a great artificer, but also for the discovery of useful facts in physics and medicine. And writers who take these diverse routes should not speak ill of each other. For I see that those who attempt to explain beauty by the divine anatomy ridicule those who imagine that the apparently fortuitous flow of certain liquids has been able to produce such a beautiful variety and that they regard them as overbold and irreverent. These others on the contrary treat the former as simple and superstitious, and compare them to those ancients who regarded the physicists as impious when they maintained that not Jupiter thundered but some material which is found in the clouds. The best plan would be to join the two ways of thinking. To use a practical comparison, we recognize and praise the ability of a workman not only when we show what designs he had in making the parts of his machine, but also when we explain the instruments which he employed in making each part, above all if these instruments are simple and ingeniously contrived. God is also a workman able enough to produce a machine still a thousand times more ingenious than is our body, by employing only certain quite simple liquids purposely composed in such a way that ordinary laws of nature alone are required to develop them so as to produce such a marvellous effect. But it is also true that this development would not take place if God were not the author of nature. Yet I find that the method of efficient causes, which goes much deeper and is in a measure more immediate and *a priori*, is also more difficult when we come to details, and I think that our philosophers are still very frequently far removed from making the most of this method. The method of final causes, however, is easier and can be frequently employed to find out important and useful truths which we should have to seek for a long time, if we were confined to that other more physical method of which anatomy is able to furnish many examples. It seems to me that Snellius, who was the first discoverer of the laws of refraction would have waited a long time before finding them if he had wished to seek out first how light was formed. But he apparently followed that method which the ancients employed for Catoptrics, that is, the method of final causes. Because, while seeking for the easiest way in which to conduct a ray of light from one given point to another given point by reflection from a given plane (supposing that that was the design of nature) they discovered the equality of the angles of incidence and reflection, as can be seen from a little treatise by Heliodorus of Larissa and also elsewhere. This principle Mons. Snellius, I believe, and afterwards independently of him, M. Fermat, applied most ingeniously to refraction. For since the rays while in the same media always maintain the same propor-

tion of sines, which in turn corresponds to the resistance of the media, it appears that they follow the easiest way, or at least that way which is the most determinate for passing from a given point in one medium to a given point in another medium. That demonstration of this same theorem which M. Descartes has given, using efficient causes, is much less satisfactory. At least we have grounds to think that he would never have found the principle by that means if he had not learned in Holland of the discovery of Snellius.

XXIII. RETURNING TO IMMATERIAL SUBSTANCES WE EXPLAIN HOW GOD ACTS UPON THE UNDERSTANDING OF SPIRITS AND ASK WHETHER ONE ALWAYS KEEPS THE IDEA OF WHAT HE THINKS ABOUT

I have thought it well to insist a little upon final causes, upon incorporeal natures and upon an intelligent cause with respect to bodies so as to show the use of these conceptions in physics and in mathematics. This for two reasons, first to purge from mechanical philosophy the impiety that is imputed to it, second, to elevate to nobler lines of thought the thinking of our philosophers who incline to materialistic considerations alone. Now, however, it will be well to return from corporeal substances to the consideration of immaterial natures and particularly of spirits, and to speak of the methods which God uses to enlighten them and to act upon them. Although we must not forget that there are here at the same time certain laws of nature in regard to which I can speak more amply elsewhere. It will be enough for now to touch upon ideas and to inquire if we see everything in God and how God is our light. First of all it will be in place to remark that the wrong use of ideas occasions many errors. For when one reasons in regard to anything, he imagines that he has an idea of it and this is the foundation upon which certain philosophers, ancient and modern, have constructed a demonstration of God that is extremely imperfect. It must be, they say, that I have an idea of God, or of a perfect being, since I think of him and we cannot think without having ideas; now the idea of this being includes all perfections and since existence is one of these perfections, it follows that he exists. But I reply, inasmuch as we often think of impossible chimeras, for example of the highest degree of swiftness, of the greatest number, of the meeting of the conchoid with its base or determinant, such reasoning is not sufficient. It is therefore in this sense that we can say that there are true and false ideas according as the thing which is in question is possible or not. And it is when he is assured of the possibility of a thing, that one can boast of having an idea of it. Therefore, the aforesaid argument proves that God exists, if he is possible. This is in fact an excellent privilege of the divine nature, to have need only of a possibility or an essence in order to actually exist, and it is just this which is called *ens a se.*

XXIV. WHAT CLEAR AND OBSCURE, DISTINCT AND CONFUSED, ADEQUATE AND INADEQUATE, INTUITIVE AND ASSUMED KNOWLEDGE IS, AND THE DEFINITION OF NOMINAL, REAL, CAUSAL AND ESSENTIAL

In order to understand better the nature of ideas it is necessary to touch somewhat upon the various kinds of knowledge. When I am able to recognize a thing among others, without being able to say in what its differences or characteristics consist, the knowledge is confused. Sometimes indeed we may know clearly, that is without being in the slightest doubt, that a poem or a picture is well or badly done because there is in it an "I know not what" which satisfies or shocks us. Such knowledge is not yet distinct. It is when I am able to explain the peculiarities which a thing has, that the knowledge is called distinct. Such is the knowledge of an assayer who discerns the true gold from the false by means of certain proofs or marks which make up the definition of gold. But distinct knowledge has degrees, because ordinarily the conceptions which enter into the definitions will themselves have need of definition, and are only known confusedly. When at length everything which enters into a definition or into distinct knowledge is known distinctly, even back to the primitive conception, I call that knowledge adequate. When my mind understands at once and distinctly

all the primitive ingredients of a conception, then we have intuitive knowledge. This is extremely rare as most human knowledge is only confused or indeed assumed. It is well also to distinguish nominal from real definition. I call a definition nominal when there is doubt whether an exact conception of it is possible; as for instance, when I say that an endless screw is a line in three dimensional space whose parts are congruent or fall one upon another. Now although this is one of the reciprocal properties of an endless screw, he who did not know from elsewhere what an endless screw was could doubt if such a line were possible, because the other lines whose ends are congruent (there are only two: the circumference of a circle and the straight line) are plane figures, that is to say they can be described *in plano*. This instance enables us to see that any reciprocal property can serve as a nominal definition, but when the property brings us to see the possibility of a thing it makes the definition real, and as long as one has only a nominal definition he cannot be sure of the consequences which he draws, because if it conceals a contradiction or an impossibility he would be able to draw the opposite conclusions. That is why truths do not depend upon names and are not arbitrary, as some of our new philosophers think. There is also a considerable difference among real definitions, for when the possibility proves itself only by experience, as in the definition of quicksilver, whose possibility we know because such a body, which is both an extremely heavy fluid and quite volatile, actually exists, the definition is merely real and nothing more. If, however, the proof of the possibility is *a priori*, the definition is not only real but also causal as for instance when it contains the possible generation of a thing. Finally when the definition, without assuming anything which requires a proof *a priori* of its possibility, carries the analysis clear to the primitive conception, the definition is perfect or essential.

XXV. IN WHAT CASES KNOWLEDGE IS ADDED TO MERE CONTEMPLATION OF THE IDEA

Now it is manifest that we have no idea of a conception when it is impossible. And in case the knowledge, where we have the idea of it, is only assumed, we do not visualize it because such a conception is known only in like manner as conceptions, internally impossible. And if it be in fact possible, it is not by this kind of knowledge that we learn its possibility. For instance, when I am thinking of a thousand or of a chiliagon, I frequently do it without contemplating the idea. Even if I say a thousand is ten times a hundred, I frequently do not trouble to think what ten and a hundred are, because I assume that I know, and I do not consider it necessary to stop just at present to conceive of them. Therefore it may well happen, as it in fact does happen often enough, that I am mistaken in regard to a conception which I assume that I understand, although it is an impossible truth or at least is incompatible with others with which I join it, and whether I am mistaken or not, this way of assuming our knowledge remains the same. It is, then, only when our knowledge is clear in regard to confused conceptions, and when it is intuitive in regard to those which are distinct, that we see its entire idea.

XXVI. IDEAS ARE ALL STORED UP WITHIN US. PLATO'S DOCTRINE OF REMINISCENCE

In order to see clearly what an idea is, we must guard ourselves against a misunderstanding. Many regard the idea as the form or the differentiation of our thinking, and according to this opinion we have the idea in our mind, in so far as we are thinking of it, and each separate time that we think of it anew we have another idea although similar to the preceding one. Some, however, take the idea as the immediate object of thought, or as a permanent form which remains even when we are no longer contemplating it. As a matter of fact our soul has the power of representing to itself any form or nature whenever the occasion comes for thinking about it, and I think that this activity of our soul is, so far as it expresses some nature, form or essence, properly the idea of the thing. This is in us, and is always in us, whether we are thinking of it or no. (Our soul expresses God and the universe and all essences as well as all existences.) This position is in accord with my principles that naturally nothing enters into our minds from outside.

It is a bad habit we have of thinking as though our minds receive certain messengers, as it were, or as if they had doors or windows. We have in our minds all those forms for all periods of time because the mind at every moment expresses all its future thoughts and already thinks confusedly of all that of which it will ever think distinctly. Nothing can be taught us of which we have not already in our minds the idea. This idea is as it were the material out of which the thought will form itself. This is what Plato has excellently brought out in his doctrine of reminiscence, a doctrine which contains a great deal of truth, provided that it is properly understood and purged of the error of pre-existence, and provided that one does not conceive of the soul as having already known and thought at some other time what it learns and thinks now. Plato has also confirmed his position by a beautiful experiment. He introduces a small boy, whom he leads by short steps, to extremely difficult truths of geometry bearing on incommensurables, all this without teaching the boy anything, merely drawing out replies by a well arranged series of questions. This shows that the soul virtually knows those things, and needs only to be reminded (animadverted) to recognize the truths. Consequently it possesses at least the idea upon which those truths depend. We may say even that it already possesses those truths, if we consider them as the relations of the ideas.

XXVII. IN WHAT RESPECT OUR SOULS CAN BE COMPARED TO BLANK TABLETS AND HOW CONCEPTIONS ARE DERIVED FROM THE SENSES

Aristotle preferred to compare our souls to blank tablets prepared for writing, and he maintained that nothing is in the understanding which does not come through the senses. This position is in accord with the popular conceptions as Aristotle's positions usually are. Plato thinks more profoundly. Such tenets or practicologies are nevertheless allowable in ordinary use somewhat in the same way as those who accept the Copernican theory still continue to speak of the rising and setting of the sun. I find indeed that these usages can be given a real meaning containing no error, quite in the same way as I have already pointed out that we may truly say particular substances act upon one another. In this same sense we may say that knowledge is received from without through the medium of the senses because certain exterior things contain or express more particularly the causes which determine us to certain thoughts. Because in the ordinary uses of life we attribute to the soul only that which belongs to it most manifestly and particularly, and there is no advantage in going further. When, however, we are dealing with the exactness of metaphysical truths, it is important to recognize the powers and independence of the soul which extend infinitely further than is commonly supposed. In order, therefore, to avoid misunderstandings it would be well to choose separate terms for the two. These expressions which are in the soul whether one is conceiving of them or not may be called ideas, while those which one conceives of or constructs may be called conceptions, *conceptus*. But whatever terms are used, it is always false to say that all our conceptions come from the so-called external senses, because those conceptions which I have of myself and of my thoughts, and consequently of being, of substance, of action, of identity, and of many others came from an inner experience.

XXVIII. THE ONLY IMMEDIATE OBJECT OF OUR PERCEPTIONS WHICH EXISTS OUTSIDE OF US IS GOD, AND IN HIM ALONE IS OUR LIGHT

In the strictly metaphysical sense no external cause acts upon us excepting God alone, and he is in immediate relation with us only by virtue of our continual dependence upon him. Whence it follows that there is absolutely no other external object which comes into contact with our souls and directly excites perceptions in us. We have in our souls ideas of everything, only because of the continual action of God upon us, that is to say, because every effect expresses its cause and therefore the essences of our souls are certain expressions, imitations or images of the divine essence, divine thought and divine will, including all the ideas which are there contained. We may say, therefore, that God is for us the only immediate external object, and that we see

things through him. For example, when we see the sun or the stars, it is God who gives to us and preserves in us the ideas and whenever our senses are affected according to his own laws in a certain manner, it is he, who by his continual concurrence, determines our thinking. God is the sun and the light of souls, *lumen illuminans omnem hominem venientem in hunc mundum*, although this is not the current conception. I think I have already remarked that during the scholastic period many believed God to be the light of the soul, *intellectus agens animae rationalis*, following in this the Holy Scriptures and the fathers who were always more Platonic than Aristotelian in their mode of thinking. The Averroists misused this conception, but others, among whom were several mystic theologians, and William of Saint Amour, also I think, understood this conception in a manner which assured the dignity of God and was able to raise the soul to a knowledge of its welfare.

XXIX. YET WE THINK DIRECTLY BY MEANS OF OUR OWN IDEAS AND NOT THROUGH GOD'S

Nevertheless I cannot approve of the position of certain able philosophers who seem to hold that our ideas themselves are in God and not at all in us. I think that in taking this position they have neither sufficiently considered the nature of substance, which we have just explained, nor the entire extension and independence of the soul which includes all that happens to it, and expresses God, and with him all possible and actual beings in the same way that an effect expresses its cause. It is indeed inconceivable that the soul should think using the ideas of something else. The soul when it thinks of anything must be affected effectively in a certain manner, and it must needs have in itself in advance not only the passive capacity of being thus affected, a capacity already wholly determined, but it must have besides an active power by virtue of which it has always had in its nature the marks of the future production of this thought, and the disposition to produce it at its proper time. All of this shows that the soul already includes the idea which is comprised in any particular thought.

XXX. HOW GOD INCLINES OUR SOULS WITHOUT NECESSITATING THEM; THAT THERE ARE NO GROUNDS FOR COMPLAINT; THAT WE MUST NOT ASK WHY JUDAS SINNED BECAUSE THIS FREE ACT IS CONTAINED IN HIS CONCEPT, THE ONLY QUESTION BEING WHY JUDAS THE SINNER IS ADMITTED TO EXISTENCE, PREFERABLY TO OTHER POSSIBLE PERSONS; CONCERNING THE ORIGINAL IMPERFECTION OR LIMITATION BEFORE THE FALL AND CONCERNING THE DIFFERENT DEGREES OF GRACE

Regarding the action of God upon the human will there are many quite different considerations which it would take too long to investigate here. Nevertheless the following is what can be said in general. God in co-operating with ordinary actions only follows the laws which he has established, that is to say, he continually preserves and produces our being so that the ideas come to us spontaneously or with freedom in that order which the concept of our individual substance carries with itself. In this concept they can be foreseen for all eternity. Furthermore, by virtue of the decree which God has made that the will shall always seek the apparent good in certain particular respects (in regard to which this apparent good always has in it something of reality expressing or imitating God's will), he, without at all necessitating our choice, determines it by that which appears most desirable. For absolutely speaking, our will as contrasted with necessity, is in a state of indifference, being able to act otherwise, or wholly to suspend its action, either alternative being and remaining possible. It therefore devolves upon the soul to be on guard against appearances, by means of a firm will, to reflect and to refuse to act or decide in certain circumstances, except after mature deliberation. It is, however, true and has been assured from all eternity that certain souls will not employ their power upon certain occasions.

But who could do more than God has done, and can such a soul complain of anything except itself? All these complaints after the deed are unjust, inasmuch as they would have been unjust before the deed. Would this soul a little before committing the sin have had the right to complain of God as though he had determined the sin. Since the determinations of God in these matters cannot be foreseen, how would the soul know that it was pre-ordained to sin unless it had already committed the sin? It is merely a question of wishing to or not wishing to, and God could not have set an easier or juster condition. Therefore all judges without asking the reasons which have disposed a man to have an evil will, consider only how far this will is wrong. But, you object, perhaps it is ordained from all eternity that I will sin. Find your own answer. Perhaps it has not been. Now then, without asking for what you are unable to know and in regard to which you can have no light, act according to your duty and your knowledge. But, some one will object; whence comes it then that this man will assuredly do this sin? The reply is easy. It is that otherwise he would not be a man. For God foresees from all time that there will be a certain Judas, and in the concept or idea of him which God has, is contained this future free act. The only question, therefore, which remains is why this certain Judas, the betrayer who is possible only because of the idea of God, actually exists. To this question, however, we can expect no answer here on earth excepting to say in general that it is because God has found it good that he should exist notwithstanding that sin which he foresaw. This evil will be more than overbalanced. God will derive a greater good from it, and it will finally turn out that this series of events in which is included the existence of this sinner, is the most perfect among all the possible series of events. An explanation in every case of the admirable economy of this choice cannot be given while we are sojourners on earth. It is enough to know the excellence without understanding it. It is here that must be recognized *altitudinem divitiarum*, the unfathomable depth of the divine wisdom, without hesitating at a detail which involves an infinite number of considerations. It is clear, however, that God is not the cause of ill. For not only after the loss of innocence by men, has original sin possessed the soul, but even before that there was an original limitation or imperfection in the very nature of all creatures, which rendered them open to sin and able to fall. There is, therefore, no more difficulty in the supralapsarian view than there is in the other

views of sin. To this also, it seems to me can be reduced the opinion of Saint Augustine and of other
authors: that the root of evil is in the negativity, that
is to say, in the lack or limitation of creatures which
God graciously remedies by whatever degree of perfection it pleases him to give. This grace of God,
whether ordinary or extraordinary has its degrees and
its measures. It is always efficacious in itself to produce a certain proportionate effect and furthermore
it is always sufficient not only to keep one from sin
but even to effect his salvation, provided that the man
co-operates with that which is in him. It has not always, however, sufficient power to overcome the inclination, for, if it did, it would no longer be limited
in any way, and this superiority to limitations is reserved to that unique grace which is absolutely efficacious. This grace is always victorious whether
through its own self or through the congruity of
circumstances.

XXXI. CONCERNING THE MOTIVES OF ELECTION; CONCERNING FAITH FORESEEN AND THE ABSOLUTE DECREE AND THAT IT ALL REDUCES TO THE QUESTION WHY GOD HAS CHOSEN AND RESOLVED TO ADMIT TO EXISTENCE JUST SUCH A POSSIBLE PERSON, WHOSE CONCEPT INCLUDES JUST SUCH A SEQUENCE OF FREE ACTS AND OF FREE GIFTS OF GRACE. THIS AT ONCE PUTS AN END TO ALL DIFFICULTIES

Finally, the grace of God is wholly unprejudiced and
creatures have no claim upon it. Just as it is not sufficient in accounting for God's choice in his dispensations of grace to refer to his absolute or conditional
prevision of men's future actions, so it is also wrong
to imagine his decrees as absolute with no reasonable motive. As concerns foreseen faith and good
works, it is very true that God has elected none but
those whose faith and charity he foresees, *quos se
fide donaturum praescivit*. The same question, however, arises again as to why God gives to some rather
than to others the grace of faith or of good works.
As concerns God's ability to foresee not only the
faith and good deeds, but also their material and predisposition, or that which a man on his part contrib-

utes to them (since there are as truly diversities on
the part of men as on the part of grace, and a man
although he needs to be aroused to good and needs
to become converted, yet acts in accordance with his
temperament),—as regards his ability to foresee
there are many who say that God, knowing what a
particular man will do without grace, that is without
his extraordinary assistance, or knowing at least what
will be the human contribution, resolves to give
grace to those whose natural dispositions are the best,
or at any rate are the least imperfect and evil. But if
this were the case then the natural dispositions in so
far as they were good would be like gifts of grace,
since God would have given advantages to some over
others; and therefore, since he would well know that
the natural advantages which he had given would
serve as motives for his grace or for his extraordinary assistance, would not everything be reduced to
his mercy? I think, therefore, that since we do not
know how much and in what way God regards natural dispositions in the dispensations of his grace, it
would be safest and most exact to say, in accordance
with our principles and as I have already remarked,
that there must needs be among possible beings the
person Peter or John whose concept or idea contains
all that particular sequence of ordinary and extraordinary manifestations of grace together with the rest
of the accompanying events and circumstances, and
that it has pleased God to choose him among an infinite number of persons equally possible for actual
existence. When we have said this there seems nothing left to ask, and all difficulties vanish. For in regard to that great and ultimate question why it has
pleased God to choose him among so great a number of possible persons, it is surely unreasonable to
demand more than the general reasons which we
have given. The reasons in detail surpass our ken.
Therefore, instead of postulating an absolute decree,
which being without reason would be unreasonable,
and instead of postulating reasons which do not succeed in solving the difficulties and in turn have need
themselves of reasons, it will be best to say with St.
Paul that there are for God's choice certain great reasons of wisdom and congruity which he follows,
which reasons, however, are unknown to mortals and
are founded upon the general order, whose goal is
the greatest perfection of the world. This is what is

meant when the motives of God's glory and of the manifestation of his justice are spoken of, as well as when men speak of his mercy, and his perfection in general; that immense vastness of wealth with which the soul of the same St. Paul was so thrilled.

XXXII. USEFULNESS OF THESE PRINCIPLES IN MATTERS OF PIETY AND OF RELIGION

In addition it seems that the thoughts which we have just explained and particularly the great principle of the perfection of God's operations and the concept of substance which includes all its changes with all its accompanying circumstances, far from injuring, serve rather to confirm religion, serve to dissipate great difficulties, to inflame souls with a divine love and to raise the mind to a knowledge of incorporeal substances much more than the present-day hypotheses. For it appears clearly that all other substances depend upon God just as our thoughts emanate from our own substances; that God is all in all and that he is intimately united to all created things, in proportion however to their perfection; that it is he alone who determines them from without by his influence, and if to act is to determine directly, it may be said in metaphysical language that God alone acts upon me and he alone causes me to do good or ill, other substances contributing only because of his determinations; because God, who takes all things into consideration, distributes his bounties and compels created beings to accommodate themselves to one another. Thus God alone constitutes the relation or communication between substances. It is through him that the phenomena of the one meet and accord with the phenomena of the others, so that there may be a reality in our perceptions. In common parlance, however, an action is attributed to particular causes in the sense that I have explained above because it is not necessary to make continual mention of the universal cause when speaking of particular cases. It can be seen also that every substance has a perfect spontaneity (which becomes liberty with intelligent substances). Everything which happens to it is a consequence of its idea or its being and nothing determines it except God only. It is for this reason that a person of exalted mind and revered saintliness may say that the soul ought often to think as if there were

only God and itself in the world. Nothing can make us hold to immortality more firmly than this independence and vastness of the soul which protects it completely against exterior things, since it alone constitutes our universe and together with God is sufficient for itself. It is as impossible for it to perish save through annihilation as it is impossible for the universe to destroy itself, the universe whose animate and perpetual expression it is. Furthermore, the changes in this extended mass which is called our body cannot possibly affect the soul nor can the dissipation of the body destroy that which is indivisible.

XXXIII. EXPLANATION OF THE RELATION BETWEEN THE SOUL AND THE BODY, A MATTER WHICH HAS BEEN REGARDED AS INEXPLICABLE OR ELSE AS MIRACULOUS; CONCERNING THE ORIGIN OF CONFUSED PERCEPTIONS

We can also see the explanation of that great mystery "the union of the soul and the body," that is to say how it comes about that the passions and actions of the one are accompanied by the actions and passions or else the appropriate phenomena of the other. For it is not possible to conceive how one can have an influence upon the other and it is unreasonable to have recourse at once to the extraordinary intervention of the universal cause in an ordinary and particular case. The following, however, is the true explanation. We have said that everything which happens to a soul or to any substance is a consequence of its concept; hence the idea itself or the essence of the soul brings it about that all of its appearances or perceptions should be born out of its nature and precisely in such a way that they correspond of themselves to that which happens in the universe at large, but more particularly and more perfectly to that which happens in the body associated with it, because it is in a particular way and only for a certain time according to the relation of other bodies to its own body that the soul expresses the state of the universe. This last fact enables us to see how our body belongs to us, without, however, being attached to our essence. I believe that those who are careful thinkers will decide favorably for our principles because of this single reason, viz., that they are able to see in what consists the relation between the soul and the body, a parallelism which appears inexplicable in any other way. We can also see that the perceptions of our senses even when they are clear must necessarily contain certain confused elements, for as all the bodies in the universe are in sympathy, ours receives the impressions of all the others, and while our senses respond to everything, our soul cannot pay attention to every particular. That is why our confused sensations are the result of a variety of perceptions. This variety is infinite. It is almost like the confused murmuring which is heard by those who approach the shore of a sea. It comes from the continual beatings of innumerable waves. If now, out of many perceptions which do not at all fit together to make one, no particular one perception surpasses the others, and if they make impressions about equally strong or equally capable of holding the attention of the soul, they can be perceived only confusedly.

XXXIV. CONCERNING THE DIFFERENCE BETWEEN SPIRITS AND OTHER SUBSTANCES, SOULS OR SUBSTANTIAL FORMS; THAT THE IMMORTALITY WHICH MEN DESIRE INCLUDES MEMORY

Supposing that the bodies which constitute a *unum per se*, as human bodies, are substances, and have substantial forms, and supposing that animals have souls, we are obliged to grant that these souls and these substantial forms cannot entirely perish, any more than can the atoms or the ultimate elements of matter, according to the position of other philosophers; for no substance perishes, although it may become very different. Such substances also express the whole universe, although more imperfectly than do spirits. The principal difference, however, is that they do not know that they are, nor what they are. Consequently, not being able to reason, they are unable to discover necessary and universal truths. It is also because they do not reflect regarding themselves that they have no moral qualities, whence it follows that undergoing a thousand transformations, as we see a caterpillar change into a butterfly, the result from a moral or practical standpoint is the same as if we said that they perished in each case, and we can indeed say it from the physical standpoint in the

same way that we say bodies perish in their dissolution. But the intelligent soul, knowing that it is and having the ability to say that word "I" so full of meaning, not only continues and exists, metaphysically far more certainly than do the others, but it remains the same from the moral standpoint, and constitutes the same personality, for it is its memory or knowledge of this ego which renders it open to punishment and reward. Also the immortality which is required in morals and in religion does not consist merely in this perpetual existence, which pertains to all substances, for if in addition there were no remembrance of what one had been, immortality would not be at all desirable. Suppose that some individual could suddenly become King of China on condition, however, of forgetting what he had been, as though being born again, would it not amount to the same practically, or as far as the effects could be perceived, as if the individual were annihilated, and a king of China were the same instant created in his place? The individual would have no reason to desire this.

XXXV. THE EXCELLENCE OF SPIRITS; THAT GOD CONSIDERS THEM PREFERABLE TO OTHER CREATURES; THAT THE SPIRITS EXPRESS GOD RATHER THAN THE WORLD, WHILE OTHER SIMPLE SUBSTANCES EXPRESS THE WORLD RATHER THAN GOD

In order, however, to prove by natural reasons that God will preserve forever not only our substance, but also our personality, that is to say the recollection and knowledge of what we are (although the distinct knowledge is sometimes suspended during sleep and in swoons) it is necessary to join metaphysics to moral considerations. God must be considered not only as the principle and the cause of all substances and of all existing things, but also as the chief of all persons or intelligent substances, as the absolute monarch of the most perfect city or republic, such as is constituted by all the spirits together in the universe, God being the most complete of all spirits at the same time that he is greatest of all beings. For assuredly the spirits are the most perfect of substances and best express the divinity. Since all the nature, purpose, virtue and function of substances is, as has been sufficiently explained, to express God and the universe, there is no room for doubting that those substances which give the expression, knowing what they are doing and which are able to understand the great truths about God and the universe, do express God and the universe incomparably better than do those natures which are either brutish and incapable of recognizing truths, or are wholly destitute of sensation and knowledge. The difference between intelligent substances and those which are not intelligent is quite as great as between a mirror and one who sees. As God is himself the greatest and wisest of spirits it is easy to understand that the spirits with which he can, so to speak, enter into conversation and even into social relations by communicating to them in particular ways his feelings and his will so that they are able to know and love their benefactor, must be much nearer to him than the rest of created things which may be regarded as the instruments of spirits. In the same way we see that all wise persons consider far more the condition of a man than of anything else however precious it may be; and it seems that the greatest satisfaction which a soul, satisfied in other respects, can have is to see itself loved by others. However, with respect to God there is this difference that his glory and our worship can add nothing to his satisfaction, the recognition of creatures being nothing but a consequence of his sovereign and perfect felicity and being far from contributing to it or from causing it even in part. Nevertheless, that which is reasonable in finite spirits is found eminently in him and as we praise a king who prefers to preserve the life of a man before that of the most precious and rare of his animals, we should not doubt that the most enlightened and most just of all monarchs has the same preference.

XXXVI. GOD IS THE MONARCH OF THE MOST PERFECT REPUBLIC COMPOSED OF ALL THE SPIRITS, AND THE HAPPINESS OF THIS CITY OF GOD IS HIS PRINCIPAL PURPOSE

Spirits are of all substances the most capable of perfection and their perfections are different in this that they interfere with one another the least, or rather they aid one another the most, for only the most virtuous can be the most perfect friends. Hence it follows that God who in all things has the greatest perfection will have the greatest care for spirits and will give not only to all of them in general, but even to each one in particular the highest perfection which the universal harmony will permit. We can even say that it is because he is a spirit that God is the originator of existences, for if he had lacked the power of will to choose what is best, there would have been no reason why one possible being should exist rather than any other. Therefore God's being a spirit himself dominates all the consideration which he may have toward created things. Spirits alone are made in his image, being as it were of his blood or as children in the family, since they alone are able to serve him of free will, and to act consciously imitating the divine nature. A single spirit is worth a whole world, because it not only expresses the whole world, but it also knows it and governs itself as does God. In this way we may say that though every substance expresses the whole universe, yet the other substances express the world rather than God, while spirits express God rather than the world. This nature of spirits, so noble that it enables them to approach divinity as much as is possible for created things, has as a result that God derives infinitely more glory from them than from the other beings, or rather than other beings furnish to spirits the material for glorifying him. This moral quality of God which constitutes him Lord and Monarch of spirits influences him so to speak personally and in a unique way. It is through this that he humanizes himself, that he is willing to suffer human woes, and that he enters into social relations with us and this consideration is so dear to him that the happy and prosperous condition of his empire which consists in the greatest possible felicity of its inhabitants, becomes supreme among his laws. Happiness is to persons what perfection is to beings. And if the dominant principle in the existence of the physical world is the decree to give it the greatest possible perfection, the primary purpose in the moral world or in the city of God which constitutes the noblest part of the universe ought to be to extend the greatest happiness possible. We must not therefore doubt that God has so ordained everything that spirits not only shall live forever, because this is unavoidable, but that they shall also preserve forever their moral quality, so that his city may never lose a person, quite in the same way that the world never loses a substance. Consequently they will always be conscious of their being, otherwise they would be open to neither reward nor punishment, a condition which is the essence of a republic, and above all of the most perfect republic where nothing can be neglected. In fine, God being at the same time the most just and the most debonnaire of monarchs, and requiring only a good will on the part of men, provided that it be sincere and intentional, his subjects cannot desire a better condition. To render them perfectly happy he desires only that they love him.

XXXVII. JESUS CHRIST HAS REVEALED TO MEN THE MYSTERY AND THE ADMIRABLE LAWS OF THE KINGDOM OF HEAVEN, AND THE GREATNESS OF THE SUPREME HAPPINESS WHICH GOD HAS PREPARED FOR THOSE WHO LOVE HIM

The ancient philosophers knew very little of these important truths. Jesus Christ alone has expressed them divinely well, and in a way so clear and simple that the dullest minds have understood them. His gospel has entirely changed the face of human affairs. It has brought us to know the kingdom of heaven, or that perfect republic of spirits which deserves to be called the city of God. He it is who has discovered to us its wonderful laws. He alone has made us see how much God loves us and with what care everything that concerns us has been provided for; how God, inasmuch as he cares for the sparrows, will not neglect reasoning beings, who are infinitely more dear to him; how all the hairs of our heads are numbered; how heaven and earth may pass away but the word of God and that which belongs to the means of our salvation will not pass away; how God has more regard for the least one among intelligent souls than for the whole machinery of the world; how we ought not to fear those who are able to destroy the body but are unable to destroy the soul, since God alone can render the soul happy or unhappy; and how the souls of the righteous are protected by his hand against all the upheavals of the universe, since God alone is able to act upon them; how none of our acts are forgotten; how everything is to be accounted for; even careless words and even a spoonful of water which is well used; in fact how everything must result in the greatest welfare of the good, for then shall the righteous become like suns and neither our sense nor our minds have ever tasted of anything approaching the joys which God has laid up for those that love him.

THE MONADOLOGY

1. The Monad, of which we shall here speak, is nothing but a *simple* substance, which enters into *compounds*. By 'simple' is meant 'without parts.'

2. And there must be *simple* substances, since there are *compounds*; for a *compound* is nothing but a collection or *aggregatum* of *simple* things.

3. Now where there are no parts, there can be neither extension nor form [figure] nor divisibility. These Monads are the real atoms of nature and, in a word, the elements of things.

4. No dissolution of these elements need be feared, and there is no conceivable way in which a *simple* substance can be destroyed by natural means.

5. For the same reason there is no conceivable way in which a *simple* substance can come into being by natural means, since it cannot be formed by the combination of parts [composition].

6. Thus it may be said that a Monad can only come into being or come to an end all at once; that is to say, it can come into being only by creation and

Translated by Robert Latta.

come to an end only by annihilation, while that which is *compound* comes into being or comes to an end by parts.

7. Further, there is no way of explaining how a Monad can be altered in *quality* or internally changed by any other created thing; since it is impossible to change the place of anything in it or to conceive in it any internal motion which could be produced, directed, increased or diminished therein, although all this is possible in the case of *compounds*, in which there are changes among the parts. The Monads have no *windows*, through which anything could come in or go out. Accidents cannot separate themselves from substances nor go about outside of them, as the 'sensible species' of the Scholastics used to do. Thus neither substance nor accident can come into a Monad from outside.

8. Yet the Monads must have some qualities, otherwise they would not even be existing things. And if *simple* substances did not differ in *quality*, there would be absolutely no means of perceiving any change in things. For what is in the *compound* can come only from the *simple* elements it contains, and the Monads, if they had no qualities, would be indistinguishable from one another, since they do not differ in quantity. Consequently, space being a plenum, each part of space would always receive, in any motion, exactly the equivalent of what it already had, and no one state of things would be discernible from another.

9. Indeed, each Monad must be different from every other. For in nature there are never two beings which are perfectly alike and in which it is not possible to find an internal difference, or at least a difference founded upon an intrinsic *quality* [denomination].

10. I assume also as admitted that every created being, and consequently the created Monad, is subject to change, and further that this change is continuous in each.

11. It follows from what has just been said, that the natural changes of the Monads come from an internal principle, since an external cause can have no influence upon their inner being.

12. But, besides the principle of the change, there must be a particular series of changes [un detail de ce qui change], which constitutes, so to speak, the specific nature and variety of the *simple* substances.

13. This particular series of changes should involve a multiplicity in the *unit* [unite] or in that which is *simple*. For, as every natural change takes place gradually, something changes and something remains unchanged; and consequently a *simple* substance must be affected and related in many ways, although it has no parts.

14. The passing condition, which involves and represents a multiplicity in the *unit* [unite] or in the *simple* substance, is nothing but what is called Perception, which is to be distinguished from Apperception or Consciousness, as will afterwards appear. In this matter the Cartesian view is extremely defective, for it treats as non-existent those *perceptions* of which we are not consciously aware. This has also led them to believe that minds [esprits] alone are Monads, and that there are no *souls* of animals nor other Entelechies. Thus, like the crowd, they have failed to distinguish between a prolonged unconsciousness and absolute death, which has made them fall again into the Scholastic prejudice of *souls* entirely separate [from bodies], and has even confirmed ill-balanced minds in the opinion that *souls* are mortal.

15. The activity of the internal principle which produces change or passage from one *perception* to another may be called Appetition. It is true that desire [l'appetit] cannot always fully attain to the whole *perception* at which it aims, but it always obtains some of it and attains to new *perceptions*.

16. We have in ourselves experience of a multiplicity in *simple* substance, when we find that the least thought of which we are conscious involves variety in its object. Thus all those who admit that the *soul* is a *simple* substance should admit this multiplicity in the Monad; and M. Bayle ought not to have found any difficulty in this, as he has done in his Dictionary, article 'Rorarius.'

17. Moreover, it must be confessed that *perception* and that which depends upon it are inexplicable on mechanical grounds, that is to say, by means of figures and motions. And supposing there were a machine, so constructed as to think, feel, and have *perception*, it might be conceived as increased in size, while keeping the same proportions, so that one might go into it as into a mill. That being so, we should, on examining its interior, find only parts which work one upon another, and never anything by which to explain a *perception*. Thus it is in a *sim-*

ple substance, and not in a *compound* or in a machine, that *perception* must be sought for. Further, nothing but this (namely, *perceptions* and their changes) can be found in a *simple* substance. It is also in this alone that all the internal activities of *simple* substances can consist.

18. All *simple* substances or created Monads might be called Entelechies, for they have in them a certain perfection (echousi to enteles); they have a certain self-sufficiency (autarkeia) which makes them the sources of their internal activities and, so to speak, incorporeal automata.

19. If we are to give the name of Soul to everything which has *perceptions* and desires [appetits] in the general sense which I have explained, then all *simple* substances or created Monads might be called *souls*; but as feeling [le sentiment] is something more than a bare *perception*, I think it right that the general name of Monads or Entelechies should suffice for *simple* substances which have *perception* only, and that the name of Souls should be given only to those in which *perception* is more distinct, and is accompanied by memory.

20. For we experience in ourselves a condition in which we remember nothing and have no distinguishable *perception*; as when we fall into a swoon or when we are overcome with a profound dreamless sleep. In this state the *soul* does not perceptibly differ from a bare Monad; but as this state is not lasting, and the *soul* comes out of it, the *soul* is something more than a bare Monad.

21. And it does not follow that in this state the *simple* substance is without any *perception*. That, indeed, cannot be, for the reasons already given; for it cannot perish, and it cannot continue to exist without being affected in some way, and this affection is nothing but its *perception*. But when there is a great multitude of little *perceptions*, in which there is nothing distinct, one is stunned; as when one turns continuously round in the same way several times in succession, whence comes a giddiness which may make us swoon, and which keeps us from distinguishing anything. Death can for a time put animals into this condition.

22. And as every present state of a *simple* substance is naturally a consequence of its preceding state, in such a way that its present is big with its future;

23. And as, on waking from stupor, we are conscious of our *perceptions*, we must have had *perceptions* immediately before we awoke, although we were not at all conscious of them; for one *perception* can in a natural way come only from another *perception*, as a motion can in a natural way come only from a motion.

24. It thus appears that if we had in our *perceptions* nothing marked and, so to speak, striking and highly-flavoured, we should always be in a state of stupor. And this is the state in which the bare Monads are.

25. We see also that nature has given heightened *perceptions* to animals, from the care she has taken to provide them with organs, which collect numerous rays of light, or numerous undulations of the air, in order, by *uniting* them, to make them have greater effect. Something similar to this takes place in smell, in taste and in touch, and perhaps in a number of other senses, which are unknown to us. And I will explain presently how that which takes place in the *soul* represents what happens in the bodily organs.

26. Memory provides the *soul* with a kind of consecutiveness, which resembles [imite] reason, but which is to be distinguished from it. Thus we see that when animals have a *perception* of something which strikes them and of which they have formerly had a similar *perception*, they are led, by means of representation in their memory, to expect what was combined with the thing in this previous *perception*, and they come to have feelings similar to those they had on the former occasion. For instance, when a stick is shown to dogs, they remember the pain it has caused them, and howl and run away.

27. And the strength of the mental image which impresses and moves them comes either from the magnitude or the number of the preceding *perceptions*. For often a strong impression produces all at once the same effect as a long-formed habit, or as many and oft-repeated ordinary *perceptions*.

28. In so far as the concatenation of their *perceptions* is due to the principle of memory alone, men act like the lower animals, resembling the empirical physicians, whose methods are those of mere practice without theory. Indeed, in three-fourths of our actions we are nothing but empirics. For instance, when we expect that there will be daylight to-morrow, we do so empirically, because it has always so

happened until now. It is only the astronomer who thinks it on *rational* grounds.

29. But it is the knowledge of *necessary* and eternal truths that distinguishes us from the mere animals and gives us Reason and the sciences, raising us to the knowledge of ourselves and of God. And it is this in us that is called the *rational soul* or mind [esprit].

30. It is also through the knowledge of *necessary* truths, and through their abstract expression, that we rise to acts of reflexion, which make us think of what is called I, and observe that this or that is within us: and thus, thinking of ourselves, we think of being, of substance, of the *simple* and the *compound*, of the immaterial, and of God Himself, conceiving that what is limited in us is in Him without limits. And these acts of reflexion furnish the chief objects of our reasonings.

31. Our reasonings are grounded upon two great principles, that of *contradiction*, in virtue of which we judge false that which involves a *contradiction*, and true that which is opposed or contradictory to the false;

32. And that of sufficient reason, in virtue of which we hold that there can be no fact real or existing, no statement true, unless there be a sufficient reason, why it should be so and not otherwise, although these reasons usually cannot be known by us.

33. There are also two kinds of truths, those of reasoning and those of fact. Truths of reasoning are *necessary* and their opposite is impossible: truths of fact are *contingent* and their opposite is possible. When a truth is *necessary*, its reason can be found by analysis, resolving it into more *simple* ideas and truths, until we come to those which are primary.

34. It is thus that in Mathematics speculative Theorems and practical Canons are reduced by analysis to Definitions, Axioms, and Postulates.

35. In short, there are *simple* ideas, of which no definition can be given; there are also *axioms* and *postulates*, in a word, primary principles, which cannot be proved, and indeed have no need of proof; and these are identical propositions, whose opposite involves an express *contradiction*.

36. But there must also be a sufficient reason for *contingent* truths or truths of fact, that is to say, for the sequence or connexion of the things which are dispersed throughout the universe of created beings, in which the analyzing into particular reasons might go on into endless detail, because of the immense variety of things in nature and the infinite division of bodies. There is an infinity of present and past forms and motions which go to make up the efficient cause of my present writing; and there is an infinity of minute tendencies and dispositions of my *soul*, which go to make its final cause.

37. And as all this detail again involves other prior or more detailed *contingent* things, each of which still needs a similar analysis to yield its reason, we are no further forward: and the sufficient or final reason must be outside of the sequence or series of particular *contingent* things, however infinite this series may be.

38. Thus the final reason of things must be in a *necessary* substance, in which the variety of particular changes exists only eminently, as in its source; and this substance we call God.

39. Now as this substance is a sufficient reason of all this variety of particulars, which are also connected together throughout; there is only one God, and this God is sufficient.

40. We may also hold that this supreme substance, which is unique, universal and *necessary*, nothing outside of it being independent of it,—this substance, which is a pure sequence of possible being, must be illimitable and must contain as much reality as is possible.

41. Whence it follows that God is absolutely perfect; for perfection is nothing but amount of positive reality, in the strict sense, leaving out of account the limits or bounds in things which are limited. And where there are no bounds, that is to say in God, perfection is absolutely infinite.

42. It follows also that created beings derive their perfections from the influence of God, but that their imperfections come from their own nature, which is incapable of being without limits. For it is in this that they differ from God. An instance of this original imperfection of created beings may be seen in the natural inertia of bodies.

43. It is farther true that in God there is not only the source of existences but also that of essences, in so far as they are real, that is to say, the source of what is real in the possible. For the understanding of

God is the region of eternal truths or of the ideas on which they depend, and without Him there would be nothing real in the possibilities of things, and not only would there be nothing in existence, but nothing would even be possible.

44. For if there is a reality in essences or possibilities, or rather in eternal truths, this reality must needs be founded in something existing and actual, and consequently in the existence of the *necessary* Being, in whom essence involves existence, or in whom to be possible is to be actual.

45. Thus God alone (or the *necessary* Being) has this prerogative that He must necessarily exist, if He is possible. And as nothing can interfere with the possibility of that which involves no limits, no negation and consequently no *contradiction*, this [His possibility] is sufficient of itself to make known the existence of God a priori. We have thus proved it, through the reality of eternal truths. But a little while ago we proved it also a posteriori, since there exist *contingent* beings, which can have their final or sufficient reason only in the *necessary* Being, which has the reason of its existence in itself.

46. We must not, however, imagine, as some do, that eternal truths, being dependent on God, are arbitrary and depend on His will, as Descartes, and afterwards M. Poiret, appear to have held. That is true only of *contingent* truths, of which the principle is fitness [*convenance*] or choice of the best, whereas *necessary* truths depend solely on His understanding and are its inner object.

47. Thus God alone is the primary *unity* or original *simple* substance, of which all created or derivative Monads are products and have their birth, so to speak, through continual fulgurations of the Divinity from moment to moment, limited by the receptivity of the created being, of whose essence it is to have limits.

48. In God there is Power, which is the source of all, also Knowledge, whose content is the variety of the ideas, and finally Will, which makes changes or products according to the principle of the best. These characteristics correspond to what in the created Monads forms the ground or basis, to the faculty of Perception and to the faculty of Appetition. But in God these attributes are absolutely infinite or perfect; and in the created Monads or the Entelechies

(or *perfectihabiae*, as Hermolaus Barbarus translated the word) there are only imitations of these attributes, according to the degree of perfection of the Monad.

49. A created thing is said to act outwardly in so far as it has perfection, and to suffer [or be passive] in relation to another, in so far as it is imperfect. Thus activity [action] is attributed to a Monad, in so far as it has distinct *perceptions*, and passivity [passion] in so far as it has *perceptions* are confused.

50. And one created thing is more perfect than another, in this, that there is found in the more perfect that which serves to explain a priori what takes place in the less perfect, and it is on this account that the former is said to act upon the latter.

51. But in *simple* substances the influence of one Monad upon another is only ideal, and it can have its effect only through the mediation of God, in so far as in the ideas of God any Monad rightly claims that God, in regulating the others from the beginning of things, should have regard to it. For since one created Monad cannot have any physical influence upon the inner being of another, it is only by this means that the one can be dependent upon the other.

52. Accordingly, among created things, activities and passivities are mutual. For God, comparing two *simple* substances, finds in each reasons which oblige Him to adapt the other to it, and consequently what is active in certain respects is passive from another point of view; active in so far as what we distinctly know in it serves to explain [*rendre raison de*] what takes place in another, and passive in so far as the explanation [*raison*] of what takes place in it is to be found in that which is distinctly known in another.

53. Now, as in the Ideas of God there is an infinite number of possible universes, and as only one of them can be actual, there must be a sufficient reason for the choice of God, which leads Him to decide upon one rather than another.

54. And this reason can be found only in the fitness [*convenance*], or in the degrees of perfection, that these worlds possess, since each possible thing has the right to aspire to existence in proportion to the amount of perfection it contains in germ.

55. Thus the actual existence of the best that wisdom makes known to God is due to this, that His

goodness makes Him choose it, and His power makes Him produce it.

56. Now this connexion or adaptation of all created things to each and of each to all, means that each *simple* substance has relations which express all the others, and, consequently, that it is a perpetual living mirror of the universe.

57. And as the same town, looked at from various sides, appears quite different and becomes as it were numerous in aspects [perspectivement]; even so, as a result of the infinite number of *simple* substances, it is as if there were so many different universes, which, nevertheless are nothing but aspects [perspectives] of a single universe, according to the special point of view of each Monad.

58. And by this means there is obtained as great variety as possible, along with the greatest possible order; that is to say, it is the way to get as much perfection as possible.

59. Besides, no hypothesis but this (which I venture to call proved) fittingly exalts the greatness of God; and this Monsieur Bayle recognized when, in his Dictionary (article *Rorarius*), he raised objections to it, in which indeed he was inclined to think that I was attributing too much to God—more than it is possible to attribute. But he was unable to give any reason which could show the impossibility of this universal harmony, according to which every substance exactly expresses all others through the relations it has with them.

60. Further, in what I have just said there may be seen the reasons a priori why things could not be otherwise than they are. For God in regulating the whole has had regard to each part, and in particular to each Monad, whose nature being to represent, nothing can confine it to the representing of only one part of things; though it is true that this representation is merely confused as regards the variety of particular things [le detail] in the whole universe, and can be distinct only as regards a small part of things, namely, those which are either nearest or greatest in relation to each of the Monads; otherwise each Monad would be a deity. It is not as regards their object, but as regards the different ways in which they have knowledge of their object, that the Monads are limited. In a confused way they all strive after [vont a] the infinite, the whole; but they are limited and differentiated through the degrees of their distinct *perceptions*.

61. And *compounds* are in this respect analogous with [symbolisent avec] *simple* substances. For all is a plenum (and thus all matter is connected together) and in the plenum every motion has an effect upon distant bodies in proportion to their distance, so that each body not only is affected by those which are in contact with it and in some way feels the effect of everything that happens to them, but also is mediately affected by bodies adjoining those with which it itself is in immediate contact. Wherefore it follows that this inter-communication of things extends to any distance, however great. And consequently every body feels the effect of all that takes place in the universe, so that he who sees all might read in each what is happening everywhere, and even what has happened or shall happen, observing in the present that which is far off as well in time as in place: sympnoia panta, as Hippocrates said. But a *soul* can read in itself only that which is there represented distinctly; it cannot all at once unroll everything that is enfolded in it, for its complexity is infinite.

62. Thus, although each created Monad represents the whole universe, it represents more distinctly the body which specially pertains to it, and of which it is the *entelechy*; and as this body expresses the whole universe through the connexion of all matter in the plenum, the *soul* also represents the whole universe in representing this body, which belongs to it in a special way.

63. The body belonging to a Monad (which is its *entelechy* or its *soul*) constitutes along with the *entelechy* what may be called a living being, and along with the *soul* what is called an animal. Now this body of living being or of an animal is always organic; for, as every Monad is, in its own way, a mirror of the universe, and as the universe is ruled according to a perfect order, there must also be order in that which represents it, i.e. in the *perceptions* of the *soul*, and consequently there must be order in the body, through which the universe is represented in the *soul*.

64. Thus the organic body of each living being is a kind of divine machine or natural automaton, which infinitely surpasses all artificial automata. For a machine made by the skill of man is not a machine in each of its parts. For instance, the tooth of a brass

wheel has parts or fragments which for us are not artificial products, and which do not have the special characteristics of the machine, for they give no indication of the use for which the wheel was intended. But the machines of nature, namely, living bodies, are still machines in their smallest parts ad infinitum. It is this that constitutes the difference between nature and art, that is to say, between the divine art and ours.

65. And the Author of nature has been able to employ this divine and infinitely wonderful power of art, because each portion of matter is not only infinitely divisible, as the ancients observed, but is also actually subdivided without end, each part into further parts, of which each has some motion of its own; otherwise it would be impossible for each portion of matter to express the whole universe.

66. Whence it appears that in the smallest particle of matter there is a world of creatures, living beings, animals, entelechies, *souls*.

67. Each portion of matter may be conceived as like a garden full of plants and like a pond full of fishes. But each branch of every plant, each member of every animal, each drop of its liquid parts is also some such garden or pond.

68. And though the earth and the air which are between the plants of the garden, or the water which is between the fish of the pond, be neither plant nor fish; yet they also contain plants and fishes, but mostly so minute as to be imperceptible to us.

69. Thus there is nothing fallow, nothing sterile, nothing dead in the universe, no chaos, no confusion save in appearance, somewhat as it might appear to be in a pond at a distance, in which one would see a confused movement and, as it were, a swarming of fish in the pond, without separately distinguishing the fish themselves.

70. Hence it appears that each living body has a dominant *entelechy*, which in an animal is the *soul*; but the members of this living body are full of other living beings, plants, animals, each of which has also its dominant *entelechy* or *soul*.

71. But it must not be imagined, as has been done by some who have misunderstood my thought, that each *soul* has a quantity or portion of matter belonging exclusively to itself or attached to it for ever, and that it consequently owns other inferior living beings, which are devoted for ever to its service. For all bodies are in a perpetual flux like rivers, and parts are entering into them and passing out of them continually.

72. Thus the *soul* changes its body only by degrees, little by little, so that it is never all at once deprived of all its organs; and there is often metamorphosis in animals, but never metempsychosis or transmigration of *souls*; nor are there *souls* entirely separate [from bodies] nor unembodied spirits [genies sans corps]. God alone is completely without body.

73. It also follows from this that there never is absolute birth [generation] nor complete death, in the strict sense, consisting in the separation of the *soul* from the body. What we call births [generations] are developments and growths, while what we call deaths are envelopments and diminutions.

74. Philosophers have been much perplexed about the origin of forms, entelechies, or *souls*; but nowadays it has become known, through careful studies of plants, insects, and animals, that the organic bodies of nature are never products of chaos or putrefaction, but always come from seeds, in which there was undoubtedly some preformation; and it is held that not only the organic body was already there before conception, but also a *soul* in this body, and, in short, the animal itself; and that by means of conception this animal has merely been prepared for the great transformation involved in its becoming an animal of another kind. Something like this is indeed seen apart from birth [generation], as when worms become flies and caterpillars become butterflies.

75. The animals, of which some are raised by means of conception to the rank of larger animals, may be called spermatic, but those among them which are not so raised but remain in their own kind (that is, the majority) are born, multiply, and are destroyed like the large animals, and it is only a few chosen ones [elus] that pass to a greater theatre.

76. But this is only half of the truth, and accordingly I hold that if an animal never comes into being by natural means [*naturellement*], no more does it come to an end by natural means; and that not only will there be no birth [generation], but also no complete destruction or death in the strict sense. And

these reasonings, made a posteriori and drawn from experience are in perfect agreement with my principles deduced a priori, as above.

77. Thus it may be said that not only the *soul* (mirror of an indestructible universe) is indestructible, but also the animal itself, though its mechanism [machine] may often perish in part and take off or put on an organic slough [des depouilles organiques].

78. These principles have given me a way of explaining naturally the union or rather the mutual agreement [conformite] of the *soul* and the organic body. The *soul* follows its own laws, and the body likewise follows its own laws; and they agree with each other in virtue of the pre-established harmony between all substances, since they are all representations of one and the same universe.

79. Souls act according to the laws of final causes through *appetitions*, ends, and means. Bodies act according to the laws of efficient causes or motions. And the two realms, that of efficient causes and that of final causes, are in harmony with one another.

80. Descartes recognized that *souls* cannot impart any force to bodies, because there is always the same quantity of force in matter. Nevertheless he was of opinion that the *soul* could change the direction of bodies. But that is because in his time it was not known that there is a law of nature which affirms also the conservation of the same total direction in matter. Had Descartes noticed this he would have come upon my system of pre-established harmony.

81. According to this system bodies act as if (to suppose the impossible) there were no *souls*, and *souls* act as if there were no bodies, and both act as if each influenced the other.

82. As regards minds [*esprits*] or *rational souls*, though I find that what I have just been saying is true of all living beings and animals (namely that animals and *souls* come into being when the world begins and no more come to an end than the world does), yet there is this peculiarity in *rational* animals, that their spermatic animalcules, so long as they are only spermatic, have merely ordinary or sensuous [sensitive] *souls*; but when those which are chosen [elus], so to speak, attain to human nature through an actual conception, their sensuous *souls* are raised to the rank of reason and to the prerogative of minds [*esprits*].

83. Among other differences which exist between ordinary *souls* and minds [*esprits*], some of which differences I have already noted, there is also this: that *souls* in general are living mirrors or images of the universe of created things, but that minds are also images of the Deity or Author of nature Himself, capable of knowing the system of the universe, and to some extent of imitating it through architectonic ensamples [*echantillons*], each mind being like a small divinity in its own sphere.

84. It is this that enables spirits [or minds-esprits] to enter into a kind of fellowship with God, and brings it about that in relation to them He is not only what an inventor is to his machine (which is the relation of God to other created things), but also what a prince is to his subjects, and, indeed, what a father is to his children.

85. Whence it is easy to conclude that the totality [*assemblage*] of all spirits [*esprits*] must compose the City of God, that is to say, the most perfect State that is possible, under the most perfect of Monarchs.

86. This City of God, this truly universal monarchy, is a moral world in the natural world, and is the most exalted and most divine among the works of God; and it is in it that the glory of God really consists, for He would have no glory were not His greatness and His goodness known and admired by spirits [*esprits*]. It is also in relation to this divine City that God specially has goodness, while His wisdom and His power are manifested everywhere.

87. As we have shown above that there is a perfect harmony between the two realms in nature, one of efficient, and the other of final causes, we should here notice also another harmony between the physical realm of nature and the moral realm of grace, that is to say, between God, considered as Architect of the mechanism [machine] of the universe and God considered as Monarch of the divine City of spirits.

88. A result of this harmony is that things lead to grace by the very ways of nature, and that this globe, for instance, must be destroyed and renewed by natural means at the very time when the government of spirits requires it, for the punishment of some and the reward of others.

89. It may also be said that God as Architect satisfies in all respects God as Lawgiver, and thus that sins must bear their penalty with them, through the order of nature, and even in virtue of the mechanical structure of things; and similarly that noble actions will attain their rewards by ways which, on the bodily side, are mechanical, although this cannot and ought not always to happen immediately.

90. Finally, under this perfect government no good action would be unrewarded and no bad one unpunished, and all should issue in the well-being of the good, that is to say, of those who are not malcontents in this great state, but who trust in Providence, after having done their duty, and who love and imitate, as is meet, the Author of all good, finding pleasure in the contemplation of His perfections, as is the way of genuine 'pure love,' which takes pleasure in the happiness of the beloved. This it is which leads wise and virtuous people to devote their energies to everything which appears in harmony with the presumptive or antecedent will of God, and yet makes them content with what God actually brings to pass by His secret, consequent and positive [decisive] will, recognizing that if we could sufficiently understand the order of the universe, we should find that it exceeds all the desires of the wisest men, and that it is impossible to make it better than it is, not only as a whole and in general but also for ourselves in particular, if we are attached, as we ought to be, to the Author of all, not only as to the architect and efficient cause of our being, but as to our master and to the final cause, which ought to be the whole aim of our will, and which can alone make our happiness.

REVIEW QUESTIONS

1. What is Leibniz's concept of substance? What attributes must it have?
2. What is a monad? What are a monad's characteristics?
3. Do monads interact? How are they related to one another? What is Leibniz's notion of "pre-established harmony"?
4. What does Leibniz say to those who think that God could have made things better than he has?
5. To Leibniz, are matter and space real? What things *are* real?

19

JOHN LOCKE

The English philosopher John Locke (1632–1704) was born in Bristol and raised as a Puritan. He was educated at Christ Church, Oxford University, where he became a tutor in Greek rhetoric and philosophy. Later he was a practicing physician and assistant to Lord Ashley, the Earl of Shaftesbury. In 1683, because of the Earl of Shaftesbury's anti-Stuart political views, Locke was forced to flee to the Netherlands. There he wrote his two great masterpieces: *An Essay Concerning Human Understanding* (published in 1689), from which our selection is taken, and *Two Treatises on Civil Government* (published in 1690). He returned to England in 1689, wrote his final work, *The Reasonableness of Christianity*, and died in 1704.

Locke's work in the theory of knowledge is the first systematic assault on Cartesian rationalism, the view that reason alone guarantees knowledge. Locke argued that if our claims to knowledge make any sense, they must be derived from the world. He rejects the rationalist notion that we have *innate ideas* (actual knowledge of metaphysical truths, such as mathematical truths, universals, and the laws of nature) because (1) there is not good deductive argument establishing the existence of such entities; (2) children and idiots do not seem to possess them; and (3) an empirical way of knowing, which seems far more reasonable, has no place for such entities.

According to Locke, the mind at birth is a *tabula rasa*, a blank slate. It is like white paper, devoid of characteristics until it receives sense perceptions. All knowledge begins with sensory experience upon which the powers of the mind operate, developing complex ideas, abstractions, and the like. In place of the absolute certainty that the rationalists sought to find, Locke says that apart from the knowledge of the self, most of what we know we know in degrees of certainty derived from inductive generalizations. For example, we see the sun rise every morning and infer that it is highly probable that it will rise tomorrow, but we cannot be absolutely certain.

Locke holds a Representational Theory of Perception in which objects in the world cause our sense organs to start processes that result in perceptual experience. We are never aware of the thing in itself, the object which is perceived and which causes the idea to arise in our mind, but only the idea or *representation* of the object. We are directly aware of the idea but in as much as the object is the cause of the idea, we may be said to be *indirectly* aware of the object itself.

Locke held a causal theory of perception in which processes in the external world impinge on the perceiver's sense organs, which in turn send messages to the brain, where they are transformed into mental events. We may diagram the Causal Theory of Perception this way:

Objects and Events in the Real World
>   (Energy coming to sense organs: insensible particles reflected from the object onto the sense organ or contacted with the sense organ)

Sense Organs
>   (Signals to brain)

Brain Event
>   (Transformation from physical to mental event)

Perceptual Experience
>   The mechanical yields the non-mechanical IDEA in the Mind

Although the process is physical and mechanistic, it yields a nonphysical result, a mental event, the perceptual experience, what will later be identified as a *percept* or *sense datum*.

Locke divides our ideas into two types: ideas of primary qualities and ideas of secondary qualities. Primary qualities are inseparable from their objects and so truly represent them. Examples of primary qualities are solidity, extension, figure, movement, and number. These are the building blocks of knowledge. Secondary qualities are not in the things themselves but are caused by primary qualities. They include colors, sounds, tastes, and touch. They are power that objects have to do certain things. Fire has the power to change liquids into gases, sugar is soluble in warm water, and glass is fragile. Solubility, flammability, and fragility are dispositional qualities in bodies, and as such cause changes in the world.

FOR FURTHER READING

Aaron, Richard I. *John Locke* (Clarendon Press, 1971).

Ayers, Michael. *Locke* (Routledge & Kegan Paul, 1991).

Bennett, Jonathan. *Locke, Berkeley, and Hume: Central Themes* (Oxford University Press, 1971).

Dunn, John. *Locke* (Oxford University Press, 1984).

Dunn, John, et al., eds. *The British Empiricists* (Oxford University Press, 1992).

Jolley, Nicholas. *Leibniz and Locke* (Oxford University Press, 1984).

Mackie, J. L. *Problems from Locke* (Oxford University Press, 1971).

Martin, C. B., and D. M. Armstrong, eds. *Locke and Berkeley: A Collection of Critical Essays* (University of Notre Dame Press, 1968).

Woolhouse, R. S. *Locke* (Harvester Press, 1983).

AN ESSAY CONCERNING HUMAN UNDERSTANDING

BOOK I

CHAPTER 1. INTRODUCTION

1. An inquiry into the understanding pleasant and useful.   Since it is the understanding, that sets man above the rest of sensible beings, and gives him all the advantage and dominion, which he has over them; it is certainly a subject, even for its nobleness, worth our labour to enquire into. The understanding, like the eye, whilst it makes us see and perceive all other things, takes no notice of itself; and it requires art and pains to set it at a distance and make it its own object. But, whatever be, the difficulties that lie in the way of this enquiry; whatever it be that keeps us so much in the dark to ourselves; sure I am, that all the light we can let in upon our minds, all the acquaintance we can make with our own understandings, will not only be very pleasant, but bring us great advantage, in directing our thoughts in the search of other things.

2. Design.   This, therefore, being my purpose, to enquire into the original, certainty, and extent of human knowledge; together with the grounds and degrees of belief, opinion, and assent; I shall not at present meddle with the physical consideration of the mind; or trouble myself to examine, wherein its essence consists, or by what motions of our spirits, or alterations of our bodies, we come to have any sensation by our organs, or any ideas in our understandings; and whether those ideas do in their formation, any, or all of them, depend on matter or no: These are speculations, which, however curious and entertaining, I shall decline, as lying out of my way in the design I am now upon. It shall suffice to my present purpose, to consider the discerning faculties of a man, as they are employed about the objects, which they have to do with: And I shall imagine I have not wholly misemployed myself in the thoughts I shall have on this occasion, if, in this historical, plain method, I can give any account of the ways, whereby our understandings come to attain those notions of things we have, and can set down any measures of the certainty of our knowledge, or the

grounds of those persuasions which are to be found amongst men, so various, different, and wholly contradictory; and yet asserted somewhere or other, with such assurance and confidence, that he that shall take a view of the opinions of mankind, observe their Opposition, and at the same time consider the fondness and devotion wherewith they are embraced, the resolution and eagerness wherewith they are maintained, may perhaps have reason to suspect, that either there is no such thing as truth at all; or that mankind hath no sufficient means to attain a certain knowledge of it.

3. Method.   It is therefore worth while to search out the bounds between opinion and knowledge; and examine by what measures, in things, whereof we have no certain knowledge, we ought to regulate our assent, and moderate our persuasions. In order whereunto, I shall pursue this following method.

First, I shall enquire into the original of those ideas, notions, or whatever else you please to call them, which a man observes, and is conscious to himself he has in his mind; and the ways whereby the understanding comes to be furnished with them.

Secondly, I shall endeavor to shew what knowledge the understanding hath by those ideas; and the certainty, evidence, and extent of it.

Thirdly, I shall make some enquiry into the nature and grounds of faith, or opinion; whereby I mean that assent, which we give to any proposition as true, of whose truth yet we have no certain knowledge; and here we shall have occasion to examine the reasons and degrees of *assent*.

4. Useful to know the extent of our comprehension.   If, by this enquiry into the nature of the understanding, I can discover the powers thereof; how far they reach; to what things they are in any degree proportionate; and where they fail us: I suppose it may be of use to prevail with the busy mind of man, to be more cautious in meddling with things exceeding its comprehension; to stop when it is at the utmost extent of its tether; and to sit down in a quiet ignorance of those things which, upon examination, are found to be beyond the reach of our capacities. We should not then perhaps be so forward, out of an affectation of an universal knowledge, to raise questions, and perplex ourselves and others with disputes about things, to which our understandings are not suited; and of which we cannot frame in our minds any clear or distinct perceptions, or whereof (as it has perhaps too often happened) we have not any notions at all. If we can find out how far the understanding can extend its view, how far it has faculties to attain certainty, and in what cases it can only judge and guess; we may learn to content ourselves with what is attainable by us in this state.

5. Our capacity proportioned to our state and concerns, to discover things useful to us. For, though the comprehension of our understandings comes exceeding short of the vast extent of things; yet we shall have cause enough to magnify the bountiful author of our being, for that proportion and degree of knowledge he has bestowed on us, so far above all the rest of the inhabitants of this our mansion. Men have reason to be well satisfied with what God hath thought fit for them, since he hath given them (as St. Peter says), whatsoever is necessary for the conveniences of life, and information of virtue; and has put within the reach of their discovery the comfortable provision for this life, and the way that leads to a better. How short soever their knowledge may come of an universal or perfect comprehension of whatsoever is, it yet secures their great concernments, that they have light enough to lead them to the knowledge of their maker, and the sight of their own duties. Men may find matter sufficient to busy their heads, and employ their hands with variety, delight, and satisfaction; if they will not boldly quarrel with their own constitution, and throw away the blessings their hands are filled with, because they are not big enough to grasp every thing. We shall not have much reason to complain of the narrowness of our minds, if we will but employ them about what may be of use to us; for of that they are very capable: And it will be an unpardonable, as well as childish peevishness, if we undervalue the advantages of our knowledge, and neglect to improve it to the ends for which it was given us, because there are some

things that are set out of the reach of it. It will be no excuse to an idle and untoward servant, who would not attend his business by candle-light, to plead that he had not broad sun-shine. The candle, that is set up in us, shines bright enough for all our purposes. The discoveries we can make with this, ought to satisfy us; and we shall then use our understandings right, when we entertain all objects in that way and proportion that they are suited to our faculties, and upon those grounds they are capable of being proposed to us, and not peremptorily, or intemperately require demonstration, and demand certainty, where probability only is to be had, and which is sufficient to govern all our concernments. If we will disbelieve every thing, because we cannot certainly know all things; we shall do as wisely as he, who would not use his legs, but sit still and perish, because he had no wings to fly. . . .

8. What idea stands for. This much I thought necessary to say concerning the occasion of this enquiry into human understanding. But, before I proceed on to what I have thought on this subject, I must here in the entrance beg pardon of my reader for the frequent use of the word "idea," which he will find in the following treatise. It being that term, which, I think, serves best to stand for whatsoever is the object of the understanding when a man thinks; I have used it to express whatever is meant by phantasm, notion, species, or whatever it is which the mind can be employed about in thinking; and I could not avoid frequently using it.

I presume it will be easily granted me, that there are such ideas in men's minds; every one is conscious of them in himself, and men's words and actions will satisfy him that they are in others. Our first enquiry then shall be, how they come into the mind.

CHAPTER 2. NO INNATE PRINCIPLES IN THE MIND

1. The way shown how we come by any knowledge, sufficient to prove it not innate. It is an established opinion amongst some men, that there are in the understanding certain innate principles; some primary notions, characters, as it were, stamped upon the mind of man, which the soul receives in its very first being; and brings into the world with it. It would be sufficient to convince unprejudiced readers of the falseness of this supposition, if I should only shew (as I hope I shall in the following parts of this discourse) how men, barely by the use of their natural faculties, may attain to all the knowledge they have, without the help of any innate impressions; and may arrive at certainty, without any such original notions or principles. For I imagine any one will easily grant, that it would be impertinent to suppose, the ideas of colours innate in a creature, to whom God hath given sight, and a power to receive them by the eyes, from external objects: And no less unreasonable would it be to attribute several truths to the impressions of nature, and innate characters, when we may observe in ourselves faculties, fit to attain as easy and certain knowledge of them, as if they were originally imprinted on the mind.

But because a man is not permitted without censure to follow his own thoughts in the search of truth, when they lead him ever so little out of the common road; I shall set down the reasons that made me doubt of the truth of that opinion, as an excuse for my mistake, if I be in one; which I leave to be considered by those who, with me, dispose themselves to embrace truth, wherever they find it.

2. General assent, the great argument. There is nothing more commonly taken for granted, than that there are certain principles, both speculative and practical, (for they speak of both), universally agreed upon by all mankind: Which therefore, they argue, must needs be the constant impressions, which the souls of men receive in their first beings, and which they bring into the world with them, as necessarily and really as they do any of their inherent faculties.

3. Universal consent proves nothing. This argument, drawn from universal consent, has this misfortune in it, that if it were true in matter of fact, that there were certain truths wherein all mankind agreed, it would not prove them innate, if there can be any other way shewn how men may come to that universal agreement, in the things they do consent in, which I presume may be done.

**4. What is, is; and it is impossible for the same thing to be, and not to be; not universally assented

to.** But, which is worse, this argument of universal consent, which is made use of to prove innate principles, seems to me a demonstration that there are none such; because there are none to which all mankind give an universal assent. I shall begin with the speculative, and instance in those magnified principles of demonstration; "Whatsoever is, is;" and "It is impossible for the same thing to be and not to be;" which, of all others, I think have the most allowed title to innate. These have so settled a reputation of maxims universally received, that it will, no doubt, be thought strange, if any one should seem to question it. But yet I take liberty to say, that these propositions are so far from having an universal assent, that there are a great part of mankind to whom they are not so much as known.

5. Not on the mind naturally imprinted, because not known to children, idiots, etc. For, first, it is evident, that all children and idiots have not the least apprehension or thought of them; and the want of that is enough to destroy that universal assent, which must needs be the necessary concomitant of all innate truths: It seeming to me near a contradiction, to say, that there are truths imprinted on the soul, which it perceives or understands not; imprinting, if it signify any thing, being nothing else, but the making certain truths to be perceived. For to imprint any thing on the mind, without the mind's perceiving it, seems to me hardly intelligible. If therefore children and idiots have souls, have minds, with those impressions upon them, they must unavoidably perceive them, and necessarily know and assent to these truths: Which since they do not, it is evident that there are no such impressions. For if they are not notions naturally imprinted, how can they be innate? and if they are notions imprinted, how can they be unknown? To say a notion is imprinted on the mind, and yet at the same time to say, that the mind is ignorant of it, and never yet took notice of it, is to make this impression nothing. No proposition can be said to be in the mind which it never yet knew, which it was never yet conscious of. For if any one may, then, by the same reason, all propositions that are true, and the mind is capable ever of assenting to, may be said to be in the mind, and to be imprinted: Since, if any one can be said to be in the mind, which it never yet knew, it must be only, because it is capable of knowing it, and so the mind is of all truths it ever shall know. Nay, thus truths may be imprinted on the mind, which it never did, nor ever shall know: For a man may live long, and die at last in ignorance of many truths, which his mind was capable of knowing, and that with certainty. So that if the capacity of knowing, be the natural impression contended for, all the truths a man ever comes to know, will, by this account, be every one of them innate; and this great point will amount to no more, but only to a very improper way of speaking; which, whilst it pretends to assert the contrary, says nothing different from those, who deny innate principles. For nobody, I think, ever denied that the mind was capable of knowing several truths. The capacity, they say, is innate, the knowledge acquired. But then to what end such contest for certain innate maxims? If truths can be imprinted on the understanding without being perceived, I can see no difference there can be, between any truths the mind is capable of knowing in respect of their original: They must all be innate, or all adventitious: In vain shall a man go about to distinguish them. He therefore that talks of innate notions in the understanding, cannot (if he intend thereby any distinct sort of truths) mean such truths to be in the understanding, as it never perceived, and is yet wholly ignorant of. For if these words (to be in the understanding) have any propriety, they signify to be understood: So that to be in the understanding, and not to be understood; to be in the mind, and never to be perceived; is all one, as to say any thing is, and is not, in the mind or understanding. If therefore these two propositions, "Whatsoever is, is," and "It is impossible for the same thing to be and not to be," are by nature imprinted, children cannot be ignorant of them; infants, and all that have souls, must necessarily have them in their understandings, know the truth of them, and assent to it.

6. That men know when they come to the use of reason, answered. To avoid this, it is usually answered, That all men know and assent to them, when they come to the use of reason, and this is enough to prove them innate. I answer,

7. Doubtful expressions, that have scarce any signification, go for clear reasons, to those who, being prepossessed, take not the pains to examine even what they themselves say. For to apply this answer with any tolerable sense to our present purpose, it must signify one of these two things; either, that, as soon as men come to the use of reason, these supposed native inscriptions come to be known, and observed by them: Or else, that the use and exercise of men's reason assists them in the discovery of these principles, and certainly makes them known to them.

8. If reason discovered them, that would not prove them innate. If they mean, that by the use of reason men may discover these principles; and that this is sufficient to prove them innate: Their way of arguing will stand thus, (viz.) that, whatever truths reason can certainly discover to us, and make us firmly assent to, those are all naturally imprinted on the mind; since that universal assent, which is made the mark of them, amounts to no more but this; that by the use of reason, we are capable to come to a certain knowledge of and assent to them, and, by this means, there will be no difference between the maxims of the mathematicians, and theorems they deduce from them; all must be equally allowed innate; they being all discoveries made by the use of reason, and truths that a rational creature may certainly come to know, if he apply his thoughts rightly that way.

9. It is false that reason discovers them. But how can these men think the use of reason necessary, to discover principles that are supposed innate, when reason (if we may believe them) is nothing else but the faculty of deducing unknown truths from principles or propositions, that are already known? That certainly can never be thought innate, which we have need of reason to discover; unless, as I have said, we will have all the certain truths that reason ever teaches us, to be innate. We may as well think the use of reason necessary to make our eyes discover visible objects, as that there should be need of reason, or the exercise thereof, to make the understanding see what is originally engraven on it, and cannot be in the understanding before it be perceived by it. So that to make a reason discover those truths, thus imprinted, is to say, that the use of reason discovers to a man what he knew before: And if men have those innate impressed truths originally, and before the use of reason, and yet are always ignorant of them till they come to the use of reason, it is in effect to say, that men know, and know them not, at the same time.

10. It will here perhaps be said, that mathematical demonstrations, and other truths that are not innate, are not assented to, as soon as proposed, wherein they are distinguished from these maxims and other innate truths. I shall have occasion to speak of assent, upon the first proposing, more particularly by and by. I shall here only, and that very readily, allow, that these maxims and mathematical demonstrations are in this different; that the one have need of reason, using of proofs, to make them out, and to gain our assent; but the other, as soon as understood, are, without any the least reasoning, embraced and assented to. But I withal beg leave to observe, that it lays open the weakness of this subterfuge, which requires the use of reason for the discovery of these general truths: Since it must be confessed, that in their discovery there is no use made of reasoning at all. And I think those, who give this answer, will not be forward to affirm that the knowledge of this maxim, "That it is impossible for the same thing to be and not to be," is a deduction of our reason. For this would be to destroy that bounty of nature they seem so fond of, whilst they make the knowledge of those principles to depend on the labour of our thoughts. For all reasoning is search, and casting about, and requires pains and application. And how can it with any tolerable sense be supposed, that what was imprinted by nature, as the foundation and guide of our reason, should need the use of reason to discover it? . . .

BOOK II

CHAPTER 1. OF IDEAS IN GENERAL, AND THEIR ORIGINAL

1. Idea is the object of thinking. Every man being conscious to himself that he thinks, and that which his mind is applied about, whilst thinking, being the ideas that are there, it is past doubt that men have in their minds several ideas, such as are those expressed by the words, Whiteness, Hardness, Sweetness, Thinking, Motion, Man, Elephant, Army, Drunken-

ness, and others. It is in the first place then to be enquired, how he comes by them. I know it is a received doctrine, that men have native ideas, and original characters, stamped upon their minds, in their very first being. This opinion I have, at large, examined already; and, I suppose, what I have said, in the foregoing book, will be much more easily admitted, when I have shewn, whence the understanding may get all the ideas it has, and by what ways and degrees they may come into the mind for which I shall appeal to every one's own observation and experience.

2. All ideas come from sensations or reflection. Let us then suppose the mind to be, as we say, white paper, void of all characters, without any ideas; how comes it to be furnished? Whence comes it by that vast store which the busy and boundless fancy of man has painted on it with an almost endless variety? Whence has it all the materials of reason and knowledge? To this I answer, in one word, from experience; in all that our knowledge is founded, and from that it ultimately derives itself. Our observation employed either about external sensible objects, or about the internal operations of our minds, perceived and reflected on by ourselves, is that which supplies our understandings with all the materials of thinking. These two are the fountains of knowledge, from whence all the ideas we have, or can naturally have, do spring.

3. The objects of sensation one source of ideas. First, Our senses, conversant about particular sensible objects, do convey into the mind several distinct perceptions of things, according to those various ways wherein those objects do affect them: And thus we come by those ideas we have of Yellow, White, Heat, Cold, Soft, Hard, Bitter, Sweet, and all those which we call sensible qualities; which when I say the senses convey into the mind, I mean, they from external objects convey into the mind what produces there those perceptions. This great source of most of the ideas we have, depending wholly upon our senses, and derived by them to the understanding, I call SENSATION.

4. The operations of our minds the other source of them. Secondly, The other fountain from which experience furnishes the understanding with ideas, is the perception of the operations of our own mind within us, as it is employed about the ideas it has got; which operations, when the soul comes to reflect on and consider, do furnish the understanding with another set of ideas, which could not be had from things without. And such are Perception, Thinking, Doubting, Believing, Reasoning, Knowing, Willing, and all the different actings of our own minds; which we being conscious of and observing in ourselves, do from these receive into our understandings as distinct ideas, as we do from bodies affecting our senses. This source of ideas every man has wholly in himself; and though it be not sense, as having nothing to do with external objects, yet it is very like it, and might properly enough be called internal sense. But as I call the other sensation, so I call this REFLECTION, the ideas it affords being such only as the mind gets by reflecting on its own operations within itself. By reflection then, in the following part of this discourse, I would be understood to mean that notice which the mind takes of its own operations, and the manner of them; by reason whereof there come to be ideas of these operations in the understanding. These two, I say, viz. external material things, as the objects of sensation; and the operations of our own minds within, as the objects of reflection; are to me the only originals from whence all our ideas take their beginnings. The term operations here I use in a large sense, as comprehending not barely the actions of the mind about its ideas, but some sort of passions arising sometimes from them, such as is the satisfaction or uneasiness arising from any thought.

5. All our ideas of the one or the other of these.   The understanding seems to me not to have the least glimmering of any ideas, which it doth not receive from one of these two. External objects furnish the mind with the ideas of sensible qualities, which are all those different perceptions they produce in us: And the mind furnishes the understanding with ideas of its own operations.

These, when we have taken a full survey of them, and their several modes, combinations, and relations, we shall find to contain all our whole stock of ideas; and that we have nothing in our minds which did not come in one of these two ways. Let any one examine his own thoughts, and thoroughly search into his understanding; and then let him tell me, whether all the original ideas he has there, are any other than of the objects of his senses, or of the operations of his mind, considered as objects of his reflection; and how great a mass of knowledge soever he imagines to be lodged there, he will, upon taking a strict view, see that he has not any idea in his mind, but what one of these two have imprinted; though perhaps, with infinite variety compounded and enlarged by the understanding, as we shall see hereafter.

6. Observable in children.   He that attentively considers the state of a child, at his first coming into the world, will have little reason to think him stored with plenty of ideas, that are to be the matter of his future knowledge: It is by degrees he comes to be furnished with them. And though the ideas of obvious and familiar qualities imprint themselves before the memory begins to keep a register of time or order, yet it is often so late before some unusual qualities come in the way, that there are few men that cannot recollect the beginning of their acquaintance with them: And if it were worth while, no doubt a child might be so ordered as to have but a very few even of the ordinary ideas, till he were grown up to a man. But all that are born into the world being surrounded with bodies that perpetually and diversely affect them; variety of ideas, whether care be taken of it or not, are imprinted on the minds of children. Light and colors are busy at hand every-where, when the eye is but open; sounds and some tangible qualities fail not to solicit their proper senses, and force an entrance to the mind; but yet, I think, it will be granted easily, that if a child were kept in a place where he never saw any other but black and white till he were a man, he would have no more ideas of scarlet or green, than he that from his childhood never tasted an oyster, or a pineapple, has of those particular relishes.

7. Men are differently furnished with these according to the different objects they converse with.   Men then come to be furnished with fewer or more simple ideas from without, according as the objects they converse with afford greater or less variety; and from the operations of their minds within, according as they more or less reflect on them. For though he that contemplates the operations of his mind, cannot but have plain and clear ideas of them; yet, unless he turn his thoughts that way, and considers them attentively, he will no more have clear and distinct ideas of all the operations of his mind, and all that may be observed therein, than he will have all the particular ideas of any landscape, or of the parts and motions of a clock, who will not turn his eyes to it, and with attention heed all the parts of it. The picture, or clock may be so placed, that they may come in his way every day; but yet he will have but a confused idea of all the parts they are made up of, till he applies himself with attention to consider them each in particular.

8. Ideas of reflection later, because they need attention. And hence we see the reason why it is pretty late before most children get ideas of the operations of their own minds; and some have not any very clear or perfect ideas of the greatest part of them all their lives: Because, though they pass there continually, yet, like floating visions, they make not deep impressions enough to leave in their mind clear, distinct, lasting ideas, till the understanding turns inward upon itself, reflects on its own operations, and makes them the objects of its own contemplation. Children when they come first into it, are surrounded with a world of new things, which, by a constant solicitation of these senses, draw the mind constantly to them, forward to take notice of new, and apt to be delighted with the variety of changing objects. Thus the first years are usually employed and diverted in looking abroad. Men's business in them is to acquaint themselves with what is to be found without: And so growing up in a constant attention to outward sensation, seldom make any considerable reflection on what passes within them till they come to be of riper years; and some scarce ever at all.

9. The soul begins to have ideas when it begins to perceive. To ask at what time a man has first any ideas, is to ask when he begins to perceive; having ideas, and perception, being the same thing. I know it is an opinion, that the soul always thinks, and that it has the actual perception of ideas in itself constantly as long as it exists; and that actual thinking is as inseparable from the soul, as actual extension is from the body; which if true, to enquire after the beginning of a man's ideas is the same as to enquire after the beginning of his soul. For by this account soul and its ideas, as body and its extension, will begin to exist both at the same time. . . .

CHAPTER 2. OF SIMPLE IDEAS

1. Uncompounded appearances. The better to understand the nature, manner, and extent of our knowledge, one thing is carefully to be observed concerning the ideas we have; and that is, that some of them are simple, and some complex.

Though the qualities that affect our senses are, in the things themselves, so united and blended, that there is no separation, no distance between them; yet it is plain, the ideas they produce in the mind enter by the senses simple and unmixed. For though the sight and touch often take in from the same object, at the same time, different ideas; as a man sees at once motion and color; the hand feels softness and warmth in the same piece of wax; yet the simple ideas, thus united in the same subject, are as perfectly distinct as those that come in by different senses: The coldness and hardness which a man feels in a piece of ice being as distinct ideas in the mind, as the smell and whiteness of a lily; or as the taste of sugar, and smell of a rose. And there is nothing can be plainer to a man, than the clear and distinct perception he has of those simple ideas; which, being each in itself uncompounded, contains in it nothing but one uniform appearance, or conception in the mind, and is not distinguishable into different ideas.

2. The mind can neither make nor destroy them. These simple ideas, the materials of all our knowledge, are suggested and furnished to the mind only by those two ways above-mentioned, viz. sensation and reflection. When the understanding is once stored with these simple ideas, it has the power to repeat, compare, and unite them, even to an almost infinite variety, and so can make at pleasure new complex ideas. But it is not in the power of the most exalted wit, or enlarged understanding, by any quickness or variety of thought, to invent or frame one new simple idea in the mind, not taken in by the ways before mentioned: Nor can any force of the understanding destroy those that are there. The dominion of man, in this little world of his own understanding, being much-what the same as it is in the great world of visible things; wherein his power, however managed by art and skill, reaches no farther than to compound and divide the materials that are made to his hand; but can do nothing towards making the least particle of new matter, or destroying one atom of what is already in being. The same inability will every one find in himself, who shall go about to fashion in his understanding any simple idea, not received in by his senses from external objects, or by reflection from the operations of his own mind about them. I would have any one try to fancy any taste, which had never affected his palate; or frame the idea of a scent he had never smelt: And when he can do this, I will also conclude that a blind man hath ideas of colors, and a deaf man true distinct notions of sounds.

3. Only the qualities that affect the sense are imaginable. This is the reason why, though we cannot believe it impossible to God to make a creature with other organs, and more ways to convey into the understanding the notice of corporeal things than those five, as they are usually counted, which he has given to man: Yet I think, it is not possible for any one to imagine any other qualities in bodies, howsoever constituted, whereby they can be taken notice of, besides sounds, tastes, smells, visible and tangible qualities. And had mankind been made but with four senses, the qualities then, which are the objects of the fifth sense, had been as far from our notice, imagination, and conception, as now any belonging to a sixth, seventh, or eighth sense, can possibly be: Which, whether yet some other creatures, in some other parts of this vast and stupendous universe, may not have, will be a great presumption to deny. He that will not set himself proudly at the top of all things, but will consider the immensity of this fabric, and the great variety that is to be found in this little and inconsiderable part of it which he has to do with, may be apt to think, that in other mansions of it there may be other and different intelligent beings, of whose faculties he has as little knowledge or apprehension, as a worm shut up in one drawer of a cabinet hath of the senses or understanding of a man: Such variety and excellency being suitable to the wisdom and power of the maker. I have here

followed the common opinion of man's having but five senses; though, perhaps, there may be justly counted more: But either supposition serves equally to my present purpose.

CHAPTER 3. OF IDEAS OF ONE SENSE

1. Division of simple ideas. The better to conceive the ideas we receive from sensation, it may not be amiss for us to consider them, in reference to the different ways whereby they make their approaches to our minds, and make themselves perceivable by us.

First, Then, there are some which come into our minds by one sense only.

Secondly, there are others that convey themselves into the mind by more senses than one.

Thirdly, Others that are had from reflection only.

Fourthly, There are some that make themselves way, and are suggested to the mind by all the ways of sensation and reflection.

We shall consider them apart under these several heads.

First, There are some ideas which have admittance only through one sense, which is peculiarly adapted to receive them. Thus light and colours, as white, red, yellow, blue, with their several degrees or shades and mixtures, as green, scarlet, purple, seagreen, and the rest, come in only by the eyes: All kinds of noises, sounds, and tones, only by the ears: The several tastes and smells, by the nose and palate. And if these organs, or the nerves, which are the conduits to convey them from without to their audience in the brain, the mind's presence-room (as I may so call it) are any of them so disordered, as not to perform their functions, they have no postern to be admitted by; no other way to bring themselves into view, and be perceived by the understanding.

The most considerable of those belonging to the touch are heat and cold, and solidity: All the rest, consisting almost wholly in the sensible configuration, as smooth and rough, or else more or less firm adhesion of the parts, as hard and soft, tough and brittle, are obvious enough.

2. Few simple ideas have names. I think, it will be needless to enumerate all the particular simple ideas, belonging to each sense. Nor indeed is it possible, if we would; there being a great many more of them belonging to most of the senses, than we have names for. The variety of smells, which are as many almost, if not more, than species of bodies in the world, do most of them want names. Sweet and stinking commonly serve our turn for these ideas, which in effect is little more than to call them pleasing or displeasing; though the smell of a rose and violet, both sweet, are certainly very distinct ideas. Nor are the different tastes, that by our palates we receive ideas of, much better provided with names. Sweet, bitter, sour, harsh, and salt, are almost all the epithets we have to denominate that numberless variety of relishes, which are to be found distinct, not only in almost every sort of creatures, but all the different parts of the same plant, fruit, or animal. The same may be said of colours and sounds. I shall therefore, in the account of simple ideas I am here giving, content myself to set down only such, as are most material to our present purpose, or are in themselves less apt to be taken notice of, though they are very frequently the ingredients of our complex ideas, amongst which, I think, I may well account solidity; which therefore I shall treat of in the next chapter.

CHAPTER 4. OF SOLIDITY

1. We receive this idea from touch. The idea of solidity we receive by our touch: And it arises from the resistance which we find in body, to the entrance of any other body into the place it possesses, till it has left it. There is no idea which we receive more constantly from sensation, than solidity. Whether we move or rest, in what posture soever we are, we always feel some thing under us that supports us, and hinders our farther sinking downwards; and the bodies which we daily handle make us perceive, that, whilst they remain between them, they do by an insurmountable force hinder the approach of the parts of our hands that press them. That which thus hinders the approach of two bodies, when they are moved one towards another, I call solidity. I will not dispute, whether this acceptation of the word solid be nearer to its original signification, than that which mathematicians use it in: It suffices, that I think the common notion of solidity will allow, if not justify, this use of it; but, if any one think it better

to call it impenetrability, he has my consent. Only I have thought the term solidity the more proper to express this idea, not only because of its vulgar use in that sense, but also because it carries some thing more of positive in it than impenetrability, which is negative, and is perhaps more a consequence of solidity, than solidity itself. This, of all other, seems the idea most intimately connected with and essential to body, so as no-where else to be found or imagined, but only in matter. And though our senses take no notice of it, but in masses of matter, of a bulk sufficient to cause a sensation in us; yet the mind, having once got this idea from such grosser sensible bodies, traces it farther; and considers it, as well as figure, in the minutest particle of matter that can exist: And finds it inseparably inherent in body, wherever or however modified.

2. Solidity fills space. This is the idea which belongs to body, whereby we conceive it to fill space. The idea of which filling of space is, that, where we imagine any space taken up by a solid substance, we conceive it so to possess it, that it excludes all other solid substances; and will for ever hinder any other two bodies, that move towards one another in a straight line, from coming to touch one another, unless it removes from between them, in a line not parallel to that which they move in. This idea of it the bodies which we ordinarily handle sufficiently furnish us with.

6. What it is. If any one asks me, what this solidity is, I send him to his senses to inform him: Let him put a flint or a foot-ball between his hands, and then endeavor to join them, and he will know. If he thinks this not a sufficient explication of solidity, what it is, and wherein it consists; I promise to tell him what it is, and wherein it consists, when he tells me what thinking is, or wherein it consists; or explains to me what extension or motion is, which perhaps seems much easier. The simple ideas we have are such as experience teaches them us, but if, beyond that, we endeavor by words to make them clearer in the mind, we shall succeed no better, than if we went about to clear up the darkness of a blind man's mind by talking; and to discourse into him the ideas of light and colours. The reason of this I shall shew in another place.

CHAPTER 5. OF SIMPLE IDEAS OF DIVERS SENSES

The ideas we get by more than one sense are of space, or extension, figure, rest, and motion; for these make perceivable impressions, both on the eyes and touch: And we can receive and convey into our minds the ideas of the extension, figure, motion, and rest of bodies, both by seeing and feeling. But having occasion to speak more at large of these in another place, I here only enumerate them.

CHAPTER 6. OF SIMPLE IDEAS OF REFLECTION

1. Simple ideas are operations of the mind about its other ideas. The mind, receiving the ideas, mentioned in the foregoing chapters, from without, when it turns its view inward upon itself, and observes its own actions about those ideas it has, takes from thence other ideas, which are as capable to be the objects of its contemplation as any of those it received from foreign things.

2. The idea of perception, and the idea of willing, we have from reflection. The two great and principal actions of the mind, which are most frequently considered, and which are so frequent, that every one that pleases may take notice of them in himself, are these two: Perception or Thinking; and Volition, or Willing. The power of thinking is called the understanding, and the power of volition is called the will; and these two powers or abilities in the mind are denominated faculties. Of some of the modes of these simple ideas of reflection, such as are Remembrance, Discerning, Reasoning, Judging, Knowledge, Faith, &c. I shall have occasion to speak hereafter.

CHAPTER 7. OF SIMPLE IDEAS OF BOTH SENSATION AND REFLECTION

1. Ideas of pleasure and pain. There be other simple ideas which convey themselves into the mind by all the ways of sensation and reflection, viz. Pleasure or Delight, and its opposite, Pain or Uneasiness; Power; Existence; Unity.

2. Mix with almost all our other ideas. Delight or uneasiness, one or other of them, join themselves to almost all our ideas, both of sensation and reflection: And there is scarce any affection of our senses from without, any retired thought of our mind within, which is not able to produce in us pleasure or pain. By pleasure and pain I would be understood to signify whatsoever delights or molests us; whether it arises from the thoughts of our minds, or any thing operating on our bodies. For whether we call it satisfaction, delight, pleasure, happiness, &c. on the one side; or uneasiness, trouble, pain, torment, anguish, misery, &c. on the other; they are still but different degrees of the same thing, and belong to the ideas of pleasure and pain, delight or uneasiness; which are the names I shall most commonly use for those two sorts of ideas.

7. Existence and unity. Existence and unity are two other ideas that are suggested to the understanding by every object without, and every idea within. When ideas are in our minds, we consider them as being actually there, as well as we consider things to be actually without us; which is, that they exist, or have existence: And whatever we can consider as one thing, whether a real being or idea, suggests to the understanding the idea of unity.

8. Power. Power also is another of those simple ideas which we receive from sensation and reflection. For observing in ourselves, that we can at pleasure move several parts of our bodies which were at rest; the effects also, that natural bodies are able to produce in one another, occurring every moment to our senses, we both these ways get the idea of power.

9. Succession. Besides these there is another idea, which, though suggested by our senses, yet is more constantly offered to us by what passes in our minds; and that is the idea of succession. For if we look immediately into ourselves, and reflect on what is observable there, we shall find our ideas always, whilst we are awake, or have any thought, passing in train, one going and another coming, without intermission.

10. Simple ideas the materials of all our knowledge. These, if they are not all, are at least (as I think) the most considerable of those simple ideas which the mind has, and out of which is made all its other knowledge: All which it receives only by the two forementioned ways of sensation and reflection.

Nor let any one think these too narrow bounds for the capacious mind of man to expatiate in, which takes its flight farther than the stars, and cannot be confined by the limits of the world; that extends its thoughts often even beyond the utmost expansion of matter, and makes excursions into that incomprehensible inane. I grant all this, but desire any one to assign any simple idea which is not received from one of those inlets before-mentioned, or any complex idea not made out of those simple ones. Nor will it be so strange to think these few simple ideas sufficient to employ the quickest thought, or largest capacity; and to furnish the materials of all that various knowledge, and more various fancies and opinions of all mankind, if we consider how many words may be made out of the various composition of twenty-four letters; or if, going one step farther, we will but reflect on the variety of combinations may be made, with barely one of the above-mentioned ideas, viz. number, whose stock is inexhaustible and truly infinite; and what a large and immense field doth extension alone afford the mathematicians?

CHAPTER 8. SOME FARTHER CONSIDERATIONS CONCERNING OUR SIMPLE IDEAS

1. Positive ideas from privative causes. Concerning the simple ideas of sensation it is to be considered that whatsoever is so constituted in nature as to be able, by affecting our senses, to cause any perception in the mind, doth thereby produce in the understanding a simple idea; which, whatever be the external cause of it, when it comes to be taken notice of by our discerning faculty, it is by the mind looked on and considered there to be a real positive idea in the understanding, as much as any other whatsoever; though perhaps the cause of it be but a privation of the subject.

2. Ideas in the mind distinguished from that in things which gives rise to them. Thus the ideas of heat and cold, light and darkness, white and black, motion and rest, are equally clear and positive ideas in the mind; though perhaps some of the causes which produce them are barely privations in subjects, from whence our senses derive those ideas. These the understanding, in its view of them, considers all as distinct positive ideas, without taking notice of the causes that produce them: Which is an enquiry not belonging to the idea, as it is in the understanding, but to the nature of the things existing without us. These are two very different things, and carefully to be distinguished; it being one thing to perceive and know the idea of white or black, and quite another to examine what kind of particles they must be, and how ranged in the superficies, to make any object appear white or black.

3. We may have ideas when we are ignorant of their physical causes. A painter or dyer, who never enquired into their causes, hath the ideas of white and black, and other colors, as clearly, perfectly, and distinctly in his understanding, and perhaps more distinctly, than the philosopher, who hath busied himself in considering their natures, and thinks he knows how far either of them is in its cause positive or privative; and the idea of black is no less positive in his mind, than that of white, however the cause of that color in the external object may be only a privation.

4. Why a privative cause in nature may occasion a positive idea. If it were the design of my present undertaking to enquire into the natural causes and manner of perception, I should offer this as a reason why a privative cause might, in some cases at least, produce a positive idea, viz. that all sensation being produced in us only by different degrees and modes of motion in our animal spirits, variously agitated by external objects, the abatement of any former motion must as necessarily produce a new sensation, as the variation or increase of it; and so introduce a new idea, which depends only on a different motion of the animal spirits in that organ.

5. Negative names need not be meaningless. But whether this be so or no, I will not here determine, but appeal to every one's own experience, whether the shadow of a man, though it consists of nothing but the absence of light (and the more the absence of light is, the more discernible is the shadow) does not, when a man looks on it, cause as clear and positive idea in his mind, as a man himself, though covered over with clear sunshine? and the picture of a shadow is a positive thing. Indeed we have negative names, which stand not directly for positive ideas, but for their absence, such as insipid, silence, nihil, &c. which words denote positive ideas, v.g. taste, sound, being, with a signification of their absence.

6. Whether any ideas are due to causes really privative. And thus one may truly be said to see darkness. For supposing a hole perfectly dark, from whence no light is reflected, it is certain one may see the figure of it, or it may be painted: Or whether the ink I write with makes any other idea, is a question. The privative causes I have here assigned of positive ideas are according to the common opinion; but in truth it will be hard to determine, whether there be really any ideas from a privative cause, till it be determined, whether rest be any more a privation than motion.

7. Ideas in the mind, qualities of bodies. To discover the nature of our ideas the better, and to discourse of them intelligibly, it will be convenient to distinguish them as they are ideas or perceptions in our minds, and as they are modifications of matter in the bodies that cause such perceptions in us: That so we may not think (as perhaps usually is done) that they are exactly the images and resemblances of some thing inherent in the subject; most of those of sensation being in the mind no more the likeness of some thing existing without us, than the names that stand for them are the likeness of our ideas, which yet upon hearing they are apt to excite in us.

8. Our ideas and the qualities of bodies. Whatsoever the mind perceives in itself, or is the immediate object of perception, thought, or understanding, that I call idea; and the power to produce any idea in our mind I call a quality of the subject wherein that power is. Thus a snow-ball having the power to produce in us the ideas of white, cold, and round, the power to produce those ideas in us, as they are in the snow-ball, I call qualities; and as they are sensations or perceptions in our understandings, I call them ideas; which ideas, if I speak of sometimes, as in the things themselves, I would be understood to mean those qualities in the objects which produce them in us.

9. Primary qualities of bodies. Qualities thus considered in bodies are, first, such as are utterly inseparable from the body, in what state soever it be; such as in all the alterations and changes it suffers, all the force can be used upon it, it constantly keeps; and such as sense constantly finds in every particle of matter which has bulk enough to be perceived, and the mind finds inseparable from every particle of matter, though less than to make itself singly be perceived by our senses, v.g. Take a grain of wheat, divide it into two parts, each part has still solidity, extension, figure, and mobility; divide it again, and it retains still the same qualities; and so divide it on till the parts become insensible, they must retain still each of them all those qualities. For division (which is all that a mill, or pestle, or any other body does upon another, in reducing it to insensible parts) can never take away either solidity, extension, figure, or mobility from any body, but only makes two or more distinct separate masses of matter, of that which was but one before: All which distinct masses, reckoned as so many distinct bodies, after division make a certain number. These I call original or primary qualities of body, which I think we may observe to produce simple ideas in us, viz. solidity, extension, figure, motion or rest, and number.

10. Secondary qualities of bodies. Secondly, such qualities which in truth are nothing in the objects themselves, but powers to produce various sensations in us by their primary qualities, i.e. by the bulk, figure, texture, and motion of their insensible parts, as colors, sounds, tastes, &c. these I call secondary qualities. To these might be added a third sort, which are allowed to be barely powers, though they are as much real qualities in the subject, as those which I, to comply with the common way of speaking, call qualities, but for distinction, secondary qualities. For the power in fire to produce a new color, or consistency, in wax or clay, by its primary qualities, is as much a quality in fire, as the power it has to produce in me a new idea or sensation of warmth or burning, which I felt not before by the same primary qualities, viz. the bulk, texture, and motion of its insensible parts.

11. How primary qualities produce their ideas. The next thing to be considered is, how bodies produce ideas in us; and that is manifestly by impulse, the only way which we can conceive bodies to operate in.

12. By motions both external and in us. If then external objects be not united to our minds, when they produce ideas therein, and yet we perceive these original qualities in such of them as singly fall under our senses, it is evident that some motion must be thence continued by our nerves, or animal spirits, by some parts of our bodies, to the brains or the seat of sensation, there to produce in our minds the particular ideas we have of them. And since the extension, figure, number, and motion of bodies, of an observable bigness, may be perceived at a distance by the sight, it is evident some singly imperceptible bodies must come from them to the eyes, and thereby convey to the brain some motion, which produces these ideas which we have of them in us.

13. How secondary. After the same manner that the ideas of these original qualities are produced in us, we may conceive that the ideas of secondary qualities are also produced, viz. by the operation of insensible particles on our senses. For it being manifest that there are bodies and good store of bodies, each whereof are so small, that we cannot, by any of our senses, discover either their bulk, figure, or motion as is evident in the particles of the air and water, and others extremely smaller than those, perhaps as much smaller than the particles of air and water, as the particles of air and water are smaller than peas or hail-stones: Let us suppose at present, that the different motions and figures, bulk and number of such particles, affecting the several organs of our senses, produce in us those different sensations, which we have from the colors and smells of bodies; v.g. that a violet, by the impulse of such insensible particles of matter of peculiar figures and bulks, and in different degrees and modifications of their motions, causes the ideas of the blue color and sweet scent of that flower, to be produced in our minds; it being no more impossible to conceive that God should annex such ideas to such motions, with which they have no similitude, than that he should annex the idea of pain to the motion of a piece of steel dividing our flesh, with which that idea hath no resemblance.

14. They depend on the primary qualities. What I have said concerning colors and smells may be understood also of tastes and sounds, and other the like sensible qualities; which, whatever reality we by mistake attribute to them, are in truth nothing in the objects themselves, but powers to produce various sensations in us, and depend on those primary qualities, viz. bulk, figure, texture, and motion of parts; as I have said.

15. Ideas of primary qualities are resemblances; of secondary, not. From whence I think it easy to draw this observation, that the ideas of primary qualities of bodies are resemblances of them, and their patterns do really exist in the bodies themselves; but the ideas, produced in us by these secondary qualities, have no resemblance of them at all. There is nothing like our ideas existing in the bodies themselves. They are in the bodies, we denominate from them, only a power to produce those sensations in us: And what is sweet, blue, or warm in idea, is but the certain bulk, figure, and motion of the insensible parts in the bodies themselves, which we call so.

16. Examples. Flame is denominated hot and light; snow, white and cold; and manna, white and sweet, from the ideas they produce in us: Which qualities are commonly thought to be the same in those bodies that those ideas are in us, the one the perfect resemblance of the other, as they are in a mirror; and it would by most men be judged very extravagant, if one should say otherwise. And yet he that will consider that the same fire, that at one distance produces in us the sensation of warmth, does at a nearer approach produce in us the far different sensation of pain, ought to bethink himself what reason he has to say, that his idea of warmth, which was produced in him by the fire, is actually in the fire; and his idea of pain, which the same fire produced in him the same way, is not in the fire. Why are whiteness and coldness in snow, and pain not, when it produces the one and the other idea in us; and can do neither, but by the bulk, figure, number, and motion of its solid parts?

17. The idea of the primary alone really exist. The particular bulk, number, figure, and motion of the parts of fire or snow are really in them, whether any one's senses perceive them or no: And therefore they may be called real qualities, because they really exist in those bodies: But light, heat, whiteness or coldness, are no more really in them, than sickness or pain is in manna. Take away the sensation of them; let not the eyes see light, or colors, nor the ears hear sounds; let the palate not taste, nor the nose smell; and all colors, tastes, odors, and sounds, as they are such particular ideas, vanish and cease, and are reduced to their causes, i.e. bulk, figure, and motion of parts.

18. Secondary exist only as modes of the primary.   A piece of manna of a sensible bulk is able to produce in us the idea of a round or square figure, and, by being removed from one place to another, the idea of motion. This idea of motion represents it as it really is in the manna moving: A circle or square are the same, whether in idea or existence, in the mind, or in the manna; and this both motion and figure are really in the manna, whether we take notice of them or no: This every body is ready to agree to. Besides, manna, by the bulk, figure, texture, and motion of its parts, has a power to produce the sensations of sickness, and sometimes of acute pains or gripings in us. That these ideas of sickness and pain are not in the manna, but effects of its operations on us, and are nowhere when we feel them not; this also every one readily agrees to. And yet men are hardly to be brought to think, that sweetness and whiteness are not really in manna; which are but the effects of the operations of manna by the motion, size, and figure of its particles on the eyes and palate; as the pain and sickness caused by manna are confessedly nothing but the effects of its operations on the stomach and guts, by the size, motion, and figure of its insensible parts (for by nothing else can a body operate, as has been proved): As if it could not operate on the eyes and palate, and thereby produce in the mind particular distinct ideas, which in itself it has not, as well as we allow it can operate on the guts and stomach, and thereby produce distinct ideas, which in itself it has not. These ideas, being all effects of the operations of manna, on several parts of our bodies, by the size, figure, number, and motion of its parts: Why those produced by the eyes and palate should rather be thought to be really in the manna, than those produced by the stomach and guts; or why the pain and sickness, ideas that are the effect of manna, should be thought to be no-where when they are not felt; and yet the sweetness and whiteness, effects of the same manna on other parts

of the body, by ways equally as unknown, should be thought to exist in the manna, when they are not seen or tasted, would need some reason to explain.

19. Examples.   Let us consider the red and white colors in porphyry: Hinder light from striking on it, and its colors vanish, it no longer produces any such ideas in us; upon the return of light, it produces these appearances on us again. Can any one think any real alterations are made in the porphyry, by the presence or absence of light; and that those ideas of whiteness and redness are really in porphyry in the light, when it is plain it has no color in the dark? It has, indeed, such a configuration of particles, both night and day, as are apt, by the rays of light rebounding from some parts of that hard stone, to produce in us the idea of redness, and from others the idea of whiteness; but whiteness or redness are not in it at any time, but such a texture, that hath the power to produce such a sensation in us. . . .

23. Three sorts of qualities in bodies.   The qualities then that are in bodies rightly considered, are of three sorts.

First, the bulk, figure, number, situation, and motion, or rest of their solid parts; those are in them, whether we perceive them or no; and when they are of that size, that we can discover them, we have by these an idea of the thing as it is in itself, as is plain in artificial things. These I call primary qualities.

Secondly, The power that is in any body, by reason of its insensible primary qualities, to operate after a peculiar manner on any of our senses, and thereby produce in us the different ideas of several colors, sounds, smells, tastes, &c. These are usually called sensible qualities.

Thirdly, the power that is in any body, by reason of the particular constitution of its primary qualities, to make such a change in the bulk, figure, texture, and motion of another body, as to make it operate on our senses differently from what it did before. Thus the sun has a power to make wax white, and fire to make lead fluid. These are usually called powers.

The first of these, as has been said, I think, may be properly called real, original, or primary qualities, because they are in the things themselves, whether they are perceived or no: And upon their different modifications it is, that the secondary qualities depend.

The other two are only powers to act differently upon other things, which powers result from the different modifications of those primary qualities.

24. The first are resemblances; the second thought resemblances, but are not; the third neither are, nor are thought so. But though the two latter sorts of qualities are powers barely, and nothing but powers, relating to several other bodies, and resulting from the different modifications of the original qualities; yet they are generally otherwise thought of. For the second sort, viz. the powers to produce several ideas in us by our senses, are looked upon as real qualities, in the things thus affecting us: But the third sort are called and esteemed barely powers, v.g. the idea of heat, or light, which we receive by our eyes or touch from the sun, are commonly thought real qualities, existing in the sun, and some thing more than mere powers in it. But when we consider the sun, in reference to wax, which it melts or blanches, we look on the whiteness and softness produced in the wax, not as qualities in the sun, but effects produced by powers in it: Whereas, if rightly considered, these qualities of light and warmth, which are perceptions in me when I am warmed, or enlightened by the sun, are no otherwise in the sun, than the changes made in the wax, when it is blanched or melted, are in the sun. They are all of them equally powers in the sun, depending on its primary qualities; whereby it is able, in the one case, so to alter the bulk, figure, texture, or motion of some of the insensible parts of my eyes or hands, as thereby to produce in me the idea of light or heat; and in the other it is able so to alter the bulk, figure, texture, or motion of the insensible parts of the wax, as to make them fit to produce in me the distinct ideas of white and fluid.

25. Why the secondary are ordinarily taken for real qualities, and not for bare powers. The reason why the one are ordinarily taken for real qualities, and the other only for bare powers, seems to be, because the ideas we have of distinct colors, sounds, &c. containing nothing at all in them of bulk, figure, or motion, we are not apt to think them the effects of these primary qualities, which appear not, to our senses, to operate in their production; and with which they have not any apparent congruity, or conceivable connexion. Hence it is that we are so forward to imagine, that those ideas are the resemblances of some thing really existing in the objects themselves: Since sensation discovers nothing of bulk, figure, or motion of parts in their production; nor can reason shew how bodies, by their bulk, figure, and motion, should produce in the mind the ideas of blue or yellow, &c. But in the other case, in the operations of bodies changing the qualities one of another, we plainly discover, that the quality produced hath commonly no resemblance with any thing in the thing producing it; wherefore we look on it as a bare effect of power. For though receiving the idea of heat, or light, from the sun, we are apt to think it is a perception and resemblance of such a quality in the sun; yet when we see wax, or a fair face, receive change of color from the sun, we cannot imagine that to be the reception or resemblance of any thing in the sun, because we find not those different colors in the sun itself. For our senses being able to observe a likeness or unlikeness of sensible qualities in two different external objects, we forwardly enough conclude the production of any sensible quality, in any subject to be an effect of bare power, and not the communication of any quality, which was really in the efficient, when we find no such sensible quality in the thing that produced it. But our senses not being able to discover any unlikeness between the idea produced in us, and the quality of the object producing it; we are apt to imagine, that our ideas are resemblances of something, in the objects, and not the effects of certain powers placed in the modification of their primary qualities, with which primary qualities the ideas produced in us have no resemblance.

26. Secondary qualities two fold; first, immediately perceivable; secondly, mediately perceivable. To conclude, beside those before mentioned primary qualities in bodies, viz. bulk, figure, extension, number, and motion of their solid parts; all the rest whereby we take notice of bodies, and distinguish them one from another, are nothing else but several powers in them depending on those primary qualities; whereby they are fitted, either by immediately operating on our bodies to produce several different ideas, or else, by operating on other bodies, so to change their primary qualities, as to render them capable of producing ideas in us, different from what before they did. The former of these, I think, may be called secondary qualities, immediately perceivable: The latter, secondary qualities, mediately perceivable.

CHAPTER 9. OF PERCEPTION

1. It is the first simple idea of reflection. Perception, as it is the first faculty of the mind exercised about our ideas; so it is the first and simplest idea we have from reflection, and is by some called thinking in general. Though thinking, in the propriety of the English tongue, signifies that sort of operation in the mind about its ideas, wherein the mind is active; where it, with some degree of voluntary attention, considers any thing. For in bare naked perception, the mind is, for the most part, only passive: And what it perceives, it cannot avoid perceiving.

2. Perception is only when the mind receives the impression. What perception is, every one will know better by reflecting on what he does himself, when he sees, hears, feels, &c. or thinks, than by any discourse of mine. Whoever reflects on what passes in his own mind, cannot miss it: And if he does not reflect, all the words in the world cannot make him have any notion of it.

3. This is certain, that whatever alterations are made in the body, if they reach not the mind; whatever impressions are made on the outward parts, if they are not taken notice of within; there is no perception. Fire may burn our bodies, with no other effect, than it does a billet, unless the motion be continued to the brain, and there the sense of heat, or idea of pain, be produced in the mind, wherein consists actual perception.

4. How often may a man observe in himself, that whilst his mind is intently employed in the contemplation of some objects, and curiously surveying some ideas that are there, it takes no notice of impressions of sounding bodies made upon the organ of hearing, with the same alteration that uses to be for the producing the idea of sound? A sufficient impulse there may be on the organ; but it not reaching the observation of the mind, there follows no

perception: And though the motion that uses to produce the idea of sound be made in the ear, yet no sound is heard. Want of sensation, in this case, is not through any defect in the organ, or that the man's ears are less affected than at other times when he does hear; but that which uses to produce the idea, though conveyed in by the usual organ, not being taken notice of in the understanding, and so imprinting no idea in the mind, there follows no sensation. So that wherever there is sense, or perception, there some idea is actually produced, and present in the understanding.

5. Children, though they have ideas in the womb, have none innate. Therefore I doubt not but children, by the exercise of their senses about objects that affect them in the womb, receive some few ideas before they are born; as the unavoidable effects, either of the bodies that environ them, or else of those wants or diseases they suffer: Amongst which (if one may conjecture concerning things not very capable of examination) I think the ideas of hunger and warmth are two; which probably are some of the first that children have, and which they scarce ever part with again.

6. But though it be reasonable to imagine that children receive some ideas before they come into the world, yet these simple ideas are far from those innate principles which some contend for, and we above have rejected. These here mentioned being the effects of sensation, are only from some affections of the body, which happen to them there, and so depend on some thing exterior to the mind: No otherwise differing in their manner of production from other ideas derived from sense, but only in the precedency of time; whereas those innate principles are supposed to be quite of another nature; not coming into the mind by any accidental alterations in, or operations on the body; but, as it were, original characters impressed upon it, in the very first moment of its being and constitution.

7. Which ideas first, is not evident. As there are some ideas which we may reasonably suppose may be introduced into the minds of children in the womb, subservient to the necessities of their life and being there; so after they are born, those ideas are the earliest imprinted which happen to be the sensible qualities which first occur to them: Amongst which, light is not the least considerable, nor of the weakest efficacy. And how covetous the mind is to be furnished with all such ideas as have no pain accompanying them, may be a little guessed, by what is observable in children new-born, who always turn their eyes to that part from whence the light comes, lay them how you please. But the ideas that are most familiar at first being various, according to the divers circumstances of children's first entertainment in the world; the order wherein the several ideas come at first into the mind is very various and uncertain also; neither is it much material to know it.

8. Ideas of sensation often changed by the judgment. We are further to consider concerning perception, that the ideas we receive by sensation are often in grown people altered by the judgment, without our taking notice of it. When we set before our eyes a round globe, of any uniform color, v.g. gold, alabaster, or jet; it is certain that the idea thereby imprinted in our mind, is of a flat circle variously shadowed, with several degrees of light and brightness coming to our eyes. But we having by use been accustomed to perceive what kind of appearance convex bodies are wont to make in us, what alterations are made in the reflections of light by the difference of the sensible figures of bodies; the judgment presently, by an habitual custom, alters the appearances into their causes; so that from that which is truly variety of shadow or color, collecting the figure, it makes it pass for a mark of figure, and frames to itself the perception of a convex figure and an uniform color; when the idea we receive from thence is only a plane variously colored, as is evident in painting. To which purpose I shall here insert a problem of that very ingenious and studious promoter of real knowledge, the learned and worthy Mr. Molineaux, which he was pleased to send me in a letter some months since; and it is this: Suppose a man born blind, and now adult, and taught by his touch to distinguish between a cube and a sphere of the same metal, and nighly of the same bigness, so as to tell, when he felt one and the other, which is the cube, which the sphere. Suppose then the cube and sphere placed on a table, and the blind man be made to see: Quaere, "whether by his sight, before he touched them, he could now distinguish and tell, which is the globe, which the cube?" to which the acute and judicious proposer answers: Not. For though he has obtained the experience of how a globe, how a cube affects his touch; yet he has not yet obtained the experience, that what affects his touch so or so, must affect his sight so or so: Or that a protuberant angle in the cube, that pressed his hand unequally, shall appear to his eye as it does in the cube. I agree with this thinking gentleman, whom I am proud to call my friend, in his answer to this problem; and am of opinion, that the blind man at first sight, would not be able with certainty to say which was the globe, which the cube, whilst he only saw them: Though he could unerringly name them by his touch, and certainly distinguish them by the difference of their figures felt. This I have set down, and leave with my reader, as an occasion for him to consider how much he may be beholden to experience, improvement, and acquired notions, where he thinks he had not the least use of, or help from them: And the rather, because this observing gentleman further adds, that having, upon the occasion of my book, proposed this to divers very ingenious men, he hardly ever met with one, that at first gave the answer to it which he thinks true, till by hearing his reasons they were convinced.

9. But this is not, I think, usual in any of our ideas, but those received by sight: Because sight, the most comprehensive of all our senses, conveying to our minds the ideas of light and colors, which are peculiar only to that sense; and also the far different ideas of space, figure, and motion, the several varieties whereof change the appearances of its proper object, viz. light and colors; we bring ourselves by use to judge of the one by the other. This, in many cases, by a settled habit, in things whereof we have frequent experience, is performed so constantly and so quick, that we take that for the perception of our sensation, which is an idea formed by our judgment; so that one, viz. that of sensation, serves only to excite the other, and is scarce taken notice of itself: As a man who reads or hears with attention and understanding, takes little notice of the characters, or sounds, but of the ideas that are excited in him by them.

10. Nor need we wonder that this is done with so little notice, if we consider how quick the actions of the mind are performed: For as itself is thought to take up no space, to have no extension; so its actions seem to require no time, but many of them seem to be crowded into an instant. I speak this in comparison to the actions of the body. Any one may easily observe this in his own thoughts, who will take the pains to reflect on them. How, as it were in an instant, do our minds with one glance see all the parts of a demonstration, which may very well be called a long one, if we consider the time it will require to put it into words, and step by step shew it another? Secondly, we shall not be so much surprised, that this is done in us with so little notice, if we consider how the facility which we get of doing things, by a custom of doing, makes them often pass in us without our notice. Habits, especially such as are begun very early, come at last to produce actions in us, which often escape our observation. How frequently do we, in a day, cover our eyes with our eye-lids, without perceiving that we are at all in the dark? Men that by custom have got the use of a by-word, do almost in every sentence pronounce sounds which, though taken notice of by others, they themselves neither hear nor observe. And therefore it is not so strange, that our mind should often change the idea of its sensation into that of its judgment, and make one serve only to excite the other without our taking notice of it.

11. Perception puts the difference between animals and inferior beings. This faculty of perception seems to me to be that, which puts the distinction betwixt the animal kingdom and the inferior parts of nature. For however vegetables have, many of them, some degrees of motion, and upon the different application of other bodies to them, do very briskly alter their figures and motions, and so have obtained the name of sensitive plants, from a motion which has some resemblance to that which in animals follows upon sensation: Yet, I suppose, it is all bare mechanism; and not otherwise produced, than the turning of a wild oat-beard, by the insinuation of the particles of moisture, or the shortening of a rope, by the affusion of water. All which is done without any sensation in the subject, or the having or receiving any ideas.

12. Perception, I believe, is in some degree in all sorts of animals; though in some, possibly, the avenues provided by nature for the reception of sensations are so few, and the perception they are received with so obscure and dull, that it comes extremely short of the quickness and variety of sensation which is in other animals; but yet it is sufficient for, and wisely adapted to, the state and condition of that sort of animals who are thus made. So that the wisdom and goodness of the Maker plainly appear in all the parts of this stupendous fabric, and all the several degrees and ranks of creatures in it.

13. We may, I think, from the make of an oyster, or cockle, reasonably conclude that it has not so many, nor so quick senses, as a man, or several other animals; nor if it had, would it, in that state and incapacity of transferring itself from one place to another, be bettered by them. What good would sight and hearing do to a creature, that cannot move itself to, or from the objects wherein at a distance it perceives good or evil? And would not quickness of sensation be an inconvenience to an animal that must lie still, where chance has once placed it; and there receive the afflux of colder or warmer, clear or foul water, as it happens to come to it?

14. But yet I cannot but think there is some small dull perception, whereby they are distinguished from perfect insensibility. And that this may be so, we have plain instances even in mankind itself. Take one, in whom decrepit old age has blotted out the memory of his past knowledge, and clearly wiped out the ideas his mind was formerly stored with; and has, by destroying his sight, hearing, and smell quite, and his taste to a great degree, stopped up almost all the passages for new ones to enter; or if there be some of the inlets yet half open, the impressions made are scarce perceived, or not at all retained. How far such an one (notwithstanding all that is boasted of innate principles) is in his knowledge, and intellectual faculties, above the condition of a cockle or an oyster, I leave to be considered. And if a man had passed sixty years in such a state, as it is possible he might, as well as three days; I wonder what difference there would have been, in any intellectual perfections, between him and the lowest degree of animals.

15. Perception the inlet of knowledge. Perception then being the first step and degree towards knowledge, and the inlet of all the materials of it; the fewer senses any man, as well as any other creature, hath, and the fewer and duller the impressions are that are made by them, and the duller the faculties are that are employed about them; the more remote are they from that knowledge, which is to be found in some men. But this being in great variety of degrees (as may be perceived amongst men) cannot certainly be discovered in the several species of animals, much less in their particular individuals. It suffices me only to have remarked here, that perception is the first operation of all our intellectual faculties, and the inlet of all knowledge in our minds. And I am apt too to imagine, that it is perception in the lowest degree of it, which puts the boundaries between animals and the inferior ranks of creatures. But this I mention only as my conjecture by the by; it being indifferent to the matter in hand, which way the learned shall determine of it.

CHAPTER 23. OF OUR COMPLEX IDEAS OF SUBSTANCES

1. Ideas *of substances how made*. The mind being, as I have declared, furnished with a great number of the simple *ideas*, conveyed in by the *senses*, as they are found in exterior things, or by *reflection* on its own operations, takes notice also, that a certain number of these simple *ideas* go constantly together; which being presumed to belong to one thing, and words being suited to common apprehensions, and made use of for quick dispatch, are called so united in one subject, by one name; which by inadvertency we are apt afterward to talk of and consider as one simple *idea*, which indeed is a complication of many *ideas* together; because, as I have said, not imagining how these simple *ideas* can subsist by themselves, we accustom ourselves, to suppose some *substratum*, wherein they do subsist, and from which they do result, which therefore we call *substance*.

2. *Our* idea *of substance in general*. So that if anyone will examine himself concerning his *notion of pure substance in general*, he will find he has no other *idea* of it at all, but only a supposition of he knows not what support of such qualities, which are capable of producing simple *ideas* in us; which qualities are commonly called accidents. If anyone should be asked, what is the subject wherein color or weight inheres, he would have nothing to say, but the solid extended parts: and if he were demanded, what is it, that solidity and extension inhere in, he would not be in a much better case, than the *Indian* before mentioned; who, saying that the world was supported by a great elephant, was asked, what the elephant rested on; to which his answer was a great tortoise: but being again pressed to know what gave support to the broad-backed tortoise, replied, something, he knew not what. And thus here, as in all other cases, where we use words without having clear and distinct *ideas*, we talk like children; who, being questioned, what such a thing is, which they know not, readily give this satisfactory answer, that it is *something;* which in truth signifies no more, when so used, either by children or men, but that they know not what; and that the thing they pretend to know, and talk of, is what they have no distinct *idea* of at all, and so are perfectly ignorant of it, and in the dark. The *idea* then we have, to which we give the general name substance, being nothing, but the supposed, but unknown support of those qualities, we find existing, which we imagine cannot subsist, *sine re substante*, without something to support them, we call that support *substantia;* which, according to the true import of the word, is in plain *English, standing under*, or *upholding*.

3. *Of the sorts of substances*. An obscure and relative *idea* of substance in general being thus made, we come to have the *ideas of particular sorts of substances*, by collecting such combinations of simple *ideas*, as are by experience and observation of men's senses taken notice of to exist together, and are therefore supposed to flow from the particular internal constitution, or unknown essence of that substance. Thus we come to have the *ideas* of a man, horse, gold, water, &c. of which substances, whether anyone has any other clear *idea*, farther than of certain simple *ideas* coexisting together, I appeal to everyone's own experience. . . . Only we must take notice, that our complex *ideas* of substances, besides all these simple *ideas* they are made up of, have always the confused *idea* of *something* to which they belong, and in which they subsist: and therefore when we speak of any sort of substance, we say it is a *thing* having such or such qualities, as body is a *thing* that is extended, figured, and capable of motion; a spirit a *thing* capable of thinking; and so hardness, friability, and power to draw iron, we say, are qualities to be found in a lodestone. These, and the like fashions of speaking intimate, that the substance is supposed always *something* besides the extension, figure, solidity, motion, thinking, or other observable *ideas*, though we know not what it is.

4. *No clear* idea *of substance in general.* Hence when we talk or think of any particular sort of corporeal substances, as *horse, stone, &c.* though the *idea*, we have of either of them, be but the complication, or collection of those several simple *ideas* of sensible qualities, which we use to find united in the thing called *horse* or *stone*, yet because we cannot conceive, how they should subsist alone, nor one in another, we suppose them existing in, and supported by some common subject; *which support we denote by the name substance*, though it be certain, we have no clear, or distinct *idea* of that *thing* we suppose a support.

5. *As clear an* idea *of spirit, as body.* The same happens concerning the operations of the mind, *viz.* thinking, reasoning, fearing, *&c.* which we concluding not to subsist of themselves, nor apprehending how they can belong to body, or be produced by it, we are apt to think these the actions of some other *substance*, which we call *spirit;* whereby yet it is evident, that having no other *idea* or notion, of matter, but *something* wherein those many sensible qualities, which affect our senses, do subsist; by supposing a substance, wherein *thinking, knowing, doubting,* and a power of moving, *&c.* do subsist, *we have as clear a notion of the substance of spirit, as we have of body;* the one being supposed to be (without knowing what it is) the *substratum* to those simple *ideas* we have from without; and the other supposed (with a like ignorance of what it is) to be the *substratum* to those operations, which we experiment in ourselves within. 'Tis plain then, that the *idea* of corporeal *substance* in matter is as remote from our conceptions, and apprehensions, as that of spiritual *substance*, or *spirit;* and therefore from our not having any notion of the *substance* of spirit, we can no more conclude its non-existence, than we can, for the same reason, deny the existence of body: it being as rational to affirm, there is no body, because we have no clear and distinct *idea* of the *substance* of matter; as to say, there is no spirit, because we have no clear and distinct *idea* of the *substance* of a spirit.

6. *Of the sorts of substances.* Whatever therefore be the secret and abstract nature of *substance* in general, all *the* ideas *we have of particular distinct sorts of substances*, are nothing but several combinations of simple *ideas*, co-existing in such, though unknown, cause of their union, as makes the whole subsist of itself. . . .

7. *Powers a great part of our complex* ideas *of substances.* . . . He has the perfectest *idea* of any of the particular sorts of *substance*, who has gathered, and put together, most of those simple *ideas*, which do exist in it, among which are to be reckoned its active powers, and passive capacities; which though not simple *ideas*, yet, in this respect, for brevity's sake, may conveniently enough be reckoned amongst them. Thus the power of drawing iron, is one of the *ideas* of the complex one of that substance we call a *lodestone*, and a power to be so drawn is a part of the complex one we call *iron;* which powers pass for inherent qualities in those subjects. . . .

8. *And why.* Nor are we to wonder, that *powers make a great part of our complex* ideas *of substances;* since their secondary qualities are those, which in most of them serve principally to distinguish substances one from another, and commonly make a considerable part of the complex *idea* of the several sorts of them. For our senses failing us, in the discovery of the bulk, texture, and figure of the minute parts of bodies, on which their real constitutions and differences depend, we are fain to make use of their secondary qualities, as the characteristical notes and marks, whereby to frame *ideas* of them in our minds, and distinguish them one from another. All which secondary qualities, as has been shown, are nothing but bare powers. . . .

9. *Three sorts of* ideas *make our complex ones of substance*. *The* ideas *that make our complex ones of corporeal substances*, are of these three sorts. *First*, the *ideas* of the primary qualities of things, which are discovered by our senses, and are in them even when we perceive them not, such are the bulk, figure, number, situation, and motion of the parts of bodies, which are really in them, whether we take notice of them or no. *Secondly*, the sensible secondary qualities, which depending on these, are nothing but the powers, those substances have to produce several *ideas* in us by our senses; which *ideas* are not in the things themselves, otherwise than as anything is in its cause. *Thirdly*, the aptness we consider in any substance, to give or receive alterations of primary qualities, as that the substance so altered, should produce in us different *ideas* from what it did before, these are called active and passive powers: all which powers, as far as we have any notice or notion of them, terminate only in sensible simple *ideas*. . . .

10. *Powers make a great part of our complex* ideas *of substances*. *Powers*, therefore, justly *make a great part of our complex* ideas *of substances*. He, that will examine his complex *idea* of gold, will find several of its *ideas*, that make it up, to be only powers, as the power of being melted, but of not spending itself in the fire; of being dissolved, in *aqua regia*, are *ideas*, as necessary to make up our complex *idea* of gold, as its color and weight: which if duly considered, are also nothing but different powers. . . .

11. *The now secondary qualities of bodies would disappear, if we could discover the primary ones of their minute parts*. Had we senses acute enough to discern the minute particles of bodies, and the real constitution on which their sensible qualities depend, I doubt not but that they would produce quite different *ideas* in us; and that which is now the yellow color of gold, would then disappear, and instead of it we should see an admirable texture of parts of a certain size and figure. This microscopes plainly discover to us: for what to our naked eyes produces a certain color, is by thus augmenting the acuteness of our senses, discovered to be quite a different thing; and the thus altering, as it were, the proportion of the bulk of the minute parts of a colored object to our usual sight, produces different *ideas*, from what it did before. . . .

12. *Our faculties of discovery suited to our state*. The infinite wise contriver of us, and all things about us, has fitted our senses, faculties, and organs, to the conveniences of life, and the business we have to do here. . . . We are furnished with faculties (dull and weak as they are) to discover enough in the creatures, to lead us to the knowledge of the creator, and the knowledge of our duty; and we are fitted well enough with abilities, to provide for the conveniences of living: these are our business in this world. But were our senses altered, and made much quicker and acuter, the appearance and outward scheme of things would have quite another face to us; and I am apt to think, would be inconsistent with our being, or at least well-being in this part of the universe, which we inhabit. . . . If our sense of hearing were but 1000 times quicker than it is, how would a perpetual noise distract us. . . . Nay, if that most instructive of our senses, seeing, were in any man 1000 or 100000 times more acute than it is now by the best microscope, things several millions of times less than the smallest object of his sight now, would then be visible to his naked eyes, and so he would come nearer the discovery of the texture and motion of the minute parts of corporeal things; and in many of them, probably get *ideas* of their internal constitutions: but then he would be in a quite different world from other people: nothing would appear the same to him, and others: the visible *ideas* of everything would be different. So that I doubt, whether he, and the rest of men, could discourse concerning the objects of sight; or have any communication about colors, their appearances being so wholly different. And, perhaps, such a quickness and tenderness of sight could not endure bright sunshine, or so much as open daylight; nor take in but a very small part of any object at once, and that too only at a very near distance. And if by the help of such microscopical eyes, (if I may so call them), a man could penetrate farther than ordinary into the secret composition, and radical texture of bodies, he would not make any great advantage by the change, if such an acute sight would not serve to conduct him to the market and exchange; if he could not see things, he was to avoid, at a convenient distance; nor distinguish things he had to do with, by those sensible qualities others do. . . .

14. Complex ideas of substance. But to return to the matter in hand, the ideas we have of substances, and the ways we come by them; I say, our specific ideas of substances are nothing else but a collection of a certain number of simple ideas, considered as united in one thing. These ideas of substances, though they are commonly simple apprehensions, and the names of them simple terms; yet in effect are complex and compounded. Thus the idea which an Englishman signifies by the name Swan, is white color, long neck, red beak, black legs, and whole feet, and all these of a certain size, with a power of swimming in the water, and making a certain kind of noise: And perhaps, to a man who has long observed this kind of bird, some other properties which all terminate in sensible simple ideas, all united in one common subject.

15. Idea of spiritual substances, as clear as of bodily substances. Besides the complex ideas we have of material sensible substances, of which I have last spoken, by the simple ideas we have taken from those operations of our own minds, which we experiment daily in ourselves, as thinking, understanding, willing, knowing, and power of beginning motion, &c. co-existing in some substance: We are able to frame the complex idea of an immaterial spirit. And thus by putting together the ideas of thinking, perceiving, liberty, and power of moving themselves, and other things, we have as clear a perception and notion of immaterial substances, as we have of material. For putting together the ideas of thinking and willing, or the power of moving or quieting corporeal motion, joined to substance of which we have no distinct idea, we have the idea of an immaterial spirit; and by putting together the ideas of coherent solid parts, and a power of being moved, joined with substance, of which likewise we have no positive idea, we have the idea of matter. The one is as clear and distinct an idea as the other: The idea of thinking, and moving a body, being as clear and distinct ideas, as the ideas of extension, solidity, and being moved. For our idea of substance is equally

obscure, or none at all in both: It is but a supposed I know not what, to support those ideas we call accidents. It is for want of reflection that we are apt to think, that our senses shew us nothing but material things. Every act of sensation, when duly considered, gives us an equal view of both parts of nature, the corporeal and spiritual. For whilst I know, by seeing or hearing, &c. that there is some corporeal being without me, the object of that sensation; I do more certainly know, that there is some spiritual being within me, that sees and hears. This, I must be convinced, cannot be the action of bare insensible matter; nor ever could be, without an immaterial thinking being. . . .

22. Idea *of soul and body compared.* Let us *compare* then our complex *idea* of an immaterial spirit, with our complex *idea* of body, and see whether there be any more obscurity in one, than in the other, and in which most. Our *idea* of body, as I think, is an extended solid substance, capable of communicating motion by impulse: and our *idea* of our soul, as a immaterial spirit, is of a substance that thinks, and has a power of exciting motion in body, by will, or thought. These, I think, are *our complex* ideas *of soul and body, as contradistinguished;* and now let us examine which has most obscurity in it, and difficulty to be apprehended. I know that people, whose thoughts are immersed in matter, and have so subjected their minds to their senses, that they seldom reflect on anything beyond them, are apt to say, they cannot comprehend a thinking thing, which, perhaps, is true; but I affirm, when they consider it well, they can no more comprehend an extended thing.

23. *Cohesion of solid parts in body, as hard to be conceived as thinking in a soul.* If anyone say, he knows not what 'tis thinks in him; he means he knows not what the substance is of that thinking thing: no more, say I, knows he what the substance is of that solid thing. Farther, if he says he knows not how he thinks; I answer, neither knows he how he is extended; how the solid parts of body are united, or cohere together to make extension. For though the pressure of the particles of air, may account for the *cohesion of several parts of matter*, that are grosser than the particles of air, and have pores less than the corpuscles of air; yet the weight, or pressure of the air, will not explain, nor can be a cause of the coherence of the particles of air themselves. And if the pressure of the aether, or any subtler matter than the air, may unite, and hold fast together the parts of a particle of air, as well as other bodies; yet it cannot make bonds for itself, and hold together the parts, that make up every the least corpuscle of that *materia subtilis.* . . .

25. I allow, it is usual for most people to wonder, how anyone should find a difficulty in what they think, they every day observe. Do we not see, will they be ready to say, the parts of bodies stick firmly together? Is there anything more common? And what doubt can there be made of it? And the like, I say, concerning *thinking,* and *voluntary motion:* do we not every moment experiment it in ourselves; and therefore can it be doubted? The matter of fact is clear, I confess; but when we would a little nearer look into it, and consider how it is done, there, I think, we are at a loss, both in the one, and the other; and can as little understand how the parts of body cohere, as how we ourselves perceive, or move. . . .

28. *Communication of motion by impulse, or by thought, equally intelligible.* Another *idea* we have of body, is the power of *communication of motion by impulse;* and of our souls, the power of *exciting motion by thought.* These *ideas,* the one of body, the other of our minds, every day's experience clearly furnishes us with: but if here again we inquire how this is done, we *are equally in the dark.* For in the communication of motion by impulse, wherein as much motion is lost to one body, as is got to the other, which is the ordinariest case, we can have no other conception, but of the passing of motion out of one body into another; which, I think, is as obscure and unconceivable, as how our minds move or stop our bodies by thought; which we every moment find they do. . . . And if we consider the active power of moving, or, as I may call it, *motivity,* it is much clearer in spirit than body; since two bodies, placed by one another at rest, will never afford us the *idea* of a power in the one to move the other, but by a borrowed motion: whereas the mind, every day, affords us *ideas* of an active power of moving of bodies; and therefore it is worth our consideration, whether active power be not the proper attribute of

spirits, and passive power of matter. Hence may be conjectured, that created spirits are not totally separate from matter, because they are both active and passive. Pure spirit, *viz.* God, is only active; pure matter is only passive; those beings that are both active and passive we may judge to partake of both. But be that as it will, I think, we have as many, and as clear *ideas* belonging to spirit, as we have belonging to body, the substance of each being equally unknown to us; and the *idea* of thinking in spirit, as clear as of extension in body; and the communication of motion by thought, which we attribute to spirit, is as evident, as that by impulse, which we ascribe to body. . . .

30. Ideas *of body and spirit compared.* So that, in short, *the idea* we have *of spirit, compared with the idea* we have *of body,* stands thus: the substance of spirit is unknown to us; and so is the substance of body, equally unknown to us: two primary qualities or properties of body, *viz.* solid coherent parts, and impulse we have distinct clear *ideas* of: so likewise we know, and have distinct clear *ideas* of two primary qualities, or properties of spirit, *viz.* thinking, and a power of action; *i.e.* a power of beginning, or stopping several thoughts or motions. We have also the *ideas* of several qualities inherent in bodies, and have the clear distinct *ideas* of them: which qualities, are but the various modifications of the extension of cohering solid parts, and their motion. We have likewise the *ideas* of several modes of thinking, *viz.* believing, doubting, intending, fearing, hoping; all which, are but the several modes of thinking. We have also the *ideas* of willing, and moving the body consequent to it, and with the body itself too; for, as has been showed, spirit is capable of motion.

31. *The notion of spirit involves no more difficulty in it, than that of body.* Lastly, if this notion of immaterial spirit may have, perhaps, some difficulties in it, not easy to be explained, we have therefore no more reason to deny, or doubt the existence of such spirits, than we have to deny, or doubt the existence of body; because the notion of body is cumbered with some difficulties very hard, and, perhaps, impossible to be explained, or understood by us. For I would fain have instanced anything in our notion of spirit more perplexed, or nearer a contradiction, than the very notion of body includes in it; the diversibility *in infinitum* of any finite extension, involving us, whether we grant or deny it, in consequences impossible to be explicated, or made in our apprehensions consistent; consequences that carry greater difficulty, and more apparent absurdity, than anything can follow from the notion of an immaterial knowing substance.

32. *We know nothing beyond our simple* ideas. Which we are not at all to wonder at, since we having but some few superficial *ideas* of things, discovered to us only by the senses from without, or by the mind, reflecting on what it experiments in itself within, have no knowledge beyond that, much less of the internal constitution, and true nature of things, being destitute of faculties to attain it. And therefore experimenting and discovering in ourselves knowledge, and the power of voluntary motion, as certainly as we experiment, or discover in things without us, the cohesion and separation of solid parts, which is the extension and motion of bodies; *we have as much reason to be satisfied with our notion of immaterial spirit, as with our notion of body; and the existence of the one, as well as the other.* For it being no more a contradiction, that thinking should exist, separate, and independent from solidity; than it is a contradiction, that solidity should exist, separate, and independent from thinking, they being both but simple *ideas,* independent one from another; and having as clear and distinct *ideas* in us of thinking, as of solidity, I know not, why we may not as well allow a thinking thing without solidity, *i.e. immaterial* to exist; as a solid thing without thinking, *i.e. matter,* to exist; especially since it is no harder to conceive how thinking should exist without matter, than how matter should think. For whensoever we would proceed beyond these simple *ideas,* we have from sensation and reflection, and dive farther into the nature of things, we fall presently into darkness and obscurity, perplexedness and difficulties; and can discover nothing farther, but our own blindness and ignorance. But whichever of these complex *ideas* be clearest, that of body, or immaterial spirit, this is evident, that the simple *ideas* that make them up, are no other than what we have received from sensation

or reflection; and so is it of all our other *ideas* of substance, even of God himself.

33. Idea *of God.* For if we examine the *idea* we have of the incomprehensible supreme being, we shall find, that we come by it the same way; and that the complex *ideas* we have both of God, and separate spirits, are made up of the simple *ideas* we receive from *reflection, v.g.* having from what we experiment in ourselves, got the *ideas* of existence and duration; of knowledge and power; of pleasure and happiness; and of several other qualities and powers, which it is better to have, than to be without; when we would frame an *idea* the most suitable we can to the supreme being, we enlarge every one of these with our *idea* of infinity; and so putting them together, make our complex *idea of God.* For that the mind has such a power of enlarging some of its *ideas,* received from sensation and reflection, has been already showed.

34. If I find, that I know some few things, and some of them, or all, perhaps, imperfectly, I can frame an *idea* of knowing twice as many; which I can double again, as often as I can add to number, and thus enlarge my *idea* of knowledge, by extending its comprehension to all things existing, or possible: the same also I can do of knowing them more perfectly; *i.e.* all their qualities, powers, causes, consequences, and relations, &c. till all be perfectly known, that is in them, or can any way relate to them, and thus frame the *idea* of infinite or boundless knowledge: the same may also be done of power, till we come to that we call infinite; and also of the duration of existence, without beginning or end; and so frame the *idea* of an eternal being: the degrees or extent, wherein we ascribe existence, power, wisdom, and all other perfection, (which we can have any *ideas* of) to that sovereign being, which we call God, being all boundless and infinite, we frame the best *idea* of him our minds are capable of; all which is done, I say, by enlarging those simple ideas, we have taken from the operations of our own minds, by reflection; or by our senses, from exterior things, to that vastness, to which infinity can extend them.

35. For it is infinity, which, joined to our *ideas* of existence, power, knowledge, &c. makes that complex *idea*, whereby we represent to ourselves the best we can, the supreme being. For though in his own essence, (which certainly we do not know, not knowing the real essence of a pebble, or a fly, or of our own selves,) God be simple and uncompounded; yet, I think, I may say we have no other *idea* of him, but a complex one of existence, knowledge, power, happiness, &c. infinite and eternal: which are all distinct *ideas*, and some of them being relative, are again compounded of others; all which being, as has been shown, originally got from *sensation* and *reflection*, go to make up the *idea* or notion we have of God.

36. *No* **ideas** *in our complex one of spirits, but those got from sensation or reflection.* This farther is to be observed, that there is no *idea* we attribute to God, bating infinity, which is not also a part of our complex *idea* of other spirits. . . .

37. *Recapitulation.* And thus we have seen, *what kind of* ideas *we have of substances of all kinds*, wherein they consist, and how we come by them. From whence, I think, it is very evident.

First, that all our *ideas* of the several sorts of substances, are nothing but collections of simple *ideas*, with a supposition of something, to which they belong, and in which they subsist; though of this supposed something, we have no clear distinct *idea* at all.

Secondly, that all the simple *ideas*, that thus united in one common *substratum* make up our complex *ideas* of several sorts of substances, are no other but such, as we have received from *sensation* or *reflection*. So that even in those, which we think, we are most intimately acquainted with, and come nearest the comprehension of, our most enlarged conceptions, cannot reach beyond those simple *ideas*. . . .

Thirdly, that most of the simple *ideas*, that make up our complex *ideas* of substances, when truly considered, are only powers, however we are apt to take them for positive qualities; *v.g.* the greatest part of the *ideas*, that make our complex *idea* of *gold*, are yellowness, great weight, ductility, fusibility, and solubility, in *aqua regia*, &c. all united together in an unknown *substratum;* all which *ideas*, are nothing else, but so many relations to other substances; and are not really in the gold, considered barely in

itself, though they depend on those real, and primary qualities of its internal constitution, whereby it has a fitness, differently to operate, and be operated on by several other substances.

BOOK IV

CHAPTER 1. OF KNOWLEDGE IN GENERAL

1. Our knowledge conversant about our ideas. Since the mind, in all its thoughts and reasonings, hath no other immediate object but its own ideas, which it alone does or can contemplate; it is evident, that our knowledge is only conversant about them.

2. Knowledge is the perception of the agreement or disagreement of two ideas. Knowledge then seems to me to be nothing but the perception of the connexion and agreement, or disagreement and repugnancy, of any of our ideas. In this alone it consists. Where this perception is, there is knowledge; and where it is not, there, though we may fancy, guess, or believe, yet we always come short of knowledge. For when we know that white is not black, what do we else but perceive that these two ideas do not agree? When we possess ourselves with the utmost security of the demonstration, that the three angles of a triangle are equal to two right ones, what do we more but perceive, that equality to two right ones does necessarily agree to, and is inseparable from the three angles of a triangle?

3. This agreement is fourfold. But to understand a little more distinctly wherein this agreement or disagreement consists, I think we may reduce it all to these four sorts: 1. Identity, or diversity; 2. Relation; 3. Co-existence, or necessary connexion; 4. Real existence.

4. First, Of Identity or Diversity. As to the first sort of agreement or disagreement, viz. identity or diversity. It is the first act of the mind, when it has any sentiments or ideas at all, to perceive its ideas; and so far as it perceives them, to know each what it is, and thereby also to perceive their difference, and that one is not another. This is so absolutely necessary, that without it there could be no knowledge, no reasoning, no imagination, no distinct thoughts, at all. By this the mind clearly and infallibly perceives each idea to agree with itself, and to be what it is; and all distinct ideas to disagree, i.e. the one not to be the other: And this it does without pains, labour, or deduction; but at first view, by its natural power of perception and distinction. And though men of art have reduced this into those general rules, "what is, is"; and "it is impossible for the same thing to be and not to be"; for ready application in all cases, wherein there may be occasion to reflect on it: Yet it is certain, that the first exercise of this faculty is about particular ideas. A man infallibly knows, as soon as ever he has them in his mind, that the ideas he calls white and round, are the very ideas they are, and that they are not other ideas which he calls red or square. Nor can any maxim or proposition in the world make him know it clearer or surer than he did before, and without any such general rule. This then is the first agreement or disagreement, which the mind perceives in its ideas; which it always perceives at first sight: And if there ever happen any doubt about it, it will always be found to be about the names, and not the ideas themselves, whose identity and diversity will always be perceived, as soon and clearly as the ideas themselves are; nor can it possibly be otherwise.

5. Secondly, Relative. The next sort of agreement or disagreement, the mind perceives in any of its ideas, may, I think, be called relative, and is nothing but the perception of the relation between any two ideas, of what kind soever, whether substances, modes, or any other. For since all distinct ideas must eternally be known not to be the same, and so be universally and constantly denied one of another, there could be no room for any positive knowledge at all, if we could not perceive any relation between our ideas, and find out the agreement or disagreement they have one with another, in several ways the mind takes of comparing them.

6. Thirdly, Of Coexistence. The third sort of agreement, or disagreement, to be found in our ideas, which the perception of the mind is employed about, is co-existence, or non-co-existence in the same subject; and this belongs particularly to substances. Thus when we pronounce concerning gold that it is fixed, our knowledge of this truth amounts to no more but

this, that fixedness, or a power to remain in the fire unconsumed, is an idea that always accompanies, and is joined with that particular sort of yellowness, weight, fusibility, malleableness, and solubility in aqua regia (royal water), which make our complex idea, signified by the word gold.

7. Fourthly, Of Real Existence. The last sort is that of actual real existence agreeing to any idea. Within these four sorts of agreement or disagreement, is, I suppose, contained all the knowledge we have, or are capable of: For all the inquiries we can make concerning any of our ideas, all that we know or can affirm concerning any of them, is, that it is, or is not, the same with some other; that it does or does not, always co-exist with some other idea in the same subject; that it has this or that relation with some other idea; or that it has a real existence without the mind. Thus "blue is not yellow"; is of identity: "two triangles upon equal bases between two parallels are equal"; is of relation: "iron is susceptible of magnetical impressions"; is of co-existence: "God is"; is of real existence. Though identity and co-existence are truly nothing but relations, yet they are such peculiar ways of agreement or disagreement of our ideas, that they deserve well to be considered as distinct heads, and not under relation in general; since they are so different grounds of affirmation and negation, as will easily appear to any one, who will but reflect on what is said in several places of this essay. I should now proceed to examine the several degrees of our knowledge, but that it is necessary first to consider the different acceptations of the word knowledge.

8. Knowledge Actual or Habitual. There are several ways wherein the mind is possessed of truth, each of which is called knowledge.

1. There is actual knowledge which is the present view the mind has of the agreement or disagreement of any of its ideas, or of the relation they have one to another.

2. A man is said to know any proposition, which having been once laid before his thoughts, he evidently perceived the agreement or disagreement of the ideas whereof it consists; and so lodged it in his memory, that whenever that proposition comes again to be reflected on, he, without doubt or hesitation,

embraces the right side, assents to, and is certain of the truth of it. This, I think, one may call habitual knowledge: And thus a man may be said to know all those truths which are lodged in his memory, by a foregoing, clear and full perception, whereof the mind is assured past doubt, as often as it has occasion to reflect on them. For our finite understandings being able to think clearly and distinctly but on one thing at once, if men had no knowledge of any more than what they actually thought on, they would all be very ignorant; and he that knew most, would know but one truth, that being all he was able to think on at one time.

9. Habitual knowledge twofold. Of habitual knowledge, there are also, vulgarly speaking, two degrees:

First, the one is of such truths laid up in the memory as, whenever they occur to the mind, it actually perceives the relation is between those ideas. And this is in all those truths whereof we have an intuitive knowledge; where the ideas themselves, by an immediate view, discover their agreement or disagreement one with another.

Secondly, The other is of such truths whereof the mind having been convinced, it retains the memory of the conviction, without the proofs. Thus a man that remembers certainly that he once perceived the demonstration, that the three angles of a triangle are equal to two right ones, is certain that he knows it, because he cannot doubt the truth of it. In his adherence to a truth, where the demonstration by which it was at first known is forgot, though a man may be thought rather to believe his memory than really to know, and this way of entertaining a truth seemed formerly to me like something between opinion and knowledge; a sort of assurance which exceeds bare belief, for that relies on the testimony of another: Yet upon a due examination I find it comes not short of perfect certainty, and is in effect true knowledge. That which is apt to mislead our first thoughts into a mistake in this matter, is, that the agreement or disagreement of the ideas in this case is not perceived, as it was at first, by an actual view of all the intermediate ideas, whereby the agreement or disagreement of those in the proposition was at first perceived; but by other intermedi-

ate ideas, that show the agreement or disagreement of the ideas contained in the proposition whose certainty we remember. For example, in this proposition, that "the three angles of a triangle are equal to two right ones," one who has seen and clearly perceived the demonstration of this truth, knows it to be true, when that demonstration is gone out of his mind; so that at present it is not actually in view, and possibly cannot be recollected: But he knows it in a different way from what he did before. The agreement of the two ideas joined in that proposition is perceived, but it is by the intervention of other ideas than those which at first produced that perception. He remembers, i.e. he knows (for remembrance is but the reviving of some past knowledge) that he was once certain of the truth of this proposition, that the three angles of a triangle are equal to two right ones. The immutability of the same relations between the same immutable things, is now the idea that shows him, that if the three angles of a triangle were once equal to two right ones, they will always be equal to two right ones. And hence he comes to be certain, that what was once true in the case, is always true; what ideas once agreed, will always agree; and consequently what he once knew to be true, he will always know to be true; as long as he can remember that he once knew it. Upon this ground it is, that particular demonstrations in mathematics afford general knowledge. If then the perception that the same ideas will eternally have the same habitudes and relations, but not a sufficient ground of knowledge, there could be no knowledge of general propositions in mathematics; for no mathematical demonstration would be any other than particular: And when a man had demonstrated any proposition concerning one triangle or circle, his knowledge would not reach beyond that particular diagram. If he would extend it farther, he must renew his demonstration in another instance, before he could know it to be true in another like triangle, and so on: By which means one could never come to the knowledge of any general propositions. Nobody, I think, can deny that Mr. Newton certainly knows any proposition, that he now at any time reads in his book, to be true; though he has not in actual view that admirable chain of intermediate ideas, whereby he at first discovered it to be true.

Such a memory as that, able to retain such a train of particulars, may be well thought beyond the reach of human faculties; when the very discovery, perception, and laying together that wonderful connexion of ideas, is found to surpass most readers' comprehension. But yet it is evident, the author himself knows the proposition to be true, remembering he once saw the connexion of those ideas, as certainly as he knows such a man wounded another, remembering that he saw him run him through. But because the memory is not always so clear as actual perception, and does in all men more or less decay in length of time, this amongst other differences is one, which shows that demonstrative knowledge is much more imperfect than intuitive. . . .

CHAPTER 2. OF THE DEGREES OF OUR KNOWLEDGE

1. Intuitive. All our knowledge consisting, as I have said, in the view the mind has of its own ideas, which is the utmost light and greatest certainty we, with our faculties, and in our way of knowledge, are capable of; it may not be amiss to consider a little the degrees of its evidence. The different clearness of our knowledge seems to me to lie in the different way of perception the mind has of the agreement or disagreement of any of its ideas. For if we will reflect on our own ways of thinking, we shall find, that sometimes the mind perceives the agreement or disagreement of two ideas immediately by themselves, without the intervention of any other: And this, I think, we may call intuitive knowledge. For in this the mind is at no pains of proving or examining, but perceives the truth, as the eye doth light, only by being directed towards it. Thus the mind perceives, that white is not black, that a circle is not a triangle, that three are more than two, and equal to one and two. Such kinds of truths the mind perceives at the first sight of the ideas together, by bare intuition, without the intervention of any other idea; and this kind of knowledge is the clearest and most certain, that human frailty is capable of. This part of knowledge is irresistible, and like bright sunshine forces itself immediately to be perceived, as soon as ever the mind turns its view that way; and leaves no room for hesitation, doubt, or examination, but the mind is presently filled with the clear light of it. It is on this intuition that depends all the certainty and evidence of all our knowledge; which certainty every one finds to be so great, that he cannot imagine, and therefore not require a greater: For a man cannot conceive himself capable of a greater certainty, than to know that any idea in his mind is such as he perceives it to be; and that two ideas wherein he perceives a difference, are different and not precisely the same. He that demands a greater certainty than this, demands he knows not what, and shows only that he has a mind to be a skeptic, without being able to be so. Certainty depends so wholly on this intuition, that in the next degree of knowledge, which I call demonstrative, this intuition is necessary in all the connexions of the intermediate ideas, without which we cannot attain knowledge and certainty.

2. Demonstrative. The next degree of knowledge is, where the mind perceives the agreement or disagreement of any ideas, but not immediately. Though wherever the mind perceives the agreement or disagreement of any of its ideas, there be certain knowledge: Yet it does not always happen, that the mind sees that agreement or disagreement which there is between them, even where it is discoverable: And in that case remains in ignorance, and at most gets no farther than a probable conjecture. The reason why the mind cannot always perceive presently the agreement or disagreement of two ideas, is, because those ideas, concerning whose agreement or disagreement the inquiry is made, cannot by the mind be so put together as to show it. In this case then, when the mind cannot so bring its ideas together, as by their immediate comparison, and as it were juxtaposition or application one to another, to perceive their agreement or disagreement, it is fain, by the intervention of other ideas (one or more, as it happens) to discover the agreement or disagreement which it searches; and this is that which we call reasoning. Thus the mind being willing to know the agreement or disagreement in bigness, between the three angles of a triangle and two right ones, cannot by an immediate view and comparing them do it: Because the three angles of a triangle cannot be brought at once, and be compared with any other one or two angles; and so of this the mind has no immediate, no intuitive knowledge. In this case the mind is fain to find out some other angles, to which the three angles of a triangle have an equality; and, finding those equal to two right ones, comes to know their equality to two right ones.

3. Depends on Proofs. Those intervening ideas which serve to show the agreement of any two others, are called proofs; and where the agreement and disagreement is by this means plainly and clearly perceived, it is called demonstration, it being shown to the understanding, and the mind made to see that it is so. A quickness in the mind to find out these intermediate ideas (that shall discover the agreement or disagreement of any other) and to apply them right, is, I suppose, that which is called sagacity.

4. But not so easy. This knowledge by intervening proofs, though it be certain, yet the evidence of it is not altogether so clear and bright, nor the assent so ready, as in intuitive knowledge. For though, in demonstration, the mind does at last perceive the agreement or disagreement of the ideas it considers; yet it is not without pains and attention: There must be more than one transient view to find it. A steady application and pursuit are required to this discovery: And there must be a progression by steps and degrees, before the mind can in this way arrive at certainty, and come to perceive the agreement or repugnancy between two ideas that need proofs and the use of reason to show it.

5. Not without precedent doubt. Another difference between intuitive and demonstrative knowledge is, that though in the latter all doubt be removed, when by the intervention of the intermediate ideas the agreement or disagreement is perceived; yet before the demonstration there was a doubt, which in intuitive knowledge cannot happen to the mind, that has its faculty of perception left to a degree capable of distinct ideas, no more than it can be a doubt to the eye (that can distinctly see white and black) whether this ink and this paper be all of a color. If there be sight in the eyes, it will at first glimpse, without hesitation, perceive the words printed on this paper different from the color of the paper: And so if the mind have the faculty of distinct perception, it will perceive the agreement or disagreement of those ideas that produce intuitive knowledge. If the eyes have lost the faculty of seeing, or the mind of perceiving, we in vain inquire after the quickness of sight in one, or clearness of perception in the other.

6. Not so clear. It is true the perception produced by demonstration is also very clear, yet it is often with a great abatement of that evident lustre and full assurance, that always accompany that which I call intuitive; like a face reflected by several mirrors one to another, where as long as it retains the similitude and agreement with the object, it produces a knowledge; but it is still in every successive reflection with a lessening of that perfect clearness and distinctness, which is in the first; till at last, after many removes, it has a great mixture of dimness, and is not at first sight so knowable, especially to weak eyes. Thus it is with knowledge made out by a long train of proof.

7. Each step must have intuitive evidence. Now, in every step reason makes in demonstrative knowledge, there is an intuitive knowledge of that agreement or disagreement it seeks with the next intermediate idea, which it uses as a proof; for if it were not so, that yet would need a proof; since without the perception of such agreement or disagreement, there is no knowledge produced. . . . This intuitive perception of the agreement or disagreement of the intermediate ideas, in each step and progression of the demonstration, must also be carried exactly in the mind, and a man must be sure that no part is left out: Which because in long deductions, and the use of many proofs, the memory does not always so readily and exactly retain; therefore it comes to pass, that this is more imperfect than intuitive knowledge, and men embrace often falsehood for demonstrations. . . .

9. Demonstration not limited to quantity. It has been generally taken for granted, that mathematics alone are capable of demonstrative certainty; but to have such an agreement or disagreement, as may intuitively be perceived, being, as I imagine, not the privilege of the ideas of number, extension, and figure alone, it may possibly be the want of due method and application in us, and not of sufficient evidence in things, that demonstration has been thought to have so little to do in other parts of knowledge, and been scarce so much as aimed at by any but mathematicians. For whatever ideas we have, wherein the mind can perceive the immediate agreement or disagreement that is between them, there the mind is capable of intuitive knowledge; and where it can perceive the agreement or disagreement of any two ideas, by an intuitive perception of the agreement or disagreement they have with any intermediate ideas, there the mind is capable of demonstration, which is not limited to ideas of extension, figure, number, and their modes.

10. Why it has been so thought. The reason why it has been generally sought for, and supposed to be only in those, I imagine has been not only the general usefulness of those sciences; but because, in comparing their equality or excess, the modes of numbers have every the least difference very clear and perceivable; and though in extension, every the least excess is not so perceptible, yet the mind has found out ways to examine and discover demonstratively the just equality of two angles, or extensions, or figures: And both these, i.e. numbers and figures, can be set down by visible and lasting marks, wherein the ideas under consideration are perfectly determined; which for the most part they are not, where they are marked only by names and words.

11. Modes of quantity demonstrable, modes of qualities not. But in other simple ideas, whose modes and differences are made and counted by degrees, and not quantity, we have not so nice and accurate a distinction of their differences, as to perceive, or find ways to measure their just equality, or the least differences. For those other simple ideas, being appearances of sensations, produced in us by the size, figure, number, and motion of minute corpuscles singly insensible; their different degrees also depend upon the variation of some, or of all those causes: Which since it cannot be observed by us in particles of matter, whereof each is too subtile to be perceived, it is impossible for us to have any exact measures of the different degrees of these simple ideas. . . .

13. Secondary Qualities not discovered by demonstration. Not knowing therefore what number of particles, nor what motion of them is fit to produce any precise degree of whiteness, we cannot demonstrate the certain equality of any two degrees of whiteness; because we have no certain standard to measure them by, nor means to distinguish every the least real difference, the only help we have being from our senses, which in this point fail us. But where the difference is so great, as to produce in the mind clearly distinct ideas, whose differences can be perfectly retained, there these ideas or colors, as we see in different kinds, as blue and red, are as capable of demonstration, as ideas of number and extension. What I have here said of whiteness and colors, I think, holds true in all secondary qualities, and their modes.

14. Sensitive knowledge of particular existence. These two, viz. intuition and demonstration, are the degrees of our knowledge; whatever comes short of one of these, with what assurance soever embraced, is but faith, or opinion, but not knowledge, at least in all general truths. There is, indeed, another perception of the mind, employed about the particular existence of finite beings without us; which going beyond bare probability, and yet not reaching perfectly to either of the foregoing degrees of certainty, passes under the name of knowledge. There can be nothing more certain, than that the idea we receive from an external object is in our minds; this is intuitive knowledge. But whether there be any thing more than barely that idea in our minds; whether we can thence certainly infer the existence of any thing without us, which corresponds to that idea, is that, hereof some men think there may be a question made; because men may have such ideas in their minds, when no such thing exists, no such object affects their senses. But yet here, I think, we are provided with an evidence, that puts us past doubting: For I ask any one, whether he be not invincibly conscious to himself of a different perception, when he looks on the sun by day, and thinks on it by night; when he actually tastes wormwood, or smells a rose, or only thinks on that savor or odor? We as plainly find the difference there is between any idea revived in our minds by our own memory, and actually coming into our minds by our senses, as we do between any two distinct ideas. If any one say, a dream may do the same thing, and all these ideas may be produced in us without any external objects; he may please to dream that I make him this answer: 1. That it is no great matter, whether I remove his scruple or no: Where all is but dream, reasoning and arguments are of no use, truth and knowledge nothing. 2. That I believe he will allow a very manifest difference between dreaming of being in the fire, and being actually in it. But yet if he be resolved to appear so sceptical, as to maintain, that what I call being actually in the fire is nothing but a dream; and that we cannot thereby certainly know, that any such thing as fire actually exists without us: I answer, that we certainly finding that pleasure or pain follows upon the application of certain objects to us, whose existence we perceive, or dream that we perceive by our senses; this certainty is as great as our happiness or misery, beyond which we have no concernment to know or to be. So that, I think, we may add to the two former sorts of knowledge this also of the existence of particular external objects, by that perception and consciousness we have of the actual entrance of ideas from them, and allow these three degrees of knowledge, viz. intuitive, demonstrative, and sensitive: In each of which there are different degrees and ways of evidence and certainty.

CHAPTER 3. OF THE EXTENT OF HUMAN KNOWLEDGE

1. Extent of our knowledge. Knowledge, as has been said, lying in the perception of the agreement or disagreement of any of our ideas, it follows from hence, That,

First, we can have knowledge no farther than we have ideas.

2. Not farther than we have ideas. Secondly, that we can have no knowledge farther than we can have perceptions of that agreement or disagreement. Which perception being, 1. Either by intuition, or the immediate comparing any two ideas; or, 2. By reason, examining the agreement or disagreement of two ideas, by the intervention of some others; or, 3. By sensation, perceiving the existence of particular things: Hence it also follows,

3. Intuitive knowledge extends itself not to all the relations of all our ideas. Thirdly, that we cannot have an intuitive knowledge, that shall extend itself to all our ideas, and all that we would know about them; because we cannot examine and per-

ceive all the relations they have one to another by juxta-position, or an immediate comparison one with another. Thus having the ideas of an obtuse and an acute angled triangle, both drawn from equal bases, and between parallels, I can, by intuitive knowledge, perceive the one not to be the other, but cannot that way know whether they be equal or no; because their agreement or disagreement in equality can never be perceived by an immediate comparing them: The difference of figure makes their parts incapable of an exact immediate application; and therefore there is need of some intervening quantities to measure them by, which is demonstration, or rational knowledge.

4. Nor demonstrative knowledge. Fourthly, it follows also, from what is above observed, that our rational knowledge cannot reach to the whole extent of our ideas: Because between two different ideas we would examine, we cannot always find such mediums, as we can connect one to another with an intuitive knowledge, in all the parts of the deduction; and wherever that fails, we come short of knowledge and demonstration.

5. Sensitive knowledge narrower than either. Fifthly, sensitive knowledge reaching no farther than the existence of things actually present to our senses, is yet much narrower than either of the former.

6. Our knowledge, therefore, narrower than either. From all which it is evident, that the extent of our knowledge comes not only short of the reality of things, but even of the extent of our own ideas. Though our knowledge be limited to our ideas, and cannot exceed them either in extent or perfection; and though these be very narrow bounds, in respect of the extent of all being, and far short of what we may justly imagine to be in some even created understandings, not tied down to the dull and narrow information, is to be received from some few, and not very acute ways of perception, such as are our senses; yet it would be well with us if our knowledge were but as large as our ideas, and there were not many doubts and inquiries concerning the ideas we have, whereof we are not, nor I believe ever shall be in this world resolved. Nevertheless I do not question but that human knowledge, under the present circumstances of our beings and constitutions, may be carried much farther than it has hitherto been, if men would sincerely, and with freedom of mind, employ all that industry and labour of thought, in improving the means of discovering truth, which they do for the coloring or support of falsehood, to maintain a system, interest, or party, they are once engaged in. But yet after all, I think I may, without injury to human perfection, be confident, that our knowledge would never reach to all we might desire to know concerning those ideas we have: Nor be able to surmount all the difficulties, and resolve all the questions that might arise concerning any of them. We have the ideas of a square, a circle, and equality; and yet, perhaps, shall never be able to find a circle equal to a square, and certainly know that it is so. We have the ideas of matter and thinking, but possibly shall never be able to know, whether any mere material being thinks, or no; it being impossible for us, by the contemplation of our own ideas, without revelation, to discover, whether omnipotency has not given to some systems of matter fitly disposed, a power to perceive and think, or else joined and fixed to matter so disposed a thinking immaterial substance: It being, in respect of our notions, not much more remote from our comprehension to conceive, that God can, if he pleases, superadd to matter a faculty of thinking, than that he should superadd to it another substance with a faculty of thinking; since we know not wherein thinking consists, nor to what sort of substances the Almighty has been pleased to give that power, which cannot be in any created being, but merely by the good pleasure and bounty of the Creator. For I see no contradiction in it, that the first eternal thinking Being or omnipotent Spirit should, if he pleased, give to certain systems of created senseless matter, put together as he thinks fit, some degrees of sense, perception, and thought: Though, as I think, I have proved, lib. iv. ch. 10, sec. 14, &c. it is no less than a contradiction to suppose matter (which is evidently in its own nature void of sense and thought) should be that eternal first-thinking being. What certainty of knowledge can any one have that some perceptions, such as, v.g. pleasure and pain, should not be in some bodies themselves, after a certain manner modified and moved, as well as that they should be in an immaterial substance, upon the motion of the parts of body? Body, as far as we can conceive, being able

only to strike and affect body; and motion, according to the utmost reach of our ideas, being able to produce nothing but motion: So that when we allow it to produce pleasure or pain, or the idea of a color or sound, we are fain to quit our reason, go beyond our ideas, and attribute it wholly to the good pleasure of our Maker. For since we must allow he has annexed effects to motion, which we can no way conceive motion able to produce, what reason have we to conclude that he could not order them as well to be produced in a subject we cannot conceive capable of them, as well as in a subject we cannot conceive the motion of matter can any way operate upon? I say not this, that I would any way lessen the belief of the soul's immateriality: I am not here speaking of probability, but knowledge; and I think not only, that it becomes the modesty of philosophy not to pronounce magisterially, where we want that evidence that can produce knowledge; but also, that it is of use to us to discern how far our knowledge does reach; for the state we are at present in, not being that of vision, we must, in many things, content ourselves with faith and probability; and in the present question, about the immateriality of the soul, if our faculties cannot arrive at demonstrative certainty, we need not think it strange. All the great ends of morality and religion are well enough secured, without philosophical proofs of the soul's immateriality; since it is evident, that he who made us at the beginning to subsist here, sensible intelligent beings, and for several years continued us in such a state, can and will restore us to the like state of sensibility in another world, and make us capable there to receive the retribution he has designed to men, according to their doings in this life. And therefore it is not of such mighty necessity to determine one way or the other, as some, over-zealous for or against the immateriality of the soul, have been forward to make the world believe. Who, either on the one side, indulging too much their thoughts, immersed altogether in matter, can allow no existence to what is not material: Or who, on the other side, finding not cogitation within the natural powers of matter, examined over and over again by the utmost intention of mind, have the confidence to conclude, that omnipotency itself cannot give perception and thought to a substance which has the modification of solidity. He that considers how hardly sensation is, in our thoughts, reconcilable to extended matter; or existence to any thing that hath no extension at all; will confess that he is very far from certainly knowing what his soul is. It is a point which seems to me to be put out of the reach of our knowledge: And he who will give himself leave to consider freely, and look into the dark and intricate part of each hypothesis, will scarce find his reason able to determine him fixedly for or against the soul's materiality. Since on which side soever he views it, either as an unextended substance, or as a thinking extended matter; the difficulty to conceive either will, whilst either alone is in his thoughts, still drive him to the contrary side. An unfair way which some men take with themselves; who, because of the inconceivableness of something they find in one, throw themselves violently into the contrary hypothesis, though altogether as unintelligible to an unbiased understanding. This serves not only to shew the weakness and the scantiness of our knowledge, but the insignificant triumph of such sort of arguments, which, drawn from our own views, may satisfy us that we can find no certainty on one side of the question; but do not at all thereby help us to truth by running into the opposite opinion, which, on examination, will be found clogged with equal difficulties. For what safety, what advantage to any one is it, for the avoiding the seeming absurdities, and to him unsurmountable rubs he meets with in one opinion, to take refuge in the contrary, which is built on something altogether as inexplicable, and as far remote from his comprehension? It is past controversy, that we have in us something that thinks; our very doubts about what it is confirm the certainty of its being, though we must content ourselves in the ignorance of what kind of being it is: And it is in vain to go about to be sceptical in this, as it is unreasonable in most other cases to be positive against the being of any thing, because we cannot comprehend its nature. For I would fain know what substance exists, that has not something in it which manifestly baffles our understandings. Other spirits, who see and know the nature and inward constitution of things, how much must they exceed us in knowledge? To which if we add larger comprehension, which enables them at one glance to see the connexion and agreement of very many ideas, and read-

ily supplies to them the intermediate proofs, which we by single and slow steps, and long poring in the dark, hardly at last find out, and are often ready to forget one before we have hunted out another: We may guess at some part of the happiness of superior ranks of spirits, who have a quicker and more penetrating sight, as well as a larger field of knowledge. But to return to the argument in hand; our knowledge, I say, is not only limited to the paucity and imperfections of the ideas we have, and which we employ it about, but even comes short of that too.

CHAPTER 11. OF OUR KNOWLEDGE OF THE EXISTENCE OF OTHER THINGS

1. Is to be had only by sensation. The knowledge of our own being we have by intuition. The existence of a God reason clearly makes known to us, as has been shown.

The knowledge of the existence of any other thing, we can have only by sensation: For there being no necessary connexion of real existence with any idea a man hath in his memory, nor of any other existence but that of God, with the existence of any particular man; no particular man can know the existence of any other being, but only when by actual operating upon him, it makes itself perceived by him. For the having the idea of any thing in our mind, no more proves the existence of that thing, than the picture of a man evidences his being in the world, or the visions of a dream make thereby a true history.

2. Instance, whiteness of this paper. It is therefore the actual receiving of ideas from without, that gives us notice of the existence of other things, and makes us know that something doth exist at that time without us, which causes that idea in us, though perhaps we neither know nor consider how it does it: For it takes not from the certainty of our senses, and the ideas we receive by them, that we know not the manner wherein they are produced: V.g. whilst I write this, I have, by the paper affecting my eyes, that idea produced in my mind, which whatever object causes, I call white; by which I know that that quality or accident (i.e. whose appearance before my eyes always causes that idea) doth really exist, and hath a being without me. And of this, the greatest assurance I can possibly have, and to which my faculties can attain, is the testimony of my eyes, which are the proper and sole judges of this thing, whose testimony I have reason to rely on as so certain, that I can no more doubt, whilst I write this, that I see white and black, and that something really exists, that causes that sensation in me, than that I write or move my hand; which is a certainty as great as human nature is capable of, concerning the existence of any thing, but a man's self alone, and of God.

3. This, though not so certain as demonstration, yet may be called knowledge, and proves the existence of things without us. The notice we have by our senses, of the existing of things without us, though it be not altogether so certain as our intuitive knowledge, or the deductions of our reason employed about the clear abstract ideas of our own minds; yet it is an assurance that deserves the name of knowledge. If we persuade ourselves, that our faculties act and inform us right, concerning the existence of those objects that affect them, it cannot pass for an ill-grounded confidence: For I think nobody can, in earnest, be so sceptical, as to be uncertain of the existence of those things which he sees and feels. At least, he that can doubt so far (whatever he may have with his own thoughts) will never have any controversy with me; since he can never be sure I say any thing contrary to his own opinion. As to myself, I think God has given me assurance enough of the existence of things without me; since by their different application I can produce in myself both pleasure and pain, which is one great concernment of my present state. This is certain; the confidence that our faculties do not herein deceive us is the greatest assurance we are capable of, concerning the existence of material beings. For we cannot act any thing but by our faculties; nor talk of knowledge itself, but by the help of those faculties, which are fitted to apprehend even what knowledge is. But besides the assurance we have from our senses themselves, that they do not err in the information they give us, of the existence of things without us, when they are affected by them, we are farther confirmed in this assurance by other concurrent reasons.

4. Because we cannot have them but by the inlets of the senses. First, it is plain those perceptions are produced in us by exterior causes affecting our senses; because those that want the organs of any sense, never can have the ideas belonging to that sense produced in their minds. This is too evident to be doubted: And therefore we cannot but be assured, that they come in by the organs of that sense, and no other way. The organs themselves, it is plain, do not produce them, for then the eyes of a man in the dark would produce colors, and his nose smell roses in the winter: But we see nobody gets the relish of a pine-apple, till he goes to the Indies, where it is, and tastes it.

5. Because an idea from actual sensation, and another from memory, are very distinct perceptions. Secondly, because sometimes I find, that I cannot avoid the having those ideas produced in my mind. For though when my eyes are shut, or windows fast, I can at pleasure recall to my mind the ideas of light, or the sun, which former sensations had lodged in my memory; so I can at pleasure lay by that idea, and take into my view that of the smell of a rose, or taste of sugar. But, if I turn my eyes at noon towards the sun, I cannot avoid the ideas, which the light, or sun, then produces in me. So that there is a manifest difference between the ideas laid up in my memory, (over which, if they were there only, I should have constantly the same power to dispose of them, and lay them by at pleasure) and those which force themselves upon me, and I cannot avoid having. And therefore it must needs be some exterior cause, and the brisk acting of some objects without me, whose efficacy I cannot resist, that produces those ideas in my mind, whether I will or no. Besides, there is nobody who doth not perceive the difference in himself between contemplating the sun, as he hath the idea of it in his memory, and actually looking upon it: Of which two, his perception is so distinct, that few of his ideas are more distinguishable one from another. And therefore he hath certain knowledge that they are not both memory, or the actions of his mind, and fancies only within him; but that actual seeing hath a cause without.

6. Pleasure and Pain, which accompanies actual sensation, accompanies not the returning of those ideas, without the external objects. Thirdly, add to this, that many of those ideas are produced in us with pain, which afterwards we remember without the least offence. Thus the pain of heat or cold, when the idea of it is revived in our minds, gives us no disturbance; which, when felt, was very troublesome, and is again, when actually repeated; which is occasioned by the disorder the external object causes in our bodies when applied to it. And we remember the pains of hunger, thirst, or the head-ache, without any pain at all; which would either never disturb us, or else constantly do it, as often as we thought of it, were there nothing more but ideas floating in our minds, and appearances entertaining our fancies, without the real existence of things affecting us from abroad. The same may be said of pleasure, accompanying several actual sensations: And though mathematical demonstration depends not upon sense, yet the examining them by diagrams gives great credit to the evidence of our sight, and seems to give it a certainty approaching to that of demonstration itself. For it would be very strange, that a man should allow it for an undeniable truth, that two angles of a figure, which he measures by lines and angles of a diagram, should be bigger one than the other; and yet doubt of the existence of those lines and angles, which by looking on he makes use of to measure that by.

7. Our senses assist one another's testimony of the existence of outward things. Fourthly, our senses in many cases bear witness to the truth of each other's report, concerning the existence of sensible things without us. He that sees a fire, may, if he doubt whether it be any thing more than a bare fancy, feel it too; and be convinced by putting his hand in it. Which certainly could never be put into such exquisite pain, by a bare idea or phantom, unless that the pain be a fancy too: Which yet he cannot, when the burn is well, by raising the idea of it, bring upon himself again.

Thus I see, whilst I write this, I can change the appearance of the paper: And by designing the letters tell before-hand what new idea it shall exhibit the very next moment, by barely drawing my pen over it: Which will neither appear (let me fancy as much as I will) if my hands stand still; or though I move my pen, if my eyes be shut: Nor when those characters are once made on the paper, can I choose afterwards but see them as they are; that is, have the ideas of such letters as I have made. Whence it is

manifest, that they are not barely the sport and play of my own imagination, when I find that the characters, that were made at the pleasure of my own thoughts, do not obey them; nor yet cease to be, whenever I shall fancy it; but continue to affect my senses constantly and regularly, according to the figures I made them. To which if we will add, that the sight of those shall, from another man, draw such sounds, as I beforehand design they shall stand for; there will be little reason left to doubt, that those words I write do really exist without me, when they cause a long series of regular sounds to affect my ears, which could not be the effect of my imagination, nor could my memory retain them in that order.

8. This certainty is as great as our condition needs. But yet, if after all this any one will be so sceptical, as to distrust his senses, and to affirm that all we see and hear, feel and taste, think and do, during our whole being, is but the series and deluding appearances of a long dream, whereof there is no reality; and therefore will question the existence of all things, or our knowledge of any thing; I must desire him to consider, that if all be a dream, then he doth but dream, that he makes the question; and so it is not much matter, that a waking man should answer him. But yet, if he pleases, he may dream that I make him this answer, that the certainty of things existing in rerum natura, when we have the testimony of our senses for it, is not only as great as our frame can attain to, but as our condition needs. For our faculties being suited not to the full extent of being, nor to a perfect, clear, comprehensive knowledge of things free from all doubt and scruple; but to the preservation of us, in whom they are; and accommodated to the use of life; they serve to our purpose well enough, if they will but give us certain notice of those things, which are convenient or inconvenient to us. For he that sees a candle burning, and hath experimented the force of its flame, by putting his finger in it, will little doubt that this is something existing without him, which does him harm, and puts him to great pain: Which is assurance enough, when no man requires greater certainty to govern his actions by, than what is as certain as his actions themselves. And if our dreamer pleases to try, whether the glowing heat of a glass furnace be barely a wandering imagination in a drowsy man's fancy; by putting his hand into it, he may perhaps be wakened into a certainty greater than he could wish, that it is something more than bare imagination. So that this evidence is as great as we can desire, being as certain to us as our pleasure or pain, i.e. happiness or misery; beyond which we have no concernment, either of knowing or being. Such an assurance of the existence of things without us is sufficient to direct us in the attaining the good, and avoiding the evil, which is caused by them; which is the important concernment we have of being made acquainted with them.

9. But reaches no farther than actual sensation. In fine then, when our senses do actually convey into our understandings any idea, we cannot but be satisfied that there doth something at that time really exist without us, which doth affect our senses, and by them give notice of itself to our apprehensive faculties, and actually produce that idea which we then perceive: And we cannot so far distrust their testimony, as to doubt, that such collections of simple ideas, as we have observed by our senses to be united together, do really exist together. But this knowledge extends as far as the present testimony of our senses, employed about particular objects that do then affect them, and no farther. For if I saw such a collection of simple ideas, as is wont to be called man, existing together one minute since, and am now alone, I cannot be certain that the same man exists now, since there is no necessary connexion of his existence a minute since, with his existence now: By a thousand ways he may cease to be, since I had the testimony of my senses for his existence. And if I cannot be certain, that the man I saw last to-day is now in being, I can less be certain that he is so, who hath been longer removed from my senses, and I have not seen since yesterday, or since the last year; and much less can I be certain of the existence of men that I never saw. And therefore though it be highly probable, that millions of men do now exist, yet, whilst I am alone writing this, I have not that certainty of it which we strictly call knowledge; though the great likelihood of it puts me past doubt, and it be reasonable for me to do several things upon the confidence that there are men (and men also of my acquaintance, with whom I have to do) now in the world: But this is but probability, not knowledge.

10. Folly to expect demonstration in every thing. Whereby yet we may observe, how foolish and vain a thing it is, for a man of a narrow knowledge, who having reason given him to judge of the different evidence and probability of things, and to be swayed accordingly; how vain, I say, it is to expect demonstration and certainty in things not capable of it; and refuse assent to very rational propositions, and act contrary to very plain and clear truths, because they cannot be made out so evident, as to surmount every the least (I will not say reason, but) pretence of doubting. He that in the ordinary affairs of life would admit of nothing but direct plain demonstration, would be sure of nothing in this world, but of perishing quickly. The wholesomeness of his meat or drink would not give him reason to venture on it: And I would fain know, what it is he could do upon such grounds, as are capable of no doubt, no objection.

REVIEW QUESTIONS

1. In his *Essay*, what is Locke's purpose? Why is his project important?
2. What is the difference between primary and secondary qualities?
3. What reasons does Locke give for rejecting the notion of innate ideas?
4. What does Locke argue is the origin of our ideas?
5. What is his view of probability?

20

❦

GEORGE BERKELEY

George Berkeley (1685–1753), an Irish philosopher and Anglican bishop, was educated at Trinity College, Dublin, where he subsequently taught. There he wrote *An Essay Towards a New Theory of Vision* (1709), *A Treatise Concerning the Principles of Human Knowledge* (1710), and *Three Dialogues Between Hylas and Philonous* (1713) from which the present selections are taken. At this time he became an Anglican priest and moved to London. In the 1720s he helped plan a college in Bermuda for sons of settlers and native Americans. In 1728 he married Anne Forster and sailed to Newport, Rhode Island, where he waited for promised government support for the college. It never came, and the college was never established. In 1731 he returned to London, where he wrote *The Theory of Vision* (1733). From 1734 to 1752 he served as Bishop of Cloyne, Ireland. A deeply committed Christian, he sought to reconcile science with his faith by proving that matter does not exist, and that the laws of physics, being God's laws, govern a universe made up of ideas.

Berkeley's fame rests on his development of a type of Idealism, better called "ideaism" or "Immaterialism," and for his incisive critique of Locke's Representationalism. It should be noted that Berkeley's Idealism is different from traditional idealism (e.g., Plato's), in that it is not rationalistic. It does not adhere to independently existing ideas, but rather it assumes an empirical foundation. It agrees with Locke that all ideas originate in sense experience, and proceeds to show that all we ever experience is ideas, our sensations or sense perceptions. The only reality there is to be known is perceivers and perceptions.

Concerning Locke's theory of knowledge, Berkeley argued, first, that the primary/secondary qualities distinction was exceedingly weak. The primary qualities are no more "in" the objects of perception than the secondary ones. Second, he argued that there were logical problems in the theory that our perceptions resembled physical objects ("an idea can be like nothing but an idea"). Third, he undermined the whole notion of substance which Locke needed to maintain his theory. What is the difference, Berkeley rhetorically asked, between a "something I know not what" (Locke's notion of substance) and nothing at all? Ultimately, Locke's Representationalism leads back to skepticism. Finally, Locke's theory was an explanatory failure. Locke asserted that ideas in the Mind were caused by mechanical actions upon our sense organs and brains. But Berkeley pointed out that this fails to explain mental events both in detail and principle: in *detail* because it was impossible to explain why a certain physical event should produce certain but quite different (in character) mental states (e.g., light waves producing the color red); in *principle* because the whole notion of dualistic interactionism was incoherent, misusing the notion of "cause." A cause makes something happen, but for this you need a notion of a WILL, agency—all causation is agent causation, but events in Nature do not make other events happen. One sees only two events in temporal succession—with regularity. But this only signals the reality of a cause; it is not the cause, for it is not an agent and exerts no will.

Berkeley held that there were only two realities: minds and mental events; ideas exist in the mind alone. All qualities are essentially secondary and have their reality by being perceived (*esse est percipi*—"To be is to be perceived"). There is no material world. Physical objects are simply mental events. "The table I write on exists, that is, I see and feel it; and if I were out of my study I should say it existed—meaning thereby that if I was in my study I might perceive it, or that some other spirit actually perceives it." All physical objects are mental phenomena that would cease to exist if they were not perceived. Why do physical objects continue to exist when no one is perceiving them? What happens to them when we are not looking at trees or mountains? Do they cease to be? No, someone is always perceiving them. God's eye keeps the world from dissolving.

> There was a young man who said, "God
> Must think it exceedingly odd
> If he finds that this tree
> Continues to be,
> While there's no one about in the quad."
> Dear Sir, your astonishment's odd
> I'm always about in the quad,
> And that's why the tree
> Continues to be,
> Since observed by,
>   Yours faithfully,
>   God

FOR FURTHER READING

Bennett, Jonathan. *Locke, Berkeley and Hume: Central Themes* (Oxford University Press, 1971).

Luce, A. A. *The Dialectic of Immaterialism: An Account of the Making of Berkeley's Principles* (Hodder and Stoughton, 1963).

Martin, C. B., and D. M. Armstrong, eds. *Locke and Berkeley: A Collection of Critical Essays* (Doubleday, 1968).

Muehlmann, Robert. *Berkeley's Ontology* (Hackett Publishing Co., 1992).

Pitcher, George. *Berkeley* (Routledge & Kegan Paul, 1977).

Turbayne, Colin, ed. *Berkeley: Critical and Interpretive Essays* (University of Minnesota Press, 1987).

Urmson, J. O. *Berkeley* (Oxford University Press, 1982).
Warnock, G. J. *Berkeley* (Penguin Books, 1953).
Winkler, Kenneth. *Berkeley: The Philosophy of Immaterialism* (Oxford University Press, 1989).

OF THE PRINCIPLES OF HUMAN KNOWLEDGE

INTRODUCTION

1. Philosophy being nothing else but the study of wisdom and truth, it may with reason be expected, that those who have spent most time and pains in it should enjoy a greater calm and serenity of mind, a greater clearness and evidence of knowledge, and be less disturbed with doubts and difficulties than other men. Yet so it is we see the illiterate bulk of mankind that walk the high-road of plain, common sense, and are governed by the dictates of Nature, for the most part easy and undisturbed. To them nothing that's familiar appears unaccountable or difficult to comprehend. They complain not of any want of evidence in their senses, and are out of all danger of becoming *sceptics*. But no sooner do we depart from sense and instinct to follow the light of a superior principle, to reason, meditate, and reflect on the nature of things, but a thousand scruples spring up in our minds, concerning those things which before we seemed fully to comprehend. Prejudices and errors of sense do from all parts discover themselves to our view; and endeavouring to correct these by reason we are insensibly drawn into uncouth paradoxes, difficulties, and inconsistences, which multiply and grow upon us as we advance in speculation; till at length, having wander'd through many intricate mazes, we find ourselves just where we were, or, which is worse, sit down in a forlorn scepticism.

2. The cause of this is thought to be the obscurity of things, or the natural weakness and imperfection of our understandings. It is said the faculties we have are few, and those designed by Nature for the support and comfort of life, and not to penetrate into the inward essence and constitution of things. Besides, the mind of man being finite, when it treats of things which partake of infinity, it is not to be wondered at, if it run into absurdities and contradictions; out of which it is impossible it should ever extricate itself, it being of the nature of infinite not to be comprehended by that which is finite.

3. But perhaps we may be too partial to ourselves in placing the fault originally in our faculties, and not rather in the wrong use we make of them. It is a hard thing to suppose, that right deductions from true principles should ever end in consequences which cannot be maintained or made consistent. We should believe that God has dealt more bountifully with the sons of men, than to give them a strong desire for that knowledge, which He had placed quite out of their reach. This were not agreeable to the wonted, indulgent methods of Providence, which, whatever appetites it may have implanted in the creatures, doth usually furnish them with such means as, if rightly made use of, will not fail to satisfy them. Upon the whole, I am inclined to think that the far greater part, if not all, of those difficulties which have hitherto amused philosophers, and blocked up the way to knowledge, are entirely owing to ourselves. That we have first raised a dust, and then complain, we cannot see.

4. My purpose therefore is, to try if I can discover what those principles are, which have introduced all that doubtfulness and uncertainty, those absurdities and contradictions into the several sects of philosophy; insomuch that the wisest men have thought our ignorance incurable, conceiving it to arise from the natural dulness and limitation of our faculties. And surely it is a work well deserving our pains, to make a strict inquiry concerning the first principles of *human knowledge,* to sift and examine them on all sides: especially since there may be some grounds to suspect that those lets and difficulties,

Reprinted from *Principles of Human Knowledge and Three Dialogues,* George Berkeley, 2009. By permission of Oxford University Press, Inc.

which stay and embarrass the mind in its search after truth, do not spring from any darkness and intricacy in the objects, or natural defect in the understanding, so much as from false principles which have been insisted on, and might have been avoided.

5. How difficult and discouraging soever this attempt may seem, when I consider how many great and extraordinary men have gone before me in the same designs: yet I am not without some hopes, upon the consideration that the largest views are not always the clearest, and that he who is short-sighted will be obliged to draw the object nearer, and may, perhaps, by a close and narrow survey discern that which had escaped far better eyes.

6. In order to prepare the mind of the reader for the easier conceiving what follows, it is proper to premise somewhat, by way of introduction, concerning the nature and abuse of language. But the unravelling this matter leads me in some measure to anticipate my design, by taking notice of what seems to have had a chief part in rendering speculation intricate and perplexed, and to have occasioned innumerable errors and difficulties in almost all parts of knowledge. And that is the opinion that the mind hath a power of framing *abstract ideas* or notions of things. He who is not a perfect stranger to the writings and disputes of philosophers, must needs acknowledge that no small part of them are spent about abstract ideas. These are in a more especial manner, thought to be the object of those sciences which go by the name of Logic and Metaphysics, and of all that which passes under the notion of the most abstracted and sublime learning, in all which one shall scarce find any question handled in such a manner, as does not suppose their existence in the mind, and that it is well acquainted with them.

7. It is agreed on all hands, that the qualities or modes of things do never really exist each of them apart by itself, and separated from all others, but are mixed, as it were, and blended together, several in the same object. But we are told, the mind being able to consider each quality singly, or abstracted from those other qualities with which it is united, does by that means frame to itself abstract ideas. For example, there is perceived by sight an object extended, coloured, and moved: this mixed or compound idea the mind resolving into its simple, constituent parts, and viewing each by itself, exclusive of the rest, does frame the abstract ideas of extension, colour, and motion. Not that it is possible for colour or motion to exist without extension: but only that the mind can frame to itself by *abstraction* the idea of colour exclusive of extension, and of motion exclusive of both colour and extension.

8. Again, the mind having observed that in the particular extensions perceived by sense, there is something common and alike in all, and some other things peculiar, as this or that figure or magnitude, which distinguish them one from another; it considers apart or singles out by itself that which is common, making thereof a most abstract idea of extension, which is neither line, surface, nor solid, nor has any figure or magnitude but is an idea entirely prescinded from all these. So likewise the mind by leaving out of the particular colours perceived by sense, that which distinguishes them one from another, and retaining that only which is common to all, makes an idea of colour in abstract which is neither red, nor blue, nor white, nor any other determinate colour. And in like manner by considering motion abstractedly not only from the body moved, but likewise from the figure it describes, and all particular directions and velocities, the abstract idea of motion is framed; which equally corresponds to all particular motions whatsoever that may be perceived by sense.

9. And as the mind frames to itself abstract ideas of qualities or modes, so does it, by the same precision or mental separation, attain abstract ideas of the more compounded beings, which include several coexistent qualities. For example, the mind having observed that Peter, James, and John resemble each other, in certain common agreements of shape and other qualities, leaves out of the complex or compounded idea it has of Peter, James, and any other particular man, that which is peculiar to each, retaining only what is common to all; and so makes an abstract idea wherein all the particulars equally partake, abstracting entirely from and cutting off all those circumstances and differences, which might determine it to any particular existence. And after this manner it is said we come by the abstract idea of *man* or, if you please, humanity or human nature; wherein it is true, there is included colour, because

there is no man but has some colour, but then it can be neither white, nor black, nor any particular colour; because there is no one particular colour wherein all men partake. So likewise there is included stature, but then it is neither tall stature nor low stature, nor yet middle stature, but something abstracted from all these. And so of the rest. Moreover, there being a great variety of other creatures that partake in some parts, but not all, of the complex idea of *man,* the mind leaving out those parts which are peculiar to men, and retaining those only which are common to all the living creatures, frameth the idea of *animal,* which abstracts not only from all particular men, but also all birds, beasts, fishes, and insects. The constituent parts of the abstract idea of animal are body, life, sense, and spontaneous motion. By *body* is meant, body without any particular shape or figure, there being no one shape or figure common to all animals, without covering, either of hair or feathers, or scales, &c. nor yet naked: hair, feathers, scales, and nakedness being the distinguishing properties of particular animals, and for that reason left out of the *abstract idea.* Upon the same account the spontaneous motion must be neither walking, nor flying, nor creeping, it is nevertheless a motion, but what that motion is, it is not easy to conceive.

10. Whether others have this wonderful faculty of *abstracting their ideas,* they best can tell: for myself I find indeed I have a faculty of imagining, or representing to myself the ideas of those particular things I have perceived and of variously compounding and dividing them. I can imagine a man with two heads or the upper parts of a man joined to the body of a horse. I can consider the hand, the eye, the nose, each by itself abstracted or separated from the rest of the body. But then whatever hand or eye I imagine, it must have some particular shape and colour. Likewise the idea of man that I frame to myself, must be either of a white, or a black, or a tawny, a straight, or a crooked, a tall, or a low, or a middle-sized man. I cannot by any effort of thought conceive the abstract idea above described. And it is equally impossible for me to form the abstract idea of motion distinct from the body moving, and which is neither swift nor slow, curvilinear nor rectilinear; and the like may be said of all other abstract general ideas whatsoever. To be

plain, I own myself able to abstract in one sense, as when I consider some particular parts or qualities separated from others, with which though they are united in some object, yet, it is possible they may really exist without them. But I deny that I can abstract one from another, or conceive separately, those qualities which it is impossible should exist so separated; or that I can frame a general notion by abstracting from particulars in the manner aforesaid. Which two last are the proper acceptations of *abstraction.* And there are grounds to think most men will acknowledge themselves to be in my case. The generality of men which are simple and illiterate never pretend to *abstract notions.* It's said they are difficult and not to be attained without pains and study. We may therefore reasonably conclude that, if such there be, they are confined only to the learned.

11. I proceed to examine what can be alleged in defence of the doctrine of abstraction, and try if I can discover what it is that inclines the men of speculation to embrace an opinion, so remote from common sense as that seems to be. There has been a late deservedly esteemed philosopher, who, no doubt, has given it very much countenance by seeming to think the having abstract general ideas is what puts the widest difference in point of understanding betwixt man and beast. 'The having of general ideas (*saith he*) is that which puts a perfect distinction betwixt man and brutes, and is an excellency which the faculties of brutes do by no means attain unto. For it is evident we observe no footsteps in them of making use of general signs for universal ideas; from which we have reason to imagine that they have not the faculty of *abstracting* or making general ideas, since they have no use of words or any other general signs. *And a little after.* Therefore, I think, we may suppose that it is in this that the species of brutes are discriminated from men, and 'tis that proper difference wherein they are wholly separated, and which at last widens to so wide a distance. For if they have any ideas at all, and are not bare machines (as some would have them) we cannot deny them to have some reason. It seems as evident to me that they do some of them in certain instances reason as that they have sense, but it is only in particular ideas, just as they receive them from their senses. They are the best of

them tied up within those narrow bounds, and have not (as I think) the faculty to enlarge them by any kind of *abstraction.' Essay on Hum. Underst.,* b. 2. c. 11. sects. 10 and 11. I readily agree with this learned author, that the faculties of brutes can by no means attain to *abstraction.* But then if this be made the distinguishing property of that sort of animals, I fear a great many of those that pass for men must be reckoned into their number. The reason that is here assigned why we have no grounds to think brutes have abstract general ideas, is that we observe in them no use of words or any other general signs; which is built on this supposition, to wit, that the making use of words, implies the having general ideas. From which it follows, that men who use language are able to abstract or generalize their ideas. That this is the sense and arguing of the author will further appear by his answering the question he in another place puts. 'Since all things that exist are only particulars, how come we by general terms?' *His answer is,* 'Words become general by being made the signs of general ideas.' *Essay on Hum. Underst.,* b. 3. c. 3. sect. 6. But it seems that a word becomes general by being made the sign, not of an abstract general idea but, of several particular ideas, any one of which it indifferently suggests to the mind. For example, when it is said *the change of motion is proportional to the impressed force,* or that *whatever has extension is divisible*; these propositions are to be understood of motion and extension in general, and nevertheless it will not follow that they suggest to my thoughts an idea of motion without a body moved, or any determinate direction and velocity, or that I must conceive an abstract general idea of extension, which is neither line, surface nor solid, neither great nor small, black, white, nor red, nor of any other determinate colour. It is only implied that whatever motion I consider, whether it be swift or slow, perpendicular, horizontal or oblique, or in whatever object, the axiom concerning it holds equally true. As does the other of every particular extension, it matters not whether line, surface or solid, whether of this or that magnitude or figure.

12. By observing how ideas become general, we may the better judge how words are made so. And here it is to be noted that I do not deny absolutely there are general ideas, but only that there are any *abstract general ideas*: for in the passages above quoted, wherein there is mention of general ideas, it is always supposed that they are formed by *abstraction*, after the manner set forth in sects. 8 and 9. Now if we will annex a meaning to our words, and speak only of what we can conceive, I believe we shall acknowledge, that an idea, which considered in itself is particular, becomes general, by being made to represent or stand for all other particular ideas of the same sort. To make this plain by an example, suppose a geometrician is demonstrating the method, of cutting a line in two equal parts. He draws, for instance, a black line of an inch in length, this which in itself is a particular line is nevertheless with regard to its signification general, since as it is there used, it represents all particular lines whatsoever; for that what is demonstrated of it, is demonstrated of all lines or, in other words, of a line in general. And as that particular line becomes general, by being made a sign, so the name *line* which taken absolutely is particular, by being a sign is made general. And as the former owes its generality, not to its being the sign of an abstract or general line, but of all particular right lines that may possibly exist, so the latter must be thought to derive its generality from the same cause, namely, the various particular lines which it indifferently denotes.

13. To give the reader a yet clearer view of the nature of abstract ideas, and the uses they are thought necessary to, I shall add one more passage out of the *Essay on Human Understanding,* which is as follows. '*Abstract ideas* are not so obvious or easy to children or the yet unexercised mind as particular ones. If they seem so to grown men, it is only because by constant and familiar use they are made so. For when we nicely reflect upon them, we shall find that general ideas are fictions and contrivances of the mind, that carry difficulty with them, and do not so easily offer themselves, as we are apt to imagine. For example, does it not require some pains and skill to form the general idea of a triangle (which is yet none of the most abstract comprehensive and difficult) for it must be neither oblique nor rectangle, neither equilateral, equicrural, nor scalenon, but *all and none* of these at once. In effect, it is something imperfect that

cannot exist, an idea wherein some parts of several different and *inconsistent* ideas are put together. It is true the mind in this imperfect state has need of such ideas, and makes all the haste to them it can, for the conveniency of communication and enlargement of knowledge, to both which it is naturally very much inclined. But yet one has reason to suspect such ideas are marks of our imperfection. At least this is enough to shew that the most abstract and general ideas are not those that the mind is first and most easily acquainted with, nor such as its earliest knowledge is conversant about', b. 4. c. 7. sect. 9. If any man has the faculty of framing in his mind such an idea of a triangle as is here described, it is in vain to pretend to dispute him out of it, nor would I go about it. All I desire is, that the reader would fully and certainly inform himself whether he has such an idea or no. And this, methinks, can be no hard task for anyone to perform. What more easy than for anyone to look a little into his own thoughts, and there try whether he has, or can attain to have, an idea that shall correspond with the description that is here given of the general idea of a triangle, which is, *neither oblique, nor rectangle, equilateral, equicrural, nor scalenon, but all and none of these at once?*

14. Much is here said of the difficulty that abstract ideas carry with them, and the pains and skill requisite to the forming them. And it is on all hands agreed that there is need of great toil and labour of the mind, to emancipate our thoughts from particular objects, and raise them to those sublime speculations that are conversant about abstract ideas. From all which the natural consequence should seem to be, that so difficult a thing as the forming abstract ideas was not necessary for *communication,* which is so easy and familiar to all sorts of men. But we are told, if they seem obvious and easy to grown men, *It is only because by constant and familiar use they are made so.* Now I would fain know at what time it is, men are employed in surmounting that difficulty, and furnishing themselves with those necessary helps for discourse. It cannot be when they are grown up, for then it seems they are not conscious of any such pains-taking; it remains therefore to be the business of their childhood. And surely, the great and multiplied labour of framing abstract notions, will be found a hard task for that tender age. Is it not a hard thing to imagine, that a couple of children cannot prate together, of their sugar-plumbs and rattles and the rest of their little trinkets, till they have first tacked together numberless inconsistencies, and so framed in their minds *abstract general ideas,* and annexed them to every common name they make use of?

15. Nor do I think them a whit more needful for the *enlargement of knowledge than for communication.* It is I know a point, must insisted on, that all knowledge and demonstration are about universal notions, to which I fully agree: but then it doth not appear to me that those notions are formed by *abstraction* in the manner premised; *universality,* so far as I can comprehend not consisting in the absolute, positive nature or conception of anything, but in the relation it bears to the particulars signified or represented by it: by virtue whereof it is that things, names, or notions, being in their own nature *particular,* are rendered *universal.* Thus when I demonstrate any proposition concerning triangles, it is to be supposed that I have in view the universal idea of a triangle; which ought not to be understood as if I could frame an idea of a triangle which was neither equilateral nor scalenon nor equicrural. But only that the particular triangle I consider, whether of this or that sort it matters not, doth equally stand for and represent all rectilinear triangles whatsoever, and is in that sense *universal.* All which seems very plain and not to include any difficulty in it.

16. But here it will be demanded, how we can know any proposition to be true of all particular triangles, except we have first seen it demonstrated of the abstract idea of a triangle which equally agrees to all? For because a property may be demonstrated to agree to some one particular triangle, it will not thence follow that it equally belongs to any other triangle, which in all respects is not the same with it. For example, having demonstrated that the three angles of an isosceles rectangular triangle are equal to two right ones, I cannot therefore conclude this affection agrees to all other triangles, which have neither a right angle, nor two equal sides. It seems therefore that, to be certain this proposition is universally true, we must either make a particular demonstration for every particular triangle, which is impossible, or once for all demonstrate it of the

abstract idea of a triangle, in which all the particulars do indifferently partake, and by which they are all equally represented. To which I answer, that though the idea I have in view whilst I make the demonstration, be, for instance, that of an isosceles rectangular triangle, whose sides are of a determinate length, I may nevertheless be certain it extends to all other rectilinear triangles, of what sort or bigness soever. And that, because neither the right angle, nor the equality, nor determinate length of the sides, are at all concerned in the demonstration. It is true, the diagram I have in view includes all these particulars, but then there is not the least mention made of them in the proof of the proposition. It is not said, the three angles are equal to two right ones, because one of them is a right angle, or because the sides comprehending it are of the same length. Which sufficiently shews that the right angle might have been oblique, and the sides unequal, and for all that the demonstration have held good. And for this reason it is, that I conclude that to be true of any obliquangular or scalenon, which I had demonstrated of a particular right-angled, equicrural triangle; and not because I demonstrated the proposition of the abstract idea of· a triangle. And here it must be acknowledged that a man may consider a figure merely as triangular, without attending to the particular qualities of the angles, or relations of the sides. So far he may abstract: but this will never prove, that he can frame an abstract general inconsistent idea of a triangle. In like manner we may consider Peter so far forth as man, or so far forth as animal, without framing the forementioned abstract idea, either of man or of animal, in as much as all that is perceived is not considered.

17. It were an endless, as well as an useless thing, to trace the Schoolmen, those great masters of abstraction, through all the manifold inextricable labyrinths of error and dispute, which their doctrine of abstract natures and notions seems to have led them into. What bickerings and controversies, and what a learned dust have been raised about those matters, and what mighty advantage hath been from thence derived to mankind, are things at this day too clearly known to need being insisted on. And it had been well if the ill effects of that doctrine were confined to those only who make the most avowed profession of it. When men consider the great pains, industry and parts, that have for so many ages been laid out on the cultivation and advancement of the sciences, and that notwithstanding all this, the far greater part of them remain full of darkness and uncertainty, and disputes that are like never to have an end, and even those that are thought to be supported by the most clear and cogent demonstrations, contain in them paradoxes which are perfectly irreconcilable to the understandings of men, and that taking all together, a small portion of them doth supply any real benefit to mankind, otherwise than by being an innocent diversion and amusement. I say, the consideration of all this is apt to throw them into a despondency, and perfect contempt of all study. But this may perhaps cease, upon a view of the false principles that have obtained in the world, amongst all which there is none, methinks, hath a more wide influence over the thoughts of speculative men, than this of abstract general ideas.

18. I come now to consider the source of this prevailing notion, and that seems to me to be language. And surely nothing of less extent than reason itself could have been the source of an opinion so universally received. The truth of this appears as from other reasons, so also from the plain confession of the ablest patrons of abstract ideas, who acknowledge that they are made in order to naming; from which it is a clear consequence, that if there had been no such thing as speech or universal signs, there never had been any thought of abstraction. See b. 3. c. 6. sect. 39 and elsewhere of *The Essay on Human Understanding*. Let us therefore examine the manner wherein words have contributed to the origin of that mistake. First then, 'tis thought that every name hath, or ought to have, one only precise and settled signification, which inclines men to think there are certain *abstract, determinate ideas,* which constitute the true and only immediate signification of each general name. And that it is by the mediation of these abstract ideas, that a general name comes to signify any particular thing. Whereas, in truth, there is no such thing as one precise and definite signification annexed to any general name, they all signifying indifferently a great number of particular ideas. All which doth evidently follow from what has been already said, and will clearly

appear to anyone by a little reflexion. To this it will be objected, that every name that has a definition, is thereby restrained to one certain signification. For example, a *triangle* is defined to be a *plane surface comprehended by three right lines;* by which that name is limited to denote one certain idea and no other. To which I answer, that in the definition it is not said whether the surface be great or small, black or white, nor whether the sides are long or short, equal or unequal, nor with what angles they are inclined to each other; in all which there may be great variety, and consequently there is no one settled idea which limits the signification of the word *triangle.* 'Tis one thing for to keep a name constantly to the same definition, and another to make it stand everywhere for the same idea: the one is necessary, the other useless and impracticable.

19. But to give a farther account how words came to produce the doctrine of abstract ideas, it must be observed that it is a received opinion, that language has no other end but the communicating our ideas, and that every significant name stands for an idea. This being so, and it being withal certain, that names, which yet are not thought altogether insignificant, do not always mark out particular conceivable ideas, it is straightway concluded that they stand for abstract notions. That there are many names in use amongst speculative men, which do not always suggest to others determinate particular ideas, is what nobody will deny. And a little attention will discover, that it is not necessary (even in the strictest reasonings) significant names which stand for ideas should, every time they are used, excite in the understanding the ideas they are made to stand for: in reading and discoursing, names being for the most part used as letters are in *algebra,* in which though a particular quantity be marked by each letter, yet to proceed right it is not requisite that in every step each letter suggest to your thoughts, that particular quantity it was appointed to stand for.

20. Besides, the communicating of ideas marked by words is not the chief and only end of language, as is commonly supposed. There are other ends, as the raising of some passion, the exciting to, or deterring from an action, the putting the mind in some particular disposition; to which the former is in many cases barely subservient, and sometimes entirely omitted, when these can be obtained without it, as I think doth not infrequently happen in the familiar use of language. I entreat the reader to reflect with himself, and see if it doth not often happen either in hearing or reading a discourse, that the passions of fear, love, hatred, admiration, disdain, and the like arise, immediately in his mind upon the perception of certain words, without any ideas coming between. At first, indeed, the words might have occasioned ideas that were fit to produce those emotions; but, if I mistake not, it will be found that when language is once grown familiar, the hearing of the sounds or sight of the characters is oft immediately attended with those passions, which at first were wont to be produced by the intervention of ideas, that are now quite omitted. May we not, for example, be affected with the promise of a *good thing,* though we have not an idea of what it is? Or is not the being threatened with danger sufficient to excite a dread, though we think not of any particular evil likely to befall us, nor yet frame to ourselves an idea of danger in abstract? If anyone shall join ever so little reflection of his own to what has been said, I believe it will evidently appear to him, that general names are often used in the propriety of language without the speaker's designing them for marks of ideas in his own, which he would have them raise in the mind of the hearer. Even proper names themselves do not seem always spoken, with a design to bring into our view the ideas of those individuals that are supposed to be marked by them. For example, when a Schoolman tells me *Aristotle hath said it,* all I conceive he means by it, is to dispose me to embrace his opinion with the deference and submission which custom has annexed to that name. And this effect may be so instantly produced in the minds of those who are accustomed to resign their judgment to the authority of that philosopher, as it is impossible any idea either of his person, writings, or reputation should go before. Innumerable examples of this kind may be given, but why should I insist on those things, which everyone's experience will, I doubt not, plentifully suggest unto him?

21. We have, I think, shewn the impossibility of *abstract ideas.* We have considered what has been said for them by their ablest patrons; and endeavoured to shew they are of no use for those ends, to which

they are thought necessary. And lastly, we have traced them to the source from whence they flow, which appears to be language. It cannot be denied that words are of excellent use, in that by their means all that stock of knowledge which has been purchased by the joint labours of inquisitive men in all ages and nations, may be drawn into the view and made the possession of one single person. But at the same time it must be owned that most parts of knowledge have been strangely perplexed and darkened by the abuse of words, and general ways of speech wherein they are delivered. Since therefore words are so apt to impose on the understanding, whatever ideas I consider, I shall endeavour to take them bare and naked into my view, keeping out of my thoughts, so far as I am able, those names which long and constant use hath so strictly united with them; from which I may expect to derive the following advantages.

22. First, I shall be sure to get clear of all controversies purely verbal; the springing up of which weeds in almost all the sciences has been a main hindrance to the growth of true and sound knowledge. Secondly, this seems to be a sure way to extricate myself out of that fine and subtle net of *abstract ideas*, which has so miserably perplexed and entangled the minds of men, and that with this peculiar circumstance, that by how much the finer and more curious was the wit of any man, by so much the deeper was he like to be ensnared, and faster held therein. Thirdly, so long as I confine my thoughts to my own ideas divested of words, I do not see how I can easily be mistaken. The objects I consider, I clearly and adequately know. I cannot be deceived in thinking I have an idea which I have not. It is not possible for me to imagine, that any of my own ideas are alike or unlike, that are not truly so. To discern the agreements or disagreements there are between my ideas, to see what ideas are included in any compound idea, and what not, there is nothing more requisite, than an attentive perception of what passes in my own understanding.

23. But the attainment of all these advantages doth presuppose an entire deliverance from the deception of words, which I dare hardly promise myself; so difficult a thing it is to dissolve an union so early begun, and confirmed by so long a habit as that betwixt words and ideas. Which difficulty seems to have been very much increased by the doctrine of *abstraction*. For so long as men thought abstract ideas were annexed to their words, it doth not seem strange that they should use words for ideas: it being found an impracticable thing to lay aside the word, and retain the abstract idea in the mind, which in itself was perfectly inconceivable. This seems to me the principal cause, why those men who have so emphatically recommended to others, the laying aside all use of words in their meditations, and contemplating their bare ideas, have yet failed to perform it themselves. Of late many have been very sensible of the absurd opinions and insignificant disputes, which grow out of the abuse of words. And in order to remedy these evils they advise well, that we attend to the ideas signified, and draw off our attention from the words which signify them. But how good soever this advice may be, they have given others, it is plain they could not have a due regard to it themselves, so long as they thought the only immediate use of words was to signify ideas, and that the immediate signification of every general name was a *determinate, abstract idea*.

24. But these being known to be mistakes, a man may with greater ease prevent his being imposed on by words. He that knows he has no other than particular ideas, will not puzzle himself in vain to find out and conceive the abstract idea, annexed to any name. And he that knows names do not always stand for ideas, will spare himself the labour of looking for ideas, where there are none to be had. It were therefore to be wished that everyone would use his utmost endeavours, to obtain a clear view of the ideas he would consider, separating from them all that dress and encumbrance of words which so much contribute to blind the judgment and divide the attention. In vain do we extend our view into the heavens, and pry into the entrails of the earth, in vain do we consult the writings of learned men, and trace the dark footsteps of antiquity; we need only draw the curtain of words, to behold the fairest tree of knowledge, whose fruit is excellent, and within the reach of our hand.

25. Unless we take care to clear the first principles of knowledge, from the embarras and delusion of words, we may make infinite reasonings upon them to no purpose; we may draw consequences from consequences, and be never the wiser. The farther we go,

we shall only lose ourselves the more irrecoverably, and be the deeper entangled in difficulties and mistakes. Whoever therefore designs to read the following sheets, I entreat him to make my words the occasion of his own thinking, and endeavour to attain the same train of thoughts in reading, that I had in writing them. By this means it will be easy for him to discover the truth or falsity of what I say. He will be out of all danger of being deceived by my words, and I do not see how he can be led into an error by considering his own naked, undisguised ideas.

PART I

I. It is evident to any one who takes a survey of the objects of human knowledge, that they are either ideas actually imprinted on the senses, or else such as are perceived by attending to the passions and operations of the mind, or lastly, ideas formed by help of memory and imagination, either compounding, dividing, or barely representing those originally perceived in the aforesaid ways. By sight I have the ideas of light and colours with their several degrees and variations. By touch I perceive, for example, hard and soft, heat and cold, motion and resistance, and of all these more and less either as to quantity or degree. Smelling furnishes me with odours; the palate with tastes; and hearing conveys sounds to the mind in all their variety of tone and composition. And as several of these are observed to accompany each other, they come to be marked by one name, and so to be reputed as one thing. Thus, for example, a certain colour, taste, smell, figure, and consistence having been observed to go together, are accounted one distinct thing, signified by the name apple. Other collections of ideas constitute a stone, a tree, a book, and the like sensible things; which, as they are pleasing or disagreeable, excite the passions of love, hatred, joy, grief, and so forth.

II. But besides all that endless variety of ideas or objects of knowledge, there is likewise something which knows or perceives them, and exercises divers operations, as willing, imagining, remembering about them. This perceiving, active being is what I call mind, spirit, soul, or myself. By which words I do not denote any one of my ideas, but a thing entirely distinct from them, wherein they exist, or, which is the same thing, whereby they are perceived; for the existence of an idea consists in being perceived.

III. That neither our thoughts, nor passions, nor ideas formed by the imagination, exist without the mind, is what every body will allow. And (to me) it seems no less evident that the various sensations or ideas imprinted on the sense, however blended or combined together (that is, whatever objects they compose), cannot exist otherwise than in a mind perceiving them. I think an intuitive knowledge may be obtained of this, by any one that shall attend to what is meant by the term exist, when applied to sensible things. The table I write on, I say, exists, that is, I see and feel it; and if I were out of my study I should say it existed, meaning thereby that if I was in my study I might perceive it, or that some other spirit actually does perceive it. There was an odour, that is, it was smelled; there was a sound, that is to say, it was heard; a colour or figure, and it was perceived by sight or touch. This is all that I can understand by these and the like expressions. For as to what is said of the absolute existence of unthinking things without any relation to their being perceived, that seems perfectly unintelligible. Their esse is percipi, nor is it possible they should have any existence, out of the minds or thinking things which perceive them.

IV. It is indeed an opinion strangely prevailing amongst men, that houses, mountains, rivers, and in a word sensible objects have an existence natural or real, distinct from their being perceived by the understanding. But with how great an assurance and acquiescence soever this principle may be entertained in the world; yet whoever shall find in his heart to call it in question, may, if I mistake not, perceive it to involve a manifest contradiction. For what are the forementioned objects but the things we perceive by sense, and what do we perceive besides our own ideas or sensations; and is it not plainly repugnant that any one of these or any combination of them should exist unperceived?

V. If we thoroughly examine this tenet, it will, perhaps, be found at bottom to depend on the doctrine of abstract ideas. For can there be a nicer strain of abstraction than to distinguish the existence of sensible objects from their being perceived, so as to conceive them existing unperceived? Light and colours, heat and cold, extension and figures, in a word the things we see and feel, what are they but so many sensations, notions, ideas, or impressions on the sense; and is it possible to separate, even in thought, any of these from perception? For my part I might as easily divide a thing from itself. I may indeed divide in my thoughts or conceive apart from each other those things which, perhaps, I never perceived by sense so divided. Thus I imagine the trunk of a human body without the limbs, or conceive the smell of a rose without thinking on the rose itself. So far I will not deny I can abstract, if that may properly be called abstraction, which extends only to the conceiving separately such objects as it is possible may really exist or be actually perceived asunder. But my conceiving or imagining power does not extend beyond the possibility of real existence or perception. Hence as it is impossible for me to see or feel any thing without an actual sensation of that thing, so is it impossible for me to conceive in my thoughts any sensible thing or object distinct from the sensation or perception of it.

VI. Some truths there are so near and obvious to the mind, that a man need only open his eyes to see them. Such I take this important one to be, to wit, that all the choir of heaven and furniture of the earth, in a word all those bodies which compose the mighty frame of the world, have not any subsistence without a mind, that their being (esse) is to be perceived or known; that consequently so long as they are not actually perceived by me, or do not exist in my mind or that of any other created spirit, they must either have no existence at all, or else subsist in the mind of some eternal spirit: it being perfectly unintelligible and involving all the absurdity of abstraction, to attribute to any single part of them an existence independent of a spirit. To be convinced of which, the reader need only reflect and try to separate in his own thoughts the being of a sensible thing from its being perceived.

VII. From what has been said, it follows, there is not any other substance than spirit, or that which perceives. But for the fuller proof of this point, let it be considered, the sensible qualities are colour, figure, motion, smell, taste, and such like, that is, the ideas perceived by sense. Now for an idea to exist in an unperceiving thing, is a manifest contradiction; for to have an idea is all one as to perceive: that therefore wherein colour, figure, and the like qualities exist, must perceive them; hence it is clear there can

be no unthinking substance or substratum of those ideas.

VIII. But say you, though the ideas themselves do not exist without the mind, yet there may be things like them whereof they are copies or resemblances, which things exist without the mind, in an unthinking substance. I answer, an idea can be like nothing but an idea; a colour or figure can be like nothing but another colour or figure. If we look but ever so little into our thoughts, we shall find it impossible for us to conceive a likeness except only between our ideas. Again, I ask whether those supposed originals or external things, of which our ideas are the pictures or representations, be themselves perceivable or no? if they are, then they are ideas, and we have gained our point; but if you say they are not, I appeal to any one whether it be sense, to assert a colour is like something which is invisible; hard or soft, like something which is intangible; and so of the rest.

IX. Some there are who make a distinction betwixt primary and secondary qualities: by the former, they mean extension, figure, motion, rest, solidity or impenetrability, and number: by the latter they denote all other sensible qualities, as colours, sounds, tastes, and so forth. The ideas we have of these they acknowledge not to be the resemblances of any thing existing without the mind or unperceived; but they will have our ideas of the primary qualities to be patterns or images of things which exist without the mind, in an unthinking substance which they call matter. By matter therefore we are to understand an inert, senseless substance, in which extension, figure and motion, do actually subsist. But it is evident from what we have already shown, that extension, figure, and motion, are only ideas existing in the mind, and that an idea can be like nothing but another idea, and that consequently neither they nor their archetypes can exist in an unperceiving substance. Hence it is plain, that the very notion of what is called matter, or corporeal substance, involves a contradiction in it.

X. They who assert that figure, motion, and the rest of the primary or original qualities, do exist without the mind, in unthinking substances, do at the same time acknowledge that colours, sounds, heat, cold, and such like secondary qualities, do not, which they tell us are sensations existing in the mind alone, that depend on and are occasioned by the different size, texture, and motion of the minute particles of matter. This they take for an undoubted truth, which they can demonstrate beyond all exception. Now if it be certain, that those original qualities are inseparably united with the other sensible qualities, and not, even in thought, capable of being abstracted from them, it plainly follows that they exist only in the mind. But I desire any one to reflect and try, whether he can, by any abstraction of thought, conceive the extension and motion of a body, without all other sensible qualities. For my own part, I see evidently that it is not in my power to frame an idea of a body extended and moved, but I must withal give it some colour or other sensible quality which is acknowledged to exist only in the mind. In short, extension, figure, and motion, abstracted from all other qualities, are inconceivable. Where therefore the other sensible qualities are, there must these be also, to wit, in the mind and nowhere else.

XI. Again, great and small, swift and slow, are allowed to exist no where without the mind, being entirely relative, and changing as the frame or position of the organs of sense varies. The extension therefore which exists without the mind, is neither great nor small, the motion neither swift nor slow, that is, they are nothing at all. But, say you, they are extension in general, and motion in general: thus we see how much the tenet of extended, moveable substances existing without the mind, depends on that strange doctrine of abstract ideas. And here I cannot but remark, how nearly the vague and indeterminate description of matter or corporeal substance, which the modern philosophers are run into by their own principles, resembles that antiquated and so much ridiculed notion of materia prima, to be met with in Aristotle and his followers. Without extension solidity cannot be conceived; since therefore it has been shown that extension exists not in an unthinking substance, the same must also be true of solidity.

XII. That number is entirely the creature of the mind, even though the other qualities be allowed to exist without, will be evident to whoever considers, that the same thing bears a different denomination of number, as the mind views it with different respects. Thus, the same extension is one, or three, or thirty-six, according as the mind considers it with reference to a yard, a foot, or an inch. Number is so visibly relative, and dependent on men's under-

standing, that it is strange to think how any one should give it an absolute existence without the mind. We say, one book, one page, one line; all these are equally units, though some contain several of the others. And in each instance it is plain, the unit relates to some particular combination of ideas arbitrarily put together by the mind.

XIII. Unity, I know, some will have to be a simple or uncompounded idea, accompanying all other ideas into the mind. That I have any such idea, answering the word unity, I do not find; and if I had, methinks I could not miss finding it; on the contrary, it should be the most familiar to my understanding, since it is said to accompany all other ideas, and to be perceived by all the ways of sensation and reflection. To say no more, it is an abstract idea.

XIV. I shall further add, that after the same manner as modern philosophers prove certain sensible qualities to have no existence in matter, or without the mind, the same thing may be likewise proved of all other sensible qualities whatsoever. Thus, for instance, it is said that heat and cold are affections only of the mind, and not at all patterns of real beings, existing in the corporeal substances which excite them, for that the same body which appears cold to one hand, seems warm to another. Now why may we not as well argue that figure and extension are not patterns or resemblances of qualities existing in matter, because to the same eye at different stations, or eyes of a different texture at the same station, they appear various, and cannot therefore be the images of any thing settled and determinate without the mind? Again, it is proved that sweetness is not really in the said thing, because, the thing remaining unaltered, the sweetness is changed into bitter, as in case of a fever or otherwise vitiated palate. Is it not as reasonable to say, that motion is not without the mind, since if the succession of ideas in the mind become swifter, the motion, it is acknowledged, shall appear slower without any alteration in any external object.

XV. In short, let any one consider those arguments which are thought manifestly to prove that colours and tastes exist only in the mind, and he shall find they may with equal force be brought to prove the same thing of extension, figure, and motion. Though it must be confessed, this method of arguing doth not so much prove that there is no extension or colour in an outward object, as that we do not know by sense which is the true extension or colour of the object. But the arguments foregoing plainly show it to be impossible that any colour or extension at all, or other sensible quality whatsoever, should exist in an unthinking subject without the mind, or in truth, that there should be any such thing as an outward object.

XVI. But let us examine a little the received opinion. It is said extension is a mode or accident of matter, and that matter is the substratum that supports it. Now I desire that you would explain what is meant by matter's supporting extension: say you, I have no idea of matter, and therefore cannot explain it. I answer, though you have no positive, yet if you have any meaning at all, you must at least have a relative idea of matter; though you know not what it is, yet you must be supposed to know what relation it bears to accidents, and what is meant by its supporting them. It is evident support cannot here be taken in its usual or literal sense, as when we say that pillars support a building: in what sense therefore must it be taken?

XVII. If we inquire into what the most accurate philosophers declare themselves to mean by material substance, we shall find them acknowledge, they have no other meaning annexed to those sounds, but the idea of being in general, together with the relative notion of its supporting accidents. The general idea of being appeareth to me the most abstract and incomprehensible of all other; and as for its supporting accidents, this, as we have just now observed, cannot be understood in the common sense of those words; it must therefore be taken in some other sense, but what that is they do not explain. So that when I consider the two parts or branches which make the signification of the words material substance, I am convinced there is no distinct meaning annexed to them. But why should we trouble ourselves any further, in discussing this material substratum or support of figure and motion, and other sensible qualities? does it not suppose they have an existence without the mind? and is not this a direct repugnancy, and altogether inconceivable?

XVIII. But though it were possible that solid, figured, moveable substances may exist without the mind, corresponding to the ideas we have of bodies,

yet how is it possible for us to know this? either we must know it by sense, or by reason. As for our senses, by them we have the knowledge only of our sensations, ideas, or those things that are immediately perceived by sense, call them what you will: but they do not inform us that things exist without the mind, or unperceived, like to those which are perceived. This the materialists themselves acknowledge. It remains therefore that if we have any knowledge at all of external things, it must be by reason, inferring their existence from what is immediately perceived by sense. But (I do not see) what reason can induce us to believe the existence of bodies without the mind, from what we perceive, since the very patrons of matter themselves do not pretend, there is any necessary connexion betwixt them and our ideas. I say, it is granted on all hands (and what happens in dreams, frenzies, and the like, puts it beyond dispute) that it is possible we might be affected with all the ideas we have now, though no bodies existed without, resembling them. Hence it is evident the supposition of external bodies is not necessary for the producing our ideas: since it is granted they are produced sometimes, and might possibly be produced always, in the same order we see them in at present, without their concurrence.

XIX. But though we might possibly have all our sensations without them, yet perhaps it may be thought easier to conceive and explain the manner of their production, by supposing external bodies in their likeness rather than otherwise; and so it might be at least probable there are such things as bodies that excite their ideas in our minds. But neither can this be said; for though we give the materialists their external bodies, they, by their own confession, are never the nearer knowing how our ideas are produced: since they own themselves unable to comprehend in what manner body can act upon spirit, or how it is possible it should imprint any idea in the mind. Hence it is evident, the production of ideas or sensations in our minds, can be no reason why we should suppose matter or corporeal substances, since that is acknowledged to remain equally inexplicable with or without this supposition. If therefore it were possible for bodies to exist without the mind, yet to hold they do so must needs be a very precarious opinion; since it is to suppose, without any reason at all, that God has created innumerable beings that are entirely useless, and serve to no manner of purpose.

XX. In short, if there were external bodies, it is impossible we should ever come to know it; and if there were not, we might have the very same reasons to think there were that we have now. Suppose, what no one can deny possible, an intelligence, without the help of external bodies, to be affected with the same train of sensations or ideas that you are, imprinted in the same order and with like vividness in his mind. I ask, whether that intelligence hath not all the reason to believe the existence of corporeal substances, represented by his ideas, and exciting them in his mind, that you can possibly have for believing the same thing? Of this there can be no question; which one consideration is enough to make any reasonable person suspect the strength of whatever arguments he may think himself to have for the existence of bodies without the mind.

XXI. Were it necessary to add any further proof against the existence of matter, after what has been said, I could instance several of those errors and difficulties (not to mention impieties) which have sprung from that tenet. It has occasioned numberless controversies and disputes in philosophy, and not a few of greater moment in religion. But I shall not enter into the detail of them in this place, as well because I think arguments a posteriori are unnecessary for confirming what has been, if I mistake not, sufficiently demonstrated a priori, as because I shall hereafter find occasion to say somewhat of them.

XXII. I am afraid I have given cause to think me needlessly prolix in handling this subject. For to what purpose is it to dilate on that which may be demonstrated with the utmost evidence in a line or two, to any one that is capable of the least reflection? it is but looking into your own thoughts, and so trying whether you can conceive it possible for a sound, or figure, or motion, or colour, to exist without the mind, or unperceived. This easy trial may make you see, that what you contend for is a downright contradiction. Insomuch that I am content to put the whole upon this issue; if you can but conceive it possible for one extended moveable substance, or in general, for any one idea, or any thing like an idea, to exist otherwise than in a mind perceiving it, I shall readily give up the cause: and as for all that compacts of external bodies which you contend for, I shall grant you its existence, though you cannot either give me any reason why you believe it exists, or assign any use to it when it is supposed to exist. I say, the bare possibility of your opinion's being true, shall pass for an argument that it is so.

XXIII. But say you, surely there is nothing easier than to imagine trees, for instance, in a park, or books existing in a closet, and nobody by to perceive them. I answer, you may so, there is no difficulty in it: but what is all this, I beseech you, more than framing in your mind certain ideas which you call books and trees, and at the same time omitting to frame the idea of any one that may perceive them? but do not you yourself perceive or think of them all the while? this therefore is nothing to the purpose; it only shows you have the power of imagining or forming ideas in your mind; but it doth not show that you can conceive it possible the objects of your thought may exist without the mind: to make out this, it is necessary that you conceive them existing unconceived or unthought-of, which is a manifest repugnancy. When we do our utmost to conceive the existence of external bodies, we are all the while only contemplating our own ideas. But the mind, taking no notice of itself, is deluded to think it can and doth conceive bodies existing unthought-of or without the mind; though at the same time they are apprehended by or exist in itself. A little attention will discover to any one the truth and evidence of what is here said, and make it unnecessary to insist on any other proofs against the existence of material substance.

XXIV. It is very obvious, upon the least inquiry into our own thoughts, to know whether it be possible for us to understand what is meant by the absolute existence of sensible objects in themselves or without the mind. To me it is evident those words mark out either a direct contradiction, or else nothing at all. And to convince others of this, I know no readier or fairer way, than to entreat they would calmly attend to their own thoughts: and if by this attention the emptiness or repugnancy of those expressions does appear, surely nothing more is requisite for their conviction. It is on this therefore that I insist, to wit, that the absolute existence of unthinking things are words without a meaning, or which include a contradiction.

This is what I repeat and inculcate, and earnestly recommend to the attentive thoughts of the reader.

XXV. All our ideas, sensations, or the things which we perceive, by whatsoever names they may be distinguished, are visibly inactive; there is nothing of power or agency included in them. So that one idea or object of thought cannot produce, or make any alteration in another. To be satisfied of the truth of this, there is nothing else requisite but a bare observation of our ideas. For since they and every part of them exist only in the mind, it follows that there is nothing in them but what is perceived. But whoever shall attend to his ideas, whether of sense or reflection, will not perceive in them any power or activity; there is therefore no such thing contained in them. A little attention will discover to us that the very being of an idea implies passiveness and inertness in it, insomuch that it is impossible for an idea to do any thing, or, strictly speaking, to be the cause of any thing: neither can it be the resemblance or pattern of any active being, as is evident from Sect. viii. Whence it plainly follows that extension, figure, and motion, cannot be the cause of our sensations. To say, therefore, that these are the effects of powers resulting from the configuration, number, motion, and size of corpuscles, must certainly be false.

XXVI. We perceive a continual succession of ideas, some are anew excited, others are changed or totally disappear. There is therefore some cause of these ideas whereon they depend, and which produces and changes them. That this cause cannot be any quality or idea or combination of ideas, is clear from the preceding section. It must therefore be a substance; but it has been shown that there is no corporeal or material substance: it remains therefore that the cause of ideas is an incorporeal active substance or spirit.

XXVII. A spirit is one simple, undivided, active being: as it perceives ideas, it is called the understanding, and as it produces or otherwise operates about them, it is called the will. Hence there can be no idea formed of a soul or spirit: for all ideas whatever, being passive and inert (vide Sect. xxv.), they cannot represent unto us, by way of image or likeness, that which acts. A little attention will make it plain to any one, that to have an idea which shall be like that active principle of motion and change of ideas, is absolutely impossible. Such is the nature of spirit, or that which acts, that it cannot be of itself perceived but only by the effects which it produceth. If any man shall doubt of the truth of what is here delivered, let him but reflect and try if he can frame the idea of any power or active being; and whether he hath ideas of two principal powers, marked by the names *will* and *understanding*, distinct from each other as well as from a third idea of substance or being in general, with a relative notion of its supporting or being the subject of the aforesaid powers, which is signified by the name soul or spirit. This is what some hold; but so far as I can see, the words will, soul, spirit, do not stand for different ideas, or in truth, for any idea at all, but for something which is very different from ideas, and which being an agent cannot be like unto, or represented by, any idea whatsoever. Though it must be owned at the same time, that we have some notion of soul, spirit, and the operations of the mind, such as willing, loving, hating, inasmuch as we know or understand the meaning of those words.

XXVIII. I find I can excite ideas in my mind at pleasure, and vary and shift the scene as oft as I think fit. It is no more than willing, and straightway this or that idea arises in my fancy: and by the same power it is obliterated, and makes way for another. This making and unmaking of ideas doth very properly denominate the mind active. Thus much is certain, and grounded on experience: but when we talk of unthinking agents, or of exciting ideas exclusive of volition, we only amuse ourselves with words.

XXIX. But whatever power I may have over my own thoughts, I find the ideas actually perceived by sense have not a like dependence on my will. When in broad day-light I open my eyes, it is not in my power to choose whether I shall see or no, or to determine what particular objects shall present themselves to my view; and so likewise as to the hearing and other senses, the ideas imprinted on them are not creatures of my will. There is therefore some other will or spirit that produces them.

XXX. The ideas of sense are more strong, lively, and distinct than those of the imagination; they have likewise a steadiness, order, and coherence, and are not excited at random, as those which are the effects of human wills often are, but in a regular train or series, the admirable connexion whereof sufficiently testifies the wisdom and benevolence of its author. Now the set rules or established methods, wherein the mind we depend on excites in us the ideas of sense, are called the laws of nature: and these we learn by experience, which teaches us that such and such ideas are attended with such and such other ideas, in the ordinary course of things.

XXXI. This gives us a sort of foresight, which enables us to regulate our actions for the benefit of life. And without this we should be eternally at a loss: we could not know how to act any thing that might procure us the least pleasure, or remove the least pain of sense. That food nourishes, sleep refreshes, and fire warms us; that to sow in the seed-time is the way to reap in the harvest, and, in general, that to obtain such or such ends, such or such means are conducive, all this we know, not by discovering any necessary connexion between our ideas, but only by the observation of the settled laws of nature, without which we should be all in uncertainty and confusion, and a grown man no more know how to manage himself in the affairs of life than an infant just born.

XXXII. And yet this consistent, uniform working, which so evidently displays the goodness and wisdom of that governing Spirit whose will constitutes the laws of nature, is so far from leading our thoughts to him, that it rather sends them a wandering after second causes. For when we perceive certain ideas of sense constantly followed by other ideas, and we know this is not of our own doing, we forthwith attribute power and agency to the ideas themselves, and make one the cause of another, than which nothing can be more absurd and unintelligible. Thus, for example, having observed that when we perceive by sight a certain round luminous figure, we at the same time perceive by touch the idea or sensation called heat, we do from thence conclude the sun to be the cause of heat. And in like manner perceiving the motion and collision of bodies to be attended with sound, we are inclined to think the latter an effect of the former.

XXXIII. The ideas imprinted on the senses by the author of nature are called real things: and those excited in the imagination, being less regular, vivid, and constant, are more properly termed ideas, or images of things, which they copy and represent. But then our sensations, be they never so vivid and distinct, are nevertheless ideas, that is, they exist in the mind, or are perceived by it, as truly as the ideas of its own framing. The ideas of sense are allowed to have more reality in them, that is, to be more strong, orderly, and coherent than the creatures of the mind: but this is no argument that they exist without the mind. They are also less dependent on the spirit, or thinking substance which perceives them, in that they are excited by the will of another and more powerful spirit: yet still they are ideas, and certainly no idea, whether faint or strong, can exist otherwise than in a mind perceiving it.

XXXIV. Before we proceed any further, it is necessary to spend some time in answering objections which may probably be made against the principles hitherto laid down. In doing of which, if I seem too prolix to those of quick apprehensions, I hope it may be pardoned, since all men do not equally apprehend things of this nature; and I am willing to be understood by every one. First then it will be objected that by the foregoing principles, all that is real and substantial in nature is banished out of the world: and instead thereof a chimerical scheme of ideas takes place. All things that exist, exist only in the mind, that is, they are purely notional. What therefore becomes of the sun, moon, and stars? What must we think of houses, rivers, mountains, trees, stones; nay, even of our own bodies? Are all these but so many chimeras and illusions on the fancy? To all which, and whatever else of the same sort may be objected, I answer, that by the principles premised, we are not deprived of any one thing in nature. Whatever we see, feel, hear, or any wise conceive or understand, remains as secure as ever, and is as real as ever. There is a rerum natura, and the distinction between realities and chimeras retains its full force. This is evident from Sect. xxix., xxx., and xxxiii., where we have shown what is meant by real things in opposition to chimeras, or ideas of our own framing; but then they both equally exist in the mind, and in that sense are like ideas.

XXXV. I do not argue against the existence of any one thing that we can apprehend, either by sense or reflection. That the things I see with mine eyes and touch with my hands do exist, really exist, I make not the least question. The only thing whose existence we deny, is that which philosophers call matter or corporeal substance. And in doing of this, there is no damage done to the rest of mankind, who, I dare say, will never miss it. The atheist indeed will want the colour of an empty name to support his impiety; and the philosophers may possibly find, they have lost a great handle for trifling and disputation. . . .

CXLV. From what hath been said, it is plain that we cannot know the existence of other spirits otherwise than by their operations, or the ideas of them excited in us. I perceive several motions, changes, and combinations of ideas, that inform me there are certain particular agents like myself, which accompany them, and concur in their production. Hence the knowledge I have of other spirits is not immediate, as is the knowledge of my ideas; but depending on the intervention of ideas, by me referred to agents or spirits distinct from myself, as effects or concomitant signs.

CXLVI. But though there be some things which convince us human agents are concerned in producing them; yet it is evident to every one, that those things which are called the works of nature, that is, the far greater part of the ideas or sensations perceived by us, are not produced by, or dependent on, the wills of men. There is therefore some other spirit that causes them, since it is repugnant that they should subsist by themselves. See Sect. xxix. But if we attentively consider the constant regularity, order, and concatenation of natural things, the surprising magnificence, beauty, and perfection of the larger, and the exquisite contrivance of the smaller parts of the creation, together with the exact harmony and correspondence of the whole, but, above all, the never enough admired laws of pain and pleasure, and the instincts or natural inclinations, appetites, and passions of animals; I say if we consider all these things, and at the same time attend to the meaning and import of the attributes, one, eternal, infinitely wise, good, and perfect, we shall clearly perceive that they belong to the aforesaid spirit, who works all in all, and by whom all things consist.

CXLVII. Hence it is evident, that God is known as certainly and immediately as any other mind or spirit whatsoever, distinct from ourselves. We may even assert, that the existence of God is far more evidently perceived than the existence of men; because the effects of nature are infinitely more numerous and considerable than those ascribed to human agents. There is not any one mark that denotes a man, or effect produced by him, which doth not more strongly evince the being of that Spirit who is the Author of nature. For it is evident that in affecting other persons, the will of man hath no other object than barely the motion of the limbs of his body; but that such a motion should be attended by, or excite any idea in the mind of another, depends wholly on the will of the Creator. He alone it is who, "upholding all things by the world of his power," maintains that intercourse between spirits, whereby they are able to perceive the existence of each other. And yet this pure and clear light, which enlightens every one, is itself invisible.

THREE DIALOGUES BETWEEN HYLAS AND PHILONOUS IN OPPOSITION TO SCEPTICS AND ATHEISTS

THE FIRST DIALOGUE

Philonous.   Good morrow, Hylas: I did not expect to find you abroad so early.

Hylas.   It is indeed something unusual: but my thoughts were so taken up with a subject I was discoursing of last night, that finding I could not sleep, I resolved to rise and take a turn in the garden.

Phil.   It happened well, to let you see what innocent and agreeable pleasures you lose every morning. Can there be a pleasanter time of the day, or a more delightful season of the year? That purple sky, those wild but sweet notes of birds, the fragrant bloom upon the trees and flowers, the gentle influence of the rising sun, these and a thousand nameless beauties of nature inspire the

Reprinted from *Principles of Human Knowledge and Three Dialogues,* George Berkeley, 2009. By permission of Oxford University Press, Inc.

soul with secret transports; its faculties too being at this time fresh and lively, are fit for these meditations, which the solitude of a garden and tranquillity of the morning naturally dispose us to. But I am afraid I interrupt your thoughts; for you seemed very intent on something.

Hyl. It is true, I was, and shall be obliged to you if you will permit me to go on in the same vein; not that I would by any means deprive myself of your company, for my thoughts always flow more easily in conversation with a friend, than when I am alone: but my request is, that you would suffer me to impart my reflections to you.

Phil. With all my heart, it is what I should have requested myself, if you had not prevented me.

Hyl. I was considering the odd fate of those men who have in all ages, through an affectation of being distinguished from the vulgar, or some unaccountable turn of thought, pretended either to believe nothing at all, or to believe the most extravagant things in the world. This however might be borne, if their paradoxes and scepticism did not draw after them some consequences of general disadvantage to mankind. But the mischief lieth here; that when men of less leisure see them who are supposed to have spent their whole time in the pursuits of knowledge, professing an entire ignorance of all things, or advancing such notions as are repugnant to plain and commonly received principles, they will be tempted to entertain suspicions concerning the most important truths, which they had hitherto held sacred and unquestionable.

Phil. I entirely agree with you, as to the ill tendency of the affected doubts of some philosophers, and fantastical conceits of others. I am even so far gone of late in this way of thinking, that I have quitted several of the sublime notions I had got in their schools for vulgar opinions. And I give it you on my word, since this revolt from metaphysical notions to the plain dictates of nature and common sense, I find my understanding strangely enlightened, so that I can now easily comprehend a great many things which before were all mystery and riddle.

Hyl. I am glad to find there was nothing in the accounts I heard of you.

Phil. Pray, what were those?

Hyl. You were represented in last night's conversation, as one who maintained the most extravagant opinion that ever entered into the mind of man, to wit, that there is no such thing as material substance in the world.

Phil. That there is no such thing as what philosophers call material substance, I am seriously persuaded: but if I were made to see any thing absurd or sceptical in this, I should then have the same reason to renounce this, that I imagine I have now to reject the contrary opinion.

Hyl. What! can any thing be more fantastical, more repugnant to common sense, or a more manifest piece of scepticism, than to believe there is no such thing as matter?

Phil. Softly, good Hylas. What if it should prove, that you who hold there is, are by virtue of that opinion a greater sceptic, and maintain more paradoxes and repugnancies to common sense, than I who believe no such thing?

Hyl. You may as soon persuade me, the part is greater than the whole, as that, in order to avoid absurdity and scepticism, I should ever be obliged to give up my opinion in this point.

Phil. Well then, are you content to admit that opinion for true, which upon examination shall appear most agreeable to common sense, and remote from scepticism?

Hyl. With all my heart. Since you are for raising disputes about the plainest things in nature, I am content for once to hear what you have to say.

Phil. Pray, Hylas, what do you mean by a sceptic?

Hyl. I mean what all men mean, one that doubts of every thing.

Phil. He then who entertains no doubt concerning some particular point, with regard to that point cannot be thought a sceptic.

Hyl. I agree with you.

Phil. Whether doth doubting consist in embracing the affirmative or negative side of a question?

Hyl. In neither; for whoever understands English, cannot but know that doubting signifies a suspense between both.

Phil. He then that denieth any point, can no more be said to doubt of it than he who affirmeth it with the same degree of assurance.

Hyl. True.

Phil. And consequently, for such his denial is no more to be esteemed a sceptic than the other.

Hyl. I acknowledge it.

Phil. How cometh it to pass then, Hylas, that you pronounce me a sceptic, because I deny what you affirm, to wit, the existence of matter? Since, for ought you can tell, I am as peremptory in my denial, as you in your affirmation.

Hyl. Hold, Philonous, I have been a little out in my definition; but every false step a man makes in discourse is not to be insisted on. I said, indeed, that a sceptic was one who doubted of every thing; but I should have added, or who denies the reality and truth of things.

Phil. What things? Do you mean the principles and theorems of sciences? but these you know are universal intellectual notions, and consequently independent of matter; the denial therefore of this doth not imply the denying them.

Hyl. I grant it. But are there no other things? What think you of distrusting the senses, of denying the real existence of sensible things, or pretending to know nothing of them? Is not this sufficient to denominate a man a sceptic?

Phil. Shall we therefore examine which of us it is that denies the reality of sensible things, or professes the greatest ignorance of them; since, if I take you rightly, he is to be esteemed the greatest sceptic?

Hyl. That is what I desire.

Phil. What mean you by sensible things?

Hyl. Those things which are perceived by the senses. Can you imagine that I mean any thing else?

Phil. Pardon me, Hylas, if I am desirous clearly to apprehend your notions, since this may much shorten our inquiry. Suffer me then to ask you this further question. Are those things only perceived by the senses which are perceived immediately? or may those things properly be said to be sensible, which are perceived mediately, or not without the intervention of others?

Hyl. I do not sufficiently understand you.

Phil. In reading a book, what I immediately perceive are the letters, but mediately, or by means of these, are suggested to my mind the notions of God, virtue, truth &c. Now that the letters are truly sensible things, or perceived by sense, there is no doubt: but I would know whether you take the things suggested by them to be so too.

Hyl. No, certainly, it were absurd to think God or virtue sensible things, though they may be signified and suggested to the mind by sensible marks, with which they have an arbitrary connexion.

Phil. It seems then, that by sensible things you mean those only which can be perceived immediately by sense.

Hyl. Right.

Phil. Doth it not follow from this, that though I see one part of the sky red, and another blue, and that my reason doth thence evidently conclude there must be some cause of that diversity of colours, yet that cause cannot be said to be a sensible thing, or perceived by the sense of seeing?

Hyl. It doth.

Phil. In like manner, though I hear variety of sounds, yet I cannot be said to hear the causes of those sounds.

Hyl. You cannot.

Phil. And when by my touch I perceive a thing to be hot and heavy, I cannot say with any truth or propriety, that I feel the cause of its heat or weight.

Hyl. To prevent any more questions of this kind, I tell you once for all, that by sensible things I mean those only which are perceived by sense, and that in truth the senses perceive nothing which they do not perceive immediately: for they make no inferences. The deducing therefore of causes or occasions from effects and appearances, which alone are perceived by sense, entirely relates to reason.

Phil. This point then is agreed between us, that sensible things are those only which are immediately perceived by sense. You will further inform me, whether we immediately perceive by sight any thing beside light, and colours, and figures: or by hearing any thing but sounds: by the palate, any thing besides tastes: by the smell, besides odours: or by the touch, more than tangible qualities.

Hyl.   We do not.

Phil.   It seems therefore, that if you take away all sensible qualities, there remains nothing sensible.

Hyl.   I grant it.

Phil.   Sensible things therefore are nothing else but so many sensible qualities, or combinations of sensible qualities.

Hyl.   Nothing else.

Phil.   Heat then is a sensible thing.

Hyl.   Certainly.

Phil.   Doth the reality of sensible things consist in being perceived? or, is it something distinct from their being perceived, and that bears no relation to the mind?

Hyl.   To exist is one thing, and to be perceived is another.

Phil.   I speak with regard to sensible things only; and of these I ask, whether by their real existence you mean a subsistence exterior to the mind, and distinct from their being perceived?

Hyl.   I mean a real absolute being, distinct from, and without any relation to their being perceived.

Phil.   Heat therefore, if it be allowed a real being, must exist without the mind.

Hyl.   It must.

Phil.   Tell me, Hylas, is this real existence equally compatible to all degrees of heat, which we perceive: or is there any reason why we should attribute it to some, and deny it others? and if there be, pray let me know that reason.

Hyl.   Whatever degree of heat we perceive by sense, we may be sure the same exists in the object that occasions it.

Phil.   What, the greatest as well as the least?

Hyl.   I tell you, the reason is plainly the same in respect of both: they are both perceived by sense; nay, the greater degree of heat is more sensibly perceived; and consequently, if there is any difference, we are more certain of its real existence than we can be of the reality of a lesser degree.

Phil.   But is not the most vehement and intense degree of heat a very great pain?

Hyl.   No one can deny it.

Phil.   And is any unperceiving thing capable of pain or pleasure?

Hyl.   No certainly.

Phil.   Is your material substance a senseless being, or a being endowed with sense and perception?

Hyl.   It is senseless without doubt.

Phil.   It cannot therefore be the subject of pain.

Hyl.   By no means.

Phil.   Nor consequently of the greatest heat perceived by sense, since you acknowledge this to be no small pain.

Hyl.   I grant it.

Phil.   What shall we say then of your external object; is it a material substance, or no?

Hyl.   It is a material substance with the sensible qualities inhering in it.

Phil.   How then can a great heat exist in it, since you own it cannot in a material substance? I desire you would clear this point.

Hyl.   Hold, Philonous; I fear I was out in yielding intense heat to be a pain. It should seem rather, that pain is something distinct from heat, and the consequence or effect of it.

Phil.   Upon putting your hand near the fire, do you perceive one simple uniform sensation, or two distinct sensations?

Hyl.   But one simple sensation.

Phil.   Is not the heat immediately perceived?

Hyl.   It is.

Phil.   And the pain?

Hyl.   True.

Phil.   Seeing therefore they are both immediately perceived at the same time, and the fire affects you only with one simple, or uncompounded idea, it follows that this same simple idea is both the intense heat immediately perceived, and the pain; and consequently, that the intense heat immediately perceived, is nothing distinct from a particular sort of pain.

Hyl.   It seems so.

Phil. Again, try in your thoughts, Hylas, if you can conceive a vehement sensation to be without pain, or pleasure.

Hyl. I cannot.

Phil. Or can you frame to yourself an idea of sensible pain or pleasure in general, abstracted from every particular idea of heat, cold, tastes, smells, &c.?

Hyl. I do not find that I can.

Phil. Doth it not therefore follow, that sensible pain is nothing distinct from those sensations or ideas, in an intense degree?

Hyl. It is undeniable; and to speak the truth, I begin to suspect a very great heat cannot exist but in a mind perceiving it.

Phil. What! are you then in that sceptical state of suspense, between affirming and denying?

Hyl. I think I may be positive in the point. A very violent and painful heat cannot exist without the mind.

Phil. It hath not therefore, according to you, any real being.

Hyl. I own it.

Phil. Is it therefore certain, that there is no body in nature really hot?

Hyl. I have not denied there is any real heat in bodies. I only say, there is no such thing as an intense real heat.

Phil. But did you not say before, that all degrees of heat were equally real: or if there was any difference, that the greater were more undoubtedly real than the lesser?

Hyl. True: but it was, because I did not then consider the ground there is for distinguishing between them, which I now plainly see. And it is this: because intense heat is nothing else but a particular kind of painful sensation; and pain cannot exist but in a perceiving being; it follows that no intense heat can really exist in an unperceiving corporeal substance. But this is no reason why we should deny heat in an inferior degree to exist in such a substance.

Phil. But how shall we be able to discern those degrees of heat which exist only in the mind, from those which exist without it?

Hyl. That is no difficult matter. You know, the least pain cannot exist unperceived; whatever therefore degree of heat is a pain, exists only in the mind. But as for all other degrees of heat, nothing obliges us to think the same of them.

Phil. I think you granted before, that no unperceiving being was capable of pleasure, any more than of pain.

Hyl. I did.

Phil. And is not warmth, or a more gentle degree of heat than what causes uneasiness, a pleasure?

Hyl. What then?

Phil. Consequently it cannot exist without the mind in any unperceiving substance, or body.

Hyl. So it seems.

Phil. Since therefore, as well those degrees of heat that are not painful, as those that are, can exist only in a thinking substance; may we not conclude that external bodies are absolutely incapable of any degree of heat whatsoever?

Hyl. On second thoughts, I do not think it so evident that warmth is a pleasure, as that a great degree of heat is a pain.

Phil. I do not pretend that warmth is as great a pleasure as heat is a pain. But if you grant it to be even a small pleasure, it serves to make good my conclusion.

Hyl. I could rather call it an indolence. It seems to be nothing more than a privation of both pain and pleasure. And that such a quality or state as this may agree to an unthinking substance, I hope you will not deny.

Phil. If you are resolved to maintain that warmth, or a gentle degree of heat, is no pleasure, I know not how to convince you otherwise, than by appealing to your own sense. But what think you of cold?

Hyl. The same that I do of heat. An intense degree of cold is a pain; for to feel a very great cold, is to perceive a great uneasiness: it cannot therefore exist without the mind; but a lesser degree of cold may, as well as a lesser degree of heat.

Phil. Those bodies therefore, upon whose application to our own we perceive a moderate degree of heat, must be concluded to have a moderate degree of heat or warmth in them: and those, upon whose application we feel a like degree of cold, must be thought to have cold in them.

Hyl. They must.

Phil. Can any doctrine be true that necessarily leads a man into an absurdity?

Hyl. Without doubt it cannot.

Phil. Is it not an absurdity to think that the same thing should be at the same time both cold and warm?

Hyl. It is.

Phil. Suppose now one of your hands hot, and the other cold, and that they are both at once put into the same vessel of water, in an intermediate state; will not the water seem cold to one hand, and warm to the other?

Hyl. It will.

Phil. Ought we not therefore by your principles to conclude, it is really both cold and warm at the same time, that is, according to your own concession, to believe an absurdity?

Hyl. I confess it seems so.

Phil. Consequently, the principles themselves are false, since you have granted that no true principle leads to an absurdity.

Hyl. But after all, can any thing be more absurd than to say, there is no heat in the fire?

Phil. To make the point still clearer; tell me, whether in two cases exactly alike, we ought not to make the same judgment?

Hyl. We ought.

Phil. When a pin pricks your finger, doth it not rend and divide the fibres of your flesh?

Hyl. It doth.

Phil. And when a coal burns your finger, doth it any more?

Hyl. It doth not.

Phil. Since therefore you neither judge the sensation itself occasioned by the pin, nor any thing like it to be in the pin; you should not, conformably to what you have now granted, judge the sensation occasioned by the fire, or any thing like it, to be in the fire.

Hyl. Well, since it must be so, I am content to yield this point, and acknowledge, that heat and cold are only sensations existing in our minds: but

there still remain qualities enough to secure the reality of external things.

Phil. But what will you say, Hylas, if it shall appear that the case is the same with regard to all other sensible qualities, and that they can no more be supposed to exist without the mind, than heat and cold?

Hyl. Then indeed you will have done something to the purpose; but that is what I despair of seeing proved.

Phil. Let us examine them in order. What think you of tastes, do they exist without the mind, or no?

Hyl. Can any man in his senses doubt whether sugar is sweet, or wormwood bitter?

Phil. Inform me, Hylas. Is a sweet taste a particular kind of pleasure or pleasant sensation, or is it not?

Hyl. It is.

Phil. And is not bitterness some kind of uneasiness or pain?

Hyl. I grant it.

Phil. If therefore sugar and wormwood are unthinking corporeal substances existing without the mind, how can sweetness and bitterness, that is, pleasure and pain, agree to them?

Hyl. Hold, Philonous; I now see what it was deluded me all this time. You asked whether heat and cold, sweetness and bitterness, were not particular sorts of pleasure and pain; to which I answered simply, that they were. Whereas I should have thus distinguished: those qualities, as perceived by us, are pleasures or pains, but not as existing in the external objects. We must not therefore conclude absolutely, that there is no heat in the fire, or sweetness in the sugar, but only that heat or sweetness, as perceived by us, are not in the fire or sugar. What say you to this?

Phil. I say it is nothing to the purpose. Our discourse proceeded altogether concerning sensible things, which you defined to be the things we immediately perceive by our senses. Whatever other qualities therefore you speak of, as distinct from these, I know nothing of them, neither do they at all belong to the point in dispute. You may indeed pretend to have discovered certain qualities which you do not perceive, and assert those insensible qualities exist in fire and sugar. But what use can be made of this to your present purpose, I am at a loss to conceive. Tell me then once more, do you acknowledge that heat and cold, sweetness and bitterness (meaning those qualities which are perceived by the senses), do not exist without the mind?

Hyl. I see it is to no purpose to hold out, so I give up the cause as to those mentioned qualities. Though I profess it sounds oddly, to say that sugar is not sweet.

Phil. But for your further satisfaction, take this along with you: that which at other times seems sweet, shall to a distempered palate appear bitter. And nothing can be plainer, than that divers persons perceive different tastes in the same food, since that which one man delights in, another abhors. And how could this be, if the taste was something really inherent in the food?

Hyl. I acknowledge I know not how.

Phil. In the next place, odours are to be considered. And with regard to these, I would fain know, whether what hath been said of tastes doth not exactly agree to them? Are they not so many pleasing or displeasing sensations?

Hyl. They are.

Phil. Can you then conceive it possible that they should exist in an unperceiving thing?

Hyl. I cannot.

Phil. Or can you imagine, that filth and ordure affect those brute animals that feed on them out of choice, with the same smells which we perceive in them?

Hyl. By no means.

Phil. May we not therefore conclude of smells, as of the other forementioned qualities, that they cannot exist in any but a perceiving substance or mind?

Hyl. I think so.

Phil. Then as to sounds, what must we think of them: are they accidents really inherent in external bodies, or not?

Hyl. That they inhere not in the sonorous bodies, is plain from hence; because a bell struck in the exhausted receiver of an air-pump, sends forth no sound. The air therefore must be thought the subject of sound.

Phil. What reason is there for that, Hylas?

Hyl. Because when any motion is raised in the air, we perceive a sound greater or lesser, in proportion to the air's motion; but without some motion in the air, we never hear any sound at all.

Phil. And granting that we never hear a sound but when some motion is produced in the air, yet I do not see how you can infer from thence, that the sound itself is in the air.

Hyl. It is this very motion in the external air, that produces in the mind the sensation of sound. For striking on the drum of the ear, it causeth a vibration, which by the auditory nerves being communicated to the brain, the soul is thereupon affected with the sensation called sound.

Phil. What! is sound then a sensation?

Hyl. I tell you, as perceived by us, it is a particular sensation in the mind.

Phil. And can any sensation exist without the mind?

Hyl. No, certainly.

Phil. How then can sound, being a sensation, exist in the air, if by the air you mean a senseless substance existing without the mind.

Hyl. You must distinguish, Philonous, between sound, as it is perceived by us, and as it is in itself; or, (which is the same thing) between the sound we immediately perceive, and that which exists without us. The former indeed is a particular kind of sensation, but the latter is merely a vibrative or undulatory motion in the air.

Phil. I thought I had already obviated that distinction by the answer I gave when you were applying it in a like case before. But to say no more of that; are you sure then that sound is really nothing but motion?

Hyl. I am.

Phil. Whatever therefore agrees to real sound, may with truth be attributed to motion.

Hyl. It may.

Phil. It is then good sense to speak of motion, as of a thing that is loud, sweet, acute, or grave.

Hyl. I see you are resolved not to understand me. Is it not evident, those accidents or modes belong only to sensible sound, or sound in the common acceptation of the word, but not to sound in the real and philosophic sense, which, as I just now told you, is nothing but a certain motion of the air?

Phil. It seems then there are two sorts of sound, the one vulgar, or that which is heard, the other philosophical and real.

Hyl. Even so.

Phil. And the latter consists in motion.

Hyl. I told you so before.

Phil. Tell me, Hylas, to which of the senses, think you, the idea of motion belongs: to the hearing?

Hyl. No, certainly, but to the sight and touch.

Phil. It should follow then, that according to you, real sounds may possibly be seen or felt, but never heard.

Hyl. Look you, Philonous, you may if you please make a jest of my opinion, but that will not alter the truth of things. I own, indeed, the inferences you draw me into sound something oddly: but common language, you know, is framed by, and for the use of the vulgar: we must not therefore wonder, if expressions adapted to exact philosophic notions, seem uncouth and out of the way.

Phil. Is it come to that? I assure you, I imagine myself to have gained no small point, since you make so light of departing from common phrases and opinions; it being a main part of our inquiry, to examine whose notions are widest of the common road, and most repugnant to the general sense of the world. But can you think it no more than a philosophical paradox, to say that real sounds are never heard, and that the idea of them is obtained by some other sense. And is there nothing in this contrary to nature and the truth of things?

Hyl. To deal ingenuously, I do not like it. And after the concessions already made, I had as well grant that sounds too have no real being without the mind.

Phil. And I hope you will make no difficulty to acknowledge the same of colours.

Hyl. Pardon me; the case of colours is very different. Can any thing be plainer, than that we see them on the objects?

Phil. The objects you speak of are, I suppose, corporeal substances existing without the mind.

Hyl. They are.

Phil. And have true and real colours inhering in them?

Hyl. Each visible object hath that colour which we see in it.

Phil. How! is there any thing visible but what we perceive by sight?

Hyl. There is not.

Phil. And do we perceive any thing by sense, which we do not perceive immediately?

Hyl. How often must I be obliged to repeat the same thing? I tell you, we do not.

Phil. Have patience, good Hylas; and tell me once more whether there is any thing immediately perceived by the senses, except sensible qualities. I know you asserted there was not: but I would now be informed, whether you still persist in the same opinion.

Hyl. I do.

Phil. Pray, is your corporeal substance either a sensible quality or made up of sensible qualities?

Hyl. What a question that is! who ever thought it was?

Phil. My reason for asking was, because in saying, each visible object hath that colour which we see in it, you make visible objects to be corporeal substances; which implies either that corporeal substances are sensible qualities, or else that there is something beside sensible qualities perceived by sight: but as this point was formerly agreed between us, and is still maintained by you, it is a clear consequence, that your corporeal substance is nothing distinct from sensible qualities.

Hyl. You may draw as many absurd consequences as you please, and endeavour to perplex the plainest things; but you shall never persuade me out of my senses. I clearly understand my own meaning.

Phil. I wish you would make me understand it too. But since you are unwilling to have your notion of corporeal substance examined, I shall urge that point no further. Only be pleased to let me know, whether the same colours which we see, exist in external bodies, or some other.

Hyl. The very same.

Phil. What! are then the beautiful red and purple we see on yonder clouds, really in them? Or do you imagine they have in themselves any other form than that of a dark mist or vapour?

Hyl. I must own, Philonous, those colours are not really in the clouds as they seem to be at this distance. They are only apparent colours.

Phil. Apparent call you them? how shall we distinguish these apparent colours from real?

Hyl. Very easily. Those are to be thought apparent, which, appearing only at a distance, vanish upon a nearer approach.

Phil. And those I suppose are to be thought real, which are discovered by the most near and exact survey.

Hyl. Right.

Phil. Is the nearest and exactest survey made by the help of a microscope, or by the naked eye?

Hyl. By a microscope, doubtless.

Phil. But a microscope often discovers colours in an object different from those perceived by the unassisted sight. And in case we had microscopes magnifying to any assigned degree; it is certain, that no object whatsoever viewed through them, would appear in the same colour which it exhibits to the naked eye.

Hyl. And what will you conclude from all this? You cannot argue that there are really and naturally no colours on objects; because by artificial managements they may be altered, or made to vanish.

Phil. I think it may evidently be concluded from your own concessions, that all the colours we see with our naked eyes, are only apparent as those on the clouds, since they vanish upon a more close and accurate inspection, which is afforded us by a microscope. Then as to what you say by way of prevention; I ask you, whether the real and natural state of an object is better discovered by a very sharp and piercing sight, or by one which is less sharp.

Hyl. By the former without doubt.

Phil. Is it not plain from dioptrics, that microscopes make the sight more penetrating, and represent objects as they would appear to the eye, in case it were naturally endowed with a most exquisite sharpness?

Hyl. It is.

Phil. Consequently the microscopical representation is to be thought that which best sets forth the real nature of the thing, or what it is in itself. The colours therefore by it perceived, are more genuine and real, than those perceived otherwise.

Hyl. I confess there is something in what you say.

Phil. Besides, it is not only possible but manifest, that there actually are animals, whose eyes are by nature framed to perceive those things, which by reason of their minuteness escape our sight. What think you of those inconceivably small animals perceived by glasses? must we suppose they are all stark blind? Or, in case they see, can it be imagined their sight hath not the same use in preserving their bodies from injuries, which appears in that of all other animals? And if it hath, is it not evident, they must see particles less than their own bodies, which will present them with a far different view in each object, from that which strikes our senses? Even our own eyes do not always represent objects to us after the same manner. In the jaundice, every one knows that all things seem yellow. Is it not therefore highly probable, those animals in whose eyes we discern a very different texture from that of ours, and whose bodies abound with different humours, do not see the same colours in every object that we do? From all of which, should it not seem to follow that all colours are equally apparent, and that none of those which we perceive are really inherent in any outward object?

Hyl. It should.

Phil. The point will be past all doubt, if you consider, that in case colours were real properties or affections inherent in external bodies, they could admit of no alteration, without some change wrought in the very bodies themselves: but is it not evident from what hath been said, that upon the use of microscopes, upon a change happening in the humours of the eye, or a variation of distance, without any manner of real alteration in the thing itself, the colours of any object are either changed, or totally disappear? Nay, all other circumstances remaining the same, change but the situation of some objects, and they shall present different colours to the eye. The same thing happens upon viewing an object in various degrees of light. And what is more known, than that the same bodies appear differently coloured by candle-light from what they do in the open day? Add to these the experiment of a prism, which, separating the heterogeneous rays of light, alters the colour of any object; and will cause the whitest to appear of a deep blue or red to the naked eye. And now tell me, whether you are still of opinion, that every body hath its true, real colour inhering in it; and if you think it hath, I would fain know further from you, what certain distance and position of the object, what peculiar texture and formation of the eye, what degree or kind of light is necessary for ascertaining that true colour, and distinguishing it from apparent ones.

Hyl. I own myself entirely satisfied, that they are all equally apparent; and that there is no such thing as colour really inhering in external bodies, but that it is altogether in the light. And what confirms me in this opinion, is, that in proportion to the light, colours are still more or less vivid; and if there be no light, then are there no colours perceived. Besides, allowing there are colours on external objects, yet how is it possible for us to perceive them? For no external body affects the mind, unless it act first on our organs of sense. But the only action of bodies is motion; and motion cannot be communicated otherwise than by impulse. A distant object therefore cannot act on the eye, nor consequently make itself or its properties perceivable to the soul. Whence it plainly follows, that it is immediately some contiguous substance, which operating on the eye occasions a perception of colours: and such is light.

Phil. How! is light then a substance?

Hyl. I tell you, Philonous, external light is nothing but a thin fluid substance, whose minute particles being agitated with a brisk motion, and in various manners reflected from the different surfaces of outward objects to the eyes, communicate different motions to the optic nerves; which being propagated to the brain, cause therein various impressions: and these are attended with the sensations of red, blue, yellow, &c.

Phil. It seems, then, the light doth no more than shake the optic nerves.

Hyl. Nothing else.

Phil. And consequent to each particular motion of the nerves the mind is affected with a sensation, which is some particular colour.

Hyl. Right.

Phil. And these sensations have no existence without the mind.

Hyl. They have not.

Phil. How then do you affirm that colours are in the light, since by light you understand a corporeal substance external to the mind?

Hyl. Light and colours, as immediately perceived by us, I grant cannot exist without the mind. But in themselves they are only the motions and configurations of certain insensible particles of matter.

Phil. Colours then, in the vulgar sense, or taken for the immediate objects of sight, cannot agree to any but a perceiving substance.

Hyl. That is what I say.

Phil. Well then, since you give up the point as to those sensible qualities, which are alone thought colours by all mankind beside, you may hold what you please with regard to those invisibles ones of the philosophers. It is not my business to dispute about them; only I would advise you to bethink yourself, whether, considering the inquiry we are upon, it be prudent for you to affirm the red and blue which we see are not real colours, but certain unknown motions and figures which no man ever did or can see, are truly so. Are not these shocking notions, and are not they subject to as many ridiculous inferences, as those you were obliged to renounce before in the case of sounds?

Hyl. I frankly own, Philonous, that it is in vain to stand out any longer. Colours, sounds, tastes, in a word, all those termed secondary qualities, have certainly no existence without the mind. But by this acknowledgment I must not be supposed to derogate any thing from the reality of matter or external objects, seeing it is no more than several philosophers maintain, who nevertheless are the furthest imaginable from denying matter. For the clearer understanding of this, you must know sensible qualities are by philosophers divided into primary and secondary. The former are extension, figure, solidity, gravity, motion, and rest. And these they hold exist really in bodies. The latter are those above enumerated; or briefly, all sensible qualities beside the primary, which they assert are only so many sensations or ideas existing no where but in the mind. But all this, I doubt not, you are already apprised of. For my part, I have been a long time sensible there was such an opinion current among philosophers, but was never thoroughly convinced of its truth till now.

Phil. You are still then of opinion, that extension and figures are inherent in external unthinking substances.

Hyl. I am.

Phil. But what if the same arguments which are brought against secondary qualities, will hold proof against these also?

Hyl. Why then I shall be obliged to think, they too exist only in the mind.

Phil. Is it your opinion, the very figure and extension which you perceive by sense, exist in the outward object or material substance?

Hyl. It is.

Phil. Have all other animals as good grounds to think the same of the figure and extension which they see and feel?

Hyl. Without doubt, if they have any thought at all.

Phil. Answer me, Hylas. Think you the senses were bestowed upon all animals for their preservation and well-being in life? or were they given to men alone for this end?

Hyl. I make no question but they have the same use in all other animals.

Phil. If so, is it not necessary they should be enabled by them to perceive their own limbs, and those bodies which are capable of harming them?

Hyl. Certainly.

Phil. A mite therefore must be supposed to see his own foot, and things equal or even less than it, as bodies of some considerable dimen-

sion; though at the same time they appear to you scarce discernible, or at best as so many visible points.

Hyl. I cannot deny it.

Phil. And to creatures less than the mite they will seem yet larger.

Hyl. They will.

Phil. Insomuch that what you can hardly discern, will to another extremely minute animal appear as some huge mountain.

Hyl. All this I grant.

Phil. Can one and the same thing be at the same time in itself of different dimensions?

Hyl. That were absurd to imagine.

Phil. But from what you have laid down it follows, that both the extension by you perceived, and that perceived by the mite itself, as likewise all those perceived by lesser animals, are each of them the true extension of the mite's foot, that is to say, by your own principles you are led into an absurdity.

Hyl. There seems to be some difficulty in the point.

Phil. Again, have you not acknowledged that no real inherent property of any object can be changed, without some change in the thing itself?

Hyl. I have.

Phil. But as we approach to or recede from an object, the visible extension varies, being at one distance ten or a hundred times greater than at another. Doth it not therefore follow from hence likewise, that it is not really inherent in the object?

Hyl. I own I am at a loss what to think.

Phil. Your judgment will soon be determined, if you will venture to think as freely concerning this quality, as you have done concerning the rest. Was it not admitted as a good argument, that neither heat nor cold was in the water, because it seemed warm to one hand, and cold to the other?

Hyl. It was.

Phil. Is it not the very same reasoning to conclude, there is no extension or figure in an object, because to one eye it shall seem little, smooth, and round, when at the same time it appears to the other, great, uneven, and angular?

Hyl. The very same. But doth this latter fact ever happen?

Phil. You may at any time make the experiment, by looking with one eye bare, and with the other through a microscope.

Hyl. I know not how to maintain it, and yet I am loath to give up extension, I see so many odd consequences following upon such a concession.

Phil. Odd, say you? After the concessions already made, I hope you will stick at nothing for its oddness. But on the other hand should it not seem very odd, if the general reasoning which includes all other sensible qualities did not also include extension? If it be allowed that no idea nor any thing like an idea can exist in an unperceiving substance, then surely it follows, that no figure or mode of extension, which we can either perceive or imagine, or have any idea of, can be really inherent in matter; not to mention the peculiar difficulty there must be, in conceiving a material substance, prior to and distinct from extension, to be the substratum of extension. Be the sensible quality what it will, figure, or sound, or colour; it seems alike impossible it should subsist in that which doth not perceive it.

Hyl. I give up the point for the present, reserving still a right to retract my opinion, in case I shall hereafter discover any false step in my progress to it.

Phil. That is a right you cannot be denied. Figures and extension being despatched, we proceed next to motion. Can a real motion in any external body be at the same time both very swift and very slow?

Hyl. It cannot.

Phil. Is not the motion of a body swift in a reciprocal proportion to the time it takes up in describing any given space? Thus a body that describes a mile in an hour, moves three times faster than it would in case it described only a mile in three hours.

Hyl. I agree with you.

Phil. And is not time measured by the succession of ideas in our minds?

Hyl. It is.

Phil. And is it not possible ideas should succeed one another twice as fast in your mind, as they do in mine, or in that of some spirit of another kind.

Hyl. I own it.

Phil. Consequently the same body may to another seem to perform its motion over any space in half the time that it doth to you. And the same reasoning will hold as to any other proportion: that is to say, according to your principles (since the motions perceived are both really in the object) it is possible one and the same body shall be really moved the same way at once, both very swift and very slow. How is this consistent either with common sense, or with what you just now granted?

Hyl. I have nothing to say to it.

Phil. Then as for solidity: either you do not mean any sensible quality by that word, and so it is beside our inquiry: or if you do, it must be either hardness or resistance. But both the one and the other are plainly relative to our senses: it being evident, that what seems hard to one animal, may appear soft to another, who hath greater force and firmness of limbs. Nor is it less plain, that the resistance I feel is not in the body.

Hyl. I own the very sensation of resistance, which is all you immediately perceive, is not in the body, but the cause of that sensation is.

Phil. But the causes of our sensations are not things immediately perceived, and therefore not sensible. This point I thought had been already determined.

Hyl. I own it was; but you will pardon me if I seem a little embarrassed: I know not how to quit my old notions.

Phil. To help you out, do but consider, that if extension be once acknowledged to have no existence without the mind, the same must necessarily be granted of motion, solidity, and gravity, since they all evidently suppose extension. It is therefore superfluous to inquire particularly concerning each of them. In denying extension, you have denied them all to have any real existence.

Hyl. I wonder, Philonous, if what you say be true, why those philosophers who deny the secondary qualities any real existence, should yet attribute it to the primary. If there is no difference between them, how can this be accounted for?

Phil. It is not my business to account for every opinion of the philosophers. But among other reasons which may be assigned for this, it seems probable, that pleasure and pain being rather annexed to the former than the latter, may be one. Heat and cold, tastes and smells, have something more vividly pleasing or disagreeable than the ideas of extension, figure, and motion, affect us with. And it being too visibly absurd to hold, that pain or pleasure can be in an unperceiving substance, men are more easily weaned from believing the external existence of the secondary, than the primary qualities. You will be satisfied there is something in this, if you recollect the difference you made between an intense and more moderate degree of heat, allowing the one a real existence, while you denied it to the other. But after all, there is no rational ground for that distinction; for surely an indifferent sensation is as truly a sensation, as one more pleasing or painful; and consequently should not any more than they be supposed to exist in an unthinking subject.

Hyl. It is just come into my head, Philonous, that I have somewhere heard of a distinction between absolute and sensible extension. Now though it be acknowledged that great and small, consisting merely in the relation which other extended beings have to the parts of our own bodies, do not really inhere in the substances themselves; yet nothing obliges us to hold the same with regard to absolute extension, which is something abstracted from great and small, from this or that particular magnitude or figure. So likewise as to motion, swift and slow are altogether relative to the succession of ideas in our own minds. But it doth not follow, because those modifications of motion exist not without the mind, that therefore absolute motion abstracted from them doth not.

Phil. Pray what is it that distinguishes one motion, or one part of extension from another? Is it not something sensible, as some degree of swiftness or slowness, some certain magnitude or figure peculiar to each?

Hyl. I think so.

Phil. These qualities therefore, stripped of all sensible properties, are without all specific and numerical differences, as the schools call them.

Hyl. They are.

Phil. That is to say, they are extension in general, and motion in general.

Hyl. Let it be so.

Phil. But it is a universally received maxim, that every thing which exists is particular. How then can motion in general, or extension in general, exist in any corporeal substance?

Hyl. It will take time to solve your difficulty.

Phil. But I think the point may be speedily decided. Without doubt you can tell, whether you are able to frame this or that idea. Now I am content to put our dispute on this issue. If you can frame in your thoughts a distinct abstract idea of motion or extension, divested of all those sensible modes, as swift and slow, great and small, round and square, and the like, which are acknowledged to exist only in the mind, I will then yield the point you contend for. But if you cannot, it will be unreasonable on your side to insist any longer upon what you have no notion of.

Hyl. To confess ingenuously, I cannot.

Phil. Can you even separate the ideas of extension and motion, from the ideas of all those qualities which they who make the distinction term secondary?

Hyl. What! is it not an easy matter, to consider extension and motion by themselves, abstracted from all other sensible qualities? Pray how do the mathematicians treat of them?

Phil. I acknowledge, Hylas, it is not difficult to form general propositions and reasonings about those qualities, without mentioning any other; and in this sense to consider or treat of them abstractedly. But how doth it follow that because I can pronounce the word motion by itself, I can form the idea of it in my mind exclusive of body? Or because theorems may be made of extension and figures, without any mention of great or small, or any other sensible mode or quality; that therefore it is possible such an abstract idea of extension, without any particular size or figure, or sensible quality, should be distinctly formed, and apprehended by the mind? Mathematicians treat of quantity, without regarding what other sensible qualities it is attended with, as being altogether indifferent to their demonstrations. But when laying aside the words, they contemplate the bare ideas, I believe you will find, they are not the pure abstracted ideas of extension.

Hyl. But what say you to pure intellect? May not abstracted ideas be framed by that faculty?

Phil. Since I cannot frame abstract ideas at all, it is plain, I cannot frame them by the help of pure intellect, whatsoever faculty you understand by those words. Besides, not to inquire into the nature of pure intellect and its spiritual objects, as virtue, reason, God, or the like, thus much seems manifest, that sensible things are only to be perceived by sense, or represented by the imagination. Figures therefore and extension, being originally perceived by sense, do not belong to pure intellect. But for your further satisfaction, try if you can frame the idea of any figure, abstracted from all particularities of size, or even from other sensible qualities.

Hyl. Let me think a little—I do not find that I can.

Phil. And can you think it possible, that should really exist in nature, which implies a repugnancy in its conception?

Hyl. By no means.

Phil. Since therefore it is impossible even for the mind to disunite the ideas of extension and motion from all other sensible qualities, doth it not follow, that where the one exist, there necessarily the other exist likewise?

Hyl. It should seem so.

Phil. Consequently the very same arguments which you admitted, as conclusive against the secondary qualities, are without any further application of force against the primary too. Besides, if you will trust your senses, is it not plain all sensible qualities co-exist, or to them appear as being in the same place? Do they ever represent a motion, or figure, as being divested of all other visible and tangible qualities?

Hyl. You need say no more on this head. I am free to own, if there be no secret error or oversight in our proceedings hitherto, that all sensible qualities are alike to be denied existence without the mind. But my fear is, that I have been too liberal in my former concessions, or overlooked some fallacy or other. In short, I did not take time to think.

Phil. For that matter, Hylas, you may take what time you please in reviewing the progress of our inquiry. You are at liberty to recover any slips you might have made, or offer whatever you have omitted, which makes for your first opinion.

Hyl. One great oversight I take to be this: that I did not sufficiently distinguish the object from the sensation. Now though this latter may not exist without the mind, yet it will not thence follow that the former cannot.

Phil. What object do you mean? The object of the senses?

Hyl. The same.

Phil. It is then immediately perceived?

Hyl. Right.

Phil. Make me to understand the difference between what is immediately perceived, and a sensation.

Hyl. The sensation I take to be an act of the mind perceiving; beside which, there is something perceived; and this I call the object. For example, there is red and yellow on that tulip. But then the act of perceiving those colours is in me only, and not in the tulip.

Phil. What tulip do you speak of? is it that which you see?

Hyl. The same.

Phil. And what do you see beside colour, figure, and extension?

Hyl. Nothing.

Phil. What you would say then is, that the red and yellow are co-existent with the extension; is it not?

Hyl. That is not all: I would say, they have a real existence without the mind, in some unthinking substance.

Phil. That the colours are really in the tulip which I see, is manifest. Neither can it be denied, that this tulip may exist independent of your mind or mine; but that any immediate object of the senses, that is, any idea, or combination of ideas, should exist in an unthinking substance, or exterior to all minds, is in itself an evident contradiction. Nor can I imagine how this follows from what you said just now, to wit that the red and yellow were on the tulip you saw, since you do not pretend to see that unthinking substance.

Hyl. You have an artful way, Philonous, of diverting our inquiry from the subject.

Phil. I see you have no mind to be pressed that way. To return then to your distinction between sensation and object; if I take you right, you distinguish in every perception two things, the one an action of the mind, the other not.

Hyl. True.

Phil. And this action cannot exist in, or belong to any unthinking thing; but whatever beside is implied in a perception, may.

Hyl. That is my meaning.

Phil. So that if there was a perception without any act of the mind, it were possible such a perception should exist in an unthinking substance.

Hyl. I grant it. But it is impossible there should be such a perception.

Phil. When is the mind said to be active?

Hyl. When it produces, puts an end to, or changes any thing.

Phil. Can the mind produce, discontinue, or change any thing but by an act of the will?

Hyl. It cannot.

Phil. The mind therefore is to be accounted active in its perceptions, so far forth as volition is included in them.

Hyl. It is.

Phil. In plucking this flower, I am active, because I do it by the motion of my hand, which was consequent upon my volition; so likewise in applying it to my nose. But is either of these smelling?

Hyl. No.

Phil. I act too in drawing the air through my nose; because my breathing so rather than otherwise, is the effect of my volition. But neither can this be called smelling: for if it were, I should smell every time I breathed in that manner.

Hyl. True.

Phil. Smelling then is somewhat consequent to all this.

Hyl. It is.

Phil. But I do not find my will concerned any further. Whatever more there is, as that I perceive such a particular smell or any smell at all, this is independent of my will, and therein I am altogether passive. Do you find it otherwise with you, Hylas?

Hyl. No, the very same.

Phil. Then as to seeing, is it not in your power to open your eyes, or keep them shut; to turn them this or that way?

Hyl. Without doubt.

Phil. But doth it in like manner depend on your will, that in looking on this flower, you perceive white rather than any other colour? Or directing your open eyes towards yonder part of the heaven, can you avoid seeing the sun? Or is light or darkness the effect of your volition?

Hyl. No, certainly.

Phil. You are then in these respects altogether passive.

Hyl. I am.

Phil. Tell me now, whether seeing consists in perceiving light and colours, or in opening and turning the eyes?

Hyl. Without doubt, in the former.

Phil. Since therefore you are in the very perception of light and colours altogether passive, what is become of that action you were speaking of, as an ingredient in every sensation? And doth it not follow from your own concessions, that the perception of light and colours, including no action in it, may exist in an unperceiving substance? And is not this a plain contradiction?

Hyl. I know not what to think of it.

Phil. Besides, since you distinguish the active and passive in every perception, you must do it in that of pain. But how is it possible that pain, be it as little active as you please, should exist in an unperceiving substance? In short, do but consider the point, and then confess ingenuously, whether light and colours, tastes, sounds, &c., are not all equally passions or sensations in the soul. You may indeed call them external objects, and give them in words what subsistence you please. But examine your own thoughts, and then tell me whether it be not as I say?

Hyl. I acknowledge, Philonous, that upon a fair observation of what passes in my mind, I can discover nothing else, but that I am a thinking being, affected with variety of sensations; neither is it possible to conceive how a sensation should exist in an unperceiving substance. But then on the other hand, when I look on sensible things in a different view, considering them as so many modes and qualities, I find it necessary to suppose a material substratum, without which they cannot be conceived to exist.

Phil. Material substratum call you it? Pray, by which of your senses came you acquainted with that being?

Hyl. It is not itself sensible; its modes and qualities only being perceived by the senses.

Phil. I presume then, it was by reflection and reason you obtained the idea of it.

Hyl. I do not pretend to any proper positive idea of it. However I conclude it exists, because qualities cannot be conceived to exist without a support.

Phil. It seems then you have only a relative notion of it, or that you conceive it not otherwise than by conceiving the relation it bears to sensible qualities.

Hyl. Right.

Phil. Be pleased therefore to let me know wherein that relation consists.

Hyl. Is it not sufficiently expressed in the term substratum, or substance?

Phil. If so, the word substratum should import, that it is spread under the sensible qualities or accidents.

Hyl. True.

Phil. And consequently under extension.

Hyl. I own it.

Phil. It is therefore somewhat in its own nature entirely distinct from extension.

Hyl. I tell you, extension is only a mode, and matter is something that supports modes. And is it not evident the thing supported is different from the thing supporting?

Phil. So that something distinct from, and exclusive of extension, is supposed to be the substratum of extension.

Hyl. Just so.

Phil. Answer me, Hylas. Can a thing be spread without extension? or is not the idea of extension necessarily included in spreading?

Hyl. It is.

Phil. Whatsoever therefore you suppose spread under any thing, must have in itself an extension distinct from the extension of that thing under which it is spread.

Hyl. It must.

Phil. Consequently every corporeal substance being the substratum of extension, must have in itself another extension by which it is qualified to be a substratum: and so on to infinity. And I ask whether this be not absurd in itself, and repugnant to what you granted just now, to wit, that the substratum was something distinct from, and exclusive of extension.

Hyl. Aye but Philonous, you take me wrong. I do not mean that matter is spread in a gross literal sense under extension. The word substratum is used only to express in general the same thing with substance.

Phil. Well then, let us examine the relation implied in the term substance. Is it not that it stands under accidents?

Hyl. The very same.

Phil. But that one thing may stand under or support another, must it not be extended?

Hyl. It must.

Phil. Is not therefore this supposition liable to the same absurdity with the former?

Hyl. You still take things in a strict literal sense: that is not fair, Philonous.

Phil. I am not for imposing any sense on your words: you are at liberty to explain them as you please. Only I beseech you, make me understand something by them. You tell me, matter supports or stands under accidents. How! is it as your legs support your body?

Hyl. No; that is the literal sense.

Phil. Pray let me know any sense, literal, or not literal, that you understand it in.—How long must I wait for an answer, Hylas?

Hyl. I declare I know not what to say. I once thought I understood well enough what was meant by matter's supporting accidents. But now the more I think on it, the less can I comprehend it; in short, I find that I know nothing of it.

Phil. It seems then you have no idea at all, neither relative nor positive, of matter; you know neither what it is in itself, nor what relation it bears to accidents.

Hyl. I acknowledge it.

Phil. And yet you asserted, that you could not conceive how qualities or accidents should really exist, without conceiving at the same time a material support of them.

Hyl. I did.

Phil. That is to say, when you conceive the real existence of qualities, you do withal conceive something which you cannot conceive.

Hyl. It was wrong, I own. But still I fear there is some fallacy or other. Pray what think you of this? It is just come into my head, that the ground of all our mistakes lies in your treating of each quality by itself. Now, I grant that each quality cannot singly subsist without the mind. Colour cannot without extension, neither can figure without some other sensible quality. But as the several qualities united or blended together form entire sensible things, nothing hinders why such things may not be supposed to exist without the mind.

Phil. Either, Hylas, you are jesting, or have a very bad memory. Though indeed we went through all the qualities by name one after another; yet my arguments, or rather your concessions no where tended to prove, that the secondary qualities did not subsist each alone by itself; but that they were not at all without the mind. Indeed in treating of figure and motion, we concluded they could not exist without the mind, because it was impossible even in thought to separate them from all secondary qualities, so as to conceive them existing by themselves. But then this was not the only argument made use of upon that oc-

casion. But (to pass by all that hath been hitherto said, and reckon it for nothing, if you will have it so) I am content to put the whole upon this issue. If you can conceive it possible for any mixture or combination of qualities, or any sensible object whatever, to exist without the mind, then I will grant it actually to be so.

Hyl. If it comes to that, the point will soon be decided. What more easy than to conceive a tree or house existing by itself, independent of, and unperceived by any mind whatsoever? I do at this present time conceive them existing after that manner.

Phil. How say you, Hylas, can you see a thing which is at the same time unseen?

Hyl. No, that were a contradiction.

Phil. Is it not as great a contradiction to talk of conceiving a thing which is unconceived?

Hyl. It is.

Phil. The tree or house therefore which you think of, is conceived by you.

Hyl. How should it be otherwise?

Phil. And what is conceived is surely in the mind.

Hyl. Without question, that which is conceived is in the mind.

Phil. How then came you to say, you conceived a house or tree existing independent and out of all minds whatsoever?

Hyl. That was, I own, an oversight; but stay, let me consider what led me into it. It is a pleasant mistake enough. As I was thinking of a tree in a solitary place, where no one was present to see it, methought that was to conceive a tree as existing unperceived or unthought of, not considering that I myself conceived it all the while. But now I plainly see, that all I can do is to frame ideas in my own mind. I may indeed conceive in my own thoughts the idea of a tree, or a house, or a mountain, but that is all. And this is far from proving, that I can conceive them existing out of the minds of all spirits.

Phil. You acknowledge then that you cannot possibly conceive how any one corporeal sensible thing should exist otherwise than in a mind?

Hyl.   I do.

Phil.   And yet you will earnestly contend for the truth of that which you cannot so much as conceive?

Hyl.   I profess I know not what to think, but still there are some scruples remain with me. Is it not certain I see things at a distance? Do we not perceive the stars and moon, for example, to be a great way off? Is not this, I say, manifest to the senses?

Phil.   Do you not in a dream too perceive those or the like objects?

Hyl.   I do.

Phil.   And have they not then the same appearance of being distant?

Hyl.   They have.

Phil.   But you do not thence conclude the apparitions in a dream to be without the mind?

Hyl.   By no means.

Phil.   You ought not therefore to conclude that sensible objects are without the mind, from their appearance or manner wherein they are perceived.

Hyl.   I acknowledge it. But doth not my sense deceive me in those cases?

Phil.   By no means. The idea or thing which you immediately perceive, neither sense nor reason inform you that it actually exists without the mind. By sense you only know that you are affected with such certain sensations of light and colours, &c. And these you will not say are without the mind.

Hyl.   True: but beside all that, do you not think the sight suggests something of outness or distance?

Phil.   Upon approaching a distant object, do the visible size and figure change perpetually, or do they appear the same at all distances?

Hyl.   They are in a continual change.

Phil.   Sight therefore doth not suggest or any way inform you, that the visible object you immediately perceive, exists at a distance, or will be perceived when you advance further onward, there being a continued series of visible objects succeeding each other, during the whole time of your approach.

Hyl.   It doth not; but still I know, upon seeing an object, what object I shall perceive after having passed over a certain distance: no matter whether it be exactly the same or no: there is still something of distance suggested in the case.

Phil.   Good Hylas, do but reflect a little on the point, and then tell me whether there be any more in it than this. From the ideas you actually perceive by sight, you have by experience learned to collect what other ideas you will (according to the standing order of nature) be affected with, after such a certain succession of time and motion.

Hyl.   Upon the whole, I take it to be nothing else.

Phil.   Now is it not plain, that if we suppose a man born blind was on a sudden made to see, he could at first have no experience of what may be suggested by sight.

Hyl.   It is.

Phil.   He would not then, according to you, have any notion of distance annexed to the things he saw; but would take them for a new set of sensations existing only in his mind.

Hyl.   It is undeniable.

Phil.   But to make it still more plain: is not distance a line turned endwise to the eye?

Hyl.   It is.

Phil.   And can a line so situated be perceived by sight?

Hyl.   It cannot.

Phil.   Doth it not therefore follow that distance is not properly and immediately perceived by sight?

Hyl.   It should seem so.

Phil.   Again, is it your opinion that colours are at a distance?

Hyl.   It must be acknowledged, they are only in the mind.

Phil.   But do not colours appear to the eye as coexisting in the same place with extension and figures?

Hyl.   They do.

Phil.   How can you then conclude from sight, that figures exist without, when you acknowledge colours do not; the sensible appearance being the very same with regard to both?

Hyl.   I know not what to answer.

Phil. But allowing that distance was truly and immediately perceived by the mind, yet it would not thence follow it existed out of the mind. For whatever is immediately perceived is an idea: and can any idea exist out of the mind?

Hyl. To suppose that were absurd: but inform me, Philonous, can we perceive or know nothing beside our ideas?

Phil. As for the rational deducing of causes from effects, that is beside our inquiry. And by the senses you can best tell, whether you perceive any thing which is not immediately perceived. And I ask you, whether the things immediately perceived, are other than your own sensations or ideas? You have indeed more than once, in the course of this conversation, declared yourself on those points; but you seem, by this last question, to have departed from what you then thought.

Hyl. To speak the truth, Philonous, I think there are two kinds of objects, the one perceived immediately, which are likewise called ideas; the other are real things or external objects perceived by the mediation of ideas, which are their images and representations. Now I own, ideas do not exist without the mind; but the latter sort of objects do. I am sorry I did not think of this distinction sooner; it would probably have cut short your discourse.

Phil. Are those external objects perceived by sense, or by some other faculty?

Hyl. They are perceived by sense.

Phil. How! is there any thing perceived by sense, which is not immediately perceived?

Hyl. Yes, Philonous, in some sort there is. For example, when I look on a picture or statue of Julius Caesar, I may be said, after a manner, to perceive him (though not immediately) by my senses.

Phil. It seems, then, you will have our ideas, which alone are immediately perceived, to be pictures of external things: and that these also are perceived by sense, inasmuch as they have a conformity or resemblance to our ideas.

Hyl. That is my meaning.

Phil. And in the same way that Julius Caesar, in himself invisible, is nevertheless perceived by sight; real things, in themselves imperceptible, are perceived by sense.

Hyl. In the very same.

Phil. Tell me, Hylas, when you behold the picture of Julius Caesar, do you see with your eyes any more than some colours and figures, with a certain symmetry and composition of the whole?

Hyl. Nothing else.

Phil. And would not a man, who had never known any thing of Julius Caesar, see as much?

Hyl. He would.

Phil. Consequently he hath his sight, and the use of it, in as perfect a degree as you.

Hyl. I agree with you.

Phil. Whence comes it then that your thoughts are directed to the Roman emperor and his are not? This cannot proceed from the sensations or ideas of sense by you then perceived; since you acknowledge you have no advantage over him in that respect. It should seem therefore to proceed from reason and memory: should it not?

Hyl. It should.

Phil. Consequently it will not follow from that instance, that any thing is perceived by sense which is not immediately perceived. Though I grant we may in one acceptation be said to perceive sensible things mediately by sense: that is, when from a frequently perceived connexion, the immediate perception of ideas by one sense suggests to the mind others perhaps belonging to another sense, which are wont to be connected with them. For instance, when I hear a coach drive along the streets, immediately I perceive only the sound; but from the experience I have had that such a sound is connected with a coach, I am said to hear the coach. It is nevertheless evident, that in truth and strictness, nothing can be heard but sound: and the coach is not then properly perceived by sense, but suggested from experience. So likewise when we are said to see a red-hot bar of iron; the solidity and heat of the iron are not the objects of sight, but suggested to the imagination by the colour and figure, which are properly perceived by that sense. In short, those things alone are actually and strictly perceived by any sense, which would have been perceived, in case that same sense had then been first conferred on us. As for other things, it is plain they are only suggested to the mind by experience grounded on former perceptions. But to return to your comparison of Caesar's picture, it is plain, if you keep to that, you must hold the real things or archetypes of our ideas are not perceived by sense, but by some internal faculty of the soul, as reason or memory. I would therefore fain know, what arguments you can draw from reason for the existence of what you call real things or material objects; or whether you remember to have seen them formerly as they are in themselves; or if you have heard or read of any one that did.

Hyl. I see, Philonous, you are disposed to raillery; but that will never convince me.

Phil. My aim is only to learn from you the way to come at the knowledge of material beings. Whatever we perceive, is perceived either immediately or mediately: by sense, or by reason and reflection. But as you have excluded sense, pray show me what reason you have to believe their existence; or what medium you can possibly make use of to prove it, either to mine or your own understanding.

Hyl. To deal ingenuously, Philonous, now I consider the point, I do not find I can give you any good reason for it. But thus much seems pretty plain, that it is at least possible such things may really exist; and as long as there is no absurdity in supposing them, I am resolved to believe as I did, till you bring good reasons to the contrary.

Phil. What! is it come to this, that you only believe the existence of material objects, and that your belief is founded barely on the possibility of its being true? Then you will have me bring reasons against it: though another would think it reasonable, the proof should lie on him who holds the affirmative. And after all, this very point which you are now resolved to maintain without any reason, is, in effect, what you have more than once, during this discourse, seen good reason to give up. But to pass over all this; if I understand you rightly, you say our ideas do not exist without the mind; but that they are

copies, images, or representations of certain originals that do.

Hyl. You take me right.

Phil. They are then like external things.

Hyl. They are.

Phil. Have those things a stable and permanent nature independent of our senses; or are they in a perpetual change, upon our producing any motions in our bodies, suspending, exerting, or altering our faculties or organs of sense.

Hyl. Real things, it is plain, have a fixed and real nature, which remains the same, notwithstanding any change in our senses, or in the posture and motion of our bodies; which, indeed, may affect the ideas in our minds, but it were absurd to think they had the same effect on things existing without the mind.

Phil. How then is it possible, that things perpetually fleeting and variable as our ideas, should be copies or images of any thing fixed and constant? or in other words, since all sensible qualities, as size, figure, colour, &c., that is, our ideas, are continually changing upon every alteration in the distance, medium, or instruments of sensation; how can any determinate material objects be properly represented or painted forth by several distinct things, each of which is so different from and unlike the rest? Or if you say it resembles some one only of our ideas, how shall we be able to distinguish the true copy from all the false ones?

Hyl. I profess, Philonous, I am at a loss. I know not what to say to this.

Phil. But neither is this all. Which are material objects in themselves, perceptible or imperceptible?

Hyl. Properly and immediately nothing can be perceived but ideas. All material things therefore are in themselves insensible, and to be perceived only by their ideas.

Phil. Ideas then are sensible, and their archetypes or originals insensible.

Hyl. Right.

Phil. But how can that which is sensible be like that which is insensible? Can a real thing in itself invisible be like a colour; or a real thing which is not audible, be like a sound? In a word, can any thing be like a sensation or idea, but another sensation or idea?

Hyl. I must own, I think not.

Phil. Is it possible there should be any doubt in the point? Do you not perfectly know your own ideas?

Hyl. I know them perfectly; since what I do not perceive or know, can be no part of my idea.

Phil. Consider therefore, and examine them, and then tell me if there be any thing in them which can exist without the mind: or if you can conceive any thing like them existing without the mind.

Hyl. Upon inquiry, I find it is impossible for me to conceive or understand how any thing but an idea can be like an idea. And it is most evident, that no idea can exist without the mind.

Phil. You are therefore by your principles forced to deny the reality of sensible things, since you made it to consist in an absolute existence exterior to the mind. That is to say, you are a downright sceptic. So I have gained my point, which was to show your principles led to scepticism.

Hyl. For the present I am, if not entirely convinced, at least silenced.

Phil. I would fain know what more you would require in order to a perfect conviction. Have you not had the liberty of explaining yourself all manner of ways? Were any little slips in discourse laid hold and insisted on? Or were you not allowed to retract or reinforce any thing you had offered, as best served your purpose? Hath not every thing you could say been heard and examined with all the fairness imaginable? In a word, have you not in every point been convinced out of your own mouth? And if you can at present discover any flaw in any of your former concessions, or think of any remaining subterfuge, any new distinction, colour, or comment whatsoever, why do you not produce it?

Hyl. A little patience, Philonous. I am at present so amazed to see myself ensnared, and as it were imprisoned in the labyrinths you have drawn me into, that on the sudden it cannot be expected I should find my way out. You must give me time to look about me, and recollect myself. . . .

[Philonous and Hylas agree to meet on the morrow.]

THE SECOND DIALOGUE

Hylas. I beg your pardon, Philonous, for not meeting you sooner. All this morning my head was so filled with our late conversation, that I had not leisure to think of the time of the day, or indeed of any thing else.

Philonous. I am glad you were so intent upon it, in hopes if there were any mistakes in your concessions, or fallacies in my reasonings from them, you will now discover them to me.

Hyl. I assure you, I have done nothing ever since I saw you, but search after mistakes and fallacies, and with that view have minutely examined the whole series of yesterday's discourse: but all in vain, for the notions it led me into, upon review appear still more clear and evident; and the more I consider them, the more irresistibly do they force my assent.

Phil. And is not this, think you, a sign that they are genuine, that they proceed from nature, and are comfortable to right reason? Truth and beauty are in this alike, that the strictest survey sets them both off to advantage. While the false lustre of error and disguise cannot endure being reviewed, or too nearly inspected.

Hyl. I own there is a great deal in what you say. Nor can any one be more entirely satisfied of the truth of those odd consequences, so long as I have in view the reasonings that lead to them. But when these are out of my thoughts, there seems on the other hand something so satisfactory, so natural and intelligible in the modern way of explaining things, that I profess I know now how to reject it.

Phil. I know not what way you mean.

Hyl. I mean the way of accounting for our sensations or ideas.

Phil. How is that?

Hyl. It is supposed the soul makes her residence in some part of the brain, from which the nerves take their rise, and are thence extended to all parts of the body: and that outward objects, by the different impressions they make on the organs of sense, communicate certain vibrative motions to the nerves; and these being filled with spirits, propagate them to the brain or seat of the soul, which according to the various impressions or traces thereby made in the brain, is variously affected with ideas.

Phil. And call you this an explication of the manner whereby we are affected with ideas?

Hyl. Why not, Philonous? have you any thing to object against it?

Phil. I would first know whether I rightly understand your hypothesis. You make certain traces in the brain to be the causes or occasions of our ideas. Pray tell me, whether by the brain you mean any sensible thing?

Hyl. What else think you I could mean?

Phil. Sensible things are all immediately perceivable; and those things which are immediately perceivable, are ideas; and these exist only in the mind. Thus much you have, if I mistake not, long since agreed to.

Hyl. I do not deny it.

Phil. The brain therefore you speak of, being a sensible thing, exists only in the mind. Now, I would fain know whether you think it reasonable to suppose, that one idea or thing existing in the mind, occasions all other ideas. And if you think so, pray how do you account for the origin of that primary idea or brain itself?

Hyl. I do not explain the origin of our ideas by that brain which is perceivable to sense, this being itself only a combination of sensible ideas, but by another which I imagine.

Phil. But are not things imagined as truly in the mind as things perceived?

Hyl. I must confess they are.

Phil. It comes therefore to the same thing; and you have been all this while accounting for ideas, by certain motions or impressions in the brain, that is, by some alterations in an idea, whether sensible or imaginable, it matters not.

Hyl. I begin to suspect my hypothesis.

Phil. Beside spirits, all that we know or conceive are our own ideas. When therefore you say, all ideas are occasioned by impressions in the brain, do you conceive this brain or no? If you do, then you talk of ideas imprinted in an idea, causing that same idea, which is absurd. If you do not conceive it, you talk unintelligibly, instead of forming a reasonable hypothesis.

Hyl. I now clearly see it was a mere dream. There is nothing in it.

Phil. You need not be much concerned at it; for after all, this way of explaining things, as you called it, could never have satisfied any reasonable man. What connexion is there between a motion in the nerves, and the sensations of sound or colour in the mind? Or how is it possible these should be the effect of that?

Hyl. But I could never think it had so little in it, as now it seems to have.

Phil. Well then, are you at length satisfied that no sensible things have a real existence; and that you are in truth an arrant sceptic?

Hyl. It is too plain to be denied.

Phil. Look! are not the fields covered with a delightful verdure? Is there not something in the woods and groves, in the rivers and clear springs, that soothes, that delights, that transports the soul? At the prospect of the wide and deep ocean, or some huge mountain whose top is lost in the clouds, or of an old gloomy forest, are not our minds filled with a pleasing horror? Even in rocks and deserts, is there not an agreeable wildness? How sincere a pleasure is it to behold the natural beauties of the earth! to preserve and renew our relish for them, is not the veil of night alternately drawn over her face, and doth she not change her dress with the seasons? How aptly are the elements disposed! What variety and use in the meanest production of nature! What delicacy, what beauty, what contrivance in animal and vegetable bodies? How exquisitely are all things suited as well to their particular ends, as to constitute opposite parts of the whole! and while they mutually aid and support, do they not also set off and illustrate each other! Raise now your thoughts from this ball of earth, to all those glorious luminaries that adorn the high arch of heaven. The motion and situation of the planets, are they not admirable for use and order. Were those (miscalled erratic) globes ever known to stray, in their repeated journeys through the pathless void? Do they not measure areas round the sun ever proportioned to the times? So fixed, so immutable are the laws by which the unseen Author of nature actuates the universe. How vivid and radiant is the lustre of the fixed stars! how magnificent and rich that negligent profusion, with which they appear to be scattered throughout the whole azure vault! yet if you take the telescope, it brings into your sight a new host of stars that escape the naked eye. Here they seem contiguous and minute, but to a nearer view immense orbs of light at various distances, far sunk in the abyss of space. Now you must call imagination to your aid. The feeble narrow sense cannot descry innumerable worlds revolving round the central fires; and in those worlds the energy of an all-perfect mind displayed in endless forms. But neither sense nor imagination are big enough to comprehend the boundless extent with all its glittering furniture. Though the labouring mind exert and strain each power to its utmost reach, there still stands out ungrasped a surplusage immeasurable. Yet all the vast bodies that compose this mighty frame, how distant and remove soever, are by some secret mechanism, some divine art and force, linked in a mutual dependence and intercourse with each other, even with this earth, which was almost slipped from my thoughts, and lost in the crowd of worlds. Is not the whole system immense, beautiful, glorious beyond expression and beyond thought? What treatment then do those philosophers deserve, who would deprive these noble and delightful scenes of all reality? How should those principles be entertained, that lead us to think all the visible beauty of the creation a false imaginary glare? To be plain, can you expect this scepticism of yours will not be thought extravagantly absurd by all men of sense?

Hyl. Other men may think as they please: but for your part you have nothing to reproach me with. My comfort is, you are as much a sceptic as I am.

Phil. There, Hylas, I must beg leave to differ from you.

Hyl. Wait! have you all along agreed to the premises, and do you now deny the conclusion, and leave me to maintain these paradoxes by myself which you led me into? This surely is not fair.

Phil. I deny that I agreed with you in those notions that led to scepticism. You indeed said, the reality of sensible things consisted in an absolute existence out of the minds of spirits, or distinct from their being perceived. And pursuant to this notion of reality, you are obliged to deny sensible things any real existence: that is, according to your own definition, you profess yourself a sceptic. But I neither said nor thought the reality of sensible things was to be defined after that manner. To me it is evident, for the reasons you allow of, that sensible things cannot exist otherwise than in a mind or spirit. Whence I conclude, not that they have no real existence, but that seeing they depend not on my thought, and have an existence distinct from being perceived by me, there must be some other mind wherein they exist. As sure therefore as the sensible world really exists, so sure is there an infinite, omnipresent Spirit who contains and supports it.

Hyl. What! this is no more than I and all Christians hold; nay, and all others too who believe there is a God, and that he knows and comprehends all things.

Phil. Ay, but here lies the difference. Men commonly believe that all things are known or perceived by God, because they believe the being of a God, whereas I, on the other side, immediately and necessarily conclude the being of a God, because all sensible things must be perceived by him.

Hyl. But so long as we all believe the same thing, what matter is it how we come by that belief?

Phil. But neither do we agree in the same opinion. For philosophers, though they acknowledge all corporeal beings to be perceived by God, yet they attribute to them an absolute subsistence distinct from their being perceived by any mind whatever, which I do not. Besides, is there no difference between saying, there is a God, therefore he perceives all things: and saying, sensible things do really exist: and if they really exist, they are necessarily perceived by an infinite mind: therefore there is an infinite mind, or God. This furnishes you with a direct and immediate demonstration, from a most evident principle, of the being of a God. Divines and philosophers had proved beyond all controversy, from the beauty and usefulness of the several parts of the creation, that it was the workmanship of God. But that setting aside all help of astronomy and natural philosophy, all contemplation of the contrivance, order, and adjustment of things, an infinite mind should be necessarily inferred from the bare existence of the sensible world, is an advantage peculiar to them only who have made this easy reflection: that the sensible world is that which we perceive by our several senses; and that nothing is perceived by the senses beside ideas; and that no idea or archetype of an idea can exist otherwise than in a mind.

You may now, without any laborious search into the sciences, without any subtilty of reason, or tedious length of discourse, oppose and baffle the most strenuous advocate for atheism. Those miserable refuges, whether in an eternal succession of unthinking causes and effects, or in a fortuitous concourse of atoms; those wild imaginations of Vanini, Hobbes, and Spinoza; in a word, the whole system of atheism, is it not entirely overthrown by this single reflection on the repugnancy included in supposing the whole, or any part, even the most rude and shapeless of the visible world, to exist without a mind? Let any one of those abettors of impiety but look into his own thoughts, and there try if he can conceive how so much as a rock, a desert, a chaos, or confused jumble of atoms; how any thing at all, either sensible or imaginable, can exist independent of a mind, and he need go no further to be convinced of his folly. Can any thing be fairer than to put a dispute on such an issue, and leave it to a man himself to see if he can conceive, even in thought, what he holds to be true in fact, and from a notional to allow it a real existence?

Hyl. It cannot be denied, there is something highly serviceable to religion in what you advance. But do you not think it looks very like a notion entertained by some eminent moderns, of seeing all things in God?

Phil. I would gladly know that opinion; pray explain it to me.

Hyl. They conceive that the soul being immaterial, is incapable of being united with material things, so as to perceive them in themselves, but that she perceives them by her union with the substance of God, which being spiritual is therefore purely intelligible, or capable of being the immediate object of a spirit's thought. Besides, the divine essence contains in it perfections correspondent to each created being; and which are, for that reason, proper to exhibit or represent them to the mind. . . .

Phil. I do not pretend to be a setter-up of new notions. My endeavours tend only to unite and place in a clearer light that truth, which was before shared between the vulgar and the philosophers: the former being of opinion, that those things they immediately perceive are the real things: and the latter, that the things immediately perceived are ideas which exist only in the mind. Which two notions put together, do in effect constitute the substance of what I advance.

Hyl. I have been a long time distrusting my senses; methought I saw things by a dim light, and through false glasses. Now the glasses are removed, and a new light breaks in upon my understanding. I am clearly convinced that I see things in their native forms; and am no longer in pain about their unknown natures or absolute existence. This is the state I find myself in at present: though indeed the course that brought me to it I do not yet thoroughly comprehend. You set out upon the same principles that Academics, Cartesians, and the like sects, usually do; and for a long time it looked as if you were advancing their philosophical scepticism; but in the end your conclusions are directly opposite to theirs.

Phil. You see, Hylas, the water of yonder fountain, how it is forced upwards, in a round column, to a certain height; at which it breaks and falls back into the bason from whence it rose: its ascent, as well as descent, proceeding from the same uniform law or principle of gravitation. Just so, the same principles which at first view lead to scepticism, pursued to a certain point, bring men back to common sense.

REVIEW QUESTIONS

1. According to Berkeley, what is the most "extravagant opinion that ever entered into the mind of man"?
2. How does Berkeley try to show that all we ever experience is ideas?
3. Why does Philonous reject the notion of a material substratum (matter that exists independently of our perceptions)?
4. Why does the world continue to exist when we are not perceiving it?
5. On what grounds does Berkeley conclude that there is a God?

21

DAVID HUME

David Hume was born in Edinburgh in 1711 into a strict Scottish Presbyterian family. He was taught at home until the age of twelve, when he entered the University of Edinburgh, where he was to pursue a legal career. Instead he fell in love with philosophy. He lost his religious faith and tended toward skepticism. Still in his early twenties he tried a career in business, but it was not suitable to his personality. He suffered exhaustion and in 1734 he traveled to France and eventually found lodging at La Fleche, Descartes' alma mater. There he argued with the Jesuits about miracles and completed his *Treatise on Human Nature*. The book was published in England in January 1739, but sold few copies and received very little attention. Hume noted in his autobiography that it "fell dead-born from the press." Today this work of the youthful Hume is considered one of the classics of philosophy. Encouraged by the success of his work *Essays Moral and Political* (1741), he decided to revise the *Treatise* and published it under the title *An Enquiry Concerning Human Understanding* (1748). The entire book is reprinted here. In 1752 Hume became the librarian to the Faculty of Advocates in Edinburgh. While in this position he wrote his famous history of England. Hume never married. He was disappointed in love, having been rejected by the woman he proposed to marry—apparently she found him obese and clumsy. He was, nevertheless, a charming man with a good sense of humor, popular at social occasions, modest, mild, and moral, a generous friend. He died of cancer of the bowel on August 25, 1776, the year of the signing of the American Declaration of Independence. Hume's final masterpiece, *Dialogues Concerning Natural Religion*, had been written around 1751 but was left unpublished until after his death. Hume apparently thought its critique of religion too dangerous to publish. It appeared in print in 1779. It is reprinted here.

HUME'S THEORY OF KNOWLEDGE

Whereas Descartes was a Rationalist, who believed that reason could discover all truth, especially metaphysical truth, Hume, like Locke, is an Empiricist, who believes that we must start with our perceptions and reason from there. Descartes was a global skeptic, doubting even mathematical truth, whereas Hume is a *local* skeptic. He does not doubt truths of mathematics or logic as well as commonsense truth (e.g., memory reports and sensory impressions), but he doubts all metaphysical propositions: the existence of God, miracles, the idea of a self, material substance, free will, cause and effect, and induction.

Hume divides perceptions into two kinds: impressions and ideas. Impressions (both internal and external, the emotions, and sense experiences) are more forceful and lively when they strike the mind, whereas ideas are the faint copies of impressions we have when we remember past experiences or reason. All sensations, feelings, and passions are impressions. All thinking consists of ideas.

Hume's most original insight consists in his skepticism about causality and inductive reasoning. Before Hume philosophers thought that there was a *necessary connection* between cause and effect. Neither Locke nor Berkeley, nor anyone else before Hume, questioned the basic principle of causality. Hume asks, What is the origin of the idea of causality? Since ideas are copies of impressions, Hume asks what impressions give us the idea of causality. None can be discovered. Certainly, there is no impression of a necessary connection. Then how does the idea arise in the mind? Hume eventually concludes that it is brought on by a habit of association at seeing two types of events in constant conjunction.

Similarly, Hume challenges our notion of induction, the belief that the future will be like the past. Hume points out that, unlike truths of reason (logical and mathematical truths), it is never contradictory to deny a matter of fact. It is not logically necessary that the earth is now rotating or revolving around the sun, nor that it will do so tomorrow. These are mere contingent truths. "That the sun will not rise tomorrow is no less intelligible a proposition, and implies no more a contradiction than the affirmation that it will rise." And if the sun's not rising is possible, what reason do we have for thinking it won't actually happen?

What is our justification for the belief regarding matters of fact? Hume asks. He replies that we justify that belief by our belief in causal laws and relationships. We believe that a causal order rooted in nature's laws operates to produce all that is. But what is the foundation of all our reasoning concerning cause and effect? Experience, Hume replies, like a good Empiricist. All our experience corroborates such relations. But, Hume relentlessly continues, "What is the foundation of all conclusions from experience?" His reply, "In reality, all arguments from experience are founded on the similarity which we discover among natural objects, and by which we are induced to expect effects similar to those which we have found to follow from such objects." Only a fool or a lunatic would pretend to dispute this faith in causality based on experience.

But only experience shows us that certain objects and events regularly give rise to a number of uniform effects. From a body of like color and consistency with bread we "expect nourishment and support. But this surely is a step of the mind," which stands in need of explanation. Reasoning from the proposition "I have always found so and so to happen in the past" to the proposition "So and so will continue to happen in the future" is a great leap that stands in need of justification.

We must admit "that the inference is not intuitive; neither is it demonstrative. Of what nature is it then? To say it is experimental is begging the question. For all inferences from

No formal deductive argument ✱

experience suppose, as their foundation, that the future will resemble the past. It is impossible, therefore, that any argument from experience can prove this resemblance of the past to the future; since all these arguments are founded on the supposition of that resemblance."

Hume shows that our belief that the future will be like the past is based on our belief in the uniformity of nature, which in turn is based on our past experience, which is an inadequate premise for arguing for the future. The argument "The uniformity of nature has been reliable in the past so it will likely be reliable in the future," is not a sound deductive argument, because the conclusion contains more information than the premises. Inductive generalizations are "ampliative," adding more data than the premises contain. Since Hume's time there have been many attempts to solve this problem of induction.

In our second selection, from the *Treatise*, Hume casts doubt on our notions of the self and personal identity.

HUME'S PHILOSOPHY OF RELIGION

Our third selection is *Dialogues Concerning Natural Religion* (1779), in which Hume critiques the teleological and cosmological arguments for the existence of God and raises the problem of evil. Hume asserts that we cannot prove the existence of God via a priori reasoning (such as the ontological argument seeks to do) because the claim that God exists is a factual claim and it is never contradictory to deny a factual claim. So one must attempt to demonstrate God's existence via a posteriori arguments, those which begin with the observation that there is a world that needs to be accounted for and that there is order which suggests a designer. But Hume argues that such a posteriori arguments are filled with insuperable problems. Hume's several criticisms have engaged philosophers for over two hundred years. I trust that they will stimulate you to work out your own answers to the problems they raise.

It may help you to know that Cleanthes, who opens the dialogue, is a natural theologian. Demea is an orthodox believer, and the skeptic Philo, who puts forth the arguments against the argument from design, seems to represent Hume's position.

FOR FURTHER READING

Ayer, A. J. *Hume* (Oxford University Press, 1981).

Bennett, Jonathan. *Locke, Berkeley and Hume: Central Themes* (Oxford University Press, 1971).

Chappell, V. C., ed. *Hume: A Collection of Critical Essays* (University of Notre Dame Press, 1968).

Flew, Anthony. *Hume's Philosophy of Belief* (Routledge & Kegan Paul, 1961).

Hendel, William. *Studies in the Philosophy of David Hume* (Princeton University Press, 1925).

Kemp Smith, N. *The Philosophy of David Hume* (Macmillan, 1941).

Mackie, J. L. *Hume's Moral Theory* (Routledge & Kegan Paul, 1980).

Mossner, E. C. *The Life of David Hume* (Clarendon Press, 1954, 1980).

Norton, David. *David Hume: Common Sense Moralist, Sceptical Metaphysician* (Princeton University Press, 1982).

Skyrms, Brian. *Choice and Chance* (Wadsworth Publishing Company, 1986).

Stove, D. C. *Probability and Hume's Induction* (Clarendon Press, 1973).

Stroud, Barry. *Hume* (Routledge & Kegan Paul, 1978).

Swinburne, Richard. *The Existence of God* (Clarendon Press, 1979).

AN ENQUIRY CONCERNING HUMAN UNDERSTANDING

SECTION I: OF THE DIFFERENT SPECIES OF PHILOSOPHY

Moral philosophy, or the science of human nature, may be treated after two different manners, each of which has its peculiar merit, and may contribute to the entertainment, instruction, and reformation of mankind. The one considers man chiefly as born for action; and as influenced in his measures by taste and sentiment; pursuing one object, and avoiding another, according to the value which these objects seem to possess, and according to the light in which they present themselves. As virtue, of all objects, is allowed to be the most valuable, this species of philosophers paint her in the most amiable colours; borrowing all helps from poetry and eloquence, and treating their subject in an easy and obvious manner, and such as is best fitted to please the imagination, and engage the affections. They select the most striking observations and instances from common life; place opposite characters in a proper contrast; and alluring us into the paths of virtue by the views of glory and happiness, direct our steps in these paths by the soundest precepts and most illustrious examples. They make us feel the difference between vice and virtue; they excite and regulate our sentiments; and so they can but bend our hearts to the love of probity and true honour, they think, that they have fully attained the end of all their labors.

The other species of philosophers consider man in the light of a reasonable rather than an active being, and endeavor to form his understanding more than cultivate his manners. They regard human nature as a subject of speculation; and with a narrow scrutiny examine it, in order to find those principles, which regulate our understanding, excite our sentiments, and make us approve or blame any particular object, action, or behavior. They think it a reproach to all literature, that philosophy should not yet have fixed, beyond controversy, the foundation of morals, reasoning, and criticism; and should for ever talk of truth and falsehood, vice and virtue, beauty and deformity, without being able to determine the source of these distinctions. While they attempt this arduous task, they are deterred by no difficulties; but proceeding from particular instances to general principles, they still push on their enquiries to principles more general, and rest not satisfied till they arrive at those original principles, by which, in every science, all human curiosity must be bounded. Though their speculations seem abstract, and even unintelligible to common readers, they aim at the approbation of the learned and the wise; and think themselves sufficiently compensated for the labour of their whole lives, if they can discover some hidden truths, which may contribute to the instruction of posterity.

It is certain that the easy and obvious philosophy will always, with the generality of mankind, have the preference above the accurate and abstruse; and by many will be recommended, not only as more agreeable, but more useful than the other. It enters more into common life; molds the heart and affections; and, by touching those principles which actuate men, reforms their conduct, and brings them nearer to that model of perfection which it describes. On the contrary, the abstruse philosophy, being founded on a turn of mind, which cannot enter into business and action, vanishes when the philosopher leaves the shade, and comes into open day; nor can its principles easily retain any influence over our conduct and behavior. The feelings of our heart, the agitation of our passions, the vehemence of our affections, dissipate all its conclusions, and reduce the profound philosopher to a mere plebeian.

This also must be confessed, that the most durable, as well as justest fame, has been acquired by the easy philosophy, and that abstract reasoners seem hitherto to have enjoyed only a momentary reputation, from the caprice or ignorance of their own age, but have not been able to support their renown with more equitable posterity. It is easy for a profound philosopher to commit a mistake in his subtile reasonings; and one mistake is the necessary parent of another, while he pushes on his consequences, and is not deterred from embracing any conclusion, by its unusual appearance, or its contradiction to popular opinion. But a philosopher, who purposes only

who will be remembered as philosopher

Be a philosopher but... still be a man.

③

to represent the common sense of mankind in more beautiful and more engaging colours, if by accident he falls into error, goes no farther; but renewing his appeal to common sense, and the natural sentiments of the mind, returns into the right path, and secures himself from any dangerous illusions. The fame of Cicero flourishes at present; but that of Aristotle is utterly decayed. La Bruyere passes the seas, and still maintains his reputation: But the glory of Malebranche is confined to his own nation, and to his own age. And Addison, perhaps, will be read with pleasure, when Locke shall be entirely forgotten.

The mere philosopher is a character, which is commonly but little acceptable in the world, as being supposed to contribute nothing either to the advantage or pleasure of society; while he lives remote from communication with mankind, and is wrapped up in principles and notions equally remote from their comprehension. On the other hand, the mere ignorant is still more despised; nor is any thing deemed a surer sign of an illiberal genius in an age and nation where the sciences flourish, than to be entirely destitute of all relish for those noble entertainments. The most perfect character is supposed to lie between those extremes; retaining an equal ability and taste for books, company, and business; preserving in conversation that discernment and delicacy which arise from polite letters; and in business, that probity and accuracy which are the natural result of a just philosophy. In order to diffuse and cultivate so accomplished a character, nothing can be more useful than compositions of the easy style and manner, which draw not too much from life, require no deep application or retreat to be comprehended, and send back the student among mankind full of noble sentiments and wise precepts, applicable to every exigence of human life. By means of such compositions, virtue becomes amiable, science agreeable, company instructive, and retirement entertaining.

ideal balance compromise

Man is a reasonable being; and as such, receives from science his proper food and nourishment: But so narrow are the bounds of human understanding, that little satisfaction can be hoped for in this particular, either from the extent or security of his acquisitions. Man is a sociable, no less than a reasonable being: But neither can he always enjoy company agreeable and amusing, or preserve the proper relish for them. Man is also an active being; and from that disposition, as well as from the various necessities of human life, must submit to business and occupation: But the mind requires some relaxation, and cannot always support its bent to care and industry. It seems, then, that nature has pointed out a mixed kind of life as most suitable to human race, and secretly admonished them to allow none of these biases to draw too much, so as to incapacitate them for other occupations and entertainments. Indulge your passion for science, says she, but let your science be human, and such as may have a direct reference to action and society. Abstruse thought and profound researches I prohibit, and will severely punish, by the pensive melancholy which they introduce, by the endless uncertainty in which they involve you, and by the cold retention which your pretended discoveries shall meet with, when communicated. Be a philosopher; but, amidst all your philosophy, be still a man.

Were the generality of mankind contented to prefer the easy philosophy to the abstract and profound, without throwing any blame or contempt on the latter, it might not be improper, perhaps, to comply with this general opinion, and allow every man to enjoy, without opposition, his own taste and sentiment. But as the matter is often carried farther, even to the absolute rejecting of all profound reasonings, or what is commonly called metaphysics, we shall now proceed to consider what can reasonably be pleaded in their behalf.

We may begin with observing, that one considerable advantage, which results from the accurate and abstract philosophy, is, its subserviency to the easy and humane; which, without the former, can never attain a sufficient degree of exactness in its sentiments, precepts, or reasonings. All polite letters are nothing but pictures of human life in various attitudes and situations; and inspire us with different sentiments, of praise or blame, admiration or ridicule, according to the qualities of the object, which they set before us. An artist must be better qualified to succeed in this undertaking, who, besides a delicate taste and a quick apprehension, possesses an accurate knowledge of the internal fabric, the operations of the understanding, the workings of the passions, and the various species of sentiment

[handwritten marginalia at top: value in accuracy — value of philosophy. made — art + calling]

which discriminate vice and virtue. How painful soever this inward search or enquiry may appear, it becomes, in some measure, requisite to those, who would describe with success the obvious and outward appearances of life and manners. The anatomist presents to the eye the most hideous and disagreeable objects; but his science is useful to the painter in delineating even a Venus or an Helen. While the latter employs all the richest colours of his art, and gives his figures the most graceful and engaging airs; he must still carry his attention to the inward structure of the human body, the position of the muscles, the fabric of the bones, and the use and figure of every part or organ. Accuracy is, in every case, advantageous to beauty, and just reasoning to delicate sentiment. In vain would we exalt the one by depreciating the other.

Besides, we may observe, in every art or profession, even those which most concern life or action, that a spirit of accuracy, however acquired, carries all of them nearer their perfection, and renders them more subservient to the interests of society. And though a philosopher may live remote from business, the genius of philosophy, if carefully cultivated by several, must gradually diffuse itself throughout the whole society, and bestow a similar correctness on every art and calling. The politician will acquire greater foresight and subtility, in the subdividing and balancing of power; the lawyer more method and finer principles in his reasonings; and the general more regularity in his discipline, and more caution in his plans and operations. The stability of modern governments above the ancient, and the accuracy of modern philosophy, have improved, and probably will still improve, by similar gradations.

Were there no advantage to be reaped from these studies, beyond the gratification of an innocent curiosity, yet ought not even this to be despised; as being one accession to those few safe and harmless pleasures, which are bestowed on human race. The sweetest and most inoffensive path of life leads through the avenues of science and learning; and whoever can either remove any obstructions in this way, or open up any new prospect, ought so far to be esteemed a benefactor to mankind. And though these researches may appear painful and fatiguing, it is with some minds as with some bodies, which

being endowed with vigorous and florid health, require severe exercise, and reap a pleasure from what, to the generality of mankind, may seem burdensome and laborious. Obscurity, indeed, is painful to the mind as well as to the eye; but to bring light from obscurity, by whatever labour, must needs be delightful and rejoicing.

But this obscurity in the profound and abstract philosophy, is objected to, not only as painful and fatiguing, but as the inevitable source of uncertainty and error. Here indeed lies the justest and most plausible objection against a considerable part of metaphysics, that they are not properly a science; but arise either from the fruitless efforts of human vanity, which would penetrate into subjects utterly inaccessible to the understanding, or from the craft of popular superstitions, which, being unable to defend themselves on fair ground, raise these entangling brambles to cover and protect their weakness. Chased from the open country, these robbers fly into the forest, and lie in wait to break in upon every unguarded avenue of the mind, and overwhelm it with religious fears and prejudices. The stoutest antagonist, if he remit his watch a moment, is oppressed. And many, through cowardice and folly, open the gates to the enemies, and willingly receive them with reverence and submission, as their legal sovereigns.

But is this a sufficient reason, why philosophers should desist from such researches, and leave superstition still in possession of her retreat? Is it not proper to draw an opposite conclusion, and perceive the necessity of carrying the war into the most secret recesses of the enemy? In vain do we hope, that men, from frequent disappointment, will at last abandon such airy sciences, and discover the proper province of human reason. For, besides, that many persons find too sensible an interest in perpetually recalling such topics; besides this, I say, the motive of blind despair can never reasonably have place in the sciences; since, however unsuccessful former attempts may have proved, there is still room to hope, that the industry, good fortune, or improved sagacity of succeeding generations may reach discoveries unknown to former ages. Each adventurous genius will still leap at the arduous prize, and find himself stimulated, rather than discouraged, by the failures of his predecessors; while he hopes that the glory of achieving so hard an adventure is reserved for him alone. The only method of freeing learning, at once, from these abstruse questions, is to enquire seriously into the nature of human understanding, and shew, from an exact analysis of its powers and capacity, that it is by no means fitted for such remote and abstruse subjects. We must submit to this fatigue, in order to live at ease ever after: and must cultivate true metaphysics with some care, in order to destroy the false and adulterate. Indolence, which, to some persons, affords a safeguard against this deceitful philosophy, is, with others, overbalanced by curiosity; and despair, which, at some moments, prevails, may give place afterwards to sanguine hopes and expectations. Accurate and just reasoning is the only catholic remedy, fitted for all persons and all dispositions; and is alone able to subvert that abstruse philosophy and metaphysical jargon, which, being mixed up with popular superstition, renders it in a manner impenetrable to careless reasoners, and gives it the air of science and wisdom.

Besides this advantage of rejecting, after deliberate enquiry, the most uncertain and disagreeable part of learning, there are many positive advantages, which result from an accurate scrutiny into the powers and faculties of human nature. It is remarkable concerning the operations of the mind, that, though most intimately present to us, yet, whenever they become the object of reflection, they seem involved in obscurity; nor can the eye readily find those lines and boundaries, which discriminate and distinguish them. The objects are too fine to remain long in the same aspect or situation; and must be apprehended in an instant, by a superior penetration, derived from nature, and improved by habit and reflection. It becomes, therefore, no inconsiderable part of science barely to know the different operations of the mind, to separate them from each other, to class them under their proper heads, and to correct all that seeming disorder, in which they lie involved, when made the object of reflection and enquiry. This task of ordering and distinguishing, which has no merit, when performed with regard to external bodies, the objects of our senses, rises in its value, when directed towards the operations of the mind, in proportion to the difficulty and labour, which we meet with in performing it. And if we can go no farther than this mental geography, or delineation of the distinct parts and powers of the mind, it is at least a satisfaction to go so far; and the more obvious this science may appear (and it is by no means obvious) the more contemptible still must the ignorance of it be esteemed, in all pretenders to learning and philosophy.

Nor can there remain any suspicion, that this science is uncertain and chimerical; unless we should entertain such a scepticism as is entirely subversive of all speculation, and even action. It cannot be doubted, that the mind is endowed with several powers and faculties, that these powers are distinct from each other, that what is really distinct to the immediate perception may be distinguished by reflection; and consequently, that there is a truth and falsehood in all propositions on this subject, and a truth and falsehood, which lie not beyond the compass of human understanding. There are many obvious distinctions of this kind, such as those between the will and understanding, the imagination and passions, which fall within the comprehension of every human creature; and the finer and more philosophical distinctions are no less real and certain, though more difficult to be comprehended. Some instances, especially late ones, of success in these enquiries, may give us a juster notion of the certainty and solidity of this branch of learning. And shall we esteem it worthy the labour of a philosopher to give us a true system of the planets, and adjust the position and order of those remote bodies; while we affect to overlook those, who, with so much success, delineate the parts of the mind, in which we are so intimately concerned?

But may we not hope, that philosophy, if cultivated with care, and encouraged by the attention of the public, may carry its researches still farther, and discover, at least in some degree, the secret springs and principles, by which the human mind is actuated in its operations? Astronomers had long contented themselves with proving, from the phenomena, the true motions, order, and magnitude of the heavenly bodies: Till a philosopher, at last, arose, who seems, from the happiest reasoning, to have also determined the laws and forces, by which the revolutions of the planets are governed and directed. The like has been performed with regard to other

" most lively thought is still inferior to the dullest sensation "

parts of nature. And there is no reason to despair of equal success in our enquiries concerning the mental powers and economy, if prosecuted with equal capacity and caution. It is probable, that one operation and principle of the mind depends on another; which, again, may be resolved into one more general and universal: And how far these researches may possibly be carried, it will be difficult for us, before, or even after, a careful trial, exactly to determine. This is certain, that attempts of this kind are every day made even by those who philosophize the most negligently: And nothing can be more requisite than to enter upon the enterprise with thorough care and attention; that, if it lie within the compass of human understanding, it may at last be happily achieved; if not, it may, however, be rejected with some confidence and security. This last conclusion, surely, is not desirable; nor ought it to be embraced too rashly. For how much must we diminish from the beauty and value of this species of philosophy, upon such a supposition? Moralists have hitherto been accustomed, when they considered the vast multitude and diversity of those actions that excite our approbation or dislike, to search for some common principle, on which this variety of sentiments might depend. And though they have sometimes carried the matter too far, by their passion for some one general principle; it must, however, be confessed, that they are excusable in expecting to find some general principles, into which all the vices and virtues were justly to be resolved. The like has been the endeavor of critics, logicians, and even politicians; Nor have their attempts been wholly unsuccessful; though perhaps longer time, greater accuracy, and more ardent application may bring these sciences still nearer their perfection. To throw up at once all pretensions of this kind may justly be deemed more rash, precipitate, and dogmatical, than even the boldest and most affirmative philosophy, that has ever attempted to impose its crude dictates and principles on mankind.

What though these reasonings concerning human nature seem abstract, and of difficult comprehension? This affords no presumption of their falsehood. On the contrary, it seems impossible, that what has hitherto escaped so many wise and profound philosophers can be very obvious and easy. And whatever

pains these researches may cost us, we may think ourselves sufficiently rewarded, not only in point of profit but of pleasure, if, by that means, we can make any addition to our stock of knowledge, in subjects of such unspeakable importance.

But as, after all, the abstractedness of these speculations is no recommendation, but rather a disadvantage to them, and as this difficulty may perhaps be surmounted by care and art, and the avoiding of all unnecessary detail, we have, in the following enquiry, attempted to throw some light upon subjects, from which uncertainty has hitherto deterred the wise, and obscurity the ignorant. Happy, if we can unite the boundaries of the different species of philosophy, by reconciling profound enquiry with clearness, and truth with novelty! And still more happy, if, reasoning in this easy manner, we can undermine the foundations of an abstruse philosophy, which seems to have hitherto served only as a shelter to superstition, and a cover to absurdity and error!

perceptions of heat, memory of sense

SECTION II: OF THE ORIGIN OF IDEAS

Every one will readily allow, that there is a considerable difference between the perceptions of the mind, when a man feels the pain of excessive heat, or the pleasure of moderate warmth, and when he afterwards recalls to his memory this sensation, or anticipates it by his imagination. These faculties may mimic or copy the perceptions of the senses; but they never can entirely reach the force and vivacity of the original sentiment. The utmost we say of them, even when they operate with greatest vigor, is, that they represent their object in so lively a manner, that we could almost say we feel or see it: But, except the mind be disordered by disease or madness, they never can arrive at such a pitch of vivacity, as to render these perceptions altogether undistinguishable. All the colours of poetry, however splendid, can never paint natural objects in such a manner as to make the description be taken for a real landscape. The most lively thought is still inferior to the dullest sensation.

We may observe a like distinction to run through all the other perceptions of the mind. A man in a fit of anger, is actuated in a very different manner from

Hume on God.

one who only thinks of that emotion. If you tell me, that any person is in love, I easily understand your meaning, and form a just conception of his situation; but never can mistake that conception for the real disorders and agitations of the passion. When we reflect on our past sentiments and affections, our thought is a faithful mirror, and copies its objects truly; but the colours which it employs are faint and dull, in comparison of those in which our original perceptions were clothed. It requires no nice discernment or metaphysical head to mark the distinction between them.

Here therefore we may divide all the perceptions of the mind into two classes or species, which are distinguished by their different degrees of force and vivacity. The less forcible and lively are commonly denominated Thoughts or Ideas. The other species want a name in our language, and in most others; I suppose, because it was not requisite for any, but philosophical purposes, to rank them under a general term or appellation. Let us, therefore, use a little freedom, and call them Impressions; employing that word in a sense somewhat different from the usual. By the term impression, then, I mean all our more lively perceptions, when we hear, or see, or feel, or love, or hate, or desire, or will. And impressions are distinguished from ideas, which are the less lively perceptions, of which we are conscious, when we reflect on any of those sensations or movements above mentioned.

Nothing, at first view, may seem more unbounded than the thought of man, which not only escapes all human power and authority, but is not even restrained within the limits of nature and reality. To form monsters, and join incongruous shapes and appearances, costs the imagination no more trouble than to conceive the most natural and familiar objects. And while the body is confined to one planet, along which it creeps with pain and difficulty; the thought can in an instant transport us into the most distant regions of the universe; or even beyond the universe, into the unbounded chaos, where nature is supposed to lie in total confusion. What never was seen, or heard of, may yet be conceived; nor is any thing beyond the power of thought, except what implies an absolute contradiction.

But though our thought seems to possess this unbounded liberty, we shall find, upon a nearer examination, that it is really confined within very narrow limits, and that all this creative power of the mind amounts to no more than the faculty of compounding, transposing, augmenting, or diminishing the materials afforded us by the senses and experience. When we think of a golden mountain, we only join two consistent ideas, gold, and mountain, with which we were formerly acquainted. A virtuous horse we can conceive; because, from our own feeling, we can conceive virtue; and this we may unite to the figure and shape of a horse, which is an animal familiar to us. In short, all the materials of thinking are derived either from our outward or inward sentiment: The mixture and composition of these belongs alone to the mind and will. Or, to express myself in philosophical language, all our ideas or more feeble perceptions are copies of our impressions or more lively ones.

To prove this, the two following arguments will, I hope, be sufficient. First, when we analyze our thoughts or ideas, however compounded or sublime, we always find, that they resolve themselves into such simple ideas as were copied from a precedent feeling or sentiment. Even those ideas, which, at first view, seem the most wide of this origin, are found, upon a nearer scrutiny, to be derived from it. The idea of God, as meaning an infinitely intelligent, wise, and good Being, arises from reflecting on the operations of our own mind, and augmenting, without limit, those qualities of goodness and wisdom. We may prosecute this enquiry to what length we please; where we shall always find, that every idea which we examine is copied from a similar impression. Those who would assert, that this position is not universally true nor without exception, have only one, and that an easy method of refuting it; by producing that idea, which, in their opinion, is not derived from this source. It will then be incumbent on us, if we would maintain our doctrine, to produce the impression or lively perception, which corresponds to it.

Secondly, If it happen, from a defect of the organ, that a man is not susceptible of any species of sensation, we always find, that he is as little susceptible of the correspondent ideas. A blind man can form no notion of colours; a deaf man of sounds. Restore either of them that sense, in which he is defi-

defining ideas

defining impression

cient; by opening this new inlet for his sensations, you also open an inlet for the ideas; and he finds no difficulty in conceiving these objects. The case is the same, if the object, proper for exciting any sensation, has never been applied to the organ. A Laplander or Negro, has no notion of the relish of wine. And though there are few or no instances of a like deficiency in the mind, where a person has never felt or is wholly incapable of a sentiment or passion that belongs to his species; yet we find the same observation to take place in a less degree. A man of mild manners can form no idea of inveterate revenge or cruelty; nor can a selfish heart easily conceive the heights of friendship and generosity. It is readily allowed, that other beings may possess many senses of which we can have no conception; because the ideas of them have never been introduced to us, in the only manner, by which an idea can have access to the mind, to wit, by the actual feeling and sensation.

There is, however, one contradictory phenomenon, which may prove, that it is not absolutely impossible for ideas to arise, independent of their correspondent impressions. I believe it will readily be allowed, that the several distinct ideas of colour, which enter by the eye, or those of sound, which are conveyed by the ear, are really different from each other; though, at the same time, resembling. Now if this be true of different colours, it must be no less so of the different shades of the same colour; and each shade produces a distinct idea, independent of the rest. For if this should be denied, it is possible, by the continual gradation of shades, to run a colour insensibly into what is most remote from it; and if you will not allow any of the means to be different, you cannot, without absurdity, deny the extremes to be the same. Suppose, therefore, a person to have enjoyed his sight for thirty years, and to have become perfectly acquainted with colours of all kinds, except one particular shade of blue, for instance, which it never has been his fortune to meet with. Let all the different shades of that colour, except that single one, be placed before him, descending gradually from the deepest to the lightest; it is plain, that he will perceive a blank, where that shade is wanting, and will be sensible, that there is a greater distance in that place between the contiguous colours than in any

other. Now I ask, whether it be possible for him, from his own imagination, to supply this deficiency, and raise up to himself the idea of that particular shade, though it had never been conveyed to him by his senses? I believe there are few but will be of opinion that he can: And this may serve as a proof, that the simple ideas are not always, in every instance, derived from the correspondent impressions; though this instance is so singular, that it is scarcely worth our observing, and does not merit, that for it alone we should alter our general maxim.

Here, therefore, is a proposition, which not only seems, in itself, simple and intelligible; but, if a proper use were made of it, might render every dispute equally intelligible, and banish all that jargon, which has so long taken possession of metaphysical reasonings, and drawn disgrace upon them. All ideas, especially abstract ones, are naturally faint and obscure: The mind has but a slender hold of them: they are apt to be confounded with other resembling ideas; and when we have often employed any term, though without a distinct meaning, we are apt to imagine it has a determinate idea, annexed to it. On the contrary, all impressions, that is, all sensations, either outward or inward, are strong and vivid: The limits between them are more exactly determined: Nor is it easy to fall into any error or mistake with regard to them. When we entertain, therefore, any suspicion, that a philosophical term is employed without any meaning or idea (as is but too frequent), we need but enquire, from what impression is that supposed idea derived? And if it be impossible to assign any, this will serve to confirm our suspicion. By bringing ideas into so clear a light, we may reasonably hope to remove all dispute, which may arise, concerning their nature and reality.

relation between terms & impression derived >

SECTION III: OF THE ASSOCIATION OF IDEAS

It is evident, that there is a principle of connexion between the different thoughts or ideas of the mind, and that, in their appearance to the memory or imagination, they introduce each other with a certain degree of method and regularity. In our more serious thinking or discourse, this is so observable, that any particular thought, which breaks in upon the regular tract or chain of ideas, is immediately remarked and rejected. And even in our wildest and most wandering reveries, nay in our very dreams, we shall find, if we reflect, that the imagination ran not altogether at adventures, but that there was still a connexion upheld among the different ideas, which succeeded each other. Were the loosest and freest conversation to be transcribed, there would immediately be observed something, which connected it in all its transitions. Or where this is wanting, the person, who broke the thread of discourse, might still inform you, that there had secretly revolved in his mind a succession of thought, which had gradually led him from the subject of conversation. Among different languages, even where we cannot suspect the least connexion or communication, it is found, that the words, expressive of ideas, the most compounded, do yet nearly correspond to each other: A certain proof, that the simple ideas, comprehended in the compound ones, were bound together by some universal principle, which had an equal influence on all mankind.

Though it be too obvious to escape observation, that different ideas are connected together; I do not find, that any philosopher has attempted to enumerate or class all the principles of association; a subject, however, that seems worthy of curiosity. To me, there appear to be only three principles of connexion among ideas, namely, Resemblance, Contiguity in time or place, and Cause or Effect.

That these principles serve to connect ideas will not, I believe, be much doubted. A picture naturally leads our thoughts to the original: The mention of one apartment in a building naturally introduces an enquiry or discourse concerning the others: and if we think of a wound, we can scarcely forbear reflecting on the pain which follows it. But that this enumeration is complete, and that there are no other principles of association, except these, may be difficult to prove to the satisfaction of the reader, or even to a man's own satisfaction. All we can do, in such cases, is to run over several instances, and examine carefully the principle, which binds the different thoughts to each other, never stopping till we render the principle as general as possible. The more instances we examine, and the more care we employ, the more assurance shall we acquire, that the enumeration, which we form from the whole, is complete and entire.

SECTION IV: SCEPTICAL DOUBTS CONCERNING THE OPERATIONS OF THE UNDERSTANDING

PART I

All the objects of human reason or enquiry may naturally be divided into two kinds, to wit, Relations of Ideas, and Matters of Fact. Of the first kind are the sciences of Geometry, Algebra, and Arithmetic; and in short, every affirmation, which is either intuitively or demonstratively certain. That the square of the hypotenuse is equal to the squares of the two sides, is a proposition, which expresses a relation between these figures. That three times five is equal to the half of thirty, expresses a relation between these numbers. Propositions of this kind are discoverable by the mere operation of thought, without dependence on what is any where existent in the universe. Though there never were a circle or triangle in nature, the truths, demonstrated by Euclid, would for ever retain their certainty and evidence.

Matters of fact, which are the second objects of human reason, are not ascertained in the same manner; nor is our evidence of their truth, however great, of a like nature with the foregoing. The contrary of every matter of fact is still possible; because it can never imply a contradiction, and is conceived by the mind with the same facility and distinctness, as if ever so conformable to reality. That the sun will not rise to-morrow is no less intelligible a proposition, and implies no more contradiction, than the affirmation, that it will rise. We should in vain, therefore, attempt to demonstrate its falsehood. Were it demonstratively false, it would imply a contradiction, and could never be distinctly conceived by the mind.

It may, therefore, be a subject worthy of curiosity, to enquire what is the nature of that evidence, which assures us of any real existence and matter of fact, beyond the present testimony of our senses, or the records of our memory. This part of philosophy, it is observable, has been little cultivated, either by the ancients or moderns; and therefore our doubts and errors, in the prosecution of so important an enquiry, may be the more excusable; while we march through such difficult paths, without any guide or direction. They may even prove useful, by exciting cu-

Cause & effect discovered by experience

riosity, and destroying that implicit faith and security, which is the bane of all reasoning and free enquiry. The discovery of defects in the common philosophy, if any such there be, will not, I presume, be a discouragement, but rather an incitement, as is usual, to attempt something more full and satisfactory, than has yet been proposed to the public.

All reasonings concerning matter of fact seem to be founded on the relation of Cause and Effect. By means of that relation alone we can go beyond the evidence of our memory and senses. If you were to ask a man, why he believes any matter of fact, which is absent; for instance, that his friend is in the country, or in France; he would give you a reason; and this reason would be some other fact; as a letter received from him, or the knowledge of his former resolutions and promises. A man, finding a watch or any other machine in a desert island, would conclude, that there had once been men in that island. All our reasonings concerning fact are of the same nature. And here it is constantly supposed, that there is a connexion between the present fact and that which is inferred from it. Were there nothing to bind them together, the inference would be entirely precarious. The hearing of an articulate voice and rational discourse in the dark assures us of the presence of some person: Why? because these are the effects of the human make and fabric, and closely connected with it. If we anatomize all the other reasonings of this nature, we shall find, that they are founded on the relation of cause and effect, and that this relation is either near or remote, direct or collateral. Heat and light are collateral effects of fire, and the one effect may justly be inferred from the other.

If we would satisfy ourselves, therefore, concerning the nature of that evidence, which assures us of matters of fact, we must enquire how we arrive at the knowledge of cause and effect.

I shall venture to affirm, as a general proposition, which admits of no exception, that the knowledge of this relation is not, in any instance, attained by reasonings a priori; but arises entirely from experience, when we find, that any particular objects are constantly conjoined with each other. Let an object be presented to a man of ever so strong natural reason and abilities; if that object be entirely new to him, he will not be able, by the most accurate examination of its sensible qualities, to discover any of its causes or effects. Adam, though his rational faculties be supposed, at the very first, entirely perfect, could not have inferred from the fluidity, and transparency of water, that it would suffocate him, or from the light and warmth of fire, that it would consume him. No object ever discovers, by the qualities which appear to the senses, either the causes which produced it, or the effects which will arise from it; nor can our reason, unassisted by experience, ever draw any inference concerning real existence and matter of fact.

This proposition, that causes and effects are discoverable, not by reason but by experience, will readily be admitted with regard to such objects, as we remember to have once been altogether unknown to us; since we must be conscious of the utter inability, which we then lay under, of foretelling, what would arise from them. Present two smooth pieces of marble to a man, who has no tincture of natural philosophy; he will never discover, that they will adhere together, in such a manner as to require great force to separate them in a direct line, while they make so small a resistance to a lateral pressure. Such events, as bear little analogy to the common course of nature, are also readily confessed to be known only by experience; nor does any man imagine that the explosion of gunpowder, or the attraction of a loadstone, could ever be discovered by arguments a priori. In like manner, when an effect is supposed to depend upon an intricate machinery or secret structure of parts, we make no difficulty in attributing all our knowledge of it to experience. Who will assert, that he can give the ultimate reason, why milk or bread is proper nourishment for a man, not for a lion or a tiger?

But the same truth may not appear, at first sight, to have the same evidence with regard to events, which have become familiar to us from our first appearance in the world, which bear a close analogy to the whole course of nature, and which are supposed to depend on the simple qualities of objects, without any secret structure of parts. We are apt to imagine, that we could discover these effects by the mere operation of our reason, without experience. We fancy, that were we brought, on a sudden, into this world, we could at first have inferred, that one Billiard-ball *effect totally different from cause*

would communicate motion to another upon impulse; and that we needed not to have waited for the event, in order to pronounce with certainty concerning it. Such is the influence of custom, that, where it is strongest, it not only covers our natural ignorance, but even conceals itself, and seems not to take place, merely because it is found in the highest degree.

But to convince us, that all the laws of nature, and all the operations of bodies without exception, are known only by experience, the following reflections may, perhaps, suffice. Were any object presented to us, and were we required to pronounce concerning the effect, which will result from it, without consulting past observation; after what manner, I beseech you, must the mind proceed in this operation? It must invent or imagine some event, which it ascribes to the object as its effect; and it is plain that this invention must be entirely arbitrary. The mind can never possibly find the effect in the supposed cause, by the most accurate scrutiny and examination. For the effect is totally different from the cause, and consequently can never be discovered in it. Motion in the second Billiard-ball is a quite distinct event from motion in the first; nor is there any thing in the one to suggest the smallest hint of the other. A stone or piece of metal raised into the air, and left without any support, immediately falls: But to consider the matter a priori, is there any thing we discover in this situation, which can beget the idea of a downward, rather than an upward, or any other motion, in the stone or metal?

And as the first imagination or invention of a particular effect, in all natural operations, is arbitrary, where we consult not experience; so must we also esteem the supposed tie or connexion between the cause and effect, which binds them together, and renders it impossible, that any other effect could result from the operation of that cause. When I see, for instance, a Billiard-ball moving in a straight line towards another; even suppose motion in the second ball should by accident be suggested to me, as the result of their contact or impulse; may I not conceive, that a hundred different events might as well follow from that cause? May not both these balls remain at absolute rest? May not the first ball return in a straight line, or leap off from the second in any line

or direction? All these suppositions are consistent and conceivable. Why then should we give the preference to one, which is no more consistent or conceivable than the rest? All our reasonings a priori will never be able to shew us any foundation for this preference.

In a word, then, every effect is a distinct event from its cause. It could not, therefore, be discovered in the cause, and the first invention or conception of it, a priori, must be entirely arbitrary. And even after it is suggested, the conjunction of it with the cause must appear equally arbitrary; since there are always many other effects, which, to reason, must seem fully as consistent and natural. In vain, therefore, should we pretend to determine any single event, or infer any cause or effect, without the assistance of observation and experience.

Hence we may discover the reason, why no philosopher, who is rational and modest, has ever pretended to assign the ultimate cause of any natural operation, or to show distinctly the action of that power, which produces any single effect in the universe. It is confessed, that the utmost effort of human reason is to reduce the principles, productive of natural phenomena, to a greater simplicity, and to resolve the many particular effects into a few general causes, by means of reasonings from analogy, experience, and observation. But as to the causes of these general causes, we should in vain attempt their discovery; nor shall we ever be able to satisfy ourselves, by any particular explication of them. These ultimate springs and principles are totally shut up from human curiosity and enquiry. Elasticity, gravity, cohesion of parts, communication of motion by impulse; these are probably the ultimate causes and principles which we shall ever discover in nature; and we may esteem ourselves sufficiently happy, if, by accurate enquiry and reasoning, we can trace up the particular phenomena to, or near to, these general principles. The most perfect philosophy of the natural kind only staves off our ignorance a little longer: As perhaps the most perfect philosophy of the moral or metaphysical kind serves only to discover larger portions of it. Thus the observation of human blindness and weakness is the result of all philosophy, and meets us, at every turn, in spite of our endeavors to elude or avoid it.

Nor is geometry, when taken into the assistance of natural philosophy, ever able to remedy this defect, or lead us into the knowledge of ultimate causes, by all that accuracy of reasoning, for which it is so justly celebrated. Every part of mixed mathematics proceeds upon the supposition, that certain laws are established by nature in her operations; and abstract reasonings are employed, either to assist experience in the discovery of these laws, or to determine their influence in particular instances, where it depends upon any precise degree of distance and quantity. Thus, it is a law of motion, discovered by experience, that the moment or force of any body in motion is in the compound ratio or proportion of its solid contents and its velocity; and consequently, that a small force may remove the greatest obstacle or raise the greatest weight, if, by any contrivance or machinery, we can increase the velocity of that force, so as to make it an overmatch for its antagonist. Geometry assists us in the application of this law, by giving us the just dimensions of all the parts and figures, which can enter into any species of machine; but still the discovery of the law itself is owing merely to experience, and all the abstract reasonings in the world could never lead us one step towards the knowledge of it. When we reason a priori, and consider merely any object or cause, as it appears to the mind, independent of all observation, it never could suggest to us the notion of any distinct object, such as its effect; much less, shew us the inseparable and inviolable connexion between them. A man must be very sagacious, who could discover by reasoning that crystal is the effect of heat, and ice of cold, without being previously acquainted with the operation of these qualities.

PART II

But we have not, yet, attained any tolerable satisfaction with regard to the question first proposed. Each solution still gives rise to a new question as difficult as the foregoing, and leads us on to farther enquiries. When it is asked, What is the nature of all our reasonings concerning matter of fact? the proper answer seems to be, that they are founded on the relation of cause and effect. When again it is asked, What is the foundation of all our reasonings and con-clusions concerning that relation? it may be replied in one word, Experience. But if we still carry on our sifting humor, and ask, What is the foundation of all conclusions from experience? this implies a new question, which may be of more difficult solution and explication. Philosophers, that give themselves airs of superior wisdom and sufficiency, have a hard task, when they encounter persons of inquisitive dispositions, who push them from every corner, to which they retreat, and who are sure at last to bring them to some dangerous dilemma. The best expedient to prevent this confusion, is to be modest in our pretensions; and even to discover the difficulty ourselves before it is objected to us. By this means, we may make a kind of merit of our very ignorance.

I shall content myself, in this section, with an easy task, and shall pretend only to give a negative answer to the question here proposed. I say then, that, even after we have experience of the operations of cause and effect, our conclusions from that experience are not founded on reasoning, or any process of the understanding. This answer we must endeavor, both to explain and to defend.

It must certainly be allowed, that nature has kept us at a great distance from all her secrets, and has afforded us only the knowledge of a few superficial qualities of objects; while she conceals from us those powers and principles, on which the influence of these objects entirely depends. Our senses inform us of the colour, weight, and consistence of bread; but neither sense nor reason can ever inform us of those qualities, which fit it for the nourishment and support of a human body. Sight or feeling conveys an idea of the actual motion of bodies; but as to that wonderful force or power, which would carry on a moving body for ever in a continued change of place, and which bodies never lose but by communicating it to others; of this we cannot form the most distant conception. But notwithstanding this ignorance of natural powers and principles, we always presume, when we see like sensible qualities, that they have like secret powers, and expect, that effects, similar to those which we have experienced, will follow from them. If a body of like colour and consistence with that bread, which we have formerly eaten, be presented to us, we make no scruple of repeating the experiment, and foresee, with certainty, like nour-

2 Kinds of reasoning

ishment and support. Now this is a process of the mind or thought, of which I would willingly know the foundation. It is allowed on all hands, that there is no known connexion between the sensible qualities and the secret powers; and consequently, that the mind is not led to form such a conclusion concerning their constant and regular conjunction, by any thing which it knows of their nature. As to past Experience, it can be allowed to give direct and certain information of those precise objects only, and that precise period of time, which fell under its cognizance: But why this experience should be extended to future times, and to other objects, which for aught we know, may be only in appearance similar; this is the main question on which I would insist. The bread, which I formerly eat, nourished me; that is, a body of such sensible qualities, was, at that time, endued with such secret powers: But does it follow, that other bread must also nourish me at another time, and that like sensible qualities must always be attended with like secret powers? The consequence seems nowise necessary. At least, it must be acknowledged, that there is here a consequence drawn by the mind; that there is a certain step taken; a process of thought, and an inference, which wants to be explained. These two propositions are far from being the same, I have found that such an object has always been attended with such an effect, and I foresee, that other objects, which are, in appearance, similar, will be attended with similar effects. I shall allow, if you please, that the one proposition may justly be inferred from the other: I know in fact, that it always is inferred. But if you insist, that the inference is made by a chain of reasoning, I desire you to produce that reasoning. The connexion between these propositions is not intuitive. There is required a medium, which may enable the mind to draw such an inference, if indeed it be drawn by reasoning and argument. What that medium is, I must confess, passes my comprehension; and it is incumbent on those to produce it, who assert, that it really exists, and is the origin of all our conclusions concerning matter of fact.

This negative argument must certainly, in process of time, become altogether convincing, if many penetrating and able philosophers shall turn their enquiries this way; and no one be ever able to discover any connecting proposition or intermediate step, which supports the understanding in this conclusion. But as the question is yet new, every reader may not trust so far to his own penetration, as to conclude, because an argument escapes his enquiry, that therefore it does not really exist. For this reason it may be requisite to venture upon a more difficult task; and enumerating all the branches of human knowledge, endeavor to shew, that none of them can afford such an argument.

All reasonings may be divided into two kinds, namely demonstrative reasoning, or that concerning relations of ideas, and moral reasoning, or that concerning matter of fact and existence. That there are no demonstrative arguments in the case, seems evident; since it implies no contradiction, that the course of nature may change, and that an object, seemingly like those which we have experienced, may be attended with different or contrary effects. May I not clearly and distinctly conceive, that a body, falling from the clouds, and which, in all other respects, resembles snow, has yet the taste of salt or feeling of fire? Is there any more intelligible proposition than to affirm, that all the trees will flourish in December and January, and decay in May and June? Now whatever is intelligible, and can be distinctly conceived, implies no contradiction, and can never be proved false by any demonstrative argument or abstract reasoning a priori.

If we be, therefore, engaged by arguments to put trust in past experience, and make it the standard of our future judgment, these arguments must be probable only, or such as regard matter of fact and real existence, according to the division above mentioned. But that there is no argument of this kind, must appear, if our explication of that species of reasoning be admitted as solid and satisfactory. We have said, that all arguments concerning existence are founded on the relation of cause and effect; that our knowledge of that relation is derived entirely from experience; and that all our experimental conclusions proceed upon the supposition, that the future will be conformable to the past. To endeavor, therefore, the proof of this last supposition by probable arguments, or arguments regarding existence, must be evidently going in a circle, and taking that for granted, which is the very point in question.

In reality, all arguments from experience are founded on the similarity, which we discover among natural objects, and by which we are induced to expect effects similar to those, which we have found to follow from such objects. And though none but a fool or madman will ever pretend to dispute the authority of experience, or to reject that great guide of human life; it may surely be allowed a philosopher to have so much curiosity at least, as to examine the principle of human nature, which gives this mighty authority to experience, and makes us draw advantage from that similarity, which nature has placed among different objects. From causes, which appear similar, we expect similar effects. This is the sum of all our experimental conclusions. Now it seems evident, that, if this conclusion were formed by reason, it would be as perfect at first, and upon one instance, as after ever so long a course of experience. But the case is far otherwise. Nothing so like as eggs; yet no one, on account of this appearing similarity, expects the same taste and relish in all of them. It is only after a long course of uniform experiments in any kind, that we attain a firm reliance and security with regard to a particular event. Now where is that process of reasoning, which, from one instance, draws a conclusion, so different from that which it infers from a hundred instances, that are nowise different from that single one? This question I propose as much for the sake of information, as with an intention of raising difficulties. I cannot find, I cannot imagine any such reasoning. But I keep my mind still open to instruction, if any one will vouchsafe to bestow it on me.

Should it be said, that, from a number of uniform experiments, we infer a connexion between the sensible qualities and the secret powers; this, I must confess, seems the same difficulty, couched in different terms. The question still recurs, on what process of argument this inference is founded? Where is the medium, the interposing ideas, which join propositions so very wide of each other? It is confessed, that the colour, consistence, and other sensible qualities of bread appear not, of themselves, to have any connexion with the secret powers of nourishment and support. For otherwise we could infer these secret powers from the first appearance of these sensible qualities, without the aid of experience; contrary to the sentiment of all philosophers, and contrary to

plain matter of fact. Here then is our natural state of ignorance with regard to the powers and influence of all objects. How is this remedied by experience? It only shows us a number of uniform effects, resulting from certain objects, and teaches us, that those particular objects, at that particular time, were endowed with such powers and forces. When a new object, endowed with similar sensible qualities, is produced, we expect similar powers and forces, and look for a like effect. From a body of like colour and consistence with bread, we expect like nourishment and support. But this surely is a step or progress of the mind, which wants to be explained. When a man says, I have found, in all past instances, such sensible qualities conjoined with such secret powers: And when he says, Similar sensible qualities will always be conjoined with similar secret powers; he is not guilty of a tautology, nor are these propositions in any respect the same. You say that the one proposition is an inference from the other. But you must confess that the inference is not intuitive; neither is it demonstrative: Of what nature is it then? To say it is experimental, is begging the question. For all inferences from experience suppose, as their foundation, that the future will resemble the past, and that similar powers will be conjoined with similar sensible qualities. If there be any suspicion, that the course of nature may change, and that the past may be no rule for the future, all experience becomes useless, and can give rise to no inference or conclusion. It is impossible, therefore, that any arguments from experience can prove this resemblance of the past to the future; since all these arguments are founded on the supposition of that resemblance. Let the course of things be allowed hitherto ever so regular; that alone, without some new argument or inference, proves not, that, for the future, it will continue so. In vain do you pretend to have learned the nature of bodies from your past experience. Their secret nature, and consequently, all their effects and influence, may change, without any change in their sensible qualities. This happens sometimes, and with regard to some objects: Why may it not happen always, and with regard to all objects? What logic, what process of argument secures you against this supposition? My practice, you say, refutes my doubts. But you mistake the purport of my question. As an agent, I am quite satisfied in the point; but as a philosopher, who has some share of curiosity, I will not say scepticism, I want to learn the foundation of this inference. No reading, no enquiry has yet been able to remove my difficulty, or give me satisfaction in a matter of such importance. Can I do better than propose the difficulty to the public, even though, perhaps, I have small hopes of obtaining a solution? We shall at least, by this means, be sensible of our ignorance, if we do not augment our knowledge.

I must confess, that a man is guilty of unpardonable arrogance, who concludes, because an argument has escaped his own investigation, that therefore it does not really exist. I must also confess, that, though all the learned, for several ages, should have employed themselves in fruitless search upon any subject, it may still, perhaps, be rash to conclude positively, that the subject must, therefore, pass all human comprehension. Even though we examine all the sources of our knowledge, and conclude them unfit for such a subject, there may still remain a suspicion, that the enumeration is not complete, or the examination not accurate. But with regard to the present subject, there are some considerations, which seem to remove all this accusation of arrogance or suspicion of mistake.

It is certain, that the most ignorant and stupid peasants, nay infants, nay even brute beasts, improve by experience, and learn the qualities of natural objects, by observing the effects, which result from them. When a child has felt the sensation of pain from touching the flame of a candle, he will be careful not to put his hand near any candle; but will expect a similar effect from a cause, which is similar in its sensible qualities and appearance. If you assert, therefore, that the understanding of the child is led into this conclusion by any process of argument or ratiocination, I may justly require you to produce that argument; nor have you any pretence to refuse so equitable a demand. You cannot say, that the argument is abstruse, and may possibly escape your enquiry; since you confess, that it is obvious to the capacity of a mere infant. If you hesitate, therefore, a moment, or if, after reflection, you produce any intricate or profound argument, you, in a manner, give up the question, and confess, that it is not reasoning which engages us to suppose the past resembling the future, and to expect similar effects from causes, which are, to appearance, similar. This is the proposition which I intended to enforce in the present section. If I be right, I pretend not to have made any mighty discovery. And if I be wrong, I must acknowledge myself to be indeed a very backward scholar; since I cannot now discover an argument, which, it seems, was perfectly familiar to me, long before I was out of my cradle.

SECTION V: SCEPTICAL SOLUTION OF THESE DOUBTS

PART I

The passion for philosophy, like that for religion, seems liable to this inconvenience, that, though it aims at the correction of our manners, and extirpation of our vices, it may only serve, by imprudent management, to foster a predominant inclination, and push the mind, with more determined resolution, towards that side, which already draws too much, by the bias and propensity of the natural temper. It is certain, that, while we aspire to the magnanimous firmness of the philosophic sage, and endeavor to confine our pleasures altogether within our own minds, we may, at last, render our philosophy like that of Epictetus, and other Stoics, only a more refined system of selfishness, and reason ourselves out of all virtue, as well as social enjoyment. While we study with attention the vanity of human life, and turn all our thoughts towards the empty and transitory nature of riches and honors, we are, perhaps, all the while, flattering our natural indolence, which, hating the bustle of the world, and drudgery of business, seeks a presence of reason to give itself a full and uncontrolled indulgence. There is, however, one species of philosophy, which seems little liable to this inconvenience, and that because it strikes in with no disorderly passion of the human mind, nor can mingle itself with any natural affection or propensity; and that is the Academic or Sceptical philosophy. The academics always talk of doubt and suspense of judgment, of danger in hasty determinations, of confining to very narrow bounds the enquiries of the understanding, and of renouncing all speculations which lie not within the limits of common life and

principle of Custom
principle of
human nature

practice. Nothing, therefore, can be more contrary than such a philosophy to the supine indolence of the mind, its rash arrogance, its lofty pretensions, and its superstitious credulity. Every passion is mortified by it, except the love of truth; and that passion never is, nor can be, carried to too high a degree. It is surprising, therefore, that this philosophy, which, in almost every instance, must be harmless and innocent, should be the subject of so much groundless reproach and obloquy. But, perhaps, the very circumstance, which renders it so innocent, is what chiefly exposes it to the public hatred and resentment. By flattering no irregular passion, it gains few partisans: By opposing so many vices and follies, it raises to itself abundance of enemies, who stigmatize it as libertine, profane, and irreligious.

Nor need we fear, that this philosophy, while it endeavors to limit our enquiries to common life, should ever undermine the reasonings of common life, and carry its doubts so far as to destroy all action, as well as speculation. Nature will always maintain her rights, and prevail in the end over any abstract reasoning whatsoever. Though we should conclude, for instance, as in the foregoing section, that, in all reasonings from experience, there is a step taken by the mind, which is not supported by any argument or process of the understanding, there is no danger, that these reasonings, on which almost all knowledge depends, will ever be affected by such a discovery. If the mind be not engaged by argument to make this step, it must be induced by some other principle of equal weight and authority; and that principle will preserve its influence as long as human nature remains the same. What that principle is, may well be worth the pains of enquiry.

Suppose a person, though endowed with the strongest faculties of reason and reflection, to be brought on a sudden into this world; he would, indeed, immediately observe a continual succession of objects, and one event following another; but he would not be able to discover any thing farther. He would not, at first, by any reasoning, be able to reach the idea of cause and effect; since the particular powers, by which all natural operations are performed, never appear to the senses; nor is it reasonable to conclude, merely because one event, in one instance, precedes another, that therefore the one is the cause,

the other the effect. Their conjunction may be arbitrary and casual. There may be no reason to infer the existence of one from the appearance of the other. And in a word, such a person, without more experience, could never employ his conjecture or reasoning concerning any matter of fact, or be assured of any thing beyond what was immediately present to his memory and senses.

Suppose again, that he has acquired more experience, and has lived so long in the world as to have observed similar objects or events to be constantly conjoined together; what is the consequence of this experience? He immediately infers the existence of one object from the appearance of the other. Yet he has not, by all his experience, acquired any idea or knowledge of the secret power, by which the one object produces the other; nor is it, by any process of reasoning, he is engaged to draw this inference. But still he finds himself determined to draw it: And though he should be convinced, that his understanding has no part in the operation, he would nevertheless continue in the same course of thinking. There is some other principle, which determines him to form such a conclusion.

This principle is Custom or Habit. For wherever the repetition of any particular act or operation produces a propensity to renew the same act or operation, without being impelled by any reasoning or process of the understanding; we always say, that this propensity is the effect of Custom. By employing that word, we pretend not to have given the ultimate reason of such a propensity. We only point out a principle of human nature, which is universally acknowledged, and which is well known by its effects. Perhaps, we can push our enquiries no farther, or pretend to give the cause of this cause; but must rest contented with it as the ultimate principle, which we can assign, of all our conclusions from experience. It is sufficient satisfaction, that we can go so far; without repining at the narrowness of our faculties, because they will carry us no farther. And it is certain we here advance a very intelligible proposition at least, if not a true one, when we assert, that, after the constant conjunction of two objects, heat and flame, for instance, weight and solidity, we are determined by custom alone to expect the one from the appearance of the other. This hypothesis seems even

all inferences from experience are effects of custom not reasoning

natural instincts

the only one, which explains the difficulty, why we draw, from a thousand instances, an inference, which we are not able to draw from one instance, that is, in no respect, different from them. Reason is incapable of any such variation. The conclusions, which it draws from considering one circle, are the same which it would form upon surveying all the circles in the universe. But no man, having seen only one body move after being impelled by another, could infer, that every other body will move after a like impulse. All inferences from experience, therefore, are effects of custom, not of reasoning.

Custom, then, is the great guide of human life. It is that principle alone, which renders our experience useful to us, and makes us expect, for the future, a similar train of events with those which have appeared in the past. Without the influence of custom, we should be entirely ignorant of every matter of fact, beyond what is immediately present to the memory and senses. We should never know how to adjust means to ends, or to employ our natural powers in the production of any effect. There would be an end at once of all action, as well as of the chief part of speculation.

But here it may be proper to remark that though our conclusions from experience carry us beyond our memory and senses, and assure us of matters of fact, which happened in the most distant places and most remote ages; yet some fact must always be present to the senses or memory, from which we may first proceed in drawing these conclusions. A man, who should find in a desert country the remains of pompous buildings, would conclude, that the country had, in ancient times, been cultivated by civilized inhabitants; but did nothing of this nature occur to him, he could never form such an inference. We learn the events of former ages from history; but then we must peruse the volumes, in which this instruction is contained, and thence carry up our inferences from one testimony to another, till we arrive at the eyewitnesses and spectators of these distant events. In a word, if we proceed not upon some fact, present to the memory or senses, our reasonings would be merely hypothetical; and however the particular links might be connected with each other, the whole chain of inferences would have nothing to support it, nor could we ever, by its means, arrive at the

knowledge of any real existence. If I ask why you believe any particular matter of fact, which you relate, you must tell me some reason; and this reason will be some other fact, connected with it. But as you cannot proceed after this manner, in infinitum, you must at last terminate in some fact, which is present to your memory or senses; or must allow that your belief is entirely without foundation.

What then is the conclusion of the whole matter? A simple one; though, it must be confessed, pretty remote from the common theories of philosophy. All belief of matter of fact or real existence is derived merely from some object, present to the memory or senses, and a customary conjunction between that and some other object. Or in other words; having found, in many instances, that any two kinds of objects, flame and heat, snow and cold, have always been conjoined together; if flame or snow be presented anew to the senses, the mind is carried by custom to expect heat or cold, and to believe, that such a quality does exist, and will discover itself upon a nearer approach. This belief is the necessary result of placing the mind in such circumstances. It is an operation of the soul, when we are so situated, as unavoidable as to feel the passion of love, when we receive benefits: or hatred, when we meet with injuries. All these operations are a species of natural instincts, which no reasoning or process of the thought and understanding is able, either to produce, or to prevent.

At this point, it would be very allowable for us to stop our philosophical researches. In most questions, we can never make a single step farther; and in all questions, we must terminate here at last, after our most restless and curious enquiries. But still our curiosity will be pardonable, perhaps commendable, if it carry us on to still farther researches, and make us examine more accurately the nature of this belief, and of the customary conjunction, whence it is derived. By this means we may meet with some explications and analogies, that will give satisfaction; at least to such as love the abstract sciences, and can be entertained with speculations, which, however accurate, may still retain a degree of doubt and uncertainty. As to readers of a different taste; the remaining part of this section is not calculated for them, and the following enquiries may well be understood, though it be neglected.

definitions of belief:

PART II

Nothing is more free than the imagination of man; and though it cannot exceed that original stock of ideas, furnished by the internal and external senses, it has unlimited power of mixing, compounding, separating, and dividing these ideas, in all the varieties of fiction and vision. It can feign a train of events, with all the appearance of reality, ascribe to them a particular time and place, conceive them as existent, and paint them out to itself with every circumstance, that belongs to any historical fact, which it believes with the greatest certainty. Wherein, therefore, consists the difference between such a fiction and belief? It lies not merely in any peculiar idea, which is annexed to such a conception as commands our assent, and which is wanting to every known fiction. For as the mind has authority over all its ideas, it could voluntarily annex this particular idea to any fiction, and consequently be able to believe whatever it pleases; contrary to what we find by daily experience. We can, in our conception, join the head of a man to the body of a horse; but it is not in our power to believe, that such an animal has ever really existed.

It follows, therefore, that the difference between fiction and belief lies in some sentiment or feeling, which is annexed to the latter, not to the former, and which depends not on the will, nor can be commanded at pleasure. It must be excited by nature, like all other sentiments; and must arise from the particular situation, in which the mind is placed at any particular juncture. Whenever any object is presented to the memory or senses, it immediately, by the force of custom, carries the imagination to conceive that object, which is usually conjoined to it; and this conception is attended with a feeling or sentiment, different from the loose reveries of the fancy. In this consists the whole nature of belief. For as there is no matter of fact which we believe so firmly, that we cannot conceive the contrary, there would be no difference between the conception assented to, and that which is rejected, were it not for some sentiment, which distinguishes the one from the other. If I see a billiard-ball moving towards another, on a smooth table, I can easily conceive it to stop upon contact. This conception implies no contradiction; but still it feels very differently from that conception, by which I represent to myself the impulse, and the communication of motion from one ball to another.

Were we to attempt a definition of this sentiment, we should, perhaps, find it a very difficult, if not an impossible task; in the same manner as if we should endeavor to define the feeling of cold or passion of anger, to a creature who never had any experience of these sentiments. Belief is the true and proper name of this feeling; and no one is ever at a loss to know the meaning of that term; because every man is every moment conscious of the sentiment represented by it. It may not, however, be improper to attempt a description of this sentiment; in hopes we may, by that means, arrive at some analogies, which may afford a more perfect explication of it. I say then, that belief is nothing but a more vivid, lively, forcible, firm, steady conception of an object, than what the imagination alone is ever able to attain. This variety of terms, which may seem so unphilosophical, is intended only to express that act of the mind, which renders realities, or what is taken for such, more present to us than fictions, causes them to weigh more in the thought, and gives them a superior influence on the passions and imagination. Provided we agree about the thing, it is needless to dispute about the terms. The imagination has the command over all its ideas, and can join and mix and vary them, in all the ways possible. It may conceive fictitious objects with all the circumstances of place and time. It may set them, in a manner, before our eyes, in their true colours, just as they might have existed. But as it is impossible, that this faculty of imagination can ever, of itself, reach belief, it is evident, that belief consists not in the peculiar nature or order of ideas, but in the manner of their conception, and in their feeling to the mind. I confess, that it is impossible perfectly to explain this feeling or manner of conception. We may make use of words, which express something near it. But its true and proper name, as we observed before, is belief; which is a term, that every one sufficiently understands in common life. And in philosophy, we can go no farther than assert, that belief is something felt by the mind, which distinguishes the ideas of the judgment from the fictions of the imagination. It gives them more weight and influence; makes them appear of greater importance; enforces them in the mind; and renders them the governing principle of our actions. I hear at present, for instance, a person's voice, with whom I am acquainted; and the sound comes as from the next room. This impression of my senses immediately conveys my thought to the person, together with all the surrounding objects. I paint them out to myself as existing at present, with the same qualities and relations, of which I formerly knew them possessed. These ideas take faster hold of my mind, than ideas of an enchanted castle. They are very different to the feeling, and have a much greater influence of every kind, either to give pleasure or pain, joy or sorrow.

Let us, then, take in the whole compass of this doctrine, and allow, that the sentiment of belief is nothing but a conception more intense and steady than what attends the mere fictions of the imagination, and that this manner of conception arises from a customary conjunction of the object with something present to the memory or senses: I believe that it will not be difficult, upon these suppositions, to find other operations of the mind analogous to it, and to trace up these phenomena to principles still more general.

We have already observed, that nature has established connexions among particular ideas, and that no sooner one idea occurs to our thoughts than it introduces its correlative, and carries our attention towards it, by a gentle and insensible movement. These principles of connexion or association we have reduced to three, namely, Resemblance, Contiguity, and Causation; which are the only bonds, that unite our thoughts together, and beget that regular train of reflection or discourse, which, in a greater or less degree, takes place among all mankind. Now here arises a question, on which the solution of the present difficulty will depend. Does it happen, in all these relations, that, when one of the objects is presented to the senses or memory, the mind is not only carried to the conception of the correlative, but reaches a steadier and stronger conception of it than what otherwise it would have been able to attain? This seems to be the case with that belief, which arises from the relation of cause and effect. And if the case be the same with the other relations or principles of

association, this may be established as a general law, which takes place in all the operations of the mind.

We may, therefore, observe, as the first experiment to our present purpose, that, upon the appearance of the picture of an absent friend, our idea of him is evidently enlivened by the resemblance, and that every passion, which that idea occasions, whether of joy or sorrow, acquires new force and vigor. In producing this effect, there concur both a relation and a present impression. Where the picture bears him no resemblance, at least was not intended for him, it never so much as conveys our thought to him: And where it is absent, as well as the person; though the mind may pass from the thought of the one to that of the other; it feels its idea to be rather weakened than enlivened by that transition. We take a pleasure in viewing the picture of a friend, when it is set before us; but when it is removed, rather choose to consider him directly, than by reflection in an image, which is equally distant and obscure.

The ceremonies of the Roman Catholic religion may be considered as instances of the same nature. The devotees of that superstition usually plead in excuse for the mummeries, with which they are upbraided, that they feel the good effect of those external motions, and postures, and actions, in enlivening their devotion and quickening their fervor, which otherwise would decay, if directed entirely to distant and immaterial objects. We shadow out the objects of our faith, say they, in sensible types and images, and render them more present to us by the immediate presence of these types, than it is possible for us to do, merely by an intellectual view and contemplation. Sensible objects have always a greater influence on the fancy than any other; and this influence they readily convey to those ideas, to which they are related, and which they resemble. I shall only infer from these practices, and this reasoning, that the effect of resemblance in enlivening the ideas is very common; and as in every case a resemblance and a present impression must concur, we are abundantly supplied with experiments to prove the reality of the foregoing principle.

We may add force to these experiments by others of a different kind, in considering the effects of contiguity as well as of resemblance. It is certain, that distance diminishes the force of every idea, and

p. 728

that, upon our approach to any object; though it does not discover itself to our senses; it operates upon the mind with an influence, which imitates an immediate impression. The thinking on any object readily transports the mind to what is contiguous; but it is only the actual presence of an object, that transports it with a superior vivacity. When I am a few miles from home, whatever relates to it touches me more nearly than when I am two hundred leagues distant; though even at that distance the reflecting on any thing in the neighborhood of my friends or family naturally produces an idea of them. But as in this latter case, both the objects of the mind are ideas; notwithstanding there is an easy transition between them; that transition alone is not able to give a superior vivacity to any of the ideas, for want of some immediate impression.

③ No one can doubt but causation has the same influence as the other two relations of resemblance and contiguity. Superstitious people are fond of the relics of saints and holy men, for the same reason, that they seek after types or images, in order to enliven their devotion, and give them a more intimate and strong conception of those exemplary lives, which they desire to imitate. Now it is evident, that one of the best relics, which a devotee could procure, would be the handiwork of a saint; and if his clothes and furniture are ever to be considered in this light, it is because they were once at his disposal, and were moved and affected by him; in which respect they are to be considered as imperfect effects, and as connected with him by a shorter chain of consequences than any of those, by which we learn the reality of his existence.

Suppose, that the son of a friend, who had been long dead or absent, were presented to us; it is evident, that this object would instantly revive its correlative idea, and recall to our thoughts all past intimacies and familiarities, in more lively colours than they would otherwise have appeared to us. This is another phenomenon, which seems to prove the principle above-mentioned.

We may observe, that, in these phenomena, the belief of the correlative object is always presupposed; without which the relation could have no effect. The influence of the picture supposes, that we believe our friend to have once existed. Contiguity to home can never excite our ideas of home, unless we believe

that it really exists. Now I assert, that this belief, where it reaches beyond the memory or senses, is of a similar nature, and arises from similar causes, with the transition of thought and vivacity of conception here explained. When I throw a piece of dry wood into a fire, my mind is immediately carried to conceive, that it augments, not extinguishes the flame. This transition of thought from the cause to the effect proceeds not from reason. It derives its origin altogether from custom and experience. And as it first begins from an object, present to the senses, it renders the idea or conception of flame more strong and lively than any loose, floating reverie of the imagination. That idea arises immediately. The thought moves instantly towards it, and conveys to it all that force of conception, which is derived from the impression present to the senses. When a sword is levelled at my breast, does not the idea of wound and pain strike me more strongly, than when a glass of wine is presented to me, even though by accident this idea should occur after the appearance of the latter object? But what is there in this whole matter to cause such a strong conception, except only a present object and a customary transition to the idea of another object, which we have been accustomed to conjoin with the former? This is the whole operation of the mind, in all our conclusions concerning matter of fact and existence; and it is a satisfaction to find some analogies, by which it may be explained. The transition from a present object does in all cases give strength and solidity to the related idea.

Here, then, is a kind of pre-established harmony between the course of nature and the succession of our ideas; and though the powers and forces, by which the former is governed, be wholly unknown to us; yet our thoughts and conceptions have still, we find, gone on in the same train with the other works of nature. Custom is that principle, by which this correspondence has been effected; so necessary to the subsistence of our species, and the regulation of our conduct, in every circumstance and occurrence of human life. Had not the presence of an object instantly excited the idea of those objects, commonly conjoined with it, all our knowledge must have been limited to the narrow sphere of our memory and senses; and we should never have been able to adjust means to ends, or employ our natural powers, either to the

nature = instinct

producing of good, or avoiding of evil. Those, who delight in the discovery and contemplation of final causes, have here ample subject to employ their wonder and admiration.

I shall add, for a further confirmation of the foregoing theory, that, as this operation of the mind, by which we infer like effects from like causes, and vice versa, is so essential to the subsistence of all human creatures, it is not probable, that it could be trusted to the fallacious deductions of our reason, which is slow in its operations; appears not, in any degree, during the first years of infancy; and at best is, in every age and period of human life, extremely liable to error and mistake. It is more conformable to the ordinary wisdom of nature to secure so necessary an act of the mind, by some instinct or mechanical tendency, which may be infallible in its operations, may discover itself at the first appearance of life and thought, and may be independent of all the labored deductions of the understanding. As nature has taught us the use of our limbs, without giving us the knowledge of the muscles and nerves, by which they are actuated; so has she implanted in us an instinct, which carries forward the thought in a correspondent course to that which she has established among external objects: though we are ignorant of those powers and forces, on which this regular course and succession of objects totally depends.

SECTION VI: OF PROBABILITY

Though there be no such thing as Chance in the world; our ignorance of the real cause of any event has the same influence on the understanding, and begets a like species of belief or opinion.

There is certainly a probability, which arises from a superiority of chances on any side; and according as this superiority increases, and surpasses the opposite chances, the probability receives a proportionable increase, and begets still a higher degree of belief or assent to that side, in which we discover the superiority. If a dye were marked with one figure or number of spots on four sides, and with another figure or number of spots on the two remaining sides, it would be more probable, that the former would turn up than the latter; though, if it had a thousand sides marked in the same manner, and only one

side different, the probability would be much higher, and our belief or expectation of the event more steady and secure. This process of the thought or reasoning may seem trivial and obvious; but to those who consider it more narrowly, it may, perhaps, afford matter for curious speculation.

It seems evident, that, when the mind looks forward to discover the event, which may result from the throw of such a dye, it considers the turning up of each particular side as alike probable; and this is the very nature of chance, to render all the particular events, comprehended in it, entirely equal. But finding a greater number of sides concur in the one event than in the other, the mind is carried more frequently to that event, and meets it oftener, in revolving the various possibilities or chances, on which the ultimate result depends. This concurrence of several views in one particular event begets immediately, by an inexplicable contrivance of nature, the sentiment of belief, and gives that event the advantage over its antagonist, which is supported by a smaller number of views, and recurs less frequently to the mind. If we allow, that belief is nothing but a firmer and stronger conception of an object than what attends the mere fictions of the imagination, this operation may, perhaps, in some measure be accounted for. The concurrence of these several views or glimpses imprints the idea more strongly on the imagination; gives it superior force and vigor; renders its influence on the passions and affections more sensible; and in a word, begets that reliance or security, which constitutes the nature of belief and opinion.

The case is the same with the probability of causes, as with that of chance. There are some causes, which are entirely uniform and constant in producing a particular effect; and no instance has ever yet been found of any failure or irregularity in their operation. Fire has always burned, and water suffocated every human creature: The production of motion by impulse and gravity is an universal law, which has hitherto admitted of no exception. But there are other causes, which have been found more irregular and uncertain; nor has rhubarb always proved a purge, or opium a soporific to every one, who has taken these medicines. It is true, when any cause fails of producing its usual effect, philosophers *mathematics — ideas clear / determinate*

ascribe not this to any irregularity in nature; but suppose, that some secret causes, in the particular structure of parts, have prevented the operation. Our reasonings, however, and conclusions concerning the event are the same as if this principle had no place. Being determined by custom to transfer the past to the future, in all our inferences; where the past has been entirely regular and uniform, we expect the event with the greatest assurance, and leave no room for any contrary supposition. But where different effects have been found to follow from causes, which are to appearance exactly similar, all these various effects must occur to the mind in transferring the past to the future, and enter into our consideration, when we determine the probability of the event. Though we give the preference to that which has been found most usual, and believe that this effect will exist, we must not overlook the other effects, but must assign to each of them a particular weight and authority, in proportion as we have found it to be more or less frequent. It is more probable, in almost every country of Europe, that there will be frost sometime in January, than that the weather will continue open throughout that whole month; though this probability varies according to the different climates, and approaches to a certainty in the more northern kingdoms. Here then it seems evident, that, when we transfer the past to the future, in order to determine the effect, which will result from any cause, we transfer all the different events, in the same proportion as they have appeared in the past, and conceive one to have existed a hundred times, for instance, another ten times, and another once. As a great number of views do here concur in one event, they fortify and confirm it to the imagination, beget that sentiment which we call belief, and give its object the preference above the contrary event, which is not supported by an equal number of experiments, and recurs not so frequently to the thought in transferring the past to the future. Let any one try to account for this operation of the mind upon any of the received systems of philosophy, and he will be sensible of the difficulty. For my part, I shall think it sufficient, if the present hints excite the curiosity of philosophers, and make them sensible how defective all common theories are in treating of such curious and such sublime subjects.

SECTION VII: OF THE IDEA OF NECESSARY CONNEXION

Cause + effect.

PART I

The great advantage of the mathematical sciences above the moral consists in this, that the ideas of the former, being sensible, are always clear and determinate, the smallest distinction between them is immediately perceptible, and the same terms are still expressive of the same ideas, without ambiguity or variation. An oval is never mistaken for a circle, nor an hyperbola for an ellipsis. The isosceles and scalenum are distinguished by boundaries more exact than vice and virtue, right and wrong. If any term be defined in geometry, the mind readily, of itself, substitutes, on all occasions, the definition for the term defined: Or even when no definition is employed, the object itself may be presented to the senses, and by that means be steadily and clearly apprehended. But the finer sentiments of the mind, the operations of the understanding, the various agitations of the passions, though really in themselves distinct, easily escape us, when surveyed by reflection; nor is it in our power to recall the original object, as often as we have occasion to contemplate it. Ambiguity, by this means, is gradually introduced into our reasonings: Similar objects are readily taken to be the same: And the conclusion becomes at last very wide of the premises.

One may safely, however, affirm, that, if we consider these sciences in a proper light, their advantages and disadvantages nearly compensate each other, and reduce both of them to a state of equality. If the mind, with greater facility, retains the ideas of geometry clear and determinate, it must carry on a much longer and more intricate chain of reasoning, and compare ideas much wider of each other, in order to reach the abstruser truths of that science. And if moral ideas are apt, without extreme care, to fall into obscurity and confusion, the inferences are always much shorter in these disquisitions, and the intermediate steps, which lead to the conclusion, much fewer than in the sciences which treat of quantity and number. In reality, there is scarcely a proposition in Euclid so simple, as not to consist of more parts, than are to be found in any moral reasoning which runs not into chimera and conceit. Where we

[handwritten margin notes: "metaphysical sciences are ambiguous"; "billiard balls: no tie between cause & effect – not infallible connection"]

trace the principles of the human mind through a few steps, we may be very well satisfied with our progress; considering how soon nature throws a bar to all our enquiries concerning causes, and reduces us to an acknowledgment of our ignorance. The chief obstacle, therefore, to our improvement in the moral or metaphysical sciences is the obscurity of the ideas, and ambiguity of the terms. The principal difficulty in the mathematics is the length of inferences and compass of thought, requisite to the forming of any conclusion. And, perhaps, our progress in natural philosophy is chiefly retarded by the want of proper experiments and phenomena, which are often discovered by chance, and cannot always be found, when requisite, even by the most diligent and prudent enquiry. As moral philosophy seems hitherto to have received less improvement than either geometry or physics, we may conclude, that, if there be any difference in this respect among these sciences, the difficulties, which obstruct the progress of the former, require superior care and capacity to be surmounted.

There are no ideas, which occur in metaphysics, more obscure and uncertain, than those of power, force, energy or necessary connexion, of which it is every moment necessary for us to treat in all our disquisitions. We shall, therefore, endeavor, in this section, to fix, if possible, the precise meaning of these terms, and thereby remove some part of that obscurity, which is so much complained of in this species of philosophy.

It seems a proposition, which will not admit of much dispute, that all our ideas are nothing but copies of our impressions, or, in other words, that it is impossible for us to think of any thing, which we have not antecedently felt, either by our external or internal senses. I have endeavored to explain and prove this proposition, and have expressed my hopes, that, by a proper application of it, men may reach a greater clearness and precision in philosophical reasonings, than what they have hitherto been able to attain. Complex ideas may, perhaps, be well known by definition, which is nothing but an enumeration of those parts or simple ideas, that compose them. But when we have pushed up definitions to the most simple ideas, and find still some ambiguity and obscurity; what resource are we then possessed of? By

what invention can we throw light upon these ideas, and render them altogether precise and determinate to our intellectual view? Produce the impressions or original sentiments, from which the ideas are copied. These impressions are all strong and sensible. They admit not of ambiguity. They are not only placed in a full light themselves, but may throw light on their correspondent ideas, which lie in obscurity. And by this means, we may, perhaps, attain a new microscope or species of optics, by which, in the moral sciences, the most minute, and most simple ideas may be so enlarged as to fall readily under our apprehension, and be equally known with the grossest and most sensible ideas, that can be the object of our enquiry.

To be fully acquainted, therefore, with the idea of power or necessary connexion, let us examine its impression; and in order to find the impression with greater certainty, let us search for it in all the sources, from which it may possibly be derived.

When we look about us towards external objects, and consider the operation of causes, we are never able, in a single instance, to discover any power or necessary connexion; any quality, which binds the effect to the cause, and renders the one an infallible consequence of the other. We only find, that the one does actually, in fact, follow the other. The impulse of one billiard-ball is attended with motion in the second. This is the whole that appears to the outward senses. The mind feels no sentiment or inward impression from this succession of objects: Consequently, there is not, in any single, particular instance of cause and effect, any thing which can suggest the idea of power or necessary connexion.

From the first appearance of an object, we never can conjecture what effect will result from it. But were the power or energy of any cause discoverable by the mind, we could foresee the effect, even without experience; and might, at first, pronounce with certainty concerning it, by the mere dint of thought and reasoning.

In reality, there is no part of matter, that does ever, by its sensible qualities, discover any power or energy, or give us ground to imagine, that it could produce any thing, or be followed by any other object, which we could denominate its effect. Solidity, extension, motion; these qualities are all complete in themselves, and never point out any other event which may result from them. The scenes of the universe are continually shifting, and one object follows another in an uninterrupted succession; but the power or force, which actuates the whole machine, is entirely concealed from us, and never discovers itself in any of the sensible qualities of body. We know, that, in fact, heat is a constant attendant of flame; but what is the connexion between them, we have no room so much as to conjecture or imagine. It is impossible, therefore, that the idea of power can be derived from the contemplation of bodies, in single instances of their operation; because no bodies ever discover any power, which can be the original of this idea.

Since, therefore, external objects as they appear to the senses, give us no idea of power or necessary connexion, by their operation in particular instances, let us see, whether this idea be derived from reflection on the operations of our own minds, and be copied from any internal impression. It may be said, that we are every moment conscious of internal power; while we feel, that, by the simple command of our will, we can move the organs of our body, or direct the faculties of our mind. An act of volition produces motion in our limbs, or raises a new idea in our Imagination. This influence of the will we know by consciousness. Hence we acquire the idea of power or energy; and are certain, that we ourselves and all other intelligent beings are possessed of power. This idea, then, is an idea of reflection, since it arises from reflecting on the operations of our own mind, and on the command which is exercised by will, both over the organs of the body and faculties of the soul.

We shall proceed to examine this pretension; and first with regard to the influence of volition over the organs of the body. This influence, we may observe, is a fact, which, like all other natural events, can be known only by experience, and can never be foreseen from any apparent energy or power in the cause, which connects it with the effect, and renders the one an infallible consequence of the other. The motion of our body follows upon the command of our will. Of this we are every moment conscious. But the means, by which this is effected; the energy, by which the will performs so extraordinary an operation; of this we are so far from being immediately

conscious, that it must for ever escape our most diligent enquiry.

For first; is there any principle in all nature more mysterious than the union of soul with body; by which a supposed spiritual substance acquires such an influence over a material one, that the most refined thought is able to actuate the grossest matter? Were we empowered, by a secret wish, to remove mountains, or control the planets in their orbit; this extensive authority would not be more extraordinary, nor more beyond our comprehension. But if by consciousness we perceived any power or energy in the will, we must know this power; we must know its connexion with the effect; we must know the secret union of soul and body, and the nature of both these substances; by which the one is able to operate, in so many instances, upon the other.

Secondly, We are not able to move all the organs of the body with a like authority; though we cannot assign any reason besides experience, for so remarkable a difference between one and the other. Why has the will an influence over the tongue and fingers, not over the heart or liver? This question would never embarrass us, were we conscious of a power in the former case, not in the latter. We should then perceive, independent of experience, why the authority of will over the organs of the body is circumscribed within such particular limits. Being in that case fully acquainted with the power or force, by which it operates, we should also know, why its influence reaches precisely to such boundaries, and no farther.

A man, suddenly struck with a palsy in the leg or arm, or who had newly lost those members, frequently endeavors, at first to move them, and employ them in their usual offices. Here he is as much conscious of power to command such limbs, as a man in perfect health is conscious of power to actuate any member which remains in its natural state and condition. But consciousness never deceives. Consequently, neither in the one case nor in the other, are we ever conscious of any power. We learn the influence of our will from experience alone. And experience only teaches us, how one event constantly follows another; without instructing us in the secret connexion, which binds them together, and renders them inseparable.

Not knowable:
Soul as creation—
something out of
nothing.

Thirdly, We learn from anatomy, that the immediate object of power in voluntary motion, is not the member itself which is moved, but certain muscles, and nerves, and animal spirits and, perhaps, something still more minute and more unknown, through which the motion is successively propagated, ere it reach the member itself whose motion is the immediate object of volition. Can there be a more certain proof that the power, by which this whole operation is performed, so far from being directly and fully known by an inward sentiment or consciousness, is, to the last degree, mysterious and unintelligible? Here the mind wills a certain event: Immediately another event, unknown to ourselves, and totally different from the one intended, is produced: This event produces another, equally unknown: Till at last, through a long succession, the desired event is produced. But if the original power were felt, it must be known: Were it known, its effect must also be known; since all power is relative to its effect. And vice versa, if the effect be not known, the power cannot be known nor felt. How indeed can we be conscious of a power to move our limbs, when we have no such power; but only that to move certain animal spirits, which, though they produce at last the motion of our limbs, yet operate in such a manner as is wholly beyond our comprehension?

We may, therefore, conclude from the whole, I hope, without any temerity, though with assurance; that our idea of power is not copied from any sentiment or consciousness of power within ourselves, when we give rise to animal motion, or apply our limbs, to their proper use and office. That their motion follows the command of the will is a matter of common experience, like other natural events: But the power or energy by which this is effected, like that in other natural events, is unknown and inconceivable.

Shall we then assert, that we are conscious of a power or energy in our own minds, when, by an act or command of our will, we raise up a new idea, fix the mind to the contemplation of it, turn it on all sides, and at last dismiss it for some other idea, when we think that we have surveyed it with sufficient accuracy? I believe the same arguments will prove, that even this command of the will gives us no real idea of force or energy.

First, It must be allowed, that, when we know a power, we know that very circumstance in the cause, by which it is enabled to produce the effect: For these are supposed to be synonymous. We must, therefore, know both the cause and effect, and the relation between them. But do we pretend to be acquainted with the nature of the human soul and the nature of an idea, or the aptitude of the one to produce the other? This is a real creation; a production of something out of nothing: Which implies a power so great, that it may seem, at first sight, beyond the reach of any being, less than infinite. At least it must be owned, that such a power is not felt, nor known, nor even conceivable by the mind. We only feel the event, namely, the existence of an idea, consequent to a command of the will: But the manner, in which this operation is performed, the power by which it is produced, is entirely beyond our comprehension.

Secondly, The command of the mind over itself is limited, as well as its command over the body; and these limits are not known by reason, or any acquaintance with the nature of cause and effect, but only by experience and observation, as in all other natural events and in the operation of external objects. Our authority over our sentiments and passions is much weaker than that over our ideas; and even the latter authority is circumscribed within very narrow boundaries. Will any one pretend to assign the ultimate reason of these boundaries, or shew why the power is deficient in one case, not in another?

Thirdly, This self-command is very different at different times. A man in health possesses more of it than one languishing with sickness. We are more master of our thoughts in the morning than in the evening: Fasting, than after a full meal. Can we give any reason for these variations, except experience? Where then is the power, of which we pretend to be conscious? Is there not here, either in a spiritual or material substance, or both, some secret mechanism or structure of parts, upon which the effect depends, and which, being entirely unknown to us, renders the power or energy of the will equally unknown and incomprehensible?

Volition is surely an act of the mind, with which we are sufficiently acquainted. Reflect upon it. Consider it on all sides. Do you find anything in it like this creative power, by which it raises from nothing

[handwritten marginalia: common nature + extraordinary phenomena at a loss to... power]

[handwritten marginalia top right: our ideas are revealed to us by God.]

[handwritten marginalia right: we don't create it ourselves]

a new idea, and with a kind of Fiat, imitates the omnipotence of its Maker, if I may be allowed so to speak, who called forth into existence all the various scenes of nature? So far from being conscious of this energy in the will, it requires as certain experience, as that of which we are possessed, to convince us, that such extraordinary effects do ever result from a simple act of volition.

The generality of mankind never find any difficulty in accounting for the more common and familiar operations of nature; such as the descent of heavy bodies, the growth of plants, the generation of animals, or the nourishment of bodies by food: But suppose, that, in all these cases, they perceive the very force or energy of the cause, by which it is connected with its effect, and is for ever infallible in its operation. They acquire, by long habit, such a turn of mind, that, upon the appearance of the cause, they immediately expect with assurance its usual attendant, and hardly conceive it possible, that any other event could result from it. It is only on the discovery of extraordinary phenomena, such as earthquakes, pestilence, and prodigies of any kind, that they find themselves at a loss to assign a proper cause, and to explain the manner, in which the effect is produced by it. It is usual for men, in such difficulties, to have recourse to some invisible intelligent principle, as the immediate cause of that event, which surprises them, and which, they think, cannot be accounted for from the common powers of nature. But philosophers, who carry their scrutiny a little farther, immediately perceive, that, even in the most familiar events, the energy of the cause is as unintelligible as in the most unusual, and that we only learn by experience the frequent Conjunction of objects, without being ever able to comprehend anything like Connexion between them. Here then, many philosophers think themselves obliged by reason to have recourse, on all occasions, to the same principle, which the vulgar never appeal to but in cases, that appear miraculous and supernatural. They acknowledge mind and intelligence to be, not only the ultimate and original cause of all things, but the immediate and sole cause of every event, which appears in nature. They pretend, that those objects, which are commonly denominated causes, are in reality nothing but occasions; and that the true and di-

rect principle of every effect is not any power or force in nature, but a volition of the Supreme Being, who wills, that such particular objects should, for ever, be conjoined with each other. Instead of saying, that one billiard-ball moves another, by a force, which it has derived from the author of nature; it is the Deity himself, they say, who, by a particular volition, moves the second ball, being determined to this operation by the impulse of the first ball: in consequence of those general laws, which he has laid down to himself in the government of the universe. But philosophers advancing still in their enquiries, discover, that, as we are totally ignorant of the power, on which depends the mutual operation of bodies, we are no less ignorant of that power, on which depends the operation of mind on body, or of body on mind; nor are we able, either from our senses or consciousness, to assign the ultimate principle in one case, more than in the other. The same ignorance, therefore, reduces them to the same conclusion. They assert, that the Deity is the immediate cause of the union between soul and body; and that they are not the organs of sense, which, being agitated by external objects, produce sensations in the mind; but that it is a particular volition of our omnipotent Maker, which excites such a sensation, in consequence of such a motion in the organ. In like manner, it is not any energy in the will, that produces local motion in our members: It is God himself, who is pleased to second our will, in itself impotent, and to command that motion, which we erroneously attribute to our own power and efficacy. Nor do philosophers stop at this conclusion. They sometimes extend the same inference to the mind itself, in its internal operations. Our mental vision or conception of ideas is nothing but a revelation made to us by our Maker. When we voluntarily turn our thoughts to any object, and raise up its image in the fancy; it is not the will which creates that idea: It is the universal Creator, who discovers it to the mind, and renders it present to us.

Thus, according to these philosophers, every thing is full of God. Not content with the principle, that nothing exists but by his will, that nothing possesses any power but by his concession: They rob nature, and all created beings, of every power, in order to render their dependence on the Deity still more sensible and immediate. They consider not, that, by this *we can't know God reflections or motivations*

theory, they diminish, instead of magnifying, the grandeur of those attributes, which they affect so much to celebrate. It argues surely more power in the Deity to delegate a certain degree of power to inferior creatures, than to produce every thing by his own immediate volition. It argues more wisdom to contrive at first the fabric of the world with such perfect foresight, that, of itself, and by its proper operation, it may serve all the purposes of providence, than if the great Creator were obliged every moment to adjust its parts, and animate by his breath all the wheels of that stupendous machine.

But if we would have a more philosophical confutation of this theory, perhaps the two following reflections may suffice.

First, It seems to me, that this theory of the universal energy and operation of the Supreme Being, is too bold ever to carry conviction with it to a man, sufficiently apprized of the weakness of human reason, and the narrow limits, to which it is confined in all its operations. Though the chain of arguments which conduct to it, were ever so logical, there must arise a strong suspicion, if not an absolute assurance, that it has carried us quite beyond the reach of our faculties, when it leads to conclusions so extraordinary, and so remote from common life and experience. We are got into fairy land, long ere we have reached the last steps of our theory; and there we have no reason to trust our common methods of argument, or to think that our usual analogies and probabilities have any authority. Our line is too short to fathom such immense abysses. And however we may flatter ourselves, that we are guided, in every step which we take, by a kind of verisimilitude and experience; we may be assured, that this fancied experience has no authority, when we thus apply it to subjects, that lie entirely out of the sphere of experience. But on this we shall have occasion to touch afterwards.

Secondly, I cannot perceive any force in the arguments, on which this theory is founded. We are ignorant, it is true, of the manner in which bodies operate on each other: Their force or energy is entirely incomprehensible: But are we not equally ignorant of the manner or force by which a mind, even the supreme mind, operates either on itself or on body? Whence, I beseech you, do we acquire any

idea of it? We have no sentiment or consciousness of this power in ourselves. We have no idea of the Supreme Being but what we learn from reflection on our own faculties. Were our ignorance, therefore, a good reason for rejecting any thing, we should be led into that principle of denying all energy in the Supreme Being as much as in the grossest matter. We surely comprehend as little the operations of one as of the other. Is it more difficult to conceive, that motion may arise from impulse, than that it may arise from volition? All we know is our profound ignorance in both cases.

PART II

But to hasten to a conclusion of this argument, which is already drawn out to too great a length: We have sought in vain for an idea of power or necessary connexion, in all the sources from which we could suppose it to be derived. It appears, that, in single instances of the operation of bodies, we never can, by our utmost scrutiny, discover any thing but one event following another; without being able to comprehend any force or power, by which the cause operates, or any connexion between it and its supposed effect. The same difficulty occurs in contemplating the operations of mind on body; where we observe the motion of the latter to follow upon the volition of the former; but are not able to observe or conceive the tie which binds together the motion and volition, or the energy by which the mind produces this effect. The authority of the will over its own faculties and ideas is not a whit more comprehensible: So that, upon the whole, there appears not, throughout all nature, any one instance of connexion, which is conceivable by us. All events seem entirely loose and separate. One event follows another; but we never can observe any tie between them. They seem conjoined, but never connected. And as we can have no idea of any thing, which never appeared to our outward sense or inward sentiment, the necessary conclusion seems to be, that we have no idea of connexion or power at all, and that these words are absolutely without any meaning, when employed either in philosophical reasonings, or common life.

But there still remains one method of avoiding this conclusion, and one source which we have not yet examined. When any natural object or event is presented, it is impossible for us, by any sagacity or penetration, to discover, or even conjecture, without experience, what event will result from it, or to carry our foresight beyond that object, which is immediately present to the memory and senses. Even after one instance or experiment, where we have observed a particular event to follow upon another, we are not entitled to form a general rule, or foretell what will happen in like cases; it being justly esteemed an unpardonable temerity to judge of the whole course of nature from one single experiment, however accurate or certain. But when one particular species of event has always, in all instances, been conjoined with another, we make no longer any scruple of foretelling one upon the appearance of the other, and of employing that reasoning, which can alone assure us of any matter of fact or existence. We then call the one object, Cause; the other, Effect. We suppose, that there is some connexion between them; some power in the one, by which it infallibly produces the other, and operates with the greatest certainty and strongest necessity.

It appears, then, that this idea of a necessary connexion among events arises from a number of similar instances, which occur, of the constant conjunction of these events; nor can that idea ever be suggested by any one of these instances, surveyed in all possible lights and positions. But there is nothing in a number of instances, different from every single instance, which is supposed to be exactly similar; except only, that after a repetition of similar instances, the mind is carried by habit, upon the appearance of one event, to expect its usual attendant, and to believe, that it will exist. This connexion, therefore, which we feel in the mind, this customary transition of the imagination from one object to its usual attendant, is the sentiment or impression, from which we form the idea of power or necessary connexion. Nothing farther is in the case. Contemplate the subject on all sides; you will never find any other origin of that idea. This is the sole difference between one instance, from which we can never receive the idea of connexion, and a number of similar instances, by which it is suggested. The first time a man saw the communication of motion by impulse, as by the shock of two billiard-balls, he could not

pronounce that the one event was connected: but only that it was conjoined with the other. After he has observed several instances of this nature, he then pronounces them to be connected. What alteration has happened to give rise to this new idea of connexion? Nothing but that he now feels these events to be connected in his imagination, and can readily foretell the existence of one from the appearance of the other. When we say, therefore, that one object is connected with another, we mean only, that they have acquired a connexion in our thought, and give rise to this inference, by which they become proofs of each other's existence: A conclusion, which is somewhat extraordinary; but which seems founded on sufficient evidence. Nor will its evidence be weakened by any general diffidence of the understanding, or sceptical suspicion concerning every conclusion, which is new and extraordinary. No conclusions can be more agreeable to scepticism than such as make discoveries concerning the weakness and narrow limits of human reason and capacity.

And what stronger instance can be produced of the surprising ignorance and weakness of the understanding, than the present? For surely, if there be any relation among objects, which it imports to us to know perfectly, it is that of cause and effect. On this are founded all our reasonings concerning matter of fact or existence. By means of it alone we attain any assurance concerning objects, which are removed from the present testimony of our memory and senses. The only immediate utility of all sciences, is to teach us, how to control and regulate future events by their causes. Our thoughts and enquiries are, therefore, every moment, employed about this relation: Yet so imperfect are the ideas which we form concerning it, that it is impossible to give any just definition of cause, except what is drawn from something extraneous and foreign to it. Similar objects are always conjoined with similar. Of this we have experience. Suitably to this experience, therefore, we may define a cause to be an object, followed by another, and where all the objects, similar to the first, are followed by objects similar to the second. Or, in other words, where, if the first object had not been, the second never had existed. The appearance of a cause always conveys the mind, by a customary transition, to the idea of the effect. Of this also we have

Cause always brings effect

cause: definition

experience. We may, therefore, suitably to this experience, form another definition of cause; and call it, an object followed by another, and whose appearance always conveys the thought to that other. *or an* But though both these definitions be drawn from circumstances foreign to the cause, we cannot remedy this inconvenience, or attain any more perfect definition, which may point out that circumstance in the cause, which gives it a connexion with its effect. We have no idea of this connexion; nor even any distinct notion what it is we desire to know, when we endeavor at a conception of it. We say, for instance, that the vibration of this string is the cause of this particular sound. But what do we mean by that affirmation? We either mean, that this vibration is followed by this sound, and that all similar vibrations have been followed by similar sounds: Or, that this vibration is followed by this sound, and that upon the appearance of one, the mind anticipates the senses, and forms immediately an idea of the other. We may consider the relation of cause and effect in either of these two lights; but beyond these, we have no idea of it.

Summary To recapitulate, therefore, the reasonings of this section: Every idea is copied from some preceding impression or sentiment; and where we cannot find any impression, we may be certain that there is no idea. In all single instances of the operation of bodies or minds, there is nothing that produces any impression, nor consequently can suggest any idea of power or necessary connexion. But when many uniform instances appear, and the same object is always followed by the same event; we then begin to entertain the notion of cause and connexion. We then feel a new sentiment or impression, to wit, a customary connexion in the thought or imagination between one object and its usual attendant; and this sentiment is the original of that idea which we seek for. For as this idea arises from a number of similar instances, and not from any single instance, it must arise from that circumstance, in which the number of instances differ from every individual instance. But this customary connexion or transition of the imagination is the only circumstance in which they differ. In every other particular they are alike. The first instance which we saw of motion, communicated by the shock of two billiard-balls (to re-

turn to this obvious illustration) is exactly similar to any instance that may, at present, occur to us; except only, that we could not, at first, infer one event from the other; which we are enabled to do at present, after so long a course of uniform experience. I know not whether the reader will readily apprehend this reasoning. I am afraid, that, should I multiply words about it, or throw it into a greater variety of lights, it would only become more obscure and intricate. In all abstract reasonings, there is one point of view, which, if we can happily hit, we shall go farther towards illustrating the subject than by all the eloquence and copious expression in the world. This point of view we should endeavor to reach, and reserve the flowers of rhetoric for subjects which are more adapted to them.

SECTION VIII: OF LIBERTY AND NECESSITY

PART I

It might reasonably be expected, in questions, which have been canvassed and disputed with great eagerness, since the first origin of science and philosophy, that the meaning of all the terms, at least, should have been agreed upon among the disputants; and our enquiries, in the course of two thousand years, been able to pass from words to the true and real subject of the controversy. For how easy may it seem to give exact definitions of the terms employed in reasoning, and make these definitions, not the mere sound of words, the object of future scrutiny and examination? But if we consider the matter more narrowly, we shall be apt to draw a quite opposite conclusion. From this circumstance alone, that a controversy has been long kept on foot, and remains still undecided, we may presume, that there is some ambiguity in the expression, and that the disputants affix different ideas to the terms employed in the controversy. For as the faculties of the mind are supposed to be naturally alike in every individual; otherwise nothing could be more fruitless than to reason or dispute together; it were impossible, if men affix the same ideas to their terms, that they could so long form different opinions of the same subject; especially when they communicate their views, and each party turn themselves on all sides, in search of arguments, which may give them the victory over their antagonists. It is true; if men attempt the discussion of questions, which lie entirely beyond the reach of human capacity, such as those concerning the origin of worlds, or the economy of the intellectual system or region of spirits, they may long beat the air in their fruitless contests, and never arrive at any determinate conclusion. But if the question regard any subject of common life and experience; nothing, one would think, could preserve the dispute so long undecided, but some ambiguous expressions, which keep the antagonists still at a distance, and hinder them from grappling with each other.

This has been the case in the long disputed question concerning liberty and necessity; and to so remarkable a degree, that, if I be not much mistaken, we shall find, that all mankind, both learned and ignorant, have always been of the same opinion with regard to this subject, and that a few intelligible definitions would immediately have put an end to the whole controversy. I own, that this dispute has been so much canvassed on all hands, and has led philosophers into such a labyrinth of obscure sophistry, that it is no wonder, if a sensible reader indulge his ease so far as to turn a deaf ear to the proposal of such a question, from which he can expect neither instruction nor entertainment. But the state of the argument here proposed may, perhaps, serve to renew his attention; as it has more novelty, promises at least some decision of the controversy, and will not much disturb his ease by any intricate or obscure reasoning.

I hope, therefore, to make it appear, that all men have ever agreed in the doctrine both of necessity and of liberty, according to any reasonable sense, which can be put on these terms; and that the whole controversy has hitherto turned merely upon words. We shall begin with examining the doctrine of necessity.

It is universally allowed that matter, in all its operations, is actuated by a necessary force, and that every natural effect is so precisely determined by the energy of its cause, that no other effect, in such particular circumstances, could possibly have resulted from it. The degree and direction of every motion is, by the laws of nature, prescribed with such exactness, that a living creature may as soon arise from the shock of two bodies, as motion, in any other degree or direction than what is actually produced by it. Would we, therefore, form a just and precise idea of necessity, we must consider whence that idea arises, when we apply it to the operation of bodies.

It seems evident, that, if all the scenes of nature were continually shifted in such a manner, that no two events bore any resemblance to each other, but every object was entirely new, without any similitude to whatever had been seen before, we should never, in that case, have attained the least idea of necessity, or of a connexion among these objects. We might say, upon such a supposition, that one object or event has followed another; not that one was produced by the other. The relation of cause and effect must be utterly unknown to mankind. Inference and reasoning concerning the operations of nature would, from that moment, be at an end; and the memory and senses remain the only canals, by which the knowledge of any real existence could possibly have access to the mind. Our idea, therefore, of necessity and causation arises entirely from the uniformity, observable in the operations of nature; where similar objects are constantly conjoined together, and the mind is determined by custom to infer the one from the appearance of the other. These two circumstances form the whole of that necessity, which we ascribe to matter. Beyond the constant conjunction of similar objects, and the consequent inference from one to the other, we have no notion of any necessity, or connexion.

If it appear, therefore, that all mankind have ever allowed, without any doubt or hesitation, that these two circumstances take place in the voluntary actions of men, and in the operations of mind; it must follow, that all mankind have ever agreed in the doctrine of necessity, and that they have hitherto disputed, merely for not understanding each other.

As to the first circumstance, the constant and regular conjunction of similar events; we may possibly satisfy ourselves by the following considerations. It is universally acknowledged, that there is a great uniformity among the actions of men, in all nations and ages, and that human nature remains still the same, in its principles and operations. The same motives always produce the same actions: The same events follow from the same causes. Ambition, avarice, self-love, vanity, friendship, generosity, public spirit; these passions, mixed in various degrees, and distributed through society, have been, from the beginning of the world, and still are, the source of all the actions and enterprises, which have ever been observed among mankind. Would you know the sentiments, inclinations, and course of life of the Greeks and Romans? Study well the temper and actions of the French and English: You cannot be much mistaken in transferring to the former most of the observations, which you have made with regard to the latter. Mankind are so much the same, in all times and places, that history informs us of nothing new or strange in this particular. Its chief use is only to discover the constant and universal principles of human nature, by showing men in all varieties of circumstances and situations, and furnishing us with materials, from which we may form our observations, and become acquainted with the regular springs of human action and behavior. These records of wars, intrigues, factions, and revolutions, are so many collections of experiments, by which the politician or moral philosopher fixes the principles of his science; in the same manner as the physician or natural philosopher becomes acquainted with the nature of plants, minerals, and other external objects, by the experiments, which he forms concerning them. Nor are the earth, water, and other elements, examined by Aristotle, and Hippocrates, more like to those, which at present lie under our observation than the men, described by Polybius and Tacitus, are to those, who now govern the world.

Should a traveller, returning from a far country, bring us an account of men, wholly different from any, with whom we were ever acquainted; men, who were entirely divested of avarice, ambition, or revenge; who knew no pleasure but friendship, generosity, and public spirit; we should immediately, from these circumstances, detect the falsehood, and prove him a liar, with the same certainty as if he had stuffed his narration with stories of centaurs and dragons, miracles and prodigies. And if we would explode any forgery in history, we cannot make use of a more convincing argument, than to prove, that the actions, ascribed to any person, are directly contrary to the course of nature, and that no human mo-

tives, in such circumstances, could ever induce him to such a conduct. The veracity of Quintus Curtius is as much to be suspected, when he describes the supernatural courage of Alexander, by which he was hurried on singly to attack multitudes, as when he describes his supernatural force and activity, by which he was able to resist them. So readily and universally do we acknowledge a uniformity in human motives and actions as well as in the operations of body.

Hence likewise the benefit of that experience, acquired by long life and a variety of business and company, in order to instruct us in the principles of human nature, and regulate our future conduct, as well as speculation. By means of this guide, we mount up to the knowledge of men's inclinations and motives, from their actions, expressions, and even gestures; and again, descend to the interpretation of their actions from our knowledge of their motives and inclinations. The general observations, treasured up by a course of experience, give us the clue of human nature, and teach us to unravel all its intricacies. Pretexts and appearances no longer deceive us. Public declarations pass for the specious coloring of a cause. And though virtue and honour be allowed their proper weight and authority, that perfect disinterestedness, so often pretended to, is never expected in multitudes and parties; seldom in their leaders; and scarcely even in individuals of any rank or station. But were there no uniformity in human actions, and were every experiment, which we could form of this kind, irregular and anomalous, it were impossible to collect any general observations concerning mankind; and no experience, however accurately digested by reflection, would ever serve to any purpose. Why is the aged husbandman more skillful in his calling than the young beginner, but because there is a certain uniformity in the operation of the sun, rain, and earth towards the production of vegetables; and experience teaches the old practitioner the rules, by which this operation is governed and directed?

We must not, however, expect, that this uniformity of human actions should be carried to such a length, as that all men, in the same circumstances, will always act precisely in the same manner, without making any allowance for the diversity of characters, prejudices, and opinions. Such a uniformity in every particular, is found in no part of nature. On the contrary, from observing the variety of conduct in different men, we are enabled to form a greater variety of maxims, which still suppose a degree of uniformity and regularity.

Are the manners of men different in different ages and countries? We learn thence the great force of custom and education, which mould the human mind from its infancy, and form it into a fixed and established character. Is the behavior and conduct of the one sex very unlike that of the other? It is thence we become acquainted with the different characters, which nature has impressed upon the sexes, and which she preserves with constancy and regularity. Are the actions of the same person much diversified in the different periods of his life, from infancy to old age? This affords room for many general observations concerning the gradual change of our sentiments and inclinations, and the different maxims, which prevail in the different ages of human creatures. Even the characters, which are peculiar to each individual, have a uniformity in their influence; otherwise our acquaintance with the persons and our observation of their conduct, could never teach us their dispositions, or serve to direct our behavior with regard to them.

I grant it possible to find some actions, which seem to have no regular connexion with any known motives, and are exceptions to all the measures of conduct, which have ever been established for the government of men. But if we would willingly know, what judgment should be formed of such irregular and extraordinary actions; we may consider the sentiments, commonly entertained with regard to those irregular events, which appear in the course of nature, and the operations of external objects. All causes are not conjoined to their usual effects, with like uniformity. An artificer, who handles only dead matter, may be disappointed of his aim, as well as the politician, who directs the conduct of sensible and intelligent agents.

The vulgar, who take things according to their first appearance, attribute the uncertainty of events to such an uncertainty in the causes as makes the latter often fail of their usual influence; though they meet with no impediment in their operation. But philosophers, observing, that, almost in every part of nature, there is contained a vast variety of springs and principles, which are hid, by reason of their minuteness or remoteness, find, that it is at least possible the contrariety of events may not proceed from any contingency in the cause, but from the secret operation of contrary causes. This possibility is converted into certainty by farther observation; when they remark, that, upon an exact scrutiny, a contrariety of effects always betrays a contrariety of causes, and proceeds from their mutual opposition. A peasant can give no better reason for the stopping of any clock or watch than to say that it does not commonly go right: But an artist easily perceives that the same force in the spring or pendulum has always the same influence on the wheels; but fails of its usual effect, perhaps by reason of a grain of dust, which puts a stop to the whole movement. From the observation of several parallel instances, philosophers form a maxim, that the connexion between all causes and effects is equally necessary, and that its seeming uncertainty in some instances proceeds from the secret opposition of contrary causes.

Thus for instance, in the human body, when the usual symptoms of health or sickness disappoint our expectation; when medicines operate not with their wonted powers; when irregular events follow from any particular cause; the philosopher and physician are not surprised at the matter, nor are ever tempted to deny, in general, the necessity and uniformity of those principles, by which the animal economy is conducted. They know, that a human body is a mighty complicated machine: That many secret powers lurk in it, which are altogether beyond our comprehension: That to us it must often appear very uncertain in its operations: And that therefore the irregular events, which outwardly discover themselves, can be no proof, that the laws of nature are not observed with the greatest regularity in its internal operations and government.

The philosopher, if he be consistent, must apply the same reasoning to the actions and volitions of intelligent agents. The most irregular and unexpected resolutions of men may frequently be accounted for by those, who know every particular circumstance of their character and situation. A person of an obliging disposition gives a peevish answer: But he has the toothache, or has not dined. A stupid fellow discovers an uncommon alacrity in his carriage: But he has met with a sudden piece of good fortune. Or even when an action, as sometimes happens, cannot be particularly accounted for, either by the person himself or by others; we know, in general, that the characters of men are, to a certain degree, inconstant and irregular. This is, in a manner, the constant character of human nature; though it be applicable, in a more particular manner, to some persons, who have no fixed rule for their conduct, but proceed in a continued course of caprice and inconstancy. The internal principles and motives may operate in a uniform manner, notwithstanding these seeming irregularities; in the same manner as the winds, rain, clouds, and other variations of the weather are supposed to be governed by steady principles; though not easily discoverable by human sagacity and enquiry.

Thus it appears, not only that the conjunction between motives and voluntary actions is as regular and uniform, as that between the cause and effect in any part of nature; but also that this regular conjunction has been universally acknowledged among mankind, and has never been the subject of dispute, either in philosophy or common life. Now, as it is from past experience, that we draw all inferences concerning the future, and as we conclude, that objects will always be conjoined together, which we find to have always been conjoined; it may seem superfluous to prove, that this experienced uniformity in human actions is a source, whence we draw inferences concerning them. But in order to throw the argument into a greater variety of lights, we shall also insist, though briefly, on this latter topic.

The mutual dependence of men is so great, in all societies, that scarce any human action is entirely complete in itself, or is performed without some reference to the actions of others, which are requisite to make it answer fully the intention of the agent. The poorest artificer, who labors alone, expects at least the protection of the magistrate, to ensure him the enjoyment of the fruits of his labour. He also expects, that, when he carries his goods to market, and offers them at a reasonable price, he shall find purchasers; and shall be able, by the money he acquires, to engage others to supply him with those commodities, which are requisite for his subsistence. In

proportion as men extend their dealings, and render their intercourse with others more complicated, they always comprehend, in their schemes of life, a greater variety of voluntary actions, which they expect, from the proper motives, to co-operate with their own. In all these conclusions, they take their measures from past experience, in the same manner as in their reasonings concerning external objects; and firmly believe, that men, as well as all the elements, are to continue, in their operations, the same, that they have ever found them. A manufacturer reckons upon the labour of his servants, for the execution of any work, as much as upon the tools, which he employs, and would be equally surprised, were his expectations disappointed. In short, this experimental inference and reasoning concerning the actions of others enters so much into human life, that no man, while awake, is ever a moment without employing it. Have we not reason, therefore, to affirm, that all mankind have always agreed in the doctrine of necessity, according to the foregoing definition and explication of it?

Nor have philosophers ever entertained a different opinion from the people in this particular. For not to mention, that almost every action of their life supposes that opinion; there are even few of the speculative parts of learning, to which it is not essential. What would become of history, had we not a dependence on the veracity of the historian, according to the experience, which we have had of mankind? How could politics be a science, if laws and forms of government had not a uniform influence upon society? Where would be the foundation of morals, if particular characters had no certain or determinate power to produce particular sentiments, and if these sentiments had no constant operation on actions? And with what presence could we employ our criticism upon any poet or polite author, if we could not pronounce the conduct and sentiments of his actors, either natural or unnatural, to such characters, and in such circumstances? It seems almost impossible, therefore, to engage, either in science or action of any kind, without acknowledging the doctrine of necessity, and this inference from motives to voluntary actions; from characters to conduct.

And indeed, when we consider how aptly natural and moral evidence link together, and form only one chain of argument, we shall make no scruple to allow, that they are of the same nature, and derived from the same principles. A prisoner, who has neither money nor interest, discovers the impossibility of his escape, as well when he considers the obstinacy of the jailer, as the walls and bars, with which he is surrounded; and, in all attempts for his freedom, chooses rather to work upon the stone and iron of the one, than upon the inflexible nature of the other. The same prisoner, when conducted to the scaffold, foresees his death as certainly from the constancy and fidelity of his guards, as from the operation of the ax or wheel. His mind runs along a certain train of ideas: The refusal of the soldiers to consent to his escape; the action of the executioner; the separation of the head and body; bleeding, convulsive motions, and death. Here is a connected chain of natural causes and voluntary actions; but the mind feels no difference between them, in passing from one link to another: Nor is less certain of the future event than if it were connected with the objects present to the memory or senses, by a train of causes, cemented together by what we are pleased to call a physical necessity. The same experienced union has the same effect on the mind, whether the united objects be motives, volition, and actions; or figure and motion. We may change the names of things; but their nature and their operation on the understanding never change.

Were a man, whom I know to be honest and opulent, and with whom I live in intimate friendship, to come into my house, where I am surrounded with my servants, I rest assured, that he is not to stab me before he leaves it, in order to rob me of my silver standish; and I no more suspect this event, than the falling of the house itself which is new, and solidly built and founded.—But he may have been seized with a sudden and unknown frenzy.—So may a sudden earthquake arise, and shake and tumble my house about my ears. I shall therefore change the suppositions. I shall say, that I know with certainty, that he is not to put his hand into the fire, and hold it there, till it be consumed: And this event, I think I can foretell with the same assurance, as that, if he throw himself out at the window, and meet with no obstruction, he will not remain a moment suspended in the air. No suspicion of an unknown frenzy can give the least possibility to the former event, which is so contrary to all the known principles of human nature. A man who at noon leaves his purse full of gold on the pavement at Charing-Cross, may as well expect that it will fly away like a feather, as that he will find it untouched an hour after. Above one half of human reasonings contain inferences of a similar nature, attended with more or less degrees of certainty, proportioned to our experience of the usual conduct of mankind in such particular situations.

I have frequently considered, what could possibly be the reason why all mankind, though they have ever, without hesitation, acknowledged the doctrine of necessity, in their whole practice and reasoning, have yet discovered such a reluctance to acknowledge it in words, and have rather strewn a propensity, in all ages, to profess the contrary opinion. The matter, I think, may be accounted for, after the following manner. If we examine the operations of body, and the production of effects from their causes, we shall find that all our faculties can never carry us farther in our knowledge of this relation, than barely to observe, that particular objects are constantly conjoined together, and that the mind is carried, by a customary transition, from the appearance of one to the belief of the other. But though this conclusion concerning human ignorance be the result of the strictest scrutiny of this subject, men still entertain a strong propensity to believe, that they penetrate farther into the powers of nature, and perceive something like a necessary connexion between the cause and the effect. When again they turn their reflections towards the operations of their own minds, and feel no such connexion of the motive and the action; they are thence apt to suppose, that there is a difference between the effects, which result from material force, and those which arise from thought and intelligence. But being once convinced, that we know nothing farther of causation of any kind, than merely the constant conjunction of objects, and the consequent inference of the mind from one to another and finding, that these two circumstances are universally allowed to have place in voluntary actions; we may be more easily led to own the same necessity common to all causes. And though this reasoning may contradict the systems of many philosophers, in ascribing necessity to the determinations of the will, we shall find, upon reflection, that they dissent from it in words only, not in their real sentiment. Necessity, according to the sense, in which it is here taken, has never yet been rejected, nor can ever, I think, be rejected by any philosopher. It may only, perhaps, be pretended, that the mind can perceive, in the operations of matter, some farther connexion between the cause and effect; and a connexion that has not place in the voluntary actions of intelligent beings. Now whether it be so or not, can only appear upon examination; and it is incumbent on these philosophers to make good their assertion, by defining or describing that necessity, and pointing it out to us in the operations of material causes.

It would seem, indeed, that men begin at the wrong end of this question concerning liberty and necessity, when they enter upon it by examining the faculties of the soul, the influence of the understanding, and the operations of the will. Let them first discuss a more simple question, namely, the operations of body and of brute unintelligent matter; and try whether they can there form any idea of causation and necessity, except that of a constant conjunction of objects, and subsequent inference of the mind from one to another. If these circumstances form, in reality, the whole of that necessity, which we conceive in matter, and if these circumstances be also universally acknowledged to take place in the operations of the mind, the dispute is at an end; at least, must be owned to be thenceforth merely verbal. But as long as we will rashly suppose, that we have some farther idea of necessity and causation in the operations of external objects; at the same time, that we can find nothing farther, in the voluntary actions of the mind; there is no possibility of bringing the question to any determinate issue, while we proceed upon so erroneous a supposition. The only method of undeceiving us, is, to mount up higher; to examine the narrow extent of science when applied to material causes; and to convince ourselves, that all we know of them, is, the constant conjunction and inference above mentioned. We may, perhaps, find, that it is with difficulty we are induced to fix such narrow limits to human understanding: But we can afterwards find no difficulty when we come to apply this doctrine to the actions of the will. For as it

is evident, that these have a regular conjunction with motives and circumstances and characters, and as we always draw inferences from one to the other, we must be obliged to acknowledge in words, that necessity, which we have already avowed, in every deliberation of our lives, and in every step of our conduct and behavior.

But to proceed in this reconciling project with regard to the question of liberty and necessity; the most contentious question, of metaphysics, the most contentious science; it will not require many words to prove, that all mankind have ever agreed in the doctrine of liberty as well as in that of necessity, and that the whole dispute, in this respect also, has been hitherto merely verbal. For what is meant by liberty, when applied to voluntary actions? We cannot surely mean, that actions have so little connexion with motives, inclinations, and circumstances, that one does not follow with a certain degree of uniformity from the other, and that one affords no inference by which we can conclude the existence of the other. For these are plain and acknowledged matters of fact. By liberty, then, we can only mean a power of acting or not acting, according to the determinations of the will; that is, if we choose to remain at rest, we may; if we choose to move, we also may. Now this hypothetical liberty is universally allowed to belong to every one, who is not a prisoner and in chains. Here then is no subject of dispute.

Whatever definition we may give of liberty, we should be careful to observe two requisite circumstances; first, that it be consistent with plain matter of fact; secondly, that it be consistent with itself. If we observe these circumstances, and render our definition intelligible, I am persuaded that all mankind will be found of one opinion with regard to it.

It is universally allowed that nothing exists without a cause of its existence, and that chance, when strictly examined, is a mere negative word, and means not any real power, which has any where, a being in nature. But it is pretended, that some causes are necessary, some not necessary. Here then is the advantage of definitions. Let any one define a cause, without comprehending, as a part of the definition, a necessary connexion with its effect; and let him shew distinctly the origin of the idea, expressed by the definition; and I shall readily give up the whole controversy. But if the foregoing explication of the matter be received, this must be absolutely impracticable. Had not objects a regular conjunction with each other, we should never have entertained any notion of cause and effect; and this regular conjunction produces that inference of the understanding, which is the only connexion, that we can have any comprehension of. Whoever attempts a definition of cause, exclusive of these circumstances, will be obliged, either to employ unintelligible terms, or such as are synonymous to the term, which he endeavors to define. And if the definition above mentioned be admitted; liberty, when opposed to necessity, not to constraint, is the same thing with chance; which is universally allowed to have no existence.

PART II

There is no method of reasoning more common, and yet none more blameable, than, in philosophical disputes, to endeavor the refutation of any hypothesis, by a pretence of its dangerous consequences to religion and morality. When any opinion leads to absurdities, it is certainly false; but it is not certain that an opinion is false, because it is of dangerous consequence. Such topics, therefore, ought entirely to be forborne; as serving nothing to the discovery of truth, but only to make the person of an antagonist odious. This I observe in general, without pretending to draw any advantage from it. I frankly submit to an examination of this kind, and shall venture to affirm, that the doctrines, both of necessity and of liberty, as above explained, are not only consistent with morality, but are absolutely essential to its support.

Necessity may be defined two ways, conformably to the two definitions of cause, of which it makes an essential part. It consists either in the constant conjunction of like objects, or in the inference of the understanding from one object to another. Now necessity, in both these senses, (which, indeed, are, at bottom, the same) has universally, though tacitly, in the schools, in the pulpit, and in common life, been allowed to belong to the will of man; and no one has ever pretended to deny, that we can draw inferences concerning human actions, and that those inferences are founded on the experienced union of like actions, with like motives, inclinations, and circumstances.

The only particular, in which any one can differ, is, that either, perhaps, he will refuse to give the name of necessity to this property of human actions: But as long as the meaning is understood, I hope the word can do no harm: Or that he will maintain it possible to discover something farther in the operations of matter. But this, it must be acknowledged, can be of no consequence to morality or religion, whatever it may be to natural philosophy or metaphysics. We may here be mistaken in asserting, that there is no idea of any other necessity or connexion in the actions of body: But surely we ascribe nothing to the actions of the mind, but what every one does, and must readily allow of. We change no circumstance in the received orthodox system with regard to the will, but only in that with regard to material objects and causes. Nothing therefore can be more innocent, at least, than this doctrine.

All laws being founded on rewards and punishments, it is supposed as a fundamental principle, that these motives have a regular and uniform influence on the mind, and both produce the good and prevent the evil actions. We may give to this influence what name we please; but, as it is usually conjoined with the action, it must be esteemed a cause, and be looked upon as an instance of that necessity, which we would here establish.

The only proper object of hatred or vengeance, is a person or creature, endowed with thought and consciousness; and when any criminal or injurious actions excite that passion, it is only by their relation to the person, or connexion with him. Actions are, by their very nature, temporary and perishing; and where they proceed not from some cause in the character and disposition of the person who performed them, they can neither redound to his honour, if good; nor infamy, if evil. The actions themselves may be blameable; they may be contrary to all the rules of morality and religion: But the person is not answerable for them; and as they proceeded from nothing in him, that is durable and constant, and leave nothing of that nature behind them, it is impossible he can, upon their account, become the object of punishment or vengeance. According to the principle, therefore, which denies necessity, and consequently causes, a man is as pure and untainted, after having committed the most horrid crime, as at the first moment of his birth, nor is his character any wise concerned in his actions; since they are not derived from it, and the wickedness of the one can never be used as a proof of the depravity of the other.

Men are not blamed for such actions, as they perform ignorantly and casually, whatever may be the consequences. Why? but because the principles of these actions are only momentary, and terminate in them alone. Men are less blamed for such actions as they perform hastily and unpremeditatedly, than for such as proceed from deliberation. For what reason? but because a hasty temper, though a constant cause or principle in the mind, operates only by intervals, and infects not the whole character. Again, repentance wipes off every crime, if attended with a reformation of life and manners. How is this to be accounted for? but by asserting, that actions render a person criminal, merely as they are proofs of criminal principles in the mind; and when, by an alteration of these principles, they cease to be just proofs, they likewise cease to be criminal. But, except upon the doctrine of necessity, they never were just proofs, and consequently never were criminal.

It will be equally easy to prove, and from the same arguments, that liberty, according to that definition above mentioned, in which all men agree, is also essential to morality, and that no human actions, where it is wanting, are susceptible of any moral qualities, or can be the objects either of approbation or dislike. For as actions are objects of our moral sentiment, so far only as they are indications of the internal character, passions, and affections; it is impossible that they can give rise either to praise or blame, where they proceed not from these principles, but are derived altogether from external violence.

I pretend not to have obviated or removed all objections to this theory, with regard to necessity and liberty. I can foresee other objections, derived from topics, which have not here been treated of. It may be said, for instance, that, if voluntary actions be subjected to the same laws of necessity with the operations of matter, there is a continued chain of necessary causes, pre-ordained and pre-determined, reaching from the original cause of all, to every single volition of every human creature. No contingency any where in the universe; no indifference; no liberty. While we act, we are, at the same time,

acted upon. The ultimate Author of all our volitions is the Creator of the world, who first bestowed motion on this immense machine, and placed all beings in that particular position, whence every subsequent event, by an inevitable necessity, must result. Human actions, therefore, either can have no moral turpitude at all, as proceeding from so good a cause; or if they have any turpitude, they must involve our Creator in the same guilt, while he is acknowledged to be their ultimate cause and author. For as a man, who fired a mine, is answerable for all the consequences, whether the train he employed be long or short; so wherever a continued chain of necessary causes is fixed, that Being, either finite or infinite, who produces the first, is likewise the author of all the rest, and must both bear the blame and acquire the praise, which belong to them. Our clear and unalterable ideas of morality establish this rule, upon unquestionable reasons, when we examine the consequences of any human action; and these reasons must still have greater force, when applied to the volitions and intentions of a Being, infinitely wise and powerful. Ignorance or impotence may be pleaded for so limited a creature as man; but those imperfections have no place in our Creator. He foresaw, he ordained, he intended all those actions of men, which we so rashly pronounce criminal. And we must therefore conclude, either that they are not criminal, or that the Deity, not man, is accountable for them. But as either of these positions is absurd and impious, it follows, that the doctrine, from which they are deduced, cannot possibly be true, as being liable to all the same objections. An absurd consequence, if necessary, proves the original doctrine to be absurd; in the same manner as criminal actions render criminal the original cause, if the connexion between them be necessary and inevitable.

This objection consists of two parts, which we shall examine separately; First, that, if human actions can be traced up, by a necessary chain, to the Deity, they can never be criminal; on account of the infinite perfection of that Being, from whom they are derived, and who can intend nothing but what is altogether good and laudable. Or, Secondly, if they be criminal, we must retract the attribute of perfection, which we ascribe to the Deity, and must acknowledge him to be the ultimate author of guilt and moral turpitude in all his creatures.

The answer to the first objection seems obvious and convincing. There are many philosophers, who, after an exact scrutiny of all the phenomena of nature, conclude, that the WHOLE, considered as one system, is, in every period of its existence, ordered with perfect benevolence; and that the utmost possible happiness will, in the end, result to all created beings, without any mixture of positive or absolute ill and misery. Every physical ill, say they, makes an essential part of this benevolent system, and could not possibly be removed, even by the Deity himself, considered as a wise agent, without giving entrance to greater ill, or excluding greater good, which will result from it. From this theory, some philosophers, and the ancient Stoics among the rest, derived a topic of consolation under all afflictions, while they taught their pupils, that those ills, under which they labored, were, in reality, goods to the universe; and that to an enlarged view, which could comprehend the whole system of nature, every event became an object of joy and exultation. But though this topic be specious and sublime, it was soon found in practice weak and ineffectual. You would surely more irritate, than appease a man, lying under the racking pains of the gout, by preaching up to him the rectitude of those general laws, which produced the malignant humors in his body, and led them through the proper canals, to the sinews and nerves, where they now excite such acute torments. These enlarged views may, for a moment, please the imagination of a speculative man, who is placed in ease and security; but neither can they dwell with constancy on his mind, even though undisturbed by the emotions of pain or passion; much less can they maintain their ground, when attacked by such powerful antagonists. The affections take a narrower and more natural survey of their object; and by an economy, more suitable to the infirmity of human minds, regard alone the beings around us, and are actuated by such events as appear good or ill to the private system.

The case is the same with moral as with physical ill. It cannot reasonably be supposed, that those remote considerations, which are found of so little efficacy with regard to one, will have a more powerful influence with regard to the other. The mind of man is so formed by nature, that, upon the appearance of certain characters, dispositions, and actions, it immediately feels the sentiment of approbation or blame; nor are there any emotions more essential to its frame and constitution. The characters, which engage our approbation, are chiefly such as contribute to the peace and security of human society; as the characters, which excite blame, are chiefly such as tend to public detriment and disturbance: Whence it may reasonably be presumed, that the moral sentiments arise, either mediately or immediately, from a reflection of these opposite interests. What though philosophical meditations establish a different opinion or conjecture; that every thing is right with regard to the WHOLE, and that the qualities, which disturb society, are, in the main, as beneficial, and are as suitable to the primary intention of nature, as those which more directly promote its happiness and welfare? Are such remote and uncertain speculations able to counterbalance the sentiments, which arise from the natural and immediate view of the objects? A man who is robbed of a considerable sum; does he find his vexation for the loss any wise diminished by these sublime reflections? Why then should his moral resentment against the crime be supposed incompatible with them? Or why should not the acknowledgment of a real distinction between vice and virtue be reconcilable to all speculative systems of philosophy, as well as that of a real distinction between personal beauty and deformity? Both these distinctions are founded in the natural sentiments of the human mind: And these sentiments are not to be controlled or altered by any philosophical theory or speculation whatsoever.

The second objection admits not of so easy and satisfactory an answer; nor is it possible to explain distinctly, how the Deity can be the mediate cause of all the actions of men, without being the author of sin and moral turpitude. These are mysteries, which mere natural and unassisted reason is very unfit to handle; and whatever system she embraces, she must find herself involved in inextricable difficulties, and even contradictions, at every step which she takes with regard to such subjects. To reconcile the indifference and contingency of human actions with prescience; or to defend absolute decrees, and yet free the Deity from being the author of sin, has been found hitherto to exceed all the power of philosophy. Happy, if she be thence sensible of her temerity, when she pries into these sublime mysteries; and leaving a scene so full of obscurities and perplexities, return, with suitable modesty, to her true and proper province, the examination of common life; where she will find difficulties enough to employ her enquiries, without launching into so boundless an ocean of doubt, uncertainty, and contradiction!

SECTION IX: OF THE REASON OF ANIMALS

All our reasonings concerning matter of fact are founded on a species of Analogy, which leads us to expect from any cause the same events, which we have observed to result from similar causes. Where the causes are entirely similar, the analogy is perfect, and the inference, drawn from it, is regarded as certain and conclusive: Nor does any man ever entertain a doubt, where he sees a piece of iron, that it will have weight and cohesion of parts; as in all other instances, which have ever fallen under his observation. But where the objects have not so exact a similarity, the analogy is less perfect, and the inference is less conclusive; though still it has some force, in proportion to the degree of similarity and resemblance. The anatomical observations, formed upon one animal, are, by this species of reasoning, extended to all animals; and it is certain, that when the circulation of the blood, for instance, is clearly proved to have place in one creature, as a frog, or fish, it forms a strong presumption, that the same principle has place in all. These analogical observations may be carried farther, even to this science, of which we are now treating; and any theory, by which we explain the operations of the understanding, or the origin and connexion of the passions in man, will acquire additional authority, if we find, that the same theory is requisite to explain the same phenomena in all other animals. We shall make trial of this, with regard to the hypothesis, by which, we have, in the foregoing discourse, endeavored to account for all experimental reasonings; and it is hoped, that this new point of view will serve to confirm all our former observations.

First, It seems evident, that animals, as well as men, learn many things from experience, and infer, that the same events will always follow from the same causes. By this principle they become acquainted with the more obvious properties of external objects, and gradually, from their birth, treasure up a knowledge of the nature of fire, water, earth, stones, heights, depths, &c., and of the effects, which result from their operation. The ignorance and inexperience of the young are here plainly distinguishable from the cunning and sagacity of the old, who have learned, by long observation, to avoid what hurt them, and to pursue what gave ease or pleasure. A horse, that has been accustomed to the field, becomes acquainted with the proper height, which he can leap, and will never attempt what exceeds his force and ability. An old greyhound will trust the more fatiguing part of the chase to the younger, and will place himself so as to meet the hare in her doubles; nor are the conjectures, which he forms on this occasion, founded in any thing but his observation and experience.

This is still more evident from the effects of discipline and education on animals, who, by the proper application of rewards and punishments, may be taught any course of action, the most contrary to their natural instincts and propensities. Is it not experience, which renders a dog apprehensive of pain, when you menace him, or lift up the whip to beat him? Is it not even experience, which makes him answer to his name, and infer, from such an arbitrary sound, that you mean him rather than any of his fellows, and intend to call him, when you pronounce it in a certain manner, and with a certain tone and accent?

In all these cases, we may observe, that the animal infers some fact beyond what immediately strikes his senses; and that this inference is altogether founded on past experience, while the creature expects from the present object the same consequences, which it has always found in its observation to result from similar objects.

Secondly, It is impossible, that this inference of the animal can be founded on any process of argument or reasoning, by which he concludes, that like events must follow like objects, and that the course of nature will always be regular in its operations. For if there be in reality any arguments of this nature, they surely lie too abstruse for the observation of such imperfect understandings; since it may well employ the utmost care and attention of a philosophic genius to discover and observe them. Animals, therefore, are not guided in these inferences by reasoning: Neither are children: Neither are the generality of mankind, in their ordinary actions and conclusions: Neither are philosophers themselves, who, in all the active parts of life, are, in the main, the same with the vulgar, and are governed by the same maxims. Nature must have provided some other principle, of more ready, and more general use and application; nor can an operation of such immense consequence in life, as that of inferring effects from causes, be trusted to the uncertain process of reasoning and argumentation. Were this doubtful with regard to men, it seems to admit of no question with regard to the brute creation; and the conclusion being once firmly established in the one, we have a strong presumption, from all the rules of analogy, that it ought to be universally admitted, without any exception or reserve. It is custom alone, which engages animals, from every object, that strikes their senses, to infer its usual attendant, and carries their imagination, from the appearance of the one, to conceive the other, in that particular manner, which we denominate belief. No other explication can be given of this operation, in all the higher, as well as lower classes of sensitive beings, which fall under our notice and observation.

But though animals learn many parts of their knowledge from observation, there are also many parts of it, which they derive from the original hand of nature; which much exceed the share of capacity they possess on ordinary occasions; and in which they improve, little or nothing, by the longest practice and experience. These we denominate Instincts, and are so apt to admire as something very extraordinary, and inexplicable by all the disquisitions of human understanding. But our wonder will, perhaps, cease or diminish; when we consider, that the experimental reasoning itself, which we possess in common with beasts, and on which the whole conduct of life depends, is nothing but a species of instinct or mechanical power, that acts in us unknown to ourselves; and in its chief operations, is not

directed by any such relations or comparisons of ideas, as are the proper objects of our intellectual faculties. Though the instinct be different, yet still it is an instinct, which teaches a man to avoid the fire; as much as that, which teaches a bird, with such exactness, the art of incubation, and the whole economy and order of its nursery.

SECTION X: OF MIRACLES

PART I

There is, in Dr. Tillotson's writings, an argument against the real presence, which is as concise, and elegant, and strong as any argument can possibly be supposed against a doctrine, so little worthy of a serious refutation. It is acknowledged on all hands, says that learned prelate, that the authority, either of the scripture or of tradition, is founded merely in the testimony of the apostles, who were eye-witnesses to those miracles of our Savior, by which he proved his divine mission. Our evidence, then, for the truth of the Christian religion is less than the evidence for the truth of our senses; because, even in the first authors of our religion, it was no greater; and it is evident it must diminish in passing from them to their disciples; nor can any one rest such confidence in their testimony, as in the immediate object of his senses. But a weaker evidence can never destroy a stronger; and therefore, were the doctrine of the real presence ever so clearly revealed in scripture, it were directly contrary to the rules of just reasoning to give our assent to it. It contradicts sense, though both the scripture and tradition, on which it is supposed to be built, carry not such evidence with them as sense; when they are considered merely as external evidences, and are not brought home to every one's breast, by the immediate operation of the Holy Spirit.

Nothing is so convenient as a decisive argument of this kind, which must at least silence the most arrogant bigotry and superstition, and free us from their impertinent solicitations. I flatter myself, that I have discovered an argument of a like nature, which, if just, will, with the wise and learned, be an everlasting check to all kinds of superstitious delusion, and consequently, will be useful as long as the world endures. For so long, I presume, will the accounts of miracles and prodigies be found in all history, sacred and profane.

Though experience be our only guide in reasoning concerning matters of fact; it must be acknowledged, that this guide is not altogether infallible, but in some cases is apt to lead us into errors. One, who in our climate, should expect better weather in any week of June than in one of December, would reason justly, and conformably to experience; but it is certain, that he may happen, in the event, to find himself mistaken. However, we may observe, that, in such a case, he would have no cause to complain of experience; because it commonly informs us beforehand of the uncertainty, by that contrariety of events, which we may learn from a diligent observation. All effects follow not with like certainty from their supposed causes. Some events are found, in all countries and all ages, to have been constantly conjoined together: Others are found to have been more variable, and sometimes to disappoint our expectations; so that, in our reasonings concerning matter of fact, there are all imaginable degrees of assurance, from the highest certainty to the lowest species of moral evidence.

A wise man, therefore, proportions his belief to the evidence. In such conclusions as are founded on an infallible experience, he expects the event with the last degree of assurance, and regards his past experience as a full proof of the future existence of that event. In other cases, he proceeds with more caution: He weighs the opposite experiments: He considers which side is supported by the greater number of experiments: To that side he inclines, with doubt and hesitation; and when at last he fixes his judgment, the evidence exceeds not what we properly call probability. All probability, then, supposes an opposition of experiments and observations, where the one side is found to overbalance the other, and to produce a degree of evidence, proportioned to the superiority. A hundred instances or experiments on one side, and fifty on another, afford a doubtful expectation of any event; though a hundred uniform experiments, with only one that is contradictory, reasonably beget a pretty strong degree of assurance. In all cases, we must balance the opposite experiments, where they are opposite, and deduct the smaller number from the greater, in order to know the exact force of the superior evidence.

To apply these principles to a particular instance; we may observe, that there is no species of reasoning more common, more useful, and even necessary to human life, than that which is derived from the testimony of men, and the reports of eye-witnesses and spectators. This species of reasoning, perhaps, one may deny to be founded on the relation of cause and effect. I shall not dispute about a word. It will be sufficient to observe, that our assurance in any argument of this kind is derived from no other principle than our observation of the veracity of human testimony, and of the usual conformity of facts to the reports of witnesses. It being a general maxim, that no objects have any discoverable connexion together, and that all the inferences, which we can draw from one to another, are founded merely on our experience of their constant and regular conjunction; it is evident, that we ought not to make an exception to this maxim in favour of human testimony, whose connexion with any event seems, in itself, as little necessary as any other. Were not the memory tenacious to a certain degree; had not men commonly an inclination to truth and a principle of probity; were they not sensible to shame, when detected in a falsehood: Were not these, I say, discovered by experience to be qualities, inherent in human nature, we should never repose the least confidence in human testimony. A man delirious, or noted for falsehood and villainy, has no manner of authority with us.

And as the evidence, derived from witnesses and human testimony, is founded on past experience, so it varies with the experience, and is regarded either as a proof or a probability, according as the conjunction between any particular kind of report and any kind of object has been found to be constant or variable. There are a number of circumstances to be taken into consideration in all judgments of this kind; and the ultimate standard, by which we determine all disputes, that may arise concerning them, is always derived from experience and observation. Where this experience is not entirely uniform on any side, it is attended with an unavoidable contrariety in our judgments, and with the same opposition and mutual destruction of argument as in every other kind of evidence. We frequently hesitate concerning the reports of others. We balance the opposite circumstances, which cause any doubt or uncertainty; and when we discover a superiority on any side, we incline to it;

but still with a diminution of assurance, in proportion to the force of its antagonist.

This contrariety of evidence, in the present case, may be derived from several different causes; from the opposition of contrary testimony; from the character or number of the witnesses; from the manner of their delivering their testimony; or from the union of all these circumstances. We entertain a suspicion concerning any matter of fact, when the witnesses contradict each other; when they are but few, or of a doubtful character; when they have an interest in what they affirm; when they deliver their testimony with hesitation, or on the contrary, with too violent asseverations. There are many other particulars of the same kind, which may diminish or destroy the force of any argument, derived from human testimony.

Suppose, for instance, that the fact, which the testimony endeavors to establish, partakes of the extraordinary and the marvelous; in that case, the evidence, resulting from the testimony, admits of a diminution, greater or less, in proportion as the fact is more or less unusual. The reason, why we place any credit in witnesses and historians, is not derived from any connexion, which we perceive a priori, between testimony and reality, but because we are accustomed to find a conformity between them. But when the fact attested is such a one as has seldom fallen under our observation, here is a contest of two opposite experiences; of which the one destroys the other, as far as its force goes, and the superior can only operate on the mind by the force, which remains. The very same principle of experience, which gives us a certain degree of assurance in the testimony of witnesses, gives us also, in this case, another degree of assurance against the fact, which they endeavor to establish; from which contradiction there necessarily arises a counterpoise, and mutual destruction of belief and authority.

I should not believe such a story were it told me by Cato; was a proverbial saying in Rome, even during the lifetime of that philosophical patriot. The incredibility of a fact, it was allowed, might invalidate so great an authority.

The INDIAN prince, who refused to believe the first relations concerning the effects of frost, reasoned justly; and it naturally required very strong testimony to engage his assent to facts, that arose from a state of nature, with which he was unacquainted, and which bore so little analogy to those events, of which he had had constant and uniform experience. Though they were not contrary to his experience, they were not conformable to it.

But in order to increase the probability against the testimony of witnesses, let us suppose, that the fact, which they affirm, instead of being only marvelous, is really miraculous; and suppose also, that the testimony, considered apart and in itself, amounts to an entire proof; in that case, there is proof against proof, of which the strongest must prevail, but still with a diminution of its force, in proportion to that of its antagonist.

A miracle is a violation of the laws of nature; and as a firm and unalterable experience has established these laws, the proof against a miracle, from the very nature of the fact, is as entire as any argument from experience can possibly be imagined. Why is it more than probable, that all men must die; that lead cannot, of itself, remain suspended in the air; that fire consumes wood, and is extinguished by water; unless it be, that these events are found agreeable to the laws of nature, and there is required a violation of these laws, or in other words, a miracle to prevent them? Nothing is esteemed a miracle, if it ever happen in the common course of nature. It is no miracle that a man, seemingly in good health, should die on a sudden: because such a kind of death, though more unusual than any other, has yet been frequently observed to happen. But it is a miracle, that a dead man should come to life; because that has never been observed, in any age or country. There must, therefore, be an uniform experience against every miraculous event, otherwise the event would not merit that appellation. And as a uniform experience amounts to a proof, there is here a direct and full proof, from the nature of the fact, against the existence of any miracle; nor can such a proof be destroyed, or the miracle rendered credible, but by an opposite proof, which is superior.

The plain consequence is (and it is a general maxim worthy of our attention), 'That no testimony is sufficient to establish a miracle, unless the testimony be of such a kind, that its falsehood would be more miraculous, than the fact, which it endeavors to establish: And even in that case there is a mutual destruction of arguments, and the superior only gives

surprise + wonder is so attractive we want to believe

us an assurance suitable to that degree of force, which remains, after deducting the inferior.' When any one tells me, that he saw a dead man restored to life, I immediately consider with myself, whether it be more probable, that this person should either deceive or be deceived, or that the fact, which he relates, should really have happened. I weigh the one miracle against the other; and according to the superiority, which I discover, I pronounce my decision, and always reject the greater miracle. If the falsehood of his testimony would be more miraculous, ② than the event which he relates; then, and not till then, can he pretend to command my belief or opinion.

PART II *miracles: no evidence*

In the foregoing reasoning we have supposed, that the testimony, upon which a miracle is founded, may possibly amount to an entire proof, and that the falsehood of that testimony would be a real prodigy: But it is easy to shew, that we have been a great deal too liberal in our concession, and that there never was a miraculous event established on so full an evidence.

① no attestation For first, there is not to be found in all history, any miracle attested by a sufficient number of men, of such unquestioned good-sense, education, and learning, as to secure us against all delusion in themselves; of such undoubted integrity, as to place them beyond all suspicion of any design to deceive others; of such credit and reputation in the eyes of mankind, as to have a great deal to lose in case of their being detected in any falsehood; and at the same time, attesting facts performed in such a public manner, and in so celebrated a part of the world, as to render the detection unavoidable: All which circumstances are requisite to give us a full assurance in the testimony of men.

Secondly. We may observe in human nature a principle, which, if strictly examined, will be found to diminish extremely the assurance, which we might, from human testimony, have, in any kind of prodigy. The maxim, by which we commonly conduct ourselves in our reasonings, is, that the objects, of which we have no experience, resemble those, of which we have; that what we have found to be most usual is always most probable; and that where there is an opposition of arguments, we ought to give the preference to such as are founded on the greatest number of past observations. But though, in proceeding by this rule, we readily reject any fact which is unusual and incredible in an ordinary degree; yet in advancing farther, the mind observes not always the same rule; but when anything is affirmed utterly absurd and miraculous, it rather the more readily admits of such a fact, upon account of that very circumstance, which ought to destroy all its authority. The passion of surprise and wonder, arising from miracles, being an agreeable emotion, gives a sensible tendency towards the belief of those events, from which it is derived. And this goes so far, that even those who cannot enjoy this pleasure immediately, nor can believe those miraculous events, of which they are informed, yet love to partake of the satisfaction at second-hand or by rebound, and place a pride and delight in exciting the admiration of others.

With what greediness are the miraculous accounts of travellers received, their descriptions of sea and land monsters, their relations of wonderful adventures, strange men, and uncouth manners? But if the spirit of religion join itself to the love of wonder, there is an end of common sense; and human testimony, in these circumstances, loses all pretensions to authority. A religionist may be an enthusiast, and imagine he sees what has no reality: He may know his narrative to be false, and yet persevere in it, with the best intentions in the world, for the sake of promoting so holy a cause: Or even where this delusion has no place, vanity, excited by so strong a temptation, operates on him more powerfully than on the rest of mankind in any other circumstances; and self-interest with equal force. His auditors may not have, and commonly have not, sufficient judgment to canvass his evidence: What judgment they have, they renounce by principle, in these sublime and mysterious subjects: Or if they were ever so willing to employ it, passion and a heated imagination disturb the regularity of its operations. Their credulity increases his impudence: And his impudence overpowers their credulity.

Eloquence, when at its highest pitch, leaves little room for reason or reflection; but addressing itself entirely to the fancy or the affections, captivates the willing hearers, and subdues their understanding. Happily, this pitch it seldom attains. But what a Tully

[handwritten marginalia: "eloquence of preacher can convince others" · "we want to believe miracles" · "human nature has 'evolved' from vulgar"]

or a Demosthenes could scarcely effect over a Roman or Athenian audience, every Capuchin, every itinerant or stationary teacher can perform over the generality of mankind, and in a higher degree, by touching such gross and vulgar passions.

The many instances of forged miracles, and prophecies, and supernatural events, which, in all ages, have either been detected by contrary evidence, or which detect themselves by their absurdity, prove sufficiently the strong propensity of mankind to the extraordinary and the marvelous, and ought reasonably to beget a suspicion against all relations of this kind. This is our natural way of thinking, even with regard to the most common and most credible events. For instance: There is no kind of report, which rises so easily, and spreads so quickly, especially in country places and provincial towns, as those concerning marriages; insomuch that two young persons of equal condition never see each other twice, but the whole neighborhood immediately join them together. The pleasure of telling a piece of news so interesting, of propagating it, and of being the first reporters of it, spreads the intelligence. And this is so well known, that no man of sense gives attention to these reports, till he find them confirmed by some greater evidence. Do not the same passions, and others still stronger, incline the generality of mankind to believe and report, with the greatest vehemence and assurance, all religious miracles?

Thirdly. It forms a strong presumption against all supernatural and miraculous relations, that they are observed chiefly to abound among ignorant and barbarous nations; or if a civilized people has ever given admission to any of them, that people will be found to have received them from ignorant and barbarous ancestors, who transmitted them with that inviolable sanction and authority, which always attend received opinions. When we peruse the first histories of all nations, we are apt to imagine ourselves transported into some new world; where the whole frame of nature is disjointed, and every element performs its operations in a different manner, from what it does at present. Battles, revolutions, pestilence, famine, and death, are never the effect of those natural causes, which we experience. Prodigies, omens, oracles, judgments, quite obscure the few natural events, that are intermingled with them. But as the former grow thinner every page, in proportion as we advance nearer the enlightened ages, we soon learn, that there is nothing mysterious or supernatural in the case, but that all proceeds from the usual propensity of mankind towards the marvelous, and that, though this inclination may at intervals receive a check from sense and learning, it can never be thoroughly extirpated from human nature.

It is strange, a judicious reader is apt to say, upon the perusal of these wonderful historians, that such prodigious events never happen in our days. But it is nothing strange, I hope, that men should lie in all ages. You must surely have seen instances enough of that frailty. You have yourself heard many such marvelous relations started, which, being treated with scorn by all the wise and judicious, have at last been abandoned even by the vulgar. Be assured, that those renowned lies, which have spread and flourished to such a monstrous height, arose from like beginnings; but being sown in a more proper soil, shot up at last into prodigies almost equal to those which they relate.

It was a wise policy in that false prophet, Alexander, who, though now forgotten, was once so famous, to lay the first scene of his impostures in Paphlagonia, where, as Lucian tells us, the people were extremely ignorant and stupid, and ready to swallow even the grossest delusion. People at a distance, who are weak enough to think the matter at all worth enquiry, have no opportunity of receiving better information. The stories come magnified to them by a hundred circumstances. Fools are industrious in propagating the imposture; while the wise and learned are contented, in general, to deride its absurdity, without informing themselves of the particular facts, by which it may be distinctly refuted. And thus the impostor above-mentioned was enabled to proceed, from his ignorant Paphlagonians, to the enlisting of votaries, even among the Grecian philosophers, and men of the most eminent rank and distinction in Rome: Nay, could engage the attention of that sage emperor Marcus Aurelius; so far as to make him trust the success of a military expedition to his delusive prophecies.

The advantages are so great, of starting an imposture among an ignorant people, that, even though the delusion should be too gross to impose on the generality of them (which, though seldom, is sometimes the case) it has a much better chance for suc-

the ignorant country people believe the marvellous

treat all miracles & stories equally

ceeding in remote countries, than if the first scene had been laid in a city renowned for arts and knowledge. The most ignorant and barbarous of these barbarians carry the report abroad. None of their countrymen have a large correspondence, or sufficient credit and authority to contradict and beat down the delusion. Men's inclination to the marvelous has full opportunity to display itself. And thus a story, which is universally exploded in the place where it was first started, shall pass for certain at a thousand miles distance. But had Alexander fixed his residence at Athens, the philosophers of that renowned mart of learning had immediately spread, throughout the whole Roman empire, their sense of the matter; which, being supported by so great authority, and displayed by all the force of reason and eloquence, had entirely opened the eyes of mankind. It is true; Lucian, passing by chance through Paphlagonia, had an opportunity of performing this good office. But, though much to be wished, it does not always happen, that every Alexander meets with a Lucian, ready to expose and detect his impostures.

I may add as a fourth reason, which diminishes the authority of prodigies, that there is no testimony for any, even those which have not been expressly detected, that is not opposed by an infinite number of witnesses; so that not only the miracle destroys the credit of testimony, but the testimony destroys itself. To make this the better understood, let us consider, that, in matters of religion, whatever is different is contrary; and that it is impossible the religions of ancient Rome, of Turkey, of Siam, and of China should, all of them, be established on any solid foundation. Every miracle, therefore, pretended to have been wrought in any of these religions (and all of them abound in miracles), as its direct scope is to establish the particular system to which it is attributed; so has it the same force, though more indirectly, to overthrow every other system. In destroying a rival system, it likewise destroys the credit of those miracles, on which that system was established; so that all the prodigies of different religions are to be regarded as contrary facts, and the evidences of these prodigies, whether weak or strong, as opposite to each other. According to this method of reasoning, when we believe any miracle of Mahomet or his successors, we have for our warrant the testimony of a

few barbarous Arabians: And on the other hand, we are to regard the authority of Titus Livius, Plutarch, Tacitus, and, in short, of all the authors and witnesses, Grecian, Chinese, and Roman Catholic, who have related any miracle in their particular religion; I say, we are to regard their testimony in the same light as if they had mentioned that Mahometan miracle, and had in express terms contradicted it, with the same certainty as they have for the miracle they relate. This argument may appear over subtile and refined; but is not in reality different from the reasoning of a judge, who supposes, that the credit of two witnesses, maintaining a crime against any one, is destroyed by the testimony of two others, who affirm him to have been two hundred leagues distant, at the same instant when the crime is said to have been committed.

One of the best attested miracles in all profane history, is that which Tacitus reports of Vespasian, who cured a blind man in Alexandria, by means of his spittle, and a lame man by the mere touch of his foot; in obedience to a vision of the god Serapis, who had enjoined them to have recourse to the Emperor, for these miraculous cures. The story may be seen in that fine historian; where every circumstance seems to add weight to the testimony, and might be displayed at large with all the force of argument and eloquence, if any one were now concerned to enforce the evidence of that exploded and idolatrous superstition. The gravity, solidity, age, and probity of so great an emperor, who, through the whole course of his life, conversed in a familiar manner with his friends and courtiers, and never affected those extraordinary airs of divinity assumed by Alexander and Demetrius. The historian, a contemporary writer, noted for candor and veracity, and withal, the greatest and most penetrating genius, perhaps, of all antiquity; and so free from any tendency to credulity, that he even lies under the contrary imputation, of atheism and profaneness: The persons, from whose authority he related the miracle, of established character for judgment and veracity, as we may well presume; eye-witnesses of the fact, and confirming their testimony, after the Flavian family was despoiled of the empire, and could no longer give any reward, as the price of a lie. Those who were present recount both even now that a lie is no longer rewarded. To which if we add the public nature of the facts, as related, it will appear, that no evidence can well be supposed stronger for so gross and so palpable a falsehood.

There is also a memorable story related by Cardinal de Retz, which may well deserve our consideration. When that intriguing politician fled into Spain, to avoid the persecution of his enemies, he passed through Saragossa, the capital of Arragon, where he was shewn, in the cathedral, a man, who had served seven years as a door-keeper, and was well known to every body in town, that had ever paid his devotions at that church. He had been seen, for so long a time, wanting a leg; but recovered that limb by the rubbing of holy oil upon the stump; and the cardinal assures us that he saw him with two legs. This miracle was vouched by all the canons of the church; and the whole company in town were appealed to for a confirmation of the fact; whom the cardinal found, by their zealous devotion, to be thorough believers of the miracle. Here the relater was also contemporary to the supposed prodigy, of an incredulous and libertine character, as well as of great genius; the miracle of so singular a nature as could scarcely admit of a counterfeit, and the witnesses very numerous, and all of them, in a manner, spectators of the fact, to which they gave their testimony. And what adds mightily to the force of the evidence, and may double our surprise on this occasion, is, that the cardinal himself, who relates the story, seems not to give any credit to it, and consequently cannot be suspected of any concurrence in the holy fraud. He considered justly, that it was not requisite, in order to reject a fact of this nature, to be able accurately to disprove the testimony, and to trace its falsehood, through all the circumstances of knavery and credulity which produced it. He knew, that, as this was commonly altogether impossible at any small distance of time and place; so was it extremely difficult, even where one was immediately present, by reason of the bigotry, ignorance, cunning, and roguery of a great part of mankind. He therefore concluded, like a just reasoner, that such an evidence carried falsehood upon the very face of it, and that a miracle supported by any human testimony, was more properly a subject of derision than of argument.

There surely never was a greater number of miracles ascribed to one person, than those, which were lately said to have been wrought in France upon the tomb of Abbe Paris, the famous Jansenist, with whose sanctity the people were so long deluded. The curing of the sick, giving hearing to the deaf, and sight to the blind, were every where talked of as the usual effects of that holy sepulchre. But what is more extraordinary; many of the miracles were immediately proved upon the spot, before judges of unquestioned integrity, attested by witnesses of credit and distinction, in a learned age, and on the most eminent theater that is now in the world. Nor is this all: A relation of them was published and dispersed every where; nor were the Jesuits, though a learned body, supported by the civil magistrate, and determined enemies to those opinions, in whose favour the miracles were said to have been wrought, ever able distinctly to refute or detect them. Where shall we find such a number of circumstances, agreeing to the corroboration of one fact? And what have we to oppose to such a cloud of witnesses, but the absolute impossibility or miraculous nature of the events, which they relate? And this surely, in the eyes of all reasonable people, will alone be regarded as a sufficient refutation.

Is the consequence just, because some human testimony has the utmost force and authority in some cases, when it relates the battle of Philippi or Pharsalia for instance; that therefore all kinds of testimony must, in all cases, have equal force and authority? Suppose that the Caesarean and Pompeian factions had, each of them, claimed the victory in these battles, and that the historians of each party had uniformly ascribed the advantage to their own side: how could mankind, at this distance, have been able to determine between them? The contrariety is equally strong between the miracles related by Herodotus or Plutarch, and those delivered by Mariana, Bede, or any monkish historian.

The wise lend a very academic faith to every report which favors the passion of the reporter; whether it magnifies his country, his family, or himself, or in any other way strikes in with his natural inclinations and propensities. But what greater temptation than to appear a missionary, a prophet, an ambassador from heaven? Who would not encounter many dan-

stories flame to life *miracles: not probable not proved*

gers and difficulties, in order to attain so sublime a character? Or if, by the help of vanity and a heated imagination, a man has first made a convert of himself, and entered seriously into the delusion; who ever scruples to make use of pious frauds, in support of so holy and meritorious a cause?

The smallest spark may here kindle into the greatest flame; because the materials are always prepared for it. The crowd hungry for gossip, the gazing populace, receive greedily, without examination, whatever soothes superstition, and promotes wonder.

How many stories of this nature, have, in all ages, been detected and exploded in their infancy? How many more have been celebrated for a time, and have afterwards sunk into neglect and oblivion? Where such reports, therefore, fly about, the solution of the phenomenon is obvious; and we judge in conformity to regular experience and observation, when we account for it by the known and natural principles of credulity and delusion. And shall we, rather than have a recourse to so natural a solution, allow of a miraculous violation of the most established laws of nature?

I need not mention the difficulty of detecting a falsehood in any private or even public history, at the place, where it is said to happen; much more when the scene is removed to ever so small a distance. Even a court of judicature, with all the authority, accuracy, and judgment, which they can employ, find themselves often at a loss to distinguish between truth and falsehood in the most recent actions. But the matter never comes to any issue, if trusted to the common method of altercation and debate and flying rumors; especially when men's passions have taken part on either side.

In the infancy of new religions, the wise and learned commonly esteem the matter too inconsiderable to deserve their attention or regard. And when afterwards they would willingly detect the cheat, in order to undeceive the deluded multitude, the season is now past, and the records and witnesses, which might clear up the matter, have perished beyond recovery.

No means of detection remain, but those which must be drawn from the very testimony itself of the reporters: And these, though always sufficient with the judicious and knowing, are commonly too fine to fall under the comprehension of the vulgar.

Upon the whole, then, it appears, that no testimony for any kind of miracle has ever amounted to a probability, much less to a proof; and that, even supposing it amounted to a proof, it would be opposed by another proof; derived from the very nature of the fact, which it would endeavor to establish. It is experience only, which gives authority to human testimony; and it is the same experience, which assures us of the laws of nature. When, therefore, these two kinds of experience are contrary, we have nothing to do but subtract the one from the other, and embrace an opinion, either on one side or the other, with that assurance which arises from the remainder. But according to the principle here explained, this subtraction, with regard to all popular religions, amounts to an entire annihilation; and therefore we may establish it as a maxim, that no human testimony can have such force as to prove a miracle, and make it a just foundation for any such system of religion.

I beg the limitations here made may be remarked, when I say, that a miracle can never be proved, so as to be the foundation of a system of religion. For I own, that otherwise, there may possibly be miracles, or violations of the usual course of nature, of such a kind as to admit of proof from human testimony; though, perhaps, it will be impossible to find any such in all the records of history. Thus, suppose, all authors, in all languages, agree, that, from the first of January 1600, there was a total darkness over the whole earth for eight days: Suppose that the tradition of this extraordinary event is still strong and lively among the people: That all travellers, who return from foreign countries, bring us accounts of the same tradition, without the least variation or contradiction: It is evident, that our present philosophers, instead of doubting the fact, ought to receive it as certain, and ought to search for the causes whence it might be derived. The decay, corruption, and dissolution of nature, is an event rendered probable by so many analogies, that any phenomenon, which seems to have a tendency towards that catastrophe, comes within the reach of human testimony, if that testimony be very extensive and uniform.

But suppose, that all the historians who treat of England, should agree, that, on the first of January 1600, Queen Elizabeth died; that both before and after her death she was seen by her physicians and the whole court, as is usual with persons of her rank; that her successor was acknowledged and proclaimed by the parliament; and that, after being interred a month, she again appeared, resumed the throne, and governed England for three years: I must confess that I should be surprised at the concurrence of so many odd circumstances, but should not have the least inclination to believe so miraculous an event. I should not doubt of her pretended death, and of those other public circumstances that followed it: I should only assert it to have been pretended, and that it neither was, nor possibly could be real. You would in vain object to me the difficulty, and almost impossibility of deceiving the world in an affair of such consequence; the wisdom and solid judgment of that renowned queen; with the little or no advantage which she could reap from so poor an artifice: All this might astonish me; but I would still reply, that the knavery and folly of men are such common phenomena, that I should rather believe the most extraordinary events to arise from their concurrence, than admit of so signal a violation of the laws of nature.

But should this miracle be ascribed to any new system of religion; men, in all ages, have been so much imposed on by ridiculous stories of that kind, that this very circumstance would be a full proof of a cheat, and sufficient, with all men of sense, not only to make them reject the fact, but even reject it without farther examination. Though the Being to whom the miracle is ascribed, be, in this case, Almighty, it does not, upon that account, become a whit more probable; since it is impossible for us to know the attributes or actions of such a Being, otherwise than from the experience which we have of his productions, in the usual course of nature. This still reduces us to past observation, and obliges us to compare the instances of the violation of truth in the testimony of men, with those of the violation of the laws of nature by miracles, in order to judge which of them is most likely and probable. As the violations of truth are more common in the testimony concerning religious miracles, than in that concerning any other matter of fact; this must diminish very much the authority of the former testimony, and make us form a general resolution, never to lend any

attention to it, with whatever specious presence it may be covered.

Lord Bacon seems to have embraced the same principles of reasoning. 'We ought,' says he, 'to make a collection or particular history of all monsters and prodigious births of productions, and in a word of every thing new, rare, and extraordinary in nature. But this must be done with the most severe scrutiny, lest we depart from truth. Above all, every relation must be considered as suspicious, which depends in any degree upon religion, as the prodigies of Livy: And no less so, every thing that is to be found in the writers of natural magic or alchemy, or such authors, who seem, all of them, to have an unconquerable appetite for falsehood and fable.'

I am the better pleased with the method of reasoning here delivered, as I think it may serve to confound those dangerous friends or disguised enemies to the Christian Religion, who have undertaken to defend it by the principles of human reason. Our most holy religion is founded on Faith, not on reason; and it is a sure method of exposing it to put it to such a trial as it is, by no means, fitted to endure. To make this more evident, let us examine those miracles, related in scripture; and not to lose ourselves in too wide a field, let us confine ourselves to such as we find in the Pentateuch, which we shall examine, according to the principles of these pretended Christians, not as the word or testimony of God himself, but as the production of a mere human writer and historian. Here then we are first to consider a book, presented to us by a barbarous and ignorant people, written in an age when they were still more barbarous, and in all probability long after the facts which it relates, corroborated by no concurring testimony, and resembling those fabulous accounts, which every nation gives of its origin. Upon reading this book, we find it full of prodigies and miracles. It gives an account of a state of the world and of human nature entirely different from the present: Of our fall from that state: Of the age of man, extended to near a thousand years: Of the destruction of the world by a deluge: Of the arbitrary choice of one people, as the favorites of heaven; and that people the countrymen of the author: Of their deliverance from bondage by prodigies the most astonishing imaginable: I desire any one to lay his hand upon his heart, and after a serious consideration declare, whether he thinks that the falsehood of such a book, supported by such a testimony, would be more extraordinary and miraculous than all the miracles it relates; which is, however, necessary to make it be received, according to the measures of probability above established.

What we have said of miracles may be applied, without any variation, to prophecies; and indeed, all prophecies are real miracles, and as such only, can be admitted as proofs of any revelation. If it did not exceed the capacity of human nature to foretell future events, it would be absurd to employ any prophecy as an argument for a divine mission or authority from heaven. So that, upon the whole, we may conclude, that the Christian Religion not only was at first attended with miracles, but even at this day cannot be believed by any reasonable person without one. Mere reason is insufficient to convince us of its veracity: And whoever is moved by Faith to assent to it, is conscious of a continued miracle in his own person, which subverts all the principles of his understanding, and gives him a determination to believe what is most contrary to custom and experience.

SECTION XI: OF A PARTICULAR PROVIDENCE AND OF A FUTURE STATE

I was lately engaged in conversation with a friend who loves sceptical paradoxes; where, though he advanced many principles, of which I can by no means approve, yet as they seem to be curious, and to bear some relation to the chain of reasoning carried on throughout this enquiry, I shall here copy them from my memory as accurately as I can, in order to submit them to the judgment of the reader.

Our conversation began with my admiring the singular good fortune of philosophy, which, as it requires entire liberty above all other privileges, and chiefly flourishes from the free opposition of sentiments and argumentation, received its first birth in an age and country of freedom and toleration, and was never cramped, even in its most extravagant principles, by any creeds, confessions, or penal statutes. For, except the banishment of Protagoras,

and the death of Socrates, which last event proceeded partly from other motives, there are scarcely any instances to be met with, in ancient history, of this bigoted jealousy, with which the present age is so much infested. Epicurus lived at Athens to an advanced age, in peace and tranquillity: Epicureans were even admitted to receive the sacerdotal character, and to officiate at the altar, in the most sacred rites of the established religion: And the public encouragement of pensions and salaries was afforded equally, by the wisest of all the Roman emperors, to the professors of every sect of philosophy. How requisite such kind of treatment was to philosophy, in her early youth, will easily be conceived, if we reflect, that, even at present, when she may be supposed more hardy and robust, she bears with much difficulty the inclemency of the seasons, and those harsh winds of calumny and persecution, which blow upon her.

You admire, says my friend, as the singular good fortune of philosophy, what seems to result from the natural course of things, and to be unavoidable in every age and nation. This pertinacious bigotry, of which you complain, as so fatal to philosophy, is really her offspring, who, after allying with superstition, separates himself entirely from the interest of his parent, and becomes her most inveterate enemy and persecutor. Speculative dogmas of religion, the present occasions of such furious dispute, could not possibly be conceived or admitted in the early ages of the world; when mankind, being wholly illiterate, formed an idea of religion more suitable to their weak apprehension, and composed their sacred tenets of such tales chiefly as were the objects of traditional belief, more than of argument or disputation. After the first alarm, therefore, was over, which arose from the new paradoxes and principles of the philosophers; these teachers seem ever after, during the ages of antiquity, to have lived in great harmony with the established superstition, and to have made a fair partition of mankind between them; the former claiming all the learned and wise, the latter possessing all the vulgar and illiterate.

It seems then, say I, that you leave politics entirely out of the question, and never suppose, that a wise magistrate can justly be jealous of certain tenets of philosophy, such as those of Epicurus, which, denying a divine existence, and consequently a providence and a future state, seem to loosen, in a great measure, the ties of morality, and may be supposed, for that reason, pernicious to the peace of civil society.

I know, replied he, that in fact these persecutions never, in any age, proceeded from calm reason, or from experience of the pernicious consequences of philosophy; but arose entirely from passion and prejudice. But what if I should advance farther, and assert, that, if Epicurus had been accused before the people, by any of the sycophants or informers of those days, he could easily have defended his cause, and proved his principles of philosophy to be as salutary as those of his adversaries, who endeavored, with such zeal, to expose him to the public hatred and jealousy?

I wish, said I, you would try your eloquence upon so extraordinary a topic, and make a speech for Epicurus, which might satisfy, not the mob of Athens, if you will allow that ancient and polite city to have contained any mob, but the more philosophical part of his audience, such as might be supposed capable of comprehending his arguments.

The matter would not be difficult, upon such conditions, replied he: And if you please, I shall suppose myself Epicurus for a moment, and make you stand for the Athenian people, and shall deliver you such an harangue as will fill all the urn with white beans, and leave not a black one to gratify the malice of my adversaries.

Very well: Pray proceed upon these suppositions.

I come hither, O ye Athenians, to justify in your assembly what I maintained in my school, and I find myself impeached by furious antagonists, instead of reasoning with calm and dispassionate inquirers. Your deliberations, which of right should be directed to questions of public good, and the interest of the commonwealth, are diverted to the disquisitions of speculative philosophy; and these magnificent, but perhaps fruitless enquiries, take place of your more familiar but more useful occupations. But so far as in me lies, I will prevent this abuse. We shall not here dispute concerning the origin and government of worlds. We shall only enquire how far such questions concern the public interest. And if I can persuade you, that they are entirely indifferent to the peace of society and security of government, I hope that you will presently send us back to our schools, there to examine, at leisure, the question, the most sublime, but, at the same time, the most speculative of all philosophy.

The religious philosophers, not satisfied with the tradition of your forefathers, and doctrine of your priests (in which I willingly acquiesce), indulge a rash curiosity, in trying how far they can establish religion upon the principles of reason; and they thereby excite, instead of satisfying, the doubts, which naturally arise from a diligent and scrutinous enquiry. They paint, in the most magnificent colours, the order, beauty, and wise arrangement of the universe; and then ask, if such a glorious display of intelligence could proceed from the fortuitous concourse of atoms, or if chance could produce what the greatest genius can never sufficiently admire. I shall not examine the justness of this argument. I shall allow it to be as solid as my antagonists and accusers can desire. It is sufficient, if I can prove, from this very reasoning, that the question is entirely speculative, and that, when, in my philosophical disquisitions, I deny a providence and a future state, I undermine not the foundations of society, but advance principles, which they themselves, upon their own topics, if they argue consistently, must allow to be solid and satisfactory.

You then, who are my accusers, have acknowledged, that the chief or sole argument for a divine existence (which I never questioned) is derived from the order of nature; where there appear such marks of intelligence and design, that you think it extravagant to assign for its cause, either chance, or the blind and unguided force of matter. You allow, that this is an argument drawn from effects to causes. From the order of the work, you infer, that there must have been project and forethought in the workman. If you cannot make out this point, you allow, that your conclusion fails; and you pretend not to establish the conclusion in a greater latitude than the phenomena of nature will justify. These are your concessions. I desire you to mark the consequences.

When we infer any particular cause from an effect, we must proportion the one to the other, and can never be allowed to ascribe to the cause any qualities, but what are exactly sufficient to produce the effect. A body of ten ounces raised in any scale may serve as a proof, that the counterbalancing weight exceeds ten ounces; but can never afford a reason that it exceeds a hundred. If the cause, assigned for any effect, be not sufficient to produce it, we must either reject that cause, or add to it such qualities as will give it a just proportion to the effect. But if we ascribe to it farther qualities, or affirm it capable of producing other effects, we can only indulge the license of conjecture, and arbitrarily suppose the existence of qualities and energies, without reason or authority.

The same rule holds, whether the cause assigned be brute unconscious matter, or a rational intelligent being. If the cause be known only by the effect, we never ought to ascribe to it any qualities, beyond what are precisely requisite to produce the effect: Nor can we, by any rules of just reasoning, return back from the cause, and infer other effects from it, beyond those by which alone it is known to us. No one, merely from the sight of one of Zeuxis's pictures, could know, that he was also a statuary or architect, and was an artist no less skillful in stone and marble than in colours. The talents and taste, displayed in the particular work before us; these we may safely conclude the workman to be possessed of. The cause must be proportioned to the effect; and if we exactly and precisely proportion it, we shall never find in it any qualities, that point farther, or afford an inference concerning any other design or performance. Such qualities must be somewhat beyond what is merely requisite for producing the effect, which we examine.

Allowing, therefore, the gods to be the authors of the existence or order of the universe; it follows, that they possess that precise degree of power, intelligence, and benevolence, which appears in their workmanship; but nothing farther can ever be proved, except we call in the assistance of exaggeration and flattery to supply the defects of argument and reasoning. So far as the traces of any attributes, at present, appear, so far may we conclude these attributes to exist. The supposition of farther attributes is mere hypothesis; much more the supposition, that, in distant regions of space or periods of time, there has been, or will be, a more magnificent display of these attributes, and a scheme of administration more suitable to such imaginary virtues. We can never be

allowed to mount up from the universe, the effect, to Jupiter, the cause; and then descend downwards, to infer any new effect from that cause; as if the present effects alone were not entirely worthy of the glorious attributes, which we ascribe to that deity. The knowledge of the cause being derived solely from the effect, they must be exactly adjusted to each other; and the one can never refer to any thing farther, or be the foundation of any new inference and conclusion.

You find certain phenomena in nature. You seek a cause or author. You imagine that you have found him. You afterwards become so enamored of this offspring of your brain, that you imagine it impossible, but he must produce something greater and more perfect than the present scene of things, which is so full of ill and disorder. You forget, that this superlative intelligence and benevolence are entirely imaginary, or, at least, without any foundation in reason; and that you have no ground to ascribe to him any qualities, but what you see he has actually exerted and displayed in his productions. Let your gods, therefore, O philosophers, be suited to the present appearances of nature: And presume not to alter these appearances by arbitrary suppositions, in order to suit them to the attributes, which you so fondly ascribe to your deities.

When priests and poets, supported by your authority, O Athenians, talk of a golden or silver age, which preceded the present state of vice and misery, I hear them with attention and with reverence. But when philosophers, who pretend to neglect authority, and to cultivate reason, hold the same discourse, I pay them not, I own, the same obsequious submission and pious deference. I ask; who carried them into the celestial regions, who admitted them into the councils of the gods, who opened to them the book of fate, that they thus rashly affirm, that their deities have executed, or will execute, any purpose beyond what has actually appeared? If they tell me, that they have mounted on the steps or by the gradual ascent of reason, and by drawing inferences from effects to causes, I still insist, that they have aided the ascent of reason by the wings of imagination; otherwise they could not thus change their manner of inference, and argue from causes to effects; presuming, that a more perfect production than the present world would be more suitable to such perfect beings as the gods, and forgetting that they have no reason to ascribe to these celestial beings any perfection or any attribute, but what can be found in the present world.

Hence all the fruitless industry to account for the ill appearances of nature, and save the honour of the gods; while we must acknowledge the reality of that evil and disorder, with which the world so much abounds. The obstinate and intractable qualities of matter, we are told, or the observance of general laws, or some such reason, is the sole cause, which controlled the power and benevolence of Jupiter, and obliged him to create mankind and every sensible creature so imperfect and so unhappy. These attributes, then, are, it seems, beforehand, taken for granted, in their greatest latitude. And upon that supposition, I own, that such conjectures may, perhaps, be admitted as plausible solutions of the ill phenomena. But still I ask; Why take these attributes for granted, or why ascribe to the cause any qualities but what actually appear in the effect? Why torture your brain to justify the course of nature upon suppositions, which, for aught you know, may be entirely imaginary, and of which there are to be found no traces in the course of nature?

The religious hypothesis, therefore, must be considered only as a particular method of accounting for the visible phenomena of the universe: But no just reasoner will ever presume to infer from it any single fact, and alter or add to the phenomena, in any single particular. If you think, that the appearances of things prove such causes, it is allowable for you to draw an inference concerning the existence of these causes. In such complicated and sublime subjects, every one should be indulged in the liberty of conjecture and argument. But here you ought to rest. If you come backward, and arguing from your inferred causes, conclude, that any other fact has existed, or will exist, in the course of nature, which may serve as a fuller display of particular attributes; I must admonish you, that you have departed from the method of reasoning, attached to the present subject, and have certainly added something to the attributes of the cause, beyond what appears in the effect; otherwise you could never, with tolerable sense or propriety, add any thing to the effect, in order to render it more worthy of the cause.

Where, then, is the odiousness of that doctrine, which I teach in my school, or rather, which I examine in my gardens? Or what do you find in this whole question, wherein the security of good morals, or the peace and order of society is in the least concerned?

I deny a providence, you say, and supreme governor of the world, who guides the course of events, and punishes the vicious with infamy and disappointment, and rewards the virtuous with honour and success, in all their undertakings. But surely, I deny not the course itself of events, which lies open to every one's enquiry and examination. I acknowledge, that, in the present order of things, virtue is attended with more peace of mind than vice, and meets with a more favorable reception from the world. I am sensible, that, according to the past experience of mankind, friendship is the chief joy of human life, and moderation the only source of tranquillity and happiness. I never balance between the virtuous and the vicious course of life; but am sensible, that, to a well disposed mind, every advantage is on the side of the former. And what can you say more, allowing all your suppositions and reasonings? You tell me, indeed, that this disposition of things proceeds from intelligence and design. But whatever it proceeds from, the disposition itself, on which depends our happiness or misery, and consequently our conduct and deportment in life, is still the same. It is still open for me, as well as you, to regulate my behavior, by my experience of past events. And if you affirm, that, while a divine providence is allowed, and a supreme distributive justice in the universe, I ought to expect some more particular reward of the good, and punishment of the bad, beyond the ordinary course of events; I here find the same fallacy, which I have before endeavored to detect. You persist in imagining, that, if we grant that divine existence, for which you so earnestly contend, you may safely infer consequences from it, and add something to the experienced order of nature, by arguing from the attributes which you ascribe to your gods. You seem not to remember, that all your reasonings on this subject can only be drawn from effects to causes; and that every argument, deduced from causes to effects, must of necessity be a gross sophism; since it is impossible for you to know any thing of the cause, but what you have antecedently, not inferred, but discovered to the full, in the effect.

But what must a philosopher think of those vain reasoners, who, instead of regarding the present scene of things as the sole object of their contemplation, so far reverse the whole course of nature, as to render this life merely a passage to something farther; a porch, which leads to a greater, and vastly different building; a prologue, which serves only to introduce the piece, and give it more grace and propriety? Whence, do you think, can such philosophers derive their idea of the gods? From their own conceit and imagination surely. For if they derived it from the present phenomena, it would never point to anything farther, but must be exactly adjusted to them. That the divinity may possibly be endowed with attributes, which we have never seen exerted; may be governed by principles of action, which we cannot discover to be satisfied: All this will freely be allowed. But still this is mere possibility and hypothesis. We never can have reason to infer any attributes, or any principles of action in him, but so far as we know them to have been exerted and satisfied.

Are there any marks of a distributive justice in the world? If you answer in the affirmative, I conclude, that, since justice here exerts itself, it is satisfied. If you reply in the negative, I conclude, that you have then no reason to ascribe justice, in our sense of it, to the gods. If you hold a medium between affirmation and negation, by saying, that the justice of the gods, at present, exerts itself in part, but not in its full extent; I answer, that you have no reason to give it any particular extent, but only so far as you see it, at present, exert itself.

Thus I bring the dispute, O Athenians, to a short issue with my antagonists. The course of nature lies open to my contemplation as well as to theirs. The experienced train of events is the great standard, by which we all regulate our conduct. Nothing else can be appealed to in the field, or in the senate. Nothing else ought ever to be heard of in the school, or in the closet. In vain would our limited understanding break through those boundaries, which are too narrow for our fond imagination. While we argue from the course of nature, and infer a particular intelligent cause, which first bestowed, and still preserves order in the universe, we embrace a principle, which is both uncertain and useless. It is uncertain; because the subject lies entirely beyond the reach of human experience. It is useless; because our knowledge of this cause being derived entirely from the course of nature, we can never, according to the rules of just reasoning, return back from the cause with any new inference, or making additions to the common and experienced course of nature, establish any new principles of conduct and behavior.

I observe (said I, finding he had finished his harangue) that you neglect not the artifice of the demagogues of old; and as you were pleased to make me stand for the people, you insinuate yourself into my favour by embracing those principles, to which, you know, I have always expressed a particular attachment. But allowing you to make experience (as indeed I think you ought) the only standard of our judgment concerning this, and all other questions of fact; I doubt not but, from the very same experience, to which you appeal, it may be possible to refute this reasoning, which you have put into the mouth of Epicurus. If you saw, for instance, a half-finished building, surrounded with heaps of brick and stone and mortar, and all the instruments of masonry; could you not infer from the effect, that it was a work of design and contrivance? And could you not return again, from this inferred cause, to infer new additions to the effect, and conclude, that the building would soon be finished, and receive all the further improvements, which art could bestow upon it? If you saw upon the sea-shore the print of one human foot, you would conclude, that a man had passed that way, and that he had also left the traces of the other foot, though effaced by the rolling of the sands or inundation of the waters. Why then do you refuse to admit the same method of reasoning with regard to the order of nature? Consider the world and the present life only as an imperfect building, from which you can infer a superior intelligence; and arguing from that superior intelligence, which can leave nothing imperfect; why may you not infer a more finished scheme or plan, which will receive its completion in some distant point of space or time? Are not these methods of reasoning exactly similar? And under what pretence can you embrace the one, while you reject the other?

The infinite difference of the subjects, replied he, is a sufficient foundation for this difference in my conclusions. In works of human art and contrivance, it is allowable to advance from the effect to the cause, and returning back from the cause, to form new inferences concerning the effect, and examine the alterations, which it has probably undergone, or may still undergo. But what is the foundation of this method of reasoning? Plainly this; that man is a being, whom we know by experience, whose motives and designs we are acquainted with, and whose projects and inclinations have a certain connexion and coherence, according to the laws which nature has established for the government of such a creature. When, therefore, we find, that any work has proceeded from the skill and industry of man; as we are otherwise acquainted with the nature of the animal, we can draw a hundred inferences concerning what may be expected from him; and these inferences will all be founded in experience and observation. But did we know man only from the single work or production which we examine, it were impossible for us to argue in this manner; because our knowledge of all the qualities, which we ascribe to him, being in that case derived from the production, it is impossible they could point to any thing farther, or be the foundation of any new inference. The print of a foot in the sand can only prove, when considered alone, that there was some figure adapted to it, by which it was produced: But the print of a human foot proves likewise, from our other experience, that there was probably another foot, which also left its impression, though effaced by time or other accidents. Here we mount from the effect to the cause; and descending again from the cause, infer alterations in the effect; but this is not a continuation of the same simple chain of reasoning. We comprehend in this case a hundred other experiences and observations, concerning the usual figure and members of that species of animal, without which this method of argument must be considered as fallacious and sophistical.

The case is not the same with our reasonings from the works of nature. The Deity is known to us only by his productions, and is a single being in the universe, not comprehended under any species or genus, from whose experienced attributes or qualities, we can, by analogy, infer any attribute or quality in him. As the universe shows wisdom and goodness, we infer wisdom and goodness. As it shows a particular degree of these perfections, we infer a particular degree of them, precisely adapted to the effect which we examine. But farther attributes or farther degrees of the same attributes, we can never be authorized to infer or suppose, by any rules of just reasoning. Now, without some such license of supposition, it is impossible for us to argue from the cause, or infer any alteration in the effect, beyond what has immediately fallen under our observation. Greater good produced by this Being must still prove a greater degree of goodness: A more impartial distribution of rewards and punishments must proceed from a greater regard to justice and equity. Every supposed addition to the works of nature makes an addition to the attributes of the Author of nature; and consequently, being entirely unsupported by any reason or argument, can never be admitted but as mere conjecture and hypothesis.

The great source of our mistake in this subject, and of the unbounded license of conjecture, which we indulge, is, that we tacitly consider ourselves, as in the place of the Supreme Being, and conclude, that he will, on every occasion, observe the same conduct, which we ourselves, in his situation, would have embraced as reasonable and eligible. But, besides that the ordinary course of nature may convince us, that almost everything is regulated by principles and maxims very different from ours; besides this, I say, it must evidently appear contrary to all rules of analogy to reason, from the intentions and projects of men, to those of a Being so different, and so much superior. In human nature, there is a certain experienced coherence of designs and inclinations; so that when, from any fact, we have discovered one intention of any man, it may often be reasonable, from experience, to infer another, and draw a long chain of conclusions concerning his past or future conduct. But this method of reasoning can never have place with regard to a Being, so remote and incomprehensible, who bears much less analogy to any other being in the universe than the sun to a waxen taper, and who discovers himself only by some faint traces or outlines, beyond which we have no authority to ascribe to him any attribute or perfection. What we imagine to be a superior perfection, may really be a defect. Or were it ever so much a perfection, the ascribing of it to the Supreme Being, where it appears not to have been really exerted, to the full, in his works, savors more of flattery and panegyric, than of just reasoning and sound philosophy. All the philosophy, therefore, in the world, and all the religion, which is nothing but a species of philosophy, will never be able to carry us beyond the usual course of experience, or give us measures of conduct and behavior different from those which are furnished by reflections on common life. No new fact can ever be inferred from the religious hypothesis; no event foreseen or foretold; no reward or punishment expected or dreaded, beyond what is already known by practice and observation. So that my apology for Epicurus will still appear solid and satisfactory; nor have the political interests of society any connexion with the philosophical disputes concerning metaphysics and religion.

There is still one circumstance, replied I, which you seem to have overlooked. Though I should allow your premises, I must deny your conclusion. You conclude, that religious doctrines and reasonings can have no influence on life, because they ought to have no influence; never considering, that men reason not in the same manner you do, but draw many consequences from the belief of a divine Existence, and suppose that the Deity will inflict punishments on vice, and bestow rewards on virtue, beyond what appear in the ordinary course of nature. Whether this reasoning of theirs be just or not, is no matter. Its influence on their life and conduct must still be the same. And, those, who attempt to disabuse them of such prejudices, may, for aught I know, be good reasoners, but I cannot allow them to be good citizens and politicians; since they free men from one restraint upon their passions, and make the infringement of the laws of society, in one respect, more easy and secure.

After all, I may, perhaps, agree to your general conclusion in favour of liberty, though upon different premises from those, on which you endeavor to found it. I think, that the state ought to tolerate every principle of philosophy; nor is there an instance, that any government has suffered in its political interests by such indulgence. There is no enthusiasm among philosophers; their doctrines are not very alluring to the people; and no restraint can be put upon their reasonings, but what must be of dangerous consequence to the sciences, and even to the state, by paving the way for persecution and oppression in points, where the generality of mankind are more deeply interested and concerned.

But there occurs to me (continued I) with regard to your main topic, a difficulty, which I shall just propose to you, without insisting on it; lest it lead into reasonings of too nice and delicate a nature. In a word, I much doubt whether it be possible for a cause to be known only by its effect (as you have all along supposed) or to be of so singular and particular a nature as to have no parallel and no similarity with any other cause or object, that has ever fallen under our observation. It is only when two species of objects are found to be constantly conjoined, that we can infer the one from the other; and were an effect presented, which was entirely singular, and could not be comprehended under any known species, I do not see, that we could form any conjecture or inference at all concerning its cause. If experience and observation and analogy be, indeed, the only guides which we can reasonably follow in inferences of this nature; both the effect and cause must bear a similarity and resemblance to other effects and causes, which we know, and which we have found, in many instances, to be conjoined with each other. I leave it to your own reflection to pursue the consequences of this principle. I shall just observe, that, as the antagonists of Epicurus always suppose the universe, an effect quite singular and unparalleled, to be the proof of a Deity, a cause no less singular and unparalleled; your reasonings, upon that supposition, seem, at least, to merit our attention. There is, I own, some difficulty, how we can ever return from the cause to the effect, and, reasoning from our ideas of the former, infer any alteration on the latter, or any addition to it.

SECTION XII: OF THE ACADEMICAL OR SCEPTICAL PHILOSOPHY

PART I

There is not a greater number of philosophical reasonings, displayed upon any subject, than those, which prove the existence of a Deity, and refute the fallacies of Atheists; and yet the most religious philosophers still dispute whether any man can be so blinded as to be a speculative atheist. How shall we reconcile these contradictions? The knights-errant, who wandered about to clear the world of dragons and giants, never entertained the least doubt with regard to the existence of these monsters.

The Sceptic is another enemy of religion, who naturally provokes the indignation of all divines and graver philosophers; though it is certain, that no man ever met with any such absurd creature, or conversed with a man, who had no opinion or principle concerning any subject, either of action or speculation. This begets a very natural question; What is meant by a sceptic? And how far it is possible to push these philosophical principles of doubt and uncertainty?

There is a species of scepticism, antecedent to all study and philosophy, which is much inculcated by Descartes and others, as a sovereign preservative against error and precipitate judgment. It recommends an universal doubt, not only of all our former opinions and principles, but also of our very faculties; of whose veracity, say they, we must assure ourselves, by a chain of reasoning, deduced from some original principle, which cannot possibly be fallacious or deceitful. But neither is there any such original principle, which has a prerogative above others, that are self-evident and convincing: Or if there were, could we advance a step beyond it, but by the use of those very faculties, of which we are supposed to be already diffident. The Cartesian doubt, therefore, were it ever possible to be attained by any human creature (as it plainly is not) would be entirely incurable; and no reasoning could ever bring us to a state of assurance and conviction upon any subject.

It must, however, be confessed, that this species of scepticism, when more moderate, may be understood in a very reasonable sense, and is a necessary preparative to the study of philosophy, by preserving a proper impartiality in our judgments, and weaning our mind from all those prejudices, which we may have imbibed from education or rash opinion. To begin with clear and self-evident principles, to advance by timorous and sure steps, to review frequently our conclusions, and examine accurately all their consequences; though by these means we shall make both a slow and a short progress in our systems; are the only methods, by which we can ever hope to reach truth, and attain a proper stability and certainty in our determinations.

There is another species of scepticism, consequent to science and enquiry, when men are supposed to have discovered, either the absolute fallaciousness of their mental faculties, or their unfitness to reach any fixed determination in all those curious subjects of speculation, about which they are commonly employed. Even our very senses are brought into dispute, by a certain species of philosophers; and the maxims of common life are subjected to the same doubt as the most profound principles or conclusions of metaphysics and theology. As these paradoxical tenets (if they may be called tenets) are to be met with in some philosophers, and the refutation of them in several, they naturally excite our curiosity, and make us enquire into the arguments, on which they may be founded.

I need not insist upon the more trite topics, employed by the sceptics in all ages, against the evidence of sense; such as those which are derived from the imperfection and fallaciousness of our organs, on numberless occasions; the crooked appearance of an oar in water; the various aspects of objects, according to their different distances; the double images which arise from the pressing one eye; with many other appearances of a like nature. These sceptical topics, indeed, are only sufficient to prove, that the senses alone are not implicitly to be depended on; but that we must correct their evidence by reason, and by considerations, derived from the nature of the medium, the distance of the object, and the disposition of the organ, in order to render them, within their sphere, the proper criteria of truth and falsehood. There are other more profound arguments against the senses, which admit not of so easy a solution.

It seems evident, that men are carried, by a natural instinct or prepossession, to repose faith in their senses; and that, without any reasoning, or even almost before the use of reason, we always suppose an external universe, which depends not on our perception, but would exist, though we and every sensible creature were absent or annihilated. Even the animal creation are governed by a like opinion, and preserve this belief of external objects, in all their thoughts, designs, and actions.

It seems also evident, that, when men follow this blind and powerful instinct of nature, they always suppose the very images, presented by the senses, to be the external objects, and never entertain any suspicion, that the one are nothing but representations of the other. This very table, which we see white, and which we feel hard, is believed to exist, independent of our perception, and to be something external to our mind, which perceives it. Our presence bestows not being on it: Our absence does not annihilate it. It preserves its existence uniform and entire, independent of the situation of intelligent beings, who perceive or contemplate it.

But this universal and primary opinion of all men is soon destroyed by the slightest philosophy, which teaches us, that nothing can ever be present to the mind but an image or perception, and that the senses are only the inlets, through which these images are conveyed, without being able to produce any immediate intercourse between the mind and the object. The table, which we see, seems to diminish, as we remove farther from it: But the real table, which exists independent of us, suffers no alteration: It was, therefore, nothing but its image, which was present to the mind. These are the obvious dictates of reason; and no man, who reflects, ever doubted, that the existences, which we consider, when we say, this house and that tree, are nothing but perceptions in the mind, and fleeting copies or representations of other existences, which remain uniform and independent.

So far, then, are we necessitated by reasoning to contradict or depart from the primary instincts of nature, and to embrace a new system with regard to the evidence of our senses. But here philosophy finds herself extremely embarrassed, when she would justify this new system, and obviate the cavils and objections of the sceptics. She can no longer plead the infallible and irresistible instinct of nature: For that led us to a quite different system, which is acknowledged fallible and even erroneous. And to justify this pretended philosophical system, by a chain of clear and convincing argument, or even any appearance of argument, exceeds the power of all human capacity.

By what argument can it be proved, that the perceptions of the mind must be caused by external objects, entirely different from them, though resembling them (if that be possible) and could not arise either from the energy of the mind itself, or from the suggestion of some invisible and unknown spirit, or from some other cause still more unknown to us? It is acknowledged, that, in fact, many of these perceptions arise not from any thing external, as in dreams, madness, and other diseases. And nothing can be more inexplicable than the manner, in which body should so operate upon mind as ever to convey an image of itself to a substance, supposed of so different, and even contrary a nature.

It is a question of fact, whether the perceptions of the senses be produced by external objects, resembling them: how shall this question be determined? By experience surely; as all other questions of a like nature. But here experience is, and must be entirely silent. The mind has never any thing present to it but the perceptions, and cannot possibly reach any experience of their connexion with objects. The supposition of such a connexion is, therefore, without any foundation in reasoning.

To have recourse to the veracity of the supreme Being, in order to prove the veracity of our senses, is surely making a very unexpected circuit. If his veracity were at all concerned in this matter, our senses would be entirely infallible; because it is not possible that he can ever deceive. Not to mention, that, if the external world be once called in question, we shall be at a loss to find arguments, by which we may prove the existence of that Being or any of his attributes.

This is a topic, therefore, in which the profounder and more philosophical sceptics will always triumph, when they endeavor to introduce an universal doubt into all subjects of human knowledge and enquiry. Do you follow the instincts and propensities of nature, may they say, in assenting to the veracity of sense? But these lead you to believe, that the very perception or sensible image is the external object. Do you disclaim this principle, in order to embrace a more rational opinion, that the perceptions are only representations of something external? You here depart from your natural propensities and more obvious sentiments; and yet are not able to satisfy your reason, which can never find any convincing argument from experience to prove, that the perceptions are connected with any external objects.

There is another sceptical topic of a like nature, derived from the most profound philosophy; which might merit our attention, were it requisite to dive so deep, in order to discover arguments and reasonings, which can so little serve to any serious purpose. It is universally allowed by modern inquirers, that all the sensible qualities of objects, such as hard, soft, hot, cold, white, black, &c. are merely secondary, and exist not in the objects themselves, but are perceptions of the mind, without any external archetype or model, which they represent. If this be allowed, with regard to secondary qualities, it must also follow, with regard to the supposed primary qualities of extension and solidity; nor can the latter be any more entitled to that denomination than the former. The idea of extension is entirely acquired from the senses of sight and feeling; and if all the qualities, perceived by the senses, be in the mind, not in the object, the same conclusion must reach the idea of extension, which is wholly dependent on the sensible ideas or the ideas of secondary qualities. Nothing can save us from this conclusion, but the asserting, that the ideas of those primary qualities are attained by Abstraction; an opinion, which, if we examine it accurately, we shall find to be unintelligible, and even absurd. An extension, that is neither tangible nor visible, cannot possibly be conceived: And a tangible or visible extension, which is neither hard nor soft, black nor white, is equally beyond the reach of human conception. Let any man try to conceive a triangle in general, which is neither Isosceles nor Scalenum, nor has any particular length or proportion of sides; and he will soon perceive the absurdity of all the scholastic notions with regard to abstraction and general ideas.

Thus the first philosophical objection to the evidence of sense or to the opinion of external existence consists in this, that such an opinion, if rested on natural instinct, is contrary to reason, and if referred to reason, is contrary to natural instinct, and at the same time carries no rational evidence with it, to convince an impartial enquirer. The second objection goes farther, and represents this opinion as contrary to reason: at least, if it be a principle of reason, that all sensible qualities are in the mind, not in the object. Bereave matter of all its intelligible qualities, both primary and secondary, you in a manner annihilate it, and leave only a certain unknown, inexplicable something, as the cause of our perceptions; a notion so imperfect, that no sceptic will think it worth while to contend against it.

PART II

It may seem a very extravagant attempt of the sceptics to destroy reason by argument and ratiocination;

yet is this the grand scope of all their enquiries and disputes. They endeavor to find objections, both to our abstract reasonings, and to those which regard matter of fact and existence.

The chief objection against all abstract reasonings is derived from the ideas of space and time; ideas, which, in common life and to a careless view, are very clear and intelligible, but when they pass through the scrutiny of the profound sciences (and they are the chief object of these sciences) afford principles, which seem full of absurdity and contradiction. No priestly dogmas, invented on purpose to tame and subdue the rebellious reason of mankind, ever shocked common sense more than the doctrine of the infinite divisibility of extension, with its consequences; as they are pompously displayed by all geometricians and metaphysicians, with a kind of triumph and exultation. A real quantity, infinitely less than any finite quantity, containing quantities infinitely less than itself, and so on in infinitum; this is an edifice so bold and prodigious, that it is too weighty for any pretended demonstration to support, because it shocks the clearest and most natural principles of human reason. But what renders the matter more extraordinary, is, that these seemingly absurd opinions are supported by a chain of reasoning, the clearest and most natural; nor is it possible for us to allow the premises without admitting the consequences. Nothing can be more convincing and satisfactory than all the conclusions concerning the properties of circles and triangles; and yet, when these are once received, how can we deny, that the angle of contact between a circle and its tangent is infinitely less than any rectilinear angle, that as you may increase the diameter of the circle in infinitum, this angle of contact becomes still less, even in infinitum, and that the angle of contact between other curves and their tangents may be infinitely less than those between any circle and its tangent, and so on, in infinitum? The demonstration of these principles seems as unexceptionable as that which proves the three angles of a triangle to be equal to two right ones, though the latter opinion be natural and easy, and the former big with contradiction and absurdity. Reason here seems to be thrown into a kind of amazement and suspense, which, without the suggestions of any sceptic, gives her a diffidence of herself, and of the ground on which she treads. She sees a full light, which illuminates certain places; but that light borders upon the most profound darkness. And between these she is so dazzled and confounded, that she scarcely can pronounce with certainty and assurance concerning any one object.

The absurdity of these bold determinations of the abstract sciences seems to become, if possible, still more palpable with regard to time than extension. An infinite number of real parts of time, passing in succession, and exhausted one after another, appears so evident a contradiction, that no man, one should think, whose judgment is not corrupted, instead of being improved, by the sciences, would ever be able to admit of it.

Yet still reason must remain restless, and unquiet, even with regard to that scepticism, to which she is driven by these seeming absurdities and contradictions. How any clear, distinct idea can contain circumstances, contradictory to itself, or to any other clear, distinct idea, is absolutely incomprehensible; and is, perhaps, as absurd as any proposition, which can be formed. So that nothing can be more sceptical, or more full of doubt and hesitation, than this scepticism itself, which arises from some of the paradoxical conclusions of geometry or the science of quantity.

The sceptical objections to moral evidence, or to the reasonings concerning matter of fact, are either popular or philosophical. The popular objections are derived from the natural weakness of human understanding; the contradictory opinions, which have been entertained in different ages and nations; the variations of our judgment in sickness and health, youth and old age, prosperity and adversity; the perpetual contradiction of each particular man's opinions and sentiments; with many other topics of that kind. It is needless to insist farther on this head. These objections are but weak. For as, in common life, we reason every moment concerning fact and existence, and cannot possibly subsist, without continually employing this species of argument, any popular objections, derived from thence, must be insufficient to destroy that evidence. The great subverter of Pyrrhonism or the excessive principles of scepticism, is action, and employment, and the oc-

cupations of common life. These principles may flourish and triumph in the schools; where it is, indeed, difficult, if not impossible, to refute them. But as soon as they leave the shade, and by the presence of the real objects, which actuate our passions and sentiments, are put in opposition to the more powerful principles of our nature, they vanish like smoke, and leave the most determined sceptic in the same condition as other mortals.

The sceptic, therefore, had better keep within his proper sphere, and display those philosophical objections, which arise from more profound researches. Here he seems to have ample matter of triumph; while he justly insists, that all our evidence for any matter of fact, which lies beyond the testimony of sense or memory, is derived entirely from the relation of cause and effect; that we have no other idea of this relation than that of two objects, which have been frequently conjoined together; that we have no argument to convince us, that objects, which have, in our experience, been frequently conjoined, will likewise, in other instances, be conjoined in the same manner; and that nothing leads us to this inference but custom or a certain instinct of our nature; which it is indeed difficult to resist, but which, like other instincts, may be fallacious and deceitful. While the sceptic insists upon these topics, he shows his force, or rather, indeed, his own and our weakness; and seems, for the time at least, to destroy all assurance and conviction. These arguments might be displayed at greater length, if any durable good or benefit to society could ever be expected to result from them.

For here is the chief and most confounding objection to excessive scepticism, that no durable good can ever result from it; while it remains in its full force and vigor. We need only ask such a sceptic, What his meaning is? And what he proposes by all these curious researches? He is immediately at a loss, and knows not what to answer. A Copernican or Ptolemaic, who supports each his different system of astronomy, may hope to produce a conviction, which will remain constant and durable, with his audience. A Stoic or Epicurean displays principles, which may not only be durable, but which have an effect on conduct and behavior. But a Pyrrhonian cannot expect, that his philosophy will have any constant influence on the mind: or if it had, that its influence would be beneficial to society. On the contrary, he must acknowledge, if he will acknowledge any thing, that all human life must perish, were his principles universally and steadily to prevail. All discourse, all action would immediately cease; and men remain in a total lethargy, till the necessities of nature, unsatisfied, put an end to their miserable existence. It is true; so fatal an event is very little to be dreaded. Nature is always too strong for principle. And though a Pyrrhonian may throw himself or others into a momentary amazement and confusion by his profound reasonings; the first and most trivial event in life will put to flight all his doubts and scruples, and leave him the same, in every point of action and speculation, with the philosophers of every other sect, or with those who never concerned themselves in any philosophical researches. When he awakes from his dream, he will be the first to join in the laugh against himself, and to confess, that all his objections are mere amusement, and can have no other tendency than to shew the whimsical condition of mankind, who must act and reason and believe; though they are not able, by their most diligent enquiry, to satisfy themselves concerning the foundation of these operations, or to remove the objections, which may be raised against them.

PART III

There is, indeed, a more mitigated scepticism or academical philosophy, which may be both durable and useful, and which may, in part, be the result of this Pyrrhonism, or excessive scepticism, when its undistinguished doubts are, in some measure, corrected by common sense and reflection. The greater part of mankind are naturally apt to be affirmative and dogmatical in their opinions; and while they see objects only on one side, and have no idea of any counterpoising argument, they throw themselves precipitately into the principles, to which they are inclined; nor have they any indulgence for those who entertain opposite sentiments. To hesitate or balance perplexes their understanding, checks their passion, and suspends their action. They are, therefore, impatient till they escape from a state, which to them is so uneasy; and they think, that they can never remove themselves far enough from it, by the violence of

their affirmations and obstinacy of their belief. But could such dogmatical reasoners become sensible of the strange infirmities of human understanding, even in its most perfect state, and when most accurate and cautious in its determinations; such a reflection would naturally inspire them with more modesty and reserve, and diminish their fond opinion of themselves, and their prejudice against antagonists. The illiterate may reflect on the disposition of the learned, who, amidst all the advantages of study and reflection, are commonly still diffident in their determinations: And if any of the learned be inclined, from their natural temper, to haughtiness and obstinacy, a small tincture of Pyrrhonism might abate their pride, by showing them, that the few advantages, which they may have attained over their fellows, are but inconsiderable, if compared with the universal perplexity and confusion, which is inherent in human nature. In general, there is a degree of doubt, and caution, and modesty, which, in all kinds of scrutiny and decision, ought for ever to accompany a just reasoner.

Another species of mitigated scepticism, which may be of advantage to mankind, and which may be the natural result of the Pyrrhonian doubts and scruples, is the limitation of our enquiries to such subjects as are best adapted to the narrow capacity of human understanding. The imagination of man is naturally sublime, delighted with whatever is remote and extraordinary, and running, without control, into the most distant parts of space and time in order to avoid the objects, which custom has rendered too familiar to it. A correct Judgment observes a contrary method, and avoiding all distant and high enquiries, confines itself to common life, and to such subjects as fall under daily practice and experience; leaving the more sublime topics to the embellishment of poets and orators, or to the arts of priests and politicians. To bring us to so salutary a determination, nothing can be more serviceable, than to be once thoroughly convinced of the force of the Pyrrhonian doubt, and of the impossibility, that any thing, but the strong power of natural instinct, could free us from it. Those who have a propensity to philosophy, will still continue their researches; because they reflect, that, besides the immediate pleasure, attending such an occupation, philosophical decisions are nothing but the reflections of common life, methodized and corrected. But they will never be tempted to go beyond common life, so long as they consider the imperfection of those faculties which they employ, their narrow reach, and their inaccurate operations. While we cannot give a satisfactory reason, why we believe, after a thousand experiments, that a stone will fall, or fire burn; can we ever satisfy ourselves concerning any determination, which we may form, with regard to the origin of worlds, and the situation of nature, from, and to eternity?

This narrow limitation, indeed, of our enquiries, is, in every respect, so reasonable, that it suffices to make the slightest examination into the natural powers of the human mind and to compare them with their objects, in order to recommend it to us. We shall then find what are the proper subjects of science and enquiry.

It seems to me, that the only objects of the abstract sciences or of demonstration are quantity and number, and that all attempts to extend this more perfect species of knowledge beyond these bounds are mere sophistry and illusion. As the component parts of quantity and number are entirely similar, their relations become intricate and involved; and nothing can be more curious, as well as useful, than to trace, by a variety of mediums, their equality or inequality, through their different appearances. But as all other ideas are clearly distinct and different from each other, we can never advance farther, by our utmost scrutiny, than to observe this diversity, and, by an obvious reflection, pronounce one thing not to be another. Or if there be any difficulty in these decisions, it proceeds entirely from the undeterminate meaning of words, which is corrected by juster definitions. That the square of the hypothenuse is equal to the squares of the other two sides, cannot be known, let the terms be ever so exactly defined, without a train of reasoning and enquiry. But to convince us of this proposition, that where there is no property, there can be no injustice, it is only necessary to define the terms, and explain injustice to be a violation of property. This proposition is, indeed, nothing but a more imperfect definition. It is the same case with all those pretended syllogistical reasonings, which may be found in every other branch of learning, except the sciences of quantity and number; and these may safely,

I think, be pronounced the only proper objects of knowledge and demonstration.

All other enquiries of men regard only matter of fact and existence; and these are evidently incapable of demonstration. Whatever is may not be. No negation of a fact can involve a contradiction. The nonexistence of any being, without exception, is as clear and distinct an idea as its existence. The proposition, which affirms it not to be, however false, is no less conceivable and intelligible, than that which affirms it to be. The case is different with the sciences, properly so called. Every proposition, which is not true, is there confused and unintelligible. That the cube root of 64 is equal to the half of 10, is a false proposition, and can never be distinctly conceived. But that Caesar, or the angel Gabriel, or any being never existed, may be a false proposition, but still is perfectly conceivable, and implies no contradiction.

The existence, therefore, of any being can only be proved by arguments from its cause or its effect; and these arguments are founded entirely on experience. If we reason a priori, any thing may appear able to produce any thing. The falling of a pebble may, for aught we know, extinguish the sun; or the wish of a man control the planets in their orbits. It is only experience, which teaches us the nature and bounds of cause and effect, and enables us to infer the existence of one object from that of another. Such is the foundation of moral reasoning, which forms the greater part of human knowledge, and is the source of all human action and behavior.

Moral reasonings are either concerning particular or general facts. All deliberations in life regard the former; as also all disquisitions in history, chronology, geography, and astronomy.

The sciences, which treat of general facts, are politics, natural philosophy, physic, chemistry, &c. where the qualities, causes and effects of a whole species of objects are enquired into.

Divinity or Theology, as it proves the existence of a Deity, and the immortality of souls, is composed partly of reasonings concerning particular, partly concerning general facts. It has a foundation in reason, so far as it is supported by experience. But its best and most solid foundation is faith and divine revelation.

Morals and criticism are not so properly objects of the understanding as of taste and sentiment. Beauty, whether moral or natural, is felt, more properly than perceived. Or if we reason concerning it, and endeavor to fix its standard, we regard a new fact, to wit, the general taste of mankind, or some such fact, which may be the object of reasoning and enquiry.

When we run over libraries, persuaded of these principles, what havoc must we make? If we take in our hand any volume; of divinity or school metaphysics, for instance; let us ask, Does it contain any abstract reasoning concerning quantity or number? No. Does it contain any experimental reasoning concerning matter of fact and existence? No. Commit it then to the flames: For it can contain nothing but sophistry and illusion.

TREATISE ON HUMAN NATURE

BOOK I: PART IV

SECTION VI: OF PERSONAL IDENTITY

There are some philosophers who imagine we are every moment intimately conscious of what we call our self; that we feel its existence and its continuance in existence; and are certain, beyond the evidence of a demonstration, both of its perfect identity and simplicity. The strongest sensation, the most violent passion, say they, instead of distracting us from this view, only fix it the more intensely, and make us consider their influence on self either by their pain or pleasure. To attempt a further proof of this were to weaken its evidence; since no proof can be derived from any fact of which we are so intimately conscious; nor is there any thing of which we can be certain if we doubt of this.

Unluckily all these positive assertions are contrary to that very experience which is pleaded for them; nor have we any idea of self, after the manner it is here explained. For, from what impression could this idea be derived? This question it is impossible to answer without a manifest contradiction and absurdity; and yet it is a question which must necessarily be answered, if we would have the idea of self pass for clear and intelligible. It must be some one impression that gives rise to every real idea. But self or person is not any one impression, but that to which our several impressions and ideas are supposed to have a reference. If any impression gives rise to the idea of self, that impression must continue invariably the same, through the whole course of our lives; since self is supposed to exist after that manner. But there is no impression constant and invariable. Pain and pleasure, grief and joy, passions and sensations succeed each other, and never all exist at the same time. It cannot therefore be from any of these impressions, or from any other, that the idea of self is derived; and consequently there is no such idea.

But further, what must become of all our particular perceptions upon this hypothesis? All these are different, and distinguishable, and separable from each other, and may be separately considered, and may exist separately, and have no need of any thing to support their existence. After what manner therefore do they belong to self, and how are they connected with it? For my part, when I enter most intimately into what I call myself, I always stumble on some particular perception or other, of heat or cold, light or shade, love or hatred, pain or pleasure. I never can catch myself at any time without a perception, and never can observe any thing but the perception. When my perceptions are removed for any time, as by sound sleep, so long am I insensible of myself, and may truly be said not to exist. And were all my perceptions removed by death, and could I neither think, nor feel, nor see, nor love, nor hate, after the dissolution of my body, I should be entirely annihilated, nor do I conceive what is further requisite to make me a perfect nonentity. If any one, upon serious and unprejudiced reflection, thinks he has a different notion of himself, I must confess I can reason no longer with him. All I can allow him is, that he may be in the right as well as I, and that we are essentially different in this particular. He may, perhaps, perceive something simple and continued, which he calls himself; though I am certain there is no such principle in me.

But setting aside some metaphysicians of this kind, I may venture to affirm of the rest of mankind, that they are nothing but a bundle or collection of different perceptions, which succeed each other with an inconceivable rapidity, and are in a perpetual flux and movement. Our eyes cannot turn in their sockets without varying our perceptions. Our thought is still more variable than our sight; and all our other senses and faculties contribute to this change: nor is there any single power of the soul, which remains unalterably the same, perhaps for one moment. The mind is a kind of theatre, where several perceptions successively make their appearance; pass, repass, glide away, and mingle in an infinite variety of postures and situations. There is properly no simplicity in it at one time, nor identity in different, whatever natural propension we may have to imagine that simplicity and identity. The comparison of the theatre must not mislead us. They are the successive perceptions only, that constitute the mind; nor have we the most distant notion of the place where these scenes are represented, or of the materials of which it is composed.

What then gives us so great a propension to ascribe an identity to these successive perceptions, and to suppose ourselves possessed of an invariable and uninterrupted existence through the whole course of our lives? In order to answer this question we must distinguish betwixt personal identity, as it regards our thought or imagination, and as it regards our passions or the concern we take in ourselves. The first is our present subject; and to explain it perfectly we must take the matter pretty deep, and account for that identity, which we attribute to plants and animals; there being a great analogy betwixt it and the identity of a self or person.

We have a distinct idea of an object that remains invariable and uninterrupted through a supposed variation of time; and this idea we call that of identity or sameness. We have also a distinct idea of several different objects existing in succession, and connected together by a close relation; and this to an accurate view affords as perfect a notion of diversity as if there was no manner of relation among the objects. But though these two ideas of identity, and a succession of related objects, be in themselves perfectly distinct, and even contrary, yet it is certain that, in our common way of thinking, they are generally confounded with each other. That action of the imagination, by which we consider the uninterrupted and invariable object, and that by which we reflect on the succession of related objects, are almost the same to the feeling; nor is there much more effort of thought required in the latter case than in the former. The relation facilitates the transition of the mind from one object to another, and renders its passage as smooth as if it contemplated one continued object. This resemblance is the cause of the confusion and mistake, and makes us substitute the notion of identity, instead of that of related objects. However at one instant we may consider the related succession as variable or interrupted, we are sure the next to ascribe to it a perfect identity, and regard it as invariable and uninterrupted. Our propensity to this mistake is so great from the resemblance above mentioned, that we fall into it before we are aware; and though we incessantly correct ourselves by reflection, and return to a more accurate method of thinking, yet we cannot long sustain our philosophy, or take off this biass from the imagination. Our last resource is to yield to it, and boldly assert that these different related objects are in effect the same, however interrupted and variable. In order to justify to ourselves this absurdity, we often feign some new and unintelligible principle, that connects the objects together, and prevents their interruption or variation. Thus we feign the continued existence of the perceptions of our senses, to remove the interruption; and run into the notion of a soul, and self, and substance, to disguise the variation. But, we may further observe, that where we do not give rise to such a fiction, our propension to confound identity with relation is so great, that we are apt to imagine something unknown and mysterious, connecting the parts, beside their relation; and this I take to be the case with regard to the identity we ascribe to plants and vegetables. And even when this does not take place, we still feel a propensity to confound these ideas, though we are not able fully to satisfy ourselves in that particular, nor find any thing invariable and uninterrupted to justify our notion of identity. Thus the controversy concerning identity is not merely a dispute of words. For when we attribute identity, in an improper sense, to variable or interrupted objects, our mistake is not confined to the expression, but is commonly attended with a fiction, either of something invariable and uninterrupted, or of something mysterious and inexplicable, or at least with a propensity to such fictions. What will suffice to prove this hypothesis to the satisfaction of every fair enquirer, is to shew, from daily experience and observation, that the objects which are variable or interrupted, and yet are supposed to continue the same, are such only as consist of a succession of parts, connected together by resemblance, contiguity, or causation. For as such a succession answers evidently to our notion of diversity, it can only be by mistake we ascribe to it an identity; and as the relation of parts, which leads us into this mistake, is really nothing but a quality, which produces an association of ideas, and an easy transition of the imagination from one to another, it can only be from the resemblance, which this act of the mind bears to that by which we contemplate one continued object, that the error arises. Our chief business, then, must be to prove, that all objects, to which we ascribe identity, without observing their invariableness and uninterruptedness, are such as consist of a succession of related objects.

In order to do this, suppose any mass of matter, of which the parts are contiguous and connected, to be placed before us; it is plain we must attribute a perfect identity to this mass, provided all the parts continue uninterruptedly and invariably the same, whatever motion or change of place we may observe either in the whole or in any of the parts. But supposing some very small or inconsiderable part to be added to the mass, or subtracted from it; though this absolutely destroys the identity of the whole, strictly speaking, yet as we seldom think so accurately, we scruple not to pronounce a mass of matter the same, where we find so trivial an alteration. The passage of the thought from the object before the change to the object after it, is so smooth and easy, that we scarce perceive the transition, and are apt to imagine, that it is nothing but a continued survey of the same object.

There is a very remarkable circumstance that attends this experiment; which is, that though the change of any considerable part in a mass of matter destroys the identity of the whole, yet we must measure the greatness of the part, not absolutely, but by its proportion to the whole. The addition or diminution of a mountain would not be sufficient to produce a diversity in a planet; though the change of a very few inches would be able to destroy the identity of some bodies. It will be impossible to account for this, but by reflecting that objects operate upon the mind, and break or interrupt the continuity of its actions, not according to their real greatness, but according to their proportion to each other; and therefore, since this interruption makes an object cease to appear the same, it must be the uninterrupted progress of the thought which constitutes the imperfect identity.

This may be confirmed by another phenomenon. A change in any considerable part of a body destroys its identity; but it is remarkable, that where the change is produced gradually and insensibly, we are less apt to ascribe to it the same effect. The reason can plainly be no other, than that the mind, in following the successive changes of the body, feels an easy passage from the surveying its condition in one moment, to the viewing of it in another, and at no particular time perceives any interruption in its actions. From which continued perception, it ascribes a continued existence and identity to the object.

But whatever precaution we may use in introducing the changes gradually, and making them proportionable to the whole, it is certain, that where the changes are at last observed to become considerable, we make a scruple of ascribing identity to such different objects. There is, however, another artifice, by which we may induce the imagination to advance a step further; and that is, by producing a reference of the parts to each other, and a combination to some common end or purpose. A ship, of which a considerable part has been changed by frequent reparations, is still considered as the same; nor does the difference of the materials hinder us from ascribing an identity to it. The common end, in which the parts conspire, is the same under all their variations, and affords an easy transition of the imagination from one situation of the body to another.

But this is still more remarkable, when we add a sympathy of parts to their common end, and suppose that they bear to each other the reciprocal relation of cause and effect in all their actions and operations. This is the case with all animals and vegetables; where not only the several parts have a reference to some general purpose, but also a mutual dependence on, and connexion with, each other. The effect of so strong a relation is, that though every one must allow, that in a very few years both vegetables and animals endure a total change, yet we still attribute identity to them, while their form, size, and substance, are entirely altered. An oak that grows from a small plant to a large tree is still the same oak, though there be not one particle of matter or figure of its parts the same. An infant becomes a man, and is sometimes fat, sometimes lean, without any change in his identity.

We may also consider the two following phenomena, which are remarkable in their kind. The first is, that though we commonly be able to distinguish pretty exactly betwixt numerical and specific identity, yet it sometimes happens that we confound them, and in our thinking and reasoning employ the one for the other. Thus, a man who hears a noise that is frequently interrupted and renewed, says it is still the same noise, though it is evident the sounds have only a specific identity or resemblance, and there is nothing numerically the same but the cause which produced them. In like manner it may be said, without breach of the propriety of language, that such a church, which was formerly of brick, fell to ruin, and that the parish rebuilt the same church of freestone, and according to modern architecture. Here neither the form nor materials are the same, nor is there any thing common to the two objects but their relation to the inhabitants of the parish; and yet this alone is sufficient to make us denominate them the same. But we must observe, that in these cases the first object is in a manner annihilated before the second comes into existence; by which means, we are never presented, in any one point of time, with the idea of difference and multiplicity; and for that reason are less scrupulous in calling them the same.

Secondly, we may remark, that though, in a succession of related objects, it be in a manner requisite that the change of parts be not sudden nor entire, in order to preserve the identity, yet where the objects are in their nature changeable and inconstant, we admit of a more sudden transition than would otherwise be consistent with that relation. Thus, as the nature of a river consists in the motion and change of parts, though in less than four-and-twenty hours these be totally altered, this hinders not the river from continuing the same during several ages. What is natural and essential to any thing is, in a

manner, expected; and what is expected makes less impression, and appears of less moment than what is unusual and extraordinary. A considerable change of the former kind seems really less to the imagination than the most trivial alteration of the latter; and by breaking less the continuity of the thought, has less influence in destroying the identity.

We now proceed to explain the nature of personal identity, which has become so great a question in philosophy, especially of late years, in England, where all the abstruser sciences are studied with a peculiar ardour and application. And here it is evident the same method of reasoning must be continued which has so successfully explained the identity of plants and animals, and ships, and houses, and of all the compounded and changeable productions either of art or nature. The identity which we ascribe to the mind of man is only a fictitious one, and of a like kind with that which we ascribe to vegetables and animal bodies. It cannot therefore have a different origin, but must proceed from a like operation of the imagination upon like objects.

But lest this argument should not convince the reader, though in my opinion perfectly decisive, let him weigh the following reasoning, which is still closer and more immediate. It is evident that the identity which we attribute to the human mind, however perfect we may imagine it to be, is not able to run the several different perceptions into one, and make them lose their characters of distinction and difference which are essential to them. It is still true that every distinct perception which enters into the composition of the mind, is a distinct existence, and is different, and distinguishable, and separable from every other perception, either contemporary or successive. But as, notwithstanding this distinction and separability, we suppose the whole train of perceptions to be united by identity, a question naturally arises concerning this relation of identity, whether it be something that really binds our several perceptions together, or only associates their ideas in the imagination; that is, in other words, whether, in pronouncing concerning the identity of a person, we observe some real bond among his perceptions, or only feel one among the ideas we form of them. This question we might easily decide, if we would recollect what has been already proved at large, that the understanding never observes any real connexion among objects, and that even the union of cause and effect, when strictly examined resolves itself into a customary association of ideas. For from thence it evidently follows, that identity is nothing really belonging to these different perceptions, and uniting them together, but is merely a quality which we attribute to them, because of the union of their ideas in the imagination when we reflect upon them. Now, the only qualities which can give ideas a union in the imagination, are these three relations above mentioned. These are the uniting principles in the ideal world, and without them every distinct object is separable by the mind, and may be separately considered, and appears not to have any more connexion with any other object than if disjoined by the greatest differences and remoteness. It is therefore on some of these three relations of resemblance, contiguity, and causation, that identity depends; and as the very essence of these relations consists in their producing an easy transition of ideas, it follows that our notions of personal identity proceed entirely from the smooth and uninterrupted progress of the thought along a train of connected ideas, according to the principles above explained.

The only question, therefore, which remains is, by what relations this uninterrupted progress of our thought is produced, when we consider the successive existence of a mind or thinking person. And here it is evident we must confine ourselves to resemblance and causation, and must drop contiguity, which has little or no influence in the present case.

To begin with resemblance; suppose we could see clearly into the breast of another, and observe that succession of perceptions which constitutes his mind or thinking principle, and suppose that he always preserves the memory of a considerable part of past perceptions, it is evident that nothing could more contribute to the bestowing a relation on this succession amidst all its variations. For what is the memory but a faculty, by which we raise up the images of past perceptions? And as an image necessarily resembles its object, must not the frequent placing of these resembling perceptions in the chain of thought, convey the imagination more easily from one link to another, and make the whole seem like the continuance of one object? In this particular, then, the memory

not only discovers the identity, but also contributes to its production, by producing the relation of resemblance among the perceptions. The case is the same, whether we consider ourselves or others.

As to causation we may observe that the true idea of the human mind, is to consider it as a system of different perceptions or different existences, which are linked together by the relation of cause and effect, and mutually produce, destroy, influence, and modify each other. Our impressions give rise to their correspondent ideas; and these ideas, in their turn, produce other impressions. One thought chases another, and draws after it a third, by which it is expelled in its turn. In this respect, I cannot compare the soul more properly to any thing than to a republic or commonwealth, in which the several members are united by the reciprocal ties of government and subordination, and give rise to other persons who propagate the same republic in the incessant changes of its parts. And as the same individual republic may not only change its members, but also its laws and constitutions; in like manner the same person may vary his character and disposition, as well as his impressions and ideas, without losing his identity. Whatever changes he endures, his several parts are still connected by the relation of causation. And in this view our identity with regard to the passions serves to corroborate that with regard to the imagination, by the making our distant perceptions influence each other, and by giving us a present concern for our past or future pains or pleasures.

As memory alone acquaints us with the continuance and extent of this succession of perceptions, it is to be considered, upon that account chiefly, as the source of personal identity. Had we no memory, we never should have any notion of causation, nor consequently of that chain of causes and effects, which constitute our self or person. But having once acquired this notion of causation from the memory, we can extend the same chain of causes, and consequently the identity of our persons beyond our memory, and can comprehend times, and circumstances, and actions, which we have entirely forgot, but suppose in general to have existed. For how few of our past actions are there, of which we have any memory? Who can tell me, for instance, what were his thoughts and actions on the 1st of January 1715, the

11th of March 1719 and the 3rd of August 1733? Or will he affirm, because he has entirely forgot the incidents of these days, that the present self is not the same person with the self of that time; and by that means overturn all the most established notions of personal identity? In this view, therefore, memory does not so much produce as discover personal identity, by showing us the relation of cause and effect among our different perceptions. It will be incumbent on those who affirm that memory produces entirely our personal identity, to give a reason why we can thus extend our identity beyond our memory.

The whole of this doctrine leads us to a conclusion, which is of great importance in the present affair, viz. that all the nice and subtle questions concerning personal identity can never possibly be decided, and are to be regarded rather as grammatical than as philosophical difficulties. Identity depends on the relations of ideas; and these relations produce identity, by means of that easy transition they occasion. But as the relations, and the easiness of the transition may diminish by insensible degrees, we have no just standard by which we can decide any dispute concerning the time when they acquire or lose a title to the name of identity. All the disputes concerning the identity of connected objects are merely verbal, except so far as the relation of parts gives rise to some fiction or imaginary principle of union, as we have already observed.

What I have said concerning the first origin and uncertainty of our notion of identity, as applied to the human mind, may be extended with little or no variation to that of simplicity. An object, whose different coexistent parts are bound together by a close relation, operates upon the imagination after much the same manner as one perfectly simple and indivisible, and requires not a much greater stretch of thought in order to its conception. From this similarity of operation we attribute a simplicity to it, and feign a principle of union as the support of this simplicity, and the centre of all the different parts and qualities of the object.

Thus we have finished our examination of the several systems of philosophy, both of the intellectual and moral world; and, in our miscellaneous way of reasoning, have been led into several topics, which will either illustrate and confirm some preceding part of this discourse, or prepare the way for our following opinions. It is now time to return to a more close examination of our subject, and to proceed in the accurate anatomy of human nature, having fully explained the nature of our judgment and understanding.

BOOK II: PART III

SECTION I: OF LIBERTY AND NECESSITY

We come now to explain the *direct* passions, or the impressions which arise immediately from good or evil, from pain or pleasure. Of this kind are, *desire and aversion, grief and joy, hope and fear.*

Of all the immediate effects of pain and pleasure, there is none more remarkable than the *will;* and though, properly speaking, it be not comprehended among the passions, yet, as the full understanding of its nature and properties is necessary to the explanation of them, we shall here make it the subject of our inquiry. I desire it may be observed, that, by the *will,* I mean nothing but *the internal impression we feel, and are conscious of, when we knowingly give rise to any new motion of our body, or new perception of our mind.* This impression, like the preceding ones of pride and humility, love and hatred, it is impossible to define, and needless to describe any further; for which reason we shall cut off all those definitions and distinctions with which philosophers are wont to perplex rather than clear up this question; and entering at first upon the subject, shall examine that long-disputed question concerning *liberty and necessity,* which occurs so naturally in treating of the will.

It is universally acknowledged that the operations of external bodies are necessary; and that, in the communication of their motion, in their attraction, and mutual cohesion, there are not the least traces of indifference or liberty. Every object is determined by an absolute fate to a certain degree and direction of its motion, and can no more depart from that precise line in which it moves, than it can convert itself into an angel, or spirit, or any superior substance. The actions therefore, of matter, are to be regarded as instances of necessary actions; and whatever is, in this respect, on the same footing with matter, must be acknowledged to be necessary. That we may know whether this be the case with the actions of the mind, we shall begin with examining matter, and considering on what the idea of a necessity in its operations are founded, and why we conclude one body or action to be the infallible cause of another.

It has been observed already, that in no single instance the ultimate connection of any objects is discoverable either by our senses or reason, and that we can never penetrate so far into the essence and construction of bodies, as to perceive the principle on which their mutual influence depends. It is their constant union alone with which we are acquainted; and it is from the constant union the necessity arises. If objects had not an uniform and regular conjunction with each other, we should never arrive at any idea of cause and effect; and even after all, the necessity which enters into that idea, is nothing but a determination of the mind to pass from one object to its usual attendant, and infer the existence of one from that of the other. Here then are two particulars which we are to consider as essential to necessity, viz. the constant *union* and the *inference* of the mind; and wherever we discover these, we must acknowledge a necessity. As the actions of matter have no necessity but what is derived from these circumstances, and it is not by any insight into the essence of bodies we discover their connection, the absence of this insight, while the union and inference remain, will never, in any case, remove the necessity. It is the observation of the union which produces the inference; for which reason it might be thought sufficient, if we prove a constant union in the actions of the mind, in order to establish the inference along with the necessity of these actions. But that I may bestow a greater force on my reasoning, I shall examine these particulars apart, and shall first prove from experience that our actions have a constant union with out motives, tempers, and circumstances, before I consider the inferences we draw from it.

To this end a very slight and general view of the common course of human affairs will be sufficient. There is no light in which we can take them that does not confirm this principle. Whether we consider mankind according to the difference of sexes, ages, governments, conditions, or methods of education; the same uniformity and regular operation of natural principles are discernible. Like causes still produce like effects; in the same manner as in the mutual action of the elements and powers of nature.

There are different trees which regularly produce fruit, whose relish is different from each other; and this regularity will be admitted as an instance of necessity and causes in external bodies. But are the products of Guienne and of Champagne more regularly different than the sentiments, actions, and passions of the two sexes, of which the one are distinguished by their force and maturity, the other by their delicacy and softness?

Are the changes of our body from infancy to old age more regular and certain than those of our mind and conduct? And would a man be more ridiculous, who would expect that an infant of four years old will raise a weight of three hundred pounds, than one who, from a person of the same age, would look for a philosophical reasoning, or a prudent and well concerted action?

We must certainly allow, that the cohesion of the parts of matter arises from natural and necessary principles, whatever difficulty we may find in explaining them: and for a like reason we must allow, that human society is founded on like principles; and our reason in the latter case is better than even that in the former; because we not only observe that men *always* seek society, but can also explain the principles on which this universal propensity is founded. For is it more certain that two flat pieces of marble will unite together, than two young savages of different sexes will copulate? Do the children arise from this copulation more uniformly, than does the parents' care for their safety and preservation? And after they have arrived at years of discretion by the care of their parents, are the inconveniences attending their separation more certain than their foresight of these inconveniences, and their care of avoiding them by a close union and confederacy?

The skin, pores, muscles, and nerves of a day-labourer, are different from those of a man of quality; so are his sentiments, actions, and manners. The different stations of life influence the whole fabric, external arid internal; and these different stations arise necessarily, because uniformly, from the necessary and uniform principles of human nature.

Men cannot live without society, and cannot be associated without government. Government makes a distinction of property, and establishes the different ranks of men. This produces industry, traffic, manufactures, lawsuits, war, leagues, alliances, voyages, travels, cities, fleets, ports, and all those other actions and objects which cause such a diversity, and at the same time maintain such an uniformity in human life.

Should a traveller, returning from a far country, tell us, that he had seen a climate in the fiftieth degree of northern latitude, where all the fruits ripen and come to perfection in the winter, and decay in the summer, after the same manner as in England they are produced and decay in the contrary seasons, he would find few so credulous as to believe him. I am apt to think a traveller would meet with as little credit, who should inform us of people exactly of the same character with those in Plato's republic on the one hand, or those in Hobbes's *Leviathan* on the other. There is a general course of nature in human actions, as well as in the operations of the sun and the climate. There are also characters peculiar to different nations and particular persons, as well as common to mankind. The knowledge of these characters is founded on the observation of an uniformity in the actions that flow from them; and this uniformity forms the very essence of necessity.

I can imagine only one way of eluding this argument, which is by denying that uniformity of human actions, on which it is founded. As long as actions have a constant union and connection with the situation and temper of the agent, however we may in words refuse to acknowledge the necessity, we really allow the thing. Now, some may perhaps find a pretext to deny this regular union and connection. For what is more capricious than human actions? What more inconstant than the desires of man? And what creature departs more widely, not only from right reason, but from his own character and disposition? An hour, a moment is sufficient to make him change from one extreme to another, and overturn what cost the greatest pain and labour to establish. Necessity is regular and certain. Human conduct is irregular and uncertain. The one therefore proceeds not from the other.

To this I reply, that in judging of the actions of men we must proceed upon the same maxims, as when we reason concerning external objects. When any phenomena are constantly and invariably conjoined together, they acquire such a connection in the imagination, that it passes from one to the other without any doubt or hesitation. But below this there are many inferior degrees of evidence and probability, nor does one single contrariety of experiment entirely destroy all our reasoning. The mind balances the contrary experiments, and, deducting the inferior from the superior, proceeds with that degree of assurance or evidence, which remains. Even when these contrary experiments are entirely equal, we remove not the notion of causes and necessity; but, supposing that the usual contrariety proceeds from the operation of contrary and concealed causes, we conclude, that the chance or indifference lies only in our judgment on account of our imperfect knowledge, not in the things themselves, which are in every case equally necessary, though, to appearance, not equally constant or certain. No union can be more constant and certain than that of some actions with some motives and characters; and if, in other cases, the union is uncertain, it is no more than what happens in the operations of body; nor can we conclude anything from the one irregularity which will not follow equally from the other.

It is commonly allowed that madmen have no liberty. But, were we to judge by their actions, these have less regularity and constancy than the actions of wise men, and consequently are further removed from necessity. Our way of thinking in this particular is, therefore, absolutely inconsistent; but is a natural consequence of these confused ideas and undefined terms, which we so commonly make use of in our reasonings, especially on the present subject.

We must now show, that, as the *union* betwixt motives and actions has the same constancy as that in any natural operations, so its influence on the understanding is also the same in *determining* us to infer the existence of one from that of another. If this shall appear, there is no known circumstance that enters into the connection and production of the actions of matter that is not to be found in all the operations of the mind; and consequently we cannot, without a manifest absurdity, attribute necessity to the one, and refuse it to the other.

There is no philosopher, whose judgment is so riveted to this fantastical system of liberty, as not to acknowledge the force of *moral evidence*, and both in speculation and practice proceed upon it as upon a reasonable foundation. Now, moral evidence is nothing but a conclusion concerning the actions of men, derived from the consideration of their motives, temper, and situation. Thus, when we see certain characters or figures described upon paper, we infer that the person who produced them would affirm such facts, the death of Cæsar, the success of Augustus, the cruelty of Nero; and, remembering many other concurrent testimonies, we conclude that those facts were once really existent, and that so many men, without any interest, would never conspire to deceive us; especially since they must, in the attempt, expose themselves to the derision of all their contemporaries, when these facts were asserted to be recently and universally known. The same kind of reasoning runs through politics, war, commerce, economy, and indeed mixes itself so entirely in human life, that it is impossible to act or subsist a moment without having recourse to it. A prince who imposes a tax upon his subjects, expects their compliance. A general who conducts an army, makes account of a certain degree of courage. A merchant looks for fidelity and skill in his factor or supercargo. A man who gives orders for his dinner, doubts not of the obedience of his servants. In short, as nothing more nearly interests us than our own actions and those of others, the greatest part of our reasonings is employed in judgments concerning them. Now I assert, that whoever reasons after this manner, does *ipso facto* believe the actions of the will to arise from necessity, and that he knows not what he means when he denies it.

All those objects, of which we call the one *cause* and the other *effect*, considered in themselves, are as distinct and separate from each other as any two things in nature; nor can we ever, by the most accurate survey of them, infer the existence of the one from that of the other. It is only from experience and the observation of their constant union, that we are able to form this inference; and even after all, the inference is nothing but the effects of custom on the imagination. We must not here be content with saying, that the idea of cause and effect arises from objects constantly united; but must affirm, that it is the very same with the idea of these objects, and that the

necessary connection is not discovered by a conclusion of the understanding, but is merely a perception of the mind. Wherever, therefore, we observe the same union, and wherever the union operates in the same manner upon the belief and opinion, we have the idea of cause and necessity, though perhaps we may avoid those expressions. Motion in one body, in all past instances that have fallen under our observation, is followed upon impulse by motion in another. It is impossible for the mind to penetrate further. From this constant union it *forms* the idea of cause and effect, and by its influence *feels* the necessity. As there is the same constancy, and the same influence, in what we call moral evidence, I ask no more. What remains can only be a dispute of words.

And indeed, when we consider how aptly *natural* and *moral* evidence cement together, and form only one chain of argument betwixt them, we shall make no scruple to allow, that they are of the same nature, and derived from the same principles. A prisoner, who has neither money nor interest discovers the impossibility of his escape, as well from the obstinacy of the gaoler, as from the walls and bars with which he is surrounded; and in all attempts for his freedom, chooses rather to work upon the stone and iron of the one, than upon the inflexible nature of the other. The same prisoner, when conducted to the scaffold, forsees his death as certainly from the constancy and fidelity of his guards, as from the operation of the axe or wheel. His mind runs along a certain train of ideas: the refusal of the soldiers to consent to his escape; the action of the executioner; the separation of the head and body, bleeding, convulsive motions, and death. Here is a connected chain of natural causes and voluntary actions; but the mind feels no difference betwixt them in passing from one link to another; nor is less certain of the future event than if it were connected with the present impressions of the memory and senses by a train of causes cemented together by what we are pleased to call a *physical necessity*. The same experienced union has the same effect on the mind, whether the united objects be motives, volitions, and actions, or figure and motion. We may change the names of things, but their nature and their operation on the understanding never change.

I dare be positive no one will ever endeavour to refute these reasonings otherwise than by altering my definitions, and assigning a different meaning to the terms of *cause, and effect, and necessity, and liberty, and chance.* According to my definitions, necessity makes an essential part of causation; and consequently liberty, by removing necessity, removes all causes, and is the very same thing with chance. As chance is commonly thought to imply a contradiction, and is at least directly contrary to experience, there are always the same arguments against liberty or free-will. If any one alters the definitions, I cannot pretend to argue with him till I know the meaning he assigns to these terms.

DIALOGUES CONCERNING NATURAL RELIGION

PAMPHILUS TO HERMIPPUS

It has been remarked, my Hermippus, that though the ancient philosophers conveyed most of their instruction in the form of dialogue, this method of composition has been little practiced in later ages, and has seldom succeeded in the hands of those who have attempted it. Accurate and regular argument, indeed, such as is now expected of philosophical enquirers, naturally throws a man into the methodical and didactic manner; where he can immediately, without preparation, explain the point at which he aims; and thence proceed, without interruption, to deduce the proofs on which it is established. To deliver a SYSTEM in conversation, scarcely appears natural; and while the dialogue-writer desires, by departing from the direct style of composition, to give a freer air to his performance, and avoid the appearance of Author and Reader, he is apt to run into a worse inconvenience, and convey the image of Pedagogue and Pupil. Or, if he carries on the dispute in the natural spirit of good company, by throwing in a variety of topics, and preserving a proper balance among the speakers, he often loses so much time in preparations and transitions, that the reader will scarcely think himself compensated, by all the graces of dialogue, for the order, brevity, and precision, which are sacrificed to them.

There are some subjects, however, to which dialogue-writing is peculiarly adapted, and where it is still preferable to the direct and simple method of composition.

Any point of doctrine, which is so obvious that it scarcely admits of dispute, but at the same time so important that it cannot be too often inculcated, seems to require some such method of handling it; where the novelty of the manner may compensate the triteness of the subject; where the vivacity of conversation may enforce the precept; and where the variety of lights, presented by various personages and characters, may appear neither tedious nor redundant.

Any question of philosophy, on the other hand, which is so obscure and uncertain, that human reason can reach no fixed determination with regard to it; if it should be treated at all, seems to lead us naturally into the style of dialogue and conversation. Reasonable men may be allowed to differ, where no one can reasonably be positive. Opposite sentiments, even without any decision, afford an agreeable amusement; and if the subject be curious and interesting, the book carries us, in a manner, into company; and unites the two greatest and purest pleasures of human life, study and society.

Happily, these circumstances are all to be found in the subject of NATURAL RELIGION. What truth so obvious, so certain, as the being of a God, which the most ignorant ages have acknowledged, for which the most refined geniuses have ambitiously striven to produce new proofs and arguments? What truth so important as this, which is the ground of all our hopes, the surest foundation of morality, the firmest support of society, and the only principle which ought never to be a moment absent from our

Reprinted from *An Enquiry Concerning Human Understanding*, ed. Peter Millican, 2008. By permission of Oxford University Press, Inc.

thoughts and meditations? But, in treating of this obvious and important truth, what obscure questions occur concerning the nature of that Divine Being, his attributes, his decrees, his plan of providence? These have been always subjected to the disputations of men; concerning these human reason has not reached any certain determination. But these are topics so interesting, that we cannot restrain our restless enquiry with regard to them; though nothing but doubt, uncertainty, and contradiction, have as yet been the result of our most accurate researches.

This I had lately occasion to observe, while I passed, as usual, part of the summer season with Cleanthes, and was present at those conversations of his with Philo and Demea, of which I gave you lately some imperfect account. Your curiosity, you then told me, was so excited, that I must, of necessity, enter into a more exact detail of their reasonings, and display those various systems which they advanced with regard to so delicate a subject as that of natural religion. The remarkable contrast in their characters still further raised your expectations; while you opposed the accurate philosophical turn of Cleanthes to the careless scepticism of Philo, or compared either of their dispositions with the rigid inflexible orthodoxy of Demea. My youth rendered me a mere auditor of their disputes; and that curiosity, natural to the early season of life, has so deeply imprinted in my memory the whole chain and connexion of their arguments, that, I hope, I shall not omit or confound any considerable part of them in the recital.

PART I

After I joined the company, whom I found sitting in Cleanthes's library, Demea paid Cleanthes some compliments on the great care which he took of my education, and on his unwearied perseverance and constancy in all his friendships. The father of Pamphilus, said he, was your intimate friend: The son is your pupil; and may indeed be regarded as your adopted son, were we to judge by the pains which you bestow in conveying to him every useful branch of literature and science. You are no more wanting, I am persuaded, in prudence, than in industry. I shall, therefore, communicate to you a maxim, which I have observed with regard to my own children, that

I may learn how far it agrees with your practice. The method I follow in their education is founded on the saying of an ancient, "That students of philosophy ought first to learn logics, then ethics, next physics, last of all the nature of the gods." This science of natural theology, according to him, being the most profound and abstruse of any, required the maturest judgment in its students; and none but a mind enriched with all the other sciences, can safely be intrusted with it.

Are you so late, says Philo, in teaching your children the principles of religion? Is there no danger of their neglecting, or rejecting altogether those opinions of which they have heard so little during the whole course of their education? It is only as a science, replied Demea, subjected to human reasoning and disputation, that I postpone the study of Natural Theology. To season their minds with early piety, is my chief care; and by continual precept and instruction, and I hope too by example, I imprint deeply on their tender minds an habitual reverence for all the principles of religion. While they pass through every other science, I still remark the uncertainty of each part; the eternal disputations of men; the obscurity of all philosophy; and the strange, ridiculous conclusions, which some of the greatest geniuses have derived from the principles of mere human reason. Having thus tamed their mind to a proper submission and self-diffidence, I have no longer any scruple of opening to them the greatest mysteries of religion; nor apprehend any danger from that assuming arrogance of philosophy, which may lead them to reject the most established doctrines and opinions.

Your precaution, says Philo, of seasoning your children's minds early with piety, is certainly very reasonable; and no more than is requisite in this profane and irreligious age. But what I chiefly admire in your plan of education, is your method of drawing advantage from the very principles of philosophy and learning, which, by inspiring pride and self-sufficiency, have commonly, in all ages, been found so destructive to the principles of religion. The vulgar, indeed, we may remark, who are unacquainted with science and profound enquiry, observing the endless disputes of the learned, have commonly a thorough contempt for philosophy; and rivet themselves the faster, by that means, in the great points of theology which have been taught them. Those who enter a little into study and enquiry, finding many appearances of evidence in doctrines the newest and most extraordinary, think nothing too difficult for human reason; and, presumptuously breaking through all fences, profane the inmost sanctuaries of the temple. But Cleanthes will, I hope, agree with me, that, after we have abandoned ignorance, the surest remedy, there is still one expedient left to prevent this profane liberty. Let Demea's principles be improved and cultivated: let us become thoroughly sensible of the weakness, blindness, and narrow limits of human reason: let us duly consider its uncertainty and endless contrarieties, even in subjects of common life and practice: let the errors and deceits of our very senses be set before us; the insuperable difficulties which attend first principles in all systems; the contradictions which adhere to the very ideas of matter, cause and effect, extension, space, time, motion; and in a word, quantity of all kinds, the object of the only science that can fairly pretend to any certainty or evidence. When these topics are displayed in their full light, as they are by some philosophers and almost all divines; who can retain such confidence in this frail faculty of reason as to pay any regard to its determinations in points so sublime, so abstruse, so remote from common life and experience? When the coherence of the parts of a stone, or even that composition of parts which renders it extended; when these familiar objects, I say, are so inexplicable, and contain circumstances so repugnant and contradictory; with what assurance can we decide concerning the origin of worlds, or trace their history from eternity to eternity?

While Philo pronounced these words, I could observe a smile in the countenance both of Demea and Cleanthes. That of Demea seemed to imply an unreserved satisfaction in the doctrines delivered: but, in Cleanthes's features, I could distinguish an air of finesse; as if he perceived some raillery or artificial malice in the reasonings of Philo.

You propose then, Philo, said Cleanthes, to erect religious faith on philosophical scepticism; and you think, that if certainty or evidence be expelled from every other subject of enquiry, it will all retire to these theological doctrines, and there acquire a superior force and authority. Whether your scepticism be as absolute and sincere as you pretend, we shall learn by and by, when the company breaks up: we shall then see, whether you go out at the door or the window; and whether you really doubt if your body has gravity, or can be injured by its fall; according to popular opinion, derived from our fallacious senses, and more fallacious experience. And this consideration, Demea, may, I think, fairly serve to abate our ill-will to this humourous sect of the sceptics. If they be thoroughly in earnest, they will not long trouble the world with their doubts, cavils, and disputes: if they be only in jest, they are, perhaps, bad railers; but can never be very dangerous, either to the state, to philosophy, or to religion.

In reality, Philo, continued he, it seems certain, that though a man, in a flush of humour, after intense reflection on the many contradictions and imperfections of human reason, may entirely renounce all belief and opinion, it is impossible for him to persevere in this total scepticism, or make it appear in his conduct for a few hours. External objects press in upon him; passions solicit him; his philosophical melancholy dissipates; and even the utmost violence upon his own temper will not be able, during any time, to preserve the poor appearance of scepticism. And for what reason impose on himself such a violence? This is a point in which it will be impossible for him ever to satisfy himself, consistently with his sceptical principles. So that, upon the whole, nothing could be more ridiculous than the principles of the ancient Pyrrhonians; if in reality they endeavoured, as is pretended, to extend, throughout, the same scepticism which they had learned from the declamations of their schools, and which they ought to have confined to them.

In this view, there appears a great resemblance between the sects of the Stoics and Pyrrhonians, though perpetual antagonists; and both of them seem founded on this erroneous maxim, That what a man can perform sometimes, and in some dispositions, he can perform always, and in every disposition. When the mind, by Stoical reflections, is elevated into a sublime enthusiasm of virtue, and strongly smit with any species of honour or public good, the utmost bodily pain and sufferings will not prevail over such a high sense of duty; and it is possible, perhaps, by its means, even to smile and exult in the midst of tortures. If this sometimes may be the case in fact and reality, much more may a philosopher, in his school, or even in his closet, work himself up to such an enthusiasm, and support in imagination the acutest pain or most calamitous event which he can possibly conceive. But how shall he support this enthusiasm itself? The bent of his mind relaxes, and cannot be recalled at pleasure; avocations lead him astray; misfortunes attack him unawares; and the philosopher sinks by degrees into the plebeian.

I allow of your comparison between the Stoics and Sceptics, replied Philo. But you may observe, at the same time, that though the mind cannot, in Stoicism, support the highest flights of philosophy, yet, even when it sinks lower, it still retains somewhat of its former disposition; and the effects of the Stoic's reasoning will appear in his conduct in common life, and through the whole tenor of his actions. The ancient schools, particularly that of Zeno, produced examples of virtue and constancy which seem astonishing to present times.

Vain Wisdom all and false Philosophy.
Yet with a pleasing sorcery could charm
Pain, for a while, or anguish; and excite
Fallacious Hope, or arm the obdurate breast
With stubborn Patience, as with triple steel.

In like manner, if a man has accustomed himself to sceptical considerations on the uncertainty and narrow limits of reason, he will not entirely forget them when he turns his reflection on other subjects; but in all his philosophical principles and reasoning, I dare not say in his common conduct, he will be found different from those, who either never formed any opinions in the case, or have entertained sentiments more favourable to human reason.

To whatever length any one may push his speculative principles of scepticism, he must act, I own, and live, and converse, like other men; and for this conduct he is not obliged to give any other reason, than the absolute necessity he lies under of so doing. If he ever carries his speculations further than this necessity constrains him, and philosophizes either on natural or moral subjects, he is allured by a certain pleasure and satisfaction which he finds in employing himself after that manner. He considers besides, that every one, even in common life, is constrained to have more or less of this philosophy; that from our earliest infancy we make continual advances in forming more general principles of conduct and reasoning; that the larger experience we acquire, and the stronger reason we are endued with, we always render our principles the more general and comprehensive; and that what we call philosophy is nothing but a more regular and methodical operation of the same kind. To philosophize on such subjects, is nothing essentially different from reasoning on common life; and we may only expect greater stability, if not greater truth, from our philosophy, on account of its exacter and more scrupulous method of proceeding.

But when we look beyond human affairs and the properties of the surrounding bodies: when we carry our speculations into the two eternities, before and after the present state of things; into the creation and formation of the universe; the existence and properties of spirits; the powers and operations of one universal Spirit existing without beginning and without end; omnipotent, omniscient, immutable, infinite, and incomprehensible: we must be far removed from the smallest tendency to scepticism not to be apprehensive, that we have here got quite beyond the reach of our faculties. So long as we confine our speculations to trade, or morals, or politics, or criticism, we make appeals, every moment, to common sense and experience, which strengthen our philosophical conclusions, and remove, at least in part, the suspicion which we so justly entertain with regard to every reasoning that is very subtile and refined. But, in theological reasonings, we have not this advantage; while, at the same time, we are employed upon objects, which, we must be sensible, are too large for our grasp, and of all others, require most to be familiarized to our apprehension. We are like foreigners in a strange country, to whom every thing must seem suspicious, and who are in danger every moment of transgressing against the laws and customs of the people with whom they live and converse. We know not how far we ought to trust our vulgar methods of reasoning in such a subject; since, even in common life, and in that province which is peculiarly appropriated to them, we cannot account for them, and are entirely guided by a kind of instinct or necessity in employing them.

All sceptics pretend, that, if reason be considered in an abstract view, it furnishes invincible arguments against itself; and that we could never retain any conviction or assurance, on any subject, were not the sceptical reasonings so refined and subtile, that they are not able to counterpoise the more solid and more natural arguments derived from the senses and experience. But it is evident, whenever our arguments lose this advantage, and run wide of common life, that the most refined scepticism comes to be upon a footing with them, and is able to oppose and counterbalance them. The one has no more weight than the other. The mind must remain in suspense between them; and it is that very suspense or balance, which is the triumph of scepticism.

But I observe, says Cleanthes, with regard to you, Philo, and all speculative sceptics, that your doctrine and practice are as much at variance in the most abstruse points of theory as in the conduct of common life. Wherever evidence discovers itself, you adhere to it, notwithstanding your pretended scepticism; and I can observe, too, some of your sect to be as decisive as those who make greater professions of certainty and assurance. In reality, would not a man be ridiculous, who pretended to reject Newton's explication of the wonderful phenomenon of the rainbow, because that explication gives a minute anatomy of the rays of light; a subject, forsooth, too refined for human comprehension? And what would you say to one, who, having nothing particular to object to the arguments of Copernicus and Galileo for the motion of the earth, should withhold his assent, on that general principle, that these subjects were too magnificent and remote to be explained by the narrow and fallacious reason of mankind?

There is indeed a kind of brutish and ignorant scepticism, as you well observed, which gives the vulgar a general prejudice against what they do not easily understand, and makes them reject every principle which requires elaborate reasoning to prove and establish it. This species of scepticism is fatal to knowledge, not to religion; since we find, that those who make greatest profession of it, give often their assent, not only to the great truths of Theism and natural theology, but even to the most absurd tenets which a traditional superstition has recommended to them. They firmly believe in witches, though they will not believe nor attend to the most simple proposition of Euclid. But the refined and philosophical sceptics fall into an inconsistence of an opposite nature. They push their researches into the most abstruse corners of science; and their assent attends them in every step, proportioned to the evidence which they meet with. They are even obliged to acknowledge, that the most abstruse and remote objects are those which are best explained by philosophy. Light is in reality anatomized. The true system of the heavenly bodies is discovered and ascertained. But the nourishment of bodies by food is still an inexplicable mystery. The cohesion of the parts of matter is still incomprehensible. These sceptics, therefore, are obliged, in every question, to consider each particular evidence apart, and proportion their assent to the precise degree of evidence which occurs. This is their practice in all natural, mathematical, moral, and political science. And why not the same, I ask, in the theological and religious? Why must conclusions of this nature be alone rejected on the general presumption of the insufficiency of human reason, without any particular discussion of the evidence? Is not such an unequal conduct a plain proof of prejudice and passion?

Our senses, you say, are fallacious; our understanding erroneous; our ideas, even of the most familiar objects, extension, duration, motion, full of absurdities and contradictions. You defy me to solve the difficulties, or reconcile the repugnancies which you discover in them. I have not capacity for so great an undertaking: I have not leisure for it: I perceive it to be superfluous. Your own conduct, in every circumstance, refutes your principles, and shews the firmest reliance on all the received maxims of science, morals, prudence, and behaviour.

I shall never assent to so harsh an opinion as that of a celebrated writer, who says, that the Sceptics are not a sect of philosophers: they are only a sect of liars. I may, however, affirm (I hope without offence), that they are a sect of jesters or railers. But for my part, whenever I find myself disposed to mirth and amusement, I shall certainly choose my entertainment of a less perplexing and abstruse nature. A comedy, a novel, or at most a history, seems a more natural recreation than such metaphysical subtilties and abstractions.

In vain would the sceptic make a distinction between science and common life, or between one science and another. The arguments employed in all, if just, are of a similar nature, and contain the same force and evidence. Or if there be any difference among them, the advantage lies entirely on the side of theology and natural religion. Many principles of mechanics are founded on very abstruse reasoning; yet no man who has any pretensions to science, even no speculative sceptic, pretends to entertain the least doubt with regard to them. The Copernican system contains the most surprising paradox, and the most contrary to our natural conceptions, to appearances, and to our very senses: yet even monks and inquisitors are now constrained to withdraw their opposition to it. And shall Philo, a man of so liberal a genius and extensive knowledge, entertain any general undistinguished scruples with regard to the religious hypothesis, which is founded on the simplest and most obvious arguments, and, unless it meets with artificial obstacles, has such easy access and admission into the mind of man?

And here we may observe, continued he, turning himself towards Demea, a pretty curious circumstance in the history of the sciences. After the union of philosophy with the popular religion, upon the first establishment of Christianity, nothing was more usual, among all religious teachers, than declamations against reason, against the senses, against every principle derived merely from human research and enquiry. All the topics of the ancient Academics were adopted by the fathers; and thence propagated for several ages in every school and pulpit throughout Christendom. The Reformers embraced the same principles of reasoning, or rather declamation; and all panegyrics on the excellency of faith, were sure to be interlarded with some severe strokes of satire against natural reason. A celebrated prelate too, of the Romish communion, a man of the most extensive learning, who wrote a demonstration of Christianity, has also composed a treatise, which contains all the cavils of the boldest and most determined Pyrrhonism. Locke seems to have been the first Christian who ventured openly to assert, that faith was nothing but a species of reason; that religion was only a branch of philosophy; and that a chain of arguments, similar to that which established any truth in morals, politics, or physics, was always employed in discovering all the principles of theology, natural and revealed. The ill use which Bayle and other libertines made of the philosophical scepticism of the fathers and first reformers, still further propagated the judicious sentiment of Mr. Locke: and it is now in a manner avowed, by all pretenders to reasoning and philosophy, that Atheist and Sceptic are almost synonymous. And as it is certain that no man is in earnest when he professes the latter principle, I would fain hope that there are as few who seriously maintain the former.

Don't you remember, said Philo, the excellent saying of Lord Bacon on this head? That a little philosophy, replied Cleanthes, makes a man an Atheist: a great deal converts him to religion. That is a very judicious remark too, said Philo. But what I have in my eye is another passage, where, having mentioned David's fool, who said in his heart there is no God, this great philosopher observes, that the Atheists nowadays have a double share of folly; for they are not contented to say in their hearts there is no God, but they also utter that impiety with their lips, and are thereby guilty of multiplied indiscretion and imprudence. Such people, though they were ever so much in earnest, cannot, methinks, be very formidable.

But though you should rank me in this class of fools, I cannot forbear communicating a remark that occurs to me, from the history of the religious and irreligious scepticism with which you have entertained us. It appears to me, that there are strong symptoms of priestcraft in the whole progress of this affair. During ignorant ages, such as those which followed the dissolution of the ancient schools, the priests perceived, that Atheism, Deism, or heresy of any kind, could only proceed from the presumptuous questioning of received opinions, and from a belief that human reason was equal to every thing. Education had then a mighty influence over the minds of men, and was almost equal in force to those suggestions of the senses and common understanding, by which the most determined sceptic must allow himself to be governed. But at present, when the influence of education is much diminished, and men, from a more open commerce of the world, have learned to compare the popular principles of different nations and ages, our sagacious divines have changed their whole system of philosophy, and talk the language of Stoics, Platonists, and Peripatetics, not that of Pyrrhonians and Academics. If we distrust human reason, we have now no other principle to lead us into religion. Thus, sceptics in one age, dogmatists in another; whichever system best suits the purpose of these reverend gentlemen, in giving them an ascendant over mankind, they are sure to make it their favourite principle, and established tenet.

It is very natural, said Cleanthes, for men to embrace those principles, by which they find they can best defend their doctrines; nor need we have any recourse to priestcraft to account for so reasonable an expedient. And, surely nothing can afford a stronger presumption, that any set of principles are true, and ought to be embraced, than to observe that they tend to the confirmation of true religion, and serve to confound the cavils of Atheists, Libertines, and Freethinkers of all denominations.

PART II

I must own, Cleanthes, said Demea, that nothing can more surprise me, than the light in which you have all along put this argument. By the whole tenor of your discourse, one would imagine that you were maintaining the Being of a God, against the cavils of Atheists and Infidels; and were necessitated to become a champion for that fundamental principle of all religion. But this, I hope, is not by any means a question among us. No man, no man at least of common sense, I am persuaded, ever entertained a serious doubt with regard to a truth so certain and self-evident. The question is not concerning the BEING, but the NATURE of GOD. This, I affirm, from the infirmities of human understanding, to be altogether incomprehensible and unknown to us. The essence of that supreme Mind, his attributes, the manner of his existence, the very nature of his duration; these, and every particular which regards so divine a Being, are mysterious to men. Finite, weak, and blind creatures, we ought to humble ourselves in his august presence; and, conscious of our frailties, adore in silence his infinite perfections, which eye hath not seen, ear hath not heard, neither hath it entered into the heart of man to conceive. They are covered in a deep cloud from human curiosity. It is profaneness to attempt penetrating through these sacred obscurities. And, next to the impiety of denying his existence, is the temerity of prying into his nature and essence, decrees and attributes.

But lest you should think that my piety has here got the better of my philosophy, I shall support my opinion, if it needs any support, by a very great authority. I might cite all the divines, almost, from the foundation of Christianity, who have ever treated of this or any other theological subject: but I shall confine myself, at present, to one equally celebrated for piety and philosophy. It is Father Malebranche, who, I remember, thus expresses himself. "One ought not so much," says he, "to call God a spirit, in order to express positively what he is, as in order to signify that he is not matter. He is a Being infinitely perfect: of this we cannot doubt. But in the same manner as we ought not to imagine, even supposing him corporeal, that he is clothed with a human body, as the Anthropomorphites asserted, under colour that that figure was the most perfect of any; so, neither ought we to imagine that the spirit of God has human ideas, or bears any resemblance to our spirit, under colour that we know nothing more perfect than a human mind. We ought rather to believe, that as he comprehends the perfections of matter without being material . . . he comprehends also the perfections of created spirits without being spirit, in the manner we conceive spirit: that his true name is, He that is; or, in other words, Being without restriction, All Being, the Being infinite and universal."

After so great an authority, Demea, replied Philo, as that which you have produced, and a thousand more which you might produce, it would appear ridiculous in me to add my sentiment, or express my approbation of your doctrine. But surely, where reasonable men treat these subjects, the question can never be concerning the Being, but only the Nature, of the Deity. The former truth, as you well observe, is unquestionable and self-evident. Nothing exists without a cause; and the original cause of this universe (whatever it be) we call God; and piously ascribe to him every species of perfection. Whoever scruples this fundamental truth, deserves every punishment which can be inflicted among philosophers, to wit, the greatest ridicule, contempt, and disapprobation. But as all perfection is entirely relative, we ought never to imagine that we comprehend the attributes of this divine Being, or to suppose that his perfections have any analogy or likeness to the perfections of a human creature. Wisdom, Thought, Design, Knowledge; these we justly ascribe to him; because these words are honorable among men, and we have no other language or other conceptions by which we can express our adoration of him. But let us beware, lest we think that our ideas anywise correspond to his perfections, or that his attributes have any resemblance to these qualities among men. He is infinitely superior to our limited view and comprehension; and is more the object of worship in the temple, than of disputation in the schools.

In reality, Cleanthes, continued he, there is no need of having recourse to that affected scepticism so displeasing to you, in order to come at this determination. Our ideas reach no further than our experience. We have no experience of divine attributes and operations. I need not conclude my syllogism. You can draw the inference yourself. And it is a pleasure to me (and I hope to you too) that just reasoning and sound piety here concur in the same conclusion, and both of them establish the adorably mysterious and incomprehensible nature of the Supreme Being.

Not to lose any time in circumlocutions, said Cleanthes, addressing himself to Demea, much less in replying to the pious declamations of Philo; I shall briefly explain how I conceive this matter. Look round the world: contemplate the whole and every part of it: you will find it to be nothing but one great machine, subdivided into an infinite number of lesser machines, which again admit of subdivisions to a degree beyond what human senses and faculties can trace and explain. All these various machines, and even their most minute parts, are adjusted to each other with an accuracy which ravishes into admiration all men who have ever contemplated them. The curious adapting of means to ends, throughout all nature, resembles exactly, though it much exceeds, the productions of human contrivance; of human designs, thought, wisdom, and intelligence. Since, therefore, the effects resemble each other, we are led to infer, by all the rules of analogy, that the causes also resemble; and that the Author of Nature is somewhat similar to the mind of man, though possessed of much larger faculties, proportioned to the grandeur of the work which he has executed. By this argument a posteriori, and by this argument alone, do we prove at once the existence of a Deity, and his similarity to human mind and intelligence.

I shall be so free, Cleanthes, said Demea, as to tell you, that from the beginning, I could not approve of your conclusion concerning the similarity of the Deity to men; still less can I approve of the mediums by which you endeavor to establish it. What! No demonstration of the Being of God! No abstract arguments! No proofs a priori! Are these, which have hitherto been so much insisted on by philosophers, all fallacy, all sophism? Can we reach no further in this subject than experience and probability? I will not say that this is betraying the cause of a Deity: but surely, by this affected candor, you give advantages to Atheists, which they never could obtain by the mere dint of argument and reasoning.

What I chiefly scruple in this subject, said Philo, is not so much that all religious arguments are by Cleanthes reduced to experience, as that they appear not to be even the most certain and irrefragable of that inferior kind. That a stone will fall, that fire will burn, that the earth has solidity, we have observed a thousand and a thousand times; and when any new instance of this nature is presented, we draw without hesitation the accustomed inference. The exact similarity of the cases gives us a perfect assurance of a similar event; and a stronger evidence is never desired nor sought after. But wherever you depart, in the least, from the similarity of the cases, you diminish proportionately the evidence; and may at last bring it to a very weak analogy, which is confessedly liable to error and uncertainty. After having experienced the circulation of the blood in human creatures, we make no doubt that it takes place in Titius and Maevius. But from its circulation in frogs and fishes, it is only a presumption, though a strong one, from analogy, that it takes place in men and other animals. The analogical reasoning is much weaker, when we infer the circulation of the sap in vegetables from our experience that the blood circulates in animals; and those, who hastily followed that imperfect analogy, are found, by more accurate experiments, to have been mistaken.

If we see a house, Cleanthes, we conclude, with the greatest certainty, that it had an architect or builder; because this is precisely that species of effect which we have experienced to proceed from that species of cause. But surely you will not affirm, that the universe bears such a resemblance to a house that we can with the same certainty infer a similar cause, or that the analogy is here entire and perfect. The dissimilitude is so striking, that the utmost you can here pretend to is a guess, a conjecture, a presumption concerning a similar cause; and how that pretension will be received in the world, I leave you to consider.

It would surely be very ill received, replied Cleanthes; and I should be deservedly blamed and detested, did I allow, that the proofs of a Deity amounted to no more than a guess or conjecture. But is the whole adjustment of means to ends in a house and in the universe so slight a resemblance? The economy of final causes? The order, proportion, and arrangement of every part? Steps of a stair are plainly contrived, that human legs may use them in mounting; and this inference is certain and infallible. Human legs are also contrived for walking and mounting; and this inference, I allow, is not altogether so certain, because of the dissimilarity which you remark; but does it, therefore, deserve the name only of presumption or conjecture?

Good God! cried Demea, interrupting him, where are we? Zealous defenders of religion allow, that the proofs of a Deity fall short of perfect evidence! And you, Philo, on whose assistance I depended in proving the adorable mysteriousness of the Divine Nature, do you assent to all these extravagant opinions of Cleanthes? For what other name can I give them? or, why spare my censure, when such principles are advanced, supported by such an authority, before so young a man as Pamphilus?

You seem not to apprehend, replied Philo, that I argue with Cleanthes in his own way; and, by showing him the dangerous consequences of his tenets, hope at last to reduce him to our opinion. But what sticks most with you, I observe, is the representation which Cleanthes has made of the argument a posteriori; and finding that that argument is likely to escape your hold and vanish into air, you think it so disguised, that you can scarcely believe it to be set in its true light. Now, however much I may dissent,

in other respects, from the dangerous principles of Cleanthes, I must allow that he has fairly represented that argument; and I shall endeavor so to state the matter to you, that you will entertain no further scruples with regard to it.

Were a man to abstract from every thing which he knows or has seen, he would be altogether incapable, merely from his own ideas, to determine what kind of scene the universe must be, or to give the preference to one state or situation of things above another. For as nothing which he clearly conceives could be esteemed impossible or implying a contradiction, every chimera of his fancy would be upon an equal footing; nor could he assign any just reason why he adheres to one idea or system, and rejects the others which are equally possible.

Again; after he opens his eyes, and contemplates the world as it really is, it would be impossible for him at first to assign the cause of any one event, much less of the whole of things, or of the universe. He might set his fancy a rambling; and she might bring him in an infinite variety of reports and representations. These would all be possible; but being all equally possible, he would never of himself give a satisfactory account for his preferring one of them to the rest. Experience alone can point out to him the true cause of any phenomenon.

Now, according to this method of reasoning, Demea, it follows, (and is, indeed, tacitly allowed by Cleanthes himself,) that order, arrangement, or the adjustment of final causes, is not of itself any proof of design; but only so far as it has been experienced to proceed from that principle. For ought we can know a priori, matter may contain the source or spring of order originally within itself as well as mind does; and there is no more difficulty in conceiving, that the several elements, from an internal unknown cause, may fall into the most exquisite arrangement, than to conceive that their ideas, in the great universal mind, from a like internal unknown cause, fall into that arrangement. The equal possibility of both these suppositions is allowed. But, by experience, we find, (according to Cleanthes,) that there is a difference between them. Throw several pieces of steel together, without shape or form; they will never arrange themselves so as to compose a watch. Stone, and mortar, and wood, without an architect, never erect a house. But the ideas in a human mind, we see, by an unknown, inexplicable economy, arrange themselves so as to form the plan of a watch or house. Experience, therefore, proves, that there is an original principle of order in mind, not in matter. From similar effects we infer similar causes. The adjustment of means to ends is alike in the universe, as in a machine of human contrivance. The causes, therefore, must be resembling.

I was from the beginning scandalized, I must own, with this resemblance, which is asserted, between the Deity and human creatures; and must conceive it to imply such a degradation of the Supreme Being as no sound Theist could endure. With your assistance, therefore, Demea, I shall endeavor to defend what you justly call the adorable mysteriousness of the Divine Nature, and shall refute this reasoning of Cleanthes, provided he allows that I have made a fair representation of it.

When Cleanthes had assented, Philo, after a short pause, proceeded in the following manner.

That all inferences, Cleanthes, concerning fact, are founded on experience; and that all experimental reasonings are founded on the supposition that similar causes prove similar effects, and similar effects similar causes; I shall not at present much dispute with you. But observe, I entreat you, with what extreme caution all just reasoners proceed in the transferring of experiments to similar cases. Unless the cases be exactly similar, they repose no perfect confidence in applying their past observation to any particular phenomenon. Every alteration of circumstances occasions a doubt concerning the event; and it requires new experiments to prove certainly, that the new circumstances are of no moment or importance. A change in bulk, situation, arrangement, age, disposition of the air, or surrounding bodies; any of these particulars may be attended with the most unexpected consequences: and unless the objects be quite familiar to us, it is the highest temerity to expect with assurance, after any of these changes, an event similar to that which before fell under our observation. The slow and deliberate steps of philosophers here, if any where, are distinguished from the precipitate march of the vulgar, who, hurried on by the smallest similitude, are incapable of all discernment or consideration.

But can you think, Cleanthes, that your usual phlegm and philosophy have been preserved in so wide a step as you have taken, when you compared to the universe houses, ships, furniture, machines, and, from their similarity in some circumstances, inferred a similarity in their causes? Thought, design, intelligence, such as we discover in men and other animals, is no more than one of the springs and principles of the universe, as well as heat or cold, attraction or repulsion, and a hundred others, which fall under daily observation. It is an active cause, by which some particular parts of nature, we find, produce alterations on other parts. But can a conclusion, with any propriety, be transferred from parts to the whole? Does not the great disproportion bar all comparison and inference? From observing the growth of a hair, can we learn any thing concerning the generation of a man? Would the manner of a leaf's blowing, even though perfectly known, afford us any instruction concerning the vegetation of a tree?

But, allowing that we were to take the operations of one part of nature upon another, for the foundation of our judgment concerning the origin of the whole, (which never can be admitted,) yet why select so minute, so weak, so bounded a principle, as the reason and design of animals is found to be upon this planet? What peculiar privilege has this little agitation of the brain which we call thought, that we must thus make it the model of the whole universe? Our partiality in our own favour does indeed present it on all occasions; but sound philosophy ought carefully to guard against so natural an illusion.

So far from admitting, continued Philo, that the operations of a part can afford us any just conclusion concerning the origin of the whole, I will not allow any one part to form a rule for another part, if the latter be very remote from the former. Is there any reasonable ground to conclude, that the inhabitants of other planets possess thought, intelligence, reason, or any thing similar to these faculties in men? When nature has so extremely diversified her manner of operation in this small globe, can we imagine that she incessantly copies herself throughout so immense a universe? And if thought, as we may well suppose, be confined merely to this narrow corner, and has even there so limited a sphere of action, with what propriety can we assign it for the original cause of all things? The narrow views of a peasant, who makes his domestic economy the rule for the government of kingdoms, is in comparison a pardonable sophism.

But were we ever so much assured, that a thought and reason, resembling the human, were to be found throughout the whole universe, and were its activity elsewhere vastly greater and more commanding than it appears in this globe; yet I cannot see, why the operations of a world constituted, arranged, adjusted, can with any propriety be extended to a world which is in its embryo state, and is advancing towards that constitution and arrangement. By observation, we know somewhat of the economy, action, and nourishment of a finished animal; but we must transfer with great caution that observation to the growth of a foetus in the womb, and still more in the formation of an animalcule in the loins of its male parent. Nature, we find, even from our limited experience, possesses an infinite number of springs and principles, which incessantly discover themselves on every change of her position and situation. And what new and unknown principles would actuate her in so new and unknown a situation as that of the formation of a universe, we cannot, without the utmost temerity, pretend to determine.

A very small part of this great system, during a very short time, is very imperfectly discovered to us; and do we then pronounce decisively concerning the origin of the whole?

Admirable conclusion! Stone, wood, brick, irons brass, have not, at this time, in this minute globe of earth, an order or arrangement without human art and contrivance; therefore the universe could not originally attain its order and arrangement, without something similar to human art. But is a part of nature a rule for another part very wide of the former? Is it a rule for the whole? Is a very small part a rule for the universe? Is nature in one situation, a certain rule for nature in another situation vastly different from the former?

And can you blame me, Cleanthes, if I here imitate the prudent reserve of Simonides, who, according to the noted story, being asked by Hiero, What God was? desired a day to think of it, and then two days more; and after that manner continually prolonged the term, without ever bringing in his definition or description? Could you even blame me, if I answered at first, that I did not know, and was sensible that this subject lay vastly beyond the reach of my faculties? You might cry out sceptic and rallier, as much as you pleased: but having found, in so many other subjects much more familiar, the imperfections and even contradictions of human reason, I never should expect any success from its feeble conjectures, in a subject so sublime, and so remote from the sphere of our observation. When two species of objects have always been observed to be conjoined together, I can infer, by custom, the existence of one wherever I see the existence of the other; and this I call an argument from experience. But how this argument can have place, where the objects, as in the present case, are single, individual, without parallel, or specific resemblance, may be difficult to explain. And will any man tell me with a serious countenance, that an orderly universe must arise from some thought and art like the human, because we have experience of it? To ascertain this reasoning, it were requisite that we had experience of the origin of worlds; and it is not sufficient, surely, that we have seen ships and cities arise from human art and contrivance.

Philo was proceeding in this vehement manner, somewhat between jest and earnest, as it appeared to me, when he observed some signs of impatience in Cleanthes, and then immediately stopped short. What I had to suggest, said Cleanthes, is only that you would not abuse terms, or make use of popular expressions to subvert philosophical reasonings. You know, that the vulgar often distinguish reason from experience, even where the question relates only to matter of fact and existence; though it is found, where that reason is properly analyzed, that it is nothing but a species of experience. To prove by experience the origin of the universe from mind, is not more contrary to common speech, than to prove the motion of the earth from the same principle. And a caviller might raise all the same objections to the Copernican system, which you have urged against my reasonings. Have you other earths, might he say, which you have seen to move? Have . . .

Yes! cried Philo, interrupting him, we have other earths. Is not the moon another earth, which we see to turn round its centre? Is not Venus another earth, where we observe the same phenomenon? Are not the revolutions of the sun also a confirmation, from analogy, of the same theory? All the planets, are they not earths, which revolve about the sun? Are not the satellites moons, which move round Jupiter and Saturn, and along with these primary planets round the sun? These analogies and resemblances, with others which I have not mentioned, are the sole proofs of the Copernican system; and to you it belongs to consider, whether you have any analogies of the same kind to support your theory.

In reality, Cleanthes, continued he, the modern system of astronomy is now so much received by all inquirers, and has become so essential a part even of our earliest education, that we are not commonly very scrupulous in examining the reasons upon which it is founded. It is now become a matter of mere curiosity to study the first writers on that subject, who had the full force of prejudice to encounter, and were obliged to turn their arguments on every side in order to render them popular and convincing. But if we peruse Galileo's famous Dialogues concerning the system of the world, we shall find, that that great genius, one of the sublimest that ever existed, first bent all his endeavors to prove, that there was no foundation for the distinction commonly made between elementary and celestial substances. The schools, proceeding from the illusions of sense, had carried this distinction very far; and had established the latter substances to be ingenerable, incorruptible, unalterable, impassible; and had assigned all the opposite qualities to the former. But Galileo, beginning with the moon, proved its similarity in every particular to the earth; its convex figure, its natural darkness when not illuminated, its density, its distinction into solid and liquid, the variations of its phases, the mutual illuminations of the earth and moon, their mutual eclipses, the inequalities of the lunar surface, &c. After many instances of this kind, with regard to all the planets, men plainly saw that these bodies became proper objects of experience; and that the similarity of their nature enabled us to extend the same arguments and phenomena from one to the other.

In this cautious proceeding of the astronomers, you may read your own condemnation, Cleanthes; or rather may see, that the subject in which you are engaged exceeds all human reason and enquiry. Can you pretend to shew any such similarity between the fabric of a house, and the generation of a universe? Have you ever seen nature in any such situation as resembles the first arrangement of the elements? Have worlds ever been formed under your eye; and have you had leisure to observe the whole progress of the phenomenon, from the first appearance of order to its final consummation? If you have, then cite your experience, and deliver your theory. . .

PART IV

It seems strange to me, said Cleanthes, that you, Demea, who are so sincere in the cause of religion, should still maintain the mysterious, incomprehensible nature of the Deity, and should insist so strenuously that he has no manner of likeness or resemblance to human creatures. The Deity, I can readily allow, possesses many powers and attributes of which we can have no comprehension: but if our ideas, so far as they go, be not just, and adequate, and correspondent to his real nature, I know not what there is in this subject worth insisting on. Is the name, without any meaning, of such mighty importance? Or how do you mystics, who maintain the absolute incomprehensibility of the Deity, differ from Sceptics or Atheists, who assert, that the first cause of all is unknown and unintelligible? Their temerity must be very great, if, after rejecting the production by a mind, I mean a mind resembling the human, (for I know of no other,) they pretend to assign, with certainty, any other specific intelligible cause: and their conscience must be very scrupulous indeed, if they refuse to call the universal unknown cause a God or Deity; and to bestow on him as many sublime eulogies and unmeaning epithets as you shall please to require of them.

Who could imagine, replied Demea, that Cleanthes, the calm philosophical Cleanthes, would attempt to refute his antagonists by affixing a nickname to them; and, like the common bigots and inquisitors of the age, have recourse to invective and declamation, instead of reasoning? Or does he not perceive, that these topics are easily retorted, and that Anthropomorphite is an appellation as invidious, and implies as dangerous consequences, as the epithet of Mystic, with which he has honored us? In reality, Cleanthes, consider what it is you assert when you represent the Deity as similar to a human mind and understanding. What is the soul of man? A composition of various faculties, passions, sentiments, ideas; united, indeed, into one self or person, but still distinct from each other. When it reasons, the ideas, which are the parts of its discourse, arrange themselves in a certain form or order; which is not preserved entire for a moment, but immediately gives place to another arrangement. New opinions, new passions, new affections, new feelings arise, which continually diversify the mental scene, and produce in it the greatest variety and most rapid succession imaginable. How is this compatible with that perfect immutability and simplicity which all true Theists ascribe to the Deity? By the same act, say they, he sees past, present, and future: his love and hatred, his mercy and justice, are one individual operation: he is entire in every point of space; and complete in every instant of duration. No succession, no change, no acquisition, no diminution. What he is implies not in it any shadow of distinction or diversity. And what he is this moment he ever has been, and ever will be, without any new judgment, sentiment, or operation. He stands fixed in one simple, perfect state: nor can you ever say, with any propriety, that this act of his is different from that other; or that this judgment or idea has been lately formed, and will give place, by succession, to any different judgment or idea.

I can readily allow, said Cleanthes, that those who maintain the perfect simplicity of the Supreme Being, to the extent in which you have explained it, are complete Mystics, and chargeable with all the consequences which I have drawn from their opinion. They are, in a word, Atheists, without knowing it. For though it be allowed, that the Deity possesses attributes of which we have no comprehension, yet ought we never to ascribe to him any attributes which are absolutely incompatible with that intelligent nature essential to him. A mind, whose acts and sentiments and ideas are not distinct and successive; one, that is wholly simple, and totally immutable, is a mind

which has no thought, no reason, no will, no sentiment, no love, no hatred; or, in a word, is no mind at all. It is an abuse of terms to give it that appellation; and we may as well speak of limited extension without figure, or of number without composition.

Pray consider, said Philo, whom you are at present inveighing against. You are honoring with the appellation of Atheist all the sound, orthodox divines, almost, who have treated of this subject; and you will at last be, yourself, found, according to your reckoning, the only sound Theist in the world. But if idolaters be Atheists, as, I think, may justly be asserted, and Christian Theologians the same, what becomes of the argument, so much celebrated, derived from the universal consent of mankind?

But because I know you are not much swayed by names and authorities, I shall endeavor to shew you, a little more distinctly, the inconveniences of that Anthropomorphism, which you have embraced; and shall prove, that there is no ground to suppose a plan of the world to be formed in the Divine mind, consisting of distinct ideas, differently arranged, in the same manner as an architect forms in his head the plan of a house which he intends to execute.

It is not easy, I own, to see what is gained by this supposition, whether we judge of the matter by Reason or by Experience. We are still obliged to mount higher, in order to find the cause of this cause, which you had assigned as satisfactory and conclusive.

If Reason (I mean abstract reason, derived from enquiries a priori) be not alike mute with regard to all questions concerning cause and effect, this sentence at least it will venture to pronounce, That a mental world, or universe of ideas, requires a cause as much, as does a material world, or universe of objects; and, if similar in its arrangement, must require a similar cause. For what is there in this subject, which should occasion a different conclusion or inference? In an abstract view, they are entirely alike; and no difficulty attends the one supposition, which is not common to both of them.

Again, when we will needs force Experience to pronounce some sentence, even on these subjects which lie beyond her sphere, neither can she perceive any material difference in this particular, between these two kinds of worlds; but finds them to be governed by similar principles, and to depend upon an equal variety of causes in their operations. We have specimens in miniature of both of them. Our own mind resembles the one; a vegetable or animal body the other. Let experience, therefore, judge from these samples. Nothing seems more delicate, with regard to its causes, than thought; and as these causes never operate in two persons after the same manner, so we never find two persons who think exactly alike. Nor indeed does the same person think exactly alike at any two different periods of time. A difference of age, of the disposition of his body, of weather, of food, of company, of books, of passions; any of these particulars, or others more minute, are sufficient to alter the curious machinery of thought, and communicate to it very different movements and operations. As far as we can judge, vegetables and animal bodies are not more delicate in their motions, nor depend upon a greater variety or more curious adjustment of springs and principles.

How, therefore, shall we satisfy ourselves concerning the cause of that Being whom you suppose the Author of Nature, or, according to your system of Anthropomorphism, the ideal world, into which you trace the material? Have we not the same reason to trace that ideal world into another ideal world, or new intelligent principle? But if we stop, and go no further; why go so far? why not stop at the material world? How can we satisfy ourselves without going on ad infinitum? And, after all, what satisfaction is there in that infinite progression? Let us remember the story of the Indian philosopher and his elephant. It was never more applicable than to the present subject. If the material world rests upon a similar ideal world, this ideal world must rest upon some other; and so on, without end. It were better, therefore, never to look beyond the present material world. By supposing it to contain the principle of its order within itself, we really assert it to be God; and the sooner we arrive at that Divine Being, so much the better. When you go one step beyond the mundane system, you only excite an inquisitive humor which it is impossible ever to satisfy.

To say, that the different ideas which compose the reason of the Supreme Being, fall into order of themselves, and by their own nature, is really to talk without any precise meaning. If it has a meaning, I would fain know, why it is not as good sense to say, that the parts of the material world fall into order of themselves and by their own nature. Can the one opinion be intelligible, while the other is not so?

We have, indeed, experience of ideas which fall into order of themselves, and without any known cause. But, I am sure, we have a much larger experience of matter which does the same; as, in all instances of generation and vegetation, where the accurate analysis of the cause exceeds all human comprehension. We have also experience of particular systems of thought and of matter which have no order; of the first in madness, of the second in corruption. Why, then, should we think, that order is more essential to one than the other? And if it requires a cause in both, what do we gain by your system, in tracing the universe of objects into a similar universe of ideas? The first step which we make leads us on for ever. It were, therefore, wise in us to limit all our enquiries to the present world, without looking further. No satisfaction can ever be attained by these speculations, which so far exceed the narrow bounds of human understanding.

It was usual with the Peripatetics, you know, Cleanthes, when the cause of any phenomenon was demanded, to have recourse to their faculties or occult qualities; and to say, for instance, that bread, nourished by its nutritive faculty, and senna purged by its purgative. But it has been discovered, that this subterfuge was nothing but the disguise of ignorance; and that these philosophers, though less ingenuous, really said the same thing with the sceptics or the vulgar, who fairly confessed that they knew not the cause of these phenomena. In like manner, when it is asked, what cause produces order in the ideas of the Supreme Being; can any other reason be assigned by you, Anthropomorphites, than that it is a rational faculty, and that such is the nature of the Deity? But why a similar answer will not be equally satisfactory in accounting for the order of the world, without having recourse to any such intelligent creator as you insist on, may be difficult to determine. It is only to say, that such is the nature of material objects, and that they are all originally possessed of a faculty of order and proportion. These are only more learned and elaborate ways of confessing our ignorance; nor has the one hypothesis any real advantage above the other, except in its greater conformity to vulgar prejudices.

You have displayed this argument with great emphasis, replied Cleanthes. You seem not sensible how easy it is to answer it. Even in common life, if I assign a cause for any event, is it any objection, Philo, that I cannot assign the cause of that cause, and answer every new question which may incessantly be started? And what philosophers could possibly submit to so rigid a rule? philosophers, who confess ultimate causes to be totally unknown; and are sensible, that the most refined principles into which they trace the phenomena, are still to them as inexplicable as these phenomena themselves are to the vulgar. The order and arrangement of nature, the curious adjustment of final causes, the plain use and intention of every part and organ; all these bespeak in the clearest language an intelligent cause or author. The heavens and the earth join in the same testimony: the whole chorus of Nature raises one hymn to the praises of its Creator. You alone, or almost alone, disturb this general harmony. You start abstruse doubts, cavils, and objections: you ask me, what is the cause of this cause? I know not; I care not; that concerns not me. I have found a Deity; and here I stop my enquiry. Let those go further, who are wiser or more enterprising.

I pretend to be neither, replied Philo: and for that very reason, I should never perhaps have attempted to go so far; especially when I am sensible, that I must at last be contented to sit down with the same answer, which, without further trouble, might have satisfied me from the beginning. If I am still to remain in utter ignorance of causes, and can absolutely give an explication of nothing, I shall never esteem it any advantage to shove off for a moment a difficulty, which, you acknowledge, must immediately, in its full force, recur upon me. Naturalists indeed very justly explain particular effects by more general causes, though these general causes themselves should remain in the end totally inexplicable; but they never surely thought it satisfactory to explain a particular effect by a particular cause, which was no more to be accounted for than the effect itself. An ideal system, arranged of itself, without a precedent design, is not a whit more explicable than a material one, which attains its order in a like manner; nor is there any more difficulty in the latter supposition than in the former.

PART V

But to shew you still more inconveniences, continued Philo, in your Anthropomorphism, please to take a new survey of your principles. Like effects prove like causes. This is the experimental argument; and this, you say too, is the sole theological argument. Now, it is certain, that the liker the effects are which are seen, and the liker the causes which are inferred, the stronger is the argument. Every departure on either side diminishes the probability, and renders the experiment less conclusive. You cannot doubt of the principle; neither ought you to reject its consequences.

All the new discoveries in astronomy, which prove the immense grandeur and magnificence of the works of Nature, are so many additional arguments for a Deity, according to the true system of Theism; but, according to your hypothesis of experimental Theism, they become so many objections, by removing the effect still further from all resemblance to the effects of human art and contrivance. For, if Lucretius, even following the old system of the world, could exclaim, Who is strong enough to rule the sum, who to hold in hand and control the mighty bridle of the unfathomable deep? Who to turn about all the heavens at one time, and warm the fruitful worlds with ethereal fires, or to be present in all places and at all times.

If Tully esteemed this reasoning so natural as to put it into the mouth of his Epicurean:

What power of mental vision enabled your master Plato to descry the vast and elaborate architectural process which, as he makes out, the deity adopted in building the structure of the universe? What method of engineering was employed? What tools and levers and derricks? What agents carried out so vast an understanding? And how were air, fire, water, and earth enabled to obey and execute the will of the architect?

If this argument, I say, had any force in former ages, how much greater must it have at present, when the bounds of Nature are so infinitely enlarged, and such a magnificent scene is opened to us? It is still more unreasonable to form our idea of so unlimited a cause from our experience of the narrow productions of human design and invention.

The discoveries by microscopes, as they open a new universe in miniature, are still objections, according to you, arguments, according to me. The further we push our researches of this kind, we are still led to infer the universal cause of all to be vastly different from mankind, or from any object of human experience and observation.

And what say you to the discoveries in anatomy, chemistry, botany? . . . These surely are no objections, replied Cleanthes; they only discover new instances of art and contrivance. It is still the image of mind reflected on us from innumerable objects. Add, a mind like the human, said Philo. I know of no other, replied Cleanthes. And the liker the better, insisted Philo. To be sure, said Cleanthes.

Now, Cleanthes, said Philo, with an air of alacrity and triumph, mark the consequences. First, By this method of reasoning, you renounce all claim to infinity in any of the attributes of the Deity. For, as the cause ought only to be proportioned to the effect, and the effect, so far as it falls under our cognizance, is not infinite; what pretensions have we, upon your suppositions, to ascribe that attribute to the Divine Being? You will still insist, that, by removing him so much from all similarity to human creatures, we give in to the most arbitrary hypothesis, and at the same time weaken all proofs of his existence.

Secondly, You have no reason, on your theory, for ascribing perfection to the Deity, even in his finite capacity, or for supposing him free from every error, mistake, or incoherence, in his undertakings. There are many inexplicable difficulties in the works of Nature, which, if we allow a perfect author to be proved a priori, are easily solved, and become only seeming difficulties, from the narrow capacity of man, who cannot trace infinite relations. But according to your method of reasoning, these difficulties become all real; and perhaps will be insisted on, as new instances of likeness to human art and contrivance. At least, you must acknowledge, that it is impossible for us to tell, from our limited views, whether this system contains any great faults, or deserves any considerable praise, if compared to other possible, and even real systems. Could a peasant, if

the Aeneid were read to him, pronounce that poem to be absolutely faultless, or even assign to it its proper rank among the productions of human wit, he, who had never seen any other production?

But were this world ever so perfect a production, it must still remain uncertain, whether all the excellences of the work can justly be ascribed to the workman. If we survey a ship, what an exalted idea must we form of the ingenuity of the carpenter who framed so complicated, useful, and beautiful a machine? And what surprise must we feel, when we find him a stupid mechanic, who imitated others, and copied an art, which, through a long succession of ages, after multiplied trials, mistakes, corrections, deliberations, and controversies, had been gradually improving? Many worlds might have been botched and bungled, throughout an eternity, ere this system was struck out; much labour lost, many fruitless trials made; and a slow, but continued improvement carried on during infinite ages in the art of world-making. In such subjects, who can determine, where the truth; nay, who can conjecture where the probability lies, amidst a great number of hypotheses which may be proposed, and a still greater which may be imagined?

And what shadow of an argument, continued Philo, can you produce, from your hypothesis, to prove the unity of the Deity? A great number of men join in building a house or ship, in rearing a city, in framing a commonwealth; why may not several deities combine in contriving and framing a world? This is only so much greater similarity to human affairs. By sharing the work among several, we may so much further limit the attributes of each, and get rid of that extensive power and knowledge, which must be supposed in one deity, and which, according to you, can only serve to weaken the proof of his existence. And if such foolish, such vicious creatures as man, can yet often unite in framing and executing one plan, how much more those deities or demons, whom we may suppose several degrees more perfect!

To multiply causes without necessity, is indeed contrary to true philosophy: but this principle applies not to the present case. Were one deity antecedently proved by your theory, who were possessed of every attribute requisite to the production of the universe; it would be needless, I own, (though not absurd,) to suppose any other deity existent. But while it is still a question, Whether all these attributes are united in one subject, or dispersed among several independent beings, by what phenomena in nature can we pretend to decide the controversy? Where we see a body raised in a scale, we are sure that there is in the opposite scale, however concealed from sight, some counterpoising weight equal to it; but it is still allowed to doubt, whether that weight be an aggregate of several distinct bodies, or one uniform united mass. And if the weight requisite very much exceeds any thing which we have ever seen conjoined in any single body, the former supposition becomes still more probable and natural. An intelligent being of such vast power and capacity as is necessary to produce the universe, or, to speak in the language of ancient philosophy, so prodigious an animal exceeds all analogy, and even comprehension.

But further, Cleanthes: men are mortal, and renew their species by generation; and this is common to all living creatures. The two great sexes of male and female, says Milton, animate the world. Why must this circumstance, so universal, so essential be excluded from those numerous and limited deities? Behold, then, the theogony of ancient times brought back upon us.

And why not become a perfect Anthropomorphite? Why not assert the deity or deities to be corporeal, and to have eyes, a nose, mouth, ears, &c.? Epicurus maintained, that no man had ever seen reason but in a human figure; therefore the gods must have a human figure. And this argument, which is deservedly so much ridiculed by Cicero, becomes, according to you, solid and philosophical.

In a word, Cleanthes, a man who follows your hypothesis is able perhaps to assert, or conjecture, that the universe, sometime, arose from something like design: but beyond that position he cannot ascertain one single circumstance; and is left afterwards to fix every point of his theology by the utmost license of fancy and hypothesis. This world, for aught he knows, is very faulty and imperfect, compared to a superior standard; and was only the first rude essay of some infant deity, who afterwards abandoned it, ashamed of his lame performance: it is the work only of some dependent, inferior deity; and is the object of derision to his superiors: it is the production of

old age and dotage in some superannuated deity; and ever since his death, has run on at adventures, from the first impulse and active force which it received from him. You justly give signs of horror, Demea, at these strange suppositions; but these, and a thousand more of the same kind, are Cleanthes's suppositions, not mine. From the moment the attributes of the Deity are supposed finite, all these have place. And I cannot, for my part, think that so wild and unsettled a system of theology is, in any respect, preferable to none at all.

These suppositions I absolutely disown, cried Cleanthes: they strike me, however, with no horror, especially when proposed in that rambling way in which they drop from you. On the contrary, they give me pleasure, when I see, that, by the utmost indulgence of your imagination, you never get rid of the hypothesis of design in the universe, but are obliged at every turn to have recourse to it. To this concession I adhere steadily; and this I regard as a sufficient foundation for religion.

PART VI

It must be a slight fabric, indeed, said Demea, which can be erected on so tottering a foundation. While we are uncertain whether there is one deity or many; whether the deity or deities, to whom we owe our existence, be perfect or imperfect, subordinate or supreme, dead or alive, what trust or confidence can we repose in them? What devotion or worship address to them? What veneration or obedience pay them? To all the purposes of life the theory of religion becomes altogether useless: and even with regard to speculative consequences, its uncertainty, according to you, must render it totally precarious and unsatisfactory.

To render it still more unsatisfactory, said Philo, there occurs to me another hypothesis, which must acquire an air of probability from the method of reasoning so much insisted on by Cleanthes. That like effects arise from like causes: this principle he supposes the foundation of all religion. But there is another principle of the same kind, no less certain, and derived from the same source of experience; that where several known circumstances are observed to be similar, the unknown will also be found similar.

Thus, if we see the limbs of a human body, we conclude that it is also attended with a human head, though hid from us. Thus, if we see, through a chink in a wall, a small part of the sun, we conclude, that, were the wall removed, we should see the whole body. In short, this method of reasoning is so obvious and familiar, that no scruple can ever be made with regard to its solidity.

Now, if we survey the universe, so far as it falls under our knowledge, it bears a great resemblance to an animal or organized body, and seems actuated with a like principle of life and motion. A continual circulation of matter in it produces no disorder: a continual waste in every part is incessantly repaired: the closest sympathy is perceived throughout the entire system: and each part or member, in performing its proper offices, operates both to its own preservation and to that of the whole. The world, therefore, I infer, is an animal; and the Deity is the SOUL of the world, actuating it, and actuated by it.

You have too much learning, Cleanthes, to be at all surprised at this opinion, which, you know, was maintained by almost all the Theists of antiquity, and chiefly prevails in their discourses and reasonings. For though, sometimes, the ancient philosophers reason from final causes, as if they thought the world the workmanship of God; yet it appears rather their favorite notion to consider it as his body, whose organization renders it subservient to him. And it must be confessed, that, as the universe resembles more a human body than it does the works of human art and contrivance, if our limited analogy could ever, with any propriety, be extended to the whole of nature, the inference seems juster in favour of the ancient than the modern theory.

There are many other advantages, too, in the former theory, which recommended it to the ancient theologians. Nothing more repugnant to all their notions, because nothing more repugnant to common experience, than mind without body; a mere spiritual substance, which fell not under their senses nor comprehension, and of which they had not observed one single instance throughout all nature. Mind and body they knew, because they felt both: an order, arrangement, organization, or internal machinery, in both, they likewise knew, after the same manner: and it could not but seem reasonable to transfer this ex-

perience to the universe; and to suppose the divine mind and body to be also coeval, and to have, both of them, order and arrangement naturally inherent in them, and inseparable from them.

Here, therefore, is a new species of Anthropomorphism, Cleanthes, on which you may deliberate; and a theory which seems not liable to any considerable difficulties. You are too much superior, surely, to systematical prejudices, to find any more difficulty in supposing an animal body to be, originally, of itself, or from unknown causes, possessed of order and organization, than in supposing a similar order to belong to mind. But the vulgar prejudice, that body and mind ought always to accompany each other, ought not, one should think, to be entirely neglected; since it is founded on vulgar experience, the only guide which you profess to follow in all these theological enquiries. And if you assert, that our limited experience is an unequal standard, by which to judge of the unlimited extent of nature; you entirely abandon your own hypothesis, and must thenceforward adopt our Mysticism, as you call it, and admit of the absolute incomprehensibility of the Divine Nature.

This theory, I own, replied Cleanthes, has never before occurred to me, though a pretty natural one; and I cannot readily, upon so short an examination and reflection, deliver any opinion with regard to it. You are very scrupulous, indeed, said Philo: were I to examine any system of yours, I should not have acted with half that caution and reserve, in starting objections and difficulties to it. However, if any thing occur to you, you will oblige us by proposing it.

Why then, replied Cleanthes, it seems to me, that, though the world does, in many circumstances, resemble an animal body; yet is the analogy also defective in many circumstances the most material: no organs of sense; no seat of thought or reason; no one precise origin of motion and action. In short, it seems to bear a stronger resemblance to a vegetable than to an animal, and your inference would be so far inconclusive in favour of the soul of the world.

But, in the next place, your theory seems to imply the eternity of the world; and that is a principle, which, I think, can be refuted by the strongest reasons and probabilities. I shall suggest an argument to this purpose, which, I believe, has not been insisted on by any writer. Those, who reason from the late origin of arts and sciences, though their inference wants not force, may perhaps be refuted by considerations derived from the nature of human society, which is in continual revolution, between ignorance and knowledge, liberty and slavery, riches and poverty; so that it is impossible for us, from our limited experience, to foretell with assurance what events may or may not be expected. Ancient learning and history seem to have been in great danger of entirely perishing after the inundation of the barbarous nations; and had these convulsions continued a little longer, or been a little more violent, we should not probably have now known what passed in the world a few centuries before us. Nay, were it not for the superstition of the Popes, who preserved a little jargon of Latin, in order to support the appearance of an ancient and universal church, that tongue must have been utterly lost; in which case, the Western world, being totally barbarous, would not have been in a fit disposition for receiving the Greek language and learning, which was conveyed to them after the sacking of Constantinople. When learning and books had been extinguished, even the mechanical arts would have fallen considerably to decay; and it is easily imagined, that fable or tradition might ascribe to them a much later origin than the true one. This vulgar argument, therefore, against the eternity of the world, seems a little precarious.

But here appears to be the foundation of a better argument. Lucullus was the first that brought cherry-trees from Asia to Europe; though that tree thrives so well in many European climates, that it grows in the woods without any culture. Is it possible, that throughout a whole eternity, no European had ever passed into Asia, and thought of transplanting so delicious a fruit into his own country? Or if the tree was once transplanted and propagated, how could it ever afterwards perish? Empires may rise and fall, liberty and slavery succeed alternately, ignorance and knowledge give place to each other; but the cherry-tree will still remain in the woods of Greece, Spain, and Italy, and will never be affected by the revolutions of human society.

It is not two thousand years since vines were transplanted into France, though there is no climate in the world more favorable to them. It is not three

centuries since horses, cows, sheep, swine, dogs, corn, were known in America. Is it possible, that during the revolutions of a whole eternity, there never arose a Columbus, who might open the communication between Europe and that continent? We may as well imagine, that all men would wear stockings for ten thousand years, and never have the sense to think of garters to tie them. All these seem convincing proofs of the youth, or rather infancy of the world; as being founded on the operation of principles more constant and steady than those by which human society is governed and directed. Nothing less than a total convulsion of the elements will ever destroy all the European animals and vegetables which are now to be found in the Western world.

And what argument have you against such convulsions? replied Philo. Strong and almost incontestable proofs may be traced over the whole earth, that every part of this globe has continued for many ages entirely covered with water. And though order were supposed inseparable from matter, and inherent in it; yet may matter be susceptible of many and great revolutions, through the endless periods of eternal duration. The incessant changes, to which every part of it is subject, seem to intimate some such general transformations; though, at the same time, it is observable, that all the changes and corruptions of which we have ever had experience, are but passages from one state of order to another; nor can matter ever rest in total deformity and confusion. What we see in the parts, we may infer in the whole; at least, that is the method of reasoning on which you rest your whole theory. And were I obliged to defend any particular system of this nature, which I never willingly should do, I esteem none more plausible than that which ascribes an eternal inherent principle of order to the world, though attended with great and continual revolutions and alterations. This at once solves all difficulties; and if the solution, by being so general, is not entirely complete and satisfactory, it is at least a theory that we must sooner or later have recourse to, whatever system we embrace. How could things have been as they are, were there not an original inherent principle of order somewhere, in thought or in matter? And it is very indifferent to which of these we give the preference. Chance has no place, on any hypothesis, sceptical or religious.

Every thing is surely governed by steady, inviolable laws. And were the inmost essence of things laid open to us, we should then discover a scene, of which, at present, we can have no idea. Instead of admiring the order of natural beings, we should clearly see that it was absolutely impossible for them, in the smallest article, ever to admit of any other disposition.

Were any one inclined to revive the ancient Pagan Theology, which maintained, as we learn from Hesiod, that this globe was governed by thirty thousand deities, who arose from the unknown powers of nature: you would naturally object, Cleanthes, that nothing is gained by this hypothesis; and that it is as easy to suppose all men animals, beings more numerous, but less perfect, to have sprung immediately from a like origin. Push the same inference a step further, and you will find a numerous society of deities as explicable as one universal deity, who possesses within himself the powers and perfections of the whole society. All these systems, then, of Scepticism, Polytheism, and Theism, you must allow, on your principles, to be on a like footing, and that no one of them has any advantage over the others. You may thence learn the fallacy of your principles. . .

PART X

It is my opinion, I own, replied Demea, that each man feels, in a manner, the truth of religion within his own breast, and, from a consciousness of his imbecility and misery, rather than from any reasoning, is led to seek protection from that Being, on whom he and all nature is dependent. So anxious or so tedious are even the best scenes of life, that futurity is still the object of all our hopes and fears. We incessantly look forward, and endeavor, by prayers, adoration, and sacrifice, to appease those unknown powers, whom we find, by experience, so able to afflict and oppress us. Wretched creatures that we are! what resource for us amidst the innumerable ills of life, did not religion suggest some methods of atonement, and appease those terrors with which we are incessantly agitated and tormented?

I am indeed persuaded, said Philo, that the best, and indeed the only method of bringing every one to a due sense of religion, is by just representations of the misery and wickedness of men. And for that purpose a talent of eloquence and strong imagery is more requisite than that of reasoning and argument. For is it necessary to prove what every one feels within himself? It is only necessary to make us feel it, if possible, more intimately and sensibly.

The people, indeed, replied Demea, are sufficiently convinced of this great and melancholy truth. The miseries of life; the unhappiness of man; the general corruptions of our nature; the unsatisfactory enjoyment of pleasures, riches, honors; these phrases have become almost proverbial in all languages. And who can doubt of what all men declare from their own immediate feeling and experience?

In this point, said Philo, the learned are perfectly agreed with the vulgar; and in all letters, sacred and profane, the topic of human misery has been insisted on with the most pathetic eloquence that sorrow and melancholy could inspire. The poets, who speak from sentiment, without a system, and whose testimony has therefore the more authority, abound in images of this nature. From Homer down to Dr. Young, the whole inspired tribe have ever been sensible, that no other representation of things would suit the feeling and observation of each individual.

As to authorities, replied Demea, you need not seek them. Look round this library of Cleanthes. I shall venture to affirm, that, except authors of particular sciences, such as chemistry or botany, who have no occasion to treat of human life, there is scarce one of those innumerable writers, from whom the sense of human misery has not, in some passage or other, extorted a complaint and confession of it. At least, the chance is entirely on that side; and no one author has ever, so far as I can recollect, been so extravagant as to deny it.

There you must excuse me, said Philo: Leibnitz has denied it; and is perhaps the first who ventured upon so bold and paradoxical an opinion; at least, the first who made it essential to his philosophical system.

And by being the first, replied Demea, might he not have been sensible of his error? For is this a subject in which philosophers can propose to make discoveries especially in so late an age? And can any man hope by a simple denial (for the subject scarcely admits of reasoning), to bear down the united testimony of mankind, founded on sense and consciousness?

And why should man, added he, pretend to an exemption from the lot of all other animals? The whole earth, believe me, Philo, is cursed and polluted. A perpetual war is kindled amongst all living creatures. Necessity, hunger, want, stimulate the strong and courageous: fear, anxiety, terror, agitate the weak and infirm. The first entrance into life gives anguish to the new-born infant and to its wretched parent: weakness, impotence, distress, attend each stage of that life: and it is at last finished in agony and horror.

Observe too, says Philo, the curious artifices of Nature, in order to embitter the life of every living being. The stronger prey upon the weaker, and keep them in perpetual terror and anxiety. The weaker too, in their turn, often prey upon the stronger, and vex and molest them without relaxation. Consider that innumerable race of insects, which either are bred on the body of each animal, or, flying about, infix their stings in him. These insects have others still less than themselves, which torment them. And thus on each hand, before and behind, above and below, every animal is surrounded with enemies, which incessantly seek his misery and destruction.

Man alone, said Demea, seems to be, in part, an exception to this rule. For by combination in society, he can easily master lions, tigers, and bears, whose greater strength and agility naturally enable them to prey upon him.

On the contrary, it is here chiefly, cried Philo, that the uniform and equal maxims of Nature are most apparent. Man, it is true, can, by combination, surmount all his real enemies, and become master of the whole animal creation: but does he not immediately raise up to himself imaginary enemies, the demons of his fancy, who haunt him with superstitious terrors, and blast every enjoyment of life? His pleasure, as he imagines, becomes, in their eyes, a crime: his food and repose give them umbrage and offence: his very sleep and dreams furnish new materials to anxious fear: and even death, his refuge from every other ill, presents only the dread of endless and innumerable woes. Nor does the wolf molest more the timid flock, than superstition does the anxious breast of wretched mortals.

Besides, consider, Demea: this very society, by which we surmount those wild beasts, our natural enemies; what new enemies does it not raise to us? What woe and misery does it not occasion? Man is the greatest enemy of man. Oppression, injustice, contempt, contumely, violence, sedition, war, calumny, treachery, fraud; by these they mutually torment each other; and they would soon dissolve that society which they had formed, were it not for the dread of still greater ills, which must attend their separation.

But though these external insults, said Demea, from animals, from men, from all the elements, which assault us, form a frightful catalogue of woes, they are nothing in comparison of those which arise within ourselves, from the distempered condition of our mind and body. How many lie under the lingering torment of diseases? Hear the pathetic enumeration of the great poet.

Intestine stone and ulcer, colic-pangs,
Demoniac frenzy, moping melancholy,
And moon-struck madness, pining atrophy,
Marasmus, and wide-wasting pestilence.
Dire was the tossing, deep the groans: DESPAIR
Tended the sick, busiest from couch to couch.
And over them triumphant DEATH his dart
Shook: but delay'd to strike, though oft invok'd
With vows, as their chief good and final hope.

The disorders of the mind, continued Demea, though more secret, are not perhaps less dismal and vexatious. Remorse, shame, anguish, rage, disappointment, anxiety, fear, dejection, despair; who has ever passed through life without cruel inroads from these tormentors? How many have scarcely ever felt any better sensations? Labour and poverty, so abhorred by every one, are the certain lot of the far greater number; and those few privileged persons, who enjoy ease and opulence, never reach contentment or true felicity. All the goods of life united would not make a very happy man; but all the ills united would make a wretch indeed; and any one of them almost (and who can be free from every one?) nay often the absence of one good (and who can possess all?) is sufficient to render life ineligible.

Were a stranger to drop on a sudden into this world, I would shew him, as a specimen of its ills, an hospital full of diseases, a prison crowded with malefactors and debtors, a field of battle strewed with carcass, a fleet foundering in the ocean, a nation languishing under tyranny, famine, or pestilence. To turn the gay side of life to him and give him a notion of its pleasures; whither should I conduct him? to a ball, to an opera, to court? He might justly think, that I was only showing him a diversity of distress and sorrow.

There is no evading such striking instances, said Philo, but by apologies, which still further aggravate the charge. Why have all men, I ask, in all ages, complained incessantly of the miseries of life? . . . They have no just reason, says one: these complaints proceed only from their discontented, repining, anxious disposition. . . . And can there possibly, I reply, be a more certain foundation of misery, than such a wretched temper?

But if they were really as unhappy as they pretend, says my antagonist, why do they remain in life? . . .

Not satisfied with life, afraid of death.

This is the secret chain, say I, that holds us. We are terrified, not bribed to the continuance of our existence.

It is only a false delicacy, he may insist, which a few refined spirits indulge, and which has spread these complaints among the whole race of mankind. . . . And what is this delicacy, I ask, which you blame? Is it any thing but a greater sensibility to all the pleasures and pains of life? and if the man of a delicate, refined temper, by being so much more alive than the rest of the world, is only so much more unhappy, what judgment must we form in general of human life?

Let men remain at rest, says our adversary, and they will be easy. They are willing artificers of their own misery. . . . No! reply I: an anxious languor follows their repose; disappointment, vexation, trouble, their activity and ambition.

I can observe something like what you mention in some others, replied Cleanthes: but I confess I feel little or nothing of it in myself, and hope that it is not so common as you represent it.

If you feel not human misery yourself, cried Demea, I congratulate you on so happy a singularity. Others, seemingly the most prosperous, have not been ashamed to vent their complaints in the most melancholy strains. Let us attend to the great, the fortunate emperor, Charles V., when, tired with human grandeur, he resigned all his extensive dominions into the hands of his son. In the last harangue which he made on that memorable occasion, he publicly avowed, that the greatest prosperities which he had ever enjoyed, had been mixed with so many adversities, that he might truly say he had never enjoyed any satisfaction or contentment. But did the retired life, in which he sought for shelter, afford him any greater happiness? If we may credit his son's account, his repentance commenced the very day of his resignation.

Cicero's fortune, from small beginnings, rose to the greatest lustre and renown; yet what pathetic complaints of the ills of life do his familiar letters, as well as philosophical discourses, contain? And suitably to his own experience, he introduces Cato, the great, the fortunate Cato, protesting in his old age, that had he a new life in his offer, he would reject the present.

Ask yourself, ask any of your acquaintance, whether they would live over again the last ten or twenty years of their lives. No! but the next twenty, they say, will be better:

And from the dregs of life, hope to receive
What the first sprightly running could not give.

Thus at last they find (such is the greatness of human misery, it reconciles even contradictions), that they complain at once of the shortness of life, and of its vanity and sorrow.

And is it possible, Cleanthes, said Philo, that after all these reflections, and infinitely more, which might be suggested, you can still persevere in your Anthropomorphism, and assert the moral attributes of the Deity, his justice, benevolence, mercy, and rectitude, to be of the same nature with these virtues in human creatures? His power we allow is infinite: whatever he wills is executed: but neither man nor any other animal is happy: therefore he does not will their happiness. His wisdom is infinite: he is never mistaken in choosing the means to any end: but the course of Nature tends not to human or animal felicity: therefore it is not established for that purpose. Through the whole compass of human knowledge, there are no inferences more certain and infallible than these. In what respect, then, do his benevolence and mercy resemble the benevolence and mercy of men?

Epicurus's old questions are yet unanswered.

Is he willing to prevent evil, but not able? then is he impotent. Is he able, but not willing? then is he malevolent. Is he both able and willing? whence then is evil?

You ascribe, Cleanthes (and I believe justly), a purpose and intention to Nature. But what, I beseech you, is the object of that curious artifice and machinery, which she has displayed in all animals? The preservation alone of individuals, and propagation of the species. It seems enough for her purpose, if such a rank be barely upheld in the universe, without any care or concern for the happiness of the members that compose it. No resource for this purpose: no machinery, in order merely to give pleasure or ease: no fund of pure joy and contentment: no indulgence, without some want or necessity accompanying it. At least, the few phenomena of this nature are over-balanced by opposite phenomena of still greater importance.

Our sense of music, harmony, and indeed beauty of all kinds, gives satisfaction, without being absolutely necessary to the preservation and propagation of the species. But what racking pains, on the other hand, arise from gouts, gravels, megrims, toothaches, rheumatisms, where the injury to the animal machinery is either small or incurable? Mirth, laughter, play, frolic, seem gratuitous satisfactions, which have no further tendency: spleen, melancholy, discontent, superstition, are pains of the same nature. How then does the Divine benevolence display itself, in the sense of you Anthropomorphites? None but we Mystics, as you were pleased to call us, can account for this strange mixture of phenomena, by deriving it from attributes, infinitely perfect, but incomprehensible.

And have you at last, said Cleanthes, smiling, betrayed your intentions, Philo? Your long agreement with Demea did indeed a little surprise me; but I find you were all the while erecting a concealed battery against me. And I must confess, that you have now fallen upon a subject worthy of your noble spirit of opposition and controversy. If you can make out the present point, and prove mankind to be unhappy or corrupted, there is an end at once of all religion. For to what purpose establish the natural attributes of the Deity, while the moral are still doubtful and uncertain?

You take umbrage very easily, replied Demea, at opinions the most innocent, and the most generally received, even amongst the religious and devout themselves: and nothing can be more surprising than to find a topic like this, concerning the wickedness and misery of man, charged with no less than Atheism and profaneness. Have not all pious divines and preachers, who have indulged their rhetoric on so fertile a subject; have they not easily, I say, given a solution of any difficulties which may attend it? This world is but a point in comparison of the universe; this life but a moment in comparison of eternity. The present evil phenomena, therefore, are rectified in other regions, and in some future period of existence. And the eyes of men, being then opened to larger views of things, see the whole connexion of general laws; and trace with adoration, the benevolence and rectitude of the Deity, through all the mazes and intricacies of his providence.

No! replied Cleanthes, No! These arbitrary suppositions can never be admitted, contrary to matter of fact, visible and uncontroverted. Whence can any cause be known but from its known effects? Whence can any hypothesis be proved but from the apparent phenomena? To establish one hypothesis upon another, is building entirely in the air; and the utmost we ever attain, by these conjectures and fictions, is to ascertain the bare possibility of our opinion; but never can we, upon such terms, establish its reality.

The only method of supporting Divine benevolence, and it is what I willingly embrace, is to deny absolutely the misery and wickedness of man. Your representations are exaggerated; your melancholy views mostly fictitious; your inferences contrary to fact and experience. Health is more common than sickness; pleasure than pain; happiness than misery. And for one vexation which we meet with, we attain, upon computation, a hundred enjoyments.

Admitting your position, replied Philo, which yet is extremely doubtful, you must at the same time allow, that if pain be less frequent than pleasure, it is infinitely more violent and durable. One hour of it is often able to outweigh a day, a week, a month of our common insipid enjoyments; and how many days, weeks, and months, are passed by several in the most acute torments? Pleasure, scarcely in one instance, is ever able to reach ecstasy and rapture; and in no one instance can it continue for any time at its highest pitch and altitude. The spirits evaporate, the nerves relax, the fabric is disordered, and the enjoyment quickly degenerates into fatigue and uneasiness. But pain often, good God, how often! rises to torture and agony; and the longer it continues, it becomes still more genuine agony and torture. Patience is exhausted, courage languishes, melancholy seizes us, and nothing terminates our misery but the removal of its cause, or another event, which is the sole cure of all evil, but which, from our natural folly, we regard with still greater horror and consternation.

But not to insist upon these topics, continued Philo, though most obvious, certain, and important; I must use the freedom to admonish you, Cleanthes, that you have put the controversy upon a most dangerous issue, and are unawares introducing a total scepticism into the most essential articles of natural and revealed theology. What! no method of fixing a just foundation for religion, unless we allow the happiness of human life, and maintain a continued existence even in this world, with all our present pains, infirmities, vexations, and follies, to be eligible and desirable! But this is contrary to every one's feeling and experience: it is contrary to an authority so established as nothing can subvert. No decisive proofs can ever be produced against this authority; nor is it possible for you to compute, estimate, and compare, all the pains and all the pleasures in the lives of all men and of all animals: and thus, by your resting the whole system of religion on a point, which, from its very nature, must for ever be uncertain, you tacitly confess, that system is equally uncertain.

But allowing you what never will be believed, at least what you never possibly can prove, that animal, or at least human happiness, in this life, exceeds its misery, you have yet done nothing: for this is not, by any means, what we expect from infinite power, infinite wisdom, and infinite goodness. Why is there any misery at all in the world? Not by chance surely. From some cause then. Is it from the intention of the Deity? But he is perfectly benevolent. Is it contrary to his intention? But he is almighty. Nothing can shake the solidity of this reasoning, so short, so clear, so decisive; except we assert, that these subjects exceed all human capacity, and that our common measures of truth and falsehood are not applicable to them; a topic which I have all along insisted on, but which you have, from the beginning, rejected with scorn and indignation.

But I will be contented to retire still from this entrenchment, for I deny that you can ever force me in it. I will allow, that pain or misery in man is compatible with infinite power and goodness in the Deity, even in your sense of these attributes: what are you advanced by all these concessions? A mere possible compatibility is not sufficient. You must prove these pure, unmixed, and uncontrollable attributes from the present mixed and confused phenomena, and from these alone. A hopeful undertaking! Were the phenomena ever so pure and unmixed, yet being finite, they would be insufficient for that purpose. How much more, where they are also so jarring and discordant!

Here, Cleanthes, I find myself at ease in my argument. Here I triumph. Formerly, when we argued concerning the natural attributes of intelligence and design, I needed all my sceptical and metaphysical subtilty to elude your grasp. In many views of the universe and of its parts, particularly the latter, the beauty and fitness of final causes strike us with such irresistible force, that all objections appear (what I believe they really are) mere cavils and sophisms; nor can we then imagine how it was ever possible for us to repose any weight on them. But there is no view of human life, or of the condition of mankind, from which, without the greatest violence, we can infer the moral attributes, or learn that infinite benevolence, conjoined with infinite power and infinite wisdom, which we must discover by the eyes of faith alone. It is your turn now to tug the laboring oar, and to support your philosophical subtilties against the dictates of plain reason and experience. . . .

REVIEW QUESTIONS

1. What are Hume's two proofs for his thesis about ideas and impressions?
2. Why is Hume skeptical about metaphysical issues?
3. In Hume's view, what is the role of custom in human life?
4. Why is causal reasoning doubtful? What does Hume mean by saying that causal relations can never be discovered by a priori argument?
5. What is Hume's solution to the problem of doubt?
6. Why does Hume say that the order, arrangement, or adjustment of final causes is not in itself proof of design?
7. Why does Hume say that we have no reason to ascribe perfection to the Deity?

22

IMMANUEL KANT

Immanuel Kant (1724–1804), who was born in a deeply pietistic Lutheran family in Konigsberg, Germany, lived in that town his entire life. At sixteen he entered the University of Konigsberg, where he studied under the tutelage of Martin Knutzen, and read works of Leibniz and Leibniz scholar Christian Wolff. After graduation he worked as a tutor, but in 1755 he was offered an unsalaried lectureship at his alma mater, receiving his fees directly from his students. He served in this capacity until 1770 when he was promoted to the chair of logic and metaphysics at the University of Konigsberg. In his inaugural address he spoke of his goal of restructuring philosophy, resolving the debate between the rationalists (e.g., Descartes, Spinoza, Leibniz, and Wolff) and the empiricists (e.g., Newton, Bacon, Locke, and Hume). For the next ten years he worked on his magnus opus, *The Critique of Pure Reason* (1781), which accomplished that goal, a Copernican revolution of the theory of knowledge. In 1783 he wrote a shorter *Prolegomena to Any Future Metaphysics* "for the benefit of teachers," and in 1785 he wrote his first major work in ethics, *Foundation for the Metaphysic of Morals.* A successor to that work appeared in 1788, *Critique of Practical Reason*, and in 1793 he published his theory of rational religion, *Religion Within the Limits of Reason Alone.*

Kant was an outstanding lecturer and excellent conversationalist, who was known for his generosity and friendliness. He lived a quiet, duty-bound, methodical life, so regular that citizens were said to have set their clocks by his walks. He would leave his home at precisely 4:30 in the afternoon and walk up and down the street on which he lived exactly eight times.

In his own lifetime Kant was recognized as one of the premier philosophers in the Western tradition. Although he wrote on virtually every philosophical topic, he made his major contributions in epistemology and ethics, represented in the selections that follow. Let us briefly examine his thought in these areas.

KANT'S THEORY OF KNOWLEDGE

Building on a mathematical model, the rationalists from Plato through Descartes to Spinoza and Leibniz argued that reason alone is the ultimate source of knowledge, that we have innate or a priori knowledge of ultimate truth which can be accessed by introspection or pure reason. On the other hand, the British empiricists Locke and Hume set forth cogent criticisms against the rationalist projects and argued that experience is the only source of knowledge. The phenomenal success of Newton (1642–1727) in physics seemed to shift the balance of evidence to the empiricists. Empirical Science, not rationalist speculation, offered the best hope of attaining knowledge of the universe.

Kant began as a rationalist but on reading Hume was struck with the cogency of his argument. Hume "woke me from my dogmatic slumbers," Kant wrote, and henceforth accepted the idea that all of our knowledge begins with experience. But Kant thought that Hume had made an invalid inference in concluding that all our knowledge arises from experience. Kant sought to demonstrate that the rationalists had an invaluable insight, which had been lost in their flamboyant speculation, that there is something determinate in the mind that causes us to know what we know.

Kant argued that the mind is so structured and empowered that it imposes interpretive categories on our experience, so that we do not simply experience the world, as the empiricists alleged, but interpret it through the constitutive mechanisms of the mind. This is sometimes called Kant's Copernican Revolution.

> Until now we have assumed that all our knowledge must conform to objects. But every attempt to extend our knowledge of objects by establishing something in regard to them a priori, by means of concepts, have, on this assumption, ended in failure. Therefore, we must see whether we may have better success in our metaphysical task if we begin with the assumption that objects must conform to our knowledge. In this way we would have knowledge of objects a priori. We should then be proceeding in the same ways as Copernicus in his revolutionary hypothesis. After he failed to make progress in explaining the movements of the heavenly bodies on the supposition that they all revolved around the observer, he decided to reverse the relationship and made the observer revolve around the heavenly body, the sun, which was at rest. A similar experiment can be done in metaphysics with regard to the intuition of objects. If our intuition must conform to the constitution of the object, I do not see how we could know anything of the object a priori, but if the object of sense must conform to the constitution of our faculty of intuition, then a priori knowledge is possible.[1]

A word is in order about a priori and a posteriori knowledge. *A priori* knowledge is that which we know *prior* to experience. It is opposed to *a posteriori* knowledge which is based on experience. You may recall that for Hume all knowledge of matters of fact was a posteriori and only analytic statements (e.g., mathematical truths or statements such as "All mothers are women") are known a priori. Kant rejects this formula. For him it is possible to have a priori matters of fact. "But though all our knowledge begins with experience, it does not follow that it all arises out of experience." Indeed, he thinks that mathematical truth is not analytic but synthetic (the predicate adds something to the subject) and that there is other synthetic a priori knowledge, such as our knowledge of time, space, causality, and the moral law.

---

[1] *Critique of Pure Reason* from the preface to the second edition, 1787, my translation.

KANT'S ETHICAL THEORY

In Kant's classic work, *Foundation for the Metaphysic of Morals*, written in 1785, he outlines his ethical system. Kant is concerned to reject those ethical theories, such as the Theory of Moral Sentiments set forth by the Scottish moralists Francis Hutcheson (1694) and David Hume (1711–1776), in which morality is contingent and hypothetical. The Moral Sentiment view is contingent in that it is based on human nature and, in particular, on our feelings or sentiments. Had we been created differently, we would have a different nature and, hence, different moral duties. Morality, on this view, consists of hypothetical imperatives in that they depend on our desires for their realization. For example, we should obey the law because we want a peaceful, orderly society. We should seek peace because it is necessary for personal happiness. The naturalistic ethicists were typically utilitarians who sought to maximize human happiness.

Kant rejects this naturalistic, utilitarian account of ethics. Ethics is not *contingent* but *absolute*, and its duties or imperatives are not *hypothetical* but *categorical* (nonconditional). Ethics is based not on feeling but on reason. It is because we are rational beings that we are valuable and capable of discovering moral laws binding on all persons at all times. As such, our moral duties are not dependent on feelings but on reason. They are unconditional, universally valid, and necessary, regardless of the possible consequences or opposition to our inclinations.

Kant's first formulation of his *categorical imperative* is, "Act only on that maxim whereby thou canst at the same time will that it would become a universal law." This imperative is given as the criterion (or second order principle) by which to judge all other principles. If we could consistently will that everyone would do some type of action, then there is an application of the categorical imperative enjoining that type of action. If we cannot consistently will that everyone would do some type of action, then that type of action is morally wrong. Kant argues, for example, that we cannot consistently will that everyone make lying-promises, for the very institution of promising entails or depends on general adherence to keeping the promise or an intention to do so.

Kant offers a second formulation of the categorical imperative: "So act as to treat humanity, whether in your own person or in that of any other, in every case as an end and never as merely a means only." Each person by virtue of his or her reason has dignity and profound worth, which entails that he or she must never be exploited or manipulated or merely used as a means to our idea of what is for the general good. Kant thought that this formulation was substantively identical with the first, but the view is controversial.

FOR FURTHER READING

Acton, Harry. *Kant's Moral Philosophy* (Macmillan, 1970).

Allison, Henry. *Kant's Transcendental Idealism* (Yale University Press, 1983).

Beck, Lewis White. *A Commentary on Kant's Critique of Practical Reason* (University of Chicago, 1960).

Beck, Lewis White, ed. *Studies in the Philosophy of Kant* (Bobbs-Merrill, 1965).

Ewing, A. C. *A Short Commentary on Kant's Critique of Pure Reason* (Methuen, 1950).

Hill, Thomas E. *Dignity and Practical Reason* (Cornell University Press, 1992).

Kemp, John. *The Philosophy of Kant* (Oxford University Press, 1968).

Kemp Smith, Norman. *A Commentary to Kant's "Critique of Pure Reason"* (Humanities Press, 1962).

(Human reason delights in construction)

Louden, Robert. *Morality and Moral Theory* (Oxford University Press, 1991).

O'Neill, Onora. *Acting on Principle: An Essay on Kantian Ethics* (Columbia University Press, 1975).

Ross, W. D. *Kant's Ethical Theory* (Clarendon Press, 1954).

Strawson, P. F. *The Bounds of Sense: An Essay on Kant's Critique of Pure Reason* (Methuen, 1966).

Sullivan, Roger. *Immanuel Kant's Moral Theory* (Cambridge University Press, 1989).

Sullivan, Roger. *An Introduction to Kant's Ethics* (Cambridge University Press, 1994).

Walker, Ralph C. S. *Kant: The Arguments of the Philosophers* (Routledge & Kegan Paul, 1978).

Walker, Ralph C. S., ed. *Kant on Pure Reason* (Oxford University Press, 1982).

Ward, Keith. *The Development of Kant's Views of Ethics* (Blackwell's, 1972).

Werkmeister, W. H. *Kant* (Open Court, 1980).

Wolff, Robert Paul, ed. *Kant* (Doubleday, 1967).

PROLEGOMENA TO ANY FUTURE METAPHYSICS

INTRODUCTION

These *Prolegomena* are destined for the use, not of pupils, but of future teachers, and even the latter should not expect that they will be serviceable for the systematic exposition of a ready-made science, but merely for the discovery of the science itself.

There are scholarly men, to whom the history of philosophy (both ancient and modern) is philosophy itself; for these the present *Prolegomena* are not written. They must wait till those who endeavor to draw from the foundation of reason itself have completed their work; it will then be the historian's turn to inform the world of what has been done. Unfortunately, nothing can be said, which in their opinion has not been said before, and truly the same prophecy applies to all future time; for since the human reason has for many centuries speculated upon innumerable objects in various ways, it is hardly to be expected that we should not be able to discover analogies for every new idea among the old sayings of past ages.

My object is to persuade all those who think Metaphysics worth studying, that it is absolutely necessary to pause a moment, and, neglecting all that has been done, to propose first the preliminary question, "Whether such a thing as metaphysics be at all possible?"

If it be a science, how comes it that it cannot, like other sciences, obtain universal and permanent recognition? If not, how can it maintain its pretensions, and keep the human mind in suspense with hopes, never ceasing, yet never fulfilled? Whether then we demonstrate our knowledge or our ignorance in this field, we must come once for all to a definite conclusion respecting the nature of this so-called science, which cannot possibly remain on its present footing. It seems almost ridiculous, while every other science is continually advancing, that in this, which pretends to be Wisdom incarnate, for whose oracle every one inquires, we should constantly move round the same spot, without gaining a single step. And so its followers having melted away, we do not find men confident of their ability to shine in other sciences venturing their reputation here, where everybody, however ignorant in other matters, may deliver a final verdict, as in this domain there is as yet no standard weight and measure to distinguish sound knowledge from shallow talk.

After all it is nothing extraordinary in the elaboration of a science, when men begin to wonder how far it has advanced, that the question should at last occur, whether and how such a science is possible? Human reason so delights in constructions, that it has several times built up a tower, and then razed it to examine the nature of the foundation. It is never too late to become wise; but if the change comes late, there is always more difficulty in starting a reform.

The question whether a science be possible, presupposes a doubt as to its actuality. But such a doubt offends the men whose whole possessions consist of

Translated by Paul Carus

this supposed jewel; hence he who raises the doubt must expect opposition from all sides. Some, in the proud consciousness of their possessions, which are ancient, and therefore considered legitimate, will take their metaphysical compendia in their hands, and look down on him with contempt; others, who never see anything except it be identical with what they have seen before, will not understand him, and everything will remain for a time, as if nothing had happened to excite the concern, or the hope, for an impending change.

Nevertheless, I venture to predict that the independent reader of these *Prolegomena* will not only doubt his previous science, but ultimately be fully persuaded, that it cannot exist unless the demands here stated on which its possibility depends, be satisfied; and, as this has never been done, that there is, as yet, no such thing as Metaphysics. But as it can never cease to be in demand[1]—since the interests of common sense are intimately interwoven with it, he must confess that a radical reform, or rather a new birth of the science after an original plan, are unavoidable, however men may struggle against it for a while.

Since the *Essays* of Locke and Leibnitz, or rather since the origin of metaphysics so far as we know its history, nothing has ever happened which was more decisive to its fate than the attack made upon it by David Hume. He threw no light on this species of knowledge, but he certainly struck a spark from which light might have been obtained, had it caught some inflammable substance and had its smouldering fire been carefully nursed and developed.

Hume started from a single but important concept in Metaphysics, viz., that of Cause and Effect (including its derivatives force and action, etc.). He challenges reason, which pretends to have given birth to this idea from herself, to answer him by what right she thinks anything to be so constituted, that if that thing be posited, something else also must necessarily be posited; for this is the meaning of the concept of cause. He demonstrated irrefutably that it was perfectly impossible for reason to think *a priori* and by means of concepts a combination involving necessity. We cannot at all see why, in consequence of the existence of one thing, another must necessarily exist, or how the concept of such a combination can arise *a priori*. Hence he inferred, that reason was altogether deluded with reference to this concept, which she erroneously considered as one of her children, whereas in reality it was nothing but a bastard of imagination, impregnated by experience, which subsumed certain representations under the Law of Association, and mistook the subjective necessity of habit for an objective necessity arising from insight. Hence he inferred that reason had no power to think such combinations, even generally, because her concepts would then be purely fictitious, and all her pretended *a priori* cognitions nothing but common experiences marked with a false stamp. In plain language there is not, and cannot be, any such thing as metaphysics at all.[2]

However hasty and mistaken Hume's conclusion may appear, it was at least founded upon investigation, and this investigation deserved the concentrated attention of the brighter spirits of his day as well as determined efforts on their part to discover, if possible, a happier solution of the problem in the sense proposed by him, all of which would have speedily resulted in a complete reform of the science.

But Hume suffered the usual misfortune of metaphysicians, of not being understood. It is positively painful to see how utterly his opponents, Reid,

---

[1] Says Horace:
Rusticus expectat, dum defluat amnis, at ille
Labitur et labetur in omne volubilis aevum.
["A rustic fellow waiteth on the shore
For the river to flow away,
But the river flows, and flows on as before,
And it flows forever and aye."]

[2] Nevertheless Hume called this very destructive science metaphysics and attached to it great value. Metaphysics and morals [he declares in the fourth part of his *Essays*] are the most important branches of science; mathematics and physics are not nearly so important. But the acute man merely regarded the negative use arising from the moderation of extravagant claims of speculative reason, and the complete settlement of the many endless and troublesome controversies that mislead mankind. He overlooked the positive injury which results, if reason be deprived of its most important prospects which can alone supply to the will the highest aim for all its endeavor.

Oswald, Beattie, and lastly Priestley, missed the point of the problem; for while they were ever taking for granted that which he doubted, and demonstrating with zeal and often with impudence that which he never thought of doubting, they so misconstrued his valuable suggestion that everything remained in its old condition, as if nothing had happened.

The question was not whether the concept of cause was right, useful, and even indispensable for our knowledge of nature, for this Hume had never doubted; but whether that concept could be thought by reason *a priori*, and consequently whether it possessed an inner truth, independent of all experience, implying a wider application than merely to the objects of experience. This was Hume's problem. It was a question concerning the *origin*, not concerning the *indispensable need* of the concept. Were the former decided, the conditions of the use and the sphere of its valid application would have been determined as a matter of course.

But to satisfy the conditions of the problem, the opponents of the great thinker should have penetrated very deeply into the nature of reason, so far as it is concerned with pure thinking—a task which did not suit them. They found a more convenient method of being defiant without any insight, viz., the appeal to *common sense*. It is indeed a great gift of God, to possess right, or (as they now call it) plain common sense. But this common sense must be shown practically, by well-considered and reasonable thoughts and words, not by appealing to it as an oracle, when no rational justification can be advanced. To appeal to common sense, when insight and science fail, and no sooner—this is one of the subtle discoveries of modern times, by means of which the most superficial ranter can safely enter the lists with the most thorough thinker, and hold his own. But as long as a particle of insight remains, no one would think of having recourse to this subterfuge. For what is it but an appeal to the opinion of the multitude, of whose applause the philosopher is ashamed, while the popular charlatan glories and confides in it? I should think that Hume might fairly have laid as much claim to common sense as Beattie, and in addition to a critical reason (such as the latter did not possess), which keeps common sense in check and prevents it from speculating, or, if speculations are under discussion, restrains the desire to decide because it cannot satisfy itself concerning its own arguments. By this means alone can common sense remain sound. Chisels and hammers may suffice to work a piece of wood, but for steel-engraving we require an engraver's needle. Thus common sense and speculative understanding are each serviceable in their own way, the former in judgments which apply immediately to experience, the latter when we judge universally from mere concepts, as in metaphysics, where sound common sense, so called in spite of the inapplicability of the word, has no right to judge at all.

I openly confess, the suggestion of David Hume was the very thing, which many years ago first interrupted my dogmatic slumber, and gave my investigations in the field of speculative philosophy quite a new direction. I was far from following him in the conclusions at which he arrived by regarding, not the whole of his problem, but a part, which by itself can give us no information. If we start from a well-founded, but undeveloped, thought, which another has bequeathed to us, we may well hope by continued reflection to advance farther than the acute man, to whom we owe the first spark of light.

I therefore first tried whether Hume's objection could not be put into a general form, and soon found that the concept of the connexion of cause and effect was by no means the only idea by which the understanding thinks the connexion of things *a priori*, but rather that metaphysics consists altogether of such connexions. I sought to ascertain their number, and when I had satisfactorily succeeded in this by starting from a single principle, I proceeded to the deduction of these concepts, which I was now certain were not deduced from experience, as Hume had apprehended, but sprang from the pure understanding. This deduction (which seemed impossible to my acute predecessor, which had never even occurred to any one else, though no one had hesitated to use the concepts without investigating the basis of their objective validity) was the most difficult task ever undertaken in the service of metaphysics; and the worst was that metaphysics, such as it then existed, could not assist me in the least, because this deduction alone can render metaphysics possible.

pure understanding

But as soon as I had succeeded in solving Hume's problem not merely in a particular case, but with respect to the whole faculty of pure reason, I could proceed safely, though slowly, to determine the whole sphere of pure reason completely and from general principles, in its circumference as well as in its contents. This was required for metaphysics in order to construct its system according to a reliable method.

But I fear that the execution of Hume's problem in its widest extent (viz., my *Critique of Pure Reason*) will fare as the problem itself fared, when first proposed. It will be misjudged because it is misunderstood, and misunderstood because men choose to skim through the book, and not to think through it—a disagreeable task, because the work is dry, obscure, opposed to all ordinary notions, moreover longwinded. I confess, however, I did not expect to hear from philosophers complaints of want of popularity, entertainment, and facility, when the existence of a highly prized and indispensable cognition is at stake, which cannot be established otherwise, than by the strictest rules of methodic precision. Popularity may follow, but is inadmissible at the beginning. Yet as regards a certain obscurity, arising partly from the diffuseness of the plan, owing to which the principal points of the investigation are easily lost sight of, the complaint is just, and I intend to remove it by the present *Prolegomena*.

The first-mentioned work, which discusses the pure faculty of reason in its whole compass and bounds, will remain the foundation, to which the *Prolegomena*, as a preliminary exercise, refer; for our critique must first be established as a complete and perfected science, before we can think of letting Metaphysics appear on the scene, or even have the most distant hope of attaining it.

We have been long accustomed to seeing antiquated knowledge produced as new by taking it out of its former context, and reducing it to system in a new suit of any fancy pattern under new titles. Most readers will set out by expecting nothing else from the *Critique*; but these *Prolegomena* may persuade him that it is a perfectly new science, of which no one has ever even thought, the very idea of which was unknown, and for which nothing hitherto accomplished can be of the smallest use, except it be

the suggestion of Hume's doubts. Yet even he did not suspect such a formal science, but ran his ship ashore, for safety's sake, landing on scepticism, there to let it lie and rot; whereas my object is rather to give it a pilot, who, by means of safe astronomical principles drawn from a knowledge of the globe, and provided with a complete chart and compass, may steer the ship safely, whither he listeth.

If in a new science, which is wholly isolated and unique in its kind, we started with the prejudice that we can judge of things by means of our previously acquired knowledge, which is precisely what has first to be called in question, we should only fancy we saw everywhere what we had already known, the expressions, having a similar sound, only that all would appear utterly metamorphosed, senseless and unintelligible, because we should have as a foundation our own notions, made by long habit a second nature, instead of the author's. But the longwindedness of the work, so far as it depends on the subject, and not the exposition, its consequent unavoidable dryness and its scholastic precision are qualities which can only benefit the science, though they may discredit the book.

Few writers are gifted with the subtlety, and at the same time with the grace, of David Hume, or with the depth, as well as the elegance, of Moses Mendelssohn. Yet I flatter myself I might have made my own exposition popular, had my object been merely to sketch out a plan and leave its completion to others, instead of having my heart in the welfare of the science, to which I had devoted myself so long; in truth, it required no little constancy, and even self-denial, to postpone the sweets of an immediate success to the prospect of a slower, but more lasting, reputation.

Making plans is often the occupation of an opulent and boastful mind, which thus obtains the reputation of a creative genius, by demanding what it cannot itself supply; by censuring, what it cannot improve; and by proposing, what it knows not where to find. And yet something more should belong to a sound plan of a general critique of pure reason than mere conjectures, if this plan is to be other than the usual declamations of pious aspirations. But pure reason is a sphere so separate and self-contained, that we cannot touch a part without affecting all the rest.

We can therefore do nothing without first determining the position of each part, and its relation to the rest; for, as our judgment cannot be corrected by anything without, the validity and use of every part depends upon the relation in which it stands to all the rest within the domain of reason.

So in the structure of an organized body, the end of each member can only be deduced from the full conception of the whole. It may, then, be said of such a critique that it is never trustworthy except it be perfectly complete, down to the smallest elements of pure reason. In the sphere of this faculty you can determine either everything or nothing.

But although a mere sketch, preceding the *Critique of Pure Reason*, would be unintelligible, unreliable, and useless, it is all the more useful as a sequel. For so we are able to grasp the whole, to examine in detail the chief points of importance in the science, and to improve in many respects our exposition, as compared with the first execution of the work.

After the completion of the work I offer here such a plan which is sketched out after an analytical method, while the work itself had to be executed in the synthetical style, in order that the science may present all its articulations, as the structure of a peculiar cognitive faculty, in their natural combination. But should any reader find this plan, which I published as the *Prolegomena to any future Metaphysics*, still obscure, let him consider that not every one is bound to study Metaphysics, that many minds will succeed very well, in the exact and even in deep sciences, more closely allied to practical experience, while they cannot succeed in investigations dealing exclusively with abstract concepts. In such cases men should apply their talents to other subjects. But he who undertakes to judge, or still more, to construct, a system of Metaphysics, must satisfy the demands here made, either by adopting my solution, or by thoroughly refuting it, and substituting another. To evade it is impossible.

In conclusion, let it be remembered that this much-abused obscurity (frequently serving as a mere pretext under which people hide their own indolence or dullness) has its uses, since all who in other sciences observe a judicious silence, speak authoritatively in metaphysics and make bold decisions, because their ignorance is not here contrasted with the knowledge of others. Yet it does contrast with sound critical principles, which we may therefore commend in the words of Virgil:

Ignavum, fucos, pecus a praesepibus arcent.[3]

PROLEGOMENA

PREAMBLE ON THE PECULIARITIES OF ALL METAPHYSICAL COGNITION

1. Of the Sources of Metaphysics

If it becomes desirable to formulate any cognition as science, it will be necessary first to determine accurately those peculiar features which no other science has in common with it, constituting its characteristics; otherwise the boundaries of all sciences become confused, and none of them can be treated thoroughly according to its nature.

The characteristics of a science may consist of a simple difference of object, or of the sources of cognition, or of the kind of cognition, or perhaps of all three conjointly. On this, therefore, depends the idea of a possible science and its territory.

First, as concerns the sources of metaphysical cognition, its very concept implies that they cannot be empirical. Its principles (including not only its maxims but its basic notions) must never be derived from experience. It must not be physical but metaphysical knowledge, viz., knowledge lying beyond experience. It can therefore have for its basis neither external experience, which is the source of physics proper, nor internal, which is the basis of empirical psychology. It is therefore *a priori* knowledge, coming from pure Understanding and pure Reason.

But so far Metaphysics would not be distinguishable from pure Mathematics; it must therefore be called pure philosophical cognition; and for the meaning of this term I refer to the *Critique of Pure Reason* (II. "Method of Transcendentalism," Chap. I., Sec. i), where the distinction between these two employments of the reason is sufficiently explained. So far concerning the sources of metaphysical cognition.

---

[3]"Bees are defending their hives against drones, those indolent creatures."

2. Concerning the Kind of Cognition Which Can Alone Be Called Metaphysical

a. *Of the distinction between Analytical and Synthetical Judgments in general.*—The peculiarity of its sources demands that metaphysical cognition must consist of nothing but *a priori* judgments. But whatever be their origin, or their logical form, there is a distinction in judgments, as to their content, according to which they are either merely explicative, adding nothing to the content of the cognition, or expansive, increasing the given cognition: the former may be called analytical, the latter synthetical, judgments.

Analytical judgments express nothing in the predicate but what has been already actually thought in the concept of the subject, though not so distinctly or with the same (full) consciousness. When I say: All bodies are extended, I have not amplified in the least my concept of body, but have only analysed it, as extension was really thought to belong to that concept before the judgment was made, though it was not expressed. This judgment is therefore analytical. On the contrary, this judgment, All bodies have weight, contains in its predicate something not actually thought in the general concept of the body; it amplifies my knowledge by adding something to my concept, and must therefore be called synthetical.

b. *The Common Principles of all Analytical Judgments is the Law of Contradiction.*—All analytical judgments depend wholly on the law of Contradiction, and are in their nature *a priori* cognitions, whether the concepts that supply them with matter be empirical or not. For the predicate of an affirmative analytical judgment is already contained in the concept of the subject, of which it cannot be denied without contradiction. In the same way its opposite is necessarily denied of the subject in an analytical, but negative, judgment, by the same law of contradiction. Such is the nature of the judgments: all bodies are extended, and no bodies are unextended (i.e., simple).

For this very reason all analytical judgments are *a priori* even when the concepts are empirical, as, for example, Gold is a yellow metal; for to know this I require no experience beyond my concept of gold as a yellow metal: it is, in fact, the very concept, and I need only analyse it, without looking beyond it elsewhere.

c. *Synthetical Judgments require a different Principle from the Law of Contradiction.*—There are synthetical *a posteriori* judgments of empirical origin; but there are also others which are proved to be certain *a priori*, and which spring from pure Understanding and Reason. Yet they both agree in this, that they cannot possibly spring from the principle of analysis, viz., the law of contradiction, alone; they require a quite different principle, though, from whatever they may be deduced, they must be subject to the law of contradiction, which must never be violated, even though everything cannot be deduced from it. I shall first classify synthetical judgments.

1. *Empirical Judgments* are always synthetical. For it would be absurd to base an analytical judgment on experience, as our concept suffices for the purpose without requiring any testimony from experience. That body is extended, is a judgment established *a priori*, and not an empirical judgment. For before appealing to experience, we already have all the conditions of the judgment in the concept, from which we have but to elicit the predicate according to the law of contradiction, and thereby to become conscious of the necessity of the judgment, which experience could not even teach us.

2. *Mathematical Judgments* are all synthetical. This fact seems hitherto to have altogether escaped the observation of those who have analysed human reason; it even seems directly opposed to all their conjectures, though incontestably certain, and most important in its consequences. For as it was found that the conclusions of mathematicians all proceed according to the law of contradiction (as is demanded by all apodeictic certainty), men persuaded themselves that the fundamental principles were known from the same law. This was a great mistake, for a synthetical proposition can indeed be comprehended according to the law of contradiction, but only by presupposing another synthetical proposition from which it follows, but never in itself.

First of all, we must observe that all proper mathematical judgments are *a priori*, and not empirical, because they carry with them necessity, which cannot be obtained from experience. But if this be not conceded to me, very good; I shall confine my assertion to *pure Mathematics*, the very notion of which implies that it contains pure *a priori* and not empirical cognitions.

It might at first be thought that the proposition $7 + 5 = 12$ is a mere analytical judgment, following from the concept of the sum of seven and five, according to the law of contradiction. But on closer examination it appears that the concept of the sum of $7 + 5$ contains merely their union in a single number, without its being at all thought what the particular number is that unites them. The concept of twelve is by no means thought by merely thinking of the combination of seven and five; and analyse this possible sum as we may, we shall not discover twelve in the concept. We must go beyond these concepts, by calling to our aid some concrete image, i.e., either our five fingers, or five points (as Segner has it in his *Arithmetic*), and we must add successively the units of the five, given in some concrete image, to the concept of seven. Hence our concept is really amplified by the proposition $7 + 5 = 12$, and we add to the first a second, not thought in it. Arithmetical judgments are therefore synthetical, and the more plainly according as we take larger numbers; for in such cases it is clear that, however closely we analyse our concepts without calling visual images to our aid, we can never find the sum by such mere dissection.

All principles of geometry are no less analytical. That a straight line is the shortest path between two points, is a synthetical proposition. For my concept of straight contains nothing of quantity, but only a quality. The attribute of shortness is therefore altogether additional, and cannot be obtained by any analysis of the concept. Here, too, visualisation must come to aid us. It alone makes the synthesis possible.

Some other principles, assumed by geometers, are indeed actually analytical, and depend on the law of contradiction; but they only serve, as identical propositions, as a method of concatenation, and not as principles, e.g., $a = a$, the whole is equal to itself, or $a + b > a$, the whole is greater than its part. And yet even these, though they are recognised as valid from mere concepts, are only admitted in mathematics, because they can be represented in some visual form. What usually makes us believe that the predicate of such apodeictic[4] judgments is already contained in

our concept, and that the judgment is therefore analytical, is the duplicity of the expression, requesting us to think a certain predicate as of necessity implied in the thought of a given concept, which necessity attaches to the concept. But the question is not what we are requested to join in thought *to* the given concept, but what we actually think together with and in it, though obscurely; and so it appears that the predicate belongs to these concepts necessarily indeed, yet not directly but indirectly by an added visualisation.

3. A Remark on the General Division of Judgments into Analytical and Synthetical

This division is indispensable, as concerns the critique of human understanding, and therefore deserves to be called classical, though otherwise it is of little use, but this is the reason why dogmatic philosophers, who always seek the sources of metaphysical judgments in Metaphysics itself, and not apart from it, in the pure laws of reason generally, altogether neglected this apparently obvious distinction. Thus the celebrated Wolf, and his acute follower Baumgarten, came to seek the proof of the principle of Sufficient Reason, which is clearly synthetical, in the principle of Contradiction. In Locke's Essay, however, I find an indication of my division. For in the fourth book (chap. iii. § 9, seq.), having discussed the various connexions of representations in judgments, and their sources, one of which he makes "identity and contradiction" (analytical judgments), and another the coexistence of representations in a subject, he confesses (§ 10) that our *a priori* knowledge of the latter is very narrow, and almost nothing. But in his remarks on this species of cognition, there is so little of what is definite, and reduced to rules, that we cannot wonder if no one, not even Hume, was led to make investigations concerning this sort of judgments. For such general and yet definite principles are not easily learned from other men, who have had them obscurely in their minds. We must hit on them first by our own reflexion, then we find them elsewhere, where we could not possibly have found them at first, because the authors themselves did not know that such an idea lay at the basis of their observations. Men who never think independently have nevertheless the

---

[4]Kant borrows the term *apodeictic* from Aristotle who uses it in the sense of "certain beyond dispute."

acuteness to discover everything, after it has been once shown them, in what was said long since, though no one ever saw it there before.

4. The General Question of the Prolegomena.— Is Metaphysics at All Possible?

Were a metaphysics, which could maintain its place as a science, really in existence; could we say, here is metaphysics, learn it, and it will convince you irresistibly and irrevocably of its truth? This question would be useless, and there would only remain that other question (which would rather be a test of our acuteness, than a proof of the existence of the thing itself), "How is the science possible, and how does reason come to attain it?" But human reason has not been so fortunate in this case. There is no single book to which you can point as you do to Euclid, and say: This is Metaphysics; here you may find the noblest objects of this science, the knowledge of a highest Being, and of a future existence, proved from principles of pure reason. We can be shown indeed many judgments, demonstrably certain, and never questioned; but these are all analytical, and rather concern the materials and the scaffolding for Metaphysics, than the extension of knowledge, which is our proper object in studying it (§ 2). Even supposing you produce synthetical judgments (such as the law of Sufficient Reason, which you have never proved, as you ought to, from pure reason *a priori*, though we gladly concede its truth), you lapse when they come to be employed for your principal object, into such doubtful assertions, that in all ages one Metaphysics has contradicted another, either in its assertions, or their proofs, and thus has itself destroyed its own claim to lasting assent. Nay, the very attempts to set up such a science are the main cause of the early appearance of scepticism, a mental attitude in which reason treats itself with such violence that it could never have arisen save from complete despair of ever satisfying our most important aspirations. For long before men began to inquire into nature methodically, they consulted abstract reason, which had to some extent been exercised by means of ordinary experience; for reason is ever present, while laws of nature must usually be discovered with labor. So Metaphysics floated to the surface, like foam, which dissolved the moment it was scooped off. But immediately there appeared

a new supply on the surface, to be ever eagerly gathered up by some, while others, instead of seeking in the depths the cause of the phenomenon, thought they showed their wisdom by ridiculing the idle labor of their neighbors.

The essential and distinguishing feature of pure mathematical cognition among all other *a priori* cognitions is, that it cannot at all proceed from concepts, but only by means of the construction of concepts (see *Critique* II., Method of Transcendentalism, chap. I., sect. I). As therefore in its judgments it must proceed beyond the concept to that which its corresponding visualisation contains, these judgments neither can, nor ought to, arise analytically, by dissecting the concept, but are all synthetical.

I cannot refrain from pointing out the disadvantage resulting to philosophy from the neglect of this easy and apparently insignificant observation. Hume being prompted (a task worthy of a philosopher) to cast his eye over the whole field of *a priori* cognitions in which human understanding claims such mighty possessions, heedlessly severed from it a whole, and indeed its most valuable, province, viz., pure mathematics; for he thought its nature, or, so to speak, the state-constitution of this empire, depended on totally different principles, namely, on the law of contradiction alone; and although he did not divide judgments in this manner formally and universally as I have done here, what he said was equivalent to this: that mathematics contains only analytical, but metaphysics synthetical, *a priori* judgments. In this, however, he was greatly mistaken, and the mistake had a decidedly injurious effect upon his whole conception. But for this, he would have extended his question concerning the origin of our synthetical judgments far beyond the metaphysical concept of Causality, and included in it the possibility of mathematics *a priori* also, for this latter he must have assumed to be equally synthetical. And then he could not have based his metaphysical judgments on mere experience without subjecting the axioms of mathematics equally to experience, a thing which he was far too acute to do. The good company into which metaphysics would thus have been brought, would have saved it from the danger of a contemptuous ill-treatment, for the thrust intended for it must have reached mathematics, which was not and could not have been Hume's intention. Thus that acute man would have been led into considerations which must needs be similar to those that now occupy us, but which would have gained inestimably by his inimitably elegant style.

Metaphysical judgments, properly so called, are all synthetical. We must distinguish judgments pertaining to metaphysics from metaphysical judgments properly so called. Many of the former are analytical, but they only afford the means for metaphysical judgments, which are the whole end of the science, and which are always synthetical. For if there be concepts pertaining to metaphysics (as, for example, that of substance), the judgments springing from simple analysis of them also pertain to metaphysics, as, for example, substance is that which only exists as subject; and by means of several such analytical judgments, we seek to approach the definition of the concept. But as the analysis of a pure concept of the understanding pertaining to metaphysics, does not proceed in any different manner from the dissection of any other, even empirical, concepts, not pertaining to metaphysics (such as: air is an elastic fluid, the elasticity of which is not destroyed by any known degree of cold), it follows that the concept indeed, but not the analytical judgment, is properly metaphysical. This science has something peculiar in the production of its *a priori* cognitions, which must therefore be distinguished from the features it has in common with other rational knowledge. Thus the judgment, that all the substance in things is permanent, is a synthetical and properly metaphysical judgment.

If the *a priori* principles, which constitute the materials of metaphysics, have first been collected according to fixed principles, then their analysis will be of great value; it might be taught as a particular part (as a *philosophia definitiva*), containing nothing but analytical judgments pertaining to metaphysics, and could be treated separately from the synthetical which constitute metaphysics proper. For indeed these analyses are not elsewhere of much value, except in metaphysics, i.e., as regards the synthetical judgments, which are to be generated by these previously analysed concepts.

The conclusion drawn in this section then is, that metaphysics is properly concerned with synthetical propositions *a priori*, and these alone constitute its

end, for which it indeed requires various dissections of its concepts, viz., of its analytical judgments, but wherein the procedure is not different from that in every other kind of knowledge, in which we merely seek to render our concepts distinct by analysis. But the generation of *a priori* cognition by concrete images as well as by concepts, [together with] synthetical propositions *a priori* in philosophical cognition, constitutes the essential subject of Metaphysics.

Weary therefore as well of dogmatism, which teaches us nothing, as of scepticism, which does not even promise us anything, not even the quiet state of a contented ignorance; disquieted by the importance of knowledge so much needed; and lastly, rendered suspicious by long experience of all knowledge which we believe we possess, or which offers itself, under the title of pure reason: there remains but one critical question on the answer to which our future procedure depends, viz., *Is Metaphysics at all possible?* But this question must be answered not by sceptical objections to the asseverations of some actual system of metaphysics (for we do not as yet admit such a thing to exist), but from the conception, as yet only problematical, of a science of this sort.

In the *Critique of Pure Reason* I have treated this question synthetically, by making inquiries into pure reason itself, and endeavoring in this source to determine the elements as well as the laws of its pure use according to principles. The task is difficult, and requires a resolute reader to penetrate by degrees into a system, based on no data except reason itself, and which therefore seeks, without resting upon any fact, to unfold knowledge from its original germs. *Prolegomena*, however, are designed for preparatory exercises—they are intended rather to point out what we have to do in order if possible to actualise a science, than to propound it. They must therefore rest upon something already known as trustworthy, from which we can set out with confidence, and ascend to sources as yet unknown, the discovery of which will not only explain to us what we knew, but exhibit a sphere of many cognitions which all spring from the same sources. The method of *Prolegomena*, especially of those designed as a preparation for future metaphysics, is consequently analytical.

But it happens fortunately, that though we cannot assume metaphysics to be an actual science, we can say with confidence that certain pure *a priori* synthetical cognitions, pure Mathematics and pure Physics are actual and given; for both contain propositions, which are thoroughly recognised as apodeictically certain partly by mere reason, partly by general consent arising from experience, and yet as independent of experience. We have therefore some at least uncontested synthetical knowledge *a priori*, and need not ask *whether* it be possible, for it is actual, but how it is possible, in order that we may deduce from the principle which makes the given knowledge possible the possibility of all the rest.

5. The General Problem: How Is Knowledge from Pure Reason Possible?

We have above learned the significant distinction between analytical and synthetical judgments. The possibility of analytical propositions was easily comprehended, being entirely founded on the law of Contradiction. The possibility of synthetical *a posteriori* judgments, of those which are gathered from experience, also requires no particular explanation; for experience is nothing but a continual synthesis of perceptions. There remain therefore only synthetical propositions *a priori*, of which the possibility must be sought or investigated, because they must depend upon other principles than the law of contradiction.

But here we need not first establish the possibility of such propositions so as to ask whether they are possible. For there are enough of them which indeed are of undoubted certainty, and as our present method is analytical, we shall start from the fact, that such synthetical but purely rational cognition actually exists; but we must now inquire into the reason of this possibility, and ask, *how* such cognition is possible, in order that we may from the principles of its possibility be enabled to determine the conditions of its use, its sphere and its limits. The proper problem upon which all depends, when expressed with scholastic precision, is therefore:

How are Synthetical Propositions a priori possible?

For the sake of popularity I have above expressed this problem somewhat differently, as an inquiry into purely rational cognition, which I could do for once without detriment to the desired comprehension, because, as we have only to do here with metaphysics and its sources, the reader will, I hope, after the foregoing remarks, keep in mind that when we speak of purely rational cognition, we do not mean analytical, but synthetical cognition.[5]

Metaphysics stands or falls with the solution of this problem: its very existence depends upon it. Let any one make metaphysical assertions with ever so much plausibility, let him overwhelm us with conclusions, if he has not previously proved able to answer this question satisfactorily, I have a right to say: this is all vain baseless philosophy and false wisdom. You speak through pure reason, and claim, as it were to create cognitions *a priori* by not only dissecting given concepts, but also by asserting connexions which do not rest upon the law of contradiction, and which you believe you conceive quite independently of all experience; how do you arrive at this, and how will you justify your pretensions? An appeal to the consent of the common sense of mankind cannot be allowed; for that is a witness whose authority depends merely upon rumor. Says Horace:

Quodcunque ostendis mihi sic, incredulus odi[6]

---

[5]It is unavoidable that as knowledge advances, certain expressions which have become classical after having been used since the Infancy of science, will be found inadequate and unsuitable and a newer and more appropriate application of the terms will give rise to confusion. [This is the case with the term "analytical."] The analytical method, so far as it is opposed to the synthetical, is very different from that which constitutes the essence of analytical propositions: it signifies only that we start from what is sought, as if it were given, and ascend to the only conditions under which it is possible. In this method we often use nothing but synthetical propositions, as in mathematical analysis, and it were better to term it the regressive method, in contradistinction to the synthetic or progressive. A principal part of Logic too is distinguished by the name of Analytics, which here signifies the logic of truth in contrast to Dialectics without considering whether the cognitions belonging to it are analytical or synthetical.

[6]"To all that which thou provest me thus I refuse to give credence and hate."

The answer to this question, though indispensable, is difficult; and though the principal reason that it was not made long ago is, that the possibility of the question never occurred to anybody, there is yet another reason, which is this that a satisfactory answer to this one question requires a much more persistent, profound, and painstaking reflexion, than the most diffuse work on Metaphysics, which on its first appearance promised immortality to its author. And every intelligent reader, when he carefully reflects what this problem requires, must at first be struck with its difficulty, and would regard it as insoluble and even impossible, did there not actually exist pure synthetical cognitions *a priori*. This actually happened to David Hume, though he did not conceive the question in its entire universality as is done here, and as must be done, should the answer be decisive for all Metaphysics. For how is it possible, says that acute man, that when a concept is given me, I can go beyond it and connect with it another, which is not contained in it, in such a manner as if the latter necessarily belonged to the former? Nothing but experience can furnish us with such connexions (thus he concluded from the difficulty which he took to be an impossibility), and all that vaunted necessity, or, what is the same thing, all cognition assumed to be *a priori*, is nothing but a long habit of accepting something as true, and hence of mistaking subjective necessity for objective.

Should my reader complain of the difficulty and the trouble which I occasion him in the solution of this problem, he is at liberty to solve it himself in an easier way. Perhaps he will then feel under obligation to the person who has undertaken for him a labor of so profound research, and will rather be surprised at the facility with which, considering the nature of the subject, the solution has been attained. Yet it has cost years of work to solve the problem in its whole universality (using the term in the mathematical sense, viz., for that which is sufficient for all cases), and finally to exhibit it in the analytical form, as the reader finds it here.

 All metaphysicians are therefore solemnly and legally suspended from their occupations till they shall have answered in a satisfactory manner the question, "How are synthetic cognitions *a priori* possible?" For the answer contains the only credentials which they must show when they have anything to offer in the name of pure reason. But if they do not possess these credentials, they can expect nothing else of reasonable people, who have been deceived so often, than to be dismissed without further ado.

If they on the other hand desire to carry on their business, not as a science, but as an art of wholesome oratory suited to the common sense of man, they cannot in justice be prevented. They will then speak the modest language of a rational belief, they will grant that they are not allowed even to conjecture, far less to know, anything which lies beyond the bounds of all possible experience, but only to assume (not for speculative use, which they must abandon, but for practical purposes only) the existence of something that is possible and even indispensable for the guidance of the understanding and of the will in life. In this manner alone can they be called useful and wise men, and the more so as they renounce the title of metaphysicians; for the latter profess to be speculative philosophers, and since, when judgments *a priori* are under discussion, poor probabilities cannot be admitted (for what is declared to be known *a priori* is thereby announced as necessary), such men cannot be permitted to play with conjectures, but their assertions must be either science, or are worth nothing at all.

It may be said, that the entire transcendental philosophy, which necessarily precedes all metaphysics, is nothing but the complete solution of the problem here propounded, in systematical order and completeness, and hitherto we have never had any transcendental philosophy; for what goes by its name is properly a part of metaphysics whereas the former science is intended first to constitute the possibility of the latter, and must therefore precede all metaphysics. And it is not surprising that when a whole science, deprived of all help from other sciences, and consequently in itself quite new, is required to answer a single question satisfactorily, we should find the answer troublesome and difficult, nay even shrouded in obscurity.

As we now proceed to this solution according to the analytical method, in which we assume that such cognitions from pure reasons actually exist, we can only appeal to two sciences of theoretical cognition (which alone is under consideration here), pure mathematics and pure natural science (physics). For these alone can exhibit to us objects in a definite and actualisable form, and consequently (if there should occur in them a cognition *a priori*) can show the truth or conformity of the cognition to the object *in concreto*, that is, its actuality, from which we could proceed to the reason of its possibility by the analytic method. This facilitates our work greatly for here universal considerations are not only applied to facts, but even start from them, while in a synthetic procedure they must strictly be derived *in abstracto* from concepts.

But, in order to rise from these actual and at the same time well-grounded pure cognitions *a priori* to such a possible cognition of the same as we are seeking, viz., to metaphysics as a science, we must comprehend that which occasions it, I mean the mere natural, though in spite of its truth still suspect, cognition *a priori* which lies at the bottom of that science, the elaboration of which without any critical investigation of its possibility is commonly called metaphysics. In a word, we must comprehend the natural conditions of such a science as a part of our inquiry, and thus the transcendental problem will be gradually answered by a division into four questions:

1. How is pure mathematics possible?
2. How is pure natural science possible?
3. How is metaphysics in general possible?
4. How is metaphysics as a science possible?

It may be seen that the solution of these problems, though chiefly designed to exhibit the essential matter of the *Critique*, has yet something peculiar, which for itself alone deserves attention. This is the search for the sources of given sciences in reason itself, so that its faculty of knowing something *a priori* may by its own deeds be investigated and measured. By this procedure these sciences gain, if not with regard to their contents, yet as to their proper use, and while they throw light on the higher question concerning their common origin, they give, at the same time, an occasion better to explain their own nature.

FIRST PART OF THE TRANSCENDENTAL PROBLEM

HOW IS PURE MATHEMATICS POSSIBLE?

6. Here is a great and established branch of knowledge, encompassing even now a wonderfully large domain and promising an unlimited extension in the future. Yet it carries with it thoroughly apodeictical certainty, i.e., absolute necessity, which therefore rests upon no empirical grounds. Consequently it is a pure product of reason, and moreover is thoroughly synthetical. [Here the question arises:]

"How then is it possible for human reason to produce a cognition of this nature entirely *a priori*?"

Does not this faculty [which produces mathematics], as it neither is nor can be based upon experience, presuppose some ground of cognition *a priori*, which lies deeply hidden, but which might reveal itself by these its effects, if their first beginnings were but diligently ferreted out?

7. But we find that all mathematical cognition has this peculiarity: it must first exhibit its concept in a visual form and indeed *a priori*, therefore in a visual form which is not empirical, but pure. Without this mathematics cannot take a single step; hence its judgments are always visual, viz., "intuitive"; whereas philosophy must be satisfied with discursive judgments from mere concepts, and though it may illustrate its doctrines through a visual figure, can never derive them from it. This observation on the nature of mathematics gives us a clue to the first and highest condition of its possibility, which is, that some non-sensuous visualisation (called pure intuition) must form its basis, in which all its concepts can be exhibited or constructed, *in concreto* and yet *a priori*. If we can find out this pure intuition and its possibility, we may thence easily explain how synthetical propositions *a priori* are possible in pure mathematics, and consequently how this science itself is possible. Empirical intuition [viz., sense-perception] enables us without difficulty to enlarge the concept which we frame of an object of intuition [or sense-perception], by new predicates, which intuition [i.e., sense perception] itself presents synthetically in experience. Pure intuition [viz., the visualisation of forms in our imagination, from

are intuit a priori objects as they appear to us not as they are—

which every thing sensual, i.e., every thought of material qualities, is excluded] does so likewise, only with this difference, that in the latter case the synthetical judgment is *a priori* certain and apodeictical, in the former, only *a posteriori* and empirically certain; because this latter contains only that which occurs in contingent empirical intuition, but the former, that which must necessarily be discovered in pure intuition. Here intuition, being an intuition *a priori*, is *before all experience*, viz., before any perception of particular objects, inseparably conjoined with its concept.

8. But with this step our perplexity seems rather to increase than to lessen. for the question now is, "How is it possible to intuit [in a visual form] anything *a priori*?" An intuition [viz., a visual sense-perception] is such a representation as immediately depends upon the presence of the object. Hence it seems impossible to intuit from the outset *a priori*, because intuition would in that event take place without either a former or a present object to refer to, and by consequence could not be intuition. Concepts indeed are such, that we can easily form some of them *a priori*, viz., such as contain nothing but the thought of an object in general; and we need not find ourselves in an immediate relation to the object. Take, for instance, the concepts of Quantity, of Cause, etc. But even these require, in order to make them understood, a certain concrete use—that is, an application to some sense-experience by which an object of them is given us. But how can the intuition of the object [its visualization] precede the object itself?

9. If our intuition [i.e., our sense-experience] were perforce of such a nature as to represent things as they are in themselves, there would not be any intuition *a priori*, but intuition would be always empirical. For I can only know what is contained in the object in itself when it is present and given to me. It is indeed even then incomprehensible how the visualising of a present thing should make me know this thing as it is in itself, as its properties cannot migrate into my faculty of representation. But even granting this possibility, a visualising of that sort would not take place *a priori*, that is, before the object were presented to me; for without this latter fact no reason of a relation between my representation and the object can be imagined, unless it depend upon a direct inspiration.

Therefore in one way only can my intuition anticipate the actuality of the object, and be a cognition *a priori*, viz.: if my intuition contains nothing but the form of sensibility, antedating in my subjectivity all the actual impressions through which I am affected by objects.

For that objects of sense can only be intuited according to this form of sensibility I can know *a priori*. Hence it follows: that propositions, which concern this form of sensuous intuition only, are possible and valid for objects of the senses; as also, conversely, that intuitions which are possible *a priori* can never concern any other things than objects of our senses.

10. Accordingly, it is only the form of sensuous intuition by which we can intuit things *a priori*, but by which we can know objects only as they appear to us (to our senses), not as they are in themselves; and this assumption is absolutely necessary if synthetical propositions *a priori* be granted as possible, or if, in case they actually occur, their possibility is to be comprehended and determined beforehand.

Now, the intuitions which pure mathematics lays at the foundation of all its cognitions and judgments which appear at once apodeictic and necessary are Space and Time. For mathematics must first have all its concepts in intuition, and pure mathematics in pure intuition, that is, it must construct them. If it proceeded in any other way, it would be impossible to make any headway, for mathematics proceeds, not analytically by dissection of concepts, but synthetically, and if pure intuition be wanting, there is nothing in which the matter for synthetical judgments *a priori* can be given. Geometry is based upon the pure intuition of space. Arithmetic accomplishes its concept of number by the successive addition of units in time; and pure mechanics especially cannot attain its concepts of motion without employing the representation of time. Both representations, however, are only intuitions; for if we omit from the empirical intuitions of bodies and their alterations (motion) everything empirical, or belonging to sensation, space and time still remain, which are therefore pure intuitions that lie *a priori* at the basis of the empirical. Hence they can never be omitted, but at the same

[handwritten margin notes: "mathematics" (top left); "time & space are sensory qualities not actual" (top right)]

time, by their being pure intuitions *a priori*, they prove that they are mere forms of our sensibility, which must precede all empirical intuition, or perception of actual objects, and conformably to which objects can be known *a priori*, but only as they appear to us.

11. The problem of the present section is therefore solved. Pure mathematics, as synthetical cognition *a priori*, is only possible by referring to no other objects than those of the senses. At the basis of their empirical intuition lies a pure intuition (of space and of time) which is *a priori*. This is possible, because the latter intuition is nothing but the mere form of sensibility, which precedes the actual appearance of the objects, in that it, in fact, makes them possible. Yet this faculty of intuiting *a priori* affects not the matter of the phenomenon (that is, the sense-element in it, for this constitutes that which is empirical), but its form, viz., space and time. Should any man venture to doubt that these are determinations adhering not to things in themselves, but to their relation to our sensibility, I should be glad to know how it can be possible to know the constitution of things *a priori*, viz., before we have any acquaintance with them and before they are presented to us. Such, however, is the case with space and time. But this is quite comprehensible as soon as both count for nothing more than formal conditions of our sensibility, while the objects count merely as phenomena; for then the form of the phenomenon, i.e., pure intuition, can by all means be represented as proceeding from ourselves, that is, *a priori*.

12. In order to add something by way of illustration and confirmation, we need only watch the ordinary and necessary procedure of geometers. All proofs of the complete congruence of two given figures (where the one can in every respect be substituted for the other) come ultimately to this that they may be made to coincide; which is evidently nothing else than a synthetical proposition resting upon immediate intuition, and this intuition must be pure, or given *a priori*, otherwise the proposition could not rank as apodeictically certain, but would have empirical certainty only. In that case, it could only be said that it is always found to be so, and holds good only as far as our perception reaches. That everywhere space (which [in its entirety] is itself no

longer the boundary of another space) has three dimensions, and that space cannot in any way have more, is based on the proposition that not more than three lines can intersect at right angles in one point; but this proposition cannot by any means be shown from concepts, but rests immediately on intuition, and indeed on pure and *a priori* intuition, because it is apodeictically certain. That we can require a line to be drawn to infinity (*in indefinitum*), or that a series of changes (for example, space traversed by motion) shall be infinitely continued, presupposes a representation of space and time, which can only attach to intuition, namely, so far as it in itself is bounded by nothing, for from concepts it could never be inferred. Consequently, the basis of mathematics actually are pure intuitions, which make its synthetical and apodeictically valid propositions possible. Hence our transcendental deduction of the notions of space and of time explains at the same time the possibility of pure mathematics. Without some such deduction its truth may be granted, but its existence could by no means be understood, and we must assume "that everything which can be given to our senses (to the external senses in space, to the internal one in time) is intuited by us as it appears to us not as it is in itself."

13. Those who cannot yet rid themselves of the notion that space and time are actual qualities inhering in things in themselves, may exercise their acumen on the following paradox. When they have in vain attempted its solution, and are free from prejudices at least for a few moments, they will suspect that the degradation of space and of time to mere forms of our sensuous intuition may perhaps be well founded.

If two things are quite equal in all respects as much as can be ascertained by all means possible, quantitatively and qualitatively, it must follow, that the one can in all cases and under all circumstances replace the other, and this substitution would not occasion the least perceptible difference. This in fact is true of plane figures in geometry; but some spherical figures exhibit, notwithstanding a complete internal agreement, such a contrast in their external relation, that the one figure cannot possibly be put in the place of the other. For instance, two spherical triangles on opposite hemispheres, which have an arc of the equator as their common base, may be quite equal, both as regards sides and angles, so that nothing is to be found in either, if it be described for itself alone and completed, that would not equally be applicable to both; and yet the one cannot be put in the place of the other (being situated upon the opposite hemisphere). Here then is an internal difference between the two triangles, which difference our understanding cannot describe as internal, and which only manifests itself by external relations in space.

But I shall adduce examples, taken from common life, that are more obvious still.

What can be more similar in every respect and in every part more alike to my hand and to my ear, than their images in a mirror? And yet I cannot put such a hand as is seen in the glass in the place of its archetype; for if this is a right hand, that in the glass is a left one, and the image or reflexion of the right ear is a left one which never can serve as a substitute for the other. There are in this case no internal differences which our understanding could determine by thinking alone. Yet the differences are internal as the senses teach, for, notwithstanding their complete equality and similarity, the left hand cannot be enclosed in the same bounds as the right one (they are not congruent); the glove of one hand cannot be used for the other. What is the solution? These objects are not representations of things as they are in themselves, and as the pure understanding would cognise them, but sensuous intuitions that is, appearances, the possibility of which rests upon the relation of certain things unknown in themselves to something else, viz., to our sensibility. Space is the form of the external intuition of this sensibility, and the internal determination of every space is only possible by the determination of its external relation to the whole space, of which it is a part (in other words, by its relation to the external sense). That is to say, the part is only possible through the whole, which is never the case with things in themselves, as objects of the mere understanding, but with appearances only. Hence the difference between similar and equal things, which are yet not congruent (for instance, two symmetric helices), cannot be made intelligible by any concept, but only by the relation to the right and the left hands which immediately refers to intuition.

Remark I

Pure Mathematics, and especially pure geometry, can only have objective reality on condition that they refer to objects of sense. But in regard to the latter the principle holds good, that our sense representation is not a representation of things in themselves, but of the way in which they appear to us. Hence it follows, that the propositions of geometry are not the results of a mere creation of our poetic imagination, and that therefore they cannot be referred with assurance to actual objects; but rather that they are necessarily valid of space, and consequently of all that may be found in space, because space is nothing else than the form of all external appearances, and it is this form alone in which objects of sense can be given. Sensibility, the form of which is the basis of geometry, is that upon which the possibility of external appearance depends. Therefore these appearances can never contain anything but what geometry prescribes to them.

It would be quite otherwise if the senses were so constituted as to represent objects as they are in themselves. For then it would not by any means follow from the conception of space, which with all its properties serves to the geometer as an *a priori* foundation, together with what is thence inferred, must be so in nature. The space of the geometer would be considered a mere fiction, and it would not be credited with objective validity, because we cannot see how things must of necessity agree with an image of them, which we make spontaneously and previous to our acquaintance with them. But if this image, or rather this formal intuition, is the essential property of our sensibility, by means of which alone objects are given to us, and if this sensibility represents not things in themselves, but their appearances: we shall easily comprehend, and at the same time indisputably prove, that all external objects of our world of sense must necessarily coincide in the most rigorous way with the propositions of geometry; because sensibility by means of its form of external intuition, viz., by space, the same with which the geometer is occupied, makes those objects at all possible as mere appearances.

It will always remain a remarkable phenomenon in the history of philosophy, that there was a time, when even mathematicians, who at the same time were philosophers, began to doubt, not of the accuracy of their geometrical propositions so far as they concerned space, but of their objective validity and the applicability of this concept itself, and of all its corollaries, to nature. They showed much concern whether a line in nature might not consist of physical points, and consequently that true space in the object might not consist of physical points, and consequently that true space in the object might consist of simple [discrete] parts, while the space which the geometer has in his mind [being continuous] cannot be such. They did not recognise that this mental space renders possible the physical space, i.e., the extension of matter; that this pure space is not at all a quality of things in themselves, but a form of our sensuous faculty of representation; and that all objects in space are mere appearances, i.e., not things in themselves but representations of our sensuous intuition. But such is the case, for the space of the geometer is exactly the form of sensuous intuition which we find *a priori* in us, and contains the ground of the possibility of all external appearances (according to their form), and the latter must necessarily and most rigidly agree with the propositions of the geometer, which he draws not from any fictitious concept, but from the subjective basis of all external phenomena, which is sensibility itself. In this and no other way can geometry be made secure as to the undoubted objective reality of its propositions against all the intrigues of a shallow Metaphysics, which is surprised at them [the geometrical propositions], because it has not traced them to the sources of their concepts.

Remark II

Whatever is given us as object, must be given us in intuition. All our intuition however takes place by means of the senses only; the understanding intuits nothing, but only reflects. And as we have just shown that the senses never and in no manner enable us to know things in themselves, but only their appearances, which are mere representations of the sensibility, we conclude that "all bodies, together with the space in which they are, must be considered nothing but mere representations in us, and exist nowhere but

in our thoughts." You will say: Is not this manifest idealism?

Idealism consists in the assertion, that there are none but thinking beings, all other things, which we think are perceived in intuition, being nothing but representations in the thinking beings, to which no object external to them corresponds in fact. Whereas I say, that things as objects of our senses existing outside us are given, but we know nothing of what they may be in themselves, knowing only their appearances, i.e., the representations which they cause in us by affecting our senses. Consequently I grant by all means that there are bodies without us, that is, things which, though quite unknown to us as to what they are in themselves, we yet know by the representations which their influence on our sensibility procures us, and which we call bodies, a term signifying merely the appearance of the thing which is unknown to us, but not therefore less actual. Can this be termed idealism? It is the very contrary.

Long before Locke's time, but assuredly since him, it has been generally assumed and granted without detriment to the actual existence of external things, that many of their predicates may be said to belong not to the things in themselves, but to their appearances, and to have no proper existence outside our representation. Heat, color, and taste, for instance, are of this kind. Now, if I go farther, and for weighty reasons rank as mere appearances the remaining qualities of bodies also, which are called primary, such as extension, place, and in general space, with all that which belongs to it (impenetrability or materiality, space, etc.)—no one in the least can adduce the reason of its being inadmissible. As little as the man who admits colors not to be properties of the object in itself, but only as modifications of the sense of sight, should on that account be called an idealist, so little can my system be named idealistic, merely because I find that more, nay,

All the properties which constitute the intuition of a body belong merely to its appearance.

The existence of the thing that appears is thereby not destroyed, as in genuine idealism, but it is only shown, that we cannot possibly know it by the senses as it is in itself.

I should be glad to know what my assertions must be in order to avoid all idealism. Undoubtedly, I should say, that the representation of space is not only perfectly conformable to the relation which our sensibility has to objects—that I have said—but that it is quite similar to the object,—an assertion in which I can find as little meaning as if I said that the sensation of red has a similarity to the property of vermilion, which in me excites this sensation.

Remark III

Hence we may at once dismiss an easily foreseen but futile objection, "that by admitting the ideality of space and of time the whole sensible world would be turned into mere sham." At first all philosophical insight into the nature of sensuous cognition was spoiled, by making the sensibility merely a confused mode of representation, according to which we still know things as they are, but without being able to reduce everything in this our representation to a clear consciousness; whereas proof is offered by us that sensibility consists, not in this logical distinction of clearness and obscurity, but in the genetical one of the origin of cognition itself. For sensuous perception represents things not at all as they are, but only the mode in which they affect our senses, and consequently by sensuous perception appearances only and not things themselves are given to the understanding for reflexion. After this necessary corrective, an objection rises from an unpardonable and almost intentional misconception, as if my doctrine turned all the things of the world of sense into mere illusion.

When an appearance is given us, we are still quite free as to how we should judge the matter. The appearance depends upon the senses, but the judgment upon the understanding, and the only question is, whether in the determination of the object there is truth or not. But the difference between truth and dreaming is not ascertained by the nature of the representations, which are referred to objects (for they are the same in both cases), but by their connexion according to those rules, which determine the coherence of the representations in the concept of an object, and by ascertaining whether they can subsist together in experience or not. And it is not the fault of the appearances if our cognition takes illusion for truth, i.e., if the intuition, by which an object is given us, is considered a concept of the thing or of its existence also, which the understanding can only think. The senses represent to us the paths of the planets as now progressive, now retrogressive, and herein is neither falsehood nor truth, because as long as we hold this path to be nothing but appearance, we do not judge of the objective nature of their motion. But as a false judgment may easily arise when the understanding is not on its guard against this subjective mode of representation being considered objective, we say they appear to move backward; it is not the senses however which must be charged with the illusion, but the understanding, whose province alone it is to give an objective judgment on appearances.

Thus, even if we did not at all reflect on the origin of our representations, whenever we connect our intuitions of sense (whatever they may contain), in space and in time, according to the rules of coherence of all cognition in experience, illusion or truth will arise according as we are negligent or careful. It is merely a question of the use of sensuous representations in the understanding, and not of their origin. In the same way, if I consider all the representations of the senses, together with their form, space and time, to be nothing but appearances, and space and time to be a mere form of the sensibility, which is not to be met with in objects out of it, and if I make use of these representations in reference to possible experience only, there is nothing in my regarding them as appearances that can lead astray or cause illusion. For all that they can correctly cohere according to rules of truth in experience. Thus all the propositions of geometry hold good of space as well as of all the objects of the senses, consequently of all possible experience, whether I consider space as a mere form of the sensibility, or as something cleaving to the things themselves. In the former case however I comprehend how I can know *a priori* these propositions concerning all the objects of external intuition. Otherwise everything else as regards all possible experience remains just as if I had not departed from the vulgar view.

But if I venture to go beyond all possible experience with my notions of space and time, which I cannot refrain from doing if I proclaim them qualities inherent in things in themselves (for what should prevent me from letting them hold good of the same things, even though my senses might be different, and unsuited to them?), then a grave error may arise due to illusion, for thus I would proclaim to be universally valid what is merely a subjective condition of the intuition of things and sure only for all objects of sense, viz., for all possible experience; I would refer this condition to things in themselves, and do not limit it to the conditions of experience.

My doctrine of the ideality of space and of time, therefore, far from reducing the whole sensible world to mere illusion, is the only means of securing the application of one of the most important cognitions (that which mathematics propounds *a priori*) to actual objects, and of preventing its being regarded as mere illusion. For without this observation it would be quite impossible to make out whether the intuitions of space and time, which we borrow from no experience, and which yet lie in our representation *a priori*, are not mere phantasms of our brain, to which objects do not correspond, at least not adequately, and consequently, whether we have been able to show its unquestionable validity with regard to all the objects of the sensible world just because they are mere appearances.

Secondly, though these my principles make appearances of the representations of the senses, they are so far from turning the truth of experience into mere illusion, that they are rather the only means of preventing the transcendental illusion, by which metaphysics has hitherto been deceived, leading to the childish endeavor of catching at bubbles, because appearances, which are mere representations, were taken for things in themselves. Here originated the remarkable event of the antimony of Reason which I shall mention by and by, and which is destroyed by the single observation, that appearance, as long as it is employed in experience, produces truth, but the moment it transgresses the bounds of experience, and consequently becomes transcendent, produces nothing but illusion.

Inasmuch, therefore, as I leave to things as we obtain them by the senses their actuality, and only limit our sensuous intuition of these things to this,

that they represent in no respect, not even in the pure intuitions of space and of time, anything more than mere appearance of those things, but never their constitution in themselves, this is not a sweeping illusion invented for nature by me. My protestation too against all charges of idealism is so valid and clear as even to seem superfluous, were there not incompetent judges, who, while they would have an old name for every deviation from their perverse though common opinion, and never judge of the spirit of philosophic nomenclature, but cling to the letter only, are ready to put their own conceits in the place of well-defined notions, and thereby deform and distort them. I have myself given this my theory the name of transcendental idealism, but that cannot authorise any one to confound it either with the empirical idealism of Descartes, (indeed, his was only an insoluble problem, owing to which he thought every one at liberty to deny the existence of the corporeal world, because it could never be proved satisfactorily), or with the mystical and visionary idealism of Berkeley, against which and other similar phantasms our *Critique* contains the proper antidote. My idealism concerns not the existence of things (the doubting of which, however, constitutes idealism in the ordinary sense), since it never came into my head to doubt it, but it concerns the sensuous representation of things, to which space and time especially belong. Of these [viz., space and time], consequently of all appearances in general, I have only shown, that they are neither things (but mere modes of representation), nor determinations belonging to things in themselves. But the word "transcendental," which with me means a reference of our cognition, i.e., not to things, but only to the cognitive faculty, was meant to obviate this misconception. Yet rather than give further occasion to it by this word, I now retract it, and desire this idealism of mine to be called critical. But if it be really an objectionable idealism to convert actual things (not appearances) into mere representations by what name shall we call him who conversely changes mere representations to things? It may, I think, be called "dreaming idealism," in contradistinction to the former, which may be called "visionary," both of which are to be refuted by my transcendental, or, better, critical idealism.

[handwritten marginalia: "Universal laws:", "not apriori", "can't know", "what belongs to thing in itself", "not aposteriori", "doesn't have", "necessary"]

SECOND PART OF THE TRANSCENDENTAL PROBLEM

HOW IS THE SCIENCE OF NATURE POSSIBLE?

14. Nature is the existence of things, so far as it is determined according to universal laws. Should nature signify the existence of things in themselves, we could never cognise it either *a priori* or *a posteriori*. Not *a priori*, for how can we know what belongs to things in themselves, since this never can be done by the dissection of our concepts (in analytical judgments)? We do not want to know what is contained in our concept of a thing (for the [concept describes what] belongs to its logical being), but what is in the actuality of the thing superadded to our concept, and by what the thing itself is determined in its existence outside the concept. Our understanding, and the conditions on which alone it can connect the determinations of things in their existence, do not prescribe any rule to things themselves; these do not conform to our understanding, but it must conform itself to them; they must therefore be first given us in order to gather these determinations from them, wherefore they would not be cognised *a priori*.

A cognition of the nature of things in themselves *a posteriori* would be equally impossible. For, if experience is to teach us laws, to which the existence of things is subject, these laws, if they regard things in themselves, must belong to them of necessity even outside our experience. But experience teaches us what exists and how it exists, but never that it must necessarily exist so and not otherwise. Experience therefore can never teach us the nature of things in themselves.

15. We nevertheless actually possess a pure science of nature in which are propounded, *a priori* and with all the necessity requisite to apodeictical propositions, laws to which nature is subject. I need only call to witness that propaedeutic [introduction] of natural science which, under the title of the universal Science of Nature, precedes all Physics (which is founded upon empirical principles). In it we have Mathematics applied to appearance, and also merely discursive principles (or those derived from concepts), which constitute the philosophical part of the pure cognition of nature. But there are several things in it, which are not quite pure and independent of empirical sources: such as the concept of *motion*, that of *impenetrability* (upon which the empirical concept of matter rests), that of *inertia*, and many others, which prevent its being called a perfectly pure science of nature. Besides, it only refers to objects of the external sense, and therefore does not give an example of a universal science of nature, in the strict sense, for such a science must reduce nature in general, whether it regards the object of the external or that of the internal sense (the object of Physics as well as Psychology), to universal laws. But among the principles of this universal physics there are a few which actually have the required universality; for instance, the propositions that "substance is permanent," and that "every event is determined by a cause according to constant laws," etc. These are actually universal laws of nature, which subsist completely *a priori*. There is then in fact a pure science of nature, and the question arises, *How is it possible?*

16. The word "nature" assumes yet another meaning, which determines the object, whereas in the former sense it only denotes the conformity to law of the determinations of the existence of things generally. If we consider it *materialiter* (i.e., in the matter that forms its objects) "nature is the complex of all the objects of experience." And with this only are we now concerned, for besides, things which can never be objects of experience, if they must be cognised as to their nature, would oblige us to have recourse to concepts whose meaning could never be given *in concreto* (by any example of possible experience). Consequently we must form for ourselves a list of concepts of their nature, the reality whereof (i.e., whether they actually refer to objects, or are mere creations of thought) could never be determined. The cognition of what cannot be an object of experience would be hyperphysical, and with things hyperphysical we are here not concerned, but only with the cognition of nature, the actuality of which can be confirmed by experience, though it [the cognition of nature] is possible *a priori* and precedes all experience.

17. The former [aspect] of nature in this narrower sense is therefore the conformity to law of all the ob-

jects of experience, and so far as it is cognised *a priori*, their necessity conformity. But it has just been shown that the laws of nature can never be cognised *a priori* in objects so far as they are considered not in reference to possible experience, but as things in themselves. And our inquiry here extends not to things in themselves (the properties of which we pass by), but to things as objects of possible experience, and the complex of these is what we properly designate as nature. And now I ask, when the possibility of a cognition of nature *a priori* is in question, whether it is better to arrange the problem thus: How can we cognise *a priori* that things as objects of experience necessarily conform to law? or thus: How is it possible to cognise *a priori* the necessary conformity to law of experience itself as regards all its objects generally?

Closely considered, the solution of the problem, represented in either way, amounts, with regard to the pure cognition of nature (which is the point of the question at issue), entirely to the same thing. For the subjective laws, under which alone an empirical cognition of things is possible, hold good of these things, as objects of possible experience (not as things in themselves, which are not considered here). Either of the following statements means quite the same:

"A judgment of observation can never rank as experience without the law that whenever an event is observed, it is always referred to some antecedent, which it follows according to a universal rule."

"Everything, of which experience teaches that it happens, must have a cause."

It is, however, more commendable to choose the first formula. For we can *a priori* and previous to all given objects have a cognition of those conditions, on which alone experience is possible, but never of the laws to which things may in themselves be subject, without reference to possible experience. We cannot therefore study the nature of things *a priori* otherwise than by investigating the conditions and the universal (though subjective) laws, under which alone such a cognition as experience (as to mere form) is possible, and we determine accordingly the possibility of things, as objects of experience. For if I should choose the second formula, and seek the conditions *a priori*, on which nature as an object of

experience is possible, I might easily fall into error, and fancy that I was speaking of nature as a thing in itself, and then move round in endless circles, in a vain search for laws concerning things of which nothing is given me.

Accordingly we shall here be concerned with experience only, and the universal conditions of its possibility which are given *a priori*. Thence we shall determine nature as the whole object of all possible experience. I think it will be understood that I here do not mean the rules of the observation of a nature that is already given, for these already presuppose experience. I do not mean how (through experience) we can study the laws of nature; for these would not then be laws *a priori*, and would yield us no pure science of nature; but [I mean to ask] how the conditions of the possibility of experience are at the same time the sources from which all the universal laws of nature must be derived.

18. In the first place we must state that, while all judgments of experience are empirical (i.e., have their ground in immediate sense-perception), vice versa, all empirical judgments are not judgments of experience, but, besides the empirical, and in general besides what is given to the sensuous intuition, particular, concepts must yet be superadded— concepts which have their origin quite *a priori* in the pure understanding, and under which every perception must be first of all subsumed and then by their means changed into experience.

Empirical judgments, so far as they have objective validity, are *judgments of experience*; but those which are only subjectively valid, I name mere *judgments of perception*. The latter require no pure concept of the understanding, but only the logical connexion of perception in a thinking subject. But the former always require, besides the representation of the sensuous intuition, particular *concepts originally begotten in the understanding*, which produce the objective validity of the judgment of experience.

All our judgments are at first merely judgments of perception; they hold good only for us (i.e., for our subject), and we do not till afterwards give them a new reference (to an object), and desire that they shall always hold good for us and in the same way for everybody else; for when a judgment agrees with an object, all judgments concerning the same object must likewise agree among themselves, and thus the objective validity of the judgment of experience signifies nothing else than its necessary universality of application. And conversely when we have reason to consider a judgment necessarily universal (which never depends upon perception, but upon the pure concept of the understanding, under which the perception is subsumed), we must consider it objective also, that is, that it expresses not merely a reference of our perception to a subject, but a quality of the object. For there would be no reason for the judgments of other men necessarily agreeing with mine, if it were not the unity of the object to which they all refer, and with which they accord; hence they must all agree with one another.

19. Therefore objective validity and necessary universality (for everybody) are equivalent terms, and though we do not know the object in itself, yet when we consider a judgment as universal, and also necessary, we understand it to have objective validity. By this judgment we cognise the object (though it remains unknown as it is in itself) by the universal and necessary connexion of the given perceptions. As this is the case with all objects of sense, judgments of experience take their objective validity not from the immediate cognition of the object (which is impossible), but from the condition of universal validity in empirical judgments, which, as already said, never rests upon empirical, or, in short, sensuous conditions, but upon a pure concept of the understanding. The object always remains unknown in itself; but when by the concept of the understanding the connexion of the representations of the object, which are given to our sensibility, is determined as universally valid, the object is determined by this relation, and it is the judgment that is objective.

To illustrate the matter: When we say, "the room is warm, sugar sweet, and wormwood bitter,"[7]—we have only subjectively valid judgments. I do not at all expect that I or any other person shall always find it as I now do; each of these sentences only expresses a relation of two sensations to the same subject, to myself, and that only in my present state of perception; consequently they are not valid of the object. Such are judgments of perception. Judgments of experience are of quite a different nature. What experience teaches me under certain circumstances, it must always teach me and everybody; and its validity is not limited to the subject nor to its state at a particular time. Hence I pronounce all such judgments as being objectively valid. For instance, when I say the air is elastic, this judgment is as yet a judgment of perception only—I do nothing but refer two of my sensations to one another. But, if I would have it called a judgment of experience, I require this connexion to stand under a condition, which makes it universally valid. I desire therefore that I and everybody else should always connect necessarily the same perceptions under the same circumstances.

20. We must consequently analyse experience in order to see what is contained in this product of the senses and of the understanding, and how the judgment of experience itself is possible. The foundation is the intuition of which I become conscious i.e., perception which pertains merely to the senses. But in the next place, there are acts of judging (which belong only to the understanding). But this judging may be twofold—first, I may merely compare perceptions and connect them in a particular state of my consciousness; or, secondly, I may connect them in consciousness generally. The former judgment is merely a judgment of perception, and of subjective validity only: it is merely a connexion of perceptions in my mental state, without reference to the object. Hence it is not, as is commonly imagined, enough for experience to compare perceptions and to connect them in consciousness through judgment; there arises no universality and necessity, for which alone

---

[7] I freely grant that these examples do not represent such judgments of perception as ever could become judgments of experience, even though a concept of the understanding were superadded, because they refer merely to feeling, which everybody knows to be merely subjective, and which of course can never be attributed to the object, and consequently never become objective. I only wished to give here an example of a judgment that is merely subjectively valid, containing no ground for universal validity, and thereby for a relation to the object. An example of the judgments of perception, which become judgments of experience by superadded concepts of the understanding, will be given in the next note.

judgments can become objectively valid and be called experience.

Quite another judgment therefore is required before perception can become experience. The given intuition must be subsumed under a concept, which determines the form of judging in general relatively to the intuition, connects its empirical consciousness of intuition in consciousness generally, and thereby procures universal validity for empirical judgments. A concept of this nature is a pure *a priori* concept of the Understanding, which does nothing but determine for an intuition the general way in which it can be used for judgments. Let the concept be that of cause, then it determines the intuition which is subsumed under it, e.g., that of air, relative to judgments in general, viz., the concept of air serves with regard to its expansion in the relation of antecedent to consequent in a hypothetical judgment. The concept of cause accordingly is a pure concept of the understanding, which is totally disparate from all possible perception, and only serves to determine the representation subsumed under it, relatively to judgments in general, and so to make a universally valid judgment possible.

Before, therefore, a judgment of perception can become a judgment of experience, it is requisite that the perception should be subsumed under some such a concept of the understanding; for instance, air ranks under the concept of causes, which determines our judgment about it in regard to its expansion as hypothetical.[8] Thereby the expansion of the air is represented not as merely belonging to the perception of the air in my present state or in several states of mine, or in the state of perception of others, but as belonging to it necessarily. The judgment, "the air is elastic," becomes universally valid, and a judgment of experience, only by certain judgments preceding it, which subsume the intuition of air under the concept of cause and effect: and they thereby determine the perceptions not merely as regards one another in me, but relatively to the form of judging in general, which is here hypothetical, and in this way they render the empirical judgment universally valid.

If all our synthetical judgments are analysed so far as they are objectively valid, it will be found that they never consist of mere intuitions connected only (as is commonly believed) by comparison into a judgment; but that they would be impossible were not a pure concept of the understanding superadded to the concepts abstracted from intuition, under which concept these latter are subsumed, and in this manner only combined into an objectively valid judgment. Even the judgments of pure mathematics in their simplest axioms are not exempt from this condition. The principle, "a straight line is the shortest between two points," presupposes that the line is subsumed under the concept of quantity, which certainly is no mere intuition, but has its seat in the understanding alone, and serves to determine the intuition (of the line) with regard to the judgments which may be made about it, relatively to their quantity, that is, to plurality (as *judicia plurativa*).[9] For under them it is understood that in a given intuition there is contained a plurality of homogeneous parts.

21. To prove, then, the possibility of experience so far as it rests upon pure concepts of the understanding *a priori*, we must first represent what belongs to judgments in general and the various func-

---

[8] As an easier example, we may take the following: "When the sun shines on the stone, it grows warm." This judgment, however often I and others may have perceived it, is a mere judgment of perception, and contains no necessity; perceptions are only usually conjoined in this manner. But if I say, "The sun warms the stone," I add to the perception a concept of the understanding, viz., that of cause, which connects with the concept of sunshine that of heat as a necessary consequence, and the synthetical judgment becomes of necessity universally valid, viz., objective, and is converted from a perception into experience.

[9] This name seems preferable to the term, *particularia*, which is used for these judgments in logic. For the latter implies the idea that they are not universal. But when I start from unity (in single judgments) and so proceed to universality, I must not [even indirectly and negatively] imply any reference to universality. I think plurality merely without universality, and not the exception from universality. This is necessary, if logical considerations shall form the basis of the pure concepts of the understanding. However, there is no need of making changes in logic.

tions of the understanding, in a complete table. For the pure concepts of the understanding must run parallel to these functions, as such concepts are nothing more than concepts of intuitions in general, so far as these are determined by one or other of these functions of judging, in themselves, that is, necessarily and universally. Hereby also the *a priori* principles of the possibility of all experience, as of an objectively valid empirical cognition, will be precisely determined. For they are nothing but propositions by which all perception is (under certain universal conditions of intuition) subsumed under those pure concepts of the understanding.

Logical Table of Judgments.

1	2
As to Quantity.	*As to Quality.*
Universal.	Affirmative.
Particular.	Negative.
Singular.	Infinite.
3	4
As to Relation.	*As to Modality.*
Categorical.	Problematical.
Hypothetical.	Assertorial.
Disjunctive.	Apodeictical.

Transcendental Table of the Pure Concepts of the Understanding.

1	2
As to Quantity.	*As to Quality.*
Unity (the Measure).	Reality.
Plurality (the Quantity).	Negation.
Totality (the Whole).	Limitation.
3	4
As to Relation.	*As to Modality.*
Substance.	Possibility.
Cause.	Existence.
Community.	Necessity.

Pure Physiological Table of the Universal Principles of the Science of Nature.

1	2
Axioms of Intuition.	Anticipations of Perception.
3	4
Analogies of Experience.	Postulates of Empirical Thinking generally.

21a. In order to comprise the whole matter in one idea, it is first necessary to remind the reader that we are discussing not the origin of experience, but of that which lies in experience. The former pertains to empirical psychology, and would even then never be adequately explained without the latter, which belongs to the critique of cognition, and particularly of the understanding.

Experience consists of intuitions, which belongs to the sensibility, and of judgments, which are entirely a work of the understanding. But the judgments, which the understanding forms alone from sensuous intuitions, are far from being judgments of experience. For in the one case the judgment connects only the perceptions as they are given in the sensuous intuition, while in the other the judgments must express what experience in general, and not what the mere perception (which possesses only subjective validity) contains. The judgment of experience must therefore add to the sensuous intuition and its logical connexion in a judgment (after it has been rendered universal by comparison) something that determines the synthetical judgment as necessary and therefore as universally valid. This can be nothing else than that concept which represents the intuition as determined in itself with regard to one form of judgment rather than another, viz., a concept of that synthetical unity of intuitions which can only be represented by a given logical function of judgments.

22. The sum of the matter is this: the business of the senses is to intuit—that of the understanding is to think. But thinking is uniting representations in one consciousness. This union originates either merely relative to the subject, and is accidental and subjective, or is absolute, and is necessary or objective. The union of representations in one consciousness is judgment. Thinking therefore is the same as judging, or referring representations to judgments in general. Hence judgments are either merely subjective, when representations are referred to a consciousness in one subject only, and united in it, or objective, when they are united in a consciousness generally, that is, necessarily. The logical functions of all judgments are but various modes of uniting representations in consciousness. But if they serve for concepts, they are concepts of their necessary union in a consciousness, and so principles of objectively valid judgments. This

union in a consciousness is either analytical, by identity, or synthetical, by the combination and addition of various representations one to another. Experience consists in the synthetical connexion of phenomena (perceptions) in consciousness, so far as this connexion is necessary. Hence the pure concepts of the understanding are those under which all perceptions must be subsumed before they can serve for judgments of experience, in which the synthetical unity of the perceptions is represented as necessary and universally valid.[10]

23. Judgments, when considered merely as the condition of the union of given representations in a consciousness, are rules. These rules, so far as they represent the union as necessary, are rules *a priori*, and so far as they cannot be deduced from higher rules, are fundamental principles. But in regard to the possibility of all experience, merely in relation to the form of thinking in it, no conditions of judgments of experience are higher than those which bring the phenomena, according to the various form of their intuition, under pure concepts of the understanding, and render the empirical judgment objectively valid. These concepts are therefore the *a priori* principles of possible experience.

The principles of possible experience are then at the same time universal laws of nature, which can be cognised *a priori*. And thus the problem in our second question, "How is the pure Science of Nature possible?" is solved. For the system which is required for the form of a science is to be met with in perfection here, because, beyond the above-mentioned formal conditions of all judgments in general offered in logic, no others are possible, and these constitute a logical system. The concepts grounded thereupon, which contain the *a priori* conditions of all synthetical and necessary judgments, accordingly constitute a transcendental system. Finally the principles, by means of which all phenomena are subsumed under these concepts, constitute a physical system, that is, a system of nature, which precedes all empirical cognition of nature, makes it even possible, and hence may in strictness be denominated the universal and pure science of nature.

24. The first one[11] of the physiological principles subsumes all phenomena, as intuitions in space and time, under the concept of Quantity, and is so far a principle of the application of Mathematics to experience. The second one subsumes the empirical element, viz., sensation, which denotes the real in intuitions, not indeed directly under the concept of quantity, because sensation is not an intuition that contains either space or time, though it places the respective object into both. But still there is between reality (sense-representation) and the zero, or total void of intuition in time, a difference which has a quantity. For between every given degree of light and of darkness, between every degree of heat and of absolute cold, between every degree of weight and of absolute lightness, between every degree of occupied space and of totally void space, diminishing degrees can be conceived, in the same manner as between consciousness and total unconsciousness (the darkness of a psychological blank) ever diminishing degrees obtain. Hence there is no perception that can prove an absolute absence of it; for instance, no psychological darkness that cannot be considered as a kind of consciousness, which is only outbalanced by a stronger consciousness. This occurs in all cases of sensation, and so the understanding can anticipate even sensations, which constitute the peculiar qual-

---

[10]But how does this proposition, "that judgments of experience contain necessity in the synthesis of perceptions," agree with my statement so often before inculcated that "experience as cognition *a posteriori* can afford contingent judgments only?" When I say that experience teaches me something I mean only the perception that lies in experience,—for example that heat always follows the shining of the sun on a stone; consequently the proposition of experience is always so far accidental. That this heat necessarily follows the shining of the sun is contained indeed in the judgment of experience (by means of the concept of cause), yet is a fact not learned by experience; for conversely experience is first of all generated by this addition of the concept of the understanding (of cause) to perception. How perception attains this addition may be seen by referring in the *Critique* itself to the section on the Transcendental faculty of Judgment.

---

[11]The three following paragraphs will hardly be understood unless reference be made to what the *Critique* itself says on the subject of the Principles; they will, however be of service in giving a general view of the Principles, and in fixing the attention on the main points.

ity of empirical representations (appearances), by means of the principle: "that they all have (consequently that what is real in all phenomena has) a degree." Here is the second application of mathematics (*mathesis intensorum*) to the science of nature.

25. About the relation of appearances merely with a view to their existence, the determination is not mathematical but dynamical, and can never be objectively valid, consequently never fit for experience, if it does not come under *a priori* principles by which the cognition of experience relative to appearances becomes even possible. Hence appearances must be subsumed under the concept of Substance, which is the foundation of all determination of existence, as a concept of the thing itself; or secondly—so far as a succession is found among phenomena, that is, an event—under the concept of an Effect with reference to Cause; or lastly—so far as coexistence is to be known objectively, that is, by a judgment of experience—under the concept of Community (action and reaction). Thus *a priori* principles form the basis of objectively valid, through empirical judgments, that is, of the possibility of experience so far as it must connect objects as existing in nature. These principles are the proper laws of nature, which may be termed dynamical.

Finally the cognition of the agreement and connexion not only of appearances among themselves in experience, but of their relation to experience in general, belongs to the judgments of experience. This relation contains either their agreement with the formal conditions, which the understanding cognises, or their coherence with the materials of the senses and of perception, or combines both into one concept. Consequently it contains Possibility, Actuality, and Necessity according to universal laws of nature; and this constitutes the physical doctrine of method, or the distinction of truth and of hypotheses, and the bounds of the certainty of the latter.

26. The third table of Principles drawn from the nature of the understanding itself after the critical method, shows an inherent perfection, which raises it far above every other table which has hitherto though in vain been tried or may yet be tried by analysing the objects themselves dogmatically. It exhibits all synthetical *a priori* principles completely

and according to one principle, viz., the faculty of judging in general, constituting the essence of experience as regards the understanding, so that we can be certain that there are no more such principles, which affords a satisfaction such as can never be attained by the dogmatical method. Yet is this not all: there is a still greater merit in it.

We must carefully bear in mind the proof which shows the possibility of this cognition *a priori*, and at the same time limits all such principles to a condition which must never be lost sight of, if we desire it not to be misunderstood, and extended in use beyond the original sense which the understanding attaches to it. This limit is that they contain nothing but the conditions of possible experience in general so far as it is subjected to laws *a priori*. Consequently I do not say, that things *in themselves* possess a quantity, that their actuality possesses a degree, their existence a connexion of accidents in a substance, etc. This nobody can prove, because such a synthetical connexion from mere concepts, without any reference to sensuous intuition on the one side, or connexion of it in a possible experience on the other, is absolutely impossible. The essential limitation of the concepts in these principles then is: That all things stand necessarily *a priori* under the aforementioned conditions, as objects of experience only.

Hence there follows secondly a specifically peculiar mode of proof of these principles: they are not directly referred to appearances and to their relations, but to the possibility of experience, of which appearances constitute the matter only, not the form. Thus they are referred to objectively and universally valid synthetical propositions, in which we distinguish judgments of experience from those of perception. This takes place because appearances, as mere intuitions, occupying a part of space and time, come under the concept of Quantity, which unites their multiplicity *a priori* according to rules synthetically. Again, so far as the perception contains, besides intuition, sensibility, and between the latter and nothing (i.e., the total disappearance of sensibility), there is an ever decreasing transition, it is apparent that that which is in appearances must have a degree, so far as it (viz., the perception) does not itself occupy any part of space or of time.[12] Still the transition to actuality from empty time or empty space is only possible in time; consequently though sensibility, as the quality of empirical intuition, can never be cognised *a priori*, by its specific difference from other sensibilities, yet it can, in a possible experience in general, as a quantity of perception be intensely distinguished from every other similar perception. Hence the application of mathematics to nature, as regards the sensuous intuition by which nature is given to us, becomes possible and is thus determined.

Above all, the reader must pay attention to the mode of proof of the principles which occur under the title of Analogies of experience. For these do not refer to the genesis of intuitions, as do the principles of applied mathematics, but to the connexion of their existence in experience; and this can be nothing but the determination of their existence in time according to necessary laws, under which alone the connexion is objectively valid, and thus becomes experience. The proof therefore does not turn on the synthetical unity in the connexion of things in themselves, but merely of perceptions, and of these not in regard to their matter, but to the determination of time and of the relation of their existence in it, according to universal laws. If the empirical determination in relative time is indeed objectively valid (i.e., experience), these universal laws contain the necessary determination of existence in time generally (viz., according to a rule of the understanding *a priori*).

In these *Prolegomena* I cannot further discuss the subject, but my reader (who has probably been long

accustomed to consider experience a mere empirical synthesis of perceptions, and hence not considered that it goes much beyond them, as it imparts to empirical judgments universal validity, and for that purpose requires a pure and *a priori* unity of the understanding) is recommended to pay special attention to this distinction of experience from a mere aggregate of perceptions, and to judge the mode of proof from this point of view.

27. Now we are prepared to remove Hume's doubt. He justly maintains, that we cannot comprehend by reason the possibility of Causality, that is, of the reference of the existence of one thing to the existence of another, which is necessitated by the former. I add, that we comprehend just as little the concept of Subsistence, that is, the necessity that at the foundation of the existence of things there lies a subject which cannot itself be a predicate of any other thing; nay, we cannot even form a notion of the possibility of such a thing (though we can point out examples of its use in experience). The very same incomprehensibility affects the Community of things, as we cannot comprehend how from the state of one thing an inference to the state of quite another thing beyond it, and *vice versa*, can be drawn, and how substances which have each their own separate existence should depend upon one another necessarily. But I am very far from holding these concepts to be derived merely from experience, and the necessity represented in them, to be imaginary and a mere illusion produced in us by long habit. On the contrary, I have amply shown, that they and the theorems derived from them are firmly established *a priori*, or before all experience, and have their undoubted objective value, though only with regard to experience.

28. Though I have no notion of such a connexion of things in themselves, that they can either exist as substances, or act as causes, or stand in community with others (as parts of a real whole), and I can just as little conceive such properties in appearances as such (because those concepts contain nothing that lies in the appearances, but only what the understanding alone must think): we have yet a notion of such a connexion of representations in our understanding, and in judgments generally; consisting in this that representations appear in one sort of

---

[12]Heat and light are in a small space just as large as to degree as in a large one; in like manner the internal representations, pain, consciousness in general, whether they last a short or a long time need not vary as to the degree. Hence the quantity is here in a point and in a moment just as great as in any space or time however great. Degrees are therefore capable of increase, but not of an intuition). Hence they can only be estimated quantitatively by the relation of 1 to 0, viz., by their capability of decreasing by infinite intermediate degrees to disappearance, or of increasing from naught through infinite gradations to a determinate sensation in a certain time. *Quantitas qualitas est gradus* [i.e., the degrees of quality is a quantity].

judgments as subject in relation to predicates, in another as reason in relation to consequences, and in a third as parts, which constitute together a total possible cognition. Besides we cognise *a priori* that without considering the representation of an object as determined in some of these respects, we can have no valid cognition of the object, and, if we should occupy ourselves about the object in itself, there is no possible attribute, by which I could know that it is determined under any of these aspects, that is, under the concept either of substance, or of cause, or (in relation to other substances) of community, for I have no notion of the possibility of such a connexion of existence. But the question is not how things in themselves, but how the empirical cognition of things is determined, as regards the above aspects of judgments in general, that is, how things, as objects of experience, can and shall be subsumed under these concepts of the understanding. And then it is clear, that I completely comprehend not only the possibility, but also the necessity of subsuming all phenomena under these concepts, that is, of using them for principles of the possibility of experience.

29. When making an experiment with Hume's problematical concept (his *crux metaphysicorum*), the concept of cause, we have, in the first place, given *a priori*, by means of logic, the form of a conditional judgment in general, i.e., we have one given cognition as antecedent and another as consequence. But it is possible, that in perception we may meet with a rule of relation, which runs thus: that a certain phenomenon is constantly followed by another (though not conversely), and this is a case for me to use the hypothetical judgment, and, for instance, to say, if the sun shines long enough upon a body, it grows warm. Here there is indeed as yet no necessity of connexion, or concept of cause. But I proceed and say, that if this proposition, which is merely a subjective connexion of perceptions, is to be a judgment of experience, it must be considered as necessary and universally valid. Such a proposition would be, "the sun is by its light the cause of heat." The empirical rule is now considered as a law, and as valid not merely of appearances but valid of them for the purposes of a possible experience which requires universal and therefore necessarily valid rules. I therefore easily comprehend the concept of cause, as a concept necessarily belonging to the mere form

of experience, and its possibility as a synthetical union of perceptions in consciousness generally; but I do not at all comprehend the possibility of a thing generally as a cause, because the concept of cause denotes a condition not at all belonging to things, but to experience. It is nothing in fact but an objectively valid cognition of appearances and of their succession, so far as the antecedent can be conjoined with the consequent according to the rule of hypothetical judgments.

30. Hence if the pure concepts of the understanding do not refer to objects of experience but to things in themselves (noumena), they have no signification whatever. They serve, as it were, only to decipher appearances, that we may be able to read them as experience. The principles which arise from their reference to the sensible world, only serve our understanding for empirical use. Beyond this they are arbitrary combinations, without objective reality: and we can neither cognise their possibility *a priori*, nor verify their reference to objects, let alone make it intelligible by any example; because examples can only be borrowed from some possible experience, consequently the objects of these concepts can be found nowhere but in a possible experience.

This complete (though to its originator unexpected) solution of Hume's problem rescues for the pure concepts of the understanding their *a priori* origin, and for the universal laws of nature their validity, as laws of the understanding, yet in such a way as to limit their use to experience, because their possibility depends solely on the reference of the understanding to experience, but with a completely reversed mode of connexion which never occurred to Hume, not by deriving them from experience, but by deriving experience from them.

This is therefore the result of all our foregoing inquiries: "All synthetical principles *a priori* are nothing more than principles of possible experience, and can never be referred to things in themselves, but to appearances as objects of experience. And hence pure mathematics as well as a pure science of nature can never be referred to anything more than mere appearances, and can only represent either that which makes experience generally possible, or else that which, as it is derived from these principles, must always be capable of being represented in some possible experience."

31. And thus we have at last something definite, upon which to depend in all metaphysical enterprises, which have hitherto, boldly enough but always at random, attempted everything without discrimination. That the aim of their exertions should be so near, struck neither the dogmatical thinkers nor those who, confident in their supposed sound common sense, started with concepts and principles of pure reason (which were legitimate and natural, but destined for mere empirical use) in quest of fields of knowledge, to which they neither knew nor could know any determinate bound, because they had never reflected nor were able to reflect on the nature or even on the possibility of such a pure understanding.

Many a naturalist of pure reason (by which I mean the man who believes he can decide in matters of metaphysics without any science) may pretend, that he long ago by the prophetic spirit of his sound sense, not only suspected, but knew and comprehended, what is here propounded with so much ado, or, if he likes, with prolix and pedantic pomp: "that with all our reason we can never reach beyond the field of experience." But when he is questioned about his rational principles individually, he must grant, that there are many of them which he has not taken from experience, and which are therefore independent of it and valid *a priori*. How then and on what grounds will he restrain both himself and the dogmatist, who makes use of these concepts and principles beyond all possible experience, because they are recognised to be independent of it? And even he, this adept in sound sense, in spite of all his assumed and cheaply acquired wisdom, is not exempt from wandering inadvertently beyond objects of experience into the field of chimeras. He is often deeply enough involved in them, though in announcing everything as mere probability, rational conjecture, or analogy, he gives by his popular language a color to his groundless pretensions.

32. Since the oldest days of philosophy inquirers into pure reason have conceived, besides the things of sense, or appearances (*phenomena*), which make up the sensible world, certain creations of the understanding called noumena, which should constitute an intelligible world. And as appearance and illusion were by those men identified (a thing which we may well excuse in an undeveloped epoch), actuality was only conceded to the creations of thought.

And we indeed, rightly considering objects of sense as mere appearances, confess thereby that they are based upon a thing in itself, though we know not this thing in its internal constitution, but only know its appearances, viz., the way in which our senses are affected by this unknown something. The understanding therefore, by assuming appearances, grants the existence of things in themselves also, and so far we may say, that the representation of such things as form the basis of phenomena, consequently of mere creations of the understanding, is not only admissible, but unavoidable.

Our critical deduction by no means excludes things of that sort (noumena), but rather limits the principles of the Aesthetic (the science of the sensibility) to this, that they shall not extend to all things, as everything would then be turned into mere appearance, but that they shall only hold good of objects of possible experience. Hereby then objects of the understanding are granted, but with the inculcation of this rule which admits of no exception: "that we neither know nor can know anything at all definite of these pure objects of the understanding, because our pure concepts of the understanding as well as our pure intuitions extend to nothing but objects of possible experience, consequently to mere things of sense, and as soon as we leave this sphere these concepts retain no meaning whatever."

33. There is indeed something seductive in our pure concepts of the understanding, which tempts us to a transcendent use,—a use which transcends all possible experience. Not only are our concepts of substance, of power, of action, of reality, and others, quite independent of experience, containing nothing of sense appearance, and so apparently applicable to things in themselves (noumena), but, what strengthens this conjecture, they contain a necessity of determination in themselves, which experience never attains. The concept of cause implies a rule, according to which one state follows another necessarily; but experience can only show us, that one state of things often, or at most, commonly, follows another, and therefore affords neither strict universality, nor necessity.

Hence the Categories seem to have a deeper meaning and import than can be exhausted by their empirical use, and so the understanding inadvertently adds for itself to the house of experience a much more extensive wing, which it fills with nothing but creatures of thought, without ever observing that it has transgressed with its otherwise lawful concepts the bounds of their use.

34. Two important, and even indispensable, though very dry, investigations had therefore become indispensable in the *Critique of Pure Reason*,—viz., the two chapters "The Schematism of the Pure Concepts of the Understanding," and "The Ground of the Distinction of All Objects in general into Phenomena and Noumena." In the former it is shown, that the senses furnish not the pure concepts of the understanding *in concreto*, but only the schedule for their use, and that the object conformable to it occurs only in experience (as the product of the understanding from materials of the sensibility). In the latter it is shown, that, although our pure concepts of the understanding and our principles are independent of experience, and despite of the apparently greater sphere of their use, still nothing whatever can be thought by them beyond the field of experience, because they can do nothing but merely determine the logical form of the judgment relative to given intuitions. But as there is no intuition at all beyond the field of the sensibility, these pure concepts, as they cannot possibly be exhibited *in concreto*, are void of all meaning; consequently all these noumena, together with their complex, the intelligible world,[13] are nothing but representation of a problem, of which the object in itself is possible, but the solution, from the nature of our understanding, totally impossible. For our understanding is not a faculty of intuition, but of the connexion of given intuitions in experience. Experience must therefore contain all the ob-

jects for our concepts; but beyond it no concepts have any significance, as there is no intuition that might offer them a foundation.

35. The imagination may perhaps be forgiven for occasional vagaries, and for not keeping carefully within the limits of experience, since it gains life and vigor by such flights, and since it is always easier to moderate its boldness, than to stimulate its languor. But the understanding which ought to *think* can never be forgiven for indulging in vagaries; for we depend upon it alone for assistance to set bounds, when necessary, to the vagaries of the imagination.

But the understanding begins its aberrations very innocently and modestly. It first elucidates the elementary cognitions, which inhere in it prior to all experience, but yet must always have their application in experience. It gradually drops these limits, and what is there to prevent it, as it has quite freely derived its principles from itself? And then it proceeds first to newly-imagined powers in nature, then to beings outside nature; in short to a world, for whose construction the materials cannot be wanting, because fertile fiction furnishes them abundantly, and though not confirmed, is never refuted, by experience. This is the reason that young thinkers are so partial to metaphysics of the truly dogmatical kind, and often sacrifice to it their time and their talents, which might be otherwise better employed.

But there is no use in trying to moderate these fruitless endeavors of pure reason by all manner of cautions as to the difficulties of solving questions so occult, by complaints of the limits of our reason, and by degrading our assertions into mere conjectures. For if their impossibility is not distinctly shown, and cognition of its own essence does not become a true science, in which the field of its right use is distinguished, so to say, with mathematical certainty from that of its worthless and idle use, these fruitless efforts will never be abandoned for good.

36. *How is Nature itself possible?* This question—the highest point that transcendental philosophy can ever reach, and to which, as its boundary and completion, it must proceed—properly contains two questions.

FIRST: How is nature at all possible in the material sense, by intuition, considered as the totality

---

[13]We speak of the "intelligible world" not (as the usual expression is) "intellectual world." For cognitions are intellectual through the understanding, and refer to our world of sense also; but objects so far as they can be represented merely by the understanding, and to which none of our sensible intuitions can refer, are termed "intelligible." But as some possible intuition must correspond to every object we would have to assume an understanding that intuits things immediately; but of such we have not the least notion, nor have we of the things of the understanding, to which it should be applied.

of appearances; how are space, time, and that which fills both—the object of sensation, in general possible? The answer is: By means of the constitution of our Sensibility, according to which it is specifically affected by objects, which are in themselves unknown to it, and totally distinct from those phenomena. This answer is given in the *Critique* itself in the transcendental Aesthetic, and in these *Prolegomena* by the solution of the first general problem.

SECONDLY: How is nature possible in the formal sense, as the totality of the rules, under which all phenomena must come, in order to be thought as connected in experience? The answer must be this: it is only possible by means of the constitution of our Understanding, according to which all the above representations of the sensibility are necessarily referred to a consciousness, and by which the peculiar way in which we think (viz., by rules), and hence experience also, are possible, but must be clearly distinguished from an insight into the objects in themselves. This answer is given in the *Critique* itself in the transcendental Logic, and in these *Prolegomena*, in the course of the solution of the second main problem.

But how this peculiar property of our sensibility itself is possible, or that of our understanding and of the apperception which is necessarily its basis and that of all thinking, cannot be further analysed or answered, because it is of them that we are in need for all our answers and for all our thinking about objects.

There are many laws of nature, which we can only know by means of experience; but conformity to law in the connexion of appearances, i.e., in nature in general, we cannot discover by any experience, because experience itself requires laws which are *a priori* at the basis of its possibility.

The possibility of experience in general is therefore at the same time the universal law of nature, and the principles of the experience are the very laws of nature. For we do not know nature but as the totality of appearances, i.e., of representations in us, and hence we can only derive the laws of its connexion from the principles of their connexion in us, that is, from the conditions of their necessary union in consciousness, which constitutes the possibility of experience.

Even the main proposition expounded throughout this section—that universal laws of nature can be distinctly cognised *a priori*—leads naturally to the proposition: that the highest legislation of nature must lie in ourselves, i.e., in our understanding, and that we must not seek the universal laws of nature in nature by means of experience, but conversely must seek nature, as to its universal conformity to law, in the conditions of the possibility of experience, which lie in our sensibility and in our understanding. For how were it otherwise possible to know *a priori* these laws, as they are not rules of analytical cognition, but truly synthetical extensions of it?

Such a necessary agreement of the principles of possible experience with the laws of the possibility of nature, can only proceed from one of two reasons: either these laws are drawn from nature by means of experience, or conversely nature is derived from the laws of the possibility of experience in general, and is quite the same as the mere universal conformity to law of the latter. The former is self-contradictory, for the universal laws of nature can and must be cognised *a priori* (that is, independent of all experience), and be the foundation of all empirical use of the understanding; the latter alternative therefore alone remains.[14]

But we must distinguish the empirical laws of nature, which always presuppose particular perceptions, from the pure or universal laws of nature, which, without being based on particular perceptions, contain merely the conditions of their necessary union in experience. In relation to the latter, nature and possible experience are quite the same, and as the conformity to law here depends upon the necessary connexion of appearances in experience (without which we cannot cognise any object what-

---

[14]Crusius alone thought of a compromise that a Spirit, who can neither err nor deceive, implanted these laws in us originally. But since false principles often intrude themselves, as indeed the very system of this man shows in not a few examples, we are involved in difficulties as to the use of such a principle in the absence of sure criteria to distinguish the genuine origin from the spurious, as we never can know certainly what the Spirit of truth or the father of lies may have instilled into us.

ever in the sensible world), consequently upon the original laws of the understanding, it seems at first strange, but is not the less certain, to say: *The understanding does not derive its laws (a priori) from, but prescribes them to, nature.*

37. We shall illustrate this seemingly bold proposition by an example, which will show, that laws, which we discover in objects of sensuous intuition (especially when these laws are cognised as necessary), are commonly held by us to be such as have been placed there by the understanding, in spite of their being similar in all points to the laws of nature, which we ascribed to experience.

38. If we consider the properties of the circle, by which this figure combines so many arbitrary determinations of space in itself, at once in a universal rule, we cannot avoid attributing a nature to this geometrical thing. Two right lines, for example, which intersect one another and the circle, howsoever they may be drawn, are always divided so that the rectangle constructed with the segments of the one is equal to that constructed with the segments of the other. The question now is: Does this law lie in the circle or in the understanding, that is, Does this figure, independently of the understanding, contain in itself the ground of the law, or does the understanding, having constructed according to its concepts (according to the quality of the radii) the figure itself, introduce into it this law of the chords cutting one another in geometrical proportion? When we follow the proofs of this law, we soon perceive, that it can only be derived from the condition on which the understanding founds the construction of this figure, and which is that of the equality of the radii. But, if we enlarge this concept, to pursue further the unity of various properties of geometrical figures under common laws, and consider the circle as a conic section, which of course is subject to the same fundamental conditions of construction as other conic sections, we shall find that all the chords which intersect within the ellipse, parabola, and hyperbola, always intersect so that the rectangles of their segments are not indeed equal, but always bear a constant ratio to one another. If we proceed still farther, to the fundamental laws of physical astronomy, we find a physical law of reciprocal attraction diffused over all material nature, the rule of which is: "that it de-

creases inversely as the square of the distance from each attracting point, i.e., as the spherical surfaces increase, over which this force spreads," which law seems to be necessarily inherent in the very nature of things, and hence is usually propounded as cognisable *a priori*. Simple as the sources of this law are, merely resting upon the relation of spherical surfaces of different radii, its consequences are so valuable with regard to the variety of their agreement and its regularity, that not only are all possible orbits of the celestial bodies conic sections, but such a relation of these orbits to each other results, that no other law of attraction, than that of the inverse square of the distance, can be imagined as fit for a cosmical system.

Here accordingly is a nature that rests upon laws which the understanding cognises *a priori* and chiefly from the universal principles of the determination of space. Now I ask:

Do the laws of nature lie in space, and does the understanding learn them by merely endeavoring to find out the enormous wealth of meaning that lies in space; or do they inhere in the understanding and in the way in which it determines space according to the conditions of the synthetical unity in which its concepts are all centered?

Space is something so uniform and as to all particular properties so indeterminate, that we should certainly not seek a store of laws of nature in it. Whereas that which determines space to assume the form of a circle or the figures of a cone and a sphere, is the understanding, so far as it contains the ground of the unity of their constructions.

The mere universal form of intuition, called space, must therefore be the substratum of all intuitions determinable to particular objects, and in it of course the condition of the possibility and of the variety of these intuitions lies. But the unity of the objects is entirely determined by the understanding, and on conditions which lie in its own nature; and thus the understanding is the origin of the universal order of nature, in that it comprehends all appearances under its own laws, and thereby first constructs, *a priori*, experience (as to its form), by means of which whatever is to be cognised only by experience, is necessarily subjected to its laws. For we are not now concerned with the nature of things in themselves, which is independent of the conditions both of our sensibility and our understanding, but with nature, as an object of possible experience, and in this case the understanding, whilst it makes experience possible, thereby insists that the sensuous world is either not an object of experience at all, or must be nature [viz., an existence of things, determined according to universal laws].

APPENDIX TO THE PURE SCIENCE OF NATURE

39. *Of the System of the Categories.* There can be nothing more desirable to a philosopher, than to be able to derive the scattered multiplicity of the concepts or the principles, which had occurred to him in concrete use, from a principle *a priori*, and to unite everything in this way in one cognition. He formerly only believed that those things, which remained after a certain abstraction, and seemed by comparison among one another to constitute a particular kind of cognitions, were completely collected; but this was only an Aggregate. Now he knows, that just so many, neither more nor less, can constitute the mode of cognition, and perceives the necessity of his division, which constitutes comprehension; and now only he has attained a *System.*

To search in our daily cognition for the concepts, which do not rest upon particular experience, and yet occur in all cognition of experience, where they as it were constitute the mere form of connexion, presupposes neither greater reflexion nor deeper insight, than to detect in a language the rules of the actual use of words generally, and thus to collect elements for a grammar. In fact both researches are very nearly related, even though we are not able to give a reason why each language has just this and no other formal constitution, and still less why an exact number of such formal determinations in general are found in it.

Aristotle collected ten pure elementary concepts under the name of Categories.[15] To these, which are also called predicaments, he found himself obliged afterwards to add five post-predicaments,[16] some of

which however (*prius, simul*, and *motus*) are contained in the former; but this random collection must be considered (and commended) as a mere hint for future inquirers, not as a regularly developed idea, and hence it has, in the present more advanced state of philosophy, been rejected as quite useless.

After long reflexion on the pure elements of human knowledge (those which contain nothing empirical), I at last succeeded in distinguishing with certainty and in separating the pure elementary notions of the Sensibility (space and time) from those of the Understanding. Thus the 7th, 8th, and 9th Categories had to be excluded from the old list. And the others were of no service to me; because there was no principle [in them], on which the understanding could be investigated, measured in its completion, and all the functions, whence its pure concepts arise, determined exhaustively and with precision.

But in order to discover such a principle, I looked about for an act of the understanding which comprises all the rest, and is distinguished only by various modifications or phases, in reducing the multiplicity of representation to the unity of thinking in general: I found this act of the understanding to consist in judging. Here then the labors of the logicians were ready at hand, though not yet quite free from defects, and with this help I was enabled to exhibit a complete table of the pure functions of the understanding, which are however undetermined in regard to any object. I finally referred these functions of judging to objects in general, or rather to the condition of determining judgments as objectively valid, and so there arose the pure concepts of the understanding, concerning which I could make certain, that these, and this exact number only, constitute our whole cognition of things from pure understanding. I was justified in calling them by their old name, *Categories*, while I reserved for myself the liberty of adding, under the title of *Predicables*, a complete list of all the concepts deducible from them, by combinations whether among themselves, or with the pure form of the appearance, i.e., space or time, or with its matter, so far as it is not yet empirically determined (viz., the object of sensation in general), as soon as a system of transcendental philosophy should be completed with the construction of which I am engaged in the *Critique of Pure Reason* itself.

---

[15]1. *Substantia.* 2. *Qualitas.* 3. *Quantitas.* 4. *Relatio.* 5. *Actio.* 6. *Passio.* 7. *Quando.* 8. *Ubi.* 9. *Situs.* 10. *Habitas.*
[16]*Oppositum, Prius, Simul, Motus, Habere.*

Now the essential point in this system of Categories, which distinguishes it from the old rhapsodical collection without any principle, and for which alone it deserves to be considered as philosophy, consists in this: that by means of it the true significance of the pure concepts of the understanding and the condition of their use could be precisely determined. For here it became obvious that they are themselves nothing but logical functions, and as such do not produce the least concept of an object, but require some sensuous intuition as a basis. They therefore only serve to determine empirical judgments, which are otherwise undetermined and indifferent as regards all functions of judging, relatively to these functions, thereby procuring them universal validity, and by means of them making judgments of experience in general possible.

Such an insight into the nature of the categories, which limits them at the same time to the mere use of experience, never occurred either to their first author, or to any of his successors; but without this insight (which immediately depends upon their derivation or deduction), they are quite useless and only a miserable list of names, without explanation or rule for their use. Had the ancients conceived such an option, doubtless the whole study of the pure rational knowledge, which under the name of metaphysics has for centuries spoiled many a sound mind, would have reached us in quite another shape, and would have enlightened the human understanding, instead of actually exhausting it in obscure and vain speculations, thereby rendering it unfit for true science.

This system of categories makes all treatment of every object of pure reason itself systematic, and affords a direction or clue how and through what points of inquiry every metaphysical consideration must proceed, in order to be complete; for it exhausts all the possible movements of the understanding, among which every concept must be classed. In like manner the table of Principles has been formulated, the completeness of which we can only vouch for by the system of the categories. Even in the division of the concepts, which must go beyond the physical application of the understanding, it is always the very same clue, which, as it must always be determined *a priori* by the same fixed points of the human understanding, always forms a closed circle. There is no doubt that the object of a pure conception either of the understanding or of reason, so far as it is to be estimated philosophically and on *a priori* principles, can in this way be completely cognised. I could not therefore omit to make use of this clue with regard to one of the most abstract ontological divisions, viz., the various distinctions of "the notions of something and of nothing," and to construct accordingly (*Critique*, B 348) a regular and necessary table of their divisions.[17]

And this system, like every other true one founded on a universal principle, shows its inestimable value in this, that it excludes all foreign concepts, which might otherwise intrude among the pure concepts of the understanding, and determines the place of every cognition. Those concepts, which under the name of "concepts of reflexion" have been likewise arranged in a table according to the clue of the categories, intrude, without having any privilege or title to be among the pure concepts of the understanding in Ontology. They are concepts of connexion, and thereby of the objects themselves, whereas the former are only concepts of a mere comparison of concepts already given, hence of quite another nature and use. By my

---

[17]On the table of the categories many neat observations may be made, for instance (1) that the third arises from the first and the second joined in one concept; (2) that in those of Quantity and of Quality there is merely a progress from unity to totality or from something to nothing (for this purpose the categories of Quality must stand thus: reality limitation total negation) without *correlata of opposita*, whereas those of Relation and of Modality have them; (3) that as in *Logic* categorical judgments are the basis of all others, so the category of Substance is the basis of all concepts of actual things; (4) that as Modality in the judgment is not a particular predicate, so by the modal concepts a determination is not superadded to things, etc., etc. Such observations are of great use. If we besides enumerate all the predicables which we can find pretty completely in any good ontology (for example, Baumgarten's), and arrange them in classes under the categories, in which operation we must not neglect to add as complete a dissection of all these concepts as possible, there will then arise a merely analytical part of metaphysics, which does not contain a single synthetical proposition, which might precede the second (the synthetical) and would by its precision and completeness be not only useful, but, in virtue of its system, be even to some extent elegant.

[handwritten margin notes: single part of whole / concepts of reason aim at / Complete. & Collective / transcend]

systematic division[18] they are saved from this confusion. But the value of my special table of the categories will be still more obvious, when we separate the table of the transcendental concepts of Reason from the concepts of the understanding. The latter being of quite another nature and origin, they must have quite another form than the former. This so necessary separation has never yet been made in any system of metaphysics for, as a rule, these rational concepts are all mixed up with the categories, like children of one family, which confusion was unavoidable in the absence of a definite system of categories.

THIRD PART OF THE MAIN TRANSCENDENTAL PROBLEM

HOW IS METAPHYSICS IN GENERAL POSSIBLE?

40. Pure mathematics and pure science of nature had no occasion for such a deduction, as we have made of both, for their own safety and certainty. For the former rests upon its own evidence; and the latter (though sprung from pure sources of the understanding) upon experience and its thorough confirmation. Physics cannot altogether refuse and dispense with the testimony of the latter; because with all its certainty, it can never, as philosophy, rival mathematics. Both sciences therefore stood in need of this inquiry, not for themselves, but for the sake of another science, metaphysics.

Metaphysics has to do not only with concepts of nature, which always find their application in experience, but also with pure rational concepts, which never can be given in any possible experience. Consequently the objective reality of these concepts (viz., that they are not mere chimeras), and the truth or falsity of metaphysical assertions, cannot be discovered or confirmed by any experience. This part of metaphysics however is precisely what constitutes its essential end, to which the rest is only a means, and thus this science is in need of such a deduction for its own sake. The third question now proposed relates therefore as it were to the root and essential difference of metaphysics, i.e., the occupation of Reason with itself, and the supposed knowledge of objects arising immediately from this incubation of its own concepts, without requiring, or indeed being able to reach that knowledge through, experience.[19]

Without solving this problem reason never is justified. The empirical use to which reason limits the pure understanding, does not fully satisfy the proper destination of the latter. Every single experience is only a part of the whole sphere of its domain, but the absolute totality of all possible experience is itself not experience. Yet it is a necessary [concrete] problem for reason, the mere representation of which requires concepts quite different from the categories, whose use is only immanent, or refers to experience, so far as it can be given. Whereas the concepts of reason aim at the completeness, i.e., the collective unity of all possible experience, and thereby transcend every given experience. Thus they become *transcendent*.

As the understanding stands in need of categories for experience, reason contains in itself the source of ideas, by which I mean necessary concepts, whose object cannot be given in any experience. The latter are inherent in the nature of reason, as the former are in that of the understanding. While the former carry with them an illusion likely to mislead, the illusion of the latter is inevitable, though it certainly can be kept from misleading us.

Since all illusion consists in holding the subjective ground of our judgments to be objective, a self-knowledge of pure reason in its transcendent (exaggerated) use is the sole preservative from the aberrations into which reason falls when it mistakes its destination, and refers that to the object transcendently, which only regards its own subject and its guidance in all immanent use.

41. The distinction of ideas, that is, of pure concepts of reason, from categories, or pure concepts of the understanding, as cognitions of a quite distinct species, origin and use, is so important a point in

---

[18]See *Critique of Pure Reason*, B 316.

[19]If we can say, that a science is actual at least in the idea of all men, as soon as it appears that the problems which lead to it are proposed to everybody by the nature of human reason, and that therefore many (though faulty) endevours are unavoidably made in its behalf, then we are bound to say that metaphysics is subjectively (and indeed necessarily) actual, and therefore we justly ask, how is it (objectively) possible.

founding a science which is to contain the system of all these *a priori* cognitions, that without this distinction metaphysics is absolutely impossible, or is at best a random, bungling attempt to build a castle in the air without a knowledge of the materials or of their fitness for any purpose. Had the *Critique of Pure Reason* done nothing but first point out this distinction, it had thereby contributed more to clear up our conception of, and to guide to our inquiry in, the field of metaphysics, than all the vain efforts which have hitherto been made to satisfy the transcendent problems of pure reason, without ever surmising that we were in quite another field than that of the understanding, and hence classing concepts of the understanding and those of reason together, as if they were of the same kind.

42. All pure cognitions of the understanding have this feature, that their concepts present themselves in experience, and their principles can be confirmed by it; whereas the transcendent cognitions of reason cannot, either as ideas, appear in experience, or as propositions ever be confirmed or refuted by it. Hence whatever errors may slip in unawares, can only be discovered by pure reason itself—a discovery of much difficulty, because this very reason naturally becomes dialectical by means of its ideas, and this unavoidable illusion cannot be limited by any objective and dogmatical researches into things, but by a subjective investigation of reason itself as a source of ideas.

43. In the *Critique of Pure Reason* it was always my greatest care to endeavor not only carefully to distinguish the several species of cognition, but to derive concepts belonging to each one of them from their common source. I did this in order that by knowing whence they originated, I might determine their use with safety, and also have the unanticipated but invaluable advantage of knowing the completeness of my enumeration, classification and specification of concepts *a priori*, and therefore according to principles. Without this, metaphysics is mere rhapsody, in which no one knows whether he has enough, or whether and where something is still wanting. We can indeed have this advantage only in pure philosophy, but of this philosophy it constitutes the very essence.

As I had found the origin of the categories in the four logical functions of all the judgments of the understanding, it was quite natural to seek the origin of the ideas in the three functions of the syllogisms

of reason. For as soon as these pure concepts of reason (the transcendental ideas) are given, they could hardly, except they be held innate, be found anywhere else, than in the same activity of reason, which, so far as it regards mere form, constitutes the logical element of the syllogisms of reason; but, so far as it represents judgments of the understanding with respect to the one or to the other form *a priori*, constitutes transcendental concepts of pure reason.

The formal distinction of syllogisms renders their division into categorical, hypothetical, and disjunctive necessary. The concepts of reason founded on them contained therefore, first, the idea of the complete subject (the substantial); secondly, the idea of the complete series of conditions; thirdly, the determination of all concepts in the idea of a complete complex of that which is possible.[20] The first idea is psychological, the second cosmological, the third theological, and, as all three give occasion to Dialectics, yet each in its own way, the division of the whole Dialectic of pure reason into its Paralogism, its Antinomy, and its Ideal, was arranged accordingly. Through this deduction we may feel assured that all the claims of pure reason are completely represented, and that none can be wanting; because the faculty of reason itself, whence they all take their origin, is thereby completely surveyed.

44. In these general considerations it is also remarkable that the ideas of reason are unlike the categories, of no service to the use of our understanding in experience, but quite dispensable, and become even an impediment to the maxims of a rational

---

[20]In disjunctive judgments we consider all possibility as divided in respect to a particular concept. By the ontological principle of the universal determination of a thing in general, I understand the principle that either the one or the other of all possible contradictory predicates must be assigned to any object. This is at the same time the principle of all disjunctive judgments, constituting the foundation of our conception of possibility, and in it the possibility of every object in general is considered as determined. This may serve as a slight explanation of the above proposition that the activity of reason in disjunctive syllogisms is formally the same as that by which it fashions the idea of a universal conception of all reality, containing in itself that which is positive in all contradictory predicates.

cognition of nature. Yet in another aspect still to be determined they are necessary. Whether the soul is or is not a simple substance, is of no consequence to us in the explanation of its phenomena. For we cannot render the notion of a simple being intelligible by any possible experience that is sensuous or concrete. The notion is therefore quite void as regards all hoped-for insight into the cause of phenomena, and cannot at all serve as a principle of the explanation of that which internal or external experience supplies. So the cosmological ideas of the beginning of the world or of its eternity (*a parte ante*) cannot be of any greater service to us for the explanation of any event in the world itself. And finally we must, according to a right maxim of the philosophy of nature, refrain from all explanations of the design of nature, drawn from the will of a Supreme Being; because this would not be natural philosophy, but an acknowledgment that we have come to the end of it. The use of these ideas, therefore, is quite different from that of those categories by which (and by the principles built upon which) experience itself first becomes possible. But our laborious analytics of the understanding would be superfluous if we had nothing else in view than the mere cognition of nature as it can be given in experience; for reason does its work, both in mathematics and in the science of nature, quite safely and well without any of this subtle deduction. Therefore our critique of the understanding combines with the ideas of pure reason for a purpose which lies beyond the empirical use of the understanding; but this we have above declared to be in this aspect totally inadmissible, and without any object or meaning. Yet there must be a harmony between that of the nature of reason and that of the understanding, and the former must contribute to the perfection of the latter, and cannot possibly upset it.

The solution of this question is as follows: Pure reason does not in its ideas point to particular objects, which lie beyond the field of experience, but only requires completeness of the use of the understanding in the system of experience. But this completeness can be a completeness of principles only, not of intuitions and of objects. In order however to represent the ideas definitely, reason conceives them after the fashion of the cognition of an object. The cognition is as far as these rules are concerned completely determined, but the object is only an idea invented for the purpose of bringing the cognition of the understanding as near as possible to the completeness represented by that idea.

Prefatory Remark to the Dialectics of Pure Reason

45. We have above shown in 33 and 34 that the purity of the categories from all admixture of sensuous determinations may mislead reason into extending their use, quite beyond all experience, to things in themselves; though as these categories themselves find no intuition which can give them meaning or sense *in concreto*, they, as mere logical functions, can represent a thing in general, but not give by themselves alone a determinate concept of anything. Such hyperbolical objects are distinguished by the appellation of noumena, or pure beings of the understanding (or better, beings of thought), such as, for example, "substance," but conceived without permanence in time, or "cause," but not acting in time, etc. Here predicates, that only serve to make the conformity-to-law of experience possible, are applied to these concepts, and yet they are deprived of all the conditions of intuition, on which alone experience is possible, and so these concepts lose all significance.

There is no danger, however, of the understanding spontaneously making an excursion so very wantonly beyond its own bounds into the field of the mere creatures of thought, without being impelled by foreign laws. But when reason, which cannot be fully satisfied with any empirical use of the rules of the understanding, as being always conditioned, requires a completion of this chain of conditions, then the understanding is forced out of its sphere. And then it partly represents objects of experience in a series so extended that no experience can grasp, partly even (with a view to complete the series) it seeks entirely beyond its noumena, to which it can attach that chain, and so, having at last escaped from the conditions of experience, make its attitude as it were final. These are then the transcendental ideas, which, though according to the true but hidden ends of the natural determination of our reason, they may aim not at extravagant concepts, but at an unbounded extension of their empirical use, yet seduce the understanding by an unavoidable illusion to a transcendent use, which, though deceitful, cannot be restrained within the bounds of experience by any resolution, but only by scientific instruction and with much difficulty.

I. The Psychological Idea[21]

46. People have long since observed, that in all substances the proper subject, that which remains after all the accidents (as predicates) are abstracted, consequently that which forms the substance of things remains unknown, and various complaints have been made concerning these limits to our knowledge. But it will be well to consider that the human understanding is not to be blamed for its inability to know the substance of things, that is, to determine it by itself, but rather for requiring to cognise it which is a mere idea definitely as though it were a given object. Pure reason requires us to seek for every predicate of a thing its proper subject, and for this subject, which is itself necessarily nothing but a predicate, its subject, and so on indefinitely (or as far as we can reach). But hence it follows, that we must not hold anything, at which we can arrive, to be an ultimate subject, and that substance itself never can be thought by our understanding, however deep we may penetrate, even if all nature were unveiled to us. For the specific nature of our understanding consists in thinking everything discursively, that is, representing it by concepts, and so by mere predicates, to which therefore the absolute subject must always be wanting. Hence all the real properties, by which we cognise bodies, are mere accidents, not excepting impenetrability, which we can only represent to ourselves as the effect of a power of which the subject is unknown to us.

Now we appear to have this substance in the consciousness of ourselves (in the thinking subject), and indeed in an immediate intuition; for all the predicates of an internal sense refer to the *ego*, as a subject, and I cannot conceive myself as the predicate of any other subject. Hence completeness in the reference of the given concepts as predicates to a subject—not merely an idea, but an object—that is, the absolute subject itself, seems to be given in experience. But this expectation is disappointed. For the ego is not a concept,[22] but only the indication of the object of the internal sense, so far as we cognise it by no further predicate. Consequently it cannot be in itself a predicate of any other thing; but just as little can it be a determinate concept of an absolute subject, but is, as in all other cases, only the reference of the internal phenomena to their unknown subject. Yet this idea (which serves very well, as a regulative principle, totally to destroy all materialistic explanations of the internal phenomena of the soul) occasions by a very natural misunderstanding a very specious argument, which, from this supposed cognition of the substance of our thinking being, infers its nature, so far as the knowledge of it falls quite without the complex of experience.

47. But though we may call this thinking self (the soul) substance, as being the ultimate subject of thinking which cannot be further represented as the predicate of another thing; it remains quite empty and without significance, if permanence—the quality which renders the concept of substances in experience fruitful—cannot be proved of it.

But permanence can never be proved of the concept of a substance, as a thing in itself, but for the purposes of experience only. This is sufficiently shown by the first Analogy of Experience,[23] and whoever will not yield to this proof may try for himself whether he can succeed in proving, from the concept of a subject which does not exist itself as the predicate of another thing, that its existence is thoroughly permanent, and that it cannot either in itself or by any natural cause originate or be annihilated. These synthetical *a priori* propositions can never be proved in themselves, but only in reference to things as objects of possible experience.

48. If therefore from the concept of the soul as a substance, we would infer its permanence, this can

---

[21] See *Critique of Pure Reason*, "The Paralogisms of Pure Reason."

[22] Were the representation of the apperception (the Ego) a concept, by which anything could be thought, it could be used as a predicate of other things or contain predicates in itself. But it is nothing more than the feeling of an existence without the least definite conception and is only the representation of that to which all thinking stands in relation (*relatione accidentis*).

[23] Cf. *Critique*, B 224.

hold good as regards possible experience only, not [of the soul] as a thing in itself and beyond all possible experience. But life is the subjective condition of all our possible experience, consequently we can only infer the permanence of the soul in life; for the death of man is the end of all experience which concerns the soul as an object of experience, except the contrary be proved, which is the very question in hand. The permanence of the soul can therefore only be proved (and no one cares for that) during the life of man, but not, as we desire to do, after death; and for this general reason, that the concept of substance, so far as it is to be considered necessarily combined with the concept of permanence, can be so combined only according to the principles of possible experience, and therefore for the purposes of experience only.[24]

49. That there is something real without us which not only corresponds, but must correspond, to our external perceptions, can likewise be proved to be not a connexion of things in themselves, but for the sake of experience. This means that there is something empirical, i.e., some phenomenon in space without us, that admits of a satisfactory proof, for we have nothing to do with other objects than those which belong to possible experience; because objects which cannot be given us in any experience, do not exist for us. Empirically without me is that which appears in space, and space, together with all the phenomena which it contains, belongs to the representations, whose connexion according to laws of experience proves their objective truth, just as the connexion of the phenomena of the internal sense provides the actuality of my soul (as an object of the internal sense). By means of external experience I am conscious of the actuality of bodies, as external phenomena in space, in the same manner as by means of the internal experience I am conscious of the existence of my soul in time, but this soul is only cognised as an object of the internal sense by phenomena that constitute an internal state, and of which the essence in itself, which forms the basis of these phenomena, is unknown. Cartesian idealism therefore does nothing but distinguish external experience from dreaming; and the conformity to law (as a criterion of its truth) of the former, from the irregularity and the false illusion of the latter. In both it presupposes space and time as conditions of the existence of objects, and it only inquires whether the objects of the external senses, which we when awake put in space, are as actually to be found in it, as the object of the internal sense, the soul, is in time; that is, whether experience carries with it sure criteria to distinguish it from imagination. This doubt, however, may easily be disposed of, and we always do so in common life by investigating the connexion of phenomena in both space and time according to universal laws of experience, and we cannot doubt, when the representation of external things throughout agrees therewith, that they constitute truthful experience. Material idealism, in which phenomena are considered as such only according to their connexion in experience, may accordingly be very easily refuted; and it is just as sure an experience, that bodies exist without us (in space), as that I myself exist according to the representation of the internal sense (in time): for the notion without us, only signifies existence in space.

---

[24]It is indeed very remarkable how carelessly metaphysicians have always passed over the principle of the permanence of substances without ever attempting a proof of it; doubtless because they found themselves abandoned by all proofs as soon as they began to deal with the concept of substance. Common sense, which felt distinctly that without this presupposition no union of perceptions in experience is possible, supplied the want by a postulate. From experience itself it never could derive such a principle, partly because substances cannot be so traced in all their alterations and dissolutions, that the matter can always be found undiminished, partly because the principle contains *necessity*, which is always the sign of an *a priori* principle. People then boldly applied this postulate to the concept of soul as a substance, and concluded a necessary continuance of the soul after the death of man (especially as the simplicity of this substance, which is inferred from the indivisibility of consciousness, secured it from destruction by dissolution). Had they found the genuine source of this principle—a discovery which requires deeper researches than they were ever inclined to make—they would have seen, that the law of the permanence of substances has place for the purposes of experience only, and hence can hold good of things so far as they are to be cognised and conjoined with others in experience, but never independently of all possible experience, and consequently cannot hold good of the soul after death.

However as the Ego in the proposition, "I am," means not only the object of internal intuition (in space), but the thing-in-itself, which is the basis of this phenomenon; [as this is the case] the question, whether bodies (as phenomena of the external sense) exist as bodies apart from my thoughts, may without any hesitation be denied in nature. But the question, whether I myself as a phenomenon of the internal sense (the soul according to empirical psychology) exist apart from my faculty of representation in time, is an exactly similar inquiry, and must likewise be answered in the negative. And in this manner everything, when it is reduced to its true meaning, is decided and certain. The formal (which I have also called transcendental) actually abolishes the material, or Cartesian, idealism. For if space be nothing but a form of my sensibility, it is as a representation in me just as actual as I myself am, and nothing but the empirical truth of the representations in it remains for consideration. But, if this is not the case, if space and the phenomena in it are something existing without us, then all the criteria of experience beyond our perception can never prove the actuality of these objects without us.

II. The Cosmological Idea[25]

50. This product of pure reason in its transcendent use is its most remarkable curiosity. It serves as a very powerful agent to rouse philosophy from its dogmatic slumber, and to stimulate it to the arduous task of undertaking a critique of reason itself.

I term this idea cosmological, because it always takes its object only from the sensible world, and does not use any other than those whose object is given to sense, consequently it remains in this respect in its native home, it does not become transcendent, and is therefore so far not mere idea; whereas, to conceive the soul as a simple substance, already means to conceive such an object (the simple) as cannot be presented to the senses. Yet the cosmological idea extends the connexion of the conditioned with its condition (whether the connexion is mathematical or dynamical) so far, that

experience never can keep up with it. It is therefore with regard to this point always an idea, whose object never can be adequately given in any experience.

51. In the first place, the use of a system of categories becomes here so obvious and unmistakable, that even if there were not several other proofs of it, this alone would sufficiently prove it indispensable in the system of pure reason. There are only four such transcendent ideas, as there are so many classes of categories; in each of which, however, they refer only to the absolute completeness of the series of the conditions for a given conditioned. In analogy to these cosmological ideas there are only four kinds of dialectical assertions of pure reason, which, as they are dialectical, thereby prove, that to each of them, on equally specious principles of pure reason, a contradictory assertion stands opposed. As all the metaphysical art of the most subtle distinction cannot prevent this opposition, it compels the philosopher to recur to the first sources of pure reason itself. This Antinomy, not arbitrarily invented, but founded in the nature of human reason, and hence unavoidable and never ceasing, contains the following four theses together with their antitheses:

1
Thesis
The world has, as to time and space,
a beginning (limit).
Antithesis
The world is, as to time and space, infinite.

2
Thesis
Everything in the world consists of
[elements that are] simple.
Antithesis
There is nothing simple, but everything is
composite.

3
Thesis
There are in the world causes through freedom.
Antithesis
There is no freedom, but all is nature.

---

[25]Cf. *Critique*, "The Antinomy of Pure Reason."

4

Thesis

In the series of the world-causes there
is some necessary Being.

Antithesis

There is nothing necessary in the world,
but in this series all is contingent.

52a. Here is the most singular phenomenon of human reason, no other instance of which can be shown in any other use. If we, as is commonly done, represent to ourselves the appearances of the sensible world as things in themselves, if we assume the principles of their combination as principles universally valid of things in themselves and not merely of experience, as is usually, nay without our *Critique*, unavoidably done, there arises an unexpected conflict, which never can be removed in the common dogmatical way; because the thesis, as well as the antithesis, can be shown by equally clear, evident, and irresistible proofs—for I pledge myself as to the correctness of all these proofs—and reason therefore perceives that it is divided with itself, a state at which the sceptic rejoices, but which must make the critical philosopher pause and feel ill at ease.

52b. We may blunder in various ways in metaphysics without any fear of being detected in falsehood. For we never can be refuted by experience if we but avoid self-contradiction, which in synthetical, though purely fictitious propositions, may be done whenever the concepts, which we connect, are mere ideas, that cannot be given (in their whole content) in experience. For how can we make out by experience, whether the world is from eternity or had a beginning, whether matter is infinitely divisible or consists of simple parts? Such concepts cannot be given in any experience, be it ever so extensive, and consequently the falsehood either of the positive or the negative proposition cannot be discovered by this touch-stone.

The only possible way in which reason could have revealed unintentionally its secret Dialectics, falsely announced as Dogmatics, would be when it were made to ground an assertion upon a universally admitted principle and to deduce the exact contrary with the greatest accuracy of inference from another which is equally granted. This is actually here the case with regard to four natural ideas of reason,

whence four assertions on the one side, and as many counter-assertions on the other arise, each consistently following from universally-acknowledged principles. Thus they reveal by the use of these principles the dialectical illusion of pure reason which would otherwise forever remain concealed.

This is therefore a decisive experiment, which must necessarily expose any error lying hidden in the assumptions of reason.[26] Contradictory propositions cannot both be false, except the concept, which is the subject of both, is self-contradictory; for example, the propositions, "a square circle is round, and a square circle is not round," are both false. For, as to the former it is false, that the circle is round, because it is quadrangular; and it is likewise false, that it is not round, that is, angular, because it is a circle. For the logical criterion of the impossibility of a concept consists in this, that if we presuppose it, two contradictory propositions both become false; consequently, as no middle between them is conceivable, nothing at all is thought by that concept.

52c. The first two antinomies, which I call mathematical, because they are concerned with the addition or division of the homogeneous, are founded on such a self-contradictory concept; and hence I explain how it happens, that both the Thesis and Antithesis of the two are false.

When I speak of objects in time and in space, it is not of things in themselves, of which I know nothing, but of things in appearance, that is, of experience, as the particular way of cognising objects which is afforded to man. I must not say of what I think in time or in space, that in itself, and independent of these my thoughts, it exists in space and in time; for

---

[26] I therefore would be pleased to have the critical reader to devote to this antimony of pure reason his chief attention, because nature itself seems to have established it with a view to stagger reason in its daring pretensions, and to force it to self-examination. For every proof, which I have given, as well of the thesis as of the antithesis, I undertake to be responsible, and thereby to show the certainty of the inevitable antinomy of reason. When the reader is brought by this curious phenomenon to fall back upon the proof of the presumption upon which it rests, he will feel himself obliged to investigate the ultimate foundation of all the cognition of pure reason with me more thoroughly.

in that case I contradict myself; because space and time, together with the appearances in them, are nothing existing in themselves and outside of my representations, but are themselves only modes of representation, and it is palpably contradictory to say, that a mere mode of representation exists without our representation. Objects of the senses therefore exist only in experience; whereas to give them a self-subsisting existence apart from experience or before it, is merely to represent to ourselves that experience actually exists apart from experience or before it.

Now if I inquire after the quantity of the world, as to space and time, it is equally impossible, as regards all my notions, to declare it infinite or to declare it finite. For neither assertion can be contained in experience, because experience either of an infinite space, or of an infinite time elapsed, or again, of the boundary of the world by a void space, or by an antecedent void time, is impossible; these are mere ideas. This quantity of the world, which is determined in either way, should therefore exist in the world itself apart from all experience. This contradicts the notion of a world of sense, which is merely a complex of the appearances whose existence and connexion occur only in our representations, that is, in experience, since this latter is not an object in itself, but a mere mode of representation. Hence it follows, that as the concept of an absolutely existing world of sense is self-contradictory, the solution of the problem concerning its quantity, whether attempted affirmatively or negatively, is always false.

The same holds good of the second antinomy, which relates to the division of phenomena. For these are mere representations, and the parts exist merely in their representation, consequently in the division, or in a possible experience where they are given, and the division reaches only as far as this latter reaches. To assume that an appearance, e.g., that of body, contains in itself before all experience all the parts, which any possible experience can ever reach, is to impute to a mere appearance, which can exist only in experience, an existence previous to experience. In other words, it would mean that mere representations exist before they can be found in our faculty of representation. Such an assertion is self-contradictory, as also every solution of our misunderstood problem, whether we maintain, that bodies in themselves consist of an infinite number of parts, or of a finite number of simple parts.

53. In the first (the mathematical) class of antinomies the falsehood of the assumption consists in representing in one concept something self-contradictory as if it were compatible (i.e., an appearance as an object in itself). But, as to the second (the dynamical) class of antinomies, the falsehood of the representation consists in representing as contradictory what is compatible; so that, as in the former case, the opposed assertions are both false, in this case, on the other hand, where they are opposed to one another by mere misunderstanding, they may both be true.

Any mathematical connexion necessarily presupposes homogeneity of what is connected (in the concept of magnitude), while the dynamical one by no means requires the same. When we have to deal with extended magnitudes, all the parts must be homogeneous with one another and with the whole: whereas in the connexion of cause and effect, homogeneity may indeed likewise be found, but is not necessary; for the concept of causality (by means of which something is posited through something else quite different from it), at all events, does not require it.

If the objects of the world of sense are taken for things in themselves, and the above laws of nature for the laws of things in themselves, the contradiction would be unavoidable. So also, if the subject of freedom were, like other objects, represented as mere appearance, the contradiction would be just as unavoidable, for the same predicate would at once be affirmed and denied of the same kind of object in the same sense. But if natural necessity is referred merely to appearances, and freedom merely to things in themselves, no contradiction arises, if we at once assume, or admit both kinds of causality, however difficult or impossible it may be to make the latter kind conceivable.

In appearance every effect is an event, or something that happens in time; it must, according to the universal law of nature, be preceded by a determination of the causality of its cause (a state), which follows according to a constant law. But this determination of the cause as causality must likewise be something that takes place or happens; the cause must have begun to act, otherwise no succession between it and the effect could be conceived. Otherwise the effect, as well as the causality of the cause, would have always existed. Therefore the determination of the cause to act must also have originated among appearances, and must consequently, as well as its effect, be an event, which must again have its cause, and so on; hence natural necessity must be the condition, on which effective causes are determined. Whereas if freedom is to be a property of certain causes of appearances, it must, as regards these, which are events, be a faculty of starting them spontaneously, that is, without the causality of the cause itself, and hence without requiring any other ground to determine its start. But then the cause, as to its causality, must not rank under time-determinations of its state, that is, it cannot be an appearance, and must be considered a thing in itself, while its effects would be only appearances.[27] If without contradiction we can think of the beings of understanding as exercising such an influence on appearances, then natural necessity will attach to all connexions of cause and effect in the sensuous world, though on the other hand, freedom can be granted to such cause, as is itself not an appearance (but the foundation of appearance). Nature therefore and freedom can without contradiction be attributed to the very same thing, but in different relations—on one side as a phenomenon, on the other as a thing in itself.

---

[27]The idea of freedom occurs only in the relation of the intellectual, as cause, to the appearance as effect. Hence we cannot attribute freedom to matter in regard to the incessant action by which it fills its space though this action takes place from an internal principle. We can likewise find no notion of freedom suitable to purely rational beings, for instance to God, so far as his action is immanent. For his action, though independent of external determining causes is determined in his eternal reason that is, in the divine *nature*. It is only if *something is to start* by an action, and so the effect occurs in the sequence of time, or in the world of sense (e.g., the beginning of the world), that we can put the question, whether the causality of the cause must in its turn have been started, or whether the cause can originate an effect without its causality itself beginning. In the former case the concept of this causality is a concept of natural necessity, in the latter that of freedom. From this the reader will see that as I explained freedom to be the faculty of starting an event spontaneously, I have exactly hit the notion which is the problem of metaphysics.

We have in us a faculty, which not only stands in connexion with its subjective determining grounds that are the natural causes of its actions, and is so far the faculty of a being that itself belongs to appearances, but is also referred to objective grounds, that are only ideas, so far as they can determine this faculty, a connexion which is expressed by the word *ought*. This faculty is called *reason*, and, so far as we consider a being (man) entirely according to this objectively determinable reason, he cannot be considered as a being of sense, but this property is that of a thing in itself, of which we cannot comprehend the possibility—I mean how the *ought* (which however has never yet taken place) should determine its activity, and can become the cause of actions, whose effect is an appearance in the sensible world. Yet the causality of reason would be freedom with regard to the effects in the sensuous world, so far as we can consider objective grounds, which are themselves ideas, as their determinants. For its action in that case would not depend upon subjective conditions, consequently not upon those of time, and of course not upon the law of nature, which serves to determine them, because grounds of reason give to actions the rule universally, according to principles, without the influence of the circumstances of either time or place.

What I adduce here is merely meant as an example to make the thing intelligible, and does not necessarily belong to our problem, which must be decided from mere concepts, independently of the properties which we meet in the actual world.

Now I may say without contradiction: that all the actions of rational beings, so far as they are appearances (occurring in any experience), are subject to the necessity of nature; but the same actions, as regards merely the rational subject and its faculty of acting according to mere reason, are free. For what is required for the necessity of nature? Nothing more than the determinability of every event in the world of sense according to constant laws, that is, a reference to cause in the appearance; in this process the thing in itself at its foundation and the causality remain unknown. But I say, that the law of nature remains, whether the rational being is the cause of the effects in the sensuous world from reason, that is, through freedom, or whether it does not determine them on grounds of reason. For, if the former is the case, the action is performed according to maxims, the effect of which as appearance is always conformable to constant laws; if the latter is the case, and the action not performed on principles of reason, it is subjected to the empirical laws of the sensibility, and in both cases the effects are connected according to constant laws; more than this we do not require or know concerning natural necessity. But in the former case reason is the cause of these laws of nature, and therefore free; in the latter the effects following according to mere natural laws of sensibility, because reason does not influence it; but reason itself is not determined on that account by the sensibility, and is therefore free in this case too. Freedom is therefore no hindrance to natural law in appearance, neither does this law abrogate the freedom of the practical use of reason, which is connected with things in themselves, as determining grounds.

Thus practical freedom, viz., the freedom in which reason possesses causality according to objectively determining grounds, is rescued and yet natural necessity is not in the least curtailed with regard to the very same effects, as appearances. The same remarks will serve to explain what we had to say concerning transcendental freedom and its compatibility with natural necessity (in the same subject, but not taken in the same reference). For, as to this, every beginning of the action of a being from objective causes regarded as determining grounds, is always a first start, though the same action is in the series of appearances only a subordinate start, which must be preceded by a state of the cause, which determines it, and is itself determined in the same manner by another immediately preceding. Thus we are able, in rational beings, or in beings generally, so far as their causality is determined in them as things in themselves, to imagine a faculty of beginning from itself a series of states, without falling into contradiction with the laws of nature. For the relation of the action to objective grounds of reason is not a time-relation; in this case that which determines the causality does not precede in time the action, because such determining grounds represent not a reference to objects of sense, e.g., to causes in the appearances, but to determining causes, as things in themselves, which do not rank under conditions of time. And in this way the action, with regard to the causality of

reason, can be considered as a first start in respect to the series of appearances, and yet also as a merely subordinate beginning. We may therefore without contradiction consider it in the former aspect as free, but in the latter (in so far as it is merely appearance) as subject to natural necessity.

As to the fourth Antinomy, it is solved in the same way as the conflict of reason with itself in the third. For, provided the cause *in* the appearance is distinguished from the cause *of* the appearance (so far as it can be thought as a thing in itself), both propositions are perfectly reconcilable: the one, that there is nowhere in the sensuous world a cause (according to similar laws of causality), whose existence is absolutely necessary; the other, that this world is nevertheless connected with a Necessary Being as its cause (but of another kind and according to another law). The incompatibility of these propositions entirely rests upon the mistake of extending what is valid merely of appearances to things in themselves, and in general confusing both in one concept.

54. This then is the proposition and this the solution of the whole antinomy, in which reason finds itself involved in the application of its principles to the sensible world. The former alone (the mere proposition) would be a considerable service in the cause of our knowledge of human reason, even though the solution might fail to fully satisfy the reader, who has here to combat a natural illusion, which has been but recently exposed to him, and which he had hitherto always regarded as genuine. For one result at least is unavoidable. As it is quite impossible to prevent this conflict of reason with itself—so long as the objects of the sensible world are taken for things in themselves, and not for mere appearances, which they are in fact—the reader is thereby compelled to examine over again the deduction of all our *a priori* cognition and the proof which I have given of my deduction in order to come to a decision on the question. This is all I require at present; for when in this occupation he shall have thought himself deep enough into the nature of pure reason, those concepts by which alone the solution of the conflict of reason is possible, will become sufficiently familiar to him. Without this preparation I cannot expect an unreserved assent even from the most attentive reader.

III. The Theological Idea[28]

55. The third transcendental Idea, which affords matter for the most important, but, if pursued only speculatively, transcendent and thereby dialectical use of reason, is the ideal of pure reason. Reason in this case does not, as with the psychological and the cosmological Ideas, begin from experience, and err by exaggerating its grounds, in striving to attain, if possible, the absolute completeness of their series. It rather totally breaks with experience, and from mere concepts of what constitutes the absolute completeness of a thing in general, consequently by means of the idea of a most perfect primal Being, it proceeds to determine the possibility and therefore the actuality of all other things. And so the mere presupposition of a Being, who is conceived not in the series of experience, yet for the purposes of experience—for the sake of comprehending its connexion, order, and unity—i.e., the idea [the notion of it], is more easily distinguished from the concept of the understanding here, than in the former cases. Hence we can easily expose the dialectical illusion which arises from our making the subjective conditions of our thinking objective conditions of objects themselves, and an hypothesis necessary for the satisfaction of our reason, a dogma. As the observations of the *Critique* on the pretensions of transcendental theology are intelligible, clear, and decisive, I have nothing more to add on the subject.

General Remark on the Transcendental Ideas

56. The objects, which are given us by experience, are in many respects incomprehensible, and many questions, to which the law of nature leads us, when carried beyond a certain point (though quite conformably to the laws of nature), admit of no answer; as for example the question: why substances attract one another? But if we entirely quit nature, or in pursuing its combinations, exceed all possible experience, and so enter the realm of mere ideas, we cannot then say that the object is incomprehensible, and that the nature of things proposes to us insoluble problems. For we are not then concerned with nature or in general with given objects, but with concepts, which have their origin merely in our reason, and with mere creations of thought; and all the problems that arise from our notions of them must be solved, because of course reason can and must give a full account of its own procedure.[29] As the psychological, cosmological, and theological Ideas are nothing but pure concepts of reason, which cannot be given in any experience, the questions which reason asks us about them are put to us not by the objects, but by mere maxims of our reason for the sake of its own satisfaction. They must all be capable of satisfactory answers, which is done by showing that they are principles which bring our use of the understanding into thorough agreement, completeness, and synthetical unity, and that they so far hold good of experience only, but of experience as a whole.

Although an absolute whole of experience is impossible, the idea of a whole of cognition according to principles must impart to our knowledge a peculiar kind of unity, that of a system, without which it is nothing but piecework, and cannot be used for proving the existence of a highest purpose (which can only be the general system of all purposes), I do not here refer only to the practical, but also to the highest purpose of the speculative use of reason.

The transcendental Ideas therefore express the peculiar application of reason as a principle of systematic unity in the use of the understanding. Yet if we assume this unity of the mode of cognition to be attached to the object of cognition, if we regard that which is merely regulative to be constitutive, and if we persuade ourselves that we can by means of these

---

[29]Herr Platner in his *Aphorisms* acutely says (§§ 728, 729), "If reason be a criterion, no concept, which is incomprehensible to human reason, can be possible. Incomprehensibility has place in what is actual only. Here incomprehensibility arises from the insufficiency of the acquired ideas." It sounds paradoxical, but is otherwise not strange to say, that in nature there is much incomprehensible (e.g., the faculty of generation) but if we mount still higher, and even go beyond nature, everything again becomes comprehensible, for we then quit entirely the objects, which can be given us, and occupy ourselves merely about ideas, in which occupation we can easily comprehend the law that reason prescribes by them to the understanding for its use in experience, because the law is the reason's own production.

Ideas enlarge our cognition transcendently, or far beyond all possible experience, while it only serves to render experience within itself as nearly complete as possible, i.e., to limit its progress by nothing that cannot belong to experience: we suffer from a mere misunderstanding in our estimate of the proper application of our reason and of its principles, and from a Dialectic, which both confuses the empirical use of reason, and also sets reason at variance with itself.

CONCLUSION

ON THE DETERMINATION OF THE BOUNDS OF PURE REASON

57. Having adduced the clearest arguments, it would be absurd for us to hope that we can know more of any object, than belongs to the possible experience of it, or lay claim to the least atom of knowledge about anything not assumed to be an object of possible experience, which would determine it according to the constitution it has in itself. For how could we determine anything in this way, since time, space, and the categories, and still more all the concepts formed by empirical experience or perception in the sensible world, have and can have no other use, than to make experience possible. And if this condition is omitted from the pure concepts of the understanding, they do not determine any object, and have no meaning whatever.

But it would be on the other hand a still greater absurdity if we conceded no things in themselves, or set up our experience for the only possible mode of knowing things, our way of beholding them in space and in time for the only possible way, and our discursive understanding for the archetype of every possible understanding; in fact if we wished to have the principles of the possibility of experience considered universal conditions of things in themselves.

Our principles, which limit the use of reason to possible experience, might in this way become transcendent, and the limits of our reason be set up as limits of the possibility of things in themselves (as Hume's dialogues may illustrate), if a careful critique did not guard the bounds of our reason with respect to its empirical use, and set a limit to its

pretensions. Scepticism originally arose from metaphysics and its licentious dialectics. At first it might, merely to favor the empirical use of reason, announce everything that transcends this use as worthless and deceitful; but by and by, when it was perceived that the very same principles that are used in experience, insensibly, and apparently with the same right, led still further than experience extends, then men began to doubt even the propositions of experience. But here there is no danger; for common sense will doubtless always assert its rights. A certain confusion, however, arose in science which cannot determine how far reason is to be trusted, and why only so far and no further, and this confusion can only be cleared up and all future relapses obviated by a formal determination, on principle, of the boundary of the use of our reason.

We cannot indeed, beyond all possible experience, form a definite notion of what things in themselves may be. Yet we are not at liberty to abstain entirely from inquiring into them; for experience never satisfies reason fully, but in answering questions, refers us further and further back, and leaves us dissatisfied with regard to their complete solution. This any one may gather from the Dialectics of pure reason, which therefore has its good subjective grounds. Having acquired, as regards the nature of our soul, a clear conception of the subject, and having come to the conviction, that its manifestations cannot be explained materialistically, who can refrain from asking what the soul really is, and, if no concept of experience suffices for the purpose, from accounting for it by a concept of reason (that of a simple immaterial being), though we cannot by any means prove its objective reality? Who can satisfy himself with mere empirical knowledge in all the cosmological questions of the duration and of the quantity of the world, of freedom or of natural necessity, since every answer given on principles of experience begets a fresh question, which likewise requires its answer and thereby clearly shows the insufficiency of all physical modes of explanation to satisfy reason? Finally, who does not see in the thorough-going contingency and dependence of all his thoughts and assumptions on mere principles of experience, the impossibility of stopping there? And who does not feel himself compelled, notwithstanding all interdictions against losing himself in transcendent ideas, to seek rest and contentment beyond all the concepts which he can vindicate by experience, in the concept of a Being, the possibility of which we cannot conceive, but at the same time cannot be refuted, because it relates to a mere being of the understanding, and without it reason must needs remain forever dissatisfied?

Bounds (in extended beings) always presuppose a space existing outside a certain definite place, and inclosing it; limits do not require this, but are mere negations, which affect a quantity, so far as it is not absolutely complete. But our reason, as it were, sees in its surroundings a space for the cognition of things in themselves, though we can never have definite notions of them, and are limited to appearances only.

As long as the cognition of reason is homogeneous, definite bounds to it are inconceivable. In mathematics and in natural philosophy human reason admits of limits, but not bounds, viz., that something indeed lies without it, at which it can never arrive, but not that it will at any point find completion in its internal progress. The enlarging of our views in mathematics, and the possibility of new discoveries, are infinite; and the same is the case with the discovery of new properties of nature, of new powers and laws, by continued experience and its rational combination. But limits cannot be mistaken here, for mathematics refers to appearances only, and what cannot be an object of sensuous contemplation, such as the concepts of metaphysics and of morals, lies entirely without its sphere, and it can never lead to them; neither does it require them. It is therefore not a continual progress and an approximation towards these sciences, and there is not, as it were, any point or line of contact. Natural science will never reveal to us the internal constitution of things, which though not appearance, yet can serve as the ultimate ground of explaining appearance. Nor does that science require this for its physical explanations. Nay even if such grounds should be offered from other sources (for instance, the influence of immaterial beings), they must be rejected and not used in the progress of its explanations. For these explanations must only be grounded upon that which as an object of sense can belong to experience, and be brought into connexion with our actual perceptions and empirical laws.

But metaphysics leads us towards bounds in the dialectical attempts of pure reason (not undertaken arbitrarily or wantonly, but stimulated hereto by the nature of reason itself). And the transcendental Ideas, as they do not admit of evasion, and are never capable of realisation, serve to point out to us actually not only the bounds of the pure use of reason, but also the way to determine them. Such is the end and the use of this natural predisposition of our reason, which has brought forth metaphysics as its favorite child, whose generation, like every other in the world, is not to be ascribed to blind chance, but to an original germ, wisely organised for great ends. For metaphysics, in its fundamental features, perhaps more than any other science, is placed in us by nature itself, and cannot be considered the production of an arbitrary choice or a casual enlargement in the progress of experience from which it is quite disparate.

Reason with all its concepts and laws of the understanding, which suffice for empirical use, i.e., within the sensible world, finds in itself no satisfaction because ever-recurring questions deprive us of all hope of their complete solution. The transcendental ideas, which have that completion in view, are such problems of reason. But it sees clearly, that the sensuous world cannot contain this completion, neither consequently can all the concepts, which serve merely for understanding the world of sense, such as space and time, and whatever we have adduced under the name of pure concepts of the understanding. The sensuous world is nothing but a chain of appearances connected according to universal laws; it has therefore no subsistence by itself; it is not the thing in itself, and consequently must point to that which contains the basis of this experience, to beings which cannot be cognised merely as phenomena, but as things in themselves. In the cognition of them alone reason can hope to satisfy its desire of completeness in proceeding from the conditioned to its conditions.

We have above (33, 34) indicated the limits of reason with regard to all cognition of mere creations of thought. Now, since the transcendental ideas have urged us to approach them, and thus have led us, as it were, to the spot where the occupied space (viz., experience) touches the void (that of which we can know nothing, viz., noumena), we can determine the bounds of pure reason. For in all bounds there is something positive (e.g., a surface is the boundary of corporeal space, and is therefore itself a space, a line is a space, which is the boundary of the surface, a point the boundary of the line, but yet always a place in space), whereas limits contain mere negations. The limits pointed out in those paragraphs are not enough after we have discovered that beyond them there still lies something (though we can never cognise what it is in itself). For the question now is, What is the attitude of our reason in this connexion of what we know with what we do not, and never shall, know? This is an actual connexion of a known thing with one quite unknown (and which will always remain so), and though what is unknown should not become the least more known—which we cannot even hope—yet the notion of this connexion must be definite, and capable of being rendered distinct.

We must therefore accept an immaterial being, a world of understanding, and a Supreme Being (all mere noumena), because in them only, as things in themselves, reason finds that completion and satisfaction, which it can never hope for in the derivation of appearances from their homogeneous grounds, and because these actually have reference to something distinct from them (and totally heterogeneous), as appearances always presuppose an object in itself, and therefore suggest its existence whether we can know more of it or not.

But as we can never cognise these beings of understanding as they are in themselves, that is, definitely, yet must assume them as regards the sensible world, and connect them with it by reason, we are at least able to think this connexion by means of such concepts as express their relation to the world of sense. Yet if we represent to ourselves a being of the understanding by nothing but pure concepts of the understanding, we then indeed represent nothing definite to ourselves, consequently our concept has no significance; but if we think it by properties borrowed from the sensuous world, it is no longer a being of understanding, but is conceived as an appearance, and belongs to the sensible world. Let us take an instance from the notion of the Supreme Being.

Our deistic conception is quite a pure concept of reason, but represents only a thing containing all realities, without being able to determine any one of them; because for that purpose an example must be taken from the world of sense, in which case we should have an object of sense only, not something quite heterogeneous, which can never be an object of sense. Suppose I attribute to the Supreme Being understanding, for instance; I have no concept of an understanding other than my own, one that must receive its perceptions by the senses, and which is occupied in bringing them under rules of the unity of consciousness. Then the elements of my concept would always lie in the appearance; I should however by the insufficiency of the appearance be necessitated to go beyond them to the concept of a being which neither depends upon appearance, nor is bound up with them as conditions of its determination. But if I separate understanding from sensibility to obtain a pure understanding, then nothing remains but the mere form of thinking without perception, by which form alone I can cognise nothing definite, and consequently no object. For that purpose I should conceive another understanding, such as would directly perceive its objects, but of which I have not the least notion; because the human understanding is discursive, and can not directly perceive, it can only cognise by means of general concepts. And the very same difficulties arise if we attribute a will to the Supreme Being; for we have this concept only by drawing it from our internal experience, and therefore from our dependence for satisfaction upon objects whose existence we require; and so the notion rests upon sensibility, which is absolutely incompatible with the pure concept of the Supreme Being.

Hume's objections to deism are weak, and affect only the proofs, and not the deistic assertion itself. But as regards theism, which depends on a stricter determination of the concept of the Supreme Being which in deism is merely transcendent, they are very strong, and as this concept is formed, in certain (in fact in all common) cases irrefutable. Hume always insists, that by the mere concept of an original being, to which we apply only ontological predicates (eternity, omnipresence, omnipotence), we think nothing definite, and that properties which can yield a concept *in concreto* must be superadded; that it is not enough to say, it is Cause, but we must explain the nature of its causality, for example, that of an understanding and of a will. He then begins his attacks on the essential point itself, i.e., theism, as he had previously directed his battery only against the proofs of deism, an attack which is not very dangerous to it in its consequences. All his dangerous arguments refer to anthropomorphism, which he holds to be inseparable from theism, and to make it absurd in itself; but if the former be abandoned, the latter must vanish with it, and nothing remain but deism, of which nothing can come, which is of no value, and which cannot serve as any foundation to religion or morals. If this anthropomorphism were really unavoidable, no proofs whatever of the existence of a Supreme Being, even were they all granted, could determine for us the concept of this Being without involving us in contradictions.

If we connect with the command to avoid all transcendent judgments of pure reason, the command (which apparently conflicts with it) to proceed to concepts that lie beyond the field of its immanent (empirical) use, we discover that both can subsist together, but only at the boundary of all lawful use of reason. For this boundary belongs as well to the field of experience, as to that of the creations of thought, and we are thereby taught, as well, how these so remarkable ideas serve merely for marking the bounds of human reason. On the one hand they give warning not boundlessly to extend cognition of experience, as if nothing but world remained for us to cognise, and yet, on the other hand, not to transgress the bounds of experience, and to think of judging about things beyond them, as things in themselves.

But we stop at this boundary if we limit our judgment merely to the relation which the world may have to a Being whose very concept lies beyond all the knowledge which we can attain within the world. For we then do not attribute to the Supreme Being any of the properties in themselves, by which we represent objects of experience, and thereby avoid dogmatic anthropomorphism; but we attribute them to his relation to the world, and allow ourselves a symbolical anthropomorphism, which in fact concerns language only, and not the object itself.

If I say that we are compelled to consider the world, as if it were the work of a Supreme Understanding and Will, I really say nothing more, than that a watch, a ship, a regiment, bears the same relation to the watchmaker, the shipbuilder, the commanding officer, as the world of sense (or whatever constitutes the substratum of this complex of appearances) does to the Unknown, which I do not hereby cognise as it is in itself, but as it is for me or in relation to the world, of which I am a part.

58. Such a cognition is one of analogy, and does not signify (as is commonly understood) an imperfect similarity of two things, but a perfect similarity of relations between two quite dissimilar things.[30] By means of this analogy, however, there remains a concept of the Supreme Being sufficiently determined *for us*, though we have left out everything that could determine it absolutely or in itself; for we determine it as regards the world and as regards ourselves, and more do we not require. The attacks which Hume makes upon those who would determine this concept absolutely, by taking the materials for so doing from themselves and the world, do not affect us; and he cannot object to us, that we have nothing left if we give up the objective anthropomorphism of the concept of the Supreme Being.

For let us assume at the outset (as Hume in his dialogues makes Philo grant Cleanthes), as a necessary hypothesis, the deistical concept of the First Being, in which this Being is thought by the mere ontological predicates of substance, of cause, etc. This must be done, because reason, actuated in the sensible world by mere conditions, which are themselves always conditional, cannot otherwise have any

---

[30]There is, e.g., an analogy between the juridical relation of human actions and the mechanical relation of motive powers. I never can do anything to another man without giving him a right to do the same to me on the same conditions; just as no mass can act with its motive power on another mass without thereby occasioning the other to react equally against it. Here right and motive power are quite dissimilar things, but in their relation there is complete similarity. By means of such an analogy I can obtain a notion of the relation of things which absolutely are unknown to me. For instance as the promotion of the welfare of children (= a) is to the love of parents (= b), so the welfare of the human species (= c) is to that unknown [quantity which is] in God (= x), which we call love; not as if it had the least similarity to any human inclination, but because we can suppose its relation to the world to be similar to that which things of the world bear one another. But the concept of relation in this case is a mere category, viz., the concept of cause which has nothing to do with sensibility.

satisfaction, and it therefore can be done without falling into anthropomorphism (which transfers predicates from the world of sense to a Being quite distinct from the world), because those predicates are mere categories, which, though they do not give a determinate concept of God, yet give a concept not limited to any conditions of sensibility. Thus nothing can prevent our predicating of this Being a causality through reason with regard to the world, and thus passing to theism, without being obliged to attribute to God in himself this kind of reason, as a property inhering in him. For as to the former, the only possible way of prosecuting the use of reason (as regards all possible experience, in complete harmony with itself) in the world of sense to the highest point, is to assume a supreme reason as a cause of all the connexions in the world. Such a principle must be quite advantageous to reason and can hurt it nowhere in its application to nature. As to the latter, reason is thereby not transferred as a property to the First Being in himself, but only to his relation to the world of sense, and so anthropomorphism is entirely avoided. For nothing is considered here but the cause of the form of reason which is perceived everywhere in the world, and reason is attributed to the Supreme Being, so far as it contains the ground of this form of reason in the world, but according to analogy only, that is, so far as this expression shows merely the relation, which the Supreme Cause unknown to us has to the world, in order to determine everything in it conformably to reason in the highest degree. We are thereby kept from using reason as an attribute for the purpose of conceiving God, but instead of conceiving the world in such a manner as is necessary to have the greatest possible use of reason according to principle. We thereby acknowledge that the Supreme Being is quite inscrutable and even unthinkable in any definite way as to what he is in himself. We are thereby kept, on the one hand, from making a transcendent use of the concepts which we have of reason as an efficient cause (by means of the will), in order to determine the Divine Nature by properties, which are only borrowed from human nature, and from losing ourselves in gross and extravagant notions, and on the other hand from deluging the contemplation of the world with hyperphysical modes of explanation according

to our notions of human reason, which we transfer to God, and so losing for this contemplation its proper application, according to which it should be a rational study of mere nature, and not a presumptuous derivation of its appearances from a Supreme Reason. The expression suited to our feeble notions is, that we conceive the world as if it came, as to its existence and internal plan, from a Supreme Reason, by which notion we both cognise the constitution, which belongs to the world itself, yet without pretending to determine the nature of its cause in itself, and on the other hand, we transfer the ground of this constitution (of the form of reason in the world) upon the relation of the Supreme Cause to the world, without finding the world sufficient by itself for that purpose.[31]

Thus the difficulties which seem to oppose theism disappear by combining with Hume's principle—"not to carry the use of reason dogmatically beyond the field of all possible experience"—this other principle, which he quite overlooked: "not to consider the field of experience as one which bounds itself in the eye of our reason." The *Critique of Pure Reason* here points out the true mean between dogmatism, which Hume combats, and skepticism, which he would substitute for it—a mean which is not like other means that we find advisable to determine for ourselves as it were mechanically (by adopting something from one side and something from the other), and by which nobody is taught a better way, but such a one as can be accurately determined on principles.

59. At the beginning of this annotation I made use of the metaphor of a boundary, in order to establish the limits of reason in regard to its suitable use. The world of sense contains merely appear-

---

[31] I may say, that the causality of the Supreme Cause holds the same place with regard to the world that human reason does with regard to its works of art. Here the nature of the Supreme Cause itself remains unknown to me: I only compare its effects (the order of the world) which I know, and their conformity to reason, to the effects of human reason which I also know; and hence I term the former reason, without attributing to it on that account that I understand in man by this term, or attaching to it anything else known to me, as its property.

ances, which are not things in themselves, but the understanding must assume these latter ones, viz., noumena. In our reason both are comprised, and the question is, How does reason proceed to set boundaries to the understanding as regards both these fields? Experience, which contains all that belongs to the sensuous world, does not bound itself; it only proceeds in every case from the conditioned to some other equally conditioned object. Its boundary must lie quite without it, and this field is that of the pure beings of the understanding. But this field, so far as the determination of the nature of these beings is concerned, is an empty space for us, and if dogmatically-determined concepts alone are in question, we cannot pass out of the field of possible experience. But as a boundary itself is something positive, which belongs as well to that which lies within, as to the space that lies without the given complex, it is still an actual positive cognition, which reason only acquires by enlarging itself to this boundary, yet without attempting to pass it; because it there finds itself to this boundary, yet without attempting to pass it; because it there finds itself in the presence of an empty space, in which it can conceive forms of things, but not things themselves. But the setting of a boundary to the field of the understanding by something, which is otherwise unknown to it, is still a cognition which belongs to reason even at this standpoint, and by which it is neither confined within the sensible, nor straying without it, but only refers, as befits the knowledge of a boundary, to the relation between that which lies without it, and that which is contained within it.

Natural theology is such a concept at the boundary of human reason, being constrained to look beyond this boundary to the Idea of a Supreme Being (and, for practical purposes to that of an intelligible world also), not in order to determine anything relatively to this pure creation of the understanding, which lies beyond the world of sense, but in order to guide the use of reason within it according to principles of the greatest possible (theoretical as well as practical) unity. For this purpose we make use of the reference of the world of sense to an independent reason, as the cause of all its connexions. Thereby we do not purely invent a being, but, as beyond the sensible world there must be something that can only

be thought by the pure understanding, we determine that something in this particular way, though only of course according to analogy.

And thus there remains our original proposition, which is the *résumé* of the whole *Critique*: "that reason by all its *a priori* principles never teaches us anything more than objects of possible experience, and even of these nothing more than can be cognised in experience." But this limitation does not prevent reason leading us to the objective boundary of experience, viz., to the reference to something which is not itself an object of experience, but is the ground of all experience. Reason does not however teach us anything concerning the thing in itself: it only instructs us as regards its own complete and highest use in the field of possible experience. But this is all that can be reasonably desired in the present case, and with which we have cause to be satisfied.

60. Thus we have fully exhibited metaphysics as it is actually given in the natural predisposition of human reason, and in that which constitutes the essential end of its pursuit, according to its subjective possibility. Though we have found, that this merely natural use of such a predisposition of our reason, if no discipline arising only from a scientific critique bridles and sets limits to it, involves us in transcendent, either apparently or really conflicting, dialectical syllogisms; and this fallacious metaphysics is not only unnecessary as regards the promotion of our knowledge of nature, but even disadvantageous to it: there yet remains a problem worthy of solution, which is to find out the natural ends intended by this disposition to transcendent concepts in our reason, because everything that lies in nature must be originally intended for some useful purpose.

Such an inquiry is of a doubtful nature; and I acknowledge, that what I can say about it is conjecture only, like every speculation about the first ends of nature. The question does not concern the objective validity of metaphysical judgments, but our natural predisposition to them, and therefore does not belong to the system of metaphysics but to anthropology.

When I compare all the transcendental Ideas, the totality of which constitutes the particular problem of natural pure reason, compelling it to quit the mere contemplation of nature, to transcend all possible experience, and in this endeavor to produce the thing (be it knowledge or fiction) called metaphysics, I think I perceive that the aim of this natural tendency is, to free our notions from the fetters of experience and from the limits of the mere contemplation of nature so far as at least to open to us a field containing mere objects for the pure understanding, which no sensibility can reach, not indeed for the purpose of speculatively occupying ourselves with them (for there we can find no ground to stand on), but because practical principles, which, without finding some such scope for their necessary expectation and hope, could not expand to the universality which reason unavoidably requires from a moral point of view.

So I find that the Psychological Idea (however little it may reveal to me the nature of the human soul, which is higher than all concepts of experience), shows the insufficiency of these concepts plainly enough, and thereby deters me from materialism, the psychological notion of which is unfit for any explanation of nature, and besides confines reason in practical respects. The Cosmological Ideas, by the obvious insufficiency of all possible cognition of nature to satisfy reason in its lawful inquiry, serve in the same manner to keep us from naturalism, which asserts nature to be sufficient for itself. Finally, all natural necessity in the sensible world is conditional, as it always presupposes the dependence of things upon others, and unconditional necessity must be sought only in the unity of a cause different from the world of sense. But as the causality of this cause, in its turn, were it merely nature, could never render the existence of the contingent (as its consequent) comprehensible, reason frees itself by means of the Theological Idea from fatalism, (both as a blind natural necessity in the coherence of nature itself, without a first principle, and as a blind causality of this principle itself), and leads to the concept of a cause possessing freedom, or of a Supreme Intelligence. Thus the transcendental Ideas serve, if not to instruct us positively, at least to destroy the rash assertions of Materialism, of Naturalism, and of Fatalism, and thus to afford scope for the moral Ideas beyond the field of speculation. These considerations, I should think, explain in some measure the natural predisposition of which I spoke.

The practical value, which a merely speculative science may have, lies without the bounds of this science, and can therefore be considered as a scholion merely, and like all scholia does not form part of the science itself. This application however surely lies within the bounds of philosophy, especially of philosophy drawn from the pure sources of reason, where its speculative use in metaphysics must necessarily be at unity with its practical use in morals. Hence the unavoidable dialectics of pure reason, considered in metaphysics, as a natural tendency, deserves to be explained not as an illusion merely, which is to be removed, but also, if possible, as a natural provision as regards its end, though this duty, a work of supererogation, cannot justly be assigned to metaphysics proper.

The solutions of these questions which are treated in the chapter on the Regulative Use of the Ideas of Pure Reason should be considered a second scholion which however has a greater affinity with the subject of metaphysics. For there certain rational principles are expounded which determine *a priori* the order of nature or rather of the understanding, which seeks nature's laws through experience. They seem to be constitutive and legislative with regard to experience, though they spring from pure reason, which cannot be considered, like the understanding, as a principle of possible experience. Now whether or not this harmony rests upon the fact, that just as nature does not inhere in appearances or in their source (the sensibility) itself, but only in so far as the latter is in relation to the understanding, as also a systematic unity in applying the understanding to bring about an entirety of all possible experience can only belong to the understanding when in relation to reason; and whether or not experience is in this way mediately subordinate to the legislation of reason: may be discussed by those who desire to trace the nature of reason even beyond its use in metaphysics, into the general principles of a history of nature; I have represented this task as important, but not attempted its solution, in the book itself.

And thus I conclude the analytical solution of the main question which I had proposed: "How is metaphysics in general possible?" by ascending from the data of its actual use in its consequences, to the grounds of its possibility.

FOUNDATION FOR THE METAPHYSIC OF MORALS

PREFACE

THE DIFFERENT BRANCHES OF PHILOSOPHY

Ancient Greek philosophy was divided into three sciences: *physics, ethics,* and *logic.* This division fits the nature of the subject perfectly, and there is no need to improve on it—except perhaps by adding the principle on which it is based. By so doing we may be able on the one hand to guarantee its completeness and on the other to determine correctly its necessary subdivisions.

All rational knowledge is either *material* and concerned with some object, or *formal* and concerned solely with the form of understanding and reason themselves—with the universal rules of thinking as such without regard to differences in its objects. Formal philosophy is called *logic*; while material philosophy, which has to do with determinate objects and with the laws to which they are subject, is in turn divided into two, since the laws in question are laws either of *nature* or of *freedom.* The science of the first is called *physics,* that of the second *ethics.* The former is also called natural philosophy, the latter moral philosophy.

Logic can have no empirical part—that is, no part in which the universal and necessary laws of thinking are based on grounds taken from experience. Otherwise it would not be logic—that is, it would not be a canon for understanding and reason, valid for all thinking and capable of demonstration. As against this, both natural and moral philosophy can each have an empirical part, since the former has to formulate its laws for nature as an object of experience, and the latter for the will of man so far as affected by nature—the first set of laws being those in accordance with which everything happens, the second being those in accordance with which everything ought to happen, although they also take into account the conditions under which what ought to happen very often does not happen.

All philosophy so far as it rests on the basis of experience can be called *empirical* philosophy. If it sets forth its doctrines as depending entirely on *a priori* principles, it can be called *pure* philosophy. The latter when wholly formal is called *logic*; but if it is confined to determinate objects of the understanding, it is then called *metaphysics.*

In this way there arises the Idea of a two-fold metaphysic—*a metaphysic of nature* and *a metaphysic of morals.* Thus physics will have its empirical part, but it will also have a rational one; and likewise ethics—although here the empirical part might be called specifically *practical anthropology,* while the rational part might properly be called *morals.*

THE NEED FOR PURE ETHICS

All industries, arts, and crafts have gained by the division of labour—that is to say, one man no longer does everything, but each confines himself to a particular task, differing markedly from others in its technique, so that he may be able to perform it with the highest perfection and with greater ease. Where tasks are not so distinguished and divided, where every man is a jack of all trades, there industry is still sunk in utter barbarism. In itself it might well be a subject not unworthy of examination, if we asked whether pure philosophy in all its parts does not demand its own special craftsman. Would it not be better for the whole of this learned industry if those accustomed to purvey, in accordance with the public taste, a mixture of the empirical and the rational in various proportions unknown even to themselves—the self-styled 'creative thinkers' as opposed to the 'hair-splitters' who attend to the purely rational part—were to be warned against carrying on at once two jobs very different in their technique, each perhaps requiring a special talent and the combination of both in one person producing mere bunglers? Here, however, I confine myself to asking

Reprinted from Immanual Kant, *Groundwork of the Metaphysics of Morals* (London: Random House, 1948), translated by H. J. Paton.

whether the nature of science does not always require that the empirical part should be scrupulously separated from the rational one, and that (empirical) physics proper should be prefaced by a metaphysic of nature, while practical anthropology should be prefaced by a metaphysic of morals—each metaphysic having to be scrupulously cleansed of everything empirical if we are to know how much pure reason can accomplish in both cases and from what sources it can by itself draw its own *a priori* teaching. I leave it an open question whether the latter business is to be conducted by all moralists (whose name is legion) or only by those who feel a vocation for the subject.

Since my aim here is directed strictly to moral philosophy, I limit my proposed question to this point only—Do we not think it a matter of the utmost necessity to work out for once a pure moral philosophy completely cleansed of everything that can only be empirical and appropriate to anthropology? That there must be such a philosophy is already obvious from the common Idea of duty and from the laws of morality. Every one must admit that a law has to carry with it absolute necessity if it is to be valid morally—valid, that is, as a ground of obligation; that the command 'Thou shalt not lie' could not hold merely for men, other rational beings having no obligation to abide by it—and similarly with all other genuine moral laws; that here consequently the ground of obligation must be looked for, not in the nature of man nor in the circumstances of the world in which he is placed, but solely *a priori* in the concepts of pure reason; and that every other precept based on principles of mere experience—and even a precept that may in a certain sense be considered universal, so far as it rests in its slightest part, perhaps only in its motive, on empirical grounds—can indeed be called a practical rule, but never a moral law.

Thus in practical knowledge as a whole, not only are moral laws, together with their principles, essentially different from all the rest in which there is some empirical element, but the whole of moral philosophy is based entirely on the part of it that is pure. When applied to man it does not borrow in the slightest from acquaintance with him (in anthropology), but gives him laws *a priori* as a rational being. These laws admittedly require in addition a power of judge-

ment sharpened by experience, partly in order to distinguish the cases to which they apply, partly to procure for them admittance to the will of man and influence over practice; for man, affected as he is by so many inclinations, is capable of the Idea of a pure practical reason, but he has not so easily the power to realize the Idea *in concreto* in his conduct of life.

A metaphysic of morals is thus indispensably necessary, not merely in order to investigate, from motives of speculation, the source of practical principles which are present *a priori* in our reason, but because morals themselves remain exposed to corruption of all sorts as long as this guiding thread is lacking, this ultimate norm for correct moral judgement. For if any action is to be morally good, it is not enough that it should *conform* to the moral law— it must also be done *for the sake of the moral law*: where this is not so, the conformity is only too contingent and precarious, since the non-moral ground at work will now and then produce actions which accord with the law, but very often actions which transgress it. Now the moral law in its purity and genuineness (and in the field of action it is precisely this that matters most) is to be looked for nowhere else than in a pure philosophy. Hence pure philosophy (that is, metaphysics) must come first, and without it there can be no moral philosophy at all. Indeed a philosophy which mixes up these pure principles with empirical ones does not deserve the name of philosophy (since philosophy is distinguished from ordinary rational knowledge precisely because it sets forth in a separate science what the latter apprehends only as confused with other things). Still less does it deserve the name of moral philosophy, since by this very confusion it undermines even the purity of morals themselves and acts against its own proper purpose.

THE PHILOSOPHY OF WILLING AS SUCH

It must not be imagined that in the propaedeutics prefixed to his moral philosophy by the celebrated *Wolff*—that is, in the '*Universal Practical Philosophy*', as he called it—we already have what is here demanded and consequently do not need to break entirely new ground. Precisely because it was supposed to be a universal practical philosophy, it has taken into consideration, not a special kind of will—not such a will as is completely determined by *a priori* principles apart from any empirical motives and so can be called a pure will—but willing as such, together with all activities and conditions belonging to it in this general sense. Because of this it differs from a metaphysic of morals in the same way as general logic differs from transcendental philosophy, the first of which sets forth the activities and rules of thinking *as such*, while the second expounds the special activities and rules of *pure* thinking—that is, of the thinking whereby objects are known completely *a priori*; for a metaphysic of morals has to investigate the idea and principles of a possible *pure* will, and not the activities and conditions of human willing as such, which are drawn for the most part from psychology. The fact that in this 'universal practical philosophy' there is also talk (though quite unjustifiably) about moral laws and duty is no objection to what I say. For the authors of this science remain true to their Idea of it on this point as well: they do not distinguish motives which, as such, are conceived completely *a priori* by reason alone and are genuinely moral, from empirical motives which understanding raises to general concepts by the mere comparison of experiences. On the contrary, without taking into account differences in their origin they consider motives only as regards their relative strength or weakness (looking upon all of them as homogeneous) and construct on this basis their concept of *obligation*. This concept is anything but moral; but its character is only such as is to be expected from a philosophy which never decides, as regards the *source* of all practical concepts, whether they arise only *a posteriori* or arise *a priori* as well.

THE AIM OF THE *GROUNDWORK*

Intending, as I do, to publish some day a metaphysic of morals, I issue this *Groundwork* in advance. For such a metaphysic there is strictly no other foundation than a critique of *pure practical reason*, just as for metaphysics there is no other foundation than the critique of pure speculative reason which I have already published. Yet, on the one hand, there is not the same extreme necessity for the former critique as for the latter, since human reason can, in matters

of morality, be easily brought to a high degree of accuracy and precision even in the most ordinary intelligence, whereas in its theoretical, but pure, activity it is, on the contrary, out and out dialectical; and, on the other hand, a critique of practical reason, if it is to be complete, requires, on my view, that we should be able at the same time to show the unity of practical and theoretical reason in a common principle, since in the end there can only be one and the same reason, which must be differentiated solely in its application. Here, however, I found myself as yet unable to bring my work to such completeness without introducing considerations of quite another sort and so confusing the reader. This is why, instead of calling it a '*Critique of Pure Practical Reason*', I have adopted the title '*Groundwork of the Metaphysic of Morals*'.

But, in the third place, since a metaphysic of morals, in spite of its horrifying title, can be in a high degree popular and suited to the ordinary intelligence, I think it useful to issue separately this preparatory work on its foundations so that later I need not insert the subtleties inevitable in these matters into doctrines more easy to understand.

The sole aim of the present *Groundwork* is to seek out and establish *the supreme principle of morality*. This by itself is a business which by its very purpose constitutes a whole and has to be separated off from every other enquiry. The application of the principle to the whole system would no doubt throw much light on my answers to this central question, so important and yet hitherto so far from being satisfactorily discussed; and the adequacy it manifests throughout would afford it strong confirmation. All the same, I had to forego this advantage, which in any case would be more flattering to myself than helpful to others, since the convenience of a principle in use and its seeming adequacy afford no completely safe proof of its correctness. They rather awaken a certain bias against examining and weighing it in all strictness for itself without any regard to its consequences.

THE METHOD OF THE *GROUNDWORK*

The method I have adopted in this book is, I believe, one which will work best if we proceed analytically from common knowledge to the formulation of its supreme principle and then back again synthetically from an examination of this principle and its origins to the common knowledge in which we find its application. Hence the division turns out to be as follows:—

1. *Chapter I*: Passage from ordinary rational knowledge of morality to philosophical.
2. *Chapter II*: Passage from popular moral philosophy to a metaphysic of morals.
3. *Chapter III*: Final step from a metaphysic of morals to a critique of pure practical reason.

CHAPTER I. PASSAGE FROM ORDINARY RATIONAL KNOWLEDGE OF MORALITY TO PHILOSOPHICAL

THE GOOD WILL

It is impossible to conceive anything at all in the world, or even out of it, which can be taken as good without qualification, except a *good will*. Intelligence, wit, judgement, and any other *talents* of the mind we may care to name, or courage, resolution, and constancy of purpose, as qualities of *temperament*, are without doubt good and desirable in many respects; but they can also be extremely bad and hurtful when the will is not good which has to make use of these gifts of nature, and which for this reason has the term '*character*' applied to its peculiar quality. It is exactly the same with *gifts of fortune*. Power, wealth, honour, even health and that complete well-being and contentment with one's state which goes by the name of '*happiness*', produce boldness, and as a consequence often over-boldness as well, unless a good will is present by which their influence on the mind—and so too the whole principle of action—may be corrected and adjusted to universal ends; not to mention that a rational and impartial spectator can never feel approval in contemplating the uninterrupted prosperity of a being graced by no touch of a pure and good will, and that consequently a good will seems to constitute the indispensable condition of our very worthiness to be happy.

Some qualities are even helpful to this good will itself and can make its task very much easier. They have none the less no inner unconditioned worth, but

rather presuppose a good will which sets a limit to the esteem in which they are rightly held and does not permit us to regard them as absolutely good. Moderation in affections and passions, self-control, and sober reflexion are not only good in many respects: they may even seem to constitute part of the *inner* worth of a person. Yet they are far from being properly described as good without qualification (however unconditionally they have been commended by the ancients). For without the principles of a good will they may become exceedingly bad; and the very coolness of a scoundrel makes him, not merely more dangerous, but also immediately more abominable in our eyes than we should have taken him to be without it.

THE GOOD WILL AND ITS RESULTS

A good will is not good because of what it effects or accomplishes—because of its fitness for attaining some proposed end: it is good through its willing alone—that is, good in itself. Considered in itself it is to be esteemed beyond comparison as far higher than anything it could ever bring about merely in order to favour some inclination or, if you like, the sum total of inclinations. Even if, by some special disfavour of destiny or by the niggardly endowment of step-motherly nature, this will is entirely lacking in power to carry out its intentions; if by its utmost effort it still accomplishes nothing, and only good will is left (not, admittedly, as a mere wish, but as the straining of every means so far as they are in our control); even then it would still shine like a jewel for its own sake as something which has its full value in itself. Its usefulness or fruitlessness can neither add to, nor subtract from, this value. Its usefulness would be merely, as it were, the setting which enables us to handle it better in our ordinary dealings or to attract the attention of those not yet sufficiently expert, but not to commend it to experts or to determine its value.

THE FUNCTION OF REASON

Yet in this Idea of the absolute value of a mere will, all useful results being left out of account in its assessment, there is something so strange that, in spite of all the agreement it receives even from ordinary reason, there must arise the suspicion that perhaps its secret basis is merely some high-flown fantasticality, and that we may have misunderstood the purpose of nature in attaching reason to our will as its governor. We will therefore submit our Idea to an examination from this point of view.

In the natural constitution of an organic being—that is, of one contrived for the purpose of life—let us take it as a principle that in it no organ is to be found for any end unless it is also the most appropriate to that end and the best fitted for it. Suppose now that for a being possessed of reason and a will the real purpose of nature were his *preservation*, his *welfare*, or in a word his *happiness*. In that case nature would have hit on a very bad arrangement by choosing reason in the creature to carry out this purpose. For all the actions he has to perform with this end in view, and the whole rule of his behaviour, would have been mapped out for him far more accurately by instinct; and the end in question could have been maintained far more surely by instinct than it ever can be by reason. If reason should have been imparted to this favoured creature as well, it would have had to serve him only for contemplating the happy disposition of his nature, for admiring it, for enjoying it, and for being grateful to its beneficient Cause—not for subjecting his power of appetition to such feeble and defective guidance or for meddling incompetently with the purposes of nature. In a word, nature would have prevented reason from striking out into a *practical use* and from presuming, with its feeble vision, to think out for itself a plan for happiness and for the means to its attainment. Nature would herself have taken over the choice, not only of ends, but also of means, and would with wise precaution have entrusted both to instinct alone.

In actual fact too we find that the more a cultivated reason concerns itself with the aim of enjoying life and happiness, the farther does man get away from true contentment. This is why there arises in many, and that too in those who have made most trial of this use of reason, if they are only candid enough to admit it, a certain degree of *misology*—that is, a hatred of reason; for when they balance all the advantage they draw, I will not say from thinking out all the arts of ordinary indulgence, but even from science (which in the last resort seems to them

to be also an indulgence of the mind), they discover that they have in fact only brought more trouble on their heads than they have gained in the way of happiness. On this account they come to envy, rather than to despise, the more common run of men, who are closer to the guidance of mere natural instinct, and who do not allow their reason to have much influence on their conduct. So far we must admit that the judgement of those who seek to moderate—and even to reduce below zero—the conceited glorification of such advantages as reason is supposed to provide in the way of happiness and contentment with life is in no way soured or ungrateful to the goodness with which the world is governed. These judgements rather have as their hidden ground the Idea of another and much more worthy purpose of existence, for which, and not for happiness, reason is quite properly designed, and to which, therefore, as a supreme condition the private purposes of man must for the most part be subordinated.

For since reason is not sufficiently serviceable for guiding the will safely as regards its objects and the satisfaction of all our needs (which it in part even multiplies)—a purpose for which an implanted natural instinct would have led us much more surely; and since none the less reason has been imparted to us as a practical power—that is, as one which is to have influence on the *will*; its true function must be to produce a *will* which is *good*, not as a *means* to some further end, but *in itself*; and for this function reason was absolutely necessary in a world where nature, in distributing her aptitudes, has everywhere else gone to work in a purposive manner. Such a will need not on this account be the sole and complete good, but it must be the highest good and the condition of all the rest, even of all our demands for happiness. In that case we can easily reconcile with the wisdom of nature our observation that the cultivation of reason which is required for the first and unconditioned purpose may in many ways, at least in this life, restrict the attainment of the second purpose—namely, happiness—which is always conditioned; and indeed that it can even reduce happiness to less than zero without nature proceeding contrary to its purpose; for reason, which recognizes as its highest practical function the establishment of a good will, in attaining this end is capable only of its own peculiar kind of contentment—contentment in

8 fulfilling a purpose which in turn is determined by reason alone, even if this fulfillment should often involve interference with the purposes of inclination.

THE GOOD WILL AND DUTY

397 We have now to elucidate the concept of a will estimable in itself and good apart from any further end. This concept, which is already present in a sound natural understanding and requires not so much to be taught as merely to be clarified, always holds the highest place in estimating the total worth of our actions and constitutes the condition of all the rest. We will therefore take up the concept of *duty*, which includes that of a good will, exposed, however, to certain subjective limitations and obstacles. These, so far from hiding a good will or disguising it, rather bring it out by contrast and make it shine forth more brightly.

THE MOTIVE OF DUTY

I will here pass over all actions already recognized as contrary to duty, however useful they may be with a view to this or that end; for about these the question does not even arise whether they could have been done *for the sake of duty* inasmuch as they are directly opposed to it. I will also set aside actions which in fact accord with duty, yet for which men have *no immediate inclination*, but perform them because impelled to do so by some other inclination.

9 For there it is easy to decide whether the action which accords with duty has been done *from duty* or from some purpose of self-interest. This distinction is far more difficult to perceive when the action accords with duty and the subject has in addition an *immediate* inclination to the action. For example, it certainly accords with duty that a grocer should not overcharge his inexperienced customer; and where there is much competition a sensible shopkeeper refrains from so doing and keeps to a fixed and general price for everybody so that a child can buy from him just as well as anyone else. Thus people are served *honestly*; but this is not nearly enough to justify us in believing that the shopkeeper has acted in this way from duty or from principles of fair dealing; his interests required him to do so. We cannot assume him to have in addition an immediate inclination towards his customers, leading him, as it were out of love, to give no man preference over another in the matter of price. Thus the action was done neither from duty nor from immediate inclination, but solely from purposes of self-interest.

On the other hand, to preserve one's life is a duty, and besides this every one has also an immediate inclination to do so. But on account of this the often anxious precautions taken by the greater part of mankind for this purpose have no inner worth, and the maxim of their action is without moral content. They do protect their lives *in conformity with duty*, 398 but not *from the motive of duty*. When on the con- 10 trary, disappointments and hopeless misery have quite taken away the taste for life; when a wretched man, strong in soul and more angered at his fate than faint-hearted or cast down, longs for death and still preserves his life without loving it—not from inclination or fear but from duty; then indeed his maxim has a moral content.

To help others where one can is a duty, and besides this there are many spirits of so sympathetic a temper that, without any further motive of vanity or self-interest, they find an inner pleasure in spreading happiness around them and can take delight in the contentment of others as their own work. Yet I maintain that in such a case an action of this kind, however right and however amiable it may be, has still no genuinely moral worth. It stands on the same footing as other inclinations—for example, the inclination for honour, which if fortunate enough to hit on something beneficial and right and consequently honourable, deserves praise and encouragement, but not esteem; for its maxim lacks moral content, namely, the performance of such actions, not from inclination, but *from duty*. Suppose then that the mind of this friend of man were overclouded by sorrows of his own which extinguished all sympathy 11 with the fate of others, but that he still had power to help those in distress, though no longer stirred by the need of others because sufficiently occupied with his own; and suppose that, when no longer moved by any inclination, he tears himself out of this deadly insensibility and does the action without any inclination for the sake of duty alone; then for the first time his action has its genuine moral worth. Still further: if nature had implanted little sympathy in this or that man's heart; if (being in other respects an honest fellow) he were cold in temperament and indifferent to the sufferings of others—perhaps because, being endowed with the special gift of patience and robust endurance in his own sufferings, he assumed the like in others or even demanded it; if such a man (who would in truth not be the worst product of nature) were not exactly fashioned by her to be a philanthropist, would he not still find in himself a source from which he might draw a worth far higher than any that a good-natured temperament can have? Assuredly he would. It is precisely in this that the worth of character begins to show—a moral worth and beyond all comparison the highest—namely, that he does good, not from inclination, but from duty.

To assure one's own happiness is a duty (at least indirectly); for discontent with one's state, in a press of cares and amidst unsatisfied wants, might easily become a great *temptation to the transgression of duty*. But here also, apart from regard to duty, all men have already of themselves the strongest and deepest inclination towards happiness, because precisely in this Idea of happiness all inclinations are combined into a sum total. The prescription for happiness is, however, often so constituted as greatly to interfere with some inclinations, and yet men cannot form under the name of 'happiness' any determinate and assured conception of the satisfaction of all inclinations as a sum. Hence it is not to be wondered at that a single inclination which is determinate as to what it promises and as to the time of its satisfaction may outweigh a wavering Idea; and that a man, for example, a sufferer from gout, may choose to enjoy what he fancies and put up with what he can—on the ground that on balance he has here at least not killed the enjoyment of the present moment because of some possibly groundless expectations of the good fortune supposed to attach to soundness of health. But in this case also, when the universal inclination towards happiness has failed to determine his will, when good health, at least for him, has not entered into his calculations as so necessary, what remains over, here as in other cases, is a law—the law of furthering his happiness, not from inclination, but from duty; and in this for the first time his conduct has a real moral worth.

It is doubtless in this sense that we should understand too the passages from Scripture in which we are commanded to love our neighbour and even our enemy. For love out of inclination cannot be commanded; but kindness done from duty—although no inclination impels us, and even although natural and unconquerable disinclination stands in our way—is *practical*, and not *pathological*, love, residing in the will and not in the propensions of feeling, in principles of action and not of melting compassion; and it is this practical love alone which can be an object of command.

THE FORMAL PRINCIPLE OF DUTY

Our second proposition is this: An action done from duty has its moral worth, *not in the purpose* to be attained by it, but in the maxim in accordance with which it is decided upon; it depends therefore, not on the realization of the object of the action, but solely on the *principle* of *volition* in accordance with which, irrespective of all objects of the faculty of desire, the action has been performed. That the purposes we may have in our actions, and also their effects considered as ends and motives of the will, can give to actions no unconditioned and moral worth is clear from what has gone before. Where then can this worth be found if we are not to find it in the will's relation to the effect hoped for from the action? It can be found nowhere but in the principle of the will, irrespective of the ends which can be brought about by such an action; for between its *a priori* principle, which is formal, and its *a posteriori* motive, which is material, the will stands, so to speak, at a parting of the ways; and since it must be determined by some principle, it will have to be determined by the formal principle of volition when an action is done from duty, where, as we have seen, every material principle is taken away from it.

REVERENCE FOR THE LAW

Our third proposition, as an inference from the two preceding, I would express thus: *Duty is the necessity to act out of reverence for the law.* For an object as the effect of my proposed action I can have an *inclination*, but *never reverence*, precisely because it is merely the effect, and not the activity, of a will. Similarly for inclination as such, whether my own or that of another, I cannot have reverence: I can at most in the first case approve, and in the second case sometimes even love—that is, regard it as favourable to my own advantage. Only something which is conjoined with my will solely as a ground and never as an effect—something which does not serve my inclination, but outweighs it or at least leaves it entirely out of account in my choice—and therefore only bare law for its own sake, can be an object of reverence and therewith a command. Now an action done from duty has to set aside altogether the influence of inclination, and along with inclination every object of the will; so there is nothing left able to determine the will except objectively the *law* and subjectively *pure reverence* for this practical law, and therefore the maxim[1] of obeying this law even to the detriment of all my inclinations.

Thus the moral worth of an action does not depend on the result expected from it, and so too does not depend on any principle of action that needs to borrow its motive from this expected result. For all these results (agreeable states and even the promotion of happiness in others) could have been brought about by other causes as well, and consequently their production did not require the will of a rational being, in which, however, the highest and unconditioned good can alone be found. Therefore nothing but the *idea of the law* in itself, *which admittedly is present only in a rational being*—so far as it, and not an expected result, is the ground determining the will—can constitute that pre-eminent good which we call moral, a good which is already present in the person acting on this idea and has not to be awaited merely from the result.[2]

---

[1] A *maxim* is the subjective principle of a volition: an objective principle (that is, one which would also serve subjectively as a practical principle for all rational beings if reason had full control over the faculty of desire) is a practical *law*.

[2] It might be urged against me that I have merely tried, under cover of the world 'reverence', to take refuge in an obscure feeling instead of giving a clearly articulated answer to the question by means of a concept of reason. Yet although reverence is a feeling, it is not a feeling *received* through outside influence, but one *self-produced* by a rational concept, and therefore specifically distinct from feelings of the first kind, all of which can be reduced to inclination or fear. What I recognize immediately as law for

The Categorical Imperative

But what kind of law can this be the thought of which, even without regard to the results expected from it, has to determine the will if this is to be called good absolutely and without qualification? Since I have robbed the will of every inducement that might arise for it as a consequence of obeying any particular law, nothing is left but the conformity of actions to universal law as such, and this alone must serve the will as its principle. That is to say, I ought never to act except in such a way *that I can also will that my maxim should become a universal law*. Here bare conformity to universal law as such (without having as its base any law prescribing particular actions) is what serves the will as its principle, and must so serve it if duty is not to be everywhere an empty delusion and a chimerical concept. The ordinary reason of mankind also agrees with this completely in its practical judgements and always has the aforesaid principle before its eyes.

Take this question, for example. May I not, when I am hard pressed, make a promise with the intention of not keeping it? Here I readily distinguish the

---

me, I recognize with reverence, which means merely consciousness of the *subordination* of my will to a law without the mediation of external influences on my senses. Immediate determination of the will by the law and consciousness of this determination is called '*reverence*', so that reverence is regarded as the *effect* of the law on the subject and not as the *cause* of the law. Reverence is properly awareness of a value which demolishes my self-love. Hence there is something which is regarded neither as an object of inclination nor as an object of fear, though it has at the same time some analogy with both. The *object* of reverence is the *law* alone—that law which we impose *on ourselves* but yet as necessary in itself. Considered as a law, we are subject to it without any consultation of self-love; considered as self-imposed it is a consequence of our will. In the first respect it is analogous to fear, in the second to inclination. All reverence for a person is properly only reverence for the law (of honesty and so on) of which that person gives us an example. Because we regard the development of our talents as a duty, we see too in a man of talent a sort of *example of the law* (the law of becoming like him by practice), and this is what constitutes our reverence for him. All moral *interest*, so-called, consists solely in *reverence* for the law.

two senses which the question can have—Is it prudent, or is it right, to make a false promise? The first no doubt can often be the case. I do indeed see that it is not enough for me to extricate myself from present embarrassment by this subterfuge: I have to consider whether from this lie there may not subsequently accrue to me much greater inconvenience than that from which I now escape, and also—since, with all my supposed *astuteness*, to foresee the consequences is not so easy that I can be sure there is no chance, once confidence in me is lost, of this proving far more disadvantageous than all the ills I now think to avoid—whether it may not be a *more prudent* action to proceed here on a general maxim and make it my habit not to give a promise except with the intention of keeping it. Yet it becomes clear to me at once that such a maxim is always founded solely on fear of consequences. To tell the truth for the sake of duty is something entirely different from doing so out of concern for inconvenient results; for in the first case the concept of the action already contains in itself a law for me, while in the second case I have first of all to look around elsewhere in order to see what effects may be bound up with it for me. When I deviate from the principle of duty, this is quite certainly bad; but if I desert my prudential maxim, this can often be greatly to my advantage, though it is admittedly safer to stick to it. Suppose I seek, however, to learn in the quickest way and yet unerringly how to solve the problem 'Does a lying promise accord with duty?' I have then to ask myself 'Should I really be content that my maxim (the maxim of getting out of a difficulty by a false promise) should hold as a universal law (one valid both for myself and others)? And could I really say to myself that every one may make a false promise if he finds himself in a difficulty from which he can extricate himself in no other way?' I then become aware at once that I can indeed will to lie, but I can by no means will a universal law of lying; for by such a law there could properly be no promises at all, since it would be futile to profess a will for future action to others who would not believe my profession or who, if they did so over-hastily, would pay me back in like coin; and consequently my maxim, as soon as it was made a universal law, would be bound to annul itself.

Thus I need no far-reaching ingenuity to find out what I have to do in order to possess a good will. Inexperienced in the course of world affairs and incapable of being prepared for all the chances that happen in it, I ask myself only 'Can you also will that your maxim should become a universal law?' Where you cannot, it is to be rejected, and that not because of a prospective loss to you or even to others, but because it cannot fit as a principle into a possible enactment of universal law. For such an enactment reason compels my immediate reverence, into whose grounds (which the philosopher may investigate) I have as yet no *insight*, although I do at least understand this much: reverence is the assessment of a worth which far outweighs all the worth of what is commended by inclination, and the necessity for me to act out of *pure* reverence for the practical law is what constitutes duty, to which every other motive must give way because it is the condition of a will good *in itself*, whose value is above all else.

ORDINARY PRACTICAL REASON

In studying the moral knowledge of ordinary human reason we have now arrived at its first principle. This principle it admittedly does not conceive thus abstractly in its universal form; but it does always have it actually before its eyes and does use it as a norm of judgement. It would be easy to show here how human reason, with this compass in hand, is well able to distinguish, in all cases that present themselves, what is good or evil, right or wrong—provided that, without the least attempt to teach it anything new, we merely make reason attend, as Socrates did, to its own principle; and how in consequence there is no need of science or philosophy for knowing what man has to do in order to be honest and good, and indeed to be wise and virtuous. It might even be surmised in advance that acquaintance with what every man is obliged to do, and so also to know, will be the affair of every man, even the most ordinary. Yet we cannot observe without admiration the great advantage which the power of practical judgement has over that of theoretical in the minds of ordinary men. In theoretical judgements, when ordinary reason ventures to depart from the laws of experience and the perceptions of sense, it falls into sheer unintelligibility and self-contradiction, or at least into a chaos of uncertainty, obscurity, and vacillation. On the practical side, however, the power of judgement first begins to show what advantages it has in itself when the ordinary mind excludes all sensuous motives from its practical laws. Then ordinary intelligence becomes even subtle—it may be in juggling with conscience or with other claims as to what is to be called right, or in trying to determine honestly for its own instruction the value of various actions; and, what is most important, it can in the latter case have as good hope of hitting the mark as any that a philosopher can promise himself. Indeed it is almost surer in this than even a philosopher, because he can have no principle different from that of ordinary intelligence, but may easily confuse his judgement with a mass of alien and irrelevant considerations and cause it to swerve from the straight path. Might it not then be more advisable in moral questions to abide by the judgement of ordinary reason and, at the most, to bring in philosophy only in order to set forth the system of morals more fully and intelligibly and to present its rules in a form more convenient for use (though still more so for disputation)— but not in order to lead ordinary human intelligence away from its happy simplicity in respect of action and to set it by means of philosophy on a new path of enquiry and instruction?

THE NEED FOR PHILOSOPHY

Innocence is a splendid thing, only it has the misfortune not to keep very well and to be easily misled. On this account even wisdom—which in itself consists more in doing and not doing than in knowing—does require science as well, not in order to learn from it, but in order to win acceptance and durability for its own prescriptions. Man feels in himself a powerful counterweight to all the commands of duty presented to him by reason as so worthy of esteem—the counterweight of his needs and inclinations, whose total satisfaction he grasps under the name of 'happiness'. But reason, without promising anything to inclination, enjoins its commands relentlessly, and therefore, so to speak, with disregard and neglect of these turbulent and seemingly equi-

table claims (which refuse to be suppressed by any command). From this there arises a *natural dialectic*—that is, a disposition to quibble with these strict laws of duty, to throw doubt on their validity or at least on their purity and strictness, and to make them, where possible, more adapted to our wishes and inclinations; that is, to pervert their very foundations and destroy their whole dignity—a result which in the end even ordinary human reason is unable to approve.

In this way the *common reason of mankind* is impelled, not by any need for speculation (which never assails it so long as it is content to be mere sound reason), but on practical grounds themselves, to leave its own sphere and take a step into the field of *practical philosophy*. It there seeks to acquire information and precise instruction about the source of its own principle, and about the correct function of this principle in comparison with maxims based on need and inclination, in order that it may escape from the embarrassment of antagonistic claims and may avoid the risk of losing all genuine moral principles because of the ambiguity into which it easily falls. Thus ordinary reason, when cultivated in its practical use, gives rise insensibly to a *dialectic* which constrains it to seek help in philosophy, just as happens in its theoretical use; and consequently in the first case as little as in the second will it anywhere else than in a full critique of our reason be able to find peace.

CHAPTER II. PASSAGE FROM POPULAR MORAL PHILOSOPHY TO A METAPHYSIC OF MORALS

THE USE OF EXAMPLES

If so far we have drawn our concept of duty from the ordinary use of our practical reason, it must by no means be inferred that we have treated it as a concept of experience. On the contrary, when we pay attention to our experience of human conduct, we meet frequent and—as we ourselves admit—justified complaints that we can adduce no certain examples of the spirit which acts out of pure duty, and that, although much may be done *in accordance with* the commands of *duty*, it remains doubtful whether it really is done *for the sake of duty* and so has a moral value. Hence at all times there have been philosophers who have absolutely denied the presence of this spirit in human actions and have ascribed everything to a more or less refined self-love. Yet they have not cast doubt on the rightness of the concept of morality. They have spoken rather with deep regret of the frailty and impurity of human nature, which is on their view noble enough to take as its rule an Idea so worthy of reverence, but at the same time too weak to follow it: the reason which should serve it for making laws it uses only to look after the interest of inclinations, whether singly or—at the best—in their greatest mutual compatibility.

In actual fact it is absolutely impossible for experience to establish with complete certainty a single case in which the maxim of an action in other respects right has rested solely on moral grounds and on the thought of one's duty. It is indeed at times the case that after the keenest self-examination we find nothing that without the moral motive of duty could have been strong enough to move us to this or that good action and to so great a sacrifice; but we cannot infer from this with certainty that it is not some secret impulse of self-love which has actually, under the mere show of the Idea of duty, been the cause genuinely determining our will. We are pleased to flatter ourselves with the false claim to a nobler motive, but in fact we can never, even by the most strenuous self-examination, get to the bottom of our secret impulsions; for when moral value is in question, we are concerned, not with the actions which we see, but with their inner principles, which we cannot see.

Furthermore, to those who deride all morality as the mere phantom of a human imagination which gets above itself out of vanity we can do no service more pleasing than to admit that the concepts of duty must be drawn solely from experience (just as out of slackness we willingly persuade ourselves that this is so in the case of all other concepts); for by so doing we prepare for them an assured triumph. Out of love for humanity I am willing to allow that most of our actions may accord with duty; but if we look more closely at our scheming and striving, we everywhere come across the dear self, which is always turning up; and it is on this that the purpose of our

actions is based—not on the strict command of duty, which would often require self-denial. One need not be exactly a foe to virtue, but merely a dispassionate observer declining to take the liveliest wish for goodness straight away as its realization, in order at certain moments (particularly with advancing years and with a power of judgement at once made shrewder by experience and also more keen in observation) to become doubtful whether any genuine virtue is actually to be encountered in the world. And then nothing can protect us against a complete falling away from our Ideas of duty, or can preserve in the soul a grounded reverence for its law, except the clear conviction that even if there never have been actions springing from such pure sources, the question at issue here is not whether this or that has happened; that, on the contrary, reason by itself and independently of all appearances commands what ought to happen; that consequently actions of which the world has perhaps hitherto given no example—actions whose practicability might well be doubted by those who rest everything on experience—are nevertheless commanded unrelentingly by reason; and that, for instance, although up to now there may have existed no loyal friend, pure loyalty in friendship can be no less required from every man, inasmuch as this duty, prior to all experience, is contained as duty in general in the Idea of a reason which determines the will by *a priori* grounds.

It may be added that unless we wish to deny to the concept of morality all truth and all relation to a possible object, we cannot dispute that its law is of such widespread significance as to hold, not merely for men, but for all *rational beings as such*—not merely subject to contingent conditions and exceptions, but *with absolute necessity*. It is therefore clear that no experience can give us occasion to infer even the possibility of such apodeictic laws. For by what right can we make what is perhaps valid only under the contingent conditions of humanity into an object of unlimited reverence as a universal precept for every rational nature? And how could laws for determining *our* will be taken as laws for determining the will of a rational being as such—and only because of this for determining ours—if these laws were merely empirical and did not have their source completely *a priori* in pure, but practical, reason?

What is more, we cannot do morality a worse service than by seeking to derive it from examples. Every example of it presented to me must first itself be judged by moral principles in order to decide if it is fit to serve as an original example—that is, as a model: it can in no way supply the prime source for the concept of morality. Even the Holy One of the gospel must first be compared with our ideal of moral perfection before we can recognize him to be such. He also says of himself: 'Why callest thou me (whom thou seest) good? There is none good (the archetype of the good) but one, that is, God (whom thou seest not)'. But where do we get the concept of God as the highest good? Solely from the *Idea* of moral perfection, which reason traces *a priori* and conjoins inseparably with the concept of a free will. Imitation has no place in morality, and examples serve us only for encouragement—that is, they set beyond doubt the practicability of what the law commands; they make perceptible what the practical law expresses more generally; but they can never entitle us to set aside their true original, which resides in reason, and to model ourselves upon examples.

POPULAR PHILOSOPHY

If there can be no genuine supreme principle of morality which is not grounded on pure reason alone independently of all experience, it should be unnecessary, I think, even to raise the question whether it is a good thing to set forth in general (*in abstracto*) these concepts which hold *a priori*, together with their corresponding principles, so far as our knowledge is to be distinguished from ordinary knowledge and described as philosophical. Yet in our days it may well be necessary to do so. For if we took a vote on which is to be preferred, pure rational knowledge detached from everything empirical—that is to say, a metaphysic of morals—or popular practical philosophy, we can guess at once on which side the preponderance would fall.

It is certainly most praiseworthy to come down to the level of popular thought when we have previously risen to the principles of pure reason and are fully satisfied of our success. This could be described as first *grounding* moral philosophy on metaphysics and subsequently winning *acceptance* for it by giving it a popular character after it has been established. But it is utterly senseless to aim at popularity in our first enquiry, upon which the whole correctness of our principles depends. It is not merely that such a procedure can never lay claim to the extremely rare merit of a truly *philosophical popularity*, since we require no skill to make ourselves intelligible to the multitude once we renounce all profundity of thought: what it turns out is a disgusting hotchpotch of second-hand observations and semi-rational principles on which the empty-headed regale themselves, because this is something that can be used in the chit-chat of daily life. Men of insight, on the other hand, feel confused by it and avert their eyes with a dissatisfaction which, however, they are unable to cure. Yet philosophers, who can perfectly well see through this deception, get little hearing when they summon us for a time from this would-be popularity in order that they may win the right to be genuinely popular only after definite insight has been attained.

We need only look at the attempts to deal with morality in this favoured style. What we shall encounter in an amazing medley is at one time the particular character of human nature (but along with this also the Idea of a rational nature as such), at another perfection, at another happiness; here moral feeling and there the fear of God; something of this and also something of that. But it never occurs to these writers to ask whether the principles of morality are to be sought at all in our acquaintance with human nature (which we can get only from experience); nor does it occur to them that if this is not so—if these principles are to be found completely *a priori* and free from empirical elements in the concepts of pure reason and absolutely nowhere else even to the slightest extent—they had better adopt the plan of separating off this enquiry altogether as pure practical philosophy or (if one may use a name so much decried) as a metaphysic[3] of morals; of bringing this

---

[3]We can, if we like, distinguish pure moral philosophy (metaphysics) from applied (applied, that is, to human nature)—just as pure mathematics is distinguished from applied mathematics and pure logic from applied logic. By this terminology we are at once reminded that moral principles are not grounded on the peculiarities of human nature, but must be established *a priori* by themselves; and

to full completeness entirely by itself; and of bidding the public which demands popularity to await in hope the outcome of this undertaking.

Nevertheless such a completely isolated metaphysic of morals, mixed with no anthropology, no theology, no physics or hyperphysics, still less with occult qualities (which might be called hypophysical), is not only an indispensable substratum of all theoretical and precisely defined knowledge of duties, but is at the same time a desideratum of the utmost importance for the actual execution of moral precepts. Unmixed with the alien element of added empirical inducements, the pure thought of duty, and in general of the moral law, has by way of reason alone (which first learns from this that by itself it is able to be practical as well as theoretical) an influence on the human heart so much more powerful than all the further impulsions[4] capable of being called up from the field of experience that in the consciousness of its own dignity reason despises these impulsions and is able gradually to become their master. In place of this, a mixed moral philosophy, compounded of impulsions from feeling and inclination and at the same time of rational concepts, must make the mind waver between motives which can be brought under no single principle and which can

411

34

yet that from such principles it must be possible to derive practical rules for human nature as well, just as it is for every kind of rational nature.

[4] I have a letter from the late distinguished Professor *Sulzer*, in which he asks me what it is that makes moral instruction so ineffective, however convincing it may be in the eyes of reason. Because of my efforts to make it complete, my answer came too late. Yet it is just this: the teachers themselves do not make their concepts pure, but—since they try to do too well by hunting everywhere for inducements to be moral—they spoil their medicine altogether by their very attempt to make it really powerful. For the most ordinary observation shows that when a righteous act is represented as being done with a steadfast mind in complete disregard of any advantage in this or in another world, and even under the greatest temptations of affliction or allurement, it leaves far behind it any similar action affected even in the slightest degree by an alien impulse and casts it into the shade: it uplifts the soul and rouses a wish that we too could act in this way. Even children of moderate age feel this impression, and duties should never be presented to them in any other way.

guide us only by mere accident to the good, but very often also to the evil.

REVIEW OF CONCLUSIONS

From these considerations the following conclusions emerge. All moral concepts have their seat and origin in reason completely *a priori*, and indeed in the most ordinary human reason just as much as in the most highly speculative: they cannot be abstracted from any empirical, and therefore merely contingent, knowledge. In this purity of their origin is to be found their very worthiness to serve as supreme practical principles, and everything empirical added to them is just so much taken away from their genuine influence and from the absolute value of the corresponding actions. It is not only a requirement of the utmost necessity in respect of theory, where our concern is solely with speculation, but is also of the utmost practical importance, to draw these concepts and laws from pure reason, to set them forth pure and unmixed, and indeed to determine the extent of this whole practical, but pure, rational knowledge— that is, to determine the whole power of pure practical reason. We ought never—as speculative philosophy does allow and even at times finds necessary—to make principles depend on the special nature of human reason. Since moral laws have to hold for every rational being as such, we ought rather to derive our principles from the general concept of a rational being as such, and on this basis to expound the whole of ethics—which requires anthropology for its *application* to man—at first independently as pure philosophy, that is, entirely as metaphysics (which we can very well do in this wholly abstract kind of knowledge). We know well that without possessing such a metaphysics it is a futile endeavour, I will not say to determine accurately for speculative judgement the moral element of duty in all that accords with duty—but that it is impossible, even in ordinary and practical usage, particularly in that of moral instruction, to base morals on their genuine principles and so to bring about pure moral dispositions and engraft them on men's minds for the highest good of the world.

In this task of ours we have to progress by natural stages, not merely from ordinary moral judge-

35

412

36

ment (which is here worthy of great respect) to philosophical judgement, as we have already done, but from popular philosophy, which goes no further than it can get by fumbling about with the aid of examples, to metaphysics. (This no longer lets itself be held back by anything empirical, and indeed—since it must survey the complete totality of this kind of knowledge—goes right to Ideas, where examples themselves fail.) For this purpose we must follow—and must portray in detail—the power of practical reason from the general rules determining it right up to the point where there springs from it the concept of duty.

IMPERATIVES IN GENERAL

Everything in nature works in accordance with laws. Only a rational being has the power to act *in accordance with his idea* of laws—that is, in accordance with principles—and only so has he a *will*. Since *reason* is required in order to derive actions from laws, the will is nothing but practical reason. If reason infallibly determines the will, then in a being of this kind the actions which are recognized to be objectively necessary are also subjectively necessary—that is to say, the will is then a power to choose *only that* which reason independently of inclination recognizes to be practically necessary, that is, to be good. But if reason solely by itself is not sufficient 37 to determine the will; if the will is exposed also to subjective conditions (certain impulsions) which do not always harmonize with the objective ones; if, in a word, the will is not *in itself* completely in accord 413 with reason (as actually happens in the case of men); then actions which are recognized to be objectively necessary are subjectively contingent, and the determining of such a will in accordance with objective laws is *necessitation*. That is to say, the relation of objective laws to a will not good through and through is conceived as one in which the will of a rational being, although it is determined by principles of reason, does not necessarily follow these principles in virtue of its own nature.

The conception of an objective principle so far as this principle is necessitating for a will is called a command (of reason), and the formula of this command is called an *Imperative*.

All imperatives are expressed by an '*ought*' (*Sollen*). By this they mark the relation of an objective law of reason to a will which is not necessarily determined by this law in virtue of its subjective constitution (the relation of necessitation). They say that something would be good to do or to leave undone; only they say it to a will which does not always do a thing because it has been informed that this is a good thing to do. The practically *good* is that which 38 determines the will by concepts of reason, and therefore not by subjective causes, but objectively—that is, on grounds valid for every rational being as such. It is distinguished from the *pleasant* as that which influences the will, not as a principle of reason valid for every one, but solely through the medium of sensation by purely subjective causes valid only for the senses of this person or that.[5]

A perfectly good will would thus stand quite as 414]39 much under objective laws (laws of the good), but it could not on this account be conceived as *necessitated* to act in conformity with law, since of itself, in accordance with its subjective constitution, it can be determined only by the concept of the good. Hence for the *divine* will, and in general for a *holy* will, there are no imperatives: '*I ought*' is here out

---

[5]The dependence of the power of appetition on sensations is called an inclination, and thus an inclination always indicates a *need*. The dependence of a contingently determinable will on principles of reason is called an *interest*. Hence an interest is found only where there is a dependent will which in itself is not always in accord with reason: to a divine will we cannot ascribe any interest. But even the human will can *take an interest* in something without therefore *acting from interest*. The first expression signifies *practical* interest in the action; the second *pathological* interest in the object of the action. The first indicates only dependence of the will on principles of reason by itself; the second its dependence on principles of reason at the service of inclination—that is to say, where reason merely supplies a practical rule for meeting the need of inclination. In the first case what interests me is the action; in the second case what interests me is the object of the action (so far as this object is pleasant to me). We have seen in Chapter I that in an action done for the sake of duty we must have regard, not to interest in the object, but to interest in the action itself and in its rational principle (namely, the law).

of place, because '*I will*' is already of itself necessarily in harmony with the law. Imperatives are in consequence only formulae for expressing the relation of objective laws of willing to the subjective imperfection of the will of this or that rational being—for example, of the human will.

CLASSIFICATION OF IMPERATIVES

All *imperatives* command either *hypothetically* or *categorically.* Hypothetical imperatives declare a possible action to be practically necessary as a means to the attainment of something else that one wills (or that one may will). A categorical imperative would be one which represented an action as objectively necessary in itself apart from its relation to a further end.

Every practical law represents a possible action as good and therefore as necessary for a subject whose actions are determined by reason. Hence all imperatives are formulae for determining an action which is necessary in accordance with the principle of a will in some sense good. If the action would be good solely as a means *to something else*, the imperative is *hypothetical*; if the action is represented as good *in itself* and therefore as necessary, in virtue of its principle, for a will which itself accords with reason, then the imperative is *categorical.*

An imperative therefore tells me which of my possible actions would be good; and it formulates a practical rule for a will that does not perform an action straight away because the action is good—whether because the subject does not always know that it is good or because, even if he did know this, he might still act on maxims contrary to the objective principles of practical reason.

A hypothetical imperative thus says only that an action is good for some purpose or other, either *possible* or *actual*. In the first case it is a *problematic* practical principle; in the second case an *assertoric* practical principle. A categorical imperative, which declares an action to be objectively necessary in itself without reference to some purpose—that is, even without any further end—ranks as an *apodeictic* practical principle.

Everything that is possible only through the efforts of some rational being can be conceived as a possible purpose of some will; and consequently there are in fact innumerable principles of action so far as action is thought necessary in order to achieve some possible purpose which can be effected by it. All sciences have a practical part consisting of problems which suppose that some end is possible for us and of imperatives which tell us how it is to be attained. Hence the latter can in general be called imperatives of *skill*. Here there is absolutely no question about the rationality or goodness of the end, but only about what must be done to attain it. A prescription required by a doctor in order to cure his man completely and one required by a poisoner in order to make sure of killing him are of equal value so far as each serves to effect its purpose perfectly. Since in early youth we do not know what ends may present themselves to us in the course of life, parents seek above all to make their children learn things *of many kinds*; they provide carefully for *skill* in the use of means to all sorts of *arbitrary* ends, of none of which can they be certain that it could not in the future become an actual purpose of their ward, while it is always *possible* that he might adopt it. Their care in this matter is so great that they commonly neglect on this account to form and correct the judgement of their children about the worth of the things which they might possibly adopt as ends.

There is, however, *one* end that can be presupposed as actual in all rational beings (so far as they are dependent beings to whom imperatives apply); and thus there is one purpose which they not only *can* have, but which we can assume with certainty that they all *do* have by a natural necessity—the purpose, namely, of *happiness*. A hypothetical imperative which affirms the practical necessity of an action as a means to the furtherance of happiness is *assertoric*. We may represent it, not simply as necessary to an uncertain, merely possible purpose, but as necessary to a purpose which we can presuppose *a priori* and with certainty to be present in every man because it belongs to his very being. Now skill in the choice of means to one's own greatest well-being can be called *prudence*[6] in the narrowest sense.

---

[6] The word 'prudence' (*Klugheit*) is used in a double sense: in one sense it can have the name of 'worldly wisdom' (*Weltklugheit*); in a second sense that of 'personal wisdom'

Thus an imperative concerned with the choice of means to one's own happiness—that is, a precept of prudence—still remains *hypothetical*: an action is commanded, not absolutely, but only as a means to a further purpose.

Finally, there is an imperative which, without being based on, and conditioned by, any further purpose to be attained by a certain line of conduct, enjoins this conduct immediately. This imperative is *categorical*. It is concerned, not with the matter of the action and its presumed results, but with its form and with the principle from which it follows; and what is essentially good in the action consists in the mental disposition, let the consequences be what they may. This imperative may be called the imperative of *morality*.

Willing in accordance with these three kinds of principle is also sharply distinguished by a *dissimilarity* in the necessitation of the will. To make this dissimilarity obvious we should, I think, name these kinds of principle most appropriately in their order if we said they were either *rules* of skill or *counsels* of prudence or *commands* (*laws*) of morality. For only *law* carries with it the concept of an *unconditioned*, and yet objective and so universally valid, *necessity*; and commands are laws which must be obeyed—that is, must be followed even against inclination. *Counsel* does indeed involve necessity, but necessity valid only under a subjective and contingent condition—namely, if this or that man counts this or that as belonging to his happiness. As against this, a categorical imperative is limited by no condition and can quite precisely be called a command, as being absolutely, although practically, necessary. We could also call imperatives of the first kind *technical* (concerned with art); of the second kind *pragmatic*[7] (concerned with well-being); of the third

---

(*Privatklugheit*). The first is the skill of a man in influencing others in order to use them for his own ends. The second is sagacity in combining all these ends to his own lasting advantage. The latter is properly that to which the value of the former can itself be traced; and of him who is prudent in the first sense, but not in the second, we might better say that he is clever and astute, but on the whole imprudent.

[7]It seems to me that the proper meaning of the word '*pragmatic*' can be defined most accurately in this way. For

kind *moral* (concerned with free conduct as such—that is, with morals).

HOW ARE IMPERATIVES POSSIBLE?

The question now arises 'How are all these imperatives possible?' This question does not ask how we can conceive the execution of an action commanded by the imperative, but merely how we can conceive the necessitation of the will expressed by the imperative in setting us a task. How an imperative of skill is possible requires no special discussion. Who wills the end, wills (so far as reason has decisive influence on his actions) also the means which are indispensably necessary and in his power. So far as willing is concerned, this proposition is analytic: for in my willing of an object as an effect there is already conceived the causality of myself as an acting cause—that is, the use of means; and from the concept of willing an end the imperative merely extracts the concept of actions necessary to this end. (Synthetic propositions are required in order to determine the means to a proposed end, but these are concerned, not with the reason for performing the act of will, but with the cause which produces the object.) That in order to divide a line into two equal parts on a sure principle I must from its ends describe two intersecting arcs—this is admittedly taught by mathematics only in synthetic propositions; but when I know that the aforesaid effect can be produced only by such an action, the proposition 'If I fully will the effect, I also will the action required for it' is analytic; for it is one and the same thing to conceive something as an effect possible in a certain way through me and to conceive myself as acting in the same way with respect to it.

If it were only as easy to find a determinate concept of happiness, the imperatives of prudence would agree entirely with those of skill and would be equally analytic. For here as there it could alike be

---

those *Sanctions* are called Pragmatic which, properly speaking, do not spring as necessary laws from the Natural Right of States, but from *forethought* in regard to the general welfare. A *history* is written pragmatically when it teaches *prudence*—that is, when it instructs the world of today how to provide for its own advantage better than, or at least as well as, the world of other times.

said 'Who wills the end, wills also (necessarily, if he accords with reason) the sole means which are in his power'. Unfortunately, however, the concept of happiness is so indeterminate a concept that although every man wants to attain happiness, he can never say definitely and in unison with himself what it really is that he wants and wills. The reason for this is that all the elements which belong to the concept of happiness are without exception empirical—that is, they must be borrowed from experience; but that none the less there is required for the idea of happiness an absolute whole, a maximum of well-being in my present, and in every future, state. Now it is impossible for the most intelligent, and at the same time most powerful, but nevertheless finite, being to form here a determinate concept of what he really wills. Is it riches that he wants? How much anxiety, envy, and pestering might he not bring in this way on his own head! Is it knowledge and insight? This might perhaps merely give him an eye so sharp that it would make evils at present hidden from him and yet unavoidable seem all the more frightful, or would add a load of still further needs to the desires which already give him trouble enough. Is it long life? Who will guarantee that it would not be a long misery? Is it at least health? How often has infirmity of body kept a man from excesses into which perfect health would have let him fall!—and so on. In short, he has no principle by which he is able to decide with complete certainty what will make him truly happy, since for this he would require omniscience. Thus we cannot act on determinate principles in order to be happy, but only on empirical counsels, for example, of diet, frugality, politeness, reserve, and so on—things which experience shows contribute most to well-being on the average. From this it follows that imperatives of prudence, speaking strictly, do not command at all—that is, cannot exhibit actions objectively as practically *necessary*; that they are rather to be taken as recommendations (*consilia*), than as commands (*praecepta*), of reason; that the problem of determining certainly and universally what action will promote the happiness of a rational being is completely insoluble; and consequently that in regard to this there is no imperative possible which in the strictest sense could command us to do what will make us happy, since happiness is an Ideal, not of reason, but of imagination—an Ideal resting merely

on empirical grounds, of which it is vain to expect that they should determine an action by which we could attain the totality of a series of consequences which is in fact infinite. Nevertheless, if we assume that the means to happiness could be discovered with certainty, this imperative of prudence would be an analytic practical proposition; for it differs from the imperative of skill only in this—that in the latter the end is merely possible, while in the former the end is given. In spite of this difference, since both command solely the means to something assumed to be willed as an end, the imperative which commands him who wills the end to will the means is in both cases analytic. Thus there is likewise no difficulty in regard to the possibility of an imperative of prudence.

Beyond all doubt, the question 'How is the imperative of *morality* possible?' is the only one in need of a solution; for it is in no way hypothetical, and consequently we cannot base the objective necessity which it affirms on any presupposition, as we can with hypothetical imperatives. Only we must never forget here that it is impossible to settle *by an example*, and so empirically, whether there is any imperative of this kind at all: we must rather suspect that all imperatives which seem to be categorical may none the less be covertly hypothetical. Take, for example, the saying 'Thou shalt make no false promises'. Let us assume that the necessity for this abstention is no mere advice for the avoidance of some further evil—as it might be said 'You ought not to make a lying promise lest, when this comes to light, you destroy your credit'. Let us hold, on the contrary, that an action of this kind must be considered as bad in itself, and that the imperative of prohibition is therefore categorical. Even so, we cannot with any certainty show by an example that the will is determined here solely by the law without any further motive, although it may appear to be so; for it is always possible that fear of disgrace, perhaps also hidden dread of other risks, may unconsciously influence the will. Who can prove by experience that a cause is not present? Experience shows only that it is not perceived. In such a case, however, the so-called moral imperative, which as such appears to be categorical and unconditioned, would in fact be only a pragmatic prescription calling attention to our advantage and merely bidding us take this into account.

We shall thus have to investigate the possibility of a *categorical* imperative entirely *a priori*, since here we do not enjoy the advantage of having its reality given in experience and so of being obliged merely to explain, and not to establish, its possibility. So much, however, can be seen provisionally—that the categorical imperative alone purports to be a practical *law*, while all the rest may be called *principles* of the will but not laws; for an action necessary merely in order to achieve an arbitrary purpose can be considered as in itself contingent, and we can always escape from the precept if we abandon the purpose; whereas an unconditioned command does not leave it open to the will to do the opposite at its discretion and therefore alone carries with it that necessity which we demand from a law.

In the second place, with this categorical imperative or law of morality the reason for our difficulty (in comprehending its possibility) is a very serious one. We have here a synthetic *a priori* practical proposition;[8] and since in theoretical knowledge there is so much difficulty in comprehending the possibility of propositions of this kind, it may readily be gathered that in practical knowledge the difficulty will be no less.

THE FORMULA OF UNIVERSAL LAW

In this task we wish first to enquire whether perhaps the mere concept of a categorical imperative may not also provide us with the formula containing the only proposition that can be a categorical imperative; for even when we know the purport of such an absolute command, the question of its possibility will still require a special and troublesome effort, which we postpone to the final chapter.

When I conceive a *hypothetical* imperative in general, I do not know beforehand what it will contain—until its condition is given. But if I conceive a *categorical* imperative, I know at once what it contains. For since besides the law this imperative contains only the necessity that our maxim[9] should conform to this law, while the law, as we have seen, contains no condition to limit it, there remains nothing over to which the maxim has to conform except the universality of a law as such; and it is this conformity alone that the imperative properly asserts to be necessary.

There is therefore only a single categorical imperative and it is this: '*Act only on that maxim through which you can at the same time will that it should become a universal law*'.

Now if all imperatives of duty can be derived from this one imperative as their principle, then even although we leave it unsettled whether what we call duty may not be an empty concept, we shall still be able to show at least what we understand by it and what the concept means.

THE FORMULA OF THE LAW OF NATURE

Since the universality of the law governing the production of effects constitutes what is properly called *nature* in its most general sense (nature as regards its form)—that is, the existence of things so far as determined by universal laws—the universal imperative of duty may also run as follows: '*Act as if the maxim of your action were to become through your will a universal law of nature.*'

ILLUSTRATIONS

We will now enumerate a few duties, following their customary division into duties towards self and du-

---

[8]Without presupposing a condition taken from some inclination I connect an action with the will *a priori* and therefore necessarily (although only objectively so—that is, only subject to the Idea of a reason having full power over all subjective impulses to action). Here we have a practical proposition in which the willing of an action is not derived analytically from some other willing already presupposed (for we do not possess any such perfect will), but is on the contrary connected immediately with the concept of the will of a rational being as something which is not contained in this concept.

---

[9]A *maxim* is a subjective principle of action and must be distinguished from an *objective principle*—namely, a practical law. The former contains a practical rule determined by reason in accordance with the conditions of the subject (often his ignorance or again his inclination): it is thus a principle on which the subject *acts*. A law, on the other hand, is an objective principle valid for every rational being; and it is a principle on which he *ought to act*—that is, an imperative.

ties towards others and into perfect and imperfect duties.[10]

1. A man feels sick of life as the result of a series of misfortunes that has mounted to the point of despair, but he is still so far in possession of his reason as to ask himself whether taking his own life may not be contrary to his duty to himself. He now applies the test 'Can the maxim of my action really become a universal law of nature?' His maxim is 'From self-love I make it my principle to shorten my life if its continuance threatens more evil than it promises pleasure'. The only further question to ask is whether this principle of self-love can become a universal law of nature. It is then seen at once that a system of nature by whose law the very same feeling whose function (*Bestimmung*) is to stimulate the furtherance of life should actually destroy life would contradict itself and consequently could not subsist as a system of nature. Hence this maxim cannot possibly hold as a universal law of nature and is therefore entirely opposed to the supreme principle of all duty.

2. Another finds himself driven to borrowing money because of need. He well knows that he will not be able to pay it back; but he sees too that he will get no loan unless he gives a firm promise to pay it back within a fixed time. He is inclined to make such a promise; but he has still enough conscience to ask 'Is it not unlawful and contrary to duty to get out of difficulties in this way?' Supposing, however, he did resolve to do so, the maxim of his action would run thus: 'Whenever I believe myself short of money, I will borrow money and promise to pay it back, though I know that this will never be done'. Now this principle of self-love or personal advantage is perhaps quite compatible with my own entire future welfare; only there remains the question 'Is it right?' I therefore transform the demand of self-love into a universal law and frame my question thus: 'How would things stand if my maxim became a universal law?' I then see straight away that this maxim can never rank as a universal law of nature and be self-consistent, but must necessarily contradict itself. For the universality of a law that every one believing himself to be in need can make any promise he pleases with the intention not to keep it would make promising, and the very purpose of promising, itself impossible, since no one would believe he was being promised anything, but would laugh at utterances of this kind as empty shams.

3. A third finds in himself a talent whose cultivation would make him a useful man for all sorts of purposes. But he sees himself in comfortable circumstances, and he prefers to give himself up to pleasure rather than to bother about increasing and improving his fortunate natural aptitudes. Yet he asks himself further 'Does my maxim of neglecting my natural gifts, besides agreeing in itself with my tendency to indulgence, agree also with what is called duty?' He then sees that a system of nature could indeed always subsist under such a universal law, although (like the South Sea Islanders) every man should let his talents rust and should be bent on devoting his life solely to idleness, indulgence, procreation, and, in a word, to enjoyment. Only he cannot possibly *will* that this should become a universal law of nature or should be implanted in us as such a law by a natural instinct. For as a rational being he necessarily wills that all his powers should be developed, since they serve him, and are given him, for all sorts of possible ends.

4. Yet a *fourth* is himself flourishing, but he sees others who have to struggle with great hardships (and whom he could easily help); and he thinks 'What does it matter to me? Let every one be as happy as Heaven wills or as he can make himself; I won't deprive him of anything; I won't even envy him; only I have no wish to contribute anything to his well-being or to his support in distress!' Now admittedly if such an attitude were a universal law of nature, mankind could get on perfectly well—better no doubt than if everybody prates about sympathy and goodwill, and even takes pains, on occasion, to practise them, but on the other hand cheats where he can, traffics in human rights, or violates them in other

---

[10]It should be noted that I reserve my division of duties entirely for a future *Metaphysic of Morals* and that my present division is therefore put forward as arbitrary (merely for the purpose of arranging my examples). Further, I understand here by a perfect duty one which allows no exception in the interests of inclination, and so I recognize among *perfect duties*, not only outer ones, but also inner. This is contrary to the accepted usage of the schools, but I do not intend to justify it here, since for my purpose it is all one whether this point is conceded or not.

ways. But although it is possible that a universal law of nature could subsist in harmony with this maxim, yet it is impossible to *will* that such a principle should hold everywhere as a law of nature. For a will which decided in this way would be in conflict with itself, since many a situation might arise in which the man needed love and sympathy from others, and in which, by such a law of nature sprung from his own will, he would rob himself of all hope of the help he wants for himself.

57

THE CANON OF MORAL JUDGEMENT

These are some of the many actual duties—or at least of what we take to be such—whose derivation from the single principle cited above leaps to the eye. We must *be able to will* that a maxim of our action should become a universal law—this is the general canon for all moral judgement of action. Some actions are so constituted that their maxim cannot even be *conceived* as a universal law of nature without contradiction, let alone be *willed* as what *ought* to become one. In the case of others we do not find this inner impossibility, but it is still impossible to *will* that their maxim should be raised to the universality of a law of nature, because such a will would contradict itself. It is easily seen that the first kind of action is opposed to strict or narrow (rigorous) duty, the second only to wider (meritorious) duty; and thus that by these examples all duties—so far as the type of obligation is concerned (not the object of dutiful action)—are fully set out in their dependence on our single principle.

424

If we now attend to ourselves whenever we transgress a duty, we find that we in fact do not will that our maxim should become a universal law—since this is impossible for us—but rather that its opposite should remain a law universally: we only take the liberty of making an *exception* to it for ourselves (or even just for this once) to the advantage of our inclination. Consequently if we weighed it all up from one and the same point of view—that of reason—we should find a contradiction in our own will, the contradiction that a certain principle should be objectively necessary as a universal law and yet subjectively should not hold universally but should admit of exceptions. Since, however, we first consider

58

our action from the point of view of a will wholly in accord with reason, and then consider precisely the same action from the point of view of a will affected by inclination, there is here actually no contradiction, but rather an opposition of inclination to the precept of reason (*antagonismus*), whereby the universality of the principle (*universalitas*) is turned into a mere generality (*generalitas*) so that the practical principle of reason may meet our maxim halfway. This procedure, though in our own impartial judgement it cannot be justified, proves none the less that we in fact recognize the validity of the categorical imperative and (with all respect for it) merely permit ourselves a few exceptions which are, as we pretend, inconsiderable and apparently forced upon us.

59

We have thus at least shown this much—that if duty is a concept which is to have meaning and real legislative authority for our actions, this can be expressed only in categorical imperatives and by no means in hypothetical ones. At the same time—and this is already a great deal—we have set forth distinctly, and determinately for every type of application, the content of the categorical imperative, which must contain the principle of all duty (if there is to be such a thing at all). But we are still not so far advanced as to prove *a priori* that there actually is an imperative of this kind—that there is a practical law which by itself commands absolutely and without any further motives, and that the following of this law is duty.

425

THE NEED FOR PURE ETHICS

For the purpose of achieving this proof it is of the utmost importance to take warning that we should not dream for a moment of trying to derive the reality of this principle from *the special characteristics of human nature.* For duty has to be a practical, unconditioned necessity of action; it must therefore hold for all rational beings (to whom alone an imperative can apply at all), and *only because of this* can it also be a law for all human wills. Whatever, on the other hand, is derived from the special predisposition of humanity, from certain feelings and propensities, and even, if this were possible, from some special bent peculiar to human reason and not

60

holding necessarily for the will of every rational being—all this can indeed supply a personal maxim, but not a law: it can give us a subjective principle—one on which we have a propensity and inclination to act—but not an objective one on which we should be *directed* to act although our every propensity, inclination, and natural bent were opposed to it; so much so that the sublimity and inner worth of the command is the more manifest in a duty, the fewer are the subjective causes for obeying it and the more those against—without, however, on this account weakening in the slightest the necessitation exercised by the law or detracting anything from its validity.

It is here that philosophy is seen in actual fact to be placed in a precarious position, which is supposed to be firm although neither in heaven nor on earth is there anything from which it depends or on which it is based. It is here that she has to show her purity as the authoress of her own laws—not as the mouthpiece of laws whispered to her by some implanted sense or by who knows what tutelary nature, all of which laws together, though they may always be better than nothing, can never furnish us with principles 426 dictated by reason. These principles must have an origin entirely and completely *a priori* and must at the same time derive from this their sovereign authority—that they expect nothing from the inclinations of men, but everything from the supremacy of the law and from the reverence due to it, or in de-61 fault of this condemn man to self-contempt and inward abhorrence.

Hence everything that is empirical is, as a contribution to the principle of morality, not only wholly unsuitable for the purpose, but is even highly injurious to the purity of morals; for in morals the proper worth of an absolutely good will, a worth elevated above all price, lies precisely in this—that the principle of action is free from all influence by contingent grounds, the only kind that experience can supply. Against the slack, or indeed ignoble, attitude which seeks for the moral principle among empirical motives and laws we cannot give a warning too strongly or too often; for human reason in its weariness is fain to rest upon this pillow and in a dream of sweet illusions (which lead it to embrace a cloud in mistake for Juno) to foist into the place of morality some misbegotten mongrel patched up from limbs of very varied ancestry and looking like anything you please, only not like virtue, to him who has once beheld her in her true shape.[11]

Our question therefore is this: 'Is it a necessary 62 law *for all rational beings* always to judge their actions by reference to those maxims of which they can themselves will that they should serve as universal laws?' If there is such a law, it must already be connected (entirely *a priori*) with the concept of the will of a rational being as such. But in order to discover this connexion we must, however much we may bristle, take a step beyond it—that is, into metaphysics, although into a region of it different from that of speculative philosophy, namely, the metaphysic of morals. In practical philosophy we are not concerned with accepting reasons for what *happens*, 427 but with accepting laws of what *ought to happen*, even if it never does happen—that is, objective practical laws. And here we have no need to set up an enquiry as to the reasons why anything pleases or displeases; how the pleasure of mere sensation differs from taste, and whether the latter differs from a universal approval by reason; whereon feelings of pleasure and displeasure are based; how from these feelings there arise desires and inclinations; and how from these in turn, with the co-operation of reason, there arise maxims. All this belongs to empirical psychology, which would constitute the second part of the doctrine of nature, if we take this doctrine to be the *philosophy of nature* so far as grounded on *em-* 63 *pirical laws*. Here, however, we are discussing objective practical laws, and consequently the relation of a will to itself as determined solely by reason. Everything related to the empirical then falls away of itself; for if *reason entirely by itself* determines conduct (and it is the possibility of this which we now wish to investigate), it must necessarily do so *a priori*.

---

[11]To behold virtue in her proper shape is nothing other than to show morality stripped of all admixture with the sensuous and of all the spurious adornments of reward or self-love. How much she then casts into the shade all else that appears attractive to the inclinations can be readily perceived by every man if he will exert his reason in the slightest—provided he has not entirely ruined it for all abstractions.

THE FORMULA OF THE END IN ITSELF

The will is conceived as a power of determining one-self to action *in accordance with the idea of certain laws.* And such a power can be found only in rational beings. Now what serves the will as a subjective ground of its self-determination is an *end*; and this, if it is given by reason alone, must be equally valid for all rational beings. What, on the other hand, contains merely the ground of the possibility of an action whose effect is an end is called a *means.* The subjective ground of a desire is an *impulsion* (*Triebfeder*); the objective ground of a volition is a *motive* (*Bewegungsgrund*). Hence the difference between subjective ends, which are based on impulsions, and objective ends, which depend on motives valid for every rational being. Practical principles are *formal* if they abstract from all subjective ends; they are *material*, on the other hand, if they are based on such ends and consequently on certain impulsions. Ends that a rational being adopts arbitrarily as *effects* of his action (material ends) are in every case only relative; for it is solely their relation to special characteristics in the subject's power of appetition which gives them their value. Hence this value can provide no universal principles, no principles valid and necessary for all rational beings and also for every volition—that is, no practical laws. Consequently all these relative ends can be the ground only of hypothetical imperatives.

Suppose, however, there were something *whose existence* has *in itself* an absolute value, something which as *an end in itself* could be a ground of determinate laws; then in it, and in it alone, would there be the ground of a possible categorical imperative—that is, of a practical law.

Now I say that man, and in general every rational being, *exists* as an end in himself, *not merely as a means* for arbitrary use by this or that will: he must in all his actions, whether they are directed to himself or to other rational beings, always be viewed *at the same time as an end.* All the objects of inclination have only a conditioned value; for if there were not these inclinations and the needs grounded on them, their object would be valueless. Inclinations themselves, as sources of needs, are so far from having an absolute value to make them desirable for

their own sake that it must rather be the universal wish of every rational being to be wholly free from them. Thus the value of all objects that can *be produced* by our action is always conditioned. Beings whose existence depends, not on our will, but on nature, have none the less, if they are non-rational beings, only a relative value as means and are consequently called *things.* Rational beings, on the other hand, are called *persons* because their nature already marks them out as ends in themselves—that is, as something which ought not to be used merely as a means—and consequently imposes to that extent a limit on all arbitrary treatment of them (and is an object of reverence). Persons, therefore, are not merely subjective ends whose existence as an object of our actions has a value *for us*: they are *objective ends*—that is, things whose existence is in itself an end, and indeed an end such that in its place we can put no other end to which they should serve *simply* as means; for unless this is so, nothing at all of *absolute* value would be found anywhere. But if all value were conditioned—that is, contingent—then no supreme principle could be found for reason at all.

If then there is to be a supreme practical principle and—so far as the human will is concerned—a categorical imperative, it must be such that from the idea of something which is necessarily an end for every one because it is an *end in itself* it forms an *objective* principle of the will and consequently can serve as a practical law. The ground of this principle is: *Rational nature exists as an end in itself.* This is the way in which a man necessarily conceives his own existence: it is therefore so far a *subjective* principle of human actions. But it is also the way in which every other rational being conceives his existence on the same rational ground which is valid also for me;[12] hence it is at the same time an *objective* principle, from which, as a supreme practical ground, it must be possible to derive all laws for the will. The practical imperative will therefore be as follows: *Act in such a way that you always treat humanity, whether in your own person or in the person of any other, never simply as a means, but always at the*

---

[12]This proposition I put forward here as a postulate. The grounds for it will be found in the final chapter.

67 *same time as an end.* We will now consider whether this can be carried out in practice.

ILLUSTRATIONS

Let us keep to our previous examples.

First, as regards the concept of necessary duty to oneself, the man who contemplates suicide will ask 'Can my action be compatible with the Idea of humanity *as an end in itself?*' If he does away with himself in order to escape from a painful situation, he is making use of a person merely as *a means* to maintain a tolerable state of affairs till the end of his life. But man is not a thing–not something to be used *merely* as a means: he must always in all his actions be regarded as an end in himself. Hence I cannot dispose of man in my person by maiming, spoiling, or killing. (A more precise determination of this principle in order to avoid all misunderstanding—for example, about having limbs amputated to save myself or about exposing my life to danger in order to preserve it, and so on—I must here forego: this question belongs to morals proper.)

Secondly, so far as necessary or strict duty to others is concerned, the man who has a mind to make a false promise to others will see at once that he is 68 intending to make use of another man *merely as a means* to an end he does not share. For the man whom I seek to use for my own purposes by such a promise cannot possibly agree with my way of behaving to him, and so cannot himself share the end of the action. This incompatibility with the principle of duty to others leaps to the eye more obviously 430 when we bring in examples of attempts on the freedom and property of others. For then it is manifest that a violator of the rights of man intends to use the person of others merely as a means without taking into consideration that, as rational beings, they ought always at the same time to be rated as ends—that is, only as beings who must themselves be able to share in the end of the very same action.[13]

Thirdly, in regard to contingent (meritorious) duty to oneself, it is not enough that an action should re- 69 frain from conflicting with humanity in our own person as an end in itself: it must also *harmonize with this end.* Now there are in humanity capacities for greater perfection which form part of nature's purpose for humanity in our person. To neglect these can admittedly be compatible with the *maintenance* of humanity as an end in itself, but not with the *promotion* of this end.

Fourthly, as regards meritorious duties to others, the natural end which all men seek is their own happiness. Now humanity could no doubt subsist if everybody contributed nothing to the happiness of others but at the same time refrained from deliberately impairing their happiness. This is, however, merely to agree negatively and not positively with *humanity as an end in itself* unless every one endeavours also, so far as in him lies, to further the ends of others. For the ends of a subject who is an end in himself must, if this conception is to have its *full* effect in me, be also, as far as possible, *my* ends.

THE FORMULA OF AUTONOMY

This principle of humanity, and in general of every rational agent, *as an end in itself* (a principle which is the supreme limiting condition of every man's freedom of action) is not borrowed from experience; 431]70 firstly, because it is universal, applying as it does to all rational beings as such, and no experience is adequate to determine universality; secondly, because in it humanity is conceived, not as an end of man (subjectively)—that is, an object which, as a matter of fact, happens to be made an end—but as an objective end—one which, be our ends what they may, must, as a law, constitute the supreme limiting condition of all subjective ends and so must spring from pure reason. That is to say, the ground for every enactment of practical law lies *objectively in the rule*

---

68 [13]Let no one think that here the trivial '*quod tibi non vis fieri, etc.*' can serve as a standard or principle. For it is merely derivative from our principle, although subject to various qualifications: it cannot be a universal law since it contains the ground neither of duties to oneself nor of duties of kindness to others (for many a man would readily agree that others should not help him if only he could be dispensed from affording help to them), nor finally of strict duties towards others; for on this basis the criminal would be able to dispute with the judges who punish him, and so on.

and in the form of universality which (according to our first principle) makes the rule capable of being a law (and indeed a law of nature); *subjectively*, however, it lies in the *end*; but (according to our second principle) the subject of all ends is to be found in every rational being as an end in himself. From this there now follows our third practical principle for the will—as the supreme condition of the will's conformity with universal practical reason—namely, the Idea *of the will of every rational being as a will which makes universal law.*

By this principle all maxims are repudiated which cannot accord with the will's own enactment of universal law. The will is therefore not merely subject to the law, but is so subject that it must be considered as also *making the law* for itself and precisely on this account as first of all subject to the law (of which it can regard itself as the author).

THE EXCLUSION OF INTEREST

Imperatives as formulated above—namely, the imperative enjoining conformity of actions to universal *supremacy* of rational beings in themselves *as ends*—did, by the mere fact that they were represented as categorical, exclude from their sovereign authority every admixture of interest as a motive. They were, however, merely *assumed* to be categorical because we were found to make this assumption if we wished to explain the concept of duty. That there were practical propositions which commanded categorically could not itself be proved, any more than it can be proved in this chapter generally; but one thing could have been done—namely, to show that in willing for the sake of duty renunciation of all interest, as the specific mark distinguishing a categorical from a hypothetical imperative, was expressed in the very imperative itself by means of some determination inherent in it. This is what is done in the present third formulation of the principle—namely, in the Idea of the will of every rational being as *a will which makes universal law.*

Once we conceive a will of this kind, it becomes clear that while a will *which is subject to law* may be bound to this law by some interest, nevertheless a will which is itself a supreme lawgiver cannot possibly as such depend on any interest; for a will which

is dependent in this way would itself require yet a further law in order to restrict the interest of self-love to the condition that this interest should itself be valid as a universal law.

Thus the *principle* that every human will is *a will which by all its maxims enacts universal law*[14]—provided only that it were right in other ways—would be *well suited* to be a categorical imperative in this respect: that precisely because of the Idea of making universal law it is *based on no interest* and consequently can alone among all possible imperatives be *unconditioned*. Or better still—to convert the proposition—if there is a categorical imperative (that is, a law for the will of every rational being), it can command us only to act always on the maxim of such a will in us as can at the same time look upon itself as making universal law; for only then is the practical principle and the imperative which we obey unconditioned, since it is wholly impossible for it to be based on any interest.

We need not now wonder, when we look back upon all the previous efforts that have been made to discover the principle of morality, why they have one and all been bound to fail. Their authors saw man as tied to laws by his duty, but it never occurred to them that he is subject only to *laws which are made by himself* and yet are *universal*, and that he is bound only to act in conformity with a will which is his own but has as nature's purpose for it the function of making universal law. For when they thought of man merely as subject to a law (whatever it might be), the law had to carry with it some interest in order to attract or compel, because it did not spring as a law from *his own* will: in order to conform with the law his will had to be necessitated by *something else* to act in a certain way. This absolutely inevitable conclusion meant that all the labour spent in trying to find a supreme principle of duty was lost beyond recall; for what they discovered was never duty, but only the necessity of acting from a certain interest. This interest might be one's own or another's; but on such a view the imperative was bound to be al-

---

[14] I may be excused from bringing forward examples to illustrate this principle, since those which were first used as illustrations of the categorical imperative and its formula can all serve this purpose here.

ways a conditioned one and could not possibly serve as a moral law. I will therefore call my principle the principle of the *Autonomy* of the will in contrast with all others, which I consequently class under *Heteronomy.*

THE FORMULA OF THE KINGDOM OF ENDS

The concept of every rational being as one who must regard himself as making universal law by all the maxims of his will, and must seek to judge himself and his actions from this point of view, leads to a closely connected and very fruitful concept— namely, that of *a kingdom of ends.*

I understand by a '*kingdom*' a systematic union of different rational beings under common laws. Now since laws determine ends as regards their universal validity, we shall be able—if we abstract from the personal differences between rational beings, and also from all the content of their private ends—to conceive a whole of all ends in systematic conjunction (a whole both of rational beings as ends in themselves and also of the personal ends which each may set before himself); that is, we shall be able to conceive a kingdom of ends which is possible in accordance with the above principles.

For rational beings all stand under the *law* that each of them should treat himself and all others, *never merely as a means*, but always *at the same time as an end in himself.* But by so doing there arises a systematic union of rational beings under common objective laws—that is, a kingdom. Since these laws are directed precisely to the relation of such beings to one another as ends and means, this kingdom can be called a kingdom of ends (which is admittedly only an Ideal).

A rational being belongs to the kingdom of ends as a *member*, when, although he makes its universal laws, he is also himself subject to these laws. He belongs to it as its *head*, when as the maker of laws he is himself subject to the will of no other.

A rational being must always regard himself as making laws in a kingdom of ends which is possible through freedom of the will—whether it be as member or as head. The position of the latter he can maintain, not in virtue of the maxim of his will alone, but only if he is a completely independent being, without needs and with an unlimited power adequate to his will.

Thus morality consists in the relation of all action to the making of laws whereby alone a kingdom of ends is possible. This making of laws must be found in every rational being himself and must be able to spring from his will. The principle of his will is therefore never to perform an action except on a maxim such as can also be a universal law, and consequently such *that the will can regard itself as at the same time making universal law by means of its maxim.* Where maxims are not already by their very nature in harmony with this objective principle of rational beings as makers of universal law, the necessity of acting on this principle is practical necessitation— that is, *duty.* Duty does not apply to the head in a kingdom of ends, but it does apply to every member and to all members in equal measure.

The practical necessity of acting on this principle—that is, duty—is in no way based on feelings, impulses, and inclinations, but only on the relation of rational beings to one another, a relation in which the will of a rational being must always be regarded as *making universal law*, because otherwise he could not be conceived as *an end in himself.* Reason thus relates every maxim of the will, considered as making universal law, to every other will and also to every action towards oneself: it does so, not because of any further motive or future advantage, but from the Idea of the *dignity* of a rational being who obeys no law other than that which he at the same time enacts himself.

THE DIGNITY OF VIRTUE

In the kingdom of ends everything has either a *price* or a *dignity.* If it has a price, something else can be put in its place as an *equivalent*; if it is exalted above all price and so admits of no equivalent, then it has a dignity.

What is relative to universal human inclinations and needs has a *market price*; what, even without presupposing a need, accords with a certain taste— that is, with satisfaction in the mere purposeless play of our mental powers—has a *fancy price* (*Affektionspreis*); but that which constitutes the sole condition under which anything can be an end in itself has not merely a relative value—that is, a price—but has an intrinsic value—that is, *dignity*.

Now morality is the only condition under which a rational being can be an end in himself; for only through this is it possible to be a law-making member in a kingdom of ends. Therefore morality, and humanity so far as it is capable of morality, is the only thing which has dignity. Skill and diligence in work have a market price; wit, lively imagination, and humour have a fancy price; but fidelity to promises and kindness based on principle (not on instinct) have an intrinsic worth. In default of these, nature and art alike contain nothing to put in their place; for their worth consists, not in the effects which result from them, not in the advantage or profit they produce, but in the attitudes of mind—that is, in the maxims of the will—which are ready in this way to manifest themselves in action even if they are not favoured by success. Such actions too need no recommendation from any subjective disposition or taste in order to meet with immediate favour and approval; they need no immediate propensity or feeling for themselves; they exhibit the will which performs them as an object of immediate reverence; nor is anything other than reason required to *impose* them upon the will, not to *coax* them from the will—which last would anyhow be a contradiction in the case of duties. This assessment reveals as dignity the value of such a mental attitude and puts it infinitely above all price, with which it cannot be brought into reckoning or comparison without, as it were, a profanation of its sanctity.

What is it then that entitles a morally good attitude of mind—or virtue—to make claims so high? It is nothing less than the *share* which it affords to a rational being *in the making of universal law*, and which therefore fits him to be a member in a possible kingdom of ends. For this he was already marked out in virtue of his own proper nature as an end in himself and consequently as a maker of laws in the kingdom of ends—as free in respect of all laws of nature, obeying only those laws which he makes himself and in virtue of which his maxims can have their part in the making of universal law (to which he at the same time subjects himself). For nothing can have a value other than that determined for it by the law. But the law-making which determines all

value must for this reason have a dignity—that is, an unconditioned and incomparable worth—for the appreciation of which, as necessarily given by a rational being, the word '*reverence*' is the only becoming expression. *Autonomy* is therefore the ground of the dignity of human nature and of every rational nature.

REVIEW OF THE FORMULAE

The aforesaid three ways of representing the principle of morality are at bottom merely so many formulations of precisely the same law, one of them by itself containing a combination of the other two. There is nevertheless a difference between them, which, however, is subjectively rather than objectively practical: that is to say, its purpose is to bring an Idea of reason nearer to intuition (in accordance with a certain analogy) and so nearer to feeling. All maxims have, in short,

1. a *form*, which consists in their universality; and in this respect the formula of the moral imperative is expressed thus: 'Maxims must be chosen as if they had to hold as universal laws of nature';
2. a *matter*—that is, an end; and in this respect the formula says: 'A rational being, as by his very nature an end and consequently an end in himself, must serve for every maxim as a condition limiting all merely relative and arbitrary ends';
3. a *complete determination* of all maxims by the following formula, namely: 'All maxims as proceeding from our own making of law ought to harmonize with a possible kingdom of ends as a kingdom of nature'.[15] This progression may be said to take place through the categories of the *unity* of the form of will (its universality); of the *multiplicity* of its matter (its

---

[15]Teleology views nature as a kingdom of ends; ethics views a possible kingdom of ends as a kingdom of nature. In the first case the kingdom of ends is a theoretical Idea used to explain what exists. In the second case it is a practical Idea used to bring into existence what does not exist but can be made actual by our conduct—and indeed to bring it into existence in conformity with this Idea.

objects—that is, its ends); and of the *totality* or completeness of its system of ends. It is, however, better if in moral *judgement* we proceed always in accordance with the strict method and take as our basis the universal formula of the categorical imperative: '*Act on the maxim which can at the same time be made a universal law*'. If, however, we wish also to secure acceptance for the moral law, it is very useful to bring one and the same action under the above-mentioned three concepts and so, as far as we can, to bring the universal formula nearer to intuition.

REVIEW OF THE WHOLE ARGUMENT

We can now end at the point from which we started out at the beginning—namely, the concept of an unconditionally good will. The *will is absolutely good* if it cannot be evil—that is, if its maxim, when made into a universal law, can never be in conflict with itself. This principle is therefore also its supreme law: 'Act always on that maxim whose universality as a law you can at the same time will'. This is the one principle on which a will can never be in conflict with itself, and such an imperative is categorical. Because the validity of the will as a universal law for possible actions is analogous to the universal interconnexion of existent things in accordance with universal laws—which constitutes the formal aspect of nature as such—we can also express the categorical imperative as follows: '*Act on that maxim which can at the same time have for its object itself as a universal law of nature*'. In this way we provide the formula for an absolutely good will.

Rational nature separates itself out from all other things by the fact that it sets itself an end. An end would thus be the matter of every good will. But in the Idea of a will which is absolutely good—good without any qualifying condition (namely, that it should attain this or that end)—there must be complete abstraction from every end that has to be *produced* (as something which would make every will only relatively good). Hence the end must here be conceived, not as an end to be produced, *but as a self-existent* end. It must therefore be conceived only negatively—that is, as an end against which we

should never act, and consequently as one which in all our willing we must never rate *merely* as a means, but always at the same time as an end. Now this end can be nothing other than the subject of all possible ends himself, because this subject is also the subject of a will that may be absolutely good; for such a will cannot without contradiction be subordinated to any other object. The principle 'So act in relation to every rational being (both to yourself and to others) that he may at the same time count in your maxim as an end in himself' is thus at bottom the same as the principle 'Act on a maxim which at the same time contains in itself its own universal validity for every rational being'. For to say that in using means to every end I ought to restrict my maxim by the condition that it should also be universally valid as a law for every subject is just the same as to say this—that a subject of ends, namely, a rational being himself, must be made the ground for all maxims of action, never *merely* as a means, but as a supreme condition restricting the use of every means—that is, always also as an end.

Now from this it unquestionably follows that every rational being, as an end in himself, must be able to regard himself as also the maker of universal law in respect of any law whatever to which he may be subjected; for it is precisely the fitness of his maxims to make universal law that marks him out as an end in himself. It follows equally that this dignity (or prerogative) of his above all the mere things of nature carries with it the necessity of always choosing his maxims from the point of view of himself—and also of every other rational being—as a maker of law (and this is why they are called persons). It is in this way that a world of rational beings (*mundus intelligibilis*) is possible as a kingdom of ends—possible, that is, through the making of their own laws by all persons as its members. Accordingly every rational being must so act as if he were through his maxims always a law-making member in the universal kingdom of ends. The formal principle of such maxims is 'So act as if your maxims had to serve at the same time as a universal law (for all rational beings)'. Thus a kingdom of ends is possible only on the analogy of a kingdom of nature; yet the kingdom of ends is possible only through maxims—that is, self-imposed rules—while nature is possible only through laws concerned with causes whose action is necessitated from without. In spite of this difference, we give to nature as a whole, even although it is regarded as a machine, the name of a 'kingdom of nature' so far as—and for the reason that—it stands in a relation to rational beings as its ends. Now a kingdom of ends would actually come into existence through maxims which the categorical imperative prescribes as a rule for all rational beings, *if these maxims were universally followed.* Yet even if a rational being were himself to follow such a maxim strictly, he cannot count on everybody else being faithful to it on this ground, nor can he be confident that the kingdom of nature and its purposive order will work in harmony with him, as a fitting member, towards a kingdom of ends made possible by himself—or, in other words, that it will favour his expectation of happiness. But in spite of this the law 'Act on the maxims of a member who makes universal laws for a merely possible kingdom of ends' remains in full force, since its command is categorical. And precisely here we encounter the paradox that without any further end or advantage to be attained the mere dignity of humanity, that is, of rational nature in man—and consequently that reverence for a mere Idea—should function as an inflexible precept for the will; and that it is just this freedom from dependence on interested motives which constitutes the sublimity of a maxim and the worthiness of every rational subject to be a law-making member in the kingdom of ends; for otherwise he would have to be regarded as subject only to the law of nature—the law of his own needs. Even if it were thought that both the kingdom of nature and the kingdom of ends were united under one head and that thus the latter kingdom ceased to be a mere Idea and achieved genuine reality, the Idea would indeed gain by this the addition of a strong motive, but never any increase in its intrinsic worth; for, even if this were so, it would still be necessary to conceive the unique and absolute lawgiver himself as judging the worth of rational beings solely by the disinterested behaviour they prescribed to themselves in virtue of this Idea alone. The essence of things does not vary with their external relations; and where there is something which, without regard to such relations, constitutes by itself the absolute worth of man, it is by this that man must also be judged by everyone whatsoever—even by the Supreme Being. Thus *morality* lies in the relation of actions to the autonomy of the will—that is, to a possible making of universal law by means of its maxims. An action which is compatible with the autonomy of the will is *permitted*; one which does not harmonize with it is *forbidden.* A will whose maxims necessarily accord with the laws of autonomy is a *holy*, or absolutely good, will. The dependence of a will not absolutely good on the principle of autonomy (that is, moral necessitation) is *obligation.* Obligation can thus have no reference to a holy being. The objective necessity to act from obligation is called *duty.*

From what was said a little time ago we can now easily explain how it comes about that, although in the concept of duty we think of subjection to the law, yet we also at the same time attribute to the person who fulfils all his duties a certain sublimity and *dignity*. For it is not in so far as he is *subject* to the law that he has sublimity, but rather in so far as, in regard to this very same law, he is at the same time its *author* and is subordinated to it only on this ground. We have also shown above how neither fear nor inclination, but solely reverence for the law, is the motive which can give an action moral worth. Our own will, provided it were to act only under the condition of being able to make universal law by means of its maxims—this ideal will which can be ours is the proper object of reverence; and the dignity of man consists precisely in his capacity to make universal law, although only on condition of being himself also subject to the law he makes.

AUTONOMY OF THE WILL *AS THE SUPREME PRINCIPLE OF MORALITY*

Autonomy of the will is the property the will has of being a law to itself (independently of every property belonging to the objects of volition). Hence the principle of autonomy is 'Never to choose except in such a way that in the same volition the maxims of your choice are also present as universal law'. That this practical rule is an imperative—that is, that the will of every rational being is necessarily bound to the rule as a condition—cannot be proved by mere analysis of the concepts contained in it, since it is a synthetic proposition. For proof we should have to go beyond knowledge of objects and pass to a critique of the subject—that is, of pure practical reason—since this synthetic proposition, as commanding apodeictically, must be capable of being known entirely *a priori*. This task does not belong to the present chapter. None the less by mere analysis of the concepts of morality we can quite well show that the above principle of autonomy is the sole principle of ethics. For analysis finds that the principle of morality must be a categorical imperative, and that this in turn commands nothing more nor less than precisely this autonomy.

HETERONOMY OF THE WILL *AS THE SOURCE OF ALL SPURIOUS PRINCIPLES OF MORALITY*

If the will seeks the law that is to determine it *anywhere else* than in the fitness of its maxims for its own making of universal law—if therefore in going beyond itself it seeks this law in the character of any of its objects—the result is always *heteronomy*. In that case the will does not give itself the law, but the object does so in virtue of its relation to the will. This relation, whether based on inclination or on rational ideas, can give rise only to hypothetical imperative: 'I ought to do something *because I will something else*'. As against this, the moral, and therefore categorical, imperative, says: 'I ought to will thus or thus, although I have not willed something else'. For example, the first says: 'I ought not to lie if I want to maintain my reputation'; while the second says: 'I ought not to lie even if so doing were to bring me not the slightest disgrace'. The second imperative must therefore abstract from all objects to this extent—they should be without any *influence* at all on the will so that practical reason (the will) may not merely administer an alien interest but may simply manifest its own sovereign authority as the supreme maker of law. Thus, for example, the reason why I ought to promote the happiness of others is not because the realization of their happiness is of consequence to myself (whether on account of immediate inclination or on account of some satisfac-

tion gained indirectly through reason), but solely because a maxim which excludes this cannot also be present in one and the same volition as a universal law.

CLASSIFICATION *OF ALL POSSIBLE PRINCIPLES OF MORALITY BASED ON THE ASSUMPTION OF HETERONOMY AS THEIR FUNDAMENTAL CONCEPT*

Here, as everywhere else, human reason in its pure use—so long as it lacks a critique—pursues every possible wrong way before it succeeds in finding the only right one.

All the principles that can be adopted from this point of view are either *empirical* or *rational*. The *first* kind, drawn from the principle of *happiness*, are based either on natural, or on moral, feeling. The *second* kind, drawn from the principle of *perfection*, are based either on the rational concept of perfection as a possible effect of our will or else on the concept of a self-existent perfection (God's will) as a determining cause of our will.

Empirical Principles of Heteronomy

Empirical principles are always unfitted to serve as a ground for moral laws. The universality with which these laws should hold for all rational beings without exception—the unconditioned practical necessity which they thus impose—falls away if their basis is taken from the *special constitution of human nature* or from the accidental circumstances in which it is placed. The principle of *personal happiness* is, however, the most objectionable, not merely because it is false and because its pretence that well-being always adjusts itself to well-being is contradicted by experience; nor merely because it contributes nothing whatever towards establishing morality, since making a man happy is quite different from making him good and making him prudent or astute in seeking his advantage quite different from making him virtuous; but because it bases morality on sensuous motives which rather undermine it and totally destroy its sublimity, inasmuch as the motives of virtue are put in the same class as those of vice and we are

91 instructed only to become better at calculation, the specific difference between virtue and vice being completely wiped out. On the other hand, moral feeling, this alleged special sense[16] (however shallow be the appeal to it when men who are unable to *think* hope to help themselves out by *feeling*, even when the question is solely one of universal law, and however little feelings, differing as they naturally do from one another by an infinity of degrees, can supply a uniform measure of good and evil—let alone that one man by his feeling can make no valid judgements at all for others)—moral feeling still remains closer to morality and to its dignity in this respect: it does virtue the honour of ascribing to her *imme-*
443 *diately* the approval and esteem in which she is held, and does not, as it were, tell her to her face that we are attached to her, not for her beauty, but only for our own advantage.

Rational Principles of Heteronomy

Among the *rational* bases of morality—those spring-
92 ing from reason—the ontological concept of *perfection* (however empty, however indefinite it is, and consequently useless for discovering in the boundless field of possible reality the maximum reality appropriate to us; and however much, in trying to distinguish specifically between the reality here in question and every other, it shows an inevitable tendency to go round in a circle and is unable to avoid covertly presupposing the morality it has to explain)—this concept none the less is better than the theological concept which derives morality from a divine and supremely perfect will; not merely because we cannot intuit God's perfection and can only derive it from our own concepts, among which that of morality is the most eminent; but because, if we

---

[16]I class the principle of moral feeling with that of happiness because every empirical principle promises a contribution to our well-being merely from the satisfaction afforded by something—whether this satisfaction is given immediately and without any consideration of advantage or is given in respect of such advantage. Similarly we must with *Hutcheson* class the principle of sympathy for the happiness of others along with the principle of moral sense as adopted by him.

do not do this (and to do so would be to give a crudely circular explanation), the concept of God's will still remaining to us—one drawn from such characteristics as lust for glory and domination and bound up with frightful ideas of power and vengefulness—would inevitably form the basis for a moral system which would be in direct opposition to morality.

Yet if I had to choose between the concept of moral sense and that of perfection in general (both of which at least do not undermine morality, though they are totally incompetent to support it as its foundation), I should decide for the latter; for this, since 93 it at least withdraws the settlement of this question from sensibility and brings it before the court of pure reason, even although it there gets no decision, does still preserve unfalsified for more precise determination the indeterminate Idea (of a will good in itself).

The Failure of Heteronomy

For the rest I believe I may be excused from a lengthy refutation of all these systems. This is so easy and is presumably so well understood even by those whose office requires them to declare themselves for one or other of these theories (since their audience will not lightly put up with a suspension of judgement) that to spend time on it would be merely superfluous labour. But what is of more interest to us here is to know that these principles never lay down anything but heteronomy as the first basis of morality and must in consequence necessarily fail in their object.

Wherever an object of the will has to be put down as the basis for prescribing a rule to determine the will, there the rule is heteronomy; the imperative is conditioned, as follows; '*If*, or *because*, you will this object, you ought to act thus or thus'; consequently it can never give a moral—that is, a categorical—command. However the object determines the will—whether by means of inclination, as in the principle of personal happiness, or by means of reason directed to objects of our possible volitions generally, as in the principle of perfection—the will never deter- 94 mines itself *immediately* by the thought of an action, but only by the impulsion which the anticipated effect of the action exercises on the will: '*I ought to do something because I will something else'*. And the basis for this must be yet a further law in me as a subject, whereby I necessarily will this 'something else'—which law in turn requires an imperative to impose limits on this maxim. The impulsion supposed to be exercised on the will of the subject, in accordance with his natural constitution, by the idea of a result to be attained by his own powers belongs to the nature of the subject—whether to his sensibility (his inclinations and taste) or to his understanding and reason, whose operation on an object is accompanied by satisfaction in virtue of the special equipment of their nature—and consequently, speaking strictly, it is nature which would make the law. This law, as a law of nature, not only must be known and proved by experience and therefore is in itself contingent and consequently unfitted to serve as an apodeictic rule of action such as a moral rule must be, but it is *always merely heteronomy of the will*: the will does not give itself the law, but an alien impulsion does so through the medium of the subject's own nature as tuned for its reception.

The Position of the Argument

An absolutely good will, whose principle must be a categorical imperative, will therefore, being undetermined in respect of all objects, contain only the *form* of *willing*, and that as autonomy. In other words, the fitness of the maxim of every good will to make itself a universal law is itself the sole law which the will of every rational being spontaneously imposes on itself without basing it on any impulsion or interest.

How such a synthetic a priori *proposition is possible* and why it is necessary—this is a problem whose solution lies no longer within the bounds of a metaphysic of morals; nor have we here asserted the truth of this proposition, much less pretended to have a proof of it in our power. We have merely shown by developing the concept of morality generally in vogue that autonomy of the will is unavoidably bound up with it or rather is its very basis. Any one therefore who takes morality to be something, and not merely a chimerical Idea without truth, must at the same time admit the principle we have put forward. This chapter, consequently,

like the first, has been merely analytic. In order to prove that morality is no mere phantom of the brain—a conclusion which follows if the categorical imperative, and with it the autonomy of the will, is true and is absolutely necessary as an *a priori* principle—we require a *possible synthetic use of pure practical reason*. On such a use we cannot venture without prefacing it by a *critique* of this power of reason itself—a critique whose main features, so far as is sufficient for our purpose, we must outline in our final chapter.

CHAPTER III. PASSAGE FROM A METAPHYSIC OF MORALS TO A CRITIQUE OF PURE PRACTICAL REASON

THE CONCEPT OF FREEDOM IS THE KEY TO EXPLAIN AUTONOMY OF THE WILL

Will is a kind of causality belonging to living beings so far as they are rational. *Freedom* would then be the property this causality has of being able to work independently of *determination* by alien causes; just as *natural necessity* is a property characterizing the causality of all non-rational beings—the property of being determined to activity by the influence of alien causes.

The above definition of freedom is *negative* and consequently unfruitful as a way of grasping its essence; but there springs from it a *positive* concept, which, as positive, is richer and more fruitful. The concept of causality carries with it that of *laws* (*Gesetze*) in accordance with which, because of something we call a cause, something else—namely, its effect—must be posited (*gesetzt*). Hence freedom of will, although it is not the property of conforming to laws of nature, is not for this reason lawless: it must rather be a causality conforming to immutable laws, though of a special kind; for otherwise a free will would be self-contradictory. Natural necessity, as we have seen, is a heteronomy of efficient causes; for every effect is possible only in conformity with the law that something else determines the efficient cause to causal action. What else then can freedom of will be but autonomy—that is, the property which will has of being a law to itself? The proposition

'Will is in all its actions a law to itself' expresses, however, only the principle of acting on no maxim other than one which can have for its object itself as at the same time a universal law. This is precisely the formula of the categorical imperative and the principle of morality. Thus a free will and a will under moral laws are one and the same.

Consequently if freedom of the will is presupposed, morality, together with its principle, follows by mere analysis of the concept of freedom. Nevertheless the principle of morality is still a synthetic proposition, namely: 'An absolutely good will is one whose maxim can always have as its content itself considered as a universal law'; for we cannot discover this characteristic of its maxim by analysing the concept of an absolutely good will. Such synthetic propositions are possible only because two cognitions are bound to one another by their connexion with a third term in which both of them are to be found. The *positive* concept of freedom furnishes this third term, which cannot, as in the case of physical causes, be the nature of the sensible world (in the concept of which there come together the concepts of something as cause and of *something else* as effect in their relation to one another). What this third term is to which freedom directs us and of which we have an Idea *a priori*, we are not yet in a position to show here straight away, nor can we as yet make intelligible the deduction of the concept of freedom from pure practical reason and so the possibility of a categorical imperative: we require some further preparation.

FREEDOM MUST BE PRESUPPOSED AS A PROPERTY OF THE WILL OF ALL RATIONAL BEINGS

It is not enough to ascribe freedom to our will, on whatever ground, unless we have sufficient reason for attributing the same freedom to all rational beings as well. For since morality is a law for us only as *rational beings*, it must be equally valid for all rational beings; and since it must be derived solely from the property of freedom, we have got to prove that freedom too is a property of the will of all rational beings. It is not enough to demonstrate freedom from certain alleged experiences of human nature (though to do this is in any case absolutely impossible and freedom can be demonstrated only *a priori*): we must prove that it belongs universally to the activity of rational beings endowed with a will. Now I assert that every being who cannot act except *under the Idea of freedom* is by this alone—from a practical point of view—really free; that is to say, for him all the laws inseparably bound up with freedom are valid just as much as if his will could be pronounced free in itself on grounds valid for theoretical philosophy.[17] And I maintain that to every rational being possessed of a will we must also lend the Idea of freedom as the only one under which he can act. For in such a being we conceive a reason which is practical—that is, which exercises causality in regard to its objects. But we cannot possibly conceive of a reason as being consciously directed from outside in regard to its judgements; for in that case the subject would attribute the determination of his power of judgement, not to his reason, but to an impulsion. Reason must look upon itself as the author of its own principles independently of alien influences. Therefore as practical reason, or as the will of a rational being, it must be regarded by itself as free; that is, the will of a rational being can be a will of his own only under the Idea of freedom, and such a will must therefore—from a practical point of view—be attributed to all rational beings.

THE INTEREST ATTACHED TO THE IDEAS OF MORALITY
Moral Interest and the Vicious Circle

We have at last traced the determinate concept of morality back to the Idea of freedom, but we have been quite unable to demonstrate freedom as some-

---

[17]This method takes it as sufficient for our purpose if freedom is presupposed merely *as an Idea* by all rational beings in their actions; and I adopt it in order to avoid the obligation of having to prove freedom from a theoretical point of view as well. For even if this latter problem is left unsettled, the same laws as would bind a being who was really free are equally valid for a being who cannot act except under the Idea of his own freedom. In this way we can relieve ourselves of the burden which weighs upon theory.

thing actual in ourselves and in human nature: we saw merely that we must presuppose it if we wish to conceive a being as rational and as endowed with consciousness of his causality in regard to actions—that is, as endowed with a will. Thus we find that on precisely the same ground we must attribute to every being endowed with reason and a will this property of determining himself to action under the Idea of his own freedom.

From the presupposition of this Idea there springs, as we further saw, consciousness of a law of action, the law that subjective principles of action—that is, maxims—must always be adopted in such a way that they can also hold as principles objectively—that is, universally—and can therefore serve for our own enactment of universal law. But why should I subject myself to this principle simply as a rational being and in so doing also subject to it every other being endowed with reason? I am willing to admit that no interest *impels* me to do so since this would not produce a categorical imperative; but all the same I must necessarily *take* an interest in it and understand how this happens; for this 'I ought' is properly an 'I will' which holds necessarily for every rational being—provided that reason in him is practical without any hindrance. For beings who, like us, are affected also by sensibility—that is, by motives of a different kind—and who do not always act as reason by itself would act, this necessity is expressed as an 'I ought,' and the subjective necessity is distinct from the objective one.

It looks as if, in our Idea of freedom, we have in fact merely taken the moral law for granted—that is, the very principle of the autonomy of the will—and have been unable to give an independent proof of its reality and objective necessity. In that case we should still have made a quite considerable gain inasmuch as we should at least have formulated the genuine principle more precisely than has been done before. As regards its validity, however, and the practical necessity of subjecting ourselves to it we should have got no further. Why must the validity of our maxim as a universal law be a condition limiting our action? On what do we base the worth we attach to this way of acting—a worth supposed to be so great that there cannot be any interest which is higher? And how does it come about that in this alone man believes

himself to feel his own personal worth, in comparison with which that of a pleasurable or painful state is to count as nothing? To these questions we should have been unable to give any sufficient answer.

We do indeed find ourselves able to take an interest in a personal characteristic which carries with it no interest in mere states, but only makes us fit to have a share in such states in the event of their being distributed by reason. That is to say, the mere fact of deserving happiness can by itself interest us even without the motive of getting a share in this happiness. Such a judgement, however, is in fact merely the result of the importance we have already assumed to belong to moral laws (when we detach ourselves from every empirical interest by our Idea of freedom). But on this basis we can as yet have no insight into the principle that we ought to detach ourselves from such interest—that is, that we ought to regard ourselves as free in our actions and yet to hold ourselves bound by certain laws in order to find solely in our own person a worth which can compensate us for the loss of everything that makes our state valuable. We do not see how this is possible nor consequently *how the moral law can be binding.*

In this, we must frankly admit, there is shown a kind of circle, from which, as it seems, there is no way of escape. In the order of efficient causes we take ourselves to be free so that we may conceive ourselves to be under moral laws in the order of ends; and we then proceed to think of ourselves as subject to moral laws on the ground that we have described our will as free. Freedom and the will's enactment of its own laws are indeed both autonomy—and therefore are reciprocal concepts—but precisely for this reason one of them cannot be used to explain the other or to furnish its ground. It can at most be used for logical purposes in order to bring seemingly different ideas of the same object under a single concept (just as different fractions of equal value can be reduced to their simplest expression).

The Two Standpoints

One shift, however, still remains open to us. We can enquire whether we do not take one standpoint when by means of freedom we conceive ourselves as causes acting *a priori*, and another standpoint when we contemplate ourselves with reference to our actions as effects which we see before our eyes.

One observation is possible without any need for subtle reflexion and, we may assume, can be made by the most ordinary intelligence—no doubt in its own fashion through some obscure discrimination of the power of judgement known to it as 'feeling.' The observation is this—that all ideas coming to us apart from our own volition (as do those of the senses) enable us to know objects only as they affect ourselves: what they may be in themselves remains unknown. Consequently, ideas of this kind, even with the greatest effort of attention and clarification brought to bear by understanding, serve only for knowledge of *appearances*, never of *things in themselves*. Once this distinction is made (it may be merely by noting the difference between ideas given to us from without, we ourselves being passive, and those which we produce entirely from ourselves, and so manifest our own activity), it follows of itself that behind appearances we must admit and assume something else which is not appearance—namely, things in themselves—although, since we can never be acquainted with these, but only with the way in which they affect us, we must resign ourselves to the fact that we can never get any nearer to them and can never know what they are in themselves. This must yield us a distinction, however rough, between the *sensible world* and the *intelligible world*, the first of which can vary a great deal according to differences of sensibility in sundry observers, while the second, which is its ground, always remains the same. Even as regards himself—so far as man is acquainted with himself by inner sensation—he cannot claim to know what he is in himself. For since he does not, so to say, make himself, and since he acquires his concept of self not *a priori* but empirically, it is natural that even about himself he should get information through sense—that is, through inner sense—and consequently only through the mere appearance of his own nature and through the way in which his consciousness is affected. Yet beyond this character of himself as a subject made up, as it is, of mere appearances he must suppose there to be something else which is

its ground—namely, his Ego as this may be constituted in itself; and thus as regards mere perception and the capacity for receiving sensations he must count himself as belonging to the *sensible world*, but as regards whatever there may be in him of pure activity (whatever comes into consciousness, not through affection of the senses, but immediately) he must count himself as belonging to the *intellectual world*, of which, however, he knows nothing further.

A conclusion of this kind must be reached by a thinking man about everything that may be presented to him. It is presumably to be found even in the most ordinary intelligence, which, as is well known, is always very much disposed to look behind the objects of the senses for something further that is invisible and is spontaneously active; but it goes on to spoil this by immediately sensifying this invisible something in its turn—that is to say, it wants to make it an object of intuition, and so by this procedure it does not become in any degree wiser.

Now man actually finds in himself a power which distinguishes him from all other things—and even from himself so far as he is affected by objects. This power is *reason*. As pure spontaneity reason is elevated even above *understanding* in the following respect. Understanding—although it too is spontaneous activity and is not, like sense, confined to ideas which arise only when we are affected by things (and therefore are passive)—understanding cannot produce by its own activity any concepts other than those whose sole service is *to bring sensuous ideas under rules* and so to unite them in one consciousness: without this employment of sensibility it would think nothing at all. Reason, on the other hand—in what are called 'Ideas'—shows a spontaneity so pure that it goes far beyond anything sensibility can offer: it manifests its highest function in distinguishing the sensible and intelligible worlds from one another and so in marking out limits for understanding itself.

Because of this a rational being must regard himself *qua intelligence* (and accordingly not on the side of his lower faculties) as belonging to the intelligible world, not to the sensible one. He has therefore two points of view from which he can regard himself and from which he can know laws governing the employment of his powers and consequently governing all his actions. He can consider himself *first*—so far as he belongs to the sensible world—to be under laws of nature (heteronomy); and *secondly*—so far as he belongs to the intelligible world—to be under laws which, being independent of nature, are not empirical but have their ground in reason alone.

As a rational being, and consequently as belonging to the intelligible world, man can never conceive the causality of his own will except under the Idea of freedom; for to be independent of determination by causes in the sensible world (and this is what reason must always attribute to itself) is to be free. To the Idea of freedom there is inseparably attached the concept of *autonomy*, and to this in turn the universal principle of morality—a principle which in Idea forms the ground for all the actions of *rational* beings, just as the law of nature does for all appearances.

The suspicion which we raised above is now removed—namely, that there might be a hidden circle in our inference from freedom to autonomy and from autonomy to the moral law; that in effect we had perhaps assumed the Idea of freedom only because of the moral law in order subsequently to infer the moral law in its turn from freedom; and that consequently we had been able to assign no ground at all for the moral law, but had merely assumed it by begging a principle which well-meaning souls will gladly concede us, but which we could never put forward as a demonstrable proposition. We see now that when we think of ourselves as free, we transfer ourselves into the intelligible world as members and recognize the autonomy of the will together with its consequence—morality; whereas when we think of ourselves as under obligation, we look upon ourselves as belonging to the sensible world and yet to the intelligible world at the same time.

HOW IS A CATEGORICAL IMPERATIVE POSSIBLE?

A rational being counts himself, *qua* intelligence, as belonging to the intelligible world, and solely *qua* efficient cause belonging to the intelligible world does he give to his causality the name of '*will*'. On the other side, however, he is conscious of himself as also a part of the sensible world, where his actions are encountered as mere appearances of this causality. Yet the possibility of these actions cannot be made intelligible by means of such causality, since with this we have no direct acquaintance; and instead these actions, as belonging to the sensible world, have to be understood as determined by other appearances—namely, by desires and inclinations. Hence, if I were solely a member of the intelligible world, all my actions would be in perfect conformity with the principle of the autonomy of a pure will; if I were solely a part of the sensible world, they would have to be taken as in complete conformity with the law of nature governing desires and inclinations—that is, with the heteronomy of nature. (In the first case they would be grounded on the supreme principle of morality; in the second case on that of happiness.) *But the intelligible world contains the ground of the sensible world and therefore also of its laws*; and so in respect of my will, for which (as belonging entirely to the intelligible world) it gives laws immediately, it must also be conceived as containing such a ground. Hence, in spite of regarding myself from one point of view as a being that belongs to the sensible world, I shall have to recognize that, *qua* intelligence, I am subject to the law of the intelligible world—that is, to the reason which contains this law in the Idea of freedom, and so to the autonomy of the will—and therefore I must look on the laws of the intelligible world as imperatives for me and on the actions which conform to this principle as duties.

And in this way categorical imperatives are possible because the Idea of freedom makes me a member of an intelligible world. This being so, if I were solely a member of the intelligible world, all my actions *would* invariably accord with the autonomy of the will; but because I intuit myself at the same time as a member of the sensible world, they *ought* so to accord. This *categorical* 'ought' presents us with a synthetic *a priori* proposition, since to my will as affected by sensuous desires there is added the Idea of the same will, viewed, however, as a pure will belonging to the intelligible world and active on its own account—a will which contains the supreme condition of the former will, so far as reason is concerned. This is roughly like the way in which concepts of the understanding, which by themselves signify nothing but the form of law in general, are added to intuitions of the sensible world and so make synthetic *a priori* propositions possible on which all our knowledge of nature is based.

The practical use of ordinary human reason confirms the rightness of this deduction. There is no one, not even the most hardened scoundrel—provided only he is accustomed to use reason in other ways—who, when presented with examples of honesty in purpose, of faithfulness to good maxims, of sympathy, and of kindness towards all (even when these are bound up with great sacrifices of advantage and comfort), does not wish that he too might be a man of like spirit. He is unable to realize such an aim in his own person—though only on account of his desires and impulses; but yet at the same time he wishes to be free from these inclinations, which are a burden to himself. By such a wish he shows that having a will free from sensuous impulses he transfers himself in thought into an order of things quite different from that of his desires in the field of sensibility; for from the fulfilment of this wish he can expect no gratification of his sensuous desires and consequently no state which would satisfy any of his actual or even conceivable inclinations (since by such an expectation the very Idea which elicited the wish would be deprived of its superiority); all he can expect is a greater inner worth of his own person. This better person he believes himself to be when he transfers himself to the standpoint of a member of the intelligible world. He is involuntarily constrained to do so by the Idea of freedom—that is, of not being dependent on *determination* by causes in the sensible world; and from this standpoint he is conscious of possessing a good will which, on his own admission, constitutes the law for the bad will belonging to him as a member of the sensible world—a law of whose authority he is aware even in transgressing it. The moral 'I ought' is thus an 'I will' for man as a member of the intelligible world; and it is conceived by him as an 'I ought' only in so far as he considers himself at the same time to be a member of the sensible world.

THE EXTREME LIMIT OF PRACTICAL PHILOSOPHY
The Antinomy of Freedom and Necessity

All men think of themselves as having a free will. From this arise all judgements that actions are such as *ought to have been done*, although they *have not been done*. This freedom is no concept of experience, nor can it be such, since it continues to hold although experience shows the opposite of those requirements which are regarded as necessary under the presupposition of freedom. On the other hand, it is just as necessary that everything which takes place should be infallibly determined in accordance with the laws of nature; and this necessity of nature is likewise no concept of experience, precisely because it carries with it the concept of necessity and so of *a priori* knowledge. The concept of nature is, however, confirmed by experience and must inevitably be presupposed if experience—that is, coherent knowledge of sensible objects in accordance with universal laws—is to be possible. Hence, while freedom is only an *Idea* of reason whose objective reality is in itself questionable, nature is a *concept of the understanding*, which proves, and must necessarily prove, its reality in examples from experience.

From this there arises a dialectic of reason, since the freedom attributed to the will seems incompatible with the necessity of nature; and although at this parting of the ways reason finds the road of natural necessity much more beaten and serviceable than that of freedom for *purposes of speculation*, yet for *purposes of action* the footpath of freedom is the only one on which we can make use of reason in our conduct. Hence to argue freedom away is as impossible for the most abstruse philosophy as it is for the most ordinary human reason. Reason must therefore suppose that no genuine contradiction is to be found between the freedom and the natural necessity ascribed to the very same human actions; for it can abandon the concept of nature as little as it can abandon that of freedom.

All the same we must at least get rid of this seeming contradiction in a convincing fashion—although we shall never be able to comprehend how freedom is possible. For if the thought of freedom is self-contradictory or incompatible with nature—a concept which is equally necessary—freedom would have to be completely abandoned in favour of natural necessity.

The Two Standpoints

From this contradiction it would be impossible to escape if the subject who believes himself free were to conceive himself *in the same sense*, or *in precisely the same relationship*, when he calls himself free as when he holds himself subject to the law of nature in respect of the same action. Hence speculative philosophy has the unavoidable task of showing at least this—that its illusion about the contradiction rests on our conceiving man in one sense and relationship when we call him free and in another when we consider him, as a part of nature, to be subject to nature's laws; and that both characteristics not merely *can* get on perfectly well together, but must be conceived as *necessarily combined* in the same subject; for otherwise we could not explain why we should trouble reason with an Idea which—even if it can *without contradiction* be combined with a different and adequately verified concept—does yet involve us in a business which puts reason to sore straits in its theoretical use. This duty is incumbent on speculative philosophy solely in order that it may clear a path for practical philosophy. Thus it is not left to the discretion of philosophers whether they will remove the seeming contradiction or leave it untouched; for in the latter case the theory on this topic becomes *bonum vacans* [unoccupied property], of which the fatalist can justifiably take possession and can chase all morality out of its supposed property, which it has no title to hold.

Nevertheless at this point we cannot yet say that the boundary of practical philosophy begins. For practical philosophy has no part in the settlement of this controversy: it merely requires speculative reason to bring to an end the dissension in which it is entangled on theoretical questions so that practical reason may have peace and security from external attacks capable of bringing into dispute the territory it seeks to cultivate.

The lawful title to freedom of will claimed even by ordinary human reason is grounded on a consciousness—and an accepted presupposition—that reason is independent of purely subjective determination by causes which collectively make up all that belongs to sensation and comes under the general name of sensibility. In thus regarding himself as intelligence man puts himself into another order of things, and into relation with determining causes of quite another sort, when he conceives himself as intelligence endowed with a will and consequently with causality, than he does when he perceives himself as a phenomenon in the sensible world (which he actually is as well) and subjects his causality to external determination in accordance with laws of nature. He then becomes aware at once that both of these can, and indeed must, take place at the same time; for there is not the slightest contradiction in holding that a *thing as an appearance* (as belonging to the sensible world) is subject to certain laws of which it is independent *as a thing* or being *in itself.* That he must represent and conceive himself in this double way rests, as regards the first side, on consciousness of himself as an object affected through the senses; as concerns the second side, on consciousness of himself as intelligence—that is, as independent of sensuous impressions in his use of reason (and so as belonging to the intelligible world).

Hence it comes about that man claims for himself a will which does not impute to itself anything appertaining merely to his desires and inclinations; and, on the other hand, that he conceives as possible through its agency, and indeed as necessary, actions which can be done only by disregarding all desires and incitements of sense. The causality of such actions lies in man as intelligence and in the laws of such effects and actions as accord with the principles of an intelligible world. Of that world he knows no more than this—that in it reason alone, and indeed pure reason independent of sensibility, is the source of law; and also that since he is there his proper self only as intelligence (while as a human being he is merely an appearance of himself), these laws apply to him immediately and categorically. It follows that incitements from desires and impulses (and therefore from the whole sensible world of nature) cannot impair the laws which govern his will as intelligence. Indeed he does not answer for the former nor impute them to his proper self—that is, to his will; but he does impute to himself the indulgence which he would show them if he admitted their influence on his maxims to the detriment of the rational laws governing his will.

There Is No Knowledge of the Intelligible World

By *thinking* itself into the intelligible world practical reason does not overstep its limits in the least: it would do so only if it sought to *intuit or feel itself* into that world. The thought in question is a merely negative one with respect to the sensible world: it gives reason no laws for determining the will and is positive only in this one point, that it combines freedom as a negative characteristic with a (positive) power as well—and indeed with a causality of reason called by us 'a will'—a power so to act that the principle of our actions may accord with the essential character of a rational cause, that is, with the condition that the maxim of these actions should have the validity of a universal law. If practical reason were also to import an *object of the will*—that is, a motive of action—from the intelligible world, it would overstep its limits and pretend to an acquaintance with something of which it has no knowledge. The concept of the intelligible world is thus only *a point of view* which reason finds itself constrained to adopt outside appearances *in order to conceive itself as practical.* To conceive itself thus would not be possible if the influences of sensibility were able to determine man; but it is none the less necessary as far as we are not to deny him consciousness of himself as intelligence and consequently as a rational cause which is active by means of reason—that is, which is free in its operation. This thought admittedly carries with it the Idea of an order and a legislation different from that of the mechanism of nature appropriate to the world of sense. It makes necessary the concept of an intelligible world (that is, of the totality of rational beings as things in themselves); but it makes not the slightest pretension to do more than conceive such a world with respect to its *formal* condition—to conceive it, that is, as conforming to the condition that the maxim of the will should have the universality of a law, and so as conforming to the autonomy of the will, which alone is compatible with freedom. In contrast with this all laws determined by reference to an object give us heteronomy, which can be found only in laws of nature and can apply only to the world of sense.

There Is No Explanation of Freedom

Reason would overstep all its limits if it took upon itself to *explain how* pure reason can be practical. This would be identical with the task of explaining *how freedom is possible.*

We are unable to explain anything unless we can bring it under laws which can have an object given in some possible experience. Freedom, however, is a mere Idea: its objective validity can in no way be exhibited by reference to laws of nature and consequently cannot be exhibited in any possible experience. Thus the Idea of freedom can never admit of full comprehension, or indeed of insight, since it can never by any analogy have an example falling under it. It holds only as a necessary presupposition of reason in a being who believes himself to be conscious of a will—that is, of a power distinct from mere appetition (a power, namely, of determining himself to act as intelligence and consequently to act in accordance with laws of reason independently of natural instincts). But where determination by laws of nature comes to an end, all *explanation* comes to an end as well. Nothing is left but *defence*—that is, to repel the objections of those who profess to have seen more deeply into the essence of things and on this ground audaciously declare freedom to be impossible. We can only show them that their pretended discovery of a contradiction in it consists in nothing but this: in order to make the law of nature apply to human actions they have necessarily had to consider man as an appearance; and now that they are asked to conceive him, *qua* intelligence, as a thing in himself as well, they continue to look upon him as an appearance in this respect also. In that case, admittedly, to exempt man's causality (that is, his will) from all the natural laws of the sensible world would, in one and the same subject, give rise to a contradiction. The contradiction would fall away if they were willing to reflect and to admit, as is reasonable, that things in themselves (although hidden) must lie behind appearances as their ground, and that we cannot require the laws of their operations to be identical with those that govern their appearances.

There Is No Explanation of Moral Interest

The subjective impossibility of *explaining* freedom of will is the same as the impossibility of finding out and making comprehensible what *interest*[18] man can take in moral laws; and yet he does in fact take such an interest. The basis of this in ourselves we call 'moral feeling'. Some people have mistakenly given out this feeling to be the gauge of our moral judgements: it should be regarded rather as the *subjective* effect exercised on our will by the law and having its objective ground in reason alone.

If we are to will actions for which reason by itself prescribes an 'ought' to a rational, yet sensuously affected, being, it is admittedly necessary that reason should have a power of *infusing* a *feeling of pleasure* or satisfaction in the fulfilment of duty, and consequently that it should possess a kind of causality by which it can determine sensibility in accordance with rational principles. It is, however, wholly

---

[18]An interest is that in virtue of which reason becomes practical—that is, becomes a cause determining the will. Hence only of a rational being do we say that he takes an interest in something: non-rational creatures merely feel sensuous impulses. Reason takes an immediate interest in an action only when the universal validity of the maxim of the action is a ground sufficient to determine the will. Such an interest alone is pure. When reason is able to determine the will only by means of some further object of desire or under the presupposition of some special feeling in the subject, then it takes only a mediate interest in the action; and since reason entirely by itself without the aid of experience can discover neither objects for the will nor a special feeling underlying the will, the latter interest would be merely empirical, and not a pure rational interest. The logical interest of reason (interest in promoting its own insight) is never immediate, but presupposes purposes for which reason can be employed.

impossible to comprehend—that is, to make intelligible *a priori*—how a mere thought containing nothing sensible in itself can bring about a sensation of pleasure or displeasure; for there is here a special kind of causality, and—as with all causality—we are totally unable to determine its character *a priori*: on this we must consult experience alone. The latter cannot provide us with a relation of cause and effect except between two objects of experience—whereas here pure reason by means of mere Ideas (which furnish absolutely no objects for experience) has to be the cause of an effect admittedly found in experience. Hence for us men it is wholly impossible to explain how and why the *universality of a maxim as a law*—and therefore morality—should interest us. This much only is certain: the law is not valid for us *because it interests us* (for this is heteronomy and makes practical reason depend on sensibility—that is to say, on an underlying feeling—in which case practical reason could never give us moral law); the law interests us because it is valid for us as men in virtue of having sprung from our will as intelligence and so from our proper self; *but what belongs to mere appearance is necessarily subordinated by reason to the character of the thing in itself.*

General Review of the Argument

Thus the question 'How is a categorical imperative possible?' can be answered so far as we can supply the sole presupposition under which it is possible—namely, the Idea of freedom—and also so far as we can have insight into the necessity of this presupposition. This is sufficient for the *practical use* of reason—that is, for conviction of the *validity of this imperative*, and so too of the moral law. But how this presupposition itself is possible is never open to the insight of any human reason. Yet, on the presupposition that the will of an intelligence is free, there follows necessarily its *autonomy* as the formal condition under which alone it can be determined. It is not only perfectly *possible* (as speculative philosophy can show) to presuppose such freedom of the will (without contradicting the principle that natural necessity governs the connexion of appearances in the sensible world); it is also *necessary*, without any further condition, for a rational being conscious of exercising causality by means of reason and so of having a will (which is distinct from desires) to make such freedom in practice—that is, in Idea—underlie all his voluntary actions as their condition. But *how* pure reason can be practical in itself without further motives drawn from some other source; that is, how the bare *principle of the universal validity of all its maxims as laws* (which would admittedly be the form of a pure practical reason) can by itself—without any matter (or object) of the will in which we could take some antecedent interest—supply a motive and create an interest which could be called purely *moral*; or, in other words, *how pure reason can be practical*—all human reason is totally incapable of explaining this, and all the effort and labour to seek such an explanation is wasted.

It is precisely the same as if I sought to fathom how freedom itself is possible as the causality of a will. There I abandon a philosophical basis of explanation, and I have no other. I could, no doubt, proceed to flutter about in the intelligible world, which still remains left to me—the world of intelligences; but although I have an *Idea* of it, which has its own good grounds, yet I have not the slightest *acquaintance* with such a world, nor can I ever attain such acquaintance by all the efforts of my natural power of reason. My Idea signifies only a 'something' that remains over when I have excluded from the grounds determining my will everything that belongs to the world of sense: its sole purpose is to restrict the principle that all motives come from the field of sensibility, by setting bounds to this field and by showing that it does not comprise all in all within itself, but that there is still more beyond it; yet with this 'more' I have no further acquaintance. Of the pure reason which conceives this Ideal, after I have set aside all matter—that is, all knowledge of objects—there remains nothing over for me except its form—namely, the practical law that maxims should be universally valid—and the corresponding conception of reason, in its relation to a purely intelligible world, as a possible efficient cause, that is, a cause determining the will. Here all sensuous motives must entirely fail; this Idea of an intelligible world would itself have to be the motive or to be that wherein reason originally took an interest. To make

this comprehensible is, however, precisely the problem that we are unable to solve.

The Extreme Limit of Moral Enquiry

Here then is the extreme limit of all moral enquiry. To determine this limit is, however, of great importance in this respect: by so doing reason may be kept, on the one hand, from searching around in the sensible world—greatly to the detriment of morality—for the supreme motive and for some interest, comprehensible indeed, but empirical; and it may be kept, on the other hand, from flapping its wings impotently, without leaving the spot, in a space that for it is empty—the space of transcendent concepts known as 'the intelligible world'—and so from getting lost among mere phantoms of the brain. For the rest, the Idea of a purely intelligible world, as a whole of all intelligences to which we ourselves belong as rational beings (although from another point of view we are members of the sensible world as well), remains always a serviceable and permitted Idea for the purposes of a rational belief, though all knowledge ends at its boundary: it serves to produce in us a lively interest in the moral law by means of the splendid ideal of a universal kingdom of *ends in themselves* (rational beings), to which we can belong as members only if we are scrupulous to live in accordance with maxims of freedom as if they were laws of nature.

CONCLUDING NOTE

The speculative use of reason *in regard to nature* leads to the absolute necessity of some supreme cause of the *world*; the practical use of reason *with respect to freedom* leads also to absolute necessity—but only to the absolute necessity *of the laws of action* for a rational being as such. Now it is an essential *principle* for every use of reason to push its knowledge to the point where we are conscious of its *necessity* (for without necessity it would not be knowledge characteristic of reason). It is an equally essential *limitation* of the same reason that it cannot have insight into the *necessity* either of what is or what happens, or of what ought to happen, except on the basis of a *condition* under which it is or happens or ought to happen. In this way, however, the satis-

128 faction of reason is merely postponed again and again by continual enquiry after a condition. Hence reason unrestingly seeks the unconditionally necessary and sees itself compelled to assume this without any means of making it comprehensible—happy enough if only it can find a concept compatible with this presupposition. Thus it is no discredit to our deduction of the supreme principle of morality, but rather a reproach which must be brought against reason as such, that it cannot make comprehensible the absolute necessity of an unconditioned practical law

(such as the categorical imperative must be). For its unwillingness to do this by means of a condition— namely, by basing this necessity on some underlying interest—reason cannot be blamed, since in that case there would be no moral law, that is, no supreme law of freedom. And thus, while we do not comprehend the practical unconditioned necessity of the moral imperative, we do comprehend its *incomprehensibility*. This is all that can fairly be asked of a philosophy which presses forward in its principles to the very limit of human reason.

CRITIQUE OF PURE REASON

B vii

PREFACE TO SECOND EDITION

Whether the treatment of such knowledge as lies within the province of reason does or does not follow the secure path of a science, is easily to be determined from the outcome. For if after elaborate preparations, frequently renewed, it is brought to a stop immediately it nears its goal; if often it is compelled to retrace its steps and strike into some new line of approach; or again, if the various participants are unable to agree in any common plan of procedure, then we may rest assured that it is very far from having entered upon the secure path of a science, and is indeed a merely random groping. In these circumstances, we shall be rendering a service to reason should we succeed in discovering the path upon which it can securely travel, even if, as a result of so doing, much that is comprised in our original aims, adopted without reflection, may have to be abandoned as fruitless.

B viii   That logic has already, from the earliest times, proceeded upon this sure path is evidenced by the fact that since Aristotle it has not required to retrace a single step, unless, indeed, we care to count as improvements the removal of certain needless subtleties or the clearer exposition of its recognised teaching, features which concern the elegance rather than the certainty of the science. It is remarkable also that to the present day this logic has not been able to advance a single step, and is thus to all appearance a closed and

completed body of doctrine. If some of the moderns have thought to enlarge it by introducing *psychological* chapters on the different faculties of knowledge (imagination, wit, etc.), *metaphysical* chapters on the origin of knowledge or on the different kinds of certainty according to difference in the objects (idealism, scepticism, etc.), or *anthropological* chapters on prejudices, their causes and remedies, this could only arise from their ignorance of the peculiar nature of logical science. We do not enlarge but disfigure sciences, if we allow them to trespass upon one another's territory. The sphere of logic is quite precisely delimited; its sole concern is to give an exhaustive exposition and a strict proof of the formal rules of all thought, whether it be *a priori* or empirical, whatever be its origin or its object, and whatever hindrances, accidental or natural, it may encounter in our minds.

B ix

That logic should have been thus successful is an advantage which it owes entirely to its limitations, whereby it is justified in abstracting—indeed, it is under obligation to do so—from all objects of knowledge and their differences, leaving the understanding nothing to deal with save itself and its form. But for reason to enter on the sure path of science is, of course, much more difficult, since it has to deal not with itself alone but also with objects. Logic, therefore, as a propaedeutic, forms, as it were, only the vestibule of the sciences; and when we are concerned with specific modes of knowledge, while logic is indeed presupposed in any critical estimate of them, yet for the actual acquiring of them we have to look to the sciences properly and objectively so called.

Now if reason is to be a factor in these sciences, something in them must be known *a priori,* and this knowledge may be related to its object in one or other of two ways, either as merely *determining* it and its concept (which must be supplied from elsewhere) or as also *making it actual.* The former is *theoretical,* the latter *practical* knowledge of reason. In both, that part in which reason determines its object completely *a priori,* namely, the *pure* part—however much or little this part may contain—must be first and separately dealt with, in case it be confounded with what comes from other sources. For it is bad management if we blindly pay out what comes in, and are not able, when the income falls into arrears, to distinguish which part of it can justify expenditure, and in which[1] line we must make reductions.

Mathematics and physics, the two sciences in which reason yields theoretical knowledge, have to determine their objects *a priori,* the former doing so quite purely, the latter having to reckon, at least partially, with sources of knowledge other than reason.

In the earliest times to which the history of human reason extends, *mathematics,* among that wonderful people, the Greeks, had already entered upon the sure path of science. But it must not be supposed that it was as easy for mathematics as it was for logic—in which reason has to deal with itself alone—to light upon, or rather to construct for itself, that royal road. On the contrary, I believe that it long remained, especially among the Egyptians, in the groping stage, and that the transformation must have been due to a *revolution* brought about by the happy thought of a single man, the experiment which he devised marking out the path upon which the science must enter, and by following which, secure progress throughout all time and in endless expansion is infallibly secured. The history of this intellectual revolution—far more important than the discovery of the passage round the celebrated Cape of Good Hope—and of its fortunate author, has not been preserved. But the fact that Diogenes Laertius, in handing down an account of these matters, names the reputed author of even the least important among the

geometrical demonstrations, even of those which, for ordinary consciousness, stand in need of no such proof, does at least show that the memory of the revolution, brought about by the first glimpse of this new path, must have seemed to mathematicians of such outstanding importance as to cause it to survive the tide of oblivion. A new light flashed upon the mind of the first man (be he Thales or some other) who demonstrated the properties of the isosceles triangle. The true method, so he found, was not to inspect what he discerned either in the figure, or in the bare concept of it, and from this, as it were, to read off its properties; but to bring out what[2] was necessarily implied in the concepts that he had himself formed *a priori,* and had put into the figure in the construction by which he presented it to himself. If he is to know anything with *a priori* certainty he must not ascribe to the figure anything save what necessarily follows from what he has himself set into it in accordance with his concept.

Natural science was very much longer in entering upon the highway of science. It is, indeed, only about a century and a half since Bacon, by his ingenious proposals, partly initiated this discovery, partly inspired fresh vigour in those who were already on the way to it. In this case also the discovery can be explained as being the sudden outcome of an intellectual revolution. In my present remarks I am referring to natural science only in so far as it is founded on *empirical* principles.

When Galileo caused balls, the weights of which he had himself previously determined, to roll down an inclined plane; when Torricelli made the air carry a weight which he had calculated beforehand to be equal to that of a definite column of water; or in more recent times, when Stahl changed metal into lime, and lime back into metal, by withdrawing something and then restoring it,[a] a light broke upon all students of nature. They learned that reason has insight only into that which it produces after a plan of its own, and that it must not allow itself to be kept, as it were, in nature's leading-strings, but must itself show the

---

[1] [Reading, with Erdmann, *von welchem* for *von welcher.*]

[2] [Reading, with Adickes, *sondern das* for *sondern durch das.*]

[a] I am not, in my choice of examples, tracing the exact course of the history of the experimental method; we have indeed no very precise knowledge of its first beginnings.

way with principles of judgment based upon fixed laws, constraining nature to give answer to questions of reason's own determining. Accidental observations, made in obedience to no previously thought-out plan, can never be made to yield a necessary law, which alone reason is concerned to discover. Reason, holding in one hand its principles, according to which alone concordant appearances can be admitted as equivalent to laws, and in the other hand the experiment which it has devised in conformity with these principles, must approach nature in order to be taught by it. It must not, however, do so in the character of a pupil who listens to everything that the teacher chooses to say, but of an appointed judge who compels the witnesses to answer questions which he has himself formulated. Even physics, therefore, owes the beneficent revolution in its point of view B xiv entirely to the happy thought, that while reason must seek in nature, not fictitiously ascribe to it, whatever as not being knowable through reason's own resources has to be learnt, if learnt at all, only from nature, it must adopt as its guide, in so seeking, that which it has itself put into nature. It is thus that the study of nature has entered on the secure path of a science, after having for so many centuries been nothing but a process of merely random groping.

Metaphysics is a completely isolated speculative science of reason, which soars far above the teachings of experience, and in which reason is indeed meant to be its own pupil. Metaphysics rests on concepts alone—not, like mathematics, on their application to intuition. But though it is older than all other sciences, and would survive even if all the rest were swallowed up in the abyss of an all-destroying barbarism, it has not yet had the good fortune to enter upon the secure path of a science. For in it reason is perpetually being brought to a stand, even when the laws into which it is seeking to have, as it professes, an *a priori* insight are those that are confirmed by our most common experiences. Ever and again we have to retrace our steps, as not leading us in the direction B xv in which we desire to go. So far, too, are the students of metaphysics from exhibiting any kind of unanimity in their contentions, that metaphysics has rather to be regarded as a battle-ground quite peculiarly suited for those who desire to exercise themselves in mock combats, and in which no participant has ever yet succeeded in gaining even so much as an inch of territory, not at least in such manner as to secure him in its permanent possession. This shows, beyond all questioning, that the procedure of metaphysics has hitherto been a merely random groping, and, what is worst of all, a groping among mere concepts.

What, then, is the reason why, in this field, the sure road lo science has not hitherto been found? Is it, perhaps, impossible of discovery? Why, in that case, should nature have visited our reason with the restless endeavour whereby it is ever searching for such a path, as if this were one of its most important concerns. Nay, more, how little cause have we to place trust in our reason, if, in one of the most important domains of which we would fain have knowledge, it does not merely fail us, but lures us on by deceitful promises, and in the end betrays us! Or if it be only that we have thus far failed to find the true path, are there any indications to justify the hope that by renewed efforts we may have better fortune than has fallen to our predecessors?

The examples of mathematics and natural science, which by a single and sudden revolution have be-B xvi come what they now are, seem to me sufficiently remarkable to suggest our considering what may have been the essential features in the changed point of view by which they have so greatly benefited. Their success should incline us, at least by way of experiment, to imitate their procedure, so far as the analogy which, as species of rational knowledge, they bear to metaphysics may permit. Hitherto it has been assumed that all our knowledge must conform to objects. But all attempts to extend our knowledge of objects by establishing something in regard to them *a priori,* by means of concepts, have, on this assumption, ended in failure. We must therefore make trial whether we may not have more success in the tasks of metaphysics, if we suppose that objects must conform to our knowledge. This would agree better with what is desired, namely, that it should be possible to have knowledge of objects *a priori,* determining something in regard to them prior to their being given. We should then be proceeding precisely on the lines of Copernicus' primary hypothesis.[3] Failing of satisfactory progress in explaining the move-

---

[3] [*mit den ersten Gedanken des Kopernikus.*]

ments of the heavenly bodies on the supposition that they all revolved round the spectator, he tried whether he might not have better success if he made the spectator to revolve and the stars to remain at rest. A similar experiment can be tried in metaphysics, as regards the *intuition* of objects. If intuition must conform to the constitution of the objects, I do not see how we could know anything of the latter *a priori;* but if the object (as object of the senses) must conform to the constitution of our faculty of intuition, I have no difficulty in conceiving such a possibility. Since I cannot rest in these intuitions if they are to become known, but must relate them as representations to something as their object, and determine this latter through them, either I must assume that the *concepts,* by means of which I obtain this determination, conform to the object, or else I assume that the objects, or what is the same thing, that the *experience* in which alone, as given objects, they can be known, conform to the concepts. In the former case, I am again in the same perplexity as to how I can know anything *a priori* in regard to the objects. In the latter case the outlook is more hopeful. For experience is itself a species of knowledge which involves understanding; and understanding has rules which I must presuppose as being in me prior to objects being given to me, and therefore as being *a priori.* They find expression in *a priori* concepts to which all objects of experience necessarily conform, and with which they must agree. As regards objects which are thought solely through reason, and indeed as necessary, but which can never—at least not in the manner in which reason thinks them—be given in experience, the attempts at thinking them (for they must admit of being thought) will furnish an excellent touchstone of what we are adopting as our new method of thought, namely, that we can know *a priori* of things only what we ourselves put into them.*b*

This experiment succeeds as well as could be desired, and promises to metaphysics, in its first part—the part that is occupied with those concepts *a priori* to which the corresponding objects, commensurate with them, can be given in experience— the secure path of a science. For the new point of view enables us to explain how there can be knowledge *a priori*; and, in addition, to furnish satisfactory proofs of the laws which form the *a priori* basis of nature, regarded as the sum of the objects of experience—neither achievement being possible on the procedure hitherto followed. But this deduction of our power of knowing *a priori,* in the first part of metaphysics, has a consequence which is startling, and which has the appearance of being highly prejudicial to the whole purpose of metaphysics, as dealt with in the second part. For we are brought to the conclusion that we can never transcend the limits of possible experience, though that is precisely what this science is concerned, above all else, to achieve. This situation yields, however, just the very experiment by which, indirectly, we are enabled to prove the truth of this first estimate of our *a priori* knowledge of reason, namely, that such knowledge has to do only with appearances, and must leave the thing in itself[5] as indeed real *per se,* but as not known by us. For what necessarily forces us to transcend the limits of experience and of all appearances is the *unconditioned,* which reason, by necessity and by right, demands in things in themselves, as required to complete the series of conditions. If, then, on the supposition that our empirical knowledge conforms to objects as things in themselves, we find that the unconditioned *cannot be thought without contradiction,* and that

B xvii

B xviii

B xix

B xx

---

b This method, modelled on that of the student of nature, consists in looking for the elements of pure reason in *what admits of confirmation or refutation by experiment.* Now the propositions of pure reason, especially if they venture out beyond all limits of possible experience, cannot be brought to the test through any experiment with their *objects,* as in natural science. In dealing with those *concepts* and *principles* which we adopt *a priori,* all that we can do is to contrive that they be used for viewing

objects from two different points of view—on the one hand, in connection with experience, as objects of the senses and of the understanding, and on the other hand, for the isolated reason that strives to transcend all[4] limits of experience, as objects which are thought merely. If, when things are viewed from this twofold standpoint, we find that there is agreement with the principle of pure reason, but that when we regard them only from a single point of view reason is involved in unavoidable self-conflict, the experiment decides in favour of the correctness of this distinction.

B xix

[4] [Reading, with Adickes, *über alle* for *über.*]

[5] [*die Sache an sich selbst.*]

when, on the other hand, we suppose that our representation of things, as they are given to us, does not conform to these things as they are in themselves, but that these objects, as appearances, conform to our mode of representation, *the contradiction vanishes*; and if, therefore, we thus find that the unconditioned is not to be met with in things, so far as we know them, that is, so far as they are given to us, but only so far as we do not know them, that is, so far as they are things in themselves, we are justified in concluding that what we at first assumed for the purposes of experiment is now definitely confirmed.[c] But when all progress in the field of the supersensible has thus been denied to speculative reason, it is still open to us to enquire whether, in the practical knowledge of reason, data may not be found sufficient to determine reason's transcendent concept of the unconditioned, and so to enable us, in accordance with the wish of metaphysics, and by means of knowledge that is possible *a priori,* though only from a practical point of view, to pass beyond the limits of all possible experience. Speculative reason has thus at least made room for such an extension; and if it must at the same time leave it empty, yet none the less we are at liberty, indeed we are summoned, to take occupation of it, if we can, by practical data of reason.[d]

This attempt to alter the procedure which has hitherto prevailed in metaphysics, by completely revolutionising it in accordance with the example set by the geometers and physicists, forms indeed the main purpose of this critique of pure speculative reason. It is a treatise on the method, not a system of the science itself. But at the same time it marks out the whole plan of the science, both as regards its limits and as regards its entire internal structure. For pure speculative reason has this peculiarity, that it can measure its powers according to the different ways in which it chooses the objects of its thinking, and can also give an exhaustive enumeration of the various ways in which it propounds its problems, and so is able, nay bound, to trace the complete outline of a system of metaphysics. As regards the first point, nothing in *a priori* knowledge can be ascribed to objects save what the thinking subject derives from itself; as regards the second point, pure reason, so far as the principles of its knowledge are concerned, is a quite separate self-subsistent unity, in which, as in an organised body, every member exists for every other, and all for the sake of each, so that no principle can safely be taken in *any one* relation, unless it has been investigated in the *entirety* of its relations to the whole employment of pure reason. Consequently, metaphysics has also this singular advantage, such as falls to the lot of no other science which deals with objects (for *logic* is concerned only with the form of thought in general), that should it, through this critique, be set upon the secure path of a science, it is capable of acquiring exhaustive knowledge of its entire field. Metaphysics has to deal only with principles, and with the limits of their employment as determined by these principles themselves, and it can therefore finish its work and bequeath it to posterity as a capital to which no addition can be made. Since it is a fundamental science, it is under obligation to achieve this completeness. We must be able to say of it: *nil actum reputans, si quid superesset agendum.*

B xxi

B xxii

B xxiii

B xxiv

---

[c] This experiment of pure reason bears a great similarity to what in chemistry is sometimes entitled the experiment of *reduction,* or more usually the *synthetic* process. The *analysis of the metaphysician* separates pure *a priori* knowledge into two very heterogeneous elements, namely, the knowledge of things as appearances, and the knowledge of things in themselves; his *dialectic* combines these two again, in *harmony* with the necessary idea of the *unconditioned* demanded by reason, and finds that this harmony can never be obtained except through the above distinction, which must therefore be accepted.

[d] Similarly, the fundamental laws of the motions of the heavenly bodies gave established certainty to what Copernicus had at first assumed only as an hypothesis, and at the same time yielded proof of the invisible force (the Newtonian attraction) which holds the universe together. The latter would have remained for ever undiscovered if Copernicus had not dared, in a manner contradictory of the senses, but yet true, to seek the observed movements, not in the heavenly bodies, but in the spectator. The change in point of view, analogous to this hypothesis, which is expounded in the *Critique,* I put forward in this preface as an hypothesis only, in order in draw attention to the character of these first attempts at such a change, which are always hypothetical. But in the *Critique* itself it will be proved, apodeictically not hypothetically, from the nature of our representations of space and time and from the elementary concepts of the understanding.

But, it will be asked, what sort of a treasure is this that we propose to bequeath to posterity? What is the value of the metaphysics that is alleged to be thus purified by criticism and established once for all? On a cursory view of the present work it may seem that its results are merely *negative,* warning us that we must never venture with speculative reason beyond the limits of experience. Such is in fact its primary use. But such teaching at once acquires a *positive* value when we recognise that the principles with which speculative reason ventures out beyond its proper limits do not in effect *extend* the employment of reason, but, as we find on closer scrutiny, inevitably *narrow* it. These principles properly belong [not to reason but] to sensibility, and when thus employed they threaten to make the bounds of sensibility coextensive with the real, and so to supplant reason in its pure (practical) employment. So far, therefore, as our Critique limits speculative reason, it is indeed *negative;* but since it thereby removes an obstacle which stands in the way of the employment of practical reason, nay threatens to destroy it, it has in reality *a positive* and very important use. At least this is so, immediately we are convinced that there is an absolutely necessary *practical* employment of pure reason—the *moral*—in which it inevitably goes beyond the limits of sensibility. Though [practical] reason, in thus proceeding, requires no assistance from speculative reason, it must yet be assured against its opposition, that reason may not be brought into conflict with itself. To deny that the service which the Critique renders is *positive* in character, would thus be like saying that the police are of no positive benefit, inasmuch as their main business is merely to prevent the violence of which citizens stand in mutual fear, in order that each may pursue his vocation in peace and security. That space and time are only forms of sensible intuition, and so only conditions of the existence of things as appearances; that, moreover, we have no concepts of understanding, and consequently no elements for the knowledge of things, save in so far as intuition can be given corresponding to these concepts; and that we can therefore have no knowledge of any object as thing in itself, but only in so far as it[6] is an object of sensible intuition, that is, an appearance—all this is proved in the analytical part of the Critique. Thus it does indeed follow that all possible speculative knowledge of reason is limited to mere objects of *experience.* But our further contention must also be duly borne in mind, namely, that though we cannot *know* these objects as things in themselves, we must yet be in position at least to *think* them as things in themselves;[e] otherwise we should be landed in the absurd conclusion that there can be appearance without anything that appears. Now let us suppose that the distinction, which our Critique has shown to be necessary, between things as objects of experience and those same things as things in themselves, had not been made. In that case all things in general, as far as they are efficient causes, would be determined by the principle of causality, and consequently by the mechanism of nature. I could not, therefore, without palpable contradiction, say of one and the same being, for instance the human soul, that its will is free and yet is subject to natural necessity, that is, is not free. For I have taken the soul in both propositions *in one and the same sense,* namely as a thing in general, that is, as a thing[7] in itself; and save by means of a preceding critique, could not have done otherwise. But if our Critique is not in error in teaching that the object is to be taken *in a twofold sense,* namely as appearance and as thing in itself; if the deduction of the concepts of understanding is valid, and the principle of causality therefore applies only to things taken in the former sense, namely, in so far as they are objects of experience—these same

B xxv

B xxvi

B xx

---

[e] To *know* an object I must be able to prove its possibility, either from its actuality as attested by experience, or *a priori* by means of reason. But I can *think* whatever I please, provided only that I do not contradict myself, that is, provided my concept is a possible thought. This suffices for the possibility of the concept, even though I may not be able to answer for there being, in the sum of all possibilities, an object corresponding to it. But something more is required before I can ascribe to such a concept objective validity, that is, real possibility; the former possibility is merely logical. This something more need not, however, be sought in the theoretical sources of knowledge; it may lie in those that are practical.

[6] [Reading, with Erdmann, *er* for *es.*]

[7] [*Sache.*]

objects, taken in the other sense, not being subject to the principle—then there is no contradiction in supposing that one and the same will is, in the appearance, that is, in its visible acts, necessarily subject to the law of nature, and so far *not free*, while yet, as belonging to a thing in itself, it is not subject to that law, and is therefore *free*. My soul, viewed from the latter standpoint, cannot indeed be known by means of speculative reason (and still less through empirical observation); and freedom as a property of a being to which I attribute effects in the sensible world, is therefore also not knowable in any such fashion. For I should then have to know such a being as determined in its existence, and yet as not determined in time—which is impossible, since I cannot support my concept by any intuition. But though I cannot *know,* I can yet *think* freedom; that is to say, the representation of it is at least not self-contradictory, provided due account be taken of our critical distinction between the two modes of representation, the sensible and the intellectual, and of the resulting limitation of the pure concepts of understanding and of the principles which flow from them.

If we grant that morality necessarily presupposes freedom (in the strictest sense) as a property of our will; if, that is to say, we grant that it yields practical principles—original principles, proper to our reason—as *a priori data* of reason, and that this would be absolutely impossible save on the assumption of freedom; and if at the same time we grant that speculative reason has proved that such freedom does not allow of being thought, then the former supposition—that made on behalf of morality—would have to give way to this other contention, the opposite of which involves a palpable contradiction. For since it is only on the assumption of freedom that the negation of morality contains any contradiction; freedom, and with it morality, would have to yield to the mechanism of nature.

Morality does not, indeed, require that freedom should be understood, but only that it should not contradict itself, and so should at least allow of being thought, and that as thus thought it should place no obstacle in the way of a free act (viewed in another relation) likewise conforming to the mechanism of nature. The doctrine of morality and the doctrine of nature may each, therefore, make good its position.

This, however, is only possible in so far as criticism has previously established our unavoidable ignorance of things in themselves, and has limited all that we can theoretically *know* to mere appearances.

This discussion as to the positive advantage of critical principles of pure reason can be similarly developed in regard to the concept of *God* and of the *simple nature* of our *soul;* but for the sake of brevity such further discussion may be omitted. [From what has already been said, it is evident that] even the *assumption*—as made on behalf of the necessary practical employment of my reason—of *God, freedom,* and *immortality* is not permissible unless at the same time speculative reason be deprived of its pretensions to transcendent insight. For in order to arrive at such insight it must make use of principles which, in fact, extend only to objects of possible experience, and which, if also applied to what cannot be an object of experience, always really change this into an appearance, thus rendering all *practical extension* of pure reason impossible. I have therefore found it necessary to deny *knowledge,* in order to make room for *faith.*[8] The dogmatism of metaphysics, that is, the preconception that it is possible to make headway in metaphysics without a previous criticism of pure reason, is the source of all that unbelief,[9] always very dogmatic, which wars against morality.

Though it may not, then, be very difficult to leave to posterity the bequest of a systematic metaphysic, constructed in conformity with a critique of pure reason, yet such a gift is not to be valued lightly. For not only will reason be enabled to follow the secure path of a science, instead of, as hitherto, groping at random, without circumspection or self-criticism; our enquiring youth will also be in a position to spend their time more profitably than in the ordinary dogmatism by which they are so early and so greatly encouraged to indulge in easy speculation about things of which they understand nothing, and into which neither they nor anyone else will ever have any insight—encouraged, indeed, to invent new ideas and opinions, while neglecting the study of the better-established sciences. But, above all, there is

---

[8] [*Glaube.*]

[9] [*Unglaube.*]

the inestimable benefit, that all objections to morality and religion will be for ever silenced, and this in Socratic fashion, namely, by the clearest proof of the ignorance of the objectors. There has always existed in the world, and there will always continue to exist, some kind of metaphysics, and with it the dialectic that is natural to pure reason. It is therefore the first and most important task of philosophy to deprive metaphysics, once and for all, of its injurious influence, by attacking its errors at their very source.

B xxxii   Notwithstanding this important change in the field of the sciences, and the *loss* of its fancied possessions which speculative reason must suffer, general human interests remain in the same privileged position as hitherto, and the advantages which the world has hitherto derived from the teachings of pure reason are in no way diminished. The loss affects only the *monopoly of the schools,* in no respect the *interests of humanity.* I appeal to the most rigid dogmatist, whether the proof of the continued existence of our soul after death, derived from the simplicity of substance, or of the freedom of the will as opposed to a universal mechanism, arrived at through the subtle but ineffectual distinctions between subjective and objective practical necessity, or of the existence of God as deduced from the concept of an *ens realissimum* (of the contingency of the changeable and of the necessity of a prime mover), have ever, upon passing out from the schools, succeeded in reaching the public mind or in exercising the slightest influence on its convictions? That has never been found to occur, and in view of the unfitness of the common human understanding for such subtle speculation, ought never to have been expected. Such widely held convictions, so far as they rest on rational grounds, are due to quite other considerations. The hope of a *future life* has its source in that notable characteristic of our nature, never to be capable of being satisfied by what is temporal (as insufficient for the capacities of its whole destination); the consciousness of *free-*
B xxxiii   *dom* rests exclusively on the clear exhibition of duties, in opposition to all claims of the inclinations; the belief in a wise and great *Author of the world* is generated solely by the glorious order, beauty, and providential care everywhere displayed in nature.

When the schools have been brought to recognise that they can lay no claim to higher and fuller insight in a matter of universal human concern than that which is equally within the reach of the great mass of men (ever to be held by us in the highest esteem), and that, as Schools of philosophy, they should limit themselves to the study of those universally comprehensible, and, for moral purposes, sufficient grounds of proof, then not only do these latter possessions remain undisturbed, but through this very fact they acquire yet greater authority. The change affects only the arrogant pretensions of the Schools, which would fain be counted the sole authors and possessors of such truths (as, indeed, they can justly claim to be in many other branches of knowledge), reserving the key to themselves, and communicating to the public their use only—*quod mecum nescit, solus vult scire videri.* At the same time due regard is paid to the more moderate claims of the speculative philosopher. He still remains the   B xxx sole authority in regard to a science which benefits the public without their knowing it, namely, the critique of reason. That critique can never become popular, and indeed there is no need that it should. For just as fine-spun arguments in favour of useful truths make no appeal to the general mind, so neither do the subtle objections that can be raised against them. On the other hand, both inevitably present themselves to everyone who rises to the height of speculation; and it is therefore the duty of the Schools, by means of a thorough investigation of the rights of speculative reason, once for all to prevent the scandal which, sooner or later, is sure to break out even among the masses, as the result of the disputes in which metaphysicians (and, as such, finally also the clergy) inevitably become involved to the consequent perversion of their teaching. Criticism alone can sever the root of *materialism, fatalism, atheism, free-thinking, fanaticism,* and *superstition,* which can be injurious universally; as well as of *idealism,* and *scepticism,* which are dangerous chiefly to the Schools, and hardly allow of being handed on to the public. If governments think proper to interfere with   B xx: the affairs of the learned, it would be more consistent with a wise regard for science as well as for mankind, to favour the freedom of such criticism, by which alone the labours of reason can be established on a firm basis, than to support the ridiculous despotism of the Schools, which raise a loud cry of public danger over the destruction of cobwebs to which the public has never paid any attention, and the loss of which it can therefore never feel.

This critique is not opposed to the *dogmatic procedure* of reason in its pure knowledge, as science, for that must always be dogmatic, that is, yield strict proof from sure principles *a priori*. It is opposed only to *dogmatism,* that is, to the presumption that it is possible to make progress with pure knowledge, according to principles, from concepts alone (those that are philosophical), as reason has long been in the habit of doing; and that it is possible to do this without having first investigated in what way and by what right reason has come into possession of these concepts. Dogmatism is thus the dogmatic procedure of pure reason, *without previous criticism of its own powers.* In withstanding dogmatism we must not allow ourselves to give free rein to that loquacious shallowness, which assumes for itself the name of popularity, nor yet to scepticism, which makes short work with all metaphysics. On the contrary, such criticism is the necessary preparation for a thoroughly grounded metaphysics, which, as science, must necessarily be developed dogmatically, according to the strictest demands of system, in such manner as to satisfy not the general public but the requirements of the Schools. For that is a demand to which it stands pledged, and which it may not neglect, namely, that it carry out its work entirely *a priori,* to the complete satisfaction of speculative reason. In the execution of the plan prescribed by the critique, that is, in the future system of metaphysics, we have therefore to follow the strict method of the celebrated Wolff, the greatest of all the dogmatic philosophers. He was the first to show by example (and by his example he awakened that spirit of thoroughness which is not extinct in Germany) how the secure progress of a science is to be attained only through orderly establishment of principles, clear determination of concepts, insistence upon strictness of proof, and avoidance of venturesome, non-consecutive steps in our inferences. He was thus peculiarly well fitted to raise metaphysics to the dignity of a science, if only

it had occurred to him to prepare the ground beforehand by a critique of the organ, that is, of pure reason itself. The blame for his having failed to do so lies not so much with himself as with the dogmatic way of thinking prevalent in his day, and with which the philosophers of his time, and of all previous times, have no right to reproach one another. Those who reject both the method of Wolff and the procedure of a critique of pure reason can have no other aim than to shake off the fetters of *science* altogether, and thus to change work into play, certainty into opinion, philosophy into philodoxy.

Now, *as regards this second edition,* I have, as is fitting, endeavoured to profit by the opportunity, in order to remove, wherever possible, difficulties and obscurity which, not perhaps without my fault, may have given rise to the many misunderstandings into which even acute thinkers have fallen in passing judgment upon my book. In the propositions themselves and their proofs, and also in the form and completeness of the [architectonic] plan, I have found nothing to alter. This is due partly to the long examination to which I have subjected them, before offering them[10] to the public, partly to the nature of the subject-matter with which we are dealing. For pure speculative reason has a structure wherein everything is an *organ,* the whole being for the sake of every part, and every part for the sake of all the others, so that even the smallest imperfection, be it a fault (error) or a deficiency, must inevitably betray itself in use. This system, will, as I hope, maintain, throughout the future, this unchangeableness. It is not self-conceit which justifies me in this confidence, but the evidence experimentally obtained through the parity of the result, whether we proceed from the smallest elements to the whole of pure reason or reverse-wise from the whole (for this also is presented to reason through its final end in the sphere of the practical) to each part. Any attempt to change even the smallest part at once gives rise to contradictions, not merely in the system, but in human reason in general. As to the mode of *exposition,* on the other hand, much still remains to be done; and in this edition I have sought to make

B xxxvii

B xxxviii

xxvi

---

10 [Reading, with Erdmann, *sie* for *es.*]

improvements which should help in removing, first, the misunderstanding in regard to the Aesthetic, especially concerning the concept of time; secondly, the obscurity of the deduction, of the concepts of understanding; thirdly, a supposed want of sufficient evidence in the proofs of the principles of pure understanding; and finally, the false interpretation placed upon the paralogisms charged against rational psychology. Beyond this point, that is, beyond the end of the first chapter of the Transcendental Dialectic, I have made no changes in the mode of exposition.*f* Time was too short to allow of further changes; and besides, I have not found among competent and impartial critics any misapprehension in regard to the remaining sections. Though I shall not venture to name these critics with the praise that is their due, the attention which I have paid to their comments will easily be recognised in the [new] passages [above mentioned]. These improvements involve, however, a small loss, not to be prevented save by making the book too voluminous, namely, that I have had to omit or abridge certain passages, which, though not indeed essential to the completeness of the whole, may yet be missed by many

B xxxix
B xl
B xli

B xlii

readers as otherwise helpful. Only so could I obtain space for what, as I hope, is now a more intelligible exposition, which, though altering absolutely nothing in the fundamentals of the propositions put forward or even in their proofs, yet here and there departs so far from the previous method of treatment, that mere interpolations could not be made to suffice. This loss, which is small and can be remedied by consulting the first edition, will, I hope, be compensated by the greater clearness of the new text. I have observed, with pleasure and thankfulness, in various published works—alike in critical reviews and in independent treatises—that the spirit of thoroughness is not extinct in Germany, but has only been temporarily overshadowed by the prevalence of a pretentiously free manner of thinking; and that the thorny paths of the Critique have not discouraged courageous and clear heads from setting themselves to master my book—a work which leads to a methodical, and as such alone enduring, and therefore most necessary, science of pure reason. To these worthy men, who so happily combine thoroughness of insight with a talent for lucid exposition—which I cannot

B xlii

B l

---

f The only addition, strictly so called, though one affecting the method of proof only, is the new refutation of psychological *idealism* (cf. below, p. 244), and a strict (also, as I believe, the only possible) proof of the objective reality of outer intuition. However harmless idealism may be considered in respect of the essential aims of metaphysics (though, in fact, it is not thus harmless), it still remains a scandal to philosophy and to human reason in general that the existence of things outside us (from which we derive the whole material of knowledge, even for our inner sense) must be accepted merely on *faith,* and that if anyone thinks good to doubt their existence, we are unable to counter his doubts by any satisfactory proof. Since there is some obscurity in the expressions used in the proof, from the third line to the sixth line, I beg to alter the passage as follows: *"But this permanent cannot be an intuition in me. For all grounds of determination of my existence which are to be met with in me are representations; and as representations themselves require a permanent distinct from them, in relation to which their change, end so my existence in the time wherein they change, may be determined."* To this proof it will probably be objected, that I am immediately conscious only of that which is in me, that is, of my

representation of outer things; and consequently that it must still remain uncertain whether outside me there is anything corresponding to it, or not. But through inner *experience* I am conscious of *my existence* in time (consequently also of its determinability in time), and this is more than to be conscious merely of my representation. It is identical with the *empirical consciousness of my existence,* which is determinable only through relation to something which, while bound up with my existence, is outside me. This consciousness of my existence in time is bound up in the way of identity[11] with the consciousness of a relation to something outside me, and it is therefore experience not invention, sense not imagination, which inseparably connects this outside something with my inner sense. For outer sense is already in itself a relation of intuition to something actual outside me, and the reality of outer sense, in its distinction from imagination, rests simply on that which is here found to take place, namely, its being inseparably bound up with inner experience, as the condition of its possibility. If, with the *intellectual consciousness* of my existence, in the representation 'I am', which accompanies all my judgments and acts of understanding, I could at the

[11] [*identisch verbunden.*]

regard myself as possessing—I leave the task of perfecting what, here and there, in its exposition, is still somewhat defective; for in this regard the danger is not that of being refuted, but of not being understood. From now on, though I cannot allow myself to enter into controversy, I shall take careful note of all suggestions, be they from friends or from opponents, for use, in accordance with this propaedeutic, in the further elaboration of the system. In the course of these labours I have advanced somewhat far in years (this month I reach my sixty-fourth year), and I must be careful with my time if I am to succeed in my proposed scheme of providing a metaphysic of nature and of morals which will confirm the truth of my Critique in the two fields, of speculative and of practical reason. The clearing up of the obscurities in the present work—they are hardly to be avoided in a new enterprise—and the defence of it as a whole, I must therefore leave to those worthy men who have made my teaching their own. A philosophical work cannot be armed at all points, like a mathematical treatise, and may there-

xliv

fore be open to objection in this or that respect, while yet the structure of the system, taken in its unity, is not in the least endangered. Few have the versatility of mind to familiarise themselves with a new system; and owing to the general distaste for all innovation, still fewer have the inclination to do so. If we take single passages, torn from their contexts, and compare them with one another, apparent contradictions are not likely to be lacking, especially in a work that is written with any freedom of expression. In the eyes of those who rely on the judgment of others, such contradictions have the effect of placing the work in an unfavourable light; but they are easily resolved by those who have mastered the idea of the whole. If a theory has in itself stability, the stresses and strains which may at first have seemed very threatening to it serve only, in the course of time, to smooth away its inequalities; and if men of impartiality, insight, and true popularity devote themselves to its exposition, it may also, in a short time, secure for itself the necessary elegance of statement.

---

same time connect a determination of my existence through *intellectual intuition,* the consciousness of a relation to something outside me would not be required. But though that intellectual consciousness does indeed come first,[12] the inner intuition, in which my existence can alone be determined, is sensible and is bound up with the condition of time. This determination, however, and therefore the inner experience itself, depends upon something permanent which is not in me, and consequently can be only in something outside me, to which I must regard myself as standing in relation. The reality of outer sense is thus necessarily bound up with inner sense, if experience in general is to be possible at all; that is, I am just as certainly conscious that there are things outside me, which are in relation to my sense, as I am conscious that I myself exist as determined in time. In order to determine to which given intuitions objects outside me actually correspond, and which therefore belong to outer *sense* (to which, and not to the faculty of imagination, they are to be ascribed), we must in each single case appeal to the rules according to which experience in general, even inner experience, is distinguished from imagination—the proposition that there is

B xli

[12] [*vorangeht.*]

such a thing as outer experience being always presupposed. This further remark may be added. The representation of something *permanent* in existence is not the same as *permanent representation.* For though the representation of [something permanent][13] may be very transitory and variable like all our other representations, not excepting those of matter, it yet refers to something permanent. This latter must therefore be an external thing distinct from all my representations, and its existence must be included in the *determination* of my own existence, constituting with it but a single experience such as would not take place even inwardly if it were not also at the same time, in part, outer. How this should be possible we are as little capable of explaining further as we are of accounting for our being able to think the abiding in time, the coexistence of which with the changing generates the concept of alteration.

[13] [Reading, with Wille, *jene for diese.*]

REVIEW QUESTIONS

1. What is Kant's "Copernican revolution" in the theory of knowledge? How is his view a dramatic departure from the past?

2. How does Kant's view of a priori and a posteriori knowledge differ from that of David Hume? What does he mean by "But though all our knowledge begins with experience, it does not follow that it all arises out of experience"?

3. For Kant, mathematical truth is not analytic but synthetic a priori. What is the difference, and why does this distinction matter?

4. What does Kant mean when he says we should always treat people as ends in themselves, never as merely a means to an end? By this principle, what kinds of behavior toward others would be impermissible?

5. What is the difference between hypothetical and categorical imperatives?

6. What is the first formulation of the Categorical Imperative? What does Kant mean by universalizing a moral maxim?

7. How does Kant's Categorical Imperative apply to the case of a lying promise? Does he allow any exceptions to a categorical imperative?

23

GEORG WILHELM FRIEDRICH HEGEL

Georg W. F. Hegel was born in Stuttgart, Germany, in 1770 and became the most prominent Continental philosopher in the nineteenth century. Taught Greek by his mother, he developed a love of Greek philosophy while still in high school. In 1788 he entered the University of Tubingen to study theology. As a student he became friends with the poet
Holderlin and the philosopher Schelling. After graduating from the university in 1793, he
became a family tutor in Bern and Frankfurt for six years. In 1799 he became an unsalaried
lecturer at the University of Jena. While there he wrote his major work, *The Phenomenology of Mind*, a portion of which is reprinted here. The work was completed just as Napoleon
launched the Battle of Jena, which closed the university. Hegel became the principal of a
high school, married, and had two sons. In 1816 he joined the faculty of Heidelberg, where
he continued to develop his ideas, publishing the *Science of Logic* (1816). In 1818 he was
appointed to the prestigious Chair of Philosophy at the University of Berlin, where he published his *Philosophy of Right* (1821). He died of cholera in 1831.

Hegel is the pivotal philosopher between Kant and Marx. He was profoundly influenced
by Kant, yet criticized him and then transformed his system into Absolute Idealism. He
himself was then subjected to the same treatment by Karl Marx, who criticized and transformed his dialectical idealism into dialectical materialism. Hegel thought that Kant had
brought philosophy to a new crisis by denying knowledge of metaphysical truth. Hegel accepted Kant's criticisms of previous rationalist thought but thought Kant had not gone far

enough. He rejected Kant's theory of knowledge, which claimed that we had no meta-physical knowledge, that we must be in ignorance regarding the thing-in-itself, ultimate re-ality. Following criticisms inaugurated by his friend Johann Fichte (1762–1814), Hegel pointed out that Kant's system contained an apparent contradiction: he says that we are both ignorant of the thing-in-itself, reality (the *noumenal world*), and that we know that it exists and *causes* our appearances. If we are ignorant of the noumenal world, how do we know that it exists at all? and how do we know that *it* causes our perceptions?

Hegel transformed Kant's categories of the mind into his system of Absolute Idealism, building a comprehensive and coherentist metaphysical system. Whereas Kant thought the categories were purely subjective, part of the structure of our minds, Hegel argued that they had objective reality.

The intricacies of Hegel's dialectical method, the overcoming internal contradictions in-herent in the triadic process of "Being-Nothingness" and "Becoming" and the resolution of the dichotomy of "Idea-Nature" in "Spirit" have challenged some of the greatest minds in Western philosophy. Hegel defines "dialectics" this way:

> There are three aspects in every thought which is logically real or true: (1) the abstract or ratio-nal form, which says what something is; (2) the dialectical negation, which says what something is not; and (3) the speculative-concrete comprehension: A is also that which it is not, A is not-A. These three aspects do not constitute three parts of logic, but are moments of everything that is logically real or true. They belong to every philosophical concept. Every concept is rational, is abstractly opposed to another, and is united in comprehension together with its opposites. This is the definition of dialectic.[1]

Take Hegel's notion of being. This is a pure category or concept that we must think, not the being of this or that, but pure being, such as we might arrive at by subtracting all other qualities from any existing object until we are left simply with its *existence*. Take this table (or pen or any object you like). Let us abstract its properties—in the case of the table, its shape, its size, its wood, its color, its hardness, and every other property it has, and leave only its bare existence. What do we have left? Mere "isness," "existence"—that which this table has in common with every other existent but which it doesn't have in common with possible but nonexistent tables, centaurs, unicorns, and so forth. Such being has in it no *de-terminations* or qualities whatsoever, for we have subtracted all of these determinations from it. It is therefore completely indeterminate, vacant, and empty. It has no content, what-soever. It is simply nothing. Being, therefore, amounts to nothing. And the pure concept of being is thus seen to contain—dialectically—the idea of nothingness. So we have deduced the idea of nothingness from the idea of being.

Of course, this doesn't mean that existing things like tables and chairs are nothing, only that being itself is identical with nothing. Since being and nothing are identical, and we can deduce one from another, we can speak of a *passage* from being to nothing—and vice versa. Nothing is an emptiness, emptiness is pure being, hence nothing is pure being. So there is a two-way traffic between the concepts, and hence we arrived at the third category, *be-coming*, the passage from being to nothing.

Hegel applies this method to history. Spirit or Mind demands an opposite, which Hegel shows to be Nature (or Matter in motion), its other. In overcoming this otherness, Spirit truly becomes itself. Nature is the other which is implicit in spirit but which is, in the first instance, opposed to it.

---

[1] *Encyclopedia of Philosophy,* p. 82.

Nature must be seen as a set of stages, leading up from inert mechanisms and mutual externality to organized life, which in its higher, animal forms is conscious and spiritual, and spirit must develop from a state in which it can understand and transform nature, and ultimately achieve the philosophico-religious understanding of itself as the immanent end of nature, thereby achieving absoluteness.

The Absolute Spirit is Hegel's interpretation of God, that which works through history, suffering and struggling to realize perfection, to find unity through plurality, to overcome alienation and bring forth the ultimate synthesis. "It is only in and through the Golgotha of the Absolute Spirit that its truth and kingdom are secured."

We will note the diverse reactions to this method and Hegel's vision in Kierkegaard and Marx.

In our selection from *The Phenomenology of Mind*, Hegel develops his dialectic of consciousness where the master finds himself in bondage to and dependent on the slave for his status and well-being. The solution is to reach a state of freedom, where there is neither oppressor nor oppressed.

FOR FURTHER READING

Kaufmann, Walter. *Hegel: Reinterpretation, Text, and Commentary* (Doubleday, 1965).

Inwood, Michael, ed. *Hegel* (Oxford University Press, 1985).

MacIntyre, Alasdair, ed. *Hegel: A Collection of Critical Essays* (University of Notre Dame Press, 1972).

Mure, G. R. *An Introduction to Hegel* (Oxford University Press, 1940).

Norman, Richard. *Hegel's Phenomenology: A Philosophical Introduction* (Brighton, 1976).

Singer, Peter. *Hegel* (Oxford University Press, 1983).

Soll, Ivan. *An Introduction to Hegel's Metaphysics* (University of Chicago, 1969).

Solomon, Robert. *From Hegel to Existentialism* (Oxford University Press, 1987).

Stace, W. T. *The Philosophy of Hegel* (Dover Reprint, 1924, 1955).

Taylor, Charles, *Hegel* (Cambridge University Press, 1975).

PHENOMENOLOGY OF SPIRIT

LORDSHIP AND BONDAGE

Self-consciousness exists in itself and for itself, in that, and by the fact that it exists for another self-consciousness; that is to say, it *is* only by being acknowledged or "recognized." The conception of this its unity in its duplication, of infinitude realizing itself in self-consciousness, has many sides to it and encloses within it elements of varied significance. Thus its moments must on the one hand be strictly kept apart in detailed distinctiveness, and, on the other, in this distinction must, at the same time, also be taken as not distinguished, or must always be accepted and understood in their opposite sense. This double meaning of what is distinguished lies in the nature of self-consciousness:—of its being infinite, or directly the opposite of the determinateness in which it is fixed. The detailed exposition of the notion of this spiritual unity in its duplication will bring before us the process of Recognition.

Self-consciousness has before it another self-consciousness; it has come outside itself. This has a

From *The Phenomenology of Mind*, trans. J.B. Baillie (1910). Reprinted with permission.

double significance. First it has lost its own self, since it finds itself as an *other* being; secondly, it has thereby sublated that other, for it does not regard the other as essentially real, but sees its own self in the other.

It must cancel this its other. To do so is the sublation of that first double meaning, and is therefore a second double meaning. First, it must set itself to sublate the other independent being, in order thereby to become certain of itself as true being, secondly, it thereupon proceeds to sublate its own self, for this other is itself.

This sublation in a double sense of its otherness in a double sense is at the same time a return in a double sense into its self. For, firstly, through sublation, it gets back itself, because it becomes one with itself again through the canceling of *its* otherness; but secondly, it likewise gives otherness back again to the other self-consciousness, for it was aware of being in the other, it cancels this its own being in the other and thus lets the other again go free.

This process of self-consciousness in relation to another self-consciousness has in this manner been represented as the action of one alone. But this action on the part of the one has itself the double significance of being at once its own action and the action of that other as well. For the other is likewise independent, shut up within itself, and there is nothing in it which is not there through itself. The first does not have the object before it only in the passive form characteristic primarily of the object of desire, but as an object existing independently for itself, over which therefore it has no power to do anything for its own behoof, if that object does not *per se* do what the first does to it. The process then is absolutely the double process of both self-consciousnesses. Each sees the other do the same as itself; each itself does what it demands on the part of the other, and for that reason does what it does only so far as the other does the same. Action from one side only would be useless, because what is to happen can only be brought about by means of both.

The action has then a *double entente* not only in the sense that it is an act done to itself as well as to the other, but also in the sense that the act *simpliciter* is the act of the one as well as of the other regardless of their distinction.

In this movement we see the process repeated which came before us as the play of forces; in the present case, however, it is found in consciousness. What in the former had effect only for us [contemplating experience], holds here for the terms themselves. The middle term is self-consciousness which breaks itself up into the extremes; and each extreme is this interchange of its own determinateness, and complete transition into the opposite. While *qua* consciousness, it no doubt comes outside itself, still, in being outside itself, it is at the same time restrained within itself, it exists for itself, and its self-externalization is for consciousness. *Consciousness* finds that it immediately is and is not another consciousness, as also that this other is for itself only when it cancels itself as existing for itself, and has self-existence only in the self-existence of the other. Each is the mediating term to the other, through which each mediates and unites itself with itself; and each is to itself and to the other an immediate self-existing reality, which, at the same time, exists thus for itself only through this mediation. They recognize themselves as mutually recognizing one another.

This pure conception of recognition, of duplication of self-consciousness within its unity, we must now consider in the way its process appears for self-consciousness. It will, in the first place, present the aspect of the disparity of the two, or the break-up of the middle term into the extremes, which, *qua* extremes, are opposed to one another, and of which one is merely recognized, while the other only recognizes.

Self-consciousness is primarily simply existence for self, self-identity by exclusion of every other from itself. It takes its essential nature and absolute object to be Ego; and in this immediacy, in this bare fact of its self-existence, it is individual. That which for it is other stands as unessential object, as object with the impress and character of negation. But the other is also a self-consciousness; an individual makes its appearance in antithesis to an individual. Appearing thus in their immediacy, they are for each other in the manner of ordinary objects. They are independent individual forms, modes of consciousness that have not risen above the bare level of life (for the existent object here has been determined as life). They are, moreover, forms of consciousness which have not yet accomplished for one another the process of absolute abstraction, of uprooting all immediate existence, and of being merely the bare, negative fact of self-identical consciousness; or, in other words, have not yet revealed themselves to each other as existing purely for themselves, i.e., as self-consciousness. Each is indeed certain of its own self, but not of the other, and hence its own certainty of itself is still without truth. For its truth would be merely that its own individual existence for itself would be shown to it to be an independent object or, which is the same thing, that the object would be exhibited as this pure certainty of itself. By the notion of recognition, however, this is not possible, except in the form that as the other is for it, so it is for the other; each in its self through its own action and again through the action of the other achieves this pure abstraction of existence for self.

The presentation of itself, however, as pure abstraction of self-consciousness consists in showing itself as a pure negation of its objective form, or in showing that it is fettered to no determinate existence, that it is not bound at all by the particularity everywhere characteristic of existence as such, and is *not* tied up with life. The process of bringing all this out involves a twofold action—action on the part of the other and action on the part of itself. In so far as it is the other's action, each aims at the destruction and death of the other. But in this there is implicated also the second kind of action, self-activity; for the former implies that it risks its own life. The relation of both self-consciousnesses is in this way so constituted that they prove themselves and each other through a life-and-death struggle. They must enter into this struggle, for they must bring their certainty of themselves, the certainty of being for themselves, to the level of objective truth, and make this a fact both in the case of the other and in their own case as well. And it is solely by risking life that freedom is obtained; only thus is it tried and proved that the essential nature of self-consciousness is not bare existence, is not the merely immediate form in which it at first makes its appearance, is not its mere absorption in the expanse of life. Rather it is thereby guaranteed that there is nothing present but what might be taken as a vanishing moment—that self-consciousness is merely pure self-existence, being-for-self. The individual, who has not staked his life,

may, no doubt, be recognized as a Person; but he has not attained the truth of this recognition as an independent self-consciousness. In the same way each must aim at the death of the other, as it risks its own life thereby; for that other is to it of no more worth than itself; the other's reality is presented to the former as an external other, as outside itself; it must cancel that externality. The other is a purely existent consciousness and entangled in manifold ways; it must view its otherness as pure existence for itself or as absolute negation.

This trial by death, however, cancels both the truth which was to result from it, and therewith the certainty of self altogether. For just as life is the natural "position" of consciousness, independence without absolute negativity, so death is the natural "negation" of consciousness, negation without independence, which thus remains without the requisite significance of actual recognition. Through death, doubtless, there has arisen the certainty that both did stake their life, and held it lightly both in their own case and in the case of the other; but that is not for those who underwent this struggle. They cancel their consciousness which had its place in this alien element of natural existence; in other words, they cancel themselves and are sublated as terms or extremes seeking to have existence on their own account. But along with this there vanishes from the play of change the essential moment, viz. that of breaking up into extremes with opposite characteristics; and the middle term collapses into a lifeless unity which is broken up into lifeless extremes, merely existent and not opposed. And the two do not mutually give and receive one another back from each other through consciousness; they let one another go quite indifferently, like things. Their act is abstract negation, not the negation characteristic of consciousness, which cancels in such a way that it preserves and maintains what is sublated, and thereby survives its being sublated.

In this experience self-consciousness becomes aware that *life* is as essential to it as pure self-consciousness. In immediate self-consciousness the simple ego is absolute object, which, however, is for us or in itself absolute mediation, and has as its essential moment substantial and solid independence. The dissolution of that simple unit is the result of the first experience; through this there is posited a pure self-consciousness, and a consciousness which is not purely for itself, but for another, i.e. as an existent consciousness, consciousness in the form and shape of thinghood. Both moments are essential, since, in the first instance, they are unlike and opposed, and their reflexion into unity has not yet come to light, they stand as two opposed forms or modes of consciousness. The one is independent, and its essential nature is to be for itself; the other is dependent, and its essence is life or existence for another. The former is the Master, or Lord, the latter the Bondsman.

The master is the consciousness that exists for *itself*; but no longer merely the general notion of existence for self. Rather, it is a consciousness existing on its own account which is mediated with itself through an other consciousness, i.e. through an other whose very nature implies that it is bound up with an independent being or with thinghood in general. The master brings himself into relation to both these moments, to a thing as such, the object of desire, and to the consciousness whose essential character is thinghood. And since the master, is (*a*) *qua* notion of self-consciousness, an immediate relation of self-existence, but (*b*) is now moreover at the same time mediation, or a being-for-self which is for itself only through an other—he [the master] stands in relation (*a*) immediately to both (*b*) mediately to each through the other. The master relates himself to the bondsman mediately through independent existence, for that is precisely what keeps the bondsman in thrall; it is his chain, from which he could not in the struggle get away, and for that reason he proved himself to be dependent, to have his independence in the shape of thinghood. The master, however, is the power controlling this state of existence, for he has shown in the struggle that he holds it to be merely something negative. Since he is the power dominating existence, while this existence again is the power controlling the other [the bondsman], the master holds, *par consequence*, the other in subordination. In the same way the master relates himself to the thing mediately through the bondsman. The bondsman being a self-consciousness in the broad sense, also takes up a negative attitude to things and cancels them; but

the thing is, at the same time, independent for him, and, in consequence, he cannot, with all his negating, get so far as to annihilate it outright and be done with it; that is to say, he merely works on it. To the master, on the other hand, by means of this mediating process, belongs the immediate relation, in the sense of the pure negation of it, in other words he gets the enjoyment. What mere desire did not attain, he now succeeds in attaining, viz. to have done with the thing, and find satisfaction in enjoyment. Desire alone did not get the length of this, because of the independence of the thing. The master, however, who has interposed the bondsman between it and himself, thereby relates himself merely to the dependence of the thing, and enjoys it without qualification and without reserve. The aspect of its independence he leaves to the bondsman, who labours upon it.

In these two moments, the master gets his recognition through an other consciousness, for in them the latter affirms itself as unessential, both by working upon the thing, and, on the other hand, by the fact of being dependent on a determinate existence; in neither case can this other get the mastery over existence, and succeed in absolutely negating it. We have thus here this moment of recognition, viz. that the other consciousness cancels itself as self-existent, and, *ipso facto*, itself does what the first does to it. In the same way we have the other moment, that this action on the part of the second is the action proper of the first; for what is done by the bondsman is properly an action on the part of the master. The latter exists only for himself, that is his essential nature; he is the negative power without qualification, a power to which the thing is naught. And he is thus the absolutely essential act in this situation, while the bondsman is not so, he is an unessential activity. But for recognition proper there is needed the moment that what the master does to the other he should also do to himself, and what the bondsman does to himself, he should do to the other also. On that account a form of recognition has arisen that is one-sided and unequal.

In all this, the unessential consciousness is, for the master, the object which embodies the truth of his certainty of himself. But it is evident that this object does not correspond to its notion; for, just where the master has effectively achieved lordship, he really finds that something has come about quite different from an independent consciousness. It is not an independent, but rather a dependent consciousness that he has achieved. He is thus not assured of self-existence as his truth; he finds that his truth is rather the unessential consciousness, and the fortuitous unessential action of that consciousness.

The truth of the independent consciousness is accordingly the consciousness of the bondsman. This doubtless appears in the first instance outside itself, and not as the truth of self-consciousness. But just as lordship showed its essential nature to be the reverse of what it wants to be, so, too, bondage will, when completed, pass into the opposite of what it immediately is: being a consciousness repressed within itself, it will enter into itself, and change round into real and true independence.

We have seen what bondage is only in relation to lordship. But it is a self-consciousness, and we have now to consider what it is, in this regard, in and for itself. In the first instance, the master is taken to be the essential reality for the state of bondage; hence, for it, the truth is the independent consciousness existing for itself, although this truth is not taken yet as inherent in bondage itself. Still, it does in fact contain within itself this truth of pure negativity and self-existence, because it has experienced this reality within it. For this consciousness was not in peril and fear for this element or that, nor for this or that moment of time, it was afraid for its entire being; it felt the fear of death, the sovereign master. It has been in that experience melted to its inmost soul, has trembled throughout its every fibre, and all that was fixed and steadfast has quaked within it. This complete perturbation of its entire substance, this absolute dissolution of all its stability into fluent continuity, is, however, the simple, ultimate nature of self-consciousness, absolute negativity, pure self-referent existence, which consequently is involved in this type of consciousness. This moment of pure self-existence is moreover a fact for it; for in the master it finds this as its object. Further, this bondsman's consciousness is not only this total dissolution in a general way; in serving and toiling the bondsman actually carries this out. By serving he cancels in every

particular aspect his dependence on and attachment to natural existence, and by his work removes this existence away.

The feeling of absolute power, however, realized both in general and in the particular form of service, is only dissolution implicitly; and albeit the fear of the lord is the beginning of wisdom, consciousness is not therein aware of being self-existent. Through work and labour, however, this consciousness of the bondsman comes to itself. In the moment which corresponds to desire in the case of the master's consciousness, the aspect of the non-essential relation to the thing seemed to fall to the lot of the servant, since the thing there retained its independence. Desire has reserved to itself the pure negating of the object and thereby unalloyed feeling of self. This satisfaction, however, just for that reason is itself only a state of evanescence, for it lacks objectivity or subsistence. Labour, on the other hand, is desire restrained and checked, evanescence delayed and postponed; in other words, labour shapes and fashions the thing. The negative relation to the object passes into the *form* of the object, into something that is permanent and remains; because it is just for the labourer that the object has independence. This negative mediating agency, this activity giving shape and form, is at the same time the individual existence, the pure self-existence of that consciousness, which now in the work it does is externalized and passes into the condition of permanence. The consciousness that toils and serves accordingly attains by this means the direct apprehension of that independent being as its self.

But again, shaping or forming the object has not only the positive significance that the bondsman becomes thereby aware of himself as factually and objectively self-existent; this type of consciousness has also a negative import, in contrast with its first moment, the element of fear. For in shaping the thing it only becomes aware of its own proper negativity, its existence on its own account, as an object, through the fact that it cancels the actual form confronting it. But this objective negative element is precisely the alien, external reality, before which it trembled. Now, however, it destroys this extraneous alien negative, affirms and sets itself up as a negative in the element of permanence, and thereby becomes for itself a self-existence being. In the master, the bondsman feels self-existence to be something external, an objective fact; in fear self-existence is present within himself; in fashioning the thing, self-existence comes to be felt explicitly as his own proper being, and he attains the consciousness that he himself exists in its own right and on its own account (an und für sich). By the fact that the form is objectified, it does not become something other than the consciousness moulding the thing through work; for just that form is his pure self-existence, which therein becomes truly realized. Thus precisely in labour where there seemed to be merely some outsider's mind and ideas involved, the bondsman becomes aware, through this rediscovery of himself by himself, of having by himself, of having and being a "mind of his own."

For this reflexion of self into self the two moments, fear and service in general, as also that of formative activity, are necessary: and at the same time both must exist in a universal manner. Without the discipline of service and obedience, fear remains formal and does not spread over the whole known reality of existence. Without the formative activity shaping the thing, fear remains inward and mute, and consciousness does not become objective for itself. Should consciousness shape and form the thing without the initial state of absolute fear, then it has a merely vain and futile "mind of its own"; for its form or negativity is not negativity per se, and hence its formative activity cannot furnish the consciousness of itself as essentially real. If it has endured not absolute fear, but merely some slight anxiety, the negative reality has remained external to it, its substance has not been through and through infected thereby. Since the entire content of its natural consciousness has not tottered and shaken, it is still inherently a determinate mode of being; having a "mind of its own" (der eigene Sinn) is simply stubbornness (Eigensinn), a type of freedom which does not get beyond the attitude of bondage. As little as the pure form can become its essential nature, so little is that form, considered as extending over particulars, a universal formative activity, an absolute notion; it is rather a piece of cleverness which has mastery within a certain range, but not over the universal power nor over the entire objective reality.

REVIEW QUESTIONS

1. What is the basic idea in Hegel's "dialectic"?
2. How does Hegel apply his dialectic (the three-part process of being-nothingness-becoming) to consciousness?
3. What is absolute idealism? What suggestions of absolute idealism can be found in the reading selection?
4. Is Hegel a skeptic? Must an absolute idealist like Hegel be a skeptic? Or does Hegel escape skepticism through his idealism. If so, how?
5. Does Hegel advance the idea that consciousness ultimately reaches a stage of absolute knowledge? If so, how is this knowledge possible?

24

ARTHUR SCHOPENHAUER

Arthur Schopenhauer (1788–1860) ranks among the great Continental philosophers who built elaborate systems of thought and developed ideas that have influenced generations of readers and writers. He was born in Danzig to wealthy, cosmopolitan parents—a successful merchant father with Enlightenment views and varied cultural interests, and an author mother who was, for a time, more famous than her son. Unlike most other thinkers of his day, he was exposed, from a young age, to a variety of cultures and ideas. He was educated in France, Britain, and Germany; was fluent in several modern and classical languages; and studied not only philosophy, but science, Hinduism, and Buddhism.

On several counts, Schopenhauer was a maverick and an eccentric. Contrary to the great rationalist philosophers who preceded him, he thinks the will more fundamental than reason. Against their belief in the possibility of achieving some ultimate good in this life or the next, he posits a universe of suffering and illusion, a troubled reality from which the only true escape is extinction. He is renowned for his pessimism, which seems all the darker when contrasted with the more affirmative thinkers in the Western tradition. Putting no stock in the West's strong Christian ethic, he instead looks to the East to nontheistic Buddhism and to asceticism (although in practice he was hardly ascetic).

Some famous philosophers (David Hume and Baruch Spinoza, for example) are admired for their social virtues and goodness of character. Not so Schopenhauer. On one hand, he was obviously a brilliant intellectual and gifted writer, but he was also a conceited, dour man given to selfishness, pettiness, and quarrels. Once he was irritated by an elderly woman's chatting outside his apartment door, so he hurled her down the stairs. She sustained permanent injuries, for which a court ordered Schopenhauer to pay her an allowance for the rest of her life. When she died years later, he wrote on her death certificate in Latin "The old woman is dead, the burden departs."

The central idea of Schopenhauer's philosophy, articulated in his masterwork *The World as Will and Representation,* is based on a distinction he derives from Immanuel Kant. In *Critique of Pure Reason,* Kant contrasts the world as it is in itself independent of our minds (the *noumena*) with the world as it appears to our perception, the realm of appearances (the *phenomena*). Kant says that the noumenal world, or the thing-in-itself, is unknowable, but Schopenhauer contends that it is none other than the Will, a mindless, timeless, universal desire or striving without purpose or direction. The noumenal world of the Will is the real world, the true substratum behind the appearances. Our individual wills—our desiring, wanting, and craving—are also real, for they are manifestations of, and are identical to, the universal Will. So the separateness of our individual wills is an illusion, just as the rest of our experience is mere phenomena.

For Schopenhauer, the cosmic Will is neither God nor the Good. It is pitiless, blind energy and the source of all suffering. The urgings of the will propel us to pointless strivings, thwarted ends, and painful illusions. Our duty is to conquer the will, to quench the fires of desire, a goal that few ever attain. We may for a moment quiet the will through aesthetic experience, but ultimately there is only one escape. Inspired by Buddhist philosophy, Schopenhauer declares that the true path requires us to extinguish all desire as the ascetic saint does, deny life, and embrace nothingness.

FOR FURTHER READING

Gardiner, Patrick. *Schopenhauer* (Penguin Books, 1967).

Hamlyn, D. W. *Schopenhauer* (Routledge and Kegan Paul, 1980).

Janaway, Christopher. *Schopenhauer: A Very Short Introduction* (Oxford University Press, 2002).

Janaway, Christopher. *Self and World in Schopenhauer's Philosophy* (Oxford University Press, 1989).

Magee, Bryan. *The Philosophy of Schopenhauer* (Oxford University Press, 1997).

Payne, E. F. J. *Arthur Schopenhauer: The World as Will and Representation,* 2 vols. (Dover Publications, 1966, 1969).

Young, Julian. *Willing and Unwilling: A Study in the Philosophy of Arthur Schopenhauer* (Martinus Nijhoff, 1987).

THE WORLD AS WILL AND REPRESENTATION

§ 17

In the first book we considered the representation only as such, and hence only according to the general form. It is true that, so far as the abstract representation, the concept, is concerned, we also obtained a knowledge of it according to its content, in so far as it has all content and meaning only through its relation to the representation of perception, without which it would be worthless and empty. Therefore, directing our attention, entirely to the representation of perception, we shall endeavour to arrive at a knowledge of its content, its more precise determinations, and the forms it presents to us. It will be of

Reprinted from *The World as Will and Representation,* trans. E. F. J. Payne, Dover Publications, 1958.

special interest for us to obtain information about its real significance, that significance, otherwise merely felt, by virtue of which these pictures or images do not march past us strange and meaningless, as they would otherwise inevitably do, but speak to us directly, are understood, and acquire an interest that engrosses our whole nature.

We direct our attention to mathematics, natural science, and philosophy, each of which holds out the hope that it will furnish a part of the information desired. In the first place, we find philosophy to be a monster with many heads, each of which speaks a different language. Of course, they are not all at variance with one another on the point here mentioned, the significance of the representation of perception. For, with the exception of the Sceptics and Idealists, the others in the main speak fairly consistently of an *object* forming the *basis* of the representation. This object indeed is different in its whole being and nature from the representation, but yet is in all respects as like it as one egg is like another. But this does not help us, for we do not at all know how to distinguish that object from the representation. We find that the two are one and the same, for every object always and eternally presupposes a subject, and thus remains representation. We then recognize also that being-object belongs to the most universal form of the representation, which is precisely the division into object and subject. Further, the principle of sufficient reason, to which we here refer, is also for us only the form of the representation, namely the regular and orderly combination of one representation with another, and not the combination of the whole finite or infinite series of representations with something which is not representation at all, and is therefore not capable of being in any way represented. We spoke above of the Sceptics and Idealists, when discussing the controversy about the reality of the external world.

Now if we look to mathematics for the desired more detailed knowledge of the representation of perception, which we have come to know only quite generally according to the mere form, then this science will tell us about these representations only in so far as they occupy time and space, in other words, only in so far as they are quantities. It will state with extreme accuracy the How-many and the How-large; but as this is always only relative, that is to say, a comparison of one representation with another, and even that only from the one-sided aspect of quantity, this too will not be the information for which principally we are looking.

Finally, if we look at the wide province of natural science, which is divided into many fields, we can first of all distinguish two main divisions. It is either a description of forms and shapes, which I call *Morphology;* or an explanation of changes, which I call *Etiology.* The former considers the permanent forms, the latter the changing matter, according to the laws of its transition from one form into another. Morphology is what we call natural history in its whole range, though not in the literal sense of the word. As botany and zoology especially, it teaches us about the various, permanent, organic, and thus definitely determined forms in spite of the incessant change of individuals; and these forms constitute a great part of the content of the perceptive representation. In natural history they are classified, separated, united, and arranged according to natural and artificial systems, and brought under concepts that render possible a survey and knowledge of them all. There is further demonstrated an infinitely fine and shaded analogy in the whole and in the parts of these forms which runs through them all (*unité de plan*),[1] by virtue of which they are like the many different variations on an unspecified theme. The passage of matter into those forms, in other words the origin of individuals, is not a main part of the consideration, for every individual springs from its like through generation, which everywhere is equally mysterious, and has so far baffled clear knowledge. But the little that is known of this finds its place in physiology, which belongs to etiological natural science. Mineralogy, especially where it becomes geology, though it belongs mainly to morphology, also inclines to this etiological science. Etiology proper includes all the branches of natural science in which the main concern everywhere is knowledge of cause and effect. These sciences teach how, according to an invariable rule, one state of matter is necessarily followed by another definite state; how one definite change necessarily conditions and brings about

---

[1] "Unity of plan." [Tr.]

another definite change; this demonstration is called *explanation.* Here we find principally mechanics, physics, chemistry, and physiology.

But if we devote ourselves to its teaching, we soon become aware that the information we are chiefly looking for no more comes to us from etiology than it does from morphology. The latter presents us with innumerable and infinitely varied forms that are nevertheless related by an unmistakable family likeness. For us they are representations that in this way remain eternally strange to us, and, when considered merely in this way, they stand before us like hieroglyphics that are not understood. On the other hand, etiology teaches us that, according to the law of cause and effect, this definite condition of matter produces that other condition, and with this it has explained it, and has done its part. At bottom, however, it does nothing more than show the orderly arrangement according to which the states or conditions appear in space and time, and teach for all cases what phenomenon must necessarily appear at this time and in this place. It therefore determines for them their position in time and space according to a law whose definite content has been taught by experience, yet whose universal form and necessity are known to us independently of experience. But in this way we do not obtain the slightest information about the inner nature of any one of these phenomena. This is called a *natural force,* and lies outside the province of etiological explanation, which calls the unalterable constancy with which the manifestation of such a force appears whenever its known conditions are present, a *law of nature.* But this law of nature, these conditions, this appearance in a definite place at a definite time, are all that it knows, or ever can know. The force itself that is manifested, the inner nature of the phenomena that appear in accordance with those laws, remain for it an eternal secret, something entirely strange and unknown, in the case of the simplest as well as of the most complicated phenomenon. For although etiology has so far achieved its aim most completely in mechanics, and least so in physiology, the force by virtue of which a stone falls to the ground, or one body repels another, is, in its inner nature, just as strange and mysterious as that which produces the movements and growth of an animal. Mechanics presupposes matter, weight, im-

penetrability, communicability of motion through impact, rigidity, and so on as unfathomable; it calls them forces of nature, and their necessary and regular appearance under certain conditions a law of nature. Only then does its explanation begin, and that consists in stating truly and with mathematical precision how, where, and when each force manifests itself, and referring to one of those forces every phenomenon that comes before it. Physics, chemistry, and physiology do the same in their province, only they presuppose much more and achieve less. Consequently, even the most perfect etiological explanation of the whole of nature would never be more in reality than a record of inexplicable forces, and a reliable statement of the rule by which their phenomena appear, succeed, and make way for one another in time and space. But the inner nature of the forces that thus appear was always bound to be left unexplained by etiology, which had to stop at the phenomenon and its arrangement, since the law followed by etiology does not go beyond this. In this respect it could be compared to a section of a piece of marble showing many different veins side by side, but not letting us know the course of these veins from the interior of the marble to the surface. Or, if I may be permitted a facetious comparison, because it is more striking, the philosophical investigator must always feel in regard to the complete etiology of the whole of nature like a man who, without knowing how, is brought into a company quite unknown to him, each member of which in turn presents to him another as his friend and cousin, and thus makes them sufficiently acquainted. The man himself, however, while assuring each person introduced of his pleasure at meeting him, always has on his lips the question: "But how the deuce do I stand to the whole company?"

Hence, about those phenomena known by us only as our representations, etiology can never give us the desired information that leads us beyond them. For after all its explanations, they still stand quite strange before us, as mere representations whose significance we do not understand. The causal connexion merely gives the rule and relative order of their appearance in space and time, but affords us no further knowledge of that which so appears. Moreover, the law of causality itself has validity only for representations, for objects of a definite class, and has meaning only when they are assumed. Hence, like these objects themselves, it always exists only in relation to the subject, and so conditionally. Thus it is just as well known when we start from the subject, i.e., *a priori,* as when we start from the object, i.e., *a posteriori,* as Kant has taught us.

But what now prompts us to make enquiries is that we are not satisfied with knowing that we have representations, that they are such and such, and that they are connected according to this or that law, whose general expression is always the principle of sufficient reason. We want to know the significance of those representations; we ask whether this world is nothing more than representation. In that case, it would inevitably pass by us like an empty dream, or a ghostly vision not worth our consideration. Or we ask whether it is something else, something in addition, and if so what that something is. This much is certain, namely that this something about which we are enquiring must be by its whole nature completely and fundamentally different from the representation; and so the forms and laws of the representation must be wholly foreign to it. We cannot, then, reach it from the representation under the guidance of those laws that merely combine objects, representations, with one another; these are the forms of the principle of sufficient reason.

Here we already see that we can never get at the inner nature of things *from without.* However much we may investigate, we obtain nothing but images and names. We are like a man who goes round a castle, looking in vain for an entrance, and sometimes sketching the façades. Yet this is the path that all philosophers before me have followed.

§ 18

In fact, the meaning that I am looking for of the world that stands before me simply as my representation, or the transition from it as mere representation of the knowing subject to whatever it may be besides this, could never be found if the investigator himself were nothing more than the purely knowing subject (a winged cherub without a body). But he himself is rooted in that world; and thus he finds himself in it as an *individual,* in other words, his

knowledge, which is the conditional supporter of the whole world as representation, is nevertheless given entirely through the medium of a body, and the affections of this body are, as we have shown, the starting-point for the understanding in its perception of this world. For the purely knowing subject as such, this body is a representation like any other, an object among objects. Its movements and actions are so far known to him in just the same way as the changes of all other objects of perception; and they would be equally strange and incomprehensible to him, if their meaning were not unravelled for him in an entirely different way. Otherwise, he would see his conduct follow on presented motives with the constancy of a law of nature, just as the changes of other objects follow upon causes, stimuli, and motives. But he would be no nearer to understanding the influence of the motives than he is to understanding the connexion with its cause of any other effect that appears before him. He would then also call the inner, to him incomprehensible, nature of those manifestations and actions of his body a force, a quality, or a character, just as he pleased, but he would have no further insight into it. All this, however, is not the case; on the contrary, the answer to the riddle is given to the subject of knowledge appearing as individual, and this answer is given in the word *Will.* This and this alone gives him the key to his own phenomenon, reveals to him the significance and shows him the inner mechanism of his being, his actions, his movements. To the subject of knowing, who appears as an individual only through his identity with the body, this body is given in two entirely different ways. It is given in intelligent perception as representation, as an object among objects, liable to the laws of these objects. But it is also given in quite a different way, namely as what is known immediately to everyone, and is denoted by the word *will.* Every true act of his will is also at once and inevitably a movement of his body; he cannot actually will the act without at the same time being aware that it appears as a movement of the body. The act of will and the action of the body are not two different states objectively known, connected by the bond of causality; they do not stand in the relation of cause and effect, but are one and the same thing, though given in two entirely different ways, first quite directly, and then in perception for the understanding. The action of the body is nothing but the act of will objectified, i.e., translated into perception. Later on we shall see that this applies to every movement of the body, not merely to movement following on motives, but also to involuntary movement following on mere stimuli; indeed, that the whole body is nothing but the objectified will, i.e., will that has become representation. All this will follow and become clear in the course of our discussion. Therefore the body, which in the previous book and in the essay *On the Principle of Sufficient Reason* I called the *immediate object,* according to the one-sided viewpoint deliberately taken there (namely that of the representation), will here from another point of view be called the *objectivity of the will.* Therefore, in a certain sense, it can also be said that the will is knowledge *a priori* of the body, and that the body is knowledge *a posteriori* of the will. Resolutions of the will relating to the future are mere deliberations of reason about what will be willed at some time, not real acts of will. Only the carrying out stamps the resolve; till then, it is always a mere intention that can be altered; it exists only in reason, in the abstract. Only in reflection are willing and acting different; in reality they are one. Every true, genuine, immediate act of the will is also at once and directly a manifest act of the body; and correspondingly, on the other hand, every impression on the body is also at once and directly an impression on the will. As such, it is called pain when it is contrary to the will, and gratification or pleasure when in accordance with the will. The gradations of the two are very different. However, we are quite wrong in calling pain and pleasure representations, for they are not these at all, but immediate affections of the will in its phenomenon, the body; an enforced, instantaneous willing or not-willing of the impression undergone by the body. There are only a certain few impressions on the body which do not rouse the will, and through these alone is the body an immediate object of knowledge; for, as perception in the understanding, the body is an indirect object like all other objects. These impressions are therefore to be regarded directly as mere representations, and hence to be excepted from what has just been said. Here are meant the affections of the purely objective senses of sight, hearing, and touch, although only in so far as their organs are affected in the specific natural way that is specially characteristic of them. This is such an exceedingly feeble stimulation of the enhanced and specifically modified sensibility of these parts that it does not affect the will, but, undisturbed by any excitement of the will, only furnishes for the understanding data from which perception arises. But every stronger or heterogeneous affection of these sense-organs is painful, in other words, is against the will; hence they too belong to its objectivity. Weakness of the nerves shows itself in the fact that the impressions which should have merely that degree of intensity that is sufficient to make them data for the understanding, reach the higher degree at which they stir the will, that is to say, excite pain or pleasure, though more often pain. This pain, however, is in part dull and inarticulate; thus it not merely causes us to feel painfully particular tones and intense light, but also gives rise generally to a morbid and hypochondriacal disposition without being distinctly recognized. The identity of the body and the will further shows itself, among other things, in the fact that every vehement and excessive movement of the will, in other words, every emotion, agitates the body and its inner workings directly and immediately, and disturbs the course of its vital functions. This is specially discussed in *The Will in Nature,* second edition, p. 27.

Finally, the knowledge I have of my will, although an immediate knowledge, cannot be separated from that of my body. I know my will not as a whole, not as a unity, not completely according to its nature, but only in its individual acts, and hence in time, which is the form of my body's appearing, as it is of every body. Therefore, the body is the condition of knowledge of my will. Accordingly, I cannot really imagine this will without my body. In the essay *On the Principle of Sufficient Reason* the will, or rather the subject of willing, is treated as a special class of representations or objects. But even there we saw this object coinciding with the subject, in other words, ceasing to be object. We then called this coincidence the miracle κατ᾽ ἐξοχήν;[2] to a certain extent the whole

---

[2] *"par excellence."* [Tr.]

of the present work is an explanation of this. In so far as I know my will really as object, I know it as body; but then I am again at the first class of representations laid down in that essay, that is, again at real objects. As we go on, we shall see more and more that the first class of representations finds its explanation, its solution, only in the fourth class enumerated in that essay, which could no longer be properly opposed to the subject as object; and that, accordingly, we must learn to understand the inner nature of the law of causality valid in the first class, and of what happens according to this law, from the law of motivation governing the fourth class.

The identity of the will and of the body, provisionally explained, can be demonstrated only as is done here, and that for the first time, and as will be done more and more in the further course of our discussion. In other words, it can be raised from immediate consciousness, from knowledge in the concrete, to rational knowledge of reason, or be carried over into knowledge in the abstract. On the other hand, by its nature it can never be demonstrated, that is to say, deduced as indirect knowledge from some other more direct knowledge, for the very reason that it is itself the most direct knowledge. If we do not apprehend it and stick to it as such, in vain shall we expect to obtain it again in some indirect way as derived knowledge. It is a knowledge of quite a peculiar nature, whose truth cannot therefore really be brought under one of the four headings by which I have divided all truth in the essay *On the Principle of Sufficient Reason,* § 29 *seqq.,* namely, logical, empirical, transcendental, and metalogical. For it is not, like all these, the reference of an abstract representation to another representation, or to the necessary form of intuitive or of abstract representing, but it is the reference of a judgement to the relation that a representation of perception, namely the body, has to that which is not a representation at all, but is *toto genere* different therefrom, namely will. I should therefore like to distinguish this truth from every other, and call it *philosophical truth* κατ᾽ ἐξοχήν. We can turn the expression of this truth in different ways and say: My body and my will are one; or, What as representation of perception I call my body, I call my will in so far as I am conscious of it in an entirely different way comparable with no other; or, My body is the *objectivity*

of my will; or, Apart from the fact that my body is my representation, it is still my will, and so on.[3]

§ 19

Whereas in the first book we were reluctantly forced to declare our own body to be mere representation of the knowing subject, like all the other objects of this world of perception, it has now become clear to us that something in the consciousness of everyone distinguishes the representation of his own body from all others that are in other respects quite like it. This is that the body occurs in consciousness in quite another way, *toto genere* different, that is denoted by the word *will.* It is just this double knowledge of our own body which gives us information about that body itself, about its action and movement following on motives, as well as about its suffering through outside impressions, in a word, about what it is, not as representation, but as something over and above this, and hence what it is *in itself.* We do not have such immediate information about the nature, action, and suffering of any other real objects.

The knowing subject is an individual precisely by reason of this special relation to the one body which, considered apart from this, is for him only a representation like all other representations. But the relation by virtue of which the knowing subject is an *individual,* subsists for that very reason only between him and one particular representation among all his representations. He is therefore conscious of this particular representation not merely as such, but at the same time in a quite different way, namely as a will. But if he abstracts from that special relation, from that twofold and completely heterogeneous knowledge of one and the same thing, then that one thing, the body, is a representation like all others. Therefore, in order to understand where he is in this matter, the knowing individual must either assume that the distinctive feature of that one representation is to be found merely in the fact that his knowledge stands in this double reference only to that one representation; that only into this one object of perception is an insight in two ways at the same time open to him;

---

[3]Cf. chap. 18 of volume 2.

and that this is to be explained not by a difference of this object from all others, but only by a difference between the relation of his knowledge to this one object and its relation to all others. Or he must assume that this one object is essentially different from all others; that it alone among all objects is at the same time will and representation, the rest, on the other hand, being mere representation, i.e., mere phantoms. Thus, he must assume that his body is the only real individual in the world, i.e., the only phenomenon of will, and the only immediate object of the subject. That the other objects, considered as mere *representations,* are like his body, in other words, like this body fill space (itself perhaps existing only as representation), and also, like this body, operate in space—this, I say, is demonstrably certain from the law of causality, which is *a priori* certain for representations, and admits of no effect without a cause. But apart from the fact that we can infer from the effect only a cause in general, not a similar cause, we are still always in the realm of the mere representation, for which alone the law of causality is valid, and beyond which it can never lead us. But whether the objects known to the individual only as representations are yet, like his own body, phenomena of a will, is, as stated in the previous book, the proper meaning of the question as to the reality of the external world. To deny this is the meaning of *theoretical egoism,* which in this way regards as phantoms all phenomena outside its own will, just as practical egoism does in a practical respect; thus in it a man regards and treats only his own person as a real person, and all others as mere phantoms. Theoretical egoism, of course, can never be refuted by proofs, yet in philosophy it has never been positively used otherwise than as a sceptical sophism, i.e., for the sake of appearance. As a serious conviction, on the other hand, it could be found only in a madhouse; as such it would then need not so much a refutation as a cure. Therefore we do not go into it any further, but regard it as the last stronghold of scepticism, which is always polemical. Thus our knowledge, bound always to individuality and having its limitation in this very fact, necessarily means that everyone can *be* only one thing, whereas he can *know* everything else, and it is this very limitation that really creates the need for philosophy. Therefore we, who for this very reason

are endeavouring to extend the limits of our knowledge through philosophy, shall regard this sceptical argument of theoretical egoism, which here confronts us, as a small frontier fortress. Admittedly the fortress is impregnable, but the garrison can never sally forth from it, and therefore we can pass it by and leave it in our rear without danger.

The double knowledge which we have of the nature and action of our own body, and which is given in two completely different ways, has now been clearly brought out. Accordingly, we shall use it further as a key to the inner being of every phenomenon in nature. We shall judge all objects which are not our own body, and therefore are given to our consciousness not in the double way, but only as representations, according to the analogy of this body. We shall therefore assume that as, on the one hand, they are representation, just like our body, and are in this respect homogeneous with it, so on the other hand, if we set aside their existence as the subject's representation, what still remains over must be, according to its inner nature, the same as what in ourselves we call *will.* For what other kind of existence or reality could we attribute to the rest of the material world? From what source could we take the elements out of which we construct such a world? Besides the will and the representation, there is absolutely nothing known or conceivable for us. If we wish to attribute the greatest known reality to the material world, which immediately exists only in our representation, then we give it that reality which our own body has for each of us, for to each of us this is the most real of things. But if now we analyse the reality of this body and its actions, then, beyond the fact that it is our representation, we find nothing in it but the will; with this even its reality is exhausted. Therefore we can nowhere find another kind of reality to attribute to the material world. If, therefore, the material world is to be something more than our mere representation, we must say that, besides being the representation, and hence in itself and of its inmost nature, it is what we find immediately in ourselves as will. I say 'of its inmost nature,' but we have first of all to get to know more intimately this inner nature of the will, so that we may know how to distinguish from it what belongs not to it itself, but to its phenomenon, which has many grades.

Such, for example, is the circumstance of its being accompanied by knowledge, and the determination by motives which is conditioned by this knowledge. As we proceed, we shall see that this belongs not to the inner nature of the will, but merely to its most distinct phenomenon as animal and human being. Therefore, if I say that the force which attracts a stone to the earth is of its nature, in itself, and apart from all representation, will, then no one will attach to this proposition the absurd meaning that the stone moves itself according to a known motive, because it is thus that the will appears in man.[4] But we will now prove, establish, and develop to its full extent, clearly and in more detail, what has hitherto been explained provisionally and generally.[5]

§ 20

As the being-in-itself of our own body, as that which this body is besides being object of perception, namely representation, the *will,* as we have said, proclaims itself first of all in the voluntary movements of this body, in so far as these movements are nothing but the visibility of the individual acts of the will. These movements appear directly and simultaneously with those acts of will; they are one and the same thing with them, and are distinguished from them only by the form of perceptibility into which they have passed, that is to say, in which they have become representation.

But these acts of the will always have a ground or reason outside themselves in motives. Yet these motives never determine more than what I will at

this time, in *this* place, in *these* circumstances, not *that* I will in general, or *what* I will in general, in other words, the maxim characterizing the whole of my willing. Therefore, the whole inner nature of my willing cannot be explained from the motives, but they determine merely its manifestation at a given point of time; they are merely the occasion on which my will shows itself. This will itself, on the other hand, lies outside the province of the law of motivation; only the phenomenon of the will at each point of time is determined by this law. Only on the presupposition of my empirical character is the motive a sufficient ground of explanation of my conduct. But if I abstract from my character, and then ask why in general I will this and not that, no answer is possible, because only the *appearance* or *phenomenon* of the will is subject to the principle of sufficient reason, not the will itself, which in this respect may be called *groundless.* Here I in part presuppose Kant's doctrine of the empirical and intelligible characters, as well as my remarks pertinent to this in the *Grundprobleme der Ethik,* pp. 48-58, and again p. 178 *seqq.* of the first edition (pp. 46-57 and 174 *seqq.* of the second). We shall have to speak about this again in more detail in the fourth book. For the present, I have only to draw attention to the fact that one phenomenon being established by another, as in this case the deed by the motive, does not in the least conflict with the essence-in-itself of the deed being will. The will itself has no ground; the principle of sufficient reason in all its aspects is merely the form of knowledge, and hence its validity extends only to the representation, to the phenomenon, to the visibility of the will, not to the will itself that becomes visible.

Now if every action of my body is an appearance or phenomenon of an act of will in which my will itself in general and as a whole, and hence my character, again expresses itself under given motives, then phenomenon or appearance of the will must also be the indispensable condition and presupposition of every action. For the will's appearance cannot depend on something which does not exist directly and only through it, and would therefore be merely accidental for it, whereby the will's appearance itself would be only accidental. But that condition is the whole body itself. Therefore this body itself must be phenomenon

---

[4]Thus we cannot in any way agree with Bacon when he (*De Augmentis Scientiarum,* 1. 4 *in fine*) thinks that all mechanical and physical movements of bodies ensue only after a preceding perception in these bodies, although a glimmering of truth gave birth even to this false proposition. This is also the case with Kepler's statement, in his essay *De Planeta Martis,* that the planets must have knowledge in order to keep to their elliptical courses so accurately, and to regulate the velocity of their motion, so that the triangles of the plane of their course always remain proportional to the time in which they pass through their bases.

[5]Cf. chap. 19 of volume 2.

of the will, and must be related to my will as a whole, that is to say, to my intelligible character, the phenomenon of which in time is my empirical character, in the same way as the particular action of the body is to the particular act of the will. Therefore the whole body must be nothing but my will become visible, must be my will itself, in so far as this is object of perception, representation of the first class. It has already been advanced in confirmation of this that every impression on my body also affects my will at once and immediately, and in this respect is called pain or pleasure, or in a lower degree, pleasant or unpleasant sensation. Conversely, it has also been advanced that every violent movement of the will, and hence every emotion and passion, convulses the body, and disturbs the course of its functions. Indeed an etiological, though very incomplete, account can be given of the origin of my body, and a somewhat better account of its development and preservation. Indeed this is physiology; but this explains its theme only in exactly the same way as motives explain action. Therefore the establishment of the individual action through the motive, and the necessary sequence of the action from the motive, do not conflict with the fact that action, in general and by its nature, is only phenomenon or appearance of a will that is in itself groundless. Just as little does the physiological explanation of the functions of the body detract from the philosophical truth that the whole existence of this body and the sum-total of its functions are only the objectification of that will which appears in this body's outward actions in accordance with motives. If, however physiology tries to refer even these outward actions, the immediate voluntary movements, to causes in the organism, for example, to explain the movement of a muscle from an affluxion of humours ("like the contraction of a cord that is wet," as Reil says in the *Archiv für Physiologie,* Vol. VI, p. 153); supposing that it really did come to a thorough explanation of this kind, this would never do away with the immediately certain truth that every voluntary movement (*functiones animates*) is phenomenon of an act of will. Now, just as little can the physiological explanation of vegetative life (*functiones naturales, vitales*), however far it may be developed, ever do away with the truth that this whole animal life, thus developing itself, is phenomenon of the will. Generally then, as

already stated, no etiological explanation can ever state more than the necessarily determined position in time and space of a particular phenomenon and its necessary appearance there according to a fixed rule. On the other hand, the inner nature of everything that appears in this way remains for ever unfathomable, and is presupposed by every etiological explanation; it is merely expressed by the name force, or law of nature, or, when we speak of actions, the name character or will. Thus, although every particular action, under the presupposition of the definite character, necessarily ensues with the presented motive, and although growth, the process of nourishment, and all the changes in the animal body take place according to necessarily acting causes (stimuli), the whole series of actions, and consequently every individual act and likewise its condition, namely the whole body itself which performs it, and therefore also the process through which and in which the body exists, are nothing but the phenomenal appearance of the will, its becoming visible, the *objectivity of the will.* On this rests the perfect suitability of the human and animal body to the human and animal will in general, resembling, but far surpassing, the suitability of a purposely made instrument to the will of its maker, and on this account appearing as fitness or appropriateness, i.e., the teleological accountability of the body. Therefore the parts of the body must correspond completely to the chief demands and desires by which the will manifests itself; they must be the visible expression of these desires. Teeth, gullet, and intestinal canal are objectified hunger; the genitals are objectified sexual impulse; grasping hands and nimble feet correspond to the more indirect strivings of the will which they represent. Just as the general human form corresponds to the general human will, so to the individually modified will, namely the character of the individual, there corresponds the individual bodily structure, which is therefore as a whole and in all its parts characteristic and full of expression. It is very remarkable that even Parmenides expressed this in the following verses, quoted by Aristotle (*Metaphysics,* iii, 5):

Ὡς γὰρ ἕκασος ἔχει κρᾶσιν μελέων πολυκάμπτων,
Τώς νόος ἀνθρώποισι παρέστηκεν τὸ γὰρ αὐτό
Ἔστιν, ὅπερ φρονέει, μελέων φύσις ἀνθρώποισι,
Καὶ πᾶσιν καὶ παντί τὸ γὰρ πλέον ἐστὶ νόημα.

(Ut enim cuique complexio membrorum flexibilium se habet, ita mens hominibus adest: idem namque est, quod sapit, membrorum natura hominibus, et omnibus et omni: quod enim plus est, intelligentia est.)[6]

§21

From all these considerations the reader has now gained in the abstract, and hence in clear and certain terms, a knowledge which everyone possesses directly in the concrete, namely as feeling. This is the knowledge that the inner nature of his own phenomenon, which manifests itself to him as representation both through his actions and through the permanent substratum of these his body, is his *will*. This will constitutes what is most immediate in his consciousness, but as such it has not wholly entered into the form of the representation, in which object and subject stand over against each other; on the contrary, it makes itself known in an immediate way in which subject and object are not quite clearly distinguished, yet it becomes known to the individual himself not as a whole, but only in its particular acts. The reader who with me has gained this conviction, will find that of itself it will become the key to the knowledge of the innermost being of the whole of nature, since he now transfers it to all those phenomena that are given

to him, not like his own phenomenon both in direct and in indirect knowledge, but in the latter solely, and hence merely in a one-sided way, as *representation* alone. He will recognize that same will not only in those phenomena that are quite similar to his own, in men and animals, as their innermost nature, but continued reflection will lead him to recognize the force that shoots and vegetates in the plant, indeed the force by which the crystal is formed, the force that turns the magnet to the North Pole, the force whose shock he encounters from the contact of metals of different kinds, the force that appears in the elective affinities of matter as repulsion and attraction, separation and union, and finally even gravitation, which acts so powerfully in all matter, pulling the stone to the earth and the earth to the sun; all these he will recognize as different only in the phenomenon, but the same according to their inner nature. He will recognize them all as that which is immediately known to him so intimately and better than everything else, and where it appears most distinctly is called *will*. It is only this application of reflection which no longer lets us stop at the phenomenon, but leads us on to the *thing-in-itself*. Phenomenon means representation and nothing more. All representation, be it of whatever kind it may, all *object*, is *phenomenon*. But only the *will* is *thing-in-itself;* as such it is not representation at all, but *toto genere* different therefrom. It is that of which all representation, all object, is the phenomenon, the visibility, the *objectivity*. It is the innermost essence, the kernel, of every particular thing and also of the whole. It appears in every blindly acting force of nature, and also in the deliberate conduct of man, and the great difference between the two concerns only the degree of the manifestation, not the inner nature of what is manifested.

---

[6]"Just as everyone possesses the complex of flexible limbs, so does there dwell in men the mind in conformity with this. For everyone mind and complex of limbs are always the same; for intelligence is the criterion." [Tr.]

Cf. chap. 20 of volume 2; also my work *Über den Willen in der Natur,* under the heads "Physiology" and "Comparative Anatomy," where the subject, here merely alluded to, has received a full and thorough treatment.

REVIEW QUESTIONS

1. What are the noumenal and phenomenal worlds? How does Schopenhauer distinguish between them? For him, is the real world knowable?
2. What does Schopenhauer's phrase "the world as will and representation" refer to?
3. What is our fundamental duty in life? Why does Schopenhauer emphasize extinction or escape into nothingness?
4. What Buddhist elements does Schopenhauer's philosophy contain?
5. What is the nature of the cosmic Will?

25

SØREN KIERKEGAARD

The Danish philosopher Søren Aabye Kierkegaard (1813–1855) is widely recognized as the father of modern existentialism. He was born in Copenhagen, Denmark, into a deeply religious, but melancholy, Lutheran family with a brilliant self-taught father, Michael, who, though a successful businessman, was haunted by guilt. Michael suspected that God had cursed him for his sins to suffer the penalty of outliving all members of his family, two wives and his seven children. Indeed, all but two children, including Søren, did precede Michael in death. Søren was the youngest child and received special nurturing from his father, playing games that were likely to expand the imagination.

In 1830 he entered the University of Copenhagen to study theology, but spent most of his time reading literature and philosophy. He left the church, joined a fraternity, and lived a debauched life, spending his father's money. His father, brokenhearted by his son's immorality, reprimanded Kierkegaard, leading to a break between them.

In 1838, after spending eight years dallying at the University, Kierkegaard experienced a religious awakening, recommitted himself to the Christian faith and was reunited with his father. He turned from his frivolous living, finished his degree within a year, and earned the equivalent of a doctorate the next year, writing a long dissertation on Socratic Irony (1841).

While finishing his degree, in 1839, Kierkegaard fell in love with Regina Olsen, who was ten years younger than he, courted her, and the next year they became engaged. Almost immediately, he realized that the relationship would never work, that he was too melancholy for her, and that the relationship would destroy both of them. He sought to break the engagement and finally, a year later in 1841, succeeded, creating a citywide scandal.

Kierkegaard escaped from the public opprobrium by journeying to Berlin, where he wrote his first book *Either-Or*, contrasting the aesthetic (Epicurean) with the ethical (Stoic-Kantian) way of life. He published the two-volume work pseudonymously (under the name of "Victor Eremita"—the victorious hermit). It soon became a best seller, and all Copenhagen wondered who this brilliant author was. Other works followed, all written under different pseudonyms—Johannes de Silentio (Silent John), Vigilius Haufniensis (Watchman of the Harbor—Copenhagen is a harbor town), Johannes Climacus (John the Climber—to eternity), and so forth, some thirty books in all. Kierkegaard published all his work at his own expense. Only his first work made him a profit.

His life was filled with constant and intense suffering. He was frustrated in love, frustrated in his vocational aspirations—he was unable to get a teaching post, suffering a severe back ailment which may have led to his premature death. He was held in disrepute by most of his community. He opposed journalist corruption and suffered at the hands of the press. Yet he found solace in a deeply religious life. His last battle was with the organized state Lutheran Church, which he accused of betraying Christ. "As a religion, organized Christianity, as it is now practiced is just about as genuine as tea made from a bit of paper which once lay in a drawer beside another bit of paper which once had been used to wrap a few dried tea leaves from which tea had already been made three times."

Most of his works centered on the questions, "How shall I live my life? "What kind of life is worth living—the aesthetic, ethical or religious?" "What does it mean to have faith?" "What does it mean to love?" "What does it mean to accept one's suffering and how can one do this?" His discussion of these questions revealed philosophical acumen and literary brilliance.

In the first set of miscellaneous writings, we get a picture of Kierkegaard struggling to find meaning in his life. He rejects the abstract system-building philosophy of his day, especially Hegel's system, and opts for a philosophy that grows out of personal experience and for which one can live and die.

In the second reading from his most philosophical work, *Concluding Unscientific Postscript* (1844), Kierkegaard sets forth a radical version of fideism in which faith not only is said to be higher than reason but, in a sense, opposed to it. Faith, not reason, is the highest virtue a human can reach; faith is necessary for the deepest fulfillment. He argues that there is something misguided in trying to base one's religious faith on objective evidence or reason. It is both useless (it won't work) and a bad thing (it detracts one from the essential task of growing in faith). He then goes on to develop a theory of subjectivity wherein faith finds an authentic home. Even if we had direct proof for theism or Christianity, we would not want it, for such objective certainty would take the venture out of the religious pilgrimage, reducing it to a set of dull mathematical certainties.

FOR FURTHER READING

Bretall, Robert, ed. *A Kierkegaard Anthology* (Modern Library, 1936).
Evans, C. Stephen. *Kierkegaard's "Fragments" and "Postscript"* (Humanities Press, 1983).
Gardiner, Patrick. *Kierkegaard* (Oxford University Press, 1988).
Kaufmann, Walter, ed. *Existentialism from Dostoevski to Sartre* (American Library, 1975).
Kierkegaard, Søren. *Concluding Unscientific Postscript* (Princeton University Press, 1946).

Kierkegaard, Søren. *Fear and Trembling*, trans. Walter Lowrie (Princeton University Press, 1954).

Krimse, Bruce. *Kierkegaard in Golden Age Denmark* (University of Indiana Press, 1990).

Lowrie, Walter. *Kierkegaard* (Oxford University Press, 1938).

Lowrie, Walter. *A Short Life of Kierkegaard* (Princeton University Press, 1942).

Pojman, Louis. *The Logic of Subjectivity* (University of Alabama Press, 1984).

Thomson, Josiah, ed. *Kierkegaard: A Collection of Critical Essays* (Anchor Books, 1972).

Westphal, Merold. *Kierkegaard's Critique of Reason and Society* (Mercer University Press, 1987).

READINGS

AN ENTRY FROM THE JOURNAL OF THE YOUNG KIERKEGAARD[1]

There is something missing in my life, and it has to do with my need to understand *what I must do*, not what I must know—except, of course, that a certain amount of knowledge is presupposed in every action. I need to understand my purpose in life, to see what God wants me to do, and this means that I must find a truth which is true for me, that I must find *that Idea for which I can live and die.*

For what would it profit me if I found the so-called 'objective truth', if I worked through all the systems of philosophy and were able to analyze them and expose their inconsistencies; what would it profit me to develop a political theory and combine all the intricate details of politics into a complete whole, and so construct a world for the exhibition of others but in which I did not live; what would it profit me if I developed the correct interpretation of Christianity in which I resolved all the internal problems, if it had no deeper significance *for me and for my life;* what would it profit me if truth stood before me cold and naked, indifferent to whether I recognized her or not, creating in me paroxysms of anxiety rather than confident devotion? I will not deny that I am presupposing an imperative of knowledge and that it can have an effect in our lives, but it *must be appropriated by me*, and this is what I now recognize as paramount. This is what my soul thirsts after as the African desert thirsts for water. This is what I lack, and why I am like a man who has just rented a house and completely furnished it but still has not found a lover with whom to share life's happiness and sorrows.

But in order to find this Idea, or better said, to find myself, it profits me nought to get involved in the world. And that is exactly the mistake I have been making! That is why I thought it would be good to plunge into the study of law, for I thought thereby to develop my mental acuity through analyzing the complications of life. Here was exactly that great mass of details wherein I would lose myself; here perhaps I could take the facts and construct a total view, an organism of theft, pursuing the darker side of the law (here a certain spirit of association is incredibly noteworthy!). Therefore I wished to become an attorney, so that by putting myself into another person's role, I could for all practical purposes find a substitute for my own life and find a certain distraction in outward events and circumstances.

The Idea was what I lacked in order *to live a complete human life* and not merely knowledge. So I could not base the development of my philosophy of life—yes, on something one calls 'objective'—on something not my own, but upon something which reaches to the deepest roots of my existence and wherein I am connected into the divine and held fast to it, even though the whole world falls apart. Yes, *this is what I lack and this is what I am striving for.*

Translated by Louis P. Pojman

[1]This entry was written by Søren Kierkegaard as a twenty-two-year-old university student on August 1, 1835, in Gilleleie on the northern coast of Denmark.

THE SAYINGS OF KIERKEGAARD

Philosophy and Christianity will never allow themselves to be united, for if I hold to the most essential element in Christianity, namely, the redemption, so that if this element is to be something vital, it must be extended over the whole person. Or must I consider a person's moral ability as impaired while viewing his cognitive faculties as unimpaired? I certainly could consider the possibility of a philosophy according to Christianity, but it would be a Christian philosophy. The relation would not be philosophy's relation to Christianity, but Christianity's relation to Christian cognition [*Papers*, Oct. 17, 1835].

There is a major opposition between Augustine and Pelagius. The first will crush all in order to raise it. The second refers itself to man as he is. The first system views Christianity in three stages: creation; the fall through sin and with it a condition of death and impotence; and a new creation, whereby man becomes placed in a position where he can choose Christianity. The other system refers itself to man as he is (Christianity adapted to the world). The importance of the theory of inspiration is seen from the first system. Here one sees the relation between the synergistic and semi-pelagian conflict. It is the same question, only that the synergistic conflict has the Augustinian system's idea of new creation as its presupposition [*Papers* 1835].

Reasons are in general very curious things. If I lack passion, I look down on them with contempt. If I have passion, they grow up into something immense [*Papers* X].

All such scientific methods became particularly dangerous and pernicious when they encroach upon the spiritual field. Plants, animals, and stars may be handled in that way, but to handle the spirit of man in such a fashion is blasphemy which only weakens moral and religious passion. And so physiology spreads out over the kingdom of plants and animals, showing more and more analogies, which are not really analogies, since man is qualitatively different from plants and animals. Just as metaphysics has supplanted theology, physics will in the end supplant ethics. The whole modern statistical approach to morality is bent in this direction [*Papers* VII].

How ridiculous men are! They do not use the liberties they already possess, but they demand those they do not have. They have freedom of thought, but they demand freedom of speech [*Either/Or I*].

Do not check your soul's flight, do not grieve the better promptings within you, do not dull your spirit with half wishes and half thoughts. Ask yourself, and

continue to ask until you find the answer. For one may have known a thing many times and acknowledged it, one may have willed a thing many times and attempted it; and yet it is only by the deep inward movements, only by the indescribable emotions of the hearts, that for the first time you are convinced that what you have known belongs to you, that no power can take it from you; for only the truth that edifies is truth for you [*Either/Or II*].

If there were no eternal consciousness in man, if at the foundation of all there lay only a wildly seething power which writhing with obscure passions produced everything that is great and everything that is insignificant, if a bottomless void never satiated lay hidden beneath all—what then would life be but despair? If such were the case, if there were no sacred bond which united mankind, if one generation arose after another like the leafage in the forest, if the human race passed through the desert, a thoughtless and fruitless activity, if an eternal oblivion were always lurking for its prey and there was no power strong enough to wrest it from its maw—how empty then and comfortless life would be! [*Fear and Trembling*, 1843].

If Hegel had written his whole logic and had written in the Preface that it was simply a thought experiment, he would have been the greatest thinker who has ever lived [*Papers*, VI].

Life can only be understood backwards, but it must be lived forward.

The only fundamental basis for understanding is that one understands only in proportion to becoming himself that which he understands [*Papers* V].

Both [proving and being convinced by an argument for the existence of God] are equally fantastic, for just as no one has ever proved the existence of God, so no one has ever been an atheist, although many have never willed to allow their knowledge of God's existence to get power over their mind. It is the same with immortality. . . . With regard to God's existence, immortality and all problems of immanence, recollection is valid; it is present in every man, only he is not aware of it; however, this in no way means that his concept is adequate [*Papers* V].

In making a choice it is not so much a question of choosing the right as of the energy, the earnest, the pathos with which one chooses. Thereby the personality is consolidated. Therefore, even if a man were to choose the wrong, he will nevertheless *discover, precisely by reason of the energy with which he chose, that he had chosen the wrong*. For the choice being made with the whole inwardness of his personality, his nature is purified and he himself brought into immediate relation with the eternal Power whose omnipotence interpenetrates the whole of existence [*Either/Or II*].

The absurd is a category, and the most developed thought is required to define the Christian absurd accurately and with conceptual correctness. The absurd is a category, the negative criterion, of the divine or of the relationship to the divine. *When the believer has faith, the absurd is not the absurd*—faith transforms it, but in every weak moment it is again more or less absurd to him. The passion of faith is the only thing which masters the absurd [*Papers*, X].

As a religion [organized Christianity] as it is now practiced is just about as genuine as tea made from a bit of paper which once lay in a drawer beside another bit of paper which once had been used to wrap up a few dried tea leaves from which tea had already been made three times [*Papers*].

Indeed, if the press were to hang a sign out like every other business, it would have to read as follows: Here people are demoralized in the shortest possible time on the largest possible scale for the smallest possible price. The lowest depths to which people can sink before God is defined by the word "Journalist." If I were a father and had a daughter who was seduced, I should not despair over her; I would hope for her salvation. But if I had a son who became a journalist, and continued to be one for five years, I would despair and give up on him [*Papers*].

CONCLUDING UNSCIENTIFIC POSTSCRIPT

The problem we are considering is not the truth of Christianity but the individual's relation to Christianity. Our discussion is not about the scholar's systematic zeal to arrange the truths of Christianity in nice tidy categories but about the individual's personal relationship to this doctrine, a relationship which is properly one of infinite interest to him. Simply stated, "I, Johannes Climacus, born in this city, now thirty years old, a decent fellow like most folk, suppose that there awaits me, as it awaits a maid and a professor, a highest good, which is called an eternal happiness. I have heard that Christianity is the way to that good, and so I ask, how may I establish a proper relationship to Christianity?"

I hear an intellectual's response to this, "What outrageous presumption! What egregious egoistic vanity in this theocentric and philosophically enlightened age, which is concerned with global history, to lay such inordinate weight on one's petty self."

I tremble at such a reproof and had I not already inured myself to these kinds of responses, I would slink away like a dog with his tail between his legs.

But I have no guilt whatsoever about what I am doing, for it is not I who is presumptuous, but, rather, it is Christianity itself which compels me to ask the question in this way. For Christianity places enormous significance on my little self, and upon every other self however insignificant it may seem, in that it offers each self eternal happiness on the condition that a proper relationship between itself and the individual is established.

Although I am still an outsider to faith, I can see that the only unpardonable sin against the majesty of Christianity is for an individual to take his relationship to it for granted. However modest it may seem to relate oneself in this way, Christianity considers such a casual attitude to be imprudent. So I must respectfully decline all theocentric helpers and the helpers' helpers who would seek to help me through a detached relationship to this doctrine. I would rather remain where I am with my infinite concern about my spiritual existence, with the problem of how I may become a Christian. For while it is not impossible for one with an infinite concern for his eternal happiness to achieve salvation, it is entirely impossible for one who has lost all sensitivity to the relationship to achieve such a state.

The objective problem is: Is Christianity true? The subjective problem is: What is the individual's relationship to Christianity? Quite simply, how may I, Johannes Climacus, participate in the happiness promised by Christianity? The problem concerns myself alone; partly because, if it is properly set forth, it will concern everyone in exactly the same way; and partly because all the other points of view take faith for granted, as trivial.

In order to make my problem clear, I shall first describe the objective problem and show how it should be treated. In this way the historical aspect will be given its due. After this I shall describe the subjective problem.

The objective problem of the truth of Christianity. From an objective point of view Christianity is a historical fact whose truth must be considered in a purely objective manner, for the modest scholar is far too objective not to leave himself outside—though as a matter of fact, he may count himself as a believer. 'Truth' in this objective sense may mean either (1) historical truth or (2) philosophical truth. As historical truth, the truth claims must be decided by a critical examination of the various sources in the same way we determine other historical claims. Considered philosophically, the doctrine that has been historically verified must be related to the eternal truth.

The inquiring, philosophical, and learned researcher raises the question of the truth, but not the subjective truth, that is, the truth as appropriated. The inquiring researcher is interested, but he is not infinitely, personally, and passionately interested in a way that relates his own eternal happiness to this truth. Far be it for the objective person to be so immodest, so presumptuous as that!

Such an inquirer must be in one of two states. Either he is already in faith convinced of the truth of Christianity—and in such a relationship he cannot be infinitely interested in the objective inquiry, since faith itself consists in being infinitely concerned with Christianity and regards every competing interest as a temptation; or he is not in faith but objectively considering the subject matter, and as such not in a condition of being infinitely interested in the question.

I mention this in order to draw your attention to what will be developed in the second part of this work, namely, that the problem of the truth of Christianity is never appropriately set forth in this objective manner, that is, it does not arise at all, since Christianity lies in decision. Let the scholarly researcher work with indefatigable zeal even to the point of shortening his life in devoted service to scholarship. Let the speculative philosopher spare neither time nor effort. They are nevertheless not personally and passionately concerned. On the contrary, they wouldn't want to be but will want to develop an objective and disinterested stance. They are only concerned about objective truth, so that the question of personal appropriation is relatively unimportant, something that will follow their findings as a matter of course. In the last analysis what matters to the individual is of minor significance. Herein precisely lies the scholar's exalted equanimity as well as the comedy of his parrotlike pedantry.

The historical point of view. When Christianity is considered through its historical documents, it becomes vital to get a trustworthy account of what Christian doctrine really is. If the researcher is infinitely concerned with his relationship to this truth, he will immediately despair, because it is patently clear that in historical matters the greatest certainty is still only an approximation, and an approximation is too weak for one to build his eternal happiness upon, since its incommensurability with eternal happiness prevents it from obtaining. So the scholar, having only a historical interest in the truth of Christianity, begins his work with tremendous zeal and contributes important research until his seventieth year. Then just fourteen days before his death he comes upon a new document that casts fresh light over one whole side of his inquiry. Such an objective personality is the antithesis of the restless concern of the subject who is infinitely interested in eternal happiness and who surely deserves to have a decisive answer to the question concerning that happiness.

When one raises the historical question of the truth of Christianity or of what is and what is not Christian truth, we come directly to the Holy Scriptures as the central document. The historical investigation focuses first on the Bible.

The holy scriptures. It is very important that the scholar secure the highest possible reliability in his work. In this regard it is important for me not to pretend that I have learning or show that I have none, for my purpose here is more important. And that is to have it understood and remembered that even with the most impressive scholarly credentials and persistence, even if all the intelligence of all the critics met in one single head, still one would get no further than an approximation. We could never show more than that there is an incommensurability between the infinite personal concern for one's eternal happiness and the reliability of the documents.

When the Scriptures are considered as the ultimate arbiter, which determines what is and what is not Christian, it becomes imperative to secure their reliability through a critical historical investigation. So we must deal here with several issues: the canonicity of each book of the Bible, their authenticity, their integrity, the trustworthiness of the authors, and finally, we must assume a dogmatic guarantee: inspiration. When one thinks of the prodigious labors that the English are devoting to digging the tunnel under the Thames, the incredible expenditure of time and effort, and how a little accident can upset the whole project for a long time, one may be able to get some idea of what is involved in the undertaking that we are describing. How much time, what diligence, what glorious acumen, what remarkable scholarship from generation to generation have been requisitioned to accomplish this work of supreme wonder! And yet a single little dialectical doubt can suddenly touch the foundations and for a long time disturb the whole project, closing the underground way to Christianity, which one has tried to establish objectively and scientifically, instead of approaching the problem as it should be approached, above ground—subjectively.

But let us assume first that the critics have established everything that scholarly theologians in their happiest moments ever dreamed to prove about the Bible. These books and no others belong to the canon. They are authentic, complete, their authors are trustworthy—it is as though every letter were divinely inspired (one cannot say more than this, for inspiration is an object of faith and is qualitatively dialectical. It cannot be reached by a quantitative increment). Furthermore, there is not the slightest contradiction in these holy writings. For let us be careful in formulating our hypothesis. If there is even a word that is problematic, the parenthesis of uncertainty begins again, and the critical philological enterprise will lead one astray. In general, all that is needed to cause us to question our findings is a little circumspection, the renunciation of every learned middle-term, which could in a twinkle of the eye degenerate into a hundred-year parenthesis.

And so it comes to pass that everything we hoped for with respect to the Scriptures has been firmly established. What follows from this? Has anyone who didn't previously have faith come a single step closer to faith? Of course not, not a single step closer. For faith isn't produced through academic investigations. It doesn't come directly at all, but, on the contrary, it is precisely in objective analysis that one loses the infinite personal and passionate concern that is the requisite condition for faith, its ubiquitous ingredient, wherein faith comes into existence.

Has anyone who had faith gained anything in terms of faith's strength and power? No, not the least. Rather, his prodigious learning which lies like a dragon at faith's door, threatening to devour it, will become a handicap, forcing him to put forth an even greater prodigious effort in fear and trembling in order not to fall into temptation and confuse knowledge with faith. Whereas faith had uncertainty as a useful teacher, it now finds that certainty is its most dangerous enemy. Take passion away and faith disappears, for certainty and passion are incompatible. Let an analogy throw light on this point. He who believes that God exists and providentially rules the world finds it easier to preserve his faith (and not a fantasy) in an imperfect world where passion is kept awake, than in an absolutely perfect world; for in such an ideal world faith is unthinkable. This is the reason that we are taught that in eternity faith will be annulled.

Now let us assume the opposite, that the opponents have succeeded in proving what they desired to establish regarding the Bible and did so with a certainty that transcended their wildest hopes. What then? Has the enemy abolished Christianity? Not a whit. Has he harmed the believer? Not at all. Has he won the right of being free from the responsibility of becoming a believer? By no means. Simply because these books are not by these authors, are not authentic, lack integrity, do not seem to be inspired (though this cannot be demonstrated since it is a matter of faith), it in no way follows that these authors have not existed, and above all it does not follow that Christ never existed. In so far as faith perdures, the believer is at liberty to assume it, just as free (mark well!); for if he accepted the content of faith on the basis of evidence, he would now be on the verge of giving up faith. If things ever came this far, the believer is somewhat to blame, for he invited the procedure and began to play into the hands of unbelief by attempting to prove the content of faith.

Here is the heart of the matter, and I come back to learned theology. For whose sake is the proof sought? Faith does not need it. Yes, it must regard it as an enemy. But when faith begins to feel ashamed, when like a young woman for whom love ceases to suffice, who secretly feels ashamed of her lover and must therefore have it confirmed by others that he really is quite remarkable, so likewise when faith falters and begins to lose its passion, when it begins to cease to be faith, then proof becomes necessary in order to command respect from the side of unbelief.

So when the subject of faith is treated objectively, it becomes impossible for a person to relate himself to the decision of faith with passion, let alone with infinitely concerned passion. It is a self-contradiction and as such comical to be infinitely concerned about what at best can only be an approximation. If in spite of this, we still preserve passion, we obtain fanaticism. For the person with infinite passionate concern every relevant detail becomes something of infinite value. The error lies not in the infinite passion but in the fact that its object has become an approximation.

As soon as one takes subjectivity away—and with it subjectivity's passion—and with passion the infinite concern—it becomes impossible to make a decision—either with regard to this problem or any other; for every decision, every genuine decision, is a subjective action. A contemplator (i.e., an objective subject) experiences no infinite urge to make a decision and sees no need for a commitment anywhere. This is the falsity of objectivity and this is the problem with the Hegelian notion of mediation

as the mode of transition in the continuous process, where nothing endures and where nothing is infinitely decided because the movement turns back on itself and again turns back; but the movement itself is a chimera and philosophy becomes wise afterwards. Objectively speaking, this method produces results in great supply, but it does not produce a single decisive result. This is as is expected, since decisiveness inheres in subjectivity, essentially in passion and maximally in the personal passion that is infinitely concerned about one's eternal happiness.

Christianity is spirit, spirit is inwardness, inwardness is subjectivity, subjectivity is essentially passion and at its maximum infinite personal and passionate concern about one's eternal happiness.

Becoming subjective. Objectively we only consider the subject matter, subjectively we consider the subject and his subjectivity, and, behold, subjectivity is precisely our subject matter. It must constantly be kept in mind that the subjective problem is not about some other subject matter but simply about subjectivity itself. Since the problem is about a decision, and all decisions lie in subjectivity, it follows that not a trace of objectivity remains, for at the moment that subjectivity slinks away from the pain and crisis of decision, the problem becomes to a degree objective. If the Introduction still awaits another work before a judgment can be made on the subject matter, if the philosophical system still lacks a paragraph, if the speaker still has a final argument, the decision is postponed. We do not raise the question of the truth of Christianity in the sense that when it has been decided, subjectivity is ready and willing to accept it. No, the question is about the subject's acceptance of it, and it must be regarded as an infernal illusion or a deceitful evasion which seeks to avoid the decision by taking an objective treatment of the subject matter and assumes that a subjective commitment will follow from the objective deliberation as a matter of course. On the contrary, the decision lies in subjectivity and an objective acceptance is either a pagan concept or one devoid of all meaning.

Christianity will give the single individual eternal happiness, a good that cannot be divided into parts but can only be given to one person at a time. Although we presuppose that subjectivity is available to be appropriated, a possibility that involves accepting this good, it is not a subjectivity without qualification, without a genuine understanding of the meaning of this good. Subjectivity's development or transformation, its infinite concentration in itself with regard to an eternal happiness—this highest good of Infinity, an eternal happiness—this is subjectivity's developed possibility. As such, Christianity protests against all objectivity and will infinitely concern itself only with subjectivity. If there is any Christian truth, it first arises in subjectivity. Objectively it does not arise at all. If its truth is only in a single person, then Christianity exists in him alone, and there is greater joy in heaven over this one than over all world history and philosophical systems which, as objective forces, are incommensurable with the Christian idea.

Philosophy teaches that the way to truth is to become objective, but Christianity teaches that the way is to become subjective, that is, to become a subject in truth. Lest we seem to be trading on ambiguities, let it be said clearly that Christianity aims at intensifying passion to its highest pitch; but passion is subjectivity and does not exist objectively at all.

Subjective truth, inwardness; truth is subjectivity. For an objective reflection the truth becomes an object, something objective, and thought points away from the subject. For subjective reflection the truth becomes a matter of appropriation, of inwardness, of subjectivity, and thought must penetrate deeper and still deeper into the subject and his subjectivity. Just as in objective reflection, when objectivity had come into being, subjectivity disappeared, so here the subjectivity of the subject becomes the final stage, and objectivity disappears. It is not for an instant forgotten that the subject is an existing individual, and that existence is a process of becoming, and that therefore the idea of truth being an identity of thought and being is a chimera of abstraction; this is not because the truth is not such an identity but because the believer is an existing individual for whom the truth cannot be such an identity as long as he exists as a temporal being.

If an existing subject really could transcend himself, the truth would be something complete for him, but where is this point outside of himself? The I = I is a mathematical point that does not exist, and in-

sofar as one would take this standpoint, he will not stand in another's way. It is only momentarily that the existential subject experiences the unity of the infinite and the finite, which transcends existence, and that moment is the moment of passion. While scribbling modern philosophy is contemptuous of passion, passion remains the highest point of existence for the individual who exists in time. In passion the existential subject is made infinite in imagination's eternity, and at the same time he is himself.

All essential knowledge concerns existence, or only that knowledge that relates to existence is essential knowledge. All knowledge that is not existential, that does not involve inward reflection, is really accidental knowledge, its degree and compass are essentially a matter of no importance. This essential knowledge that relates itself essentially to the existing individual is not to be equated with the above-mentioned abstract identity between thought and being. But it means that knowledge must relate itself to the knower, who is essentially an existing individual, and therefore all essential knowledge essentially relates itself to existence, to that which exists. But all ethical and all ethical-religious knowledge has this essential relationship to the existence of the knower.

In order to elucidate the difference between the objective way of reflection and the subjective way, I shall now show how subjective reflection makes its way back into inwardness. The highest point of inwardness in an existing person is passion, for passion corresponds to truth as a paradox, and the fact that the truth becomes a paradox is grounded in its relation to an existing individual. The one corresponds to the other. By forgetting that we are existing subjects, we lose passion and truth ceases to be a paradox, but the knowing subject begins to lose his humanity and becomes fantastic and the truth likewise becomes a fantastic object for this kind of knowledge.

When the question of truth is put forward in an objective manner, reflection is directed objectively to the truth as an object to which the knower is related. The reflection is not on the relationship but on whether he is related to the truth. If that which he is related to is the truth, the subject is in the truth. When the question of truth is put forward in a subjective manner, reflection is directed subjectively to the individual's relationship. If the relation's HOW is in truth, the individual is in truth, even if the WHAT to which he is related is not true.

We may illustrate this by examining the knowledge of God. Objectively the reflection is on whether the object is the true God; subjectively reflection is on whether the individual is related to a *what* in such a way that his relationship in truth is a God-relationship. On which side does the truth lie? Ah, let us not lean towards mediation and say, it is on neither side but in the mediation of both of them.

The existing individual who chooses the objective way enters upon the entire approximation process that is supposed to bring God into the picture. But this in all eternity cannot be done because God is Subject and therefore exists only for the subjective individual in inwardness. The existing individual who chooses the subjective way comprehends instantly the entire dialectical difficulty involved in having to use some time, perhaps a long time, in order to find God objectively. He comprehends this dialectical difficulty in all its pain because every moment without God is a moment lost—so important is the matter of being related to God. In this way God certainly becomes a postulate but not in the useless sense in which it is often taken. It becomes the only way in which an existing individual comes into a relation with God—when the dialectical contradiction brings passion to the point of despair and helps him embrace God with the category of despair (faith). Now the postulate is far from being arbitrary or optional. It becomes a life-saving necessity, so that it is no longer simply a postulate, but rather the individual's postulation of the existence of God is a necessity.

Now the problem is to calculate on which side there is the most truth: *either* the side of one who seeks the true God objectively and pursues the approximate truth of the God-idea *or* the side of one who is driven by infinite concern for his relationship to God. No one who has not been corrupted by science can have any doubt in the matter.

If one who lives in a Christian culture goes up to God's house, the house of the true God, with a true conception of God, with knowledge of God and prays—but prays in a false spirit; and one who lives in an idolatrous land prays with the total passion of the infinite, although his eyes rest on the image of an idol; where is there most truth? The one prays in truth to God, although he worships an idol. The other prays in untruth to the true God and therefore really worships an idol.

When a person objectively inquires about the problem of immortality and another person embraces it as an uncertainty with infinite passion, where is there most truth, and who really has the greater certainty? The one has entered into an inexhaustible approximation, for certainty of immortality lies precisely in the subjectivity of the individual. The other is immortal and fights against his uncertainty.

Let us consider Socrates. Today everyone is playing with some proof or other. Some have many, some fewer. But Socrates! He put the question objectively in a hypothetical manner: "*if* there is immortality." Compared to the modern philosopher with three proofs for immortality, should we consider Socrates a doubter? Not at all. On this little *if* he risks his entire life, he dares to face death, and he has directed his life with infinite passion so that the *if* is confirmed—*if* there is immortality. Is there any better proof for life after death? But those who have the three proofs do not at all pattern their lives in conformity with the idea. If there is an immortality, it must feel disgust over their lackadaisical manner of life. Can any better refutation be given of the three proofs? These crumbs of uncertainty helped Socrates because they hastened the process along, inciting the passions. The three proofs that others have are of no help at all because they are dead to the spirit, and the fact that they need three proofs proves that they are spiritually dead. The Socratic ignorance that Socrates held fast with the entire passion of his inwardness was an expression of the idea that eternal truth is related to an existing individual, and that this will be in the form of a paradox as long as he exists; and yet it is just possible that there is more truth in Socratic ignorance than is contained in the "objective truth" of the philosophical systems, which flirts with the spirit of the times and cuddles up to associate professors.

The objective accent falls on *what* is said; the subjective accent falls on *how* it is said. This distinction is valid even for aesthetics and shows itself in the notion that what may be objectively true may in the mouth of certain people become false. This distinction is illustrated by the saying that the difference between the older days and our day is that in the old days only a few knew the truth while in ours all know it, except that the inwardness towards it is in inverse proportion to the scope of its possession. Aesthetically the contradiction that the truth becomes error in certain mouths is best understood comically. In the ethical-religious domain the accent is again on the *how*. But this is not to be understood as referring to decorum, modulation, delivery, and so on, but to the individual's relationship to the proposition, the way he relates himself to it. Objectively it is a question simply about the content of the proposition, but subjectively it is a question of inwardness. At its maximum this inward *how* is the passion of infinity and the passion of the infinite is itself the truth. But since the passion of the infinite is exactly subjectivity, subjectivity is the truth. Objectively there is no infinite decision or commitment, and so it is objectively correct to annul the difference between good and evil as well as the law of noncontradiction and the difference between truth and untruth. Only in subjectivity is there decision and commitment, so that to seek this in objectivity is to be in error. It is the passion of infinity that brings forth decisiveness, not its content, for its content is precisely itself. In this manner the subjective *how* and subjectivity are the truth.

But the *how* that is subjectively emphasized because the subject is an existing individual is also subject to a temporal dialectic. In passion's decisive moment, where the road swings off from the way to objective knowledge, it appears that the infinite decision is ready to be made. But in that moment the existing individual finds himself in time, and the subjective *how* becomes transformed into a striving, a striving that is motivated by and is repeatedly experienced in the decisive passion of the infinite. But this is still a striving.

When subjectivity is truth, subjectivity's definition must include an expression for an opposition to objectivity, a reminder of the fork in the road, and this expression must also convey the tension of inwardness. Here is such a definition of truth: *the objective uncertainty, held fast in an appropriation process of the most passionate inwardness is the truth*, the highest truth available for an existing person. There where the way swings off (and where that is cannot be discovered objectively but only subjectively), at that place objective knowledge is annulled. Objectively speaking he has only uncertainty, but precisely there the infinite passion of inwardness is intensified, and truth is precisely the adventure to choose objective uncertainty with the passion of inwardness.

When I consider nature in order to discover God, I do indeed see his omnipotence and wisdom, but I see much more that disturbs me. The result of all this is objective uncertainty, but precisely here is the place for inwardness because inwardness apprehends the objective uncertainty with the entire passion of infinity. In the case of mathematical statements objectivity is already given, but because of the nature of mathematics, this truth is existentially indifferent.

Now the above definition of truth is an equivalent description of faith. Without risk there is no faith. Faith is precisely the contradiction between the infinite passion of inwardness and objective uncertainty. If I can grasp God objectively, I do not believe, but because I cannot know God objectively, I must have faith, and if I will preserve myself in faith, I must constantly be determined to hold fast to the objective uncertainty, so as to remain out upon the ocean's deep, over seventy thousand fathoms of water, and still believe.

In the sentence 'subjectivity, inwardness is truth', we see the essence of Socratic wisdom, whose immortal service is exactly to have recognized the essential meaning of existence, that the knower is an *existing* subject, and for this reason in his ignorance Socrates enjoyed the highest relationship to truth within paganism. This is a truth that speculative philosophy unhappily again and again forgets: that the knower is an existing subject. It is difficult enough to recognize this fact in our objective age, long after the genius of Socrates.

When subjectivity, inwardness, is the truth, the truth becomes objectively determined as a paradox, and that it is paradoxical is made clear by the fact that subjectivity is truth, for it repels objectivity, and the expression for the objective repulsion is the intensity and measure of inwardness. The paradox is the objective uncertainty, which is the expression for the passion of inwardness, which is precisely the truth. This is the Socratic principle. The eternal, essential truth, that is, that which relates itself essentially to the individual because it concerns his existence (all other knowledge is, Socratically speaking, accidental, its degree and scope being indifferent), is a paradox. Nevertheless, the eternal truth is not essentially in itself paradoxical, but it becomes so by relating itself to an existing individual. Socratic ignorance is the expression of this objective uncertainty, the inwardness of the existential subject is the truth. To anticipate what I will develop later, Socratic ignorance is an analogy to the category of the absurd, only that there is still less objective certainty in the absurd, and therefore infinitely greater tension in its inwardness. The Socratic inwardness that involves existence is an analogy to faith, except that this inwardness is repulsed not by ignorance but by the absurd, which is infinitely deeper. Socratically the eternal, essential truth is by no means paradoxical in itself, but only by virtue of its relation to an existing individual.

Subjectivity, inwardness, is the truth. Is there a still more inward expression for this? Yes, there is. If subjectivity is seen as the truth, we may posit the opposite principle: that subjectivity is untruth, error. Socratically speaking, subjectivity is untruth if it fails to understand that subjectivity is truth and desires to understand itself objectively. But now we are presupposing that subjectivity in becoming the truth has a difficulty to overcome in as much as it is in untruth. So we must work backwards, back to inwardness. Socratically, the way back to the truth takes place through recollection, supposing that we have memories of that truth deep within us.

Let us call this untruth of the individual 'sin'. Seen from eternity the individual cannot be in sin, nor can he be eternally presupposed as having been in sin. So it must be that he becomes a sinner by coming into existence (for the beginning point is that subjectivity is untruth). He is not born as a sinner in the sense that he is sinful before he is born, but he is born in sin and as a sinner. We shall call this state *original sin.* But if existence has acquired such power over him, he is impotent to make his way back to eternity through the use of his memory (supposing that there is truth in the Platonic idea that we may discover truth through recollection). If it was already paradoxical that the eternal truth related itself to an existing individual, now it is absolutely

paradoxical that it relates itself to such an individual. But the more difficult it is for him through memory to transcend existence, the more inwardness must increase in intense passion, and when it is made impossible for him, when he is held so fast in existence that the back door of recollection is forever closed to him through sin, then his inwardness will be the deepest possible.

Subjectivity is truth. Through this relationship between the eternal truth and the existing individual the paradox comes into existence. Let us now go further and suppose that the eternal truth is essentially a paradox. How does this paradox come into existence? By juxtaposing the eternal, essential truth with temporal existence. When we set them together within the truth itself, the truth becomes paradoxical. The eternal truth has come into time. This is the paradox. If the subject is hindered by sin from making his way back to eternity by looking inward through recollection, he need not trouble himself about this, for now the eternal essential truth is no longer behind him, but it is in front of him, through its being in existence or having existed, so that if the individual does not *existentially* get hold of the truth, he will never get hold of it.

It is impossible to accentuate existence more than this. When the eternal truth is related to an existing individual, truth becomes a paradox. The paradox repels the individual because of the objective uncertainty and ignorance towards inwardness. But since this paradox in itself is not paradoxical, it does not push the spirit far enough. For without risk there is no faith, and the greater the risk the greater the faith, and the more objective reliability, the less inwardness (for inwardness is precisely subjectivity). Indeed, the less objective reliability, the deeper becomes the possible inwardness. When the paradox is in itself paradoxical, it repels the individual by the power of the absurd, and the corresponding passion, which is produced in the process, is faith. But subjectivity, inwardness, is truth, for otherwise we have forgotten the Socratic contribution; but there is no more striking expression for inwardness than when the retreat from existence through recollection back to eternity is made impossible; and when the truth as paradox encounters the individual who is caught in the vice-grip of sin's anxiety and suffering, but who is also aware of the tremendous risk involved in faith—when he nevertheless makes the leap of faith—this is subjectivity at its height.

When Socrates believed in the existence of God, he held fast to an objective uncertainty in passionate inwardness, and in that contradiction, in that risk faith came into being. Now it is different. Instead of the objective uncertainty, there is objective certainty about the object—certainty that it is absurd, and it is, again, faith that holds fast to that object in passionate inwardness. Compared with the gravity of the absurd, Socratic ignorance is a joke, and compared with the strenuosity of faith in believing the paradox, Socratic existential inwardness is a Greek life of leisure.

What is the absurd? The absurd is that the eternal truth has entered time, that God has entered existence, has been born, has grown, and so on, has become precisely like any other human being, quite indistinguishable from other humans. The absurd is precisely by its objective repulsion the measure of the inwardness of faith. Suppose there is a man who desires to have faith. Let the comedy begin. He desires to obtain faith with the help of objective investigation and what the approximation process of evidential inquiry yields. What happens? With the help of the increment of evidence the absurd is transformed to something else; it becomes probable, it becomes more probable still, it becomes perhaps highly and overwhelmingly probable. Now that there is respectable evidence for the content of his faith, he is ready to believe it, and he prides himself that his faith is not like that of the shoemaker, the tailor, and the simple folk, but comes after a long investigation. Now he prepares himself to believe it. Any proposition that is almost probable, reasonably probable, highly and overwhelmingly probable, is something that is almost known and as good as known, highly and overwhelmingly known—but it is not believed, not through faith; for the absurd is precisely faith's object and the only positive attitude possible in relation to it is faith and not knowledge.

Christianity has declared itself to be the eternal that has entered time, that has proclaimed itself as the *paradox* and demands faith's inwardness in relation to that which is a scandal to the Jews and folly to the Greeks—and as absurd to the understanding. It is impossible to say this more strongly than by saying: subjectivity is truth, and objectivity is repelled by it—by virtue of the absurd.

Subjectivity culminates in passion. Christianity is the paradox; paradox and passion belong together as a perfect match, and the paradox is perfectly suited to one whose situation is to be in the extremity of existence. Indeed, there never has been found in all the world two lovers more suited to each other than passion and paradox, and the strife between them is a lover's quarrel, when they argue about which one first aroused the other's passion. And so it is here. The existing individual by means of the paradox has come to the extremity of existence. And what is more wonderful for lovers than to be granted a long time together with each other without anything disturbing their relationship except that which makes it more inwardly passionate? And this is what is granted to the unspeculative understanding between the passion and paradox, for they will dwell harmoniously together in time and be changed first in eternity.

But the speculative philosopher views things altogether differently. He believes but only to a certain degree. He puts his hand to the plow but quickly looks about for something to know. From a Christian perspective it is hard to see how he could reach the highest good in this manner.

REVIEW QUESTIONS

1. What is Kierkegaard's definition of truth?
2. What is the highest virtue a human can reach?
3. What does Kierkegaard mean by "Without risk there is no faith"?
4. Can a person achieve faith through objective inquiries into the existence of God? Why or why not?
5. What is faith's object?

26

JOHN STUART MILL

John Stuart Mill (1806–1873), one of the most important British philosophers of the nineteenth century, was born in London and educated by his father, James Mill, a first-rate philosopher in his own right, learning Greek at the age of three and Latin at the age of eight. By the time he was fourteen, he had received a thorough classic education at home. He began work as a clerk for the East India Company at the age of seventeen and eventually became a director of the company. Influenced by the work of Jeremy Bentham (1748–1832), he embraced utilitarianism and ardently worked for social reform. However, a crisis of meaning occurred in his twenty-second year. Mill describes it in his *Autobiography*. One day in 1826 he experienced a "dull state of nerves, such as everybody is occasionally liable to," when the following question occurred to him:

> Suppose that all your objects in life were realized; that all the changes in institutions and opinions which you are looking forward to, could be completely effected at this very instant: would this be a great joy and happiness to you? An irrepressible self-consciousness distinctly answered, "No!" At this my heart sank within me: the whole foundation on which my life was constructed fell down. All my happiness was to have been founded in the continual pursuit of this end. The end had ceased to charm, and how could there ever again be any interest in the means? I seemed to have nothing left to live for.

Mill went through a period of deep depression lasting several months. Eventually, he was restored to full emotional health and pursued his tasks with renewed vigor.

When he was twenty-five, Mill became close friends with Harriet Taylor, a married woman. Their mutual devotion and intimacy, though apparently Platonic, caused a scandal in a society where the only approved intimacy between the opposite sexes was familial, either as married couples or as brother and sister. After Harriet's husband died, Mill married her (1851). Harriet's ideas changed Mill's, and Mill regarded her as the most profound mind he had ever known. Mill claims that much of the credit for his work *On Liberty* (1859) goes to her. His arguments in *The Subjection of Women* (1861) show her influence.

Mill was a prolific writer. His *A System of Logic* (1848) is one of the most original works on inductive logic ever written. His *Utilitarianism* (1861) (presented here) is the classic work on the topic. Mill was elected to Parliament in 1865. A man with an independent and penetrating mind, he fought for woman's suffrage, the rights of blacks in Jamaica, Irish land reform, the retention of capital punishment, and weighted votes for the better informed over the less educated ("It is not useful, but hurtful, that the constitution of the country should declare ignorance to be entitled to as much political power as knowledge").

Our first selection is his classic work *Utilitarianism.* Mill defends utilitarianism, a form of consequentialist ethics, against more rule-bound *deontological* systems, the sort of system represented by Kant's categorical imperative in the *Foundation for the Metaphysic of Morals.* Traditionally, two major types of ethical systems have dominated the field, one in which the locus of value is the act or kind of act, the other in which the locus of value is the outcome or consequences of the act. The former type of theory is called *deontological* (from the Greek *deon* which means 'duty'), and the latter is called *teleological* (from the Greek *telos* which means 'end' or 'goal').

That is, the standard of right or wrong action for the teleologists is the comparative consequences of the available actions. That act is right which produces the best consequences. Whereas the deontologist is concerned only with the rightness of the act itself, the teleologist asserts that there is no such thing as an act having intrinsic worth. While there is something intrinsically bad about lying for the deontologist, the only thing wrong with lying for the teleologist is the bad consequences it produces. If you can reasonably calculate that lying will do even slightly more good than telling the truth, you have an obligation to lie.

Mill wrote *Utilitarianism* in response to criticisms about Jeremy Bentham's hedonistic version of utilitarianism, which failed to differentiate between kinds and quality of pleasure, and so received the name of "pig philosophy." Mill meets this charge by substituting a more complex theory of happiness for Bentham's undifferentiated pleasure.

In our second reading, *On Liberty,* Mill attempts to ground liberty in a utilitarian ethic. He argues for "utility in the largest sense, grounded on the permanent interests of man as a progressive being," from there defends the freedom of the individual to do whatever one likes so long as one is not interfering with the rights of others. He warns against the "tyranny of the majority" which can unjustifiably coerce liberty. The only grounds for interfering with another individual is to protect others from harm.

In our final essay, *The Subjection of Women,* he argues that powerful moral and prudential reasons exist for affording women equal education and, in general, equal opportunities with men.

FOR FURTHER READING

Britton, Karl. *John Stuart Mill* (Dover, 1969).

Donner, Wendy. *The Liberal Self: John Stuart Mill's Moral and Political Philosophy* (Cornell University Press, 1991).

Himmelfarb, Gertrude. *On Liberty and Liberalism: The Case of John Stuart Mill* (Knopf, 1974).

McCloskey, H. J. *John Stuart Mill: A Critical Study* (Macmillan, 1971).

Ryan, Alan. *J. S. Mill* (Routledge & Kegan Paul, 1974).

Schneewind, J., ed. *Mill: A Collection of Critical Essays* (Anchor Doubleday, 1968).

Sen, A., and B. Williams, eds. *Utilitarianism and Beyond* (Cambridge University Press, 1982).

Smart, J. J. C., and Bernard Williams. *Utilitarianism: For and Against* (Cambridge University Press, 1973).

Ten, C. L. *Mill on Liberty* (Oxford University Press, 1980).

UTILITARIANISM

CHAPTER I. GENERAL REMARKS

There are few circumstances among those which make up the present condition of human knowledge, more unlike what might have been expected, or more significant of the backward state in which speculation on the most important subjects still lingers, than the little progress which has been made in the decision of the controversy respecting the criterion of right and wrong. From the dawn of philosophy, the question concerning the summum bonum, or, what is the same thing, concerning the foundation of morality, has been accounted the main problem in speculative thought, has occupied the most gifted intellects, and divided them into sects and schools, carrying on a vigorous warfare against one another. And after more than two thousand years the same discussions continue, philosophers are still ranged under the same contending banners, and neither thinkers nor mankind at large seem nearer to being unanimous on the subject, than when the youth Socrates listened to the old Protagoras, and asserted (if Plato's dialogue be grounded on a real conversation) the theory of utilitarianism against the popular morality of the so-called sophist.

It is true that similar confusion and uncertainty, and in some cases similar discordance, exist respecting the first principles of all the sciences, not excepting that which is deemed the most certain of them, mathematics; without much impairing, generally indeed without impairing at all, the trustworthiness of the conclusions of those sciences. An apparent anomaly, the explanation of which is, that the detailed doctrines of a science are not usually deduced from, nor depend for their evidence upon, what are called its first principles. Were it not so, there would be no science more precarious, or whose conclusions were more insufficiently made out, than algebra; which derives none of its certainty from what are commonly taught to learners as its elements, since these, as laid down by some of its most eminent teachers, are as full of fictions as English law, and of mysteries as theology. The truths which are ultimately accepted as the first principles of a science, are really the last results of metaphysical analysis, practiced on the elementary notions with which the science is conversant; and their relation to the science is not that of foundations to an edifice, but of roots to a tree, which may perform their office equally well though they be never dug down to and exposed to light. But though in science the particular truths precede the general theory, the contrary might be expected to be the case with a practical art, such as morals or legislation. All action is for the sake of some end, and rules of action, it seems natural to suppose, must take their whole character and colour from the end to which they are subservient. When we engage in a pursuit, a clear and precise conception of what we are pursuing would seem to be the first thing we need, instead of the last we are to look forward to. A test of right and wrong must be the means, one would think, of ascertaining what is right or wrong, and not a consequence of having already ascertained it.

The difficulty is not avoided by having recourse to the popular theory of a natural faculty, a sense or instinct, informing us of right and wrong. For—besides that the existence of such a moral instinct is itself one of the matters in dispute—those believers in it who have any pretensions to philosophy, have been obliged to abandon the idea that it discerns what is right or wrong in the particular case in hand, as our other senses discern the sight or sound actually present. Our moral faculty, according to all those of its interpreters who are entitled to the name of thinkers, supplies us only with the general principles of moral judgments; it is a branch of our reason, not of our sensitive faculty; and must be looked to for the abstract doctrines of morality, not for perception of it in the concrete. The intuitive, no less than what may be termed the inductive, school of ethics, insists on the necessity of general laws. They both agree that the morality of an individual action is not a question of direct perception, but of the application of a law to an individual case. They recognize also, to a great extent, the same moral laws; but differ as to their evidence, and the source from which they derive their authority. According to the one opinion, the principles of morals are evident a priori, requiring nothing to command assent, except that the meaning of the terms be understood. According to the other doctrine, right and wrong, as well as truth and falsehood, are questions of observation and experience. But both hold equally that morality must be deduced from principles; and the intuitive school affirm as strongly as the inductive, that there is a science of morals. Yet they seldom attempt to make out a list of the a priori principles which are to serve as the premises of the science; still more rarely do they make any effort to reduce those various principles to one first principle, or common ground of obligation. They either assume the ordinary precepts of morals as of a priori authority, or they lay down as the common groundwork of those maxims, some generality much less obviously authoritative than the maxims themselves, and which has never succeeded in gaining popular acceptance. Yet to support their pretensions there ought either to be some one fundamental principle or law, at the root of all morality, or if there be several, there should be a determinate order of precedence among them; and the one principle, or the rule for deciding between the various principles when they conflict, ought to be self-evident.

To inquire how far the bad effects of this deficiency have been mitigated in practice, or to what extent the moral beliefs of mankind have been vitiated or made uncertain by the absence of any distinct recognition of an ultimate standard, would imply a complete survey and criticism of past and present ethical doctrine. It would, however, be easy to show that whatever steadiness or consistency these moral beliefs have attained, has been mainly due to the tacit influence of a standard not recognized. Although the non-existence of an acknowledged first principle has made ethics not so much a guide as a consecration of men's actual sentiments, still, as men's sentiments, both of favour and of aversion, are greatly influenced by what they suppose to be the effects of things upon their happiness, the principle of utility, or as Bentham latterly called it, the greatest happiness principle, has had a large share in forming the moral doctrines even of those who most scornfully reject its authority. Nor is there any school of thought which refuses to admit that the influence of actions on happiness is a most material and even predominant consideration in many of the details of morals, however unwilling to acknowledge it as the fundamental principle of morality, and the source of moral obligation. I might go much further, and say that to all those a priori moralists who deem it necessary to argue at all, utilitarian arguments are indispensable. It is not my present purpose to criticize these thinkers; but I cannot help referring, for illustration, to a systematic treatise by one of the most illustrious of them, the Metaphysics of Ethics, by Kant. This remarkable man, whose system of thought will long remain one of the landmarks in the history of philosophical speculation, does, in the treatise in question, lay down an universal first principle as the origin and ground of moral obligation; it is this:—'So act, that the rule on which thou actest would admit of being adopted as a law by all rational beings.' But when he begins to deduce from this precept any of the actual duties of morality, he fails, almost grotesquely, to show that there would be any contradiction, any logical (not to say physical) impossibility, in the adoption by all rational beings of the most outrageously immoral rules of conduct. All he shows is that the consequences of their universal adoption would be such as no one would choose to incur.

On the present occasion, I shall, without further discussion of the other theories, attempt to contribute something towards the understanding and appreciation of the Utilitarian or Happiness theory, and towards such proof as it is susceptible of. It is evident that this cannot be proof in the ordinary and popular meaning of the term. Questions of ultimate ends are not amenable to direct proof. Whatever can be proved to be good, must be so by being shown to be a means to something admitted to be good without proof. The medical art is proved to be good, by its conducing to health; but how is it possible to prove that health is good? The art of music is good, for the reason, among others, that it produces pleasure; but what proof is it possible to give that pleasure is good? If, then, it is asserted that there is a comprehensive formula, including all things which are in themselves good, and that whatever else is good, is not so as an end, but as a mean, the formula may be accepted or rejected, but is not a subject of what is commonly understood by proof. We are not, however, to infer that its acceptance or rejection must depend on blind impulse, or arbitrary choice. There is a larger meaning of the word proof, in which this question is as amenable to it as any other of the disputed questions of philosophy. The subject is within the cognizance of the rational faculty; and neither does that faculty deal with it solely in the way of intuition. Considerations may be presented capable of determining the intellect either to give or withhold its assent to the doctrine; and this is equivalent to proof.

We shall examine presently of what nature are these considerations; in what manner they apply to the case, and what rational grounds, therefore, can be given for accepting or rejecting the utilitarian formula. But it is a preliminary condition of rational acceptance or rejection, that the formula should be correctly understood. I believe that the very imperfect notion ordinarily formed of its meaning, is the chief obstacle which impedes its reception; and that could it be cleared, even from only the grosser misconceptions, the question would be greatly simplified, and a large proportion of its difficulties removed. Before, therefore, I attempt to enter into the philosophical grounds which can be given for assenting to the utilitarian standard, I shall offer some illustrations of the doctrine itself; with the view of showing more clearly what it is, distinguishing it from what it is not, and disposing of such of the practical objections to it as either originate in, or are closely connected with, mistaken interpretations of its meaning. Having thus prepared the ground, I shall afterwards endeavor to throw such light as I can upon the question, considered as one of philosophical theory.

CHAPTER II. WHAT UTILITARIANISM IS

A passing remark is all that needs be given to the ignorant blunder of supposing that those who stand up for utility as the test of right and wrong, use the term in that restricted and merely colloquial sense in which utility is opposed to pleasure. An apology is due to the philosophical opponents of utilitarianism, for even the momentary appearance of confounding them with any one capable of so absurd a misconception; which is the more extraordinary, inasmuch as the contrary accusation, of referring everything to pleasure, and that too in its grossest form, is another of the common charges against utilitarianism: and, as has been pointedly remarked by an able writer, the same sort of persons, and often the very same persons, denounce the theory 'as impracticably dry when the word utility precedes the word pleasure, and as too practically voluptuous when the word pleasure precedes the word utility.' Those who know anything about the matter are aware that every writer, from Epicurus to Bentham, who maintained the theory of utility, meant by it, not something to be contradistinguished from pleasure, but pleasure itself, together with exemption from pain; and instead of opposing the useful to the agreeable or the ornamental, have always declared that the useful means these, among other things. Yet the common herd, including the herd of writers, not only in newspapers and periodicals, but in books of weight and pretension, are perpetually falling into this shallow mistake. Having caught up the word utilitarian, while knowing nothing whatever about it but its sound, they habitually express by it the rejection, or the neglect, of pleasure in some of its forms; of beauty, of ornament, or of amusement. Nor is the term thus ignorantly misapplied solely in disparagement, but occasionally in compliment; as though it implied superiority to frivolity and the mere pleasures of the moment. And this perverted use is the only one in which the word is popularly known, and the one from which the new generation are acquiring their sole notion of its meaning. Those who introduced the word, but who had for many years discontinued it as a distinctive appellation, may well feel themselves called upon to resume it, if by doing so they can hope to contribute anything towards rescuing it from this utter degradation.

The creed which accepts as the foundation of morals, Utility, or the Greatest Happiness Principle, holds that actions are right in proportion as they tend to promote happiness, wrong as they tend to produce the reverse of happiness. By happiness is intended pleasure, and the absence of pain; by unhappiness, pain, and the privation of pleasure. To give a clear view of the moral standard set up by the theory, much more requires to be said; in particular, what things it includes in the ideas of pain and pleasure; and to what extent this is left an open question. But these supplementary explanations do not affect the theory of life on which this theory of morality is grounded namely, that pleasure, and freedom from pain, are the only things desirable as ends; and that all desirable things (which are as numerous in the utilitarian as in any other scheme) are desirable either for the pleasure inherent in themselves, or as means to the promotion of pleasure and the prevention of pain.

Now, such a theory of life excites in many minds, and among them in some of the most estimable in feeling and purpose, inveterate dislike. To suppose that life has (as they express it) no higher end than pleasure—no better and nobler object of desire and pursuit—they designate as utterly mean and grovelling; as a doctrine worthy only of swine, to whom the followers of Epicurus were, at a very early period, contemptuously likened; and modern holders of the doctrine are occasionally made the subject of equally polite comparisons by its German, French, and English assailants.

When thus attacked, the Epicureans have always answered, that it is not they, but their accusers, who represent human nature in a degrading light; since the accusation supposes human beings to be capable of no pleasures except those of which swine are capable. If this supposition were true, the charge could not be gainsaid, but would then be no longer an imputation; for if the sources of pleasure were precisely

the same to human beings and to swine, the rule of life which is good enough for the one would be good enough for the other. The comparison of the Epicurean life to that of beasts is felt as degrading, precisely because a beast's pleasures do not satisfy a human being's conceptions of happiness. Human beings have faculties more elevated than the animal appetites, and when once made conscious of them, do not regard anything as happiness which does not include their gratification. I do not, indeed, consider the Epicureans to have been by any means faultless in drawing out their scheme of consequences from the utilitarian principle. To do this in any sufficient manner, many Stoic, as well as Christian elements require to be included. But there is no known Epicurean theory of life which does not assign to the pleasures of the intellect, of the feelings and imagination, and of the moral sentiments, a much higher value as pleasures than to those of mere sensation. It must be admitted, however, that utilitarian writers in general have placed the superiority of mental over bodily pleasures chiefly in the greater permanency, safety, uncostliness, &c., of the former—that is, in their circumstantial advantages rather than in their intrinsic nature. And on all these points utilitarians have fully proved their case; but they might have taken the other, and, as it may be called, higher ground, with entire consistency. It is quite compatible with the principle of utility to recognize the fact, that some kinds of pleasure are more desirable and more valuable than others. It would be absurd that while, in estimating all other things, quality is considered as well as quantity, the estimation of pleasures should be supposed to depend on quantity alone.

If I am asked, what I mean by difference of quality in pleasures, or what makes one pleasure more valuable than another, merely as a pleasure, except its being greater in amount, there is but one possible answer. Of two pleasures, if there be one to which all or almost all who have experience of both give a decided preference, irrespective of any feeling of moral obligation to prefer it, that is the more desirable pleasure. If one of the two is, by those who are competently acquainted with both, placed so far above the other that they prefer it, even though knowing it to be attended with a greater amount of discontent, and would not resign it for any quantity of the other pleasure which their nature is capable of, we are justified in ascribing to the preferred enjoyment a superiority in quality, so far outweighing quantity as to render it, in comparison, of small account.

Now it is an unquestionable fact that those who are equally acquainted with, and equally capable of appreciating and enjoying, both, do give a most marked preference to the manner of existence which employs their higher faculties. Few human creatures would consent to be changed into any of the lower animals, for a promise of the fullest allowance of a beast's pleasures; no intelligent human being would consent to be a fool, no instructed person would be an ignoramus, no person of feeling and conscience would be selfish and base, even though they should be persuaded that the fool, the dunce, or the rascal is better satisfied with his lot than they are with theirs. They would not resign what they possess more than he, for the most complete satisfaction of all the desires which they have in common with him. If they ever fancy they would, it is only in cases of unhappiness so extreme, that to escape from it they would exchange their lot for almost any other, however undesirable in their own eyes. A being of higher faculties requires more to make him happy, is capable probably of more acute suffering, and is certainly accessible to it at more points, than one of an inferior type; but in spite of these liabilities, he can never really wish to sink into what he feels to be a lower grade of existence. We may give what explanation we please of this unwillingness; we may attribute it to pride, a name which is given indiscriminately to some of the most and to some of the least estimable feelings of which mankind are capable; we may refer it to the love of liberty and personal independence, an appeal to which was with the Stoics one of the most effective means for the inculcation of it; to the love of power, or to the love of excitement, both of which do really enter into and contribute to it: but its most appropriate appellation is a sense of dignity, which all human beings possess in one form or other, and in some, though by no means in exact, proportion to their higher faculties, and which is so essential a part of the happiness of those in whom it is strong, that nothing which conflicts with it could be, otherwise than momentarily, an object of desire

to them. Whoever supposes that this preference takes place at a sacrifice of happiness—that the superior being, in anything like equal circumstances, is not happier than the inferior—confounds the two very different ideas, of happiness, and content. It is indisputable that the being whose capacities of enjoyment are low, has the greatest chance of having them full satisfied; and a highly-endowed being will always feel that any happiness which he can look for, as the world is constituted, is imperfect. But he can learn to bear its imperfections, if they are at all bearable; and they will not make him envy the being who is indeed unconscious of the imperfections, but only because he feels not at all the good which those imperfections qualify. It is better to be a human being dissatisfied than a pig satisfied; better to be Socrates dissatisfied than a fool satisfied. And if the fool, or the pig, is of a different opinion, it is because they only know their own side of the question. The other party to the comparison knows both sides.

It may be objected, that many who are capable of the higher pleasures, occasionally, under the influence of temptation, postpone them to the lower. But this is quite compatible with a full appreciation of the intrinsic superiority of the higher. Men often, from infirmity of character, make their election for the nearer good, though they know it to be the less valuable; and this no less when the choice is between two bodily pleasures, than when it is between bodily and mental. They pursue sensual indulgences to the injury of health, though perfectly aware that health is the greater good. It may be further objected, that many who begin with youthful enthusiasm for everything noble, as they advance in years sink into indolence and selfishness. But I do not believe that those who undergo this very common change, voluntarily choose the lower description of pleasures in preference to the higher. I believe that before they devote themselves exclusively to the one, they have already become incapable of the other. Capacity for the nobler feelings is in most natures a very tender plant, easily killed, not only by hostile influences, but by mere want of sustenance; and in the majority of young persons it speedily dies away if the occupations to which their position in life has devoted them, and the society into which it has thrown them, are not favorable to keeping that higher capacity in exercise. Men lose their high aspirations as they lose their intellectual tastes, because they have not time or opportunity for indulging them; and they addict themselves to inferior pleasures, not because they deliberately prefer them, but because they are either the only ones to which they have access, or the only ones which they are any longer capable of enjoying. It may be questioned whether any one who has remained equally susceptible to both classes of pleasures, ever knowingly and calmly preferred the lower; though many, in all ages, have broken down in an ineffectual attempt to combine both.

From this verdict of the only competent judges, I apprehend there can be no appeal. On a question what is the best worth having of two pleasures, or which of two modes of existence is the most grateful to the feelings, apart from its moral attributes and from its consequences, the judgment of those who are qualified by knowledge of both, or, if they differ, that of the majority among them, must be admitted as final. And there needs be the less hesitation to accept this judgment respecting the quality of pleasures, since there is no other tribunal to be referred to even on the question of quantity. What means are there of determining which is the acutest of two pains, or the intensest of two pleasurable sensations, except the general suffrage of those who are familiar with both? Neither pains nor pleasures are homogeneous, and pain is always heterogeneous with pleasure. What is there to decide whether a particular pleasure is worth purchasing at the cost of a particular pain, except the feelings and judgment of the experienced? When, therefore, those feelings and judgment declare the pleasures derived from the higher faculties to be preferable in kind, apart from the question of intensity, to those of which the animal nature, disjoined from the higher faculties, is susceptible, they are entitled on this subject to the same regard.

I have dwelt on this point, as being a necessary part of a perfectly just conception of Utility or Happiness, considered as the directive rule of human conduct. But it is by no means an indispensable condition to the acceptance of the utilitarian standard; for that standard is not the agent's own greatest happiness, but the greatest amount of happiness altogether; and if it may possibly be doubted whether a noble character is always the happier for its nobleness, there can be no doubt that it makes other people happier, and that the world in general is immensely a gainer by it. Utilitarianism, therefore, could only attain its end by the general cultivation of nobleness of character, even if each individual were only benefited by the nobleness of others, and his own, so far as happiness is concerned, were a sheer deduction from the benefit. But the bare enunciation of such an absurdity as this last, renders refutation superfluous.

According to the Greatest Happiness Principle, as above explained, the ultimate end, with reference to and for the sake of which all other things are desirable (whether we are considering our own good or that of other people), is an existence exempt as far as possible from pain, and as rich as possible in enjoyments, both in point of quantity and quality; the test of quality, and the rule for measuring it against quantity, being the preference felt by those who in their opportunities of experience, to which must be added their habits of self-consciousness and self-observation, are best furnished with the means of comparison. This, being, according to the utilitarian opinion, the end of human action, is necessarily also the standard of morality; which may accordingly be defined, the rules and precepts for human conduct, by the observance of which an existence such as has been described might be, to the greatest extent possible, secured to all mankind; and not to them only, but, so far as the nature of things admits, to the whole sentient creation.

Against this doctrine, however, arises another class of objectors, who say that happiness, in any form, cannot be the rational purpose of human life and action; because, in the first place, it is unattainable: and they contemptuously ask, What right hast thou to be happy? a question which Mr. Carlyle clenches by the addition, What right, a short time ago, hadst thou even to be? Next, they say, that men can do without happiness; that all noble human beings have felt this, and could not have become noble but by learning the lesson of Entsagen, or renunciation; which lesson, thoroughly learnt and submitted to, they affirm to be the beginning and necessary condition of all virtue.

The first of these objections would go to the root of the matter were it well founded; for if no happiness is to be had at all by human beings, the attainment of it cannot be the end of morality, or of any rational conduct. Though, even in that case, something might still be said for the utilitarian theory; since utility includes not solely the pursuit of happiness, but the prevention or mitigation of unhappiness; and if the former aim be chimerical, there will be all the greater scope and more imperative need for the latter, so long at least as mankind think fit to live, and do not take refuge in the simultaneous act of suicide recommended under certain conditions by Novalis. When, however, it is thus positively asserted to be impossible that human life should be happy, the assertion, if not something like a verbal quibble, is at least an exaggeration. If by happiness be meant a continuity of highly pleasurable excitement, it is evident enough that this is impossible. A state of exalted pleasure lasts only moments, or in some cases, and with some intermissions, hours or days, and is the occasional brilliant flash of enjoyment, not its permanent and steady flame. Of this the philosophers who have taught that happiness is the end of life were as fully aware as those who taunt them. The happiness which they meant was not a life of rapture; but moments of such, in an existence made up of few and transitory pains, many and various pleasures, with a decided predominance of the active over the passive, and having as the foundation of the whole, not to expect more from life than it is capable of bestowing. A life thus composed, to those who have been fortunate enough to obtain it, has always appeared worthy of the name of happiness. And such an existence is even now the lot of many, during some considerable portion of their lives. The present wretched education, and wretched social arrangements, are the only real hindrance to its being attainable by almost all.

The objectors perhaps may doubt whether human beings, if taught to consider happiness as the end of life, would be satisfied with such a moderate share of it. But great numbers of mankind have been satisfied with much less. The main constituents of a satisfied life appear to be two, either of which by itself is often found sufficient for the purpose: tranquillity, and excitement. With much tranquillity, many find that they can be content with very little pleasure: with much excitement, many can reconcile themselves to a considerable quantity of pain. There is assuredly no inherent impossibility in enabling even the mass of mankind to unite both; since the two are so far

from being incompatible that they are in natural alliance, the prolongation of either being a preparation for, and exciting a wish for, the other. It is only those in whom indolence amounts to a vice, that do not desire excitement after an interval of repose; it is only those in whom the need of excitement is a disease, that feel the tranquillity which follows excitement dull and insipid, instead of pleasurable in direct proportion to the excitement which preceded it. When people who are tolerably fortunate in their outward lot do not find in life sufficient enjoyment to make it valuable to them, the cause generally is, caring for nobody but themselves. To those who have neither public nor private affections, the excitements of life are much curtailed, and in any case dwindle in value as the time approaches when all selfish interests must be terminated by death: while those who leave after them objects of personal affection, and especially those who have also cultivated a fellow-feeling with the collective interests of mankind, retain as lively an interest in life on the eve of death as in the vigor of youth and health. Next to selfishness, the principal cause which makes life unsatisfactory is want of mental cultivation. A cultivated mind—I do not mean that of a philosopher, but any mind to which the fountains of knowledge have been opened, and which has been taught, in any tolerable degree, to exercise its faculties—finds sources of inexhaustible interest in all that surrounds it; in the objects of nature, the achievements of art, the imaginations of poetry, the incidents of history, the ways of mankind past and present, and their prospects in the future. It is possible, indeed, to become indifferent to all this, and that too without having exhausted a thousandth part of it; but only when one has had from the beginning no moral or human interest in these things, and has sought in them only the gratification of curiosity.

Now there is absolutely no reason in the nature of things why an amount of mental culture sufficient to give an intelligent interest in these objects of contemplation, should not be the inheritance of every one born in a civilized country. As little is there an inherent necessity that any human being should be a selfish egotist, devoid of every feeling or care but those which centre in his own miserable individuality. Something far superior to this is sufficiently common even now, to give ample earnest of what the human species may be made. Genuine private affections, and a sincere interest in the public good, are possible, though in unequal degrees, to every rightly brought up human being. In a world in which there is so much to interest, so much to enjoy, and so much also to correct and improve, every one who has this moderate amount of moral and intellectual requisites is capable of an existence which may be called enviable; and unless such a person, through bad laws, or subjection to the will of others, is denied the liberty to use the sources of happiness within his reach, he will not fail to find this enviable existence, if he escape the positive evils of life, the great sources of physical and mental suffering—such as indigence, disease, and the unkindness, worthlessness, or premature loss of objects of affection. The main stress of the problem lies, therefore, in the contest with these calamities, from which it is a rare good fortune entirely to escape; which, as things now are, cannot be obviated, and often cannot be in any material degree mitigated. Yet no one whose opinion deserves a moment's consideration can doubt that most of the great positive evils of the world are in themselves removable, and will, if human affairs continue to improve, be in the end reduced within narrow limits. Poverty, in any sense implying suffering, may be completely extinguished by the wisdom of society, combined with the good sense and providence of individuals. Even that most intractable of enemies, disease, may be indefinitely reduced in dimensions by good physical and moral education, and proper control of noxious influences; while the progress of science holds out a promise for the future of still more direct conquests over this detestable foe. And every advance in that direction relieves us from some, not only of the chances which cut short our own lives, but, what concerns us still more, which deprive us of those in whom our happiness is wrapped up. As for vicissitudes of fortune, and other disappointments connected with worldly circumstances, these are principally the effect either of gross imprudence, of ill-regulated desires, or of bad or imperfect social institutions. All the grand sources, in short, of human suffering are in a great degree, many of them almost entirely, conquerable by human care and effort; and though their removal is grievously slow—though a long succession of generations will

perish in the breach before the conquest is completed, and this world becomes all that, if will and knowledge were not wanting, it might easily be made—yet every mind sufficiently intelligent and generous to bear a part, however small and inconspicuous, in the endeavor, will draw a noble enjoyment from the contest itself, which he would not for any bribe in the form of selfish indulgence consent to be without.

And this leads to the true estimation of what is said by the objectors concerning the possibility, and the obligation, of learning to do without happiness. Unquestionably it is possible to do without happiness; it is done involuntarily by nineteen-twentieths of mankind, even in those parts of our present world which are least deep in barbarism; and it often has to be done voluntarily by the hero or the martyr, for the sake of something which he prizes more than his individual happiness. But this something, what is it, unless the happiness of others, or some of the requisites of happiness? It is noble to be capable of resigning entirely one's own portion of happiness, or chances of it: but, after all, this self-sacrifice must be for some end; it is not its own end; and if we are told that its end is not happiness, but virtue, which is better than happiness, I ask, would the sacrifice be made if the hero or martyr did not believe that it would earn for others immunity from similar sacrifices? Would it be made if he thought that his renunciation of happiness for himself would produce no fruit for any of his fellow creatures, but to make their lot like his, and place them also in the condition of persons who have renounced happiness? All honour to those who can abnegate for themselves the personal enjoyment of life, when by such renunciation they contribute worthily to increase the amount of happiness in the world; but he who does it, or professes to do it, for any other purpose, is no more deserving of admiration than the ascetic mounted on his pillar. He may be an inspiriting proof of what men can do, but assuredly not an example of what they should.

Though it is only in a very imperfect state of the world's arrangements that any one can best serve the happiness of others by the absolute sacrifice of his own, yet so long as the world is in that imperfect state, I fully acknowledge that the readiness to make such a sacrifice is the highest virtue which can be found in man. I will add, that in this condition of the world, paradoxical as the assertion may be, the conscious ability to do without happiness gives the best prospect of realizing such happiness as is attainable. For nothing except that consciousness can raise a person above the chances of life, by making him feel that, let fate and fortune do their worst, they have not power to subdue him: which, once felt, frees him from excess of anxiety concerning the evils of life, and enables him, like many a Stoic in the worst times of the Roman Empire, to cultivate in tranquillity the sources of satisfaction accessible to him, without concerning himself about the uncertainty of their duration, any more than about their inevitable end.

Meanwhile, let utilitarians never cease to claim the morality of self-devotion as a possession which belongs by as good a right to them, as either to the Stoic or to the Transcendentalist. The utilitarian morality does recognize in human beings the power of sacrificing their own greatest good for the good of others. It only refuses to admit that the sacrifice is itself a good. A sacrifice which does not increase, or tend to increase, the sum total of happiness, it considers as wasted. The only self-renunciation which it applauds, is devotion to the happiness, or to some of the means of happiness, of others; either of mankind collectively, or of individuals within the limits imposed by the collective interests of mankind.

I must again repeat, what the assailants of utilitarianism seldom have the justice to acknowledge, that the happiness which forms the utilitarian standard of what is right in conduct, is not the agent's own happiness, but that of all concerned. As between his own happiness and that of others, utilitarianism requires him to be as strictly impartial as a disinterested and benevolent spectator. In the golden rule of Jesus of Nazareth, we read the complete spirit of the ethics of utility. To do as one would be done by, and to love one's neighbor as oneself, constitute the ideal perfection of utilitarian morality. As the means of making the nearest approach to this ideal, utility would enjoin, first, that laws and social arrangements should place the happiness, or (as speaking practically it may be called) the interest, of every individual, as nearly as possible in harmony with the inter-

est of the whole; and secondly, that education and opinion, which have so vast a power over human character, should so use that power as to establish in the mind of every individual an indissoluble association between his own happiness and the good of the whole; especially between his own happiness and the practice of such modes of conduct, negative and positive, as regard for the universal happiness prescribes: so that not only he may be unable to conceive the possibility of happiness to himself, consistently with conduct opposed to the general good, but also that a direct impulse to promote the general good may be in every individual one of the habitual motives of action, and the sentiments connected therewith may fill a large and prominent place in every human being's sentient existence. If the impugners of the utilitarian morality represented it to their own minds in this its true character, I know not what recommendation possessed by any other morality they could possibly affirm to be wanting to it: what more beautiful or more exalted developments of human nature any other ethical system can be supposed to foster, or what springs of action, not accessible to the utilitarian, such systems rely on for giving effect to their mandates.

The objectors to utilitarianism cannot always be charged with representing it in a discreditable light. On the contrary, those among them who entertain anything like a just idea of its disinterested character, sometimes find fault with its standard as being too high for humanity. They say it is exacting too much to require that people shall always act from the inducement of promoting the general interests of society. But this is to mistake the very meaning of a standard of morals, and to confound the rule of action with the motive of it. It is the business of ethics to tell us what are our duties, or by what test we may know them; but no system of ethics requires that the sole motive of all we do shall be a feeling of duty; on the contrary, ninety-nine hundredths of all our actions are done from other motives, and rightly so done, if the rule of duty does not condemn them. It is the more unjust to utilitarianism that this particular misapprehension should be made a ground of objection to it, inasmuch as utilitarian moralists have gone beyond almost all others in affirming that the motive has nothing to do with the morality of the action, though much with the worth of the agent. He who saves a fellow creature from drowning does what is morally right, whether his motive be duty, or the hope of being paid for his trouble: he who betrays the friend that trusts him, is guilty of a crime, even if his object be to serve another friend to whom he is under greater obligations. But to speak only of actions done from the motive of duty, and in direct obedience to principle: it is a misapprehension of the utilitarian mode of thought, to conceive it as implying that people should fix their minds upon so wide a generality as the world, or society at large. The great majority of good actions are intended, not for the benefit of the world, but for that of individuals, of which the good of the world is made up; and the thoughts of the most virtuous man need not on these occasions travel beyond the particular persons concerned, except so far as is necessary to assure himself that in benefiting them he is not violating the rights—that is, the legitimate and authorized expectations—of any one else. The multiplication of happiness is, according to the utilitarian ethics, the object of virtue: the occasions on which any person (except one in a thousand) has it in his power to do this on an extended scale, in other words, to be a public benefactor, are but exceptional; and on these occasions alone is he called on to consider public utility; in every other case, private utility, the interest or happiness of some few persons, is all he has to attend to. Those alone the influence of whose actions extends to society in general, need concern themselves habitually about so large an object. In the case of abstinences indeed— of things which people forbear to do, from moral considerations, though the consequences in the particular case might be beneficial—it would be unworthy of an intelligent agent not to be consciously aware that the action is of a class which, if practiced generally, would be generally injurious, and that this is the ground of the obligation to abstain from it. The amount of regard for the public interest implied in this recognition, is no greater than is demanded by every system of morals; for they all enjoin to abstain from whatever is manifestly pernicious to society.

The same considerations dispose of another reproach against the doctrine of utility, founded on a still grosser misconception of the purpose of a standard of morality, and of the very meaning of the words right and wrong. It is often affirmed that utilitarianism renders men cold and unsympathizing; that it chills their moral feelings towards individuals; that it makes them regard only the dry and hard consideration of the consequences of actions, not taking into their moral estimate the qualities from which those actions emanate. If the assertion means that they do not allow their judgment respecting the rightness or wrongness of an action to be influenced by their opinion of the qualities of the person who does it, this is a complaint not against utilitarianism, but against having any standard of morality at all; for certainly no known ethical standard decides an action to be good or bad because it is done by a good or a bad man, still less because done by an amiable, a brave, or a benevolent man, or the contrary. These considerations are relevant, not to the estimation of actions, but of persons; and there is nothing in the utilitarian theory inconsistent with the fact that there are other things which interest us in persons besides the rightness and wrongness of their actions. The Stoics, indeed, with the paradoxical misuse of language which was part of their system, and by which they strove to raise themselves above all concern about anything but virtue, were fond of saying that he who has that has everything; that he, and only he, is rich, is beautiful, is a king. But no claim of this description is made for the virtuous man by the utilitarian doctrine. Utilitarians are quite aware that there are other desirable possessions and qualities besides virtue, and are perfectly willing to allow to all of them their full worth. They are also aware that a right action does not necessarily indicate a virtuous character, and that actions which are blameable often proceed from qualities entitled to praise. When this is apparent in any particular case, it modifies their estimation, not certainly of the act, but of the agent. I grant that they are, notwithstanding, of opinion, that in the long run the best proof of a good character is good actions; and resolutely refuse to consider any mental disposition as good, of which the predominant tendency is to produce bad conduct. This makes them unpopular with many people; but it is an unpopularity which they must share with every one who regards the distinction between right and wrong in a serious light; and the reproach is not one which a conscientious utilitarian need be anxious to repel.

If no more be meant by the objection than that many utilitarians look on the morality of actions, as measured by the utilitarian standard, with too exclusive a regard, and do not lay sufficient stress upon the other beauties of character which go towards making a human being loveable or admirable, this may be admitted. Utilitarians who have cultivated their moral feelings, but not their sympathies nor their artistic perceptions, do fall into this mistake; and so do all other moralists under the same conditions. What can be said in excuse for other moralists is equally available for them, namely, that if there is to be any error, it is better that it should be on that side. As a matter of fact, we may affirm that among utilitarians as among adherents of other systems, there is every imaginable degree of rigidity and of laxity in the application of their standard: some are even puritanically rigorous, while others are as indulgent as can possibly be desired by sinner or by sentimentalist. But on the whole, a doctrine which brings prominently forward the interest that mankind have in the repression and prevention of conduct which violates the moral law, is likely to be inferior to no other in turning the sanctions of opinion against such violations. It is true, the question, What does violate the moral law? is one on which those who recognize different standards of morality are likely now and then to differ. But difference of opinion on moral questions was not first introduced into the world by utilitarianism, while that doctrine does supply, if not always an easy, at all events a tangible and intelligible mode of deciding such differences.

It may not be superfluous to notice a few more of the common misapprehensions of utilitarian ethics, even those which are so obvious and gross that it might appear impossible for any person of candor and intelligence to fall into them: since persons, even of considerable mental endowments, often give themselves so little trouble to understand the bearings of any opinion against which they entertain a prejudice, and men are in general so little conscious of this voluntary ignorance as a defect, that the vulgarest misunderstandings of ethical doctrines are continually met with in the deliberate writings of persons of the greatest pretensions both to high principle and to philosophy. We not uncommonly hear the doctrine of utility inveighed against as a godless doctrine. If it be necessary to say anything at all against so mere an assumption, we may say that the question depends upon what idea we have formed of the moral character of the Deity. If it be a true belief that God desires, above all things, the happiness of his creatures, and that this was his purpose in their creation, utility is not only not a godless doctrine, but more profoundly religious than any other. If it be meant that utilitarianism does not recognize the revealed will of God as the supreme law of morals, I answer, that an utilitarian who believes in the perfect goodness and wisdom of God, necessarily believes that whatever God has thought fit to reveal on the subject of morals, must fulfil the requirements of utility in a supreme degree. But others besides utilitarians have been of opinion that the Christian revelation was intended, and is fitted, to inform the hearts and minds of mankind with a spirit which should enable them to find for themselves what is right, and incline them to do it when found, rather than to tell them, except in a very general way, what it is: and that we need a doctrine of ethics, carefully followed out, to interpret to us the will of God. Whether this opinion is correct or not, it is superfluous here to discuss; since whatever aid religion, either natural or revealed, can afford to ethical investigation, is as open to the utilitarian moralist as to any other. He can use it as the testimony of God to the usefulness or hurtfulness of an given course of action, by as good a right as others can use it for the indication of a transcendental law, having no connexion with usefulness or with happiness.

Again, Utility is often summarily stigmatized as an immoral doctrine by giving it the name of Expediency, and taking advantage of the popular use of that term to contrast it with Principle. But the Expedient, in the sense in which it is opposed to the Right, generally means that which is expedient for the particular interest of the agent himself; as when a minister sacrifices the interest of his country to keep himself in place. When it means anything better than this, it means that which is expedient for some immediate object, some temporary purpose, but which violates a rule whose observance is expedient in a much higher degree. The Expedient, in this sense, instead of being the same thing with the useful, is a branch of the hurtful. Thus, it would often be expedient, for the purpose of getting over some momentary embarrassment, or attaining some object immediately useful to ourselves or others, to tell a lie. But inasmuch as the cultivation in ourselves of a sensitive feeling on the subject of veracity, is one of the most useful, and the enfeeblement of that feeling one of the most hurtful, things to which our conduct can be instrumental; and inasmuch as any, even unintentional, deviation from truth, does that much towards weakening the trustworthiness of human assertion, which is not only the principal support of all present social well-being, but the insufficiency of which does more than any one thing that can be named to keep back civilization, virtue, everything on which human happiness on the largest scale depends; we feel that the violation, for a present advantage, of a rule of such transcendent expediency, is not expedient, and that he who, for the sake of a convenience to himself or to some other individual, does what depends on him to deprive mankind of the good, and inflict upon them the evil, involved in the greater or less reliance which they can place in each other's word, acts the part of one of their worst enemies. Yet that even this rule, sacred as it is, admits of possible exceptions, is acknowledged by all moralists; the chief of which is when the withholding of some fact (as of information from a malefactor, or of bad news from a person dangerously ill) would preserve some one (especially a person other than oneself) from great and unmerited evil, and when the withholding can only be effected by denial. But in order that the exception may not extend itself beyond the need, and may have the least possible effect in weakening reliance on veracity, it ought to be recognized, and, if possible, its limits defined; and if the principle of utility is good for anything, it must be good for weighing these conflicting utilities against one another, and marking out the region within which one or the other preponderates.

Again, defenders of utility often find themselves called upon to reply to such objections as this—that there is not time, previous to action, for calculating and weighing the effects of any line of conduct on the general happiness. This is exactly as if any one were to say that it is impossible to guide our conduct by Christianity, because there is not time, on every occasion on which anything has to be done, to read through the Old and New Testaments. The answer to the objection is, that there has been ample time, namely, the whole past duration of the human species. During all that time mankind have been learning by experience the tendencies of actions; on which experience all the prudence, as well as all the morality of life, is dependent. People talk as if the commencement of this course of experience had hitherto been put off, and as if, at the moment when some man feels tempted to meddle with the property or life of another, he had to begin considering for the first time whether murder and theft are injurious to human happiness. Even then I do not think that he would find the question very puzzling; but, at all events, the matter is now done to his hand. It is truly a whimsical supposition that if mankind were agreed in considering utility to be the test of morality, they would remain without any agreement as to what is useful, and would take no measures for having their notions on the subject taught to the young, and enforced by law and opinion. There is no difficulty in proving any ethical standard whatever to work ill, if we suppose universal idiocy to be conjoined with it; but on any hypothesis short of that, mankind must by this time have acquired positive beliefs as to the effects of some actions on their happiness; and the beliefs which have thus come down are the rules of morality for the multitude, and for the philosopher until he has succeeded in finding better. That philosophers might easily do this, even now, on many subjects; that the received code of ethics is by no means of divine right; and that mankind have still much to learn as to the effects of actions on the general happiness, I admit, or rather, earnestly maintain. The corollaries from the principle of utility, like the precepts of every practical art, admit of indefinite improvement, and, in a progressive state of the human mind, their improvement is perpetually going on. But to consider the rules of morality as improvable, is one thing; to pass over the intermediate generalizations entirely, and endeavor to test each individual action directly by the first principle, is another. It is a strange notion that the acknowledgment of a first principle is inconsistent with the admission of secondary ones. To inform a traveller respecting the place of his ultimate destination, is not to forbid the use of landmarks and direction-posts on the way. The proposition that happiness is the end and aim of morality, does not mean that no road ought to be laid down to that goal, or that persons going thither should not be advised to take one direction rather than another. Men really ought to leave off talking a kind of nonsense on this subject, which they would neither talk nor listen to on other matters of practical concernment. Nobody argues that the art of navigation is not founded on astronomy, because sailors cannot wait to calculate the Nautical Almanac. Being rational creatures, they go to sea with it ready calculated; and all rational creatures go out upon the sea of life with their minds made up on the common questions of right and wrong, as well as on many of the far more difficult questions of wise and foolish. And this, as long as foresight is a human quality, it is to be presumed they will continue to do. Whatever we adopt as the fundamental principle of morality, we require subordinate principles to apply it by: the impossibility of doing without them, being common to all systems, can afford no argument against any one in particular: but gravely to argue as if no such secondary principles could be had, and as if mankind had remained till now, and always must remain, without drawing any general conclusions from the experience of human life, is as high a pitch, I think, as absurdity has ever reached in philosophical controversy.

The remainder of the stock arguments against utilitarianism mostly consist in laying to its charge the common infirmities of human nature, and the general difficulties which embarrass conscientious persons in shaping their course through life. We are told that an utilitarian will be apt to make his own particular case an exception to moral rules, and, when under temptation, will see an utility in the breach of a rule, greater than he will see in its observance. But is utility the only creed which is able to furnish us with excuses for evil doing, and means of cheating our own conscience? They are afforded in abundance by all doctrines which recognize as a fact in morals the existence of conflicting considerations; which all doctrines do, that have been believed by sane persons. It is not the fault of any creed, but of the complicated nature of human affairs, that rules of conduct cannot be so framed as to require no exceptions, and that hardly any kind of action can safely be laid down as either always obligatory or always condemnable. There is no ethical creed which does not temper the rigidity of its laws, by giving a certain latitude, under the moral responsibility of the agent, for accommodation to peculiarities of circumstances; and under every creed, at the opening thus made, self-deception and dishonest casuistry get in. There exists no moral system under which there do not arise unequivocal cases of conflicting obligation. These are the real difficulties, the knotty points both in the theory of ethics, and in the conscientious guidance of personal conduct. They are overcome practically with greater or with less success according to the intellect and virtue of the individual; but it can hardly be pretended that any one will be the less qualified for dealing with them, from possessing an ultimate standard to which conflicting rights and duties can be referred. If utility is the ultimate source of moral obligations, utility may be invoked to decide between them when their demands are incompatible. Though the application of the standard may be difficult, it is better than none at all: while in other systems, the moral laws all claiming independent authority, there is no common umpire entitled to interfere between them; their claims to precedence one over another rest on little better than sophistry, and unless determined, as they generally are, by the unacknowledged influence of considerations of utility, afford a free scope for the action of personal desires and partialities. We must remember that only in these cases of conflict between secondary principles is it requisite that first principles should be appealed to. There is no case of moral obligation in which some secondary principle is not involved; and if only one, there can seldom be any real doubt which one it is, in the mind of any person by whom the principle itself is recognized.

CHAPTER III. OF THE ULTIMATE SANCTION OF THE PRINCIPLE OF UTILITY

The question is often asked, and properly so, in regard to any supposed moral standard—What is its sanction? what are the motives to obey it? or more specifically, what is the source of its obligation? whence does it derive its binding force? It is a necessary part of moral philosophy to provide the answer to this question; which, though frequently assuming the shape of an objection to the utilitarian morality, as if it had some special applicability to that above others, really arises in regard to all standards. It arises, in fact, whenever a person is called on to adopt a standard, or refer morality to any basis on which he has not been accustomed to rest it. For the customary morality, that which education and opinion have consecrated, is the only one which presents itself to the mind with the feeling of being in itself obligatory; and when a person is asked to believe that this morality derives its obligation from some general principle round which custom has not thrown the same halo, the assertion is to him a paradox; the supposed corollaries seem to have a more binding force than the original theorem; the superstructure seems to stand better without, than with, what is represented as its foundation. He says to himself, I feel that I am bound not to rob or murder, betray or deceive; but why am I bound to promote the general happiness? If my own happiness lies in something else, why may I not give that the preference?

If the view adopted by the utilitarian philosophy of the nature of the moral sense be correct, this difficulty will always present itself, until the influences which form moral character have taken the same hold of the principle which they have taken of some of the consequences—until, by the improvement of education, the feeling of unity with our fellow creatures shall be (what it cannot be doubted that Christ intended it to be) as deeply rooted in our character, and to our own consciousness as completely a part of our nature, as the horror of crime is in an ordinarily well-brought up young person. In the mean time, however, the difficulty has no peculiar application to the doctrine of utility, but is inherent in every attempt to analyse morality and reduce it to principles; which, unless the principle is already in men's minds invested with as much sacredness as any of its applications, always seems to divest them of a part of their sanctity.

The principle of utility either has, or there is no reason why it might not have, all the sanctions which belong to any other system of morals. Those sanctions are either external or internal. Of the external

sanctions it is not necessary to speak at any length. They are, the hope of favour and the fear of displeasure from our fellow creatures or from the Ruler of the Universe, along with whatever we may have of sympathy or affection for them, or of love and awe of Him, inclining us to do his will independently of selfish consequences. There is evidently no reason why all these motives for observance should not attach themselves to the utilitarian morality, as completely and as powerfully as to any other. Indeed, those of them which refer to our fellow creatures are sure to do so, in proportion to the amount of general intelligence; for whether there be any other ground of moral obligation than the general happiness or not, men do desire happiness; and however imperfect may be their own practice, they desire and commend all conduct in others towards themselves, by which they think their happiness is promoted. With regard to the religious motive, if men believe, as most profess to do, in the goodness of God, those who think that conduciveness to the general happiness is the essence, or even only the criterion, of good, must necessarily believe that it is also that which God approves. The whole force therefore of external reward and punishment, whether physical or moral, and whether proceeding from God or from our fellow men, together with all that the capacities of human nature admit, of disinterested devotion to either, become available to enforce the utilitarian morality, in proportion as that morality is recognized; and the more powerfully, the more the appliances of education and general cultivation are bent to the purpose.

So far as to external sanctions. The internal sanction of duty, whatever our standard of duty may be, is one and the same—a feeling in our own mind; a pain, more or less intense, attendant on violation of duty, which in properly-cultivated moral natures rises, in the more serious cases, into shrinking from it as an impossibility. This feeling, when disinterested, and connecting itself with the pure idea of duty, and not with some particular form of it, or with any of the merely accessory circumstances, is the essence of Conscience; though in that complex phenomenon as it actually exists, the simple fact is in general all encrusted over with collateral associations, derived from sympathy, from love, and still more from fear; from all the forms of religious feeling; from the recollections of childhood and of all our past life; from self-esteem, desire of the esteem of others, and occasionally even self-abasement. This extreme complication is, I apprehend, the origin of the sort of mystical character which, by a tendency of the human mind of which there are many other examples, is apt to be attributed to the idea of moral obligation, and which leads people to believe that the idea cannot possibly attach itself to any other objects than those which, by a supposed mysterious law, are found in our present experience to excite it. Its binding force, however, consists in the existence of a mass of feeling which must be broken through in order to do what violates our standard of right, and which, if we do nevertheless violate that standard, will probably have to be encountered afterwards in the form of remorse. Whatever theory we have of the nature or origin of conscience, this is what essentially constitutes it.

The ultimate sanction, therefore, of all morality (external motives apart) being a subjective feeling in our own minds, I see nothing embarrassing to those whose standard is utility, in the question, what is the sanction of that particular standard? We may answer, the same as of all other moral standards—the conscientious feelings of mankind. Undoubtedly this sanction has no binding efficacy on those who do not possess the feelings it appeals to; but neither will these persons be more obedient to any other moral principle than to the utilitarian one. On them morality of any kind has no hold but through the external sanctions. Meanwhile the feelings exist, a fact in human nature, the reality of which, and the great power with which they are capable of acting on those in whom they have been duly cultivated, are proved by experience. No reason has ever been shown why they may not be cultivated to as great intensity in connexion with the utilitarian, as with any other rule of morals.

There is, I am aware, a disposition to believe that a person who sees in moral obligation a transcendental fact, an objective reality belonging to the province of 'Things in themselves,' is likely to be more obedient to it than one who believes it to be entirely subjective, having its seat in human consciousness only. But whatever a person's opinion may be on this point of Ontology, the force he is re-

ally urged by is his own subjective feeling, and is exactly measured by its strength. No one's belief that Duty is an objective reality is stronger than the belief that God is so; yet the belief in God, apart from the expectation of actual reward and punishment, only operates on conduct through, and in proportion to, the subjective religious feeling. The sanction, so far as it is disinterested, is always in the mind itself; and the notion therefore of the transcendental moralists must be, that this sanction will not exist in the mind unless it is believed to have its root out of the mind; and that if a person is able to say to himself, This which is restraining me, and which is called my conscience, is only a feeling in my own mind, he may possibly draw the conclusion that when the feeling ceases the obligation ceases, and that if he find the feeling inconvenient, he may disregard it, and endeavor to get rid of it. But is this danger confined to the utilitarian morality? Does the belief that moral obligation has its seat outside the mind make the feeling of it too strong to be got rid of? The fact is so far otherwise, that all moralists admit and lament the ease with which, in the generality of minds, conscience can be silenced or stifled. The question, Need I obey my conscience? is quite as often put to themselves by persons who never heard of the principle of utility, as by its adherents. Those whose conscientious feelings are so weak as to allow of their asking this question, if they answer it affirmatively, will not do so because they believe in the transcendental theory, but because of the external sanctions.

It is not necessary, for the present purpose, to decide whether the feeling of duty is innate or implanted. Assuming it to be innate, it is an open question to what objects it naturally attaches itself; for the philosophic supporters of that theory are now agreed that the intuitive perception is of principles of morality, and not of the details. If there be anything innate in the matter, I see no reason why the feeling which is innate should not be that of regard to the pleasures and pains of others. If there is any principle of morals which is intuitively obligatory, I should say it must be that. If so, the intuitive ethics would coincide with the utilitarian, and there would be no further quarrel between them. Even as it is, the intuitive moralists, though they believe that there are other intuitive moral obligations, do already believe this to be one; for they unanimously hold that a large portion of morality turns upon the consideration due to the interests of our fellow creatures. Therefore, if the belief in the transcendental origin of moral obligation gives any additional efficacy to the internal sanction, it appears to me that the utilitarian principle has already the benefit of it.

On the other hand, if, as is my own belief, the moral feelings are not innate, but acquired, they are not for that reason the less natural. It is natural to man to speak, to reason, to build cities, to cultivate the ground, though these are acquired faculties. The moral feelings are not indeed a part of our nature, in the sense of being in any perceptible degree present in all of us; but this, unhappily, is a fact admitted by those who believe the most strenuously in their transcendental origin. Like the other acquired capacities above referred to, the moral faculty, if not a part of our nature, is a natural outgrowth from it; capable, like them, in a certain small degree, of springing up spontaneously; and susceptible of being brought by cultivation to a high degree of development. Unhappily it is also susceptible, by a sufficient use of the external sanctions and of the force of early impressions, of being cultivated in almost any direction: so that there is hardly anything so absurd or so mischievous that it may not, by means of these influences, be made to act on the human mind with all the authority of conscience. To doubt that the same potency might be given by the same means to the principle of utility, even if it had no foundation in human nature, would be flying in the face of all experience.

But moral associations which are wholly of artificial creation, when intellectual culture goes on, yield by degrees to the dissolving force of analysis: and if the feeling of duty, when associated with utility, would appear equally arbitrary; if there were no leading department of our nature, no powerful class of sentiments, with which that association would harmonize, which would make us feel it congenial, and incline us not only to foster it in others (for which we have abundant interested motives), but also to cherish it in ourselves; if there were not, in short, a natural basis of sentiment for utilitarian morality, it might well happen that his association also, even after it had been implanted by education, might be analysed away.

But there is this basis of powerful natural sentiment; and this it is which, when once the general happiness is recognized as the ethical standard, will constitute the strength of the utilitarian morality. This firm foundation is that of the social feelings of mankind; the desire to be in unity with our fellow creatures, which is already a powerful principle in human nature, and happily one of those which tend to become stronger, even without express inculcation, from the influences of advancing civilization. The social state is at once so natural, so necessary, and so habitual to man, that, except in some unusual circumstances or by an effort of voluntary abstraction, he never conceives himself otherwise than as a member of a body; and this association is riveted more and more, as mankind are further removed from the state of savage independence. Any condition, therefore, which is essential to a state of society, becomes more and more an inseparable part of every person's conception of the state of things which he is born into, and which is the destiny of a human being. Now, society between human beings, except in the relation of master and slave, is manifestly impossible on any other footing than that the interests of all are to be consulted. Society between equals can only exist on the understanding that the interests of all are to be regarded equally. And since in all states of civilization, every person, except an absolute monarch, has equals, every one is obliged to live on these terms with somebody; and in every age some advance is made towards a state in which it will be impossible to live permanently on other terms with anybody. In this way people grow up unable to conceive as possible to them a state of total disregard of other people's interests. They are under a necessity of conceiving themselves as at least abstaining from all the grosser injuries, and (if only for their own protection) living in a state of constant protest against them. They are also familiar with the fact of co-operating with others, and proposing to themselves a collective, not an individual, interest, as the aim (at least for the time being) of their actions. So long as they are co-operating, their ends are identified with those of others; there is at least a temporary feeling that the interests of others are their own interests. Not only does all strengthening of social ties, and all healthy growth of society, give to each individual a stronger personal interest in practically consulting the welfare of others; it also leads him to identify his feelings more and more with their good, or at least with an ever greater degree of practical consideration for it. He comes, as though instinctively, to be conscious of himself as a being who of course pays regard to others. The good of others becomes to him a thing naturally and necessarily to be attended to, like any of the physical conditions of our existence. Now, whatever amount of this feeling a person has, he is urged by the strongest motives both of interest and of sympathy to demonstrate it, and to the utmost of his power encourage it in others; and even if he has none of it himself, he is as greatly interested as any one else that others should have it. Consequently the smallest germs of the feeling are laid hold of and nourished by the contagion of sympathy and the influences of education; and a complete web of corroborative association is woven round it, by the powerful agency of the external sanctions. This mode of conceiving ourselves and human life, as civilization goes on, is felt to be more and more natural. Every step in political improvement renders it more so, by removing the sources of opposition of interest, and levelling those inequalities of legal privilege between individuals or classes, owing to which there are large portions of mankind whose happiness it is still practicable to disregard. In an improving state of the human mind, the influences are constantly on the increase, which tend to generate in each individual a feeling of unity with all the rest; which feeling, if perfect, would make him never think of, or desire, any beneficial condition for himself, in the benefits of which they are not included. If we now suppose this feeling of unity to be taught as a religion, and the whole force of education, of institutions, and of opinion, directed, as it once was in the case of religion, to make every person grow up from infancy surrounded on all sides both by the profession and by the practice of it, I think that no one, who can realize this conception, will feel any misgiving about the sufficiency of the ultimate sanction for the Happiness morality. To any ethical student who finds the realization difficult, I recommend, as a means of facilitating it, the second of M. Comte's two principal works, the Systeme de Politique Positive. I entertain the strongest objections to the system of politics and morals set forth in that treatise; but I think it has superabundantly shown the possibility of giving to the service of humanity, even without the aid of belief in a Providence, both the psychical power and the social efficacy of a religion; making it take hold of human life, and colour all thought, feeling, and action, in a manner of which the greatest ascendancy ever exercised by any religion may be but a type and foretaste; and of which the danger is, not that it should be insufficient, but that it should be so excessive as to interfere unduly with human freedom and individuality.

Neither is it necessary to the feeling which constitutes the binding force of the utilitarian morality on those who recognize it, to wait for those social influences which would make its obligation felt by mankind at large. In the comparatively early state of human advancement in which we now live, a person cannot indeed feel that entireness of sympathy with all others, which would make any real discordance in the general direction of their conduct in life impossible; but already a person in whom the social feeling is at all developed, cannot bring himself to think of the rest of his fellow creatures as struggling rivals with him for the means of happiness, whom he must desire to see defeated in their object in order that he may succeed in his. The deeply-rooted conception which every individual even now has of himself as a social being, tends to make him feel it one of his natural wants that there should be harmony between his feelings and aims and those of his fellow creatures. If differences of opinion and of mental culture make it impossible for him to share many of their actual feelings—perhaps make him denounce and defy those feelings—he still needs to be conscious that his real aim and theirs do not conflict; that he is not opposing himself to what they really wish for, namely, their own good, but is, on the contrary, promoting it. This feeling in most individuals is much inferior in strength to their selfish feelings, and is often wanting altogether. But to those who have it, it possesses all the characters of a natural feeling. It does not present itself to their minds as a superstition of education, or a law despotically imposed by the power of society, but as an attribute which it would not be well for them to be without. This conviction is the ultimate sanction of the greatest happiness morality. This it is which makes any mind, of well-developed feelings, work with, and not against, the outward motives to care for others, afforded by what I have called the external sanctions; and when those sanctions are wanting, or act in an opposite direction, constitutes in itself a powerful internal binding force, in proportion to the sensitiveness and thoughtfulness of the character; since few but those whose mind is a moral blank, could bear to lay out their course of life on the plan of paying no regard to others except so far as their own private interest compels.

CHAPTER IV. OF WHAT SORT OF PROOF THE PRINCIPLE OF UTILITY IS SUSCEPTIBLE

It has already been remarked, that questions of ultimate ends do not admit of proof, in the ordinary acceptation of the term. To be incapable of proof by reasoning is common to all first principles; to the first premises of our knowledge, as well as to those of our conduct. But the former, being matters of fact, may be the subject of a direct appeal to the faculties which judge of fact—namely, our senses, and our internal consciousness. Can an appeal be made to the same faculties on questions of practical ends? Or by what other faculty is cognizance taken of them?

Questions about ends are, in other words, questions about what things are desirable. The utilitarian doctrine is, that happiness is desirable, and the only thing desirable, as an end; all other things being only desirable as means to that end. What ought to be required of this doctrine—what conditions is it requisite that the doctrine should fulfil—to make good its claim to be believed?

The only proof capable of being given that an object is visible, is that people actually see it. The only proof that a sound is audible, is that people hear it:

and so of the other sources of our experience. In like manner, I apprehend, the sole evidence it is possible to produce that anything is desirable, is that people do actually desire it. If the end which the utilitarian doctrine proposes to itself were not, in theory and in practice, acknowledged to be an end, nothing could ever convince any person that it was so. No reason can be given why the general happiness is desirable, except that each person, so far as he believes it to be attainable, desires his own happiness. This, however, being a fact, we have not only all the proof which the case admits of, but all which it is possible to require, that happiness is a good: that each person's happiness is a good to that person, and the general happiness, therefore, a good to the aggregate of all persons. Happiness has made out its title as one of the ends of conduct, and consequently one of the criteria of morality.

But it has not, by this alone, proved itself to be the sole criterion. To do that, it would seem, by the same rule, necessary to show, not only that people desire happiness, but that they never desire anything else. Now it is palpable that they do desire things which, in common language, are decidedly distinguished from happiness. They desire, for example, virtue, and the absence of vice, no less really than pleasure and the absence of pain. The desire of virtue is not as universal, but it is as authentic a fact, as the desire of happiness. And hence the opponents of the utilitarian standard deem that they have a right to infer that there are other ends of human action besides happiness, and that happiness is not the standard of approbation and disapprobation.

But does the utilitarian doctrine deny that people desire virtue, or maintain that virtue is not a thing to be desired? The very reverse. It maintains not only that virtue is to be desired, but that it is to be desired disinterestedly, for itself. Whatever may be the opinion of utilitarian moralists as to the original conditions by which virtue is made virtue; however they may believe (as they do) that actions and dispositions are only virtuous because they promote another end than virtue; yet this being granted, and it having been decided, from considerations of this description, what is virtuous, they not only place virtue at the very head of the things which are good as means to the ultimate end, but they also recognize as a psychological fact the possibility of its being, to the individual, a good in itself, without looking to any end beyond it; and hold, that the mind is not in a right state, not in a state conformable to Utility, not in the state most conducive to the general happiness, unless it does love virtue in this manner—as a thing desirable in itself, even although, in the individual instance, it should not produce those other desirable consequences which it tends to produce, and on account of which it is held to be virtue. This opinion is not, in the smallest degree, a departure from the Happiness principle. The ingredients of happiness are very various, and each of them is desirable in itself, and not merely when considered as swelling an aggregate. The principle of utility does not mean that any given pleasure, as music, for instance, or any given exemption from pain, as for example health, are to be looked upon as means to a collective something termed happiness, and to be desired on that account. They are desired and desirable in and for themselves; besides being means, they are a part of the end. Virtue, according to the utilitarian doctrine, is not naturally and originally part of the end, but it is capable of becoming so; and in those who love it disinterestedly it has become so, and is desired and cherished, not as a means to happiness, but as a part of their happiness.

To illustrate this farther, we may remember that virtue is not the only thing, originally a means, and which if it were not a means to anything else, would be and remain indifferent, but which by association with what it is a means to, comes to be desired for itself, and that too with the utmost intensity. What, for example, shall we say of the love of money? There is nothing originally more desirable about money than about any heap of glittering pebbles. Its worth is solely that of the things which it will buy; the desires for other things than itself, which it is a means of gratifying. Yet the love of money is not only one of the strongest moving forces of human life, but money is, in many cases, desired in and for itself; the desire to possess it is often stronger than the desire to use it, and goes on increasing when all the desires which point to ends beyond it, to be compassed by it, are falling off. It may be then said truly, that money is desired not for the sake of an end, but as part of the end. From being a means to happiness,

it has come to be itself a principal ingredient of the individual's conception of happiness. The same may be said of the majority of the great objects of human life—power, for example, or fame; except that to each of these there is a certain amount of immediate pleasure annexed, which has at least the semblance of being naturally inherent in them; a thing which cannot be said of money. Still, however, the strongest natural attraction, both of power and of fame, is the immense aid they give to the attainment of our other wishes; and it is the strong association thus generated between them and all our objects of desire, which gives to the direct desire of them the intensity it often assumes, so as in some characters to surpass in strength all other desires. In these cases the means have become a part of the end, and a more important part of it than any of the things which they are means to. What was once desired as an instrument for the attainment of happiness, has come to be desired for its own sake. In being desired for its own sake it is, however, desired as part of happiness. The person is made, or thinks he would be made, happy by its mere possession; and is made unhappy by failure to obtain it. The desire of it is not a different thing from the desire of happiness, any more than the love of music, or the desire of health. They are included in happiness. They are some of the elements of which the desire of happiness is made up. Happiness is not an abstract idea, but a concrete whole; and these are some of its parts. And the utilitarian standard sanctions and approves their being so. Life would be a poor thing, very ill provided with sources of happiness, if there were not this provision of nature, by which things originally indifferent, but conducive to, or otherwise associated with, the satisfaction of our primitive desires, become in themselves sources of pleasure more valuable than the primitive pleasures, both in permanency, in the space of human existence that they are capable of covering, and even in intensity.

Virtue, according to the utilitarian conception, is a good of this description. There was no original desire of it, or motive to it, save its conduciveness to pleasure, and especially to protection from pain. But through the association thus formed, it may be felt a good in itself, and desired as such with as great intensity as any other good; and with this difference between it and the love of money, of power, or of fame, that all of these may, and often do, render the individual noxious to the other members of the society to which he belongs, whereas there is nothing which makes him so much a blessing to them as the cultivation of the disinterested love of virtue. And consequently, the utilitarian standard, while it tolerates and approves those other acquired desires, up to the point beyond which they would be more injurious to the general happiness than promotive of it, enjoins and requires the cultivation of the love of virtue up to the greatest strength possible, as being above all things important to the general happiness.

It results from the preceding considerations, that there is in reality nothing desired except happiness. Whatever is desired otherwise than as a means to some end beyond itself, and ultimately to happiness, is desired as itself a part of happiness, and is not desired for itself until it has become so. Those who desire virtue for its own sake, desire it either because the consciousness of it is a pleasure, or because the consciousness of being without it is a pain, or for both reasons united; as in truth the pleasure and pain seldom exist separately, but almost always together, the same person feeling pleasure in the degree of virtue attained, and pain in not having attained more. If one of these gave him to pleasure, and the other no pain, he would not love or desire virtue, or would desire it only for the other benefits which it might produce to himself or to persons whom he cared for.

We have now, then, an answer to the question, of what sort of proof the principle of utility is susceptible. If the opinion which I have now stated is psychologically true—if human nature is so constituted as to desire nothing which is not either a part of happiness or a means of happiness, we can have no other proof, and we require no other, that these are the only things desirable. If so, happiness is the sole end of human action, and the promotion of it the test by which to judge of all human conduct; from whence it necessarily follows that it must be the criterion of morality, since a part is included in the whole.

And now to decide whether this is really so; whether mankind do desire nothing for itself but that which is a pleasure to them, or of which the absence is a pain; we have evidently arrived at a question of fact and experience, dependent, like all similar questions, upon evidence. It can only be determined by practiced self-consciousness and self-observation, assisted by observation of others. I believe that these sources of evidence, impartially consulted, will declare that desiring a thing and finding it pleasant, aversion to it and thinking of it as painful, are phenomena entirely inseparable, or rather two parts of the same phenomenon; in strictness of language, two different modes of naming the same psychological fact: that to think of an object as desirable (unless for the sake of its consequences), and to think of it as pleasant, are one and the same thing; and that to desire anything, except in proportion as the idea of it is pleasant, is a physical and metaphysical impossibility.

So obvious does this appear to me, that I expect it will hardly be disputed: and the objection made will be, not that desire can possibly be directed to anything ultimately except pleasure and exemption from pain, but that the will is a different thing from desire; that a person of confirmed virtue, or any other person whose purposes are fixed, carries out his purposes without any thought of the pleasure he has in contemplating them, or expects to derive from their fulfilment; and persists in acting on them, even though these pleasures are much diminished, by changes in his character or decay of his passive sensibilities, or are outweighed by the pains which the pursuit of the purposes may bring upon him. All this I fully admit, and have stated it elsewhere, as positively and emphatically as any one. Will, the active phenomenon, is a different thing from desire, the state of passive sensibility, and though originally an offshoot from it, may in time take root and detach itself from the parent stock; so much so, that in the case of an habitual purpose, instead of willing the thing because we desire it, we often desire it only because we will it. This, however, is but an instance of that familiar fact, the power of habit, and is nowise confined to the case of virtuous actions. Many indifferent things, which men originally did from a motive of some sort, they continue to do from habit. Sometimes this is done unconsciously, the consciousness coming only after the action: at other times with conscious volition, but volition which has become habitual, and is put into operation by the force of habit, in opposition perhaps to the deliberate preference, as often happens with those who have contracted habits of vicious or hurtful indulgence. Third and last comes the case in which the habitual act of will in the individual instance is not in contradiction to the general intention prevailing at other times, but in fulfilment of it; as in the case of the person of confirmed virtue, and of all who pursue deliberately and consistently any determinate end. The distinction between will and desire thus understood, is an authentic and highly important psychological fact; but the fact consists solely in this—that will, like all other parts of our constitution, is amenable to habit, and that we may will from habit what we no longer desire for itself, or desire only because we will it. It is not the less true that will, in the beginning, is entirely produced by desire; including in that term the repelling influence of pain as well as the attractive one of pleasure. Let us take into consideration, no longer the person who has a confirmed will to do right, but him in whom that virtuous will is still feeble, conquerable by temptation, and not to be fully relied on; by what means can it be strengthened? How can the will to be virtuous, where it does not exist in sufficient force, be implanted or awakened? Only by making the person desire virtue—by making him think of it in a pleasurable light, or of its absence in a painful one. It is by associating the doing right with pleasure, or the doing wrong with pain, or by eliciting and impressing and bringing home to the person's experience the pleasure naturally involved in the one or the pain in the other, that it is possible to call forth that will to be virtuous, which, when confirmed, acts without any thought of either pleasure or pain. Will is the child of desire, and passes out of the dominion of its parent only to come under that of habit. That which is the result of habit affords no presumption of being intrinsically good; and there would be no reason for wishing that the purpose of virtue should become independent of pleasure and pain, were it not that the influence of the pleasurable and painful associations which prompt to virtue is not sufficiently to be depended on for unerring constancy of action until it has acquired the support of habit. Both in feeling and in conduct, habit is the only thing which imparts certainty; and it is because of the importance to others of being able to rely absolutely on one's feelings and

conduct, and to oneself of being able to rely on one's own, that the will to do right ought to be cultivated into this habitual independence. In other words, this state of the will is a means to good, not intrinsically a good; and does not contradict the doctrine that nothing is a good to human beings but in so far as it is either itself pleasurable, or a means of attaining pleasure or averting pain.

But if this doctrine be true, the principle of utility is proved. Whether it is so or not, must now be left to the consideration of the thoughtful reader.

CHAPTER V. ON THE CONNEXION BETWEEN JUSTICE AND UTILITY

In all ages of speculation, one of the strongest obstacles to the reception of the doctrine that Utility or Happiness is the criterion of right and wrong, has been drawn from the idea of Justice. The powerful sentiment, and apparently clear perception, which that word recalls with a rapidity and certainty resembling an instinct, have seemed to the majority of thinkers to point to an inherent quality in things; to show that the Just must have an existence in Nature as something absolute, generically distinct from every variety of the Expedient, and, in idea, opposed to it, though (as is commonly acknowledged) never, in the long run, disjoined from it in fact.

In the case of this, as of our other moral sentiments, there is no necessary connexion between the question of its origin, and that of its binding force. That a feeling is bestowed on us by Nature, does not necessarily legitimate all its promptings. The feeling of justice might be a peculiar instinct, and might yet require, like our other instincts, to be controlled and enlightened by a higher reason. If we have intellectual instincts, leading us to judge in a particular way, as well as animal instincts that prompt us to act in a particular way, there is no necessity that the former should be more infallible in their sphere than the latter in theirs: it may as well happen that wrong judgments are occasionally suggested by those, as wrong actions by these. But though it is one thing to believe that we have natural feelings of justice, and another to acknowledge them as an ultimate criterion of conduct, these two opinions are very closely connected in point of fact. Mankind are always predisposed to believe that any subjective feeling, not otherwise accounted for, is a revelation of some objective reality. Our present object is to determine whether the reality, to which the feeling of justice corresponds, is one which needs any such special revelation; whether the justice or injustice of an action is a thing intrinsically peculiar, and distinct from all its other qualities, or only a combination of certain of those qualities, presented under a peculiar aspect. For the purpose of this inquiry, it is practically important to consider whether the feeling itself, of justice and injustice, is sui generis like our sensations of colour and taste, or a derivative feeling, formed by a combination of others. And this it is the more essential to examine, as people are in general willing enough to allow, that objectively the dictates of justice coincide with a part of the field of General Expediency; but inasmuch as the subjective mental feeling of Justice is different from that which commonly attaches to simple expediency, and, except in extreme cases of the latter, is far more imperative in its demands, people find it difficult to see, in Justice, only a particular kind or branch of general utility, and think that its superior binding force requires a totally different origin.

To throw light upon this question, it is necessary to attempt to ascertain what is the distinguishing character of justice, or of injustice: what is the quality, or whether there is any quality, attributed in common to all modes of conduct designated as unjust (for justice, like many other moral attributes, is best defined by its opposite), and distinguishing them from such modes of conduct as are disapproved, but without having that particular epithet of disapprobation applied to them. If in everything which men are accustomed to characterize as just or unjust, some one common attribute or collection of attributes is always present, we may judge whether this particular attribute or combination of attributes would be capable of gathering round it a sentiment of that peculiar character and intensity by virtue of the general laws of our emotional constitution, or whether the sentiment is inexplicable, and requires to be regarded as a special provision of Nature. If we find the former to be the case, we shall, in resolving this question, have resolved also the main problem: if the

latter, we shall have to seek for some other mode of investigating it.

To find the common attributes of a variety of objects, it is necessary to begin by surveying the objects themselves in the concrete. Let us therefore advert successively to the various modes of action, and arrangements of human affairs, which are classed, by universal or widely spread opinion, as Just or as Unjust. The things well known to excite the sentiments associated with those names, are of a very multifarious character. I shall pass them rapidly in review, without studying any particular arrangement.

In the first place, it is mostly considered unjust to deprive any one of his personal liberty, his property, or any other thing which belongs to him by law. Here, therefore, is one instance of the application of the terms just and unjust in a perfectly definite sense, namely, that it is just to respect, unjust to violate, the legal rights of any one. But this judgment admits of several exceptions, arising from the other forms in which the notions of justice and injustice present themselves. For example, the person who suffers the deprivation may (as the phrase is) have forfeited the rights which he is so deprived of: a case to which we shall return presently. But also,

Secondly; the legal rights of which he is deprived, may be rights which ought not to have belonged to him; in other words, the law which confers on him these rights, may be a bad law. When it is so, or when (which is the same thing for our purpose) it is supposed to be so, opinions will differ as to the justice or injustice of infringing it. Some maintain that no law, however bad, ought to be disobeyed by an individual citizen; that his opposition to it, if shown at all, should only be shown in endeavoring to get it altered by competent authority. This opinion (which condemns many of the most illustrious benefactors of mankind, and would often protect pernicious institutions against the only weapons which, in the state of things existing at the time, have any chance of succeeding against them) is defended, by those who hold it, on grounds of expediency; principally on that of the importance, to the common interest of mankind, of maintaining inviolate the sentiment of submission to law. Other persons, again, hold the directly contrary opinion, that any law, judged to be bad, may blamelessly be disobeyed, even though it be not judged to be unjust, but only inexpedient; while others would confine the license of disobedience to the case of unjust laws; but again, some say, that all laws which are inexpedient are unjust; since every law imposes some restriction on the natural liberty of mankind, which restriction is an injustice, unless legitimated by tending to their good. Among these diversities of opinion, it seems to be universally admitted that there may be unjust laws, and that law, consequently, is not the ultimate criterion of justice, but may give to one person a benefit, or impose on another an evil, which justice condemns. When, however, a law is thought to be unjust, it seems always to be regarded as being so in the same way in which a breach of law is unjust, namely, by infringing somebody's right; which, as it cannot in this case be a legal right, receives a different appellation, and is called a moral right. We may say, therefore, that a second case of injustice consists in taking or withholding from any person that to which he has a moral right.

Thirdly, it is universally considered just that each person should obtain that (whether good or evil) which he deserves; and unjust that he should obtain a good, or be made to undergo an evil, which he does not deserve. This is, perhaps, the clearest and most emphatic form in which the idea of justice is conceived by the general mind. As it involves the notion of desert, the question arises, what constitutes desert? Speaking in a general way, a person is understood to deserve good if he does right, evil if he does wrong; and in a more particular sense, to deserve good from those to whom he does or has done good, and evil from those to whom he does or has done evil. The precept of returning good for evil has never been regarded as a case of the fulfilment of justice, but as one in which the claims of justice are waved, in obedience to other considerations.

Fourthly, it is confessedly unjust to break faith with any one: to violate an engagement, either express or implied, or disappoint expectations raised by our own conduct, at least if we have raised those expectations knowingly and voluntarily. Like the other obligations of justice already spoken of, this one is not regarded as absolute, but as capable of being overruled by a stronger obligation of justice on the other side; or by such conduct on the part of the person concerned as is deemed to absolve us from our obligation to him, and to constitute a forfeiture of the benefit which he has been led to expect.

Fifthly, it is, by universal admission, inconsistent with justice to be partial; to show favour or preference to one person over another, in matters to which favour and preference do not properly apply. Impartiality, however, does not seem to be regarded as a duty in itself, but rather as instrumental to some other duty; for it is admitted that favour and preference are not always censurable, and indeed the cases in which they are condemned are rather the exception than the rule. A person would be more likely to be blamed than applauded for giving his family or friends no superiority in good offices over strangers, when he could do so without violating any other duty; and no one thinks it unjust to seek one person in preference to another as a friend, connexion, or companion. Impartiality where rights are concerned is of course obligatory, but this is involved in the more general obligation of giving to every one his right. A tribunal, for example, must be impartial, because it is bound to award, without regard to any other consideration, a disputed object to the one of two parties who has the right to it. There are other cases in which impartiality means, being solely influenced by desert; as with those who, in the capacity of judges, preceptors, or parents, administer reward and punishment as such. There are cases, again, in which it means, being solely influenced by consideration for the public interest; as in making a selection among candidates for a government employment. Impartiality, in short, as an obligation of justice, may be said to mean, being exclusively influenced by the considerations which it is supposed ought to influence the particular case in hand; and resisting the solicitation of any motives which prompt to conduct different from what those considerations would dictate.

Nearly allied to the idea of impartiality, is that of equality; which often enters as a component part both into the conception of justice and into the practice of it, and, in the eyes of many persons, constitutes its essence. But in this, still more than in any other case, the notion of justice varies in different persons, and always conforms in its variations to their notion of utility. Each person maintains that equality is the dictate of justice, except where he thinks that expediency requires inequality. The justice of giving equal protection to the rights of all, is maintained by those who support the most outrageous inequality in the rights themselves. Even in slave countries it is theoretically admitted that the rights of the slave, such as they are, ought to be as sacred as those of the master; and that a tribunal which fails to enforce them with equal strictness is wanting in justice; while, at the same time, institutions which leave to the slave scarcely any rights to enforce, are not deemed unjust, because they are not deemed inexpedient. Those who think that utility requires distinctions of rank, do not consider it unjust that riches and social privileges should be unequally dispensed; but those who think this inequality inexpedient, think it unjust also. Whoever thinks that government is necessary, sees no injustice in as much inequality as is constituted by giving to the magistrate powers not granted to other people. Even among those who hold levelling doctrines, there are as many questions of justice as there are differences of opinion about expediency. Some Communists consider it unjust that the produce of the labour of the community should be shared on any other principle than that of exact equality; others think it just that those should receive most whose needs are greatest; while others hold that those who work harder, or who produce more, or whose services are more valuable to the community, may justly claim a larger quota in the division of the produce. And the sense of natural justice may be plausibly appealed to in behalf of every one of these opinions.

Among so many diverse applications of the term Justice, which yet is not regarded as ambiguous, it is a matter of some difficulty to seize the mental link which holds them together, and on which the moral sentiment adhering to the term essentially depends. Perhaps, in this embarrassment, some help may be derived from the history of the word, as indicated by its etymology.

In most, if not in all, languages, the etymology of the word which corresponds to Just, points to an origin connected either with positive law, or with that which was in most cases the primitive form of law—authoritative custom. *Justum* is a form of *jussum*, that which has been ordered. *Jus* is of the same origin. [*Dikaion*] comes from [*dike*], of which the principal meaning, at least in the historical ages of Greece, was a suit at law. Originally, indeed, it meant only the mode or manner of doing things, but it early came to mean the prescribed manner; that which the recognized authorities, patriarchal, judicial, or political, would enforce. *Recht*, from which came right and righteous, is synonymous with law. The original meaning indeed of *recht* did not point to law, but to physical straightness; as wrong and its Latin equivalents meant twisted or tortuous; and from this it is argued that right did not originally mean law, but on the contrary law meant right. But however this may be, the fact that *recht* and *droit* became restricted in their meaning to positive law, although much which is not required by law is equally necessary to moral straightness or rectitude, is as significant of the original character of moral ideas as if the derivation had been the reverse way. The courts of justice, the administration of justice, are the courts and the administration of law. *La justice*, in French, is the established term for judicature. There can, I think, be no doubt that the *idee mere*, the primitive element, in the formation of the notion of justice, was conformity to law. It constituted the entire idea among the Hebrews, up to the birth of Christianity; as might be expected in the case of a people whose laws attempted to embrace all subjects on which precepts were required, and who believed those laws to be a direct emanation from the Supreme Being. But other nations, and in particular the Greeks and Romans, who knew that their laws had been made originally, and still continued to be made, by men, were not afraid to admit that those men might make bad laws; might do, by law, the same things, and from the same motives, which, if done by individuals without the sanction of law, would be called unjust. And hence the sentiment of injustice came to be attached, not to all violations of law, but only to violations of such laws as ought to exist, including such as ought to exist but do not; and to laws themselves, if supposed to be contrary to what ought to be law. In this manner the idea of law and of its injunctions was still predominant in the notion of justice, even when the laws actually in force ceased to be accepted as the standard of it.

It is true that mankind consider the idea of justice and its obligations as applicable to many things which neither are, nor is it desired that they should be, regulated by law. Nobody desires that laws should interfere with the whole detail of private life; yet every one allows that in all daily conduct a person may and does show himself to be either just or unjust. But even here, the idea of the breach of what ought to be law, still lingers in a modified shape. It would always give us pleasure, and chime in with our feelings of fitness, that acts which we deem unjust should be punished, though we do not always think it expedient that this should be done by the tribunals. We forego that gratification on account of incidental inconveniences. We should be glad to see just conduct enforced and injustice repressed, even in the minutest details, if we were not, with reason, afraid of trusting the magistrate with so unlimited an amount of power over individuals. When we think that a person is bound in justice to do a thing, it is an ordinary form of language to say, that he ought to be compelled to do it. We should be gratified to see the obligation enforced by anybody who had the power. If we see that its enforcement by law would be inexpedient, we lament the impossibility, we consider the impunity given to injustice as an evil, and strive to make amends for it by bringing a strong expression of our own and the public disapprobation to bear upon the offender. Thus the idea of legal constraint is still the generating idea of the notion of justice, though undergoing several transformations before that notion, as it exists in an advanced state of society, becomes complete.

The above is, I think, a true account, as far as it goes, of the origin and progressive growth of the idea of justice. But we must observe, that it contains, as yet, nothing to distinguish that obligation from moral obligation in general. For the truth is, that the idea of penal sanction, which is the essence of law, enters not only into the conception of injustice, but into that of any kind of wrong. We do not call anything wrong, unless we mean to imply that a person ought to be punished in some way or other for doing it; if not by law, by the opinion of his fellow creatures; if not by opinion, by the reproaches of his own conscience. This seems the real turning point of the distinction between morality and simple expediency. It is a part of the notion of Duty in every one of its forms, that a person may rightfully be compelled to fulfil it. Duty is a thing which may be exacted from a person, as one exacts a debt. Unless we think that it might be exacted from him, we do not call it his

duty. Reasons of prudence, or the interest of other people, may militate against actually exacting it; but the person himself, it is clearly understood, would not be entitled to complain. There are other things, on the contrary, which we wish that people should do, which we like or admire them for doing, perhaps dislike or despise them for not doing, but yet admit that they are not bound to do; it is not a case of moral obligation; we do not blame them, that is, we do not think that they are proper objects of punishment. How we come by these ideas of deserving and not deserving punishment, will appear, perhaps, in the sequel; but I think there is no doubt that this distinction lies at the bottom of the notions of right and wrong; that we call any conduct wrong, or employ, instead, some other term of dislike or disparagement, according as we think that the person ought, or ought not, to be punished for it; and we say that it would be right to do so and so, or merely that it would be desirable or laudable, according as we would wish to see the person whom it concerns, compelled, or only persuaded and exhorted, to act in that manner.

This, therefore, being the characteristic difference which marks off, not justice, but morality in general, from the remaining provinces of Expediency and Worthiness; the character is still to be sought which distinguishes justice from other branches of morality. Now it is known that ethical writers divide moral duties into two classes, denoted by the ill-chosen expressions, duties of perfect and of imperfect obligation; the latter being those in which, though the act is obligatory, the particular occasions of performing it are left to our choice; as in the case of charity or beneficence, which we are indeed bound to practise, but not towards any definite person, nor at any prescribed time. In the more precise language of philosophic jurists, duties of perfect obligation are those duties in virtue of which a correlative right resides in some person or persons; duties of imperfect obligation are those moral obligations which do not give birth to any right. I think it will be found that this distinction exactly coincides with that which exists between justice and the other obligations of morality. In our survey of the various popular acceptations of justice, the term appeared generally to involve the idea of a personal right—a claim on the part of one or more individuals, like that which the law gives when it confers a proprietary or other legal right.

Whether the injustice consists in depriving a person of a possession, or in breaking faith with him, or in treating him worse than he deserves, or worse than other people who have no greater claims, in each case the supposition implies two things—a wrong done, and some assignable person who is wronged. Injustice may also be done by treating a person better than others; but the wrong in this case is to his competitors, who are also assignable persons. It seems to me that this feature in the case—a right in some person, correlative to the moral obligation—constitutes the specific difference between justice, and generosity or beneficence. Justice implies something which it is not only right to do, and wrong not to do, but which some individual person can claim from us as his moral right. No one has a moral right to our generosity or beneficence, because we are not morally bound to practise those virtues towards an given individual. And it will be found with respect to this as with respect to every correct definition, that the instances which seem to conflict with it are those which most confirm it. For if a moralist attempts, as some have done, to make out that mankind generally, though not any given individual, have a right to all the good we can do them, he at once, by that thesis, includes generosity and beneficence within the category of justice. He is obliged to say, that our utmost exertions are due to our fellow creatures, thus assimilating them to a debt; or that nothing less can be a sufficient return for what society does for us, thus classing the case as one of gratitude; both of which are acknowledged cases of justice. Wherever there is a right, the case is one of justice, and not of the virtue of beneficence: and whoever does not place the distinction between justice and morality in general, where we have now placed it, will be found to make no distinction between them at all, but to merge all morality in justice.

Having thus endeavored to determine the distinctive elements which enter into the composition of the idea of justice, we are ready to enter on the inquiry, whether the feeling, which accompanies the idea, is attached to it by a special dispensation of nature, or whether it could have grown up, by any known laws, out of the idea itself; and in particular, whether it can have originated in considerations of general expediency.

I conceive that the sentiment itself does not arise from anything which would commonly, or correctly, be termed an idea of expediency; but that though the sentiment does not, whatever is moral in its does.

We have seen that the two essential ingredients in the sentiment of justice are, the desire to punish a person who has done harm, and the knowledge or belief that there is some definite individual or individuals to whom harm has been done.

Now it appears to me, that the desire to punish a person who has done harm to some individual, is a spontaneous outgrowth from two sentiments, both in the highest degree natural, and which either are or resemble instincts; the impulse of self-defence, and the feeling of sympathy.

It is natural to resent, and to repel or retaliate, any harm done or attempted against ourselves, or against those with whom we sympathize. The origin of this sentiment it is not necessary here to discuss. Whether it be an instinct or a result of intelligence, it is, we know, common to all animal nature; for every animal tries to hurt those who have hurt, or who it thinks are about to hurt, itself or its young. Human beings, on this point, only differ from other animals in two particulars. First, in being capable of sympathizing, not solely with their offspring, or, like some of the more noble animals, with some superior animal who is kind to them, but with all human, and even with all sentient, beings. Secondly, in having a more developed intelligence, which gives a wider range to the whole of their sentiments, whether self-regarding or sympathetic. By virtue of his superior intelligence, even apart from his superior range of sympathy, a human being is capable of apprehending a community of interest between himself and the human society of which he forms a part, such that any conduct which threatens the security of the society generally, is threatening to his own, and calls forth his instinct (if instinct it be) of self-defence. The same superiority of intelligence, joined to the power of sympathizing with human beings generally, enables him to attach himself to the collective idea of his tribe, his country, or mankind, in such a manner that any act hurtful to them rouses his instinct of sympathy, and urges him to resistance.

The sentiment of justice, in that one of its elements which consists of the desire to punish, is thus,

I conceive, the natural feeling of retaliation or vengeance, rendered by intellect and sympathy applicable to those injuries, that is, to those hurts, which wound us through, or in common with, society at large. This sentiment, in itself, has nothing moral in it; what is moral is, the exclusive subordination of it to the social sympathies, so as to wait on and obey their call. For the natural feeling tends to make us resent indiscriminately whatever any one does that is disagreeable to us; but when moralized by the social feeling, it only acts in the directions conformable to the general good: just persons resenting a hurt to society, though not otherwise a hurt to themselves, and not resenting a hurt to themselves, however painful, unless it be of the kind which society has a common interest with them in the repression of.

It is no objection against this doctrine to say, that when we feel our sentiment of justice outraged, we are not thinking of society at large, or of any collective interest, but only of the individual case. It is common enough certainly, though the reverse of commendable, to feel resentment merely because we have suffered pain; but a person whose resentment is really a moral feeling, that is, who considers whether an act is blameable before he allows himself to resent it—such a person, though he may not say expressly to himself that he is standing up for the interest of society, certainly does feel that he is asserting a rule which is for the benefit of others as well as for his own. If he is not feeling this—if he is regarding the act solely as it affects him individually—he is not consciously just; he is not concerning himself about the justice of his actions. This is admitted even by anti-utilitarian moralists. When Kant (as before remarked) propounds as the fundamental principle of morals, 'So act, that thy rule of conduct might be adopted as a law by all rational beings,' he virtually acknowledges that the interest of mankind collectively, or at least of mankind indiscriminately, must be in the mind of the agent when conscientiously deciding on the morality of the act. Otherwise he uses words without a meaning: for, that a rule even of utter selfishness could not possibly be adopted by all rational beings—that there is an insuperable obstacle in the nature of things to its adoption—cannot be even plausibly maintained. To give any meaning to Kant's principle, the sense put upon it must be, that we ought to shape our conduct by a rule which all rational beings might adopt with benefit to their collective interest.

To recapitulate: the idea of justice supposes two things; a rule of conduct, and a sentiment which sanctions the rule. The first must be supposed common to all mankind, and intended for their good. The other (the sentiment) is a desire that punishment may be suffered by those who infringe the rule. There is involved, in addition, the conception of some definite person who suffers by the infringement; whose rights (to use the expression appropriated to the case) are violated by it. And the sentiment of justice appears to me to be, the animal desire to repel or retaliate a hurt or damage to oneself, or to those with whom one sympathizes, widened so as to include all persons, by the human capacity of enlarged sympathy, and the human conception of intelligent self-interest. From the latter elements, the feeling derives its morality; from the former, its peculiar impressiveness, and energy of self-assertion.

I have, throughout, treated the idea of a right residing in the injured person, and violated by the injury, not as a separate element in the composition of the idea and sentiment, but as one of the forms in which the other two elements clothe themselves. These elements are, a hurt to some assignable person or persons on the one hand, and a demand for punishment on the other. An examination of our own minds, I think, will show, that these two things include all that we mean when we speak of violation of a right. When we call anything a person's right, we mean that he has a valid claim on society to protect him in the possession of it, either by the force of law, or by that of education and opinion. If he has what we consider a sufficient claim, on whatever account, to have something guaranteed to him by society, we say that he has a right to it. If we desire to prove that anything does not belong to him by right, we think this done as soon as it is admitted that society ought not to take measures for securing it to him, but should leave it to chance, or to his own exertions. Thus, a person is said to have a right to what he can earn in fair professional competition; because society ought not to allow any other person to hinder him from endeavoring to earn in that manner as much as he can. But he has not a right to three hundred a-year, though he may happen to be earning it; because society is not called on to provide that he shall earn that sum. On the contrary, if he owns ten thousand pounds three per cent stock, he has a right to three hundred a-year; because society has come under an obligation to provide him with an income of that amount.

To have a right, then, is, I conceive, to have something which society ought to defend me in the possession of. If the objector goes on to ask why it ought, I can give him no other reason than general utility. If that expression does not seem to convey a sufficient feeling of the strength of the obligation, nor to account for the peculiar energy of the feeling, it is because there goes to the composition of the sentiment, not a rational only but also an animal element, the thirst for retaliation; and this thirst derives its intensity, as well as its moral justification, from the extraordinarily important and impressive kind of utility which is concerned. The interest involved is that of security, to every one's feelings the most vital of all interests. Nearly all other earthly benefits are needed by one person, not needed by another; and many of them can, if necessary, be cheerfully foregone, or replaced by something else; but security no human being can possibly do without; on it we depend for all our immunity from evil, and for the whole value of all and every good, beyond the passing moment; since nothing but the gratification of the instant could be of any worth to us, if we could be deprived of everything the next instant by whoever was momentarily stronger than ourselves. Now this most indispensable of all necessaries, after physical nutriment, cannot be had, unless the machinery for providing it is kept unintermittedly in active play. Our notion, therefore, of the claim we have on our fellow-creatures to join in making safe for us the very groundwork of our existence, gathers feelings round it so much more intense than those concerned in any of the more common cases of utility, that the difference in degree (as is often the case in psychology) becomes a real difference in kind. The claim assumes that character of absoluteness, that apparent infinity, and incommensurability with all other considerations, which constitute the distinction between the feeling of right and wrong and that of ordinary expediency and inexpediency. The feelings concerned are so powerful, and we count so positively on finding a responsive feeling in others (all being alike interested), that ought and should grow into must, and recognized indispensability becomes a moral necessity, analogous to physical, and often not inferior to it in binding force.

If the preceding analysis, or something resembling it, be not the correct account of the notion of justice; if justice be totally independent of utility, and be a standard per se, which the mind can recognize by simple introspection of itself; it is hard to understand why that internal oracle is so ambiguous, and why so many things appear either just or unjust, according to the light in which they are regarded.

We are continually informed that Utility is an uncertain standard, which every different person interprets differently, and that there is no safety but in the immutable, ineffaceable, and unmistakable dictates of Justice, which carry their evidence in themselves, and are independent of the fluctuations of opinion. One would suppose from this that on questions of justice there could be no controversy; that if we take that for our rule, its application to any given case could leave us in as little doubt as a mathematical demonstration. So far is this from being the fact, that there is as much difference of opinion, and as fierce discussion, about what is just, as about what is useful to society. Not only have different nations and individuals different notions of justice, but in the mind of one and the same individual, justice is not some one rule, principle, or maxim, but many, which do not always coincide in their dictates, and in choosing between which, he is guided either by some extraneous standard, or by his own personal predilections.

For instance, there are some who say, that it is unjust to punish any one for the sake of example to others; that punishment is just, only when intended for the good of the sufferer himself. Others maintain the extreme reverse, contending that to punish persons who have attained years of discretion, for their own benefit, is despotism and injustice, since if the matter at issue is solely their own good, no one has a right to control their own judgment of it; but that they may justly be punished to prevent evil to others, this being an exercise of the legitimate right of self-defence. Mr. Owen, again, affirms that it is unjust to punish at all; for the criminal did not make his own character; his education, and the circumstances which surround him, have made him a criminal, and for these he is not responsible. All these opinions are extremely plausible; and so long as the question is argued as one of justice simply, without going down to the principles which lie under justice and are the source of its authority, I am unable to see how any of these reasoners can be refuted. For in truth every one of the three builds upon rules of justice confessedly true. The first appeals to the acknowledged injustice of singling out an individual, and making him a sacrifice, without his consent, for other people's benefit. The second relies on the acknowledged justice of self-defence, and the admitted injustice of forcing one person to conform to another's notions of what constitutes his good. The Owenite invokes the admitted principle, that it is unjust to punish any one for what he cannot help. Each is triumphant so long as he is not compelled to take into consideration any other maxims of justice than the one he has selected; but as soon as their several maxims are brought face to face, each disputant seems to have exactly as much to say for himself as the others. No one of them can carry out his own notion of justice without trampling upon another equally binding. These are difficulties; they have always been felt to be such; and many devices have been invented to turn rather than to overcome them. As a refuge from the last of the three, men imagined what they called the freedom of the will; fancying that they could not justify punishing a man whose will is in a thoroughly hateful state, unless it be supposed to have come into that state through no influence of anterior circumstances. To escape from the other difficulties, a favorite contrivance has been the fiction of a contract, whereby at some unknown period all the members of society engaged to obey the laws, and consented to be punished for any disobedience to them; thereby giving to their legislators the right, which it is assumed they would not otherwise have had, of punishing them, either for their own good or for that of society. This happy thought was considered to get rid of the whole difficulty, and to legitimate the infliction of punishment, in virtue of another received maxim of justice, *Volenti non fit injuria;* that is not unjust which is done with the consent of the person who is supposed to be hurt by it. I need hardly remark, that even if the consent were not a mere fiction, this maxim is not superior in au-

thority to the others which it is brought in to supersede. It is, on the contrary, an instructive specimen of the loose and irregular manner in which supposed principles of justice grow up. This particular one evidently came into use as a help to the coarse exigencies of courts of law, which are sometimes obliged to be content with very uncertain presumptions, on account of the greater evils which would often arise from any attempt on their part to cut finer. But even courts of law are not able to adhere consistently to the maxim, for they allow voluntary engagements to be set aside on the ground of fraud, and sometimes on that of mere mistake or misinformation.

Again, when the legitimacy of inflicting punishment is admitted, how many conflicting conceptions of justice come to light in discussing the proper apportionment of punishment to offences. No rule on this subject recommends itself so strongly to the primitive and spontaneous sentiment of justice, as the lex talionis, an eye for an eye and a tooth for a tooth. Though this principle of the Jewish and of the Mahomedan law has been generally abandoned in Europe as a practical maxim, there is, I suspect, in most minds, a secret hankering after it; and when retribution accidentally falls on an offender in that precise shape, the general feeling of satisfaction evinced, bears witness how natural is the sentiment to which this repayment in kind is acceptable. With many the test of justice in penal infliction is that the punishment should be proportioned to the offence; meaning that it should be exactly measured by the moral guilt of the culprit (whatever be their standard for measuring moral guilt): the consideration, what amount of punishment is necessary to deter from the offence, having nothing to do with the question of justice, in their estimation: while there are others to whom that consideration is all in all; who maintain that it is not just, at least for man, to inflict on a fellow-creature, whatever may be his offences, any amount of suffering beyond the least that will suffice to prevent him from repeating, and others from imitating, his misconduct.

To take another example from a subject already once referred to. In a co-operative industrial association, is it just or not that talent or skill should give a title to superior remuneration? On the negative side of the question it is argued, that whoever does the best he can, deserves equally well, and ought not in justice to be put in a position of inferiority for no fault of his own; that superior abilities have already advantages more than enough, in the admiration they excite, the personal influence they command, and the internal sources of satisfaction attending them, without adding to these a superior share of the world's goods; and that society is bound in justice rather to make compensation to the less favored, for this unmerited inequality of advantages, than to aggravate it. On the contrary side it is contended, that society receives more from the more efficient laborer; that his services being more useful, society owes him a larger return for them; that a greater share of the joint result is actually his work, and not to allow his claim to it is a kind of robbery; that if he is only to receive as much as others, he can only be justly required to produce as much, and to give a smaller amount of time and exertion, proportioned to his superior efficiency. Who shall decide between these appeals to conflicting principles of justice? Justice has in this case two sides to it, which it is impossible to bring into harmony, and the two disputants have chosen opposite sides; the one looks to what it is just that the individual should receive, the other to what it is just that the community should give. Each, from his own point of view, is unanswerable; and any choice between them, on grounds of justice, must be perfectly arbitrary. Social utility alone can decide the preference.

How many, again, and how irreconcilable, are the standards of justice to which reference is made in discussing the repartition of taxation. One opinion is, that payment to the State should be in numerical proportion to pecuniary means. Others think that justice dictates what they term graduated taxation; taking a higher percentage from those who have more to spare. In point of natural justice a strong case might be made for disregarding means altogether, and taking the same absolute sum (whenever it could be got) from every one: as the subscribers to a mess, or to a club, all pay the same sum for the same privileges, whether they can all equally afford it or not. Since the protection (it might be said) of law and government is afforded to, and is equally required by all, there is no injustice in making all buy it at the same price. It is reckoned justice, not injustice, that a dealer should charge to all customers the same price for the same article, not a price varying according to their means of payment. This doctrine, as applied to taxation, finds no advocates, because it conflicts strongly with men's feelings of humanity and perceptions of social expediency; but the principle of justice which it invokes is as true and as binding as those which can be appealed to against it. Accordingly, it exerts a tacit influence on the line of defence employed for other modes of assessing taxation. People feel obliged to argue that the State does more for the rich than for the poor, as a justification for its taking more from them: though this is in reality not true, for the rich would be far better able to protect themselves, in the absence of law or government, than the poor, and indeed would probably be successful in converting the poor into their slaves. Others, again, so far defer to the same conception of justice, as to maintain that all should pay an equal capitation tax for the protection of their persons (these being of equal value to all), and an unequal tax for the protection of their property, which is unequal. To this others reply, that the all of one man is as valuable to him as the all of another. From these confusions there is no other mode of extrication than the utilitarian.

Is, then, the difference between the Just and the Expedient a merely imaginary distinction? Have mankind been under a delusion in thinking that justice is a more sacred thing than policy, and that the latter ought only to be listened to after the former has been satisfied? By no means. The exposition we have given of the nature and origin of the sentiment, recognizes a real distinction; and no one of those who profess the most sublime contempt for the consequences of actions as an element in their morality, attaches more importance to the distinction than I do. While I dispute the pretensions of any theory which sets up an imaginary standard of justice not grounded on utility, I account the justice which is grounded on utility to be the chief part, and incomparably the most sacred and binding part, of all morality. Justice is a name for certain classes of moral rules, which concern the essentials of human well-being more nearly, and are therefore of more absolute obligation, than any other rules for the guidance of life; and the notion which we have found to be of the essence of the idea of justice, that of a right residing in an individual, implies and testifies to this more binding obligation.

The moral rules which forbid mankind to hurt one another (in which we must never forget to include wrongful interference with each other's freedom) are more vital to human well-being than any maxims, however important, which only point out the best mode of managing some department of human affairs. They have also the peculiarity, that they are the main element in determining the whole of the social feelings of mankind. It is their observance which alone preserves peace among human beings: if obedience to them were not the rule, and disobedience the exception, every one would see in every one else a probable enemy, against whom he must be perpetually guarding himself. What is hardly less important, these are the precepts which mankind have the strongest and the most direct inducements for impressing upon one another. By merely giving to each other prudential instruction or exhortation, they may gain, or think they gain, nothing: in inculcating on each other the duty of positive beneficence they have an unmistakable interest, but far less in degree: a person may possibly not need the benefits of others; but he always needs that they should not do him hurt. Thus the moralities which protect every individual from being harmed by others, either directly or by being hindered in his freedom of pursuing his own good, are at once those which he himself has most at heart, and those which he has the strongest interest in publishing and enforcing by word and deed. It is by a person's observance of these, that his fitness to exist as one of the fellowship of human beings, is tested and decided; for on that depends his being a nuisance or not to those with whom he is in contact. Now it is these moralities primarily, which compose the obligations of justice. The most marked cases of injustice, and those which give the tone to the feeling of repugnance which characterizes the sentiment, are acts of wrongful aggression, or wrongful exercise of power over some one; the next are those which consist in wrongfully withholding from him something which is his due; in both cases, inflicting on him a positive hurt, either in the form of direct suffering, or of the privation of some good which he had reasonable ground, either of a physical or of a social kind, for counting upon.

The same powerful motives which command the observance of these primary moralities, enjoin the punishment of those who violate them; and as the impulses of self-defence, of defence of others, and of vengeance, are all called forth against such persons, retribution, or evil for evil, becomes closely connected with the sentiment of justice, and is universally included in the idea. Good for good is also one of the dictates of justice; and this, though its social utility is evident, and though it carries with it a natural human feeling, has not at first sight that obvious connexion with hurt or injury, which, existing in the most elementary cases of just and unjust, is the source of the characteristic intensity of the sentiment. But the connexion, though less obvious, is not less real. He who accepts benefits, and denies a return of them when needed, inflicts a real hurt, by disappointing one of the most natural and reasonable of expectations, and one which he must at least tacitly have encouraged, otherwise the benefits would seldom have been conferred. The important rank, among human evils and wrongs, of the disappointment of expectation, is shown in the fact that it constitutes the principal criminality of two such highly immoral acts as a breach of friendship and a breach of promise. Few hurts which human beings can sustain are greater, and none wound more, than when that on which they habitually and with full assurance relied, fails them in the hour of need; and few wrongs are greater than this mere withholding of good; none excite more resentment, either in the person suffering, or in a sympathizing spectator. The principle, therefore, of giving to each what they deserve, that is, good for good as well as evil for evil, is not only included within the idea of Justice as we have defined it, but is a proper object of that intensity of sentiment, which places the Just, in human estimation, above the simply Expedient.

Most of the maxims of justice current in the world, and commonly appealed to in its transactions, are simply instrumental to carrying into effect the principles of justice which we have now spoken of. That a person is only responsible for what he has done voluntarily, or could voluntarily have avoided; that it is unjust to condemn any person unheard; that the punishment ought to be proportioned to the offence, and the like, are maxims intended to prevent the just principle of evil for evil from being perverted to the infliction of evil without that justification. The greater part of these common maxims have come into use from the practice of courts of justice, which have been naturally led to a more complete recognition and elaboration than was likely to suggest itself to others, of the rules necessary to enable them to fulfil their double function, of inflicting punishment when due, and of awarding to each person his right.

That first of judicial virtues, impartiality, is an obligation of justice, partly for the reason last mentioned; as being a necessary condition of the fulfilment of the other obligations of justice. But this is not the only source of the exalted rank, among human obligations, of those maxims of equality and impartiality, which, both in popular estimation and in that of the most enlightened, are included among the precepts of justice. In one point of view, they may be considered as corollaries from the principles already laid down. If it is a duty to do to each according to his deserts, returning good for good as well as repressing evil by evil, it necessarily follows that we should treat all equally well (when no higher duty forbids) who have deserved equally well of us, and that society should treat all equally well who have deserved equally well of it, that is, who have deserved equally well absolutely. This is the highest abstract standard of social and distributive justice; towards which all institutions, and the efforts of all virtuous citizens, should be made in the utmost possible degree to converge. But this great moral duty rests upon a still deeper foundation, being a direct emanation from the first principle of morals, and not a mere logical corollary from secondary or derivative doctrines. It is involved in the very meaning of Utility, or the Greatest-Happiness Principle. That principle is a mere form of words without rational signification, unless one person's happiness, supposed equal in degree (with the proper allowance made for kind), is counted for exactly as much as another's. Those conditions being supplied, Bentham's dictum, 'everybody to count for one, nobody for more than one,' might be written under the principle of utility as an explanatory commentary. The equal claim of everybody to happiness in the estimation of the moralist and the legislator, involves an equal claim to all the means of happiness, except in so far as the inevitable

conditions of human life, and the general interest, in which that of every individual is included, set limits to the maxim; and those limits ought to be strictly construed. As every other maxim of justice, so this, is by no means applied or held applicable universally; on the contrary, as I have already remarked, it bends to every person's ideas of social expediency. But in whatever case it is deemed applicable at all, it is held to be the dictate of justice. All persons are deemed to have a right to equality of treatment, except when some recognized social expediency requires the reverse. And hence all social inequalities which have ceased to be considered expedient, assume the character not of simple inexpediency, but of injustice, and appear so tyrannical, that people are apt to wonder how they ever could have been tolerated; forgetful that they themselves perhaps tolerate other inequalities under an equally mistaken notion of expediency, the correction of which would make that which they approve seem quite as monstrous as what they have at last learnt to condemn. The entire history of social improvement has been a series of transitions, by which one custom or institution after another, from being a supposed primary necessity of social existence, has passed into the rank of an universally stigmatized injustice and tyranny. So it has been with the distinctions of slaves and freemen, nobles and serfs, patricians and plebeians; and so it will be, and in part already is, with the aristocracies of colour, race, and sex.

It appears from what has been said, that justice is a name for certain moral requirements, which, regarded collectively, stand higher in the scale of social utility, and are therefore of more paramount obligation, than any others; though particular cases may occur in which some other social duty is so important, as to overrule any one of the general maxims of justice. Thus, to save a life, it may not only be allowable, but a duty, to steal, or take by force, the necessary food or medicine, or to kidnap, and compel to officiate, the only qualified medical practitioner. In such cases, as we do not call anything justice which is not a virtue, we usually say, not that justice must give way to some other moral principle, but that what is just in ordinary cases is, by reason of that other principle, not just in the particular case. By this useful accommodation of language, the character of indefeasibility attributed to justice is kept up, and we are saved from the necessity of maintaining that there can be laudable injustice.

The considerations which have now been adduced resolve, I conceive, the only real difficulty in the utilitarian theory of morals. It has always been evident that all cases of justice are also cases of expediency: the difference is in the peculiar sentiment which attaches to the former, as contradistinguished from the latter. If this characteristic sentiment has been sufficiently accounted for; if there is no necessity to assume for it any peculiarity of origin; if it is simply the natural feeling of resentment, moralized by being made coextensive with the demands of social good; and if this feeling not only does but ought to

exist in all the classes of cases to which the idea of justice corresponds; that idea no longer presents itself as a stumbling-block to the utilitarian ethics. Justice remains the appropriate name for certain social utilities which are vastly more important, and therefore more absolute and imperative, than any others are as a class (though not more so than others may be in particular cases); and which, therefore, ought to be, as well as naturally are, guarded by a sentiment not only different in degree, but also in kind; distinguished from the milder feeling which attaches to the mere idea of promoting human pleasure or convenience, at once by the more definite nature of its commands, and by the sterner character of its sanctions.

ON LIBERTY

The grand, leading principle, towards which every argument unfolded in these pages directly converges, is the absolute and essential importance of human development in its richest diversity.

—*WILHELM VON HUMBOLDT: Sphere and Duties of Government.*

CHAPTER I. INTRODUCTORY

The subject of this Essay is not the so-called Liberty of the Will, so unfortunately opposed to the misnamed doctrine of Philosophical Necessity; but Civil, or Social Liberty: the nature and limits of the power which can be legitimately exercised by society over the individual. A question seldom stated, and hardly ever discussed, in general terms, but which profoundly influences the practical controversies of the age by its latent presence, and is likely soon to make itself recognized as the vital question of the future. It is so far from being new, that, in a certain sense, it has divided mankind, almost from the remotest ages; but in the stage of progress into which the more civilized portions of the species have now entered, it presents itself under new conditions, and requires a different and more fundamental treatment.

The struggle between Liberty and Authority is the most conspicuous feature in the portions of history

with which we are earliest familiar, particularly in that of Greece, Rome, and England. But in old times this contest was between subjects, or some classes of subjects, and the Government. By liberty, was meant protection against the tyranny of the political rulers. The rulers were conceived (except in some of the popular governments of Greece) as in a necessarily antagonistic position to the people whom they ruled. They consisted of a governing One, or a governing tribe or caste, who derived their authority from inheritance or conquest, who, at all events, did not hold it at the pleasure of the governed, and whose supremacy men did not venture, perhaps did not desire, to contest, whatever precautions might be taken against its oppressive exercise. Their power was regarded as necessary, but also as highly dangerous; as a weapon which they would attempt to use against their subjects, no less than against external enemies. To prevent the weaker members of the community from being preyed upon by innumerable vultures, it was needful that there should be an animal of prey stronger than the rest, commissioned to keep them down. But as the king of the vultures would be no less bent upon preying on the flock than any of the minor harpies, it was indispensable to be in a perpetual attitude of defence against his beak and claws. The aim, therefore, of patriots was to set limits to the power which the ruler should be suffered to exercise over the community; and this limitation was what they meant by liberty. It was attempted in two ways. First, by obtaining a recognition of certain immunities, called political liberties or rights, which it was to be regarded as a breach of duty in the ruler to infringe, and which if he did infringe, specific resistance, or general rebellion, was held to be justifiable. A second, and generally a later expedient, was the establishment of constitutional checks, by which the consent of the community, or of a body of some sort, supposed to represent its interests, was made a necessary condition to some of the more important acts of the governing power. To the first of these modes of limitation, the ruling power, in most European countries, was compelled, more or less, to submit. It was not so with the second; and, to attain this, or when already in some degree possessed, to attain it more completely, became everywhere the principal object of the lovers of liberty. And so long as mankind were content to combat one enemy by another, and to be ruled by a master, on condition of being guaranteed more or less efficaciously against his tyranny, they did not carry their aspirations beyond this point.

A time, however, came, in the progress of human affairs, when men ceased to think it a necessity of nature that their governors should be an independent power, opposed in interest to themselves. It appeared to them much better that the various magistrates of the State should be their tenants or delegates, revocable at their pleasure. In that way alone, it seemed, could they have complete security that the powers of government would never be abused to their disadvantage. By degrees this new demand for elective and temporary rulers became the prominent object of the exertions of the popular party, wherever any such party existed; and superseded, to a considerable extent, the previous efforts to limit the power of rulers. As the struggle proceeded for making the ruling power emanate from the periodical choice of the ruled, some persons began to think that too much importance had been attached to the limitation of the power itself. That (it might seem) was a resource against rulers whose interests were habitually opposed to those of the people. What was now wanted was, that the rulers should be identified with the people; that their interest and will should be the interest and will of the nation. The nation did not need to be protected against its own will. There was no fear of its tyrannizing over itself. Let the rulers be effectually responsible to it, promptly removable by it, and it could afford to trust them with power of which it could itself dictate the use to be made. Their power was but the nation's own power, concentrated, and in a form convenient for exercise. This mode of thought, or rather perhaps of feeling, was common among the last generation of European liberalism, in the Continental section of which it still apparently predominates. Those who admit any limit to what a government may do, except in the case of such governments as they think ought not to exist, stand out as brilliant exceptions among the political thinkers of the Continent. A similar tone of sentiment might by this time have been prevalent in our own country, if the circumstances which for a time encouraged it, had continued unaltered.

But, in political and philosophical theories, as well as in persons, success discloses faults and infirmities which failure might have concealed from observation. The notion, that the people have no need to limit their power over themselves, might seem axiomatic, when popular government was a thing only dreamed about, or read of as having existed at some distant period of the past. Neither was that notion necessarily disturbed by such temporary aberrations as those of the French Revolution, the worst of which were the work of an usurping few, and which, in any case, belonged, not to the permanent working of popular institutions, but to a sudden and convulsive outbreak against monarchical and aristocratic despotism. In time, however, a democratic republic came to occupy a large portion of the earth's surface, and made itself felt as one of the most powerful members of the community of nations; and elective and responsible government became subject to the observations and criticisms which wait upon a great existing fact. It was now perceived that such phrases as 'self-government,' and 'the power of the people over themselves,' do not express the true state of the case. The 'people' who exercise the power are not always the same people with those over whom it is exercised; and the 'self-government' spoken of is not the government of each by himself, but of each by all the rest. The will of the people, moreover, practically means the will of the most numerous or the most active part of the people; the majority, or those who succeed in making themselves accepted as the majority; the people, consequently, may desire to oppress a part of their number; and precautions are as much needed against this as against any other abuse of power. The limitation, therefore, of the power of government over individuals loses none of its importance when the holders of power are regularly accountable to the community, that is, to the strongest party therein. This view of things, recommending itself equally to the intelligence of thinkers and to the inclination of those important classes in European society to whose real or supposed interests democracy is adverse, has had no difficulty in establishing itself; and in political speculations 'the tyranny of the majority' is now generally included among the evils against which society requires to be on its guard.

Like other tyrannies, the tyranny of the majority was at first, and is still vulgarly, held in dread, chiefly as operating through the acts of the public authorities. But reflecting persons perceived that when society is itself the tyrant—society collectively, over the separate individuals who compose it—its means of tyrannizing are not restricted to the acts which it may do by the hands of its political functionaries. Society can and does execute its own mandates: and if it issues wrong mandates instead of right, or any mandates at all in things with which it ought not to meddle, it practices a social tyranny more formidable than many kinds of political oppression, since, though not usually upheld by such extreme penalties, it leaves fewer means of escape, penetrating much more deeply into the details of life, and enslaving the soul itself. Protection, therefore, against the tyranny of the magistrate is not enough: there needs protection also against the tyranny of the prevailing opinion and feeling; against the tendency of society to impose, by other means than civil penal-ties, its own ideas and practices as rules of conduct on those who dissent from them; to fetter the development, and, if possible, prevent the formation, of any individuality not in harmony with its ways, and compel all characters to fashion themselves upon the model of its own. There is a limit to the legitimate interference of collective opinion with individual independence: and to find that limit, and maintain it against encroachment, is as indispensable to a good condition of human affairs, as protection against political despotism. . . .

The object of this Essay is to assert one very simple principle, as entitled to govern absolutely the dealings of society with the individual in the way of compulsion and control, whether the means used be physical force in the form of legal penalties, or the moral coercion of public opinion. That principle is, that the sole end for which mankind are warranted, individually or collectively, in interfering with the liberty of action of any of their number, is self-protection. That the only purpose for which power can be rightfully exercised over any member of a civilized community, against his will, is to prevent harm to others. His own good, either physical or moral, is not a sufficient warrant. He cannot rightfully be compelled to do or forbear because it will be better for him to do so, because it will make him happier, because, in the opinions of others, to do so would be wise, or even right. These are good reasons for remonstrating with him, or reasoning with him, or persuading him, or entreating him, but not for compelling him, or visiting him with any evil in case he do otherwise. To justify that, the conduct from which it is desired to deter him, must be calculated to produce evil to some one else. The only part of the conduct of any one, for which he is amenable to society, is that which concerns others. In the part which merely concerns himself, his independence is, of right, absolute. Over himself, over his own body and mind, the individual is sovereign.

It is, perhaps, hardly necessary to say that this doctrine is meant to apply only to human beings in the maturity of their faculties. We are not speaking of children, or of young persons below the age which the law may fix as that of manhood or womanhood. Those who are still in a state to require being taken care of by others, must be protected against their own actions as well as against external injury. For the same reason, we may leave out of consideration those backward states of society in which the race itself may be considered as in its nonage. The early difficulties in the way of spontaneous progress are so great, that there is seldom any choice of means for overcoming them; and a ruler full of the spirit of improvement is warranted in the use of any expedients that will attain an end, perhaps otherwise unattainable. Despotism is a legitimate mode of government in dealing with barbarians, provided the end be their improvement, and the means justified by actually effecting that end. Liberty, as a principle, has no application to any state of things anterior to the time when mankind have become capable of being improved by free and equal discussion. Until then, there is nothing for them but implicit obedience to an Akbar or a Charlemagne, if they are so fortunate as to find one. But as soon as mankind have attained the capacity of being guided to their own improvement by conviction or persuasion (a period long since reached in all nations with whom we need here concern ourselves), compulsion, either in the direct form or in that of pains and penalties for non-compliance, is no longer admissible as a means to their own good, and justifiable only for the security of others.

It is proper to state that I forgo any advantage which could be derived to my argument from the idea of abstract right, as a thing independent of utility. I regard utility as the ultimate appeal on all ethical questions; but it must be utility in the largest sense, grounded on the permanent interests of man as a progressive being. Those interests, I contend, authorize the subjection of individual spontaneity to external control, only in respect to those actions of each, which concern the interest of other people. If any one does an act hurtful to others, there is a prima facie case for punishing him, by law, or, where legal penalties are not safely applicable, by general disapprobation. There are also many positive acts for the benefit of others which he may rightfully be compelled to perform; such as, to give evidence in a court of justice; to bear his fair share in the common defence, or in any other joint work necessary to the interest of the society of which he enjoys the protection; and to perform certain acts of individual beneficence, such as saving a fellow-creature's life,

or interposing to protect the defenceless against ill-usage, things which whenever it is obviously a man's duty to do, he may rightfully be made responsible to society for not doing. A person may cause evil to others not only by his actions but by his inaction, and in either case he is justly accountable to them for the injury. The latter case, it is true, requires a much more cautious exercise of compulsion than the former. To make any one answerable for doing evil to others, is the rule; to make him answerable for not preventing evil, is, comparatively speaking, the exception. Yet there are many cases clear enough and grave enough to justify that exception. In all things which regard the external relations of the individual, he is de jure amenable to those whose interests are concerned, and if need be, to society as their protector. There are often good reasons for not holding him to the responsibility; but these reasons must arise from the special expediencies of the case: either because it is a kind of case in which he is on the whole likely to act better, when left to his own discretion, than when controlled in any way in which society have it in their power to control him; or because the attempt to exercise control would produce other evils, greater than those which it would prevent. When such reasons as these preclude the enforcement of responsibility, the conscience of the agent himself should step into the vacant judgment seat, and protect those interests of others which have no external protection; judging himself all the more rigidly, because the case does not admit of his being made accountable to the judgment of his fellow-creatures.

But there is a sphere of action in which society, as distinguished from the individual, has, if any, only an indirect interest; comprehending all that portion of a person's life and conduct which affects only himself, or if it also affects others, only with their free, voluntary, and undeceived consent and participation. When I say only himself, I mean directly, and in the first instance: for whatever affects himself, may affect others through himself; and the objection which may be grounded on this contingency, will receive consideration in the sequel. This, then, is the appropriate region of human liberty. It comprises, first, the inward domain of consciousness; demanding liberty of conscience, in the most comprehensive sense; liberty of thought and feeling; absolute freedom of opinion and sentiment on all subjects, practical or speculative, scientific, moral, or theological. The liberty of expressing and publishing opinions may seem to fall under a different principle, since it belongs to that part of the conduct of an individual which concerns other people; but, being almost of as much importance as the liberty of thought itself, and resting in great part on the same reasons, is practically inseparable from it. Secondly, the principle requires liberty of tastes and pursuits; of framing the plan of our life to suit our own character; of doing as we like, subject to such consequences as may follow: without impediment from our fellow-creatures, so long as what we do does not harm them, even though they should think our conduct foolish, perverse, or wrong. Thirdly, from this liberty of each individual, follows the liberty, within the same limits, of combination among individuals; freedom to unite, for any purpose not involving harm to others: the persons combining being supposed to be of full age, and not forced or deceived.

No society in which these liberties are not, on the whole, respected, is free, whatever may be its form of government; and none is completely free in which they do not exist absolute and unqualified. The only freedom which deserves the name, is that of pursuing our own good in our own way, so long as we do not attempt to deprive others of theirs, or impede their efforts to obtain it. Each is the proper guardian of his own health, whether bodily, or mental and spiritual. Mankind are greater gainers by suffering each other to live as seems good to themselves, than by compelling each to live as seems good to the rest.

Though this doctrine is anything but new, and, to some persons, may have the air of a truism, there is no doctrine which stands more directly opposed to the general tendency of existing opinion and practice. Society has expended fully as much effort in the attempt (according to its lights) to compel people to conform to its notions of personal, as of social excellence. The ancient commonwealths thought themselves entitled to practise, and the ancient philosophers countenanced, the regulation of every part of private conduct by public authority, on the ground that the State had a deep interest in the whole bodily and mental discipline of every one of its cit-izens; a mode of thinking which may have been admissible in small republics surrounded by powerful enemies, in constant peril of being subverted by foreign attack or internal commotion, and to which even a short interval of relaxed energy and self-command might so easily be fatal, that they could not afford to wait for the salutary permanent effects of freedom. In the modern world, the greater size of political communities, and above all, the separation between spiritual and temporal authority (which placed the direction of men's consciences in other hands than those which controlled their worldly affairs), prevented so great an interference by law in the details of private life; but the engines of moral repression have been wielded more strenuously against divergence from the reigning opinion in self-regarding, then even in social matters; religion, the most powerful of the elements which have entered into the formation of moral feeling, having almost always been governed either by the ambition of a hierarchy, seeking control over every department of human conduct, or by the spirit of Puritanism. And some of those modern reformers who have placed themselves in strongest opposition to the religions of the past, have been noway behind either churches or sects in their assertion of the right of spiritual domination: M. Comte, in particular, whose social system, as unfolded in his Systeme de Politique Positive, aims at establishing (though by moral more than by legal appliances) a despotism of society over the individual, surpassing anything contemplated in the political ideal of the most rigid disciplinarian among the ancient philosophers.

Apart from the peculiar tenets of individual thinkers, there is also in the world at large an increasing inclination to stretch unduly the powers of society over the individual, both by the force of opinion and even by that of legislation: and as the tendency of all the changes taking place in the world is to strengthen society, and diminish the power of the individual, this encroachment is not one of the evils which tend spontaneously to disappear, but, on the contrary, to grow more and more formidable. The disposition of mankind, whether as rulers or as fellow-citizens, to impose their own opinions and inclinations as a rule of conduct on others, is so energetically supported by some of the best and by some of the worst feelings incident to human nature, that it is hardly ever kept under restraint by anything but want of power; and as the power is not declining, but growing, unless a strong barrier of moral conviction can be raised against the mischief, we must expect, in the present circumstances of the world, to see it increase.

It will be convenient for the argument, if, instead of at once entering upon the general thesis, we confine ourselves in the first instance to a single branch of it, on which the principle here stated is, if not fully, yet to a certain point, recognized by the current opinions. This one branch is the Liberty of Thought: from which it is impossible to separate the cognate liberty of speaking and of writing. Although these liberties, to some considerable amount, form part of the political morality of all countries which profess religious toleration and free institutions, the grounds, both philosophical and practical, on which they rest, are perhaps not so familiar to the general mind, nor so thoroughly appreciated by many even of the leaders of opinion, as might have been expected. Those grounds, when rightly understood, are of much wider application than to only one division of the subject, and a thorough consideration of this part of the question will be found the best introduction to the remainder. Those to whom nothing which I am about to say will be new, may therefore, I hope, excuse me, if on a subject which for now three centuries has been so often discussed, I venture on one discussion more.

CHAPTER II. OF THE LIBERTY OF THOUGHT AND DISCUSSION

The time, it is to be hoped, is gone by, when any defence would be necessary of the 'liberty of the press' as one of the securities against corrupt or tyrannical government. No argument, we may suppose, can now be needed, against permitting a legislature or an executive, not identified in interest with the people, to prescribe opinions to them, and determine what doctrines or what arguments they shall be allowed to hear. This aspect of the question, besides, has been so often and so triumphantly enforced by preceding writers, that it needs not be specially insisted on in this place. Though the law of England, on the sub-

ject of the press, is as servile to this day as it was in the time of the Tudors, there is little danger of its being actually put in force against political discussion, except during some temporary panic, when fear of insurrection drives ministers and judges from their propriety; and, speaking generally, it is not, in constitutional countries, to be apprehended, that the government, whether completely responsible to the people or not, will often attempt to control the expression of opinion, except when in doing so it makes itself the organ of the general intolerance of the public. Let us suppose, therefore, that the government is entirely at one with the people, and never thinks of exerting any power of coercion unless in agreement with what it conceives to be their voice. But I deny the right of the people to exercise such coercion, either by themselves or by their government. The power itself is illegitimate. The best government has no more title to it than the worst. It is as noxious, or more noxious, when exerted in accordance with public opinion, than when in opposition to it. If all mankind minus one, were of one opinion, and only one person were of the contrary opinion, mankind would be no more justified in silencing that one person, than he, if he had the power, would be justified in silencing mankind. Were an opinion a personal possession of no value except to the owner; if to be obstructed in the enjoyment of it were simply a private injury, it would make some difference whether the injury was inflicted only on a few persons or on many. But the peculiar evil of silencing the expression of an opinion is, that it is robbing the human race; posterity as well as the existing generation; those who dissent from the opinion, still more than those who hold it. If the opinion is right, they are deprived of the opportunity of exchanging error for truth: if wrong, they lose, what is almost as great a benefit, the clearer perception and livelier impression of truth, produced by its collision with error.

It is necessary to consider separately these two hypotheses, each of which has a distinct branch of the argument corresponding to it. We can never be sure that the opinion we are endeavoring to stifle is a false opinion; and if we were sure, stifling it would be an evil still.

First: the opinion which it is attempted to suppress by authority may possibly be true. Those who desire to suppress it, of course deny its truth; but they are not infallible. They have no authority to decide the question for all mankind, and exclude every other person from the means of judging. To refuse a hearing to an opinion, because they are sure that it is false, is to assume that their certainty is the same thing as absolute certainty. All silencing of discussion is an assumption of infallibility. Its condemnation may be allowed to rest on this common argument, not the worse for being common.

Unfortunately for the good sense of mankind, the fact of their fallibility is far from carrying the weight in their practical judgment, which is always allowed to it in theory; for while every one well knows himself to be fallible, few think it necessary to take any precautions against their own fallibility, or admit the supposition that any opinion, of which they feel very certain, may be one of the examples of the error to which they acknowledge themselves to be liable. Absolute princes, or others who are accustomed to unlimited deference, usually feel this complete confidence in their own opinions on nearly all subjects. People more happily situated, who sometimes hear their opinions disputed, and are not wholly unused to be set right when they are wrong, place the same unbounded reliance only on such of their opinions as are shared by all who surround them, or to whom they habitually defer: for in proportion to a man's want of confidence in his own solitary judgment, does he usually repose, with implicit trust, on the infallibility of 'the world' in general. And the world, to each individual, means the part of it with which he comes in contact; his party, his sect, his church, his class of society: the man may be called, by comparison, almost liberal and large-minded to whom it means anything so comprehensive as his own country or his own age. Nor is his faith in this collective authority at all shaken by his being aware that other ages, countries, sects, churches, classes, and parties have thought, and even now think, the exact reverse. He devolves upon his own world the responsibility of being in the right against the dissentient worlds of other people; and it never troubles him that mere accident has decided which of these numerous worlds is the object of his reliance, and that the same causes which make him a Churchman in London, would have made him a Buddhist or a Confucian in

Pekin. Yet it is as evident in itself, as any amount of argument can make it, that ages are no more infallible than individuals; every age having held many opinions which subsequent ages have deemed not only false but absurd; and it is as certain that many opinions, now general, will be rejected by future ages, as it is that many, once general, are rejected by the present.

The objection likely to be made to this argument, would probably take some such form as the following. There is no greater assumption of infallibility in forbidding the propagation of error, than in any other thing which is done by public authority on its own judgment and responsibility. Judgment is given to men that they may use it. Because it may be used erroneously, are men to be told that they ought not to use it at all? To prohibit what they think pernicious, is not claiming exemption from error, but fulfilling the duty incumbent on them, although fallible, of acting on their conscientious conviction. If we were never to act on our opinions, because those opinions may be wrong, we should leave all our interests uncared for, and all our duties unperformed. An objection which applies to all conduct, can be no valid objection to any conduct in particular. It is the duty of governments, and of individuals, to form the truest opinions they can; to form them carefully, and never impose them upon others unless they are quite sure of being right. But when they are sure (such reasoners may say), it is not conscientiousness but cowardice to shrink from acting on their opinions, and allow doctrines which they honestly think dangerous to the welfare of mankind, either in this life or in another, to be scattered abroad without restraint, because other people, in less enlightened times, have persecuted opinions now believed to be true. Let us take care, it may be said, not to make the same mistake: but governments and nations have made mistakes in other things, which are not denied to be fit subjects for the exercise of authority: they have laid on bad taxes, made unjust wars. Ought we therefore to lay on no taxes, and, under whatever provocation, make no wars? Men, and governments, must act to the best of their ability. There is no such thing as absolute certainty, but there is assurance sufficient for the purposes of human life. We may, and must, assume our opinion to be true for the guidance of our own conduct: and it is assuming no more when we forbid bad men to pervert society by the propagation of opinions which we regard as false and pernicious.

I answer, that it is assuming very much more. There is the greatest difference between presuming an opinion to be true, because, with every opportunity for contesting it, it has not been refuted, and assuming its truth for the purpose of not permitting its refutation. Complete liberty of contradicting and disproving our opinion, is the very condition which justifies us in assuming its truth for purposes of action; and on no other terms can a being with human faculties have any rational assurance of being right.

When we consider either the history of opinion, or the ordinary conduct of human life, to what is it to be ascribed that the one and the other are no worse than they are? Not certainly to the inherent force of the human understanding; for, on any matter not self-evident, there are ninety-nine persons totally incapable of judging of it, for one who is capable; and the capacity of the hundredth person is only comparative; for the majority of the eminent men of every past generation held many opinions now known to be erroneous, and did or approved numerous things which no one will now justify. Why is it, then, that there is on the whole a preponderance among mankind of rational opinions and rational conduct? If there really is this preponderance—which there must be unless human affairs are, and have always been, in an almost desperate state—it is owing to a quality of the human mind, the source of everything respectable in man either as an intellectual or as a moral being, namely, that his errors are corrigible. He is capable of rectifying his mistakes, by discussion and experience. Not by experience alone. There must be discussion, to show how experience is to be interpreted. Wrong opinions and practices gradually yield to fact and argument: but facts and arguments, to produce any effect on the mind, must be brought before it. Very few facts are able to tell their own story, without comments to bring out their meaning. The whole strength and value, then, of human judgment, depending on the one property, that it can be set right when it is wrong, reliance can be placed on it only when the means of setting it right are kept constantly at hand. In the case of any person whose judgment is really deserving of confidence, how has it become so? Because he has kept his mind open to criticism of his opinions and conduct. Because it has been his practice to listen to all that could be said against him; to profit by as much of it as was just, and expound to himself, and upon occasion to others, the fallacy of what was fallacious. Because he has felt, that the only way in which a human being can make some approach to knowing the whole of a subject, is by hearing what can be said about it by persons of every variety of opinion, and studying all modes in which it can be looked at by every character of mind. No wise man ever acquired his wisdom in any mode but this; nor is it in the nature of human intellect to become wise in any other manner. The steady habit of correcting and completing his own opinion by collating it with those of others, so far from causing doubt and hesitation in carrying it into practice, is the only stable foundation for a just reliance on it: for, being cognizant of all that can, at least obviously, be said against him, and having taken up his position against all gainsayers—knowing that he has sought for objections and difficulties, instead of avoiding them, and has shut out no light which can be thrown upon the subject from any quarter—he has a right to think his judgment better than that of any person, or any multitude, who have not gone through a similar process. . . .

It is not too much to require that what the wisest of mankind, those who are best entitled to trust their own judgment, find necessary to warrant their relying on it, should be submitted to by that miscellaneous collection of a few wise and many foolish individuals, called the public. The most intolerant of churches, the Roman Catholic Church, even at the canonization of a saint, admits, and listens patiently to, a 'devil's advocate.' The holiest of men, it appears, cannot be admitted to posthumous honors, until all that the devil could say against him is known and weighed. If even the Newtonian philosophy were not permitted to be questioned, mankind could not feel as complete assurance of its truth as they now do. The beliefs which we have most warrant for, have no safeguard to rest on, but a standing invitation to the whole world to prove them unfounded. If the challenge is not accepted, or is accepted and the attempt fails, we are far enough from certainty still; but we have done the best that the existing state of human reason admits of; we have neglected nothing that could give the truth a chance of reaching us: if the lists are kept open, we may hope that if there be a better truth, it will be found when the human mind is capable of receiving it; and in the meantime we may rely on having attained such approach to truth, as is possible in our own day. This is the amount of certainty attainable by a fallible being, and this the sole way of attaining it.

Strange it is, that men should admit the validity of the arguments for free discussion, but object to their being 'pushed to an extreme;' not seeing that unless the reasons are good for an extreme case, they are not good for any case. Strange that they should imagine that they are not assuming infallibility, when they acknowledge that there should be free discussion on all subjects which can possibly be doubtful, but think that some particular principle or doctrine should be forbidden to be questioned because it is so certain, that is, because they are certain that it is certain. To call any proposition certain, while there is any one who would deny its certainty if permitted, but who is not permitted, is to assume that we ourselves, and those who agree with us, are the judges of certainty, and judges without hearing the other side.

In the present age—which has been described as 'destitute of faith, but terrified at scepticism'—in which people feel sure, not so much that their opinions are true, as that they should not know what to do without them—the claims of an opinion to be protected from public attack are rested not so much on its truth, as on its importance to society. There are, it is alleged, certain beliefs, so useful, not to say indispensable to well-being, that it is as much the duty of governments to uphold those beliefs, as to protect any other of the interests of society. In a case of such necessity, and so directly in the line of their duty, something less than infallibility may, it is maintained, warrant, and even bind, governments, to act on their own opinion, confirmed by the general opinion of mankind. It is also often argued, and still oftener thought, that none but bad men would desire to weaken these salutary beliefs; and there can be nothing wrong, it is thought, in restraining bad men, and prohibiting what only such men would wish to practise. This mode of thinking makes the justification of restraints on discussion not a question of the truth of doctrines, but of their usefulness; and flatters itself by that means to escape the responsibility

of claiming to be an infallible judge of opinions. But those who thus satisfy themselves, do not perceive that the assumption of infallibility is merely shifted from one point to another. The usefulness of an opinion is itself matter of opinion; as disputable, as open to discussion, and requiring discussion as much, as the opinion itself. There is the same need of an infallible judge of opinions to decide an opinion to be noxious, as to decide it to be false, unless the opinion condemned has full opportunity of defending itself. And it will not do to say that the heretic may be allowed to maintain the utility or harmlessness of his opinion, though forbidden to maintain its truth. The truth of an opinion is part of its utility. If we would know whether or not it is desirable that a proposition should be believed, is it possible to exclude the consideration of whether or not it is true? In the opinion, not of bad men, but of the best men, no belief which is contrary to truth can be really useful: and can you prevent such men from urging that plea, when they are charged with culpability for denying some doctrine which they are told is useful, but which they believe to be false? Those who are on the side of received opinions, never fail to take all possible advantage of this plea; you do not find them handling the question of utility as if it could be completely abstracted from that of truth: on the contrary, it is, above all, because their doctrine is the 'truth,' that the knowledge or the belief of it is held to be so indispensable. There can be no fair discussion of the question of usefulness, when an argument so vital may be employed on one side, but not on the other. And in point of fact, when law or public feeling do not permit the truth of an opinion to be disputed, they are just as little tolerant of a denial of its usefulness. The utmost they allow is an extenuation of its absolute necessity, or of the positive guilt of rejecting it. . . .

Mankind can hardly be too often reminded, that there was once a man named Socrates, between whom and the legal authorities and public opinion of his time, there took place a memorable collision. Born in an age and country abounding in individual greatness, this man has been handed down to us by those who best knew both him and the age, as the most virtuous man in it; while we know him as the head and prototype of all subsequent teachers of virtue, the source equally of the lofty inspiration of Plato and the judicious utilitarianism of Aristotle, 'i maestri di color che sanno,' the two headsprings of ethical as of all other philosophy. This acknowledged master of all the eminent thinkers who have since lived—whose fame, still growing after more than two thousand years, all but outweighs the whole remainder of the names which make his native city illustrious—was put to death by his countrymen, after a judicial conviction, for impiety and immorality. Impiety, in denying the gods recognized by the State; indeed his accuser asserted (see the Apologia) that he believed in no gods at all. Immorality, in being, by his doctrines and instructions, a 'corruptor of youth.' Of these charges the tribunal, there is every ground for believing, honestly found him guilty, and condemned the man who probably of all then born had deserved best of mankind, to be put to death as a criminal.

To pass from this to the only other instance of judicial iniquity, the mention of which, after the condemnation of Socrates, would not be an anti-climax: the event which took place on Calvary rather more than eighteen hundred years ago. The man who left on the memory of those who witnessed his life and conversation, such an impression of his moral grandeur, that eighteen subsequent centuries have done homage to him as the Almighty in person, was ignominiously put to death, as what? As a blasphemer. Men did not merely mistake their benefactor; they mistook him for the exact contrary of what he was, and treated him as that prodigy of impiety, which they themselves are now held to be, for their treatment of him. The feelings with which mankind now regard these lamentable transactions, especially the later of the two, render them extremely unjust in their judgment of the unhappy actors. These were, to all appearance, not bad men—not worse than men commonly are, but rather the contrary; men who possessed in a full, or somewhat more than a full measure, the religious, moral, and patriotic feelings of their time and people: the very kind of men who, in all times, our own included, have every chance of passing through life blameless and respected. The high-priest who rent his garments when the words were pronounced, which, according to all the ideas of his country, constituted the blackest guilt, was in all probability quite as sincere in his horror and indignation, as the generality of respectable and pious

men now are in the religious and moral sentiments they profess; and most of those who now shudder at his conduct, if they had lived in his time, and been born Jews, would have acted precisely as he did. Orthodox Christians who are tempted to think that those who stoned to death the first martyrs must have been worse men than they themselves are, ought to remember that one of those persecutors was Saint Paul. . . .

Aware of the impossibility of defending the use of punishment for restraining irreligious opinions . . . the enemies of religious freedom, when hard pressed, occasionally accept this consequence, and say, with Dr. Johnson, that the persecutors of Christianity were in the right; that persecution is an ordeal through which truth ought to pass, and always passes successfully, legal penalties being, in the end, powerless against truth, though sometimes beneficially effective against mischievous errors. This is a form of the argument for religious intolerance, sufficiently remarkable not to be passed without notice.

A theory which maintains that truth may justifiably be persecuted because persecution cannot possibly do it any harm, cannot be charged with being intentionally hostile to the reception of new truths; but we cannot commend the generosity of its dealing with the persons to whom mankind are indebted for them. To discover to the world something which deeply concerns it, and of which it was previously ignorant; to prove to it that it had been mistaken on some vital point of temporal or spiritual interest, is as important a service as a human being can render to his fellow-creatures, and in certain cases, as in those of the early Christians and of the Reformers, those who think with Dr. Johnson believe it to have been the most precious gift which could be bestowed on mankind. That the authors of such splendid benefits should be requited by martyrdom; that their reward should be to be dealt with as the vilest of criminals, is not, upon this theory, a deplorable error and misfortune, for which humanity should mourn in sackcloth and ashes, but the normal and justifiable state of things. The propounder of a new truth, according to this doctrine, should stand, as stood, in the legislation of the Locrians, the proposer of a new law, with a halter round his neck, to be instantly tightened if the public assembly did not, on hearing his reasons, then and there adopt his proposition. People who defend this mode of treating benefactors, cannot be supposed to set much value on the benefit; and I believe this view of the subject is mostly confined to the sort of persons who think that new truths may have been desirable once, but that we have had enough of them now.

But, indeed, the dictum that truth always triumphs over persecution, is one of those pleasant falsehoods which men repeat after one another till they pass into commonplaces, but which all experience refutes. History teems with instances of truth put down by persecution. If not suppressed for ever, it may be thrown back for centuries. To speak only of religious opinions: the Reformation broke out at least twenty times before Luther, and was put down. Arnold of Brescia was put down. Fra Dolcino was put down. Savonarola was put down. The Albigeois were put down. The Vaudois were put down. The Lollards were put down. The Hussites were put down. Even after the era of Luther, wherever persecution was persisted in, it was successful. In Spain, Italy, Flanders, the Austrian empire, Protestantism was rooted out; and, most likely, would have been so in England, had Queen Mary lived, or Queen Elizabeth died. Persecution has always succeeded, save where the heretics were too strong a party to be effectually persecuted. No reasonable person can doubt that Christianity might have been extirpated in the Roman Empire. It spread, and became predominant, because the persecutions were only occasional, lasting but a short time, and separated by long intervals of almost undisturbed propagandism. It is a piece of idle sentimentality that truth, merely as truth, has any inherent power denied to error, of prevailing against the dungeon and the stake. Men are not more zealous for truth than they often are for error, and a sufficient application of legal or even of social penalties will generally succeed in stopping the propagation of either. The real advantage which truth has, consists in this, that when an opinion is true, it may be extinguished once, twice, or many times, but in the course of ages there will generally be found persons to rediscover it, until some one of its reappearances falls on a time when from favorable circumstances it escapes persecution until it has made such head as to withstand all subsequent attempts to suppress it. . . .

Let us now pass to the second division of the argument, and dismissing the supposition that any of the received opinions may be false, let us assume them to be true, and examine into the worth of the manner in which they are likely to be held, when their truth is not freely and openly canvassed. However unwillingly a person who has a strong opinion may admit the possibility that his opinion may be false, he ought to be moved by the consideration that however true it may be, if it is not fully, frequently, and fearlessly discussed, it will be held as a dead dogma, not a living truth.

There is a class of persons (happily not quite so numerous as formerly) who think it enough if a person assents undoubtingly to what they think true, though he has no knowledge whatever of the grounds of the opinion, and could not make a tenable defence of it against the most superficial objections. Such persons, if they can once get their creed taught from authority, naturally think that no good, and some harm, comes of its being allowed to be questioned. Where their influence prevails, they make it nearly impossible for the received opinion to be rejected wisely and considerately, though it may still be rejected rashly and ignorantly; for to shut out discussion entirely is seldom possible, and when it once gets in, beliefs not grounded on conviction are apt to give way before the slightest semblance of an argument. Waving, however, this possibility—assuming that the true opinion abides in the mind, but abides as a prejudice, a belief independent of, and proof against, argument—this is not the way in which truth ought to be held by a rational being. This is not knowing the truth. Truth, thus held, is but one superstition the more, accidentally clinging to the words which enunciate a truth.

If the intellect and judgment of mankind ought to be cultivated, a thing which Protestants at least do not deny, on what can these faculties be more appropriately exercised by any one, than on the things which concern him so much that it is considered necessary for him to hold opinions on them? If the cultivation of the understanding consists in one thing more than in another, it is surely in learning the grounds of one's own opinions. Whatever people believe, on subjects on which it is of the first importance to believe rightly, they ought to be able to defend against at least the common objections. But, some one may say, 'Let them be taught the grounds of their opinions. It does not follow that opinions must be merely parroted because they are never heard controverted. Persons who learn geometry do not simply commit the theorems to memory, but understand and learn likewise the demonstrations; and it would be absurd to say that they remain ignorant of the grounds of geometrical truths, because they never hear any one deny, and attempt to disprove them.' Undoubtedly: and such teaching suffices on a subject like mathematics, where there is nothing at all to be said on the wrong side of the question. The peculiarity of the evidence of mathematical truths is, that all the argument is on one side. There are no objections, and no answers to objections. But on every subject on which difference of opinion is possible, the truth depends on a balance to be struck between two sets of conflicting reasons. Even in natural philosophy, there is always some other explanation possible of the same facts; some geocentric theory instead of heliocentric, some phlogiston instead of oxygen; and it has to be shown why that other theory cannot be the true one: and until this is shown, and until we know how it is shown, we do not understand the grounds of our opinion. But when we turn to subjects infinitely more complicated, to morals, religion, politics, social relations, and the business of life, three-fourths of the arguments for every disputed opinion consist in dispelling the appearances which favour some opinion different from it. The greatest orator, save one, of antiquity, has left it on record that he always studied his adversary's case with as great, if not with still greater, intensity than even his own. What Cicero practiced as the means of forensic success, requires to be imitated by all who study any subject in order to arrive at the truth. He who knows only his own side of the case, knows little of that. His reasons may be good, and no one may have been able to refute them. But if he is equally unable to refute the reasons on the opposite side; if he does not so much as know what they are, he has no ground for preferring either opinion. The rational position for him would be suspension of judgment, and unless he contents himself with that, he is either led by authority, or adopts, like the generality of the world, the side to which he feels most inclination. Nor is it enough that he should hear the arguments of adversaries from his own teachers, presented as they state them, and accompanied by what they offer as refutations. That is not the way to do justice to the arguments, or bring them into real contact with his own mind. He must be able to hear them from persons who actually believe them; who defend them in earnest, and do their very utmost for them. He must know them in their most plausible and persuasive form; he must feel the whole force of the difficulty which the true view of the subject has to encounter and dispose of; else he will never really possess himself of the portion of truth which meets and removes that difficulty. Ninety-nine in a hundred of what are called educated men are in this condition; even of those who can argue fluently for their opinions. Their conclusion may be true, but it might be false for anything they know: they have never thrown themselves into the mental position of those who think differently from them, and considered what such persons may have to say; and consequently they do not, in any proper sense of the word, know the doctrine which they themselves profess. They do not know those parts of it which explain and justify the remainder; the considerations which show that a fact which seemingly conflicts with another is reconcilable with it, or that, of two apparently strong reasons, one and not the other ought to be preferred. All that part of the truth which turns the scale, and decides the judgment of a completely informed mind, they are strangers to; nor is it ever really known, but to those who have attended equally and impartially to both sides, and endeavored to see the reasons of both in the strongest light. So essential is this discipline to a real understanding of moral and human subjects, that if opponents of all important truths do not exist, it is indispensable to imagine them, and supply them with the strongest arguments which the most skillful devil's advocate can conjure up.

To abate the force of these considerations, an enemy of free discussion may be supposed to say, that there is no necessity for mankind in general to know and understand all that can be said against or for their opinions by philosophers and theologians. That it is not needful for common men to be able to expose all the misstatements or fallacies of an ingenious opponent. That it is enough if there is always some-body capable of answering them, so that nothing likely to mislead uninstructed persons remains unre-futed. That simple minds, having been taught the ob-vious grounds of the truths inculcated on them, may trust to authority for the rest, and being aware that they have neither knowledge nor talent to resolve every difficulty which can be raised, may repose in the assurance that all those which have been raised have been or can be answered, by those who are spe-cially trained to the task.

Conceding to this view of the subject the utmost that can be claimed for it by those most easily sat-isfied with the amount of understanding of truth which ought to accompany the belief of it; even so, the argument for free discussion is no way weak-ened. For even this doctrine acknowledges that mankind ought to have a rational assurance that all objections have been satisfactorily answered; and how are they to be answered if that which requires to be answered is not spoken? or how can the an-swer be known to be satisfactory, if the objectors have no opportunity of showing that it is unsatisfac-tory? If not the public, at least the philosophers and theologians who are to resolve the difficulties, must make themselves familiar with those difficulties in their most puzzling form; and this cannot be ac-complished unless they are freely stated, and placed in the most advantageous light which they admit of. The Catholic Church has its own way of dealing with this embarrassing problem. It makes a broad separa-tion between those who can be permitted to receive its doctrines on conviction, and those who must ac-cept them on trust. Neither, indeed, are allowed any choice as to what they will accept; but the clergy, such at least as can be fully confided in, may ad-missibly and meritoriously make themselves ac-quainted with the arguments of opponents, in order to answer them, and may, therefore, read heretical books; the laity, not unless by special permission, hard to be obtained. This discipline recognizes a knowledge of the enemy's case as beneficial to the teachers, but finds means, consistent with this, of denying it to the rest of the world: thus giving to the elite more mental culture, though not more mental freedom, than it allows to the mass. By this device it succeeds in obtaining the kind of mental superior-ity which its purposes require; for though culture without freedom never made a large and liberal mind, it can make a clever nisi prius advocate of a cause. But in countries professing Protestantism, this resource is denied; since Protestants hold, at least in theory, that the responsibility for the choice of a re-ligion must be borne by each for himself, and can-not be thrown off upon teachers. Besides, in the pres-ent state of the world, it is practically impossible that writings which are read by the instructed can be kept from the uninstructed. If the teachers of mankind are to be cognizant of all that they ought to know, every-thing must be free to be written and published with-out restraint.

If, however, the mischievous operation of the ab-sence of free discussion, when the received opinions are true, were confined to leaving men ignorant of the grounds of those opinions, it might be thought that this, if an intellectual, is no moral evil, and does not affect the worth of the opinions, regarded in their influence on the character. The fact, however, is, that not only the grounds of the opinion are forgotten in the absence of discussion, but too often the meaning of the opinion itself. The words which convey it, cease to suggest ideas, or suggest only a small por-tion of those they were originally employed to com-municate. Instead of a vivid conception and a living belief, there remain only a few phrases retained by rote; or, if any part, the shell and husk only of the meaning is retained, the finer essence being lost. The great chapter in human history which this fact occu-pies and fills, cannot be too earnestly studied and meditated on.

It is illustrated in the experience of almost all eth-ical doctrines and religious creeds. They are all full of meaning and vitality to those who originate them, and to the direct disciples of the originators. Their meaning continues to be felt in undiminished strength, and is perhaps brought out into even fuller consciousness, so long as the struggle lasts to give the doctrine or creed an ascendancy over other creeds. At last it either prevails, and becomes the general opinion, or its progress stops; it keeps pos-session of the ground it has gained, but ceases to spread further. When either of these results has be-come apparent, controversy on the subject flags, and gradually dies away. The doctrine has taken its place, if not as a received opinion, as one of the admitted sects or divisions of opinion: those who hold it have generally inherited, not adopted it; and conversion from one of these doctrines to another, being now an exceptional fact, occupies little place in the thoughts of their professors. Instead of being, as at first, constantly on the alert either to defend themselves against the world, or to bring the world over to them, they have subsided into acquiescence, and neither listen, when they can help it, to arguments against their creed, nor trouble dissentients (if there be such) with arguments in its favour. From this time may usually be dated the decline in the living power of the doctrine. We often hear the teachers of all creeds lamenting the difficulty of keeping up in the minds of believers a lively apprehension of the truth which they nominally recognize, so that it may penetrate the feelings, and acquire a real mastery over the conduct. No such difficulty is complained of while the creed is still fighting for its existence: even the weaker combatants then know and feel what they are fighting for, and the difference between it and other doctrines; and in that period of every creed's existence, not a few persons may be found, who have realized its fundamental principles in all the forms of thought, have weighed and considered them in all their important bearings, and have experienced the full effect on the character, which belief in that creed ought to produce in a mind thoroughly imbued with it. But when it has come to be an hereditary creed, and to be received passively, not actively—when the mind is no longer compelled, in the same degree as at first, to exercise its vital powers on the questions which its belief presents to it, there is a progressive tendency to forget all of the belief except the formularies, or to give it a dull and torpid assent, as if accepting it on trust dispensed with the necessity of realizing it in consciousness, or testing it by personal experience; until it almost ceases to connect itself at all with the inner life of the human being. Then are seen the cases, so frequent in this age of the world as almost to form the majority, in which the creed remains as it were outside the mind, incrusting and petrifying it against all other influences addressed to the higher parts of our nature; manifesting its power by not suffering any fresh and living conviction to get in, but itself doing nothing for the mind or heart, except standing sentinel over them to keep them vacant.

To what an extent doctrines intrinsically fitted to make the deepest impression upon the mind may remain in it as dead beliefs, without being ever realized in the imagination, the feelings, or the understanding, is exemplified by the manner in which the majority of believers hold the doctrines of Christianity. By Christianity I here mean what is accounted such by all churches and sects—the maxims and precepts contained in the New Testament. These are considered sacred, and accepted as laws, by all professing Christians. Yet it is scarcely too much to say that not one Christian in a thousand guides or tests his individual conduct by reference to those laws. The standard to which he does refer it, is the custom of his nation, his class, or his religious profession. He has thus, on the one hand, a collection of ethical maxims, which he believes to have been vouchsafed to him by infallible wisdom as rules for his government; and on the other, a set of every-day judgments and practices, which go a certain length with some of those maxims, not so great a length with others, stand in direct opposition to some, and are, on the whole, a compromise between the Christian creed and the interests and suggestions of worldly life. To the first of these standards he gives his homage; to the other his real allegiance. All Christians believe that the blessed are the poor and humble, and those who are ill-used by the world; that it is easier for a camel to pass through the eye of a needle than for a rich man to enter the kingdom of heaven; that they should judge not, lest they be judged; that they should swear not at all; that they should love their neighbor as themselves; that if one take their cloak, they should give him their coat also; that they should take no thought for the morrow; that if they would be perfect, they should sell all that they have and give it to the poor. They are not insincere when they say that they believe these things. They do believe them, as people believe what they have always heard lauded and never discussed. But in the sense of that living belief which regulates conduct, they believe these doctrines just up to the point to which it is usual to act upon them. The doctrines in their integrity are serviceable to pelt adversaries with; and it is understood that they are to be put forward (when possible) as the reasons for whatever people do that they think laudable. But any one who reminded them that the maxims require an infinity of things which they never even think of doing, would gain nothing but to be classed among those very unpopular characters who affect to be better than other people. The doctrines have no hold on ordinary believers—are not a power in their minds. They have an habitual respect for the sound of them, but no feeling which spreads from the words to things signified, and forces the mind to take them in, and make them conform to the formula. Whenever conduct is concerned, they look round for Mr. A and B to direct them how far to go in obeying Christ.

Now we may be well assured that the case was not thus, but far otherwise, with the early Christians. Had it been thus, Christianity never would have expanded from an obscure sect of the despised Hebrews into the religion of the Roman empire. When their enemies said, 'See how these Christians love one another' (a remark not likely to be made by anybody now), they assuredly had a much livelier feeling of the meaning of their creed than they have ever had since. And to this cause, probably, it is chiefly owing that Christianity now makes so little progress in extending its domain, and after eighteen centuries, is still nearly confined to Europeans and the descendants of Europeans. Even with the strictly religious, who are much in earnest about their doctrines, and attach a greater amount of meaning to many of them than people in general, it commonly happens that the part which is thus comparatively active in their minds is that which was made by Calvin, or Knox, or some such person much nearer in character to themselves. The sayings of Christ coexist passively in their minds, producing hardly any effect beyond what is caused by mere listening to words so amiable and bland. There are many reasons, doubtless, why doctrines which are the badge of a sect retain more of their vitality than those common to all recognized sects, and why more pains are taken by teachers to keep their meaning alive; but one reason certainly is, that the peculiar doctrines are more questioned, and have to be oftener defended against open gainsayers. Both teachers and learners go to sleep at their post, as soon as there is no enemy in the field.

The same thing holds true, generally speaking, of all traditional doctrines—those of prudence and knowledge of life, as well as of morals or religion. All languages and literatures are full of general observations on life, both as to what it is, and how to conduct oneself in it; observations which everybody knows, which everybody repeats, or hears with acquiescence, which are received as truisms, yet of which most people first truly learn the meaning, when experience, generally of a painful kind, has made it a reality to them. How often, when smarting under some unforeseen misfortune or disappointment, does a person call to mind some proverb or common saying, familiar to him all his life, the meaning of which, if he had ever before felt it as he does now, would have saved him from the calamity. There are indeed reasons for this, other than the absence of discussion: there are many truths of which the full meaning cannot be realized, until personal experience has brought it home. But much more of the meaning even of these would have been understood, and what was understood would have been far more deeply impressed on the mind, if the man had been accustomed to hear it argued pro and con by people who did understand it. The fatal tendency of mankind to leave off thinking about a thing when it is no longer doubtful, is the cause of half their errors. A contemporary author has well spoken of 'the deep slumber of a decided opinion.'

But what! (it may be asked) Is the absence of unanimity an indispensable condition of true knowledge? Is it necessary that some part of mankind should persist in error, to enable any to realize the truth? Does a belief cease to be real and vital as soon as it is generally received—and is a proposition never thoroughly understood and felt unless some doubt of it remains? As soon as mankind have unanimously accepted a truth, does the truth perish within them? The highest aim and best result of improved intelligence, it has hitherto been thought, is to unite mankind more and more in the acknowledgment of all important truths: and does the intelligence only last as long as it has not achieved its object? Do the fruits of conquest perish by the very completeness of the victory?

I affirm no such thing. As mankind improve, the number of doctrines which are no longer disputed or doubted will be constantly on the increase: and the well-being of mankind may almost be measured by the number and gravity of the truths which have reached the point of being uncontested. The cessation, on one question after another, of serious controversy, is one of the necessary incidents of the consolidation of opinion; a consolidation as salutary in the case of true opinions, as it is dangerous and noxious when the opinions are erroneous. But though this gradual narrowing of the bounds of diversity of opinion is necessary in both senses of the term, being at once inevitable and indispensable, we are not therefore obliged to conclude that all its consequences must be beneficial. The loss of so important an aid to the intelligent and living apprehension of a truth, as is afforded by the necessity of explaining it to, or defending it against, opponents, though not sufficient to outweigh, is no trifling drawback from, the benefit of its universal recognition. Where this advantage can no longer be had, I confess I should like to see the teachers of mankind endeavoring to provide a substitute for it; some contrivance for making the difficulties of the question as present to the learner's consciousness, as if they were pressed upon him by a dissentient champion, eager for his conversion.

But instead of seeking contrivances for this purpose, they have lost those they formerly had. The Socratic dialectics, so magnificently exemplified in the dialogues of Plato, were a contrivance of this description. They were essentially a negative discussion of the great questions of philosophy and life, directed with consummate skill to the purpose of convincing any one who had merely adopted the commonplaces of received opinion, that he did not understand the subject—that he as yet attached no definite meaning to the doctrines he professed; in order that, becoming aware of his ignorance, he might be put in the way to attain a stable belief, resting on a clear apprehension both of the meaning of doctrines and of their evidence. The school disputations of the middle ages had a somewhat similar object. They were intended to make sure that the pupil understood his own opinion, and (by necessary correlation) the opinion opposed to it, and could enforce the grounds of the one and confute those of the other. These last-mentioned contests had indeed the incur-

able defect, that the premises appealed to were taken from authority, not from reason; and, as a discipline in the mind, they were in every respect inferior to the powerful dialectics which formed the intellects of the 'Socratici viri:' but the modern mind owes far more to both than it is generally willing to admit, and the present modes of education contain nothing which in the smallest degree supplies the place either of the one or of the other. A person who derives all his instruction from teachers or books, even if he escape the besetting temptation of contenting himself with cram, is under no compulsion to hear both sides; accordingly it is far from a frequent accomplishment, even among thinkers, to know both sides; and the weakest part of what everybody says in defence of his opinion, is what he intends as a reply to antagonists. It is the fashion of the present time to disparage negative logic—that which points out weaknesses in theory or errors in practice, without establishing positive truths. Such negative criticism would indeed be poor enough as an ultimate result; but as a means to attaining any positive knowledge or conviction worthy the name, it cannot be valued too highly; and until people are again systematically trained to it, there will be few great thinkers, and a low general average of intellect, in any but the mathematical and physical departments of speculation. On any other subject no one's opinions deserve the name of knowledge, except so far as he has either had forced upon him by others, or gone through of himself, the same mental process which would have been required of him in carrying on an active controversy with opponents. That, therefore, which when absent, it is so indispensable, but so difficult, to create, how worse than absurd it is to forego, when spontaneously offering itself! If there are any persons who contest a received opinion, or who will do so if law or opinion will let them, let us thank them for it, open our minds to listen to them, and rejoice that there is some one to do for us what we otherwise ought, if we have any regard for either the certainty or the vitality of our convictions, to do with much greater labour for ourselves.

It still remains to speak of one of the principal causes which make diversity of opinion advantageous, and will continue to do so until mankind shall have entered a stage of intellectual advancement which at present seems at an incalculable distance. We have hitherto considered only two possibilities: that the received opinion may be false, and some other opinion, consequently, true; or that, the received opinion being true, a conflict with the opposite error is essential to a clear apprehension and deep feeling of its truth. But there is a commoner case then either of these; when the conflicting doctrines, instead of being one true and the other false, share the truth between them; and the nonconforming opinion is needed to supply the remainder of the truth, of which the received doctrine embodies only a part. Popular opinions, on subjects not palpable to sense, are often true, but seldom or never the whole truth. They are a part of the truth; sometimes a greater, sometimes a smaller part, but exaggerated, distorted, and disjoined from the truths by which they ought to be accompanied and limited. Heretical opinions, on the other hand, are generally some of these suppressed and neglected truths, bursting the bonds which kept them down, and either seeking reconciliation with the truth contained in the common opinion, or fronting it as enemies, and setting themselves up, with similar exclusiveness, as the whole truth. The latter case is hitherto the most frequent, as, in the human mind, one-sidedness has always been the rule, and many-sidedness the exception. Hence, even in revolutions of opinion, one part of the truth usually sets while another rises. Even progress, which ought to superadd, for the most part only substitutes, one partial and incomplete truth for another; improvement consisting chiefly in this, that the new fragment of truth is more wanted, more adapted to the needs of the time, than that which it displaces. Such being the partial character of prevailing opinions, even when resting on a true foundation, every opinion which embodies somewhat of the portion of truth which the common opinion omits, ought to be considered precious, with whatever amount of error and confusion that truth may be blended. No sober judge of human affairs will feel bound to be indignant because those who force on our notice truths which we should otherwise have overlooked, overlook some of those which we see. Rather, he will think that so long as popular truth is one-sided, it is more desirable than otherwise that unpopular truth should have one-sided asserters too; such being usu-

ally the most energetic, and the most likely to compel reluctant attention to the fragment of wisdom which they proclaim as if it were the whole.

Thus, in the eighteenth century, when nearly all the instructed, and all those of the uninstructed who were led by them, were lost in admiration of what is called civilization, and of the marvels of modern science, literature, and philosophy, and while greatly overrating the amount of unlikeness between the men of modern and those of ancient times, indulged the belief that the whole of the difference was in their own favour; with what a salutary shock did the paradoxes of Rousseau explode like bombshells in the midst, dislocating the compact mass of one-sided opinion, and forcing its elements to recombine in a better form and with additional ingredients. Not that the current opinions were on the whole farther from the truth than Rousseau's were; on the contrary, they were nearer to it; they contained more of positive truth, and very much less of error. Nevertheless there lay in Rousseau's doctrine, and has floated down the stream of opinion along with it, a considerable amount of exactly those truths which the popular opinion wanted; and these are the deposit which was left behind when the flood subsided. The superior worth of simplicity of life, the enervating and demoralizing effect of the trammels and hypocrisies of artificial society, are ideas which have never been entirely absent from cultivated minds since Rousseau wrote; and they will in time produce their due effect, though at present needing to be asserted as much as ever, and to be asserted by deeds, for words, on this subject, have nearly exhausted their power.

In politics, again, it is almost a commonplace, that a party of order or stability, and a party of progress or reform, are both necessary elements of a healthy state of political life; until the one or the other shall have so enlarged its mental grasp as to be a party equally of order and of progress, knowing and distinguishing what is fit to be preserved from what ought to be swept away. Each of these modes of thinking derives its utility from the deficiencies of the other; but it is in a great measure the opposition of the other that keeps each within the limits of reason and sanity. Unless opinions favorable to democracy and to aristocracy, to property and to equality, to co-operation and to competition, to luxury and to abstinence, to sociality and individuality, to liberty and discipline, and all the other standing antagonisms of practical life, are expressed with equal freedom, and enforced and defended with equal talent and energy, there is no chance of both elements obtaining their due; one scale is sure to go up, and the other down. Truth, in the great practical concerns of life, is so much a question of the reconciling and combining of opposites, that very few have minds sufficiently capacious and impartial to make the adjustment with an approach to correctness, and it has to be made by the rough process of a struggle between combatants fighting under hostile banners. On any of the great open questions just enumerated, if either of the two opinions has a better claim than the other, not merely to be tolerated, but to be encouraged and countenanced, it is the one which happens at the particular time and place to be in a minority. That is the opinion which, for the time being, represents the neglected interests, the side of human wellbeing which is in danger of obtaining less than its share. I am aware that there is not, in this country, any intolerance of differences of opinion on most of these topics. They are adduced to show, by admitted and multiplied examples, the universality of the fact, that only through diversity of opinion is there, in the existing state of human intellect, a chance of fair play to all sides of the truth. When there are persons to be found, who form an exception to the apparent unanimity of the world on any subject, even if the world is in the right, it is always probable that dissentients have something worth hearing to say for themselves, and that truth would lose something by their silence.

It may be objected, 'But some received principles, especially on the highest and most vital subjects, are more than half-truths. The Christian morality, for instance, is the whole truth on that subject, and if any one teaches a morality which varies from it, he is wholly in error.' As this is of all cases the most important in practice, none can be fitter to test the general maxim. But before pronouncing what Christian morality is or is not, it would be desirable to decide what is meant by Christian morality. If it means the morality of the New Testament, I wonder that any one who derives his knowledge of this from the book itself, can suppose that it was announced, or intended, as a complete doctrine of morals. The Gospel always refers to a pre-existing morality, and confines its precepts to the particulars in which that morality was to be corrected, or superseded by a wider and higher; expressing itself, moreover, in terms most general, often impossible to be interpreted literally, and possessing rather the impressiveness of poetry or eloquence than the precision of legislation. To extract from it a body of ethical doctrine, has never been possible without eking it out from the Old Testament, that is, from a system elaborate indeed, but in many respects barbarous, and intended only for a barbarous people. St. Paul, a declared enemy to this Judaical mode of interpreting the doctrine and filling up the scheme of his Master, equally assumes a pre-existing morality, namely that of the Greeks and Romans; and his advice to Christians is in a great measure a system of accommodation to that; even to the extent of giving an apparent sanction to slavery. What is called Christian, but should rather be termed theological, morality, was not the work of Christ or the Apostles, but is of much later origin, having been gradually built up by the Catholic church of the first five centuries, and though not implicitly adopted by moderns and Protestants, has been much less modified by them than might have been expected. For the most part, indeed, they have contented themselves with cutting off the additions which had been made to it in the middle ages, each sect supplying the place by fresh additions, adapted to its own character and tendencies. That mankind owe a great debt to this morality, and to its early teachers, I should be the last person to deny, but I do not scruple to say of it, that it is, in many important points, incomplete and one-sided, and that unless ideas and feelings, not sanctioned by it, had contributed to the formation of European life and character, human affairs would have been in a worse condition than they now are. Christian morality (so called) has all the characters of a reaction; it is, in great part, a protest against Paganism. Its ideal is negative rather than positive; passive rather than active; Innocence rather than Nobleness; Abstinence from Evil, rather than energetic Pursuit of Good: in its precepts (as has been well said) 'thou shalt not' predominates unduly over 'thou shalt.' In its horror of sensuality, it made an idol of asceticism, which has been gradually compromised away into one of legality. It holds out the hope of heaven and the threat of hell, as the appointed and appropriate motives to a virtuous life: in this falling far below the best of the ancients, and doing what lies in it to give to human morality an essentially selfish character, by disconnecting each man's feelings of duty from the interests of his fellow-creatures, except so far as a self-interested inducement is offered to him for consulting them. It is essentially a doctrine of passive obedience; it inculcates submission to all authorities found established; who indeed are not to be actively obeyed when they command what religion forbids, but who are not to be resisted, far less rebelled against, for any amount of wrong to ourselves. And while, in the morality of the best Pagan nations, duty to the State holds even a disproportionate place, infringing on the just liberty of the individual; in purely Christian ethics, that grand department of duty is scarcely noticed or acknowledged. It is in the Koran, not the New Testament, that we read the maxim—'A ruler who appoints any man to an office, when there is in his dominions another man better qualified for it, sins against God and against the State.' What little recognition the idea of obligation to the public obtains in modern morality, is derived from Greek and Roman sources, not from Christian; as, even in the morality of private life, whatever exists of magnanimity, highmindedness, personal dignity, even the sense of honour, is derived from the purely human, not the religious part of our education, and never could have grown out of a standard of ethics in which the only worth, professedly recognized, is that of obedience.

I am as far as any one from pretending that these defects are necessarily inherent in the Christian ethics, in every manner in which it can be conceived, or that the many requisites of a complete moral doctrine which it does not contain, do not admit of being reconciled with it. Far less would I insinuate this of the doctrines and precepts of Christ himself. I believe that the sayings of Christ are all, that I can see any evidence of their having been intended to be; that they are irreconcilable with nothing which a comprehensive morality requires; that everything which is excellent in ethics may be brought within them, with no greater violence to their language than has been done to it by all who have attempted to deduce from them any practical system of conduct whatever. But it is quite consistent with this, to believe that they contain, and were meant to contain, only a part of the truth; that many essential elements of the highest morality are among the things which are not provided for, nor intended to be provided for, in the recorded deliverances of the Founder of Christianity, and which have been entirely thrown aside in the system of ethics erected on the basis of those deliverances by the Christian Church. And this being so, I think it a great error to persist in attempting to find in the Christian doctrine that complete rule for our guidance, which its author intended it to sanction and enforce, but only partially to provide. I believe, too, that this narrow theory is becoming a grave practical evil, detracting greatly from the value of the moral training and instruction, which so many well-meaning persons are now at length exerting themselves to promote. I much fear that by attempting to form the mind and feelings on an exclusively religious type, and discarding those secular standards (as for want of a better name they may be called) which heretofore coexisted with and supplemented the Christian ethics, receiving some of its spirit, and infusing into it some of theirs, there will result, and is even now resulting, a low, abject, servile type of character, which, submit itself as it may to what it deems the Supreme Will, is incapable of rising to or sympathizing in the conception of Supreme Goodness. I believe that other ethics than any which can be evolved from exclusively Christian sources, must exist side by side with Christian ethics to produce the moral regeneration of mankind; and that the Christian system is no exception to the rule, that in an imperfect state of the human mind, the interests of truth require a diversity of opinions. It is not necessary that in ceasing to ignore the moral truths not contained in Christianity, men should ignore any of those which it does contain. Such prejudice, or oversight, when it occurs, is altogether an evil; but it is one from which we cannot hope to be always exempt, and must be regarded as the price paid for an inestimable good. The exclusive pretension made by a part of the truth to be the whole, must and ought to be protested against; and if a reactionary impulse should make the protestors unjust in their turn, this one-sidedness, like the other, may be lamented, but must be tolerated. If Christians would teach infidels to be just to Christianity, they should themselves be just to infidelity. It can do truth no service to blink the fact, known to all who have the most ordinary acquaintance with literary history, that a large portion of the noblest and most valuable moral teaching has been the work, not only of men who did not know, but of men who knew and rejected, the Christian faith.

I do not pretend that the most unlimited use of the freedom of enunciating all possible opinions would put an end to the evils of religious or philosophical sectarianism. Every truth which men of narrow capacity are in earnest about, is sure to be asserted, inculcated, and in many ways even acted on, as if no other truth existed in the world, or at all events none that could limit or qualify the first. I acknowledge that the tendency of all opinions to become sectarian is not cured by the freest discussion, but is often heightened and exacerbated thereby; the truth which ought to have been, but was not, seen, being rejected all the more violently because proclaimed by persons regarded as opponents. But it is not on the impassioned partisan, it is on the calmer and more disinterested bystander, that this collision of opinions works its salutary effect. Not the violent conflict between parts of the truth, but the quiet suppression of half of it, is the formidable evil; there is always hope when people are forced to listen to both sides; it is when they attend only to one that errors harden into prejudices, and truth itself ceases to have the effect of truth, by being exaggerated into falsehood. And since there are few mental attributes more rare than that judicial faculty which can sit in intelligent judgment between two sides of a question, of which only one is represented by an advocate before it, truth has no chance but in proportion as every side of it, every opinion which embodies any fraction of the truth, not only finds advocates, but is so advocated as to be listened to.

We have now recognized the necessity to the mental well-being of mankind (on which all their other well-being depends) of freedom of opinion, and freedom of the expression of opinion, on four distinct grounds; which we will now briefly recapitulate.

First, if any opinion is compelled to silence, that opinion may, for aught we can certainly know, be true. To deny this is to assume our own infallibility.

Secondly, though the silenced opinion be an error, it may, and very commonly does, contain a portion of truth; and since the general or prevailing opinion on any subject is rarely or never the whole truth, it is only by the collision of adverse opinions that the remainder of the truth has any chance of being supplied.

Thirdly, even if the received opinion be not only true, but the whole truth; unless it is suffered to be, and actually is, vigorously and earnestly contested, it will, by most of those who receive it, be held in the manner of a prejudice, with little comprehension or feeling of its rational grounds. And not only this, but, fourthly, the meaning of the doctrine itself will be in danger of being lost, or enfeebled, and deprived of its vital effect on the character and conduct: the dogma becoming a mere formal profession, inefficacious for good, but cumbering the ground, and preventing the growth of any real and heartfelt conviction, from reason or personal experience.

Before quitting the subject of freedom of opinion, it is fit to take some notice of those who say, that the free expression of all opinions should be permitted, on condition that the manner be temperate, and do not pass the bounds of fair discussion. Much might be said on the impossibility of fixing where these supposed bounds are to be placed; for if the test be offence to those whose opinion is attacked, I think experience testifies that this offence is given whenever the attack is telling and powerful, and that every opponent who pushes them hard, and whom they find it difficult to answer, appears to them, if he shows any strong feeling on the subject, an intemperate opponent. But this, though an important consideration in a practical point of view, merges in a more fundamental objection. Undoubtedly the manner of asserting an opinion, even though it be a true one, may be very objectionable, and may justly incur severe censure. But the principal offences of the kind are such as it is mostly impossible, unless by accidental self-betrayal, to bring home to conviction. The gravest of them is, to argue sophistically, to suppress facts or arguments, to misstate the elements of the case, or misrepresent the opposite opinion. But all this, even to the most aggravated degree, is so continually done in perfect good faith, by persons who are not considered, and in many other respects may not deserve to be considered, ignorant or incompetent, that it is rarely possible on adequate grounds conscientiously to stamp the misrepresentation as morally culpable; and still less could law presume to interfere with this kind of controversial misconduct. With regard to what is commonly meant by intemperate discussion, namely invective, sarcasm, personality, and the like, the denunciation of these weapons would deserve more sympathy if it were ever proposed to interdict them equally to both sides; but it is only desired to restrain the employment of them against the prevailing opinion: against the unprevailing they may not only be used without general disapproval, but will be likely to obtain for him who uses them the praise of honest zeal and righteous indignation. Yet whatever mischief arises from their use, is greatest when they are employed against the comparatively defenceless; and whatever unfair advantage can be derived by any opinion from this mode of asserting it, accrues almost exclusively to received opinions. The worst offence of this kind which can be committed by a polemic, is to stigmatize those who hold the contrary opinion as bad and immoral men. To calumny of this sort, those who hold any unpopular opinion are peculiarly exposed, because they are in general few and uninfluential, and nobody but themselves feels much interested in seeing justice done them; but this weapon is, from the nature of the case, denied to those who attack a prevailing opinion: they can neither use it with safety to themselves, nor, if they could, would it do anything but recoil on their own cause. In general, opinions contrary to those commonly received can only obtain a hearing by studied moderation of language, and the most cautious avoidance of unnecessary offence, from which they hardly ever deviate even in a slight degree without losing ground: while unmeasured vituperation employed on the side of the prevailing opinion, really does deter people from professing contrary opinions, and from listening to those who profess them. For the interest, therefore, of truth and justice, it is far more important to restrain this employment of vituperative language than the other; and, for example, if it were necessary to choose, there would be much more need to discourage offensive attacks on infidelity, than on religion. It is, however, obvious that law and authority have

no business with restraining either, while opinion ought, in every instance, to determine its verdict by the circumstances of the individual case; condemning every one, on whichever side of the argument he places himself, in whose mode of advocacy either want of candor, or malignity, bigotry, or intolerance of feeling manifest themselves; but not inferring these vices from the side which a person takes, though it be the contrary side of the question to our own: and giving merited honour to every one, whatever opinion he may hold, who has calmness to see and honesty to state what his opponents and their opinions really are, exaggerating nothing to their discredit, keeping nothing back which tells, or can be supposed to tell, in their favour. This is the real morality of public discussion: and if often violated, I am happy to think that there are many controversialists who to a great extent observe it, and a still greater number who conscientiously strive towards it.

CHAPTER III. OF INDIVIDUALITY, AS ONE OF THE ELEMENTS OF WELL-BEING

Such being the reasons which make it imperative that human beings should be free to form opinions, and to express their opinions without reserve; and such the baneful consequences to the intellectual, and through that to the moral nature of man, unless this liberty is either conceded, or asserted in spite of prohibition; let us next examine whether the same reasons do not require that men should be free to act upon their opinions—to carry these out in their lives, without hindrance, either physical or moral, from their fellow-men, so long as it is at their own risk and peril. This last proviso is of course indispensable. No one pretends that actions should be as free as opinions. On the contrary, even opinions lose their immunity, when the circumstances in which they are expressed are such as to constitute their expression a positive instigation to some mischievous act. An opinion that corn-dealers are starvers of the poor, or that private property is robbery, ought to be unmolested when simply circulated through the press, but may justly incur punishment when delivered orally to an excited mob assembled before the house of a corn-dealer, or when handed about among the same mob in the form of a placard. Acts, of whatever kind, which, without justifiable cause, do harm to others, may be, and in the more important cases absolutely require to be, controlled by the unfavorable sentiments, and, when needful, by the active interference of mankind. The liberty of the individual must be thus far limited; he must not make himself a nuisance to other people. But if he refrains from molesting others in what concerns them, and merely acts according to his own inclination and judgment in things which concern himself, the same reasons which show that opinion should be free, prove also that he should be allowed, without molestation, to carry his opinions into practice at his own cost. That mankind are not infallible; that their truths, for the most part, are only half-truths; that unity of opinion, unless resulting from the fullest and freest comparison of opposite opinions, is not desirable, and diversity not an evil, but a good, until mankind are much more capable than at present of recognizing all sides of the truth, are principles applicable to men's modes of action, not less than to their opinions. As it is useful that while mankind are imperfect there should be different opinions, so is it that there should be different experiments of living; that free scope should be given to varieties of character, short of injury to others; and that the worth of different modes of life should be proved practically, when any one thinks fit to try them. It is desirable, in short, that in things which do not primarily concern others, individuality should assert itself. Where, not the person's own character, but the traditions or customs of other people are the rule of conduct, there is wanting one of the principal ingredients of human happiness, and quite the chief ingredient of individual and social progress.

In maintaining this principle, the greatest difficulty to be encountered does not lie in the appreciation of means towards an acknowledged end, but in the indifference of persons in general to the end itself. If it were felt that the free development of individuality is one of the leading essentials of wellbeing; that it is not only a co-ordinate element with all that is designated by the terms civilization, instruction, education, culture, but is itself a necessary part and condition of all those things; there would

be no danger that liberty should be undervalued, and the adjustment of the boundaries between it and social control would present no extraordinary difficulty. But the evil is, that individual spontaneity is hardly recognized by the common modes of thinking, as having any intrinsic worth, or deserving any regard on its own account. The majority, being satisfied with the ways of mankind as they now are (for it is they who make them what they are), cannot comprehend why those ways should not be good enough for everybody; and what is more, spontaneity forms no part of the ideal of the majority of moral and social reformers, but is rather looked on with jealousy, as a troublesome and perhaps rebellious obstruction to the general acceptance of what these reformers, in their own judgment, think would be best for mankind. Few persons, out of Germany, even comprehend the meaning of the doctrine which Wilhelm Von Humboldt, so eminent both as a savant and as a politician, made the text of a treatise—that 'the end of man, or that which is prescribed by the eternal or immutable dictates of reason, and not suggested by vague and transient desires, is the highest and most harmonious development of his powers to a complete and consistent whole;' that, therefore, the objects 'towards which every human being must ceaselessly direct his efforts, and on which especially those who design to influence their fellow-men must ever keep their eyes, is the individuality of power and development;' that for this there are two requisites, 'freedom, and variety of situations;' and that from the union of these arise 'individual vigor and manifold diversity,' which combine themselves in 'originality.'

Little, however, as people are accustomed to a doctrine like that of Von Humboldt, and surprising as it may be to them to find so high a value attached to individuality, the question, one must nevertheless think, can only be one of degree. No one's idea of excellence in conduct is that people should do absolutely nothing but copy one another. No one would assert that people ought not to put into their mode of life, and into the conduct of their concerns, any impress whatever of their own judgment, or of their own individual character. On the other hand, it would be absurd to pretend that people ought to live as if nothing whatever had been known in the world before they came into it; as if experience has as yet done nothing towards showing that one mode of existence, or of conduct, is preferable to another. Nobody denies that people should be so taught and trained in youth, as to know and benefit by the ascertained results of human experience. But it is the privilege and proper condition of a human being, arrived at the maturity of his faculties, to use and interpret experience in his own way. It is for him to find out what part of recorded experience is properly applicable to his own circumstances and character. The traditions and customs of other people are, to a certain extent, evidence of what their experience has taught them; presumptive evidence, and as such, have a claim to his deference: but, in the first place, their experience may be too narrow; or they may not have interpreted it rightly. Secondly, their interpretation of experience may be correct, but unsuitable to him. Customs are made for customary circumstances, and customary characters; and his circumstances or his character may be uncustomary. Thirdly, though the customs be both good as customs, and suitable to him, yet to conform to custom, merely as custom, does not educate or develop in him any of the qualities which are the distinctive endowment of a human being. The human faculties of perception, judgment, discriminative feeling, mental activity, and even moral preference, are exercised only in making a choice. He who does anything because it is the custom, makes no choice. He gains no practice either in discerning or in desiring what is best. The mental and moral, like the muscular powers, are improved only by being used. The faculties are called into no exercise by doing a thing merely because others do it, no more than by believing a thing only because others believe it. If the grounds of an opinion are not conclusive to the person's own reason, his reason cannot be strengthened, but is likely to be weakened, by his adopting it: and if the inducements to an act are not such as are consentaneous to his own feelings and character (where affection, or the rights of others, are not concerned) it is so much done towards rendering his feelings and character inert and torpid, instead of active and energetic.

He who lets the world, or his own portion of it, choose his plan of life for him, has no need of any other faculty than the ape-like one of imitation. He who chooses his plan for himself, employs all his faculties. He must use observation to see, reasoning and judgment to foresee, activity to gather materials for decision, discrimination to decide, and when he has decided, firmness and self-control to hold to his deliberate decision. And these qualities he requires and exercises exactly in proportion as the part of his conduct which he determines according to his own judgment and feelings is a large one. It is possible that he might be guided in some good path, and kept out of harm's way, without any of these things. But what will be his comparative worth as a human being? It really is of importance, not only what men do, but also what manner of men they are that do it. Among the works of man, which human life is rightly employed in perfecting and beautifying, the first in importance surely is man himself. Supposing it were possible to get houses built, corn grown, battles fought, causes tried, and even churches erected and prayers said, by machinery—by automatons in human form—it would be a considerable loss to exchange for these automatons even the men and women who at present inhabit the more civilized parts of the world, and who assuredly are but starved specimens of what nature can and will produce. Human nature is not a machine to be built after a model, and set to do exactly the work prescribed for it, but a tree, which requires to grow and develop itself on all sides, according to the tendency of the inward forces which make it a living thing.

It will probably be conceded that it is desirable people should exercise their understandings, and that an intelligent following of custom, or even occasionally an intelligent deviation from custom, is better than a blind and simply mechanical adhesion to it. To a certain extent it is admitted, that our understanding should be our own: but there is not the same willingness to admit that our desires and impulses should be our own likewise; or that to possess impulses of our own, and of any strength, is anything but a peril and a snare. Yet desires and impulses are as much a part of a perfect human being, as beliefs and restraints: and strong impulses are only perilous when not properly balanced; when one set of aims and inclinations is developed into strength, while others, which ought to co-exist with them, remain weak and inactive. It is not because men's desires are strong that they act ill; it is because their consciences are weak. There is no natural connexion between strong impulses and a weak conscience. The natural connexion is the other way. To say that one person's desires and feelings are stronger and more various than those of another, is merely to say that he has more of the raw material of human nature, and is therefore capable, perhaps of more evil, but certainly of more good. Strong impulses are but another name for energy. Energy may be turned to bad uses; but more good may always be made of an energetic nature, than of an indolent and impassive one. Those who have most natural feeling, are always those whose cultivated feelings may be made the strongest. The same strong susceptibilities which make the personal impulses vivid and powerful, are also the source from whence are generated the most passionate love of virtue, and the sternest self-control. It is through the cultivation of these, that society both does its duty and protects its interests: not by rejecting the stuff of which heroes are made, because it knows not how to make them. A person whose desires and impulses are his own—are the expression of his own nature, as it has been developed and modified by his own culture—is said to have a character. One whose desires and impulses are not his own, has no character, no more than a steam-engine has a character. If, in addition to being his own, his impulses are strong, and are under the government of a strong will, he has an energetic character. Whoever thinks that individuality of desires and impulses should not be encouraged to unfold itself, must maintain that society has no need of strong natures—is not the better for containing many persons who have much character—and that a high general average of energy is not desirable.

In some early states of society, these forces might be, and were, too much ahead of the power which society then possessed of disciplining and controlling them. There has been a time when the element of spontaneity and individuality was in excess, and the social principle had a hard struggle with it. The difficulty then was, to induce men of strong bodies or minds to pay obedience to any rules which required them to control their impulses. To overcome this difficulty, law and discipline, like the Popes struggling against the Emperors, asserted a power over the whole man, claiming to control all his life in order to control his character—which society had not found any other sufficient means of binding. But society has now fairly got the better of individuality; and the danger which threatens human nature is not the excess, but the deficiency, of personal impulses and preferences. Things are vastly changed, since the passions of those who were strong by station or by personal endowment were in a state of habitual rebellion against laws and ordinances, and required to be rigorously chained up to enable the persons within their reach to enjoy any particle of security. In our times, from the highest class of society down to the lowest, every one lives as under the eye of a hostile and dreaded censorship. Not only in what concerns others, but in what concerns only themselves, the individual or the family do not ask themselves—what do I prefer? or, what would suit my character and disposition? or, what would allow the best and highest in me to have fair play, and enable it to grow and thrive? They ask themselves, what is suitable to my position? what is usually done by persons of my station and pecuniary circumstances? or (worse still) what is usually done by persons of a station and circumstances superior to mine? I do not mean that they choose what is customary, in preference to what suits their own inclination. It does not occur to them to have any inclination, except for what is customary. Thus the mind itself is bowed to the yoke: even in what people do for pleasure, conformity is the first thing thought of; they like in crowds; they exercise choice only among things commonly done: peculiarity of taste, eccentricity of conduct, are shunned equally with crimes: until by dint of not following their own nature, they have no nature to follow: their human capacities are withered and starved: they become incapable of any strong wishes or native pleasures, and are generally without either opinions or feelings of home growth, or properly their own. Now is this, or is it not, the desirable condition of human nature?

It is so, on the Calvinistic theory. According to that, the one great offence of man is self-will. All the good of which humanity is capable, is comprised in obedience. You have no choice; thus you must do, and no otherwise: 'whatever is not a duty, is a sin.'

Human nature being radically corrupt, there is no redemption for any one until human nature is killed within him. To one holding this theory of life, crushing out any of the human faculties, capacities, and susceptibilities, is no evil: man needs no capacity, but that of surrendering himself to the will of God: and if he uses any of his faculties for any other purpose but to do that supposed will more effectually, he is better without them. This is the theory of Calvinism; and it is held, in a mitigated form, by many who do not consider themselves Calvinists; the mitigation consisting in giving a less ascetic interpretation to the alleged will of God; asserting it to be his will that mankind should gratify some of their inclinations; of course not in the manner they themselves prefer, but in the way of obedience, that is, in a way prescribed to them by authority; and, therefore, by the necessary conditions of the case, the same for all.

In some such insidious form there is at present a strong tendency to this narrow theory of life, and to the pinched and hidebound type of human character which it patronizes. Many persons, no doubt, sincerely think that human beings thus cramped and dwarfed, are as their Maker designed them to be; just as many have thought that trees are a much finer thing when clipped into pollards, or cut out into figures of animals, than as nature made them. But if it be any part of religion to believe that man was made by a good Being, it is more consistent with that faith to believe, that this Being gave all human faculties that they might be cultivated and unfolded, not rooted out and consumed, and that he takes delight in every nearer approach made by his creatures to the ideal conception embodied in them, every increase in any of their capabilities of comprehension, of action, or of enjoyment. There is a different type of human excellence from the Calvinistic; a conception of humanity as having its nature bestowed on it for other purposes than merely to be abnegated. 'Pagan self-assertion' is one of the elements of human worth, as well as 'Christian self-denial.' There is a Greek ideal of self-development, which the Platonic and Christian ideal of self-government blends with, but does not supersede. It may be better to be a John Knox than an Alcibiades, but it is better to be a Pericles than either; nor would a Pericles, if we had one in these days, be without anything good which belonged to John Knox.

It is not by wearing down into uniformity all that is individual in themselves, but by cultivating it and calling it forth, within the limits imposed by the rights and interests of others, that human beings become a noble and beautiful object of contemplation; and as the works partake the character of those who do them, by the same process human life also becomes rich, diversified, and animating, furnishing more abundant aliment to high thoughts and elevating feelings, and strengthening the tie which binds every individual to the race, by making the race infinitely better worth belonging to. In proportion to the development of his individuality, each person becomes more valuable to himself, and is therefore capable of being more valuable to others. There is a greater fullness of life about his own existence, and when there is more life in the units there is more in the mass which is composed of them. As much compression as is necessary to prevent the stronger specimens of human nature from encroaching on the rights of others, cannot be dispensed with; but for this there is ample compensation even in the point of view of human development. The means of development which the individual loses by being prevented from gratifying his inclinations to the injury of others, are chiefly obtained at the expense of the development of other people. And even to himself there is a full equivalent in the better development of the social part of his nature, rendered possible by the restraint put upon the selfish part. To be held to rigid rules of justice for the sake of others, develops the feelings and capacities which have the good of others for their object. But to be restrained in things not affecting their good, by their mere displeasure, develops nothing valuable, except such force of character as may unfold itself in resisting the restraint. If acquiesced in, it dulls and blunts the whole nature. To give any fair play to the nature of each, it is essential that different persons should be allowed to lead different lives. In proportion as this latitude has been exercised in any age, has that age been noteworthy to posterity. Even despotism does not produce its worst effects, so long as individuality exists under it; and whatever crushes individuality is despotism, by whatever name it may be called, and whether it professes to be enforcing the will of God or the injunctions of men.

Having said that Individuality is the same thing with development, and that it is only the cultivation of individuality which produces, or can produce, well-developed human beings, I might here close the argument: for what more or better can be said of any condition of human affairs, than that it brings human beings themselves nearer to the best thing they can be? or what worse can be said of any obstruction to good, than that it prevents this? Doubtless, however, these considerations will not suffice to convince those who most need convincing; and it is necessary further to show, that these developed human beings are of some use to the undeveloped—to point out to those who do not desire liberty, and would not avail themselves of it, that they may be in some intelligible manner rewarded for allowing other people to make use of it without hindrance.

In the first place, then, I would suggest that they might possibly learn something from them. It will not be denied by anybody, that originality is a valuable element in human affairs. There is always need of persons not only to discover new truths, and point out when what were once truths are true no longer, but also to commence new practices, and set the example of more enlightened conduct, and better taste and sense in human life. This cannot well be gainsaid by anybody who does not believe that the world has already attained perfection in all its ways and practices. It is true that this benefit is not capable of being rendered by everybody alike: there are but few persons, in comparison with the whole of mankind, whose experiments, if adopted by others, would be likely to be any improvement on established practice. But these few are the salt of the earth; without them, human life would become a stagnant pool. Not only is it they who introduce good things which did not before exist; it is they who keep the life in those which already existed. If there were nothing new to be done, would human intellect cease to be necessary? Would it be a reason why those who do the old things should forget why they are done, and do them like cattle, not like human beings? There is only too great a tendency in the best beliefs and practices to degenerate into the mechanical; and unless there were a succession of persons whose ever-recurring

originality prevents the grounds of those beliefs and practices from becoming merely traditional, such dead matter would not resist the smallest shock from anything really alive, and there would be no reason why civilization should not die out, as in the Byzantine Empire. Persons of genius, it is true, are, and are always likely to be, a small minority; but in order to have them, it is necessary to preserve the soil in which they grow. Genius can only breathe freely in an atmosphere of freedom. Persons of genius are, ex vi termini, more individual than any other people— less capable, consequently, of fitting themselves, without hurtful compression, into any of the small number of molds which society provides in order to save its members the trouble of forming their own character. If from timidity they consent to be forced into one of these molds, and to let all that part of themselves which cannot expand under the pressure remain unexpanded, society will be little the better for their genius. If they are of a strong character, and break their fetters, they become a mark for the society which has not succeeded in reducing them to commonplace, to point at with solemn warning as 'wild,' 'erratic,' and the like; much as if one should complain of the Niagara river for not flowing smoothly between its banks like a Dutch canal.

I insist thus emphatically on the importance of genius, and the necessity of allowing it to unfold itself freely both in thought and in practice, being well aware that no one will deny the position in theory, but knowing also that almost every one, in reality, is totally indifferent to it. People think genius a fine thing if it enables a man to write an exciting poem, or paint a picture. But in its true sense, that of originality in thought and action, though no one says that it is not a thing to be admired, nearly all, at heart, think that they can do very well without it. Unhappily this is too natural to be wondered at. Originality is the one thing which unoriginal minds cannot feel the use of. They cannot see what it is to do for them: how should they? If they could see what it would do for them, it would not be originality. The first service which originality has to render them, is that of opening their eyes: which being once fully done, they would have a chance of being themselves original. Meanwhile, recollecting that nothing was ever yet done which some one was not the first to do, and that all good things which exist are the fruits of originality, let them be modest enough to believe that there is something still left for it to accomplish, and assure themselves that they are more in need of originality, the less they are conscious of the want.

In sober truth, whatever homage may be professed, or even paid, to real or supposed mental superiority, the general tendency of things throughout the world is to render mediocrity the ascendant power among mankind. In ancient history, in the middle ages, and in a diminishing degree through the long transition from feudality to the present time, the individual was a power in himself; and if he had either great talents or a high social position, he was a considerable power. At present individuals are lost in the crowd. In politics it is almost a triviality to say that public opinion now rules the world. The only power deserving the name is that of masses, and of governments while they make themselves the organ of the tendencies and instincts of masses. This is as true in the moral and social relations of private life as in public transactions. Those whose opinions go by the name of public opinion, are not always the same sort of public: in America they are the whole white population; in England, chiefly the middle class. But they are always a mass, that is to say, collective mediocrity. And what is a still greater novelty, the mass do not now take their opinions from dignitaries in Church or State, from ostensible leaders, or from books. Their thinking is done for them by men much like themselves, addressing them or speaking in their name, on the spur of the moment, through the newspapers. I am not complaining of all this. I do not assert that anything better is compatible, as a general rule, with the present low state of the human mind. But that does not hinder the government of mediocrity from being mediocre government. No government by a democracy or a numerous aristocracy, either in its political acts or in the opinions, qualities, and tone of mind which it fosters, ever did or could rise above mediocrity, except in so far as the sovereign. Many have let themselves be guided (which in their best times they always have done) by the counsels and influence of a more highly gifted and instructed One or Few. The initiation of all wise or noble things, comes and must come from individuals; generally at first from some one indi-vidual. The honour and glory of the average man is that he is capable of following that initiative; that he can respond internally to wise and noble things, and be led to them with his eyes open. I am not countenancing the sort of 'hero-worship' which applauds the strong man of genius for forcibly seizing on the government of the world and making it do his bidding in spite of itself. All he can claim is, freedom to point out the way. The power of compelling others into it, is not only inconsistent with the freedom and development of all the rest, but corrupting to the strong man himself. It does seem, however, that when the opinions of masses of merely average men are everywhere become or becoming the dominant power, the counterpoise and corrective to that tendency would be, the more and more pronounced individuality of those who stand on the higher eminences of thought. It is in these circumstances most especially, that exceptional individuals, instead of being deterred, should be encouraged in acting differently from the mass. In other times there was no advantage in their doing so, unless they acted not only differently, but better. In this age, the mere example of nonconformity, the mere refusal to bend the knee to custom, is itself a service. Precisely because the tyranny of opinion is such as to make eccentricity a reproach, it is desirable, in order to break through that tyranny, that people should be eccentric. Eccentricity has always abounded when and where strength of character has abounded; and the amount of eccentricity in a society has generally been proportional to the amount of genius, mental vigor, and moral courage which it contained. That so few now dare to be eccentric, marks the chief danger of the time.

I have said that it is important to give the freest scope possible to uncustomary things, in order that it may in time appear which of these are fit to be converted into customs. But independence of action, and disregard of custom, are not solely deserving of encouragement for the chance they afford that better modes of action, and customs more worthy of general adoption, may be struck out; nor is it only persons of decided mental superiority who have a just claim to carry on their lives in their own way. There is no reason that all human existence should be constructed on some one or some small number of patterns. If a person possesses any tolerable amount of common sense and experience, his own mode of laying out his existence is the best, not because it is the best in itself, but because it is his own mode. Human beings are not like sheep; and even sheep are not undistinguishably alike. A man cannot get a coat or a pair of boots to fit him, unless they are either made to his measure, or he has a whole warehouseful to choose from: and is it easier to fit him with a life than with a coat, or are human beings more like one another in their whole physical and spiritual conformation than in the shape of their feet? If it were only that people have diversities of taste, that is reason enough for not attempting to shape them all after one model. But different persons also require different conditions for their spiritual development; and can no more exist healthily in the same moral, than all the variety of plants can in the same physical, atmosphere and climate. The same things which are helps to one person towards the cultivation of his higher nature, are hindrances to another. The same mode of life is a healthy excitement to one, keeping all his faculties of action and enjoyment in their best order, while to another it is a distracting burden, which suspends or crushes all internal life. Such are the differences among human beings in their sources of pleasure, their susceptibilities of pain, and the operation on them of different physical and moral agencies, that unless there is a corresponding diversity in their modes of life, they neither obtain their fair share of happiness, nor grow up to the mental, moral, and aesthetic stature of which their nature is capable. Why then should tolerance, as far as the public sentiment is concerned, extend only to tastes and modes of life which extort acquiescence by the multitude of their adherents? Nowhere (except in some monastic institutions) is diversity of taste entirely unrecognized; a person may, without blame, either like or dislike rowing, or smoking, or music, or athletic exercises, or chess, or cards, or study, because both those who like each of these things, and those who dislike them, are too numerous to be put down. But the man, and still more the woman, who can be accused either of doing 'what nobody does,' or of not doing 'what everybody does,' is the subject of as much depreciatory remark as if he or she had committed some

grave moral delinquency. Persons require to possess a title, or some other badge of rank, or of the consideration of people of rank, to be able to indulge somewhat in the luxury of doing as they like without detriment to their estimation. To indulge somewhat, I repeat: for whoever allow themselves much of that indulgence, incur the risk of something worse than disparaging speeches—they are in peril of a commission de lunatico, and of having their property taken from them and given to their relations.

There is one characteristic of the present direction of public opinion, peculiarly calculated to make it intolerant of any marked demonstration of individuality. The general average of mankind are not only moderate in intellect, but also moderate in inclinations: they have no tastes or wishes strong enough to incline them to do anything unusual, and they consequently do not understand those who have, and class all such with the wild and intemperate whom they are accustomed to look down upon. Now, in addition to this fact which is general, we have only to suppose that a strong movement has set in towards the improvement of morals, and it is evident what we have to expect. In these days such a movement has set in; much has actually been effected in the way of increased regularity of conduct, and discouragement of excesses; and there is a philanthropic spirit abroad, for the exercise of which there is no more inviting field than the moral and prudential improvement of our fellow-creatures. These tendencies of the times cause the public to be more disposed than at most former periods to prescribe general rules of conduct, and endeavor to make every one conform to the approved standard. And that standard, express or tacit, is to desire nothing strongly. Its ideal of character is to be without any marked character; to maim by compression, like a Chinese lady's foot, every part of human nature which stands out prominently, and tends to make the person markedly dissimilar in outline to commonplace humanity.

As is usually the case with ideals which exclude one-half of what is desirable, the present standard of approbation produces only an inferior imitation of the other half. Instead of great energies guided by vigorous reason, and strong feelings strongly controlled by a conscientious will, its result is weak feelings and weak energies, which therefore can be kept in outward conformity to rule without any strength either of will or of reason. Already energetic characters on any large scale are becoming merely traditional. There is now scarcely any outlet for energy in this country except business. The energy expended in this may still be regarded as considerable. What little is left from that employment, is expended on some hobby; which may be a useful, even a philanthropic hobby, but is always some one thing, and generally a thing of small dimensions. The greatness of England is now all collective: individually small, we only appear capable of anything great by our habit of combining; and with this our moral and religious philanthropists are perfectly contented. But it was men of another stamp than this that made England what it has been; and men of another stamp will be needed to prevent its decline.

The despotism of custom is everywhere the standing hindrance to human advancement, being in unceasing antagonism to that disposition to aim at something better than customary, which is called, according to circumstances, the spirit of liberty, or that of progress or improvement. The spirit of improvement is not always a spirit of liberty, for it may aim at forcing improvements on an unwilling people; and the spirit of liberty, in so far as it resists such attempts, may ally itself locally and temporarily with the opponents of improvement; but the only unfailing and permanent source of improvement is liberty, since by it there are as many possible independent centers of improvement as there are individuals. The progressive principle, however, in either shape, whether as the love of liberty or of improvement, is antagonistic to the sway of Custom, involving at least emancipation from that yoke; and the contest between the two constitutes the chief interest of the history of mankind. The greater part of the world has, properly speaking, no history, because the despotism of Custom is complete. This is the case over the whole East. Custom is there, in all things, the final appeal; justice and right mean conformity to custom; the argument of custom no one, unless some tyrant intoxicated with power, thinks of resisting. And we see the result. Those nations must once have had originality; they did not start out of the ground populous, lettered, and versed in many of the arts of life; they made themselves all this, and were then the greatest and most powerful nations of the world. What are they now? The subjects or dependents of tribes whose forefathers wandered in the forests when theirs had magnificent palaces and gorgeous temples, but over whom custom exercised only a divided rule with liberty and progress. A people, it appears, may be progressive for a certain length of time, and then stop: when does it stop? When it ceases to possess individuality. If a similar change should befall the nations of Europe, it will not be in exactly the same shape: the despotism of custom with which these nations are threatened is not precisely stationariness. It proscribes singularity, but it does not preclude change, provided all change together. We have discarded the fixed costumes of our forefathers; every one must still dress like other people, but the fashion may change once or twice a year. We thus take care that when there is change it shall be for change's sake, and not from any idea of beauty or convenience; for the same idea of beauty or convenience would not strike all the world at the same moment, and be simultaneously thrown aside by all at another moment. But we are progressive as well as changeable: we continually make new inventions in mechanical things, and keep them until they are again superseded by better; we are eager for improvement in politics, in education, even in morals, though in this last our idea of improvement chiefly consists in persuading or forcing other people to be as good as ourselves. It is not progress that we object to; on the contrary, we flatter ourselves that we are the most progressive people who ever lived. It is individuality that we war against: we should think we had done wonders if we had made ourselves all alike; forgetting that the unlikeness of one person to another is generally the first thing which draws the attention of either to the imperfection of his own type, and the superiority of another, or the possibility, by combining the advantages of both, of producing something better than either. We have a warning example in China—a nation of much talent, and, in some respects, even wisdom, owing to the rare good fortune of having been provided at an early period with a particularly good set of customs, the work, in some measure, of men to whom even the most enlightened European must accord, under certain limitations, the title of sages and philosophers.

They are remarkable, too, in the excellence of their apparatus for impressing, as far as possible, the best wisdom they possess upon every mind in the community, and securing that those who have appropriated most of it shall occupy the posts of honour and power. Surely the people who did this have discovered the secret of human progressiveness, and must have kept themselves steadily at the head of the movement of the world. On the contrary, they have become stationary—have remained so for thousands of years; and if they are ever to be farther improved, it must be by foreigners. They have succeeded beyond all hope in what English philanthropists are so industriously working at—in making a people all alike, all governing their thoughts and conduct by the same maxims and rules; and these are the fruits. The modern regime of public opinion is, in an unorganized form, what the Chinese educational and political systems are in an organized; and unless individuality shall be able successfully to assert itself against this yoke, Europe, notwithstanding its noble antecedents and its professed Christianity, will tend to become another China.

What is it that has hitherto preserved Europe from this lot? What has made the European family of nations an improving, instead of a stationary portion of mankind? Not any superior excellence in them, which, when it exists, exists as the effect, not as the cause; but their remarkable diversity of character and culture. Individuals, classes, nations, have been extremely unlike one another: they have struck out a great variety of paths, each leading to something valuable; and although at every period those who travelled in different paths have been intolerant of one another, and each would have thought it an excellent thing if all the rest could have been compelled to travel his road, their attempts to thwart each other's development have rarely had any permanent success, and each has in time endured to receive the good which the others have offered. Europe is, in my judgment, wholly indebted to this plurality of paths for its progressive and many-sided development. But it already begins to possess this benefit in a considerably less degree. It is decidedly advancing towards the Chinese ideal of making all people alike. M. de Tocqueville, in his last important work, remarks how much more the Frenchmen of the present day resemble one another, than did those even of the last generation. The same remark might be made of Englishmen in a far greater degree. In a passage already quoted from Wilhelm von Humboldt, he points out two things as necessary conditions of human development, because necessary to render people unlike one another; namely, freedom, and variety of situations. The second of these two conditions is in this country every day diminishing. The circumstances which surround different classes and individuals, and shape their characters, are daily becoming more assimilated. Formerly, different ranks, different neighborhoods, different trades and professions, lived in what might be called different worlds; at present, to a great degree in the same. Comparatively speaking, they now read the same things, listen to the same things, see the same things, go to the same places, have their hopes and fears directed to the same objects, have the same rights and liberties, and the same means of asserting them. Great as are the differences of position which remain, they are nothing to those which have ceased. And the assimilation is still proceeding. All the political changes of the age promote it, since they all tend to raise the low and to lower the high. Every extension of education promotes it, because education brings people under common influences, and gives them access to the general stock of facts and sentiments. Improvements in the means of communication promote it, by bringing the inhabitants of distant places into personal contact, and keeping up a rapid flow of changes of residence between one place and another. The increase of commerce and manufactures promotes it, by diffusing more widely the advantages of easy circumstances, and opening all objects of ambition, even the highest, to general competition, whereby the desire of rising becomes no longer the character of a particular class, but of all classes. A more powerful agency than even all these, in bringing about a general similarity among mankind, is the complete establishment, in this and other free countries, of the ascendancy of public opinion in the State. As the various social eminences which enabled persons entrenched on them to disregard the opinion of the multitude, gradually become levelled; as the very idea of resisting the will of the public, when it is positively known that they have a will, disappears more and more from the minds of practical politicians; there ceases to be any social support for nonconformity—any substantive power in society, which, itself opposed to the ascendancy of numbers, is interested in taking under its protection opinions and tendencies at variance with those of the public.

The combination of all these causes forms so great a mass of influences hostile to Individuality, that it is not easy to see how it can stand its ground. It will do so with increasing difficulty, unless the intelligent part of the public can be made to feel its value—to see that it is good there should be differences, even though not for the better, even though, as it may appear to them, some should be for the worse. If the claims of Individuality are ever to be asserted, the time is now, while much is still wanting to complete the enforced assimilation. It is only in the earlier stages that any stand can be successfully made against the encroachment. The demand that all other people shall resemble ourselves, grows by what it feeds on. If resistance waits till life is reduced nearly to one uniform type, all deviations from that type will come to be considered impious, immoral, even monstrous and contrary to nature. Mankind speedily become unable to conceive diversity, when they have been for some time unaccustomed to see it.

CHAPTER IV. OF THE LIMITS TO THE AUTHORITY OF SOCIETY OVER THE INDIVIDUAL

What, then, is the rightful limit to the sovereignty of the individual over himself? Where does the authority of society begin? How much of human life should be assigned to individuality, and how much to society?

Each will receive its proper share, if each has that which more particularly concerns it. To individuality should belong the part of life in which it is chiefly the individual that is interested; to society, the part which chiefly interests society.

Though society is not founded on a contract, and though no good purpose is answered by inventing a contract in order to deduce social obligations from it, every one who receives the protection of society owes a return for the benefit, and the fact of living in society renders it indispensable that each should be bound to observe a certain line of conduct towards the rest. This conduct consists first, in not injuring the interests of one another; or rather certain interests, which, either by express legal provision or by tacit understanding, ought to be considered as rights; and secondly, in each person's bearing his share (to be fixed on some equitable principle) of the labors and sacrifices incurred for defending the society or its members from injury and molestation. These conditions society is justified in enforcing at all costs to those who endeavor to withhold fulfillment. Nor is this all that society may do. The acts of an individual may be hurtful to others, or wanting in due consideration for their welfare, without going the length of violating any of their constituted rights. The offender may then be justly punished by opinion, though not by law. As soon as any part of a person's conduct affects prejudicially the interests of others, society has jurisdiction over it, and the question whether the general welfare will or will not be promoted by interfering with it, becomes open to discussion. But there is no room for entertaining any such question when a person's conduct affects the interests of no persons besides himself, or needs not affect them unless they like (all the persons concerned being of full age, and the ordinary amount of understanding). In all such cases there should be perfect freedom, legal and social, to do the action and stand the consequences. . . .

The distinction here pointed out between the part of a person's life which concerns only himself, and that which concerns others, many persons will refuse to admit. How (it may be asked) can any part of the conduct of a member of society be a matter of indifference to the other members? No person is an entirely isolated being; it is impossible for a person to do anything seriously or permanently hurtful to himself, without mischief reaching at least to his near connexions, and often far beyond them. If he injures his property, he does harm to those who directly or indirectly derived support from it, and usually diminishes, by a greater or less amount, the general resources of the community. If he deteriorates his bodily or mental faculties, he not only brings evil upon all who depended on him for any portion of their happiness, but disqualifies himself for rendering the services which he owes to his fellow creatures generally; perhaps becomes a burden on their affection or benevolence; and if such conduct were very frequent, hardly any offence that is committed would detract more from the general sum of good. Finally, if by his vices or follies a person does no direct harm to others, he is nevertheless (it may be said) injurious by his example; and ought to be compelled to control himself, for the sake of those whom the sight or knowledge of his conduct might corrupt or mislead.

And even (it will be added) if the consequences of misconduct could be confined to the vicious or thoughtless individual, ought society to abandon to their own guidance those who are manifestly unfit for it? If protection against themselves is confessedly due to children and persons under age, is not society equally bound to afford it to persons of mature years who are equally incapable of self-government? If gambling, or drunkenness, or incontinence, or idleness, or uncleanliness, are as injurious to happiness, and as great a hindrance to improvement, as many or most of the acts prohibited by law, why (it may be asked) should not law, so far as is consistent with practicability and social convenience, endeavor to repress these also? And as a supplement to the unavoidable imperfections of law, ought not opinion at least to organize a powerful police against these vices, and visit rigidly with social penalties those who are known to practise them? There is no question here (it may be said) about restricting individuality, or impeding the trial of new and original experiments in living. The only things it is sought to prevent are things which have been tried and condemned from the beginning of the world until now; things which experience has shown not to be useful or suitable to any person's individuality. There must be some length of time and amount of experience, after which a moral or prudential truth may be regarded as established: and it is merely desired to prevent generation after generation from falling over the same precipice which has been fatal to their predecessors.

I fully admit that the mischief which a person does to himself may seriously affect, both through their sympathies and their interests, those nearly connected with him, and in a minor degree, society at large. When, by conduct of this sort, a person is led to violate a distinct and assignable obligation to any other person or persons, the case is taken out of the self-regarding class, and becomes amenable to moral disapprobation in the proper sense of the term. If, for example, a man, through intemperance or extravagance, becomes unable to pay his debts, or, having undertaken the moral responsibility of a family, becomes from the same cause incapable of supporting or educating them, he is deservedly reprobated, and might be justly punished; but it is for the breach of duty to his family or creditors, not for the extravagance. If the resources which ought to have been devoted to them, had been diverted from them for the most prudent investment, the moral culpability would have been the same. George Barnwell murdered his uncle to get money for his mistress, but if he had done it to set himself up in business, he would equally have been hanged. Again, in the frequent case of a man who causes grief to his family by addiction to bad habits, he deserves reproach for his unkindness or ingratitude; but so he may be cultivating habits not in themselves vicious, if they are painful to those with whom he passes his life, or who from personal ties are dependent on him for their comfort. Whoever fails in the consideration generally due to the interests and feelings of others, not being compelled by some more imperative duty, or justified by allowable self-preference, is a subject of moral disapprobation for that failure, but not for the cause of it, nor for the errors, merely personal to himself, which may have remotely led to it. In like manner, when a person disables himself, by conduct purely self-regarding, from the performance of some definite duty incumbent on him to the public, he is guilty of a social offence. No person ought to be punished simply for being drunk; but a soldier or a policeman should be punished for being drunk on duty. Whenever, in short, there is a definite damage, or a definite risk of damage, either to an individual or to the public, the case is taken out of the province of liberty, and placed in that of morality or law.

But with regard to the merely contingent, or, as it may be called, constructive injury which a person causes to society, by conduct which neither violates any specific duty to the public, nor occasions perceptible hurt to any assignable individual except himself; the inconvenience is one which society can afford to bear, for the sake of the greater good of human freedom. If grown persons are to be punished for not taking proper care of themselves, I would rather it were for their own sake, than under pretence of preventing them from impairing their capacity of rendering to society benefits which society does not pretend it has a right to exact. But I cannot consent to argue the point as if society had no means of bringing its weaker members up to its ordinary standard of rational conduct, except waiting till they do something irrational, and then punishing them, legally or morally, for it. Society has had absolute power over them during all the early portion of their existence: it has had the whole period of childhood and nonage in which to try whether it could make them capable of rational conduct in life. The existing generation is master both of the training and the entire circumstances of the generation to come; it cannot indeed make them perfectly wise and good, because it is itself so lamentably deficient in goodness and wisdom; and its best efforts are not always, in individual cases, its most successful ones; but it is perfectly well able to make the rising generation, as a whole, as good as, and a little better than, itself. If society lets any considerable number of its members grow up mere children, incapable of being acted on by rational consideration of distant motives, society has itself to blame for the consequences. Armed not only with all the powers of education, but with the ascendancy which the authority of a received opinion always exercises over the minds who are least fitted to judge for themselves; and aided by the natural penalties which cannot be prevented from falling on those who incur the distaste or the contempt of those who know them; let not society pretend that it needs, besides all this, the power to issue commands and enforce obedience in the personal concerns of individuals, in which, on all principles of justice and policy, the decision ought to rest with those who are to abide the consequences. Nor is there anything which tends more to discredit and frustrate the better means of influencing conduct, than a resort to the worse. If there be among those whom it is attempted to coerce into prudence or temperance, any of the material of which vigorous and independent characters are made, they will infallibly rebel against the yoke. No such person will ever feel that others have a right to control him in his concerns, such as they have to prevent him from injuring them in theirs; and it easily comes to be considered a mark of spirit and courage to fly in the face of such usurped authority, and do with ostentation the exact opposite of what it enjoins; as in the fashion of grossness which succeeded, in the time of Charles II, to the fanatical moral intolerance of the Puritans. With respect to what is said of the necessity of protecting society from the bad example set to others by the vicious or the self-indulgent; it is true that bad example may have a pernicious effect, especially the example of doing wrong to others with impunity to the wrong-doer. But we are now speaking of conduct which, while it does no wrong to others, is supposed to do great harm to the agent himself: and I do not see how those who believe this, can think otherwise than that the example, on the whole, must be more salutary than hurtful, since, if it displays the misconduct, it displays also the painful or degrading consequences which, if the conduct is justly censured, must be supposed to be in all or most cases attendant on it.

But the strongest of all the arguments against the interference of the public with purely personal conduct, is that when it does interfere, the odds are that it interferes wrongly, and in the wrong place. On questions of social morality, of duty to others, the opinion of the public, that is, of an overruling majority, though often wrong, is likely to be still oftener right; because on such questions they are only required to judge of their own interests; of the manner in which some mode of conduct, if allowed to be practiced, would affect themselves. But the opinion of a similar majority, imposed as a law on the minority, on questions of self-regarding conduct, is quite as likely to be wrong as right; for in these cases public opinion means, at the best, some people's opinion of what is good or bad for other people; while very often it does not even mean that; the public, with the most perfect indifference, passing over the pleasure or convenience of those whose conduct they censure, and considering only their own preference. There are many who consider as an injury to themselves any conduct which they have a distaste for, and resent it as an outrage to their feelings; as a religious bigot, when charged with disregarding the religious feelings of others, has been known to retort that they disregard his feelings, by persisting in their abominable worship or creed. But there is no parity between the feeling of a person for his own opinion, and the feeling of another who is offended at his holding it; no more than between the desire of a thief to take a purse, and the desire of the right owner to keep it. And a person's taste is as much his own peculiar concern as his opinion or his purse. It is easy for any one to imagine an ideal public, which leaves the freedom and choice of individuals in all uncertain matters undisturbed, and only requires them to abstain from modes of conduct which universal experience has condemned. But where has there been seen a public which set any such limit to its censorship? or when does the public trouble itself about universal experience? In its interferences with personal conduct it is seldom thinking of anything but the enormity of acting or feeling differently from itself; and this standard of judgment, thinly disguised, is held up to mankind as the dictate of religion and philosophy, by nine-tenths of all moralists and speculative writers. These teach that things are right because they are right; because we feel them to be so. They tell us to search in our own minds and hearts for laws of conduct binding on ourselves and on all others. What can the poor public do but apply these instructions, and make their own personal feelings of good and evil, if they are tolerably unanimous in them, obligatory on all the world?

The evil here pointed out is not one which exists only in theory; and it may perhaps be expected that I should specify the instances in which the public of this age and country improperly invests its own preferences with the character of moral laws. I am not writing an essay on the aberrations of existing moral feeling. That is too weighty a subject to be discussed parenthetically, and by way of illustration. Yet examples are necessary, to show that the principle I maintain is of serious and practical moment, and that I am not endeavoring to erect a barrier against imaginary evils. And it is not difficult to show, by abundant instances, that to extend the bounds of what may be called moral police, until it encroaches on the most unquestionably legitimate liberty of the individual, is one of the most universal of all human propensities.

CHAPTER V. APPLICATIONS

The principles asserted in these pages must be more generally admitted as the basis for discussion of details, before a consistent application of them to all the various departments of government and morals can be attempted with any prospect of advantage. The few observations I propose to make on questions of detail, are designed to illustrate the principles, rather than to follow them out to their consequences. I offer, not so much applications, as specimens of application; which may serve to bring into greater clearness the meaning and limits of the two maxims which together form the entire doctrine of this Essay, and to assist the judgment in holding the balance between them, in the cases where it appears doubtful which of them is applicable to the case.

The maxims are, first, that the individual is not accountable to society for his actions, in so far as these concern the interests of no person but himself. Advice, instruction, persuasion, and avoidance by other people if thought necessary by them for their own good, are the only measures by which society can justifiably express its dislike or disapprobation of his conduct. Secondly, that for such actions as are prejudicial to the interests of others, the individual is accountable, and may be subjected either to social or to legal punishment, if society is of opinion that the one or the other is requisite for its protection.

In the first place, it must by no means be supposed, because damage, or probability of damage, to the interests of others, can alone justify the interference of society, that therefore it always does justify such interference. In many cases, an individual, in pursuing a legitimate object, necessarily and therefore legitimately causes pain or loss to others, or intercepts a good which they had a reasonable hope of obtaining. Such oppositions of interest between individuals often arise from bad social institutions, but are unavoidable while those institutions last; and some would be unavoidable under any institutions. Whoever succeeds in an overcrowded profession, or in a competitive examination; whoever is preferred to another in any contest for an object which both desire, reaps benefit from the loss of others, from their wasted exertion and their disappointment. But it is, by common admission, better for the general interest of mankind, that persons should pursue their objects undeterred by this sort of consequences. In other words, society admits no right, either legal or moral, in the disappointed competitors, to immunity from this kind of suffering; and feels called on to interfere, only when means of success have been employed which it is contrary to the general interest to permit—namely, fraud or treachery, and force.

Again, trade is a social act. Whoever undertakes to sell any description of goods to the public, does what affects the interest of other persons, and of society in general; and thus his conduct, in principle, comes within the jurisdiction of society: accordingly, it was once held to be the duty of governments, in all cases which were considered of importance, to fix prices, and regulate the processes of manufacture. But it is now recognized, though not till after a long struggle, that both the cheapness and the good quality of commodities are most effectually provided for by leaving the producers and sellers perfectly free, under the sole check of equal freedom to the buyers for supplying themselves elsewhere. This is the so-called doctrine of Free Trade, which rests on grounds different from, though equally solid with, the principle of individual liberty asserted in this Essay. Restrictions on trade, or on production for purposes of trade, are indeed restraints; and all restraint, qua restraint, is an evil: but the restraints in question affect only that part of conduct which society is competent to restrain, and are wrong solely because they do not really produce the results which it is desired to produce by them. As the principle of individual liberty is not involved in the doctrine of Free Trade, so neither is it in most of the questions which arise respecting the limits of that doctrine; as for example, what amount of public control is admissible for the prevention of fraud by adulteration; how far sanitary precautions, or arrangements to protect workpeople employed in dangerous occupations, should be enforced on employers. Such questions involve considerations of liberty, only in so far as leaving people to themselves is always better, caeteris paribus, than controlling them: but that they may be legitimately controlled for these ends, is in principle undeniable. On the other hand, there are questions relating to interference with trade, which are essentially questions of liberty; such as the Maine Law, already touched upon; the prohibition of the importation of opium into China; the restriction of the sale of poisons; all cases, in short, where the object of the interference is to make it impossible or difficult to obtain a particular commodity. These interferences are objectionable, not as infringements on the liberty of the producer or seller, but on that of the buyer.

One of these examples, that of the sale of poisons, opens a new question; the proper limits of what may be called the functions of police, how far liberty may legitimately be invaded for the prevention of crime, or of accident. It is one of the undisputed functions of government to take precautions against crime before it has been committed, as well as to detect and punish it afterwards. The preventive function of government, however, is far more liable to be abused, to the prejudice of liberty, than the punitory function; for there is hardly any part of the legitimate freedom of action of a human being which would not admit of being represented, and fairly too, as increasing the facilities for some form or other of delinquency. Nevertheless, if a public authority, or even a private person, sees any one evidently preparing to commit a crime, they are not bound to look on inactive until the crime is committed, but may interfere to prevent it. If poisons were never bought or used for any purpose except the commission of murder, it would be right to prohibit their manufacture and sale. They may, however, be wanted not only for innocent but for useful purposes, and restrictions cannot be imposed in the one case without operating in the other. Again, it is a proper office of public authority to guard against accidents. If either a public officer or any one else saw a person attempting to cross a bridge which had been ascertained to be unsafe, and there were no time to warn him of his danger, they might seize him and turn him back, without any real infringement of his liberty; for liberty consists in doing what one desires, and he does not desire to fall into the river. Nevertheless, when there is not a certainty, but only a danger of mischief, no one but the person himself can judge of the sufficiency of the motive which may prompt him to incur the risk: in this case, therefore (unless he is a child, or delirious, or in some state of excitement or absorption incompatible with the full use of the reflecting faculty), he ought, I conceive, to be only warned of the danger; not forcibly prevented from exposing himself to it. Similar considerations, applied to such a question as the sale of poisons, may enable us to decide which among the possible modes of regulation are or are not contrary to principle. Such a precaution, for example, as that of labelling the drug with some word expressive of its dangerous character, may be enforced without violation of liberty: the buyer cannot wish not to know that the thing he possesses has poisonous qualities. But to require in all cases the certificate of a medical practitioner, would make it sometimes impossible, always expensive, to obtain the article for legitimate uses. The only mode apparent to me, in which difficulties may be thrown in the way of crime committed through this means, without any infringement, worth taking into account, upon the liberty of those who desire the poisonous substance for other purposes, consists in providing what, in the apt language of Bentham, is called 'preappointed evidence.' This provision is familiar to every one in the case of contracts. It is usual and right that the law, when a contract is entered into, should require as the condition of its enforcing performance, that certain formalities should be observed, such as signatures, attestation of witnesses, and the like, in order that in case of subsequent dispute, there may be evidence to prove that the contract was really entered into, and that there was nothing in the circumstances to render it legally invalid: the effect being, to throw great obstacles in the way of fictitious contracts, or contracts made in circumstances which, if known, would destroy their validity. Precautions of a similar nature might be enforced in the sale of articles adapted to be instruments of crime. The seller, for example, might be required to enter in a register the exact time of the transaction, the name and address of the buyer, the precise quality and quantity sold; to ask the purpose for which it was wanted, and record the answer he received. When there was no medical prescription, the presence of some third person might be required, to bring home the fact to the purchaser, in case there should afterwards be reason to believe that the article had been applied to criminal purposes. Such regulations would in general be no material impediment to obtaining the article, but a very considerable one to making an improper use of it without detection.

The right inherent in society, to ward off crimes against itself by antecedent precautions, suggests the obvious limitations to the maxim, that purely self-regarding misconduct cannot properly be meddled with in the way of prevention or punishment. Drunkenness, for example, in ordinary cases, is not a fit subject for legislative interference; but I should deem it perfectly legitimate that a person, who had once been convicted of any act of violence to others under the influence of drink, should be placed under a special legal restriction, personal to himself; that if he were afterwards found drunk, he should be liable to a penalty, and that if when in that state he committed another offence, the punishment to which he would be liable for that other offence should be increased in severity. The making himself drunk, in a person whom drunkenness excites to do harm to others, is a crime against others. So, again, idleness, except in a person receiving support from the public, or except when it constitutes a breach of contract, cannot without tyranny be made a subject of legal punishment; but if, either from idleness or from any other avoidable cause, a man fails to perform his legal duties to others, as for instance to support his children, it is no tyranny to force him to fulfil that obligation, by compulsory labour, if no other means are available.

Again, there are many acts which, being directly injurious only to the agents themselves, ought not to be legally interdicted, but which, if done publicly, are a violation of good manners, and coming thus within the category of offences against others, may rightfully be prohibited. Of this kind are offences against decency; on which it is unnecessary to dwell, the rather as they are only connected indirectly with our subject, the objection to publicity being equally strong in the case of many actions not in themselves condemnable, nor supposed to be so.

There is another question to which an answer must be found, consistent with the principles which have been laid down. In cases of personal conduct supposed to be blameable, but which respect for liberty precludes society from preventing or punishing, because the evil directly resulting falls wholly on the agent; what the agent is free to do, ought other persons to be equally free to counsel or instigate? This question is not free from difficulty. The case of a person who solicits another to do an act, is not strictly a case of self-regarding conduct. To give advice or offer inducements to any one, is a social act, and may, therefore, like actions in general which affect others, be supposed amenable to social control. But a little reflection corrects the first impression, by showing that if the case is not strictly within the definition of individual liberty, yet the reasons on which the principle of individual liberty is grounded, are applicable to it. If people must be allowed, in whatever concerns only themselves, to act as seems best to themselves at their own peril, they must equally be free to consult with one another about what is fit to be so done; to exchange opinions, and give and receive suggestions. Whatever it is permitted to do, it must be permitted to advise to do. The question is doubtful, only when the instigator derives a personal benefit from his advice; when he makes it his occupation, for subsistence or pecuniary gain, to promote what society and the State consider to be an evil. Then, indeed, a new element of complication is introduced; namely, the existence of classes of persons with an interest opposed to what is considered as the public weal, and whose mode of living is grounded on the counteraction of it. Ought this to be interfered with, or not? Fornication, for example, must be tolerated, and so must gambling; but should a person be free to be a pimp, or to keep a gambling-house? The case is one of those which lie on the exact boundary line between two principles, and it is not at once apparent to which of the two it properly belongs. There are arguments on both sides. On the side of toleration it may be said, that the fact of following anything as an occupation, and living or profiting by the practice of it, cannot make that criminal which would otherwise be admissible; that the act should either be consistently permitted or consistently prohibited; that if the principles which we have hitherto defended are true, society has no business, as society, to decide anything to be wrong which concerns only the individual; that it cannot go beyond dissuasion, and that one person should be as free to persuade, as another to dissuade. In opposition to this it may be contended, that although the public, or the State, are not warranted in authoritatively deciding, for purposes of repression or punishment, that such or such conduct affecting only the interests of the individual is good or bad, they are fully justified in assuming, if they regard it as bad, that its being so or not is at least a disputable question: That, this being supposed, they cannot be acting wrongly in endeavoring to exclude the influence of solicitations which

are not disinterested, of instigators who cannot possibly be impartial—who have a direct personal interest on one side, and that side the one which the State believes to be wrong, and who confessedly promote it for personal objects only. There can surely, it may be urged, be nothing lost, no sacrifice of good, by so ordering matters that persons shall make their election, either wisely or foolishly, on their own prompting, as free as possible from the arts of persons who stimulate their inclinations for interested purposes of their own. Thus (it may be said) though the statutes respecting unlawful games are utterly indefensible—though all persons should be free to gamble in their own or each other's houses, or in any place of meeting established by their own subscriptions, and open only to the members and their visitors—yet public gambling-houses should not be permitted. It is true that the prohibition is never effectual, and that, whatever amount of tyrannical power may be given to the police, gambling-houses can always be maintained under other pretenses; but they may be compelled to conduct their operations with a certain degree of secrecy and mystery, so that nobody knows anything about them but those who seek them; and more than this, society ought not to aim at. There is considerable force in these arguments. I will not venture to decide whether they are sufficient to justify the moral anomaly of punishing the accessory, when the principal is (and must be) allowed to go free; of fining or imprisoning the procurer, but not the fornicator, the gambling-house keeper, but not the gambler. Still less ought the common operations of buying and selling to be interfered with on analogous grounds. Almost every article which is bought and sold may be used in excess, and the sellers have a pecuniary interest in encouraging that excess; but no argument can be founded on this, in favour, for instance, of the Maine Law; because the class of dealers in strong drinks, though interested in their abuse, are indispensably required for the sake of their legitimate use. The interest, however, of these dealers in promoting intemperance is a real evil, and justifies the State in imposing restrictions and requiring guarantees which, but for that justification, would be infringements of legitimate liberty.

A further question is, whether the State, while it permits, should nevertheless indirectly discourage conduct which it deems contrary to the best interests of the agent; whether, for example, it should take measures to render the means of drunkenness more costly, or add to the difficulty of procuring them by limiting the number of the places of sale. On this as on most other practical questions, many distinctions require to be made. To tax stimulants for the sole purpose of making them more difficult to be obtained, is a measure differing only in degree from their entire prohibition; and would be justifiable only if that were justifiable. Every increase of cost is a prohibition, to those whose means do not come up to the augmented price; and to those who do, it is a penalty laid on them for gratifying a particular taste. Their choice of pleasures, and their mode of expending their income, after satisfying their legal and moral obligations to the State and to individuals, are their own concern, and must rest with their own judgment. These considerations may seem at first sight to condemn the selection of stimulants as special subjects of taxation for purposes of revenue. But it must be remembered that taxation for fiscal purposes is absolutely inevitable; that in most countries it is necessary that a considerable part of that taxation should be indirect; that the State, therefore, cannot help imposing penalties, which to some persons may be prohibitory, on the use of some articles of consumption. It is hence the duty of the State to consider, in the imposition of taxes, what commodities the consumers can best spare; and a fortiori, to select in preference those of which it deems the use, beyond a very moderate quantity, to be positively injurious. Taxation, therefore, of stimulants, up to the point which produces the largest amount of revenue (supposing that the State needs all the revenue which it yields) is not only admissible, but to be approved of.

The question of making the sale of these commodities a more or less exclusive privilege, must be answered differently, according to the purposes to which the restriction is intended to be subservient. All places of public resort require the restraint of a police, and places of this kind peculiarly, because offences against society are especially apt to originate there. It is, therefore, fit to confine the power of selling these commodities (at least for consumption on the spot) to persons of known or vouched-for respectability of conduct; to make such regulations respecting hours of opening and closing as may be requisite for public surveillance, and to withdraw the license if breaches of the peace repeatedly take place through the connivance or incapacity of the keeper of the house, or if it becomes a rendezvous for concocting and preparing offences against the law. Any further restriction I do not conceive to be, in principle, justifiable. The limitation in number, for instance, of beer and spirit houses, for the express purpose of rendering them more difficult of access, and diminishing the occasions of temptation, not only exposes all to an inconvenience because there are some by whom the facility would be abused, but is suited only to a state of society in which the laboring classes are avowedly treated as children or savages, and placed under an education of restraint, to fit them for future admission to the privileges of freedom. This is not the principle on which the laboring classes are professedly governed in any free country; and no person who sets due value on freedom will give his adhesion to their being so governed, unless after all efforts have been exhausted to educate them for freedom and govern them as freemen, and it has been definitively proved that they can only be governed as children. The bare statement of the alternative shows the absurdity of supposing that such efforts have been made in any case which needs be considered here. It is only because the institutions of this country are a mass of inconsistencies, that things find admittance into our practice which belong to the system of despotic, or what is called paternal, government, while the general freedom of our institutions precludes the exercise of the amount of control necessary to render the restraint of any real efficacy as a moral education.

It was pointed out in an early part of this Essay, that the liberty of the individual, in things wherein the individual is alone concerned, implies a corresponding liberty in any number of individuals to regulate by mutual agreement such things as regard them jointly, and regard no persons but themselves. This question presents no difficulty, so long as the will of all the persons implicated remains unaltered; but since that will may change, it is often necessary, even in things in which they alone are concerned, that they should enter into engagements with one another; and when they do, it is fit, as a general rule, that those engagements should be kept. Yet, in the laws, probably, of every country, this general rule has some exceptions. Not only persons are not held to engagements which violate the rights of third parties, but it is sometimes considered a sufficient reason for releasing them from an engagement, that it is injurious to themselves. In this and most other civilized countries, for example, an engagement by which a person should sell himself, or allow himself to be sold, as a slave, would be null and void; neither enforced by law nor by opinion. The ground for thus limiting his power of voluntarily disposing of his own lot in life, is apparent, and is very clearly seen in this extreme case. The reason for not interfering, unless for the sake of others, with a person's voluntary acts, is consideration for his liberty. His voluntary choice is evidence that what he so chooses is desirable, or at the least endurable, to him, and his good is on the whole best provided for by allowing him to take his own means of pursuing it. But by selling himself for a slave, he abdicates his liberty; he foregoes any future use of it beyond that single act. He therefore defeats, in his own case, the very purpose which is the justification of allowing him to dispose of himself. He is no longer free; but is thenceforth in a position which has no longer the presumption in its favour, that would be afforded by his voluntarily remaining in it. The principle of freedom cannot require that he should be free not to be free. It is not freedom, to be allowed to alienate his freedom. . . .

A person should be free to do as he likes in his own concerns, but he ought not to be free to do as he likes in acting for another, under the pretext that the affairs of the other are his own affairs. The State, while it respects the liberty of each in what specially regards himself, is bound to maintain a vigilant control over his exercise of any power which it allows him to possess over others. The obligation is almost entirely disregarded in the case of the family relations—a case, in its direct influence on human happiness, more important than all others taken together. The almost despotic power of husbands over wives needs not be enlarged upon here, because nothing more is needed for the complete removal of the evil than that wives should have the same rights and should receive the protection of law in the same manner as all other persons; and because, on this subject, the defenders of established injustice do not avail themselves of the plea of liberty but stand forth

openly as the champions of power. It is in the case of children that misapplied notions of liberty are a real obstacle to the fulfillment by the State of its duties. One would almost think that a man's children were supposed to be literally, and not metaphorically, a part of himself, so jealous is opinion of the smallest interference of law with his absolute and exclusive control over them, more jealous than of almost any interference with his own freedom of action: so much less do the generality of mankind value liberty than power. Consider, for example, the case of education. Is it not almost a self-evident axiom that the State should require and compel the education, up to certain standard, of every human being who is born its citizen? Yet who is there that is not afraid to recognize and assert this truth? Hardly anyone, indeed, will deny that it is one of the most sacred duties of the parents, after summoning a human being into the world, to give to that being an education fitting him to perform his part well in life toward others and towards himself. But while this is unanimously declared to be the father's duty, scarcely anybody, in this country, will bear to hear of obliging him to perform it. Instead of his being required to make an exertion or sacrifice for securing education to his child, it is left to his choice to accept it or not when it is provided gratis! It still remains unrecognized that to bring a child into existence without a fair prospect of being able, not only to provide food for its body, but instruction and training for its mind is a moral crime, both against the unfortunate offspring and against society; and that if the parent does not fulfill this obligation, the State ought to see it fulfilled at the charge, as far as possible, of the parent. . . .

The worth of a State, in the long run, is the worth of the individuals composing it; and a State which postpones the interests of *their* mental expansion and elevation to a little more of administrative skill, or of that semblance of it which practice gives in the details of business; a State which dwarfs its men, in order that they may be more docile instruments in its hands even for the beneficial purposes—will find that with small men no great thing can really be accomplished; and that the perfection of machinery to which it has sacrificed everything will in the end avail it nothing, for want of the vital power which, in order that the machine might work more smoothly, it has preferred to banish.

THE SUBJECTION OF WOMEN

CHAPTER I

The object of this Essay is to explain as clearly as I am able, the grounds of an opinion which I have held from the very earliest period when I had formed any opinions at all on social or political matters, and which, instead of being weakened or modified, has been constantly growing stronger by the progress of reflection and the experience of life: That the principle which regulates the existing social relations between the two sexes—the legal subordination of one sex to the other—is wrong in itself, and now one of the chief hindrances to human improvement; and that it ought to be replaced by a principle of perfect equality, admitting no power or privilege on the one side, nor disability on the other. . . .

The generality of a practice is in some cases a strong presumption that it is, or at all events once was, conducive to laudable ends. This is the case, when the practice was first adopted, or afterwards kept up, as a means to such ends, and was grounded on experience of the mode in which they could be most effectually attained. If the authority of men over women, when first established, had been the result of a conscientious comparison between different modes of constituting the government of society; if, after trying various other modes of social organization—the government of women over men, equality between the two, and such mixed and divided modes of government as might be invented—it had been decided, on the testimony of experience, that the mode in which women are wholly under the rule of men, having no share at all in public concerns, and each in private being under the legal obligation of obedience to the man with whom she has associated her destiny, was the arrangement most conducive to the happiness and well being of both; its general adoption might then be fairly thought to be some evidence that, at the time when it was adopted, it was the best: though even then the considerations which recommended it may, like so many other primeval social facts of the greatest importance, have subsequently, in the course of ages, ceased to exist. But the state of the case is in every respect the reverse of this. In

the first place, the opinion in favour of the present system, which entirely subordinates the weaker sex to the stronger, rests upon theory only; for there never has been trial made of any other: so that experience, in the sense in which it is vulgarly opposed to theory, cannot be pretended to have pronounced any verdict.

And in the second place, the adoption of this system of inequality never was the result of deliberation, or forethought, or any social ideas, or any notion whatever of what conduced to the benefit of humanity or the good order of society. It arose simply from the fact that from the very earliest twilight of human society, every woman (owing to the value attached to her by men, combined with her inferiority in muscular strength) was found in a state of bondage to some man. Laws and systems of polity always begin by recognising the relations they find already existing between individuals. They convert what was a mere physical fact into a legal right, give it the sanction of society, and principally aim at the substitution of public and organized means of asserting and protecting these rights, instead of the irregular and lawless conflict of physical strength. Those who had already been compelled to obedience became in this manner legally bound to it. Slavery, from being a mere affair of force between the master and the slave, became regularized and a matter of compact among the masters, who, binding themselves to one another for common protection, guaranteed by their collective strength the private possessions of each, including his slaves. In early times, the great majority of the male sex were slaves, as well as the whole of the female. And many ages elapsed, some of them ages of high cultivation, before any thinker was bold enough to question the rightfulness, and the absolute social necessity, either of the one slavery or of the other. By degrees such thinkers did arise: and (the general progress of society assisting) the slavery of the male sex has, in all the countries of Christian Europe at least (though, in one of them, only within the last few years) been at length abolished, and that of the female sex has been gradually changed into a milder form of dependence.

But this dependence, as it exists at present, is not an original institution, taking a fresh start from considerations of justice and social expediency—it is the primitive state of slavery lasting on, through successive mitigations and modifications occasioned by the same causes which have softened the general manners, and brought all human relations more under the control of justice and the influence of humanity. It has not lost the taint of its brutal origin. No presumption in its favour, therefore, can be drawn from the fact of its existence. The only such presumption which it could be supposed to have, must be grounded on its having lasted till now, when so many other things which came down from the same odious source have been done away with. And this, indeed, is what makes it strange to ordinary ears, to hear it asserted that the inequality of rights between men and women has no other source than the law of the strongest. . . .

Some will object, that a comparison cannot fairly be made between the government of the male sex and the forms of unjust power which I have adduced in illustration of it, since these are arbitrary, and the effect of mere usurpation, while it on the contrary is natural. But was there ever any domination which did not appear natural to those who possessed it? There was a time when the division of mankind into two classes, a small one of masters and numerous one of slaves, appeared, even to the most cultivated minds, to be a natural, and the only natural, condition of the human race. No less an intellect, and one which contributed no less to the progress of human thought, than Aristotle, held this opinion without doubt or misgiving; and rested it on the same premises on which the same assertion in regard to the dominion of men over women is usually based, namely that there are different natures among mankind, free natures, and slave natures; that the Greeks were of a free nature, the barbarian races of Thracians and Asiatics of a slave nature. But why need I go back to Aristotle? Did not the slaveowners of the Southern United States maintain the same doctrine, with all the fanaticism with which men cling to the theories that justify their passions and legitimate their personal interests? Did they not call heaven and earth to witness that the dominion of the white man over the black is natural, that the black race is by nature incapable of freedom, and marked out for slavery? some even going so far as to say that the freedom of manual labourers is an unnatural order of things anywhere. Again, the theorists of absolute monarchy have always affirmed it to be the only natural form of government; issuing from the patriarchal, which was the primitive and spontaneous form of society, framed on the model of the paternal, which is anterior to society itself, and, as they contend, the most natural authority of all. Nay, for that matter, the law of force itself, to those who could not plead any other, has always seemed the most natural of all grounds for the exercise of authority.

Conquering races hold it to be Nature's own dictate that the conquered should obey the conquerors, or, as they euphoniously paraphrase it, that the feebler and more unwarlike races should submit to the braver and manlier. The smallest acquaintance with human life in the middle ages, shows how supremely natural the dominion of the feudal nobility over men of low condition appeared to the nobility themselves, and how unnatural the conception seemed, of a person of the inferior class claiming equality with them, or exercising authority over them. It hardly seemed less so to the class held in subjection. The emancipated serfs and burgesses, even in their most vigorous struggles, never made any pretension to a share of authority; they only demanded more or less of limitation to the power of tyrannizing over them. So true is it that unnatural generally means only uncustomary, and that everything which is usual appears natural. The subjection of women to men being a universal custom, any departure from it quite naturally appears unnatural. But how entirely, even in this case, the feeling is dependent on custom, appears by ample experience. Nothing so much astonishes the people of distant parts of the world, when they first learn anything about England, as to be told that it is under a queen: the thing seems to them so unnatural as to be almost incredible. To Englishmen this does not seem in the least degree unnatural, because they are used to it; but they do feel it unnatural that women should be soldiers or members of Parliament. In the feudal ages, on the contrary, war and politics were not thought unnatural to women, because not unusual; it seemed natural that women of the privileged classes should be of manly character, inferior in nothing but bodily strength to their husbands and fathers. The independence of women seemed rather less unnatural to the Greeks than to other ancients, on account of the fabulous Amazons (whom they believed to be historical), and the partial example afforded by the Spartan women; who, though no less subordinate by law than in other Greek states, were more free in fact, and being trained to bodily exercises in the same manner with men, gave ample proof that they were not naturally disqualified for them. There can be little doubt that Spartan experience suggested to Plato, among many other of his doctrines, that of the social and political equality of the two sexes.

But, it will be said, the rule of men over women differs from all these others in not being a rule of force: it is accepted voluntarily; women make no complaint, and are consenting parties to it. In the first place, a great number of women do not accept it. Ever since there have been women able to make their sentiments known by their writings (the only mode of publicity which society permits to them), an increasing number of them have recorded protests against their present social condition: and recently many thousands of them, headed by the most eminent women known to the public, have petitioned Parliament for their admission to the Parliamentary Suffrage.

The claim of women to be educated as solidly, and in the same branches of knowledge, as men, is urged with growing intensity, and with a great prospect of success; while the demand for their admission into professions and occupations hitherto closed against them, becomes every year more urgent. . . .

It must be remembered, also, that no enslaved class ever asked for complete liberty at once. When Simon de Montfort called the deputies of the commons to sit for the first time in Parliament, did any of them dream of demanding that an assembly, elected by their constituents, should make and destroy ministries, and dictate to the king in affairs of state? No such thought entered into the imagination of the most ambitious of them. The nobility had already these pretensions; the commons pretended to nothing but to be exempt from arbitrary taxation, and from the gross individual oppression of the king's

officers. It is a political law of nature that those who are under any power of ancient origin, never begin by complaining of the power itself, but only of its oppressive exercise. There is never any want of women who complain of ill usage by their husbands. There would be infinitely more, if complaint were not the greatest of all provocatives to a repetition and increase of the ill usage. It is this which frustrates all attempts to maintain the power but protect the woman against its abuses. In no other case (except that of a child) is the person who has been proved judicially to have suffered an injury, replaced under the physical power of the culprit who inflicted it. Accordingly wives, even in the most extreme and protracted cases of bodily ill usage, hardly every dare avail themselves of the laws made for their protection: and if, in a moment of irrepressible indignation, or by the interference of neighbours, they are induced to do so, their whole effort afterwards is to disclose as little as they can, and to beg off their tyrant from his merited chastisement.

All causes, social and natural, combine to make it unlikely that women should be collectively rebellious to the power of men. They are so far in a position different from all other subject classes, that their masters require something more from them than actual service. Men do not want solely the obedience of women, they want their sentiments. All men, except the most brutish, desire to have, in the woman most nearly connected with them, not a forced slave but a willing one, not a slave merely, but a favourite. They have therefore put everything in practice to enslave their minds. The masters of all other slaves rely, for maintaining obedience, on fear; either fear of themselves, or religious fears. The masters of women wanted more than simple obedience, and they turned the whole force of education to effect their purpose. All women are brought up from the very earliest years in the belief that their ideal of character is the very opposite to that of men; not self-will, and government by self-control, but submission, and yielding to the control of others. All the moralities tell them that it is the duty of women, and all the current sentimentalities that it is their nature, to live for others; to make complete abnegation of themselves, and to have no life but in their affections. And by their affections are meant the only ones they are allowed to have—those to the men with whom they are connected, or to the children who constitute an additional and indefeasible tie between them and a man.

When we put together three things—first, the natural attraction between opposite sexes; secondly, the wife's entire dependence on the husband, every privilege or pleasure she has being either his gift, or depending entirely on his will; and lastly, that the principal object of human pursuit, consideration, and all objects of social ambition, can in general be sought or obtained by her only through him, it would be a miracle if the object of being attractive to men had not become the polar star of feminine education and formation of character. And, this great means of influence over the minds of women having been acquired, an instinct of selfishness made men avail themselves of it to the utmost as a means of holding women in subjection, by representing to them meekness, submissiveness, and resignation of all individual will into the hands of a man, as an essential part of sexual attractiveness. Can it be doubted that any of the other yokes which mankind have succeeded in breaking, would have subsisted till now if the same means had existed, and had been as sedulously used, to bow down their minds to it? If it had been made the object of the life of every young plebeian to find personal favour in the eyes of some patrician, of every young serf with some seigneur; if domestication with him, and a share of his personal affections, had been held out as the prize which they all should look out for, the most gifted and aspiring being able to reckon on the most desirable prizes; and if, when this prize had been obtained, they had been shut out by a wall of brass from all interests not centering in him, all feelings and desires but those which he shared or inculcated; would not serfs and seigneurs, plebeians and patricians, have been as broadly distinguished at this day as men and women are? and would not all but a thinker here and there, have believed the distinction to be a fundamental and unalterable fact in human nature? . . .

The least that can be demanded is, that the question should not be considered as prejudged by existing fact and existing opinion, but open to discussion on its merits, as a question of justice and expediency: the decision on this, as on any of the other social arrangements of mankind, depending on what an enlightened estimate of tendencies and consequences may show to be most advantageous to humanity in general, without distinction of sex. And the discussion must be a real discussion, descending to foundations, and not resting satisfied with vague and general assertions. It will not do, for instance, to assert in general terms, that the experience of mankind has pronounced in favour of the existing system. Experience cannot possibly have decided between two courses, so long as there has only been experience of one. If it be said that the doctrine of the equality of the sexes rests only on theory, it must be remembered that the contrary doctrine also has only theory to rest upon. All that is proved in its favour by direct experience, is that mankind have been able to exist under it, and to attain the degree of improvement and prosperity which we now see; but whether that prosperity has been attained sooner, or is now greater, than it would have been under the other system, experience does not say. . . .

Neither does it avail anything to say that the nature of the two sexes adapts them to their present functions and position, and renders these appropriate to them. Standing on the ground of common sense and the constitution of the human mind, I deny that any one knows, or can know, the nature of the two sexes, as long as they have only been seen in their present relation to one another. If men had ever been found in society without women, or women without men, or if there had been a society of men and women in which the women were not under the control of the men, something might have been positively known about the mental and moral differences which may be inherent in the nature of each. What is now called the nature of women is an eminently artificial thing—the result of forced repression in some directions, unnatural stimulation in others. It may be asserted without scruple, that no other class of dependents have had their character so entirely distorted from its natural proportions by their relation with their masters; for, if conquered and slave races have been, in some respects, more forcibly repressed, whatever in them has not been crushed down by an iron heel has generally been let alone, and if left with any liberty of development, it has developed itself according to its own laws; but in the case of women, a hot-house and stove cultivation has always been carried on of some of the capabilities of their nature, for the benefit and pleasure of their masters. . . .

Of all difficulties which impede the progress of thought, and the formation of well-grounded opinions on life and social arrangements, the greatest is now the unspeakable ignorance and inattention of mankind in respect to the influences which form human character. Whatever any portion of the human species now are, or seem to be, such, it is supposed, they have a natural tendency to be: even when the most elementary knowledge of the circumstances in which they have been placed, clearly points out the causes that made them what they are. Because a cottier deeply in arrears to his landlord is not industrious, there are people who think that the Irish are naturally idle. Because constitutions can be overthrown when the authorities appointed to execute them turn their arms against them, there are people who think the French incapable of free government. Because the Greeks cheated the Turks, and the Turks only plundered the Greeks, there are persons who think that the Turks are naturally more sincere: and because women, as is often said, care nothing about politics except their personalities, it is supposed that the general good is naturally less interesting to women than to men. History, which is now so much better understood than formerly, teaches another lesson: if only by showing the extraordinary susceptibility of human nature to external influences, and the extreme variableness of those of its manifestations which are supposed to be most universal and uniform. But in history, as in travelling, men usually see only what they already had in their own minds; and few learn much from history, who do not bring much with them to its study.

Hence, in regard to that most difficult question, what are the natural differences between the two sexes—a subject on which it is impossible in the present state of society to obtain complete and correct knowledge—while almost everybody dogmatizes upon it, almost all neglect and make light of the only means by which any partial insight can be obtained into it. This is, an analytic study of the most important department of psychology, the laws of the influence of circumstances on character. For, however great and apparently ineradicable the moral and intellectual differences between men and women might be, the evidence of their being natural differences could only be negative. Those only could be inferred to be natural which could not possibly be artificial—the residuum, after deducting every characteristic of either sex which can admit of being explained from education or external circumstances. The profoundest knowledge of the laws of the formation of character is indispensable to entitle any one to affirm even that there is any difference, much more what the difference is, between the two sexes considered as moral and rational beings; and since no one, as yet, has that knowledge, (for there is hardly any subject which, in proportion to its importance, has been so little studied), no one is thus far entitled to any positive opinion on the subject. Conjectures are all that can at present be made; conjectures more or less probable, according as more or less authorized by such knowledge as we yet have of the laws of psychology, as applied to the formation of character.

Even the preliminary knowledge, what the differences between the sexes now are, apart from all question as to how they are made what they are, is still in the crudest and most incomplete state. Medical practitioners and physiologists have ascertained, to some extent, the differences in bodily constitution; and this is an important element to the psychologist: but hardly any medical practitioner is a psychologist. Respecting the mental characteristics of women; their observations are of no more worth than those of common men. It is a subject on which nothing final can be known, so long as those who alone can really know it, women themselves, have given but little testimony, and that little, mostly suborned. It is easy to know stupid women. Stupidity is much the same all the world over. A stupid person's notions and feelings may confidently be inferred from those which prevail in the circle by which the person is surrounded. Not so with those whose opinions and feelings are an emanation from their own nature and faculties. It is only a man here and there who has any tolerable knowledge of the character even of the women of his own family. I do not mean, of their capabilities; these nobody knows, not even themselves, because most of them have never been called out. I mean their actually existing thoughts and feelings. Many a man thinks he perfectly understands women, because he has had amatory relations with several, perhaps with many of them. If he is a good observer, and his experience extends to quality as well as quantity, he may have learnt something of one narrow department of their nature—an important department, no doubt. But of all the rest of it, few persons are generally more ignorant, because there are few from whom it is so carefully hidden. The most favourable case which a man can generally have for studying the character of a woman, is that of his own wife: for the opportunities are greater, and the cases of complete sympathy not so unspeakably rare. And in fact, this is the source from which any knowledge worth having on the subject has, I believe, generally come. But most men have not had the opportunity of studying in this way more than a single case: accordingly one can, to an almost laughable degree, infer what a man's wife is like, from his opinions about women in general. To make even this one case yield any result, the woman must be worth knowing, and the man not only a competent judge, but of a character so sympathetic in itself, and so well adapted to hers, that he can either read her mind by sympathetic intuition, or has nothing in himself which makes her shy of disclosing it.

Hardly anything, I believe, can be more rare than this conjunction. It often happens that there is the most complete unity of feeling and community of interests as to all external things, yet the one has as little admission into the internal life of the other as if they were common acquaintance. Even with true affection, authority on the one side and subordination on the other prevent perfect confidence. Though nothing may be intentionally withheld, much is not shown. In the analogous relation of parent and child, the corresponding phenomenon must have been in the observation of every one. As between father and son, how many are the cases in which the father, in spite of real affection on both sides, obviously to all the world does not know, nor suspect, parts of the son's character familiar to his companions and equals. The truth is, that the position of looking up

to another is extremely unpropitious to complete sincerity and openness with him. The fear of losing ground in his opinion or in his feelings is so strong, that even in an upright character, there is an unconscious tendency to show only the best side, or the side which, though not the best, is that which he most likes to see: and it may be confidently said that thorough knowledge of one another hardly ever exists, but between persons who, besides being intimates, are equals. How much more true, then, must all this be, when the one is not only under the authority of the others, but has it inculcated on her as a duty to reckon everything else subordinate to his comfort and pleasure, and to let him neither see nor feel anything coming from her, except what is agreeable to him. All these difficulties stand in the way of a man's obtaining any thorough knowledge even of the one woman whom alone, in general, he has sufficient opportunity of studying. When we further consider that to understand one woman is not necessarily to understand any other woman; that even if he could study many women of one rank, or of one country, he would not thereby understand women of other ranks or countries; and even if he did, they are still only the women of a single period of history; we may safely assert that the knowledge which men can acquire of women, even as they have been and are, without reference to what they might be, is wretchedly imperfect and superficial, and always will be so, until women themselves have told all that they have to tell.

And this time has not come; nor will it come otherwise than gradually. It is but of yesterday that women have either been qualified by literary accomplishments, or permitted by society, to tell anything to the general public. As yet very few of them dare tell anything, which men, on whom their literary success depends, are unwilling to hear. Let us remember in what manner, up to a very recent time, the expression, even by a male author, of uncustomary opinions, or what are deemed eccentric feelings, usually was, and in some degree still is, received; and we may form some faint conception under what impediments a woman, who is brought up to think custom and opinion her sovereign rule, attempts to express in books anything drawn from the depths of her own nature. . . . The greater part of what women write about women is mere sycophancy to men. In the case of unmarried women, much of it seems only intended to increase their chance of a husband. Many, both married and unmarried, overstep the mark, and inculcate a servility beyond what is desired or relished by any man, except the very vulgarest. But this is not so often the case as, even at a quite late period, it still was. Literary women are becoming more freespoken, and more willing to express their real sentiments. Unfortunately, in this country especially, they are themselves such artificial products, that their sentiments are compounded of a small element of individual observation and consciousness, and a very large one of acquired associations. This will be less and less the case, but it will remain true to a great extent, as long as social institutions do not admit the same free development of originality in women which is possible to men. When that time comes, and not before, we shall see, and not merely hear, as much as it is necessary to know of the nature of women, and the adaptation of other things to it. . . .

One thing we may be certain of—that what is contrary to women's nature to do, they never will be made to do by simply giving their nature free play. The anxiety of mankind to interfere in behalf of nature, for fear lest nature should not succeed in effecting its purpose, is an altogether unnecessary solicitude. What women by nature cannot do, it is quite superfluous to forbid them from doing. What they can do, but not so well as the men who are their competitors, competition suffices to exclude them from; since nobody asks for protective duties and bounties in favour of women; it is only asked that the present bounties and protective duties in favour of men should be recalled. If women have a greater natural inclination for some things than for others, there is no need of laws or social inculcation to make the majority of them do the former in preference to the latter. Whatever women's services are most wanted for, the free play of competition will hold out the strongest inducements to them to undertake. And, as the words imply, they are most wanted for the things for which they are most fit; by the apportionment of which to them, the collective faculties of the two sexes can be applied on the whole with the greatest sum of valuable result.

The general opinion of men is supposed to be, that the natural vocation of a woman is that of a wife and mother. I say, is supposed to be, because, judging from acts—from the whole of the present constitution of society—one might infer that their opinion was the direct contrary. They might be supposed to think that the alleged natural vocation of women was of all things the most repugnant to their nature; insomuch that if they are free to do anything else— if any other means of living, or occupation of their time and faculties, is open, which has any chance of appearing desirable to them—there will not be enough of them who will be willing to accept the condition said to be natural to them. If this is the real opinion of men in general, it would be well that it should be spoken out. I should like to hear somebody openly enunciating the doctrine (it is already implied in much that is written on the subject)—"It is necessary to society that women should marry and produce children. They will not do so unless they are compelled. Therefore it is necessary to compel them." The merits of the case would then be clearly defined. It would be exactly that of the slaveholders of South Carolina and Louisiana. "It is necessary that cotton and sugar should be grown. White men cannot produce them. Negroes will not, for any wages which we choose to give. Ergo they must be compelled." An illustration still closer to the point is that of impressment. Sailors must absolutely be had to defend the country. It often happens that they will not voluntarily enlist. Therefore there must be the power of forcing them. How often has this logic been used! and, but for one flaw in it, without doubt it would have been successful up to this day. But it is open to the retort—First pay the sailors the honest value of their labour. When you have made it as well worth their while to serve you, as to work for other employers, you will have no more difficulty than others have in obtaining their services. To this there is no logical answer except "I will not:" and as people are now not only ashamed, but are not desirous, to rob the labourer of his hire, impressment is no longer advocated. Those who attempt to force women into marriage by closing all other doors against them, lay themselves open to a similar retort. If they mean what they say, their opinion must evidently be, that men do not render the married condition so desirable to women, as to induce them to accept it for its own recommendations. It is not a sign of one's thinking the boon one offers very attractive, when one allows only Hobson's choice, "that or none." . . . .

CHAPTER III

On the other point which is involved in the just equality of women, their admissibility to all the functions and occupations hitherto retained as the monopoly of the stronger sex. . . . I believe that their disabilities elsewhere are only clung to in order to maintain their subordination in domestic life; because the generality of the male sex cannot yet tolerate the idea of living with an equal. Were it not for that, I think that almost every one, in the existing state of opinion in politics and political economy, would admit the injustice of excluding half the human race from the greater number of lucrative occupations, and from almost all high social functions; ordaining from their birth either that they are not, and cannot by any possibility become, fit for employments which are legally open to the stupidest and basest of the other sex, or else that however fit they may be, those employments shall be interdicted to them, in order to be preserved for the exclusive benefit of males. In the last two centuries, when (which was seldom the case) any reason beyond the mere existence of the fact was thought to be required to justify the disabilities of women, people seldom assigned as a reason their inferior mental capacity; which, in times when there was a real trial of personal faculties (from which all women were not excluded) in the struggles of public life, no one really believed in. The reason given in those days was not women's unfitness, but the interest of society, by which was meant the interest of men: just as the raison d'etat, meaning the convenience of the government, and the support of existing authority, was deemed a sufficient explanation and excuse for the most flagitious crimes. In the present day, power holds a smoother language, and whomsoever it oppresses, always pretends to do so for their own good: accordingly, when anything is forbidden to women, it is thought necessary to say, and desirable to believe, that they are incapable of doing it, and that they depart from their real path of success and happiness when they aspire to it. But to make this reason plausible (I do not say valid), those by whom it is urged must be prepared to carry it to a much greater length than any one ventures to do in the face of present experience.

It is not sufficient to maintain that women on the average are less gifted than men on the average, with certain of the higher mental faculties, or that a smaller number of women than of men are fit for occupations and functions of the highest intellectual character. It is necessary to maintain that no women at all are fit for them, and that the most eminent women are inferior in mental faculties to the most mediocre of the men on whom those functions at present devolve. For if the performance of the function is decided either by competition, or by any mode of choice which secures regard to the public interest, there needs be no apprehension that any important employments will fall into the hands of women inferior to average men, or to the average of their male competitors. The only result would be that there would be fewer women than men in such employments; a result certain to happen in any case, if only from the preference always likely to be felt by the majority of women for the one vocation in which there is nobody to compete with them. Now, the most determined depreciator of women will not venture to deny, that when we add the experience of recent times to that of ages past, women, and not a few merely, but many women, have proved themselves capable of everything, perhaps without a single exception, which is done by men, and of doing it successfully and creditably. The utmost that can be said is, that there are many things which none of them have succeeded in doing as well as they have been done by some men—many in which they have not reached the very highest rank. But there are extremely few, dependent only on mental faculties, in which they have not attained the rank next to the highest. Is not this enough, and much more than enough, to make it a tyranny to them, and a detriment to society, that they should not be allowed to compete with men for the exercise of these functions? Is it not a mere truism to say, that such functions are often filled by men far less fit for them than numbers of women, and who would be beaten by women in any fair field of competition? What difference does it make that there may be men somewhere, fully employed about other things, who may be still better qualified for the things in question than these women? Does not this take place in all competitions? Is there so great a superfluity of men fit for high duties, that society can afford to reject the service of any competent person? Are we so certain of always finding a man made to our hands for any duty or function of social importance which falls vacant, that we lose nothing by putting a ban upon one-half of mankind, and refusing beforehand to make their faculties available, however distinguished they may be? And even if we could do without them, would it be consistent with justice to refuse to them their fair share of honour and distinction, or to deny to them the equal moral right of all human beings to choose their occupation (short of injury to others) according to their own preferences, at their own risk? Nor is the injustice confined to them: it is shared by those who are in a position to benefit by their services. To ordain that any kind of persons shall not be physicians, or shall not be advocates, or shall not be members of parliament, is to injure not them only, but all who employ physicians or advocates or elect members of parliament, and who are deprived of the stimulating effect of greater competition on the exertions of the competitors, as well as restricted to a narrower range of individual choice.

It will perhaps be sufficient if I confine myself, in the details of my argument, to functions of a public nature: since, if I am successful as to those, it probably will be readily granted that women should be admissible to all other occupations to which it is at all material whether they are admitted or not. . . .

With regard to the fitness of women, not only to participate in elections, but themselves to hold offices or practise professions involving important public responsibilities; I have already observed that this consideration is not essential to the practical question in dispute: since any woman, who succeeds in an open profession, proves by that very fact that she is qualified for it. And in the case of public offices, if the political system of the country is such as to exclude unfit men, it will equally exclude unfit women: while if it is not, there is no additional evil in the fact that the unfit persons whom it admits may be either women or men. As long therefore as it is

acknowledged that even a few women may be fit for these duties, the laws which shut the door on those exceptions cannot be justified by any opinion which can be held respecting the capacities of women in general. But, though this last consideration is not essential, it is far from being irrelevant. An unprejudiced view of it gives additional strength to the arguments against the disabilities of women, and reinforces them by high considerations of practical utility.

Let us at first make entire abstraction to all psychological considerations tending to show, that any of the mental differences supposed to exist between women and men are but the natural effect of the differences in their education and circumstances, and indicate no radical difference, far less radical inferiority, of nature. Let us consider women only as they already are, or as they are known to have been; and the capacities which they have already practically shown. What they have done, that at least, if nothing else, it is proved that they can do. When we consider how sedulously they are all trained away from, instead of being trained towards, any of the occupations or objects reserved for men, it is evident that I am taking a very humble ground for them, when I rest their case on what they have actually achieved. For, in this case, negative evidence is worth little, while any positive evidence is conclusive. It cannot be inferred to be impossible that a woman should be a Homer, or an Aristotle, or a Michael Angelo, or a Beethoven, because no woman has yet actually produced works comparable to theirs in any of those lines of excellence. This negative fact at most leaves the question uncertain, and open to psychological discussion. But it is quite certain that a woman can be a Queen Elizabeth, or a Deborah, or a Joan of Arc, since this is not inference, but fact. Now it is a curious consideration, that the only things which the existing law excludes women from doing, are the things which they have proved that they are able to do. There is no law to prevent a woman from having written all the plays of Shakspeare, or composed all the operas of Mozart. But Queen Elizabeth or Queen Victoria, had they not inherited the throne, could not have been intrusted with the smallest of the political duties, of which the former showed herself equal to the greatest.

If anything conclusive could be inferred from experience, without psychological analysis, it would be that the things which women are not allowed to do are the very ones for which they are peculiarly qualified; since their vocation for government has made its way, and become conspicuous, through the very few opportunities which have been given; while in the lines of distinction which apparently were freely open to them, they have by no means so eminently distinguished themselves. We know how small a number of reigning queens history presents, in comparison with that of kings. Of this smaller number a far larger proportion have shown talents for rule; though many of them have occupied the throne in difficult periods. It is remarkable, too, that they have, in a great number of instances, been distinguished by merits the most opposite to the imaginary and conventional character of women: they have been as much remarked for the firmness and vigour of their rule, as for its intelligence. When, to queens and empresses, we add regents, and viceroys of provinces, the list of women who have been eminent rulers of mankind swells to a great length. This fact is so undeniable, that some one, long ago, tried to retort the argument, and turned the admitted truth into an additional insult, by saying that queens are better than kings, because under kings women govern, but under queens, men.

It may seem a waste of reasoning to argue against a bad joke; but such things do affect people's minds; and I have heard men quote this saying, with an air as if they thought that there was something in it. At any rate, it will serve as well as anything else for a starting point in discussion. I say, then, that it is not true that under kings, women govern. Such cases are entirely exceptional: and weak kings have quite as often governed ill through the influence of male favourites, as of female. When a king is governed by a woman merely through his amatory propensities, good government is not probable, though even then there are exceptions. But French history counts two kings who have voluntarily given the direction of affairs during many years, the one to his mother, the other to his sister: one of them, Charles VIII., was a mere boy, but in doing so he followed the intentions of his father Louis XI., the ablest monarch of his age. The other, Saint Louis, was the best, and one of the

most vigorous rulers, since the time of Charlemagne. Both these princesses ruled in a manner hardly equalled by any prince among their contemporaries. The emperor Charles V., the most politic prince of his time, who had as great a number of able men in his service as a ruler ever had, and was one of the least likely of all sovereigns to sacrifice his interest to personal feelings, made two princesses of his family successively Governors of the Netherlands, and kept one or other of them in that post during his whole life, (they were afterwards succeeded by a third). Both ruled very successfully, and one of them, Margaret of Austria, was one of the ablest politicians of the age. So much for one side of the question. Now as to the other. When it is said that under queens men govern, is the same meaning to be understood as when kings are said to be governed by women? Is it meant that queens choose as their instruments of government, the associates of their personal pleasures? The case is rare even with those who are as unscrupulous on the latter point as Catherine II.: and it is not in these cases that the good government, alleged to arise from male influence, is to be found. If it be true, then, that the administration is in the hands of better men under a queen than under an average king, it must be that queens have a superior capacity for choosing them; and women must be better qualified than men both for the position of sovereign, and for that of chief minister; for the principal business of a prime minister is not to govern in person, but to find the fittest persons to conduct every department of public affairs. The more rapid insight into character, which is one of the admitted points of superiority in women over men, must certainly make them, with anything like parity of qualifications in other respects, more apt than men in that choice of instruments, which is nearly the most important business of every one who has to do with governing mankind. Even the unprincipled Catherine de' Medici could feel the value of a Chancellor de l'Hopital. But it is also true that most great queens have been great by their own talents for government, and have been well served precisely for that reason. They retained the supreme direction of affairs in their own hands: and if they listened to good advisers, they gave by that fact the strongest proof that their judgment fitted them for dealing with the great questions of government.

Is it reasonable to think that those who are fit for the greater functions of politics, are incapable of qualifying themselves for the less? Is there any reason in the nature of things, that the wives and sisters of princes should, whenever called on, be found as competent as the princes themselves to their business, but that the wives and sisters of statesmen, and administrators, and directors of companies, and managers of public institutions, should be unable to do what is done by their brothers and husbands? The real reason is plain enough; it is that princesses, being more raised above the generality of men by their rank than placed below them by their sex, have never been taught that it was improper for them to concern themselves with politics; but have been allowed to feel the liberal interest natural to any cultivated human being, in the great transactions which took place around them, and in which they might be called on to take a part. The ladies of reigning families are the only women who are allowed the same range of interests and freedom of development as men; and it is precisely in their case that there is not found to be any inferiority. Exactly where and in proportion as women's capacities for government have been tried, in that proportion have they been found adequate.

This fact is in accordance with the best general conclusions which the world's imperfect experience seems as yet to suggest, concerning the peculiar tendencies and aptitudes characteristic of women, as women have hitherto been. I do not say, as they will continue to be; for, as I have already said more than once, I consider it presumption in any one to pretend to decide what women are or are not, can or cannot be, by natural constitution. They have always hitherto been kept, as far as regards spontaneous development, in so unnatural a state, that their nature cannot but have been greatly distorted and disguised; and no one can safely pronounce that if women's nature were left to choose its direction as freely as men's, and if no artificial bent were attempted to be given to it except that required by the conditions of human society, and given to both sexes alike, there would be any material difference, or perhaps any difference at all, in the character and capacities which would unfold themselves. I shall presently show, that even the least contestable of the differences which now exist, are such as may very well have been pro-duced merely by circumstances, without any difference of natural capacity. But, looking at women as they are known in experience, it may be said of them, with more truth than belongs to most other generalizations on the subject, that the general bent of their talents is towards the practical. This statement is conformable to all the public history of women, in the present and the past. It is no less borne out by common and daily experience. Let us consider the special nature of the mental capacities most characteristic of a woman of talent. They are all of a kind which fits them for practice, and makes them tend towards it. What is meant by a woman's capacity of intuitive perception? It means, a rapid and correct insight into present fact. It has nothing to do with general principles. Nobody ever perceived a scientific law of nature by intuition, nor arrived at a general rule of duty or prudence by it. These are results of slow and careful collection and comparison of experience; and neither the men nor the women of intuition usually shine in this department, unless, indeed, the experience necessary is such as they can acquire by themselves. For what is called their intuitive sagacity makes them peculiarly apt in gathering such general truths as can be collected from their individual means of observation. When, consequently, they chance to be as well provided as men are with the results of other people's experience, by reading and education (I use the word chance advisedly, for, in respect to the knowledge that tends to fit them for the greater concerns of life, the only educated women are the self-educated), they are better furnished than men in general with the essential requisites of skillful and successful practice. Men who have been much taught, are apt to be deficient in the sense of present fact; they do not see, in the facts which they are called upon to deal with, what is really there, but what they have been taught to expect. This is seldom the case with women of any ability. Their capacity of "intuition" preserves them from it. With equality of experience and of general faculties, a woman usually sees much more than a man of what is immediately before her. Now this sensibility to the present, is the main quality on which the capacity for practice, as distinguished from theory, depends. To discover general principles, belongs to the speculative faculty: to discern and discriminate the particular cases in which they are and are not applicable, constitutes practical talent: and for this, women as they now are have a peculiar aptitude. I admit that there can be no good practice without principles, and that the predominant place which quickness of observation holds among a woman's faculties, makes her particularly apt to build over-hasty generalizations upon her own observation; though at the same time no less ready in rectifying those generalizations, as her observation takes a wider range. But the corrective to this defect, is access to the experience of the human race; general knowledge—exactly the thing which education can best supply. A woman's mistakes are specifically those of a clever self-educated man, who often sees what men trained in routine do not see, but falls into errors for want of knowing things which have long been known. Of course he has acquired much of the pre-existing knowledge, or he could not have got on at all; but what he knows of it he has picked up in fragments and at random, as women do.

But this gravitation of women's minds to the present, to the real, to actual fact, while in its exclusiveness it is a source of errors, is also a most useful counteractive of the contrary error. The principal and most characteristic aberration of speculative minds as such, consists precisely in the deficiency of this lively perception and ever-present sense of objective fact. For want of this, they often not only overlook the contradiction which outward facts oppose to their theories, but lose sight of the legitimate purpose of speculation altogether, and let their speculative faculties go astray into regions not peopled with real beings, animate or inanimate, even idealized, but with personified shadows created by the illusions of metaphysics or by the mere entanglement of words, and think these shadows the proper objects of the highest, the most transcendent, philosophy. Hardly anything can be of greater value to a man of theory and speculation who employs himself not in collecting materials of knowledge by observation, but in working them up by processes of thought into comprehensive truths of science and laws of conduct, than to carry on his speculations in the companionship, and under the criticism, of a really superior woman. There is nothing comparable to it for keeping his thoughts within the limits of real things, and

the actual facts of nature. A woman seldom runs wild after an abstraction. The habitual direction of her mind to dealing with things as individuals rather than in groups, and (what is closely connected with it) her more lively interest in the present feelings of persons, which makes her consider first of all, in anything which claims to be applied to practice, in what manner persons will be affected by it—these two things make her extremely unlikely to put faith in any speculation which loses sight of individuals, and deals with things as if they existed for the benefit of some imaginary entity, some mere creation of the mind, not resolvable into the feelings of living beings. Women's thoughts are thus as useful in giving reality to those of thinking men, as men's thoughts in giving width and largeness to those of women. In depth, as distinguished from breadth, I greatly doubt if even now, women, compared with men, are at any disadvantage. . . .

CHAPTER IV

He who would rightly appreciate the worth of personal independence as an element of happiness, should consider the value he himself puts upon it as an ingredient of his own. There is no subject on which there is a greater habitual difference of judgment between a man judging for himself, and the same man judging for other people. When he hears others complaining that they are not allowed freedom of action—that their own will has not sufficient influence in the regulation of their affairs—his inclination is, to ask, what are their grievances? what positive damage they sustain? and in what respect they consider their affairs to be mismanaged? and if they fail to make out, in answer to these questions, what appears to him a sufficient case, he turns a deaf ear, and regards their complaint as the fanciful querulousness of people whom nothing reasonable will satisfy. But he has a quite different standard of judgment when he is deciding for himself. Then, the most unexceptionable administration of his interests by a tutor set over him, does not satisfy his feelings: his personal exclusion from the deciding authority appears itself the greatest grievance of all, rendering it superfluous even to enter into the question of mismanagement. It is the same with nations. What citizen of a free country would listen to any offers of good and skillful administration, in return for the abdication of freedom? Even if he could believe that good and skillful administration can exist among a people ruled by a will not their own, would not the consciousness of working out their own destiny under their own moral responsibility be a compensation to his feelings for great rudeness and imperfection in the details of public affairs? Let him rest assured that whatever he feels on this point, women feel in a fully equal degree. Whatever has been said or written, from the time of Herodotus to the present, of the ennobling influence of free government—the nerve and spring which it gives to all the faculties, the larger and higher objects which it presents to the intellect and feelings, the more unselfish public spirit, and calmer and broader views of duty, that it engenders, and the generally loftier platform on which it elevates the individual as a moral, spiritual, and social being—is every particle as true of women as of men. Are these things no important part of individual happiness? Let any man call to mind what he himself felt on emerging from boyhood—from the tutelage and control of even loved and affectionate elders—and entering upon the responsibilities of manhood. Was it not like the physical effect of taking off a heavy weight, or releasing him from obstructive, even if not otherwise painful, bonds? Did he not feel twice as much alive, twice as much a human being, as before? And does he imagine that women have none of these feelings? But it is a striking fact, that the satisfactions and mortifications of personal pride, though all in all to most men when the case is their own, have less allowance made for them in the case of other people, and are less listened to as a ground or a justification of conduct, than any other natural human feelings; perhaps because men compliment them in their own case with the names of so many other qualities, that they are seldom conscious how mighty an influence these feelings exercise in their own lives. No less large and powerful is their part, we may assure ourselves, in the lives and feelings of women. Women are schooled into suppressing them in their most natural and most healthy direction, but the internal principle remains, in a different outward form. An active and energetic mind, if denied liberty, will seek for power: refused the command of itself, it will assert its personality by attempting to control others. To allow to any human beings no existence of their own but what depends on others, is giving far too high a premium on bending others to their purposes. Where liberty cannot be hoped for, and power can, power becomes the grand object of human desire; those to whom others will not leave the undisturbed management of their own affairs, will compensate themselves, if they can, by meddling for their own purposes with the affairs of others. Hence also women's passion for personal beauty, and dress and display; and all the evils that flow from it, in the way of mischievous luxury and social immorality. The love of power and the love of liberty are in eternal antagonism. Where there is least liberty, the passion for power is the most ardent and unscrupulous. The desire of power over others can only cease to be a depraving agency among mankind, when each of them individually is able to do without it: which can only be where respect for liberty in the personal concerns of each is an established principle.

But it is not only through the sentiment of personal dignity, that the free direction and disposal of their own faculties is a source of individual happiness, and to be fettered and restricted in it, a source of unhappiness, to human beings, and not least to women. There is nothing, after disease, indigence, and guilt, so fatal to the pleasurable enjoyment of life as the want of a worthy outlet for the active faculties. Women who have the cares of a family, and while they have the cares of a family, have this outlet, and it generally suffices for them: but what of the greatly increasing number of women, who have had no opportunity of exercising the vocation which they are mocked by telling them is their proper one? What of the women whose children have been lost to them by death or distance, or have grown up, married, and formed homes of their own? There are abundant examples of men who, after a life engrossed by business, retire with a competency to the enjoyment, as they hope, of rest, but to whom, as they are unable to acquire new interests and excitements that can replace the old, the change to a life of inactivity brings ennui, melancholy, and premature death. Yet no one thinks of the parallel case of so many worthy and devoted women, who, having paid that they are told is their debt to society—having brought up a family blamelessly to manhood and womanhood—having kept a house as long as they had a house needing to be kept—are deserted by the sole occupation for which they have fitted themselves; and remain with undiminished activity but with no employment for it, unless perhaps a daughter or daughter-in-law is willing to abdicate in their favour the discharge of the same functions in her younger household. Surely a hard lot for the old age of those who have worthily discharged, as long as it was given to them to discharge, what the world accounts their only social duty. Of such women, and of those others to whom this duty has not been committed at all—many of whom pine through life with the consciousness of thwarted vocations, and activities which are not suffered to expand—the only resources, speaking generally, are religion and charity. But their religion, though it may be one of feeling, and of ceremonial observance, cannot be a religion of action, unless in the form of charity. For charity many of them are by nature admirably fitted; but to practise it usefully, or even without doing mischief, requires the education, the manifold preparation, the knowledge and the thinking powers, of a skillful administrator. There are few of the administrative functions of government for which a person would not be fit, who is fit to bestow charity usefully. In this as in other cases (pre-eminently in that of the education of children), the duties permitted to women cannot be performed properly, without their being trained for duties which, to the great loss of society, are not permitted to them. And here let me notice the singular way in which the question of women's disabilities is frequently presented to view, by those who find it easier to draw a ludicrous picture of what they do not like, than to answer the arguments for it. When it is suggested that women's executive capacities and prudent counsels might sometimes be found valuable in affairs of state, these lovers of fun hold up to the ridicule of the world, as sitting in parliament or in the cabinet, girls in their teens, or young wives of two or three and twenty, transported bodily, exactly as they are, from the drawing-room to the House of Commons. They forget that males are not usually selected at this early age for a seat in Parliament, or for responsible political functions. Common sense would tell them that if such trusts were confided to women, it would be to such as having no special vocation for married life, or preferring another employment of their faculties (as many women even now prefer to marriage some of the few honorable occupations within their reach), have spent the best years of their youth in attempting to qualify themselves for the pursuits in which they desire to engage; or still more frequently perhaps, widows or wives of forty or fifty, by whom the knowledge of life and faculty of government which they have acquired in their families, could by the aid of appropriate studies be made available on a less contracted scale. There is no country of Europe in which the ablest men have not frequently experienced, and keenly appreciated, the value of the advice and help of clever and experienced women of the world, in the attainment both of private and of public objects; and there are important matters of public administration to which few men are equally competent with such women; among others, the detailed control of expenditure. But what we are now discussing is not the need which society has of the services of women in public business, but the full and hopeless life to which it so often condemns them, by forbidding then to exercise the practical abilities which many of them are conscious of, in any wider field than one which to some of them never was, and to others is no longer, open. If there is anything vitally important to the happiness of human beings, it is that they should relish their habitual pursuit. This requisite of an enjoyable life is very imperfectly granted, or altogether denied, to a large part of mankind; and by its absence many a life is a failure, which is provided, in appearance, with every requisite of success. But if circumstances which society is not yet skillful enough to overcome, render such failures often for the present inevitable, society need not itself inflict them. The injudiciousness of parents, a youth's own inexperience, or the absence of external opportunities for the congenial vocation, and their presence for an uncongenial, condemn numbers of men to pass their lives in doing one thing reluctantly and ill, when there are other things which they could have done well and happily. But on women this sentence is imposed by actual law, and by customs equivalent to law. What, in unenlightened societies, colour, race, religion, or in the case of a conquered country, nationality, are to some men, sex is to all women; a peremptory exclusion from almost all honorable occupations, but either such as cannot be fulfilled by others, or such as those others do not think worthy of their acceptance. Sufferings arising from causes of this nature usually meet with so little sympathy, that few persons are aware of the great amount of unhappiness even now produced by the feeling of a wasted life. The case will be even more frequent, as increased cultivation creates a greater and greater disproportion between the ideas and faculties of women, and the scope which society allows to their activity.

When we consider the positive evil caused to the disqualified half of the human race by their disqualification—first in the loss of the most inspiriting and elevating kind of personal enjoyment, and next in the weariness, disappointment, and profound dissatisfaction with life, which are so often the substitute for it; one feels that among all the lessons which men require for carrying on the struggle against the inevitable imperfections of their lot on earth, there is no lesson which they more need, than not to add to the evils which nature inflicts, by their jealous and prejudiced restrictions on one another. Their vain fears only substitute other and worse evils for those which they are idly apprehensive of: while every restraint on the freedom of conduct of any of their human fellow creatures (otherwise than by making them responsible for any evil actually caused by it), dries up pro tanto the principal fountain of human happiness, and leaves the species less rich, to an inappreciable degree, in all that makes life valuable to the individual human being.

REVIEW QUESTIONS

1. How does Mill define utilitarianism?
2. What does Mill mean by "It is better to be a human being dissatisfied than a pig satisfied; better to be Socrates dissatisfied than a fool satisfied"?
3. According to Mill, in what ways can the experience of happiness vary?
4. In Mill's view, who is to be the judge of the desirability of different forms of pleasure?
5. What is Mill's "proof" of the truth of utilitarianism?
6. For Mill, what is the sole justification of society's interfering in the lives of its members? What are some unjustified reasons?
7. What are the areas of life covered by the principle of liberty?

27

FRIEDRICH NIETZSCHE

Friedrich Nietzsche (1844–1900) was a German philosopher who has played a major role in contemporary intellectual development. Descended through both of his parents from Christian ministers, Nietzsche was brought up in a pious German Lutheran home and was known as "the little Jesus" by his schoolmates. He studied theology at the University of Bonn and philology at Leipzig, becoming an atheist in the process. At the age of twenty-four he was appointed professor of classical philology at the University of Basel in Switzerland, where he taught for ten years until forced by ill health to retire. Eventually he became mentally ill. He died on August 25, 1900.

Nietzsche believes that the fundamental creative force that motivates all creation is the will to power. We all seek to affirm ourselves, to flourish and dominate. Since we are essentially unequal in ability, it follows that the fittest will survive and be victorious in the contest with the weaker and the baser. There is great aesthetic beauty in the noble spirit coming to fruition, but this process is hampered by Judeo-Christian morality, which Nietzsche labels "slave morality." Slave morality, which is the invention of jealous priests, envious and resentful of the power of the noble, prescribes that we give up the will to power and excellence and become meek and mild, that we believe the lie of all humans having equal worth. In our reading, Nietzsche also refers to this as the ethics of resentment.

Nietzsche's ideas of inegalitarian ethics are based on his notion of the death of God. God plays no vital role in our culture—except as a protector of the slave morality, including the idea of equal worth of all persons. If we recognize that there is no rational basis for believing in God, we will see that the whole edifice of slave morality must crumble and with it the notion of equal worth. In its place will arise the morality of the noble person based on the virtues of the high courage, discipline, and intelligence, in the pursuit of self-affirmation and excellence.

We begin with some aphorisms, then his famous description of the madman who announces the death of God (from *Joyful Wisdom*), and then to longer passages from *Beyond Good and Evil, Twilight of the Idols*, and *The Anti-Christ*.

FOR FURTHER READING

Copleston, F. C. *Friedrich Nietzsche, A Philosopher of Culture* (Barnes & Noble, 1975).
Danto, Arthur. *Nietzsche as Philosopher* (Macmillan, 1965).
Hollingdale, R. J. *Nietzsche* (Routledge & Kegan Paul, 1973).
Kaufmann, W. *Nietzsche, Philosopher, Psychologist, Anti-Christ* (Princeton University Press, 1968).
Nietzsche, Friedrich. *The Complete Works of Nietzsche*, ed. Oscar Levy (Foulis, 1910).
Nietzsche, Friedrich. *The Portable Nietzsche*, ed. Walter Kaufmann (Viking Press, 1954).
Richardson, John. *Nietzsche's System* (Oxford University Press, 1996).
Solomon, Robert C., and Kathleen M. Higgins, eds. *Reading Nietzsche* (Oxford University Press, 1988).
Stern, J. P. *A Study of Nietzsche* (Cambridge University Press, 1977).

APHORISMS

THOUGHTS ON THE MEANING OF LIFE

"Man would sooner have the Void for his purpose than be void of Purpose."

"Hegel says, 'That at the bottom of history, and particularly of world history, there is a final aim, and that this has actually been realized in it and is being realized—the plan of Providence—that there is reason in history: that is to be shown philosophically and this as altogether necessary.' [This is balderdash] My life has no aim and this is evident even from the accidental nature of its origin. That I can posit an aim for myself is another matter. But a state has no aim; we alone give it an aim."

"Whatever does not kill me makes me stronger."

TRUTH AND UNTRUTH

"A belief, however necessary it may be for the preservation of a species, has nothing to do with truth."

"The falseness of a judgment is not for us necessarily an objection to a judgment. The question is to what extent it is life-promoting, life-preserving, species preserving, perhaps even species cultivating.

To recognize untruth as a condition of life—that certainly means resisting accustomed value feelings in a dangerous way; and a philosophy that risks this would by that token alone place itself beyond good and evil." (*Beyond Good and Evil*, 4).

BEYOND GOOD AND EVIL

"To speak of right and wrong per se makes no sense at all. No act of violence, rape, exploitation, destruction, is intrinsically *unjust*, since life itself is violent, rapacious, exploitative, and destructive and cannot be conceived otherwise." (*Genealogy of Morals*, 208)

WILL TO POWER

What is good? All that enhances the feeling of power, the Will to Power, and the power itself in man. What is bad?—All that proceeds from weakness. What is happiness?—The feeling that power is increasing—that resistance has been overcome.

Not contentment, but more power; not peace at any price but war; not virtue, but competence (virtue in the Renaissance sense, *virtu*, free from moralistic acid). The first principle of our humanism: The weak and the failures shall perish. They ought even to be helped to perish.

What is more harmful than any vice?—Practical sympathy and pity for all the failures and all the weak: Christianity.

STYLE AND CHARACTER

One thing is needful.—To give style to one's character—a great and rare art! It is practiced by those who survey all the strengths and weaknesses of their nature and then fit them into an artist plan until every one of them appears as art and reason and even weaknesses delight the eye. Here a large mass of second nature has been added; there a piece of original nature has been removed—both times through long practice and daily work at it. Here the ugly that could not be removed is concealed; there it has been reinterpreted and made sublime. Much that is vague and resisted shaping has been saved and exploited for distant views. . . . In the end, when the work is finished, it becomes evident how the constraint of a single taste governed and formed everything large and small. Whether this taste was good or bad is less important than one might suppose, if only it was a single taste!

THE ÜBERMENSCH (SUPERMAN)

We immoralists make it a point of honor to be affirmers. More and more our eyes have opened to that economy which needs and knows how to utilize all that the holy witlessness of the priest, of the diseased reason of the priest, rejects—that economy in the law of life which finds an advantage even in the disgusting species of the prigs, the priests, the virtuous. What advantage? Be we ourselves, we immoralists, are the answer.

ON INTERPRETATION

Everything is Interpretation: Against positivism, which halts at phenomena—Against those who say "There are only facts," I say, "No, facts are precisely what there is not, only interpretations." We cannot establish any fact *in itself*. Perhaps it is folly to want to do such a thing.

"Everything is subjective," you say; but even here we have interpretation. The "subject" is not something given. It is something added and invented and projected behind what there is. Finally, is it necessary to posit an interpreter behind the interpretation? Even this is invention, hypothesis.

Insofar as the word "knowledge" has any meaning, the world is knowable; but it is *interpretable* otherwise. It has no meaning behind it, but countless meanings.

PERSPECTIVISM

It is our needs that interpret the world; our drives and their For and Against. Every drive is a kind of lust to rule; each one has its perspective that it would like to compel all other drives to accept as a norm.

ETERNAL RECURRENCE

What if a demon crept after thee into thy loneliness one day or night, and said to thee: "This life, as thou livest it at present, and hast lived it, thou must live it once more, and also innumerable times; and there will be nothing new in it, but every pain and every joy and every thought and every sigh, and all the unspeakably small and great in thy life must come to thee again, and all in the same series and sequence—and similarly, this spider and this moonlight among the trees, and similarly this moment and I myself. The eternal sandglass of existence will ever be turned once more, and thou with it, thou speck of dust!"

Wouldst thou not throw thyself down and gnash thy teeth, and curse the demon that so spake? Or hast thou experienced a tremendous moment in which thou wouldst answer him: "Thou art a god, and never did I hear anything so divine!"

If that thought acquired power over thee as thou art, it would transform thee, and perhaps crush thee; the question with regard to all and everything: "Dost thou want this once more, and also or innumerable times?" would lie as the heaviest burden upon thy activity. Or how wouldst thou have to become favorably inclined to thyself and to life, so as to long for nothing more ardently than for this last eternal sanctioning and sealing? (*The Gay Science,* 270–71)

JOYFUL WISDOM

THE MADMAN AND THE DEATH OF GOD

Have you ever heard of the madman who on a bright morning lighted a lantern and ran to the market-place calling out unceasingly: "I seek God! I seek God!"—As there were many people standing about who did not believe in God, he caused a great deal of amusement. Why! is he lost? said one. Has he strayed away like a child? said another. Or does he keep himself hidden? Is he afraid of us? Has he taken a sea-voyage? Has he emigrated?—the people cried out laughingly, all in a hubbub. The insane man jumped into their midst and transfixed them with his glances. "Where is God gone?" he called out. "I mean to tell you! *We have killed him,*—you and I! We are all his murderers! But how have we done it? How were we able to drink up the sea? Who gave us the sponge to wipe away the whole horizon? What did we do when we loosened this earth from its sun? Whither does it now move? Whither do we move? Away from all suns? Do we not dash on unceasingly? Backwards, sideways, forewards, in all directions? Is there still an above and below? Do we not stray, as through infinite nothingness? Does not empty space breathe upon us? Has it not become colder? Does not night come on continually, darker and darker? Shall we not have to light lanterns in the morning? Do we not hear the noise of the gravediggers who are burying God? Do we not smell the divine putrefaction?—for even Gods putrefy! God is dead! God remains dead! And we have killed him! How shall we console ourselves, the most murderous of all murderers? The holiest and the mightiest that the world has hitherto possessed, has bled to death under our knife,—who will wipe the blood from us? With what water could we cleanse ourselves? What lustrums, what sacred games shall we have to devise? Is not the magnitude of this deed too great for us? Shall we not ourselves have to become Gods, merely to seem worthy of it? There never was a greater event,—and on account of it, all who are born after us belong to a higher history than any history hitherto!"—Here the madman was silent and looked again at his hearers; they also were silent and looked at him in surprise. At last he threw his lantern on the ground, so that it broke in pieces and was extinguished. "I come too early," he then said, "I am not yet at the right time. This prodigious event is still on its way, and is traveling,—it has not yet reached men's ears. Lightning and thunder need time, the light of the stars needs time, deeds need time, even after they are done, to be seen and heard. This deed is as yet further from them than the furthest star,—*and yet they have done it!*"—It is further stated that the madman made his way into different churches on the same day, and there intoned his *Requiem aeternam deo*. When led out and called to account, he always gave the reply: "What are these churches now, if they are not the tombs and monuments of God?"— . . .

BEYOND GOOD AND EVIL

WHAT IS NOBLE?

Every elevation of the type "man," has hitherto been the work of an aristocratic society and so it will always be—a society believing in a long scale of gradations of rank and differences of worth among human beings, and requiring slavery in some form or other. Without the *pathos of distance*, such as grows out of the incarnated difference of classes, out of the constant outlooking and downlooking of the ruling caste on subordinates and instruments, and out of their equally constant practice of obeying and commanding, of keeping down and keeping at a distance—that other more mysterious pathos could never have arisen, the longing for an ever new widening of distance within the soul itself, the formation of ever higher, rarer, further, more extended, more comprehensive states, in short, just the elevation of the type "man," the continued "self-surmounting of man," to use a moral formula in a supermoral sense. To be sure, one must not resign oneself to any humanitarian illusions about the history of the origin of an aristocratic society (that is to say, of the preliminary condition for the elevation of the type "man"): the truth is hard. Let us acknowledge unprejudicedly how ever higher civilisation hitherto has *originated!* Men with a still natural nature, barbarians in every terrible sense of the word, men of prey, still in possession of unbroken strength of will and desire for power, threw themselves upon weaker, more moral, more peaceful races (perhaps trading or cattle-rearing communities), or upon old mellow civilisations in which the final vital force was flickering out in brilliant fireworks of wit and depravity. At the commencement, the noble caste was always the barbarian caste: their superiority did not consist first of all in their physical, but in their psychical power—they were more *complete* men (which at every point also implies the same as "more complete beasts").

Corruption—as the indication that anarchy threatens to break out among the instincts, and that the foundation of the emotions, called "life," is convulsed—is something radically different according to the organisation in which it manifests itself. When, for instance, an aristocracy like that of France at the beginning of the Revolution, flung away its privileges with sublime disgust and sacrificed itself to an excess of its moral sentiments, it was corruption:—it was really only the closing act of the corruption which had existed for centuries, by virtue of which that aristocracy had abdicated step by step its lordly prerogatives and lowered itself to a *function* of royalty (in the end even to its decoration and paradedress). The essential thing, however, in a good and healthy aristocracy is that it should *not* regard itself as a function either of the kingship or the commonwealth, but as the *significance* and highest justification thereof—that it should therefore accept with a good conscience the sacrifice of a legion of individuals, who, *for its sake*, must be suppressed and reduced to imperfect men, to slaves and instruments. Its fundamental belief must be precisely that society is *not* allowed to exist for its own sake, but only as a foundation and scaffolding, by means of which a select class of beings may be able to elevate themselves to their higher duties, and in general to a

higher *existence:* like those sun-seeking climbing plants in Java—they are called *Sipo Matador,*—which encircle an oak so long and so often with their arms, until at last, high above it, but supported by it, they can unfold their tops in the open light, and exhibit their happiness.

To refrain mutually from injury, from violence, from exploitation, and put one's will on a par with that of others: this may result in a certain rough sense in good conduct among individuals when the necessary conditions are given (namely, the actual similarity of the individuals in amount of force and degree of worth, and their co-relation within one organisation). As soon, however, as one wished to take this principle more generally, and if possible even as *the fundamental principle of society*, it would immediately disclose what it really is—namely, a Will to the *denial* of life, a principle of dissolution and decay. Here one must think profoundly to the very basis and resist all sentimental weakness: life itself is *essentially* appropriation, injury, conquest of the strange and weak, suppression, severity, obtrusion of peculiar forms, incorporation, and at the least, putting it mildest, exploitation;—but why should one for ever use precisely these words on which for ages a disparaging purpose has been stamped? Even the organisation within which, as was previously supposed, the individuals treat each other as equal—it takes place in every healthy aristocracy—must itself, if it be a living and not a dying organisation, do all that towards other bodies, which the individuals within it refrain from doing to each other: it will have to be the incarnated Will to Power, it will endeavour to grow, to gain ground, attract to itself and acquire ascendency—not owing to any morality or immorality, but because it *lives*, and because life *is* precisely Will to Power. On no point, however, is the ordinary consciousness of Europeans more unwilling to be corrected than on this matter; people now rave everywhere, even under the guise of science, about coming conditions of society in which "the exploiting character" is to be absent:—that sounds to my ears as if they promised to invent a mode of life which should refrain from all organic functions. "Exploitation" does not belong to a depraved, or imperfect and primitive society: it belongs to the *nature* of the living being as a primary organic function; it is a consequence of the intrinsic Will to Power, which is precisely the Will to Life.—Granting that as a theory this is a novelty—as a reality it is the *fundamental fact* of all history: let us be so far honest towards ourselves!

MASTER AND SLAVE MORALITY

In a tour through the many finer and coarser moralities which have hitherto prevailed or still prevail on the earth, I found certain traits recurring regularly together, and connected with one another, until finally two primary types revealed themselves to me, and a radical distinction was brought to light. There is *master-morality* and *slave-morality;*—I would at once add, however, that in all higher and mixed civilisations, there are also attempts at the reconciliation of the two moralities; but one finds still oftener the confusion and mutual misunderstanding of them, indeed, sometimes their close juxtaposition—even in the same man, within one soul. The distinctions of moral values have either originated in a ruling caste, pleasantly conscious of being different from the ruled—or among the ruled class, the slaves and dependents of all sorts. In the first case, when it is the rulers who determine the conception "good," it is the exalted, proud disposition which is regarded as the distinguishing feature, and that which determines the order of rank. The noble type of man separates from himself the beings in whom the opposite of this exalted, proud disposition displays itself: he despises them. Let it at once be noted that in this first kind of morality the antithesis "good" and "bad" means practically the same as "noble" and "despicable";—the antithesis "good" and "*evil*" is of a different origin. The cowardly, the timid, the insignificant, and those thinking merely of narrow utility are despised; moreover, also, the distrustful, with their constrained glances, the self-abasing, the dog-like kind of men who let themselves be abused, the mendicant flatterers, and above all the liars:—it is a fundamental belief of all aristocrats that the common people are untruthful. "We truthful ones"—the nobility in ancient Greece called themselves. It is obvious that everywhere the designations of moral value were at first applied to *men*, and were only derivatively and at a later period applied to *actions;* it is a gross mistake, therefore, when historians of morals start with

questions like, "Why have sympathetic actions been praised?" The noble type of man regards *himself* as a determiner of values; he does not require to be approved of; he passes the judgment: "What is injurious to me is injurious in itself"; he knows that it is he himself only who confers honour on things; he is a *creator of values*. He honours whatever he recognises in himself: such morality is self-glorification. In the foreground there is the feeling of plenitude, of power, which seeks to overflow, the happiness of high tension, the consciousness of a wealth which would fain give and bestow:—the noble man also helps the unfortunate, but not—or scarcely—out of pity, but rather from an impulse generated by the superabundance of power. The noble man honours in himself the powerful one, him also who has power over himself, who knows how to speak and how to keep silence, who takes pleasure in subjecting himself to severity and hardness, and has reverence for all that is severe and hard. "Wotan placed a hard heart in my breast," says an old Scandinavian Saga: it is thus rightly expressed from the soul of a proud Viking. Such a type of man is even proud of *not* being made for sympathy; the hero of the Saga therefore adds warningly: "He who has not a hard heart when young, will never have one." The noble and brave who think thus are the furthest removed from the morality which sees precisely in sympathy, or in acting for the good of others, or in *désintéressement*, the characteristic of the moral; faith in oneself, pride in oneself, a radical enmity and irony towards "selflessness," belong as definitely to noble morality, as do a careless scorn and precaution in presence of sympathy and the "warm heart."—It is the powerful who *know* how to honour, it is their art, their domain for invention. The profound reverence for age and for tradition—all law rests on this double reverence,—the belief and prejudice in favour of ancestors and unfavourable to newcomers, is typical in the morality of the powerful; and if, reversely, men of "modern ideas" believe almost instinctively in "progress" and the "future," and are more and more lacking in respect for old age, the ignoble origin of these "ideas" has complacently betrayed itself thereby. A morality of the ruling class, however, is more especially foreign and irritating to present-day taste in the sternness of its principle that one has duties only to one's equals; that one may act towards beings of a lower rank, towards all that is foreign, just as seems good to one, or "as the heart desires," and in any case "beyond good and evil": it is here that sympathy and similar sentiments can have a place. The ability and obligation to exercise prolonged gratitude and prolonged revenge—both only within the circle of equals,—artfulness in retaliation, *raffinement* of the idea in friendship, a certain necessity to have enemies (as outlets for the emotions of envy, quarrelsomeness, arrogance—in fact, in order to be a good *friend*): all these are typical characteristics of the noble morality, which, as has been pointed out, is not the morality of "modern ideas," and is therefore at present difficult to realise and also to unearth and disclose.—It is otherwise with the second type of morality, *slave-morality.* Supposing that the abused, the oppressed, the suffering, the unemancipated, the weary, and those uncertain of themselves, should moralise, what will be the common element in their moral estimates? Probably a pessimistic suspicion with regard to the entire situation of man will find expression, perhaps a condemnation of man, together with his situation. The slave has an unfavourable eye for the virtues of the powerful; he has a scepticism and distrust, a *refinement* of distrust of everything "good" that is there honoured—he would fain persuade himself that the very happiness there is not genuine. On the other hand, *those* qualities which serve to alleviate the existence of sufferers are brought into prominence and flooded with light; it is here that sympathy, the kind, helping hand, the warm heart, patience, diligence, humility, and friendliness attain to honour; for here these are the most useful qualities, and almost the only means of supporting the burden of existence. Slave-morality is essentially the morality of utility. Here is the seat of the origin of the famous antithesis "good" and "evil":—power and dangerousness are assumed to reside in the evil, a certain dreadfulness, subtlety, and strength, which do not admit of being despised. According to slave-morality, therefore, the "evil" man arouses fear; according to master-morality, it is precisely the "good" man who arouses fear and seeks to arouse it, while the bad man is regarded as the despicable being. The contrast attains its maximum when, in accordance with

the logical consequences of slave-morality, a shade of depreciation—it may be slight and well-intentioned—at last attaches itself to the "good" man of this morality; because, according to the servile mode of thought, the good man must in any case be the *safe* man: he is good-natured, easily deceived, perhaps a little stupid, *un bonhomme.* Everywhere that slave-morality gains the ascendency, language shows a tendency to approximate the significations of the words "good" and "stupid."—A last fundamental difference: the desire for *freedom,* the instinct for happiness and the refinements of the feeling of liberty belong as necessarily to slave-morals and morality, as artifice and enthusiasm in reverence and devotion are the regular symptoms of an aristocratic mode of thinking and estimating.—Hence we can understand without further detail why love *as a passion*—it is our European specialty—must absolutely be of noble origin; as is well known, its invention is due to the Provençal poet-cavaliers, those brilliant, ingenious men of the "*gai saber,*" to whom Europe owes so much, and almost owes itself. . . .

There is an *instinct for rank,* which more than anything else is already the sign of a *high* rank; there is a *delight* in the *nuances* of reverence which leads one to infer noble origin and habits. The refinement, goodness, and loftiness of a soul are put to a perilous test when something passes by that is of the highest rank, but is not yet protected by the awe of authority from obtrusive touches and incivilities: something that goes its way like a living touchstone, undistinguished, undiscovered, and tentative, perhaps voluntarily veiled and disguised. He whose task and practice it is to investigate souls, will avail himself of many varieties of this very art to determine the ultimate value of a soul, the unalterable, innate order of rank to which it belongs: he will test it by its *instinct for reverence. Différence engendre haine* [Difference engenders hate.—ED.]: the vulgarity of many a nature spurts up suddenly like dirty water, when any holy vessel, any jewel from closed shrines, any book bearing the marks of great destiny, is brought before it; while on the other hand, there is an involuntary silence, a hesitation of the eye, a cessation of all gestures, by which it is indicated that a soul *feels* the nearness of what is worthiest of respect. . . .

The revolt of the slaves in morals begins in the very principle of *resentment* becoming creative and giving birth to values—a resentment experienced by creatures who, deprived as they are of the proper outlet of action, are forced to find their compensation in an imaginary revenge. While every aristocratic morality springs from a triumphant affirmation of its own demands, the slave morality says "no" from the very outset to what is "outside itself," "different from itself," and "not itself": and this "no" is its creative deed. This reversal of the valuing standpoint—this *inevitable* gravitation to the objective instead of back to the subjective—is typical of "resentment": the slave-morality requires as the condition of its existence an external and objective world, to employ physiological terminology, it requires objective stimuli to be capable of action at all—its action is fundamentally a reaction. The contrary is the case when we come to the aristocrat's system of values: it acts and grows spontaneously, it merely seeks its antithesis in order to pronounce a more grateful and exultant "yes" to its own self;—its negative conception, "low," "vulgar," "bad," is merely a pale late-born foil in comparison with its positive and fundamental conception (saturated as it is with life and passion), of "we aristocrats, we good ones, we beautiful ones, we happy ones."

When the aristocratic morality goes astray and commits sacrilege on reality, this is limited to that particular sphere with which it is *not* sufficiently acquainted—a sphere, in fact, from the real knowledge of which it disdainfully defends itself. It misjudges, in some cases, the sphere which it despises, the sphere of the common vulgar man and the low people: on the other hand, due weight should be given to the consideration that in any case the mood of contempt, of disdain, of superciliousness, even on the supposition that it *falsely* portrays the object of its contempt, will always be far removed from that degree of falsity which will always characterise the attacks—in effigy, of course—of the vindictive hatred and revengefulness of the weak in onslaughts on their enemies. In point of fact, there is in contempt too strong an admixture of nonchalance, of casualness, of boredom, of impatience, even of personal exultation, for it to be capable of distorting its victim into a real caricature or a real monstrosity. Attention again should be paid to the almost benevolent *nuances* which, for instance, the Greek nobility imports into all the words by which it distinguishes the common people from itself; note how continuously a kind of pity, care, and consideration imparts its honeyed *flavour*, until at last almost all the words which are applied to the vulgar man survive finally as expressions for "unhappy," "worthy of pity"...—and how, conversely, "bad," "low," "unhappy" have never ceased to ring in the Greek ear with a tone in which "unhappy" is the predominant note: this is a heritage of the old noble aristocratic morality, which remains true to itself even in contempt.... The "well-born" simply *felt* themselves the "happy"; they did not have to manufacture their happiness artificially through looking at their enemies, or in cases to talk and lie themselves into happiness (as is the custom with all resentful men); and similarly, complete men as they were, exuberant with strength, and consequently *necessarily* energetic, they were too wise to dissociate happiness from action—activity becomes in their minds necessarily counted as happiness (that is the etymology of $\varepsilon\hat{\upsilon}\ \pi\rho\acute{\alpha}\tau\tau\varepsilon\iota\nu$)—all in sharp contrast to the "happiness" of the weak and the oppressed, with their festering venom and malignity, among whom happiness appears essentially as a narcotic, a deadening, a quietude, a peace, a "Sabbath," an enervation of the mind and relaxation of the limbs,—in short, a purely *passive* phenomenon. While the aristocratic man lives in confidence and openness with himself ($\gamma\varepsilon\nu$-$\nu\alpha\hat{\iota}o\varsigma$, "noble-born," emphasises the nuance "sincere," and perhaps also "naïf"), the resentful man, on the other hand, is neither sincere nor naïf, nor honest and candid with himself. His soul *squints*; his mind loves hidden crannies, tortuous paths and backdoors, everything secret appeals to him as *his* world, *his* safety, *his* balm; he is past master in silence, in not forgetting, in waiting, in provisional self-depreciation and self-abasement. A race of such *resentful* men will of necessity eventually prove more *prudent* than any aristocratic race, it will honour prudence on quite a distinct scale, as, in fact, a paramount condition of existence, while prudence among aristocratic men is apt to be tinged with a delicate flavour of luxury and refinement; so among them it plays nothing like so integral a part as that complete certainty of function of the governing *unconscious* instincts, or as indeed a certain lack of prudence, such as a vehement and valiant charge, whether against danger or the enemy, or as those ecstatic bursts of rage, love, reverence, gratitude, by which at all times noble souls have recognised each other. When the resentment of the aristocratic man manifests itself, it fulfils and exhausts itself in an immediate reaction, and consequently instills no *venom:* on the other hand, it never manifests itself at all in countless instances, when in the case of the feeble and weak it would be inevitable. An inability to take seriously for any length of time their enemies, their disasters, their *misdeeds*—that is the sign of the full strong natures who possess a superfluity of moulding plastic force, that heals completely and produces forgetfulness: a good example of this in the modern world is Mirabeau, who had no memory for any insults and meannesses which were practised on him, and who was only incapable of forgiving because he forgot. Such a man indeed shakes off with a shrug many a worm which would have buried itself in another; it is only in characters like these that we see the possibility (supposing, of course, that there is such a possibility in the world) of the real "*love* of one's enemies." What respect for his enemies is found, forsooth, in an aristocratic man—and such a reverence is already a bridge to love! He insists on having his enemy to himself as his distinction. He tolerates no other enemy but a man in whose character there is nothing to despise and *much* to honour! On the other hand, imagine the "enemy" as the resentful man conceives him—and it is here exactly that we see his work, his creativeness; he has conceived "the evil enemy," the "evil one," and indeed that is the root idea from which he now evolves as a contrasting and corresponding figure a "good one," himself—his very self!

The method of this man is quite contrary to that of the aristocratic man, who conceives the root idea "good" spontaneously and straight away, that is to say, out of himself, and from that material then creates for himself a concept of "bad"! This "bad" of aristocratic origin and that "evil" out of the cauldron of unsatisfied hatred—the former an imitation, an "extra," an additional nuance; the latter, on the other hand, the original, the beginning, the essential act in the conception of a slave-morality—these two words "bad" and "evil," how great a difference do they make, in spite of the fact that they have an identical contrary in the idea "good." But the idea "good" is *not* the same: much rather let the question be asked, "Who is really evil according to the meaning of the morality of resentment?" In all sternness let it be answered thus:—*just* the good man of the other morality, just the aristocrat, the powerful one, the one who rules, but who is distorted by the venomous eye of resentfulness, into a new colour, a new signification, a new appearance. This particular point we would be the last to deny: the man who learnt to know those "good" ones only as enemies, learnt at the same time not to know them only as "*evil enemies*," and the same men who . . . were kept so rigorously in bounds through convention, respect, custom, and gratitude, though much more through mutual vigilance and jealousy, . . . these men who in their relations with each other find so many new ways of manifesting consideration, self-control, delicacy, loyalty, pride, and friendship, these men are in reference to what is outside their circle (where the foreign element, a *foreign* country, begins), not much better than beasts of prey, which have been let loose. They enjoy their freedom from all social control, they feel that in the wilderness they can give vent with impunity to that tension which is produced by enclosure and imprisonment in the peace of society, they *revert* to the innocence of the beast-of-prey conscience, like jubilant monsters, who perhaps come from a ghostly bout of murder, arson, rape, and torture, with bravado and a moral equanimity, as though merely some wild student's prank had been played, perfectly convinced that the poets have now an ample theme to sing and celebrate. It is impossible not to recognise at the core of all these aristocratic races the beast of prey; the magnificent *blonde brute*, avidly rampant for spoil and victory; this hidden core needed an outlet from time to time, the beast must get loose again, must return into the wilderness—the Roman, Arabic, German, and

Japanese nobility, the Homeric heroes, the Scandinavian Vikings, are all alike in this need. It is the aristocratic races who have left the idea "Barbarian" on all the tracks in which they have marched; nay, a consciousness of this very barbarianism, and even a pride in it, manifests itself even in their highest civilisation (for example, when Pericles says to his Athenians in that celebrated funeral oration, "Our audacity has forced a way over every land and sea, rearing everywhere imperishable memorials of itself for *good* and for *evil*"). This audacity of aristocratic races, mad, absurd, and spasmodic as may be its expression; the incalculable and fantastic nature of their enterprises, . . . their nonchalance and contempt for safety, body, life, and comfort, their awful joy and intense delight in all destruction, in all the ecstasies of victory and cruelty,—all these features become cystallised, for those who suffered thereby in the picture of the "barbarian," of the "evil enemy," perhaps of the "Goth" and of the "Vandal." The profound, icy mistrust which the German provokes, as soon as he arrives at power,—even at the present time,—is always still an aftermath of that inextinguishable horror with which for whole centuries Europe has regarded the wrath of the blonde Teuton beast . . .

. . . One may be perfectly justified in being always afraid of the blonde beast that lies at the core of all aristocratic races, and in being on one's guard: but who would not a hundred times prefer to be afraid, when one at the same time admires, than to be immune from fear, at the cost of being perpetually obsessed with the loathsome spectacle of the distorted, the dwarfed, the stunted, the envenomed? And is that not our fate? What produces to-day our repulsion towards "man"?—for we *suffer* from "man," there is no doubt about it. It is not fear; it is rather that we have nothing more to fear from men; it is that the worm "man" is in the foreground and pullulates; it is that the "tame man," the wretched mediocre and unedifying creature, has learnt to consider himself a goal and a pinnacle, an inner meaning, an historic principle, a "higher man"; yes, it is that he has a certain right so to consider himself, in so far as he feels that in contrast to that excess of deformity, disease, exhaustion, and effeteness whose odour is beginning to pollute present-day Europe, he at any rate has achieved a relative success, he at any rate still says "yes" to life.

GOODNESS AND THE WILL TO POWER

What is good?—All that enhances the feeling of power, the Will to Power, and the power itself in man. What is bad?—All that proceeds from weakness. What is happiness?—The feeling that power is increasing—that resistance has been overcome.

Not contentment, but more power; not peace at any price but war; not virtue, but competence (virtue in the Renaissance sense, *virtu*, free from all moralistic acid). The first principle of our humanism: The weak and the failures shall perish. They ought even to be helped to perish.

What is more harmful than any vice?—Practical sympathy and pity for all the failures and all the weak: Christianity.

Christianity is the religion of pity. Pity opposes the noble passions which heighten our vitality. It has a depressing effect, depriving us of strength. As we multiply the instances of pity we gradually lose our strength of nobility. Pity makes suffering contagious and under certain conditions it may cause a total loss of life and vitality out of all proportion to the magnitude of the cause. . . . Pity is the practice of nihilism.

TWILIGHT OF THE IDOLS

MAXIMS AND MISSILES

1. Idleness is the parent of all psychology. What? Is psychology then a—vice?

2. Even the pluckiest among us has but seldom the courage of what he really knows.

3. Aristotle says that in order to live alone, a man must be either an animal or a god. The third alternative is lacking: a man must be both—a *philosopher*.

4. "All truth is simple."—Is not this a double lie?

5. Once for all I wish to be blind to many things—Wisdom sets bounds even to knowledge.

6. A man recovers best from his exceptional nature—his intellectuality—by giving his animal instincts a chance.

7. Which is it? Is man only a blunder of God? Or is God only a blunder of man?

8. *From the military school of life.*—That which does not kill me, makes me stronger.

9. Help thyself, then everyone will help thee. A principle of neighbour-love.

10. A man should not play the coward to his deeds. He should not repudiate them once he has performed them. Pangs of conscience are indecent.

11. Can a donkey be tragic?—To perish beneath a load that one can neither bear nor throw off? This is the case of the Philosopher.

12. If a man knows the wherefore of his existence, then the manner of it can take care of itself. Man does not aspire to happiness; only the Englishman does that.

13. Man created women—out of what? Out of a rib of his god,—of his "ideal."

14. What? Art thou looking for something? Thou wouldst fain multiply thyself tenfold, a hundredfold? Thou seekest followers? Seek ciphers!

15. Posthumous men, like myself, are not so well understood as men who reflect their age, but they are heard with more respect. In plain English: we are never understood—hence our authority.

16. *Among women.*—"Truth? Oh, you do not know truth! Is it not an outrage on all our *pudeurs?*"—

17. There is an artist after my own heart, modest in his needs: he really wants only two things, his bread and his art—*panem et Circen.*

18. He who knows not how to plant his will in things at least endows them with some meaning: that is to say, he believes that a will is already present in them. (A principle of faith.)

19. What? Ye chose virtue and the heaving breast, and at the same time ye squint covetously at the advantages of the unscrupulous.—But with virtue ye renounce all "advantages" . . . (to be nailed to an Antisemite's door).

20. The perfect woman perpetrates literature as if it were a petty vice: as an experiment, *en passant*, and looking about her all the while to see whether anybody is noticing her, hoping that somebody *is* noticing her.

21. One should adopt only those situations in which one is in no need of sham virtues, but rather, like the tight-rope dancer on his tight rope, in which one must either fall or stand—or escape.

22. "Evil men have no songs."[1]—How is it that the Russians have songs?

23. "German intellect"; for eighteen years this has been a *contradictio in adjecto.*

---

[1]This is a reference to Seume's poem "*Die Gesänge*," the first verse of which is:—

> "*Wo man singet, lass dich ruhig nieder,*
> *Ohne Furcht, was man im Lande glaubt;*
> *Wo man singet, wird kein Mensch beraubt:*
> *Bösewichter haben keine Lieder.*"

(Wherever people sing thou canst safely settle down without a qualm as to what the general faith of the land may be. Wherever people sing, no man is ever robbed; *rascals have no songs.*) Popular tradition, however, renders the lines thus:—

> "*Wo man singt, da lass dich ruhig nieder;*
> *Böse Menschen* [evil men] *haben keine Lieder.*"
> —TR.

24. By seeking the beginnings of things, a man becomes a crab. The historian looks backwards: in the end he also *believes* backwards.

25. Contentment preserves one even from catching cold. Has a woman who knew that she was well-dressed ever caught cold?—No, not even when she had scarcely a rag to her back.

26. I distrust all systematisers, and avoid them. The will to a system, shows a lack of honesty.

27. Man thinks woman profound—why? Because he can never fathom her depths. Woman is not even shallow.

28. When woman possesses masculine virtues, she is enough to make you run away. When she possesses no masculine virtues, she herself runs away.

29. "How often conscience had to bite in times gone by! What good teeth it must have had! And today, what is amiss?"—A dentist's question.

30. Errors of haste are seldom committed singly. The first time a man always does too much. And precisely on that account he commits a second error, and then he does too little.

31. The trodden worm curls up. This testifies to its caution. It thus reduces its chances of being trodden upon again. In the language of morality: Humility.—

32. There is such a thing as a hatred of lies and dissimulation, which is the outcome of a delicate sense of humour; there is also the selfsame hatred but as the result of cowardice, in so far as falsehood is forbidden by Divine law. Too cowardly to lie. . . .

33. What trifles constitute happiness! The sound of a bagpipe. Without music life would be a mistake. The German imagines even God as a songster.

34. *On ne peut penser et écrire qu'assis* (G. Flaubert). Here I have got you, you nihilist! A sedentary life is the real sin against the Holy Spirit. Only those thoughts that come by walking have any value.

35. There are times when we psychologists are like horses, and grow fretful. We see our own shadow rise and fall before us. The psychologist must look away from himself if he wishes to see anything at all.

36. Do we immoralists injure virtue in any way? Just as little as the anarchists injure royalty. Only since they have been shot at do princes sit firmly on their thrones once more. Moral: *morality must be shot at.*

37. Thou runnest *ahead?*—Dost thou do so as a shepherd or as an exception? A third alternative would be the fugitive. . . . First question of conscience.

38. Art thou genuine or art thou only an actor? Art thou a representative or the thing represented, itself? Finally, art thou perhaps simply a copy of an actor? . . . Second question of conscience.

39. *The disappointed man speaks:*—I sought for great men, but all I found were the apes of their ideal.

40. Art thou one who looks on, or one who puts his own shoulder to the wheel?—Or art thou one who looks away, or who turns aside? . . . Third question of conscience.

41. Wilt thou go in company, or lead, or go by thyself? . . . A man should know what he desires, and that he desires something.—Fourth question of conscience.

42. They were but rungs in my ladder, on them I made my ascent:—to that end I had to go beyond them. But they imagined that I wanted to lay myself to rest upon them.

43. What matters it whether I am acknowledged to be right! I am much too right. And he who laughs best to-day, will also laugh last.

44. The formula of my happiness: a Yea, a Nay, a straight line, a *goal.* . . .

THE PROBLEM OF SOCRATES

1. In all ages the wisest have always agreed in their judgment of life: *it is no good.* At all times and places the same words have been on their lips,—words full of doubt, full of melancholy, full of weariness of life, full of hostility to life. Even Socrates' dying words were:—"To live—means to be ill a long while: I owe a cock to the God Æsculapius." Even

Socrates had had enough of it. What does that prove? What does it point to? Formerly people would have said (—oh, it has been said, and loudly enough too; by our Pessimists loudest of all!): "In any case there must be some truth in this! The *consensus sapientium* is a proof of truth."—Shall we say the same to-day? *May* we do so? "In any case there must be some sickness here," we make reply. These great sages of all periods should first be examined more closely! Is it possible that they were, everyone of them, a little shaky on their legs, effete, rocky, decadent? Does wisdom perhaps appear on earth after the manner of a crow attracted by a slight smell of carrion?

2. This irreverent belief that the great sages were decadent types, first occurred to me precisely in regard to that case concerning which both learned and vulgar prejudice was most opposed to my view. I recognised Socrates and Plato as symptoms of decline, as instruments in the disintegration of Hellas, as pseudo-Greek, as anti-Greek ("The Birth of Tragedy," 1872). That *consensus sapientium*, as I perceived ever more and more clearly, did not in the least prove that they were right in the matter on which they agreed. It proved rather that these sages themselves must have been alike in some physiological particular, in order to assume the same negative attitude towards life—in order to be bound to assume that attitude. After all, judgments and valuations of life, whether for or against, cannot be true: their only value lies in the fact that they are symptoms; they can be considered only as symptoms,—*per se* such judgments are nonsense. You must therefore endeavour by all means to reach out and try to grasp this astonishingly subtle axiom, *that the value of life cannot be estimated.* A living man cannot do so, because he is a contending party, or rather the very object in the dispute, and not a judge; nor can a dead man estimate it—for other reasons. For a philosopher to see a problem in the value of life, is almost an objection against him, a note of interrogation set against his wisdom—a lack of wisdom. What? Is it possible that all these great sages were not only decadents, but that they were not even wise? Let me however return to the problem of Socrates.

3. To judge from his origin, Socrates belonged to the lowest of the low: Socrates was mob. You know, and you can still see it for yourself, how ugly he was.

But ugliness, which in itself is an objection, was almost a refutation among the Greeks. Was Socrates really a Greek? Ugliness is not infrequently the expression of thwarted development, or of development arrested by crossing. In other cases it appears as a decadent development. The anthropologists among the criminal specialists declare that the typical criminal is ugly: *monstrum in fronte, monstrum in animo.* But the criminal is a decadent.[1] Was Socrates a typical criminal?—At all events this would not clash with that famous physiognomist's judgment which was so repugnant to Socrates' friends. While on his way through Athens a certain foreigner who was no fool at judging by looks, told Socrates to his face that he was a monster, that his body harboured all the worst vices and passions. And Socrates replied simply: "You know me sir!"—

4. Not only are the acknowledged wildness and anarchy of Socrates' instincts indicative of decadence, but also that preponderance of the logical faculties and that malignity of the mis-shapen which was his special characteristic. Neither should we forget those aural delusions which were religiously interpreted as "the demon of Socrates." Everything in his is exaggerated, *buffo*, caricature, his nature is also full of concealment, of ulterior motives, and of underground currents. I try to understand the idiosyncrasy from which the Socratic equation:—Reason = Virtue = Happiness, could have arisen: the weirdest equation ever seen, and one which was essentially opposed to all the instincts of the older Hellenes.

5. With Socrates Greek taste veers round in favour of dialectics: what actually occurs? In the first place a noble taste is vanquished: with dialectics the mob comes to the top. Before Socrates' time, dialectical manners were avoided in good society: they were regarded as bad manners, they were compromising. Young men were cautioned against them. All such proffering of one's reasons was looked upon with suspicion. Honest things like honest men do not carry their reasons on their sleeve in such fashion. It

---

[1] It should be borne in mind that Nietzsche recognised two types of criminals,—the criminal from strength, and the criminal from weakness. This passage alludes to the latter, Aphorism 45, p. 103, alludes to the former.—Tr.

is not good form to make a show of everything. That which needs to be proved cannot be worth much. Wherever authority still belongs to good usage, wherever men do not prove but command, the dialectician is regarded as a sort of clown. People laugh at him, they do not take him seriously. Socrates was a clown who succeeded in making men take him seriously: what then was the matter?

6. A man resorts to dialectics only when he has no other means to hand. People know that they excite suspicion with it and that it is not very convincing. Nothing is more easily dispelled than a dialectical effect: this is proved by the experience of every gathering in which discussions are held. It can be only the last defence of those who have no other weapons. One must require to extort one's right, otherwise one makes no use of it. That is why the Jews were dialecticians. Reynard the Fox was a dialectician: what?—and was Socrates one as well?

7. Is the Socratic irony an expression of revolt, of mob resentment? Does Socrates, as a creature suffering under oppression, enjoy his innate ferocity in the knife-thrusts of the syllogism? Does he wreak his revenge on the noblemen he fascinates?—As a dialectician a man has a merciless instrument to wield; he can play the tyrant with it: he compromises when he conquers with it. The dialectician leaves it to his opponent to prove that he is no idiot: he infuriates, he likewise paralyses. The dialectician cripples the intellect of his opponent. Can it be that dialectics was only a form of revenge in Socrates?

8. I have given you to understand in what way Socrates was able to repel: now it is all the more necessary to explain how he fascinated.—One reason is that he discovered a new kind of *Agon*, and that he was the first fencing-master in the best circles in Athens. He fascinated by appealing to the combative instinct of the Greeks,—he introduced a variation into the contests between men and youths. Socrates was also a great erotic.

9. But Socrates divined still more. He saw right through his noble Athenians; he perceived that his case, his peculiar case, was no exception even in his time. The same kind of degeneracy was silently preparing itself everywhere: ancient Athens was dying out. And Socrates understood that the whole world needed him,—his means, his remedy, his spe-

cial artifice for self-preservation. Everywhere the instincts were in a state of anarchy; everywhere people were within an ace of excess: the *monstrum in animo* was the general danger. "The instincts would play the tyrant; we must discover a counter-tyrant who is stronger than they." On the occasion when that physiognomist had unmasked Socrates, and had told him what he was—a crater full of evil desires, the great Master of Irony let fall one or two words more, which provide the key to his nature. "This is true," he said, "but I overcame them all." How did Socrates succeed in mastering himself? His case was at bottom only the extreme and most apparent example of a state of distress which was beginning to be general: that state in which no one was able to master himself and in which the instincts turned one against the other. As the extreme example of this state, he fascinated—his terrifying ugliness made him conspicuous to every eye: it is quite obvious that he fascinated still more as a reply, as a solution, as an apparent cure of this case.

10. When a man finds it necessary, as Socrates did, to create a tyrant out of reason, there is no small danger that something else wishes to play the tyrant. Reason was then discovered as a saviour; neither Socrates nor his "patients" were at liberty to be rational or not, as they pleased; at that time it was *de rigueur*, it had become a last shift. The fanaticism with which the whole of Greek thought plunges into reason, betrays a critical condition of things: men were in danger; there were only two alternatives: either perish or else be absurdly rational. The moral bias of Greek philosophy from Plato onward, is the outcome of a pathological condition, as is also its appreciation of dialectics. Reason = Virtue = Happiness, simply means: we must imitate Socrates, and confront the dark passions permanently with the light of day—the light of reason. We must at all costs be clever, precise, clear: all yielding to the instincts, to the unconscious, leads downwards.

11. I have now explained how Socrates fascinated: he seemed to be a doctor, a Saviour. Is it necessary to expose the errors which lay in his faith in "reason at any price"?—It is a piece of self-deception on the part of philosophers and moralists to suppose that they can extricate themselves from degeneration by merely waging war upon it. They cannot

thus extricate themselves: that which they choose as a means, as the road to salvation, is in itself again only an expression of degeneration—they only modify its mode of manifesting itself: they do not abolish it. Socrates was a misunderstanding. *The whole of the morality of amelioration—that of Christianity as well—was a misunderstanding.* The most blinding light of day: reason at any price; life made clear, cold, cautious, conscious, without instincts, opposed to the instincts, was in itself only a disease, another kind of disease—and by no means a return to "virtue," to "health," and to happiness. To be obliged to fight the instincts—this is the formula of degeneration: as long as life is in the ascending line, happiness is the same as instinct.

12. —Did he understand this himself, this most intelligent of self-deceivers? Did he confess this to himself in the end, in the wisdom of his courage before death. Socrates wished to die. Not Athens, but his own hand gave him the draught of hemlock; he drove Athens to the poisoned cup. "Socrates is not a doctor," he whispered to himself, "death alone can be a doctor here. . . . Socrates himself has only been ill a long while."

"REASON" IN PHILOSOPHY

1. You ask me what all idiosyncrasy is in philosophers? . . . For instance their lack of the historical sense, their hatred even of the idea of Becoming, their Egyptianism. They imagine that they do honour to a thing by divorcing it from history *sub specie æterni,*—when they make a mummy of it. All the ideas that philosophers have treated for thousands of years, have been mummied concepts; nothing real has ever come out of their hands alive. These idolaters of concepts merely kill and stuff things when they worship,—they threaten the life of everything they adore. Death, change, age, as well as procreation and growth, are in their opinion objections,— even refutations. That which is cannot evolve; that which evolves *is* not. Now all of them believe, and even with desperation, in Being. But, as they cannot lay hold of it, they try to discover reasons why this privilege is withheld from them. "Some merely apparent quality, some deception must be the cause of

our not being able to ascertain the nature of Being: where is the deceiver?" "We have him," they cry rejoicing, "it is sensuality!" These senses, *which in other things are so immoral*, cheat us concerning the true world. Moral: we must get rid of the deception of the senses, of Becoming, of history, of falsehood.—History is nothing more than the belief in the senses, the belief in falsehood. Moral: we must say "no" to everything in which the senses believe: to all the rest of mankind: all that belongs to the "people." Let us be philosophers, mummies, monotono-theists, grave-diggers!—And above all, away with the *body,* this wretched *idée fixe* of the senses, infected with all the faults of logic that exist, refuted, even impossible, although it be impudent enough to pose as if it were real!

2. With a feeling of great reverence I except the name of *Heraclitus.* If the rest of the philosophic gang rejected the evidences of the senses, because the latter revealed a state of multifariousness and change, he rejected the same evidence because it revealed things as if they possessed permanence and unity. Even Heraclitus did an injustice to the senses. The latter lie neither as the Eleatics believed them to lie, nor as he believed them to lie,—they do not lie at all. The interpretations we give to their evidence is what first introduces falsehood into it; for instance the lie of unity, the lie of matter, of substance and of permanence. Reason is the cause of our falsifying the evidence of the senses. In so far as the senses show us a state of Becoming, of transiency, and of change, they do not lie. But in declaring that Being was an empty illusion, Heraclitus will remain eternally right. The "apparent" world is the only world: the "true world" is no more than a false adjunct thereto.

3. And what delicate instruments of observation we have in our senses! This human nose, for instance, of which no philosopher has yet spoken with reverence and gratitude, is, for the present, the most finely adjusted instrument at our disposal: it is able to register even such slight changes of movement as the spectroscope would be unable to record. Our scientific triumphs at the present day extend precisely so far as we have accepted the evidence of our senses,— as we have sharpened and armed them, and learned to follow them up to the end. What remains is abortive

and not yet science—that is to say, metaphysics, theology, psychology, epistemology, or formal science, or a doctrine of symbols, like logic and its applied form mathematics. In all these things reality does not come into consideration at all, even as a problem; just as little as does the question concerning the general value of such a convention of symbols as logic.

4. The other idiosyncrasy of philosophers is no less dangerous; it consists in confusing the last and the first things. They place that which makes its appearance last—unfortunately! for it ought not to appear at all!—the "highest concept," that is to say, the most general, the emptiest, the last cloudy streak of evaporating reality, at the beginning as the beginning. This again is only their manner of expressing their veneration: the highest thing must not have grown out of the lowest, it must not have grown at all. . . . Moral: everything of the first rank must be *causa sui*. To have been derived from something else, is as good as an objection, it sets the value of a thing in question. All superior values are of the first rank, all the highest concepts—that of Being, of the Absolute, of Goodness, of Truth, and of Perfection; all these things cannot have been evolved, they must therefore be *causa sui*. All these things cannot however be unlike one another, they cannot be opposed to one another. Thus they attain to their stupendous concept "God." The last, most attenuated and emptiest thing is postulated as the first thing, as the absolute cause, as *ens realissimum*. Fancy humanity having to take the brain diseases of morbid cobweb-spinners seriously!—And it has paid dearly for having done so.

5. —Against this let us set the different manner in which we (—you observe that I am courteous enough to say "we") conceive the problem of the error and deceptiveness of things. Formerly people regarded change and evolution in general as the proof of appearance, as a sign of the fact that something must be there that leads us astray. To-day, on the other hand, we realise that precisely as far as the rational bias forces us to postulate unity, identity, permanence, substance, cause, materiality and being, we are in a measure involved in error, driven necessarily to error; however certain we may feel, as the result of a strict examination of the matter, that the error lies here. It is just the same here as with the motion of the sun: In its case it was our eyes that were wrong; in the matter of the concepts above mentioned it is our language

itself that pleads most constantly in their favour. In its origin language belongs to an age of the most rudimentary forms of psychology: if we try to conceive of the first conditions of the metaphysics of language, *i.e.*, in plain English, of reason, we immediately find ourselves in the midst of a system of fetichism. For here, the doer and his deed are seen in all circumstances, will is believed in as a cause in general; the ego is taken for granted, the ego as Being, and as substance, and the faith in the ego as substance is projected into all things—in this way, alone, the concept "thing" is created. Being is thought into and insinuated into everything as cause; from the concept "ego," alone, can the concept "Being" proceed. At the beginning stands the tremendously fatal error of supposing the will to be something that actuates,—a faculty. Now we know that it is only a word.[1] Very much later, in a world a thousand times more enlightened, the assurance, the subjective certitude, in the handling of the categories of reason came into the minds of philosophers as a surprise. They concluded that these categories could not be derived from experience,—on the contrary, the whole of experience rather contradicts them. *Whence do they come therefore?* In India, as in Greece, the same mistake was made: "we must already once have lived in a higher world (—instead of in a much lower one, which would have been the truth!), we must have been divine, for we possess reason!" . . . Nothing indeed has exercised a more simple power of persuasion hitherto than the error of Being, as it was formulated by the Eleatics for instance: in its favour are every word and every sentence that we utter!—Even the opponents of the Eleatics succumbed to the seductive powers of their concept of Being. Among others there was Democritus in his discovery of the atom. "Reason" in language!—oh what a deceptive old witch it has been! I fear we shall never be rid of God, so long as we still believe in grammar.

6. People will feel grateful to me if I condense a point of view, which is at once so important and so new, into four theses: by this means I shall facilitate comprehension, and shall likewise challenge contradiction.

---

[1]Nietzsche here refers to the concept "free will" of the Christians; this does not mean that there is no such thing as will—that is to say a powerful determining force from within.—Tr.

Proposition One. The reasons upon which the apparent nature of "this" world have been based, rather tend to prove its reality,—any other kind of reality defies demonstration.

Proposition Two. The characteristics with which man has endowed the "true Being" of things, are the characteristics of non-Being, of *nonentity*. The "true world" has been erected upon a contradiction of the real world; and it is indeed an apparent world, seeing that it is merely a *moralo-optical* delusion.

Proposition Three. There is no sense in spinning yarns about another world, provided, of course, that we do not possess a mighty instinct which urges us to slander, belittle, and cast suspicion upon this life: in this case we should be avenging ourselves on this life with the phantasmagoria of "another," of a "better" life.

Proposition Four. To divide the world into a "true" and an "apparent" world, whether after the manner of Christianity or of Kant (after all a Christian in disguise), is only a sign of decadence,—a symptom of *degenerating* life. The fact that the artist esteems the appearance of a thing higher than reality, is no objection to this statement. For "appearance" signifies once more reality here, but in a selected, strengthened and corrected form. The tragic artist is no pessimist,—he says *Yea* to everything questionable and terrible, he is Dionysian.

HOW THE "TRUE WORLD" ULTIMATELY BECAME A FABLE

THE HISTORY OF AN ERROR

1. The true world, attainable to the sage, the pious man and the man of virtue,—he lives in it, *he is it*.

    (The most ancient form of the idea was relatively clever, simple, convincing. It was a paraphrase of the proposition "I, Plato, am the truth.")

2. The true world which is unattainable for the moment, is promised to the sage, to the pious man and to the man of virtue ("to the sinner who repents").

    (Progress of the idea: it becomes more subtle, more insidious, more evasive,—*it becomes a woman*, it becomes Christian.)

3. The true world is unattainable, it cannot be proved, it cannot promise anything; but even as a thought, alone, it is a comfort, an obligation, a command.

    (At bottom this is still the old sun; but seen through mist and scepticism: the idea has become sublime, pale, northern, Königsbergian.[2])

4. The true world—is it unattainable? At all events it is unattained. And as unattained it is also *unknown*. Consequently it no longer comforts, nor saves, nor constrains: what could something unknown constrain us to?

    (The grey of dawn. Reason stretches itself and yawns for the first time. The cock-crow of positivism.)

5. The "true world"—an idea that no longer serves any purpose, that no longer constrains one to anything,—a useless idea that has become quite superfluous, consequently an exploded idea: let us abolish it!

    (Bright daylight; breakfast; the return of common sense and of cheerfulness; Plato blushes for shame and all free-spirits kick up a shindy.)

6. We have suppressed the true world: what world survives? the apparent world perhaps? . . . Certainly not! *In abolishing the true world we have also abolished the world of appearance!*

    (Noon; the moment of the shortest shadows; the end of the longest error; mankind's zenith; *Incipit Zarathustra*.)

MORALITY AS THE ENEMY OF NATURE

1. There is a time when all passions are simply fatal in their action, when they wreck their victims with the weight of their folly,—and there is a later period, a very much later period, when they marry with the spirit, when they "spiritualise" themselves.

---

[2]Kant was a native of Königsberg and lived there all his life. Did Nietzsche know that Kant was simply a Scotch Puritan, whose family had settled in Germany?

Formerly, owing to the stupidity inherent in passion, men waged war against passion itself: men pledged themselves to annihilate it,—all ancient moral-mongers were unanimous on this point, "*il faut tuer les passions.*" The most famous formula for this stands in the New Testament, in that Sermon on the Mount, where, let it be said incidentally, things are by no means regarded *from a height*. It is said there, for instance, with an application to sexuality: "if thy eye offend thee, pluck it out": fortunately no Christian acts in obedience to this precept. To annihilate the passions and desires, simply on account of their stupidity, and to obviate the unpleasant consequences of their stupidity, seems to us to-day merely an aggravated form of stupidity. We no longer admire those dentists who extract teeth simply in order that they may not ache again. On the other hand, it will be admitted with some reason, that on the soil from which Christianity grew, the idea of the "spiritualisation of passion" could not possibly have been conceived. The early Church, as everyone knows, certainly did wage war against the "intelligent," in favour of the "poor in spirit." In these circumstances how could the passions be combated intelligently? The Church combats passion by means of excision of all kinds: its practice, its "remedy," is *castration*. It never inquires "how can a desire be spiritualised, beautified, deified?"—In all ages it has laid the weight of discipline in the process of extirpation (the extirpation of sensuality, pride, lust of dominion, lust of property, and revenge).—But to attack the passions at their roots, means attacking life itself at its source: the method of the Church is hostile to life.

2. The same means, castration and extirpation, are instinctively chosen for waging war against a passion, by those who are too weak of will, too degenerate, to impose some sort of moderation upon it; by those natures who, to speak in metaphor (—and without metaphor), need *la Trappe*, or some kind of ultimatum of war, a *gulf* set between themselves and a passion. Only degenerates find radical methods indispensable: weakness of will, or more strictly speaking, the inability not to react to a stimulus, is in itself simply another form of degeneracy. Radical and mortal hostility to sensuality, remains a suspicious symptom: it justifies one in being suspicious of the general state of one who goes to such extremes.

Moreover, that hostility and hatred reach their height only when such natures no longer possess enough strength of character to adopt the radical remedy, to renounce their inner "Satan." Look at the whole history of the priests, the philosophers, and the artists as well: the most poisonous diatribes against the senses have not been said by the impotent, nor by the ascetics; but by those impossible ascetics, by those who found it necessary to be ascetics.

3. The spiritualisation of sensuality is called *love:* it is a great triumph over Christianity. Another triumph is our spiritualisation of hostility. It consists in the fact that we are beginning to realise very profoundly the value of having enemies: in short that with them we are forced to do and to conclude precisely the reverse of what we previously did and concluded. In all ages the Church wished to annihilate its enemies: we, the immoralists and Anti-christs, see our advantage in the survival of the Church. Even in political life, hostility has now become more spiritual,—much more cautious, much more thoughtful, and much more moderate. Almost every party sees its self-preservative interests in preventing the Opposition from going to pieces; and the same applies to politics on a grand scale. A new creation, more particularly, like the new Empire, has more need of enemies than friends: only as a contrast does it begin to feel necessary, only as a contrast does it *become* necessary. And we behave in precisely the same way to the "inner enemy": in this quarter too we have spiritualised enmity, in this quarter too we have understood its value. A man is productive only in so far as he is rich in contrasted instincts; he can remain young only on condition that his soul does not begin to take things easy and to yearn for peace. Nothing has grown more alien to us than that old desire—the "peace of the soul," which is the aim of Christianity. Nothing could make us less envious than the moral cow and the plump happiness of a clean conscience. The man who has renounced war has renounced a grand life. In many cases, of course, "peace of the soul" is merely a misunderstanding,—it is something *very different* which has failed to find a more honest name for itself. Without either circumlocution or prejudice I will suggest a few cases. "Peace of the soul" may for instance be the sweet effulgence of rich animality in the realm of moral-

ity (or religion). Or the first presage of weariness, the first shadow that evening, every kind of evening, is wont to cast. Or a sign that the air is moist, and that winds are blowing up from the south. Or unconscious gratitude for a good digestion (sometimes called "brotherly love"). Or the serenity of the convalescent, on whose lips all things have a new taste, and who bides his time. Or the condition which follows upon a thorough gratification of our strongest passion, the well-being of unaccustomed satiety. Or the senility of our will, of our desires, and of our vices. Or laziness, coaxed by vanity into togging itself out in a moral garb. Or the ending of a state of long suspense and of agonising uncertainty, by a state of certainty, of even terrible certainty. Or the expression of ripeness and mastery in the midst of a task, of a creative work, of a production, of a thing willed, the calm breathing that denotes that "freedom of will" has been attained. Who knows?—maybe *The Twilight of the Idols* is only a sort of "peace of the soul."

4. I will formulate a principle. All naturalism in morality—that is to say, every sound morality is ruled by a life instinct,—any one of the laws of life is fulfilled by the definite canon "thou shalt," "thou shalt not," and any sort of obstacle or hostile element in the road of life is thus cleared away. Conversely, the morality which is antagonistic to nature—that is to say, almost every morality that has been taught, honoured and preached hitherto, is directed precisely against the life-instincts,—it is a condemnation, now secret, now blatant and impudent, of these very instincts. Inasmuch as it says "God sees into the heart of man," it says Nay to the profoundest and most superior desires of life and takes God as the enemy of life. The saint in whom God is well pleased, is the ideal eunuch. Life terminates where the "Kingdom of God" begins.

5. Admitting that you have understood the villainy of such a mutiny against life as that which has become almost sacrosanct in Christian morality, you have fortunately understood something besides; and that is the futility, the fictitiousness, the absurdity and the falseness of such a mutiny. For the condemnation of life by a living creature is after all but the symptom of a definite kind of life: the question as to whether the condemnation is justified or the re-

verse is not even raised. In order even to approach the problem of the value of life, a man would need to be placed outside life, and moreover know it as well as one, as many, as all in fact, who have lived it. These are reasons enough to prove to us that this problem is an inaccessible one to us. When we speak of values, we speak under the inspiration, and through the optics of life: life itself urges us to determine values: life itself values through us when we determine values. From which it follows that even that morality which is antagonistic to life, and which conceives God as the opposite and the condemnation of life, is only a valuation of life—of what life? of what kind of life? But I have already answered this question: it is the valuation of declining, of enfeebled, of exhausted and of condemned life. Morality, as it has been understood hitherto—as it was finally formulated by Schopenhauer in the words "The Denial of the Will to Life," is the instinct of degeneration itself, which converts itself into an imperative: it says: "Perish!" It is the death sentence of men who are already doomed.

6. Let us at last consider how exceedingly simple it is on our part to say: "Man should be thus and thus!" Reality shows us a marvellous wealth of types, and a luxuriant variety of forms and changes: and yet the first wretch of a moral loafer that comes along cries "No! Man should be different!" He even knows what man should be like, does this sanctimonious prig: he draws his own face on the wall and declares: "*ecce homo!*" But even when the moralist addresses himself only to the individual and says "thus and thus shouldst thou be!" he still makes an ass of himself. The individual in his past and future is a piece of fate, one law the more, one necessity the more for all that is to come and is to be. To say to him "change thyself," is tantamount to saying that everything should change, even backwards as well. Truly these have been consistent moralists, they wished man to be different, *i.e.*, virtuous; they wished him to be after their own image,—that is to say sanctimonious humbugs. And to this end they denied the world! No slight form of insanity! No modest form of immodesty! Morality, in so far as it condemns *per se*, and *not* out of any aim, consideration or motive of life, is a specific error, for which no one should feel any mercy, a degenerate idiosyncrasy, that has done an

unutterable amount of harm. We others, we immoralists, on the contrary, have opened our hearts wide to all kinds of comprehension, understanding and approbation.[3] We do not deny readily, we glory in saying yea to things. Our eyes have opened ever wider and wider to that economy which still employs and knows how to use to its own advantage all that which the sacred craziness of priests and the morbid reason in priests, rejects; to that economy in the law of life which draws its own advantage even out of the repulsive race of bigots, the priests and the virtuous,—what advantage?—But we ourselves, we immoralists, are the reply to this question.

THE FOUR GREAT ERRORS

1. The error of the confusion of cause and effect.—There is no more dangerous error than to confound the effect with the cause: I call this error the intrinsic perversion of reason. Nevertheless this error is one of the most ancient and most recent habits of mankind. In one part of the world it has even been canonised; and it bears the name of "Religion" and "Morality." Every postulate formulated by religion and morality contains it. Priests and the promulgators of moral laws are the promoters of this perversion of reason.—Let me give you an example. Everybody knows the book of the famous Cornaro, in which he recommends his slender diet as the recipe for a long, happy and also virtuous life. Few books have been so widely read, and to this day many thousand copies of it are still printed annually in England. I do not doubt that there is scarcely a single book (the Bible of course excepted) that has worked more mischief, shortened more lives, than this well-meant curiosity. The reason of this is the confusion of effect and cause. This worthy Italian saw the cause of his long life in his diet: whereas the prerequisites of long life, which are exceptional slowness of mo-

lecular change, and a low rate of expenditure in energy, were the cause of his meagre diet. He was not at liberty to eat a small or a great amount. His frugality was not the result of free choice, he would have been ill had he eaten more. He who does not happen to be a carp, however, is not only wise to eat well, but is also compelled to do so. A scholar of the present day, with his rapid consumption of nervous energy, would soon go to the dogs on Cornaro's diet. *Crede experto.*—

2. The most general principle lying at the root of every religion and morality, is this: "Do this and that and avoid this and that—and thou wilt be happy. Otherwise—." Every morality and every religion is this Imperative—I call it the great original sin of reason,—*immortal unreason.* In my mouth this principle is converted into its opposite—first example of my "Transvaluation of all Values": a well-constituted man, a man who is one of "Nature's lucky strokes," *must* perform certain actions and instinctively fear other actions; he introduces the element of order, of which he is the physiological manifestation, into his relations with men and things. In a formula: his virtue is the consequence of his good constitution. Longevity and plentiful offspring are not the reward of virtue, virtue itself is on the contrary that retardation of the metabolic process which, among other things, results in a long life and in plentiful offspring, in short in *Cornarism.* The Church and morality say: "A race, a people perish through vice and luxury." My reinstated reason says: when a people are going to the dogs, when they are degenerating physiologically, vice and luxury (that is to say, the need of ever stronger and more frequent stimuli such as all exhausted natures are acquainted with) are bound to result. Such and such a young man grows pale and withered prematurely. His friends say this or that illness is the cause of it. I say: the fact that he became ill, the fact that he did not resist illness, was in itself already the outcome of impoverished life, of hereditary exhaustion. The newspaper reader says: such and such a party by committing such an error will meet its death. My superior politics say: a party that can make such mistakes, is in its last agony—it no longer possesses any certainty of instinct. Every mistake is in every sense the sequel to degeneration of the instincts, to disintegration

---

[3]*Cf.* Spinoza, who says in the *Tractatus politicus* (1677), Chap. I, § 4: "*Sedulo curavi, humanas actiones non ridere, non lugere, neque detestari, sed intelligere*" ("I have carefully endeavoured not to deride, or deplore, or detest human actions, but to understand them.").—Tr.

of the will. This is almost the definition of evil, Everything valuable is instinct—and consequently easy, necessary, free. Exertion is an objection, the god is characteristically different from the hero (in my language: light feet are the first attribute of divinity).

3. The error of false causality. In all ages men have believed that they knew what a cause was: but whence did we derive this knowledge, or more accurately, this faith in the fact that we know? Out of the realm of the famous "inner facts of consciousness," not one of which has yet proved itself to be a fact. We believed ourselves to be causes even in the action of the will; we thought that in this matter at least we caught causality red-handed. No one doubted that all the *antecedentia* of an action were to be sought in consciousness, and could be discovered there—as "motive"—if only they were sought. Otherwise we should not be free to perform them, we should not have been responsible for them. Finally who would have questioned that a thought is caused? that the ego causes the thought? Of these three "facts of inner consciousness" by means of which causality seemed to be guaranteed, the first and most convincing is that of the will as cause; the conception of consciousness ("spirit") as a cause, and subsequently that of the ego (the "subject") as a cause, were merely born afterwards, once the causality of the will stood established as "given," as a fact of experience. Meanwhile we have come to our senses. To-day we no longer believe a word of all this. The "inner world" is full of phantoms and will-o'-the-wisps: the will is one of these. The will no longer actuates, consequently it no longer explains anything—all it does is to accompany processes; it may even be absent. The so-called "motive" is another error. It is merely a ripple on the surface of consciousness, a side issue of the action, which is much more likely to conceal than to reveal the *antecedentia* of the latter. And as for the ego! It has become legendary, fictional, a play upon words: it has ceased utterly and completely from thinking, feeling, and willing! What is the result of it all? There are no such things as spiritual causes. The whole of popular experience on this subject went to the devil! That is the result of it all. For we had blissfully abused that experience, we had built the world upon it as a world of causes, as a world of will, as a world of spirit. The most antiquated and most traditional psychology has been at work here, it has done nothing else: all phenomena were deeds in the light of this psychology, and all deeds were the result of will; according to it the world was a complex mechanism of agents, an agent (a "subject") lay at the root of all things. Man projected his three "inner facts of consciousness," the will, the spirit, and the ego in which he believed most firmly, outside himself. He first deduced the concept Being out of the concept Ego, he supposed "things" to exist as he did himself, according to his notion of the ego as cause. Was it to be wondered at that later on he always found in things only that which he had laid in them?—The thing itself, I repeat, the concept thing was merely a reflex of the belief in the ego as cause. And even your atom, my dear good Mechanists and Physicists, what an amount of error, of rudimentary psychology still adheres to it!—Not to speak of the "thing-in-itself," of the *horrendum pudendum* of the metaphysicians! The error of spirit regarded as a cause, confounded with reality! And made the measure of reality! And called *God!*

4. The Error of imaginary Causes. Starting out from dreamland, we find that to any definite sensation, like that produced by a distant cannon shot for instance, we are wont to ascribe a cause after the fact (very often quite a little romance in which the dreamer himself is, of course, the hero). Meanwhile the sensation becomes protracted like a sort of continuous echo, until, as it were, the instinct of causality allows it to come to the front rank, no longer however as a chance occurrence, but as a thing which has some meaning. The cannon shot presents itself in a *causal* manner, by means of an apparent reversal in the order of time. That which occurs last, the motivation, is experienced first, often with a hundred details which flash past like lightning, and the shot is the *result*. What has happened? The ideas suggested by a particular state of our senses, are misinterpreted as the cause of that state. As a matter of fact we proceed in precisely the same manner when we are awake. The greater number of our general sensations—every kind of obstacle, pressure, tension, explosion in the interplay of the organs, and more particularly the condition of the *nervus*

sympathicus—stimulate our instinct of causality: we will have a reason which will account for our feeling thus or thus,—for feeling ill or well. We are never satisfied by merely ascertaining the fact that we feel thus or thus: we admit this fact—we become conscious of it—only when we have attributed it to some kind of motivation. Memory, which, in such circumstances unconsciously becomes active, adduces former conditions of a like kind, together with the causal interpretations with which they are associated,—but not their real cause. The belief that the ideas, the accompanying processes of consciousness, have been the causes, is certainly produced by the agency of memory. And in this way we become *accustomed* to a particular interpretation of causes which, truth to tell, actually hinders and even utterly prevents the investigation of the proper cause.

5. The Psychological Explanation of the above Fact. To trace something unfamiliar back to something familiar, is at once a relief, a comfort and a satisfaction, while it also produces a feeling of power. The unfamiliar involves danger, anxiety and care,—the fundamental instinct is to get rid of these painful circumstances. First principle: any explanation is better than none at all. Since, at bottom, it is only a question of shaking one's self free from certain oppressive ideas, the means employed to this end are not selected with overmuch punctiliousness: the first idea by means of which the unfamiliar is revealed as familiar, produces a feeling of such comfort that it is "held to be true." The proof of happiness ("of power") is the criterion of truth. The instinct of causality is therefore conditioned and stimulated by the feeling of fear. Whenever possible, the question "why?" should not only educe the cause as cause, but rather a certain kind of cause— a comforting, liberating and reassuring cause. The first result of this need is that something known or already experienced, and recorded in the memory, is posited as the cause. The new factor, that which has not been experienced and which is unfamiliar, is excluded from the sphere of causes. Not only do we try to find a certain kind of explanation as the cause, but those kinds of explanations are selected and preferred which dissipate most rapidly the sensation of strangeness, novelty and unfamiliarity,—in fact the most ordinary explanations. And the result is that a

certain manner of postulating causes tends to predominate ever more and more, becomes concentrated into a system, and finally reigns supreme, to the complete exclusion of all other causes and explanations. The banker thinks immediately of business, the Christian of "sin," and the girl of her love affair. . . .

7. The Error of Free-Will. At present we no longer have any mercy upon the concept "free-will": we know only too well what it is—the most egregious theological trick that has ever existed for the purpose of making mankind "responsible" in a theological manner,—that is to say, to make mankind dependent upon theologians. I will now explain to you only the psychology of the whole process of inculcating the sense of responsibility. Wherever men try to trace responsibility home to anyone, it is the instinct of punishment and of the desire to judge which is active. Becoming is robbed of its innocence when any particular condition of things is traced to a will, to intentions and to responsible actions. The doctrine of the will was invented principally for the purpose of punishment,—that is to say, with the intention of tracing guilt. The whole of ancient psychology, or the psychology of the will, is the outcome of the fact that its originators, who were the priests at the head of ancient communities, wanted to create for themselves a right to administer punishments—or the right for God to do so. Men were thought of as "free" in order that they might be judged and punished—in order that they might be held guilty: consequently every action had to be regarded as voluntary, and the origin of every action had to be imagined as lying in consciousness (—in this way the most fundamentally fraudulent character of psychology was established as the very principle of psychology itself). Now that we have entered upon the opposite movement, now that we immoralists are trying with all our power to eliminate the concepts of guilt and punishment from the world once more, and to cleanse psychology, history, nature and all social institutions and customs of all signs of those two concepts, we recognise no more radical opponents than the theologians, who with their notion of "a moral order of things," still continue to pollute the innocence of Becoming with punishment and guilt. Christianity is the metaphysics of the hangman.

8. What then, alone, can our teaching be?—That no one gives man his qualities, neither God, society, his parents, his ancestors, nor himself (—this nonsensical idea which is at last refuted here, was taught as "intelligible freedom" by Kant, and perhaps even as early as Plato himself). No one is responsible for the fact that he exists at all, that he is constituted as he is, and that he happens to be in certain circumstances and in a particular environment. The fatality of his being cannot be divorced from the fatality of all that which has been and will be. This is not the result of an individual intention, of a will, of an aim, there is no attempt at attaining to any "ideal man," or "ideal happiness" or "ideal morality" with him,—it is absurd to wish him to be careering towards some sort of purpose. *We in*vented the concept "purpose"; in reality purpose is altogether lacking. One is necessary, one is a piece of fate, one belongs to the whole, one is in the whole,—there is nothing that could judge, measure, compare, and condemn our existence, for that would mean judging, measuring, comparing and condemning the whole. *But there is nothing outside the whole!* The fact that no one shall any longer be made responsible, that the nature of existence may not be traced to a *causa prima*, that the world is an entity neither as a sensorium nor as a spirit—*this alone is the great deliverance*,—thus alone is the innocence of Becoming restored. . . . The concept "God" has been the greatest objection to existence hitherto. . . . We deny God, we deny responsibility in God: thus alone do we save the world.—

THE ANTI-CHRIST

1. Let us look each other in the face. We are hyperboreans,—we know well enough how far outside the crowd we stand. "Thou wilt find the way to the Hyperboreans neither by land nor by water": Pindar already knew this much about us. Beyond the north, the ice, and death—*our life, our happiness.* . . . We discovered happiness; we know the way; we found the way out of thousands of years of labyrinth. Who *else* would have found it?—Not the modern man, surely?—"I do not know where I am or what I am to do; I am everything that knows not where it is or what to do,"—sighs the modern man. We were made quite ill by *this* modernity,—with its indolent peace, its cowardly compromise, and the whole of the virtuous filth of its Yea and Nay. This tolerance and *largeur de cœur* which "forgives" everything because it "understands" everything, is a Sirocco for us. We prefer to live amid ice than to be breathed upon by modern virtues and other southerly winds! . . . We were brave enough; we spared neither ourselves nor others: but we were very far from knowing whither to direct our bravery. We were becoming gloomy; people called us fatalists. *Our fate*—it was the abundance, the tension and the storing up of power. We thirsted for thunderbolts and great deeds; we kept at the most respectful distance from the joy of the weakling, from "resignation." . . . Thunder was in our air, that part of nature which we are, became overcast—*for we had no direction*. The formula of our happiness: a Yea, a Nay, a straight line, a goal.

2. What is good? All that enhances the feeling of power, the Will to Power, and power itself in man. What is bad?—All that proceeds from weakness. What is happiness?—The feeling that power is *increasing*,—that resistance has been overcome.

Not contentment, but more power; not peace at any price, but war; not virtue, but efficiency[1] (virtue in the Renaissance sense, *virt_*, free from all moralic acid). The weak and the botched shall perish: first principle of our humanity. And they ought even to be helped to perish.

What is more harmful than any vice?—Practical sympathy with all the botched and the weak—Christianity.

3. The problem I set in this work is not what will replace mankind in the order of living beings (—

---

[1]The German "Tüchtigkeit" has a nobler ring than our word "efficiency."—Tr.

Man is an *end*—); but, what type of man must be *reared*, must be *willed*, as having the highest value, as being the most worthy of life and the surest guarantee of the future.

This more valuable type has appeared often enough already: but as a happy accident, as an exception, never as *willed*. He has rather been precisely the most feared; hitherto he has been almost the terrible in itself;—and from out the very fear he provoked there arose the will to rear the type which has now been reared, *attained*: the domestic animal, the gregarious animal, the sick animal man,—the Christian.

4. Mankind does *not* represent a development towards a better, stronger or higher type, in the sense in which this is supposed to occur to-day. "Progress" is merely a modern idea—that is to say, a false idea.[2] The modern European is still far below the European of the Renaissance in value. The process of evolution does not by any means imply elevation, enhancement and increasing strength.

On the other hand isolated and individual cases are continually succeeding in different places on earth, as the outcome of the most different cultures, and in these a *higher type* certainly manifests itself: something which by the side of mankind in general, represents a kind of superman. Such lucky strokes of great success have always been possible and will perhaps always be possible. And even whole races, tribes and nations may in certain circumstances represent such *lucky strokes*.

5. We must not deck out and adorn Christianity: it has waged a deadly war upon this *higher* type of man, it has set a ban upon all the fundamental instincts of this type, and has distilled evil and the devil himself out of these instincts:—the strong man as the typical pariah, the villain. Christianity has sided with everything weak, low, and botched; it has made an ideal out of *antagonism* towards all the self-preservative instincts of strong life: it has corrupted even the reason of the strongest intellects, by teaching that the highest values of intellectuality are sinful, misleading and full of temptations. The most lamenta-

ble example of this was the corruption of Pascal, who believed in the perversion of his reason through original sin, whereas it had only been perverted by his Christianity.

6. A painful and ghastly spectacle has just risen before my eyes. I tore down the curtain which concealed mankind's *corruption*. This word in my mouth is at least secure from the suspicion that it contains a moral charge against mankind. It is—I would fain emphasise this again—free from moralic acid: to such an extent is this so, that I am most thoroughly conscious of the corruption in question precisely in those quarters in which hitherto people have aspired with most determination to "virtue" and to "godliness." As you have already surmised, I understand corruption in the sense of *decadence*. What I maintain is this, that all the values upon which mankind builds its highest hopes and desires are *decadent* values.

I call an animal, a species, an individual corrupt, when it loses its instincts, when it selects and *prefers* that which is detrimental to it. A history of the "higher feelings," of "human ideals"—and it is not impossible that I shall have to write it—would almost explain why man is so corrupt. Life itself, to my mind, is nothing more nor less than the instinct of growth, of permanence, of accumulating forces, of power: where the will to power is lacking, degeneration sets in. My contention is that all the highest values of mankind *lack* this will,—that the values of decline and of *nihilism* are exercising the sovereign power under the cover of the holiest names.

7. Christianity is called the religion of *pity*.—Pity is opposed to the tonic passions which enhance the energy of the feeling of life: its action is depressing. A man loses power when he pities. By means of pity the drain on strength which suffering itself already introduces into the world is multiplied a thousand-fold. Through pity, suffering itself becomes infectious; in certain circumstances it may lead to a total loss of life and vital energy, which is absurdly out of proportion to the magnitude of the cause (—the case of the death of the Nazarene). This is the first standpoint; but there is a still more important one. Supposing one measures pity according to the value of the reactions it usually stimulates, its danger to life appears in a much more telling light. On the whole,

---

[2]*Cf.* Disraeli: "But enlightened Europe is not happy. Its existence is a fever which it calls progress. Progress to what?" ("Tancred," Book III., Chap. vii.).—TR.

pity thwarts the law of development which is the law of selection. It preserves that which is ripe for death, it fights in favour of the disinherited and the condemned of life; thanks to the multitude of abortions of all kinds which it maintains in life, it lends life itself a sombre and questionable aspect. People have dared to call pity a virtue (—in every *noble* culture it is considered as a weakness—); people went still further, they exalted it to *the* virtue, the root and origin of all virtues,—but, of course, what must never be forgotten is the fact that this was done from the standpoint of a philosophy which was nihilistic, and on whose shield the device *The Denial of Life* was inscribed. Schopenhauer was right in this respect: by means of pity, life is denied and made *more worthy of denial*,—pity is the *praxis* of Nihilism. I repeat, this depressing and infectious instinct thwarts those instincts which aim at the preservation and enhancement of the valuelife: by *multiplying* misery quite as much as by preserving all that is miserable, it is the principal agent in promoting decadence,—pity exhorts people to nothing, to *nonentity!* But they do not say "*nonentity*," they say "Beyond," or "God," or "the true life"; or Nirvana, or Salvation, or Blessedness, instead. This innocent rhetoric, which belongs to the realm of the religio-moral idiosyncrasy, immediately appears to be *very much less innocent* if one realises what the tendency is which here tries to drape itself in the mantle of sublime expressions—the tendency of hostility to life. Schopenhauer was hostile to life: that is why he elevated pity to a virtue. . . . Aristotle, as you know, recognised in pity a morbid and dangerous state, of which it was wise to rid one's self from time to time by a purgative: he regarded tragedy as a purgative. For the sake of the instinct of life, it would certainly seem necessary to find some means of lancing any such morbid and dangerous accumulation of pity, as that which possessed Schopenhauer (and unfortunately the whole of our literary and artistic decadence as well, from St Petersburg to Paris, from Tolstoi to Wagner), if only to make it *burst.* . . . Nothing is more unhealthy in the midst of our unhealthy modernity, than Christian pity. To be doctors *here*, to be inexorable *here*, to wield the knife effectively *here*,—all this is our business, all this is *our* kind of love to our fellows, this is what makes *us* philosophers, us hyperboreans!— —

8. It is necessary to state whom we regard as our antithesis:—the theologians, and all those who have the blood of theologians in their veins—the whole of our philosophy. . . . A man must have had his very nose upon this fatality, or better still he must have experienced it in his own soul; he must almost have perished through it, in order to be unable to treat this matter lightly (—the free-spiritedness of our friends the naturalists and physiologists is, in my opinion, a *joke*,—what they lack in these questions is passion, what they lack is having suffered from these questions—). This poisoning extends much further than people think: I unearthed the "arrogant" instinct of the theologian, wherever nowadays people feel themselves idealists,—wherever, thanks to superior antecedents, they claim the right to rise above reality and to regard it with suspicion. . . . Like the priest the idealist has every grandiloquent concept in his hand (—and not only in his hand!), he wields them all with kindly contempt against the "understanding," the "senses," "honours," "decent living," "science"; he regards such things as *beneath* him, as detrimental and seductive forces, upon the face of which, "the Spirit" moves in pure absoluteness:—as if humility, chastity, poverty, in a word *holiness*, had not done incalculably more harm to life hitherto, than any sort of horror and vice. . . . Pure spirit is pure falsehood. . . . As long as the priest, the *professional* denier, calumniator and poisoner of life, is considered as the *highest* kind of man, there can be no answer to the question, what *is* truth? Truth has already been turned topsy-turvy, when the conscious advocate of nonentity and of denial passes as the representative of "truth."

9. It is upon this theological instinct that I wage war. I find traces of it everywhere. Whoever has the blood of theologians in his veins, stands from the start in a false and dishonest position to all things. The pathos which grows out of this state, is called *Faith:* that is to say, to shut one's eyes once and for all, in order not to suffer at the sight of incurable falsity. People convert this faulty view of all things into a moral, a virtue, a thing of holiness. They endow their distorted vision with a good conscience,—they claim that no *other* point of view is any longer of value, once theirs has been made sacrosanct with the names "God," "Salvation," "Eternity." I unearthed

the instinct of the theologian everywhere: it is the most universal, and actually the most subterranean form of falsity on earth. That which a theologian considers true, *must* of necessity be false: this furnishes almost the criterion of truth. It is his most profound self-preservative instinct which forbids reality ever to attain to honour in any way, or even to raise its voice. Whithersoever the influence of the theologian extends, *valuations* are topsy-turvy, and the concepts "true" and "false" have necessarily changed places: that which is most deleterious to life, is here called "true," that which enhances it, elevates it, says Yea to it, justifies it and renders it triumphant, is called "false." . . . If it should happen that theologians, *via* the "conscience" either of princes or of the people, stretch out their hand for power, let us not be in any doubt as to what results there from each time, namely:—the will to the end, the *nihilistic* will to power. . . .

10. Among Germans I am immediately understood when I say, that philosophy is ruined by the blood of theologians. The Protestant minister is the grandfather of German philosophy, Protestantism itself is the latter's *peccatum originale*. Definition of Protestantism: the partial paralysis of Christianity—and of reason. . . . One needs only to pronounce the word "Tübingen Seminary," in order to understand what German philosophy really is at bottom, *i.e.:*—theology *in disguise*. . . . The Swabians are the best liars in Germany, they lie innocently. . . . Whence came all the rejoicing with which the appearance of Kant was greeted by the scholastic world of Germany, three-quarters of which consist of clergymen's and schoolmasters' sons? Whence came the German conviction, which finds an echo even now, that Kant inaugurated a change for the *better?* The theologian's instinct in the German scholar divined what had once again been made possible. . . . A back-staircase leading into the old ideal was discovered, the concept "true world," the concept morality as the *essence* of the world (—those two most vicious errors that have ever existed!), were, thanks to a subtle and wily scepticism, once again, if not demonstrable, at least no longer *refutable*. . . . Reason, the *prerogative* of reason, does not extend so far. . . . Out of reality they had made "appearance"; and an absolutely false world—that of being—had been de-

clared to be reality. Kant's success is merely a theologian's success. Like Luther, and like Leibniz, Kant was one brake the more upon the already squeaky wheel of German uprightness.

11. One word more against Kant as a *moralist*. A virtue *must* be *our* invention, our most personal defence and need: in every other sense it is merely a danger. That which does not constitute a condition of our life, is merely harmful to it: to possess a virtue merely because one happens to respect the concept "virtue," as Kant would have us do, is pernicious. "Virtue," "Duty," "Goodness in itself," goodness stamped with the character of impersonality and universal validity—these things are mere mental hallucinations, in which decline the final devitalisation of life and Kœnigsbergian Chinadom find expression. The most fundamental laws of preservation and growth, demand precisely the reverse, namely:—that each should discover *his* own virtue, his own Categorical Imperative. A nation goes to the dogs when it confounds its concept of duty with the general concept of duty. Nothing is more profoundly, more thoroughly pernicious, than every impersonal feeling of duty, than every sacrifice to the Moloch of abstraction.—Fancy no one's having thought Kant's Categorical Imperative *dangerous to life!* . . . The instinct of the theologist alone took it under its wing!—An action stimulated by the instinct of life, is proved to be a proper action by the happiness that accompanies it: and that nihilist with the bowels of a Christian dogmatist regarded happiness as an *objection*. . . . What is there that destroys a man more speedily than to work, think, feel, as an automaton of "duty," without internal promptings, without a profound personal predilection, without joy? This is the recipe *par excellence* of decadence and even of idiocy. . . . Kant became an idiot.—And he was the contemporary of Goethe! This fatal spider was regarded as *the* German philosopher,—is still regarded as such! . . . I refrain from saying what I think of the Germans. . . . Did Kant not see in the French Revolution the transition of the State from the inorganic to the *organic* form? Did he not ask himself whether there was a single event on record which could be explained otherwise than as a moral faculty of mankind; so that by means of it, "mankind's tendency towards good," might be *proved* once and for

all? Kant's reply: "that is the Revolution." Instinct at fault in anything and everything, hostility to nature as an instinct, German decadence made into philosophy—*that is Kant!*

12. Except for a few sceptics, the respectable type in the history of philosophy, the rest do not know the very first pre-requisite of intellectual uprightness. They all behave like females, do these great enthusiasts and animal prodigies,—they regard "beautiful feelings" themselves as arguments, the "heaving breast" as the bellows of divinity, and conviction as the *criterion* of truth. In the end, even Kant, with "Teutonic" innocence, tried to dress this lack of intellectual conscience up in a scientific garb by means of the concept "practical reason." He deliberately invented a kind of reason which at times would allow one to dispense with reason, that is to say when "morality," when the sublime command "thou shalt," makes itself heard. When one remembers that in almost all nations the philosopher is only a further development of the priestly type, this heirloom of priesthood, this *fraud towards one's self*, no longer surprises one. When a man has a holy lifetask, as for instance to improve, save, or deliver mankind, when a man bears God in his breast, and is the mouthpiece of imperatives from another world,—with such a mission he stands beyond the pale of all merely reasonable valuations. He is even sanctified by such a taste, and is already the type of a higher order! What does a priest care about science! He stands too high for that!—And until now the priest has *ruled!*—He it was who determined the concept "true and false."

13. Do not let us undervalue the fact that we *ourselves*, we free spirits, are already a "transvaluation of all values," an incarnate declaration of war against all the old concepts "true" and "untrue" and of a triumph over them. The most valuable standpoints are always the last to be found: but the most valuable standpoints are the methods. All the methods and the first principles of our modern scientific procedure, had for years to encounter the profoundest contempt: association with them meant exclusion from the society of decent people—one was regarded as an "enemy of God," as a scoffer at truth and as "one possessed." With one's scientific nature, one belonged to the Chandala. We have had the whole feeling of

mankind against us; hitherto their notion of that which ought to be truth, of that which ought to serve the purpose of truth: every "thou shalt," has been directed against us. . . . Our objects, our practices, our calm, cautious distrustful manner—everything about us seemed to them absolutely despicable and beneath contempt. After all, it might be asked with some justice, whether the thing which kept mankind blindfolded so long, was not an aesthetic taste: what they demanded of truth was a *picturesque* effect, and from the man of science what they expected was that he should make a forcible appeal to their senses. It was our *modesty* which ran counter to their taste so long . . . And oh! how well they guessed this, did these divine turkey-cocks!—

14. We have altered our standpoint. In every respect we have become more modest. We no longer derive man from the "spirit," and from the "godhead"; we have thrust him back among the beasts. We regard him as the strongest animal, because he is the craftiest: one of the results thereof is his intellectuality. On the other hand we guard against the vain pretension, which even here would fain assert itself: that man is the great *arri_re pens_e* of organic evolution! He is by no means the crown of creation; beside him, every other creature stands at the same stage of perfection. . . . And even in asserting this we go a little too far; for, relatively speaking, man is the most botched and diseased of animals, and he has wandered furthest from his instincts. Be all this as it may, he is certainly the most *interesting!* As regards animals, Descartes was the first, with really admirable daring, to venture the thought that the beast was *machina,* and the whole of our physiology is endeavouring to prove this proposition. Moreover, logically we do not set man apart, as Descartes did: the extent to which man is understood to-day goes only so far as he has been understood mechanistically. Formerly man was given "free will," as his dowry from a higher sphere; nowadays we have robbed him even of will, in view of the fact that no such faculty is any longer known. The only purpose served by the old word "will," is to designate a result, a sort of individual reaction which necessarily follows upon a host of partly discordant and partly harmonious stimuli:—the will no longer "effects" or "moves" anything. . . . Formerly people thought that man's con-

sciousness, his "spirit," was a proof of his lofty origin, of his divinity. With the idea of perfecting man, he was conjured to draw his senses inside himself, after the manner of the tortoise, to cut off all relations with terrestrial things, and to divest himself of his mortal shell. Then the most important thing about him, the "pure spirit," would remain over. Even concerning these things we have improved our standpoint. Consciousness, "spirit," now seems to us rather a symptom of relative imperfection in the organism, as an experiment, a groping, a misapprehension, an affliction which absorbs an unnecessary quantity of nervous energy. We deny that anything can be done perfectly so long as it is done consciously. "Pure spirit" is a piece of "pure stupidity": if we discount the nervous system, the senses and the "mortal shell," we have miscalculated—that it is all! . . .

15. In Christianity, neither morality nor religion comes in touch at all with reality. Nothing but imaginary *causes* (God, the soul, the ego, spirit, free will—or even non-free will); nothing but imaginary *effects* (sin, salvation, grace, punishment, forgiveness of sins). Imaginary beings are supposed to have intercourse (God, spirits, souls); imaginary Natural History (anthropocentric: total lack of the notion "natural causes"); an imaginary *psychology* (nothing but misunderstandings of self, interpretations of pleasant or unpleasant general feelings; for instance of the states of the *nervus sympathicus*, with the help of the sign language of a religio-moral idiosyncrasy,—repentance, pangs of conscience, the temptation of the devil, the presence of God); an imaginary teleology (the Kingdom of God, the Last Judgment, Everlasting Life).—This purely fictitious world distinguishes itself very unfavourably from the world of dreams: the latter *reflects* reality, whereas the former falsifies, depreciates and denies it. Once the concept "nature" was taken to mean the opposite of the concept God, the word "natural" had to acquire the meaning of abominable,—the whole of that fictitious world takes its root in the hatred of nature (—reality!—), it is the expression of profound discomfiture in the presence of reality. . . . *But this explains everything.* What is the only kind of man who has reasons for wriggling out of reality by lies? The man who suffers from reality. But in order to suffer

from reality one must be a bungled portion of it. The preponderance of pain over pleasure is the *cause* of that fictitious morality and religion: but any such preponderance furnishes the formula for decadence.

16. A criticism of the Christian concept of God inevitably leads to the same conclusion.—A nation that still believes in itself, also has its own God. In him it honours the conditions which enable it to remain uppermost,—that is to say, its virtues. It projects its joy over itself, its feeling of power, into a being, to whom it can be thankful for such things. He who is rich, will give of his riches: a proud people requires a God, unto whom it can *sacrifice* things. . . . Religion, when restricted to these principles, is a form of gratitude. A man is grateful for his own existence; for this he must have a God.—Such a God must be able to benefit and to injure him, he must be able to act the friend and the foe. He must be esteemed for his good as well as for his evil qualities. The monstrous castration of a God by making him a God only of goodness, would lie beyond the pale of the desires of such a community. The evil God is just as urgently needed as the good God: for a people in such a form of society certainly does not owe its existence to toleration and humaneness. . . . What would be the good of a God who knew nothing of anger, revenge, envy, scorn, craft, and violence?— who had perhaps never experienced the rapturous *ardeurs* of victory and of annihilation? No one would understand such a God: why should one possess him?—Of course, when a people is on the road to ruin; when it feels its belief in a future, its hope of freedom vanishing for ever; when it becomes conscious of submission as the most useful quality, and of the virtues of the submissive as self-preservative measures, then its God must also modify himself. He then becomes a tremulous and unassuming sneak; he counsels "peace of the soul," the cessation of all hatred, leniency and "love" even towards friend and foe. He is for ever moralising, he crawls into the heart of every private virtue, becomes a God for everybody, he retires from active service and becomes a Cosmopolitan. . . . Formerly he represented a people, the strength of a people, everything aggressive and desirous of power lying concealed in the heart of a nation: now he is merely the good God. . . . In very truth Gods have no other alterna-

tive, they are *either* the Will to Power—in which case they are always the Gods of whole nations,—or, on the other hand, the incapacity for power—in which case they necessarily become good.

17. Wherever the Will to Power, no matter in what form, begins to decline, a physiological retrogression, decadence, always supervenes. The godhead of *decadence*, shorn of its masculine virtues and passions is perforce converted into the God of the physiologically degraded, of the weak. Of course they do not call themselves the weak, they call themselves "the good." . . . No hint will be necessary to help you to understand at what moment in history the dualistic fiction of a good and an evil God first became possible. With the same instinct by which the subjugated reduce their God to "Goodness in itself," they also cancel the good qualities from their conquerer's God; they avenge themselves on their masters by diabolising the latter's God.—The *good God* and the devil as well:—both the abortions of decadence.—How is it possible that we are still so indulgent towards the simplicity of Christian theologians to-day, as to declare with them that the evolution of the concept God, from the "God of Israel," the God of a people, to the Christian God, the quintessence of all goodness, marks a *step forward?*—But even Renan does this. As if Renan had a right to simplicity! Why the very contrary stares one in the face. When the pre-requisites of *ascending* life, when everything strong, plucky, masterful and proud has been eliminated from the concept of God, and step by step he has sunk down to the symbol of a staff for the weary, of a last straw for all those who are drowning; when he becomes the pauper's God, the sinner's God, the sick man's God *par excellence*, and the attribute "Saviour," "Redeemer," remains *over* as the one essential attribute of divinity: what does such a metamorphosis, such an abasement of the godhead imply?—Undoubtedly, "the kingdom of God" has thus become larger. Formerly all he had was his people, his "chosen" people. Since then he has gone travelling over foreign lands, just as his people have done; since then he has never rested anywhere: until one day he felt at home everywhere, the Great Cosmopolitan,—until he got the "greatest number," and half the world on his side. But the God of the "greatest number," the democrat among gods, did not become a proud heathen god notwithstanding: he remained a Jew, he remained the God of the back streets, the God of all dark corners and hovels, of all the unwholesome quarters of the world! . . . His universal empire is now as ever a netherworld empire, an infirmary, a subterranean empire, a ghetto-empire. . . . And he himself is so pale, so weak, so decadent. . . . Even the palest of the pale were able to master him—our friends the metaphysicians, those albinos of thought. They spun their webs around him so long that ultimately he was hypnotised by their movements and himself became a spider, a metaphysician. Thenceforward he once more began spinning the world out of his inner being—*sub specie Spinozæ,*—thenceforward he transfigured himself into something ever thinner and ever more anaemic, became "ideal," became "pure spirit," became "*absolutum,*" and "thing-in-itself." . . . *The decline and fall of a god:* God became the "thing-in-itself.". . .

REVIEW QUESTIONS

1. For Nietzsche, how is Judeo-Christian morality a hindrance to the will to power? Why does he call this ethic "slave morality"?
2. What point is Nietzsche trying to make with the parable of the death of God?
3. According to Nietzsche, what is the first principle of humanism?
4. Why does Nietzsche say that morality is the enemy of nature? Why does he think that the church is hostile to life?
5. What are the four great errors?

Part Four

THE

CONTEMPORARY

PERIOD

28

CHARLES SANDERS PEIRCE

Charles Sanders Peirce (1839–1914), born in Cambridge, the son of a Harvard University mathematician, was a scientist and philosopher. He received his M.A. in mathematics and chemistry, and worked for three years at the Harvard astronomical observatory. From 1861 to 1891 he was associated with the U.S. Coastal and Geodetic Survey. He also lectured at Johns Hopkins University but was never a permanent member of the faculty. Although he deplored the popularization of his thought by William James, James was a loyal friend who introduced Peirce's theories to the intellectual public. Peirce is primarily known for having identified a third type of reasoning in addition to the two standard forms, deduction and induction, which he named "abduction," and which has subsequently been known as reasoning to the best explanation. He is also the father of *pragmatism* (from the Greek word *pragma*, meaning act or deed), which emphasizes the practical nature of philosophy.

In the 1870s Peirce published a series in *Popular Science Monthly*, one of which was "The Fixation of Belief," which is reprinted next. The essay argues that the function of coming to believe something is to relieve the disturbance of uncertainty and doubt. He distinguishes four ways of coming to a settled belief about some issue or subject matter: the methods of tenacity, authority, natural preferences, and science, the method that Peirce prefers.

FOR FURTHER READING

Ayer, A. J. *Origins of Pragmatism: Studies in the Philosophy of Charles Sanders Peirce and William James* (Macmillan, 1968).
Kuklick, Bruce. *The Rise of American Philosophy* (Yale University Press, 1977).
Murphy, John. *Pragmatism: From Peirce to Davidson* (Westview Press, 1990).

Peirce, C. S. *Essays in the Philosophy of Science* (Liberal Arts Library, 1957).
Quine, W. V., and Joseph Ullian. *The Web of Belief*, 2nd ed. (Random House, 1978).
Scheffler, Israel. *Four Pragmatists* (Humanities Press, 1974).
Smith, John. *The Spirit of American Philosophy* (Oxford University Press, 1963).

THE FIXATION OF BELIEF

1. SCIENCE AND LOGIC

358. Few persons care to study logic, because everybody conceives himself to be proficient enough in the art of reasoning already. But I observe that this satisfaction is limited to one's own ratiocination, and does not extend to that of other men.

359. We come to the full possession of our power of drawing inferences, the last of all our faculties; for it is not so much a natural gift as a long and difficult art. The history of its practice would make a grand subject for a book. The medieval schoolman, following the Romans, made logic the earliest of a boy's studies after grammar, as being very easy. So it was as they understood it. Its fundamental principle, according to them, was, that all knowledge rests either on authority or reason; but that whatever is deduced by reason depends ultimately on a premiss derived from authority. Accordingly, as soon as a boy was perfect in the syllogistic procedure, his intellectual kit of tools was held to be complete.

360. To Roger Bacon, that remarkable mind who in the middle of the thirteenth century was almost a scientific man, the schoolmen's conception of reasoning appeared only an obstacle to truth. He saw that experience alone teaches anything—a proposition which to us seems easy to understand, because a distinct conception of experience has been handed down to us from former generations; which to him likewise seemed perfectly clear, because its difficulties had not yet unfolded themselves. Of all kinds of experience, the best, he thought, was interior illumination, which teaches many things about Nature which the external senses could never discover, such as the transubstantiation of bread.

361. Four centuries later, the more celebrated Bacon, in the first book of his *Novum Organum*, gave his clear account of experience as something which must be open to verification and reëxamination. But, superior as Lord Bacon's conception is to earlier notions, a modern reader who is not in awe of his grandiloquence is chiefly struck by the inadequacy of his view of scientific procedure. That we have only to make some crude experiments, to draw up briefs of the results in certain blank forms, to go through these by rule, checking off everything disproved and setting down the alternatives, and that thus in a few years physical science would be finished up—what an idea! "He wrote on science like a Lord Chancellor," indeed, as Harvey, a genuine man of science said.

362. The early scientists, Copernicus, Tycho Brahe, Kepler, Galileo, Harvey, and Gilbert, had methods more like those of their modern brethren. Kepler undertook to draw a curve through the places of Mars, and to state the times occupied by the planet in describing the different parts of that curve; but perhaps his greatest service to science was in impressing on men's minds that this was the thing to be done if they wished to improve astronomy; that they were not to content themselves with inquiring whether one system of epicycles was better than another but that they were to sit down to the figures and find out what the curve, in truth, was. He accomplished this by his incomparable energy and courage, blundering along in the most inconceivable way (to us), from one irrational hypothesis to another, until, after trying twenty-two of these, he fell, by the mere exhaustion of his invention, upon the orbit which a mind well furnished with the weapons of modern logic would have tried almost at the outset.

363. In the same way, every work of science great enough to be well remembered for a few generations affords some exemplification of the defective state of the art of reasoning of the time when it was written; and each chief step in science has been a lesson in logic. It was so when Lavoisier and his contempo-

raries took up the study of Chemistry. The old chemist's maxim had been, "Lege, lege, lege, labora, ore, et relege." Lavoisier's method was not to read and pray, but to dream that some long and complicated chemical process would have a certain effect, to put it into practice with dull patience, after its inevitable failure, to dream that with some modification it would have another result, and to end by publishing the last dream as a fact: his way was to carry his mind into his laboratory, and literally to make of his alembics and cucurbits instruments of thought, giving a new conception of reasoning as something which was to be done with one's eyes open, in manipulating real things instead of words and fancies.

364. The Darwinian controversy is, in large part, a question of logic. Mr. Darwin proposed to apply the statistical method to biology. The same thing has been done in a widely different branch of science, the theory of gases. Though unable to say what the movements of any particular molecule of gas would be on a certain hypothesis regarding the constitution of this class of bodies, Clausius and Maxwell were yet able, eight years before the publication of Darwin's immortal work, by the application of the doctrine of probabilities, to predict that in the long run such and such a proportion of the molecules would, under given circumstances, acquire such and such velocities; that there would take place, every second, such and such a relative number of collisions, etc.; and from these propositions were able to deduce certain properties of gases, especially in regard to their heat-relations. In like manner, Darwin, while unable to say what the operation of variation and natural selection in any individual case will be, demonstrates that in the long run they will, or would, adapt animals to their circumstances. Whether or not existing animal forms are due to such action, or what position the theory ought to take, forms the subject of a discussion in which questions of fact and questions of logic are curiously interlaced.

2. GUIDING PRINCIPLES

365. The object of reasoning is to find out, from the consideration of what we already know, something else which we do not know. Consequently, reasoning is good if it be such as to give a true con-

clusion from true premises, and not otherwise. Thus, the question of validity is purely one of fact and not of thinking. A being the facts stated in the premises and B being that concluded, the question is, whether these facts are really so related that if A were B would generally be. If so, the inference is valid; if not, not. It is not in the least the question whether, when the premises are accepted by the mind, we feel an impulse to accept the conclusion also. It is true that we do generally reason correctly by nature. But that is an accident; the true conclusion would remain true if we had no impulse to accept it; and the false one would remain false, though we could not resist the tendency to believe in it.

366. We are, doubtless, in the main logical animals, but we are not perfectly so. Most of us, for example, are naturally more sanguine and hopeful than logic would justify. We seem to be so constituted that in the absence of any facts to go upon we are happy and selfsatisfied; so that the effect of experience is continually to contract our hopes and aspirations. Yet a lifetime of the application of this corrective does not usually eradicate our sanguine disposition. Where hope is unchecked by any experience, it is likely that our optimism is extravagant. Logicality in regard to practical matters (if this be understood, not in the old sense, but as consisting in a wise union of security with fruitfulness of reasoning) is the most useful quality an animal can possess, and might, therefore, result from the action of natural selection; but outside of these it is probably of more advantage to the animal to have his mind filled with pleasing and encouraging visions, independently of their truth; and thus, upon unpractical subjects, natural selection might occasion a fallacious tendency of thought.

367. That which determines us, from given premises, to draw one inference rather than another, is some habit of mind, whether it be constitutional or acquired. The habit is good or otherwise, according as it produces true conclusions from true premises or not; and an inference is regarded as valid or not, without reference to the truth or falsity of its conclusion specially, but according as the habit which determines it is such as to produce true conclusions in general or not. The particular habit of mind which governs this or that inference may be formulated in

a proposition whose truth depends on the validity of the inferences which the habit determines; and such a formula is called a *guiding principle* of inference. Suppose, for example, that we observe that a rotating disk of copper quickly comes to rest when placed between the poles of a magnet, and we infer that this will happen with every disk of copper. The guiding principle is, that what is true of one piece of copper is true of another. Such a guiding principle with regard to copper would be much safer than with regard to many other substances—brass, for example.

368. A book might be written to signalize all the most important of these guiding principles of reasoning. It would probably be, we must confess, of no service to a person whose thought is directed wholly to practical subjects, and whose activity moves along thoroughly-beaten paths. The problems that present themselves to such a mind are matters of routine which he has learned once for all to handle in learning his business. But let a man venture into an unfamiliar field, or where his results are not continually checked by experience, and all history shows that the most masculine intellect will ofttimes lose his orientation and waste his efforts in directions which bring him no nearer to his goal, or even carry him entirely astray. He is like a ship in the open sea, with no one on board who understands the rules of navigation. And in such a case some general study of the guiding principles of reasoning would be sure to be found useful.

369. The subject could hardly be treated, however, without being first limited; since almost any fact may serve as a guiding principle. But it so happens that there exists a division among facts, such that in one class are all those which are absolutely essential as guiding principles, while in the others are all which have any other interest as objects of research. This division is between those which are necessarily taken for granted in asking why a certain conclusion is thought to follow from certain premises, and those which are not implied in such a question. A moment's thought will show that a variety of facts are already assumed when the logical question is first asked. It is implied, for instance, that there are such states of mind as doubt and belief—that a passage from one to the other is possible, the object of thought remaining the same, and that this transition is subject to some rules by which all minds are alike bound. As

these are facts which we must already know before we can have any clear conception of reasoning at all, it cannot be supposed to be any longer of much interest to inquire into their truth or falsity. On the other hand, it is easy to believe that those rules of reasoning which are deduced from the very idea of the process are the ones which are the most essential; and, indeed, that so long as it conforms to these it will, at least, not lead to false conclusions from true premises. In point of fact, the importance of what may be deduced from the assumptions involved in the logical question turns out to be greater than might be supposed, and this for reasons which it is difficult to exhibit at the outset. The only one which I shall here mention is, that conceptions which are really products of logical reflection, without being readily seen to be so, mingle with our ordinary thoughts, and are frequently the causes of great confusion. This is the case, for example, with the conception of quality. A quality, as such, is never an object of observation. We can see that a thing is blue or green, but the quality of being blue and the quality of being green are not things which we see; they are products of logical reflections. The truth is, that common-sense, or thought as it first emerges above the level of the narrowly practical, is deeply imbued with that bad logical quality to which the epithet *metaphysical* is commonly applied; and nothing can clear it up but a severe course of logic.

3. DOUBT AND BELIEF

370. We generally know when we wish to ask a question and when we wish to pronounce a judgment, for there is a dissimilarity between the sensation of doubting and that of believing.

371. But this is not all which distinguishes doubt from belief. There is a practical difference. Our beliefs guide our desires and shape our actions. The Assassins, or followers of the Old Man of the Mountain, used to rush into death at his least command, because they believed that obedience to him would insure everlasting felicity. Had they doubted this, they would not have acted as they did. So it is with every belief, according to its degree. The feeling of believing is a more or less sure indication of there being established

in our nature some habit which will determine our actions. Doubt never has such an effect.

372. Nor must we overlook a third point of difference. Doubt is an uneasy and dissatisfied state from which we struggle to free ourselves and pass into the state of belief; while the latter is a calm and satisfactory state which we do not wish to avoid, or to change to a belief in anything else. On the contrary, we cling tenaciously, not merely to believing, but to believing just what we do believe.

373. Thus, both doubt and belief have positive effects upon us, though very different ones. Belief does not make us act at once, but puts us into such a condition that we shall behave in some certain way, when the occasion arises. Doubt has not the least such active effect, but stimulates us to inquiry until it is destroyed. This reminds us of the irritation of a nerve and the reflex action produced thereby; while for the analogue of belief, in the nervous system, we must look to what are called nervous associations— for example, to that habit of the nerves in consequence of which the smell of a peach will make the mouth water.

4. THE END OF INQUIRY

374. The irritation of doubt causes a struggle to attain a state of belief. I shall term this struggle *Inquiry*, though it must be admitted that this is sometimes not a very apt designation.

375. The irritation of doubt is the only immediate motive for the struggle to attain belief. It is certainly best for us that our beliefs should be such as may truly guide our actions so as to satisfy our desires; and this reflection will make us reject every belief which does not seem to have been so formed as to insure this result. But it will only do so by creating a doubt in the place of that belief. With the doubt, therefore, the struggle begins, and with the cessation of doubt it ends. Hence, the sole object of inquiry is the settlement of opinion. We may fancy that this is not enough for us, and that we seek, not merely an opinion, but a true opinion. But put this fancy to the test, and it proves groundless; for as soon as a firm belief is reached we are entirely satisfied, whether the belief be true or false. And it is clear

that nothing out of the sphere of our knowledge can be our object, for nothing which does not affect the mind can be the motive for mental effort. The most that can be maintained is, that we seek for a belief that we shall *think* to be true. But we think each one of our beliefs to be true, and, indeed, it is mere tautology to say so.

That the settlement of opinion is the sole end of inquiry is a very important proposition. It sweeps away, at once, various vague and erroneous conceptions of proof. A few of these may be noticed here.

376.

1. Some philosophers have imagined that to start an inquiry it was only necessary to utter a question whether orally or by setting it down on paper, and have even recommended us to begin our studies with questioning everything! But the mere putting of a proposition into the interrogative form does not stimulate the mind to any struggle after belief. There must be a real and living doubt, and without this all discussion is idle.

2. It is a very common idea that a demonstration must rest on some ultimate and absolutely indubitable propositions. These, according to one school, are first principles of a general nature; according to another, are first sensations. But, in point of fact, an inquiry, to have that completely satisfactory result called demonstration, has only to start with propositions perfectly free from all actual doubt. If the premisses are not in fact doubted at all, they cannot be more satisfactory than they are.

3. Some people seem to love to argue a point after all the world is fully convinced of it. But no further advance can be made. When doubt ceases, mental action on the subject comes to an end; and, if it did go on, it would be without a purpose.

5. METHODS OF FIXING BELIEF

377. If the settlement of opinion is the sole object of inquiry, and if belief is of the nature of a habit, why should we not attain the desired end, by taking as answer to a question any we may fancy, and con-

stantly reiterating it to ourselves, dwelling on all which may conduce to that belief, and learning to turn with contempt and hatred from anything that might disturb it? This simple and direct method is really pursued by many men. I remember once being entreated not to read a certain newspaper lest it might change my opinion upon free-trade. "Lest I might be entrapped by its fallacies and misstatements," was the form of expression. "You are not," my friend said, "a special student of political economy. You might, therefore, easily be deceived by fallacious arguments upon the subject. You might, then, if you read this paper, be led to believe in protection. But you admit that free-trade is the true doctrine; and you do not wish to believe what is not true." I have often known this system to be deliberately adopted. Still oftener, the instinctive dislike of an undecided state of mind, exaggerated into a vague dread of doubt, makes men cling spasmodically to the views they already take. The man feels that, if he only holds to his belief without wavering, it will be entirely satisfactory. Nor can it be denied that a steady and immovable faith yields great peace of mind. It may, indeed, give rise to inconveniences, as if a man should resolutely continue to believe that fire would not burn him, or that he would be eternally damned if he received his *ingesta* otherwise than through a stomach-pump. But then the man who adopts this method will not allow that its inconveniences are greater than its advantages. He will say, "I hold steadfastly to the truth, and the truth is always wholesome." And in many cases it may very well be that the pleasure he derives from his calm faith overbalances any inconveniences resulting from its deceptive character. Thus, if it be true that death is annihilation, then the man who believes that he will certainly go straight to heaven when he dies, provided he have fulfilled certain simple observances in this life, has a cheap pleasure which will not be followed by the least disappointment. A similar consideration seems to have weight with many persons in religious topics, for we frequently hear it said, "Oh, I could not believe so-and-so, because I should be wretched if I did." When an ostrich buries its head in the sand as danger approaches, it very likely takes the happiest course. It hides the danger, and then calmly says there is no danger, and, if it

feels perfectly sure there is none, why should it raise its head to see? A man may go through life, systematically keeping out of view all that might cause a change in his opinions, and if he only succeeds—basing his method, as he does, on two fundamental psychological laws—I do not see what can be said against his doing so. It would be an egotistical impertinence to object that his procedure is irrational, for that only amounts to saying that his method of settling belief is not ours. He does not propose to himself to be rational, and, indeed, will often talk with scorn of man's weak and illusive reason. So let him think as he pleases.

378. But this method of fixing belief, which may be called the method of tenacity, "will be unable to hold its ground in practice." The social impulse is against it. The man who adopts it will find that other men think differently from him, and it will be apt to occur to him, in some saner moment, that their opinions are quite as good as his own, and this will shake his confidence in his belief. This conception, that another man's thought or sentiment may be equivalent to one's own, is a distinctly new step, and a highly important one. It arises from an impulse too strong in man to be suppressed, without danger of destroying the human species. Unless we make ourselves hermits, we shall necessarily influence each other's opinions; so that the problem becomes how to fix belief, not in the individual merely, but in the community.

379. Let the will of the state act, then, instead of that of the individual. Let an institution be created which shall have for its object to keep correct doctrines before the attention of the people, to reiterate them perpetually, and to teach them to the young; having at the same time power to prevent contrary doctrines from being taught, advocated, or expressed. Let all possible causes of a change of mind be removed from men's apprehensions. Let them be kept ignorant, lest they should learn of some reason to think otherwise than they do. Let their passions be enlisted, so that they may regard private and unusual opinions with hatred and horror. Then, let all men who reject the established belief be terrified into silence. Let the people turn out and tar-and-feather such men, or let inquisitions be made into the manner of thinking of suspected persons, and when they

are found guilty of forbidden beliefs, let them be subjected to some signal punishment. When complete agreement could not otherwise be reached, a general massacre of all who have not thought in a certain way has proved a very effective means of settling opinion in a country. If the power to do this be wanting, let a list of opinions be drawn up, to which no man of the least independence of thought can assent, and let the faithful be required to accept all these propositions, in order to segregate them as radically as possible from the influence of the rest of the world.

This method has, from the earliest times, been one of the chief means of upholding correct theological and political doctrines, and of preserving their universal or catholic character. In Rome, especially, it has been practiced from the days of Numa Pompilius to those of Pius Nonus. This is the most perfect example in history; but wherever there is a priesthood—and no religion has been without one—this method has been more or less made use of. Wherever there is an aristocracy, or a guild, or any association of a class of men whose interests depend, or are supposed to depend, on certain propositions, there will be inevitably found some traces of this natural product of social feeling. Cruelties always accompany this system; and when it is consistently carried out, they become atrocities of the most horrible kind in the eyes of any rational man. Nor should this occasion surprise, for the officer of a society does not feel justified in surrendering the interests of that society for the sake of mercy, as he might his own private interests. It is natural, therefore, that sympathy and fellowship should thus produce a most ruthless power.

380. In judging this method of fixing belief, which may be called the method of authority, we must, in the first place, allow its immeasurable mental and moral superiority to the method of tenacity. Its success is proportionately greater; and, in fact, it has over and over again worked the most majestic results. The mere structures of stone which it has caused to be put together—in Siam, for example, in Egypt, and in Europe—have many of them a sublimity hardly more than rivaled by the greatest works of Nature. And, except the geological epochs, there are no periods of time so vast as those which are measured by some of these organized faiths. If we scrutinize the matter closely, we shall find that there has not been one of their creeds which has remained always the same; yet the change is so slow as to be imperceptible during one person's life, so that individual belief remains sensibly fixed. For the mass of mankind, then, there is perhaps no better method than this. If it is their highest impulse to be intellectual slaves, then slaves they ought to remain.

381. But no institution can undertake to regulate opinions upon every subject. Only the most important ones can be attended to, and on the rest men's minds must be left to the action of natural causes. This imperfection will be no source of weakness so long as men are in such a state of culture that one opinion does not influence another—that is, so long as they cannot put two and two together. But in the most priest-ridden states some individuals will be found who are raised above that condition. These men possess a wider sort of social feeling; they see that men in other countries and in other ages have held to very different doctrines from those which they themselves have been brought up to believe; and they cannot help seeing that it is the mere accident of their having been taught as they have, and of their having been surrounded with the manners and associations they have, that has caused them to believe as they do and not far differently. Nor can their candour resist the reflection that there is no reason to rate their own views at a higher value than those of other nations and other centuries; thus giving rise to doubts in their minds.

382. They will further perceive that such doubts as these must exist in their minds with reference to every belief which seems to be determined by the caprice either of themselves or of those who originated the popular opinions. The willful adherence to a belief, and the arbitrary forcing of it upon others, must, therefore, both be given up. A different new method of settling opinions must be adopted, that shall not only produce an impulse to believe, but shall also decide what proposition it is which is to be believed. Let the action of natural preferences be unimpeded, then, and under their influence let men, conversing together and regarding matters in different lights, gradually develop beliefs in harmony with natural causes. This method resembles that by which

conceptions of art have been brought to maturity. The most perfect example of it is to be found in the history of metaphysical philosophy. Systems of this sort have not usually rested upon any observed facts, at least not in any great degree. They have been chiefly adopted because their fundamental propositions seemed "agreeable to reason." This is an apt expression; it does not mean that which agrees with experience, but that which we find ourselves inclined to believe. Plato, for example, finds it agreeable to reason that the distances of the celestial spheres from one another should be proportional to the different lengths of strings which produce harmonious chords. Many philosophers have been led to their main conclusions by considerations like this; but this is the lowest and least developed form which the method takes, for it is clear that another man might find Kepler's theory, that the celestial spheres are proportional to the inscribed and circumscribed spheres of the different regular solids, more agreeable to *his* reason. But the shock of opinions will soon lead men to rest on preferences of a far more universal nature. Take, for example, the doctrine that man only acts selfishly—that is, from the consideration that acting in one way will afford him more pleasure than acting in another. This rests on no fact in the world, but it has had a wide acceptance as being the only reasonable theory.

383. This method is far more intellectual and respectable from the point of view of reason than either of the others which we have noticed. Indeed, as long as no better method can be applied, it ought to be followed, since it is then the expression of instinct which must be the ultimate cause of belief in all cases. But its failure has been the most manifest. It makes of inquiry something similar to the development of taste; but taste, unfortunately, is always more or less a matter of fashion, and accordingly metaphysicians have never come to any fixed agreement, but the pendulum has swung backward and forward between a more material and a more spiritual philosophy, from the earliest times to the latest. And so from this, which has been called the *a priori* method, we are driven, in Lord Bacon's phrase, to a true induction. We have examined into this *a priori* method as something which promised to deliver our opinions from their accidental and capricious element.

But development, while it's a process which eliminates the effect of some casual circumstances, only magnifies that of others. This method, therefore, does not differ in a very essential way from that of authority. The government may not have lifted its finger to influence my convictions; I may have been left outwardly quite free to choose, we will say, between monogamy and polygamy, and, appealing to my conscience only, I may have concluded that the latter practice is in itself licentious. But when I come to see that the chief obstacle to the spread of Christianity among a people of as high culture as the Hindoos has been a conviction of the immorality of our way of treating women, I cannot help seeing that, though governments do not interfere, sentiments in their development will be very greatly determined by accidental causes. Now, there are some people, among whom I must suppose that my reader is to be found, who, when they see that any belief of theirs is determined by any circumstance extraneous to the facts, will from that moment not merely admit in words that that belief is doubtful, but will experience a real doubt of it, so that it ceases in some degree at least to be a belief.

384. To satisfy our doubts, therefore, it is necessary that a method should be found by which our beliefs may be determined by nothing human, but by some external permanency—by something upon which our thinking has no effect. Some mystics imagine that they have such a method in a private inspiration from on high. But that is only a form of the method of tenacity, in which the conception of truth as something public is not yet developed. Our external permanency would not be external, in our sense, if it was restricted in its influence to one individual. It must be something which affects, or might affect, every man. And, though these affections are necessarily as various as are individual conditions, yet the method must be such that the ultimate conclusion of every man shall be the same. Such is the method of science. Its fundamental hypothesis, restated in more familiar language, is this: There are Real things, whose characters are entirely independent of our opinions about them; those Reals affect our senses according to regular laws, and, though our sensations are as different as are our relations to the objects, yet, by taking advantage of the

laws of perception, we can ascertain by reasoning how things really and truly are; and any man, if he have sufficient experience and he reason enough about it, will be led to the one True conclusion. The new conception here involved is that of Reality. It may be asked how I know that there are any Reals. If this hypothesis is the sole support of my method of inquiry, my method of inquiry must not be used to support my hypothesis. The reply is this: 1. If investigation cannot be regarded as proving that there are Real things, it at least does not lead to a contrary conclusion; but the method and the conception on which it is based remain ever in harmony. No doubts of the method, therefore, necessarily arise from its practice, as is the case with all the others. 2. The feeling which gives rise to any method of fixing belief is a dissatisfaction at two repugnant propositions. But here already is a vague concession that there is some *one* thing which a proposition should represent. Nobody, therefore, can really doubt that there are Reals, for, if he did, doubt would not be a source of dissatisfaction. The hypothesis, therefore, is one which every mind admits. So that the social impulse does not cause men to doubt it. 3. Everybody uses the scientific method about a great many things, and only ceases to use it when he does not know how to apply it. 4. Experience of the method has not led us to doubt it, but, on the contrary, scientific investigation has had the most wonderful triumphs in the way of settling opinion. These afford the explanation of my not doubting the method or the hypothesis which it supposes; and not having any doubt, nor believing that anybody else whom I could influence has, it would be the merest babble for me to say more about it. If there be anybody with a living doubt upon the subject, let him consider it.

385. To describe the method of scientific investigation is the object of this series of papers. At present I have only room to notice some points of contrast between it and other methods of fixing belief.

This is the only one of the four methods which presents any distinction of a right and a wrong way. If I adopt the method of tenacity, and shut myself out from all influences, whatever I think necessary to doing this, is necessary according to that method. So with the method of authority: the state may try to put down heresy by means which, from a scientific

point of view, seem very ill—calculated to accomplish its purposes; but the only test *on that method* is what the state thinks; so that it cannot pursue the method wrongly. So with the *a priori* method. The very essence of it is to think as one is inclined to think. All metaphysicians will be sure to do that, however they may be inclined to judge each other to be perversely wrong. The Hegelian system recognizes every natural tendency of thought as logical, although it be certain to be abolished by countertendencies. Hegel thinks there is a regular system in the succession of these tendencies, in consequence of which, after drifting one way and the other for a long time, opinion will at last go right. And it is true that metaphysicians do get the right ideas at last; Hegel's system of Nature represents tolerably the science of his day; and one may be sure that whatever scientific investigation shall have put out of doubt will presently receive *a priori* demonstration on the part of the metaphysicians. But with the scientific method the case is different. I may start with known and observed facts to proceed to the unknown; and yet the rules which I follow in doing so may not be such as investigation would approve. The test of whether I am truly following the method is not an immediate appeal to my feelings and purposes, but, on the contrary, itself involves the application of the method. Hence it is that bad reasoning as well as good reasoning is possible; and this fact is the foundation of the practical side of logic.

386. It is not to be supposed that the first three methods of settling opinion present no advantage whatever over the scientific method. On the contrary, each has some peculiar convenience of its own. The *a priori* method is distinguished for its comfortable conclusions. It is the nature of the process to adopt whatever belief we are inclined to, and there are certain flatteries to the vanity of man which we all believe by nature, until we are awakened from our pleasing dream by rough facts. The method of authority will always govern the mass of mankind; and those who wield the various forms of organized force in the state will never be convinced that dangerous reasoning ought not to be suppressed in some way. If liberty of speech is to be untrammeled from the grosser forms of constraint, then uniformity of opinion will be secured by a moral terrorism to which

the respectability of society will give its thorough approval. Following the method of authority is the path of peace. Certain non-conformities are permitted; certain others (considered unsafe) are forbidden. These are different in different countries and in different ages; but, wherever you are, let it be known that you seriously hold a tabooed belief, and you may be perfectly sure of being treated with a cruelty less brutal but more refined than hunting you like a wolf. Thus, the greatest intellectual benefactors of mankind have never dared, and dare not now, to utter the whole of their thought; and thus a shade of *prima facie* doubt is cast upon every proposition which is considered essential to the security of society. Singularly enough, the persecution does not all come from without; but a man torments himself and is oftentimes most distressed at finding himself believing propositions which he has been brought up to regard with aversion. The peaceful and sympathetic man will, therefore, find it hard to resist the temptation to submit his opinions to authority. But most of all I admire the method of tenacity for its strength, simplicity, and directness. Men who pursue it are distinguished for their decision of character, which becomes very easy with such a mental rule. They do not waste time in trying to make up their minds what they want, but, fastening like lightning upon whatever alternative comes first, they hold to it to the end, whatever happens, without an instant's irresolution. This is one of the splendid qualities which generally accompany brilliant, unlasting success. It is impossible not to envy the man who can dismiss reason, although we know how it must turn out at last

387. Such are the advantages which the other methods of settling opinion have over scientific investigation. A man should consider well of them; and then he should consider that, after all, he wishes his opinions to coincide with the fact, and that there is no reason why the results of those three first methods should do so. To bring about this effect is the prerogative of the method of science. Upon such considerations he has to make his choice—a choice which is far more than the adoption of any intellectual opinion, which is one of the ruling decisions of his life, to which, when once made, he is bound to

adhere. The force of habit will sometimes cause a man to hold on to old beliefs, after he is in a condition to see that they have no sound basis. But reflection upon the state of the case will overcome these habits, and he ought to allow reflection its full weight. People sometimes shrink from doing this, having an idea that beliefs are wholesome which they cannot help feeling rest on nothing. But let such persons suppose an analogous though different case from their own. Let them ask themselves what they would say to a reformed Mussulman who should hesitate to give up his old notions in regard to the relations of the sexes; or to a reformed Catholic who should still shrink from reading the Bible. Would they not say that these persons ought to consider the matter fully, and clearly understand the new doctrine, and then ought to embrace it, in its entirety? But, above all, let it be considered that what is more wholesome than any particular belief is integrity of belief, and that to avoid looking into the support of any belief from a fear that it may turn out rotten is quite as immoral as it is disadvantageous. The person who confesses that there is such a thing as truth, which is distinguished from falsehood simply by this, that if acted on it should, on full consideration, carry us to the point we aim at and not astray, and then, though convinced of this, dares not know the truth and seeks to avoid it, is in a sorry state of mind indeed.

Yes, the other methods do have their merits: a clear logical conscience does cost something—just as any virtue, just as all that we cherish, costs us dear. But we should not desire it to be otherwise. The genius of a man's logical method should be loved and reverenced as his bride, whom he has chosen from all the world. He need not contemn the others; on the contrary, he may honor them deeply, and in doing so he only honors her the more. But she is the one that he has chosen, and he knows that he was right in making that choice. And having made it, he will work and fight for her, and will not complain that there are blows to take, hoping that there may be as many and as hard to give, and will strive to be the worthy knight and champion of her from the blaze of whose splendors he draws his inspiration and his courage.

REVIEW QUESTIONS

1. What is the method of fixing belief that Peirce calls the method of tenacity? What is the method of authority? What are the disadvantages of these two methods?
2. How does the method of science differ from other methods of fixing belief? What does Peirce mean by the method of science being the only one "which presents any distinction of a right and a wrong way"?
3. What does Peirce mean by "what is more wholesome than any particular belief is integrity of belief"?
4. What is the object of reasoning? When is reasoning good?
5. What is the a priori method? What are its drawbacks?

29

WILLIAM JAMES

William James (1842–1910) was an American philosopher and psychologist, born in New York City and educated at Harvard, the brother of Henry James, the novelist. James struggled through much of his life with ill heath. He studied science, medicine, and philosophy in France and Germany, earning a medical degree from Harvard in 1869, where he taught as a psychology instructor. In 1890 he published *Principles of Psychology*, a compendious textbook in experimental psychology. But his interests were more philosophical than scientific, so eventually he moved into the philosophy department at Harvard, where he taught for many years. Throughout his early years, he was assailed by doubts over freedom of the will and the existence of God and developed the philosophy of pragmatism, in part as a response to these difficulties. Pragmatism originated with James's friend Charles Peirce (Chapter 28) but underwent crucial changes and popularization in the hands of James. James wrote: "The whole function of philosophy ought to be to find out what definite difference it will make to you and me, at definite instants of our life, if this world-formula or that world-formula be the true one."

His principal works are *The Will to Believe* (1897), reprinted here; *The Varieties of Religious Experience* (1902); *Pragmatism, A New Name for Some Old Ways of Thinking* (1907), from which a selection is taken; and *Essays in Radical Empiricism* (1912).

In our first reading, *The Will to Believe*, James argues that life would be greatly impoverished if we confined our beliefs to such a Scrooge-like epistemology as W. K. Clifford proposes: "It is wrong always, everywhere, and for anyone, to believe anything upon insufficient evidence." In everyday life, where the evidence for important propositions is often unclear, we must live by faith or cease to act at all. While we may not make leaps of faith just anywhere, sometimes practical considerations force us to make a decision regarding propositions which do not have their true value written on their faces. "Belief" is defined as a live, momentous, optional hypothesis, on which we cannot avoid a decision, for not to choose is, in effect, to choose against the hypothesis. James claims that religion may be such an optional hypothesis for many people, and where it is, the individual has the right to believe the better story rather than the worse. To do so, one must will to believe what the evidence alone is inadequate to support.

The second reading is from *Pragmatism*. After a brief introduction to Pragmatism by way of a fascinating example of resolving a dispute about the correct characterization of a squirrel's behavior, James sets forth his view of truth. He holds that truth is dynamic rather that static and is to be defined in terms of beliefs that are useful or satisfying. Unlike the "intellectualists" (James's characterization of the traditional static approaches to the question of truth, viz., the correspondence theorists) truth is in process, still becoming, and changing. Yesterday's truth is today's falsehood, and today's truth is tomorrow's half-truth. What really matters is what you can *do* with an idea, what difference it makes to your life, its cash-value. His famous definition of truth is this: " 'The true' . . . is only the expedient in the way of our thinking, just as 'the right' is only the expedient in the way of our behaving" (by 'expedient' James means prudent or suitable to achieve success). Philosophers have debated the significance of this statement, especially what James meant by the phrase that truth is expedient "in the long run and on the whole." Bertrand Russell will present a radically different view (see Chapter 30).

FOR FURTHER READING

Ayer, A. J. *Origins of Pragmatism: Studies in the Philosophy of Charles Sanders Peirce and William James* (Macmillan, 1968).

James, William. *Pragmatism* (Longmans, Green & Co., 1907).

Kuklick, Bruce. *The Rise of American Philosophy* (Yale University Press, 1977).

McDermott, John, ed. *The Writings of William James* (Random House, 1967).

Murphy, John. *Pragmatism: From Peirce to Davidson* (Westview Press, 1990).

Myers, G. E. *William James: His Life and Thought* (Yale University Press, 1986).

Perry, R. B. *The Thought and Character of William James*, 2 vols. (Harper, 1935).

Quine, W. V., and Joseph Ullian. *The Web of Belief*, 2nd ed. (Random House, 1978).

Scheffler, Israel. *Four Pragmatists* (Humanities Press, 1974).

Smith, John. *The Spirit of American Philosophy* (Oxford University Press, 1963).

Wild, John. *The Radical Empiricism of William James* (Greenwood Press, 1980).

THE WILL TO BELIEVE

I

Let us give the name of hypothesis to anything that may be proposed to our belief; and just as the electricians speak of live and dead wires, let us speak of any hypothesis as either *live* or *dead*. A live hypothesis is one which appeals as a real possibility to him to whom it is proposed. If I ask you to believe in the Mahdi, the notion makes no electric connection with your nature—it refuses to scintillate with any credibility at all. As an hypothesis it is completely dead. To an Arab, however (even if he be not one of the Madhi's followers), the hypothesis is among the mind's possibilities: It is alive. This shows that deadness and liveness in an hypothesis are not intrinsic properties, but relations to the individual thinker. They are measured by his willingness to act. The maximum of liveness in an hypothesis means willingness to act irrevocably. Practically, that means belief; but there is some believing tendency wherever there is willingness to act at all.

Next, let us call the decision between two hypotheses an *option*. Options may be of several kinds. They may be first, *living* or *dead;* secondly, *forced* or *avoidable;* thirdly, *momentous* or *trivial;* and for our purposes we may call an option a *genuine* option when it is of the forced, living, and momentous kind.

1. A living option is one in which both hypotheses are live ones. If I say to you: "Be a theosophist or be a Mohammedan," it is probably a dead option, because for you neither hypothesis is likely to be alive. But if I say: "Be an agnostic or be a Christian," it is otherwise: trained as you are, each hypothesis makes some appeal, however small, to your belief.

2. Next, if I say to you: "Choose between going out with your umbrella or without it," I do not offer you a genuine option, for it is not forced. You can easily avoid it by not going out at all. Similarly, if I say, "Either love me or hate me," "Either call my theory true or call it false," your option is avoidable. You may remain indifferent to me, neither loving nor hating, and you may decline to offer any judgment as to my theory. But if I say, "Either accept this truth or go without it," I put on you a forced option, for there is no standing place outside of the alternative. Every dilemma based on a complete logical disjunction, with no possibility of not choosing, is an option of this forced kind.

3. Finally, if I were Dr. Nansen and proposed to you to join my North Pole expedition, your option would be momentous; for this would probably be your similar opportunity, and your choice now would either exclude you from the North Pole sort of immortality altogether or put at least the chance of it into your hands. He who refuses to embrace a unique opportunity loses the prize as surely as if he tried and failed. *Per contra*, the option is trivial when the opportunity is not unique, when the stake is insignificant, or when the decision is reversible if it later prove unwise. Such trivial options abound in the scientific life. A chemist finds an hypothesis live enough to spend a year in its verification: he believes in it to that extent. But if his experiments prove inconclusive either way, he is quit for his loss of time, no vital harm being done.

It will facilitate our discussion if we keep all these distinctions well in mind.

II

The next matter to consider is the actual psychology of human opinion. When we look at certain facts, it seems as if our passional and volitional nature lay at the root of all our convictions. When we look at others, it seems as if they could do nothing when the intellect had once said its say. Let us take the latter facts up first.

Does it not seem preposterous on the very face of it to talk of our opinions being modifiable at will? Can our will either help or hinder our intellect in its perceptions of truth? Can we, by just willing it, believe that Abraham Lincoln's existence is a myth, and that the portraits of him in *McClure's Magazine* are all of some one else? Can we, by any effort of our will, or by any strength of wish that it were true, believe ourselves well and about when we are roaring with rheumatism in bed, or feel certain that the sum of the two one-dollar bills in our pocket must be a hundred dollars? We can *say* any of these things, but we are absolutely impotent to believe them; and of just such things is the whole fabric of the truths that we do believe in made up—matters of fact, immediate or remote, as Hume said, and relations between ideas, which are either there or not there for us if we see them so, and which if not there cannot be put there by any action of our own.

In Pascal's *Thoughts* there is a celebrated passage known in literature as Pascal's wager. In it he tries to force us into Christianity by reasoning as if our concern with truth resembled our concern with the stakes in a game of chance. Translated freely his words are these: You must either believe or not believe that God is—which will you do? Your human reason cannot say. A game is going on between you and the nature of things which at the day of judgment will bring out either heads or tails. Weigh what your gains and your losses would be if you should stake all you have on heads, or God's existence: if you win in such case, you gain eternal beatitude; if you lose, you lose nothing at all. If there were an infinity of chances, and only one for God in this wager, still you ought to stake your all on God; for though you surely risk a finite loss by this procedure, any finite loss is reasonable, even a certain one is reasonable, if there is but the possibility of infinite gain. Go, then, and take holy water, and have masses said; belief will come and stupefy your scruples. . . . Why should you not? At bottom, what have you to lose?

You probably feel that when religious faith expresses itself thus, in the language of the gamingtable, it is put to its last trumps. Surely Pascal's own personal belief in masses and holy water had far other springs; and this celebrated page of his is but an argument for others, a last desperate snatch at a weapon against the hardness of the unbelieving heart. We feel that a faith in masses and holy water adopted wilfully after such a mechanical calculation would lack the inner soul of faith's reality; and if we were ourselves in the place of the Deity, we should probably take particular pleasure in cutting off believers of this pattern from their infinite reward. It is evident that unless there be some preexisting tendency to believe in masses and holy water, the option offered to the will by Pascal is not a living option. Certainly no Turk ever took to masses and holy water on its account; and even to us Protestants these means of salvation seem such foregone impossibilities that Pascal's logic, invoked for them specifically, leaves us unmoved. As well might the Mahdi write to us, saying, "I am the Expected One whom God has created in his effulgence. You shall be infinitely happy if you confess me; otherwise you shall be cut off from the light of the sun. Weigh, then, your infinite gain if I am genuine against your finite sacrifice if I am not!" His logic would be that of Pascal; but he would vainly use it on us, for the hypothesis he offers us is dead. No tendency to act on it exists in us to any degree.

The talk of believing by our volition seems, then, from one point of view, simply silly. From another point of view it is worse than silly, it is vile. When one turns to the magnificent edifice of the physical sciences, and sees how it was reared; what thousands of disinterested moral lives of men lie buried in its mere foundations; what patience and postponement, what choking down of preference, what submission to the icy laws of outer fact are wrought into its very stones and mortar; how absolutely impersonal it stands in its vast augustness—then how besotted and contemptible seems every little sentimentalist who comes blowing his voluntary smoke-wreaths, and pretending to decide things from out of his private dream! Can we wonder if those bred in the rugged and manly school of science should feel like spewing such subjectivism out of their mouths? The whole system of loyalties which grow up in the schools of science go dead against its toleration; so that it is only natural that those who have caught the scientific fever should pass over to the opposite extreme, and write sometimes as if the incorruptibly truthful intellect ought positively to prefer bitterness and unacceptableness to the heart in its cup.

It fortifies my soul to know
That though I perish, Truth is so

sings Clough, while Huxley exclaims: "My only consolation lies in the reflection that, however bad our posterity may become, so far as they hold by the plain rule of not pretending to believe what they have no reason to believe, because it may be to their advantage so to pretend [the word 'pretend' is surely here redundant], they will not have reached the lowest depth of immorality." And that delicious *enfant terrible* Clifford writes: "Belief is desecrated when given to unproved and unquestioned statements for the solace and private pleasure of the believer. . . . Whoso would deserve well of his fellows in this matter will guard the purity of his belief with a very fanaticism of jealous care, lest at any time it should rest on an unworthy object, and catch a stain which can never be wiped away. . . . If [a] belief has been accepted on insufficient evidence [even though the belief be true, as Clifford on the same page explains] the pleasure is a stolen one. . . . It is sinful because it is stolen in defiance of our duty to mankind. That duty is to guard ourselves from such beliefs as from a pestilence which may shortly master our own body and then spread to the rest of the town. . . . It is wrong always, everywhere, and for every one, to believe anything upon insufficient evidence."

III

All this strikes one as healthy, even when expressed, as by Clifford, with somewhat too much of robustious pathos in the voice. Free will and simple wishing do seem, in the matter of our credences, to be only fifth wheels to the coach. Yet if any one should thereupon assume that intellectual insight is what remains after wish and will and sentimental preference have taken wing, or that pure reason is what then settles our opinions, he would fly quite as directly in the teeth of the facts.

It is only our already dead hypotheses that our willing nature is unable to bring to life again. But what has made them dead for us is for the most part a previous action of our willing nature of an antagonistic kind. When I say "willing nature," I do not mean only such deliberate volitions as may have set up habits of belief that we cannot now escape from—I mean all such factors of belief as fear and hope, prejudice and passion, imitation and partisanship, the circumpressure of our caste and set. As a matter of fact we find ourselves believing, we hardly know how or why. Mr. Balfour gives the name of "authority" to all those influences, born of the intellectual climate, that make hypotheses possible or impossible for us, alive or dead. Here in this room, we all of us believe in molecules and the conservation of energy, in democracy and necessary progress, in Protestant Christianity and the duty of fighting for "the doctrine of the immortal Monroe," all for no reasons worthy of the name. We see into these matters with no more inner clearness, and probably with much less, than any disbeliever in them might possess. His unconventionality would probably have some grounds to show for its conclusions; but for us, not insight, but the *prestige* of the opinions, is what makes the spark shoot from them and light up our sleeping magazines of faith. Our reason is quite satisfied, in nine hundred and ninety-nine cases out of every thousand of us, if it can find a few arguments that will do to recite in case our credulity is criticized by some one else. Our faith is faith in some one else's faith, and in the greatest matters this is the most the case. . . .

Evidently, then, our non-intellectual nature does influence our convictions. There are passional tendencies and volitions which run before and others which come after belief, and it is only the latter that

are too late for the fair; and they are not too late when the previous passional work has been already in their own direction. Pascal's argument, instead of being powerless, then seems a regular clincher, and is the last stroke needed to make our faith in masses and holy water complete. The state of things is evidently far from simple; and pure insight and logic, whatever they might do ideally, are not the only things that really do produce our creeds.

IV

Our next duty, having recognized this mixedup state of affairs, is to ask whether it be simply reprehensible and pathological, or whether, on the contrary, we must treat it as a normal element in making up our minds. The thesis I defend is, briefly stated, this: *Our passional nature not only lawfully may, but must, decide an option between propositions, whenever it is a genuine option that cannot by its nature be decided on intellectual grounds; for to say, under such circumstances, "Do not decide, but leave the question open," is itself a passional decision—just like deciding yes or no—and is attended with the same risk of losing the truth. . . .*

VII

One more point, small but important, and our preliminaries are done. There are two ways of looking at our duty in the matter of opinion—ways entirely different, and yet ways about whose difference the theory of knowledge seems hitherto to have shown very little concern. *We must know the truth; and we must avoid error*—these are our first and great commandments as would-be knowers; but they are not two ways of stating an identical commandment, they are two separable laws. Although it may indeed happen that when we believe the truth A, we escape as an incidental consequence from believing the falsehood B, it hardly ever happens that by merely disbelieving B we necessarily believe A. We may in escaping B fall into believing other falsehoods, C or D, just as bad as B; or we may escape B by not believing anything at all, not even A.

Believe truth! Shun error!—these, we see, are two materially different laws; and by choosing between them we may end by coloring differently our whole intellectual life. We may regard the chase for truth as paramount, and the avoidance of error as secondary; or we may, on the other hand, treat the avoidance of error as more imperative, and let truth take its chance. Clifford, in the instructive passage which I have quoted, exhorts us to the latter course. Believe nothing, he tells us, keep your mind in suspense forever, rather than by closing it on insufficient evidence incur the awful risk of believing lies. You, on the other hand, may think that the risk of being in error is a very small matter when compared with the blessings of real knowledge, and be ready to be duped many times in your investigation rather than postpone indefinitely the chance of guessing true. I myself find it impossible to go with Clifford. We must remember that these feelings of our duty about either truth or error are in any case only expressions of our passional life. Biologically considered, our minds are as ready to grind out falsehood as veracity, and he who says, "Better go without belief forever than believe a lie!" merely shows his own preponderant private horror of becoming a dupe. He may be critical of many of his desires and fears, but this fear he slavishly obeys. He cannot imagine any one questioning its binding force. For my own part, I have also a horror of being duped; but I can believe that worse things than being duped may happen to a man in this world: so Clifford's exhortation has to my ears a thoroughly fantastic sound. It is like a general informing his soldiers that it is better to keep out of battle forever than to risk a single wound. Not so are victories either over enemies or over nature gained. Our errors are surely not such awfully solemn things. In a world where we are so certain to incur them in spite of all our caution, a certain lightness of heart seems healthier than this excessive nervousness on their behalf. At any rate, it seems the fittest thing for the empiricist philosopher.

VIII

And now, after all this introduction, let us go straight at our question. I have said, and now repeat it, that not only as a matter of fact do we find our passional nature influencing us in our opinions, but that there are some options between opinions in which this in-

fluence must be regarded both as an inevitable and as a lawful determinant of our choice.

I fear here that some of you my hearers will begin to scent danger, and lend an inhospitable ear. Two first steps of passion you have indeed had to admit as necessary—we must think so as to avoid dupery, and we must think so as to gain truth; but the surest path to those ideal consummations, you will probably consider, is from now onwards to take no further passional step.

Well, of course, I agree as far as the facts will allow. Wherever the option between losing truth and gaining it is not momentous, we can throw the chance of *gaining truth* away, and at any rate save ourselves from any chance of *believing falsehood*, by not making up our minds at all till objective evidence has come. In scientific questions, this is almost always the case; and even in human affairs in general, the need of acting is seldom so urgent that a false belief to act on is better than no belief at all. Law courts, indeed, have to decide on the best evidence attainable for the moment, because a judge's duty is to make law as well as to ascertain it, and (as a learned judge once said to me) few cases are worth spending much time over: the great thing is to have them decided on *any* acceptable principle, and got out of the way. But in our dealings with objective nature we obviously are recorders, not makers, of the truth; and decisions for the mere sake of deciding promptly and getting on to the next business would be wholly out of place. Throughout the breadth of physical nature facts are what they are quite independently of us, and seldom is there any such hurry about them that the risks of being duped by believing a premature theory need be faced. The questions here are always trivial options, the hypotheses are hardly living (at any rate not living for us spectators), the choice between believing truth or falsehood is seldom forced. The attitude of sceptical balance is therefore the absolutely wise one if we would escape mistakes. What difference, indeed, does it make to most of us whether we have or have not a theory of the Röntgen rays, whether we believe or not in mind-stuff, or have a conviction about the causality of conscious states? It makes no difference. Such options are not forced on us. On every account it is better not to make them, but still keep weighing reasons *pro et contra* with an indifferent hand.

I speak, of course, here of the purely judging mind. For purposes of discovery such indifference is to be less highly recommended, and science would be far less advanced than she is if the passionate desires of individuals to get their own faiths confirmed had been kept out of the game. See for example the sagacity which Spencer and Weismann now display. On the other hand, if you want an absolute duffer in an investigation, you must, after all, take the man who has no interest whatever in its results: he is the warranted incapable, the positive fool. The most useful investigator, because the most sensitive observer, is always he whose eager interest in one side of the question is balanced by an equally keen nervousness lest he become deceived. Science has organized this nervousness into a regular *technique*, her so-called method of verification; and she has fallen so deeply in love with the method that one may even say she has ceased to care for truth by itself at all. It is only truth as technically verified that interests her. The truth of truths might come in merely affirmative form, and she would decline to touch it. Such truth as that, she might repeat with Clifford, would be stolen in defiance of her duty to mankind. Human passions, however, are stronger than technical rules. "*Le coeur a ses raisons,*" as Pascal says, "*que la raison ne connait pas,*" and however indifferent to all but the bare rules of the game the umpire, the abstract intellect, may be, the concrete players who furnish him the materials to judge of are usually, each one of them, in love with some pet "live hypothesis" of his own. Let us agree, however, that wherever there is no forced option, the dispassionately judicial intellect with no pet hypothesis, saving us, as it does, from dupery at any rate, ought to be our ideal.

The question next arises: Are there not somewhere forced options in our speculative questions, and can we (as men who may be interested at least as much in positively gaining truth as in merely escaping dupery) always wait with impunity till the coercive evidence shall have arrived? It seems *a priori* improbable that the truth should be so nicely adjusted to our needs and powers as that. In the great boardinghouse of nature, the cakes and the butter and the syrup seldom come out so even and leave the plates so clean. Indeed, we should view them with scientific suspicion if they did.

IX

Moral questions immediately present themselves as questions whose solution cannot wait for sensible proof. A moral question is a question not of what sensibly exists, but of what is good, or would be good if it did exist. Science can tell us what exists; but to compare the *worths*, both of what exists and of what does not exist, we must consult not science, but what Pascal calls our heart. . . .

Turn now from these wide questions of good to a certain class of questions of fact, questions concerning personal relations, states of mind between one man and another. *Do you like me or not?*—for example. Whether you do or not depends, in countless instances, on whether I meet you halfway, am willing to assume that you must like me, and show you trust and expectation. The previous faith on my part in your liking's existence is in such cases what makes your liking come. But if I stand aloof, and refuse to budge an inch until I have objective evidence, until you shall have done something apt, as the absolutists say, *ad extorquendum assensum meum*, ten to one your liking never comes. How many women's hearts are vanquished by the mere sanguine insistence of some man that they *must* love him! He will not consent to the hypothesis that they cannot. The desire for a certain kind of truth here brings about that special truth's existence; and so it is in innumerable cases of other sorts. . . . And where faith in a fact can help create the fact, that would be an insane logic which should say that faith running ahead of scientific evidence is the "lowest kind of immorality" into which a thinking being can fall. Yet such is the logic by which our scientific absolutists pretend to regulate our lives!

X

In truths dependent on our personal action, then, faith based on desire is certainly a lawful and possibly an indispensable thing.

But now, it will be said, these are all childish human cases, and have nothing to do with great cosmical matters, like the question of religious faith. Let us then pass on to that. Religions differ so much in their accidents that in discussing the religious question we must make it very generic and broad. What then do we now mean by the religious hypothesis? Science says things are; morality says some things are better than other things; and religion says essentially two things.

First, she says that the best things are the more eternal things, the overlapping things, the things in the universe that throw the last stone, so to speak, and say the final word. "Perfection is eternal"—this phrase of Charles Secrétan seems a good way of putting this first affirmation of religion, an affirmation which obviously cannot yet be verified scientifically at all.

The second affirmation of religion is that we are better off even now if we believe her first affirmation to be true.

Now, let us consider what the logical elements of this situation are *in case the religious hypothesis in both its branches be really true.* (Of course, we must admit that possibility at the outset. If we are to discuss the question at all, it must involve a living option. If for any of you religion be a hypothesis that cannot, by any living possibility, be true, then you need go no farther. I speak to the "saving remnant" alone.) So proceeding, we see, first, that religion offers itself as a *momentous* option. We are supposed to gain, even now, by our belief, and to lose by our non-belief, a certain vital good. Secondly, religion is a *forced* option, so far as that good goes. We cannot escape the issue by remaining sceptical and waiting for more light, because, although we do avoid error in that way *if religion be untrue,* we lose the good, *if it be true,* just as certainly as if we positively chose to disbelieve. It is as if a man should hesitate indefinitely to ask a certain woman to marry him because he was not perfectly sure that she would prove an angel after he brought her home. Would he not cut himself off from that particular angel-possibility as decisively as if he went and married some one else? Scepticism, then, is not avoidance of option; it is option of a certain particular kind of risk. *Better risk loss of truth than chance of error*—that is your faithvetoer's exact position. He is actively playing his stake as much as the believer is; he is backing the field against the religious hypothesis, just as the believer is backing the religious hypothesis against the field. To preach scepticism to us as a duty until

"sufficient evidence" for religion be found, is tantamount therefore to telling us, when in presence of the religious hypothesis, that to yield to our fear of its being error is wiser and better than to yield to our hope that it may be true. It is not intellect against all passions, then; it is only intellect with one passion laying down its law. And by what, forsooth, is the supreme wisdom of this passion warranted? Dupery for dupery, what proof is there that dupery through hope is so much worse than dupery through fear? I, for one, can see no proof; and I simply refuse obedience to the scientist's command to imitate his kind of option, in a case where my own stake is important enough to give me the right to choose my own form of risk. If religion be true and the evidence for it be still insufficient, I do not wish, by putting your extinguisher upon my nature (which feels to me as if it had after all some business in this matter), to forfeit my sole chance in life of getting upon the winning side—that chance depending, of course, on my willingness to run the risk of acting as if my passional need of taking the world religiously might he prophetic and right.

All this is on the supposition that it really may be prophetic and right, and that, even to us who are discussing the matter, religion is a live hypothesis which may be true. Now, to most of us religion comes in a still further way that makes a veto on our active faith even more illogical. The more perfect and more eternal aspect of the universe is represented in our religions as having personal form. The universe is no longer a mere *It* to us, but a *Thou,* if we are religious; and any relation that may be possible from person to person might be possible here. For instance, although in one sense we are passive portions of the universe, in another we show a curious autonomy, as if we were small active centers on our own account. We feel, too, as if the appeal of religion to us were made to our own active goodwill, as if evidence might be forever withheld from us unless we met the hypothesis halfway. To take a trivial illustration: just as a man who in a company of gentlemen made no advances, asked a warrant for every concession, and believed no one's word without proof, would cut himself off by such churlishness from all the social rewards that a more trusting spirit would earn—so here, one who should shut himself up in snarling logicality and try to make the gods extort his recognition willy-nilly, or not get it at all, might cut himself off forever from his only opportunity of making the gods' acquaintance. This feeling, forced on us we know not whence that by obstinately believing that there are gods (although not to do so would be so easy both for our logic and our life) we are doing the universe the deepest service we can, seems part of the living essence of the religious hypothesis. If the hypothesis *were* true in all its parts, including this one, then pure intellectualism, with its veto on our making willing advances, would be an absurdity; and some participation of our sympathetic nature would be logically required. I therefore, for one, cannot see my way to accepting the agnostic rules for truth-seeking, or wilfully agree to keep my willing nature out of the game. I cannot do so for this plain reason, that *a rule of thinking which would absolutely prevent me from acknowledging certain kinds of truth if those kinds of truth were really there, would be an irrational rule*. That for me is the long and short of the formal logic of the situation, no matter what the kinds of truth might materially be.

I confess I do not see how this logic can be escaped. But sad experience makes me fear that some of you may still shrink from radically saying with me, *in abstracto*, that we have the right to believe at our own risk any hypothesis that is live enough to tempt our will. I suspect, however, that if this is so, it is because you have got away from the abstract logical point of view altogether, and are thinking (perhaps without realizing it) of some particular religious hypothesis which for you is dead. The freedom to "believe what we will" you apply to the case of some patent superstition; and the faith you think of is the faith defined by the schoolboy when he said, "Faith is when you believe something that you know ain't true." I can only repeat that this is misapprehension. *In concreto*, the freedom to believe can only cover living options which the intellect of the individual cannot by itself resolve; and living options never seem absurdities to him who has them to consider. When I look at the religious question as it really puts itself to concrete men, and when I think of all the possibilities which both practically and theoretically it involves, then this command that we shall put a stopper on our heart, instincts, and courage, and *wait*—acting of course meanwhile more or less as if religion were not true—till doomsday, or till such time as our intellect and senses working together may have raked in evidence enough—this command, I say, seems to me the queerest idol ever manufactured in the philosophic cave. Were we scholastic absolutists, there might be more excuse. If we had an infallible intellect with its objective certitudes, we might feel ourselves disloyal to such a perfect organ of knowledge in not trusting to it exclusively, in not waiting for its releasing word. But if we are empiricists, if we believe that no bell in us tolls to let us know for certain when truth is in our grasp, then it seems a piece of idle fantasticality to preach so solemnly our duty of waiting for the bell. Indeed we *may* wait if we will—I hope you do not think that I am denying that—but if we do so, we do so at our peril as much as if we believed. In either case we *act*, taking our life in our hands. No one of us ought to issue vetoes to the other, nor should we bandy words of abuse. We ought, on the contrary, delicately and profoundly to respect one another's mental freedom: then only shall we bring about the intellectual republic; then only shall we have that spirit of inner tolerance without which all our outer tolerance is soulless, and which is empiricism's glory; then only shall we live and let live, in speculative as well as in practical things.

I began by a reference to Fitz-James Stephen; let me end by a quotation from him. "What do you think of yourself? What do you think of the world? . . . These are questions with which all must deal as it seems good to them. They are riddles of the Sphinx, and in some way or other we must deal with them. . . . In all important transactions of life we have to take a leap in the dark. . . . If we decide to leave the riddles unanswered, that is a choice; if we waver in our answer, that, too, is a choice: but whatever choice we make, we make it at our peril. If a man chooses to turn his back altogether on God and the future, no one can prevent him; no one can show beyond reasonable doubt that he is mistaken. If a man thinks otherwise and acts as he thinks, I do not see that any one can prove that he is mistaken. Each must act as he thinks best; and if he is wrong, so much the worse for him. We stand on a mountain pass in the midst of whirling snow and blinding mist, through which we get glimpses now and then of paths which may be deceptive. If we stand still we shall be frozen to death. If we take the wrong road we shall be dashed to pieces. We do not certainly know whether there is any right one. What must we do? 'Be strong and of a good courage.' Act for the best, hope for the best, and take what comes.

. . . If death ends all, we cannot meet death better."

PRAGMATISM

WHAT PRAGMATISM MEANS

Some years ago, being with a camping party in the mountains, I returned from a solitary ramble to find every one engaged in a ferocious metaphysical dispute. The *corpus* of the dispute was a squirrel—a live squirrel supposed to be clinging to one side of a treetrunk; while over against the tree's opposite side a human being was imagined to stand. This human witness tries to get sight of the squirrel by moving rapidly round the tree, but no matter how fast he goes, the squirrel moves as fast in the opposite direction, and always keeps the tree between himself and the man, so that never a glimpse of him is caught. The resultant metaphysical problem now is this: *Does the man go round the squirrel or not?* He goes round the tree, sure enough, and the squirrel is on the tree; but does he go round the squirrel? In the unlimited leisure of the wilderness, discussion had been worn threadbare. Everyone had taken sides, and was obstinate; and the numbers on both sides were even. Each side, when I appeared therefore appealed to me to make it a majority. Mindful of the scholastic adage that whenever you meet a contradiction you must make a distinction, I immediately sought and found one, as follows: "Which party is right," I said, "depends on what you *practically mean* by 'going round' the squirrel. If you mean passing from the north of him to the east, then to the south, then to the west, and then to the north of him again, obviously the man does go round him, for he occupies these successive positions. But if on the contrary you mean being first in front of him, then on the right of him, then behind him, then on his left, and finally in front again, it is quite as obvious that the man fails to go round him, for by the compensating movements the squirrel makes, he keeps his belly turned towards the man all the time, and his back turned away. Make the distinction, and there is no occasion for any farther dispute. You are both right and both wrong according as you conceive the verb 'to go round' in one practical fashion or the other."

Although one or two of the hotter disputants called my speech a shuffling evasion, saying they wanted no quibbling or scholastic hairsplitting, but meant just plain honest English 'round,' the majority seemed to think that the distinction had assuaged the dispute.

I tell this trivial anecdote because it is a peculiarly simple example of what I wish now to speak of as *the pragmatic method.* The pragmatic method is primarily a method of settling metaphysical disputes that otherwise might be interminable. Is the world one or many?—fated or free?—material or spiritual?—here are notions either of which may or may not hold good of the world; and disputes over such notions are unending. The pragmatic method in such cases is to try to interpret each notion by tracing its respective practical consequences. What difference would it practically make to any one if this notion rather than that notion were true? If no practical difference whatever can be traced, then the alternatives mean practically the same thing, and all dispute is idle. Whenever a dispute is serious, we ought to be able to show some practical difference that must follow from one side or the other's being right.

A glance at the history of the idea will show you still better what pragmatism means. The term is derived from the same Greek word $\pi\rho\alpha\gamma\mu\alpha$, meaning action, from which our words 'practice' and 'practical' come. It was first introduced into philosophy by Mr. Charles Peirce in 1878. In an article entitled

'How to Make Our Ideas Clear,' in the 'Popular Science Monthly' for January of that year[1] Mr. Peirce, after pointing out that our beliefs are really rules for action, said that, to develop a thought's meaning, we need only determine what conduct it is fitted to produce: that conduct is for us its sole significance. And the tangible fact at the root of all our thought-distinctions, however subtle, is that there is no one of them so fine as to consist in anything but a possible difference of practice. To attain perfect clearness in our thoughts of an object, then, we need only consider what conceivable effects of a practical kind the object may involve—what sensations we are to expect from it, and what reactions we must prepare. Our conception of these effects, whether immediate or remote, is then for us the whole of our conception of the object, so far as that conception has positive significance at all.

This is the principle of Peirce, the principle of pragmatism. It lay entirely unnoticed by any one for twenty years, until I, in an address before Professor Howison's philosophical union at the university of California, brought it forward again and made a special application of it to religion. By that date (1898) the times seemed ripe for its reception. The word 'pragmatism' spread, and at present it fairly spots the pages of the philosophic journals. On all hands we find the 'pragmatic movement' spoken of, sometimes with respect, sometimes with contumely, seldom with clear understanding. It is evident that the term applies itself conveniently to a number of tendencies that hitherto have lacked a collective name, and that it has 'come to stay.'

To take in the importance of Peirce's principle, one must get accustomed to applying it to concrete cases. I found a few years ago that Ostwald, the illustrious Leipzig chemist, had been making perfectly distinct use of the principle of pragmatism in his lectures on the philosophy of science, though he had not called it by that name.

"All realities influence our practice," he wrote me, "and that influence is their meaning for us. I am accustomed to put questions to my classes in this way: In what respects would the world be different if this alternative or that were true? If I can find nothing that would become different, then the alternative has no sense."

That is, the rival views mean practically the same thing, and meaning, other than practical, there is for us none. Ostwald in a published lecture gives this example of what he means. Chemists have long wrangled over the inner constitution of certain bodies called 'tautomerous.' Their properties seemed equally consistent with the notion that an instable hydrogen atom oscillates inside of them, or that they are instable mixtures of two bodies. Controversy raged, but never was decided. "It would never have begun," says Ostwald, "if the combatants had asked themselves what particular experimental fact could have been made different by one or the other view being correct. For it would then have appeared that no difference of fact could possibly ensue; and the quarrel was as unreal as if, theorizing in primitive times about the raising of dough by yeast, one party should have invoked a 'brownie,' while another insisted on an 'elf' as the true cause of the phenomenon."[2]

It is astonishing to see how many philosophical disputes collapse into insignificance the moment you subject them to this simple test of tracing a concrete consequence. There can *be* no difference anywhere that doesn't *make* a difference elsewhere—no difference in abstract truth that doesn't express itself in a difference in concrete fact and in conduct consequent upon that fact, imposed on somebody, somehow, somewhere, and somewhen. The whole function of philosophy ought to be to find out what definite difference it will make to you and me, at definite instants of our life, if this world-formula or that world-formula be the true one.

---

[1] Translated in the *Revue Philosophique* for January, 1879 (vol. vii).

[2] 'Theorie und Praxis,' *Zeitsch. des Oesterreichischen Ingenieur u. Architecten-Vereines*, 1905, Nr. 4 u. 6. I find a still more radical pragmatism than Ostwald's in an address by Professor W. S. Franklin: "I think that the sickliest notion of physics, even if a student gets it, is that it is 'the science of masses, molecules, and the ether.' And I think that the healthiest notion, even if a student does not wholly get it, is that physics is the science of the ways of taking hold of bodies and pushing them!" (*Science*, January 2, 1903.)

There is absolutely nothing new in the pragmatic method. Socrates was an adept at it. Aristotle used it methodically. Locke, Berkeley, and Hume made momentous contributions to truth by its means. Shadworth Hodgson keeps insisting that realities are only what they are 'known as.' But these forerunners of pragmatism used it in fragments: they were preluders only. Not until in our time has it generalized itself, become conscious of a universal mission, pretended to a conquering destiny. I believe in that destiny, and I hope I may end by inspiring you with my belief.

Pragmatism represents a perfectly familiar attitude in philosophy, the empiricist attitude, but it represents it, as it seems to me, both in a more radical and in a less objectionable form than it has ever yet assumed. A pragmatist turns his back resolutely and once for all upon a lot of inveterate habits dear to professional philosophers. He turns away from abstraction and insufficiency, from verbal solutions, from bad *a priori* reasons, from fixed principles, closed systems, and pretended absolutes and origins. He turns towards concreteness and adequacy, towards facts, towards action and towards power. That means the empiricist temper regnant and the rationalist temper sincerely given up. It means the open air and possibilities of nature, as against dogma, artificiality, and the pretence of finality in truth.

At the same time it does not stand for any special results. It is a method only. But the general triumph of that method would mean an enormous change in what I called in my last lecture the 'temperament' of philosophy. Teachers of the ultra-rationalistic type would be frozen out, much as the courtier type is frozen out in republics, as the ultramontane type of priest is frozen out in protestant lands. Science and metaphysics would come much nearer together, would in fact work absolutely hand in hand.

Metaphysics has usually followed a very primitive kind of quest. You know how men have always hankered after unlawful magic, and you know what a great part in magic *words* have always played. If you have his name, or the formula of incantation that binds him, you can control the spirit, genie, afrite, or whatever the power may be. Solomon knew the names of all the spirits, and having their names, he held them subject to his will. So the universe has always appeared to the natural mind as a kind of enigma, of which the key must be sought in the shape of some illuminating or power-bringing word or name. That word names the universe's *principle*, and to possess it is after a fashion to possess the universe itself. 'God,' 'Matter,' 'Reason,' 'the Absolute,' 'Energy,' are so many solving names. You can rest when you have them. You are at the end of your metaphysical quest.

But if you follow the pragmatic method, you cannot look on any such word as closing your quest. You must bring out of each word its practical cash-value, set it at work within the stream of your experience. It appears less as a solution, then, than as a program for more work, and more particularly as an indication of the ways in which existing realities may be *changed*.

Theories thus become instruments, not answers to enigmas, in which we can rest. We don't lie back upon them, we move forward, and, on occasion, make nature over again by their aid. Pragmatism unstiffens all our theories, limbers them up and sets each one at work. Being nothing essentially new, it harmonizes with many ancient philosophic tendencies. It agrees with nominalism for instance, in always appealing to particulars; with utilitarianism in emphasizing practical aspects; with positivism in its disdain for verbal solutions, useless questions and metaphysical abstractions.

All these, you see, are *anti-intellectualist* tendencies. Against rationalism as a pretension and a method pragmatism is fully armed and militant. But, at the outset, at least, it stands for no particular results. It has no dogmas, and no doctrines save its method. As the young Italian pragmatist Papini has well said, it lies in the midst of our theories, like a corridor in a hotel. Innumerable chambers open out of it. In one you may find a man writing an atheistic volume; in the next some one on his knees praying for faith and strength; in a third a chemist investigating a body's properties. In a fourth a system of idealistic metaphysics is being excogitated; in a fifth the impossibility of metaphysics is being shown. But they all own the corridor, and all must pass through it if they want a practicable way of getting into or out of their respective rooms.

No particular results then, so far, but only an attitude of orientation, is what the pragmatic method means. *The attitude of looking away from first things, principles, 'categories,' supposed necessities; and of looking towards last things, fruits, consequences, facts.*

So much for the pragmatic method! You may say that I have been praising it rather than explaining it to you, but I shall presently explain it abundantly enough by showing how it works on some familiar problems. Meanwhile the word pragmatism has come to be used in a still wider sense, as meaning also a certain *theory of truth*. I mean to give a whole lecture to the statement of that theory, after first paving the way, so I can be very brief now. But brevity is hard to follow, so I ask for your redoubled attention for a quarter of an hour. If much remains obscure, I hope to make it clearer in the later lectures.

One of the most successfully cultivated branches of philosophy in our time is what is called inductive logic, the study of the conditions under which our sciences have evolved. Writers on this subject have begun to show a singular unanimity as to what the laws of nature and element of fact mean, when formulated by mathematicians, physicist and chemists. When the first mathematical, logical, and natural uniformities, the first *laws*, were discovered, men were so carried away by the clearness, beauty and simplification that resulted, that they believed themselves to have deciphered authentically the eternal thoughts of the Almighty. His mind also thundered and reverberated in syllogisms. He also thought in conic sections, squares and roots and ratios, and geometrized like Euclid. He made Kepler's laws for the planets to follow; he made velocity increase proportionally to the time in falling bodies; he made the law of the sines for light to obey when refracted; he established the classes, orders, families and genera of plants and animals, and fixed the distances between them. He thought the archetypes of all things, and devised their variations; and when we rediscover any one of these his wondrous institutions, we seize his mind in its very literal intention.

But as the sciences have developed farther, the notion has gained ground that most, perhaps all, of our laws are only approximations. The laws themselves, moreover, have grown so numerous that there is no counting them; and so many rival formulations are proposed in all the branches of science that investigators have become accustomed to the notion that no theory is absolutely a transcript of reality, but that any one of them may from some point of view be useful. Their great use is to summarize old facts and to lead to new ones. They are only a man-made language, a conceptual shorthand, as some one calls them, in which we write our reports of nature; and languages, as is well known, tolerate much choice of expression and many dialects.

Thus human arbitrariness has driven divine necessity from scientific logic. If I mention the names of Sigwart, Mach, Ostwald, Pearson, Milhaud, Poincaré, Duhem, Ruyssen, those of you who are students will easily identify the tendency I speak of, and will think of additional names.

Riding now on the front of this wave of scientific logic Messrs. Schiller and Dewey appear with their pragmatistic account of what truth everywhere signifies. Everywhere, these teachers say, 'truth' in our ideas and beliefs means the same thing that it means in science. It means, they say, nothing but this, *that ideas (which themselves are but parts of our experience) become true just in so far as they help us to get into satisfactory relation with other parts of our experience*, to summarize them and get about among them by conceptual short-cuts instead of following the interminable succession of particular phenomena. Any idea upon which we can ride, so to speak; any idea that will carry us prosperously from any one part of our experience to any other part, linking things satisfactorily, working securely, simplifying, saving labor; is true for just so much, true in so far forth, true *instrumentally*. This is the 'instrumental' view of truth taught so successfully at Chicago, the view that truth in our ideas means their power to 'work,' promulgated so brilliantly at Oxford.

Messrs. Dewey, Schiller and their allies, in reaching this general conception of all truth, have only followed the example of geologists, biologists and philologists. In the establishment of these other sciences, the successful stroke was always to take some simple process actually observable in operation—as denudation by weather, say, or variation from parental type, or change of dialect by incorporation of new words and pronunciations—and then to generalize it, making it apply to all times, and produce great results by summating its effects through the ages.

The observable process which Schiller and Dewey particularly singled out for generalization is the familiar one by which any individual settles into *new opinions*. The process here is always the same. The individual has a stock of old opinions already, but he meets a new experience that puts them to a strain. Somebody contradicts them; or in a reflective moment he discovers that they contradict each other; or he hears of facts with which they are incompatible; or desires arise in him which they cease to satisfy. The result is an inward trouble to which his mind till then had been a stranger, and from which he seeks to escape by modifying his previous mass of opinions. He saves as much of it as he can, for in this matter of belief we are all extreme conservatives. So he tries to change first this opinion, and then that (for they resist change very variously), until at last some new idea comes up which he can graft upon the ancient stock with a minimum of disturbance of the latter, some idea that mediates between the stock and the new experience and runs them into one another most felicitously and expediently.

This new idea is then adopted as the true one. It preserves the older stock of truths with a minimum of modification, stretching them just enough to make them admit the novelty, but conceiving that in ways as familiar as the case leaves possible. An *outrée* explanation, violating all our preconceptions, would never pass for a true account of a novelty. We should scratch round industriously till we found something less excentric. The most violent revolutions in an individual's beliefs leave most of his old order standing. Time and space, cause and effect, nature and history, and one's biography remain untouched. New truth is always a go-between, a smoother-over of transitions. It marries old opinion to new fact so as ever to show a minimum of jolt, a maximum of continuity. We hold a theory true just in proportion to its success in solving this 'problem of maxima and minima.' But success in solving this problem is eminently a matter of approximation. We say this theory solves it on the whole more satisfactorily than that theory; but that means more satisfactorily to ourselves, and individuals will emphasize their points of satisfaction differently. To a certain degree, therefore, everything here is plastic.

The point I now urge you to observe particularly is the part played by the older truths. Failure to take account of it is the source of much of the unjust criticism levelled against pragmatism. Their influence is absolutely controlling. Loyalty to them is the first principle—in most cases it is the only principle; for by far the most usual way of handling phenomena so novel that they would make for a serious re-arrangement of our preconception is to ignore them altogether, or to abuse those who bear witness for them.

You doubtless wish examples of this process of truth's growth, and the only trouble is their super-abundance. The simplest case of new truth is of course the mere numerical addition of new kinds of facts, or of new single facts of old kinds, to our experience—an addition that involves no alteration in the old beliefs. Day follows day, and its contents are simply added. The new contents themselves are not true, they simply *come* and *are*. Truth is *what we say about* them, and when we say that they have come, truth is satisfied by the plain additive formula.

But often the day's contents oblige a rearrangement. If I should now utter piercing shrieks and act like a maniac on this platform, it would make many of you revise your ideas as to the probable worth of my philosophy. 'Radium' came the other day as part of the day's content, and seemed for a moment to contradict our ideas of the whole order of nature, that order having come to be identified with what is called the conservation of energy. The mere sight of radium paying heat away indefinitely out of its own pocket seemed to violate that conservation. What to think? If the radiations from it were nothing but an escape of unsuspected 'potential' energy, pre-existent inside of the atoms, the principle of conservation would be saved. The discovery of 'helium' as the radiation's outcome, opened a way to this belief. So Ramsay's view is generally held to be true, because, although it extends our old ideas of energy, it causes a minimum of alteration in their nature.

I need not multiply instances. A new opinion counts as 'true' just in proportion as it gratifies the individual's desire to assimilate the novel in his experience to his beliefs in stock. It must both lean on old truth and grasp new fact; and its success (as I said a moment ago) in doing this, is a matter for the individual's appreciation. When old truth grows, then, by new truth's addition, it is for subjective reasons. We are in the process and obey the reasons. That new idea is truest which performs most felicitously its function of satisfying our double urgency. It makes itself true, gets itself classed as true, by the way it works; grafting itself then upon the ancient body of truth, which thus grows much as a tree grows by the activity of a new layer of cambium.

Now Dewey and Schiller proceed to generalize this observation and to apply it to the most ancient parts of truth. They also once were plastic. They also were called true for human reasons. They also mediated between still earlier truths and what in those days were novel observations. Purely objective truth, truth in whose establishment the function of giving human satisfaction in marrying previous parts of experience with newer parts played no rôle whatever, is nowhere to be found. The reasons why we call things true is the reason why they *are* true, for 'to be true' *means* only to perform this marriage-function.

The trail of the human serpent is thus over everything. Truth independent; truth that we *find* merely; truth no longer malleable to human need; truth incorrigible, in a word; such truth exists indeed superabundantly—or is supposed to exist by rationalistically minded thinkers; but then it means only the dead heart of the living tree, and its being there means only that truth also has its paleontology, and its 'prescription,' and may grow stiff with years of veteran service and petrified in men's regard by sheer antiquity. But how plastic even the oldest truths nevertheless really are has been vividly shown in our day by the transformation of logical and mathematical ideas, a transformation which seems even to be invading physics. The ancient formulas are reinterpreted as special expressions of much wider principles, principles that our ancestors never got a glimpse of in their present shape and formulation.

Mr. Schiller still gives to all this view of truth the name of 'Humanism,' but, for this doctrine too, the name of pragmatism seems fairly to be in the ascendant, so I will treat it under the name of pragmatism in these lectures.

Such then would be the scope of pragmatism— first, a method; and second, a genetic theory of what is meant by truth. And these two things must be our future topics.

What I have said of the theory of truth will, I am sure, have appeared obscure and unsatisfactory to most of you by reason of its brevity. I shall make amends for that hereafter. In a lecture on 'common sense' I shall try to show what I mean by truths grown petrified by antiquity. In another lecture I shall expatiate on the idea that our thoughts become true in proportion as they successfully exert their go-between function. In a third I shall show how hard it is to discriminate subjective from objective factors in Truth's development. You may not follow me wholly in these lectures; and if you do, you may not wholly agree with me. But you will, I know, regard me at least as serious, and treat my effort with respectful consideration.

You will probably be surprised to learn, then, that Messrs. Schiller's and Dewey's theories have suffered a hailstorm of contempt and ridicule. All rationalism has risen against them. In influential quarters Mr. Schiller, in particular, has been treated like an impudent schoolboy who deserves a spanking. I should not mention this, but for the fact that it throws so much sidelight upon that rationalistic temper to which I have opposed the temper of pragmatism. Pragmatism is uncomfortable away from facts. Rationalism is comfortable only in the presence of abstractions. This pragmatist talk about truths in the plural, about their utility and satisfactoriness, about the success with which they 'work,' etc., suggests to the typical intellectualist mind a sort of coarse lame second-rate makeshift article of truth. Such truths are not real truth. Such tests are merely subjective. As against this, objective truth must be something non-utilitarian, haughty, refined, remote, august, exalted. It must be an absolute correspondence of our thoughts with an equally absolute reality. It must be what we *ought* to think unconditionally. The conditioned ways in which we *do* think are so much irrelevance and matter for psychology. Down with psychology, up with logic, in all this question!

See the exquisite contrast of the types of mind! The pragmatist clings to facts and concreteness, observes truth at its work in particular cases, and generalizes. Truth, for him, becomes a class-name for all sorts of definite working-values in experience. For the rationalist it remains a pure abstraction, to the bare name of which we must defer. When the pragmatist undertakes to show in detail just *why* we must defer, the rationalist is unable to recognize the concretes from which his own abstraction is taken. He accuses us of *denying* truth; whereas we have only sought to trace exactly why people follow it and always ought to follow it. Your typical ultra-abstractionist fairly shudders at concreteness: other things equal, he positively prefers the pale and spectral. If the two universes were offered, he would always choose the skinny outline rather than the rich thicket of reality. It is so much purer, clearer, nobler.

I hope that as these lectures go on, the concreteness and closeness to facts of the pragmatism which they advocate may be what approves itself to you as its most satisfactory peculiarity. It only follows here the example of the sister-sciences, interpreting the unobserved by the observed. It brings old and new harmoniously together. It converts the absolutely empty notion of a static relation of 'correspondence' (what that may mean we must ask later) between our minds and reality, into that of a rich and active commerce (that any one may follow in detail and understand) between particular thoughts of ours, and the great universe of other experiences in which they play their parts and have their uses.

But enough of this at present? The justification of what I say must be postponed. I wish now to add a word in further explanation of the claim I made at our last meeting, that pragmatism may be a happy harmonizer of empiricist ways of thinking with the more religious demands of human beings.

Men who are strongly of the fact-loving temperament, you may remember me to have said, are liable to be kept at a distance by the small sympathy with facts which that philosophy from the present-day fashion of idealism offers them. It is far too intellectualistic. Old fashioned theism was bad enough, with its notion of God as an exalted monarch, made up of a lot of unintelligible or preposterous 'attributes'; but, so long as it held strongly by the argument from design, it kept some touch with concrete realities. Since, however, Darwinism has once for all displaced design from the minds of the 'scientific,' theism has lost that foothold; and some kind of an immanent or pantheistic deity working *in* things rather than above them is, if any, the kind recommended to our contemporary imagination. Aspirants to a philosophic religion turn, as a rule, more hopefully nowadays towards idealistic pantheism than towards the older dualistic theism, in spite of the fact that the latter still counts able defenders.

But, as I said in my first lecture, the brand of pantheism offered is hard for them to assimilate if they are lovers of facts, or empirically minded. It is the absolutistic brand, spurning the dust and reared upon pure logic. It keeps no connexion whatever with concreteness. Affirming the Absolute Mind, which is its substitute for God, to be the rational presupposition of all particulars of fact, whatever they may be, it remains supremely indifferent to what the particular facts in our world actually are. Be they what they may, the Absolute will father them. Like the sick lion in Esop's fable, all footprints lead into his den, but *nulla vestigia retrorsum*. You cannot redescend into the world of particulars by the Absolute's aid, or deduce any necessary consequences of detail important for your life from your idea of his nature. He gives you indeed the assurance that all is well with *Him*, and for his eternal way of thinking; but thereupon he leaves you to be finitely saved by your own temporal devices.

Far be it from me to deny the majesty of this conception, or its capacity to yield religious comfort to a most respectable class of minds. But from the human point of view, no one can pretend that it doesn't suffer from the faults of remoteness and abstractness. It is eminently a product of what I have ventured to call the rationalistic temper. It disdains empiricism's needs. It substitutes a pallid outline for the real world's richness. It is dapper, it is noble in the bad sense, in the sense in which to be noble is to be inapt for humble service. In this real world of sweat and dirt, it seems to me that when a view of things is 'noble,' that ought to count as a presumption against its truth, and as a philosophic disqualification. The prince of darkness may be a gentleman, as we are told he is, but whatever the God of earth and heaven is, he can surely be no gentleman. His menial services are needed in the dust of our human trials, even more than his dignity is needed in the empyrean.

Now pragmatism, devoted though she be to facts, has no such materialistic bias as ordinary empiricism labors under. Moreover, she has no objection whatever to the realizing of abstractions, so long as you get about among particulars with their aid and they actually carry you somewhere. Interested in no conclusions but those which our minds and our experiences work out together, she has no *a priori* prejudices against theology. *If theological ideas prove to have a value for concrete life, they will be true, for pragmatism, in the sense of being good for so much. For how much more they are true, will depend entirely on their relations to the other truths that also have to be acknowledged.*

What I said just now about the Absolute, of transcendental idealism, is a case in point. First, I called it majestic and said it yielded religious comfort to a class of minds, and then I accused it of remoteness and sterility. But so far as it affords such comfort, it surely is not sterile; it has that amount of value; it performs a concrete function. As a good pragmatist, I myself ought to call the Absolute true 'in so far forth,' then; and I unhesitatingly now do so.

But what does *true in so far forth* mean in this case? To answer, we need only apply the pragmatic method. What do believers in the Absolute mean by saying that their belief affords them comfort? They mean that since, in the Absolute finite evil is 'overruled' already, we may, therefore, whenever we wish, treat the temporal as if it were potentially the eternal, be sure that we can trust its outcome, and, without sin, dismiss our fear and drop the worry of our finite responsibility. In short, they mean that we have a right ever and anon to take a moral holiday, to let the world wag in its own way, feeling that its issues are in better hands than ours and are none of our business.

The universe is a system of which the individual members may relax their anxieties occasionally, in which the don't-care mood is also right for men, and moral holidays in order,—that, if I mistake not, is part, at least, of what the Absolute is 'known-as,' that is the great difference in our particular experiences which his being true makes, for us, that is his cash-value when he is pragmatically interpreted. Farther than that the ordinary lay-reader in philosophy who thinks favorably of absolute idealism does not venture to sharpen his conceptions. He can use the Absolute for so much, and so much is very precious. He is pained at hearing you speak incredulously of the Absolute, therefore, and disregards your criticisms because they deal with aspects of the conception that he fails to follow.

If the Absolute means this, and means no more than this, who can possibly deny the truth of it? To deny it would be to insist that men should never relax, and that holidays are never in order.

I am well aware how odd it must seem to some of you to hear me say that an idea is 'true' so long as to believe it is profitable to our lives. That it is *good*, for as much as it profits, you will gladly admit. If what we do by its aid is good, you will allow the idea itself to be good in so far forth, for we are the better for possessing it. But is it not a strange misuse of the word 'truth,' you will say, to call ideas also 'true' for this reason?

To answer this difficulty fully is impossible at this stage of my account. You touch here upon the very central point of Messrs. Schiller's, Dewey's, and my own doctrine of truth, which I can not discuss with detail until my sixth lecture. Let me now say only this, that truth is *one species of good*, and not, as is usually supposed, a category distinct from good, and co-ordinate with it. *The true is the name of whatever proves itself to be good in the way of belief, and good, too, for definite, assignable reasons.* Surely you must admit this, that if there were *no* good for life in true ideas, or if the knowledge of them were positively disadvantageous and false ideas the only useful ones, then the current notion that truth is divine and precious, and its pursuit a duty, could never have grown up or become a dogma. In a world like that, our duty would be to *shun* truth, rather. But in this world, just as certain foods are not only agreeable to our taste, but good for our teeth, our stomach, and our tissues; so certain ideas are not only agreeable to think about, or agreeable as supporting other ideas that we are fond of, but they are also helpful in life's practical struggles. If there be any life that it is really better we should lead, and if there be any idea which, if believed in, would help us to lead that life, then it would be really *better for us* to believe in that idea, *unless, indeed, belief in it incidentally clashed with other greater vital benefits.*

'What would be better for us to believe'! This sounds very like a definition of truth. It comes very near to saying 'what we *ought* to believe': and in *that* definition none of you would find any oddity. Ought we ever not to believe what it is *better for us* to believe? And can we then keep the notion of what is better for us, and what is true for us, permanently apart?

Pragmatism says no, and I fully agree with her. Probably you also agree, so far as the abstract statement goes, but with a suspicion that if we practically did believe everything that made for good in our own personal lives, we should be found indulging all kinds of fancies about this world's affairs, and all kinds of sentimental superstitions about a world hereafter. Your suspicion here is undoubtedly well founded, and it is evident that something happens when you pass from the abstract to the concrete that complicates the situation.

I said just now that what is better for us to believe is true *unless the belief incidentally clashes with some other vital benefit.* Now in real life what vital benefits is any particular belief of ours most liable to clash with? What indeed except the vital benefits yielded by *other beliefs* when these prove incompatible with the first ones? In other words, the greatest enemy of any one of our truths may be the rest of our truths. Truths have once for all this desperate instinct of self-preservation and of desire to extinguish whatever contradicts them. My belief in the Absolute, based on the good it does me, must run the gauntlet of all my other beliefs. Grant that it may be true in giving me a moral holiday. Nevertheless, as I conceive it,—and let me speak now confidentially, as it were, and merely in my own private person,—it clashes with other truths of mine whose benefits I hate to give up on its account. It happens to be associated with a kind of logic of which I am the enemy, I find that it entangles me in metaphysical paradoxes that are inacceptable, etc., etc. But as I have enough trouble in life already without adding the trouble of carrying these intellectual inconsistencies, I personally just give up the Absolute. I just *take* my moral holidays; or else as a professional philosopher, I try to justify them by some other principle.

If I could restrict my notion of the Absolute to its bare holiday-giving value, it wouldn't clash with my other truths. But we can not easily thus restrict our hypotheses. They carry supernumerary features, and these it is that clash so. My disbelief in the Absolute means then disbelief in those other supernumerary features, for I fully believe in the legitimacy of taking moral holidays.

You see by this what I meant when I called pragmatism a mediator and reconciler and said, borrowing the word from Papini, that she 'unstiffens' our theories. She has in fact no prejudices whatever, no obstructive dogmas, no rigid canons of what shall count as proof. She is completely genial. She will entertain any hypothesis, she will consider any evidence. It follows that in the religious field she is at a great advantage both over positivistic empiricism, with its anti-theological bias, and over religious rationalism, with its exclusive interest in the remote, the noble, the simple, and the abstract in the way of conception.

In short, she widens the field of search for God. Rationalism sticks to logic and the empyrean. Empiricism sticks to the external senses. Pragmatism is willing to take anything, to follow either logic or the senses and to count the humblest and most personal experiences. She will count mystical experiences if they have practical consequences. She will take a God who lives in the very dirt of private fact—if that should seem a likely place to find him.

Her only test of probable truth is what works best in the way of leading us, what fits every part of life best and combines with the collectivity of experience's demands, nothing being omitted. If theological ideas should do this, if the notion of God, in particular, should prove to do it, how could pragmatism possibly deny God's existence? She could see no meaning in treating as 'not true' a notion that was pragmatically so successful. What other kind of truth could there be, for her, than all this agreement with concrete reality?

PRAGMATISM'S CONCEPTION OF TRUTH

I fully expect to see the pragmatist view of truth run through the classic stages of a theory's career. First, you know, a new theory is attacked as absurd; then it is admitted to be true, but obvious and insignificant; finally it is seen to be so important that its adversaries claim that they themselves discovered it. Our doctrine of truth is at present in the first of these three stages, with symptoms of the second stage having begun in certain quarters. I wish that this lecture might help it beyond the first stage in the eyes of many of you.

Truth, as any dictionary will tell you, is a property of certain of our ideas. It means their "agreement," as falsity means their "disagreement," with "reality." Pragmatists and intellectualists both accept this definition as a matter of course. They begin to quarrel only after the question is raised as to what may precisely be meant by the term "agreement," and what by the term "reality," when reality is taken as something for our ideas to agree with.

In answering these questions the pragmatists are more analytic and painstaking, the intellectualists more offhand and irreflective. The popular notion is that a true idea must copy its reality. Like other popular views, this one follows the analogy of the most usual experience. Our true ideas of sensible things do indeed copy them. Shut your eyes and think of yonder clock on the wall, and you get just such a true picture or copy of its dial. But your idea of its "works" (unless you are a clockmaker) is much less of a copy, yet it passes muster, for it in no way clashes with the reality. Even though it should shrink to the mere word "works," that word still serves you truly; and when you speak of the "time-keeping function" of the clock, or of its spring's "elasticity," it is hard to see exactly what your ideas can copy.

You perceive that there is a problem here. Where our ideas cannot copy definitely their object, what does agreement with that object mean? Some idealists seem to say that they are true whenever they are what God means that we ought to think about that subject. Others hold the copy-view all through, and speak as if our ideas possessed truth just in proportion as they approach to being copies of the Absolute's eternal way of thinking.

These views, you see, invite pragmatistic discussion. But the great assumption of the intellectualists is that truth means essentially an inert static relation. When you've got your true idea of anything, there's an end of the matter. You're in possession; you *know*; you have fulfilled your thinking destiny. You are where you ought to be mentally; you have obeyed your categorical imperative; and nothing more need follow on that climax of your rational destiny. Epistemologically you are in stable equilibrium.

Pragmatism, on the other hand, asks its usual question. "Grant an idea or belief to be true," it says, "what concrete difference will its being true make in any one's actual life? How will the truth be realized? What experiences will be different from those which would obtain if the belief were false? What, in short, is the truth's cash-value in experiential terms?"

The moment pragmatism asks this question, it sees the answer: *True ideas are those that we can assimilate, validate, corroborate and verify. False ideas are those that we cannot.* That is the practical difference it makes to us to have true ideas, that, therefore, is the meaning of truth, for it is all that truth is known-as.

This thesis is what I have to defend. The truth of an idea is not a stagnant property inherent in it. Truth *happens* to an idea. It *becomes* true, is *made* true by events. Its verity *is* in fact an event, a process: the process namely of its verifying itself, its veri-*fication*. Its validity is the process of its valid-*ation*.

But what do the words verification and validation themselves pragmatically mean? They again signify certain practical consequences of the verified and validated idea. It is hard to find any one phrase that characterizes these consequences better than the ordinary agreement-formula—just such consequences being what we have in mind whenever we say that our ideas "agree" with reality. They lead us, namely, through the acts and other ideas which they instigate, into or up to, or towards, other parts of experience with which we feel all the while—such feeling being among our potentialities—that the original ideas remain in agreement. The connexions and transitions come to us from point to point as being progressive, harmonious, satisfactory. This function of agreeable leading is what we mean by an idea's verification. . . .

. . . The possession of true thoughts means everywhere the possession of invaluable instruments of action; and that our duty to gain truth, so far from being a blank command from out of the blue, or a "stunt" self-imposed by our intellect, can account for itself by excellent practical reasons.

The importance to human life of having true beliefs about matters of fact is a thing too notorious.

We live in a world of realities that can be infinitely useful or infinitely harmful. Ideas that tell us which of them to expect count as the true ideas in all this primary sphere of verification, and the pursuit of such ideas is a primary human duty. The possession of truth, so far from being here an end in itself, is only a preliminary means towards other vital satisfactions. If I am lost in the woods and starved, and find what looks like a cow-path, it is of the utmost importance that I should think of a human habitation at the end of it, for if I do so and follow it, I save myself. The true thought is useful here because the house which is its object is useful. The practical value of true ideas is thus primarily derived from the practical importance of their objects to us. Their objects are, indeed, not important at all times. I may on another occasion have no use for the house; and then my idea of it, however verifiable, will be practically irrelevant, and had better remain latent. Yet since almost any object may some day become temporarily important, the advantage of having a general stock of *extra* truths, of ideas that shall be true of merely possible situations, is obvious. We store such extra truths away in our memories, and with the overflow we fill our books of reference. Whenever such an extra truth becomes practically relevant to one of our emergencies, it passes from cold-storage to do work in the world and our belief in it grows active. You can say of it then either that "it is useful because it is true" or that "it is true because it is useful." Both these phrases mean exactly the same thing, namely that here is an idea that gets fulfilled and can be verified. True is the name for whatever idea starts the verification-process, useful is the name for its completed function in experience. True ideas would never have been singled out as such, would never have acquired a class-name, least of all a name suggesting value, unless they had been useful from the outset in this way.

From this simple cue pragmatism gets her general notion of truth as something essentially bound up with the way in which one moment in our experience may lead us towards other moments which it will be worth while to have been led to. Primarily, and on the common-sense level, the truth of a state of mind means this function of *a leading that is worth while*. When a moment in our experience, of any kind whatever, inspires us with a thought that is true, that

means that sooner or later we dip by that thought's guidance into the particulars of experience again and make advantageous connexion with them. This is a vague enough statement, but I beg you to retain it, for it is essential.

Our experience meanwhile is all shot through with regularities. One bit of it can warn us to get ready for another bit, can "intend" or be "significant of" that remoter object. The object's advent is the significance's verification. Truth, in these cases, meaning nothing but eventual verification, is manifestly incompatible with waywardness on our part. Woe to him whose beliefs play fast and loose with the order which realities follow in his experience; they will lead him nowhere or else make false connexions.

By "realities" or "objects" here, we mean either things of common sense, sensibly present, or else common-sense relations, such as dates, places, distances, kinds, activities. Following our mental image of a house along the cow-path, we actually come to see the house; we get the image's full verification. *Such simply and fully verified leadings are certainly the originals and prototypes of the truth-process.* Experience offers indeed other forms of truth-process, but they are all conceivable as being primary verifications arrested, multiplied or substituted one for another.

Take, for instance, yonder object on the wall. You and I consider it to be a "clock," altho no one of us has seen the hidden works that make it one. We let our notion pass for true without attempting to verify. If truths mean verification-process essentially, ought we then to call such unverified truths as this abortive? No, for they form the overwhelmingly large number of the truths we live by. Indirect as well as direct verifications pass muster. Where circumstantial evidence is sufficient, we can go without eye-witnessing. Just as we here assume Japan to exist without ever having been there, because it *works* to do so, everything we know conspiring with the belief, and nothing interfering, so we assume that thing to be a clock. We *use* it as a clock, regulating the length of our lecture by it. The verification of the assumption here means its leading to no frustration or contradiction. Verif*iability* of wheels and weights and pendulum is as good as verification. For one truth-process completed there are a million in our lives that function in this state of nascency. They turn us *towards* direct verification; lead us into the *surroundings* of the objects they envisage; and then, if everything runs on harmoniously, we are so sure that verification is possible that we omit it, and are usually justified by all that happens.

Truth lives, in fact, for the most part on a credit system. Our thoughts and beliefs "pass," so long as nothing challenges them, just as banknotes pass so long as nobody refuses them. But this all points to direct face-to-face verifications somewhere, without which the fabric of truth collapses like a financial system with no cashbasis whatever. You accept my verification of one thing, I yours of another. We trade on each other's truth. But beliefs verified concretely by *somebody* are the posts of the whole superstructure.

Another great reason—besides economy of time—for waiving complete verification in the usual business of life is that all things exist in kinds and not singly. Our world is found once for all to have that peculiarity. So that when we have once directly verified our ideas about one specimen of a kind, we consider ourselves free to apply them to other specimens without verification. A mind that habitually discerns the kind of thing before it, and acts by the law of the kind immediately, without pausing to verify, will be a "true" mind in ninety-nine out of a hundred emergencies, proved so by its conduct fitting everything it meets, and getting no refutation.

Indirectly or only potentially verifying processes may thus be true as well as full verification-processes. They work as true processes would work, give us the same advantages, and claim our recognition for the same reasons. . . .

[James returns to the notion that truth is an agreement with reality.]

Here it is that pragmatism and intellectualism begin to part company. Primarily, no doubt, to agree means to copy, but we saw that the mere word "clock" would do instead of a mental picture of its works, and that of many realities our ideas can only be symbols and not copies. "Past time," "power," "spontaneity"—how can our mind copy such realities?

To "agree" in the widest sense with a reality *can only mean to be guided either straight up to it or into its surroundings, or to be put into such working touch with it as to handle either it or something con-* *nected with it better than if we disagreed.* Better either intellectually or practically! And often agreement will only mean the negative fact that nothing contradictory from the quarter of that reality comes to interfere with the way in which our ideas guide us elsewhere. To copy a reality is, indeed, one very important way of agreeing with it, but it is far from being essential. The essential thing is the process of being guided. Any idea that helps us to *deal*, whether practically or intellectually, with either the reality or its belongings, that doesn't entangle our progress in frustrations, that *fits*, in fact, and adapts our life to the reality's whole setting, will agree sufficiently to meet the requirement. It will hold true of that reality.

Thus, *names* are just as "true" or "false" as definite mental pictures are. They set up similar verification-processes, and lead to fully equivalent practical results.

All human thinking gets discursified; we exchange ideas; we lend and borrow verifications, get them from one another by means of social intercourse. All truth thus gets verbally built out, stored up, and made available for every one. Hence, we must *talk* consistently just as we must *think* consistently: for both in talk and thought we deal with kinds. Names are arbitrary, but once understood they must be kept to. We mustn't now call Abel "Cain" or Cain "Abel." If we do, we ungear ourselves from the whole book of Genesis, and from all its connexions with the universe of speech and fact down to the present time. We throw ourselves out of whatever truth that entire system of speech and fact may embody.

The overwhelming majority of our true ideas admit of no direct or face-to-face verification—those of past history, for example, as of Cain and Abel. The stream of time can be remounted only verbally, or verified directly by the present prolongations or effects of what the past harbored. Yet if they agree with these verbalities and effects, we can know that our ideas of the past are true. *As true as past time itself was*, so true was Julius Caesar, so true were antediluvian monsters all in their proper dates and settings. That past time itself was, is guaranteed by its coherence with everything that's present. True as the present *is*, the past *was* also.

Agreement thus turns out to be essentially an affair of leading—leading that is useful because it is into quarters that contain objects that are important. True ideas lead us into useful verbal and conceptual quarters as well as directly up to useful sensible termini. They lead to consistency, stability and flowing human intercourse. They lead away from excentricity and isolation, from foiled and barren thinking. The untrammelled flowing of the leading-process, its general freedom from clash and contradiction, passes for its indirect verification; but all roads lead to Rome, and in the end and eventually, all true processes must lead to the face of directly verifying sensible experiences *somewhere*, which somebody's ideas have copied.

Such is the large loose way in which the pragmatist interprets the word agreement. He treats it altogether practically. He lets it cover any process of conduction from a present idea to a future terminus, provided only it run prosperously. It is only thus that "scientific" ideas, flying as they do beyond common sense, can be said to agree with their realities. It is, as I have already said, *as if* reality were made of ether, atoms or electrons, but we mustn't think so literally. The term "energy" doesn't even pretend to stand for anything "objective." It is only a way of measuring the surface of phenomena so as to string their changes on a simple formula.

Yet in the choice of these man-made formulas we cannot be capricious with impunity any more than we can be capricious on the common-sense practical level. We must find a theory that will *work;* and that means something extremely difficult; for our theory must mediate between all previous truths and certain new experiences. It must derange common sense and previous belief as little as possible, and it must lead to some sensible terminus or other that can be verified exactly. To "work" means both these things; and the squeeze is so tight that there is little loose play for any hypothesis. Our theories are wedged and controlled as nothing else is. Yet sometimes alternative theoretic formulas are equally compatible with all the truths we know, and then we choose between them for subjective reasons. We choose the kind of theory to which we are already partial; we follow "elegance" or "economy." Clerk-Maxwell somewhere says it would be "poor scientific taste" to choose the more

complicated of two equally well-evidenced conceptions; and you will all agree with him. Truth in science is what gives us the maximum possible sum of satisfactions, taste included, but consistency both with previous truth and with novel fact is always the most imperious claimant. . . .

Our account of truth is an account of truths in the plural, of processes of leading, realized *in rebus,*[3] and having only this quality in common, that they *pay.* They pay by guiding us into or towards some part of a system that dips at numerous points into sense-percepts, which we may copy mentally or not, but with which at any rate we are now in the kind of commerce vaguely designated as verification. Truth for us is simply a collective name for verification-processes, just as health, wealth, strength, etc., are names for other processes connected with life, and also pursued because it pays to pursue them. Truth is *made,* just as health, wealth and strength are made, in the course of experience.

Here rationalism is instantaneously up in arms against us. I can imagine a rationalist to talk as follows:

"Truth is not made," he will say; "it absolutely obtains, being a unique relation that does not wait upon any process, but shoots straight over the head of experience, and hits its reality every time. Our belief that yon thing on the wall is a clock is true already, altho no one in the whole history of the world should verify it. The bare quality of standing in that transcendent relation is what makes any thought true that possesses it, whether or not there be verification. You pragmatists put the cart before the horse in making truth's being reside in verification-processes. These are merely signs of its being, merely our lame ways of ascertaining after the fact, which of our ideas already has possessed the wondrous quality. The quality itself is timeless, like all essences and natures. Thoughts partake of it directly, as they partake of falsity or of irrelevancy. It can't be analyzed away into pragmatic consequences."

The whole plausibility of this rationalist tirade is due to the fact to which we have already paid so much attention. In our world, namely, abounding as it does in things of similar kinds and similarly asso-

---

[3][in things]

ciated, one verification serves for others of its kind, and one great use of knowing things is to be led not so much to them as to their associates, especially to human talk about them. The quality of truth, obtaining *ante rem*,[4] pragmatically means, then, the fact that in such a world innumerable ideas work better by their indirect or possible than by their direct and actual verification. Truth *ante rem* means only verifiability, then; or else it is a case of the stock rationalist trick of treating the *name* of a concrete phenomenal reality as an independent prior entity, and placing it behind the reality as its explanation. . . .

In the case of "wealth" we all see the fallacy. We know that wealth is but a name for concrete processes that certain men's lives play a part in, and not a natural excellence found in Messrs. Rockefeller and Carnegie, but not in the rest of us.

Like wealth, "health" also lives *in rebus*. It is a name for processes, as digestion, circulation, sleep, etc., that go on happily, tho in this instance we are more inclined to think of it as a principle and to say the man digests and sleeps so well *because* he is so healthy.

With "strength" we are, I think, more rationalistic still, and decidedly inclined to treat it as an excellence pre-existing in the man and explanatory of the herculean performances of his muscles.

With "truth" most people go over the border entirely, and treat the rationalistic account as self-evident. But really all these words in *th* are exactly similar. Truth exists *ante rem* just as much and as little as the other things do.

The scholastics, following Aristotle, made much of the distinction between habit and act. Health *in actu* means, among other things, good sleeping and digesting. But a healthy man need not always be sleeping, or always digesting, any more than a wealthy man need be always handling money, or a strong man always lifting weights. All such qualities sink to the status of "habits" between their times of exercise; and similarly truth becomes a habit of certain of our ideas and beliefs in their intervals of rest from their verifying activities. But those activities are the root of the whole matter, and the condition of there being any habit to exist in the intervals.

"The true," to put it very briefly, is only the expedient in the way of our thinking, just as "the right" is only the expedient in the way of our behaving. Expedient in almost any fashion; and expedient in the long run and on the whole of course; for what meets expediently all the experience in sight won't necessarily meet all further experiences equally satisfactorily. Experience, as we know, has ways of *boiling over*, and making us correct our present formulas.

The "absolutely" true, meaning what no further experience will ever alter, is that ideal vanishing-point towards which we imagine that all our temporary truths will some day converge. It runs on all fours with the perfectly wise man, and with the absolutely complete experience; and, if these ideals are ever realized, they will all be realized together. Meanwhile we have to live today by what truth we can get today, and be ready tomorrow to call it falsehood. Ptolemaic astronomy, Euclidean space, Aristotelian logic, Scholastic metaphysics, were expedient for centuries, but human experience has boiled over those limits, and we now call these things only relatively true, or true within those borders of experience. "Absolutely" they are false; for we know that those limits were casual, and might have been transcended by past theorists just as they are by present thinkers.

When new experiences lead to retrospective judgments, using the past tense, what these judgments utter *was* true, even tho no past thinker had been led there. We live forwards, a Danish thinker [Kierkegaard] has said, but we understand backwards. The present sheds a backward light on the world's previous processes. They may have been truth-processes for the actors in them. They are not so for one who knows the latter revelations of the story.

This regulative notion of a potential better truth to be established later, possibly to be established some day absolutely, and having powers of retroactive legislation, turns its face, like all pragmatist notions, towards concreteness of fact, and towards the future. Like the half-truths, the absolute truth will have to be *made*, made as a relation incidental to the growth of a mass of verification-experience, to which the half-true ideas are all along contributing their quota.

---

[4][before the thing]

I have already insisted on the fact that truth is made largely out of previous truths. Men's beliefs at any time are so much experience *funded*. But the beliefs are themselves parts of the sum total of the world's experience, and become matter, therefore, for the next day's funding operations. So far as reality means experienceable reality, both it and the truths men gain about it are everlastingly in process of mutation—mutation towards a definite goal, it may be—but still mutation.

Mathematicians can solve problems with two variables. On the Newtonian theory, for instance, acceleration varies with distance, but distance also varies with acceleration. In the realm of truth-processes facts come independently and determine our beliefs provisionally. But these beliefs make us act, and as fast as they do so, they bring into sight or into existence new facts which re-determine the beliefs accordingly. So the whole coil and ball of truth, as it rolls up, is the product of a double influence.

Truths emerge from facts; but they dip forward into facts again and add to them; which facts again create or reveal new truth (the word is indifferent) and so on indefinitely. The "facts" themselves meanwhile are not *true*. They simply *are*. Truth is the function of the beliefs that start and terminate among them. . . .

The case is like a snowball's growth, due as it is to the distribution of the snow on the one hand, and to the successive pushes of the boys on the other, with these factors co-determining each other incessantly. . . .

I am well aware how odd it must seem to some of you to hear me say that an idea is "true" so long as to believe it is profitable to our lives. That it is *good*, for as much as it profits, you will gladly admit. If what we do by its aid is good, you will allow the idea itself to be good in so far forth, for we are the better for possessing it. But is it not a strange misuse of the word "truth," you will say, to call ideas also "true" for this reason? . . .

REVIEW QUESTIONS

1. What does James mean by *live* or *dead* hypotheses? What does he mean by a *genuine option*?
2. Can we make something true simply by believing it to be true? Why or why not? Does James make this claim?
3. Does James believe that it is always wrong to believe anything on insufficient evidence? As he sees it, what are the risks of refusing to make a leap of faith?
4. What is James's argument against philosophers who believe in the correspondence theory of truth?
5. How does James define true and false ideas?

30

BERTRAND RUSSELL

Bertrand Russell was born in England in 1872, the godson of John Stuart Mill. His parents died when he was three, and he was brought up by his deeply religious grandmother. He studied mathematics and philosophy and later taught at Cambridge University. He traveled widely, to China and Russia, as well as to the United States, where he taught for a brief period. His work covers virtually all areas of philosophical inquiry, from logic through philosophy of religion and philosophy of mind to ethics. He made major contributions to logic, especially with his *Principia Matematica* (written with Alfred North Whitehead), philosophy of language, and epistemology.

Russell received the Nobel Prize for Literature in 1950.

Though he never was a doctrinaire pacifist, Russell's opposition to World War I and the Vietnam War, which he regarded as senseless slaughters, led to loss of his Cambridge fellowship and two imprisonments—on the last occasion at the age of ninety-four. An agnostic, he debated the Jesuit philosopher Father F. C. Copleston on the existence of God. He was asked what he would say to God, when, after death, he was asked by God why he didn't believe in Him. Russell replied, "God, why did you make the evidence for your existence so insufficient?" He died in 1970 at the age of ninety-seven.

Our first reading, from *The Problems of Philosophy*, is one of the most succinct, insightful outlines of the central notions of epistemology. Russell wrote in his preface, "In the following pages I have confined myself in the main to those problems of philosophy in regard to which I thought it possible to say something positive and constructive, since merely negative criticism seemed out of place. For this reason, theory of knowledge occupies a larger space than metaphysics in the present volume, and some topics much discussed by philosophers are treated very briefly, if at all." In the first few chapters Russell defends a Lockean (see John Locke, Chapter 19) or representationalist view of sense perception, holding that there is a real world but that we never know it directly. Of special importance is his defense of the Correspondence theory of truth (chapter XII), which may be contrasted with William James's Pragmatic theory of truth (see James, Chapter 29).

In our last selection, "A Free Man's Worship," Russell attempts to find meaning and morality in a life or world without God or a transcendental being. The world, Russell laments, is an absurd, godless tragedy, in which nature, omnipotent but blind, has brought forth rational, purposeful children who are superior to their mother, and as such can discover moral ideals with which to sustain themselves in this ultimately meaningless existence. Morality doesn't need religion for legitimation.

FOR FURTHER READING

Ayer, A. J. *Bertrand Russell* (University of Chicago Press, 1988).
Clark, R. *The Life of Bertrand Russell* (De Capo Press, 1990).
Russell, Bertrand. *The Autobiography of Bertrand Russell* (Allen & Unwin, 1961).
Russell, Bertrand. *A History of Western Philosophy* (Random House, 1945).
Russell, Bertrand. *Human Knowledge* (Simon & Schuster, 1962).
Sainsbury, M. *Russell* (Routledge & Kegan Paul, 1979).
Schilpp, P. A., ed. *The Philosophy of Bertrand Russell* (Harper & Row, 1963).

THE PROBLEMS OF PHILOSOPHY

CHAPTER I. APPEARANCE AND REALITY

Is there any knowledge in the world which is so certain that no reasonable man could doubt it? This question, which at first sight might not seem difficult, is really one of the most difficult that can be asked. When we have realized the obstacles in the way of a straightforward and confident answer, we shall be well launched on the study of philosophy—for philosophy is merely the attempt to answer such ultimate questions, not carelessly and dogmatically, as we do in ordinary life and even in the sciences, but critically after exploring all that makes such questions puzzling, and after realizing all the vagueness and confusion that underlie our ordinary ideas.

In daily life, we assume as certain many things which, on a closer scrutiny, are found to be so full of apparent contradictions that only a great amount of thought enables us to know what it is that we really may believe. In the search for certainty, it is natural to begin with our present experiences, and in some sense, no doubt, knowledge is to be derived from them. But any statement as to what it is that our immediate experiences make us know is very likely to be wrong. It seems to me that I am now sitting in a chair, at a table of a certain shape, on which I see sheets of paper with writing or print. By turning my head I see out of the window buildings and clouds and the sun. I believe that the sun is about ninety-three million miles from the earth; that it is a hot globe many times bigger than the earth; that, owing to the earth's rotation, it rises every morning, and will continue to do so for an indefinite time in the future. I believe that, if any other normal person comes into my room, he will see the same chairs and tables and books and papers as I see, and that the table which I see is the same as the table which I feel pressing against my arm. All this seems to be so evident as to be hardly worth stating, except in answer to a man who doubts whether I know anything. Yet all this may be reasonably doubted, and all of it requires much careful discussion before we can be sure that we have stated it in a form that is wholly true.

To make our difficulties plain, let us concentrate attention on the table. To the eye it is oblong, brown and shiny, to the touch it is smooth and cool and hard; when I tap it, it gives out a wooden sound. Any one else who sees and feels and hears the table will agree with this description, so that it might seem as if no difficulty would arise; but as soon as we try to be more precise our troubles begin. Although I believe that the table is 'really' of the same colour all over, the parts that reflect the light look much brighter than the other parts, and some parts look white because of reflected light. I know that, if I move, the parts that reflect the light will be different, so that the apparent distribution of colours on the table will change. It follows that if several people are looking at the table at the same moment, no two of them will see exactly the same distribution of colours, because no two can see it from exactly the same point of view, and any change in the point of view makes some change in the way the light is reflected.

For most practical purposes these differences are unimportant, but to the painter they are all-important: the painter has to unlearn the habit of thinking that things seem to have the colour which common sense says they 'really' have, and to learn the habit of seeing things as they appear. Here we have already the beginning of one of the distinctions that cause most trouble in philosophy—the distinction between 'appearance' and 'reality', between what things seem to be and what they are. The painter wants to know what things seem to be, the practical man and the philosopher want to know what they are; but the philosopher's wish to know this is stronger than the practical man's, and is more troubled by knowledge as to the difficulties of answering the question.

To return to the table. It is evident from what we have found, that there is no colour which preemi-

nently appears to be the colour of the table, or even of any one particular part of the table—it appears to be of different colours from different points of view, and there is no reason for regarding some of these as more really its colour than others. And we know that even from a given point of view the colour will seem different by artificial light, or to a colour-blind man, or to a man wearing blue spectacles, while in the dark there will be no colour at all, though to touch and hearing the table will be unchanged. This colour is not something which is inherent in the table, but something depending upon the table and the spectator and the way the light falls on the table. When, in ordinary life, we speak of the colour of the table, we only mean the sort of colour which it will seem to have to a normal spectator from an ordinary point of view under usual conditions of light. But the other colours which appear under other conditions have just as good a right to be considered real; and therefore, to avoid favouritism, we are compelled to deny that, in itself, the table has any one particular colour.

The same thing applies to the texture. With the naked eye one can see the grain, but otherwise the table looks smooth and even. If we looked at it through a microscope, we should see roughnesses and hills and valleys, and all sorts of differences that are imperceptible to the naked eye. Which of these is the 'real' table? We are naturally tempted to say that what we see through the microscope is more real, but that in turn would be changed by a still more powerful microscope. If, then, we cannot trust what we see with the naked eye, why should we trust what we see through a microscope? Thus, again, the confidence in our senses with which we began deserts us.

The shape of the table is no better. We are all in the habit of judging as to the 'real' shapes of things, and we do this so unreflectingly that we come to think we actually see the real shapes. But, in fact, as we all have to learn if we try to draw, a given thing looks different in shape from every different point of view. If our table is 'really' rectangular, it will look, from almost all points of view, as if it had two acute angles and two obtuse angles. If opposite sides are parallel, they will look as if they converged to a point away from the spectator; if they are of equal length, they will look as if the nearer side were longer. All these things are not commonly noticed in looking at a table, because experience has taught us to construct the 'real' shape from the apparant shape, and the 'real' shape is what interests us as practical men. But the 'real' shape is not what we see; it is something inferred from what we see. And what we see is constantly changing in shape as we move about the room; so that here again the senses seem not to give us the truth about the table itself, but only about the appearance of the table.

Similar difficulties arise when we consider the sense of touch. It is true that the table always gives us a sensation of hardness, and we feel that it resists pressure. But the sensation we obtain depends upon how hard we press the table and also upon what part of the body we press with; thus the various sensations due to various pressures or various parts of the body cannot be supposed to reveal directly any definite property of the table, but at most to be signs of some property which perhaps causes all the sensations, but is not actually apparent in any of them. And the same applies still more obviously to the sounds which can be elicited by rapping the table.

Thus it becomes evident that the real table, if there is one, is not the same as what we immediately experience by sight or touch or hearing. The real table, if there is one, is not immediately known to us at all, but must be an inference from what is immediately known. Hence, two very difficult questions at once arise; namely, (1) Is there a real table at all? (2) If so, what sort of object can it be?

It will help us in considering these questions to have a few simple terms of which the meaning is definite and clear. Let us give the name of 'sense-data' to the things that are immediately known in sensation: such things as colours, sounds, smells, hardnesses, roughnesses, and so on. We shall give the name 'sensation' to the experience of being immediately aware of these things. Thus, whenever we see a colour, we have a sensation of the colour, but the colour itself is a sense-datum, not a sensation. The colour is that of which we are immediately aware, and the awareness itself is the sensation. It is plain that if we are to know anything about the table, it must be by means of the sense-data—brown colour, oblong shape, smoothness, etc.—which we associate with the table; but, for the reasons which have been given, we cannot say that the table is the

sense-data, or even that the sense-data are directly properties of the table. Thus a problem arises as to the relation of the sense-data to the real table, supposing there is such a thing.

The real table, if it exists, we will call a 'physical object'. Thus we have to consider the relation of sense-data to physical objects. The collection of all physical objects is called 'matter'. Thus our two questions may be re-stated as follows: (1) Is there any such thing as matter? (2) If so, what is its nature?

The philosopher who first brought prominently forward the reasons for regarding the immediate objects of our senses as not existing independently of us was Bishop Berkeley (1685–1753). His *Three Dialogues between Hylas and Philonous, in Opposition to Sceptics and Atheists*, undertake to prove that there is no such thing as matter at all, and that the world consists of nothing but minds and their ideas. Hylas has hitherto believed in matter, but he is no match for Philonous, who mercilessly drives him into contradictions and paradoxes, and makes his own denial of matter seem, in the end, as if it were almost common sense. The arguments employed are of very different value: some are important and sound, others are confused or quibbling. But Berkeley retains the merit of having shown that the existence of matter is capable of being denied without absurdity, and that if there are any things that exist independently of us they cannot be the immediate objects of our sensations.

There are two different questions involved when we ask whether matter exists, and it is important to keep them clear. We commonly mean by 'matter' something which is opposed to 'mind', something which we think of as occupying space and as radically incapable of any sort of thought or consciousness. It is chiefly in this sense that Berkeley denies matter; that is to say, he does not deny that the sense-data which we commonly take as signs of the existence of the table are really signs of the existence of something independent of us, but he does deny that this something is nonmental, that it is neither mind nor ideas entertained by some mind. He admits that there must be something which continues to exist when we go out of the room or shut our eyes, and that what we call seeing the table does really give us reason for believing in something which persists even when we are not seeing it. But he thinks that this something cannot be radically different in nature from what we see, and cannot be independent of seeing altogether, though it must be independent of our seeing. He is thus led to regard the 'real' table as an idea in the mind of God. Such an idea has the required permanence and independence of ourselves, without being—as matter would otherwise be—something quite unknowable, in the sense that we can only infer it, and can never be directly and immediately aware of it.

Other philosophers since Berkeley have also held that, although the table does not depend for its existence upon being seen by me, it does depend upon being seen (or otherwise apprehended in sensation) by some mind—not necessarily the mind of God, but more often the whole collective mind of the universe. This they hold, as Berkeley does, chiefly because they think there can be nothing real—or at any rate nothing known to be real except minds and their thoughts and feelings. We might state the argument by which they support their view in some such way as this: 'Whatever can be thought of is an idea in the mind of the person thinking of it; therefore nothing can be thought of except ideas in minds; therefore anything else is inconceivable, and what is inconceivable cannot exist.'

Such an argument, in my opinion, is fallacious; and of course those who advance it do not put it so shortly or so crudely. But whether valid or not, the argument has been very widely advanced in one form or another; and very many philosophers, perhaps a majority, have held that there is nothing real except minds and their ideas. Such philosophers are called 'idealists'. When they come to explaining matter, they either say, like Berkeley, that matter is really nothing but a collection of ideas, or they say, like Leibniz (1646–1716), that what happens as matter is really a collection of more or less rudimentary minds.

But these philosophers, though they deny matter as opposed to mind, nevertheless, in another sense, admit matter. It will be remembered that we asked two questions; namely, (1) Is there a real table at all? (2) If so, what sort of object can it be? Now both Berkeley and Leibniz admit that there is a real table, but Berkeley says it is certain ideas in the mind of God, and Leibniz says it is a colony of souls. Thus both of them answer our first question in the affirmative and only diverge from the views of ordinary mortals in their answer to our second question. In fact, almost all philosophers seem to be agreed that there is a real table. They almost all agree that, however much our sense-data—colour, shape, smoothness, etc.—may depend upon us, yet their occurrence is a sign of something existing independently of us, something differing, perhaps, completely from our sense-data whenever we are in a suitable relation to the real table.

Now obviously this point in which the philosophers are agreed—the view that there is a real table, whatever its nature may be is vitally important, and it will be worth while to consider what reasons there are for accepting this view before we go on to the further question as to the nature of the real table. Our next chapter, therefore, will be concerned with the reasons for supposing that there is a real table at all.

Before we go farther it will be well to consider for a moment what it is that we have discovered so far. It has appeared that, if we take any common object of the sort that is supposed to be known by the senses, what the senses immediately tell us is not the truth about the object as it is apart from us, but only the truth about certain sense-data which, so far as we can see, depend upon the relations between us and the object. Thus what we directly see and feel is merely 'appearance', which we believe to be a sign of some 'reality' behind. But if the reality is not what appears, have we any means of knowing whether there is any reality at all? And if so, have we any means of finding out what it is like?

Such questions are bewildering, and it is difficult to know that even the strangest hypotheses may not be true. Thus our familiar table, which has roused but the slightest thoughts in us hitherto, has become a problem full of surprising possibilities. The one thing we know about it is that it is not what it seems. Beyond this modest result, so far, we have the most complete liberty of conjecture. Leibniz tells us it is a community of souls: Berkeley tells us it is an idea in the mind of God; sober science, scarcely less wonderful, tells us it is a vast collection of electric charges in violent motion.

Among these surprising possibilities, doubt suggests that perhaps there is no table at all. Philosophy, if it cannot answer so many questions as we could wish, has at least the power of asking questions which increase the interest of the world, and show the strangeness and wonder lying just below the surface even in the commonest things of daily life.

CHAPTER II. THE EXISTENCE OF MATTER

In this chapter we have to ask ourselves whether, in any sense at all, there is such a thing as matter. Is there a table which has a certain intrinsic nature, and continues to exist when I am not looking, or is the table merely a product of my imagination, a dream-table in a very prolonged dream? This question is of the greatest importance. For if we cannot be sure of the independent existence of objects, we cannot be sure of the independent existence of other people's bodies, and therefore still less of other people's minds, since we have no grounds for believing in their minds except such as are derived from observing their bodies. Thus if we cannot be sure of the independent existence of objects, we shall be left alone in a desert—it may be that the whole outer world is nothing but a dream, and that we alone exist. This is an uncomfortable possibility; but although it cannot be strictly proved to be false, there is not the slightest reason to suppose that it is true. In this chapter we have to see why this is the case.

Before we embark upon doubtful matters, let us try to find some more or less fixed point from which to start. Although we are doubting the physical existence of the table, we are not doubting the existence of the sense-data which made us think there was a table; we are not doubting that, while we look, a certain colour and shape appear to us, and while we press, a certain sensation of hardness is experienced by us. All this, which is psychological, we are not calling in question. In fact, whatever else may be doubtful, some at least of our immediate experiences seem absolutely certain.

Descartes (1596–1650), the founder of modern philosophy, invented a method which may still be used with profit—the method of systematic doubt. He determined that he would believe nothing which he did not see quite clearly and distinctly to be true. Whatever he could bring himself to doubt, he would

doubt, until he saw reason for not doubting it. By applying this method he gradually became convinced that the only existence of which he could be quite certain was his own. He imagined a deceitful demon, who presented unreal things to his senses in a perpetual phantasmagoria; it might be very improbable that such a demon existed, but still it was possible, and therefore doubt concerning things perceived by the senses was possible.

But doubt concerning his own existence was not possible, for if he did not exist, no demon could deceive him. If he doubted, he must exist; if he had any experiences whatever, he must exist. Thus his own existence was an absolute certainty to him. 'I think, therefore I am,' he said (Cogito, ergo sum); and on the basis of this certainty he set to work to build up again the world of knowledge which his doubt had laid in ruins. By inventing the method of doubt, and by showing that subjective things are the most certain, Descartes performed a great service to philosophy, and one which makes him still useful to all students of the subject.

But some care is needed in using Descartes' argument. 'I think, therefore I am' says rather more than is strictly certain. It might seem as though we were quite sure of being the same person to-day as we were yesterday, and this is no doubt true in some sense. But the real Self is as hard to arrive at as the real table and does not seem to have the absolute, convincing certainty that belongs to particular experiences. When I look at my table and see a certain brown colour, what is quite certain at once is not 'I am seeing a brown colour', but rather, 'a brown colour is being seen'. This of course involves something (or somebody) which (or who) sees the brown colour; but it does not of itself involve that more or less permanent person whom we call 'I'. So far as immediate certainty goes, it might be that the something which sees the brown colour is quite momentary, and not the same as the something which has some different experience the next moment.

Thus it is our particular thoughts and feelings that have primitive certainty. And this applies to dreams and hallucinations as well as to normal perceptions: when we dream or see a ghost, we certainly do have the sensations we think we have, but for various reasons it is held that no physical object corresponds to these sensations. Thus the certainty of our knowledge of our own experiences does not have to be limited in any way to allow for exceptional cases. Here, therefore, we have, for what it is worth, a solid basis from which to begin our pursuit of knowledge.

The problem we have to consider is this: Granted that we are certain of our own sense-data, have we any reason for regarding them as signs of the existence of something else, which we can call the physical object? When we have enumerated all the sense-data which we should naturally regard as connected with the table have we said all there is to say about the table, or is there still something else—something not a sense-datum, something which persists when we go out of the room? Common sense unhesitatingly answers that there is. What can be bought and sold and pushed about and have a cloth laid on it, and so on, cannot be a mere collection of sense-data. If the cloth completely hides the table, we shall derive no sense-data from the table, and therefore, if the table were merely sense-data, it would have ceased to exist, and the cloth would be suspended in empty air, resting, by a miracle, in the place where the table formerly was. This seems plainly absurd; but whoever wishes to become a philosopher must learn not to be frightened by absurdities.

One great reason why it is felt that we must secure a physical object in addition to the sense-data, is that we want the same object for different people. When ten people are sitting round a dinner-table, it seems preposterous to maintain that they are not seeing the same tablecloth, the same knives and forks and spoons and glasses. But the sense-data are private to each separate person; what is immediately present to the sight of one is not immediately present to the sight of another: they all see things from slightly different points of view, and therefore see them slightly differently. Thus, if there are to be public neutral objects, which can be in some sense known to many different people, there must be something over and above the private and particular sense-data which appear to various people. What reason, then, have we for believing that there are such public neutral objects?

The first answer that naturally occurs to one is that, although different people may see the table slightly differently, still they all see more or less similar things when they look at the table, and the variations in what they see follow the laws of perspective and reflection of light, so that it is easy to arrive at a permanent object underlying all the different people's sense-data. I bought my table from the former occupant of my room; I could not buy his sense-data, which died when he went away, but I could and did buy the confident expectation of more or less similar sense-data. Thus it is the fact that different people have similar sense-data, and that one person in a given place at different times has similar sense-data, which makes us suppose that over and above the sense-data there is a permanent public object which underlies or causes the sense-data of various people at various times.

Now in so far as the above considerations depend upon supposing that there are other people besides ourselves, they beg the very question at issue. Other people are represented to me by certain sense-data, such as the sight of them or the sound of their voices, and if I had no reason to believe that there were physical objects independent of my sense-data, I should have no reason to believe that other people exist except as part of my dream. Thus, when we are trying to show that there must be objects independent of our own sense-data, we cannot appeal to the testimony of other people, since this testimony itself consists of sense-data, and does not reveal other people's experiences unless our own sense-data are signs of things existing independently of us. We must therefore, if possible, find, in our own purely private experiences, characteristics which show, or tend to show, that there are in the world things other than ourselves and our private experiences.

In one sense it must be admitted that we can never prove the existence of things other than ourselves and our experiences. No logical absurdity results from the hypothesis that the world consists of myself and my thoughts and feelings and sensations, and that everything else is mere fancy. In dreams a very complicated world may seem to be present, and yet on waking we find it was a delusion; that is to say, we find that the sense-data in the dream do not appear to have corresponded with such physical objects as we should naturally infer from our sense-data. (It is true that, when the physical world is assumed, it is possible to find physical causes for the sense-data in dreams: a door banging, for instance, may cause us to dream of a naval engagement. But although, in this case, there is a physical cause for the sense-data, there is not a physical object corresponding to the sense-data in the way in which an actual naval battle would correspond.) There is no logical impossibility in the supposition that the whole of life is a dream, in which we ourselves create all the objects that come before us. But although this is not logically impossible, there is no reason whatever to suppose that it is true; and it is, in fact, a less simple hypothesis, viewed as a means of accounting for the facts of our own life, than the common-sense hypothesis that there really are objects independent of us, whose action on us causes our sensations.

The way in which simplicity comes in from supposing that there really are physical objects is easily seen. If the cat appears at one moment in one part of the room, and at another in another part, it is natural to suppose that it has moved from the one to the other, passing over a series of intermediate positions. But if it is merely a set of sense-data, it cannot have ever been in any place where I did not see it; thus we shall have to suppose that it did not exist at all while I was not looking, but suddenly sprang into being in a new place. If the cat exists whether I see it or not, we can understand from our own experience how it gets hungry between one meal and the next; but if it does not exist when I am not seeing it, it seems odd that appetite should grow during non-existence as fast as during existence. And if the cat consists only of sense-data, it cannot be hungry, since no hunger but my own can be a sense-datum to me. Thus the behaviour of the sense-data which represent the cat to me, though it seems quite natural when regarded as an expression of hunger, becomes utterly inexplicable when regarded as mere movements and changes of patches of colour, which are as incapable of hunger as triangle is of playing football.

But the difficulty in the case of the cat is nothing compared to the difficulty in the case of human beings. When human beings speak—that is, when we hear certain noises which we associate with ideas, and simultaneously see certain motions of lips and expressions of face—it is very difficult to suppose that what we hear is not the expression of a thought, as we know it would be if we emitted the same sounds. Of course similar things happen in dreams, where we are mistaken as to the existence of other

people. But dreams are more or less suggested by what we call waking life, and are capable of being more or less accounted for on scientific principles if we assume that there really is a physical world. Thus every principle of simplicity urges us to adopt the natural view, that there really are objects other than ourselves and our sense-data which have an existence not dependent upon our perceiving them.

Of course it is not by argument that we originally come by our belief in an independent external world. We find this belief ready in ourselves as soon as we begin to reflect: it is what may be called an instinctive belief. We should never have been led to question this belief but for the fact that, at any rate in the case of sight, it seems as if the sense-datum itself was instinctively believed to be the independent object, whereas argument shows that the object cannot be identical with the sense-datum. This discovery, however—which is not at all paradoxical in the case of taste and smell and sound, and only slightly so in the case of touch—leaves undiminished our instinctive belief that there are objects corresponding to our sense-data. Since this belief does not lead to any difficulties, but on the contrary tends to simplify and systematize our account of our experiences, there seems no good reason for rejecting it. We may therefore admit—though with a slight doubt derived from dreams—that the external world does really exist, and is not wholly dependent for its existence upon our continuing to perceive it.

The argument which has led us to this conclusion is doubtless less strong than we could wish, but it is typical of many philosophical arguments, and it is therefore worth while to consider briefly its general character and validity. All knowledge, we find, must be built up upon our instinctive beliefs, and if these are rejected, nothing is left. But among our instinctive beliefs some are much stronger than others, while many have, by habit and association, become entangled with other beliefs, not really instinctive, but falsely supposed to be part of what is believed instinctively.

Philosophy should show us the hierarchy of our instinctive beliefs, beginning with those we hold most strongly, and presenting each as much isolated and as free from irrelevant additions as possible. It should take care to show that, in the form in which they are finally set forth, our instinctive beliefs do not clash, but form a harmonious system. There can never be any reason for rejecting one instinctive belief except that it clashes with others; thus, if they are found to harmonize, the whole system becomes worthy of acceptance.

It is of course possible that all or any of our beliefs may be mistaken, and therefore all ought to be held with at least some slight element of doubt. But we cannot have reason to reject a belief except on the ground of some other belief. Hence, by organizing our instinctive beliefs and their consequences, by considering which among them is most possible, if necessary, to modify or abandon, we can arrive, on the basis of accepting as our sole data what we instinctively believe, at an orderly systematic organization of our knowledge, in which, though the possibility of error remains, its likelihood is diminished by the interrelation of the parts and by the critical scrutiny which has preceded acquiescence.

This function, at least, philosophy can perform. Most philosophers, rightly or wrongly, believe that philosophy can do much more than this—that it can give us knowledge, not otherwise attainable, concerning the universe as a whole, and concerning the nature of ultimate reality. Whether this be the case or not, the more modest function we have spoken of can certainly be performed by philosophy, and certainly suffices, for those who have once begun to doubt the adequacy of common sense, to justify the arduous and difficult labours that philosophical problems involve.

CHAPTER III. THE NATURE OF MATTER

In the preceding chapter we agreed, though without being able to find demonstrative reasons, that it is rational to believe that our sense-data—for example, those which we regard as associated with my table—are really signs of the existence of something independent of us and our perceptions. That is to say, over and above the sensations of colour, hardness, noise, and so on, which make up the appearance of the table to me, I assume that there is something else, of which these things are appearances. The colour ceases to exist if I shut my eyes, the sensation of hardness ceases to exist if I remove my arm from

contact with the table, the sound ceases to exist if I cease to rap the table with my knuckles. But I do not believe that when all these things cease the table ceases. On the contrary, I believe that it is because the table exists continuously that all these sense-data will reappear when I open my eyes, replace my arm, and begin again to rap with my knuckles. The question we have to consider in this chapter is: What is the nature of this real table, which persists independently of my perception of it?

To this question physical science gives an answer, somewhat incomplete it is true, and in part still very hypothetical, but yet deserving of respect so far as it goes. Physical science, more or less unconsciously, has drifted into the view that all natural phenomena ought to be reduced to motions. Light and heat and sound are all due to wave-motions, which travel from the body emitting them to the person who sees light or feels heat or hears sound. That which has the wave-motion is either ether or 'gross matter', but in either case is what the philosopher would call matter. The only properties which science assigns to it are position in space, and the power of motion according to the laws of motion. Science does not deny that it may have other properties; but if so, such other properties are not useful to the man of science, and in no way assist him in explaining the phenomena.

It is sometimes said that 'light is a form of wave-motion', but this is misleading, for the light which we immediately see, which we know directly by means of our senses, is not a form of wave-motion, but something quite different—something which we all know if we are not blind, though we cannot describe it so as to convey our knowledge to a man who is blind. A wave-motion, on the contrary, could quite well be described to a blind man, since he can acquire a knowledge of space by the sense of touch; and he can experience a wave-motion by a sea voyage almost as well as we can. But this, which a blind man can understand, is not what we mean by light: we mean by light just that which a blind man can never understand, and which we can never describe to him.

Now this something, which all of us who are not blind know, is not, according to science, really to be found in the outer world: it is something caused by the action of certain waves upon the eyes and nerves and brain of the person who sees the light. When it is said that light is waves, what is really meant is that waves are the physical cause of our sensations of light. But light itself, the thing which seeing people experience and blind people do not, is not supposed by science to form any part of the world that is independent of us and our senses. And very similar remarks would apply to other kinds of sensations.

It is not only colours and sounds and so on that are absent from the scientific world of matter, but also space as we get it through sight or touch. It is essential to science that its matter should be in a space, but the space in which it is cannot be exactly the space we see or feel. To begin with, space as we see it is not the same as space as we get it by the sense of touch; it is only by experience in infancy that we learn how to touch things we see, or how to get a sight of things which we feel touching us. But the space of science is neutral as between touch and sight; thus it cannot be either the space of touch or the space of sight.

Again, different people see the same object as of different shapes, according to their point of view. A circular coin, for example, though we should always judge it to be circular, will look oval unless we are straight in front of it. When we judge that it is circular, we are judging that it has a real shape which is not its apparent shape, but belongs to it intrinsically apart from its appearance. But this real shape, which is what concerns science, must be in a real space, not the same as anybody's apparent space. The real space is public, the apparent space is private to the percipient. In different people's private spaces the same object seems to have different shapes; thus the real space, in which it has its real shape, must be different from the private spaces. The space of science, therefore, though connected with the spaces we see and feel, is not identical with them, and the manner of its connexion requires investigation.

We agreed provisionally that physical objects cannot be quite like our sense-data, but may be regarded as causing our sensations. These physical objects are in the space of science, which we may call 'physical' space. It is important to notice that, if our sensations are to be caused by physical objects, there must be a physical space containing these objects and our sense-organs and nerves and brain. We get a sensation of touch from an object when we are in contact with it; that is to say, when some part of our body occupies a place in physical space quite close to the space occupied by the object. We see an object (roughly speaking) when no opaque body is between the object and our eyes in physical space. Similarly, we only hear or smell or taste an object when we are sufficiently near to it, or when it touches the tongue, or has some suitable position in physical space relatively to our body. We cannot begin to state what different sensations we shall derive from a given object under different circumstances unless we regard the object and our body as both in one physical space, for it is mainly the relative positions of the object and our body that determine what sensations we shall derive from the object.

Now our sense-data are situated in our private spaces, either the space of sight or the space of touch or such vaguer spaces as other senses may give us. If, as science and common sense assume, there is one public all-embracing physical space in which physical objects are, the relative positions of physical objects in physical space must more or less correspond to the relative positions of sense-data in our private spaces. There is no difficulty in supposing this to be the case. If we see on a road one house nearer to us than another, our other senses will bear out the view that it is nearer; for example, it will be reached sooner if we walk along the road. Other people will agree that the house which looks nearer to us is nearer; the ordnance map will take the same view; and thus everything points to a spatial relation between the houses corresponding to the relation between the sense-data which we see when we look at the houses. Thus we may assume that there is a physical space in which physical objects have spatial relations corresponding to those which the corresponding sense-data have in our private spaces. It is this physical space which is dealt with in geometry and assumed in physics and astronomy.

Assuming that there is physical space, and that it does thus correspond to private spaces, what can we know about it? We can know only what is required in order to secure the correspondence. That is to say, we can know nothing of what it is like in itself, but we can know the sort of arrangement of physical objects which results from their spatial relations. We can know, for example, that the earth and moon and sun are in one straight line during an eclipse, though we cannot know what a physical straight line is in itself, as we know the look of a straight line in our visual space. Thus we come to know much more about the relations of distances in physical space than about the distances themselves; we may know that one distance is greater than another, or that it is along the same straight line as the other, but we cannot have that immediate acquaintance with physical distances that we have with distances in our private spaces, or with colours or sounds or other sense-data. We can know all those things about physical space which a man born blind might know through other people about the space of sight; but the kind of things which a man born blind could never know about the space of sight we also cannot know about physical space. We can know the properties of the relations required to preserve the correspondence with sense-data, but we cannot know the nature of the terms between which the relations hold.

With regard to time, our feeling of duration or of the lapse of time is notoriously an unsafe guide as to the time that has elapsed by the clock. Times when we are bored or suffering pain pass slowly, times when we are agreeably occupied pass quickly, and times when we are sleeping pass almost as if they did not exist. Thus, in so far as time is constituted by duration, there is the same necessity for distinguishing a public and a private time as there was in the case of space. But in so far as time consists in an order of before and after, there is no need to make such a distinction; the time-order which events seem to have is, so far as we can see, the same as the time-order which they do have. At any rate no reason can be given for supposing that the two orders are not the same. The same is usually true of space: if a regiment of men are marching along a road, the shape of the regiment will look different from different points of view, but the men will appear arranged in the same order from all points of view. Hence we regard the order as true also in physical space, whereas the shape is only supposed to correspond to the physical space so far as is required for the preservation of the order.

In saying that the time-order which events seem to have is the same as the time-order which they really have, it is necessary to guard against a possible misunderstanding. It must not be supposed that the various states of different physical objects have the same time-order as the sense-data which constitute the perceptions of those objects. Considered as physical objects, the thunder and lightning are simultaneous; that is to say, the lightning is simultaneous with the disturbance of the air in the place where the disturbance begins, namely, where the lightning is. But the sense-datum which we call hearing the thunder does not take place until the disturbance of the air has travelled as far as to where we are. Similarly, it takes about eight minutes for the sun's light to reach us; thus, when we see the sun we are seeing the sun of eight minutes ago. So far as our sense-data afford evidence as to the physical sun they afford evidence as to the physical sun of eight minutes ago; if the physical sun had ceased to exist within the last eight minutes, that would make no difference to the sense-data which we call 'seeing the sun'. This affords a fresh illustration of the necessity of distinguishing between sense-data and physical objects.

What we have found as regards space is much the same as what we find in relation to the correspondence of the sense-data with their physical counterparts. If one object looks blue and another red, we may reasonably presume that there is some corresponding difference between the physical objects; if two objects both look blue, we may presume a corresponding similarity. But we cannot hope to be acquainted directly with the quality in the physical object which makes it look blue or red. Science tells us that this quality is a certain sort of wave-motion, and this sounds familiar, because we think of wave-motions in the space we see. But the wave-motions must really be in physical space, with which we have no direct acquaintance; thus the real wave-motions have not that familiarity which we might have supposed them to have. And what holds for colours is closely similar to what holds for other sense-data. Thus we find that, although the relations of physical objects have all sorts of knowable properties, derived from their correspondence with the relations of sense-data, the physical objects themselves remain unknown in their intrinsic nature, so far at least as can be discovered by means of the senses. The question remains whether there is any other method of discovering the intrinsic nature of physical objects.

The most natural, though not ultimately the most defensible, hypothesis to adopt in the first instance, at any rate as regards visual sense-data, would be that, though physical objects cannot, for the reasons we have been considering, be exactly like sense-data, yet they may be more or less like. According to this view, physical objects will, for example, really have colours, and we might, by good luck, see an object as of the colour it really is. The colour which an object seems to have at any given moment will in general be very similar, though not quite the same, from many different points of view; we might thus suppose the 'real' colour to be a sort of medium colour, intermediate between the various shades which appear from the different points of view.

Such a theory is perhaps not capable of being definitely refuted, but it can be shown to be groundless. To begin with, it is plain that the colour we see depends only upon the nature of the light-waves that strike the eye, and is therefore modified by the medium intervening between us and the object, as well as by the manner in which light is reflected from the object in the direction of the eye. The intervening air alters colours unless it is perfectly clear, and any strong reflection will alter them completely. Thus the colour we see is a result of the ray as it reaches the eye, and not simply a property of the object from which the ray comes. Hence, also, provided certain waves reach the eye, we shall see a certain colour, whether the object from which the waves start has any colour or not. Thus it is quite gratuitous to suppose that physical objects have colours, and therefore there is no justification for making such a supposition. Exactly similar arguments will apply to other sense-data.

It remains to ask whether there are any general philosophical arguments enabling us to say that, if matter is real, it must be of such and such a nature. As explained above, very many philosophers, perhaps most, have held that whatever is real must be in some sense mental, or at any rate that whatever we can know anything about must be in some sense mental. Such philosophers are called 'idealists'. Idealists tell us that what appears as matter is really something mental; namely, either (as Leibniz held) more or less rudimentary minds, or (as Berkeley contended) ideas in the minds which, as we should commonly say, 'perceive' the matter. Thus idealists deny the existence of matter as something intrinsically different from mind, though they do not deny that our sense-data are signs of something which exists independently of our private sensations. In the following chapter we shall consider briefly the reasons—in my opinion fallacious—which idealists advance in favour of their theory.

CHAPTER IV. IDEALISM

The word 'idealism' is used by different philosophers in somewhat different senses. We shall understand by it the doctrine that whatever exists, or at any rate whatever can be known to exist, must be in some sense mental. This doctrine, which is very widely held among philosophers, has several forms, and is advocated on several different grounds. The doctrine is so widely held, and so interesting in itself, that even the briefest survey of philosophy must give some account of it.

Those who are unaccustomed to philosophical speculation may be inclined to dismiss such a doctrine as obviously absurd. There is no doubt that common sense regards tables and chairs and the sun and moon and material objects generally as something radically different from minds and the contents of minds, and as having an existence which might continue if minds ceased. We think of matter as having existed long before there were any minds, and it is hard to think of it as a mere product of mental activity. But whether true or false, idealism is not to be dismissed as obviously absurd.

We have seen that, even if physical objects do have an independent existence, they must differ very widely from sense-data, and can only have a correspondence with sense-data, in the same sort of way in which a catalogue has a correspondence with the things catalogued. Hence common sense leaves us completely in the dark as to the true intrinsic nature of physical objects, and if there were good reason to regard them as mental, we could not legitimately reject this opinion merely because it strikes us as strange. The truth about physical objects must be strange. It may be unattainable, but if any philosopher believes that he has attained it, the fact that what he offers as the truth is strange ought not to be made a ground of objection to his opinion.

The grounds on which idealism is advocated are generally grounds derived from the theory of knowledge, that is to say, from a discussion of the conditions which things must satisfy in order that we may be able to know them. The first serious attempt to establish idealism on such grounds was that of Bishop Berkeley. He proved first, by arguments which were largely valid, that our sense-data cannot be supposed to have an existence independent of us, but must be, in part at least, 'in' the mind, in the sense that their existence would not continue if there were no seeing or hearing or touching or smelling or tasting. So far, his contention was almost certainly valid, even if some of his arguments were not so. But he went on to argue that sense-data were the only things of whose existence our perceptions could assure us, and that to be known is to be 'in' a mind, and therefore to be mental. Hence he concluded that nothing can ever be known except what is in some mind, and that whatever is known without being in my mind must be in some other mind.

In order to understand his argument, it is necessary to understand his use of the word 'idea'. He gives the name 'idea' to anything which is immediately known, as, for example, sense-data are known. Thus a particular colour which we see is an idea; so is a voice which we hear, and so on. But the term is not wholly confined to sense-data. There will also be things remembered or imagined, for with such things also we have immediate acquaintance at the moment of remembering or imagining. All such immediate data he calls 'ideas'.

He then proceeds to consider common objects, such as a tree, for instance. He shows that all we know immediately when we 'perceive' the tree consists of ideas in his sense of the word, and he argues that there is not the slightest ground for supposing that there is anything real about the tree except what is perceived. Its being, he says, consists in being perceived: in the Latin of the schoolmen its 'esse' is 'percipi'. He fully admits that the tree must continue to exist even when we shut our eyes or when no human being is near it. But this continued existence, he says, is due to the fact that God continues to perceive it; the 'real' tree, which corresponds to what we called the physical object, consists of ideas in the mind of God, ideas more or less like those we have when we see the tree, but differing in the fact that they are permanent in God's mind so long as the tree

continues to exist. All our perceptions, according to him, consist in a partial participation in God's perceptions, and it is because of this participation that different people see more or less the same tree. Thus apart from minds and their ideas there is nothing in the world, nor is it possible that anything else should ever be known, since whatever is known is necessarily an idea.

There are in this argument a good many fallacies which have been important in the history of philosophy, and which it will be as well to bring to light. In the first place, there is a confusion engendered by the use of the word 'idea'. We think of an idea as essentially something in somebody's mind, and thus when we are told that a tree consists entirely of ideas, it is natural to suppose that, if so, the tree must be entirely in minds. But the notion of being 'in' the mind is ambiguous. We speak of bearing a person in mind, not meaning that the person is in our minds, but that a thought of him is in our minds. When a man says that some business he had to arrange went clean out of his mind, he does not mean to imply that the business itself was ever in his mind, but only that a thought of the business was formerly in his mind, but afterwards ceased to be in his mind. And so when Berkeley says that the tree must be in our minds if we can know it, all that he really has a right to say is that a thought of the tree must be in our minds. To argue that the tree itself must be in our minds is like arguing that a person whom we bear in mind is himself in our minds. This confusion may seem too gross to have been really committed by any competent philosopher, but various attendant circumstances rendered it possible. In order to see how it was possible, we must go more deeply into the question as to the nature of ideas.

Before taking up the general question of the nature of ideas, we must disentangle two entirely separate questions which arise concerning sense-data and physical objects. We saw that, for various reasons of detail, Berkeley was right in treating the sense-data which constitute our perception of the tree as more or less subjective, in the sense that they depend upon us as much as upon the tree, and would not exist if the tree were not being perceived. But this is an entirely different point from the one by which Berkeley seeks to prove that whatever can be immediately known must be in a mind. For this purpose arguments of detail as to the dependence of sense-data upon us are useless. It is necessary to prove, generally, that by being known, things are shown to be mental. This is what Berkeley believes himself to have done. It is this question, and not our previous question as to the difference between sense-data and the physical object, that must now concern us.

Taking the word 'idea' in Berkeley's sense, there are two quite distinct things to be considered whenever an idea is before the mind. There is on the one hand the thing of which we are aware—say the colour of my table—and on the other hand the actual awareness itself, the mental act of apprehending the thing. The mental act is undoubtedly mental, but is there any reason to suppose that the thing apprehended is in any sense mental? Our previous arguments concerning the colour did not prove it to be mental; they only proved that its existence depends upon the relation of our sense organs to the physical object—in our case, the table. That is to say, they proved that a certain colour will exist, in a certain light, if a normal eye is placed at a certain point relatively to the table. They did not prove that the colour is in the mind of the percipient.

Berkeley's view, that obviously the colour must be in the mind, seems to depend for its plausibility upon confusing the thing apprehended with the act of apprehension. Either of these might be called an 'idea'; probably either would have been called an idea by Berkeley. The act is undoubtedly in the mind; hence, when we are thinking of the act, we readily assent to the view that ideas must be in the mind. Then, forgetting that this was only true when ideas were taken as acts of apprehension, we transfer the proposition that 'ideas are in the mind' to ideas in the other sense, i.e. to the things apprehended by our acts of apprehension. Thus, by an unconscious equivocation, we arrive at the conclusion that whatever we can apprehend must be in our minds. This seems to be the true analysis of Berkeley's argument, and the ultimate fallacy upon which it rests.

This question of the distinction between act and object in our apprehending of things is vitally important, since our whole power of acquiring knowledge is bound up with it. The faculty of being acquainted with things other than itself is the main characteristic of a mind. Acquaintance with objects essentially consists in a relation between the mind and something other than the mind; it is this that constitutes the mind's power of knowing things. If we say that the things known must be in the mind, we are either unduly limiting the mind's power of knowing, or we are uttering a mere tautology. We are uttering a mere tautology if we mean by 'in the mind' the same as by 'before the mind', i.e. if we mean merely being apprehended by the mind. But if we mean this, we shall have to admit that what, in this sense, is in the mind, may nevertheless be not mental. Thus when we realize the nature of knowledge, Berkeley's argument is seen to be wrong in substance as well as in form, and his grounds for supposing that 'ideas'—i.e. the objects apprehended—must be mental, are found to have no validity whatever. Hence his grounds in favour of idealism may be dismissed. It remains to see whether there are any other grounds.

It is often said, as though it were a self-evident truism, that we cannot know that anything exists which we do not know. It is inferred that whatever can in any way be relevant to our experience must be at least capable of being known by us; whence it follows that if matter were essentially something with which we could not become acquainted, matter would be something which we could not know to exist, and which could have for us no importance whatever. It is generally also implied, for reasons which remain obscure, that what can have no importance for us cannot be real, and that therefore matter, if it is not composed of minds or of mental ideas, is impossible and a mere chimaera.

To go into this argument fully at our present stage would be impossible, since it raises points requiring a considerable preliminary discussion; but certain reasons for rejecting the argument may be noticed at once. To begin at the end: there is no reason why what cannot have any practical importance for us should not be real. It is true that, if theoretical importance is included, everything real is of some importance to us, since, as persons desirous of knowing the truth about the universe, we have some interest in everything that the universe contains. But if this sort of interest is included, it is not the case that matter has no importance for us, provided it exists even if we cannot know that it exists. We can, obviously, suspect that it may exist, and wonder whether it does; hence it is connected with our desire for knowledge, and has the importance of either satisfying or thwarting this desire.

Again, it is by no means a truism, and is in fact false, that we cannot know that anything exists which we do not know. The word 'know' is here used in two different senses. (1) In its first use it is applicable to the sort of knowledge which is opposed to error, the sense in which what we know is true, the sense which applies to our beliefs and convictions, i.e. to what are called judgements. In this sense of the word we know that something is the case. This sort of knowledge may be described as knowledge of truths. (2) In the second use of the word 'know' above, the word applies to our knowledge of things, which we may call acquaintance. This is the sense in which we know sense-data. (The distinction involved is roughly that between savoir and connaitre in French, or between wissen and kennen in German.)

Thus the statement which seemed like a truism becomes, when re-stated, the following: 'We can never truly judge that something with which we are not acquainted exists.' This is by no means a truism, but on the contrary a palpable falsehood. I have not the honour to be acquainted with the Emperor of China, but I truly judge that he exists. It may be said, of course, that I judge this because of other people's acquaintance with him. This, however, would be an irrelevant retort, since, if the principle were true, I could not know that any one else is acquainted with him. But further: there is no reason why I should not know of the existence of something with which nobody is acquainted. This point is important, and demands elucidation.

If I am acquainted with a thing which exists, my acquaintance gives me the knowledge that it exists. But it is not true that, conversely, whenever I can know that a thing of a certain sort exists, I or some one else must be acquainted with the thing. What happens, in cases where I have true judgement without acquaintance, is that the thing is known to me by description, and that, in virtue of some general principle, the existence of a thing answering to this description can be inferred from the existence of something with which I am acquainted. In order to understand this point fully, it will be well first to deal with the difference between knowledge by acquaintance and knowledge by description, and then to consider what knowledge of general principles, if any, has the same kind of certainty as our knowledge of the existence of our own experiences. These subjects will be dealt with in the following chapters.

CHAPTER V. KNOWLEDGE BY ACQUAINTANCE AND KNOWLEDGE BY DESCRIPTION

In the preceding chapter we saw that there are two sorts of knowledge: knowledge of things, and knowledge of truths. In this chapter we shall be concerned exclusively with knowledge of things, of which in turn we shall have to distinguish two kinds. Knowledge of things, when it is of the kind we call knowledge by acquaintance, is essentially simpler than any knowledge of truths, and logically independent of knowledge of truths, though it would be rash to assume that human beings ever, in fact, have acquaintance with things without at the same time knowing some truth about them. Knowledge of things by description, on the contrary, always involves, as we shall find in the course of the present chapter, some knowledge of truths as its source and ground. But first of all we must make clear what we mean by 'acquaintance' and what we mean by 'description'.

We shall say that we have acquaintance with anything of which we are directly aware, without the intermediary of any process of inference or any knowledge of truths. Thus in the presence of my table I am acquainted with the sense-data that make up the appearance of my table—its colour, shape, hardness, smoothness, etc.; all these are things of which I am immediately conscious when I am seeing and touching my table. The particular shade of colour that I am seeing may have many things said about it—I may say that it is brown, that it is rather dark, and so on. But such statements, though they make me know truths about the colour, do not make me know the colour itself any better than I did before: so far as concerns knowledge of the colour itself, as opposed to knowledge of truths about it, I know the colour perfectly and completely when I see it, and no further knowledge of it itself is even theoretically possible. Thus the sense-data which make up the appearance of my table are things with which I have acquaintance, things immediately known to me just as they are.

My knowledge of the table as a physical object, on the contrary, is not direct knowledge. Such as it is, it is obtained through acquaintance with the sense-data that make up the appearance of the table. We have seen that it is possible, without absurdity, to doubt that there is a table at all, whereas it is not possible to doubt the sense-data. My knowledge of the table is of the kind which we shall call 'knowledge by description'. The table is 'the physical object which causes such-and-such sense-data'. This describes the table by means of the sense-data. In order to know anything at all about the table, we must know truths connecting it with things with which we have acquaintance: we must know that 'such-and-such sense-data are caused by a physical object'. There is no state of mind in which we are directly aware of the table; all our knowledge of the table is really knowledge of truths, and the actual thing which is the table is not, strictly speaking, known to us at all. We know a description and we know that there is just one object to which this description applies, though the object itself is not directly known to us. In such a case, we say that our knowledge of the object is knowledge by description.

All our knowledge, both knowledge of things and knowledge of truths, rests upon acquaintance as its foundation. It is therefore important to consider what kinds of things there are with which we have acquaintance.

Sense-data, as we have already seen, are among the things with which we are acquainted; in fact, they supply the most obvious and striking example of knowledge by acquaintance. But if they were the sole example, our knowledge would be very much more restricted than it is. We should only know what is now present to our senses: we could not know anything about the past—not even that there was a past—nor could we know any truths about our sense-data, for all knowledge of truths, as we shall show, demands acquaintance with things which are of an essentially different character from sense-data, the things which are sometimes called 'abstract ideas', but which we shall call 'universals'. We have there-

fore to consider acquaintance with other things besides sense-data if we are to obtain any tolerably adequate analysis of our knowledge.

The first extension beyond sense-data to be considered is acquaintance by memory. It is obvious that we often remember what we have seen or heard or had otherwise presented to our senses, and that in such cases we are still immediately aware of what we remember, in spite of the fact that it appears as past and not as present. This immediate knowledge by memory is the source of all our knowledge concerning the past: without it, there could be no knowledge of the past by inference, we should never know that there was anything past to be inferred.

The next extension to be considered is acquaintance by introspection. We are not only aware of things, but we are often aware of being aware of them. When I see the sun, I am often aware of my seeing the sun; thus 'my seeing the sun' is an object with which I have acquaintance. When I desire food, I may be aware of my desire for food; thus 'my desiring food' is an object with which I am acquainted. Similarly we may be aware of our feeling pleasure or pain, and generally of the events which happen in our minds. This kind of acquaintance, which may be called self-consciousness, is the source of all our knowledge of mental things. It is obvious that it is only what goes on in our own minds that can be thus known immediately. What goes on in the minds of others is known to us through our perception of their bodies, that is, the sense-data in us which are associated with their bodies. But for our acquaintance with the contents of our own minds, we should be unable to imagine the minds of others, and therefore we could never arrive at the knowledge that they have minds. It seems natural to suppose that self-consciousness is one of the things that distinguish men from animals: animals, we may suppose, though they have acquaintance with sense-data, never become aware of this acquaintance. I do not mean that they doubt whether they exist, but that they have never become conscious of the fact that they have sensations and feelings, nor therefore of the fact that they, the subjects of their sensations and feelings, exist.

We have spoken of acquaintance with the contents of our minds as self-consciousness, but it is not, of course, consciousness of our self: it is consciousness of particular thoughts and feelings. The question whether we are also acquainted with our bare selves, as opposed to particular thoughts and feelings, is a very difficult one, upon which it would be rash to speak positively. When we try to look into ourselves we always seem to come upon some particular thought or feeling, and not upon the 'I' which has the thought or feeling. Nevertheless there are some reasons for thinking that we are acquainted with the 'I', though the acquaintance is hard to disentangle from other things. To make clear what sort of reason there is, let us consider for a moment what our acquaintance with particular thoughts really involves.

When I am acquainted with 'my seeing the sun', it seems plain that I am acquainted with two different things in relation to each other. On the one hand there is the sense-datum which represents the sun to me, on the other hand there is that which sees this sense-datum. All acquaintance, such as my acquaintance with the sense-datum which represents the sun, seems obviously a relation between the person acquainted and the object with which the person is acquainted. When a case of acquaintance is one with which I can be acquainted (as I am acquainted with my acquaintance with the sense-datum representing the sun), it is plain that the person acquainted is myself. Thus, when I am acquainted with my seeing the sun, the whole fact with which I am acquainted is 'Self-acquainted-with-sense-datum'.

Further, we know the truth 'I am acquainted with this sense-datum'. It is hard to see how we could know this truth, or even understand what is meant by it, unless we were acquainted with something which we call 'I'. It does not seem necessary to suppose that we are acquainted with a more or less permanent person, the same to-day as yesterday, but it does seem as though we must be acquainted with that thing, whatever its nature, which sees the sun and has acquaintance with sense-data. Thus, in some sense it would seem we must be acquainted with our Selves as opposed to our particular experiences. But the question is difficult, and complicated arguments can be adduced on either side. Hence, although acquaintance with ourselves seems probably to occur, it is not wise to assert that it undoubtedly does occur.

We may therefore sum up as follows what has been said concerning acquaintance with things that exist. We have acquaintance in sensation with the data of the outer senses, and in introspection with the data of what may be called the inner sense—thoughts, feelings, desires, etc.; we have acquaintance in memory with things which have been data either of the outer senses or of the inner sense. Further, it is probable, though not certain, that we have acquaintance with Self, as that which is aware of things or has desires towards things.

In addition to our acquaintance with particular existing things, we also have acquaintance with what we shall call universals, that is to say, general ideas such as whiteness, diversity, brotherhood, and so on. Every complete sentence must contain at least one word which stands for a universal, since all verbs have a meaning which is universal. We shall return to universals later on, in Chapter IX; for the present, it is only necessary to guard against the supposition that whatever we can be acquainted with must be something particular and existent. Awareness of universals is called conceiving, and a universal of which we are aware is called a concept.

It will be seen that among the objects with which we are acquainted are not included physical objects (as opposed to sense-data), nor other people's minds. These things are known to us by what I call 'knowledge by description', which we must now consider.

By a 'description' I mean any phrase of the form 'a so-and-so' or 'the so-and-so'. A phrase of the form 'a so-and-so' I shall call an 'ambiguous' description; a phrase of the form 'the so-and-so' (in the singular) I shall call a 'definite' description. Thus 'a man' is an ambiguous description, and 'the man with the iron mask' is a definite description. There are various problems connected with ambiguous descriptions, but I pass them by, since they do not directly concern the matter we are discussing, which is the nature of our knowledge concerning objects in cases where we know that there is an object answering to a definite description, though we are not acquainted with any such object. This is a matter which is concerned exclusively with definite descriptions. I shall therefore, in the sequel, speak simply of 'descriptions' when I mean 'definite descriptions'. Thus a description will mean any phrase of the form 'the so-and-so' in the singular.

We say that an object is 'known by description' when we know that it is 'the so-and-so', i.e. when we know that there is one object, and no more, having a certain property; and it will generally be implied that we do not have knowledge of the same object by acquaintance. We know that the man with the iron mask existed, and many propositions are known about him; but we do not know who he was. We know that the candidate who gets the most votes will be elected, and in this case we are very likely also acquainted (in the only sense in which one can be acquainted with some one else) with the man who is, in fact, the candidate who will get most votes; but we do not know which of the candidates he is, i.e. we do not know any proposition of the form 'A is the candidate who will get most votes' where A is one of the candidates by name. We shall say that we have 'merely descriptive knowledge' of the so-and-so when, although we know that the so-and-so exists, and although we may possibly be acquainted with the object which is, in fact, the so-and-so, yet we do not know any proposition 'A is the so-and-so', where A is something with which we are acquainted.

When we say 'the so-and-so exists', we mean that there is just one object which is the so-and-so. The proposition 'A is the so-and-so' means that A has the property so-and-so, and nothing else has. 'Mr. A. is the Unionist candidate for this constituency' means 'Mr. A. is a Unionist candidate for this constituency, and no one else is'. 'The Unionist candidate for this constituency exists' means 'some one is a Unionist candidate for this constituency, and no one else is'. Thus, when we are acquainted with an object which is the so-and-so, we know that the so-and-so exists; but we may know that the so-and-so exists when we are not acquainted with any object which we know to be the so-and-so, and even when we are not acquainted with any object which, in fact, is the so-and-so.

Common words, even proper names, are usually really descriptions. That is to say, the thought in the mind of a person using a proper name correctly can generally only be expressed explicitly if we replace the proper name by a description. Moreover, the description required to express the thought will vary for different people, or for the same person at different times. The only thing constant (so long as the name is rightly used) is the object to which the name applies. But so long as this remains constant, the particular description involved usually makes no difference to the truth or falsehood of the proposition in which the name appears.

Let us take some illustrations. Suppose some statement made about Bismarck. Assuming that there is such a thing as direct acquaintance with oneself, Bismarck himself might have used his name directly to designate the particular person with whom he was acquainted. In this case, if he made a judgement about himself, he himself might be a constituent of the judgement. Here the proper name has the direct use which it always wishes to have, as simply standing for a certain object, and not for a description of the object. But if a person who knew Bismarck made a judgement about him, the case is different. What this person was acquainted with were certain sense-data which he connected (rightly, we will suppose) with Bismarck's body. His body, as a physical object, and still more his mind, were only known as the body and the mind connected with these sense-data. That is, they were known by description. It is, of course, very much a matter of chance which characteristics of a man's appearance will come into a friend's mind when he thinks of him; thus the description actually in the friend's mind is accidental. The essential point is that he knows that the various descriptions all apply to the same entity, in spite of not being acquainted with the entity in question.

When we, who did not know Bismarck, make judgement about him, the description in our minds will probably be some more or less vague mass of historical knowledge—far more, in most cases, than is required to identify him. But, for the sake of illustration, let us assume that we think of him as 'the first Chancellor of the German Empire'. Here all the words are abstract except 'German'. The word 'German' will, again, have different meanings for different people. To some it will recall travels in

Germany, to some the look of Germany on the map, and so on. But if we are to obtain a description which we know to be applicable, we shall be compelled, at some point, to bring in a reference to a particular with which we are acquainted. Such reference is involved in any mention of past, present, and future (as opposed to definite dates), or of here and there, or of what others have told us. Thus it would seem that, in some way or other, a description known to be applicable to a particular must involve some reference to a particular with which we are acquainted, if our knowledge about the thing described is not to be merely what follows logically from the description. For example, 'the most long-lived of men' is a description involving only universals, which must apply to some man, but we can make no judgements concerning this man which involve knowledge about him beyond what the description gives. If, however, we say, 'The first Chancellor of the German Empire was an astute diplomatist', we can only be assured of the truth of our judgement in virtue of something with which we are acquainted—usually a testimony heard or read. Apart from the information we convey to others, apart from the fact about the actual Bismarck, which gives importance to our judgement, the thought we really have contains the one or more particulars involved, and otherwise consists wholly of concepts.

All names of places—London, England, Europe, the Earth, the Solar System—similarly involve, when used, descriptions which start from some one or more particulars with which we are acquainted. I suspect that even the Universe, as considered by metaphysics, involves such a connexion with particulars. In logic on the contrary, where we are concerned not merely with what does exist, but with whatever might or could exist or be, no reference to actual particulars is involved.

It would seem that, when we make a statement about something only known by description, we often intend to make our statement, not in the form involving the description, but about the actual thing described. That is to say, when we say anything about Bismarck, we should like, if we could, to make the judgement which Bismarck alone can make, namely, the judgement of which he himself is a constituent. In this we are necessarily defeated, since the actual Bismarck is unknown to us. But we know that

there is an object B, called Bismarck, and that B was an astute diplomatist. We can thus describe the proposition we should like to affirm, namely, 'B was an astute diplomat', where B is the object which was Bismarck. If we are describing Bismarck as 'the first Chancellor of the German Empire', the proposition we should like to affirm may be described as 'the proposition asserting, concerning the actual object which was the first Chancellor of the German Empire, that this object was an astute diplomatist'. What enables us to communicate in spite of the varying descriptions we employ is that we know there is a true proposition concerning the actual Bismarck, and that however we may vary the description (so long as the description is correct) the proposition described is still the same. This proposition, which is described and is known to be true, is what interests us; but we are not acquainted with the proposition itself, and do not know it, though we know it is true.

It will be seen that there are various stages in the removal from acquaintance with particulars: there is Bismarck to people who knew him; Bismarck to those who only know of him through history; the man with the iron mask; the longest-lived of men. These are progressively further removed from acquaintance with particulars; the first comes as near to acquaintance as is possible in regard to another person; in the second, we shall still be said to know 'who Bismarck was'; in the third, we do not know who was the man with the iron mask, though we can know many propositions about him which are not logically deducible from the fact that he wore an iron mask; in the fourth, finally, we know nothing beyond what is logically deducible from the definition of the man. There is a similar hierarchy in the region of universals. Many universals like many particulars, are only known to us by description. But here, as in the case of particulars, knowledge concerning what is known by description is ultimately reducible to knowledge concerning what is known by acquaintance.

The fundamental principle in the analysis of propositions containing descriptions is this: Every proposition which we can understand must be composed wholly of constituents with which we are acquainted.

We shall not at this stage attempt to answer all the objections which may be urged against this fundamental principle. For the present, we shall merely point out that, in some way or other, it must be possible to meet these objections, for it is scarcely conceivable that we can make a judgement or entertain a supposition without knowing what it is that we are judging or supposing about. We must attach some meaning to the words we use, if we are to speak significantly and not utter mere noise; and the meaning we attach to our words must be something with which we are acquainted. Thus when, for example, we make a statement about Julius Caesar, it is plain that Julius Caesar himself is not before our minds, since we are not acquainted with him. We have in mind some description of Julius Caesar: 'the man who was assassinated on the Ides of March', 'the founder of the Roman Empire', or, merely 'the man whose name was Julius Caesar'. (In this last description, Julius Caesar is a noise or shape with which we are acquainted.) Thus our statement does not mean quite what it seems to mean, but means something involving, instead of Julius Caesar, some description of him which is composed wholly of particulars and universals with which we are acquainted.

The chief importance of knowledge by description is that it enables us to pass beyond the limits of our experience. In spite of the fact that we can only know truths which are wholly composed of terms which we have experienced in acquaintance, we can yet have knowledge by description of things which we have never experienced. In view of the very narrow range of our immediate experience, this result is vital, and until it is understood, much of our knowledge must remain mysterious and therefore doubtful.

CHAPTER VI. ON INDUCTION

In almost all our previous discussions we have been concerned in the attempt to get clear as to our data in the way of knowledge of existence. What things are there in the universe whose existence is known to us owing to our being acquainted with them? So far, our answer has been that we are acquainted with our sense-data, and, probably, with ourselves. These we know to exist. And past sense-data which are remembered are known to have existed in the past. This knowledge supplies our data.

But if we are to be able to draw inferences from these data—if we are to know of the existence of matter, of other people, of the past before our individual memory begins, or of the future, we must know general principles of some kind by means of which such inferences can be drawn. It must be known to us that the existence of some one sort of thing, A, is a sign of the existence of some other sort of thing, B, either at the same time as A or at some earlier or later time, as, for example, thunder is a sign of the earlier existence of lightning. If this were not known to us, we could never extend our knowledge beyond the sphere of our private experience; and this sphere, as we have seen, is exceedingly limited. The question we have now to consider is whether such an extension is possible, and if so, how it is effected.

Let us take as an illustration a matter about which none of us, in fact, feel the slightest doubt. We are all convinced that the sun will rise to-morrow. Why? Is this belief a mere blind outcome of past experience, or can it be justified as a reasonable belief? It is not easy to find a test by which to judge whether a belief of this kind is reasonable or not, but we can at least ascertain what sort of general beliefs would suffice, if true, to justify the judgement that the sun will rise to-morrow, and the many other similar judgements upon which our actions are based.

It is obvious that if we are asked why we believe the sun will rise to-morrow, we shall naturally answer, 'Because it always has risen every day'. We have a firm belief that it will rise in the future, because it has risen in the past. If we are challenged as to why we believe that it will continue to rise as heretofore, we may appeal to the laws of motion: the earth, we shall say, is a freely rotating body, and such bodies do not cease to rotate unless something interferes from outside, and there is nothing outside to interfere with the earth between now and to-morrow. Of course it might be doubted whether we are quite certain that there is nothing outside to interfere, but this is not the interesting doubt. The interesting doubt is as to whether the laws of motion will remain in operation until to-morrow. If this doubt is raised, we find ourselves in the same position as when the doubt about the sunrise was first raised.

The only reason for believing that the laws of motion remain in operation is that they have operated hitherto, so far as our knowledge of the past enables us to judge. It is true that we have a greater body of evidence from the past in favour of the laws of motion than we have in favour of the sunrise, because the sunrise is merely a particular case of fulfillment of the laws of motion, and there are countless other particular cases. But the real question is: Do any number of cases of a law being fulfilled in the past afford evidence that it will be fulfilled in the future? If not, it becomes plain that we have no ground whatever for expecting the sun to rise to-morrow, or for expecting the bread we shall eat at our next meal not to poison us, or for any of the other scarcely conscious expectations that control our daily lives. It is to be observed that all such expectations are only probable; thus we have not to seek for a proof that they must be fulfilled, but only for some reason in favour of the view that they are likely to be fulfilled.

Now in dealing with this question we must, to begin with, make an important distinction, without which we should soon become involved in hopeless confusions. Experience has shown us that, hitherto, the frequent repetition of some uniform succession or coexistence has been a cause of our expecting the same succession or coexistence on the next occasion. Food that has a certain appearance generally has a certain taste, and it is a severe shock to our expectations when the familiar appearance is found to be associated with an unusual taste. Things which we see become associated, by habit, with certain tactile sensations which we expect if we touch them; one of the horrors of a ghost (in many ghost-stories) is that it fails to give us any sensations of touch. Uneducated people who go abroad for the first time are so surprised as to be incredulous when they find their native language not understood.

And this kind of association is not confined to men; in animals also it is very strong. A horse which has been often driven along a certain road resists the attempt to drive him in a different direction. Domestic animals expect food when they see the person who feeds them. We know that all these rather crude expectations of uniformity are liable to be misleading. The man who has fed the chicken every day throughout its life at last wrings its neck instead, showing that more refined views as to the uniformity of nature would have been useful to the chicken.

But in spite of the misleadingness of such expectations, they nevertheless exist. The mere fact that something has happened a certain number of times causes animals and men to expect that it will happen again. Thus our instincts certainly cause us to believe the sun will rise to-morrow, but we may be in no better a position than the chicken which unexpectedly has its neck wrung. We have therefore to distinguish the fact that past uniformities cause expectations as to the future, from the question whether there is any reasonable ground for giving weight to such expectations after the question of their validity has been raised.

The problem we have to discuss is whether there is any reason for believing in what is called 'the uniformity of nature'. The belief in the uniformity of nature is the belief that everything that has happened or will happen is an instance of some general law to which there are no exceptions. The crude expectations which we have been considering are all subject to exceptions, and therefore liable to disappoint those who entertain them. But science habitually assumes, at least as a working hypothesis, that general rules which have exceptions can be replaced by general rules which have no exceptions. 'Unsupported bodies in air fall' is a general rule to which balloons and aeroplanes are exceptions. But the laws of motion and the law of gravitation, which account for the fact that most bodies fall, also account for the fact that balloons and aeroplanes can rise; thus the laws of motion and the law of gravitation are not subject to these exceptions.

The belief that the sun will rise to-morrow might be falsified if the earth came suddenly into contact with a large body which destroyed its rotation; but the laws of motion and the law of gravitation would not be infringed by such an event. The business of science is to find uniformities, such as the laws of motion and the law of gravitation, to which, so far as our experience extends, there are no exceptions. In this search science has been remarkably successful, and it may be conceded that such uniformities have held hitherto. This brings us back to the question: Have we any reason, assuming that they have always held in the past, to suppose that they will hold in the future?

It has been argued that we have reason to know that the future will resemble the past, because what was the future has constantly become the past, and has always been found to resemble the past, so that we really have experience of the future, namely of times which were formerly future, which we may call past futures. But such an argument really begs the very question at issue. We have experience of past futures, but not of future futures, and the question is: Will future futures resemble past futures? This question is not to be answered by an argument which starts from past futures alone. We have therefore still to seek for some principle which shall enable us to know that the future will follow the same laws as the past.

The reference to the future in this question is not essential. The same question arises when we apply the laws that work in our experience to past things of which we have no experience—as, for example, in geology, or in theories as to the origin of the Solar system. The question we really have to ask is: 'When two things have been found to be often associated, and no instance is known of the one occurring without the other, does the occurrence of one of the two, in a fresh instance, give any good ground for expecting the other?' On our answer to this question must depend the validity of the whole of our expectations as to the future, the whole of the results obtained by induction, and in fact practically all the beliefs upon which our daily life is based.

It must be conceded, to begin with, that the fact that two things have been found often together and never apart does not, by itself, suffice to prove demonstratively that they will be found together in the next case we examine. The most we can hope is that the oftener things are found together, the more probable it becomes that they will be found together another time, and that, if they have been found together often enough, the probability will amount almost to certainty. It can never quite reach certainty, because we know that in spite of frequent repetitions there sometimes is a failure at the last, as in the case of the chicken whose neck is wrung. Thus probability is all we ought to seek.

It might be urged, as against the view we are advocating, that we know all natural phenomena to be subject to the reign of law, and that sometimes, on the basis of observation, we can see that only one law can possibly fit the facts of the case. Now to this

view there are two answers. The first is that, even if some law which has no exceptions applies to our case, we can never, in practice, be sure that we have discovered that law and not one to which there are exceptions. The second is that the reign of law would seem to be itself only probable, and that our belief that it will hold in the future, or in unexamined cases in the past, is itself based upon the very principle we are examining.

The principle we are examining may be called the principle of induction, and its two parts may be stated as follows:

(a) When a thing of a certain sort A has been found to be associated with a thing of a certain other sort B, and has never been found dissociated from a thing of the sort B, the greater the number of cases in which A and B have been associated, the greater is the probability that they will be associated in a fresh case in which one of them is known to be present;

(b) Under the same circumstances, a sufficient number of cases of association will make the probability of a fresh association nearly a certainty, and will make it approach certainty without limit.

As just stated, the principle applies only to the verification of our expectation in a single fresh instance. But we want also to know that there is a probability in favour of the general law that things of the sort A are always associated with things of the sort B, provided a sufficient number of cases of association are known, and no cases of failure of association are known. The probability of the general law is obviously less than the probability of the particular case, since if the general law is true, the particular case must also be true, whereas the particular case may be true without the general law being true. Nevertheless the probability of the general law is increased by repetitions, just as the probability of the particular case is. We may therefore repeat the two parts of our principle as regards the general law, thus:

(a) The greater the number of cases in which a thing the sort A has been found associated with a thing the sort B, the more probable it is (if no cases of failure of association are known) that A is always associated with B;

(b) Under the same circumstances, a sufficient number of cases of the association of A with B will make it nearly certain that A is always associated with B, and will make this general law approach certainty without limit.

It should be noted that probability is always relative to certain data. In our case, the data are merely the known cases of coexistence of A and B. There may be other data, which might be taken into account, which would gravely alter the probability. For example, a man who had seen a great many white swans might argue by our principle, that on the data it was probable that all swans were white, and this might be a perfectly sound argument. The argument is not disproved by the fact that some swans are black, because a thing may very well happen in spite of the fact that some data render it improbable. In the case of the swans, a man might know that colour is a very variable characteristic in many species of animals, and that, therefore, an induction as to colour is peculiarly liable to error. But this knowledge would be a fresh datum, by no means proving that the probability relatively to our previous data had been wrongly estimated. The fact, therefore, that things often fail to fulfill our expectations is no evidence that our expectations will not probably be fulfilled in a given case or a given class of cases. Thus our inductive principle is at any rate not capable of being disproved by an appeal to experience.

The inductive principle, however, is equally incapable of being proved by an appeal to experience. Experience might conceivably confirm the inductive principle as regards the cases that have been already examined; but as regards unexamined cases, it is the inductive principle alone that can justify any inference from what has been examined to what has not been examined. All arguments which, on the basis of experience, argue as to the future or the unexperienced parts of the past or present, assume the inductive principle; hence we can never use experience to prove the inductive principle without begging the question. Thus we must either accept the inductive principle on the ground of its intrinsic evidence, or forgo all justification of our expectations about the future. If the principle is unsound, we have no reason to expect the sun to rise to-morrow, to expect bread to be more nourishing than a stone, or to expect that if we throw ourselves off the roof we shall fall. When we see what looks like our best friend approaching us, we shall have no reason to suppose that his body is not inhabited by the mind of our worst enemy or of some total stranger. All our conduct is based upon associations which have worked in the past, and which we therefore regard as likely to work in the future; and this likelihood is dependent for its validity upon the inductive principle.

The general principles of science, such as the belief in the reign of law, and the belief that every event must have a cause, are as completely dependent upon the inductive principle as are the beliefs of daily life. All such general principles are believed because mankind have found innumerable instances of their truth and no instances of their falsehood. But this affords no evidence for their truth in the future, unless the inductive principle is assumed.

Thus all knowledge which, on a basis of experience tells us something about what is not experienced, is based upon a belief which experience can neither confirm nor confute, yet which, at least in its more concrete applications, appears to be as firmly rooted in us as many of the facts of experience. The existence and justification of such beliefs—for the inductive principle, as we shall see, is not the only example—raises some of the most difficult and most debated problems of philosophy. We will, in the next chapter, consider briefly what may be said to account for such knowledge, and what is its scope and its degree of certainty.

CHAPTER VII. ON OUR KNOWLEDGE OF GENERAL PRINCIPLES

We saw in the preceding chapter that the principle of Induction, while necessary to the validity of all arguments based on experience, is itself not capable of being proved by experience, and yet is unhesitatingly believed by every one, at least in all its concrete applications. In these characteristics the principle of induction does not stand alone. There are a number of other principles which cannot be proved or disproved by experience, but are used in arguments which start from what is experienced.

Some of these principles have even greater evidence than the principle of induction, and the knowledge of them has the same degree of certainty as the knowledge of the existence of sense-data. They constitute the means of drawing inferences from what is given in sensation; and if what we infer is to be true, it is just as necessary that our principles of inference should be true as it is that our data should be true. The principles of inference are apt to be overlooked because of their very obviousness—the assumption involved is assented to without our realizing that it is an assumption. But it is very important to realize the use of principles of inference, if a correct theory of knowledge is to be obtained; for our knowledge of them raises interesting and difficult questions.

In all our knowledge of general principles, what actually happens is that first of all we realize some particular application of the principle, and then we realize the particularity is irrelevant, and that there is a generality which may equally truly be affirmed. This is of course familiar in such matters as teaching arithmetic: 'two and two are four' is first learnt in the case of some particular pair of couples, and then in some other particular case, and so on, until at last it becomes possible to see that it is true of any pair of couples. The same thing happens with logical principles. Suppose two men are discussing what day of the month it is. One of them says, 'At least you will admit that if yesterday was the 15th to-day must the 16th.' 'Yes', says the other, 'I admit that.' 'And you know', the first continues, 'that yesterday was the 15th, because you dined with Jones, and your diary will tell you that was on the 15th.' 'Yes', says the second; 'therefore to-day is the 16th.'

Now such an argument is not hard to follow; and if it is granted that its premisses are true in fact, no one deny that the conclusion must also be true. But it depends for its truth upon an instance of a general logical principle. The logical principle is as follows: 'Suppose it known that if this is true, then that is true. Suppose it also known that this is true, then it follows that that is true.' When it is the case that if this is true, that is true, we shall say that this 'implies' that, that that 'follows from' this. Thus our principle states that if this implies that, and this is true, then that is true. In other words, 'anything implied by a proposition is true', or 'whatever follows from a true proposition is true'.

This principle is really involved—at least, concrete instances of it are involved—in all demonstra-

tions. Whenever one thing which we believe is used to prove something else, which we consequently believe, this principle is relevant. If any one asks: 'Why should I accept the results of valid arguments based on true premisses?' we can only answer by appealing to our principle. In fact, the truth of the principle is impossible to doubt, and its obviousness is so great that at first sight it seems almost trivial. Such principles, however, are not trivial to the philosopher, for they show that we may have indubitable knowledge which is in no way derived from objects of sense.

The above principle is merely one of a certain number of self-evident logical principles. Some at least of these principles must be granted before any argument or proof becomes possible. When some of them have been granted, others can be proved, though these others, so long as they are simple, are just as obvious as the principles taken for granted. For no very good reason, three of these principles have been singled out by tradition under the name of 'Laws of Thought'.

They are as follows:

1. The law of identity: 'Whatever is, is.'
2. The law of contradiction: 'Nothing can both be and not be.'
3. The law of excluded middle: 'Everything must either be or not be.'

These three laws are samples of self-evident logical principles, but are not really more fundamental or more self-evident than various other similar principles: for instance, the one we considered just now, which states that what follows from a true premise is true. The name 'laws of thought' is also misleading, for what is important is not the fact that we think in accordance with these laws, but the fact that things behave in accordance with them; in other words, the fact that when we think in accordance with them we think truly. But this is a large question, to which we return at a later stage.

In addition to the logical principles which enable us to prove from a given premiss that something is *certainly* true, there are other logical principles which enable us to prove, from a given premiss, that there is a greater or less probability that something is true. An example of such principles—perhaps the most important example—is the inductive principle, which we considered in the preceding chapter.

One of the great historic controversies in philosophy is the controversy between the two schools called respectively 'empiricists' and 'rationalists'. The empiricists—who are best represented by the British philosophers, Locke, Berkeley, and Hume—maintained that all our knowledge is derived from experience; the rationalists—who are represented by the continental philosophers of the seventeenth century, especially Descartes and Leibniz—maintained that, in addition to what we know by experience, there are certain 'innate ideas' and 'innate principles', which we know independently of experience. It has now become possible to decide with some confidence as to the truth or falsehood of these opposing schools. It must be admitted, for the reasons already stated, that logical principles are known to us, and cannot be themselves proved by experience, since all proof presupposes them. In this, therefore, which was the most important point of the controversy, the rationalists were in the right.

On the other hand, even that part of our knowledge which is logically independent of experience (in the sense that experience cannot prove it) is yet elicited and caused by experience. It is on occasion of particular experiences that we become aware of the general laws which their connexions exemplify. It would certainly be absurd to suppose that there are innate principles in the sense that babies are born with a knowledge of everything which men know and which cannot be deduced from what is experienced. For this reason, the word 'innate' would not now be employed to describe our knowledge of logical principles. The phrase 'a priori' is less objectionable, and is more usual in modern writers. Thus, while admitting that all knowledge is elicited and caused by experience, we shall nevertheless hold that some knowledge is a priori, in the sense that the experience which makes us think of it does not suffice to prove it, but merely so directs our attention that we see its truth without requiring any proof from experience.

There is another point of great importance, in which the empiricists were in the right as against the rationalists. Nothing can be known to exist except by the help of experience. That is to say, if we wish to prove that something of which we have no direct experience exists, we must have among our premisses the existence of one or more things of which we have direct experience. Our belief that the Emperor of China exists, for example, rests upon testimony, and testimony consists, in the last analysis, of sense-data seen or heard in reading or being spoken to. Rationalists believed that, from general consideration as to what must be, they could deduce the existence of this or that in the actual world. In this belief they seem to have been mistaken. All the knowledge that we can acquire a priori concerning existence seems to be hypothetical: it tells us that if one thing exists, another must exist, or, more generally, that if one proposition is true another must be true. This is exemplified by principles we have already dealt with, such as 'if this is true, and this implies that, then that is true', of 'if this and that have been repeatedly found connected, they will probably be connected in the next instance in which one of them is found.' Thus the scope and power of a priori principles is strictly limited. All knowledge that something exists must be in part dependent on experience. When anything is known immediately, its existence is known by experience alone; when anything is proved to exist, without being known immediately, both experience and a priori principles must be required in the proof. Knowledge is called empirical when it rests wholly or partly upon experience. Thus all knowledge which asserts existence is empirical, and the only a priori knowledge concerning existence is hypothetical, giving connexions among things that exist or may exist, but not giving actual existence.

A priori knowledge is not all of the logical kind we have been hitherto considering. Perhaps the most important example of non-logical a priori knowledge is knowledge as to ethical value. I am not speaking of judgements as to what is useful or as to what is virtuous, for such judgements do require empirical premisses; I am speaking of judgements as to the intrinsic desirability of things. If something is useful, it must be useful because it secures some end, the end must, if we have gone far enough, be valuable on its own account, and not merely because it is useful for some further end. Thus all judgements as to what is useful depend upon judgements as to what has value on its own account.

We judge, for example, that happiness is more desirable than misery, knowledge than ignorance, goodwill than hatred, and so on. Such judgements must, in part at least, be immediate and a priori. Like our previous a priori judgements, they may be elicited by experience, and indeed they must be; for it seems not possible to judge whether anything is intrinsically valuable unless we have experienced something of the same kind. But it is fairly obvious that they cannot be proved by experience; for the fact that a thing exists or does not exist cannot prove either that it is good that it should exist or that it is bad. The pursuit of this subject belongs to ethics, where the impossibility of deducing what ought to be from what is has to established. In the present connexion, it is only important to realize that knowledge as to what is intrinsically of value is a priori in the same sense in which logic is a priori, namely in the sense that the truth of such knowledge can be neither proved nor disproved by experience.

All pure mathematics is a priori, like logic. This is strenuously denied by the empirical philosophers, who maintained that experience was as much the source of our knowledge of arithmetic as of our knowledge of geography. They maintained that by the repeated experience of seeing two things and two other things, and finding that altogether they made four things, we were led by induction to the conclusion that two things and two other things would always make four things altogether. If, however, this were the source of our knowledge that two and two are four we should proceed differently, in persuading ourselves of its truth, from the way in which we do actually proceed. In fact, a certain number of instances are needed to make us think of two abstractly, rather than of two coins or two books or two people, or two of any other specified kind. But as soon as we are able to divest our thoughts of irrelevant particularity, we become able to see the general principle that two and two are four; any one instance is seen to be typical and the examination of other instances becomes unnecessary.

The same thing is exemplified in geometry. If we want to prove some property of all triangles, we draw some one triangle and reason about it; but we can avoid making use of any property which it does not share with all other triangles, and thus, from our par-

ticular case, we obtain a general result. We do not, in fact, feel our certainty that two and two are four increased by fresh instances, because, as soon as we have seen the truth of this proposition, our certainty becomes so great as to be incapable of growing greater. Moreover, we feel some quality of necessity about the proposition 'two and two are four', which is absent from even the best attested empirical generalizations. Such generalizations always remain mere facts: we feel that there might be a world in which they were false, though in the actual world they happen to be true. In any possible world, on the contrary, we feel that two and two would be four: this is not a mere fact, but a necessity to which everything actual and possible must conform.

The case may be made clearer by considering a genuinely empirical generalization, such as 'All men are mortal.' It is plain that we believe this proposition, in the first place, because there is no known instance of men living beyond a certain age, and in the second place because there seem to be physiological grounds for thinking that an organism such as a man's body must sooner or later wear out. Neglecting the second ground, and considering merely our experience of men's mortality, it is plain that we should not be content with one quite clearly understood instance of a man dying, whereas, in the case of 'two and two are four', one instance does suffice, when carefully considered, to persuade us that the same must happen in any other instance. Also we can be forced to admit, on reflection, that there may be some doubt, however slight, as to whether all men are mortal. This may be made plain by the attempt to imagine two different worlds, in one of which there are men who are not mortal, while in the other two and two make five. When Swift invites us to consider the race of Struldbugs who never die, we are able to acquiesce in imagination. But a world where two and two make five seems quite on a different level. We feel that such a world, if there were one, would upset the whole fabric of our knowledge and reduce us to utter doubt.

The fact is that, in simple mathematical judgements such as 'two and two are four', and also in many judgements of logic, we can know the general proposition without inferring it from instances, although some instance is usually necessary to make clear to us what the general proposition means. This is why there is real utility in the process of deduction, which goes from the general to the general, or from the general to the particular, as well as in the process of induction, which goes from the particular to the particular, or from the particular to the general. It is an old debate among philosophers whether deduction ever gives new knowledge. We can now see that in certain cases, at least, it does do so. If we already know that two and two always make four, and we know that Brown and Jones are two, and so are Robinson and Smith, we can deduce that Brown and Jones and Robinson and Smith are four. This is new knowledge, not contained in our premises, because the general proposition, 'two and two are four', never told us there were such people as Brown and Jones and Robinson and Smith, and the particular premises do not tell us that there were four of them, whereas the particular proposition deduced does tell us both these things.

But the newness of the knowledge is much less certain if we take the stock instance of deduction that is always given in books on logic, namely, 'All men are mortal; Socrates is a man, therefore Socrates is mortal.' In this case, what we really know beyond reasonable doubt is that certain men, A, B, C, were mortal, since, in fact, they have died. If Socrates is one of these men, it is foolish to go the roundabout way through 'all men are mortal' to arrive at the conclusion that probably Socrates is mortal. If Socrates is not one of the men on whom our induction is based, we shall still do better to argue straight from our A, B, C, to Socrates, than to go round by the general proposition, 'all men are mortal'. For the probability that Socrates is mortal is greater, on our data, than the probability that all men are mortal. (This is obvious, because if all men are mortal, so is Socrates; but if Socrates is mortal, it does not follow that all men are mortal.) Hence we shall reach the conclusion that Socrates is mortal with a greater approach to certainty if we make our argument purely inductive than if we go by way of 'all men are mortal' and then use deduction.

This illustrates the difference between general propositions known a priori, such as 'two and two are four', and empirical generalizations such as 'all men are mortal'. In regard to the former, deduction is the right mode of argument, whereas in regard to the latter, induction is always theoretically preferable, and warrants a greater confidence in the truth of our conclusion, because all empirical generalizations are more uncertain than the instances of them.

We have now seen that there are propositions known a priori, and that among them are the propositions of logic and pure mathematics, as well as the fundamental propositions of ethics. The question which must next occupy us is this: How is it possible that there should be such knowledge? And more particularly, how can there be knowledge of general propositions in cases where we have not examined all the instances, and indeed never can examine them all, because their number is infinite? These questions, which were first brought prominently forward by the German philosopher Kant (1724–1804), are very difficult, and historically very important.

CHAPTER VIII. HOW A PRIORI KNOWLEDGE IS POSSIBLE

Immanuel Kant is generally regarded as the greatest of the modern philosophers. Though he lived through the Seven Years War and the French Revolution, he never interrupted his teaching of philosophy at Konigsberg in East Prussia. His most distinctive contribution was the invention of what he called the 'critical' philosophy, which, assuming as a datum that there is knowledge of various kinds, inquired how such knowledge comes to be possible, and deduced, from the answer to this inquiry, many metaphysical results as to the nature of the world. Whether these results were valid may well be doubted. But Kant undoubtedly deserves credit for two things: first, for having perceived that we have a priori knowledge which is not purely 'analytic', i.e. such that the opposite would be self-contradictory; and secondly, for having made evident the philosophical importance of the theory of knowledge.

Before the time of Kant, it was generally held that whatever knowledge was a priori must be 'analytic'. What this word means will be best illustrated by examples. If I say, 'A bald man is a man', 'A plane figure is a figure', 'A bad poet is a poet', I make a purely analytic judgement: the subject spoken about is given as having at least two properties, of which one is singled out to be asserted of it. Such propositions as the above are trivial, and would never be enunciated in real life except by an orator preparing the way for a piece of sophistry. They are called 'analytic' because the predicate is obtained by merely analysing the subject. Before the time of Kant it was thought that all judgements of which we could be certain a priori were of this kind: that in all of them there was a predicate which was only part of the subject of which it was asserted. If this were so, we should be involved in a definite contradiction if we attempted to deny thinking that could be known a priori. 'A bald man is not bald' would assert and deny baldness of the same man, and would therefore contradict itself. Thus according to the philosophers before Kant, the law of contradiction, which asserts that nothing can at the same time have and not have a certain property, sufficed to establish the truth of all a priori knowledge.

Hume (1711–1776), who preceded Kant, accepting the usual view as to what makes knowledge a priori, discovered that, in many cases which had previously been supposed analytic, and notably in the case of cause and effect, the connexion was really synthetic. Before Hume, rationalists at least had supposed that the effect could be logically deduced from the cause, if only we had sufficient knowledge. Hume argued—correctly, as would now be generally admitted—that this could not be done. Hence he inferred the far more doubtful proposition that nothing could be known a priori about the connexion of cause and effect. Kant, who had been educated in the rationalist tradition, was much perturbed by Hume's skepticism, and endeavoured to find an answer to it. He perceived that not only the connexion of cause and effect, but all the propositions of arithmetic and geometry, are 'synthetic' i.e. not analytic: in all these propositions, no analysis of the subject will reveal the predicate. His stock instance was the proposition $7 + 5 = 12$. He pointed out, quite truly, that 7 and 5 have to be put together to give 12: the idea of 12 is not contained in them, nor even in the idea of adding them together. Thus he was led to the conclusion that all pure mathematics, though a priori, is synthetic; and this conclusion raised a new problem of which he endeavoured to find the solution.

The question which Kant put at the beginning of his philosophy, namely 'How is pure mathematics possible?' is an interesting and difficult one, to which every philosophy which is not purely sceptical must find some answer. The answer of the pure empiricists, that our mathematical knowledge is derived by induction from particular instances, we have already seen to be inadequate, for two reasons: first, that the validity of the inductive principle itself cannot be proved by induction; secondly, that the general propositions of mathematics, such as 'two and two always make four', can obviously be known with certainty by consideration of a single instance, and gain nothing by enumeration of other cases in which they have been found to be true. Thus our knowledge of the general propositions of mathematics (and the same applies to logic) must be accounted for otherwise than our (merely probable) knowledge of empirical generalizations such as 'all men are mortal'.

The problem arises through the fact that such knowledge is general, whereas all experience is particular. It seems strange that we should apparently be able to know some truths in advance about particular things of which we have as yet no experience; but it cannot easily be doubted that logic and arithmetic will apply to such things. We do not know who will be the inhabitants of London a hundred years hence; but we know that any two of them and any other two of them will make four of them. This apparent power of anticipating facts about things of which we have no experience is certainly surprising. Kant's solution of the problem, though not valid in my opinion, is interesting. It is, however, very difficult, and is differently understood by different philosophers. We can, therefore, only give the merest outline of it, and even that will be thought misleading by many exponents of Kant's system.

What Kant maintained was that in all our experience there are two elements to be distinguished, the one due to the object (i.e. to what we have called the 'physical object'), the other due to our own nature. We saw, in discussing matter and sense-data, that the physical object is different from the associated sense-data, and that the sense-data are to be regarded as resulting from an interaction between the physical object and ourselves. So far, we are in agreement with Kant. But what is distinctive of Kant is the way in which he apportions the shares of ourselves and the physical object respectively. He considers that the crude material given in sensation—the colour, hardness etc.—is due to the object, and that what we supply is the arrangement in space and time, and all the relations between sense-data which result from comparison or from considering one as the cause of the other or in any other way. His chief reason in favour of this view is that we seem to have a priori knowledge as to space and time and causality and comparison, but not as to the actual crude material of sensation. We can be sure, he says, that anything we shall ever experience must show the characteristics affirmed of it in our a priori knowledge, because these characteristics are due to our own nature, and therefore nothing can ever come into our experience without acquiring these characteristics.

The physical object, which he calls the 'thing in itself',[1] he regards as essentially unknowable; what can be known is the object as we have it in experience, which he calls the 'phenomenon'. The phenomenon, being a joint product of us and the thing in itself, is sure to have those characteristics which are due to us, and is therefore sure to conform to our a priori knowledge. Hence this knowledge, though true of all actual and possible experience, must not be supposed to apply outside experience. Thus in spite of the existence of a priori knowledge, we cannot know anything about the thing in itself or about what is not an actual or possible object of experience. In this way he tries to reconcile and harmonize the contentions of the rationalists with the arguments of the empiricists.

Apart from minor grounds on which Kant's philosophy may be criticized, there is one main objection which seems fatal to any attempt to deal with the problem of a priori knowledge by his method. The thing to be accounted for is our certainty that the facts must always conform to logic and arithmetic. To say that logic and arithmetic are contributed by us does not account for this. Our nature is as much a fact of the existing world as anything, and there can be no certainty that it will remain constant. It might happen, if Kant is right, that to-morrow our nature would

so change as to make two and two become five. This possibility seems never to have occurred to him, yet it is one which utterly destroys the certainty and universality which he is anxious to vindicate for arithmetical propositions. It is true that this possibility, formally, is inconsistent with the Kantian view that time itself is a form imposed by the subject upon phenomena, so that our real Self is not in time and has no to-morrow. But he will still have to suppose that the time-order of phenomena is determined by characteristics of what is behind phenomena, and this suffices for the substance of our argument.

Reflection, moreover, seems to make it clear that, if there is any truth in our arithmetical beliefs, they must apply to things equally whether we think of them or not. Two physical objects and two other physical objects must make four physical objects, even if physical objects cannot be experienced. To assert this is certainly within the scope of what we mean when we state that two and two are four. Its truth is just as indubitable as the truth of the assertion that two phenomena and two other phenomena make four phenomena. Thus Kant's solution unduly limits the scope of a priori propositions, in addition to failing in the attempt at explaining their certainty.

Apart from the special doctrines advocated by Kant, it is very common among philosophers to regard what is a priori as in some sense mental, as concerned rather with the way we must think than with any fact of the outer world. We noted in the preceding chapter the three principles commonly called 'laws of thought'. The view which led to their being so named is a natural one, but there are strong reasons for thinking that it is erroneous. Let us take as an illustration the law of contradiction. This is commonly stated in the form 'Nothing can both be and not be', which is intended to express the fact that nothing can at once have and not have a given quality. Thus, for example, if a tree is a beech it cannot also be not a beech; if my table is rectangular it cannot also be not rectangular, and so on.

Now what makes it natural to call this principle a law of thought is that it is by thought rather than by outward observation that we persuade ourselves of its necessary truth. When we have seen that a tree is a beech, we do not need to look again in order to ascertain whether it is also not a beech; thought alone

---

[1]Kant's 'thing in itself' is identical in definition with the physical object, namely, it is the cause of sensations. In the properties deduced from the definition it is not identical, since Kant held (in spite of some inconsistency as regards cause) that we can know that none of the categories are applicable to the 'thing in itself'.

makes us know that this is impossible. But the conclusion that the law of contradiction is a law of thought is nevertheless erroneous. What we believe, when we believe the law of contradiction, is not that the mind is so made that it must believe the law of contradiction. This belief is a subsequent result of psychological reflection, which presupposes the belief in the law of contradiction. The belief in the law of contradiction is a belief about things, not only about thoughts. It is not, e.g., the belief that if we think a certain tree is a beech, we cannot at the same time think that it is not a beech; it is the belief that if a tree is a beech, it cannot at the same time be not a beech. Thus the law of contradiction is about things, and not merely about thoughts; and although belief in the law of contradiction is a thought, the law of contradiction itself is not a thought, but a fact concerning the things in the world. If this, which we believe when we believe the law of contradiction, were not true of the things in the world, the fact that we were compelled to think it true would not save the law of contradiction from being false; and this shows that the law is not a law of thought.

A similar argument applies to any other a priori judgement. When we judge that two and two are four, we are not making a judgement about our thoughts, but about all actual or possible couples. The fact that our minds are so constituted as to believe that two and two are four, though it is true, is emphatically not what we assert when we assert that two and two are four. And no fact about the constitution of our minds could make it true that two and two are four. Thus our a priori knowledge, if it is not erroneous, is not merely knowledge about the constitution of our minds, but is applicable to whatever the world may contain, both what is mental and what is non-mental.

The fact seems to be that all our a priori knowledge is concerned with entities which do not, properly speaking exist, either in the mental or in the physical world. These entities are such as can be named by parts of speech which are not substantives; they are such entities as qualities and relations. Suppose, for instance, that I am in my room. I exist, and my room exists; but does 'in' exist? Yet obviously the word 'in' has a meaning; it denotes a relation which holds between me and my room. This relation is something, although we cannot say that it exists in the same sense in which I and my room exist. The relation 'in' is something which we can think about and understand, for, if we could not understand it, we could not understand the sentence 'I am in my room'. Many philosophers, following Kant, have maintained that relations are the work of the mind, that things in themselves have no relations, but that the mind brings them together in one act of thought and thus produces the relations which it judges them to have.

This view, however, seems open to objections similar to those which we urged before against Kant. It seems plain that it is not thought which produces the truth of the proposition 'I am in my room'. It may be true that an earwig is in my room, even if neither I nor the earwig nor any one else is aware of this truth; for this truth concerns only the earwig and the room, and does not depend upon anything else. Thus relations, as we shall see more fully in the next chapter, must be placed in a world which is neither mental nor physical. This world is of great importance to philosophy, and in particular to the problems of a priori knowledge. In the next chapter we shall proceed to develop its nature and its bearing upon the questions with which we have been dealing. . . .

CHAPTER XII. TRUTH AND FALSEHOOD

Our knowledge of truths, unlike our knowledge of things, has an opposite, namely error. So far as things are concerned, we may know them or not know them, but there is no positive state of mind which can be described as erroneous knowledge of things, so long, at any rate, as we confine ourselves to knowledge by acquaintance. Whatever we are acquainted with must be something; we may draw wrong inferences from our acquaintance, but the acquaintance itself cannot be deceptive. Thus there is no dualism as regards acquaintance. But as regards knowledge of truths, there is a dualism. We may believe what is false as well as what is true. We know that on very many subjects different people hold different and incompatible opinions: hence some beliefs must be erroneous. Since erroneous beliefs are often held just as strongly as true beliefs, it becomes a difficult question how they are to be distinguished from true beliefs. How are we to know, in a given case, that our belief is not erroneous? This is a question of the very greatest difficulty, to which no completely satisfactory answer is possible. There is, however, a preliminary question which is rather less difficult, and that is: What do we mean by truth and falsehood? It is this preliminary question which is to be considered in this chapter.

In this chapter we are not asking how we can know whether a belief is true or false: we are asking what is meant by the question whether a belief is true or false. It is to be hoped that a clear answer to this question may help us to obtain an answer to the question what beliefs are true, but for the present we ask only 'What is truth?' and 'What is falsehood?' not 'What beliefs are true?' and 'What beliefs are false?' It is very important to keep these different questions entirely separate, since any confusion between them is sure to produce an answer which is not really applicable to either.

There are three points to observe in the attempt to discover the nature of truth, three requisites which any theory must fulfill.

1. Our theory of truth must be such as to admit of its opposite, falsehood. A good many philosophers have failed adequately to satisfy this condition: they have constructed theories according to which all our thinking ought to have been true, and have then had the greatest difficulty in finding a place for falsehood. In this respect our theory of belief must differ from our theory of acquaintance, since in the case of acquaintance it was not necessary to take account of any opposite.

2. It seems fairly evident that if there were no beliefs there could be no falsehood, and no truth either, in the sense in which truth is correlative to falsehood. If we imagine a world of mere matter, there would be no room for falsehood in such a world, and although it would contain what may be called 'facts', it would not contain any truths, in the sense in which truths are things of the same kind as falsehoods. In fact, truth and falsehood are properties of beliefs and statements: hence a world of mere matter, since it would contain no beliefs or statements, would also contain no truth or falsehood.

3. But, as against what we have just said, it is to be observed that the truth or falsehood of a belief always depends upon something which lies outside the belief itself. If I believe that Charles I died on the scaffold, I believe truly, not because of any intrinsic quality of my belief, which could be discovered by merely examining the belief, but because of an historical event which happened two and a half centuries ago. If I believe that Charles I died in his bed, I believe falsely: no degree of vividness in my belief, or of care in arriving at it, prevents it from being false, again because of what happened long ago, and not because of any intrinsic property of my belief. Hence, although truth and falsehood are properties of beliefs, they are properties dependent upon the relations of the beliefs to other things, not upon any internal quality of the beliefs.

The third of the above requisites leads us to adopt the view—which has on the whole been commonest among philosophers—that truth consists in some form of correspondence between belief and fact. It is, however, by no means an easy matter to discover a form of correspondence to which there are no irrefutable objections. By this partly—and partly by the feeling that, if truth consists in a correspondence of thought with something outside thought, thought can never know when truth has been attained—many philosophers have been led to try to find some definition of truth which shall not consist in relation to something wholly outside belief. The most important attempt at a definition of this sort is the theory that truth consists in coherence. It is said that the mark of falsehood is failure to cohere in the body of our beliefs, and that it is the essence of a truth to form part of the completely rounded system which is The Truth.

There is, however, a great difficulty in this view, or rather two great difficulties. The first is that there is no reason to suppose that only one coherent body of beliefs is possible. It may be that, with sufficient imagination, a novelist might invent a past for the world that would perfectly fit on to what we know, and yet be quite different from the real past. In more scientific matters, it is certain that there are often two or more hypotheses which account for all the known facts on some subject, and although, in such cases, men of science endeavour to find facts which will rule out all the hypotheses except one, there is no reason why they should always succeed.

In philosophy, again, it seems not uncommon for two rival hypotheses to be both able to account for all the facts. Thus, for example, it is possible that life is one long dream, and that the outer world has only that degree of reality that the objects of dreams have; but although such a view does not seem inconsistent with known facts, there is no reason to prefer it to the common-sense view, according to which other people and things do really exist. Thus coherence as the definition of truth fails because there is no proof that there can be only one coherent system.

The other objection to this definition of truth is that it assumes the meaning of 'coherence' known, whereas, in fact, 'coherence' presupposes the truth of the laws of logic. Two propositions are coherent when both may be true, and are incoherent when one at least must be false. Now in order to know whether two propositions can both be true, we must know such truths as the law of contradiction. For example, the two propositions, 'this tree is a beech' and 'this tree is not a beech', are not coherent, because of the law of contradiction. But if the law of contradiction itself were subjected to the test of coherence, we should find that, if we choose to suppose it false, nothing will any longer be incoherent with anything else. Thus the laws of logic supply the skeleton or framework within which the test of coherence applies, and they themselves cannot be established by this test.

For the above two reasons, coherence cannot be accepted as giving the meaning of truth, though it is often a most important test of truth after a certain amount of truth has become known.

Hence we are driven back to correspondence with fact as constituting the nature of truth. It remains to define precisely what we mean by 'fact', and what is the nature of the correspondence which must subsist between belief and fact, in order that belief may be true.

In accordance with our three requisites, we have to seek a theory of truth which (1) allows truth to have an opposite, namely falsehood, (2) makes truth a property of beliefs, but (3) makes it a property wholly dependent upon the relation of the beliefs to outside things.

The necessity of allowing for falsehood makes it impossible to regard belief as a relation of the mind to a single object, which could be said to be what is believed. If belief were so regarded, we should find

that, like acquaintance, it would not admit of the opposition of truth and falsehood, but would have to be always true. This may be made clear by examples. Othello believes falsely that Desdemona loves Cassio. We cannot say that this belief consists in a relation to a single object, 'Desdemona's love for Cassio', for if there were such an object, the belief would be true. There is in fact no such object, and therefore Othello cannot have any relation to such an object. Hence his belief cannot possibly consist in a relation to this object.

It might be said that his belief is a relation to a different object, namely 'that Desdemona loves Cassio'; but it is almost as difficult to suppose that there is such an object as this, when Desdemona does not love Cassio, as it was to suppose that there is 'Desdemona's love for Cassio'. Hence it will be better to seek for a theory of belief which does not make it consist in a relation of the mind to a single object.

It is common to think of relations as though they always held between two terms, but in fact this is not always the case. Some relations demand three terms, some four, and so on. Take, for instance, the relation 'between'. So long as only two terms come in, the relation 'between' is impossible: three terms are the smallest number that render it possible. York is between London and Edinburgh; but if London and Edinburgh were the only places in the world, there could be nothing which was between one place and another. Similarly jealousy requires three people: there can be no such relation that does not involve three at least. Such a proposition as 'A wishes B to promote C's marriage with D' involves a relation of four terms; that is to say, A and B and C and D all come in, and the relation involved cannot be expressed otherwise than in a form involving all four. Instances might be multiplied indefinitely, but enough has been said to show that there are relations which require more than two terms before they can occur.

The relation involved in judging or believing must, if falsehood is to be duly allowed for, be taken to be a relation between several terms, not between two. When Othello believes that Desdemona loves Cassio, he must not have before his mind a single object, 'Desdemona's love for Cassio', or 'that Desdemona loves Cassio', for that would require that there should be objective falsehoods, which subsist independently of any minds; and this, though not logically refutable, is a theory to be avoided if possible. Thus it is easier to account for falsehood if we take judgement to be a relation in which the mind and the various objects concerned all occur severally; that is to say, Desdemona and loving and Cassio must all be terms in the relation which subsists when Othello believes that Desdemona loves Cassio. This relation, therefore, is a relation of four terms, since Othello also is one of the terms of the relation. When we say that it is a relation of four terms, we do not mean that Othello has a certain relation to Desdemona, and has the same relation to loving and also to Cassio. This may be true of some other relation than believing; but believing, plainly, is not a relation which Othello has to each of the three terms concerned, but to all of them together: there is only one example of the relation of believing involved, but this one example knits together four terms. Thus the actual occurrence, at the moment when Othello is entertaining his belief, is that the relation called 'believing' is knitting together into one complex whole the four terms Othello, Desdemona, loving, and Cassio. What is called belief or judgement is nothing but this relation of believing or judging, which relates a mind to several things other than itself. An act of belief or of judgement is the occurrence between certain terms at some particular time, of the relation of believing or judging.

We are now in a position to understand what it is that distinguishes a true judgement from a false one. For this purpose we will adopt certain definitions. In every act of judgement there is a mind which judges, and there are terms concerning which it judges. We will call the mind the subject in the judgement, and the remaining terms the objects. Thus, when Othello judges that Desdemona loves Cassio, Othello is the subject, while the objects are Desdemona and loving and Cassio. The subject and the objects together are called the constituents of the judgement. It will be observed that the elation of judging has what is called a 'sense' or 'direction'. We may say, metaphorically, that it puts its objects in a certain order, which we may indicate by means of the order of the words in the sentence. (In an inflected language, the same thing will be indicated by inflections, e.g., by the difference between nominative and accusative.) Othello's judgement that Cassio loves

Desdemona differs from his judgement that Desdemona loves Cassio, in spite of the fact that it consists of the same constituents, because the relation of judging places the constituents in a different order in the two cases. Similarly, if Cassio judges that Desdemona loves Othello, the constituents of the judgement are still the same, but their order is different. This property of having a 'sense' or 'direction' is one which the relation of judging shares with all other relations. The 'sense' of relations is the ultimate source of order and series and a host of mathematical concepts; but we need not concern ourselves further with this aspect.

We spoke of the relation called 'judging' or 'believing' as knitting together into one complex whole the subject and the objects. In this respect, judging is exactly like every other relation. Whenever a relation holds between two or more terms, it unites the terms into a complex whole. If Othello loves Desdemona, there is such a complex whole as 'Othello's love for Desdemona'. The terms united by the relation may be themselves complex, or may be simple, but the whole which results from their being united must be complex. Wherever there is a relation which relates certain terms, there is a complex object formed of the union of those terms; and conversely, wherever there is a complex object, there is a relation which relates its constituents. When an act of believing occurs, there is a complex, in which 'believing' is the uniting relation, and subject and objects are arranged in a certain order by the 'sense' of the relation of believing. Among the objects, as we saw in considering 'Othello believes that Desdemona loves Cassio', one must be a relation—in this instance, the relation 'loving'. But this relation, as it occurs in the act of believing, is not the relation which creates the unity of the complex whole consisting of the subject and the objects. The relation 'loving', as it occurs in the act of believing, is one of the objects—it is a brick in the structure, not the cement. The cement is the relation 'believing'. When the belief is true, there is another complex unity, in which the relation which was one of the objects of the belief relates the other objects. Thus, e.g., if Othello believes truly that Desdemona loves Cassio, then there is a complex unity, 'Desdemona's love for Cassio', which is composed exclusively of the objects of the belief, in the same order as they had in the belief, with the relation which was one of the objects occurring now as the cement that binds together the other objects of the belief. On the other hand, when a belief is false, there is no such complex unity composed only of the objects of the belief. If Othello believes falsely that Desdemona loves Cassio, then there is no such complex unity as 'Desdemona's love for Cassio'.

Thus a belief is *true* when it *corresponds* to a certain associated complex, and *false* when it does not. Assuming, for the sake of definiteness, that the objects of the belief are two terms and a relation, the terms being put in a certain order by the 'sense' of the believing, then if the two terms in that order are united by the relation into a complex, the belief is true; if not, it is false. This constitutes the definition of truth and falsehood that we were in search of. Judging or believing is a certain complex unity of which a mind is a constituent; if the remaining constituents, taken in the order which they have in the belief, form a complex unity, then the belief is true; if not, it is false.

Thus although truth and falsehood are properties of beliefs, yet they are in a sense extrinsic properties, for the condition of the truth of a belief is something not involving beliefs, or (in general) any mind at all, but only the objects of the belief. A mind, which believes, believes truly when there is a corresponding complex not involving the mind, but only its objects. This correspondence ensures truth, and its absence entails falsehood. Hence we account simultaneously for the two facts that beliefs (a) depend on minds for their *existence*, and (b) do not depend on minds for their *truth*.

We may restate our theory as follows: If we take such a belief as 'Othello believes that Desdemona loves Cassio', we will call Desdemona and Cassio the object-terms, and loving the object-relation. If there is a complex unity 'Desdemona's love for Cassio', consisting of the object-terms related by the object-relation in the same order as they have in the belief, then this complex unity is called the fact corresponding to the belief. Thus a belief is true when there is a corresponding fact, and is false when there is no corresponding fact.

It will be seen that minds do not create truth or falsehood. They create beliefs, but when once the beliefs are created, the mind cannot make them true or false, except in the special case where they concern future things which are within the power of the person believing, such as catching trains. What makes a belief true is a fact, and this fact does not (except in exceptional cases) in any way involve the mind of the person who has the belief.

Having now decided what we mean by truth and falsehood, we have next to consider what ways there are of knowing whether this or that belief is true or false. This consideration will occupy the next chapter. . . .

CHAPTER XV. THE VALUE OF PHILOSOPHY

Having now come to the end of our brief and very incomplete review of the problems of philosophy, it will be well to consider, in conclusion, what is the value of philosophy and why it ought to be studied. It is the more necessary to consider this question, in view of the fact that many men, under the influence of science or of practical affairs, are inclined to doubt whether philosophy is anything better than innocent but useless trifling, hair-splitting distinctions, and controversies on matters concerning which knowledge is impossible.

This view of philosophy appears to result, partly from a wrong conception of the ends of life, partly from a wrong conception of the kind of goods which philosophy strives to achieve. Physical science, through the medium of inventions, is useful to innumerable people who are wholly ignorant of it; thus the study of physical science is to be recommended, not only, or primarily, because of the effect on the student, but rather because of the effect on mankind in general. Thus utility does not belong to philosophy. If the study of philosophy has any value at all for others than students of philosophy, it must be only indirectly, through its effects upon the lives of those who study it. It is in these effects, therefore, if anywhere, that the value of philosophy must be primarily sought.

But further, if we are not to fail in our endeavour to determine the value of philosophy, we must first free our minds from the prejudices of what are wrongly called 'practical' men. The 'practical' man, as this word is often used, is one who recognizes only material needs, who realizes that men must have food for the body, but is oblivious of the necessity of providing food for the mind. If all men were well off, if poverty and disease had been reduced to their lowest possible point, there would still remain much to be done to produce a valuable society; and even in the existing world the goods of the mind are at least as important as the goods of the body. It is exclusively among the goods of the mind that the value of philosophy is to be found; and only those who are not indifferent to these goods can be persuaded that the study of philosophy is not a waste of time.

Philosophy, like all other studies, aims primarily at knowledge. The knowledge it aims at is the kind of knowledge which gives unity and system to the body of the sciences, and the kind which results from a critical examination of the grounds of our convictions, prejudices, and beliefs. But it cannot be maintained that philosophy has had any very great measure of success in its attempts to provide definite answers to its questions. If you ask a mathematician, a mineralogist, a historian, or any other man of learning, what definite body of truths has been ascertained by his science, his answer will last as long as you are willing to listen. But if you put the same question to a philosopher, he will, if he is candid, have to confess that his study has not achieved positive results such as have been achieved by other sciences. It is true that this is partly accounted for by the fact that, as soon as definite knowledge concerning any subject becomes possible, this subject ceases to be called philosophy, and becomes a separate science. The whole study of the heavens, which now belongs to astronomy, was once included in philosophy; Newton's great work was called 'the mathematical principles of natural philosophy'. Similarly, the study of the human mind, which was a part of philosophy, has now been separated from philosophy and has become the science of psychology. Thus, to a great extent, the uncertainty of philosophy is more apparent than real: those questions which are already capable of definite answers are placed in the sciences, while those only to which, at present, no definite answer can be given, remain to form the residue which is called philosophy.

This is, however, only a part of the truth concerning the uncertainty of philosophy. There are many questions—and among them those that are of the profoundest interest to our spiritual life—which, so far as we can see, must remain insoluble to the human intellect unless its powers become of quite a different order from what they are now. Has the universe any unity of plan or purpose, or is it a fortuitous concourse of atoms? Is consciousness a permanent part of the universe, giving hope of indefinite growth in wisdom, or is it a transitory accident on a small planet on which life must ultimately become impossible? Are good and evil of importance to the universe or only to man? Such questions are asked by philosophy, and variously answered by various philosophers. But it would seem that, whether answers be otherwise discoverable or not, the answers suggested by philosophy are none of them demonstrably true. Yet, however slight may be the hope of discovering an answer, it is part of the business of philosophy to continue the consideration of such questions, to make us aware of their importance, to examine all the approaches to them, and to keep alive that speculative interest in the universe which is apt to be killed by confining ourselves to definitely ascertainable knowledge.

Many philosophers, it is true, have held that philosophy could establish the truth of certain answers to such fundamental questions. They have supposed that what is of most importance in religious beliefs could be proved by strict demonstration to be true. In order to judge of such attempts, it is necessary to take a survey of human knowledge, and to form an opinion as to its methods and its limitations. On such a subject it would be unwise to pronounce dogmatically; but if the investigations of our previous chapters have not led us astray, we shall be compelled to renounce the hope of finding philosophical proofs of religious beliefs. We cannot, therefore, include as part of the value of philosophy any definite set of answers to such questions. Hence, once more, the value of philosophy must not depend upon any supposed body of definitely ascertainable knowledge to be acquired by those who study it.

The value of philosophy is, in fact, to be sought largely in its very uncertainty. The man who has no tincture of philosophy goes through life imprisoned in the prejudices derived from common sense, from the habitual beliefs of his age or his nation, and from convictions which have grown up in his mind without the co-operation or consent of his deliberate reason. To such a man the world tends to become definite, finite, obvious; common objects rouse no questions, and unfamiliar possibilities are contemptuously rejected. As soon as we begin to philosophize, on the contrary, we find, as we saw in our opening chapters, that even the most everyday things lead to problems to which only very incomplete answers can be given. Philosophy, though unable to tell us with certainty what is the true answer to the doubts which it raises, is able to suggest many possibilities which enlarge our thoughts and free them from the tyranny of custom. Thus, while diminishing our feeling of certainty as to what things are, it greatly increases our knowledge as to what they may be; it removes the somewhat arrogant dogmatism of those who have never travelled into the region of liberating doubt, and it keeps alive our sense of wonder by showing familiar things in an unfamiliar aspect.

Apart from its utility in showing unsuspected possibilities, philosophy has a value—perhaps its chief value—through the greatness of the objects which it contemplates, and the freedom from narrow and personal aims resulting from this contemplation. The life of the instinctive man is shut up within the circle of his private interests: family and friends may be included, but the outer world is not regarded except as it may help or hinder what comes within the circle of instinctive wishes. In such a life there is something feverish and confined, in comparison with which the philosophic life is calm and free. The private world of instinctive interests is a small one, set in the midst of a great and powerful world which must, sooner or later, lay our private world in ruins. Unless we can so enlarge our interests as to include the whole outer world, we remain like a garrison in a beleaguered fortress, knowing that the enemy prevents escape and that ultimate surrender is inevitable. In such a life there is no peace, but a constant strife between the insistence of desire and the powerlessness of will. In one way or another, if our life is to be great and free, we must escape this prison and this strife.

One way of escape is by philosophic contemplation. Philosophic contemplation does not, in its widest survey, divide the universe into two hostile camps—friends and foes, helpful and hostile, good and bad—it views the whole impartially. Philosophic

contemplation, when it is unalloyed, does not aim at proving that the rest of the universe is akin to man. All acquisition of knowledge is an enlargement of the Self, but this enlargement is best attained when it is not directly sought. It is obtained when the desire for knowledge is alone operative, by a study which does not wish in advance that its objects should have this or that character, but adapts the Self to the characters which it finds in its objects. This enlargement of Self is not obtained when, taking the Self as it is, we try to show that the world is so similar to this Self that knowledge of it is possible without any admission of what seems alien. The desire to prove this is a form of self-assertion and, like all self-assertion, it is an obstacle to the growth of Self which it desires, and of which the Self knows that it is capable. Self-assertion, in philosophic speculation as elsewhere, views the world as a means to its own ends; thus it makes the world of less account than Self, and the Self sets bounds to the greatness of its goods. In contemplation, on the contrary, we start from the not-Self, and through its greatness the boundaries of Self are enlarged; through the infinity of the universe the mind which contemplates it achieves some share in infinity.

For this reason greatness of soul is not fostered by those philosophies which assimilate the universe to Man. Knowledge is a form of union of Self and not-Self; like all union, it is impaired by dominion, and therefore by any attempt to force the universe into conformity with what we find in ourselves. There is a widespread philosophical tendency towards the view which tells us that Man is the measure of all things, that truth is man-made, that space and time and the world of universals are properties of the mind, and that, if there be anything not created by the mind, it is unknowable and of no account for us. This view, if our previous discussions were correct, is untrue; but in addition to being untrue, it has the effect of robbing philosophic contemplation of all that gives it value, since it fetters contemplation to Self. What it calls knowledge is not a union with the not-Self, but a set of prejudices, habits, and desires, making an impenetrable veil between us and the world beyond. The man who finds pleasure in such a theory of knowledge is like the man who never leaves the domestic circle for fear his word might not be law.

The true philosophic contemplation, on the contrary, finds its satisfaction in every enlargement of the not-Self, in everything that magnifies the objects contemplated, and thereby the subject contemplating. Everything, in contemplation, that is personal or private, everything that depends upon habit, self-interest, or desire, distorts the object, and hence impairs the union which the intellect seeks. By thus making a barrier between subject and object, such personal and private things become a prison to the intellect.

The free intellect will see as God might see, without a here and now, without hopes and fears, without the trammels of customary beliefs and traditional prejudices, calmly, dispassionately, in the sole and exclusive desire of knowledge—knowledge as impersonal, as purely contemplative, as it is possible for man to attain. Hence also the free intellect will value more the abstract and universal knowledge into which the accidents of private history do not enter, than the knowledge brought by the senses, and dependent, as such knowledge must be, upon an exclusive and personal point of view and a body whose sense-organs distort as much as they reveal.

The mind which has become accustomed to the freedom and impartiality of philosophic contemplation will preserve something of the same freedom and impartiality in the world of action and emotion.

It will view its purposes and desires as parts of the whole, with the absence of insistence that results from seeing them as infinitesimal fragments in a world of which all the rest is unaffected by any one man's deeds. The impartiality which, in contemplation, is the unalloyed desire for truth, is the very same quality of mind which, in action, is justice, and in emotion is that universal love which can be given to all, and not only to those who are judged useful or admirable. Thus contemplation enlarges not only the objects of our thoughts, but also the objects of our actions and our affections: it makes us citizens of the universe, not only of one walled city at war with all the rest. In this citizenship of the universe consists man's true freedom, and his liberation from the thraldom of narrow hopes and fears.

Thus, to sum up our discussion of the value of philosophy; Philosophy is to be studied, not for the sake of any definite answers to its questions since no definite answers can, as a rule, be known to be true, but rather for the sake of the questions themselves; because these questions enlarge our conception of what is possible, enrich our intellectual imagination and diminish the dogmatic assurance which closes the mind against speculation; but above all because, through the greatness of the universe which philosophy contemplates, the mind also is rendered great, and becomes capable of that union with the universe which constitutes its highest good.

A FREE MAN'S WORSHIP

This essay was written in 1903 during one of Russell's deepest personal crises. It shows his attempt to find meaning and morality in life, and is a classic essay on humanistic perspective.

The world, says Russell, is an absurd, godless tragedy in which nature, omnipotent but blind, has brought forth rational children who are superior to their mother, and as such can discover moral ideals with which to sustain themselves in this ultimately meaningless existence. Morality doesn't need religion for legitimation.

To Dr. Faustus in his study Mephistopheles told the history of the Creation, saying,

The endless praises of the choirs of angels had begun to grow wearisome; for, after all, did he not deserve their praise? Had he not given them endless joy? Would it not be more amusing to obtain undeserved praise, to be worshiped by beings whom he

tortured? He smiled inwardly, and resolved that the great drama should be performed.

For countless ages the hot nebula whirled aimlessly through space. At length it began to take shape, the central mass threw off planets, the planets cooled, boiling seas and burning mountains heaved and tossed, from black masses of cloud hot sheets of rain deluged the barely solid crust. And now the first germ of life grew in the depths of the ocean and developed rapidly in the fructifying warmth into vast forest trees, huge ferns springing from the damp mold, sea monsters breeding, fighting, devouring, and passing away. And from the monsters, as the play unfolded itself, Man was born, with the power of thought, the knowledge of good and evil, and the cruel thirst for worship. And Man saw that all is passing in this mad, monstrous world, that all is struggling to snatch, at any cost, a few brief moments of life before Death's inexorable decree. And Man said, "There is a hidden purpose, could we but fathom it, and the purpose is good; for we must reverence something, and in the visible world there is nothing worthy of reverence." And Man stood aside from the struggle, resolving that God intended harmony to come out of chaos by human efforts. And when he followed the instincts which God had transmitted to him from his ancestry of beasts of prey, he called it Sin, and asked God to forgive him. But he doubted whether he could be justly forgiven, until he invented a divine Plan by which God's wrath was to have been appeased. And seeing the present was bad, he made it yet worse, that thereby the future might be better. And he gave God thanks for the strength that enabled him to forgo even the joys that were possible. And God smiled; and when he saw that Man had become perfect in renunciation and worship, he sent another sun through the sky, which crashed into Man's sun; and all returned again to nebula.

"Yes," he murmured, "it was a good play; I will have it performed again."

Such, in outline, but even more purposeless, more void of meaning, is the world which science presents for our belief. Amid such a world, if anywhere, our ideals henceforward must find a home. That man is the product of causes which had no prevision of the end they were achieving; that his origin, his growth, his hopes and fears, his loves and his beliefs, are but the outcome of accidental collocations of atoms; that no fire, no heroism, no intensity of thought and feeling, can preserve an individual life beyond the grave; that all the labors of the ages, all the devotion, all the inspiration, all the noonday brightness of human genius, are destined to extinction in the vast death

of the solar system, and that the whole temple of man's achievement must inevitably be buried beneath the debris of a universe in ruins—all these things, if not quite beyond dispute, are yet so nearly certain that no philosophy which rejects them can hope to stand. Only within the scaffolding of these truths, only on the firm foundation of unyielding despair, can the soul's habitation henceforth be safely built.

How, in such an alien and inhuman world, can so powerless a creature as man preserve his aspirations untarnished? A strange mystery it is that nature, omnipotent but blind, in the revolutions of her secular hurryings through the abysses of space, has brought forth at last a child, subject still to her power, but gifted with sight, with knowledge of good and evil, with the capacity of judging all the works of his unthinking mother. In spite of death, the mark and seal of the parental control, man is yet free, during his brief years, to examine, to criticize, to know, and in imagination to create. To him alone, in the world with which he is acquainted, this freedom belongs; and in this lies his superiority to the resistless forces that control his outward life.

The savage, like ourselves, feels the oppression of his impotence before the powers of nature; but having in himself nothing that he respects more than power, he is willing to prostrate himself before his gods, without inquiring whether they are worthy of his worship. Pathetic and very terrible is the long history of cruelty and torture, of degradation and human sacrifice, endured in the hope of placating the jealous gods: surely, the trembling believer thinks, when what is most precious has been freely given, their lust for blood must be appeased, and more will not be required. The religion of Moloch—as such creeds may be generally called—is in essence the cringing submission of the slave, who dare not, even in his heart, allow the thought that his master deserves no adulation. Since the independence of ideals is not yet acknowledged, power may be freely worshiped and receive an unlimited respect, despite its wanton infliction of pain.

But gradually, as morality grows bolder, the claim of the ideal world begins to be felt; and worship, if it is not to cease, must be given to gods of another kind than those created by the savage. Some, though they feel the demands of the ideal, will still consciously reject them, still urging that naked power is worthy of worship. Such is the attitude inculcated in God's answer to Job out of the whirlwind: the divine power and knowledge are paraded, but of the divine goodness there is no hint. Such also is the attitude of those who, in our own day, base their morality upon the struggle for survival, maintaining that the survivors are necessarily the fittest. But others, not content with an answer so repugnant to the moral sense, will adopt the position which we have become accustomed to regard as specially religious, maintaining that, in some hidden manner, the world of fact is really harmonious with the world of ideals. Thus man created God, all-powerful and all-good, the mystic unity of what is and what should be.

But the world of fact, after all, is not good; and, in submitting our judgment to it, there is an element of slavishness from which our thoughts must be purged. For in all things it is well to exalt the dignity of man, by freeing him as far as possible from the tyranny of nonhuman power. When we have realized that power is largely bad, that man, with his knowledge of good and evil, is but a helpless atom in a world which has no such knowledge, the choice is again presented to us: Shall we worship force, or shall we worship goodness? Shall our God exist and be evil, or shall he be recognized as the creation of our own conscience?

The answer to this question is very momentous and affects profoundly our whole morality. The worship of force, to which Carlyle and Nietzsche and the creed of militarism have accustomed us, is the result of failure to maintain our own ideals against a hostile universe: it is itself a prostrate submission to evil, a sacrifice of our best to Moloch. If strength indeed is to be respected, let us respect rather the strength of those who refuse that false "recognition of facts" which fails to recognize that facts are often bad. Let us admit that, in the world we know, there are many things that would be better otherwise, and that the ideals to which we do and must adhere are not realized in the realm of matter. Let us preserve our respect for truth, for beauty, for the ideal of perfection which life does not permit us to attain, though none of these things meet with the approval of the unconscious universe. If power is bad, as it

seems to be, let us reject it from our hearts. In this lies man's true freedom: in determination to worship only the God created by our own love of the good, to respect only the heaven which inspires the insight of our best moments. In action, in desire, we must submit perpetually to the tyranny of outside forces; but in thought, in aspiration, we are free, free from our fellow men, free from the petty planet on which our bodies impotently crawl, free even, while we live, from the tyranny of death. Let us learn, then, that energy of faith which enables us to live constantly in the vision of the good; and let us descend, in action, into the world of fact, with that vision always before us.

When first the opposition of fact and ideal grows fully visible, a spirit of fiery revolt, of fierce hatred of the gods, seems necessary to the assertion of freedom. To defy with Promethean constancy a hostile universe, to keep its evil always in view, always actively hated, to refuse no pain that the malice of power can invent, appears to be the duty of all who will not bow before the inevitable. But indignation is still a bondage, for it compels our thoughts to be occupied with an evil world; and in the fierceness of desire from which rebellion springs there is a kind of self-assertion which it is necessary for the wise to overcome. Indignation is a submission of our thoughts but not of our desires; the Stoic freedom in which wisdom consists is found in the submission of our desires but not of our thoughts. From the submission of our desires springs the virtue of resignation; from the freedom of our thoughts springs the whole world of art and philosophy, and the vision of beauty by which, at last, we half reconquer the reluctant world. But the vision of beauty is possible only to unfettered contemplation, to thoughts not weighted by the load of eager wishes; and thus freedom comes only to those who no longer ask of life that it shall yield them any of those personal goods that are subject to the mutations of time.

Although the necessity of renunciation is evidence of the existence of evil, yet Christianity, in preaching it, has shown a wisdom exceeding that of the Promethean philosophy of rebellion. It must be admitted that, of the things we desire, some, though they prove impossible, are yet real goods; others, however, as ardently longed for, do not form part of a fully purified ideal. The belief that what must be renounced is bad, though sometimes false, is far less often false than untamed passion supposes; and the creed of religion, by providing a reason for proving that it is never false, has been the means of purifying our hopes by the discovery of many austere truths.

But there is in resignation a further good element: even real goods, when they are unattainable, ought not to be fretfully desired. To every man comes, sooner or later, the great renunciation. For the young, there is nothing unattainable; a good thing desired with the whole force of a passionate will, and yet impossible, is to them not credible. Yet, by death, by illness, by poverty, or by the voice of duty, we must learn, each one of us, that the world was not made for us, and that, however beautiful may be the things we crave, Fate may nevertheless forbid them. It is the part of courage, when misfortune comes, to bear without repining the ruin of our hopes, to turn away our thoughts from vain regrets. This degree of submission to power is not only just and right: it is the very gate of wisdom.

But passive renunciation is not the whole of wisdom; for not by renunciation alone can we build a temple for the worship of our own ideals. Haunting foreshadowings of the temple appear in the realm of imagination, in music, in architecture, in the untroubled kingdom of reason, and in the golden sunset magic of lyrics, where beauty shines and glows, remote from the touch of sorrow, remote from the fear of change, remote from the failures and disenchantments of the world of fact. In the contemplation of these things the vision of heaven will shape itself in our hearts, giving at once a touchstone to judge the world about us and an inspiration by which to fashion to our needs whatever is not incapable of serving as a stone in the sacred temple.

Except for those rare spirits that are born without sin, there is a cavern of darkness to be traversed before that temple can be entered. The gate of the cavern is despair, and its floor is paved with the gravestones of abandoned hopes. There self must die; there the eagerness, the greed of untamed desire, must be slain, for only so can the soul be freed from the empire of Fate. But out of the cavern, the Gate of Renunciation leads again to the daylight of wisdom, by whose radiance a new insight, a new joy, a new tenderness, shine forth to gladden the pilgrim's heart.

When, without the bitterness of impotent rebellion, we have learned both to resign ourselves to the outward rule of Fate and to recognize that the nonhuman world is unworthy of our worship, it becomes possible at last so to transform and refashion the unconscious universe, so to transmute it in the crucible of imagination, that a new image of shining gold replaces the old idol of clay. In all the multiform facts of the world—in the visual shapes of trees and mountains and clouds, in the events of the life of man, even in the very omnipotence of death—the insight of creative idealism can find the reflection of a beauty which its own thoughts first made. In this way mind asserts its subtle mastery over the thoughtless forces of nature. The more evil the material with which it deals, the more thwarting to untrained desire, the greater is its achievement in inducing the reluctant rock to yield up its hidden treasures, the prouder its victory in compelling the opposing forces to swell the pageant of its triumph. Of all the arts, tragedy is the proudest, the most triumphant; for it builds its shining citadel in the very center of the enemy's country, on the very summit of his highest mountain; from its impregnable watchtowers, his camps and arsenals, his columns and forts, are all revealed; within its walls the free life continues, while the legions of death and pain and despair, and all the servile captains of tyrant Fate, afford the burghers of that dauntless city new spectacles of beauty. Happy those sacred ramparts, thrice happy the dwellers on that all-seeing eminence. Honor to those brave warriors who, through countless ages of warfare, have preserved for us the priceless heritage of liberty and have kept undefiled by sacrilegious invaders the home of the unsubdued.

But the beauty of tragedy does but make visible a quality which, in more or less obvious shapes, is present always and everywhere in life. In the spectacle of death, in the endurance of intolerable pain, and in the irrevocableness of a vanished past, there is a sacredness, an overpowering awe, a feeling of the vastness, the depth, the inexhaustible mystery of existence, in which, as by some strange marriage of pain, the sufferer is bound to the world by bonds of sorrow. In these moments of insight, we lose all eagerness of temporary desire, all struggling and striving for petty ends, all care for the little trivial things that, to a superficial view, make up the common life of day by day; we see, surrounding the narrow raft illumined by the flickering light of human comradeship, the dark ocean on whose rolling waves we toss for a brief hour; from the great night without, a chill blast breaks in upon our refuge; all the loneliness of humanity amid hostile forces is concentrated upon the individual soul, which must struggle alone, with what of courage it can command, against the whole weight of a universe that cares nothing for its hopes and fears. Victory, in this struggle with the powers of darkness, is the true baptism into the glorious company of heroes, the true initiation into the overmastering beauty of human existence. From that awful encounter of the soul with the outer world, renunciation, wisdom, and charity are born; and with their birth a new life begins. To take into the inmost shrine of the soul the irresistible forces whose puppets we seem to be—death and change, the irrevocableness of the past, and the powerlessness of man before the blind hurry of the universe from vanity to vanity— to feel these things and know them is to conquer them.

This is the reason why the past has such magical power. The beauty of its motionless and silent pictures is like the enchanted purity of late autumn, when the leaves, though one breath would make them fall, still glow against the sky in golden glory. The past does not change or strive; like Duncan, after life's fitful fever it sleeps well; what was eager and grasping, what was petty and transitory, has faded away; the things that were beautiful and eternal shine out of it like stars in the night. Its beauty, to a soul not worthy of it, is unendurable; but to a soul which has conquered Fate it is the key of religion.

The life of man, viewed outwardly, is but a small thing in comparison with the forces of nature. The slave is doomed to worship Time and Fate and Death, because they are greater than anything he finds in himself, and because all his thoughts are of things which they devour. But, great as they are, to think

of them greatly, to feel their passionless splendor, is greater still. And such thought makes us free men; we no longer bow before the inevitable in Oriental subjection, but we absorb it and make it a part of ourselves. To abandon the struggle for private happiness, to expel all eagerness of temporary desire, to burn with passion for eternal things—this is emancipation, and this is the free man's worship. And this liberation is effected by contemplation of Fate; for Fate itself is subdued by the mind which leaves nothing to be purged by the purifying fire of time.

United with his fellow men by the strongest of all ties, the tie of a common doom, the free man finds that a new vision is with him always, shedding over every daily task the light of love. The life of man is a long march through the night, surrounded by invisible foes, tortured by weariness and pain, toward a goal that few can hope to reach, and where none may tarry long. One by one, as they march, our comrades vanish from our sight, seized by the silent orders of omnipotent death. Very brief is the time in which we can help them, in which their happiness or misery is decided. Be it ours to shed sunshine on their path, to lighten their sorrows by the balm of sympathy, to give them the pure joy of a never-tiring affection, to strengthen failing courage, to instill faith in hours of despair. Let us not weigh in grudging scales their merits and demerits, but let us think only of their need—of the sorrows, the difficulties, perhaps the blindnesses, that make the misery of their lives; let us remember that they are fellow sufferers in the same darkness, actors in the same tragedy with ourselves. And so, when their day is over, when their good and their evil have become eternal by the immortality of the past, be it ours to feel that, where they suffered, where they failed, no deed of ours was the cause; but wherever a spark of the divine fire kindled in their hearts, we were ready with encouragement, with sympathy, with brave words in which high courage glowed.

Brief and powerless is man's life; on him and all his race the slow, sure doom falls pitiless and dark. Blind to good and evil, reckless of destruction, omnipotent matter rolls on its relentless way; for man, condemned today to lose his dearest, tomorrow himself to pass through the gate of darkness, it remains only to cherish, ere yet the blow fall, the lofty thoughts that ennoble his little day; disdaining the coward terrors of the slave of Fate, to worship at the shrine that his own hands have built; undismayed by the empire of chance, to preserve a mind free from the wanton tyranny that rules his outward life; proudly defiant of the irresistible forces that tolerate, for a moment, his knowledge and his condemnation, to sustain alone, a weary but unyielding Atlas, the world that his own ideals have fashioned despite the trampling march of unconscious power.

REVIEW QUESTIONS

1. What is Russell's argument for the correspondence theory of truth?
2. In Russell's view, what is the value of philosophy, and why should it be studied?
3. On what grounds does Russell reject Berkeley's idealism?
4. What is Russell's view on the historic controversy between empiricists and rationalists?
5. Does Russell believe that moral values are possible in a godless universe? What is the "free man's worship"?

31

G. E. MOORE

G. E. Moore (1873–1958) was a professor of philosophy at Cambridge University and one of the leading philosophers of the first half of the twentieth century. As a student at Cambridge University, he was a close acquaintance, though more a rival than a friend, of Bertrand Russell. He was also the leader of the Bloomsbury group of writers and artists that included such illustrious intellectuals as John Maynard Keynes, Leonard and Virginia Woolf, and Lytton Strachey. He was editor of the British philosophy journal *Mind* from 1921 to 1947 and was appointed to the Order of Merit in 1951. Perhaps his most influential work is *Principia Ethica* (1903) where he argues for the indefinability of "good."

Moore was a defender of common sense against skeptics and others who derided our ordinary beliefs. He argued that there is a vast amount of shared knowledge about the world, expressible in ordinary language and about which we can be quite certain. In this essay—which is a combination of two of his articles, "A Defence of Common Sense" and "Proof of the External World"—Moore argues that skepticism is decisively refuted by common sense. The essence of the argument is as follows:

1. If skepticism is true, we do not have knowledge of the external world.
2. But we do have knowledge of the external world (Moore gives many examples).

Therefore

3. Skepticism is false.

FOR FURTHER READING

Baldwin, Thomas. *G. E. Moore* (London, 1990).

Copleston, F. C. *Contemporary Philosophy* (Newman Press, 1963).

Moore, G. E. *Philosophical Papers* (George Allen & Unwin, 1959).

Moore, G. E. *Some Main Problems of Philosophy* (Collier Books, 1962).

Passmore, John. *A Hundred Years of Philosophy* (Macmillan, 1957).

Schilpp, P. A., ed. *The Philosophy of G.E. Moore* (Open Court, 1942).

PHILOSOPHICAL PAPERS

A DEFENSE OF COMMON SENSE

In what follows I have merely tried to state, one by one, some of the most important points in which my philosophical position differs from positions which have been taken up by *some* other philosophers. It may be that the points which I have had room to mention are not really the most important, and possibly some of them may be points as to which no philosopher has ever really differed from me. But, to the best of my belief, each is a point as to which many have really differed; although (in most cases, at all events) each is also a point as to which many have agreed with me.

I

The first point is a point which embraces a great many other points. And it is one which I cannot state as clearly as I wish to state it, except at some length. The method I am going to use for stating it is this. I am going to begin by enunciating, under the heading (1), a whole long list of propositions, which may seem, at first sight, such obvious truisms as not to be worth stating: they are, in fact, a set of propositions, every one of which (in my own opinion) I *know*, with certainty, to be true. I shall, next, under the heading (2), state a single proposition which makes an assertion about a whole set of *classes* of propositions—each class being defined, as the class consisting of all propositions which resemble *one* of

the propositions in (1) in a certain respect. (2), therefore, is a proposition which could not be stated, until the list of propositions in (1), or some similar list, had already been given. (2) is itself a proposition which may seem such an obvious truism as not to be worth stating: and it is also a proposition which (in my own opinion) I know, with certainty, to be true. But, nevertheless, it is, to the best of my belief, a proposition with regard to which many philosophers have, for different reasons, differed from me; even if they have not directly denied (2) itself, they have held views incompatible with it. My first point, then, may be said to be that (2), together with all its implications, some of which I shall expressly mention, is true.

(1) I begin, then, with my list of truisms, every one of which (in my own opinion) I *know*, with certainty, to be true. The propositions to be included in this list are the following:

There exists at present a living human body, which is *my* body. This body was born at a certain time in the past, and has existed continuously ever since, though not without undergoing changes; it was, for instance, much smaller when it was born, and for some time afterwards, than it is now. Ever since it was born, it has been either in contact with or not far from the surface of the earth; and, at every moment since it was born, there have also existed many other things, having shape and size in three dimensions (in the same familiar sense in which it has), from which it has been *at various distances* (in the

Reprinted from G.E. Moore, *Philosophical Papers* (London: George Allen & Unwin, 1959) by permission of Timothy Moore.

familiar sense in which it is now at a distance both from that mantelpiece and from that bookcase, and at a greater distance from the bookcase than it is from the mantelpiece); also there have (very often, at all events) existed some other things of this kind with which it was *in contact* (in the familiar sense in which it is now in contact with the pen I am holding in my right hand and with some of the clothes I am wearing). Among the things which have, in this sense, formed part of its environment (i.e. have been either in contact with it, or at *some* distance from it, however *great*) there have, at every moment since its birth, been large numbers of other living human bodies, each of which has, like it, (*a*) at some time been born, (*b*) continued to exist from some time after birth, (*c*) been, at every moment of its life after birth, either in contact with or not far from the surface of the earth; and many of these bodies have already died and ceased to exist. But the earth had existed also for many years before my body was born; and for many of these years, also, large numbers of human bodies had, at every moment, been alive upon it; and many of these bodies had died and ceased to exist before it was born. Finally (to come to a different class of propositions), I am a human being, and I have, at different times since my body was born, had many different experiences, of each of many different kinds: e.g. I have often perceived both my own body and other things which formed part of its environment, including other human bodies; I have not only perceived things of this kind, but have also observed facts about them, such as, for instance, the fact which I am now observing, that that mantelpiece is at present nearer to my body than that bookcase; I have been aware of other facts, which I was not at the time observing, such as, for instance, the fact, of which I am now aware, that my body existed yesterday and was then also for some time nearer to that mantelpiece than to that bookcase; I have had expectations with regard to the future, and many beliefs of other kinds, both true and false; I have thought of imaginary things and persons and incidents, in the reality of which I did not believe; I have had dreams; and I have had feelings of many different kinds. And, just as my body has been the body of a human being, namely myself, who has, during his lifetime, had many experiences of each of these

(and other) different kinds; so, in the case of very many of the other human bodies which have lived upon the earth, each has been the body of a different human being, who has, during the lifetime of that body, had many different experiences of each of these (and other) different kinds.

(2) I now come to the single truism which, as will be seen, could not be stated except by reference to the whole list of truisms, just given in (1). This truism also (in my own opinion) I *know*, with certainty, to be true; and it is as follows:

In the case of *very many* (I do not say *all*) of the human beings belonging to the class (which includes myself) defined in the following way, i.e. as human beings who have had human bodies, that were born and lived for some time upon the earth, and who have, during the lifetime of those bodies, had many different experiences of each of the kinds mentioned in (1), it is true that each has frequently, during the life of his body, known, with regard to *him*self or *his* body, and with regard to some time earlier than any of the times at which I wrote down the propositions in (1), a proposition *corresponding* to each of the propositions in (1), in the sense that it asserts with regard to *himself* or *his* body and the earlier time in question (namely, in each case, the time at which he knew it), just what the corresponding proposition in (1) asserts with regard to *me* or *my* body and the time at which I wrote that proposition down.

In other words what (2) asserts is only (what seems an obvious enough truism) that each of *us* (meaning by 'us', very many human beings of the class defined) has frequently *known*, with regard to *him*self or *his* body and the time at which he knew it, everything which, in writing down my list of propositions in (1), I was claiming to know about *my*self or *my* body and the time at which I wrote that proposition down, i.e. just as *I* knew (when I wrote it down) 'There exists at present a living human body which is my body', so each of us has frequently known with regard to himself and some other time the different but corresponding proposition, which *he* could *then* have properly expressed by, 'There exists *at present* a human body which is *my* body'; just as *I* know 'Many human bodies other than mine have before now lived on the earth', so each of us has frequently known the different but corresponding proposition 'Many human bodies other than *mine* have before *now* lived on the earth'; just as *I* know 'Many human beings other than myself have before now perceived, and dreamed, and felt', so each of *us* has frequently known the different but corresponding proposition 'Many human beings other than *myself* have before *now* perceived, and dreamed, and felt'; and so on, in the case of *each* of the propositions enumerated in (1). . . .

PROOF OF AN EXTERNAL WORLD

In the preface to the second edition of Kant's *Critique of Pure Reason* some words occur, which, in Professor Kemp Smith's translations, are rendered as follows:

> It still remains a scandal to philosophy . . . that the existence of things outside of us . . . must be accepted merely on *faith*, and that, if anyone thinks good to doubt their existence, we are unable to counter his doubts by any satisfactory proof.[1]

It seems clear from these words that Kant thought it a matter of some importance to give a proof of 'the existence of things outside of us' or perhaps rather (for it seems to me possible that the force of the German words is better rendered in this way) of 'the existence of *the* things outside of us'; for had he not thought it important that a proof should be given, he would scarcely have called it a 'scandal' that no proof had been given. And it seems clear also that he thought that the giving of such a proof was a task which fell properly within the province of philosophy; for, if it did not, the fact that no proof had been given could not possibly be a scandal to *philosophy*.

Now, even if Kant was mistaken in both of these two opinions, there seems to me to be no doubt whatever that it is a matter of some importance and also a matter which falls properly within the province of

philosophy, to discuss the question what sort of proof, if any, can be given of 'the existence of things outside of us'. And to discuss this question was my object when I began to write the present lecture. But I may say at once that, as you will find, I have only, at most, succeeded in saying a very small part of what ought to be said about it.

The words 'it . . . remains a scandal to philosophy . . . that we are unable . . .' would, taken strictly, imply that, at the moment at which he wrote them, Kant himself was unable to produce a satisfactory proof of the point in question. But I think it is unquestionable that Kant himself did not think that he personally was at the time unable to produce such a proof. On the contrary, in the immediately preceding sentence, he has declared that he has, in the second edition of his *Critique*, to which he is now writing the Preface, given a 'rigorous proof' of this very thing; and has added that he believes this proof of his to be 'the only possible proof'. It is true that in this preceding sentence he does not describe the proof which he has given as a proof of 'the existence of things outside of us' or of 'the existence of the things outside of us', but describes it instead as a proof of 'the objective reality of outer intuition'. But the context leaves no doubt that he is using these two phrases, 'the objective reality of outer intuition' and 'the existence of things (*or* 'the things') outside of us', in such a way that whatever is a proof of the first is also necessarily a proof of the second. We must, therefore, suppose that when he speaks as if *we* are unable to give a satisfactory proof, he does not mean to say that he himself, as well as others, is *at the moment* unable; but rather that, until he discovered the proof which he has given, both he himself and everybody else *were* unable. Of course, if he is right in thinking that he has given a satisfactory proof, the state of things which he describes came to an end as soon as his proof was published. As soon as that happened, anyone who read it was able to give a satisfactory proof by simply repeating that which Kant had given, and the 'scandal' to philosophy had been removed once for all.

If, therefore, it were certain that the proof of the point in question given by Kant in the second edition is a satisfactory proof, it would be certain that at least one satisfactory proof can be given; and all

---

[1] B xxxix, note: Kemp Smith, p. 34. The German words are 'so bleibt es immer ein Skandal de Philosophie . . . , das Dasein der Dinge ausser uns . . . bloss auf *Glauben* annehmen zu müssen, und wenn es jemand einfällt es zu bezweifeln, ihm keinin genugtuenden Beweis entgegenstellen zu können'.

that would remain of the question which I said I proposed to discuss would be, firstly, the question as to what *sort* of a proof this of Kant's is, and secondly the question whether (contrary to Kant's own opinion) there may not perhaps be other proofs, of the same or of a different sort, which are also satisfactory. But I think it is by no means certain that Kant's proof is satisfactory. I think it is by no means certain that he did succeed in removing once for all the state of affairs which he considered to be a scandal to philosophy. And I think, therefore, that the question whether it is possible to give *any* satisfactory proof of the point in question still deserves discussion.

But what is the point in question? I think it must be owned that the expression 'things outside of us' is rather an odd expression, and an expression the meaning of which is certainly not perfectly clear. It would have sounded less odd if, instead of 'things outside of us' I had said 'external things', and perhaps also the meaning of this expression would have seemed to be clearer; and I think we make the meaning of 'external things' clearer still if we explain that this phrase has been regularly used by philosophers as short for 'things external to *our minds*'. The fact is that there has been a long philosophical tradition, in accordance with which the three expressions 'external things', 'things external to *us*', and 'things external to *our minds*' have been used as equivalent to one another, and have, each of them, been used as if they needed no explanation. The origin of this usage I do not know. It occurs already in Descartes; and since he uses the expressions as if they needed no explanation, they had presumably been used with the same meaning before. Of the three, it seems to me that the expression 'external to *our minds*' is the clearest, since it at least makes clear that what is meant is not 'external to *our bodies*'; whereas both the other expressions might be taken to mean this: and indeed there has been a good deal of confusion, even among philosophers, as to the relation of the two conceptions 'external things' and 'things external to *our bodies*'. But even the expression 'things external to our minds' seems to me to be far from perfectly clear; and if I am to make really clear what I mean by 'proof of the existence of things outside of us', I cannot do it by merely saying that by 'outside of us' I mean 'external to our minds'. . . .

But now, if to say of anything, e.g. my body, that it is external to *my* mind, means merely that from a proposition to the effect that it existed at a specified time, there in no case follows the further proposition that *I* was having an experience at the time in question, then to say of anything that it is external to *our* minds, will mean similarly that from a proposition to the effect that it existed at a specified time, it in no case follows that any of *us* were having experiences at the time in question. And if by *our* minds be meant, as is, I think, usually meant, the minds of human beings living on the earth, then it will follow that any pains which animals may feel, any after-images they may see, any experiences they may have, though not external to *their* minds, yet are external to *ours*. And this at once makes plain how different is the conception 'external to our minds' from the conception 'to be met with in space'; for, of course, pains which animals feel or after-images which they see are no more to be met with in space than are pains which *we* feel or after-images which *we* see. From the proposition that there are external objects—objects that are not in any of *our* minds, it does *not* follow that there are things to be met with in space; and hence 'external to our minds' is not a mere synonym for 'to be met with in space': that is to say, 'external to our minds' and 'to be met with in space' are two different conceptions. And the true relation between these conceptions seems to me to be this. We have already seen that there are ever so many kinds of 'things', such that, in the case of each of these kinds, from the proposition that there is at least one thing of that kind there *follows* the proposition that there is at least one thing to be met with in space: e.g. this follows from 'There is at least one star', from 'There is at least one human body', from 'There is at least one shadow', etc. And I think we can say that of every kind of thing of which this is true, it is also true that from the proposition that there is at least one 'thing' of that kind there *follows* the proposition that there is at least one thing external to our minds: e.g. from 'There is at least one star' there follows not only 'There is at least one thing to be met with in space' but also 'There is at least one external thing', and similarly in all other cases. My reason for saying this is as follows. Consider any kind of thing, such that anything of that kind, if there is anything of it, must be 'to be met with in space':

e.g. consider the kind 'soap-bubble'. If I say of anything which I am perceiving, 'That is a soap-bubble', I am, it seems to me, certainly implying that there would be no contradiction in asserting that it existed before I perceived it and that it will continue to exist, even if I cease to perceive it. This seems to me to be part of what is meant by saying that it is a real soap-bubble, as distinguished, for instance, from an hallucination of a soap-bubble. Of course, it by no means follows, that if it really is a soap-bubble, it did in fact exist before I perceived it or will continue to exist after I cease to perceive it: soap-bubbles are an example of a kind of 'physical object' and 'thing to be met with in space', in the case of which it is notorious that particular specimens of the kind often do exist only so long as they are perceived by a particular person. But a thing which I perceive would not be a soap-bubble unless its existence at any given time were *logically independent* of my perception of it at that time; unless that is to say, from the proposition, with regard to a particular time, that it existed at that time, it *never* follows that I perceived it at that time. But, if it is true that it would not be a soap-bubble, unless it *could* have existed at any given time without being perceived by me at that time, it is certainly also true that it would not be a soap-bubble, unless it *could* have existed at any given time, without its being true that I was having any experience of any kind at the time in question: it would not be a soap-bubble, unless, whatever time you take, from the proposition that it existed at that time it does *not* follow that I was having any experience at that time. That is to say, from the proposition with regard to anything which I am perceiving that it is a soap-bubble, there *follows* the proposition that it is external to *my* mind. But if, when I say that anything which I perceive is a soap-bubble, I am implying that it is external to *my* mind, I am, I think, certainly also implying that it is also external to all other minds: I am implying that it is not a thing of a sort such that things of that sort *can* only exist at a time when somebody is having an experience. I think, therefore, that from any proposition of the form 'There's a soap-bubble!' there does really *follow* the proposition 'There's an external object!' 'There's an object external to *all* our minds!' And, if this is true of the kind 'soap-bubble', it is certainly also true of any other kind

(including the kind 'unicorn') which is such that, if there are any things of that kind, it follows that there are *some* things to be met with in space.

I think, therefore, that in the case of all kinds of 'things', which are such that if there is a pair of things, both of which are of one of these kinds, or a pair of things one of which is of one of them and one of them of another, then it will follow at once that there are some things to be met with in space, it is true also that if I can prove that there are a pair of things, one of which is of one of these kinds and another of another, or a pair both of which are of one of them, then I shall have proved *ipso facto* that there are at least two 'things outside of us'. That is to say, if I can prove that there exist now both a sheet of paper and a human hand, I shall have proved that there are now 'things outside of us'; if I can prove that there exist now both a shoe and sock, I shall have proved that there are not 'things outside of us'; etc.; and similarly I shall have proved it, if I can prove that there exist now two sheets of paper, or two human hands, or two shoes, or two socks, etc. Obviously, then, there are thousands of different things such that, if, at any time, I can prove any one of them, I shall have proved the existence of things outside of us. Cannot I prove any of these things?

It seems to me that, so far from its being true, as Kant declares to be his opinion, that there is only one possible proof of the existence of things outside of us, namely the one which he has given, I can now give a large number of different proofs, each of which is a perfectly rigorous proof; and that at many other times I have been in a position to give many others. I can prove now, for instance, that two human hands exist. How? By holding up my two hands, and saying, as I make a certain gesture with the right hand, 'Here is one hand', and adding, as I make a certain gesture with the left, 'and here is another'. And if, by doing this, I have proved *ipso facto* the existence of external things, you will all see that I can also do it now in numbers of other ways: there is no need to multiply examples.

But did I prove just now that two human hands were then in existence? I do want to insist that I did; that the proof which I gave was a perfectly rigorous one; and that it is perhaps impossible to give a better or more rigorous proof of anything whatever. Of course, it would not have been a proof unless three conditions were satisfied; namely (1) unless the pre-miss which I adduced as proof of the conclusion was different from the conclusion I adduced it to prove; (2) unless the premiss which I adduced was some-thing which I *knew* to be the case, and not merely something which I believed but which was by no means certain, or something which, though in fact true, I did not know to be so; and (3) unless the con-clusion did really follow from the premiss. But all these three conditions were in fact satisfied by my proof. (1) The premiss which I adduced in proof was quite certainly different from the conclusion, for the conclusion was merely 'Two human hands exist at this moment'; but the premiss was something far more specific than this—something which I ex-pressed by showing you my hands, making certain gestures, and saying the words 'Here is one hand, and here is another'. It is quite obvious that the two were different, because it is quite obvious that the conclusion might have been true, even if the premiss had been false. In asserting the premiss I was as-serting much more than I was asserting in asserting the conclusion. (2) I certainly did at the moment *know* that which I expressed by the combination of certain gestures with saying the words 'There is one hand and here is another'. I *knew* that there was one hand in the place indicated by combining a certain gesture with my first utterance of 'here' and that there was another in the different place indicated by combining a certain gesture with my second utter-ance of 'here'. How absurd it would be to suggest that I did not know it, but only believed it, and that perhaps it was not the case! You might as well sug-gest that I do not know that I am now standing up and talking—that perhaps after all I'm not, and that it's not quite certain that I am! And finally (3) it is quite certain that the conclusion did follow from the premiss. This is as certain as it is that if there is one hand here and another here *now*, then it follows that there are two hands in existence *now*.

My proof, then, of the existence of things outside of us did satisfy three of the conditions necessary for a rigorous proof. Are there any other conditions nec-essary for a rigorous proof, such that perhaps it did not satisfy one of them? Perhaps there may be; I do not know; but I do want to emphasize that, so far as I can see, we all of us do constantly take proofs of

this sort as absolutely conclusive proofs of certain conclusions—as finally settling certain questions, as to which we were previously in doubt. Suppose, for instance, it were a question whether there were as many as three misprints on a certain page in a cer-tain book. A says there are, B is inclined to doubt it. How could A prove that he is right? Surely he *could* prove it by taking the book, turning to the page, and pointing to three separate places on it, saying 'There's one misprint here, another here, and another here': surely that is a method by which it *might* be proved! Of course, A would not have proved, by do-ing this that there were at least three misprints on the page in question, unless it was certain that there was a misprint in each of the places to which he pointed. But to say that he *might* prove it in this way, is to say that it *might* be certain that there was. And if such a thing as that could ever be certain, then as-suredly it was certain just now that there was one hand in one of the two places I indicated and another in the other.

I did, then, just now, give a proof that there were *then* external objects; and obviously, if I did, I could *then* have given many other proofs of the same sort that there were external objects *then*, and could now give many proofs of the same sort that there are ex-ternal objects *now*.

But, if what I am asked to do is to prove that ex-ternal objects have existed *in the past*, then I can give many different proofs of this also, but proofs which are in important respects of a different *sort* from those just given. And I want to emphasize that, when Kant says it is a scandal not to be able to give a proof of the existence of external objects, a proof of their existence in the past would certainly *help* to remove the scandal of which he is speaking. He says that, if it occurs to anyone to question their existence, we ought to be able to confront him with a satisfactory proof. But by a person who questions their existence, he certainly means not merely a person who ques-tions whether any exist at the moment of speaking, but a person who questions whether any have *ever* existed; and a proof that some have existed in the past would certainly therefore be relevant to *part* of what such a person is questioning. How then can I prove that there have been external objects in the past? Here is one proof. I can say: 'I held up two hands above this desk not very long ago; therefore two hands existed not very long ago; therefore at least two external objects have existed at some time in the past, Q.E.D.' This is a perfectly good proof, provided I *know* what is asserted in the premiss. But I *do* know that I held up two hands above this desk not very long ago. As a matter of fact, in this case you all know it too. There's no doubt whatever that I did. Therefore I have given a perfectly conclusive proof that external objects have existed in the past; and you will all see at once that, if this is a conclusive proof, I could have given many others of the same sort, and could now give many others. But it is also quite obvious that this sort of proof differs in important respects from the sort of proof I gave just now that there were two hands existing *then*.

I have, then, given two conclusive proofs of the existence of external objects. The first was a proof that two human hands existed at the time when I gave the proof; the second was a proof that two human hands had existed at a time previous to that at which I gave the proof. These proofs were of a different sort in important respects. And I pointed out that I could have given, then, many other conclusive proofs of both sorts. It is also obvious that I could give many others of both sorts now. So that, if these are the sort of proof that is wanted, nothing is easier than to prove the existence of external objects.

But now I am perfectly well aware that, in spite of all that I have said, many philosophers will still feel that I have not given any satisfactory proof of the point in question. And I want briefly, in conclusion, to say something as to why this dissatisfaction with my proofs should be felt.

One reason why, is, I think, this. Some people understand 'proof of an external world' as including a proof of things which I haven't attempted to prove and haven't proved. It is not quite easy to say *what* it is that they want proved—*what* it is that is such that unless they got a proof of it, they would not say that they had a proof of the existence of external things; but I can make an approach to explaining what they want by saying that if I had proved the propositions which I used as *premises* in my two proofs, then they would perhaps admit that I had proved the existence of external things, but, in the absence of such a proof (which, of course, I have

neither given nor attempted to give), they will say that I have not given what they mean by a proof of the existence of external things. In other words, they want a proof of what I assert *now* when I hold up my hands and say 'Here's one hand and here's another'; and, in the other case, they want a proof of what I assert *now* when I say 'I did hold up two hands above this desk just now'. Of course, what they really want is not merely a proof of these two propositions, but something like a general statement as to how *any* propositions of this sort may be proved. This, of course, I haven't given; and I do not believe it can be given: if this is what is meant by proof of the existence of external things, I do not believe that any proof of the existence of external things is possible. Of course, in some cases what might be called a proof of propositions which seem like these can be got. If one of you suspected that one of my hands was artificial he might be said to get a proof of my proposition 'Here's one hand, and here's another', by coming up and examining the suspected hand close up, perhaps touching and pressing it, and so establishing that it really was a human hand. But I do not believe that any proof is possible in nearly all cases. How am I to prove now that 'Here's one hand, and here's another? I do not believe I can do it. In order to do it, I should need to prove for one thing, as Descartes pointed out, that I am not now dreaming. But how can I prove that I am not? I have, no doubt, conclusive reasons for asserting that I am not now dreaming; I have conclusive evidence that I am awake: but that is a very different thing from being able to prove it. I could not tell you what all my evidence is; and I should require to do this at least, in order to give you a proof.

But another reason why some people would feel dissatisfied with my proofs is, I think, not merely that they want a proof of something which I haven't proved, but that they think that, if I cannot give such extra proofs, then the proofs that I have given are not conclusive proofs at all. And this, I think, is a definite mistake. They would say: 'If you cannot prove your premiss that here is one hand and here is another, then you do not know it. But you yourself have admitted that, if you did not know it, then your proof was not conclusive. Therefore your proof was not, as you say it was, a conclusive proof.' This view that, if I cannot prove such things as these, I do not know them, is, I think, the view that Kant was expressing in the sentence which I quoted at the beginning of this lecture, when he implies that so long as we have no proof of the existence of external things, their existence must be accepted merely on *faith*. He means to say, I think, that if I cannot prove that there is a hand here, I must accept it merely as a matter of faith—I cannot know it. Such a view, though it has been very common among philosophers, can, I think, be shown to be wrong—though shown only by the use of premises which are not known to be true, unless we do know of the existence of external things. I can know things, which I cannot prove; and among things which I certainly did know, even if (as I think) I could not prove them, were the premisses of my two proofs. I should say, therefore, that those, if any, who are dissatisfied with these proofs merely on the ground that I did not know their premisses, have no good reason for their dissatisfaction.

REVIEW QUESTIONS

1. What is Moore's argument for the proposition that we have knowledge of the external world?
2. What does Moore mean by the phrase "external to our minds"?
3. What is Moore's ultimate proof of the existence of things outside of him?
4. What are Moore's three conditions that any rigorous proof must satisfy?
5. What does Moore mean by his distinction between having conclusive evidence that he is awake and being able to prove it?

32

LUDWIG WITTGENSTEIN

Ludwig Wittgenstein (1889–1951) was born in Vienna into a wealthy, highly cultured family. His father was a Jew who had converted to Protestantism, his mother a Roman Catholic, in which religion Wittgenstein was brought up. Wittgenstein went to study engineering at the University of Manchester. Having read the work of Bertrand Russell, in 1912 he transferred to Cambridge University, where Russell was teaching, to study under him. Russell soon realized that his student was a genius and also an extremely eccentric and intense young man. Russell relates the following story about his pupil.

> At the end of his first term at Cambridge he came to me and said, "Will you please tell me whether I am a complete idiot or not?" I replied, "My dear fellow, I don't know. Why are you asking me?" He said, "Because, if I am a complete idiot, I shall become an aeronaut; but if not, I shall become a philosopher." I told him to write something during the vacation on some philosophical subject and I would then tell him whether he was a complete idiot or not. At the beginning of the following term he brought me the fulfillment of this suggestion. After reading only one sentence, I said to him, "No, you must not become an aeronaut."[1]

Wittgenstein returned to Austria to serve in the Austrian army during the First World War. He was captured by the Italians and spent time in a prisoner-of-war camp, where he finished writing his first work, *Tractatus Logico-Philosophicus* (1919). The work was to show the logical relationship between language and the world, to show what could and could not be said. He writes in the preface:

---

[1]Bertrand Russell, *Portraits from Memory* (George Allen & Unwin, 1956), 26–27.

The book deals with the problems of philosophy, and shows, I believe, that the reason why these problems are posed is that the logic of our language is misunderstood. The whole sense of the book might be summed up in the following words: what can be said at all can be said clearly, and what we cannot talk about we must pass over in silence.

A selection from this work is reprinted next.

After the war, he worked as a schoolmaster and gardener in a monastery before returning to Cambridge in 1929. There he submitted the *Tractatus* as his PhD dissertation. Russell and G. E. Moore were his examiners. He was appointed a lecturer at Cambridge and continued in that capacity until his death in 1951. His second book, *Philosophical Investigations*, was published posthumously in 1953.

Wittgenstein came to reject the reasoning of the *Tractatus*, believing his solution of giving logical structure to language solved the problem of how language related to the world. In this second work, Wittgenstein denies his earlier views that words have essences and that propositions have pictorial form which reflects the world. Instead he claimed that languages were various games that occurred within different cultures or forms of life. Philosophy cannot provide foundations for knowledge in general but only shows us that our practices are justified within forms of life. "Philosophy may in no way interfere with the actual use of language; it can in the end only describe it. For it cannot give it any foundation either. It leaves everything as it is."

FOR FURTHER READING

Ayer, A. J. *Wittgenstein* (University of Chicago, 1986).

Grayling, A. C. *Wittgenstein* (Oxford University Press, 1988).

Hacker, P. M. S. *Wittgenstein's Position in Twentieth Century Analytic Philosophy* (Oxford University Press, 1996).

Kenny, Anthony. *Wittgenstein* (Harvard University Press, 1974).

Malcolm, Norman. *Ludwig Wittgenstein: A Memoir* (Oxford University Press, 1958).

Monk, Ray. *Ludwig Wittgenstein: The Duty of Genius* (Free Press, 1990).

Rundle, Bede. *Wittgenstein on Language: Meaning, Use and Truth* (Blackwell, 1990).

Wittgenstein, Ludwig. *Tractatus Logico-Philosophicus*, trans. D. Pears and B. McGuiness (Routledge & Kegan Paul, 1961).

TRACTATUS LOGICO-PHILOSOPHICUS

PREFACE

Perhaps this book will be understood only by someone who has himself already had the thoughts that are expressed in it—or at least similar thoughts.—So it is not a textbook.—Its purpose would be achieved if it gave pleasure to one person who read and understood it.

The book deals with the problems of philosophy, and shows, I believe, that the reason why these problems are posed is that the logic of our language is misunderstood. The whole sense of the book might be summed up in the following words: what can be said at all can be said clearly, and what we cannot talk about we must pass over in silence.

Thus the aim of the book is to draw a limit to thought, or rather—not to thought, but to the expressing of thoughts: for in order to be able to draw a limit to thought, we should have to find both sides of the limit thinkable (i.e. we should have to be able to think what cannot be thought).

It will therefore only be in language that the limit can be drawn, and what lies on the other side of the limit will simply be nonsense.

I do not wish to judge how far my efforts coincide with those of other philosophers. Indeed, what I have written here makes no claim to novelty in detail, and the reason why I give no sources is that it is a matter of indifference to me whether the thoughts that I have had have been anticipated by someone else.

I will only mention that I am indebted to Frege's great works and to the writings of my friend Mr. Bertrand Russell for much of the stimulation of my thoughts.

If this work has any value, it consists in two things: the first is that thoughts are expressed in it, and on this score the better the thoughts are expressed—the more the nail has been hit on the head—the greater will be its value.—Here I am conscious of having fallen a long way short of what is possible. Simply because my powers are too slight for the accomplishment of the task.—May others come and do it better.

On the other hand the *truth* of the thoughts that are here communicated seems to me unassailable and definitive. I therefore believe myself to have found, on all essential points, the final solution of the problems. And if I am not mistaken in this belief, then the second thing in which the value of this work consists is that it shows how little is achieved when these problems are solved.

LANGUAGE AS PICTURE

1[1]   The world is all that is the case.

1.1   The world is the totality of facts, not of things.

---

[1]The decimal numbers assigned to the individual propositions indicate the logical importance of the propositions, the stress laid on them in my exposition. The propositions *n*.1, *n*.2, *n*.3, etc. are comments of proposition no. *n*; the propositions *n.m*1, *n.m*2, etc. are comments on proposition no. *n.m*; and so on. Text of Footnote.

1.11   The world is determined by the facts, and by their being *all* the facts.

1.12   Totality of facts determines what is the case, and also whatever is not the case.

1.13   The facts in logical space are the world.

1.2   The world divides into facts.

1.21   Each item can be the case or not the case while everything else remains the same.

2   What is the case—a fact—is existence of states of affairs.

2.01   A state of affairs (a state of things) is a combination of objects (things).

2.011   It is essential to things that they should be possible constituents of states of affairs.

2.012   In logic nothing is accidental: if a thing can occur in a state of affairs, the possibility of the state of affairs must be written into the thing itself.

2.0121   It would seem to be a sort of accident, if it turned out that a situation would fit a thing that could already exist entirely on its own.

If things can occur in states of affairs, this possibility must be in them from the beginning.

(Nothing in the province of logic can be merely possible. Logic deals with every possibility and all possibilities are its facts.)

Just as we are quite unable to imagine spatial objects outside space or temporal objects outside time, so too there is no object that we can imagine excluded from the possibility of combining with others.

If I can imagine objects combined in states of affairs, I cannot imagine them excluded from the *possibility* of such combinations.

2.0122   Things are dependent in so far as they can occur in all *possible* situations, but this form of independence is a form of connexion with states of affairs, a form of dependence. (It is impossible for words to appear in two different roles: by themselves, and in propositions.)

2.0123   If I know an object I also know its possible occurrences in states of affairs.

(Every one of these possibilities must be part of the nature of the object.)

A new possibility cannot be discovered later.

2.01231 If I am to know an object, though I need not know its external properties, I must know all its internal properties.

2.0124 If all objects are given, then at the same time all *possible* states of affairs are also given.

2.013 Each thing is, as it were, in a space of possible states of affairs. This space I can imagine empty, but I cannot imagine the thing without the space.

2.0131 A spatial object must be situated in infinite space. (A spatial point is an argument-place.)

A speck in the visual field, though it need not be red, must have some colour: it is, so to speak, surrounded by colour-space. Notes must have *some* pitch, objects of the sense of touch *some* degree of hardness, and so on.

2.014 Objects contain the possibility of all situations.

2.0141 The possibility of its occurring in states of affairs is the form of an object.

2.02 Objects are simple.

2.0201 Every statement about complexes can be resolved into a statement about their constituents and into the propositions that describe the complexes completely.

2.021 Objects make up the substance of the world. That is why they cannot be composite.

2.0211 If the world had no substance, then whether a proposition had sense would depend on whether another proposition was true.

2.0212 In that case we could not sketch any picture of the world (true or false).

2.022 It is obvious that an imagined world, however different it may be from the real one, must have *something*—a form—in common with it.

2.023 Objects are just what constitute this unalterable form.

2.0231 The substance of the world *can* only determine a form, and not any material properties. For it is only by means of propositions that material properties are represented—only by the configuration of objects that they are produced.

2.0232 In a manner of speaking, objects are colourless.

2.0233 If two objects have the same logical form, the only distinction between them, apart from their external properties, is that they are different.

2.02331 Either a thing has properties that nothing else has, in which case we can immediately use a description to distinguish it from the others and refer to it; or, on the other hand, there are several things that have the whole set of their properties in common, in which case it is quite impossible to indicate one of them.

For if there is nothing to distinguish a thing, I cannot distinguish it, since otherwise it would be distinguished after all.

2.024 Substance is what subsists independently of what is the case.

2.025 It is form and content.

2.0251 Space, time, and colour (being coloured) are forms of objects.

2.026 There must be objects, if the world is to have an unalterable form.

2.027 Objects, the unalterable, and the subsistent are one and the same.

2.0271 Objects are what is unalterable and subsistent; their configuration is what is changing and unstable.

2.0272 The configuration of objects produces states of affairs.

2.03 In a state of affairs objects fit into one another like the links of a chain.

2.031 In a state of affairs objects stand in a determinate relation to one another.

2.032 The determinate way in which objects are connected in a state of affairs is the structure of the state of affairs.

2.033 Form is the possibility of structure.

2.034 The structure of a fact consists of the structures of states of affairs.

2.04 The totality of existing states of affairs is the world.

2.05 The totality of existing states of affairs also determines which states of affairs do not exist.

2.06 The existence and non-existence of states of affairs is reality. (We also call the existence of states of affairs a positive fact, and their non-existence a negative fact.)

2.061 States of affairs are independent of one another.

2.062 From the existence or non-existence of one state of affairs it is impossible to infer the existence or non-existence of another.

2.063 The sum-total of reality is the world.

2.1 We picture facts to ourselves.

2.11 A picture presents a situation in logical space, the existence and non-existence of states of affairs.

2.12 A picture is a model of reality.

2.13 In a picture objects have the elements of the picture corresponding to them.

2.131 In a picture the elements of the picture are the representatives of objects.

2.14 What constitutes a picture is that its elements are related to one another in a determinate way.

2.141 A picture is a fact.

2.15 The fact that the elements of a picture are related to one another in a determinate way represents that things are related to one another in the same way.

Let us call this connexion of its elements the structure of the picture, and let us call the possibility of this structure the pictorial form of the picture.

2.151 Pictorial form is the possibility that things are related to one another in the same way as the elements of a picture.

2.1511 *That* is how a picture is attached to reality; it reaches right out to it.

2.1512 It is laid against reality like a measure.

2.15121 Only the end-points of the graduating lines actually *touch* the object that is to be measured.

2.1513 So a picture, conceived in this way, also includes the pictorial relationship, which makes it into a picture.

2.1514 The pictorial relationship consists of the correlations of the picture's elements with things.

2.1515 These correlations are, as it were, the feelers of the picture's elements, with which the picture touches reality.

2.16 If a fact is to be a picture, it must have something in common with what it depicts.

2.161 There must be something identical in a picture and what it depicts, to enable the one to be a picture of the other at all.

2.17 What a picture must have in common with reality, in order to be able to depict it—correctly or incorrectly—in the way it does, is its pictorial form.

2.171 A picture can depict any reality whose form it has.

A spatial picture can depict anything spatial, a coloured one anything coloured, etc.

2.172 A picture cannot, however, depict its pictorial form: it displays it.

2.173 A picture represents its subject from a position outside it. (Its standpoint is its representational form.) That is why a picture represents its subject correctly or incorrectly.

2.174 A picture cannot, however, place itself outside its representational form.

2.18 What any picture, of whatever form, must have in common with reality, in order to be able to depict it—correctly or incorrectly—in any way at all, is logical form, i.e. the form of reality.

2.181 A picture whose pictorial form is logical form is called logical picture.

2.182 Every picture is *at the same time* a logical one. (On the other hand, not every picture is, for example, a spatial one.)

2.19 Logical pictures can depict the world.

2.2 A picture has logico-pictorial form in common with what it depicts.

2.201 A picture depicts reality by representing a possibility of existence and non-existence of states of affairs.

2.202 A picture represents a possible situation in logical space.

2.203 A picture contains the possibility of the situation that it represents.

2.21 A picture agrees with reality or fails to agree; it is correct or incorrect, true or false.

2.22 What a picture represents it represents independently of its truth or falsity, by means of its pictorial form.

2.221 What a picture represents is its sense.

2.222 The agreement or disagreement of its sense with reality constitutes its truth or falsity.

2.223 In order to tell whether a picture is true or false we must compare it with reality.

2.224 It is impossible to tell from the picture alone whether it is true or false.

2.225 There are no pictures that are true a priori.

3 A logical picture of facts is a thought.

3.001 'A state of affairs is thinkable': what this means is that we can picture it to ourselves.

3.01 The totality of true thoughts is a picture of the world.

3.02 A thought contains the possibility of the situation of which it is the thought. What is thinkable is possible too.

3.03 Thought can never be of anything illogical, since, if it were, we should have to think illogically.

3.031 It used to be said that God could create anything except what would be contrary to the laws of logic.—The truth is that we could not *say* what an 'illogical' world would look like.

3.032 It is as impossible to represent in language anything that 'contradicts logic' as it is in geometry to represent by its co-ordinates a figure that contradicts the laws of space, or to give the co-ordinates of a point that does not exist.

3.0321 Though a state of affairs that would contravene the laws of physics can be represented by us spatially, one that would contravene the laws of geometry cannot.

3.04 If a thought were correct a priori, it would be a thought whose possibility ensured its truth.

3.05 A priori knowledge that a thought was true would be possible only if its truth were recognizable from the thought itself (without anything to compare it with).

3.1 In a proposition a thought finds an expression that can be perceived by the senses.

3.11 We use the perceptible sign of a proposition (spoken or written, etc.) as a projection of a possible situation.

The method of projection is to think of the sense of the proposition.

3.12 I call the sign with which we express a thought a propositional sign.—And a proposition is a propositional sign in its projective relation to the world.

3.13 A proposition includes all that the projection includes, but not what is projected.

Therefore, though what is projected is not itself included, its possibility is.

A proposition, therefore, does not actually contain its sense, but does contain the possibility of expressing it.

('The content of a proposition' means the content of a proposition that has sense.)

A proposition contains the form, but not the content, of its sense.

3.14 What constitutes a propositional sign is that in it its elements (the words) stand in a determinate relation to one another.

A propositional sign is a fact.

3.141 A proposition is not a blend of words.— (Just as a theme in music is not a blend of notes.)

A propositional is articulate.

3.142 Only facts can express a sense, a set of names cannot.

3.143 Although a propositional sign is a fact, this is obscured by the usual form of expression in writing or print.

For in a printed proposition, for example, no essential difference is apparent between a propositional sign and a word.

(That is what made it possible for Frege to call a proposition a composite name.)

3.1431 The essence of a propositional sign is very clearly seen if we imagine one composed of spatial objects (such as tables, chairs, and books) instead of written signs.

3.1432 Instead of, 'The complex sign "aRb" says that a stands to b in the relation R', we ought to put, 'That "a" stands to "b" in a certain relation says *that aRb*.'

3.144 Situations can be described but not *given names*.

(Names are like points; propositions like arrows—they have sense.)

3.2 In a proposition a thought can be expressed in such a way that elements of the propositional sign correspond to the objects of the thought.

3.201 I call such elements 'simple signs', and such a proposition 'completely analysed'.

3.202 The simple signs employed in propositions are called names.

3.203 A name means an object. The object is its meaning. ('*A*' is the same sign as '*A*'.)

3.21 The configuration of objects in a situation corresponds to the configuration of simple signs in the propositional sign.

3.22 In a proposition a name is the representative of an object.

3.221 Objects can only be *named*. Signs are their representatives. I can only speak *about* them: I cannot *put them into words*. Propositions can only say *how* things are, not *what* they are.

3.23 The requirement that simple signs be possible is the requirement that sense be determinate.

3.24 A proposition about a complex stands in an internal relation to a proposition about a constituent of the complex.

A complex can be given only by its description, which will be right or wrong. A proposition that mentions a complex will not be nonsensical, if the complex does not exist, but simply false.

When a propositional element signifies a complex, this can be seen from an indeterminateness in the propositions in which it occurs. In such cases we *know* that the proposition leaves something undetermined. (In fact the generality-sign *contains* a prototype.)

The contraction of a symbol for a complex into a simple symbol can be expressed in a definition.

3.25 A proposition has one and only one complete analysis.

3.251 What a proposition expresses it expresses in a determinate manner, which can be set out clearly: a proposition is articulated.

3.26 A name cannot be dissected any further by means of a definition: it is a primitive sign.

3.261 Every sign that has a definition signifies *via* the signs that serve to define it; and the definitions point the way.

Two signs cannot signify in the same manner if one is primitive and the other is defined by means of primitive signs. Names *cannot* be anatomized by means of definitions. (This cannot be done to any sign that has a meaning independently and on its own.)

3.262 What signs fail to express, their application shows. What signs slur over, their application says clearly.

3.263 The meanings of primitive signs can be explained by means of elucidations. Elucidations are propositions that contain the primitive signs. So they can only be understood if the meanings of those signs are already known.

3.3 Only propositions have sense; only in the nexus of a proposition does a name have meaning.

3.31 I call any part of a proposition that characterizes its sense an expression (or a symbol).

(A proposition is itself an expression.)

Everything essential to their sense that propositions can have in common with one another is an expression.

An expression is the mark of a form and a content.

3.311 An expression presupposes the forms of all the propositions in which it can occur. It is the common characteristic mark of a class of propositions.

3.312 It is therefore presented by means of the general form of the propositions that it characterizes.

In fact, in this form the expression will be *constant* and everything else *variable*.

3.313 Thus an expression is presented by means of a variable whose values are the propositions that contain the expression.

(In the limiting case the variable becomes a constant, the expression becomes a proposition.)

I call such a variable a 'propositional variable'.

3.314 An expression has meaning only in a proposition. All variables can be construed as propositional variables.

(Even variable names.)

3.315 If we turn a constituent of a proposition into a variable, there is a class of propositions all of which are values of the resulting variable proposition. In general, this class too will be dependent on the meaning that our arbitrary conventions have given to parts of the original proposition. But if all the signs in it that have arbitrarily determined meanings are turned into variables, we shall still get a class of this kind. This one, however, is not dependent on any convention, but solely on the nature of the proposition. It corresponds to a logical form—a logical prototype.

3.316 What values a propositional variable may take is something that is stipulated.

The stipulation of values *is* the variable.

3.317 To stipulate values for a propositional variable is *to give the propositions* whose common characteristic the variable is.

The stipulation is a description of those propositions.

The stipulation will therefore be concerned only with symbols, not with their meaning.

And the *only* thing essential to the stipulation is *that it is merely a description of symbols and states nothing about what is signified.*

How the description of the propositions is produced is not essential.

3.318 Like Frege and Russell I construe a proposition as a function of the expressions contained in it.

6.362 What can be described can also happen: and what the law of causality is meant to exclude cannot even be described.

6.363 The procedure of induction consists in accepting as true the *simplest* law that can be reconciled with our experiences.

6.3631 This procedure, however, has no logical justification but only a psychological one.

It is clear that there are no grounds for believing that the simplest eventuality will in fact be realized.

6.36311 It is an hypothesis that the sun will rise tomorrow: and this means that we do not *know* whether it will rise.

6.37 There is no compulsion making one thing happen because another has happened. The only necessity that exists is *logical* necessity.

6.371 The whole modern conception of the world is founded on the illusion that the so-called laws of nature are the explanations of natural phenomena.

6.372 Thus people today stop at the laws of nature, treating them as something inviolable, just as God and Fate were treated in past ages.

And in fact both are right and both wrong: though the view of the ancients is clearer in so far as they have a clear and acknowledged terminus, while the modern system tries to make it look as if *everything* were explained.

6.373 The world is independent of my will.

6.374 Even if all that we wish for were to happen, still this would only be a favour granted by fate, so to speak: for there is no *logical* connexion between the will and the world, which would guarantee it, and the supposed physical connexion itself is surely not something that we could will.

6.375 Just as the only necessity that exists is *logical* necessity, so too the only impossibility that exists is *logical* impossibility.

6.3751 For example, the simultaneous presence of two colours at the same place in the visual field is impossible, in fact logically impossible, since it is ruled out by the logical structure of colour.

Let us think how this contradiction appears in physics: more or less as follows—a particle cannot have two velocities at the same time; that is to say, it cannot be in two places at the same time; that is to say, particles that are in different places at the same time cannot be identical.

(It is clear that the logical product of two elementary propositions can neither be a tautology nor a contradiction. The statement that a point in the visual field has two different colours at the same time is a contradiction.)

6.4 All propositions are of equal value.

6.41 The sense of the world must lie outside the world. In the world everything is as it is, and everything happens as it does happen: *in* it no value exists—and if it did exist, it would have no value.

If there is any value that does have values, it must lie outside the whole sphere of what happens and is the case. For all that happens and is the case is accidental.

What makes it non-accidental cannot lie *within* the world, since if it did it would itself be accidental.

It must lie outside the world.

6.42 So too it is impossible for there to be propositions of ethics.

Propositions can express nothing that is higher.

6.421 It is clear that ethics cannot be put into words.

Ethics is transcendental.

(Ethics and aesthetics are one and the same.)

6.422 When an ethical law of the form, 'Thou shalt . . .', is laid down, one's first thought is, 'And what if I do not do it?' It is clear, however, that ethics has nothing to do with punishment and reward in the usual sense of the terms. So our question about the *consequences* of an action must be unimportant.—At least those consequences should not be events. For there must be something right about the question we posed. There must indeed be some kind of ethical reward and ethical punishment, but they must reside in the action itself.

(And it is also clear that the reward must be something pleasant and the punishment something unpleasant.)

6.423 It is impossible to speak about the will in so far as it is the subject of ethical attributes.

And the will as a phenomenon is of interest only to psychology.

6.43 If the good or bad exercise of the will does alter the world, it can alter only the limits of the world, not the facts—not what can be expressed by means of language.

In short the effect must be that it becomes an altogether different world. It must, so to speak, wax and wane as a whole.

The world of the happy man is a different one from that of the unhappy man.

6.431 So too at death the world does not alter, but comes to an end.

6.4311 Death is not an event in life: we do not live to experience death.

If we take eternity to mean not infinite temporal duration but timelessness, then eternal life belongs to those who live in the present.

Our life has no end in just the way in which our visual field has no limits.

6.4312 Not only is there no guarantee of the temporal immortality of the human soul, that is to say of its eternal survival after death; but, in any case, this assumption completely fails to accomplish the purpose for which it has always been intended. Or is some riddle solved by my surviving for ever? Is not this eternal life itself as much of a riddle as our present life? The solution of the riddle of life in space and time lies *outside* space and time.

(It is certainly not the solution of any problems of natural science that is required.)

6.432 *How* things are in the world is a matter of complete indifference for what is higher. God does not reveal himself *in* the world.

6.4321 The facts all contribute only to settling the problem, not to its solution.

6.44 It is not *how* things are in the world that is mystical, but *that* it exists.

6.45 To view the world sub specie aeterni is to view it as a whole—a limited whole.

Feeling the world as a limited whole—it is this that is mystical.

6.5 When the answer cannot be put into words, neither can the question be put into words.

The riddle does not exist.

If a question can be framed at all, it is also *possible* to answer it.

6.51 Scepticism is *not* irrefutable, but obviously nonsensical when it tries to raise doubts where no questions can be asked.

For doubt can exist only where a question exists, a question only where an answer exists, and an answer only where something *can be said.*

6.52 We feel that even when all *possible* scientific questions have been answered, the problems of life remain completely untouched. Of course there are then no questions left, and this itself is the answer.

6.521 The solution of the problem of life is seen in the vanishing of the problem.

(Is not this the reason why those who have found after a long period of doubt that the sense of life became clear to them have then been unable to say what constituted sense?)

6.522 There are, indeed, things that cannot be put into words. They *make themselves manifest.* They are what is mystical.

6.53 The correct method in philosophy would really be the following: to say nothing except what can be said, i.e. propositions of natural science—i.e. something that has nothing to do with philosophy—and then, whenever someone else wanted to say something metaphysical, to demonstrate to him that he had failed to give a meaning to certain signs in his propositions. Although it would not be satisfying to the other person—he would not have the feeling that we were teaching him philosophy—*this* method would be the only strictly correct one.

6.54 My propositions serve as elucidations in the following way: anyone who understands me eventually recognizes them as nonsensical, when he has used them—as steps—to climb up beyond them. (He must, so to speak, throw away the ladder after he has climbed up it.)

He must transcend these propositions, and then he will see the world aright.

7 What we cannot speak about we must pass over in silence.

PHILOSOPHICAL INVESTIGATIONS

1. "When they (my elders) named some object, and accordingly moved towards something, I saw this and I grasped that the thing was called by the sound they uttered when they meant to point it out. Their intention was shewn by their bodily movements, as it were the natural language of all peoples: the expression of the face, the play of the eyes, the movement of other parts of the body, and the tone of voice which expresses our state of mind in seeking, having, rejecting, or avoiding something. Thus, as I heard words repeatedly used in their proper places in various sentences, I gradually learnt to understand what objects they signified; and after I had trained my mouth to form these signs, I used them to express my own desires." [Augustine, *Confessions*, I.8]

These words, it seems to me, give us a particular picture of the essense of human language. It is this: the individual words in language name objects—sentences are combinations of such names.—In this picture of language we find the roots of the following idea: Every word has a meaning. This meaning is correlated with the word. It is the object for which the word stands.

Philosophical Investigations by Ludwig Wittgenstein, translated by Anscombe. Reprinted by permission of Blackwell Publishers and Prentice-Hall, Inc., Upper Saddle River, NJ. (© 1953).

Augustine does not speak of there being any difference between kinds of word. If you describe the learning of language in this way you are, I believe, thinking primarily of nouns like "table", "chair", "bread", and of people's names, and only secondarily of the names of certain actions and properties; and of the remaining kinds of word as something that will take care of itself.

Now think of the following use of language: I send someone shopping. I give him a slip marked "five red apples". He takes the slip to the shopkeeper, who opens the drawer marked "apples"; then he looks up the word "red" in a table and finds a colour sample opposite it; then he says the series of cardinal numbers—I assume that he knows them by heart—up to the word "five" and for each number he takes an apple of the same colour as the sample out of the drawer.——It is in this and similar ways that one operates with words.——"But how does he know where and how he is to look up the word 'red' and what he is to do with the word 'five'?"——Well, I assume that he *acts* as I have described. Explanations come to an end somewhere.—But what is the meaning of the word "five"?—No such thing was in question here, only how the word "five" is used.

2. That philosophical concept of meaning has its place in a primitive idea of the way language functions. But one can also say that it is the idea of a language more primitive than ours.

Let us imagine a language for which the description given by Augustine is right. The language is meant to serve for communication between a builder A and an assistant B. A is building with building-stones: there are blocks, pillars, slabs and beams. B has to pass the stones, and that in the order in which A needs them. For this purpose they use a language consisting of the words "block", "pillar", "slab", "beam". A calls them out;—B brings the stone which he has learnt to bring at such-and-such a call.——Conceive this as a complete primitive language.

3. Augustine, we might say, does describe a system of communication; only not everything that we call language is this system. And one has to say this in many cases where the question arises "Is this an appropriate description or not?" The answer is: "Yes, it is appropriate, but only for this narrowly circumscribed region, not for the whole of what you were claiming to describe."

It is as if someone were to say: "A game consists in moving objects about on a surface according to certain rules . . ."—and we replied: You seem to be thinking of board games, but there are others. You can make your definition correct by expressly restricting it to those games.

4. Imagine a script in which the letters were used to stand for sounds, and also as signs of emphasis and punctuation. (A script can be conceived as a language for describing sound-patterns.) Now imagine someone interpreting that script as if there were simply a correspondence of letters to sounds and as if the letters had not also completely different functions. Augustine's conception of language is like such an over-simple conception of the script.

5. If we look at the example in §1, we may perhaps get an inkling how much this general notion of the meaning of a word surrounds the working of language with a haze which makes clear vision impossible. It disperses the fog to study the phenomena of language in primitive kinds of application in which one can command a clear view of the aim and functioning of the words.

A child uses such primitive forms of language when it learns to talk. Here the teaching of language is not explanation, but training.

6. We could imagine that the language of §2 was the *whole* language of A and B; even the whole language of a tribe. The children are brought up to perform *these* actions, to use *these* words as they do so, and to react in *this* way to the words of others.

An important part of the training will consist in the teacher's pointing to the objects, directing the child's attention to them, and at the same time uttering a word; for instance, the word "slab" as he points to that shape. (I do not want to call this "ostensive definition", because the child cannot as yet *ask* what the name is. I will call it "ostensive teaching of words".——I say that it will form an important part of the training, because it is so with human beings; not because it could not be imagined otherwise.) This ostensive teaching of words can be said to establish an association between the word and the thing. But what does this mean? Well, it may mean various things; but one very likely thinks first of all that a picture of the object comes before the child's mind when it hears the word. But now, if this does happen—is it the purpose of the word?—Yes, it *may* be the purpose.—I can imagine such a use of words (of series of sounds). (Uttering a word is like striking a note on the keyboard of the imagination.) But in the language of §2 it is *not* the purpose of the words to evoke images. (It may, of course, be discovered that that helps to attain the actual purpose.)

But if the ostensive teaching has this effect,—am I to say that it effects an understanding of the word? Don't you understand the call "Slab!" if you act upon it in such-and-such a way?—Doubtless the ostensive teaching helped to bring this about; but only together with a particular training. With different training the same ostensive teaching of these words would have effected a quite different understanding.

"I set the brake up by connecting up rod and lever."—Yes, given the whole of the rest of the mechanism. Only in conjunction with that is it a brake-lever, and separated from its support it is not even a lever; it may be anything, or nothing.

7. In the practice of the use of language (2) one party calls out the words, the other acts on them. In instruction in the language the following process will occur: the learner *names* the objects; that is, he utters the word when the teacher points to the stone.—And there will be this still simpler exercise: the pupil repeats the words after the teacher—both of these being processes resembling language.

We can also think of the whole process of using words in (2) as one of those games by means of which children learn their native language. I will call these games "language-games" and will sometimes speak of a primitive language as a language-game.

And the processes of naming the stones and of repeating words after someone might also be called language-games. Think of much of the use of words in games like ring-a-ring-a-roses.

I shall also call the whole, consisting of language and the actions into which it is woven, the "language-game".

8. Let us now look at an expansion of language (2). Besides the four words "block", "pillar", etc., let it contain a series of words used as the shopkeeper in (1) used the numerals (it can be the series of letters of the alphabet); further, let there be two words,

which may as well be "there" and "this" (because this roughly indicates their purpose), that are used in connexion with a pointing gesture; and finally a number of colour samples. A gives an order like: "d—slab—there". At the same time he shews the assistant a colour sample, and when he says "there" he points to a place on the building site. From the stock of slabs B takes one for each letter of the alphabet up to "d", of the same colour as the sample, and brings them to the place indicated by A.—On other occasions A gives the order "this—there". At "this" he points to a building stone. And so on.

9. When a child learns this language, it has to learn the series of 'numerals' a, b, c, . . . by heart. And it has to learn their use.—Will this training include ostensive teaching of the words?—Well, people will, for example, point to slabs and count: "a, b, c slabs".—Something more like the ostensive teaching of the words "block", "pillar", etc. would be the ostensive teaching of numerals that serve not to count but to refer to groups of objects that can be taken in at a glance. Children do learn the use of the first five or six cardinal numerals in this way.

Are "there" and "this" also taught ostensively?—Imagine how one might perhaps teach their use. One will point to places and things—but in this case the pointing occurs in the *use* of the words too and not merely in learning the use.—

10. Now what do the words of this language *signify*?—What is supposed to shew what they signify, if not the kind of use they have? And we have already described that. So we are asking for the expression "This word signifies *this*" to be made a part of the description. In other words the description ought to take the form: "The word . . . . signifies . . . .".

Of course, one can reduce the description of the use of the word "slab" to the statement that this word signifies this object. This will be done when, for example, it is merely a matter of removing the mistaken idea that the word "slab" refers to the shape of building-stone that we in fact call a "block"—but the kind of '*referring*' this is, that is to say the use of these words for the rest, is already known.

Equally one can say that the signs "a", "b", etc. signify numbers; when for example this removes the mistaken idea that "a", "b", "c", play the part actually played in language by "block", "slab", "pillar".

And one can also say that "c" means this number and not that one; when for example this serves to explain that the letters are to be used in the order a, b, c, d, etc. and not in the order a, b, d, c.

But assimilating the descriptions of the uses of words in this way cannot make the uses themselves any more like one another. For, as we see, they are absolutely unlike.

11. Think of the tools in a tool-box: there is a hammer, pliers, a saw, a screw-driver, a rule, a glue-pot, glue, nails and screws.—The functions of words are as diverse as the functions of these objects. (And in both cases there are similarities.)

Of course, what confuses us is the uniform appearance of words when we hear them spoken or meet them in script and print. For their *application* is not presented to us so clearly. Especially when we are doing philosophy!

12. It is like looking into the cabin of a locomotive. We see handles all looking more or less alike. (Naturally, since they are all supposed to be handled.) But one is the handle of a crank which can be moved continuously (it regulates the opening of a valve); another is the handle of a switch, which has only two effective positions, it is either off or on; a third is the handle of a brake-lever, the harder one pulls on it, the harder it brakes; a fourth, the handle of a pump: it has an effect only so long as it is moved to and fro.

13. When we say: "Every word in language signifies something" we have so far said *nothing whatever*; unless we have explained exactly *what* distinction we wish to make. (It might be, of course, that we wanted to distinguish the words of language (8) from words 'without meaning' such as occur in Lewis Carroll's poems, or words like "Lilliburlero" in songs.)

14. Imagine someone's saying: "*All* tools serve to modify something. Thus the hammer modifies the position of the nail, the saw the shape of the board, and so on."—And what is modified by the rule, the glue-pot, the nails?—"Our knowledge of a thing's length, the temperature of the glue, and the solidity of the box."——Would anything be gained by this assimilation of expressions?—

15. The word "to signify" is perhaps used in the most straightforward way when the object signified is marked with the sign. Suppose that the tools A uses in building bear certain marks. When A shews his assistant such a mark, he brings the tool that has that mark on it.

It is in this and more or less similar ways that a name means and is given to a thing.—It will often prove useful in philosophy to say to ourselves: naming something is like attaching a label to a thing.

16. What about the colour samples that A shews to B: are they part of the *language*? Well, it is as you please. They do not belong among the words; yet when I say to someone: "Pronounce the word 'the'", you will count the second "the" as part of the sentence. Yet it has a role just like that of a colour-sample in a language-game (8); that is, it is a sample of what the other is meant to say.

It is most natural, and causes least confusion, to reckon the samples among the instruments of the language.

((Remark on the reflexive pronoun "*this* sentence".))

17. It will be possible to say: In language (8) we have different *kinds of word*. For the functions of the word "slab" and the word "block" are more alike than those of "slab" and "d". But how we group words into kinds will depend on the aim of the classification,—and on our own inclination.

Think of the different points of view from which one can classify tools or chess-men.

18. Do not be troubled by the fact that languages (2) and (8) consist only of orders. If you want to say that this shews them to be incomplete, ask yourself whether our language is complete;—whether it was so before the symbolism of chemistry and the notation of the infinitesimal calculus were incorporated in it; for these are, so to speak, suburbs of our language. (And how many houses or streets does it take before a town begins to be a town?) Our language can be seen as an ancient city: a maze of little streets and squares, of old and new houses, and of houses with additions from various periods; and this surrounded by a multitude of new boroughs with straight regular streets and uniform houses.

19. It is easy to imagine a language consisting only of orders and reports in battle.—Or a language consisting only of questions and expressions for answering yes and no. And innumerable others.——

And to imagine a language means to imagine a form of life.

But what about this: is the call "Slab!" in example (2) a sentence or a word?—If a word, surely it has not the same meaning as the like-sounding word of our ordinary language, for in §2 it is a call. But if a sentence, it is surely not the elliptical sentence: "Slab!" of our language.——As far as the first question goes you can call "Slab!" a word and also a sentence; perhaps it could be appropriately called a 'degenerate sentence' (as one speaks of a degenerate hyperbola); in fact it *is* our 'elliptical' sentence.—But that is surely only a shortened form of the sentence "Bring me a slab", and there is no such sentence in example (2).—But why should I not on the contrary have called the sentence "Bring me a slab" a *lengthening* of the sentence "Slab!"?—Because if you shout "Slab!" you really mean: "Bring me a slab".—But how do you do this: how do you *mean that* while you *say* "Slab!"? Do you say the unshortened sentence to yourself? And why should I translate the call "Slab!" into a different expression in order to say what someone means by it? And if they mean the same thing—why should I not say: "When he says 'Slab!' he means 'Slab!' "? Again, if you can mean "Bring me the slab", why should you not be able to mean "Slab!"?——But when I call "Slab!", then what I want is, *that he should bring me a slab*!——Certainly, but does 'wanting this' consist in thinking in some form or other a different sentence from the one you utter?—

20. But now it looks as if when someone says "Bring me a slab" he could mean this expression as *one* long word corresponding to the single word "Slab!"——Then can one mean it sometimes as one word and sometimes as four? And how does one usually mean it?——I think we shall be inclined to say: we mean the sentence as *four* words when we use it in contrast with other sentences such as "*Hand* me a slab", "Bring *him* a slab", "Bring *two* slabs", etc.; that is, in contrast with sentences containing the separate words of our command in other combinations.——But what does using one sentence in contrast with others consist in? Do the others, perhaps, hover before one's mind? *All* of them? And *while* one is saying the one sentence, or before, or afterwards?—No. Even if such an explanation rather

tempts us, we need only think for a moment of what actually happens in order to see that we are going astray here. We say that we use the command in contrast with other sentences because *our language* contains the possibility of those other sentences. Someone who did not understand our language, a foreigner, who had fairly often heard someone giving the order: "Bring me a slab!", might believe that this whole series of sounds was one word corresponding perhaps to the word for "building-stone" in his language. If he himself had then given this order perhaps he would have pronounced it differently, and we should say: he pronounces it so oddly because he takes it for a *single* word.——But then, is there not also something different going on in him when he pronounces it,—something corresponding to the fact that he conceives the sentence as a *single* word?——Either the same thing may go on in him, or something different. For what goes on in you when you give such an order? Are you conscious of its consisting of four words *while* you are uttering it? Of course you have a *mastery* of this language—which contains those other sentences as well—but is this having a mastery something that *happens* while you are uttering the sentence?—And I have admitted that the foreigner will probably pronounce a sentence differently if he conceives it differently; but what we call his wrong conception *need* not lie in anything that accompanies the utterance of the command.

The sentence is 'elliptical', not because it leaves out something that we think when we utter it, but because it is shortened—in comparison with a particular paradigm of our grammar.—Of course one might object here: "You grant that the shortened and the unshortened sentence have the same sense.—What is this sense, then? Isn't there a verbal expression for this sense?"——But doesn't the fact that sentences have the same sense consist in their having the same *use*?—(In Russian one says "stone red" instead of "the stone is red"; do they feel the copula to be missing in the sense, or attach it in *thought*?)

21. Imagine a language-game in which A asks and B reports the number of slabs or blocks in a pile, or the colours and shapes of the building-stones that are stacked in such-and-such a place.—Such a report might run: "Five slabs". Now what is the difference

between the report or statement "Five slabs" and the order "Five slabs!"?—Well, it is the part which uttering these words plays in language-game. No doubt the tone of voice and the look with which they are uttered, and much else besides, will also be different. But we could also imagine the tone's being the same—for an order and a report can be spoken in a *variety* of tones of voice and with various expressions of face—the difference being only in the application. (Of course, we might use the words "statement" and "command" to stand for grammatical forms of sentence and intonations; we do in fact call "Isn't the weather glorious to-day?" a question, although it is used as a statement.) We could imagine a language in which *all* statements had the form and tone of rhetorical questions; or every command the form of the question "Would you like to . . .?". Perhaps it will then be said: "What he says has the form of a question but is really a command",—that is, has the function of a command in the technique of using the language. (Similarly one says "You will do this" not as a prophecy but as a command. What makes it the one or the other?)

22. Frege's idea that every assertion contains an assumption, which is the thing that is asserted, really rests on the possibility found in our language of writing every statement in the form: "It is asserted that such-and-such is the case."—But "that such-and-such is the case" is *not* a sentence in our language—so far it is not a *move* in the language-game. And if I write, not "It is asserted that . . . .", but "It is asserted: such-and-such is the case", the words "It is asserted" simply become superfluous.

We might very well also write every statement in the form of a question followed by a "Yes"; for instances: "Is it raining? Yes!: Would this shew that every statement contained a question?

Of course we have the right to use an assertion sign in contrast with a question-mark, for example, or if we want to distinguish an assertion from a fiction or a supposition. It is only a mistake if one thinks that the assertion consists of two actions, entertaining and asserting (assigning the truth-value, or something of the kind), and that in performing these actions we follow the propositional sign roughly as we sing from the musical score. Reading the written sentence loud or soft is indeed comparable with

singing from a musical score, but '*meaning*' (thinking) the sentence that is read is not.

Frege's assertion sign marks the *beginning of the sentence*. Thus its function is like that of the full-stop. It distinguishes the whole period from a clause *within* the period. If I hear someone say "it's raining" but do not know whether I have heard the beginning and end of the period, so far this sentence does not serve to tell me anything.

23. But how many kinds of sentence are there? Say assertion, question, and command?—There are *countless* kinds: countless different kinds of use of what we call "symbols", "words", "sentences". And this multiplicity is not something fixed, given once for all; but new types of language, new language-games, as we may say, come into existence, and others become obsolete and get forgotten. (We can get a *rough picture* of this from the changes in mathematics.)

Here the term "language-*game*" is meant to bring into prominence the fact that the *speaking* of language is part of an activity, or of a form of life.

Review the multiplicity of language-games in the following examples, and in others:

Giving orders, and obeying them—

Describing the appearance of an object, or giving its measurements—

Constructing an object from a description (a drawing)—

Reporting an event—

Speculating about an event—

Forming and testing a hypothesis—

Presenting the results of an experiment in tables and diagrams—

Making up a story; and reading it—

Play-acting—

Singing catches—

Guessing riddles—

Making a joke; telling it—

Solving a problem in practical arithmetic—

Translating from one language into another—

Asking, thanking, cursing, greeting, praying.

—It is interesting to compare the multiplicity of the tools in language and of the ways they are used, the multiplicity of kinds of word and sentence, with what logicians have said about the structure of language. (Including the author of the *Tractatus Logico-Philosophicus*.)

24. If you do not keep the multiplicity of language-games in view you will perhaps be inclined to ask questions like: "What is a question?"—Is it the statement that I do not know such-and-such, or the statement that I wish the other person would tell me . . . .? Or is it the description of my mental state of uncertainty?—And is the cry "Help!" such a description?

Think how many different kinds of thing are called "description": description of a body's position by means of its co-ordinates; description of a facial expression; description of a sensation of touch; of a mood.

Of course it is possible to substitute the form of statement or description for the usual form of question: "I want to know whether . . . ." or "I am in doubt whether . . . ."—but this does not bring the different language-games any closer together.

The significance of such possibilities of transformation, for example of turning all statements into sentences beginning "I think" or "I believe" (and thus, as it were, into descriptions of *my* inner life) will become clearer in another place. (Solipsism.)

25. It is sometimes said that animals do not talk because they lack the mental capacity. And this means: "they do not think, and that is why they do not talk." But—they simply do not talk. Or to put it better: they do not use language—if we except the most primitive forms of language.—Commanding, questioning, recounting, chatting, are as much a part of our natural history as walking, eating, drinking, playing.

LANGUAGE AS LANGUAGE-GAMES

65. Here we come up against the great question that lies behind all these considerations.—For someone might object against me: "You take the easy way out! You talk about all sorts of language-games, but have nowhere said that the essence of a language-game, and hence of language, is: what is common to all these activities, and what makes them into language or parts of language. So you let yourself off the very part of the investigation that once gave you yourself most headache, the part about the *general form of propositions and of language*."

And this is true.—Instead of producing something common to all that we call language, I am saying that these phenomena have no one thing in common which makes us use the same word for all,—but that they are *related* to one another in many different ways. And it is because of this relationship, or these relationships, that we call them all "language." I will try to explain this.

66. Consider for example the proceedings that we call "games". I mean board-games, card-games, ball-games, Olympic games, and so on. What is common to them all?—Don't say: "There *must* be something common, or they would not be called 'games'—but *look and see* whether there is anything common to all.—For if you look at them you will not see something that is common to *all*, but similarities, relationships, and a whole series of them at that. To repeat: don't think, but look!—Look for example at board-games, with their multifarious relationships. Now pass to card-games; here you find many correspondences with the first group, but many common features drop out, and others appear. When we pass next to ball-games, much that is common is retained, but much is lost.—Are they all 'amusing'? Compare chess with noughts and crosses. Or is there always winning and losing, or competition between players? Think of patience. In ball games there is winning and losing; but when a child throws his ball at the wall and catches it again, this feature has disappeared. Look at the parts played by skill and luck; and at the difference between skill in chess and skill in tennis. Think now of games like ring-a-ring-a-roses; here is the element of amusement, but how many other characteristic features have disappeared! And we can go through the many, many other groups of games in the same way; can see how similarities crop up and disappear.

And the result of this examination is: we see a complicated network of similarities overlapping and criss-crossing: sometimes overall similarities, sometimes similarities of detail.

67. I can think of no better expression to characterize these similarities than "family resemblances"; for the various resemblances between members of a family: build, features, colour of eyes, gait, temperament, etc. etc. overlap and criss-cross in the same way.—And I shall say: 'games' form a family.

And for instance the kinds of number form a family in the same way. Why do we call something a "number"? Well, perhaps because it has a—direct—relationship with several things that have hitherto been called number; and this can be said to give it an indirect relationship to other things we call the same name. And we extend our concept of number as in spinning a thread we twist fibre on fibre. And the strength of the thread does not reside in the fact that some one fibre runs through its whole length, but in the overlapping of many fibres.

But if someone wished to say: "There is something common to all these constructions—namely the disjunction of all their common properties"—I should reply: Now you are only playing with words. One might as well say: "Something runs through the whole thread—namely the continuous overlapping of those fibres".

68. "All right: the concept of number is defined for you as the logical sum of these individual inter-related concepts: cardinal numbers, rational numbers, real numbers, etc.; and in the same way the concept of a game as the logical sum of a corresponding set of sub-concepts."—It need not be so. For I *can* give the concept 'number' rigid limits in this way, that is, use the word "number" for a rigidly limited concept, but I can also use it so that the extension of the concept is *not* closed by a frontier. And this is how we do use the word "game". For how is the concept of a game bounded? What still counts as a game and what no longer does? Can you give the boundary? No. You can *draw* one; for none has so far been drawn. (But that never troubled you before when you used the word "game".)

"But when the use of the word is unregulated, the 'game' we play with it is unregulated."—It is not everywhere circumscribed by rules; but no more are there any rules for how high one throws the ball in tennis, or how hard; yet tennis is a game for all that and has rules too.

69. How should we explain to someone what a game is? I imagine that we should describe *games* to him, and we might add: "This *and similar things* are called 'games'." And do we know any more about it ourselves? Is it only other people whom we cannot tell exactly what a game is?—But this is not ignorance. We do not know the boundaries because

none have been drawn. To repeat, we can draw a boundary—for a special purpose. Does it take that to make the concept usable? Not at all! (Except for that special purpose.) No more than it took the definition: 1 pace = 75 cm. to make the measure of length 'one pace' usable. And if you want to say "But still, before that it wasn't an exact measure", then I reply: very well, it was an inexact one.—Though you still owe me a definition of exactness.

70. "But if the concept 'game' is uncircumscribed like that, you don't really know what you mean by a 'game'."—When I give the description: "The ground was quite covered with plants"—do you want to say I don't know what I am talking about until I can give a definition of a plant?

My meaning would be explained by, say, a drawing and the words "The ground looked roughly like this." Perhaps I even say "it looked *exactly* like this."—Then were just *this* grass and *these* leaves there, arranged just like this? No, that is not what it means. And I should not accept any picture as exact in *this* sense.

Someone says to me: "Shew the children a game." I teach them gaming with dice, and the other says "I didn't mean that sort of game." Must the exclusion of the game with dice have come before his mind when he gave me the order? (Note added by Wittgenstein.)

71. One might say that the concept 'game' is a concept with blurred edges.—"But is a blurred concept a concept at all?—Is an indistinct photograph a picture of a person at all? Is it even always an advantage to replace an indistinct picture by a sharp one? Isn't the indistinct one often exactly what we need?

Frege compares a concept to an area and says that an area with vague boundaries cannot be called an area at all. This presumably means that we cannot do anything with it.—But is it senseless to say: "Stand roughly there"? Suppose that I were standing with someone in a city square and said that. As I say it I do not draw any kind of boundary, but perhaps point with my hand—as if I were indicating a particular *spot*. And this is just how one might explain to someone what a game is. One gives examples and intends them to be taken in a particular way.—I do not, however, mean by this that he is supposed to see in those examples that common thing which I—for some reason—was unable to express; but that he is now to *employ* those examples in a particular way. Here giving examples is not an *indirect* means of explaining—in default of a better. For any general definition can be misunderstood too. The point is that *this* is how we play the game. (I mean the language-game with the word "game.")

72. *Seeing what is common.* Suppose I shew someone various multicoloured pictures, and say: "The colour you see in all these is called 'yellow ochre'."—This is a definition, and the other will get to understand it by looking for and seeing what is common to the pictures. Then he can look *at*, can point *to*, the common thing.

Compare with this a case in which I shew him figures of different shapes all painted the same colour, and say: "What these have in common is called 'yellow ochre'."

And compare this case: I shew him samples of different shades of blue and say: "The colour that is common to all these is what I call 'blue'."

73. When someone defines the names of colours for me by pointing to samples and saying "This colour is called 'blue', this 'green' . . ." this case can be compared in many respects to putting a table in my hands, with the words written under the colour-samples.—Though this comparison may mislead in many ways.—One is now inclined to extend the comparison: to have understood the definition means to have in one's mind an idea of the thing defined, and that is a sample or picture. So if I am shewn various different leaves and told "This is called a 'leaf'," I get an idea of the shape of a leaf, a picture of it in my mind.—But what does the picture of a leaf look like when it does not shew us any particular shape, but 'what is common to all shapes of leaf'? Which shade is the 'sample in my mind' of the colour green—the sample of what is common to all shades of green.

"But might there not be such 'general' samples? Say a schematic leaf, or a sample of *pure* green?"—Certainly there might. But for such a schema to be understood as a *schema*, and not as the shape of a particular leaf, and for the slip of pure green to be

understood as a sample of all that is greenish and not as a sample of pure green—this in turn resides in the way the samples are used.

Ask yourself: what *shape* must the sample of the colour green be? Should it be rectangular? Or would it then be the sample of a green rectangle?—So should it be 'irregular' in shape? And what is to prevent us then from regarding it—that is, from using it—only as a sample of irregularity of shape?

74. Here also belongs the idea that if you see this leaf as a sample of the 'leaf shape in general' you *see* it differently from someone who regards it as, say, a sample of this particular shape. Now this might well be so—though it is not so—for it would only be to say that, as a matter of experience, if you *see* the leaf in a particular way, you use it in such-and-such a way or according to such-and-such rules. Of course, there is such a thing as seeing in *this* way or *that*; and there are also cases where whoever sees a sample like *this* will in general use it in *this* way, and whoever sees it otherwise in another way. For example, if you see the schematic drawing of a cube as a plane figure consisting of a square and two rhombi you will, perhaps, carry out the order "Bring me something like this" differently from someone who sees the picture three-dimensionally.

75. What does it mean to know what a game is? What does it mean, to know it and not be able to say it? Is this knowledge somehow equivalent to an unformulated definition? So that if it were formulated I should be able to recognize it as the expression of my knowledge? Isn't my knowledge, my concept of a game, completely expressed in the explanations that I could give? That is, in my describing examples of various kinds of game; shewing how all sorts of other games can be constructed on the analogy of these; saying that I should scarcely include this or this among games; and so on.

76. If someone were to draw a sharp boundary I could not acknowledge it as the one that I too always wanted to draw, or had drawn in my mind. For I did not want to draw one at all. His concept can then be said to be not the same as mine, but akin to it. The kinship is that of two pictures, one of which consists of colour patches with vague contours, and the other of patches similarly shaped and distributed, but with

clear contours. The kinship is just as undeniable as the difference.

77. And if we carry this comparison still further it is clear that the degree to which the sharp picture *can* resemble the blurred one depends on the latter's degree of vagueness. For imagine having to sketch a sharply defined picture 'corresponding' to a blurred one. In the latter there is a blurred red rectangle: for it you put down a sharply defined one. Of course—several such sharply defined rectangles can be drawn to correspond to the indefinite one.—But if the colours in the original merge without a hint of any outline won't it become a hopeless task to draw a sharp picture corresponding to the blurred one? Won't you then have to say: "Here I might just as well draw a circle or heart as a rectangle, for all the colours merge. Anything—and nothing—is right."—And this is the position you are in if you look for definitions corresponding to our concepts in aesthetics or ethics.

In such a difficulty always ask yourself: How did we *learn* the meaning of this word ("good" for instance)? From what sort of examples? in what language-games? Then it will be easier for you to see that the word must have a family of meanings.

REVIEW QUESTIONS

1. How does Wittgenstein sum up the basic idea of his *Tractatus Logico-Philosophicus*?
2. What is his theory regarding "language as picture"?
3. What does Wittgenstein mean by "language games" and "forms of life"?
4. According to Wittgenstein, can philosophy provide foundations for knowledge? Why or why not?
5. Does he propose a form of relativism, the notion that truth is relative to particular persons, frameworks, or cultures?

33

EDMUND HUSSERL

Edmund Husserl (1859–1938) was born in Moravia (now the Czech Republic). After attending the University of Leipzig where he studied mathematics and science, he went to Vienna to study under Franz Brentano, who awakened his thought in philosophical psychology. Brentano held that a basic form of consciousness is *intentionality*. All thought and desire is *about* something. One never just thinks or desires but thinks or desires something, even though the object may be vague and amorphous. Husserl developed Brentano's ideas, centering his studies on the nature or *phenomenology* of consciousness. He is considered the father of phenomenology, the basic ideas of which are outlined in the selection that follows.

In 1916 he became a professor at the University of Freiburg, Germany, where he remained until his retirement in 1929. During the last five years of his life, he was barred from public activities because of his Jewish ancestry.

In our selection from *Ideas: General Introduction to Pure Phenomenology* (1913) Husserl focuses on his notion of phenomenological (or *eidetic*) reduction: all acts must be reduced to an essence of *eidos* (essential idea). The perceiver must perform an *epoche*, that is, suspend judgment on the existence of the objects of consciousness. For example, I should not focus on whether the computer before me really exists but on the essential features of the experience itself. He describes this as "bracketing" the experience. For Husserl, I am neither a thinking substance (as Descartes thought) nor a bundle of perceptions (as Hume thought) nor an embodied soul (as Plato thought), but a pure transcendental ego, a consciousness that cannot be bracketed, but transcends its intentional object.

The main criticism of Husserl's program is that it entails solipsism, the idea that the only thing which really exists is the self or ego—all else being uncertain. Husserl tried to answer this objection by explaining how one transcendental ego can experience other such egos.

FOR FURTHER READING

Dreyfus, Hubert, ed. *Husserl, Intentionality and Cognitive Science* (MIT Press, 1982).

Husserl, Edmund. *Ideas: General Introduction to Pure Phenomenology*, trans. W. R. Gibson (Allen & Unwin, 1931).

Kockelman, Joseph. *Edmund Husserl's Phenomenology* (Humanities Press, 1978).

Kolakowski, Leszek. *Husserl and the Search for Certitude* (University of Chicago Press, 1987).

Solomon, Robert, ed. *Phenomenology and Existentialism* (Harper & Row, 1972).

Speigelberg, Herbert. *The Phenomenological Movement*, 2 vols. (Martinus Nijhoff, 1960).

Stapleton, Timothy J. *Husserl and Heidegger* (SUNY Press, 1983).

IDEAS: GENERAL INTRODUCTION TO PURE PHENOMENOLOGY

THE THESIS OF THE NATURAL STANDPOINT AND ITS SUSPENSION

THE WORD OF THE NATURAL STANDPOINT: I AND MY WORLD ABOUT ME

Our first outlook upon life is that of natural human beings, imagining, judging, feeling, willing, "*from the natural standpoint.*" Let us make clear to ourselves what this means in the form of simple meditations which we can best carry on in the first person.

I am aware of a world, spread out in space endlessly, and in time becoming and become, without end. I am aware of it, that means, first of all, I discover it immediately, intuitively, I experience it. Through sight, touch, hearing, etc., in the different ways of sensory perception, corporeal things somehow spatially distributed are *for me simply there*, in verbal or figurative sense "present," whether or not I pay them special attention by busying myself with them, considering, thinking, feeling, willing. Animal beings also, perhaps men, are immediately there for me; I look up, I see them, I hear them coming towards me, I grasp them by the hand; speaking with them, I understand immediately what they are sensing and thinking, the feelings that stir them, what they wish or will. They too are present as realities in my field of intuition, even when I pay them no attention. But it is not necessary that they and other objects likewise should be present precisely in my *field of perception*. For me real objects are there, definite, more or less familiar, agreeing with what is actually perceived without being themselves perceived or even intuitively present. I can let my attention wander from the writing-table I have just seen and observed, through the unseen portions of the room behind my back to the verandah, into the garden, to the children in the summer-house, and so forth, to all the objects concerning which I precisely "know" that they are there and yonder in my immediate co-perceived surroundings—a knowledge which has nothing of conceptual thinking in it, and first changes into clear intuiting with the bestowing of attention, and even then only partially and for the most part very imperfectly.

But not even with the added reach of this intuitively clear or dark, distinct or indistinct *co-present* margin, which forms a continuous ring around the actual field of perception, does that world exhaust itself which in every waking moment is in some conscious measure "present" before me. It reaches rather in a fixed order of being the limitless beyond. What is actually perceived, and what is more or less clearly co-present and determinate (to some extent at least), is partly pervaded, partly girt about with a *dimly apprehended depth or fringe of indeterminate reality*. I can pierce it with rays from the illuminating focus of attention with varying success. Determining representations, dim at first, then livelier, fetch me something out, a chain of such recollections takes shape, the circle of determinacy extends ever farther, and eventually so far that the connexion with the actual field of perception as the *immediate* environment is established. But in general the issue is a different one: an empty mist of dim indeterminacy gets studded over with intuitive possibilities or presumptions, and only the "form" of the world as "world" is foretokened. Moreover, the zone of indeterminacy is infinite. The misty horizon that can never be completely outlined remains necessarily there.

As it is with the world in its ordered being as a spatial present—the aspect I have so far been considering—so likewise is it with the world in respect to its *ordered being in the succession of time*. This world now present to me, and in every waking "now" obviously so, has its temporal horizon, infinite in both directions, its known and unknown, its intimately alive and its unalive past and future. Moving freely within the moment of experience which brings what is present into my intuitional grasp, I can follow up these connexions of the reality which immediately surrounds me. I can shift my standpoint in space and time, look this way and that, turn temporally forwards and backwards; I can provide for myself constantly new and more or less clear and meaningful perceptions and representations, and images also more or less clear, in which I make intuitable to myself whatever can possibly exist really or supposedly in the steadfast order of space and time.

In this way, when consciously awake, I find myself at all times, and without my ever being able to change this, set in relation to a world which, through its constant changes, remains one and ever the same. It is continually "present" for me, and I myself am a member of it. Therefore this world is not there for me as a mere *world of facts and affairs*, but, with the same immediacy, as a *world of values, a world of goods*, a *practical world*. Without further effort on my part I find the things before me furnished not only with the qualities that befit their positive nature, but with value-characters such as beautiful or ugly, agreeable or disagreeable, pleasant or unpleasant, and so forth. Things in their immediacy stand there as objects to be used, the "table" with its "books," the "glass to drink from," the "vase," the "piano," and so forth. These values and practicalities, they too belong to *the constitution of the "actually present" objects as such*, irrespective of my turning or not turning to consider them or indeed any other objects. The same considerations apply of course just as well to the men and beasts in my surroundings as to "mere things." They are my "friends" or my "foes," my "servants" or "superiors," "strangers" or "relatives," and so forth.

THE "COGITO." MY NATURAL WORLD-ABOUT-ME AND THE IDEAL WORLDS-ABOUT-ME

It is then to this world, *the world in which I find myself and which is also my world-about-me*, that the complex forms of my manifold and shifting *spontaneities* of consciousness stand related: observing in the interests of research the bringing of meaning into conceptual form through description; comparing and distinguishing, collecting and counting, presupposing and inferring, the theorizing activity of consciousness, in short, in its different forms and stages. Related to it likewise are the diverse acts and states of sentiment and disapproval, joy and sorrow, desire and aversion, hope and fear, decision and action. All these, together with the sheer acts of the Ego, in which I become acquainted with the world as *immediately* given me, through spontaneous tendencies to turn towards it and to grasp it, are included under the one Cartesian expression: *Cogito*. In the natural urge of life I live continually in *this fundamental form of all "wakeful" living*, whether in addition I do or do not assert the *cogito*, and whether I am or am not "reflectively" concerned with the Ego and the *cogitare*. If I am so concerned, a new *cogito* has become livingly active, which for its part is not reflected upon, and so not objective for me.

I am present to myself continually as someone who perceives, represents, thinks, feels, desires, and so forth; and *for the most part* herein I find myself related in present experience to the fact-world which is constantly about me. But I am not always so related, not every *cogito* in which I live has for its *cogitatum* things, men, objects or contents of one kind or another. Perhaps I am busied with pure numbers and the laws they symbolize: nothing of this sort is present in the world about me, this world of "real fact." And yet the world of numbers also is there for me, as the field of objects with which I am arithmetically busied; while I am thus occupied some numbers or constructions of a numerical kind will be at the focus of vision, girt by an arithmetical horizon partly defined, partly not; but obviously this being-there-for-me, like the being there at all, is something very different from this. *The arithmetical world is there for me only when and so long as I occupy the arithmetical standpoint.* But the *natural* world, the world in the ordinary sense of the word, is *constantly there for me*, so long as I live naturally and look in its direction. I am then at the *"natural standpoint,"* which is just another way of stating the same thing. And there is no need to modify these conclusions when I proceed to appropriate to myself the arithmetical world, and other similar "worlds," by adopting the corresponding standpoint. The natural world *still remains "present,"* I am at the natural standpoint after as well as before, and in this respect *undisturbed by the adoption of new standpoints.* If my *cogito* is active *only* in the worlds proper to the new standpoints, the natural world remains unconsidered; it is now the background for my consciousness as act, but it is *not the encircling sphere within which an arithmetical world finds its true and proper place.* The two worlds are present together but *disconnected*, apart, that is, from their relation to the Ego, in virtue of which I can freely direct my glance or my acts to the one or to the other.

THE "OTHER" EGO-SUBJECT AND THE INTERSUBJECTIVE NATURAL WORLD-ABOUT-ME

Whatever holds good for me personally, also holds good, as I know, for all other men whom I find present in my world-about-me. Experiencing them as men, I understand and take them as Ego-subjects, units like myself, and related to their natural surroundings. But this in such wise that I apprehend the world-about-them and the world-about-me objectively as one and the same world, which differs in each case only through affecting consciousness differently. Each has his place whence he sees the things that are present, and each enjoys accordingly different appearances of the things. For each, again, the fields of perception and memory actually present are different, quite apart from the fact that even that which is here intersubjectively known in common is

known in different ways, is differently apprehended, shows different grades of clearness, and so forth. Despite all this, we come to understandings with our neighbours, and set up in common an objective spatio-temporal fact-world as *the world about us that is there for us all, and to which we ourselves none the less belong.*

THE GENERAL THESIS OF THE NATURAL STANDPOINT

That which we have submitted towards the characterization of what is given to us from the natural standpoint, and thereby of the natural standpoint itself, was a piece of pure description *prior to all "theory."* In these studies we stand bodily aloof from all theories, and by "theories" we here mean anticipatory ideas of every kind. Only as facts of our environment, not as agencies for uniting facts validly together, do theories concern us at all. But we do not set ourselves the task of continuing the pure description and raising it to a systematically inclusive and exhaustive characterization of the data, in their full length and breadth, discoverable from the natural standpoint (or from any standpoint, we might add, that can be knit up with the same in a common consent). A task such as this can and must—as scientific—be undertaken, and it is one of extraordinary importance, although so far scarcely noticed. Here it is not ours to attempt. For us who are striving towards the entrance-gate of phenomenology all the necessary work in this direction has already been carried out; the few features pertaining to the natural standpoint which we need are of a quite general character, and have already figured in our descriptions, and been sufficiently *and fully clarified.* We even made a special point of securing this full measure of clearness.

We emphasize a most important point once again in the sentences that follow: I find continually present and standing over against me the one spatio-temporal fact-world to which I myself belong, as do all other men found in it and related in the same way to it. This "fact-world," as the world already tells us, I find to *be out there*, and also *take it just as it gives itself to me as something that exists out there.* All doubting and rejecting of the data of the natural world leaves standing the *general thesis of the natural standpoint*. "The" world is as fact-world always there; at the most it is at odd points "other" than I supposed, this or that under such names as "illusion," "hallucination," and the like, must be struck *out of it*, so to speak; but the "it" remains ever, in the sense of the general thesis, a world that has its being out there. To know it more comprehensively, more trustworthily, more perfectly than the naïve lore of experience is able to do, and to solve all the problems of scientific knowledge which offer themselves upon its ground, that is the goal of the *sciences of the natural standpoint*.

RADICAL ALTERATION OF THE NATURAL THESIS "DISCONNEXION," "BRACKETING"

Instead now of remaining at this standpoint, we propose to alter it radically. Our aim must be to convince ourselves of the possibility of this alteration on grounds of principle.

The General Thesis according to which the real world about me is at all times known not merely in a general way as something apprehended, but as a fact-world *that has its being out there*, does *not* consist of course *in an act proper*, in an articulated judgment *about existence*. It is and remains something all the time the standpoint is adopted, that is, it endures persistently during the whole course of our life of natural endeavour. What has been at any time perceived clearly, or obscurely made present, in short everything out of the world of nature through experience and prior to any thinking, bears in its totality and in all its articulated sections the character "present" "out there," a character which can function essentially as the ground of support for an explicit (predicative) existential judgment which is in agreement with the character it is grounded upon. If we express that same judgment, we know quite well that in so doing we have simply put into the form of a statement and grasped as a predication what already lay somehow in the original experience, or lay there as the character of something "present to one's hand."

We can treat the potential and unexpressed thesis exactly as we do the thesis of the explicit judgment. A procedure of this sort, *possible at any time*, is, for instance, *the attempt to doubt everything* which

Descartes, with an entirely different end in view, with the purpose of setting up an absolutely indubitable sphere of Being, undertook to carry through. We link on here, but add directly and emphatically that this attempt to doubt everything should serve us *only as a device of method*, helping us to stress certain points which by its means, as though secluded in its essence, must be brought clearly to light.

The attempt to doubt everything has its place in the realm of our *perfect freedom*. We can *attempt to doubt* anything and everything, however convinced we may be concerning what we doubt, even though the evidence which seals our assurance is completely adequate.

Let us consider what is essentially involved in an act of this kind. He who attempts to doubt is attempting to doubt "Being" of some form or other, or it may be Being expanded into such predicative forms as "It is," "It is this or thus," and the like. The attempt does not affect the form of Being itself. He who doubts, for instance, whether an object, whose Being he does not doubt, is constituted in such and such a way doubts *the way it is constituted*. We can obviously transfer this way of speaking from the doubting to the *attempt* at doubting. It is clear that we cannot doubt the Being of anything, and in the same act of consciousness (under the unifying form of simultaneity) bring what is substantive to this Being under the terms of the Natural Thesis, and so confer upon it the character of "being actually there" (*vorhanden*). Or to put the same in another way: we cannot at once doubt and hold for certain one and the same quality of Being. It is likewise clear that the *attempt* to doubt any object of awareness in respect of it *being actually there necessarily conditions a certain suspension (Aufhebung) of the thesis*; and it is precisely this that interests us. It is not a transformation of the thesis into its antithesis, of positive into negative; it is also not a transformation into presumption, suggestion, indecision, doubt (in one or another sense of the word); each shifting indeed is not at our free pleasure. *Rather is it something quite unique. We do not abandon the thesis we have adopted, we make no change in our conviction*, which remains in itself what it is so long as we do not introduce new motives of judgment, which we precisely refrain from doing. And yet the thesis undergoes a modification—whilst remaining in itself what it is, *we set it as it were "out of action,"* we *"disconnect it," "bracket it."* It still remains there like the bracketed in the bracket, like the disconnected outside the connexional system. We can also say: The thesis is experience as lived (*Erlebnis*), *but we make "no use" of it*, and by that, of course, we do not indicate privation (as when we say of the ignorant that he makes no use of a certain thesis); in this case rather, as with all parallel expressions, we are dealing with indicators that point to a definite but *unique form of consciousness*, which clamps on to the original simple thesis (whether it actually or even predicatively *posits* existence or not), and transvalues it in a quite peculiar way. *This transvaluing is a concern of our full freedom, and is opposed to all cognitive attitudes* that would set themselves up as coordinate with the *thesis*, and yet within the unity of "simultaneity" remain incompatible with it, as indeed it is in general with all attitudes whatsoever in the strict sense of the word.

In *the attempt to doubt* applied to a thesis which, as we presuppose, is certain and tenaciously held, the "disconnexion" takes place in and with a modification of the antithesis, namely with the "*supposition*" (*Ansetzung*) *of Non-Being*, which is thus the partial basis of the attempt to doubt. With Descartes this is so markedly the case that one can say that his universal attempt at doubt is just an attempt at universal denial. We disregard this possibility here, we are not interested in every analytical component of the attempt to doubt, nor therefore in its exact and completely sufficing analysis. *We extract only the phenomenon of "bracketing" or "disconnexion,"* which is obviously not limited to that of the attempt to doubt, although it can be detached from it with special ease, but can appear *in other contexts also*, and with no less ease *independently*. In relation to every thesis and wholly uncoerced we can use this *peculiar ἐποχή*, (*epokhe*—abstention), *a certain refraining from judgment which is compatible with the unshaken and unshakable because of the self-evidencing conviction of Truth*. The thesis is "put out of action," bracketed, it passes off into the modified status of a "bracketed thesis," and the judgment *simpliciter* into "*bracketed judgment*."

Naturally one should not simply identify this consciousness with that of "mere supposal," that nymphs, for instance, are dancing in a ring; for thereby *no disconnecting* of a living conviction that goes on living takes place, although from another side the close relation of the two forms of consciousness lies clear. Again, we are not concerned here with supposal in the sense of "*assuming*" or *taking for granted*, which in the equivocal speech of current usage may also be expressed in the words: "I suppose (I make the assumption) that it is so and so."

Let us add further that nothing hinders us *from speaking bracketing correlatively* also, in respect of *an objectivity to be posited*, what ever be the region or category to which it belongs. What is meant in this case is that *every thesis related to this objectivity* must be *disconnected* and changed into its bracketed counterpart. On closer view, moreover, the "bracketing" image is from the outset better suited to the sphere of the object, just as the expression "to put out of action" better suits the sphere of the Act or of Consciousness.

THE PHENOMENOLOGICAL ἐποχή

We can now let the universal ἐποχή, (*epokhe*—abstention) in the sharply defined and novel sense we have given to it step into the place of the Cartesian attempt at universal doubt. But on good grounds we *limit* the universality of this ἐποχή. For were it as inclusive as it is in general capable of being, then since every thesis and every judgment can be modified freely to any extent, and every objectivity that we can judge or criticize can be bracketed, no field would be left over for unmodified judgments, to say nothing of a science. But our design is just to discover a new scientific domain, such as might be won precisely *through the method of bracketing*, though only through a definitely limited form of it.

The limiting consideration can be indicated in a word.

We put out of action the general thesis which belongs to the essence of the natural standpoint, we place in brackets whatever it includes respecting the nature of Being: *this entire natural world therefore* which is continually "there for us," "present to our hand," and will ever remain there, is a "fact-world" of which we continue to be conscious, even though it pleases us to put it in brackets.

If I do this, as I am fully free to do, I do *not* then *deny* this "world," as though I were a sophist, *I do not doubt that it is there* as though I were a sceptic; but I use the "phenomenological" ἐποχή, which *completely bars me from using any judgment that concerns spatio-temporal existence (Dasein).*

Thus *all sciences which relate to this natural world,* though they stand never so firm to me, though they fill me with wondering admiration, though I am far from any thought of objecting to them in the least degree, *I disconnect them all, I make absolutely no use of their standards, I do not appropriate a single one of the propositions that enter into their systems, even though their evidential value is perfect, I take none of them, no one of them serves me for a foundation*—so long, that is, as it is understood, in the way these sciences themselves understand it, as a truth *concerning the realities* of this world. *I may accept it only after I have placed it in the bracket.* That means: only in the modified consciousness of the judgment as it appears in disconnexion, and *not as it figures within the science as its proposition, a proposition which claims to be valid and whose validity I recognize and make use of.*

The ἐποχή here in question will not be confined with that which positivism demands, and against which, as we were compelled to admit, it is itself an offender. We are not concerned at present with removing the preconceptions which trouble the pure positivity (*Sachlichkeit*) of research, with the constituting of a science "free from theory" and "free from metaphysics" by bringing all the grounding back to the immediate data, nor with the means of reaching such ends, concerning whose value there is indeed no question. What *we* demand lies along another line. The whole world as placed within the nature-setting and presented in experience as real, taken completely "free from all theory," just as it is in reality experienced, and made clearly manifest in and through the linkings of our experiences, has now no validity for us, it must be set in brackets, untested indeed but also uncontested. Similarly all theories and sciences, positivistic or otherwise, which relate to this world, however good they may be, succumb to the same fate.

CONSCIOUSNESS AND NATURAL REALITY

INTIMATION CONCERNING "PURE" OR "TRANSCENDENTAL CONSCIOUSNESS" AS PHENOMENOLOGICAL RESIDUUM

We have learnt to understand the meaning of the phenomenological ἐποχή (epokhe—abstention), but we are still quite in the dark as to its serviceability. In the first place it is not clear to what extent the limitation of the total field of the ἐποχή, as discussed in the previous pages, involves a real narrowing of its general scope. *For what can remain over when the whole world is bracketed, including ourselves and all our thinking (cogitare)?*

Since the reader already knows that the interest which governs these "Meditations" concerns a new eidetic science, he will indeed at first expect the world as fact to succumb to the disconnexion, but not *the world as Eidos,* nor any other sphere of Essential Being. The disconnecting of the world does not as a matter of fact mean the disconnecting of the number series, for instance, and the arithmetic relative to it.

However, we do not take this path, nor does our goal lie in its direction. That goal we could also refer to as *the winning of a new region of Being, the distinctive character of which has not yet been defined,* a region of *individual* Being, like every genuine region. We must leave the sequel to teach us what that more precisely means.

We proceed in the first instance by showing up simply and directly what we see; and since the Being to be thus shown up is neither more nor less than that which we refer to on essential grounds as "pure experiences (*Erlebnisse*)" "pure consciousness" with its pure "correlates of consciousness," and on the other side its "pure Ego," we observe that it is from *the Ego, the* consciousness, *the* experience as given to us from the natural standpoint, that we take our start.

I, the real human being, am a real object like others in the natural world. I carry out *cogitationes,* "acts of consciousness" in both a narrower and a wider sense, and these acts, as belonging to this human subject, are events of the same natural world. And all my remaining experiences (*Erlebnisse*) likewise, out of whose changing stream the specific acts of the Ego shine forth in so distinctive a way, glide into one another, enter into combinations, and are being incessantly modified. Now in its *widest connotation* the expression "*consciousness*" (then indeed less suited for its purpose) includes *all* experiences (*Erlebnisse*), and entrenched in the natural standpoint as we are even in our scientific thinking, grounded there in habits that are most firmly established since they have never misled us, we take all these data of psychological reflexion as real world-events, as the experiences (*Erlebnisse*) of animal beings. So natural is it to us to see them only in this light that, though acquainted already with the possibility of a change of standpoint, and on the search for the new domain of objects, we fail to notice that it is from out these centres of experience (*Erlebnisse*) themselves that through the adoption of the new standpoint the new domain emerges. Connected with this is the fact that instead of keeping our eyes turned towards these centres of experience, we turned them away and sought the new objects in the ontological realms of arithmetic, geometry, and the like, whereby indeed nothing truly new has to be won.

Thus we fix our eyes steadily upon the sphere of Consciousness and study what it is that we find immanent in *it*. At first, without having yet carried out the phenomenological suspensions of the element of judgment, we subject this sphere of Consciousness in its essential nature to a systematic though in no sense exhaustive analysis. What we lack above all is a certain general insight into the essence of *consciousness in general*, and quite specially also of consciousness, so far as in and through its essential Being, the "natural" fact-world comes to be known. In these studies we go so far as is needed to furnish the full insight at which we have been aiming, to wit, *that Consciousness in itself has a being of its own which in its absolute uniqueness of nature remains unaffected by the phenomenological disconnexion.* It therefore remains over as a "*phenomenological residuum*," as a region of Being which is in principle unique, and can become in fact the field of a new science—the science of Phenomenology.

Through this insight the "phenomenological" *ἐποχή* will for the first time deserve its name; to exercise it in full consciousness of its import will turn out to be the necessary operation which *renders* "*pure*" *consciousness accessible to us, and subsequently the whole phenomenological region.* And thus we shall be able to understand why this region and the new science attached to it was fated to remain unknown. From the natural standpoint nothing can be seen except the natural world. So long as the possibility of the phenomenological standpoint was not grasped, and the method of relating the objectivities which emerge therewith to a primordial form of apphension had not been devised, the phenomenological world must needs have remained unknown, and indeed barely divined at all.

We would add yet the following to our terminology: Inportant motives which have their ground in epistemological requirements justify us in referring to "pure" consciousness, of which much is yet to be said, also as *transcendental consciousness*, and the operation through which it is acquired as *transcendental ἐποχή*. On grounds of method this operation will split up into different steps of "disconnexion" or "bracketing," and thus our method will assume the character of a graded reduction. For this reason we propose to speak, and even preponderatingly, of *phenomenological reductions* (though, in respect of their unity as a whole, we would speak in unitary form of *the* phenomenological reduction). From the epistemological viewpoint we would also speak of transcendental reductions. Moreover, these and *all* our terms must be understood exclusively in accordance with the sense which *our* presentations indicate for them, but not in any other one which history or the terminological habits of the reader may favour.

THE ESSENCE OF CONSCIOUSNESS AS THEME OF INQUIRY

We start with a series of observations within which we are not troubled with any phenomenological *ἐποχή*. We are directed to an "outer world," and, without forsaking the natural standpoint, reflect psychologically on our Ego and its experience (*Erleben*). We busy ourselves, precisely as we have done if we had never heard of the new viewpoint, with *the essential nature of "the consciousness of something,"* following, for instance, our consciousness of the existence of material things, living bodies and men, or that of technical and literary works, and so forth. We adhere to our general principle that each individual event has its essence that can be grasped in its eiditic purity, and in this purity must belong to a field available to eidetic inquiry. In accordance herewith the universal fact of nature conveyed by the words "I am," "I think," "I have a world over against me," and the like, has also its essential content, and it is on this exclusively that we now intend to concentrate. Thus we rehearse to ourselves by way of illustration certain conscious experiences chosen at random, and in their individuality just as they are in their natural setting as real facts of human life, and we make these present to ourselves through memory or in the free play of fancy. On the ground of illustrations such as these, which we assume to be presented with perfect clearness, we grasp and fix in adequate ideation the pure essences that interest us. The individual facts, the fact-character of the natural world in general, thereby escapes our theoretical scrutiny—as in all cases where our inquiry is purely eidetic.

We limit still further the theme of our inquiry. Its title ran: Consciousness, or more distinctly *Conscious experience (Erlebnis) in general*, to be taken in an extremely wide sense about whose exact definition we are fortunately not concerned. Exact definitions do not lie at the threshold of analysis of the kind we are here making, but are a later result involving great labour. As starting-point we take consciousness in a pregnant sense which suggests itself at once, most simply indicated through the Cartesian *cogito*, "I think." As is known Descartes understood this in a sense so wide as to include every case of "I perceive, I remember, I fancy, I judge, feel, desire, will," and all experiences of the Ego that in any way resemble the foregoing, in all the countless fluctuations of their special patterns. The Ego itself to which they are all related, spontaneous, in receptive or any other "attitude," and indeed the Ego in any and every sense, we leave at first out of consideration. We shall be concerned with it later, and fundamentally. For the present there is sufficient other material to serve as support for our analysis and grasp of the essential. And we shall find ourselves forthwith referred thereby to enveloping connexions of experience which compel us to widen our conception of a conscious experience beyond this circle of specific *cogitationes*.

We shall consider conscious experiences *in the concrete fullness and entirety* with which they figure in their concrete context—the *stream of experience*—and to which they are closely attached through their own proper essence. It then becomes evident that every experience in the stream which our reflexion can lay hold on has *its own essence open to intuition*, a "content" which can be considered in its *singularity in and for itself*. We shall be concerned to grasp this individual content of the *cogitatio* in its *pure* singularity, and to describe it in its general features, excluding everything which is not to be found in the *cogitatio* as it is in itself. We must likewise describe the *unity of consciousness* which is demanded *by the intrinsic nature of the cogitationes*, and so necessarily demanded that they could not be without this unity.

THE COGITO AS "ACT." THE MODAL FORM OF MARGINAL ACTUALITY

Let us start with an example. In front of me, in the dim light, lies this white paper. I see it, touch it. This perceptual seeing and touching of the paper as the full concrete experience *of* the paper that lies here as given in truth precisely with this relative lack of clearness, with this imperfect definition, appearing to me from this particular angle—is a *cogitatio*, a conscious experience. The paper itself with its objective qualities, its extension in space, its objective position in regard to that spatial thing I call my body, is not *cogitatio*, but *cogitatum*, not perceptual experience, but something perceived. Now that which is perceived can itself very well be a conscious experience; but it is evident that an object such as a material thing, this paper, for instance, as given in perceptual exerience, is in principle other than an experience, a being of a completely different kind.

Before pursuing this point farther, let us amplify the illustration. In perception properly so-called, as an explicit awareness (*Gewahren*), I am turned towards the object, to the paper, for instance, I apprehend it as being this here and now. The apprehension is a singling out, every perceived object having a background in experience. Around and about the paper lie books, pencils, ink-well, and so forth, and these in a certain sense are also "perceived," perceptually there, in the "field of intuition"; but whilst I was turned towards the paper there was no turning in their direction, nor any apprehending of them, not even in a secondary sense. They appeared and yet were not singled out, were not posited on their own account. Every perception of a thing has such a zone of *background intuitions* (or background awarenesses, if "intuiting" already includes the state of being turned towards), and this also is a "*conscious experience*," or more briefly a "consciousness *of*" all indeed that in point of fact lies in the co-perceived objective "background." We are not talking here of course of that which is to be found as an "objective" element in the objective space to which the background in question may belong, of all the things and thing-like events which a valid and progressive experience may establish there. What we say applies exclusively to that zone of consciousness which belongs to the model essence of a perception as "being turned towards an object," and further to that which belongs to the proper essence of this zone itself. But it is here implied that certain modifications of the original experience are possible, which we refer to as a free turning of the "look"—not precisely nor merely of the physical but of the "*mental look*"—from the paper at first *descried* to objects which had already appeared before of which we had been "implicitly" aware, and whereof *subsequent* to the directing of one's look thither we are explicitly aware, perceiving them "attentitively," or "noticing them near by."

We are aware of things not only in perception, but also consciously in recollections, in representations similar to recollections, and also in the free play of fancy, and this in "clear intuition" it may be, or without noticeable perceptibility after the manner of "dim" presentations; they float past us in different "characterizations" as real, possible, fancied, and so forth. All that we have stated concerning perceptual experiences holds good, obviously, of these other experiences, essentially different as they are. We shall not think of confusing the *objects of which we are aware* under these forms of consciousness (the fancy-shaped nymphs, for instance) with the conscious experiences themselves which are a consciousness *of* them. Then, again, we know that it is the essence of all such experiences—taking the same, as always, in their concrete fullness—to show that remarkable modification which transfers consciousness in the *mode of actual orientation* to consciousness in the *mode of non-actuality* and conversely. At the one time the experience is, so to speak "*explicitly*" aware of its objective content, at the other implicitly and merely *potentially*. The objective factor, whether in perception, memory, or fancy, may already be appearing to us, but *our mental gaze is not yet "directed" towards it*, not even in a secondary sense, to say nothing of being "busied" with it in some special way.

Similar remarks apply to all and any of the *cogitationes* in the sense illustrated by Descartes' use of the term, to all experiences of thought, feeling and will, except that, as will be emphasized (in the next paragraph), the "directedness towards," the "being turned towards," which is the distinctive mark of focal actuality, does not coincide, as in the favourite because simplest examples of sensory presentations, with singling out and noting the objects we are aware of. It is also obviously true of all such experiences that the focal is girt about with a "zone" of the marginal; *the stream of experience can never consist wholly of focal actualities*. These indeed determine, in a very general sense which must be extended beyond the circle of our illustrations, and through the contrast with marginal actualities already drawn, the *pregnant* meaning of the expression "cogito," "I have *consciousness* of something," "I perform an *act* of consciousness." In order to keep this well-established concept purely separate, we propose to reserve for it exclusively the Cartesian expressions *cogito* and *cogitationes*, unless through some addition, such as "marginal" or the like, we expressly indicate the modified use we are making of the term.

We can define a "*wakeful*" Ego as one that within its stream of experience is continually conscious in the specific form of the *cogito*; which, of course, does not mean that it can and does bring these experiences persistently or in general to predicative expression. Ego-subjects include animals. But, according to what we have said above, it belongs to the essence of the stream of experience of a wakeful Self that the continuously prolonged chain of *cog-

itationes is constantly enveloped in a medium of dormant actuality (*Inaktualität*), which is ever prepared to pass off into the wakeful mode (*Aktualität*), as conversely the wakeful into the dormant.

INTENTIONAL EXPERIENCE. EXPERIENCE IN GENERAL

However drastic the change which the experiences of a wakeful Consciousness undergo in their transition into the dormant state, the experiences as modified share the essential nature of the original experiences in an important respect. It belongs as a general feature to the essence of every actual *cogito* to be a consciousness *of* something. But according to what we have already said, the *modified cogitatio is likewise and in its own way Consciousness*, and *of the same* something as with the corresponding unmodified consciousness. Thus the essential property of Consciousness in its general form is preserved in the modification. All experiences which have these essential properties in common are also called "*internal experiences*" (acts in the *very wide sense* of the *Logical Studies*); in so far as they are a consciousness of something they are said to be "*intentionally related*" to this something.

We must, however, be quite clear on this point that *there is no question here of a relation between a psychological event—called experience (Erlebnis)—and some other real existent (Dasein)—called Object*—or of a *psychological connexion* obtaining between the one and the other *in objective reality*. On the contrary, we are concerned with experiences in their essential purity, with *pure essences*, and with that which is *involved in* the essence "*a priori*," in *unconditioned necessity*.

That an experience is the consciousness of something: a fiction, for instance, the fiction of this or that centaur; a perception, the perception of its "real" object; a judgment, the judgment concerning its subject-matter, and so forth, this does not relate to the experimental fact as lived within the world, more specifically within some given psychological context, but to the pure essence grasped ideationally as pure idea. In the very essence of an experience lies determined not only *that*, but also *whereof* it is a consciousness, and in what determinate or indeterminate

sense it is this. So too in the essence of consciousness as dormant lies included the variety of wakeful *cogitationes*, into which it can be differentiated through the modification we have already referred to as "the noticing of what was previously unnoticed."

Under *experiences* in the *widest sense* we understand whatever is to be found in the stream of experience, not only therefore intentional experiences, *cogitationes* actual and potential taken in their full concreteness, but all the real (*reellen*) phases to be found in this stream and in its concrete sections.

For it is easily seen that *not every real phase* of the concrete unity of an intentional experience has itself the *basic character of intentionality*, the property of being a "consciousness of something." This is the case, for instance, with all sensory data, which play so great a part in the perceptive intuitions of things. In the experience of the perception of this white paper, more closely in those components of it related to the paper's quality of whiteness, we discover through properly directed noticing the sensory datum "white." This "whiteness" is something that belongs inseparably to the essence of the concrete perception, as a *real* (*reelles*) concrete constitutive portion of it. As the content which presents the whiteness of the paper as it appears to us it is the *bearer of* an intentionality, but not itself a consciousness of something. The same holds good of other data of experience, of the so-called *sensory feelings*, for instance. We shall be speaking of these at greater length in a later context.

THE "DIRECTEDNESS" OF THE PURE EGO IN THE *COGITO*, AND THE NOTICING THAT APPREHENDS

Though we are unable at this point to proceed farther with our descriptive analysis of intentional experiences in their essential nature, we would single out certain aspects as noteworthy in relation to further developments. If an intentional experience is actual, carried out, that is, after the manner of the *cogito*, the subject "directs" itself within it towards the intentional object. To the *cogito* itself belongs an immanent "glancing-towards" the object, a directedness which from another side springs forth from the "Ego," which can therefore never be absent. This glancing of the Ego towards something is in harmony with the act involved, perceptive in perception, fanciful in fancy, approving in approval, volitional in will, and so forth. This means, therefore, that this having in one's glance, in one's mental eye, which belongs to the *essence* of the *cogito*, to the act as such, is not in itself in turn a proper act, and in particular should not be confused with a perceiving (in however wide a sense this term be used), or with any other types of act related to perceptions. It should be noticed that *intentional* object of a consciousness (understood as the latter's full correlate) is by no means to be identified with *apprehended* object. We are accustomed without further thought to include the being apprehended in the concept of the object (of that generally which stands over against the subject), since in so far as we think of it and say something *about* it, we have made it into an object in the sense of something apprehended. In the widest sense of the world, apprehending an object (*Erfassen*) coincides with mindfully heeding it (*achten*), and noting its nature (*bemerken*), whether attentively as a special case, or cursorily, provided at least that these expressions are used in their customary sense. *This heeding or apprehending is not to be identified with the modus of "cogito" in general*, that of actuality, but seen more closely, with a *special act-modus* which every consciousness or every act which does not yet possess it can assume. Should it do this, its intentional object is not only known in a general way and brought within the directed glance of the mind, but is an apprehended and noted object. A turning towards a Thing, to be sure, cannot take place otherwise than in the way of apprehension, and the same holds good of all *objectivities that are "plainly presentable"*: here a turning towards (be it even in fancy) is *eo ipso* an "apprehending" and a "heeding." But in the act of valuation we are turned towards values, in acts of joy to the enjoyed, in acts of love to the beloved, in acting to the action, and *without* apprehending all this. The intentional object rather, that which is valued, enjoyed, beloved, hoped as such, the action as action, first becomes an apprehended object through a distinctively *"objectifying"* turn of *thought*. If one is turned towards some matter absorbed in appreciation, the apprehension of the matter is no doubt included in the total attitude; but it is

not the *mere* matter in general, but the matter *values* or the *value* which is (and the point will concern us more in detail later on) *the complete intentional correlate of the act of valuation*. Thus *"to be turned in appreciation towards some matter"* does not already imply *"having"* the value *"for object"* in the special sense of object apprehended, as indeed we must have the object if we are to predicate anything of it; and similarly in regard to all logical acts which are related to it.

Thus in acts like those of appreciation we have an *intentional object in a double sense*: we must distinguish between the *"subject matter"* pure and simple and the *full intentional object*, and corresponding to this, a *double intentio*, a two-fold directedness. If we are directed towards some matter in an act of appreciation, the direction towards the matter in question is a noting and apprehending of it; but we are "directed"—only not in an apprehending way—also to the value. Not merely the *representing of the matter* in question, but also the *appreciating* which includes this representing, has the modus of actuality.

But we must hasten to add that it is only in respect of simple acts of valuation that the matter stands so simply. In general, acts of sentiment and will are consolidated upon a higher level, and the intentional objectivity also differentiates itself accordingly: there is also a complicating of the ways in which the objects included in the unitary total objectivity come under the directed mental glance. But in any case the following main propositions hold good:

In every act some mode of heeding (Achtsamkeit) holds sway. But wherever it is not the plain consciousness of a subject-matter, wherever some further "attitude towards" the subject-matter is grounded in such consciousness, subject-matter and full intentional object ("subject-matter" and "value," for instance), likewise heeding the object and mentally scrutinizing it, separate out the one from the other. But at the same time the possibility of a modification remains an essential property of these grounded acts, a modification whereby their full intentional objects become noticed, and in this sense *"represented"* objects, which now, from their side, become capable of serving as bases for explanations, relations, conceptual renderings, and predications. Thanks to this objectification we find facing us in natural setting, and therefore *as members of the natural world*, not natural things merely, but values and practical objects of every kind, cities, streets with street-lighting arrangements, dwellings, furniture, works of art, books, tools and so forth. . . .

CONSCIOUSNESS AND NATURAL REALITY. THE VIEW OF THE "MAN IN THE STREET"

All the essential characteristics of experience and consciousness which we have reached are for us necessary steps towards the attainment of the end which is unceasingly drawing us on, the discovery, namely, of the essence of that *"pure" consciousness* which is to fix the limits of the phenomenological field. Our inquiries were eidetic; but the individual instances of the essences we have referred to as experience, stream of experience, "consciousness" in all its senses, belonged as real events to the natural world. To that extent we have not abandoned the ground of the natural standpoint. Individual consciousness is interwoven with the *natural world* in a *twofold* way: it is some *man's* consciousness, or that of some *man* or *beast*, and in a large number at least of its particularizations it is a consciousness of this world. *In respect now of this intimate attachment with the real world, what is meant by saying that consciousness has an essence "of its own,"* that with other consciousness it constitutes a self-contained *connexion determined purely through this, its own essence,* the connexion, namely, of the stream of consciousness? Moreover, since we can interpret consciousness in the widest sense to cover eventually whatever the concept of experience includes, the question concerns the experience-stream's own essential nature and that of all its components. To what extent, in the first place, must the *material world* be fundamentally different in kind, *excluded from the experience's own essential nature*? And if it is this, if over against all consciousness and the essential being proper to it, it is that which is *"foreign"* and *"other,"* how can consciousness be *interwoven* with it, and consequently with the whole world that is alien to consciousness? For it is easy to convince oneself that the material world is not just any portion of the natural world, but its fundamental stratum to which all

other real being is *essentially* related. It still fails to include the souls of men and animals; and the new factor which these introduce is first and foremost their "experiencing" together with their conscious relationship to the world surrounding them. *But here consciousness and thinghood form a connected whole*, connected within the particular psychological unities which we call *animalia*, and in the last resort within the *real unity of the world as a whole.* Can the unity of a whole be other than made one through the essential proper nature of its parts, which must therefore have some *community of essence* instead of a fundamental heterogeneity?

To be clear, let us seek out the ultimate sources whence the general thesis of the world which I adopt when taking up the natural standpoint draws its nourishment, thereby enabling me as a conscious being to discover over against me an existing world of things, to ascribe to myself in this world a body, and to find for myself within this world a proper place. This ultimate source is obviously *sensory experience.* For our purpose, however, it is sufficient to consider *sensory perception*, which in a certain proper sense plays among experiencing acts the part of an original experience, whence all other experiencing acts draw a chief part of their power to serve as a ground. Every perceiving consciousness has this peculiarity, that it is the consciousness of *the embodied (leibhaftigen) self-presence of an individual object*, which on its own side and in a pure logical sense of the term is an individual or some logico-categorical modification of the same. In our own instance, that of sensory perception, or, in distincter terms, perception of a world of things, the logical individual is the Thing; and it is sufficient for us to treat the perception of things as representing all other perceptions (of properties, processes, and the like).

The natural wakeful life of our Ego is a continuous perceiving, actual or potential. The world of things and our body within it are continuously present to our perception. How then does and can *Consciousness itself* separate out as a *concrete thing in itself*, from that within it, of which we are conscious, namely, the *perceived being, "standing over against"* consciousness *"in and for itself"*?

I meditate first as would the man "in the street." I see and grasp the thing itself in its bodily reality.

It is true that I sometimes deceive myself, and not only in respect of the perceived constitution of the thing, but also in respect of its being there at all. I am subject to an illusion or hallucination. The perception is not then "genuine." But if it is, if, that is, we can "confirm" its presence in the actual context of experience, eventually with the help of correct empirical thinking, then the perceived thing *is real* and itself really given, and that bodily in perception. Here perceiving considered simply as consciousness, and apart from the body and the bodily organs, appears as something in itself essenceless, an empty looking of an empty "Ego" towards the object itself which comes into contact with it in some astonishing way.

"PRIMARY" AND "SECONDARY" QUALITIES. THE BODILY GIVEN THING "MERE APPEARANCE" OF THE "PHYSICALLY TRUE"

If as a "man in the street" misled by sensibility I have indulged the inclination to spin out such thoughts as these, now, as a "man of science," I call to mind the familiar distinction between *secondary* and *primary* qualities, according to which the specific qualities of sense should be "merely subjective" and only the geometrico-physical qualities "objective." The colour and sound of a thing, its smell, its taste, and so forth, though they appear to cleave to the thing "bodily" as though belonging to its essence, are not themselves and as they appear to be, real, but mere "signs" of certain primary qualities. But if I recall familiar theories of Physics, I see at once that the meaning of such much-beloved propositions can hardly be the one which the words warrant: as though really only the "specific" sensory qualities of the perceived thing were mere appearance; which would come to saying that the "primary" qualities which remain after the *subtraction* of these same sensory qualities belonged to the same thing as it objectively and truly is, together with other such qualities which did not show forth as appearance. So understood, the old Berkeleian objection would hold good, namely, that extension, this essential nucleus of corporeality and all primary qualities, is unthinkable apart from the secondary qualities. Rather *the whole essential content of the perceived thing*, all that is present in the body, with all its qualities and all that can ever

be perceived, *is "mere appearance,"* and the *"true thing" is that of physical science*. When the latter defines the given thing exclusively through concepts such as atoms, ions, energies, and so forth, and in every case as space-filling processes whose sole *characteristica* are mathematical expressions, its reference is to *something that transcends the whole content of the thing as present to us in bodily form*. It cannot therefore mean even the thing as lying in natural sensible space; in other words, its physical space cannot be the space of the world of bodily perception: otherwise it would also fall under the Berkeleian objection.

The *"true Being"* would therefore be entirely and *fundamentally something that is defined otherwise than as that which is given in perception as corporeal reality*, which is given exclusively through its sensory determinations, among which must also be reckoned the sensori-spatial. *The thing as strictly experienced gives the mere "this," an empty X which becomes the bearer of mathematical determinations, and of the corresponding mathematical formulae* and exists not in perceptual space, but in an *"objective space,"* of which the former is the mere "symbol," *a Euclidean manifold of three dimensions that can be only symbolically represented*.

Let us then accept this. Let that which is given bodily in any perception be, as is taught there, "mere appearance," in principle "merely subjective," and yet no empty illusion. Yet that which is given in perception serves in the rigorous method of natural science for the valid determination, open to anyone to carry out and to verify through his own insight of that transcendent being whose "symbol" it is. The sensory content of that which is given in perception itself continues indeed to be reckoned as other than the true thing as it is in itself, but the *substratum*, the bearer (the empty X) of the perceived determinations still continues to count as that which is determined through exact method in the form of physical predicates. *All physical knowledge serves accordingly, and in the reverse sense, as an indicator of the course of possible experiences with the sensory things found in them and the occurrences in which they figure*. Thus it helps us to find our way about in the world of actual experience in which we all live and act.

THE REAL NATURE OF PERCEPTION AND ITS TRANSCENDENT OBJECT

All this being presupposed, *what is it, we ask, that belongs to the concrete real nature (reellen Bestande) of the perception itself, as cogitatio?* Not the physical thing, as is obvious: radically transcendent as it is, transcendent over against the whole "world of appearance." But *even the latter*, though we refer to it habitually as "merely subjective," does not belong in all its detail of things and events to the real nature of perception, but is opposed to it as "transcendent." Let us consider this more closely. We have indeed already spoken of the transcendence of the thing, but only in passing. It concerns us now to win a deeper insight into *the relation of the transcendent to the Consciousness* that knows it, and to see how this mutual connexion, which has its own riddles, is to be understood.

We shut off the whole of physics and the whole domain of theoretical thought. We remain within the framework of plain intuition and the syntheses that belong to it, including perception. It is then evident that intuition and the intuited, perception and the thing perceived, though essentially related to each other, are in principle and of necessity *not really (reell) and essentially one and united.*

We start by taking an example. Keeping this table steadily in view as I go round it, changing my position in space all the time, I have continually the consciousness of the bodily presence out there of this one and self-same table, which in itself remains unchanged throughout. But the perception of the table is one that changes continuously, it is a continuum of changing perceptions. I close my eyes. My other senses are inactive in relation to the table. I have now no perception of it. I open my eyes, and the perception returns. The perception? Let us be more accurate. Under no circumstances does it return to me individually the same. Only the table is the same, known as identical through the synthetic consciousness which connects the new perception with the recollection. The perceived thing can be, without being perceived, without my being aware of it even as potential only (in the way of inactuality, as previously described), and perhaps without itself changing at all. But the perception itself is what it is within the steady flow of consciousness, and is itself constantly in flux; the per-

ceptual now is ever passing over into the adjacent consciousness of the just-past, a new now simultaneously gleams forth, and so on. The perceived thing in general, and all its parts, aspects, and phases, whether the quality be primary or secondary, are necessarily transcendent to the perception, and on the same grounds everywhere. The colour of the thing seen is not in principle a real phase of the consciousness of colour; it appears, but even while it is appearing the appearance can and *must* be continually changing, as experience shows. The *same* colour appears "in" continuously varying patterns of *perspective colour-variations.* Similarly for every sensory quality and likewise for every spatial shape! One and the same shape (given *as* bodily the same) appears continuously ever again "in another way," in ever-differing perspective variations of shape. That is a necessary state of things, and it has obviously a more general bearing. For it is only in the interests of simplicity that we have illustrated our point by reference to a thing that appears unchanged in perception. The transfer to changes of any other sort is a perfectly simple proceeding.

An empirical consciousness of a self-same thing that looks "all-round" its object, and in so doing is continually confirming the unity of its own nature, essentially and necessarily possesses a manifold system of continuous patterns of appearance and perspective variations, in and through which all objective phases of the bodily self-given which appear in perception manifest themselves perspectively in definite continua. Every determinate feature has *its own* system of perspective variations; and for each of these features, as for the thing as a whole, the following holds good, namely, that it remains one and the same for the consciousness that in grasping it unites recollection and fresh perception synthetically together, despite interruption in the continuity of the course of actual perception. . . .

INDUBITABILITY OF IMMANENT, DUBITABILITY OF TRANSCENDENT PERCEPTION

From all this important consequences follow. Every immanent perception necessarily guarantees the existence (*Existenz*) of its object. If reflective apprehension is directed to my experience, I apprehend an absolute Self whose existence (*Dasein*) is, in principle, undeniable, that is, the insight that it does not exist is, in principle, impossible; it would be nonsense to maintain the possibility of an experience *given in such a way not* truly existing. The stream of experience which is mine, namely, of the one who is thinking, may be to ever so great an extent uncomprehended, unknown in its past and future reaches, yet so soon as I glance towards the flowing life and into the real present it flows through, and in so doing grasp myself as the pure subject of this life (what that means will expressly concern us at a later stage), I say forthwith and because I must: *I am*, this life is, I live: *cogito*.

To every stream of experience, and to every Ego as such, there belongs, in principle, the possibility of securing this self-evidence: each of us bears in himself the warrant of this absolute existence (*Dasein*) as a fundamental possibility. But is it not conceivable, one might ask, that an Ego might have only fancies in its stream of experience, that the latter might consist of nothing beyond fictive intuitions? Such an Ego would thus discover only fictive *cogitationes*; its reflexions, by the very nature of this experiential medium, would be exclusively reflexions within the imagination. But that is obvious nonsense. That which floats before the mind may be a mere fiction; the floating itself, the fiction-producing consciousness, is not itself imagined, and the possibility of a perceiving reflexion which lays hold on absolute existence belongs to its essence as it does to every experience. No nonsense lies in the possibility that all alien consciousness which I posit in the experience of empathy does not exist. But *my* empathy and my consciousness in general is given in a primordial and absolute sense, not only essentially but existentially. This privileged position holds only for oneself and for the stream of experience to which the self is related; here only is there, and must there be, anything of the nature of immanent perception.

In contrast to this, it is, as we know, an essential feature of the thing-world that no perception, however perfect it may be, gives us anything absolute within its domain; and with this the following is essentially connected, namely, that every experience (*Erfahrung*), however far it extends, leaves open the possibility that what is given, despite the persistent consciousness of its bodily self-presence, does *not* exist. It is an essentially valid law that *existence in the form of a thing is never demanded as necessary by virtue of its givenness*, but in a certain way is always *contingent*. That means: It can always happen that the further course of experience will compel us to abandon what has already been set down and justified *in the light of empirical canons of rightness*. It was, so we afterwards say, mere illusion, hallucination, merely a coherent dream, and the like. Moreover, in this sphere of given data the open possibility remains of changes in apprehension, the turning of an appearance over into one which cannot unite with it harmoniously, and therewith an influence of later empirical positions on early ones whereby the intentional objects of these earlier positings suffer, so to speak, a posthumous reconstruction—eventualities which in the sphere of subject-experience (*Erlebnis*) are essentially excluded. In the absolute sphere, opposition, illusion, and being-otherwise have no place. It is a sphere of the absolutely established (*absoluter Position*).

In every way, then, it is clear that everything which is there for me in the world of things is on grounds of principle *only a presumptive reality*; that *I myself*, on the contrary, for whom it is there (excluding that which is imputed to the thing-world "by me"), I myself or my experience in its actuality am *absolute* Reality (*Wirklichkeit*), given through a positing that is unconditioned and simply indissoluble.

The thesis of my pure Ego and its personal life, which is "necessary" and plainly indubitable, thus stands opposed to the thesis of the world which is "contingent." All corporeally given thing-like entities can also not be, no corporeally given experiencing can also not be: that is the essential law, which defines this necessity and that contingency.

Obviously then the ontic necessity of the actual present experiencing is no pure essential necessity, that is, no pure eidetic specification of an essential law; it is the necessity of a fact (*Faktum*), and called "necessity" because an essential law is involved in the fact, and here indeed in its existence as such. The ideal possibility of a reflexion which has the essential character of a self-evident unshakeable *existential* thesis has its ground in the essential nature of a pure Ego *in general* and of an experiencing *in general*.

The reflexions in which we have been indulging also make it clear that no proofs drawn from the empirical consideration of the world can be conceived which could assure us with absolute certainty of the world's existence. The world is not doubtful in the sense that there are rational grounds which might be pitted against the tremendous force of unanimous experiences, but in the sense that a doubt is *thinkable*, and this is so because the possibility of non-Being is in principle never excluded. Every empirical power, be it ever so great, can be gradually outweighed and overcome. Nothing is thereby altered in the absolute Being of experiences, indeed these remain presupposed in all this all the time.

With this conclusion our study has reached its climax. We have won the knowledge we needed. In the essential connexions it has revealed to us already involved the most important of the premises on which depend those inferences we would draw concerning the detachability in principle of the whole natural world from the domain of consciousness, the sphere in which experiences have their being; inferences in which, as we can readily convince ourselves, a central, though not fully developed, thought of the quite otherwise oriented meditations of Descartes comes at last to its own. To reach our final goal we shall need indeed to add in the sequel a few supplementary discussions, which for the rest will not trouble us too much. Meanwhile let us draw our conclusions provisionally within a compass of limited bearing.

REVIEW QUESTIONS

1. What is the general thesis of "the natural standpoint"?
2. What does Husserl mean by "bracketing"?
3. What is Husserl's attitude toward science?
4. Does Husserl's view entail solipsism? Why or why not?
5. What does Husserl mean by experiencing the world "free from all theory"? Is it possible to experience the world this way?

34

MARTIN HEIDEGGER

Martin Heidegger (1889–1976) was born in Messkirch, an agricultural community in southwest Germany. He entered the seminary to become a Jesuit priest, but was soon attracted to philosophy and transferred to the University of Freiburg. There he studied under Edmund Husserl (see Chapter 33). After graduation he became a professor at the University of Marburg, where he wrote his famous *Being and Time* (1927) and became a colleague of two of the leading Protestant theologians of the twentieth century, Rudolf Bultmann and Paul Tillich, both of whom he significantly influenced. In 1928 he was chosen as Husserl's successor at the University of Freiburg and was elected Rector of the University in 1933. For a brief period he was a member of the Nazi party, believing that it offered the best hope for the renewal of the nation. Although his reputation has been sullied by his brief support of the Nazis, there is no evidence that he shared Nazi fanatical beliefs. To his credit, he became disillusioned with the party and resigned the Rectorship and his party membership. After the war, he retired to the Black Forest where he spent his days writing. In the meantime, his work had attracted worldwide attention, and philosophers came from many countries to visit him in his mountain home.

Heidegger's thought is concerned with the question of the meaning of *being*, the question which he claims motivated the inquiries of the first philosophers but which had become neglected by subsequent philosophers. Some, such as Gilbert Ryle, would say it is a "pseudo question," for being is not a thing but a word referring to concepts that are instantiated. Heidegger disagrees and holds that we intuitively realize that there is something in the idea that a common reality underlies all reality. He then asks, Is there a particular being that is particularly suited to inquire into the meaning of being? His existential philosophy is a response to that question. Since human beings experience openness to the future and have a measure of freedom and responsibility, the question of who he is, is inescapable for him; but this question, if pursued in a correct manner, leads with equal inescapability into the question of Being in general. As Heidegger says in our reading, "Each of us is grazed at least once, perhaps more than once, by the hidden power of this question, even if he is not aware of what is happening to him."

The central question in the essay before us, "The Fundamental Question of Metaphysics," is "Why is there anything at all, rather than nothing?" Some may dismiss this as a nonsensical question, but that only shows that it is so primordial and, perhaps, unanswerable, that it seems pointless to raise it. Yet it leads us to wonder—What is the explanation of reality, of the universe, of our being here? According to Heidegger, wondering about this basic ontological question opens oneself up to the presence of Being. Heidegger traces the quest for Being back to the ancient Greeks, especially Parmenides.

Following his teacher Husserl, Heidegger uses the phenomenological method of drawing attention to salient features of experience (the phenomena), awakening us to patterns of reality that we have ignored.

FOR FURTHER READING

Guignon, C., ed. *The Cambridge Companion to Heidegger* (Cambridge University Press, 1993).

Heidegger, Martin. *Being and Time*, trans. Edward Robinson and John Macquarrie (Harper & Row, 1962).

Macquarrie, John. *Martin Heidegger* (Lutterworth Press, 1968).

Olafson, Frederick. *Heidegger and the Philosophy of Mind* (Yale University Press, 1987).

Richardson, J. *Existential Phenomenology: A Heideggerian Critique of the Cartesian Project* (Oxford University Press, 1986).

Shahan, Robert, and J. N. Mohanty, eds. *Thinking About Being: Aspects of Heidegger's Thought* (Oklahoma University Press, 1984).

Solomon, Robert, ed. *Phenomenology and Existentialism* (Harper & Row, 1972).

Speigelberg, Herbert. *The Phenomenological Movement*, 2 vols. (Martinus Nijhoff, 1960).

Stapleton, Timothy J. *Husserl and Heidegger* (SUNY Press, 1983).

THE FUNDAMENTAL QUESTION OF METAPHYSICS

Why are there essents[1] rather than nothing? That is the question. Clearly it is no ordinary question. "Why are there essents, why is there anything at all, rather than nothing?"—obviously this is the first of all questions, though not in a chronological sense. Individuals and peoples ask a good many questions in the course of their historical passage through time. They examine, explore, and test a good many things before they run into the question "Why are there essents rather than nothing?" Many men never encounter this question, if by encounter we mean not merely to hear and read about it as an interrogative formulation but to ask the question, that is, to bring it about, to raise it, to feel its inevitability.

---

[1]"Essents" = "existents," "things that are."

Reprinted from Martin Heidegger's *Introduction to Metaphysics*, translated by Ralph Mannheim (1959) by permission from Yale University Press. © Yale University Press.

And yet each of us is grazed at least once, perhaps more than once, by the hidden power of this question, even if he is not aware of what is happening to him. The question looms in moments of great despair, when things tend to lose all their weight and all meaning becomes obscured. Perhaps it will strike but once like a muffled bell that rings into our life and gradually dies away. It is present in moments of rejoicing, when all the things around us are transfigured and seem to be there for the first time, as if it might be easier to think they are not than to understand that they are and are as they are. The question is upon us in boredom, when we are equally removed from despair and joy, and everything about us seems so hopelessly commonplace that we no longer care whether anything is or is not—and with this the question "Why are there essents rather than nothing?" is evoked in a particular form.

But this question may be asked expressly, or, unrecognized as a question, it may merely pass through our lives like a brief gust of wind; it may press hard upon us, or, under one pretext or another, we may thrust it away from us and silence it. In any case it is never the question that we ask first in point of time.

But it is the first question in another sense—in regard to rank. This may be clarified in three ways. The question "Why are there essents rather than nothing?" is first in rank for us first because it is the most far reaching, second because it is the deepest, and finally because it is the most fundamental of all questions.

It is the widest of all questions. It confines itself to no particular essent of whatever kind. The question takes in everything, and this means not only everything that is present in the broadest sense but also everything that ever was or will be. The range of this question finds its limit only in nothing, in that which simply is not and never was. Everything that is not nothing is covered by this question, and ultimately even nothing itself; not because it is *something*, since after all we speak of it, but because it *is* nothing. Our question reaches out so far that we can never go further. We do not inquire into this and that, or into each essent in turn, but from the very outset into the essent as a whole, or, as we say for reasons to be discussed below: into the essent as such in its entirety.

This broadest of questions is also the deepest: Why are there essents . . . ? Why, that is to say, on what ground? from what source does the essent derive? on what ground does it stand? The question is not concerned with particulars, with what essents are and of what nature at any time, here and there, with how they can be changed, what they can be used for, and so on. The question aims at the ground of what is insofar as it is. To seek the ground is to try to get to the bottom; what is put in question is thus related to the ground. However, since the question is a question, it remains to be seen whether the ground arrived at is really a ground, that is, whether it provides a foundation; whether it is a primal ground ⟨Ur-grund⟩; or whether it fails to provide a foundation and is an abyss ⟨Ab-grund⟩; or whether the ground is neither one nor the other but presents only a perhaps necessary appearance of foundation—in other words, it is a nonground ⟨Un-grund⟩. Be that as it may, the ground in question must account for the being of the essent as such. This question "why" does not look for causes that are of the same kind and on the same level as the essent itself. This "why" does not move on any one plane but penetrates to the "underlying" ⟨"zu-grunde" liegend⟩ realms and indeed to the very last of them, to the limit; turning away from the surface, from all shallowness, it strives toward the depths; this broadest of all questions is also the deepest.

Finally, this broadest and deepest question is also the most fundamental. What do we mean by this? If we take the question in its full scope, namely the essent as such in its entirety, it readily follows that in asking this question we keep our distance from every particular and individual essent, from every this and that. For we mean the essent as a whole, without any special preference. Still, it is noteworthy that in this questioning *one* kind of essent persists in coming to the fore, namely the men who ask the question. But the question should not concern itself with any particular essent. In the spirit of its unrestricted scope, all essents are of equal value. An elephant in an Indian jungle "is" just as much as some chemical combustion process at work on the planet Mars, and so on.

Accordingly, if our question "Why are there essents rather than nothing?" is taken in its fullest sense, we must avoid singling out any special, particular essent, including man. For what indeed is man? Consider the earth within the endless darkness of space in the universe. By way of comparison it is a tiny grain of sand; between it and the next grain of its own size there extends a mile or more of emptiness; on the surface of this grain of sand there lives a crawling, bewildered swarm of supposedly intelligent animals, who for a moment have discovered knowledge.[2] And what is the temporal extension of a human life amid all the millions of years? Scarcely a move of the second hand, a breath. Within the essent as a whole there is no legitimate ground for singling out this essent which is called mankind and to which we ourselves happen to belong.

But whenever the essent as a whole enters into this question, a privileged, unique relation arises between it and the act of questioning. For through this questioning the essent as a whole is for the first time opened up *as such* with a view to its possible ground, and in the act of questioning it is kept open. In relation to the essent as such in its entirety the asking of the question is not just any occurrence within the realm of the essent, like the falling of raindrops for example. The question "why" may be said to confront the essent as a whole, to break out of it, though never completely. But that is exactly why the act of questioning is privileged. Because it confronts the essent as a whole, but does not break loose from it, the content of the question reacts upon the questioning itself. Why the why? What is the ground of this question "why" which presumes to ask after the ground of the essent as a whole? Is the ground asked for in *this* why not merely a foreground—which would imply that the sought-for ground is again an essent? Does not the "first" question nevertheless come first in view of the intrinsic rank of the question of being and its modulations?

To be sure, the things in the world, the essents, are in no way affected by our asking of the question "Why are there essents rather than nothing?" Whether we ask it or not, the planets move in their orbits, the sap of life flows through plant and animal.

But *if* this question is asked and if the act of questioning is really carried out, the content and the object of the question react inevitably on the act of questioning. Accordingly this questioning is not just any occurrence but a privileged happening that we call an *event*.

This question and all the questions immediately rooted in it, the questions in which this one question unfolds—this question "why" is incommensurable with any other. It encounters the search for its own why. At first sight the question "Why the why?" looks like a frivolous repetition ad infinitum of the same interrogative formulation, like an empty and unwarranted brooding over words. Yes, beyond a doubt, that is how it looks. The question is only whether we wish to be taken in by this superficial look and so regard the whole matter as settled, or whether we are capable of finding a significant event in this recoil of the question "why" upon itself.

But if we decline to be taken in by surface appearances we shall see that this question "why," this question as to the essent as such in its entirety, goes beyond any mere playing with words, provided we possess sufficient intellectual energy to make the question actually recoil into its "why"—for it will not do so of its own accord. In so doing we find out that this privileged question "why" has its ground in a leap through which man thrusts away all the previous security, whether real or imagined, of his life. The question is asked only in this leap; it *is* the leap; without it there is no asking. What "leap" means here will be elucidated later. Our questioning is not yet the leap; for this it must undergo a transformation; it still stands perplexed in the face of the essent. Here it may suffice to say that the leap in this questioning opens up its own source—with this leap the question arrives at its own ground. We call such a leap, which opens up its own source, the original source or origin ⟨Ur-sprung⟩, the finding of one's own ground. It is because the question "Why are there essents rather than nothing?" breaks open the ground for all authentic questions and is thus at the origin ⟨Ursprung⟩ of them all that we must recognize it as the most fundamental of all questions.

It is the most fundamental of questions because it is the broadest and deepest, and conversely.

In this threefold sense the question is the first in rank—first, that is, in the order of questioning within the domain which this first question opens, defining

---

[2]Cf. Nietzsche, *Über Wahrheit und Lüge im aussermoralischen Sinne.* 1873 *Nachlass.*

its scope and thus founding it. Our question is the *question* of all authentic questions, i.e. of all self-questioning questions, and whether consciously or not it is necessarily implicit in every question. No questioning and accordingly no single scientific "problem" can be fully intelligible if it does not include, i.e. ask, the question of all questions. Let us be clear about this from the start: it can never be objectively determined whether anyone, whether we, really ask this question, that is whether we make the leap, or never get beyond a verbal formula. In a historical setting that does not recognize questioning as a fundamental human force, the question immediately loses its rank.

Anyone for whom the Bible is divine revelation and truth has the answer to the question "Why are there essents rather than nothing?" even before it is asked: everything that is, except God himself, has been created by Him. God himself, the increate creator, "is." One who holds to such faith can in a way participate in the asking of our question, but he cannot really question without ceasing to be a believer and taking all the consequences of such a step. He will only be able to act "as if" . . . On the other hand a faith that does not perpetually expose itself to the possibility of unfaith is no faith but merely a convenience: the believer simply makes up his mind to adhere to the traditional doctrine. This is neither faith nor questioning, but the indifference of those who can busy themselves with everything, sometimes even displaying a keen interest in faith as well as questioning.

What we have said about security in faith as one position in regard to the truth does not imply that the biblical "In the beginning God created heaven and earth" is an answer to our question. Quite aside from whether these words from the Bible are true or false for faith, they can supply no answer to our question because they are in no way related to it. Indeed, they cannot even be brought into relation with our question. From the standpoint of faith our question is "foolishness."

Philosophy is this very foolishness. A "Christian philosophy" is a round square and a misunderstanding. There is, to be sure, a thinking and questioning elaboration of the world of Christian experience, i.e. of faith. That is theology. Only epochs which no longer fully believe in the true greatness of the task of theology arrive at the disastrous notion that philosophy can help to provide a refurbished theology if not a substitute for theology, which will satisfy the needs and tastes of the time. For the original Christian faith philosophy is foolishness. To philosophize is to ask "Why are there essents rather than nothing?" Really to ask the question signifies: a daring attempt to fathom this unfathomable question by disclosing what it summons us to ask, to push our questioning to the very end. Where such an attempt occurs there is philosophy.

It would not serve our purpose to begin our discussion with a detailed report on philosophy. But there are a few things that all must know who wish to concern themselves with philosophy. They can be briefly stated.

All essential philosophical questioning is necessarily untimely. This is so because philosophy is always projected far in advance of its time, or because it connects the present with its antecedent, with what *initially* was. Philosophy always remains a knowledge which not only cannot be adjusted to a given epoch but on the contrary imposes its measure upon its epoch.

Philosophy is essentially untimely because it is one of those few things that can never find an immediate echo in the present. When such an echo seems to occur, when a philosophy becomes fashionable, either it is no real philosophy or it has been misinterpreted and misused for ephemeral and extraneous purposes.

Accordingly, philosophy cannot be directly learned like manual and technical skills; it cannot be directly applied, or judged by its usefulness in the manner of economic or other professional knowledge.

But what is useless can still be a force, perhaps the only real force. What has no immediate echo in everyday life can be intimately bound up with a nation's profound historical development, and can even anticipate it. What is untimely will have its own times. This is true of philosophy. Consequently there is no way of determining once and for all what the task of philosophy is, and accordingly what must be expected of it. Every state and every beginning of its development bears within it its own law. All that can be said is what philosophy cannot be and cannot accomplish.

A question has been stated: "Why are there essents rather than nothing?" We have claimed first place for this question and explained in what sense it is regarded as first.

We have not even begun to ask the question itself, but have digressed into a discussion about it. Such a digression is indispensable. For this question has nothing in common with our habitual concerns. There is no way of familiarizing ourselves with this question by a gradual transition from the things to which we are accustomed. Hence it must, as it were, be singled out in advance, presented. Yet in introducing the question and speaking of it, we must not postpone, let alone forget, the questioning itself.

Here then let us conclude our preliminary remarks.

Every essential form of spiritual life is marked by ambiguity. The less commensurate it is with other forms, the more it is misinterpreted.

Philosophy is one of the few autonomous creative possibilities and at times necessities of man's historical being-there.[3] The current misinterpretations of philosophy, all of which have some truth about them, are legion. Here we shall mention only two, which are important because of the light they throw on the present and future situation of philosophy. The first misinterpretation asks too much of philosophy. The second distorts its function.

Roughly speaking, philosophy always aims at the first and last grounds of the essent, with particular emphasis on man himself and on the meaning and goals of human being-there. This might suggest that philosophy can and must provide a foundation on which a nation will build its historical life and culture. But this is beyond the power of philosophy. As a rule such excessive demands take the form of a belittling of philosophy. It is said, for example: Because metaphysics did nothing to pave the way for the revolution it should be rejected. This is no clever than saying that because the carpenter's bench is useless for flying it should be abolished. Philosophy can never *directly* supply the energies and create the opportunities and methods that bring about a historical change; for one thing, because philosophy is always the concern of the few. Which few? The creators, those who initiate profound transformations. It spreads only indirectly, by devious paths that can never be laid out in advance, until at last, at some future date, it sinks to the level of a commonplace; but by then it has long been forgotten as original philosophy.

What philosophy essentially can and must be is this: a thinking that breaks the paths and opens the perspectives of the knowledge that sets the norms and hierarchies, of the knowledge in which and by which a people fulfills itself historically and culturally, the knowledge that kindles and necessitates all inquiries and thereby threatens all values.

The second misinterpretation involves a distortion of the function of philosophy. Even if philosophy can provide no foundation for a culture, the argument goes, it is nevertheless a cultural force, whether because it gives us an over-all, systematic view of what is, supplying a useful chart by which we may find our way amid the various possible things and realms of things, or because it relieves the sciences of their work by reflecting on their premises, basic concepts, and principles. Philosophy is expected to promote and even to accelerate—to make easier as it were—the practical and technical business of culture.

But—it is in the very nature of philosophy never to make things easier but only more difficult. And this not merely because its language strikes the everyday understanding as strange if not insane. Rather, it is the authentic function of philosophy to challenge historical being-there and hence, in the last analysis, being pure and simple. It restores to things, to the essents, their weight (being). How so? Because the challenge is one of the essential prerequisites for the birth of all greatness, and in speaking of greatness we are referring primarily to the works and destinies of nations. We can speak of historical destiny only where an authentic knowledge of things dominates man's being-there. And it is philosophy that opens up the paths and perspectives of such knowledge.

The misinterpretations with which philosophy is perpetually beset are promoted most of all by people

---

[3]The word "Dasein" is ordinarily translated as "existence." It is used in "normal," popular discourse. But Heidegger breaks it into its components "Da" "there" and "Sein" "being," and puts his own definition on it. In general he means man's conscious, historical existence in the world, which is always projected into a there beyond its here. The German word Dasein has often been carried over into translations; the English strikes me as preferable.

of our kind, that is, by professors of philosophy. It is our customary business—which may be said to be justified and even useful—to transmit a certain knowledge of the philosophy of the past, as part of a general education. Many people suppose that this is philosophy itself, whereas at best it is the technique of philosophy.

In correcting these two misinterpretations I cannot hope to give you at one stroke a clear conception of philosophy. But I do hope that you will be on your guard when the most current judgments and even supposed observations assail you unawares. Such judgments are often disarming, precisely because they seem so natural. You hear remarks such as "Philosophy leads to nothing," "You can't do anything with philosophy," and readily imagine that they confirm an experience of your own. There is no denying the soundness of these two phrases, particularly common among scientists and teachers of science. Any attempt to refute them by proving that after all it does "lead to something" merely strengthens the prevailing misinterpretation to the effect that the everyday standards by which we judge bicycles or sulphur baths are applicable to philosophy.

It is absolutely correct and proper to say that "You can't do anything with philosophy." It is only wrong to suppose that this it the last word on philosophy. For the rejoinder imposes itself: granted that *we* cannot do anything with philosophy, might not philosophy, if we concern ourselves with it, do something *with us*? So much for what philosophy is not.

At the outset we stated a question: "Why are there essents rather than nothing?" We have maintained that to ask this question is to philosophize. When in our thinking we open our minds to this question, we first of all cease to dwell in any of the familiar realms. We set aside everything that is on the order of the day. Our question goes beyond the familiar and the things that have their place in everyday life. Nietzsche once said (*Werke, 7,* 269): "A philosopher is a man who never ceases to experience, see, hear, suspect, hope, and dream extraordinary things . . ."

To philosophize is to inquire into the *extra*-ordinary. But because, as we have just suggested, this questioning recoils upon itself, not only what is asked after is extraordinary but also the asking itself. In other words: this questioning does not lie along the way so that we bump into it one day unexpect-

edly. Nor is it part of everyday life: there is no requirement or regulation that forces us into it; it gratifies no urgent or prevailing need. The questioning itself is "out of order." It is entirely voluntary, based wholly and uniquely on the mystery of freedom, on what we have called the leap. The same Nietzsche said: "Philosophy . . . is a voluntary living amid ice and mountain heights" (*Werke, 15,* 2). To philosophize, we may now say, is an extra-ordinary inquiry into the extra-ordinary.

In the age of the earliest and crucial unfolding of Western philosophy among the Greeks, who first raised the authentic question of the essent as such in its entirety, the essent was called *physis*. This basic Greek word for the essent is customarily translated as "nature." This derives from the Latin translation, *natura,* which properly means "to be born," "birth." But with this Latin translation the original meaning of the Greek word *physis* is thrust aside, the actual philosophical force of the Greek word is destroyed. This is true not only of the Latin translation of *this* word but of all other Roman translations of the Greek philosophical language. What happened in this translation from the Greek into the Latin is not accidental and harmless; it marks the first stage in the process by which we cut ourselves off and alienated ourselves from the original essence of Greek philosophy. The Roman translation was later taken over by Christianity and the Christian Middle Ages. And the Christian Middle Ages were prolonged in modern philosophy, which, moving in the conceptual world of the Middle Ages, coined those representations and terms by means of which we still try to understand the beginnings of Western philosophy. These beginnings are regarded as something that present-day philosophers have supposedly transcended and long since left behind them.

But now let us skip over this whole process of deformation and decay and attempt to regain the unimpaired strength of language and words; for words and language are not wrappings in which things are packed for the commerce of those who write and speak. It is in words and language that things first come into being and are. For this reason the misuse of language in idle talk, in slogans and phrases, destroys our authentic relation to things. What does the word *physis* denote? It denotes self-blossoming emergence (e.g. the blossoming of a rose), opening up, unfolding, that which manifests itself in such unfolding and perseveres and endures in it; in short, the realm of things that emerge and linger on. According to the dictionary *phyein* means to grow or make to grow. But what does growing mean? Does it imply only to increase quantitatively, to become more and larger?

Physis as emergence can be observed everywhere, e.g. in celestial phenomena (the rising of the sun), in the rolling of the sea, in the growth of plants, in the coming forth of man and animal from the womb. But *physis*, the realm of that which arises, is not synonymous with these phenomena, which today we regard as part of "nature." This opening up and inward-jutting-beyond-itself ⟨in-sich-aus-sich-hinausstehen⟩ must not be taken as a process among other processes that we observe in the realm of the essent. *Physis* is being itself, by virtue of which essents become and remain observable.

The Greeks did not learn what *physis* is through natural phenomena, but the other way around: it was through a fundamental poetic and intellectual experience of being that they discovered what they had to call *physis*. It was this discovery that enabled them to gain a glimpse into nature in the restricted sense. Hence *physis* originally encompassed heaven as well as earth, the stone as well as the plant, the animal as well as man, and it encompassed human history as a work of men and the gods; and ultimately and first of all, it meant the gods themselves as subordinated to destiny. *Physis* means the power that emerges and the enduring realm under its sway. This power of emerging and enduring includes "becoming" as well as "being" in the restricted sense of inert duration. *Physis* is the process of a-rising, of emerging from the hidden, whereby the hidden is first made to stand.

But if, as is usually done, *physis* is taken not in the original sense of the power to emerge and endure, but in the later and present signification of nature; and if moreover the motion of material things, of the atoms and electrons, of what modern physics investigates as *physis*, is taken to be the fundamental manifestation of nature, then the first philosophy of the Greeks becomes a nature philosophy, in which all things are held to be of a material nature. In this case the beginning of Greek philosophy, as is perfectly proper for a beginning according to the com-

mon-sense view, gives the impression of what we, once again in Latin, designate as primitive. Thus the Greeks become essentially a higher type of Hottentot, whom modern science has left far behind. Disregarding the lesser absurdities involved in this view of the beginning of Western philosophy as something primitive, we need only say this: those who put forward such an interpretation forget that what is under discussion is philosophy, one of man's few great achievements. But what is great can only begin great. Its beginning is in fact that greatest thing of all. A small beginning belongs only to the small, whose dubious greatness it is to diminish all things; small are the beginning of decay, though it may later become great in the sense of the enormity of total annihilation.

The great begins great, maintains itself only through the free recurrence of greatness within it, and if it is great ends also in greatness. So it is with the philosophy of the Greeks. It ended in greatness with Aristotle. Only prosaic common sense and the little man imagine that the great must endure forever, and equate this duration with eternity.

The Greeks called the essent as a whole *physis*. But it should be said in passing that even within Greek philosophy a narrowing of the word set in forthwith, although the original meaning did not vanish from the experience, knowledge, and orientation of Greek philosophy. Knowledge of its original meaning still lives on in Aristotle, when he speaks of the grounds of the essent as such (see *Metaphysics,* I, 1003 a 27).

But this narrowing of *physis* in the direction of "physics" did not occur in the way that we imagine today. We oppose the psychic, the animated, the living, to the "physical." But for the Greeks all this belonged to *physis* and continued to do so even after Aristotle. They contrasted it with what they called *thesis*, thesis, ordinance, or *nomos*, law, rule in the sense of *ethos*. This, however, denotes not mere norms but mores, based on freely accepted obligations and traditions; it is that which concerns free behavior and attitudes, the shaping of man's historical being, the *ethos* which under the influence of morality was later degraded to the ethical.

The meaning of *physis* is further restricted by contrast with *technē*—which denotes neither art nor technology but a knowledge, the ability to plan and organize freely, to master institutions (cf. Plato's *Phaedrus*). *Technē* is creating, building in the sense of a deliberate pro-ducing. (It would require a special study to explain what is essentially the same in *physis* and *technē*). The physical was opposed to the historical, a domain which for the Greeks was part of the originally broader concept of *physis*. But this has nothing whatever to do with a naturalistic interpretation of history. The realm of being as such and as a whole is *physis*—i.e. its essence and character are defined as that which emerges and endures. It is experienced primarily through what in a way imposes itself most immediately on our attention, and this was the later, narrower sense of *physis: ta physei onta, ta physika*, nature. If the question concerning *physis* in general was asked at all, i.e. if it was asked: What is the realm of being as such? it was primarily *ta physei onta* that gave the point of departure. Yet from the very outset the question could not dwell in this or that realm of nature, inanimate bodies, plants, animals, but had to reach out beyond *ta physika*.

In Greek, "beyond something" is expressed by the word *meta*. Philosophical inquiry into the realm of being as such is *meta ta physika*; this inquiry goes beyond the essent, it is metaphysics. Here it is not important to follow the genesis and history of this term in detail.

Accordingly, the question to which we have given first rank, "Why are there essents rather than nothing?" is the fundamental question of metaphysics. Metaphysics is a name for the pivotal point and core of all philosophy.

[In this introduction our treatment of the entire subject has been intentionally superficial and hence essentially vague. According to our explanation of the word *physis*, it signifies the being of the essent. If the questioning is *peri physeōs*, if it concerns the being of the essent, then the discussion has gone beyond *physis*, beyond "physics" in the ancient sense, and essentially beyond *ta physika*, beyond essents, and deals with being. From the very first "physics" has determined the essence and history of metaphysics. Even in the doctrines of being as pure act (Thomas Aquinas), as absolute concept (Hegel), as eternal recurrence of the identical will to power (Nietzsche), metaphysics has remained unalterably "physics."]

But the inquiry into being as such is of a different nature and origin.

Within the purview of metaphysics and thinking on its level, we can, to be sure, consider the question about being as such as merely a mechanical repetition of the question about the essent as such. In this case the question about being as such is just another transcendental question, though one of a higher order. But this reinterpretation of the question about being as such bars the road to its appropriate unfolding.

However, this new interpretation comes readily to mind; it is bound to suggest itself, particularly as we have spoken in *Sein und Zeit* of a "transcendental horizon." But the "transcendental" there intended is not that of the subjective consciousness; rather, it defines itself in terms of the existential-ecstatic temporality of human being-there. Yet the reinterpretation of the question of being as such tends to take the same form as the question of the essent as such, chiefly because the essential origin of the question of the existent as such and with it the essence of metaphysics remain obscure. And this draws all questions that are in any way concerned with being into the indeterminate.

In the present attempt at an "introduction to metaphysics" I shall keep this confused state of affairs in mind.

In the current interpretation the "question of being" signifies the inquiry into the essent as such (metaphysics). But from the standpoint of *Sein und Zeit*, the "question of being" means the inquiry into being as such. This signification of the title is also the appropriate one from the standpoint of the subject matter and of linguistics; for the "question of being" in the sense of the metaphysical question regarding the essent as such does *not inquire* thematically into being. In this way of asking, being remains forgotten.

But just as ambiguous as the "question of being" referred to in the title is what is said about "forgetfulness of being." It is pointed out—quite correctly—that metaphysics inquires into the being of the essent and that it is therefore an obvious absurdity to impute a forgetfulness of being to metaphysics.

But if we consider the question of being in the sense of an inquiry into being as such, it becomes clear to anyone who follows our thinking that being *as such* is precisely hidden from metaphysics, and remains forgotten—and so radically that the forgetfulness of being, which itself falls into forgetfulness, is the unknown but enduring impetus to metaphysical questioning.

If for the treatment of the "question of being" in the indeterminate sense we choose the name "metaphysics," then the title of the present work is ambiguous. For at first sight the questioning seems to remain within the sphere of the assent as such, yet at the very first sentence it strives to depart from this sphere in order to consider and inquire into another realm. Actually the title of the work is deliberately ambiguous.

The fundamental question of this work is of a different kind from the leading question of metaphysics. Taking what was said in *Sein und Zeit* (pp. 21 f. and 37 f.) as a starting point, we inquired into the *"disclosure of being."* "Disclosure of being" means the unlocking of what forgetfulness of being closes and hides. And it is through this questioning that a light first falls on the *essence* of metaphysics that had hitherto also been hidden.

"Introduction to metaphysics" means accordingly: an introduction to the asking of the fundamental question. But questions and particularly fundamental questions do not just occur like stones and water. Questions are not found ready-made like shoes and clothes and books. Questions *are*, and are only as they are actually asked. A leading into the asking of the fundamental questions is consequently not a going to something that lies and stands somewhere; no, this leading-to must first awaken and create the questioning. The leading is itself a questioning advance, a preliminary questioning. It is a leading for which in the very nature of things there can be no following. When we hear of disciples, "followers," as in a school of philosophy for example, it means that the nature of questioning is misunderstood. Such schools can exist only in the domain of scientific and technical work. Here everything has its definite hierarchical order. This work is also an indispensable part of philosophy and has today been lost. But the best technical ability can never replace the actual power of seeing and inquiring and speaking.

"Why are there essents rather than nothing?" That is the question. To state the interrogative sentence, even in a tone of questioning, is not yet to question. To repeat the interrogative sentence several times in succession does not necessarily breathe life into the questioning; on the contrary, saying the sentence over and over may well dull the questioning.

But even though the interrogative sentence is not the question and not the questioning, it must not be taken as a mere linguistic form of communication, as though, for example, the interrogative sentence were only a statement "about" a question. When I say to you "Why are these essents rather than nothing?" the purpose of my speaking and questioning is not to communicate to you the fact that a process of questioning is now at work within me. The spoken interrogative sentence can of course be interpreted in this way, but this means precisely that the questioning has not been heard. In this case you do not join me in questioning, nor do you question yourself. No sign of a questioning attitude or state of mind is awakened. Such a state of mind consists in a *willing* to know. Willing—that is no mere wishing or striving. Those who wish to know also seem to question; but they do not go beyond the stating of the question; they stop precisely where the question begins. To question is to will to know. He who wills, he who puts his whole existence into a will, *is* resolved. Resolve does not shift about; it does not shirk, but acts from out of the moment and never stops. Re-solve is no mere decision to act, but the crucial beginning of action that anticipates and reaches through all action. To will is to be resolved. [The essence of willing is here carried back to determination ⟨Ent-schlossen-heit, unclosedness⟩. But the essence of resolve lies in the opening, the coming-out-of-cover ⟨Ent-borgenheit⟩ of human being-there into the clearing of being, and not in a storing up of energy for "action." See *Sein und Zeit*, § 44 and § 60. But its relation to being is of letting-be. The idea that all willing should be grounded in letting-be offends the understanding. See my lecture *Vom Wesen der Wahrheit*, 1930.]

But to know means: to be able to stand in the truth. Truth is the manifestness of the essent. To know is accordingly the ability to stand ⟨stehen⟩ in the manifestness of the essent, to endure ⟨bestehen⟩ it. Merely to have information, however abundant, is not to know. Even if curricula and examination requirements concentrate this information into what is of the greatest practical importance, it still does not amount to knowledge. Even if this information, pruned down to the most indispensable needs, is "close to life," its possession is not knowledge. The man who possesses such information and has learned a few practical tricks, will still be perplexed in the presence of real reality, which is always different from what the philistine means by down-to-earth; he will always be a bungler. Why? Because he has no knowledge, for to know means *to be able to learn.*

In the common-sense view, to be sure, knowledge belongs to the man who has no further need to learn because he has finished learning. No, only that man is knowing who understands that he must keep learning over and over again and who above all, on the basis of this understanding, has attained to the point where he is always *able to learn.* This is much more difficult than to possess information.

Ability to learn presupposes ability to inquire. Inquiry is the willing-to-know analyzed above: the resolve to be able to stand in the openness of the essent. Since we are concerned with the asking of the question that is first in rank, clearly the willing as well as the knowing is of a very special kind. So much the less will the interrogative sentence, even if it is uttered in an authentically questioning tone and even if the listener joins in the questioning, exhaustively reproduce the question. The questioning, which indeed is sounded in the interrogative sentence but which is still enclosed, wrapped up in the words, remains to be unwrapped. The questioning attitude must clarify and secure itself in this process, it must be consolidated by training.

Our next task lies in the development of the question "Why are there essents rather than nothing?" In what direction can it be asked? First of all the question is accessible in the interrogative sentence, which gives a kind of approximation of it. Hence its linguistic formulation must be correspondingly broad and loose. Let us consider our sentence in this respect. "Why are there essents rather than nothing?" The sentence has a caesura. "Why are there essents?" With these words the question is actually asked. The formulation of the question includes: 1) a definite indication of what is put into question, of what is *questioned*: 2) an indication of what the

question is about, of what is asked. For it is clearly indicated what the question is about, namely the essent. What is asked after, that which is asked, is the why, i.e. the ground. What follows in the interrogative sentence, "rather than nothing," is only an appendage, which may be said to turn up of its own accord if for purposes of introduction we permit ourselves to speak loosely, a turn of phrase that says nothing further about the question or the object of questioning, an ornamental flourish. Actually the question is far more unambiguous and definite without such an appendage, which springs only from the prolixity of loose discourse. "Why are there essents?" The addition "rather than nothing" is dropped not only because we are striving for a strict formulation of the question but even more because it says nothing. For why should we go on to ask about nothing? Nothing is simply nothing. Here there is nothing more to inquire about. And above all, in talking about nothing or nothingness, we are not making the slightest advance toward the knowledge of the essent.

He who speaks of nothing does not know what he is doing. In speaking of nothing he makes it into a something. In speaking he speaks against what he intended. He contradicts himself. But discourse that contradicts itself offends against the fundamental rule of discourse (*logos*), against "logic." To speak of nothing is illogical. He who speaks and thinks illogically is unscientific. But he who goes so far as to speak of nothing in the realm of philosophy, where logic has its very home, exposes himself most particularly to the accusation of offending against the fundamental rule of all thinking. Such a speaking about nothing consists entirely of meaningless propositions. Moreover: he who takes the nothing seriously is allying himself with nothingness. He is patently promoting the spirit of negation and serving the cause of disintegration. Not only is speaking of nothing utterly repellent to thought; it also undermines all culture and all faith. What disregards the fundamental law of thought and also destroys faith and the will to build is pure nihilism.

On the basis of such considerations we shall do well, in our interrogative sentence, to cross out the superfluous words "rather than nothing" and limit the sentence to the simple and strict form: "Why are there essents?"

To this there would be no objection if . . . if in formulating our question, if altogether, in the asking of this question, we were as free as it may have seemed to us up to this point. But in asking this question we stand in a tradition. For philosophy has always, from time immemorial, asked about the ground of what is. With this question it began and with this question it will end, provided that it ends in greatness and not in an impotent decline. Ever since the question about the essent began, the question about the nonessent, about nothing, has gone side by side with it. And not only outwardly, in the manner of a by-product. Rather, the question about nothing has been asked with the same breadth, depth, and originality as the question about the essent. The manner of asking about nothing may be regarded as a gauge and hallmark for the manner of asking about the essent.

· If we bear this in mind, the interrogative sentence uttered in the beginning, "Why are there essents rather than nothing?" seems to express the question about the essent far more adequately than the abbreviated version. It is not looseness of speech or prolixity that leads us to mention nothing. Nor is it an invention of ours; no, it is only strict observance of the original tradition regarding the meaning of the fundamental question.

Still, this speaking of nothing remains in general repellent to thought and in particular demoralizing. But what if both our concern for the fundamental rules of thought and our fear of nihilism, which both seem to counsel against speaking of nothing, should be based on a misunderstanding? And this indeed is the case. True, this misunderstanding is not accidental. It is rooted in long years of failure to understand the question about the essent. And this failure to understand arises from an increasingly hardened forgetfulness of being.

For it cannot be decided out of hand whether logic and its fundamental rules can, altogether, provide a standard for dealing with the question about the essent as such. It might be the other way around. Perhaps the whole body of logic as it is known to us, perhaps all the logic that we treat as a gift from heaven, is grounded in a very definite answer to the question about the essent; perhaps, in consequence, all thinking which solely follows the laws of thought prescribed by traditional logic is incapable from the very start of even understanding the question about the essent by its own resources, let alone actually unfolding the question and guiding it toward an answer. Actually it is only an appearance of strict, scientific method when we invoke the principle of contradiction and logic in general, in order to prove that all thinking and speaking about nothing are contradictory and therefore meaningless. In such a contention "logic" is regarded as a court of justice, established for all eternity, whose rights as first and last authority no rational man will impugn. Anyone who speaks against logic is therefore tacitly or explicitly accused of irresponsibility. And the mere accusation is taken as a proof and an argument relieving one of the need for any further, genuine reflection.

It is perfectly true that we cannot talk about nothing, as though it were a thing like the rain outside or a mountain or any object whatsoever. In principle, nothingness remains inaccessible to science. The man who wishes truly to speak about nothing must of necessity become unscientific. But this is a misfortune only so long as one supposes that scientific thinking is the only authentic rigorous thought, and that it alone can and must be made into the standard of philosophical thinking. But the reverse is true. All scientific thought is merely a derived form of philosophical thinking, which proceeded to freeze into its scientific cast. Philosophy never arises out of science or through science and it can never be accorded equal rank with the sciences. No, it is prior in rank, and not only "logically" or in a table representing the system of the sciences. Philosophy stands in a totally different realm and order. Only poetry stands in the same order as philosophy and its thinking, though poetry and thought are not the same thing. To speak of nothing will always remain a horror and an absurdity for science. But aside from the philosopher, the poet can do so—and not because, as common sense supposes, poetry is without strict rules, but because the spirit of poetry (only authentic and great poetry is meant) is essentially superior to the spirit that prevails in all mere science. By virtue of this superiority the poet always speaks as though the essent were being expressed and invoked for the first time. Poetry, like the thinking of the philosopher, has always so much world space to spare that in it each thing—a tree, a mountain, a house, the cry of a bird—loses all indifference and commonplaceness.

Authentic speaking about nothing always remains extraordinary. It cannot be vulgarized. It dissolves if it is placed in the cheap acid of a merely logical intelligence. Consequently true discourse about nothing can never be immediate like the description of a picture for example. Here I should like to cite a passage from one of Knut Hamsun's last works, *The Road Leads On*. The work forms a whole with *Vagabonds* and *August*. It describes the last years and end of this August, who embodies the uprooted modern man who can do everything equally well yet who cannot lose his ties with the extraordinary, because even in his weakness and despair he remains authentic and superior. In his last days August is alone in the high mountains. And the poet says: "Here he sits between his ears and all he hears is emptiness. An amusing conception, indeed. On the sea there were both motion and sound, something for the ear to feed upon, a chorus of waters. Here nothingness meets nothingness and the result is zero, not even a hole. Enough to make one shake one's head, utterly at a loss."[4]

We see that there is something very interesting about nothing. Let us then go back to our interrogative sentence; let us ask it through, and see whether this "rather than nothing" is merely a meaningless appendage or whether it does not have an essential meaning even in our provisional statement of the question.

Let us begin with the abbreviated, seemingly simpler, and ostensibly stricter form of the question: "Why are there essents?" When we inquire in this way, we start from the essent. The essent *is*. It is given, it confronts us; accordingly, it is to be found at any time, and it is, in certain realms, known to us. Now this essent, from which we start, is immediately questioned as to its ground. The questioning advances immediately toward a ground. Such a method is only an extension and enlargement, so to speak, of a method practiced in everyday life. Somewhere in the vineyard, for example, the vine-disease occurs; something incontestably present. We ask: where

does it come from, where and what is the reason for it, the ground? Similarly the essent as a whole is present. We ask: where and what is the ground? This manner of questioning is represented in the simple formula: Why are there essents? Where and what is their ground? Tacitly we are asking after another and higher kind of essent. But here the question is not by any means concerned with the essent as such and as a whole.

But if we put the question in the form of our original interrogative sentence: "Why are there essents rather than nothing?" this addition prevents us in our questioning from beginning directly with an unquestionably given essent and, having scarcely begun, from continuing on to another expected essent as a ground. Instead this essent, through questioning, is held out into the possibility of nonbeing. Thereby the why takes on a very different power and penetration. Why is the essent torn away from the possibility of nonbeing? Why does it not simply keep falling back into nonbeing? Now the essent is no longer that which just happens to be present; it begins to waver and oscillate, regardless of whether or not we recognize the essent in all certainty, regardless of whether or not we apprehend it in its full scope. Henceforth the essent as such oscillates, insofar as we draw it into the question. The swing of the pendulum extends to the extreme and sharpest contrary possibility, to nonbeing and nothingness. And the search for the why undergoes a parallel change. It does not aim simply at providing an also present ground and explanation for what is present; now a ground is sought which will explain the emergence of the essent as an overcoming of nothingness. The ground that is now asked after is the ground of the decision for the essent over against nothingness, or more precisely, the ground for the oscillation of the essent, which sustains and unbinds us, half being, half not being, which is also why we can belong entirely to no thing, not even to ourselves; yet being-there ⟨Dasein⟩ is in every case mine.

[The qualification "in every case mine" means that being-there is allotted to me in order that my self should be being-there. But being-there signifies: care of the ecstatically manifested being of the essent as such, not only of human being. Being-there is "in every case mine"; this means neither "posited

---

[4]Knut Hamsun, *The Road Leads On* (Coward-McCann, 1934), p. 508. Trans. Eugene Gay-Tifft.

through me" nor "apportioned to an individual ego." Being-there is *itself* by virtue of its essential relation to being in general. That is the meaning of the sentence that occurs frequently in *Sein und Zeit*: Being-there implies awareness of being.]

It is already becoming clearer that this "rather than nothing" is no superfluous appendage to the real question, but is an essential component of the whole interrogative sentence, which as a whole states an entirely different question from that intended in the question "Why are there essents?" With our question we place ourselves in the essent in such a way that it loses its self-evident character *as the essent*. The essent begins to waver between the broadest and most drastic extremes: "either essents—or nothing"—and thereby the questioning itself loses all solid foundation. Our questioning being-there is suspended, and in this suspense is nevertheless self-sustained.

But the essent is not changed by our questioning. It remains what it is and as it is. Our questioning is after all only a psycho-spiritual process in us which, whatever course it may take, cannot in any way affect the essent itself. True, the essent remains as it is manifested to us. But it cannot slough off the problematic fact that it might also *not* be what it is and as it is. We do not experience this possibility as something that we add to the essent by thinking; rather, the essent itself elicits this possibility, and in this possibility reveals itself. Our questioning only opens up the horizon, in order that the essent may dawn in such questionableness.

We still know far too little about the process of such questioning, and what we do know is far too crude. In this questioning we seem to belong entirely to ourselves. Yet it is this questioning that moves us into the open, provided that in questioning it transform itself (which all true questioning does), and cast a new space over everything and into everything.

The main thing is not to let ourselves be led astray by over-hasty theories, but to experience things as they are on the basis of the first thing that comes to hand. This piece of chalk has extension; it is a relatively solid, grayish white thing with a definite shape, and apart from all that, it is a thing to write with. This particular thing has the attribute of lying here;

but just as surely, it has the attitude of potentially not lying here and not being so large. The possibility of being guided along the blackboard and of being used up is not something that we add to the thing by thought. Itself, as this essent, is in this possibility; otherwise it would not be chalk as a writing material. Correspondingly, every essent has in it this potentiality in a different way. This potentiality belongs to the chalk. It has in itself a definite aptitude for a definite use. True, we are accustomed and inclined, in seeking this potentiality in the chalk, to say that we cannot see or touch it. But that is a prejudice, the elimination of which is part of the unfolding of our question. For the present our question is only to open up the essent in its wavering between nonbeing and being. Insofar as the essent resists the extreme possibility of nonbeing, it stands in being, but it has never caught up with or overcome the possibility of nonbeing.

We suddenly find ourselves speaking of the nonbeing and being of the essent, without saying how this being or nonbeing is related to the essent. Are the two terms the same? The essent and its being? What, for example, is "the essent" in this piece of chalk? The very question is ambiguous, because the word "the essent" can be understood in two respects, like the Greek *to on*. The essent means first *that* which is at any time, in particular this grayish white, so-and-so-shaped, light, brittle mass. But "the essent" also means that which "brings it about," so to speak, that this thing is an essent rather than a nonessent, that which constitutes its being if it *is*. In accordance with this twofold meaning of the word "the essent," the Greek *to on* often has the second significance, not the essent itself, not that which is, but "is-ness," essentness, being. Over against this, "the essent" in the first sense signifies all or particular essent things themselves, in respect to themselves and not to their is-ness, their *ousia*.

The first meaning of *to on* refers to *ta onta* (entia), the second to *to einai* (esse). We have listed what the essent is in the piece of chalk. This was relatively easy to do. It was also easy to see that the object named can also *not* be, that this chalk need ultimately not be here and not be. What then is being in distinction to what can stand in being or fall back into nonbeing—what is being in distinction to the essent? Is it the same as the essent? We ask the question once again. But in the foregoing we did not list being; we listed only material mass, grayish-white light, so-and-so-shaped, brittle. But where is the being situated? It must belong to the chalk, for this chalk *is*.

We encounter the essent everywhere; it sustains and drives us, enhances and fills us, elevates and disappoints us; but with all this, where is, and wherein consists, the being of the essent? One might reply: this distinction between the essent and its being may occasionally have an importance from the standpoint of language and even of meaning; this distinction can be effected in mere thought, i.e. in ideas and opinions, but is it certain that anything essent in the essent corresponds to the distinction? And even this merely cogitated distinction is questionable; for it remains unclear *what* is to be thought under the name of "being." Meanwhile it suffices to know the essent and secure our mastery over it. To go further and introduce being as distinct from it is artificial and leads to nothing.

We have already said a certain amount about this frequent question: What comes of such distinctions? Here we are going to concentrate on our undertaking. We ask: "Why are there essents rather than nothing?" And in this question we seemingly stick to the essent and avoid all empty brooding about being. But what really are we asking? Why the essent as such is. We are asking for the ground of the essent: that it is and is what it is, and that there is not rather nothing. Fundamentally we are asking about being. But how? We are asking about the being of the essent. We are questioning the essent in regard to its being.

But if we persevere in our questioning we shall actually be questioning forward, asking about being in respect to its ground, even if this question remains undeveloped and it remains undecided whether being itself is not in itself a ground and a sufficient ground. If we regard this question of being as the first question in order of rank, should we ask it without knowing how it stands with being and how being stands in its distinction to the essent? How shall we inquire into, not to say find, the ground for the being of the essent, if we have not adequately considered and understood being itself? This undertaking would be just as hopeless as if someone were to try to bring out the cause and ground of a fire, and yet claim that he need not worry about the actual course of the fire or examine the scene of it.

Thus it transpires that the question "Why are there essents rather than nothing?" compels us to ask the preliminary question: "How does it stand with being?"

Here we are asking about something which we barely grasp, which is scarcely more than the sound of a word for us, and which puts us in danger of serving a mere word idol when we proceed with our questioning. Hence it is all the more indispensable that we make it clear from the very outset how it stands at present with being and with our understanding of being. And in this connection the main thing is to impress it on our experience that we cannot immediately grasp the being of the essent itself, either through the essent or in the essent—or anywhere else.

A few examples may be helpful. Over there, across the street, stands the high school building. An essent. We can look over the building from all sides, we can go in and explore it from cellar to attic, and note everything we encounter in that building: corridors, staircases, schoolrooms, and their equipment. Everywhere we find essents and we even find them in a very definite arrangement. Now where is the being of this high school? For after all it *is*. The building *is*. If anything belongs to this essent, it is its being; yet we do not find the being inside it.

Nor does the being consist in the fact that we look at the essent. The building stands there even if we do not look at it. We can find it only because it already *is*. Moreover, this building's being does not by any means seem to be the same for everyone. For us, who look at it or ride by, it is different than for the pupils who sit in it; not because they see it only from within but because for them this building really is what it is and as it is. You can, as it were, smell the being of this building in your nostrils. The smell communicates the being of this essent far more immediately and truly than any description or inspection could ever do. But on the other hand the building's being is not based on this odor that is somewhere in the air.

How does it stand with being? Can you see being? We see essents; this chalk for example. But do we see being as we see color and light and shade? Or do we hear, smell, taste, feel being? We hear the motorcycle racing through the street. We hear the grouse gliding through the forest. But actually we hear only the whirring of the motor, the sound the grouse makes. As a matter of fact it is difficult to describe even the pure sound, and we do not ordinarily do so, because it is *not* what we commonly hear. [From the standpoint of sheer sound] we always hear *more*. We hear the flying bird, even though strictly speaking we should say: a grouse is nothing audible, it is no manner of tone that fits into a scale. And so it is with the other senses. We touch velvet, silk; we see them directly as this and that kind of essent, the one different from the other. Wherein lies and wherein consists being?

But we must take a wider look around us and consider the lesser and greater circle within which we spend our days and hours, wittingly and unwittingly, a circle whose limits shift continuously and which is suddenly broken through.

A heavy storm coming up in the mountains "is," or what here amounts to the same thing, "was" during the night. Wherein consists its being?

A distant mountain range under a broad sky . . . It "is." Wherein consists the being? When and to whom does it reveal itself? To the traveler who enjoys the landscape, or to the peasant who makes his living in it and from it, or to the meteorologist who is preparing a weather report? Who of these apprehends being? All and none. Or is what these men apprehend of the mountain range under the great sky only certain aspects of it, not the mountain range itself as it "is" as such, not that wherein its actual being consists? Who may be expected to apprehend this being? Or is it a non-sense, contrary to the sense of being, to inquire after what is in itself, behind those aspects? Does the being lie in the aspects?

The door of an early romanesque church is an essent. How and to whom is its being revealed? To the connoisseur of art, who examines it and photographs it on an excursion, or to the abbot who on a holiday passes through this door with his monks, or to the children who play in its shadow on a summer's day? How does it stand with the being of this essent?

A state—*is*. By virtue of the fact that the state police arrest a suspect, or that so-and-so-many typewriters are clattering in a government building, taking down the words of ministers and state secretaries? Or "is" the state in a conversation between the chancellor and the British foreign minister? The state *is*. But where is being situated? Is it situated anywhere at all?

A painting by Van Gogh. A pair of rough peasant shoes, nothing else. Actually the painting represents nothing. But as to what *is* in that picture, you are immediately alone with it as though you yourself were making your way wearily homeward with your hoe on an evening in late fall after the last potato fires have died down. What *is* here? The canvas? The brush strokes? The spots of color?

What in all these things we have just mentioned is the being of the essent? We run (or stand) around in the world with our silly subtleties and conceit. But where in all this is being?

All the things we have named *are* and yet—when we wish to apprehend being, it is always as though we were reaching into the void. The being after which we inquire is almost like nothing, and yet we have always rejected the contention that the essent in its entirety *is not*.

But being remains unfindable, almost like nothing, or ultimately *quite* so. Then, in the end, the word "being" is no more than an empty word. It means nothing real, tangible, material. Its meaning is an unreal vapor. Thus in the last analysis Nietzsche was perfectly right in calling such "highest concepts" as being "the last cloudy streak of evaporating reality." Who would want to chase after such a vapor, when the very term is merely a name for a great fallacy! "Nothing indeed has exercised a more simple power of persuasion hitherto than the error of Being . . ."[5]

"Being"—a vapor and a fallacy? What Nietzsche says here of being is no random remark thrown out in the frenzy of preparation for his central, never finished work. No, this was his guiding view of being from the earliest days of his philosophical effort. It is the fundamental support and determinant of his philosophy. Yet even now this philosophy holds its

---

[5] *The Twilight of Idols*, Nietzsche's Complete Works, Edinburgh and London, *16* (1911), 19, 22.

ground against all the crude importunities of the scribblers who cluster round him more numerous with each passing day. And so far there seems to be no end in sight to this abuse of Nietzche's work. In speaking here of Nietzsche, we mean to have nothing to do with all that—or with blind hero worship for that matter. The task in hand is too crucial and at the same time too sobering. It consists first of all, if we are to gain a true grasp of Nietzsche, in bringing his accomplishment to a full unfolding. Being a vapor, a fallacy? If this were so, the only possible consequence would be to abandon the question "Why are there essents as such and as a whole, rather than nothing?" For what good is the question if what it inquires into is only a vapor and a fallacy?

Does Nietzsche speak the truth? Or was he himself only the last victim of a long process of error and neglect, but as such the unrecognized witness to a new necessity?

Is it the fault of being that it is so involved? is it the fault of the word that it remains so empty? or are we to blame that with all our effort, with all our chasing after the essent, we have fallen out of being? And should we not say that the fault did not begin with us, or with our immediate or more remote ancestors, but lies in something that runs through Western history from the very beginning, a happening which the eyes of all the historians in the world will never perceive, but which nevertheless happens, which happened in the past and will happen in the future? What if it were possible that man, that nations in their greatest movements and traditions, are linked to being and yet had long fallen out of being, without knowing it, and that this was the most powerful and most central cause of their decline? (See *Sein und Zeit*, § 38, in particular pp. 179 f.)

We do not ask these questions incidentally, and still less do they spring from any particular outlook or state of mind; no, they are questions to which we are driven by that preliminary question which sprang necessarily from our main question "How does it stand with being?"—a sober question perhaps, but assuredly a very useless one. And yet a *question, the* question: is "being" a mere word and its meaning a vapor or is it the spiritual destiny of the Western world?

This Europe, in its ruinous blindness forever on the point of cutting its own throat, lies today in a great pincers, squeezed between Russia on one side and America on the other. From a metaphysical point of view, Russia and America are the same; the same dreary technological frenzy, the same unrestricted organization of the average man. At a time when the farthermost corner of the globe has been conquered by technology and opened to economic exploitation; when any incident whatever, regardless of where or when it occurs, can be communicated to the rest of the world at any desired speed; when the assassination of a king in France and a symphony concert in Tokyo can be "experienced" simultaneously; when time has ceased to be anything other than velocity, instantaneousness, and simultaneity, and time as history has vanished from the lives of all peoples; when a boxer is regarded as a nation's great man; when mass meetings attended by millions are looked on as a triumph—then, yes then, through all this turmoil a question still haunts us like a specter: What for?—Whither?—And what then?

The spiritual decline of the earth is so far advanced that the nations are in danger of losing the last bit of spiritual energy that makes it possible to see the decline (taken in relation to the history of "being"), and to appraise it as such. This simple observation has nothing to do with *Kulturpessimismus*, and of course it has nothing to do with any sort of optimism either; for the darkening of the world, the flight of the gods, the destruction of the earth, the transformation of men into a mass, the hatred and suspicion of everything free and creative, have assumed such proportions throughout the earth that such childish categories as pessimism and optimism have long since become absurd.

We are caught in a pincers. Situated in the center, our nation incurs the severest pressure. It is the nation with the most neighbors and hence the most endangered. With all this, it is the most metaphysical of nations. We are certain of this vocation, but our people will only be able to wrest a destiny from it if *within itself* it creates a resonance, a possibility of resonance for this vocation, and takes a creative view of its tradition. All this implies that this nation, as a historical nation, must move itself and thereby the history of the West beyond the center of their future "happening" and into the primordial realm of the powers of being. If the great decision regarding

Europe is not to bring annihilation, that decision must be made in terms of new spiritual energies unfolding historically from out of the center.

To ask "How does it stand with being"? means nothing less than to recapture, to repeat ⟨wiederholen⟩, the beginning of our historical-spiritual existence, in order to transform it into a new beginning. This is possible. It is indeed the crucial form of history, because it begins in the fundamental event. But we do not repeat a beginning by reducing it to something past and now known, which need merely be imitated; no, the beginning must be begun again, more radically, with all the strangeness, darkness, insecurity that attend a true beginning. Repetition as we understand it is anything but an improved continuation with the old methods of what has been up to now.

The question "How is it with being?" is included as a preliminary question in our central question "Why are there essents rather than nothing?" If we now begin to look into that which is questioned in our preliminary question, namely being, the full truth of Nietzsche's dictum is at once apparent. For if we look closely, what more is "being" to us than a mere word, an indeterminate meaning, intangible as a vapor? Nietzsche's judgment, to be sure, was meant in a purely disparaging sense. For him "being" is a delusion that should never have come about. Is "being," then, indeterminate, vague as a vapor? It is indeed. But we do not mean to sidestep this fact. On the contrary, we must see how much of a fact it is if we are to perceive its full implication.

Our questioning brings us into the landscape we must inhabit as a basic prerequisite, if we are to win back our roots in history. We shall have to ask why this fact, that for us "being" is no more than a word and a vapor, should have arisen precisely today, or whether and why it has existed for a long time. We must learn to see that this fact is not as harmless as it seems at first sight. For ultimately what matters is not that the word "being" remains a mere sound and its meaning a vapor, but that we have fallen away from what this word says and for the moment cannot find our way back; that it is for this and no other reason that the word "being" no longer applies to anything, that everything, if we merely take hold of it, dissolves like a tatter of cloud in the sunlight.

Because this is so—that is why we ask about being. And we *ask* because we know that truths have never fallen into any nation's lap. The fact that people still cannot and do not wish to understand this question, even if it is asked in a still more fundamental form, deprives the question of none of its cogency.

Of course we can, seemingly with great astuteness and perspicacity, revive the old familiar argument to the effect that "being" is the most universal of concepts, that it covers anything and everything, even the nothing which also, in the sense that it is thought or spoken, "is" something. Beyond the domain of this most universal concept "being," there is, in the strictest sense of the word, nothing more, on the basis of which being itself could be more closely determined. The concept of being is an ultimate. Moreover, there is a law of logic that says: the more comprehensive a concept is—and what could be more comprehensive than the concept of "being"?—the more indeterminate and empty is its content.

For every normally thinking man—and we all should like to be normal men—this reasoning is immediately and wholly convincing. But the question now arises: does the designation of being as the most universal concept strike the essence of being, or is it not from the very outset such a misinterpretation that all questioning becomes hopeless? This then is the question: can being be regarded only as the most universal concept which inevitably occurs in all special concepts, or is being of an entirely different essence, and hence anything but an object of "ontology," provided we take this word in its traditional sense?

The word "ontology" was first coined in the seventeenth century. It marks the development of the traditional doctrine of the essent into a discipline of philosophy and a branch of the philosophical system. But the traditional doctrine was an academic classification and ordering of what for Plato and Aristotle and again for Kant was a question, though no longer to be sure a primordial one. And it is in this sense that the word "ontology" is used today. Under this title each school of philosophy has set up and described a branch within its system. But we can also take the word "ontology" in the "broadest sense," "without reference to ontological directions and tendencies" (cf. *Sein und Zeit*, p. 11 top). In this case "ontology" signifies the endeavor to make being manifest itself, and to do so by way of the question "how does it stand with being?" (and not only with the essent as such). But since thus far this question has not even been heard, let alone echoed; since it has been expressly rejected by the various schools of academic philosophy, which strive for an "ontology" in the traditional sense, it may be preferable to dispense in the future with the terms "ontology" and "ontological." Two modes of questioning which, as we now see clearly, are worlds apart, should not bear the same name.

We ask the questions "how does it stand with being?" "What is the meaning of being?" *not* in order to set up an ontology on the traditional style, much less to criticize the past mistakes of ontology. We are concerned with something totally different: to restore man's historical being-there—and that always includes our own future being-there in the totality of the history allotted to us—to the domain of being, which it was originally incumbent on man to open up for himself. All this, to be sure, in the limits within which philosophy can accomplish anything.

Out of the fundamental question of metaphysics, "Why are there essents rather than nothing?" we have separated the preliminary question, "How does it stand with being?" The relation between the two questions requires clarification, for it is of a special kind. Ordinarily a preliminary question is dealt with before and outside the main question, though in reference to it. But, in principle, philosophical questions are never dealt with as though we might some day cast them aside. Here the preliminary question is not by any means outside of the main question; rather, it is the flame which burns as it were in the asking of the fundamental question; it is the flaming center of all questioning. That is to say: it is crucial for the first asking of the fundamental question that in asking its *preliminary* question we derive the decisive fundamental attitude that is here essential. That is why we have related the question of being to the destiny of Europe, where the destiny of the earth is being decided—while our own historic being there proves to be the center for Europe itself.

The question is:

Is being a mere word and its meaning a vapor, or does what is designated by the word "being" hold within it the historical destiny of the West?

To many ears the question may sound violent and exaggerated: for one might in a pinch suppose that a discussion of the question of being might be related in some very remote and indirect way to the decisive historical question of the earth, but assuredly not that the basic position and attitude of our questioning might be directly determined by the history of the human spirit on earth. And yet this relationship exists. Since our purpose is to set in motion the asking of the preliminary question, we must now show that, and to what extent, the asking of this question is an immediate and fundamental factor in the crucial historical question. For this demonstration it is necessary to anticipate an essential insight in the form of an assertion.

We maintain that this preliminary question and with it the fundamental question of metaphysics are historical questions through and through. But do not metaphysics and philosophy thereby become a historical science? Historical science after all investigates the temporal, while philosophy investigates the timeless. Philosophy is historical only insofar as it—like every work of the spirit—realizes itself in time. But in this sense the designation of metaphysical questioning as historical cannot characterize metaphysics, but merely expresses something obvious. Accordingly, the assertion is either meaningless and superfluous or else impossible, because it creates an amalgam of two fundamentally different kinds of science: philosophy and historical science.

In answer to this it must be said:

1. Metaphysics and philosophy are not sciences at all, and the fact that their questioning is basically historical cannot make them so.

2. Historical science does not determine a fundamental relation to history, but always presupposes such a relation. It is only for this reason that historical science can distort men's relation to history, which itself is always historical; or misinterpret it and degrade it to a mere knowledge of antiquities; or else deal with crucial fields in the light of this once established relation to history, and so produce cogent history. A historical relation between our historical being-there and history may become an object of knowledge and mark an advanced state of knowledge; but it need not. Moreover, all relations to history cannot be scientifically objectified and

given a place in science, and it is precisely the essential ones that cannot. Historical science can never produce the historical relation to history. It can only illuminate a relation once supplied, ground it in knowledge, which is indeed an absolute necessity for the historical being-there of a wise people, and not either an "advantage" or a "disadvantage." Because it is only in philosophy—*as distinguished from all science*—that essential relations to the realm of what is take shape, this relation *can*, indeed *must*, for us today be a fundamentally historical one.

But for an understanding of our assertion that the "metaphysical" asking of the preliminary question is historical through and through, it is above all necessary to consider this: for us history is not synonymous with the past; for the past is precisely what is no longer happening. And much less is history the merely contemporary, which never happens but merely "passes," comes and goes by. History as happening is an acting and being acted upon which pass through the *present*, which are determined from out of the future, and which take over the past. It is precisely the present that vanishes in happening.

Our asking of the fundamental question of metaphysics is historical because it opens up the process of human being-there in its essential relations—i.e. its relations to the essent as such and as a whole—opens it up to unasked possibilities, futures, and at the same time binds it back to its past beginning, so sharpening it and giving it weight in its present. In this questioning our being-there is summoned to its history in the full sense of the word, called to history and to a decision in history. And this not after the fact, in the sense that we draw ethical, ideological lessons from it. No, the basic attitude of the questioning is in itself historical; it stands and maintains itself in happening, inquiring out of happening for the sake of happening.

But we have not yet come to the essential reason why this inherently historical asking of the question about being is actually an integral part of history on earth. We have said that the world is darkening. The essential episodes of this darkening are: the flight of the gods, the destruction of the earth, the standardization of man, the pre-eminence of the mediocre.

What do we mean by world when we speak of a darkening of the world? World is always world of the *spirit*. The animal has no world nor any environment ⟨Umwelt⟩. Darkening of the world means emasculation of the spirit, the disintegration, wasting away, repression, and misinterpretation of the spirit. We shall attempt to explain the emasculation of the spirit in one respect, that of misinterpretation. We have said: Europe lies in a pincers between Russia and America, which are metaphysically the same, namely in regard to their world character and their relation to the spirit. What makes the situation of Europe all the more catastrophic is that this enfeeblement of the spirit originated in Europe itself and—though prepared by earlier factors—was definitively determined by its own spiritual situation in the first half of the nineteenth century. It was then that occurred what is popularly and succinctly called the "collapse of German idealism." This formula is a kind of shield behind which the already dawning spiritlessness, the dissolution of the spiritual energies, the rejection of all original inquiry into grounds and men's bond with the grounds, are hidden and masked. It was not German idealism that collapsed; rather, the age was no longer strong enough to stand up to the greatness, breadth, and originality of that spiritual world, i.e. truly to realize it, for to realize a philosophy means something very different from applying theorems and insights. The lives of men began to slide into a world which lacked that depth from out of which the essential always comes to man and comes back to man, so compelling him to become superior and making him act in conformity to a rank. All things sank to the same level, a surface resembling a blind mirror that no longer reflects, that casts nothing back. The prevailing dimension became that of extension and number. Intelligence no longer meant a wealth of talent, lavishly spent, and the command of energies, but only what could be learned by everyone, the practice of a routine, always associated with a certain amount of sweat and a certain amount of show. In America and in Russia this development grew into a boundless etcetera of indifference and always-the-sameness—so much so that the quantity took on a quality of its own. Since then the domination in those countries of a cross section of the indifferent mass has become something more than a dreary accident. It has become an active onslaught that destroys all rank and every world-creating impulse of the spirit, and calls it a lie. This is the onslaught of what we call the demonic (in the sense of destructive evil). There are many indications of the emergence of this demonism, identical with the increasing helplessness and uncertainty of Europe against it and within itself. One of these signs is the emasculation of the spirit through misinterpretation; we are still in the midst of this process. This misinterpretation of the spirit may be described briefly in four aspects.

1. The crux of the matter is the reinterpretation of the spirit as *intelligence*, or mere cleverness in examining and calculating given things and the possibility of changing them and complementing them to make new things. This cleverness is a matter of mere talent and practice and mass division of labor. The cleverness itself is subject to the possibility of organization, which is never true of the spirit. The attitude of the littérateur and esthete is merely a late consequence and variation of the spirit falsified into intelligence. Mere intelligence is a semblance of spirit, masking its absence.

2. The spirit falsified into intelligence thus falls to the level of a tool in the service of others, a tool the manipulation of which can be taught and learned. Whether this use of intelligence relates to the regulation and domination of the material conditions of production (as in Marxism) or in general to the intelligent ordering and explanation of everything that is present and already posited at any time (as in positivism), or whether it is applied to the organization and regulation of a nation's vital resources and race—in any case the spirit as intelligence becomes the impotent superstructure of something else, which, because it is without spirit or even opposed to the spirit, is taken for the actual reality. If the spirit is taken as intelligence, as is done in the most extreme form of Marxism, then it is perfectly correct to say, in defense against it, that in the order of the effective forces of human being-there, the spirit, i.e. intelligence, must always be ranked below healthy physical activity and character. But this order becomes false once we understand the true essence of the spirit. For all true power and beauty of the body, all sureness and boldness in combat, all authenticity and inventiveness of the understanding, are grounded

in the spirit and rise or fall only through the power or impotence of the spirit. The spirit is the sustaining, dominating principle, the first and the last, not merely an indispensable third factor.

3. As soon as the misinterpretation sets in that degrades the spirit to a tool, the energies of the spiritual process, poetry and art, statesmanship and religion, become subject to *conscious* cultivation and planning. They are split into branches. The spiritual world becomes culture and the individual strives to perfect himself in the creation and preservation of this culture. These branches become fields of free endeavor, which sets its own standards and barely manages to live up to them. These standards of production and consumption are called values. The cultural values preserve their meaning only by restricting themselves to an autonomous field: poetry for the sake of poetry, art for the sake of art, science for the sake of science.

Let us consider the example of science, which is of particular concern to us here at the university. The state of science since the turn of the century—it has remained unchanged despite a certain amount of house cleaning—is easy to see. Though today two seemingly different conceptions of science seem to combat one another—science as technical, practical, professional knowledge and science as cultural value per se—both are moving along the same downgrade of misinterpretation and emasculation of the spirit. They differ only in this: in the present situation the technical, practical conception of science as specialization can at least lay claim to frank and clear consistency, while the reactionary interpretation of science as a culture value, now making its reappearance, seeks to conceal the impotence of the spirit behind an unconscious lie. The confusion of spiritlessness can even go so far as to lead the upholders of the technical, practical view of science to profess their belief in science as a cultural value; then the two understand each other perfectly in the same spiritlessness. We may choose to call the institution where the specialized sciences are grouped together for purposes of teaching and research a university, but this is no more than a name; the "university" has ceased to be a fundamental force for unity and responsibility. What I said here in 1929, in my inaugural address, is still true of the German university:

"The scientific fields are still far apart. Their subjects are treated in fundamentally different ways. Today this hodgepodge of disciplines is held together only by the technical organization of the universities and faculties and preserves what meaning it has only through the practical aims of the different branches. The sciences have lost their roots in their essential ground." (*Was ist Metaphysik?* 1929, p. 8.) Science today in all its branches is a technical, practical business of gaining and transmitting information. An awakening of the spirit cannot take its departure from such science. It is itself in need of an awakening.

4. The last misinterpretation of the spirit is based on the above-mentioned falsifications which represent the spirit as intelligence, and intelligence as a serviceable tool which, along with its product, is situated in the realm of culture. In the end the spirit as utilitarian intelligence and the spirit as culture become holiday ornaments cultivated along with many other things. They are brought out and exhibited as a proof that there is *no* intention to combat culture or favor barbarism. In the beginning Russian Communism took a purely negative attitude but soon went over to propagandist tactics of this kind.

In opposition to this multiple misinterpretation of the spirit, we define the essence of the spirit briefly as follows (I shall quote from the address I delivered on the occasion of my appointment as rector, because of its succinct formulation): "Spirit is neither empty cleverness nor the irresponsible play of the wit, nor the boundless work of dismemberment carried on by the practical intelligence; much less is it world-reason; no, spirit is a fundamental, knowing resolve toward the essence of being." (Rektoratsrede, p. 13.) Spirit is the mobilization of the powers of the essent as such and as a whole. Where spirit prevails, the essent as such becomes always and at all times more essent. Thus the inquiry into the essent as such and as a whole, the asking of the question of being, is one of the essential and fundamental conditions for an awakening of the spirit and hence for an original world of historical being-there. It is indispensable if the peril of world darkening is to be forestalled and if our nation in the center of the Western world is to take on its historical mission. Here we can explain

only in these broad outlines why the asking of the question of being is in itself through and through historical, and why, accordingly, our question as to whether being will remain a mere vapor for us or become the destiny of the West is anything but an exaggeration and a rhetorical figure.

But if our question about being has this essential and decisive character, we must above all take an absolutely serious view of *the fact* that gives the question its immediate necessity, the fact that for us being has become little more than a mere word and its meaning an evanescent vapor. This is not the kind of fact which merely confronts us as something alien and other, which we need merely note as an occurrence. It is a fact in which we stand. It is a state of our being-there. And by state, of course, I do not mean a quality that can be demonstrated only psychologically. Here state means our entire constitution, the way in which we ourselves are constituted in regard to being. Here we are not concerned with psychology but with our history in an essential respect. When we call it a "fact" that being for us is a mere word and vapor, we are speaking very provisionally. We are merely holding fast, establishing something which has not yet been thought through, for which we still have no locus, even if it looks as though this something were an occurrence among us, here and now, or "in" us, as we like to say.

One would like to integrate the individual fact that for us being remains no more than an empty word and an evanescent vapor with the more general fact that many words, and precisely the essential ones, are in the same situation; that the language in general is worn out and used up—an indispensable but masterless means of communication that may be used as one pleases, as indifferent as a means of public transport, as a street car which everyone rides in. Everyone speaks and writes away in the language, without hindrance and above all *without danger*. That is certainly true. And only a very few are capable of thinking through the full implications of this misrelation and unrelation of present-day being-there to language.

But the emptiness of the word "being," the total disappearance of its appellative force, is not merely a particular instance of the general exhaustion of language; rather, the destroyed relation to being as such is the actual reason for the general misrelation to language.

The organizations for the purification of the language and defense against its progressive barbarization are deserving of respect. But such efforts merely demonstrate all the more clearly that we no longer know what is at stake in language. Because the destiny of language is grounded in a nation's *relation* to *being*, the question of being will involve us deeply in the question of language. It is more than an outward accident that now, as we prepare to set forth, in all its implication, the fact of the evaporation of being, we find ourselves compelled to take linguistic considerations as our starting point.

REVIEW QUESTIONS

1. Why does Heidegger think that the nature of being is the most fundamental of all questions?
2. According to Heidegger, why is Christianity incapable of answering the question "Why is there something rather than nothing?"?
3. On what grounds does Heidegger assert that a common reality (being) underlies all reality?
4. Does Heidegger disagree with Nietzsche on the importance of the question of being? If so, how?
5. What does he mean by "a darkening of the world"?

35

JEAN-PAUL SARTRE

Jean-Paul Sartre (1905–1980) was born in Paris and was a teacher in a French high school. He served in the French army during World War II, was captured by the Germans, and spent time in a prison camp reading German philosophers (especially Hegel, Husserl, and Heidegger). After the war, Sartre's plays, novels, and philosophical work, especially *Being and Nothingness* (1943), set him apart as Europe's premier existentialist. Later Sartre combined existentialism with Marxism, though he never joined the Communist party.

Here is Paul Johnson's description of the impact of Sartre and the essay we are about to read on French society:

> [On October 29, 1945 shortly after the end of the war], at the Club Maintenant, Jean-Paul Sartre delivered a lecture, "Existentialism is a Humanism." Here was the new Paris. This occasion . . . was packed. Men and women fainted, fought for chairs, smashing thirty of them, shouted and barracked. It coincided with the launching of Sartre's new review, *Les Temps Modernes*, in which he argued that literary culture, plus the haute couture of the fashion shops, were the only things France now had left—a symbol of Europe, really—and he produced Existentialism to give people a bit of dignity and to preserve their individuality in the midst of degradation and absurdity. The response was overwhelming. As his consort, Simone de Beauvoir, put it, "We were astounded by the furor we caused." Existentialism was remarkably un-Gallic; hence perhaps, its attractiveness. Sartre was half-Alsacian (Albert Schweitzer was his cousin) and he was brought up in the house of his grandfather, Karl Schweitzer. His culture was as much German as French. He was essentially a product of the Berlin school and especially Heidegger, from whom most of his ideas derived. . . . Thus Existentialism was a French cultural import, which Paris then reexported to Germany, its country of origin, in a sophisticated and vastly more attractive guise.[1]

---

[1]Paul Johnson, *Modern Times*, (Harper & Row, 1983), p. 575f.

In our first selection, "Bad Faith," from *Being and Nothingness*, Sartre contrasts "bad faith" with authenticity (good faith). He argues that any attempt to deny our freedom, to identify ourselves with our roles in society, our gender, race, or religion, is to act in bad faith. Authenticity is to acknowledge one's freedom at every moment of existence.

In our second selection, "Existentialism and Humanism," Sartre sets forth the broader principles of atheistic existentialism: that we are completely free; that since there is no God to give us an essence, we must create our own essence; that we are completely responsible for our actions, and are responsible for everyone else too; that because of the death of God and the human predicament, which leaves us totally free to create our values and our world, we must exist in anguish, forlornness, and despair. Yet there is a certain celebration and optimism in knowing that we are creators of our own values.

In this essay you will come across Sartre's notion that "existence precedes essence." This is a difficult idea, but he seems to mean something like the following. If you have an idea of something in your mind first and then create it, we would say that the idea (essence) of the thing precedes the actuality or existence of it. But if the thing existed before any idea of it, then its existence precedes its essence. If there were a God who created us, who had us in mind, we would have an essence (in terms of a function or purpose) and our existence would succeed our essence, but since, according to Sartre, there is no God to create us, we simply find ourselves existing and must create our own essence (i.e., give ourselves a function or purpose).

FOR FURTHER READING

Barrett, William. *Irrational Man* (Doubleday, 1958).

Caws, Peter. *Sartre* (Routledge, Chapman and Hall, 1984).

Kaufmann, Walter, ed. *Existentialism from Dostoevsky to Sartre* (New American Library, 1975).

Murdoch, Iris. *Sartre, Romantic Rationalist* (Viking Penguin, 1987).

Sartre, Jean Paul. *Being and Nothingness*, trans. H. Barnes (Philosophical Library, 1956).

Sartre, Jean Paul. *Existentialism and Human Emotions*, trans. B. Frechtman (Philosophical Library, 1947).

Schilpp, P. A. *The Philosophy of Jean-Paul Sartre* (Open Court, 1981).

Silverman, Hugh, and Frederick Elliston, eds. *Jean-Paul Sartre: Contemporary Approaches to His Philosophy* (Duquesne University Press, 1980).

BEING AND NOTHINGNESS

BAD FAITH

I. BAD FAITH AND FALSEHOOD

The human being is not only the being by whom *négattés* are disclosed in the world; he is also the one who can take negative attitudes with respect to himself. In our Introduction we defined consciousness as "a being such that in its being, its being is in question in so far as this being implies a being other than itself." But now that we have examined the meaning of "the question," we can at present also write the formula thus: "Consciousness is a being, the nature

Reprinted from Jean Paul Sartre, *Being and Nothingness*, translated by Hazel Barnes (1956) by permission of Philosophical Library.

of which is to be conscious of the nothingness of its being." In a prohibition or a veto, for example, the human being denies a future transcendence. But this negation is not explicative. My consciousness is not restricted to *envisioning a négatité*. It constitutes itself in its own flesh as the nihilation of a possibility. For that reason it must arise in the world as a *No*; it is as a No that the slave first apprehends the master, or that the prisoner who is trying to escape sees the guard who is watching him. There are even men (*e.g.*, caretakers, overseers, gaolers), whose social reality is uniquely that of the No, who will live and die, having forever been only a No upon the earth. Others, so as to make the No a part of their very subjectivity, establish their human personality as a perpetual negation. This is the meaning and function of what Scheler calls "the man of resentment"—in reality, the No. But there exist more subtle behaviors, the description of which will lead us further into the inwardness of consciousness. Irony is one of these. In irony a man annihilates what he posits within one and the same act; he leads us to believe in order not to be believed; he affirms to deny and denies to affirm; he creates a positive object but it has no being other than its nothingness. Thus attitudes of negation toward the self permit us to raise a new question: What are we to say is the being of man who has the possibility of denying himself? But it is out of the question to discuss the attitude of "self-negation" in its universality. The kinds of behavior which can be ranked under this heading are too diverse; we risk retaining only the abstract form of them. It is best to choose and to examine one determined attitude which is essential to human reality and which is such that consciousness instead of directing its negation outward turns it toward itself. This attitude, it seems to me, is *bad faith* (*mauvaise foi*).

Frequently this is identified with falsehood. We say indifferently of a person that he shows signs of bad faith or that he lies to himself. We shall willingly grant that bad faith is a lie to oneself, on condition that we distinguish the lie to oneself from lying in general. Lying is a negative attitude, we will agree to that. But this negation does not bear on consciousness itself; it aims only at the transcendent. The essence of the lie implies in fact that the liar actually is in complete possession of the truth which

he is hiding. A man does not lie about what he is ignorant of; he does not lie when he spreads an error of which he himself is the dupe; he does not lie when he is mistaken. The ideal description of the liar would be a cynical consciousness, affirming truth within himself, denying it in his words, and denying that negation as such. Now this double negative attitude rests on the transcendent; the fact expressed is transcendent since it does not exist, and the original negation rests on a *truth*; that is, on a particular type of transcendence. As for the inner negation which I effect correlatively with the affirmation for myself of the truth, this rests on *words*; that is, on an event in the world. Furthermore the inner disposition of the liar is positive; it could be the object of an affirmative judgment. The liar intends to deceive and he does not seek to hide this intention from himself nor to disguise the translucency of consciousness; on the contrary, he has recourse to it when there is a question of deciding secondary behavior. It explicitly exercises a regulatory control over all attitudes. As for his flaunted intention of telling the truth ("I'd never want to deceive you! This is true! I swear it!")—all this, of course, is the object of an inner negation, but also it is not recognized by the liar as *his* intention. It is played, imitated, it is the intention of the character which he plays in the eyes of his questioner, but this character, precisely because he *does not exist*, is a transcendent. Thus the lie does not put into the play the inner structure of present consciousness; all the negations which constitute it bear on objects which by this fact are removed from consciousness. The lie then does not require special ontological foundation, and the explanations which the existence of negation in general requires are valid without change in the case of deceit. Of course we have described the ideal lie; doubtless it happens often enough that the liar is more or less the victim of his lie, that he half persuades himself of it. But these common, popular forms of the lie are also degenerate aspects of it; they represent intermediaries between falsehood and bad faith. The lie is a behavior of transcendence.

The lie is also a normal phenomenon of what Heidegger calls the *"mit-sein."*[1] It presupposes my existence, the existence of the *Other*, my existence

---

[1] Tr. A "being-with" others in the world.

for the Other, and the existence of the Other *for* me. Thus there is no difficulty in holding that the liar must make the project of the lie in entire clarity and that he must possess a complete comprehension of the lie and of the truth which he is altering. It is sufficient that an overall opacity hide his intentions from the *Other*; it is sufficient that the Other can take the lie for truth. By the lie consciousness affirms that it exists by nature as *hidden from the Other*; it utilizes for its own profit the ontological duality of myself and myself in the eyes of the Other.

The situation can not be the same for bad faith if this, as we have said, is indeed a lie to oneself. To be sure, the one who practices bad faith is hiding a displeasing truth or presenting as truth a pleasing untruth. Bad faith then has in appearance the structure of falsehood. Only what changes everything is the fact that in bad faith it is from myself that I am hiding the truth. Thus the duality of the deceiver and the deceived does not exist here. Bad faith on the contrary implies in essence the unity of a *single* consciousness. This does not mean that it can not be conditioned by the *mit-sein* like all other phenomena of human reality, but the *mit-sein* can call forth bad faith only by presenting itself as *a situation* which bad faith permits surpassing; bad faith does not come from outside to human reality. One does not undergo his bad faith; one is not infected with it; it is not a *state*. But consciousness affects itself with bad faith. There must be an original intention and a project of bad faith; this project implies a comprehension of bad faith as such and a pre-reflective apprehension (of) consciousness as affecting itself with bad faith. It follows first that the one to whom the lie is told and the one who lies are one and the same person, which means that I must know in my capacity as deceiver the truth which is hidden from me in my capacity as the one deceived. Better yet I must know the truth very exactly *in order* to conceal it more carefully—and this not at two different moments, which at a pinch would allow us to re-establish a semblance of duality—but in the unitary structure of a single project. How then can the lie subsist if the duality which conditions it is suppressed?

To this difficulty is added another which is derived from the total translucency of consciousness. That which affects itself with bad faith must be conscious (of) its bad faith since the being of consciousness is consciousness of being. It appears then that I must be in good faith, at least to the extent that I am conscious of my bad faith. But then this whole psychic system is annihilated. We must agree in fact that if I deliberately and cynically attempt to lie to myself, I fail completely in this undertaking; the lie falls back and collapses beneath my look; it is ruined *from behind* by the very consciousness of lying to myself which pitilessly constitutes itself well within my project as its very condition. We have here an *evanescent* phenomenon which exists only in and through its own differentiation. To be sure, these phenomena are frequent and we shall see that there is in fact an "evanescence" of bad faith, which, it is evident, vacillates continually between good faith and cynicism: Even though the existence of bad faith is very precarious, and though it belongs to the kind of psychic structures which we might call *metastable*, it presents nonetheless an autonomous and durable form. It can even be the normal aspect of life for a very great number of people. A person can *live* in bad faith, which does not mean that he does not have abrupt awakenings to cynicism or to good faith, but which implies a constant and particular style of life. Our embarrassment then appears extreme since we can neither reject nor comprehend bad faith.

II. PATTERNS OF BAD FAITH

If we wish to get out of this difficulty, we should examine more closely the patterns of bad faith and attempt a description of them. This description will permit us perhaps to fix more exactly the conditions for the possibility of bad faith; that is, to reply to the questions we raised at the outset: "What must be the being of man if he is to be capable of bad faith?"

Take the example of a woman who has consented to go out with a particular man for the first time. She knows very well the intentions which the man who is speaking to her cherishes regarding her. She knows also that it will be necessary sooner or later for her to make a decision. But she does not want to realize the urgency; she concerns herself only with what is respectful and discreet in the attitude of her companion. She does not apprehend this conduct as an attempt to achieve what we call "the first approach"; that is, she does not want to see possibilities of temporal development which his conduct presents. She restricts this behavior to what is in the present; she does not wish to read in the phrases which he addresses to her anything other than their explicit meaning. If he says to her, "I find you so attractive!" she disarms this phrase of its sexual background; she attaches to the conversation and to the behavior of the speaker, the immediate meanings, which she images as objective qualities. The man who is speaking to her appears to her sincere and respectful as the table is round or square, as the wall coloring is blue or gray. The qualities thus attached to the person she is listening to are in this way fixed in a permanence like that of things, which is no other than the projection of the strict present of the qualities into the temporal flux. This is because she does not quite know what she wants. She is profoundly aware of the desire which she inspires, but the desire cruel and naked would humiliate and horrify her. Yet she would find no charm in a respect which would be only respect. In order to satisfy her, there must be a feeling which is addressed wholly to her *personality*—i.e., to her full freedom—and which would be a recognition of her freedom. But at the same time this feeling must be wholly desire; that is, it must address itself to her body as object. This time then she refuses to apprehend the desire for what it is; she does not even give it a name; she recognizes it only to the extent that it transcends itself toward admiration, esteem, respect and that it is wholly absorbed in the more refined forms which it produces, to the extent of no longer figuring anymore as a sort of warmth and density. But then suppose he takes her hand. This act of her companion risks changing the situation by calling for an immediate decision. To leave the hand there is to consent in herself to flirt, to engage herself. To withdraw it is to break the troubled and unstable harmony which gives the hour its charm. The aim is to postpone the moment of decision as long as possible. We know what happens next; the young woman leaves her hand there, but she *does not notice* that she is leaving it. She does not notice because it happens by chance that she is at this moment all intellect. She draws her companion up to the most lofty regions of sentimental speculation; she speaks of Life, of her life, she shows herself in her essential aspect—a personality, a consciousness. And during this time the divorce of the body from the soul is accomplished; the hand rests

inert between the warm hands of her companion—neither consenting nor resisting—a thing.

We shall say that this woman is in bad faith. But we see immediately that she uses various procedures in order to maintain herself in this bad faith. She has disarmed the actions of her companion by reducing them to being only what they are; that is, to existing in the mode of the in-itself. But she permits herself to enjoy his desire, to the extent that she will apprehend it as not being what it is, will recognize its transcendence. Finally while sensing profoundly the presence of her own body—to the point of being aroused, perhaps—she realizes herself as *not being* her own body, and she contemplates it as though from above as a passive object to which events can *happen* but which can neither provoke them nor avoid them because all its possibilities are outside of it. What unity do we find in these various aspects of bad faith? It is a certain art of forming contradictory concepts which unite in themselves both an idea and the negation of that idea. The basic concept which is thus engendered utilizes the double property of the human being, who is at once a *facticity* and a *transcendence*. These two aspects of human reality are and ought to be capable of a valid coordination. But bad faith does not wish either to coordinate them or to surmount them in a synthesis. Bad faith seeks to affirm their identity while preserving their differences. It must affirm facticity as *being* transcendence and transcendence as *being* facticity, in such a way that at the instant when a person apprehends the one, he can find himself abruptly faced with the other.

We can find the prototype of formulae of bad faith in certain famous expressions which have been rightly conceived to produce their whole effect in a spirit of bad faith. Take for example the title of a work by Jacques Chardonne, *Love Is Much More than Love*. We see here how unity is established between *present* love in its facticity—"the contact of two skins," sensuality, egoism, Proust's mechanism of jealousy, Adler's battle of the sexes, *etc.*—and love as transcendence—Mauriac's "river of fire," the longing for the infinite, Plato's *eros*, Lawrence's deep cosmic intuition, *etc.* Here we leave facticity to find ourselves suddenly beyond the present and the factual condition of man, beyond the psychological, in the heart of metaphysics. On the other hand, the title of a play by Sarment, *I Am Too Great for My-*

self, which also presents characters in bad faith, throws us first into full transcendence in order suddenly to imprison us within the narrow limits of our factual essence. We will discover this structure again in the famous sentence: "He has become what he was" or in its no less famous opposite: "Eternity at last changes each man into himself." It is well understood that these various formulae have only the appearance of bad faith; they have been conceived in this paradoxical form explicitly to shock the mind and discountenance it by an enigma. But it is precisely this appearance which is of concern to us. What counts here is that the formulae do not constitute new, solidly structured ideas; on the contrary, they are formed so as to remain in perpetual disintegration and so that we may slide at any time from naturalistic present to transcendence and *vice versa*.

We can see the use which bad faith can make of these judgments which all aim at establishing that I am not what I am. If I were only what I *am*, I could, for example, seriously consider an adverse criticism which someone makes of me, question myself scrupulously, and perhaps be compelled to recognize the truth in it. But thanks to transcendence, I am not subject to all that I am. I do not even have to discuss the justice of the reproach. As Suzanne says to Figaro, "To prove that I am right would be to recognize that I can be wrong." I am on a plane where no reproach can touch me since what I really am is my transcendence. I flee from myself, I escape myself, I leave my tattered garment in the hands of the fault-finder. But the ambiguity necessary for bad faith comes from the fact that I affirm here that I *am* my transcendence in the mode of being of a thing. It is only thus, in fact, that I can feel that I escape all reproaches. It is in the sense that our young woman purifies the desire of anything humiliating by being willing to consider it only as pure transcendence, which she avoids even naming. But inversely "I Am Too Great for Myself," while showing our transcendence changed into facticity, is the source of an infinity of excuses for our failures or our weaknesses. Similarly the young coquette maintains transcendence to the extent that the respect, the esteem manifested by the actions of her admirer are already on the plane of the transcendent. But she arrests this transcendence, she glues it down with all the facticity of the present; respect is nothing other than respect, it is an arrested surpassing which no longer surpasses itself toward anything.

But although this *metastable* concept of "transcendence-facticity" is one of the most basic instruments of bad faith, it is not the only one of its kind. We can equally well use another kind of duplicity derived from human reality which we will express roughly by saying that its being-for-itself implies complementarily a being-for-others. Upon any one of my conducts it is always possible to converge two looks, mine and that of the Other. The conduct will not present exactly the same structure in each case. But as we shall see later, as each look perceives it, there is between these two aspects of my being, no difference between appearance and being—as if I were to my self the truth of myself and as if the Other possessed only a deformed image of me. The equal dignity of being, possessed by my being-for-others and by my being-for-myself, permits a perpetually disintegrating synthesis and a perpetual game of escape from the for-itself to the for-others and from the for-others to the for-itself. We have seen also the use which our young lady made of our being-in-the-midst-of-the-world—*i.e.*, of our inert presence as a passive object among other objects—in order to relieve herself suddenly from the functions of her being-in-the-world—that is, from the being which causes there to be a world by projecting itself beyond the world towards its own possibilities. Let us note finally the confusing syntheses which play on the nihilating ambiguity of these temporal ekstases, affirming at once that I am what I have been (the man who deliberately *arrests himself* at one period in his life and refuses to take into consideration the later changes) and that I am not what I have been (the man who in the face of reproaches or rancor dissociates himself from his past by insisting on his freedom and on his perpetual re-creation). In all these concepts, which have only a transitive role in the reasoning and which are eliminated from the conclusion (like the imaginaries in the computations of physicists), we find again the same structure. We have to deal with human reality as a being which is what it is not and which is not what it is.

But what exactly is necessary in order for these concepts of disintegration to be able to receive even a pretence of existence, in order for them to be able to appear for an instant to consciousness, even in a process of evanescence? A quick examination of the idea of sincerity, the antithesis of bad faith, will be very instructive in this connection. Actually sincerity presents itself as a demand and consequently is not a *state*. Now what is the ideal to be attained in this case? It is necessary that a man be *for himself* only what he *is*. But is this not precisely the definition of the in-itself—or if you prefer—the principle of identity? To posit as an ideal the being of things, is this not to assert by the same stroke that this being does not belong to human reality and that the principle of identity, far from being a universal axiom universally applied, is only a synthetic principle enjoying a merely regional universality? Thus in order that the concepts of bad faith can put us under illusion at least for an instant, in order that the candor of "pure hearts" (*cf.* Gide, Kessel) can have validity for human reality as an ideal, the principle of identity must not represent a constitutive principle of human reality and human reality must not be necessarily what it is but must be able to be what it is not. What does this mean?

If man is what he is, bad faith is forever impossible and candor ceases to be his ideal and becomes instead his being. But is man what he is? And more generally, how can he *be* what he is when he exists as consciousness of being? If candor or sincerity is a universal value, it is evident that the maxim "one must be what one is" does not serve solely as a regulating principle for judgments and concepts by which I express what I am. It posits not merely an ideal of knowing but an ideal of *being*; it proposes for us an absolute equivalent of being with itself as a prototype of being. In this sense it is necessary that we *make ourselves* what we are. But what *are we* then if we have the constant obligations to make ourselves what we are, if our mode of being is having the obligation to be what we are?

Let us consider this waiter in the café. His movement is quick and forward, a little too precise, a little too rapid. He comes toward the patrons with a step a little too quick. He bends forward a little too eagerly; his voice, his eyes express an interest a little too solicitous for the order of the customer. Finally there he returns, trying to imitate in his walk the inflexible stiffness of some kind of automaton while carrying his tray with the recklessness of a tight-rope-walker by putting it in a perpetually unstable, perpetually broken equilibrium which he perpetually re-establishes by a light movement of the arm and hand. All his behavior seems to us a game. He applies himself to chaining his movements as if they were mechanisms, the one regulating the other; his gestures and even his voice seem to be mechanisms; he gives himself the quickness and pitiless rapidity of things. He is playing, he is amusing himself. But what is he playing? We need not watch long before we can explain it: he is playing at *being* a waiter in a café. There is nothing there to surprise us. The game is a kind of marking out and investigation. The child plays with his body in order to explore it, to take inventory of it; the waiter in the café plays with his condition in order to *realize* it. This obligation is not different from that which is imposed on all tradesmen. Their condition is wholly one of ceremony. The public demands of them that they realize it as a ceremony; there is the dance of the grocer, of the tailor, of the auctioneer, by which they endeavor to persuade their clientele that they are nothing but a grocer, an auctioneer, a tailor. A grocer who dreams is offensive to the buyer, because such a grocer is not wholly a grocer. Society demands that he limit himself to his function as a grocer, just as the soldier at attention makes himself into a soldier-thing with a direct regard which does not see at all, which is no longer meant to see, since it is the rule and not the interest of the moment which determines the point he must fix his eyes on (the sight "fixed at ten paces"). There are indeed many precautions to imprison a man in what he is, as if we lived in perpetual fear that he might escape from it, that he might break away and suddenly elude his condition.

In a parallel situation, from within, the waiter in the café can not be immediately a café waiter in the sense that this inkwell *is* an inkwell, or the glass is a glass. It is by no means that he can not form reflective judgments or concepts concerning his condition. He knows well what it "means": the obligation of getting up at five o'clock, of sweeping the floor of the shop before the restaurant opens, of starting the coffee pot going, *etc.* He knows the rights which it allows: the right to the tips, the right to belong to a union, *etc.* But all these concepts, all these judgments refer to the transcendent. It is a matter of abstract possibilities, of rights and duties conferred on a "person possessing rights." And it is precisely this person *who I have to be* (if I am the waiter in question) and who I am not. It is not that I do not wish to be this person or that I want this person to be different. But rather there is no common measure between his being and mine. It is a "representation" for others and for myself, which means that I can be he only in *representation*. But if I represent myself as him, I am not he; I am separated from him as the object from the subject, separated *by nothing*, but this nothing isolates me from him. I can not be he, I can only play *at being* him; that is, imagine to myself that I am he. And thereby I affect him with nothingness. In vain do I fulfill the functions of a café waiter. I can be he only in the neutralized mode, as the actor is Hamlet, by mechanically making the *typical gestures* of my state and by aiming at myself as an imaginary café waiter through those gestures taken as an "analogue." What I attempt to realize is a being-in-itself of the café waiter, as if it were not just in my power to confer their value and their urgency upon my duties and the rights of my position, as if it were not my free choice to get up each morning at five o'clock or to remain in bed, even though it meant getting fired. As if from the very fact that I sustain this role in existence I did not transcend it on every side, as if I did not constitute myself as one *beyond* my condition. Yet there is no doubt that I *am* in a sense a café waiter—otherwise could I not just as well call myself a diplomat or a reporter? But if I am one, this can not be in the mode of being in-itself. I am a waiter in the mode of *being what I am not*.

Furthermore we are dealing with more than mere social positions; I am never any one of my attitudes, any one of my actions. The good speaker is the one who *plays* at speaking, because he can not *be speaking*. The attentive pupil who wishes to *be* attentive, his eyes riveted on the teacher, his ears wide open, so exhausts himself in playing the attentive role that he ends up by no longer hearing anything. Perpetually absent to my body, to my acts, I am despite myself that "divine absence" of which Valéry speaks. I can not say either that I *am* here or that I *am* not here, in the sense that we say "that box of matches

is on the table"; this would be to confuse my "being-in-the-world" with a "being-in-the-midst-of-the-world." Nor that I *am* standing, nor that I *am* seated; this would be to confuse my body with the idiosyncratic totality of which it is only one of the structures. On all sides I escape being and yet—I am. . . .

Consciousness of the Other is what it is not.

Furthermore the being of my own consciousness does not appear to be as the consciousness of the Other. It *is* because it makes itself, since its being is consciousness of being. But this means that making sustains being; consciousness has to be its own being, it is never sustained by being; it sustains being in the heart of subjectivity, which means once again that it is inhabited by being but that it is not being: *consciousness is not what it is.*

Under these conditions what can be the significance of the ideal of sincerity except as a task impossible to achieve, of which the very meaning is in contradiction with the structure of my consciousness. To be sincere, we said, is to be what one is. That supposes that I am not originally what I am. But here naturally Kant's "You ought, therefore you can" is implicitly understood. I can *become* sincere; this is what my duty and my effort to achieve sincerity imply. But we definitely establish that the original structure of "not being what one is" renders impossible in advance all movement toward being in itself or "being what one is." And this impossibility is not hidden from consciousness; on the contrary, it is the very stuff of consciousness; it is the embarrassing constraint which we constantly experience; it is our very incapacity to recognize ourselves, to constitute ourselves as being what we are. It is this necessity which means that, as soon as we posit ourselves as a certain being, by a legitimate judgment, based on inner experience or correctly deduced from a *priori* or empirical premises, then by that very positing we surpass this being—and that not toward another being but toward emptiness, toward *nothing*.

How then can we blame another for not being sincere or rejoice in our own sincerity since this sincerity appears to us at the same time to be impossible? How can we in conversation, in confession, in introspection, even attempt sincerity since the effort will be by its very nature be doomed to failure and since at the very time when we announce it we have a prejudicative comprehension of its futility? In introspection I try to determine exactly what I am, to make up my mind to be my true self without delay—even though it means consequently to set about searching for ways to change myself. But what does this mean if not that I am constituting myself as a thing? Shall I determine the ensemble of purposes and motivations which have pushed me to do this or that action? But this is already to postulate a causal determinism which constitutes the flow of my states of consciousness as a succession of physical states. Shall I uncover in myself "drives," even though it be to affirm them in shame? But is this not deliberately to forget that these drives are realized with my consent, that they are not forces of nature but that I lend them their efficacy by a perpetually renewed decision concerning their value. Shall I pass judgment on my character, on my nature? Is this not to veil from myself at that moment what I know only too well, that I thus judge a past to which by definition my present is not subject? The proof of this is that the same man who in sincerity posits that he is what in actuality he was, is indignant at the reproach of another and tries to disarm it by asserting that he can no longer be what he was. We are readily astonished and upset when the penalties of the court affect a man who in his new freedom *is no longer* the guilty person he was. But at the same time we require of this man that he recognize himself as *being* this guilty one. What then is sincerity except precisely a phenomenon of bad faith? Have we not shown indeed that in bad faith human reality is constituted as a being which is what it is not and which is not what it is?

Let us take an example: A homosexual frequently has an intolerable feeling of guilt, and his whole existence is determined in relation to this feeling. One will readily foresee that he is in bad faith. In fact it frequently happens that this man, while recognizing his homosexual inclination, while avowing each and every particular misdeed which he has committed, refuses with all his strength to consider himself "*a paederast.*" His case is always "different," peculiar; there enters into it something of a game, of chance, of bad luck; the mistakes are all in the past; they are explained by a certain conception of the beautiful which women can not satisfy; we should see in them the results of a restless search, rather than the manifestations of a deeply rooted tendency, etc., etc. Here is assuredly a man in bad faith who borders on the comic since, acknowledging all the facts which are imputed to him, he refuses to draw from them the conclusion which they impose. His friend, who is his most severe critic, becomes irritated with this duplicity. The critic asks only one thing—and perhaps then he will show himself indulgent: that the guilty one recognize himself as guilty, that the homosexual declare frankly—whether humbly or boastfully matters little—"I am a paederast." We ask here: Who is in bad faith? The homosexual or the champion of sincerity?

The homosexual recognizes his faults, but he struggles with all his strength against the crushing view that his mistakes constitute for him a *destiny*. He does not wish to let himself be considered as a thing. He has an obscure but strong feeling that an homosexual is not an homosexual as this table is a table or as this red-haired man is red-haired. It seems to him that he has escaped from each mistake as soon as he has posited it and recognized it; he even feels that the psychic duration by itself cleanses him from each misdeed, constitutes for him an undetermined future, causes him to be born anew. Is he wrong? Does he not recognize in himself the peculiar, irreducible character of human reality? His attitude includes then an undeniable comprehension of truth. But at the same time he needs this perpetual rebirth, this constant escape in order to live; he must constantly put himself beyond reach in order to avoid the terrible judgment of collectivity. Thus he plays on the word *being*. He would be right actually if he understood the phrase, "I am not a paederast" in the sense of "I am not what I am." That is, if he declared to himself, "To the extent that a pattern of conduct is defined as the conduct of a paederast and to the extent that I have adopted this conduct, I am a paederast. But to the extent that human reality can not be finally defined by patterns of conduct, I am not one." But instead he slides surreptitiously towards a different connotation of the word "being." He understands "not being" in the sense of "not-being-in-itself." He lays claim to "not being a paederast" in the sense in which this table *is not* an inkwell. He is in bad faith.

But the champion of sincerity is not ignorant of the transcendence of human reality, and he knows how at need to appeal to it for his own advantage. He makes use of it even and brings it up in the present argument. Does he not wish, first in the name of sincerity, then of freedom, that the homosexual reflect on himself and acknowledge himself as an homosexual? Does he not let the other understand that such a confession will win indulgence for him? What does this mean if not that the man who will acknowledge himself as an homosexual will no longer be the same as the homosexual whom he acknowledges being and that he will escape into the region of freedom and of good will? The critic asks the man then to be what he is in order no longer to be what he is. It is the profound meaning of the saying, "A sin confessed is half pardoned." The critic demands of the guilty one that he constitute himself as a thing, precisely in order no longer to treat him as a thing. And this contradiction is constitutive of the demand of sincerity. Who can not see how offensive to the Other and how reassuring for me is a statement such as, "He's just a paederast," which removes a disturbing freedom from a trait and which aims at henceforth constituting all the acts of the Other as consequences following strictly from his essence. That is actually what the critic is demanding of his victim—that he constitute himself as a thing, that he should entrust his freedom to his friend as a fief, in order that the friend should return it to him subsequently—like a suzerain to his vassal. The champion of sincerity is in bad faith to the degree that in order to reassure himself, he pretends to judge, to the extent that he demands that freedom as freedom constitute itself as a thing. We have here only one episode in that battle to the death of consciousnesses which Hegel calls "the relation of the master and the slave." A person appeals to another and demands that in the name of his nature as consciousness he should radically destroy himself as consciousness, but while making this appeal he leads the other to hope for a rebirth beyond this destruction.

Very well, someone will say, but our man is abusing sincerity, playing one side against the other. We should not look for sincerity in the relation of the *Mit-sein* but rather where it is pure—in the relations of a person with himself. But who can not see that

objective sincerity is constituted in the same way? Who can not see that the sincere man constitutes himself as a thing in order to escape the condition of a thing by the same act of sincerity? The man who confesses that he is evil has exchanged his disturbing "freedom-for-evil" for an inanimate character of evil; he *is* evil, he clings to himself, he is what he is. But by the same stroke, he escapes from that *thing*, since it is he who contemplates it, since it depends on him to maintain it under his glance or to let it collapse in an infinity of particular acts. He derives a *merit* from his sincerity, and the deserving man is not the evil man as he is evil but as he is beyond his evilness. At the same time the evil is disarmed since it is nothing, save on the plane of determinism, and since in confessing it, I posit my freedom in respect to it; my future is virgin; everything is allowed to me.

Thus the essential structure of sincerity does not differ from that of bad faith since the sincere man constitutes himself as what he is *in order not to be it*. This explains the truth recognized by all that one can fall into bad faith through being sincere. As Valéry pointed out, this is the case with Stendhal. Total, constant sincerity as a constant effort to adhere to oneself is by nature a constant effort to dissociate oneself from oneself. A person frees himself from himself by the very act by which he makes himself an object for himself. To draw up a perpetual inventory of what one is means constantly to redeny oneself and to take refuge in a sphere where one is no longer anything but a pure, free regard. The goal of bad faith, as we said, is to put oneself out of reach; it is an escape. Now we see that we must use the same terms to define sincerity. What does this mean?

In the final analysis the goal of sincerity and the goal of bad faith are not so different. To be sure, there is a sincerity which bears on the past and which does not concern us here; I am sincere if I confess *having had* this pleasure or that intention. We shall see that if this sincerity is possible, it is because in his fall into the past, the being of man is constituted as a being-in-itself. But here our concern is only with the sincerity which aims at itself in present immanence. What is its goal? To bring me to confess to myself what I am in order that I may finally coincide with my being; in a word, to cause myself to be, in the mode of the in-itself, what I am in the mode of "not being what I am." Its assumption is that fundamentally I am already, in the mode of the in-itself, what I have to be. Thus we find at the base of sincerity a continual game of mirror and reflection, a perpetual passage from the being which is what it is, to the being which is not what it is and inversely from the being which is not what it is to the being which is what it is. And what is the goal of bad faith? To cause me to be what I am, in the mode of "not being what one is," or not to be what I am in the mode of "being what one is." We find here the same game of mirrors. In fact in order for me to have an intention of sincerity, I must at the outset simultaneously be and not be what I am. Sincerity does not assign to me a mode of being or a particular quality, but in relation to that quality it aims at making me pass from one mode of being to another mode of being. This second mode of being, the ideal of sincerity, I am prevented by nature from attaining; and at the very moment when I struggle to attain it, I have a vague prejudicative comprehension that I shall not attain it. But all the same, in order for me to be able to conceive an intention in bad faith, I must have such a nature that within my being I escape from my being. If I were sad or cowardly in the way in which this inkwell is an inkwell, the possibility of bad faith could not even be conceived. Not only should I be unable to escape from my being; I could not even imagine that I could escape from it. But if bad faith is possible by virtue of a simple project, it is because so far as my being is concerned, there is no difference between being and non-being if I am cut off from my project.

Bad faith is possible only because sincerity is conscious of missing its goal inevitably, due to its very nature. I can try to apprehend myself as "*not being cowardly*," when I am so, only on condition that the "being cowardly" is itself "in question" at the very moment when it exists, on condition that it is itself *one* question, that at the very moment when I wish to apprehend it, it escapes me on all sides and annihilates itself. The condition under which I can attempt an effort in bad faith is that in one sense, I am not this coward which I do not wish to be. But if I were not cowardly in the simple mode of not-being-what-one-is-not, I would be "in good faith" by de-

claring that I am not cowardly. Thus this inapprehensible coward is evanescent; in order for me not to be cowardly, I must in some way also be cowardly. That does not mean that I must be "a little" cowardly, in the sense that "a little" signifies "to a certain degree cowardly—and not cowardly to a certain degree." No. I must at once both be and not be totally and in all respects a coward. Thus in this case bad faith requires that I should not be what I am; that is, that there be an imponderable difference separating being from non-being in the mode of being of human reality.

But bad faith is not restricted to denying the qualities which I possess, to not seeing the being which I am. It attempts also to constitute myself as being what I am not. It apprehends me positively as courageous when I am not so. And that is possible, once again, only if I am what I am not; that is, if non-being in me does not have being even as non-being. Of course necessarily I *am not* courageous; otherwise bad faith would not be *bad* faith. But in addition my effort in bad faith must include the ontological comprehension that even in my usual being what I *am*, I am not it really and that there is no such difference between the being of "being-sad," for example— which I am in the mode of not being what I am—and the "non-being" of not-being-courageous which I wish to hide from myself. Moreover it is particularly requisite that the very negation of being should be itself the object of a perpetual nihilation, that the very meaning of "non-being" be perpetually in question in human reality. If I were not courageous in the way in which this inkwell is not a table; that is, if I were isolated in my cowardice, propped firmly against it, incapable of putting it in relation to its opposite, if I were not capable of *determining* myself as cowardly—that is, to deny courage to myself and thereby to escape my cowardice in the very moment that I posit it—if it were not on principle *impossible* for me to coincide with my *not-being-courageous* as well as with my being-courageous—then any project of bad faith would be prohibited me. Thus in order for bad faith to be possible, sincerity itself must be in bad faith. The condition of the possibility for bad faith is that human reality, in its most immediate being, in the intrastructure of the pre-reflective *cogito*, must be what it is not and not be what it is.

III. THE "FAITH" OF BAD FAITH

We have indicated for the moment only those conditions which render bad faith conceivable, the structures of being which permit us to form concepts of bad faith. We can not limit ourselves to these considerations; we have not yet distinguished bad faith from falsehood. The two-faced concepts which we have described would without a doubt be utilized by a liar to discountenance his questioner, although their two-faced quality being established on the being of a man and not on some empirical circumstance, can and ought to be evident to all. The true problem of bad faith stems evidently from the fact that bad faith is *faith*. It can not be either a cynical lie or certainty—if certainty is the intuitive possession of the object. But if we take belief as meaning the adherence of being to its object when the object is not given or is given indistinctly, then bad faith is belief; and the essential problem of bad faith is a problem of belief.

How can we believe by bad faith in the concepts which we forge expressly to persuade ourselves? We must note in fact that the project of bad faith must be itself in bad faith. I am not only in bad faith at the end of my effort when I have constructed my two-faced concepts and when I have persuaded myself. In truth, I have not persuaded myself; to the extent that I could be so persuaded, I have always been so. And at the very moment when I was disposed to put myself in bad faith, I of necessity was in bad faith with respect to this same disposition. For me to have represented it to myself as bad faith would have been cynicism; to believe it sincerely innocent would have been in good faith. The decision to be in bad faith does not dare to speak its name; it believes itself and does not believe itself in bad faith; it believes itself and does not believe itself in good faith. It is this which from the upsurge of bad faith, determines the later attitude and, as it were, the *Weltanschauung* of bad faith.

Bad faith does not hold the norms and criteria of truth as they are accepted by the critical thought of good faith. What it decides first, in fact, is the nature of truth. With bad faith a truth appears, a method of thinking, a type of being which is like that of objects; the ontological characteristic of the world of bad faith with which the subject suddenly surrounds

himself is this: that here being is what it is not, and is not what it is. Consequently a peculiar type of evidence appears; *non-persuasive* evidence. Bad faith apprehends evidence but it is resigned in advance to not being fulfilled by this evidence, to not being persuaded and transformed into good faith. It makes itself humble and modest; it is not ignorant, it says, that faith is decision and that after each intuition, it must decide and *will what it is*. Thus bad faith in its primitive project and in its coming into the world decides on the exact nature of its requirement. It stands forth in the firm resolution *not to demand too much*, to count itself satisfied when it is barely persuaded, to force itself in decisions to adhere to uncertain truths. This original project of bad faith is a decision in bad faith on the nature of faith. Let us understand clearly that there is no question of a reflective, voluntary decision, but of a spontaneous determination of our being. One *puts oneself* in bad faith as one goes to sleep and one is in bad faith as one dreams. Once this mode of being has been realized, it is as difficult to get out of it as to wake oneself up; bad faith is a type of being in the world, like waking or dreaming, which by itself tends to perpetuate itself, although its structure is of the *metastable* type. But bad faith is conscious of its structure, and it has taken precautions by deciding that the metastable structure is the structure of being and that non-persuasion is the structure of all convictions. It follows that if bad faith is faith and if it includes in its original project its own negation (it determines itself to be not quite convinced in order to convince itself that I am what I am not), then to start with, a faith which wishes itself to be not quite convinced must be possible. What are the conditions for the possibility of such a faith?

I believe that my friend Pierre feels friendship for me. I believe it in *good faith*. I believe it but I do not have for it any self-evident intuition, for the nature of the object does not lend itself to intuition. I *believe it*; that is, I allow myself to give into all impulses to trust it; I decide to believe in it, and to maintain myself in this decision; I conduct myself, finally, as if I were certain of it—and all this in the synthetic unity of one and the same attitude. This which I define as good faith is what Hegel would call the *immediate*. It is simple faith. Hegel would demonstrate at once that the immediate calls for mediation and that belief by becoming *belief for itself*, passes to the state of non-belief. If I *believe* that my friend Pierre likes me, this means that his friendship appears to me as the meaning of all his acts. Belief is a particular consciousness of *the meaning* of Pierre's acts. But if I know that I believe, the belief appears to me as pure subjective determination without external correlative. This is what makes the very word "to believe" a term utilized indifferently to indicate the unwavering firmness of belief ("My God, I believe in you") and its character as disarmed and strictly subjective ("Is Pierre my friend? I do not know; I believe so.") But the nature of consciousness is such that in it the mediate and the immediate are one and the same being. To believe is to know that one believes, and to know that one believes is no longer to believe. Thus to believe is not to believe any longer because that is only to believe—this in the unity of one and the same nonthetic self-consciousness. To be sure, we have here forced the description of the phenomenon by designating it with the word to *know*; non-thetic consciousness is not to *know*. But it is in its very translucency at the origin of all knowing. Thus the non-thetic consciousness (of) believing is destructive of belief. But at the same time the very law of the pre-reflective *cogito* implies that the being of believing ought to be the consciousness of believing.

Thus belief is a being which questions its own being, which can realize itself only in its destruction, which can manifest itself to itself only by denying itself. It is a being for which to be is to appear and to appear is to deny itself. To believe is not-to-believe. We see that reason for it; the being of consciousness is to exist by itself, then to make itself be and thereby to pass beyond itself. In this sense consciousness is perpetually escaping itself, belief becomes non-belief, the immediate becomes mediation, the absolute becomes relative, and the relative becomes absolute. The ideal of good faith (to believe what one believes) is, like that of sincerity (to be what one is), an ideal of being-in-itself. Every belief is a belief that falls short; one never wholly believes what one believes. Consequently the primitive project of bad faith is only the utilization of this self-destruction of the fact or consciousness. If every belief in good faith is an impossible belief, then there is a place for every impossible belief. My inability

to *believe* that I am courageous will not discourage me since every belief involves not quite believing. I shall define this impossible belief as *my* belief. To be sure, I shall not be able to hide from myself that I believe in order not to believe and that I do not believe *in order to* believe. But the subtle, total annihilation of bad faith by itself can not surprise me; it exists at the basis of all faith. What is it then? At the moment when I wish to believe myself courageous I *know* that I am a coward. And this certainly would come to destroy my belief. But *first*, I *am* not any more courageous than cowardly, if we are to understand this in the mode of being of the-in-itself. In the second place, I do not *know* that I am courageous; such a view of myself can be accompanied only by *belief*, for it surpasses pure reflective certitude. In the third place, it is very true that bad faith does not succeed in believing what it wishes to believe. But it is precisely as the acceptance of not believing what it believes that it is bad faith. Good faith wishes to flee the "not-believing-what-one-believes" by finding refuge in being. Bad faith flees being by taking refuse in "not-believing-what-one-believes." It has disarmed all beliefs in advance—those which it would like to take hold of and, by the same stroke, the others, those which it wishes to flee. In *willing* this self-destruction of belief, from which science escapes by searching for evidence, it ruins the beliefs which are opposed to it, which reveal themselves as *being only* belief. Thus we can better understand the original phenomenon of bad faith.

In bad faith there is no cynical lie nor knowing preparation for deceitful concepts. But the first act of bad faith is to flee what it can not flee, to flee what it is. The very project of flight reveals to bad faith an inner disintegration in the heart of being, and it is this disintegration which bad faith wishes to be. In truth, the two immediate attitudes which we can take in the face of our being are conditioned by the very nature of this being and its immediate relation with the in-itself. Good faith seeks to flee the inner disintegration of my being in the direction of the in-itself which it should be and is not. Bad faith seeks to flee the in-itself by means of the inner disintegration of my being. But it denies this very disintegration as it denies that it is itself bad faith. Bad faith seeks by means of "not-being-what-one is" to escape from the in-itself which I am not in the mode of being what one is not. It denies itself as bad faith and aims at the in-itself which I am not in the mode of "not-being-what-one-is not."[2] If bad faith is possible, it is because it is an immediate, permanent threat to every project of the human being; it is because consciousness conceals in its being a permanent risk

of bad faith. The origin of this risk is the fact that the nature of conscious simultaneously is to be what it is not and not to be what it is. In the light of these remarks we can now approach the ontological study of consciousness, not as the totality of the human being, but as the instantaneous nucleus of this being.

---

[2]If it is indifferent whether one is in good or in bad faith, because bad faith reapprehends good faith and slides to the very origin of the project of good faith, that does not mean

that we can not radically escape bad faith. But this supposes a self-recovery of being which was previously corrupted. This self-recovery we shall call authenticity, the description of which has no place here.

EXISTENTIALISM AND HUMANISM

What is meant by the term *existentialism*?

Most people who use the word would be rather embarrassed if they had to explain it, since, now that the word is all the rage, even the work of a musician or painter is being called existentialist. . . . It seems that for want of an advance-guard doctrine analogous to surrealism, the kind of people who are eager for scandal and flurry turn to this philosophy which in other respects does not at all serve their purposes in this sphere.

Actually, it is the least scandalous, the most austere of doctrines. It is intended strictly for specialists and philosophers. Yet it can be defined easily. What complicates matters is that there are two kinds of existentialists; first, those who are Christian, among whom I would include Jaspers and Gabriel Marcel, both Catholic; and on the other hand, the atheistic existentialists, among whom I class Heidegger, and then the French existentialists and myself. What they have in common is that they think that existence precedes essence, or, if you prefer, that subjectivity must be the starting point.

Just what does that mean? Let us consider some object that is manufactured, for example, a book or paper-cutter: here is an object which has been made by an artisan whose inspiration came from a concept. He referred to the concept of what a paper-

cutter is and likewise to a known method of production, which is part of the concept, something which is, by and large, a routine. Thus, the paper-cutter is at once an object produced in a certain way and, on the other hand, one having a specific use; and one cannot postulate a man who produces a paper-cutter but does not know what it is used for. Therefore, let us say that, for the paper-cutter, essence—that is, the ensemble of both the production routines and the properties which enable it to be both produced and defined—precedes existence. Thus, the presence of the paper-cutter or book in front of me is determined. Therefore, we have here a technical view of the world whereby it can be said that production precedes existence.

When we conceive God as the Creator, He is generally thought of as a superior sort of artisan. Whatever doctrine we may be considering, whether one like that of Descartes or that of Leibnitz, we always grant that will more or less follows understanding or, at the very least, accompanies it, and that when God creates He knows exactly what He is creating. Thus, the concept of man in the mind of God is comparable to the concept of paper-cutter in the mind of the manufacturer, and, following certain techniques and a conception, God produces man, just as the artisan, following a definition and a technique, makes a

Reprinted from Jean Paul Sartre, *Existentialism*, translated by Bernard Frechtman (1947) by permission of Philosophical Library.

paper-cutter. Thus, the individual man is the realization of a certain concept in the divine intelligence.

In the eighteenth century, the atheism of the *philosophes* discarded the idea of God, but not so much for the notion that essence precedes existence. To a certain extent, this idea is found everywhere; we find it in Diderot, in Voltaire, and even in Kant. Man has a human nature; this human nature, which is the concept of the human, is found in all men, which means that each man is a particular example of a universal concept, man. In Kant, the result of this universality is that the wild-man, the natural man, as well as the bourgeois, are circumscribed by the same definition and have the same basic qualities. Thus, here too the essence of man precedes the historical existence that we find in nature.

Atheistic existentialism, which I represent, is more coherent. It states that if God does not exist, there is at least one being in whom existence precedes essence, a being who exists before he can be defined by any concept, and that this being is man, or, as Heidegger says, human reality. What is meant here by saying that existence precedes essence? It means that, first of all, man exists, turns up, appears on the scene, and, only afterwards, defines himself. If man, as the existentialist conceives him, is indefinable, it is because at first he is nothing. Only afterward will he be something, and he himself will have made what he will be. Thus, there is no human nature, since there is no God to conceive it. Not only is man what he conceives himself to be, but he is also only what he wills himself to be after this thrust toward existence.

Man is nothing else but what he makes of himself. Such is the first principle of existentialism. It is also what is called subjectivity, the name we are labeled with when charges are brought against us. But what do we mean by this, if not that man has a greater dignity than a stone or table? For we mean that man first exists, that is, that man first of all is the being in the future. Man is at the start a plan which is aware of itself, rather than a patch of moss, a piece of garbage, or a cauliflower; nothing exists prior to this plan; there is nothing in heaven; man will be what he will have planned to be. Not what he will want to be. Because by the word "will" we generally mean a conscious decision, which is subsequent to what we have already made of ourselves. I may want to belong to a politi-

cal party, write a book, get married; but all that is only a manifestation of an earlier, more spontaneous choice that is called "will." But if existence really does precede essence, man is responsible for what he is. Thus, existentialism's first move is to make every man aware of what he is and to make the full responsibility of his existence rest on him. And when we say that a man is responsible for himself, we do not only mean that he is responsible for his own individuality, but that he is responsible for all men.

The word subjectivism has two meanings, and our opponents play on the two. Subjectivism means, on the one hand, that an individual chooses and makes himself; and, on the other, that it is impossible for man to transcend human subjectivity. The second of these is the essential meaning of existentialism. When we say that man chooses his own self, we mean that every one of us does likewise; but we also mean by that that in making this choice he also chooses all men. In fact, in creating the man that we want to be, there is not a single one of our acts which does not at the same time create an image of man as we think he ought to be. To choose to be this or that is to affirm at the same time the value of what we choose, because we can never choose evil. We always choose the good, and nothing can be good for us without being good for all.

If, on the other hand, existence precedes essence, and if we grant that we exist and fashion our image at one and the same time, the image is valid for everybody and for our whole age. Thus, our responsibility is much greater than we might have supposed, because it involves all mankind. If I am a workingman and choose to join a Christian trade-union rather than be a communist, and if by being a member I want to show that the best thing for man is resignation, that the kingdom of man is not of this world, I am not only involving my own case—I want to be resigned for everyone. As a result, my action has involved all humanity. To take a more individual matter, if I want to marry, to have children; even if this marriage depends solely on my own circumstances or passion or wish, I am involving all humanity in monogamy and not merely myself. Therefore, I an responsible for myself and for everyone else. I am creating a certain image of man of my own choosing. In choosing myself, I choose man.

This helps us understand what the actual content is of such rather grandiloquent words as anguish, forlornness, despair. As you will see, it's all quite simple.

First, what is meant by anguish? The existentialists say at once that man is anguish. What that means is this: the man who involves himself and who realizes that he is not only the person he chooses to be, but also a law-maker who is, at the same time, choosing all mankind as well as himself, cannot help escape the feeling of his total and deep responsibility. Of course, there are many people who are not anxious; but we claim that they are hiding their anxiety, that they are fleeing from it. Certainly, many people believe that when they do something, they themselves are the only ones involved, and when someone says to them, "What if everyone acted that way?" they shrug their shoulders and answer, "Everyone doesn't act that way." But really, one should always ask himself, "What would happen if everybody looked at things that way?" There is no escaping this disturbing thought except by a kind of double-dealing. A man who lies and makes excuses for himself by saying "not everybody does that," is someone with an uneasy conscience, because the act of lying implies that a universal value is conferred upon the lie.

Anguish is evident even when it conceals itself. This is the anguish that Kierkegaard called the anguish of Abraham. You know the story: an angel has ordered Abraham to sacrifice his son; if it really were an angel who has come and said, "You are Abraham, you shall sacrifice your son," everything would be all right. But everyone might first wonder, "Is it really an angel, and am I really Abraham? What proof do I have?" . . .

Now, I'm not being singled out as an Abraham, and yet at every moment I'm obliged to perform exemplary acts. For every man, everything happens as if all mankind had its eyes fixed on him and were guiding itself by what he does. And every man ought to say to himself, "Am I really the kind of man who has the right to act in such a way that humanity might guide itself by my actions?" And if he does not say that to himself, he is masking his anguish.

There is no question here of the kind of anguish which would lead to quietism, to inaction. It is a matter of a simple sort of anguish that anybody who has had responsibilities is familiar with. For example, when a military officer takes the responsibility for an attack and sends a certain number of men to death, he chooses to do so, and in the main he alone makes the choice. Doubtless, orders come from above, but they are too broad; he interprets them, and on this interpretation depend the lives of ten or fourteen or twenty men. In making a decision he cannot help having a certain anguish. All leaders know this anguish. That doesn't keep them from acting; on the contrary, it is the very condition of their action. For it implies that they envisage a number of possibilities, and when they choose one, they realize that it has value only because it is chosen. We shall see that this kind of anguish, which is the kind that existentialism describes, is explained, in addition, by a direct responsibility to the other men whom it involves. It is not a curtain separating us from action, but is part of action itself.

When we speak of forlornness, a term Heidegger was fond of, we mean only that God does not exist and that we have to face all the consequences of this. The existentialist is strongly opposed to a certain kind of secular ethics which would like to abolish God with the least possible expense. About 1880, some French teachers tried to set up a secular ethics which went something like this: God is a useless and costly hypothesis; we are discarding it, but meanwhile, in order for there to be an ethics, a society, a civilization, it is essential that certain values be taken seriously and that they be considered as having an *a priori* existence. It must be obligatory, *a priori*, to be honest, not to lie, not to beat your wife, to have children, etc., etc. So we're going to try a little device which will make it possible to show that values exist all the same, inscribed in a heaven of ideas, though otherwise God does not exist. In other words—and this, I believe, is the tendency of everything called reformism in France—nothing will be changed if God does not exist. We shall find ourselves with the same norms of honesty, progress, and humanism, and we shall have made of God an outdated hypothesis which will peacefully die off by itself.

The existentialist, on the contrary, thinks it very distressing that God does not exist, because all possibility of finding values in a heaven of ideas disappears along with Him; there can be no longer an *a priori* Good, since there is no infinite and perfect consciousness to think it. Nowhere is it written that the Good exists, that we must be honest, that we must not lie; because the fact is we are on a plane where there are only men. Dostoievsky said, "If God didn't exist, everything would be possible." That is the very starting point of existentialism. Indeed, everything is permissible if God does not exist, and as a result man is forlorn, because neither within him nor without does he find anything to cling to. He can't start making excuses for himself.

If existence really does precede essence, there is no explaining things away by reference to a fixed and given human nature. In other words, there is no determinism, man is free, man is freedom. On the other hand, if God does not exist, we find no values or commands to turn to which legitimize our conduct. So, in the bright realm of values, we have no excuse behind us, no justification before us. We are alone, with no excuses.

That is the idea I shall try to convey when I say that man is condemned to be free. Condemned, because he did not create himself, yet, in other respects is free; because, once thrown into the world, he is responsible for everything he does. The existentialist does not believe in the power of passion. He will never agree that a sweeping passion is a ravaging torrent which fatally leads a man to certain acts and is therefore an excuse. He thinks that man is responsible for his passion.

The existentialist does not think that man is going to help himself by finding in the world some omen by which to orient himself. Because he thinks that man will interpret the omen to suit himself. Therefore, he thinks that man, with no support and no aid, is condemned every moment to invent man. Ponge, in a very fine article, has said, "Man is the future of man." That's exactly it. But if it is taken to mean that this future is recorded in heaven, that God sees it, then it is false, because it would really no longer be a future. If it is taken to mean that, whatever a man may be, there is a future to be forged, a virgin future before him, then this remark is sound. But then we are forlorn.

To give you an example which will enable you to understand forlornness better, I shall cite the case of one of my students who came to see me under the following circumstances: his father was on bad terms with his mother, and, moreover, was inclined to be a collaborationist; his older brother had been killed in the German offensive of 1940, and the young man, with somewhat immature but generous feelings, wanted to avenge him. His mother lived alone with him, very much upset by the half-treason of her husband and the death of her older son; the boy was her only consolation.

The boy was faced with the choice of leaving for England and joining the Free French Forces—that is, leaving his mother behind—or remaining with his mother and helping her to carry on. He was fully aware that the woman lived only for him and that his going-off—and perhaps his death—would plunge her into despair. He was also aware that every act that he did for his mother's sake was a sure thing, in the sense that it was helping her to carry on, whereas every effort he made toward going off and fighting was an uncertain move which might run aground and prove completely useless; for example, on his way to England he might, while passing though Spain, be detained indefinitely in a Spanish camp; he might reach England or Algiers and be stuck in an office at a desk job. As a result, he was faced with two very different kinds of action: one, concrete, immediate, but concerning only one individual; the other concerned an incomparably vaster group, a national collectivity, but for that very reason was dubious, and might be interrupted en route. And, at the same time, he was wavering between two kinds of ethics. On the one hand, an ethics of sympathy, of personal devotion; on the other, a broader ethics, but one whose efficacy was more dubious. He had to choose between the two.

Who could help him choose? Christian doctrine? No. Christian doctrine says, "Be charitable, love your neighbor, take the more rugged path, etc., etc." But which is the more rugged path? Whom should he love as a brother? The fighting man or his mother? Which does the greater good, the vague act of fighting in a group, or the concrete one of helping a particular human being to go on living? Who can decide *a priori*? Nobody. No book of ethics can tell him. The Kantian ethics says, "Never treat any person as a means, but as an end." Very well, if I stay with my mother, I'll treat her as an end and not as a means; but by virtue of this very fact, I'm running the risk of treating the people around me who are fighting, as means; and, conversely, if I go to join those who are fighting, I'll be treating them as an end, and, by doing that, I run the risk of treating my mother as a means.

If values are vague, and if they are always too broad for the concrete and specific case that we are considering, the only thing left for us is to trust our instincts. That's what this young man tried to do; and when I saw him, he said, "In the end, feeling is what counts. I ought to choose whichever pushes me in one direction. If I feel that I love my mother enough to sacrifice everything else for her—my desire for vengeance, for action, for adventure—then I'll stay with her. If, on the contrary, I feel that my love for my mother isn't enough, I'll leave."

But how is the value of a feeling determined? What gives his feeling for his mother value? Precisely the fact that he remained with her. I may say that I like so-and-so well enough to sacrifice a certain amount of money for him, but I may say so only if I've done it. I may say, "I love my mother well enough to remain with her" if I have remained with her. The only way to determine the value of this affection is, precisely, to perform an act which confirms and defines it. But, since I require this affection to justify my act, I find myself caught in a vicious circle. . . .

As for despair, the term has a very simple meaning. It means that we shall confine ourselves to reckoning only with what depends upon our will, or on the ensemble of probabilities which make our action possible. When we want something, we always have to reckon with probabilities. I may be counting on the arrival of a friend. The friend is coming by rail or street-car; this supposes that the train will arrive on schedule, or that the street-car will not jump the track. I am left in the realm of possibility; but possibilities are to be reckoned with only to the point where my action comports with the ensemble of these possibilities, and no further. The moment the possibilities I am considering are not rigorously involved by my action, I ought to disengage myself from them, because no God, no scheme, can adapt the world and its possibilities to my will. When

Descartes said, "Conquer yourself rather than the world," he meant essentially the same thing.

The Marxists to whom I have spoken reply, "You can rely on the support of others in your action, which obviously has certain limits because you're not going to live forever. That means: rely on both what others are doing elsewhere to help you, in China, in Russia, and what they will do later on, after your death, to carry on the action and lead it to its fulfillment, which will be the revolution. You even *have* to rely upon that, otherwise you're immortal." I reply at once that I will always rely on fellow fighters insofar as these comrades are involved with me in a common struggle, in the unity of a party or a group in which I can more or less make my weight felt; that is, one whose ranks I am in as a fighter and whose movements I am aware of at every moment. In such a situation, relying on the unity and will of the party is exactly like counting on the fact that the train will arrive on time or that the car won't jump the track. But, given that man is free and that there is no human nature for me to depend on, I cannot count on men whom I do not know by relying on human goodness or man's concern for the good of society. I don't know what will become of the Russian revolution; I may make an example of it to the extent that at the present time it is apparent that the proletariat plays a part in Russia that it plays in no other nation. But I can't swear that this will inevitably lead to a triumph of the proletariat. I've got to limit myself to what I see.

Given that men are free, and that tomorrow they will freely decide what man will be, I cannot be sure that, after my death, fellow fighters will carry on my work to bring it to its maximum perfection. Tomorrow, after my death, some men may decide to set up Facism, and the others may be cowardly and muddled enough to let them do it. Fascism will then be the human reality, so much the worse for us.

Actually, things will be as man will have decided they are to be. Does that mean that I should abandon myself to quietism? No. First, I should involve myself; then, act on the old saying, "Nothing ventured, nothing gained." Nor does it mean that I shouldn't belong to a party, but rather that I shall have no illusions and shall do what I can. For example, suppose I ask myself, "Will socialization, as such, ever come about?" I know nothing about it. All I know is that I'm going to do everything in my power to bring it about. Beyond that, I can't count on anything. Quietism is the attitude of people who say, "Let others do what I can't do." The doctrine I am presenting is the very opposite of quietism, since it declares, "There is no reality except in action." Moreover, it goes further, since it adds, "Man is nothing else than his plan; he exists only to the extent that he fulfills himself; he is, therefore, nothing else than the ensemble of his acts, nothing else than his life."

REVIEW QUESTIONS

1. What does Sartre mean by saying that responsibility for our actions involves being responsible for everyone? How does he answer those who deny this thesis?
2. What does Sartre mean by "we are condemned to be free"?
3. What is his notion of anguish? Why must we experience it?
4. What is his notion of forlornness? Why must we experience it?
5. What does Sartre mean by "bad faith"?

36

A. J. AYER

Alfred Jules Ayer (1910–1989) was born in London, the son of immigrant parents. He attended Eton and Christ Church, Oxford University, where he studied under Gilbert Ryle. When he was twenty-six he traveled to Vienna to meet Moritz Schlick, the leader of the Vienna Circle, a group of Logical Positivists. On his return to Oxford he wrote his most famous book, *Language, Truth and Logic*, a selection of which is reprinted here. He later became a professor at University College, London University, before returning to Oxford in 1960 to take up the Wykeham Professorship of Logic, where he taught until a short time before his death in 1989. A lifelong atheist, he astounded the public several months before his death with a report of a mystical experience. His heart had stopped for four minutes, during which time "I was confronted by a red light, exceedingly bright, and also very painful, even when I turned away from it. I was aware that this light was responsible for the government of the universe."[1]

Ayer was England's most prominent Logical Positivist. That philosophy, which had its roots in Hume's empiricism, like Hume, rejected metaphysics as nonsense. Its driving idea was that for a sentence to be meaningful, it must be verifiable in principle by experience. So my statement that atoms exist, though not observable by human senses, could conceivably be, if we had instruments to bring them to human consciousness. We must be able somehow to point to it. But moral and theological statements cannot be verified. Statements such as "Telling the truth is good" or "Killing innocents is bad" can't be observed. That is, we can observe a lie or a killing, but we can't observe the "goodness" or "badness"

---

[1]"What I Saw When I Was Dead . . ." *Spectator* July 16, 1988, reprinted in *The Philosophy of A. J. Ayer*, ed. L. E. Hahn (Open Court, 1992), p. 48.

which are predicated of these subject terms. Ayer would reduce the value sentences to emotive expressions, such as "Telling the truth—Hurrah!" and "Killing Innocents—Boo!" Theological assertions such as "God exists" are simply nonsense, since they fail to express the conditions under which one could verify such claims. In the selection presented here, Ayer sets forth to eliminate all metaphysical discourse.

FOR FURTHER READING

Achinstein, Peter, and Stephen Barker. *The Legacy of Logical Positivism* (Johns Hopkins Press, 1969).

Ashby, R. W. "Logical Positivism," in D. J. O'Connor, ed. *A Critical History of Western Philosophy* (Free Press, 1964).

Ayer, A. J., ed. *Logical Positivism* (Free Press, 1959).

Ayer, A. J. *Language, Truth and Logic* (Dover, 1936).

Gower, Barry, ed. *Logical Positivism in Perspective: Essays on "Language, Truth and Logic"* (Croom Helm, 1987).

Hahn, Lewis, ed. *The Philosophy of A. J. Ayer* (Open Court, 1992).

Macdonald, Graham, and Crispin Wright, eds. *Fact, Science and Morality: Essays on A. J. Ayer's "Language, Truth and Logic"* (Blackwell, 1987).

LANGUAGE, TRUTH AND LOGIC

PREFACE TO FIRST EDITION

The views which are put forward in this treatise derive from the doctrines of Bertrand Russell and Wittgenstein, which are themselves the logical outcome of the empiricism of Berkeley and David Hume. Like Hume, I divide all genuine propositions into two classes: those which, in his terminology, concern "relations of ideas," and those which concern "matters of fact." The former class comprises the *a priori* propositions of logic and pure mathematics, and these I allow to be necessary and certain only because they are analytic. That is, I maintain that the reason why these propositions cannot be confuted in experience is that they do not make any assertion about the empirical world, but simply record our determination to use symbols in a certain fashion. Propositions concerning empirical matters of fact, on the other hand, I hold to be hypotheses, which can be probable but never certain. And in giving an account of the method of their validation I claim also to have explained the nature of truth.

To test whether a sentence expresses a genuine empirical hypothesis, I adopt what may be called a modified verification principle. For I require of an empirical hypothesis, not indeed that it should be conclusively verifiable, but that some possible sense-experience should be relevant to the determination of its truth or falsehood. If a putative proposition fails to satisfy this principle, and is not a tautology, then I hold that it is metaphysical, and that, being metaphysical, it is neither true nor false but literally senseless. It will be found that much of what ordinarily passes for philosophy is metaphysical according to this criterion, and, in particular, that it can not be significantly asserted that there is a non-empirical world of values, or that men have immortal souls, or that there is a transcendent God.

As for the propositions of philosophy themselves, they are held to be linguistically necessary, and so analytic. And with regard to the relationship of philosophy and empirical science, it is shown that the philosopher is not in a position to furnish speculative truths, which would, as it were, compete with the hypotheses of science, nor yet to pass *a priori* judgements upon the validity of scientific theories, but that his function is to clarify the propositions of science by exhibiting their logical relationships, and by defining the symbols which occur in them. Consequently I maintain that there is nothing in the nature of philosophy to warrant the existence of conflicting philosophical "schools." And I attempt to substantiate this by providing a definitive solution of the problems which have been the chief sources of controversy between philosophers in the past.

The view that philosophizing is an activity of analysis is associated in England with the work of G.E. Moore and his disciples. But while I have learned a great deal from Professor Moore, I have reason to believe that he and his followers are not prepared to adopt such a thoroughgoing phenomenalism as I do, and that they take a rather different view of the nature of philosophical analysis. The philosophers with whom I am in the closest agreement are those who compose the "Viennese circle," under the leadership of Moritz Schlick, and are commonly known as logical positivists. And of these I owe most to Rudolf Carnap. Further, I wish to acknowledge my indebtedness to Gilbert Ryle, my original tutor in philosophy, and to Isaiah Berlin, who have discussed with me every point in the argument of this treatise, and made many valuable suggestions, although they both disagree with much of what I assert. . . .

CHAPTER 1: THE ELIMINATION OF METAPHYSICS

The traditional disputes of philosophers are, for the most part, as unwarranted as they are unfruitful. The surest way to end them is to establish beyond question what should be the purpose and method of a philosophical enquiry. And this is by no means so difficult a task as the history of philosophy would lead one to suppose. For if there are any questions which science leaves it to philosophy to answer, a straightforward process of elimination must lead to their discovery.

We may begin by criticising the metaphysical thesis that philosophy affords us knowledge of a real-

ity transcending the world of science and common sense. Later on, when we come to define metaphysics and account for its existence, we shall find that it is possible to be a metaphysician without believing in a transcendent reality; for we shall see that many metaphysical utterances are due to the commission of logical errors, rather than to a conscious desire on the part of their authors to go beyond the limits of experience. But it is convenient for us to take the case of those who believe that it is possible to have knowledge of a transcendent reality as a starting-point for our discussion. The arguments which we use to refute them will subsequently be found to apply to the whole of metaphysics.

One way of attacking a metaphysician who claimed to have knowledge of a reality which transcended the phenomenal world would be to enquire from what premises his propositions were deduced. Must he not begin, as other men do, with the evidence of his senses? And if so, what valid process of reasoning can possibly lead him to the conception of a transcendent reality? Surely from empirical premises nothing whatsoever concerning the properties, or even the existence, of anything super-empirical can legitimately be inferred. But this objection would be met by a denial on the part of the metaphysician that his assertions were ultimately based on the evidence of his senses. He would say that he was endowed with a faculty of intellectual intuition which enabled him to know facts that could not be known through sense-experience. And even if it could be shown that he was relying on empirical premises, and that his venture into a non-empirical world was therefore logically unjustified, it would not follow that the assertions which he made concerning this non-empirical world could not be true. For the fact that a conclusion does not follow from its putative premise is not sufficient to show that it is false. Consequently one cannot overthrow a system of transcendent metaphysics merely by criticising the way in which it comes into being. What is required is rather a criticism of the nature of the actual statements which comprise it. And this is the line of argument which we shall, in fact, pursue. For we shall maintain that no statement which refers to a "reality" transcending the limits of all possible sense-experience can possibly have any literal significance; from which it must follow that the labours of those who have striven to describe such a reality have all been devoted to the production of nonsense.

It may be suggested that this is a proposition which has already been proved by Kant. But although Kant also condemned transcendent metaphysics, he did so on different grounds. For he said that the human understanding was so constituted that it lost itself in contradictions when it ventured out beyond the limits of possible experience and attempted to deal with things in themselves. And thus he made the impossibility of a transcendent metaphysic not, as we do, a matter of logic, but a matter of fact. He asserted, not that our minds could not conceivably have had the power of penetrating beyond the phenomenal world, but merely that they were in fact devoid of it. And this leads the critic to ask how, if it is possible to know only what lies within the bounds of sense-experience, the author can be justified in asserting that real things do exist beyond, and how he can tell what are the boundaries beyond which the human understanding may not venture, unless he succeeds in passing them himself. As Wittgenstein says, "in order to draw a limit to thinking, we should have to think both sides of this limit,"[1] a truth to which Bradley gives a special twist in maintaining that the man who is ready to prove that metaphysics is impossible is a brother metaphysician with a rival theory of his own.[2]

Whatever force these objections may have against the Kantian doctrine, they have none whatsoever against the thesis that I am about to set forth. It cannot here be said that the author is himself overstepping the barrier he maintains to be impassable. For the fruitlessness of attempting to transcend the limits of possible sense-experience will be deduced, not from a psychological hypothesis concerning the actual constitution of the human mind, but from the rule which determines the literal significance of language. Our charge against the metaphysician is not that he attempts to employ the understanding in a field where it cannot profitably venture, but that he produces sentences which fail to conform to the conditions under which alone a sentence can be literally significant. Nor are we ourselves obliged to talk nonsense in order to show that all sentences of a certain type are necessarily devoid of literal significance. We need only formulate the criterion which enables us to test whether a sentence expresses a genuine proposition about a matter of fact, and then point out that the sentences under consideration fail to satisfy it. And this we shall now proceed to do. We shall first of all formulate the criterion in somewhat vague terms, and then give the explanations which are necessary to render it precise.

The criterion which we use to test the genuineness of apparent statements of fact is the criterion of verifiability. We say that a sentence is factually significant to any given person, if, and only if, he knows how to verify the proposition which it purports to express—that is, if he knows what observations would lead them, under certain conditions, to accept the proposition as being true, or reject it as being false. If, on the other hand, the putative proposition is of such a character that the assumption of its truth, or falsehood, is consistent with any assumption whatsoever concerning the nature of his future experience, then, as far as he is concerned, it is, if not a tautology, a mere pseudoproposition. The sentence expressing it may be emotionally significant to him; but it is not literally significant. And with regard to questions the procedure is the same. We enquire in every case what observations would lead us to answer the question, one way or the other; and, if none can be discovered, we must conclude that the sentence under consideration does not, as far as we are concerned, express a genuine question, however strongly its grammatical appearance may suggest that it does.

As the adoption of this procedure is an essential factor in the argument of this book, it needs to be examined in detail.

In the first place, it is necessary to draw a distinction between practical verifiability, and verifiability in principle. Plainly we all understand, in many cases believe, propositions which we have not in fact taken steps to verify. Many of these are propositions which we could verify if we took enough trouble. But there remain a number of significant propositions, concerning matters of fact, which we could not

[1] *Tractatus Logico-Philosophicus*, Preface.
[2] Bradley, *Appearance and Reality*, 2nd ed., p. 1.

verify even if we chose; simply because we lack the practical means of placing ourselves in the situation where the relevant observations could be made. A simple and familiar example of such a proposition is the proposition that there are mountains on the farther side of the moon. No rocket has yet been invented which would enable me to go and look at the farther side of the moon, so that I am unable to decide the matter by actual observation. But I do know what observations would decide it for me, if, as is theoretically conceivable, I were once in a position to make them. And therefore I say that the proposition is verifiable in principle, if not in practice, and is accordingly significant. On the other hand, such a metaphysical pseudo-proposition as "the Absolute enters into, but is itself incapable of, evolution and progress," is not even in principle verifiable. For one cannot conceive of an observation which would enable one to determine whether the Absolute did, or did not, enter into evolution and progress. Of course it is possible that the author of such a remark is using English words in a way in which they are not commonly used by English-speaking people, and that he does, in fact, intend to assert something which could be empirically verified. But until he makes us understand how the proposition that he wishes to express would be verified, he fails to communicate anything to us. And if he admits, as I think the author of the remark in question would have admitted, that his words were not intended to express either a tautology or a proposition which was capable, at least in principle, of being verified, then it follows that he has made an utterance which has no literal significance even for himself.

A further distinction which we must make is the distinction between the "strong" and the "weak" sense of the term "verifiable." A proposition is said to be verifiable, in the strong sense of the term, if, and only if, its truth could be conclusively established in experience. But it is verifiable, in the weak sense, if it is possible for experience to render it probable. In which sense are we using the term when we say that a putative proposition is genuine only if it is verifiable?

It seems to me that if we adopt conclusive verifiability as our criterion of significance, as some positivists have proposed, our argument will prove too much. Consider, for example, the case of general propositions of law—such propositions, namely, as "arsenic is poisonous"; "all men are mortal"; "a body tends to expand when it is heated." It is of the very nature of these propositions that their truth cannot be established with certainty by any finite series of observations. But if it is recognised that such general propositions of law are designed to cover an infinite number of cases, then it must be admitted that they cannot, even in principle, be verified conclusively. And then, if we adopt conclusive verifiability as our criterion of significance, we are logically obligated to treat these general propositions of law in the same fashion as we treat the statements of the metaphysician.

In face of this difficulty, some positivists have adopted the heroic course of saying that these general propositions are indeed pieces of nonsense, albeit an essentially important type of nonsense. But here the introduction of the term "important" is simply an attempt to hedge. It serves only to mark the authors' recognition that their view is somewhat too paradoxical, without in any way removing the paradox. Besides, the difficulty is not confined to the case of general propositions of law, though it is there revealed most plainly. It is hardly less obvious in the case of propositions about the remote past. For it must surely be admitted that, however strong the evidence in favour of historical statements may be, their truth can never become more than highly probable. And to maintain that they also constituted an important, or unimportant, type of nonsense would be unplausible, to say the very least. Indeed, it will be our contention that no proposition, other than a tautology, can possibly be anything more than a probable hypothesis. And if this is correct, the principle that a sentence can be factually significant only if it expresses what is conclusively verifiable is self-stultifying as a criterion of significance. For it leads to the conclusion that it is impossible to make a significant statement of fact at all.

Nor can we accept the suggestion that a sentence should be allowed to be factually significant if, and only if, it expresses something which is definitely confutable by experience. Those who adopt this course assume that, although no finite series of observations is ever sufficient to establish the truth of a hypothesis beyond all possibility of doubt, there are crucial cases in which a single observation, or series of observations, can definitely confute it. But, as we shall show later on, this assumption is false. A hypothesis cannot be conclusively confuted any more than it can be conclusively verified. For when we take the occurrence of certain observation as proof that a given hypothesis is false, we presuppose the existence of certain conditions. And though, in any given case, it may be extremely improbable that this assumption is false, it is not logically impossible. We shall see that there need be no self-contradiction in holding that some of the relevant circumstances are other than we have taken them to be, and consequently that the hypothesis has not really broken down. And if it is not the case that any hypothesis can be definitely confuted, we cannot hold that the genuineness of a proposition depends on the possibility of its definite confutation.

Accordingly, we fall back on the weaker sense of verification. We say that the question that must be asked about any putative statement of fact is not, Would any observations make its truth or falsehood logically certain? but simply, Would any observations be relevant to the determination of its truth or falsehood? And it is only if a negative answer is given to this second question that we conclude that the statement under consideration is nonsensical.

To make our position clearer, we may formulate it in another way. Let us call a proposition which records an actual or possible observation an experiential proposition. Then we may say that it is the mark of a genuine factual proposition, not that it should be equivalent to an experiential proposition, or any finite number of experiential propositions, but simply that some experiential propositions can be deduced from it in conjunction with certain other premises without being deducible from those other premises alone.

This criterion seems liberal enough. In contrast to the principle of conclusive verifiability, it clearly does not deny significance to general propositions or to propositions about the past. Let us see what kinds of assertion it rules out.

A good example of the kind of utterance that is condemned by our criterion as being not even false but nonsensical would be the assertion that the world of sense-experience was altogether unreal. It must,

of course, be admitted that our senses do sometimes deceive us. We may, as the result of having certain sensations, expect certain other sensations to be obtainable which are, in fact, not obtainable. But, in all such cases, it is further sense-experience that informs us of the mistakes that arise out of sense-experience. We say that the senses sometimes deceive us, just because the expectations to which our sense-experiences give rise do not always accord with what we subsequently experience. That is, we rely on our senses to substantiate or confute the judgements which are based on our sensations. And therefore the fact that our perceptual judgements are sometimes found to be erroneous has not the slightest tendency to show that the world of sense-experience is unreal. And, indeed, it is plain that no conceivable observation, or series of observations, could have any tendency to show that the world revealed to us by sense-experience was unreal. Consequently, anyone who condemns the sensible world as a world of mere appearance, as opposed to reality, is saying something which, according to our criterion of significance, is literally nonsensical.

An example of a controversy which the application of our criterion obliges us to condemn as fictitious is provided by those who dispute concerning the number of substances that there are in the world. For it is admitted both by monists, who maintain that reality is one substance, and by pluralists, who maintain that reality is many, that it is impossible to imagine any empirical situation which would be relevant to the solution of their dispute. But if we are told that no possible observation could give any probability either to the assertion that reality was one substance or to the assertion that it was many, then we must conclude that neither assertion is significant. We shall see later on that there are genuine logical and empirical questions involved in the dispute between monists and pluralists. But the metaphysical question concerning "substance" is ruled out by our criterion as spurious.

A similar treatment must be accorded to the controversy between realists and idealists, in its metaphysical aspect. A simple illustration, which I have made use of in a similar argument elsewhere, will help to demonstrate this. Let us suppose that a picture is discovered and the suggestion made that it was painted by Goya. There is a definite procedure for dealing with such a question. The experts examine the picture to see in what way it resembles the accredited works of Goya, and to see if it bears any marks which are characteristic of a forgery; they look up contemporary records for evidence of the existence of such a picture, and so on. In the end, they may still disagree, but each one knows what empirical evidence would go to confirm or discredit his opinion. Suppose, now, that these men have studied philosophy, and some of them proceed to maintain that this picture is a set of ideas in the perceiver's mind, or in God's mind, others that it is objectively real. What possible experience could any of them have which would be relevant to the solution of this dispute one way or the other? In the ordinary sense of the term "real," in which it is opposed to "illusory," the reality of the picture is not in doubt. The disputants have satisfied themselves that the picture is real, in this sense, by obtaining a correlated series of sensations of sight and sensations of touch. Is there any similar process by which they could discover whether the picture was real, in the sense in which the term "real" is opposed to "ideal"? Clearly there is none. But, if that is so, the problem is fictitious according to our criterion. This does not mean that the realist-idealist controversy may be dismissed without further ado. For it can legitimately be regarded as a dispute concerning the analysis of existential propositions, and so as involving a logical problem which, as we shall see, can be definitively solved. What we have just shown is that the question at issue between idealists and realists becomes fictitious when, as is often the case, it is given a metaphysical interpretation.

There is no need for us to give further examples of the operation of our criterion of significance. For our object is merely to show that philosophy, as a genuine branch of knowledge, must be distinguished from metaphysics. We are not now concerned with the historical question how much of what has traditionally passed for philosophy is actually metaphysical. We shall, however, point out later on that the majority of the "great philosophers" of the past were not essentially metaphysicians, and thus reassure those who would otherwise be prevented from adopting our criterion by considerations of piety.

As to the validity of the verification principle . . . it will be shown that all propositions which have factual content are empirical hypotheses; and that the function of an empirical hypothesis is to provide a rule for the anticipation of experience. And this means that every empirical hypothesis must be relevant to some actual, or possible, experience, so that a statement which is not relevant to any experience is not an empirical hypothesis, and accordingly has no factual content. But this is precisely what the principle of verifiability asserts.

It should be mentioned here that the fact that the utterances of the metaphysician are nonsensical does not follow simply from the fact that they are devoid of factual content. It follows from that fact, together with the fact that they are not *a priori* propositions. . . . *a priori* propositions, which have always been attractive to philosophers on account of their certainty, owe this certainty to the fact that they are tautologies. We may accordingly define a metaphysical sentence as a sentence which purports to express a genuine proposition, but does, in fact, express neither a tautology nor an empirical hypothesis. And as tautologies and empirical hypotheses form the entire class of significant propositions, we are justified in concluding that all metaphysical assertions are nonsensical. Our next task is to show how they come to be made.

The use of the term "substance," to which we have already referred, provides us with a good example of the way in which metaphysics mostly comes to be written. It happens to be the case that we cannot, in our language, refer to the sensible properties of a thing without introducing a word or phrase which appears to stand for the thing itself as opposed to anything which may be said about it. And, as a result of this, those who are infected by the primitive superstition that to every name a single real entity must correspond assume that it is necessary to distinguish logically between the thing itself and any, or all, of its sensible properties. And so they employ the term "substance" to refer to the thing itself. But from the fact that we happen to employ a single word to refer to a thing, and make that word the grammatical subject of the sentences in which we refer to the sensible appearances of the thing, it does not by any means follow that the thing itself is a "simple entity," or that it cannot be defined in terms of the totality of its appearances. It is true that in talking of "its" appearances we appear to distinguish the thing from the appearances, but that is simply an accident of linguistic usage. Logical analysis shows that what makes these "appearances" the "appearances of" the same thing is not their relationship to an entity other than themselves, but their relationship to one another. The metaphysician fails to see this because he is misled by a superficial grammatical feature of his language.

A simpler and clearer instance of the way in which a consideration of grammar leads to metaphysics is the case of the metaphysical concept of Being. The origin of our temptation to raise questions about Being, which no conceivable experience would enable us to answer, lies in the fact that, in our language, sentences which express existential propositions and sentences which express attributive propositions may be of the same grammatical form. For instance, the sentences "Martyrs exist" and "Martyrs suffer" both consist of a noun followed by an intransitive verb, and the fact that they have grammatically the same appearance leads one to assume that they are of the same logical type. It is seen that in the proposition "Martyrs suffer," the members of a certain species are credited with a certain attribute, and it is sometimes assumed that the same thing is true of such a proposition as "Martyrs exist." If this were actually the case, it would, indeed, be as legitimate to speculate about the Being of martyrs as it is to speculate about their suffering. But, as Kant pointed out, existence is not an attribute. For, when we ascribe an attribute to a thing, we covertly assert that it exists: so that if existence were itself an attribute, it would follow that all positive existential propositions were tautologies, and all negative existential propositions self-contradictory; and this is not the case. So that those who raise questions about Being which are based on the assumption that existence is an attribute are guilty of following grammar beyond the boundaries of sense.

A similar mistake has been made in connection with such propositions as "Unicorns are fictitious." Here again the fact that there is a superficial grammatical resemblance between the English sentences "Dogs are faithful" and "Unicorns are fictitious," and between the corresponding sentences in other languages, creates the assumption that they are of the same logical type. Dogs must exist in order to have the property of being faithful, and so it is held that unless unicorns in some way existed they could not have the property of being fictitious. But, as it is plainly self-contradictory to say that fictitious objects exist, the device is adopted of saying that they are real in some non-empirical sense—that they have a mode of real being which is different from the mode of being of existent things. But since there is no way of testing whether an object is real in this sense, as there is for testing whether it is real in the ordinary sense, the assertion that fictitious objects have a special non-empirical mode of real being is devoid of all literal significance. It comes to be made as a result of the assumption that being fictitious is an attribute. And this is a fallacy of the same order as the fallacy of supposing that existence is an attribute, and it can be exposed in the same way.

In general, the postulation of real non-existent entities results from the superstition, just now referred to, that, to every word or phrase that can be the grammatical subject of a sentence, there must somewhere be a real entity corresponding. For as there is no place in the empirical world for many of these "entities," a special non-empirical world is invoked to house them. To this error must be attributed, not only the utterances of a Heidegger, who bases his metaphysics on the assumption that "Nothing" is a name which is used to denote something peculiarly mysterious, but also the prevalence of such problems as those concerning the reality of propositions and universals whose senselessness, though less obvious, is no less complete.

These few examples afford a sufficient indication of the way in which most metaphysical assertions come to be formulated. They show how easy it is to write sentences which are literally nonsensical without seeing that they are nonsensical. And thus we see that the view that a number of the traditional "problems of philosophy" are metaphysical, and consequently fictitious, does not involve any incredible assumptions about the psychology of philosophers.

Among those who recognise that if philosophy is to be accounted a genuine branch of knowledge it must be defined in such a way as to distinguish it from metaphysics, it is fashionable to speak of the metaphysician as a kind of misplaced poet. As his statements have no literal meaning, they are not subject to any criteria of truth or falsehood: but they may still serve to express, or arouse, emotion, and thus be subject to ethical or aesthetic standards. And it is suggested that they may have considerable value, as means of moral inspiration, or even as works of art. In this way, an attempt is made to compensate the metaphysician for his extrusion from philosophy.

I am afraid that this compensation is hardly in accordance with his deserts. The view that the metaphysician is to be reckoned among the poets appears to rest on the assumption that both talk nonsense. But this assumption is false. In the vast majority of cases the sentences which are produced by poets do have literal meaning. The difference between the man who uses language scientifically and the man who uses it emotively is not that the one produces sentences which are incapable of arousing emotion, and the other sentences which have no sense, but that the one is primarily concerned with the expression of true propositions, the other with the creation of a work of art. Thus, if a work of science contains true and important propositions, its value as a work of science will hardly be diminished by the fact that they are inelegantly expressed. And similarly, a work of art is not necessarily the worse for the fact that all the propositions comprising it are literally false. But to say that many literary works are largely composed of falsehoods is not to say that they are composed of pseudo-propositions. It is, in fact, very rare for a literary artist to produce sentences which have no literal meaning. And where this does occur, the sentences are carefully chosen for their rhythm and balance. If the author writes nonsense, it is because he considers it most suitable for bringing about the effects for which his writing is designed.

The metaphysician, on the other hand, does not intend to write nonsense. He lapses into it through being deceived by grammar, or through committing errors of reasoning, such as that which leads to the view that the sensible world is unreal. But it is not the mark of a poet simply to make mistakes of this sort. There are some, indeed, who would see in the fact that the metaphysician's utterances are senseless a reason against the view that they have aesthetic value. And, without going so far as this, we may safely say that it does not constitute a reason for it.

It is true, however, that although the greater part of metaphysics is merely the embodiment of humdrum errors, there remain a number of metaphysical passages which are the work of genuine mystical feeling; and they may more plausibly be held to have moral or aesthetic value. But, as far as we are concerned, the distinction between the kind of metaphysics that is produced by a philosopher who has been duped by grammar, and the kind that is produced by a mystic who is trying to express the inexpressible, is of no great importance: what is important to us is to realise that even the utterances of the metaphysician who is attempting to expound a vision are literally senseless; so that henceforth we may pursue our philosophical researches with as little regard for them as for the more inglorious kind of metaphysics which comes from a failure to understand the workings of our language.

REVIEW QUESTIONS

1. What is the central idea of Ayer's logical positivism?
2. On what grounds does Ayer reject metaphysics as nonsense?
3. What is the test of whether a sentence expresses a genuine empirical hypothesis?
4. What is Ayer's view of the notion of substance, of idealism, and of religious claims?
5. What does Ayer think of the concept of Being?

37

THOMAS NAGEL

Thomas Nagel is professor of philosophy at New York University and the author of several works in ethics and philosophy of mind, including *The View from Nowhere* (1986). Much of Nagel's work involves showing the incongruities between objective and subjective perspectives, especially between the scientific explanation of humanness and our subjective experience of it. Something vital is lost in the reduction of mental states to brain states.

In this article Nagel argues against the view that the objective perspective is the correct one. He contends that the peculiarity of the subjective character experience is that increased objectivity actually takes us further from its real nature.

FOR FURTHER READING

Acton, Harry. *Kant's Moral Philosophy* (Macmillan, 1970).

Baier, Kurt. *The Moral Point of View* (Cornell University Press, 1958).

Broad, C. D. *Five Types of Ethical Theory* (Routledge and Kegan Paul, 1930).

Donagan, Alan. *The Theory of Morality* (University of Chicago Press, 1977). A comprehensive deontological account of ethical theory.

Feldman, Fred. *Introductory Ethics* (Prentice-Hall, 1978), chaps. 7 and 8. A clear and critical exposition.

Gewirth, Alan. *Reason and Morality* (University of Chicago, 1978). Important but advanced.

Harris, C. E. *Applying Moral Theories* (Wadsworth, 1986), chap. 7. An excellent exposition of contemporary deontological theories, especially of Gewirth's work.

Hill, Tom. *Dignity and Practical Reason* (Cornell University Press, 1992).

Kant, Immanuel. *Critique of Practical Reason*, trans. Lewis White Beck (Bobbs-Merrill, 1956).

Kant, Immanual. *Foundations of the Metaphysic of Morals*, trans. Lewis White Beck (Bobbs-Merrill, 1959).

Korgaard, Christine. *Creating the Kingdom of Ends* (Cambridge University Press, 1995).

Louden, Robert. *Morality and Moral Theory* (Oxford University Press, 1991). A sophisticated contemporary account combining Kantian and virtue ethics.

Nagel, Thomas. *Mortal Questions* (Cambridge University Press, 1979).

Nagel, Thomas. *Other Minds* (Oxford University Press, 1995).

Nagel, Thomas. *The Possibility of Altruism* (Oxford University Press, 1970).

Nagel, Thomas. *The View from Nowhere* (Oxford University Press, 1986).

O'Neill, Onora. *Acting on Principle: An Essay on Kantian Ethics* (Columbia University Press, 1975).

O'Neill, Onora. *Constructions of Reason* (Cambridge University Press, 1989).

Raphael, D. D. *Moral Philosophy* (Oxford University Press, 1981), chap. 6.

Ross, W. D. *Kant's Ethical Theory* (Clarendon Press, 1954).

Ward, Keith. *The Development of Kant's Views of Ethics* (Blackwell, 1972).

Wolff, Robert P. *The Autonomy of Reason: A Commentary on Kant's "Groundwork of the Metaphysic of Morals"* (Harper & Row, 1973).

WHAT IS IT LIKE TO BE A BAT?

Consciousness is what makes the mind-body problem really intractable. Perhaps that is why current discussions of the problem give it little attention or get to it obviously wrong. The recent wave of reductionist euphoria has produced several analyses of mental phenomena and mental concepts designed to explain the possibility of some variety of materialism, psychophysical identification, or reduction. But the problems dealt with are those common to this type of reduction and other types, and what makes the mind-body problem unique, and unlike the water–H$_2$O problem or the Turing machine–IBM machine problem or the lightning–electrical discharge problem or the gene–DNA problem or the oak tree–hydrocarbon problem, is ignored. Every reductionist has his favorite analogy from modern science. It is most unlikely that any of these unrelated examples of successful reduction will shed light on the relation of mind to brain. But philosophers share the general human weakness for explanations of what is incomprehensible in terms suited for what is familiar and well understood, though entirely different. This has led to the acceptance of implausible accounts of the mental largely because they would permit familiar kinds of reduction. I shall try to explain why the usual examples do not help us to understand the relation between mind and body—why, indeed, we have at present no conception of what an explanation of the physical nature of a mental phenomenon would be. Without consciousness the mind-body problem would be much less interesting. With consciousness it seems hopeless. The most important and characteristic feature of conscious mental phenomena is very poorly understood. Most reductionist theories do not even try to explain it. And careful examination will show that no currently available concept of reduction is applicable to it. Perhaps a new theoretical form can be devised for the purpose, but such a solution, if it exists, lies in the distant intellectual future.

Conscious experience is a widespread phenomenon. It occurs at many levels of animal life, though we cannot be sure of its presence in the simpler organisms, and it is very difficult to say in general what provides evidence of it. (Some extremists have been prepared to deny it even of mammals other than man.) No doubt it occurs in countless forms totally unimaginable to us, on other planets in other solar systems throughout the universe. But no matter how the form may vary, the fact that an organism has conscious experience *at all* means, basically, that there is something it is like to *be* that organism. There may

From Thomas Nagel, "What Is It Like to Be a Bat," in *Philosophical Review* (October 1974). Reprinted by permission of the author. Footnotes edited.

be further implications about the form of the experience; there may even (though I doubt it) be implications about the behavior of the organism. But fundamentally an organism has conscious mental states if and only if there is something that it is like to *be* that organism— something it is like *for* the organism.

We may call this the subjective character of experience. It is not captured by any of the familiar, recently devised reductive analyses of the mental, for all of them are logically compatible with its absence. It is not analyzable in terms of any explanatory system of functional states, or intentional states, since these could be ascribed to robots or automata that behaved like people though they experienced nothing. It is not analyzable in terms of the causal role of experiences in relation to typical human behavior—for similar reasons. I do not deny that conscious mental states and events cause behavior, nor that they may be given functional characterizations. I deny only that this kind of thing exhausts their analysis. Any reductionist program has to be based on an analysis of what is to be reduced. If the analysis leaves something out, the problem will be falsely posed. It is useless to base the defense of materialism on any analysis of mental phenomena that fails to deal explicitly with their subjective character. For there is no reason to suppose that a reduction which seems plausible when no attempt is made to account for consciousness can be extended to include consciousness. Without some idea, therefore, of what the subjective character of experience is, we cannot know what is required of physicalist theory.

While an account of the physical basis of mind must explain many things, this appears to be the most difficult. It is impossible to exclude the phenomenological features of experience from a reduction in the same way that one excludes the phenomenal features of an ordinary substance from a physical or chemical reduction of it—namely, by explaining them as effects on the minds of human observers. If physicalism is to be defended, the phenomenological features must themselves be given a physical account. But when we examine their subjective character it seems that such a result is impossible. The reason is that every subjective phenomenon is es-

sentially connected with a single point of view, and it seems inevitable that an objective, physical theory will abandon that point of view.

Let me first try to state the issue somewhat more fully than by referring to the relation between the subjective and the objective. This is far from easy. Facts about what it is like to be an X are very peculiar, so peculiar that some may be inclined to doubt their reality, or the significance of claims about them. To illustrate the connexion between subjectivity and a point of view, and to make evident the importance of subjective features, it will help to explore the matter in relation to an example that brings out clearly the divergence between the two types of conception, subjective and objective.

I assume we all believe that bats have experience. After all, they are mammals, and there is no more doubt that they have experience than that mice or pigeons or whales have experience. I have chosen bats instead of wasps or flounders because if one travels too far down the phylogenetic tree, people gradually shed their faith that there is experience there at all. Bats, although more closely related to us than those other species, nevertheless present a range of activity and a sensory apparatus so different from ours that the problem I want to pose is exceptionally vivid (though it certainly could be raised with other species). Even without the benefit of philosophical reflection, anyone who has spent some time in an enclosed space with an excited bat knows what it is to encounter a fundamentally *alien* form of life.

I have said that the essence of the belief that bats have experience is that there is something that it is like to be a bat. Now we know that most bats (the microchiroptera, to be precise) perceive the external world primarily by sonar, or echolocation, detecting the reflections, from objects within range, of their own rapid, subtly modulated, high-frequency shrieks. Their brains are designed to correlate the outgoing impulses with the subsequent echoes, and the information thus acquired enables bats to make precise discrimination of distance, size, shape, motion, and texture comparable to those we make by vision. But bat sonar, though clearly a form of perception, is not similar in its operation to any sense that we possess, and there is no reason to suppose that it is subjectively like anything we can experience or imagine. This appears to create difficulties for the notion of what it is like to be a bat. We must consider whether any method will permit us to extrapolate to the inner life of the bat from our own case,[1] and if not, what alternative methods there may be for understanding the notion.

Our own experience provides the basic material for our imagination, whose range is therefore limited. It will not help to try to imagine that one has webbing on one's arms, which enables one to fly around at dusk and dawn catching insects in one's mouth; that one has very poor vision, and perceives the surrounding world by a system of reflected high-frequency sound signals; and that one spends the day hanging upside down by one's feet in an attic. Insofar as I can imagine this (which is not very far), it tells me only what it would be like for *me* to behave as a bat behaves. But that is not the question. I want to know what it is like for a *bat* to be a bat. Yet if I try to imagine this, I am restricted to the resources of my own mind, and those resources are inadequate to the task. I cannot perform it either by imagining additions to my present experience, or by imagining segments gradually subtracted from it, or by imagining some combination of additions, subtractions, and modifications.

To the extent that I could look and behave like a wasp or a bat without changing my fundamental structure, my experiences would not be anything like the experiences of those animals. On the other hand, it is doubtful that any meaning can be attached to the supposition that I should possess the internal neurophysiological constitution of a bat. Even if I could by gradual degrees be transformed into a bat, nothing in my present constitution enables me to imagine what the experiences of such a future stage of myself thus metamorphosed would be like. The best evidence would come from the experiences of bats, if we only knew what they were like.

So if extrapolation from our own case is involved in the idea of what it is like to be a bat, the extrap-

olation must be incompletable. We cannot form more than a schematic conception of what it *is* like. For example, we may ascribe general *types* of experience on the basis of the animal's structure and behavior. Thus we describe bat sonar as a form of three-dimensional forward perception; we believe that bats feel some versions of pain, fear, hunger, and lust, and that they have other, more familiar types of perception besides sonar. But we believe that these experiences also have in each case a specific subjective character, which it is beyond our ability to conceive. And if there is conscious life elsewhere in the universe, it is likely that some of it will not be describable even in the most general experiential terms available to us.[2] (The problem is not confined to exotic cases, however, for it exists between one person and another. The subjective character of the experience of a person deaf and blind from birth is not accessible to me, for example, nor presumably is mine to him. This does not prevent us each from believing that the other's experience has such a subjective character.)

If anyone is inclined to deny that we can believe in the existence of facts like this whose exact nature we cannot possibly conceive, he should reflect that in contemplating the bats we are in much the same position that intelligent bats or Martians[3] would occupy if they tried to form a conception of what it was like to be us. The structure of their own minds might make it impossible for them to succeed, but we know they would be wrong to conclude that there is not anything precise that it is like to be us: that only certain general types of mental state could be ascribed to us (perhaps perception and appetite would be concepts common to us both; perhaps not). We know they would be wrong to draw such a skeptical conclusion because we know what it is like to be us. And we know that while it includes an enormous amount of variation and complexity, and while

---

[1] By "our own case," I do not mean just "my own case," but rather the mentalistic ideas that we apply unproblematically to ourselves and other human beings.

[2] Therefore the analogical form of the English expression "what it is *like*" is misleading. It does not mean "what (in our experience) it *resembles*," but rather "how it is for the subject himself."

[3] Any intelligent extraterrestrial beings totally different from us.

we do not possess the vocabulary to describe it adequately, its subjective character is highly specific, and in some respects describable in terms that can be understood only by creatures like us. The fact that we cannot expect ever to accommodate in our language a detailed description of Martian or bat phenomenology should not lead us to dismiss as meaningless the claim that bats and Martians have experiences fully comparable in richness of detail to our own. It would be fine if someone were to develop concepts and a theory that enabled us to think about those things, but such an understanding may be permanently denied to us by the limits of our nature. And to deny the reality or logical significance of what we can never describe or understand is the crudest form of cognitive dissonance.

This brings us to the edge of a topic that requires much more discussion than I can give it here: namely, the relation between facts on the one hand and conceptual schemes or systems of representation on the other. My realism about the subjective domain in all its forms implies a belief in the existence of facts beyond the reach of human concepts. Certainly it is possible for a human being to believe that there are facts which humans never *will* possess the requisite concepts to represent or comprehend. Indeed, it would be foolish to doubt this, given the finiteness of humanity's expectations. After all, there would have been transfinite numbers even if everyone had been wiped out by the Black Death before Cantor discovered them. But one might also believe that there are facts which *could* not ever be represented or comprehended by human beings, even if the species lasted for ever—simply because our structure does not permit us to operate with concepts of the requisite type. This impossibility might even be observed by other beings, but it is not clear that the existence of such beings, or the possibility of their existence, is a precondition of the significance of the hypothesis that there are humanly inaccessible facts. (After all, the nature of beings with access to humanly inaccessible facts is presumably itself a humanly inaccessible fact.) Reflection on what it is like to be a bat seems to lead us, therefore, to the conclusion that there are facts that do not consist in the truth of propositions expressible in a human

language. We can be compelled to recognize the existence of such facts without being able to state or comprehend them.

I shall not pursue this subject, however. Its bearing on the topic before us (namely, the mind-body problem) is that it enables us to make a general observation about the subjective character of experience. Whatever may be the status of facts about what it is like to be a human being, or a bat, or a Martian, these appear to be facts that embody a particular point of view.

I am not adverting here to the alleged privacy of experience to its possessor. The point of view in question is not one accessible only to a single individual. Rather it is a *type*. It is often possible to take up a point of view other than one's own, so the comprehension of such facts is not limited to one's own case. There is a sense in which phenomenological facts are perfectly objective: One person can know or say of another what the quality of the other's experience is. They are subjective, however, in the sense that even this objective ascription of experience is possible only for someone sufficiently similar to the object of ascription to be able to adopt his point of view—to understand the ascription in the first person as well as in the third, so to speak. The more different from oneself the other experiencer is, the less success one can expect with this enterprise. In our own case we occupy the relevant point of view, but we will have as much difficulty understanding our own experience properly if we approach it from another point of view as we would if we tried to understand the experience of another species without taking up *its* point of view.

This bears directly on the mind-body problem. For if the facts of experience—facts about what it is like *for* the experiencing organism—are accessible only from one point of view, then it is a mystery how the true character of experiences could be revealed in the physical operation of that organism. The latter is a domain of objective facts *par excellence*— the kind that can be observed and understood from many points of view and by individuals with differing perceptual systems. There are no comparable imaginative obstacles to the acquisition of knowledge about bat neurophysiology by human scientists,

and intelligent bats or Martians might learn more about the human brain than we ever will.

This is not by itself an argument against reduction. A Martian scientist with no understanding of visual perception could understand the rainbow, or lightning, or clouds as physical phenomena, though he would never be able to understand the human concepts of rainbow, lightning, or cloud, or the place these things occupy in our phenomenal world. The objective nature of the things picked out by these concepts could be apprehended by him because, although the concepts themselves are connected with a particular point of view and a particular visual phenomenology, the things apprehended from that point of view are not: They are observable from the point of view but external to it; hence they can be comprehended from other points of view also, either by the same organisms or by others. Lightning has an objective character that is not exhausted by its visual appearance, and this can be investigated by a Martian without vision. To be precise, it has a *more* objective character than is revealed in its visual appearance. In speaking of the move from subjective characterization, I wish to remain noncommittal about the existence of an end point, the completely objective intrinsic nature of the thing, which one might or might not be able to reach. It may be more accurate to think of objectivity as a direction in which the understanding can travel. And in understanding a phenomenon like lightning, it is legitimate to go as far away as one can from a strictly human viewpoint.

In the case of experience, on the other hand, the connexion with a particular point of view seems much closer. It is difficult to understand what could be meant by the *objective* character of an experience, apart from the particular point of view from which its subject apprehends it. After all, what would be left of what it was like to be a bat if one removed the viewpoint of the bat? But if experience does not have, in addition to its subjective character, an objective nature that can be apprehended from many different points of view, then how can it be supposed that a Martian investigating my brain might be observing physical processes which were my mental processes (as he might observe physical processes which were bolts of lightning), only from a different point of view? How, for that matter, could a human physiologist observe them from another point of view?[4]

We appear to be faced with a general difficulty about psychophysical reduction. In other areas the process of reduction is a move in the direction of greater objectivity, toward a more accurate view of the real nature of things. This is accomplished by reducing our dependence on individual or species-specific points of view toward the object of investigation. We describe it not in terms of the impressions it makes on our senses, but in terms of its more general effects and of properties detectable by means other than the human senses. The less it depends on a specifically human viewpoint, the more objective is our description. It is possible to follow this path because although the concepts and ideas we employ in thinking about the external world are initially applied from a point of view that involves our perceptual apparatus, they are used by us to refer to things beyond themselves—toward which we *have* the phenomenal point of view. Therefore we can abandon it in favor of another, and still be thinking about the same things.

Experience itself, however, does not seem to fit the pattern. The idea of moving from appearance to reality seems to make no sense here. What is the analogue in this case to pursuing a more objective understanding of the same phenomena by abandoning the initial subjective viewpoint toward them in favour of another that is more objective but concerns the same thing? Certainly it *appears* unlikely that we will get closer to the real nature of human experience by leaving behind the particularity of our human point of view and striving for a description in terms accessible to beings that could not imagine what it was like to be us. If the subjective character of experience is fully comprehensible only from one

---

[4]The problem is not just that when I look at the *Mona Lisa*, my visual experience has a certain quality, no trace of which is to be found by someone looking into my brain. For even if he did observe there a tiny image of the *Mona Lisa*, he would have no reason to identify it with the experience.

point of view, then any shift to greater objectivity—that is, less attachment to a specific viewpoint—does not take us nearer to the real nature of the phenomenon: It takes us farther away from it. In a sense, the seeds of this objection to the reducibility of experience are already detectable in successful cases of reduction; for in discovering sound to be, in reality, a wave phenomenon in air or other media, we leave behind one viewpoint to take up another, and the auditory, human or animal viewpoint that we leave behind remains unreduced. Members of radically different species may both understand the same physical events in objective terms, and this does not require that they understand the phenomenal forms in which those events appear to the senses of members of the other species. Thus it is a condition of their referring to a common reality that their more particular viewpoints are not part of the common reality that they both apprehend. The reduction can succeed only if the species-specific viewpoint is omitted from what is to be reduced.

But while we are right to leave this point of view aside in seeking a fuller understanding of the external world, we cannot ignore it permanently, since it is the essence of the internal world, and not merely a point of view on it. Most of the neobehaviorism of recent philosophical psychology results from the effort to substitute an objective concept of mind for the real thing, in order to have nothing left over which cannot be reduced. If we acknowledge that a physical theory of mind must account for the subjective character of experience, we must admit that no presently available conception gives us a clue how this could be done. The problem is unique. If mental processes are indeed physical processes, then there is something it is like, intrinsically, to undergo certain physical processes. What it is for such a thing to be the case remains a mystery.

What moral should be drawn from these reflections, and what should be done next? It would be a mistake to conclude that physicalism must be false. Nothing is proved by the inadequacy of physicalist hypotheses that assume a faulty objective analysis of mind. It would be truer to say that physicalism is a position we cannot understand because we do not at present have any conception of how it might be true. Perhaps it will be thought unreasonable to require such a conception as a condition of understanding. After all, it might be said, the meaning of physicalism is clear enough: Mental states are states of the body; mental events are physical events. We do not know *which* physical states and events they are, but that should not prevent us from understanding the hypothesis. What could be clearer than the words "is" and "are"?

But I believe it is precisely this apparent clarity of the word "is" that is deceptive. Usually, when we are told that X is Y we know *how* it is supposed to be true, but that depends on a conceptual or theoretical background and is not conveyed by the "is" alone. We know how both "X" and "Y" refer, and the kinds of things to which they refer, and we have a rough idea how the two referential paths might converge on a single thing, be it an object, a person, a process, an event or whatever. But when the two terms of the identification are very disparate it may not be so clear how it could be true. We may not have even a rough idea of how the two referential paths could converge, or what kind of things they might converge on, and a theoretical framework may have to be supplied to enable us to understand this. Without the framework, an air of mysticism surrounds the identification.

This explains the magical flavor of popular presentations of fundamental scientific discoveries, given out as propositions to which one must subscribe without really understanding them. For example, people are now told at an early age that all matter is really energy. But despite the fact that they know what "is" means, most of them never form a conception of what makes this claim true, because they lack the theoretical background.

At the present time the status of physicalism is similar to that which the hypothesis that matter is energy would have had if uttered by a pre-Socratic philosopher. We do not have the beginnings of a conception of how it might be true. In order to understand the hypothesis that a mental event is a physical event, we require more than an understanding of the word "is." The idea of how a mental and a physical term might refer to the same thing is lacking, and the usual analogies with theoretical identification in other fields fail to supply it. They fail because if we construe the reference of mental terms to physical events on the usual model, we either get a reappearance of separate subjective events as the effects through which mental reference to physical events is secured, or else we get a false account of how mental terms refer (for example, a causal behaviorist one).

Strangely enough, we may have evidence for the truth of something we cannot really understand. Suppose a caterpillar is locked in a sterile safe by someone unfamiliar with insect metamorphosis, and weeks later the safe is reopened, revealing a butterfly. If the person knows that the safe has been shut the whole time, he has reason to believe that the butterfly is or was once the caterpillar, without having any idea in what sense this might be so. (One possibility is that the caterpillar contained a tiny winged parasite that devoured it and grew into the butterfly.) It is conceivable that we are in such a position with regard to physicalism. Donald Davidson has argued that if mental events have physical causes and effects, they must have physical descriptions. He holds that we have reason to believe this even though we do not—and in fact *could* not—have a general psychophysical theory. His argument applies to intentional mental events, but I think we also have some reason to believe that sensations are physical processes, without being in a position to understand how. Davidson's position is that certain physical events have irreducibly mental properties, and perhaps some view describable in this way is correct. But nothing of which we can now form a conception corresponds to it; nor have we any idea what a theory would be like that enabled us to conceive of it. Very little work has been done on the basic question (from which mention of the brain can be entirely omitted) whether any sense can be made of experiences having an objective character at all. Does it make sense, in other words, to ask what my experiences are *really* like, as opposed to how they appear to me? We cannot genuinely understand the hypothesis that their nature is captured in a physical description unless we understand the more fundamental idea that they *have* an objective nature (or that objective processes can have a subjective nature). I should like to close with a speculative proposal. It may be possible to approach the gap between subjective and objective from another direction. Setting aside temporarily the relation between the mind and the brain, we can pursue a more objective understanding of the mental in its own right. At present we are completely unequipped to think about the subjective character of experience without relying on the imagination—without taking up the point of view of the experiential subject. This should be regarded as a challenge to form new concepts and devise a new method—an objective phenomenology not dependent on empathy or the imagination. Though presumably it would not capture everything, its goal would be to describe, at least in part, the subjective character of experiences in a form comprehensible to beings incapable of having those experiences.

We would have to develop such a phenomenology to describe the sonar experiences of bats; but it would also be possible to begin with humans. One might try, for example, to develop concepts that could be used to explain to a person blind from birth what it was like to see. One would reach a blank wall eventually, but it should be possible to devise a method of expressing in objective terms much more than we can at present, and with much greater precision. The loose intermodal analogies—for example, "Red is like the sound of a trumpet"—which crop up in discussions of this subject are of little use. That should be clear to anyone who has both heard a trumpet and seen red. But structural features of perception might be more accessible to objective description, even though something would be left out. And concepts alternative to those we learn in the first person may enable us to arrive at a kind of understanding even of our own experience which is denied us by the very ease of description and lack of distance that subjective concepts afford.

Apart from its own interest, a phenomenology that is in this sense objective may permit questions about the physical basis of experience to assume a more intelligible form. Aspects of subjective experience that admitted this kind of objective description might be better candidates for objective explanations of a more familiar sort. But whether or not this guess is correct, it seems unlikely that any physical theory of mind can be contemplated until more thought has been given to the general problem of subjective and objective. Otherwise we cannot even pose the mind-body problem without sidestepping it.

REVIEW QUESTIONS

1. What point is Nagel trying to make with the bat example?
2. How does the nature of subjective experience count against reductive theories of mind?
3. Does Nagel's argument suggest that mental states cannot be identical with brain states? Is his argument sound?
4. Can knowledge of what it is like to be a bat be acquired through scientific investigation? Why or why not?
5. What is Nagel's verdict on physicalism?

38

PHILIPPA FOOT

Philippa Foot is professor emeritus of the University of California at Los Angeles and a fellow at Sommerville College, Oxford University. She has written important articles in moral theory, including this selection. Here she argues that Kant is wrong in viewing morality as categorical rather than hypothetical. Kant has been credited by the vast majority of ethicists, even those who disagree with him on other issues, with establishing the necessity of grounding moral judgments in categorical imperatives, rather than in hypothetical ones. Moral judgments are objectively necessary—not a mere means to achieve something one desires, as prudential judgments are. Foot argues that Kant seems to be wrong here, and that the categorical aspect of morality may stem more from the way it is taught than the way it really is. Nonetheless, while taking a certain transcendence away from morality, a morality based on hypothetical considerations may still be adequate and important and true.

FOR FURTHER READING

Foot, Philippa. *Virtues and Vices* (Basil Blackwell, 1978).
Foot, Philippa., ed. *Theories of Ethics* (Oxford University Press, 1967).
Louden, Robert. *Morality and Moral Theory* (Oxford University Press, 1991).
Pincoffs, Edmund. *Quandries and Virtues* (University of Kansas Press, 1986).
Pojman, Louis, ed. *Ethical Theory* (Wadsworth Publishing Co., 2002).

MORALITY AS A SYSTEM OF HYPOTHETICAL IMPERATIVES

There are many difficulties and obscurities in Kant's moral philosophy, and few contemporary moralists will try to defend it all. Many, for instance, agree in rejecting Kant's derivation of duties from the mere form of the law expressed in terms of a universally legislative will. Nevertheless, it is generally supposed, even by those who would not dream of calling themselves his followers, that Kant established one thing beyond doubt—namely, the necessity of distinguishing moral judgments from hypothetical imperatives. That moral judgments cannot be hypothetical imperatives has come to seem an unquestionable truth. It will be argued here that it is not.

In discussing so thoroughly Kantian a notion as that of the hypothetical imperative, one naturally begins by asking what Kant himself meant by a hypothetical imperative, and it may be useful to say a little about the idea of an imperative as this appears in Kant's works. In writing about imperatives Kant seems to be thinking at least as much of statements about what ought to be or should be done, as of injunctions expressed in the imperative mood. He even describes as an imperative the assertion that it would be "good to do or refrain from doing something"[1] and explains that for a will that "does not always do something simply because it is presented to it as a good thing to do" this has the force of a command of reason. We may therefore think of Kant's imperatives as statements to the effect that something ought to be done or that it would be good to do it.

The distinction between hypothetical imperatives and categorical imperatives, which plays so important a part in Kant's ethics, appears in characteristic form in the following passages from the *Foundations of the Metaphysic of Morals*:

All imperatives command either hypothetically or categorically. The former present the practical necessity of a possible action as a means to achieving something else which one desires (or which one may possibly desire). The categorical imperative would be one which presented an action as of itself objectively necessary, without regard to any other end.[2]

If the action is good only as a means to something else, the imperative is hypothetical; but if it is thought of as good in itself, and hence as necessary in a will which of itself conforms to reason as the principle of this will, the imperative is categorical.[3]

The hypothetical imperative, as Kant defines it, "says only that the action is good to some purpose" and the purpose, he explains, may be possible or actual. Among imperatives related to actual purposes Kant mentions rules of prudence, since he believes that all men necessarily desire their own happiness. Without committing ourselves to this view it will be useful to follow Kant in classing together as "hypothetical imperatives" those telling a man what he ought to do because (or if) he wants something and those telling him what he ought to do on grounds of self-interest. Common opinion agrees with Kant in insisting that a moral man must accept a rule of duty whatever his interests or desires.

Having given a rough description of the class of Kantian hypothetical imperatives it may be useful to point to the heterogeneity within it. Sometimes what a man should do depends on his passing inclination, as when he wants his coffee hot and should warm the jug. Sometimes it depends on some long-term project, when the feelings and inclinations of the moment are irrelevant. If one wants to be a respectable

---

[1] Immanuel Kant, *Foundations of the Metaphysic of Morals*, L. W. Beck, trans. (Bobbs-Merrill, 1959), sec. II.

[2] Ibid.

[3] Ibid.

Reprinted with permission from *Philosophical Review* 84(1972): 305–316. Philippa Foot added the following footnote in 1987: "I now think that this paper shows a mistaken bias in favor of a Humean theory of reasons for action. But its question, 'Why is it rational to follow moral rules but not those of etiquette?' still seems to need an answer."

philosopher one should get up in the mornings and do some work, though just at that moment when one should do it the thought of being a respectable philosopher leaves one cold. It is true nevertheless to say of one, at that moment, that one wants to be a respectable philosopher, and this can be the foundation of a desire-dependent hypothetical imperative. The term "desire" as used in the original account of the hypothetical imperative was meant as a grammatically convenient substitute for "want," and was not meant to carry any implication of inclination rather than long-term aim or project. Even the word "project," taken strictly, introduces undesirable restrictions. If someone is devoted to his family or his country or to any cause, there are certain things he wants, which may then be the basis of hypothetical imperatives, without either inclinations or projects being quite what is in question. Hypothetical imperatives should already be appearing as extremely diverse; a further important distinction is between those that concern an individual and those that concern a group. The desires on which a hypothetical imperative is dependent may be those of one man, or may be taken for granted as belonging to a number of people engaged in some common project or sharing common aims.

Is Kant right to say that moral judgements are categorical, not hypothetical, imperatives? It may seem that he is, for we find in our language two different uses of words such as "should" and "ought," apparently corresponding to Kant's hypothetical and categorical imperatives, and we find moral judgements on the "categorical" side. Suppose, for instance, we have advised a traveller that he should take a certain train, believing him to be journeying to his home. If we find that he has decided to go elsewhere, we will most likely have to take back what we said: the "should" will now be unsupported and in need of support. Similarly, we must be prepared to withdraw our statement about what he should do if we find that the right relation does not hold between the action and the end—that it is either no way of getting what he wants (or doing what he wants to do) or not the most eligible among possible means. The use of "should" and "ought" in moral contexts is, however, quite different. When we say that a man should do something and intend a moral judgement we do not

have to back up what we say by considerations about his interests or his desires; if no such connexion can be found the "should" need not be withdrawn. It follows that the agent cannot rebut an assertion about what, morally speaking, he should do by showing that the action is not ancillary to his interests or desires. Without such a connexion the "should" does not stand unsupported and in need of support; the support that it requires is of another kind.

There is, then, one clear difference between moral judgements and the class of "hypothetical imperatives" so far discussed. In the latter "should" is "used hypothetically," in the sense defined, and if Kant were merely drawing attention to this piece of linguistic usage his point would easily be proved. But obviously Kant meant more than this; in describing moral judgements as non-hypothetical—that is, categorical imperatives—he is ascribing to them a special dignity and necessity which this usage cannot give. Modern philosophers follow Kant in talking, for example, about the "unconditional requirement" expressed in moral judgements. These, they say, tell us what we have to do whatever our interests or desires, and by their inescapability they are distinguished from hypothetical imperatives.

The problem is to find proof for this further feature of moral judgements. If anyone fails to see the gap that has to be filled it will be useful to point out to him that we find "should" used non-hypothetically in some non-moral statements to which no one attributes the special dignity and necessity conveyed by the description "categorical imperative." For instance, we find this non-hypothetical use of "should" in sentences enunciating rules of etiquette, as, for example, that an invitation in the third person should be answered in the third person, where the rule does not fail to apply to someone who has his own good reasons for ignoring this piece of nonsense, or who simply does not care about what, from the point of view of etiquette, he should do. Similarly, there is a non-hypothetical use of "should" in contexts where something like a club rule is in question. The club secretary who has told a member that he should not bring ladies into the smoking-room does not say, "Sorry, I was mistaken" when informed that this member is resigning tomorrow and cares nothing about his reputation in the club. Lacking a connexion with the agent's desires or interests, this "should" does not stand "unsupported and in need of support"; it requires only the backing of the rule. This use of "should" is therefore "non-hypothetical" in the sense defined.

It follows that if a hypothetical use of "should" gave a hypothetical imperative, and a non-hypothetical use of "should" a categorical imperative, then "should" statements based on rules of etiquette, or rules of a club would be categorical imperatives. Since this would not be accepted by defenders of the categorical imperative in ethics, who would insist that these other "should" statements give hypothetical imperatives, they must be using this expression in some other sense. We must therefore ask what they mean when they say that "You should answer . . . in the third person" is a hypothetical imperative. Very roughly the idea seems to be that one may reasonably ask why anyone should bother about what should (from the point of view of etiquette) be done, and that such considerations deserve no notice unless reason is shown. So although people give as their reason for doing something the fact that it is required by etiquette, we do not take this consideration as in itself giving us reason to act. Considerations of etiquette do not have any automatic reasongiving force, and a man might be right if he denied that he had reason to do "what's done."

This seems to take us to the heart of the matter, for, by contrast, it is supposed that moral considerations necessarily give reasons for acting to any man. The difficulty is, of course, to defend this proposition which is more often repeated than explained. Unless it is said, implausibly, that all "should" or "ought" statements give reasons for acting, which leaves the old problem of assigning a special categorical status to moral judgement, we must be told what it is that makes the moral "should" relevantly different from the "shoulds" appearing in normative statements of other kinds.[4] Attempts have sometimes been made to show that some kind of irrationality is involved in ignoring the "should" of morality: in saying "Immoral—so what?" as one says "Non comme il faut— so what?" But as far as I can see these have all rested on some illegitimate assumption, as, for instance, of thinking that the amoral man, who agrees that some piece of conduct is immoral but takes no notice of that, is inconsistently disregarding a rule of conduct that he has accepted; or again of thinking it inconsistent to desire that others will not do to one what one proposes to do to them. The fact is that the man who rejects morality because he sees no reason to obey its rules can be convicted of villainy but not of inconsistency. Nor will his action necessarily be irrational. Irrational actions are those in which a man in some way defeats his own purposes, doing what is calculated to be disadvantageous or to frustrate his ends. Immorality does not necessarily involve any such thing.

It is obvious that the normative character of moral judgement does not guarantee its reasongiving force. Moral judgements are normative, but so are judgements of manners, statements of club rules, and many others. Why should the first provide reasons for acting as the others do not? In every case it is because there is a background of teaching that the non-hypothetical "should" can be used. The behaviour is required, not simply recommended, but the question remains as to why we should do what we are required to do. It is true that moral rules are often enforced much more strictly than the rules of etiquette, and our reluctance to press the non-hypothetical

---

[4] To say that moral considerations are called reasons is blatantly to ignore the problem.

In the case of etiquette or club rules it is obvious that the non-hypothetical use of "should" has resulted in the loss of the usual connexion between what one should do and what one has reason to do. Someone who objects that in the moral case a man cannot be justified in restricting his practical reasoning in this way, since every moral "should" gives reasons for acting, must face the following dilemma. Either it is possible to create reasons for acting simply by putting together any silly rules and introducing a non-hypothetical "should," or else the non-hypothetical "should" does not necessarily imply reasons for acting. If it does not necessarily imply reasons for acting we may ask why it is supposed to do so in the case of morality. Why cannot the indifferent amoral man say that for him "shouldm" gives no reason for acting, treating "shouldm" as most of us treat "shouldc"? Those who insist that "shouldm" is categorical in this second "reason-giving" sense do not seem to realise that they never prove this to be so. They sometimes say that moral considerations "just do" give reasons for acting, without explaining why some devotee of etiquette could not say the same about the rules of etiquette.

"should" of etiquette may be one reason why we think of the rules of etiquette as hypothetical imperatives. But are we then to say that there is nothing behind the idea that moral judgements are categorical imperatives but the relative stringency of our moral teaching? I believe that this may have more to do with the matter than the defenders of the categorical imperatives would like to admit. For if we look at the kind of thing that is said in its defence we may find ourselves puzzled about what the words can even mean unless we connect them with the feelings that this stringent teaching implants. People talk, for instance, about the "binding force" of morality, but it is not clear what this means if not that we feel ourselves unable to escape. Indeed the "inescapability" of moral requirements is often cited when they are being contrasted with hypothetical imperatives. No one, it is said, escapes the requirements of ethics by having or not having particular interests or desires. Taken in one way this only reiterates the contrast between the "should" of morality and the hypothetical "should," and once more places morality alongside of etiquette. Both are inescapable in that behaviour does not cease to offend against either morality or etiquette because the agent is indifferent to their purposes and to the disapproval he will incur by flouting them. But morality is supposed to be inescapable in some special way and this may turn out to be merely the reflection of the way morality is taught. Of course, we must try other ways of expressing the fugitive thought. It may be said, for instance, that moral judgements have a kind of necessity since they tell us what we "must do" or "have to do" whatever our interests and desires. The sense of this is, again, obscure. Sometimes when we use such expressions we are referring to physical or mental compulsion. (A man has to go along if he is pulled by strong men and he has to give in if tortured beyond endurance.) But it is only in the absence of such conditions that moral judgements apply. Another and more common sense of the words is found in sentences such as "I caught a bad cold and had to stay in bed" where a penalty for acting otherwise is in the offing. The necessity of acting morally is not, however, supposed to depend on such penalties. Another range of examples, not necessarily having to do with penalties, is found where there is an unquestioned acceptance of some project or role, as when a nurse tells us that she has to make her rounds at a certain time, or we say that we have to run for a certain train. But these too are irrelevant in the present context, since the acceptance condition can always be revoked.

No doubt it will be suggested that it is in some other sense of the words "have to" or "must" that one has to or must do what morality demands. But why should one insist that there must be such a sense when it proves so difficult to say what it is? Suppose that what we take for a puzzling thought were really no thought at all but only the reflection of our feelings about morality? Perhaps it makes no sense to say that we "have to" submit to the moral law, or that morality is "inescapable" in some special way. For just as one may feel as if one is falling without believing that one is moving downward, so one may feel as if one has to do what is morally required without believing oneself to be under physical or psychological compulsion, or about to incur a penalty if one does not comply. No one thinks that if the word "falling" is used in a statement reporting one's sensations it must be used in a special sense. But this kind of mistake may be involved in looking for the special sense in which one "has to" do what morality demands. There is no difficulty about the idea that we feel we have to behave morally, and given the psychological conditions of the learning of moral behaviour it is natural that we should have such feelings. What we cannot do is quote them in support of the doctrine of the categorical imperative. It seems, then, that in so far as it is backed up by statements to the effect that the moral law is inescapable, or that we do have to do what is morally required of us, it is uncertain whether the doctrine of the categorical imperative even makes sense.

The conclusion we should draw is that moral judgements have no better claim to be categorical imperatives than do statements about matters of etiquette. People may indeed follow either morality or etiquette without asking why they should do so, but equally well they may not. They may ask for reasons and may reasonably refuse to follow either if reasons are not to be found.

It will be said that this way of viewing moral considerations must be totally destructive of morality, because no one could ever act morally unless he accepted such considerations as in themselves sufficient reason for action. Actions that are truly moral must be done "for their own sake," "because they are right," and not for some ulterior purpose. This argument we must examine with care, for the doctrine of the categorical imperative has owed much to its persuasion.

Is there anything to be said for the thesis that a truly moral man acts "out of respect for the moral law" or that he does what is morally right because it is morally right? That such propositions are not prima facie absurd depends on the fact that moral judgement concerns itself with a man's reasons for acting as well as with what he does. Law and etiquette require only that certain things are done or left undone, but no one is counted as charitable if he gives alms "for the praise of men," and one who is honest only because it pays him to be honest does not have the virtue of honesty. This kind of consideration was crucial in shaping Kant's moral philosophy. He many times contrasts acting out of respect for the moral law with acting from an ulterior motive, and what is more from one that is selfinterested. In the early *Lectures on Ethics* he gave the principle of truth-telling under a system of hypothetical imperatives as that of not lying if it harms one to lie. In the *Metaphysic of Morals* he says that ethics cannot start from the ends which a man may propose to himself, since these are all "selfish."[5] In the *Critique of Practical Reason* he argues explicitly that when acting not out of respect for moral law but "on a material maxim" men do what they do for the sake of pleasure or happiness.

> All material practical principles are, as such, of one and the same kind and belong under the general principle of self-love or one's own happiness.[6]

Kant, in fact, was a psychological hedonist[7] in respect of all actions except those done for the sake of the moral law, and this faulty theory of human nature was one of the things preventing him from seeing that moral virtue might be compatible with the rejection of the categorical imperative.

If we put this theory of human action aside, and allow as ends the things that seem to be ends, the picture changes. It will surely be allowed that quite apart from thoughts of duty a man may care about the suffering of others, having a sense of identification with them, and wanting to help if he can. Of course he must want not the reputation of charity, nor even a gratifying role helping others, but, quite simply, their good. If this is what he does care about, then he will be attached to the end proper to the virtue of charity and a comparison with someone acting from an ulterior motive (even a respectable ulterior motive) is out of place. Nor will the conformity of his action to the rule of charity be merely contingent. Honest action may happen to further a man's career; charitable actions do not happen to further the good of others.[8]

Can a man accepting only hypothetical imperatives possess other virtues besides that of charity? Could he be just or honest? This problem is more complex because there is no end related to such virtues as the good of others is related to charity. But what reason could there be for refusing to call a man a just man if he acted justly because he loved truth and liberty, and wanted every man to be treated with a certain respect? And why should the truly honest man not follow honesty for the sake of the good that honest dealing brings to men? Of course, the usual difficulties can be raised about the rare case in which no good is foreseen from an individual act of honesty. But it is not evident that a man's desires could not give him reason to act honestly even here. He wants to live openly and in good faith with his neighbours; it is not all the same to him to lie and conceal.

If one wants to know whether there could be a truly moral man who accepted moral principles as hypothetical rules of conduct, as many people accept rules of etiquette as hypothetical rules of conduct, one must consider the right kind of example. A man who demanded that morality should be brought under the heading of self-interest would not be a good candidate, nor would anyone who was ready to be

---

[5]Immanuel Kant, *Metaphysic of Morals*, Pt. II, Introduction, sec. II.

[6]Immanuel Kant, *Critique of Practical Reason*, trans. L. W. Beck, p. 133.

[7]One who believes that actions are performed to gain pleasure or avoid pain.

---

[8]It is not, of course, necessary that charitable actions should succeed in helping others; but when they do so they do not happen to do so, since that is necessarily their aim. (Footnote added, 1977.)

charitable or honest only so long as he felt inclined. A cause such as justice makes strenuous demands, but this is not peculiar to morality, and men are prepared to toil to achieve many ends not endorsed by morality. That they are prepared to fight so hard for moral ends—for example, for liberty and justice—depends on the fact that these are the kinds of ends that arouse devotion. To sacrifice a great deal for the sake of etiquette one would need to be under the spell of the emphatic "ought." One could hardly be devoted to behaving *comme il faut.*

In spite of all that has been urged in favour of the hypothetical imperative in ethics, I am sure that many people will be unconvinced and will argue that one element essential to moral virtue is still missing. This missing feature is the recognition of a duty to adopt those ends which we have attributed to the moral man. We have said that he does care about others, and about causes such as liberty and justice; that it is on this account that he will accept a system of morality. But what if he never cared about such things, or what if he ceased to care? Is it not the case that he ought to care? This is exactly what Kant would say, for though at times he sounds as if he thought that morality is not concerned with ends, at others he insists that the adoption of ends such as the happiness of others is itself dictated by morality.[9] How is this proposition to be regarded by one who rejects all talk about the binding force of the moral law? He will agree that a moral man has moral ends and cannot be indifferent to matters such as suffering and injustice. Further, he will recognise in the statement that one ought to care about these things a correct application of the non-hypothetical moral "ought" by which society is apt to voice its demands. He will not, however, take the fact that he ought to have certain ends as in itself reason to adopt them. If he himself is a moral man then he cares about such things, but not "because he ought." If he is an amoral man he may deny that he has any reason to trouble his head over this or any other moral demand. Of course he may be mistaken, and his life as well as others' lives may be most sadly spoiled by his selfishness. But this is not what is urged by those who think they can close the matter by an emphatic use of "ought." My argument is that they are relying on an illusion, as if trying to give the moral "ought" a magic force.[10]

This conclusion may, as I said, appear dangerous and subversive of morality. We are apt to panic at the thought that we ourselves, or other people, might stop caring about the things we do care about, and we feel that the categorical imperative gives us some control over the situation. But it is interesting that the people of Leningrad were not struck by the thought that only the contingent fact that other citizens shared their loyalty and devotion to the city stood between them and the Germans during the terrible years of the siege. Perhaps we should be less troubled than we are by fear of defection from the moral cause; perhaps we should even have less reason to fear it if people thought of themselves as volunteers banded together to fight for liberty and justice and against inhumanity and oppression. It is often felt, even if obscurely, that there is an element of deception in the official line about morality. And while some have been persuaded by talk about the authority of the moral law, others have turned away with a sense of distrust.

[9]Kant, *Metaphysic of Morals*, Pt. II, sec. XXX.

[10]See G. E. M. Anscombe, "Modern Moral Philosophy," *Philosophy* (1958). My view is different from Miss Anscombe's, but I have learned from her.

REVIEW QUESTIONS

1. What is a categorical imperative? A hypothetical imperative?
2. On what point does Foot think Kant is wrong?
3. What is her argument to show that Kant is mistaken?
4. What does Foot mean by "morality as a system of hypothetical imperatives"? How would such a system apply to actual cases?
5. How does Foot respond to the question of whether a man accepting only hypothetical imperatives could possess moral virtues?

39

❧

NELSON GOODMAN

Nelson Goodman (1906–1998) until his retirement was professor of philosophy at Harvard University. In this selection, taken from his book *Fact, Fiction, and Forecast*, Goodman argues that besides Hume's puzzle over induction, there is a second problem: what are the rules for deciding which properties are projectable into the future? Why does seeing another black raven confirm our hypothesis that all ravens are black or that the next raven we see will be black but the seeing of three bachelors in a room not count as evidence that tomorrow we will see three bachelors in this room? Inventing a new color term *grue*, made up from our color terms *green* and *blue*, Goodman illustrates the problem of projectability.

FOR FURTHER READING

Elgin, Catherine. *With Reference to Reference* (Hackett Publishing Co., 1983).
Goodman, Nelson. *Fact, Fiction and Forecast* (Harvard University Press, 1983).
Goodman, Nelson. *Problems and Projects* (Hackett Publishing Co., 1972).
Goodman, Nelson. *Ways of Worldmaking* (Hackett Publishing Co., 1978).
Mitchell, W. J. T. *Iconology* (University of Chicago Press, 1986).
Scheffler, I. *The Anatomy of Inquiry* (Hackett Publishing Co., 1981).

FACT, FICTION, AND FORECAST

THE NEW RIDDLE OF INDUCTION

Confirmation of a hypothesis by an instance depends rather heavily upon features of the hypothesis other than its syntactical form. That a given piece of copper conducts electricity increases the credibility of statements asserting that other pieces of copper conduct electricity, and thus confirms the hypothesis that all copper conducts electricity. But the fact that a given man now in this room is a third son does not increase the credibility of statements asserting that other men now in this room are third sons, and so does not confirm the hypothesis that all men now in this room are third sons. Yet in both cases our hypothesis is a generalization of the evidence statement. The difference is that in the former case the hypothesis is a *lawlike* statement; while in the latter case, the hypothesis is a merely contingent or accidental generality. Only a statement that is *lawlike*—regardless of its truth or falsity or its scientific importance—is capable of receiving confirmation from an instance of it; accidental statements are not. Plainly, then, we must look for a way of distinguishing lawlike from accidental statements.

So long as what seems to be needed is merely a way of excluding a few odd and unwanted cases that are inadvertently admitted by our definition of confirmation, the problem may not seem very hard or very pressing. We fully expect that minor defects will be found in our definition and that the necessary refinements will have to be worked out patiently one after another. But some further examples will show that our present difficulty is of a much graver kind.

Suppose that all emeralds examined before a certain time *t* are green.[1] At time *t*, then, our observations support the hypothesis that all emeralds are green; and this is in accord with our definition of confirmation. Our evidence statements assert that emerald *a* is green, that emerald *b* is green, and so on; and each confirms the general hypothesis that all emeralds are green. So far, so good.

Now let me introduce another predicate less familiar than "green". It is the predicate "grue" and it applies to all things examined before *t* just in case they are green but to other things just in case they are blue. Then at time *t* we have, for each evidence statement asserting that a given emerald is green, a parallel evidence statement asserting that that emerald is grue. And that statements that emerald *a* is grue, that emerald *b* is grue, and so on, will each confirm the general hypothesis that all emeralds are grue. Thus according to our definition, the prediction that all emeralds subsequently examined will be green and the prediction that all will be grue are alike confirmed by evidence statements describing the same observations. But if an emerald subsequently examined is grue, it is blue and hence not green. Thus although we are well aware which of the two incompatible predictions is genuinely confirmed, they are equally well confirmed according to our present definition. Moreover, it is clear that if we simply choose an appropriate predicate, then on the basis of these same observations we shall have equal confirmation, by our definition, for any prediction whatever about other emeralds—or indeed about anything else.[2] As in our earlier example, only the predictions subsumed under lawlike hypotheses are

[1] Although the example used is different, the argument to follow is substantially the same as that set forth in my note 'A Query on Confirmation' [*Journal of Philosophy*, XLIII (1946), 383–385.]

[2] For instance, we shall have equal confirmation, by our present definition, for the prediction that roses subsequently examined will be blue. Let "emerose" apply just to emeralds examined before time *t*, and to roses examined later. Then all emeroses so far examined are grue, and this confirms the hypothesis that all emeroses are grue and hence the prediction that roses subsequently examined will be blue. The problem raised by such antecedents has been little noticed, but is no easier to meet than that raised by similarly perverse consequents.

genuinely confirmed; but we have no criterion as yet for determining lawlikeness. And now we see that without some criterion, our definition not merely includes a few unwanted cases, but is so completely ineffectual that it virtually excludes nothing. We are left once again with the intolerable result that anything confirms anything. This difficulty cannot be set aside as an annoying detail to be taken care of in due course. It has to be met before our definition will work at all.

Nevertheless, the difficulty is often slighted because on the surface there seem to be easy ways of dealing with it. Sometimes, for example, the problem is thought to be much like the paradox of the ravens. We are here again, it is pointed out, making tacit and illegitimate use of information outside the stated evidence: the information, for example, that different samples of one material are usually alike in conductivity, and the information that different men in a lecture audience are usually not alike in the number of their older brothers. But while it is true that such information is being smuggled in, this does not by itself settle the matter as it settles the matter of the ravens. There the point was that when the smuggled information is forthrightly declared, its effect upon the confirmation of the hypothesis in question is immediately and properly registered by the definition we are using. On the other hand, if to our initial evidence we add statements concerning the conductivity of pieces of other materials or concerning the number of older brothers of members of other lecture audiences, this will not in the least affect the confirmation, according to our definition, of the hypothesis concerning copper or of that concerning other lecture audiences. Since our definition is insensitive to the bearing upon hypotheses of evidence so related to them, even when the evidence is fully declared, the difficulty about accidental hypotheses cannot be explained away on the ground that such evidence is being surreptitiously taken into account.

A more promising suggestion is to explain the matter in terms of the effect of this other evidence not directly upon the hypothesis in question but *in*directly through other hypotheses that *are* confirmed, according to our definition, by such evidence. Our information about other materials does by our defi-

nition confirm such hypotheses as that all pieces of iron conduct electricity, that no pieces of rubber do, and so on; and these hypotheses, the explanation runs, impart to the hypothesis that all pieces of copper conduct electricity (and also to the hypothesis that none do) the character of lawlikeness—that is, amenability to confirmation by direct positive instances when found. On the other hand, our information about other lecture audiences *dis*confirms many hypotheses to the effect that all the men in one audience are third sons, or that none are; and this strips any character of lawlikeness from the hypothesis that all (or the hypothesis that none) of the men in *this* audience are third sons. But clearly if this course is to be followed, the circumstances under which hypotheses are thus related to one another will have to be precisely articulated.

The problem, then, is to define the relevant ways in which such hypotheses must be alike. Evidence for the hypothesis that all iron conducts electricity enhances the lawlikeness of the hypothesis that all zirconium conducts electricity, but does not similarly affect the hypothesis that all the objects on my desk conduct electricity. Wherein lies the difference? The first two hypotheses fall under the broader hypothesis—call it "H"—that every class of things of the same material is uniform in conductivity; the first and third fall only under some such hypothesis as—call it "K"—that every class of things that are either all of the same material or all on a desk is uniform in conductivity. Clearly the important difference here is that evidence for a statement affirming that one of the classes covered by H has the property in question increases the credibility of any statement affirming that another such class has this property; while nothing of the sort holds true with respect to K. But this is only to say that H is lawlike and K is not. We are faced anew with the very problem we are trying to solve: the problem of distinguishing between lawlike and accidental hypotheses.

The most popular way of attacking the problem takes its cue from the fact that accidental hypotheses seem typically to involve some spatial or temporal restriction, or reference to some particular individual. They seem to concern the people in some particular room, or the objects on some particular person's desk; while lawlike hypotheses characteristically concern all ravens or all pieces of copper whatsoever. Complete generality is thus very often supposed to be a sufficient condition of lawlikeness; but to define this complete generality is by no means easy. Merely to require that the hypothesis contain no term naming, describing, or indicating a particular thing or location will obviously not be enough. The troublesome hypothesis that all emeralds are grue contains no such term; and where such a term does occur, as in hypotheses about men in *this room*, it can be suppressed in favor of some predicate (short or long, new or old) that contains no such term but applies only to exactly the same things. One might think, then, of excluding not only hypotheses that actually contain terms for specific individuals but also all hypotheses that are equivalent to others that do contain such terms. But, as we have just seen, to exclude only hypotheses of which *all* equivalents contain such terms is to exclude nothing. On the other hand, to exclude all hypotheses that have *some* equivalent containing such a term is to exclude everything; for even the hypothesis

All grass is green

has as an equivalent

All grass in London or elsewhere is green.

The next step, therefore, has been to consider ruling out predicates of certain kinds. A syntactically universal hypothesis is lawlike, the proposal runs, if its predicates are 'purely qualitative' or 'nonpositional'.[3] This will obviously accomplish nothing if a purely qualitative predicate is then conceived either as one that is equivalent to some expression free of terms for specific individuals, or as one that is equivalent to no expression that contains such a term; for this only raises again the difficulties just pointed out. The claim appears to be rather that at

least in the case of a simple enough predicate we can readily determine by direct inspection of its meaning whether or not it is purely qualitative. But even aside from obscurities in the notion of 'the meaning' of a predicate, this claim seems to me wrong. I simply do not know how to tell whether a predicate is qualitative or positional, except perhaps by completely begging the question at issue and asking whether the predicate is 'well-behaved'—that is, whether simple syntactically universal hypotheses applying it are lawlike.

This statement will not go unprotested. "Consider", it will be argued, "the predicates 'blue' and 'green' and the predicate 'grue' introduced earlier, and also the predicate 'bleen' that applies to emeralds examined before time *t* just in case they are blue and to other emeralds just in case they are green. Surely it is clear", the argument runs, "that the first two are purely qualitative and the second two are not; for the meaning of each of the latter two plainly involves reference to a specific temporal position." To this I reply that indeed I do recognize the first two as well-behaved predicates admissible in lawlike hypotheses, and the second two as ill-behaved predicates. But the argument that the former but not the latter are purely qualitative seems to me quite unsound. True enough, if we start with "blue" and "green," then "grue" and "bleen" will be explained in terms of "blue" and "green" and a temporal term. But equally truly, if we start with "grue" and "bleen," then "blue" and "green" will be explained in terms of "grue" and "bleen" and a temporal term; "green", for example, applies to emeralds examined before time *t* just in case they are grue, and to other emeralds just in case they are bleen. Thus qualitativeness is an entirely relative matter and does not by itself establish any dichotomy of predicates. This relativity seems to be completely overlooked by those who contend that the qualitative character of a predicate is a criterion for its good behavior.

Of course, one may ask why we need worry about such unfamiliar predicates as "grue" or about accidental hypotheses in general, since we are unlikely to use them in making predictions. If our definition works for such hypotheses as are normally employed, isn't that all we need? In a sense, yes; but only in the sense that we need no definition, no

---

[3] Carnap took this course in his paper 'On the Application of Inductive Logic', *Philosophy and Phenomenological Research*, vol. 8 (1947), pp. 133–47, which is in part a reply to my 'A Query on Confirmation'. The discussion was continued in my note 'On Infirmities of Confirmation Theory', *Philosophy and Phenomenological Research*, vol. 8 (1947), pp. 149–51; and in Carnap's 'Reply to Nelson Goodman', same journal, same volume, pp. 461–2.

theory of induction, and no philosophy of knowledge at all. We get along well enough without them in daily life and in scientific research. But if we seek a theory at all, we cannot excuse gross anomalies resulting from a proposed theory by pleading that we can avoid them in practice. The odd cases we have been considering are clinically pure cases that, though seldom encountered in practice, nevertheless display to best advantage the symptoms of a widespread and destructive malady.

We have so far neither any answer nor any promising clue to an answer to the question what distinguishes lawlike or confirmable hypotheses from accidental or non-confirmable ones; and what may at first have seemed a minor technical difficulty has taken on the stature of a major obstacle to the development of a satisfactory theory of confirmation. It is this problem that I call the new riddle of induction.

At the beginning of this lecture, I expressed the opinion that the problem of induction is still unsolved, but that the difficulties that face us today are not the old ones; and I have tried to outline the changes that have taken place. The problem of justifying induction has been displaced by the problem of defining confirmation, and our work upon this has left us with the residual problem of distinguishing between confirmable and non-confirmable hypotheses. One might say roughly that the first question was "Why does a positive instance of a hypothesis give any grounds for predicting further instances?"; that the newer question was "What is a positive instance of a hypothesis?"; and that the crucial remaining question is "What hypotheses are confirmed by their positive instances?"

The vast amount of effort expended on the problem of induction in modern times has thus altered our afflictions but hardly relieved them. The original difficulty about induction arose from the recognition that anything may follow upon anything. Then, in attempting to define confirmation in terms of the converse of the consequence relation, we found ourselves with the distressingly similar difficulty that our definition would make any statement confirm any other. And now, after modifying our definition drastically, we still get the old devastating result that any statement will confirm any statement.

Until we find a way of exercising some control over the hypotheses to be admitted, our definition makes no distinction whatsoever between valid and invalid inductive inferences.

The real inadequacy of Hume's account lay not in his descriptive approach but in the imprecision of his description. Regularities' inexperience, according to him, give rise to habits of expectation; and thus it is predictions conforming to past regularities that are normal or valid. But Hume overlooks the fact that some regularities do and some do not establish such habits; that predictions based on some regularities are valid while predictions based on other regularities are not. Every word you have heard me say has occurred prior to the final sentence of this lecture; but that does not, I hope, create any expectation that every word you will hear me say will be prior to that sentence. Again, consider our case of emeralds. All those examined before time t are green; and this leads us to expect, and confirms the prediction, that the next one will be green. But also, all those examined are grue; and this does not lead us to expect, and does not confirm the prediction, that the next one will be grue. Regularity in greenness confirms the prediction of further cases; regularity in grueness does not. To say that valid predictions are those based on past regularities, without being able to say *which* regularities, is thus quite pointless. Regularities are where you find them, and you can find them anywhere. As we have seen, Hume's failure to recognize and deal with this problem has been shared even by his most recent successors.

As a result, what we have in current confirmation theory is a definition that is adequate for certain cases that so far can be described only as those for which it is adequate. The theory works where it works. A hypothesis is confirmed by statements related to it in the prescribed way provided it is so confirmed. This is a good deal like having a theory that tells us that the area of a plane figure is one-half the base times the altitude, without telling us for what figures this holds. We must somehow find a way of distinguishing lawlike hypotheses, to which our definition of confirmation applies, from accidental hypotheses, to which it does not.

Today I have been speaking solely of the problem of induction, but what has been said applies equally to the more general problem of projection. As pointed out earlier, the problem of prediction from past to future cases is but a narrower version of the problem of projecting from any set of cases to others. We saw that a whole cluster of troublesome problems concerning dispositions and possibility can be reduced to this problem of projection. That is why the new riddle of induction, which is more broadly the problem of distinguishing between projectible and non-projectible hypotheses, is as important as it is exasperating.

Our failures teach us, I think, that lawlike or projectible hypotheses cannot be distinguished on any merely syntactical grounds or even on the ground that these hypotheses are somehow purely general in meaning.

REVIEW QUESTIONS

1. What is the "new riddle of induction"?
2. What is the "intolerable result" that Goodman highlights?
3. According to Goodman, what new problem has displaced the old problem of justifying induction?
4. What does he mean by "We must somehow find a way to distinguish lawlike hypotheses . . . from accidental hypotheses"?
5. What point does Goodman make with the example of the color term *grue*?

40

JOHN RAWLS

John Rawls (1921–2002), perhaps the most important political philosopher in the twentieth century, was educated at Princeton University and taught at Cornell and Harvard universities. No twentieth-century work in moral and political philosophy has had a greater influence on our generation than Rawls's *A Theory of Justice* (1971). Robert Nisbett calls it the "long awaited successor to Rousseau's *Social Contract*, the Rock on which the Church of Equality can properly be founded in our time." In scope and power it rivals the classics of Hobbes, Locke, and Rousseau. Fundamentally a strong form of liberal egalitarianism, it seeks to justify the welfare state. We have included, as our final reading in this book of classics, Rawls's earlier essay, "Justice as Fairness" (1955), which outlines the central ideas later to become developed in *A Theory of Justice.*

In "Justice as Fairness," Rawls sets forth a hypothetical contract theory in which participants decide on practices acknowledged "to be fair [and] bind themselves by the duty of fair play to follow the rules when it comes their turn to do so, and this implies a limitation on their pursuit of self-interest in particular cases." Parties to the contract are to act as rationally self-interested agents, and choose the basic principles which will govern their society. Rawls thinks that these conditions ensure objectivity and impartiality of judgment. He calls the system "Justice as Fairness," because he seeks a contract on whose fairness all parties will agree. In effect, the parties to the contract should choose the kind of principles they could live with if their enemies were assigning them positions in society. Rawls argues that they would choose the following two principles:

1. Everyone will have an equal right to the most extensive liberty compatible with similar liberty for others.

2. "Inequalities are arbitrary unless it is reasonable to expect that they will work out for everyone's advantage, and provided the positions and offices to which they attach, or from which they may be gained, are open to all. These principles express justice as a complex of three ideas: liberty, equality and reward for services contributing to the common good."

It might be pointed out that this two-part second principle will be transformed in *A Theory of Justice*, where Rawls introduces the *difference* principle. The second principle will become:

2. Social and economic inequalities must satisfy two conditions:

a. They are to the greatest benefit of the least advantaged ("the difference principle").
b. They are attached to positions open to all under conditions of fair equality of opportunity.

Rawls's egalitarianism is more fully developed in *A Theory of Justice*, but it is present in the article, at least in outline. He believes that each minimally rational human being, who has a conception of the good (a value system), and is able to act justly, is valuable and equally so. He now states the main idea of his theory. Yet inequalities are justified if they work for the good of all. In his book, of course, that is not sufficient. They must aid the least well off in order to be justified.

Here is how Rawls states his aim in *A Theory of Justice:*

My aim is to present a conception of justice which generalizes and carries to a higher level of abstraction the familiar theory of the social contract as found, say, in Locke, Rousseau, and Kant. In order to do this we are not to think of the original contract as one to enter a particular society or to set up a particular form of government. Rather, the guiding idea is that the principles of justice for the basic structure of society are the object of the original agreement. They are the principles that free and rational persons concerned to further their own interests would accept in an initial position of equality as defining the fundamental terms of their association. These principles are to regulate all further agreements; they specify the kinds of social cooperation that can be entered into and the forms of government that can be established. This way of regarding the principles of justice I shall call *justice as fairness.*

Thus we are to imagine that those who engage in social cooperation choose together, in one joint act, the principles which are to assign basic rights and duties and to determine the division of social benefits. Men are to decide in advance how they are to regulate their claims against one another and what is to be the foundation charter of their society. Just as each person must decide by rational reflection what constitutes his good, that is, the system of ends which it is rational for him to pursue, so a group of persons must decide once and for all what is to count among them as just and unjust. The choice which rational men would make in this hypothetical situation of equal liberty, assuming for the present that this choice problem has a solution, determines the principle of justice.

In *justice as fairness* the original position of equality corresponds to the state of nature in the traditional theory of the social contract. This original position is not, of course, thought of as an actual historical state of affairs, much less as a primitive condition of culture. It is understood as a purely hypothetical situation characterized so as to lead to a certain conception of justice. Among the essential features of this situation is that no one knows his place in society, his class position or social status, nor does any one know his fortune in the distribution of natural assets and abilities, his intelligence, strength, and the like. I shall even assume that the parties do not know their conceptions of the good or their special psychological propensities. The principles of justice are chosen behind the *veil of ignorance.* This ensures that no one is advantaged or disadvantaged in the choice of principles by the outcome of natural chance or the contingency of social circumstances. Since all are similarly situated and no one is able to design principles to favor his particular condition, the principles of justice are the result of a fair agreement or bargain. For given the circumstances of the original position, the symmetry of everyone's relations to each other, this initial situation is fair between individuals as moral persons, that is, as rational beings with their own ends and capable, I shall assume, of a sense of justice. The *original position* is, one might say, the appropriate initial status quo, and thus the fundamental agreements reached in it are fair. This explains the propriety of the name "justice as fairness": it conveys the idea that the principles of justice are agreed to in an initial situation that is fair. . . .

Finally, Rawls argues that not only is the principle of fairness not a utilitarian principle but it is opposed to utilitarianism, because maximal utility may not be sought if it imposes unfair burdens on the less well off. Persons have rights which even the good of the society may not override.

FOR FURTHER READING

Barry, Brian. *Theories of Justice* (University of California Press, 1989).

Daniels, Norman, ed. *Reading Rawls: Critical Studies of A Theory of Justice* (Basil Blackwell, 1975).

Kukathas, Chandran, and Philip Pettit. *Rawls: A Theory of Justice and Its Critics* (Stanford University Press, 1990).

Kymlicka, Will. *Contemporary Political Theory: An Introduction* (Oxford University Press, 1990).

Nozick, Robert. *Anarchy, State and Utopia* (Basic Books, 1974). A Libertarian critique of Rawls.

Pogge, Thomas. *Realizing Rawls* (Cornell University Press, 1989).

Rawls, John. *Political Liberalism* (Columbia University Press, 1994).

Rawls, John. *A Theory of Justice* (Harvard University Press, 1971).

Sandel, Michael. *Liberalism and the Limits of Justice* (Cambridge University Press, 1982).

Sterba, James, ed. *Justice: Alternative Political Perspectives*, 2nd ed. (Wadsworth Publishing Company, 1992). Contains a useful set of readings.

Wolff, Robert Paul. *Understanding Rawls* (Princeton University Press, 1977).

JUSTICE AS FAIRNESS

1. It might seem at first sight that the concepts of justice and fairness are the same, and that there is no reason to distinguish them, or to say that one is more fundamental than the other. I think that this impression is mistaken. In this paper I wish to show that the fundamental idea in the concept of justice is fairness; and I wish to offer an analysis of the concept of justice from this point of view. To bring out the force of this claim, and the analysis based upon it, I shall then argue that it is this aspect of justice for which utilitarianism, in its classical form, is unable to account, but which is expressed, even if misleadingly, by the ideas of the social contract.

To start with I shall develop a particular conception of justice by stating and commenting upon two principles which specify it, and by considering the circumstances and conditions under which they may be thought to arise. The principles defining this conception, and the conception itself are, of course, familiar. It may be possible, however, by using the notion of fairness as a framework, to assemble and to look at them in a new way. Before stating this

"Justice as Fairness," *Philosophical Review*, 1955, reprinted by permission of the author.

conception, however, the following preliminary matters should be kept in mind.

Throughout I consider justice only as a virtue of social institutions, or what I shall call practices.[1] The principles of justice are regarded as formulating restrictions as to how practices may define positions and offices, and assign thereto powers and liabilities, rights and duties. Justice as a virtue of particular actions or of persons I do not take up at all. It is important to distinguish these various subjects of justice, since the meaning of the concept varies according to whether it is applied to practices, particular actions, or persons. These meanings are, indeed, connected, but they are not identical. I shall confine my discussion to the sense of justice as applied to practices, since this sense is the basic one. Once it is understood, the other senses should go quite easily.

Justice is to be understood in its customary sense as representing but *one* of the many virtues of social institutions, for these may be antiquated, inefficient, degrading, or any number of other things, without being unjust. Justice is not to be confused with an all-inclusive vision of a good society; it is only one part of any such conception. It is important, for example, to distinguish that sense of equality which is an aspect of the concept of justice from that sense of equality which belongs to a more comprehensive social ideal. There may well be inequalities which one concedes are just, or at least not unjust, but which, nevertheless, one wishes, on other grounds, to do away with. I shall focus attention, then, on the usual sense of justice in which it is essentially the elimination of arbitrary distinctions and the establishment, within the structure of a practice, of a proper balance between competing claims.

Finally, there is no need to consider the principles discussed below as *the* principles of justice. For the moment it is sufficient that they are typical of a family of principles normally associated with the concept of justice. The way in which the principles of this family resemble one another, as shown by the background against which they may be thought to arise, will be made clear by the whole of the subsequent argument.

2. The conception of justice which I want to develop may be stated in the form of two principles as follows: first, each person participating in a practice, or affected by it, has an equal right to the most extensive liberty compatible with a like liberty for all; and second, inequalities are arbitrary unless it is reasonable to expect that they will work out for everyone's advantage, and provided the positions and offices to which they attach, or from which they may be gained, are open to all. These principles express justice as a complex of three ideas: liberty, equality, and reward for services contributing to the common good.[2]

The term "person" is to be construed variously depending on the circumstances. On some occasions it will mean human individuals, but in others it may refer to nations, provinces, business firms, churches, teams, and so on. The principles of justice apply in all these instances, although there is a certain logical priority to the case of human individuals. As I

---

[1] I use the word "practice" throughout as a sort of technical term meaning any form of activity specified by a system of rules which defines offices, roles, moves, penalties, defenses, and so on, and which gives the activity its structure. As examples one may think of games and rituals, trials and parliaments, markets and systems of property. I have attempted a partial analysis of the notion of a practice in a paper "Two Concepts of Rules" *Philosophical Review* LXIV (1955) 3–32.

[2] These principles are of course well-known in one form or another and appear in many analyses of justice even where the writers differ widely on other matters. Thus if the principle of equal liberty is commonly associated with Kant (see *The Philosophy of Law*, tr. by W. Hastie, Edinburgh, 1887, pp. 56 f.), it may be claimed that it can also be found in J. S. Mill's *On Liberty* and elsewhere, and in many other liberal writers. Recently H. L. A. Hart has argued for something like it in his paper "Are There Any Natural Rights?," *Philosophical Review*, LXIV (1955), 175–191. The injustice of inequalities which are not won in return for a contribution to the common advantage is, of course, widespread in political writings of all sorts. The conception of justice here discussed is distinctive, if at all, only in selecting these two principles in this form; but for another similar analysis, see the discussion by W. D. Lamont, *The Principles of Moral Judgment* (Oxford, 1946), ch. v.

shall use the term "person," it will be ambiguous in the manner indicated.

The first principle holds, of course, only if other things are equal: that is, while there must always be a justification for departing from the initial position of equal liberty (which is defined by the pattern of rights and duties, powers and liabilities, established by a practice), and the burden of proof is placed on him who would depart from it, nevertheless, there can be, and often there is, a justification for doing so. Now, that similar particular cases, as defined by a practice, should be treated similarly as they arise, is part of the very concept of a practice; it is involved in the notion of an activity in accordance with rules.[3] The first principle expresses an analogous conception, but as applied to the structure of practices themselves. It holds, for example, that there is a presumption against the distinctions and classifications made by legal systems and other practices to the extent that they infringe on the original and equal liberty of the persons participating in them. The second principle defines how this presumption may be rebutted.

It might be argued at this point that justice requires only an equal liberty. If, however, a greater liberty were possible for all without loss or conflict, then it would be irrational to settle on a lesser liberty. There is no reason for circumscribing rights unless their exercise would be incompatible, or would render the practice defining them less effective. Therefore no serious distortion of the concept of justice is likely to follow from including within it the concept of the greatest equal liberty.

The second principle defines what sorts of inequalities are permissible; it specifies how the presumption laid down by the first principle may be put aside. Now by inequalities it is best to understand not *any* differences between offices and positions, but differences in the benefits and burdens attached to them either directly or indirectly, such as prestige and wealth, or liability to taxation and compulsory

services. Players in a game do not protest against there being different positions, such as batter, pitcher, catcher, and the like, nor to there being various privileges and powers as specified by the rules; nor do the citizens of a country object to there being the different offices of government such as president, senator, governor, judge, and so on, each with their special rights and duties. It is not differences of this kind that are normally thought of as inequalities, but differences in the resulting distribution established by a practice, or made possible by it, of the things men strive to attain or avoid. Thus they may complain about the pattern of honors and rewards set up by a practice (e.g., the privileges and salaries of government officials) or they may object to the distribution of power and wealth which results from the various ways in which men avail themselves of the opportunities allowed by it (e.g., the concentration of wealth which may develop in a free price system allowing large entrepreneurial or speculative gains).

It should be noted that the second principle holds that an inequality is allowed only if there is reason to believe that the practice with the inequality, or resulting in it, will work for the advantage of *every* party engaging in it. Here it is important to stress that *every* party must gain from the inequality. Since the principle applies to practices, it implies that the representative man in every office or position defined by a practice, when he views it as a going concern, must find it reasonable to prefer his condition and prospects with the inequality to what they would be under the practice without it. The principle excludes, therefore, the justification of inequalities on the grounds that the disadvantages of those in one position are outweighed by the greater advantages of those in another position. This rather simple restriction is the main modification I wish to make in the utilitarian principle as usually understood. When coupled with the notion of a practice, it is a restriction of consequence,[4] and one which some utilitari-

---

[3] This point was made by Sidgwick, *Methods of Ethics*, 6th ed. (London, 1901), Bk. III, ch. v, sec. 1. It has recently been emphasized by Sir Isaiah Berlin in a symposium, "Equality," *Proceedings of the Aristotelian Society*, n.s. LVI (1955–56), 305 f.

[4] In the paper referred to above, footnote 2, I have tried to show the importance of taking practices as the proper subject of the utilitarian principle. The criticisms of so-called "restricted utilitarianism" by J. J. C. Smart, "Extreme and Restricted Utilitarianism," *Philosophical Quarterly*, VI

ans, e.g., Hume and Mill, have used in their discussions of justice without realizing apparently its significance, or at least without calling attention to it.[5] Why it is a significant modification of principle, changing one's conception of justice entirely, the whole of my argument will show.

Further, it is also necessary that the various offices to which special benefits or burdens attach are

---

(1956), 344–354, and by H. J. McCloskey, "An Examination of Restricted Utilitarianism," *Philosophical Review*, LXVI (1957), 466–485, do not affect my argument. These papers are concerned with the very general proposition, which is attributed (with what justice I shall not consider) to S. E. Toulmin and P. H. Nowell-Smith (and in the case of the latter paper, also, apparently, to me); namely, the proposition that particular moral actions are justified by appealing to moral rules, and moral rules in turn by reference to utility. But clearly I meant to defend no such view. My discussion of the concept of rules as maxims is an explicit rejection of it. What I did argue was that, in the *logically special* case of practices (although actually quite a common case) where the rules have special features and are not moral rules at all but legal rules or rules of games and the like (except, perhaps, in the case of promises), there is a peculiar force to the distinction between justifying particular actions and justifying the system of rules themselves. Even then I claimed only that restricting the utilitarian principle to practices as defined strengthened it. I did not argue for the position that this amendment alone is sufficient for a complete defense of utilitarianism as a general theory of morals. In this paper I take up the question as to how the utilitarian principle itself must be modified, but here, too, the subject of inquiry is not all of morality at once, but a limited topic, the concept of justice.

[5] It might seem as if J. S. Mill, in paragraph 36 of Chapter v of *Utilitarianism*, expressed the utilitarian principle in this modified form, but in the remaining two paragraphs of the chapter, and elsewhere, he would appear not to grasp the significance of the change. Hume often emphasizes that *every* man must benefit. For example, in discussing the utility of general rules, he holds that they are requisite to the "well-being of every individual"; from a stable system of property "every individual person must find himself a gainer in balancing the account. . . ." "Every member of society is sensible of this interest; everyone expresses this sense to his fellows along with the resolution he has taken of squaring his actions by it on the conditions that others will do the same." *A Treatise of Human Nature*, Bk. III, Pt. II, Section II, paragraph 22.

open to all. It may be, for example, to the common advantage, as just defined, to attach special benefits to certain offices. Perhaps by doing so the requisite talent can be attracted to them and encouraged to give its best efforts. But any offices having special benefits must be won in a fair competition in which contestants are judged on their merits. If some offices were not open, those excluded would normally be justified in feeling unjustly treated, even if they benefited from the greater efforts of those who were allowed to compete for them. Now if one can assume that offices are open, it is necessary only to consider the design of practices themselves and how they jointly, as a system, work together. It will be a mistake to focus attention on the varying relative positions of particular persons, who may be known to us by their proper names, and to require that each such change, as a once for all transaction viewed in isolation, must be in itself just. It is the system of practices which is to be judged, and judged from a general point of view: unless one is prepared to criticize it from the standpoint of a representative man holding some particular office, one has no complaint against it.

3. Given these principles one might try to derive them from a priori principles of reason, or claim that they were known by intuition. These are familiar enough steps and, at least in the case of the first principle, might be made with some success. Usually, however, such arguments, made at this point, are unconvincing. They are not likely to lead to an understanding of the basis of the principles of justice, not at least as principles of justice. I wish, therefore, to look at the principles in a different way.

Imagine a society of persons amongst whom a certain system of practices is *already* well established. Now suppose that by and large they are mutually self-interested; their allegiance to their established practice is normally founded on the prospect of self-advantage. One need not assume that, in all senses of the term "person," the persons in this society are mutually self-interested. If the characterization as mutually self-interested applies when the line of division is the family, it may still be true that members of families are bound by ties of sentiment and affection and willingly acknowledge duties in contradiction to self-interest. Mutual self-interestedness in the relations between families, nations, churches, and the like, is commonly associated with intense loyalty and devotion on the part of individual members. Therefore, one can form a more realistic conception of this society if one thinks of it as consisting of mutually self-interested families, or some other association. Further, it is not necessary to suppose that these persons are mutually self-interested under all circumstances, but only in the usual situations in which they participate in their common practices.

Now suppose also that these persons are rational: they know their own interests more or less accurately; they are capable of tracing out the likely consequences of adopting one practice rather than another; they are capable of adhering to a course of action once they have decided upon it; they can resist present temptations and the enticements of immediate gain; and the bare knowledge or perception of the difference between their condition and that of others is not, within certain limits and in itself, a source of great dissatisfaction. Only the last point adds anything to the usual definition of rationality. This definition should allow, I think, for the idea that a rational man would not be greatly downcast from knowing, or seeing, that others are in a better position than himself, unless he thought their being so was the result of injustice, or the consequence of letting chance work itself out for no useful common purpose, and so on. So if these persons strike us as unpleasantly egoistic, they are at least free in some degree from the fault of envy.[6]

Finally, assume that these persons have roughly similar needs and interests, or needs and interests in various ways complementary, so that fruitful cooperation amongst them is possible; and suppose that they are sufficiently equal in power and ability to

guarantee that in normal circumstances none is able to dominate the others. This condition (as well as the other) may seem excessively vague; but in view of the conception of justice to which the argument leads, there seems no reason for making it more exact here.

Since these persons are conceived as engaging in their common practices, which are already established, there is no question of our supposing them to come together to deliberate as to how they will set these practices up for the first time. Yet we can imagine that from time to time they discuss with one another whether any of them has a legitimate complaint against their established institutions. Such discussions are perfectly natural in any normal society. Now suppose that they have settled on doing this in the following way. They first try to arrive at the principles by which complaints, and so practices themselves, are to be judged. Their procedure for this is to let each person propose the principles upon which he wishes these complaints to be tried with the understanding that, if acknowledged, the complaints of others will be similarly tried, and that no complaints will be heard at all until everyone is roughly of one mind as to how complaints are to be judged. They each understand further that the principles proposed and acknowledged on this occasion are binding on future occasions. Thus each will be wary of proposing a principle which would give him a peculiar advantage, in his present circumstances, supposing it to be accepted. Each person knows that he will be bound by it in future circumstances the peculiarities of which cannot be known and which might well be such that the principle is then to his disadvantage. The idea is that everyone should be required to make *in advance* a firm commitment which others also may reasonably be expected to make, and that no one be given the opportunity to tailor the canons of a legitimate complaint to fit his own special condition, and then to discard them when they no longer suit his purpose. Hence each person will propose principles of a general kind which will, to a large degree, gain their sense from the various applications to be made of them, the particular circumstances of which being as yet unknown. These principles will express the conditions in accordance with which each is the

[6]It is not possible to discuss here this addition to the usual conception of rationality. If it seems peculiar, it may be worth remarking that it is analogous to the modification of the utilitarian principle which the argument as a whole is designed to explain and justify. In the same way that the satisfaction of interests, the representative claims of which violate the principles of justice, is not reason for having a practice (see sec. 7), unfounded envy, within limits, need not to be taken into account.

least unwilling to have his interests limited in the design of practices, given the competing interests of the others, on the supposition that the interests of others will be limited likewise. The restrictions which would so arise might be thought of as those a person would keep in mind if he were designing a practice in which his enemy were to assign him his place.

The two main parts of this conjectural account have a definite significance. The character and respective situations of the parties reflect the typical circumstances in which questions of justice arise. The procedure whereby principles are proposed and acknowledged represents constraints, analogous to those of having a morality, whereby rational and mutually self-interested persons are brought to act reasonably. Thus the first part reflects the fact that questions of justice arise when conflicting claims are made upon the design of a practice and where it is taken for granted that each person will insist, as far as possible, on what he considers his rights. It is typical of cases of justice to involve persons who are pressing on one another their claims, between which a fair balance or equilibrium must be found. On the other hand, as expressed by the second part, having a morality must at least imply the acknowledgment of principles as impartially applying to one's own conduct as well as to another's, and moreover principles which may constitute a constraint, or limitation, upon the pursuit of one's own interests. There are, of course, other aspects of having a morality: the acknowledgment of moral principles must show itself in accepting a reference to them as reasons for limiting one's claims, in acknowledging the burden of providing a special explanation, or excuse, when one acts contrary to them, or else in showing shame and remorse and a desire to make amends, and so on. It is sufficient to remark here that having a morality is analogous to having made a firm commitment in advance; for one must acknowledge the principles of morality even when to one's disadvantage.[7] A

man whose moral judgments always coincided with his interests could be suspected of having no morality at all.

Thus the two parts of the foregoing account are intended to mirror the kinds of circumstances in which questions of justice arise and the constraints which having a morality would impose upon persons so situated. In this way one can see how the acceptance of the principles of justice might come about, for given all these conditions as described, it would be natural if the two principles of justice were to be acknowledged. Since there is no way for anyone to win special advantages for himself, each might consider it reasonable to acknowledge equality as an initial principle. There is, however, no reason why they should regard this position as final; for if there are inequalities which satisfy the second principle, the immediate gain which equality would allow can be considered as intelligently invested in view of its future return. If, as is quite likely, these inequalities work as incentives to draw out better efforts, the members of this society may look upon them as concessions to human nature: they, like us, may think that people ideally should want to serve one another. But as they are mutually self-interested, their acceptance of these inequalities is merely the acceptance of the relations in which they actually stand, and a recognition of the motives which lead them to engage in their common practices. *They* have no title to complain of one another. And so provided that the conditions of the principle are met, there is no reason why they should not allow such inequalities. Indeed, it would be short-sighted of them not to do so, and could result, in most cases, only from their being dejected by the bare knowledge, or perception, that others are better situated. Each person will, however, insist on an advantage to himself, and so on a common advantage, for none is willing to sacrifice anything for the others.

These remarks are not offered as a proof that persons so conceived and circumstanced would settle on

---

[7]The idea that accepting a principle as a moral principle implies that one generally acts on it, failing a special explanation, has been stressed by R. M. Hare, *The Language of Morals* (Oxford, 1952). His formulation of it needs to be modified, however, along the lines suggested by P. L.

Gardiner, "On Assenting to a Moral Principle," *Proceedings of the Aristotelian Society*, n.s. LV (1955), 23–44. See also C. K. Grant, "Akrasia and the Criteria of Assent to Practical Principles," *Mind*, LXV (1956), 400–407, where the complexity of the criteria for assent is discussed.

the two principles, but only to show that these principles could have such a background, and so can be viewed as those principles which mutually self-interested and rational persons, when similarly situated and required to make in advance a firm commitment, could acknowledge as restrictions governing the assignment of rights and duties in their common practices, and thereby accept as limiting their rights against one another. The principles of justice may, then, be regarded as those principles which arise when the constraints of having a morality are imposed upon parties in the typical circumstances of justice.

4. These ideas are, of course, connected with a familiar way of thinking about justice which goes back at least to the Greek Sophists, and which regards the acceptance of the principles of justice as a compromise between persons of roughly equal power who would enforce their will on each other if they could, but who, in view of the equality of forces amongst them and for the sake of their own peace and security, acknowledge certain forms of conduct insofar as prudence seems to require. Justice is thought of as a pact between rational egoists the stability of which is dependent on a balance of power and a similarity of circumstances.[8] While the

previous account is connected with this tradition, and with its most recent variant, the theory of games,[9] it differs from it in several important respects which, to forestall misinterpretations, I will set out here.

First, I wish to use the previous conjectural account of the background of justice as a way of analyzing the concept. I do not want, therefore, to be interpreted as assuming a general theory of human motivation: when I suppose that the parties are mutually self-interested, and are not willing to have their (substantial) interests sacrificed to others, I am referring to their conduct and motives as they are taken for granted in cases where questions of justice ordinarily arise. Justice is the virtue of practices where there are assumed to be competing interests and conflicting claims, and where it is supposed that persons will press their rights on each other. That persons are mutually self-interested in certain situations and for certain purposes is what gives rise to the question of justice in practices covering those circumstances. Amongst an association of saints, if such a community could really exist, the disputes about justice could hardly occur; for they would all work selflessly together for one end, the glory of God as defined by their common religion, and reference to this end would settle every question of right. The justice of practices does not come up until there are several different parties (whether we think of these as individuals, associations, or nations and so on, is irrelevant) who do press their claims on one another, and

---

[8] Perhaps the best known statement of this conception is that given by Glaucon at the beginning of Book II of Plato's *Republic*. Presumably it was, in various forms, a common view among the Sophists; but that Plato gives a fair representation of it is doubtful. See K. R. Popper, *The Open Society and Its Enemies*, rev. ed. (Princeton, 1950), pp. 112–118. Certainly Plato usually attributes to it a quality of manic egoism which one feels must be an exaggeration; on the other hand, see the Melian Debate in Thucydides, *The Peloponnesian War*, Book V, ch. VII, although it is impossible to say to what extent the views expressed there reveal any current philosophical opinion. Also in this tradition are the remarks of Epicurus on justice in *Principal Doctrines*, XXXI–XXXVIII. In modern times elements of the conception appear in a more sophisticated form in Hobbes *The Leviathan* and in Hume *A Treatise of Human Nature*, Book III, Pt. II, as well as in the writings of the school of natural law such as Pufendorf's *De jure naturae et gentium*. Hobbes and Hume are especially instructive. For Hobbes's argument see Howard Warrender's

The Political Philosophy of Hobbes (Oxford, 1957). W. J. Baumol's *Welfare Economics and the Theory of the State* (London, 1952) is valuable in showing the wide applicability of Hobbes's fundamental idea (interpreting his natural law as principles of prudence), although in this book it is traced back only to Hume's *Treatise*.

[9] See J. von Neumann and O. Morgenstern, *The Theory of Games and Economic Behavior*, 2nd ed. (Princeton, 1947). For a comprehensive and not too technical discussion of the developments since, see R. Duncan Luce and Howard Raiffa, *Games and Decisions: Introduction and Critical Survey* (New York, 1957). Chs. VI and XIV discuss the developments most obviously related to the analysis of justice.

who do regard themselves as representatives of interests which deserve to be considered. Thus the previous account involves no general theory of human motivation. Its intent is simply to incorporate into the conception of justice the relations of men to one another which set the stage for questions of justice. It makes no difference how wide or general these relations are, as this matter does not bear on the analysis of the concept.

Again, in contrast to the various conceptions of the social contract, the several parties do not establish any particular society or practice; they do not covenant to obey a particular sovereign body or to accept a given constitution.[10] Nor do they, as in the theory of games (in certain respects a marvelously sophisticated development of this tradition), decide on individual strategies adjusted to their respective circumstances in the game. What the parties do is to *jointly* acknowledge certain *principles* of appraisal relating to their common *practices* either as already established or merely proposed. They accede to standards of judgment, not to a given practice; they do not make any specific agreement, or bargain, or adopt a particular strategy. The subject of their acknowledgment is, therefore, very general indeed; it is simply the acknowledgment of certain principles of judgment, fulfilling certain general conditions, to be used in criticizing the arrangement of their common affairs. The relations of mutual self-interest between the parties who are similarly circumstanced mirror the conditions under which questions of justice arise, and the procedure by which the principles of judgment are proposed and acknowledged reflects the constraints of having a morality. Each aspect, then, of the preceding hypothetical account serves the purpose of bringing out a feature of the notion of justice. One could, if one liked, view the principles of justice as the "solution" of this highest order "game" of adopting, subject to the procedure described, principles of argument for all coming particular "games" whose peculiarities one can in no

way foresee. But this comparison, while no doubt helpful, must not obscure the fact that this highest order "game" is of a special sort.[11] Its significance is that its various pieces represent aspects of the concept of justice.

---

[10] For a general survey see J. W. Gough, *The Social Contract*, 2nd ed. (Oxford, 1957), and Otto von Gierke, *The Development of Political Theory*, tr. by B. Freyd (London, 1939), Pt. II, ch. 11.

[11] The difficulty one gets into by a mechanical application of the theory of games to moral philosophy can be brought out by considering among several possible examples, R. B. Braithwaite's study, *Theory of Games as a Tool for the Moral Philosopher* (Cambridge, 1955). On the analysis there given, it turns out that the fair division of playing time between Matthew and Luke depends on their preferences, and these in turn are connected with the instruments they wish to play. Since Matthew has a threat advantage over Luke, arising purely from the fact that Matthew, the trumpeter, prefers both of them playing at once to neither of them playing, whereas Luke, the pianist, prefers silence to cacophony, Matthew is allotted 26 evenings of play to Luke's 17. If the situation were reversed, the threat advantage would be with Luke. See p. 36 f. But now we have only to suppose that Matthew is a jazz enthusiast who plays the drums, and Luke a violinist who plays sonatas, in which case it will be fair, on this analysis, for Matthew to play whenever and as often as he likes, assuming, of course, as it is plausible to assume, that he does not care whether Luke plays or not. Certainly something has gone wrong. To each according to his threat advantage is hardly the principle of fairness. What is lacking is the concept of morality, and it must be brought into the conjectural account in some way or other. In the text this is done by the form of the procedure whereby principles are proposed and acknowledged (Section 3). If one starts directly with the particular case as known, and if one accepts as given and definitive the preferences and relative positions of the parties, whatever they are, it is impossible to give an analysis of the moral concept of fairness. Braithwaite's use of the theory of games, insofar as it is intended to analyze the concept of fairness, is, I think, mistaken. This is not, of course, to criticize in any way the theory of games as a mathematical theory, to which Braithwaite's book certainly contributes, nor as an analysis of how rational (and amoral) egoists might behave (and so as an analysis of how people sometimes actually do behave). But it is to say that if the theory of games is to be used to analyze moral concepts, its formal structure must be interpreted in a special and general manner as indicted in the text. Once we do this, though, we are in touch again with a much older tradition.

Finally, I do not, of course, conceive the several parties as necessarily coming together to establish their common practices for the first time. Some institutions may, indeed, be set up *de novo*; but I have framed the preceding account so that it will apply when the full complement of social institutions already exists and represents the result of a long period of development. Nor is the account in any way fictitious. In any society where people reflect on their institutions they will have an idea of what principles of justice would be acknowledged under the conditions described, and there will be occasions when questions of justice are actually discussed in this way. Therefore if their practices do not accord with these principles, this will affect the quality of their social relations. For in this case there will be some recognized situations wherein the parties are mutually aware that one of them is being forced to accept what the other would concede is unjust. The foregoing analysis may then be thought of as representing the actual quality of relations between persons as defined by practices accepted as just. In such practices the parties will acknowledge the principles on which it is constructed, and the general recognition of this fact shows itself in the absence of resentment and in the sense of being justly treated. Thus one common objection to the theory of the social contract, its apparently historical and fictitious character, is avoided.

5. That the principles of justice may be regarded as arising in the manner described illustrates an important fact about them. Not only does it bring out the idea that justice is a primitive moral notion in that it arises once the concept of morality is imposed on mutually self-interested agents similarly circumstanced, but it emphasizes that, fundamental to justice, is the concept of fairness which relates to right dealing between persons who are cooperating with or competing against one another, as when one speaks of fair games, fair competition, and fair bargains. The question of fairness arises when free persons, who have no authority over one another, are engaging in a joint activity and amongst themselves settling or acknowledging the rules which define it and which determine the respective shares in its benefits and burdens. A practice will strike the parties as fair if none feels that, by participating in it, they

or any of the others are taken advantage of, or forced to give in to claims which they do not regard as legitimate. This implies that each has a conception of legitimate claims which he thinks it reasonable for others as well as himself to acknowledge. If one thinks of the principles of justice as arising in the manner described, then they do define this sort of conception. A practice is just or fair, then, when it satisfies the principles which those who participate in it could propose to one another for mutual acceptance under the afore-mentioned circumstances. Persons engaged in a just, or fair, practice can face one another openly and support their respective positions, should they appear questionable, by reference to principles which it is reasonable to expect each to accept.

It is this notion of the possibility of mutual acknowledgment of principles by free persons who have no authority over one another which makes the concept of fairness fundamental to justice. Only if such acknowledgment is possible can there be true community between persons in their common practices; otherwise their relations will appear to them as founded to some extent on force. If, in ordinary speech, fairness applies more particularly to practices in which there is a choice whether to engage or not (e.g., in games, business competition), and justice to practices in which there is no choice (e.g., in slavery), the element of necessity does not render the conception of mutual acknowledgment inapplicable, although it may make it much more urgent to change unjust than unfair institutions. For one activity in which one can always engage is that of proposing and acknowledging principles to one another supposing each to be similarly circumstanced; and to judge practices by the principles so arrived at is to apply the standard of fairness to them.

Now if the participants in a practice accept its rules as fair, and so have no complaint to lodge against it, there arises a prima facie duty (and a corresponding prima facie right) of the parties to each other to act in accordance with the practice when it falls upon them to comply. When any number of persons engage in a practice, or conduct a joint undertaking according to rules, and thus restrict their liberty, those who have submitted to these restrictions when required have the right to a similar acquiescence on the part of those who have benefited by their submission. These conditions will obtain if a practice is correctly acknowledged to be fair, for in this case all who participate in it will benefit from it. The rights and duties so arising are special rights and duties in that they depend on previous actions voluntarily undertaken, in this case on the parties having engaged in a common practice and knowingly accepted its benefits.[12] It is not, however, an obligation which presupposes a deliberate performative act in the sense of a promise, or contract, and the like.[13] An unfortunate mistake of proponents of the idea of the social contract was to suppose that political obligation does require some such act, or at least to use language which suggests it. It is sufficient that one has knowingly participated in and accepted the benefits of a practice acknowledged to be fair. This prima facie obligation may, of course, be overridden: it may happen, when it comes one's turn to follow a rule, that other considerations will justify not doing so. But one cannot, in general, be released from this obligation by denying the justice of the practice only when it falls on one to obey. If a person rejects a practice, he should, so far as possible, declare his intention in advance, and avoid participating in it or enjoying its benefits.

This duty I have called that of fair play, but it should be admitted that to refer to it in this way is, perhaps, to extend the ordinary notion of fairness. Usually acting unfairly is not so much the breaking of any particular rule, even if the infraction is difficult to detect (cheating), but taking advantage of loop-holes or ambiguities in rules, availing oneself of unexpected or special circumstances which make it impossible to enforce them, insisting that rules be enforced to one's advantage when they should be suspended, and more generally, acting contrary to the intention of a practice. It is for this reason that

one speaks of the sense of fair play: acting fairly requires more than simply being able to follow rules; what is fair must often be felt, or perceived, one wants to say. It is not, however, an unnatural extension of the duty of fair play to have it include the obligation which participants who have knowingly accepted the benefits of their common practice owe to each other to act in accordance with it when their performance falls due; for it is usually considered unfair if someone accepts the benefits of a practice but refuses to do his part in maintaining it. Thus one might say of the tax-dodger that he violates the duty of fair play: he accepts the benefits of government but will not do his part in releasing resources to it; and members of labor unions often say that fellow workers who refuse to join are being unfair: they refer to them as "free riders," as persons who enjoy what are the supposed benefits of unionism, higher wages, shorter hours, job security, and the like, but who refuse to share in its burdens in the form of paying dues, and so on.

The duty of fair play stands beside other prima facie duties such as fidelity and gratitude as a basic moral notion; yet it is not to be confused with them.[14] These duties are all clearly distinct, as would be obvious from their definitions. As with any moral duty, that of fair play implies a constraint on self-interest in particular cases; on occasion it enjoins conduct which a rational egoist strictly defined would not decide upon. So while justice does not require of anyone that he sacrifice his interests in that *general*

---

[12] For the definition of this prima facie duty, and the idea that it is a special duty, I am indebted to H. L. A. Hart. See his paper "Are There Any Natural Rights?," *Philosophical Review*, LXIV (1955), 185 f.

[13] The sense of "performative" here is to be derived from J. L. Austin's paper in the symposium, "Other Minds," *Proceedings of the Aristotelian Society*, Supplementary Volume (1946), pp. 170–174.

---

[14] This, however, commonly happens. Hobbes, for example, when invoking the notion of a "tacit covenant," appeals not to the natural law that promises should be kept but to his fourth law of nature, that of gratitude. On Hobbes's shift from fidelity to gratitude, see Warrender, *op. cit.*, pp. 51–52, 233–237. While it is not serious criticism of Hobbes, it would have improved his argument had he appealed to the duty of fair play. On his premises he is perfectly entitled to do so. Similarly, Sidgwick thought that a principle of justice, such as every man ought to receive adequate requital for his labor, is like gratitude universalized. See *Methods of Ethics*, Bk. III, ch. v, Sec. 5. There is a gap in the stock of moral concepts used by philosophers into which the concept of the duty of fair play fits quite naturally.

position and procedure whereby the principles of justice are proposed and acknowledged, it may happen that in particular situations, arising in the context of engaging in a practice, the duty of fair play will often cross his interests in the sense that he will be required to forego particular advantages which the peculiarities of his circumstances might permit him to take. There is, of course, nothing surprising in this. It is simply the consequence of the firm commitment which the parties may be supposed to have made, or which they would make, in the general position, together with the fact that they have participated in and accepted the benefits of a practice which they regard as fair.

Now the acknowledgment of this constraint in particular cases, which is manifested in acting fairly or wishing to make amends, feeling ashamed, and the like, when one has evaded it, is one of the forms of conduct by which participants in a common practice exhibit their recognition of each other as persons with similar interests and capacities. In the same way that, failing a special explanation, the criterion for the recognition of suffering is helping one who suffers, acknowledging the duty of fair play is a necessary part of the criterion for recognizing another as a person with similar interests and feelings as oneself.[15] A person who never under any circumstances showed a wish to help others in pain would show, at the same time, that he did not recognize that they were in pain; nor could he have any feelings of affection or friendship for anyone; for having these feelings implies, failing special circumstances, that

he comes to their aid when they are suffering. Recognition that another is a person in pain shows itself in sympathetic action; this primitive natural response of compassion is one of those responses upon which the various forms of moral conduct are built.

Similarly, the acceptance of the duty of fair play by participants in a common practice is a reflection in each person of the recognition of the aspirations and interests of the others to be realized by their joint activity. Failing a special explanation, their acceptance of it is a necessary part of the criterion for their recognizing one another as persons with similar interests and capacities, as the conception of their relations in the general position supposes them to be. Otherwise they would show no recognition of one another as persons with similar capacities and interests, and indeed, in some cases perhaps hypothetical, they would not recognize one another as persons at all, but as complicated objects involved in a complicated activity. To recognize another as a person one must respond to him and act towards him in certain ways; and these ways are intimately connected with the various prima facie duties. Acknowledging these duties in *some* degree, and so having the elements of morality, is not a matter of choice, or of intuiting moral qualities, or a matter of expression of feelings or attitudes (the three interpretations between which philosophical opinion frequently oscillates); it is simply the possession of one of the forms of conduct in which the recognition of others as persons is manifested.

These remarks are unhappily obscure. Their main purpose here, however, is to forestall, together with the remarks in Section 4, the misinterpretation that, on the view presented, the acceptance of justice and the acknowledgment of the duty of fair play depends in every day life solely on there being a *de facto* balance of forces between the parties. It would indeed be foolish to underestimate the importance of such a balance in securing justice; but it is not the only basis thereof. The recognition of one another as persons with similar interests and capacities engaged in a common practice must, failing a special explanation, show itself in the acceptance of the principles of justice and the acknowledgment of the duty of fair play.

The conception at which we have arrived, then, is that the principles of justice may be thought of as

---

[15]I am using the concept of criterion here in what I take to be Wittgenstein's sense. See *Philosophical Investigations* (Oxford, 1953); and Norman Malcolm's review, "Wittgenstein's *Philosophical Investigations,*" *Philosophical Review*, LXIII (1954), 543–547. That the response of compassion, under appropriate circumstances, is part of the criterion for whether or not a person understands what "pain" means, is, I think, in the *Philosophical Investigations*. The view in the text is simply an extension of this idea. I cannot, however, attempt to justify it here. Similar thoughts are to be found, I think, in Max Schelere, *The Nature of Sympathy*, tr. by Peter Heath (New Haven, 1954). His way of writing is often so obscure that I cannot be certain.

arising once the constraints of having a morality are imposed upon rational and mutually self-interested parties who are related and situated in a special way. A practice is just if it is in accordance with the principles which all who participate in it might reasonably be expected to propose or to acknowledge before one another when they are similarly circumstanced and required to make a firm commitment in advance without knowledge of what will be their peculiar condition, and thus when it meets standards which the parties could accept as fair should occasion arise for them to debate its merits. Regarding the participants themselves, once persons knowingly engage in a practice which they acknowledge to be fair and accept the benefits of doing so, they are bound by the duty of fair play to follow the rules when it comes their turn to do so, and this implies a limitation on their pursuit of self-interest in particular cases.

Now one consequence of this conception is that, where it applies, there is no moral value in the satisfaction of a claim incompatible with it. Such a claim violates the conditions of reciprocity and community amongst persons, and he who presses it, not being willing to acknowledge it when pressed by another, has no grounds for complaint when it is denied; whereas he against whom it is pressed can complain. As it cannot be mutually acknowledged it is a resort to coercion; granting the claim is possible only if the party can compel acceptance of what the other will not admit. But it makes no sense to concede claims the denial of which cannot be complained of in preference to claims the denial of which can be objected to. Thus in deciding on the justice of a practice it is not enough to ascertain that it answers to wants and interests in the fullest and most effective manner. For if any of these conflict with justice, they should not be counted, as their satisfaction is no reason at all for having a practice. It would be irrelevant to say, even if true, that it resulted in the greatest satisfaction of desire. In tallying up the merits of a practice one must toss out the satisfaction of interests the claims of which are incompatible with the principles of justice.

6. The discussion so far has been excessively abstract. While this is perhaps unavoidable, I should now like to bring out some of the features of the conception of justice as fairness by comparing it with the conception of justice in classical utilitarianism as represented by Bentham and Sidgwick, and its counterpart in welfare economics. This conception assimilates justice to benevolence and the latter in turn to the most efficient design of institutions to promote the general welfare. Justice is a kind of efficiency.[16]

Now it is said occasionally that this form of utilitarianism puts no restrictions on what might be a just assignment of rights and duties in that there might be circumstances which, on utilitarian grounds, would justify institutions highly offensive to our ordinary sense of justice. But the classical utilitarian conception is not totally unprepared for this objection. Beginning with the notion that the general happiness can be represented by a social utility function consisting of a sum of individual utility functions with identical weights (this being the meaning of the maxim that each counts for one and no more than

_____

[16]While this assimilation is implicit in Bentham's and Sidgwick's moral theory, explicit statements of it as applied to justice are relatively rare. One clear instance in *The Principles of Morals and Legislation* occurs in ch. x, footnote 2 to section XL: ". . . justice, in the only sense in which it has a meaning, is an imaginary personage, feigned for the convenience of discourse, whose dictators are the dictates of utility, applied to certain particular cases. Justice, then, is nothing more than an imaginary instrument, employed to forward on certain occasions, and by certain means, the purposes of benevolence. The dictates of justice are nothing more than a part of the dictates of benevolence, which, on certain occasions, are applied to certain subjects. . . ." Likewise in *The Limits of Jurisprudence Refined*, ed. by C. W. Everett (New York, 1945), pp. 117 f., Bentham criticizes Grotius for denying that justice derives from utility; and in *The Theory of Legislation*, ed. by C. K. Ogden (London, 1931), p. 3, he says that he uses the words "just" and "unjust" along with other words "simply as collective terms including the ideas of certain pains or pleasures." That Sidgwick's conception of justice is similar to Bentham's is admittedly not evident from his discussion of justice in Book III, ch. v. of *Methods of Ethics*. But it follows, I think, from the moral theory he accepts. Hence C. D. Broad's criticisms of Sidgwick in the matter of distributive justice in *Five Types of Ethical Theory* (London, 1930), pp. 249–253, do not rest on a misinterpretation.

one),[17] it is commonly assumed that the utility functions of individuals are similar in all essential respects. Differences between individuals are ascribed to accidents of education and upbringing, and they should not be taken into account. This assumption, coupled with that of diminishing marginal utility, results in a prima facie case for equality, e.g., of equality in the distribution of income during any given period of time, laying aside indirect effects on the future. But even if utilitarianism is interpreted as having such restrictions built into the utility function, and even if it is supposed that these restrictions have in practice much the same result as the application of the principles of justice (and appear, perhaps, to be ways of expressing these principles in the language of mathematics and psychology), the fundamental idea is very different from the conception of justice as fairness. For one thing, that the principles of justice should be accepted is interpreted as the contingent result of a higher order administrative decision. The form of this decision is regarded as being similar to that of an entrepreneur deciding how much to produce of this or that commodity in view of its marginal revenue, or to that of someone distributing goods to needy persons according to the relative urgency of their wants. The choice between practices is thought of as being made on the basis of the allocation of benefits and burdens to individuals (these being measured by the present capitalized value of their utility over the full period of the practice's existence), which results from the distribution of rights and duties established by a practice.

Moreover, the individuals receiving these benefits are not conceived as being related in any way: they represent so many different directions in which limited resources may be allocated. The value of assigning resources to one direction rather than another depends solely on the preferences and interests of individuals as individuals. The satisfaction of desire has its value irrespective of the moral relations between persons, say as members of a joint undertaking, and of the claims which, in the name of these interests, they are prepared to make on one another;[18] and it is this value which is to be taken into account by the (ideal) legislator who is conceived as adjusting the rules of the system from the center so as to maximize the value of the social utility function.

It is thought that the principles of justice will not be violated by a legal system so conceived provided these executive decisions are correctly made. In this

---

[17] This maxim is attributed to Bentham by J. S. Mill in *Utilitarianism*, ch. v, paragraph 36. I have not found it in Bentham's writings, nor seen such a reference. Similarly James Bonar, *Philosophy and Political Economy* (London, 1893), p. 234 n. But it accords perfectly with Bentham's ideas. See the hitherto unpublished manuscript in David Baumgardt, *Bentham and the Ethics of Today* (Princeton, 1952), Appendix IV. For example, "the total value of the stock of pleasure belonging to the whole community is to be obtained by multiplying the number expressing the value of it as respecting any one person, by the number expressing the multitude of such individuals" (p. 556).

[18] An idea essential to the classical utilitarian conception of justice. Bentham is firm in his statement of it: "It is only upon that principle [the principle of asceticism], and not from the principle of utility, that the most abominable pleasure which the vilest of malefactors ever reaped from his crime would be reprobed, if it stood alone. The case is, that it never does stand alone; but is necessarily followed by such a quantity of pain (or, what comes to the same thing, such a chance for a certain quantity of pain) that the pleasure in comparison of it, is as nothing: and this is true and sole, but perfectly sufficient, reason for making it a ground for punishment" (*The Principles of Morals and Legislation*, ch. 11, sec. iv. See also ch. x, sec. x, footnote 1). The same point is made in *The Limits of Jurisprudence Defined*, pp. 115 f. Although much recent welfare economics, as found in such important works as I. M. D. Little, *A Critique of Welfare Economics*, 2nd ed. (Oxford, 1957) and K. J. Arrow, *Social Choice and Individual Values* (New York, 1951), dispenses with the idea of cardinal utility, and uses instead the theory of ordinal utility as stated by J. R. Hicks, *Value and Capital*, 2nd ed. (Oxford, 1946), Pt. I, it assumes with utilitarianism that individual preferences have value as such, and so accepts the idea being criticized here. I hasten to add, however, that this is no objection to it as a means of analyzing economic policy, and for that purpose it may, indeed, be a necessary simplifying assumption. Nevertheless it is an assumption which cannot be made in so far as one is trying to analyze moral concepts, especially the concept of justice, as economists would, I think, agree. Justice is usually regarded as a separate and distinct part of any comprehensive criterion of economic policy. See, for example, Tibor Scitovsky, *Welfare and Competition* (London, 1952), pp. 59–69, and Little, *op. cit.*, cs. vii.

fact the principles of justice are said to have their derivation and explanation; they simply express the most important general features of social institutions in which the administrative problem is solved in the best way. These principles have, indeed, a special urgency because, given the facts of human nature, so much depends on them; and this explains the peculiar quality of the moral feelings associated with justice.[19] This assimilation of justice to a higher order executive decision, certainly a striking conception, is central to classical utilitarianism; and it also brings out its profound individualism, in one sense of this ambiguous word. It regards persons as so many *separate* directions in which benefits and burdens may be assigned; and the value of the satisfaction or dissatisfaction of desire is not thought to depend in any way on the moral relations in which individuals stand, or on the kinds of claims which they are willing, in the pursuit of their interests, to press on each other.

7. Many social decisions are, of course, of an administrative nature. Certainly this is so when it is a matter of social utility in what one may call its ordinary sense: that is, when it is a question of the efficient design of social institutions for the use of common means to achieve common ends. In this case either the benefits and burdens may be assumed to be impartially distributed, or the question of distribution is misplaced, as in the instance of maintaining public order and security or national defense. But as an interpretation of the basis of the principles of justice, classical utilitarianism is mistaken. It *permits* one to argue, for example, that slavery is unjust on the grounds that the advantages to the slaveholder as slaveholder do not counterbalance the disadvantages to the slave and to society at large burdened by a comparatively inefficient system of labor. Now the conception of justice as fairness, when applied to the practice of slavery with its offices of slaveholder and slave, would not allow one to consider the advantages of the slaveholder in the first place. As that office is not in accordance with principles which could be mutually acknowledged, the gains accruing to the slaveholder, assuming them to exist, cannot be

counted as in *any* way mitigating the injustice of the practice. The question whether these gains outweigh the disadvantages to the slave and to society cannot arise, since in considering the justice of slavery these gains have no weight at all which requires that they be overridden. Where the conception of justice as fairness applies, slavery is *always* unjust.

I am not, of course, suggesting the absurdity that the classical utilitarians approved of slavery. I am only rejecting a type of argument which their view allows them to use in support of their disapproval of it. The conception of justice as derivative from efficiency implies that judging the justice of a practice is always, in principle at least, a matter of weighing up advantages and disadvantages, each having an intrinsic value or disvalue as the satisfaction of interests, irrespective of whether or not these interests necessarily involve acquiescence in principles which could not be mutually acknowledged. Utilitarianism cannot account for the fact that slavery is always unjust, nor for the fact that it would be recognized as irrelevant in defeating the accusation of injustice for one person to say to another, engaged with him in a common practice and debating its merits, that nevertheless it allowed of the greatest satisfaction of desire. The charge of injustice cannot be rebutted in this way. If justice were derivative from a higher order executive efficiency, this would not be so.

But now, even if it is taken as established that, so far as the ordinary conception of justice goes, slavery is always unjust (that is, slavery by definition violates commonly recognized principles of justice), the classical utilitarian would surely reply that these principles, as other moral principles subordinate to that of utility, are only generally correct. It is simply for the most part true that slavery is less efficient than other institutions; and while common sense may define the concept of justice so that slavery is unjust, nevertheless, where slavery would lead to the greatest satisfaction of desire, it is not wrong. Indeed, it is then right, and for the very same reason that justice, as ordinarily understood, is usually right. If, as ordinarily understood, slavery is always unjust, to this extent the utilitarian conception of justice might be admitted to differ from that of common moral opinion. Still the utilitarian would want to hold

---

[19] See J. S. Mill's argument in *Utilitarianism*, ch. v, pars. 16–25.

that, as a matter of moral principle, his view is correct in giving no special weight to considerations of justice beyond that allowed for by the general presumption of effectiveness. And this, he claims, is as it should be. The every day opinion is morally in error, although, indeed, it is a useful error, since it protects rules of generally high utility.

The question, then, relates not simply to the analysis of the concept of justice as common sense defines it, but the analysis of it in the wider sense as to how much weight considerations of justice, as defined, are to have when laid against other kinds of moral considerations. Here again I wish to argue that reasons of justice have a *special* weight for which only the conception of justice as fairness can account. Moreover, it belongs to the concept of justice that they do have this special weight. While Mill recognized that this was so, he thought that it could be accounted for by the special urgency of the moral feelings which naturally support principles of such high utility. But it is a mistake to resort to the urgency of feeling; as with the appeal to intuition, it manifests a failure to pursue the question far enough. The special weight of considerations of justice can be explained from the conception of justice as fairness. It is only necessary to elaborate a bit what has already been said as follows.

If one examines the circumstances in which a certain tolerance of slavery is justified, or perhaps better, excused, it turns out that these are of a rather special sort. Perhaps slavery exists as an inheritance from the past and it proves necessary to dismantle it piece by piece; at times slavery may conceivably be an advance on previous institutions. Now while there may be some excuse for slavery in special conditions, it is never an excuse for it that it is sufficiently advantageous to the slaveholder to outweigh the disadvantages to the slave and to society. A person who argues in this way is not perhaps making a wildly irrelevant remark; but he is guilty of a moral fallacy. There is disorder in his conception of the ranking of moral principles. For the slaveholder, by his own admission, has no moral title to the advantages which he receives as a slaveholder. He is no more prepared than the slave to acknowledge the principle upon which is founded the respective positions in which they both stand. Since slavery does not accord with principles which they could mutually acknowledge, they each may be supposed to agree that it is unjust: it grants claims which it ought not to grant and in doing so denies claims which it ought not to deny. Amongst persons in a general position who are debating the form of their common practices, it cannot, therefore, be offered as a reason for a practice that, in conceding these very claims that ought to be denied, it nevertheless meets existing interests more effectively. By their very nature the satisfaction of these claims is without weight and cannot enter into any tabulation of advantages and disadvantages.

Furthermore, it follows from the concept of morality that, to the extent that the slaveholder recognizes his position via-à-vis the slave to be unjust, he would not choose to press his claims. His not wanting to receive his special advantages is one of the ways in which he shows that he thinks slavery is unjust. It would be fallacious for the legislator to suppose, then, that it is a ground for having a practice that it brings advantages greater than disadvantages, if those for whom the practice is designed, and to whom the advantages flow, acknowledge that they have no moral title to them and do not wish to receive them.

For these reasons the principles of justice have a special weight; and with respect to the principle of the greatest satisfaction of desire, as cited in the general position amongst those discussing the merits of their common practices, the principles of justice have an absolute weight. In this sense they are not contingent; and this is why their force is greater than can be accounted for by the general presumption (assuming that there is one) of the effectiveness, in the utilitarian sense, of practices which in fact satisfy them.

If one wants to continue using the concepts of classical utilitarianism, one will have to say, to meet this criticism, that at least the individual or social utility functions must be so defined that no value is given to the satisfaction of interests the representative claims of which violate the principles of justice. In this way it is no doubt possible to include these principles within the form of the utilitarian conception; but to do so is, of course, to change its inspiration altogether as a moral conception. For it is to incorporate within it principles which cannot be understood on the basis of a higher order executive decision aiming at the greatest satisfaction of desire.

It is worth remarking, perhaps, that this criticism of utilitarianism does not depend on whether or not the two assumptions, that of individuals having similar utility functions and that of diminishing marginal utility, are interpreted as psychological propositions to be supported or refuted by experience, or as moral and political principles expressed in a somewhat technical language. There are, certainly, several advantages in taking them in the latter fashion.[20] For one thing, one might say that this is what Bentham and others really meant by them, at least as shown by how they were used in arguments for social reform. More importantly, one could hold that the best way to defend the classical utilitarian view is to interpret these assumptions as moral and political principles. It is doubtful whether, taken as psychological propositions, they are true of men in general as we know them under normal conditions. On the other hand, utilitarians would not have wanted to propose them merely as practical working principles of legislation, or as expedient maxims to guide reform, given the egalitarian sentiments of modern society.[21] When pressed they might well have invoked the idea of a more or less equal capacity of men in relevant respects if given an equal chance in a just society. But if the argument above regarding slavery is correct, then granting these assumptions as moral and political principles makes no difference. To view individuals as equally fruitful lines for the allocation of benefits, even as a matter of moral principle, still leaves the mistaken notion that the satisfaction of desire has value in itself irrespective of the relations between persons as members of a common practice, and irrespective of the claims upon one another which the satisfaction of interests represents. To see the error of this idea one must give up the conception of justice as an executive decision altogether and refer to the notion of justice as fairness: that participants in a common practice be regarded as having an original and equal liberty and that their common practices be considered unjust unless they accord with principles which persons so circumstanced and related could freely acknowledge before one another, and so could accept as fair. Once the emphasis is put upon the concept of the mutual recognition of principles by participants in a common practice the rules of which are to define their several relations and give form to their claims on one another, then it is clear that the granting of a claim the principle of which could not be acknowledged by each in the general position (that is, in the position in which the parties propose and acknowledge principles before one another) is not a reason for adopting a practice. Viewed in this way, the background of the claim is seen to exclude it from consideration; that it can represent a value in itself arises from the conception of individuals as separate lines for the assignment of benefits, as isolated persons who stand as claimants on an administrative or benevolent largesse. Occasionally persons do so stand to one another; but this is not the general case, nor, more importantly, is it the case when it is a matter of the justice of practices themselves in which participants stand in various relations to be appraised in accordance with standards which they may be expected to acknowledge before one another. Thus however mistaken the notion of the social contract may be as history, and however far it may overreach itself as a general theory of social and political obligation, it does express, suitably interpreted, an essential part of the concept of justice.[22]

---

[20] See D. G. Ritchie, *Natural Rights* (London, 1894), pp. 95 ff., 249 ff. Lionel Robbins has insisted on this point on several occasions. See *An Essay on the Nature and Significance of Economic Science*, 2nd ed. (London, 1935), pp. 134–43, "Interpersonal Comparisons of Utility: A Comment," *Economic Journal*, XLVIII (1938), 635–41, and more recently, "Robertson on Utility and Scope," *Economica*, n.s. XX (1953), 108 f.

[21] As Sir Henry Maine suggested Bentham may have regarded them. See *The Early History of Institutions* (London, 1875), pp. 398 ff.

[22] Thus Kant was not far wrong when he interpreted the original contract merely as an "Idea of Reason"; yet he still thought of it as a *general* criterion of right and as providing a general theory of political obligation. See the second part of the essay, "On the Saying 'That may be right in theory but has no value in practice' " (1793), in *Kant's Principles of Politics*, tr. by W. Hastie (Edinburgh, 1891). I have drawn on the contractarian tradition not for a general theory of political obligation but to clarify the concept of justice.

8. By way of conclusion I should like to make two remarks: first, the original modification of the utilitarian principle (that it require of practices that the offices and positions defined by them be equal unless it is reasonable to suppose that the representative man in *every* office would find the inequality to his advantage), slight as it may appear at first sight, actually has a different conception of justice standing behind it. I have tried to show how this is so by developing the concept of justice as fairness and by indicating how this notion involves the mutual acceptance, from a general position, of the principles on which a practice is founded, and how this in turn requires the exclusion from consideration of claims violating the principles of justice. Thus the slight alteration of principle reveals another family of notions, another way of looking at the concept of justice.

Second, I should like to remark also that I have been dealing with the *concept* of justice. I have tried to set out the kinds of principles upon which judgments concerning the justice of practices may be said to stand. The analysis will be successful to the degree that it expresses the principles involved in these judgments when made by competent persons upon deliberation and reflection.[23] Now every people may be supposed to have the concept of justice, since in the life of every society there must be at least some relations in which the parties consider themselves to be circumstanced and related as the concept of justice as fairness requires. Societies will differ from one another not in having or in failing to have this notion but in the range of cases to which they apply it and in the emphasis which they give to it as compared with other moral concepts.

A firm grasp of the concept of justice itself is necessary if these variations, and the reasons for them, are to be understood. No study of the development of moral ideas and of the differences between them is more sound than the analysis of the fundamental moral concepts upon which it must depend. I have tried, therefore, to give an analysis of the concept of justice which should apply generally, however large a part the concept may have in a given morality, and which can be used in explaining the course of men's thoughts about justice and its relations to other moral concepts. How it is to be used for this purpose is a large topic which I cannot, of course, take up here. I mention it only to emphasize that I have been dealing with the concept of justice itself and to indicate what use I consider such an analysis to have.

---

[23] For a further discussion of the idea expressed here, see my paper, "Outline of a Decision Procedure for Ethics," in the *Philosophical Review*, LX (1951), 177–197. For an analysis, similar in many respects but using the notion of the ideal observer instead of that of the considered judgment of a competent person, see Roderick Firth, "Ethical Absolutism and the Ideal Observer," *Philosophy and Phenomenological Research*, XII (1952), 317–345. While the similarities between these two discussions are more important than the differences, an analysis based on the notion of a considered judgment of a competent person, as it is based on a kind of judgment, may prove more helpful in understanding the features of moral judgment than an analysis based on the notion of an ideal observer, although this remains to be shown. A man who rejects the conditions imposed on a considered judgment of a competent person could no longer profess to *judge* at all. This seems more fundamental than his rejecting the conditions of observation, for these do not seem to apply, in an ordinary sense, to making a moral judgment.

REVIEW QUESTIONS

1. What does Rawls say about the relative importance of the individual versus the welfare of society?
2. What is the level of ignorance of the parties in the original position? How deep is their ignorance?
3. Why does Rawls choose the device of a veil of ignorance? What is its purpose?
4. How does Rawls deal with accidents and natural endowments of people?
5. What are the two principles that Rawls says we would choose behind the veil of ignorance?